THE NATIONAL ROLL OF THE GREAT WAR.

The National Roll of the Great War

One of the most sought-after sets of reference books of the First World War is the *National Roll of the Great War*. The National Publishing Company attempted, shortly after hostilities ceased, to compile a brief biography of as many participants in the War as possible. The vast majority of entries refer to combatants who survived the Great War and the *National Roll* is often the only source of information available. Fourteen volumes were completed on a regional basis; **the Naval & Military Press has compiled a fifteenth volume which contains an alphabetic index to the fourteen now republished volumes**.

The National Roll - complete 15 vol. set	ISBN: 1 847340 33 4	£285.00
Section I - London	ISBN: 1 847340 34 2	£22.00
Section II - London	ISBN: 1 847340 35 0	£22.00
Section III - London	ISBN: 1 847340 36 9	£22.00
Section IV - Southampton	ISBN: 1 847340 37 7	£22.00
Section V - Luton	ISBN: 1 847340 38 5	£22.00
Section VI - Birmingham	ISBN: 1 847340 39 3	£22.00
Section VII - London	ISBN: 1 847340 40 7	£22.00
Section VIII - Leeds	ISBN: 1 847340 41 5	£22.00
Section IX - Bradford	ISBN: 1 847340 42 3	£22.00
Section X - Portsmouth	ISBN: 1 847340 43 1	£22.00
Section XI - Manchester	ISBN: 1 847340 44 X	£22.00
Section XII - Bedford & Northampton	ISBN: 1 847340 45 8	£22.00
Section XIII - London	ISBN: 1 847340 46 6	£22.00
Section XIV - Salford	ISBN: 1 847340 47 4	£22.00
Section XV - Index to all 14 volumes	ISBN: 1 847340 48 2	£22.00

The Naval & Military Press Ltd

Unit 10, Ridgewood Industrial Park, Uckfield,
East Sussex, TN22 5QE, England
Tel: 01825 749494   Fax: 01825 765701
www.naval-military-press.com
www.military-genealogy.com

THE NATIONAL ROLL
OF THE GREAT WAR
1914-1918

CONTAINED WITHIN
THE PAGES OF THIS
VOLUME WILL BE
FOUND THE NAMES
AND RECORDS OF
SERVICE OF THOSE
WHO HELPED TO
SECURE VICTORY FOR
THE EMPIRE DURING
THE GREAT WAR OF
1914-1918.

THE
NAVAL &
MILITARY
PRESS LTD
2006

Published by

The Naval & Military Press Ltd

Unit 10, Ridgewood Industrial Park,

Uckfield, East Sussex,

TN22 5QE England

Tel: +44 (0) 1825 749494

Fax: +44 (0) 1825 765701

www.naval-military-press.com

www.military-genealogy.com

*In reprinting in facsimile from the original, any imperfections are inevitably reproduced
and the quality may fall short of modern type and cartographic standards.*

FOREWORD

AND SHORT OUTLINE OF THE PART
PLAYED BY BRITAIN IN THE GREAT WAR.

WHEN we quietly consider what the Great War, with its gains and losses, its cares and anxieties, has taught us, we are at once struck by the splendid heroism of all who took part in it. Many by reason of special qualities of mind or soul stand out more prominently than the rest; but the names and deeds of others, who toiled no less meritoriously, are officially left unsung.

Yet it is well, if only for purely personal and family reasons, that there should be some abiding record of the self-sacrificing services of all men and women who answered their Country's call in her hour of need, and who, whether on land, or sea, or in the air, in hospital, or camp, or workshop, were ready to lay down life itself, if need be, that Britain might live and Right prevail over Might.

It is for this reason primarily that the present " National Roll of the Great War " was projected. In these pages will be found records of devotion and patriotism of which the individual, the family, and the nation have every reason to be proud.

1914. This foreword, besides recording our gratitude to all who toiled for the Empire, may also serve a subsidiary purpose by providing a sketch of the part which Britain played in the war which burst on the World in the Summer of 1914. Space does not allow us to follow the course of the negotiations which preceded the outbreak, or to explain the aims of Germany. Suffice it to say that her long projected design of rushing through Belgium on France in one overwhelming flood was foiled by the gallantry of the Allies in August and September. Our share in that struggle is told in the records of " The Contemptible Little Army " that fought at Mons, the Marne, the Aisne and Ypres.

1915. Our campaign in 1915 opened with the Battle of Neuve Chapelle, and in quick succession followed those at St. Éloi, Hill 60, Ypres, and Festubert. In the Autumn we gained a temporary success at Loos, and at one time Lens was almost ours, but when Winter set in, our lines were much the same as they had been a year before. We now began to realize, in a way we had not done hitherto, the greatness of the task to which we had set our hands. Our failure in the East had taught us the lesson that in the West and on the Sea lay our hopes of victory.

v

1916   Early in 1916 the fortune of war swayed for and against us at Loos, Ypres and Vimy Ridge, while the Germans were making their great effort at Verdun. Their protracted attack on that fortress failed, while their attempt to take command of the Sea was crushed by our Naval victory in the Battle of Jutland. Our great effort in 1916 was the Somme Offensive, which opened in July, and continued with varying success until November

1917.   Early in 1917 we reaped to some extent the benefit of our efforts of the preceding year, and a German retirement on a long line of the front took place, which by the middle of March gave us Bapaume and Péronne. On Easter Monday we attacked along the Vimy Ridge, and before Arras. Monchy-le-Preux was captured, Bailleul and several villages near Lens fell into our hands, and by May 17th we had taken Bullecourt. In June came our victory at Messines, and from July to November we fought the series of engagements round St. Julien, Pilkem, Hooge, Polygon Wood and Passchendaele, which go by the name of the third Battle of Ypres. At the same time severe fighting was going on near Lens, and this was followed in November and December by the first Battle of Cambrai, which opened auspiciously, but left us with little gained in the end.

1918.   The year 1918 opened with the great German Offensive, which was designed to end the struggle before the full weight of the American help could tell in our favour. It broke upon the Allied lines between the Scarpe and the Oise on March 21st, and for a time carried everything before it ; but Arras and Amiens remained in our possession. On April 9th the Germans made another effort on the Lys front, from La Bassée to Armentières. Desperate fighting occurred around Bailleul, Passchendaele, Kemmel and Givenchy, but in spite of our severe losses, Ludendorff failed to break through.

At the end of May the Germans made yet another attempt along the Aisne, and captured Soissons, Dormans and many villages. Their last effort began on July 15th along the Marne, east and west of Rheims. They achieved some success at first, but on July 18th the Allied counter-stroke began. Blow followed blow in quick succession, and Soissons and Beaumont-Hamel, that had been lost in the Spring, were now recovered. On August 21st the Battle of Bapaume opened, and concurrently with it the Battle of the Scarpe was going on. Towards the end of September the Battles of Cambrai and Ypres began, and our victories began seriously to jeopardise the enemy's lines of communication Eastwards. Le Cateau was entered on October 10th ; Ostend, Lille and Douai fell into Allied hands and within a few days the Belgian coast was freed. In November our successes still continued in the Battle of the Sambre, and the enemy retreated rapidly towards Mons and Maubeuge. Mons was entered at dawn on November 11th, 1918, and at 11 a.m. fighting ceased.

GALLIPOLI.   During 1915 we anxiously followed the course of our venture in the Dardanelles. Weighty reasons prompted it, and we hoped that our combined forces would be able to make their way to Constantinople, and by so doing would relieve the pressure on Russia, as well as remove the danger that threatened Egypt.

Unhappily, however, the successes at Anzac and Krithia and the later landing at Suvla Bay could not be followed up ; the Naval forces could not force their way through the Narrows ; and reluctantly we had to admit failure and evacuate the Peninsula.

EGYPT.

Early in the war the Turks made several unsuccessful attacks on the Canal Zone, while on the Western Frontiers of Egypt the Senussi were repulsed at Mersa, Matruh and Agagia. In August 1916 another Turkish attack was crushed at Romani, and six months later the enemy were again defeated at Magdhaba and Rafa. Henceforward Egypt became the base for offensive operations against the Turks in Palestine. Gaza was first attacked in March 1917, and again in April, but it was not captured until November, after General Allenby had previously taken Beersheba. Shortly afterwards Jaffa fell into our hands, and on December 9th Jerusalem surrendered, to be followed by Jericho in February. Hostilities were resumed in September, 1918, and by the end of October we were masters of Acre, Haifa, Damascus, Tripolis and Aleppo.

MESOPOTAMIA

Indian detachments reached Mesopotamia in November 1914, and occupied Basra and Kurma on the Tigris. Amara, higher up the river, was captured in June 1915, and Kut-el-Amara in September. General Townshend's forces then proceeded towards Baghdad, but their way was barred at Ctesiphon, and finding it impossible to break through the Turkish lines they retired on Kut, where in April 1916 they surrendered. In December 1916 a better organised offensive began, which in 1917 and 1918 captured Kut, Baghdad, Tekrit and Mosul.

SALONIKA.

Our troops on this front came from Gallipoli in December 1915, too late to stem the Bulgarian Advance against Serbia, but in August 1916 they began a general offensive along the Doiran front, and in September advanced across the Struma. Before the close of the year Monastir was recovered. In 1917 we were mainly concerned in the Doiran Advance, and in 1918 in a similar operation along the Vardar, which on September 30th ended in the victory of the Allies and the Armistice with Bulgaria.

AFRICA.

The Germans in Togoland were overcome by August 27th, 1914, while those in the Cameroons held out only one month longer. German South-West Africa proved more difficult to reduce owing to political complications, but it eventually surrendered to General Botha in July 1915. In East Africa the Germans kept up the struggle with success whilst hostilities continued in Europe, and ceased fighting on November 14th, 1918, in compliance with the terms of the Armistice.

THE NAVY.

The work of the Navy throughout the war was of boundless importance. Not only did she take command of the Seas in August 1914, but she kept it to the end. Of the Battles of Heligoland, Coronel and the Falkland Islands in 1914, the Dogger Bank and the Dardanelles in 1915, Jutland in 1916, the bombardments of Zeebrugge and Ostend in 1917, and the raids on Zeebrugge and Durazzo in 1918 the public have full information ; but of the smaller engagements in almost all waters of the globe, few have as yet any accurate knowledge.

ROYAL AIR FORCE. Still less do we know, except in a general way, of the work of the Royal Air Force, which arose in 1918 from the union of the R.F.C. and the R.N.A.S. Handicapped at first by lack of men and material, they soon became a highly efficient body, and proved of incalculable value to both the Army and the Navy. The heroic deeds of Major McCudden, Captain Leefe Robinson, Captain Ball, Lieutenant Warneford and many others, will for ever live in our memory.

The National Roll makes no claim to being a complete book of reference—in fact no such record could be compiled—but it may safely claim to supply a wonderful memorial of splendid services, truly worthy of the thankful remembrance of a grateful Empire.

To all who, by their Faith and Courage, helped to bring Victory to our Arms, we dedicate this book.

THE EDITOR.

1, York Place, Baker Street,
London, W.1.

———

THE NATIONAL ROLL OF THE
1914   GREAT WAR   1918

SECTION VII.

A

ABBETT, H., Private, R.A.M.C.
After joining in June 1916, in a line regiment, he was transferred to the R.A.M.C., and crossed to the Western Front in 1917. He rendered valuable medical service with his Corps in many important engagements, and was gassed near Cambrai. After returning to England he was demobilised in February 1920, and holds the General Service and Victory Medals.
19, Nealdon Street, Landor Road, S.W.9.   Z1002B

ABBETT, W., Rifleman, King's Royal Rifle Corps.
He joined in April 1918, while still under military age, and was going through his course of training when hostilities ceased. He was afterwards drafted to the Army of Occupation in Germany and rendered valuable services at Cologne and Dusseldorf. After his return to England he was demobilised in March 1920.
19, Nealdon Street, Landor Road, S.W.9.   Z1002A

ABBOTT, E. A., Private, South Wales Borderers.
Joining in February 1916, he was sent to France later in the year on the completion of his training. Whilst overseas he took part in many engagements of importance, including those at Vimy Ridge, the Ancre and Arras, and was wounded. After his recovery he went back to the lines, and was killed in action at Cambrai on November 26th, 1917. He was entitled to the General Service and Victory Medals.
7, Stockdale Road, Wandsworth Road, S.W.8.   Z1006

ABBOTT, F., L/Corporal, East Surrey Regiment.
He volunteered in August 1914, and was shortly afterwards drafted to the Western Front, where he fought in the important Battles of Loos, the Somme, Ypres, Passchendaele, Lens and Cambrai. In the last action he was badly wounded, but after hospital treatment in England returned to France and subsequently rendered valuable service as Traffic Controller. He was demobilised in 1920, after being six years with the Colours. and holds the 1914 Star, and the General Service and Victory Medals.
17, Lubeck Street, Battersea, S.W.11.   Z1003

ABBOTT, H. (M.S.M.), Sergt., Grenadier Guards.
A serving soldier, who enlisted in 1896, he crossed to France with the British Expeditionary Force at the outbreak of war. He remained overseas for four years, during which time he fought in many important engagements, notably the Retreat from Mons, and the Battles of Ypres and the Somme. He was awarded the Meritorious Service Medal for consistently good work in the Field, and after his return to England in 1918, was engaged on important duties as master shoemaker, in which capacity he was still serving at Pirbright in 1920. In addition to the decoration won in the Field, he holds the Mons Star, and the General Service and Victory Medals.
16A, Tennyson Street, Wentworth Street, S.W.8.   Z1005

ABEL, J., Sapper, R.E.
He volunteered in May 1915, and after his training served at various stations on important duties with his unit. He rendered valuable services in connection with telephones, and in the band, but was not successful owing to physical unfitness, in obtaining his transfer overseas before the cessation of hostilities. He was demobilised in October 1918. He had previously served for twelve years, over eight of which he spent in India.
12, Minnow Street, Walworth, S.E.17.   Z1000

ABEL, R., L/Cpl., Prince of Wales Leinster Regt.
He volunteered in the R.F.A. in 1915, but was shortly afterwards discharged owing to being under age. He subsequently re-enlisted and after the completion of his training was sent to the Western Front, where he took part in many important engagements. He returned home and was demobilised in 1919, and holds the General Service and Victory Medals.
97, Ingrave Street, Battersea, S.W.11.   Z1001

ABERDEEN, G., Private, Royal Fusiliers.
He volunteered in October 1915, and proceeded to France in the following year. He took part in numerous engagements, including those of Vimy Ridge, Passchendaele, and Beaumont-Hamel, and was wounded. In 1917 he was transferred to Italy, and served in the campaign against the Austrians, but in the following year returned to the Western Front, and was in action during the Retreat and Advance. He holds the General Service and Victory Medals, and was demobilised in March 1919.
26A, Avenue Road, Camberwell, S.E.5.   Z3288A

ABERY, F. H., Leading Aircraftsman, R.A.F.
He joined in November 1917, and after his training was engaged in important duties which called for a high degree of technical skill. He rendered valuable services, but was not able to secure his transfer to any battle area before the signing of the Armistice. He was demobilised in November 1919.
21, Alexandra Road, Southfield Road, Chiswick, W.4.   7681

ABSOLOM, A. J., Private, Oxfordshire and Buckinghamshire Light Infantry.
He joined in February 1917, and was drafted to France in January of the following year. He took part in various engagements on the Somme and Cambrai Fronts, and was wounded. After the Armistice he was transferred to Egypt, where he served at Tanta on important duties with his unit. He returned home and was demobilised in May 1919, and holds the General Service and Victory Medals.
36, Warrior Road, Camberwell, S.E.5.   Z1007A

ADAMS, A. H., Private (Signaller), 10th London Regt.
He joined in March 1916, and after completing his training was sent to the Western Front in the same year. He took part in the severe fighting in the Battles of the Somme, and Arras, and in other important engagements, and was wounded. He was demobilised in May 1919, and holds the General Service and Victory Medals.
69, Farmer's Road, Camberwell, S.E.5.   Z1008

ADAMS, B., Leading Stoker, R.N., H.M.S. "Conqueror."
He was serving at the outbreak of war, and was engaged with the Grand Fleet in the North Sea. He took part in the Battles of Jutland and Heligoland Bight, and was also engaged on important patrol and convoy duties until hostilities ceased. He was still serving in 1920, and holds the 1914–15 Star, and the General Service and Victory Medals.
176, Farmer's Road, Camberwell, S.E.5.   Z1010A

ADAMS, C., Gunner, R.F.A.
He joined in 1916, and in the following year, after completing his training, was drafted to Salonika, where he took an active part in numerous engagements on the Doiran front, and in the Advance on Vardar. He was demobilised in February 1919 after returning home, and holds the General Service and Victory Medals.
16, Love Lane, Stockwell Road, S.W.9.   Z1015

ADAMS, E., A.B., R.N., H.M.S. "Iris."
He joined in August 1917, and was engaged in the North Sea on H.M.S. "Iris" on important mine-sweeping duties. He rendered valuable services until after hostilities ceased, and was demobilised in April 1919, holding the General Service and Victory Medals.
12, Cologne Road, Battersea, S.W.11.   Z1014

ADAMS, G. H., Rifleman, 18th London Regiment (London Irish Rifles) and Private, M.G.C.
He volunteered in July 1915, and after his training was drafted in 1916 to Egypt. Later he proceeded to Palestine, where he took part with General Allenby's Forces in many important engagements up to the taking of Jerusalem. He was demobilised in October 1919, after his return to England, and holds the General Service and Victory Medals.
176, Farmer's Road, Camberwell, S.E.5.   Z1010C

ADAMS, H. H., Private, 25th London Regt. (Cyclists).
He attested at the commencement of hostilities, and was rejected, but in 1917 was called up and drafted to Egypt in the following year. He served with General Allenby's Forces in the Offensive on Palestine, and was in action at Jericho, and in various subsequent engagements. He returned home and was demobilised in 1919, and holds the General Service and Victory Medals.
5, Headley Street, Nunhead, S.E.15.   Z6133

ADAMS, J. E., Rifleman, 21st London Regiment (1st Surrey Rifles).
Joining in March 1917, he was sent to France in June of the same year. He took part in various engagements, and was killed in action near Messines on August 30th, 1917. He was entitled to the General Service and Victory Medals.
84, Wickersley Road, Lavender Hill, S.W.11.   Z1013

ADAMS, J. L., Gunner, R.F.A.
Volunteering in September 1914, he was drafted overseas in the following year, and whilst in France fought at La Bassée and Loos, and was wounded and invalided home. On recovery he returned to the fighting area, and was in action at Ypres, Passchendaele, and various other engagements with the Trench Mortar Batteries until the close of the war. He was demobilised in February 1919, and holds the 1914–15 Star, and the General Service and Victory Medals.
70, Copeland Road, Peckham Rye, S.E.15.   Z5555

ADAMS, J. T., Cpl., 3rd (King's Own) Hussars.
He was serving at the outbreak of war and was immediately afterwards sent to the Western Front, where he took part in the severe fighting in the Retreat from Mons and in many other engagements, and was twice wounded. In 1915 he was transferred to Egypt, and later Palestine. He took an active part in various engagements in General Allenby's campaign, including those leading up to the capture of Jerusalem. He was demobilised in June 1919, and holds the Mons Star, and the General Service and Victory Medals.
176, Farmer's Road, Camberwell, S.E.5.   Z1010B

ADAMS, J. T., Private, 6th South Staffordshire Regt.
He joined in September 1916, and in the following February was drafted to France. After taking part in several engagements he died gloriously on the Field of Battle at Cambrai on December 17th, 1917. He was entitled to the General Service and Victory Medals.
" He died the noblest death a man may die.
     Fighting for God and right and liberty."
12C, Lewis Trust Buildings, Warner Road, Camberwell, S.E.5.   Z5867

ADAMS, R. J., Gunner, 136th Battery, R.F.A.
Mobilised from the Reserve at the outbreak of war he proceeded overseas in the following year. Whilst in France he took part in many notable engagements until the conclusion of hostilities, and was gassed. In June 1919 he returned home and was demobilised, holding the 1914–15 Star, and the General Service and Victory Medals.
38, Cator Street, Peckham, S.E.15.   Z4388

ADAMS, W., Private, 1st Queen's (Royal West Surrey Regiment).
He enlisted in March 1914, and on the outbreak of war was drafted to the Western Front, where he took part in the Retreat from Mons and the Battles of the Marne, the Aisne and Neuve Chapelle and was wounded. He was later transferred to Italy and served in the Offensive of 1918. He returned home and was sent to Ireland, where he was still serving in 1920. He holds the Mons Star, and the General Service and Victory Medals.
112, Avenue Road, Camberwell, S.E.5.   Z1012A

ADAMS, W. A. (M.M.), Driver, R.F.A.
He volunteered in April 1915, and after his training was drafted to the Western Front, where he took part in the severe fighting at Ypres, Loos, the Somme and in many other engagements of importance until hostilities ceased. He was awarded the Military Medal for bravery in the Field, and also holds the 1914–15 Star, and the General Service and Victory Medals. He was demobilised in March 1919.
37A, Stainford Road, Battersea, S.W.11.   Z1169

ADAMS, W. H., Corporal Shoeing Smith, R.F.A.
He volunteered in November 1914, and in February of the following year was drafted to the Western Front, where he took part in numerous engagements, including those at Ypres, the Somme and Arras. While attending to his horses he met with an accident which necessitated his being invalided home. He was demobilised in March 1919, and holds the 1914–15 Star, and the General Service and Victory Medals.
6, Torrens Street, Clapham, S.W.4.   Z1009

ADAMS, W. R., Private, Bedfordshire and Hertfordshire Regiments.
Joining in November 1917 he was drafted to France in the same year. He took part in the severe fighting at Cambrai Ypres and various other engagements. He returned home and after further valuable service at Ripon was demobilised in March 1920, holding the General Service and Victory Medals.
87, Robertson Street, Wandsworth Road, S.W.8.   Z1011

ADDRISON, F. A., Private, 5th Queen's (Royal West Surrey Regiment).
He joined in August 1916, and in the following January was drafted to Mesopotamia, where he did valuable work at Basra, Hit, Mosul and other places for three years, and was for a time engaged in important duties on the staff. He was demobilised in February 1920, after his return to England, and holds the General Service and Victory Medals.
3, Comber Grove, Camberwell, S.E.5.   Z1170

AINSWORTH, C., A.B., Merchant Marine, H.M.S. " Highland Leader."
He joined in March 1917, and was posted to H.M.S. " Highland Leader." In this and other vessels he was engaged on important patrol duties in the North and many other seas. He was demobilised in May 1919, and holds the General Service and the Mercantile Marine War Medals.
32, Lockington Road, Battersea Park Road, S.W.8.   Z1016

ALBERT, A. T. (M.M.), Pte., Highland Light Infantry.
He enlisted in 1910, and proceeding on the declaration of hostilities took part in the Retreat from Mons. He also served at Neuve Chapelle, St. Julien 60, and many subsequent engagements, and in 1915 was awarded the Military Medal for distinguished bravery in the Field. He was demobilised in March 1919, after over four and a half years' service, and holds in addition to the Military Medal, the Mons Star, and the General Service and Victory Medals.
25, Meyrick Road, Battersea, S.W.11.   Z1017

ALDERMAN, F. W., Gunner, R.F.A. and L/Cpl., 21st London Regiment.
Volunteering in November 1914, he proceeded to France on the completion of his training. Whilst in this theatre of war he was in action at Roclincourt, Arras, Vimy Ridge, St. Eloi, St. Quentin and many other places. In 1917 he was drafted to Salonika and served on the Doiran and Vardar fronts. In the following year he crossed to Egypt and did much valuable service at Ismailia and Kantara before joining the expedition into Palestine. While there he fought at Beersheba, Gaza, Jerusalem, Bethlehem, Jericho, the Jordan, Es Salt and Ammon, where he was wounded. After his return to England he was demobilised in May 1919, and holds the General Service and Victory Medals.
45, Stonhouse Street, Clapham, S.W.4.   Z1016

ALDERMAN, W., Gunner, R.F.A. and R.G.A.
He volunteered in May 1915, and in March of the following year was drafted to the Western Front, where he took part in the severe fighting at the Somme, Beaumont-Hamel, Messines and in many other engagements. He was later transferred to the R.G.A. Anti-Aircraft Section, and served in the Retreat and Advance of 1918. He was demobilised in February 1919, and holds the General Service and Victory Medals.
137, Cronin Road, Peckham, S.E.15.   Z5310

ALDERSLEY, C. H., Rifleman, Royal Irish Rifles.
Joining in February 1916 he went through his course of training, and in the following June was drafted to France. While there he took part in many engagements of importance, including those at Albert, Vimy Ridge, the Somme, Arras and Ypres, and served also in the Retreat and Advance of 1918. He was severely wounded in the hand at Cambrai, and lost four of his fingers in consequence. He was discharged as unfit for further service in February 1919, and holds the General Service and Victory Medals.
26, Northampton Place, Walworth, S.E.17.   Z2903B

ALDERTON, C. (M.S.M.), Sapper, R.E.
He volunteered in September 1914, and in the following year was drafted to the Western Front, where he served in numerous engagements, including those of Ypres, Loos, the Somme, and Cambrai, and was gassed. He was awarded the Meritorious Service Medal for devotion to duty, and also holds the 1914–15 Star, and the General Service and Victory Medals, and was demobilised in July 1919.
4, Eythorne Road, Stockwell, S.W.9.   Z3416B. Z3417B

ALDERTON, F., Sergt., R.F.A.
He volunteered in April 1915, and in the same year was drafted to the Western Front, where he served in various engagements, including those at Vimy Ridge, the Somme, Ypres and Poperinghe. He was demobilised in August 1919, and holds the 1914–15 Star, and the General Service and Victory Medals.
4, Eythorne Road, Stockwell, S.W.9.   Z3416A. Z3417A

ALDOUS, A., Rifleman, 21st London Regiment (1st Surrey Rifles).
He volunteered in April 1915, and later in the same year was drafted to France. Whilst in this theatre of war he fought at Ypres, Loos, Vimy Ridge, the Somme and Beaumont-Hamel, and was wounded. After his recovery he was drafted to Egypt, and served with the British Forces in the Advance through Palestine. Being again severely wounded in action he was invalided to hospital in Egypt, and later in England. He was demobilised in March 1919, and holds the General Service and Victory Medals.
12, Arlesford Road, Landor Road, S.W.9. Z1168

ALDRIDGE, T., Private, 20th London Regiment.
Joining in March 1916, he proceeded in July of the same year to the Western Front. There he fought in many engagements, including those of the Somme, Ypres and Cambrai, and was wounded and gassed. He was invalided home, but on recovery returning to the fighting area took part in the Retreat and Advance of 1918, during which he was again wounded. In October 1919 he was demobilised, and holds the General Service and Victory Medals.
43, Harris Street, Camberwell, S.E.5. Z4389B

ALDRIDGE, W., Gunner, R.F.A.
He volunteered in February 1915, and in the same year was drafted to the Western Front, where he took part in numerous engagements, including the Battles of Arras and the Somme, where he was wounded in March 1918, during the Retreat. On his recovery he took part in the Advance and after the Armistice proceeded to Germany with the Army of Occupation, and served at Cologne until July 1919, when he returned to England, and was demobilised, holding the 1914-15 Star, and the General Service and Victory Medals.
24, Kay Road, Landor Road, S.W.9. Z1018

ALEXANDER, A., Guardsman, Coldstream Guards.
A serving soldier who enlisted in June 1906, he was sent to France on the declaration of war, and took part in the engagements at Mons, Le Cateau, Maubeuge and the Marne. He was twice wounded in action, and was taken prisoner in September 1914. After being in captivity in Germany until after the Armistice, he was released and was demobilised in March 1919. He holds the Mons Star, and the General Service and Victory Medals.
33, Dalyell Road, Landor Road, S.W.9. Z1034

ALEXANDER, F., Rifleman, 20th King's Royal Rifle Corps.
He joined in September 1918, and after the conclusion of his training was drafted to France. At a later date he proceeded to Germany with the Army of Occupation and did much valuable service there until February 1920, when he returned home and was demobilised.
118, Maysoule Road, Battersea, S.W.11. Z1035

ALEXANDER, F. H., Private, Queen's (Royal West Surrey Regiment).
He joined in 1916, and in the same year proceeded to the Western Front, where he took part in the fierce fighting on the Somme. He died gloriously on the Field of battle at Ploegsteert Wood on August 12th, 1916, after being in France only a few months. He was entitled to the General Service and Victory Medals.
  "A valiant soldier with undaunted heart, he breasted life's last hill."
19, Crawshay Road, Stockwell, S.W.9. Z4390

ALFORD, J., Private, 8th Queen's (Royal West Surrey Regiment).
After volunteering in November 1915, he went through his course of training, and in 1916 crossed to France. He saw much severe fighting at Vermelles, Armentières and Hulluch, and was badly injured by an explosion. After considerable hospital treatment in France, and at home, he was discharged in August 1917, as medically unfit for further duty. He holds the General Service and Victory Medals.
2, Gladstone Terrace, Battersea, S.W.8. Z2805

ALGATE, W. C., Private, 17th Royal Fusiliers.
He joined in June 1916, and in the following November, on completing his training was drafted to France, where he served in the Somme area until 1919. He suffered throughout his service from ill-health, and was demobilised in March 1919. He holds the General Service and Victory Medals.
50, Robertson Street, Clapham, S.W.8. Z1020

ALLBRIGHT, V., Gunner, R.G.A.
He volunteered in November 1915, and in the following year was drafted to France where he did good work as a gunner in numerous engagements, especially in the Advance of 1918. After the Armistice was signed he proceeded to Germany with the Army of Occupation, remaining until his demobilisation in August 1919. He holds the General Service and Victory Medals.
26, Bognor Street, Wandsworth Road, S.W.8. Z1021A

ALLCHIN, C. D., Driver, R.F.A.
Volunteering in 1914, he was sent to France in February of the following year. He took part in many important engagements, including those at Hill 60, Ypres, Festubert, Loos, Vimy Ridge, the Somme, Bullecourt and Cambrai, and in the Retreat and Advance of 1918. He was demobilised in March 1919, holding the 1914-15 Star, and the General Service and Victory Medals.
11, Atwell Street, Rye Lane, S.E.15. Z5311

ALLCHURCH, H. F. W., Corporal, Tank Corps.
He volunteered in April 1915, and in the same month was drafted to France, where he did much valuable work in the mechanical department of the Tank Corps at Etaples. Later he was sent to Egypt, and thence to Palestine, where he fought in the three Battles of Gaza, and in many other engagements. He was present at the entry into Jerusalem. He afterwards returned to France, and was then sent home to be demobilised in June 1919. He holds the 1914-15 Star, and the General Service and Victory Medals.
55, St. John's Hill Grove, Battersea, S.W.11. Z1022

ALLCHURCH, H. S., Signalman, R.N.V.R.
He joined the Navy on attaining military age in September 1917, and after much valuable service in the North Sea, proceeded on a trawler to Italy. He was subsequently posted to H.M.S. "Queen," in which he served as a Signalman until October 1919, when he was demobilised after his return to England. He holds the General Service and Victory Medals.
129, Tyneham Road, Lavender Hill, S.W.11. Z1023

ALLDEN, B., Driver, R.F.A.
He volunteered in January 1915, at the age of sixteen and a half, and in the following July was drafted to the Western Front. During his service in France he was in action at the Somme, Ypres and Arras, and in various subsequent engagements until the cessation of hostilities. He was demobilised in February 1919, and holds the 1914-15 Star, and the General Service and Victory Medals.
61, Mayall Road, Herne Hill, S.E.24. Z1787

ALLDEN, W. B., Pioneer, R.E.
He joined in March 1918, and after having completed his training served at various stations on important duties with his unit. He rendered valuable services, but was not successful in obtaining his transfer overseas prior to the cessation of hostilities. He was demobilised in December 1918.
88, Geneva Road, Coldharbour Lane, Stockwell, S.W.9. Z3054A

ALLEN, A. B., Corporal, Labour Corps.
He volunteered in 1915, and later in the same year was drafted to France, where he served for a time in the Ypres sector. Owing to a breakdown in health he returned to England in the following year and was afterwards engaged on important duties in connection with the manufacture and repair of Army boots until 1919, when he was demobilised. He holds the 1914-15 Star, and the General Service and Victory Medals.
11, Chalmer's Street, Wandsworth Road, S.W.8. Z1031

ALLEN, A. E., A.B., R.N., H.M.S. "Lark," "Silk," and "North Star."
He joined in May 1909, and on the outbreak of war was stationed at Harwich, but was immediately ordered to sea, and on August 5th, 1914, was in action in the engagement in which the German mine-layer "Königin Luise" was sunk. Later he took part in the Battles of Heligoland Bight, the Dogger Bank, and Jutland, and also served in the Zeebrugge raid, during which H.M.S. "North Star," in which he was serving, was sunk. Fortunately he was amongst the rescued, but he had received such severe shock that he was rendered unfit for further service, and returned to England and was discharged in February 1919. He holds the 1914-15 Star, and the General Service and Victory Medals.
16, Clock Place, Hampden Street, Walworth Road, Walworth, S.E.17. Z26128

ALLEN, A. H., Rifleman, Rifle Brigade and Trench Mortar Battery.
After joining in 1916, he went through his course of training, and later in the year on its completion was drafted to the Western Front. He served with a Trench Mortar Battery in the Battles of the Somme and Ypres, and was killed in action on September 20th, 1917. He was buried near Gheluvelt, and was entitled to the General Service and Victory Medals.
117, Barlow Street, Walworth, S.E.17. Z1028A

ALLEN, B., Driver, R.A.S.C. (H.T.)
Mobilised on the declaration of war he almost immediately embarked for the Western Front, and served in the Battle of Mons, where he was wounded. He was invalided home and on recovery returned to the fighting line, and served with the 46th Division in many engagements until the Armistice. Returning home in April 1919 he was demobilised, holding the Mons Star, and the General Service and Victory Medals.
28, Pentridge Street, Peckham, S.E.15. Z5558

ALLEN, C. J., Rifleman, King's Royal Rifle Corps.
Joining in May 1917 he proceeded to the Western Front in the following January. Whilst overseas he took part in much of the severe fighting in the Arras sector, and in many other engagements, including that of Cambrai. He suffered from dysentery, and was invalided home. On his recovery he was drafted to India, where in 1920 he was still serving. He holds the General Service and Victory Medals.
87B, Albany Road, Camberwell, S.E.5. Z5557

ALLEN, F., Rifleman, Rifle Brigade.
He joined in June 1916, and in the same year was drafted to the Western Front. During his service in France he was in action at the Ancre, Ypres and Bullecourt, and in many later engagements. He was twice wounded and was taken prisoner in the Allied Advance in November 1918. After captivity in Germany for a short time he was repatriated, and subsequently demobilised in September 1919. He holds the General Service and Victory Medals.
1, Bolton Street, Camberwell, S.E.5. Z1025

ALLEN, F. C., Private, Queen's Own (Royal West Kent Regiment).
He joined in July 1916, and in the same year was drafted to Mesopotamia. Whilst in this theatre of war he took part in the engagements at Samara, Kut-el-Amara, Baghdad, Mosul and Tekrit, and for a time suffered from an illness which kept him in hospital. He returned home and was demobilised in May 1919, and holds the General Service and Victory Medals.
27, St. Alphonsus Road, Clapham, S.W.4. Z1027

ALLEN, F. J., Driver, R.F.A.
He volunteered in December 1914, and in November of the following year was drafted to France. Whilst in this theatre of war he did excellent work as a driver for his Battery at Loos, Albert, Ploegsteert Wood, Vimy Ridge, the Somme, Arras, Ypres and Cambrai, and in many subsequent engagements in the Retreat and Advance of 1918. He was demobilised in December 1918, and holds the 1914-15 Star, and the General Service and Victory Medals.
15, Duffield Street, Battersea, S.W.11. Z1029B

ALLEN, H., Private, 1st East Surrey Regiment.
He volunteered in February 1916, and in the following September was drafted to France. While overseas he took part in very severe fighting near Ypres, and was seriously wounded in October of the same year. After his recovery he was transferred to the Royal Defence Corps, and rendered valuable service at various stations on important defence duties until February 1919, when he was demobilised. He holds the General Service and Victory Medals.
19, Horseman Street, Camberwell, S.E.5. Z1024A

ALLEN, H. G., Private, Labour Corps.
He joined in 1916, and after his training was completed was engaged at his depôt on important duties with his unit. He rendered valuable services, but was not successful in obtaining his transfer overseas before the cessation of hostilities. He was demobilised in 1919.
26, Arlesford Road, Stockwell, S.W.9. Z1568D. Z1569D

ALLEN, J., Rifleman, King's Royal Rifle Corps.
He joined in November 1916, and after his training was drafted with his Regiment to India, where he served on important duties until he was sent to Salonika. Whilst in this theatre of war he fought in many important engagements, and frequently during his service in the East suffered from malaria. He was demobilised on his return to England in September 1919, and holds the General Service and Victory Medals.
15, Duffield Street, Battersea, S.W.11. Z1029A

ALLEN, J. K., Driver, R.F.A.
He volunteered at the outbreak of war, and in November of the same year was drafted to France, where he did good work as a driver in numerous engagements. He was present at the Battles of Neuve Chapelle, Ypres, Ploegsteert Wood, the Somme, Arras, the Ancre, Bullecourt, Vermelles and Passchendaele Ridge, and was gassed. In consequence of severe illness he was invalided home, and after much treatment in hospital was eventually discharged in October 1918 as medically unfit for further duty. He holds the 1914 Star, and the General Service and Victory Medals.
47, Gloucester Road, Peckham, S.E.15. Z5869B

ALLEN, S. H., Private, 5th Essex Regiment.
He volunteered in July 1915, and in the following November was drafted to Egypt, where he saw much service. He took part in the engagements at Agagia, Sollum, Jifjaffa, Katia, El Fasher, Romani and Magdhaba, and also fought in the Offensive in Palestine under General Allenby at Rafa and Gaza, and was present at the fall of Jerusalem. He returned home and was demobilised in March 1919, and holds the 1914-15 Star, and the General Service and Victory Medals.
8, Smyrks Road, Walworth, S.E.17. Z1026

ALLEN, R. A., Driver, R.F.A.
Volunteering in July 1915, he was afterwards drafted to the Western Front. During his service in France he did good work as a driver in various sectors, but suffered from shell-shock, and was invalided home to hospital. He was discharged as medically unfit for further military duty in July 1916, and holds the General Service and Victory Medals.
79, Bramber Road, West Kensington, W.14. 15720B

ALLEN, S. A., L/Corporal, Royal Fusiliers.
He volunteered in May 1915, and after the completion of his training was drafted to France. While on that front he fought at Arras, and in many other engagements, and was wounded in action. Later he was sent to Malta, and after a period of service there returned to France until March 1919, when he returned home and was demobilised. He holds the General Service and Victory Medals.
15, Duffield Street, Battersea, S.W.11. Z1029C

ALLEN, T. R., Private, 1st Royal Irish Fusiliers.
Joining in the Queen's in August 1917, he was afterwards transferred to the Royal Irish Fusiliers, and on the completion of his training was drafted to the Western Front. He took part in many important engagements in the Retreat of the Allies in 1918, and was taken prisoner in July. After five months' captivity in Germany he was repatriated and was demobilised in January 1919, holding the General Service and Victory Medals.
11, Kinglake Street, Walworth, S.E.17. Z1030

ALLEN, W. C., Private, 23rd London Regiment.
He joined the 23rd London Regiment in April 1914, and was mobilised at the outbreak of war. After serving at various stations on important duties he was drafted to France in November 1916. During his service on the Western Front, he fought at Arras, Messines, Ypres and Cambrai, and in August 1918, was wounded and taken prisoner in action at Bray, near Albert. During his captivity in Germany, he was employed in making railway trucks, and loading up German aeroplanes with bombs. He was repatriated in February 1919, and demobilised in the same month, holding the General Service and Victory Medals.
2, Bennerley Road, Battersea, S.W.11. Z1171

ALLEN, W. G., 1st Air Mechanic, R.A.F. (late R.F.C.)
He joined in November 1916, and after having completed his training was sent to Canada as a drill instructor to the Canadian Army. He rendered valuable services, but was not able to obtain his transfer to a fighting front owing to physical disability. He was demobilised in February 1919.
9, Copeland Road, Peckham Rye, S.E.15. Z5556A

ALLEN, W. H., Sergt. R.F.A.
He volunteered in September 1914, and in April of the following year was drafted to France, where he was in action at Ypres and Loos. He was unfortunately killed by shrapnel in the Battle of Loos on October 24th, 1915, and was entitled to the 1914-15 Star, and the General Service and Victory Medals.
"A costly sacrifice upon the altar of freedom."
9, Wivenhoe Road, Peckham, S.E.15. Z5870

ALLINGTON, C., Gunner, R.G.A.
He joined in February 1916, and after his training was engaged at Aldershot and other stations on important duties with his Battery until 1918, when he was drafted to the Western Front. While overseas he served in various sectors and did much valuable work until hostilities ceased. He was demobilised in January 1919, and holds the General Service and Victory Medals.
24, Gladstone Terrace, Battersea Park Road, S.W.8. Z1032

ALLSO, J., Petty Officer, R.N., H.M.S. "Conqueror."
He was serving at the outbreak of war and throughout the course of hostilities was engaged with the Grand Fleet in the North Sea. He took part in the Battle of Jutland and was in the "Reserve" at the Dogger Bank. He was also employed on special control work and in escorting food ships arriving from the United States of America. He was demobilised in February 1919, and holds the 1914-15 Star, and the General Service with (two clasps) and Victory Medals.
8, Alfreton Street, Walworth, S.E.17. Z1033

ALLSOPP, C. W. J., Steward, H.M.T. "Durham Castle" and "Saxon."
He volunteered in July 1915, and rendered valuable services until the end of the war in connection with the transport of troops to and from America, Africa and Australia. He holds the Mercantile Marine, and the General Service and Victory Medals, and was still serving in 1920.
4, Radnor Street, King's Road, S.W.3. X23016

ALMOND, J. R., Private, Labour Corps.
He joined in 1916, and after his training was drafted to France in the same year. He was engaged on road construction and other important duties with his unit and rendered valuable services. After the Armistice he proceeded with the Army of Occupation to Germany. After his return to England he was demobilised in October 1919, holding the General Service and Victory Medals.
81, Westmacott Street, Camberwell, S.E.5. Z3989

ALSEPT, A. G., Private, 15th (The King's) Hussars.
He was mobilised in August 1914, and in the next month was drafted to France, where he served in many sectors, including those of the Somme and Ypres. In 1916 he was discharged from causes due to his service, but in August 1918, he rejoined in the Royal Army Service Corps, and after the Armistice proceeded to Germany, where he remained until May 1919, when he was demobilised. He holds the 1914 Star, and the General Service and Victory Medals.
7, Northlands Street, Camberwell, S.E.5.   L6135

ALSOP, F. W., Private, 24th London Regiment.
He volunteered in June 1915, and in the following October was sent overseas. During his service in France he fought in various engagements, including those at Ypres, and on the Somme, where he was wounded and invalided home. On recovery he rejoined his unit in France in April 1917, and was again severely wounded, at Vimy Ridge, in the following July. He was sent back to hospital in England and after treatment was eventually invalided out of the Service in May 1919. He holds the 1914-15 Star, nd the General Service and Victory Medals. 40, Lilford Road, Camberwell S.E.5.   Z6134

AMENT, H. C., Private, R.A.S.C.
He enlisted in August 1913, and was sent to France in August 1914. He served at Mons, La Bassée, and in many other engagements, and in 1916 was sent home for a course of training. He afterwards proceeded to Mesopotamia, where he rendered valuable service. He was demobilised in June 1919, holding the Mons Star, and the General Service and Victory Medals.
23, Sandover Road, Albany Road, Camberwell. S.E.5.   Z5312

AMES, H. C., Petty Officer, Royal Naval Division.
He volunteered in 1914, and in March 1915 was sent to Gallipoli, where he did good service until the evacuation in December of the same year. He was afterwards transferred to France, and during the voyage his vessel was torpedoed. He took part in many engagements, including those in the Beaumont-Hamel and Cambrai sectors, and was mentioned in Despatches for his good work. He was invalided home in consequence of being gassed twice, and discharged as medically unfit for further service in January 1919. He holds the 1914-15 Star, and the General Service and Victory Medals.
22, Oberstein Road, Battersea, S.W.11.   Z1037

AMES, O. (M.M.), Driver, R.F.A.
He volunteered in October 1914, at the age of sixteen, and served on important duties with his Battery until December 1916, when he was drafted to France. While overseas he took part in the severe fighting at Arras, Messines, Ypres, Lens, Cambrai and the Somme, and also served in the Retreat and Advance of 1918, and was twice wounded. After the Armistice he was drafted to Germany with the Army of Occupation, and on his return home was demobilised in May 1919. He was awarded the Military Medal for conspicuous bravery in the Field, when horses stampeded, and also holds the General Service and Victory Medals.
42, Santley Street, Ferndale Road, S.W.4.   Z1036

AMEY, A. E., Private, Queen's (Royal West Surrey Regiment).
He joined in September 1917, and after his training was drafted to France. He was in action at Cambrai and afterwards contracting dysentery, was sent down to the Base. On his recovery he returned to the front line. He later proceeded with the Army of Occupation to Germany. He was demobilised in November 1919, and holds the General Service and Victory Medals.
13, Atherton Street, Battersea, S.W.11.   Z1038B

AMEY, A. G., Private, East Surrey Regiment.
He volunteered in September 1914, and in the following year was drafted to the Western Front, where he took part in numerous engagements, including those at St. Eloi, Ypres, Loos, Messines and Cambrai, and was severely gassed. He was invalided home and subsequently discharged as medically unfit for further service in August 1918. He holds the 1914-15 Star, and the General Service and Victory Medals.
45, Stockdale Road, Wandsworth Road, S.W.8.   Z1039

AMEY, W., Pte., 2nd London Regt. (Royal Fusiliers).
He joined in March 1916, and completing his training was sent to the Western Front. He took part in the severe fighting at Cambrai, and was badly wounded. He was invalided home and demobilised in November 1918, and holds the General Service and Victory Medals.
13, Atherton Street, Battersea, S.W.11.   Z1038A

AMOR, F. T., Gunner, R.F.A.
Volunteering in February 1915, he was sent to France in July of the same year. He took part in numerous engagements of importance, including those at Givenchy, Armentières, Ypres and the Somme, and was wounded and gassed. He was invalided home and discharged as medically unfit for further military duty in November 1918, and holds the 1914-15 Star, and the General Service and Victory Medals.
21, Elfin Road, Camberwell, S.E.5   Z1040

ANDERSON, A., Private, R.A.S.C. and Royal Warwickshire Regiment.
He volunteered in August 1914, and was sent to France in the same month. He served on important transport duties with the R.A.S.C. for two years, and was then transferred to the Royal Warwickshire Regiment, in which he served as a stretcher bearer in numerous engagements. He later proceeded to India, where he was still serving in 1920, and holds the 1914 Star, and the General Service and Victory Medals.
33, Salisbury Row, Walworth, S.E.17.   Z1042A

ANDERSON, A. J., Gunner, R.F.A.
He joined in April 1916, and in September of the same year was drafted to Mesopotamia, where he took part in numerous engagements, including those at Kut-el-Amara, the Turkish rout in February 1917, and the capture of Baghdad, Ramadieh and Baghdadie. He returned home and was demobilised in January 1919, and holds the General Service and Victory Medals.
33, Lavender Road, Battersea, S.W.11.   Z1041

ANDERSON, R., Shoeing Smith, R.F.A.
He volunteered in May 1915, and was drafted to the Western Front in the same year. He took part in the severe fighting on the Somme and was killed by shell fire in action on July 25th, 1916. He was entitled to the 1914-15 Star, and the General Service and Victory Medals.
9, Nealdon Street, Landor Road, S.W.9.

ANDERSON, R. H. T., Driver, R.F.A.
He volunteered at the outbreak of war, and proceeded to France in March 1915. During his service there he was in action at Loos and the Somme, and was afterwards drafted to Salonika. After much good work as a driver in various operations on the Balkan front, he was sent to Egypt, and served throughout the Palestine Offensive until the Armistice. He returned home and was demobilised in April 1919, and holds the 1914-15 Star, and the General Service and Victory Medals.
41, Flaxman Road, Camberwell, S.E.5.   Z5871

ANDERSON, R. J., Sapper, R.E.
He joined in May 1916, and on the completion of his training was drafted overseas. Whilst on the Western Front he was in action at the Somme, Cambrai and many other engagements until hostilities ceased. In March 1919, he returned home and was demobilised, holding the General Service and Victory Medals.
90, East Surrey Grove, Peckham, S.E.15.   Z5025

ANDERSON, W., Driver, R.F.A.
He volunteered in November 1914, and was sent to France in September of the following year, and served in the Arras and Albert sectors for two months, after which he was transferred to Salonika. Here he served in various engagements on the Doiran front, and also in the Advance into Bulgaria. During his service in this theatre of war he suffered from malarial fever. He holds the 1914-15 Star, and the General Service and Victory Medals, and was still serving in 1920.
95, Lavender Road, Battersea, S.W.11.   Z1043

ANDREW, F. W., Sapper, R.E.
He volunteered in May 1915, and in the same year was drafted to France. Whilst overseas he was engaged on important duties in connection with the operations, and was frequently in the forward areas, notably at Loos, Ypres, the Somme, Arras, and the Retreat and Advance of 1918. He returned home, and was demobilised in March 1919, and holds the 1914-15 Star, and the General Service and Victory Medals.
36, Gordon Road, Nunhead, S.E.15.   Z6132

ANDREW, W. J., Sapper, R.E.
He joined in December 1916, and in January of the following year was drafted to France. Whilst there he was engaged in the construction of the light railways on the Somme, and also helped to convey ammunition and troops to the fighting areas. Later he met with an accident and was invalided home. In October 1918 he was discharged as medically unfit, and holds the General Service and Victory Medals.
102, Warriner Gardens, Battersea, S.W.11.   Z1045

ANDREWS, A. H., Rifleman, Royal Irish Rifles.
He joined in February 1917, and was sent to Ireland to complete his training. In June of the same year he proceeded to the Western Front, he met with an accident, and was invalided home. On recovery he was again drafted overseas, and whilst en route his ship was torpedoed, but fortunately he was rescued and finally landed in France. He took part in the heavy fighting on the Somme, and was wounded during the Retreat on March 27th, 1918. He was invalided home, and in September of the same year was discharged as medically unfit, and holds the General Service and Victory Medals.
29, Hasker Street, Chelsea, S.W.3.   24866

ANDREWS, C., Gunner, R.G.A.

He volunteered in August 1914, and in May of the following year was drafted to the Western Front. There he fought in many notable battles, including those of Festubert, Loos, Vimy Ridge, the Somme, Arras, Messines, Ypres, Cambrai and Bapaume, and was twice wounded. He holds the 1914-15 Star, and the General Service and Victory Medals, and in 1920 was still serving.

64, Bagshot Street, Walworth, S.E.17.   Z1048

ANDREWS, C. G., Private, M.G.C.

He volunteered in March 1915, and in September of the same year was drafted to the Western Front, where he took part in various engagements, including those at Loos, Ploegsteert Wood, Arras, Messines and Ypres. He was killed in action at Ypres on August 22nd, 1917, and was entitled to the 1914-15 Star, and the General Service and Victory Medals.

"Steals on the ear the distant triumph song."

8, Claude Road, Peckham Rye, S.E.15.   Z5709

ANDREWS, C. H., Private, 4th Royal Fusiliers.

He volunteered in September 1914, and after a period of training proceeded to the Western Front. There he took part in the fighting in various sectors, including the Somme, Arras, and Ypres, where he was wounded. In January 1919, he was demobilised, and holds the General Service and Victory Medals.

15, Vicarage Road, Camberwell, S.E.5.   Z1786

ANDREWS, D. W., Sapper, R.E.

He volunteered in March 1915, and in the same year was drafted to France, where he was engaged in laying mines, and fixing barbed wire entanglements. Later he took part in the fighting at Arras, and the Somme, and was killed in action at Hamel in March 1918. He was entitled to the 1914-15 Star, and the General Service and Victory Medals.

65, Camilla Road, Rotherhithe, S.E.16.   Z26344A

ANDREWS, F. J., Driver, R.A.S.C. (M.T.)

He volunteered in May 1915, and in the same year was drafted to France, where he was engaged in transporting anti-aircraft guns to various sectors of the front. After the cessation of hostilities, he proceeded with the Army of Occupation to Germany, remaining there until he returned home and was demobilised in June 1919, holding the 1914-15 Star, and the General Service and Victory Medals.

65, Camilla Road, Rotherhithe, S.E.16.   Z26344B

ANDREWS, G., B.S.M., R.H.A.

Volunteering in November 1915, he was drafted early in the following year to the Western Front. Whilst there he took part in the fighting at Ypres, the Somme, Arras, and Cambrai, and was severely gassed and invalided to England. On recovery he was sent to India and later to Mesopotamia, where he saw much active service. In November 1919, he returned to England and was demobilised. He holds the General Service and Victory Medals.

11, Montefiore Street, Wandsworth Road, S.W.8.   Z1050A

ANDREWS, G. E., Driver, R.A.S.C.

He joined in May 1918, and after his training was drafted to Egypt in the same year. He was engaged in the transport of supplies and water to the troops in Palestine under General Allenby, and rendered valuable services. He returned home and was demobilised in 1919, and holds the General Service and Victory Medals.

33, Russell Road, Peckham, S.E.15.   Z5313A

ANDREWS, S. W., Private, Middlesex Regiment.

He volunteered in January 1915, and on the completion of his training was drafted to the Western Front. Whilst there he took part in the fighting at Loos and Ypres, and was severely wounded, and invalided home. He was discharged as medically unfit in April 1916, and holds the 1914-15 Star, and the General Service and Victory Medals.

7, Urswick Road, Battersea, S.W.11.   Z1051

ANDREWS, H. G., Corporal, R.A.M.C.

He volunteered in October 1915, and in August of the following year was drafted to the Western Front. There he saw much service on the Somme, and at Armentières with various Field Ambulances. After the Armistice he served at No. 11 Stationary Hospital until demobilised in August 1919. He holds the General Service and Victory Medals.

2, Tintern Street, Ferndale Road, S.W.4.   Z1046B

ANDREWS, T. R., Pte., Royal Warwickshire Regt.

He joined in October 1916, and on the completion of his training was drafted to Mesopotamia, where he saw much active service. In 1918 he took part in the Evacuation of Baku, later proceeding to Constantinople. He returned to England, and was demobilised in January 1920, and holds the General Service and Victory Medals.

86, Cabul Road, Battersea, S.W.11.   Z1047

ANDREWS, J., Rifleman, 1/12th London Regiment (The Rangers).

He joined in February 1916, and in the April of same year was drafted to the Western Front. He was in action at Vimy Ridge, the Somme, Bullecourt, Messines, the 3rd Battle of Ypres, where he was severely wounded, necessitating the amputation of a leg. He was invalided home and discharged in February 1919, and holds the General Service and Victory Medals.

58, Elsted Street, Walworth, S.E.17.   Z1049

ANDREWS, W. J. E., Private, 7th Buffs (East Kent Regiment).

He joined in November 1917, and proceeded to France in the following April. He served in numerous engagements, and was in action on the Somme, and was taken prisoner. Whilst in captivity he was forced to work behind the German lines at Cambrai. In November 1918 he was released and returning to England was demobilised in the following March, holding the General Service and Victory Medals.

18, Elmington Road, Camberwell, S.E.5.   Z3052

ANGELL, A. E., Corporal, East Surrey Regiment.

Volunteering in July 1915, he proceeded overseas early in the following year, and whilst in France was in action on the Somme, and at Vimy Ridge, Lens, Ypres, Cambrai, and elsewhere. In 1917 he was drafted to Egypt, and served with General Allenby's forces in the Advance to Palestine, and was present at the entry into Jerusalem. After the Armistice he returned home, but in 1920 was still serving. He holds the General Service and Victory Medals.

20, Dartnell Road, Camberwell, S.E.5.   Z5559

ANNELLS, A. J., Driver, R.A.S.C.

Having previously served in the South African war, he volunteered in May 1915, and was speedily drafted to the East. He served under General Allenby in the Advance through Egypt into Palestine. In August 1919, he returned home and was demobilised, and holds the Queen's and King's South African Medals, and the General Service and Victory Medals.

44, Stainforth Road, Battersea, S.W.11.   Z1763

ANSDELL, E., Private, 13th Sherwood Foresters.

Joining in September 1916, he proceeded to Ireland to complete his training, and was later, in February 1917, drafted to the Western Front. Whilst in this theatre of war he fought in various engagements, and was wounded three times, and on March 21st, 1918, was taken prisoner. He was held in captivity until after the Armistice, when he was released and returning to England was demobilised in September 1919, and holds the General Service and Victory Medals.

46, Stanton Street, Peckham, S.E.15.   Z5207

ANSELL, J. (M.S.M.), R.Q.M.S., 7th Wiltshire Regt.

He had previously served in the Dorsetshire Regiment for thirteen years, and had fought throughout the South African war, and on the outbreak of hostilities rejoined at the age of forty-four years. He proceeded to France in September 1915, and took part in the Battle of Loos, and in the following November was drafted to Salonika. Whilst in this theatre of war he was engaged in the operations on the Vardar and Doiran fronts, including the first Battle of Doiran. In May 1918, he returned to France, and served in the Retreat and Advance of that year. He was mentioned in Despatches for his devotion to duty in the Advance, and was also awarded the Meritorious Service Medal for sustained good work throughout. He holds in addition to the Meritorious Service Medal, the Queen's and King's South African Medals (with seven clasps), the 1914-15 Star, and the General Service and Victory Medals. He was demobilised in February 1919.

11, Elam Street, Camberwell, S.E.5.   Z6136

ANSET, W. H., Sergt., 1st Life Guards and Grenadier Guards.

He volunteered in September 1914, and in October of the same year was drafted overseas. He served in France with the 1st Life Guards, but was later transferred to the Grenadier Guards, and took part in the Battles of the Somme, Arras, Cambrai, and many others. In 1918 he proceeded to East Africa, and served there until March 1919, when he returned home and was demobilised, holding the 1914 Star, and the General Service and Victory Medals.

29, Southampton Street, Camberwell, S.E.5.   Z4391

ANSLEY, J. E. A., Sapper, R.E.

Volunteering in 1914 he was later drafted to the Dardanelles and attached to the Naval Division, took part with H.M.S. "Collingwood" in the landing at Gallipoli. He rendered valuable services as a wireless operator, and on June 5th, 1915, was killed in action. He was entitled to the 1914-15 Star, and the General Service and Victory Medals.

7, Ingrave Street, Battersea, S.W.11.   Z1052

ANSTEE, A., Shoeing Smith, R.F.A.
He volunteered in December 1914, and in March of the following year proceeded to the Western Front. There he took part in the fighting at Neuve Chapelle, Ypres, and Festubert. Shortly afterwards he was drafted to Mesopotamia, and in this theatre of war saw much service at Kut-el-Amara, and on the Tigris. In September 1919 he returned home and was demobilised, and holds the 1914-15 Star, General Service and Victory Medals.
257, East Street, Walworth, S.E.17.　　　Z1053

ANSTEY, A. (Junior), Driver, R.F.A.
Volunteering in 1914 he was drafted in the following year to the Western Front. Whilst there he took part in the heavy fighting on the Somme and at Arras, Ypres, and in many other engagements until the conclusion of hostilities. He then served with the Army of Occupation in Germany until April 1919, when he was demobilised, holding the 1914-15 Star, and the General Service and Victory Medals.
12, Mina Road, Walworth, S.E.17.　　　Z1054

ANSTY, G. H., Rflmn., Rifle Brigade, Pte., Tank Corps.
Volunteering in September 1914, he proceeded to the Western Front in March of the following year. In this theatre of war he took part in the fierce fighting on the Somme, and at Ypres, and Arras. Later he was transferred to the Tank Corps, with which he rendered valuable service. Whilst overseas he was twice wounded. He was demobilised in March 1919, and holds the 1914-15 Star, and the General Service and Victory Medals.
19, Trafalgar Street, Walworth, S.E.17.　　　Z27327B

ANTHONY, A. J., Private, Welch Regiment.
He volunteered in December 1915, and in August of the following year was drafted to France with the 38th Division. He took part in much of the heavy fighting in the Ypres sector, and on the Somme and Ancre fronts until the conclusion of hostilities. He was demobilised in January 1919, and holds the General Service and Victory Medals.
141, Wickersley Road, Battersea, S.W.11.　　　Z1055

ANTHONY, G., Private, Labour Corps and 4th Northamptonshire Regiment.
Joining in November 1916, he was sent to France in April of the following year. Upon his arrival in France he unfortunately met with a severe accident which necessitated his removal to hospital, and later, to England. He was discharged in February 1919, as medically unfit for further service, and holds the General Service and Victory Medals.
149, Albert Road, Peckham, S.E.15.　　　Z5707

ANWELL, P. W., Sapper, R.E.
He joined in June 1917, and on the completion of his training served at various stations on the East Coast on defence duties. He rendered valuable services, but was not successful in obtaining his transfer overseas before the cessation of hostilities. He was demobilised in March 1919.
47, Hargwyne Street, Stockwell Road, S.W.9.　　　Z1637A

ANWELL, R. W., Private, Durham Light Infantry.
He attested in September 1915, but was not called up until the following year. He was then, after a period of training drafted to Salonika, where he was principally engaged at the Base on police and guard duties, being unfit for service in the trenches. He returned home for demobilisation in April 1919, and holds the General Service and Victory Medals.
2, Kimberley Road, Landor Road, S.W.9.　　　Z1056

APARK, E. W., Trooper, Surrey Lancers (Queen Mary's Regiment).
He volunteered in 1914, and was drafted to the Western Front in the same year. He took part in the engagements at La Bassée, Ypres, Neuve Chapelle, Hill 60, Festubert and Loos, and at the end of 1915 was drafted to Mesopotamia. Here he served in the campaign against the Turks, and was in action in numerous battles. Later, contracting malaria, he was invalided home, and in 1919 was demobilised, holding the 1914 Star, and the General Service and Victory Medals.
4, Shamrock Street, Clapham, S.W.4.　　　Z1057

APLIN, E., Corporal, 9th (Queen's Royal) Lancers.
He volunteered in August 1914, and was almost immediately drafted to the Western Front, where he took part in numerous engagements. On March 26th, 1918, he was killed in action on the Somme, during the German Offensive. He was entitled to the 1914 Star, and the General Service and Victory Medals.
40, Westbury Street, Wandsworth Road, S.W.8.　　　Z1058B

APLIN, J. W., Driver, R.H.A.
He was called up from the Reserve in August 1914, and in the same year was drafted to the Western Front, where he took part in the Battles of Ypres, Neuve Chapelle, Loos, the Somme, Arras, and Cambrai. Returning to England after the cessation of hostilities he was demobilised in March 1919, and holds the 1914 Star, and the General Service and Victory Medals.
11, Westbury Street, Wandsworth Road, S.W.8.　　　Z1059

APLIN, V. J. (Miss) Special War Worker.
In August 1914, this lady accepted an important appointment at Messrs. Waring and Gillow's Aircraft Factory, where she was engaged on responsible work in connection with the construction of aeroplanes. Throughout her service with the firm the manner in which she carried out her arduous duties was worthy of the highest commendation.
40, Westbury Street, Wandsworth Road, S.W.8.　　　Z1058A

APPELMAN, G. A., Gunner, R.G.A.
He volunteered in September 1914, and in the following March was drafted to the Western Front, where he took part in numerous engagements. In October 1915, he was transferred to Mesopotamia, and fought in the campaign against the Turks, and was present at the capture of Kut-el-Amara. Later he died on board H.M.H.S. "Assaye" on December 31st, 1918, whilst en route for Malta. He was entitled to the 1914-15 Star, and the General Service and Victory Medals.
12, Caspian Street, Camberwell, S.E.5.　　　Z3051

APPLEBEE, H. J., Pioneer, R.E.
He joined in August 1916, and in the following November was drafted to the Western Front, where he was employed with the Special Gas Section at Beaumont-Hamel, Bourlon Wood, Amiens, and St. Omer. He also served in the Advance of 1918, and after the conclusion of hostilities returned to England, and was demobilised in March 1919 holding the General Service and Victory Medals.
12, Comyn Road, Battersea, S.W.11.　　　Z1778　1779B

APPLEBY, A. J., Trooper, Derbyshire Dragoons.
He joined in October 1916, and after having completed his training served at various stations on important duties until October 1918, when he was drafted to Russia. Here he took part in numerous engagements and was wounded. In November 1919, he returned to England, and was demobilised holding the General Service and Victory Medals
89, Wickersley Road, Lavender Hill, S.W.11.　　　Z1060

APPLEGATE, G., Private, M.G.C.
He joined in June 1916, and in the same year was drafted to France, where he took part in numerous engagements, including the Battles of Ypres and Amiens. During the Retreat of 1918 he was twice wounded and was invalided home, but on his recovery returned to the Western Front, where he continued to serve until February 1919, when he was demobilised. He holds the General Service and Victory Medals.
23, Sterndale Road, Wandsworth Road, S.W.8.　　　Z1061

APPLIN, F., Private, Northumberland Fusiliers and Sapper, R.E.
He volunteered in May 1915, and after his training served with his unit at various stations on important coastal defence duties. He rendered valuable services, but was not successful in obtaining his transfer overseas before the end of the war, owing to medical unfitness. In 1919 he was demobilised.
18, Russell Grove, Vassall Road, S.W.9.　　　Z5026A

APPS, J. H., A.B. (Seaman Gunner), Royal Navy.
He joined in May 1916, and was posted to H.M.S. "Courageous" in which vessel he served in many minor engagements. He was also engaged on important escort duties and in conveying supplies to the various theatres of war, later being present at the surrender of the German Fleet at Scapa Flow. In January 1919 he returned home and was demobilised, holding the General Service and Victory Medals.
102, St. George's Road, Peckham, S.E.15.　　　Z5560

ARCHER, B. W., Private, R.A.S.C.
He volunteered in May 1915, and in the same year was drafted to the Western Front, where he was present at engagments on the Somme and at Arras and Ypres. He continued his service in France until December 1919, when he returned to England and was demobilised.
90, Somerleyton Road, Coldharbour Lane, S.W.9.　　　Z3055A

ARCHER, C. E., Private, 16th Manchester Regt.
He joined in August 1917, and on completion of his training was drafted to France in the following May. He served in the Retreat and Advance of 1918 and was in action at Ypres and Voormezeele. On the conclusion of hostilities he returned to England, and in February 1919 was demobilised, holding the General Service and Victory Medals.
19, Henley Road, Battersea, S.W.11.　　　Z1065A

ARCHER, J. A., Private., 8th (King's Royal Irish) Hussars.
He volunteered in August 1914, and after serving in Ireland for some time was drafted to France in 1916. He took part in the engagements at Ypres, the Somme, Péronne and Cambrai, where he was wounded, and was invalided home. On his recovery he returned to the Western Front, where he continued to serve until the cessation of hostilities, after which he was again sent to Ireland, where he remained until demobilised in March 1919. He holds the General Service and Victory Medals.
53, Stockdale Road, Wandsworth Road, S.W.8.　　　Z1064A

ARCHER, L. C., Band Sergt., Scots Guards.

He was serving at the outbreak of war, and on several occasions during the period of hostilities visited the Western Front with the Band. He holds the 1914-15 Star, and the General Service, Victory, and Long Service and Good Conduct Medals, and was still with the Colours in 1920, having served for twenty-eight years.
21, Broadhinton Road, Clapham, S.W.4. Z1062A

ARCHER, L. C. (M.M.), Sergt.-Instructor, Scots Gds.

He volunteered in June 1915 at sixteen and a half years of age, and on completion of his training served at various stations on important duties with his unit until March 1918, when he was drafted to the Western Front. He was in action on the Somme and at Amiens, and served in the Retreat and Advance. During his service overseas he was awarded the Military Medal for conspicuous bravery in rescuing the wounded. Later he was severely wounded himself and was invalided home. On his recovery he rejoined his unit, and in 1920 was still serving. He holds, in addition to the Military Medal, the General Service and Victory Medals.
21, Broadhinton Road, Clapham, S.W.4. Z1062B

ARCHER, R. G., Sapper, R.E.

He joined in April 1917, and after his training was stationed at Plymouth, where he served with the 1/5th Devonshire Electric Light Co. as electrician in charge of the searchlight of the coastal defences. He rendered valuable services in this connection until September 1919, when he was demobilised.
4, Connaught Mansions, Bromell's Road, Clapham, S.W.4. Z1063

ARCHER, T. H., Private, 24th London Regiment (The Queen's.)

He was mobilised from the National Reserve in November 1914, having previously served in the R.G.A. for twelve years, and for nearly a year was engaged on important duties guarding the railways. Later he was taken ill and died at the 3rd London General Hospital on November 25th, 1915.
19, Henley Street, Battersea, S.W.11 Z1065B

ARCHER, W. J., Driver, R.A.S.C.

Volunteering in August 1914, he proceeded to France in the following month. He rendered valuable services at Mons, the Marne, the Aisne, La Bassée, Neuve Chapelle, Ypres, Cambrai and in many engagements in the Retreat and Advance of 1918, and afterwards served with the Army of Occupation in Germany. He was demobilised in May 1919, holding the Mons Star, and the General Service and Victory Medals.
37, Chumleigh Street, Camberwell, S.E.5. Z5314A

ARGENT, F., Private, Royal Fusiliers and Leading Aircraftsman, R.A.F.

He volunteered in August 1915, and after serving at various stations in England was drafted to Ireland, where he was engaged on important duties, which required a high degree of technical skill. He rendered valuable services, but was not successful in obtaining his transfer to a theatre of war prior to the cessation of hostilities. He was demobilised in March 1919, and has since joined the Royal Irish Constabulary.
18, Brisbane Street, Camberwell, S.E.5. Z3053

ARIS, E. G., Sergt., M.G.C.

He joined in February 1916, and in the same year proceeded to France, where he took part in various engagements. In July 1917 he was drafted to the East and saw much service in Mesopotamia, being present in the engagements on the Dialah River and before Baghdad. He returned home, and was demobilised in November 1919, and holds the General Service and Victory Medals.
25A, Avenue Road, Camberwell, S.E.5. 1066C

ARIS, F., Air Mechanic, R.A.F.

He joined in May 1919, and on the completion of his training was drafted to Mesopotamia, where he did much valuable service that required considerable technical skill. He was still serving there in 1920.
25A, Avenue Road, Camberwell, S.E.5. 1066B

ARKELL, S. J., Gunner, R.F.A.

He volunteered in July 1915, and in the following March was drafted to France. During his service on the Western Front he fought at Armentières, the Somme and Ypres and other later engagements, and was gassed on three occasions. He was demobilised in April 1919 after returning home, and holds the General Service and Victory Medals.
29, Gloucester Road, Peckham, S.E.15. Z5872

ARMITAGE, E. G. T., Rifleman, 6th London Regiment (Rifles).

He volunteered in May 1915, and served on important duties with his unit until December 1916, when he was sent to France. He was engaged as a stretcher-bearer and took part in numerous engagements, including those on the Somme and at Arras, Ypres and Cambrai. He was taken prisoner near Cambrai in March 1918. On his release, he returned home and was demobilised in March 1919, and holds the General Service and Victory Medals.
18, Sears Street, Camberwell, S.E.5. Z5706

ARMSBY, T. E. (M.M.), Private, Labour Corps.

He joined in June 1917, and was speedily drafted to France. He rendered valuable service in many engagements, including those at Messines, Lens, the Somme and in the Retreat and Advance of 1918, and was gassed. He was awarded the Military Medal for conspicuous bravery in the Field when working a machine gun to cover the Retreat at Epéhy, and also holds the General Service and Victory Medals. In December 1919 he was demobilised.
192, Bridge Road, Battersea, S.W.11. Z1067

ARMSTRONG, F. W., Corporal, R.A.S.C.

Volunteering in August 1914, he was almost immediately drafted to the Western Front. There he served during the Retreat from Mons, and in the Battles of Le Cateau, the Marne, La Bassée, Neuve Chapelle, Hill 60 and Ypres. He was invalided home and discharged as unfit for military duty in May 1916. He holds the Mons Star, and the General Service and Victory Medals.
26, Nelson Row, Clapham, S.W.4. Z1069

ARMSTRONG, J. W., Sapper, R.E.

He joined in May 1916, and in the following year was drafted to German East Africa. Whilst serving near Dar-es-Salaam he contracted malaria and after being in hospital for a considerable time was invalided to England. On his recovery he was engaged on important duties at home until demobilised in April 1919. He holds the General Service and Victory Medals.
23, Pitcairn Street, Wandsworth Road, S.W.8. Z1068

ARMSTRONG, P., Rflmn., King's Royal Rifle Corps.

Joining in 1917 he proceeded overseas in the same year, and whilst in France took part in many engagements, including those of Vimy Ridge, Bullecourt, Ypres and the Retreat and Advance of 1918. After the Armistice he was sent to Germany with the Army of Occupation, and served there until demobilised in 1919. He holds the General Service and Victory Medals. 8, Baker Street, Brixton Road, S.W.9. Z5208

ARMSTRONG, W. P., Private, 4th Royal Fusiliers.

Volunteering in August 1914, he proceeded in the same month to the Western Front, where he took part in severe fighting, and was killed in action at La Bassée on October 26th, 1914. He was entitled to the 1914 Star, and the General Service and Victory Medals.
43, Havil Street, Camberwell, S.E.5. Z3418

ARNILL, H. J., Private, 23rd London Regiment.

Volunteering in August 1914, he was drafted on the completion of his training to the Western Front. There he took part in the fighting at Ypres, Vimy Ridge, the Somme, Arras, Cambrai and the Retreat and Advance of 1918, and was wounded and gassed. He holds the 1914-15 Star, and the General Service and Victory Medals, and was demobilised in 1919.
5, Stockwell Grove, Stockwell, S.W.9. Z1070

ARNOLD, C. W., Private, Royal Welch Fusiliers.

He joined in July 1916, and in November of the same year was drafted to Salonika. In this theatre of war he took part in many notable engagements until the conclusion of hostilities. Later he served in Turkey with the Army of Occupation until March 1919, when he returned home for demobilisation. He holds the General Service and Victory Medals.
38, Wayford Street, Battersea, S.W.11. Z1072

ARNOLD, E. W. (D.C.M.), Sergt., R.F.A.

He volunteered in June 1915, and in March of the following year was drafted to France. There he took part in the heavy fighting at the Somme, Arras, Vimy Ridge and Ypres. He was awarded the Distinguished Conduct Medal for conspicuous gallantry in the Field when aiding a neighbouring gun crew at Avesnes, and also holds the General Service and Victory Medals. In March 1919 he was demobilised.
158, Beresford Street, Camberwell, S.E.5. Z1071

ARNOULD, R. H., Private, Queen's Own (Royal West Kent) Regiment.

He volunteered in September 1914, and in the following July was drafted to the Western Front, where he fought in numerous engagements. He was killed in action on July 1st, 1917, and was entitled to the 1914-15 Star, and the General Service and Victory Medals.
33, Alfred Street, Bermondsey, S.E.1. 26948A

ARTIS, H. J., Private, 1st Norfolk Regiment.

A Reservist, he was mobilised in August 1914, and was almost immediately drafted to the Western Front. Whilst there he took part in the Battles of La Bassée, Ypres, the Somme, Arras and various other engagements. Later he proceeded to Italy with the 5th Division and fought on the Piave front, but returned to France in time for the Retreat and Advance of 1918. In February 1919 he was demobilised, holding the 1914 Star, and the General Service and Victory Medals.
21, Tidemore Street, Battersea Park Road, S.W.8. Z1073

ARY, R. W., Aircraftsman, R.A.F.
He joined in January 1917, and early in the following year, on completion of his training, was drafted to Mesopotamia, where he was engaged on highly important duties. For a short time he was in hospital at Baghdad through ill-health, but on his recovery returned to his unit, and served with it until his demobilisation in May 1920. He holds the General Service and Victory Medals.
62, Este Road, Battersea, S.W.11. Z1074

ASH, A. G., A.B., Royal Navy.
Volunteering in August 1915, he was posted to H.M.S. " Commonwealth," and took part in the Naval operations at the Dardanelles up to the Evacuation of the Peninsula. He also saw much valuable service off Ostend and Dunkirk with the Dover Patrol until the close of hostilities, and was present at the bombardment of Zeebrugge. He was demobilised in June 1919, and holds the 1914–15 Star, and the General Service and Victory Medals.
30, Gladstone Street, Battersea Park Road, S.W.8. Z1075A

ASH, F. T., Gunner, R.F.A.
He volunteered in November 1914, and after his training served on important duties with his unit at various stations. In November 1916 he contracted pneumonia, from which he subsequently died.
6, Arlesford Road, Landor Road, S.W.9. Z3342A

ASH, G. E., Rifleman, 1st Surrey Rifles.
Volunteering in August 1914, he proceeded in the following year to France. There served with the 47th Division in many engagements, including that of Vimy Ridge, where he was wounded. On his recovery he returned to the fighting line and fought in the Battle of Cambrai, and was again wounded. He was demobilised in February 1919, and holds the 1914–15 Star, and the General Service and Victory Medals.
102, St. George's Road, Peckham, S.E.15. Z5561

ASHBY, A., Private, 6th North Staffordshire Regt.
Volunteering in 1915 he completed his course of training and later proceeded to France. Whilst there he fought in many notable battles, including those of the Somme and the Retreat and Advance of 1918, during which he was taken prisoner. He was released after the Armistice and demobilised in February 1919, holding the 1914–15 Star, and the General Service and Victory Medals.
231, Haslam Place, Peckham, S.E.15. Z5027

ASHBY, G., B.S.M., R.F.A.
An old soldier, who had served in the South African War, he volunteered in December 1914, and after being retained for important duties at home was drafted to the Western Front in 1916. There he took part in the fierce fighting at Vimy Ridge, the Somme, Arras, Bullecourt, Passchendaele, Cambrai, Ypres and various other engagements until hostilities ceased. In February 1919 he returned home and was demobilised, holding the Queen's and King's South African Medals, and the General Service and Victory Medals.
6, Mordaunt Street, Stockwell, S.W.9. Z1076

ASHDOWN, A. E. (M.M.), Sergt., Tank Corps.
He volunteered in February 1916, and in the same year was sent overseas. During his service in France he was in action at the Somme, Arras, Vimy Ridge, Bullecourt and Cambrai. On May 3rd, 1917, he was awarded the Military Medal for great gallantry in bringing back his tank to the field of action to rescue the wounded, whilst he himself was wounded. He holds, in addition to the Military Medal, the General Service and Victory Medals, and was demobilised in February 1919.
82, Evelina Road, Peckham, S.E.15. Z5873

ASHDOWN, J. G., Private, 21st Middlesex Regt.
He volunteered in September 1915, and in December of the same year was drafted to Salonika. There he took part in much severe fighting on the Vardar, Doiran and Struma fronts, and was also present at the Capture of Monastir. Whilst in the East he suffered from malaria. In February 1919 he returned home and was demobilised, holding the 1914–15 Star, and the General Service and Victory Medals.
100, Aylesbury Road, Walworth, S.E.17. Z1077

ASHFORD, R. H. S., A.B., R.N., H.M.S. "Conqueror."
He volunteered in December 1915, and was posted to H.M.S. " Conqueror." While with this ship he was engaged until the end of the war on important duties with the Grand Fleet in the North Sea and other waters, and took part in the Battle of Jutland. He was demobilised in July 1920, and holds the 1914–15 Star, and the General Service and Victory Medals.
12, Shepherd's Place, Upper Kennington Lane, S.E.11. Z23850

ASHLEY, J. W., Private, M.G.C.
He joined in February 1917, and early in the following year was drafted to the Western Front, where he was in action on the Somme. He also took part in the Retreat and Advance of 1918. After the Armistice he proceeded with the Army of Occupation to Germany. He was demobilised in October 1919, and holds the General Service and Victory Medals.
10, New Church Road, Camberwell, S.E.5. Z5705

ASHLEY, C., Sapper, R.E.
He volunteered in November 1915, and after his training was engaged on important duties with his unit until March 1918, when he was sent to France. He saw heavy fighting on the Arras sector and was engaged on various duties in connection with his branch of the Service. He afterwards proceeded with the Army of Occupation to Germany. He was demobilised in May 1919, and holds the General Service and Victory Medals.
160, Albert Road, Peckham, S.E.15. Z5708A

ASHLEY, W., Private, 14th London Regiment (London Scottish).
He volunteered in November 1915, and in the following year was drafted to the Western Front, where he took part in severe fighting on the Somme and at Arras and Ypres, and was wounded and gassed. He was invalided home and discharged in September 1918, owing to his wounds, and holds the General Service and Victory Medals.
160, Albert Road, Peckham, S.E.15. Z5708B

ASHLEY, W., Private, King's Own (Yorkshire Light Infantry).
He joined in June 1916, and in the following year, on the completion of his training was drafted to the Western Front. Whilst in this theatre of war he fought in many notable battles, including those at Ypres, Passchendaele, Lens, Cambrai and the Somme. On April 13th, 1918, he died from the effects of gas poisoning. He was entitled to the General Service and Victory Medals.
9, Charleston Street, Walworth, S.E.17. Z1079

ASHMAN, C., Private, R.G.A.
He joined in June 1916, and after completing his training served at various stations on important duties with the anti-aircraft section. He rendered valuable services, but was unable to obtain his transfer overseas before the conclusion of hostilities. In 1919 he was demobilised.
32, Ceylon Street, Battersea Park Road, S.W.8. Z1080

ASHTON, A., Sergt., 8th Yorkshire Regiment.
Volunteering in August 1914, he proceeded to France in January of the following year. Whilst in this seat of war he took part in the Battles of Neuve Chapelle, Ypres, Loos, the Somme, Bullecourt, Messines, Lens and various other engagements. Being afterwards drafted to Italy, he saw much service on the Piave and the Asiago Plateaux, and for his excellent work he was mentioned in Despatches by the Commander-in-Chief of the British Forces in Italy. Whilst overseas he was wounded three times. He holds the 1914–15 Star, and the General Service and Victory Medals, and was demobilised in February 1919.
50, Elsted Street, Walworth, S.E.17. Z1082

ASHTON, A., Corporal, R.A.S.C. (M.T.)
He volunteered in January 1915, and in May of the same year was drafted to France. He rendered valuable service in the Ypres sector and in many other parts of the fighting areas, as the driver of a motor conveying ammunition to the lines. He also served for a time in Germany. In June 1919 he returned home and was demobilised, holding the 1914–15 Star, and the General Service and Victory Medals.
50, Sterndale Road, Wandsworth Road, S.W.8. Z1083

ASHWELL, A. E., Stoker, R.N.R.
A Reservist, he was mobilised at the outbreak of war, and immediately proceeded to Antwerp with the Naval Brigade. After the operations there ceased he was interned in Holland until the cessation of hostilities. He returned home and was demobilised in November 1918, holding the 1914 Star, and the General Service and Victory Medals.
18, Power Street, Wandsworth Road, S.W.8. Z1084

ASHWORTH, C. E., Rifleman, Rifle Brigade.
He joined in March 1916, and in December of the same year was drafted to France. Whilst there he fought in many notable Battles, including that of Arras, and was badly wounded at Passchendaele. After being in hospital for a long time he was discharged in May 1918 as medically unfit for further duty. He holds the General Service and Victory Medals.
13, Angle Street, Walworth, S.E.17. Z1085

ASHWORTH, F. (M.M.), Corporal, R.F.A.
Mobilised at the outbreak of war, he was almost immediately drafted to the Western Front. There he was in action at Mons, the Marne, the Aisne, La Bassée, Vimy Ridge, Arras, Ypres, Lens, Messines and the Retreat and Advance of 1918. During his service he was badly wounded and suffered severely from shell-shock. He was invalided home, and after receiving hospital treatment was discharged as medically unfit in March 1919. In 1916 he was awarded the Military Medal for conspicuous bravery in rescuing a Sergeant under heavy shell fire, and he also holds the Mons Star, and the General Service and Victory Medals.
40, Somerleyton Road, Coldharbour Lane, S.W.9. Z4392

ASKEY, A. E., Private, 23rd Middlesex Regiment.
He joined in September 1918, and after a brief training was drafted to France, where he took part in the last engagement before the conclusion of hostilities. Afterwards he served in Germany with the Army of Occupation, returning home for demobilisation in February 1920. He holds the General Service and Victory Medals.
139, Dorset Road, Clapham Road, S.W.8.   Z1078A

ASKEY, H. G., Gunner, R.F.A.
Volunteering in February 1915, he was drafted in the same year to the Western Front. Whilst there he took part in the heavy fighting at Ypres, Loos and the Somme. Shortly afterwards he proceeded to Salonika and did good service on the Vardar front. He subsequently took an active part in General Allenby's campaign in Palestine, and entered Jerusalem. On his voyage home he died on July 4th, 1919, in hospital at Toronto through causes due to his service. He was entitled to the 1914-15 Star, and the General Service and Victory Medals.
139, Dorset Road, Clapham Road, S.W.8.   Z1078B

ASLETT, A., Corporal, Northumberland Fusiliers.
Volunteering in October 1915, he was sent to India in the following year and served principally at Delhi. Later he was drafted to Mesopotamia, where he saw much service, remaining there until the conclusion of the war. He was demobilised in May 1919, and holds the General Service and Victory Medals.
4, Cancell Road, Brixton Road, S.W.9.   Z5209

ASLET, W., Pte., Devonshire Regt. and Labour Corps.
Volunteering in 1915, he was drafted to France later in the same year. He fought in the Battle of Arras, and being severely wounded in action near Béthune was invalided home. On his recovery he was retained for home service, being medically unfit for trench warfare. He was engaged on important duties in guarding German prisoners and in agricultural work. He was demobilised in 1919, and holds the 1914-15 Star, and the General Service and Victory Medals.
5, Sondes Street, Walworth, S.E.17.

ASTELL, A. E., Cpl., 20th King's Royal Rifle Corps.
He joined in 1916, and on the completion of his training proceeded to France in 1917. There he took part in the Battles of Arras, Ypres and Cambrai, and various engagements in the Retreat and Advance of 1918. Later he went to Germany with the Army of Occupation and served there until June 1919, when he returned home for demobilisation. He holds the General Service and Victory Medals.
7, Tennyson Street, Wentworth Road, S.W.8.   Z1081

ATKINS, A. H., Private, 15th Loyal North Lancashire Regiment.
Joining in 1916, he proceeded to France on the completion of his training. Whilst in this theatre of war he fought in many notable engagements until almost the close of hostilities. He was killed in action in October 1918, during the Advance of that year. He was entitled to the General Service and Victory Medals.
"His memory is cherished with pride."
117, Cator Street, Peckham, S.E.15.   Z4393A

ATKINS, A. R., Gunner, R.F.A.
Volunteering in February 1915, he was drafted on the completion of his training to the Western Front, and took part in much of the heavy fighting on the Somme. On March 4th, 1917, he died gloriously on the field of battle at Combles after two years' service. He was entitled to the 1914-15 Star, and the General Service and Victory Medals.
"The path of duty was the way to glory."
117, Cator Street, Peckham, S.E.15.   Z4393B

ATKINS, H. A., Gunner, R.F.A.
He volunteered in October 1915, and after completing his course of training was drafted to the Western Front. He rendered valuable services in many important engagements, including those of Albert, Vimy Ridge, the Somme, Arras, Bullecourt, Messines, Ypres, Passchendaele, and Cambrai. He was severely gassed in the second Battle of the Somme in 1918, and was in consequence invalided home. After protracted treatment in King's College Hospital he died on November 2nd, 1919. He was entitled to the General Service and Victory Medals.
60, Chatham Street, Walworth, S.E.17.   Z1088A

ATKINS, T. G., Driver, R.F.A.
He volunteered in May 1915, and in the same year was drafted to the Western Front, where he took part in severe fighting on the Somme and in many other engagements. He also served in the Retreat and Advance of 1918, and was in action on numerous occasions. He was demobilised in March 1919, and holds the 1914-15 Star, and the General Service and Victory Medals.
18, Tradescent Road, South Lambeth Road, S.W.8.   Z1087A

ATKINS, W., Private, Northumberland Fusiliers.
Joining in June 1916, he was drafted to the Western Front on completion of his training and took part in the fighting in the Albert sector. Later, owing to ill-health, he was invalided home. On his recovery he returned to France and was engaged on various duties until February 1919, when he was demobilised, holding the General Service and Victory Medals. 11, Auckland Road, Battersea, S.W.11.   Z1086

ATKINSON, A. E, A.B., R.N., H.M.S. "Enterprise" and "Merlin."
He volunteered in August 1915, and served in the Mediterranean. He was engaged in chasing enemy submarines and convoying troopships and merchantmen, and rendered valuable services. He was still serving in 1920, and holds the 1914-15 Star, and the General Service and Victory Medals.
21, Moat Place, Stockwell, S.W.9.   Z1089B

ATKINSON, C. H., Gunner, R.G.A.
He joined in August 1917, and in the same year was drafted to the Western Front, where he took part in various engagements, including those at Lens, Cambrai, the Somme and the Marne. He also served in the Retreat and Advance of 1918, and after the Armistice proceeded with the Army of Occupation to Germany. He was demobilised in August 1919, and holds the General Service and Victory Medals.
194, Stewarts Road, Battersea Park Road, S.W.8.   Z1091

ATKINSON, F. G., Sergt., R.E. and Labour Corps.
He volunteered in February 1915, and was sent to the Western Front in the same year. After serving in France for six months he was drafted to Salonika, where he was in action on the Doiran and Struma fronts, and took part in the Balkan campaign. During his service in the East he contracted malaria and was invalided home and discharged in 1918, but re-enlisted later in the same year in the Labour Corps, and was engaged in superintending the Chinese coolies in France. He was demobilised in February 1919, and holds the 1914-15 Star, and the General Service and Victory Medals.
21, Moat Place, Stockwell, S.W.9.   Z1089A

ATKINSON, F. G. (Junior), Petty Officer, R.N., H.M.S. "Niobe," "Centaur" and "Dolphin," also H.M. Submarine 53 and 45.
He enlisted in 1910, and during the war was engaged on patrol and submarine duties in the North Sea. He also took part in various actions off the German coast and Heligoland, and was for a time employed on mine-laying. He rendered valuable services, and was demobilised in December 1919, holding the 1914-15 Star, and the General Service and Victory Medals.
70, Claylands Road, Clapham Road, S.W.8.   Z1090

ATKINSON, J., Rflmn., 3rd King's Royal Rifle Corps.
Volunteering in August 1914, he was sent to France in January of the following year. He took part in severe fighting at Ypres, Festubert and Loos, and was wounded and invalided home. In 1916 he was drafted to India, where he was engaged with the Oxfordshire and Buckinghamshire Light Infantry on various important duties. He was demobilised in February 1919, and holds the 1914-15 Star, and the General Service and Victory Medals.
9, Prescott Place, Little Manor Street, Clapham, S.W.4. Z1092

ATTRIDGE, F., A.B., Royal Navy, Harwich Force, Dover Patrol.
He was mobilised in August 1914, and was posted to H.M.S. "Lucifer." He took part in the Battles of Heligoland Bight and Dogger Bank, and also served in the Zeebrugge Raid, and various other engagements. He was also for a time employed on patrol duties, and rendered valuable services. He was demobilised in March 1919, and holds the 1914-15 Star, and the General Service and Victory Medals.
10, Alfred Cottages, Bolney Street, Dorset Road, S.W.8. Z1093

AUSTIN, E. J. (D.C.M.), Grdsmn., Grenadier Guards.
He was serving at the outbreak of war and was sent to France immediately afterwards. He took part in severe fighting during the Retreat from Mons, and also fought on the Marne and the Aisne, and at Ypres, Neuve Chapelle, Loos, the Somme, Beaumont-Hamel, and many other engagements, and was wounded. He was awarded the Distinguished Conduct Medal for conspicuous gallantry in repairing wires under heavy fire, and also holds the Mons Star, and the General Service and Victory Medals, and was demobilised in April 1920.
32, Aliwal Road, Battersea, S.W.11.   Z1098

AUSTIN, G. D., Driver, R.F.A.
He volunteered in November 1914, and in August of the following year was drafted to the Western Front. He took part in severe fighting at Loos, Lens, Ypres, and Cambrai, and also served in the Retreat and Advance of 1918. He was demobilised in February 1919, and holds the 1914-15 Star, and the General Service and Victory Medals.
19, Gonsalva Road, Wandsworth Road, S.W.8.   Z1094

AUSTIN, G. H., Corporal, 5th Middlesex Regiment.
He was serving at the outbreak of war, having previously fought in the South African campaign, and was sent to France in August 1914. He took part in the Retreat from Mons, and was wounded, and also served at Loos, and Cambrai, and in the Retreat and Advance of 1918, during which he was gassed. He was demobilised in February 1919, and holds the Queen's South African Medal, the Mons Star, and the General Service and Victory Medals.
19, Gladstone Street, Battersea Park Road, S.W.8.   Z1095B

AUSTIN, H., Private, R.A.S.C. (M.T.)
He volunteered in August 1915, and in September of the same year was drafted to the Western Front where he served in numerous engagements, including those at Festubert, Loos, Ypres, the Somme, and Cambrai. During his service overseas he suffered with trench fever. He was demobilised in August 1919, and holds the 1914-15 Star, and the General Service and Victory Medals.
55, Rowena Crescent, Battersea, S.W.11.   Z1097

AUSTIN, W. J., Musician, R.M.L.I.
Having previously served in the South African campaign he was mobilised in August 1914, and was posted to the Chatham Division. He served with the Grand Fleet, with which he was engaged on important duties, and rendered valuable services. He was demobilised in February 1919, and holds the Queen's South African Medals (with three clasps), and the General Service, Victory, Long Service, and Good Conduct Medals.
16, Coronation Buildings, Lambeth, S.W.8.   Z1096

AVERN, S. H., Private, Royal Fusiliers.
He volunteered in July 1915, and in the same year was drafted to the Western Front. During his service in France he fought at Loos, the Ancre, Ypres, and Cambrai, and was severely wounded in the Somme sector in 1917. He was sent home to hospital, and later invalided out of the Service in September 1918. He holds the 1914-15 Star, and the General Service and Victory Medals.
19, Arlesford Road, Landor Road, S.W.9.   Z1099

AVERY, W. R., Rifleman, 6th London Regt. (Rifles)
Volunteering in September 1914, he was drafted in the following year to the Western Front, where he took part in the severe fighting at Festubert and Loos. He was blown up by the explosion of a mine, and being seriously injured was invalided home. He was discharged as medically unfit for further service in 1919, and holds the 1914-15 Star, and the General Service and Victory Medals.
28, Mysore Road, Battersea, S.W.11.   Z4001B

AXWORTHY, A. F., Ship's Cook, Merchant Service, s.s. "Durham Castle" and "Valdovia."
Previously to joining the Merchant Service, which he did in February 1917, he occupied an important position at Messrs. Vernon's Flour Mills, and whilst working there was blown up in an explosion, but fortunately escaped serious injury. On joining his ship he proceeded to Egypt, and thence to Salonika, and later to India. He holds the Merchant Service War Medal and the General Service and Victory Medals, and was still serving in 1920.
52, Old Paradise Street, Kennington, S.E.11.   Z25779

AYERS, A., Rifleman, Rifle Brigade, attached 8th London Regiment (Post Office Rifles).
He joined in May 1917, and in the following November was drafted to the Western Front. During his service in France he fought in the third Battle of Ypres, on the Somme, and in the third Battle of the Aisne, and was later severely wounded in the Albert sector. He was invalided home to hospital, and after his recovery was demobilised in January 1919. He holds the General Service and Victory Medals.
36, Doddington Grove, Battersea, S.W.11.   Z1100

AYLES, G. T., Driver, R.F.A.
He volunteered in February 1915, and was drafted to France in the following year. Whilst in this theatre of war he served in various engagements on the Somme, and later in the year was sent to Salonika, where he was in action on the Balkan front in the Vardar sector. In 1918 he proceeded to Egypt, and thence to Palestine, where he did good work with his Battery at Jericho and Tripoli. He returned home and was demobilised in July 1919, and holds the General Service and Victory Medals.
11, Grimscott Street, Bermondsey, S.E.1.   25973B

AYLES, J. A., L/Corporal, 2nd Hampshire Regt.
He volunteered in November 1915, and in the following April was drafted to France. Here he fought at Arras, and in the third Battle of Ypres, where he was severely wounded in action in July 1917. He was invalided home to hospital, and discharged as medically unfit for further duty in October 1917, and holds the General Service and Victory Medals.
11, Grimscott Street, Grange Road, S.E.1.   25973A

AYLES, J. A., Gunner, R.F.A.
He joined in June 1916 and in the following November was drafted to France, and shortly afterwards to Italy, where he was in action on the Piave in December 1917. He returned to the Western Front at the end of the following March, and took part in the Battles of the Somme, the Marne, Bapaume, Havrincourt, and Cambrai. During this period he was twice gassed, but continued his service until February 1919, when he was demobilised. He holds the General Service and Victory Medals.   55, Elsted Street, Walworth, S.E.17.   Z1101

AYLESBURY, A., Private, R.A.S.C. (M.T.)
He joined in August 1917, and embarked for France in the same month. He served in various sectors on important duties in connection with the Motor Transport, notably at Cambrai, where he was severely wounded and gassed in November 1917. He was invalided home and died from his injuries on November 29th. He was entitled to the General Service and Victory Medals.
" Whilst we remember, the Sacrifice is not in vain."
56, Blakes Road, Peckham Grove. S.E.15.   Z5868

AYLESBURY, W. C., Gunner, 47th Battery, R.F.A.
Mobilised at the outbreak of war he almost immediately proceeded to France and took part in the Retreat from Mons. He also fought in many other battles, including those at Ypres, St. Eloi, and Arras, until the conclusion of hostilities. He returned home in February 1919, and was demobilised, holding the Mons Star, and the General Service and Victory Medals.
4, Grennard Road, Peckham, S.E.15.   Z5562

AYLWARD, J. W., Private, R.A.S.C. (M.T.)
Joining in May 1916, he was drafted shortly afterwards to France. There he served as a driver with the motor transport, conveying food supplies to the various fighting areas. He suffered from shell-shock while serving on the Somme Front, and was invalided home, but on recovery returned to France, and remained there until March 1919, when he was demobilised. He holds the General Service and Victory Medals.
27, Cunard Street, Camberwell, S.E.5.   Z5028

AYLWARD, W. G., Private, R.A.M.C.
Volunteering in November 1914, he was drafted to France in June 1916, and served in many sectors of the Western Front on important Field Ambulance duties, notably on the Somme, and at Arras. Later in 1917 he proceeded to Salonika and Egypt, and rendered valuable services in both of these theatres of war. He returned home and was demobilised in July 1919, and holds the General Service and Victory Medals.
21, Bonnington Square, South Lambeth Road, S.W.8. Z110

B

BABBAGE, A. J., Private, R.A.S.C. and Labour Corps.
He volunteered in April 1915, at forty-three years of age, and was engaged at Aldershot on important duties with his unit. He rendered valuable services, but falling seriously ill he was discharged in June 1916 as medically unfit for further service.
24, Pulross Road, Stockwell, S.W.9.   Z1103A

BABBAGE, C. V., Driver, R.A.S.C. (M.T.)
He joined in December 1917, and early in the following year was drafted to France, where he did good service in the Somme sector, and at Amiens, Bapaume, Béthune, Bullecourt, and many engagements in the Retreat and Advance of 1918. After the signing of the Armistice he fell ill, and after treatment in hospital in France and England, was demobilised in March 1919. He holds the General Service and Victory Medals.
24, Pulross Road, Stockwell, S.W.9.   Z1103B

BABBS, H. C., Private, 23rd London Regiment.
Mobilised at the commencement of hostilities he took part in the Retreat from Mons, and in the Battles of Ypres, and Loos, where he was wounded. After his recovery he fought on the Somme, and was again wounded, but proceeded later to Egypt and served in the Offensive on Palestine under General Allenby. Whilst in this theatre of war he was in action at Gaza, and was present at the capture of Jericho, and in subsequent engagements until the cessation of hostilities. After returning home he was demobilised in 1919, and holds the Mons Star, and the General Service and Victory Medals.
98, Wadhurst Road, Wandsworth Road, S.W.8.   Z1608B

BABBS, J. F., Private, R.A.M.C.
Volunteering in November 1915, he was drafted to Salonika in August of the following year, and served in the advanced areas with the 66th Field Ambulance with the Greek Forces. He was also engaged as stretcher-bearer with our men, and did excellent work in this important and dangerous duty. He returned home and was demobilised in April 1919, and holds the General Service and Victory Medals.
33, Darwin Buildings, Barlow Street, Walworth, S.E.17. Z1104

BACON, A. V., Leading Cook, R.N., H.M.S. " King Edward VII."
Having served in the Royal Navy since January 1912 he was sent at the outbreak of war to the North Sea with the Grand Fleet. His ship, H.M.S. " King Edward VII," was torpedoed and sunk by enemy action off the North Coast of Scotland in 1916, but he was fortunately among the saved. He also did much valuable convoy work in the Mediterranean and Adriatic, and off the coast of Russia. In 1920 he was still serving at the Royal Naval Barracks at Portsmouth, and holds the 1914–15 Star, and the General Service and Victory Medals.
16, Medlar Street, Camberwell, S.E.5.   Z1173

BACON, W. G., Pte., 6th South Staffordshire Regt.
He joined in September 1916, and in the following February was drafted to France. Here he took part in many important engagements, including those at Arras, Vimy Ridge, Bullecourt, Cambrai, and the second Battle of the Somme. He was reported missing on March 21st, 1918, and was later presumed to have been killed in action on that date. He was entitled to the General Service and Victory Medals.
37, Kimberley Road, Landor Road, S.W.9.   Z1105

BADCOCK, E. C., Private, 2nd Royal Fusiliers.
He volunteered in 1915, and in the same year was drafted to the Western Front, where he took part in numerous engagements, including those at Armentières, Festubert, Vimy Ridge, the Somme, Arras, and Lens. He also served in the Retreat and Advance of 1918, and later proceeded with the Army of Occupation to Germany. He was demobilised in March 1919, and holds the 1914–15 Star, and the General Service and Victory Medals.
16, Russell Road, Peckham, S.E.15.   Z5315

BADGER, A. C., C.S.M., 13th Royal Fusiliers.
He volunteered in October 1914, and was later drafted to the Western Front. During his service in France he fought in the Battle of the Somme, and at Pozières, was very severely wounded and twice buried by shell explosions. He was invalided home and discharged in March 1917 in consequence of his wounds. He holds the 1914–15 Star, and the General Service and Victory Medals.
106, Claxton Grove, Hammersmith, W.6.   13436A

BADGER, F. (M.M.), 2nd Lieutenant, 3rd City of London Regiment (Royal Fusiliers).
As a Private in the Territorials he was mobilised at the outbreak of war, and in October 1914 was drafted to France, where he served with distinction in the Battles of Neuve Chapelle, Ypres, Festubert, Loos, Messines and Cambrai, and was present at the entry into Mons, on November 11th, 1918. After being promoted to sergeant's rank, he was recommended for a commission. He was awarded the Military Medal for great bravery in the Field, and in addition holds the 1914 Star, and the General Service and Victory Medals. He was demobilised in April 1919, after over four and a half years' service.
11, St. Philip Street, Battersea Park, S.W.8.   Z1106

BADGER, T., Corporal, R.E.
He joined in 1916 with the London Electric Engineering Company of the Royal Engineers, and after his training was engaged on important and responsible duties with the searchlights at various stations. He rendered valuable services, but was not able to secure his transfer overseas before the cessation of hostilities, and was demobilised in March 1919.
29, Bramfield Road, Wandsworth Common, S.W.11. Z1766

BADGER, W., L/Corporal, 2nd Royal Fusiliers.
A serving soldier, who had previously been engaged on important garrison duties in India, he was mobilised at the outbreak of war. He was drafted to Gallipoli in 1915, and after taking part in several engagements was killed in action there on August 22nd of the same year. He was entitled to the 1914–15 Star, and the General Service and Victory Medals.
106, Claxton Grove, Hammersmith, W.6.   13436B

BADSTEVENER, J. W., Gunner, R.F.A.
He volunteered in December 1914, and on the completion of his training in 1915 proceeded overseas. Whilst in France he was in action at many engagements, including those of Neuve Chapelle, Hill 60, Ypres, Loos, and the Somme, also acting as a signaller with the R.F.A. In February 1919, he returned home and was demobilised holding the 1914–15 Star, and the General Service and Victory Medals.
4, East Surrey Grove, Peckham, S.E.15.   Z5211

BAGLEY, H., Private, Labour Corps.
He joined in April 1917, and was drafted to France in the latter part of the same year. During his service on the Western Front he did valuable work in various sectors, but unfortunately contracted pneumonia, from which he died abroad on November 12th, 1918. He was entitled to the General Service and Victory Medals.
103, Acton Lane, Chiswick, W.4.   6363B

BAGLEY, J. H., Private, R.A.S.C.
A Reservist, he was mobilised in August 1914, and was almost immediately drafted to France, where he rendered valuable service in the Retreat from Mons. He was also present at many engagements in various sectors of the Western Front, until 1917, when he was discharged on account of service. He holds the Mons Star, and the General Service and Victory Medals.
103, Acton Lane, Chiswick, W.4.   6363A

BAGLIN, E. A., Private, Royal Marine Engineers.
He volunteered in January 1915, and after his training served at various coastal stations on important special duties in connection with the submarine mine service. He rendered valuable services of a highly skilled nature until after the close of hostilities, and was demobilised in February 1919, holding the General Service and Victory Medals.
49, Flint Street, Walworth, S.E.17.   Z1107A

BAGLIN, G., Private, 23rd London Regiment.
He joined in March 1916, and in the following July was drafted to France, where he saw much service. He took part in the fighting at the Somme, Arras, Vimy Ridge, Messines, Lens, Cambrai, the second Battle of the Somme, and in many engagements which followed until October 1918, when he was unfortunately killed in action near Arras. He was entitled to the General Service and Victory Medals.
49, Flint Street, Walworth, S.E.7.   Z1107B

BAGSHAW, R. L., Private, East Surrey Regiment.
He volunteered in February 1915, and later in the same year after completing his training, was drafted overseas. During his service in France he fought in the Somme and Ypres sectors, and was unhappily killed by the explosion of a shell in February 1916. He was entitled to the General Service and Victory Medals.
26, Henshaw Street, Walworth, S.E.17.   Z1108

BAGWELL, A., Corporal, Queen's Own (Royal West Kent Regiment).
Mobilised in August 1914, he was almost immediately drafted overseas, and took part in the Retreat from Mons. He also fought in the Battles of the Marne, La Bassée, Ypres, Neuve Chapelle, Hill 60, the second Battle of Ypres, Festubert, Loos, Albert, Vimy Ridge, and the first Battle of the Somme. He was severely wounded in this engagement in September 1916, and was invalided home to hospital. After being under treatment for about eighteen months until February 1918 he was discharged as medically unfit for further military service. He holds the Mons Star, and the General Service and Victory Medals.
102, Ferndale Road, Clapham, S.W.4.   Z1109

BAILEY, A., Gunner, R.F.A.
He volunteered in October 1915, and was drafted overseas in the following April. During his service in France he was engaged in much heavy fighting in various sectors of the Western Front, including Armentières, the Somme, Metz Wood, Lens, Arras, Delville Wood, Vimy Ridge, Bullecourt, and Bapaume. He was gassed in action at Armentières on March 19th, 1918, and was invalided home, but returned again to France after three months. In May 1919 he was demobilised and holds the General Service and Victory Medals.
91, Hubert Grove, Landor Road, S.W.9.   Z1114B

BAILEY, C., Private, Queen's Own (Royal West Kent Regiment).
He volunteered in June 1915, and after his training served for a time on important duties with his unit. In August 1916, after crossing to France he was transferred to a Trench Mortar Battery, and after taking part in many important engagements was killed in action at Cambrai on November 20th, 1917. He was entitled to the General Service and Victory Medals.
49, Rockingham Street, Southwark, S.E.1.   Z25389B

BAILEY, G., Private, 12th King's (Liverpool Regt.)
A serving soldier since May 1913, he was sent to the Western Front in May 1917. While in France he fought at Arras, Ypres, Passchendaele, Cambrai, the Somme, and St. Quentin, and was gassed in action near Lens in May 1918. After the Armistice he proceeded to Germany with the Army of Occupation, and was stationed on the Rhine until February 1919, when he was discharged. He holds the General Service and Victory Medals.
91, Hubert Grove, Landor Road, S.W.9.   Z1114A

BAILEY, G. R., Private, 7th Buffs (East Kent Regt.)
He volunteered in 1914, and in the following year was sent overseas. During his service in France he took part in the Battle of the Somme, and was gassed, and later killed in action on May 4th, 1917. He was mentioned in Despatches for his gallantry, and was awarded a Certificate to that effect. He was entitled to the 1914–15 Star, and the General Service and Victory Medals.
14, Redmore Road, Hammersmith, W.6.   11623A

BAILEY, H., Private, 1st Middlesex Regiment.
He attested in 1916, and two years later was called up for military service and sent to the Western Front in October. While overseas he served on the Maubeuge and Cambrai fronts, and was severely wounded near Le Cateau. After considerable hospital treatment he returned to England and was demobilised in October 1919, holding the General Service and Victory Medals.
103, Stonhouse Street, Clapham, S.W.4.   Z1116B

BAILEY, H. A., Corporal, R.E.
He volunteered in February 1915, and after his training was drafted to the Western Front. During his service overseas he took part in many important engagements. He returned home and was demobilised in January 1919, and holds the 1914-15 Star, and the General Service and Victory Medals.
23, Ramsay Road, Acton, W.3.   6383B

BAILEY, H. H., Private, Suffolk Regiment and Lancashire Fusiliers.
He volunteered in November 1915, and in the following year was drafted to France. During his service on the Western Front he fought in the Battle of the Somme, and after being severely wounded in August 1916, was invalided home. After his recovery he was retained on home duties, and did excellent work at the Manchester docks. He was demobilised in March 1919 and holds the General Service and Victory Medals.
16, Darwin Buildings, Walworth, S.E.17.   Z1111

BAILEY, H. J., R.S.M., Grenadier Guards.
He was mobilised at the outbreak of war, and was drafted to the Western Front, where he took a distinguished part in many important engagements in various sectors of the line. During his service he was in action at Ypres, and was severely wounded and twice buried by shell explosion. In April 1919, he was demobilised after his return home, and holds the 1914-15 Star, and the General Service and Victory Medals.
6, Wellesley Avenue, Hammersmith, W.6.   11569

BAILEY, H. J., Rifleman, Royal Irish Rifles.
After joining in February 1917, and passing through his course of training, he was drafted to France in May. He took a prominent part in many important engagements, including the Battles of Ypres, and Cambrai, and many operations in the Retreat and Advance of the Allies. He fell in action near Courtrai on October 23rd, and was buried at Vichte. He was entitled to the General Service and Victory Medals.
" His life for his country."
76, Harris Street, Camberwell, S.E.5.   Z4394

BAILEY, J., Private, Labour Corps.
He volunteered in June 1915, and in the same year was drafted to the Western Front, where he was engaged on important duties at Rouen in connection with the transport of munitions and supplies to the front lines. After the cessation of hostilities he returned to England, and in 1919 was demobilised, holding the 1914-15 Star, and the General Service and Victory Medals.
57, Lingham Street, Clapham Road, S.W.9.   Z1113

BAILEY, J. W., Private, Queen's (Royal West Surrey Regiment).
He joined in August 1916, and in the same year proceeded to Salonika, where he took part in many important operations on the Doiran, Struma, and Vardar fronts. During his service he suffered severely from malaria, and was in hospital at Taranto, Marseilles, and at home on arrival. After a period of home service he was demobilised in September 1919, and holds the General Service and Victory Medals.
12, Power Street, Wandsworth Road, S.W.8.   Z1115

BAILEY, P., Private, Royal Fusiliers.
He joined in 1916, and later in the same year was drafted to France, where he fought in many important engagements, including those at the Somme, the Ancre, Beaumont-Hamel, Ypres, Passchendaele and Lens. He was wounded and taken prisoner in the second battle of the Somme in 1918, and was in captivity in Germany for about nine months. He was released and demobilised in December of the same year, and holds the General Service and Victory Medals.
103, Stonhouse Street, Clapham, S.W.4.   Z1116A

BAILEY, W., Private, R.A.M.C.
He was serving at the commencement of hostilities, and was immediately drafted to France, where he served in the advanced areas on important ambulance duties in the Retreat from Mons, and in many later engagements. Whilst carrying out his duties in the Battle of the Somme he was mortally wounded, and died of his injuries on August 24th, 1916. He was buried at Beaucourt Military Cemetery. He was entitled to the Mons Star, and the General Service and Victory Medals.
49, Rockingham Street, Southwark, S.E.1.   Z25389A

BAILEY, V. C., Private, R.A.S.C. (M.T.)
Volunteering in January 1915, he was drafted to France four months later, and was engaged on important transport duties at Dunkirk and Calais until after hostilities ceased. He rendered valuable services, and was demobilised after four years with the Colours in July 1919. He holds the 1914-15 Star, and the General Service and Victory Medals.
2, Bradmore Park Road, Hammersmith, W.6.   11115

BAILEY, W., Driver, R.A.S.C. (M.T.)
He joined in June 1917, and in October of the same year was drafted to the Western Front. Attached to the 58th Division Ammunition Column, he served in many sectors until the conclusion of hostilities, afterwards being engaged on various important duties in connection with supplies. In May 1919 he was demobilised and holds the General Service and Victory Medals.
4, South Island Place, Brixton Road, S.W.9.   Z5217B.Z5218B

BAILEY, W. G., Corporal, R.A.F.
He joined in March 1916, and in the following June embarked for France. During his service in this theatre of war he rendered valuable service at the Somme, Vimy Ridge, Passchendaele, and in various later engagements. He was attached to the Observation Balloon Section until the Armistice. He was then sent to Germany with the Army of Occupation, and was stationed on the Rhine until demobilised on his return home in June 1919. He holds the General Service and Victory Medals.
101, Honeywell Road, Wandsworth Common, S.W.11.   Z1792

BAILEY, W. J., Private, Royal Fusiliers.
A serving soldier, he was mobilised at the outbreak of war, and in April 1915 was sent to the Dardanelles, where he took part in the Landing in Gallipoli, and was wounded. On his recovery he was drafted to France, and while fighting at Arras was again wounded. On rejoining his unit he was wounded in two other engagements, but was able to return to the fighting areas. He returned home and was demobilised in March 1919, and holds the 1914-15 Star, and the General Service and Victory Medals.
4, Bolingbroke Road, Battersea, S.W.11.   Z1112B

BAILEY, W. R., Driver, R.F.A.
Volunteering at the outbreak of war, he was sent to France on the completion of his training, and was engaged on important duties as a driver for the Royal Field Artillery in many notable engagements. Later he was drafted to Salonika, and afterwards to Egypt, where he was similarly employed until the cessation of hostilities. He was twice wounded in action during his service overseas. In 1919 he was demobilised after his return to England, and holds the General Service and Victory Medals.
109, Brackenbury Road, Hammersmith, W.6.   10710

BAILEY, W. R., A.B., R.N., T.B.D. " Ullswater."
He joined the Navy in August 1917, before attaining military age, and after training was posted to the Torpedo Boat Destroyer " Ullswater." He served in many seas and after taking part in the Raid on Zeebrugge, was on board the " Ullswater " when she was torpedoed off the coast of Holland. He was transferred to H.M.S. " Swallow," in which vessel he continued to serve until after the cessation of hostilities. He was demobilised in 1919, and holds the General Service and Victory Medals.
23, Lockington Road, Battersea Park Road, S.W.8.   Z1110

BAILEY, W. T., Rifleman, Rifle Brigade.
Volunteering in November 1914, he was sent to France on the completion of his training. After taking part in many important engagements he was unfortunately killed in the fierce fighting at Loos, at the end of September 1915. He was entitled to the 1914-15 Star, and the General Service and Victory Medals. 5, Laundry Road, Hammersmith, W.6.   15343

BAIN, G., Pte., Queen's (Royal West Surrey Regt).
He joined in April 1916, and was drafted to France in August of the same year. He took part in various important engagements, including those on the Somme, and was killed in action at Pozières on November 3rd, 1916. He was entitled to the General Service and Victory Medals.
36, Binns Road, Chiswick, W.4.   5417

BAINBRIDGE, F. G., Private, 2nd London Regiment (Royal Fusiliers) and West Yorkshire Regiment.
He was mobilised on the outbreak of war and in November 1914, was drafted to Egypt, and thence to Malta. In April 1915, he was sent to the Dardanelles, and served at Gallipoli until the Evacuation of the Peninsula. He was then transferred to Salonika, where he fought in the Balkan Campaign. Later he proceeded to the Western Front, where he was in action at Beaumont-Hamel, Arras, Vimy Ridge, Bullecourt, Messines, Bourlon Wood, and St. Quentin, and was present during the Retreat and Advance of 1918. He holds the 1914-15 Star, and the General Service and Victory Medals. and was demobilised in February 1919.
7, Pulross Road, Brixton Road, S.W.9.   Z1117

BAINBRIDGE, H. G., Pte., 2nd Gloucestershire Regt.
He volunteered in 1914, and in the following year was sent to the Western Front. He took part in various engagements including that at Ypres, and was killed in action near Hill 60 on May 6th 1915. He was entitled to the 1914-15 Star, and the General Service and Victory Medals.
59, Edithna Street, Landor Road, S.W.9. Z1145

BAINBRIDGE, H. J., Pte., 2nd Gloucestershire Regt.
He volunteered in September 1914, and in the following January was drafted to France, where he took part in numerous engagements, including those of Ypres, Festubert, Fromelles and Armentières. He was killed in action at Ypres on May 6th 1916, and was entitled to the 1914-15 Star, and the General Service and Victory Medals.
7, Pulross Road, Brixton Road, S.W.9. Z3498

BAINBRIDGE, W. R., Corporal, R.E. (R.O.D.)
He volunteered in July 1915, and after his training was drafted to the Western Front. He was engaged in various sectors on the construction of railways during his period of service overseas, and rendered valuable services. He was demobilised in April 1919, and holds the General Service and Victory Medals.
106, Antrobus Road, Chiswick, W.4. 6053

BAKER, A. A., Gunner, R.F.A.
Volunteering in April 1915, he was sent to France in December of the same year. He took part in numerous engagements, including those on the Somme, and at Arras, Ypres, and Passchendaele, and also served in the Retreat and Advance of 1918. After the Armistice he proceeded to Germany, where he served with the Army of Occupation at Cologne until he was demobilised in May 1919. He holds the 1914-15 Star, and the General Service and Victory Medals.
47, St. John's Hill Grove, Battersea, S.W. 11. Z1131

BAKER, A. C., Gunner, R.F.A.
He volunteered in 1915, and in the same year was drafted to the Western Front. He took part in severe fighting at Festubert, the Somme, Arras, Ypres, and in many other important engagements, and was wounded and invalided home. On his recovery he was drafted as garrison duty until 1919, when he returned home and was demobilised, holding the 1914-15 Star, and the General Service and Victory Medals.
59, Barlow Street, Walworth, S.E.17. Z1123

BAKER, A. E., Rifleman, King's Royal Rifle Corps.
He volunteered in February 1915, and in the same year was drafted to France, where he was in action at Ypres, Hooge, and Loos, and was severely wounded. He was invalided home and in 1918 was discharged as medically unfit for further service. In 1919 he re-joined, however, and served in France with the Graves Registration Section until 1920, when he returned home and was demobilised, holding the 1914-15 Star, and the General Service and Victory Medals.
42, Saltoun Road, Brixton, S.W.2. Z3060

BAKER, A. E., Trooper, 3rd (Prince of Wales') Dragoon Guards.
He was serving at the outbreak of war, and was sent to France immediately afterwards, and was killed in action during severe fighting in the Retreat from Mons in 1914. He was entitled to the Mons Star, and the General Service and Victory Medals.
84, Cranbrook Road, Chiswick, W.4. 5388B

BAKER, A. G., Private, R.A.S.C. (M.T.)
Volunteering in December 1914, he was in the same month sent to the Western Front, where he was present at numerous engagements. He was chiefly employed in the transport of ammunition and supplies to the various fronts and rendered valuable services. He was demobilised in May 1919, holding the 1914-15 Star, and the General Service and Victory Medals.
86B, Queen's Road, Battersea, S.W.8. Z1130

BAKER, B., Private, R.A.S.C. (M.T.)
He volunteered in November 1914, and after his training served on important duties with his unit. He was not successful in obtaining his transfer overseas owing to being medically unfit, and was discharged in March 1915.
56, Dalyell Road, Landor Road, S.W.9. Z1127C

BAKER, B., Driver and Farrier, R.F.A.
He joined in May 1916, and in the same year was drafted to the Western Front, where he took part in numerous engagements, including those on the Somme, and at Arras, Ypres, Béthune, Bapaume, and elsewhere. He also served in the Retreat and Advance of 1918, and after the conclusion of hostilities returned to England, and was demobilised in January 1919. He holds the General Service and Victory Medals.
2, Content Street, Walworth, S.E.17. Z1119

BAKER, B. T., Private, R.A.S.C. (M.T.)
He volunteered in April 1915, and was drafted to the Western Front in the same month. He served in various engagements including those at Ypres, Loos, Vimy Ridge, the Somme, Arras, Passchendaele, Lens, and Cambrai, and also took part in the Retreat and Advance of 1918, and was wounded. He afterwards proceeded with the Army of Occupation to Germany, where he was still serving in 1920, and holds the 1914-15 Star, and the General Service and Victory Medals.
36, Smyrks Road, Walworth, S.E.17. Z1133

BAKER, C. F., Sapper, R.E.
He joined in July 1918, and after his training served at various stations on important duties with his unit. He rendered valuable services but was not successful in obtaining his transfer overseas before the cessation of hostilities. He was demobilised in February 1919.
2, Carthew Road, Hammersmith, W.6. 10724

BAKER, E., Driver, R.F.A.
Volunteering in April 1915, he was sent to France in the same year. He took part in severe fighting at Vimy Ridge, the Somme, Arras, Ypres, Passchendaele, and in various other engagements, and also served in the Retreat and Advance of 1918, and was wounded. He was demobilised in January 1919, and holds the 1914-15 Star, and the General Service and Victory Medals.
8, New Road, Battersea Park Road, S.W.8. Z1132B

BAKER, F., Corporal, East Surrey Regiment.
He was in the Army in India on the outbreak of war, and on coming to the Western Front in 1915, fought with the 85th Division at Ypres, and in other engagements. In 1916 he was drafted to Salonika where he did good service until the cessation of hostilities in many operations on the Struma and Doiran fronts. During his service there he suffered badly from malaria. After his return to England he was demobilised in April 1919, and holds the 1914-15 Star, and the General Service and Victory Medals.
37, Crawshay Road, Stockwell, S.W.9. Z4395C

BAKER, F., Private, 1st Welch Regiment.
He joined in August 1916, and was drafted to Salonika in November of the same year. He took part in various engagements on the Doiran, Struma and Monastir fronts, and also served in the Advance on the Vardar. Contracting malaria he was invalided home, and in February 1919 was demobilised holding the General Service and Victory Medals.
96, Sabine Road, Battersea, S.W.11. Z1124

BAKER, F. W., Corporal, R.A.S.C. (M.T.)
Mobilised in 1914 he was shortly afterwards sent to France where he served in numerous engagements, including those at Mons, Ypres and Loos, and was also engaged as a motor driver in the transport of ammunition and supplies to various sectors. He was afterwards transferred to Italy, where he was again in action. Later he returned to France, and took part in the Retreat and Advance of 1918. He was demobilised in April 1919, and holds the Mons Star and the General Service and Victory Medals.
82, Mysore Road, Lavender Hill, S.W.11. Z4002A

BAKER, F. W., Driver, R.F.A.
He volunteered in August 1914, having previously served, and was drafted to India in the same year. In 1915 he was transferred to Salonika, where he served in various engagements in the Balkan campaign. After the cessation of hostilities he returned home and was demobilised in March 1919, holding the 1914-15 Star, and the General Service, Victory, and Long Service and Good Conduct Medals.
5, Bridgman Road, Chiswick, W.4. 6618

BAKER, H. (D.C.M.), Sergt., Oxfordshire and Buckinghamshire Light Infantry.
Volunteering in September 1914, he was sent to France in the following year. He took part in severe fighting in many important engagements and was twice wounded, and was awarded the Distinguished Conduct Medal for bravery in the Field. He also holds the 1914-15 Star, and the General Service and Victory Medals. He was invalided home in 1918, and was discharged in the same year as medically unfit for further service. 6, Anley Road, West Kensington, W.14. 11816B

BAKER, H., Private, R.A.M.C.
He volunteered in July 1915, and in the following year was drafted to the Western Front where he was engaged in various sectors on important hospital duties and rendered valuable services. He returned home and was demobilised in January 1919, and holds the General Service and Victory Medals.
27, Yeovil Street, Wandsworth Road, S.W.8. Z1135

BAKER, H. G. Signalman, R.N., H.M.S. "Prince George" and "King Orry."
He volunteered in 1915, and served with the Grand Fleet in the North Sea, where he was engaged on important duties and rendered valuable services. He was also at Scapa Flow when the surrendered German Fleet arrived. He was demobilised in May 1919, and holds the General Service and Victory Medals.
173, Ingrave Road, Battersea, S.W.11. Z1129

BAKER, H. H., Private, R.A.S.C. (Labour Section).
Volunteering in March 1915, he was sent to France in the following month. He served in various sectors on important duties with his unit and rendered valuable services. He returned home and was demobilised in January 1919, holding the 1914-15 Star, and the General Service and Victory Medals. 5, Warrior Road, Camberwell, S.E.5. Z1125C

BAKER, H. J. W., Private, 2nd Middlesex Regt.
Joining in February 1917, he was drafted to the Western Front in the following year. He took part in the Retreat and Advance of 1918, and after only ten weeks' service in France was reported missing, and is presumed to have been killed in action. He was entitled to the General Service and Victory Medals. 13, Porson Street, Wandsworth Road, S.W.8. Z1122A

BAKER, H. J. W. (Senior), Private, Labour Corps and Queen's (Royal West Surrey Regiment).
He joined in February 1917, and was afterwards drafted to the Western Front. He was engaged during the Retreat and Advance of 1918 on special duties with the R.E. on road repairing and other important work and rendered valuable services. During his service overseas he met with an accident which resulted in an injury to his ankle. He was demobilised in February 1919, and holds the General Service and Victory Medals. 13, Porson Street, Wandsworth Road, S.W.8. Z1122B

BAKER, J., Rifleman, Rifle Brigade.
He joined in June 1917, and after completing his training proceeded to France in the following January. He took part in several operations on that Front, and was wounded and taken prisoner in March 1918 in the Battle of the Somme. He had been previously wounded at St. Quentin, and was also hit while being taken to hospital. After the Armistice he was repatriated, and was demobilised in September 1919, holding the General Service and Victory Medals. 12, Elmington Road, Camberwell, S.E.5. Z4369

BAKER, J. C. S., Driver, R.F.A.
He was serving at the outbreak of war, and was shortly after sent to the Western Front, where he took part in the severe fighting at the Battles of Mons, Ypres, Vimy Ridge, and in other engagements. He was wounded near Ypres in December 1915, and after being invalided home was discharged in July 1916, owing to his injuries. He holds the Mons Star and the General Service and Victory Medals. 40. Cowan Street, Camberwell, S.E.5. Z5030

BAKER, J. W., Corporal, R.F.A.
He volunteered in November 1914, and after a period of training was drafted to the Western Front, where he took part in severe fighting at Neuve Chapelle, Festubert, Loos, the Somme, Ypres, Passchendaele, and other engagements. He also served in the Retreat and Advance of 1918, and afterwards proceeded with the Army of Occupation to Germany. He was demobilised in April 1919, and holds the 1914-15 Star, and the General Service and Victory Medals. 12830 4, Yeldham Buildings, Yeldham Road, Hammersmith, W.6.

BAKER, P. C., Sergt., R.A.S.C.
He was mobilised in August 1914, and was drafted to the Western Front in the same month. He was engaged throughout the war in the transport of ammunition and supplies to the various fronts and rendered valuable services. He was demobilised in August 1919, holding the 1914 Star, and the General Service and Victory Medals. 18, Kinglake Street, Walworth, S.E.17. Z1120

BAKER, P. E., A.B., Royal Naval Division.
He volunteered in August 1914, and was posted to H.M.S. "Benbow," and proceeded direct to Antwerp, where he served during the Siege. On the surrender of the city he escaped to Holland, where he was interned until the Armistice. He returned home and was demobilised in January 1919, and holds the 1914 Star, and the General Service and Victory Medals. 63, Aldbridge Street, Walworth, S.E.17. Z1118

BAKER, T., Corporal, R.E.
He volunteered in August 1914, and in the same year was sent to France with the Queen's Own (Royal West Kent Regiment). He took part in severe fighting in various engagements, and was wounded at Ypres. He was afterwards transferred to the Royal Engineers, and was engaged as an acetylene welder in France, and rendered valuable services. He was demobilised in January 1919, and holds the 1914 Star, and the General Service and Victory Medals. 48, Beaufoy Road, Lavender Hill, S.W.11. Z1134

BAKER, W., Private, R.A.V.C.
He joined in December 1916, and in January of the following year was sent to Salonika. He was engaged with the Mobile Section in taking horses up to the various fronts, often under heavy fire. Contracting malaria he was invalided home and was discharged as medically unfit for further service in September 1919, holding the General Service and Victory Medals. 9, Osborne Street, Walworth, S.E.17. Z1121

BAKER, T., Rifleman, 2nd Rifle Brigade.
Joining in March 1917, he went through a course of training and afterwards served on important duties with his unit until April of the following year, when he was drafted to the Western Front. He took part in severe fighting in the Somme, Marne, Amiens, and Ypres areas, and was wounded. He was taken prisoner at Villers Bretonneux, and whilst in captivity was employed by the enemy in conveying ammunition to the front lines and bringing back the wounded. On his release he returned home, and was demobilised in November 1918, holding the General Service and Victory Medals. 18, Wye Street, Battersea, S.W.11. Z1128

BAKER, W. H., Pte., M.G.C. and Sherwood Foresters.
He attested in December 1915, and after being called up in September 1916, went through his training until February 1917, when he was drafted to the Western Front. He took an active part in the severe fighting at Vimy Ridge, Arras, Messines, Ypres, Passchendaele, and Cambrai. In November 1917, he contracted trench fever and was invalided home, but on his recovery he returned to France in September 1918, after being transferred to the Machine Gun Corps, and again went into action. He was demobilised in February 1919, holding the General Service and Victory Medals. 185B, Cator Street, Peckham, S.E.15. Z5029

BAKEWELL, H., Trooper, 1st (Royal) Dragoons.
Having enlisted in March 1912 he was mobilised on the outbreak of hostilities and immediately sent to France, where he took a prominent part in many important engagements right through the war, including those at Mons, La Bassée, Ypres, Neuve Chapelle, Loos, the Somme, Arras, Bullecourt, and the Retreat and Advance of the Allies in 1918. After returning home he was demobilised in March 1919, and holds the Mons Star, and the General Service and Victory Medals. 81, Arthur Road, Brixton Road, S.W.9. Z4397

BALDRY, E. E., Driver, R.H.A. and R.F.A.
Volunteering in November 1914, he was drafted in the following year to the Western Front. Whilst there he took part in the fierce fighting at Hill 60, Ypres, Loos, the Somme, Arras, Vimy Ridge, Lens, Albert, Bapaume, Delville Wood and various other engagements. Later he proceeded to India, and was stationed at Meerut, where he contracted small pox. On his recovery he went to Mesopotamia, where he saw much service until the close of the campaign. When about to return to England he was drafted to the North West Frontier of India, and assisted in the suppression of the Afghan rising. After his return home he was demobilised in October 1919, and holds the 1914-15 Star, the General Service and Victory Medals, and the India General Service Medal (with Clasp, Afghanistan, N.W. Frontier, 1919.) 8, Hillery Road, Walworth, S.E.17. Z1136

BALDRY, W., Private, Dorset Regiment.
A Reservist, he was mobilised in August 1914, and proceeded to the Western Front early in the following year. There he fought in many battles of importance, including those of Neuve Chapelle, Vimy Ridge, the Somme and Ypres, and was seriously wounded. He returned home and after being in hospital for a considerable time was demobilised in December 1919, holding the 1914-15 Star, and the General Service and Victory Medals. In March 1920 he died as a result of wounds received in action. 10, Bolton Street, Camberwell, S.E.5. Z1137

BALDWIN, J. H., Corporal, Royal Fusiliers.
He volunteered in February 1915, and after his training was drafted to the Dardanelles, where he took part in the landing at Suvla Bay, and subsequently suffered from dysentery. Afterwards he proceeded to France, where he saw much active service. At Ploegsteert Wood he was severely gassed and invalided home, but on his recovery he returned to the fighting area, and was wounded at Sailly. Later he served in Ireland until demobilised in July 1919. He holds the 1914-15 Star, and the General Service and Victory Medals. 54, Blondel Street, Battersea, S.W.11. Z1138

BALL, A. J., Corporal, R.A.S.C. (M.T.)
Volunteering in October 1914, he was drafted in November of the same year to the Western Front. There he was engaged on important duties at repairing depôts in various sectors, and rendered valuable services until after fighting ceased. In March 1919 he returned home and was demobilised, holding the 1914 Star, and the General Service and Victory Medals. 51, Aldbridge Street, Walworth, S.E.17. Z1140A

BALL, E. C., Rifleman, King's Royal Rifle Corps.
Volunteering in November 1914, he was sent to France in May of the following year. He took part in severe fighting at Ypres, and was seriously wounded. He was invalided home and discharged as medically unfit for further service in October 1916, and holds the 1914-15 Star, and the General Service and Victory Medals. 40, Geneva Road, Brixton Road, S.W.9. Z3431

BALL, G., Rifleman, 16th London Regiment (Queen's Westminster Rifles).
Volunteering in August 1915, he was drafted to the Western Front in January of the following year, and took part in severe fighting at Bullecourt, and in numerous other engagements. During the operations near Bapaume his Battalion was surrounded, and he was reported missing. He was afterwards presumed to have been killed in action on August 28th, 1918, and was entitled to the General Service and Victory Medals.
"A valiant soldier with undaunted heart he breasted Life's last hill."
61, Calmington Road, Camberwell, S.E.5.   Z5316

BALL, H. G., Trooper, West Somerset Hussars.
He joined in February 1917, and on the completion of his training in the following year was drafted to the Western Front, where he fought in the last stages of the war. Later he proceeded to Egypt, and did good service there for about twelve months. In March 1920 he returned home and was demobilised, holding the General Service and Victory Medals.
36, Portland Street, Walworth, S.E.17.

BALL, H. W., Private, R.A.S.C.
He volunteered in May 1915, and for a time was retained on important military duties at various stations. Later he was drafted to Salonika, where he also did much valuable work until his return to England. He was discharged in June 1918 in consequence of his service, and holds the 1914–15 Star, and the General Service and Victory Medals.
36, Portland Street, Walworth, S.E.17.

BALL, H. W., Private, M.G.C.
He joined in November 1917, and in August of the following year after the completion of his training proceeded to France. There he took part in the fighting at Péronne, and was unfortunately killed in action in September 1918, after being overseas only one month. He was entitled to the General Service and Victory Medals.
15, Dashwood Road, Wandsworth Road, S.W.8.   Z1142

BALL, J., Private, R.A.S.C. (F.A.)
Volunteering in October 1914, he proceeded to Ireland for his training, and in 1916 was drafted to France. There he served with the 113th Field Ambulance at Ypres, the Somme and many other important engagements, and was gassed. In June 1919 he returned home and was demobilised, holding the General Service and Victory Medals.
11, Latchmere Road, Battersea, S.W.11.   Z1139

BALL, J. W., Rifleman, King's Royal Rifle Corps.
Joining in June 1916 he completed his course of training, and in the following September was drafted to the Western Front. He took an active part in the Somme Offensive in the Autumn of that year, and was unfortunately killed in action on December 22nd, 1916. He was entitled to the General Service and Victory Medals.
"Great deeds cannot die."
79, Akerman Road, Brixton Road, S.W.9.   Z4399B. Z4400B

BALL, P. H., Gunner, R.N., H.M.S. "Benbow."
He volunteered in August 1915, and served with the Grand Fleet in the North Sea. He was in action in various engagements and also on patrol duties. He was discharged as medically unfit for further service in January 1920, and holds the 1914–15 Star, and the General Service and Victory Medals.
16, Sandover Road, Camberwell, S.E.5.   Z5317B

BALL, S. J., Private, Suffolk Regiment.
He joined in April 1916, and in October of the same year proceeded overseas. He was principally engaged on important guard duties during his service on the Western Front, and did much valuable work. He returned home and was demobilised in December 1918, holding the General Service and Victory Medals.
19, Cornbury Street, Walworth, S.E.17.   Z1141

BALL, W. E., Private, 24th London Regt. (Queen's).
Volunteering in May 1915, he was drafted in July of the following year to France, and afterwards into Salonika, in both of which fighting areas he saw much active service. Later he proceeded to Egypt, and remained there until March 1919, when he returned home for demobilisation. He holds the General Service and Victory Medals.
36, Bridgman Road, Chiswick, W.4.   6275

BALL, W. H., Private, 2nd East Lancashire Regt.
He joined the Army in 1905, and shortly after the outbreak of war proceeded to France, where he fought at Le Cateau and Ypres in 1914, and was wounded and captured at Loos in September 1915. Still suffering from his injuries he was brought to England in September 1919, and three months later, after hospital treatment, was discharged. He holds the 1914 Star, and the General Service and Victory Medals.
12, Broomgrove Road, Stockwell, S.W.9.   Z4398

BALLARD, A., L/Cpl., 20th King's Royal Rifle Corps.
He volunteered in November 1915, and was sent to France in the following March, and took part in severe fighting on the Somme, and at Arras, Ypres and Cambrai. He also served in the Retreat and Advance of 1918, and returning to England after the cessation of hostilities was demobilised in April 1919, holding the General Service and Victory Medals.
20, Hazelmere Road, Peckham, S.E.15.   Z5901

BALLARD, J. T., Corporal, R.F.A.
He volunteered in May 1915, and after the completion of his training crossed to France in the following June. He took a prominent part in many important operations from that date onwards, and was unfortunately killed with several others in a dug-out on September 15th, 1918. He was entitled to the 1914–15 Star, and the General Service and Victory Medals.
"Nobly striving, he nobly fell that we might live."
52, Cater Street, Peckham, S.E.15.   Z4401

BALLARD, W., Private, R.A.S.C. (M.T.)
He volunteered in November 1914, and was almost immediately drafted to the Western Front. There he rendered valuable service in the fierce fighting on the Somme, and in many other engagements, until the conclusion of hostilities. He was demobilised in April 1919, and holds the 1914 Star, and the General Service and Victory Medals.
35, Kent Road, Chiswick, W.4.   6887

BALLER, G. F., Private, Essex Regiment.
He joined in November 1916, and after his training was retained for a time on important duties in England. In May 1918 he was drafted to France, and took part in the fighting at Merville, Lille, Armentières, and various other places until the cessation of hostilities. In June 1919 he returned home and was demobilised, holding the General Service and Victory Medals.
27, Bramfield Road, Wandsworth Common. S.W.11.   Z1764

BALMFORTH, J. E., Driver, R.F.A.
Volunteering in April 1915, he was drafted in November of the same year to the Western Front. While there he took part in fierce fighting on the Somme, at Arras, Kemmel, Passchendaele, Cambrai and in various other engagements, until the cessation of hostilities. In January 1919 he returned home, and was demobilised, holding the 1914–15 Star, and the General Service and Victory Medals.
166, Grosvenor Terrace, Camberwell, S.E.5.   Z1143

BAMBERY, J., Private, Labour Corps.
He joined in July 1917, and was soon drafted to the Western Front, where he was engaged in trench digging, burial work, and various other important duties until November 1919, when he returned home for demobilisation. He holds the General Service and Victory Medals.
22, Lingham Street, Stockwell, S.W.9.   Z1144

BAMBRIDGE, S. H., Pte., 5th (Royal Irish) Lancers.
Volunteering in August 1914, he served until December 1916 in Ireland. He then proceeded to France, and there rendered excellent service as a Signaller in many notable battles, including those of Beaumont-Hamel, Arras, Vimy Ridge, Ypres, Passchendaele, the Somme, Cambrai, Armentières, Amiens, and the Retreat and Advance of 1918. After the Armistice he proceeded to Germany with the Army of Occupation and was stationed at Cologne. During his service he was seriously injured by being thrown from his horse, and was in hospital for four months. He was demobilised in October 1919, and holds the General Service and Victory Medals. 20, Carfax Square, Clapham Park Rd., S.W.4. Z1146

BANDY, J. D., Pioneer, R.E.
Volunteering in March 1915, he was sent to the Western Front in the following year. He rendered valuable service in the Somme sector, and was wounded. He unfortunately died from injuries received accidentally in the course of his duties on August 3rd, 1916, and was entitled to the General Service and Victory Medals.
"He passed out of the sight of men by the path of duty and self-sacrifice."
20, Tindal Street, Lothian Road, S.W.9.   Z5031

BANFIELD, A., Special War Worker.
In order to release a man for the Army this lady was engaged on highly important dairy duties, and other public services throughout the war. The manner in which she performed her trying work gave entire satisfaction.
69, Rylston Road, Fulham, S.W.6.   16180B

BANFIELD, H., Gunner, R.F.A.
He joined in November 1916, and after serving in Ireland at various stations was sent to the Western Front in February 1918. Whilst overseas he took part in many engagements in the Retreat and Advance, including those at Soissons, Amiens, Bapaume, the Scarpe, Epéhy, Cambrai and Le Cateau. He was demobilised in April 1919, and holds the General Service and Victory Medals.
27, Nunhead Crescent, Peckham, S.E.15.   Z6140

BANFIELD, J. G., 1st Class Aircraftsman, R.A.F. (late R.N.A.S.)
He joined the R.N.A.S. in November 1917, and early in the following year was drafted to Egypt. There he saw much service at Alexandria, and was attached to the motor boats service on patrol work for the seaplanes. He returned home and was demobilised in December 1919, and holds the General Service and Victory Medals.
3, Montholme Road, Wandsworth Common, S.W.11.   Z1791

BANFIELD, P. A., Bombardier, R.G.A.
He joined in May 1916, and in the following year was drafted to the Western Front. While there he took part in much severe fighting at the Somme, Ypres, Arras, Messines and Bullecourt. He suffered from shell-shock in October 1917, and was invalided home. In August 1919 he was discharged as medically unfit for further duty, and holds the King's Certificate, and the General Service and Victory Medals.
18, Seneca Road, Sandmere Road, Clapham. S.W.4.   Z1147

BANGS, E. J., Private, 17th Essex Regiment.
After joining in June 1918, he went through his course of training and was engaged on important duties with his unit. He was not successful in securing his transfer to a fighting front before the cessation of hostilities, but rendered valuable coastal defence services, and was demobilised in February 1919.
105, Smyrks Road, Walworth, S.E.17.   Z1148

BANHAM, H. A., Pte., Duke of Cornwall's Light Infantry.
After joining in August 1914, and completing his training he proceeded to the Western Front in November 1915. He took a prominent part in the engagements at Albert, the Somme and Givenchy, where he was badly wounded. After his recovery he returned to the lines, and was subsequently killed in action in the Battle of Cambrai on November 30th, 1917. He was entitled to the 1914-15 Star, and the General Service and Victory Medals.
134, Lavender Road, Battersea, S.W.11.   Z1149

BANKS, B. A., Special War Worker.
During the whole course of the war he was engaged on highly responsible duties at Messrs. Vanderville's Munition Works at Acton. He acted as chief clerk in this important business, and rendered services of a most valuable nature.
149, St. Alban's Avenue, Chiswick, W.4.   T7877

BANKS, F., Pte., Duke of Cornwall's Light Infantry.
He volunteered in February 1915, and in the following June, after completing his training, proceeded to France. After only a few days' service overseas he was unfortunately killed by shell explosion at Festubert on June 18th, 1915. He was entitled to the 1914-15 Star, and the General Service and Victory Medals.
17, Kennard Street, Battersea, S.W.11.   Z1150

BANKS, F., Rifleman, 5th London Regt. (London Rifle Brigade) and Rifle Brigade.
He joined in April 1918, and after his training served at various stations on important duties with his unit. He rendered valuable services, but was not successful in obtaining his transfer overseas before the cessation of hostilities. He was demobilised in October 1919.
59, Sussex Road, Coldharbour Lane, S.W.9.   Z3432A

BANKS, F., Private, R.A.O.C.
Volunteering in January 1915, he was drafted to the Western Front in the following April, and served overseas until after the cessation of hostilities. He was engaged with his unit in many sectors of the Front, particularly Ypres and the Somme, and rendered valuable services throughout. After his return home he was demobilised in December 1919, and holds the 1914-15 Star, and the General Service and Victory Medals.
34, Eastbury Grove, Chiswick, W.4.   5466

BANKS, J. H., Private, Labour Corps.
He joined in August 1916, and in March of the following year was drafted to the Western Front with the 21st London Regiment (1st Surrey Rifles.) He contracted dysentery, and afterwards was transferred to the Labour Corps, with which he served on the Ypres and Arras fronts. In July 1918 he was invalided home. He was discharged in consequence of his services in February 1919, and holds the General Service and Victory Medals.
7A, Victory Square, Camberwell, S.E.5.   Z5563

BANKS, V., Sergt., 2nd East Surrey Regiment.
He joined in June 1918, and after the completion of his training proceeded to Russia, where he held the responsible position of chief intelligence clerk at Riga, and rendered valuable services. In 1920 he was still serving there.
15, Brackenbury Road, Hammersmith, W.6.   11645

BANKS, W. G., Private, R.A.V.C.
Joining in 1916, he went through a course of training, and afterwards served on important duties with his unit at various stations. He rendered valuable services, but was not successful in obtaining his transfer overseas before the cessation of hostilities. He was demobilised in September 1919.
59, Sussex Road, Coldharbour Lane, S.W.9.   Z3432B

BANNING, A. (Mrs.), Special War Worker.
From May until October 1916, this lady was engaged as wardmaid and laundress at the Horton War Hospital, Epsom, and the Brook Military Hospital, Woolwich, and carried out her important and varied duties with great care and efficiency.
17, Sedan Street, Walworth, S.E.17.   Z1151B

BANNING, A. E., Sapper, R.E.
Volunteering in April 1915, he completed his course of training and was drafted to Egypt, where he was engaged on important guard duties and building operations. In 1916 he proceeded to France, and rendered valuable services with his unit in the Somme area, and at Hill 60, Ypres, Arras and Loos, and during the Retreat and Advance of 1918. After the Armistice he returned to England, and was demobilised in January 1919, holding the 1914-15 Star, and the General Service and Victory Medals.
17, Sedan Street, Walworth, S.E.17.   Z1151A

BANTING, E., Private, Middlesex Regt. (Labour Bn).
He joined in June 1916, and until 1919 was engaged at various stations on important duties with his unit. Owing to physical unfitness he was not successful in securing his transfer to a fighting front, but he rendered valuable services until demobilised in September 1919.
142, Stewart's Road, Battersea Park Road, S.W.8.   Z1152

BARBARY, W. J., Corporal, R.A.S.C.
He volunteered in June 1915, and after completing his training was drafted to France in the following year. While on this Front he was engaged on transport service in various parts of the line, particularly at Ypres, the Somme, Albert, Péronne and Cambrai, and also did valuable work in the Retreat and Advance of 1918. After returning to England he was demobilised in March 1919, and holds the General Service and Victory Medals.
43, Longhedge Street, Battersea, S.W.11.   Z1153

BARBER, A. G., Gunner, R.F.A.
He volunteered soon after the outbreak of hostilities, and in January 1915, was drafted to the Western Front. He took an active part in many important engagements until the close of the war, including those at Ypres, the Somme, Loos, Arras, and the Retreat and Advance of 1918. After the Armistice he went to Germany with the Army of Occupation and did valuable service at Cologne until his return home for demobilisation in February 1919. He holds the 1914-15 Star, and the General Service and Victory Medals.
8, D'Eynsford Road, Camberwell Green, S.E.5.   Z1783

BARBER, B. A., Private, Labour Corps.
He joined in January 1916, and later in the year proceeded to the Western Front, where he was engaged until the close of hostilities in trench digging and burial duties in connection with many operations of importance, including those of the Retreat and Advance of 1918. He returned home and was demobilised in February 1919, holding the General Service and Victory Medals.
25, Broughton Street, Battersea Park, S.W.8.   Z1155

BARBER, H. E., Sapper, R.E.
He volunteered in November 1914, and after the completion of his training was drafted to the Western Front, where he rendered valuable services with his unit in the Battles of St. Eloi, Loos, the Somme, the Ancre, and in the Retreat and Advance of 1918. He also took part in several bombing raids. On one occasion he was badly gassed and was blind for a time, but fortunately recovered his sight later. After his return home he was demobilised in May 1919, holding the 1914-15 Star, and the General Service and Victory Medals.
137, Queen's Road, Walworth, S.E.17   Z2688C

BARBER, O. J., Gunner, R.G.A.
He volunteered in November 1915, and upon the completion of his training was drafted to France in January 1916. From that time onward he did valuable service with his Battery in various sectors of our line and took part in many important engagements until hostilities ceased. Returning home in February 1919, he was demobilised in the following month, and holds the General Service and Victory Medals.
85, Brackenbury Road, Hammersmith, W.6.   10721

BARBER, P., Special War Worker.
During the whole period of the war he was engaged on work of great National importance at Messrs. Wilkinson's Factory, Acton, where he was employed as a sword and bayonet grinder. He carried out his highly responsible duties with the utmost care and efficiency.
14, Quick Road, Chiswick, W.4.   5671A

BARBER, J. R., Private, 12th Essex Regiment.

He came over from Canada to fight for England and volunteered in September 1914. After being retained on important duties with his unit he was drafted to France in 1916, and for some time served at Calais. Subsequently he did good work at Poperinghe and Ypres, and was transferred to the 1st Suffolk Regiment. His health then broke down and after being invalided home he was engaged on important duties in Cambridgeshire until his demobilisation in March 1919. He holds the General Service and Victory Medals.

12, Trollope Street, Battersea Park, S.W.8.   Z1157

BARBER, T. H., Pte., Loyal North Lancashire Regt.

After volunteering in November 1914, he went through his course of training, and was retained at various stations on important duties until 1916, when he proceeded to France. He fought in the Somme Offensive of that year, and in the Battle of Ypres in 1917. In consequence of a severe wound he was then invalided to England, but on his recovery returned to France and fought in the Retreat and Advance of 1918. After the Armistice he went to Germany with the Army of Occupation, and on his return home was demobilised in December 1919. He holds the General Service and Victory Medals.

21, Latchmere Road, Battersea, S.W.11.   Z1156

BARBER, T. J., Sergt., King's Royal Rifle Corps.

After volunteering in November 1914, he was drafted to the Western Front in February 1915, From that time forward he took a prominent part in many of the chief engagements, including those at Neuve Chapelle, Ypres, Loos, Vimy Ridge, the Somme, Lens, Cambrai and the Retreat and Advance of the Allies in 1918. During his service he was wounded on three occasions. After returning to England he was demobilised in February 1919, and holds the 1914-15 Star, and the General Service and Victory Medals.

92, Nelson Row, High Street, Clapham, S.W.4.   Z1158

BARBER, W., Rflmn., King's Royal Rifle Corps and Private, 24th London Regiment (The Queen's).

He was serving in the 24th London Regiment at the outbreak of war, but later was transferred to the King's Royal Rifle Corps, and in 1915 proceeded overseas. Whilst in France he fought in various battles and at Hill 60 was severely wounded He was invalided to hospital, and subsequently succumbed to his injuries on May 4th, 1915. He was entitled to the 1914-15 Star, and the General Service and Victory Medals.

"Whilst we remember the Sacrifice is not in vain."

7, Albion House, Amelia Street, Walworth, S.E.17.   26132

BARBER, W. S., Private, East Surrey and 23rd London Regiments.

He volunteered in May 1915, and later in the year on the completion of his training proceeded to France. He took part in the Battles of Loos, and many other engagements, and was killed in action in the Somme Offensive on September 16th, 1916. He was entitled to the 1914-15 Star, and the General Service and Victory Medals.

25, Broughton Road, Battersea Park, S.W.8.   Z1154

BARBER, W. P., Private, Royal Fusiliers.

Joining in June 1916, he passed through his training, and in November of the same year was drafted to the Western Front. After five months' service overseas, during which he fought in many operations in the Somme and Ypres areas, he was invalided home through serious illness, and in August 1917 was discharged as medically unfit for further military duty. He holds the General Service and Victory Medals.

25, Plough Road, Battersea, S.W.11.   Z1159

BARBER, W. W., Rifleman, Rifle Brigade.

He volunteered in August 1914, and was almost immediately drafted to France, and took part in the Retreat from Mons. He also fought in the Battle of the Aisne, where he died gloriously on the field of action on September 13th. He was entitled to the Mons Star, and the General Service and Victory Medals.

"Great deeds cannot die."

76, Kirkwood, Road, Nunhead S.E.15.   Z6139

BARBET, W. G., Armourer, R.N., H.M.S. "Walpole."

He joined in January 1916, and was posted to H.M.S. "Walpole" and served on important escort duties in the North Sea and Baltic. He holds the General Service and Victory Medals, and was demobilised in June 1919.

11, Shirley Road, Bedford Park, W.4.   7622

BARBET, W. J., Special War Worker.

In 1914 he accepted an important appointment at Messrs. Du Cros', Acton, where he was engaged on responsible work in connection with the manufacture of shells. Later he left this firm to take up the position of assistant manager at Messrs. Cubitts'. With both of these firms he rendered most valuable services in the production of that vital necessity for our Armies in the Field—munitions.

11, Shirley Road, Bedford Park, W.4.   7623

BARBURY, F. A., Gunner, R.F.A. and Private, South Wales Borderers.

He joined in February 1916, and in the same year proceeded to France. Whilst overseas he fought in numerous important engagements, including those on the Somme and at Cambrai, where he was wounded. He was invalided home to hospital, and after his recovery rejoined his unit in France, and served in the Retreat and Advance of 1918. He was demobilised in March of the succeeding year, and holds the General Service and Victory Medals.

3, Southwell Terrace, Lewis Road, Camberwell, S.E.5.   Z6148

BARCLAY, J. F., A.B., R.N., H.M.S. "Shakespeare."

He volunteered in August 1915, and served with the minesweepers, and on patrol duties. During his service he was in action in numerous engagements, and in 1920 was still with his ship. He holds the General Service and Victory Medals.

57, Speke Road, Battersea, S.W.11.   Z1160

BARDELL, A., Pte., Oxfordshire and Buckinghamshire Light Infantry and Royal Sussex Regt.

He volunteered in August 1914, and was immediately drafted to the Western Front, where he took part in the Retreat from Mons and was wounded. On his recovery he fought in numerous other engagements in France, until drafted to Russia. Here he served in the campaign against the Bolshevists until August 1919, when he returned to England, and was demobilised. He holds the Mons Star, and the General Service and Victory Medals, and a Russian Decoration.

73, Whellock Road, Chiswick, W.4.   T7521A

BARDELL, W., Private (Signaller), Oxfordshire and Buckinghamshire Light Infantry.

He volunteered in 1915, and in the same year was drafted to the Western Front, where he took part in the Battle of Arras and numerous other engagements, and was twice wounded. After the cessation of hostilities he proceeded to Germany with the Army of Occupation and served at Cologne until November 1919, when he returned to England and was demobilised, holding the 1914-15 Star, and the General Service and Victory Medals.

73, Whelland Road, Chiswick, W.4.   T7521B

BARHAM, A., Sergt., R.F.A.

He was serving in India at the outbreak of war and at the end of 1914 was drafted to Mesopotamia, where he took part in the campaign against the Turks. Later he was transferred to Egypt, and served with the forces operating in Palestine under General Allenby's command. In 1919 he was sent to Ireland, where he was still serving in 1920. He holds the 1914-15 Star, and the General Service and Victory Medals.

29, Mundella Road, Wandsworth Road, S.W.8.   Z1161B

BARHAM, F., Bombardier, R.F.A.

He was serving in India on the outbreak of war and in 1915 was drafted to Mesopotamia, where he took part in the campaign against the Turks and was in action in numerous engagements. After the cessation of hostilities he returned to England, and in 1919 was demobilised. holding the 1914-15 Star, and the General Service and Victory Medals.

29, Mundella Road, Wandsworth Road, S.W.8.   Z1161A

BARHAM, R. S., Sergt., Canadian Overseas Forces.

Volunteering in August 1914, he was drafted to the Western Front in the following year. Whilst in this theatre of war he fought in many Battles, including those at Ypres, Arras, and the Somme, and was twice wounded. He was invalided home in 1917 in consequence, and after his recovery was demobilised in June 1919, holding the 1914-15 Star, and the General Service and Victory Medals.

48, Handforth Road, Brixton Road, S.W.9.   Z5216

BARKER, A. W., Pte., Loyal North Lancashire Regt.

He joined in December 1916, and in the following year was drafted to France, where he was in action at Lens and Cambrai. He was gassed and later wounded during the Retreat of 1918, but on his recovery served in the Advance of that year. He holds the General Service and Victory Medals, and was demobilised in December 1919.

74, Aylesbury Road, Walworth, S.E.17.   Z1165

BARKER, C., Driver, R.A.S.C.

He joined in November 1918, and after his training served at various stations on important duties with his unit. He rendered valuable services, but owing to the cessation of hostilities before he had completed his training, was unable to obtain his transfer overseas. He was demobilised in October 1919.

10, Landseer Street, Battersea, S.W.11.   Z1162

BARKER, C. (M.S.M.), Sergt., 1st Grenadier Guards.

He was serving at the outbreak of war, and was drafted to the Western Front in August 1914. He took part in the Retreat from Mons and in the engagements at Ypres and Vimy Ridge and was wounded. He was awarded the Meritorious Service Medal for his consistently good work, and in addition holds the Mons Star, and the General Service and Victory Medals, and was demobilised in July 1920.

25, Queen's Square, Battersea Park, S.W.8.   Z1166

BARKER, E. E., Pte., East Surrey Regt., Highland Light Infantry and M.G.C.
He volunteered in August 1915, at fourteen years of age, and was drafted to the Western Front in the following January. He was in action at Ploegsteert, and on the Somme, and was wounded and invalided home. On his recovery he was sent to Ireland, but returned to France in March 1918, and took part in the Advance of that year. He holds the General Service and Victory Medals, and was demobilised in March 1919.
134, Speke Road, Battersea, S.W.11.   Z1163

BARKER, E. W., Rifleman, 1st Rifle Brigade.
He joined in April 1916, and three months later after passing through his course of training proceeded to France, where he did valuable work as a signaller in many important engagements, including those at the Somme, Beaumont-Hamel, Vimy Ridge, Bullecourt, Passchendaele, and the Retreat and Advance of 1918. After returning to England he was demobilised in 1919, holding the General Service and Victory Medals.
9, Love Lane, Stockwell Road, S.W.9.   Z4403

BARKER, G. E., Driver, R.F.A. and Sapper, R.E.
He volunteered in January 1915, and in the following year was drafted to France. Here he served in the Somme and Messines sectors, and took part in the Retreat and Advance of 1918. Later he was transferred to the R.E., and did valuable work on the railways. He holds the General Service and Victory Medals, and was demobilised in 1919.
21, Pitcairn Street, Wandsworth Road, S.W.8.   Z1164

BARKER, H., Private, 7th London Regiment.
He volunteered in April 1915, and was drafted to the Western Front, where he took part in numerous engagements. He was killed in action at Delville Wood during the Somme Offensive on September 15th, 1916, and was entitled to the General Service and Victory Medals.
76, St. Dunstan's Road, Hammersmith, W.6.   13538

BARKER, J., Rifleman, 6th London Regt. (Rifles.)
He joined in July 1916, and after having completed his training was drafted to the Western Front, where he took part in numerous engagements. He was killed in action during the Battle of Arras on May 6th, 1917, and was entitled to the General Service and Victory Medals.
7, Beryl Road, Hammersmith, W.6.   12785

BARKER, J. C., Private, Bedfordshire Regiment.
He joined in February 1917, and in January of the following year was drafted to the Western Front, where he took part in the severe fighting at Ypres and Cambrai, and in the Retreat of 1918. He was wounded at Ypres in May 1918, and invalided home. On his recovery he was engaged on important duties with his unit until he was demobilised in February 1919, holding the General Service and Victory Medals.
44, Grenard Road, Peckham, S.E.15.   Z5564A. Z5565A

BARKER, J. R., Gunner and Saddler, R.F.A.
He volunteered in July 1915, and was drafted to the Western Front in the following February. He served at Ypres and in the Somme and Arras sectors and was in action in numerous engagements. On the cessation of hostilities he returned to England, and in July 1919 was demobilised, holding the General Service and Victory Medals.
9, Torrens Street, Ferndale Road, S.W.4.   Z1167

BARLOW, A., Private, 10th Queen's (Royal West Surrey Regiment).
He joined in April 1917, and after having completed his training was drafted to the Western Front. Here he took part in numerous engagements, and was wounded in action. After the Armistice he proceeded to Germany with the Army of Occupation, with which he was still serving on the Rhine in 1920. He holds the General Service and Victory Medals.
82, Beryl Road, Hammersmith, W.6.   13426B

BARLOW, A., Private, 2nd Royal Fusiliers.
He volunteered in September 1914, and after having completed his training was drafted to the Western Front. Here he took part in numerous engagements and was killed in action at Ypres on August 20th 1918. He was entitled to the 1914-15 Star, and the General Service and Victory Medals.
82, Beryl Road, Hammersmith, W.6.   13426A

BARLOW, H. J. (M.M.), Cpl., The Royal Canadian Regiment and R.A.F.
He volunteered in August 1914, and was drafted to Bermuda, where he served until the following year, when he was sent to the Western Front. Here he was in action at Kemmel, Vimy Ridge, the Somme, Arras, Passchendaele and Lens. He was awarded the Military Medal for conspicuous gallantry at Ypres in June 1916, and later was transferred to the Royal Air Force, and served as a pilot until his demobilisation, which took place in February 1919. He also holds the 1914-15 Star, and the General Service and Victory Medals.   Z1184
5, Clarence Mansions, Bromells Road, Clapham, S.W.4.

BARLOW, J., Gunner, R.F.A.
He volunteered in May 1915, and later in the same year was drafted to the Western Front, where he was in action on the Somme and at Ypres, and in numerous other engagements. Returning to England he was discharged in February 1917 in consequence of his service. He holds the 1914-15 Star, and the General Service and Victory Medals.
5, Ingelow Road, Battersea Park, S.W.8.   Z1172

BARNES, E., Corporal, R.E.
He volunteered in 1914, and was sent to France in the following year. He took part in numerous engagements, including those at Loos, the Somme, Arras, Bullecourt, Messines, Lens and Cambrai. He also served in the Retreat and Advance of 1918, was killed in action at Le Cateau on November 5th, 1918, and was entitled to the 1914-15 Star, and the General Service and Victory Medals.
" His life for his Country, his soul to God."
18, Arden Street, Battersea Park Road, S.W.8.   Z5702D

BARNES, H., Driver, R.H.A.
He was serving at the outbreak of war, and was shortly afterwards sent to France. He took part in severe fighting in the Retreat from Mons, and at Ypres, the Somme, and in many other engagements. He also served in the Retreat and Advance of 1918, and afterwards proceeded with the Army of Occupation to Germany. He was discharged in 1920, holding the Mons Star, and the General Service and Victory Medals.
18, Arden Street, Battersea Park Road, S.W.8.   Z5702C

BARNES, H. C., 1st Air Mechanic, R.A.F.
He joined in July 1916, and was almost immediately drafted to the Western Front. Whilst in this theatre of war he rendered valuable service and was engaged as a sail maker, and on other various highly important duties. In April 1919, he returned to England, and was demobilised, holding the General Service and Victory Medals.
29, Bramfield Road, Battersea, S.W.11.   Z1765

BARNES, M. (Miss), Special War Worker.
From 1916 until September 1919, this lady was engaged on the production of munitions. For six months she worked at Messrs. Johnson's Filling Factory, Southwark, and afterwards at Messrs. Higgs & Hills' Factory, Lambeth, where she was engaged for three years on doping work. Her duties were carried out with great care and efficiency.
62, Sheepcote Lane, Battersea, S.W.11.   Z1185A

BARNES, W., Sergt., R.F.A.
Volunteering in August 1914, he was speedily drafted to the Western Front. Whilst there he took part in much heavy fighting in the Ypres, Somme, and Cambrai sectors. On one occasion he was blown up and seriously wounded by shell explosion and invalided home. After being in hospital for a considerable period he was discharged as medically unfit in November 1918. He holds the 1914-15 Star, and the General Service and Victory Medals.   Z1187A
33, Priory Grove, Lansdowne Road, South Lambeth. S.W.8.

BARNES, W. H., Private, West Yorkshire Regiment.
Volunteering in 1914, he was sent to the Dardanelles in the following year and served there until the Evacuation. He was next transferred to Egypt, and thence to France, where he took part in severe fighting on the Somme and at Arras and Ypres. He also served in the North Russian Expedition, and whilst overseas was three times wounded. He was demobilised in 1919, holding the 1914-15 Star, and the General Service and Victory Medals.
18, Arden Street, Battersea Park Road, S.W.8.   Z5702A

BARNES, W. J., Private, R.A.S.C. (M.T.)
He volunteered in 1915, and was drafted to France in the same year. He served in many sectors whilst engaged on the transport of supplies and did much good work with his unit. He returned home and was demobilised in 1919, holding the 1914-15 Star, and the General Service and Victory Medals.
18, Arden Street, Battersea Park Road, S.W.8.   Z5702B

BARNES, W. P., Signaller, R.F.A.
He was serving in India at the outbreak of war and returned to England. Later he was drafted to the Dardanelles, where he took part in the Landing in April 1915, and was wounded. On his recovery, after treatment in Egypt, he proceeded to France, and while taking part in the fierce fighting on the Somme was gassed on July 31st, 1916. After his discharge from hospital he was retained on home duties until demobilised in February 1919. He holds the 1914-15 Star, and the General Service and Victory Medals.
4, Thessaly Square, Wandsworth Road, S.W.8.   Z1186

BARNETT, A. J., 1st Class Stoker, R.N.
He joined in November 1917, and on the conclusion of his training was posted to H.M.S. "Acasta." On board this ship he was engaged on convoy and other highly dangerous duties in the Atlantic until the conclusion of hostilities. He was demobilised in March 1919, and holds the General Service and Victory Medals.
11, Perrers Road, Hammersmith, W.6.   11135C

BARNETT, B. J., Private, 2nd Royal Fusiliers.

Volunteering in May 1915, he was drafted in July of the same year to France. Whilst there he took part in the Battles of the Somme, Arras and Ypres, and was twice wounded. After being in hospital for some time at home he was discharged as medically unfit for further service in February 1918, and holds the 1914-15 Star, and the General Service and Victory Medals.

53, Mordaunt Street, Stockwell, S.W.9. Z1188A

BARNETT, F. J., Corporal, R.E.

Volunteering in August 1914, he was drafted on the completion of his training to the Western Front. He rendered valuable services with his unit in connection with many notable engagements until the conclusion of hostilities, and was wounded on two occasions. In March 1919 he returned to England, and was demobilised, holding the 1914-15 Star, and the General Service and Victory Medals.

11, Perrers Road, Hammersmith, W.6. 11135B

BARNETT, J., Driver, R.A.S.C. (M.T.)

He volunteered in August 1915, and after his training served at various stations on important defence duties. He rendered valuable services, but was not successful in obtaining his transfer overseas before the cessation of hostilities. In January 1919 he was demobilised.

11, Perrers Road, Hammersmith, W.6. 11135A

BARNETT, S., Private, Sherwood Foresters.

He was in the Army at the outbreak of hostilities, and was almost immediately drafted to the Western Front. Whilst overseas he fought in the memorable Retreat from Mons, and in the Battles of the Marne, the Aisne and La Bassée, and was taken prisoner. During his captivity in Germany he was employed on the canals. He holds the Mons Star, and the General Service and Victory Medals, and was discharged in December 1918, after his return from Germany.

120, Darwin Buildings, Crail Row, Walworth, S.E.17. Z1189

BARNETT, W. E., P.O., R.N., H.M.S. "Hermione."

Mobilised in August 1914, he first saw service in the North Sea, where he took part in the engagement in the Heligoland Bight. Four months later he fought in the Battle of the Falkland Islands, and was afterwards engaged in the defence of the Suez Canal. In 1917, he returned to the North Sea, and from that year until the war ceased did important patrol and escort duties. He was demobilised in January 1919, holding the 1914-15 Star, and the General Service and Victory Medals.

57, St. Lawrence Road, Brixton Road, S.W.9. Z4402

BARNFIELD, J., Rifleman, 12th London Regiment (Rangers).

He was mobilised in 1914, and was shortly afterwards sent to France, where he took part in numerous engagements, including those in the Retreat from Mons, and at Ypres, Hill 60, Loos, Vimy Ridge, the Somme, Beaumont-Hamel, Passchendaele and Cambrai. He also served in the Retreat and Advance of 1918, and was wounded at Le Cateau in October of that year. He was invalided home and discharged as medically unfit for further service in 1919, holding the Mons Star, and the General Service and Victory Medals.

13, McKerrell Road, Peckham, S.E.15. Z5720

BARNSLEY, W. C., Gunner, R.F.A. and Private, Bedfordshire Regiment.

Volunteering in August 1914, he was drafted to France in the following year and took part in severe fighting at Ypres, Festubert, Loos, Vimy Ridge and Arras. He was killed in action at Ypres in July 1917, and was entitled to the 1914-15 Star, and the General Service and Victory Medals.

11, Mostyn Road, Brixton, S.W.9. Z3429

BARON, A. E., Pte., Tank Corps (Technical Dept.)

He volunteered in June 1915, and in November of the same year was drafted to the Western Front. He took part in various engagements, including those at Albert, Vermelles, Vimy Ridge, the Somme, Arras Bullecourt, Messines, Ypres and Cambrai. He was also in action in the Retreat and Advance of 1918. During the earlier part of his service he was in the King's Royal Rifle Corps, and was transferred to the Tank Corps later. He was demobilised in January 1919, holding the 1914-15 Star, and the General Service and Victory Medals.

195, Albert Road, Peckham, S.E.15. Z5719

BARRACLOUGH, J. P., Private, R.A.M.C.

Volunteering in October 1915, he proceeded to France in May of the following year. Whilst there he was engaged with the Field Ambulance, and served at the Somme, Ypres, Arras, Cambrai and Passchendaele. In 1917 he was drafted to Italy but later returned to France. Whilst overseas he was wounded three times. In January 1919 he was demobilised and holds the General Service and Victory Medals.

44, Ingelow Road, Battersea Park, S.W.8. Z1190A

BARRATT, A. B., Private, 2nd Queen's (Royal West Surrey Regiment).

He joined in January 1916, and in the same year proceeded to France, where he took part in numerous engagements. He was killed in action in May 1917, and was entitled to the General Service and Victory Medals.

70, Westmacott Street, Camberwell, S.E.5. Z3059A

BARRATT, G. (Miss), Member, W.R.A.F.

She volunteered for service in the W.R.A.F. in September 1918, and for over a year was engaged on important clerical duties at Kidbrooke. During her service she met with a serious accident which unfortunately resulted in the amputation of one of her legs. She was demobilised in October 1919, after having performed her duties with great care and efficiency. 34, Mostyn Road, Brixton Road, S.W.9. Z4404

BARRATT, H. T., Private, 23rd London Regiment.

He volunteered in May 1915, and in the same year was drafted to France. Whilst on this Front he fought in many notable battles, including those of the Somme, Arras, Vimy Ridge, Ypres, and Passchendaele, and was gassed. He was invalided home and after being in hospital was discharged in 1917, medically unfit for further service. He holds the 1914-15 Star, and the General Service and Victory Medals.

28, Grant Road, Battersea, S.W.11. Z119

BARRELL, A., Private, 7th Middlesex Regiment.

He joined in March 1917, and after his training was drafted to the Western Front. Whilst there he took part in many important engagements, including those at Messines, Ypres and Lens, and on April 24th, 1918 was reported missing, but later was presumed to have been killed on that date. He was entitled to the General Service and Victory Medals.

63, Sterndale Road, Wandsworth Road, S.W.8. Z1194A

BARRELL, W., Private, R.A.S.C.

Volunteering in September 1914, he was later drafted to the Dardanelles, where he served until they Evacuation of the Peninsula. Later, he proceeded to Salonika where he did good service on the Vardar and other fronts. He was afterwards transferred to Mesopotamia and Egypt with the Motor Transport, in which he did splendid work. He returned home after much varied service in the East, and was demobilised in August 1919, holding the 1914-15 Star, and the General Service and Victory Medals.

63, Sterndale Road, Wandsworth Road, S.W.8. Z1194B

BARRETT, A., L/Corporal, King's Royal Rifles and East Lancashire Regiment.

He joined in 1916, and in the same year proceeded to France. He took part in the heavy fighting at the Battles of the Somme, Arras and Ypres, and many other notable battles until the conclusion of hostilities. In 1919 he was demobilised after returning home, and holds the General Service and Victory Medals.

287, East Street, Walworth, S.E.17. Z1193

BARRETT, A. J., L/Cpl., 5th Canadian Mounted Rifles.

Volunteering in June 1915, he was drafted to France in May of the following year. Whilst overseas he took part in many battles of importance, including that of the Somme, and on August 26th, 1918 was unhappily killed in action near Arras. He was entitled to the General Service and Victory Medals.

101, St. Alban's Avenue, Chiswick, W.4. 7967B

BARRETT, C. T., Private, 4th Royal Berkshire Regt. and Aircraftsman, R.A.F.

He joined in February 1916, and in August of the same year was drafted to France, where he fought in the Battle of the Somme, afterwards being invalided home through ill-health. In April 1917 he returned to the fighting line, was wounded and sent to hospital. On recovery he was transferred to the R.A.F. in which he served until demobilised in February 1919. He holds the General Service and Victory Medals.

29, Chryssell Road, Brixton Road, S.W.9. Z5221

BARRETT, F., Private, 1st Queen's (Royal West Surrey Regiment).

Mobilised in August 1914, he was almost immediately drafted to the Western Front. There he took part in the Retreat from Mons, and the Battles of Le Cateau, the Marne and the Aisne, La Bassée, Ypres and Givenchy, where he was wounded. After being in hospital for two months he returned to the lines and fought in many notable battles, including those of Neuve Chapelle, Hill 60, Loos, Vimy Ridge, the Somme, where he was again wounded. After his recovery he took part in the operations at Arras, Bullecourt, Passchendaele, Cambrai and in the Retreat and Advance of 1918, during which he was gassed. In March 1919 he was demobilised, and holds the Mons Star, and the General Service and Victory Medals.

37, Surrey Square, Walworth, S.E.17. Z1192

BARRETT, F., Rifleman, King's Royal Rifle Corps.
He was in the Army at the outbreak of hostilities, and was shortly afterwards drafted to the Western Front. Whilst in this theatre of war he fought in many great battles, including those at Mons, Ypres and the Somme, and was killed in action on July 10th, 1916. He was entitled to the Mons Star, and the General Service and Victory Medals.
15, Nasmyth Street, Hammersmith, W.6. 11229

BARRETT, F. (M.S.M.), Sergt., R.F.A.
Having previously served in India and Ireland, he volunteered in August 1914, and was speedily drafted to the Western Front. There he fought in the memorable Retreat from Mons, and at Loos, the Somme, Arras and many other engagements until hostilities ceased. He was awarded the Meritorious Service Medal for his consistent work and devotion to duty, and holds in addition the Mons Star, and the General Service and Victory Medals. In July 1919 he was demobilised.
37, Cardross Street, Hammersmith, W.6. 11189A

BARRETT, H., Private, 10th Middlesex Regiment.
He volunteered in February 1915, and on the completion of his training was drafted to the Dardanelles, where he served until the Evacuation of the Peninsula. Shortly afterwards he proceeded to Egypt and saw much service in this seat of war. He was then invalided home, but on his recovery returned to the East and remained there until demobilised in July 1919. He holds the 1914-15 Star, and the General Service and Victory Medals.
37, Cardross Street, Hammersmith, W.6. 11189C

BARRETT, H. C., Corporal, 7th London Regiment.
Volunteering in May 1915, he was drafted on the completion of his training to the Western Front. While overseas he fought in many notable battles until hostilities ceased, including that of the Somme. In January 1919 he returned home and was demobilised, holding the General Service and Victory Medals.
St. Alban's Avenue, Chiswick, W.4. 7967A

BARRETT, T., Private, 10th Middlesex Regiment.
Volunteering in November 1915, he was drafted on the completion of his training to India. There he rendered much valuable service at various stations. He returned to England and was demobilised in November 1919. He holds the General Service and Victory Medals.
37, Cardross Street, Hammersmith, W.6. 11189B

BARRON, A. F., Cpl., East Surrey and Queen's (Royal West Surrey) Regiments.
He volunteered in October 1914, and was retained on various important duties until January 1916, when he was sent to Mesopotamia, and took part in various operations in the attempt to relieve Kut. He afterwards proceeded to India and was engaged in the suppression of the North West Frontier Rising. Whilst on service overseas he contracted malaria, and also met with a serious accident. He returned home and was demobilised in October 1919, holding the General Service and Victory Medals, and the India General Service Medal (with clasp, Afghanistan, N.W. Frontier 1919).
61, Beaufoy Road, Lavender Hill, S.W.11. Z1195A, Z1196A

BARRY, A., Driver, R.F.A.
He volunteered in September 1914, and in the following year was drafted to the Western Front, where he took part in the engagements at Loos, the Somme, Arras, Ypres, and Cambrai. He also served in the Advance of 1918. Owing to ill-health he was invalided home and in March 1919 was discharged, holding the 1914-15 Star, and the General Service and Victory Medals. X27558, X12110
57, Netherwood Road, West Kensington, W.14.

BARRY, J., Private, Northamptonshire Regiment.
He volunteered in August 1914, and in June of the following year was sent to France, where he took part in numerous engagements, including those at the Somme, Arras and Cambrai, where he was wounded. He was unfortunately killed in action on March 27th, 1918, and was entitled to the 1914-15 Star, and the General Service and Victory Medals.
"His life for his Country."
11, Albany Road, Camberwell, S.E.5. Z5566B

BARTER, J., Bmdr., R.M.A., H.M.S. "Resolution."
He joined in June 1916, and saw much service in the North Sea, where he was twice, when on trawlers, torpedoed. He was also on escort duty at the surrender of the German Fleet on November 21st, 1918. He was demobilised in March 1919, and holds the General Service and Victory Medals.
91, Hubert Road, Stockwell, S.W.9. Z1114C

BARTER, W. J. H., Sergt., R.A.F.
He volunteered in June 1915, and in the following year was drafted to the Western Front. He was reported missing after a flying raid on July 2nd, 1916, over the Somme, and was presumed to have been killed on that date. He was entitled to the General Service and Victory Medals.
36, Shorncliffe Road, Walworth, S.E.17. Z1197

BARTLETT, H., Rifleman, 17th London Regiment (Rifles).
He volunteered in August 1914, but after a time was discharged. Later he rejoined in November 1915, and in the following October was drafted to the Western Front, where he took part in engagements at Arras, Messines and Bourlon Wood. He also served in the Retreat and Advance of 1918, and was wounded. He holds the General Service and Victory Medals, and was demobilised in February 1919.
35, Henshaw Street, Walworth, S.E.17. Z3388A

BARTLETT, J. R., Sergt., R.A.F.
He volunteered in November 1914, and served on important duties with his Squadron until August 1916, when he was drafted to German East Africa. While there he was engaged on highly responsible work, and rendered valuable services. He returned home in March 1918, and was still serving in 1920. He holds the General Service and Victory Medals.
64, Chiswick Lane, Chiswick, W.4. 5625

BARTON, R. H., Private, Royal Fusiliers.
He joined in March 1916, and was sent to the Western Front in the same year. He took part in severe fighting at Albert, the Somme, Arras, Ypres and Cambrai, and also served in the Retreat and Advance of 1918. He was demobilised in January 1919, and holds the General Service and Victory Medals. 12, Vivian Road, Peckham, S.E.15. Z5874

BARTON, W. H., Sapper, R.E.
He joined in August 1917, and after his training was engaged on special duties with his unit. He rendered valuable services, but was not successful in obtaining his transfer overseas owing to his medical unfitness. He was discharged in January 1918 on medical grounds.
115, Neate Street, Camberwell, S.E.5. Z5032

BARTON, W. H., Gunner, R.F.A.
Having previously served in the South African campaign, he volunteered in August 1914, and in the following year was drafted to the Western Front, where he took part in many engagements of importance. He was wounded at Albert in 1916, and invalided home, but on his recovery returned to France and was again in action. He was demobilised in May 1919, and holds the Queen's and King's South African Medals, the 1914-15 Star, and the General Service and Victory Medals. 30, Este Road, Battersea, S.W.11. Z1198

BARTRAM, J. T. (M.M.), Sergt., Rifle Brigade.
He volunteered in December 1915, and in the following August was drafted to the Western Front and fought in the Offensive on the Somme, and at Ypres. Later he was again in action on the Somme, at Cambrai and in various engagements in the Retreat and Advance of 1918. He was wounded three times during his service, and was awarded the Military Medal on March 21st 1918, for distinguished gallantry and devotion to duty in the Field, and also won a Bar in a later engagement. He was demobilised in March 1919, and holds in addition to the Military Medal, the 1914-15 Star, and the General Service and Victory Medals. Z1209
13, Rowena Crescent, Candahar Road, Battersea, S.W.11.

BASLEY A., Driver, British Red Cross Society.
He joined in October 1916, and in November of the same year proceeded to France, where he was engaged on various important Red Cross duties, and rendered valuable services until after the close of hostilities. He was awarded the Croix de Guerre for his excellent work, and also holds the General Service and Victory Medals. He returned home and was demobilised in February 1919.
4, Dorchester Grove, Chiswick, W.4. 5631A

BASLEY, J. J., Sapper, R.E.
He volunteered in 1915, and after his training was engaged at various stations on important duties with his unit. He was not successful in obtaining his transfer overseas on account of his medical unfitness for active service, but rendered valuable services until his discharge in 1917.
2, Burgoyne Road, Stockwell, S.W.9. Z1199

BASLEY, R. H., Special War Worker.
In May 1915 this lady volunteered for work of National importance, and from that date until November 1918 was engaged at the Hayes Munition Factory. By reason of her care and efficiency she rose to be forewoman in the 18-pounder Filling Room, and throughout her services did excellent work.
4, Dorchester Grove, Chiswick, W.4. 5631B

BASON, W., Private, R.A.S.C. (M.T.)
Volunteering in October 1915 he was sent to France in the same year. He was engaged as a motor driver and served at Loos, Vimy Ridge, the Somme, Beaumont-Hamel, Arras, Messines, Ypres, Cambrai and in the Retreat and Advance of 1918. He was chiefly employed on the supply of water to the troops in the line, and rendered valuable services. He was demobilised in 1919, and holds the 1914-15 Star, and the General Service and Victory Medals.
22, Prideaux Road, Stockwell, S.W.9. Z1200

BASSAM, F. G., A.B., R.N., H.M.S. T.B.D. "Nith."
He volunteered in August 1914, and served with the Grand
Fleet in the North Sea. He was engaged throughout the
war on torpedo boats doing convoy and patrol duty, and
rendered valuable services. He was demobilised in February
1919, and holds the 1914–15 Star, and the General Service
and Victory Medals.
8, Medlar Street, Camberwell, S.E.5.   Z1174

BASSEY, C. A., Private, 13th Middlesex Regiment.
Volunteering in February 1915, he was drafted the same
year to the Western Front. There he was in action at Loos,
St. Eloi, Ypres and in many other battles, including that of the
Somme, where he was wounded. He was sent to hospital
in France, later being invalided to England, and after receiving
hospital treatment was discharged as medically unfit in April
1917. He holds the 1914–15 Star, and the General Service
and Victory Medals.
59, Jocelyn Street, Peckham, S.E.15.   Z5212

BASTIN, A. T., Rifleman, Rifle Brigade.
He joined in August 1918, and after his training was engaged
on important duties with his unit. He rendered valuable
services, but was not successful in obtaining his transfer overseas before the cessation of hostilities. He was demobilised
in February 1919.
15, Pitcairn Street, Wandsworth Road, S.W.8.   Z1201A

BATCHELOR, C. R., Corporal, Rifle Brigade.
After volunteering in November 1915, and completing his
training he was drafted to the Western Front in the following
year. He took part in much severe fighting at Albert, Vimy
Ridge, the Somme, Arras, Bullecourt, Passchendaele, Cambrai
and the Retreat and Advance of 1918. He was demobilised
in March 1919, holding the General Service and Victory Medals.
188, East Surrey Grove, Peckham, S.E.15.   Z5033

BATCHELOR, G., Gunner, R.G.A.
Joining in June 1917, he was drafted to the Western Front in
the same year. He took part in various important engagements, including that at Ypres, where he was wounded and
was invalided home. He was discharged as medically unfit
for further service in January 1919, and holds the General
Service and Victory Medals.
30, Clayton Road, Peckham, S.E.15.   Z5879

BATCHELOR, W. S., Gunner (Shoeing-Smith), R.F.A.
He volunteered in October 1914, and after his training was
drafted in 1915 to the Western Front, where he took part in
numerous engagements, including those at Ypres, Loos,
the Somme, Arras and Cambrai, and the Retreat and Advance
of 1918. In the last week of the fighting he fell ill, and unfortunately died on November 9th, 1918. He was entitled
to the 1914–15 Star, and the General Service and Victory
Medals.
19, Mosedale Street, S.E.5.   Z1775

BATE, H. A., A.B., R.N., H.M.S. "Minotaur."
He volunteered in August 1914, and was engaged with the
Grand Fleet. He took part in the Battle of Jutland and
also served on patrol duties in the North Sea and on guard
duties at Scapa Flow. He was still serving in the Atlantic
Fleet in 1920, and holds the 1914–15 Star, and the General
Service and Victory Medals.
4, Stockwell Grove, Stockwell, S.W. 9.   Z1202B

BATEMAN, W., Private, R.A.O.C.
He volunteered in November 1915, and after his training was
drafted to the Western Front, where he served as a fitter in
the gun repairing shops. His duties demanded a high degree
of technical skill and he rendered valuable services, often being
under heavy fire. He was demobilised in July 1919, and
holds the 1914–15 Star, and the General Service and Victory
Medals.
26, Rosemary Road, Peckham, S.E.15.   Z5318

BATES, G. A., Private, R.A.S.C. (H.T.)
He joined in December 1916, and in the following year was
drafted to the Western Front, where he served at Dieppe,
Le Havre, Rouen, Ypres, Vimy Ridge, Amiens, Armentières
and Cambrai. After the cessation of hostilities he returned
to England and in May 1919 was demobilised, holding the
General Service and Victory Medals.
79, Sussex Road, Coldharbour Lane, S.W.9.   Z3058A

BATES, H., C.S.M., Royal Fusiliers.
He was serving in India at the outbreak of war, and in 1915
proceeded to the Dardanelles, where he rendered valuable
services and was wounded in action. On his recovery he was
transferred to France, and took a distinguished part in numerous engagements, and was three times wounded. He was
demobilised in April 1919, and holds the 1914–15 Star, and
the General Service and Victory Medals.
4, Aldbridge Street, Walworth, S.E.17.   Z1207

BATES, H. C., Rifleman, 17th Rifle Brigade.
He joined in February 1917, and after his training was engaged
at various stations on important duties with his unit. He
rendered valuable services, but was not successful in obtaining
his transfer overseas before the cessation of hostilities, owing
to his medical unfitness. He was demobilised in February
1919.
131, Warham Street, Camberwell, S.E.5.   Z1206B

BATES, H. J. R., Private, 1st Queen's Own (Royal West Kent Regiment).
Having previously served, he re-enlisted in August 1914, and
was sent to France in December of the same year. He took
part in the severe fighting at Hill 60, where he was wounded
and invalided home. On his recovery he returned to France,
and was engaged at Festubert, Loos, the Somme and Ypres.
He returned to England in December 1917, and was discharged
in consequence of his services. He holds the 1914–15 Star,
and the General Service and Victory Medals.
45, Gwynne Road, Battersea, S.W.11.   Z1203

BATES, J. V., Driver, R.F.A.
Volunteering in October 1914, he proceeded to Egypt early
in the following year. He took part afterwards in many
important engagements in Palestine, including those at Jaffa
and preceding the taking of Jerusalem. He returned home
and was still serving in 1920, holding the 1914–15 Star, and
the General Service and Victory Medals.
131, Warham Street, Camberwell, S.E.5.   Z1206A

BATES, S. H., Sapper, R.E. and Pte., Labour Corps.
Joining in February 1918, he was drafted to France in the
same year. He was later transferred to the Labour Corps
and was engaged at the 3rd Army Headquarters on the
Somme front, and at Péronne and Bapaume on important
duties. He rendered much valuable service until demobilised
in December 1919, holding the General Service and Victory
Medals.
16, Edithna Street, Stockwell, S.W.9.   Z1205

BATES, W., L/Corporal, Duke of Cornwall's Light Infantry.
He volunteered in September 1914, and was sent to the Western
Front in the same year. He took part in the severe fighting
at Ypres, and in many other engagements, and was unfortunately killed in action on November 9th, 1915. He was entitled to the 1914–15 Star, and the General Service and Victory
Medals.
19, St. Andrew's Street, Wandsworth Road, S.W.8.   Z1204

BATES, W. S., Private, 13th Middlesex Regiment.
He was mobilised in 1914, and shortly afterwards was sent to
France, where he took part in the heavy fighting at Mons,
the Marne, the Aisne, Hill 60, Ypres, Loos, St. Eloi, Albert
and the Somme. He was killed in action on the Somme on
August 16th, 1916, and was entitled to the Mons Star, and the
General Service and Victory Medals.
    "Honour to the immortal dead who gave their youth
       that the world might grow old in peace."
18, Myatt Road, Stockwell, S.W.9.   Z5036

BATESON, T., Driver, R.A.S.C. (M.T.)
He was mobilised from the Reserve at the commencement of
hostilities, and was soon drafted to the Western Front. During
his service in France, which lasted until the close of the war,
he was engaged on important duties with the Motor Transport
Section in conveying rations and ammunition to the troops,
and served at Vimy Ridge and in many subsequent engagements. After the Armistice he advanced into Germany with
the Army of Occupation. He was demobilised in May 1919,
after nearly five years with the Colours, and holds the 1914–15
Star, and the General Service and Victory Medals.
84, Rayleigh Road, W. Kensington, W.14.   12080

BATH, G., Pte., Queen's (Royal West Surrey Regt.)
He volunteered in July 1915, and in the following May was
drafted to France. He took part in the engagements at
Ploegsteert Wood and the Somme in 1916, and was wounded.
In the following year he fought at Messines, where he was
again severely wounded in June. On his recovery after
treatment in England he rejoined his unit in France, and was
captured in the Battle of Ypres. Released after the Armistice
in November 1918 he returned to England and served on
various important duties until his demobilisation in April
1919. He holds the General Service and Victory Medals.
48, Palmerston Street, Battersea, S.W.11.   Z1208

BATHURST, W. T., Pte., 18th Middlesex Regiment.
He volunteered in May 1915, and in the following November
was drafted to France, where he served for three years and
three months, and took part in numerous important engagements until the cessation of hostilities. He was demobilised
in 1919 after his return to England, and holds the General
Service and Victory Medals.
26, Antrobus Road, Chiswick, W.4.   T6902B

BATHURST, F. H. (Miss), Special War Worker
For nearly three years of the war this lady was engaged on important duties at the Park Royal Munition Works, where she held a responsible post as a bullet-gauger. She rendered valuable services, and her work was highly appreciated.
26, Antrobus Road, Chiswick, W.4. T6902A

BATSON, A. E., Gunner, R.G.A.
He joined in November 1916, and after completing his training, was drafted to Italy in the following year. After only five months' service in this theatre of war he was unhappily killed in action on September 6th, 1917. He was entitled to the General Service and Victory Medals.
27, Cardross Street, Hammersmith, W.6. 11574A

BATT, W. J., Stoker Petty Officer, R.N., H.M.S. "Commonwealth."
He had previously enlisted in the Navy in 1909, and at the outbreak of war was posted to H.M.S. "Triumph." In 1915 he was sent to the Dardanelles and took part in all the Naval operations in the campaign until the Evacuation of the Peninsula. During his service he was transferred to H.M.S. "Wolverine," which was sunk while he was absent from her, and later to H.M.S. "Commonwealth," and cruised in the Mediterranean on important patrol duties until the cessation of hostilities. In 1920 he was still serving, and holds the 1914-15 Star, and the General Service and Victory Medals.
26, Cologne Road, Battersea, S.W.11. Z1210

BATTAMS, R. E., Air Mechanic, R.A.F.
He joined in October 1917, and after his training was engaged at various stations on important duties, which demanded a high degree of technical skill. He rendered valuable services, but was not successful in obtaining his transfer overseas before the cessation of hostilities, and was demobilised in April 1919. 35, Quick Road, Chiswick, W.4. 5695

BATTEN, W. J., Air Mechanic, R.A.F.
Volunteering at the outbreak of hostilities, he was drafted to the Western Front in the same year. During his service in France he took part in many engagements, including those at the Somme, Ypres, Cambrai and other operations in the Retreat and Advance of 1918, and was twice wounded in action. He was demobilised in November 1919, after over five years' service with the Colours, and holds the 1914 Star, and the General Service and Victory Medals.
31, Priory Grove, Lansdowne Road, S.W.8. Z1211A

BATTERSBY, H., Private, R.A.M.C.
He joined in May 1917, and after his training was engaged at large Military Hospitals in Blackpool and elsewhere on important duties in attendance on the wounded. Owing to medical reasons he was unable to secure his transfer overseas while hostilities continued, and was demobilised in November 1919, after rendering much valuable service. Z1213
22, Darwin Buildings, Barlow Street, Walworth, S.E.17.

BATTLEY, A. E., Private, East Surrey Regiment.
He was mobilised at the outbreak of war, and was shortly afterwards drafted to France, where he served for about a year, and fought in the Retreat from Mons and the first Battle of Ypres. Suffering from rheumatic fever he was afterwards invalided home and was discharged in September 1915 as medically unfit for further duty. He holds the Mons Star, and the General Service and Victory Medals.
18, Tradescant Road, South Lambeth Road, S.W.8. Z1212A

BATTS, A., Corporal, 9th London Regiment (Queen Victoria's Rifles).
He volunteered in April 1915, and in the following month was drafted to the Western Front, where he took part in numerous engagements, including those on the Somme and at Arras, Ypres and Cambrai, where he was wounded and was invalided home. On his recovery he returned to France and served in the Retreat and Advance of 1918, and was gassed and again invalided home. Returning to France he proceeded with the Army of Occupation to Germany, with which he served until demobilised in September 1919. He holds the 1914-15 Star, and the General Service and Victory Medals.
48, Pepler Road, Peckham, S.E.15. Z3427

BATTY, G. G. A., Private, 23rd London Regiment.
He was mobilised with the London Territorial Forces at the outbreak of war, and was drafted to France in March 1915. After taking part in several important operations he was unfortunately killed in action at Givenchy in May of the same year after only ten weeks' service overseas. He was entitled to the 1914-15 Star, and the General Service and Victory Medals. 15, Este Road, Battersea, S.W.11. Z1214

BAUGH, E. E., Rifleman, 6th London Regt. (Rifles).
Volunteering in June 1915, he was drafted to France in April of the following year, and took part in the severe fighting at the Somme and in other engagements. He was killed in action on the Somme on October 6th, 1916, and was entitled to the General Service and Victory Medals.
"Great deeds cannot die."
173, Albany Road, Camberwell, S.E.5. Z5567

BAUGHEN, G. R., Private, R.A.F. (late R.N.A.S.)
After joining in September 1916, and completing his training he was engaged on patrol duties in the English Channel between Eastbourne and Dunkirk, and rendered valuable services. He later served on important duties at various stations with his Squadron, and did much valuable work in assisting Concert Parties in their entertainments for the troops. He was demobilised in March 1919, and holds the General Service and Victory Medals.
32, Geneva Road, Coldharbour Lane, Brixton, S.W.9. Z3990

BAULCH, W. E., Rifleman, 6th London Regt. (Rifles).
He was serving at the outbreak of war and was immediately afterwards sent to the Western Front where he took part in the Battles of Mons, La Bassée, Ypres, Neuve Chapelle, St. Eloi, Hill 60, and Festubert After being severely wounded he was invalided home and was discharged as medically unfit for further service in May 1916. He holds the Mons Star, and the General Service and Victory Medals.
35, Mayall Road, Herne Hill, S.E.24. Z3991

BAVERSTOCK, T., Private, 4th Middlesex Regt.
He volunteered in August 1915, and after his training was completed, served at various stations on important duties with his unit. He rendered valuable services, but was not able to secure his transfer overseas before the cessation of hostilities. He was demobilised in July 1919 after nearly four years' service.
48, Rothschild Road, Chiswick, W.4. 6290

BAVIN, F., Sergt., 6th Royal Fusiliers.
He was serving in India at the outbreak of war, and was drafted to the Western Front. He took part in the severe fighting at the Battles of the Marne, the Aisne, the first and second engagements at Ypres, and the Somme, and was three times wounded. He was invalided home in consequence, and after treatment in hospital was discharged as medically unfit for further service in September 1917. He holds the 1914 Star, and the General Service and Victory Medals.
65, Henry Street, Kennington, S.E.11. TZ24136

BAWDEN, A., Private, Argyll and Sutherland Highlanders.
Volunteering at the commencement of hostilities he was drafted to Malta, where he was stationed for a year and eight months. He was then sent to Salonika, and took part in numerous important engagements throughout the Balkan campaign until the cessation of hostilities. He was demobilised on his return to England in March 1919, and holds the General Service and Victory Medals.
27, Sulgrave Road, Hammersmith, W.6. 12220

BAWDEN, F., Private, 2nd London Regt. (Royal Fusiliers).
He volunteered early in August 1914, and afterwards was drafted to Malta, where he was stationed for three months. He was then sent to Gallipoli, and took part in many important engagements throughout the campaign until the Evacuation of the Peninsula. He afterwards proceeded to France, where he fought in numerous battles and suffered from severe shell-shock in 1916. In May of the following year he was seriously wounded in the Battle of Arras, and was invalided home. He was subsequently discharged as medically unfit for further duty in November 1917, and holds the 1914-15 Star, and the General Service and Victory Medals.
27, Sulgrave Road, Hammersmith, W.6. 12218

BAXTER, H. W., Pte., 9th Northamptonshire Regt.
He joined in June 1916, and after serving at various stations on important defence duties was drafted in 1918 to France, where he was engaged in many sectors until the conclusion of hostilities. He was demobilised in February 1919, and holds the General Service and Victory Medals.
12, Alexandra Road, Southfield Road, Chiswick, W.4. 7678

BAXTER, J., Pte., 10th, 22nd and 31st Royal Fusiliers, 21st Middlesex and 9th Northants Regiment.
He volunteered in July 1915, and served on important duties with his unit until November of the following year, when he was drafted to the Western Front, where he took part in various engagements. He returned home and was demobilised in November 1918, and holds the General Service and Victory Medals.
22, Rumsey Road, Stockwell, S.W.9. Z5717B

BAYLEY, A. W., 1st and 5th Dragoon Guards.
He was mobilised in 1914, and was shortly afterwards sent to the Western Front, where he took part in severe fighting at Mons, the Marne, the Aisne, Ypres, Loos, the Somme, and Arras. He afterwards proceeded with the Army of Occupation to Germany, where he served until April 1919, when he returned to England and was demobilised, holding the Mons Star, and the General Service and Victory Medals.
15, Pilkington Road, Peckham, S.E.15. Z5891

BAYLIS, W., L/Corporal, 23rd Royal Fusiliers.
He volunteered in November 1915, and in the following year was sent overseas. During his service he fought in the Battle of the Somme, and was wounded in action. On his recovery he took part in the engagements at Arras and Ypres, and was again wounded in the Retreat in March 1918. He was invalided home, and after prolonged treatment was discharged as medically unfit for further duty in March 1919. He holds the General Service and Victory Medals.
88, Home Road, Battersea, S.W.11.   Z1215A

BAYNES, E., Private, East Surrey Regiment.
Mobilised at the outbreak of hostilities, he was almost immediately drafted to the Western Front, and served in the Battles of Mons, the Marne, Ypres, and later at Arras. During his service in France he was severely gassed, but after his recovery returned to the fighting line and took part in many engagements until the conclusion of the war. He was demobilised in 1920, and holds the Mons Star, and the General Service and Victory Medals.
13, Tisdale Place, Walworth, S.E.17.   Z1216B

BAYSTON, G., Shoeing-Smith, R.F.A.
He volunteered in September 1914, and was in 1915 drafted to France, where he served at Loos, Givenchy, Grandecourt and the Somme. In 1916 he was sent to Salonika, and was present in the Allied operations on the Struma and the Vardar fronts. Later he proceeded to Egypt, and after being stationed at Alexandria, advanced into Palestine with General Allenby's Forces, fighting in the Battle of Jaffa, and before the fall of Jerusalem. He returned home and was demobilised in July 1919, and holds the 1914-15 Star, and the General Service and Victory Medals.
1, Oakridge Cottages, Hutten Road, Kennington, S.E.11.   Z25518A

BAYSTON, J. W., Private, 2nd London Regiment (Royal Fusiliers).
He volunteered in September 1914, and in the following year was drafted to the Dardanelles, and after service there, to Egypt in September. After about a year's service in Egypt and Salonika he was sent to the Western Front in September 1916, and in the same year was unfortunately killed in action near Delville Wood. He was entitled to the 1914-15 Star, and the General Service and Victory Medals, and his relatives hold the King's Certificate.
1, Oakridge Cottages, Hutten Road, Kennington, S.E.11.   25518B

BAZZI, J. H., Gunner, R.G.A.
He joined in June 1916, and was drafted to France in the following year. During his service on the Western Front he did good work as a Gunner at Bullecourt, and in various engagements in the Retreat of 1918, and was two months in hospital with a serious illness. In January 1919 he was demobilised and holds the General Service and Victory Medals.
35, Lochaline Street, Hammersmith, W.6.   13258

BEACH, W. A., Private, Labour Corps.
He joined in December 1916, and after his training was sent to the Western Front. Whilst in this theatre of war he was attached to the Royal Field Artillery, and did valuable work during operations at Arras, Messines, Ypres, and Passchendaele. He was also engaged on special duties in the Retreat and Advance of 1918, and remained in France until after the cessation of hostilities. He was demobilised in September 1919, and holds the General Service and Victory Medals.
35, Tracey Street, Kennington, S.E.11.   TZ25319B

BEADLE, G. E., Driver, R.A.S.C. (M.T.)
He joined in 1916, and at the conclusion of his training in the following year was sent to Mesopotamia, where he was engaged on important duties in connection with the transport of supplies to the forward areas. He was demobilised in March 1920, after his return to England, and holds the General Service and Victory Medals.
42, Cork Street, Camberwell, S.E.5.   Z1788

BEADLE, W., 2nd Corporal, R.E.
He joined in May 1917, and upon completing his training was sent to the Western Front. In this theatre of war he did valuable work in many important sectors, and also served throughout the Retreat and Advance of 1918. He holds the General Service and Victory Medals, and was demobilised in March 1920, after his return to England.
53, Cork Street, Camberwell, S.E.5.   Z1789C

BEAL, C., Air Mechanic, R.A.F.
He joined in June 1916, and after his training in Scotland crossed to France. Here he served with his Squadron in many important sectors, including those of the Somme, Arras, and Ypres, and also in the Retreat and Advance of 1918, during which he was engaged on important duties which called for much technical skill. He was demobilised on his return to England in March 1919, and holds the General Service and Victory Medals.
26, Fenwick Place, Landor Street, S.W.9.   Z1217C

BEALE, G. J., Private, Royal Berkshire Regiment.
Volunteering in April 1915 he was sent to France in October of the same year. He took part in numerous engagements, including those at Loos, Vimy Ridge, the Somme, and the Ancre. He was invalided home owing to shell-shock in November 1916, and discharged in consequence in December 1917. He holds the 1914-15 Star, and the General Service and Victory Medals.
207, Cator Street, Peckham, S.E.15.   Z5037A

BEALE, H., Private, Leicestershire Regt. and R.A.F.
He volunteered in July 1915, and in the following year was drafted to the Western Front, where he took part in numerous engagements, including those on the Somme, and at Arras and Ypres. Contracting trench fever he was invalided home, and on his recovery was transferred to the Royal Air Force and returned to France, where he served until 1919, when he was demobilised. He holds the General Service and Victory Medals.
88, Somerleyton Road, Coldharbour Lane, Brixton, S.W.9.   Z3062

BEALES, J. S., 1st Class Petty Officer, R.N.
Volunteering in August 1914, he was posted to H.M.S. "Formidable," which vessel was engaged on important duties in the North Sea. On January 1st, 1915, his ship was torpedoed and sunk in the English Channel, and he was unfortunately drowned. He was entitled to the 1914-15 Star, and the General Service and Victory Medals.
20, Wansey Street, Walworth, S.E.17.   Z1218

BEAMAN, J. J., Trooper, King Edward's Horse (The King's Oversea Dominions Regiment).
He joined in January 1918, and at the conclusion of his training was engaged on duties of an important nature with his unit. He was unable to secure his transfer overseas before the termination of hostilities, but rendered valuable services until he was demobilised in January 1919.
39, Councillor Street, Camberwell, S.E.5.   Z1175

BEAN, W., Rifleman, King's Royal Rifle Corps.
Joining in 1916, he was sent overseas on completing his training early in the following year. During his service in France he fought at Bullecourt, the Somme, and in the Retreat and Advance of 1918 until hostilities ceased. He was demobilised on his return to England in February 1919, and holds the General Service and Victory Medals.
70, Mayall Road, Herne Hill, S.E.24.   Z1773A

BEANEY, H., Private, R.A.S.C.
He volunteered in December 1914, and in the same month was sent to France, there he served in various engagements, including those at Neuve Chapelle, Loos, and Vimy Ridge. He was engaged in taking horses up to the front lines, and rendered valuable services. He was demobilised in February 1919, and holds the 1914-15 Star, and the General Service and Victory Medals.
1, Secretan Road, Camberwell, S.E.5.   Z5319

BEANEY, J. R. S., Private, 9th Royal Fusiliers.
He joined in February 1917, and in January of the following year was sent to France, where he took part in severe fighting at Arras and the Somme, and in many other engagements, and was wounded and invalided home. On his recovery he was drafted to Egypt, and served there until he returned home and was demobilised in January 1919. He holds the General Service and Victory Medals.
45, Blakes Road, Peckham, S.E.15.   Z5883

BEARD, A., Gunner, R.F.A.
Volunteering in May 1915, he was sent to France three months later. Subsequently he was engaged in the fighting at Loos, Albert, Vimy Ridge, the Somme, Arras, Messines Ridge, Ypres, Passchendaele, Lens, and Cambrai, but in 1918 returned to England in consequence of ill-health. He was invalided out of the Service in March of that year, and holds the 1914-15 Star, and the General Service and Victory Medals.
23, Congreve Street, Walworth, S.E.17.   Z1219

BEARD, F., Gunner, R.F.A.
He volunteered in 1915, and during his service on the Western Front, which lasted for over three years, was engaged as a saddler with his Battery, in many important sectors. He also fought in the Retreat and Advance of 1918, and returning to England at the termination of hostilities, was demobilised in 1919. He holds the 1914-15 Star, and the General Service and Victory Medals.
27, Pitcairn Street, Wandsworth Road, S.W.8.   Z1222C

BEARD, S., Driver, R.F.A.
He volunteered in May 1915, and in that year was drafted to the Western Front upon completing his training. Whilst overseas he did excellent work with his Battery during operations at Ypres, the Somme and Cambrai, and on one occasion was blown up and buried by a shell explosion. In 1918 he was invalided home owing to serious illness, and was demobilised in February 1919. He holds the 1914-15 Star, and the General Service and Victory Medals.
20, Medwin Street, Ferndale Road, S.W.4.   Z1221

BEARD, S. A., Private, R.A.S.C.

He joined in 1916, and was sent to France on completing his training in the same year. Whilst in this theatre of war he did important work with his unit in connection with the transport of supplies, and was present during fighting at Ypres, and Armentières. In 1917 he was gassed, and in consequence returned to England, and was invalided out of the Service in November of that year. He holds the 1914-15 Star, and the General Service and Victory Medals. Z1220 1222D
68, Wadhurst Road, Wandsworth Road, S.W.8.

BEARD, W., Sergt. (Signaller), M.G.C.

Volunteering in May 1915, he was sent to the Western Front in the following year. He served in various engagements, including those at Hooge, Festubert, and Givenchy, and was later transferred to Mesopotamia, where he was present at the fall of Baghdad. In 1919 he proceeded to India, and served on the Afghanistan Frontier. He returned home and was demobilised in November 1919, holding the General Service, Victory, and India General Service Medals (with Clasp, Afghanistan, 1919, N.W. Frontier).
62, Dalwood Street, Camberwell, S.E.5. Z3424

BEARD, W., Cpl., 16th (The Queen's) Lancers.

He enlisted in 1911, and when war broke out was stationed in Ireland. Crossing immediately to France, he served in the Retreat from Mons, in which he was severely wounded and invalided home. After his recovery he returned to the Western Front, and subsequently fought in many important engagements, including that at Cambrai, where he was again wounded. He was demobilised in 1919, and holds the Mons Star, and the General Service and Victory Medals.
27, Pitcairn Street, Wandsworth Road, S.W.8. Z1222B

BEARMAN, F., Private, 2nd Royal Fusiliers.

He enlisted in 1908, and was serving in India at the outbreak of war. In 1915 he proceeded to Gallipoli and took part in the Landing and the three Battles of Krithia. In August 1915, he was badly wounded at Chunuk Bair, and after being invalided home was discharged in December of the same year owing to his injuries. He holds the 1914-15 Star, and the General Service and Victory Medals.
20, Myatt Road, Stockwell, S.W.9. Z5039C

BEASLEY, J., A.B., Royal Navy.

Volunteering in August 1914, he was posted to H.M.S. "Glory," which was engaged on patrol and convoy duties in Canadian waters until 1915, when she proceeded to the Dardanelles. Here he served with his ship throughout the Gallipoli campaign during which he took part in several actions, and was afterwards engaged on important work in the White Sea. He holds the 1914-15 Star, and the General Service and Victory Medals, and was demobilised on his return to England in February 1919.
4, Andulus Road, Landor Road, S.W.9. Z1223

BEAUCHAMP, A. J., Driver, R.F.A.

He volunteered in the Queen's at the outbreak of hostilities, and after being transferred to the R.F.A. was drafted early in 1915 to Gallipoli. He took an active part with his Battery in many of the severe engagements there until November, when he was invalided home, suffering badly from shell-shock. After considerable hospital treatment he was discharged in June 1916 as medically unfit for further service. He holds the 1914-15 Star, and the General Service and Victory Medals.
107, Trafalgar Road, Peckham, S.E.15. Z4405

BEAUMONT, A., Pte., The Buffs (East Kent Regt.)

He joined in 1916, and after his training served for nearly three years in Mesopotamia, where he took part in several engagements, notably in the Advance on Baghdad. He did valuable work with his unit throughout, and was demobilised on his return to England in 1919. He holds the General Service and Victory Medals.
55, Emu Road, Battersea Park, S.W.8. Z1225

BEAUMONT, W., Corporal, Grenadier Guards.

Volunteering in September 1914, he was early in 1915 drafted to the Western Front, and fought at Neuve Chapelle, St. Eloi, Hill 60, Ypres, Festubert, and Loos, where he was wounded. He was then invalided home, and after being in hospital for four months, was sent to his depôt, where he was retained on special duties until August 1916, when he returned to France. On his arrival he proceeded to the Somme sector, where operations were then in progress, and was again severely wounded. He was sent to a hospital in York, and had his right leg amputated. After nine months' treatment he was invalided out of the Service in May 1917, and holds the 1914-15 Star, and the General Service and Victory Medals. Z1224
2, Marlborough Mansions, Bromell's Road, Clapham, S.W.4.

BEAVEN, E. V., Private, East Lancashire Regt.

Joining in August 1916, he was sent to the Western Front at the conclusion of his training, and after taking part in several engagements, was unfortunately killed in action on September 27th, 1918, during the Advance of the Allies. He was entitled to the General Service and Victory Medals.
55, Ivy Crescent, Chiswick, W.4. 5877A

BEAVEN, G. J., Gunner, R.F.A.

Joining in July 1916, he was sent to the Western Front a month later. Whilst in this theatre of war, he fought in many important engagements until hostilities ceased, and was wounded. He was demobilised on his return to England in March 1919, and holds the General Service and Victory Medals.
144, Duke Road, Chiswick, W.4. 5664A

BEAVEN, M. E. (Mrs.), Special War Worker.

This lady rendered valuable services during the recent war at the Chiswick Tram Depôt, where she was engaged as an examiner of shells, and carried out these important and responsible duties in a most efficient manner.
144, Duke Road, Chiswick, W.4. 5664B

BEAVER, S. G., Corporal, R.H.A.

A serving soldier, who enlisted in 1911, he was in India when war broke out, and left for the Western Front. He was subsequently engaged in the fighting at Neuve Chapelle, Festubert, Loos, and Albert, and in 1916 was drafted to Mesopotamia. In this theatre of war he again fought in many important engagements, notably at Kut-el-Amara, where he was severely wounded, and was afterwards in hospital at Basra for three months. After his recovery he again went into action, and took part in the defeat of the Turks at Ramadieh, and in the capture of Tekrit. Later he was sent to Egypt, where he was training for a pilot in the Royal Air Force, and afterwards saw service in India. Returning to England, he was placed on the Reserve in December 1919, and holds the 1914 Star, and the General Service and Victory Medals.
5, Auckland Road, Battersea, S.W.11. Z1226

BEAVIS, A. M. D., Corporal, R.A.S.C. (M.T.)

He joined in 1917, and being sent to the Western Front in the same year, served at Ypres, Passchendaele, Cambrai, the Somme, Albert, and Amiens. He was engaged as a motor driver in the transport of supplies, and rendered valuable services. After the Armistice he proceeded with the Army of Occupation to Germany. He was demobilised in March 1920, holding the General Service and Victory Medals.
44, Patmos Road, Brixton, S.W.9. Z5036

BEAVIS, W., Corporal, R.A.O.C.

He was an old volunteer, and when war broke out offered his services, but was rejected on medical grounds. On applying a second time however, he was accepted for home service in the Royal Army Ordnance Corps in July 1916. For almost three years he did valuable work in many capacities with his unit, and was stationed at various places in England until June 1919, when he was demobilised.
2, Colworth Grove, Walworth, S.E.17. Z1227

BECK, A. E., Private, 1st London Regiment (Royal Fusiliers).

He joined in June 1916, and after his training in the following year was drafted overseas. Whilst in France he took part in much of the fighting at Bapaume, Monchy, Arras, Bullecourt, and in June 1917, was wounded at Fontaine Les Croiselles. After receiving hospital treatment he was discharged as medically unfit in June 1918. He holds the General Service and Victory Medals.
118, Sussex Road, Coldharbour Lane, S.W.9. Z5204A

BECK, F. C., Driver, R.F.A.

He volunteered in October 1914, and after his training served on important duties with the 5th London Brigade, R.F.A., until June 1916, when he was drafted to the Western Front, where he took part in various engagements, including those on the Somme, and at Arras. In 1918 he was wounded at Kemmel Hill and invalided home, and was discharged as medically unfit for further service in December 1918, holding the General Service and Victory Medals.
77, Ethelred Road, Kennington, S.E.11. Z24817

BECK, F. J., Gunner, R.F.A.

He volunteered in September 1914, and was drafted to the Western Front in the same year. He took part in severe fighting on the Marne, and the Aisne, and at La Bassée, Ypres, St. Eloi, the Somme, Arras, and Cambrai, and various other engagements. He was demobilised in January 1919, and holds the 1914-15 Star, and the General Service and Victory Medals.
31, Tunstall Road, Brixton Road, S.W.9. Z1795

BECK, S. J., Private, 14th London Regt. (London Scottish).

Joining in January 1916, he proceeded to France in July of the same year. Whilst in this theatre of war he saw much service, and was in action at Gommecourt, the Somme, Arras, Bullecourt, and the Retreat and Advance of 1918. In September 1919, he returned home and was demobilised holding the General Service and Victory Medals.
118, Sussex Road, Coldharbour Lane, S.W.9. Z5204B

BECKER, H., Special War Worker.
Having been rejected for the Army on account of defective
eyesight, he was engaged in the manufacture of bombs at
Havre and Harfleur from 1914 to 1916, also assisting in the
transport of munitions to France. He was afterwards employed at Woolwich Arsenal, where he rendered valuable
services until the cessation of hostilities.
4, Nealdon Street, Landor Road, S.W.9.   Z1228

BECKER, J., Sapper, R.E.
He joined in February 1917, and in the next month proceeded
to France, where he did much valuable service with the 22nd
Light Railway Section in many important sectors of the line,
including those of Dickebusch, Cambrai, Bullecourt, and
Passchendaele. He went through the Retreat of the Allies
at Ham in March, 1918, and was gassed on one occasion. He
was afterwards transferred to the Royal Ordnance Depôt, in
which he served until his return home for demobilisation in
March 1919. He holds the General Service and Victory Medals.
42, Coleman Road, Camberwell, S.E.5.   Z4406

BECKET, E., 2nd Corporal, R.E.
Volunteering in May 1915, he was drafted to France in October
of the same year, and was in action at Loos, afterwards proceeding to Egypt. Later he was sent to Salonika, and took
part in the fighting on the Doiran, Struma, and Vardar fronts.
Whilst in the East he contracted malaria, and after the cessation of hostilities returned home and was demobilised in May
1919, holding the 1914–15 Star, and the General Service and
Victory Medals.
41, Lothian Road, Camberwell New Road, S.W.9.   Z5215

BECKETT, C., Pte., 2/5th South Staffordshire Regt.
He joined in October 1916, and in the following February was
drafted to France. In this theatre of war he took part in
many engagements, including those at Ypres, Arras, Passchendaele and Cambrai, where he was wounded. On recovery he
was again in action and was badly gassed at Condé three days
before the Armistice. He was discharged in February 1919,
and died through the effects of gas poisoning on April 29th,
1920. He was entitled to the General Service and Victory
Medals.
        " The path of duty was the way to glory."
53, Gloucester Road, Peckham, S.E.15.   Z5896

BECKETT, F. E., Private, East Surrey Regiment.
Joining in March 1916, he was drafted to France in the same
year. He took part in heavy fighting on the Somme, and also
served in the Retreat and Advance of 1918. He returned
home and was demobilised in February 1919, and holds the
General Service and Victory Medals.
14, Neate Street, Camberwell, S.E.5.   Z5320

BECKETT, G., Private, R.M.L.I.
Joining in 1916, he was drafted to France in the same year, and
served at Dunkirk, and various other places. He was engaged
in unloading munitions from ships, and in other important
duties and rendered valuable services. He was demobilised
in 1919, holding the General Service and Victory Medals.
23, Havelock Terrace, Battersea Park Road, S.W.8.   Z1229

BECKETT, H. D., Gunner, R.G.A.
Volunteering in December 1915, he was afterwards sent to
India. He was engaged at Quetta, Rawal Pindi, and various
other stations on important duties with his Battery, and
rendered valuable services. He returned home and was
demobilised in December 1918, holding the General Service
and Victory Medals.
53, Bridgman Road, Chiswick, W.4.   7010

BECKHAM, A., L/Corporal, East Surrey Regiment.
He was serving at the outbreak of war, and was shortly afterwards sent to France, and took part in the Retreat from Mons.
He was also in the Battle of Neuve Chapelle, where he was
severely wounded, and was invalided home. Later he was
discharged, owing to his injuries in August 1915, and holds the
Mons Star, and the General Service and Victory Medals.
60, Harling Street, Camberwell, S.E.5.   Z5321

**BEDFORD, A. R., Rifleman, Cameronians (Scottish
Rifles) and Private, Royal Defence Corps.**
He joined in October 1916, and after his training served at
various stations on important duties with his unit. He
rendered valuable services, but was not successful in obtaining
his transfer overseas before the cessation of hostilities, owing
to being overage for duty abroad. He was demobilised in
March 1919.
42, Ferndale Road, Clapham, S.W.4.   Z1231

BEDFORD, G. F. E., Worker, Q.M.A.A.C.
She joined the Q.M.A.A.C., and served at various stations on
important duties with her unit. She rendered valuable services
and carried out her work in a highly efficient manner until
December 1918, when she was demobilised.
98, Wycliffe Road, Lavender Hill, S.W.11.   Z1230B

**BEDFORD, C. A., Private, Queen's (Royal West
Surrey Regiment).**
Volunteering in June 1915, he was sent to France in May of
the following year. He took part in various engagements,
including those at Ploegsteert Wood, the Somme, Messines,
and Ypres, and was twice wounded and gassed. In December
1917, he was transferred to the Italian front, where he fought
in the campaign against the Austrians. He returned home
and was demobilised in March 1919, and holds the General
Service and Victory Medals.
98, Wycliffe Road, Lavender Hill, S.W.11.   Z1230A

**BEDFORD, F., Lieutenant, 25th Bn. Australian
Imperial Forces (2nd Divn.)**
He volunteered as a private in February 1915, and in July of
the same year was sent to Gallipoli, where he served until the
Evacuation. He was afterwards transferred to the Western
Front, and was promoted to commissioned rank for efficiency.
He took part in numerous engagements, including those of
Vimy Ridge, the Somme and Lens, and was twice wounded.
He was invalided to England, and in January 1919 was dis-
charged as medically unfit for further service, holding the
1914–15 Star, and the General Service and Victory Medals.
104, Dalyell Road, Landor Road, S.W.9.   Z1232

BEDFORD, W., Private, R.A.V.C.
He joined in 1916, and was quickly drafted to France, where
he served at Vermelles, Vimy Ridge, Passchendaele, and
Cambrai. He was then transferred to Italy, and saw much
fighting on the Piave. He returned home, and was demobilised
in 1919, holding the General Service and Victory Medals.
181, Gordon Road, Peckham, S.E.15.   Z5878

BEDINGHAM, F. J., Bombardier, R.G.A.
He joined in June 1916, and in February of the following year
was drafted to the Western Front, where he took part in severe
fighting at Arras, Messines, and Cambrai. He also served in
the Retreat and Advance of 1918, and after the Armistice
proceeded with the Army of Occupation to Germany, where he
served at Cologne until September 1919, when he returned
home, and was demobilised. He holds the General Service
and Victory Medals.
5, Oberstein Road, Battersea, S.W.11.   Z1233

**BEDMAN, W. J., A./C.S.M., 23rd London Regiment
and Royal Defence Corps.**
He volunteered in September 1914, and served at various
stations as drill instructor, and in guarding prisoners. He
rendered valuable services, but was not successful in obtaining
his transfer overseas before the cessation of hostilities. He
was demobilised in July 1919.
18, Park Place, Clapham, S.W.4.   Z1234

BEDWELL, A. E., Pioneer, King's Royal Rifle Corps.
He volunteered in October 1915, and in January of the following year was drafted to the Western Front, where he took part
in many important engagements, including those at Poperinghe,
the Somme, Albert, Bray, Beaumont-Hamel, and many others,
and was wounded. He was then invalided home and was
discharged owing to his injuries in July 1917, holding the
General Service and Victory Medals.
11, Hornby Road, Peckham, S.E.15.   Z5038

BEDWELL, G., Corporal, 1st Middlesex Regiment.
He was mobilised in 1914, and was shortly afterwards sent to
France, where he took part in severe fighting in the Retreat
from Mons, and at Ypres, Neuve Chapelle, and numerous
other engagements, and was wounded. He also served in the
Retreat and Advance of 1918, and returning to England after
the cessation of hostilities, was demobilised in 1919, holding
the Mons Star, and the General Service and Victory Medals.
10, Tennyson Street, Wentworth Road, S.W.8.   Z1238C

BEDWIN, H., Sergt., M.G.C.
He volunteered in August 1914, and was sent to France in
February of the following year. He took part in severe fighting
at St. Eloi, Ypres, Festubert, Loos, Vimy Ridge, the Somme,
the Ancre, Passchendaele, Lens and Cambrai, and also served
in the Retreat and Advance of 1918. He was mentioned in
Despatches for conspicuous gallantry by Sir Douglas Haig on
November 8th, 1918. Holding the 1914 Star, and the General
Service and Victory Medals, he was demobilised in January
1919.
20, Knowsley Road, Battersea, S.W.11.   Z1236 1235

BEECHEY, F. E., Driver, R.F.A.
He volunteered in January 1915, and in March of the same
year was sent to France, where he served in numerous engagements, including those at Neuve Chapelle, Laventie, Vimy
Ridge, the Somme, Beaumont-Hamel, Lens, Arras, Cambrai
and elsewhere. He also took part in the Retreat and Advance
of 1918, and was gassed. He was invalided home, and was
demobilised in March 1919, holding the 1914–15 Star, and the
General Service and Victory Medals.
16, Wadding Street, Walworth, S.E.11.   Z1239

BEECHING, S. T. N., Rifleman, King's Royal Rifle Corps.
He joined in June 1917, and was drafted to the Western Front in the same year. He took part in severe fighting on the Somme and at Arras and Ypres, and was killed in action at Wytschaete on August 4th, 1918. He was entitled to the General Service and Victory Medals.
64, Mordaunt Street, Stockwell, S.W.9. Z1240

BEER, F., Private, Queen's (Royal West Surrey Regiment) and Labour Corps.
Joining in January 1916, he was sent to France in the same year. He took part in many important engagements, including that at Ypres, where he was killed in action on October 4th, 1917. He was entitled to the General Service and Victory Medals.
110, Surrey Lane, Bridge Road West, Battersea, S.W.11. Z27564A

BEER, M. (Mrs.), Special War Worker.
During the war this lady held an important appointment at Messrs. Hardingham's Star Works, Battersea, where she was engaged on responsible work in connection with the manufacture of aeroplane ribs. Her services proved of the utmost value to the firm, and she carried out her duties in an exemplary manner.
110, Surrey Lane, S.W.11. Z27564B

BEER, T. H., Sergt., R.M.L.I.
He was serving on the outbreak of war, having previously taken part in the South African campaign, and was posted for duty with the Grand Fleet in the North Sea. Later he was engaged on escort duties to India and took part in the capture of a Turkish Island in the Red Sea. He holds the Queen's South African Medal and the 1914-15 Star, and the General Service and Victory Medals, and was demobilised in March 1919 after twenty-three years' service.
9, Gilbert Road, Kennington, S.E.11. Z27249

BEESON, C. J. E., Pte., 11th Queen's (Royal West Surrey Regiment).
He volunteered in November 1915, and after his training served on important duties with his unit. He was not successful in obtaining his transfer overseas owing to being medically unfit, and was discharged in May 1916 on account of his physical disabilities.
3, Short Road, Chiswick, W.4. 5831B

BEGENT, A., Gunner, R.G.A.
He volunteered in 1915, and after his training was drafted to the Western Front, where he took part in severe fighting at Neuve Chapelle, Loos, the Somme, Arras, Cambrai, St. Quentin and in many other engagements, and was wounded. He also served in the Retreat and Advance of 1918. He was demobilised in 1919, holding the 1914-15 Star, and the General Service and Victory Medals.
66, Glenthorne Road, Hammersmith, W.6. 11811B

BEGENT, A. E., Special War Worker.
He was engaged at Park Royal, Willesden, in filling shells and other important work. His duties were carried out with great efficiency, and he received high commendation for his valuable services during the war.
66, Glenthorne Road, Hammersmith, W.6. 11811A

BEHR, C., Private, Middlesex Regiment.
He joined in June 1918, and after his training served at various stations on important duties with his unit. He rendered valuable services, but was not successful in obtaining his transfer overseas before the cessation of hostilities. He was demobilised in February 1919.
75, Farmer's Road, Camberwell, S.E.5. 1241A

BEHR, C. T., Private, R.A.M.C.
He enlisted in July 1912, and immediately after the outbreak of war was sent to the Western Front. During his period of service overseas he was engaged in various sectors on important hospital duties with his unit and rendered valuable services. He was demobilised in February 1919, holding the Mons Star, and the General Service and Victory Medals.
75, Farmers Road, Camberwell, S.E.5. 1241B

BELBEN, T., Rifleman, King's Royal Rifle Corps.
Joining in July 1916, he was drafted to Italy in the following year. He took part in various actions on the Piave front and in 1918 was transferred to France, where he was present in the Retreat and was wounded and taken prisoner and sent to Germany. He unhappily died of his wounds whilst in captivity, and was entitled to the General Service and Victory Medals.
"Whilst we remember, the Sacrifice is not in vain."
99, Rosemary Road, Peckham, S.E.15. Z5323

BELCHER, J. C., Gunner, R.F.A.
He volunteered in January 1915, and in the same year proceeded to the Western Front. There he fought in many battles, including those of the Somme, Ypres, Arras and Bapaume, and was severely gassed. He was invalided home, and after being in hospital for a considerable period was discharged as medically unfit in August 1917. He holds the 1914-15 Star, and the General Service and Victory Medals.
36, Eltham Street, Walworth, S.E.17. Z1242

BELL, F. H., Private, Royal Scots Greys.
He was serving at the outbreak of war, and at once proceeded to the Western Front. There he took part in the Retreat from Mons and the Battles of the Marne, Ypres, Neuve Chapelle, Loos, the Somme and Cambrai, and in the Advance of 1918, during which he acted as a messenger. Later he went to Germany with the Army of Occupation. In April 1919 he returned to England and was placed on the Reserve, and holds the Mons Star, and the General Service and Victory Medals.
131, Grant Road, Battersea, S.W.11. Z1244B

BELL, J. S., Private, Royal Berkshire Regiment.
He volunteered in April 1915, and in August of the same year proceeded to France. Whilst there he fought at Hulluch, Festubert and Loos, and on October 13th, 1915 was reported missing, and is presumed to have been killed in action. He was entitled to the 1914-15 Star, and the General Service and Victory Medals.
13, Nardel Terrace, Alvey Street, Walworth, S.E.17. Z1245

BELLAIRS, A., Private, 1/19th London Regiment.
He joined in July 1917, and after a period of training was drafted to France. There he took part in many engagements and was gassed on the Somme. He also fought at Arras, Ypres, Cambrai, and was wounded and invalided home. He was demobilised in February 1919, and holds the General Service and Victory Medals.
53, Gloucester Road, Peckham, S.E.15. Z5897

BELLAMY, J., A.B., R.N., H.M.S. "Dolphin."
He was in the Navy at the outbreak of war, and throughout the war rendered valuable service chiefly in the North Sea, where he took part in several engagements whilst serving on submarines. He was still serving in 1920, and holds the 1914-15 Star, and the General Service and Victory Medals.
265, Mayall Road, Herne Hill, S.E.24. Z3992

BELLIS, A., L/Corporal, 3rd Middlesex Regiment.
Volunteering in August 1914, he served for a time on important duties in England. Later he proceeded to France and during the Advance of 1918 was wounded. After being in hospital for some months he was, on his recovery, drafted to Ireland, and afterwards to Germany with the Army of Occupation. He holds the General Service and Victory Medals, and in 1920 was still serving.
26, Dorset Road, Clapham Road, S.W.8. Z1246

BELSEY, J. H., L/Corporal, R.A.S.C. (M.T.)
He volunteered in April 1915, and in the following year proceeded to German East Africa, where he contracted malaria and dysentery and was invalided home. In 1917 he was drafted to France and served in various engagements, including the Somme and Cambrai. He was demobilised in May 1919, and holds the General Service and Victory Medals.
270, Albert Road, Peckham, S.E.15. Z5721B

BELTON, A., Private, R.A.F.
He joined in July 1918, and after a brief training proceeded to France. Here he served with the transport section of the R.A.F., being unfit for service in the trenches. He returned home, and was demobilised in February 1919, and holds the General Service and Victory Medals.
20, St. John's Hill Grove, Battersea, S.W.11. Z1247

BELTON, G. H., Private, R.A.M.C.
Volunteering in October 1915, he was drafted on the completion of his training to the Western Front. In this theatre of war he took part in the fighting at Loos, Béthune and many other places, and suffered from severe shell-shock. He was invalided home and in May 1918 was discharged as medically unfit, and holds the General Service and Victory Medals.
117, St. Albans Avenue, Chiswick, W.4. 7968

BENEST, W., Gunner, R.F.A.
Volunteering in January 1915, he proceeded to France in the same month. There he took part in the fighting at Hill 60, Ypres, Loos, Vimy Ridge, the Somme and Cambrai, and in the Retreat and Advance of 1918. Later he served with the Army of Occupation in Germany until demobilised in January 1919. He holds the 1914-15 Star, and the General Service and Victory Medals.
129, Grant Road, Battersea, S.W.11 Z1248

BENFIELD, A. W., Private, 2/10th London Regt.
He joined in 1917, and in the same year was drafted to the Western Front. Whilst there he took part in the fighting at Cambrai and in the Retreat and Advance of 1918, during which he was wounded. He returned to England, and after receiving hospital treatment was demobilised in 1919, holding the General Service and Victory Medals.
83, Wadhurst Road, Wandsworth Road, S,.W.8.   Z1785B

BENFIELD, H. J., Driver, R.F.A.
Volunteering in August 1915, he was in the same year drafted to the Western Front, where he took part in many important engagements, including those at Ypres, Festubert, Loos, Vimy Ridge, the Somme, Arras and Messines. He was, unfortunately, killed in action on the Somme on April 12th, 1918, and was entitled to the 1914-15 Star, and the General Service and Victory Medals.
16, Draycourt Place, Camberwell, S.E.5.   Z3993

BENFORD, J. M. L., Lieut., Sherwood Foresters.
Already a Sergt.-Major at the outbreak of war in August 1914, he immediately proceeded to France and fought at Mons. He also played a prominent part in the Battles of the Marne (I and II), Neuve Chapelle, Ypres (I and II), Loos, the Somme (I and II), Passchendaele, Cambrai, the Aisne, Epéhy and Mons (II), and was three times wounded in action. He was five times mentioned in Despatches and was awarded the Belgian Croix de Guerre and granted a commission on the Field for conspicuous bravery and devotion to duty. In April 1919 he returned to his depôt, where he served until transferred to the Reserve of Officers in February 1920. He also holds the India Medal, 1895 (with clasps Malakand, 1897, Punjab Frontier 1897-8, and Tirah 1897-8), the Mons Star, the General Service and Victory Medals, and the Long Service and Good Conduct Medals.
Syston, Leicester.   Z6131

BENIFER, E., Private, Suffolk Regiment.
He volunteered in August 1915, and after his training served at various stations on guard and other important duties. He rendered valuable services, but was not able to obtain a transfer overseas owing to his being overage for duty abroad. In November 1918 he was demobilised.
9, Knowsley Road, Battersea, S.W.11.   Z1237

BENIT, S. J., Rifleman, 13th Rifle Brigade.
Volunteering in September 1914, he was drafted overseas in July of the following year. He took part in many notable battles, including those of Ypres, Festubert, Loos, Vimy Ridge, the Somme, Arras, Messines, Ypres, Cambrai and others. He was taken prisoner on April 4th, 1918, and kept in captivity until December 1918, when he was released and repatriated. In January 1919 he was demobilised, and holds the 1914-15 Star, and the General Service and Victory Medals.
105, Smyrks Road, Old Kent Road, S.E.17.   Z1249

BENNETT, A., Private, 24th Queen's (Royal West Surrey Regiment).
Volunteering in August 1914, he was drafted overseas in the following year. Whilst in France he took part in the fighting at Festubert and Givenchy and was killed in action on June 7th, 1915, after only a few months' active service. He was entitled to the 1914-15 Star, and the General Service and Victory Medals.
19, Sedan Street, Walworth, S.E.17.   Z1255

BENNETT, B. (Mrs.), Special War Worker.
From November 1916 until the cessation of hostilities this lady held an important position at Hayes Filling Factory. She was engaged on dangerous work in connection with shell filling and fuses, and carried out her duties with great care and efficiency.
43, Raynham Road, Hammersmith, W.6.   11607B

BENNETT, C., Private, Argyll and Sutherland Highlanders and Labour Corps.
He joined in April 1916, and early in the following year was drafted to the Western Front, where he took part in much of the heavy fighting on the Somme. Shortly afterwards he was invalided home through ill-health, and on recovery was transferred to the Labour Corps. He then returned to France and was principally engaged in conveying supplies to the lines. In February 1919 he was demobilised, and holds the General Service and Victory Medals.
10, Combermere Road, Stockwell, S.W.9.   Z1254

BENNETT, C. H., Driver, R.A.S.C. (M.T.)
Volunteering in October 1915, he was drafted in the following year to the Western Front. There he saw much service at Ypres, the Somme, Arras, Bapaume, Béthune, Amiens and Armentières, and also served in the Retreat and Advance of 1918, being principally engaged in conveying supplies and ammunition to the fighting areas. He was demobilised in April 1919, and holds the General Service and Victory Medals.
38, Edithna Street, Landor Road, S.W.9.   Z1253

BENNETT, G. H., Driver, R.F.A.
He volunteered in May 1915, and after completing his training served for a time on important duties in England. In January 1917 he proceeded to France and took part in many notable battles, including those of Arras, Ypres, St. Quentin, Armentières, Cambrai, Amiens, Bapaume, and the Retreat and Advance of 1918. He was demobilised in July 1919, and holds the General Service and Victory Medals.
52, Westmoreland Road, Walworth, S.E.17.   Z1256A

BENNETT, L. S., L/Corporal, The Queen's (Royal West Surrey Regiment).
He joined in June 1916, and in the following year was drafted to France, where he was in action at Vimy Ridge, and was wounded and invalided home. On his recovery he returned to the Western Front and again saw heavy fighting at Vimy Ridge, where he fell in action on September 29th, 1917. He was entitled to the General Service and Victory Medals.
"Great deeds cannot die."
141, Denmark Road, Camberwell, S.E.5.   Z5889A

BENNETT, R. G., Guardsman, 2nd Coldstream Guards.
He was mobilised in August 1914, and was sent to France in the same month. He took part in severe fighting at Mons, Ypres, Vimy Ridge, Arras, Cambrai, and in numerous other engagements, and was wounded. He returned home and was demobilised in February 1919, and holds the Mons Star, and the General Service and Victory Medals.
37, Wells Place, Camberwell, S.E.5.   Z3421

BENNETT, R. J., Gunner, R.G.A.
He joined in February 1916, and was drafted to the Western Front in the same year. He took part in numerous engagements, including those at Ploegsteert Wood and Ypres, and also served in the Retreat and Advance of 1918. He was demobilised in June 1919, holding the General Service and Victory Medals.
18, Ada Road, Camberwell, S.E.5.   Z3420

BENNETT, W., Leading Telegraphist, R.N.
He enlisted in March 1914, and at the outbreak of war was serving on H.M.S. "Powerful" at Devonport. Later he was posted to H.M.S. "King George 5th," and in this ship took part in the naval engagement off Dogger Bank and in the Battle of Jutland, afterwards cruising in the North Sea until demobilised in November 1919. He holds the 1914-15 Star, and the General Service and Victory Medals.
2, Milford Street, Wandsworth Road, S.W.8.   Z1252

BENNETT, W., Private, Northumberland Fusiliers.
Having previously served in the South African war, he rejoined in March 1916. Owing to medical unfitness he was not successful in obtaining his transfer overseas, but was engaged on important duties with his unit at various stations until discharged in November 1917. He holds the Queen's and King's South African Medals.
29, Horsman Street, Camberwell, S.E.5.   Z1250

BENNETT, W. G., Pte., 7th City of London Regt.
Volunteering in May 1915, he was drafted in the same year to the Western Front. Whilst there he took part in the fighting at Arras, Ypres, Cambrai, the Somme and St. Quentin, and was wounded twice. In April 1918 he was invalided home, and in the following January was demobilised. He holds the 1914-15 Star, and the General Service and Victory Medals.
43, Raynham Road, Hammersmith, W.6.   11607A

BENNETT, W. H., Gunner, R.G.A.
He joined in 1917, and in the same year was drafted overseas. He took part in many engagements on the Western Front, including those on the Somme, Arras, Ypres, and in the Retreat and Advance of 1918. He holds the General Service and Victory Medals, and was demobilised in 1919.
16, Mina Road, Walworth, S.E.17.   Z1251

BENNEY, E., Private, 2nd Bedfordshire Regiment.
He joined in March 1917, and was drafted to France on the completion of his training. He did valuable service for two years on the Western Front, mainly in the Somme sector, and was wounded during this period. He was demobilised in September 1919, holding the General Service and Victory Medals.
91, Fielding Road, Bedford Park, W.4.   7658B

BENNEY, G., Driver, R.A.S.C. (M.T.)
He joined in 1916, and on the completion of his training was engaged at his depôt on important duties in connection with motor transport. He rendered valuable services, but was unable to obtain his transfer overseas while hostilities continued, and on medical grounds was invalided out of the Army in 1918.
91, Fielding Road, Bedford Park, W.4.   7658A

BENNIE, J., Telegraphist (Wireless), R.N., H.M.S. "Curlew."
He joined in May 1917, and served with the Grand Fleet in the North Sea. He took part in the Battle of Jutland and the bombardment of Ostend. He also served with the Harwich Patrol and was engaged in Russian waters. He was still serving in 1920, and holds the General Service and Victory Medals.
148, Albert Road, Peckham, S.E.15.   Z5722

BENSON, J., Private, M.G.C.
He was mobilised in August 1914, and quickly drafted to France. In this seat of war he took part in the Battles of Mons, Ypres, Loos, the Somme, Arras, Cambrai, and in the Retreat of 1918, during which he was taken prisoner. He was held in captivity at Gustron Camp in Germany until after the Armistice, when he returned home and was demobilised in February 1919. He holds the Mons Star, and the General Service and Victory Medals.
2, Pomfret Road, Camberwell, S.E.5.   Z5886

BENTON, A., Private, 1st Canadian Regiment.
He joined in 1916, and on the conclusion of his training proceeded to the Western Front in 1917. He took an active part in many operations on the Somme Front, and was unfortunately killed in action in 1917. He was entitled to the General Service and Victory Medals.
   "He died the noblest death a man may die,
      Fighting for God and right and liberty."
16, Santley Street, Stockwell, S.W.9.   Z4407A

BENTON, W., Private, East Surrey Regiment.
A serving soldier, who had enlisted in 1908, he was mobilised at the outbreak of hostilities, and in the following year was drafted to the Dardanelles. He took an active part in many severe engagements, and was killed in action there before the close of the campaign. He was entitled to the 1914-15 Star, and the General Service and Victory Medals.
   "The path of duty was the way to glory."
16, Santley Street, Stockwell, S.W.9.   Z4407B

BENTZ, H. V., Rifleman, 5th London Regiment (London Rifle Brigade).
He joined in 1916, and in the following year was drafted to France. There he took part in much heavy fighting in the Somme and Arras sectors, and in the Advance of 1918. He was unhappily killed in action at Cambrai on October 11th, 1918, and was entitled to the General Service and Victory Medals.
   "Whilst we remember, the Sacrifice is not in vain."
36, McKerrell Road, Peckham, S.E.15.   Z5892

BERNARD, J. C., Sapper, R.E.
Volunteering in February 1915, he was sent to the Western Front later in the same year. During his service in France he was engaged on important duties in connection with the operations and was in action at Loos, Arras and Ypres, where he was wounded. He was invalided home, but after his recovery was sent to Germany with the Army of Occupation, and stationed at Cologne until July 1919, when he returned home, and was demobilised. He holds the 1914-15 Star, and the General Service and Victory Medals.
11, Atherton Street, Battersea, S.W.11.   Z1257

BERRY, F., Private, 8th Seaforth Highlanders.
Volunteering in December 1915, he was drafted to the Western Front in the following year. He took part in much severe fighting at St. Eloi, Albert, Vermelles, Vimy Ridge, the Somme, Beaumont-Hamel, Cambrai, Bapaume and other engagements. He fell fighting at Bapaume on August 22nd, 1918, and was there buried. He was entitled to the General Service and Victory Medals.
   "And doubtless he went in splendid company."
20, Wyatt Road, Brixton, S.W.9.   Z5039A

BERRY, J. A., Sergt., Mounted Military Police.
A serving soldier, he was mobilised at the outbreak of war, and almost immediately sent to France, where he took part in the Retreat from Mons. He was in action also at Ypres in 1915, and in many important engagements in the Somme sector throughout the war. He returned home and was discharged as time-expired in April 1919, having served seventeen years with the Colours, and holds the Mons Star, the General Service and Victory Medals, and the Croix de Guerre, which was conferred upon him by the French for distinguished services.
12, Stewart's Road, Battersea Park Road, S.W.8.   Z1258

BERRYMAN, T. H., Driver, R.A.S.C. (M.T.)
He joined in January 1916, and in the same year was drafted overseas. Attached to the Supply Column he served in many sectors of the Western Front and did valuable work. In March 1919 he was demobilised, holding the General Service and Victory Medals.
38, South Island Place, Brixton Road, S.W.9.   Z5219

BESFORD, E., Private, R.A.O.C.
He joined in September 1916, and in the same year was drafted to Salonika, where he was engaged until 1919 on important duties as a saddler with the Royal Army Ordnance Corps. He contracted malaria, and in consequence was invalided home. After his recovery he did valuable service at home until his demobilisation in September 1919. He holds the General Service and Victory Medals.
29, Sedan Street, Walworth, S.E.17.   Z1710C

BESSANT, A. R., Private, 24th Queen's (Royal West Surrey Regiment).
He volunteered in 1914, and after his training was engaged at various stations on important duties with his unit. He did much valuable work, but owing to medical reasons was unfit for overseas service, and was discharged in May 1916.
7, Heyford Avenue, South Lambeth Road, S.W.8.   Z1259

BEST, A., Special War Worker.
For a year of the war he held a responsible post under the Navy and Army Canteen Board, Knightsbridge. He was engaged on important duties at head ticket inspector for all canteens and travelled throughout the country. His services were highly appreciated until his retirement in November 1918.
42, Eastbury Grove, Chiswick, W.4.   5469A

BEST, B. M. (Mrs.), Special War Worker.
From April 1917 to April 1918 this lady was engaged on work of National importance as a book-keeper for the Navy and Army Canteens Board, Knightsbridge. She carried out her important duties with great care and efficiency.
42, Eastbury Grove, Chiswick, W.4.   5469B

BEST, E. A., Private, 5th East Surrey Regiment.
He joined in February 1916, and in the same year proceeded to India, where he was stationed until 1917, when he was drafted to Mesopotamia. Whilst in this theatre of war he fought in many important engagements, and was in hospital owing to severe illness. He returned home, and was demobilised in September 1919, and holds the General Service and Victory Medals.
14, Milford Street, Wandsworth Road, S.W.8.   Z1260B

BEST, G. E., A.B., R.N., H.M.S. "Vernon."
He was mobilised at the outbreak of war, and was posted to H.M.S. "Vernon." Whilst in this ship he fought in the Battle of Heligoland Bight, and in 1915 proceeded to the Dardanelles, where he served for a time. He was afterwards engaged on mine-sweeping duties in the North Sea and the Mediterranean until 1918. In the following year he was demobilised and holds the 1914-15 Star, the General Service, Victory, and Long Service and Good Conduct Medals.
28, Kirkwood Road, Nunhead, S.E.15.   Z6138B

BEST, H., Driver, R.E.
He volunteered in April 1915, and on the completion of his training was drafted to the Western Front, where he served until hostilities ceased. During this period he was frequently engaged in the forward areas whilst operations were in progress, and did excellent work as a driver in the Royal Engineers. He was demobilised in February 1919, after returning home, and holds the General Service and Victory Medals.
25, Redmore Road, Hammersmith, W.6.   12782A

BEST, H. C., Corporal, R.A.O.C.
He joined in March 1916, and after his training was retained on important duties in the Armourer's Department, where he was engaged as a storeman. He rendered valuable services, but was not successful in obtaining his transfer overseas before the conclusion of hostilities, and was demobilised in December 1919.
14, Milford Street, Wandsworth Road, S.W.8.   Z1260D

BEST, H. T., Private, R.A.S.C. (Remounts).
He joined in December 1917, and in the following January was drafted overseas. He was stationed at the depôt at Boulogne and was chiefly engaged in taking remounts up the line until the cessation of hostilities. In January 1919 he returned home, and was demobilised, and holds the General Service and Victory Medals.
14, Milford Street, Wandsworth Road, S.W.8.   Z1260A

BEST, S. T., Private, Monmouthshire Regiment.
He volunteered in January 1915, and in November of the same year was drafted to the Western Front, where he took part in severe fighting at Albert, Vermelles and Vimy Ridge. He was then sent home, being under age, but returning later, he served in the engagements at Arras, Bullecourt, Ypres, Cambrai and the Somme, and also in the Retreat and Advance of 1918. After the Armistice he proceeded with the Army of Occupation to Germany. He was still serving in 1920, and holds the 1914-15 Star, and the General Service and Victory Medals.
25, Atwell Road, Rye Lane, S.E.5.   Z5324B

BEST, T. V., Gunner (Signaller), R.G.A.
Joining in March 1917, he went through his course of training
and was afterwards drafted to the Western Front. He did
valuable work for his Battery as a Signaller in many important engagements until hostilities ceased, and after his
return home was demobilised in February 1919. He holds
the General Service and Victory Medals.
25, Redmore Road, Hammersmith, W.6.   12782B

BEST, W., Corporal, 4th East Surrey Regiment.
He volunteered in August 1914, and was sent to France in
February of the following year, and took part in severe fighting.
He died gloriously on the Field of Battle at Neuve Chapelle
on March 9th, 1915, and was entitled to the 1914-15 Star,
and the General Service and Victory Medals.
              " His life for his Country."
25, Atwell Road, Peckham, S.E.15.   Z5324A

BEST, W. R., Private, 1st Lancashire Fusiliers.
He joined in June 1917, and was sent to the Western Front in
the following year. During his service in France he fought in
many important engagements in the Retreat and Advance of
1918, and was wounded in action. He was invalided home
in consequence, and on his recovery was transferred to the
Royal Army Service Corps and drafted to Salonika, where he
remained until February 1920. He then returned home and
was demobilised, holding the General Service and Victory
Medals.
14, Milford Street, Wandsworth Road, S.W.8.   Z1260C

BESTLEY, F., Private, R.A.M.C.
He joined in May 1918, and in the following September was
drafted to France. During his service on the Western Front
he was engaged on important duties in connection with the
wounded at many military hospitals, including that at Etaples.
He was demobilised in April 1919, after returning home, and
holds the General Service and Victory Medals.
1, Comber Grove, Camberwell, S.E.5.   Z1176

BETHELL, F., Private, R.A.O.C.
He joined in 1916, and in the following year was drafted to
Egypt. At Kantara and Alexandria he was engaged on
special duties with the Royal Army Ordnance Corps until
hostilities ceased. He returned home in November 1918, but
after a year was redrafted to Egypt. He holds the General
Service and Victory Medals.
43, Stanley Street, Battersea Park, S.W.8.   Z1261A

BETTIS, H. J., Driver, R.F.A.
He volunteered in June 1915, and after his training served on
important duties with his unit until 1917, when he was drafted
to the Western Front, and took part in much severe fighting
on the Arras and Somme fronts. He also served in the Retreat
and Advance of 1918, and afterwards proceeded with the Army
of Occupation to Germany. While serving there he was
presented with the Belgian Croix de Guerre, and he also holds
the General Service and Victory Medals. He was demobilised
in June 1919.
4, Brisbane Street, Camberwell, S.E.5.   Z5040

BETTS, G. W., Stoker, R.N., H.M.S. " Devonshire."
He joined the Navy in August 1916, and for nearly three years
was engaged in H.M.S. " Devonshire " on important and
dangerous duties, convoying food supply ships to and from
various ports in Canada, the United States, the Bermudas and
Cuba, and frequently passing through mine infested areas
during these voyages. He was demobilised in June 1919, and
holds the General Service and Victory Medals.
45, Bonnington Square, South Lambeth Road, S.W.8.   1262

BEVAN, E. E., Air Mechanic, R.A.F.
He attested in 1916, but was not called up until June 1918,
when after a brief training he was drafted to France. There
he was engaged on important duties as a wingmaker with the
Royal Air Force. Whilst serving at Lille he contracted pneumonia, and was in hospital for a time. In March 1919, he
returned home and was demobilised holding the General
Service and Victory Medals.
10, Farrar Street, Stockwell, S.W.9.   Z5220

BEW, A. E., Private, 26th Middlesex Regiment.
He joined in June 1916, and having completed his training was
drafted to Salonika, where he was engaged in various sectors of
the Balkan Front, and took part in many important operations.
He unfortunately contracted enteric fever and died on September 30th, 1918. He was entitled to the General Service and
Victory Medals.
2, Richford Street, Hammersmith, W.6.   10452A

BEW, W., Private, 7th London Regiment.
After his mobilisation in August 1914, he was soon drafted
to the Western Front. During his service in France he fought
in numerous engagements of importance in various sectors, and
was wounded and gassed in action. He was demobilised in
March 1919, after his return home, and holds the 1914 Star,
and the General Service and Victory Medals.
2, Richford Street, Hammersmith, W.6.   10452C

**BEW, W. F., Pte., 2nd London Regt. (Royal Fusiliers)
and Rifleman, 18th London Regt. (London Irish
Rifles).**
He volunteered in August 1914, and after his training was
drafted to France, where he served with distinction as a sharp-
shooter. He took part in many important engagements, and
being twice severely wounded in action, was invalided home.
He unfortunately died in hospital at Cheltenham on August
31st, 1918, and was entitled to the General Service and
Victory Medals.
2, Richford Street, Hammersmith, W.6.   10452B

BEWS, F. W., A.B., R.N., H.M.S. " Diligence."
He volunteered in August 1914, and served with the Grand
Fleet in the North Sea. He was engaged on patrol duties, and
also in repairing damaged ships after they had been in action.
He was demobilised in September 1919, holding the 1914-15
Star, and the General Service and Victory Medals.
26, Russell Road, Peckham, S.E.15.   Z5325

BEWSEY, W. S., 1st Class W.O., R.A.F. (late R.F.C.)
He volunteered in August 1914, and in the following year was
drafted to the Western Front, where he was engaged on important aircraft duties at St. Omer. He afterwards returned
to England, and was stationed at Farnborough Aerodrome on
similar work. Early in 1919 he proceeded to India and served
on the North West Frontier during the Afghan Risings. He
contracted malaria while in India, and was invalided home to
hospital and was demobilised in December 1919. He holds
the 1914-15 Star, the General Service and Victory Medals, and
the India General Service Medals (with clasp Afghanistan
N.W. Frontier, 1919).
3, St. Alphonsus Road, Clapham, S.W.4.   Z1464

BIBBS, C. S., Private, R.A.S.C. (M.T.)
He volunteered in May 1915, and was sent to France in the
same month. He was attached to the Indian Cavalry, and was
engaged on important duties in connection with the water
supply, and served in many sectors including Péronne, Ypres,
Albert, Béthune, Loos, Lens, and Poperinghe, and also in the
Retreat and Advance of 1918. He was demobilised in January
1919, holding the 1914-15 Star, and the General Service and
Victory Medals.
7, Treherne Road, Stockwell, S.W.9.   Z3435

BICKNELL, F. T., Driver, R.F.A.
H volunteered at the commencement of hostilities, and after
his training was drafted to the Western Front, where he fought
in many important engagements up to the cessation of hostilities
He was demobilised on his return to England in May 1919, and
holds the 1914-15 Star, and the General Service and Victory
Medals. 6, Brackley Terrace, Chiswick, W.4.   5432B

BIDEN, E. L., Private, Somerset Light Infantry.
Joining in October 1916, he was drafted, after having completed
his training, to the Western Front, and was wounded during the
severe fighting at Ypres. He was invalided home, but on
recovery returned to the firing line, and was in action until the
cessation of hostilities. Shortly afterwards he proceeded to
Germany with the Army of Occupation, serving there until
demobilised in November 1919. He holds the General Service
and Victory Medals.
29, Russell Street, Brixton Road, S.W.9.   Z5222

BIGENT, H. G. C., 1st Class Aircraftsman, R.A.F.
He joined in June 1916, and at the conclusion of his training
was engaged with his Squadron on important duties, which
demanded a high degree of technical knowledge and skill. He
was unable to secure his transfer overseas before the termination of hostilities, but rendered valuable services until demobilised in June 1919.
7, Tabor Road, Hammersmith, W.6.   11207

BIGGS, A. L., Gunner, R.F.A.
He volunteered in October 1915, and in the following year
proceeded to the Western Front. In this theatre of war he
took part in many engagements, including those at Vimy
Ridge, the Somme, Arras, Lens, Passchendaele, Cambrai,
Amiens, and the Retreat and Advance of 1918. He was
demobilised in 1919, and holds the General Service and Victory
Medals.
22, Scylla Road, Peckham, S.E.15.   Z5876B

**BIGGS, J. M., Sergt.-Drummer, 2nd Queen's (Royal
West Surrey Regiment).**
A serving soldier, he was drafted to the Western Front on the
outbreak of hostilities, and fought in the Battle of, and subsequent Retreat from, Mons. In October 1914, he was taken
prisoner, and was sent to Mettlenburg Camp, where he remained
until his repatriation in December 1918, when he rejoined his
unit. Later he was sent to India, where in 1920 he was still
serving. He holds the Mons Star, and the General Service and
Victory Medals, and in addition a Medal awarded by Queen
Mary to prisoners of war.
74, Ingleton Street, Brixton Road, S.W.9.   Z1264

BIGGS, S. H. (D.C.M.), Sergt., 21st London Regt. (1st Surrey Rifles).
He volunteered in August 1914, and in the following year proceeded to France. He took part in the Battles of Ypres, Loos, Vimy Ridge, the Somme, Messines, Lens, Passchendaele, Cambrai, and the Retreat and Advance of 1918, during which he was wounded and invalided home. He was awarded the Distinguished Conduct Medal for conspicuous gallantry and devotion to duty in the Field. He was demobilised in December 1919, and also holds the 1914–15 Star, and the General Service and Victory Medals.
22, Scylla Road, Peckham, S.E.15.   Z5876A

BIGLEY, T. F., Private, Royal Fusiliers.
He volunteered in October 1914, but at the conclusion of his training at Dover and Nuneaton, was found to be physically unfit for further military duties, and was invalided out of the Service in January 1915.
10, Dieppe Street, West Kensington, W.14.   16254A

BIGNOLD, A., Gunner, R.F.A.
Volunteering in October 1914, he obtained his training at Woolwich, and in the following year was sent to the Western Front. He was engaged in the fighting at Hill 60, Ypres, Festubert, and Messines Ridge, where he was severely wounded, and was in consequence invalided home. After his recovery he returned to France, and took part in many more engagements, and was again wounded and gassed. Returning to England, he was demobilised in February 1919, and holds the 1914–15 Star, and the General Service and Victory Medals.
15K, Victoria Dwellings, Battersea Park Road, Lambeth, S.W.8.   Z1266

BILHAM, G., Trooper, Surrey Lancers.
He volunteered in November 1914, and on the completion of his training was drafted to France early in 1915. After serving there for ten months, during which he was in action at Ypres, and Loos, he sailed for Egypt, and in February 1916, was transferred to Salonika. While there he took part in many operations on the Doiran and Struma fronts until hostilities ceased. Owing to a severe attack of malaria he was invalided home and discharged in March 1919, as medically unfit for further military duty. He holds the 1914–15 Star, and the General Service and Victory Medals.
49, Bennerley Road, Wandsworth Common, S.W.11.   Z4408

BILLERS, J., A.B., Royal Navy.
Having previously served for sixteen years, he was mobilised at the outbreak of hostilities, and was posted to H.M.S. "Abercrombie." This ship took part in several Naval engagements during the war, and he was wounded on one occasion. He distinguished himself as a gunner during his service. He holds the 1914–15 Star, and the General Service and Victory Medals, and was demobilised in March 1919.
40, Porten Road, West Kensington, W.14.   T12481A

BILLERS, W. G., Gunner, R.F.A.
He volunteered in August 1914, and after completing his training was drafted to the Western Front. Whilst in this theatre of war he fought in many important engagements, notably those at the Somme, Ypres, and Cambrai, and did valuable work with his unit throughout. He was demobilised in May 1919, and holds the 1914 Star, and the General Service and Victory Medals.
40, Porten Road, West Kensington, W.14.   T12481B

BILLSON, G., L/Cpl., 4th East Surrey Regiment.
He volunteered in October 1914, and in the following year was drafted to the Western Front, where he took part in numerous engagements, including those at Albert, Ypres, the Somme, and Arras. He was severely wounded in September 1916, and invalided home, and was discharged in September 1917 as medically unfit for further service. He holds the 1914–15 Star, and the General Service and Victory Medals.
50, Bournemouth Road, Peckham, S.E.15.   Z5326

BIRCH, A. (M.S.M.), C.S.M., 2nd Grenadier Guards.
A serving soldier, who enlisted in 1898, he was drafted to the Western Front at the outbreak of war, and took part in the Retreat from Mons, and the Battles of the Marne, and the Aisne. He also fought at Neuve Chapelle, Cambrai, and in many other important sectors until hostilities ceased, and was awarded the Meritorious Service Medal for consistently good work in the Field. In addition he holds the Khedive's Sudan and the British Sudan Medals, the Queen's South African Medal, the Mons Star, and the General Service and Victory Medals. He was demobilised in May 1919.
100A, Ingelow Road, Battersea Park, S.W.8.   Z1269

BIRCH, E., Private, R.A.S.C.
He volunteered in December 1914, and after his training was drafted to the Western Front, where he rendered valuable service with the Supply Column in many sectors for the remaining period of hostilities. He was demobilised on his return to England in March 1919, and holds the General Service and Victory Medals.
65, Faroe Road, West Kensington, W.14.   12453C

BIRCH, R. H., Private, R.M.L.I.
Called from the Reserve at the outbreak of hostilities, he was immediately posted to the Grand Fleet, and subsequently served in various patrol ships in the North Sea. Frequently passing through mine infested areas he had many escapes, and on one occasion his vessel was torpedoed in the Mediterranean. He did valuable work until his demobilisation, in July 1919 and holds the 1914–15 Star, and the General Service and Victory Medals.
6, Holden Street, Battersea, S.W.11.   Z1268

BIRCH, W. S., Private, Wiltshire Regiment.
Mobilised at the commencement of war, he was quickly drafted to the Western Front, and served in the Retreat from Mons, and the Battles of the Marne and the Aisne. Whilst in action at Ypres, he was wounded and taken prisoner, and during his captivity was interned in various camps, including one at Munster. He was employed in many capacities, chiefly in stone breaking, and in work at a saw-mill, and on his release after the cessation of hostilities returned to England, and was demobilised early in 1919. He holds the Mons Star, and the General Service and Victory Medals.
312, Battersea Park Road, Battersea, S.W.11.   Z1267

BIRD, C., Special War Worker.
Owing to the importance of the work upon which he was engaged with the Metropolitan Railway Company, he could not be released for military service. Throughout the war he was employed on special duties of a responsible nature, and rendered valuable services.
46, Leamore Street, Hammersmith, W.6.   12608

BIRD, C. J., Private, Essex Regiment.
He volunteered in September 1914, and until June 1915, when he was transferred to the Essex Regiment, served with the Royal Field Artillery as an Instructor at Ipswich. Afterwards he was stationed at Felixstowe for a time, and in 1916 was sent to France, where he took part in several engagements in the Arras area, and three months later was wounded. He was invalided home, and after his recovery was engaged at his depôt until demobilised in February 1919. He holds the General Service and Victory Medals.
35, Portslade Road, Wandsworth Road, S.W.8.   Z1271

BIRD, E. G., Private, 9th Royal Fusiliers.
He volunteered in August 1915, and after rendering valuable service at various stations, was drafted to the Western Front at the beginning of 1918. He took part in many important engagements in the final stages of the war, including those at the Somme and Cambrai, and was wounded in action. After the Armistice he was drafted to Mesopotamia, where in 1920 he was still serving. He holds the General Service and Victory Medals.
4, Shepherd's Place, Upper Kennington Lane, S.E.11.   Z23852

BIRD, G. S., Private, Queen's (Royal West Surrey Regiment).
Joining in January 1916, he was sent to France on completing his training, and was stationed for a time at Calais and Boulogne. Later he was sent to a fighting area, and after taking part in several engagements, advanced into Germany with the Army of Occupation at the termination of hostilities. He was demobilised in November 1919, and holds the General Service and Victory Medals.
37, Heath Road, Wandsworth Road, S.W.8.   Z1272

BIRD, J., Private, Labour Corps.
He volunteered in 1914, but until he was sent to France in 1917, was engaged on special duties at Tidworth. Whilst overseas, he was engaged in road repairing, and other important work, which he carried out chiefly in the Cambrai sector. He also served in the Retreat and Advance of 1918. He holds the General Service and Victory Medals, and was demobilised in September 1919.
1, Corunna Terrace, New Road, S.W.8.   Z1273

BIRD, T. J., Private, 13th East Surrey Regiment.
Joining in February 1916, he was sent to France in May of the same year. He took part in the severe fighting on the Somme, and in other engagements. He fell fighting on the Somme on August 8th, 1916, and was entitled to the General Service and Victory Medals.
"A costly sacrifice upon the altar of freedom."
108, Cronin Road, Peckham, S.E.15.   Z5570C

BIRD, W., A.B., Royal Navy.
Volunteering at the commencement of hostilities, he was posted to H.M.S. "Southampton." With this vessel he was engaged on important duties in the North Sea, and took part in several Naval actions, including that of Heligoland Bight, in which he was wounded. After remaining in his ship until 1916, he was invalided to King's College Hospital, where, it was found necessary to amputate one of his legs. He unfortunately died after the operation, in the latter part of 1918. He was entitled to the 1914–15 Star, and the General Service and Victory Medals.
21, Irving Grove, Stockwell Road, S.W.9.   Z2090B

BIRD, W., Special War Worker.
Being ineligible for military service, he was engaged on work of National importance at Newcastle-on-Tyne. For a considerable period of the war he worked there as an electrician in connection with ship-building, and in this capacity rendered services of a most valuable nature.
35, Acorn Street, Camberwell, S.E.5.   Z1790

BIRD, W., Gunner, R.F.A.
He joined in December 1916, and after his training was sent in the following March to the Western Front, where he served for two years. During this time he did good work with his Battery in the Battles of the Somme, Arras, Vimy Ridge, Cambrai, and Béthune, where he was gassed. He holds the General Service and Victory Medals, and was demobilised in January 1919.
26, Kitson Road, Camberwell, S.E.5.   Z1270

BIRDSEYE, J., Special War Worker.
He was engaged at Messrs. Waring and Gillows', the White City, in the manufacture of military equipment. His duties which were of a responsible nature were carried out with great care and efficiency, and he received high commendation for his valuable services.
45, Havelock Road, Hammersmith, W.6.   12016B

BIRDSEYE, M. (Mrs.), Special War Worker.
This lady volunteered her services and was offered a post at Messrs. Waring and Gillow's Munition Works, at the White City. She was engaged in the manufacture of military equipment. Her duties were carried out in a most efficient manner, and she rendered valuable services during the war.
45, Havelock Road, Hammersmith, W. 6.   12016A

BIRKETT, C. A., Corporal, R.M.L.I.
He joined in 1917, and after a period of service in Scotland, was engaged on important and dangerous patrol and mine-sweeping duties in the North Sea. He unfortunately met with a serious accident which caused his discharge in 1919, as medically unfit for further service. He holds the General Service and Victory Medals. 2, Vivian Road, Peckham, S.E.15.   Z5875

BIRKS, J. E., Private, 24th Queen's (Royal West Surrey Regiment).
He volunteered in August 1914, and in March of the following year was drafted to the Western Front, where he took part in numerous engagements including those at Vimy Ridge, the Somme, Arras, Ypres, Lens, and Cambrai. During his service overseas he was wounded at Givenchy and was sent to England for treatment. On his recovery he returned to France, where he continued to serve until January 1919, when he was demobilised, holding the 1914–15 Star, and the General Service and Victory Medals.
71, Darwin Buildings, Barlow Street, Walworth, S.E.17. Z1274

BIRRELL, D., Private, R.A.S.C. (M.T.)
Volunteering in December 1914, he was drafted to France in the same month. He was engaged as a motor driver in the transport of ammunition and supplies to the various fronts including those of the Marne, the Aisne, Ypres, Loos, the Somme and Arras, He also served in the Retreat and Advance of 1918, and afterwards proceeded with the Army of Occupation to Germany. During his service he was wounded on one occasion. He was demobilised in April 1919, holding the 1914–15 Star, and the General Service and Victory Medals.
21, Neate Street, Camberwell, S.E.5.   Z5041

BISHOP, A., Private, South Staffordshire Regiment.
He volunteered in March 1915, and in the following year was sent overseas, and during his service on the Western Front fought in various engagements in the Somme sector. He gave his life for the freedom of England in the Battle of Arras in May 1917, and was entitled to the General Service and Victory Medals.
"Great deeds cannot die.
They with the sun and moon renew their light for ever."
38, Parkstone Road, Peckham, S.E.15.   Z6143A

BISHOP, A. W., Private, Welch Regiment.
He joined in April 1916, and was shortly afterwards drafted to France. During his service overseas he took part in several engagements in the Somme Offensive, and in August 1916, was wounded and sustained severe shell shock in the fierce fighting at Delville Wood. He was invalided home to hospital and was subsequently discharged as medically unfit for service in June 1917. He holds the General Service and Victory Medals.
81, Clayton Road, Peckham, S.E.15.   5894C

BISHOP, E. H., Gunner, R.F.A.
He joined in October 1916, and in the following year was drafted to India, where he was engaged at various stations on important duties with his unit. While serving there he became seriously ill and unfortunately died at Mhow, on October 27th, 1918. He was entitled to the General Service and Victory Medals.
"He joined the great white company of valiant souls."
36, Tindal Street, Brixton, S.W.9.   Z5042A

BISHOP, F., 1st Class Air Mechanic, R.N.A.S.
Volunteering in February 1915, he was sent to Salonika in the following year after the completion of his course of training. He took part in many important engagements on the Doiran and Struma fronts in the Balkan campaign, and rendered valuable services. He returned home and was demobilised in December 1918, holding the General Service and Victory Medals.
51, Tindal Street, Brixton, S.W.9.   Z5042B

BISHOP, G. D., 1st Class Stoker, R.N., H.M.S. "Black Prince."
He was in the Navy at the outbreak of war and served in various ships with the Grand Fleet in the North Sea. He was afterwards sent to the Dardanelles where he was wounded in action. He was invalided home and discharged in September 1916 as medically unfit for further service and died on January 17th, 1919. He was entitled to the 1914–15 Star, and the General Service and Victory Medals.
1, Comber Grove, Camberwell, S.E.5.   Z1177

BISHOP, J. J., Rifleman, 9th King's Royal Rifle Corps.
He volunteered in February 1915, and in the same year was drafted to France, where he took part in much heavy fighting, and was wounded at Hooge. On his recovery he was again in action and was unfortunately killed at Ypres whilst on outpost duty on February 11th, 1916. He was entitled to the 1914–15 Star, and the General Service and Victory Medals.
"His memory is cherished with pride."
81, Clayton Road, Peckham, S.E.15.   Z5894A

BISHOP, R. (M.M.), Lieutenant, M.G.C.
He volunteered in September 1914, and was afterwards sent to the Western Front, where he took part in numerous engagements and was wounded. He was awarded the Military Medal for bravery in the Field, and was gazetted to a commission for efficiency. Later he was taken prisoner and died of wounds, while in captivity, in April 1918. He was entitled to the General Service and Victory Medals.
1, Beryl Road, Hammersmith, W.6.   12784A

BISHOP, S. A., A.B., R.N.V.R.
He volunteered in June 1915, and later in the same year was drafted to France. In this theatre of war he took part in many engagements, including those on the Somme, and was wounded and invalided to hospital. On his recovery he returned to France, and was in action at Arras, Ypres, Cambrai, and in the Retreat and Advance of 1918. He was demobilised in January 1919, and holds the 1914–15 Star, and the General Service and Victory Medals.
45, Flaxman Road, Camberwell, S.E.5.   Z5887

BISHOP, S. F. (M.M.), Driver, R.F.A.
He volunteered in August 1914, and was immediately afterwards sent to France, where he took part in severe fighting at Mons, and on the Marne, the Aisne, the Somme, and in many other important engagements, and was severely gassed at Ypres. In 1917 he was transferred to Italy, where he served in various actions on the Piave, and was wounded. He was awarded the Military Medal for bravery in the Field, and also holds the Mons Star, and the General Service and Victory Medals. He was demobilised in April 1919.
25, Treherne Road, Stockwell, S.W.9.   Z3433

BISHOP, S. G. C., Driver, R.F.A.
He volunteered in September 1914, and in the following year proceeded to France. Whilst in this theatre of war he did good work as a driver at Loos, and Armentières, where he was wounded. After his recovery he served on the Ypres front, and in the Battle of Menin Road. In October 1917, he was drafted to Italy, where he was again wounded at Montello, in the succeeding January. He continued his service until April 1919, when he returned home and was demobilised in the following month. He holds the 1914–15 Star and the General Service and Victory Medals.
81, Clayton Road, Peckham, S.E.15.   5894D

BISHOP, T. R., Private, Buffs (East Kent Regt.)
He volunteered in August 1914, and in July 1916 was drafted overseas. During his service in France he fought in various engagements, and was wounded at Albert in 1917, and at Thiépval during the Offensive on the Somme in the following year. He was invalided to hospital in England, and was discharged in December 1918, holding the 1914–15 Star, and the General Service and Victory Medals.
81, Clayton Road, Peckham, S.E.15.   5894B

BISHOP, W. H., Private, 7th London Regiment.
He joined in July 1916, and after his training was drafted to the Western Front, where he took part in severe fighting in various important engagements. He was killed in action on December 3rd, 1916, and was entitled to the General Service and Victory Medals.
26, Redmore Road, Hammersmith, W.6.   11618A

BISHOP, W. H., L/Corporal, Queen's Own (Royal West Kent Regiment).
He volunteered in August 1914, and in March of the following year was drafted to France, where he took part in numerous engagements, including those on the Somme, and at Arras and Cambrai, and elsewhere. In 1917 he was invalided home with trench fever, and on his recovery served on important duties with his unit at various stations until he was demobilised in March 1919, holding the 1914-15 Star, and the General Service and Victory Medals.
133, Heath Road, Wandsworth Road, S.W.8.   Z1277

BISNELL, W., C.S.M., 12th East Surrey Regiment.
He was mobilised at the outbreak of war, and was for some time afterwards engaged on important duties as an Instructor of recruits at Saltash, Cornwall. In 1917 he was sent to Italy, where he rendered much valuable service. A year later he was drafted to France, and whilst taking part in the final Advance, received a severe wound at Havrincourt Wood, of which he unfortunately died on September 8th, 1918. He was entitled to the General Service and Victory Medals.
18, Abyssinia Road, Battersea, S.W.11.   Z1265

BITTEN, J., P.O., R.N., H.M.S. "Excellent."
He was mobilised in August 1914, and was appointed Gunnery Instructor at Portsmouth on H.M.S. "Excellent." He was engaged in training recruits and rendered valuable services. He afterwards proceeded to Gibraltar, where he remained until he was demobilised in March 1919.
75, Ingrave Street, Battersea, S.W.11.   Z1278

BLABER, J., Special War Worker.
He was engaged on special war work at Woolwich Arsenal for five years in the research department. His duties, which were of a most important nature, were carried out in a highly commendable manner, and he rendered valuable services during the war. He died on March 20th, 1919.
78, Faroe Road, West Kensington, W.14.   T12187C

BLACK, A. T., Sergt., R.G.A.
He joined in 1916, and after his training was drafted to the Western Front. He took part in severe fighting on the Somme and at Cambrai and in other important engagements, and was wounded and invalided home. He was demobilised in February 1919, and holds the General Service and Victory Medals.
65, Army Street, Clapham, S.W.4.   Z1280

BLACKBURN, E. A., Private, R.A.S.C. (M.T.)
He attested in December 1915, and was called up in February 1917, and proceeded to France in the following month. He served in the Arras, Ypres, and Somme sectors, and was present during the Retreat and Advance of 1918. He returned to England in December 1919, and was demobilised, holding the General Service and Victory Medals.
7, Pulross Road, Stockwell, S.W.9.   Z3499

BLACKFORD, J. H. (M.M.), Private, 6th Queen's Own (Royal West Kent Regiment).
He joined in November 1917, and after a course of training was drafted to the Western Front, where he took part in various engagements, including those at Ypres, and St. Quentin, where he was wounded. He was awarded the Military Medal for bravery in the Field, and also holds the General Service and Victory Medals. He was demobilised in October 1919.
30, Verona Street, Battersea, S.W.11.   Z1279

BLACKMAN, E. G., Corporal, R.A.S.C.
He volunteered in November 1914, and was immediately afterwards sent to France, where he served in various engagements, including Neuve Chapelle, the Somme, Ypres and many others. He also took part in the Retreat and Advance of 1918. He was demobilised in February 1919, and holds the 1914 Star, and the General Service and Victory Medals.
39, Gladstone Terrace, Battersea Park Road, S.W.8. Z1282

BLACKMAN, E. R., 1st Class Stoker, R.N., H.M.S. "Fawn."
He was serving at the outbreak of war and was engaged with the Torpedo Boat Squadron. He assisted in the sinking of the German submarine S33. He, unfortunately, lost his life on submarine L10 off the Dutch coast on October 4th, 1918, and was entitled to the 1914-15 Star, and the General Service and Victory Medals.
"A costly sacrifice upon the altar of freedom."
15, Victory Square, Camberwell, S.E.5.   Z5569A

BLACKSHAW, T. H., Driver, R.F.A.
Volunteering in October 1914, he was sent to France in September of the following year. He took part in numerous engagements, including those at Vimy Ridge, the Somme, Arras and Ypres, and was wounded. He was demobilised in January 1919, and holds the 1914-15 Star, and the General Service and Victory Medals.
20, Elfin Road, Camberwell, S.E.5.   Z1283

BLACKWELL, C., Pte., The Buffs (East Kent Regt.)
He volunteered in August 1914, and was immediately afterwards sent to the Western Front, where he took part in severe fighting during the Retreat from Mons. In 1915 he was transferred to Mesopotamia and was in action on various Fronts. He was demobilised in February 1919, and holds the Mons Star, and the General Service and Victory Medals.
18, Badsworth Road, Camberwell, S.E.5.   Z1784

BLACKWELL, J., Private, 5th Royal Fusiliers.
He was mobilised in August 1914, and in the following November was sent to the Western Front. He took part in severe fighting in numerous engagements, and was wounded and later died of his injuries in June 1915. He was entitled to the 1914 Star, and the General Service and Victory Medals.
54, Heath Road, Wandsworth Road, S.W.8.   Z1602B

BLAKE, A., Private, Sherwood Foresters.
He joined in October 1916, and was sent to France in June of the following year. He took part in various engagements in the Ypres sector and sustained shell-shock. He was invalided home and eventually discharged in February 1919, and holds the General Service and Victory Medals. Z5710
6, Chester Buildings, Lomond Grove, Camberwell, S.E.5.

BLAKE, A. H., Rifleman, Royal Irish Rifles.
He joined in February 1917, and after his training was sent to the Western Front, where he took part in various engagements, including those at Ypres and Passchendaele. He was reported missing during the Advance of 1918, and is presumed to have been killed in action on September 16th of that year. He was entitled to the General Service and Victory Medals.
4A, Claxton Grove, Hammersmith, W.6.   13536

BLAKE, G., Private, 2nd Royal Fusiliers.
He volunteered in August 1914, and in the following year was sent to the Dardanelles, where he took part in severe fighting and was wounded and invalided home. On his recovery he was drafted to France in 1917 and served in numerous engagements. He was demobilised in April 1919, and holds the 1914-15 Star, and the General Service and Victory Medals.
9, Russell Street, Battersea, S.W.11.   Z1284

BLAKE, G. E. W., L/Cpl., 9th Duke of Wellington's (West Riding Regiment).
He joined in 1916, and in the same year was drafted to the Western Front, where he took part in many engagements, including those on the Somme and at Ypres. He was killed in action near Cambrai in 1918, and was entitled to the General Service and Victory Medals.
8, Lollard Street, Kennington, S.E.11.   TZ25861C

BLAKE, G. J., Private, 66th Canadian Infantry.
He volunteered in 1915, and proceeded to the Western Front in June of the following year and took part in many important engagements, including that at Vimy Ridge. He fell fighting at Cambrai in November 1917, and was entitled to the General Service and Victory Medals.
"The path of duty was the way to glory."
121, Villa Street, Walworth, S.E.17.   27452D

BLAKE, H., Sapper, R.E.
He joined in August 1917, and after his training served at various stations on important duties with his unit. He rendered valuable services, but was not successful in obtaining his transfer overseas before the cessation of hostilities, owing to being medically unfit for duty abroad. He was demobilised in December 1919.
62, Merrow Street, Walworth, S.E.17.   27452B

BLAKE, J., Seaman Gunner, R.N., H.M.S. "Ajax."
He enlisted in 1894, and served with the Grand Fleet in the North Sea and took part in the Battle of Jutland and various other engagements. He was afterwards sent to the Mediterranean, and was on board H.M.S. "Russell" when that vessel was sunk near Malta. Fortunately, he was rescued and was still serving on H.M.S. "Ajax" in 1920. He holds the 1914-15 Star, and the General Service and Victory Medals.
17, Latchmere Street, Battersea, S.W.11.   Z1285

BLAKE, J. S., Sergt., R.A.M.C.
He volunteered in February 1915, and was drafted to France in the following year. He served in various engagements, including those at Arras and Ypres and was taken prisoner on the Somme in March 1918. On his release he returned home and was demobilised in March 1919, holding the General Service and Victory Medals.
35, Chantry Road, Stockwell, S.W.9.   Z1287

BLAKE, J. W., Rifleman, Rifle Brigade and M.G.C.
He joined in 1916, and proceeded to the Western Front in the same year. He took part in the heavy fighting at Arras, the Somme and in many other important engagements, and was wounded and taken prisoner during the Retreat of 1918. On his release he returned home, and was demobilised in 1919, and holds the General Service and Victory Medals.
8, Lollard Street, Kennington, S.E.11.   TZ25861B

BLAKE, J. W., Sergt., Duke of Cornwall's Light Infantry.
He was mobilised in August 1914, and was immediately afterwards sent to France. He took part in severe fighting in the Retreat from Mons and in the Battle of Ypres and many other engagements. He was killed in action in December 1915, and was entitled to the Mons Star, and the General Service and Victory Medals.
"Great deeds cannot die."
121, Villa Street, Walworth, S.E.17. 27452C

BLAKE, W. B., Private, 10th Middlesex Regiment.
He joined in January 1916, and after his training was sent to India, where he served at various stations on important duties with his unit. Owing to his health breaking down he was invalided home and discharged as medically unfit for further service in September 1917, holding the General Service and Victory Medals.
136, Southfield Road, Bedford Park, W.4. 7545

BLAKE, W. J. C., Bandsman, Royal Sussex Regt.
He joined in September 1918, and after his training served on important duties with his unit until the following year, when he was drafted to the Army of Occupation in Germany. He returned home and was demobilised in April 1920, but has since rejoined in the Welch Guards.
16, Stewart's Road, Battersea Park Road, S.W.8. Z1286

BLANCH, J. A., Lieutenant, Royal Fusiliers and Suffolk Regiment.
He volunteered in March 1915, and in November of the same year was drafted to the Western Front, where he saw much active service. He was taken prisoner in March 1918, and was held in captivity until December of that year. In November 1919 he was demobilised and holds the General Service and Victory Medals.
44, Montgomery Road, Chiswick, W.4. 6881C

BLANCH, J. R., 2nd Corporal, R.E.
He volunteered in November 1915, and after his training served for a time on important duties at various stations with his unit. In March 1918 he was drafted to Salonika, and in this theatre of war took part in many engagements. He returned home and was demobilised in March 1919, and holds the General Service and Victory Medals.
44, Montgomery Road, Chiswick, W.4. 6881A

BLANCH, S. F., Private, R.A.S.C. (M.T.)
He joined in November 1917, and in April of the following year proceeded to the Western Front. In this theatre of war he saw much active service in various sectors. He holds the General Service and Victory Medals, and in 1920 was still serving. 44, Montgomery Road, Chiswick, W.4. 6881B

BLAZEY, A. L. (Miss), Special War Worker.
During the war this lady was engaged at South Kensington Post Office, thus releasing a man for military service. She carried out her duties in an entirely satisfactory manner.
13, Humbolt Road, Hammersmith, W.6. 15302

BLOOMFIELD, A., Signalman, R.N.
He enlisted in January 1913, and at the outbreak of war was posted to H.M.S. "Indomitable." On board this ship he took part in the engagement off Heligoland, the Naval operations at the Dardanelles, and the Battle of Jutland. Afterwards he served on highly dangerous duties in the North Sea until the conclusion of hostilities. He holds the 1914 Star, and the General Service and Victory Medals, and in 1920 was still serving.
21, Montefiore Street, Wandsworth Road, S.W.8. Z1288C

BLOOMFIELD, A. A. (D.C.M.), Sergt.-Major, Royal Warwickshire Regiment.
He volunteered in May 1915, having previously served in the Boer War, and was drafted in the same year to Egypt and served at Khartoum, Alexandria and various other places in this theatre of war. Whilst there he contracted malaria, and after being in hospital for some time returned to England and was demobilised in February 1919. He holds the Distinguished Conduct Medal, which he won in the South African campaign, and the Queen's and King's South African, General Service and Victory Medals.
21, Montefiore Street, Wandsworth Road, S.W.8. Z1288A

BLOOMFIELD, G., Special War Worker.
This lady was engaged at Messrs. Gwynnes, Chiswick, for eighteen months during the war, on highly important work in connection with the manufacture of aeroplanes. The manner in which she carried out her duties gave entire satisfaction.
35, Cranbrook Road, Chiswick, W.4. 5351B

BLOOMFIELD, M., Special War Worker.
From 1916 until 1920 this lady was engaged with the R.A.P.C. at Hounslow Barracks. She rendered valuable services and her good work was much appreciated.
35, Cranbrook Road, Chiswick, W.4. 5351C

BLOOMFIELD, L., Special War Worker.
For two years during the war this lady held an important position at Messrs. Gwynnes', Chiswick, where she was engaged on important work in connection with aeroplane construction. She carried out her duties with great care and efficiency.
35, Cranbrook Road, Chiswick, W.4. 5351A

BLOOMFIELD, S., Private, Middlesex Regiment.
He joined in June 1918, and after his training served at various stations on important duties with his unit. He rendered valuable services, but was not successful in obtaining his transfer overseas before the cessation of hostilities. He was demobilised in January 1919.
21, Montefiore Street, Wandsworth Road, S.W.8. Z1288B

BLOOR, P. J., Sergt., Northumberland Fusiliers.
Volunteering in May 1915, he was drafted, in the same year to the Western Front. There he took part in many important engagements, including those of Ypres, the Somme, the Retreat and Advance of 1918, during which time he was wounded. He returned home and was demobilised in February 1919, and holds the 1914-15 Star, and the General Service and Victory Medals.
5, Urswick Road, Battersea, S.W.11. Z1289

BLOW, W. R., Private, R.A.S.C.
He joined in August 1916, and on the completion of his training proceeded to the Western Front. He served at Beaumont-Hamel, Vimy Ridge, Bullecourt, Messines, Ypres, the Somme, Cambrai and in the Retreat and Advance of 1918. He returned home, and was demobilised in November 1919, and holds the General Service and Victory Medals.
26, Kimberley Road, Landor Road, S.W.9. Z1291

BLOWS, J. H., Corporal, 12th Queen's (Royal West Surrey Regiment).
He joined in February 1917, and in the same year proceeded overseas. Attached to the Labour Corps, he served in many notable engagements on the Western Front, including those at Arras, St. Eloi and Vimy Ridge. In February 1919 he returned home, and was demobilised, holding the General Service and Victory Medals.
59, Sterndale Road, Wandsworth Road, S.W.8. Z1290

BLUMSUM, J. C., Private, Queen's (Royal West Surrey Regiment).
He joined in September 1917, and on the completion of his training was drafted to the Western Front. There he took part in the fighting in the Somme sector, and at Cambrai, where he was wounded. He was invalided home, and after receiving hospital treatment was discharged as medically unfit in November 1918. He holds the General Service and Victory Medals.
8, Caskell Street, Clapham, S.W.4. Z1292

BLUNTACH, A., Corporal, King's Liverpool Regt.
He joined in November 1917, on attaining military age, and in February of the following year was drafted to the Western Front. There he was in action on the Somme, the Marne, at Amiens, Bapaume, Cambrai and in other engagements until the conclusion of hostilities. He was demobilised in February 1919, and holds the General Service and Victory Medals.
48, Bagshot Street, Walworth, S.E.17. Z1293D Z1294D

BLUNTACH, A., Leading Stoker, R.N.
Volunteering in June 1915, he was posted to H.M.S. "Russell," which was shortly afterwards mined and sunk near Gibraltar. Fortunately, he was rescued and was transferred to H.M.S. "Weymouth." Later this ship also struck a mine and was severely damaged, but he escaped injury. Later he served on the "Emperor of India," and was engaged on patrol and convoy duties in all seas until demobilised in June 1920. He holds the 1914-15 Star, and the General Service and Victory Medals.
48, Bagshot Street, Walworth, S.E.17. Z1293C Z1294C

BLUNTACH, E., Stoker, R.N.
Volunteering in August 1914, he was posted to H.M.T.B.D. No. 11, and served on patrol duties in the North Sea. On March 6th, 1916, his boat was mined and he was drowned. He was entitled to the 1914-15 Star, and the General Service and Victory Medals.
48, Bagshot Street, Walworth, S.E.17. Z1293B Z1294B

BLUNTACH, W. B., Rflmn., King's Royal Rifle Corps.
He joined in March 1917, and in July of the same year proceeded overseas. He was in action at Lens and Cambrai, but was invalided home through ill-health. On recovery he returned to France and was killed in action at Bapaume on August 20th, 1918. He was entitled to the General Service and Victory Medals.
48, Bagshot Street, Walworth, S.E.17. Z1293A Z1294A

BOARDER, J., Rflmn., The Cameronians (Scottish Rifles), Pte., Queen's (Royal West Surrey Regt).
He volunteered in September 1914, and was drafted to France in the following year. He took part in severe fighting at Albert, the Somme, and in many other engagements, and was wounded. He returned home and was demobilised in February 1919, holding the 1914-15 Star, and the General Service and Victory Medals.
186, St. George's Road, Peckham, S.E.15. Z5715

BOAS, D., Gunner, R.F.A.
He joined in 1916, and proceeded to France in the following year. He took part in numerous engagements, including those at Arras, Messines, Ypres and Cambrai, and was wounded and gassed. He was invalided home, and on his recovery was demobilised in 1919, holding the General Service and Victory Medals.
29, Mostyn Road, Brixton Road, S.W.9. Z3428

BOATWRIGHT, G. A., Master Mariner, Merchant Service.
He joined the Merchant Service in August 1914, and was posted to the s.s. " Mary and Kate," which vessel was engaged with the Grand Fleet in the North Sea on important convoy and other duties during the whole course of the war. He holds the General Service and Mercantile Marine War Medals, and in 1920 was still serving in the Merchant Service.
49, Farmer's Road, Camberwell, S.E.5. Z1295

BODDINGTON, H. M., Private, R.A.S.C.
He volunteered in April 1915, and on the completion of his training was drafted in the same year to Egypt, where he saw much service. He was engaged on important transport duties in the forward areas and was present at many engagements. Owing to ill-health he returned to England, and after a period of hospital treatment was invalided out of the Service in April 1919. He holds the 1914-15 Star, and the General Service and Victory Medals.
15, Ingrave Street, Battersea, S.W.11. Z1296A

BOLSTER, A., Private, R.A.S.C.
Volunteering in 1914, he was drafted in the following year to the Western Front. There he was engaged on various important duties with the Labour Corps in all sectors. He returned home, and in 1919 was invalided out of the Service through ill-health. He holds the 1914-15 Star, and the General Service and Victory Medals.
185, Stewart's Road, Battersea Park Road, S.W.8. Z1297B

BOLSTER, E., Driver, "C" Battery, 14th Brigade, R.F.A.
He volunteered in April 1915, and in December of the same year was drafted to France. There he was in action on the Somme, and at Beaumont-Hamel, Arras, Vimy Ridge, Messines, Ypres, Cambrai, Maubeuge and many other engagements until the cessation of hostilities. Later he served with the Army of Occupation at Cologne until March 1919, when he returned home, and was demobilised. He holds the 1914-15 Star, and the General Service and Victory Medals.
12, Landseer Street, Battersea, S.W.11. Z1298A

BOLSTER, P., Private, R.A.S.C.
Volunteering in 1914, he was drafted in the following year to Egypt, where he saw much service. He was engaged on important duties until 1919, when he returned to England and was demobilised. He holds the 1914-15 Star, and the General Service and Victory Medals.
185, Stewart's Road, Battersea Park Road, S.W.8. Z1297A

BOLTON, C. H., Private, Royal Fusiliers.
He joined in August 1916, and in the following year was drafted to the Western Front, where he was in action at Ypres, Passchendaele, Amiens, and the Somme, and was twice wounded. He was taken prisoner at St. Quentin and was held in captivity until after the Armistice, when he was released and returned to England. He holds the General Service and Victory Medals, and was demobilised in October 1919.
87, Sussex Road, Coldharbour Lane, S.W.9. Z3061

BOLTON, F. C., Bandsman, Royal Munster Fusiliers.
He enlisted in October 1903, and at the outbreak of war proceeded to the Western Front, and took part in the Battle of Mons. On August 27th, 1914, he was taken prisoner and sent to Sennenlager, where he remained until May 1916, when he was sent to Russia, remaining there until December 1917. He then returned to Saxony and worked in the coalfields until his release in December 1918. He holds the 1914 Star, and the General Service and Victory Medals, and was demobilised in April 1919.
52, Gaskell Street, Clapham, S.W.4. Z1300

BOLTON, G., Rifleman, 3rd Rifle Brigade.
He joined in August 1916, and after his training proceeded to the Western Front in the same year. Whilst there he took part in many notable battles, including those of Vimy Ridge, the Ancre and Ypres. He returned home in February 1919, and was demobilised, holding the General Service and Victory Medals.
6, Auckland Road, Battersea, S.W.11. Z1299

BOLTON, T. E., 1st Class Aircraftsman, R.A.F. (late R.N.A.S.)
He joined in September 1916, in the R.N.A.S. and served on the East Coast. He was afterwards drafted to Mudros, where he took part in the operations against the German warships "Goeben" and "Breslau." He was demobilised in February 1919, holding the General Service and Victory Medals.
12, Westmacott Street, Camberwell, S.E.5. Z3422

BOND, A. B., Private, 10th London Regiment.
He attested in February 1915, and was called up in September 1917. He was retained on home defence until early in 1918, when he was drafted to France and served on important duties in various sectors of the Western Front until the cessation of hostilities. In March 1919 he was demobilised after his return to England, and holds the General Service and Victory Medals.
3, Dalyell Road, Landor Road, S.W.9. Z1302

BOND, C. E., Telegraphist, R.N., H.M.S. "Impregnable" and "Barham."
He joined the Navy at the age of only fifteen, and a half years, and was in training when the Armistice was signed. Later he was posted to H.M.S. "Impregnable" and was sent to the Mediterranean, where in 1920 he was still serving.
10, Hillery Road, Walworth, S.E.17. Z1303A

BOND, G. W., Sergt., 25th London Regt. (Cyclists').
He joined in January 1917, and was immediately drafted to India, where he served on important garrison duties at Rawal Pindi, the Punjab and on the Afghan Frontier. He returned home and was demobilised in November 1919, and holds the General Service and Victory Medals.
20, Arlesford Road, Landor Road, S.W.9. Z1304

BOND, H., Private, Middlesex Regiment and 2nd London Regiment (Royal Fusiliers).
He volunteered in August 1914, and in the following year was drafted to the Western Front, where he saw much service. He fought in the Battles of the Somme, and at Albert, Arras, Ypres, Passchendaele, Armentières, Amiens, Bapaume and Béthune, and in various other engagements in the Retreat and Advance of 1918. He was demobilised in February 1919, and holds the 1914-15 Star, and the General Service and Victory Medals.
21, Eltham Street, Walworth, S.E.17. Z1301B

BOND, J. F., Pte., Oxfordshire and Buckinghamshire Light Infantry.
He attested in 1915, but was not called up for service until June 1918. Three months later he was drafted to France. In this theatre of war he served in the fourth Battle of Ypres, and in the engagements which followed, until the cessation of hostilities. In May 1919 he was sent to the East, and was engaged on important duties at Damascus and Cairo until his return in March 1920, when he was demobilised. He holds the General Service and Victory Medals.
40, Latchmere Grove, Battersea, S.W.11. Z1306

BOND, T. J., 2nd Lieutenant, R.A.F., 104th Squadron.
He joined in October 1917, at seventeen years of age, and was sent to the Western Front in the following year. There he saw much flying service as an observer, and took part in bombing raids over the enemy lines. During one of these he was mortally wounded and succumbed to his injuries on September 13th, 1918. He was entitled to the General Service and Victory Medals.
10, Hillery Road, Walworth, S.E.17. Z1303B

BOND, W., Pte., Duke of Cornwall's Light Infantry.
He volunteered in September 1914, and in the following year proceeded to France, where he saw much service. He fought in numerous important battles, including those at Hill 60, Ypres and Loos, and in subsequent engagements in the Retreat and Advance of 1918, and was gassed. He was demobilised in December 1918, and holds the 1914-15 Star, and the General Service and Victory Medals.
172, Farmer's Road, Camberwell, S.E.5. Z1305

BONE, J. E., Bombardier, R.F.A.
He volunteered in January 1916, and in the following May was drafted to France. Here he served in various sectors and fought on the Somme, and at Arras, Ypres and Cambrai, and in numerous subsequent engagements until the cessation of hostilities. He returned home and was demobilised in July 1919, and later died on September 13th, 1920. He was entitled to the General Service and Victory Medals.
6, Kitson Road, Camberwell, S.E.5. Z1307

BONKEN, A. W., Private, Labour Corps.
He volunteered in December 1915, and after his training served at various stations on important agricultural duties. He rendered valuable services, but was not successful in obtaining his transfer overseas before the cessation of hostilities, and was discharged through causes due to his service in October 1918. 40, Rolls St., Battersea, S.W.Z11.   1308

BONNER, F. J., Gunner, R.F.A.
Mobilised in August 1914, he immediately proceeded overseas, and took part in the Retreat from Mons, and in the Battles of the Marne, the Aisne, La Bassée and Ypres. He was also in action on the Somme, and at Arras, Messines and Cambrai, and in many subsequent engagements in the Retreat and Advance of 1918, and was three times wounded and twice gassed. In 1920 he was serving with the British Forces stationed in Turkey, and holds the Mons Star, and the General Service and Victory Medals.
6, Flint Street, Walworth, S.E.17.   Z1309

BONNER, J., Private, 4th South Lancashire Regt.
He joined in May 1916, and in the following year was drafted to France, where he served for two years. During this period he contracted fever and was for a time in hospital. He was demobilised in February 1919, and holds the General Service and Victory Medals.   12074C 12075C
72, Rayleigh Road, West Kensington, W.14.   12073C

BONNER, H. (Mrs.), Special War Worker.
For fifteen months during the war this lady was engaged on important work, first at Messrs. Blake's, Wood Lane, Shepherd's Bush, where she carried out dangerous duties in filling shells, and later at another factory, where she served in the gas bag department. She carried out all her duties with great care and efficiency.   12073A 12074A
72, Rayleigh Road, West Kensington, W.14.   12075A

BONNER, S. (Miss), Special War Worker.
This lady held a responsible post at Messrs. Blake's Munition Factory at Shepherd's Bush, for two and a half years. She was engaged on highly dangerous duties in the T.N.T. department, and carried out her work with great care and efficiency.
72, Rayleigh Road, West Kensington, W.14.   12073B
                                            12074B 12075B

BONNICK, A. H., Sapper, R.E. (R.O.D.)
He volunteered in November 1914, and two years later was drafted to Egypt, where he was at first stationed at Kantara. Later he served in the British Advance through Palestine, and was engaged on important duties in connection with the operations at Ludd and Haifa and in various other sectors. He returned home, and was demobilised in June 1919, and holds the General Service and Victory Medals.
89, Heath Road, Wandsworth Road, S.W.8.   Z1310.

BOOKER, G. (M.M.), Private, Duke of Cornwall's Light Infantry and M.G.C.
He was serving at the outbreak of war, and in the same month was sent to the Western Front, where he took part in numerous important engagements, including those at Mons, Le Cateau and Ypres. He was awarded the Military Medal for conspicuous bravery in the Field, in assisting in the saving of several men and two guns. He later proceeded to North Russia, and fought in various engagements against the Bolsheviks, Returning home he was drafted to Ireland, where he was still serving in 1920, and he holds in addition to the Military Medal, the Mons Star and the General Service and Victory Medals.   151, Grange Road, Bermondsey S.E.1.   TZ27071B

BOOM, M. D., Private, M.G.C.
He volunteered in June 1915, and later in the same year was drafted to France, where he was in action at Loos and took part in the Battles of the Somme, Arras, and Cambrai. He also served in the Retreat and Advance of 1918, and after the cessation of hostilities returned to England and was demobilised in May 1919, holding the 1914-15 Star, and the General Service and Victory Medals
70, Westmacott Street, Camberwell, S E 5   Z3059B

BOON L. E., Pioneer, R.E.
He joined in April 1918, and on the completion of his training was about to proceed to Mesopotamia, when the Armistice was signed. With the cessation of hostilities, however, he was retained in England on important duties with his unit until demobilised in April 1919
80, Wickersley Road, Lavender Hill, S W 11   Z1311

BOON, S. P., Driver, R.A.S.C.
He volunteered in September 1914, and in the following month was drafted to the Western Front, but returned home shortly afterwards. In February 1915 he again proceeded to France and rendered valuable services with the 47th Division at Armentières, Givenchy, Festubert, the Somme, Ypres, and several other places. He was badly wounded, and after being invalided home was discharged in February 1917, owing to his injuries He holds the 1914 Star, and the General Service and Victory Medals.
57, The Albany, Albany Road, Camberwell, S.E.5.   Z3994

BOOT, E. G., Sapper, R.E.
He joined in March 1917, and after his training was completed was drafted to India, where he served on the North West Frontier in the operations against the Afghans During his two years' service in the East, he suffered from malarial fever He returned to England in December 1919, and was demobilised, holding the India General Service Medal (with clasp, Afghanistan N.W. Frontier, 1919), and the General Service and Victory Medals
30, Venn Street, Clapham, S.W.4.   Z1312

BOOTH, A., Private, 8th Royal Berkshire Regiment.
He volunteered in September 1914, and in the following June was drafted to France. After taking part in several engagements he was killed in action in the Battle of Loos on September 25th, 1915, and was entitled to the 1914-15 Star, and the General Service and Victory Medals.
164, Duke Road, Chiswick, W.4.   5599A

BOOTH, J., Special War Worker.
He volunteered in September 1915, for work of National importance, and was engaged in the repairing of torpedo boat destroyers and ships which had been torpedoed, with Messrs. Fletcher, Son, and Fernell, Union Dock, Limehouse. He did excellent work, and in 1920 was still an employe of the firm.
164, Duke Road, Chiswick, W.4.   5599B

BORAMAN, M., Sapper, R.E.
He joined in 1916, and after his training served at various stations on important duties. He was engaged on experimental work in connection with the production of ammunition and in the course of his duties was gassed. He rendered valuable services, but was unable to obtain his transfer overseas owing to being medically unfit for duty abroad. He was demobilised in December 1918.
3, Abyssinia Road, Battersea, S.W.11.   Z1313

BOREHAM, J., L/Cpl., 11th Royal Sussex Regt.
He joined in February 1916, and after his training was drafted to the Western Front, where he took part in the severe fighting round Ypres, and in other important engagements. He was afterwards invalided home, through illness contracted while on service, and was discharged as medically unfit for further duty in May 1917. He holds the General Service and Victory Medals.
88, East Surrey Grove, Peckham, S.E.15.   Z5043

BOREHAM, T., Sergt., R.A.O.C.
He joined in April 1917, and after a period of training served at various stations on important duties with his unit. He was unable to obtain a transfer overseas owing to his being medically unfit, but rendered valuable services until his demobilisation in September 1919.
147, Gloucester Road, Peckham, S.E.15.   Z5882

BORRETT, A. H., Private, 10th Queen's (Royal West Surrey Regiment) and Royal Scots.
He volunteered in November 1915, and in March of the following year was drafted to the Western Front, where he took part in various engagements, and was wounded and invalided home. On his recovery he was sent to Ireland in 1917, but returned to France in the following year and was killed in action during the Advance on August 1st, 1918. He was entitled to the General Service and Victory Medals.
69, Tyer's Street, Kennington, S.E.11.   Z25084B

BORRETT, G. F., Private, M.G.C.
He volunteered in September 1914, and after serving on important duties at several home stations was drafted to France in January 1916. Whilst in this theatre of war he took part in various engagements, including the Battle of the Somme, where he was killed in action on June 7th, 1916. He was entitled to the General Service and Victory Medals.
69, Tyer's Street, Kennington, S.E.11.   Z25084A

BOSHER, A. G., Rifleman, 14th Rifle Brigade.
He joined in May 1916, and in the following August was drafted to France, where he was in action in the Somme sector, and was severely wounded in September of the same year. He was sent to hospital in France and invalided home in 1917, and after prolonged treatment was demobilised in March 1919. He holds the General Service and Victory Medals.
160, Stewart's Road, Battersea Park Road, S.W.8.   Z1314

BOSS, A., L/Corporal, Coldstream Guards.
He was called up from the Reserve on the outbreak of war, and was drafted to the Western Front in August 1914, He took part in the Retreat from Mons, and the Battles of the Marne and Aisne, and was also in action at La Bassée, Ypres, Neuve Chapelle and Richebourg, where he was severely wounded. He was invalided home, and in December 1915 was discharged as medically unfit for further service. He holds the Mons Star, and the General Service and Victory Medals.
52, Smyrk's Road, Walworth, S.E.17.   Z3286A

BOSTOCK, H., Rifleman, Rifle Brigade.
He joined in March 1917, and was sent to France in the same year. He took part in numerous engagements, including those at Arras and Cambrai, and also served in the Retreat and Advance of 1918. During his service in France he was wounded at La Bassée and gassed at Cambrai. He was demobilised in October 1919, holding the General Service and Victory Medals.
57, Pepler Road, Peckham, S.E.15.   Z3426

BOSTWICK, T. J., Rifleman, 7th King's Royal Rifle Corps.
He volunteered in April 1915, and in the following year was drafted to the Western Front. There he took part in heavy fighting at Loos, St. Eloi, Vermelles, the Somme, Arras and Ypres. On December 4th, 1917, he gallantly fell in action at Passchendaele, and was entitled to the General Service and Victory Medals.
" His life for his Country."
15, Huguenot Road, Peckham Rye, S.E.15.   Z5900

BOSWELL, J., Pte., 1st Duke of Cornwall's Light Infantry and M.G.C.
He was mobilised in August 1914, and was almost immediately drafted to the Western Front, where he fought in the Retreat from Mons. He served also on the Marne, the Aisne, and at Ypres, Arras, Passchendaele Ridge, St. Quentin, Bapaume, Béthune and Péronne, and in many other engagements in the Retreat and Advance of 1918. He was discharged in April 1919, as medically unfit for further duty, and holds the Mons Star, and the General Service and Victory Medals.
25, Sedan Street, Walworth, S.E.17.   Z1315

BOTELL, T. A., Sergt., R.F.A.
He volunteered in March 1915, and was in the year following drafted to the Western Front. Whilst in this theatre of war he fought in many battles, notably those of Albert, Vimy Ridge, the Somme, Arras, Bullecourt, Messines, Ypres and Passchendaele. In August 1917, he was invalided home to a hospital in Yorkshire, suffering from fever, and remained under treatment for some months. On his recovery he was retained for important home duties, and after the termination of hostilities was sent to Turkey, where in 1920 he was still serving. He holds the General Service and Victory Medals.
58, Chatham Street, Walworth, S.E.17.   Z1316

BOTELL, W. L., Private, Royal Warwickshire Regt.
He joined in February 1916, and in the following August was sent to the Western Front, where he took part in the Somme Offensive. Later he saw service in Italy, and did excellent work with his unit on the Piave and the Asiago Plateaux. He was demobilised on his return to England in February 1919, and holds the General Service and Victory Medals.
58, Chatham Street, Walworth, S.E.17.   Z1317

BOUCHER, L. J. (M.M.), Sergt., 22nd London Regt. (Queen's).
He volunteered in October 1914, and joined the 22nd London Regiment. In March 1915, after a short period of training, he was drafted to the Western Front, and first went into action at Neuve Chapelle, subsequently taking part in the fighting on the Somme, and at Ypres, Arras, High Wood, Givenchy, Festubert, Béthune, Bapaume, Delville Wood, Vimy Ridge, and in many other sectors. His excellent work in the Field soon won for him promotion to the rank of Sergeant, and he was awarded the Military Medal on October 18th 1916, for an act of distinguished gallantry whilst in action at Aucourtle-Abbage. He was also recommended for the Distinguished Conduct Medal. In March 1918 he was taken prisoner during the German Offensive, and as the result of ill-treatment was seriously ill on arriving at the prison camp. He recovered, however, and after the Armistice escaped from Munster to Austria, and was repatriated in December of the same year. He was demobilised in January 1919, and in addition to the Decoration won in the Field, holds the 1914–15 Star, and the General Service and Victory Medals.
16, Aldbridge Street, Walworth, S.E.17.   Z1318

BOUD, D. M. (Miss), Member, W.R.A.F.
She joined in March 1916, and during her service in the W.R.A.F., did good work in many capacities, chiefly as a storekeeper, and on important clerical duties. She also worked for a time as an armature winder. She rendered valuable service until her resignation in June 1918.
263, Eversleigh Road, Battersea, S.W.11.   Z1320C

BOUD, F. E., Rifleman, 18th London Regiment (London Irish Rifles).
He volunteered in November 1915, and in February of the following year was drafted to the Western Front, where he took part in many important engagements, including those at Albert, the Somme, Bourlon Wood and Cambrai. He also served in the Retreat and Advance of 1918. He was demobilised in February 1919, after returning home, and holds the General Service and Victory Medals.
54, Jardin Street, Camberwell S.E.5.   Z5044

BOUD, H., Private, Royal Defence Corps.
Being ineligible for service with the Colours, he joined the Royal Defence Corps in August 1914. After a period of training he was engaged in guarding munition factories, and other important duties with his unit, and did valuable work. He was discharged in February 1918, through causes due to his service. 262, Eversleigh Road, Battersea, S.W.11.   Z1320B

BOUD, W. A., Wheeler, R.A.S.C. (M.T.)
He volunteered in March 1915, and in the following July was sent to the Western Front. During his service in this theatre of war he acted as wheeler, and in this capacity was present at many engagements, including those at the Somme, Vimy Ridge, Arras, Cambrai, Messines and Passchendaele. In October 1918, however, he was severely injured in a bombing raid at Bourlon Wood, and was in consequence invalided home. He was demobilised in March 1919, and holds the 1914–15 Star, and the General Service and Victory Medals.
14, Kitson Road, Camberwell, S.E.5.   Z1319

BOUD, W. E., Private, R.A.M.C.
Volunteering in September 1914, he was sent to the Western Front on completing his training in the following March. Whilst overseas he served as a stretcher-bearer with the 47th Division, and in this capacity was present at many engagements. In 1917 he was severely gassed at Cambrai, and after being in a Base hospital for some time was invalided home. After his recovery he returned to France, where he remained until the termination of hostilities. He holds the 1914–15 Star, and the General Service and Victory Medals, and was demobilised in June 1919.
263, Eversleigh Road, Battersea, S.W.11.   Z1320A

BOULT, W. P., Special War Worker.
He volunteered for military service, but, owing to physical disabilities, was rejected. He was afterwards engaged at Woolwich Arsenal examining tools and on other work. He also did duty with the aircraft section in the working of signal lights for aeroplanes, and rendered valuable services during the war. 4, St. John's Hill Grove, Battersea, S.W.11. Z1321

BOULTER, D. G., Private, Seaforth Highlanders.
He volunteered in April 1915, and in the following August crossed to France. Subsequently he fought at Loos, St. Eloi, Vimy Ridge, the Somme, Messines, and Passchendaele Ridge, and in October 1917 was severely wounded. He was then invalided home, but after his recovery in January 1918, returned to the Western Front, where he served until the termination of hostilities. He then advanced into Germany with the Army of Occupation. He was demobilised on his return to England in February 1919, and holds the 1914–15 Star, and the General Service and Victory Medals.
63, Plough Road, Battersea, S.W.11.   Z1329

BOULTER, R., Driver, R.F.A.
Volunteering in April 1915, he was drafted to the Dardanelles in the following July, and served in the landing at Suvla Bay, and in the engagements which followed. After the Evacuation of the Peninsula, he was drafted to Egypt, and thence to France, where he was engaged in the Battles of the Somme, Vimy Ridge, Ypres and Cambrai, and in the Retreat and Advance of 1918. He was demobilised on his return to England in February 1919, and holds the 1914–15 Star, and the General Service and Victory Medals.
63, Plough Road, Battersea, S.W.11.   Z1322

BOUND, S., Corporal, Royal Irish Regiment.
A serving soldier, he was engaged on duties of an important nature in India until December 1914, when he was sent to France. He fought in the Battles of Hill 60 and Ypres, and in June 1915, returned wounded to England. After his recovery he was sent to his depôt in Ireland, and later rendered valuable services in the suppression of the Sinn Fein riots of 1916. In June of that year, he was invalided out of the Army, and holds the 1914–15 Star, and the General Service and Victory Medals.
41, Vardens Road, Battersea, S.W.11.   Z1323

BOURNE, J. H. De Pledge, L/Cpl., King's Royal Rifle Corps.
Joining in 1916, he was sent to France after a short course of training. For ten months he did valuable work with his unit overseas, and fought in several important battles, including those of Vimy Ridge and Arras. On June 12th, 1917, he was unfortunately killed in action. He was entitled to the General Service and Victory Medals.
15, Gayville Road, Wandsworth Common, S.W.11. Z1793B

BOURNER, A., Private, R.A.S.C.
He volunteered in November 1914, and in January of the following year was drafted to the Western Front, where he served in various engagements, including those at Hill 60, Ypres and Cambrai. In July 1915, he was invalided home with shellshock, and was eventually discharged through the same cause in May 1917. He holds the 1914–15 Star, and the General Service and Victory Medals.
2, New Church Road, Camberwell, S.E.5.   Z5712

BOURNER, A., Air Mechanic, R.A.F.
He joined in June 1918, and after his training was engaged on important duties, which demanded a high degree of technical skill. During an aerial test he met with an accident, in which he sustained severe injuries, and after being for some weeks in hospital, was transferred to the Motor Transport section of the R.A.F. He was unable to secure his transfer overseas before the termination of hostilities, but did valuable work until he was demobilised in June 1919.
5, Colworth Grove, Walworth, S.E.17.　　　Z1324

BOW, A., Gunner, R.F.A.
Volunteering in May 1915, he was sent overseas at the conclusion of his training. During his service on the Western Front he fought in several of the principal engagements, notably those at Ypres, Arras and Albert, but was unfortunately killed during a bombing raid on June 3rd, 1918. He was buried at the Gwalia British Cemetery, near Poperinghe, and was entitled to the 1914-15 Star, and the General Service and Victory Medals.
16, Seneca Road, Sandmere Road, S.W.4.　　　Z1325A

BOW, A. T., Private, Queen's (Royal West Surrey Regiment) and Gunner, R.F.A.
He joined the Queen's in April 1918, and after his training was engaged as a Lewis gunner on duties of an important nature at various stations with his unit. He was unable to secure his transfer overseas before the termination of hostilities, but after his demobilisation rejoined into the R.F.A., and was drafted to India, where in 1920 he was still serving.
16, Seneca Road, Sandmere Road, S.W.4.　　　Z1325C

BOWDERY, W., Private, R.A.S.C. (M.T.)
He joined in June 1916, and after his training was sent for three months to the Western Front, where he was engaged on important duties in the forward areas. In 1917 he was drafted to Egypt, and during the voyage out on May 4th, his ship H.M.T. "Transylvania" was sunk by a submarine in the Mediterranean. Fortunately he was rescued, and was able to continue his journey. Subsequently he did valuable work with his unit during the Palestine campaign, and was present at many engagements, notably those at Gaza, Jaffa and Jerusalem, where in consequence of a severe illness, he had to undergo an operation. In June 1918 he returned to England, and was invalided out of the Service in the following August. He holds the General Service and Victory Medals.
11, Elsted Street, Walworth, S.E.17.　　　Z1326A

BOWDERY, W. (Junior), Pte., Argyll and Sutherland Highlanders.
He volunteered at the age of sixteen, in June 1915, and in September 1917 was sent to the Western Front, where he fought in several important engagements, including the second Battle of the Somme, and was severely wounded. In consequence he was invalided home, but on his recovery five months later returned to France, and served in the concluding operations of the war. He was demobilised in May 1919, and holds the General Service and Victory Medals.
11, Elsted Street, Walworth, S.E.17.　　　Z1326B

BOWDITCH, E. J., Stoker Petty Officer, R.N.
He enlisted in 1909, and throughout the recent war served on board H.M.S. "Skipjack," which was engaged on important mine-sweeping duties in the North Sea. He was in the engagement off Scarborough, and was frequently in action with enemy submarines. After the Armistice, his vessel was shipwrecked near the Dardanelles, but he was saved. In 1920 he was serving in the patrol boat "P. 59." and holds the 1914-15 Star, and the General Service and Victory Medals.
147, Battersea Bridge Road, Battersea, S.W.11.　　　Z1327A

BOWDITCH, F. C., Private, 2nd Royal Fusiliers.
He joined in February 1916, and a year later was sent to France. In this theatre of war he fought in several engagements, including those at Arras, Bullecourt and Vimy Ridge, and whilst in action at Vermelles, received a severe wound, of which he died in hospital at Abbeville on May 17th, 1917. He was entitled to the General Service and Victory Medals.
147, Battersea Bridge Road, Battersea, S.W.11.　　　Z1327B

BOWLER, A. C., Bombardier, R.F.A.
He joined in August 1916, and in the following year was drafted to Italy, where he saw much service on the Piave. Later he proceeded to the Western Front, and was in action at Amiens, Bapaume, and the Scarpe, and in the Advance of 1918, afterwards going to Germany with the Army of Occupation. In October 1919 he was demobilised and holds the General Service and Victory Medals.
57, Russell Street, Brixton Road, S.W.9.　　　Z5223

BOWLES, J. W., Private, 23rd London Regiment.
He volunteered in July 1915, and after a course of training was transferred to important work in connection with the output of munitions. Later he was sent to Scotland for further training, preparatory to being drafted overseas, and in 1917 embarked in H.M.T. "Aragon" for Egypt. On December 30th, 1917, this vessel was torpedoed and sunk off Alexandria, and he was unfortunately drowned. He was entitled to the General Service and Victory Medals.
115, Sabine Road, Battersea, S.W.11.　　　Z1328

BOWLEY, F. C., Private, 24th London Regt. (The Queen's).
He enlisted in May 1911, and proceeded to the Western Front in March 1915. While there he took part in many engagements until October 1915, when he was severely wounded and invalided home. In May 1916 he was discharged as a time-expired soldier, but in April 1917 he was again called up for service. Three months later he was finally discharged as medically unfit for further duty owing to his earlier injuries. He holds the 1914-15 Star, and the General Service and Victory Medals.
48, Warrior Road, Camberwell, S.E.5.　　　Z4409B

BOWLEY, F. W., Private, R.A.S.C.
After volunteering in April 1915, he finished his course of training and proceeded to France in the following July. While overseas he did valuable transport work in many engagements until almost the close of the war, including those at the Somme, and in the Retreat and Advance of 1918. Owing to severe illness he was invalided to England in October of that year, and was subsequently discharged as unfit for further service. He holds the 1914-15 Star, and the General Service and Victory Medals.
48, Warrior Road, Camberwell, S.E.5.　　　Z4409A

BOWMAN, S., Driver, R.A.S.C. (M.T.)
He volunteered in November 1915, and in the following year was drafted to the Western Front. Whilst in this theatre of war he was engaged with the Mechanical Transport conveying supplies to the forward areas, during the Battles of the Somme, Messines, Ypres, Passchendaele, and many other engagements. After the cessation of hostilities he went into Germany with the Army of Occupation. He was demobilised in February 1919, and holds the General Service and Victory Medals.
1, Denmark Road, Camberwell, S.E.5.　　　Z5888

BOWMAN, S., 1st Class Air Mechanic, R.A.F.
He joined in September 1917, and after his training served at various stations on important duties with his unit. He was engaged as a carpenter and carried out his work with great efficiency. He rendered valuable services, but was not successful in obtaining his transfer overseas before the cessation of hostilities. He was demobilised in January 1919.
46, Stainforth Road, Battersea, S.W.11.　　　Z5571

BOWN, B., Sergt., Queen's (Royal West Surrey Regiment.
He volunteered in September 1915, joining in the 6th Royal Sussex Regiment, but was later transferred to the Royal West Surrey. After his training he was drafted to Egypt, where he took part in several minor engagements until the commencement of the Palestine campaign, in which he also fought. In March 1918 he was sent to the Western Front, and there fought in the Retreat of that year, and in the subsequent Advance. He was demobilised on his return to England in March 1919, and holds the General Service and Victory Medals.
31, Edithna Street, Landor Road, S.W.9.　　　Z1330

BOWN, C., B.Q.M.S., R.F.A.
He volunteered in January 1915, and was drafted to the Western Front in the same year. He took part in numerous engagements, including those at St. Eloi, Albert, the Somme, Arras, Ypres, St. Quentin, and Amiens, and was wounded. He was invalided home, and on his recovery returned to France and served in the Retreat and Advance of 1918. He was demobilised in June 1919, and holds the 1914-15 Star, and the General Service and Victory Medals.
53, Tindal Street, Lothian Road, S.W.9.　　　Z5328

BOWN, W., Driver, R.F.A.
He joined in November 1917, and at the conclusion of his training was sent to the Western Front, and took part in the Advance of 1918. After the cessation of hostilities he served for a time with the Army of Occupation in Germany. He was demobilised in August 1919, and holds the General Service and Victory Medals.
35, Mundella Road, Wandsworth Road, S.W.8.　　　Z2180B

BOWSHER, S. F., A.B., Royal Navy.
Volunteering in February 1915, he was posted to H.M.S. "Carnarvon." He served in this vessel on important convoy duties, escorting food, munition and troopships to and from Canada, the United States, and the West Indies. Later he was transferred to the mine-sweeper "Spanker," in which he was engaged in the North Sea and the English Channel until after the termination of hostilities. He was demobilised in February 1919, and holds the 1914-15 Star, and the General Service and Victory Medals.
12, Duffield Street, Battersea, S.W.11.　　　Z1332

BOWRING, F., Private, R.A.M.C.
Joining in 1916, he was sent overseas in the same year. He was engaged on important duties at the 6th Stationary Hospital whilst in France, but in October 1919 unfortunately died at Antwerp of an illness which he contracted while in the Service. He was entitled to the General Service and Victory Medals.
41, Priory Grove, Lansdowne Road, S.W.8.　　　Z1331B

BOWRING, H., Sergt., R.A.S.C.

He enlisted in 1911, and during the recent war saw service until hostilities ceased in German East, West and South Africa, when he did valuable work in connection with the transport of supplies. He was demobilised in December 1919, and holds the 1914-15 Star, and the General Service and Victory Medals.

41, Priory Grove, Lansdowne Road, S.W.8.   Z1331A

BOWYER, S. T., Sergt., Queen's Own (Royal West Kent Regiment).

A serving soldier, he was drafted to the Western Front in August 1914, and took part in the Retreat from Mons, and the Battles of Le Cateau, Neuve Chapelle, Hill 60, and Arras. During his service in France he was wounded on three occasions. Later he was transferred to Italy, and remained there doing good work with his unit, until after the cessation of hostilities. He was discharged after returning to England in March 1919, and holds the Mons Star, and the General Service and Victory Medals.

8, Ponsonby Terrace, Grosvenor Road, S.W.1.   Z23208

BOXHALL, H., Private, East Surrey Regiment.

Volunteering in August 1914, he was quickly drafted to the Western Front, where he fought in many of the principal engagements, and was twice wounded. In 1918 he was discharged, but re-enlisted, and on returning to France served in the concluding operations of the war. Afterwards he was sent with the Relief Force to Russia, and did valuable work there with his unit for some time. He then returned to England and was again discharged, but re-enlisted a second time, and in 1920 was still serving in Ireland. He holds the 1914-15 Star, and the General Service and Victory Medals.

24, Bognor Street, Wandsworth Road, S.W.8.   Z1333

BOYLE, G. W., Private, Welch Guards.

Joining in May 1916, he was sent to the Western Front at the conclusion of his training. After taking part in several engagements, including those at the Somme, and Arras, he was unfortunately killed in action at Ypres on July 31st, 1917. He was entitled to the General Service and Victory Medals.

24, Shorncliffe Road, Old Kent Road, S.E.1.   Z1334B

BOYNE, C., L/Corporal, 7th East Surrey Regiment.

Volunteering in 1914, he was sent to the Western Front at the conclusion of his training. His service in this theatre of war lasted for two years, during which time he fought in many important battles, including those of the Somme, Ypres and Arras. In 1917 he was mentioned in Despatches for his courageous conduct and devotion to duty whilst acting as a Lewis gunner. He was severely wounded at Monchy, and after protracted hospital treatment was invalided out of the Service in 1919. He holds the General Service and Victory Medals.

65, Barlow Street, Walworth, S.E.17.   Z1336

BRACKLEY, I., Private, East Surrey Regiment.

Volunteering in December 1915, he was sent to France in September of the following year, and was transferred to the 8th Royal Fusiliers. He took part in the severe fighting at the Somme, Arras, Vimy Ridge, and many later battles. After the Armistice he proceeded with the Army of Occupation to Germany. He was demobilised in March 1919, after returning home, and holds the General Service and Victory Medals.

66, Beaufoy Road, Lavender Hill, S.W.11.   Z1178

BRACKSTONE, C. A., Private, Bedfordshire Regt.

Volunteering in 1915, he was sent to France in the following year. He took part in numerous engagements of importance while overseas, and was gassed. He afterwards contracted fever, and was invalided home. On his recovery he was engaged on important duties with his unit until he was demobilised in June 1919. He holds the General Service and Victory Medals.

240, Cator Street, Peckham, S.E.15.   Z5045

BRACKWELL, W., Pte., 13th East Surrey Regt.

He volunteered in 1915, and was going through his course of training at Whitley Camp when he contracted a serious illness, from which he unfortunately died on April 27th, 1916.

46, Gonsalva Road, Wandsworth Road, S.W.8.   Z1337

BRADBERRY, E. T., Rifleman, King's Royal Rifle Corps.

He volunteered in 1914, and was drafted to France in the following year. He took part in the severe fighting at the Somme, Arras, Ypres, and in many other engagements, and was wounded early in 1918. After being invalided home, he was demobilised in 1919, holding the 1914-15 Star, and the General Service and Victory Medals.

12, Raywood Street, Battersea Park Road, S.W.8.   Z1338

BRADBURY, J. E., Gunner, R.G.A.

Volunteering in June 1915, he was sent to France in December of the same year. He took part in the heavy fighting at Arras, Vimy Ridge, Messines, Cambrai, and in many important engagements in the Retreat and Advance of 1918. He was demobilised in February 1919, after his return home, and holds the 1914-15 Star, and the General Service and Victory Medals.

6, Namur Terrace, Alvey Street, Walworth, S.E.17.   Z1339

BRADEN, J., Sergt., 2nd East Lancashire Regt.

He was in the Army at the outbreak of war, and in November 1914 proceeded to France. There he fought in many battles, including those of Neuve Chapelle, the Somme and Arras. He was wounded three times and twice invalided home, and on each occasion on recovery he returned to his unit in France. He remained overseas until March 1919, when he was sent to Ireland, where in 1920 he was still serving. He holds the 1914 Star, and the General Service and Victory Medals.

7, Latchmere Grove, Battersea, S.W.11.   Z1363

BRADFORD, W. E., Private, R.A.S.C. (M.T.)

He joined in October 1916, and after his training was retained with his unit until 1918, when he was sent to France. He was engaged in the Somme area on important transport duties and rendered valuable services. He also did excellent work in repairing and testing engines at various stations. He was demobilised in October 1919, holding the General Service and Victory Medals.

14, Ingleton Street, Brixton, S.W.9.   Z1761

BRADFORD, W. H., Pte., 2nd Essex Regiment.

Volunteering in March 1915, he was sent to France in the following year. After being in action on the Somme, he contracted an illness in consequence of which he was invalided home. On his recovery he returned to France in March 1918, and while taking part in the Retreat of that year was unfortunately killed in action near the Aisne on June 16th 1918. He was entitled to the General Service and Victory Medals. 20, Henley Street, Battersea, S.W.11.   Z1340

BRADLEY, J., L/Cpl., 5th Royal Berkshire Regt.

He volunteered in August 1914, and after having served at various stations with his unit was drafted to France early in the following year. He took part in numerous engagements, including the Battle of the Somme, Beaumont-Hamel and Arras. He was captured by the Germans, and kept in captivity until November 1918. He escaped to Metz immediately after the Armistice, and after making his way to our troops, returned to England in December. He was demobilised in January 1919, and holds the 1914-15 Star, and the General Service and Victory Medals.

68, Tyers Street, Kennington, S.E.11.   Z25146

BRADLEY, W. L., Rifleman, 12th London Regt. (Rangers).

He joined in January 1916, and after his training was sent to the Western Front, where he took part in the severe fighting on the Somme, and at Arras and Bullecourt. He was unfortunately killed in the last named battle in May 1917, and was entitled to the General Service and Victory Medals.

3, Biscay Road, Hammersmith, W.6.   12798

BRADSHAW, W., Driver, R.F.A.

He volunteered in December 1914, and was drafted to the Western Front in October of the following year. He took part in the heavy fighting in the Battles of Vimy Ridge, the Somme, Messines and Ypres. He was gassed at Ypres, and after being invalided home was discharged as medically unfit for further service in February 1918. He holds the 1914-15 Star, and the General Service and Victory Medals.

127, York Road, Battersea, S.W.11.   Z1342

BRADY, W., Cpl., 1st and 2nd Hampshire Regts.

An old soldier who had served in the 9th Lancers and the 2nd Life Guards, and had taken part in the Afghan War of 1878-79 under Lord Roberts, he volunteered in December 1914 for further service. He was engaged in the Military Forwarding Department and frequently crossed to France in charge of parcels. After rendering much valuable service he was discharged in August 1916 owing to ill-health. He holds the Afghanistan Medal, 1878-9, and Roberts' Star, the 1914-15 Star, General Service and Victory and Long Service and Good Conduct Medals, and the Life Saving Medal and Certificate for saving a boy from drowning.   Z1343B

43, Broadhinton Road, Clapham, S.W.4.   Z1344B

BRADY, W. A., Captain, Royal Fusiliers, transferred to Indian Army.

He volunteered in January 1915, and was gazetted Second Lieutenant in the Royal Fusiliers. In 1916 he was drafted to the Balkan front, and took part in many severe engagements there until August 1917, when he was transferred to the Indian Army, and posted to a Sikh Regiment. He has since been promoted to the rank of Captain, and in 1920 was still serving in India. He holds the General Service and Victory Medals.

43, Broadhinton Road, Clapham, S.W.4.   Z1343A Z1344A

BRAGG, J. S. H., Driver, R.E.
He volunteered in July 1915, and after his training was drafted to the Western Front, where he took part in various engagements of importance, including those of the Somme, Arras, Armentières, and many others. He was demobilised in January 1919 after returning home, and holds the General Service and Victory Medals.
7, Carlton Road, Chiswick, W.4.　　　　6647

BRAHAM, F., Q.M.S., R.G.A.
He enlisted in 1909, and was sent to France shortly after the outbreak of war. He took part in the severe fighting in the Retreat from Mons and in the Battle of Ypres, and many other engagements, and was gassed. Later he was transferred to Salonika and served on the Vardar front and at Monastir, and contracted malaria. He next proceeded to Egypt, and afterwards to Palestine, where he took part in the Battle of Gaza and the capture of Jerusalem, and Aleppo. He was demobilised in February 1919, holding the 1914–15 Star, and the General Service and Victory Medals.
38, Bonnington Square, Lambeth Road, S.W.8.　　Z1345

BRAIDMAN, A., Member, W.R.A.F.
She volunteered in 1914, and was engaged at Regent's Park on clerical duties during the whole period of the war. Her work, which was of a responsible nature, was carried out with great care and efficiency until she was demobilised in March 1919.
111, Sulgrave Road, Hammersmith, W.6.　　11774A

BRAIDMAN, J., Corporal, R.A.S.C.
He joined in April 1916, and after his training was drafted to the Western Front. He was engaged in many sectors of the line on important transport duties with his unit, and rendered valuable services until hostilities ceased. After returning home he was demobilised in August 1919, holding the General Service and Victory Medals.
111, Sulgrave Road, Hammersmith, W.6.　　11774B

BRAIDWOOD, A. J., Gunner, R.G.A.
Joining in 1918, he was drafted to the Western Front in the same year. He was chiefly employed as a despatch rider, and served in various engagements until the end of the war, including those at the Somme and Ypres. He was demobilised in 1919, holding the General Service and Victory Medals.
295, East Street, Walworth, S.E.17.　　Z1346

BRAINT, H. S., A.B., R.N., H.M.S. "Temeraire."
He enlisted in 1911, and was on H.M.S. "Exmouth" at the outbreak of war. He afterwards saw much service in the North Sea with the Grand Fleet, and took part in many engagements of importance. He was still serving in 1920, and holds the 1914–15 Star, and the General Service and Victory Medals.
31, Milford Street, Wandsworth Road, S.W.8.　　Z1347

BRAITHWAITE, H. G., Private, Labour Corps.
He joined in July 1918, and after his training served on important duties with his unit at various stations. He rendered valuable services, but was unable to secure his transfer overseas prior to the cessation of hostilities. He was demobilised in February 1919.
19, Sterndale Road, Wandsworth Road, S.W.8.　　Z3296B

BRAMBLEY, W., Private, 13th East Surrey Regt.
He volunteered in June 1915, and in February of the following year after the completion of his training was drafted to the Western Front, where he took part in the severe fighting on the Somme and in many other engagements, and was unfortunately killed in action on April 24th, 1917. He was entitled to the General Service and Victory Medals.
39, Newcomen Road, Battersea, S.W.11.　　Z1348

BRANAGH, T., Private, 1st Worcestershire Regt. and King's Own (Royal Lancaster Regiment).
He was serving at the outbreak of war, and in the following year was drafted to the Western Front, where he took part in much severe fighting at Hooge, Festubert, Ploegsteert Wood, Armentières and Poperinghe. In 1918 he was transferred to Salonika, and served on the Struma front. Having contracted malaria and dysentery he was invalided home and was discharged in March 1919 as medically unfit for further service. He holds the 1914–15 Star, and the General Service and Victory Medals.
137, Stonhouse Street, Clapham, S.W.4.　　Z1349

BRANCHER, J. J., Bombardier, R.G.A.
He joined in January 1916, and in the following April proceeded to France, where he took part in many engagements, including those at Ypres, the Somme, Cambrai and Armentières. After the cessation of hostilities, he went into Germany with the Army of Occupation. He was demobilised in September 1919, and holds the General Service and Victory Medals.
17, Gloucester Road, Peckham, S.E.15.　　Z5880A

BRANCHER, P. E., Sergt., Army Cyclist Corps.
He joined in September 1916, and in the following year proceeded to the Western Front, where he saw much heavy fighting in various sectors. He took part in the Battles of Vimy Ridge, Ypres, Cambrai, the Somme and Vermelles and other engagements until the cessation of hostilities, and was then sent with the Army of Occupation into Germany. He was demobilised on his return home in December 1919, and holds the General Service and Victory Medals.
17, Gloucester Road, Peckham, S.E.15.　　Z5880B

BRANCHETT, A., Petty Officer, R.N.
Enlisting in 1902 he served on H.M.S. "Agincourt," "Kent," "Inflexible" and several others. He took part in the Battle of Jutland, and in various other engagements, and was also engaged in mine-sweeping. In 1919 he volunteered for service with the North Russian Expeditionary Force. and after serving against the Bolshevists returned home and was demobilised in March 1919, holding the 1914–15 Star, and the General Service and Victory Medals.
52, Pepper Street, Southwark, S.E.1.　　Z3425

BRANDON, C., Private, Loyal North Lancashire Regt.
Joining in May 1919, he went through a course of training, and was afterwards drafted to Malta, where, in 1920, he was still engaged on important duties with his unit.
6, The Parade, Lambeth Walk, S.E.11.　　25689B

BRANDON, J., Private, North Staffordshire Regt.
He joined in 1916, and after completing his training was drafted to the Western Front in the same year. He took part in much heavy fighting on the Somme, and in other important engagements, and was unfortunately killed in action in April 1917. He was entitled to the General Service and Victory Medals.
6, The Parade, Lambeth Walk, S.E.11.　　Z25689A

BRANFORD, J., Private, Labour Corps.
Having been previously rejected several times on account of his heatlh, he was accepted in June 1917, and after his training served at various stations on important duties with his unit. He rendered valuable services, but was not successful in obtaining his transfer overseas before the cessation of hostilities. He was demobilised in June 1919.
49, Bennerley Road, Wandsworth Common, S.W.11.　　Z1179

BRANSGROVE, H. S., Sapper, R.E.
Volunteering in November 1915, he was sent to India in May of the following year, and thence to Mesopotamia in 1917, and entered Baghdad with General Maude. He afterwards returned to India and was engaged at Poona on the Frontier on important duties with his unit. He was demobilised in January 1920, and holds the General Service and Victory Medals.
65, Cobourg Road, Camberwell, S.E.5.　　Z5329

BRAUTIGAM, D., L/Corporal, Royal Fusiliers.
After joining in April 1917, and completing his training, he was drafted to the Western Front in the same year. During his service overseas he served at Etaples, Boulogne, Calais and other places on important duties with his unit and did much valuable work. He was demobilised in November 1919, holding the General Service and Victory Medals.
13, Stockdale Road, Wandsworth Road, S.W.8.　　Z1350

BRAY, L. E., Corporal, 8th Middlesex Regiment.
He volunteered in August 1914, and in the following June was drafted to the Western Front, where he fought at the Battle of Loos and was wounded. He was also in action on the Somme and at Arras, where he was wounded for the second time and invalided home. He was discharged in 1918, and holds the 1914–15 Star, and the General Service and Victory Medals.
15, Industry Terrace, Brixton Road, S.W.9.　　Z2991B

BRAZIER, A., Gunner, R.F.A.
He volunteered in September 1914, and in the following May was drafted to the Western Front, and later in the same year to Salonika, where he took part in much severe fighting on the Struma and Doiran fronts, and was wounded. In 1917 he was sent to Egypt and afterwards to Palestine, and served in many engagements until the campaign closed, including those leading up to the taking of Jerusalem. He was demobilised in June 1919, and holds the 1914–15 Star, and the General Service and Victory Medals.
, Palmerston Street, Battersea, S.W.11.　　Z1351C

BRAZIER, C. P., Private, Queen's (Royal West Surrey Regiment).
Mobilised in August 1914, he was sent to France in the same month, and took part in the severe fighting at Mons, Le Cateau, the Marne and the Aisne, where he was seriously wounded. On his recovery he was engaged on important home duties with his unit, being no longer fit for service overseas. He was discharged owing to his injuries in September 1917, holding the Mons Star, and the General Service and Victory Medals.
11, Glendall Street, Ferndale Road, S.W.9.　　Z1352

BRAZIER, H. A., Private, East Surrey Regiment.

He joined in 1909, and was serving in India at the outbreak of war. In January he reached France and afterwards took part in many operations, in one of which near Ypres, he was wounded. He was unfortunately killed in action at Hill 60, in April 1915, and was entitled to the 1914–15 Star, and the General Service and Victory Medals.

8, Palmerston Street, Battersea, S.W.11.   Z1351A

BRAZIER, J. H., Driver, R.F.A.

Volunteering in March 1915, he was sent to France in February of the following year. He took part in numerous engagements, including those on the Somme and at Arras, Ypres, Cambrai and Fleurbaix, and also served in the Retreat and Advance of 1918. He was demobilised in April 1919, and holds the General Service and Victory Medals.

3, Brunswick Road, Camberwell, S.E.5.   Z3419

BRAZIER, W. L., Rifleman, 12th London Regiment (Rangers).

Joining in December 1917, he was drafted to the Western Front in May of the following year, and took part in the Retreat and Advance of the Allies. He afterwards proceeded to Germany with the Army of Occupation. After his return to England he was demobilised in October 1919, holding the General Service and Victory Medals.

8, Palmerston Street, Battersea, S.W.11.   Z1351B

BREACH, H. G., Signalman, R.N., H.M.S. "Benbow."

He enlisted in April 1914, and served with the Grand Fleet in the North Sea. He took part in the Battle of Jutland, and in many other engagements, and was still serving in 1920. He holds the 1914–15 Star, and the General Service and Victory Medals.

40, Porter Road, Hammersmith, W.6.   12479B

BREAM, J. H., Trooper, Royal Wiltshire Hussars (Prince of Wales' Own Royal Regt.), and Private 6th Wiltshire Regt.

Volunteering in November 1915, he proceeded to the Western Front in the following year. Whilst there he took part in the fighting at Ypres and was severely gassed and invalided to Boulogne. Later he was sent to hospital in England and finally was discharged as medically unfit in September 1918. He holds the King's Certificate and the General Service and Victory Medals.

12, Combermere Road, Stockwell, S.W.9.   Z1353

BREEDEN, H. W., Sapper, R.E.

Mobilised at the outbreak of war he served for a time on important duties in England. In January 1916 he was drafted to Salonika, where he saw much service and did valuable work on the lines of communication. Later in 1917 he proceeded to France, and served on the Somme, and at Ypres and various other places until the conclusion of hostilities. He was demobilised in March 1919, and holds the General Service and Victory Medals.

37, Lockington Road, Battersea Park Road, S.W.8.   Z1354

BREHME, A. F., Gnr., R.F.A. and Pte., Labour Corps.

He joined in October 1916, and in the following year proceeded to France, where he was engaged on important duties in connection with road construction and also on the transport of rations to the fighting areas. In February 1919 he returned home and was demobilised, holding the General Service and Victory Medals.

11, Shorncliffe Road, Walworth, S.E.17.   Z1355

BRENT, T. H. V., Private, East Surrey Regiment.

He volunteered in July 1915, and in June of the following year was sent to France, where he took part in severe fighting on the Ancre Front and at Bullecourt. He also served in the Retreat and Advance of 1918, and was in action at Havrincourt, Epéhy and Cambrai, and was wounded. He was demobilised in February 1919, and holds the General Service and Victory Medals.

6, Bennerley Road, Battersea, S.W.11.   Z5713

BRERETON, E., Driver, R.F.A.

Volunteering in March 1915, he was sent to France in the following year. He took part in numerous engagements of importance, including those on the Somme, at Vimy Ridge, Bullecourt, and Ypres, where he was wounded. He also took part in the Retreat and Advance of 1918. He was demobilised in April 1919, and holds the General Service and Victory Medals. 36, Moncrieff Street, Peckham, S.E.15.   Z5572

BRETT, E. C., Private, R.A.O.C.

He volunteered in February 1915, and in the same year proceeded to France. He served in many notable battles, including those of Ypres, Cambrai and St. Quentin and in numerous other engagements, until the conclusion of hostilities. He was demobilised in February 1919, and holds the 1914–15 Star, and the General Service and Victory Medals.

39, Angel Road, Hammersmith, W.6.   12487A

BRETT, H. W., L/Corporal, M.G.C.

He joined in January 1917, and in the same year was drafted overseas. He took part in many engagements on the Western Front, including those at Arras, Cambrai and the Somme, where he was taken prisoner on March 21st, 1918. At the conclusion of hostilities he was released, and in January 1919, was demobilised, holding the General Service and Victory Medals. 5, Shannon Grove, Brixton Road, S.W.9.   Z1794

BREWER, A., Private, R.A.S.C. (M.T.)

Volunteering in August 1914, he was drafted to the Western Front in the same year, and was present at numerous engagements, including those at Ypres and St. Eloi. In 1916 he was sent to Salonika, where he served on the Vardar. Whilst in the East he suffered from malaria and after seven months' service in this theatre of war returned to France. There he was engaged on important duties in the Somme, Arras and Amiens sectors, and served at Cambrai during the Advance of 1918. He holds the 1914–15 Star, and the General Service and Victory Medals, and was demobilised in December 1918.

46, Tindal Street, Lothian Street, S.W.9.   Z5224

BREWER, A. E., Corporal, Middlesex Regiment.

He volunteered in September 1914, and in the same year was drafted to India. He served at various stations on important duties with his unit, and rendered valuable services. He returned home and was demobilised in September 1919, and holds the General Service and Victory Medals.

34, Bradmore Park Road, Hammersmith, W.6.   10620C

BREWER, H., Private, Northumberland Fusiliers.

He joined in June 1916, and in November of the same year was drafted to France. There he took part in many important engagements, including those at Arras and Cambrai and in the Advance of 1918. Whilst overseas he was twice wounded, on one occasion being invalided to England for a time and on recovery returning to his unit. After the cessation of hostilities he served in Germany with the Army of Occupation until September 1919, when he was demobilised, holding the General Service and Victory Medals.

11, Auckland Road, Battersea, S.W.11.   Z1356

BREWER, W. G., Private, R.A.M.C.

He was mobilised in August 1914, and was shortly afterwards sent to the Western Front, where he served in various engagements. He died gloriously on the field of battle in July 1918, and was entitled to the 1914 Star, and the General Service and Victory Medals.

"His memory is cherished with pride."

36, Bradmore Park Road, Hammersmith, W.6.   10620B

BREWER, W. J., Private, Middlesex Regiment.

Volunteering in 1915, he was drafted to the Western Front in the same year. Whilst in this theatre of war he took part in many notable battles, and in July 1917 was killed in action. He was entitled to the 1914–15 Star, and the General Service and Victory Medals.

36, Bradmore Park Road, Hammersmith, W.6.   10620A

BREWSTER, W. E., Private, Bedford Regiment.

Volunteering in June 1915, he was drafted in the same year to India, where he was engaged on important duties with his unit at Delhi. In June 1918, he died of sunstroke, and was entitled to the 1914–15 Star, and the General Service and Victory Medals.

41, Kay Road, Stockwell, S.W.9.   Z1358

BREWSTER, W. J., Mechanic, R.A.S.C. (M.T.)

Mobilised in August 1914, he proceeded to France in the same month, and served in the memorable Retreat from Mons. He did valuable work in the advanced workshops, and was present at engagements at La Bassée, Ypres, Loos, Vimy Ridge, the Somme and Messines. After the conclusion of hostilities he returned to England and in May 1919 was demobilised, holding the 1914–15 Star, and the General Service and Victory Medals.

11, Shellwood Road, Battersea, S.W.11.   Z1357

BRIANT, F. L., Flight Sergt., R.A.F.

Mobilised in August 1914, he was almost immediately drafted to the Western Front. Whilst there he was present in the Retreat from Mons and the Battles of Le Cateau, the Marne and Aisne, La Bassée and Ypres. In February 1915, he met with an accident and was invalided home, and on his recovery served on important duties at various stations. He was about to proceed to France for the second time when the Armistice was signed, but in consequence of the cessation of hostilities, was retained in England, and was engaged on important work at No. 2 Stores Depôt, Regent's Park, until February 1920, when he was demobilised. He holds the Mons Star, and the General Service and Victory Medals.

1, Marlborough Mansions, Bromell's Road, Clapham, S.W.4.   Z1359

BRIDGE, P. A., Gunner, R.F.A.
He volunteered in March 1915, and in December of the same year was drafted to the Western Front, where he took part in the Battle of the Somme. There he was wounded and invalided home, but on his recovery returned to France in 1917, and while in action at Ypres, was again wounded and sent home, In August 1918 he went overseas for the third time, and served in some of the last operations of the war. After returning home he was demobilised in March 1919, holding the 1914-15 Star, and the General Service and Victory Medals.
14, Lisford Street, Peckham, S.E.15.   Z5046

BRIDGE, W. A., Rifleman, 12th Royal Irish Rifles.
He joined in October 1916, and in January of the following year was drafted to the Western Front. Whilst there he fought in the engagements at Arras, Messines, and Ypres, and in 1918 was taken prisoner at St. Quentin. Whilst in captivity in Germany he died on June 30th, 1918 in consequence of the ill-treatment which he received at the hands of the enemy. He was entitled to the General Service and Victory Medals.
16, Matthew's Street, Battersea, S.W.11.   Z1786

BRIDGEMAN, W. T. H., Rifleman, Royal Irish Rifles.
He joined in December 1916, and in the following year was sent to France, where he took part in heavy fighting at Messines, Ypres, Passchendaele, Cambrai, Kemmel and Menin Road. He also served in the Retreat and Advance of 1918, and afterwards proceeded with the Army of Occupation to Germany. He was demobilised in December 1919, and holds the General Service and Victory Medals.
47, Goldie Street, Camberwell, S.E.5.   Z5330

BRIDGER, J., Rifleman, King's Royal Rifle Corps.
He joined in May 1918, and after his training served on important duties at various stations. He rendered valuable service, but was not successful in obtaining his transfer overseas before the cessation of hostilities, but after the Armistice was sent to Germany with the Army of Occupation. He returned home and was demobilised in January 1920.
9, Townsend Street, Walworth, S.E.17.   Z1360A

BRIDGES, F. G., Private, Norfolk Regiment.
He volunteered in September 1914. but after ten months' service was discharged. Later he rejoined and was transferred to the Norfolk Regiment, and was drafted to India, where he served with the Military Police for four and a half years. In May 1920 he returned home and was demobilised, holding the General Service and Victory Medals.
21, Newcomen Road, Battersea, S.W.11.   Z1361C

BRIDGES, W., Sergt., 1st King's Dragoon Guards.
He was mobilised in August 1914, and was sent to France in the same year with the composite Regiment of 1st Life Guards, and served at Ypres. In 1915 he was transferred to the 1st King's Dragoon Guards, and fought at Péronne and Bapaume, after which he proceeded to India in 1917, and took part in various actions in Afghanistan. He returned home and was discharged as time expired in November 1919, holding the 1914 Star, and the General Service and Victory Medals, also the India General Service Medal (with clasp Afghanistan, N.W. Frontier, 1919).
102, Brayard's Road, Peckham, S.E.15.   Z5331

BRIDGES, W. K., Gunner, R.F.A.
Volunteering in January 1915, he was drafted to France in March of the same year. Whilst in this theatre of war he took part in many engagements, including those at Vimy Ridge and on the Somme. On one occasion he was blown up by the explosion of a shell, and suffering from shock was invalided home, where after receiving hospital treatment he was discharged as medically unfit in December 1918. He holds the 1914-15 Star, and the General Service and Victory Medals.
21, Newcomen Road, Battersea, S.W.11.   Z1361A

BRIDGES, W. S., Driver, R.F.A.
He volunteered in January 1915, and in March of the same year proceeded overseas. He served in many engagements on the Western Front, including those at Loos and on the Somme. After the conclusion of hostilities he returned to England and in 1920 was still serving on Salisbury Plain. He holds the 1914-15 Star, and the General Service and Victory Medals.
21, Newcomen Road, Battersea, S.W.11   Z1361B

BRIDGES, W. S., Driver, R.F.A.
Volunteering in August 1914, he proceeded to France in the same year. Whilst in this theatre of war he took part in much of the heavy fighting at Loos, on the Somme, at Arras, Messines, Ypres, and in other engagements until the cessation of hostilities He holds the 1914 Star, and the General Service and Victory Medals, and in 1920 was still serving.
77, Grant Road Battersea, S.W.11.   Z1362

BRIGDEN, J., Private, 1st Monmouth Regiment.
He joined in 1916, and in the same year was drafted overseas. He fought in many battles on the Western Front, including those of Ypres and Cambrai and was wounded three times. In 1919 he returned home and was demobilised, holding the General Service and Victory Medals.
1, Pitman Street, Camberwell, S.E.5.   Z1364

BRIGGS, C., Private, Royal Fusiliers.
Mobilised in August 1914, he was drafted in the same year to France. Whilst there he fought in many notable battles, and in August 1917 was killed in action. He was entitled to the 1914 Star, and the General Service and Victory Medals.
70, Rothschild Road, Chiswick, W.4.   6280A

BRIGGS, F., Trooper, Fife and Forfar Dragoons and Hertfordshire Dragoons.
He volunteered in January 1915, and later in the same year sailed for Egypt, but his vessel was torpedoed during the voyage. He was fortunately rescued and after ten months in hospital at Malta, proceeded to Egypt, where he saw much active service, and was wounded in action, and suffered from malaria. He returned home for demobilisation in February 1919, and holds the General Service and Victory Medals.
86, Blake's Road, Peckham Grove, S.E.15.   Z5902B

BRIGGS, R. G., Private, Argyll and Sutherland Highlanders.
Volunteering in 1915 he was drafted on the completion of his training to the Western Front. During his service overseas, which lasted for over two years, he was wounded and was invalided home. In 1919 he was demobilised, and holds the General Service and Victory Medals.
70, Rothschild Road, Chiswick, W.4.   6280B

BRIGHT, D., Private, R.A.S.C. (M.T.)
He volunteered in August 1914, and in the same year proceeded to the Western Front. He was principally engaged in conveying supplies and ammunition to the fighting areas, and was present at many engagements. Later he was reported missing, and is believed to have been killed in action. He was entitled to the 1914 Star, and the General Service and Victory Medals. 143, Ingrave Street, Battersea, S.W.11.   Z1365B

BRIGHT, J., Private, Buffs (East Kent Regiment).
He volunteered in September 1914, and in the same year was drafted overseas. Whilst on the Western Front he took part in many engagements, including those at Ypres and on the Somme, where he was wounded. He was invalided to Ireland on recovery, returning to France, where during the latter part of his service he was engaged in guarding German prisoners. In 1919 he was demobilised and holds the 1914 Star, and the General Service and Victory Medals.
143, Ingrave Street, Battersea, S.W.11.   Z1365C

BRIGHT, J. A., Private, R.A.S.C.
He volunteered in December 1915, and in August of the following year was drafted to the Western Front. There he was engaged on important transport and other duties, and was wounded by shrapnel. In December 1919 he returned home and was demobilised, holding the General Service and Victory Medals. 33, Salisbury Row, Walworth, S.E.17.   Z1042B

BRIGHT, T., Private, Middlesex Regiment.
Volunteering in August 1915, he was drafted early in the following year to the Western Front. There he fought in many battles and was killed in action on the Somme on October 29th, 1916. He was entitled to the General Service and Victory Medals. 143, Ingrave Street, Battersea, S.W.11.   Z1365A

BRIMMER, T. A., Sapper, R.E.
Volunteering in March 1915, he was drafted to the Western Front in the same year. He was engaged in the R.E. Signal Section in numerous engagements, including those at Albert, the Somme, Arras and Ypres, and did much gallant service. He returned home and was demobilised in March 1919, holding the 1914-15 Star, and the General Service and Victory Medals.
30, Myatt Road, Stockwell, S.W.9.   Z5047

BRINKLER, J. A., Driver, R.A.S.C.
Having enlisted in August 1910, he was drafted to the Western Front shortly after the outbreak of war four years later, and there took part in the Battles of Givenchy, Ypres and Festubert and many other important engagements. He was unhappily killed in action during the Somme Offensive on July 20th, 1916, and was entitled to the 1914 Star, and the General Service and Victory Medals.
" Whilst we remember the Sacrifice is not in vain."
10, Khyber Road, Battersea, S.W.11.   Z1366B

BRINKLER, J. J., Driver, R.F.A. and Private, Labour Corps.
He volunteered in September 1914, and after his training was engaged on important duties at various stations until May 1915, when he was invalided out of the Army. He re-enlisted, however, in 1916, and shortly afterwards proceeded to the Western Front, where he was engaged on important duties in various sectors. He was demobilised on his return home in 1919, and holds the General Service and Victory Medals.
10, Khyber Road, Battersea, S.W.11.   Z1366A

BRINKLEY, R. L., Private, 22nd London Regiment (The Queen's).
He joined in August 1917, and after completing his training was drafted to France in the following May. He served in various important engagements and was wounded in action. He returned home and was demobilised in January 1919, and holds the General Service and Victory Medals.
91, Battersea Bridge Road, Battersea, S.W.11.   Z1367

BRITTON, A. H., Bombardier, R.F.A.
He volunteered in July 1915, and in the following November was drafted to France During his service on the Western Front, he was in action on the Somme, and at Albert, Poperinghe and Ypres, and in many subsequent engagements until the cessation of hostilities. He was demobilised in March 1919, and holds the 1914-15 Star, and the General Service and Victory Medals.
15, Frere Street, Battersea, S.W.11.   Z1368

BRITTON, J., Corporal, 8th Middlesex Regiment.
He volunteered in May 1915, and after his training was sent to France, where he took part in numerous engagements, and was twice wounded. He also served in Malta and Egypt, He was demobilised in February 1919, holding the 1914-15 Star, and the General Service and Victory Medals.
53, Western Road, Ealing, W.5.   10567B

BRITTON, J. J., Private, 1st East Surrey Regiment.
He joined in June 1916, and in the same year was drafted to the Western Front. During his service in France he fought in several engagements, but was unfortunately killed in action at Béthune in February 1917. He was entitled to the General Service and Victory Medals.
11, Carlton Road, Chiswick, W.4.   6646B

BRITTON, J. R., Private, Essex Regiment.
He joined in August 1918, and was attached to the Royal Defence Corps. He was engaged in Scotland in charge of German prisoners and on other important duties with his unit, and rendered valuable services. He was demobilised in March 1919.
53, Western Road, Ealing, W.5.   10567A

BRITTON, W. C., Corporal, Royal Irish Regiment.
Volunteering in November 1915, he was drafted to Salonika, and fought in many important engagements on the Balkan and Macedonian fronts Later he was sent to Palestine, where he served with General Allenby's Forces in the campaign against the Turks. Finally he proceeded to Mesopotamia, and was killed in action in an engagement on March 10th, 1918. He was entitled to the General Service and Victory Medals.
11, Carlton Road, Chiswick, W.4.   6646A

BROADHURST, A. C., Sergt., R.A.M.C.
He joined the Army in 1896, and during the late war was engaged on highly important medical duties with his unit at various stations. In spite of many efforts he was not successful, owing to his age, in securing his transfer to a fighting front before hostilities ceased, but he rendered valuable services until demobilised in 1919.
8, Myatt Road, Stockwell, S.W.9.   Z4410A

BROADHURST, A. J., Rifleman, 1st Rifle Brigade.
After earlier attempts to join voluntarily he was called up on attaining military age in 1917. On the conclusion of his training at Aldershot he was engaged on important duties with his unit until after the Armistice, when he proceeded to Germany with the Army of Occupation In 1920 he returned home and was demobilised, after rendering much valuable service.
8, Myatt Road, Stockwell, S.W.9.   Z4410B

BROADRIBB, J., Driver, R.F.A.
He joined in February 1916, and in the following May was drafted to the Western Front, and took part in severe fighting on the Somme and at Arras, Vimy Ridge, Ypres and Cambrai. He also served in the Retreat and Advance of 1918, and afterwards proceeded with the Army of Occupation to Germany. He was demobilised in September 1919, and holds the General Service and Victory Medals.
4, New Church Road, Camberwell, S.E.5.   Z5711A

BROCKETT, J. T., Private, R.A.S.C. (H.T.)
He was mobilised in August 1914, having previously fought in the Boer war, and was sent to the Western Front shortly afterwards. He served in numerous engagements, including those at Mons, the Marne, the Aisne, La Bassée, Ypres, St. Eloi, Hill 60, Vimy Ridge, Albert, Arras, Passchendaele and others. He was also present in the Retreat and Advance of 1918, and returning to England after the cessation of hostilities, was demobilised in January 1919, holding the Queen's and King's South African Medals, the Mons Star, and the General Service and Victory Medals.
51, Tindal Street, Lothian Road, S.W.9.   Z5333

BROCKWELL, W. J., Rifleman, Rifle Brigade.
He joined in March 1917, and after serving on important duties at various stations was drafted to the Western Front in November of the same year. He fought at the Battles of Ypres and Cambrai in the engagements of Fins and Sorel, and in various subsequent operations in the Retreat and Advance of 1918. He was demobilised in December 1919, and holds the General Service and Victory Medals.
59, Ascalon Street, Battersea Park Road, S.W.8.   Z1369

BROMHEAD, R., Chief Electrical Artificer, R.N.
He was serving at the outbreak of hostilities, and at once went to sea in H.M.S. "Invincible." He took part in many important Naval engagements, including those of Heligoland Bight, the Falkland Islands, and was unfortunately killed in action in the Battle of Jutland on May 31st, 1916. He was entitled to the 1914-15 Star, and the General Service and Victory Medals.
"His life for his Country, his Soul to God."
11, Coleman Road, Camberwell, S.E.5.   Z4411

BROMLEY, A. J., Private, 10th London Regiment.
He joined in May 1917, and in August of the same year was drafted to France, and took part in severe fighting at Cambrai and Péronne, and was wounded in September 1918. In 1919 he was transferred to Egypt, where he was engaged in various important duties. He was demobilised in January 1920, and holds the General Service and Victory Medals.
170, Cronin Road, Peckham, S.E.15.   Z5334

BRONS, C., Private, Middlesex Regiment.
Volunteering in May 1915, he was sent to France in the same year. He took part in many important engagements, including those on the Somme and at Armentières. He was demobilised in February 1919, holding the 1914-15 Star, and the General Service and Victory Medals.
9, Odell Street, Camberwell, S.E.5.   Z5335B

BROOKE, A., Private, R.M.L.I., H.M.S. "New Zealand."
He was mobilised in August 1914, and was posted to H.M.S. "New Zealand." Whilst in this vessel he served with the Grand Fleet Battle Cruiser Squadron in the Battles of Dogger Bank and Jutland, and in the bombardment of Ostend. He was also engaged with his ship on important and dangerous convoy duties in the North Sea off the coasts of Norway and Sweden, and Cromarty, and at Scapa Flow and Queensferry. In June 1919 he was demobilised, and holds the 1914-15 Star, and the General Service and Victory Medals.
65, Darwin Street, Walworth, S.E.17.   Z1370

BROOKE, W. V., Rifleman, Royal Irish Rifles.
Volunteering in May 1915, he was drafted to the Western Front in the following August. During his service in France he fought at Ypres, Givenchy, Festubert, Fricourt, Mametz, High Wood, and the Battle of the Somme. He was transferred to the 1st Inniskilling Fusiliers, and was in action at Guillemont and Cambrai, where he was buried by the explosion of a shell in September 1918, and invalided home to hospital. In the following month, October 1918, he was discharged as permanently disabled, and holds the 1914-15 Star, and the General Service and Victory Medals.
49, Kamballa Road, Battersea, S.W.11.   Z1383

BROOKER, E., Air Mechanic, R.A.F.
He joined in 1917, and after his training served at various stations on important duties which demanded a high degree of technical skill, and was also for a time engaged on Police work. He rendered valuable services, but owing to the loss of an eye, was unable to proceed overseas. He was demobilised in June 1919.   20, Latchmere Street, Battersea, S.W.11.   Z1372

BROOKER, G., Gunner, R.F.A. (Trench Mortar Battery).
Volunteering in January 1915, he embarked for France in the following April and served at Vimy Ridge, Loos and the Somme, where he was wounded in July 1916. After his recovery he was again fighting at Ypres and Cambrai, and in many subsequent engagements, including Amiens, and the Retreat and Advance of 1918, until December of the same year, when he was demobilised. He re-enlisted however in the following May, in the Royal Army Service Corps, and was engaged on important duties at various stations until the following October, when he was discharged as medically unfit for further service. He holds the 1914-15 Star, and the General Service and Victory Medals.
13, Barmore Street, Battersea, S.W.11.   Z1371

BROOKER, W. J., Private, 75th Canadian Regt.
He volunteered in October 1915, and came over to England with the 75th Canadians, and proceeded to the Western Front. During his service in France he took part in various engagements, and was later killed in heavy fighting in the Somme sector on October 23rd, 1916. He was entitled to the 1914-15 Star, and the General Service and Victory Medals.
19, Bolton Street, Camberwell, S.E.5.   Z1373B

BROOKES, F. T. G., Driver, R.H.A.
A serving soldier, he was mobilised at the outbreak of war, and shortly afterwards was drafted to France. There he fought at Neuve Chapelle, Ypres, the Somme and Cambrai, and in numerous subsequent engagements in the Retreat and Advance of 1918. His time expired in 1915, but he voluntarily rejoined early in the following year, and served until the cessation of hostilities. He was demobilised in March 1919, and holds the 1914 Star, and the General Service and Victory Medals. 19, Bolton Street, Camberwell, S.E.5.　　Z1373A

BROOKMAN, R., Private, 2nd Middlesex Regiment.
Volunteering in February 1915, he was sent to the Western Front in the same year, and fought in various important engagements, including those at Vimy Ridge and Ploegsteert Wood. He was severely wounded near Neuve Chapelle and invalided home to hospital, and after treatment was discharged as physically unfit for further duty in June 1917. He holds the 1914-15 Star, and the General Service and Victory Medals.　　　　　　　　　　　　　　Z1374
34, Gladstone Terrace, Battersea Park Road, S.W.8.

BROOKS, A., Corporal, 4th Buffs (East Kent Regt.)
He volunteered in September 1915, and after his training embarked for France, where he served for four and a half years. During this period he fought in numerous important engagements in various sectors of the Western Front until the conclusion of hostilities. He was demobilised in December 1919, and holds the General Service and Victory Medals. 89, Grant Road, Battersea, S.W.11.　　　　Z1378

BROOKS, A. S., Private, 2nd South Lancashire Regt.
Having previously enlisted in September 1902, and served in India, he was on the Reserve when war broke out, and was immediately mobilised and drafted to France in August 1914. Whilst in this theatre of war he fought in the Retreat from Mons, and was wounded at La Bassée. At the latter end of 1917 he was again wounded and taken prisoner in an engagement, and was held in captivity in Germany until released in December of the following year, when he was repatriated and demobilised. He holds the Mons Star, and the General Service and Victory Medals.
139, Maysoule Road, Battersea, S.W.11.　　　Z1385

BROOKS, A. W., Rifleman, King's Royal Rifle Corps and Private, R.A.S.C.
He attested in 1917, on attaining military age, and was called up in the following year. After his training, which included a special course of signalling, he proceeded to Germany with the Army of Occupation, and served there until March 1920, when he returned to England and was demobilised.
11, Longhedge Street, Battersea, S.W.11.　　Z1380

BROOKS, B., Private, R.A.S.C. (M.T.)
Volunteering in March 1915, he was sent in the same year to the Dardanelles, where he served in the Landing at Suvla Bay, and in the subsequent operations until the Evacuation of the Peninsula. He was then drafted to Egypt, but contracting malaria very severely, was invalided home. In 1916 he was drafted to France, and was present in the engagements on the Somme, and at Messines, Ypres, Béthune, Péronne, and the final operations until the cessation of hostilities. He was demobilised in July 1919, and holds the 1914-15 Star, and the General Service and Victory Medals.
10, Hillery Road, Walworth, S.E.17.　　　　Z1382

BROOKS, E., Private, Suffolk Regiment.
He volunteered in December 1915, and in the following year was drafted to France. During his service on the Western Front he fought on the Somme, and at Ypres and Cambrai, and in many other engagements in the Retreat and Advance of 1918, and was wounded. After the cessation of hostilities he proceeded to Germany with the Army of Occupation, was stationed on the Rhine until January 1919, when he returned to England and was demobilised. He holds the General Service and Victory Medals.
7, Montefiore Road, Wandsworth Road, S.W.8.　Z1384

BROOKS, F., Rifleman, Rifle Brigade.
He joined in May 1916, and in the same year was drafted to France. There he served at Vimy Ridge, the Somme, Beaumont-Hamel, Ypres, Passchendaele and Cambrai. He was also frequently in action in the Retreat and Advance of 1918. In December of the following year he returned home and was demobilised, and holds the General Service and Victory Medals. 76, Gordon Road, Nunhead, S.E.15.　Z6141A. Z6142A

BROOKS, F. H., Ordinary Seaman, Mercantile Marine Reserve, H.M.S. "Victorian."
He joined in July 1918, and after his training was posted to H.M.S. "Victorian," and whilst on board this vessel was engaged on important and dangerous duties in convoying American and Colonial troops to the Western Front. Throughout his service he was in the danger zone, his ship frequently passing through mine-infested areas. He was demobilised in February 1920, and holds the General Service Medal, and the Mercantile Marine War Medal.
28, Comus Place, Walworth, S.E.17.　　　　Z1379

BROOKS, F. J., Private, East Surrey Regiment.
Volunteering in September 1914, he was drafted overseas in the following year, and fought at Ypres and Loos, where he was severely wounded. He was invalided home to hospital, and after his recovery was retained on home service until demobilised in March 1919. He holds the 1914-15 Star, and the General Service and Victory Medals.
77, Hargwyne Street, Stockwell Road, S.W.9.　Z1381B

BROOKS, I. J., Private, 11th Middlesex Regiment.
He volunteered in November 1914, and was sent to the Western Front on the completion of his training. He fought in the engagements at Ypres and Loos, and was killed in action in the heavy fighting at Beaumont-Hamel on the Somme on July 1st, 1916. He was entitled to the 1914-15 Star, and the General Service and Victory Medals.
7, Montefiore Street, Wandsworth Road, S.W.8.　Z1375

BROOKS, J. E., Rifleman, 10th Rifle Brigade.
He volunteered in 1915, and in the same year was drafted to France. Whilst in this theatre of war he fought at Hill 60, Loos, Vimy Ridge, Bullecourt and Beaumont-Hamel, and was severely wounded at Arras, in May 1917. He was invalided home to hospital and subsequently discharged as medically unfit for further duty in June 1919. He holds the General Service and Victory Medals.
76, Gordon Road, Nunhead, S.E.15.　　Z6141C. Z6142C

BROOKS, J. H., Private, Tank Corps.
He joined in 1917, and was trained in the 1st London Regiment, and later was transferred to the Tank Corps School of Instruction. He did good work, but owing to being medically unfit for duty abroad was unable to secure a transfer overseas, and in April 1919 was invalided out of the service.
18, Chalmers Street, Wandsworth Road, S.W.8.　Z1376

BROOKS, R. M., Private, Royal Sussex Regiment.
He joined in 1916, and served on important duties in the erecting and painting of military huts. until the cessation of hostilities. Owing to being medically unfit for duty abroad, he was unable to obtain his transfer overseas, and was demobilised in 1919.
76, Gordon Road, Nunhead, S.E.15.　　Z6141D. Z6142D

BROOKS, S. H., Corporal, R.E.
He volunteered in June 1915, and in November of the same year was sent to the Dardanelles, where he was in action until the Evacuation. In 1916 he was transferred to Mesopotamia and was engaged in the attempt to relieve Kut, also at Um-el-Hannah, Sanna-i-Yat, the Tigris, Kut, Baghdad, and in other engagements. During his service in this theatre of war he contracted malaria. He was demobilised in March 1919, holding the 1914-15 Star, and the General Service and Victory Medals. 69, Moncrieff Street, Peckham, S.E.15.　Z5573

BROOKS, S. W., Rifleman (Machine Gunner), 21st London Regiment (Surrey Rifles.)
He volunteered in 1915, and in the same year was drafted to France. During his service on the Western Front he fought at Hill 60, Loos, Vermelles, Ploegsteert Wood, Vimy Ridge and Bullecourt. On June 9th, 1917, he gave his life for his Country at Messines, and was entitled to the 1914-15 Star, and the General Service and Victory Medals.
" He passed out of the sight of men by the path of duty and self-sacrifice."
76, Gordon Road, Nunhead, S.E.15.　Z6141B. Z6142B

BROOKS, W. J. (M.S.M.), Rifleman, Rifle Brigade.
He joined in June 1916, and in the following October was drafted overseas. During his service in France he fought in the Battles of the Somme, Arras, Vimy Ridge, Cambrai, and in the engagements which followed, and was present at the historic entry into Mons on Armistice Day. In August 1918 he was awarded the Meritorious Service Medal for sustained good work, and holds in addition the General Service and Victory Medals. He was demobilised in September 1919.
58, Bonnington Square, South Lambeth Road, S.W.8. Z1377

BROOKSON, A. W., Private, Norfolk Regiment.
He joined in 1918, and after his training served on important duties at various stations in England, and later in Ireland. He was afterwards drafted to India, where he was still serving in 1920.
39, Park Crescent, Clapham Park Road, S.W.4.　Z1386

BROOM, B., Sergt., 10th Middlesex Regiment.
He volunteered in July 1915, and after his training served at various stations on important duties, and was mainly engaged in drilling recruits. He rendered valuable services, but was not able to secure a transfer overseas, and was demobilised in March 1919. 46, Bridgman Road, Chiswick, W.4. 6265A

BROOM, H., A.B., R.N., H.M.S. "Victory."
He volunteered in October 1915, and after his training was posted to H.M.S. "Powerful" with which he served until May 1916, when he was transferred to H.M.S. "Royal Oak." Whilst in this ship he took part in the Battle of Jutland, and later was engaged on hazardous patrol duties in the North Sea. In October 1919 he was again transferred to H.M.S. "Valorous" and sent to the Baltic, and after his return he was finally posted to H.M.S. "Victory" in which vessel he was still serving in 1920. He holds the General Service and Victory Medals.
121, Grant Road, Battersea, S.W.19.   Z1389A

BROOM, L. (Mrs.), Special War Worker.
For nearly three years during the war this lady was engaged on work of National importance at Messrs. Spicer Brothers, Newington Causeway. Her duties consisted in the manufacture of anti-gas masks, and she gave great satisfaction by her efficiency in carrying out this responsible work.
96, Darwin Street, Walworth, S.E.17.   Z1387A

BROOM, S., Private, 4th Royal Fusiliers.
He volunteered in September 1914, and in the following February was drafted to France. There he fought in the engagements at Hill 60, where he was gassed in action, and Ypres, and in many subsequent battles until the conclusion of hostilities, and was wounded. He was demobilised in November 1919, and holds the 1914–15 Star, and the General Service and Victory Medals.
46, Bridgman Road, Chiswick, W.4.   6265B

BROOM, W., Private, King's Own (Royal Lancaster Regiment).
He joined in February 1916, and in the following September was drafted to France, and whilst in this theatre of war fought at Beaumont-Hamel. On March 28th, 1917, he was taken prisoner, and was held in captivity in Germany until his release in December 1918, when he was repatriated. After two months' leave he served at Monmouth guarding German prisoners until he was demobilised in October 1919. He holds the General Service and Victory Medals.
96, Darwin Street, Walworth, S.E.17.   Z1387B

BROOMFIELD, W. R., Air Mechanic, R.A.F.
He joined in 1918, and after his training served at various stations on important clerical duties with the Royal Air Force. He did good work, but owing to the cessation of hostilities was unable to serve overseas, and was demobilised in 1919.
32, Raywood Street, Battersea Park Road, S.W.8.   Z1390A

BROOMFIELD, W. R. J., Rifleman, King's Royal Rifle Corps.
He volunteered in May 1915, and in the following year was drafted to the Western Front. During his service in France he fought on the Somme, and at Givenchy, Ypres and Beaumont-Hamel, and was subsequently invalided home with trench fever. After his recovery he was engaged on guard and other important duties at various home stations, and was demobilised in April 1919. He holds the General Service and Victory Medals.
32, Raywood Street, Battersea Park Road, S.W.8.   Z1390B

BROWN, A., Private, 11th Middlesex Regiment.
Having previously served in the East Surrey Regiment, he re-enlisted in August 1914, and was sent to France in the same month. He took part in the severe fighting at Loos, Albert and the Somme, and was wounded in September 1916. After his recovery he rejoined his unit and proceeded to Malta, where he stayed until demobilised in March 1919. He holds the 1914 Star, and the General Service and Victory Medals. 3, Lisford Street, Peckham, S.E.15.   Z5048

BROWN, A., Private, 5th Middlesex Regiment.
He joined in 1918, before attaining military age, and after his training served at his depôt on important duties. He did good work but was unable to obtain his transfer overseas, owing to being under age for service abroad. He was demobilised in 1919.
187, Bollo Bridge Road, Acton, W.3.   6864B

BROWN, A., Sergt., Queen's (Royal West Surrey Regiment).
Volunteering in November 1915, he was drafted to France in the following year, and saw much service. He took part in the heavy fighting on the Somme, and at Arras and Ypres, and in many subsequent engagements in the Retreat and Advance of 1918, and was three times wounded. In April 1920 he was demobilised, and holds the General Service and Victory Medals.
103, Ingelow Road, Battersea Park Road, S.W.8.   Z1393A

BROWN, A. A., Private, 24th London Regt. (The Queen's).
He volunteered in February 1915, when only seventeen years of age, and after his training was completed was drafted to France in the same year. He fought at Givenchy, and was killed in action at Festubert on May 26th, 1915. He was entitled to the 1914–15 Star, and the General Service and Victory Medals.
82, Ascalon Street, Battersea Park Road, S.W.8.   Z1391

BROWN, A. C., Air Mechanic, R.A.F.
He joined in July 1916, and in the following August was drafted to France. There he served in the Battles of the Somme, Ypres, and Cambrai, and was wounded. After his recovery he was again in action at various later engagements, until the cessation of hostilities, after which he returned home, and was demobilised in April 1919. He holds the General Service and Victory Medals.
37, Park View Crescent, New Southgate, N.11.   5017B

BROWN, A. E., Private, Highland Light Infantry.
He volunteered in July 1915, and after his training was sent to France, where he took part in severe fighting on the Somme, and in various other engagements. He was unfortunately killed in action on October 23rd, 1916, and was entitled to the General Service and Victory Medals.
"Steals on the ear the distant triumph song."
174, St. George's Road, Peckham, S.E.15.   TZ5714A

BROWN, A. E., Rifleman, King's Royal Rifle Corps and Private, R.A.S.C.
Volunteering in October 1915, he crossed to France in the following June, and while there took an active part in the Battles of the Somme, Ypres, Messines, Passchendaele, and Langemarck. In consequence of wounds received at Cambrai in November 1917, he was invalided home and after his recovery he was transferred to the R.A.S.C., with which he did valuable service as a blacksmith in England, and with the Army of Occupation in Germany. He was demobilised in September 1919, and holds the General Service and Victory Medals. 40, Mostyn Road, Brixton, S.W.9.   Z4412B

BROWN, A. E., Private, Lancashire Fusiliers.
Volunteering in November 1914, he was drafted to France in the same year, and served on important transport duties at Boulogne and Etaples. In 1915 he was sent to Egypt, and thence to Salonika, where he was engaged in various sectors of the Doiran front. He returned to France in 1918, and served throughout the final Advance. He was demobilised in April 1919, and holds the 1914 Star, and the General Service and Victory Medals.
37, Comus Place, Walworth, S.E.17.   Z1399A

BROWN, A. G., Private, M.G.C.
He volunteered in January 1915, and in the following April was drafted to France. During his service on the Western Front, he took part in the fighting on the Somme, and was killed in action on July 25th, 1916. He was entiled to the 1914–15 Star, and the General Service and Victory Medals.
6, Alacross Road, Ealing, W.5.   8905B

BROWN, A. J., Gunner, R.F.A.
He volunteered in August 1914, and in the following year was drafted to France, where he did good work as a gunner in various sectors. He served at Albert, Ypres, the Somme, Arras and Cambrai, and was wounded near Cambrai in May 1918. After his recovery he was again in action in the final operations, and was present at the entry into Mons at dawn on Armistice Day. He was demobilised in 1919, and holds the 1914–15 Star, and the General Service and Victory Medals.
40, Nealden Street, Landor Street, S.W.9.   Z1400

BROWN, A. T., Gunner, R.G.A. and Pte., Military Police.
Having enlisted in 1902, he was called up from the Reserve on the outbreak of war in August 1914, and in the following March was sent to the Western Front. There he took part in the Battles of Neuve Chapelle, Ypres, Festubert and Loos, and other engagements until the cessation of hostilities, and was discharged in January 1919. He re-enlisted in August of that year, and in 1920 was serving with the Military Police. He holds the 1914–15 Star, and the General Service and Victory Medals. 47, Gloucester Road, Peckham, S.E.15.   Z5869A

BROWN, A. W., Rifleman, Rifle Brigade.
He joined in August 1916, and being sent to France in the same year served there as a Lewis gunner. He took part in many important engagements, including those at the Somme, Vimy Ridge, Arras and Ypres. He was wounded at Vimy Ridge, and in 1918 was gassed and contracted fever. After being invalided home he was demobilised in January 1919, holding the General Service and Victory Medals.
6, Russell Grove, Brixton, S.W.9.   Z5050

BROWN, C. H., Gunner, R.G.A.
He volunteered in October 1914, and was sent to France, and during his service on the Western Front did good work as a gunner at Ypres and Arras, and in many subsequent engagements until the cessation of hostilities. He then advanced into Germany with the Army of Occupation, with which he served until he was demobilised in February 1919. He holds the General Service and Victory Medals.
48, Gorden Road, Chase Side, Enfield.   10019B

BROWN, C. G., Private, R.A.S.C. (Remounts) and 5th Hampshire Regiment.

He volunteered in June 1915, and at first served in the Royal Army Service Corps. He was engaged in taking horses and mules to and from France until 1917, when he was transferred to the Hampshire Regiment and sent to India, where he suffered much from malaria. He also served in Egypt for a short time, and was in action at Tripoli and Aleppo in the Palestine campaign. He was demobilised in April 1919, holding the General Service and Victory Medals.

64, Geneva Road, Coldharbour Lane, S.W.9. Z5049

BROWN, C. W., Sergt., 23rd London Regiment.

He volunteered in September 1914, and in June 1916 was drafted to France, where he served in various sectors of the Western Front. In January 1917 he was sent to Salonika, and later to Palestine where he took part in the campaign against the Turks, and was wounded. Returning home he was demobilised in July 1919, and holds the General Service and Victory Medals.

1, Darien Road, Battersea, S.W.11. Z1180

BROWN, C. W., Rifleman, 12th City of London Regiment (Rangers).

He joined in November 1917, and after his training served at various stations on important duties with his unit. He rendered valuable services, but was not able, on medical grounds, to obtain a transfer overseas, and was demobilised in November 1919.

23, Amies Street, Battersea, S.W.11. Z1395A

BROWN, E. A., Air Mechanic, R.A.F. (late R.F.C.)

He joined in June 1916, and after his training was drafted to the Western Front. During his service in France he was engaged on important duties on the Somme, and at Arras, and in other sectors. He was chiefly employed on the repairing and testing of aeroplane engines, and did good work with his Squadron. In September 1919 he was demobilised, and holds the General Service and Victory Medals.

32, Bellefields Road, Stockwell Road, S.W.9. Z1401

BROWN, E. E., Driver, R.A.S.C. (Remount Section).

He joined in March 1917, and in the following year proceeded to France. Whilst overseas he was engaged on important duties in the Remount Service, and the transport section of his Corps. He returned to England and was demobilised in November 1919, and holds the General Service and Victory Medals.

90, Kenbury Street, Camberwell, S.E.5. Z6147B

BROWN, E. M. (Miss), Special War Worker.

This lady was engaged from October 1916 until December 1919 on important duties at the War Office, where she held a responsible position in the Army Medical Supply Department. She carried out her work with care and efficiency, and in a manner worthy of the highest commendation.

16, Brackley Terrace, Chiswick, W.4. 5434A

BROWN, F., Private, 23rd London Regiment.

He volunteered in May 1915, and in the following year was drafted to the Western Front. During his service in France he was in action at Hill 60, and was severely wounded and invalided home. He was discharged as medically unfit for further service in 1918, and holds the General Service and Victory Medals.

37, Beaufoy Road, Lavender Hill, S.W.11. Z1404

BROWN, F., Sergt., Tank Corps.

He volunteered in July 1915, and after training with the Infantry proceeded to France in the following year. After taking part in the Battle of the Somme he was transferred to the Tank Corps, and fought in the chief engagements until March 1918, including those of Ypres, Lens (where he was wounded) and Cambrai. He then came home and was subsequently engaged as Sergeant-Instructor of English and American Tank Officers. After his demobilisation he rejoined in February 1919, and in 1920 was still serving. He holds the General Service and Victory Medals.

46, Treherne Road, Brixton, S.W.9. Z4415

BROWN, F. H., Pte., Queen's (Royal West Surrey Regiment).

Volunteering in June 1915, he went through a course of training and afterwards proceeded to France, where he took part in severe fighting on the Somme, and at Arras, Polygon Wood, and in other engagements, and was wounded. He was reported missing on August 10th, 1917, and was presumed to have been killed in action on that date. He was entitled to the General Service and Victory Medals.

"Thinking that remembrance, though unspoken, may
reach him where he sleeps."

174, St. George's Road, Peckham, S.E.15. Z5714B

BROWN, F., Private, R.A.S.C. (M.T.)

He volunteered in May 1915, and was sent to Egypt in the same year, and served with the 48th Siege Battery, Royal Garrison Artillery in the Sahara. He was later drafted to France, and was engaged on important transport duties at Cambrai, the Somme, Poperinghe, Ypres, and in other sectors of the Western Front. He was demobilised in April 1920, and holds the 1914-15 Star, and the General Service and Victory Medals.

24, Gladstone Terrace, Battersea Park Road, S.W.8. Z1398

BROWN, G., Gunner, R.F.A.

He volunteered in June 1915, and in the same year was drafted to the Western Front, where he took part in numerous engagements, including those at Loos, the Somme, Cambrai, and Laventie. He also served in the Retreat and Advance of 1918, and was twice wounded. He was demobilised in July 1919, and holds the 1914-15 Star, and the General Service and Victory Medals.

59, Goldie Street, Camberwell, S.E.5. Z5336

BROWN, G., Pte., Queen's (Royal West Surrey Regt.)

He volunteered in 1915, and in the same year was drafted to France. During his service on the Western Front he fought at Ypres, and on the Somme, and was killed in action on July 3rd, 1916. He was entitled to the 1914-15 Star, and the General Service and Victory Medals.

217, East Street, Walworth, S.E.17. Z1408

BROWN, G. H., Private, R.M.L.I.

Joining in August 1916, he proceeded to the Western Front in the following month, and was wounded immediately on going into action. Later he took part in the Battle of Cambrai, and many other important engagements in various sectors, and, on his return to England in March 1919, was demobilised. He holds the General Service and Victory Medals.

21, Blake's Road, Peckham Grove, S.E.15. Z5881

BROWN, G. J. H., Pte., R.A.S.C. (Supply Column.)

He joined in March 1917, and after the completion of his training was engaged on important duties in connection with food supplies at various stations. He did excellent work but was not successful in obtaining a transfer overseas before the cessation of hostilities. He was demobilised in August 1920.

90, Kenbury Street, Camberwell, S.E.5. Z6147A

BROWN, G. J., 1st Class Petty Officer, R.N., H.M.S. "Iron Duke."

He was serving at the outbreak of war on H.M.S. "Essex" with the Grand Fleet in the North Sea, and took part in various engagements. He was afterwards transferred to H.M.S. "Iron Duke," and was again in action. He was still serving in the last named vessel off the Turkish Coast in 1920, and holds the 1914-15 Star, and the General Service and Victory Medals.

41, Graylands Road, Peckham, S.E.15. Z5716

BROWN, G. S., Corporal, R.E.

He volunteered in September 1914, and in the same month was drafted to the Western Front. He served in many sectors and took part in numerous engagements, including those at Ypres, the Somme, Arras, Cambrai, and the Retreat and Advance of 1918, and later proceeded with the Army of Occupation to Germany, and was stationed at Cologne, He returned home and was demobilised in December 1919, and holds the 1914 Star, and the General Service and Victory Medals.

4, Lapford Place, off Upper Kennington Lane, S.E.11, Vauxhall. Z25310C

BROWN, G. T., Air Mechanic, R.N.A.S.

He volunteered in May 1915, but during the course of his training his health broke down, and he was in consequence invalided out of the Service in the following November.

71, Manor Street, Clapham, S.W.4. Z1405

BROWN, H. G., Rifleman, Rifle Brigade.

He first volunteered in June 1915, and joined the 10th Queen's (Royal West Surrey Regiment), and after his training did excellent work in the regimental band, which was mainly engaged in playing for recruiting purposes. In February 1916, however, he was discharged as under military age, but in September of the following year he re-enlisted in the Rifle Brigade, and embarked for France in the succeeding February. Whilst serving on the Somme as a Machine Gunner, he was severely wounded in action on March 21st, 1918, and was invalided to hospital, but later succumbed to his injuries on June 2nd of the same year. He was entitled to the General Service and Victory Medals.

106, Wycliffe Road, Lavender Hill, S.W.11. Z1407

BROWN, H. G., Private, Highland Light Infantry.

He volunteered in July 1915, and in the following year was sent to France. He took part in severe fighting on the Somme and in other engagements. He was wounded on the Somme, and suffered the amputation of a leg. He was invalided home and discharged, on account of his disability, in 1917, and holds the General Service and Victory Medals.

174, St. George's Road, Peckham, S.E.15. Z5714C

BROWN, H. V., Private, R.A.S.C., and Rifleman, Rifle Brigade.
He volunteered in May 1915, and, after his training, was sent to France, where he took part in various engagements, including those at Vimy Ridge, the Somme, Ypres, and Passchendaele. He also served in the Retreat and Advance of 1918, and was wounded. He was demobilised in January 1919, holding the 1914–15 Star, and the General Service and Victory Medals. 174, St. George's Road, Peckham, S.E.15.   Z5714D

BROWN, I. W., Sapper, R.E.
He volunteered in February 1915, and in the following September was drafted to France. Whilst in this theatre of war he was engaged on important duties in connection with the operations, and was frequently in the forward areas, notably at Albert, Loos, Vermelles, Ploegsteert Wood, Vimy Ridge, and the Somme. Later he was sent to Salonika, and served in the Allied Offensive on the Doiran front, in the Advance across the Struma, and in the recapture of Monastir. Finally he proceeded to Egypt, and after taking part in several engagements, unfortunately contracted diphtheria, and died at El Arish on November 29th, 1917. He was entitled to the 1914–15 Star, and the General Service and Victory Medals. 94, Nelson's Row, Clapham, S.W.4.   Z1402

BROWN, J., Private, 4th Middlesex Regiment.
He was mobilised from the Reserve in August 1914, and was quickly sent to the Western Front, where he took part in the severe fighting at Mons, the Marne, the Aisne, and Neuve Chapelle. Being severely gassed during his service he was invalided home and discharged as medically unfit for further duty in February 1916. He holds the Mons Star, and the General Service and Victory Medals. 59, Cowan Street, Albany Road, Camberwell, S.E.5.   Z5051

BROWN, J. (Miss), Special War Worker.
During the war this lady rendered valuable services at several munition works. From 1914 to 1915 she held a responsible position as an overseer at Hayes Arsenal, and later was engaged on important and dangerous duties at a private munition factory in Suffolk. Subsequently she worked at Chiswick on the manufacture of aeroplane wings until January 1919. She carried out her duties throughout with commendable efficiency, and her services were highly appreciated. 77, Eastbury Grove, Chiswick, W.4.   9926A

BROWN, J., Special War Worker.
For over five years during the war he was engaged on work of National importance at Messrs. Barker and Co.'s Aircraft Works at Shepherd's Bush. He served as a turner on important and highly skilled duties and did excellent work throughout. 98, Tremadoc Road, Clapham, S.W.4.   Z1394

BROWN, J. E., Private, 18th Middlesex Regiment.
He volunteered in May 1915, and in the following November was drafted to France. During his service on the Western Front he was in action at Loos and Vimy Ridge, and later fell fighting on June 22nd, 1916. He was entitled to the 1914–15 Star, and the General Service and Victory Medals. 26, Hargwyne Street, Stockwell Road, S.W.9.   Z1403

BROWN, J. J., C.S.M., 1st Irish Guards.
He had previously served throughout the South African War, and at the outbreak of hostilities in August 1914, he immediately rejoined and was drafted to France where he took part in the Retreat from Mons. He also served on the Marne and the Aisne, and at Neuve Chapelle, and was then invalided home owing to an injury. Later he was engaged on conducting reinforcements of troops to France until the cessation of hostilities. He holds the Queen's and King's South African Medals, the Mons Star, and the General Service and Victory Medals, and was demobilised in December 1919. 20, Broughton Street, Battersea Park, S.W.8.   Z1392A

BROWN, J. R., Private, Army Cyclist Corps.
He volunteered in October 1914, and in the following July was drafted overseas. During his service in France he was in action at Loos, Albert, Vimy Ridge, the Somme, Beaumont-Hamel, Arras, Messines, Bullecourt, Ypres, Lens, and Cambrai. In November 1917, he was sent to Italy and served in the operations on the Piave until the cessation of hostilities. Whilst overseas he was twice wounded and gassed, and was invalided home to hospital for a time, but rejoined his unit on recovery. He was demobilised in February 1919, and holds the 1914–15 Star, and the General Service and Victory Medals. 26, Charleston Street, Walworth, S.E.17.   Z1411

BROWN, J. T. J., Driver, R.F.A.
He enlisted in September 1912, and at the outbreak of war was drafted to France. He took part in the Retreat from Mons, and the Battles of the Marne and Aisne, Ypres, Neuve Chapelle, Festubert, Vimy Ridge, the Somme, and many others including the Retreat and Advance of 1918. Shortly after the Armistice he contracted influenza, and was invalided to hospital in England, and on his recovery was demobilised in January 1919. He holds the Mons Star, and the General Service and Victory Medals. 15, Stanton Street, Peckham, S.E.15.   Z5214A

BROWN, J. W., Driver, R.A.S.C. (M.T.)
He volunteered in August 1915, and in the same year was drafted to France and served in many sectors of the Western Front on important duties connected with the motor transport. He was present at the Battles of the Somme and Ypres, and in various other engagements until the cessation of hostilities. In January 1919 he was demobilised, and holds the 1914–15 Star, and the General Service and Victory Medals. 98, Sheepcote Lane, Battersea, S.W.11.   Z1410

BROWN, J. W., Gunner, R.F.A.
He volunteered in October 1915, and early in the following year was drafted to France. There he did good work as a gunner with his Battery in many engagements, including those on the Somme, and at Arras, Vimy Ridge, and Ypres, and in various later operations until the conclusion of the war. He was demobilised in September 1919, and holds the General Service and Victory Medals. 28, Cavendish Grove, Wandsworth Road, S.W.8.   Z1396

BROWN, M. (Miss), Special War Worker.
For three years during the war this lady held a responsible position in the Army Post Office at Regent's Park, London. She rendered valuable services and carried out her duties in a highly efficient manner until relinquishing her appointment in 1919. 20, Broughton Street, Battersea Park, S.W.8.   Z1392C

BROWN, N., Corporal, 2nd East Surrey Regiment.
He joined in February 1919, and after his training was drafted to South Russia, and served on the Black Sea littoral. In 1920 he was in England with his unit, and was about to proceed to Mesopotamia. 20, Broughton Street, Battersea Park, S.W.8.   Z1392B

BROWN, P. E., Corporal, 11th Essex Regiment.
He volunteered in September 1914, and proceeded to France in August of the following year. He was wounded in an engagement in September 1915, and after his recovery was frequently in action until September 1916, when he gave his life for King and Country during the severe fighting at Loos on the 25th of that month. He was entitled to the 1914–15 Star, and the General Service and Victory Medals. 51, Plough Road, Battersea, S.W.11.   Z1397

BROWN, R., Lieutenant, R.A.F.
He volunteered at the outbreak of war, and in the following February was drafted to the Western Front. During his service in France he was twice wounded, and severely injured when his machine crashed and fell behind the Belgian lines. He was demobilised in March 1919, and holds the 1914–15 Star, and the General Service and Victory Medals. 51, Kingswood Road, Chiswick, W.4.   T6794B

BROWN, R. C., L/Corporal, R.A.S.C. (M.T.)
He volunteered in May 1915, and proceeded to France in February of the following year. He served in various sectors, including those of the Somme, Albert, Cambrai, and Ypres, and in March 1918 was attached to the French Army and engaged on Secret Service duties. He was demobilised in February 1919, and holds the General Service and Victory Medals, and also a French Decoration. 12, Elmington Terrace, Camberwell, S.E.5.   Z3423

BROWN, S., Rifleman, King's Royal Rifle Corps.
He volunteered in March 1915, and proceeded to France in the following year. He took part in various engagements, including those on the Somme and at Ypres. In 1917 he was transferred to Italy, where he was again in action, but in 1918 returned to France and was taken prisoner in March of that year. On his release he returned home, and was demobilised in January 1919, holding the General Service and Victory Medals. 26, Domville Grove, Camberwell, S.E.5.   Z5574

BROWN, S. G., Driver, R.F.A.
He volunteered in August 1914, and after completing his training in Ireland was drafted to the Western Front in the following November. He took an active part in the Battles of St. Eloi, Ypres, Loos, the Somme, Cambrai, and in many engagements in the Retreat and Advance of 1918. Suffering badly from shell-shock he was treated in hospital, but on his recovery rejoined his unit. After his return home he was demobilised in January 1919, and holds the 1914–15 Star, and the General Service and Victory Medals. 133, Cator Street, Peckham, S.E.15.   Z4413

BROWN, T., Bombardier, R.F.A.
He volunteered in March 1915, and in July of the same year was drafted to the Western Front, where he took part in numerous engagements, including those at Loos, Vimy Ridge, the Somme, Beaumont-Hamel, Arras, Bullecourt, Ypres, Passchendaele, Cambrai, the Marne and many others in the Retreat and Advance of 1918, and was once wounded. He was demobilised in April 1919, holding the 1914–15 Star, and the General Service and Victory Medals. 64, Geneva Road, Brixton, S.W.9.   Z5049B

BROWN, T., Private, Labour Corps.

He joined in May 1918, and in the following July was drafted to France, where he served on important duties mainly in connection with the interment of the dead. In October 1919 he was severely injured in an accident, and was invalided home and succumbed to his injuries in the following July. He was entitled to the General Service and Victory Medals.
116, Speke Road, Battersea, S.W.11.   Z1409

BROWN, T. H., R.Q.M.S., R.E.

Volunteering in October 1914, he proceeded to the Dardanelles in the following year, and took part in the Landing at Suvla Bay, and in the engagements which followed until the Evacuation of the Peninsula. He was then drafted to Egypt and served on important duties at Cairo, Alexandria, and Kantara, and afterwards served in Palestine with General Allenby's Forces, and was present at the fall of Jerusalem. He returned home and was demobilised in March 1920, and holds the 1914–15 Star, and the General Service and Victory Medals.
4, Lapford Place, off Upper Kennington Lane, Battersea, S.E.11.   Z25310B

BROWN, T. W., Private, R.A.S.C. and Labour Corps.

He volunteered in April 1915, and in May of the same year was drafted to the Western Front, where he was engaged on various important duties and rendered valuable services. In June 1916 he was invalided home, and in August of the same year was discharged as medically unfit for further service, and holds the 1914–15 Star, and the General Service and Victory Medals.
4, Lapford Place, off Upper Kennington Lane, Battersea, S.E.11.   Z25310A

BROWN, W., Private, 23rd London Regiment.

Volunteering in November 1914, he completed his training, and in 1915 proceeded to France, where he fought in the Battles of Neuve Chapelle, Ypres, Loos, St. Eloi, and Vimy Ridge. He was subsequently sent to England for service in home training camps, and in June 1917 was discharged. He holds the 1914–15 Star and the General Service and Victory Medals.
6, Moat Place, Stockwell, S.W.9.   Z4414

BROWN, W., Rflmn., Cameronians (Scottish Rifles.)

He joined in April 1916, and after his training served on important duties with his unit until November 1917, when he was drafted to the Western Front. He took part in the severe fighting at Cambrai, and in other engagements. He afterwards became ill, and being transferred to the Labour Corps, again served in various engagements. He was demobilised in May 1919, and holds the General Service and Victory Medals.
108, Newchurch Road, Camberwell, S.E.5.   5575A

BROWN, W. C., Private, King's Own (Yorkshire Light Infantry).

He volunteered in 1915, and in the following year was drafted to the Western Front, where he was engaged in the Somme and Ypres sectors in charge of prisoners and other important duties. He also served in the Retreat and Advance of 1918. He was demobilised in January 1919, and holds the General Service and Victory Medals.
65, Arthur Road, Brixton Road, S.W.9.   Z3430

BROWN, W. E. A. (M.M.), Private, 1st Royal Welch Fusiliers.

He volunteered in April 1915, and after having completed his training was drafted overseas in January of the following year. Whilst there he fought with distinction on the Somme, and in July 1916 was awarded the Military Medal for conspicuous bravery in the Field. In November of the same year he died gloriously on the field of battle at Ploegsteert Wood. He was entitled to the General Service and Victory Medals.
"A costly sacrifice upon the altar of freedom."
15, Stanton Street, Peckham, S.E.15.   Z5214B

BROWN, W. G., Rifleman, King's Royal Rifle Corps.

He volunteered in June 1915, and in the following March was drafted overseas. During his service in France he fought at Vimy Ridge, the Somme, and Ypres, and was three times wounded, and later severely gassed and invalided home. He was discharged as medically unfit in January 1918, but re-enlisted in the following month, and in 1920 was serving in India. He holds the General Service and Victory Medals.
23, Amies Street, Battersea, S.W.11.   Z1395B

BROWN, W. H., Corporal, 23rd London Regiment.

He was mobilised at the outbreak of war and was drafted to the Western Front, and served in various engagements. Later he was sent home and discharged as time-expired, but rejoined as drill Instructor and returned to France. He was afterwards frequently in action in many important battles, and was killed in the Advance in August 1918. He was entitled to the 1914 Star, and the General Service and Victory Medals.
17, Ægis Grove, Battersea Park Road, S.W.8.   Z1406

BROWN, W. R., 1st Class Stoker, R.N., H.M.S. "King Alfred."

He joined in February 1916, and served during the war with the Grand Fleet in the North Sea. He took part in the Battle of Zeebrugge, and in various other engagements. He was demobilised in February 1919. In April of the same year he re-enlisted in the 11th (Prince Albert's Own) Hussars, and was sent to Egypt, and afterwards to India, where he took part in the Afghanistan campaign of 1919. He returned home and was discharged owing to defective eyesight in July 1919, and holds the General Service and Victory Medals, and the India General Service Medal (with clasp Afghanistan, N.W. Frontier 1919). 108, Newchurch Road, Camberwell, S.E.5.   5575B

BROWNE, A. W. (M.M.), Corporal, 11th Field Ambulance, Australian Imperial Forces.

He joined in Australia in May 1916, and in the same year came to England. In 1917 he was drafted to the Western Front, and fought with distinction at Ypres, Messines, and Cambrai, and other engagements until the war ceased, and was wounded. He was awarded the Military Medal for conspicuous bravery on the Field, and also holds the General Service and Victory Medals. In May 1919 he was demobilised.
57, Gonsalva Road, Battersea Park, S.W.8.   Z1412

BROWNING, A. G., Driver, R.A.S.C. (M.T.)

Volunteering in December 1915, he was drafted in March of the following year to the Western Front. Whilst there he served with the 5th Division at the Somme, Arras, Poperinghe, Ypres, and many other places. In November 1917 he proceeded to Italy, but afterwards returned to France and took part in the Retreat and Advance of 1918. After the Armistice he proceeded to Germany with the Army of Occupation, and was demobilised in August 1919, holding the General Service and Victory Medals.
147, Lavender Road, Battersea, S.W.11.   Z1413

BROWNLIE, A. J., A.B., Royal Navy.

He joined in July 1918, and was posted to H.M.S. "Concord," in which cruiser he served in many waters on important duties. He was engaged for a time in conveying our prisoners of war from Germany. He holds the General Service and Victory Medals, and in 1920 was still serving.
5, Lockington Road, Battersea Park Road, S.W.8.   Z1415

BRUCE, A., Special War Worker.

He volunteered for service in the Army eleven times, but was rejected on medical grounds. In June 1916, he joined the French Red Cross Society, Knightsbridge, and from that date rendered excellent services as a warehouseman at their depôt, in charge of the forwarding of supplies to hospitals in France. He remained at this post until April 1920, and was highly valued for his carefulness and attention to duty.
4, Sussex Grove, Loughborough Park, S.W.9.   Z4416

BRUCE, H. T., Rflmn., 11th London Regt. and Pte., Oxfordshire & Buckinghamshire Light Infantry.

Joining in November 1916, he was drafted to France in the following year. He took part in numerous engagements, including those at Arras, Vimy Ridge, Ypres, Passchendaele, Cambrai, Bapaume, and in many others in the Retreat and Advance of 1918. He afterwards proceeded with the Army of Occupation to Germany, and did much valuable service at Cologne until demobilised in March 1919. He holds the General Service and Victory Medals.
83, Sussex Road, Coldharbour Lane, S.W.9.   Z5052

BRUNIGES, G. W., Gunner, R.F.A.

He volunteered in August 1914, and served on important duties with his unit until December of the following year, when he was drafted to the Western Front. He took part in severe fighting at the Somme, and at Arras, Ypres, Cambrai, Dickebusch, Bourlon Wood, and Béthune, and also served in the Retreat and Advance of 1918. He was demobilised in February 1919, and holds the 1914–15 Star, and the General Service and Victory Medals.
22, Dartnell Road, Camberwell, S.E.5.   Z5337

BRUSH, E. E., Trooper, 1st King's Own (Norfolk Dragoons).

He volunteered in November 1915, and after his training served at various stations on important duties with his unit. He rendered valuable services but was not successful in obtaining his transfer overseas before the cessation of hostilities. He was demobilised in February 1919.
166, Cronin Road, Peckham, S.E.15.   Z5338

BRYAN, E., Private, Royal Fusiliers.

After being engaged at Messrs. Du Cros' Works, Acton, on very important munition duties as a charge hand, he joined in 1917, and on the completion of his training was drafted to the Western Front. During his service overseas, which lasted about twelve months, he took part in numerous battles of importance until the conclusion of hostilities. He holds the General Service and Victory Medals, and in 1920, was still serving. 130, Cranbrook Road, Chiswick, W.4.   8356A

BRYANT, A. C., 2nd Aircraftsman, R.A.F.
He joined in May 1918, and after his training was engaged on important duties with his unit. He had previously served with the V.A.D., and acted as hospital orderly and stretcher bearer. He rendered valuable services, but was not successful in obtaining his transfer overseas before the cessation of hostilities. In September 1919 he was demobilised.
2, St. Alphonsus Road, Clapham, S.W.4. Z1417

BRYANT, A. W. K., Special War Worker.
Being exempt from the Army he was engaged on duties of National importance in Munition Works at Chelsea. He served there from 1914 until the conclusion of hostilities as a tool maker, and carried out his duties in a thoroughly efficient manner. 36, Birley Street, Battersea, S.W.11. Z1418A

BRYANT, A. V., Rifleman, 16th King's Royal Rifle Corps.
Volunteering in September 1914, he proceeded to France on the completion of his training in October 1915. Whilst in this theatre of war he took part in many notable battles, including those at Loos, the Somme, and High Wood, where he was wounded and gassed. He was invalided home, and after considerable hospital treatment was discharged in May 1917, as medically unfit for further service. He holds the 1914-15 Star, and the General Service and Victory Medals, and in 1919 re-joined for two years.
36, Birley Street, Battersea, S.W.11. Z1418B

BRYANT, F., Private, Royal Welch Fusiliers.
Volunteering in April 1915, he was drafted to France in September of the same year. He took part in severe fighting at the Battle of Loos, where he was wounded, and later unfortunately succumbed to his injuries on November 25th, 1915. He was entitled to the 1914-15 Star, and the General Service and Victory Medals.
"A costly sacrifice upon the altar of freedom."
26, Longcroft Road, Camberwell, S.E.5. Z5340A

BRYANT, G. Private, M.G.C.
He joined in August 1917, and in September of the following year on the conclusion of his training was drafted to France. There he took part in several engagements in the Advance of the Allies, and in October was reported wounded and missing, and later was presumed to have been killed in action. He was entitled to the General Service and Victory Medals.
17, Kennard Street, Battersea, S.W.11. Z1416B

BRYANT, G. A. S., Rifleman, Rifle Brigade and Private, Labour Corps.
Joining in August 1916, he was sent to the Western Front in December of the same year, and took part in much severe fighting in the Arras sector. In consequence of illness, which unfitted him for the line, he was transferred to the Labour Corps, and was engaged on various important duties, until discharged in May 1918, owing to his physical disabilities. He holds the General Service and Victory Medals.
75, Moncrieff Street, Rye Lane, S.E.15. Z5576

BRYANT, J., Private, 10th Middlesex Regiment.
Volunteering in August 1914, he was on the completion of his training drafted to India in the following October. He saw much valuable service on the Frontier, and at Lucknow. He remained overseas until the conclusion of hostilities. He returned to England, and in December 1919 was demobilised, holding the General Service and Victory Medals.
37, Windmill Road, Chiswick, W.4. 8814A

BRYANT, P., Private, Bedfordshire Regiment and Labour Corps.
Volunteering in May 1915, he was engaged on the completion of his training on important duties with his unit. He also served in various parts of the country on the Prisoners of War Staff. He rendered valuable services, but was not successful in obtaining his transfer overseas before the cessation of hostilities. In March 1919 he was demobilised.
17, Kennard Street, Battersea, S.W.11. Z1416A

BRYANT, W., Corporal, 1st Queen's (Royal West Surrey Regiment).
He was mobilised in August 1914, and shortly afterwards was sent to the Western Front, where he took part in severe fighting at Mons, the Marne, and was twice wounded. He was taken prisoner in October 1914, and after being interned in various camps in Germany was sent to Switzerland on account of ill-health. He later returned home and was discharged as unfit for further service in November 1917. He holds the Mons Star, and the General Service and Victory Medals.
25, Tindal Street, Lothian Road, S.W.9. Z5339

BRYANT, W. T., Private, 10th Middlesex Regiment.
Volunteering in August 1914, he was drafted on the completion of his training in the following October, to India, where he served until the conclusion of the war at Lucknow and various other stations. In December 1919 he returned home and was demobilised holding the General Service and Victory Medals.
37, Windmill Road, Chiswick, W.4. 8814B

BRYSON, W. R., Sapper, R.E.
Volunteering in October 1915, he was drafted to the Western Front in the following year. Whilst in this theatre of war he rendered much valuable service at the Somme, Arras, and Ypres. During the German Offensive of 1918 he was taken prisoner and kept in captivity for eight months. Repatriated after the Armistice he was demobilised, and holds the General Service and Victory Medals.
82, Sandmere Road, Clapham, S.W.4. Z1767A

BUCK, J. W., Corporal (Saddler), R.F.A.
Volunteering in August 1914, he was drafted to the Dardanelles in 1915. He was present at the landing at Gallipoli and took part in many engagements until the Evacuation of the Peninsula. He then proceeded to Egypt, where he served for a short time, before being transferred to France. There he fought at Ypres, Arras, Cambrai, and in the Retreat and Advance of 1918. In April 1919 he was demobilised holding the 1914-15 Star, and the General Service and Victory Medals.
22, Gonsalva Road, Wandsworth Road, S.W.8. Z1419

BUCKELL, E. (Mrs.), Special War Worker.
From 1915 until October 1918, this lady was engaged on work of great importance in the manufacture of gas-masks at a Clapham Munition Factory. She carried out her very responsible duties under great pressure, and with the utmost care and efficiency.
1, Newman Street, Battersea, S.W.11. Z1420A

BUCKELL, H. (Miss), Special War Worker.
In 1916 this lady accepted a responsible appointment at the Munition Factory, Clapham, where she was engaged on vitally important work in connection with the manufacture of gas-masks. The efficient and expeditious manner in which she carried out her work was worthy of high praise. She resigned her post in December 1918.
1, Newman Street, Battersea, S.W.11. Z1420B

BUCKEY, W., Corporal, R.F.A.
He volunteered in August 1914, and in the following year was drafted to the Western Front, where he was in action at Ypres, and on the Somme. In 1916 he was transferred to Italy, and took part in the campaign against the Austrians, serving in the Piave sector. After the conclusion of hostilities he returned to England. and in 1919 was demobilised, holding the 1914-15 Star, and the General Service and Victory Medals.
64, Somerleyton Road, Coldharbour Lane, S.W.9. Z3063A

BUCKLEY, J., Trooper, 6th Dragoon Guards.
Mobilised from the Reserve at the outbreak of war, he was speedily drafted to the Western Front. There he fought in the Retreat from Mons, the Battles of the Marne, the Somme, Ypres, Arras, Cambrai, and many other notable engagements until the conclusion of hostilities. In February 1919 he returned home, and was demobilised, holding the Mons Star, and the General Service and Victory Medals.
3, Tidbury Street, Battersea, Park Road, S.W.8. Z1421

BUCKNELL, J. H., Rflmn., 11th London Regt.(Rifles) and 21st London Regt. (1st Surrey Rifles).
Volunteering in January 1915, he was retained with his unit on important duties after the completion of his training. On proceeding to France in 1917 he took part in the Battles of Arras, Albert, Ypres, Passchendaele, and many important engagements in the Retreat and Advance of 1918, and was gassed. He returned home in February 1919, and was demobilised holding the General Service and Victory Medals. Later he re-joined the Army in the Welch Guards.
14, Combermere Road, Stockwell, S.W.9. Z1422

BUDD, J., Rifleman, Rifle Brigade.
He enlisted in March 1909, and at the outbreak of war was drafted to the Western Front. He fought in the Retreat from Mons, and in the Battles of the Aisne, Armentières, Ypres, and Hooge, where he was badly wounded. He was invalided home and after receiving hospital treatment was discharged as medically unfit for further duties in July 1916. He holds the Mons Star, and the General Service and Victory Medals.
190, Farmer's Road, Camberwell, S.E.5. Z1423

BUDDEN, A., Sapper, R.E.
Volunteering in August 1914, he proceeded to the Dardanelles in the following year, and rendered valuable services at Suvla Bay and other engagements until the Evacuation of the Peninsula. He was then drafted to Mesopotamia, and was with the Relief Force which entered Kut. Later he was sent to Persia, and thence to Russia, and was principally engaged in supervising native labour. He returned home and in July 1919 was demobilised, holding the 1914-15 Star, and the General Service and Victory Medals.
26, Cobbett Street, Dorset Road, S.W.8. Z1424

BUDDLE, T. J., Driver, R.A.S.C. (M.T.)
He joined in September 1917, and for a time served on important transport duties at various stations with his unit. He then proceeded to Ireland and afterwards to France, where he saw much service in the concluding stages of the war. In February 1920 he returned home and was demobilised, holding the General Service and Victory Medals.
2, Horsman Street, Camberwell, S.E.5. Z1425A

BUGG, P. O., Corporal, 12th Rifle Brigade.
He volunteered in August 1914, and was immediately drafted to the Western Front, where he served in the Retreat from Mons, and the Battles of the Aisne and Ypres, where he was wounded. He was invalided home, but on his recovery returned to France and was in action at Vimy Ridge, Arras and the Somme, where he was again wounded and sent to hospital in England. He holds the Mons Star. and the General Service and Victory Medals, and was demobilised in 1919.
4, Tappersfield Road, Nunhead, Peckam, S.E.15.   Z6680

BUIST, R. H., Sergt., Sherwood Foresters.
He volunteered in 1915, and in July of the following year proceeded overseas. During his service on the Western Front he took part in the Battles of the Somme, and was badly wounded. On his recovery after treatment at home he returned to France, and in March 1918 was taken prisoner on the Cambrai front. After being in captivity for nine months he was repatriated, and in 1919 was demobilised, holding the General Service and Victory Medals.
10, Chantrey Road, Stockwell, S.W.9.   Z1426

BULL, E. A., Pte., Royal Sussex Regt. and R.A.V.C.
He joined in July 1918, and on the completion of his training served on important home defence duties until the cessation of hostilities. He was then drafted to Germany with the Army of Occupation, and was stationed at Cologne on responsible guard duties at various outposts. In August 1919, he returned to England, and was subsequently demobilised in April of the following year.
90, Kenbury Street, Camberwell, S.E.5.   Z6146

BULL, H., L/Corporal, 12th Middlesex Regiment.
Mobilised in October 1914, he was shortly afterwards drafted to France, where he took an active part in the Battles of Ypres, the Somme, Arras, Messines, Cambrai, and was wounded twice. In the Retreat of 1918 he was unfortunately killed in action on March 24th. He was entitled to the 1914-15 Star, and the General Service and Victory Medals.
1, Dean's Buildings, Flint Street, Walworth, S.E.17.   Z1427

BULLARD, J., Gunner, R.G.A.
He volunteered in November 1915, and in April of the following year proceeded to the Western Front. There he took part in many engagements, including those at Vimy Ridge, the Somme, Beaumont-Hamel, Arras, Cambrai, and the Retreat and Advance of 1918. On one occasion he was wounded, but on his recovery returned to his Battery. He was demobilised in February 1919, and holds the General Service and Victory Medals.
55, Darwin Street, Walworth, S.E.17.   Z1428

BULLEN, A. E., Pte., 2nd Northumberland Fusiliers.
He joined in September 1916, after being previously rejected, and was engaged on various important duties with his unit. He was not successful in obtaining his transfer overseas, and was discharged as medically unfit for further services in March 1917.
9, Brymer Road, Camberwell, S.E.5.   Z5578C

BULLEN, C. W., Driver, R.F.A.
He joined in August 1916, and in January of the following year was drafted to the Western Front, where he took part in numerous engagements of importance, including those at Arras, Vimy Ridge, and Cambrai, and in the Retreat and Advance of 1918. He was demobilised in June 1919, and holds the General Service and Victory Medals.
9, Brymer Road, Camberwell S.E.5.   Z5578D

BULLEN, R. B., Rifleman, Rifle Brigade.
He joined in May 1918, and after going through a course of training proceeded after the Armistice with the Army of Occupation to Germany. He returned home and was demobilised in October 1919.
9, Brymer Road, Camberwell, S.E.5.   Z5578B

BULLOCK, E. W., Private, Royal Fusiliers, Durham Light Infantry and R.A.F. (late R.F.C.)
He joined in 1916, and on the completion of his training was drafted overseas. He saw much service in many important engagements on the Western Front, and was gassed twice and wounded. In 1919 he was demobilised after his return to England, and holds the General Service and Victory Medals.
105, Ferndale Road, Clapham, S.W.4.   Z1430A

BULLOCK, J. A., Rifleman, Rifle Brigade.
He volunteered in August 1914, and after his training was engaged at various stations on important duties with his unit. He rendered valuable services, but on medical grounds was unable to secure his transfer overseas. He was discharged in January 1916.
15, Shorncliffe Road, Walworth, S.E.17.   Z1429B

BULLOCK, J. R., Private, 6th Dorsetshire and 9th Devonshire Regiments.
Volunteering in September 1914, he was drafted in the following year to the Western Front, where he took part in the Battles of Hill 60, Ypres, Albert, the Somme, Delville Wood, Bullecourt, and many others. In 1917 he proceeded to Italy, and did excellent service during the campaign on the Piave. On returning to France he fought in the Offensive of 1918. He was gassed on one occasion during his service overseas. In June 1919 he returned home, and was demobilised, holding the 1914-15 Star, and the General Service and Victory Medals.
15, Shorncliffe Road, Walworth Road, S.E.17.   Z1429A

BULLOCK, R. T., Rflmn., King's Royal Rifle Corps.
Volunteering in November 1914, he was sent to France in September of the following year. He took part in many important engagements, including those at Loos, and was wounded. He was invalided home with shell shock, and gas poisoning, and was discharged as medically unfit for further service in January 1919, holding the 1914-15 Star, and the General Service and Victory Medals.
27, Secretan Road, Camberwell, S.E.5.   Z5341

BULLOCK, S. L., Driver, R.F.A.
Five months after volunteering in October 1915, he was drafted to France, where he saw severe fighting in various sectors of the Front. He served through the Battles of the Somme, Vimy Ridge, Ypres, and Passchendaele, and many other important engagements in this theatre of war, and was wounded in action near Cambrai in March 1918, and was also gassed. He was demobilised in June 1919, and holds the 1914-15 Star, and the General Service and Victory Medals.
54, Foreign Street, Camberwell, S.E.5.   Z5884

BULMER, E., Driver, R.F.A.
He volunteered in December 1915, and in the following year was sent to France, where he took part in severe fighting at Vimy Ridge, the Somme, Arras, Ypres, and Albert. He also served in the Retreat and Advance of 1918. He was demobilised in August 1919, and holds the General Service and Victory Medals.   24, Sandover Road, Camberwell, S.E.5.   Z5342

BUMSTEAD, W. R., Private, R.E. (Signal Section).
He joined in May 1916, and in January of the following year proceeded overseas. Whilst in France he served as a signaller, and did excellent work in keeping up communication often under heavy fire. In February 1919 he returned to England, and was demobilised, holding the General Service and Victory Medals.
30, Rowena Crescent, Battersea, S.W.11..   Z1432

BUNCE, F. H., Private, Duke of Cornwall's Light Infantry.
Volunteering in April 1915, he was drafted in the same year to the Western Front. There he took part in the fierce fighting on the Somme, and on August 31st, 1916, was wounded. He was invalided home, and on September 16th died at Netley from the effects of his injuries. He was entitled to the 1914-15 Star, and the General Service and Victory Medals.
7, Victoria Place, Priory Grove, S.W.8.   Z1434

BUNCE, G. H., Driver, R.A.S.C.
He volunteered in the Infantry in April 1915, and was later transferred to the R.A.S.C. On the completion of his training he was drafted to the Western Front in 1917, and in this theatre of war served in many engagements, including those at Ypres, and Passchendaele. Being badly wounded he was invalided home, and was discharged as medically unfit for further service in March 1920. He holds the 1914-15 Star, and the General Service and Victory Medals.
16D, Victoria Dwellings, Battersea, S.W.11.   Z1433

BUNSTEAD, P. S., Rifleman, 21st London Regiment (1st Surrey Rifles).
He volunteered in August 1914, and after rendering valuable services with his unit, was drafted to France in 1916, where he took part in the fighting in the Arras Sector. Shortly afterwards he proceeded to Salonika, and was present at the engagements on the Vardar and Doiran fronts. He was then sent to Egypt and served in the Palestine campaign under General Allenby at Beersheba, and Aleppo, and was present at the entry into Jerusalem. In April 1919 he was demobilised after his return home, and holds the General Service and Victory Medals.
6, Ingleton Street, Brixton Road, S.W.9.   Z1762A

BUNTON, A. A., Private, Middlesex Regiment.
He joined in April 1918 in the 9th Royal Fusiliers, and after being transferred to the Middlesex Regiment was drafted to France where he served with distinction in many of the final engagements of the war, including those at the Aisne, the Marne and Ypres. After returning home he was demobilised in January 1920, and holds the General Service and Victory Medals.
20, Lewis Road, Camberwell, S.E.5.   Z6145B

BUNTON, W. J., Cpl., 24th London Regt. (Queen's).
Volunteering in November 1915, he shortly afterwards proceeded to the Western Front and took an active part in the Somme Offensive in 1916. Later in that year he was drafted to Mesopotamia, and after valuable service there was transferred to the Egyptian front. He took part in the Palestine campaign under General Allenby, and after entering Jerusalem in December 1917, fell fighting near Jericho on March 9th, 1918. He was entitled to the 1914-15 Star, and the General Service and Victory Medals.
" The path of duty was the way to glory."
20, Lewis Road, Camberwell, S.E.5. Z6145A

BURBAGE, B., Special War Worker.
For three years of the war he was engaged at the Waverley Motor Factory, Willesden, on important work in connection with the manufacture of engines for air-craft. He carried out his duties with great care and efficiency.
35, Perrers Road, Hammersmith, W.6. T11523C

BURBAGE, F. J., Air Mechanic, R.A.F.
He joined in January 1916, and after his training was drafted overseas. He served with the Mobile Squadron at their base at Vendôme, and did valuable work. At the conclusion of hostilities he proceeded to Germany with the Army of Occupation, remaining there until July 1919, when he returned home, and was demobilised. He holds the General Service and Victory Medals.
35, Perrers Road, Hammersmith, W.6. T11523A

BURBAGE, W. H., 1st Air Mechanic, R.A.F.
Volunteering in April 1915, he was drafted overseas in May of the same year. He was present at many engagements on the Western Front, including those at Neuve Chapelle, Ypres, Arras, and the entry into Mons in 1918. He was demobilised in February 1919, and holds the 1914-15 Star, and the General Service and Victory Medals.
35, Perrers Road, Hammersmith, W.6. T11523B

BURDEN, A., Corporal, R.A.F.
He joined in June 1916, and in the following September was drafted to Salonika, where he was engaged on important duties with his unit during the Balkan campaign. After the cessation of hostilities he returned to England, and in March 1919 was demobilised, holding the General Service and Victory Medals.
40, Chatto Road, Battersea, S.W.11. Z3057

BURDETT, A., Private, 10th London Regt. and M.G.C.
He joined in June 1916, and after a period of training was drafted to France. There he took part in the severe fighting at Ypres and Passchendaele, and in various other engagements on the Western Front. In 1918 he was transferred to the Machine Gun Corps, and on May 30th of that year was unfortunately killed in action. He was entitled to the General Service and Victory Medals.
" And doubtless he went in splendid company."
B Block, 5, Jubilee Buildings, Gerridge Street, Westminster Bridge Road. Z25065

BURDETT, A. E., Driver, R.A.S.C. (M.T.).
Shortly after volunteering in August 1914, he was drafted to the Western Front, where he was engaged on transport duties, conveying food and munitions to the forward areas. He contracted double pneumonia whilst in France, was invalided home, and in May 1916 was discharged as medically unfit for further service. He holds the 1914 Star, and the General Service and Victory Medals.
47, Castlemain Road, Peckham, S.E.15. Z5898

BURDETT, T., Driver, R.A.S.C.
He joined the Royal Field Artillery in 1916, but was shortly afterwards transferred to the Royal Army Service Corps. In 1917 he proceeded to the East, and afterwards served in the Advance into Palestine. He did much good work at Gaza and Jerusalem, and remained in that theatre of war until 1919, when he returned to England and was demobilised. He holds the General Service and Victory Medals.
67, Farmer's Road, Camberwell, S.E.5. Z1435

BURDETT, T. R., Rifleman, Rifle Brigade.
Volunteering in September 1914, he proceeded overseas in May of the following year. Whilst in France he took part in the fighting at St. Eloi, and fell in action near Ypres on August 9th, 1915. He was entitled to the 1914-15 Star, and the General Service and Victory Medals.
" His life for his Country, his Soul to God."
74, Aylesbury Road, Walworth, S.E.17. Z27600

BURGESS, A. D., 1st Class Air Mechanic, R.A.F.
He joined in September 1917, and after his training was engaged on important duties with his Squadron. His work which demanded a high degree of skill was carried out with great care, and he rendered valuable services, but was not successful in obtaining his transfer overseas before the cessation of hostilities. In June 1920 he was sent to India.
2, Neate Street, Camberwell, S.E.5. 5053C

BURGESS, C. E., Lieutenant, R.F.A.
He was serving at the outbreak of war, and in January of the following year proceeded to the Western Front, and took part in severe fighting at the 2nd Battle of Ypres, and on the Somme. He was mentioned in Despatches in the " London Gazette," August 28th, 1919, for services in connection with anti-aircraft defences in England. He was still serving in 1920, and holds the 1914-15 Star and the General Service and Victory Medals.
22, Speenham Road, Stockwell, S.W.9. Z5718A

BURGESS, E. J. F., Private, Suffolk Regiment.
He joined in September 1917, and after his training was drafted to the Western Front. Whilst there he took part in many important engagements, including those at Loos, Arras, Armentières, and later was engaged in guarding German prisoners. In February 1919 he was demobilised after returning home, and holds the General Service and Victory Medals.
5, Church Road, Hammersmith, W.6. 11127A

BURGESS, G., Stoker, R.N.
He enlisted in September 1910, and after the outbreak of war in August 1914, served in H.M.S. " Dreadnought " in many waters. He was also engaged on various duties in several submarines, took part in many Naval engagements, and assisted in sinking an enemy submarine. He holds the 1914 Star, and the General Service and Victory, Medals and in 1920 was still at sea in H.M. Submarine L25.
86, Blake's Road, Peckham Grove, S.E.15. Z5902A

BURGESS, G. J. (Senior), Air Mechanic, R.A.F.
He joined in June 1918, and after his training was engaged on important duties with his unit. He was engaged as a driver and rendered valuable services, but was not successful in obtaining his transfer overseas before the cessation of hostilities. He was demobilised in February 1919.
2, Neate Street, Camberwell, S.E.5. 5053B

BURGESS, G. J. (Junior), 1st Class Petty Officer, R.N., H.M.S. " Victory."
He joined the Navy in September 1909, and during the war did excellent service with the Grand Fleet in the North Sea. He was engaged for a time in mine-sweeping on H.M.S. " Thetis " and was on H.M.S. " Dreadnought " when she sank the German Submarine U. 29. He was still serving on a submarine in 1920, and holds the 1914-15 Star, and the General Service and Victory Medals.
2, Neate Street, Camberwell, S.E.5. 5053A

BURGESS, H. A. G., L/Cpl., 11th Worcestershire Regt.
He volunteered in June 1915, and on the completion of his training proceeded overseas. Whilst in France he took part in much fighting on the Somme, and at other engagements. Later he was drafted to the East, and saw service in Egypt and Salonika, and was wounded. He returned home in March 1919, and was demobilised, holding the 1914-15 Star, and the General Service and Victory Medals.
5, Church Street, Hammersmith, W.6. 11127B

BURGESS, J. H., Private, R.A.S.C. (Remounts).
Volunteering in December 1915, he was immediately drafted overseas. During his service on the Western Front he was engaged on important Regimental duties, and did much valuable work. For a time he was in hospital through ill-health. In May 1919 he was demobilised, after returning to England, and holds the 1914-15 Star, and the General Service and Victory Medals.
56, Wycliffe Road, Lavender Hill, S.W.11. Z1181

BURGESS, R. W. (D.C.M.), C.Q.M.S., East Surrey Regiment.
He volunteered in September 1914, and in June of the following year proceeded to the Western Front. Whilst in this theatre of war he took part in many important engagements, including the Battles of Ypres, Festubert, Arras and Vimy Ridge, and was wounded in action in the Somme Offensive of July 1916. He was awarded the Distinguished Conduct Medal for conspicuous bravery and devotion to duty in the Field at Vimy Ridge, and holds also the 1914-15 Star, and the General Service and Victory Medals. He was demobilised in May 1919.
33D, Lewis Trust Buildings, Warner Road, Camberwell, S.E.5. Z5890

BURLES, A. R., Rifleman, 5th London Regiment (London Rifle Brigade).
He volunteered in November 1915, and early in the following year was drafted to the Western Front. There he took part in many important engagements until hostilities ceased, including those at Ypres and Cambrai, and was gassed. In January 1919 he returned home and was demobilised, holding the General Service and Victory Medals.
39, Angel Road, Hammersmith, W.6. 12487B

BURLEY, R., Special War Worker.
He was specially exempted from military service on account of his exceptional qualifications and technical skill in connection with the manufacture of shells, and throughout the war rendered valuable services in the production of munitions. On three occasions he was seriously injured in the course of his duties, but continued his work until after the cessation of hostilities.
263, Guiness Buildings, Glasshouse Street, Vauxhall Walk, S.E.11.   Z24317

BURLS, F. A., Private, Royal Berkshire Regiment.
He was mobilised in August 1914, and was immediately afterwards sent to France, where he took part in severe fighting at Mons, the Marne, the Aisne, La Bassée and Ypres. He was twice wounded and invalided home, and in March 1916 was discharged as medically unfit for further service, holding the Mons Star, and the General Service and Victory Medals.
1, Combermere Road, Stockwell, S.W.9.   Z1436

BURLS, H. G., Gunner, R.F.A.
Volunteering in April 1915, he was sent to the Western Front in the same year. He took part in many important engagements, including those on the Somme, and was wounded. He also served in the Retreat and Advance of 1918, and was killed in action at Cambrai in October of that year. He was entitled to the 1914-15 Star, and the General Service and Victory Medals.
25, Moat Place, Stockwell, S.W.9.   Z1437B

BURLS, W. A., Private (Signaller), 4th (Queen's Own) Hussars.
He was serving at the outbreak of war and was immediately afterwards sent to France, where he took part in severe fighting in the Retreat from Mons, and on the Marne and the Aisne, and at St. Eloi, Ypres, Festubert, the Somme and Arras, and was wounded at Hooge. He also served in the Retreat and Advance and was mentioned in Despatches for conspicuous gallantry at Villers Bretonneux in August 1918. He was demobilised in May 1919, and holds the Mons Star, and the General Service and Victory Medals.
25, Moat Place, Stockwell, S.W.9.   Z1437A

BURNELL, C. E., Private, R.A.M.C.
He volunteered in September 1915, and after his training served on important duties with his unit until December of the following year, when he was drafted to the Western Front. He was engaged in various sectors, including the Somme and Amiens on hospital work and rendered valuable services. After the Armistice he went with the Army of Occupation to Germany, where he remained until May 1919, when he returned home and was demobilised. He holds the General Service and Victory Medals.
11, Radnor Terrace, South Lambeth Road, S.W.8.   TZ27541

BURNELL, W., Sapper, R.E.
He joined in August 1916, and after his training served at various stations on important duties with his unit. He rendered valuable services, but was not successful in obtaining his transfer overseas before the cessation of hostilities. He was demobilised in February 1919.
56, Cabul Road, Battersea, S.W.11.   Z1182

BURNS, E., Private, 23rd London Regiment.
He volunteered in November 1914, and after going through a course of training served on important duties with his unit at various stations and rendered valuable services. He was about to proceed overseas, but was suddenly taken ill and died on November 15th, 1916.
65, Ingrave Road, Battersea, S.W.11.   Z1438

BURNS, G., Corporal, R.E. (R.O.D.)
After volunteering in September 1914, and completing his training he was sent to France. He was engaged on railway duties conveying troops to and from the various fronts, and rendered valuable services. During his service overseas he was wounded, was invalided home, and in July 1918 was discharged as medically unfit for further service, holding the 1914-15 Star, and the General Service and Victory Medals.
52, Weybridge Street, Battersea, S.W.11.   Z1439

BURNS, W. T., Driver, R.F.A.
He volunteered in October 1914, and was sent to France in January of the following year. He took part in numerous engagements, including those at Neuve Chapelle, Loos, the Somme and Ypres, and was twice wounded and gassed. In 1916 he proceeded to Salonika, where he contracted malaria and was invalided home, and was later engaged on transport duties. He was demobilised in March 1919, holding the 1914-15 Star, and the General Service and Victory Medals.
75, Cronin Road, Peckham, S.E.15.   Z5344

BURRAGE, G. E., Trooper, 4th (Royal Irish) Dragoon Guards.
Volunteering in September 1914, he went through a course of training and afterwards served on various important duties with his unit until February 1919, when he was discharged as medically unfit for further services.
27, Thorncroft Street, Wandsworth Road, S.W.8. Z1440A

BURRAGE, R. A., Trooper, 4th (Royal Irish) Dragoon Guards.
He volunteered in September 1914, and in February of the following year was drafted to the Western Front, where he took part in severe fighting at Vimy Ridge, the Somme, Cambrai, and in many other important engagements, and was wounded in April 1918. He was demobilised in February 1919, holding the 1914-15 Star, and the General Service and Victory Medals.
27, Thorncroft Street, Wandsworth Road, S.W.8. Z1440B

BURRAGE, V., Private, Queen's Own (Royal West Kent Regiment).
He joined in March 1917, and after his training served on important duties with his unit until March of the following year, when he was drafted to France. He was in action in many sectors, including those of the Somme and Cambrai, and took part in numerous important engagements. He was killed near Cambrai in October 1918, and was entitled to the General Service and Victory Medals.
27, Thorncroft Street, Wandsworth Road, S.W.8. Z1440C

BURRAGE, W. C., Pte., 7th Northamptonshire Regt.
He volunteered in October 1914, and in the same year proceeded to France as a Driver in the R.A.S.C. He was present at many important engagements, including those on the Somme and at Ypres, and Cambrai and was wounded and invalided home. On his recovery he was transferred to the Northamptonshire Regiment and returned to France, where he took part in the Retreat and Advance of 1918. He was demobilised in March 1919, and holds the 1914 Star, and the General Service and Victory Medals.
45, Montifiore Street, Battersea, S.W.8.   Z1441

BURREE, E., Pte., Queen's (Royal West Surrey Regt.)
Volunteering in October 1914, he was sent to France in March of the following year. He took part in severe fighting, and was wounded at Loos and invalided home. On his recovery he returned to France, where he was killed in action on the Somme in July 1916. He was entitled to the 1914-15 Star, and the General Service and Victory Medals.
26, Newman Street, Battersea, S.W.11.   Z1442

BURREE, G., Private, 13th Royal Fusiliers.
Volunteering in November 1914, he was drafted to France in the same year. He took part in severe fighting at Neuve Chapelle, Ypres, Loos, the Somme, Arras, Cambrai and in other engagements, and also served in the Retreat and Advance of 1918. During his service in France he was three times wounded, and after the cessation of hostilities returned home and was demobilised in March 1919, holding the 1914-15 Star, and the General Service and Victory Medals.
6, Porson Street, Wandsworth Road, S.W.8.   Z1444A

BURREE, T. H., Petty Officer (Stoker), R.N., H.M.S. "Triumph."
He was serving at the outbreak of war in the North Sea, and was engaged in mine-sweeping and also took part in several engagements. In 1915 he proceeded to the Dardanelles and was present during the Landing of the troops at Gallipoli, and was on board H.M.S. "Triumph" when that vessel was sunk. Fortunately, he was amongst the saved and was still serving in 1920. He holds the 1914-15 Star, and the General Service and Victory Medals.
6, Porson Street, Wandsworth Road, S.W.8.   Z1444C

BURRELL, A. F., Gunner, R.G.A.
He joined in 1916, and was in the same year drafted to France, where he took part in numerous engagements, including those on the Somme and at Ypres, Passchendaele, Cambrai and Amiens. He also served in the Retreat and Advance of 1918, and during his service in France suffered from trench fever. He was demobilised in 1919, and holds the General Service and Victory Medals.
226, Elmhurst Mansions, Clapham, S.W.4.   Z1443

BURRIDGE, W. E., Private, R.A.S.C. (M.T.).
He joined in November 1916, but during his training proved physically unfit for the strain of military service owing to lung trouble. After medical treatment in Bermondsey Military Hospital, he was discharged in February 1917.
28, Philip Road, Peckham, S.E.15.   Z6137

BURROWS, A. E., Trimmer, Royal Navy.
Joining in 1917, he was posted to H.M.S. " Actaeon," in which he served until the cessation of hostilities, engaged on important mine-sweeping duties in the North Sea. After his demobilisation in 1919 he joined the R.H.A. and was stationed in Ireland in 1920. He holds the General Service and Victory Medals.
19, Hubert Grove, Landor Road, S.W.9.   Z1445B

BURROWS, A. T., Private, Queen's Own (Royal West Kent Regiment).
Although under military age he volunteered in September 1914, and early in the following year was sent to the Western Front. In this theatre of war he fought in many important engagements, and was so severely wounded as to necessitate his return to England. On his recovery he was re-drafted to France and was subsequently killed in action near Albert on October 25th, 1916, during the Somme Offensive. He was entitled to the 1914–15 Star, and the General Service and Victory Medals.
14, St. Alphonsus Road, Clapham, S.W.4.   Z1446B

BURROWS, A. W., Private, R.A.S.C.
He joined in March 1916, and during his service on the Western Front did valuable work with his unit in connection with the transport of supplies to our troops in the forward areas. He was demobilised on his return to England in March 1919, and holds the General Service and Victory Medals.
140, Sulgrave Road, Hammersmith, W.6.   11823B

BURROWS, G., Trooper, Lancashire Hussars.
He volunteered in November 1915, and after his training served in Scotland on important duties with his unit. He rendered valuable services, but was not successful in obtaining his transfer overseas on account of his medical unfitness for active service. He was discharged in July 1916 owing to his physical disabilities.   Z5343
3, Harling Cottages, Harling Street, Camberwell, S.E.5.

BURROWS, J. C., Private, Royal Fusiliers and Sapper, R.E.
He joined the Royal Fusiliers in May 1918, and after his training, which he received at Newmarket, was transferred to the R.E. and sent to France. In the capacity of Signaller, he did excellent work in many important sectors during the closing stages of the war, and after the termination of hostilities, advanced into Germany with the Army of Occupation, with which he was still serving at Cologne in 1920. He holds the General Service and Victory Medals.
14, St. Alphonsus Road, Clapham, S.W.4.   Z1446A

BURROWS, M. A. (Mrs.), Special War Worker.
This lady volunteered to release a man for the Colours, and was subsequently engaged at the West Kensington Post Office, where for two years she held an important post. She carried out the duties thus incurred in a thoroughly efficient manner and rendered war service of a valuable nature.
140, Sulgrave Road, Hammersmith, W.6.   11823A

BURROWS, R. A., Rflmn., King's Royal Rifle Corps.
Joining in 1916, he was drafted to the Western Front at the conclusion of his training. Whilst overseas he was in continuously heavy fighting until he was unfortunately killed in action in September 1918, towards the end of the Advance of that year. He was entitled to the General Service and Victory Medals. 19, Hubert Grove, Landor Road, S.W.9. Z1445A

BURT, W. H., Rifleman, King's Royal Rifle Corps.
Volunteering in November 1915, he proceeded to France in January of the following year and there saw much severe fighting. He took part in the Battles of St. Eloi, the Somme, Arras, Vimy Ridge, Ypres, Passchendaele, Cambrai, Bapaume, and Havrincourt and many other important engagements until the cessation of hostilities. He was demobilised on his return home in October 1919, and holds the General Service and Victory Medals.
72, Scylla Road, Peckham, S.E.15.   Z5877

BURTENSHAW, F. H., Driver, R.A.S.C.
He joined in February 1917, and after his training was engaged on important transport work in various parts of England. Owing to being medically unfit for duty abroad he was unable to secure his transfer to a theatre of war, but nevertheless, did valuable work until he was demobilised in March 1919.
22, Camellia Street, Wandsworth Road, S.W.8.   Z1447

BURTON, L. C., Pte., 24th London Regt. (Queen's).
He volunteered in May 1915, and after his training was drafted to Egypt, where he fought in several minor engagements, and was wounded. Later he saw service in Salonika and France, where he also did good work, and was demobilised on his return to England in February 1919. He holds the General Service and Victory Medals.
75, Farmer's Road, Camberwell, S.E.5.   1241C

BURTON, A. E., Pioneer, R.E.
He volunteered in September 1914, and at the conclusion of his training was engaged on important electrical work at Southampton until 1916, when he was sent to France. During his service in this theatre of war, he did valuable work with his unit in the forward areas, and was present at the Battles of the Somme, Ypres and Arras. After the Retreat and Advance of 1918, in which he also took part, he was sent with the Army of Occupation to Germany, where he served for some months. He was demobilised in July 1919, and holds the General Service and Victory Medals.
1, Trott Street, Battersea, S.W.11.   Z1448

BURTON, H. (D.C.M.), Bombardier, R.F.A.
He was in India, when war broke out, and left immediately for the Western Front. He fought in the final stages of the Retreat from Mons and the subsequent Battles of the Marne, the Aisne, Festubert, Loos and the Somme, and was twice wounded. Later he was transferred to German East Africa, where he again took part in several important engagements, and was wounded for the third time. During his service he was awarded the Distinguished Conduct Medal for conspicuous gallantry and devotion to duty, and in addition holds the Queen's and King's South African Medals, the Mons Star, and the General Service and Victory Medals. He was discharged in July 1918, and had completed fifteen years' service with the Colours.
9, Patience Road, Battersea, S.W.11.   Z1450

BURTON, H. C., L/Corporal, 1st London Regiment (Royal Fusiliers).
He volunteered in August 1914, and after his training served on important duties with his unit at various stations. In January 1918, however, he was drafted to the Western Front, where he acted as despatch bearer, and also took an active part in several engagements, including those on the Somme and at Amiens and Cambrai, and in the final Retreat and Advance. He was demobilised on his return to England in March 1919, and holds the General Service and Victory Medals.
35, Solon Road, Acre Lane, S.W.2.   Z1449B

BURTON, J. J., Sergt., Armoured Car Section.
Volunteering in December 1914, he joined up in Canada, and came over to England with one of the first contingents. He was later drafted to the Western Front, and in the course of his service there rose to the rank of Regimental Sergeant-Major, which he forfeited on transferring to the Armoured Car Section. He was subsequently promoted to the rank of Sergeant, and did valuable work during operations in many important sectors until the termination of hostilities, when he advanced into Germany with the Army of Occupation. He holds the 1914–15 Star, and the General Service and Victory Medals, and was demobilised on his return to England in February 1919.
35, Solon Road, Acre Lane, S.W.2.   Z1449A

BURTON, W. B., Private, Middlesex Regiment.
He joined on attaining military age in January 1918, and two months later was sent to the Western Front, where he fought in the Retreat and Advance of that year. During the latter part of his service in France, he was wounded and was in consequence for a time in hospital. He was demobilised in April 1919, and holds the General Service and Victory Medals.
35, Solon Road, Acre Lane, S.W.2.   Z1449C

BURVILL, C. (M.M.), Rifleman, 6th London Regt.
He joined in August 1916, and was sent to France immediately upon the completion of his training. Subsequently he fought in many important battles, notably those of the Somme, Arras, Ypres, St. Quentin, Messines and St. Eloi, and in the Advance at Cambrai in 1917, in which he was severely wounded. During his service he was mentioned in Despatches for his splendid work, and was awarded the Military Medal for an act of conspicuous bravery, in carrying a comrade into safety through a barbed wire entanglement. He returned to England in 1918, and in June of that year was invalided out of the Service. In addition to the decoration won in the Field, he holds the General Service and Victory Medals.
15, Hubert Grove, Landor Road, S.W.9.   Z1451B

BURVILL, H. R., Private, 22nd Manchester Regt.
He volunteered in April 1915, joining in the 16th Middlesex Regiment, and was later transferred to the Manchester Regiment. After his training, he was drafted to the Western Front, but in February 1916, after taking part in several engagements, was invalided home through ill-health. After his recovery, however, he returned to France, where he again went into action, and on September 2nd, 1916, was killed near Albert during the Somme Offensive. He was entitled to the 1914–15 Star, and the General Service and Victory Medals.
15, Hubert Grove, Landor Road, S.W.9.   Z1451A

BUSBY, A. G. E. (M.M.), Sergt., 10th Queen's (Royal West Surrey Regiment).

He volunteered in October 1915, and in the same month was sent to the Western Front. Whilst in this theatre of war he fought at Ploegsteert Wood, the Somme and Flers, and was then sent to Italy, where he did valuable work during operations on the Piave. Later he returned to France and again took part in many important engagements. In September 1917 he was awarded the Military Medal for conspicuous gallantry in capturing an enemy machine-gun single-handed, and in bombing ten German gunners. He also showed great initiative in leading his Platoon into action when his Officer had fallen, successfully reaching the objective and taking a number of prisoners. During his service he was wounded, but remained overseas until after the termination of hostilities. He was demobilised in January 1919, and in addition to the decoration won in the Field, holds the General Service and Victory Medals.
48, Wayford Street, Battersea, S.W.11. Z1452

BUSH, C. H., Gunner, R.F.A.

He volunteered in January 1915, and in June of that year proceeded to the Western Front. Whilst in this theatre of war he fought in many important engagements, including the Battle of Cambrai, was wounded in action in the second Battle of Ypres and again on the Somme. He unhappily died of wounds on March 26th, 1918, and was entitled to the 1914-15 Star, and the General Service and Victory Medals.
"His life for his country, his soul to God."
73, Kenbury Street, Camberwell, S.E.5. Z5885

BUSH, E., R.S.M., R.F.A.

A serving soldier, having enlisted in 1902, he was sent to the Western Front at the outbreak of hostilities, and fought in the Retreat from Mons and the Battle of the Marne. In 1915, owing to ill-health, he was invalided home, and after his recovery, being physically unfit for further foreign service, was engaged on important clerical duties at the War Office. In 1918 he was mentioned in Despatches for consistently good work, and in 1920 was still serving. He holds the Mons Star, and the General Service and Victory Medals.
64, Lollard Street, Kennington, S.E.11. T25765

BUSH, T. R., Driver, R.F.A.

When war broke out he was serving in India, where he afterwards remained until 1918, engaged upon duties of an important nature. He was then sent to Mesopotamia, and subsequently took an active part in several important engagements, including those at Baghdad. Returning to England in 1919, he was demobilised in April of that year, and holds the General Service and Victory Medals.
8, Beech Street, Dorset Road, S.W.8. Z1454A

BUSH, W., Private, R.A.S.C.

He volunteered in January 1915, and after his training served on the Western Front until the termination of hostilities. During this period he did important work with his unit in connection with the issue of rations and ammunition to the troops in the forward areas, and in carrying out these duties was frequently exposed to heavy fire. On his return to England he contracted an illness, and was in consequence for some time in hospital, before he was discharged in February 1919. He holds the 1914-15 Star, and the General Service and Victory Medals.
64, Landseer Street, Battersea, S.W.11. Z1453

BUSHBY, T. W., Rflmn., King's Royal Rifle Corps.

He joined in May 1916, and was drafted to the Western Front in the same year, and took part in severe fighting on the Somme, and at Arras, Ypres, Menin Road, and in many other engagements. He was demobilised in February 1919, and holds the General Service and Victory Medals.
232, Neate Street, Camberwell, S.E.5. Z5345

BUSHBY, W. A., Driver, R.A.S.C.

He joined in May 1916, and after his training served on important duties with his unit and rendered valuable services. He was unfortunately kicked by a mule, which resulted in his death on September 16th, 1916.
"His memory is cherished with pride."
35, Chumleigh Road, Camberwell, S.E.5. Z5314B

BUSHEL, H. J. (M.M.), Gunner, R.F.A.

Volunteering in September 1914, he crossed to France in the following January. He was engaged in the fighting at Neuve Chapelle, Hill 60, Ypres, Loos, and in many other important sectors, and was gassed. In 1917 he was awarded the Military Medal for conspicuous bravery and devotion to duty in the Field, and in addition holds the 1914-15 Star, and the General Service and Victory Medals. He was demobilised on his return to England in June 1919.
66, Meyrick Road, Battersea, S.W.11. Z1455

BUSSEY, R. C., Private, R.M.L.I.

He volunteered in April 1915, and was later drafted to the Western Front, where he fought in several important engagements, notably those at Passchendaele Ridge, Messines, Cambrai and the Somme. In November 1917 he returned wounded to England, and after protracted treatment at various hospitals, was invalided out of the Service in October 1918. He holds the General Service and Victory Medals.
24, Horsman Street, Camberwell, S.E.5. Z1456

BUTCHER, E. J., A.B., Royal Navy.

He was in the Navy when war broke out, having joined in 1900. In 1914 he was transferred to H.M.S. "Marshal Ney," with which vessel he proceeded to the Dardanelles, and subsequently took part in several Naval actions, in one of which he was wounded. Later his ship participated in the Battle of Jutland, in which he was again wounded, and was invalided to Chatham, where he underwent protracted treatment. He holds the National Life Saving Medal, the China (1900) and the Queen's South African Medal, the 1914-15 Star, and the General Service and Victory Medals, and was discharged in January 1919.
38, Doris Street, Kennington, S.E.11. TZ25186

BUTCHER J., Sergt., R.E. (I.W.T.)

He volunteered in August 1914, and was speedily drafted to the Western Front. Whilst in this theatre of war he took part in numerous engagements, including those at Beaulieu and Armentières. Owing to ill-health, he was invalided home in 1915, and on recovery was sent to Mesopotamia, where he again saw much active service. He was taken prisoner in March 1917 by the U38, whilst carrying out engineer's duties on a ship near Algiers. On his release in December 1918, he returned home and was demobilised in January 1919. He holds the 1914 Star, and the General Service and Victory Medals. 103, Vauxhall Street, Kennington, S.E.11. Z24146

BUTCHER, W., Private, R.M.L.I.

He was serving at the outbreak of the late war, having enlisted in 1908, and in the early stages of hostilities was engaged on important duties with units of the North Sea Fleet. Whilst on his way to the Eastern Mediterranean, aboard H.M.S. "Alanza," he unhappily died on November 12th, 1916 from illness brought on by exposure during his service. He was entitled to the 1914-15 Star, and the General Service and Victory Medals. "Great deeds cannot die."
28, Kirkwood Road, Peckham, S.E.15. Z6138A

BUTLER, W., Private, R.A.S.C. (M.T.)

Volunteering in June 1915, he was drafted to France in the same year. He was engaged in various sectors on the transport of supplies, until December 1917, when he was taken ill and invalided home. He was discharged in June 1918, as medically unfit for further service, and holds the 1914-15 Star, and the General Service and Victory Medals.
20, Sandover Road, Camberwell, S.E.5. Z5346

BUTTEN, W., Gunner, R.F.A.

Volunteering in September 1914, he was sent to the Western Front early in the following year. Whilst overseas he fought in many important sectors, notably those of the Somme, Arras and Ypres. In July 1916 he was severely wounded, and on returning to England, underwent protracted hospital treatment before he was invalided out of the Service in 1917. He holds the 1914-15 Star, and the General Service and Victory Medals. 48, Barlow Street, Walworth, S.E.17. Z1461

BUTEUX, A. R., Private, King's Shropshire Light Infantry.

Volunteering in April 1915, he was sent to the Western Front three months later. Subsequently he fought in many important engagements, and in August 1917 was taken prisoner, being held in captivity for eighteen months. Released early in 1919 he returned to England and was demobilised, and holds the 1914-15 Star, and the General Service and Victory Medals.
40, Wayford Street, Battersea, S.W.11. Z1460B

BUTEUX, W. S., Private, East Surrey Regiment.

He volunteered in September 1914, and after his training was sent to the Western Front, where he fought in many important engagements, notably that on the Somme, and was wounded. Later he was drafted to Salonika, and after taking part in several battles there contracted malaria, and was in consequence for some time in hospital. He was demobilised on his return to England in 1919, and holds the 1914-15 Star, and the General Service and Victory Medals.
40, Wayford Street, Battersea, S.W.11. Z1460A

BUTLER, A., Corporal, R.E.

He joined in May 1916, and a year later was sent to the Western Front, where he was engaged on important duties in connection with the Inland Water Transport, and was also present at the Battles of Arras and Cambrai. In the course of his service, he contracted a severe form of pneumonia, of which he subsequently died on February 22nd, 1919. He was entitled to the General Service and Victory Medals.
182, Sheepcote Lane, Battersea, S.W.11. Z1459

BUTLER, A. E., Private, 20th London Regiment.
Volunteering in January 1915, he was drafted to the Western Front six months later. After taking part in several important engagements, including that at Cambrai, he was killed in action at Flesquières on March 24th, 1918, during the German Offensive. He is buried near Bapaume, and was entitled to the 1914–15 Star, and the General Service and Victory Medals.
36, Cunnington Street, Chiswick, W.4. 6880A

BUTLER, B., Petty Officer, R.N.
When war broke out, he was on board H.M.S. "Itchen," in the North Sea. With this ship he subsequently took part in several Naval engagements, notably the Battles of Heligoland Bight and Jutland. On July 6th, 1917 his vessel was torpedoed and sunk. Fortunately he was saved, and was afterwards posted to H.M.S. "Legion," in which he served in the Mediterranean until the termination of hostilities. He was demobilised in 1920, and holds the 1914–15 Star, and the General Service and Victory Medals.
32, Bagshot Street, Walworth, S.E.17. Z1457A

BUTLER, C. E., A.B., Royal Navy.
He volunteered at the age of fourteen in August 1914, and after training was posted to H.M.S. "Queen Mary," in which he eventually lost his life, when she was sunk in the Battle of Jutland on May 31st, 1916. He was entitled to the 1914–15 Star, and the General Service and Victory Medals.
103, Queen Street, Hammersmith, W.6. Z12790B

BUTLER, E., Private, R.A.S.C.
Volunteering in April 1915, he was drafted to the Western Front in the same month. During his overseas service, he did valuable work in many capacities, which included that of a transport driver. He was also attached for a time to the R.E., and the Ammunition and Supply Columns. He was demobilised on his return to England in December 1918, and holds the 1914–15 Star, and the General Service and Victory Medals.
36, Cunnington Street, Chiswick, W.4. 6880B

BUTLER, E. J., L/Corporal, 1st Border Regiment.
A serving soldier, he was engaged upon important duties until the early part of the following year, when he was sent to the Dardanelles. With the 29th Division, he took part in the Ladings at Gallipoli and Suvla Bay, and was later severely wounded at Anafarta Ridge. After the Evacuation of the Peninsula, he was drafted to France, and acting as team leader with the Machine Gun Corps, was wounded at Ypres and at Villers-Bretonneux. Later he served with the 8th Division in the Ardennes sector, and was subsequently taken prisoner at Berry-au-Bac in May 1918. On his release at the termination of hostilities he rejoined his unit, and in 1920 was still serving. He holds the 1914–15 Star, and the General Service and Victory Medals.
12, Neville Street, Vauxhall, S.E.11. Z25444

BUTLER, G. H., Private, Royal Fusiliers.
An ex-soldier, with a previous record of service in India, he volunteered in August 1914. He was later drafted to the Western Front, where he fought almost continuously until he was killed in action at Hill 60, on May 4th, 1915. He was entitled to the 1914–15 Star, and the General Service and Victory Medals.
103, Queen Street, Hammersmith, W.6. 12790A

BUTLER, H. C., Sapper, R.E.
Mobilised with the Territorials, he was engaged on duties of an important nature until he was sent to the Western Front in January 1915. In the capacity of signaller, he took part in several important engagements, including those at Ypres, Armentières and St. Quentin, and throughout his overseas service, which lasted for over three years, did valuable work with his unit. He holds the 1914–15 Star, and the General Service and Victory Medals, and was demobilised in April 1919.
28, Kitson Road, Camberwell, S.E.5. Z1458

BUTLER, H. F., Driver, R.F.A
He volunteered in January 1915, and in the following October was sent to the Western Front, where he served for over three years. During this time he did valuable work with his unit during operations in many important sectors, notably in that of Loos, and was severely wounded. He was then sent home and in February 1919 was invalided out as unfit for further military service, and holds the 1914–15 Star, and the General Service and Victory Medals.
42, Wycliffe Road, Lavender Hill,, S.W.11. Z1183

BUTT, A. E., Private, R.A.S.C. (M.T.).
He attested in 1915, but did not join up until 1916, and after going through his training served on important duties with his unit until 1918, when he was drafted to the Western Front, where he was engaged in the transport of ammunition and supplies to the various sectors of the firing line, including those of Cambrai and the Somme. He was demobilised in 1919, and holds the General Service and Victory Medals.
105, Ferndale Road, Clapham, S.W.4. Z1430B

BUTT, J. G., 2nd Lieutenant, R.A.F.
Joining in 1915, he proceeded in the following year to the Eastern Front, and served in Salonika and Egypt. He took part in many important actions in the air, and his Squadron brought down numerous enemy machines. He returned to England and was demobilised in 1919, and holds the General Service and Victory Medals.
10, Solon New Road, Bedford Road, S.W.4. Z1462

BUTTIVANT, H. W., Rifleman, 12th London Regt. (Rangers).
He volunteered in November 1915, and after his training was drafted to the Western Front. Here he took part in severe fighting at St. Eloi, Albert, Ploegsteert Wood, the Somme and Beaumont-Hamel, where he was gassed and invalided home. On his recovery he returned to France and fought at Passchendaele and Cambrai, and was gassed for the second time during the Retreat of March 1918, on the Somme. He was sent to hospital in England, and in January 1919 was discharged as medically unfit for further service, holding the 1914–15 Star, and the General Service and Victory Medals.
9, Clarence Street, Clapham, S.W.4. Z1463

BUXTON, R. G. M., Private, R.A.O.C.
Volunteering in January 1915, he was drafted to Egypt in the same year. He was engaged as a carpenter on important work with his unit, and rendered valuable services. Later contracting malaria he was invalided home and was discharged as medically unfit for further service in 1916, holding the 1914–15 Star, and the General Service and Victory Medals.
50, Andulus Road, Stockwell, S.W.9. Z1465B

BYATT, A. W. (M.M.), Queen's (Royal West Surrey Regiment).
Joining in February 1916, he was sent to France in the following year, and took part in severe fighting at Vimy Ridge and in other engagements. He also served in the Retreat and Advance of 1918, being in action at Le Cateau and Epéhy, and was twice gassed. He was mentioned in Despatches for gallantry and was awarded the Military Medal for bravery in the Field during a gas attack. He also holds the General Service and Victory Medals, and was demobilised in November 1919.
2, Creek Street, Battersea, S.W.11. Z1466

BYERS, G. H., Private. Queen's Own (Royal West Kent Regiment).
He was serving at the outbreak of war, and early in the following year was drafted to the Western Front, where he took part in several engagements, including those on the Somme. In 1916 he was transferred to Mesopotamia, where he was again in action. He was demobilised in March 1919, and holds the 1914–15 Star, and the General Service and Victory Medals.
166, Beresford Street, Camberwell, S.E.5. Z1467

BYHAM, A. G., Bombardier, R.F.A. and R.G.A.
He volunteered in September 1915, and after his training served on important duties with his Battery until June 1917, when he was sent to the Western Front, where he took part in severe fighting at Vimy Ridge, Messines, Ypres, Passchendaele, Cambrai, and in other engagements. He also served as a range finder for anti-aircraft guns. He was demobilised in June 1919, and holds the General Service and Victory Medals.
41, North Street, Clapham, S.W.4. Z1388B

BYHAM, H. W., Driver, R.F.A.
Volunteering in September 1915, he was drafted to the Western Front in May of the following year. He took part in numerous engagements, including those at Vimy Ridge, the Somme, Arras, Bullecourt, Messines, Ypres, Passchendaele and others. In November 1917 he was transferred to Italy and was in action on the Piave. In February 1918 he returned to France, and served in the Retreat and Advance of 1918. He was killed in action near Ypres on October 2nd, 1918, and was entitled to the General Service and Victory Medals.
41, North Street, Clapham, S.W.4. Z1388A

BYHAM, V. M. (Miss), Special War Worker.
This lady worked in connection with the British Red Cross Society, and was engaged in the needlework department at Victoria, S.W., in making bandages, bed socks, pyjamas and other articles for the sick and wounded at the various hospitals. She rendered valuable services until the conclusion of hostilities.
41, North Street, Clapham, S.W.4. Z1388C

BYRNE, R. T., Corporal, R.A.S.C.
He had served in the South African War in 1901-02, with the R.A.S.C., and volunteered in April 1915. From that date onwards he was engaged on important duties in charge of stores at the 2nd Reserve Home Transport Depôt, Blackheath. He rendered valuable services, but was not successful in securing his transfer overseas while hostilities lasted, and was demobilised in August 1919. He holds the Queen's South African Medal.
46, Lilford Road, Camberwell, S.E.5. Z6144

BYRON, J., Cpl., Westmoreland and Cumberland Hussars.
He joined in November 1916, having been previously rejected, and after his training served at various stations on important duties with his unit. He rendered valuable services, but was not successful in obtaining his transfer overseas before the cessation of hostilities. He was demobilised in January 1919.
19, Kay Road, Stockwell, S.W.9.   Z1468

BYWATERS, H. E., Driver, R.F.A.
A Reservist, he was called to the Colours in August 1914, and was immediately drafted to the Western Front, where he fought in the Battle of Mons. Later he took part in the Battles of the Marne, the Aisne, Ypres, Albert, Arras, Passchendaele, St. Quentin, Bapaume and Amiens, and many other engagements, and also served through the Retreat and Advance of 1918. He was discharged in April 1919, and holds the Mons Star, and the General Service and Victory Medals.
52, Clayton Road, Peckham, S.E.15.   Z5893

C

CABLE, G. (Mrs.), Special War Worker.
From December 1915 until January 1920 this lady rendered valuable service in the employ of the Clapham Post Office, thus releasing a man for military service. Her duties were carried out in an efficient manner and she was commended for her patriotic work.
2, Lillieshall Road, Clapham, S.W.4.   Z1469A

CABLE, W. J., Private, Royal Berkshire Regiment.
Volunteering in September 1914, he was drafted in the following year to the Western Front, where he served for about two months. In January 1916 he proceeded to the East and took part in the fighting on the Vardar, Doiran and Struma fronts. He was invalided to hospital through ill-health and was at Taranto for about one month, going thence to Rouen and finally to England. On recovery he was engaged on special home duties until demobilised in February 1919. He holds the 1914–15 Star and the General Service and Victory Medals.
2, Lillieshall Road, Clapham, S.W.4.   Z1469B

CACKETT, F., Leading Signalman, H.M.S. "King Edward VII."
He was in the Navy at the outbreak of War and served in H.M.S. "King Edward VII." during the naval operations at Gallipoli, the Battle of Jutland and the bombardment of Zeebrugge. Shortly afterwards this vessel was torpedoed, but fortunately he was rescued and transferred to H.M.S. "Dominion." He also served in H.M.S. "Princess Royal" and "Europa" and later on a Torpedo Boat Destroyer. He holds the General Service and Victory Medals, and in 1920 was still serving.
21, Smyrks Road, Walworth, S.E.17.   Z1470A
                                                      Z1471A

CACKETT, W. G., Private, 2nd Northamptonshire Regiment.
He joined in March 1918 and after his training served on important duties at various stations with his unit. He rendered valuable services, but was not successful in obtaining his transfer overseas until after the cessation of hostilities. He was then drafted to India and in 1920 was still serving.   Z1470B
21, Smyrks Road, Walworth, S.E.17.   Z1471B

CAHILL, A., L/Corporal, 4th Buffs (East Kent Regt.)
He joined in August 1916 and in the following year was drafted overseas. Whilst in France he took part in the fighting at Arras and at various other engagememts. In 1918 he was invalided home through ill-health, and after receiving hospital treatment was demobilised in 1919. He holds the General Service and Victory Medals.
13, Lambourne Road, Wandsworth, S.W.4.   Z1472

CAHILL, V. J., Ambulance Driver, Canadian Red Cross.
He joined in July 1917 at 15½ years of age and in the same year proceeded overseas. He served with the Section Sanitaire Anglaise at Verdun, the Argonne and Cambrai on ambulance work, and was twice gassed. He was invalided home, and on recovery served in England on important duties for a time, later returning to France with the Graves Registration Section with which he remained until demobilised in December 1919. He holds the General Service and Victory Medals.
97, Villa Street, Walworth, S.E.17.   Z27450

CAINE, T., Gunner, R.F.A.
He joined in October 1916 and in the following year proceeded to the Western Front. There he was in action in many engagements, including those of Ypres, the Somme and the Retreat and Advance of 1918. In February 1919 he returned home, and was demobilised, holding the General Service and Victory Medals.
10, Kibworth Street, Dorset Road, S.W.8.   Z1473A

CAIRNS, H., Private, 24th London Regiment (The Queen's).
Mobilised in August 1914 he was speedily drafted to the Western Front. Whilst in this theatre of war he fought at Neuve Chapelle, the Somme, Ypres, Cambrai and in many other engagements. He was wounded at Loos and invalided home, and after receiving hospital treatment was discharged as medically unfit in March 1916. He holds the 1914–15 Star and the General Service and Victory Medals.
159, Heath Road, Wandsworth Road, S.W.8.   Z1474

CAKEBREAD, A. E. W., Private, R.A.S.C. (M.T.)
Mobilised in August 1914 he was almost immediately drafted to the Western Front. There he served in the Retreat from Mons, the Battles of the Marne and Aisne, La Bassée, Ypres, the Somme, Messines, Arras, Lens, Cambrai and many other engagements, including the Retreat and Advance of 1918. He returned home in January 1919, and was demobilised, holding the Mons Star and the General Service and Victory Medals.
3, Aylesbury Road, Walworth, S.E.17.   Z1475B

CAKEBREAD, W., 1st Air Mechanic, R.A.F.
Volunteering in May 1915, he proceeded overseas in March of the following year. Whilst in France he did valuable work in the motor shops, and was also engaged on special reconnoitring duties. In September 1919 he returned home, and was demobilised, holding the General Service and Victory Medals.
3, Aylesbury Road, Walworth, S.E.17.   Z1475A

CAKEBREAD, W. E., Pte., 1st Seaforth Highlanders.
He enlisted in May 1914 and proceeded to France in March of the following year. He served in this theatre of war until 1916, when he was drafted to the East. There he was present at the Relief of Kut, the capture of Baghdad, and in many other engagements in this area. Whilst overseas he was twice wounded. He holds the 1914–15 Star and the General Service and Victory Medals, and in 1920 was still serving.
3, Aylesbury Road, Walworth, S.E.17.   Z1475C

CALCUTT, A. J., Private, M.G.C.
He was mobilised in August 1914 and in the following year was drafted to the Dardanelles and took part in the landing at Suvla Bay and the Evacuation of the Peninsula. Later he proceeded to Egypt and served with General Allenby's Forces in Palestine at Gaza and Jerusalem. Whilst overseas he contracted malaria and was in hospital for a considerable time. He returned home in April 1919, and was demobilised, holding the 1914–15 Star, and the General Service and Victory Medals.
1, Pulross Road, Brixton Road, S.W.9.   Z1476

CALDWELL, H., Private, R.A.V.C.
He volunteered in June 1915 and was drafted to Egypt in that year. He rendered valuable services attending to sick and wounded horses during the War and was employed on many fronts. He served at Salonika in 1916, in Italy in 1917, and later in France till 1919. Holding the 1914–15 Star, and the General Service and Victory Medals, he was demobilised in March, 1919.
17, Over Place, Princes Road, Kennington, S.E.11.   Z25461

CALLAWAY, W. J., Private, R.A.O.C. and South Staffordshire Regiment.
He volunteered in October 1915 and was drafted to France in the following month. He was stationed at Le Havre for about ten months and shortly afterwards was transferred to the South Staffordshire Regiment, with which he took part in the fighting at Arras. In March 1917 he was taken prisoner and six months later he died as result of ill-treatment received at the hands of the enemy. He was entitled to the 1914–15 Star. and the General Service and Victory Medals.
13, Frances Street, Battersea, S.W.11.   Z1477

CALLF, J., Private, Queen's Own (Royal West Kent Regiment).
Volunteering in August 1915, he was drafted to Egypt in the following year and later served with General Allenby's forces in Palestine, taking part in the engagements at Jerusalem, Jericho, Tripoli and Aleppo. During his service in this theatre of war he was wounded and after the cessation of hostilities returned home and in June 1919 was demobilised, holding the General Service and Victory Medals.
12, Alfreton Street, Walworth, S.E.17.   Z1478

CALLINGHAM, W. E., Corporal, 3rd Coldstream Guards.
He joined in August 1917 on attaining military age, and on the completion of his training was drafted to France. He was in action in the Second Battle of Cambrai and the engagement on the Sambre, and after the conclusion of hostilities proceeded to Germany with the Army of Occupation, remaining there until November 1919, when he returned home for demobilisation. He holds the General Service and Victory Medals.
11, Matthews Street, Battersea, S.W.11.   Z1479

CALLIS, T., Gunner, R.F.A.

He volunteered in September 1914 and on the completion of his training in 1915 was drafted to Gallipoli, where he served with the mountain batteries at Cape Helles and other places until the evacuation of the Peninsula, when he returned to England. He was then engaged on important duties at various stations until demobilised in 1919. He holds the 1914-15 Star and the General Service and Victory Medals.

15, Ingrave Street, Battersea, S.W.11. Z1296B

CALLOWAY, H., Sapper, R.E.

He volunteered in September 1914 and in February of the following year was drafted to the Western Front. He served at Neuve Chapelle, Hill 60, Ypres and Festubert on important postal duties, and later proceeded to Salonika, where he remained until 1917, when he contracted malaria and was invalided home. On recovery he was engaged on important duties at various stations until demobilised in April 1919. He holds the 1914-15 Star and the General Service and Victory Medals.

58, Elsted Street, Walworth, S.E.17. Z1480

CALNAN, H. (Mrs.), Special War Worker.

For four-and-a-half years during the War this lady held an important position at the Army Pay Office, Hounslow, where she carried out her duties in a most efficient manner and gave entire satisfaction.

31, Duke Road, Chiswick, W.4. 5687A

CALNAN, H. J., Rifleman, Royal Irish Rifles.

He joined in October 1916 and after his training served at various stations on important duties with his unit. He rendered valuable services, but was not successful in obtaining his transfer overseas before the cessation of hostilities. In October 1919 he was demobilised.

31, Duke Road, Chiswick, W.4. 5687B

CAMBRIDGE, J., Sergt., 12th Hampshire Regiment.

Volunteering in September 1914, he proceeded to France on the completion of his training in 1915. Whilst in this theatre of war he fought on the Somme and in other engagements. Later he was drafted to Salonika and saw much active service on the Doiran front. He was killed in action on April 24th, 1917, and was entitled to the 1914-15 Star and the General Service and Victory Medals.

165, Ingrave Street, Battersea, S.W.11. Z1481

CAMERON, N. B., Private, 4th (Queen's Own) Hussars.

He enlisted in September 1902 and on the outbreak of War had already seen much foreign service. In August 1914 he was drafted to the Western Front and was in action at Neuve Chapelle, Ypres and Festubert, and was seriously wounded in July 1915 by the explosion of a shell. He was invalided home and after receiving hospital treatment was discharged as medically unfit in December 1915. He holds the 1914 Star, and the General Service and Victory Medals.

5, Pountney Road, Lavender Hill, S.W.11. Z1482

CAMP, E. H., Air Mechanic, R.A.F.

He joined in July 1916 and in the same year was drafted to Salonika, where he served for two years on important duties on the Struma front, and in many engagements in the Balkan Campaign. During this period he suffered severely from malaria and was sent to hospital in Salonika and later to Malta and thence invalided home. He was discharged as medically unfit for further service in June 1918, and holds the General Service and Victory Medals.

Tindal Street, Lothian Road, S.W.9. Z5235

CAMPBELL, H. W. (Senior), Sapper, R.E., and Private, R.D.C.

He volunteered in December 1914 and after his training was drafted to the Western Front. Later he was transferred to the R.D.C. and was engaged on important duties in connection with the repatriation of disabled prisoners of war. He was demobilised in February 1919, and holds the 1914-15 Star and the General Service and Victory Medals.

71, Westmacott Street, Camberwell, S.E.5. Z3995A

CAMPBELL, H. W. (Junior), Private, Queen's (Royal West Surrey Regiment).

Volunteering in August 1915, he was drafted in the following year to the Western Front. There he took part in the fierce fighting on the Somme and was killed in action in September, 1916. He was entitled to the General Service and Victory Medals.

"Great deeds cannot die."

71, Westmacott Street, Camberwell, S.E.5. Z3995B

CAMPBELL, R., Private, 3rd Essex Regiment.

Joining in March 1916 he proceeded overseas in the following year. Whilst in France he fought in many battles, including those of Arras, Messines, Ypres, Cambrai and the Retreat of 1918, and was unfortunately killed in action near the Aisne on April 11th, 1918. He was entitled to the General Service and Victory Medals.

"His memory is cherished with pride."

107, Darwin Street, Walworth, S.E.17. Z1485

CAMPBELL, R., L/Corporal, Royal Fusiliers.

He volunteered in April 1915 and on the completion of his training proceeded to the Western Front. There he fought in many engagements and was three times wounded and on two occasions was invalided home, but on recovery returned to his unit. He was demobilised in February 1919, and holds the General Service and Victory Medals.

50, Stewart's Road, Battersea Park Road, S.W.8. Z1844

CAMPBELL, S. J., Private, King's Own (Royal Lancaster Regiment).

He enlisted in 1907 and in 1915 was drafted from India to the Western Front. Whilst there he took part in the fighting at Neuve Chapelle, and was wounded and taken prisoner. He was held in captivity until February 1918, when he was released and discharged as medically unfit for further service. He holds the 1914-15 Star and the General Service and Victory Medals.

52, Stewart's Road, Battersea Park Road, S.W.8. Z1483

CAMPION, E. L., Corporal, Queen's (Royal West Surrey Regiment).

Volunteering in September 1914, he was drafted in the following year to the Western Front. There he served with his Regiment as a bomb thrower and was severely wounded at Loos in September 1915 and suffered the loss of his right arm. After being in hospital for some considerable time he was discharged as medically unfit in March 1915. He holds the 1914-15 Star and the General Service and Victory Medals.

31, Auckland Road, Battersea, S.W.11. Z1486

CANE, J. F. W., Sergt., Queen's (Royal West Surrey Regiment).

He was in the Navy at the outbreak of War and took part in the defence of Antwerp, during which he was wounded, and awarded the Croix de Guerre for conspicuous bravery. He was invalided home and after receiving hospital treatment was discharged. Later, however, he joined the Army and after rendering valuable services was again discharged in 1916 as medically unfit for further service. In addition to the Croix de Guerre he holds the 1914-15 Star and the General Service and Victory Medals.

24, Patmore Street, Wandsworth Road, S.W.8. Z1488B

CANFIELD, Q. (Mrs.), Special War Worker.

This lady was engaged at the Ailsa Craig Works, Kew, in the shell department, and later at Woolwich Arsenal as an examiner. Her duties which were of a responsible nature were carried out with great care and efficiency and she rendered valuable services during the War.

2, Quick Road, Chiswick, W.4. 5677A

CANFIELD, W., Driver, R.F.A., and Private, R.A.V.C.

He volunteered in April 1915 and was drafted to the Western Front in the same month. He served in many important engagements, including those at Arras, Ypres and Cambrai, and returning home in August 1918 was discharged in consequence of his services. He holds the 1914-15 Star and the General Service and Victory Medals.

8, Quick Road, Chiswick, W.4. 5677B

CANHAM, A. H., Private., R.A.S.C., and Air Mechanic, R.A.F.

He joined in 1916 and in the same year was drafted to the Western Front and served in the Somme and Arras sectors. He was engaged in motor transport duties in conveying supplies to the various fronts and rendered valuable services. He was later transferred to the R.A.F., with which he served until demobilised in 1919. He holds the General Service and Victory Medals.

35, Mordaunt Street, Stockwell, S.W.9. Z1489C

CANHAM, G. H., Rifleman, 16th London Regiment (Queen's Westminster Rifles).

He volunteered in March 1915 and was drafted to the Western Front in the following year. He took part in several important engagements and was killed in action on the Somme on September 10th, 1916. He was entitled to the General Service and Victory Medals.

35, Mordaunt Street, Stockwell, S.W.9. Z1489A

CANHAM, W. J., Air Mechanic, R.F.A.

He volunteered in December 1914 and after his training served on important duties with his unit until 1916, when he was drafted to the Western Front and was present at the Battle of the Somme. Later in the following year he was transferred to Salonika and thence to Egypt. He afterwards served in Palestine and was in the Advance on Jerusalem. He was demobilised in 1919, holding the General Service and Victory Medals.

35, Mordaunt Street, Stockwell, S.W.9. Z1489B

CANNON, A., Rifleman, 8th London Regiment (Post Office Rifles).

He joined in 1918 and after his training served on important duties with his unit. He rendered valuable services but was not successful in obtaining his transfer overseas before the cessation of hostilities. He was demobilised in 1919.
21, McKerrell Road, Peckham, S.E.15.   Z5920C

CANNON, F. E., Driver, R.F.A.

He volunteered in July 1915 and in March of the following year was drafted to the Western Front, where he took part in numerous engagements, including those at Vimy Ridge, the Somme, Arras, Ypres, Passchendaele and Cambrai. He was demobilised in February 1919, and holds the General Service and Victory Medals.
42, Smyrk's Road, Walworth, S.E.17.   Z1492

CANNON, H. H., Private, 2nd London Regiment (Royal Fusiliers).

He joined in 1916 and was sent to France in the same year and took part in severe fighting at Vimy Ridge, the Somme, Beaumont-Hamel, Bullecourt, Ypres and Cambrai. He was unfortunately killed in action on March 28th, 1918, and was entitled to the General Service and Victory Medals.
" And doubtless went in splendid company."
21, McKerrell Road, Peckham, S.E.15.   Z5920B

CANNON, H. J., Corporal, 4th Royal Fusiliers.

He enlisted in August 1913 and immediately after the outbreak of War was sent to France. He took part in severe fighting in the Retreat from Mons and was in action on the Aisne and at La Bassée, Ypres, Givenchy, Festubert and many other engagements, and was four times wounded. He was invalided home and discharged as medically unfit in August 1917, and holds the Mons Star, and the General Service and Victory Medals.
31, Everett Street, Nine Elms Lane, S.W.8.   Z1490

CANNON, J., Corporal, R.N.D. (Drake Battalion).

He volunteered in 1914 and was sent to Gallipoli, where he took part in the landing in 1915 and was wounded. He was invalided home, but on his recovery proceeded to France in 1916 and served at Vimy Ridge, the Somme and Passchendaele and was again wounded and sent to hospital in England. He was demobilised in 1919, and holds the 1914-15 Star, and the General Service and Victory Medals.
21, McKerrell Road, Peckham, S.E.15.   Z5920A

CANNON, J., Rifleman, 1st King's Royal Rifle Corps.

He was called up from the Reserve in August 1914 and at once proceeded to France, where he fought in the Retreat from Mons and was taken prisoner in the Battle of the Aisne. After internment in many camps during his four years' captivity he was repatriated after the Armistice and demobilised in December, 1918. He holds the Mons Star, and the General Service and Victory Medals.
9, Brymer Street, Camberwell, S.E.5.   Z5578C

CANNON, J., Private, Royal Fusiliers.

He volunteered in August 1914 and shortly afterwards was sent to Malta, where he served on important duties with unit until April 1916, when he was transferred to France. He took part in severe fighting on the Somme and was wounded and suffered the loss of his left arm. He was invalided home and discharged owing to this disability in April 1917, and holds the General Service and Victory Medals.
66, Stainforth Road, Battersea, S.W.11.   Z1769

CANNON, S. W., Corporal, R.A.S.C.

He volunteered in November 1914 and after his training served on important duties with his unit until January 1916, when he was drafted to Salonika, where he served in the Balkan Campaign and was wounded. Later he contracted malaria and was invalided home in March 1918, and on his recovery was stationed at Woolwich. In the following October he was taken suddenly ill and died. He was entitled to the General Service and Victory Medals.
51, Lavender Road, Battersea, S.W.11.   Z1493

CANNON, T. E., Corporal, R.E.

He joined in November 1916 and after his training served at various stations on important duties with his unit. He rendered valuable services but was not successful in obtaining his transfer overseas before the cessation of hostilities. He was demobilised in July, 1919.
18, Kennard Street, Battersea Park Road, S.W.11.   Z1491

CANNON, W. J., Private, 10th London Regiment.

Volunteering in 1915 he was sent to the Dardanelles in the same year. He took part in various engagements and was wounded and invalided home. On his recovery he proceeded to Egypt and thence to Palestine. He was killed in action at Gaza, and was entitled to the 1914-15 Star, and the General Service and Victory Medals.
2, Raywood Street, Battersea Park Road, S.W.8.   Z1494

CANTELL, F., Sergeant, Queen's (Royal West Surrey Regiment).

He was mobilised at the outbreak of War, having previously served in India and China, and was sent to France in September, 1914. He took part in severe fighting at St. Eloi, the Somme and in many other engagements, and later contracting dysentery was invalided home and discharged as medically unfit for further service in October 1918. He holds the 1914 Star, and the General Service and Victory Medals.
12, Tipthorpe Road, Lavender Hill, S.W.11.   Z1495

CANTY, T. (M.M.), Driver, R.F.A.

Volunteering in March 1915 he was sent to France in December of the same year. He took part in numerous engagements, including those at Vimy Ridge, the Somme, the Ancre, Arras, Ypres and Cambrai, and in 1917 was transferred to Italy. Here he served in the campaign against the Austrians and was in action on the Piave. He was awarded the Military Medal for conspicuous bravery in bringing up ammunition on pack mules under heavy shell fire, and also holds the 1914-15 Star, and the General Service and Victory Medals. He was demobilised in February 1919.
24, Benfield Street, Battersea, S.W.11.   Z1496

CAPON, E., L/Corporal, 5th Royal Berkshire Regiment.

He volunteered in September 1914 and in May of the following year was drafted to the Western Front, where he took part in severe fighting at St. Eloi, Ypres and Loos. He was killed in action at St. Eloi on May 17th, 1916, and was entitled to the 1914-15 Star and the General Service and Victory Medals.
" His life for his Country, his Soul to God."
12, White Square, Clapham, S.W.4.   Z1497

CAPP, W., L/Corporal, R.F.A.

He joined in 1916 and after his training served at various stations on important duties with his Battery. He rendered valuable services but was not successful in obtaining his transfer overseas before the cessation of hostilities. He was demobilised in 1919.
85, Wadhurst Road, Wandsworth Road, S.W.8.   Z1498B

CAPSEY, G., Private, Bedfordshire Regiment.

Volunteering in August 1914 he shortly afterwards proceeded to Africa, where he served at various places for nearly three years. He was invalided home in 1917, suffering from sunstroke, and was for some time in hospital at Woolwich. He was discharged as medically unfit for further service in 1917, and holds the 1914-15 Star, and the General Service and Victory Medals.
54, Heaton Road, Peckham Rye, S.E.15.   Z5736B

CAPSEY, G. E., Private, Royal Welch Fusiliers.

He enlisted in 1903 and, on the outbreak of War in August 1914, was serving in China, where he was engaged on important duties at various places. After three years' active service he was unfortunately killed in 1917, and was entitled to the General Service and Victory Medals.
" His memory is cherished with pride."
54, Heaton Road, Peckham Rye, S.E.15.   Z5736A

CARDY, F. R., Guardsman, Coldstream Guards.

Shortly after volunteering in March 1915 he was drafted to the Western Front, where he saw severe fighting at Givenchy and many other places and fought in the Somme Offensive. He was killed in action on September 15th, 1916, and was entitled to the 1914-15 Star, and the General Service and Victory Medals.
" Nobly striving,
He nobly fell that we might live."
154, Albert Road, Peckham, S.E.15.   Z5741

CAREY, C. A., Private, 24th London Regiment (The Queen's).

He volunteered in September 1914 and after completing his training served on important duties with his unit until July 1916, when he was sent to France and took part in severe fighting on the Somme. In November of the same year he was transferred to Salonika and thence to Egypt. He afterwards proceeded to Palestine, where he served in many engagements, including those at Jerusalem, Jericho and Tripoli. He was demobilised in February 1919, holding the General Service and Victory Medals.
7, Charleston Street, Walworth, S.E.17.   Z1499

CAREY, H., Private, Surrey Lancers (Queen Mary's Regiment).

He volunteered in August 1914 and served on important duties with his unit until 1917, when he was drafted to Salonika. Here he served in the Balkan Campaign and took part in various engagements on the Doiran and Vardar Fronts. During his service in the East he contracted malaria and was in hospital for a time. He returned to England, and was demobilised in May 1919, and holds the General Service and Victory Medals.
34, Sussex Road, Coldharbour Lane, S.W.9.   Z1781

CAREY, W., Private, R.A.M.C.

A Reservist, he was called to the Colours in August 1914 and was immediately drafted to the Western Front, where he took an active part in many engagements until July 1915. He was then engaged on clerical work at Rouen for a few months and in 1916 served at the 36th Casualty Clearing Station in the Somme sector. In the following January he was transferred to Arras and later served in the 3rd Army Headquarters until April 1919, when he was discharged. He holds the 1914 Star, and the General Service and Victory Medals.

30, Graylands Road, Peckham, S.E.15. Z5734

CAREY, W. J., Private R.A.S.C., and Essex Regt.

Volunteering in August 1914 he crossed to France in the R.A.S.C. with the first Expeditionary Force, and was wounded at the Battle of the Marne. On his recovery after treatment at home he returned to the Western Front, and later proceeded to Salonika, where he took part in many of the principal engagements. In 1917 he was transferred to Egypt and afterwards fought under General Allenby in the Palestine Campaign, during which he was wounded in action at Aleppo. He was also present at the entry into Jerusalem. He was demobilised in March 1919, and holds the 1914 Star, and the General Service and Victory Medals.

8, Neate Street, Camberwell, S.E.5. Z5055A

CARLESS, R., Corporal, R.A.S.C., and Labour Corps.

He joined in July 1917 and after his training was engaged on important duties at various stations with his unit. He rendered valuable services but was not successful in obtaining a transfer overseas until the cessation of hostilities. He had previously served for two years in the South African Campaign, and holds the Queen's South African Medal.

38, Tindal Street, Lothian Road, S.W.9. Z5236

CARLOSS, F. A., 1st Class Air Mechanic, R.A.F.

Joining in June 1917, he was drafted to Egypt in October of the same year. Here he was engaged with various Squadrons in many parts on important duties. His work, which demanded a high degree of technical skill, was carried out in a most efficient manner and he rendered valuable services. He was demobilised in September 1919, and holds the General Service and Victory Medals.

70, Speke Road, Battersea, S.W.11. Z1500

CARMICHAEL, F., Gunner, R.F.A.

He volunteered in December 1914 and in the following year proceeded to Salonika. There he saw much severe fighting during the Balkan Campaign and took part in many engagements on the Vardar, Doiran and Struma fronts, serving also at the capture of Monastir. He was later stationed for a time in Egypt before returning to England for demobilisation in January 1919. He holds the 1914-15 Star and the General Service and Victory Medals.

5, Claude Road, Peckham Rye, S.E.15. Z5745A

CARMICHAEL, J., L/Corporal, 8th London Regt. (Post Office Rifles).

Volunteering in 1914, he was sent to France in the following year and there took part in severe fighting in various sectors of the Front. He served through the Battles of Ypres, Loos, the Somme, Cambrai and Epéhy and many other important engagements until the cessation of hostilities, when he proceeded with the Army of Occupation into Germany. He was demobilised on his return home in January 1919, and holds the 1914-15 Star, and the General Service and Victory Medals.

5, Claude Road, Peckham Rye, S.E.15. Z5745B

CARMOODY, T. H., Gunner, R.F.A.

Volunteering in April 1915, he was drafted to the Western Front in November of the same year and there saw much severe fighting, taking part in important engagements in various sectors. He fell fighting at Albert on July 26th, 1916, during the Somme Offensive, and was entitled to the 1914-15 Star and the General Service and Victory Medals.

"The path of duty was the way to glory."

5, Ewell Place, Camberwell, S.E.5. Z5727

CARNEY, J. P., Driver, R.F.A.

Volunteering in September 1915, he was drafted to France in June of the following year. He took part in many important engagements, including those on the Somme and at Messines, Ypres and Passchendaele, and also served in the Retreat and Advance of 1918. He was demobilised in February 1919, and holds the General Service and Victory Medals.

66, Webb's Road, Battersea, S.W.11. Z1803

CARPENTER, A. J., L/Corporal, 6th London Regiment (Rifles), and King's Royal Rifle Corps.

He joined in July 1915 and was sent to France in the following year and took part in severe fighting on the Somme and at Ypres, Cambrai and Armentières. He was reported missing on November 30th, 1917 and is believed to have been killed in action on that date. He was entitled to the General Service and Victory Medals.

"His life for his Country, his Soul to God."

30, Gloucester Road, Peckham, S.E.15. Z5907B

CARPENTER, C., Private, R.A.V.C.

He joined in January 1916 and after his training served at various stations on important duties with his unit. He was engaged in looking after sick horses and rendered valuable services, but was not successful in obtaining his transfer overseas before the cessation of hostilities. He was demobilised in March 1919, and holds the General Service and Victory Medals.

72, Scylla Road, Peckham, S.E.15. Z5905

CARPENTER, H. G., Leading Seaman, R.N., "Submarine E.4."

On the outbreak of War he was serving on board H.M.S. "King George V.," but later was transferred to the Submarine E4 and was engaged on patrol duties in the North Sea. On August 14th, 1916, his vessel was in collision with E16 and he was unfortunately killed. He was entitled to the 1914-15 Star, and the General Service and Victory Medals.

"Whilst we remember the Sacrifice was not in vain."

33, Gloucester Road, Peckham. S.E.15. Z5907C

CARPENTER, T. C., 1st Air Mechanic, R.A.F.

He volunteered in August 1914 at the age of 15 and in the following month was sent to the Western Front with the King's Royal Rifle Corps. He took part in severe fighting on the Marne and the Aisne, and at La Bassée, Hooge, Neuve Chapelle, Loos, Ploegsteert Wood, Vimy Ridge and the Somme, and was twice wounded. He was afterwards transferred to the R.A.F. and took part in numerous raids over the enemy's lines, on three occasions being brought down but fortunately escaping serious injury. He was demobilised in June 1919, holding the 1914 Star, and the General Service and Victory Medals.

200, Westmorland Road, Walworth, S.E.17. Z1501

CARPENTER, W. M., Bombardier, R.F.A.

He volunteered in May 1915 and was sent to France in December of the same year. He took part in numerous engagements, including those at Vimy Ridge, the Somme, Arras, Ypres and Passchendaele, and was gassed. After his recovery he returned to his unit and was again in action. He was demobilised in June, 1919, holding the 1914-15 Star, and the General Service and Victory Medals.

33, Gloucester Road, Peckham. S.E.15. Z5907A

CARR, A. E. J., Sergt., 11th Queen's (Royal West Surrey Regiment).

He volunteered in October 1914 and in the following year was drafted to the Western Front and took part in severe fighting on the Somme. He died gloriously on the field of battle on the Somme in 1916, and was entitled to the 1914-15 Star, and the General Service and Victory Medals.

"Steals on the ear the distant triumph song."

75, Stonehouse Street, Clapham. S.W.4 Z1504

CARR, F., Sergt., 3rd Worcestershire Regiment.

Already in the Army when War broke out in August 1914, he proceeded to the Western Front in the following year. There he took part in the Battles of Ypres, the Somme, Arras, Passchendaele, St Quentin and Cambrai, and many other important engagements, and was severely wounded in action in the Retreat of 1918. He was invalided from the Army in January 1919, and holds the 1914-15 Star, and the General Service and Victory Medals.

59, Bournemouth Road, Rye Lane, S.E.15. Z5740

CARR, W. H., Private (Fitter), R.A.S.C. (M.T.)

He volunteered in August 1914 and in the same year was drafted to the Western Front. He served in the Retreat from Mons and was also present at numerous other engagements. He returned home and was demobilised in February 1919, and holds the Mons Star, and the General Service and Victory Medals.

7, St. Philip Street, Battersea Park, S.W.8. Z1503

CARROLL, J., Sergt., R.A.F.

He volunteered in 1915 and proceeded to France in the following year. Whilst in this theatre of war he served at Arras and was engaged as an observer in the Kite Balloon Section. After the cessation of hostilities he returned to England and in January 1919 was demobilised, holding the General Service and Victory Medals.

37, Rutland Street, South Lambeth, S.W.8. Z1505

CARROLL, J. D., Private, R.A.S.C.

He volunteered in 1915 and during his service on the Western Front, which lasted for nearly three years, served in many important sectors, including those of Ypres, the Somme and Arras, engaged in loading and unloading munitions of war at railheads and dumps. He was demobilised in 1919, and holds the 1914-15 Star, and the General Service and Victory Medals.

21, Broomsgrove Road, Stockwell Road. S.W.9. Z4417

CARROLL, W. H., Private, Royal Berkshire Regt.

Volunteering in August 1914 he served on important duties with his unit until the following year, when he was sent to France, where he took part in severe fighting. He was unfortunately killed at Loos on September 25th, 1915, and was entitled to the 1914-15 Star, and the General Service and Victory Medals.

"Thinking that remembrance, though unspoken, may reach him where he sleeps."

1, Rushcroft Road, Brixton, S.W.2. Z1804

CARTER, A., Rifleman, 3rd Rifle Brigade.
Joining in March 1916 he proceeded to France in November of the same year. He took part in severe fighting on the Ancre Front and at Bullecourt, Ypres, Passchendaele and the Aisne. He also served in the Retreat and Advance of 1918 and was wounded at Cambrai in September of that year. He was invalided home and on his recovery served in England until demobilised in May 1919. He holds the General Service and Victory Medals.
12, Grant Road, Battersea, S.W.11.   Z1510A

CARTER, A. E., Private, Oxfordshire and Buckinghamshire Light Infantry.
He volunteered in April 1915 and in the same year was sent to Mesopotamia, where he served in various engagements, including those at Kut-el-Amara, Um-el-Hannah and Baghdad. He was demobilised in December 1919, and holds the 1914-15 Star, and the General Service and Victory Medals.
110, Albert Road, Peckham, S.E.15.   Z5923

CARTER, A. J., Private, R.A.S.C.
He volunteered in April 1915 and in October of the same year was drafted to Mesopotamia and thence to Egypt, where he was engaged on transport duties. In December 1916 he was transferred to the Western Front and served on similar work at Dunkirk and Boulogne. He was demobilised in January 1919, and holds the 1914-15 Star and the General Service and Victory Medals.
12, Grant Road, Battersea, S.W.11.   Z1510B

CARTER, A. L., Private, King's Shropshire Light Infantry.
He enlisted in November 1907 and in 1914 was drafted to the Western Front, where he took part in various important engagements, including that at Ypres, and was severely wounded. He was invalided home and discharged as medically unfit in April 1916, and holds the 1914 Star, and the General Service and Victory Medals.
71, Barlow Street, Walworth, S.E.17.   Z1508

CARTER, C. A., Private, 1st Queen's (Royal West Surrey Regiment) & 7th Gloucestershire Regt.
He enlisted in May 1908 and in November 1914 was sent to France, where he took part in severe fighting at La Bassée and on the Somme, and was wounded and invalided home. On his recovery he was drafted to Mesopotamia and served at Kut, Baghdad and other places. After the Armistice he proceeded to Constantinople, where he served until June 1919, when he returned home and was demobilised, holding the 1914 Star, and the General Service and Victory Medals.
4, Elmington Road, Camberwell, S.E.5.   Z3068

CARTER, C. J., Rifleman, Rifle Brigade.
He volunteered in April 1915 and after his training served at various stations on important duties with his unit. He rendered valuable services but was not successful in obtaining his transfer overseas on account of being medically unfit. He was discharged in February 1916.
9, K Block, Victoria Buildings, Battersea Park Road, S.W.8
Z1512

CARTER, E. (Miss), Special War Worker.
During the war this lady was engaged on work of National importance at the Royal Arsenal, Woolwich. She held an important post as an examiner of fuses, and carried out her responsible duties in a thoroughly efficient manner until her health broke down, and she was obliged to resign in March 1917.
12, Tindal Street, Lothian Road, S.W.9.   Z5054

CARTER, E., 2nd Lieutenant, R.F.A.
He enlisted in September 1901 and proceeded to the Western Front in August, 1914. He took part in heavy fighting at Mons, the Marne, the Aisne, Ypres and Neuve Chapelle, and was gazetted to a Commission in June 1915 in recognition of his splendid services. He died gloriously on the field of battle at Loos on September 25th, 1915, and was entitled to the Mons Star, and the General Service and Victory Medals.
"Nobly striving,
He nobly fell that we might live."
17, Winstead Street, Battersea, S.W.11.   Z1513

CARTER, E. J., Private, 23rd London Regiment.
He volunteered in May 1915 and in the following August was drafted to the Western Front, where he took part in various engagements, including those at Loos, Vimy Ridge, the Somme, Bullecourt, Ypres and Cambrai. He also served in the Retreat and Advance of 1919, and holds the 1914-15 Star, and the General Service and Victory Medals.
14, Abyssinia Road, Battersea, S.W.11.   Z1507

CARTER, F., Private, Tank Corps.
He joined in 1916 and on the completion of his training was drafted to France in 1917. While overseas he did excellent work as a machine gunner at Arras, Cambrai, the Somme and in the Retreat and Advance of 1918. Being badly wounded at Cambrai in September 1918 he was invalided and after several months' hospital treatment returned to his unit and was subsequently demobilised in March 1920. He holds the General Service and Victory Medals.
83, Tappesfield Road, Peckham, S.E.15.   Z6596

CARTER, G. W., Sergt., 3rd East Surrey Regiment.
He re-enlisted at the outbreak of War and in January of the following year was drafted to the Western Front, where he took part in severe fighting at Ypres, Hill 60, Vimy Ridge, Arras and in other engagements. In 1917 he was wounded and invalided home. He was discharged in December of that year as medically unfit, and holds the 1914-15 Star, and the General Service and Victory Medals.
5, Westhall Road, Camberwell, S.E.5.   Z1511

CARTER, O. E. (M.M.), Corporal, Royal Fusiliers.
Volunteering in 1914 he was drafted to France in the following year. He took part in many important engagements, including those at Ypres, Neuve Chapelle, St. Eloi, Hill 60, Loos, the Somme and Passchendaele, and was three times wounded. He was awarded the Military Medal for bravery in the Field, and also holds the 1914-15 Star, and the General Service and Victory Medals. He was demobilised in March 1919.
13, Stanley Street, Battersea Park, S.W.8.   Z1509C

CARTER, S., Petty Officer, Royal Navy.
He enlisted in 1905 and during the recent War served in H.M.S. "Newcastle," "Scythe," "Courageous" and "Orama." In 1914 and 1915 he was engaged with his ship on special duties in Chinese waters, and afterwards in patrolling the Pacific Ocean. For a further period of years he served with the North Sea Patrol, and in 1918 was invalided to the Chatham Military Hospital, where he was for some time under treatment for consumption, which he contracted in the course of his service. He was discharged as medically unfit for further duty in 1919, and holds the 1914-15 Star, and the General Service and Victory Medals.
49, Elliott Road, Stockwell, S.W.9.   Z4413

CARTER, W. J., Private, Royal Fusiliers.
He volunteered in February 1915 and in the same year proceeded to the Western Front, where he saw a few months' severe fighting and took part in the Battle of Loos. In October of the same year he was transferred to the East and, after a few weeks' service in Egypt, went into action at Salonika. He returned to France in January 1918 and took part in the Allied Retreat, when he was gassed and invalided home. On his recovery in September of that year, he was again drafted to the Western Front and saw much further heavy fighting before the cessation of hostilities. He was demobilised on his return home in March 1919, and holds the 1914-15 Star, and the General Service and Victory Medals.
66, Geneva Road, Coldharbour Lane, S.W.9.   Z5744

CARTWRIGHT, C., Driver, R.F.A.
He volunteered in November 1914 and in the following year was drafted to France, where he did good work as a driver in the Royal Field Artillery in various engagements, notably at Loos, Arras, Ypres and the Somme. He was demobilised in May 1919, and holds the 1914-15 Star, and the General Service and Victory Medals.
63, Westmacott Street, Camberwell, S.E.5.   Z3996A

CARTWRIGHT, E. (Miss), Special War Worker.
During the war this lady was engaged on important duties as a wallet manufacturer in connection with gas masks at Messrs. Spicers, Borough High Street. She did excellent work and on relinquishing her post in December 1918, after the cessation of hostilities, was highly commended for her skill and efficiency.
65, Westmacott Street, Camberwell, S.E.5.   Z3996B

(V.C.) CARTWRIGHT, G., Private, 33rd Battalion Australian Imperial Forces.
Volunteering at Elsinore, Australia, in December 1915 he proceeded to the Western Front in 1916 and served there for two years. During this period he played a conspicuous part in the fighting and was three times wounded and gassed. He was awarded the Victoria Cross for supreme gallantry and devotion to duty during an attack near Bouchavesnes on August 31st, 1918. Two companies of his Battalion were held up by a withering machine gun fire but Private Cartwright with a sublime disregard for personal safety advanced towards the gun and successively shot three Germans who attempted to man it. Then, throwing a bomb, he rushed on the post and captured the gun together with nine of the enemy. This glorious act of gallantry had a most inspiring effect on our troops and the line advanced. He received his decoration from H.M. the King at Buckingham Palace on March 8th, 1919, and in addition holds the General Service and Victory Medals. He was demobilised in June 1919 and returned to Australia.
65, Westmacott Street, Camberwell, S.E.5.   5413

CARVELL, W. A., Private, Royal Fusiliers.
Volunteering in November 1914 he was soon drafted to the Western Front, and saw much service. He fought in the Battles of Neuve Chapelle, St. Eloi, Ypres, the Somme, Arras and Cambrai, and in various later engagements. During his service overseas he was wounded five times and also gassed in action. He returned home and was demobilised in April 1919, and holds the 1914-15 Star, and the General Service and Victory Medals.
16, Randall Street, Battersea, S.W.11.   Z1514

CASPARD, S., Driver, R.G.A.

Volunteering in April 1915 he crossed to France in the following November. During his service he fought at Loos, Vimy Ridge, Ypres, the Somme and Armentières, and also in the Retreat and Advance of 1918. When hostilities ended he was sent to England for leave, at the conclusion of which he returned to France. On April 5th, 1919, he was unfortunately run over by a motor lorry at Lille and killed. He was entitled to the 1914-15 Star, and the General Service and Victory Medals.

35, Harling Street, Camberwell, S.E.5 Z5347

CASEY, W., Private, 2nd Queen's (Royal West Surrey Regiment).

He volunteered in August 1915 and in the following year was sent overseas and served in various engagements in France until 1917, when he was drafted to Italy. Whilst in this theatre of war he fought in the operations on the Piave and on the Asiago Plateaux, and in the second great offensive on the Piave in 1918. He remained in Italy until after the Armistice was signed, and unhappily died on his return home in 1919. He was entitled to the General Service and Victory Medals.

24, Offley Road, Brixton Road, S.W.9. Z5254

CASS, W. G., Private, 4th Middlesex Regiment.

Three months after volunteering in March 1915 he was drafted to France, where he saw much severe fighting in various sectors of the Front. After taking part in the Battle of Ypres and many other important engagements, he was very severely wounded in action on the Somme. He unfortunately died on the following day, September 29th, 1916, and was entitled to the 1914-15 Star, and the General Service and Victory Medals.

"Honour to the immortal dead who gave their youth that the world might grow old in peace."

17, Cator Street, Peckham, S.E.15. Z5735B

CASTLE, A. E., Private, 1st Queen's (Royal West Surrey Regiment).

He was mobilised at the outbreak of war and was almost immediately sent to France, where he took part in the Retreat from Mons and was wounded. After his recovery he served in other early engagements, and was killed in action at La Bassée on October 23rd, 1914. He was entitled to the Mons Star, and the General Service and Victory Medals.

87, Gwynne Road, Battersea, S.W.11. Z1515A

CASTLE, A. H. C., Private, 15th Hampshire Regt.

He joined in March 1917 and after his training served at various stations on important duties with his unit. In 1918 he was drafted to France and fought in numerous engagements during the Retreat and Advance of that year, including those of the Marne, Amiens and Bapaume, and was three times wounded. He was demobilised in February 1919, and holds the General Service and Victory Medals.

111, Lavender Road, Battersea, S.W.11. Z1516

CASTLE, G., Private, Queen's (Royal West Surrey Regiment).

He joined in October 1916 and early in the following year was drafted to France. Whilst in this theatre of war he took part in many important battles, including those on the Somme and at Arras and Cambrai, and in various subsequent engagements. He was demobilised in September 1919, and holds the General Service and Victory Medals.

16, Vicarage Road, Camberwell, S.E.5. Z1800

CASTLETON, H. W., Private, 1st Suffolk Regt.

He volunteered in November 1914 and in the following January was drafted to France. There he served only one month and was then taken prisoner in an engagement near Arras in February 1915. He was held in captivity in Germany for nearly four years, and after his release and repatriation was demobilised in February 1919. He holds the 1914-15 Star, and the General Service and Victory Medals.

27, Westhall Road, Camberwell, S.E.5. Z1517

CASTLING, H. A., Rflmn., King's Royal Rifle Corps.

He joined in August 1916 and in the following November was drafted to the Western Front. During his service in France he fought on the Ancre and at Arras, Vimy Ridge, Messines and Bullecourt. Afterwards he was reported missing and was later presumed to have been killed in action on July 10th, 1917. He was entitled to the General Service and Victory Medals.

"Great deeds cannot die."

7, Elsted Street, Walworth, S.E.17. Z1518

CATCHPOLE, W. H., Private, 13th East Surrey Regt., M.G.C. and 1st Wiltshire Regt., and Rifleman, Rifle Brigade.

He volunteered in July 1915 at the age of sixteen years and in the following year was drafted to France, where he fought at Hulluch and Albert, and was wounded. He was invalided home and after his recovery was transferred to the 1st Wiltshire Regiment and returned to the Western Front. He gave his life for King and Country on April 3rd, 1918, and was entitled to the 1914-15 Star, and the General Service and Victory Medals.

"His memory is cherished with pride."

20, Newby Street, Wandsworth Road, S.W.8. Z1519

CATLIN, E. S., Sapper, R.E.

Mobilised in September 1914 he crossed to France in the same month and did important work as a motor despatch rider during the Battles of the Marne and the Aisne. He also served at Loos, where he was gassed in September 1915, at Ypres and in the Somme Offensive, during which he was again gassed, and was subsequently under treatment at Rouen for some time. He was demobilised in March 1919 on returning to England, and holds the 1914 Star, and the General Service and Victory Medals.

22, Calmington Road, Camberwell, S.E.5. Z5348

CATMULL, H., Driver, R.E.

He volunteered in October 1914 and in January 1916 was drafted to the Western Front, where he saw much severe fighting. He took part in the first and second Battles of the Somme and many minor engagements, and was wounded in action in the Retreat of 1918. He was in hospital for a short time in France and later served through the Advance, fighting in the second Battles of Le Cateau and Mons. He was demobilised in February 1919, and holds the General Service and Victory Medals.

181, Albert Road, Peckham, S.E.15. Z5738

CATTERMOLE, F. C., 1st Air Mechanic, R.A.F.

He joined in January 1916 and in the same year was drafted to Russia. Whilst in this theatre of war he served on important and skilled duties with his Squadron, and was mentioned in Despatches for his excellent work. In 1917 he returned to England but shortly afterwards was sent to France, where he was in action until the cessation of hostilities. He holds the General Service and Victory Medals.

1, Bognor Street, Wandsworth Road, S.W.8. Z1617A

CATTON, W. A., Private, 5th Suffolk Regiment.

He was serving at the outbreak of war and in 1915 proceeded to Gallipoli, where he took part in the Landing at Suvla Bay and was wounded. He was invalided home and was discharged as medically unfit for further service in July 1917, holding the 1914-15 Star and the General Service and Victory Medals.

7, D Block, Lewis Trust Buildings, Camberwell, S.E.5. Z5918

CAVE, H. C. (M.M.), Sapper, R.E.

He was mobilised at the outbreak of war, and was almost immediately drafted to France and took part in the Retreat from Mons. Later he was sent to the Dardanelles and served in the Gallipoli Campaign. On the Evacuation of the Peninsula he returned to the Western Front and took part in the Battles of the Somme, Ypres and Cambrai, and was four times wounded. He was awarded the Military Medal for conspicuous gallantry and devotion to duty on the Field, and also holds the Mons Star, and the General Service and Victory Medals. In 1920 he was still serving with the Colours.

63, Stockdale Road, Wandsworth Road, S.W.8. Z1487B

CAVILLA, R. J., Rifleman, 21st London Regiment (1st Surrey Rifles).

He volunteered early in 1915 at the age of sixteen and was drafted to France two years later. Whilst overseas he fought in several important engagements, and in the Retreat and Advance of 1918, towards the close of which he was wounded and gassed. After being invalided home he was demobilised in 1919, and holds the General Service and Victory Medals.

56, Bournemouth Road, Rye Lane, S.E.15. Z5349

CAWSON, R. J., 1st Air Mechanic, R.A.F.

He joined in May 1916 and after his training served at a School of Aerial Gunnery on important special duties which demanded a high degree of technical proficiency. He did excellent work and, owing to his ability in this branch of service, was unable to secure a transfer overseas. He was demobilised in 1919.

2, Tasman Road, Landor Road, S.W.9. Z1520

CHADD, B., Sergt., 9th Norfolk Regiment.

He volunteered in October 1914 and in August 1915 was sent to France, where he took part in severe fighting at Loos and in various other engagements. He fell fighting at the Battle of the Somme on October 18th, 1916, and was entitled to the 1914-15 Star, and the General Service and Victory Medals.

"His life for his Country, his Soul to God."

35, Blake's Road, Peckham, S.E.15. Z5909

CHADWICK, G., Corporal, R.F.A.

He volunteered in October 1914 and in the following March was sent to the Western Front. Here he fought in many important battles, including those at Neuve Chapelle, St. Eloi, Hill 60, Ypres, Festubert, Loos, Albert, Vimy Ridge, the Somme, Arras, Messines and Cambrai. In March 1918, during the Retreat, he was very severely gassed in action and was invalided home to hospital. Unfortunately he died from the effects on July 15th, 1918, and was entitled to the 1914-15 Star, and the General Service and Victory Medals.

"A costly sacrifice upon the altar of freedom."

16, Wooler Street, Walworth, S.E.17. Z1521C

CHADWICK, J. J., Corporal, 18th London Regt., London Irish Rifles and R.A.P.C.

He volunteered in November 1915 and after his training served at various stations on important duties in the Clerical Department of the Quartermaster's Stores. He was later transferred to the Royal Army Pay Corps and rendered valuable services in this unit until demobilised in March, 1919.
16, Wooler Street, Walworth, S.E.17.   Z1521A

CHADWICK, R. K. (Miss), Special War Worker.

From 1916 onwards this lady voluntarily devoted her time to assisting at the Munitions' Canteen at Farnborough. The services which she rendered in this connection were greatly appreciated.
16, Wooler Street, Walworth, S.E.17.   Z1521B

CHAFFE, G. F., Private, Queen's (Royal West Surrey Regiment).

Volunteering in September 1915 he was sent to France on the completion of his training in May 1916. He took part in the fighting in the Battles of the Somme and Ypres, and was severely wounded. He was invalided home to hospital, and was discharged as physically unfit for further military service in December 1917. He holds the General Service and Victory Medals.
23, Sheepcote Lane, Battersea, S.W.11.   Z1522B

CHAFFE, W. H., Leading Stoker, Royal Navy.

A serving sailor, since July 1910, he was posted for duty with his ship in the North Sea on the outbreak of War. He was in action in the Battle of Jutland and in all the important operations at sea, including the Raid on Zeebrugge. After the cessation of hostilities he returned home and in 1920 was discharged as time-expired. He holds the 1914–15 Star, and the General Service and Victory Medals.
23, Sheepcote Lane, Battersea, S.W.11.   Z1522A

CHAINEY, C., L/Corporal, 2nd Dorsetshire Regt.

He volunteered in 1914 and in the following year was drafted to the Dardanelles and after valuable service there to the Western Front. During his service in France he was in action in numerous engagements and was severely wounded during the Battle of the Somme and later reported missing. Afterwards he was presumed to have been killed in action on July 1st, 1916. He was entitled to the 1914–15 Star, and the General Service and Victory Medals.
"The path of duty was the way to glory."
49, Seaham Street, Wandsworth Road, S.W.8.   Z1523A

CHAINEY, F., Private, 2nd Buffs (East Kent Regiment).

Volunteering in 1914, at the outbreak of hostilities, he was drafted to France at the conclusion of his training in the following year. He served in the Battle of Ypres, and was taken prisoner at Arras and sent to Germany. There he was held in captivity until the Armistice, when he was released and returning to England was demobilised in 1919, holding the 1914–15 Star, and the General Service and Victory Medals.
49, Seaham Street, Wandsworth Road, S.W.8.   Z1523B

CHAINEY, G., Gunner, R.F.A.

He was serving in India at the outbreak of war and was drafted to Mesopotamia in the following year. After valuable service there he proceeded to France and did excellent work as a Gunner in numerous important engagements until the cessation of hostilities. He was demobilised in March 1919, and holds the 1914–15 Star, and the General Service and Victory Medals.
49, Seaham Street, Wandsworth Road, S.W.8.   Z1523C

CHALK, J. K., Private, Royal Marine Light Infantry.

He was serving at the outbreak of war, having enlisted in the Royal Marines in 1897. He was posted to H.M.S. "Victorious," with which he served until April 1915, when he was transferred to H.M.S. "Sirius." Whilst in these vessels he was engaged on patrolling duties off the Belgian Coast. He also served in France for a time. After the cessation of hostilities he was demobilised in February 1919, and holds the 1914–15 Star, and the General Service and Victory Medals.
76, Este Road, Battersea, S.W.11.   Z1524

CHALKER, A., A.B., R.N., H.M.S. "Ajax."

He had joined the Navy in 1912, and at the outbreak of hostilities was sent to the North Sea, where his ship was engaged on dangerous patrol duties. He also took part with H.M.S. "Ajax" in the Battle of Jutland and the Raid on Zeebrugge, and in subsequent important Naval operations. He was discharged from the Navy in 1919, and has since joined the Mercantile Marine. He holds the 1914–15 Star, and the General Service and Victory Medals.
22, Porson Street, Wandsworth, S.W.8.   Z1502A

CHALLINOR, J. J., Staff-Sergt., 10th Canadian Regt.

He volunteered in August 1914 and was drafted to France with the first Canadian contingent. During his service on the Western Front he fought in many important engagements, including those at Neuve Chapelle, St. Eloi, Hill 60 and Ypres, and was severely gassed. He was invalided home, and subsequently succumbed in August 1915. He was entitled to the 1914–15 Star, and the General Service and Victory Medals.
"His memory is cherished with pride."
16, Acanthus Road, Lavender Hill, S.W.11.   Z1525

CHAMBERLAIN, C., Private, Middlesex Regiment.

He volunteered in November 1915 and in the same year was drafted to Mesopotamia and whilst in this theatre of war took part in the Relief of Kut and in the Capture of Baghdad. Later he proceeded to Egypt and served in the Palestine Campaign with General Allenby's Forces, being present at the entry into Jerusalem. He was demobilised after his return to England in October 1919, and holds the 1914–15 Star, and the General Service and Victory Medals.
9, Clarence Street, Clapham, S.W.4.   Z1526

CHAMBERLIN, J. E., 1st Class Petty Officer, R.N., H.M.S. "Sapphire."

He volunteered at the outbreak of war and was posted to H.M.S. "Sapphire" and sent to the North Sea. Whilst on board this ship he took part in various engagements, including the Naval operations in the Dardanelles, where he served in covering the landing of the troops in Gallipoli. He holds the 1914–15 Star, and the General Service and Victory Medals, and in 1920 was still serving.
30, Bellefields Road, Stockwell Road, S.W.9.   Z1527

CHAMBERLAIN, T. H., Driver, R.F.A.

He volunteered in 1914 and after six months' service was discharged as physically unfit. However, he rejoined in September 1916, and three days later was sent to France. He was in action in the Battle of the Somme, and at Vimy Ridge and numerous other engagements, and was gassed. During the fighting at Ypres a shell exploded amongst his gun team and he was kicked by a wounded horse and severely injured. He was invalided home and after eighteen months' treatment in hospital was discharged as medically unfit for further service in February 1919. He holds the General Service and Victory Medals.
2, Wesley Place, Newington Butts, S.E.11.   Z26173

CHAMBERS, E., Driver, R.F.A.

Volunteering in January 1915 he was sent to the Western Front in the following October. During his service in France he took part in the engagements at Albert, Vimy Ridge, the Somme, Beaumont-Hamel, Arras, Messines, Ypres and Bullecourt, and was severely wounded at Ypres in 1917. He was invalided to hospital for about seven months, and was subsequently discharged as unfit for further military duty in February 1918. He holds the 1914–15 Star, and the General Service and Victory Medals.
155, Chatham Place, Walworth, S.E.17.   Z1529

CHAMBERS, T., Cook, R.N., H.M.S. "Norman."

He volunteered in August 1914 and was posted as ship's cook to H.M.S. "Norman," which was engaged in conveying troops to Salonika, Egypt and Mesopotamia. He was later employed on the hospital ship "Valdovina," which was carrying wounded from the Eastern Front. He was demobilised in May 1919, and holds the General Service, Victory and Mercantile Marine War Medals.
155, Chatham Street, Walworth, S.E.17.   Z1528

CHAMMINGS, H. F., Rifleman, 10th King's Royal Rifle Corps.

Volunteering in May 1915 he crossed to France later in the year and took part in many important engagements, including those at Loos and Ploegsteert Wood. He was wounded and taken prisoner near Zillebeke in August 1916, and remained in German hands until the Armistice, when he was repatriated. He was demobilised in January 1919, holding the 1914–15 Star, and the General Service and Victory Medals.
96, Copeland Road, Peckham, S.E.15.   Z5579

CHAMP, W. H., Private, M.G.C.

Joining in June 1917 he was sent to the Western Front in the following May. He took part in many important engagements during the concluding stages of the War, and afterwards advanced into Germany with the Army of Occupation. He holds the General Service and Victory Medals, and was demobilised on his return to England in September 1919.
22, Tennyson Street, Wentworth Road, S.W.8.   Z1530

CHAMPION (Mrs.), Special War Worker.

This lady volunteered in order to release a man for service with the Colours, and throughout the War held an important and responsible post at Victoria Station, carrying out the duties thus incurred in a thoroughly capable and efficient manner.
48, Gonsalva Road, Wandsworth Road, S.W.8.   Z1532J

CHAMPION, G. F., Gunner, R.G.A.
Volunteering in December 1914 he was sent to France early in the following year. Whilst overseas he took an active part in many important engagements, including the Retreat and Advance of 1918, and was wounded. After the termination of hostilities he returned to England, and in 1920 was serving with his unit on Salisbury Plain. He holds the 1914–15 Star, and the General Service and Victory Medals.
48, Gonsalva Road, Wandsworth Road, S.W.8.   Z1532B

CHAMPION, H., Private, R.A.S.C., and Labour Corps.
He volunteered in February 1915 and was sent to France in the same month. Throughout his service overseas he was engaged on important duties in connection with the unloading of food supplies for our troops, and in this capacity was stationed at Boulogne, Calais, Rouen and Dickebusch. Owing to illhealth, he returned to England in July 1918, and in the following November was invalided out of the Service. He holds the 1914–15 Star, and the General Service and Victory Medals.
78, Smyrk's Road, Walworth, S.E. 17.   Z1531

CHAMPION, J. E., Driver, R.E.
He volunteered in March 1915 and during his service on the Western Front did valuable work as an engine driver on the light railway conveying troops, ammunition and rations to the forward areas. On one occasion he was wounded. He was demobilised on his return to England in March, 1919, and holds the 1914–15 Star, and the General Service and Victory Medals.
48, Gonsalva Road, Wandsworth Road, S.W.8.   Z1532A

CHAMPION, J. W., Leading Seaman, R.N.
Having enlisted in 1910 he was in the Navy when war broke out, and from 1914 until after the cessation of hostilities served on board H.M.S. "Royal Oak." With this ship he took part in several Naval battles, notably that of Jutland, and was also engaged on important patrol duties. He holds the 1914–15 Star, and the General Service and Victory Medals, and in 1920 was still serving.
48, Gonsalva Road, Wandsworth Road, S.W.8.   Z1532C

CHAMPKINS, E. M. (M.S.M.), Gunner, R.F.A., and Private, Labour Corps.
He volunteered in August 1915 and after his training was engaged on duties of an important nature with his unit. He was unable to secure his transfer overseas, but nevertheless rendered valuable services, for which he was awarded the Meritorious Service Medal. He was demobilised in December 1918.
73A, Silverthorne Road, Wandsworth Road, S.W.8.   Z1533

CHANCE, S. J., Private, 1st Welch Regiment.
Joining in May 1916 he was sent to Salonika three months later and subsequently fought in many important engagements on that Front, including the Advance across the Struma. He returned to England in 1918, and in September of the following year was demobilised. He holds the General Service and Victory Medals.
5, Coleman Road, Camberwell, S.E.5.   Z4419

CHANDLER, F. J., Rifleman, King's Royal Rifle Corps.
Joining in 1916 he was drafted to the Western Front at the conclusion of his training, and after taking part in many of the principal battles, was killed in action near Bapaume on August 21st, 1918, during the Advance of that year. He was entitled to the General Service and Victory Medals.
10, Dieppe Street, West Kensington, W.14.   16254B

CHANDLER, G. A., L/Corporal, Bedfordshire Regt.
He volunteered at the commencement of hostilities and early in 1915 was sent to the Western Front. During his service in this theatre of war he fought in many important engagements, but was unfortunately killed in action at Loos in September 1915. He was entitled to the 1914–15 Star, and the General Service and Victory Medals.
92, Minford Gardens, West Kensington, W.14.   11566A

CHANDLER, J. E. J., Rifleman, Rifle Brigade.
He joined in December 1916 and at the conclusion of his training was sent to the Western Front. His overseas' service lasted for only a few months, however, owing to ill-health, and on his return to England in November 1917 he was discharged. He holds the General Service and Victory Medals.
92, Minford Gardens, West Kensington, W.14.   11566B

CHANDLER, S. F., Air Mechanic, R.A.F.
He joined in July 1916 and after his training was engaged on duties of an important nature, which demanded much technical knowledge and skill. In December 1918 he was sent to Mesopotamia, where he was engaged in repairing and keeping in order aeroplanes ready for flight, and was present at engagements at Baghdad and Kut. He was demobilised on his return to England in September 1919, and holds the General Service and Victory Medals.
1, Albert Mansions, Bromell's Road, Clapham, S.W.4.   Z1534

CHANDLER, W. F., A.B., Royal Navy.
He volunteered in December 1915 and after his training proceeded on board the "Macedonia" to German East Africa, where he subsequently served for two years. During this time he was engaged on special duties in connection with the loading of ships with coal, and on his return to England in February 1918 was discharged. He holds the General Service and Victory Medals.
29, Runham Street, Walworth, S.E.17.   Z1535

CHANNER, J. A., Private, 5th Essex Regiment.
He joined in June 1916 and after his training was engaged on important agricultural duties at various stations. Owing to ill-health he was unable to secure his transfer overseas, but nevertheless did valuable work until he was demobilised in March 1919.
326, East Street, Walworth, S.E.17.   Z1536

CHANTRY, B., Private, Royal Fusiliers.
He joined in May 1917 and in the following January was sent to the Western Front. Subsequently he fought in several important engagements, including those on the Somme, at Bapaume and Cambrai. In March 1918 he was gassed and also suffered from shell-shock, and was in consequence for some time in hospital. After his recovery, however, he rejoined his unit and served in the concluding stages of the War. He was demobilised on his return to England in March 1919, and holds the General Service and Victory Medals.
15J, Peabody Estate, Rodney Road, Walworth, S.E.17.   Z1537

CHAPMAN, A. G., Private, 17th Royal Fusiliers.
He joined in May 1918, after having been previously engaged on important munition work, and in the following September was sent to the Western Front, where he fought in the Battles of Cambrai and Ypres and other engagements in the Advance of that year. After the termination of hostilities he was sent with the Army of Occupation to Cologne, and on his return to England in November 1919 was demobilised. He holds the General Service and Victory Medals.
25, Harris Street, Camberwell, S.E.5.   Z4421

CHAPMAN, A. J., Rifleman, 6th London Regiment.
Mobilised with the Territorials at the outbreak of war he was quickly drafted to the Western Front, where he took part in the Retreat from Mons and the engagements which followed. During his overseas service he was wounded three times, and was taken prisoner in the Advance of 1918. After his release in November 1918 he returned to England and was demobilised, and holds the Mons Star, and the General Service and Victory Medals.
46, Smyrk's Road, Walworth, S.E.17.   Z1539

CHAPMAN, F., Private, 23rd London Regiment.
He volunteered in July 1915 and after his training was drafted to the Western Front, where he fought in engagements at Hill 60, Ypres, Loos, St. Eloi and Vermelles. Later he saw service in Salonika and did valuable work with his unit during operations on the Doiran front. He was demobilised on his return to England in December 1918, and holds the 1914–15 Star, and the General Service and Victory Medals.
26, Clarence Street, Clapham, S.W.4.   Z1541

CHAPMAN, J., Private, Yorkshire Regiment.
Volunteering in October 1914 he was sent to the Western Front early in the following year. He took part in several engagements in this theatre of war, notably those at Ypres, the Somme and Arras, but later was admitted into hospital in consequence of an illness contracted in the service. After his recovery he was retained at the Base and was engaged on special guard duties until the termination of hostilities. He was demobilised on his return to England in January 1919, and holds the 1914–15 Star, and the General Service and Victory Medals.
50, Bellefield Road, Stockwell Road, S.W.9.   Z1538A

CHAPMAN, J. H., Rifleman, 17th London Regiment (Rifles).
He joined in February 1918 and after his training was engaged on duties of an important nature with his unit. He was not successful in obtaining his transfer overseas before the termination of hostilities, but nevertheless rendered valuable services until he was demobilised in October 1919.
45, Maysoule Road, Battersea, S.W.11.   Z1543

CHAPMAN, L. J., Sergt.-Major, Army Gymnastic Staff.
He volunteered at the commencement of hostilities and early in 1915 was drafted overseas. During his service in France he was attached to the Australian Army as an Instructor, and also went into action with it on the Somme and at Ypres and Arras. Throughout the War he did valuable work, and was demobilised in 1919. He holds the 1914–15 Star, and the General Service and Victory Medals.
98, Sandmere Road, Clapham, S.W.4.   Z1770

CHAPMAN, W., Private, 24th London Regiment (Queen's).
Volunteering in November 1915 he was drafted to the Western Front in the following June, and was engaged on important duties in connection with rations and supplies. Later, in the same capacity, he served in Salonika, Egypt and Palestine, where he did valuable work throughout that campaign. He was demobilised on his return to England in February 1919, and holds the General Service and Victory Medals.
32, Edmund Street, Camberwell, S.E.5.　　Z4420

CHAPMAN, W. J., Corporal, R.E.
Volunteering in November 1915 he was drafted to the Western Front in the following year. Whilst overseas he was engaged on important duties, chiefly in connection with the Inland Water Transport, and in this capacity rendered valuable services He was demobilised in March 1919, and holds the General Service and Victory Medals.
43, Ingelow Road, Battersea Park, S.W.8.　　Z1540

CHAPPELL, A. W., Private, Royal Fusiliers.
He volunteered in August 1914 and after his training served for the remaining period of hostilities in France, where he fought in most of the principal engagements. He was demobilised on his return to England in February 1919, and holds the 1914-15 Star, and the General Service and Victory Medals.
28, Rockley Road, West Kensington, W.14.　　11815C

CHAPPELL, J. E., Driver, R.F.A.
He volunteered on two occasions at the commencement of War, but was each time claimed out by his parents on account of his being under age. In 1917, however, he again joined, and after his training was engaged on important duties at various stations with his unit. He was unable to secure his transfer overseas before the termination of hostilities, but afterwards was sent with the Army of Occupation to Cologne, where he served until November 1919. He was demobilised a month later.
5, Denyer Street, Chelsea, S.W.3.　　TX24098

CHAPPELL, J. E., Private, Queen's Own (Royal West Kent Regiment).
He was mobilised in August 1914 and was shortly afterwards sent to France, where he took part in severe fighting at Mons, the Marne, Ypres, Festubert and Arras. In 1917 he was transferred to Italy and was in action on the Piave front. He was demobilised in February 1919, and holds the Mons Star, and the General Service and Victory Medals.
48, Parkstone Road, Peckham, S.E.15.　　Z6156

CHAPPELL, J. G., L/Corporal, Queen's (Royal West Surrey Regiment).
Volunteering in November 1914 he was sent to France at the conclusion of his training and fought at Ypres and the Somme. In 1917 he was transferred to Salonika and served in the Balkan Campaign, and in operations on the Vardar and Struma fronts. He was then drafted to Egypt, and thence to Palestine, where he took part in several important engagements under General Allenby, notably those on the Jordan and Beersheba and in the Capture of Jerusalem. He was demobilised on returning to England in June 1919, and holds the General Service and Victory Medals.
16, Sedan Street, Walworth, S.E.17.　　Z1544B

CHAPPELL, J. H., Sergt., Queen's (Royal West Surrey Regiment).
He volunteered in September 1914 and, until he was sent to France in 1916, was retained for important home duties. Subsequently he fought in several engagements on that Front, and was later sent to Salonika, where he did valuable work during operations on the Vardar and Struma fronts. In 1918 he was transferred to Egypt, and thence to Palestine, and served in several important engagements under General Allenby. He received a severe wound whilst in action at Beersheba, which unhappily proved fatal on March 30th, 1918. He was entitled to the General Service and Victory Medals.
"The path of duty was the way to glory."
16, Sedan Street, Walworth, S.E.17.　　Z1544A

CHAPPLE, H. (Mrs.), Member V.A.D.
This lady offered her services in July 1915 and was given an appointment at the Eastbourne Military Hospital, later being transferred to Summerdown Camp. Her efforts at relieving the sick under her care proved unfailing, and the way in which she carried out her, often very arduous, duties was greatly appreciated. She was discharged in December 1918.
86, Duke's Avenue, Chiswick, W.4.　　5692A

CHAPPLE, H., Captain, R.E.
Volunteering in July 1915 he proceeded to the Western Front on completion of his training and served with the Tunnelling Company at Ypres and numerous other engagements. He was killed in action on December 30th, 1917, and was entitled to the 1914-15 Star, and the General Service and Victory Medals.
"His life for his country."
86, Duke's Avenue, Chiswick, W.4.　　5269B

CHARD, J. R., Private, 10th Essex Regiment.
Joining in September 1917 he was drafted to the Western Front on the completion of his training in the following April. Unhappily he was killed in action on April 26th during the German Offensive after but a few days' service. He was entitled to the General Service and Victory Medals.
"Steals on the ear the distant triumph song."
86, Neate Street, Camberwell, S.E.5.　　Z5057A

CHARD, W. E., Sergt., Royal Irish Rifles.
An ex-soldier, with a previous record of sixteen years' service with the Colours, he volunteered in August 1914, but was unable to secure his transfer overseas, owing to physical unfitness. He did valuable work in Ireland as an Instructor to recruits until he was demobilised in August 1919.
86, Neate Street, Camberwell, S.E.5.　　Z5057B

CHARKER, T., Private, 2nd East Surrey Regiment.
Volunteering in 1915 he was drafted overseas in the following year. In the course of his service on the Western Front he fought in many important engagements, and after the Retreat and Advance, in which he also took part, went with the Army of Occupation into Germany, where in 1920 he was still serving. He holds the General Service and Victory Medals.
22, Byam Street, Townmead Road, S.W.6.　　16180A

CHARLES, G., Bombardier, R.F.A.
He volunteered in November 1914 and early in the following year was sent to France. Whilst in this theatre of war he was engaged on special duties as an observer, and in this capacity served on the Somme, at Arras and Cambrai. In 1917, however, he returned to England, where he carried out similar work until the termination of hostilities. He holds the 1914-15 Star, and the General Service and Victory Medals, and in 1920 was stationed in Scotland.
21, Camellia Street, Wandsworth Road, S.W.8.　　Z1545A

CHARLES, HILDA, Member V.A.D.
This lady volunteered in September 1916 and for two years served at the 98th London Military Hospital. During this time she did valuable work, which was greatly appreciated by all who benefited by her efforts. She was discharged in September 1918.
11, Prebend Gardens, Chiswick, W.4.　　5445A

CHARLES, MILDRED, Member V.A.D.
From March 1916 until March 1919 this lady served at the 98th London Hospital. She carried out her duties, which were often of an arduous nature, with much zeal, and her efforts were greatly appreciated.
11, Prebend Gardens, Chiswick, W.4.　　5445B

CHARLES, W., Corporal, R.F.A.
He volunteered in January 1915 and later in that year was sent to the Western Front, where he took part in various important engagements. He was transferred to Salonika shortly afterwards and whilst in this theatre of war saw much heavy fighting on the Doiran front. He returned home on the cessation of hostilities and in 1920 was still with his Battery in Ireland. He holds the 1914-15 Star, and the General Service and Victory Medals.
2, Victory Square, Camberwell, S.E.5.　　Z5725

CHARMAN, A. R., Private, 24th London Regiment (Queen's).
Volunteering in June 1915 he was sent to France at the conclusion of his training in the following January. Whilst in this theatre of war he took part in many important engagements and did much valuable work with his unit. He died gloriously on the field of battle on October 2nd, 1916. He was entitled to the General Service and Victory Medals.
"His life for his Country, his Soul to God."
115, New Church Road, Camberwell, S.E.5.　　Z4422

CHARMAN, F. E., Sergt., R.E.
He volunteered in August 1914 and in the same year proceeded to the Western Front. Whilst there he served with the Royal Warwickshire Regiment in the Retreat from Mons and the Battles of the Somme, Neuve Chapelle, Ypres, Hill 60 and Cambrai, and was gassed. Later he was discharged but afterwards rejoined in the R.E., and in 1920 was serving, in Turkey. He holds the Mons Star, and the General Service and Victory Medals.
24, Prairie Street, Battersea Park, S.W.8.　　Z1546

CHARMAN, H., Private, Duke of Cornwall's Light Infantry.
He joined in February 1917 and on the completion of his training was drafted to the Western Front. There he was in action in the Retreat of 1918 and was wounded and invalided home. On his recovery he proceeded to Germany with the Army of Occupation, with which he served until November 1919, when he was returned to England and was demobilised, holding the General Service and Victory Medals.
25, Wayford Street, Battersea, S.W.11.　　Z1547A

CHARMAN, J., Private, 23rd London Regiment.

Volunteering in April 1915 he was drafted on the completion of his training to the Western Front, where he took part in numerous engagements, including that of Cambrai. Shortly afterwards he proceeded to the East and saw much service in Salonika and Palestine, and was wounded and invalided to hospital in Alexandria. On recovery he was sent to France and was again wounded. In February 1919 he was demobilised, and holds the General Service and Victory Medals.

25, Wayford Street, Battersea, S.W.11. Z1547B

CHART, A. E., Driver, R.A.S.C. (M.T.)

Volunteering at the commencement of hostilities he was quickly drafted to France, and served in the Retreat from Mons and many of the subsequent engagements, including those at Ypres, Vimy Ridge, the Somme and Cambrai. He was engaged on important duties in connection with the food supply column and in this capacity did valuable work until the termination of hostilities, when he was sent with the Army of Occupation to Germany. He was demobilised in March 1919 after his return to England, and holds the Mons Star, and the General Service and Victory Medals.

11, Bonsor Street, Camberwell, S.E.5. Z4423

CHART, H. J., Private, 1st Hampshire Regiment.

He volunteered in December 1915 and after his training proceeded to France in 1917. Whilst in this theatre of war he was in action in many battles, including those of Messines and Ypres, and in 1918 was gassed at Sanctuary Wood. He was invalided home and after receiving hospital treatment was discharged in May 1918, holding the General Service and Victory Medals.

38, Doddington Grove, Battersea, S.W.11. Z1549

CHART, H. R., L/Corporal, 4th South Wales Borderers.

He joined in January 1916 and in the same year was drafted to Mesopotamia. He was wounded in action at Amara, and whilst on his way to the dressing station was again hit by Turkish snipers. He was sent to hospital at Bazra and later to Calcutta, finally being invalided to England. After receiving hospital treatment he was discharged in August 1918, and holds the General Service and Victory Medals.

23, Combermere Road, Stockwell, S.W.9. Z1548A

CHASMAR, F. A., Rifleman, 11th Rifle Brigade.

He volunteered in February 1915 and in the following year was drafted to France, where he took part in various engagements. He fell fighting on the Somme on September 18th, 1916, and was entitled to the General Service and Victory Medals.

"A costly sacrifice upon the altar of Freedom."

11, Hillery Road, Walworth, S.E.17. Z1550

CHASTON, G., Private, 10th Queen's (Royal West Surrey Regiment).

Volunteering in November 1915 he proceeded to the Western Front in May of the following year. Whilst in this theatre of war he took part in much of the heavy fighting in the Ypres sector and was killed in action in July 1917. He was entitled to the General Service and Victory Medals.

"He died the noblest death a man may die,
Fighting for God and right and liberty."

54, Heath Road, Wandsworth Road, S.W.8. Z1551

CHATER, D., Private, Northamptonshire Regt.

He volunteered in March 1915 and in August of the same year was drafted to the Western Front. There he took part in many notable battles, including those at Loos, Vimy Ridge, the Somme, Messines, Passchendaele, Cambrai, Amiens and Epéhy, where he was wounded in September 1918. He was invalided to England and on his recovery served on special home duties until demobilised in January 1919. Having previously served in the South African Campaign he holds the Queen's and King's South African Medals, and the 1914–15 Star, and the General Service and Victory Medals.

103, Lavender Road, Battersea, S.W.11. Z1552

CHATTERTON, J., Sergt., 2/5th North Staffordshire Regiment.

Volunteering in November 1914 he proceeded to France in 1916. Whilst there he fought in many important engagements and on March 21st, 1918, was taken prisoner. He was held in captivity until November of that year, when he was released and repatriated. He was demobilised later in the same month, holding the General Service and Victory Medals.

102, Duke Road, Chiswick, W.4. 5662A

CHAVE, C. H., Rifleman, 12th London Regiment (The Rangers).

Volunteering in July 1915 he was drafted to the Western Front in August of the same year. In this theatre of war he was in action at Loos, Albert, Vimy Ridge, the Somme and many other engagements. He suffered from shell-shock and was invalided home, and after being in hospital for some time was discharged as medically unfit for further service in November 1917. He holds the 1914–15 Star, and the General Service and Victory Medals.

8, Cross Street, Clapham, S.W.4. Z1553

CHEADLE, E. T., Private, M.G.C.

Joining in March 1916 he was drafted overseas in the following year. During his service on the Western Front he fought at Arras, Lens and the Somme, and in the Retreat and Advance of 1918, during which time he was wounded. In February 1919 he returned home and was demobilised, and holds the General Service and Victory Medals.

7, Arlesford Road, Landor Road, S.W.9. Z1554

CHEESE, A. A., Private, 2nd East Surrey Regiment.

Volunteering in March 1915 he was sent to Salonika on completion of his training. Whilst in this theatre of war he did valuable work with his unit during operations on the Struma and Vardar fronts, and remained overseas until after the cessation of hostilities. He was demobilised in March 1919, and holds the 1914–15 Star, and the General Service and Victory Medals. Z4590B

27, Cork Street, Camberwell, S.E.5. Z4591B

CHEESMAN, W., Private, 11th Queen's (Royal West Surrey Regiment).

Volunteering in November 1915 he was drafted in December of the same year to the Western Front. There he took part in the fighting at Loos, St. Eloi, Ploegsteert Wood, Vimy Ridge, the Somme, Arras and Ypres, and was wounded. Later he served with the Labour Corps on important duties behind the lines. In July 1919 he was demobilised, and holds the 1914–15 Star, and the General Service and Victory Medals.

134, Dalvell Road, Landor Road, S.W.9. Z1555

CHENERY, H. J., 1st Class Petty Officer, R.N.

He was in the Navy at the outbreak of War and served in H.M.S. "Chatham" and various other vessels, including mine-layers. He took part in the Naval operations at the Landing and Evacuation of Gallipoli and served in the North Sea with the Grand Fleet on important duties. He holds the 1914 Star, and the General Service and Victory Medals, and in 1920 was serving on board H.M.S. "Surprise."

7, Sansom Street, Camberwell, S.E.5. Z3067

CHERRILL, J., L/Corporal, Royal Inniskilling Fusiliers.

He enlisted in 1911 and at the outbreak of War was serving in India. Later he proceeded to Mesopotamia and took part in the Capture of Baghdad and in many other engagements in that theatre of war, and was wounded twice. He contracted pneumonia and subsequently died on April 17th, 1917. He was entitled to the General Service and Victory Medals.

"His memory is cherished with pride."

63, Orb Street, Walworth, S.E.17. Z1557

CHERRILL, R. E., C.Q.M.S., 8th London Regiment (Post Office Rifles).

He joined in January 1916 and was drafted to the Western Front in the following December. Whilst overseas he was engaged in the fighting in many important battles, notably those of Ypres, Achiet-le-Grand and Bullecourt, where in July 1918 he was wounded. Remaining in France, however, he served throughout the final Advance through Bussy and Patte d'Oie until the Armistice. On his return to England in September 1919 he was demobilised, and holds the General Service and Victory Medals.

12, Dowlas Street, Camberwell, S.E.5. Z4424

CHERRY, C. F., Corporal, 4th Middlesex Regiment.

He joined in July 1918 and after his training served at various stations on important duties with his unit. He rendered valuable services, but was not successful in obtaining his transfer overseas before the cessation of hostilities. Later he was drafted to Gibraltar, and in 1920 was still serving.

43, Coronation Buildings, South Lambeth, S.W.8. Z1558

CHESHIRE, W. C., Driver, R.F.A.

Having previously served in the South African War he volunteered in April 1915 and after a brief training served in Ireland on garrison duties. He was unable to obtain his transfer to the fighting area owing to medical unfitness. In February 1919 he was demobilised.

48, Sussex Road, Coldharbour Lane, S.W.9. Z1782B

CHESSUN, C. J., Bombardier, R.F.A.

Volunteering in September 1914 he was drafted on the completion of his training to the Western Front and was in action in many engagements, including those of Loos, Ypres and the Somme. In 1917 he was wounded and invalided to hospital, and in April 1919 was discharged as medically unfit. He holds the 1914–15 Star, and the General Service and Victory Medals.

48, Park Grove, Battersea, S.W.11. Z1559

CHEVAL, W., Private, 1st King's Shropshire Light Infantry.

Mobilised at the outbreak of War he was almost immediately drafted overseas. Whilst in France he took part in the fighting on the Marne and Aisne, and at Ypres, Festubert, Loos, Vimy Ridge, Arras, Cambrai and many other notable engagements, and was four times wounded. He holds the 1914 Star and the General Service and Victory Medals, and was demobilised in March 1919.

33, Mayall Road, Herne Hill, S.E.24. 1806

CHEVERTON, H., Private, Welch Regiment.

He joined in June 1916 and after his training was drafted first to Mesopotamia and afterwards to Salonika, where he did excellent work with his unit during operations against the Bulgars and Austrians. He returned to England in the latter part of 1918, and in October of that year was discharged through causes due to his service. He holds the General Service and Victory Medals.

5, Odell Street, Camberwell, S.E.5. Z5350

CHIDGEY, G. W., Rifleman, King's Royal Rifle Corps.

Mobilised in August 1914 he proceeded overseas in September of the same year. Whilst in this theatre of war he was in action at Neuve Chapelle, St. Eloi, Ypres, Festubert, Loos, Albert, Vimy Ridge, Arras and Messines, and was killed by the explosion of a shell in October 1917. He was entitled to the 1914 Star, and the General Service and Victory Medals.

"His life for his Country, his soul to God."

10A, Madron Street, Walworth, S.E.17. Z1560

CHILD, J. J. H., Rifleman, 1/11th London Regt. (Finsbury Rifles).

He volunteered in January 1915 and in the following year was sent to the Dardanelles, where he took part in various engagements and was wounded. In 1917 he was transferred to France and was engaged in heavy fighting at Ypres, Passchendaele, Lens and Cambrai. He was killed in action at Cambrai on December 12th, 1917 and was entitled to the General Service and Victory Medals.

38, Marshall Street, Southwark, S.E.1. TZ25209A

CHILD, M. J., Member W.R.A.F.

She joined in August 1918. Being a tailoress by trade she was engaged in the repair and alteration of uniforms. She carried out her duties in a most efficient manner and was complimented for her good work. She was demobilised in July 1919.

38, Marshall Street, Southwark, S.E.1. TZ25209B

CHILDS, H. E., Air Mechanic, R.A.F.

He joined in January 1918 and was shortly afterwards drafted to the Western Front, where he was engaged on important duties with his Squadron, and was wounded. After the cessation of hostilities he proceeded to Germany with the Army of Occupation, and in March 1919 was demobilised, holding the General Service and Victory Medals.

49, Camillia Street, Wandsworth Road, S.W.8. Z1561

CHILDS, W., Sapper, R.E.

Volunteering in February 1915 he was sent overseas in the same year. He served in many engagements, and was severely gassed at Hill 60 and invalided home. On recovery he remained in England on important duties, being medically unfit for service in the trenches. In September 1919 he was demobilised, and holds the 1914-15 Star, and the General Service and Victory Medals.

25A, Avenue Road, Camberwell, S.E.5. 1066A

CHILLMAN, A., L/Corporal, King's Royal Rifle Corps.

Volunteering in 1914 he was drafted on the completion of his training in 1915 to the Western Front. There he fought in many battles, including those at Ypres, the Somme and Loos, and was wounded and invalided to hospital at the Base. On recovery he returned to the fighting line and took part in the Retreat and Advance of 1918. He holds the 1914-15 Star, and the General Service and Victory Medals, and in 1920 was serving in India.

27, Pitcairn Street, Wandsworth, S.W.8. Z1222A

CHIPLING, W. E., Gunner, R.F.A.

Volunteering in November 1914 he proceeded to France in September of the following year and took part in severe fighting at Loos and the Somme. He was wounded and invalided home and on his recovery was sent to Mesopotamia, where he served in various engagements. He was also in Persia for a time. He returned to England and was demobilised in April 1920, holding the 1914-15 Star, and the General Service and Victory Medals.

4, Southwell Terrace, Lewis Road, Camberwell, S.E.5. Z6158

CHIPPS, W. H., Private, Royal Sussex Regiment.

He volunteered in 1915 and in the same year proceeded to the Western Front, where he served in many engagements. In February 1916 he was invalided home and discharged as medically unfit owing to ill-health. He holds the 1914-15 Star, and the General Service and Victory Medals.

40, Avenue Road, Camberwell, S.E.5. Z1563A

CHISWELL, V. D. (Mrs.), Special War Worker.

From September 1916 until February 1919 this lady was engaged on important work at Woolwich Arsenal. For some time she served as a cartridge examiner, later being employed in the manufacture of cases. She carried out her duties with care and efficiency, and the services which she rendered were of the utmost value.

37, Mansion Street, Camberwell, S.E.5. Z1562B

CHISWELL, J. R., Driver, R.F.A., 37th Battery, 5th Division.

Mobilised at the outbreak of War he was almost immediately drafted overseas with the Expeditionary Force. He took part in the fighting in the Retreat from Mons and in the Battles of the Marne and Aisne, Ypres, Hill 60, Festubert, Loos, the Somme and Arras. In November 1917 he proceeded to Italy, where he saw much service on the Piave, but afterwards returned to France and served there until the Armistice. He was demobilised in February 1919, and holds the Mons Star, and the General Service and Victory Medals.

37, Mansion Street, Camberwell, S.E.5. Z1562A

CHIVERS, A. C., Corporal, 27th Royal Fusiliers.

Volunteering in June 1915 he was sent to East Africa in the following year and took part in various engagements. He returned home in 1917 and in the same year proceeded to France and served in the Retreat and Advance of 1918. He was demobilised in 1918, holding the 1914-15 Star, and the General Service and Victory Medals.

56, Gordon Road, Peckham, S.E.15. Z6154

CHOAT, F., Sergt., R.A.F. (R.N.A.S.)

He volunteered in September 1915 and in January of the following year was drafted to the Western Front, where he was engaged with No. 11 Kite Balloon Section, R.N.A.S., at Nieuport, operating on the sand dunes. In 1917 he returned home and served on important duties with his Squadron until he was demobilised in February 1919, holding the General Service and Victory Medals.

14, Nunhead Crescent, S.E.15. Z6151A

CHOAT, H., Leading Aircraftsman, R.A.F. (late R.N.A.S.)

Volunteering in August 1915 he was sent to France in May of the following year and served between Verdun and Belfort with No. 3 Wing, R.N.A.S., attached to the French Army. He was engaged in various bombing raids into enemy territory. He returned home in June 1917 and was engaged on important work until he was demobilised in April 1919. He holds the General Service and Victory Medals.

14, Nunhead Crescent, S.E.15. Z6151B

CHOPPING, C. J., Private, R.A.M.C.

He joined in April 1916 and served in the 3rd London General Hospital tending the sick and wounded from the Front until May 1918, when he was drafted to France, where he was engaged on important medical duties at Etaples Hospital until the cessation of hostilities. He was demobilised in February 1919, and holds the General Service and Victory Medals.

70, Plough Road, Battersea, S.W.11. Z1564A

CHOPPING, J., Driver, R.A.S.C. (M.T.)

He volunteered in July 1915 and after his training was engaged on important duties at various stations. He was not successful in obtaining his transfer to the Front but, nevertheless, rendered very valuable services until 1919, when he was demobilised.

116, Lothian Road, Camberwell New Road, S.W.9. Z5743

CHOWN, E. M. (Miss), Worker, Q.M.A.A.C.

Having previously been engaged on responsible and dangerous munition work for two-and-a-half years, she joined the Q.M.A.A.C. in June 1918. After a period of training she was drafted to France and was there engaged on important duties at Le Havre and Boulogne, where she did much good work. She was demobilised in December 1919, and holds the General Service and Victory Medals.

53, Henley Street, Battersea, S.W.11. Z1565

CHRISTIE, C. H., Corporal, King's Royal Rifle Corps.

He joined in June 1916 and in the following October was drafted to France. After taking part in several previous engagements he sustained severe shell-shock at Messines and was invalided to hospital. Subsequently he was engaged at Headquarters until his return home in September 1919, when he was demobilised. He holds the General Service and Victory Medals.

23, Mayall Road, Herne Hill, S.E.24. Z1805

CHUBB, W. G., Rifleman, Rifle Brigade.

He joined in June 1916 and in November of the following year proceeded to Salonika. There he saw much severe fighting on the Struma and Doiran fronts until the cessation of hostilities and was then transferred to Russia, where he served at Batum. Later he was invalided home suffering from malaria and dysentery and was finally demobilised in November 1919, holding the General Service and Victory Medals.

96, Gloucester Road, Peckham, S.E.15. Z5731

CHURCH, A. B., Corporal, Royal Sussex Regiment.

He volunteered in November 1914 and was engaged on coastal defence duties until February 1916, when he was drafted to India. There he served on important duties at several stations and was made overseer of the Army Clothing Depôts at Jalandhar, Alipore. He returned home and was demobilised in August 1919, and holds the General Service and Victory Medals.

7, Pountney Road, Lavender Hill, S.W.11. Z1566B

CHURCH, A. H., Private, 7th City of London Regt.
He joined in May 1916 and after a short training was drafted to France in the same year. After only a brief period on the Western Front he gave his life for the freedom of England in the Battle of the Somme on September 17th, 1916. He was entitled to the General Service and Victory Medals.
  " He died the noblest death a man may die,
    Fighting for God and right and liberty."
54, Yeldham Road, Hammersmith, W.6. 12827B

CHURCH, D. A. (Miss), Special War Worker.
During the War this lady was engaged on important duties in the Royal Army Clothing Department at the Skating Rink, Holland Park. She carried out her work with care and efficiency and her services were much appreciated.
54, Yeldham Road, Hammersmith, W.6. 12827C

CHURCH, G. E., Driver, R.H.A. and R.F.A.
He volunteered in November 1914 and in the following year was sent to Egypt and served in the Suez Canal zone at Kantara and Ismailia. Later he was drafted to Salonika, where he did excellent work as a driver throughout the operations on the Struma and Doiran fronts. He then proceeded to France and took part in various engagements, including those on the Somme and at Arras and Ypres and several later battles until the cessation of hostilities. He holds the 1914–15 Star, and the General Service and Victory Medals, and was demobilised in March 1919.
90, Somerleyton Road, Coldharbour Lane, S.W.9. Z3064

CHURCH, H. J., Rifleman and Private, 11th London Regiment (Rifles) and Dublin Fusiliers.
He volunteered in December 1915 and in the following year was drafted to France and whilst in this theatre of war fought in the Battle of the Somme and was wounded. He was invalided home to hospital but on his recovery was transferred to the Dublin Fusiliers and sent to Egypt, where he took part in numerous engagements. During his service in the East he suffered from malarial fever. Later, returning to the Western Front, he served in various engagements up to the Armistice, and was afterwards demobilised in February 1919. He holds the General Service and Victory Medals.
117, Villa Street, Walworth, S.E.17. 2745

CHURCH, J. W. G., Sergt., R.B.
He joined in July 1917 and rapidly rose to the rank of Sergeant, which he attained at the early age of eighteen years. In February 1919 he embarked for Germany and served with the Army of Occupation on the Rhine, acting as Quartermaster-Sergeant until March 1920, when he returned home and was demobilised.
7, Pountney Road, Lavender Hill, S.W.11. Z1566A

CHURCH, S. W., Private, 3rd King's Own (Hussars).
He was mobilised at the outbreak of War and almost immediately drafted to France, where he took part in the Retreat from Mons. He also served at Armentières, the Somme and Ypres, and was twice wounded in action. In September 1918 he was taken prisoner in the second Battle of Cambrai and was sent to a German Camp, where he was held in captivity until released after the Armistice. In 1920 he was still serving, and holds the Mons Star, and the General Service and Victory Medals.
54, Yeldham Road, Hammersmith, W.6. 12827A

CHURCHER, A. E., Private, R.A.S.C. (M.T.)
He volunteered at the outbreak of War and was almost immediately drafted to France and served in the Retreat from Mons. Throughout his service, which lasted from 1914 until 1919, he was engaged on important transport duties conveying supplies of food and ammunition to the front line troops. He was present at numerous battles, including those at Hill 60, Loos, Vimy Ridge, the Somme, Arras, Ypres and Cambrai, and in many of the later operations in the Retreat and Advance of 1918, during which time he was wounded. Returning to England he was demobilised in 1919, and holds the Mons Star, and the General Service and Victory Medals.
26, Arlesford Road, Landor Road, S.W.9. Z1568E
                                            Z1569E

CHURCHER, A. G., Sapper, R.E.
He volunteered in May 1915 and in the same year was drafted to France. During his service on the Western Front he was engaged on important road construction duties and was frequently in the forward areas, notably at Ypres and in the Somme sector. In September 1919 he returned home and was demobilised, and holds the 1914–15 Star, and the General Service and Victory Medals.
26, Arlesford Road, Landor Road, S.W.9. Z1568C
                                          Z1569C

CHURCHER, E. H., C.S.M., 4th Australian Infantry
He volunteered in 1914 and in the same year was drafted overseas. During his services in France he fought at Hill 60, Festubert, Loos, Ypres, Vimy Ridge and the Somme and was severely wounded in action, his injury necessitating the amputation of one of his legs. He was invalided to hospital in England and discharged as medically unfit in 1919. He holds the 1914 Star, and the General Service and Victory Medals. Z1568A
26, Arlesford Road, Landor Road, S.W.9. Z1569A

CHURCHER, E. J., Private, Canadian Regiment.
He volunteered in 1915 and was drafted to France in the following year. During his service on the Western Front he was engaged on Military Police duties. He was unfortunately killed in action on September 10th, 1917, and was entitled to the General Service and Victory Medals.
  " He passed out of the sight of men by the path of duty and self sacrifice." Z1568B
26, Arlesford Road, Landor Road, S.W.9. Z1569B

CHURCHER, L. C., Private, Royal Irish Regiment.
He joined in February 1917 and on the completion of his training served at various stations until drafted to France. Here he did good work in several engagements until the Armistice was signed in November 1918. Unhappily he died of the prevailing influenza a fortnight later. He was entitled to the General Service and Victory Medals.
  " His memory is cherished with pride."
64, Landseer Street, Battersea, S.W.11. Z1567

CHURCHILL, A., Trooper, County of London Yeomanry, and Pte., Northumberland Fusiliers.
He joined in November 1916 and after his training served at various stations on important duties with his unit. He rendered valuable services but was not successful in obtaining his transfer overseas on account of medical unfitness. He was discharged in November 1918 and unfortunately died on January 26th, 1919.
  " He joined the great white company of valiant souls."
39, Albert Road, Peckham, S.E.15. Z5928

CLACK, A., Gunner, R.G.A.
After mobilisation on the outbreak of War he quickly crossed to the Western Front and was actively engaged in the Battles of Mons, the Marne, the Aisne, Neuve Chapelle, Ypres, Loos, Festubert and the Somme. During his service overseas he was gassed. In September 1917 he was released in order to take up his duties with the L.C.C. Fire Brigade, in which he did valuable service during many subsequent air-raids. He holds the Mons Star, and the General Service and Victory Medals.
12, Domville Grove, Camberwell, S.E.5. Z5580

CLACK, G. L., Corporal, The Queen's (West Surrey Regiment) and Bedfordshire Regiment.
He joined in May 1916 and was drafted to the Western Front in August of the same year. After first serving in a Highland Regiment he was transferred to the Queen's and later to the Bedfordshire Regiment, and fought in many important engagements, including those on the Somme, and at Arras and Ypres. He was wounded and invalided home to hospital for a short period, rejoining his unit in France after his recovery. He holds the General Service and Victory Medals, and in 1920 was still serving with the Colours.
1, Allardyce Street, Ferndale Road, S.W.4. Z1570

CLACK, I. T. H., Sergt., Bedfordshire Regiment.
He volunteered in August 1914 and in the following year was drafted to the Western Front. During his service in France he fought at Loos, Vermelles, Ploegsteert and Vimy Ridge, and was then invalided home to hospital owing to ill-health and remained under treatment for twelve months. After his recovery he was sent to India, where he served on important garrison duties for about two years. He returned home and was demobilised in March 1919, and holds the 1914–15 Star, and the General Service and Victory Medals.
42, Geneva Road, Coldharbour Lane, S.W.9. Z3445

CLAGGETT, A. G., Air Mechanic, R.A.F.
He volunteered in 1915 and after his training served at various stations on important duties with his Squadron. He was engaged in the repair of aeroplanes and rendered valuable services but was not successful in obtaining his transfer overseas before the cessation of hostilities. He was demobilised in 1919.
38, McKerrell Road, Peckham, S.E.15. Z5921

CLARIDGE, C. F., Private, Royal Fusiliers.
He volunteered in February 1915 and in the same year was drafted to France. After taking part in the fighting in various engagements he was severely wounded near Ypres on August 21st, 1916. He was sent home to hospital and discharged as totally disabled in the following September. He holds the 1914–15 Star, and the General Service and Victory Medals.
13, Southfield Road, Bedford Park, W.4. 7792A

CLARIDGE, F., Sergt.-Instructor, R.M.L.I.
He rejoined at the outbreak of hostilities, having previously served in the South African War, and was engaged on important duties as Sergeant Instructor at Plymouth, and afterwards served with the Fleet in the North Sea. He rendered valuable services throughout the War and was demobilised in January 1919. He holds the General Service and Victory, and the Long Service and Good Conduct Medals.
Rose Villa, Burlington Lane, Chiswick, W.4. 5835B

CLARIDGE, H. V., Corporal, 6th Dragoon Guards (Carabiniers).

He was mobilised at the outbreak of war and crossing immediately to France fought in the Retreat from Mons and in many later engagements until hostilities ceased, including those at the Marne, Ypres, Arras, Cambrai and the Retreat and Advance of 1918. After the Armistice he was drafted to Ireland, where in 1920 he was still serving. He holds the Mons Star, and the General Service and Victory Medals.

30, Copeland Road, Peckham, S.E.15.   Z5581

CLARK, A. A., Private, 1st Royal Fusiliers.

He joined in April 1918 in the 5th Bedfordshire Regiment and on completion of his training was engaged on important duties with his unit. He was not successful in securing his draft overseas while hostilities lasted, and in January 1919 was transferred to the 1st Suffolk Regiment. After his demobilisation he re-enlisted in the Royal Fusiliers in March 1919 and from the following August to November served with the Army of Occupation in Germany. In 1920 he was still in the Army.

57, Ascalon Street, Battersea Park Road, S.W.8.   Z1577C
                                                       Z1578C

CLARK, C., Private, 7th Middlesex Regiment.

He joined in 1917 and on the conclusion of his training was engaged with his unit on important defence duties. He was not successful in securing his transfer overseas prior to the cessation of hostilities, but after the Armistice was drafted to Germany with the Army of Occupation. In 1920 he was still serving.

1, Yeldham Buildings, Hammersmith, W.6.   12808A

CLARK, E. C., Private, City of London Volunteer Regiment.

Being unfit for the regular army owing to physical weakness he joined the Volunteers in 1915 and for the following four years rendered valuable services. He was employed as a machine gunner during enemy air-raids and did much other good work until his demobilisation in 1919. He holds the King's Certificate for his services.

8, Circular Road, Falmouth Road, S.E.1.   Z25453

CLARK, E. H., Private, 8th Queen's (Royal West Surrey Regiment).

He volunteered in September 1914 and early in the following year was drafted to the Western Front. He took part in many engagements, including those at Loos and the Somme, and was wounded and taken prisoner in September 1916. On his release he returned home and was discharged as medically unfit for further service in January 1919. He holds the 1914–15 Star, and the General Service and Victory Medals.

27, Warham Street, Camberwell, S.E.5.   Z1576

CLARK, E. T., Private, 3rd London Regiment (Royal Fusiliers).

He volunteered in June 1915 and after his training was retained on important duties with his unit until April 1918, when he was drafted to the Western Front. He served in the Retreat and Advance of that year and was in action at Amiens, Bapaume, Havrincourt, Cambrai and Ypres, and was twice wounded. He was demobilised in February 1919, holding the General Service and Victory Medals.

4, Charleston Street, Walworth, S.E.17.   Z1575

CLARK, E. W., Rifleman, 21st London Regiment (1st Surrey Rifles).

He was serving in the Territorial Force at the outbreak of War and proceeded to France early in the following year. He took part in the severe fighting in many important engagements, including that at Loos, where he was seriously wounded in October 1915 and lost the sight of his left eye. After being invalided home he was discharged as medically unfit for further service in July 1916, and holds the 1914–15 Star, and the General Service and Victory Medals.

27, Warham Street, Camberwell, S.E.5.   Z1579

CLARK, F. A., Bombardier, R.F.A.

A serving soldier since April 1914 he was sent to the Western Front in the following March. During his service in France he fought at Givenchy, Hill 60, Ypres, Loos, Vimy Ridge, the Somme, Arras, Messines, Passchendaele, Cambrai, Bapaume and Havrincourt and was wounded. He was invalided home to hospital and was subsequently demobilised in April 1919. He holds the 1914–15 Star, and the General Service and Victory Medals.

10, Chryssell Road, Brixton Road, S.W.9.   Z5232

CLARK, F. A., Petty Officer, R.N., H.M.S. "Hogue" and "Duchess of Devonshire."

He was mobilised from the Reserve in August 1914 and served with the Grand Fleet in the North Sea. He took part in the Battle of Heligoland Bight and was on board H.M.S. "Hogue" when that vessel was torpedoed. He did valuable service at Scapa Flow and was also engaged on important convoy duty in the Channel. He was demobilised in February 1919, holding the 1914–15 Star, and the General Service and Victory Medals.

24, Combermere Road, Stockwell, S.W.9.   Z1580

CLARK, G., L/Corporal, Queen's (Royal West Surrey Regiment).

Volunteering in September 1914, after his training he was retained on important duties with his unit until he was drafted to France. He took part in many engagements, and gave his life for King and Country on the Somme on November 3rd, 1916. He was entitled to the General Service and Victory Medals.

"Whilst we remember the sacrifice is not in vain."   Z1581

29, Kinglake Street, Walworth, S.E.17.   Z1583C

CLARK, G. A., A/Bombardier, R.F.A.

He volunteered in May 1915 and proceeded to France in the same year. He took part in numerous engagements of importance, including those at Albert, the Somme, Arras, Bullecourt, Ypres and Passchendaele, and was wounded and invalided home. On his recovery he returned to France and served in the Retreat and Advance of 1918. He was demobilised in March 1919, holding the 1914–15 Star, and the General Service and Victory Medals.

171, South Street, Walworth, S.E.17.   Z1574

CLARK, G. J., Gunner, R.H.A.

He was mobilised in August 1914 and was shortly afterwards sent to the Western Front, where he took part in the severe fighting at Mons, the Marne, La Bassée, Ypres, Loos, Albert, Vimy Ridge and the Somme. He was killed in action on the Somme on September 5th, 1916, and was entitled to the Mons Star, and the General Service and Victory Medals.

"His life for his country."

95, Westmoreland Road, Walworth, S.E.17.   Z1584

CLARK, G. E., Private, R.A.S.C. (M.T.)

He volunteered in January 1915 and after his training served on the Western Front until the termination of hostilities. During this time he did excellent work with his unit in connection with the transport of food, water and munitions to the forward areas, especially in the Arras and Somme sectors. After the Armistice he was sent with the Army of Occupation to Germany, and was demobilised on his return to England in May 1919. He holds the 1914–15 Star, and the General Service and Victory Medals.

41, Myatt Road, Stockwell, S.W.9.   Z4425

CLARK, H., A.B., Royal Naval Division.

He volunteered in 1914 and in the following year being drafted to the Dardanelles took part in the chief operations until the Evacuation of the Peninsula. In 1916 he was transferred to France, where he again rendered valuable services. He fell fighting on the Somme on November 13th, 1916, and was entitled to the 1914–15 Star, and the General Service and Victory Medals.

"Great deeds cannot die."

48, Bedford Street, Walworth, S.E.17.   Z1583B

CLARK, H. A., Rifleman, 17th London Regt. (Rifles).

Joining in February 1918 he was drafted to France in August of the same year. He took part in many important engagements in the last stages of hostilities, including those at Cambrai and Menin Wood. He returned home and was demobilised in November 1919, holding the General Service and Victory Medals.

23, Barmore Street, Battersea, S.W.11.   Z1586B

CLARK, H. R. (M.M.), Corporal, Queen's (Royal West Surrey Regiment).

He volunteered in 1914 and was sent to France in the same year. He served as a machine gunner and took part in many engagements, including those at the Somme, Arras and Ypres. He was unfortunately killed in action in February 1918. He was awarded the Military Medal in 1917 for great bravery and devotion in the Field, standing by his gun after most of his comrades had been killed or wounded. He was also entitled to the 1914 Star, and the General Service and Victory Medals.

"His memory is cherished with pride."

6, Beddome Street, Walworth, S.E.17.   Z1572

CLARK, H. T., Corporal, 1st Cheshire Regiment.

He volunteered in December 1914 and after his training was drafted to the Western Front, where he took part in many important engagements and was twice wounded. He fell fighting gallantly in the Advance of the Allies near Arras on August 23rd, 1918, and was entitled to the General Service and Victory Medals.

"A costly sacrifice upon the altar of freedom."

4, Banim Street, Hammersmith, W.6.   11123B

CLARK, L. M. (Mrs.), Special War Worker.

This lady was engaged throughout the war at St. George's Hospital, Hyde Park Corner, thereby releasing a man for military service. Her duties, which were of a responsible nature, were carried out with great care and efficiency.

4, Banim Street, Hammersmith, W.6.   11123C

CLARK, R., Sergt., Queen's (Royal West Surrey Regiment).

He enlisted in November 1912 in the Royal Fusiliers and shortly after the outbreak of War was sent with the 6th Division to the Western Front, where he took part in numerous engagements, including those at the Marne, Ypres, St. Eloi and Hill 60, and was wounded at Ploegsteert Wood. In November 1916 he proceeded to German East Africa, and after much distinguished service was wounded in action at Beho Beho. In January 1918 he was invalided home and was transferred to the Queen's Royal West Surrey Regiment, in which he was still serving in 1920. He holds the 1914 Star, and the General Service and Victory Medals.

57, Ascalon Street, Battersea Park Road, S.W.8.　Z1577B
Z1578B

CLARK, R., Sergt.-Drummer, 2nd London Regiment (Royal Fusiliers).

He volunteered in August 1914 and shortly afterwards proceeded to Malta. In 1915 he was transferred to France, where he took part in numerous engagements, including those at Ypres, St. Eloi, Festubert, Vimy Ridge, the Somme, Beaumont-Hamel, Messines, Ypres and Cambrai. He also served in the Retreat and Advance of 1918 and was wounded. He was mentioned in Despatches for gallantry in the Field in September 1916. He was demobilised in February 1919, and holds the 1914-15 Star and the General Service and Victory Medals.

54, Holden Street, Battersea, S.W.11.　Z1571

CLARK, R., Chief Stoker, R.N., H.M.S. "Tyne."

He volunteered in August 1914 and saw much service on Motor Launches 201 and 362 and on H.M.S. "Tyne" of the 8th Flotilla. He was engaged on patrol and other important duties in the North Sea and throughout the war rendered valuable services. He served for twenty-two years in the Royal Navy previous to the War, and has the Long Service and Good Conduct Medal. He also holds the 1914-15 Star, and the General Service and Victory Medals. He was demobilised in February 1919.

Latchmere Hotel, Battersea, S.W.11.　Z1573

CLARK, S., Driver, R.F.A.

He volunteered in March 1915 and in the same year was drafted to the Western Front, where he took part in various engagements, including those on the Somme and at Arras and Bapaume, and was gassed and invalided home. He was discharged as medically unfit for further service in December 1917, and holds the 1914-15 Star, and the General Service and Victory Medals.

6, Pomfret Road, Camberwell, S.E.5.　Z5912

CLARK, S. C., Private, King's Own Yorkshire Light Infantry.

He joined in September 1916 and was sent to France in the following year and took part in severe fighting in the Arras sector. He was unfortunately killed in action on May 10th, 1917, and was entitled to the General Service and Victory Medals.

"Thinking that remembrance, though unspoken, may reach him where he sleeps."

45, Phillips Road, Peckham, S.E.15.　Z5904

CLARK, S. G. (M.M.), Corporal, 21st London Regiment (1st Surrey Rifles).

He joined in July 1916 and in the same year was sent to the Western Front, where he served at Ypres for about a year and was wounded in July 1917. He was invalided to hospital at the Base, and after two months' treatment rejoined his unit and fought at Cambrai, and in various engagements in the Retreat and Advance of 1918. He was awarded the Military Medal for conspicuous bravery in action in the Somme sector on August 24th, 1918, and was afterwards again wounded and invalided home to hospital. He was demobilised in January 1919, and holds in addition to the Military Medal, the General Service and Victory Medals.

31, Russell Street, Brixton Road, S.W.9.　Z5233

CLARK, T. V., Rifleman, 21st London Regiment (1st Surrey Rifles).

He volunteered in April 1915 and was sent to France in October of the same year and took part in various engagements and was wounded and invalided home. In 1916 he was transferred to the 3rd Cambridgeshire Regiment and later to the R.A.S.C. and was engaged as a clerk on important work until he was demobilised in September 1919. He holds the 1914-15 Star, and the General Service and Victory Medals.

77, Clayton Road, Peckham, S.E.15.　Z6149

CLARK, W., Corporal, 4th (Royal Irish) Dragoon Guards.

He was mobilised in August 1914 and was shortly afterwards sent to France, where he took part in the severe fighting at Mons, the Aisne and Messines. Being severely wounded and also suffering from shell-shock he was invalided home and was discharged after protracted treatment as medically unfit for further service in March 1915. He holds the Mons Star, and the General Service and Victory Medals, and was one of seven brothers who served in the War.

48, Bedford Street, Walworth, S.E.17.　Z1583A

CLARK, T., Private, Queen's Own (Royal West Kent Regiment).

He enlisted in February 1913 and shortly after the outbreak of War was sent to France. He took an active part in the severe fighting at Mons, Le Cateau, the Marne, the Aisne, La Bassée, Neuve Chapelle and Ypres, and in many other important engagements. In 1915 he was transferred to Mesopotamia and was engaged in the Expedition for the Relief of General Townshend at Kut-el-Amara and was wounded. He unfortunately died of his wounds at Basra on April 17th, 1916, and was entitled to the Mons Star, and the General Service and Victory Medals.

" He died the noblest death a man may die, fighting for God and right and liberty."　Z1577A
57, Ascalon Street, Battersea Park Road, S.W.8.　Z1578A

CLARK, T. M., Private, R.A.S.C. (M.T.)

He volunteered in April 1915 and at the conclusion of his training was drafted to the Western Front. During his service overseas he was engaged in transporting ammunition to the forward areas, and did valuable work in this capacity at the Battles of the Somme, Ypres, Passchendaele and Arras, and in the Retreat of March 1918, when he was severely wounded. After being for some time in Hospital at Rouen he was invalided home and was demobilised on his recovery in March 1919. He holds the 1914-15 Star, and the General Service and Victory Medals.

15, Tindal Street, Lothian Road, S.W.9.　Z5351

CLARK, W. E., Private, Royal Welch Fusiliers.

He volunteered in January 1915 and in the same year was drafted to France, where he took part in severe fighting. He was reported missing on September 25th, 1915, and is believed to have been killed in action in the Somme sector on that date. He was entitled to the 1914-15 Star, and the General Service and Victory Medals.

"He passed out of the sight of men by the path of duty and self-sacrifice."

61, Clayton Road, Peckham, S.E.15.　Z5922

CLARK, W. E., Sergt., Cameron Highlanders.

Having previously served through the South African War he rejoined in June 1916. Being medically unfit for active service he was engaged as a drill instructor and in conducting drafts to France, and rendered valuable services. He was demobilised in January 1919, and holds the Queen's and King's South African Medals with eight clasps, and the General Service and Victory Medals.

1, Murray Building, Burnett Street, Vauxhall, S.E.11. TZ24528

CLARK, W. F. E., Private, 11th Royal Fusiliers.

He joined in April 1917 and in February of the following year was drafted to France and took part in severe fighting on the Somme. He was unfortunately killed in action near St. Quentin on March 22nd, 1918, and was entitled to the General Service and Victory Medals.

"His life for his Country, his Soul to God."

37, Nunhead Crescent, S.E.15.　Z6150

CLARK, W. H., Private, 9th (Queen's Royal) Lancers.

Having previously served for five years he re-enlisted in August 1914 and shortly afterwards was sent to France, where he took part in the severe fighting at Mons and in several other engagements. He was invalided home through illness and discharged as medically unfit for further service in December 1916. He holds the Mons Star, and the General Service and Victory Medals.

31, Waterloo Street, Hammersmith, W. 6.　12598A

CLARKE, A., L/Corporal, 24th London Regiment (The Queen's).

He was mobilised at the outbreak of War with the Territorials and signed on for foreign service, but owing to being transferred to the 2nd Battalion was not able to proceed overseas. He served instead on important duties in recruiting for Kitchener's Army and rendered valuable services. In March 1916 he was discharged owing to defective eyesight. He then took up a position at the General Post Office, where he did good work. He afterwards attempted to re-enlist but the Post Office authorities would not consent to release him. He holds the Territorial Force Efficiency Medal.

41, Ingleton Street, Brixton Road, S.W.9.　Z1796

CLARKE, A. J., Rifleman, King's Royal Rifle Corps.

He joined in November 1917 and in the following March was drafted to France, where he served for thirteen months. During this period he was severely wounded and was invalided to hospital in Scotland. He was demobilised in April 1919, and holds the General Service and Victory Medals.

24, Church Path, Hammersmith, W.6.　19393B

CLARKE, B., Gunner, R.F.A., and L/Corporal, R.E. (Signals).

He volunteered in May 1915 and in the following March was drafted to France. During his service on the Western Front he was in action on the Somme, and at Beaumont-Hamel, Messines, Ypres, Passchendaele, Cambrai, Amiens, Havrincourt and Epéhy, and the engagements which followed until the cessation of hostilities. He was demobilised in February 1919, and holds the General Service and Victory Medals.

9, Jocelyn Street, Peckham, S.E.15.　Z5225B

CLARKE, C. G., Private, Royal Fusiliers.
He volunteered in November 1914 and in the following year
was drafted to France. There he served in many important
engagements, including those on the Somme and Ancre, and at
Ypres and Passchendaele. He died gloriously on the field of
battle at Polygon Wood in July 1917, and was entitled to the
1914-15 Star, and the General Service and Victory Medals.
"A valiant soldier, with undaunted heart he breasted Life's last
hill." 26, Cambridge Street, Camberwell, S.E.5. Z1590A

CLARKE, E., Private, Lancashire Fusiliers.
He was serving at the outbreak of War and was almost
immediately drafted to France and took part in the Retreat
from Mons. He was in action also in various subsequent engagements on the Western Front before proceeding to Salonika
and whilst in this theatre of war he served in numerous operations
on the Balkan Front until the Armistice. He was demobilised
in April 1919, and holds the 1914 Star, and the General Service
and Victory Medals.
10, Trafalgar Street, Walworth, S.E.17. Z27335

CLARKE, E. C., L/Corporal, 6th Middlesex Regt.
He joined in March 1917 and was sent to the Western Front.
During his service in France he fought at Cambrai and Bullecourt,
and was severely wounded and invalided home to hospital
After a period of treatment he was discharged as medically unfit
for further duty in March 1918. He holds the General Service
and Victory Medals.
64, Park Crescent, Clapham Park Road, S.W.4. Z1588A

CLARKE, E. H., Sapper, R.E.
He volunteered in November 1915 and in the following year
was drafted to France. Whilst in this theatre of war he served
on the Somme. At the end of 1916 he was sent to Salonika
with the 60th Division, and thence to Egypt. Later he was
with General Allenby's Forces in the Advance through Palestine.
During his service in the East he suffered from malaria. He
returned home and was demobilised in August 1919, and holds
the General Service and Victory Medals.
64, Park Crescent, Clapham Park Road, S.W.4. Z1588B

CLARKE, F., Private, Black Watch.
He joined in 1916 and in the same year was drafted to France,
where he fought in the Battle of the Somme and later at Cambrai.
After the signing of the Armistice he proceeded to Germany
with the Army of Occupation and in 1920 was still serving.
He holds the General Service and Victory Medals.
106, Rayleigh Road, West Kensington, W.14. 12043C

CLARKE, F. E. (M.M.), Sergt., R.F.A.
He volunteered in April 1915 and was sent to the Western Front
three months later. In the course of his service overseas he
fought in the Battles of Loos, the Somme and Ypres, and many
later operations until fighting ceased, and was awarded the
Military Medal for conspicuous bravery in rescuing a machine
gun from the enemy during the Battle of Cambrai in 1917.
In addition he holds the 1914-15 Star, and the General Service
and Victory Medals, and was demobilised on his return to England
in 1919. 123, Landor Road, Clapham Road, S.W.9. Z5056A

**CLARKE, F. J., L/Corporal, R.E., and Royal
Berkshire Regiment.**
He volunteered in September 1914 and in the following year
was drafted to France. During his service on the Western
Front he fought at St. Eloi, Albert, Vimy Ridge, the Somme,
Beaumont-Hamel and Arras, where he was wounded. He
was invalided home to hospital and on his recovery returned to
France and was engaged with the Gas Section of the Royal
Engineers on the Cambrai front. He was demobilised in
February 1919, and holds the 1914-15 Star, and the General
Service and Victory Medals.
Park Crescent, Clapham Park Road, S.W.4. Z1588C

CLARKE, H. C., Private, Durham Light Infantry.
He joined in August 1916 and was almost immediately drafted
to Salonika. Whilst in this theatre of war he fought in the
general offensive on the Doiran front, in the Advance across the
Struma, and in the recapture of Monastir. He was also in
action in the second Advance in the Doiran sector and in the Vardar battles. He then proceeded to Russia, where he took part in
the campaign against the Bolshevists. Whilst serving on
this front he was for a short time in hospital with malaria.
He returned home and was demobilised in December 1919,
and holds the General Service and Victory Medals.
16, Cross Street, Clapham, S.W.4. Z1589

**CLARKE, J. O. R., Private, 10th Queen's (Royal
West Surrey Regiment).**
He volunteered in December 1915 and in the following March
was drafted to France, where he saw considerable service. He
was severely wounded in the Battle of the Somme, and after
his recovery was sent to Italy in November 1917. Whilst in
this theatre of war he took part in the operations on the Piave
and on the Asiago Plateaux, and subsequently returned to
France. During his service overseas he was wounded three
times. He was demobilised in March 1919, and holds the General
Service and Victory Medals.
29, Rowena Crescent, Battersea, S.W.11. Z1591

CLARKE, G., Driver, R.F.A.
He joined in July 1916 and after his training was completed
served at various stations on important duties with his Battery.
He rendered valuable services, but was not able, on medical
grounds, to obtain a transfer overseas, and was demobilised in
March 1919.
257 Mayall Road, Herne Hill, S.E.24. Z3997B
Z3998B

CLARKE, J., Private, Royal Fusiliers.
He volunteered in 1914 and after a short training was sent to
France and was in action in several early engagements. He
gave his life for his country at Messines on January 21st, 1915,
and was entitled to the 1914 Star, and the General Service and
Victory Medals.
"Whilst we remember, the sacrifice was not in vain."
106, Rayleigh Road, West Kensington, W.14. 12044A

CLARKE, R., Corporal, Royal Fusiliers.
He volunteered in September 1914 and after a brief training was
drafted to France in the same year. After fighting in several
early engagements he died gloriously on the field of battle at
La Bassée on May 21st, 1915. He was entitled to the 1914
Star, and the General Service and Victory Medals.
"Nobly striving
He nobly fell that we might live."
106, Rayleigh Road, West Kensington, W.14. 12044B

CLARKE, S. S., Private, 6th Dorsetshire Regiment.
We volunteered in April 1915 and in the following year was
drafted to France. After serving only a few weeks on the
Western Front he was unhappily killed in action in the fierce
encounter at Delville Wood on July 12th, 1916. He was entitled
to the General Service and Victory Medals.
"Great deeds cannot die:
They with the sun and moon renew their light for ever."
13, Shorncliffe Road, Old Kent Road, S.E.1. Z1587

CLARKE, T., Pioneer, R.E.
He volunteered in September 1915 and was drafted to the Western
Front in the following June. During his service in France he
was engaged on important duties in connection with the operations and was frequently in the forward areas. Owing to ill-
health he was invalided home and was discharged as medically
unfit for further military duty in June 1916. He then volunteered
for work on munitions at Woolwich Arsenal, and was unfortunately
severely injured in a serious accident and died from the effects
of his injuries in 1917. He was entitled to the 1914-15 Star,
and the General Service and Victory Medals.
4, Alfred Tenements, The Parade, Lambeth Walk, S.E.11. Z2568I

**CLARKE, W., Private, Middlesex Regiment, and
Labour Corps.**
He joined in November 1916 and after his training was completed
served on important duties at various stations until July 1917,
when he was transferred to the Labour Corps and sent to France
in the following November. He was engaged on important
duties at the Clearing Station in Paris, and unfortunately was
killed in an enemy air-raid on January 31st, 1918. He was
entitled to the General Service and Victory Medals.
"His life for his Country."
23, Barmore Street, Battersea, S.W.11. Z1586C

CLARKE, W., Private, Royal Fusiliers.
He was mobilised in August 1914 and was almost immediately
drafted to France and served in the memorable Retreat from
Mons. He was in action also in several other early engagements,
and in November 1914 was taken prisoner. After nearly four
years' captivity in Germany he died on October 1st, 1918. He
was entitled to the Mons Star, and the General Service and
Victory Medals.
"Thinking that remembrance, though unspoken, may reach
him where he sleeps."
106, Rayleigh Road, West Kensington, W.14. 12044C

**CLARKE, W. G., Sergt., 6th London Regiment,
and King's Royal Rifle Corps.**
Volunteering in 1914 he was afterwards drafted to the Western
Front, where he fought in many important engagements, notably
those round La Bassée, Ypres and Festubert. In September 1915
he was severely wounded in action at Loos and was in consequence
invalided to a Military Hospital in Brighton. He was discharged
as medically unfit for further service in August 1916, and holds
the 1914-15 Star, and the General Service and Victory Medals.
123, Landor Road, Clapham Road, S.W.9. Z5056B

CLARKE, W. H., Gunner, R.F.A.
He volunteered in 1914 and was sent to the Western Front
in the following year. During his service in France he did
excellent work as a gunner at Ypres and on the Somme and in
various other sectors. He was wounded and for a time was in
hospital at the Base. After his recovery he rejoined his Battery
and was in action throughout the Retreat and Advance. He
returned home and was demobilised in May 1919, and holds the
1914-15 Star, and the General Service and Victory Medals.
3, Newby Street, Wandsworth Road, S.W.8. Z1592A

CLARKSON, E. F., Sapper, R.E.
He joined in February 1917 and in the following year was drafted to France. There he was engaged on important duties in connection with the operations and was frequently in the forward areas, notably on the Somme and at Ypres and Cambrai, and in the subsequent engagements until the Armistice was signed. He was demobilised in March 1919, and holds the General Service and Victory Medals.
15, Heath Road, Wandsworth Road, S.W.8.   Z1593B

CLARKSON, T., 2nd Lieutenant, R.A.F.
He was mobilised at the outbreak of War and was sent to the Western Front in 1915. During his service in France he was wounded at Givenchy and was also in action at Ypres, where he was gassed, and High Wood, where he was again wounded. After his recovery he served at Cambrai and in various engagements in the Retreat of 1918. He was demobilised in May 1919, and holds the 1914–15 Star, and the General Service and Victory Medals. 15, Heath Road, Wandsworth Road, S.W.8.   Z1593A

CLARKSON, W., Driver, R.A.S.C. (M.T.)
He volunteered in 1915 and in the same year was sent overseas. During his service in France he did good work as a driver at Ypres, Loos, the Somme and Merville, and in numerous subsequent engagements until the cessation of hostilities. He was attached for the greater part of the time to the 12th Divisional Ammunition Park, and returning to England was demobilised in 1919. He holds the 1914–15 Star, and the General Service and Victory Medals. 68, Faraday Street, Walworth, S.E.17.   Z1594

CLAXTON, A. B. C., Pte., 1/8th Middlesex Regt.
He joined the Army in March 1916, and in the following November was sent to the Western Front, where he was gassed shortly after his arrival. He was in hospital for a time but returned to the firing line and was again in action. Gassed a second time, he was invalided to England and was eventually discharged as unfit owing to gas-poisoning in February 1919. He holds the General Service and Victory Medals, and the King's Scroll.
14, Garden Street, Vauxhall Bridge Road, S.W.1.   Z23154

CLAXTON, A. W., Special War Worker.
Being ineligible for service with the Colours he obtained work of National importance at Messrs. Napiers, Acton, where he was engaged as a viewer of aeroplanes. During his service he joined the St. John Ambulance Society, and when proficient was able to render valuable aid when necessity arose in the firm.
20, Alexandra Road, Southfield Road, Chiswick, W.4.   7676A

CLAXTON, D. C. (Miss), Special War Worker.
During the War this lady was engaged on important work in connection with fuses at Messrs. Vandervells, Acton. In the course of her service she attained a high degree of efficiency in this branch of the work and proved invaluable to the firm.
20, Alexandra Road, Southfield Road, Chiswick, W.4.   7676B

CLAXTON, W., Private, R.A.S.C.
Joining in September 1916 he was sent overseas in the same month. During his service on the Western Front he did valuable work with his unit in many important sectors, including those of Arras, Vimy Ridge, the Somme, Ypres, Cambrai, Armentières and St. Quentin. After the final Retreat and Advance, in which he also took part, he served with the Army of Occupation in Germany. He was demobilised on his return to England in September 1919, and holds the General Service and Victory Medals. 60, Chatham Street, Walworth, S.E.17.   Z1088B

CLAYSON, A. V. G., Private, 12th Suffolk Regiment.
He volunteered in November 1914 and at the conclusion of his training was sent to the Western Front, where he fought in many important engagements, including those at Ypres, Neuve Chapelle, Festubert and Loos. Later he was drafted to Mesopotamia and thence to India. During his service he was wounded on five occasions, and after receiving treatment at various hospitals was invalided home and discharged in August 1918. He holds the 1914–15 Star, and the General Service and Victory Medals. 54, Gwynne Road, Battersea, S.W.11.   Z1595

CLAYTON, G. E., Private, 2nd Royal Fusiliers.
He joined in July 1916 and in the following October embarked for France. There he took part in several engagements, being a trained sniper. He was unfortunately killed whilst in the front line at Ypres on January 25th, 1917, and was entitled to the General Service and Victory Medals.
123, Blake's Road, Peckham Grove, S.E.15.   Z5930

CLAYTON, H. E., Private, M.G.C.
Volunteering in March 1915 he joined in the 19th London Regiment and was later transferred to the Machine Gun Corps. In the following month he was drafted to the Western Front, where he subsequently fought in many important battles, notably those of Loos, Albert, the Somme, Arras, Messines and Cambrai. He also served in the Retreat and Advance of 1918 and was wounded. After the cessation of hostilities he went with the Relief Force to Russia and did good work with his unit until January 1919, when he was taken prisoner. Released in 1920 he returned to England and was demobilised in April of that year. He holds the 1914–15 Star, and the General Service and Victory Medals.
2, Anne's Buildings, Aylesbury Road, Walworth, S.E.17.   Z1599

CLAYTON, J., Private, 1/23rd London Regiment.
He joined in 1916 and being over age for foreign service was retained after his training for important home duties, which he carried out at various stations. In 1918, however, he was discharged and was afterwards engaged on special munition work until after the termination of hostilities.
21, Barmore Street, Battersea, S.W.11.   Z1598B

CLAYTON, J. A., Private, 23rd London Regiment.
Volunteering in 1915 he was drafted to France early in the following year. Whilst overseas he fought in many of the principal engagements, including those at Ypres and Arras. In 1918 he was severely wounded in action and after being invalided home was for some time in hospital. He was discharged in February 1919, and holds the General Service and Victory Medals. 21, Barmore Street, Battersea, S.W.11.   Z1598C

CLAYTON, J. A., Private, 23rd London Regiment.
He joined in 1916 and after his training, which he obtained at Clapham and Winchester, was drafted to France. Whilst in this theatre of war he fought in many notable engagements, including those at Ypres and the Somme, where he was twice wounded. He remained overseas, however, until after the termination of hostilities and was demobilised on his return to England in 1919. He holds the General Service and Victory Medals.
2, Lithgow Street, Battersea, S.W.11.   Z1597B

CLAYTON, P. S., L/Corporal, 2/19th London Regt.
He volunteered in June 1915 and in September 1916 was sent to France, where he was severely wounded in action on the Somme. He was invalided home, but on his recovery in November 1917 was sent to Egypt and thence to Palestine. Whilst in this theatre of war he was attached for a time to the Royal Irish Rifles and took part in many important engagements. He also served for eight months with the Military Foot Police and as Assistant Provost Marshal's Clerk at Port Said. Returning to England he was demobilised in November 1919, and holds the General Service and Victory Medals.
45, Tredescant Road, South Lambeth Road, S.W.8.   Z1596

CLAYTON, W. E., Private, Bedfordshire Regiment.
He joined in 1917 and on completing his training was sent to the Western Front, where he subsequently fought in several engagements. He fell fighting on October 24th of the same year, and was entitled to the General Service and Victory Medals. 2, Lithgow Street, Battersea, S.W.11.   Z1597A

CLAYTON, W. E., Private, 11th Suffolk Regiment.
Volunteering in 1915 he was sent to France early in the following year and took part in many of the principal engagements, including those on the Somme and at Ypres. He gave his life for the freedom of England in the Battle of Cambrai on October 24th, 1918. He was entitled to the General Service and Victory Medals. 21, Barmore Street, Battersea, S.W.11.   Z1598A

CLEMENTS, A. E. (D.C.M., M.M.), Sergt., Tank Corps.
Volunteering in 1914, he was sent to France early in the following year, but, after serving with the 22nd London Regiment at Givenchy, was sent to England owing to his being under age. He was then transferred to the Machine Gun Corps, in which he was engaged as an Instructor until 1917, when he was again drafted to the Western Front. In this theatre of war he subsequently served with the Tank Corps and was in the same year awarded the Distinguished Conduct Medal for gallantry in the Field. He showed great courage and contempt of danger in all the engagements in which he took part and on October 4th, 1918, he was awarded the Military Medal for a further act of conspicuous bravery and devotion to duty whilst in action at Ramecourt. On the following day he died gloriously on the field of battle. He was entitled to the 1914–15 Star, and the General Service and Victory Medals.
"He joined the great white company of valiant souls."
40, Thurlow Street, Walworth, S.E.17.   Z1601B

CLEMENTS, E. J. (M.M.), Gunner, R.F.A.
He volunteered early in 1915 and after his training served on the Western Front for over three years. During this time he took an active part in many of the principal engagements, including those at Arras and Ypres. Throughout his service he did splendid work with his Battery, and was awarded the Military Medal for bravery and devotion to duty whilst in action on the Somme during the German Offensive in 1918. In addition he holds the 1914–15 Star, and the General Service and Victory Medals, and was demobilised on his return to England in 1919.
46, Thurlow Street, Walworth, S.E.17.   Z1601A

CLEMENTS, J., Private, 13th Middlesex Regiment.
Volunteering in September 1914 he was sent to the Western Front in the following March. He fought at Neuve Chapelle, Hill 60, Loos, Albert, Ypres, Vimy Ridge, the Somme and Cambrai and in the Retreat and Advance of 1918, and on three occasions was wounded. Returning to England he was invalided out of the Service in December 1918, and holds the 1914–15 Star, and the General Service and Victory Medals.
15, Townsend Street, Walworth, S.E.17.   Z1600

CLEVERLY, F. E., Private, M.G.C.

Called up from the Reserve he was engaged on duties of an important nature until early in 1915, when he was sent to the Western Front. Whilst in this theatre of war he fought in many important engagements, including those of the Somme and Cambrai, where in March 1918 he was severely wounded. He then returned to England and in March 1920 was invalided out of the Service. He is still under treatment. He holds the 1914-15 Star, and the General Service and Victory Medals.
54, Heath Road, Wandsworth Road, S.W.8.   Z1602A

CLEWER, H. S., Driver, R.F.A.

He volunteered in August 1914 and after his training served on the Western Front for a year, during which time he took part in several of the principal engagements, including those of St. Eloi and Ypres. He was then drafted to Salonika and did excellent work with his Battery in the operations on the Struma, Vardar and Doiran fronts. Returning to England in February 1919 he was demobilised in the following April, and holds the 1914-15 Star, and the General Service and Victory Medals.
98, Westmorland Road, Walworth, S.E.17.   Z1603

CLIFF, J., Private, M.G.C.

He volunteered in November 1915 at the age of only fifteen years and on the completion of his training was drafted to the Western Front. After taking part in several engagements he died gloriously on the field of battle in the Somme sector on July 20th, 1916. He was entitled to the General Service and Victory Medals.
" Honour to the immortal dead who gave their youth that the
    world might grow old in peace."
58, St. Dunstan's Road, Hammersmith, W.6.   13529A

CLIFF, T., Private, R.A.S.C.

He volunteered in June 1915 and during his service on the Western Front was engaged on important transport work. In this capacity he did valuable work with his unit until hostilities ceased and was present at engagements in many sectors, notably those of Ypres, Passchendaele and Poperinghe. He holds the General Service and Victory Medals, and was demobilised in March, 1919.
58, St. Dunstan's Road, Hammersmith, W.6.   13529B

CLIFFORD, J., Corporal, 5th (Prince Charlotte of Wales') Dragoon Guards.

A serving soldier, who enlisted in October 1911, he was drafted to France immediately upon the outbreak of War and took part in the Retreat from Mons and the Battles of the Marne and Le Cateau. He also fought at La Bassée, Ypres, St. Eloi, Hill 60 and Festubert, where he was so severely wounded as to necessitate his return to England. For seven months he was under treatment in the London Hospital and was afterwards retained on home duties until February 1918, when in consequence of ill-health following wounds he was invalided out of the Service. He holds the Mons Star, and the General Service and Victory Medals.
5, Glendall Street, Ferndale Road, S.W.9.   Z1604

CLIFFORD, T., A.B., Royal Navy.

He joined in November 1916 and was in training at Chatham until the following January, when he was posted to H.M.S. " Centaur." This vessel served on important duties with the North Sea Patrol, and was also engaged in the Battle of Heligoland, and in several actions with enemy submarines. She was subsequently mined and badly damaged, and after returning to the Base he was transferred to H.M.S. " Curacoa," in which he served until the cessation of hostilities. He was demobilised in April 1919, and holds the General Service and Victory Medals.
60, Elstead Street, Walworth, S.E.17.   Z1605

CLIFT, A. E. (M.M.), Gunner, R.F.A.

Mobilised at the outbreak of hostilities he was sent to the Western Front in March 1915 and fought at Fleurbaix, St. Eloi, Hill 60, Ypres, Festubert, Loos, Albert, the Somme, Ploegsteert Wood, Arras, Messines and St. Quentin. Later he was drafted to Italy, where he again took part in much heavy fighting, and in 1918 returned to France and served in the Retreat and Advance of 1918, during which he was awarded the Military Medal for bravery and devotion to duty. After the termination of hostilities he was sent to Germany with the Army of Occupation, and was demobilised on his return to England in May 1919. He holds in addition to the decoration won on the Field the 1914-15 Star, and the General Service and Victory Medals.
162, Peabody Avenue, Ebury Bridge, Pimlico, S.W.1.   Z23301

CLIFTON, W. G., Private, 5th Argyll and Sutherland Highlanders.

Volunteering in April 1915 he was sent to Egypt in the following January, and after taking part in several minor engagements there proceeded to Palestine. In this theatre of war he fought in the Battles of Gaza and was present at the Capture of Jerusalem. He was transferred to France in 1918 and served throughout the Retreat and Advance of the Allies. Returning to England after the termination of hostilities he was demobilised in January 1919, and holds the General Service and Victory Medals.
184, Farmer's Road, Camberwell, S.E.5.   Z1606

CLINTON, J. F., Trooper, 6th Dragoon Guards (Carabiniers).

Volunteering in August 1914 he was sent to France two months later. His service in this theatre of war lasted for over four years, during which time he took part in many notable battles, including those of Ypres, Loos, Albert, the Somme, Arras, Passchendaele and Cambrai, and the Retreat and Advance of 1918. He was demobilised in November of the following year, and holds the 1914 Star, and the General Service and Victory Medals.
10, Hopwood Street, Walworth, S.E.17.   23309B

CLODE, A. B., L/Corporal, R.G.A.

He joined in April 1916 and served for two years in the Island of Inchkeith as an Instructor and Mess Caterer, and in other important duties with his Battery. When on draft for France he was detained for instructional purposes and rendered most valuable services in this way until August 1919, when he was demobilised. He was one of eight brothers who served their country in the War, the youngest of whom unfortunately died.
9, Auckland Road, Battersea, S.W.11.   Z1607

CLODE, J., Rifleman, Rifle Brigade.

He was mobilised in August 1914 and was shortly afterwards sent to France, where he took part in severe fighting at Mons, Le Cateau, the Marne, La Bassée, Ypres, Neuve Chapelle, St. Eloi and Hill 60, and was wounded at Ypres in 1915. He was invalided home and was discharged in May 1916 as medically unfit for further service, and holds the Mons Star, and the General Service and Victory Medals.
12, Nunhead Green, S.E.15.   Z6152

CLOKE, E. J., Driver, R.F.A.

He volunteered in September 1914 and in the following year was drafted to the Western Front, where he served for a short time in the Ypres sector. Afterwards he was transferred to Egypt and thence to Salonika, where he saw much service on the Struma, Doiran and Vardar fronts until hostilities ceased. He was demobilised in December 1918, holding the 1914-15 Star, and the General Service and Victory Medals.
98, Wadhurst Road, New Battersea Park Road, S.W.8.   Z1608A

CLOVER, F., Private, R.A.S.C. (M.T.)

Volunteering in March 1915 he was sent to France in the same year. He rendered valuable service in many important engagements, including those at the Somme, Arras, Vimy Ridge, Ypres, Passchendaele and Cambrai, and also took part in the Retreat and Advance of 1918. He was demobilised in 1919, holding the 1914-15 Star, and the General Service and Victory Medals.
30, Thurlow Street, Walworth, S.E.17.   Z1609

CLOW, E. H., A/Q.M.S., Middlesex Regiment attached to R.F.A.

He joined in January 1916 and was engaged at Woolwich in the R.F.A. Record Office. He rendered valuable services but was not successful in obtaining his transfer overseas before the cessation of hostilities on account of his medical unfitness for active service. He was demobilised in March 1920.
9, Combermere Road, Stockwell, S.W.9.   Z1610

CLOWSLEY, A., Private, 5th Hampshire Regiment.

He was mobilised with the Territorials at the outbreak of War and was sent to Scotland, where he was engaged on special duties. He rendered valuable services but was not successful in obtaining his transfer overseas on account of his medical unfitness for active service. He was discharged in 1917 owing to his physical disabilities.
13, Patmore Street, Wandsworth Road, S.W.8.   Z1611

CLUNN, A., Private, East Surrey Regiment.

He joined in March 1916 and at the conclusion of his training in the September following was sent to the Western Front. In the course of his service he fought in many of the principal battles, including those of the Somme, Ypres, Passchendaele Ridge and Cambrai, and did valuable work. He was in turn attached to the Northumberland Fusiliers, the Norfolk Regiment and the Labour Corps. Towards the close of hostilities he was invalided home in consequence of ill-health and on his recovery in February 1919 was demobilised. He holds the General Service and Victory Medals.
119, Akerman Road, Brixton Road, S.W.9.   Z4426

COAD, E. A., Private, 3rd South African Infantry Regiment.

He volunteered in 1914 with General Botha's Commando and took an active part in the German East African Campaign. He was afterwards transferred to England and subsequently to Egypt in 1916. Later in the same year he proceeded to France. He fell fighting at Delville Wood on July 18th, 1916, and was entitled to the 1914-15 Star, and the General Service and Victory Medals.
" The path of duty was the way to glory."
14, Peardon Street, Wandsworth Road, S.W.8.   Z1612

COALES, L. D. (Miss), Special War Worker.
This lady was engaged for nearly five years with Messrs. Dewrance and Co., Ltd., Electrical Engineers, Great Dover Street, S.E., in the manufacture of pressure gauges for ships and aeroplanes. The work, which was of a most important nature, was carried out in a commendable manner, and she rendered valuable services during the War.
7, Flinton Street, Walworth, S.E.17.   Z1613A

COALES, N. (Miss), Special War Worker.
From January 1915 until September 1919 this lady was engaged on duties of vital importance at Messrs. Dewrance & Co.'s Works, Great Dover Street. She was employed in making pressure gauges for aeroplanes and ships, and performed her delicate work with the utmost care and skill.
7, Flinton Street, Walworth, S.E.17.   Z1613B

COATES, W. H., Rifleman, 18th London Regiment (London Irish Rifles).
He volunteered in 1915 and at the conclusion of his training was sent to the Western Front, where he fought in several important engagements and was severely wounded. Invalided to a hospital in England he was for some time under treatment, but on his recovery returned to France. Subsequently he again went into action and died gloriously on the field of battle on March 26th, 1918, during the German Offensive. He was entitled to the 1914-15 Star, and the General Service and Victory Medals.
"He passed out of the sight of men by the path of duty and self-sacrifice."
79, East Surrey Grove, Peckham, S.E.15.   Z5058

COATH, S. R. G., Sapper, R.E.
Volunteering in November 1915 he was sent to France in April of the following year. He took part in many important engagements, including those at St. Eloi, Albert, Vermelles, Vimy Ridge and the Somme. In December 1916 he was transferred to Egypt and later proceeded to Palestine, where he rendered valuable service at Rafa, Gaza, Jerusalem, Jericho, Tripoli and Aleppo. He was demobilised in July 1919, holding the General Service and Victory Medals.
25, Ranelagh Road, Pimlico, S.W.1.   Z2757B

COBB, R., Rifleman, 17th London Regiment (Rifles).
He volunteered in October 1915 and in January of the following year was drafted to the Western Front, where he took part in the severe fighting at Ypres and on the Ancre front. He was wounded and invalided home in January 1917, but on his recovery was engaged on important home duties with his unit until he was demobilised in May 1919. He holds the General Service and Victory Medals.
15, Barmore Street, Battersea, S.W.11.   Z1614

COBBOLD, H. (Senior), Rifleman, Rifle Brigade.
He had previously served in the Suffolk Regiment during the South African War and in India. On the outbreak of War he re-enlisted in the Rifle Brigade and was engaged on important duties with his unit until 1916, when he volunteered for service in India. He was demobilised in January 1919, holding the Queen's South African, and the General Service and Victory Medals. He unfortunately died in October 1919 through illness contracted during the War.
"His memory is cherished with pride."
7, Wycliffe Road, Battersea, S.W.11.   Z1615A

COBBOLD, H. W. C., Private, East Surrey Regiment.
He joined in April 1918 and in October of the same year was drafted to France. After a few weeks he proceeded with the Army of Occupation to Germany, where he remained until September 1919. Having re-enlisted for a further term of service he was sent to Turkey in January 1920. He holds the General Service and Victory Medals.
7, Wycliffe Road, Battersea, S.W.11.   Z1615B

COCKERTON, H. C., 1st Air Mechanic, R.A.F.
He joined in March 1917 and after his training was drafted to the Western Front, where he was engaged on important duties in connection with the repairing of damaged machines at various aerodromes. In this capacity he did valuable work until after the termination of hostilities and was demobilised on his return to England in November 1919. He holds the General Service and Victory Medals.
24, Langton Road, Vassall Road, S.W.9.   Z5059

COCKMAN, J., L/Corporal, R.E. (Signals).
He was mobilised in August 1914 with the R.A.M.C. and was transferred to the R.E. in September of the same year. In March 1915 he crossed to France, where he took part in numerous engagements, including those at Givenchy, Loos, Vimy Ridge, the Somme, Messines and Cambrai. He also rendered valuable service in the Retreat and Advance of 1918. He was demobilised in April 1919, holding the 1914-15 Star, and the General Service and Victory Medals.
70, Lavender Road, Battersea, S.W.11.   Z1618

COCKMAN, M. (Mrs.), Special War Worker.
This lady for nearly three years was engaged by the London General Omnibus Company as a bus conductress thereby releasing a man for the Army. She carried out her duties in an exemplary manner and rendered valuable services during the War.
30, Mansion Street, Camberwell, S.E.5.   Z1616B

COCKMAN, O. L., Private, King's Own Yorkshire Light Infantry.
After joining in January 1916 and completing his training he was drafted to France in the same year. He took part in the severe fighting at Arras, Ypres and in many other engagements, and was badly gassed in March 1918. He was demobilised in February 1919, holding the General Service and Victory Medals. He unfortunately died through the effects of the gas poisoning on July 7th, 1920.
"He joined the great white company of valiant souls."
30, Mansion Street, Camberwell, S.E.5.   Z1616A

COCKS, G. F., Gunner (Saddler), R.F.A.
Volunteering in February 1915 he was drafted to the Western Front in the same year. He took part in numerous engagements, including those at Ypres, Loos, the Somme and the Ancre, and also served in the Retreat and Advance of 1918. He was demobilised in March 1919, holding the 1914-15 Star, and the General Service and Victory Medals.
10, Draycourt Place, Camberwell, S.E.5.   Z3999

COE, G. H., Driver, R.E.
He re-enlisted in August 1914 and in the following year proceeded to France, where he rendered valuable services in many engagements of importance, including those at Hooge, Loos, the Somme, Ypres, Passchendaele, Lens, Cambrai and the Retreat and Advance of 1918. He returned to England and was demobilised in May 1919, holding the 1914-15 Star, and the General Service and Victory Medals.
9, Copeland Road, Peckham, S.E.15.   Z5588C

COFFIELD, G., 1st Air Mechanic, R.A.F. (late R.N.A.S.)
He joined in May 1916 and after his training served at various stations on important duties with his Squadron. He was engaged as leading electrician, and his work, which demanded a high degree of technical skill, was carried out with great efficiency. He was not successful in obtaining his transfer overseas before the cessation of hostilities, and was demobilised in January 1919.
61, Villa Street, Walworth, S.E.17.   Z1619

COFFIN, A., Gunner, R.F.A.
Shortly after volunteering in June 1915 he was sent to the Western Front, where he saw severe fighting in various sectors. He took part in the Battles of Arras, Lens and St. Quentin and many minor engagements in this theatre of war and also fought in the Advance of 1918. He was demobilised on his return home in July 1919, and holds the 1914-15 Star, and the General Service and Victory Medals.
3, Sussex Road, Coldharbour Lane, S.W.9.   Z5742B

COFFIN, J., Private, 1/4th Royal Berkshire Regt., and 1/5th Staffordshire Regt.
He joined in November 1916 and in the following year was drafted to the Western Front. There he took part in many important engagements, including those of the Somme, Arras, Albert, Ypres, Messines, Bourlon Wood, Delville Wood, Amiens and in the Advance of 1918. He was demobilised in November 1919, and holds the General Service and Victory Medals.
3, Sussex Road, Coldharbour Lane, S.W.9.   Z5742A

COLBOURNE, G., Rifleman, 16th London Regiment (Queen's Westminster Rifles), and Private, M.G.C.
He joined in October 1916 and after completing his training was in the following year sent to the Western Front, where he took part in the severe fighting at Arras, Bullecourt, Messines, Lens and Cambrai. He also fought in the Retreat and Advance of 1918. In August 1919 he was transferred to Egypt, and after his return home was demobilised in May 1920, holding the General Service and Victory Medals.
51, Darwin Street, Walworth, S.E.17.   Z1620

COLE, A. H., C.P.O., R.N., H.M.S. "Bulwark."
He enlisted in 1908 and at the outbreak of War was serving on H.M.S. "Bulwark" with the Grand Fleet in the North Sea. He became seriously ill soon afterwards and was discharged as medically unfit for further service in September 1914, and holds the 1914-15 Star, and the General Service and Victory Medals. He afterwards volunteered for further service, but was rejected on medical grounds.
18, Hubert Grove, Stockwell, S.W.9.   Z1622

COLE, C., Sapper, R.E.
He joined in June 1917 and after his training served at various stations on important coastal duties. He was also engaged on repairing boots for the troops and rendered valuable services. He was not successful in obtaining a transfer overseas before the cessation of hostilities, and was demobilised in January 1919.
1A, Clifton Square, Peckham, S.E.15.   Z5924

COLE, C. D., Air Mechanic, R.A.F. (late R.N.A.S.)

Joining in 1916 he was drafted in the same year to the Western Front and served with the Independent Air Force. He was engaged at Dunkirk and other places in the repair of aero-engines and on patrol duties over the enemy lines until hostilities ceased. He was demobilised in 1919, and holds the General Service and Victory Medals.
68, Faraday Street, Walworth, S.E.17.   Z1624

COLE, G., Corporal, R.E. (I.W.T.)

He volunteered in July 1915 and in September of the same year was sent to the Western Front. He was engaged with the Inland Water Transport until hostilities ended in conveying ammunition and supplies to the various Fronts by barge and rendered valuable services. He also served in Dunkirk and Calais during the raids. He was demobilised in January 1919, and holds the 1914-15 Star, and the General Service and Victory Medals.
11, Lombard Road, Battersea, S.W.11.   Z1623

COLE, H. C., Private, King's (Liverpool Regiment).

He volunteered in December 1915 and after completing his training was retained on important duties with his unit until 1917, when he was sent to the Western front. While there he took part in the severe fighting on many battle fronts, and after being wounded was invalided home. He was discharged owing to his injuries in January 1920, and holds the General Service and Victory Medals.
49, Wayford Street, Battersea, S.W.11.   Z1625

COLE, J., Private, Royal Fusiliers.

He joined in 1917 after having previously served with the Essex Regiment in India, and was engaged on important duties until the end of the War. He rendered valuable clerical services in the Army Pay Office, Hounslow, but was not successful in obtaining his transfer overseas before the cessation of hostilities. He was demobilised in December 1919.
95, Battersea Bridge Road, Battersea, S.W.11.   Z1621B

COLE, J. A., Driver, R.A.S.C. (M.T.)

Volunteering in May 1915 he crossed to France in the following March. Whilst overseas he did valuable work as a transport driver at Ypres, Arras, the Somme and other places, and was present at many notable engagements. After the termination of hostilities he advanced into Germany with the Army of Occupation, and was demobilised in May 1919 on his return to England. He holds the General Service and Victory Medals.
118, Cronin Road, Peckham, S.E.15.   Z5352

COLE, S. M. (Miss), Special War Worker.

From November 1917 this lady was engaged on clerical work of great importance by the Navy and Army Canteens Board. She carried out her responsible duties with great care and accuracy and rendered valuable services. She was still serving in 1920.
21, Dale Street, Chiswick, W.4.   T5342B

COLE, W. R., Private, 29th Middlesex Regiment.

Joining in February 1917 he was sent to France in August of the same year. He took part in the Battle of Cambrai and also rendered valuable service in the Retreat and Advance of 1918. He was demobilised in February 1919 after returning home, and holds the General Service and Victory Medals.
21, Dale Street, Chiswick, W.4.   T5342A

COLEMAN, A. E., Private, R.A.S.C.

Volunteering in February 1915 he was drafted to France in the same month. He was engaged in many sectors on important duties with his unit and rendered valuable services. In 1918 he was invalided home owing to shell-shock and on his recovery was sent to Ireland, where he remained until he was demobilised in February 1919. He holds the 1914-15 Star, and the General Service and Victory Medals.
20, Lubeck Street, Battersea, S.W.11.   Z1626

COLEMAN, A. W., Air Mechanic, R.A.F. (Balloon Section).

He joined in November 1917 and in the following February was sent to Gibraltar, where he was engaged on important coastal defence and submarine patrol duties. He was demobilised in March 1919, and holds the General Service and Victory Medals.
29, Albert Road, Peckham, S.E.15.   Z5927B

COLEMAN, H., Private, 3rd Royal Fusiliers, and 11th Royal Welch Fusiliers.

Volunteering in April 1915 he was sent to France in the same year. He took part in the severe fighting at Givenchy and was afterwards transferred to Egypt. After a short stay there he proceeded to Salonika and was in action on the Struma and Doiran fronts. He was severely wounded in September 1918 on the Doiran front and invalided to Malta. He also suffered from malaria during his service in the East. He was demobilised in February 1919 after his return home, and holds the 1914-15 Star, and the General Service and Victory Medals.
48, Edithna Street, Stockwell, S.W.9.   Z1627

COLEMAN, C., Private, R.A.S.C. (H.T.)

He volunteered in September 1914 and shortly afterwards was drafted to the Western Front. He was engaged on important transport and supply duties with his unit in many sectors and rendered valuable services until the close of the War. He returned home and was demobilised in February 1919, holding the 1914 Star, and the General Service and Victory Medals.
70, Faroe Road, West Kensington, W.14.   T12186B

COLEMAN, H., Rifleman, 16th London Regiment (Queen's Westminster Rifles).

He volunteered in November 1915 and in July of the following year was drafted to France. After only two months' service on the Western Front he was reported missing during the Battle of the Somme on September 10th, 1916. He was afterwards presumed to have been killed in action on that date, and was entitled to the General Service and Victory Medals.
"His life for his Country, his Soul to God."
29, Albert Road, Peckham, S.E.15.   Z5927A

COLEMAN, H. A., Driver, R.F.A.

Volunteering in June 1915 he proceeded to France in January 1916 and took an active part in the Battles of Vimy Ridge, the Somme, Arras, Messines, Ypres and Passchendaele. He was severely wounded in the Ypres sector in September 1917 and after being invalided home was discharged in May 1918 as unfit for further duty. He holds the General Service and Victory Medals.
28, Cronin Road, Peckham, S.E.15.   Z5582

COLEMAN, W., Rifleman, King's Royal Rifle Corps.

He volunteered in September 1914 and after completing his training was drafted to the Western Front, where he took part in much severe fighting in many important engagements and was severely wounded at Loos. He was invalided home and discharged owing to his injuries in July 1918, holding the 1914-15 Star and the General Service and Victory Medals.
70, Faroe Road, West Kensington, W.14.   T12186C

COLERIDGE, E. R. C., Private, R.A.S.C. (M.T.)

Joining in November 1916 he was sent to France in the same month. Whilst in this theatre of war he did valuable work as a transport and ambulance driver in many important sectors, including those of Cambrai, Ypres, Passchendaele and Bullecourt. He was demobilised in February 1919 after his return to England, and holds the General Service and Victory Medals.
102, Trafalgar Road, Peckham, S.E.15.   Z3444A

COLES, A. B., Gunner, R.F.A., and Private, R.A.S.C.

Volunteering in November 1914 he was drafted to the Western Front in the following September. During his service overseas he fought in the Battles of Loos, the Somme, Arras and Ypres, where he was so badly gassed as to necessitate his return to England for treatment. On his recovery he was transferred to the R.A.S.C. and served on important duties at various stations until February 1919, when he was discharged. He holds the 1914-15 Star, and the General Service and Victory Medals.
224, Grosvenor Terrace, Camberwell, S.E.5.   Z1628

COLES, A. W., Air Mechanic, R.A.F.

He volunteered in November 1915 and after completing his training was drafted to Egypt in July 1916. Throughout his service he was engaged on important duties, which called for a high degree of technical knowledge and skill, and did valuable work. He was demobilised in 1919 after returning home, and holds the General Service and Victory Medals.
36, Arthur Road, Brixton Road, S.W.9.   Z3069

COLES, F. L., Private, 4th Royal Fusiliers.

He joined in August 1918 in the King's Royal Rifle Corps and proceeded to France with his Regiment and then to Cologne with the Army of Occupation. In 1919 he returned to England, and was transferred to the 4th Royal Fusiliers, and in September of the same year sailed for Mesopotamia, where he was engaged on important duties as a despatch rider. In 1920 he was still serving, and holds the General Service and Victory Medals.
49, Denmark Road, Camberwell, S.E.5.   Z5919

COLES, J. J., Corporal, Royal Fusiliers.

He joined in September 1916 and at the conclusion of his training was sent to the Western Front. Whilst in this theatre of war he took part in many important engagements, including those at the Somme, Arras and Albert, until, on account of his age, he returned to England. He was discharged in July 1918, and holds the General Service and Victory Medals.
77, Avenue Road, Camberwell, S.E.5.   Z1629A

COLES, S. J., Private, R.M.L.I., H.M.S. "Cressy" and "Campania."

He was serving at the outbreak of War in H.M.S. "Cressy," and was in that vessel when she was torpedoed in the North Sea in September 1914. After being in the water for about four hours he was fortunately rescued. Later he was in the "Campania" when she was in a collision but happily he was picked up without having sustained serious injury. He was still serving in 1920, and holds the 1914-15 Star, and the General Service and Victory Medals.
54, Gordon Road, Peckham, S.E.15.   Z6153

COLLETT, W. R., Rifleman, Rifle Brigade.

Joining in June 1916 he was sent to the Western Front at the conclusion of his training and fought at St. Eloi and the Somme. He gave his life for King and country at the Battle of Arras on May 12th, 1917. He was entitled to the General Service and Victory Medals.

"He died the noblest death a man may die,
Fighting for God, and right, and liberty."
75, Tasman Road, Landor Road, S.W.9. Z1630

COLLEY, J., Gunner, R.G.A.

He volunteered in November 1914 and after his training served on important duties with his unit until August 1916, when he was drafted to Egypt. In this theatre of war he took part in several minor engagements and later was sent to Palestine. In this Campaign he fought at Magdhaba, Rafa, Sieva and Gaza, and was present at the Capture of Jerusalem, Jericho, Tripoli and Aleppo. He was demobilised on his return to England in September 1919, and holds the General Service and Victory Medals.
85, Beckway Street, Walworth, S.E.17. Z1631

COLLIER, E. A., Corporal, R.A.V.C.

He volunteered in August 1914 and during his service on the Western Front, which lasted for practically the whole period of War, was engaged on veterinary duties of an important nature in connection with sick and wounded horses. He holds the Mons Star, and the General Service and Victory Medals, and was demobilised in 1919 after his return to England.
4, Bolingbroke Road, Battersea, S.E.11. Z1112A

COLLIER, G. W., Bandsman, Royal Navy.

Having joined the Navy in 1901 he was serving on board H.M.S. "Natal" when war broke out and subsequently took part in several Naval actions. Unhappily he lost his life when his ship was destroyed by an internal explosion in Cromarty Firth on December 31st, 1915. He was entitled to the 1914-15 Star, and the General Service and Victory Medals.
"His memory is cherished with pride."
7, Sterndale Road, Wandsworth Road, S.W.8. 1632B

COLLIER, P. W., Corporal, Royal Fusiliers.

He joined in October 1916 and in the following April was drafted to France. There he took part in many engagements, including the Battles of the Somme, Ypres, Vimy Ridge and Cambrai. He was killed in action in August 1918, and was entitled to the General Service and Victory Medals.
"A costly sacrifice upon the altar of freedom."
19, Sears Street, Camberwell, S.E.5. Z5724

COLLINGRIDGE, W., Sergt., 2nd East Surrey Regt.

He joined in the 21st London Regiment in October 1916 and in the course of his training was transferred to the 16th Worcestershire and the 2nd East Surrey Regiments. During his service he was engaged on important duties in many different capacities at Frinton, Barrow, Cardiff, Swindon and other places, and although he was unable to secure his transfer overseas before the termination of hostilities, did valuable work until January 1920, when in consequence of ill-health he was discharged.
5, Inworth Street, Battersea, S.W.11. Z1633

COLLINGS, P., Sapper, R.E.

He volunteered in 1914 and was drafted to France in the following year. Whilst serving on the Western Front he was engaged on important duties in connection with the operations and was frequently in the front lines, notably at Lens, Loos, St. Quentin, Delville Wood and Messines. He was demobilised in May 1919, and holds the 1914-15 Star, and the General Service and Victory Medals.
30, Handforth Road, Brixton Road, S.W.9. Z5229A

COLLINGS, S. B., Rifleman, Royal Irish Rifles.

He joined in 1916 and in the following year was drafted to France, where he served in the Somme sector and at Messines Ridge. Later contracting trench fever he was invalided home to hospital. After his recovery he was employed on responsible clerical duties in the Military Hospital at Birmingham being medically unfit for further active service. He was demobilised in July 1919, and holds the General Service and Victory Medals.
30, Handforth Road, Brixton Road, S.W.9. Z5229B

COLLINGS, W. J., Private, 5th Gordon Highlanders.

He volunteered in May 1915 and after his training was engaged on agricultural and timber-felling duties of an important nature at various stations with his unit. He was not successful in obtaining his transfer to a theatre of war before the cessation of hostilities, but rendered valuable services until his demobilisation in March 1919.
44, North Street, Clapham, S.W.4. Z1634

COLLINS, E., Sapper, R.E.

Volunteering in February 1915 he proceeded to France on the completion of his training and was engaged at Vimy Ridge and Arras. Afterwards he was drafted to Salonika and saw much service on the Doiran and Vardar fronts, going thence to Palestine and serving under General Allenby at Beersheba, Jerusalem, Jericho and in the Jordan Valley. He returned home in August 1919 and was demobilised, holding the General Service and Victory Medals.
33, Rozel Road, Wandsworth Road, S.W.4. Z1638B

COLLINS, E., Private, Royal Fusiliers.

He joined in 1918 and in the same year was drafted to the Western Front, where he served in the Somme and Arras sectors. He afterwards proceeded with the Army of Occupation to Germany. He was demobilised in 1920, and holds the General Service and Victory Medals.
21, Beddome Street, Walworth, S.E.17. Z1642A

COLLINS, F., Private, Somerset Light Infantry.

He volunteered in February 1915 and in the same year was drafted overseas. Whilst in France he fought in many battles, including those of Festubert, Loos, Vimy Ridge and on the Somme. He was killed in action near Ypres on August 8th, 1916, and was entitled to the 1914-15 Star, and the General Service and Victory Medals.
"A valiant soldier, with undaunted heart he breasted Life's last hill."
12, Tidemore Street, Battersea Park Road, S.W.8. Z1636A

COLLINS, F., Corporal, 2nd Dragoon Guards (Queen's Bays).

He was in the Army at the outbreak of War and almost immediately proceeded overseas. He took part in the fighting on many sectors of the Western Front during the whole of the War and after the cessation of hostilities was drafted to Germany with the Army of Occupation, where in 1920 he was still serving. He holds the 1914 Star, and the General Service and Victory Medals.
29, Stonehill Road, Chiswick, W.4. 6068A

COLLINS, H., Private, Royal Sussex Regiment.

Volunteering in November 1914 he was drafted on the completion of his training to the Western Front. Whilst there he fought in several battles and was seriously wounded by shrapnel. He was invalided home in consequence and after receiving hospital treatment was discharged in 1915 as medically unfit for further duty. He holds the 1914-15 Star, and the General Service and Victory Medals.
29, Stonehill Road, Chiswick, W.4. 6068C

COLLINS, H. J., Trooper, 2nd Dragoon Guards (Queen's Bays).

He was in the Army at the outbreak of War and was immediately drafted overseas. He gave his life for the freedom of England on September 1st, 1914, in the memorable Retreat from Mons. He was entitled to the Mons Star, and the General Service and Victory Medals.
"His life for his country, his soul to God."
29, Stonehill Road, Chiswick, W.4. 6068B

COLLINS, H. J., Private, Royal Naval Division.

He joined in September 1918 and was engaged on important duties with his unit. He was not successful in obtaining his transfer overseas before the cessation of hostilities and in November 1918 was demobilised.
9, Kingswood Road, Chiswick, W.4. T6299B

COLLINS, J. H., Corporal, Border Regiment.

He was in the Army at the outbreak of War and was immediately drafted to France. There he fought in the memorable Retreat from Mons, the Battles of Le Cateau, the Marne, the Aisne, Hill 60, Ypres and the Somme Offensive, where he was wounded. He was invalided to England, but on his recovery returned to the fighting line. He took part in the Battle of Cambrai in 1917 and the Retreat and Advance and was again wounded at Albert. After his discharge from hospital he was engaged on important duties as a Machine-gun Instructor until May 1919, when he was placed on the Reserve. He holds the Mons Star, and the General Service and Victory Medals.
19, Barmore Street, Battersea, S.W.11. Z1640

COLLINS, J. J., R.S.M., R.E.

Mobilised from the Reserve at the outbreak of War he was almost immediately drafted to France. There he did valuable service in the Field Service Section in the Retreat from Mons, the Battles of the Marne, the Aisne, La Bassée, Ypres, Neuve Chapelle, Hill 60, the Somme, Arras and many other engagements until the close of the War. He then proceeded to Germany with the Army of Occupation and was stationed at Cologne. In 1920 he was still serving in Ireland and holds the Mons Star and the General Service and Victory Medals.
12, Exon Street, Walworth, S.E.17. Z1643

COLLINS, J. W., Private, Leicestershire Regiment; and Labour Corps.

He joined in July 1916 and in August of the same year proceeded to France. There he did valuable service in many notable engagements until hostilities ceased, including those at Arras, Messines, Ypres, Lens and Cambrai. In October 1919 he returned home and was demobilised, holding the General Service and Victory Medals.
7, Benfield Street, Battersea, S.W.11. Z1635

COLLINS, R., Gunner, R.F.A.

Volunteering in November 1914 he was drafted after having completed his training to the Western Front, where he was in action at the Somme and Arras. He then proceeded to Salonika and took part in the fighting on the Struma and Doiran fronts. Going thence to Egypt he afterwards served under General Allenby in the Advance to Jerusalem and fought at Beersheba, Gaza, the Jordan and Damascus. He returned home in June 1919 and was demobilised, holding the General Service and Victory Medals.

33, Rozel Road, Wandsworth Road, S.W.4.　　　Z1638A

COLLINS, R., Private, 2nd Queen's (Royal West Surrey Regiment).

Mobilised at the outbreak of War he crossed to France in August and fought in the Battle of and Retreat from Mons and the Battle of the Aisne. He gave his life for King and country at Ypres, where he fell fighting on November 17th, 1914. He was entitled to the Mons Star, and the General Service and Victory Medals.　　　"Great deeds cannot die."

16, Godman Road, Peckham, S.E.15.　　　Z5353

COLLINS, R. L., Driver, R.A.S.C.

Mobilised at the outbreak of War he was drafted in September of the same year to Malta, where he was engaged on important duties until April 1916. He then proceeded to Salonika and in this theatre of war saw much service until the cessation of hostilities. He returned home and was demobilised in April 1919, holding the General Service and Victory Medals.

33, Rozel Road, Wandsworth Road, S.W.4.　　　Z1638C

COLLINS, S., Air Mechanic, R.A.F.

He joined in 1916 and in the same year was drafted to the Western Front, where he served in the Arras and Somme sectors. He also served in Belgium. After the Armistice he proceeded with the Army of Occupation to Germany. He was demobilised in 1919, and holds the General Service and Victory Medals.

21, Beddome Street, Walworth, S.E.17.　　　Z1642B

COLLINS, S. H., Private, Labour Corps.

After volunteering several times and being rejected he joined in September 1918 and was speedily drafted overseas. Whilst in France he did good work at Albert, the Somme and Cambrai in the advance of 1918 and was principally engaged on special duties with the Re-interment Corps. In December 1919 he returned home and was demobilised, holding the General Service and Victory Medals.

57, Surrey Square, Walworth, S.E.17.　　　Z1639

COLLINS, S. W., Private, Queen's Own (Royal West Kent Regiment).

Volunteering in September 1914 in the "Buffs" he proceeded a year later to France, where he was severely wounded at Loos, in his first engagement. He was invalided home, but in April 1916 returned to the Western Front, and later went into action on the Somme, where operations were then in progress. At the end of July however he was again sent to England suffering from fever, and on his recovery in August was transferred to the Queen's Own and re-drafted to France. He subsequently fought at Arras, Cambrai and the Somme, and in the Retreat of 1918, but in May of that year in consequence of continued ill-health returned to England, and was demobilised in February 1919. He holds the 1914-15 Star, and the General Service and Victory Medals.

185B, Cator Street, Peckham, S.E.15.　　　Z5060

COLLINS, T. B., Rifleman, 18th London Regiment (London Irish Rifles).

He volunteered in September 1914 and on the completion of his training proceeded to France in 1916. Whilst there he served at the Somme and Beaumont-Hamel, and afterwards was drafted to Egypt. Later he saw much service in the Advance through Palestine, in which he was wounded. In consequence of his severe injuries he died in May 1918. He was entitled to the General Service and Victory Medals.

"Honour to the immortal dead who gave their youth that the world might grow old in peace."

70, Coronation Buildings, South Lambeth Road, S.W.8. Z1644B

COLLINS, W., Private, 57th Battalion Australian Expeditionary Force.

Volunteering at the outbreak of War he left Australia for France in August 1914 and subsequently fought in many important engagements. In 1915 he was drafted to the Dardanelles and took part in the Landing at Gallipoli and the engagements which followed. After the Evacuation of the Peninsula he returned to France and was wounded. He was then sent back to Australia, but in 1917 was re-drafted to the Western Front, where he was again in action and was wounded. He was demobilised in November 1919, and holds the 1914-15 Star, and the General Service and Victory Medals.

133, Rosemary Road, Peckham, S.E.15.　　　Z5354

COLLINS, T. W., Corporal, R.E.

Volunteering in February 1915 he was drafted in May of the same year to the Western Front. There he rendered valuable service with his unit at the Somme, Arras, Cambrai, Béthune, St. Quentin and in many other sectors until the close of War. He returned home in March 1919 and was demobilised, holding the 1914-15 Star, and the General Service and Victory Medals.

9, Kingswood Road, Chiswick, W.4.　　　T6299C

COLLINS, W., Driver, R.F.A.

Volunteering in August 1915 he was sent to the Western Front in the following February. During his service overseas he fought in several important engagements, but in September 1918, owing to loss of speech following shell-shock, he was invalided home and transferred to the R.A.S.C. Subsequently he did valuable agricultural work in Cornwall until he was demobilised in January 1919. He holds the General Service and Victory Medals.

135, New Church Road, Camberwell, S.E.5.　　　Z4428

COLLINS, W., Sapper, R.E.

Mobilised from the Reserve at the outbreak of war he was immediately drafted to the Western Front and served in the Retreat from Mons and the Battles of the Marne and the Aisne. He was also engaged in the heavy fighting at Arras, Ypres, Cambrai and was severely wounded and lost a leg. After protracted treatment in hospital he was discharged in July 1920 as medically unfit for further service. He holds the Queen's and King's South African Medals, the Mons Star, and the General Service and Victory Medals.

11, Page Street, Westminster, S.W.1.　　　TZ23583

COLLINS, W. J., Private, R.A.S.C., and King's Own Yorkshire Light Infantry.

He volunteered in April 1915 and in the same year was drafted overseas. He served for two years in many sectors of the Western Front on important transport duties, and was afterwards transferred to the Infantry and with them took part in numerous engagements until hostilities ceased. He was demobilised in January 1919, and holds the 1914-15 Star, and the General Service and Victory Medals.

16, Bolney Street, Dorset Road, S.W.8.　　　Z1641

COLLMAN, W. H. A., Sapper, R.E.

He volunteered in January 1915 and was sent to the Western Front in the same year. He took part in numerous engagements, including those at Arras, Ypres, Bullecourt and Cambrai, and was engaged in laying cables. He was demobilised in February 1919, holding the 1914-15 Star, and the General Service and Victory Medals.

36, Mayall Road, Herne Hill, S.E.24.　　　Z6155

COLLOM, W. T., Rifleman, King's Royal Rifle Corps.

He volunteered in November 1914 and proceeded to France in the following year. Whilst overseas he served in numerous important engagements and was in action at the Battle of Loos. He fell fighting on March 14th, 1916, and was entitled to the 1914-15 Star, and the General Service and Victory Medals.

"His life for his Country, his Soul to God."

14, Pitcairn Street, Wandsworth Road, S.W.8.　　　Z1645

COLLYER, G. W., Sergt., R.F.A.

He volunteered in September 1914 with the Royal Field Artillery, 52nd Army Brigade, and landed in France in May of the following year. He served in many important engagements, including those at Loos, the Somme, Vimy Ridge and various subsequent operations in the Retreat and Advance of 1918. He was demobilised in June 1919, and holds the 1914-15 Star, and the General Service and Victory Medals.

36, Wickersley Road, Lavender Hill, S.W.11.　　　Z3290B

COLQUHOUN, J., Driver, R.F.A.

He volunteered in March 1915 and in the following December was drafted to France. Here he did good work as a driver at Loos, the Somme, Albert, Messines, Arras, Ypres and Cambrai, and in many subsequent engagements in the Retreat and Advance of 1918. He was demobilised in January 1919, and holds the General Service and Victory Medals.

1, High Park Crescent, Aylesbury Road, Walworth, S.E.17. Z1646

COMAN, C. H., Q.M.S., 2nd Lincolnshire Regt.

He had served for twenty-one years previous to the late War and was called up from the Reserve in August 1914. He took a distinguished part in many engagements in the Gallipoli Campaign, where he fell fighting for King and Country on August 9th, 1915. He held the Soudan and the Queen's and King's South African Medals, and was also entitled to the 1914-15 Star, and the General Service and Victory Medals.

"The path of duty was the way to glory."

210, Albert Road, Peckham, S.E.15.　　　Z5584

COMB, T. J., Gunner, R.F.A.
He joined in January 1918 and was shortly afterwards drafted to France, where he took part in the Retreat and Advance. He died gloriously on the field of battle on October 11th, 1918, and was entitled to the General Service and Victory Medals.
"Great deeds cannot die."
151, St. George's Road, Peckham, S.E.15. Z5730

COMPTON, E. S., Private, Queen's (Royal West Surrey Regiment).
He volunteered in August 1914 and after his training served at various stations on important duties with his unit. He rendered valuable services but was not successful in obtaining his transfer overseas owing to his being medically unfit for duty abroad. He was discharged in December 1915 and was afterwards engaged on important work at the Royal Arsenal.
205, J Block, Guinness' Buildings, Page's Walk, Grange Road, S.E.1. Z26371

COMPTON, F. W., 1st Class Petty Officer, R.N., H.M.S. "Diamond."
He joined in 1918 and was posted to H.M.S. "Diamond" and sent to the North Sea, where he served on important patrol duties with the Grand Fleet. His ship was also engaged in various operations, and later he was employed on experimental work in connection with naval warfare. He was demobilised in 1920, and holds the General Service and Victory Medals.
57, Elmington Road, Camberwell, S.E.5. Z3442C

COMPTON, W., Private, Royal Berkshire Regiment.
He joined in September 1916 and in January of the following year was drafted to the Western Front. During his service in France he fought at Arras, Bullecourt, Ypres and St. Quentin, and in 1918 was sent to Egypt and stationed at Alexandria. He returned home and was demobilised in December 1919, and holds the General Service and Victory Medals.
26, Rollo Street, Battersea, S.W.11. Z1648

CONNELL, J., Private, Royal Defence Corps.
He had previously served throughout the South African War and in August 1914 was mobilised from the Reserve. During his service he was engaged on important duties in connection with the guarding of the railway lines and later was employed at various detention camps for German prisoners. He rendered valuable services and was demobilised in February 1919. He holds the Queen's and King's South African Medals.
15, Rowena Crescent, Battersea, S.W.11. Z1649

CONNELL, J. W., Private, Queen's (Royal West Surrey Regiment).
He joined in September 1916 and in the following December was drafted to Salonika. Whilst in this theatre of war he was engaged in various sectors in many important operations and was severely wounded in action in 1917. He returned to England and was demobilised in February 1919, and holds the General Service and Victory Medals.
15, Thorncroft Street, Wandsworth Road, S.W.8. Z1650

CONNETT, W., Sapper, R.E. (Army Post Office)
He volunteered in February 1915 and on the completion of his training was drafted to France and was engaged on important duties in connection with the Army Post Office. He was demobilised in August 1919, and holds the General Service and Victory Medals.
65, Faroe Road, West Kensington, W.14. 12453B

CONOLLY, C. H., Corporal, City of London Lancers (Rough Riders).
He volunteered in August 1914 and in the following April was sent to Egypt. There he served in various minor engagements until he was invalided home to hospital suffering from dysentery. After his recovery he was engaged on important Home Defence duties until September 1916, when he was discharged as medically unfit for further military service. He holds the 1914-15 Star, and the General Service and Victory Medals.
83, Manor Street, Clapham S.W.4. Z1652

CONNOLLY, F., Private, R.A.M.C.
He was mobilised in August 1914 and was almost immediately drafted to France, where he served in the Retreat from Mons. He was present also at the Battles of the Aisne, Ypres, Neuve Chapelle, Loos and Vimy Ridge, and in the operations on the Somme in 1918. He was demobilised in March 1919, and holds the 1914-15 Star, and the General Service and Victory Medals.
44, Goulden Street, Battersea, S.W.11. Z1651

CONNOR, E. (Mrs.), Gang Supervisor, Land Army, attached R.A.S.C.
After the death of her husband and brother in the war she joined the Land Army in April 1918 and served on important agricultural duties until the following October. She was then transferred to the Forage Company and attached to the Royal Army Service Corps, in which, owing to her ability and energy, she was promoted to the rank of gang supervisor. She rendered valuable services until she was demobilised in October 1919.
33, Alfred Street, Bermondsey, S.E.1. 26498C

CONNOR, I., Pioneer, R.E.
He was serving at the outbreak of War and was drafted to France in April 1915. During his service on the Western Front he was mainly engaged on stretcher bearing duties. In January 1917 he was sent to Mesopotamia but unfortunately later contracted a severe illness and died on July 22nd of the same year. He was entitled to the 1914-15 Star, and the General Service and Victory Medals.
"A costly sacrifice upon the altar of freedom."
23, Alfred Street, Bermondsey, S.E.1. 26948B

CONOLLY, S. E., Corporal, 3rd London Yeomanry.
He joined in November 1916 and on the completion of his training was engaged with his unit on important duties, chiefly in the Q.M.S. Stores, at stations in Ireland. He was not successful in securing his transfer to a fighting front before hostilities ceased, but rendered valuable services until his demobilisation in February 1919.
102, St. George's Road, Peckham, S.E.15. Z5585

CONS, A., Rifleman, 6th London Regiment (Rifles).
Volunteering in August 1914 he was sent to the Western Front in the following March and fought at Neuve Chapelle, St. Eloi, Givenchy, Ypres, Festubert and Loos, where he was severely wounded. He was then invalided home and after fourteen months' treatment in King George's Hospital was discharged in November 1916 as physically unfit for further service. He holds the 1914-15 Star, and the General Service and Victory Medals.
3, Geneva Terrace, Coldharbour Lane, S.W.9. Z4429A

CONS, S., Sapper, R.E.
Although under age he volunteered in June 1915 and after his training was engaged on special duties until he was sent to France in October, 1916. He subsequently served on duties of an important nature in the forward areas, and was present at the Battles of Arras, Vimy Ridge, Ypres, Cambrai and the Somme, and in the Retreat and Advance of 1918. He was demobilised after his return to England in May 1919, and holds the General Service and Victory Medals.
3, Geneva Terrace, Coldharbour Lane, S.W.9. Z4429C

CONS, W. R., Gunner, R.F.A.
He volunteered in August 1914 and from the following March until the termination of hostilities served on the Western Front. Whilst in this theatre of war he was engaged in the fighting at Neuve Chapelle, Hill 60, Ypres, Loos, Vermelles, Ploegsteert Wood, Vimy Ridge, the Somme, Beaumont-Hamel, Arras, Bullecourt, Messines and Cambrai, and in the Retreat and Advance of 1918, and did valuable work with his Battery throughout. He was demobilised on his return to England in March 1919, and holds the 1914-15 Star, and the General Service and Victory Medals.
3, Geneva Terrace, Coldharbour Lane, S.W.9. Z4429B

CONSTABLE, G. T., Sergt., 2/5th Sherwood Foresters.
He volunteered in June 1915 and in February of the following year was drafted to the Western Front, where he saw much severe fighting. After taking part in the Battles of Ypres, Passchendaele, Armentières and Cambrai he was invalided to hospital suffering from shell-shock, but on his recovery re-joined his unit in the firing line. He returned home for demobilisation in November 1919, and holds the General Service and Victory Medals.
45, Gloucester Road, Peckham, S.E.15. Z5926

CONSTABLE, J. E., Rifleman, 1st Royal Irish Rifles.
Joining in February 1917 he crossed to France in May and took part in several important engagements, including those at Arras and Vimy Ridge. He gave his life for the freedom of England after only ten weeks' foreign service at the Battle of Ypres on August 16th, 1917. He was entitled to the General Service and Victory Medals.
"His memory is cherished with pride."
49, Cronin Road, Peckham, S.E.15. Z5355

CONWAY, W. B., Private, R.A.S.C. (M.T.)
He volunteered in September 1914 and was immediately drafted to the Western Front. During his service in France he did excellent work as a driver, conveying supplies of food and ammunition to the front lines. He was present at numerous important engagements, including those at La Bassée, Ypres, Neuve Chapelle, the second Battle of Ypres, Festubert, Loos, Vimy Ridge, the Somme, Messines, Lens, Cambrai, Amiens and Bapaume. He was demobilised in April 1919, and holds the 1914 Star, and the General Service and Victory Medals.
60, Elsted Street, Walworth, S.E.17. Z1653

COOK, A., C.Q.M.S., 6th Queen's (Royal West Surrey Regiment).
He volunteered in August 1914 having previously served for seven years in India and was engaged as Drill Instructor to recruits at various stations. He rendered valuable services in this capacity throughout the period of hostilities and was demobilised after four-and-a-half years' service in April 1919. He holds the Long Service and Good Conduct Medal.
15, St. Alphonsus Road, Clapham, S.W.4. Z1661

COOK, A., L/Corporal, King's Royal Rifle Corps.

He volunteered in December 1915 and after his training was promoted to the rank of Lance-Corporal in March 1917 and sent to France in the following August. He fought at Messines and Ypres, where he was severely wounded in September, when his whole section was put out of action by heavy enemy bombardment. He was also buried by the explosion of a shell but managed to extricate himself and was sent to hospital at Poperinghe and later invalided home, where he was under treatment in several hospitals. He was discharged in March 1918 as medically unfit for further duty, and holds the General Service and Victory Medals.

52, Mawbey Road, Old Kent Road, S.E.1.   1797

COOK, A. F., Private, 2nd Seaforth Highlanders.

A serving soldier since May 1912 he was sent to the Western Front at the outbreak of hostilities and fought in the Retreat from Mons and was wounded. After his recovery he took part in the second Battle of Ypres, where he was again severely wounded. He was invalided home in July 1915 and subsequently served on important duties in Scotland until demobilised in March 1919. He holds the Mons Star, and the General Service and Victory Medals.

44, Balfern Grove, Chiswick, W.4.   5478A

COOK, A. T. W., Rifleman, Rifle Brigade.

He volunteered in 1914 and was drafted to the Western Front in the following year. During his service in France he fought at Ypres and was severely wounded in the Battle of the Somme. He was invalided home to hospital and subsequently succumbed to his injuries in July 1916. He was entitled to the 1914-15 Star, and the General Service and Victory Medals.

"Whilst we remember, the sacrifice is not in vain."

23, Brooklands Road, South Lambeth, S.W.8.   Z1659C

COOK, A. W., Rifleman, 21st London Regiment (1st Surrey Rifles).

He joined in August 1917 and in April of the following year was drafted to the Western Front. Whilst in this theatre of war he saw much severe fighting in various sectors and took part in the Battles of Amiens and the Menin Road, and many other important engagements. He was demobilised in March 1919, but immediately re-enlisted in the 2nd East Surrey Regiment and was drafted to Turkey, where he was still serving in 1920. He holds the General Service and Victory Medals.

14, Fendick Road, Peckham, S.E.15.   Z5910

COOK, C., Sergt., Queen's (Royal West Surrey Regiment).

He volunteered in November 1914 and rendered very valuable service as an Instructor at various depôts during the continuance of war. He was afterwards engaged on special duties in connection with demobilisation until he was himself demobilised in March 1919. He had many years' service with the Colours, and holds the Queen's and King's South African Medals.

45, St. Alban's Street, Kennington, S.E.11.   Z26987A

COOK, C. A., Signaller, R.F.A.

He volunteered in April 1915 and proceeded to France in the same year and saw much service. He fought at Ypres, Nieuport, the Somme, Lens, Arras, Vimy Ridge, Cambrai and Messines, and various subsequent engagements. He was gassed in 1917 at Ypres, and again in 1918. He returned home the day before the Armistice and was demobilised in the following February. He holds the 1914-15 Star, and the General Service and Victory Medals.   108, Speke Road, Battersea, S.W.11.   Z1660C

COOK, C. H., Rifleman, 21st London Regiment (1st Surrey Rifles).

He volunteered in November 1914 and after his training was retained on important duties with his unit until 1916, when he was drafted to the Western Front. The hardships of war, however, were too much for his strength and after being seriously ill he was discharged in June 1916 as physically unfit for further service. He holds the General Service and Victory Medals.

23, Parkstone Road, Peckham, S.E.15.   Z5586

COOK, E. E., Private, 6th Cheshire Regiment.

Joining in January 1916 he was sent soon to France. During his service overseas, which lasted for three years, he fought in many important battles, notably those of the Somme, Arras, Bullecourt, Vimy Ridge and Beaumont-Hamel, and in the Retreat and Advance of 1918. He was demobilised after his return to England in August 1919, and holds the General Service and Victory Medals.

72, Harris Street, Camberwell, S.E.5.   Z4430

COOK, E. R., Bombardier, R.F.A.

He volunteered in 1915 and in the following year was drafted to France, where he fought in various engagements, including those on the Somme and at Ypres. He was wounded in the Battle of Arras and sent to hospital at Boulogne. After his recovery he was again in action at Passchendaele and in the engagements which followed in the Retreat and Advance of 1918. He was demobilised in 1919, and holds the General Service and Victory Medals.

23, Brooklands Road, South Lambeth, S.W.8.   Z1659A

COOK, F., Private, 10th London Regiment, and R.D.C.

He volunteered in May 1915 and after his training was transferred from the London Regiment to the Royal Defence Corps. He was engaged on important duties in guarding German prisoners of war at various detention camps and was discharged in consequence of his service in November 1917.

1, Claxton Grove, Hammersmith, W.6.   13535A

COOK, F. W., Private, R.A.V.C.

He joined in September 1916 and in the same year was drafted to France, where he served for three years. He was engaged on important duties in connection with his Corps at Forges-les-Eaux, Abbeville, Rouen and many other stations. He rendered valuable services and was demobilised in May 1919, and holds the General Service and Victory Medals.

42, Bolton Street, Camberwell, S.E.5.   Z1657

COOK, J., Gunner, R.F.A.

He volunteered in August 1914 and in the following year was sent overseas. Whilst in France he did good work as a gunner at Ypres and on the Somme and in many engagements in the Retreat and Advance of 1918. He was gassed and wounded in the fighting during that year, and was invalided home and subsequently demobilised in February 1919. He holds the 1914-15 Star, and the General Service and Victory Medals.

45, St. Alban's Street, Kennington, S.E.11.   Z26987B

COOK, J., Private, Royal Fusiliers.

Volunteering in 1915 he was drafted overseas in the same year and served in many important engagements in the Somme, Ypres and Arras sectors, and in the final operations of the War. He was demobilised in 1919, and holds the 1914-15 Star, and the General Service and Victory Medals.

25, Henshaw Street, Walworth, S.E.17.   Z1654B

COOK, J. W., Corporal, Middlesex Regiment, and Labour Corps.

He joined in May 1917 and in the same year was drafted to France. During his service on the Western Front he was engaged on important duties in connection with the upkeep of roads and the loading and unloading of waggons, notably in the Retreat of 1918. He was demobilised in October 1919, and holds the General Service and Victory Medals.

108, Speke Road, Battersea, S.W.11.   Z1660A

COOK, J. W., Private, Royal Sussex Regiment.

He joined in 1917 at eighteen years of age and after his training served at various stations on important duties with his unit. He did excellent work but was not able to secure a transfer overseas and was demobilised in 1919.

23, Brooklands Road, South Lambeth, S.W.8.   Z1659B

COOK, J. W., Private, Labour Corps.

He joined in April 1916 and in the same year was drafted overseas. During his service in France he was engaged on important duties at Ypres, Albert, Amiens and Hardecourt, and at various other stations until February 1919, when he was demobilised. He holds the General Service and Victory Medals.

15, Sidney Road, Stockwell Road, S.W.9.   Z1655

COOK, M. F. (M.S.M.), Sergt.-Major, R.G.A.

He volunteered in 1914 and after his training was completed was drafted in 1916 to the Western Front. Whilst in this theatre of war he saw much service and was engaged in many battles in various sectors, including those of the Somme and Cambrai. After the Armistice he returned home and then volunteered to serve in the British Military Mission to South Russia in October 1919. He returned home in the course of the following year and was demobilised. He was awarded the Meritorious Service Medal for his consistently good work in France and Russia, and holds in addition the General Service and Victory Medals.

12, Arlesford Road, Landor Road, S.W.9.   Z1662

COOK, P. H., Private, Duke of Cornwall's Light Infantry.

Volunteering in June 1915, in the following October he was drafted to France. Whilst in this theatre of war he was in action at Loos, Vermelles, Vimy Ridge, Beaumont-Hamel, Bullecourt, Messines, Ypres and Passchendaele. In 1917 he was sent to Italy and served on the Piave, the Asiago Plateaux and the last Offensive against the Austrians in 1918. He was demobilised after his return to England in February 1919, and holds the 1914-15 Star, and the General Service and Victory Medals.

8, Wansey Street, Walworth, S.E.17.   Z1658A

COOK, P. M. A. (Mrs.), Special War Worker.

During the war this lady was engaged on special clerical duties at the Australian Headquarters, Horseferry Road, Westminster. She did excellent work from September 1917 to August 1918 and gave entire satisfaction to the authorities.

44, Balfern Grove, Chiswick, W.4.   5478B

COOK, R., Private, Royal Inniskilling Fusiliers, and Gunner, M.G.C.

He volunteered in October 1915 and in the following mo th was sent overseas. After serving only two weeks in France he died gloriously on the field of battle in November 1915. He was entitled to the 1914-15 Star, and the General Service and Victory Medals.
"A valiant soldier, with undaunted heart he breasted Life's last hill."
25, Henshaw Street, Walworth, S.E.17. Z1654A

COOK, R. W., Private, R.A.S.C. (M.T.)

He joined in July 1916 and was drafted to Mesopotamia in the following year. He served with General Maude's Forces in the Campaign against the Turks and fought at Baghdad. Later he contracted small-pox and died after only two days' illness. He was entitled to the General Service and Victory Medals.
"His memory is cherished with pride."
30, Handforth Road, Brixton Road, S.W.9. Z5228

COOK, S. W., Driver, R.A.S.C.

He volunteered in August 1914 and in the following November was drafted to France. Whilst in this theatre of war he served in many engagements in various sectors of the Western Front until the cessation of hostilities. He was demobilised in January 1919, and holds the 1914 Star, and the General Service and Victory Medals.
38, Benfield Street, Battersea, S.W.11. TZ1656

COOK, T. F. W., Rifleman, 3rd Rifle Brigade.

He was mobilised from the Reserve at the outbreak of War and almost immediately drafted to France, where he took part in the Retreat from Mons. He died fighting during the Retreat, and was entitled to the Mons Star, and the General Service and Victory Medals.
"He died the noblest death a man may die,
Fighting for God, and right and liberty."
24, Patmore Street, Wandsworth Road, S.W.8. Z1488A

COOK, W. A., Private, M.G.C.

He joined in May 1918 and shortly afterwards proceeded to the Western Front, where he took part in many important engagements during the final stages of the war. Later he was sent with the Army of Occupation into Germany and finally returned to England for demobilisation in April 1920. He holds the General Service and Victory Medals.
108, Speke Road, Battersea, S.W.11. Z1660B

COOK, W. G., Private, 1st Norfolk Regiment.

He joined in April 1916 and after his training was drafted to the Western Front in June 1918. During his service in France he fought in the Cambrai sector until September 29th, 1918, when he gave his life for the freedom of England at Gouzeaucourt. He was entitled to the General Service and Victory Medals.
"Nobly striving,
He nobly fell that we might live."
140, Heath Road, Wandsworth Road, S.W.8. Z1663

COOK, W. J., Private, 4th Middlesex Regiment.

He volunteered in 1915 and proceeded in the same year to the Western Front, where he took part in the fighting at Ypres and the Somme. Unhappily he was killed in action at Arras in April 1917. He was entitled to the 1914-15 Star, and the General Service and Victory Medals.
"A costly sacrifice upon the altar of freedom."
23, Brooklands Road, South Lambeth, S.W.8. Z1659D

COOKE, A., Shoeing Smith, R.A.S.C. (Remounts).

Volunteering in January 1915 he was drafted to Egypt in the following year and served for three years on important duties as a shoeing smith. He returned home and was demobilised in July 1919, and holds the 1914-15 Star, and the General Service and Victory Medals.
57, Fletcher Road, Chiswick, W.4. 46C

COOKE, A. S., Private, Royal Defence Corps.

Being medically unfit for active service he joined the R.D.C. in January 1915 and after the completion of his training was engaged on important duties in connection with the examination of passports. He rendered valuable services throughout and was demobilised in March 1919.
43, Purser's Cross Road, Fulham Road, S.W.6. X20052

COOKE, F., Private, M.G.C.

He volunteered in January 1915, proceeded to the Dardanelles and served throughout the Gallipoli operations until the Evacuation of the Peninsula. He was then drafted to the Western Front and fought in various engagements, including the Battle of Arras, and was four times wounded. He was demobilised in 1918, and holds the 1914-15 Star, and the General Service and Victory Medals.
57, Fletcher Road, Chiswick, W.4. 6346A

COOKE, G., Staff-Sergt., 18th Hussars.

He enlisted in September 1912 and in 1915 was drafted to the Western Front, where he took part in numerous engagements and was severely gassed. On his recovery he was transferred to the Army Provost Staff and was engaged on important military prison duties until September 1919, when he was demobilised. He holds the 1914-15 Star, and the General Service and Victory Medals.
1, Gladstone Street, Wyvil Street, S.W.8. Z1664

COOKE, P., Sergt., R.F.A.

He was mobilised in August 1914 and in the following year was drafted to France. There he fought in the Battle of Cambrai and in many engagements in the Retreat and Advance of 1918. After the cessation of hostilities he returned to England and in January 1919 was demobilised, holding the 1914-15 Star, and the General Service and Victory Medals.
57, Fletcher Road, Chiswick, W.4. 6346B

COOKSEY, A. E., Private, Hampshire Regiment.

Volunteering in 1914 he proceeded to France on the completion of his training and fought in the Battle of Ypres and other engagements, in which he was wounded. On his recovery he was drafted to the Dardanelles and fought in the later engagements up to the Evacuation of the Peninsula. He afterwards returned to France and while fighting in the Somme Offensive was severely wounded. He was subsequently discharged in 1916 as medically unfit for further service, and holds the 1914-15 Star, and the General Service and Victory Medals.
146, Robertson Street, Wandsworth Road, S.W.8. Z1665

COOMBER, A. J., Private, 1st Queen's Own (Royal West Kent Regiment).

Mobilised from the Reserve at the outbreak of war he was immediately drafted overseas. Whilst in France he fought in the Retreat from Mons and in the Battles of Ypres and Hill 60, where he was wounded and reported missing. He was presumed to have been killed in action there on April 18th, 1915, and was entitled to the Mons Star, and the General Service and Victory Medals.
"The path of duty was the way to glory."
63, Greyhound Road, Hammersmith, W.6. T15026B

COOMBES, B., Driver, R.F.A.

Joining in September 1916 he proceeded overseas in January of the following year. Whilst in France he fought at Arras, Vimy Ridge, Bullecourt, Messines, Ypres, Cambrai, the Somme, Amiens, Bapaume, the Scarpe and in many other battles until the cessation of hostilities. He was then drafted to Germany with the Army of Occupation and served there until September 1919, when he was demobilised. He holds the General Service and Victory Medals.
27, Alvey Street, Walworth, S.E.17. Z1667A

COOMBES, F. E., Private, R.A.M.C.

He joined in October 1916 and in April of the following year was drafted to the Western Front. There he served at Abbeville Stationary Hospital as orderly and did splendid work until the close of war. He then proceeded with the Army of Occupation to Cologne, where he remained until March 1920. On his return home he was demobilised, holding the General Service and Victory Medals.
23, Clovelly Road, Chiswick, W.4. T6596A

COOMBES, GLADYS (Miss), Special War Worker.

During the war this lady was engaged at the Royal Arsenal, Woolwich, on work of National importance. She was employed in the Canteens as Chief Cashier, in which capacity she rendered very valuable services.
96, Gloucester Road, Peckham, S.E. 15. Z5733C

COOMBES, GRACE (Miss), Special War Worker.

From 1917 until the Armistice this lady was engaged at the Small Arms Factory, Royal Arsenal, Woolwich, on work of the utmost importance. She was employed in the filling of cartridges, which work called for skilful and careful handling. She carried out these duties in a very efficient manner and rendered valuable services.
96, Gloucester Road, Peckham, S.E.15. Z5733A

COOMBES, G. A., L/Corporal, R.F.A.

He volunteered in January 1915 and in the following June was drafted to France, where he took part in the Battle of Loos. He was then transferred to Salonika and thence to Egypt and Palestine, where he served with General Allenby's Forces in the capture of Jericho and other important engagements. Later he returned to France and was again in action until hostilities ceased. He was demobilised in August 1919, and holds the 1914-15 Star, and the General Service and Victory Medals.
96, Gloucester Road, Peckham, S.E.15. Z5733B

COOMBES, W. E., Driver, R.F.A.

He volunteered in October 1915 and in March of the following year proceeded to the Western Front. Whilst in this theatre of war he took part in many important engagements, including the Battles of the Somme, Messines, Ypres and Passchendaele, and also served with a flying column. He was demobilised on his return home in June 1919, and holds the General Service and Victory Medals.
53, Blake's Road, Peckham Grove, S.E.15. Z5903

COOMBES, R. J., Corporal, 4th Rifle Brigade, Army Cyclist Corps and 1st Royal Munster Fusiliers.

He was on Indian service at the outbreak of war having enlisted in 1906 and in December 1914 was drafted to the Western Front. There he took part in much heavy fighting at Ypres, the Somme, Arras and in many other great battles. He died gloriously on the field of battle in Flanders on April 4th, 1918, whilst serving as Lewis Gunner with the Royal Munster Fusiliers. He was entitled to the 1914-15 Star, and the General Service and Victory Medals.
"A valiant soldier, with undaunted heart he breasted Life's last hill."
23, Clovelly Road, Chiswick, W.4.   T6596B

COOMBS, F. G., Private, Royal Sussex Regiment.

Volunteering in November 1914 he proceeded overseas on the completion of his training in 1915. Whilst in France he fought in several engagements and was killed in action on May 9th, 1915 at Richebourg. He was entitled to the 1914-15 Star, and the General Service and Victory Medals.
"He passed out of the sight of men by the path of duty and self-sacrifice."
115, Farmer's Road, Camberwell, S.E.5.   Z1666B

COOMBS, F. S., Ordinary Seaman, R.N.

He joined in 1916 and saw much service in H.M.S. "Shannon" and "Erebus" in the North Sea with the Grand Fleet. He was also engaged for a time in Russian waters conveying food and ammunition to the various ports. He holds the General Service and Victory Medals, and in 1920 was still serving.
28, Caithness Road, West Kensington, W.14.   12448B

COOMBS, R., Corporal, R.A.S.C. (M.T.)

He joined in May 1916 and after having completed his training proceeded in December of the following year to France. There he was present at many engagements of importance, including those of the Somme, Amiens, Cambrai and Ypres, and at the entry into Mons in November 1918. After the conclusion of hostilities he was drafted to Germany with the Army of Occupation and served there until October 1919, when he was demobilised. He holds the General Service and Victory Medals.
26, North Street, Lambeth, S.E.1.   26088

COOMBS, W. J., Sergt., Queen's (Royal West Surrey Regt.), and 1st Royal Fusiliers.

Mobilised in August 1914 he was speedily drafted to the Western Front and was in action at Mons, Loos and many other battles until the close of the war. Whilst overseas he was wounded three times and suffered from shell-shock. In March 1919 he returned home and was demobilised, holding the Mons Star, and the General Service and Victory Medals.
28, Caithness Road, West Kensington, W.14.   12448A

COOPER, A. H., Private, R.A.V.C.

Volunteering in December 1914 he was speedily drafted to France, where he saw much service and did valuable work in attendance on sick and wounded horses. He was invalided home through ill-health and after considerable hospital treatment was discharged as medically unfit for further duty in February 1919. He holds the 1914-15 Star, and the General Service and Victory Medals.
68, Weybridge Street, Battersea, S.W.11.   Z1677

COOPER, C. F., Corporal, 4th Dragoon Guards (Royal Irish).

Mobilised in August 1914 he immediately embarked for France and was in action at Mons, La Bassée and Neuve Chapelle. He was severely wounded in the last mentioned engagements and invalided to England. After prolonged hospital treatment he was discharged as medically unfit for further service, and holds the Mons Star and the General Service and Victory Medals.
38, Mossbury Road, Lavender Hill, S.W.11.   Z1678

COOPER, C. R., Private, R.A.S.C., and M.G.C.

Volunteering in September 1914 he was speedily drafted in the R.A.S.C. to the Western Front. Whilst there he did valuable service in many battles, including those at the Marne, the Aisne, Neuve Chapelle, Hill 60, Festubert, Loos, Arras, Messines, Passchendaele and Cambrai. During the Retreat and Advance of 1918 he acted as a machine gunner and was gassed on one occasion. He returned home in June 1919 and was demobilised, holding the General Service and Victory Medals.
153, Beresford Street, Camberwell, S.E.5.   Z1672

COOPER, E. E., Rifleman, King's Royal Rifle Corps.

He was mobilised with the Territorial Forces on the declaration of war but was rejected as medically unfit. He immediately volunteered in the King's Royal Rifles and after completing his training embarked for France in 1915. Whilst in this theatre of war he fought in the Battle of the Somme and was unfortunately killed in action at Thiepval on September 3rd, 1916. He was entitled to the 1914-15 Star, and the General Service and Victory Medals.
"His life for his Country, his Soul to God."
15, Porson Street, Wandsworth Road, S.W.8.   Z1673C

COOPER, E. G., R.Q.M.S., R.G.A.

Serving at the outbreak of war he was drafted to German East Africa, where he remained until 1916, when he was transferred to France. Whilst in this theatre of war he was in action in numerous important engagements until the cessation of hostilities. He returned to England and was demobilised in July 1919, and holds the 1914-15 Star, and the General Service and Victory Medals.
43, Ramsay Road, Acton, W.3.   6391A

COOPER, E. S., Corporal, R.A.S.C.

Volunteering in August 1914 he proceeded overseas on the completion of his training in the following year. Whilst on the Western Front he was present at many notable engagements, including those of Neuve Chapelle and Loos, and did valuable transport work until the cessation of hostilities. In February 1919 he returned home and was demobilised, holding the 1914-15 Star, and the General Service and Victory Medals.
20, Cambridge Street, Camberwell, S.E.5.   Z1679

COOPER, G. E., Special War Worker.

Being ineligible for service with the Colours he volunteered in January 1916 for work of National importance at the Royal Arsenal, Woolwich. He held an important and responsible post in charge of a section of workers in the T.N.T. department and did work of an extremely valuable nature for three years. He resigned in February 1919.
134, Wells Street, Camberwell, S.E.5.   Z4431

COOPER, G. P., Rifleman, Rifle Brigade.

He joined in June 1917 and after his training was engaged on important duties with his unit. He was unable to obtain his transfer overseas before the cessation of hostilities but in 1919 proceeded to India. There he served in the Afghanistan Campaign and in consequence of a serious injury to his head was invalided home. He was discharged in June 1920, holding the India General Service Medal (with clasp, Afghanistan, North-West Frontier, 1919).
76, Ingleton Street, Brixton Road, S.W.9.   Z1669A

COOPER, H. A., Driver, R.A.S.C.

He volunteered in December 1914 and on the completion of his training proceeded overseas. Whilst in France he did excellent service in many engagements, including those of Ypres, Neuve Chapelle, Loos, Hill 60, the Somme, Arras and the Retreat and Advance of 1918, and was gassed. He returned home and was demobilised in February 1919, holding the 1914-15 Star, and the General Service and Victory Medals.
12, Mantua Street, Battersea, S.W.11.   Z1668

COOPER, H. E., Private, Devonshire Regiment.

He volunteered in 1914 and in the following year crossed to France, where he was in action at Ypres and the Somme, and was wounded. On his recovery after treatment at home he returned to the fighting area and served at Cambrai and in many engagements, including the Retreat and Advance of 1918. He holds the 1914-15 Star, and the General Service and Victory Medals, and in 1919 was demobilised.
28, Brooklands Road, South Lambeth, S.W.8.   Z1671

COOPER, J., 1st Class Stoker, Royal Navy, H.M.S. "Warspite."

He was in the Navy at the outbreak of war and from 1914 until after the termination of hostilities served with the Grand Fleet in the North Sea. With his ship he took part in several Naval engagements, including the Battle of Jutland, and did valuable work. He was demobilised in June 1919, and holds the 1914-15 Star, and the General Service and Victory Medals.
15, Sandover Road, Camberwell, S.E.5.   Z5357

COOPER, J., Saddler, R.F.A.

He volunteered at the outbreak of hostilities and was drafted to Mesopotamia in the following year. During his service on the Eastern front he fought under General Aylmer and took part in the Advance on Kut and in the Capture of Baghdad. He returned home and was discharged in consequence of his service in September 1918, and holds the 1914-15 Star, and the General Service and Victory Medals.
43, Ramsay Road, Acton, W.3.   6391B

COOPER, J. A., Private, R.A.M.C.

He volunteered in July 1915 and in January of the following year proceeded to the Western Front. Attached to the 35th Division he did splendid work with the Field Ambulance and was present at the engagements at Albert, Vimy Ridge, the Somme, Arras and others until August 1917. He then served in the Hospital Ship "Dunluce Castle" until demobilised in May 1919. He holds the General Service and Victory Medals.
98, Smyrk's Road, Walworth, S.E.17.   1676A

COOPER, J. T., Private, Royal Marine Light Infantry

He enlisted in 1904 and at the outbreak of war was in H.M.S. "Diamond," in which vessel he saw much service in the North Sea with the Grand Fleet until May 1918. He was then transferred to H.M. Monitor "Terror" and served in it until demobilised in May 1919. He holds the 1914-15 Star, and the General Service and Victory Medals.
23, Abercrombie Street, Battersea, S.W.11.   Z1675

COOPER, J. C., Private, 18th (Queen Mary's Own) Hussars.

Mobilised from the Reserve at the outbreak of war he was quickly sent to the Western Front and fought in the Retreat from Mons and the Battles of Ypres, La Bassée and Hill 60. Unhappily he was killed in action on May 26th, 1915, whilst taking part in operations in the Ypres sector. He was entitled to the Mons Star, and the General Service and Victory Medals.
"The path of duty was the way to glory."
30, Sandover Road, Camberwell, S.E.5. Z5358

COOPER, S., Private, 22nd Middlesex Regiment.

Volunteering in March 1915 he was retained on various important duties in England and in 1917 proceeded overseas. He saw active service in many sectors of the Western Front and did valuable work. Whilst abroad he was transferred to the Labour Corps and with them was engaged on important duties until he returned home for demobilisation in January 1919. He holds the General Service and Victory Medals.
41, Stockdale Road, Wandsworth Road, S.W.8. Z1673B

COOPER, S., L/Corporal, Royal Buckinghamshire Hussars.

Joining in 1916 he was sent on completing his training to the Western Front, where he fought in several engagements, including those at Loos, Vimy Ridge and the Somme. Later he was invalided home suffering from pneumonia, of which he unhappily died in King's College Hospital on November 26th, 1918. He was entitled to the General Service and Victory Medals.
"His memory is cherished with pride."
Pasley Road, Walworth, S.E.17. Z27038

COOPER, W., Private, R.A.S.C., and Queen's (Royal West Surrey Regiment).

He volunteered in November 1915 and in February of the following year was sent to France, where he met with a serious accident, being kicked by a mule, and was invalided home. In 1917 he proceeded to India and thence to Mesopotamia, where he took part in various engagements. He was demobilised in April 1919, and holds the General Service and Victory Medals.
38, Charleston Street, Walworth, S.E.17. Z1674

COOPER, W., Private, Welch Regiment.

Mobilised at the outbreak of war he immediately proceeded to France and fought in the Retreat from Mons and the Battle of the Marne, during which he was wounded. He was invalided home and after receiving hospital treatment was discharged as medically unfit for further duty in January 1915. He holds the Mons Star, and the General Service and Victory Medals.
10, Stockdale Road, Wandsworth Road, S.W.8. Z1670

COOPER, W. R., Private, 10th Middlesex Regiment.

He volunteered in November 1915 and after having completed his training proceeded to France in March 1917. Whilst in this theatre of war he took part in many engagements until August 1918, including those at the Somme, Ypres and Passchendaele Ridge. In May 1919 he returned home and was demobilised, holding the General Service and Victory Medals.
25, Binns' Road, Chiswick, W.4. 5411

COOTE, C. J., Private, 23rd London Regiment.

He was mobilised in August 1914 and after being engaged on important defence duties with his unit was drafted in 1917 to France and was transferred to the 3rd London Regiment (Royal Fusiliers). He took part in the severe fighting at Bullecourt and fell fighting there on May 10th, 1917. He was entitled to the General Service and Victory Medals.
"Whilst we remember the sacrifice is not in vain."
127, Grant Road, Battersea, S.W.11. Z1681A

COOTE, T. W., Private, Labour Corps.

He volunteered in September 1914 and was posted to the 23rd London Regiment. In March of the following year he was drafted to France, where he took part in numerous engagements, including those at Neuve Chapelle, Festubert, Loos, Vimy Ridge. He was taken ill in August 1916 and invalided home but on his recovery returned to France in December 1916 and was in action at Messines, Passchendaele and Cambrai. He was afterwards transferred to the Labour Corps and was engaged on hospital duties at Havre until he was demobilised in March 1919. He holds the 1914-15 Star, and the General Service and Victory Medals.
127, Grant Road, Battersea, S.W.11. Z1681B

COOTE, W. S., Private, R.A.S.C.

He joined in June 1916 and after his training served at various stations on important duties with his unit. He rendered valuable services but was not successful in obtaining his transfer overseas before the cessation of hostilities owing to his low medical category. He was still serving in 1920.
59, Bullen Street, Battersea, S.W.11. Z1680

COPPARD, E. E., Private, Royal Army Pay Corps.

He volunteered in July 1915 and, after a period of training, served on important duties in the Army Accounts Offices. He was not successful in obtaining a transfer overseas but rendered valuable services until his discharge as medically unfit in 1917.
8, Bournemouth Road, Peckham, S.E.15. Z5739A

COPPARD, C. R., Private, 3/6th City of London Regiment, and M.G.C.

He volunteered in August 1915 at sixteen years of age and, after a period of training, was drafted to France. There he took part in engagements on the Somme and at Arras, Ypres, Vimy Ridge and Cambrai, and was five times wounded in action. He was discharged in 1918 as medically unfit for further service, and holds the General Service and Victory Medals.
8, Bournemouth Road, Peckham, S.E.15. Z5739C

COPPARD, E. G., Sapper, R.E.

He volunteered in August 1914 and on completing his training in the following year was drafted to the Dardanelles. There he served with the Royal Engineers as a Wireless Operator and took part in many engagements. After the Evacuation of the Gallipoli Peninsula he served in Egypt and Palestine and was in action at the fall of Jerusalem and Beersheba. In 1920 he was still serving, and holds the 1914-15 Star, and the General Service and Victory Medals.
8, Bournemouth Road, Peckham, S.E.15. Z5739B

COPPARD, F. S., Rifleman, Rifle Brigade.

He joined in May 1918 at the age of seventeen years and served at various stations with his unit. Owing to the early cessation of hostilities he was not successful in obtaining a transfer overseas, but rendered valuable service and in 1920 was still in the Army.
8, Bournemouth Road, Peckham, S.E.15. Z5739D

COPPER, C. T., Private, Durham Light Infantry.

He joined in April 1917 and after completing his training was engaged with his unit on important duties until September 1918. He was then sent to North Russia and served at Archangel until September of the following year. He was demobilised in November 1919, holding the General Service and Victory Medals.
47, Riverhall Street, Wandsworth Road, S.W.8. Z1647

COPPIN, A. H., Private, Dorsetshire and Loyal North Lancashire Regiments and R.A.M.C.

He volunteered in 1914 and in the following year was drafted to the Western Front. He took part in the severe fighting at St. Eloi, Hill 60, Ypres, Festubert, Loos and Ploegsteert. In 1916 he was transferred to the Loyal North Lancashire Regiment and was sent to East Africa. Later he was transferred to the R.A.M.C. and proceeded to Egypt, where he served under General Murray and was wounded. He also fought at Le Cateau in the last phase of hostilities. He was demobilised in 1919, holding the 1914-15 Star, and the General Service and Victory Medals.
10, Industry Terrace, Brixton, S.W.9. Z1772A

COPPIN, W. R., Private, Buffs (East Kent Regt.)

He volunteered in January 1915 and in the following May was drafted to the Western Front, where he took part in the severe fighting at Ypres. Three days after landing he was unfortunately killed in action there on May 24th, 1915, and was entitled to the 1914-15 Star, and the General Service and Victory Medals.
"The path of duty was the way to glory."
10, Industry Terrace, Brixton Road, S.W.9. Z1772B

COPPING, H., Private, R.A.S.C. (M.T.)

He joined in June 1917 and after his training served at various stations in Ireland on important duties with his unit. He rendered valuable services but was not successful in obtaining his transfer to a theatre of war while hostilities continued. He was demobilised in March 1920.
30A, Curwen Road, Shepherd's Bush, W.12. T9129A

COPPOCK, F. C., L/Corporal, 8th London Regiment (Post Office Rifles).

Shortly after joining in September 1916 he was drafted to France, where he was engaged on important duties whilst attached to the Signal Section of the R.E. He saw service at Béthune, Arras and Rouen, and many other places, was in action in several engagements and was gassed whilst in this theatre of war. He was demobilised in October 1919, and holds the General Service and Victory Medals.
88, Blake's Road, Peckham Grove, S.E.15. Z5929

COPSEY, C. G., Corporal, R.A.S.C. (M.T.)

He volunteered in April 1915 and was drafted to Salonika in the same year. He was engaged as a motor driver in the transport of supplies on the Doiran front and also served as a motor cyclist despatch-bearer. He afterwards proceeded to Constantinople. He was demobilised in April 1919, holding the 1914-15 Star, and the General Service and Victory Medals.
36, Deynsford Road, Camberwell, S.E.5. Z1774B

COPSEY, H. S., Sapper, R.E. (Signals).

Joining in February 1917 he was drafted to the Western Front in the same year. He took part in numerous engagements, including those on the Somme front, and also served in the Retreat and Advance of 1918. After the Armistice he proceeded with the Army of Occupation to Germany. He was demobilised in March 1920 after returning home, and holds the General Service and Victory Medals.
36, Deynsford Road, Camberwell, S.E.5. Z1774A

CORBEN, A. S., Sergt., 16th London Regiment (Queen's Westminster Rifles).

He volunteered in September 1914 and joined the Royal Fusiliers. In 1915 he was sent to Egypt and afterwards served in Gallipoli. In the following year he proceeded to France and after being transferred to the 16th London Regiment (Queen's Westminster Rifles) took part in the heavy fighting on the Somme. He fell fighting at Leuze Wood on September 10th, 1916, and was entitled to the 1914–15 Star, and the General Service and Victory Medals.

"Great deeds cannot die."

71, Farmer's Road, Camberwell, S.E.5. Z1682

CORBET, G. J., Pioneer, R.E. (Postal Section).

He volunteered in September 1915 and in April of the following year was sent to the Western Front. He served at Le Havre, Arras, Ypres and Rouen. He was engaged in travelling with the mails and rendered valuable services. He also took part in the Retreat and Advance of 1918. He was demobilised in April 1919, and holds the General Service and Victory Medals.

6, Harley Street, Battersea, S.W.11. Z1683

CORBETT, C., Private, Sherwood Foresters.

After joining in March 1917 and completing his training he was drafted to the Western Front, where he took part in numerous engagements, including those on the Somme Front and at Ypres and Passchendaele, and the Retreat and Advance of 1918. He was wounded in October and after being invalided home was discharged in August 1919 owing to his injuries. He holds the General Service and Victory Medals.

80, Haselrigge Road, Clapham, S.W.4. Z1684A

CORBETT, E. J., Gunner, R.G.A.

Having previously served in the South African Campaign he volunteered in September 1914 and was drafted to the Western Front, where he took part in severe fighting on the Somme and at Cambrai and in many other engagements. He was demobilised in February 1919, and holds the Queen's South African Medal (with two clasps), the 1914–15 Star, and the General Service and Victory Medals.

88, Kenbury Street, Camberwell, S.E.5. Z6157

CORBETT, R. A., Private, Queen's (Royal West Surrey Regiment).

Volunteering in December 1914 he crossed to the Western Front in the following year and there took a prominent part in the severe fighting at Ypres, the Somme and Arras. He gave his life for King and Country at Ypres on May 19th, 1917, and was entitled to the 1914–15 Star, and the General Service and Victory Medals.

"His memory is cherished with pride."

80, Haselrigge Road, Clapham, S.W.4. Z1684C

CORBETT, T. L., Private, Australian Imperial Forces.

He volunteered in August 1914 and in the following year proceeded to Gallipoli, where he took part in the Landing and in several other engagements up to the Evacuation. He was then sent to France and took part in much severe fighting on the Somme and in other engagements. After being severely wounded at Cambrai in 1918 he was discharged in 1919 and sent back to Australia. He holds the 1914–15 Star, and the General Service and Victory Medals.

80, Haselrigge Road, Clapham, S.W.4. Z1684B

CORBEY, T. H., Corporal, R.F.A.

Having enlisted in 1906 he was mobilised at the outbreak of war and was shortly afterwards sent to the Western Front, where he took part in the heavy fighting in the Retreat from Mons and at Hill 60, Ypres, Vimy Ridge, the Somme and Arras. He afterwards took part in the Retreat and Advance of 1918. During his service in France he was twice wounded. He was still serving in 1920, and holds the Mons Star, and the General Service and Victory Medals.

16, Mantua Street, Battersea, S.W.11. Z1685

CORBY, H. E., Sapper, R.E.

Joining in September 1916 he was drafted to the Western Front in the following December. He took part in numerous engagements, including those at the Somme, Arras and Cambrai, and also served in the Retreat and Advance of 1918. He was demobilised in March 1919 after returning home, and holds the General Service and Victory Medals.

94, Harris Street, Camberwell, S.E.5. Z3441A

CORBY, R. T., Private, R.A.S.C. (M.T.)

He volunteered in September 1917 and in the same year was sent to the Western Front. He was engaged in driving a caterpillar tractor in the transport of supplies from the base at Rouen and rendered valuable services. He was demobilised in 1920 on his return to England, and holds the General Service and Victory Medals.

94, Harris Street, Camberwell, S.E.5. Z3441B

CORDELL, W. F. E., Sergt., 1st East Lancashire Regiment.

He enlisted in 1912 and shortly after the outbreak of war was sent to France. He took part in the severe fighting at Mons, the Marne, the Aisne and Ypres, in which he was wounded and invalided home. In 1915 after his recovery he was drafted to Egypt and in the following year was transferred to France, where he took part in further engagements, including those at the Somme, Arras and Ypres. During his service overseas he was wounded four times. He was demobilised in February 1919, and holds the Mons Star, and the General Service and Victory Medals.

142, Lavender Road, Battersea, S.W.11. Z1686A

CORNACHIA, C. J., L/Corporal, 2nd London Regt. (Royal Fusiliers).

He volunteered in February 1915 and after completing his training was sent to France in August of the same year. He took part in numerous engagements, including those at Loos, Vimy Ridge, the Somme and Ypres. He was afterwards transferred to German East Africa, where he was again in action. While there he contracted malaria and after being invalided to Cape Town was sent back to England. He was discharged in October 1918, and holds the 1914–15 Star, and the General Service and Victory Medals.

226, St. George's Road, Peckham, S.E.15. Z3443

CORNELL, H. E., Private, Middlesex Regiment.

He joined in 1917 and in April of the following year was drafted to France. He gave his life for the freedom of England in the Battle of Villers-Brétonneux on April 24th, 1918, and was buried there. He was entitled to the General Service and Victory Medals.

"He died the noblest death a man may die."

27, Saltoun Road, Brixton, S.W.2. Z3066

CORNISH, E., Musician, Scots Guards.

He enlisted in 1898 and was serving in London at the outbreak of war. In 1916 he was sent to France with the Scots Guards Band and served in many different parts of the line. He later proceeded to Italy and was on duty for a time in Rome. He was demobilised in 1919 after his return home, and holds the General Service and Victory Medals.

51, Emu Road, Battersea Park, S.W.8. Z1689

CORNISH, H., Air Mechanic, R.A.F.

Volunteering in November 1915 he was sent to the Western Front in the following year. He was engaged as an Air Mechanic at various stations in France and Belgium with his Squadron and carried out duties which demanded a high degree of technical skill. He was demobilised in April 1919 after returning home, and holds the General Service and Victory Medals.

74, Este Road, Battersea, S.W.11. Z1687

CORSTON, W. N. E., Seaman Gunner, Royal Navy.

He was already in the Navy, having enlisted in November 1913. He afterwards proceeded to the Dardanelles in H.M.S. "Lord Nelson," which took part in several Naval actions, and covered the landing of the troops on the Gallipoli Peninsula. This ship also participated in the sinking of the "Breslau" on January 20th, 1918. While with his ship in Grecian waters he was wounded in action and returned to England. After his recovery he was posted to H.M.S. "Endeavour," which was engaged on special service, and was later transferred to H.M.S. "Comet." This vessel was subsequently torpedoed and sunk by a submarine in the Mediterranean on August 6th, 1918, but he was rescued by an Italian boat and conveyed to Taranto, where he remained for some time. He then sailed to South America and was demobilised on his return in June 1919. He holds the 1914–15 Star, and the General Service and Victory Medals.

19, Godman Road, Peckham, S.E.15. Z5359

COSBY, H. D., Special War Worker.

He was engaged from November 1916 to November 1918 as an aeroplane fusilage erector at Messrs. Lyons' Aeroplane Factory, Medar Street, Camberwell. His work, which demanded a high degree of skill, was carried out in a most efficient manner and he rendered valuable services.

109, Villa Street, Walworth, S.E.17. Z27447A

COSBY, H. W., Driver, R.F.A.

He volunteered in August 1915 and after his training served at various stations on important duties. Owing to an accident during his training he was rendered unfit for military duties overseas and in December 1916 he was discharged as medically unfit for further service.

109, Villa Street, Walworth, S.E.17. Z27447B

COSGRAVE, G., Pioneer, R.E.

A serving soldier, having enlisted in November 1910, he was sent to the Western Front immediately upon the outbreak of hostilities and served in the Retreat from Mons and the Battles of the Marne, Ypres, the Somme, Albert, Loos and Arras. He was engaged on important duties with his unit throughout and did valuable work until January 1918, when he returned to England and was discharged. He holds the Mons Star, and the General Service and Victory Medals.

30, Temple Road, Chiswick, W.4. 6084B

COSIER, E., 1st Air Mechanic, R.A.F.

He joined in April 1916 and after his training saw service in France and Egypt. On each of these fronts he was engaged on important duties, which called for much technical knowledge and skill, and did valuable work with his Squadron until after the cessation of hostilities. He was demobilised in June 1919, and holds the General Service and Victory Medals.

48, Tabor Road, Hammersmith, W.6. 11648C

COSIER, E. (M.S.M.), Staff-Sergt., R.A.S.C. (M.T.)

Volunteering in August 1914 he obtained his training at various stations in England and afterwards served in France and Italy. He did valuable work with his unit in connection with the transport of supplies to the forward areas and was awarded the Meritorious Service Medal for consistently good work. In addition he holds the 1914-15 Star, and the General Service and Victory Medals, and was demobilised in April 1919.

48, Tabor Road, Hammersmith, W.6. 11648B

COSIER, P., Corporal, 2nd Dragoon Guards (Queen's Bays).

A serving soldier, having enlisted in January 1910, he was drafted to France in 1914 and served on that Front for four years. During this time he fought in many of the principal engagements and in 1918 was so severely wounded as to necessitate his return to England. He was invalided out of the Service in October of that year, and holds the 1914 Star, and the General Service and Victory Medals.

48, Tabor Road, Hammersmith, W.6. 11648A

COSSOM, L. A., Corporal, R.G.A.

Joining in January 1917 he was sent to the Western Front two months later. He subsequently did valuable work with his Battery during operations at Ypres and Cambrai, and in the Retreat and Advance of 1918, remaining overseas until the termination of hostilities. He holds the General Service and Victory Medals, and was demobilised in November 1919 after his return to England.

61, Winstead Street, Battersea, S.W.11. Z1690

COSTELLA, T., A.B., R.N., H.M.S. "Chatham."

He was already in the Navy when war broke out in August 1914 and served in H.M.S. "Chatham" in many waters. He took part in the Battle of Heligoland Bight and in a destroyer action in the North Sea in November 1916. Later he was engaged in conveying Australian and American troops to and from the various theatres of war and on one occasion his ship was torpedoed. He was discharged in March 1919, and holds the 1914-15 Star, and the General Service and Victory Medals.

27, D Block, Lewis Trust Buildings, Warner Road, Camberwell, S.E.5. Z5917

COTTER, J., Sergt., R.G.A.

Volunteering in November 1914 he was drafted to the Western Front in the following May. He fought in many important engagements, notably those at St. Eloi, Festubert, Loos, Vimy Ridge, Beaumont-Hamel, Bullecourt, the Somme and St. Quentin and in the Retreat and Advance of 1918. During his service he was awarded the Belgian Croix de Guerre for conspicuous bravery and devotion to duty whilst in action in Belgium. After the termination of hostilities he served for a time with the Army of Occupation in Germany, being stationed at Bonn. He holds the 1914-15 Star, and the General Service and Victory Medals, and was demobilised in April 1919 after his return to England.

196, East Street, Walworth, S.E.17. Z1691

COTTER, W. J., Trumpeter, R.G.A.

He volunteered at the age of sixteen in February 1915 and in the following May was drafted to the Western Front. Whilst in this theatre of war he acted as a despatch rider, in which capacity he did splendid work and served at St. Eloi, Festubert, Loos, Vimy Ridge, the Somme, Beaumont-Hamel and in many other important sectors. After the Retreat and Advance of 1918, in which he also took part, he was sent with the Army of Occupation to Germany and was later transferred to India, where in 1920 he was still serving. He holds the 1914-15 Star, and the General Service and Victory Medals.

196, East Street, Walworth, S.E.17. Z1692A

COTTER, W. M. (Miss), Special War Worker.

This lady did important work during the war. She was engaged at the Oxo Co., Ltd., Southwark, S.E., where she packed and labelled boxes of this product in readiness for transport to our troops in the various theatres of war, thus rendering valuable national service.

196, East Street, Walworth, S.E.17. Z1692B

COTTINGHAM, J., Private, 1st Border Regiment.

He was serving in India at the outbreak of war, having enlisted in 1912, and in the following year was drafted to the Dardanelles, where he saw much severe fighting and was wounded in action. On recovery he proceeded to France and took part in many important engagements, including those on the Somme, at Arras and Vimy Ridge, and in the Retreat and Advance of 1918. He was placed on the Reserve in 1919, and holds the 1914-15 Star, and the General Service and Victory Medals.

6, Victory Square, Camberwell, S.E.5. Z5726

COTTINGHAM, T., Driver, R.F.A.

He volunteered many times in the early part of the war but was rejected on medical grounds. Attesting under the Derby Scheme in November 1915, however, he was called up in the following January, but at the conclusion of his training in April 1916 was found to be physically unfit and was invalided out of the Service.

21, Cross Street, Clapham, S.W.4. Z1693

COTTON, A. G., Private, R.A.S.C. (H.T.)

He joined in March 1916 and in the following January crossed to France. During his service overseas he was engaged on important transport duties in the forward areas and was present at several important engagements, including those at Arras, Vimy Ridge, Bullecourt, Messines, Ypres, Lens, Cambrai, the Somme and Havrincourt Wood. He was demobilised in March 1919 after his return to England, and holds the General Service and Victory Medals.

33, Gaskell Street, Larkhall Lane, S.W.4. Z1695B

COTTON, D. H., Leading Aircraftsman, R.A.F.

He volunteered in July 1915 and on completing his training in the following December was sent to the Western Front. Whilst in this theatre of war he served in the testing section of the aircraft park, in which he was engaged on duties of an important nature, which called for much technical knowledge and skill. He returned to England in August 1920, when he was demobilised, and holds the 1914-15 Star, and the General Service and Victory Medals.

1, Gray's Place, Hutton Road, Lambeth, S.E.11. TZ23464

COTTON, E. J., Rifleman, Royal Irish Rifles, and Private, Queen's (Royal West Surrey Regiment).

He was mobilised in August 1914 and immediately drafted to France. There he took part in the Retreat from Mons and the Battles of Ypres, Loos, Vimy Ridge and the Somme, and was badly wounded and invalided home in 1917. He was discharged in August 1918 as medically unfit for further service, and holds the Mons Star, and the General Service and Victory Medals.

54, Heaton Road, Peckham, S.E.15. Z5737

COTTON, F. C., C.Q.M.S., R.E.

Being released from the Post Office in March 1916 he joined in the Royal Engineers and after a course of training was engaged on important duties in connection with telephone and telegraphic communications. He was not successful in obtaining his transfer overseas before the termination of hostilities but rendered valuable services until he was demobilised in February 1919.

14, Gambetta Street, Wandsworth Road, S.W.8. Z1694

COTTON, H. L., Gunner, R.F.A.

He volunteered in May 1915 and in February of the following year proceeded to France, where he saw much severe fighting. He took part in the Battles of the Somme, Arras, Vimy Ridge and Messines, and many other important engagements and was wounded in action near Ypres in August 1917. He was consequently invalided from the Army in May 1918, and holds the General Service and Victory Medals.

19, Sear's Street, Camberwell, S.E.5. Z5723

COTTON, R. L., A.B., Royal Navy.

He was already in the Navy, and when war broke out was on board H.M.S. "Iron Duke." Later he was transferred to H.M.S. "Gipsy," which vessel was subsequently engaged in actions off the Belgian Coast. In December 1918 he was transferred to Portsmouth and thence to a generating station at Port Edgar in Scotland, where he was engaged on duties of an important nature. He did valuable work until December 1919, when he was discharged through causes due to his service. He holds the 1914-15 Star, and the General Service and Victory Medals.

30, Plough Road, Battersea, S.W.11. Z1696

COTTON, T., Private, 12th Suffolk Regiment.

Volunteering in September 1915 he was drafted overseas in the following July. Throughout his service on the Western Front he did valuable work with his unit and took part in the Battles of the Somme, Arras, Messines, Ypres, Passchendaele and Cambrai. He was taken prisoner during the second Battle of the Somme in 1918 and worked behind the German lines until he was repatriated at the termination of hostilities. He holds the General Service and Victory Medals, and was demobilised in April 1919.

33, Gaskell Street, Larkhall Lane, S.W.4. Z1695D

COTTON, W., Private, Royal Berkshire Regiment.

Volunteering at the commencement of hostilities he crossed to France in January 1915 and whilst on that front took an active part in many of the principal engagements, notably those at Cambrai and the Somme. During his service he was wounded and invalided home on four occasions, and after his last return to the Western Front fought in the Retreat and Advance of 1918. He then served with the Army of Occupation in Germany and was demobilised in April 1919 after his return to England. He holds the 1914-15 Star, and the General Service and Victory Medals.

33, Gaskell Street, Larkhall Lane, S.W.4. Z1695C

COULMAN, J., Sapper, R.E.
A serving soldier, he was drafted to the Western Front immediately upon the declaration of war and served in the Retreat from Mons and many of the engagements which followed, including those at Vimy Ridge, the Somme, Bullecourt and Ypres, where he was wounded. From 1916 until 1919 he was in Salonika, where he was engaged on duties of an important nature in the forward areas. He was demobilised in May 1919 on his return to England, and holds the Mons Star, and the General Service and Victory Medals.
33, Lockington Road, Battersea Park Road, S.W.8.   Z1697

COULSON, A. H., Driver, R.F.A.
Volunteering in August 1914 he went through his course of training and rendered valuable services with his Battery until 1917, when he proceeded to India. While there he did excellent work on the Afghanistan frontier against the hill tribes, and suffered much from malaria. He returned home and was demobilised in 1919, holding the General Service and Victory Medals, and the India General Service Medal (with clasp, Afghanistan, North-West Frontier, 1919).
31, Brayard's Road, Peckham, S.E.15.   Z5587B

COULSON, A. L., Gunner, R.F.A.
After joining in February 1917 he was quickly drafted to France and took an active part in the Battles of Arras, Messines, Ypres, Lens, Passchendaele, Cambrai, Péronne, Bapaume and many other engagements in the Offensives of 1918. After the Armistice he proceeded to Germany with the Army of Occupation and rendered valuable service there until his return home for demobilisation in 1919. He holds the General Service and Victory Medals.
31, Brayard's Road, Peckham, S.E.15.   Z5587A

COULSON, R., Battery Q.M. Sergt., R.F.A.
He volunteered in 1915 and in the same year was drafted to France, where he rendered valuable service in different sectors. He took part in several actions, including those at Hill 60, Ypres, the Somme, Arras and Vimy Ridge, and served until the cessation of hostilities, after which he returned to England and was demobilised in 1919. He holds the 1914-15 Star, and the General Service and Victory Medals.
11, Wesley Place, Newington Butts, S.E.11.   Z26169

COULSTON, J., Private, Queen's (Royal West Surrey Regiment).
Volunteering in August 1914 he joined in the R.A.S.C. and after his training was drafted to France, where for two years he was engaged on important transport duties. In the course of his service he was transferred to the Queen's (Royal West Surrey Regiment) and fought with his unit in several battles, including those of Ypres and the Somme. He fell fighting at Vimy Ridge on April 10th, 1917, and was entitled to the 1914 Star, and the General Service and Victory Medals.
"A valiant soldier, with undaunted heart, he breasted Life's last hill."
23, Stendale Road, Wandsworth Road, S.W.8.   Z1698

COURTNEIDGE, A. J., Rifleman, Cameronians (Scottish Rifles).
Joining in March 1916 he crossed to France three months later. He was subsequently engaged in the fighting at Arras, Vimy Ridge, Ypres and Passchendaele, where he was wounded and gassed in July 1917. Later he returned to England and after protracted treatment in hospital at Cambridge was invalided out of the Service in February 1919. He holds the General Service and Victory Medals.
77, Farmer's Road, Camberwell, S.E.5.   Z1699

COURTNEY, W. G., Private, 8th Buffs (East Kent Regiment).
Volunteering in September 1914 he obtained his training at Shoreham and in the following August was drafted overseas. On his arrival in France he was sent to the Loos sector, where operations were then in progress, and where he was unfortunately killed in action in September 1915. He was entitled to the 1914-15 Star, and the General Service and Victory Medals.
"Whilst we remember the sacrifice is not in vain."
26, Ægis Grove, Battersea Park Road, S.W.8.   Z1700

COUSINS, H. W., Private, 11th Queen's (Royal West Surrey Regiment).
He volunteered in June 1915 and in the following year was drafted to the Western Front, where he served until 1917. During this time he fought in several engagements, including those at Ypres, Messines and the Somme, and was then sent to Italy, where he did valuable work with his unit in operations on the Piave. After the termination of hostilities he was sent with the Army of Occupation to Germany and was demobilised in 1919 after his return to England. He holds the General Service and Victory Medals.
6, The Triangle, Clapham, S.W.4.   Z1701

COVE, D., Private, R.A.S.C.
Volunteering in May 1915 he was sent to the Western Front in the same month and was subsequently engaged on important duties in connection with the loading and unloading of munitions of war. In July 1917 he was invalided home and discharged in consequence of ill-health and later died in June 1920. He was an ex-service man, having previously enlisted in the East Surrey Regiment in 1882, and at the time of his discharge had completed thirty-eight years with the Colours. He was entitled to the 1914-15 Star, and the General Service and Victory Medals.
"His memory is cherished with pride."
12, Stainforth Road, Battersea, S.W.11.   Z1777

COWDEROY, C., Rifleman, King's Royal Rifle Corps.
He volunteered in 1915 and on the completion of his training served at various stations on important duties with his unit. He did good work but was unable to proceed overseas owing to being medically unfit for duty abroad and was discharged in 1916 as the result of illness contracted whilst in the service.
3, Cancell Road, Brixton Road, S.W.9.   Z5230B

COWDEROY, W. A., Driver, R.A.S.C. (M.T.)
He volunteered in August 1914, having previously served in the South African War from 1899 till 1902. He was soon drafted to France and was engaged in all sectors of the Western Front, where he did good work as a transport driver. In 1916 he was sent to German East Africa and during his service there was taken ill and was in consequence invalided home and discharged in 1917. He holds the Queen's and King's South African Medals, the 1914 Star, and the General Service and Victory Medals.
3, Cancell Road, Brixton Road, S.W.9.   Z5230A

COWDERY, C., Corporal, 1st Life Guards.
He volunteered in August 1914 and during his service on the Western Front, which lasted for practically the whole period of the war, fought in many of the principal battles, including those of Ypres, Arras and Armentières. He was still serving in 1920, and holds the 1914 Star, and the General Service and Victory Medals.
139, St. Albans Avenue, Chiswick, W.4.   7876B

COWDERY, F. (M.C.), Lieutenant, 23rd Middlesex Regiment.
He volunteered in September 1914 and after his training saw service in France and Italy. On each of these fronts he fought with distinction in many of the principal battles and was awarded the Military Cross for an act of distinguished gallantry and devotion to duty in the Field. In addition he holds the General Service and Victory Medals, and was demobilised in November 1919 on his return to England.
139, St. Albans Avenue, Chiswick, W.4.   7876C

COWDERY, H., Sapper, R.E.
He joined in April 1916 and after his training was drafted to the Western Front, where he was engaged on duties of an important nature in the forward areas. He was invalided home and discharged in October 1917 through causes due to his service, and holds the General Service and Victory Medals.
139, St. Albans Avenue, Chiswick, W.4.   7876A

COWELL, E., Driver, R.F.A.
He volunteered in November 1914 and in the following September was drafted to the Western Front, where he served for over two years. During this time he did valuable work with his Battery in operations at Loos, Neuve Chapelle, Vimy Ridge, Albert, the Somme, Ypres, Passchendaele and Arras, and in 1918, on being sent to Italy, served on the Piave. He was demobilised in April 1919 on his return to England, and holds the 1914-15 Star, and the General Service and Victory Medals.
45, Comus Place, Walworth, S.E.17.   Z1776

COWELL, W., Private, 2nd Essex Regiment.
After twenty-one years' previous service he rejoined voluntarily in September 1914 and in the following April was drafted to the Dardenelles, where he did excellent work in many operations. He was unfortunately killed in action at Suvla Bay on August 6th, 1915, and was entitled to the 1914-15 Star, and the General Service and Victory Medals.
"Great deeds cannot die ;
They with the sun and moon renew their light for ever."
9, Copeland Road, Peckham, S.E.15.   Z5588A

COWLIN, E. M. (Mrs.), Special War Worker.
This lady offered her services for work of National importance and was engaged by Messrs. Wilkinson at their sword factory. Her duties, which consisted of the chamfering of bayonet points, were of a most important nature, and were carried out in a most efficient and commendable manner.
66, Church Path, Acton Green, W.4.   6320B

COWLIN, F. A., Special War Worker.
Being ineligible for service with the Colours he obtained work of National importance at the Aircraft Works of Messrs. Ogston, Acton. Here he was engaged on duties of an important nature, which demanded a high degree of technical knowledge and skill, and did valuable work throughout the period of hostilities.
66, Church Path, Acton Green, W.4.   6320A

COX, C. A., Private, R.A.S.C. (M.T.)
He volunteered in May 1915 and in the same year was drafted to the Western Front, where he served for over three-and-a-half years and was engaged on important duties in connection with the motor transports in numerous sectors of the front. In January 1919 he was demobilised, and holds the 1914-15 Star, and the General Service and Victory Medals.
95, Yeldham Road, Hammersmith, W.6.   13242B

COX, C. G., Private, 17th Essex Regiment.
He joined in June 1918 and on the completion of his training was engaged on important coastal defence and other duties with his unit. He was not successful in obtaining his transfer overseas before hostilities ceased but rendered much valuable service until his demobilisation in January 1919.
74, Grenard Road, Peckham, S.E.15.   Z5589

COX, D. R., Rifleman, 18th London Regiment (London Irish Rifles).
He volunteered at the outbreak of war at the age of forty-two years, having previously served in the South African War and in India. He was engaged on important coastal defence duties at various stations and rendered valuable services for nearly three years, at the end of which time he was discharged in 1917. He holds the Queen's South African Medal and the India General Service Medal.
14, Crossford Street, Stockwell Green, S.W.9.   Z1703

COX, E. C. (M.S.M.), R.S.M., 24th London Regiment (The Queen's).
He was mobilised with the Territorials at the outbreak of war and in August 1916 was sent overseas. During his service in France he fought on the Somme and at Ypres, and was then transferred to the 2nd Army School of Musketry as Sergeant-Major until his demobilisation in January 1919. In June 1918 he was awarded the Meritorious Service Medal for consistently good work, and also holds the Territorial Efficiency, and the General Service and Victory Medals.
89, Lothian Road, Camberwell New Road, S.W.9.   Z5227

COX, E. F. J., Rifleman, Rifle Brigade.
He joined in June 1918 on attaining military age and after his training was completed was drafted to France in the following October. After the cessation of hostilities he advanced into Germany with the Army of Occupation and served on important duties guarding the bridge heads at Cologne and other places. He was demobilised in March 1920 on returning to England, and holds the General Service and Victory Medals.
93, Chatham Road, Wandsworth Common, S.W.11.   Z1802

COX, F. W., Special War Worker.
During the war he was engaged on important special duties as an electrician at Halton Camp from January to December 1917, and from April 1918 to December in the same year at Plymouth Camp, Cattewater. He rendered skilled and valuable services during this period.
28, Annandell Road, Chiswick, W.4.   5441C

COX, H. F., Driver, R.A.S.C.
He volunteered in May 1915 and crossed to France in the following September. His service overseas lasted for over three years, during which time he did important transport work conveying rations, guns, bridges and other munitions of war to the forward areas and working for a time with the R.E. He was demobilised in August 1919 on his return to England, and holds the 1914-15 Star, and the General Service and Victory Medals.
46, Jocelyn Street, Peckham, S.E.15.   Z5360

COX, H. W., Rifleman, 8th London Regiment (Post Office Rifles).
He joined on attaining military age in June 1918 and was still in training when hostilities ceased. He did valuable work during his service and was engaged on important guard duties at Ripon and Aldershot. He was demobilised in November 1918.
38, Elliott Road, Stockwell, S.W.9.   Z4433B

COX, J., Private, 21st (Empress of India's) Lancers, and M.G.C.
He enlisted in June 1914 and twelve months later was drafted to the Western Front. There he saw much heavy fighting with the M.G.C. and took part in many important engagements until the cessation of hostilities. He was then sent with the Army of Occupation into Germany, where he was stationed at Cologne until October 1919. He holds the 1914-15 Star, and the General Service and Victory Medals, and in 1920 was still with his unit in India.
30, Gloucester Road, Peckham, S.E.15.   Z5732B

COX, P. (Miss), Member, W.R.A.F.
She joined in September 1918 and served with the W.R.A.F. for fourteen months. During this time she was engaged as a telephonist at a Stores Depôt at Greenwich and as a clerk at Kidbrooke, and did valuable work in each of these capacities. She was demobilised in November 1919.
38, Elliott Road, Stockwell, S.W.9.   Z4433A

COX, R. C., Pte., Royal Sussex and East Surrey Regts.
He joined in April 1916 and after his training proceeded overseas in the same year and took part in the heavy fighting in the Battle of the Somme, where he was severely wounded in action. He was invalided to hospital at Wimereux and was afterwards sent home, and after prolonged treatment in various hospitals was discharged as physically unfit for further military duty in February 1919. He holds the King's Certificate, and the General Service and Victory Medals.
30, Shorncliffe Road, Old Kent Road, S.E.1.   Z1702

COX, S. E., Bombardier, R.F.A.
He volunteered in June 1915 and at the conclusion of his training saw service in France, especially in the Somme area, and in Salonika and Russia. On each of these fronts he did valuable work with his Battery during military operations. He was demobilised in August 1919 after his return to England, and holds the General Service and Victory Medals.
11, Sandover Road, Camberwell, S.E.5.   Z5361

COX, T. J., Private, 8th Sherwood Foresters.
He joined on attaining military age in June 1916 and was sent to the Western Front in the following March. Subsequently he went into action and fell fighting in the vicinity of Arras on April 7th, 1917. He is buried near St. Quentin, and was entitled to the General Service and Victory Medals.
"His life for his Country, his Soul to God."
13, Southampton Street, Camberwell, S.E.5.   Z4432

COX, W. G., Private, Oxfordshire and Buckingham-shire Light Infantry.
He volunteered in September 1914 and in the same year embarked for France. During his service on the Western Front he did excellent work as a bomber at Ypres, the Somme, where he was gassed, and Arras, and in various subsequent engagements until the cessation of hostilities. He was demobilised in 1919, and holds the 1914-15 Star, and the General Service and Victory Medals.
22, Northall Street, Stockwell, S.W.9.   Z1704A

COXHEAD, E., Sergt., R.F.A. (T.F.)
He re-enlisted in August 1914 and in March of the following year proceeded to the Western Front. There he saw much heavy fighting, took part in the Battles of Neuve Chapelle, Festubert, Loos, the Somme, Vimy Ridge and Cambrai, and many other important engagements, and was wounded in action in the Somme Offensive in October 1916. He was demobilised on his return home in March 1919, and holds the 1914-15 Star, and the General Service and Victory Medals.
8, Crawford Street, Camberwell, S.E.5.   Z5915
          Z5916

COXHEAD, G., A.B., R.N., H.M.S. "Cordelia."
He joined in May 1917 and was posted to H.M.S. "Cordelia," on board which vessel he served with the Grand Fleet in the North Sea. He was engaged on important patrol duties off Zeebrugge and various other places until the cessation of hostilities and in 1920 was still at sea. He holds the General Service and Victory Medals.
8, Crawford Street, Camberwell, S.E.5.   Z5914

COXWELL, A. F., Rifleman, Rifle Brigade.
He volunteered in January 1916 and in the same year embarked for France. Whilst in this theatre of war he was in action in the Battle of the Somme, and at Arras and Ypres, where he was gassed in 1917. He was invalided home to hospital and after his recovery and a few months on home service rejoined his unit in France. He then took part in the Advance of 1918 and was severely wounded in the second Battle of Cambrai. He was again invalided home to hospital and demobilised in February 1919. He holds the General Service and Victory Medals.
17, Treherne Road, Stockwell, S.W.9.   Z3434

CRABB, W., Private, 19th Middlesex Regiment.
He volunteered in May 1915 and in the following year was drafted to France. There he fought in the engagements on the Somme, at High Wood, Delville Wood, Trones Wood, Flers, Combles, Ypres and Dixmude. He was then transferred to the Labour Corps after having suffered from fever contracted on duty and was demobilised on his return home in January 1919. He holds the General Service and Victory Medals.
24, Gonsalva Road, Wandsworth Road, S.W.8.   Z1705

CRACKNELL, J., 1st Air Mechanic, R.A.F.
He joined in July 1916 and on completing his training was engaged on important duties as a motor-transport driver at many of our chief aerodromes. He was unable to secure his transfer overseas before the termination of hostilities but did valuable work until he was demobilised in March 1919.
111, Akerman Road, Brixton Road, S.W.9.   Z4435

CRACKNELL, E., Gunner, R.F.A., and Pioneer, R.E.
He volunteered in May 1915 and embarked for France with the Royal Field Artillery and was later transferred to the Royal Engineers. He was then on special duties with the Gas Inspection Corps until the Armistice was signed. He was demobilised in February 1919, and holds the General Service and Victory Medals.
9, Bognor Street, Wandsworth Road, S.W.8.   Z1708

CRACKNELL, A. H., Corporal, 16th London Regiment (Queen's Westminster Rifles).
He volunteered in August 1914 and in 1916 was drafted to France and thence to Salonika. Later he was sent to Palestine, where he served with General Allenby's Forces in many engagements and was wounded. On recovery he returned to the Western Front and was again very severely wounded in action near Arras. He was demobilised in February 1919, and holds the General Service and Victory Medals.
40, South Island Place, Brixton Road, S.W.9. Z5231

CRACKNELL, H., Rifleman, 21st London Regiment (1st Surrey Rifles).
Joining in April 1916 he was sent to Salonika in July 1917 and served there for some months attached to the 9th Entrenching Battalion. He then proceeded to Egypt, but unfortunately contracting dysentery in hospital for some time at Port Said and Alexandria. On his recovery he rejoined his unit and subsequently fought in the Palestine Campaign under General Allenby. In consequence of continued ill-health he was again invalided to hospital and later to a convalescent camp at Mustapha. He afterwards did service with the Labour Corps and the R.A.F. in Alexandria, and, after being confined to hospital for a further period, was sent to England and discharged as physically unfit in October 1918. He holds the General Service and Victory Medals.
46, Treherne Road, Stockwell, S.W.9. Z4434

CRACKNELL, R., Shoeing Smith, R.F.A.
He volunteered in October 1914 and in the following year proceeded to France, where he served in various engagements in many sectors of the Western Front. He was mainly engaged on shoeing-smith duties during his service overseas and did excellent work. In January 1919 he was demobilised, and holds the 1914-15 Star, and the General Service and Victory Medals.
186, Farmer's Road, Camberwell, S.E.5. Z1707A

CRACKNELL, T., Rifleman, King's Royal Rifle Corps
He joined in August 1916 and in the following December was sent to France. Here he was engaged in the fighting in the Battle of the Somme, where he was wounded. After his recovery he served in the third Battle of Ypres and in many subsequent engagements. He was demobilised in August 1919, and holds the General Service and Victory Medals.
2, Sandford Row, Walworth, S.E.17. Z1706A

CRACKNELL, T. R., Private, 11th Middlesex Regt.
He volunteered in August 1914 and in the following February was sent to the Western Front. During his service in France he fought in many important engagements, including those of Ypres, the Somme and Arras, and also served in the Retreat and Advance of 1918, and was gassed. He was demobilised in December 1918, and holds the 1914-15 Star, and the General Service and Victory Medals.
2, Sandford Row, Walworth, S.E.17. Z1706B

CRAFT, C., Gunner, R.G.A, and Private, R.A.S.C. (M.T.)
He was mobilised from the Reserve at the outbreak of war and was almost immediately drafted to France, where he took part in the Retreat from Mons. He also served on the Marne and the Aisne, and was severely gassed at Béthune in 1917 and sent home to hospital. After his recovery he was transferred to the Royal Army Service Corps and was engaged on important transport duties conveying provisions to various camps. He was demobilised in March 1919, and holds the Mons Star, and the General Service and Victory Medals.
12, Sedan Street, Walworth, S.E.17. Z1710A

CRAFT, C., Driver, R.F.A.
He volunteered in 1915 and in the same year was drafted to the Western Front. There he did good work as a driver in numerous engagements, including those on the Somme, and at Ypres, Arras, Albert, St. Quentin, Péronne, Bapaume and the subsequent final operations. He was demobilised in August 1919, and holds the 1914-15 Star, and the General Service and Victory Medals.
12, Sedan Street, Walworth, S.E.17. Z1710B

CRAFTER, H. P., Gunner, R.F.A.
He volunteered in September 1915 and in the following December proceeded overseas. During his service in France he fought in the Battle of the Somme and at Beaumont-Hamel, and in August 1918 was wounded and gassed at Amiens. He was invalided to hospital in England and was subsequently discharged in March 1919. He holds the 1914-15 Star, and the General Service and Victory Medals.
75, Latchmere Road, Battersea, S.W.11. Z1709

CRAIG, J. (Mrs.), Special War Worker.
This lady volunteered her services during the war and was engaged at Messrs. Beardmore's Munition Works, Park Heath, Glasgow. There she carried out responsible and dangerous duties shell filling until the war was concluded. Her services, which were efficiently rendered, were highly appreciated by the Firm.
154, The Grove, Hammersmith, W.6. 10343B

CRAIG, R. C., Special War Worker.
For three years during the war he was engaged at the Lancashire Steel Works on bridge buildings which were designed for France. He afterwards served at Messrs. Beardmore's Munition Factory at Glasgow, where he was employed on the manufacture of parts for guns until the end of the war. He did excellent work and carried out all his duties with skill.
154, The Grove, Hammersmith, W.6. 10343A

CRAKER, H. E., Corporal, 8th Duke of Cornwall's Light Infantry.
Volunteering in September 1914 he was drafted in August of the following year to France and served in the Somme area until November of that year. He then proceeded to Salonika and took part in the fighting on the Vardar and Doiran fronts and in many other engagements in that campaign. In February 1919 he was demobilised after returning home, and holds the 1914-15 Star, and the General Service and Victory Medals.
20, Bonnington Square, South Lambeth Road, S.W.8. Z1711

CRANE, C., Private, 1st Lancashire Fusiliers.
He volunteered in August 1914 and was sent to France immediately upon completing his training. Subsequently he fought in several engagements, notably those at Hill 60 and Loos. He returned to England in consequence of being severely gassed at Ypres and was invalided out of the service in 1917. He holds the 1914 Star, and the General Service and Victory Medals.
6, Draycout Place, Camberwell, S.E.5. Z4436

CRANE, F. C., Gunner, R.F.A.
He volunteered in October 1914 and in December of the following year was drafted to the Western Front, where he subsequently fought in many engagements, notably those at the Somme, Arras and Cambrai, and the Offensives of 1918. In 1917 he was severely gassed and on May 30th, 1919, died from the effects whilst stationed at Douai. He was entitled to the 1914-15 Star, and the General Service and Victory Medals.
"Steals on the ear the distant triumph song."
25, Sandover Road, Camberwell, S.E.5. Z5362

CRANE, J., L/Corporal, 23rd Royal Fusiliers.
He volunteered in April 1915 and after his training served at various stations on important duties with his unit. He rendered valuable services but both on account of his age and his health was not able to obtain a transfer overseas and was demobilised in February 1919. Later he rejoined, however, in the Labour Corps and proceeded to France on duties in connection with the burial of the dead.
19, Lothian Road, Camberwell New Road, S.W.9. Z5226

CRANSTON, J. A., A.B., Merchant Service.
He joined the Merchant Service in 1912 and served with the Royal Navy after his ship was chartered by the Admiralty at the outbreak of war. Throughout the period of hostilities he did valuable work in various vessels and frequently passed through submarine and mine infested areas. He returned to shore in January 1920, when he was discharged, and holds the General Service and Mercantile Marine War Medals.
24, Blondel Street, Battersea, S.W.11. Z2335

CRASKE, E. W., Sapper, R.E., and Air Mechanic, R.A.F.
He volunteered in September 1914 and after having completed his training was drafted to the Western Front. He rendered valuable service in the Battles of Ypres, the Somme, Arras and Cambrai, and many others until the close of the war. He returned home and was demobilised in January 1919, holding the 1914-15 Star, and the General Service and Victory Medals.
156, The Grove, Hammersmith, W.6. 10344A

CRASKE, H. (Mrs.), Special War Worker.
For two-and-a-half years during the war this lady was engaged at the White City, Shepherd's Bush, on important work in connection with the manufacture of gas bags and military tents. She did excellent work and carried out her duties in a highly commendable manner until November 1918.
156, The Grove, Hammersmith, W.6. 10344B

CRASKE, S. W., 1st Class Petty Officer, R.N.
He joined the Navy in July 1897 and during the war was engaged on important patrol duties in the North Sea. He was also employed on escorting troopships to and from the fighting areas and in convoying food and ammunition vessels. He was discharged in consequence of his service in February 1916, and holds the Long Service and Good Conduct Medal, the 1914-15 Star, and the General Service and Victory Medals.
178, Eversleigh Road, Battersea, S.W.11. Z1712

CRAWFORD, C., L/Corporal, M.G.C. (Infantry).
He volunteered in December 1915 and after his training was drafted to Mesopotamia in August 1917. Whilst there he took part in the Capture of Tekrit and in all operations in that seat of war up to the Capture of Mosul in November 1918. He remained in the East until February 1920, when he returned home and was demobilised. He holds the General Service and Victory Medals.
6, Shellwood Road, Battersea, S.W.11. Z1714

CRAWFORD, W. H., Guardsman, 3rd Grenadier Guards.
Mobilised from the Reserve at the outbreak of war he was drafted with the Expeditionary Force to France and was in action at Mons, the Marne, the Aisne, Neuve Chapelle, Hill 60, Ypres, Festubert and Loos, where he was severely wounded. After hospital treatment in England he was discharged as a time-expired man and afterwards unhappily died of his injuries in 1918. He was entitled to the Mons Star, and the General Service and Victory Medals.
"His life for his Country."
48, Broughton Street, Battersea Park, S.W.8. Z1713A

CRAWLEY, D., Private, 2nd East Yorkshire Regt.
He volunteered in August 1914 after many years' earlier Colour service and was drafted to the Dardanelles. He was present at the Landing at Suvla Bay and after the Evacuation of the Peninsula proceeded to Egypt. After taking part in the Battle of Gaza in the Palestine campaign he was sent to France and fought at the Somme and Cambrai in the Retreat and Advance of 1918. In February 1919 he was demobilised, and holds the 1914-15 Star, and the General Service and Victory Medals.
12, Rozel Road, Wandsworth Road, S.W.4. Z1715

CRAY, H., Sergt., Cheshire Regiment.
Volunteering in November 1914 he proceeded in the following March to the Western Front. There he fought in many battles, including those at Ypres, Festubert, Loos, Vimy Ridge, the Somme, Arras, Cambrai and the Retreat and Advance of 1918, and was wounded. In April 1919 he was demobilised, and holds the 1914-15 Star, and the General Service and Victory Medals.
25, Townley Street, Walworth, S.E.17. Z1716

CREAK, W. F. (Senior), Private, Black Watch.
Volunteering in August 1914 he proceeded to the Western Front on the completion of his training and fought at Ypres and Ploegsteert Wood. On one occasion he was buried in the trenches for several hours by the explosion of a shell. In April 1916 he was discharged in consequence of his service, and holds the 1914-15 Star, and the General Service and Victory Medals.
77, Whellock Road, Chiswick, W.4. 7520A

CREAK, W. F. (Junior), Private, Canadian Expeditionary Force.
He joined in February 1916 and after having completed his training was drafted to the Western Front. There he took part in many battles, including those at Vimy Ridge, Arras, and in the Retreat and Advance of 1918, and on one occasion was wounded. In October 1919 he returned home, and was demobilised, holding the General Service and Victory Medals.
77, Whellock Road, Chiswick, W.4. 7520B

CREASEY, C., A.B., R.N., H.M.S. "Edinburgh."
He joined on attaining eighteen years of age in November 1916 and was posted to H.M.S. "Edinburgh," on board which vessel he served with the Grand Fleet in the North Sea. Engaged on various duties he took part in important operations in these waters until the cessation of hostilities and in November 1919 was invalided from the Navy owing to defective hearing. He holds the General Service and Victory Medals.
172, St. George's Road, Peckham, S.E.15. Z5729A

CREASEY, C., Leading Seaman, R.N.
He was already in the Navy when war broke out in August 1914 and later was engaged on escort and other important duties in H.M.S. "Africa." He served off the African Coast, in the Black Sea and in many other waters during the period of hostilities and in 1920 was still at sea in H.M.S. "Stuart." He holds the 1914-15 Star, and the General Service and Victory Medals.
172, St. George's Road, Peckham, S.E.15. Z5729B

CREASEY, H., Private, 10th Hampshire Regiment.
Volunteering in February 1915 in the Bedfordshire Regiment he was in the course of his training transferred to the Hampshire Regiment. In the following September he was drafted to Salonika, and three months later was twice wounded and taken prisoner. Whilst in captivity in Bulgarian hands he suffered badly from malaria but ultimately recovered. Returning to England on being released after the Armistice he was demobilised in February 1919, and holds the 1914-15 Star, and the General Service and Victory Medals.
108, Cator Street, Peckham, S.E.15. Z4437

CREASEY, W. A., A.B., R.N.
He volunteered in February 1915 and served in many vessels, including H.M.S. "Marlborough," "Africa" and "Canada." He was engaged on convoy and other duties in many waters and took part in the Battle of Jutland and various minor engagements until the cessation of hostilities. He holds the 1914-15 Star, and the General Service and Victory Medals, and in 1920 was still at sea. 208, St. George's Road, Peckham, S.E.15. Z5728

CREATES, E. J., Driver, R.F.A.
He volunteered in April 1915 and in the same year was drafted overseas. Whilst in France he took part in much of the heavy fighting at Ypres and the Somme. He was unfortunately killed in action on July 14th, 1916, and was entitled to the 1914-15 Star, and the General Service and Victory Medals.
"A costly sacrifice upon the altar of freedom."
33, Henshaw Street, Walworth, S.E.17. Z1771

CREED, S., Private, 9th Loyal North Lancashire Regiment.
Volunteering in December 1915 he was drafted on the completion of his training in the following year to the Western Front. There he was in action at the Somme, Arras, Albert, Passchendaele, Delville Wood and St. Quentin, and was severely wounded at Ypres in 1918. He was invalided home and after hospital treatment was discharged in November 1918 as medically unfit. He holds the General Service and Victory Medals.
42, Fenwick Place, Stockwell, S.W.9. Z1718

CREER, P. (M.M.), Driver, R.F.A.
He joined in October 1916 and in the following January was drafted to Egypt. He served with General Allenby in the Palestine Campaign at Gaza and other engagements, and was present at the Entry into Jerusalem. Whilst in the East he was wounded. In 1918 he proceeded to France and fought in various engagements until the conclusion of hostilities and was again wounded. He was awarded the Military Medal while serving in the East for conspicuous bravery in laying communication wires under heavy fire when attached to the R.E., and also holds the General Service and Victory Medals. He was demobilised in January 1919.
90, Beresford Street, Camberwell Road, S.E.5. Z1719

CREIGHTON, F., Driver, R.A.S.C. (M.T.)
He volunteered in November 1914 and was soon drafted to the Western Front. Whilst there he was engaged on important transport duties and in conveying the wounded to hospital after the Battles on the Somme, Passchendaele, Armentières, Ypres and others. In May 1919 he returned home and was demobilised, holding the 1914 Star, and the General Service and Victory Medals. 21, Warham Street, Camberwell, S.E.5. Z1720

CRESSWELL, H., Private, Middlesex Regiment, and Sapper, R.E.
Volunteering in 1915 he proceeded in the same year to the Western Front. There he was in action at Ypres and the Somme, and was wounded. On his recovery he returned to the fighting line and took part in several engagements until he was again wounded in the Advance of 1918. In May 1919 he returned home and was demobilised, holding the 1914-15 Star, and the General Service and Victory Medals.
72, Stewart's Road, Battersea Park Road, S.W.8. Z1721

CREW, W., Driver, R.F.A.
Having previously served in the Egyptian and the South African Wars he volunteered in August 1914 and was speedily drafted to France. There he took part in the Retreat from Mons and the Battles of the Marne, the Aisne and Ypres. In 1916 he proceeded to Salonika, where he saw much service until the cessation of hostilities. Whilst overseas he was wounded twice. He returned home and was demobilised in 1919, holding the Egyptian Medal (1882), the Khedive Star, the Queen's South African Medal, the Mons Star, and the General Service and Victory Medals.
9, Revesby Street, Walworth, S.E.17. Z17

CRIBB, T., Private, M.G.C.
He joined in June 1916 and in the following December was drafted to the Western Front. In this theatre of war he was in action in many engagements and being severely wounded at Elverdinghe on August 19th, 1917, unfortunately died while being conveyed to the dressing station. He was entitled to the General Service and Victory Medals.
"He died the noblest death a man may die,
Fighting for God, and right, and liberty."
90, Ascalon Street, Battersea Park Road, S.W.8. Z1723

CRICKMAY, S., Sergt., Essex Regiment.
Joining in 1916 he was drafted on the completion of his training to the Western Front. Whilst there he fought at the Somme and Arras, and in 1917 proceeded to Salonika. After seeing much service there he proceeded to Egypt and served under General Allenby throughout his Palestine Campaign. He remained in the East until April 1920, when he returned home and was demobilised, holding the General Service and Victory Medals.
43, Buller Street, Battersea, S.W.11. Z1724

CRIPPS, E. G., Trooper, 4th (Royal Irish) Dragoon Guards.
He joined in May 1918 and at the conclusion of his training served with the 17th and 10th London Regiments and the 5th Rifle Brigade on important duties. He was not successful in obtaining his transfer overseas before the termination of hostilities, but was afterwards engaged in escorting German prisoners to Le Havre. He was demobilised in November 1919.
27, Campana Road, Parson's Green, S.W.6. Z19922

CRIPPS, F. H., Rifleman, Rifle Brigade.
He joined in 1916 and after completing a period of training was engaged on important duties at various stations. Owing to ill-health he was unable to obtain his transfer overseas and after rendering valuable services with his unit was invalided from the Army in 1919, suffering from the effects of pneumonia contracted during his military service.
41, Philip Road, Peckham, S.E.15. Z5903

CRIPPS, J. A. (M.M.), Private, R.A.S.C. (M.T.)
Volunteering in May 1915, he proceeded to France in February of the following year. Whilst in this theatre of war he served with distinction in many notable engagements, including those at Albert, Vimy Ridge, Arras, Ypres, Cambrai, St. Quentin and Amiens, and did splendid work. He was awarded the Military Medal for conspicuous bravery in bringing in the gassed and wounded under heavy shell fire, and in addition holds the General Service and Victory Medals. He was demobilised in March 1919.
13, Palmerston Street, Battersea, S.W.11   Z1725

CRISP, A. G., Gunner, R.F.A.
Volunteering in June 1915 he was drafted in the following year to France. He took part in many engagements, including those at the Somme, Arras, Ypres, Passchendaele and Cambrai, and acted as a signaller during his service overseas. In March 1918 he was taken prisoner in the German Offensive and after being in captivity for about nine months was repatriated and demobilised in 1919. He holds the General Service and Victory Medals.
63, Stonhouse Street, Clapham, S.W.4.   Z1726C

CRISP, P. G., Sergt., R.F.A.
Mobilised in August 1914, he almost immediately embarked for France and took part in the Retreat from Mons, the Battles of the Marne, the Aisne, the Somme, Arras, Messines, Ypres, Cambrai and other engagements until the close of war. He also did valuable work as an Instructor in Signalling. Whilst overseas he was wounded twice, but on his recovery returned to his unit. In March 1919 he returned home and was demobilised, holding the Mons Star, and the General Service and Victory Medals.
16, Vicarage Road, Camberwell, S.E.5.   1799

CROAD, F. W., Private, Queen's (Royal West Surrey Regiment).
He joined in 1917 and after his training was engaged at various stations on important duties with his unit. He rendered valuable services but on account of his youth was not successful in obtaining his transfer overseas before the cessation of hostilities. He was demobilised in 1919.
8, Khyber Road, Battersea, S.W.11.   Z1727

CROCKER, E., Private, Worcestershire Regiment.
Mobilised from the Reserve at the outbreak of hostilities he was quickly drafted to the Western Front and fought in the Retreat from Mons and the Battles of Ypres and Givenchy. He also served at Festubert, Neuve Chapelle, Ploegsteert Wood and Loos, where he was buried alive by shell explosion in September 1916. Returning then to England he was invalided out of the Service in May 1917, and holds the Mons Star, and the General Service and Victory Medals.
111, Brayard's Road, Peckham, S.E.15.   Z5363

CROCKFORD, A., Leading Stoker, R.N., H.M.S. "Hecla.
He was serving at the outbreak of hostilities and during the war saw much service with the Grand Fleet in the North Sea. He was in the "Eden" in 1915 when she was run into in the Channel and was one of the minority who were saved. He also did good service in other ships until hostilities ceased. He was still serving, on board H.M.S. "Hecla," in 1920, and holds the 1914-15 Star, and the General Service and Victory Medals.
295, Mayall Road, Herne Hill, S.E.24.   Z3446B

CROCOME, W., Driver, R.F.A.
He joined in November 1916 and a year later was drafted to the Western Front, where he took part in numerous engagements of importance, including those at Cambrai and the Somme. He also served with distinction in the Retreat and Advance of 1918 and afterwards proceeded with the Army of Occupation to Germany. He was demobilised in October 1919, holding the General Service and Victory Medals.
71, Mysore Road, Battersea, S.W.11.   Z1801

CROFT, F. G., Private, 1st Devonshire Regiment.
He was mobilised from the Reserve in August 1914 and shortly afterwards was sent to France, where he took part in the severe fighting at the Aisne, La Bassée, Hill 60, Ypres, the Somme, Arras, Delville Wood, Passchendaele and many other engagements. He afterwards proceeded to Italy, but returning to France in 1918 served in the Retreat and Advance of that year. During his service in France he was wounded and gassed. He was demobilised in August 1919, and holds the 1914 Star, and the General Service and Victory Medals.
19, Latchmere Road, Battersea, S.W.11.   Z1729

CROFT, H., Corporal, Royal Irish Regiment.
Mobilised in August 1914 he proceeded to the Western Front in time to take part in the Battle of, and Retreat from, Mons. After serving also through the Battles of the Marne and the Aisne he was taken prisoner at La Bassée in October 1914 and for three-and-a-half years was held in captivity in Germany. He was then interned in Holland until the cessation of hostilities and on his return home was demobilised in March 1919. He holds the Mons Star, and the General Service and Victory Medals.
142, Coronation Buildings, South Lambeth Road, S.W.8.   Z1728

CROKER, S. W., Gunner, R.F.A.
Joining in 1917 he was drafted to the Western Front later in the same year. He took part in numerous important engagements with his Battery in the Retreat and Advance of 1918. He returned home and was demobilised in February 1919, holding the General Service and Victory Medals.
225, Mayall Road, Herne Hill, S.E.24.   Z1771

CROMBIE, A., Private, Labour Corps.
Joining in February 1917 he proceeded to France in the following month and there served in various sectors of the Front. He was engaged on road-making and other important duties at Dickebusch, Passchendaele and Arras, and did much good work until his demobilisation in February 1919. He holds the General Service and Victory Medals.
18, Foreign Street, Camberwell, S.E.5.   Z5911

CRONIN, H. E., Private, Bedfordshire Regiment.
He joined in May 1918 and after his training in Norfolk was drafted to France in December of the same year. He afterwards proceeded with the Army of Occupation to Germany and did much valuable service there. He returned home and was demobilised in April 1920.
25, Speke Road, Battersea, S.W.11.   Z2376

CRONIN, H. W., Private, Norfolk Regiment, and M.G.C.
He volunteered in 1914 and early in the following year was sent to the Western Front. He fought in several important engagements, including those near Ypres, and in 1916 was severely wounded in action during the Somme Offensive. Invalided home to hospital he underwent protracted treatment, and in October 1918 was discharged as medically unfit for further duty. He holds the 1914-15 Star, and the General Service and Victory Medals.
37, Sanson Street, Camberwell, S.E.5.   Z4438

CROOK, A., Air Mechanic, R.A.F. (late R.N.A.S.)
He joined in 1917 and after the completion of his training was engaged in testing engines and other important duties with his Squadron. He also served on patrol duties over the North Sea and on one occasion came down in the sea and was three hours in the water before being rescued. He was demobilised in 1919, and holds the General Service and Victory Medals.
82, Faraday Street, Walworth, S.E.17.   Z1731A

CROOK, C. J., Driver, R.F.A.
Volunteering in May 1915 at the age of fourteen he was sent to France in the same year. He took part in numerous engagements of importance, including those at Loos, the Somme, the Ancre, Arras and Cambrai. He was invalided home in 1918 with fever, and discharged in June 1919. He holds the 1914-15 Star, and the General Service and Victory Medals.
28, Priory Road, Wandsworth Road, S.W.8.   Z1732B

CROOK, E. L., Driver, R.A.S.C. (M.T.)
He joined in January 1916 and after his training was engaged with the Red Cross Society at Bessington War Hospital and rendered valuable services. In 1918 he proceeded to France, where he was present at various engagements in the Cambrai area and was wounded. He was invalided home, and discharged owing to his injuries, but afterwards re-enlisted and was still serving in 1920, holding the General Service and Victory Medals.
28, Priory Road, Wandsworth Road, S.W.8.   Z1732A

CROOK, F. C., Boy Telegraphist, R.N., H.M.S. "Dunedin."
He joined as a boy in the Royal Navy in 1916 and after his training served with the Grand Fleet in the North Sea. He was engaged on important duties and rendered valuable services. He was still serving in 1920 on board H.M.S. "Dunedin" in the Home Fleet, and holds the General Service and Victory Medals.
28, Priory Road, Wandsworth Road, S.W.8.   Z1732C

CROOK, G. W., Staff-Sergt. Farrier, 4th (Queen's Own) Hussars.
He volunteered in September 1914 and served as Farrier Sergt.-Major in Ireland on important duties with his unit. He rendered valuable services, but was not successful in obtaining his transfer to a theatre of war. He was seriously injured by a kick from a horse, and was in consequence discharged in October 1918.
170, Mayall Road, Herne Hill, S.E.24.   1807

CROOK, W., L/Corporal, 6th London Regiment.
Volunteering in August 1915 he was sent to the Western Front in the same year after completing his training. He took part in much severe fighting at Loos, the Somme, Arras, Ypres and Lens, and also served in the Retreat and Advance of 1918. He was demobilised in 1919 after his return home, and holds the 1914-15 Star, and the General Service and Victory Medals.
82, Faraday Street, Walworth, S.E.17.   Z1731B

CROSS, A. E., Driver, R.F.A.
Having previously served in the Army since 1899 he volunteered in August 1914 and was sent to France in the following month. He took part in the severe fighting at Mons, the Marne, the Aisne, Ypres, Hill 60, Festubert, Loos and in many other engagements in the Ypres area until June 1918, when he returned to England. He was discharged in consequence of his services in September 1918, and holds the Mons Star, and the General Service and Victory Medals.
36, Morrison Street, Battersea, S.W.11. Z1733

CROSS, A. S., Sergt., M.G.C.
He volunteered in November 1915 and in the same month was drafted to Lapland and thence to Asia Minor, where he served with the Armoured Car Brigade attached to the Russian Army during the campaign against the Turks. Later he was transferred to Roumania and thence to Galicia, where he took part in the Retreat from Lemberg. Afterwards he was made prisoner by the Bolshevists, but in April 1918 was released and sent to Murmansk and was there when the British Forces captured Romanoff. He was then sent to England and posted to the M.G.C. and was later drafted to Mesopotamia. There he served on the Tigris, and was also in Persia for a time until 1919, when he returned to England and was demobilised, holding the Russian Order of St. Stanislaus, and the General Service and Victory Medals.
4, Whellock Road, Chiswick, W.4. 5701A

CROSS, H., Leading Signalman, R.N., H.M.S. "Newcastle."
He enlisted in March 1901 and at the outbreak of war was serving with the Grand Fleet in the North Sea. He took part in the Battles of Heliogoland Bight and Jutland, and was in action in the Dardanelles. He was also engaged on patrol and convoy duties until demobilised in January 1919. He was awarded the Albert Gallantry Medal for saving life at sea in 1911, and also holds the 1914-15 Star, and the General Service and Victory Medals.
21, Broughton Street, Battersea Park, S.W.8. Z1735

CROSS, J. A., Corporal, Durham Light Infantry, and Labour Corps.
He joined in July 1916 and was drafted to the Western Front in the same year. He served in the Ypres and Arras sectors, and in the Retreat and Advance of 1918. He was also engaged for some time on railway reconstruction work and on important orderly-room duties. He was at Brandhock camp when it was bombed during a German air raid in October 1917. He was demobilised in February 1919, and holds the General Service and Victory Medals.
64, Edithna Street, Stockwell, S.W.9. Z1734

CROSS, W. G., Driver, R.A.S.C.
He volunteered in September 1914 and in November of the same year was drafted to the Western Front, where he served in numerous engagements, including those at Loos, Albert, the Somme, Ypres, Passchendaele, Cambrai and Lens. He also took part in the Retreat and Advance of 1918. He was blown up in an explosion in November 1918 and was incapacitated for several weeks. He was demobilised in April 1919, and holds the 1914-15 Star, and the General Service and Victory Medals.
39, Searle's Road, New Kent Road, S.E.1. Z1798

CROSSWELL, F. G., Guardsman, Coldstream Guards.
Volunteering in September 1914 he was sent to France in January of the following year. He took part in the severe fighting in many important engagements until June 1916, when he was wounded and lost his right arm. He was invalided home and discharged in January 1917 owing to his physical disabilities, holding the 1914-15 Star, and the General Service and Victory Medals.
8, Brussels Road, Battersea, S.W.11. Z1736

CROUCH, A., Private, 1st East Surrey Regiment.
Called up from the Reserve at the declaration of war he was immediately drafted to the Western Front and took part in the Retreat from Mons and many of the engagements which followed. Later he was taken prisoner and after being for some time in an internment camp at Doeberitz was sent to work in the coal mines in Russia. He was repatriated and demobilised in December 1918, and holds the Mons Star and the General Service and Victory Medals.
33, St. Alphonsus Road, Clapham, S.W.4. Z1737

CROUCH, C. E. (Mrs.), née HASTIE, Special War Worker.
This lady rendered much valuable service during the recent war. She was engaged for four months in the production of shells at Messrs. Du Cros', Acton, for twelve months in shell filling at Messrs. Blake's, Shepherd's Bush, and for fifteen months in a similar capacity at Messrs. Baker's, Willesden. She carried out her important duties in a most capable manner which was worthy of high commendation.
14, Redmore Road, Hammersmith, W.6. 11622A

CROUCH, A. R., Sergt., R.F.A.
He volunteered in September 1915 and during his service on the Western Front, which lasted for three years, fought in many important battles, notably those of the Somme and Cambrai and was wounded and gassed. On his return to England in February 1919 he was demobilised, and holds the General Service and Victory Medals.
14, Redmore Road, Hammersmith, W.6. 11622B

CROUT, T. W., Driver, R.F.A.
Volunteering in October 1915 he was drafted to the Western Front early in 1916 and did excellent work as a driver whilst operations were in progress on the Somme, at Arras and Ypres. During his service he was mentioned in Despatches for remaining with his horses under very heavy fire, although he was gassed and wounded. He holds the General Service and Victory Medals, and was demobilised in March 1919 after his return to England.
22, Bournemouth Road, Rye Lane, S.E.15. Z5364

CROW, E. (Mrs.), Special War Worker.
This lady was employed for a considerable period of the war at Messrs. Spicer & Sons', Bermondsey Street, S.E. She was engaged as a machinist in connection with the production of gas masks and in this capacity did excellent work throughout her service, which terminated in March 1919.
213, Sayer Street, Walworth, S.E.17. Z1739A

CROW, H. C., Private, 24th London Regt. (Queen's).
Volunteering in August 1914 he was sent to the Western Front in the following February and fought in the Battles of Neuve Chapelle, St. Eloi and Ypres. He died gloriously on the field of battle at Givenchy on May 26th, 1915, and was entitled to the 1914-15 Star, and the General Service and Victory Medals.
"Great deeds cannot die."
213, Sayer Street, Walworth, S.E.17. Z1739B

CROW, J. E., Sapper, R.E.
He joined in 1917 and after his training was engaged on duties of an important nature in connection with telegraphy. He was considered indispensable in this branch of the service and on this account was unable to obtain his transfer to a theatre of war. He did valuable work until he was demobilised in March 1919.
213, Sayer Street, Walworth, S.E.17. Z1739C

CROW, J. G., L/Corporal, 3rd York and Lancaster Regiment.
A serving soldier, he was in India when war broke out and landed in France in January 1915. He subsequently fought in several battles, including that of Ypres, and was wounded twice and gassed. Invalided home in April of that year he underwent protracted treatment in hospital and in April 1916 was discharged. Two years later he died from the effects of his wounds. He was entitled to the 1914-15 Star, and the General Service and Victory Medals.
"His memory is cherished with pride."
2, Berkley Street, Kennington, S.E.11. Z25865

CROW, T. F., Special War Worker.
Being ineligible for service with the Colours he obtained work of National importance at the Mark Brown Wharf, where he was engaged on duties of an important nature in connection with the loading and unloading of transport ships. In this capacity he did valuable work until October 1919, when he resigned.
213, Sayer Street, Walworth, S.E.17. Z1739D

CROWE, F., Gunner, R.F.A.
He volunteered in December 1914 and after a period of training proceeded to the Western Front in 1916. There he took part in many important engagements, including the Battles of the Somme, Arras, Bullecourt and Ypres, and other engagements until sent home suffering from shell-shock. He was invalided from the Army in March 1918, and holds the General Service and Victory Medals.
11, Foreign Street, Camberwell, S.E.5. Z5913

CROWE, H., Private, 1/2nd Royal Fusiliers.
Joining in August 1916 he obtained his training at Salisbury Plain and in the same year was drafted to France. He was subsequently engaged in the fighting on the Somme, at Ypres and in many other sectors. Whilst in action at Vimy Ridge he was severely wounded in the left leg and later suffered its amputation. Unfortunately he died from the effects on May 6th, 1917. He is buried at Etaples Cemetery, and was entitled to the General Service and Victory Medals.
"His life for his Country, his Soul to God."
108, Sheepcote Lane, Battersea, S.W.11. Z1738

CROWHURST, G. H., Driver, R.F.A.
He volunteered in May 1915 and after his training was drafted to France, where he served for over three years. During this time he fought in several important engagements, notably those at Loos, the Somme, St. Eloi, St. Quentin, Armentières, Bullecourt, Péronne and Messines, and in the Retreat and Advance of 1918. He was demobilised in June 1919 after his return to England, and holds the 1914-15 Star, and the General Service and Victory Medals.
24, Sussex Road, Coldharbour Lane, S.W.9. Z1780

CROXSON, E., Sergt., R.G.A.

Volunteering in August 1914 he was sent to the Western Front three months later. During his service overseas he did valuable work with his Battery, principally in the Ypres sector, and was wounded. On returning to England in May 1919 he was demobilised, but later re-enlisted in the R.A.S.C. and in 1920 was still serving. He holds the 1914 Star, and the General Service and Victory Medals.

19, Elmington Road, Camberwell, S.E.5.   Z4439B

CROYDON, S., Rifleman, King's Royal Rifle Corps.

He volunteered in May 1915 and until 1917, when he was drafted to France, was engaged on duties of an important nature with his unit. After taking part in several important engagements he was wounded and taken prisoner at the second Battle of the Somme in 1918. During his captivity he was sent to work with German farmers at Oldenburg and was released after the cessation of hostilities. He was demobilised in January 1919, and holds the General Service and Victory Medals.

15, Godman Road, Peckham, S.E.15.   Z5365

CRUMP, R., Private, 2nd Staffordshire Regiment.

Volunteering in September 1915 he was sent to France early in the following year and was subsequently engaged in the fighting on the Somme and at Arras, Ypres and Cambrai. He also served in the Retreat and Advance of 1918, but in September of that year was invalided home in consequence of ill-health and was in hospital until the following November. He was demobilised in February 1919, and holds the General Service and Victory Medals.

4, Horsman Street, Camberwell, S.E.5.   Z1740

CRUMP, S., Corporal, Tank Corps.

Joining in February 1916 he crossed to France in September of that year. He did valuable work with his unit during operations at Arras, Vimy Ridge, Ypres, Passchendaele and Cambrai, and in the Retreat and Advance of 1918, remaining overseas until early in 1919. He was demobilised in November, and holds the General Service and Victory Medals.

83, Lavender Road, Battersea, S.W.11.   Z1741A

CRUSE, A. C., 1st Air Mechanic, R.A.F.

Volunteering in January 1915 he was sent to Egypt a month later and served on board various seaplane-carrying ships. Whilst in H.M.S. " Ben-my-Chree " on January 11th, 1917, she was sunk in action off the coast of Asia Minor, but he, fortunately, was rescued. Later he was engaged on duties of an important technical nature at the Seaplane Base at Port Said. He holds the 1914-15 Star, and the General Service and Victory Medals, and was demobilised in September 1919 on his return to England. 8, Flinton Street, Walworth, S.E.17.   Z1742C

CRUTCHLOW, T., Private, R.A.S.C. (M.T.)

Volunteering in March 1915 he was sent to France in the same month. Whilst overseas he was engaged on duties of an important nature in connection with the transport of food supplies to the forward areas, and was present at many of the principal battles. He was demobilised in January 1920, and holds the 1914-15 Star, and the General Service and Victory Medals.

17, Smyrke's Road, Walworth, S.E.17.   Z1743B

CRUTCHLOW, W., Private, Queen's Own (Royal West Kent Regiment).

He volunteered at the commencement of hostilities and crossed to France in March 1915. During his service overseas he fought at St. Eloi, Ypres, Festubert, Loos, Vimy Ridge and the Somme, where in September 1916 he was severely wounded. Invalided home he underwent protracted hospital treatment, and in March 1917 was discharged as physically unfit. He holds the 1914-15 Star, and the General Service and Victory Medals.

17, Smyrke's Road, Walworth, S.E.17.   Z1743

CUDD, F., Private, West Yorkshire Regiment.

He volunteered in August 1914 and after his training was drafted to the Western Front. During his service he fought in a number of the principal engagements, including those at Neuve Chapelle, Hill 60, Ypres, Festubert, Loos and the Somme, and was wounded. He was unfortunately killed in action in April 1918 during the German Offensive of that year. He was entitled to the 1914-15 Star, and the General Service and Victory Medals.

"Nobly striving,
He nobly fell that we might live."

66, Acorn Street, Camberwell, S.E.5.   Z4440B

CUFF, H. J., Private and Rifleman, M.G.C. and King's Royal Rifle Corps.

Joining in January 1917 he crossed to France three months later and was subsequently in action at Arras, Vimy Ridge, Bullecourt, Messines, Ypres and Passchendaele. In August 1917 he was invalided home in consequence of ill-health and after being in hospital at Stockport for some months was sent to his depôt, where he was then transferred to the Machine Gun Corps, in which he returned to France. During the German Offensive in March 1918, however, he was again taken ill and after being for a time in hospital at Rouen was sent to England and discharged as physically unfit in October of that year. He holds the General Service and Victory Medals.

86, Chatham Street, Walworth, S.E.17.   Z1744

CUFFLEY, J. R., A.B., Royal Navy.

He volunteered in January 1915 and after his training was posted to H.M.S. " London," which vessel was subsequently engaged on important patrol duties in the North Sea. Later he was transferred to H.M.S. " Parker," and in 1920 was still serving. He holds the 1914-15 Star, and the General Service and Victory Medals.

18, Mundella Road, Wandsworth Road, S.W.8.   Z1745

CULHAM, J. W., Sapper, R.E.

He joined in April 1916 and after a period of training was engaged on important ferrying duties, loading and unloading trains for France. Being medically unfit for active service he was unable to obtain his transfer to the front but, nevertheless, did much good work until demobilised in January 1919.

19, Evelina Road, Peckham, S.E.15.   Z5906

CULLUM, D., Private, R.A.S.C.

Volunteering in November 1914 he crossed to France in the same month and served on important transport duties during the Battle of La Bassée, in which he was gassed in May 1915. For some time he remained in hospital in France and was later invalided to Paignton in Devonshire, where he remained until he was discharged as medically unfit in November of the same year. He holds the 1914 Star, and the General Service and Victory Medals.

48, Henley Street, Battersea, S.W.11.   Z1746

CULLUM, F. C., 1st Air Mechanic, R.A.F.

He joined in November 1916 and at the conclusion of his training was engaged on important duties which demanded a high degree of technical skill. He was unable to secure his transfer overseas before the termination of hostilities, but nevertheless did valuable work until he was demobilised in 1918.

57, Wellington Road, Battersea, S.W.11.   Z1747A

CULWICK, W. J., Private, 8th Buffs (East Kent Regiment), and M.G.C.

He volunteered in September 1914 and early in the following year was sent to the Western Front, where he fought in the Battles of Ypres and Loos. Whilst in action in the vicinity of Ypres he received severe wounds, to which he unfortunately succumbed on June 3rd, 1916. He was entitled to the 1914-15 Star, and the General Service and Victory Medals.

"And doubtless he went in splendid company."

5, Neate Street, Camberwell, S.E.5.   Z5061

CUNNINGHAM, L., Pte., 1st and 2nd Royal Fusiliers.

A serving soldier, having enlisted in April 1913, he was retained for important home duties until 1917, when he was drafted to France. In this theatre of war he fought at Ypres, where he was so severely gassed as to necessitate his return to England. On his recovery, however, he returned to the Western Front and took part in engagements at Loos, Lens and Cambrai, and was wounded. Later he was sent to England, and in February 1919, in consequence of his wounds, was invalided out of the Service. He holds the General Service and Victory Medals.

3, Lilac Place, Kennington, S.E.11.   Z24799B

CUNNINGHAM, W., Private, Royal Fusiliers.

Volunteering in February 1915 he was sent to the Dardanelles in the following July and served in the Landing at Suvla Bay and in the engagements which followed. After the Evacuatio of the Peninsula he was transferred to the Western Front, and on July 1st, 1916, fell fighting near Ypres. He was entitled to the 1914-15 Star, and the General Service and Victory Medals.

"A costly sacrifice upon the altar of freedom."

23, Alsace Street, Walworth, S.E.17.   1748

CUNNINGHAM, W. T., Guardsman, Scots Guards.

Having enlisted in 1912 he was serving at the outbreak of war and immediately crossed to France, where he fought in the Retreat from Mons and the Battles of the Marne, the Aisne and Ypres. He gave his life for the freedom of England in the Battle of Neuve Chapelle on March 12th, 1915, and was entitled to the Mons Star, and the General Service and Victory Medals.

"Thinking that remembrance, though unspoken, may reach
him where he sleeps."

3, Lilac Place, Kennington, S.E.11.   Z24799A

CURD, A., Sergt., Military Mounted Police.

He volunteered in January 1915 and in the following December sailed for France. During his service on the Western Front he did excellent work until he was demobilised after four-and-a-half years' service in July 1919. He holds the 1914-15 Star, and the General Service and Victory Medals.

150, Battersea Park Road, Battersea, S.W.11.   Z1749

CURD, J., Gunner, R.F.A.

He volunteered in March 1915 and in December of the same year was drafted to France. There he was mainly engaged as a shoeing smith and served in various sectors of the Western Front. In April 1918 whilst rescuing horses from an exposed and dangerous position he was unfortunately killed in action by shell fire. He was entitled to the 1914-15 Star, and the General Service and Victory Medals.

"The path of duty was the way to glory."

9B, Madron Street, Walworth, S.E.17.   Z1750

CURNICK, A. E., Private, R.A.M.C.
He volunteered in 1915 and after his training was drafted to Egypt, where he was stationed at Alexandria hospital in charge of mental patients. He did excellent work and carried out his arduous duties with great care and skill. He returned home, and was demobilised in September 1919, and holds the General Service and Victory Medals.
12, Elwell Road, Larkhall Lane, S.W.4.   Z1751

CURR, H. E. A., Sergt., R.F.A.
He volunteered in October 1914 and was drafted overseas in the following February. During his service in France he took part in many important engagements, including those at Neuve Chapelle, Ypres, Loos, the Somme, Arras and Cambrai. He was demobilised in February 1919, and holds the 1914-15 Star, and the General Service and Victory Medals.
29, Cambridge Street, Camberwell, S.E.5.   Z1752B

CURR, L. E. (M.M.), Corporal, R.E.
He volunteered in August 1914 and on the completion of his training was drafted to the Western Front. During his service in France he fought in many engagements, and was severely wounded at Arras in May 1917 and invalided home to hospital. He was discharged as medically unfit for further duty in the following November, and died as the result of his injuries on April 12th, 1920. He was awarded the Military Medal for conspicuous gallantry in action and devotion to duty on the Field, and was entitled in addition to the 1914-15 Star, and the General Service and Victory Medals.
"His life for his Country, his Soul to God."
29, Cambridge Street, Camberwell, S.E.5.   Z1752A

CURSONS, J. T., Shoeing Smith, R.F.A.
He volunteered in January 1915 and after his training served at various stations on important duties as a shoeing smith. He did excellent work but was not successful in obtaining a transfer overseas before the cessation of hostilities and was discharged in consequence of his services in October 1917.
27, Dorchester Grove, Chiswick, W.4.   5381B

CURSONS, A. M. (Mrs.), Special War Worker.
From April 1916 until July 1919 this lady was engaged at Messrs. Gwynne's Aircraft Works at Chiswick as a driller. She carried out her duties, which demanded great care and exactitude, with skill, and was specially selected to be presented to Queen Mary when Her Majesty visited the works in April 1917.
27, Dorchester Grove, Chiswick, W.4.   5381A

CURTIS, C., Gunner, R.F.A.
Mobilised from the Reserve at the outbreak of war he was almost immediately drafted to the Western Front, and served at Mons, Le Cateau, the Marne and Aisne, Ypres, Neuve Chapelle, Festubert, Loos, the Somme, the Ancre, Bullecourt, Ypres and Passchendaele. Later he proceeded to Italy, where he did valuable service at the Piave, Asiago and the Tagliamento, and was wounded. He holds the Mons Star, and the General Service and Victory Medals, and in 1920 was still serving.
13, Palmerston Street, Battersea, S.W.11.   Z1755

CURTIS, G., Private, 2nd Middlesex Regiment.
He volunteered in August 1914 and after having completed his training was drafted to the Western Front, where he fought in many important battles. He was unfortunately killed in action in July 1917, and was entitled to the General Service and Victory Medals.
"Whilst we remember the sacrifice is not in vain."
45, Richford Street, Hammersmith, W.6.   10689A

CURTIS, G. J., Private, R.A.V.C.
He joined in March 1917 and after his training served at various stations on important duties with his unit. He rendered valuable services in attendance on sick horses and in training remounts but was not successful in obtaining his transfer overseas before the conclusion of hostilities. In 1920 he was still serving.
60, Thurlow Street, Walworth, S.E.17.   Z1754B

CURTIS, J., Air Mechanic, R.A.F. (late R.N.A.S.)
Volunteering in 1915 he proceeded to the Western Front in the following year. Whilst in this theatre of war he was engaged at Ypres, the Somme, Messines, and the Retreat and Advance of 1918 on important aeroplane duties. After the cessation of hostilities he was sent with the Army of Occupation to Cologne. He remained there until 1919, when he returned home and was demobilised, holding the General Service and Victory Medals.
11, Patmore Street, Wandsworth Road, S.W.8.   Z1753

CURTIS, W., Rifleman, 17th London Regt. (Rifles).
He volunteered in March 1915 at 16 years of age and after his training was drafted to the Western Front. Whilst there he fought in many battles but was unfortunately killed in action in October 1916. He was entitled to the General Service and Victory Medals.
"Honour to the immortal dead who gave their youth
that the world might grow old in peace."
45, Richford Street, Hammersmith, W.6.   10689B

CUSSENS, T. E., Air Mechanic, R.A.F.
He joined in 1916 and after his training was engaged on important duties at various stations with his Squadron. Later he was drafted to Dunkirk and served there until the conclusion of hostilities, repairing and testing engines. He did valuable work and in 1919 returned home and was demobilised, holding the General Service and Victory Medals.
295, East Street, Walworth, S.E.17.   Z1756

CUTHBERT, H., Private, R.D.C.
Having previously served in the South African War he volunteered in November 1914 and was engaged on important guard and other duties at various stations. Later he was invalided to hospital through ill-health and in April 1918 was discharged as medically unfit, subsequently dying on July 23rd, 1918. He held the Queen's and King's South African Medals.
"He passed out of the sight of men by the path
of duty and self-sacrifice."
325, Eversleigh Road, Battersea, S.W.11.   Z1757

CUTHBERT, W., Pte., 24th London Regt. (Queen's).
He joined in November 1917 and after having completed his training proceeded overseas in the following year. He took part in many engagements on the Western Front and at Albert was severely wounded and invalided home. After being in hospital some considerable time he was demobilised in 1919, holding the General Service and Victory Medals.
95, Hubert Grove, Landor Road, S.W.9.   Z1758

CUTHBERTSON, A. A., A.B., Royal Navy.
Joining in August 1917 he was posted to H.M. Destroyer "Swallow," in which he served in Chinese waters until 1919. He then returned to England for leave and shortly afterwards proceeded to Russia, where he took part in operations against the Bolshevists. At the close of the Campaign he was sent with his ship to Turkish waters, in which he was serving in 1920. He holds the General Service and Victory Medals.
17, Neate Street, Camberwell, S.E.5.   Z5062A

CUTHBERTSON, F. W., Pte., 8th East Surrey Regt.
Volunteering in August 1914 he crossed to France early in the following year. He took part in many important engagements in this theatre of war and did excellent work as a sniper and despatch rider. Whilst at an observation post at Vaux Wood a French soldier, with whom he was sharing duty, was killed, and he courageously carried him back to our lines at great personal risk. He died gloriously, at the age of twenty-two, on the field of battle on July 1st, 1916, during the Somme Offensive. He was entitled to the 1914-15 Star, and the General Service and Victory Medals.
"A valiant soldier, with undaunted heart
he breasted Life's last hill."
17, Neate Street, Camberwell, S.E.5.   Z5062B

CUTTING, E. J., Corporal, R.F.A.
Joining in January 1916 he was sent to Egypt at the conclusion of his training and subsequently fought at Katia and Romani. Later he was sent to Palestine and after fighting at Rafa was severely wounded during the first Battle of Gaza. He was treated in hospital in Egypt but on his recovery rejoined his Battery and took part in several other engagements, including the Capture of Jerusalem. He was demobilised on his return to England in January 1919, and holds the General Service and Victory Medals.
28, Myatt Road, Stockwell, S.W.9.   Z5074C

CUTTING, F., Private, Lincolnshire Regiment, and Bedfordshire Regiment.
He joined in February 1917 and after having completed his training was drafted overseas in the following June. Whilst in France he fought in many battles and was twice wounded. He was demobilised in January 1919, and holds the General Service and Victory Medals.
35, Dale Street, Chiswick, W.4.   T5340A

CUTTING, H. A., 1st Air Mechanic, R.A.F.
He joined in June 1918 and after his training served at Dover in the Experimental Station on important work in connection with the bombardment of Zeebrugge. He rendered valuable services and remained there until May 1919, when he was demobilised.
43, Longhedge Street, Battersea, S.W.11.   Z1759

CUTTING, J., Driver, R.E.
Volunteering in April 1915 he was drafted in the following September to the Western Front. Whilst there he served in many notable engagements, including those of Ypres, the Somme, Arras, Albert, and in the Retreat and Advance of 1918. He returned home and was demobilised in July 1919, holding the General Service and Victory Medals.
35, Dale Street, Chiswick, W.4.   T5340B

CUTTS, E., Pte., Queen's (Royal West Surrey Regt).
He joined in September 1918 and on the completion of his training was drafted with the Army of Occupation to Germany, serving there until March 1920, when he returned to England for his demobilisation.
73, Battersea Bridge Road, Battersea, S.W.8.   Z1760A

CUTTS, F. G., Gunner (Signaller), R.G.A.

He joined in June 1917, having previously attempted to enlist and been rejected, and after completing his training was drafted in the following November to France. There he fought in many notable battles, including those of the Somme, Cambrai and the Advance of 1918. He also acted as Signaller whilst overseas. In January 1919 he returned home and was demobilised, holding the General Service and Victory Medals.
73, Battersea Bridge Road, Battersea S.W.11.   Z1760B

D

DACHTLER, F. W., L/Corporal, R.E.

Volunteering in June 1915 he was sent to the Western Front in the following January and served there for upwards of four years. During this period he fought in the Battles of the Somme, Arras, Albert, Vimy Ridge, Bullecourt, Messines, Lens, Cambrai, Amiens and Bapaume, and was wounded. He was demobilised in February 1919, and holds the General Service and Victory Medals.
19, Aldbridge Street, Walworth, S.E.17.   Z1808A

DACHTLER, R. J., Private, Bedfordshire Regiment.

He joined in April 1918 on attaining military age and after his training served at various stations on important duties with his Battalion. He did good work but was not successful in obtaining his transfer overseas before the close of the war. In January 1919, however, he was drafted to Germany to the Army of Occupation and was employed on guard and other duties until the following year. He was demobilised in April 1920.
19, Aldbridge Street, Walworth, S.E.17.   Z1808B

DACK, R. P., Private, 3rd, 17th and 10th Worcestershire Regiment.

Joining in May 1917 he crossed to France in the following March and was quickly sent up to Kemmel Hill, where operations were then in progress. He also fought in many other important engagements, including those at Epernay, Rheims, Soissons, Château Thierry, Cambrai and Valenciennes, and was wounded on two occasions. Whilst overseas he was attached to the Flying Column strengthening the line wherever danger was greatest. He was demobilised in September 1919 after a period of service in the Army of Occupation in Germany, and holds the General Service and Victory Medals.
80, Henley Street, Battersea, S.W.11.   Z6193

DACKOMBE, J., Private, 2nd Welch Regiment.

He volunteered in April 1915 and in the following year proceeded to the Western Front. He took a prominent part with his unit in several important engagements, including those at Martinpuich, Flers, High Wood, Delville Wood and Mametz Wood, and was twice wounded. He returned to England for medical treatment and was subsequently discharged in July 1917 unfit for further service. He holds the General Service and Victory Medals.
51, Westmacott Street, Camberwell, S.E.5.   Z3072

DADDS, T. E., Private, Essex Regiment.

Joining in December 1916 he completed his training and serving in the Signal Section of his Battalion was engaged on important coastal defence duties on the East Coast. He also served in Ireland and did excellent work but was unable to obtain a transfer to a theatre of war before the cessation of hostilities, and was demobilised in June 1919.
37, Surrey Square, Walworth, S.E.17.   Z1809

DAFFEY, W. A., Signalman, Royal Navy.

Volunteering in June 1915 he was posted to H.M.S. "Tyne," which vessel was engaged on patrol and minesweeping duties in the North Sea. He also served in H.M.S. "Ophelia" and was aboard her when she sank the German submarine U.B. 83. He holds the 1914-15 Star, and the General Service and Victory Medals, and in 1920 was still serving.
8, Graham Road, Chiswick, W.4.   6611

DAGWELL, C. J., Special War Worker.

He offered his services for work of National importance during the war and from January 1915 until December 1918 was employed as a tool maker at the Batt Munition Factory, Penge, and afterwards at the National Aircraft Works, Croydon. He rendered valuable services throughout.
1, Exon Street, Walworth, S.E.17.   Z1810A

DAGWELL, M. R. (Mrs.), Special War Worker.

This lady offered her services for work of National importance and was employed by the National Aircraft Works, Waddon, Croydon, from May 1918 until the following December. She was engaged on important work in connection with the making of aeroplane parts and discharged her duties in a thoroughly capable and efficient manner.
1, Exon Street, Walworth, S.E.17.   Z1810B

DAINS, E. E., Driver, R.F.A.

He volunteered in July 1915 and in the following March proceeded overseas. Serving on the Western Front he was in action in many important engagements, including the Battles of the Somme, Albert and Ypres, and was gassed. Rejoining his Battery he fought in the Retreat and Advance of 1918, and, returning to England in May 1919, was demobilised in the following month. He holds the General Service and Victory Medals.
20, Amies Street, Battersea, S.W.11.   Z1811

DAINTON, W. J., Private, R.A.S.C. (M.T.)

Volunteering in May 1915 he was later drafted to Salonika and was engaged on important duties as a motor mechanic and did valuable work in that capacity. He also saw service in Egypt. He contracted malaria and was sent home and, after spending some time in hospital, was discharged as medically unfit for further service in February 1919, and holds the General Service and Victory Medals.
12, Ceylon Road, West Kensington, W.14.   12233

DAINTREE, W., Rifleman, 9th London Regiment (Queen Victoria's Rifles).

Joining in July 1916 he was sent to the Western Front in the following November. During his service in this theatre of war he was engaged in severe fighting and fought in many important operations. He was killed in action at the Battle of Arras on April 14th, 1917, and was entitled to the General Service and Victory Medals.
16, Barmore Street, Battersea, S.W.11.   Z1812B

DAINTY, A., Sergt., 1st London Regiment (Royal Fusiliers).

He joined in August 1916 and four months later embarked for France. In the course of his service on the Western Front he fought in the Battles of Vimy Ridge, Bullecourt, Messines, Passchendaele and Cambrai, and, owing to ill-health, was sent to hospital at Rouen. He was demobilised in November 1919, and holds the General Service and Victory Medals.
49, Comyn Road, Battersea, S.W.11.   Z1813

DALE, A., Air Mechanic, R.A.F.

Joining in February 1918 he completed his training and served with his Squadron at various aerodromes. Engaged on important duties as a rigger he did valuable work but was unable to secure a transfer overseas before the termination of hostilities and in 1920 was still serving.
15, Stockwell Grove, Stockwell, S.W.9.   Z1814D

DALE, G. H., Private, Royal Marines.

He volunteered in November 1914 and in the following April embarked for Gallipoli and fought at the first Landing on the Peninsula and in other engagements, and was severely wounded. Invalided to England he received medical treatment at Gosport and Roehampton hospitals and was eventually discharged as medically unfit for further service in May 1916. He holds the 1914-15 Star, and the General Service and Victory Medals.
15, Stockwell Grove, Stockwell, S.W.9.   Z1814A

DALE, J., Private, 13th London Regiment (Kensingtons).

He joined in January 1918 and in the following July was sent to the Western Front. Whilst overseas he was in action during the Retreat and Advance of 1918, and after the signing of the Armistice served on guard and other important duties. Returning to England for demobilisation in December 1919, he holds the General Service and Victory Medals.
15, Stockwell Grove, Stockwell, S.W.9.   Z1814C

DALE, S., Private, Royal Fusiliers.

Joining in 1916 he completed his training and served at various stations with his Battalion until drafted to France in June 1918. In this theatre of war he took part in several important engagements during the Retreat and Advance and was killed in action near Albert on August 30th, 1918. He was entitled to the General Service and Victory Medals.
15, Stockwell Grove, Stockwell, S.N.9.   Z1814B

DALLEN, H., Private, R.A.S.C. (M.T.)

He volunteered in August 1915 and proceeding overseas two months later served in France throughout the war. He was engaged on important duties in connection with the transport of ammunition and supplies to the forward areas and rendered valuable services. Demobilised in February 1919, he holds the 1914-15 Star, and the General Service and Victory Medals.
74, Overstone Road, Hammersmith, W.6.   11631

DALLINGER, J. R., Private, 12th East Surrey Regt.

He joined in September 1916 and, drafted to France shortly afterwards, fought in the Battles of the Somme, Arras and Ypres, and was wounded. Sent to Italy on recovery he was in action during the Austrian Advance of 1917, and returned to the Western Front in 1918 and was in action in the Retreat and Advance. He was killed in action on October 22nd, 1918, and was entitled to the General Service and Victory Medals.
6, Cromwell House, Vauxhall Walk, Kennington, S.E.11 Z24482A

DALLISON, T., Private, 6th Border Regiment.
He volunteered in August 1914 and was sent overseas in the
following year. Serving in Gallipoli he fought in the first Landing
and in several other operations on the Peninsula until wounded
in August 1915. Invalided home on account of his injuries he
was subsequently discharged as medically unfit for further service
in August 1916, and holds the 1914–15 Star, and the General
Service and Victory Medals.
39, Sandover Road, Camberwell, S.E.5. Z5375

DALTON, A., Gunner, R.F.A.
Volunteering in October 1914 he was sent to the Western Front
in the following August and served there for upwards of four
years. He was in action in the Battles of Loos, Vermelles,
Ploegsteert Wood, the Somme, Ypres, Passchendaele, Lens,
Cambrai, and during the Retreat and Advance of 1918. Returning home for demobilisation in May 1919, he holds the 1914–15
Star, and the General Service and Victory Medals.
106, Mina Road, Walworth, S.E.17. Z1816A

**DALTON, C., Corporal (Bandsman), The Queen's
(Royal West Surrey Regiment).**
He volunteered in May 1915 and proceeding to France two
months later was in action in the Battle of Loos and other engagements until sent to Salonika in the following October. After
serving for a time in the Balkans he was drafted to Egypt, where he
remained until the end of the war. During his service overseas
he did good work as Corporal of the stretcher bearers and acted
as Doctor's Orderly at various dressing stations. He was
demobilised on his return home in July 1919, and holds the
1914–15 Star, and the General Service and Victory Medals.
234, East Street, Walworth, S.E.17. Z1817C

**DALTON, H. G., Private (Bandsman), The Queen's
(Royal West Surrey Regiment).**
He volunteered in July 1915 and on the conclusion of his training
was engaged on important duties with his unit. Owing to age
and physical unfitness he was not sent overseas and was discharged
in consequence in May 1917.
234, East Street, Walworth, S.E.17. Z1817A

DALTON, H. G. W., 1st Air Mechanic, R.A.F.
Volunteering in July 1915 he was engaged with his Squadron
in Scotland until sent to the Western Front a year later. During
his service he was engaged at various aerodromes on work which
called for a high degree of technical knowledge and skill, and rendered valuable services. He returned home for demobilisation in
February 1919, and holds the General Service and Victory
Medals.
234, East Street, Walworth, S.E.17. Z1817B

DALTON, J. C., Driver, R.F.A.
He volunteered in December 1915 and served with his Battery
at various depôts until drafted to Mesopotamia in September
1917. He fought in several important engagements, including
those at Tekrit and Talat Shergat, and was present at the Occupation of Mosul. Returning home he was demobilised in May
1919, and holds the General Service and Victory Medals.
150. Stewart's Road, Battersea Park Road, S.W.8. Z1815

**DALTON, P. E., Private, 1/4th London Regiment
(Royal Fusiliers).**
Volunteering in 1915 he was sent to the Western Front in the
same year and served in the Lewis Gun Section of his Company.
He was in action in the Battles of Arras, Ypres, Albert,
Armentières, Passchendaele, Bullecourt and in other engagements,
and was wounded. He also fought during the Retreat and
Advance of 1918. Demobilised in February 1919, he holds the
1914–15 Star, and the General Service and Victory Medals.
119, South Street, Walworth, S.E.17. Z1818

DALTON, R., Rifleman, King's Royal Rifle Corps.
Joining in June 1917 on attaining military age he completed
his training and was engaged on important duties with his unit
at various depôts. He rendered valuable services but was
unable to secure a transfer to a theatre of war before the cessation
of hostilities. In July 1919, however, he was sent to India,
where he was still serving in 1920.
106, Mina Road, Walworth, S.E.17. Z1816B

DANCE, A. T., Private, 1st East Yorkshire Regt.
He volunteered in September 1914 and at the conclusion of his
training proceeded to the Western Front, where he was engaged
on important duties with his unit. He was in action in many
important engagements and was wounded and taken prisoner.
He died in captivity in Germany in 1918, and was entitled to the
1914–15 Star, and the General Service and Victory Medals.
12, Claybrook Road, Hammersmith, W.6. 13422

DANCE, T., Driver, R.A.S.C.
Volunteering in August 1914 he was sent to the Western Front
in the same year and served throughout the war. He was
engaged on important duties in connection with the transport
of ammunition and supplies to the forward areas, and was present
at the Battles of Loos, Arras and the Somme. Returning
home for demobilisation in February 1919, he holds the 1914
Star, and the General Service and Victory Medals.
15, Westmacott Street, Camberwell, S.E.5. Z3439

DANIEL, G. L., Corporal, Gordon Highlanders.
He joined in June 1916 and in the following year embarked
for France. He was in action in the Battles of Arras, Ypres,
St. Quentin and was wounded at Cambrai on November 20th,
1917. Rejoining his unit on recovery he served until the end
of hostilities and, sent with the Army of Occupation into Germany,
was stationed at Cologne and other towns on the Rhine. He
was demobilised in September 1919, and holds the General
Service and Victory Medals.
8, Medwin Street, Ferndale Road, S.W.4. Z1819

DANIELS, C., Sergt., M.G.C.
A regular soldier, having enlisted in 1903, he was serving in
India when war broke out and was sent to the Western Front
later in 1914. He took an active part in several battles and was
gassed and wounded. Returning to the Field on recovery
he was taken prisoner on March 21st, 1918, during the Retreat
from Cambrai, and during his captivity in Germany worked in
a crucible factory. He was released after the Armistice and
returning to England was demobilised in February 1919. He
holds the 1914 Star, and the General Service and Victory
Medals. 23, St. Philip Street, Battersea Park, S.W.8. Z1822

DANIELS, F. G., Private, Labour Corps.
Joining in November 1917 he proceeded overseas in the following
year and saw much service on the Western Front. He was
engaged in the transport of ammunition to the forward areas and
on trench digging and other work during operations, including
the Battles of the Somme and Ypres. He was demobilised in
February 1919, and holds the General Service and Victory
Medals.
18, Goldsboro' Road, Wandsworth Road, S.W.8. Z1823

DANIELS, G. H., Private, 2/23rd London Regiment.
He volunteered in August 1914 and embarking for the Western
Front in the following January fought in several engagements
until sent to Palestine in 1917. He was in action in many
operations during the British Advance through Palestine and
served there until the end of hostilities. He returned to England
for demobilisation in January 1919, and holds the 1914–15 Star,
and the General Service and Victory Medals.
9, Lubeck Street, Battersea, S.W.11. Z1821

DANIELS, W. T. G., Leading Seaman, Royal Navy.
He enlisted in 1893 and, mobilised when war broke out, was
shortly afterwards sent to Belgium. Serving with the Fleet
Reserve he took part in several operations on the Belgian Coast
and was gassed and wounded, and on recovery was sent to
Egypt in 1915. He was engaged on special duties on the Suez
Canal and in the same year proceeded to Mesopotamia, where
he did valuable work for over two years. He then served with
the Grand Fleet until after hostilities ceased. Discharged
in April 1919, he holds the 1914 Star, and the General Service
and Victory Medals in addition to Medals for the South African
Campaign. 91, Wickersley Road, Lavender Hill, S.W.11. Z1820

DARBY, W., Rifleman, Royal Irish Rifles.
He volunteered in July 1915 and in the same year embarked
for the Western Front, where he fought in the Battles of the
Somme, Arras and Ypres. Invalided home in 1917 owing to
illness he received medical treatment and on recovery served
with his unit at various depôts until the end of the war. He
was demobilised in 1919, and holds the 1914–15 Star, and the
General Service and Victory Medals.
83, Sandmere Road, Clapham, S.W.4. Z1824

DARE, F., Private, 23rd London Regiment.
He joined in June 1916 and in December of the same year was
drafted to the Western Front. Here he was in action in several
important battles, including those of Ypres, the Somme, Arras
and the Ancre. He was badly gassed in the third Battle of the
Aisne in June 1918 and was invalided home for treatment.
On recovery he was discharged as medically unfit for further
service in December 1918. He holds the General Service and
Victory Medals.
1, Broomgrove Road, Stockwell, S.W.9. Z4441

DARK, H. J., Bombardier, R.F.A.
Volunteering in August 1915 he was sent to the Western Front
in the same year and was in action in the Battles of the Somme,
Arras and Ypres. He was later drafted to Italy and fought in
this theatre of war until the termination of hostilities.
Demobilised on his return home in April 1919, he holds the
1914–15 Star, and the General Service and Victory Medals.
5, Cardross Street, Hammersmith, W.6. 11571

**DARKE, F. E., Rifleman, 17th London Regiment
(Rifles).**
He volunteered in 1915 and after serving at home for a time was
drafted to Salonika in 1917. He was in action on the Doiran
front and contracted malaria. On recovery he proceeded to
Egypt and fought at Gaza and Jerusalem during the British
Advance through Palestine. In August 1918 he was sent to
France and was engaged on important guard duties until
demobilised in 1919. He holds the General Service and Victory
Medals.
5, Heaton Road, Peckham Rye, S.E.15. Z5935

DARKE, H. W. L., Private, 29th M.G.C.
He joined in March 1917 and was drafted to France after completing his training. During his service overseas he was engaged in heavy fighting until severely wounded in the Battle of Armentières. Invalided to hospital in England in consequence of his injuries his right leg had to be amputated and after receiving medical treatment he was discharged as physically unfit for further service in October 1919. He holds the General Service and Victory Medals.
28, Linden Gardens, Chiswick, W.4.   5876

DARLEY, H. L., Trooper, 5th (Princess Charlotte of Wales') Dragoon Guards.
Volunteering at the outbreak of war he was immediately drafted to France. Whilst on the Western Front he fought in the Retreat from Mons and many subsequent engagements. Owing to ill-health he was invalided to England early in 1915 and on recovery served on home duties until demobilised in May 1919. He holds the Mons Star, and the General Service and Victory Medals.
59c, Lewis Buildings, Warner Road, Camberwell, S.E.5.   Z5945

DARLING, J., Sergt., 2/23rd London Regiment.
Volunteering in June 1915 he embarked for France a year later and served on the Western Front until December 1916. He was then drafted to Salonika, where he was in action in the Advance on the Doiran front and in other operations in the Balkans. In May 1917 he proceeded to Egypt and fought at the Battle of Gaza and in the Capture of Jericho and Jerusalem, and was severely wounded in the Jordan Valley in March 1918. Sent to hospital in England in consequence of his injuries he lost a leg by amputation and was invalided out of the Service in February 1919. He holds the General Service and Victory Medals.
157, Lavender Road, Battersea, S.W.11.   Z1825

DART, J. H., Sergt., Middlesex Regiment.
He volunteered in September 1914 and in the following year was sent to Salonika, where he served with his Battalion and was engaged in the fighting in many battles on the Vardar front. During his service in this theatre of war he contracted malaria and was in hospital for a time. In 1918 he was drafted with the Relief Force to Russia and remained there until 1919. He returned to England and was demobilised later in that year, and holds the 1914-15 Star, and the General Service and Victory Medals.
16, Mundella Road, Wandsworth Road, S.W.8.   Z1827

DARTNELL, E., Rifleman, King's Royal Rifle Corps.
He joined in August 1916 and in the following March was drafted to France. Whilst on the Western Front he was in action at the Battles of Ypres, the Somme, Passchendaele and Cambrai, where he was taken prisoner in November 1917. He was held captive in Germany until after the cessation of hostilities. He was then repatriated and demobilised in November 1919, and holds the General Service and Victory Medals.
33, Westhall Road, Camberwell, S.E.5.   Z1826

DARVILL, G., A.B., Royal Navy.
He was serving in H.M.S. "Formidable" when war broke out and was fortunately rescued though wounded when his ship was torpedoed in January 1915, whilst engaged on patrol duties in the North Sea. Transferred to H.M.S. "Abercrombie" his ship served in the bombardment of Kavala and in action against the "Goeben" and "Breslau," and in operations supporting General Allenby's Advance through Palestine. After the Armistice he was engaged on mine-sweeping duties in German waters. He was invalided out of the Service in June 1920, and holds the 1914-15 Star, and the General Service and Victory Medals.
13, Secretan Road, Camberwell, S.E.5.   Z5366

DARVILL, G. F., Private, 21st Middlesex Regiment.
Joining in June 1916 he was drafted overseas on completion of his training. During his service on the Western Front he was engaged in much heavy fighting and was unfortunately killed in action at the Battle of Cambrai on November 24th, 1917. He was entitled to the General Service and Victory Medals.
44, Cranbrook Road, Chiswick, W.4.   5363

DARVILL, H., Private, 1st and 2nd London Regiment (Royal Fusiliers).
He joined in 1916 and in the same year proceeded to France. During his service in this theatre of war he fought in the Battles of Ypres and Loos and in many other important engagements, and was gassed and suffered from shell-shock. Sent to England in 1917 for hospital treatment he was invalided out of the Service in 1918, and holds the General Service and Victory Medals.
20, Westmacott Street, Camberwell, S.E.5.   Z3437

DAVALL, A. F., Stevedore, Surrey Docks.
He was engaged at the Surrey Docks from 1906 and owing to the nature of his work was exempted from serving with the Colours. During the war he rendered valuable services loading and unloading munitions of war, frequently working very long hours. In 1920 he was still employed at the Docks.
15, Pilkington Road, Peckham, S.E.15.   Z5938

DAVEY, A., Trooper, 1st (Royal) Dragoons and King Edward's Horse.
He joined in December 1916 and three months later was sent to the Western Front. He fought at the Battles of Ypres, the Somme, Cambrai and in the Retreat and Advance of 1918. After the cessation of hostilities he was transferred to the 6th Dragoon Guards (Carabiniers) and served with the Army of Occupation on the Rhine until demobilised in December 1919. He holds the General Service and Victory Medals.   Z1841A
5, Smyrk's Road, Walworth, S.E.17.   Z1842A

DAVEY, A. G. (M.S.M.), Sergt., R.F.A., R.G.A.
Mobilised from the Army Reserve on the outbreak of war he was drafted to France in December 1914 and took an active part in the Battles of Neuve Chapelle, Ypres, Loos and other engagements, and was awarded the Meritorious Service Medal for consistently good work in the Field. Sent to Egypt in 1916 he served there and in Palestine until February 1919. He was demobilised in March 1919, and holds the 1914-15 Star, and the General Service and Victory Medals.
95, Brackenbury Road, Hammersmith, W.6.   10713

DAVEY, C., Gunner, R.F.A.
He volunteered in 1915 and in the following year was sent to France. Whilst on the Western Front he fought in the Battles of Ypres, Loos, Vimy Ridge, Passchendaele, Cambrai, and in the Retreat and Allied Advance of 1918. He was demobilised in February 1919, and holds the General Service and Victory Medals.   Z1841B
5, Smyrk's Road, Walworth, S.E.17.   Z1842B

DAVEY, E., L/Corporal (Queen's Own) Royal West Kent Regiment.
He volunteered in October 1914 and in the following year proceeded overseas. During his service on the Western Front he was engaged in heavy fighting and was severely wounded at the first Battle of the Somme. He was invalided to England on July 2nd, 1916, but subsequently died from the effects of his wounds in Reading hospital and was buried in Nunhead Cemetery. He was entitled to the 1914-15 Star, and the General Service and Victory Medals.
72, Avenue Road, Camberwell, S.E.5.   Z1840

DAVEY, F. R., Sapper, R.E.
He volunteered in August 1914 and in the same year was sent to Egypt, where he served in the canal zone until 1916. He was then transferred to the Western Front and was engaged on important duties whilst heavy fighting was in progress and was wounded at the third Battle of Ypres on July 5th, 1917. He was invalided home to hospital and on recovery was discharged unfit for further service in February 1919. He holds the 1914-15 Star, and the General Service and Victory Medals.
15, Arthur Road, Brixton Road, S.W.9.   Z4442

DAVEY, J. T., Special War Worker.
He offered his services for work of National importance and was engaged during the period of the war at Messrs. Napier's Works, Acton. He rendered valuable services, acting as foreman in the wood department in connection with aircraft construction, and efficiently carried out his duties.
21, Strauss Road, Chiswick, W.4.   7320

DAVEY, T., Rifleman, King's Royal Rifle Corps.
He joined in January 1917 and was quickly drafted to the Western Front, where he subsequently fought in several engagements. He gave his life for King and Country at the Battle of Arras on May 13th, 1917, and was buried in the British Cemetery near the place where he was killed. He was entitled to the General Service and Victory Medals.
"Whilst we remember the sacrifice is not in vain."
16, Lewis Road, Camberwell, S.E.5.   Z6159

DAVEY, W., Private, East Surrey Regiment.
He volunteered in November 1915 and proceeded overseas in the following March. Whilst in France he fought in the Battle of Arras and was severely wounded in action at the Battle of the Somme in 1916. He was invalided home and on recovery served with the Labour Corps on special duties until demobilised in February 1919. He holds the General Service and Victory Medals.   Z1841C
5, Smyrk's Road, Walworth, S.E.17.   Z1842C

DAVIDSON, E., Corporal, 1st East Surrey Regiment.
A Reservist he was mobilised at the outbreak of war and sent to France in April 1915. He fought at the Battle of Ypres, and was wounded and gassed in the Battle of the Somme at Delville Wood in July 1916. He was invalided to England and on recovery rejoined his Battalion in the Field and was in action at the Capture of Vimy Ridge. Taken prisoner at Fresnoy on May 8th, 1917, he suffered many hardships during his captivity until released in January 1919. He was demobilised in the following April and holds the Queen's South African Medal, the 1914-15 Star, and the General Service and Victory Medals.
40, Darley Road, Wandsworth Common, S.W.11.   Z1828

DAVIDSON, E., A.B., " Anson " Battalion, R.N.D.
Volunteering in May 1915 he was shortly afterwards drafted to the Dardanelles. He was in action in many engagements at Gallipoli until wounded in November 1915. On recovery he was sent to France and fought at the Battles of Arras, Ypres, the Somme, the Ancre and in many others. He was demobilised in March 1919, and holds the 1914-15 Star, and the General Service and Victory Medals.
2, Tintern Street, Ferndale Road, S.W.4. Z1046A

DAVIDSON, E., 1st Air Mechanic, R.A.F. (late R.F.C.)
He volunteered for service with the Colours on several occasions but was rejected; however he joined the Royal Flying Corps in January 1917 and later in the same year was sent to France. He was engaged with his Squadron on important clerical duties until the end of the war. He did excellent work and returned to England after the cessation of hostilities and was demobilised in 1920. He holds the General Service and Victory Medals.
85, Sandmere Road, Clapham, S.W.4. Z1863A

DAVIDSON, E. I., Corporal, R.A.M.C.
He volunteered in September 1914 and, sent to Egypt six months later, served there until the end of hostilities. During this period he was engaged on ambulance duties at the 15th General Hospital at Alexandria and was employed on hospital ships carrying sick and wounded troops from the Dardanelles to England. He also served for a time on the Italian front, and returning to England for demobilisation in August 1919, holds the 1914-15 Star, and the General Service and Victory Medals.
51, Attwell Road, Rye Lane, S.E.15. Z5369

DAVIDSON, R. A., Sergt., Coldstream Guards.
A Reservist he was mobilised at the outbreak of hostilities and drafted to France in August 1914. He fought in the Retreat from Mons and the subsequent Battles of the Marne, the Aisne, Ypres, La Bassée, Neuve Chapelle, St. Eloi, Arras, Vimy Ridge Amiens, Cambrai and others. Owing to ill-health he was invalided to England and later transferred to the Liverpool Scottish and served for a time in Ireland on special duties. He was demobilised in January 1919, and holds the Mons Star, and the General Service and Victory Medals.
29, Parkstone Road, Peckham, S.E.15. Z5590

DAVIDSON, W. J., L/Corporal, 18th London Regiment (London Irish Rifles).
He volunteered in August 1914 and was drafted to France in 1916. Whilst on the Western Front he fought at the Battle of Somme and in the following year was sent to Salonika, where he was in action on the Struma front. He later proceeded to Egypt and served under General Allenby in the Advance through Palestine and was present at the Occupation of Jerusalem. He was transferred to the Royal Air Force and served in India on the North West Frontier during the risings in Afghanistan. He contracted malaria and returned to England, and after receiving medical treatment was discharged in 1919. He holds the General Service and Victory Medals, also the India General Service Medal (with clasp, Afghanistan, North West Frontier, 1919).
85, Sandmere Road, Clapham, S.W.4. Z1863B

DAVIES, A., Bombardier, R.F.A.
He volunteered in April 1915 and in the same year proceeded overseas. Whilst on the Western Front he fought in the first Battle of the Somme, and was wounded in September 1916. He was invalided to England, and on recovery it was found that he was under military age, he was therefore retained on home duties until demobilised in February 1919. He holds the 1914-15 Star, and the General Service and Victory Medals.
100, Kenbury Street, Camberwell, S.E.5. Z5941

DAVIES, C., Private, 12th Norfolk Regiment.
He joined in July 1917 and during his training served for a time in Ireland. In June 1918 he proceeded to the Western Front and took part in much fighting until taken prisoner at Ploegsteert Wood in September 1918. He suffered many privations during his captivity and was repatriated in December 1918. He holds the General Service and Victory Medals, and was demobilised in October 1919.
47, Hornby Road, Peckham, S.E.15. Z5931

DAVIES, C. F., Rifleman, 11th London Regiment (Rifles), and Air Mechanic, R.A.F.
He joined in June 1916 and at the conclusion of his training was engaged on important duties with his unit at various stations. He did very good work, but was unable to secure his transfer overseas before hostilities ceased, and was demobilised in March 1919.
56, Aldbridge Street, Walworth, S.E.17. Z1829B

DAVIES, E. (Mrs.), Special War Worker.
During the war for a period of nearly three years this lady was engaged on work of National importance at Messrs. E. Lazenby and Sons'. She carried out her duties in an efficient manner and was much appreciated for her good work.
56, Aldbridge Street, Walworth, S.E.17. Z1829A

DAVIES, E. A., Private, Buffs (East Kent Regiment).
He joined in February 1917 and in the following September was sent to France. During his service on the Western Front he fought in many engagements and was taken prisoner on March 21st, 1918. He suffered many privations and died whilst a prisoner of war in Germany on July 7th, 1918. He was entitled to the General Service and Victory Medals.
37, Cambridge Street, Camberwell, S.E.5. Z1839A

DAVIES, G. (Miss), Worker, Q.M.A.A.C.
She joined in 1917 and at the completion of her training served on important duties at various stations. She did good work, but was unsuccessful in obtaining her transfer overseas, and was demobilised in 1919.
24, Cardross Street, Hammersmith, W.6. 11520

DAVIES, H. W., Private, Machine Gun Corps.
He joined in November 1916 and in the following year was sent to East Africa, where he served with his unit until 1918. He was then drafted to France and was in action in various battles during the final operations of the war, and was wounded. After the Armistice he went with the Army of Occupation into Germany, and returning to England was demobilised in November 1919. He holds the General Service and Victory Medals.
5, Westbury Street, Wandsworth Road, S.W.8. Z1830A

DAVIES, I., Gunner, R.F.A.
Volunteering at the outbreak of war he was almost immediately drafted to France. He fought in the Retreat from Mons and the subsequent Battles of Le Cateau, La Bassée, Ypres, Neuve Chapelle, Loos, Vermelles, Vimy Ridge, the Somme and Arras. Severely wounded in April 1917 he was sent to England and after receiving hospital treatment was invalided out of the Service in September 1918. He holds the Mons Star, and the General Service and Victory Medals.
3, Perseverance Grove, High Street, Clapham, S.W.4. Z1833

DAVIES, J. C., Gunner, R.F.A., and Private, R.A.V.C.
A serving soldier he was mobilised at the outbreak of war and was drafted to France in March 1915. He was in action at the Battles of St. Eloi, Ypres, Festubert, Loos, Albert, Vermelles, Vimy Ridge, the Somme, and was wounded near Ypres in October 1916. He was invalided to England and on recovery was transferred to the Royal Army Veterinary Corps and served on home duties until demobilised in January 1919. He holds the 1914-15 Star, and the General Service and Victory Medals.
22, Dalyell Road, Landor Road, S.W.9. Z1832

DAVIES, J. E., Private, 2nd Norfolk Regiment.
He joined in March 1916 and was almost immediately sent to Mesopotamia, where he was in action at Kut-el-Amara and served in various other engagements in that theatre of war until the cessation of hostilities. During his service in the Middle East he suffered from malaria and was in hospital many times. He was demobilised in August 1919 after returning to England, and holds the General Service and Victory Medals.
17, Granfield Street, Battersea, S.W.11. Z1837

DAVIES, J. E., Private, R.A.S.C. (M.T.)
He volunteered in November 1914 and in the same month was sent overseas. Whilst on the Western Front he was engaged in taking ammunition and supplies to the front line trenches and was present at many battles, including those at Ypres, Neuve Chapelle, Hill 60, Loos, Vimy Ridge, the Somme, Arras, Bullecourt, Messines, Lens, Cambrai, Bapaume and in the Retreat and Advance of 1918. He was demobilised in April 1919, and holds the 1914 Star, and the General Service and Victory Medals. 7, Rushcroft Road, Brixton, S.W.2. Z1831

DAVIES, K. H., 2nd Lieutenant, Queen's (Royal West Surrey Regiment).
He was mobilised with the Territorials at the outbreak of war and was immediately sent to France. He fought in the Retreat from Mons and was wounded, and on recovery was in action in many subsequent battles and was again wounded at Ypres in 1915. He was granted a Commission in June 1917, and took a prominent part in much fighting until demobilised in June 1919. He holds the Mons Star, and the General Service and Victory Medals.
122, Dalyell Road, Landor Road, S.W.9. Z1834

DAVIES, S., Driver, R.E.
He joined in June 1917 and was later sent to France. Whilst on the Western Front he was engaged on special duties as an engine driver carrying troops, ammunition and supplies to the front lines, and was constantly under heavy shell fire. He was demobilised in March 1919, and holds the General Service and Victory Medals.
5, Westbury Street, Wandsworth Road, S.W.8. Z1830B

DAVIES, S. F., Corporal, R.E.
He joined in 1916 and shortly afterwards was drafted to Egypt. He was engaged on special duties with the Railway Operative Department and did very good work with his unit in this theatre of war. He returned to England and was demobilised in November 1919, and holds the General Service and Victory Medals.
27A, Goldsboro' Road, Wandsworth Road, S.W.8. Z1835A

DAVIES, W., Rifleman, 21st London Regiment (1st Surrey Rifles).

He was mobilised with the Territorials at the outbreak of war and was drafted to France in March 1915. He took part in the fighting in various sectors, and fought at the Battles of the Somme, Ypres, Vimy Ridge, Messines, Passchendaele and in the Retreat and Advance of 1918, and was present at the entry into Mons in November 1918. He was demobilised in February 1919, and holds the 1914-15 Star, and the General Service and Victory Medals.

9, Comber Grove, Camberwell, S.E.5.　　Z1843

DAVIES, W., Private, 4th Royal Fusiliers.

He volunteered in January 1915 and in the following year was drafted to France. Whilst on the Western Front he was engaged in many battles, including those of Ypres, Arras, the Somme, and in the Retreat and Advance of 1918. He was demobilised in March 1919, and holds the General Service and Victory Medals.

5, Lilac Place, Off Prince's Road, Kennington, S.E.11.　Z24776

DAVIES, W. A., 1st Class Air Mechanic, R.A.F.

He joined in July 1917 and in the following year was sent to France. Whilst on the Western Front he served in Belgium and after the Armistice at Lille with his Squadron on special duties as a fitter, and returned to England in July 1919. He holds the General Service and Victory Medals, and was still serving in 1920.

80, Elmhurst Mansions, Edgeley Road, Clapham, S.W.4. Z1838A

DAVIES, W. A., Rifleman, Rifle Brigade.

He joined in April 1918 and at the conclusion of his training served on important duties with his unit at various stations. He did good work, but was unable to secure his transfer overseas before the end of the war, and was demobilised in February 1919.

7E, Theatre Street, Lavender Hill, S.W.11.　　Z1836

DAVIES, W. H., Gunner, R.H.A.

He volunteered in December 1914 and in the following September was sent to France. He fought in the Battle of Loos, and was later sent to Salonika, where he was engaged in the fighting on the Vardar and Doiran fronts. He contracted pneumonia and subsequently died on November 15th, 1918. He was entitled to the 1914-15 Star, and the General Service and Victory Medals.

37, Cambridge Street, Camberwell, S.E.5.　　Z1839B

DAVIS, A. (Mrs.), Special War Worker.

This lady volunteered her services for work of National importance during the war and worked at Messrs. Blake's Munition Works, Shepherd's Bush, engaged on the manufacture of T.N.T. pellets for fuses. Later she was employed in making haversacks at Messrs. Waring & Gillow's, and rendered valuable services throughout.

86, Rayleigh Road, West Kensington, W.14.　　12066B

DAVIS, A. H., A.B., Royal Navy.

He was serving in the Royal Navy when war broke out, having joined in 1911, and was engaged on patrol and other duties in the North Sea and other waters during the war. He served in H.M.S. "Antrim," "Trinidad" and "Goshawk," and took part in the Battles of Heligoland Bight and Jutland, and the operations in the Dardanelles, and the Bombardment of Zeebrugge, He was demobilised in July 1920, and holds the 1914-15 Star, and the General Service and Victory Medals.

7, Silcote Road, Camberwell, S.E.5.　　Z5367

DAVIS, C. G., Corporal, Rifle Brigade.

He volunteered in August 1914 and was drafted to France in the following year. Whilst on the Western Front he was engaged in the fighting at the Battles of St. Eloi, Loos, Neuve Chapelle, Vermelles, Ploegsteert Wood, Ypres, the Somme and Cambrai, and was wounded. During his service he acted as a Bombing Instructor for a time. He was demobilised in January 1919, and holds the 1914-15 Star, and the General Service and Victory Medals.

29, Pensbury Street, Wandsworth Road, S.W.8.　　Z1855

DAVIS, C. T. W., Rifleman, King's Royal Rifle Corps.

He joined in September 1918 but was unable to complete his training in time to obtain his transfer overseas prior to the cessation of hostilities. He proceeded to France in March 1919 and in the following month was drafted to the Army of Occupation in Germany, and was engaged on guard and other important duties. He returned to England and was demobilised in March 1920.

87, Wickersley Road, Lavender Hill, S.W.11.　　Z1857

DAVIS, D., Private, Royal Fusiliers.

Volunteering in August 1914 he was sent to the Western Front and fought during the Retreat from Mons, where he was taken prisoner. He was held in captivity at Wittenberg in Prussia until after the Armistice, and repatriated. He was demobilised in January 1919, and holds the Mons Star, and the General Service and Victory Medals.

49, New Road, Battersea Park Road, S.W.8.　　Z1859

DAVIS, E. C. N., Sergt., R.E.

Mobilised at the commencement of hostilities he completed his training and served at various stations as Gas N.C.O. until drafted to France in 1917. Here he was engaged on important duties in the forward areas, and was under fire in the Battles of Arras and various other engagements during the Retreat and Advance of 1918. He was demobilised in May 1919, and holds the General Service and Victory Medals.

36, Bullen Street, Battersea, S.W.11.　　Z1854

DAVIS, E. R., Private, 23rd London Regiment.

Volunteering in December 1915 he was sent to France in the following year and was in action in many important engagements, including those at Ypres, Arras and Hill 60. He was gassed during the fighting at Ypres and, invalided to England, received hospital treatment. He was ultimately discharged unfit for further military service in December 1917, and holds the General Service and Victory Medals.

14, Shorncliffe Road, Old Kent Road, S.E.1.　　Z1860

DAVIS, F. (Miss), Special War Worker.

Volunteering for work of National importance this lady rendered valuable services at Messrs. Lyons, Cadby Hall, Kensington, engaged on important work in connection with food production, and discharged her duties in a most efficient and satisfactory manner.

86, Rayleigh Road, West Kensington, W.14.　　12066C

DAVIS, F. V., Special War Worker.

He offered his services for work of National importance and from 1915 until 1917 was employed at Messrs. French & Son's factory, Clapham, engaged in the manufacture of surgical instruments. He joined the 23rd London Regiment in 1917, but, discovered to be under military age, was discharged. He then worked at Messrs. Cogwell & Harrison's small-arms works for six months and afterwards at Messrs. Sibley's factory making aeroplane parts until the cessation of hostilities.　Z1845-6

18, Amies Street, Battersea, S.W.11.　　5977

DAVIS, G. A., Driver, R.F.A.

He volunteered in October 1915 and embarked for the Western Front in the following year and was in action in the Battles of the Somme, Ypres, Arras, Armentières, Messines and throughout the German Offensive and subsequent Allied Advance in 1918. He was demobilised in January 1919, and holds the General Service and Victory Medals.

72, Stewart's Road, Battersea Park Road, S.W.8.　　Z1844

DAVIS, G. D., Private, R.A.M.C. (Field Ambulance).

Mobilised at the declaration of war he proceeded to the Western Front in the following October and was engaged on important ambulance duties in the front lines during the Battles of La Bassée, Ypres, Neuve Chapelle, Hill 60, Festubert and Loos. Transferred to Salonika in August 1915 he served in many sectors and did good work. During his service in this theatre of war he suffered from malaria, and returning to England was demobilised in March 1919, and holds the 1914-15 Star, and the General Service and Victory Medals.

31, Amies Street, Battersea, S.W.11.　　Z1845-6
　　5977

DAVIS, G. S., Rifleman, 18th Rifle Brigade.

Volunteering in October 1914 and completing his training was stationed at various depôts until he embarked for India in November of the following year. During his service there he served at various garrison towns engaged on guard and other important duties. He returned to England and was demobilised in May 1919, and holds the General Service and Victory Medals.

18, Amies Street, Battersea, S.W.11.　　Z1845-6B
　　5977

DAVIS, H., Engine-room Artificer, Royal Navy.

He joined the service in 1914 and was posted to H.M.S. "Retard," which vessel was engaged on patrol and other important duties in the North Sea with the Grand Fleet and had many encounters with the German Fleet. He was discharged in March 1919, and holds the 1914-15 Star, and the General Service and Victory Medals.

243, Beresford Street, Camberwell, S.E.5.　　Z1861A

DAVIS, H., Private, 4th Royal Scots Fusiliers.

Joining in August 1916 he was drafted to the Egyptian Expeditionary Force two months later and served there until the following May. Transferred to France he fought in many important engagements, including those at Ypres, and in the German Offensive and Allied Advance in 1918. He was demobilised in March 1919, and holds the General Service and Victory Medals.

18, Kennard Street, Battersea, S.W.11.　　Z1850

DAVIS, H., Gunner, Royal Marine Artillery.

He enlisted in December 1912 and aboard H.M.S. "Royal Sovereign" saw much service throughout the war. His ship served with the Grand Fleet in the North Sea and took part in the engagement at Heligoland Bight, and was also engaged on important duties in the Mediterranean Sea, and after the Armistice was stationed at Constantinople. He was still serving in 1920, and holds the 1914-15 Star, and the General Service and Victory Medals.

61, St. Mark's Road, Camberwell, S.E.5.　　Z1856

DAVIS, H., Driver, R.F.A.
He volunteered in January 1915 and proceeded to the Western Front in June 1916 and was in action in the Somme sector and in many other engagements. In December 1916 he was transferred to Salonika and served in the offensives on the Doiran, Struma and Monastir fronts and in the following June was sent to Egypt. On the Palestine front he fought in the Battle of Gaza and in many battles during the Advance into Syria in 1918. He returned to England and was demobilised in July 1919, and holds the General Service and Victory Medals.
14, Dalyell Road, Landor Road, S.W.9.   Z1858

DAVIS, H. T., Rifleman, 18th Rifle Brigade.
He joined in October 1914 and in November of the following year was sent to Mesopotamia. In this theatre of war he took part in much fighting and served at Basra. He proceeded to India in April 1919, and later returned to England, and was demobilised in July of that year. He holds the 1914-15 Star, and the General Service and Victory Medals.
87c, Albany Road, Camberwell, S.E.5.   Z5591

DAVIS, J., Private, R.A.S.C. (M.T.)
Volunteering in September 1914 he proceeded to France later and served in the forward areas on important duties connected with the transport of supplies. He was present at the Battles of Ypres, Loos, Neuve Chapelle, Armentières and at many engagements in the Retreat and Advance of 1918. He was demobilised in 1919, and holds the 1914-15 Star, and the General Service and Victory Medals.
86, Rayleigh Road, West Kensington, W.14.   12066A

DAVIS, J., Corporal, R.E.
Volunteering in 1914 he proceeded overseas at a later date. During his service on the Western Front he fought in many important engagements, including those at Ypres, Arras, the Somme and Cambrai, where he was wounded, and received treatment in hospital at Rouen. Later he returned to England and died in 1918 from cancer. He was entitled to the 1914-15 Star, and the General Service and Victory Medals.
31, Rutland Street, Wilcox Road, S.W.8.   Z1852

DAVIS, J. A., Sergt., 20th London Regiment.
Volunteering in April 1915 he served with his unit at home for a time and embarked for France in November 1916. Whilst overseas he fought in the Battles of Arras, Ypres, Vimy Ridge, Messines and was wounded at Lens in August 1917. Sent to hospital in England on account of his injuries he was discharged as medically unfit for further service in October 1918, and holds the General Service and Victory Medals.
17, Attwell Road, Rye Lane, S.E.15.   Z5368

DAVIS, J. E., Air Mechanic, R.A.F.
Joining in July 1918 after completing his training he served at various aerodromes on important duties which called for a high degree of technical skill. He was not able to secure his transfer overseas before hostilities ceased owing to medical unfitness. He died suddenly on November 11th, 1918.
74, Geneva Road, Coldharbour Lane, S.W.9.   Z3078

DAVIS, J. S., Gunner, R.G.A.
A serving soldier he was stationed at Gibraltar at the outbreak of war and was sent to France in 1916. He fought in many important engagements, and was badly gassed and invalided to England. On recovery he was drafted to West Africa and saw much service. Contracting malaria he was invalided home, and was discharged unfit for further service in February 1920, and holds the General Service and Victory Medals.
18, Amies Street, Battersea, S.W.11.   Z1845-46A
5977

DAVIS, J. H. (D.C.M.), R.S.M., Northumberland Fusiliers and York and Lancaster Regiment.
A reservist he was mobilised in September 1914 and embarked for the Dardanelles in the following year and was in action at the Landing at Suvla Bay and in the subsequent engagements until the Evacuation of the Peninsula. Proceeding to Egypt he served in the Canal zone until sent to France in 1917, where he fought at Poziéres, the Somme, Arras, Beaumont-Hamel and was wounded. On recovery he was drafted to Italy and saw heavy fighting on the Piave front. He later returned to England and served at various stations as R.S.M. to the 9th Russian Labour Battalion. He was demobilised in April 1919, and holds the Distinguished Conduct Medal, which was awarded him in the Boer War for conspicuous gallantry and devotion to duty in the Field, the Queen's and King's South African Medals, and the 1914-15 Star, and the General Service and Victory Medals.
169, South Street, Walworth, S.E.17.   Z1851

DAVIS, L. J., Gunner, R.G.A.
He joined in 1916 and early in the following year was drafted to the Western Front, where he served in numerous engagements, and was gassed at Valenciennes on November 2nd, 1918. Returning home for demobilisation on the troopship " Marragansett," this ship was wrecked off the Isle of Wight, but he was saved. He was demobilised in February 1919, and holds the General Service and Victory Medals.
217, Alderminster Road, Bermondsey, S.E.1.   Z26254

DAVIS, O. (Mrs.), Special War Worker.
This lady offered her services for work of National importance and from 1915 until the cessation of hostilities rendered excellent services with the Land Army and in the Forage Department of the R.A.S.C. She discharged her duties in a most efficient and satisfactory manner.
243, Beresford Street, Camberwell Road, S.E.5.   Z1861B

DAVIS, R., Driver, R.F.A.
He volunteered in December 1915 and in January of 1917 proceeded to the Western Front. He took a prominent part in many important engagements, including those of Vimy Ridge, Passchendaele, Cambrai, and was injured in an accident during the Battle of Ypres. He returned to England in July 1917, and after receiving medical treatment rejoined his Battery in the Field in the following March. He saw further fighting in the Retreat and Advance of 1918, and on the cessation of hostilities served with the Army of Occupation in Germany. He was demobilised in October 1919, and holds the General Service and Victory Medals.
11, Camden Street, Peckham, S.E.15.   Z5238

DAVIS, S. C., Electrician, Royal Navy.
He volunteered in September 1914 and was posted to H.M.S. " Glory," which vessel was engaged on important patrol duties in the North Sea and other waters. Sent to Russia in 1917 he served in several engagements against the Turkish and Bulgarian forces and did valuable work until hostilities ceased. He was demobilised in February 1919, and holds the 1914-15 Star, and the General Service and Victory Medals.
24, Neate Street, Camberwell, S.E.5.   Z5063

DAVIS, T. F., Shoeing Smith, R.F.A.
Volunteering in June 1915 he was sent to the Western Front in the following January and saw much service. He was in action in the Battles of the Somme, Loos, Vimy Ridge, Arras, Cambrai and in many other engagements in the Retreat and Advance of 1918. Owing to ill-health he returned to England, and was discharged as medically unfit for further service in May 1919. He subsequently died in the following October, and was entitled to the General Service and Victory Medals.
110, Hartington Road, Wandsworth Road, S.W.8.   Z1848

DAVIS, W. A., Private, Northamptonshire Regiment.
Joining in September 1916 he embarked for the Western Front in the same year and fought in the Battle of Ypres and other important engagements. He was wounded at Lens and sent to England for hospital treatment. He was discharged in March 1919 as medically unfit for further service, and holds the General Service and Victory Medals.
41, Dalwood Street, Camberwell, S.E.5.   Z3438

DAVIS, W. A., Private, East Surrey Regiment and Labour Corps (675 H.S. Employment Company).
He joined in July 1916 and on completion of his training served at various stations on important duties with his unit. Medically unfit he was unable to obtain his transfer to a theatre of war, but rendered excellent services until demobilised in March 1919.
36, Pulross Road, Brixton Road, S.W.9.   Z1847

DAVIS, W. C., Sapper, R.E.
He volunteered at the outbreak of hostilities and embarked for France in the following year. Here he served in the forward areas engaged on important duties connected with operations during the progress of the Battles of Loos, Hill 60, the Somme, Arras, and throughout the Retreat and Advance of 1918. He died in November from sickness contracted on service, and was entitled to the 1914-15 Star, and the General Service and Victory Medals.
36, Bullen Street, Battersea, S.W.11.   Z1853

DAVIS, W. H., Private, 1st Gloucestershire Regiment.
Volunteering in August 1914 he proceeded to France and fought in the Retreat from Mons, and in the Battles of Landrecies, Ypres, Loos, Richbourg, Mount Kemmel, Neuve Chapelle, and in the German Offensive and subsequent Allied Advance in 1918. He was wounded four times during his service overseas, and was demobilised in November 1919, and holds the Mons Star, and the General Service and Victory Medals.
32, Stockdale Road, Wandsworth Road, S.W.8.   Z1849

DAVISON, J. R., Private, 23rd London Regiment.
He volunteered in 1915 and in the following year was sent to the Western Front. In this theatre of war he fought in many important engagements, including the Battle of Arras, where he was wounded. He was invalided to England and in consequence of his injuries one of his thumbs had to be amputated. He was eventually discharged unfit for further war service in 1917, and holds the General Service and Victory Medals.
24, Wyvil Road, Wandsworth Road, S.W.8.   Z1862

DAW, A. A., Private, 2nd Royal Fusiliers.

He joined in January 1917 and in the same year proceeded to France. During his service on the Western Front he was engaged in the fighting in many battles, including those at Arras, Ypres and Cambrai. He was also in action in the Retreat and Advance of 1918, and after the conclusion of hostilities returned home, and was demobilised in September 1919. He holds the General Service and Victory Medals.

36, Brisbane Street, Camberwell, S.E.5.　　　Z3073

DAWES, C. W., Gunner, R.F.A.

He volunteered in November 1914 and shortly afterwards was drafted to the Western Front, where he was engaged in severe fighting in the Battles of Ypres, Neuve Chapelle, Hill 60, Loos, Albert, Vimy Ridge, Arras, Bullecourt, Messines and Ypres. He was reported missing on July 31st, 1917, and later was presumed to have been killed in action on that date. He was entitled to the 1914-15 Star, and the General Service and Victory Medals.

27, White Square, Clapham, S.W.4.　　　Z1865

DAWES, G., Private, 1st Royal Berkshire Regiment.

He volunteered in August 1914 and two months later was sent to France, where he did good work with his Battalion and fought in many engagements. Owing to ill-health he was invalided home, and after undergoing treatment was invalided out of the Service in April 1915. He holds the 1914-15 Star, and the General Service and Victory Medals.

43, Reckitt Road, Chiswick, W.4.　　　5829A

DAWES, W. F., Private, York and Lancaster Regiment.

He volunteered in October 1915 and after completing his period of training was drafted to Salonika in the following January. In this theatre of war he was engaged in severe fighting in many parts of the line until the close of the war, and after returning home was demobilised in June 1919. He holds the General Service and Victory Medals.

43, Reckitt Road, Chiswick, W.4.　　　5829B

DAWES, W. J. A., Rifleman, 21st London Regiment (1st Surrey Rifles).

He volunteered in September 1915 and four months later proceeded to France. During his service on the Western Front he played an important part with his unit in some severe fighting, and was wounded in action. After recovery he was sent to Salonika early in 1917 and fought on the Macedonian front for a time. He also saw service in Egypt. Returning home he was demobilised in July 1919, and holds the General Service and Victory Medals.

3, Cantire Place, Councillor Street, Camberwell, S.E.5.　　Z1864

DAWKINS, A., Private, 9th Middlesex Regiment.

He joined in July 1916 and after completing his training served with his Battalion on special duties until drafted to France in 1918. He took an active part with his unit in some severe fighting during the final operations of the war and on the cessation of hostilities went into Germany with the Army of Occupation and was stationed at Cologne. He returned to England in 1920, and was demobilised in April of that year, and holds the General Service and Victory Medals.

1, Tweed Street, Battersea Park Road, S.W.8.　　Z1867B

DAWKINS, G., Rifleman, 9th London Regiment (Queen Victoria's Rifles).

He volunteered in January 1915 and in the same year was drafted to France. Whilst on the Western Front he served with his unit in many important engagements and was in action on the Somme and at Arras, where he was severely wounded. He was invalided home and after receiving medical treatment was discharged in June 1918 as physically unfit for further service. He holds the 1914-15 Star, and the General Service and Victory Medals.

1, Tweed Street, Battersea Park Road, S.W.8.　　Z1867A

DAWKINS, G. J., Corporal, Royal Sussex Regiment and R.A.M.C.

He joined in July 1918 on attaining military age and after a course of training served with his unit on important duties at various stations. He was not successful in obtaining his transfer overseas before hostilities ceased. After the Armistice, however, he was sent to Germany to the Army of Occupation and remained there until 1920. He returned to England and was demobilised in March of that year.

24, Moat Place, Stockwell Road, S.W.9.　　Z1866

DAWS, D. H. A., Private, Norfolk Regiment.

He enlisted in July 1914 and was later claimed out of the Service. He, however, rejoined in 1916 and proceeded to France in the following year and was in action in many engagements, including those of Ypres and Arras, and was severely wounded in May 1918. Invalided home he underwent hospital treatment and was discharged unfit for further service in September 1918. He holds the General Service and Victory Medals.

6, Frere Street, Battersea, S.W.11.　　　Z1863

DAWS, H., Leading Seaman, Royal Navy.

He joined the Service in 1910 and was mobilised on the outbreak of war. Aboard H.M.S. "Cressy" he served with the Grand Fleet in the North Sea and took an important part in many Naval engagements, including those of Jutland and Heligoland Bight, and during his service his ship was three times torpedoed. He holds the 1914-15 Star, and the General Service and Victory Medals, and was still serving in 1920.

2, Harley Street, Battersea, S.W.11.　　　Z1869

DAWSON, F. M., Rifleman, King's Royal Rifle Corps.

He volunteered in September 1914 and in the following year was drafted to France. There he fought in many important engagements, including those of Ypres, Arras and the Somme. He was reported to have been taken prisoner at Cambrai in 1917, but was afterwards found killed in action during that battle. He was entitled to the 1914-15 Star, and the General Service and Victory Medals.

41, Seaham Street, Wandsworth Road, S.W.8.　　Z1870

DAWSON, H., Gunner, Canadian Artillery.

Volunteering in the Canadian Artillery in August 1914 he was drafted to France in the same month and served in the early engagements of the war, including the Battles of La Bassée and Vimy Ridge. He fell fighting at Ypres in September 1918, and was entitled to the 1914 Star, and the General Service and Victory Medals.

"And doubtless he went in splendid company."

13, Lidgate Road, Peckham, S.E.15.　　　Z5748A

DAWSON, H. G., Sergt., R.A.O.C.

He joined in June 1916 and was drafted to the Western Front two months later and was in action on the Somme, at Arras, Ypres and many important engagements during the German Offensive and subsequent Allied Advance of 1918. After the Armistice he served at various stations in France until returning to England for demobilisation in November 1919. He holds the General Service and Victory Medals.

29, Bullen Street, Battersea, S.W.11.　　　1871

DAWSON, J., Driver, R.F.A.

He volunteered in August 1914 and was almost immediately sent to France, where he was in action during the Retreat from Mons, and in the Battles of Ypres and Loos. Drafted to Italy he served in the Advance on the Piave, and returning to the Western Front fought in the Battle of Bullecourt and was wounded in March 1917. Returning to his Battery on recovery he took part in several engagements and was unfortunately killed near Albert on August 23rd, 1918, and was entitled to the 1914 Star, and the General Service and Victory Medals.

Courage, bright hopes, and a myriad dreams, splendidly given."

13, Lidgate Road, Peckham, S.E.15.　　　Z5748B

DAWSON, W. J., Special Constable, T. Division.

He offered his services in January 1915 and was employed on important duties in the Chiswick district. He rendered excellent services but, owing to ill-health, he was discharged in January of the following year.

17, Brackley Road, Chiswick, W.4.　　　5434B

DAY, A., Corporal, 16th Middlesex Regiment.

He volunteered in October 1914 and was drafted overseas in the following year. During his service overseas he fought in many important engagements, including those at Loos, Vimy Ridge, the Somme and in the Retreat and Advance of 1918. He was demobilised in January 1919, and holds the 1914-15 Star, and the General Service and Victory Medals.

50, Stanley Street, Battersea Park, S.W.8.　　Z1872

DAY, A., Rifleman, 15th London Regt. (Civil Service Rifles), and Pte., London Regt. (Royal Fusiliers).

He joined in December 1917 and was drafted to the Western Front the same month. Here he saw much service in many parts of the line, fighting in various engagements during the German Offensive and subsequent Allied Advance in 1918, and was wounded. Returning to England he received medical treatment and was invalided out of the Service in September 1918, and holds the General Service and Victory Medals.

3, Doris Street, Kennington, S.E.11.　　Z25319A

DAY, A. J., Special War Worker.

He offered his services for work of National importance and from August 1914 was employed at Gwynne's Factory, Chiswick, Hammersmith engaged in manufacturing the component parts of aero-engines. He rendered excellent services throughout, and was still employed on work of a similar nature in 1920.

24, Annandale Road, Chiswick, W.4.　　　5440B

DAY, A. W., Assistant Steward, Merchant Service.

He joined in June 1918 and was posted to H.M.S. "Corinthic," which vessel was employed on special transport duties to New York. He also did good work aboard H.M.S. "Ionic" and in various coasting boats. He was demobilised in June 1919, and holds the General Service, and the Mercantile Marine War Medals. In 1920 he was serving in the Army with the 2nd King's Shropshire Light Infantry.

2, Clifton Square, Peckham, S.E.15.　　　Z5933

DAY, C. (D.C.M. and M.S.M.), Sergt., R.E.
Volunteering in September 1914 he proceeded to the Western Front in the following April. During his service on the Western Front he was in action on the Somme, at Ypres, Vimy Ridge, Ploegsteert, Poperinghe, Amiens, and in the Retreat and Advance of 1918. He was awarded the Distinguished Conduct Medal for conspicuous bravery and devotion to duty in the Field in October 1918. He also holds the Meritorious Service Medal for consistent good work, and the 1914-15 Star, the General Service and Victory Medals. He was demobilised in February 1919.
21, Flaxman Road, Camberwell, S.E.5.   Z5944

DAY, E. (Mrs.), Special War Worker.
This lady volunteered for work of National importance and was employed at the War Office engaged on important duties. Later she worked at the Vauxhall Gas Works attending to the furnaces, work of a very arduous nature. She rendered excellent services throughout, discharging her duties in a thoroughly efficient and satisfactory manner.
2, Nealdon Street, Landor Road, S.W.9.   Z1874B

DAY, G. T., Private, R.A.S.C.
He had seen much service in the Army, having fought in the South African War and the Chitrai Campaign, and volunteered in August 1914. He served at home training recruits for the New Armies and was sent to France in December 1914. He rendered valuable services on the Western Front and in the following month was invalided home owing to illness. He died in St. Thomas's Hospital, London, on February 15th, 1915. He held the 3rd India General Service Medal (1895-98), and the Queen's and King's South African Medals, and was entitled to the 1914-15 Star, and the General Service and Victory Medals.
"His memory is cherished with pride."
76, St. George's Road, Peckham, S.E.15.   Z5376

DAY, J., Gunner, R.G.A.
Mobilised in August 1914 he was sent to the Western Front in the same month and fought in various engagements during the Retreat from Mons, and was severely wounded. He returned to England and after protracted hospital treatment was invalided out of the Service in July 1916. He holds the Mons Star, and the General Service and Victory Medals.
25, Dean's Buildings, Flint Street, Walworth, S.E.17.   Z1873

DAY, J., Pte., 3rd Queen's (Royal West Surrey Regt).
Volunteering in April 1915 he completed his training and was drafted to the Western Front later in the same year and fought in many engagements of note, including those on the Somme. He made the supreme sacrifice, being killed in action at Loos on October 12th, 1915, and was entitled to the 1914-15 Star, and the General Service and Victory Medals.
2, Nealdon Street, Landor Road, S.W.9.   Z1874A

DAY, J. W. F., Private, Royal Fusiliers.
He joined in May 1918 and concluding his training was stationed at various depôts with his unit, engaged on guard and other important duties. He was unsuccessful in obtaining his transfer to a theatre of war prior to the cessation of hostilities but rendered valuable services until demobilised in December 1918.
194, Beresford Street, Camberwell, Road S.E.5.   Z1875

DAY, S., Special War Worker.
Volunteering for work of National importance he was employed at Gwynne's Factory, Chiswick, and rendered valuable services in the manufacture of the component parts of aero-engines. He carried out his work in an efficient and satisfactory manner and was still employed there in 1920.
24, Annandale Road, Chiswick, W.4.   5440A

DAY, W., Rifleman, 6th London Regiment (Rifles) and King's Royal Rifle Corps.
He volunteered in September 1914 and proceeding to France in the following year served in several engagements, and was wounded in the Battle of Loos in September, 1915. Rejoining his unit on recovery he was in action in the Battles of Vermelles, Vimy Ridge, the Somme and was again wounded at Ypres in January 1917 and sent home on account of his injuries. After receiving hospital treatment he was invalided out of the service in April 1917, and in addition to the Queen's South African Medal holds the 1914-15 Star, and the General Service and Victory Medals.
28, Sandover Road, Camberwell, S.E.5.   Z5370

DEAN, A. H., Gunner, R.F.A.
Volunteering in September 1914 a year later he proceeded to the Western Front and served there for upwards of four years. During this period he was in action in the Battles of Loos, the Somme, Arras, Ypres, Vimy Ridge, Cambrai, and in the Retreat and Advance of 1918. He returned home at the end of hostilities, was demobilised in March 1919, and holds the 1914-15 Star, and the General Service and Victory Medals.
7, Arlington Grove, Neate Street, Camberwell, S.E.5.   Z5064A

DEAN, C. J., Gunner, R.F.A.
He volunteered in September 1914 and, sent to France in the following September, fought in the Battle of Loos. Proceeding to Salonika later in 1915 he served during the Advance across the Vardar and on the Doiran front, and returned to the Western Front in 1917. He was in action at Ypres and Cambrai, and in engagements during the Retreat and Advance of 1918. He was demobilised in June 1919, and holds the 1914-15 Star, and the General Service and Victory Medals.
7, Arlington Grove, Neate Street, Camberwell, S.E.5.   Z5064B

DEAN, F., Corporal, 24th London Regiment (Queen's), and R.M. Labour Corps.
He was called up from the National Reserve in August 1914 and served at various stations with his unit on important duties until June 1916, when he was sent to France. He served in many sectors and rendered valuable services. He previously served in the Tirah Campaign of 1897-8 and in the South African War. He was demobilised in November 1919, and holds the India General Service Medal, the Queen's and King's South African Medals (with five clasps), and the General Service and Victory Medals.
45, Riley Street, Bermondsey, S.E.1.   TZ27444

DEAN, F., Gunner, R.F.A.
He volunteered in October 1914 and in the following August was sent to France. He fought at the Battles of Loos, Vimy Ridge, the Somme, Beaumont-Hamel, the Ancre, Bullecourt, and Cambrai, and was transferred to the Tank Corps in June 1918. He then served at Ypres, Lille, Le Cateau and during the final operations of the war. He was demobilised in February 1919, and holds the 1914-15 Star, and the General Service and Victory Medals.
54, Blake's Road, Peckham Grove, S.E.15.   Z5934

DEAN, W., Sapper, R.E.
Joining the 2nd Wiltshire Regiment in December 1917 he embarked for France in the following July and fought in the Battle of Cambrai and in numerous engagements during the Retreat and Advance of 1918. He was later transferred to the Royal Engineers and served with that Corps until his demobilisation in December 1920. He holds the General Service and Victory Medals.
7, Arlington Grove, Neate Street, Camberwell, S.E.5.   Z5064C

DEAR, A. E., Private, 23rd Lancashire Fusiliers.
He joined in April 1916 and was sent to France in the following August and took part in many important engagements and fought throughout the German Offensive and subsequent Allied Advance of 1918. He died in December 1918 whilst still overseas from an illness contracted on service, and was entitled to the General Service and Victory Medals.
40, Cardross Street, Hammersmith, W.6.   11517A

DEAR, F. G., Private, 1st Cheshire Regiment.
Joining in June 1915 he was drafted to France in the following May and was in action in many important engagements, including those at Leventie, the Somme, St. Quentin and in the Ypres salient. Owing to ill-health he was invalided to England and received hospital treatment. On recovery he returned to the Western Front and fought throughout the German Offensive and Allied Advance in 1918. He was demobilised in March 1919, and holds the General Service and Victory Medals.
3, Ethel Street, Walworth, S.E.17.   Z1877

DEAR, J., Private, Middlesex Regiment.
Volunteering in September 1914 he embarked for the Western Front later in the same year and saw much service in various parts of the line. He fought in many important engagements and was in action throughout the German Offensive and subsequent Allied Advance in 1918. He was demobilised in October 1919, and holds the 1914 Star, and the General Service and Victory Medals.
40, Cardross Street, Hammersmith, W.6.   11517B

DEATHE, R. J., Private, 2nd London Regiment (Royal Fusiliers) and Air Mechanic, R.A.F.
He volunteered at the declaration of war and embarked for Malta in September 1914 and served there until sent to France in the following January. He fought in the Battles of Neuve Chapelle, St. Eloi, Hill 60, Ypres, Festubert and Loos, and in many other engagements, and was wounded. Transferred to the R.A.F. on recovery he did excellent work as a wireless operator from 1916 until the cessation of hostilities, and returning to England was demobilised in February 1919. He holds the 1914-15 Star, and the General Service and Victory Medals.
138, Tyneham Road, Lavender Hill, S.W.11.   Z1878A

DEATHE, S. C., Driver, R.F.A.
Volunteering in January 1916 he concluded his training and served at various stations engaged on important duties with his unit. He was unsuccessful in obtaining his transfer overseas prior to the cessation of hostilities but rendered excellent services until demobilised in January 1919.
138, Tyneham Road, Lavender Hill, S.W.11.   Z1878B

DE ATHE, W. D., Gunner, R.F.A., and Corporal, 21st London Regiment (1st Surrey Rifles) and Labour Corps.

He volunteered in October 1914 and proceeded to France later in the same year and served there until invalided to England, when he was discharged from the Service as unfit. Re-enlisting in the 21st London Regiment he was stationed at various depôts engaged on important recruiting duties and was later transferred to the Labour Corps. He rendered valuable services until invalided out of the Army in November 1917, and holds the 1914-15 Star, and the General Service and Victory Medals.
90, Sussex Road, Coldharbour Lane, S.W.9.　　　Z1876

DEAVIN, W., Pte., Royal Berkshire Regt. and R.D.C.

He was mobilised and sent to the Western Front at the outbreak of hostilities and fought in the Retreat from Mons and the engagements at the Marne, Cambrai and the Somme, and in the first, second and third Battles of Ypres, and was wounded. On recovery he rejoined his unit and was in action in the German Offensive and Allied Advance in 1918, and was again wounded at Amiens. Invalided to England he received hospital treatment and on recovery was engaged on important guard duties at various prisoner of war camps until demobilised in June 1919. He holds the Mons Star, and the General Service and Victory Medals.
31, Aldbridge Street, Walworth, S.E.17.　　　Z1879

DEETMAN, A., Private, Bedfordshire Regiment.

He joined in February 1917 and on the completion of his training was engaged on important duties with his Battalion at home. He rendered valuable services but was unable to secure a transfer overseas before the cessation of hostilities and was demobilised in September 1919.
63, Broadwater Road, Tottenham, N.17.　　　Z5545C

DEFFEE, E. S., Private, 2/4th Queen's (Royal West Surrey Regiment).

He joined in March 1917 and twelve months later was sent overseas. He fought in engagements during the German Offensive of 1918 and was wounded. After recovery he returned to the front line trenches and was in action in the Allied Advance, and proceeded to Germany after the Armistice and served with the Army of Occupation. He was demobilised in March 1919 but shortly afterwards re-enlisted and in 1920 was serving in Persia. He holds the General Service and Victory Medals.
96, St. George's Road, Peckham, S.E.15.　　　Z5592

DEGAVINO, P. C., Private, R.A.S.C. (M.T.)

Volunteering in April 1915 he embarked for the Dardanelles almost immediately and was present at the first Landing and the Battles of Krithia and in the subsequent heavy fighting until the Evacuation of the Peninsula. Proceeding to Salonika he served on the Struma, Vardar and Monastir fronts, engaged on important transport duties in the forward areas. He returned to England and was demobilised in June 1919, and holds the 1914-15 Star, and the General Service and Victory Medals.
21, Basnett Road, Lavender Hill, S.W.11.　　　Z1880

DELAHUNT, J. C., Private, 13th London Regiment (Kensingtons).

Joining in April 1916 he embarked for the Western Front three months later and fought in many important engagements. He made the supreme sacrifice, being killed in action on October 7th, 1916, during the first British offensive on the Somme. He was entitled to the General Service and Victory Medals.
23, Newcomen Road, Battersea, S.W.11.　　　Z1881

DELL, J. A., Pte., Queen's (Royal West Surrey Regt).

Volunteering in August 1914 he was drafted to France in the following April. There he served in many sectors where heavy fighting was in progress and was severely gassed and wounded at Armentières in 1916. Invalided to England he received hospital treatment and was discharged unfit for further military service in June 1917. He holds the 1914-15 Star, and the General Service and Victory Medals.
19, Tradescant Road, South Lambeth Road, S.W.8.　　　Z1882

DELLAR, A., Rifleman, 21st London Regiment (1st Surrey Rifles).

He joined in July 1918 and on the completion of his training was engaged with his unit on important coastal defence duties in the Eastern counties and did excellent work. Owing to illness he was sent to hospital and died on December 8th, 1918.
187, Beresford Street, Camberwell Road, S.E.5.　　　Z1883B

DELLAR, A. S., Rifleman, 52nd Rifle Brigade.

Joining in April 1918 he completed his training and served with his Battalion at various stations. He rendered valuable services, but was not successful in securing a transfer overseas before the end of the war. After the Armistice he was sent into Germany with the Army of Occupation and stationed at Cologne. He returned home, and was demobilised in February 1920.
187, Beresford Street, Camberwell Road, S.E.5.　　　Z1883A

DELLER, B., Rifleman, 10th King's Royal Rifle Corps.

He joined in July 1916, and proceeding to the Western Front in the following month, was in action in many battles. He was reported missing during an engagement on November 30th, 1917, but was later found to have been taken prisoner. Held in captivity at Friedrichsfeld Wesel Camp in Germany he was released after the Armistice and repatriated. He was demobilised in March 1919, and holds the General Service and Victory Medals.
19, Over Place, Prince's Road, Kennington, S.E.11.　　TZ25462B

DELLER, F. B., Special War Worker.

He volunteered for work of National importance during the war and was engaged by Messrs. Prince & Co., Southwick, from January 1917 to March 1919. During this period he served as a sawyer and was employed in making parts for aeroplane wings. He did good work throughout.
338c, East Street, Walworth, S.E.17.　　　Z1884C

DELLER, J. C., Private, R.A.S.C.

Volunteering in May 1915 he was sent to France almost immediately and was engaged on important transport duties throughout the war. He was present at the Battles of the Somme, Arras, Cambrai, Bullecourt and Amiens, and many other engagements. Returning to England after the Armistice he was demobilised in March 1919, and holds the 1914-15 Star, and the General Service and Victory Medals.
19, Over Place, Prince's Road, Kennington, S.E.11.　　TZ25462A

DELLER, S. J. T., Private, 52nd Royal Sussex Regiment.

He joined in May 1918 on attaining military age, and after his training was engaged with his unit on important duties. He was unable to obtain a transfer to a theatre of war before the cessation of hostilities. After the Armistice he was sent into Germany with the Army of Occupation and stationed at Cologne. He was subsequently drafted to Mesopotamia, and in 1920 was still serving there.
338c, East Street, Walworth, S.E.17.　　　Z1884B

DELOCHE, T. F., Rifleman, Rifle Brigade.

He volunteered in January 1916 and was sent overseas two months later. Serving with his Battalion on the Western Front he was in action in several engagements on the Somme, and was twice wounded and invalided home for treatment in 1917. Returning to France he served in many operations until the close of the war, and was demobilised in July 1919. He holds the General Service and Victory Medals.
8, Beckway Street, Walworth, S.E.17.　　　Z1885

DEMPSEY, A. J., L/Corporal, 11th Middlesex Regt.

He volunteered in November 1914 and in June of the following year was sent to France. He was actively engaged in many important battles, including those of Loos, Vermelles, the Somme, Beaumont-Hamel, and Arras, during which he was unfortunately killed in action on April 17th, 1917. He was entitled to the 1914-15 Star, and the General Service and Victory Medals.
"Great deeds cannot die."
10, Myatt Road, Brixton, S.W.9.　　　Z4443A

DEMPSEY, F., Driver, R.F.A.

He volunteered in May 1915 and in the following October embarked for France. Whilst overseas he fought in the Battles of Loos, Festubert, Albert, Vimy Ridge, the Somme, Arras, Cambrai, and during the Retreat of 1918, and was gassed in April of that year. He was demobilised in July 1919, and holds the 1914-15 Star, and the General Service and Victory Medals.
23, Dean's Buildings, Walworth, S.E.17.　　　Z1886

DENHAM, H., Private, Loyal North Lancashire Regiment and R.A.S.C.

Enlisting in July 1913 he was mobilised on the outbreak of war and later sent to the Western Front and actively engaged with his Battalion throughout the course of hostilities. He was in action at the Battles of Neuve Chapelle, Hill 60, Festubert, Loos, Arras, Ypres, the Somme, Vimy Ridge, Ploegsteert Wood and Messines, and was gassed in 1918. After the Armistice he was sent to Ireland and returning to England was demobilised in January 1920. He holds the 1914 Star, and the General Service and Victory Medals.
57, Farmer's Road, Camberwell, S.E.5.　　　Z1887

DENLEY, G. A., Private, M.G.C.

Volunteering in July 1915 he proceeded to France three months later and served during the Battles of Loos, the Somme and Ypres, and was wounded and sent to hospital in England. On recovery he was sent to Italy in 1916 and fought in several operations until the cessation of hostilities. Returning home for demobilisation in October 1919, he holds the 1914-15 Star, and the General Service and Victory Medals.
108, Surrey Lane, Battersea, S.W.11.　　　5703

DENMAN, F. A., Private, Labour Corps.
He volunteered at the outbreak of war, but being physically unfit was rejected. He joined the 25th London Regiment in February 1917, and was later transferred to the Labour Corps. With this unit he did excellent work at various stations, but was unable to obtain his transfer overseas before the Armistice. He was demobilised in March 1919.
15, Castlemaine Road, Peckham, S.E.15.   Z5935

DENN, H. G., Pioneer, R.E.
Volunteering in 1914 he proceeded to France in the following year and was engaged on important duties in connection with operations in various sectors. He was present at many notable engagements and was killed in action near Vimy Ridge on June 28th, 1916, and was entitled to the 1914-15 Star, and the General Service and Victory Medals.
31, Kimpton Road, Camberwell, S.E.5.   Z1888

DENNE, V. P., Corporal, 21st London Regiment (1st Surrey Rifles) and R.A.F.
A Territorial he was mobilised when war broke out and served with his unit at home for a time. Transferred to the R.F.C. in August 1916 he was drafted to France in the following month and there served with his Squadron in the Somme, Ypres and Cambrai sectors and was invalided home to hospital suffering from gas-poisoning. After receiving medical treatment he was discharged as medically unfit for further service in January 1919. and holds the General Service and Victory Medals
27, D'Eynsford Road, Camberwell Green, S.E.5.   Z1889

DENNING, G., Rifleman, 12th London Regiment (Rangers).
He joined in August 1917 and after his training served at various stations on important duties with his Battalion. He did very good work, but owing to physical disability was not successful in obtaining his transfer overseas and was invalided out of the Service in February 1918.
80, Calor Street, Peckham, S.E.15.   Z4444C

DENNINGTON, E. (D.C.M.), Sergt., Queen's Own (Royal West Kent Regiment).
Volunteering in August 1914 he was sent to France with the First Expeditionary Force and fought during the Retreat from Mons and several subsequent engagements, and was wounded at Hill 60 in April 1915. Returning to the Field on recovery he was awarded the Distinguished Conduct Medal in May 1916 for conspicuous gallantry and devotion to duty in holding a trench with eleven men against heavy enemy attacks and rescuing comrades buried by a shell explosion in International Trench at Ypres. He was again wounded in the Battle of Passchendaele in 1917, and a third time at Valenciennes in 1918. He was invalided home to hospital and on recovery was demobilised in February 1919. He holds the Mons Star, and the General Service and Victory Medals.
129, Cobourg Road, Camberwell, S.E.5.   Z5371

DENNIS, W., Private, Royal Fusiliers.
A serving soldier he was mobilised on the declaration of war and almost immediately proceeded to France. He fought in the Retreat from Mons and at the Battle of Ypres, and was wounded and sent to hospital. In 1915 he was drafted to Gallipoli, where he served for a time and was later sent to Serbia and took part in the Retreat of the Serbian Army, during which he became detached from his Regiment. When found he was in a very precarious condition and, admitted to hospital, died from the effects of exposure. He was entitled to the Mons Star, and the General Service and Victory Medals.
29, Treherne Road, Stockwell, S.W.9.   Z3080

DENNISON, W., Driver, R.F.A.
He volunteered in April 1915 and embarked for the Western Front in the following December. Whilst overseas he was engaged in heavy fighting in the Battles of the Somme, Ancre, Vermelles, Vimy Ridge, Ypres, Cambrai and during the Retreat and Advance of 1918. He was demobilised in January 1919, and holds the 1914-15 Star, and the General Service and Victory Medals.
81, D'Eynsford Road, Camberwell Green, S.E.5.   Z1890

DENNY, W., Driver, R.F.A.
Mobilised from the Reserve in August 1914 he was sent to France in the same month and was in action during the Retreat from Mons, and in the Battles of Ypres and Loos. In June 1916 he returned to England and served on home service duties until discharged on account of service in June 1917. He holds the Mons Star, and the General Service and Victory Medals.
10, Rockingham Street, S.E.1.   TZ25357

DENT, A. J., Corporal, 4th (Queen's Own) Hussars.
He volunteered in October 1915 and on completion of his training was engaged on important duties with his unit at various stations in Ireland. He rendered valuable services, but was unsuccessful in obtaining a transfer to a theatre of war before the cessation of hostilities, and was demobilised in January 1919.
95, Kelmscott Road, Battersea, S.W.11.   Z3077

DENT, H. G., Private, M.G.C.
He joined in September 1917 when seventeen and a half years of age, and in the following May embarked for France. He was in action in the Battles of the Aisne, the Marne, Amiens, Bapaume, Havrincourt, Cambrai, Ypres and La Cateau, and on the termination of hostilities was sent with the Army of Occupation into Germany. Returning home for demobilisation in November 1919, he holds the General Service and Victory Medals.
27, Attwell Road, Rye Lane, S.E.15.   Z5374B

DENT, H. D., Private, 11th (Prince Albert's Own) Hussars.
A Regular soldier who had served in the Egyptian and South African Wars he volunteered in August 1914 and was drafted three months later to France. There he served in the Battles of Ypres (I, II and III), Festubert, Loos, Vermelles, Ploegsteert Wood, Vimy Ridge, the Somme, Arras, Bullecourt, Messines, Lens and during the Retreat and Advance of 1918. Transferred to the Royal Army Veterinary Corps he was engaged in the removal of sick and wounded horses from the forward areas until invalided home owing to illness. After treatment he was discharged as medically unfit for further service in September 1918, and in addition to the Egyptian Medal 1882, the Khedive Star, and the Queen's and King's South African Medals, holds the 1914 Star, and the General Service and Victory Medals.
27, Attwell Road, Rye Lane, S.E.15.   Z5374A

DENTRY, B., L/Corporal, 10th Queen's (Royal West Surrey Regiment).
Volunteering in August 1914 he was drafted to the Western Front in the same month and took part in several important engagements, including the Battle of Neuve Chapelle. He was unfortunately killed in action on May 18th, 1915, and buried at Choques, and was entitled to the 1914 Star, and the General Service and Victory Medals.
48, Broughton Street, Battersea Park, S.W.8.   Z1713D

DENWOOD, W., Driver, R.A.S.C. (M.T.)
He volunteered in November 1915 and was drafted overseas two months later. He served in France on transport duties during engagements in the Somme, Arras and other sectors and in conveying sick and wounded from the forward areas. He was sent to Salonika in 1917 and there rendered valuable services during the final operations in the Balkans. Returning home he was demobilised in July 1919, and holds the General Service and Victory Medals.
29, Loncroft Road, Camberwell, S.E.5.   Z5372

DENYER, A. W., Sergt., R.E.
He joined in March 1916 and after completing his training was engaged on important duties with his unit at several depôts. He rendered valuable services, but was unable to secure his transfer overseas before the end of the war, and was demobilised in January 1919.
9, Dashwood Road, Wandsworth Road, S.W.8.   Z1891

DESALEUX, A., Sapper, R.E.
Volunteering in March 1915 he embarked for France six months later and served throughout the war. During this period he was engaged on light railway construction and in laying tracks for guns, and was present at the Battles of Arras, Albert and Vimy Ridge. He was buried by a shell explosion in the course of operations and on recovery served with the signal section until hostilities ceased. Demobilised in May 1919, he holds the 1914-15 Star, and the General Service and Victory Medals.
41, Riverhall Street, Wandsworth Road, S.W.8.   Z1892

DEVANE, E. (Mrs.), Special War Worker.
This lady offered her services for work of National importance and was employed by the Park Royal Factory from 1916 until 1918. Acting as an Inspectress of fuses she performed her duties in a thoroughly capable and efficient manner and was afterwards engaged on important clerical work in the War Trade Department, Queen Anne's Gate.
15, Shirley Road, Chiswick, W.4.   7662B

DEVANE, J., Captain, 2nd London Regiment (Royal Fusiliers).
Volunteering in August 1914 he was later sent to the Western Front and served until the cessation of hostilities. During this period he took an important part in numerous engagements, and was gassed. He returned home for demobilisation in December 1918, and holds the 1914-15 Star, and the General Service and Victory Medals.
15, Shirley Road, Chiswick, W.4.   7662A

DEVILLE, M. (Mrs.), Special War Worker.
During the war this lady offered her services for work of National importance and was employed by Messrs. Waring & Gillow, White City. She was engaged in the manufacture of transport covers and carried out her duties in an efficient and capable manner .
106, Rayleigh Road, West Kensington, W.14.   12043B

DEVILLE, S., Private, Tank Corps.
Joining in 1917 he was drafted to the Western Front after completing his training and fought in the Battles of the Somme, Dixmude, Cambrai, and in the Retreat and Advance of 1918. On the conclusion of hostilities he was sent into Germany with the Army of Occupation and returned home for demobilisation in 1920. He holds the General Service and Victory Medals.
106, Rayleigh Road, West Kensington, W.14. 12043A

DEVITT, J., Sergt., 3rd London Regiment (Royal Fusiliers).
A Territorial, he was mobilised on the outbreak of war and sent overseas in 1915. Serving on the Western Front he fought in the Battles of Ypres, Festubert, Loos, the Somme, and during the Retreat and Advance of 1918. He returned to England for demobilisation in January 1919, and holds the 1914-15 Star, and the General Service and Victory Medals.
48, Russell Street, Battersea, S.W.11. Z1893

DEWEY, W. C., Driver, R.A.S.C.
He was mobilised from the Reserve on the outbreak of war. Sent to France in the Duke of Cornwall's Light Infantry in August 1914, he fought in the Battles of Ypres, Hill 60 and Loos, and was slightly wounded. He was later transferred to the Royal Army Service Corps and with this unit was engaged on important duties in connection with the transport of supplies to the firing line and did good work until the close of the war. Demobilised in April 1919, he holds the 1914 Star, and the General Service and Victory Medals.
172, St. George's Road, Peckham, S.E.15. Z5747

DEWSNAP, S. E., Rifleman, 16th London Regiment (Queen's Westminster Rifles).
He joined in March 1917 and was later sent to France, where he was in action at the Battles of Bullecourt and Passchendaele, and was wounded and gassed at Villers Bretonneux. On recovery he rejoined his Battalion in the Field and was again wounded in action. He was demobilised in March 1919, and holds the General Service and Victory Medals.
74, Landseer Street, Battersea, S.W.11. Z1894

DEXTER, E., Private, Queen's (Royal West Surrey Regiment), and Sapper, R.E.
He volunteered in March 1915 and in the same year proceeded to France. Whilst on the Western Front he fought at the Battle of the Somme and was wounded in March 1915. On recovery he was again in action and was wounded a second time in May 1916 at Ploegsteert Wood. In 1917 he was transferred to the Royal Engineers, with which unit he did good work in many parts of the line until hostilities ceased. He was demobilised in March 1920, and holds the 1914-15 Star, and the General Service and Victory Medals.
93, Robertson Street, Wandsworth Road, S.W.8. Z1895

DIBBENS, E., Driver, R.A.S.C.
He joined in October 1916 and in the following year was sent to France. He was engaged with his unit on special duties at Péronne, Cambrai and Verdun, and, attached to the 4th Division Cavalry, did good work taking ammunition and supplies to the front lines. He returned to England in 1918 and was discharged on account of service in September of that year, and holds the General Service and Victory Medals.
61, New Road, Battersea Park Road, S.W.8. Z1896

DIBBLIN, S. A., Private, Scots Guards.
He joined in March 1916 and in the following August was sent to France. He was engaged in much fighting on the Western Front, but owing to illness was sent home and discharged unfit for further service in October 1916. He rejoined, however, in March 1917 in the Royal Field Artillery, and was engaged on important home duties until demobilised in January 1919. He holds the General Service and Victory Medals.
25, Ranelagh Road, Pimlico Road, S.W.1. Z2757A

DIBLEY, H. W., Pioneer, R.E.
He volunteered in January 1915 and in the same year was sent to France. Whilst on the Western Front he served on special work with his unit at the Battles of Ypres, the Somme, Arras and in numerous other engagements. He was severely gassed near Ypres, and later died from the effects of gas-poisoning on January 9th, 1919. He was entitled to the 1914-15 Star, and the General Service and Victory Medals.
9, Ruskin Street, Wandsworth Road, S.W.8. Z1897

DIBLEY, J., Driver, R.F.A.
He volunteered in April 1915 and was drafted to France in the same year. He fought in many battles, including those of Arras, Ypres, Vimy Ridge and Lens, and in the German Offensive and Allied Advance of 1918. He returned to England after the cessation of hostilities and was demobilised in January 1919, and holds the 1914-15 Star, and the General Service and Victory Medals.
30, Henshaw Street, Walworth, S.E.17. Z1898

DIBSDALE, C. N. G., Gunner, R.F.A.
He joined in May 1916 and in the following September was sent overseas. He served in Mesopotamia for a time and, contracting malaria, was sent to India, where he remained for about six months. He was drafted to the Western Front in March 1918, and during the fighting in the second Battle of the Somme was wounded. After receiving hospital treatment at Rouen he returned to the firing line and was in action in many engagements until the close of the war. He then served with the Army of Occupation in Germany and was stationed at Cologne. He was demobilised in January 1920, and holds the General Service and Victory Medals.
3A, Wooler Street, Walworth, S.E.17. Z1899

DICK, J., A.B. Gunner, Royal Navy.
He volunteered at the outbreak of war and was posted to H.M.S. "Courageous." His ship was engaged in the fighting at the Battles of Heligoland Bight, Falkland Islands and Jutland, and was also in action in Russian waters. He holds the 1914-15 Star, and the General Service and Victory Medals, and was still serving in 1920.
62A, Nelson Row, High Street, Clapham, S.W.4. Z1900

DICKEN, E. W., Air Mechanic, R.A.F.
He joined in April 1917 and in the same year was sent to France. He was stationed at Dunkirk Aerodrome and was engaged on important duties attached to the Headquarters Staff and did very good work. He was demobilised in February 1919, and holds the General Service and Victory Medals.
20, Aytoun Road, Brixton Road, S.W.9. Z3079

DICKENSON, A. G., Private, R.A.S.C. (M.T.)
He volunteered in March 1915 and in the following August was sent to France. During his service on the Western Front he was engaged on important duties with the Intelligence Department and did very good work. After the Armistice he proceeded to Germany with the Army of Occupation, where he served until 1919. He returned to England and was demobilised in June of that year, and holds the 1914-15 Star, and the General Service and Victory Medals.
54, Bradmore Park Road, Hammersmith, W.6. 10618A

DICKENSON, H. H., 1st Air Mechanic, R.A.F.
He joined in April 1918 and was later sent to France. Whilst in this theatre of war he was engaged with his Squadron on important duties as magneto repairer and did very good work. On the cessation of hostilities he went with the Army of Occupation into Germany and served there for a time. He was demobilised in October 1919, and holds the General Service and Victory Medals.
54, Bradmore Park Road, Hammersmith, W.6. 10618B

DICKER, A. C., Private, 12th Manchester Regiment.
He joined in January 1917 and in the following year was sent to France. Whilst on the Western Front he was in action in the second Battle of the Somme and on the Ancre. Subsequently he was wounded at Metz. He was taken to hospital, but his injuries were so severe as to necessitate the amputation of a leg and he was invalided out of the Service in March 1918. He holds the General Service and Victory Medals.
32, Falcon Terrace, Battersea, S.W.11. Z1902

DICKER, A. E., Private, Hampshire Regiment.
He joined in November 1916 and in the following June was sent to Egypt. He was stationed at Cairo, Khartoum and other places, and served in the Sudan. During 1918 he was wounded in action. He returned to England and was demobilised in April 1920, and holds the General Service and Victory Medals.
12, Beech Street, Dorset Road, S.W.8. Z1901A

DICKER, F. J., Private, 4th London Regiment (Royal Fusiliers).
He joined in April 1917 and at the close of his training was drafted overseas in the following July. During his brief service on the Western Front he was engaged in much heavy fighting in the Ypres sector, where he was unfortunately killed in action on August 16th, 1917. He was entitled to the General Service and Victory Medals.
8, Beech Street, Dorset Road, S.W.8. Z1454B

DICKER, R. J., Leading Stoker, Royal Navy.
He was serving at the outbreak of war aboard H.M.S. "Waveney." His ship was engaged on important patrol duties on the East Coast, and did very good work there throughout the course of hostilities. He was demobilised in March 1919, and holds the 1914-15 Star, and the General Service and Victory Medals.
12, Beech Street, Dorset Road, S.W.8. Z1901B

DICKINSON, A., Corporal, R.A.S.C. (Remounts).
He joined in December 1916 and at the conclusion of his training was engaged on important transport duties to and from France. He crossed to France about twenty-four times and had many narrow escapes, being frequently in danger from enemy submarines. He did very good work and was demobilised in July 1919, and holds the General Service and Victory Medals.
64, Dorothy Road, Lavender Hill, S.W.11. Z1903

DICKINSON, A., Private, Bedfordshire Regiment.
He joined in August 1918 on attaining military age and at the conclusion of his training was drafted overseas in January 1919. He served with the Army of Occupation in Germany and was stationed at Cologne. He was demobilised in August 1919.
10, Bonnington Square, South Lambeth Road, S.W.8. Z1904

DICKINSON, A. G., Private, Royal Munster Fusiliers.
He volunteered in September 1914 and in the following August proceeded overseas. He was engaged in the fighting at Salonika and was wounded in January 1916. He received hospital treatment and on recovery returned to the front line trenches. He later contracted malaria and was invalided to hospital in Salonika, where he unhappily died on November 24th, 1916. He was entitled to the 1914-15 Star, and the General Service and Victory Medals.
87, Draycott Avenue, Chelsea, S.W.3. X24220C

DICKINSON, J. T., Gunner, R.F.A.
A serving soldier he was drafted overseas at the outbreak of war and served on the Western Front. He fought in the Retreat from Mons, and the subsequent Battles of the Marne, the Aisne, Ypres, Neuve Chapelle, Hill 60, St. Eloi, Festubert, Loos, Vimy Ridge, Albert, Beaumont-Hamel, the Somme, Passchendaele and the final Advance. During his long period of service he was once wounded. He was demobilised in April 1919, and holds the Mons Star, and the General Service and Victory Medals.
19, Henley Street, Battersea, S.W.11. Z1906A

DICKINSON, W. P., Driver, R.A.S.C. (H.T.)
He volunteered in September 1914 and in the following March proceeded to France. In this theatre of war he was engaged on important duties in many sectors, including those of Béthune, Neuve Chapelle, Ypres, Festubert, Loos, Albert, Vimy Ridge, the Somme, Arras, Bullecourt, Cambrai, Amiens and Bapaume. Owing to ill-health he was invalided to England and after receiving hospital treatment served on home duties until demobilised in February 1919. He holds the 1914-15 Star, and the General Service and Victory Medals.
87, Draycott Avenue, Chelsea, S.W.3. X24220B

DICKSON, A., Petty Officer, Royal Navy.
He volunteered at the outbreak of war and was posted to H.M.S. Pembroke." His ship was engaged in the fighting in the Dardanelles and supported the Landing and Evacuation of Gallipoli. He later served with the Naval Division in the Battle of the Somme, and also was in action at Vimy Ridge and Arras. Being wounded at Beaumont-Hamel he was sent to England and in June 1918 was invalided out of the Service. He holds the 1914-15 Star, and the General Service and Victory Medals.
22, Milford Street, Wandsworth Road, S.W.8. Z1907

DICKSON, F. E., Private, Royal Dublin Fusiliers.
He volunteered in June 1915 and at the conclusion of his training served on important duties with his unit at various stations. He did excellent work but was unsuccessful in obtaining his transfer overseas, and was demobilised in February 1919.
103, Smyrk's Road, Walworth, S.E.17. Z1909A

DICKSON, G., Private, Royal Berkshire Regiment.
He volunteered in September 1914 and in December of the same year was sent to France. Whilst on the Western Front he fought in the desperate encounter at Hill 60, and also at Neuve Chapelle, Ypres and Loos. Returning from leave at Xmas 1915 he was again in action at Loos, where he was unfortunately killed in March 1916. He was entitled to the 1914-15 Star, and the General Service and Victory Medals.
"His memory is cherished with pride."
44, Russell Street, Battersea, S.W.11. Z1910B

DICKSON, H., Gunner, R.F.A.
He joined in November 1916 and in the following March was sent to India. He was engaged on important duties with his unit at various stations and served in the fighting on the North West Frontier, where he contracted malaria. He returned home and was demobilised in November 1919, and holds the General Service and Victory Medals, and the India General Service Medal (with clasp, Afghanistan, North West Frontier, 1919). 44, Russell Street, Battersea, S.W.11. Z1910C

DICKSON, H., Sergt., Chinese Labour Corps.
He volunteered in May 1915 and having completed his training served with his Battalion in training recruits until drafted to France in August 1917. Whilst on the Western Front he fought in the Battles of Lens, Cambrai, the Somme (II), Amiens, Bapaume, Cambrai (II) and the final Advance into Germany. He was demobilised in February 1919, and holds the General Service and Victory Medals.
2, Prescott Place, Little Manor Street, Clapham, S.W.4. Z1908

DICKSON, T., Sergt., R.E.
He volunteered in February 1915 and in the following September was drafted overseas. During his service on the Western Front he fought in the Loos and Festubert sectors. He was severely wounded on Messines Ridge in June 1917 and was sent to hospital in England. Upon recovery he was retained on home service until he was demobilised in March 1919. He holds the 1914-15 Star, and the General Service and Victory Medals.
44, Russell Street, Battersea, S.W.11. Z1911

DICKSON, W., Private, Buffs (East Kent Regiment).
He volunteered in January 1915 and after a brief training was sent overseas in the following April. He fought in many important battles on the Western Front, including those of Ypres and Festubert. He was unfortunately killed in action at Loos in January 1916. He was entitled to the 1914-15 Star, and the General Service and Victory Medals.
44, Russell Street, Battersea, S.W.11. Z1910A

DIDCOCK, D. J., Gunner, R.F.A., and Corporal, M.G.C. and Tank Corps.
He volunteered in April 1915 and in the following November was drafted to France with the Tank Corps. He was in action in several important engagements, including those at Ploegsteert Wood, Vimy Ridge, Arras, Bullecourt and on the Somme. Invalided home owing to illness in 1917 he was in hospital for a considerable time and on recovery served with his unit on home service duties until demobilised in March 1919. He had previously served with the R.F.A. on the N.W. Frontier of India in 1908, and in addition to the 5th Indian General Service Medal for 1908, holds the 1914-15 Star, and the General Service and Victory Medals.
12, Orkney Street, Battersea, S.W.11. 3494

DIDCOCK, E. J., Sergt., Rifle Brigade.
Volunteering in August 1914 he proceeded to France in the following year and took an active part in the Battles of Ypres, Arras, Passchendaele, Messines, St. Quentin, and was wounded at Hooge on September 25th, 1915. On recovery he rejoined his Battalion in the Field and after fighting in many engagements was again wounded on March 23rd, 1918, during the German Offensive. He was reported killed in action, but three months afterwards was found to have been taken prisoner on that date. Repatriated after the Armistice he was discharged on account of service in November 1919, and holds the 1914-15 Star, and the General Service and Victory Medals.
45, Heath Road, Wandsworth Road, S.W.8. 3493A

DIDCOCK, F. J., Rifleman, King's Royal Rifle Corps.
Joining in June 1916 he was sent overseas four months later and saw much service on the Western Front. He fought in many important engagements, including those of Beaumont Hamel, Kemmel Hill and Arras, and was drafted to Italy in November 1917. Whilst on the Italian front he served through the Advance on the Piave and returned to France in March 1918. He was killed in action near Ypres in April 1918, and was entitled to the General Service and Victory Medals.
12, Orkney Street, Battersea, S.W.11. 3495

DIDCOCK, P. E., Rifleman, Rifle Brigade.
He joined in July 1916 and was sent to the Western Front in the following November and fought in the Battles of the Somme and Ypres, and several other engagements. He was severely wounded at Zonnebeke on August 14th, 1917, and sent to hospital in England. After receiving medical treatment he was invalided out of the Service in March 1918, and holds the General Service and Victory Medals.
66, Ravenswood Road, Balham, S.W.12. 3493B

DIGGENS, J., Staff-Sergt., R.E.
Volunteering in August 1914 he was drafted overseas in the following July and served in various sectors of the Western Front. He was engaged in bridging, wiring and making trenches and gun emplacements during the Battles of the Somme, Arras, Ypres and Passchendaele, and was severely wounded near Arras in July 1918. Invalided home for medical treatment he was discharged on account of service in January 1919. His ability and devotion to duty won for him promotion to the rank of Staff-Sergt. in 1916. He holds the 1914-15 Star, and the General Service and Victory Medals.
51, Wells Place, Camberwell, S.E.5. Z3436

DIGNUM, J. W., Gunner, R.H.A.
He volunteered in 1916 and in November of the same year was drafted to Mesopotamia, where he served as a signaller and took part in the engagements at Kut-el-Amara, the Tigris, the capture of Baghdad and Tekrit, and the occupation of Mosul. He returned to England in 1919, and was demobilised in April of that year, and holds the General Service and Victory Medals.
7, Santley Street, Brixton, S.W.4. 4445B

DIGNUM, R. R., Rifleman, 8th London Regiment (Post Office Rifles).
He volunteered in November 1915 and in the same year was sent to France. Whilst on the Western Front he was engaged in the fighting in many important battles and was unfortunately killed in action at the Battle of Vimy Ridge on April 10th, 1916. He was entitled to the 1914-15 Star, and the General Service and Victory Medals.
"The path of duty was the way to glory."
7, Santley Street, Brixton, S.W.4. 4445A

DIGNUM, W. G., A.B., Royal Navy.

He joined the Service in 1911 and at the outbreak of hostilities was mobilised, and aboard H.M.S. P.19 joined the Grand Fleet and was engaged in the North Sea on patrol and other important duties. His ship was also in action at the Dardanelles, and later had various encounters with the German Fleet off Dunkirk. He also served in various destroyers and minesweepers during the war, and in 1920 was serving in H.M.S. "Tempest." He holds the 1914-15 Star, and the General Service and Victory Medals.

64, Este Road, Battersea, S.W.11.   Z1912

DILLON, A. C., Pioneer, R.E., and Rifleman, Rifle Brigade.

He volunteered in August 1914 and after undergoing training was sent to the Western Front in September of the following year. He took an active part with his Battalion in severe fighting and fought at the Battles of Loos, Ypres, the Somme and Arras. Demobilised in June 1919, he holds the 1914-15 Star, and the General Service and Victory Medals.

50 Santley Road, Ferndale Road, S.W.14.   Z1913

DIMMOCK, E. W., Staff-Sergt., R.F.A.

He volunteered in August 1914 and two months later was drafted to the Western Front, where he was engaged in severe fighting at Ypres, Armentières and the Somme. In 1917 he was sent to Italy and was in action on the Piave and remained there until the signing of the Armistice. He was demobilised in January 1919, and holds the 1914 Star, and the General Service and Victory Medals.

49, Dawlish Street, Wilcox Road, S.W.8.   Z1914

DINMORE, J. A., Sapper, R.E.

He joined in 1916 and after completing his training was engaged on important duties with his unit on the South coast. He did very good work, but owing to medical unfitness for general service was unable to secure a transfer to a theatre of war, and was invalided out of the Army in November 1919.

197, Cator Street, Peckham, S.E.15.   Z5065

DIVERS, F. G., L/Corporal, Wiltshire Regiment.

He volunteered in 1914 and in the following year was sent to Gallipoli and was in action at the Landing at Suvla Bay. He was reported missing on August 10th, 1915, and was later presumed to have been killed in action during the fighting at Chocolate Hill on that date. He was entitled to the 1914-15 Star, and the General Service and Victory Medals.

82, Faraday Street, Walworth, S.E.17.   Z1915

DIXON, C., Private, Royal Sussex Regiment.

He joined in December 1917 and after his training served at various stations on important duties with his unit. He rendered valuable services, but was unsuccessful in obtaining his transfer overseas before the cessation of hostilities. He was demobilised in December 1919.

187, Brook Street, Kennington, S.E.11.   Z4524A

DIXON, E., Private, R.F.A.

He volunteered in November 1914 and in the same year was sent to the Western Front, where he fought in many of the principal engagements, including those of Ypres, Neuve Chapelle, Loos, Vimy Ridge, the Somme, Beaumont-Hamel, Arras, and was almost continuously in action during the Retreat and Advance of 1918. He was demobilised in that year and holds the 1914-15 Star, and the General Service and Victory Medals.

20, Hargwyne Street, Stockwell Road, S.W.9.   Z1916

DIXON, E. C., Rifleman, Rifle Brigade.

He volunteered in August 1914 and after completion of his training was engaged on important duties at home for a time. In 1916 he was sent to France and was in action with his unit on the Somme, at Ypres and Arras, and was badly gassed. On recovery he remained with his Battalion until the end of the war. He then returned to England, and was demobilised in 1919, and holds the General Service and Victory Medals.

100, Hubert Grove, Landor Road, S.W.9.   1917

DIXON, H., Corporal, R.E.

A Territorial he was mobilised on the outbreak of war and in the same year was sent to France. He saw much heavy fighting at the Retreat from Mons, and in the Battles of Arras, the Somme and Ypres, being engaged in mining, wiring and other duties, and during his service was wounded and gassed. He was demobilised in March 1919, and holds the Mons Star, and the General Service and Victory Medals.

48, Robertson Street, Wandsworth Road, S.W.8.   Z1918

DIXON, J. C., Private, Oxfordshire and Buckinghamshire Light Infantry.

He volunteered in August 1914 and shortly afterwards was drafted to the Western Front. He fought in the Retreat from Mons and the subsequent Battles of Ypres, Cambrai, the Somme and Arras, and after the cessation of hostilities was sent to Germany with the Army of Occupation and remained there until 1919. He returned home and was demobilised in March of that year, and holds the Mons Star, and the General Service and Victory Medals.

39, Yeldham Road, Hammersmith, W.6.   012802A

DIXON, L. (Mrs.), Special War Worker.

This lady offered her services for work of National importance during the war, and for eighteen months was employed at Messrs. Blake's munition factory on duties connected with the filling and soldering of shells. She was also engaged on special work in the T.N.T. room and throughout rendered valuable services.

39, Yeldham Road, Hammersmith, W.6.   12802B

DIXON, R., Gunner, R.G.A.

He joined in March 1915 and in the same year was sent to France. Whilst in this theatre of war he fought in many important engagements and during the Battle of the Somme was blown up by a mine explosion. He was invalided to England, and after receiving treatment was discharged as medically unfit for further service in August 1917. He holds the 1914-15 Star, and the General Service and Victory Medals.

44, Longhedge Street, Battersea, S.W.11.   Z1919

DIXON, S. T., Private, 3rd Gloucestershire Regiment.

He volunteered in September 1914 and in the following April was drafted to the Western Front. In this theatre of war he fought in many severely contested engagements, including those of Ypres, Hill 60 and Hooge. He was unfortunately killed in action on April 18th, 1915, and was entitled to the 1914-15 Star, and the General Service and Victory Medals

29, Verona Street, Battersea, S.W.11.   Z1920

DIXON, T., Private, Machine Gun Corps.

He joined in 1917 and in the same year was drafted to the Western Front. He was in action with his unit in many engagements, including those on the Somme, at Ypres and Arras. He was wounded during the German Offensive of 1918, and after receiving hospital treatment in England was demobilised in 1919. He holds the General Service and Victory Medals.

21, Henshaw Street, Walworth, S.E.17.   Z1921

DIXON, W. G., Private, Royal Fusiliers.

He volunteered in August 1914 and later in the same year was sent to France. He fought in many engagements, including those of the Aisne, Ypres, Armentières, the Somme and La Bassée. In 1915 he was drafted to the Dardanelles and was in action at the Landing at Suvla Bay, and many other engagements on the Peninsula. In the following year he proceeded to Egypt and served in the Canal zone for a time. He then returned to the Western Front and was severely wounded on the Somme. He was invalided home, and after receiving hospital treatment was discharged in April 1918 as physically unfit for further service. He holds the 1914 Star, and the General Service and Victory Medals.

5, Chatham Street, S.E.17.   Z1922

DOBIE, A. E, Private, 1/23rd London Regiment.

He volunteered in August 1914 and early in the following year was drafted to the Western Front. He served with his Battalion in many important engagements in this theatre of war, and was killed in action at Givenchy on May 25th, 1915. He was entitled to the 1914-15 Star, and the General Service and Victory Medals.

4A, Verona Street, Battersea, S.W.11.   Z1923B

DOBIE, S. S., Private, 10th Queen's (Royal West Surrey Regiment).

He volunteered in October 1915 and in the following year was sent to France. Whilst on the Western Front he was engaged in the fighting in many important battles, including those of the Somme and Passchendaele. He was unfortunately killed in action at the latter place on February 24th, 1917, and was entitled to the General Service and Victory Medals.

4A, Verona Street, Battersea, S.W.11.   Z1923A

DOBSON, C. H., Private, R.A.M.C.

Mobilised from the Reserve on the outbreak of war he served during the Retreat from Mons and in the Battle of the Aisne. He was wounded near Ypres in November 1914 and invalided home. Returning to the Western Front in the following month he did excellent work with his unit at Festubert, Loos, Passchendaele, Cambrai, on the Somme and during the Retreat and Advance of 1918. He was wounded at Boesinghe in July 1917 and at Arras in December 1918, and on the conclusion of hostilities was sent with the Army of Occupation into Germany. He was demobilised in June 1919. He served with the Guards Division throughout, and holds the Mons Star, and the General Service and Victory Medals.

114, Bramfield Road, Wandsworth Common, S.W.1.   Z3076

DOBSON, G E., Squadron Sergt.-Major Instructor, 14th (King's) Hussars.

A serving soldier he was stationed in India when war broke out and was engaged in the training of recruits for the United Provinces Light Horse and did valuable work in that capacity. Returning to England in November 1918 he was discharged on account of service in April 1920, and falling ill unfortunately died on the 28th day of the same month. He had served in the Army for upwards of twenty-four years, and fought in the South African War, and in addition to the Queen's and King's Medals (with four Clasps) for that campaign, was entitled to the General Service and Victory Medals.

"He joined the great white company of valiant souls."

12, Brynmaer Road, Battersea, S.W.12.   Z1924

DODD, A. M., Member W.R.A.F.
She joined in April 1917 and after completing a course of training was engaged on important clerical duties with her unit. She rendered valuable services, but was not sent overseas, and was demobilised in September 1919.
77, Carthew Road, Hammersmith, W.6. 10707B

DODD, E. F. S., Rifleman, 16th London Regiment (Queen's Westminster Rifles).
Joining in August 1917 he crossed to France in the following June and was in action almost continuously until August 1918, when he was severely wounded during the Advance of the Allies. After being for some time in hospital at Rouen and Bristol he was invalided out of the Service in August 1920. He holds the General Service and Victory Medals.
21, Elam Street, Camberwell, S.E.5. Z6160

DODD, E. G., Bombardier, R.F.A.
He volunteered in November 1914 and in September of the following year was drafted to France, where he fought at Loos, Arras, Delville Wood and Bapaume. He was badly gassed at Mametz Wood in February 1917, and invalided home. After hospital treatment he was discharged unfit for further service in September 1918. He holds the 1914-15 Star, and the General Service and Victory Medals.
54, Foreign Street, Camberwell, S.E.5. Z5932

DODD, F. W., Private, M.G.C.
He joined in November 1916 and in June of the following year was sent overseas. Serving with his unit on the Western Front he was engaged on important duties in various sectors and took part in several notable engagements until the cessation of hostilities. He was demobilised in February 1919, and holds the General Service and Victory Medals.
77, Carthew Road, Hammersmith, W.6. 10707A

DODDINGTON, J. R., Chief Petty Officer, Royal Navy.
Mobilised on the outbreak of war he served aboard H.M. Monitor "Abercrombie" and took part in the operations at Ostend. He was afterwards transferred to H.M.S. "Cynthia," which vessel was engaged on important patrol duties in the North Sea and other waters, and was in action in the Dardanelles. He holds the 1914-15 Star, and the General Service and Victory Medals, and in 1920 was still serving.
6, Aldbridge Street, Walworth, S.E.17. Z1925A

DOE, W. A., Rifleman, King's Royal Rifle Corps, and Private, R.A.S.C.
He joined in May 1918 and after completing his training was engaged on important duties with his unit at various depôts. He rendered valuable services but was unsuccessful in obtaining a transfer overseas, for owing to illness he was sent to hospital and discharged as medically unfit for further service in February 1919.
73, Sussex Road, Coldharbour Lane, S.W.9. Z3074

DOIDGE, W. H., Private, 14th (King's) and 20th Hussars.
He joined in March 1918 and in the following October, on attaining military age, he proceeded overseas. He served in Egypt and Palestine and did excellent work with his unit and was later sent to Turkey. In 1920 he was still serving, and holds the General Service and Victory Medals.
4, Hubert Grove, Landor Road, S.W.9. Z1926

DOLDING, A. J., Sapper, R.E.
He volunteered in January 1915 and embarking for France in the following September served on important duties during the Battles of Loos, Vimy Ridge, the Somme, Messines, Ypres, Passchendaele and was wounded at Ypres on September 20th, 1917. Sent home to hospital owing to his injuries he had his left arm amputated and was subsequently discharged as physically unfit for further service in January 1919. He holds the 1914-15 Star, and the General Service and Victory Medals.
27, Graylands Road, Peckham, S.E.15. Z5749

DOLLING, F. E. (Mrs.), Special War Worker.
This lady volunteered her services since she was desirous of releasing a man for military service. For more than four-and-a-half years she acted as a motor driver and rendered most valuable services in that capacity until the end of the war.
25, Masbro' Road, West Kensington, W.14. 12013A

DOLLING, J. W. J., Guardsman, 3rd Grenadier Guards.
Joining in May 1917 he completed his training and was engaged on important duties with his unit at various stations. He rendered valuable service but was unable to obtain a transfer to a theatre of war before the conclusion of hostilities and was demobilised in February 1919.
25, Masbro' Road, West Kensington, W.14. 12013B

DONALD, F. A., Private, R.A.M.C.
He joined in March 1916 and was engaged on hospital duties at home until sent to France in 1918. Whilst overseas he served with the Field Ambulance during the Battles of St. Quentin and Cambrai and other operations of the Advance. He was demobilised in February 1920, and holds the General Service and Victory Medals.
2, Cherwell Street, Battersea Park, S.W.8. Z1927

DONLEVY, G. T., Private, 18th Middlesex Regt.
He volunteered in the 1st County of London Yeomanry (Middlesex, Duke of Cambridge's Hussars) in December 1915 and was engaged on important duties with his unit on the East Coast until April 1918. He was then transferred to the 18th Middlesex Regiment and sent to France, where he served in the forward areas in the Ypres and Somme sectors until the cessation of hostilities. He was demobilised in March 1919, and holds the General Service and Victory Medals.
86, Plough Road, Battersea, S.W.11. Z1928

DONOGHUE, W., Corporal, Rifle Brigade, and Northumberland Fusiliers.
Volunteering in 1915 he proceeded overseas in the following year and saw much service on the Western Front. Whilst in this theatre of war he fought in the Battles of the Somme, Arras, Messines, Nieuport and Ypres, and was taken prisoner on January 31st, 1918, at Houthulst Forest. Released from captivity in December 1918 he was demobilised in the following August, and holds the General Service and Victory Medals.
68, Henshaw Street, Walworth, S.E.17. Z1929

DONOVAN, J., Corporal, R.A.S.C. (M.T.)
He volunteered in February 1915 and embarked in the following month for the Western Front. There he was engaged on important transport duties during the Battles of La Bassée, Loos, Arras, Ypres and the Somme, and was wounded in 1916 at Ypres and again in 1917. He was later in charge of "caterpillars" attached to the R.G.A. and did good work in the operations of the final stages of the war. Demobilised in June 1919, he holds the 1914-15 Star, and the General Service and Victory Medals.
66, The Grove, South Lambeth Road, S.W.8. Z1930

DOREY, M. (Mrs.), Special War Worker.
During the war this lady offered her services for work of National importance and for over a year was engaged at the Park Royal Munition Factory. She was employed in the shell filling department and carried out her dangerous duties in a highly efficient manner throughout.
66, Weston Road, Chiswick, W.4. 5838C

DOREY, P. E. (Miss), Special War Worker.
Offering her services for work of National importance this lady did excellent work during the war. She was engaged on important duties in the Inspection Bond Department at the Park Royal Munitions Factory and after a year's service there was employed by Messrs. Whiteheads, Ltd., Richmond, where she served as a fitter of aero-engines and carried out her duties to the satisfaction of her employers.
66, Weston Road, Chiswick, W.4. 5838A

DOREY, R. A., Special War Worker.
For upwards of two years during the war he was employed by Messrs. Whiteheads, Ltd., Richmond, in their aircraft works. He was engaged as a fitter of aero-engines, work calling for a high degree of technical knowledge and skill, and gave every satisfaction throughout his service.
66, Weston Road, Chiswick, W.4. 5838B

DORRELL, E. E., Private, Labour Corps.
Joining in May 1917, on attaining military age, he was sent to the Western Front in the following April. He was engaged on road-making and other duties in the forward areas whilst fighting was in progress, and was wounded in August 1918. On recovery he contracted influenza and died on October 22nd, 1918, and was buried at Etaples. He was entitled to the General Service and Victory Medals.
40, Harvey Road, Camberwell, S.E.5. Z1932

DORRELL, H. E., Signalman, Royal Navy.
Volunteering in April 1915, when sixteen years of age, he was posted to H.M.S. "Boadicea." His ship was engaged on important patrol duties in the North Sea and was in action at the Battle of Jutland. Sent to hospital owing to illness he was transferred to H.M.S. "Agamemnon," which vessel was sent to the Mediterranean on special duties. He holds the 1914-15 Star, and the General Service and Victory Medals, and in 1920 was still serving.
8, Union Street, Larkhall Lane, S.W.4. Z1931

DORSETT, J. T., Private, 8th Devonshire Regiment.
Volunteering in May 1915 he embarked for the Western Front in the same year and served there until the end of the war. During this time he fought in the Battles of Neuve Chapelle, Loos, the Somme, Arras and in several engagements in the Retreat and Advance of 1918. He was demobilised in January 1919, and holds the 1914-15 Star, and the General Service and Victory Medals.
32, Redmore Road, Hammersmith, W.6. T11600A

DORSETT, F. J., Ambulance Driver, British and French Red Cross.
He joined in 1917 when sixteen years of age and was sent to Salonika after completing a course of training. He did valuable work as an ambulance driver throughout the Balkan Campaign. After hostilities ceased he returned to England and enlisted in the Buffs (East Kent Regiment) in June 1919. In 1920 he was serving with his Battalion in India, and holds the Red Cross Certificate of Merit.
32, Redmore Road, Hammersmith, W.6.   T11600B

DORSETT, W. J., Driver, R.F.A.
He volunteered in the 11th London Regiment (Rifles) in August 1914, but was discharged on medical grounds five months later. Re-enlisting in the R.A.S.C. in 1916, in the following year he was transferred to the R.F.A. and sent to France. He was in action on the Somme and in the Battles of Ypres, Péronne, Messines, Lille and Passchendaele, and after the Armistice served with the Army of Occupation in Germany. He returned home for demobilisation in February 1920, and holds the General Service and Victory Medals.
32, Redmore Road, Hammersmith, W.6.   11601

DOSS, W. G., Private, Royal Marines.
He was mobilised at the outbreak of war and, aboard H.M.S. "Agamemnon," served at the Landing at Gallipoli in 1915 and in other naval engagements in this theatre of war. He also served in H.M.S. "Hibernia," which vessel did good work in the Mediterranean Sea and other waters. He holds the 1914-15 Star, and the General Service and Victory Medals, and was demobilised in 1919.
29, Wivenhoe Road, Peckham, S.E.15.   Z5937

DOSSETT, F. W., Private, 16th Middlesex Regt.
He joined in May 1916 and in the following September was drafted to France. He took part in many engagements, including those at Arras and Vimy Ridge. He gave his life for the freedom of England during the fighting at Vimy Ridge on April 18th, 1917, and was entitled to the General Service and Victory Medals.
"Steals on the ear, the distant triumph song."
81, Blake's Road, Peckham, S.E.15.   Z5946

DOUBLE, C., Private, 2nd Queen's (Royal West Surrey Regiment).
Volunteering in August 1915 he proceeded to Salonika a year later and served in the Advance on the Doiran front and in other engagements until sent to hospital suffering from malaria. Rejoining his unit he was subsequently drafted to Constantinople and was engaged on guard and police duties for a time. He returned home for demobilisation in November 1919, and holds the General Service and Victory Medals.
44, St. George's Road, Peckham, S.E.15.   Z5373

DOUBLE, R. M., Private, West Yorkshire Regiment.
He joined in November 1916 and in the following year proceeded to France. Whilst in this theatre of war he was in action in several notable engagements, including the Battles of Arras, Lens, the Somme and was wounded at Cambrai in 1917. Admitted to hospital in France he was subsequently sent home and discharged on account of service in February 1918. He holds the General Service and Victory Medals.
15, Arlesford Road, Landor Road, S.W.9.   Z1934

DOUGHTY, F. L., Gunner, R.F.A.
He volunteered in September 1914 and in June of the following year was drafted to Gallipoli, where he served with his Battery in much heavy fighting. Owing to illness he was sent home in January 1916, and six months later proceeded to France and was engaged in heavy fighting on the Somme and at Ypres, and was wounded. Invalided to hospital in England in 1917, on recovery he served with his Battery at home until demobilised in March 1919. He holds the 1914-15 Star, and the General Service and Victory Medals.
40, Chatham Road, Wandsworth Common, S.W.11.   Z1935

DOUGHTY, W. G., Sapper, R.E.
He joined in September 1916 and on completing his training was engaged on important home defence duties at various stations. He did valuable work as a Signaller but was not sent overseas owing to ill-health and was discharged in consequence in November 1917.
69, Dashwood Road, Wandsworth Road, S.W.8.   Z1936

DOUGLAS, C. T., 1st Class Stoker, Royal Navy.
He volunteered in June 1915 and served in H.M.S. "Leonidas" and afterwards in H.M.S. "Springbok" during the course of hostilities. His ship was engaged on important duties with the Harwich Patrol off the East Coast and he did excellent work until the end of the war. He holds the 1914-15 Star, and the General Service and Victory Medals, and in 1920 was still serving.
50, Ingrave Street, Battersea, S.W.11.   Z1937D

DOUGLAS, C. W., Prte., 5th North Staffordshire Regt.
He joined in September 1916 and was drafted overseas in the following April. Serving on the Western Front he took part in the Battles of Arras and Ypres and in several operations during the German Offensive of 1918. He was unfortunately killed in action on April 17th, 1918, and was entitled to the General Service and Victory Medals.
50, Ingrave Street, Battersea, S.W.11.   Z1937A

DOUGLAS, F. A., Lieutenant, R.A.F.
Joining in 1917 he completed his training and served on important duties which called for a high degree of technical skill until his embarkation for France in October 1918. Here he was actively engaged and on the cessation of hostilities was sent with the Army of Occupation into Germany, returning home for demobilisation in September 1919. He holds the General Service and Victory Medals.
50, Ingrave Street, Battersea, S.W.11.   Z1937B

DOUGLAS, G. W., A.B., Royal Navy.
Having joined the Royal Navy in January 1914 he was mobilised on the outbreak of war and served aboard H.M.S. "Warrior." Attached to the Grand Fleet his ship was engaged on important duties in the North Sea and was in action at the Battle of Jutland. He was later transferred to H.M.S. "Nizam." He holds the 1914-15 Star, and the General Service and Victory Medals and in 1920 was still serving.
50 Ingrave Street, Battersea, S.W.11.   Z1937C

DOUGLAS, P. W. (M.M.), Corporal, 11th Queen's (Royal West Surrey Regiment).
Volunteering in June 1915 he was sent to France in the following year and fought in the Battles of the Somme, Ypres, Albert and other important engagements, and was awarded the Military Medal for conspicuous gallantry at Messines on June 7th, 1917. Whilst acting as Brigade Observer he secured valuable information of enemy plans. He was later drafted to Italy and served in various operations on the Piave. Returning to the Western Front in 1918 he was in action during the Retreat and Advance, and was gassed and wounded near Courtrai and invalided home. He received medical treatment and was demobilised in January 1919, and holds the General Service and Victory Medals.
71, Sussex Road, Coldharbour Lane, S.W.9.   Z3070

DOUGLAS, W., Private, Queen's (Royal West Surrey Regiment).
He volunteered in August 1915 and in the following year was sent to the Western Front. Here he fought in many engagements, including those at Arras, Ypres and during the fierce fighting at Dickebusch was severely wounded. He was sent to England and subsequently invalided out of the Service in August 1917. He holds the General Service and Victory Medals.
23, Pilkington Road, Peckham, S.E.15.   Z5940

DOUNING, C., Driver, R.A.S.C.
Volunteering in May 1915 he was drafted to the Western Front in the same year and served on important transport duties during the Battles of Neuve Chapelle, Ypres, Loos and the Somme, and was three times wounded. After being seriously wounded on Vimy Ridge he was sent to hospital in England and invalided out of the Service. He holds the 1914-15 Star, and the General Service and Victory Medals.
14, Auckland Road, Battersea, S.W.11.   Z3287A

DOUTHWAITE, A., Signalman, Royal Navy.
Joining in July 1917 he was posted to H.M.S. "Petunia," which vessel served with the Mediterranean Fleet and was engaged on important mine-sweeping and escort duties during the whole period of the war. His ship frequently passed through mine-infested areas and had many narrow escapes. He holds the General Service and Victory Medals, and was demobilised in May 1920.
34, Amies Street, Battersea, S.W.11.   Z1938B

DOUTHWAITE, A. G., Private, 23rd London Regt.
He volunteered in January 1915 and two months later proceeded to France. Whilst on the Western Front he was engaged in heavy fighting in several notable battles. When all the Officers of his unit were casualties he was last seen leading his Battalion into action on the Somme and was reported missing on September 6th, 1916. He was later presumed to have made the supreme sacrifice on that date, and was entitled to the 1914-15 Star, and the General Service and Victory Medals.
34, Amies Street, Battersea, S.W.11.   Z1938C

DOUTHWAITE, C. E., Private, 23rd London Regt.
Volunteering in May 1915 he completed his training and was engaged on important duties with his unit until sent to France in March 1918. He fought at Arras and La Bassée, and was wounded and sent to hospital at the Base. Returning to the Field on recovery in May 1918 he was in action in the Battle of Cambrai and other concluding engagements of the war, and was wounded a second time in November 1918. He returned to England and was demobilised in March 1919, and holds the General Service and Victory Medals.
34, Amies Street, Battersea, S.W.11.   Z1938A

DOVE, F. R., Driver, R.F.A.

He volunteered in December 1914 and embarked for the Western Front in the following year. He was in action in many important engagements, including those at Cambrai, the Somme and Ypres. He also fought in the German Offensive and subsequent Allied Advance of 1918, and was wounded. On recovery he served at the Base until he returned to England and was demobilised in January 1919, and holds the 1914-15 Star, and the General Service and Victory Medals.

95A, Ingelow Road, Battersea Park, S.W.8.   Z1939

DOWDESWELL, W. C., Leading Stoker, Royal Navy.

He joined the service in October 1916 and was posted to H.M.S. "Berwick," which ship was engaged on patrol and other important duties in the North Sea and other waters. He also served in H.M.S. "Perdita." This vessel rendered valuable services mine-laying and had several narrow escapes whilst passing through mine-infested areas. He was wounded during one of the encounters his ship had with the enemy, and after hostilities ceased he returned to shore and was demobilised in May 1919. He holds the General Service and Victory Medals.

19, Bagshot Street, Walworth, S.E.17.   Z1941

DOWDESWELL, W. G., Driver, R.A.S.C.

He joined the Royal Navy in January 1901 and was discharged in November 1910. He then joined the National Reserve and in 1914 was transferred to the Special Reserve. Mobilised at the outbreak of hostilities he was sent to the Western Front later in 1914 and fought at La Bassée, Festubert and was gassed at Kemmel in November 1916. Invalided to England he received hospital treatment and was discharged unfit for further service in March 1918. He holds the 1914 Star, and the General Service and Victory Medals.

207, Eversleigh Road, Battersea, S.W.11.   Z1940

DOWDING, A., Q.M.S., Royal Fusiliers.

Mobilised at the commencement of hostilities he proceeded overseas shortly afterwards. During his service on the Western Front he fought in many important engagements in various parts of the line and was in action during the German Offensive and subsequent Allied Advance in 1918, and was gassed. He was demobilised in May 1919, and holds the 1914-15 Star, and the General Service and Victory Medals.

21, Seaham Street, Wandsworth Road, S.W.8.   Z1942

DOWDING, L. G., Private, 1/13th London Regiment (Kensingtons).

Joining in 1917 he embarked for France later in the same year and was in action in various sectors and fought throughout the German Offensive and Allied Advance of 1918, and was wounded. On recovery he was sent to Germany with the Army of Occupation and was stationed on the Rhine. Returning to England he was demobilised in 1919, and holds the General Service and Victory Medals.

71, Wadhurst Road, Wandsworth Road, S.W.8.   Z1943

DOWLING, H. L., Private, 2nd Oxfordshire and Buckinghamshire Light Infantry.

He enlisted in February 1903 and at the outbreak of war was stationed in India. He proceeded to Mesopotamia in 1914 and fought in many important engagements. He contracted sickness whilst serving in the Persian Gulf and subsequently died. He was entitled to the 1914-15 Star, and the General Service and Victory Medals.

30, Newby Street, Wandsworth Road, S.W.8.   Z1944B

DOWLING, J. E., Private, Queen's (Royal West Surrey Regiment).

He joined in March 1917 and was sent to the Western Front later in the same year and fought in many important battles, including those at Arras, Albert, Passchendaele, St. Quentin, St. Eloi, and in the Retreat and Advance of 1918. He was demobilised in March 1919, and holds the General Service and Victory Medals. 3, Sandmere Gardens, Clapham, S.W.4.   Z1945

DOWNING, F. M., Private, Royal Fusiliers and Guardsman, Grenadier Guards.

Volunteering in March 1915 on completion of his training he served at various stations until drafted to the Western Front in 1917. Here he was in action almost continuously, fighting in many important engagements, and was wounded at Maubeuge. Invalided home he was discharged in January 1919 after a protracted course of hospital treatment, and holds the General Service and Victory Medals.

194, Farmer's Road, Camberwell, S.E.5.   Z1946A

DOWSETT, H. H., Rifleman, 11th Rifle Brigade.

Joining in May 1917 he was drafted overseas four months later and was in action in many important engagements. He was wounded and taken prisoner at the Battle of Cambrai on November 30th, 1917, and during his captivity in Germany worked on a farm. Repatriated after the Armistice he was discharged on account of service in May 1919, and holds the General Service and Victory Medals.

210, Cator Street, Peckham, S.E.15.   Z5066

DOYLE, H., Private, Middlesex Regiment.

He joined in October 1916 and was sent to France in the following year and fought in many engagements, including those at Arras and Vimy Ridge, and was in action throughout the Retreat and Advance of 1918. He was demobilised shortly after the Armistice but later re-enlisted for a further period of service. He was serving in Egypt in 1920, and holds the General Service and Victory Medals.

35, Farmer's Road, Camberwell, S.E.5.   Z1947

DOYLE, J., Special Constable, W.C. Division.

He volunteered his services during the war as a Special Constable and from the outbreak of hostilities rendered excellent services generally assisting the police. He was also engaged on special duties during air-raids. He discharged his duties in a most satisfactory and efficient manner and in 1920 was still serving.

53, Yeldham Road, Hammersmith, W.6.   13243A

DOYLE, L., Corporal, Scots Guards.

He joined in 1917 on attaining military age, and after completing his training served at various depôts with his unit engaged on guard and other important duties. He was unsuccessful in obtaining his transfer to a theatre of war prior to the cessation of hostilities, but rendered valuable services until demobilised in 1919.

53, Yeldham Road, Hammersmith, W.6.   13243B

(V.C.) DRAKE, A., Corporal, 8th Rifle Brigade.

He volunteered at the outbreak of war and shortly afterwards proceeded to the Western Front, where he saw much heavy fighting. On November 23rd, 1915, whilst he was on night patrol with a party consisting of an officer and two other men in "No man's land" at La Brique the enemy opened fire and wounded the officer and a man. Corporal Drake remained to attend to them with the utmost disregard of personal safety whilst the survivor went for help. When this arrived Corporal Drake was found dead and riddled with bullets lying across the officer, whose wounds had been bandaged and who was eventually rescued. For this heroic deed of self-sacrifice he was awarded posthumously the Victoria Cross and the decoration was presented to his father by H.M. the King on November 16th, 1916. When he was killed Corporal Drake was only twenty-two years old. In addition to the Victoria Cross he was entitled to the 1914 Star, and the General Service and Victory Medals.

"Greater love hath no man than this,
That he lay down his life for his friends."

25, Sidney Road, Stockwell, S.W.9.   1188B

DRAKE, F. C., Driver, R.A.S.C. (M.T.)

Joining in June 1917 he proceeded to Italy later in the same year. During his service in this theatre of war he was engaged on important duties in the forward areas of the Piave front transporting ammunition and supplies and rendered excellent services throughout. He returned to England and was demobilised in March 1920, and holds the General Service and Victory Medals.

56, Pulross Road, Brixton Road, S.W.9.   Z1949

DRAKE, G. W. E., Flight-Sergt., R.A.F.

He enlisted in the 7th Dragoon Guards in September 1888 and after twelve years' service was transferred to the 1st Life Guards and served with this Regiment until 1909, when he was discharged on completing 21 years' service. He enlisted in the Sussex Yeomanry in November 1910 and was discharged as medically unfit on August 5th, 1914. He joined the R.A.F. as A/Corporal in July 1918 and was promoted to Flight Sergeant in the following December, and rendered excellent services at various aerodromes. He was still serving in 1920.

5A, Theatre Street, Lavender Hill, S.W.11.   Z1951

DRAKE, H., Private, R.A.O.C.

He joined in July 1917 and was drafted to the Western Front later in the same year and served in the forward areas during the German Offensive and subsequent Allied Advance of 1918, and did excellent work. He met with an accident in the course of his duties, breaking a leg, and invalided to England received hospital treatment and was subsequently demobilised in October 1919. He holds the General Service and Victory Medals.

27, Trollope Street, Battersea Park, S.W.8.   Z1948

DRAKE, H. E., Private, Labour Corps.

He joined in October 1916 and on completion of his training was stationed at various depôts employed on special duties. He was unsuccessful in obtaining his transfer overseas prior to the cessation of hostilities, but rendered valuable services engaged on important agricultural work until demobilised in December 1918.

10, Kennard Street, Battersea, S.W.11.   Z1952

DRAKE, H. J., Sapper, R.E.

Volunteering in March 1915 he embarked for the Western Front in the following September. During his service overseas he served in various sectors engaged on important duties connected with operations and was present at the fighting at the Somme, Arras, Ypres and during the Retreat and Advance of 1918. He was demobilised in January 1919, and holds the 1914-15 Star, and the General Service and Victory Medals.

31, Edithna Street, Landor Road, S.W.9.   Z1950

DRAKE, W. S., Sapper, R.E.

He joined in December 1916 and proceeded to the Western Front in the following year and served in the Battles of Cambrai, Ypres, Loos, Lille, Béthune and Armentières, and in many other engagements. He also saw fighting in the German Offensive and Allied Advance in 1918, and returning to England was demobilised in March 1919. He holds the General Service and Victory Medals.

51, Kingswood Road, Chiswick, W.4.　　　　T6794C

DRAPER, A. L. (Mrs.), Special War Worker.

This lady offered her services for work of National importance and from August 1917 until February 1919 rendered excellent services, engaged on work of an arduous nature in the employ of the S.E. & C.R. She discharged her duties in an efficient and satisfactory manner.

28, Sussex Road, Coldharbour Lane, S.W.9.　　　Z1953B

DRAPER, C. G., Private, 2nd Queen's (Royal West Surrey Regiment) and Labour Corps.

Volunteering in May 1915 he was sent to France later in the same year and fought at the Battles of Béthune, Bapaume, Armentières, Passchendaele, Vimy Ridge and was invalided home owing to ill-health. On recovery he returned to France and was wounded at the Hindenburg line and returned to England. After receiving hospital treatment he was again sent to the Western Front and transferred to the Labour Corps and was engaged on important guard duties at prisoners-of-war camps until demobilised in February 1919. He holds the 1914-15 Star, and the General Service and Victory Medals.

28, Sussex Road, Coldharbour Lane, S.W.9.　　　Z1953A

DRAPER, G. W., Private, 22nd London Regiment (The Queen's).

Joining in March 1917 he proceeded overseas in the following February. During his service on the Western Front he fought in many engagements during the German Offensive and Allied Advance of 1918, including the Battles at Ypres and Cambrai, and was present at the capture of Lille and the entry of Mons at dawn on November 11th, 1918. He was demobilised in June 1919, and holds the General Service and Victory Medals.

5, Hopwood Street, Walworth, S.E.17.　　　　Z1956

DRAPER, H., Driver, R.A.S.C. (H.T.)

A serving soldier he was mobilised and sent to the Western Front on the outbreak of war and served throughout the Retreat from Mons and in the Battles of the Somme, Ypres, Vimy Ridge, engaged on important transport duties. He also was present at the fighting in the German Offensive and Allied Advance of 1918 and was demobilised in June 1919. He holds the Mons Star, and the General Service and Victory Medals.

31, Warham Street, Camberwell, S.E.5.　　　　Z1954

DRAPER, W. H., Rifleman, 5th Rifle Brigade.

Joining in June 1916 he embarked for the Balkan theatre of war later in the same year. Here he fought in many sectors of the Struma and Doiran fronts, and was in action in the Struma Offensive. He was wounded in 1917 and on recovery rejoined his unit and fought throughout the final Allied Advance. He returned home and was demobilised in December 1919, and holds the General Service and Victory Medals.

141, Tyneham Road, Lavender Hill, S.W.11.　　　Z1955

DRESCH, W. V., Private, R.A.O.C. and Essex Regiment.

He volunteered in December 1915 and on completion of his training served at various stations until drafted to France in 1917. Here he fought in the Battles of La Bassée, Merville, Béthune and in many other engagements, and throughout the Retreat and Advance of 1918. He was demobilised in March 1919, and holds the General Service and Victory Medals

91, Sandwere Road, Clapham, S.W.4.　　　　Z1957

DREW, P. W., Driver, R.A.S.C. (M.T.)

He joined in April 1917 and embarked for the Western Front in the following year and served at various stations on transport and other important duties until the cessation of hostilities. He then proceeded into Germany with the Army of Occupation and was stationed at Cologne until he returned to England and was demobilised in December 1919. He holds the General Service and Victory Medals.

225, Mayall Road, Herne Hill, S.E.24.　　　　Z1771B

DRINKWATER, A. T., Private, 13th York and Lancaster Regiment.

Volunteering in August 1914 he was drafted to Gallipoli in the following year and fought at the Landing at Suvla Bay and in other operations until the Evacuation of the Peninsula. Sent to Egypt early in 1916 he proceeded to France later in that year and was in action at Hébuterne, Hazebrouck, Ploegsteert Wood and was wounded at Neuve Chapelle. On recovery he did excellent work as Brigade runner at the 93rd Infantry Brigade Headquarters until the cessation of hostilities. He was demobilised in January 1919, and holds the 1914-15 Star, and the General Service and Victory Medals.

32, Henley Street, Battersea, S.W.11.　　　　Z1958

DRISCOLL, C., Gunner, R.F.A.

He volunteered in August 1914 and in May of the following year was sent to the Western Front. There he played a prominent part in many important engagements, including those on the Somme, at Arras, Ypres, Cambrai and was badly gassed at Arras in January 1918. He was invalided home, and after spending some time in hospital was discharged as medically unfit for further service in March 1918. He holds the 1914-1 Star, and the General Service and Victory Medals.

10, Thorncroft Street, Wandsworth Road, S.W.8.　Z1960B

DRISCOLL, D. J., Sergt., R.G.A.

He was mobilised in August 1914 and was almost immediately drafted to the Western Front. There he was in action in many engagements, including the Retreat from Mons, and the Battles of the Aisne, the Marne, Ypres, Neuve Chapelle, Loos, Albert, Vimy Ridge and many others until wounded at Cambrai in 1918. On recovery he rejoined his Battery and was still serving in 1920, and holds the Mons Star, and the General Service and Victory Medals.

97, Westmorland Road, Walworth, S.E.17.　　　Z1961B

DRISCOLL, P., Chief Petty Officer, Royal Navy.

He was mobilised from the Reserve in August 1914 and posted to H.M.S. "Implacable," which vessel was engaged with the Grand Fleet in the North Sea on patrol and other important duties. His ship was also in action at the Dardanelles and did valuable work in covering the landing of troops in that theatre of war. He was demobilised in November 1919, and holds the 1914-15 Star, and the General Service and Victory Medals.

10, Thorncroft Street, Wandsworth Road, S.W.8.　Z1960A

DRISCOLL, T. E., Private, 1st Bedfordshire Regt.

He volunteered in September 1914 and in the following March was sent to France. In this theatre of war he was engaged in fighting in many sectors and fought at the Battles of La Bassée, Ypres, Neuve Chapelle, Ypres (II), Festubert, Loos, Albert and Vimy Ridge. He was unfortunately killed in action on the Somme on July 27th, 1916, and was entitled to the 1914-15 Star, and the General Service and Victory Medals.

97, Westmorland Road, Walworth, S.E.17.　　Z19613C

DRISCOLL, W., Sergt., 23rd London Regiment.

He volunteered in August 1914 and in the following year proceeded to France, where he took a prominent part in many important engagements, including those of Cambrai, Somme, Hill 60 and Festubert. He was wounded at Cambrai and after recovery returned to the firing line and was unfortunately killed in action in the German Offensive on March 21st, 1918. He was entitled to the 1914-15 Star, and the General Service and Victory Medals.

220, Beresford Street, Camberwell, S.E.5.　　　Z1959A

DRIVER, H., A.B., Royal Navy.

He joined the Service in 1897 and on the outbreak of war, aboard H.M.S. "Aboukir," served with the Grand Fleet under Admiral Jellicoe. His ship was torpedoed and sunk on September 22nd, 1914, and after remaining in the water for some time he was picked up by H.M.S. "Cressy," which vessel was later torpedoed and sunk on the same day and he was unfortunately drowned. He was entitled to the 1914-15 Star, and the General Service and Victory Medals.

9, St. Philip Street, Battersea Park, S.W.8.　　Z1962A

DRUCE, J. S., Private, 13th East Yorkshire Regt.

He volunteered in November 1915 and early in the following year was drafted to the Western Front, where he took part in the Battles of Ypres, the Somme, Cambrai, Valenciennes, Neuve Chapelle and many other engagements. On the cessation of hostilities he returned home and was demobilised in March 1919, and holds the General Service and Victory Medals.

45, Bolton Street, Camberwell, S.E.5.　　　Z1963A

DRUCE, W. J., Rifleman, King's Royal Rifle Corps.

He joined in December 1916 and on completion of his training was sent to France. There he played a prominent part in many engagements, including those of Arras, Armentières, Ypres and many others during the Retreat and Advance of 1918. He was demobilised in January 1919, and holds the General Service and Victory Medals.

45, Bolton Street, Camberwell, S.E.5.　　　Z1963B

DRUMMOND, H. C., Private, 1st Wiltshire Regt.

He volunteered in March 1915 and in the following month proceeded to the Western Front. There he was engaged with his unit in fierce fighting in the Battles of the Somme, Arras, Bullecourt, Cambrai and several others. On the cessation of hostilities he returned to England and was demobilised in March 1919. He holds the 1914-15 Star, and the General Service and Victory Medals.

22, Camellia Street, Wandsworth Road, S.W.8.　Z1964

DRUMMOND, J. F., Sergt., 3rd Buffs (East Kent Regiment).

He was mobilised from the Reserve in August 1914 and was immediately drafted to France, where he served through the Retreat from Mons and in many important engagements which followed. He was unfortunately killed in action in April 1917, and was entitled to the Mons Star, and the General Service and Victory Medals.

88, Fielding Road, Acton, W.4.　　　　7661A

DRUMMOND, S. B., Sergt., 18th London Regiment (London Irish Rifles).
He volunteered in 1915 and on completion of his training was drafted to Egypt. In this theatre of war he served with his Battalion in many important engagements during the Advance through Syria. He was unfortunately killed in action on December 23rd, 1916, and was entitled to the General Service and Victory Medals.
88, Fielding Road, Acton, W.4.   7661B

DRUMMY, P., Pte., 21st (Empress of India's)Lancers.
A Reservist he was mobilised at the outbreak of war and drafted to France. Whilst on the Western Front he was engaged in much fighting in various sectors. Owing to ill-health he was invalided to England and received hospital treatment, and was subsequently discharged medically unfit for further service in January 1915. He holds the 1914 Star, and the General Service and Victory Medals.
36, Oberstein Road, Battersea, S.W.11.   Z1965

DRYE, F. G., Rifleman, The Cameronians (Scottish Rifles).
He joined in February 1917 and was later drafted overseas. He served on the Western Front and took part in many battles and engagements until the cessation of hostilities. He then returned to England and was demobilised in September 1919, and holds the General Service and Victory Medals.   Z1966A
19, Stansfield Road, Stockwell Road, S.W.9.   Z1967A

DRYWOOD, F. H., Guardsman, 2nd Coldstream Guards.
Volunteering in January 1915 he was drafted to France in April of the following year. Whilst in this theatre of war he fought at the Battle of Ypres and was severely wounded. He was invalided to England and after receiving hospital treatment served on home duties until demobilised in July 1919 being medically unfit for further service overseas. He holds the General Service and Victory Medals.
76, Grenard Road, Peckham, S.E.15.   Z5593

DUBBER, R., Private, 2nd Queen's (Royal West Surrey Regiment).
A serving soldier he was drafted overseas shortly after the outbreak of war. Whilst on the Western Front he was engaged in many battles, including those at Ypres, Bray, Mametz Wood, Fricourt and Delville Wood. He was wounded in action near Ypres in November 1914, and again at the Battle of the Somme in July 1916. He was demobilised in August 1919, and holds the 1914 Star, and the General Service and Victory Medals.
6, Granby Buildings, Broad Street, Lambeth Walk, S.E.11. Z24431

DUCK, A., Private, Machine Gun Corps (Cavalry).
He was serving in India at the outbreak of war and was immediately drafted to France, where he took part in the final stages in the Retreat from Mons and fought in the Battles of the Aisne, La Bassée, Ypres, Neuve Chapelle, St. Eloi, Festubert, Loos and the Somme, and was gassed at Bapaume in September 1916. He was later sent to Mesopotamia and was in action at Ramadieh, Tekrit and Baghdad. He was demobilised in May 1919, and holds the Mons Star, and the General Service and Victory Medals.
20, Middleton Road, Battersea, S.W.11.   Z1968

DUCK, G., Private, 1st Royal Fusiliers.
A Reservist he was mobilised at the outbreak of war and was quickly drafted to France. While in this theatre of war he was engaged in much heavy fighting and was wounded three times. He was unfortunately killed in action at the Battle of Ypres on June 7th, 1915. He was entitled to the 1914 Star, and the General Service and Victory Medals.
75, Brackenbury Road, Hammersmith, W.6.   10717A

DUCK, H., L/Corporal, 4th Royal Fusiliers.
Volunteering at the outbreak of war he was engaged with his Battalion on important duties until drafted to the Western Front. He fought in many battles, notably in those at Arras and Béthune, and was unhappily killed in action at St. Quentin in April 1918. He was entitled to the General Service and Victory Medals.
75, Brackenbury Road, Hammersmith, W.6.   10717B

DUCKETT, H. E., Private, 1st East Surrey Regiment.
He volunteered in September 1914 and was immediately sent overseas. During his service on the Western Front he was engaged in the fighting at Festubert, Loos and Hill 60, where he was wounded. He was subsequently killed in action in the vicinity of Loos in December 1915. He was entitled to the 1914 Star, and the General Service and Victory Medals.
"His memory is cherished with pride."
62, Sheepcote Lane, Battersea, S.W.11.   Z1185B

DUCKETT, J. E., Private, R.A.M.C.
He volunteered in June 1915 and in the following year was sent to France. He was engaged with his unit in the Ypres, Arras and Albert sectors, and was afterwards sent to Salonika, where he served as stretcher bearer. He was afterwards drafted to Egypt and was in action in the British Advance through Palestine. He contracted malaria and was sent to Egypt and on recovery was employed on home duties until demobilised in August 1919. He holds the General Service and Victory Medals.
27, Loughboro' Street, Kennington, S.E.11.   Z25471

DUDDERIDGE, C., Private, Machine Gun Corps.
He joined in 1917 and in the following year was sent to France. Whilst in this theatre of war he was engaged in much fighting and was taken prisoner at Armentières in April 1918. He suffered many privations during his captivity until released after the signing of the Armistice. He was demobilised in 1919, and holds the General Service and Victory Medals.
99, Thorparch Road, Wandsworth Road, S.W.8.   Z1969A

DUDDERIDGE, H., Private, 23rd London Regiment.
Serving at the outbreak of war he was employed on special work until drafted to France in 1916. He fought in many battles, including those on the Somme, at Arras, Vimy Ridge, Armentières and Ypres. He was twice mentioned in Despatches for his conspicuous service in the Field, and was twice wounded. He was demobilised in January 1919, and holds the General Service and Victory Medals.
99, Thorparch Road, Wandsworth Road, S.W.8.   Z1969B

DUDDERIDGE, J., Rifleman, Rifle Brigade.
Volunteering at the outbreak of war he was drafted to France in 1915. Whilst on the Western Front he fought in many engagements and was wounded on the Somme and also on another occasion. He was unhappily killed in action in the vicinity of Cambrai on October 8th, 1918, and was buried in a cemetery on the south side of Cambrai. He was entitled to the 1914–15 Star, and the General Service and Victory Medals.
99, Thorparch Road, Wandsworth Road, S.W.8.   Z1969C

DUDLEY, W. G., Hydrophone Operator, R.N.V.R.
He joined in January 1918 and was posted to H.M.T.B.D "Phœbe," which was engaged on special service in the North Sea. His duties were connected with the detection of hostile submarines and were of a technical and highly responsible character. He was demobilised in January 1919, and holds the General Service and Victory Medals.
57, Heath Road, Wandsworth Road, S.W.8.   Z1970A

DUFFELL, A. J., Private, Durham Light Infantry.
He joined in October 1916 and in the following year was sent to Salonika. He was engaged in the fighting during the Bulgarian Offensive of 1918, and was later sent to Russia, where he was engaged in guarding oil wells against Bolshevik attacks. He was demobilised in September 1919, and holds the General Service and Victory Medals.
47, Cork Street, Camberwell, S.E.5.   Z1972

DUFFIELD, J. W., Private, Royal Fusiliers.
He joined in October 1916 and in the following January was drafted overseas. During his service on the Western Front he was engaged in the fighting at Arras, Vimy Ridge and Bullecourt. He subsequently was in action at Messines, where he was unfortunately killed in June 1917. He was entitled to the General Service and Victory Medals.
3, Morecambe Street, Walworth, S.E.17.   Z1971

DUGDALE, A. R., Private, Queen's Own (Royal West Kent Regiment).
He joined in May 1916 on attaining military age and in February of the following year was drafted to Egypt. He served in many engagements during the Advance through Palestine, and was sent to France in 1918. Whilst on the Western Front he took part in the Allied Advance into Germany and was demobilised after the cessation of hostilities. He rejoined in June 1919 and was still serving in 1920. He holds the General Service and Victory Medals.
6A, Granby Buildings, Broad Street, Lambeth Walk, S.E.11. Z24428

DUGGAN, J., Bandsman, 1st Oxfordshire and Buckinghamshire Light Infantry.
A serving soldier, he was stationed in India at the commencement of hostilities and was drafted to Mesopotamia. He fought in many engagements of note and was taken prisoner at the Capture of Kut-el-Amara. He subsequently died in captivity owing to hardships and exposure, and was entitled to the General Service and Victory Medals.
37, Montgomery Road, Chiswick, W.4.   6901A

DUKE, F. C., Private, Royal Fusiliers.

He volunteered in June 1915 and was shortly afterward drafted overseas and saw much service in various sectors of the Western Front until wounded in 1916. On recovery he proceeded to East Africa and fought in many important engagements. In 1917, returning to France, he was in action at Arras and throughout the German Offensive and Allied Advance of 1918. After the cessation of hostilities he was sent into Germany with the Army of Occupation and served there until, returning to England, he was demobilised in February 1919. He holds the 1914-15 Star and the General Service and Victory Medals.
20, Church Road, Battersea, S.W.11.   Z1973

DUKE, G., Corporal, 8th East Surrey Regiment.

He volunteered in February 1915 and was sent to France four months later and fought in many important engagements, including those at the Somme, Ypres, Arras and Cambrai. He was also in action throughout the German Offensive and subsequent Allied Advance in 1918, and was three times wounded during his service overseas. He was demobilised in March 1919, and holds the 1914-15 Star, and the General Service and Victory Medals.
13, Westhall Road, Camberwell, S.E.5.   Z1974

DUKE, W. G., Private, 4th (Queen's Own) Hussars.

A serving soldier, having enlisted in May 1912, he was mobilised at the outbreak of war and drafted to France in August 1914. He fought in the Retreat from Mons and the subsequent Battles of Ypres, Loos, the Somme, Arras and was wounded at Epéhy in June 1917. He was sent to England, where he received hospital treatment and on recovery returned to the Western Front. He took part in the Retreat and Advance of 1918, and after the signing of the Armistice proceeded to Germany with the Army of Occupation and was stationed at Cologne. Demobilised in May 1919, he holds the Mons Star, and the General Service and Victory Medals.
2, Pomfret Road, Camberwell, S.E.5.   Z5942

DULAKE, S. H., Driver, R.F.A.

He volunteered in October 1914 and embarking for France in the following May served with his Battery in the Battles of Loos, Vimy Ridge, the Somme, Arras, Monchy and Cambrai. He was also in action on the Aisne, and at Amiens, Epéhy and other places during the Retreat and Advance of 1918. He was demobilised in January 1919, and holds the 1914-15 Star, and the General Service and Victory Medals.
79, Trafalgar Road, Peckham, S.E.15.   Z3440

DUNCAN, E. E. E., Private, Argyll and Sutherland Highlanders.

He volunteered in October 1914 and at the conclusion of his training was engaged on important duties with his unit at various stations. He did good work, but owing to medical unfitness was unable to secure his transfer overseas and was demobilised in January 1919.
19, Flaxman Road, Camberwell, S.E.5.   Z5943

DUNCAN, R. J., British Red Cross Society.

Prior to the war he served in the Royal Navy for a number of years and on the outbreak of hostilities volunteered in the British Red Cross Society. He acted as a cook at King George's Hospital, Stamford Street, Waterloo, and rendered valuable services in that capacity for upwards of five years. Demobilised in 1919, he holds the Egyptian Medal (1882-89) and Khedive's Star, the India General Service Medal with Clasp, Burma, 1885-87) and the West African Medal (1890-1900).
47, Paradise Street, Lambeth, S.E.11.   Z25757

DUNCOMBE, H., Private, Labour Corps.

He joined in March 1917 and in the same month was drafted to the Western Front, where he did good work until the termination of hostilities. He was engaged on road making, on ammunition dumps and in the transport of supplies to the forward areas in various sectors. Demobilised in February 1919, he holds the General Service and Victory Medals.
117, Culvert Road, Battersea, S.W.11.   Z1975

DUNK, E., Driver, R.F.A.

Volunteering in October 1915 he was drafted to the Western Front in the following May. He there took part in many important engagements and served in various sectors until the cessation of hostilities. After the Armistice he returned to England and was demobilised in March 1919. He holds the General Service and Victory Medals.
28, Rockley Road, West Kensington, W.14.   11815A

DUNK, H. W., L/Corporal, Royal Dublin Fusiliers.

He volunteered in September 1914 and in the following year proceeded to Gallipoli. He fought in the Landing at Suvla Bay and in several other operations on the Peninsula until invalided home owing to illness. On recovery he was sent to the Western Front early in 1916 and was engaged in heavy fighting in the Somme sector. He was killed in action near Albert in March 1916, and was entitled to the 1914-15 Star, and the General Service and Victory Medals.
130, Aylesbury Road, Walworth, S.E.17.   Z1976

DUNKLEY, A., Corporal, 8th London Regiment (Post Office Rifles).

Volunteering in 1914 he was sent to the Western Front in the following year and took part in the Battles of Ypres and the Somme, where he was wounded and in consequence invalided to hospital in England. Rejoining his unit after recovery he was in action in several engagements during the Retreat and Advance of 1918. He returned home for demobilisation in 1919, and holds the 1914-15 Star, and the General Service and Victory Medals.
8, Mundella Road, Wandsworth, S.W.8.   Z1978

DUNKLEY, J. C., Private, Royal Fusiliers.

He volunteered in February 1915 and proceeded to France in the following year, where he served in various sectors and took part in the operations on the Somme. He was unfortunately killed in action on July 1st, 1916, near Gommecourt and was buried in that village. He was entitled to the General Service and Victory Medals.
55, Motley Street, Wandsworth Road, S.W.8.   Z1977

DUNN, C., Private, 1st Devonshire Regiment.

Joining in February 1918 he completed his training and was engaged on important duties with his unit. He rendered valuable services but was unsuccessful in obtaining a transfer to a theatre of war before the termination of hostilities and in February 1920 was sent to Ireland, where he was still serving later in that year.
9, Sugden Street, Camberwell, S.E.5.   Z5746A

DUNN, D., Leading Stoker, Royal Navy.

He was serving in the Royal Navy aboard H.M.S. "Champion" when war broke out and rendered valuable services throughout the course of hostilities. His ship was in action in the Battles off the Falkland Islands, Heligoland Bight, Dogger Bank, the Kattegat, Jutland and in the operations at Ostend, and was on special duty at Scapa Flow. After the Armistice he was transferred to H.M.S. "Ajax" and in 1920 was serving in that vessel in the Mediterranean. He holds the 1914-15 Star, and the General Service and Victory Medals (with four clasps).
29, Darwin Street, Walworth, S.E.17.   Z1979

DUNN, H. S., Private, Royal Fusiliers.

Volunteering in January 1915 he was drafted to the Western Front later in that year and fought in several engagements, including the actions at Hill 60, the Somme and Ypres. He was severely wounded at Bullecourt and invalided home to hospital. After his recovery he was transferred to the R.A.S.C. and on account of his wounds was retained by that unit on home service. He was demobilised in June 1919, and holds the 1914-15 Star, and the General Service and Victory Medals.
210, Beresford Street, Camberwell Road, S.E.5.   Z1980

DUNN, J., A.B., Royal Navy.

He joined in October 1916 and was posted to H.M.S. "Boadicea," which vessel was engaged on important mine-laying duties in the North Sea and off the East Coast. With his ship he served in the fighting at Heligoland Bight and during the Raid on Zeebrugge. He was demobilised in January 1919, and holds the General Service and Victory Medals.
37, McKerrell Road, Peckham, S.E.15.   Z5939

DUNN, W., Private, 2/5th Lincolnshire Regiment.

He volunteered in November 1915 and embarking for the Western Front in the following year was engaged in heavy fighting in the Battles of the Somme, Arras and other operations, and was taken prisoner at Hardecourt in April 1917. Held in captivity at Freidrichsfeld Camp in Germany he was repatriated after the Armistice and demobilised in December 1918. He holds the General Service and Victory Medals.
9, Sugden Street, Camberwell, S.E.5.   Z5746B

DUNN, W., Private, R.A.S.C.

Joining in 1916 he was sent to France on the completion of his training and served until the end of the war. Whilst overseas he was engaged on important duties in connection with the transport of supplies to the advanced areas and rendered valuable services. He returned home for demobilisation in March 1919, and holds the General Service and Victory Medals.
91, Fielding Road, Bedford Park, W.4.   7658C

DURBRIDGE, M. (Miss), Special War Worker.

This lady offered her services after the outbreak of war and was engaged by Messrs. Clisby, Falcon Road, Battersea, for important work in connection with rationing. She carried out her duties with a high degree of efficiency for three years and rendered valuable services.
80, Henley Street, Battersea, S.W.11.   Z6194

DURGAN, G. C., Private, R.A.V.C.

Volunteering in November 1915 he proceeded to the Western Front in the following year and was engaged on important duties in the 7th and 8th Veterinary Hospitals at Amiens and Rouen. He served until the end of hostilities and was then sent with the Army of Occupation to Germany and stationed at Cologne. He was demobilised in October 1919 on his return to England, and holds the General Service and Victory Medals.
54, Pullcross Road, Brixton Road, S.W.9.   Z1982

DURHAM, H. A., Rifleman, 5th Rifle Brigade.
He joined in 1917 and after completing his training was sent to the Western Front, where he was engaged in heavy fighting in various sectors and was in action in many important battles during the Retreat and Advance of 1918. He returned to England after the Armistice and was demobilised in 1919, and holds the General Service and Victory Medals.
120, East Surrey Grove, Peckham, S.E.15.   Z5237

DURRANT, W. J., Sergt., 2nd Queen's (Royal West Surrey Regiment).
He volunteered in February 1915 and four months later embarked for France, where he was in action during the Battle of the Somme and in many other important engagements. In June 1917 he was sent to Italy and was engaged on important duties in that theatre of war until his return home owing to illness. Admitted to hospital he died from the effects of his illness and was buried at Forest Hill Cemetery. He was entitled to the 1914–15 Star, and the General Service and Victory Medals.
17, Brisbane Street, Camberwell, S.E.5.   Z3071

DUTFIELD, E. D., A.B., Royal Navy.
Volunteering in August 1915 he was posted to H.M.S. " Queen " and served aboard that vessel in the Mediterranean, the Dardanelles and other waters. His ship had several encounters with enemy vessels off the Italian Coast and was in action during the operations in the Dardanelles. Demobilised in June 1919, he holds the 1914–15 Star, and the General Service and Victory Medals.
37, Spencer Street, Battersea, S.W.11.   Z1983A

DUTFIELD, S. J., A.B., Royal Navy.
He volunteered in August 1915 and served in several ships during the war. Posted to H.M.S. " Queen " he was aboard that vessel while she was in action off the Italian Coast. She was also engaged in the bombardment of the forts in the Dardanelles and was on special duty in other waters. He was demobilised in June 1919, and holds the 1914–15 Star, and the General Service and Victory Medals.
37, Spencer Street, Battersea, S.W.11.   Z1983B

DUTTON, A., Private, 3rd Middlesex Regiment.
Joining the London Cyclist Battalion in December 1916 he was shortly afterwards drafted to India and there took part in the Waziristan Campaign on the North-West Frontier. In March 1919 whilst still in India he re-engaged in the 3rd Middlesex Regiment and the following month returned to England. After a short period of home service he was sent to Germany with the Army of Occupation and in 1920 was still serving. He holds the General Service and Victory Medals.
13, Henry Street, Kennington, S.E.11.   Z24765

DWYER, E., Rifleman, King's Royal Rifle Corps.
Volunteering in August 1914 he proceeded to the Western Front in the following December and served in various sectors. He was engaged in heavy fighting until severely wounded in the Battle of Loos and invalided to hospital in England. He was discharged on account of his wounds in February 1916 being medically unfit for further service. He holds the 1914–15 Star, and the General Service and Victory Medals.
12, Byam Street, Townmead Road, S.W.6.   21311A

DWYER, E. (Junior), Private, Middlesex Regiment.
He joined in November 1916 on attaining military age and in the following March embarked for France. Whilst in this theatre of war he was in action during several engagements, including the Battles of Arras, Ypres and Cambrai, and suffered from shell-shock, as a result of which he was admitted to hospital. He returned home for demobilisation in November 1919, and holds the General Service and Victory Medals.
12, Byam Street, Townmead Road, S.W.6.   21311B

DYE, A., Private, 7th Royal Fusiliers.
Joining in January 1917 he was sent overseas in the following December and saw much service on the Western Front. He was engaged in many operations with his Battalion in various sectors and fought in the Battle of the Somme and during the Retreat and Advance of 1918. Returning to England after the Armistice he served at home for a time and again proceeded to France, where he was still serving in 1920. He holds the General Service and Victory Medals.
28, Henley Street, Battersea, S.W.11.   Z1985

DYE, A. E., Rifleman, Rifle Brigade.
He volunteered in March 1915 and later in the same year embarked for France. There he was in action in the Battles of Loos, St. Eloi and Ypres, and severely wounded at Hooge. Admitted into hospital at Etaples he was sent to the Base on recovery and later to England, where he served until discharged on account of service in September 1918. He holds the 1914–15 Star, and the General Service and Victory Medals.
27, Dorset Road, Clapham Road, S.W.8.   Z1984

DYE, D. T., Rifleman, 13th King's Royal Rifle Corps·
Volunteering in September 1914 he was drafted to France in the following January and fought in the Battles of Neuve Chapelle, Hill 60, Ypres, Vimy Ridge and the Somme. He was sent to Italy in November 1917 and served in the Advance on the Piave and on the Asiago Plateaux, and returning to the Western Front took part in several operations until the cessation of hostilities. He was demobilised in March 1919, and holds the 1914–15 Star, and the General Service and Victory Medals.
82, Nelson's Row, Clapham, S.W.4.   Z1986

DYE, E. J., Private, Queen's (Royal West Surrey Regiment).
He volunteered in November 1914 and in the following August embarked for France. Whilst in this theatre of war he fought in the Battle of Loos and other important engagements and owing to illness was invalided home in July 1916. Transferred to the Royal Scots in February 1917 he served with that Regiment in Ireland until his demobilisation in April 1919. He holds the 1914–15 Star, and the General Service and Victory Medals.
26, Chumleigh Street, Camberwell, S.E.5.   Z5067

DYMOND, H. E., Private, East Lancashire Regiment
He volunteered in March 1915 and three months later proceeded to the Western Front. There he was engaged in heavy fighting in the Battles of Loos, Ypres, Albert, Vimy Ridge, the Somme, Arras, Lens, Cambrai, and during the Retreat and Advance of 1918. During his service he was wounded near Ypres in 1917. He was demobilised in April 1919, and holds the 1914–15 Star, and the General Service and Victory Medals.
87, Darwin Street, Walworth, S.E.17.   Z1987

DYMOTT, W. J., 1st Air Mechanic, R.A.F.
Volunteering in April 1915 in the R.N.A.S. he completed his training and was then engaged with his Squadron on important coastal defence duties in the Eastern Counties. Later he was engaged on duties in connection with the searchlights at the Naval Base, Lowestoft. He rendered valuable services and owing to his duties was unable to obtain a transfer overseas. In January 1919 he was demobilised.
97, Battersea Bridge Road, S.W.11.   Z1988

DYNE, F. G., Rifleman, 17th London Regiment (Rifles).
He joined in May 1918 and on completion of his training served with his Battalion at various stations on important duties. He did much good work but was not successful in obtaining his transfer overseas before the cessation of hostilities. After the Armistice however he was sent to France on November 19th, 1918, and was employed on special work until the following year. He returned home and was demobilised in March 1920.
25, Gratton Road, West Kensington, W.14.   T12183B

DYNE, L., Rifleman, 2nd Rifle Brigade.
He joined in March 1917 and in the following December was sent to the Western Front. Whilst in this theatre of war he served with his Regiment in various sectors and was engaged in much severe fighting until the end of the war, and was gassed. He returned to England in December 1919 and was still serving in 1920. He holds the General Service and Victory Medals.
25, Gratton Road, West Kensington, W.14.   T12183B

E

EADE, A. G., L/Corporal, 8th Queen's (Royal West Surrey Regiment) and Labour Corps.
He joined in February 1917, and was sent overseas in the same month. Whilst on the Western Front he served in many important engagements, and was gassed and wounded on July 12th, 1918, in the Loos sector. Transferred to the Labour Corps on recovery he did valuable work building ammunition sheds at Vendecourt Wood, and laying light railways at Vermelles. He was demobilised in March 1919, and holds the General Service and Victory Medals.
32, Henley Street, Battersea, S.W.11.   Z1989

EADE, E. A., Gunner, R.F.A.
A serving soldier, he was drafted to France in 1914, shortly after the outbreak of hostilities. He took part in the Retreat from Mons, and the subsequent Battles of the Aisne and Ypres, being wounded on one occasion. He returned to England at the close of his long period of service, and was eventually discharged in May 1920. He holds the Mons Star, and the General Service and Victory Medals.
22, Rollo Street, Battersea, S.W.11.   Z1990

EADES, A., Rifleman, Rifle Brigade.

He joined in 1918, having served in the Boer war, and was drafted to France. Whilst in this theatre of war he was engaged in much heavy fighting, and was reported missing during the Allied Advance of 1918, and was later presumed to have been killed in action. He held the Queen's and King's South African Medals, and was entitled to the General Service and Victory Medals.

6, Porson Street, Wandsworth Road, S.W.8.   Z1444B

EAGAN, C., Petty Officer, R.A.F. (late R.N.A.S.)

He joined in June 1916, and being drafted to France in the same month was engaged in many parts of the line on the construction of aeroplane hangars. He returned to England in May 1917, and was stationed at various aerodromes, where he rendered excellent services until demobilised in June 1919. He holds the General Service and Victory Medals, and the Queen's and King's South African Medals for service in the Boer war.

9, Hazelmere Road, Peckham, S.E.15.   Z5953

EAGLE, J., 1st Air Mechanic, R.A.F.

He volunteered in February 1916, and embarked for the Western Front in the following month. He served in various sectors, including those of Albert, Vermelles, Messines, Ypres, the Somme and Cambrai, and saw much fighting during the Retreat and Advance of 1918. He was demobilised in July 1919, and holds the General Service and Victory Medals.

59, Albert Road, Peckham, S.E.15.   Z5954B

EAGLE, J., Special War Worker.

He volunteered in the early part of the war, but being ineligible for military service owing to medical unfitness joined the British Red Cross Depôt at Peckham in January 1916. He rendered valuable services in attendance on the sick and wounded, until after the cessation of hostilities, and discharged his duties in a most efficient and satisfactory manner.

59, Albert Road, Peckham, S.E.15.   Z5954A

EAGLEN, L. E. A. W., Rifleman, 21st London Regt. (1st Surrey Rifles).

Volunteering on the outbreak of war, he shortly afterwards proceeded to France, and fought in the Retreat from Mons, and the Battles of the Marne, the Aisne and Loos. He was severely wounded in the Ypres Salient in November 1915, and after hospital treatment and a period of light duty was invalided out of the Service in 1917. He holds the Mons Star, and the General Service and Victory Medals.

151, Gordon Road, Nunhead, S.E.15.   Z5947

EAMES, W. H., Driver, R.A.S.C.

He volunteered in October 1914, and from the following August until January 1916, was engaged on important transport duties on the Western Front, especially round Albert. He was then drafted to Egypt, and later served in the Palestine campaign, during which he was attached to the Royal Engineers taking pontoons to the forward areas, and was present at the Battles of Gaza and Jaffa. In April 1918 he returned to France, and did valuable work in connection with the supply of food to the troops, during the Retreat and Advance of that year. He was demobilised in July 1919, and holds the 1914–15 Star, and the General Service and Victory Medals.

16, Nunhead Green, Peckham, S.E.15.   Z6165

EARL, A. J., L/Corporal, Seaforth Highlanders.

He volunteered in December 1915, and in the following March was sent overseas. He fought in many engagements on the Western Front, including those at Ypres, on the Somme, and at Arras. At one period he served with the King's Royal Rifles. He was demobilised in February 1919, and holds the General Service and Victory Medals.

2, Glendall Street, Ferndale Road, S.W.9.   Z1991

EARL, F. G., Private, 1st Gloucestershire Regt.

Having previously served in the South African war, he re-enlisted in August 1914, and was immediately sent to France. He fought in numerous engagements until severely wounded at Ypres on October 31st, 1914. He was sent to hospital in England, and after receiving treatment was invalided out of the Service in June 1915. He holds the Queen's South African Medal, the 1914 Star, and the General Service and Victory Medals.

155, Hartington Road, Wandsworth Road, S.W.8.   Z1993

EARL, T., A.B., Royal Navy.

He was called up from the Reserve in April 1915, and after a period of home service was posted to H.M.S. "Queen." His ship was engaged in mine-sweeping off the Coast of Italy, and later in patrolling Egyptian waters. On recovering from malaria he served aboard H.M.T.B.D. "Liberty," which was engaged in mine-sweeping in the Persian Gulf. He was demobilised in May 1919, and holds the General Service and Victory Medals.

84, Sussex Road, Coldharbour Lane, S.W.9.   Z1992

EARL, W. J., Corporal, 2nd Queen's Own (Royal West Kent Regiment).

He was serving at the outbreak of war, and in January 1915 was drafted to Mesopotamia. In this theatre of war he took part in many engagements, and was wounded on three occasions. He returned to England in 1919, and was discharged in August of that year, having completed twenty-one years' service with the Colours. He holds the Queen's and King's South African Medals, the 1914–15 Star and the General Service and Victory Medals.

155, Hartington Road, Wandsworth Road, S.W.8.   Z1994

EARLE, E., Corporal, 20th Middlesex Regiment.

He joined in April 1917, on attaining military age, and was shortly afterwards drafted to France. He fought in many battles, including those at Ypres (III), Lens, Cambrai, Amiens, Bapaume, and the final Allied Advance of 1918. He was demobilised in November 1919, and holds the General Service and Victory Medals.

117, Chatham Street, Walworth, S.E.17.   Z1995

EARNEY, J., Private, Royal Fusiliers.

He volunteered in September 1914, and twelve months later was drafted to France. During his service on the Western Front he was engaged in the desperate fighting at Loos and St. Eloi, and also in the Battle of the Somme, where he was severely wounded. He was invalided to England in September 1916, and after receiving hospital treatment was discharged in September 1917, being medically unfit for further service. He holds the 1914–15 Star, and the General Service and Victory Medals.

20, Lavender Road, Battersea, S.W.11.   Z1996

EARTHY, C. A., L/Cpl., King's Royal Rifle Corps.

He joined in June 1916, and in the following August was sent to France. He fought in the Battles of the Somme I., Messines, Ypres, and Passchendaele. He was drafted in 1917 to Italy, where he took part in the fighting on the Piave, but in 1918 was sent again to the Western Front. He was in action at Cambrai, and was wounded and taken prisoner on March 23rd, 1918, during the Retreat. He was released after the signing of the Armistice, and was demobilised in September, holding the General Service and Victory Medals.

47, Heygate Street, Walworth, S.E.17.   Z1997

EASTER, G. H., 1st Stoker, R.N.

He was serving at the outbreak of war, and was engaged during the whole period of hostilities on highly dangerous work aboard Mystery Ships and Destroyers, the latter being employed on special convoy duties in many waters, including the North and Irish Seas. He holds the 1914–15 Star, and the General Service and Victory Medals, and was still serving in 1920. 41, Portslade Road, Wandsworth Road, S.W.8. Z1999

EASTER, R. J., Shoeing Smith, R.F.A.

He volunteered in May 1915, and in the following month was sent overseas. Whilst on the Western Front he served with the 12th Division at Arras and Ypres, and also in the Retreat and subsequent Advance of 1918. Towards the end of his service he was gassed and was sent to hospital at Ypres and Caux. He was demobilised in January 1919, and holds the 1914–15 Star, and the General Service and Victory Medals.

26, Renfrew Road, Kennington, S.E.11.   27386

EASTER, W. G., Private, M.G.C.

Joining in August 1916, he was sent in the following November to France. Whilst in this theatre of war, he fought in many engagements, but was unfortunately killed in action at St. Julien on July 31st, 1917. He was entitled to the General Service and Victory Medals.

"His life for his Country."

55, Cork Street, Camberwell, S.E.5.   Z1998A

EASTHER, H., Private, King's Shropshire Light Infantry.

He was serving at the outbreak of war, and was immediately drafted to France. He fought in the Retreat from Mons, and the subsequent Battles of the Marne and Ypres, and was wounded at St. Eloi. After being wounded a second time on the Somme, he took part in the operations at Arras, Vimy Ridge, and Passchendaele, and was wounded a third time at Cambrai. Upon his recovery he was transferred to the Royal Army Service Corps, but after serving for a short time he was discharged as medically unfit in February 1919. He holds the Mons Star, and the General Service and Victory Medals. 103, Mayall Road, Herne Hill, S.E.24.   Z2000

EASTLAND, W., Pte., Queen's Own (Royal West Kent Regiment).

He volunteered in 1915, and in the same year was drafted to Mesopotamia. In this theatre of war he was engaged in much heavy fighting in various sectors until the cessation of hostilities. Owing to illness he was invalided to hospital at Basra, where he unfortunately died on January 29th, 1919. He was entitled to the 1914–15 Star, and the General Service and Victory Medals.

"His life for his Country, his Soul to God."

32, Prairie Street, Battersea Park, S.W.8.   Z2001

EASTMAN, W., Private, Northumberland Fusiliers.
He joined in February 1916, and shortly afterwards was sent overseas. He fought in many sectors of the Western Front until taken prisoner at Armentières. He suffered many privations during his captivity until his release after the signing of the Armistice; he was demobilised in 1919, and holds the General Service and Victory Medals.
18 Basnett Road, Lavender Hill S.W.11. Z2002

EASTON, H. C., Sergt., 2nd Queen's (Royal West Surrey Regiment).
Mobilised from the Reserve at the outbreak of war, he was immediately drafted to the Western Front, and fought in the Retreat from Mons, and the Battles of the Marne, La Bassée and Ypres, where he was severely wounded. He was invalided home, but after his recovery returned to France, and was in action at Loos, Albert, Vimy Ridge, the Somme, Arras, Messines, Lens and Cambrai. In May 1918 he was discharged on completion of his period of service, and holds the Queen's and King's South African Medals, the Mons Star, and the General Service and Victory Medals.
14, Minnow Street, Walworth, S.E.17. Z2003

EASTON, T. C., Driver, R.F.A.
He joined in May 1917, and in the following October was sent to Mesopotamia. In this theatre of war he served at Amara Kut and Baghdad, and was present at the capture of Tekrit, thus taking part in the great engagements on the course of the Tigris. He returned to England after the cessation of hostilities, and was demobilised in February 1920, and holds the General Service and Victory Medals.
2A, Smith Street, Camberwell, S.E.5. Z2004

EATON, W. S., Private, 51st Bedfordshire Regiment.
He joined in May 1918, and at the conclusion of his training was drafted overseas. He served in Germany with the Army of Occupation, and was stationed on the Rhine. He was chiefly engaged in guarding German prisoners, and on out-post duty. He was demobilised in March 1920.
10, Cator Street, Peckham, S.E.15. Z4446

EDDELS, J., Corporal, Royal Marines.
Joining the Royal Army Service Corps in March 1915, he proceeded overseas in the same month and served on the Western Front for over a year. He was then transferred to the Royal Marines, and was engaged in the supervision of guns being sent to the Western Front. He was later engaged on transport duties to Russia, and was stationed with his ship in the Baltic. He was demobilised in November 1919, and holds the 1914-15 Star, and the General Service and Victory Medals.
23, Cunard Street, Camberwell, S.E.5. Z5068A

EDDELS, J. J., Pte., 10th Queen's (Royal West Surrey Regiment).
He volunteered in September 1915, and embarking for France four months later served there for a period of three years. During this period he fought in the Battles of the Somme, Arras, Ypres, and was wounded in August 1917. Returning to the Field on recovery, he was wounded again on March 22nd, 1918 on the Somme, and for the third time in the following September, during the Allied Advance. Invalided to hospital in England he was discharged as medically unfit for further service in February 1919, and in 1920 was still under medical treatment. He holds the General Service and Victory Medals.
23, Cunard Street, Camberwell, S.E.5. Z5068B

EDE, J. A., Rifleman, King's Royal Rifle Corps and Private, South Wales Borderers.
He joined in 1916, and after his training served in France for upwards of two years. During this time he was engaged in the fighting at the Somme, Arras, Passchendaele, Cambrai, Havrincourt Wood, and in the Retreat and Advance of 1918, and did good work as a Signaller. On one occasion he was gassed, but remained overseas until after the termination of hostilities. He was demobilised in 1919, and holds the General Service and Victory Medals.
21, Kirkwood Road, Nunhead, S.E.15. Z6164

EDEN, J. W., Private, 3/10th Middlesex Regiment.
Joining in May 1916, he was shortly afterwards sent to France. During his service on the Western Front he fought in many engagements and battles. He gave his life for the freedom of England in the Battle of Ypres on October 4th, 1917. He was entitled to the General Service and Victory Medals.
"A valiant soldier, with undaunted heart he breasted Life's last hill."
7, Overstone Road, Hammersmith, W.6. 11188B

EDEN, W. B., Rflmn, 17th London Regt. (Rifles).
He joined in June 1918, and was shortly afterwards sent to France. Whilst on the Western Front, he was engaged on important duties with his unit, being stationed at Boulogne. He was demobilised in October 1919, and holds the General Service and Victory Medals.
7, Overstone Road, Hammersmith, W.6. 11188A

EDGAR, E., Private, M.G.C.
Volunteering in July 1915, he was shortly afterwards drafted to the Western Front, and there took part in numerous engagements, including the Battles of Loos, St. Eloi, Albert, Ploegsteert Wood, the Somme, and the Retreat and Advance of 1918, during which he was gassed at Cambrai. After the Armistice he returned to England and was demobilised in January 1919. He holds the 1914-15 Star, and the General Service and Victory Medals.
3, Russell Road, Peckham, S.E.15. Z5377

EDGE, J. P. M., Private, 7th London Regiment.
He volunteered in October 1914, and in the following year proceeded overseas. He served for a time on the Western Front, where he was recommended for the Distinguished Conduct Medal for gallantry in the Field at Loos. He was afterwards drafted to Egypt and Salonika, and during the campaign in Palestine was wounded. He also served in Mesopotamia, but was invalided home and eventually discharged as medically unfit for further service in April 1918. He holds the 1914-15 Star, and the General Service and Victory Medals.
1, Viceroy Road, Guildford Road, S.W.8. Z2005

EDIS, E. C., Private, 1st Royal Inniskilling Fusiliers.
He was mobilised from the Reserve on the outbreak of war, and drafted to the Western Front in December 1915. Whilst overseas he fought in many important engagements, including the Battles of Albert, Arras, Ypres and Cambrai, and during operations at Passchendaele rendered valuable services in taking ammunition and supplies to the firing lines. He was demobilised in March 1919, and holds the 1914-15 Star, and the General Service and Victory Medals.
17, Mayall Road, Herne Hill, S.E.24. Z5069

EDMETT, B., Private, 2nd Somerset Light Infantry.
He volunteered in May 1915, and in the following February was drafted to India, where he saw considerable service with his Battalion and took part in the fighting on the North West Frontier. He returned to England after the signing of the Armistice and was demobilised in January 1920. He holds the India General Service Medal (with clasp, Afghanistan, N.W. Frontier, 1919), and the General Service and Victory Medals.
162, Cronin Road, Peckham, S.E.15. Z5378

EDMONDS, F., Trooper, Surrey Lancers (Queen Mary's Regiment).
Volunteering in October 1914, he crossed to France early in 1915, and was subsequently engaged in the fighting at Ypres and Loos. In 1916 he was transferred to Salonika, and did valuable work with his unit, during operations on the Struma and Doiran fronts. Early in 1918 he returned to France and served in the concluding stages of the war, after which he advanced into Germany with the Army of Occupation. He was demobilised in May 1919, after his return to England, and holds the 1914-15 Star, and the General Service and Victory Medals.
7A, Tunstall Road, Brixton Road, S.W.9. Z6166B

EDMONDS, G., Bombardier, R.F.A.
Volunteering in October 1915, he was sent to the Western Front early in the following year and took part in several important engagements, including those at Arras and Albert. He died gloriously on the Field of battle at Vimy Ridge in April 1917, and was entitled to the General Service and Victory Medals.
"Great deeds cannot die."
7A, Tunstall Road, Brixton Road, S.W.9. Z6166A

EDMONDS, J., Driver, R.F.A.
Volunteering in October 1914, he was drafted in the following year to France. During a long period of service he took part in the Battles of Ypres, Arras, Albert, Armentières, Bullecourt and others. Whilst on the Somme he contracted trench fever. He was invalided to England, and on his recovery was demobilised in February 1919. He holds the 1914-15 Star, and the General Service and Victory Medals.
53, Villa Street, Walworth, S.E.17. Z2006

EDMONDS, S. J., Sapper, R.E.
He volunteered in January 1915, having previously served in the South African War, and at the conclusion of his training was engaged on home defence at various stations with his unit. He did excellent work, but owing to ill-health he was invalided out of the Service in August 1918. He holds the Queen's and King's South African Medals.
8, Westbury Street, Wandsworth Road, S.W.8. Z2007

EDNEY, J. A., Gunner, R.F.A.
He volunteered in February 1915, and in the following November was drafted to India, thence to Mesopotamia. In this theatre of war he served in many engagements until July 1918, when he was invalided to hospital with dysentery, to which he unfortunately succumbed on July 17th, 1918. He was entitled to the 1914-15 Star, and the General Service and Victory Medals.
"His memory is cherished with pride."
114, Cator Street, Peckham, S.E.15. Z4447A

EDNEY, J. E., Rifleman, 26th London Regiment.
He joined in 1916, and proceeded overseas in the same year. During his service on the Western Front he was engaged in much fighting in various sectors until severely wounded in October 1917. He was taken to the Base hospital where he unfortunately died on November 1st, of that year. He was entitled to the General Service and Victory Medals.
" Whilst we remember the Sacrifice is not in vain."
114, Cator Street, Peckham, S.E.15.   Z4447B

EDNEY, J. H., Private, R.A.S.C.
Volunteering in April 1915, he was engaged with his unit on special transport duties at various stations. He did excellent work, but owing to ill-health was unable to obtain his transfer overseas, and was invalided out of the Service in October 1917.
114, Cator Street, Peckham, S.E.15.   Z4447C

EDRIDGE, H. J., Pte., Royal Inniskilling Fusiliers.
He joined in November 1916, and was immediately drafted to France. In this theatre of war he fought in many engagements, including those at Messines, and in the vicinity of Cambrai. He gave his life for King and Country at Cambrai, on November 13th, 1917, and was buried near the town. He was entitled to the General Service and Victory Medals.
" Great deeds cannot die."
37, Mostyn Road, Brixton S.W.9.   Z3449

EDWARD, F., Sergt., R.E. and Coldstream Guards.
Volunteering at the outbreak of hostilities, he was drafted to France in 1915. In this theatre of war he served in various sectors and was engaged in the fighting at Ypres, and on the Somme, and was wounded four times and gassed. He was demobilised in 1919, and holds the 1914–15 Star, and the General Service and Victory Medals.
69, Somerleyton Road, Coldharbour Lane, S.W.9.   Z3448A

EDWARD, H., Private, R.A.M.C.
He volunteered in 1915, and served with his unit at various stations until drafted to France in 1917. Whilst on the Western Front he was engaged on important duties in the Somme, Ypres and Arras sectors, and did very good work at the Casualty Clearing Stations, and was twice gassed. He was demobilised in 1919, and holds the General Service and Victory Medals.
69, Somerleyton Road, Coldharbour Lane, S.W.9.
     Z3448B

EDWARD, W., Private, R.A.S.C.
He volunteered in 1915, and in the same year was sent overseas. During his service on the Western Front he did very good work transporting rations and supplies to the front line trenches, and was constantly under heavy shell fire. He was demobilised in 1919, and holds the 1914–15 Star, and the General Service and Victory Medals.
69, Somerleyton Road, Coldharbour Lane, S.W.9.   Z3448C

EDWARDS, A. V., Gunner, R.F.A. and R.G.A.
He volunteered in January 1915, and in the same year was sent to France. He fought at Arras, Albert, Vimy Ridge, St. Quentin, the Somme and Ypres, but being badly gassed was invalided to England. On his recovery he was transferred to the Royal Garrison Artillery, and served on home defence duties until demobilised in February 1919. He holds the 1914–15 Star, and the General Service and Victory Medals.
51, Nursery Row, Brandon Street, Walworth, S.E.17.   2013

EDWARDS, B., Lieutenant, R.F.A.
He joined in 1916, and in the same year proceeded overseas. During his service on the Western Front he took a distinguished part in many engagements, including those during the Retreat and Advance of 1918, and was mentioned in Despatches in March 1918, for consistently good work in the Field. He died gloriously on the Field of Battle in the following September. He was entitled to the General Service and Victory Medals.
" A costly sacrifice upon the altar of freedom."
94, Hubert Grove, Landor Road, S.W.9.   Z2014

EDWARDS, C., Private. R.A.S.C. (M.T.)
Volunteering in October 1914, he was immediately drafted overseas. He served on important transport duties in many engagements on the Western Front, including those of the Somme, and was frequently under shell fire. He was demobilised in March 1919, and holds the 1914 Star, and the General Service and Victory Medals.
16, Alexandra Road, Kensington, W.14.   12085A

EDWARDS, C. H., Private, R.A.M.C.
He joined in March 1917, and in the following October was drafted to France. He was engaged with his unit on important duties tending the sick and wounded at the Base Hospital at Rouen, and he did very good work. He was demobilised in January 1919, and holds the General Service and Victory Medals.
51, Lavender Road, Battersea, S.W.11.   Z2010

EDWARDS, E., Driver, R.F.A.
Volunteering in August 1914, he was drafted to France in the same year, fought at the Battles of La Bassée, Ypres, where he was wounded in November 1914, Neuve Chapelle, Hill 60, Festubert, St. Eloi, and many others until hostilities ceased. He was present at the entry into Mons on November 11th, 1918. He later served with the Army of Occupation in Germany, and was stationed on the Rhine. He was demobilised in June 1919, and holds the 1914 Star, and the General Service and Victory Medals.
21, Nursery Street, Wandsworth Road, S.W.8.   Z2011A

EDWARDS, F., Rifleman, King's Royal Rifle Corps.
Volunteering in September 1915, he proceeded to the Western Front in the following year, and fought in several battles, including those of the Somme, Arras and Ypres. He was killed in action on December 29th, 1917, during the Battle of Cambrai, and was entitled to the General Service and Victory Medals.
" A valiant soldier, with undaunted heart he breasted life's last hill."
16, Victory Square, Camberwell, S.E.5.   Z5750

EDWARDS, J., L/Corporal, 4th Royal Fusiliers.
A Reservist, who had previously served in India, Somaliland and Thibet, during the Frontier War, he was mobilised in August 1914. He was drafted to France at once, and fought in the Retreat from Mons. He was wounded at La Bassée, but on his recovery rejoined his unit in the firing line. He gave his life for King and Country on June 18th, 1915, and was entitled to the Mons Star, and the General Service and Victory Medals.
" Great deeds cannot die.
They with the sun and moon renew their light for ever."
92, Clayton Road, Peckham, S.E.15.   Z6161

EDWARDS, J. C., Driver, R.A.S.C. (M.T.)
He volunteered in August 1915, and in the following October was sent to France. In this theatre of war he served on important duties with his Unit in various sectors, including those of the Somme, Bapaume, Vimy Ridge, Arras and Cambrai, and was wounded in 1918. He was demobilised in July 1919, and holds the 1914–15 Star, and the General Service and Victory Medals.
45, Lockington Road, Battersea Park Road, S.W.8.
     Z2009

EDWARDS, J. W., Rifleman, Rifle Brigade.
Volunteering in 1914, he served on important duties at various stations until drafted to France in 1916. He fought in many Battles, including those at Ypres, Loos, and the Somme, and was severely wounded. He was invalided to England, and after hospital treatment was discharged from the Service in 1917. He holds the General Service and Victory Medals.
28, Church Road, Battersea, S.W.11.   Z2012

EDWARDS, J. W., Driver, R.H.A.
He volunteered in 1915, and was later sent to France, where he served with his Battery and was in action in many engagements, and was wounded in 1917. On recovery he was sent to Egypt, where he was in action during the Advance through Palestine. After hostilities ceased he returned to England, and was demobilised in May 1919. He holds the General Service and Victory Medals.
21, Spencer Street, Battersea, S.W.11.   Z2008C

EDWARDS, P., Private, R.M.L.I.
He was serving at the outbreak of hostilities, and was later drafted to the Western Front, where he was in action at the Battles of Ypres, Cambrai and the Somme, and later, sent to West Africa, was engaged in much heavy fighting in that theatre of war. He also served aboard ship in various Naval engagements. He holds the 1914–15 Star, and the General Service and Victory Medals, and was still serving in 1920.
23, Pepler Road, Peckham, S.E.15.   Z3447

EDWARDS, R. G., Corporal, 37th Royal Fusiliers.
He joined in June 1916, and in the following month proceeded to France. In this theatre of war he served with his unit on important duties in various sectors, including those of Albert, Péronne, the Somme, and during the Retreat and Advance of 1918. He was demobilised in January 1919, and holds the General Service and Victory Medals.
6, Anley Road, West Kensington, W.14.   11816A

EDY, C., Corporal, R.E.
Volunteering in 1915, he was drafted in the same year to the Western Front. There he served in various sectors, and was engaged on important duties with his unit, and was in action at Loos, Vimy Ridge, the Somme, Beaumont-Hamel, Ypres, Cambrai and in the Retreat and Advance of 1918. He was demobilised in August 1919, and holds the 1914–15 Star, and the General Service and Victory Medals.
32, Oakden Street, Kennington, S.E.11.   Z27229

EDY, F. A., Private, Royal Defence Corps.
He joined in May 1918, being ineligible for service with the Colours, and at the conclusion of his training was engaged with his unit on special duties at various stations, and did very good work. He was demobilised in February 1919.
24, Linden Gardens, Chiswick, W.4. 5690A

EDY, J. C., Sergt., 13th London Regt. (Kensingtons).
He volunteered in August 1914, and was later sent overseas. He fought in many battles on the Western Front, and was afterwards drafted to Salonika, where he was engaged in much fighting until he proceeded to Egypt, and was in action in the Advance through Palestine, and was wounded. He returned to England, and was demobilised in July 1919, and holds the General Service and Victory Medals.
24, Linden Gardens, Chiswick, W.4. 5690C

EDY, W. A., Private, H.A.C.
Volunteering in August 1915, he was later sent overseas. During his service on the Western Front he was engaged in much fighting and fought in many important battles, and was wounded. He was invalided to England, and after receiving medical treatment was discharged on account of service in November 1916, and holds the General Service and Victory Medals.
24, Linden Gardens, Chiswick, W.4. 5690B

EELES, A., Rifleman, 12th London Regt. (Rangers).
He joined in September 1916, and early in the following year was drafted to France. In this theatre of war he fought in many engagements with his Battalion and was severely wounded at the Battle of Arras. Unfortunately his injuries proved fatal, and he died on April 20th, 1917. He was entitled to the General Serrvice and Victoy Medals.
" A costly sacrifice upon the altar of freedom."
48, St. Philip Street, Battersea Park ,S.W.8. Z2015

EELES, B. J., Private, 8th East Surrey Regiment.
He volunteered in September 1914, and in the following year was drafted to France. Whilst on the Western Front he fought in many engagements, including those at Ypres, and on the Somme. Owing to ill-health in 1916, he was invalided to England where he received hospital treatment, and on recovery returned to France and rejoined his Battalion in the firing line, and again fought in many engagements. In October 1917 he gave his life for King and Country during operations on the Somme. He was entitled to the 1914-15 Star, and the General Service and Victory Medals.
" He died the noblest death a man may die,
Fighting for God and right and liberty."
11, Chalmers Street, Wandsworth Road, S.W.8. Z2016

EGERTON, H., Corporal, R.A.F.
He joined in March 1917, having previously rendered valuable services as a Special Constable. He was drafted to France in August 1918, and was engaged with his Squadron on special duties as storeman at various aerodromes on the Western Front. He did very good work and was demobilised in April 1919. He holds the General Service and Victory Medals.
77, Hillier Road, Wandsworth Common, S.W.11. Z3081

EGGLETON, W. C., 1st Class Stoker, R.N.
He joined the Royal Navy in January 1913, and at the outbreak of war was serving in H.M.S. " Cochrane." His ship was engaged on special duties with the Grand Fleet in the North Sea, and took part in the Battle of Jutland and had many narrow escapes. He holds the 1914-15 Star, and the General Service and Victory Medals, and was serving in submarine service in 1920.
179, Warham Street, Camberwell, S.E.5. Z2017

EGLINGTON, H. J., L/Cpl., 21st London Regiment (1st Surrey Rifles).
Volunteering in July 1915, he was drafted to France in the following year. During his service on the Western Front he was engaged in fighting at the Battles of the Somme, Ypres, Péronne, Cambrai, and the Retreat and Allied Advance of 1918. After the cessation of hostilities he served with the Army of Occupation on the Belgian Frontier, and was stationed at Namur. He was demobilised in February 1919, and holds the General Service and Victory Medals.
64, Somerleyton Road, Coldharbour Lane, S.W.9. Z3063B

ELAM, S. S., Private, Volunteer Training Corps.
Being ineligible for service with the Colours he joined the Volunteer Training Corps in June 1916, and at the conclusion of his training was engaged with his unit on important duties at various stations. He did very good work during air raids and was demobilised in December 1919.
100, St. George's Road, Peckham, S.E.15. Z5594

ELCOMBE-BREACH, C. B., A.B., Royal Navy.
He joined in December 1916, and at the conclusion of his training was posted to H.M.S. " Sapphire." His ship was employed on special patrol and convoy duties off the coasts of India and in other waters, and later on service in the Black Sea. He holds the General Service and Victory Medals, and was still serving in 1920.
40, Porten Road, W. Kensington, W.14. 12479C

ELDERFIELD, W. R., Gunner, R.F.A.
He was mobilised with the Territorials at the outbreak of war, and early in 1915 was drafted to France. Whilst on the Western Front he was in action at the Battles of the Somme, Arras, Ypres, Cambrai and was wounded in the vicinity of Arras in 1918. He was invalided to England, and on recovery served on home duties until demobilised in January 1919. He holds the 1914-15 Star, and the General Service and Victory Medals.
120, Beresford Street, Camberwell, S.E.5. Z2018

ELDRIDGE, G., Gunner, R.F.A.
He volunteered in 1915, and on completing his training served at various stations with his unit, engaged on important guard and other duties. He did good work, but was found to be medically unfit, and was invalided out of the Service later in 1915.
29, Urswicke Road, Battersea, S.W.11. Z2019

ELEY, E., Private, Royal Fusiliers.
Volunteering in September 1914, he proceeded overseas three months later. During his service on the Western Front he was in action in many important engagements, including those at Neuve Chapelle, Hill 60, Ypres (II), and Loos, where he was wounded. Admitted into hospital he subsequently died from his injuries in September 1915, and was entitled to the 1914-15 Star, and the General Service and Victory Medals.
" A costly sacrifice upon the altar of freedom."
52, Elsted Street, Walworth, S.E.17. Z2020B

ELGOOD, C. F., Driver, R.F.A.
Volunteering in May 1915, he shortly afterwards embarked for the Western Front, and fought in the Battles of Ypres (II), Ploegsteert, the Somme, Messines, Passchendaele, Cambrai, and throughout the German Offensive and subsequent Allied Advance of 1918. He returned to England and was demobilised in June 1919, and holds the 1914-15 Star, and the General Service and Victory Medals.
6, Barmore Street, Battersea, S.W.11. Z2021

ELKINS, W. E., Driver, R.F.A.
Volunteering in August 1914, he was drafted to France in the following February, and fought in many important engagements in all parts of the line, and was wounded on the Somme front. On recovery he rejoined his unit and was in action throughout the Retreat and Advance of 1918, and was demobilised in March 1919. He holds the 1914-15 Star, and the General Service and Victory Medals.
144, Duke Road, Chiswick, W.4. 5664C

ELLEN, A. W., A.B., Royal Navy.
He joined the Service in October 1912, and on the declaration of hostilities was posted to H.M.S. " Birkenhead," in which he was in action in the Battles of Heligoland Bight and the Dogger Bank. Later he was transferred to H.M.S. " Liverpool " and was in this ship when she fought in the Battle of Jutland, and later did good work on patrol and other duties. He was serving in 1920 aboard H.M.S. " Ursula," and holds the 1914-15 Star, and the General Service and Victory Medals.
56, Hornby Road, Peckham, S.E.15. Z5948

ELLENS, J. H., Gunner, R.F.A.
He joined in November 1917, and on completion of his training served at various stations until drafted overseas in the following May. He was in action in many engagements during the German Offensive, and was unfortunately killed in action in Flanders in July 1918. He was entitled to the General Service and Victory Medals.
" He died the noblest death a man may die,
Fighting for God and right and liberty."
16, Camellia Street, Wandsworth Road, S.W.8. Z2022

ELLER, F. A., Pte., Queen's (Royal West Surrey Regiment).
He volunteered in September 1914, and in the following year was sent to France. During his service on the Western Front he fought in many engagements, including the Battles of Ypres, Loos, Vermelles, Vimy Ridge, the Somme and Arras. Owing to ill-health he was admitted to hospital at Rouen, and was later sent to England and invalided out of the Service in October 1916. He holds the 1914-15 Star, and the General Service and Victory Medals.
36, Longcroft Road, Camberwell, S.E.5. Z5379

ELLERINGTON, H., Private, R.A.S.C. (M.T.)
He volunteered in 1914, and later in the same year was drafted to France. Here he served on important transport duties in the forward areas, and was present at the Retreat from Mons and the subsequent Battles of the Marne, the Aisne, Arras and the Somme. Owing to ill-health he was invalided to England, and discharged as medically unfit for further service in 1916. He then volunteered for work of National importance and was engaged at Winchester Wireless Schools until the end of the war. He holds the Mons Star, and the General Service and Victory Medals.
11, Baker Street, Brixton, S.W.9. Z5239

ELLERY, J., L/Cpl., King's Royal Rifle Corps.
He joined in November 1916, and embarked for the Western Front in the following May. He saw much service in various parts of the line, and was wounded at Messines. Admitted into hospital at Wimereux he subsequently succumbed to his injuries in June 1917, and was entitled to the General Service and Victory Medals.
"The path of duty was the way to glory."
16, Kersley Street, Battersea, S.W.11. Z2023

ELLICOTT, S. A., Leading Aircraftsman, R.A.F.
He joined in 1916, on attaining military age and at the conclusion of his training was drafted to Egypt. He was engaged with his Squadron at various aerodromes on special duties connected with the assembling of aero engines and in the repair shops, and he did excellent work. He returned to England in 1918 and was stationed at Sheffield for a time. He was later sent to Henlow, and in 1920 was still serving there. He holds the General Service and Victory Medals.
51, Copeland Road, Peckham Rye, S.E.15. Z5596

ELLINGHAM, C. J., Seaman, Merchant Service.
He joined the Merchant Service in May 1905, and throughout the War served in various ships which were engaged on important transport duties from England to France, and other theatres of war. He was aboard the "Dundee" when she was torpedoed and sunk on January 31st, 1917, and was also serving in the "Silverdale" when she was sunk on February 9th, 1918, but he was fortunately rescued. He rendered valuable services and in 1920 was still serving. He holds the General Service and Mercantile Marine War Medals.
47, Riverhall Street, Wandsworth Road, S.W.8. Z2024

ELLIOT, C. J., Sergt., King's Own (Royal Lancaster Regiment).
A serving soldier, he was mobilised at the outbreak of hostilities and served at various depôts on important instructional duties to the recruits of the New Armies. He was unsuccessful in obtaining his transfer overseas, but rendered excellent services until discharged in March 1919. He holds the Queen's and King's South African Medals for service in the Boer War, and the Indian General Service Medal for service on the North Western Frontier.
38, Searles Road, New Kent Road, S.E.1. Z2025

ELLIOT, E. J., 2nd Lieutenant, R.A.S.C. (M.T.)
Volunteering in October 1914, he was sent to the Western Front in the same year, and there took part in many engagements including the actions at Ypres, the Somme and Passchendaele. In July 1917, when a Sergeant, he was mentioned in Despatches for devotion to duty, and excellent work in taking charge of the 157th Siege Battery Ammunition Column in the Ypres sector. In April 1918 he was gassed at Marles-les-Mines, and in the following September left his unit to take up a Commission. He was demobilised in January 1920, and holds the 1914-15 Star, and the General Service and Victory Medals.
109, Brayard's Road, Peckham, S.E.15. 5380A

ELLIOT, E. P., Corporal, R.A.P.C.
He joined in February 1918, and was engaged on clerical duties at Woolwich, where he rendered valuable services with his unit. Owing to ill-health he was unable to obtain his transfer overseas, and was subsequently demobilised in December 1919.
109, Brayard's Road, Peckham, S.E.15. 5380B

ELLIOTT, F., Orderly, V.A.D.
He volunteered in 1915, and served at various hospitals engaged on important duties attending to the sick and wounded troops. He was for the most part employed on night duty, and rendered valuable services during air-raids. He was discharged in 1919.
9, Galena Road, Hammersmith, W.6. 11810B

ELLIOTT, F. C., Private, Queen's (Royal West Surrey Regiment).
He joined in 1918, and completing his training, was stationed at various depôts on guard and other important duties with his unit. He rendered excellent services, but despite his efforts, was unsuccessful in obtaining his transfer overseas prior to the signing of the Armistice. After the cessation of hostilities, however, he embarked for France and proceeded into Germany with the Army of Occupation and served on the Rhine until 1920. He then returned to England, and was demobilised later in the year.
9, Galena Road, Hammersmith, W.6. 11810A

ELLIOTT, G. W., Corporal, R.A.S.C. (M.T.)
Joining in May 1917, he was sent to the Western Front later in the same year, and served in the forward areas engaged on duties connected with the transport of ammunition and supplies to the front lines. He was present at heavy fighting throughout the German Offensive and Allied Advance of 1918, and did excellent work. Returning to England he was demobilised in March 1919, and holds the General Service and Victory Medals.
68, Glenthorne Road, Hammersmith, W.6. 11802B

ELLIOTT, J., Private, 3rd Royal Fusiliers.
He volunteered in August 1914, and early in the following year was drafted to the Western Front. Here he fought in many important battles, including that of Hill 60, and was severely wounded in March 1915. Invalided to England he received hospital treatment and was discharged unfit for further service in April 1915. He holds the 1914-15 Star, and the General Service and Victory Medals.
67, Portslade Road, Wandsworth Road, S.W.8. Z2026

ELLIOTT, J. B. G., 2nd Lieutenant, 8th London Regt. (Post Office Rifles) and Royal Fusiliers.
He volunteered in August 1914, and was drafted to the Western Front shortly afterwards, and fought in many engagements, including those at Festubert and Loos, and was granted a commission for devotion to duty and gallantry in the Field. He was gazetted to the Royal Fusiliers, and was in action in many parts of the line. He made the supreme sacrifice, being killed in action in Flanders on August 16th, 1917, and was entitled to the 1914-15 Star, and the General Service and Victory Medals.
"His life for his Country."
32, Spencer Street, Battersea, S.W.11. Z2027

ELLIOTT, J. H., Staff-Sergt., 7th R.A.V.C.
Volunteering at the outbreak of hostilities he was almost immediately drafted to France, where he served with his unit on important duties, tending the sick and wounded horses. He did very good work until demobilised in April 1919, and holds the 1914 Star, and the General Service and Victory Medals.
36, Moncrieff Street, Rye Lane, S.E.15. Z5595

ELLIOTT, R., Special War Worker.
Ineligible for service with the Colours on account of his age, he volunteered for work of National importance, and was employed by Messrs. Harbrow, Builders and Contractors. He was sent to Mudros in 1915, and was engaged in erecting hospitals and huts on the island during the operations at Gallipoli. He returned to England in 1916, having rendered valuable services.
43, Bournemouth Road, Rye Lane, S.E.15. Z5751B

ELLIS, A. H., Trooper, 10th Australian Light Horse.
He volunteered at the outbreak of war, and embarked for Egypt in the following year. He fought in many engagements during the Advance through Sinai and Palestine, and was present at the capture of Jerusalem. He was unfortunately killed in action on May 3rd, 1918, and was entitled to the 1914-15 Star, and the General Service and Victory Medals.
"Steals on the ear the distant triumph song."
1, Colworth Grove, Walworth, S.E.17. Z2028

ELLIS, C., Driver, R.F.A.
He volunteered at the commencement of hostilities, and until sent to the Western Front in February 1917, was engaged on home defence duties of an important nature. Whilst overseas, he was in action at Arras, Vimy Ridge, Messines Ridge, Passchendaele, Cambrai, the Somme, Bapaume and Havrincourt Wood. In June 1918 he was taken prisoner at Villers-Bretonneux, but in a counter attack by the Australians he was recovered. He was demobilised in February 1919, after returning to England, and holds the General Service and Victory Medals.
21, Evelina Road, Peckham, S.E.15. Z6162A
Z6163A

ELLIS, C. J., Bombardier, R.F.A.
He volunteered in April 1915, and embarked for France later in the same year. During his service on the Western Front he was in action at Arras, Albert, Lens, Loos, Hill 60 and Vimy Ridge. Owing to ill-health he was invalided to hospital and on recovery returned to the front lines, and was again engaged in heavy fighting. Later, whilst on leave in England he was ill, and after protracted hospital treatment was discharged unfit for further service in June 1918. He holds the 1914-15 Star, and the General Service and Victory Medals.
28, Shorncliffe Road, Old Kent Road, S.E.1. Z1334A

ELLIS, C. R. J., Fitter, R.F.A.
He enlisted in 1899, and after being mobilised at the commencement of hostilities was drafted to Mesopotamia in 1915. He fought in many important engagements, and was taken prisoner at the Battle of Kut-el-Amara in December 1915. He unhappily died in captivity in October 1916, and was entitled to the 1914-15 Star, and the General Service and Victory Medals.
"His life for his Country, his soul to God."
14, D Block, Lewis Trust Buildings, Warner Road, Camberwell, S.E.5. Z5950

ELLIS, G., L/Corporal, 7th London Regiment.
Volunteering in June 1915, he proceeded to France later in the same year, and saw much service in all parts of the line, fighting in many important engagements. He was unfortunately killed in action on November 30th, 1917, and was entitled to the 1914–15 Star, and the General Service and Victory Medals.
" Thinking that remembrance, though unspoken, may reach
              him where he sleeps."
50, Tabor Road, Hammersmith, W.6.   11562B

ELLIS, H., Sergt., Rifle Brigade.
He volunteered in September 1914, and in the following June was sent to France where he served for upwards of four years. He acted as Sergeant Shoemaker in his Battalion, and rendered valuable services during the Battles of La Bassée, the Somme, Ypres and Vimy Ridge. He was demobilised in March 1919, and holds the 1914–15 Star, and the General Service and Victory Medals. Previous to the war he had completed twelve years' service with the Colours.
6, Scars Street, Camberwell, S.E.5.   Z5752

ELLIS, R., Gunner, R.F.A.
Mobilised from the Army Reserve on the declaration of war he was sent to France shortly afterwards, and fought in the Retreat from Mons, and the Battles of Neuve Chapelle, Ypres, Ploegsteert Wood and Arras. He was discharged on account of service in August 1915, having been in the Army since 1902. He also saw service in the South African War, and holds the Mons Star. and the General Service and Victory Medals.
209, Cator Street, Peckham, S.E.5.   Z5070

ELLIS, R. J., Private, R.A.S.C. (M.T.)
Joining in January 1917, he was almost immediately sent to France. During his service on the Western Front he was attached to the R.G.A. and R.F.A. on special duties in the Somme and Cambrai sectors. He also took part in the Retreat and Advance of 1918, and later proceeded to Germany with the Army of Occupation. He was demobilised in August 1919, and holds the General Service and Victory Medals.
60, Jocelyn Street, Peckham, S.E.15.   Z5381

ELLISON, T. H., Sergt., 9th Worcestershire Regt.
Volunteering in August 1914, he was sent to the Dardanelles in the following year, and was in action in heavy fighting on the Peninsula. Owing to ill-health he was invalided to hospital, and on recovery was drafted to Mesopotamia in 1917, and fought in many important engagements, and was wounded at Kut and also at Baghdad, and was invalided to India. Returning to England he was demobilised in March 1919, and holds the 1914–15 Star, and the General Service and Victory Medals.
28, Sheepcote Lane, Battersea, S.W.11.   Z2029

ELLS, T., Gunner, R.G.A.
Volunteering in September 1914, he proceeded to the Western Front in the early part of 1915, and fought in many important engagements including those at Ypres, the Somme, Arras and Loos. Transferred to India in 1917, he was in action in the North Western Frontier in Afghanistan. He returned to England and was demobilised in November 1919, and holds the 1914–15 Star, and the General Service and Victory Medals, also the India General Service Medal (with clasp Afghanistan, North Western Frontier, 1919).
20, Mundella Road, Wandsworth Road, S.W.8.   Z2030

ELLSON, J., Sapper, R.E.
He joined in June 1916, and embarked for the Western Front later. During his service overseas he served in the forward areas, engaged on important duties and saw heavy fighting on the Ypres, Somme and Cambrai fronts, and throughout the Retreat and Advance of 1918, and was wounded at Bapaume in September of that year. On recovery he was sent into Germany with the Army of Occupation, and stationed at Cologne. He was demobilised in October 1919, and holds the General Service and Victory Medals.
25, Ceylon Street, Battersea Park Road, S.W.8.   Z2031

ELMER, W. S., Trooper, City of London Lancers (Rough Riders).
Joining in June 1917, he was drafted to the Western Front later in the year. He fought in many parts of the line, and was in action at Cambrai. Owing to ill-health he was invalided to England, and on recovery was stationed at various depôts until demobilised in July 1919. He holds the General Service and Victory Medals.
21, Peveril Street, Battersea, S.W.11.   2032A

ELSDON, F., Gunner R.F.A. and Sapper, R.E.
He volunteered in August 1914, and shortly afterwards proceeded to France, and was in action in the Retreat from Mons, and at the Battles of the Marne, the Aisne, Ypres, Loos, Neuve Chapelle and Arras, and was twice wounded. He was gassed in 1916, and returning to England received hospital treatment and was discharged as unfit for further service later in the same year. He re-enlisted in 1918, for a further term of service, and was stationed at various depôts until demobilised in November 1919. He holds the Mons Star, and the General Service and Victory Medals.
10, Revesby Street, Walworth, S.E.17.   Z2033

ELSEY, F. Private, 3rd Middlesex Regiment.
Volunteering early in 1915, he was drafted to France in February of that year, and fought in the Battles of Ypres and Loos, and was then sent to Italy, where he was engaged in the fighting on the Piave. He later served in Egypt, Salonika and Mesopotamia, and returning home in 1919 was demobilised in April of that year. He holds the 1914–15 Star, and the General Service and Victory Medals.
4, Copeland Avenue, Peckham Rye, S.E.15.   Z5597

ELSEY, J., Private, R.A.S.C.
Volunteering in January 1915, he was sent to the Western Front later in the same year, and served in the forward areas on important duties, transporting ammunition and supplies to the front lines. He was also stationed at Boulogne and other Bases, and did good work. He was demobilised in January 1919, and holds the 1914–15 Star, and the General Service and Victory Medals.
31, Tidemore Street, Battersea Park Road, S.W.8.   Z2034A

ELSOM, C., Private, Lancashire Fusiliers.
He joined in 1918, on attaining military age, and completing his training was drafted to France. He fought on the Ypres and Somme fronts, and in many other sectors during the German Offensive and subsequent Allied Advance in 1918. He proceeded to Egypt after the cessation of hostilities, and was engaged on garrison duties there until he returned to England, and was demobilised in 1920. He holds the General Service and Victory Medals.
46, Henshaw Street, Walworth, S.E.17.   Z2035A

ELSOM, W. Private, 24th Queen's (Royal West Surrey Regiment).
Volunteering in 1915, he embarked for the Western Front in the following year, and fought in many important engagements, including those at Arras and the Somme. He was unfortunately killed in action at Ypres on June 7th, 1917, and was entitled to the General Service and Victory Medals.
              " Nobly striving,
He nobly fell, that we might live."
46, Henshaw Street, Walworth, S.E.17.   Z2035B

ELSON, R., Private, East Surrey Regiment.
Joining in July 1916, he was sent to France three months later and saw much service in many parts of the line, fighting at the Battles of the Somme, Arras, and throughout the German Offensive and subsequent Allied Advance in 1918. He was demobilised in March 1919, and holds the General Service and Victory Medals.
24, Thorncroft Street, Wandsworth Road, S.W.8.   Z2036

ELWORTHY, R. F., Gunner, R.F.A.
Volunteering in January 1915, he was drafted overseas in the same year, and served on the Western Front throughout the war. During this period he took part in several engagements, including the Battles of the Somme, Arras and Ypres. He was demobilised in 1919, and holds the 1914–15 Star, and the General Service and Victory Medals.
61, Bournemouth Road, Rye Lane, S.E.15.   Z5753

ELY, J., Private, Queen's (Royal West Surrey Regt.)
He volunteered in August 1914, and proceeded to France later in the same year, and fought in many engagements, including the Battles of Ypres (I), Neuve Chapelle, Hill 60, and Ypres (II). He gave his life for King and Country at Loos on September 25th, 1915, and was entitled to the 1914–15 Star, and the General Service and Victory Medals.
" He passed out of the sight of men by the path of duty and
              self sacrifice."
51, Sterndale Road, Wandsworth Road, S.W.8.   Z2037

ELY, J., Sergt., Rifle Brigade.
Volunteering in 1915, he was sent to France in August of that year, and was in action in various sectors, fighting in the Ypres salient, and in many important engagements. He was blown up by the explosion of a shell, and returning to England received hospital treatment, and was subsequently invalided out of the Service in 1917. He holds the 1914–15 Star and the General Service and Victory Medals.
93, Thorparch Road, Wandsworth Road, S.W.8.   Z2038

EMANUEL, C. A., Private, 4th Middlesex Regiment.
Joining in June 1917, he was drafted to the Western Front in December of the same year, and was engaged in heavy fighting on the Somme, and in many other parts of the line. He was in action throughout the German Offensive in 1918, and was wounded in August during the Allied Advance. He returned to England and on recovery served at various stations until demobilised in October 1919, and holds the General Service and Victory Medals.
11, Dean's Buildings, Walworth, S.E.17.   Z2040

EMBLEN, W., Corporal, Middlesex Regiment.
Volunteering in 1915, he embarked for the Balkan theatre of war in the following year and served in various sectors and was wounded on the Vardar. Invalided to Malta, he received medical treatment, and on recovery proceeded to France in 1917, and fought in the Battles of Ypres and Cambrai, and throughout the Retreat and Advance of 1918. He was demobilised shortly after the cessation of hostilities, and holds the General Service and Victory Medals.
99, Ferndale Road, Clapham, S.W.4.   Z2041

EMBLETON, J. W. (D.C.M.), B.S.M., R.F.A.
Having previously served for twenty-one years in the Army and having fought in South Africa, he volunteered in September 1914, and was sent to France in the following year. He was in action in the Battles of Loos, Armentières and the Somme, and was sent back to England to train recruits for the New Armies. Returning to France he served in several engagements, and was awarded the Distinguished Conduct Medal on July 9th, 1917 for conspicuous bravery and devotion to duty in the Field. He was discharged as medically unfit for further service in February 1918, and in addition to the Queen's and King's South African Medals, holds the 1914–15 Star, and the General Service and Victory Medals.
139, Wells Street, Camberwell, S.E.5.   Z5071

EMBUREY, F. G., Private, Queen's (Royal West Surrey Regiment).
Volunteering in November 1914, he proceeded overseas in the following year. During his service in France, he took part in many engagements, including that at Festubert, and was wounded. On recovery, rejoining his Regiment, he was in action on the Somme and was again wounded at High Wood. He returned to England and after protracted hospital treatment was invalided out of the Service in September 1917. He holds the 1914–15 Star, and the General Service and Victory Medals.
20, Avenue Road, Camberwell, S.E.5.   Z2042B

EMERY, W., Private, R.A.S.C. (M.T.)
Volunteering in April 1915, he was drafted to the Western Front in the following month. Whilst in France he served in the Ypres sector for a considerable period, being engaged with the Ammunition Column. He was frequently under heavy shell-fire when employed in the dangerous duty of carrying ammunition to the gun line. In January 1919 he was demobilised and holds the 1914–15 Star, and the General Service and Victory Medals.
9, Cronin Road, Peckham, S.E.15.   Z5382

EMMETT, J. T., Private, 2nd Border Regiment.
Mobilised from the Army Reserve at the outbreak of hostilities, he proceeded to Belgium in October 1914, and was present at the Evacuation of Antwerp. He fought at La Bassée and Ypres (I), where he was wounded. He returned to the front lines, and was in action at Ypres (II), Festubert and Loos, in which engagements he was captured by the Germans, stripped of his clothing and ordered to find his way back to the British lines. He rejoined his unit, and later gave his life for the freedom of England, whilst on patrol on November 25th, 1915. He was entitled to the 1914 Star, and the General Service and Victory Medals.
"Steals on the ear the distant triumph song."
5, Globe Court, Ethelred Street, Kennington, S.E.11.   Z25588

EMMETT, W. (D.C.M.), Sergt., 16th Middlesex Regt.
Volunteering in March 1915, he was drafted to the Western Front in the following November, and fought at the Battles of Givenchy, Ploegsteert, the Somme, Vimy Ridge, and throughout the German Offensive and Allied Advance in 1918. He was twice wounded during his service overseas, and was awarded the Distinguished Conduct Medal for conspicuous gallantry and devotion to duty in the Field. He was demobilised in February 1919, and holds the 1914–15 Star, and the General Service and Victory Medals.
5, Currie Road, Battersea, S.W.11.   Z2043

EMONSON, C. G., Private, Royal Fusiliers.
He volunteered in August 1914, and in the following year was sent to the Western Front. He fought throughout the war, and took part in many important engagements, and after the cessation of hostilities, returned to England and was demobilised in July 1919. He holds the 1914–15 Star, and the General Service and Victory Medals.
37, Tabor Road, Hammersmith, W.6.   11154B

EMONSON, H., L/Corporal, R.A.S.C.
He volunteered in June 1915, and later in the same year was drafted to France, where he saw much service, and was engaged on important transport duties in the forward areas whilst fighting was in progress. He returned to England when hostilities ceased, and was demobilised in December 1918, and holds the 1914–15 Star, and the General Service and Victory Medals.
37, Tabor Road, Hammersmith, W.6.   11154A

ENDERSBY, W., Sergt., 2nd Suffolk Regiment.
He was mobilised in August 1914, and proceeded almost immediately with his Regiment to the Western Front. Here he took a prominent part in the fierce fighting in the Retreat from Mons, and was unfortunately taken prisoner on August 26th. He remained in captivity for three and a half years, and on his release was sent home and subsequently demobilised in February 1919. He holds the Mons Star, and the General Service and Victory Medals.
"Wooloomooloo," 100, Wellington Road, Bush Hill Park. 8084

ERSSER, W. T., Rifleman, 6th London Regt. (Rifles).
He volunteered in June 1915, and four months later was sent to the Western Front. Here he served with his Battalion in many parts of the line, and fought in many important engagements. He was taken prisoner on November 30th, 1917 at the Battle of Cambrai, and died whilst a prisoner of war in Germany on June 9th, 1918. He was entitled to the 1914–15 Star, and the General Service and Victory Medals.
110, Boyson Road, Walworth, S.E.17.   Z2039

ESCUDIER, G., Private, R.A.S.C.
He joined in March 1916, and in the same year was drafted to France. In this theatre of war he served in various sectors and was employed on important duties at [the rail heads, at Rouen, Calais and Le Havre, and on the cessation of hostilities went to Germany, where he served with the Army of Occupation. He was demobilised in November 1919, and holds the General Service and Victory Medals.
25, Barmore Street, Battersea, S.W.11.   Z2046

ESSERY, W., Driver, R.E.
He joined in June 1917, and after completing his training was engaged on important duties at various stations with his unit. He rendered valuable services, but was not successful in obtaining his transfer overseas owing to physical unfitness. He was demobilised in February 1919.
35, Trott Street, Battersea, S.W.11.   Z2047

ESTOLL, C. M. (M.C.), Sergt.-Major, 8th East Surrey Regiment.
He volunteered in August 1914, and in June of the following year was drafted to the Western Front. Here he fought in many fierce battles, including those of the Somme, Arras, and Ypres, and was wounded in action at Armentières in August 1916, and on the Somme four months later. On recovery he saw further fighting, and at Passchendaele was awarded the Croix de Guerre for conspicuous bravery in the Field. He was also awarded the Military Cross for gallantry and devotion to duty at Ypres. He was demobilised in March 1919, and also holds the 1914–15 Star, and the General Service and Victory Medals.
2, Kennard Street, Battersea, S.W.11.   Z2048

ETHERIDGE, A. E., L/Corporal, 1/1st Staffordshire Hussars (Queen's Own Royal Regiment).
He joined in May 1917, and after a period of training was drafted to Egypt. In this theatre of war he served in several important engagements, including the capture of Jericho. On the cessation of hostilities he served with the Army of Occupation until 1919, when he was sent home and demobilised in November of that year. He holds the General Service and Victory Medals.
11C, Theatre Street, Battersea, S.W.11.   Z2044

ETHERINGTON, E. C., Sergt., 6th London Regiment (Rifles).
He volunteered in February 1915, and after performing important duties at home was in 1917 drafted to the Western Front. Here he took part in severe fighting at Cambrai, and was gassed. He was invalided to England for treatment, and on recovery served at various stations with his Battalion until demobilised in February 1919. He holds the General Service and Victory Medals.   Z2045
152, Elmhurst Mansions, Edgeley Road, Clapham, S.W.4.

EVANS, A. E., Gunner, R.F.A.
He volunteered in April 1915, and proceeded to the Western Front in October of the same year. Whilst in France he served with distinction in the Battles of Loos, Albert, Arras, Messines and Ypres, and was severely wounded in action on the Somme in 1917. He was invalided home, but later died in Colchester Hospital from the effects of his injuries on October 12th, 1917. He was entitled to the 1914–15 Star, and the General Service and Victory Medals.
7, Williams' Grove, Walworth, S.E.17.   Z2051

EVANS, A. G., Bombardier, R.F.A.

He volunteered in November 1914, and proceeding overseas in the following July served with his Battery during the Battles of Loos, Armentières, Arras, Bray, and was severely wounded at Contalmaison on July 7th, 1916. Sent to hospital in England he received protracted medical treatment, and was invalided out of the Service in March 1918. He holds the 1914–15 Star, and the General Service and Victory Medals.
48, Jardin Street, Camberwell, S.E.5. Z5073

EVANS, C., Rifleman, 18th London Regiment (London Irish Rifles).

Joining in September 1916, he embarked for France three months later, and fought in many important engagements, including those at Messines, Passchendaele, Ypres and Cambrai, where he was gassed in November 1917. After receiving medical treatment in England he was ultimately discharged in June 1918, as unfit for further service. He holds the General Service and Victory Medals.
12, Graylands Road, Peckham, S.E.15. Z5952

EVANS, C. H. J., Stoker Petty Officer, R.N.

He joined the service in 1908, and at the outbreak of hostilities was mobilised, and aboard H.M.S. " Colossus " served with the Grand Fleet in the North Sea, and was in action at the Battle of Jutland in May 1916. Transferred to H.M.S. " Dalhousie " his ship was sent to Mesopotamia, and stationed at Basra in the Persian Gulf, was engaged on special patrol duties. In 1917, he returned to England, and was posted to H.M.S. " Valkyrie " which vessel was employed in the North Sea, and was torpedoed and sunk on December 22nd, 1917, but he was fortunately saved. He then served in H.M.S. " Flying Fox " on convoying duties between England and France until the close of the war. He was discharged on account of service in June 1920, and holds the 1914–15 Star, and the General Service and Victory Medals.
9, Mawbey Street, South Lambeth Road, S.W.8. Z2053

EVANS, E., Pte., 3rd London Regt. (Royal Fusiliers).

He volunteered in November 1915, and was drafted to France in November 1917. He took part in the fighting at the Battles of Ypres, Peolcappelle, and St. Quentin, and during the German Offensive of 1918, was taken prisoner on March 23rd, 1918. He was made to work in the German front lines and was held in captivity until December 1918. He was then repatriated and demobilised in March of the following year, and holds the General Service and Victory Medals.
3, Domville Grove, Camberwell, S.E.5. Z5598

EVANS, E. C., Private, 9th Yorkshire Regiment.

He volunteered in February 1916, and in the same year was drafted to the Italian front, where he was engaged in much fighting on the Piave. He was sent to France in 1917, and was in action in many battles and fought in the Retreat and Advance of 1918. He was unfortunately killed in action on October 5th, 1918, and was entitled to the General Service and Victory Medals.
84, Chiswick Lane, Chiswick, W.4. T5616A

EVANS, F., Private, 2nd Bedfordshire Regiment.

Joining in February 1918, he was sent to the Western Front in the following July and was engaged on guard and other important duties at Prisoners of War Camps at Abbeville, Arras, Péronne and other places. On the cessation of hostilities he proceeded into Germany with the Army of Occupation, and served on the Rhine until his return home for demobilisation in November 1919. He holds the General Service and Victory Medals.
13, Northampton Place, Walworth, S.E.17. Z2056A

EVANS, G., Trooper, 1st (King's) Dragoon Guards.

He joined in September 1916, and was drafted to the Western Front in the following year. He was in action at Arras, Ypres, the Somme, Vimy Ridge, Cambrai, and throughout the German Offensive and Allied Advance of 1918. After the Armistice he was sent into Germany with the Army of Occupation until his return to England for demobilisation in April 1919. He holds the General Service and Victory Medals.
1, Foreign Street, Camberwell, S.E.5. 95945

EVANS, G., Private, 7th Queen's (Royal West Surrey Regiment).

He volunteered in January 1916, and a year later was drafted overseas. Serving with his unit on the Western Front he was in action in many important engagements, including the Battles of the Somme, Albert and Ypres, and was wounded at Albert in 1917, and in the vicinity of Bapaume in the following year. He was later transferred to the Labour Corps and did good work in France until the end of hostilities. He was demobilised in February 1919, and holds the General Service and Victory Medals.
34, Totteridge Road, Battersea, S.W.11. Z2052

EVANS, H., Pte., 1st London Regt. (Royal Fusiliers).

He joined in September 1916, and after completing his training served with his unit on the South Coast on important garrison duties. He did good work, but was not sent overseas owing to physical unfitness, and having met with an accident whilst on duty, which incapacitated him for further service, was invalided out of the Army in 1918.
85, Sandmere Road, Clapham, S.W.4. Z2061

EVANS, H., Private, 9th East Surrey Regiment.

He volunteered in October 1914, and in the following October was drafted to France, where he served throughout the war. During this period he fought in many notable engagements, including the Battles of the Somme, Armentières, Ypres and Hooge. He returned home for demobilisation in May 1919, and holds the 1914–15 Star, and the General Service and Victory Medals.
78, Coninsworth Road, Wandsworth Road, S.W.8. Z2055

EVANS, H. W., Gunner, R.F.A.

Volunteering in August 1915, he embarked for France in the following March and took part in the Battles of Loos, the Somme, Arras, Ypres, Beaumont-Hamel, and in several engagements during the Retreat and Advance of 1918. He was unhappily killed in action on September 6th, 1918, and was entitled to the General Service and Victory Medals.
" A valiant soldier, with undaunted heart he breasted Life's last hill."
13, Northampton Place, Walworth, S.E.17. Z2056A

EVANS, J., Sergt., 2nd East Yorkshire Regiment.

After eleven years' service in the Army, during which he fought in the Boer war, and served in India, he volunteered in September 1915. On completion of his training he acted as a Machine Gun Instructor at various depôts, and did valuable work in training recruits for the new Armies. He was demobilised in January 1910.
67, Graylands Road, Peckham, S.E.15. Z5754

EVANS, J. C. J., L/Cpl., 2nd South Lancashire Regt.

He was mobilised from the Army Reserve in August 1914, and sent to France shortly afterwards. He took part in the Retreat from Mons and in the subsequent heavy fighting. He was reported missing on September 14th, 1914, but was later reported to have been killed in action on that date.
" He died the noblest death a man may die,
Fighting for God, and right and liberty."
61, Jardin Street, Camberwell, S.E.5. Z5072

EVANS, M. (Miss), Special War Worker.

This lady volunteered for work of National importance, and from November 1916 to November 1918 was employed by the Park Royal Filling Factory. She was engaged in pellet-making, filling fuses and detonators, and also worked in the soldering department, and discharged her duties, which were of a highly dangerous character, in a thoroughly capable and efficient manner.
11, Palmerston Street, Battersea, S.W.11. Z2059

EVANS, M. P. (Mrs.), Member, W.R.A.F.

She joined in July 1918, and during her service was engaged on important duties in connection with the testing of aero-engine plugs, and the manufacture of parachutes. She carried out her duties, which were of a highly technical nature, with energy and zeal, and won the commendation of her employers. She was demobilised in January 1919.
11, Palmerston Street, Battersea, S.W.11. Z2058

EVANS, P., Private, Royal Fusiliers.

Joining in June 1916, he was sent overseas in the following December, and saw service in various sectors of the Western Front. He fought in the Battles of Arras, Vimy Ridge, Ypres, Bullecourt, Messines, Havrincourt, Amiens and Bapaume, and was unfortunately killed in action near Le Cateau in October 1918. He was entitled to the General Service and Victory Medals.
" Whilst we remember, the sacrifice is not in vain."
51, Aldbridge Street, Walworth, S.E.17. Z1140B

EVANS, R., Driver, R.F.A.

Mobilised from the Army Reserve on the outbreak of war, he was almost immediately drafted to France, and engaged in heavy fighting during the Retreat from Mons. He was also in action in the Battles of La Bassée, Hill 60, Ypres, Festubert and Loos, and was gassed on the Somme. Sent to hospital in England he returned to the Field on recovery, and was again gassed during the closing operations of the war. He returned to England for demobilisation in January 1919, and holds the Mons Star, and the General Service and Victory Medals.
114, Chatham Road, Wandsworth Common, S.W.11. Z2050A

EVANS, R. (Junior), Sapper, R.E.

He volunteered in January 1915, and in the same year proceeded to France. In the course of his service he was in action
in several important engagements, including the Battles of
Arras, Albert, Ypres and the Somme. He returned to England
for demobilisation in May 1919, and holds the 1914-15 Star,
and the General Service and Victory Medals.
114, Chatham Road, Wandsworth Common, S.W.11.

Z2050B

EVANS, R. H., Rifleman, 9th London Regt. (Queen Victoria's Rifles).

He volunteered in May 1915, and in the same year embarked
for the Western Front, and served there for upwards of three
years. During this period he was engaged on important
duties in various sectors and fought in several operations,
and was wounded at Menin Road. Sent to hospital in England,
he received medical treatment and on recovery served with
his unit at home, and was demobilised in February 1919,
and holds the 1914-15 Star, and the General Service and
Victory Medals.
84, Chiswick Lane, W.4.   T5616B

EVANS, V. F., Gunner, R.F.A.

Serving in India at the outbreak of war he was shortly afterwards drafted to France and engaged in heavy fighting during
the Retreat from Mons, and in the Battles of Le Cateau,
Festubert, the Somme, and Arras. He was unfortunately
killed in action on April 17th, 1917, and was entitled to the
Mons Star, and the General Service and Victory Medals.
    "His life for his Country, his soul to God."
26, Randall Street, Battersea, S.W.11.   Z2054A

EVANS, W., Pte., 22nd Queen's (Royal West Surrey Regt.) and Surrey Lancers (Queen Mary's Regt.)

He volunteered in April 1915, and on completing his training
was stationed at various depôts with his unit for guard and
other important duties. Later he rendered valuable services
whilst employed on agricultural work in Suffolk. He was
unsuccessful in obtaining his transfer overseas owing to medical
unfitness, and was demobilised in April 1919.
56, Clayton Road, Peckham, S.E.15.   Z5951

EVANS, W. A., Private, R.A.M.C.

He joined in March 1917, and in the following month proceeded
to the Western Front. He served with his unit on special
duties on the Somme, at St. Omer, Merville, Ypres, Verdun,
La Bassée, St. Quentin, and during the Allied Advance of
1918. He was demobilised in September 1919, and holds
the General Service and Victory Medals.
9, Copeland Road, Peckham Rye, S.E.15.   Z5588B

EVANS, W. J., Driver, R.A.S.C.

A Territorial, he was mobilised when war was declared and
proceeded to the Western Front in March 1915. Serving on
important transport duties throughout the course of hostilities
he was present at numerous battles, including those of Ypres,
Festubert, Loos, Vimy Ridge, Beaumont-Hamel, Passchendaele,
Cambrai, and during the Retreat and Advance of 1918. Demobilised in March 1919, he later rejoined the Territorials,
and holds the 1914-15 Star, and the General Service and
Victory Medals.
11, Palmerston Street, Battersea, S.W.11.   Z2060

EVANS, W. S., Air Mechanic, R.A.F.

He volunteered in January 1916, and on the conclusion of
his training was engaged with his Squadron at various aerodromes in England and Scotland. He rendered valuable
services on work of a highly technical nature, but was unable
to secure a transfer to a theatre of war before hostilities
ceased, and was demobilised in November 1919.
24, Wheatsheaf Lane, South Lambeth Road, S.W.8.   Z2057

EVE, W., Sergt., Irish Guards.

He volunteered in June 1915, and in the same year proceeded
to France. Whilst on the Western Front he fought in many
engagements, notably the Battles of the Somme, Arras, Cambrai, and during the Retreat and Advance of 1918. He was
wounded three times during his service overseas, and after
the Armistice returned to England. He was demobilised
in February 1919, and holds the 1914-15 Star, and the General
Service and Victory Medals.
17, Priory Road, Wandsworth Road, S.W.8.   Z2062

EVELING, R. E., Private, R.A.S.C. (Remounts).

Volunteering in November 1914, he was drafted to France in
the same month and served there for four years. During this
period he was present at the Battles of Neuve Chapelle, Loos,
Albert, the Somme, Arras, Ypres, Lens, Cambrai, and in the
Retreat and Advance of 1918, and was engaged in training
horses for active service. He was demobilised in March 1919,
and holds the 1914-15 Star, and the General Service and
Victory Medals.
25, Deans Buildings, Flint Street, Walworth, S.E.17.
                                                   Z1873B

EVEREST, H. C., Lieut., Northumberland Fusiliers.

Volunteering in the Life Guards in November 1915, he was
granted a Commission after fourteen months' service and
proceeded to Egypt in July 1916. He served in the East
for a time and was then drafted to France, where he fought
in several engagements, and during the Retreat and Advance
of 1918. After the Armistice he was sent into Germany
with the Army of Occupation, and stationed at Cologne. He
returned to England for demobilisation in April 1920, and holds
the General Service and Victory Medals.
160, St. George's Road, Peckham S.E.15.   Z5755

EVEREST, T. F., Cpl., New Zealand Field Artillery.

He volunteered in September 1914, and was sent to Gallipoli
in the following year. He took part in heavy fighting at the
Landing on the Peninsula, and in the operations until the
Evacuation, and was then sent to France. He was twice
wounded in action on the Western Front, and sent home in
consequence of his injuries. Discharged on account of service
in April 1918, he holds the 1914-15 Star, and the General Service and Victory Medals.
Rose Villa, Burlington Lane, Chiswick, W.4.   5835A

EVERETT, R. H., Corporal, Middlesex Regiment.

He volunteered in March 1915, and served for a time with his
Battalion but being under age was discharged a year later.
On attaining military age he rejoined in January 1917, and was
drafted to the Western Front in February of the following
year. He fought in various sectors during the Retreat and
Allied Advance, and was present at the entry into Mons at
dawn on November 11th, 1918. He was demobilised in April
1919, and holds the General Service and Victory Medals.
96, Grenard Road, Peckham, S.E.15.   Z5599

EVERITT, T., Private, Middlesex Regiment.

Volunteering in May 1915, he embarked for France in the
following December and fought in several engagements. He
was unfortunately killed in action near Loos in February 1916,
and buried in the British Military Cemetery at Fosse 8, in the
vicinity of Béthune, and was entitled to the 1914-15 Star, and
the General Service and Victory Medals.
    "Great deeds cannot die."
187, Trafalgar Street, Walworth, S.E.17.   Z27146

EVERITT, W., Guardsman, Scots Guards.

He enlisted in 1902, and mobilised on the outbreak of war, was
drafted to the Western Front in September 1914. He was
engaged in heavy fighting in the Battles of the Marne and the
Aisne, and was killed in action in January 1915. He was
entitled to the 1914 Star, and the General Service and Victory
Medals.
    "His memory is cherished with pride."
34, Gideon Road, Lavender Hill, S.W.11.   Z2063

EVES, A. G., Corporal, R.F.A.

Volunteering in August 1914, he was sent overseas in the
following year, and saw much service on the Western Front.
He was in action in several important engagements, including
those of Ypres, Festubert, Vimy Ridge, and was wounded on
the Somme in 1917. He was invalided to hospital in England,
and on recovery served on important duties at Home. He
was demobilised in March 1919, and holds the 1914-15 Star,
and the General Service Medals.
30, Priory Road, Wandsworth Road, S.W.8.   Z2064A

EVES, A. W., A/Staff Sergt., R.A.O.C.

He volunteered in September 1914, and in the following April
proceeded to the Western Front. Attached to the 8th Durham
Light Infantry he was in action soon after his arrival in France,
and was severely wounded at Vlamertinghe on April 27th,
1915. He died from the effects of his injuries two days later,
and was entitled to the 1914-15 Star, and the General Service
and Victory Medals.
    "His memory is cherished with pride."
78, Kelmscott Road, Battersea, S.W.11.   Z3082

EYRE, E., Pte., Queen's (Royal West Surrey Regt.)

He joined in 1916, and, drafted to France in the same year,
saw much fighting until the termination of hostilities. He
was engaged with his Battalion in various parts of the line,
and fought in the Battles of the Somme, the Ancre, and at
Vimy Ridge, and later served at Lille. On his return home
he was discharged on account of service in March 1919, and
holds the General Service and Victory Medals.
19, Nursery Street, Wandsworth Road, S.W.8.   Z2065

F

FABIAN, F. (Mrs.), Special War Worker.

This lady volunteered for work of National importance during
the war, and was employed by the Park Royal Munition Factory
from November 1915, until December 1916. She was engaged
on important duties in connection with the production of
ammunition, and throughout rendered valuable services.
44, Kent Road, Chiswick, W.4.   6782A

FABIAN, J., Private, 9th Royal Fusiliers.
He volunteered in May 1915, and in the following November proceeded to the Western Front. Whilst overseas he took an active part in numerous engagements, and was wounded in the vicinity of Ypres in March 1916. Sent home in consequence of his injuries he was discharged as medically unfit for further service in 1916, and holds the 1914–15 Star, and the General Service and Victory Medals.
44, Kent Road, Chiswick, W.4.   6782B

FAGAN, M., Sapper, R.E.
Volunteering in November 1915, in the Queen's (Royal West Surrey Regiment), he was sent to France in the following May and was in action in the Battles of the Somme, Ploegsteert, St. Eloi, and was wounded near Vimy Ridge. He was invalided home, and on recovery was drafted to Egypt with the Leinster Regiment, and served during the British Advance through Palestine, and was present at the fall of Jerusalem. Owing to illness he was invalided to hospital, and on recovery was transferred to the Royal Engineers, and served with that unit until the end of hostilities. Returning home for demobilisation in August 1919, he holds the General Service and Victory Medals.
14, Winstead Street, Battersea, S.W.11.   Z2066

FAGG, G. W., Gunner, R.F.A.
Mobilised from the Reserve on the declaration of war he embarked for the Western Front in 1914, and served there for upwards of five years. During this period he fought in the Battles of the Somme, Arras, Ypres, High Wood, Beaumont-Hamel, Delville Wood, and was wounded at Cambrai, and badly gassed near Albert. He was demobilised in March 1919, and holds the 1914 Star, and the General Service and Victory Medals.
89, Priory Grove, Lansdowne Road, S.W.8.   Z2067

FAIRBANK, A. E., Stoker Petty Officer, R.N.
He joined the Royal Navy in 1911, and when war broke out was serving in H.M.S. "Indefatigable." His ship took part in the Naval operations at the Dardanelles, and was in action in the Battle of Jutland. He was unfortunately killed during this engagement, and was entitled to the 1914–15 Star, and the General Service and Victory Medals.
"Great deeds cannot die."
8, Blondel Street, Battersea, S.W.11.   Z2068

FAIRBROTHER, A. V., Pte., 13th East Surrey Regt.
Volunteering in August 1915, he proceeded overseas in the following June, and saw service in various sectors of the Western Front. There he was engaged in heavy fighting in the Battles of the Somme, Arras, Ypres, Bullecourt, Bourlon Wood, and was wounded and taken prisoner at Armentières on April 9th, 1918. Repatriated in December 1918, he was demobilised in the following March, and holds the General Service and Victory Medals.
34, Peardon Street, Wandsworth Road, S.W.8.   Z2069

FAIRCLOUGH, C., Stoker, R.N.
He joined in June 1916, and served in H.M.S. "Glenogle," "Conqueror," and "Devenna." Sent to Boulogne he was engaged on important coast defence duties, and in guarding submarines, and rendered valuable services until invalided home owing to injuries sustained in an accident. He was discharged in consequence in September 1917, and holds the General Service and Victory Medals.
15, Parkstone Road, Peckham, S.E.15.   Z5759

FAIRCLOUGH, F., Private, Royal Irish Fusiliers.
Joining in May 1916, he was sent to Ireland, and after training proceeded to the Western Front. During his service in this theatre of war he was in action in several important engagements, and was wounded in the Advance of 1918. Sent home on account of his injuries he received hospital treatment, and was discharged as medically unfit for further service in April 1919. He holds the General Service and Victory Medals.
28, Landseer Street, Battersea, S.W.11.   Z2072

FAIRCLOUGH, H., Sergt., Middlesex Regiment.
He joined in July 1916, and on the completion of his training was engaged on important duties with his unit at various depôts. Acting as Quarter-Master-Sergeant, he rendered valuable services, but was unsuccessful in obtaining a transfer overseas before the conclusion of hostilities, and was demobilised in October 1919.
14, Rumsey Road, Stockwell Road, S.W.9.   Z2070

FAIRCLOUGH, W. R., Driver, R.A.S.C.
He volunteered in October 1914, and proceeding overseas in the following year served in France until the termination of hostilities. He was engaged on important duties in connection with the transport of ammunition and supplies during the Battles of the Somme and Cambrai, and in the Retreat and Advance of 1918. Demobilised in March 1919, he holds the 1914–15 Star, and the General Service and Victory Medals.
45, Bolton Street, Camberwell, S.E.5.   Z2071

FAIRFAX, T. H., Rifleman, 6th King's Royal Rifle Corps.
He joined in May 1916, and after completing his training was transferred to the Royal Marines, with whom he was engaged on guard and other duties in connection with home defence. He rendered valuable services but was unable to obtain a transfer overseas owing to medical unfitness for general service. He was demobilised in July 1919.
30, Foreign Street, Camberwell, S.E.5.   Z5959

FAIRHALL, F., Rflmn., King's Royal Rifle Corps.
He volunteered in January 1916, and in the following month was drafted to the Western Front. In the course of his service he fought in the Battles of the Somme and Bullecourt, and was taken prisoner at Cambrai in November 1917. He effected his escape from Germany on November 9th, 1918, and after many hardships arrived in England a fortnight later. Demobilised in February 1919, he holds the General Service and Victory Medals.
53, Corunna Road, New Road, S.W.8.   Z2074

FAIRHALL, F. C., Pte., 22nd Queen's (Royal West Surrey Regiment).
He volunteered in August 1914, and after completing his training was engaged on important duties with his unit at various stations. He did excellent work in connection with home defence measures, but was not sent overseas owing to ill-health, and was discharged in consequence in February 1915.
21, Dashwood Road, Wandsworth Road, S.W.8.   Z2073

FAIRHALL, H. J., Cpl., 18th (Queen Mary's Own) Hussars.
A serving soldier, having enlisted in September 1904, he was mobilised on the outbreak of war and drafted to France shortly afterwards. He was engaged as a cyclist despatch rider at Head Quarters, and did excellent work during the Retreat from Mons. He was later in action in the Battles of Ypres, the Somme, Arras, Vimy Ridge, and in several engagements during the Retreat and Advance of 1918, and was wounded at Le Cateau. Returning home, he was discharged on account of service in April 1919, and holds the Mons Star, and the General Service and Victory Medals.
14, Corunna Road, New Road, S.W.8.   Z2075

FAIRMAN, J. A., Private, 8th East Surrey Regt.
Volunteering in September 1914, he proceeded to France in the following March, and fought in the Battles of Neuve Chapelle, Hill 60, Ypres, Festubert, Loos, Vermelles, and Vimy Ridge. He fell fighting on the Somme on July 1st, 1916, and was entitled to the 1914–15 Star, and the General Service and Victory Medals.
"His life for his Country, his Soul to God."
94, Dalyell Road, Landor Road, S.W.9.   Z2076

FAIRMAN, J. D., Shoeing Smith, R.F.A.
He was mobilised from the Reserve on the declaration of war, and sent to France shortly afterwards. He took part in the Retreat from Mons, and in the Battles of La Bassée, Ypres, St. Eloi and Loos. Sent to Mesopotamia in 1916, he served in the relief of Kut, the Battle of Kut-el-Amara, and in several other engagements. On his return to England at the end of hostilities, he was discharged as medically unfit for further service in May 1919, and holds the Mons Star, and the General Service and Victory Medals.
75, Cator Street, Peckham, S.E.15.   Z4448

FAIRWEATHER, W. S., Sergt., R.A.M.C. and R.A.P.C.
Volunteering in February 1916, he embarked for the Western Front in the following year, and did valuable work with the Field Ambulance during the Battles of the Somme and Arras. Owing to illness he was sent to Etaples, and on recovery was engaged at General Headquarters at Rouen on clerical duties until transferred to the Royal Army Pay Corps at Wimereux. Taken ill whilst on leave in England he was admitted to hospital, and on recovery was demobilised in April 1919. He holds the General Service and Victory Medals.
20, Rozel Road, Wandsworth Road, S.W.4.   Z2077

FAITH, C. F. W., Rflmn, 21st London Regt. (1st Surrey Rifles) and Lieut., East Surrey Regt.
He volunteered in August 1914, and in March of the following year was sent to the Western Front, where he fought in the Battles of Neuve Chapelle, Ypres, Festubert, Loos, Vimy Ridge, and the Somme. Returning home in February 1917, he obtained his commission four months later, and was sent to Italy in November 1917. He saw much fighting on the Piave and Asiago Plateaux, until the end of the war. He holds the 1914–15 Star, and the General Service and Victory Medals.
33, Lothian Road, N. Brixton, S.W.9.   Z5241A

FAITH, W. H., Pte., 14th London Regt. (London Scottish).
He joined in March 1917, at the age of 16½ years, and five months later was drafted to the Western Front, where he was in action at the Battle of Cambrai. His parents claimed him out of the Army, on account of his age, and he returned to England and was discharged in October 1918. He has since joined the Merchant Service. He holds the General Service and Victory Medals.
33, Lothian Road, N. Brixton, S.W.9.   Z5241

FAITHFULL, G., Private, 13th London Regiment (Kensingtons).
He joined in 1916, and proceeding to the Western Front in the same year was engaged on important duties in various parts of the line. He was in action in the Battles of Vimy Ridge, Cambrai, Bourlon Wood, and was wounded at Albert, and sent home for medical treatment. He was demobilised in 1919, and holds the General Service and Victory Medals.
25, Arden Street, Battersea Park Road, S.W.8.   Z2078

FAITHFUL, J.W., Rflmn., King's Royal Rifle Corps.
Joining in 1917, he completed his training, and was engaged on guard and other important duties at various prisoners of war detention camps. He rendered valuable services, but was unable to obtain a transfer overseas before the cessation of hostilities, and was demobilised in 1919.
36, Redmore Road, Hammersmith, W.6.   11604

FARLEY. D. F., A.B., Royal Navy.
He was serving in the Royal Navy when war broke out, aboard H.M.S. "Hawke," but was not in her when she was sunk on October 15th, 1914. On October 5th 1914, he was sent with the British Naval Division to Antwerp. Posted later to H.M.S. "Hazel" he served aboard that ship during the operations in the Dardanelles. His ship was also engaged on special duties in the North and Mediterranean Seas, and in the Atlantic and Pacific Oceans. He was discharged on account of service in October 1917, and holds the 1914 Star, and the General Service and Victory Medals.
3, Stockdale Road, Wandsworth Road, S.W.8.   Z2080

FARLEY. J., Private, South Wales Borderers.
Mobilised on the outbreak of war and sent to France with the first Expeditionary Force, he was in action during the Retreat from Mons, and in the Battles of the Marne, the Aisne, Arras and Ypres. He also fought at Albert, Passchendaele, Vimy Ridge, Lens and in several of the engagements during the Retreat and Advance of 1918. Returning home for demobilisation in April 1919, he holds the Mons Star, and the General Service and Victory Medals.
12, Sussex Road, Coldharbour Lane, S.W.9.   Z2079

FARLEY, L., Private, 19th London Regiment.
He volunteered in May 1915, and at the conclusion of his training served with his Battalion on special duties at various stations. He did excellent work as bombing Instructor, but was not successful in obtaining his transfer overseas before the close of the war. He was demobilised in November 1919. 39, Grenard Road, Peckham, S.E.15.   Z5600

FARMER, A. C., Driver, R.F.A.
He was mobilised in August 1914, and in March of the following year was sent to France. He fought in various sectors of the Western Front, and was in action in the Battles of Hill 60, Ypres, Festubert, Vimy Ridge, the Somme, and Cambrai. After the Armistice he went into Germany with the Army of Occupation, and remained there until discharged in June 1919, He holds the 1914-15 Star, and the General Service and Victory Medals.
32, South Island Place, Brixton Road, S.W.9.   Z5243–4B

FARMER, F. W., 1st Air Mechanic, R.A.F.
Volunteering in September 1915, he was in the following year drafted to India, where he served with his Squadron at many important stations, including Tankári, Bannu and Kohát and took part in the operations on the North West Frontier. In December 1919 he returned to England and was demobilised. He holds the India General Service Medal (with clasp Afghanistan, N.W. Frontier, 1919), and the General Service and Victory Medals.
90, Brayard's Road, Peckham, S.E.15.   Z5383–4A

FARMER, J. R., 1st Air Mechanic, R.A.F.
In April 1918 upon reaching military age he joined the Royal Air Force, and was stationed at the Central Flying School, Upavon. Owing to the early cessation of hostilities he was not successful in securing his transfer overseas, but rendered excellent services until his demobilisation in May 1919.
90, Brayard's Road, Peckham, S.E.15.   Z5383–4B

FARNFIELD, J., Corporal, R.A.S.C. (M.T.)
He joined in 1916, and in the following year was drafted to Egypt, where he served for two years. During this period he was engaged at Kantara and other places on important duties in connection with the transport of supplies to the forward areas, and also served on the lines of communication. He was demobilised in 1919, on his return to England, and holds the General Service and Victory Medals.   Z2081B
27, Victoria Terrace, 152, Queen's Road, Battersea, S.W.8

FARNFIELD, L., Sergt., 18th London Regiment (London Irish Rifles).
Volunteering in 1914, he completed a course of training, and was engaged on important duties as an Instructor of recruits for the New Armies, and did valuable work in that capacity. He was not sent to a theatre of war owing to medical unfitness for general service, and was discharged in consequence in 1916.
27, Victoria Terrace, Queen's Road, Battersea Park, S.W.8.   Z2081A

FARNHAM, A., Private, Wiltshire Regiment.
Volunteering in December 1914, he proceeded overseas in the following year, and served in various sectors of the Western Front. He was engaged in heavy fighting in the Battles of Ypres and St. Eloi and was wounded at Loos. Returning to the Field on recovery he was in action in numerous engagements, including the Battle of the Somme, and was wounded on three other occasions. He was sent home to hospital on account of his injuries and invalided out of the Service in 1917, and holds the 1914-15 Star, and the General Service and Victory Medals.
23, Motley Street, Wandsworth Road, S.W.8.   Z2082

FARR, A., Corporal, R.M.L.I.
A serving soldier, having enlisted in June 1903, he was mobilised on the outbreak of war, and in 1915 was posted to H.M.S. "Havelock," which vessel was sent to the Dardanelles and took an active part in the Naval operations in that theatre of war. On the Evacuation of the Peninsula he was drafted to the Western Front, and there fought in several engagements until the cessation of hostilities. Returning home for demobilisation in January 1919, he holds the 1914-15 Star, and the General Service and Victory Medals.
23, Ivy Crescent, Bollo Lane, Chiswick, W.4.   5853A

FARR, A. J., Private, 2nd Yorkshire Regiment.
He joined in September 1916, and in the following year was sent overseas. During his service on the Western Front he fought in many engagements, and was in action at Ypres. He was reported missing on August 16th, 1917, and was later presumed to have been killed in action on that date. He was entitled to the General Service and Victory Medals.
    "He died the noblest death a man may die,
    Fighting for God and right and liberty."
119, St. George's Road, Peckham, S.E.15.   Z5601

FARR, R., L/Corporal, Royal Fusiliers.
He enlisted in 1910, and at the outbreak of war was stationed in India. In 1914, he was drafted to Gallipoli, and fought in many important engagements in that theatre of war. Invalided to England on account of ill-health, he received hospital treatment, and subsequently died on November 14th, 1915.
    "And doubtless he went in splendid company."
23, Ivy Crescent, Bollo Lane, Chiswick, W.4.   5853B

FARRANT, F. W., Driver, R.F.A.
He volunteered in December 1915, and in the following year was drafted overseas. Attached to a flying column he served in the Battles of the Somme, Arras, Ypres, Albert, Béthune, Bullecourt and in several engagements during the Retreat and Advance of 1918. He was demobilised in October 1919 after returning home, and holds the General Service and Victory Medals.
53, Clayton Road, Peckham, S.E.15.   Z5955

FARRANT, H. J., Corporal, 10th Essex Regiment.
He volunteered in September 1914, and in the following July proceeded to the Western Front, and fought in the Battles of the Somme, Delville Wood, Trones Wood, and was twice wounded at Thiepval. Rejoining his unit he was in charge of a machine-gun section, and was mentioned in Despatches on March 10th, 1917, and again on March 21st, 1918, for gallantry and devotion to duty in the Field in holding the enemy in check for sixteen hours during the German Offensive. He also fought in the Allied Advance, and gave his life for King and Country at Morlancourt, on August 6th, 1918, and was entitled to the 1914-15 Star, and the General Service and Victory Medals.
    "A costly sacrifice upon the altar of freedom."
19, Marville Road, Fulham, S.W.6.   Z4329-30-31A

FARRANT, J. E,, Private, 1/2nd Bedfordshire Regt.
He joined in July 1918, and on the conclusion of his training was engaged on guard and other important duties at various prisoners of war detention camps. He rendered valuable services, but was unable to obtain a transfer overseas owing to medical unfitness for general service, and was demobilised in November 1919.
22, Rowallan Road, Munster Road, S.W.6.   Z4329-30-31D

FARRANT, R. J., L/Corporal, 3rd and 10th Essex Regiment.
Volunteering in September 1914, he was sent overseas in the following July, and saw much service on the Western Front. He was in action at Albert, Bray, Maricourt and during engagements in the Somme sector, and was wounded in the Battle of Delville Wood on July 19th, 1916. Sent home on account of his injuries he was discharged as medically unfit for further service in October 1917, and holds the 1914-15 Star, and the General Service and Victory Medals.
19, Marville Road, Fulham, S.W.6. Z4329-30-31C

FARRANT, T. W. G., Sergt., R.A.M.C. (T.)
Volunteering in March 1915, he was drafted to the Western Front two months later and rendered valuable services with the Field Ambulance during the Battles of Ypres, Loos, the Somme and in many other engagements. After the Armistice he was sent with the Army of Occupation into Germany, and was stationed at Cologne. He returned to England for demobilisation in July 1919, and holds the 1914-15 Star, and the General Service and Victory Medals.
3, Brookville Road, Dawes Road, S.W.6. Z4329-30-31B

FARRANT, W. J. C., Private, East Surrey Regt.
Volunteering in December 1914, he was drafted to France in the following June, and fought in the Battle of Ypres and other engagements until sent to Salonika three months later. After considerable service in the Balkans he returned to the Western Front, and taking part in many operations during the Advance of 1918, was wounded near Albert. He was demobilised in February 1919, and holds the 1914-15 Star, and the General Service and Victory Medals.
79, Weybridge Street, Battersea, S.W.11. Z2083

FARRELL, C. B., C.S.M., 2nd South Lancashire Regiment.
A serving soldier, he was mobilised at the outbreak of hostilities, and embarked for France in November 1914. He was in action in many engagements, including the first and second Battles of Ypres. Owing to a fall from his horse he broke his thigh and complications arising he was invalided to England but subsequently died at Edmonton Hospital on April 15th, 1916. He was entitled to the 1914 Star, and the General Service and Victory Medals.
66, Dalyell Road, Landor Road, S.W.9. Z2085

FARRELL, F., Pte., 2nd Prince of Wales' Leinster Regiment.
A serving soldier, he was mobilised at the commencement of the war, and proceeded overseas in September 1914. During his service on the Western Front he fought in many important engagements, and was taken prisoner at Armentières in November 1914. He was held in captivity until after the cessation of hostilities, and then repatriated. He was still serving in 1920, and holds the 1914 Star, and the General Service and Victory Medals.
103, Sandmere Road, Clapham, S.W.4. Z2084B

FARRELL, F. J., Corporal, Royal Irish Rifles.
Mobilised in August 1914, he embarked for France and fought in the Retreat from Mons, and at the Battle of Le Cateau and in many other important engagements. Owing to ill-health he returned to England and after receiving hospital treatment was invalided out of the Service in May 1915. He holds the Mons Star, and the General Service and Victory Medals.
66, Dalyell Road, Landor Road, S.W.9. Z2085A

FARRELL, J., Sergt., 1st London Regiment (Royal Fusiliers).
He volunteered in September 1914, and embarked for the Dardanelles in August of the following year, and was in action at the Landing at Suvla Bay, at the capture of Chunuk Bair, and in the ensuing fighting until the Evacuation of the Peninsula. Transferred to France he fought in the Battles of Vimy Ridge and the Somme, and was wounded and returned to England. On recovery he was sent to Woolwich, and passed as a Staff Armourer Sergeant. He later served in Ireland at various stations, and was demobilised in November 1919 holding the 1914-15 Star, and the General Service and Victory Medals.
66, Dalyell Road, Landor Road, S.W.9. Z2085C

FARRELL, J., Private, 2nd Connaught Rangers.
A Reservist, he was mobilised at the commencement of hostilities and drafted to the Western Front in October 1914, was in action in various parts of the line and fought in many important engagements. He was reported missing in April 1915, and later was presumed to have been killed in action at Ypres. He was entitled to the 1914 Star, and the General Service and Victory Medals.
" Thinking that remembrance, though unspoken, may reach him where he sleeps."
103, Sandmere Road, Clapham, S.W.4. Z2084C

FARRELL, L., Pte., R.A.S.C. and Rflmn., 17th King's Royal Rifle Corps.
He volunteered in January 1916, and proceeded to France seven months later. During his service overseas he was engaged in heavy fighting in various sectors and was severely wounded in the Ypres salient during the German offensive. Admitted into hospital he subsequently succumbed to his injuries on April 17th, 1918. He was entitled to the General Service and Victory Medals.
" His memory is cherished with pride."
103, Sandmere Road, Clapham, S.W.4. Z2084D

FARRINGTON, D., Private, 1st Northumberland Fusiliers.
Volunteering in November 1915, he served at various stations until drafted to France in the following March. Here he was engaged on important duties at the Base and rendered excellent services throughout. He returned to England and was demobilised in February 1919, and holds the General Service and Victory Medals.
3, Madron Street, Walworth, S.E.17. Z2086

FARROW, H., Bombardier, R.F.A.
Volunteering in November 1914, he was sent to France in the following July, and fought in many important engagements, including those at the Somme and Ypres. In 1917, transferred to Italy, he served at various stations until returning to England he was demobilised in February 1919, and holds the 1914-15 Star, and the General Service and Victory Medals.
3, Tidbury Street, Battersea Park Road, S.W.8. Z2087B

FARROW, H. A., Private, Queen's Own (Royal West Kent Regiment).
Joining in June 1916, he completed his training and was stationed at various depôts until drafted to the Western Front in April 1918. He was in action in many parts of the line during the German offensive and subsequent Allied advance and was wounded in October 1918. He subsequently died from the effects of his injuries on November 3rd, 1918. He was entitled to the General Service and Victory Medals.
" He passed out of the sight of men by the path of duty and self-sacrifice." ·
3, Tidbury Street, Battersea Park Road, S.W.8. Z2087A

FARWIG, H. F., L/Corporal, 1st London Regiment (Royal Fusiliers).
Volunteering in August 1914, he was drafted to the Western Front in the following year and fought in many engagements, including those at Neuve Chapelle, Hill 60, Ypres, Loos and St. Eloi. He was killed in action on the Somme on September 15th, 1916, and was entitled to the 1914-15 Star, and the General Service and Victory Medals.
" Nobly striving,
He nobly fell that we might live."
36, St. Lawrence Road, Brixton Road, S.W.9. Z4450

FAULKNER. A. J., Private, 10th Queen's (Royal West Surrey Regiment).
He volunteered in November 1915 at the age of sixteen, and in the same year was sent to the Western Front, where he took part in many engagements, including those at Neuve Chapelle and Hill 60. He was reported missing in September 1916 in the first Battle of the Somme, and later was presumed to have been killed in action. He was entitled to the 1914-15 Star, and the General Service and Victory Medals.
" Honour to the immortal dead who gave their youth that the world might grow old in peace."
21, Tyers Street, Kennington, S.E.11. Z25080A

FAULKNER, G. F., Rifleman, 17th King's Royal Rifle Corps.
Volunteering in May 1915, he was sent to the Western Front later in the same year, and fought at the Battles of Loos, St. Eloi, Vermelles, Vimy Ridge and the Somme. He was taken prisoner in March 1918 during the German offensive and escaped from Germany two days before the cessation of hostilities. He returned to England in November 1918, and was demobilised in the following March, and holds the 1914-15 Star, and the General Service and Victory Medals.
20, Motley Street, Wandsworth Road, S.W.8. Z2089

FAULKNER, J., Petty Officer, R.N.
He joined the Service in July 1914, and mobilised on the outbreak of war, was posted to H.M.S. " Illustrious," which vessel was engaged on patrol and other important duties in the North Sea and was in action off the Belgian coast. He was demobilised in August 1919, and holds the 1914-15 Star, and the General Service and Victory Medals.
3, Verona Street, Battersea, S.W.11. Z2088

FAULKNER, T. J., L/Corporal, 1/24th London Regt. (The Queen's) and M.G.C.

He volunteered in August 1914, and was sent to the Western Front in March of the following year and was in action at the Battles of the Somme, Loos, Albert and many other engagements. He died gloriously on the field of battle at Vermelles in December 1917, and was entitled to the 1914-15 Star, and the General Service and Victory Medals.

"And doubtless he went in splendid company."

21, Tyers Street, Kennington, S.E.11.   Z25080B

FAULKNER, W. A., L/Corporal, Labour Corps.

He joined in February 1917, and proceeded to France in the following month and in the forward areas engaged on important duties as canteen manager. He rendered excellent services throughout, and returning to England was demobilised in February 1919. He holds the General Service and Victory Medals.

17, Rockley Road, West Kensington, W.14.   11872

FAULKNER, W. H., Sapper, R.E.

He joined in March 1916, and embarked for the Western Front in the following year. During his service overseas he was present at the Battles of Arras, Ypres and the Somme, and did excellent work engaged on duties in connection with operations in the forward areas. He also served throughout the Retreat and Advance of 1918, and was demobilised in January 1919. He holds the General Service and Victory Medals.

21, Irving Grove, Stockwell Road, S.W.9.   Z2090A

FAUX, A. H., Pte., 13th North Staffordshire Regt.

He joined in July 1916, and was drafted to the Western Front shortly afterwards. He saw much service in various sectors and fought in many important engagements and throughout the German offensive and subsequent Allied Advance of 1918. He returned to England, and was demobilised in July 1919, and holds the General Service and Victory Medals.

3, Brackley Terrace, Chiswick, W.4.   5431A

FAUX, C. H., Sapper, R.E.

Volunteering in December 1915, he was drafted to the Western Front in the following May, and was engaged on important duties in connection with the maintenance of the lines of communication. He was under fire in many important engagements and was wounded, and on recovery served throughout the Retreat and Advance of 1918, and was demobilised in May 1919. He holds the General Service and Victory Medals.

13, Dalyell Road, Landor Road, S.W.9.   Z2091

FAWCETT, J. A., Private, 2/1st Norfolk Regiment.

He joined in August 1918, and owing to his being over military age was not drafted to a theatre of war on the completion of his training. He was sent to Ireland, where he was engaged on important duties with his Battalion until his demobilisation in December 1918.

246, Albert Road, Peckham, S.E.15.   Z5761A

FAWCETT, L. H., Rflmn., 18th London Regiment (London Irish Rifles).

Mobilised on the outbreak of war, he was engaged on important duties with his unit until sent to France in 1916. He served on the Western Front for a time and was drafted to Salonika later in the same year. He proceeded to Egypt in 1917 and took part in several engagements during the British Advance through Palestine. He gave his life for King and Country at Jerusalem in December 1917, and was entitled to the General Service and Victory Medals.

"Whilst we remember the Sacrifice is not in vain."

246, Albert Road, Peckham, S.E.15.   Z5761B

FAY, J., Sergt., 2/7th London Regiment.

Joining in November 1916, he was sent to France on completing his training. Here he was in action in many sectors and fought in many important engagements, including the Battles of Bullecourt and Passchendaele. Later he served at Rouen and Havre, engaged on cooking and other important duties at various prisoners of war camps. He was demobilised in January 1919, and holds the General Service and Victory Medals.

24, Cornwall Grove, Chiswick, W.4.   T5612B

FAZACKERLEY, R., Special War Worker.

He offered his services for work of National importance in 1914, and until 1918 was engaged on the production of munitions, and did good work. He also rendered valuable services in the Motor Volunteers, conveying sick and wounded troops to the hospitals.

7, Cottage Grove, Bedford Road, S.W.9.   Z2092

FELLS, F. R. G. (M.M.), Sergt., R.F.A.

He volunteered in December 1914, and embarked for the Western Front in the following year, and was in action on the Somme and at Loos. Later in 1915 he was drafted to Salonika and fought in various sectors on the Struma and Doiran fronts and was twice wounded and also suffered from malaria. He was awarded the Military Medal and the Serbian Cross for gallantry and devotion to duty in the Field. Returning to England he was demobilised in June 1919, and also holds the 1914-15 Star, and the General Service and Victory Medals.

36, Thornton Street, Brixton Road, S.W.9.   Z2094

FELSTEAD, F. W., Driver, R.F.A.

A serving soldier, he was mobilised at the outbreak of war, and drafted to France fought in the Retreat from Mons, and at the Battles of Ypres, Loos, Vimy Ridge, the Somme I and II, Bullecourt and throughout the German offensive and Allied Advance of 1918. He was demobilised in March 1919, and holds the Mons Star, and the General Service and Victory Medals.

92, Nelson Row, High Street, Clapham, S.W.4.   Z1158A

FELSTEAD, H. C., Driver, R.F.A,

Volunteering in 1914, he proceeded to the Balkan Front in the following year, and was in action on the Struma and Strumnitza and in various other sectors of that theatre of war. He fought throughout the final Allied Advance in 1918, and returning to England was demobilised in 1919. He holds the 1914-15 Star, and the General Service and Victory Medals.

16, Blendon Row, Walworth, S.E.17.   Z2095

FELSTEAD, H. E., Private, R.A.M.C.

A Reservist, he was mobilised and drafted to the Western Front at the commencement of the war and served in the Retreat from Mons, where he was taken prisoner on August 26th, 1914. He was held in captivity for sixteen months, when, owing to ill-health, he was repatriated. He then served at various hospitals until demobilised in February 1919. He holds the Mons Star, and the General Service and Victory Medals.

17, St. Andrew's Street, Wandsworth Road, S.W.8.   Z2096A

FENNELL, H. J., Private, R.A.S.C. (M.T.)

He joined H.M. Forces in 1918, after having been rejected on five previous occasions, and, completing his training, was stationed at various depôts on important duties. Owing to ill-health he was unsuccessful on obtaining his transfer to a theatre of war, but rendered excellent services until demobilised in November 1919. Prior to joining the Colours he served as a Special Constable in the "M" Division for three years.

8, Osborne Street, Walworth, S.E.17.   Z2097

FENNINGS, F. C., Private, R.A.S.C. (M.T.)

Joining in March 1916, he embarked for the Western Front two months later and fought in many engagements, including those at Vermelles, Ploegsteert, Vimy Ridge, Messines, Lens, Bapaume, the Somme (I and II), and throughout the German Offensive and Allied Advance of 1918, and was wounded. He was demobilised in October 1919, and holds the General Service and Victory Medals.

216, East Street, Walworth, S.E.17.   Z2098

FERGOOD, E. W., Gunner, R.F.A.

He volunteered in October 1914, and in the following year was drafted to the Western Front, and during his service overseas took part in many engagements. He was killed in action during the Advance of 1918, and was entitled to the 1914-15 Star, and the General Service and Victory Medals.

"He joined the great white company of valiant souls."

8, Elim Street, Bermondsey, S.E.1.   TZ25845

FEWTRELL, G. S., Rifleman, 21st London Regt. (1st Surrey Rifles).

Volunteering in July 1915, he completed his training and was stationed at various depôts engaged on guard and other important duties with his unit. Owing to ill-health he was unable to obtain his transfer overseas, but did excellent work until demobilised in February 1919.

24, Westhall Road, Camberwell, S.E.5.   Z2099

FIELD, P. R., Corporal, Bedfordshire Regiment.

Volunteering in 1914, he was sent to France in the following year, and was in action in many engagements, including those at Ypres and the Somme. He was severely wounded at Loos, and returning to England, received hospital treatment. On recovery he was transferred to the Labour Corps, and after serving at various stations was demobilised in 1919. He holds the 1914-15 Star, and the General Service and Victory Medals.

14, Chalmers Street, Wandsworth Road, S.W.8   Z2100

FIELD, W. J., Air Mechanic, R.A.F.

He joined in December 1917, and proceeded to France in the same month. During his service overseas he served at various aerodromes with the Observation Balloon Section and did excellent work throughout the Retreat and Advance of 1918. He was demobilised in February 1919, and holds the General Service and Victory Medals.

176, Farmer's Road, Camberwell, S.E.5.   Z1010D

FIELDER, B. E., Pte., Royal Warwickshire Regt.

He volunteered in November 1914, and on completion of his training was stationed at various depôts until drafted to Mesopotamia in the following year. He served in various parts of the line, and was in action in many important engagements. He was unfortunately killed in action on April 9th, 1916, and was entitled to the 1914-15 Star, and the General Service and Victory Medals.

"Courage, bright hopes, and a myriad dreams, splendidly given."

50, Tabor Road, Hammersmith, W.6.   11562A

FIELDING, A., L/Corporal, 2nd Dorsetshire Regt.

Joining in May 1916, he embarked for Mesopotamia in September of the same year and was engaged in heavy fighting in various sectors. Transferred to Egypt in August 1917, he fought in many engagements of note during the British Advance through Palestine into Syria, and was wounded. He returned to England and was demobilised in October 1919, and holds the General Service and Victory Medals.

17, Morrison Street, Battersea, S.W.11.   Z2101

FIELDING, W. H., Bombardier, R.F.A.

Volunteering in March 1915, he proceeded to France in the following October and was in action at the Battles of La Bassée, the Somme, Passchendaele, Vimy Ridge and many engagements during the German offensive and subsequent Allied Advance of 1918. After the Armistice he proceeded into Germany with the Army of Occupation and served there until demobilised in January 1919. He holds the 1914-15 Star, and the General Service and Victory Medals.

14, Belham Street, Camberwell, S.E.5.   Z2102

FILLIS, C., Pte., Queen's (Royal West Surrey Regt).

He volunteered in September 1914, and was sent to the Western Front three months later. During his service he fought in the Battles of Neuve Chapelle, Hill 60, Ypres II, Loos, Lens, Arras, and throughout the Retreat of 1918. He was gassed in July 1918, and invalided to England, received hospital treatment. He was discharged in September of that year, unfit for further service, and holds the 1914-15 Star, and the General Service and Victory Medals.

3, Comus Place, Walworth, S.E.17.   Z2103

FILLIS, J., Gunner, R.F.A.

Volunteering in January 1915, he embarked for France later in that year, and was in action in many important engagements, including those at Loos, Ypres, the Somme, Vimy Ridge, St. Quentin, Festubert and in the German offensive and Allied Advance in 1918. He was demobilised in April 1919, and holds the 1914-15 Star, and the General Service and Victory Medals.

9, Treherne Road, Stockwell, S.W.9.   Z3455

FINBOW, F., Rifleman, Rifle Brigade.

He volunteered in September 1914, and proceeded to France in the following February. During his service overseas he fought in the Battles at Neuve Chapelle, St. Eloi, Ypres II, Festubert, Vermelles, Vimy Ridge, Loos and in many other engagements. He was reported missing on August 18th, 1916, and later was presumed to have been killed in action on that date. He was entitled to the 1914-15 Star, and the General Service and Victory Medals.

" A valiant soldier, with undaunted heart, he breasted Life's last hill."

16, Wansey Street, Walworth, S.E.17.   Z2104

FINCH, F., Private, R.A.S.C. (M.T.)

He volunteered in August 1914, and was almost immediately drafted to the Western Front. He was employed on special transport duties in many important engagements, including the Retreat from Mons, and the Battles of the Marne, the Aisne, Ypres, La Bassée, Neuve Chapelle and Hill 60. He did valuable work throughout the campaign, and was demobilised in February 1919, and holds the Mons Star, and the General Service and Victory Medals.

8, Prescott Place, Little Manor Street, Clapham, S.W.4.   Z2105

FINCH, F. B., Private, 9th East Surrey Regiment.

He joined in June 1916, and early in the following year was sent to the Western Front, in which theatre of war he was engaged in many fierce battles, including those of Ypres, Hill 60 and St. Quentin. He gave his life for King and Country on the Somme front on June 13th, 1917. He was entitled to the General Service and Victory Medals.

" Great deeds cannot die."

35, Rozel Road, Clapham, S.W.4.   Z2107A

FINCH, F. J., Private, Labour Corps.

He volunteered in January 1916, and in May of the following year was sent to France, where he served with his unit on salvage and other important duties. He also took an active part in the Retreat and Advance of 1918, and after hostilities ceased returned to England, and was demobilised in February 1919. He holds the General Service and Victory Medals.

20, Newman Street, Battersea, S.W.11.   Z2106

FINCH, H. T., Cpl., 368th H.S. Coy., Labour Corps.

He joined in November 1918, and after serving in various stations with his unit at home, was sent to France, where he did work of an important nature with the Chinese Labour Company. On the cessation of hostilities he returned to England and was demobilised in November 1919.

35, Rozel Road, Clapham, S.W.4.   Z2107B

FINCH, R., Private, 26th Queen's (Royal West Surrey Regiment).

He joined in March 1917, and was shortly afterwards drafted to France, where he was actively engaged in heavy fighting at Arras, Amiens, Bullecourt, and St. Quentin. He also saw much service in the Retreat and Advance of 1918. He returned to England in October 1918, and was demobilised in January of the following year and holds the General Service and Victory Medals.

67, Beaufoy Road, Battersea, S.W.11.   Z2108

FINCH, T., Private, The Middlesex Regiment.

He volunteered in October 1914, and early in the following year was drafted to the Western Front. There he fought in many engagements, and was badly wounded at Dickebusch on February 14th, 1915. He was invalided home, and after spending some time in hospital was eventually discharged as medically unfit for further service in June 1915. He holds the 1914-15 Star, and the General Service and Victory Medals.

21, Eltham Street, Walworth, S.W.17.   Z1301A

FINDON, W. H., C.S.M., 23rd London Regiment.

He was mobilised in August 1914, and served at various stations on important duties with his Battalion. He rendered valuable services as a physical training and musketry Instructor but was not successful in obtaining his transfer overseas before hostilities ceased. He was discharged on account of service in October 1918.

32, South Island Place, Stockwell, S.W.9.   Z5243-4A

FINEMORE, W. G. J., Private, R.A.S.C.

Although over military age he volunteered in 1915, and in the following year proceeded to France, where he was engaged on important duties in connection with the transport of ammunition and supplies to the forward areas in the Somme, Arras, and Ypres sectors. He also served in various canteens and in hospital ships bringing the sick and wounded to England. He was demobilised in 1919, and holds the General Service and Victory Medals.

31, McKerrell Road, Peckham, S.E.15.   Z5961

FINN, J., Private, 1st Royal Fusiliers.

He was mobilised from the Reserve in August 1914, and in September of the same year, was drafted to the Western Front. Here he was engaged in much severe fighting, and fought in in the Retreat from Mons, and in many of the principal battles which followed, and was twice wounded. He was unfortunately killed in action on October 13th, 1918, and was entitled to the Mons Star, and the General Service and Victory Medals.

" His life for his Country, his soul to God."

18, Joubert Street, Battersea, S.W.11.   Z2109

FISH, S., Air Mechanic, R.A.F.

He joined in August 1916, and after a period of service at home was drafted to Egypt a year later. Here he served on important duties with the Balloon Section at Cairo, and Alexandria, and remained in that theatre of war until the cessation of hostilities. He returned home and was demobilised in November 1919, and holds the General Service and Victory Medals.

31, Bullen Street, Battersea, S.W.11.   Z2111

FISH, C., Private, R.A.S.C.

He volunteered in April 1915, and later in the same year proceeded to France. He was employed on special duties in the forward areas and was present at many engagements, including those at Ypres and Arras. Owing to illness he was invalided to hospital in England, and after protracted medical treatment was discharged from the Service in February 1918. He subsequently died in May 1920, and was entitled to the 1914-15 Star, and the General Service and Victory Medals.

" Steals on the ear the distant triumph song."

34, Bonnington Square, South Lambeth Road, S.W.8.   2110

FISH, T. F., Private, R.A.S.C.

Volunteering in September 1915, he was later drafted to Gallipoli, and did valuable work during the Evacuation of the Peninsula. He then proceeded to the Western Front and there served on important transport duties in the Battles of Arras, Ypres, the Somme, Cambrai, and in other engagements during the Retreat and Advance of 1918. He returned home for demobilisation in January 1919, and holds the 1914-15 Star, and the General Service and Victory Medals.

28, Myatt Road, Stockwell, S.W.9. Z5074B

FISH, T. F. (Junior), 1st Class Petty Officer, R.N.

Already serving in the Royal Navy when war broke out he was posted to H.M.S. " Orvieto " and served on mine-laying duties in the Heligoland Bight and other waters. He also served in H.M.S. " Intrepid " and " Titania " and during his service these vessels had frequent encounters with enemy craft. Owing to impaired vision he was invalided out of the Service in September 1919, and holds the 1914-15 Star, and the General Service and Victory Medals.

28, Myatt Road, Stockwell, S.W.9. Z5074A

FISHER, A., Cpl., 23rd London Regt. (The Queen's).

He volunteered in August 1914, and in January of the following year proceeded with his unit to the Western Front. Here he served in heavy fighting in various parts of the line, and was in action in many engagements. He was later sent to Egypt, and fought in the Advance through Palestine, and died gloriously on the Field of Battle at Jerusalem in December 1917. He was entitled to the 1914-15 Star, and the General Service and Victory Medals.

" Thinking that remembrance, though unspoken, may reach
him where he sleeps."

17, Duffield Street, Battersea, S.W.11. Z2117

FISHER, F., Stoker, Royal Navy.

He joined in January 1917, and was shortly afterwards posted to H.M.S. " Lion," in which vessel he served with the Grand Fleet in the North Sea. His ship also served on special duties at Scapa Flow, and on patrol and convoy work in various waters, and had many encounters with enemy craft. He was demobilised in January 1919, and holds the General Service and Victory Medals.

15, Townsend Street, Walworth, S.E.17. Z2112

FISHER, G. H., C.Q.M.S., M.G.C.

He volunteered in August 1914, and was posted to the Duke of Wellington's (West Riding Regiment), with which unit he did good work, and was later transferred to the Machine Gun Corps. In April 1916 he was drafted to the Western Front, and engaged in heavy fighting, was unhappily killed in action during the Battle of the Somme on July 27th, 1916. He was entitled to the General Service and Victory Medals.

" Nobly striving,
He nobly fell that we might live."

22, Odger Street, Battersea, S.W.11. Z2116

FISHER, H. L., Private, 2nd Border Regiment.

He joined in November 1916, and early in the following year was sent to the Western Front. He fought in many important engagements, including those of the Somme, Arras, Ypres, and Passchendaele, and later in 1917 was drafted to Italy. In this theatre of war he was engaged in severe fighting on the Piave, and after hostilities ceased returned to England and was demobilised in January 1919. He holds the General Service and Victory Medals.

44, Handforth Road, Brixton Road, S.W.9. Z5242

FISHER, R. T., Private, 11th Essex Regiment.

He volunteered in September 1914, and in August of the following year proceeded to the Western Front, and was shortly afterwards engaged in heavy fighting at the Battle of the Somme (where he was wounded in September, 1916), Cambrai, Ypres, and many other places. He was wounded a second time at Loos in April 1917, and invalided to England received protracted hospital treatment. He was eventually discharged as medically unfit for further service in January 1918 and holds the 1914-15 Star, and the General Service and Victory Medals.

84, Robertson Street, Wandsworth Road, S.W.8. Z2113

FISHER, W. E., 1st Class Stoker, R.N.

He volunteered in November 1915, and was shortly afterwards posted to H.M.S. " Revenge." He served in this ship with the Grand Fleet in the North Sea and took part in the Battle of Jutland, and other engagements, and did valuable work throughout the war. He was demobilised in June 1919, and holds the General Service and Victory Medals.

23, Basnett Road, Lavender Hill, S.W.11. Z2115

FISHER, W. J., Private, R.A.S.C. (M.T.)

He volunteered in September 1914, and in the following August was sent to France. In this theatre of war he saw much service, and was in action at the Battles of Ypres and Loos. Invalided home owing to illness contracted on service, on recovery he was sent to Mesopotamia, where he served on important transport duties until 1918. He was then drafted to India, and was employed there on similar duties for a time. He returned to England for demobilisation in July 1919, and holds the 1914-15 Star, and the General Service and Victory Medals.

53, Tyneham Road, Battersea, S.W.11. Z2114

FITCH, A. G., Private, 6th South Staffordshire Regt.

Joining in September 1916, he was drafted to France in February of the following year. Whilst on the Western Front he was engaged in heavy fighting at the Battles of Arras, Vimy Ridge, Bullecourt, Messines, Ypres, and Cambrai. He was reported missing on November 30th, 1917, and was later presumed to have been killed in action on that date. He was entitled to the General Service and Victory Medals.

" The path of duty was the way to glory."

70, Geneva Road, Coldharbour Lane, S.W.9 Z3084

FITZJOHN, A., Pte., Royal Fusiliers and Flight Sergt., R.A.F.

Volunteering in September 1914, he was later sent overseas, and stationed at Malta, was engaged on garrison duties for a time. Owing to ill-health he was invalided to hospital, and on recovery was transferred to the Royal Air Force. He returned to England and served on important clerical duties at the Records Office of this unit until demobilised in January 1919. He holds the General Service and Victory Medals.

117, Darwin's Buildings, Crail Row, Walworth, S.E.17. Z2118A

FITZJOHN, W. J., Leading Seaman, R.N.

He was serving at the outbreak of war aboard H.M.S. " Weymouth," which vessel was engaged on important patrol and other duties off the coasts of Africa. In November 1914 his ship was engaged with the " Konigsberg " in the Rufiji River, German East Africa, and in this action he gave his life for King and Country. He was entitled to the 1914-15 Star, and the General Service and Victory Medals.

" Great deeds cannot die,
They with the sun and moon renew their light for ever."

117, Darwin Buildings, Crail Row, Walworth, S.E.17. Z2118B

FITZMAURICE, R. M., A.B., Royal Navy.

He joined the Royal Navy in 1912, and when war broke out was serving aboard H.M.S. " Agamemnon," which ship took part in the Naval operations in the Dardanelles and served there until the Evacuation of the Peninsula. Transferred later to H.M.S. " Europa " his ship was engaged on important patrol duties in the North Sea until the end of hostilities. In 1920 he was serving in H.M.S. " Swallow " in the Black Sea, and holds the 1914-15 Star, and the General Service and Victory Medals.

2, Knox Road, Battersea, S.W.11. Z5704B

FITZMAURICE, T. F., Rflmn, King's Royal Rifle Corps.

Joining in November 1916, on attaining military age, he embarked for Italy in the following year, and was in action in the Advance on the Piave, and was gassed. Sent home early in 1918, he received hospital treatment for some months and was invalided out of the Service in November of the same year. He holds the General Service and Victory Medals.

2, Knox Road, Battersea, S.W.11. Z5704C

FITZPATRICK, A. T., Driver, R.A.S.C. (M.T.)

He volunteered in September 1914, and in the following month was sent to France. In this theatre of war he was engaged in driving a Red Cross Ambulance car, and was present at the Battles of La Bassée, Ypres, the Somme, Ploegsteert, Passchendaele, and Vimy Ridge. He later served with the Army of Occupation in Germany, and was stationed at Cologne, Bonn, and Spa. He was demobilised in May 1919, and holds the 1914 Star, and the General Service and Victory Medals.

37, Elmington Road, Camberwell, S.E.5. Z4451B

FITZPATRICK, T., Private, R.A.S.C.

He joined in August 1916, and served with his unit at various stations until drafted to France in March 1918. During his service overseas he was employed on important duties in the Battles of Ypres and Vimy Ridge, and did very good work. He was discharged on account of service in November 1918, and holds the General Service and Victory Medals.

37, Elmington Road, Camberwell, S.E.5. Z4451C

FIVEASH, G. T., Gunner, R.G.A.

Volunteering in October 1914, he was drafted to the Western Front in the following February. He there took part in numerous engagements including the actions at Neuve Chapelle, Hill 60, Festubert, Loos, and the Somme. In October 1918, during the final advance he was wounded near Arras, and sent to hospital, where he remained until his return to England for demobilisation in February 1919. He holds the 1914-15 Star, and the General Service and Victory Medals.

22, Dartnell Road, Camberwell, S.E.5. Z5386

FLACK, E. J., Corporal, R.A.M.C.

He volunteered in January 1915, and later was sent to France, and served in various parts of the line engaged on important duties attending to sick and wounded troops. He was present at many important engagements, and was frequently under fire during the German Offensive and subsequent Allied Advance of 1918. He was demobilised in November 1919, and holds the General Service and Victory Medals.

45, Sulgrave Road, Hammersmith, W.6. 12104B

FLACK, H., Private, R.A.S.C.
Volunteering in June 1915, he was drafted to France in the following month, and served in the forward areas on important duties, and was present at the Battles of Loos, Vimy Ridge, the Somme, Messines, and Ypres. He was demobilised in February 1919, and held the 1914-15 Star, and the General Service and Victory Medals. Owing to ill-health he died on January 29th, 1920.
"His memory is cherished with pride."
43, Charleston Street, Walworth, S.E.17. Z2119

FLACK, L. W. (M.M.), Rifleman, King's Royal Rifle Corps.
He joined in September 1916, and was shortly afterwards drafted to France. Here he was in action in various parts of the line, and fought in many engagements. He was awarded the Military Medal for conspicuous gallantry and devotion to duty in the Field. Returning to England he was demobilised in February 1920, and also holds the General Service and Victory Medals.
45, Sulgrave Road, Hammersmith, W.6. 12104A

FLACK, W., Private, R.A.S.C. (M.T.)
He volunteered in June 1915, and in the following year was sent to France. He was in action at the Battles of the Somme, Beaumont-Hamel, and Ypres, and after serving at Dunkirk for a time, was drafted to Italy in 1917, and was present at the fighting on the Piave. In 1918 he returned to the Western Front, and was engaged on important transport duties during the Retreat and Allied Advance of 1918. After the Armistice he was sent into Germany with the Army of Occupation, and was stationed at Cologne, until he returned to England for demobilisation in July 1919. He holds the General Service and Victory Medals.
43, Broadhinton Road, Clapham, S.W.4. Z1343C Z1344C

FLAIN, R., Private, 5th Sherwood Foresters.
He joined in October 1916, and in the following March proceeded to the Western Front. During his service overseas he was engaged in heavy fighting in various sectors. On June 1st, 1917, he gave his life for the freedom of England in the Battle of Arras. He was entitled to the General Service and Victory Medals.
"Nobly striving,
He nobly fell that we might live."
47, Warrior Road, Camberwell, S.E.5. Z2120

FLANNIGAN, T. M., A.B., Royal Navy.
He was mobilised in September 1914, having previously served in the Royal Navy, and was engaged on special duties at various ports, and also at the Admiralty. He rendered valuable services, but was retained for duties ashore owing to medical unfitness, and was invalided out of the Service in September 1919.
24, Gladstone Street, Battersea Park Road, S.W.8. Z2121

FLATT, C. H., Pte., 13th London Regt. (Kensingtons).
He joined in December 1917, and at the conclusion of his training was engaged with his Battalion on important duties at various depôts. He did good work, but was unsuccessful in obtaining his transfer overseas, prior to the cessation of hostilities, and was demobilised in March 1920.
2, Claybrook Road, Hammersmith, W.6. 13425C

FLATT, W. W., Private, 13th London Regiment (Kensingtons).
Volunteering in January 1915, he was later sent to France. In this theatre of war he fought in various sectors and was in action in many important engagements. He died gloriously in action on the field of battle at Cambrai on December 1st, 1917, and was entitled to the General Service and Victory Medals.
"He passed out of the sight of men by the path of duty and self-sacrifice."
2, Claybrook Road, Hammersmith, W.6. 13425A

FLEMING, G. S., Rifleman, 1/9th London Regiment (Queen Victoria's Rifles).
He joined in August 1916, and in December of the same year was sent to France, where he was engaged in heavy fighting in many parts of the line. He gave his life for King and Country at Polygon Wood, in the Ypres Salient, on August 16th, 1917. He was entitled to the General Service and Victory Medals.
"And doubtless he went in splendid company."
55, Elmington Road, Camberwell, S.E.5. Z3453

FLEMING, J. G., Guardsman, Coldstream Guards.
Volunteering in 1914, he served with his unit on important duties at various stations, until drafted to France in 1917. He was in action in many engagements, and during heavy fighting in the Ypres salient was severely wounded and blinded. Returning to England, he received medical treatment at St. Dunstan's Hospital, and was subsequently invalided out of the Service in 1916. He holds the General Service and Victory Medals.
56, Brandon Street, Walworth, S.E.17. Z2122

FLEMMING, B. (Mrs.), C.S. Leader (Mobile), W.R.A.F. (25th Squadron).
She joined in December 1917, and served on important duties at Dover aerodrome with her Squadron, until drafted to France, where she was engaged at Maresquel, Marquise, and Arques Aerodromes on special work, and after the Armistice proceeded into Germany with the Army of Occupation, and was stationed at Cologne. She was demobilised in December 1919, and holds the General Service and Victory Medals.
27, Combermere Road, Stockwell, S.W.9. Z2123B

FLEMMING, H. W., Rifleman, 1st Rifle Brigade.
A Reservist, he was mobilised at the outbreak of war, and was almost immediately sent to France. He fought in the Retreat from Mons, and was wounded and taken prisoner, and suffered many privations during his captivity in Germany. Released after the Signing of the Armistice, he was demobilised in December 1918, and holds the Mons Star, and the General Service and Victory Medals.
27, Combermere Road, Stockwell, S.W.9. Z2123A

FLETCHER, C., Driver, R.F.A.
Volunteering in May 1915, he proceeded to the Western Front in the same year and served throughout the rest of the war. He was in action in several important engagements, including the Battles of the Somme, Ypres, and Arras. Returning to England on the cessation of hostilities he was demobilised in July 1919, and holds the 1914-15 Star, and the General Service and Victory Medals.
105, Barlow Street, Walworth, S.E.17. Z2124B

FLETCHER, E. (Mrs.), Special War Worker.
This lady was engaged on work of National importance from 1915 until 1918 at the British Rubber Works, Acton Vale, and at the Park Royal Munition Factory. Her duties, which were in connection with the filling and stamping of shells, were carried out with efficiency and skill, and she received high commendation for her valuable services.
33, Graham Road, Chiswick, W.4. T6581A

FLETCHER, F., Private, 1st East Surrey Regiment.
A serving soldier, he was mobilised and embarked for France at the outbreak of war, and fought in the Retreat from Mons, at the Battle of the Marne, and was wounded at La Bassée in October 1914. He was sent to England and on recovery returned to the Western Front in March 1915, and was again wounded at St. Eloi, and, invalided home, received hospital treatment. He rejoined his Battalion in the front lines in July 1916, and was wounded a third time in the Battle of the Somme in September 1916. He was again invalided to England, and transferred to the Labour Corps on recovery, and served on special duties with this unit until transferred to the Royal Defence Corps in November 1918. He was then employed in guarding prisoners of war until demobilised in March 1919. He re-enlisted for a further term of service in the Royal Army Service Corps in the following May, but was discharged as medically unfit for further service in October of the same year. He holds the Mons Star, and the General Service and Victory Medals.
12, Barmore Street, Battersea, S.W.11. Z2128D

FLETCHER, G. R., Private, 1st London Regiment (Royal Fusiliers).
Joining in 1916, he was drafted to the Western Front in the same year and fought in the Battles of the Somme and Ypres, and was wounded. On his recovery after treatment in England he proceeded to German East Africa in 1918, and there served in numerous operations until the end of hostilities. He was demobilised in January 1919, on his return home, and holds the General Service and Victory Medals.
105, Barlow Street, Walworth, S.E.17. Z2124A

FLETCHER, J. T., Corporal, 1st Royal Fusiliers.
Volunteering in August 1914, he proceeded overseas in the following November and fought in many engagements on the Western Front, including those at Hill 60, Ypres, Armentières, the Somme, and Messines. He was severely wounded in the Battle of the Somme in September 1916, and, invalided to England, received hospital treatment. He was subsequently discharged unfit for further service in March 1917, and holds the 1914 Star, and the General Service and Victory Medals.
78, Robertson Street, Wandsworth Road, S.W.8. Z2127

FLETCHER, W. H., Lieut., King's Royal Rifle Corps
He was mobilised with the Reservists at the outbreak of hostilities, and sent to the Western Front in November 1914. During his service overseas he was in action in many battles, including those of the Somme, Ypres, Vimy Ridge, Arras, and was wounded at Delville Wood in June 1916. On recovery he rejoined his Battalion and was engaged in the fighting at Cambrai, and throughout the German Offensive, and subsequent Allied Advance of 1918. He was demobilised in October 1919, and holds the 1914 Star, and the General Service and Victory Medals.
7, Thorncroft Street, Wandsworth Road, S.W.8. Z2125

FLETCHER, F. C., Private, 2/2nd Scottish Horse.
He joined in September 1917, and at the conclusion of his training was drafted to Ireland, where he served on important duties with his unit. He did very good work, but was unable to obtain his transfer to a theatre of war, and was demobilised in March 1920.
24, Cornbury Street, Walworth, S.E.17.   Z2126

FLETCHER, T. W., Driver, R.F.A.
He was mobilised at the outbreak of war, and almost immediately proceeded to France, where he fought in the Retreat from Mons, and in the subsequent Battles of Ypres, Arras, the Somme, Armentières and Poperinghe, and was twice wounded. He was invalided to hospital in England and was invalided out of the Service in January 1919. He holds the Mons Star, and the General Service and Victory Medals.
33, Graham Road, Chiswick, W.4.   T6581B

FLEXMAN, A. E., Sapper, R.E.
Volunteering in 1915, he embarked for the Western Front in the same year and served in various sectors. He was engaged in building bridges and other constructional work on the lines of communication in the forward areas, and was present at the Battles of Ypres and Loos. He was unfortunately killed on July 1st, 1916, in the Battle of the Somme, and was entitled to the 1914-15 Star, and the General Service and Victory Medals.
"Great deeds cannot die."
62, Heaton Road, Peckham Rye, S.E.15.   Z5957A

FLEXMAN, A. J., Private, East Surrey Regiment.
He volunteered in August 1914, and proceeding to France in the following year was engaged in the heavy fighting at Neuve Chapelle. He gave his life for the freedom of England in the Battle of Hill 60 on April 25th 1915, and was entitled to the 1914-15 Star, and the General Service and Victory Medals.
"His memory is cherished with pride."
62, Heaton Road, Peckham Rye, S.E.15.   Z5957B

FLEXMAN, E. L., Private, 2nd Hampshire Regt.
Volunteering in September 1914, he was sent to France in the following year, and after serving there for a time proceeded to Salonika in 1915. Whilst in the Balkans he took part in the Advance across the Struma and in the Serbian Retreat, and was mentioned in Despatches in March 1916 for conspicuous bravery and devotion to duty in the Field. Returning to France in 1917, he fought in several engagements and was wounded at Bailleul on September 4th, 1918. He was demobilised in March 1919, and holds the 1914-15 Star, the General Service and Victory Medals, and a Serbian decoration.
154, Albert Road, Peckham, S.E.15.   Z5962

FLEXON, S., Private, R.A.M.C.
He volunteered in September 1914, and proceeding to Gallipoli early in the following year served there until the Evacuation of the Peninsula. He was then sent to Egypt and later to Mesopotamia. After a period of service in these theatres of war he was drafted to the Western Front in 1916, and was engaged with the Field Ambulance during the Battle of the Somme, Vimy Ridge, Bullecourt, Ypres, and in the Retreat and Advance of 1918. On the conclusion of hostilities he was sent with the Army of Occupation into Germany, and returned to England for demobilisation in March 1919. He holds the 1914-15 Star, and the General Service and Victory Medals.
13, Wells Street, Camberwell, S.E.5.   Z5075

FLINT, F. H., 1st Class Petty Officer, R.N.
Volunteering at the outbreak of war he was posted to H.M.S. "Pembroke," which vessel was engaged on patrol and other important duties off the East and South Coasts. He did good work, and owing to ill-health was invalided out of the Service in February 1918. He holds the 1914-15 Star, and the General Service and Victory Medals.
43, Hargwyne Street, Stockwell Road, S.W.9.   Z2130

FLINT, G. A., Gunner, R.F.A.
He volunteered in February 1915, and later in the same year was sent to France. In this theatre of war he was in action at Loos, St. Eloi, Albert, the Somme, and Ypres, and was badly gassed. He returned to England after the cessation of hostilities, and was demobilised in January 1919. He holds the 1914-15 Star, and the General Service and Victory Medals.
27, Wheatsheaf Lane, S. Lambeth Road, S.W.8.   Z2132

FLINT, P., Pte., Queen's (Royal West Surrey Regt.)
He joined in April 1917, and later in the same year was sent overseas. During his service on the Western Front he fought at Lens, Cambrai, and in many other engagements, and throughout did very good work as a Lewis gunner. He gave his life for the freedom of England in the heavy fighting at Ypres on January 28th, 1918, and was entitled to the General Service and Victory Medals.
"Courage, bright hopes, and a myriad dreams, splendidly given."
17, Priory Road, S. Lambeth, S.W.8.   Z2131

FLINTHAM, J., Private, Queen's (Royal West Surrey Regiment).
He joined in July 1916, and in the following October was sent to Salonika. He fought in many engagements on the Doiran front, and after the Armistice proceeded to Bulgaria, and thence to Constantinople. During his service overseas he suffered from malaria and returning to England was demobilised in March 1919, and holds the General Service and Victory Medals.
3i, Block, Victoria Dwellings, Battersea Park Road, S.W.11.   Z2133

FLOOD, B. A., Private, Labour Corps.
He volunteered in November 1915, and shortly afterwards proceeded overseas. He was engaged with his unit on important duties in many sectors of the Western Front including those of Ypres and Arras. He returned to England after the cessation of hostilities, and was demobilised in March 1919, and holds the General Service and Victory Medals.
13, Severus Road, Battersea, S.W.11.   Z2135

FLOREY, R. J., Sergt., 6th London Regt. (Rifles).
He volunteered at the outbreak of war, and served at various stations as musketry Instructor until drafted to France in 1917. Whilst on the Western Front he was engaged in the fighting at Ypres, Arras, the Somme, Cambrai, and in the Retreat and Advance of 1918, and was wounded in September of that year. He was invalided to England, and on recovery was employed on home duties until demobilised in February 1919. He holds the General Service and Victory Medals.
28, Moncrieff Road, Rye Lane, S.E.15.   Z5603

FLOWER, F. J., Private, R.A.M.C.
Joining in May 1917, he served with his unit at various stations on important duties, after completing his training. He did very good work as a stretcher bearer and medical orderly at many hospitals, but was unable to secure his transfer overseas before the close of the war, and was demobilised in November 1919.
135, St. George's Road, Peckham, S.E.15.   Z5604

FLOYD, W. G., Driver, R.F.A.
Volunteering in January 1915, and later in the year drafted to France, he fought in many engagements, including those at Ypres and on the Somme. In 1916, he was sent to Salonika, and was in action on the Vardar front until hostilities ceased. He returned to England and was demobilised in 1919, and holds the 1914-15 Star, and the General Service and Victory Medals.
9, Brookland Road, S. Lambeth, S.W.8.   Z2136

FLYNN, J., Private, R.A.S.C.
He volunteered in August 1914, and was drafted overseas two months later. Whilst on the Western Front he was engaged in the transport of ammunition and supplies during the Battles of the Somme, Ypres, Arras, Cambrai, and in other engagements and was wounded in 1917. He was sent home to hospital after receiving medical treatment, and was discharged unfit for further service in 1918, and holds the 1914-15 Star, and the General Service and Victory Medals.
25A, Sears Street, Camberwell, S.E.5.   Z5757

FLYNN, W. J., Driver, R.E.
He volunteered in July 1915, and in the following June embarked for France. Whilst in this theatre of war he was engaged on important duties with his unit in various sectors, and six months later proceeded to Salonika, where he served on the Vardar, Struma, and Doiran fronts. He was drafted to Egypt in 1917, and took part in the operations during the British Advance through Palestine. He returned to England after the signing of the Armistice, and was demobilised in July 1919. He holds the General Service and Victory Medals.
98, Avenue Road, Camberwell, S.E.5.   Z2137A Z5306A

FOGERTY, E. W., Bombardier, R.F.A.
He was mobilised in August 1914, and was almost immediately sent to France. He fought in the Retreat from Mons, and in the Battles of Ypres, the Somme, and Arras, and was wounded. On recovery, transferred to Salonika, he served in many parts of the line, and contracting malaria received hospital treatment at the Base. He rejoined his Battery in the firing line and took part in the final operations in the Balkans in 1918. He was demobilised in March 1919, and holds the Mons Star, and the General Service and Victory Medals.
13, Treherne Road, Stockwell, S.W.9.   Z3456B

FOGERTY, H. E., Bombardier, R.F.A.
He was mobilised at the outbreak of war, and proceeded to France shortly afterwards, and was engaged in heavy fighting, in the Retreat from Mons, and the Battles of Arras, the Somme Ypres, Festubert, Passchendaele, Bapaume, Loos, Lens, and Cambrai, where he was severely wounded in November 1918. He was invalided to hospital, and on recovery was demobilised in October 1919, and holds the Mons Star, and the General Service and Victory Medals.
13, Treherne Road, Stockwell, S.W.9.   3456A

FOLEY, A. J., Private, M.G.C.
He joined in April 1918, and at the conclusion of his training was engaged with his unit on important duties at various depôts. He did good work, but was unable to secure his transfer overseas prior to the cessation of hostilities, and was demobilised in 1919.
19, Eastbury Grove, Chiswick, W.4. 5609B

FOLEY, D., Private, 1st Northamptonshire Regt.
He was mobilised from the Army Reserve at the outbreak of war, and drafted to France. He fought in the Retreat from Mons, at the Battles of the Marne, the Aisne, La Bassée, Ypres, Neuve Chapelle, St. Eloi, Festubert, and the Somme. He was seriously wounded on July 19th, 1916, and invalided to hospital, where his injuries proved so severe that it was necessary to amputate one of his legs. He was discharged from the Service in the following October, and holds the Mons Star, and the General Service and Victory Medals.
19, Smyrk's Road, Walworth, S.E.17. Z2138

FOLEY, F. W. G., Private, 1st East Surrey Regt.
He joined in 1916, and later embarked for the Western Front. In this theatre of war he took part in heavy fighting in various sectors, and was in action in many important engagements. He gave his life for King and Country near Vimy Ridge on May 8th, 1917, and was entitled to the General Service and Victory Medals.
"He joined the great white company of valiant souls."
19, Eastbury Grove, Chiswick, W.4. 5609A

FOLKERD, F. W., Corporal, Royal Marines.
He enlisted in 1902, and was mobilised at the outbreak of hostilities and posted to H.M.S. "Leviathan," which vessel was engaged in the Battle off the Dogger Bank and was later employed on patrol and convoy duties on the trade routes to the West Indies until the end of the war. He was demobilised in March 1919, and holds the 1914-15 Star, and the General Service and Victory Medals.
46, Elliott Road, Stockwell, S.W.9. Z4452

FOLLAND, T. J., A.B., Royal Navy.
He volunteered in May 1915, and was posted to H.M.S. (T.B.D.) "Lyra." His ship was engaged in the Mediterranean Sea on submarine patrol duties and had many narrow escapes. He later returned to England and served on coastal duties until demobilised in May 1920. He holds the 1914-15 Star, and the General Service and Victory Medals.
73, Hubert Grove, Landor Road, S.W.9. Z2139A

FOLLETT, J. P., Pte., East Surrey Regiment and 2nd Gloucestershire Regiment.
He volunteered in June 1915, and was shortly afterwards transferred to the Gloucestershire Regiment and did good work as a signaller. In 1918 he was drafted to France, and was engaged in the fighting on the Somme, and in various other sectors. Owing to ill-health he returned to England in September of the same year, and on recovery was sent to India in October 1919, where he was still serving in 1920. He holds the General Service and Victory Medals.
93, Smyrk's Road, Walworth, S.E.17. Z2140

FOOT, R. F. G., L/Cpl., 5th King's Royal Rifle Corps.
He joined in May 1918, and at the conclusion of his training was sent to France. He was engaged with his Battalion on important guard and escort duties at various prisoners of war camps and did very good work. He was demobilised in November 1919, and holds the General Service and Victory Medals.
26, Sheepcote Lane, Battersea, S.W.11. Z2141

FORD, A. E., Sergt., York and Lancaster Regiment.
A serving soldier, he was mobilised on the outbreak of war and sent to the Western Front. He was engaged in the fighting in the Retreat from Mons and the subsequent Battles of the Aisne, the Marne, Ypres and several others, and was badly gassed in 1916. He was invalided home, and on recovery rendered valuable services as an Instructor. Contracting an illness whilst serving he was invalided to hospital and died in February 1919. He was entitled to the 1914-15 Star, and the General Service and Victory Medals.
"He passed out of the sight of men by the path of duty and self-sacrifice."
44, Bagshot Street, Walworth, S.E.17. Z2142B

FORD, A., Private, M.G.C.
He volunteered in February 1915, and in the following September was drafted to France. During his service in this theatre of war he was engaged in heavy fighting, and later was transferred to Salonika, and was in action in several engagements. He remained in the Balkans until the close of the war, and returning to England was demobilised in June 1919. He holds the 1914-15 Star, and the General Service and Victory Medals.
61, Bennerley Road, Wandsworth Common, S.W.11. Z2146

FORD, A. R., Air Mechanic, R.A.F.
He joined in January 1918, and after his training was sent to Ireland, where he rendered valuable services as a coppersmith until the cessation of hostilities. He unfortunately was not successful in obtaining a transfer to a theatre of war, and was demobilised in May 1919.
63, Wayford Street, Battersea, S.W.11. Z2143

FORD, E., Private, 36th Royal Fusiliers.
He joined in May 1916, and two months later proceeded to the Western Front, where he fought in many engagements, including those on the Somme and at Bapaume. Owing to ill-health he was sent home for hospital treatment in 1917, and on discharge from hospital was invalided out of the Service in March of that year. He holds the General Service and Victory Medals.
2, Brymer Road, Camberwell, S.E.5. Z5605

FORD, F., Gunner, R.G.A.
He joined in July 1917, and during the same year was sent to the Western Front. Here he was in action with his Battery in many important engagements, including the Battles of the Somme, Ypres and Arras. He also fought in the Retreat and Advance of 1918. He returned home, and in June 1919 was demobilised, and holds the General Service and Victory Medals. 15, Alsace Street, Walworth, S.E.17. Z2145

FORD, F. G., Gunner, R.G.A.
He joined in 1917, and in the same year was sent to the Western Front, where he saw much service. He was in action in many notable engagements, including the Battles of the Somme and Ypres, until the cessation of hostilities. He returned to England and was demobilised in 1918, and holds the General Service and Victory Medals.
44, Bagshot Street, Walworth, S.E.17. Z2142B

FORD, G., Gunner, R.F.A.
He volunteered in May 1915, and early in the following year was sent to Mesopotamia, where he took a prominent part with his Battery in most of the important engagements in that theatre of war and did excellent work until the Armistice. He returned home, and was demobilised in April 1919, and holds the General Service and Victory Medals.
46, Priory Road, Chiswick, W.4. 6708

FORD, J. S. W., L/Cpl., 24th London Regt. (The Queen's).
He volunteered in August 1915, and in October of the same year was drafted to the Western Front. Here he fought with his unit in many important battles, including those of Ypres, Loos, Hill 60, the Somme, High Wood, Arras, and Vimy Ridge, where he was wounded. On recovery he served in the Retreat and Advance of 1918. He returned home and was demobilised in January 1919, and holds the General Service and Victory Medals.
17B, Doris Street, Kennington, S.E.11. Z25320

FORD, L. C., Rifleman, Rifle Brigade.
He volunteered in 1915, and in the same year was drafted to France. He was in action in many battles on the Western Front, including those of the Somme, Ypres, and Arras, and was wounded at Ypres in 1916. On recovery he rejoined his Battalion in the Field and was again wounded and gassed on the Somme in 1917. He later returned to the firing line and served until the end of the war. He then returned home, and was demobilised in January 1919, and holds the 1914-15 Star, and the General Service and Victory Medals.
44, Bagshot Street, Walworth, S.E.17. Z2142A

FORD, T., Private, 23rd East Surrey Regiment.
He joined in July 1917, and after his training served at various stations on important duties with his unit. He rendered valuable services, but was not successful in obtaining his transfer overseas before the cessation of hostilities. He was demobilised in January 1919.
11, Abyssinia Road, Battersea, S.W.11. Z2144

FORD, W. L., L/Cpl., 9th Cameronians (Scottish Rifles).
He volunteered in August 1914, and in October of the following year was drafted to the Western Front, where he fought in many engagements, including those of Le Cateau, St. Eloi, Hill 60, Ypres and Festubert. During his service overseas he was twice wounded at La Bassée, again at Ypres in September 1917, and a fourth time at St. Quentin in March 1918. He returned home and was discharged in May 1919, and holds the 1914-15 Star, and the General Service and Victory Medals.
3, Arneway Street, Westminster, S.W.1. Z24737

FOREMAN, F. W., Petty Officer, Merchant Service.
Joining in January 1918, he was posted to H.M.S. "Aquitania" and served in that ship for nearly two years. His vessel was engaged on important duties in connection with the transport of American troops to the Western Front and of sick and wounded Canadian soldiers to Halifax. He was demobilised in September 1919, and holds the Mercantile Marine War, and the General Service Medals.
3, Torrens Street, Ferndale Road, S.W.4. Z2147

FOREMAN, F. W. (M.M.), Sergt., R.F.A.

Mobilised from the Army Reserve on the outbreak of war and shortly afterwards drafted to France, he took a prominent part in the Battles of the Marne, Ypres, Neuve Chapelle and the Somme, and was mentioned in Despatches for devotion to duty and consistently good work at Ypres on December 19th, 1915, and March 16th, 1916, and for conspicuous gallantry in action on September 15th, 1916. He also fought at Vermelles, Hill 70, Cambrai and was wounded at Queant during the Retreat from Cambrai. Rejoining his unit he served in the Advance of 1918. He was awarded the Military Medal on October 7th, 1916, for conspicuous gallantry and devotion to duty during the Battle of the Somme, and also holds the 1914 Star, and the General Service and Victory Medals. He was demobilised in March 1919.
275, Eversleigh Road, Battersea, S.W.11.   Z2148

FORREST, H. V., Private, 10th Royal Scots.

He volunteered in April 1915, and was sent overseas in the following year. Serving with his Battalion in various sectors of the Western Front, he was in action in many engagements and was drafted to Russia in 1918. He was taken prisoner by the Bolsheviks on September 3rd, 1918, and held in captivity until his repatriation in April 1920. He was demobilised in July 1920, and holds the General Service and Victory Medals.
92, Tennyson Street, Wentworth Road, S.W.8.   Z2150

FORREST, J., Private, 1st Queen's (Royal West Surrey Regiment).

Volunteering in August 1914, he embarked for France in the same month and was engaged in heavy fighting during the Retreat from Mons and in the Battles of the Marne, the Aisne, La Bassée, Ypres and Loos. He was wounded at High Wood in 1916 during the action on the Somme and again at Ypres in the following year. He also took part in the Battles of Albert, Arras, Messines and Cambrai and in several engagements during the Retreat and Advance of 1918. He was demobilised in June 1919, and holds the Mons Star, and the General Service and Victory Medals.
7 High Park Crescent, Walworth, S.E.17.   Z2151

FORREST, M., Leading Stoker, R.N.

Volunteering in 1914, he was posted to submarine " G14 " and, attached to the Grand Fleet, was engaged on important submarine patrol duties in the North Sea. He took part in several engagements, and was killed in action on January 23rd, 1917. He was entitled to the 1914-15 Star, and the General Service and Victory Medals.
"His life for his Country."
70, Thurlow Street, Walworth, S.E.17.   Z2149

FORREST, S., Private, East Surrey Regiment.

He volunteered in September 1914, and proceeding overseas in the following year served in France until the cessation of hostilities. During this period he fought in many engagements, including the Battles of Loos, Arras, Ypres, Cambrai and those of the Retreat and Advance of 1918. He was demobilised in January 1919, and holds the 1914-15 Star, and the General Service and Victory Medals.
92, Tennyson Street, Wentworth Road, S.W.8.   Z2150C

FORREST, S. H., Rflmn., 6th London Regt. (Rifles).

Volunteering in April 1915, he was drafted to the Western Front in the following year, and was in action in many important engagements, including the Battles of Ypres and Cambrai, and was twice wounded. Taken prisoner he died of fever on December 22nd, 1918, during his captivity in Germany. He was entitled to the General Service and Victory Medals.
"The path of duty was the way to glory."
92, Tennyson Street, Wentworth Road, S.W.8.   Z2150B

FORSDYKE, C. E., Corporal. Royal Fusiliers.

He volunteered in 1914, and in the following year embarked for France. There he fought in the Battles of the Somme, Ypres, Arras and other engagements. He was sent to Salonika in 1917, and whilst in that theatre of war served as Battalion Scout, in which capacity he did excellent work during the advance across the Struma until invalided home owing to malaria. After treatment he served with his unit at home, and was demobilised in 1919. He holds the 1914-15 Star, and the General Service and Victory Medals.
16, Boundary Lane, Walworth, S.E.17.   Z26208A

FORSDYKE, J., 1st Class Stoker, R.N.

He joined the Royal Navy in 1911, and was posted to submarine " K5 " on the outbreak of war, and, attached to the Grand Fleet, was engaged on submarine patrol duties in the North Sea and off the Belgian coast, and also escorted transports across the Channel. Transferred on the cessation of hostilities to H.M.S. " Renown " he served aboard that ship throughout the Prince of Wales' tour into Canada and America, and later to Australia and New Zealand. He holds the 1914-15 Star, and the General Service and Victory Medals, and in 1920 was still serving.
16, Boundary Lane, Walworth, S.E.17.   Z26208B

FORSTER, B., Driver, R.F.A.

He volunteered in March 1915, and proceeded to the Western Front three months later. Serving with his Battery in various parts of the line he was in action in the Battles of the Somme, Arras, La Bassée, Ypres and Cambrai. During the Advance of 1918 he was wounded and gassed, and in consequence invalided home. He was demobilised in July 1919, and holds the 1914-15 Star, and the General Service and Victory Medals.
8, Clayton Buildings, Little East Street, Kennington, S.E.11.   Z25667

FORSTER, W. G., Gunner, R.G.A.

He volunteered in November 1914, and after completing his training served with the anti-aircraft section at various places on the coast. He was retained on this duty for some considerable time, but finally secured his transfer to the Western Front, where he served during the concluding stages of the war and did excellent work. He returned home for demobilisation in February 1919, and holds the General Service and Victory Medals.
10, Cunnington Street, Chiswick, W.4.   T6882

FORSYTH, G., Gunner, R.H.A.

He was mobilised from the Army Reserve on the declaration of war and drafted overseas in February 1915. Serving with with his Battery on the Western Front he took part in many engagements, including the Battles of Arras, Ypres, the Somme and in the Retreat and Advance of 1918. After the Armistice he was sent to Germany with the Army of Occupation. He returned home for demobilisation in March 1919, and holds the 1914-15 Star, and the General Service and Victory Medals. He had served for upwards of seventeen years, five of which he spent in India.
130, Lollard Street, Kennington, S.E.11.   Z25432

FORT, W. S., Private, Middlesex Regiment.

Volunteering in July 1915, he completed his training, and was engaged on important duties with his unit until his embarkation for France in 1917. Whilst on the Western Front he served in various sectors and took part in heavy fighting in many important battles. He fell fighting near Amiens on May 20th, 1918, and was buried in the Daours Cemetery. He was entitled to the General Service and Victory Medals.
"Whilst we remember the Sacrifice is not in vain."
6, Clovelly Road, Chiswick, W.4.   634

FORWARD, E. R., Private, 7th London Regiment.

Joining in November 1916, he was sent to the Western Front two months later and served there until the conclusion of hostilities. In the course of his service he was in action in the Battles of Arras, Vimy Ridge, Ypres, Bullecourt, Passchendaele and Cambrai, and was wounded in September 1918. He returned to England for demobilisation in January 1919, and holds the General Service and Victory Medals.
5, Lockington Road, Battersea Park Road, S.W.8. Z2153

FOSKETT, A. H., Sergt., R.H.A. and R.F.A.

Volunteering in August 1914, he embarked for France in the following November and served throughout the war. He was engaged with his Battery in heavy fighting in various parts of the British line and did valuable service. He was mentioned in Despatches for delivering a message to another battery under great difficulties, and in spite of being thrown from his horse. Discharged on account of service in January 1919, he holds the 1914 Star, and the General Service and Victory Medals.
16, Stonehill Road, Chiswick, W.4.   6061

FOSKETT, A. W. (M.M.), Rifleman, King's Royal Rifle Corps.

Joining in March 1916, he proceeded to the Western Front in the following year, and was in action in several engagements, including the Battles of Lens and Cambrai. He was awarded the Military Medal for conspicuous bravery and devotion to duty in delivering Despatches under heavy fire in spite of wounds. Sent home on account of his injuries in 1917, he remained on home service until his embarkation for India in 1919. In addition to the Military Medal he holds the General Service and Victory Medals. and in 1920 was still serving abroad.
43, Cologne Road, Battersea, S.W.11.   Z2154

FOSTER, A. E., Rifleman, King's Royal Rifle Corps.

He volunteered in November 1915, and after completing his training was sent to the Western Front. During his service in this theatre of war he fought in several important engagements, was wounded on the Somme in November 1917, and again at Cambrai a year later. For his excellent work at Cambrai he was mentioned in Despatches. Later he was transferred to the Machine Gun Corps and served with that unit until the end of hostilities. Demobilised in November 1919, he holds the General Service and Victory Medals.
21, Randall Street, Battersea, S.W.11.   Z2158A

FOSTER, A. T., Cpl., 24th London Regt. (The Queen's)

Volunteering in December 1915, he proceeded to Salonika a year later and was in action on Lake Doiran. He was sent to hospital owing to illness, and on recovery was drafted to Egypt. Taking part in the British Advance through Palestine, he was present at the capture of Jericho and wounded in the course of operations in the Jordan Valley. Drafted to the Western Front, he fought in the Battles of the Somme, Cambrai and during the Retreat and Advance of 1918. He was demobilised in January 1919, and holds the General Service and Victory Medals.

8, Geneva Terrace, Coldharbour Lane, S.W.9. Z4453

FOSTER, C. H., Rifleman, King's Royal Rifle Corps.

He volunteered in November 1915, and drafted overseas early in the following year served on the Western Front throughout the war. He fought in the Battles of St. Eloi, Albert, Vimy Ridge, the Somme, the Ancre, Arras and Cambrai. Owing to an injury sustained during the Retreat of 1918 he was invalided home. Returning to France he was engaged on guard duties at various detention camps for German prisoners until his demobilisation in March 1919. He holds the General Service and Victory Medals.

20, Arlesford Road, Landor Road, S.W.9. Z2157A

FOSTER, G., Corporal, King's Royal Rifle Corps.

Volunteering in December 1915, he embarked for France in the following August and served there until the end of hostilities. Whilst overseas he was in action in the Battles of the Somme, Beaumont-Hamel, Beaucourt, Arras, Vimy Ridge and many other engagements, and was wounded during the third Battle of Ypres. He holds the General Service and Victory Medals, and was demobilised in February 1919.

40, Elsted Street, Walworth, S.E.17. Z2155

FOSTER, G. W., Private, 13th Middlesex Regt.

He volunteered in November 1914, and proceeding overseas four months later, did much service on the Western Front. He was engaged in heavy fighting in the Battles of Ypres, Loos, Vimy Ridge, the Somme, Arras, Cambrai and during the Retreat and Advance of 1918. On the conclusion of hostilities he was sent to Egypt, and in 1920 was still serving. He holds the 1914-15 Star, and the General Service and Victory Medals.

37, Smyrk's Road, Walworth, S.E.17. Z2159B

FOSTER, H. F., Private, 8th Loyal North Lancashire Regiment.

He joined in September 1916, and was sent to France in the following January. In the course of his service on the Western Front he fought in several important engagements, including the Battles of Vimy Ridge and Ypres. He was unfortunately killed in action on August 1st, 1917, and was entitled to the General Service and Victory Medals.

"His life for his Country, his soul to God."

56, Treherne Road, Stockwell, S.W.9. Z4505B

FOSTER, H. W., Driver, R.A.S.C.

Joining in December 1916, he was drafted overseas on the completion of his training and served on the Western Front. He was engaged on important duties in connection with the transport of ammunition and supplies to the firing line and did valuable work until the termination of hostilities. He holds the General Service and Victory Medals, and was demobilised in November 1919.

21, Randall Street, Battersea, S.W.11. Z2158B

FOSTER, J., Private, 1st Essex Regiment.

He joined in 1916, and embarking for the Western Front in the same year was engaged in heavy fighting in several battles, including those of the Somme, Arras and Cambrai and during the Retreat and Advance of 1918. He was unhappily killed in action on November 4th, 1918, and was entitled to the General Service and Victory Medals.

"Great deeds cannot die."

21, Sears Street, Camberwell, S.E.5. Z5756

FOSTER, Kate, G., Special War Worker.

Volunteering for work of National importance this lady served as a postwoman from July 1916 to February 1919. Her duties were carried out in a thoroughly efficient and capable manner throughout this period, thereby releasing a man for war service.

20, Arlesford Road, Landor Road, S.W.9. Z2157B

FOSTER, R. H., L/Cpl., 3rd Worcestershire Regt.

Volunteering on the outbreak of war he was almost immediately drafted to France and was engaged in fierce fighting in the Retreat from Mons. He gave his life for the freedom of England in the Battle of La Bassée on October 21st, 1914. He was entitled to the Mons Star, and the General Service and Victory Medals.

"Steals on the ear the distant triumph song."

40, Mysore Road, Lavender Hill, S.W.11. Z2156A

FOSTER, W. T. (D.C.M.), Sergt., R.E.

He volunteered in 1914, and proceeding to France in the following year was engaged on important duties during the Battles of Ypres and Loos. He was awarded the Distinguished Conduct Medal for conspicuous bravery and devotion to duty in laying wires under heavy shell fire. Severely wounded, he lost a leg by amputation and was discharged as physically unfit for further service in 1917. In addition to the D.C.M. he holds the 1914-15 Star, and the General Service and Victory Medals.

40, Mysore Road, Lavender Hill, S.W.11. Z2156B

FOULDS, A. V., Sergt., M.G.C.

Volunteering on the outbreak of war he was drafted to Egypt in the following year and fought in several engagements during the British Advance through Palestine. He was, unfortunately killed in action on November 5th, 1917, when assisting to bring in the wounded. He was entitled to the 1914-15 Star, and the General Service and Victory Medals.

"Thinking that remembrance, though unspoken, may reach him where he sleeps."

61, Fletcher Road, Chiswick, W.4. 6347

FOULSHAM, F. A., Private, Royal Fusiliers.

Joining in June 1917, on attaining military age, he completed his training and was engaged on important duties with his unit at various depôts. He rendered valuable services, but was unable to obtain a transfer overseas before the cessation of hostilities owing to medical unfitness for general service. He was demobilised in March 1919.

22, Geneva Road, Coldharbour Lane, S.W.9. Z3454B

FOULSHAM, H. A. K., Pte., Middlesex Regiment.

He volunteered in August 1914, and in the following February embarked for France, where he took part in many engagements, including the Battles of Neuve Chapelle, St. Eloi, Ypres, Festubert and Loos. During the German attack at Albert in April 1916, he was blown up by the explosion of a mine and as a result was sent to hospital in England and eventually discharged as medically unfit for further service. In 1918, however, he rejoined in the Royal Air Force and served at Pulham, Norfolk, where owing to an accident during the release of an airship, he was seriously injured and on November 25th, 1918, died from his injuries. He was entitled to the 1914-15 Star, and the General Service and Victory Medals.

"Whilst we remember the sacrifice is not in vain."

22, Geneva Road, Coldharbour Lane, S.W.9. Z3454A

FOUNTAIN, A. H., L/Cpl., Royal Munster Fusiliers.

Volunteering in August 1915, he completed his training, and served at various stations until drafted to Italy in December 1917. He fought in many sectors of the Piave front and was in action during the Allied Advance of 1918, and was wounded. He returned to England, and was demobilised in March 1919, and holds the General Service and Victory Medals.

41, Bullen Street, Battersea, S.W.11. Z2161A

FOUNTAIN, A. R., Seaman, Merchant Service.

He joined in April 1915 at the age of fourteen in the Union Castle Line, and throughout the war served in various ships, which were engaged in carrying stores and provisions from England to South Africa, Australia, New Zealand and America. He was still serving in 1920, and holds the General Service and Mercantile Marine War Medals.

54, Comber Grove, Camberwell New Road, S.E.5. Z2160A

FOUNTAIN, C. T., Pte., 10th Queen's (West Surrey Regiment).

He volunteered in December 1915, and embarked for the Western Front in the following June. He was in action in many parts of the line and fought in the Battle of the Somme. He gave his life for King and Country in the Ypres salient on August 15th, 1916, and was entitled to the General Service and Victory Medals.

"Great deeds cannot die."

41, Bullen Street, Battersea, S.W.11. Z2161C

FOUNTAIN, J., Saddler, Bombardier, R.F.A.

Volunteering in October 1914, he proceeded to France five months later, and was in action at the Battles of Ypres, La Bassée, Hill 60, the Somme, Arras, and throughout the German offensive of 1918. He died gloriously on the Field of battle on August 15th, 1918, during the Allied Advance, and was entitled to the 1914-15 Star, and the General Service and Victory Medals.

"His life for his Country."

41, Bullen Street, Battersea, S.W.11. Z2161B

FOUNTAIN, J. W., Rifleman, 21st London Regt. (1st Surrey Rifles).

He volunteered in August 1914, and was sent to France in the following March, and fought in many important engagements, including those at Hill 60, Festubert and Givenchy. He gave his life for the freedom of England in the Battle of Vimy Ridge on May 15th, 1916, and was entitled to the 1914-15 Star, and the General Service and Victory Medals.

"His life for his Country, his Soul to God."

54, Comber Grove, Camberwell New Road, S.E.5. Z2160B

FOWLE, A. J., Pte., Middlesex Regt., Rflmn., 18th London Regt. (London Irish Rifles), and Pte., Devonshire Regt.

He volunteered in January 1916, and proceeding to France in the same year, was in action at Bullecourt and Delville Wood. In 1917 he was discovered to be under age, and was sent home and discharged. Shortly afterwards he rejoined and returning to France took part in the engagements at Béthune and the Somme and fought throughout the Retreat and Advance of 1918. He returned home and was demobilised in November 1919, and holds the General Service and Victory Medals.
20, Neville Street, Vauxhall, S.E.11. TZ25443A

FOWLE, H., Pte., Middlesex Regt., and 1st Air Mechanic, R.A.F.

He volunteered in February 1915, and, drafted to India in the same year, was engaged in the fighting in Afghanistan, on the North-Western Frontier, and was also on duty during the Amritsar riots. He returned to England, and was demobilised in November 1919, and holds the India General Service Medal (with clasp, Afghanistan, N.W. Frontier 1919), and the General Service and Victory Medals.
20, Neville Street, Vauxhall, S.E.11. TZ25443B

FOWLER, A., Rifleman, Rifle Brigade.

He volunteered in February 1916, and embarked for the Western Front shortly afterwards, and during his service overseas was engaged in heavy fighting in many sectors. He was unfortunately killed in action during the first British Offensive on the Somme in July 1916, and was entitled to the General Service and Victory Medals.
" His memory is cherished with pride."
38, St. Philip Street, Battersea Park, S.W.8. Z2167

FOWLER, A. J., Private, R.A.O.C.

Volunteering in September 1915, he proceeded to the Western Front in January 1917. Transferred to the Norfolk Regiment he served in the advanced areas and fought in many engagements. He gave his life for the freedom of England in the Battle of Kemmel Hill in April 1917, and was entitled to the General Service and Victory Medals.
" A costly sacrifice upon the altar of freedom."
30, Wayford Street, Battersea, S.W.11. Z2166B

FOWLER, A. J., A.B., Royal Navy.

He joined the Service in 1915, and was posted to H.M.S. " Conquest," which vessel was engaged on important duties until mined in 1917. He was then transferred to H.M.S. " Dragon," and saw much service abroad this ship whilst she was patrolling in the North Sea and other waters. He was still serving in 1920, and holds the 1914-15 Star, and the General Service and Victory Medals.
11, Rowena Crescent, Battersea, S.W.11. Z2168A

FOWLER, C., Private, Royal Fusiliers.

He volunteered in 1915, and was drafted to German East Africa later in that year. He was in Driscoll's Scouts and fought in many engagements. Contracting malaria, he was invalided to England, and after receiving hospital treatment was discharged unfit for further service in May 1918. He holds the 1914-15 Star, and the General Service and Victory Medals.
33, Thornton Street, Brixton Road, S.W.9. Z2163

FOWLER, E. G., Sergt., R.A.S.C.

Volunteering in August 1914, he embarked for the Dardanelles in the following year, and served in many engagements there until the Evacuation of the Peninsula. Transferred to German East Africa in 1916, he was employed on important transport duties whilst operations were in progress during the British Advance through this territory. He returned to England, and was demobilised in 1919, and holds the 1914-15 Star, and the General Service and Victory Medals.
11, Rowena Crescent, Battersea, S.W.11. Z2168A

FOWLER, E. T., Air Mechanic, R.A.F.

Joining in September 1916, he was drafted to the Western Front in the following August and served at various aerodromes engaged on important duties with the Observation Balloon Section. He gave his life for King and Country at Ypres on October 2nd, 1917, and was entitled to the General Service and Victory Medals.
" The path of duty was the way to glory."
30, Wayford Street, Battersea, S.W.11. Z2166A

FOWLER, F. J., Corporal, R.F.A.

He volunteered in August 1914, and embarked for the Western Front in the following month. He was in action in numerous engagements, including those at Neuve Chapelle, Loos, Ypres II, Albert, Vimy Ridge, the Somme, and throughout the German Offensive and Allied Advance of 1918. He was demobilised in March 1919, and holds the 1914 Star, and the General Service and Victory Medals.
140, Aylesbury Road, Walworth, S.E.17. Z2165B

FOWLER, F. B., Corporal, Royal Defence Corps.

Ineligible for service with the Colours on account of his age, he joined the Royal Defence Corps at the outbreak of hostilities and was stationed at various depôts on guard and other important duties. He rendered valuable services throughout the period of the war, and was demobilised in March 1919.
140, Aylesbury Road, Walworth, S.E.17. Z2162A

FOWLER, J. E., Rifleman, King's Royal Rifle Corps.

Volunteering in March 1915 at the age of fifteen, he was drafted to France six months later, and fought in many engagements, including those at Loos, Albert, the Somme, Arras. He was also in action in the German Offensive of 1918 and during the progress of the subsequent Allied Advance was taken prisoner. Repatriated after the cessation of hostilities he was demobilised in June 1919, and holds the 1914-15 Star, and the General Service and Victory Medals.
140, Aylesbury Road, Walworth, S.E.17. Z2162B

FOWLER, J. T., Sergt.-Dummer, Royal Welch Fusiliers.

He volunteered in November 1914, and embarked for the Western Front in the following year. During his service overseas he fought at Loos, the Somme, in the Ypres salient, and was also in action throughout the Retreat and Advance of 1918, and was wounded three times. After the Armistice he proceeded into Germany with the Army of Occupation and served there until 1919. He returned to England and was demobilised in February of that year, and holds the 1914-15 Star, and the General Service and Victory Medals.
26, Cambridge Street, Camberwell, S.E.5. Z1590B

FOWLER, W. D., Private, Tank Corps.

Mobilised at the commencement of hostilities, he proceeded to Malta, and completed his training at that station. Drafted to France in January 1915, he fought at Loos, Neuve Chapelle, Ypres, the Somme, Arras, and in the German Offensive and Allied Advance of 1918, and was wounded. He was demobilised in 1919, and holds the 1914-15 Star, and the General Service and Victory Medals.
11, Rowena Crescent, Battersea, S.W.11. Z2168B

FOWLER, W. E., Special War Worker.

He offered his services for work of National importance in August 1914, and until December 1919 worked at Messrs. Barker and Co.'s, Ltd., Notting Hill, engaged on work connected with the manufacture of aeroplane parts. He discharged his duties with the utmost efficiency and gave complete satisfaction.
61, St. Philip Street, Battersea, S.W.8. Z2164

FOWLES, W. E., Private, R.A.S.C. (H.T.)

He joined in 1916, and after completing his training served as a driver in the Horse Transport at various depôts at home. He rendered valuable services but was unable to secure his transfer to a theatre of war before the cessation of hostilities. He was, however, sent to Russia in August 1919, and returning to England in 1920 was admitted to hospital with fever. He was discharged in May of the same year, and holds the General Service and Victory Medals.
5, Headley Street, Nunhead, S.E.15. Z6167

FOX, B., Rifleman, King's Royal Rifle Corps.

Joining in January 1917, he was sent to France five months later, and fought in the Battles of Arras and Bullecourt, and was wounded. Invalided to hospital in England, he rejoined his unit in January 1918, and was in action at Ypres and Cambrai, and during the German Offensive, and was twice wounded. After the Armistice he proceeded into Germany with the Army of Occupation, and returning home for demobilisation in May 1919, holds the General Service and Victory Medals.
11, Frances Street, Battersea, S.W.11. Z2169

FOX, H., Stoker, 1st Class Petty Officer, R.N.

He was serving in the Royal Navy at the outbreak of hostilities, having joined in 1902, and was mobilised in August 1914. Attached to the Grand Fleet his ship, H.M.S. " Cressy " was engaged on important submarine patrol duties in the North Sea. He was unfortunately drowned on September 22nd, 1914, when the " Cressy " was torpedoed and sunk off the Hook of Holland, within a fortnight of his completing twelve years' service. He was entitled to the 1914-15 Star, and the General Service and Victory Medals.
" He passed out of the sight of men by the path of duty and self sacrifice."
48, Broughton Street, Battersea Park, S.W.8. Z1713B

FOX, J. E. W., Special War Worker.

Volunteering for work of National importance at the outbreak of war, he acted as a checker of ammunition and supplies at Nine Elms Goods Depôt from August 1914 until November 1918. He discharged his responsible duties in a thoroughly capable and efficient manner, and to the satisfaction of the authorities.
8, Loughboro' Street, Kennington, S.E.11. Z25496

FOX, J., 1st Class Stoker, R.N.

Joining the Royal Navy in 1908, he was mobilised on the outbreak of war and served in H.M.S. Torpedo Boat Destroyer " Tipperary." Attached to the Grand Fleet his ship was engaged on important patrol duties in the North Sea, and was in action in the Battle of Jutland. He fell fighting in this battle in May 1916, and was entitled to the 1914-15 Star, and the General Service and Victory Medals.

"Great deeds cannot die."

29, Caldew Street, Camberwell, S.E.5.   Z5763B

FRAME, A. E., Rifleman, 21st London Regiment (1st Surrey Rifles).

He volunteered in 1914, and proceeding to France in the following year, took an active part in the Battles of Neuve Chapelle, Hill 60, Ypres, Loos, Hooge, the Somme and Arras. Severely wounded at Vimy Ridge, he was invalided home and in consequence of his injuries his left leg had to be amputated. He received medical treatment until discharged as physically unfit for further service in April 1920, and holds the 1914-15 Star, and the General Service and Victory Medals.

55, Paradise Street, Lambeth, S.E.11.   25755

FRAMPTON, C., Cadet, 15th London Regiment (Civil Service Rifles).

Volunteering in 1915, he embarked for the Western Front in June of the following year, and saw much service in the Arras sector, until drafted to Salonika in December 1916. He was in action during the Advance on the Doiran and Vardar fronts and proceeded to Egypt in June 1917. Serving in the Advance through Palestine he fought in the Battles of Beersheba and Aleppo, and in operations resulting in the fall of Jerusalem, and was wounded. He returned home, and was undergoing a course of training for promotion to commissioned rank at the time of his demobilisation in 1919. He holds the General Service and Victory Medals.

76, Sandmere Road, Clapham, S.W.4.   Z2170B

FRAMPTON, L. J., Rifleman, 5th London Regiment (London Rifle Brigade).

He volunteered in September 1914, and in the following year was drafted to the Western Front. Whilst in this theatre of war he fought in several important engagements including the Battle of Arras, and was severely wounded at Ypres. Sent home on account of his injuries he was in hospital for over a year, and was invalided out of the Service in April 1916. He holds the 1914-15 Star, and the General Service and Victory Medals, and in 1920 was still receiving medical treatment.

76, Sandmere Road, Clapham, S.W.4.   Z2170A

FRAMPTON, W. E., Rifleman, 2/16th London Regt. (Queen's Westminster Rifles).

Volunteering in December 1915, he was sent overseas in the following year, and was engaged on important duties with his unit on the Western Front, and was in action in many battles. He died gloriously on the Field of battle at Vimy Ridge on October 16th, 1916, and was entitled to the General Service and Victory Medals.

"And doubtless he went in splendid company."

4, Rothschild Road, Chiswick, W.4.   6767

FRANCE, A., Air Mechanic, R.A.F.

Volunteering in August 1914, he was sent overseas in the following year, and served on the Western Front for four years. During this period he rendered valuable services as a driver on commissariat duties, and returned to England in February 1919. He was still serving in 1920 and holds the 1914-15 Star, and the General Service and Victory Medals.

6, Neate Street, Camberwell, S.E.5.   Z5067

FRANCES, S. A., 1st Class Stoker, R.N.

He joined in June 1916, and after completing his training was posted to H.M.S. " Alexander " in which vessel he served for upwards of three years. His ship was engaged on ice breaking and other important duties in North Russia until the conclusion of hostilities. He was demobilised in June 1919, and holds the General Service and Victory Medals.

25, Dorchester Grove, Chiswick, W.4.   5379B

FRANCIS, A., Private, Royal Fusiliers.

Joining in August 1916, he was drafted to the Western Front in the following December, and fought in several engagements including the Battle of the Somme. He fell fighting at Oppy Wood in April 1917, and was entitled to the General Service and Victory Medals.

"Courage, bright hopes, and a myriad dreams, splendidly given."

38, Heath Road, Wandsworth Road, S.W.8.   Z2173

FRANCIS, A. J., Rifleman, Rifle Brigade.

He joined in June 1916, and in the following year embarked for France. Whilst in this theatre of war he served in the Battles of Messines, Ypres, Lens, the Somme and Cambrai, and was wounded at Ypres in 1917. He was unhappily killed on April 4th, 1918, during the German Offensive in the vicinity of Cambrai, and was entitled to the General Service and Victory Medals.

"He joined the great white company of valiant souls."

17, Darwin Street, Walworth, S.E.17.   Z2177

FRANCIS, G. A., Gunner, R.F.A.

Enlisting in 1906, he was mobilised when war broke out and proceeded to France shortly afterwards. He was twice wounded in the early engagements and taken prisoner on August 26th, 1914, in the Battle of Le Cateau. After the Armistice he was released from captivity in Germany in 1918, and returning home was demobilised in February 1919. He holds the 1914 Star, and the General Service and Victory Medals.

65, Cranbrook Road, Chiswick, W.4.   5359

FRANCIS, J., Private, 1st Oxfordshire and Buckinghamshire Light Infantry.

A serving soldier, he was mobilised on the outbreak of hostilities, and engaged on important duties with his unit until sent to Mesopotamia in February 1916. Taking part in operations in the relief of Kut he fought in the three heavy attacks at Sanna-i-Yat, and was then drafted to India, where he was in action on the North West Frontier. Returning home for demobilisation he holds the General Service and Victory Medals, and the India General Service Medal (with clasp, Afghanistan, N.W. Frontier, 1919).

33, Everett Street, Nine Elms Lane, S.W.8.   Z4003

FRANCIS, R., Lieutenant, Suffolk Regiment.

Joining as a Rifleman in the King's Royal Rifle Corps in 1916, he was granted a commission in the Suffolk Regiment, and embarked for France in the following year. He fought in the Offensive on the Somme, and was wounded and taken prisoner at the Battle of Bullecourt. He was held in captivity in Germany until the signing of the Armistice, and returning to England was demobilised in February 1919, and holds the General Service and Victory Medals.

28, Mysore Road, Lavender Hill S.W.11.   Z4001A

FRANCIS, R. H., 2nd Lieut., King's Shropshire Light Infantry.

Volunteering in August 1914, he proceeded overseas in the following January and served on the Western Front. He was in action in the Battles of Neuve Chapelle, Ypres, the Somme and Arras, and was wounded. Rejoining his unit on recovery he was taken prisoner during the Retreat of 1918 and held in captivity in Germany. Repatriated on the conclusion of hostilities, he was demobilised in March 1919, and holds the 1914-15 Star, and the General Service and Victory Medals.

8, Harley Street, Battersea, S.W.11.   Z2172

FRANCIS, W., L/Corporal, R.A.S.C. (M.T.)

He volunteered in August 1914, and after a period of service in Ireland was drafted to the Western Front in the same year. He was engaged on important duties in connection with the transport of ammunition and supplies to the firing line, and did valuable work until sent home owing to ill-health in September 1917. Admitted into hospital he received medical treatment and was invalided out of the Service in May 1918, and holds the 1914-15 Star, and the General Service and Victory Medals.

4, Akers Street, Walworth, S.E.17.   Z2171

FRANKLIN, A., Sergt., 3rd London Regt. (Royal Fusiliers).

A Territorial, he was mobilised when war broke out, and proceeding to Gallipoli in April 1915, fought in the first Landing on the Peninsula, in the Battles of Krithia and Suvla Bay, and in the capture of Chunuk Bair. Sent to Egypt in 1916, he served there and was invalided home on account of ill-health in 1917. He was discharged as medically unfit for further service later in that year, and holds the 1914-15 Star, and the General Service and Victory Medals.

31, Alfreton Street, Walworth, S.E.17.   Z2174A

FRANKLIN, A. C., Pte., 2nd Worcestershire Regt.

He volunteered in October 1914, and after completing his training served in Ireland until 1916, in which year he embarked for France. Whilst on the Western Front, he was in action in the Battles of Albert and Vimy Ridge, and was wounded on the Somme in 1917. Returning to the firing line on recovery he fought at Arras, Cambrai, was wounded again in the Advance of 1918. He holds the General Service and Victory Medals, and was demobilised in May 1919.

31, Alfreton Street, Walworth, S.E.17.   Z2174B

FRANKLIN, A. E., Stoker, R.N.

Joining in February 1916, he was posted to H.M.S. " Marlborough," and served in that vessel throughout the course of hostilities. His ship was attached to the Grand Fleet and was in action in the Battle of Jutland, and was also engaged on patrol and special convoy duties in the North Sea. Seriously injured in an accident during his service he was sent to hospital and subsequently discharged as medically unfit for further service in September 1919. He holds the General Service and Victory Medals.

31, Alfreton Street, Walworth, S.E.17.   Z2174C

FRANKLIN, G. J., Private, 1st Middlesex Regiment.
He volunteered in April 1915, and five months later embarked for the Western Front. Serving in various sectors of this theatre of war he took part in many important engagements, and was wounded in the Battle of the Somme on July 15th, 1916. On recovery he returned to his unit, and was engaged on important duties until discharged on account of service in September 1918. He holds the 1914-15 Star, and the General Service and Victory Medals.
48, Binns Road, Chiswick, W.4.   5373C

FRANKLIN, G. J. W., Pte., 2nd Middlesex Regiment.
Volunteering in January 1915, he was sent overseas in the following month and served in various sectors of the Western Front. He was engaged on important duties with his Battalion and was buried by a shell explosion during an engagement at Vermelles. Suffering from shell shock he was invalided home and discharged as medically unfit for further service in November 1915, and holds the 1914-15 Star, and the General Service and Victory Medals.
48, Binns Road, Chiswick, W.4.   5373B

FRANKLIN, H., Special War Worker.
During the whole period of the war he was engaged on work of National importance in connection with the transport of munitions. He did excellent work and received high commendation for the services he rendered.
15, Calmington Road, Camberwell, S.E.5.   Z5387

FRANKLIN, J., Private, R.A.S.C. (M.T.)
Volunteering in September 1914, he was drafted to the Western Front in the same month and served during the Retreat from Mons, and in the Battles of the Aisne, Ypres, Arras, Albert, Bapaume. He was engaged in transporting troops and ammunition and supplies to the firing line, and was wounded in September 1918 during the Advance. After being sent to a Base Hospital he was transferred to England, and and on his recovery served with his unit at home. He was demobilised in February 1919, and holds the Mons Star, and the General Service and Victory Medals.
47, Clayton Road, Peckham S.E.15.   Z5956

FRANKS, G., L/Corporal, 11th Queen's (Royal West Surrey Regiment).
He volunteered in July 1915, and drafted to France in the following May fought in several important engagements, including the Battle of the Somme, and was wounded at Messines in June 1917, and invalided home. After protracted hospital treatment he was discharged as medically unfit for further service in May 1918, and holds the General Service and Victory Medals.
28, Kennard Street, Battersea, S.W.11.   Z2175

FRANKS, H., Private, Dorsetshire Regiment.
Mobilised on the outbreak of war he proceeded to France shortly afterwards, and took part in heavy fighting in the Retreat from Mons, and the Battles of Le Cateau and Festubert. He gave his life for King and Country at Neuve Chapelle on March 12th, 1915, and was entitled to the Mons Star, and the General Service and Victory Medals.
"A valiant soldier, with undaunted heart he breasted life's last hill."
25, Randall Street, Battersea, S.W.11.   Z2176B

FRANKS, L., Private, R.A.M.C.
He joined in 1918, on attaining military age, and on the conclusion of his training was engaged as a hospital orderly. He rendered valuable services, but was unsuccessful in obtaining a transfer to a theatre of war before the cessation of hostilities, and was demobilised in 1920. From 1914 until joining the Colours he did much useful work during air raids as a Boy Scout.
25, Randall Street, Battersea, S.W.11.   Z2176A

FRASER, H. J. (Jun.), Gunner, R.M.A.
He was serving when war broke out in August 1914, and was engaged on dangerous and important duties throughout the course of hostilities. His ship H.M.S. "St. Vincent" was attached to the Grand Fleet, and was in action in the Battle of Jutland. He was transferred to H.M.S. "Renown" and served aboard that vessel until the Armistice. He holds the 1914-15 Star, and the General Service and Victory Medals, and in 1920 was still serving.
128, Trafalgar Street, Walworth, S.E.17.   Z27340C

FRASER, H. J., L/Corporal, Royal Defence Corps.
A Territorial with several years' service he volunteered in the 3rd East Surrey Regiment in April 1915, and after transfer to the 33rd Royal Fusiliers Labour Corps proceeded to France in 1916. He was engaged on important duties in connection with operations in the forward areas, and was wounded at Poperinghe in April 1918, and invalided home. On recovery he was transferred to the Royal Defence Corps, and served with that unit until demobilised in February 1919. He holds the General Service and Victory Medals, and the Territorial Force Efficiency Medal.
128, Trafalgar Street, Walworth, S.E.17.   Z27340A

FRASER, J. C., Trooper, City of London Lancers (Rough Riders) and Private, M.G.C.
He volunteered in September 1914, and was sent to Egypt in the following year. Whilst overseas, he took part in many operations during General Allenby's Advance through Palestine in 1918, and was then drafted to France. There he was in action in the Allied Advance and served until the cessation of hostilities. He was wounded in the course of his service, and demobilised in February 1919, holding the 1914-15 Star, and the General Service and Victory Medals.
128, Trafalgar Street, Walworth, S.E.17.   Z27340B

FRASER, S., Gunner, R.F.A. and R.G.A.
Volunteering in 1914, he completed his training and served with his Battery in the Eastern Counties on important duties in connection with coast defence measures. He was also engaged on guard and other duties at large munition factories and prisoners of war camps. He did valuable work, but was unable to obtain a transfer overseas before the end of the war, and was demobilised in 1919.
24, Bagshot Street, Walworth, S.E.17.   Z2198

FRASER, W. (D.C.M., M.M.), 1st King's (Liverpool) Regiment.
A Regular soldier, having enlisted in 1903, he was mobilised on the declaration of war, and sent to France with the first Expeditionary Force. He took a prominent part in the heavy fighting during the Retreat from Mons, and the Battles of the Marne, Ypres, Festubert, and was wounded at Loos in September 1915. Rejoining his unit he was later in action near Cambrai, and again wounded, and invalided home. During his service overseas he was awarded the Distinguished Conduct Medal and bar, and the Military Medal and bar, for conspicuous gallantry and devotion to duty in the Field. Demobilised in January 1919, he also holds the Mons Star, and the General Service and Victory Medals.
20D, Victoria Dwellings, Battersea Park, S.W.8.   Z2178

FRASER, W. A., Driver, R.E. (Signals).
He volunteered in August 1914, and embarking for the Western Front in the following March was engaged on important duties in the Signal section of his unit. He was present in the Battles of Ypres, Festubert and Loos, but sustaining shell-shock was invalided home in September 1915. He returned to France in October 1916, but owing to medical unfitness for Field service was engaged on light duties until the end of the war. He was demobilised in January 1919, and holds the 1914-15 Star, and the General Service and Victory Medals.
73, Gloucester Road, Peckham, S.E.15.   Z5963B

FREELAND, A., Rifleman, King's Royal Rifle Corps.
Serving in the Merchant Service when war broke out, he volunteered for service with the Colours in July 1915, and embarked for the Western Front in the following year. Whilst overseas he fought in the Battles of Arras, Albert and was wounded at Delville Wood in 1917. Sent to hospital in France he was later transferred to England, and after treatment at various hospitals was invalided out of the Service in August 1917. He holds the General Service and Victory Medals, and the Mercantile Marine Medal.
63, Sussex Road, Coldharbour Lane, S.W.9.   Z3452

FREEMAN, C. J. (M.M.), Corporal, R.E. (R.O.D.)
He joined in April 1916, and embarked for France three months later, and was engaged in the forward areas on important duties connected with the railway transport of ammunition and supplies. He was awarded the Military Medal for conspicuous gallantry and devotion to duty in the Field in rescuing wounded under heavy shell fire at Bapaume. He was demobilised in October 1919, and holds the General Service and Victory Medals.
9, Wells Crescent, Camberwell, S.E.5.   Z3450

FREEMAN, G., Gunner, R.G.A.
He joined in May 1916, and was sent to the Western Front later in that year. During his service overseas he fought in many important engagements, including those at the Somme, Ypres and Cambrai. He died gloriously on the Field of battle at the second Battle of the Aisne in May 1918, and was entitled to the General Service and Victory Medals.
"His life for his Country, his soul to God."
63, Acorn Street, Camberwell, S.E.5.   Z2181

FREEMAN, F. R. (M.M.), Sapper, R.E.
Mobilised at the outbreak of hostilities, and drafted to France with the first Expeditionary Force, he served in the Retreat from Mons, the Battles of Ypres, Vimy Ridge, Loos, Hill 60, the Somme, Cambrai, and was mentioned in Despatches and awarded the Military Medal for gallantry and devotion to duty in the Field on November 13th, 1916. He saw much fighting during the German Offensive of 1918, and was severely wounded at Lys on August 1st in the Allied Advance, and died four days later from his injuries. He was entitled to the Mons Star, and the General Service and Victory Medals.
"Great deeds cannot die,
They with the Sun and Moon renew their light for ever."
24, Medlar Street, Camberwell, S.E.5.   Z2179B

FREEMAN, G. Driver, R.E. (Signal Section).
He joined in 1917, and later embarked for Italy, where he served until transferred to the Egyptian Expeditionary Force. On the Palestine front he was engaged on important duties, transporting supplies to the front lines, and rendered excellent services. He returned to England and was demobilised in February 1918, and holds the General Service and Victory Medals.
35, Mundella Road, Wandsworth Road, S.W.8.   Z2180A

FREEMAN, G. W. V., Corporal, 12th King's Royal Rifle Corps.
Volunteering in February 1916, he proceeded to the Western Front on the completion of his training and was in action in various engagements, including those at Cambrai, Ypres, Arras, Lens, Loos, and throughout the Retreat and Advance of 1918, and was wounded three times. He was demobilised in January 1919, and holds the General Service and Victory Medals.
28, Chiswick Lane, W.4.   5693

FREEMAN, H. F., Private, Devonshire Regiment, Norfolk Regiment and Royal Fusiliers.
Joining in March 1917, he was shortly afterwards sent to France where he was in action on the Somme, and at Passchendaele, being wounded during that engagement. He was invalided home, but after recovery returned to France, and was again wounded during a night attack near Béthune. He was again sent to England, and after a period in hospital volunteered for service in Russia, where he was in action against the Bolshevists. In November 1919 he returned home, and was demobilised. He holds the General Service and Victory Medals.
43, Tindal Street, Lothian Road, S.W.9.   Z5388A

FREEMAN, T. A., Rifleman, King's Royal Rifle Corps.
He joined in May 1918, and at the conclusion of his training served with his unit on special work until drafted to Germany with the Army of Occupation. He served at Cologne on important duties as Signaller until his return to England for demobilisation in February 1920.
43, Tindal Street, Lothian Road, S.W.9.   Z5388B

FREEMAN, W., Gunner, R.G.A.
Volunteering in 1915, he completed his training, and served at various stations with his unit engaged on important anti-aircraft duties. He was unsuccessful in obtaining his transfer overseas, but rendered excellent services until demobilised in 1919.
24, Medlar Street, Camberwell, S.E.5.   Z2179A

FREEMAN, W. T., A.B., Royal Navy.
A Reservist, he was mobilised at the commencement of hostilities, and drafted to Mesopotamia, where he served aboard H.M.S. " Cranefly " and was in action in various engagements, including those at Kut-el-Amara and Baghdad. Returning to England in April 1917, he was posted to H.M.S. " Courageous," which ship was engaged on patrol and other important duties until the cessation of hostilities. He was still serving in 1920, and holds the 1914-15 Star, and the General Service and Victory Medals.
24, Medlar Street, Camberwell, S.E.5.   Z2179C

FREER, S. E. (Mrs.), Special War Worker.
This lady volunteered for work of National importance, and for two and a half years during the war held a responsible position at Messrs. Davisons' Munition Factory, engaged on important duties in connection with the manufacture of aeroplane parts. She rendered valuable services and discharged her duties in a most efficient and satisfactory manner.
16, Banim Street, Hammersmith, W.6.   11621A

FREER, W. G., Private, Labour Corps.
He joined in October 1916, and shortly afterwards was drafted to France. Here he served in various parts of the line engaged on important duties, and was present at the Battles of Cambrai and Albert. He returned to England after the cessation of hostilities, and was demobilised in March 1919, and holds the General Service and Victory Medals.
16, Banim Street, Hammersmith, W.6.   11621B

FREESTONE, A. W., Private, R.A.S.C. (M.T.)
He joined in July 1915, and later embarked for the Western Front, where he served in the forward areas on important ambulance and other duties, and was present at many important engagements. He returned to England and was demobilised in February 1919, and held the General Service and Victory Medals. He died at a later date owing to sickness contracted whilst on service.
    " His memory is cherished with pride."
11, Creek Street, Battersea, S.W.11.   Z2188

FRENCH, A. E., Private, Labour Corps.
Volunteering in January 1916, he was sent overseas in the same year. Whilst on the Western Front he was engaged in making roads and on general fatigue duties, and did very good work with his Company in the Cambrai sector. He later proceeded to Germany with the Army of Occupation, and was stationed at Cologne. He holds the General Service and Victory Medals, and was demobilised in September 1919.
148, Mayall Road, Herne Hill, S.E.24.   Z5606

FRENCH, A. R., Driver, R.F.A.
He volunteered in September 1914, and was drafted to Mesopotamia in the following year, and fought in many engagements, including those of Kut-el-Amara, Ctesiphon. the capitulation of Kut, and in various successful operations on the Tigris. He died gloriously on the Field of Battle at Tekrit on November 5th, 1917, and was entitled to the 1914-15 Star, and the General Service and Victory Medals.
    " A valiant soldier, with undaunted heart he breasted Life's last hill."
24, Townsend Street, Walworth, S.E.17.   Z2182

FRENCH, A. R., Rifleman, 5th London Regiment (London Rifle Brigade).
Joining in September 1916 on attaining military age, he was sent to France in the following year and served in various sectors. He was in action in several important engagements, including the Battles of the Somme, Ypres and Cambrai, and did much good work until the conclusion of hostilities. He was demobilised in October 1919, and holds the General Service and Victory Medals.
52, Foreign Street, Camberwell, S.E.5.   Z5958A

FRENCH, E., Bombardier, R.F.A.
Volunteering in August 1914, from the Army Reserve, he was sent to France almost immediately and fought in the Retreat from Mons, and in many important engagements in the Ypres salient. He was wounded at St. Eloi in 1916, and after receiving medical treatment rejoined his unit and was in action in many parts of the line and throughout the Retreat and Advance of 1918. He was demobilised in April 1919, and holds the Mons Star, and the General Service and Victory Medals.
95, Latchmere Road, Battersea, S.W.11.   Z2185

FRENCH, G., L/Corporal, Queen's (Royal West Surrey Regiment).
He volunteered in August 1914, and two months later was drafted to France, where he served until sent to Gallipoli in 1915. Taking part in the Landing on the Peninsula he fought in several other operations, and was wounded. After the Evacuation he proceeded to the Western Front, and was in action in many important engagements until hostilities ceased. He was demobilised in March 1919, and holds the 1914-15 Star, and the General Service and Victory Medals.
154, St. George's Road, Peckham, S.E.15.   Z5758

FRENCH, H.. A.B., Royal Navy.
He was serving in H.M.S. " Bacchante," at the outbreak of hostilities, and during the war his ship was engaged on patrol and other important duties and was also engaged in the Battle of the Narrows and did good work covering the Landing of the Allies at the Dardanelles. Returning to the North Sea in 1916, this vessel rendered valuable services escorting convoys, and mine-sweeping until the cessation of hostilities. He was demobilised in February 1919, and holds the 1914-15 Star, and the General Service and Victory Medals.
74, Geneva Road, Coldharbour Lane, S.W.9.   Z3083

FRENCH, J. (Sen.), Private, Welch Regiment.
He volunteered in 1915, and in the following year embarked for the Western Front. Whilst in this theatre of war he was engaged in much heavy fighting on the Somme, and was gassed and wounded there. He was invalided to hospital in England, and on recovery served with a Labour Company until his demobilisation in February 1919. He holds the General Service and Victory Medals.
37, Seaham Street, Wandsworth Road, S.W.8.   Z6195B

FRENCH, J. (Jun.), Private, M.G.C.
He joined in March 1918, on attaining military age, and on the conclusion of his training was engaged on important duties with his unit. He rendered valuable services, but was unsuccessful in obtaining his transfer overseas before the termination of the war, and was demobilised in February 1919.
37, Seaham Street, Wandsworth Road, S.W.8.   Z6195A

FRENCH, J., A.B., Royal Navy.
He joined in July 1916, and was posted to H.M.S. " Antrim," which ship was patrolling in the Western Ocean from the West Indian station, and also was engaged on escorting duties. Later transferred to the North Sea, this vessel rendered valuable services until the close of the war. He was demobilised in February 1919, and holds the General Service and Victory Medals.
11, Ostend Place, Walworth Road, S.E.17.   Z26150A

FRENCH, R., Private, Royal Fusiliers.
He joined in September 1917, on attaining military age, and was drafted to the Western Front in March of the following year. He was engaged on important duties with his Battalion during the closing stages of the war, and did excellent work. He was demobilised in October 1919, and holds the General Service and Victory Medals.
52, Foreign Street, Camberwell, S.E.5.　　　　Z5958B

FRENCH, R., Sapper, R.E.
He volunteered in May 1915, and embarked for France five months later. He served in the forward areas engaged on important duties connected with operations, and was present at many engagements, including those at Arras, Ypres, the Somme, and in the Retreat and Advance of 1918. He was demobilised in February 1919, and holds the 1914-15 Star, and the General Service and Victory Medals.
126, Stewart's Road, Battersea Park Road, S.W.8.　　Z2184

FRENCH, S. H., L/Cpl., 25th Middlesex Regiment.
He volunteered in March 1915, and in the following November proceeded to the Western Front. He was in action at various engagements and was wounded at Loos in January 1916. On recovery he rejoined his unit and fought at St. Eloi, Albert, Vimy Ridge, the Somme, where he was again wounded. After receiving medical treatment he returned to the front lines, and saw heavy fighting at the Ancre, Beaumont-Hamel, Arras, Bullecourt, Messines, and was severely wounded in the third Battle of Ypres in July 1917. Invalided to England he received protracted hospital treatment, but died from the effects of his injuries on October 11th, 1917.
"Honour the immortal dead, who gave their youth that
　　the world might grow old in peace."
10, Mundella Road, Wandsworth Road, S.W.8.　　Z2183

FRENCH, W. H., R.Q.M.S., 11th Queen's (Royal West Surrey Regiment).
Volunteering in September 1914, he was retained at home training the recruits of the New Armies until he proceeded to France in April 1917. He was in action at Ploegsteert, Vimy Ridge, the Somme, Beaumont-Hamel, Messines, Cambrai, Verdun, and throughout the Retreat and Advance of 1918, and was present at the entry into Mons on November 11th, 1918, and was wounded three times during his service overseas, at Verdun, Vimy Ridge and Ypres (III). He was sent with the Army of Occupation into Germany and served there until demobilised in April 1920, and holds the General Service and Victory Medals.
123, Mayall Road, Herne Hill, S.E.24.　　　Z2187

FRENCH, W. J., Gunner, R.F.A.
He volunteered in October 1914, and embarked for the Western Front in the following year, and was in action in the Loos sector for three months. Transferred to the Balkan theatre of war, he fought in many engagements on the Vardar, Struma, and Doiran fronts. He contracted malaria whilst on service, and invalided to England was discharged in March 1918. He subsequently died in 1920 from a recurrence of the fever, and was entitled to the 1914-15 Star, and the General Service and Victory Medals.
"His memory is cherished with pride."
34, Thornton Street, Brixton Road, S.W.9.　　Z2186

FRETTON, E. A., Gunner, R.F.A.
A Regular soldier, he was mobilised and sent to France at the commencement of hostilities, and was in action throughout the Retreat from Mons, and in the Battles of the Marne, the Aisne and Loos. Transferred to Salonika in 1915, he was retained at the Base, owing to ill-health, and was engaged on guard and other important duties. He returned to England and was demobilised in May 1919, and holds the Mons Star, and the General Service and Victory Medals.
105, Aylesbury Road, Walworth, S.E.17.　　Z2189

FRETWELL, R., L/Sergt., 7th Queen's (Royal West Surrey Regiment).
Volunteering in August 1915, he was drafted to the Western Front in the following April. During his service overseas he fought in many parts of the line, and was wounded in July 1916. On recovery, he returned to the front lines and was almost continuously in action until he gave his life for King and Country at Combles in September 1916. He was entitled to the General Service and Victory Medals.
"Great deeds cannot die,
They with the Sun and Moon renew their light for ever."
8, Corunna Road, New Road, S.W.8.　　Z2190B

FRETWELL, A., Private, 15th Devonshire Regt.
He volunteered in May 1915, and was sent to France in the following year, and fought in many engagements, including that on the Somme, and was wounded. He returned to England and received hospital treatment, and on recovery served at various stations on guard and other important duties until demobilised in March 1919. He holds the General Service and Victory Medals.
8, Corunna Road, New Road, S.W.8.　　Z2190

FREWER, H. V., Guardsman, Coldstream Guards.
Volunteering at the commencement of hostilities, he embarked for the Western Front in the following year and fought at Ypres, Neuve Chapelle, Festubert, Hill 60, St. Quentin, St. Eloi, Loos, Givenchy, Vimy Ridge and La Bassée, where he was wounded in the head and lost the sight of his left eye. Invalided to England he received medical treatment, and on recovery was transferred to the Military Police, and served in this capacity until discharged unfit for further service in July 1916. He holds the 1914-15 Star, and the General Service and Victory Medals.
103, Sussex Road, Coldharbour Lane, S.W.9.　　Z3085

FRIDAY, T. C., Driver, R.F.A.
He was mobilised in August 1914, and in the following March was drafted to the Western Front, where he took part in the fierce fighting at Ypres, Festubert, and Loos. Owing to illness he subsequently returned to England, and while awaiting discharge died at home in June 1916 of typhoid fever, contracted whilst on service in France. He was entitled to the 1914-15 Star, and the General Service and Victory Medals.
"And doubtless he went in splendid company."
16, Fifth Avenue, Queen's Park Estate, W.10.　　X18323

FRIEND, T. H., Gunner, R.F.A.
Volunteering in 1914, he was drafted to France in the following year, and served in the Battles of Hill 60 and Loos. After being sent to Salonika in 1915, he was engaged with his Battery in various operations during the Advance across the Struma, and on Lake Doiran, and was present at the capture of Monastir. Owing to injuries to his knee he was invalided home and demobilised in January 1919. He holds the 1914-15 Star, and the General Service and Victory Medals.
38, Gordon Road, Nunhead, S.E.15.　　Z6168

FRISBY, P. F., Private, Labour Corps.
Having previously been unsuccessful in his attempt to join the Colours owing to medical unfitness, he enlisted in 1918, and was drafted to the Western Front in the same year. He was engaged on important trench digging and other duties in the forward areas, and did good work during the final operations of the war. He was demobilised in 1919, and holds the General Service and Victory Medals.
10, McKerrell Road, Peckham, S.E.15.　　Z5760

FRISWELL, T. W., Private, R.A.S.C.
He volunteered in 1915, and later in the same year proceeded to the Western Front. Here he was employed as a driver, and later as a wheelwright, and rendered valuable services until the end of the war. He returned to England and was demobilised in March 1919, and holds the 1914-15 Star, and the General Service and Victory Medals.
7, Mundella Road, Wandsworth Road, S.W.8.　　Z2191

FRITH, F., Pte., 10th Queen's (Royal West Surrey Regiment).
He volunteered in November 1915, and in May of the following year was drafted to the Western Front. He fought in several important engagements, including those of the Somme, Ypres, and Armentières, and was badly wounded on the Somme in October 1916. He was invalided home, and after protracted hospital treatment, was discharged as medically unfit for further service in July 1917. He holds the General Service and Victory Medals.
35, Dashwood Road, Wandsworth Road, S.W.8.　　Z2192

FROGLEY, T., Driver, R.F.A. and Gunner, T.M.B.
He volunteered in 1915, and in the following year was sent to the Western Front. Whilst in this theatre of war, he fought in several engagements, including those of Festubert, the Somme, Arras and Ypres. In 1918 he was sent to Italy and took an active part in the fighting on the Asiago and Piave fronts. After the Armistice he returned to England and was demobilised in 1919. He holds the General Service and Victory Medals.
108, Faraday Street, Walworth, S.E.17.　　Z2193

FROOME, T., Private, 1st Middlesex Regiment.
He was mobilised in August 1914, and proceeded to the Western Front. He fought in many fierce engagements, including the Retreat from Mons, and the Battles of the Marne, Le Bassée, Ypres, Loos, Albert and the Somme, where he was badly gassed. He subsequently died from the effects of gas poisoning on August 21st, 1916, and was entitled to the Mons Star, and the General Service and Victory Medals.
"His life for his Country, his Soul to God."
52, Elsted Street, Walworth, S.E.17.　　Z2020A

FROST, A. (Mrs.), Special War Worker.
This lady offered her services for work of National importance during the war, and for a period of eighteen months was engaged as checker in the Goods Department of the South Eastern and Chatham Railway, thus releasing a man for military service. She did very good work throughout.
14, Exon Street, Walworth, S.E.17.　　Z2195B

FROST, H., Guardsman, 1st Grenadier Guards.

He volunteered in January 1916, and in the following year proceeded to the Western Front, He saw much fighting in this theatre of war and fought in several engagements, including the Battle of Cambrai and those during the Retreat and Advance of 1918, and was gassed. Invalided to England he received medical treatment, and on recovery was demobilised in March 1919. He holds the General Service and Victory Medals.
11, Mosedale Street, Camberwell, S.E.5. Z2194

FROST, H., Shoeing Smith, R.H.A.

He was mobilised in August 1914, and almost immediately drafted to the Western Front, where he served through the Retreat from Mons and many of the principal engagements, which followed, including those of the Marne, Le Cateau, the Aisne, La Bassée, Ypres, St. Eloi, Hill 60, Festubert, Loos, Albert, Vimy Ridge, and the Somme. In 1917 he was invalided home, and on discharge from hospital was employed on important duties with the Anti-Aircraft Guns on the East coast. He was demobilised in September 1919, and holds the Mons Star, and the General Service and Victory Medals.
14, Exon Street, Walworth, S.E.17. Z2195A

FROST, L. F., Corporal, 3rd Worcestershire Regt.

He volunteered in March 1916, and in January of the following year was sent to Italy. Here he took part in many important engagements on the Piave, and was wounded. On recovery he was again in action on this front during the Offensive of 1918, and was wounded a second time. He returned to England for hospital treatment, and on recovery was sent to Ireland, where he served on special duties until demobilised in September 1919. He holds the General Service and the Victory Medals.
153, Bridge Road, Battersea, S.W.11. Z2196B

FROST, W. H., Bombardier, R.F.A.

He volunteered in October 1914, and in the following March was sent to France. During his service on the Western Front he fought in many important battles, including those of Loos, Festubert, the Somme, and was badly wounded at Ypres in 1917. He was invalided home for treatment, and on recovery rejoined his Battery in the Field and was in action in the Retreat and Advance of 1918, and was gassed. He returned to England in 1919, and was demobilised in June of that year, and holds the 1914-15 Star, and the General Service and Victory Medals.
153, Bridge Road, Battersea, S.W.11. Z2196A

FROUD, G., Private, Cambridgeshire Regiment.

He volunteered in 1915, and in the following year was drafted to France. He fought at Arras, Ypres, the Somme and Cambrai, and also took part in the Retreat and subsequent Allied Advance of 1918. He returned to England after the signing of the Armistice, and was demobilised in 1919, and holds the General Service and Victory Medals. Z2197
12, Frances Street, Battersea, S.W.11.

FRYER, C. W., Saddler, R.F.A.

Volunteering in July 1915, he was drafted to France in the following March, and was engaged in the fighting at Ypres, Loos, Albert, the Somme, and Vimy Ridge. He died gloriously on the Field of battle at Ypres on January 12th, 1917. He was entitled to the General Service and Victory Medals.
"A costly sacrifice upon the altar of freedom."
28, Runham Street, Walworth, S.E.17. Z2199B

FRYER, P. E., Driver, R.A.S.C.

Mobilised as a Reservist at the outbreak of hostilities he was drafted to France in September 1914. He was engaged with his unit on the Marne and the Aisne, and at La Bassée, Ypres, Neuve Chapelle, St. Eloi and Festubert, being frequently under shell fire. He was sent to India in December 1915, but was invalided to hospital, where he subsequently died in September 1916. He was entitled to the 1914 Star, and the General Service and Victory Medals.
"Thinking that remembrance, though unspoken, may reach him where he sleeps."
12, Akers Street, Walworth, S.E.17. Z2200C

FULCHER, A., Private, 8th Buffs (East Kent Regt.)

He volunteered in November 1914, and in September of the following year was drafted to France. He was engaged in the heavy fighting at the Battle of Loos, where he was wounded and reported missing on September 28th of that year. He was later presumed to have been killed in action on that date. He was entitled to the 1914-15 Star, and the General Service and Victory Medals.
"His life for his Country, his Soul to God."
36, Glycena Road, Lavender Hill, S.W.11. Z2201A

FULCHER, H. W., Corporal, R.A.S.C.

Volunteering in August 1914, he was engaged with his unit on special duties at various stations. He did very good work, but was not successful in obtaining his transfer overseas. Owing to ill-health he was invalided to hospital, where he died in July 1918.
"His memory is cherished with pride."
6, Brackley Terrace, Chiswick, W.4. 5432A

FULFORD, E. H., Seaman, Merchant Service.

He was serving at the outbreak of hostilities aboard H.M.S. "Beacon Grange," which vessel was engaged on special transport duties to and from France, and had many narrow escapes, his ships being twice torpedoed by enemy submarines. He was demobilised in February 1920, and holds the General Service and Mercantile Marine War Medals.
24, Richford Street, Hammersmith, W.6. 10453C

FULLBROOK, J. T., A.B., Royal Navy.

He was serving at the outbreak of hostilities aboard H.M.S. "Venus," which ship during the war was engaged on special patrol duties in the North and Irish Seas, and in the Atlantic Ocean, and later proceeding to China, served there until 1918. With his ship he was then sent to German East Africa, where he remained until 1919. He was discharged in June of that year, and holds the 1914-15 Star, and the General Service and Victory Medals.
39, Harling Street, Camberwell, S.E.5. Z5389

FULLER, A. F., Private, Royal Fusiliers.

Joining in September 1916, he was drafted in the following October to France. On account of ill-health he served on special duties with his Battalion in the rear, and did excellent work in road construction and building hutments. He was demobilised in March 191·, and holds the General Service and Victory Medals.
2, Sussex Grove, Loughborough Park, S.W.9. Z4454A

FULLER, B., Rifleman, 8th London Regiment (Post Office Rifles) and 14th Royal Irish Rifles.

He joined in May 1916, and in June of the following year was sent to France,. He served with his Battalion in various parts of the line, and fought in many important engagements. He was severely wounded in action at Ypres in September 1917, and in consequence of his injuries one of his legs had to be amputated. He returned to England and died on September 19th, 1917, in Leicester Hospital, and was buried in Forest Hill Cemetery. He was entitled to the General Service and Victory Medals.
"The path of duty was the way to glory."
59, East Surrey Grove, Peckham, S.E.15. Z5240

FULLER, F. H., L/Sergt., 1st Manchester Regt.

He volunteered in November 1915, and at the conclusion of his training served on important duties at various stations until drafted to India in January 1918. In the following September he proceeded to China, where he served with his Battalion until he was demobilised in February 1920. He holds the General Service and Victory Medals.
35, Cologne Road, Battersea, S.W.11. Z2202

FULLER, W., L/Corporal, Military Mounted Police.

Having previously served with the Colours, he re-enlisted in August 1914, and was drafted to France. He was engaged on important duties with his unit and did very good work, but owing to his being over military age he was discharged in June 1915. He holds the Egyptian Medal (1882), the Khedive's Star, the 1914-15 Star, and the General Service and Victory Medals.
99, St. Mark's Road, Camberwell, S.E.5. Z2204

FULLER, W. F., Driver, R.F.A.

He volunteered in February 1915, and in the following September proceeded overseas. He served in many sectors of the Western Front, and was engaged in many battles, including those of Ypres (II), Loos, and Albert. He gave his life for King and Country near Vimy Ridge, during heavy fighting on July 21st, 1916. He was entitled to the 1914-15 Star, and the General Service and Victory Medals.
"A valiant soldier, with undaunted heart he breasted Life's last hill."
136, Aylesbury Road, Walworth, S.E.17. Z2203

FULLER, W. H., L/Corporal, Royal Defence Corps.

He volunteered in July 1915, being ineligible for service overseas, and at the conclusion of his training served on special work in connection with coastal defence, rendering valuable services. He also served for a time in Ireland until demobilised in January 1919.
136, Dalyell Road, Landor Road, S.W.9. Z2205

FULLJAMES, H. G., Sapper, R.E. (A.I.F.)

He volunteered in October 1914, and in April of the following year was sent to the Dardanelles. He served at Gallipoli from April until September 1915, when he was severely wounded, and invalided to England. He remained for a long period in hospital, but unfortunately succumbed in January 1918. He was entitled to the 1914-15 Star, and the General Service and Victory Medals.
"Whilst we remember, the Sacrifice is not in vain."
17, Wells Place, Camberwell, S.E.5. Z3451B

FULLJAMES, L. J. (M.M.), Private, R.A.M.C.
He volunteered in September 1914, and in the following May
was drafted to the Western Front, where he served with
distinction on the Somme and at Cambrai. He was awarded
the Military Medal for the gallantry he displayed in bringing
in the wounded under heavy shell-fire, and for a further
act of bravery was awarded a Bar to the Medal in 1917.
Whilst carrying wounded comrades into safety he was unhappily killed at Varennes in July 1918. He was entitled to
the 1914–15 Star, and the General Service and Victory Medals.
"Greater love hath no man than this, that a man lay down
             his life for his friends."
17, Wells Place, Camberwell, S.E.5.   Z3451A

FURBER, A. W., Private, Royal Berkshire Regt.
A serving soldier, he was drafted to France at the outbreak
of war, and fought in the Retreat from Mons. Owing to
ill-health he was invalided to hospital, and on recovery proceeded to Salonika, where he fought on the Vardar front, and
was wounded. He subsequently returned to England, and
was demobilised in 1919, holding the Mons Star, and the
General Service and Victory Medals.
16, Chalmers Street, Wandsworth, Road, S.W.8.   Z2206

FURGUSON, J. J., Rifleman, Rifle Brigade.
Volunteering in March 1915, he was drafted overseas three
months later, and during his service in France fought in many
engagements, including those at Ypres, the Somme, Cambrai,
and was three times wounded. He was demobilised
in February 1919, and holds the 1914–15 Star, and the General
Service and Victory Medals.
117, Cronin Road, Peckham, S.E.15.   Z5607A

FURSEY, E., Private, 8th East Surrey Regiment.
He volunteered in September 1914, and in the following August
was sent to France. He served with his Battalion in various
parts of the line and was engaged in much heavy fighting in
many notable battles. He gave his life for the freedom of
England near Arras on November 27th, 1915, and was entitled
to the 1914–15 Star, and the General Service and Victory
Medals.
"A valiant soldier, with undaunted heart he breasted Life's
             last hill."
80, St. George's Road, Peckham, S.E.15.   Z5608

FURZER, W., Private, R.A.S.C. (M.T.)
He joined in October 1916, and at the conclusion of his training
was engaged on special transport duties at various stations
with his unit, until drafted to the Western Front in July
1918. He served as an ambulance driver, and did very
good work in many sectors until after the signing of the Armistice, when he proceeded to Germany with the Army of
Occupation. He was demobilised in March 1920, and holds
the General Service and Victory Medals.
9, Pountney Road, Lavender Hill, S.W.11.   Z2207

FUSSEY, S., Corporal, R.E.
Volunteering at the outbreak of war, he was sent to the Western
Front in February of the following year. He was engaged
with his unit on special duties in many sectors, including
those of Arras, Ypres (II), Loos and Cambrai, and was gassed.
He was sent to the Base hospital, and on recovery rejoined
his Unit. After being again in hospital he was demobilised
in December 1918, holding the 1914–15 Star, and the General
Service and Victory Medals.
9, Russell Street, Battersea, S.W.11.   Z2208

G

GABLE, A. E. T., Sapper, R.E.
He volunteered in February 1915, and was almost immediately
sent to the Western Front. During his service in this theatre
of war he was engaged on important mining operations at
Messines Ridge and elsewhere. He returned home for demobilisation in January 1919. He holds the 1914–15 Star, and
the General Service and Victory Medals.
3, Poyntz Road, Battersea, S.W.11.   Z2209

**GADD, S. W., Trooper, 6th Dragoon Guards
(Carabiniers).**
He was mobilised from the Reserve when war broke out, and
almost immediately proceeded to France. There he was
engaged in heavy fighting during the Retreat from Mons,
and in several subsequent engagements. Owing to illness he
was invalided home in 1915, and after medical treatment
served with his unit on home defence duties. He was demobilised in January 1919, and holds the Mons Star, and the General
Service and Victory Medals.
139, Heath Road, Wandsworth Road, S.W.8.   Z2210

GADD, F., Private, 10th Northamptonshire Regt.
Volunteering in December 1915, he was drafted overseas n
the following year and saw much service in France and Flanders. He took part in several important engagements, including the Battles of Ypres, Passchendaele and Armentières,
and served with his unit until the conclusion of hostilities.
He was demobilised in March 1919, and holds the General
Service and Victory Medals.
23, Edithna Street, Landor Road, S.W.9.   Z2211

GADDES, T., L/Corporal, M.F.P.
Volunteering in 1915, he was drafted to France in the same
year in the Middlesex Regiment, with which unit he was in
action in several important engagements. He was later
transferred to the Military Foot Police, and was engaged on
important duties in various sectors until the conclusion of
hostilities. Demobilised in November 1918, he holds the
1914–15 Star, and the General Service and Victory Medals.
37, Everett Street, Nine Elms Lane, S.W.8.   Z2212

**GAFFEE, E., Private, King's Own (Yorkshire
Light Infantry).**
A serving soldier, he proceeded to the Western Front shortly
after the commencements of hostilities, and fought in many
engagements, including the Battle of Ypres. Owing to ill-
health he was invalided home in 1915, and received hospital
treatment, but on recovery returned to France. He was
in action at the Somme, Ypres, Messines Le Sars, and was
again invalided to England in July 1917. From this time until
his demobilisation in 1919 he remained on home service. He
holds the 1914–15 Star, and the General Service and Victory
Medals.
56, Bournemouth Road, Rye Lane, S.E.15.   Z5390

GAIGER, W. G. A., Driver, R.A.S.C. (M.T.)
He volunteered in March 1915, and proceeding to Egypt
in the same year served there for a time and was sent to
Salonika. He was engaged on transport duties throughout
the course of operations in the Balkans, and did excellent
work. Returning to England for demobilisation in March
1919, he holds the 1914–15 Star, and the General Service and
Victory Medals.
6, Thessaly Square, Wandsworth Road, S.W.8.   Z2213

**GAINS, H., Trooper, 2nd County of London Yeo-
manry (Westminster Dragoons).**
Volunteering in November 1915, he embarked for the Western
Front in the following April, and took part in the Battles of
the Somme, Ypres, Passchendaele, the Marne, Amiens,
Bapaume, Havrincourt, Bourlon Wood and Oppy. He also
served in the Machine Gun Corps, the Tank Corps, the York
and Lancaster Regiment and the Labour Corps. He was
demobilised in 1919, and holds the General Service and Victory
Medals.
69, Mostyn Road, Brixton Road, S.W.9.   Z3463

GAINS, J., Sapper, R.E.
A serving soldier, having enlisted in December 1912, he was
mobilised on the declaration of war, and sent to France with
the first Expeditionary Force. He was in action during the
Retreat from Mons and several other engagements. Suffering
from shell-shock he was sent home in 1918, and invalided out
of the Service in the same year. He holds the Mons Star,
and the General Service and Victory Medals.
133, New Road, Battersea Park Road, S.W.8.   Z2214A

GALBRAITH, F. A. G., Bombardier, R.G.A.
He volunteered in January 1915, and was drafted to France
six months later. He was engaged in heavy fighting in the
Battles of Ypres (II), Loos and Albert, and was wounded in
the Somme sector in April 1916. After his recovery he was
again in action on Vimy Ridge, and at Arras. He also took
part in several engagements during the Retreat and Advance
of 1918. He was demobilised in March 1919, and holds the
1914–15 Star, and the General Service and Victory Medals.
102, Aylesbury Road, Walworth, S.E.17.   Z2215

GALE, A. R., Private, Royal Scots.
Volunteering in April 1915, he was sent to the Western Front
shortly afterwards, and saw service in various sectors. He
fought in many engagements, and was gassed and wounded
during the Battles of Loos in September 1915. Admitted to
hospital in France, he was later invalided home and discharged
ou account of service in April 1917. He holds the 1914–15
Star, and the General Service and Victory Medals.
5, Renshaw Street, Wandsworth Road, S.W.8.   Z2216

GALE, J. W., Driver, R.F.A.
He volunteered in November 1914, and proceeding overseas
three months later served on the Western Front for nearly
four years. During this period he was in action in the Battles
of Neuve Chapelle, St. Eloi, Hill 60, Ypres, Festubert, Loos,
Albert, Vimy Ridge and the Somme, Beaumont-Hamel,
Cambrai, Amiens, and the Marne, and was wounded. He
was demobilised in February 1919, and holds the 1914–15
Star, and the General Service and Victory Medals.
2, Waxwell Terrace, Westminster Bridge Road, S.E.1.
                                              TZ26083

GALE, R., Gunner, R.F.A.
He volunteered in January 1915, and in the following December embarked for France. Whilst in this theatre of war he served at Loos, Vimy Ridge and Mont Kemmel, and was severely wounded during the Battle of Ypres in 1917. Sent to hospital in England, he was invalided out of the Service in September 1917. He holds the 1914-15 Star, and the General Service and Victory Medals.
17, Lock's Square, Walworth, S.E.17.   Z2217

GALLANT, A. C., Private, R.A.M.C.
He joined in 1916, and on the completion of his training was engaged on important ambulance duties at several hospitals in England. He rendered valuable services but was unable to obtain a transfer overseas owing to medical unfitness, and was demobilised in August 1919.
105, Chatham Road, Wandsworth Common, S.W.11.   Z2218B

GALLANT, W. J., Private, Buffs (East Kent Regt).
Joining in June 1916, he was drafted to the Western Front in the same year, and served throughout the war. He did good work with his Battalion in various sectors and took part in many important battles, returning home at the end of hostilities. Re-enlisting for a further period of service he was sent to India, and in 1920 was still stationed there. He holds the General Service and Victory Medals.
105, Chatham Road, Wandsworth Common, S.W.11.   Z2218A

GALLARD, P. T., Bombardier, R.F.A.
He volunteered in 1915, and proceeding to France in the same year served in various sectors. He fought in the Battles of Ypres, Arras and the Somme, and was temporarily buried owing to the explosion of a shell. He was subsequently in action at Cambrai, and in several other engagements. He is entitled to the 1914-15 Star, and the General Service and Victory Medals.
13, Rutland Street, Wilcox Road, S.W.8.   Z2219

GALLERY, A., A.B., Royal Navy.
He joined the Service in 1904, and was serving aboard H.M.S. T.B.D " Renard " at the outbreak of war. His ship was engaged on important patrol duties and later was in action in the Naval operations at the Dardanelles. In 1916 he was transferred to H.M.S. " Royal Oak," in which vessel he was in action at the Battle of Jutland in May 1916. He continued to serve with his ship until the cessation of hostilities, and was demobilised in June 1919. He holds the 1914-15 Star, and the General Service and Victory Medals.
183, Cronin Road, Peckham, S.E.15.   Z5391

GALLEY, C. A., 1st Class Petty Officer, R.N.
Mobilised on the outbreak of war, he was posted to H.M.S. " Aquarius." His ship was in action in the Battle of the Falkland Islands, and was engaged on important duties in Italian waters. He took part in the landing parties in many engagements on the Italian front, and was wounded three times. He had previously served with the Naval Brigade in South Africa, and in China, and in addition to medals for those campaigns, holds the 1914-15 Star, and the General Service and Victory Medals.
84, Cranbrook Road, Chiswick, W.4.   5388A

GALLIN, A., Private, 22nd Middlesex Regiment.
He joined in July 1915, and being unfit for service overseas was employed at many ports loading ammunition and other war material for various theatres of war. He rendered valuable services, and was engaged on this important work until demobilised in February 1919.
93, Rosemary Road, Peckham, S.E.15.   Z5392

GALLOWAY, J., Private, Queen's Own Cameron Highlanders.
He volunteered in September 1914, and was sent to France in the following year. He was in action in several important engagements, and was wounded in the Battle of Loos in September 1915, on the Somme in February 1916, and at Arras in the following August. He was blown up by a shell at Ypres on July 31st, 1917, and invalided home. After medical treatment he was discharged in April 1918 as medically unfit for further service, and holds the 1914-15 Star, and the General Service and Victory Medals.
19, Brisbane Street, Camberwell, S.E.5.   Z5077

GAMBLE, R., L/Corporal, 22nd London Regiment (The Queen's).
Volunteering in November 1914, he completed his training, and was engaged on important police duties for two years. He was then transferred to the Royal Irish Rifles, and served in Ireland until drafted to France in May 1918. He returned to England on the conclusion of hostilities, and was invalided out of the Army in December 1918, and holds the General Service and Victory Medals.
105, Smyrk's Road, Walworth, S.E.17.   Z2222A

GAMBIE, A. J., Sapper, Royal Marine Engineers.
He joined in March 1918, and after completing his training was engaged with his unit at various depôts in the Southern Counties on important coastal defence duties. He was, however, unable to secure his transfer to a theatre of war before hostilities ceased, and was demobilised in March 1919.
19, Hillery Road, Walworth, S.E.1 .   Z2221

GAMBRILL, S. A. A., Gunner, R.F.A.
He was serving in India when war broke out, and proceeding to Mesopotamia saw much service in that theatre of war. He was twice wounded in the course of operations, and after his second wound was invalided home. He underwent protracted medical treatment and was eventually discharged as medically unfit for further service in October 1917. He holds the 1914-15 Star, and the General Service and Victory Medals.
27, Nunhead Crescent, Peckham, S.E.15.   Z6192

GANDER, C., Private, Royal Sussex Regiment.
He joined in August 1917, and was sent overseas in the following April. He took part in heavy fighting on the Somme, but after nine days' active service was posted as missing. He was later presumed to have been killed in action. He was entitled to the General Service and Victory Medals.
" A valiant soldier, with undaunted heart, he breasted life's
last hill."
3, Weybridge Street, Battersea, S.W.11.   Z2223

GANDER, D., Bombardier, R.F.A.
Volunteering in January 1915, he was drafted to the Western Front in the same year. He served with his Battery in the Battle of Festubert, and was wounded at Loos in 1915. Rejoining his Battery he was in action in the Somme and Ypres sectors, and was wounded at Ypres in 1916, and again in the following year. He was demobilised in June 1919, and holds the 1914-15 Star, and the General Service and Victory Medals, and having re-enlisted was sent to India, where he was serving in 1920.
84, Henley Street, Battersea, S.W.11.   Z2224

GANN, J. A., Private, 7th Duke of Cornwall's Light Infantry.
He volunteered in April 1915, and embarked for the Western Front in the following September. In the course of his service he fought in several engagements, including the Battles of Poperinghe and the Somme, and was wounded at St. Jean on November 23rd, 1915. He was discharged as medically unfit for further service in July 1916, and holds the 1914-15 Star, and the General Service and Victory Medals.
55, Elliotts Row, St. George's Road, S.E.11.   Z26891

GANNON, H. G. (D.C.M.), Sergt., 1st Hampshire Regt.
Mobilised from the Army Reserve when war was declared, he proceeded to France shortly afterwards, and fought during the Retreat from Mons, and in the Battles of the Marne, the Aisne and Ypres, and was wounded at Ploegsteert Wood in December 1914. He subsequently fought in the Battles of Ypres and Passchendaele, and was awarded the Distinguished Conduct Medal for conspicuous bravery in bombing a dug-out and taking twenty-eight prisoners and two machine guns. He was discharged in June 1918, on account of service, and in addition to the Queen's South African Medal with clasp, holds the Mons Star, and the General Service and Victory Medals.
91, Tyneham Road, Lavender Hill, S.W.11.   Z2225A

GANNON, M. E. (Mrs.), Forewoman, Q.M.A.A.C.
She joined in September 1917, and was engaged as a Hostel Forewoman at Farnborough for upwards of nine months. During her service she did valuable work, discharging the duties of her position in a capable and efficient manner.
91, Tyneham Road, Lavender Hill, S.W.11.   Z2225B

GARBUTT, J. A., Sergt., 6th Queen's (Royal West Surrey Regiment).
Volunteering in November 1915, he was sent to France in the following year. Whilst on the Western Front, he was in action at the Battles of Ypres, Albert, the Somme, Bullecourt, and in the Retreat and Advance of 1918. He was demobilised in January 1919, and holds the General Service and Victory Medals.
48, Claude Road, Peckham Rye, S.E.15.   Z5771

GARDENER, A. E., Gunner, R.G.A.
He joined in November 1917, and embarking for the Western Front four months later served until the cessation of hostilities. During this period he was in action on the Somme, the Marne and in several engagements in the Retreat from Cambrai. Suffering from shell shock, he was discharged as medically unfit for further service in February 1919, and holds the General Service and Victory Medals.
26, Freemantle Street, Walworth, S.E.17.   Z2226A

GARDENER, A. T., Private, Royal Marines.
He joined in June 1917, after twenty seven years' service in the Royal Navy, and on the completion of his training was engaged on coastal defence in the Southern Counties. He was not sent overseas owing to medical unfitness for general service, and was discharged in consequence in August 1917.
10, William's Grove, Walworth, S.E.17.　　　　Z2227

GARDENER, P. T., Private, Hampshire Regiment and R.A.V.C.
A Territorial, he was mobilised on the outbreak of war, and drafted to India in 1914. He returned home in 1916, on the completion of his period of service. Rejoining in the same year he was sent back to India in the R.A.V.C., and proceeded from there to Mesopotamia. Engaged on important duties in this theatre of operations he was present at the capture of Baghdad. He was demobilised in September 1919, on his return to England, and holds the General Service and Victory Medals.
26, Freemantle Street, Walworth, S.E.17.　　　　Z2226B

GARDENER, W. H., Pte., 2nd Royal Berkshire Regt.
He was mobilised in August 1914, and almost immediately drafted to France, where he was engaged in heavy fighting during the Retreat from Mons, the Battles of the Marne and the Aisne, and was wounded. Returning after hospital treatment to the Western Front in March 1915, he fought in the Battles of Ypres and Festubert, and fell fighting at Loos on September 25th, 1914. He was entitled to the Mons Star, and the General Service and Victory Medals.
"Whilst we remember, the Sacrifice is not in vain."
26, Freemantle Street, Walworth, S.E.17.　　　　Z2226C

GARDINER, E. M., Member, W.R.A.F.
She joined in January 1918, and was stationed at the Royal Air Force Depôt at Kenley, where she was engaged in the workshops on duties in connection with the repairing of aeroplanes. She rendered valuable services, and was demobilised in September 1919.
44, North Street, Clapham, S.W.4.　　　　Z2229C

GARDINER, G. H., Rifleman, 21st London Regt. (1st Surrey Rifles).
He enlisted in October 1913, and on the declaration of war was mobilised and sent to the Western Front in March of the following year. He fought in many important engagements, including those on the Somme, and at Arras. He was then transferred to the Macedonian front, where he saw much service. Sent to Egypt in 1917, he was in action during the Advance through the Holy Land, and took part in the Battles of Sheria Wells, Nebi Samwil, Jerusalem, and Es Salt. He returned home and was demobilised in June 1919, and holds the 1914-15 Star, and the General Service and Victory Medals.
100, Farmer's Road, Camberwell, S.E.5.　　　　Z2228

GARDINER, H. E., Special Constable.
He was called up with the Reserves in August 1914, and served at Snow Hill on patrol, observation and other important duties, during air raids of the war. He rendered valuable services throughout the course of the war, and in 1920 was still serving with the City of London Police Reserve.
17, Parkstone Road, Peckham, S.E.15.　　　　Z5768A

GARDINER, H. W. H., Private, R.A.M.C.
He joined in February 1918, and after his training served at various hospitals on important duties with his unit. He rendered valuable services in attending to sick and wounded troops, but was not successful in obtaining his transfer overseas before the cessation of hostilities, owing to medical unfitness. He was demobilised in February 1919.
37, Rozel Road, Clapham, S.W.4.　　　　Z2230

GARDINER, J., L/Corporal, 17th Middlesex Regt.
He volunteered in February 1915, and in the following November proceeded overseas. Whilst on the Western Front he fought at Loos, Vimy Ridge, the Somme, the Ancre, and Beaumont-Hamel, where he was severely wounded in December 1916. After hospital treatment in England he was discharged as medically unfit for further service in May 1917. He holds the 1914-15 Star, and the General Service and Victory Medals.
90, Scylla Road, Peckham, S.E.15.　　　　Z5964

GARDINER, L. (Mrs.), Special War Worker.
This lady offered her services for work of National importance during the war and in March 1915, was employed at Woolwich until August 1918. She was engaged on important work in the Dockyard Equipment Stores, and carried out her duties with great care and efficiency.
17, Parkstone Road, Peckham, S.E.15.　　　　Z5768B

GARDINER, M. J. (Mrs.), Special War Worker.
This lady offered her services for work of National importance during the war and for a period of four years was engaged on special duties at the Admiralty, where she gave entire satisfaction to the authorities.
44, North Street, Wandsworth Road, S.W.4.　　　　Z2229B

GARDINER, R. W., Driver, R.F.A.
He volunteered in July 1915, and was sent to France in March of the following year. He fought in many fierce battles, including those of Loos, St. Eloi, Albert, Vimy Ridge, the Somme, the Ancre, Arras, Bullecourt, Messines, Ypres, Passchendaele and Armentières, and was also in action in the Retreat and Advance of 1918, and was gassed. After hospital treatment at Boulogne he returned home and was demobilised in June 1919. He holds the General Service and Victory Medals.
44, North Street, Wandsworth Road, S.W.4.　　　　Z2229A

GARDNER, F. M., Driver, R.F.A.
He volunteered in February 1915, and was sent to France three months later, where he fought at Ypres and Cambrai, and in many other important engagements. In 1916, he was transferred to Salonika, and was in action in various sectors, and was wounded, losing the sight of his right eye in May 1918. He returned to England and was demobilised in April 1919, and holds the 1914-15 Star, and the General Service and Victory Medals.
21, Sandover Road, Camberwell, S.E.5.　　　　Z5393

GARDNER, S., Private, Royal Warwickshire Regt.
He volunteered in August 1914, and proceeding almost immediately to France, he joined in the Retreat from Mons, and was wounded. During a long period of service he fought at Ypres, Loos, and the Somme, also took part in the Allied Advance of 1918. He was demobilised in January 1919, and holds the Mons Star, and the General Service and Victory Medals.
68, Harling Street, Camberwell, S.E.5.　　　　Z5394

GARE, F., Gunner, R.F.A.
He volunteered in December 1914, and early in the following year proceeded to the Western Front. He was in action in many important engagements, including the Battles of the Somme, Ypres, and Arras. In 1916, transferred to Salonika, he was engaged in much fighting on the Doiran Front for nearly two years. He was then sent to Egypt, where he saw much service and fought at the Battles of Gaza, Jerusalem and Aleppo. He returned home and was demobilised in July 1919, and holds the 1914-15 Star, and the General Service and Victory Medals.
9, Nealdon Street, Landor Road, S.W.9.　　　　Z2312

GARE, T. W., Cadet, R.A.F.
He joined in July 1918, and after serving at various stations, undergoing instruction for promotion to commissioned rank, was unable to complete his training owing to the cessation of hostilities. He did very good work and was demobilised in December 1918.
21, Nursery Row, Walworth, S.E.17.　　　　Z2231

GARGINI, J., Private, 7th London Regiment.
He joined in August 1916, and later in the same year was sent to France, where he played a prominent part, fighting in the Battles of Ypres, Arras, Vimy Ridge, Bullecourt, Menin Road, and Cambrai. He was twice wounded and on each occasion returned to England for hospital treatment. He was demobilised in February 1919, and holds the General Service and Victory Medals.
105, Akerman Road, Brixton Road, S.W.9.　　　　Z4455

GARLAND, R. M., Rifleman, Rifle Brigade, Pte., Labour Corps, and Air Mechanic, R.A.F.
He joined in June 1916, and in March of the following year was sent to the Western Front. In this theatre of war he was engaged in severe fighting in the Battles of the Somme, Lens and Loos, and was blown up by the explosion of a shell, and sustained shell-shock. He was invalided to hospital and on recovery was transferred to the Labour Corps, and later to the R.A.F. He remained overseas until after the close of the war, and returning home in 1919 was demobilised in March of that year. He holds the General Service and Victory Medals.
46, Handforth Road, S.W.9.　　　　Z5248

GARLETT, C. A., Private, M.G.C. and R.A.M.C.
He joined in 1917, and later in the same year was drafted to the Western Front. During his service overseas he was engaged in heavy fighting in the Battles of the Somme, Ypres, and Arras, and in 1918, was transferred to the R.A.M.C. He served with this unit on hospital trains, attending to sick and wounded troops and in this capacity rendered valuable services until the close of the war. He then proceeded to Germany with the Army of Occupation, and returning home in 1919, was demobilised later in that year. He holds the General Service and Victory Medals.
13, Tisdale Place, Walworth, S.E.17.　　　　Z1216A

GARMEY, F. G., A.B., Royal Navy.
He volunteered in 1915, and was posted to H.M.S. "Ophelia," which vessel was engaged on special patrol and convoy duties in the North Sea, and took part in the Battle of Heligoland Bight. During his service at sea, he did very good work as a Signaller. He was demobilised in 1919, and holds the 1914-15 Star, and the General Service and Victory Medals.
15, Solon New Road, Bedford Road, S.W.4.　　　　Z2232

GARMSTON, A. S., Driver, R.F.A.
He joined in 1915, and later in that year embarked for the Western Front. During a long and varied period of service he was in action at Hill 60, and fought also in the Battles of Ypres II and III, the Somme, Beaumont-Hamel, Cambrai I and II, and throughout the German Offensive and subsequent Allied Advance of 1918. He remained in France until he was demobilised in December 1919, and holds the 1914-15 Star, and the General Service and Victory Medals.
5, Godman Road, Peckham, S.E.15. Z5395B

GARMSTON, G. S., Corporal, R.F.A.
Volunteering in 1915, and proceeding overseas later in the same year, he fought at Loos, Vermelles, Vimy Ridge, the Somme, Arras, and in the Ypres salient. He also was in action in the German Offensive of 1918, and was wounded. Returning to England, he recived hospital treatment, and on recovery was attached to the Royal Army Pay Crops, and served with this branch of the Service until demobilised in 1920. He holds the 1914-15 Star, and the General Service and Victory Medals.
5, Godman Road, Peckham, S.E.15. Z5395C

GARMSTON, H., Private, 15th Queen's (Royal West Surrey Regt.)
Volunteering in August 1914, he was quickly drafted to France. He fought at Mons, and in the following Retreat and was severely wounded. Invalided to England, he received a protracted course of hospital treatment, and was finally discharged in 1916, as unfit for further service. He holds the Mons Star, and the General Service and Victory Medals.
5, Godman Road, Peckham, S.E.15. Z5395A

GARNER, S. (M M.), Corporal, Norfolk Regiment.
He volunteered in November 1914, and in the following year was drafted to the Western Front, where he remained until 1919. During this period he was in action in numerous engagements, including the Battle of Loos, and the Retreat and Advance of 1918. He was awarded the Military Medal for conspicuous bravery and devotion to duty in the Field, whilst attending to the wounded under heavy shell fire, and was himself three times wounded. He also holds the 1914-15 Star, and the General Service and Victory Medals, and was demobilised in February 1919.
38, Clovelly Road, Chiswick, W.4. 6607C

GARNSEY, W. G., Bombardier, R.G.A.
Volunteering in September 1915, he proceeded to France in March 1916, and fought in many sectors. He was in action in the Battles of Messines Ridge, Ypres, and during the Retreat and subsequent Advance of 1918. He was demobilised in 1919, and holds the General Service and Victory Medals.
43, Reform Street, Battersea, S.W.11. Z2233

GARRAD, R. W., Private, R.A.S.C. (M.T.)
He volunteered in February 1916, and in the following year was sent to Egypt, where he served for a time. He was later drafted to Salonika and in this theatre of war was present during the fighting on the Doiran and Vardar fronts, and contracted malaria. He was invalided to hospital, and on recovery rejoined his unit in the front line, and served until the end of the war. He was demobilised in April 1919, and holds the General Service and Victory Medals.
99, Crail Row, Walworth, S.E.17. Z2234

GARRETT, W. S., Private, R.A.S.C. (Remounts).
He joined in June 1917, and at the conclusion of his training was engaged on important duties as a shoeing smith at various stations, and attached to the R.A.V.C., did very good work. He was later employed in taking remounts from Southampton to Le Havre until hostilities ceased. He holds the General Service and Victory Medals.
41, Corunna Road, New Road, S.W.8. Z2235

GARROD, W. A., Rflmn., King's Royal Rifle Corps.
He joined in June 1916, and embarked for the Balkan front in the following October, In this theatre of war he was in action in several minor engagements and in the Advance on the Doiran front. In March 1918, he was invalided to England suffering from malaria. Upon his recovery in September 1918, he was drafted to France, where he fought at Havrincourt, and in various battles of the Allied Advance. He was demobilised in August 1919, and holds the General Service and Victory Medals.
120, Cronin Road, Peckham, S.E.15. Z5396

GARWOOD, A. J., Private, 7th Border Regiment.
He joined in June 1916, and in the following October was drafted to the Western Front, where he fought in many engagements, including those in the Arras sector. He was seriously wounded in action near Arras, but unhappily his injuries proved fatal, and he died on April 23rd, 1917. He was entitled to the General Service and Victory Medals.
"And doubtless he went in splendid company."
22, Blewitt Street, Walworth, S.E.17. Z2236

GASKIN, A., Pioneer, R.E.
He joined in May 1918, and on the completion of his training served with his unit on important duties at various stations. He rendered valuable services, but was unable to obtain his transfer overseas, before the close of the war, and was demobilised in December 1918.
32, Montgomery Road, Chiswick, W.4. 6764A

GASKIN, A. T., Private, 1/19th London Regiment.
He volunteered in April 1915, and later proceeded overseas. He was engaged with his unit in various sectors of the Western Front, and was taken prisoner. He remained in captivity in Germany until the signing of the Armistice, when he was released and returned to England. He was demobilised in February 1919, and holds the General Service and Victory Medals.
32, Montgomery Road, Chiswick, W.4. 6764B

GASWORTHY, E. (Mrs.), Special War Worker.
During the war this lady offered her services for work of National importance, and for a period of over two years was engaged at Messrs. Leslie Ray's Munition Factory, and at Messrs. Peacock's Aeroplane Factory, Wandsworth. Her duties which were in connection with making accumulator boxes and joining and varnishing wings and ribs of aeroplanes, were carried out with care and efficiency, and she was highly commended.
13, Park Place, Clapham Park Road, S.W.4. Z2222A

GASWORTHY, J. W., Private, Gordon Highlanders and R.A.S.C. (Remounts).
He volunteered in June 1915, and in the following year was sent to France. He was engaged in the fighting on the Somme, at Ypres, Arras, Passchendaele, Vimy Ridge, St. Quentin, St. Eloi, Bullecourt, Givenchy, Bourlon Wood, and in the Retreat and Advance of 1918, and was twice gassed. Owing to ill-health he was invalided to hospital in England, and on recovery was transferred to the Royal Army Service Corps in September 1918, and served on home duties until demobilised in March 1919. He holds the General Service and Victory Medals.
13, Park Place, Clapham Park Road, S.W.4. Z2220B

GATES, W. C., Private, M.G.C.
He joined in August 1917, and in the following December proceeded overseas. He fought in many battles, including those of the Somme, Arras, and Cambrai, and was taken prisoner in March 1918. He was held in captivity until after the signing of the Armistice, during which time he suffered many privations, and returning to England was demobilised in February 1920. He holds the General Service and Victory Medals.
3, Cavendish Grove, Wandsworth Road, S.W.8. Z2238

GATHERCOLE, H. F., Rifleman, 9th London Regt. (Queen Victoria's Rifles).
He joined in November 1917, and in the following year was drafted to the Western Front. He was in action in various sectors, and took part in many battles until the cessation of hostilities. He then proceeded to Germany with the Army of Occupation, and was stationed at Cologne. He was demobilised in October 1919, and holds the General Service and Victory Medals.
4, Victoria Place, Priory Grove, S.W.8. Z2240

GAVIN, W., Corporal (Shoeing Smith), R.F.A.
He volunteered in June 1915, and in March of the following year proceeded to France. Whilst on the Western Front he was engaged with his Battery on important duties as shoeing smith during the fighting at Ypres, the Somme, Passchendaele, and the Retreat and Advance of 1918. He was demobilised in March 1919, and holds the General Service and Victory Medals.
16, Castlemaine Road, Peckham, S.E.15. Z5973

GAVIS, A., L/Corporal, Middlesex Regt.
Volunteering in September 1914, he was sent to the Western Front later in the same year. He fought in many important engagements, including those of Arras, the Somme and Cambrai. He also took part in the Retreat and Advance of 1918. He was twice wounded in 1917-18 at Ypres. He was demobilised in January 1919, and holds the 1914 Star, and the General Service and Victory Medals.
131, Cobourg Road, Camberwell, S.E.5. Z5397

GAY, F. A., Private, Durham Light Infantry.
Joining in August 1916, he was sent to Salonika in the same year. Whilst in this theatre of war he was engaged in the fighting with his Battalion during the operations in the Balkans, and fought on the Struma front, and contracting malaria was in hospital for a time. He was demobilised in August 1919, after returning to England, and holds the General Service and Victory Medals.
12, Venn Street, Clapham, S.W.4. Z2241

GEAKE, F. C., Driver, R.A.S.C.

He was mobilised with the Reservists at the outbreak of hostilities, and drafted in August 1914 to France. He served in the Retreat from Mons, and the subsequent Battles of Ypres and Loos. He gave his life for King and Country near the Somme on November 22nd, 1915, and was buried at Corbie Cemetery. He was entitled to the Mons Star, and the General Service and Victory Medals.

"He passed out of the sight of men, by the path of duty and self-sacrifice."

42, Pepler Road, Peckham, S.E.15.   Z3461

GEAKE, W. S., Gunner, R.F.A.

Volunteering in September 1914, he was sent to France in February of the following year. During his service on the Western Front he was in action at Hill 60, Ypres, the Somme, Beaumont-Hamel, Arras, Vimy Ridge, Cambrai, and in the German Offensive and subsequent Allied Advance of 1918. He was demobilised in March 1919, and holds the 1914-15 Star, and the General Service and Victory Medals.

34, Falcon Terrace, Battersea, S.W.11.   Z2242

GEAL, E., Private, R.A.S.C. (M.T.)

He joined in January 1917, and in June of the following year proceeded overseas. Whilst in France he was engaged with his unit on important duties at Ypres, Zonnebeke, Poelcapelle, and Hazebrouck, carrying ammunition and rations to the front line trenches, and was constantly under shell fire. He was demobilised in August 1919, and holds the General Service and Victory Medals.

24, Gayville Road, Wandsworth Common, S.W.11.   Z2243

GEAR, A., Private, 48th Royal Fusiliers.

Volunteering at the outbreak of hostilities he was almost immediately sent to France. He fought in the Retreat from Mons, and was wounded at Le Cateau. He was invalided to England for hospital treatment, and on recovery returned to the Western Front, where he took part in the fighting at Hill 60, and Ypres, and was again wounded. He returned to England and was subsequently invalided out of the Service in July 1916. He holds the Mons Star, and the General Service and Victory Medals.

2, Eaton Road, Loughborough Park, S.W.9.   Z4456

GEAR, W., Sergt., Rifle Brigade and Labour Corps.

He joined in 1916, and at the conclusion of his training served with his Battalion on Home Service duties until drafted to France in 1918. Whilst on the Western Front he was engaged with his unit on important duties during the Allied Advance, and was frequently under shell fire. He returned to England after the signing of the Armistice, and was demobilised in February 1919, and holds the General Service and Victory Medals.

37, Wyvil Road, Wandsworth Road, S.W.8.   Z2244

GEARD, E. C. S., Rifleman, 8th London Regt. (Post Office Rifles).

He was mobilised with the Territorials at the outbreak of war, and in March 1915 was drafted to France. Here he took part in much fighting at the Battle of Festubert, and gave his life for King and Country on May 26th, 1915. He was entitled to the 1914-15 Star, and the General Service and Victory Medals.

"A valiant soldier, with undaunted heart he breasted Life's last hill."

14, Park Road, Battersea, S.W.11.   Z2245A

GEARD, S. T., Sapper, R.E. (Postal Section).

He joined in April 1918, on attaining military age, and at the conclusion of his training was engaged on important duties with his unit at various stations. He did good work, but was not successful in obtaining his transfer overseas before the close of the war. In 1919, however, he was drafted to Egypt, where he served on postal duties until the following year. He returned to England and was demobilised in February 1920.

14, Park Road, Battersea, S.W.11.   Z2245B

GEARING, A., Private, Duke of Cornwall's Light Infantry.

A Reservist, he was mobilised at the outbreak of hostilities, and sent to Ireland, where he did important work as Musketry Instructor. He also served at various stations in England on special duties with his unit, but owing to ill-health was not successful in obtaining his transfer to a theatre of war, and was discharged in March 1917.

23, Combermere Road, Stockwell, S.W.9.   Z1548B

GEARING, A., Private, 6th Royal Fusiliers.

He joined in May 1918, and in the following month proceeded overseas. During his service on the Western Front he was engaged in much fighting and was wounded near Ypres. He was invalided to England, and after receiving hospital treatment was demobilised in February 1919. He holds the General Service and Victory Medals.

73, Graylands Road, Peckham, S.E.15.   Z5767

GEAVES, J., Private, 19th London Regiment and Sapper, R.E.

He joined in February 1917, and later in the same year proceeded overseas. He was engaged in the fighting in various sectors, and was wounded and gassed at Cambrai. He was invalided to England, and on recovery was transferred to the Royal Engineers and returned to the Western Front, where he served with his unit whilst operations were in progress during the Allied Advance of 1918. He was demobilised in January 1919, but later, re-enlisted and served for a further period of twelve months. He holds the General Service and Victory Medals.

66, Speke Road, Battersea, S.W.11.   Z2246

GEER, P. J., Private, 23rd London Regiment.

Volunteering in September 1914, he was drafted to the Western Front in March 1915. During his service in this theatre of war he fought at the Battle of Givenchy, and was severely wounded. He was sent to hospital in England in June of the same year, and was eventually invalided out of the Service in August 1916. He holds the 1914-15 Star, and the General Service and Victory Medals.

48, Broughton Street, Battersea Park, S.W.8.   Z2247

GEEVES, E., Rifleman, Rifle Brigade.

He volunteered in September 1914, and in the same year proceeded overseas. Whilst on the Western Front he fought at Ploegsteert Wood, and Ypres, and was wounded. On recovery he returned to the firing line, and was again wounded. He was then invalided to England, and subsequently discharged as medically unfit for further service in September 1916. He holds the 1914-15 Star, and the General Service and Victory Medals.

14, Goldsboro' Road, Wandsworth Road, S.W.8.   Z2248

GEORGE, A. A., Private, R.A.S.C. (M.T.)

He volunteered in August 1914, and was almost immediately sent to France. Whilst on the Western Front he was engaged with his unit in the Retreat from Mons, and the subsequent Battles of the Marne, the Aisne, Hill 60, Loos, Vimy Ridge, the Somme, Beaumont-Hamel, and Beaucourt. He was gassed at the second Battle of the Somme in April 1918, and invalided to England, and after receiving hospital treatment was eventually discharged unfit for further service in January 1919. He holds the Mons Star, and the General Service and Victory Medals.

39, Baker Street, Brixton Road, S.W.9.   Z5247

GEORGE, F., Private, 51st Devonshire Regiment.

He joined in March 1918, and at the conclusion of his training served with his unit on important home defence duties. He did good work, but was unable to secure his transfer overseas until after the cessation of hostilities. He was then sent to Germany with the Army of Occupation, and was stationed on the Rhine. He returned home in 1920, and was demobilised in March of that year.

140, Sulgrave Road, Hammersmith, W.6.   T11822A

GEORGE, F. C., Rifleman, Rifle Brigade.

He joined in 1917, and in March of that year proceeded overseas. During his service on the Western Front he took part in many engagements, and did very good work with his Battalion. He gave his life for the freedom of England in July 1917 near Hill 60, and was entitled to the General Service and Victory Medals.

"And doubtless he went in splendid company."

27A, Goldsboro' Road, Wandsworth Road, S.W.8.   Z1835B

GEORGE, H., Special War Worker.

During the whole period of the war he was engaged on special work at Messrs. Clement and Talbot's Works, North Kensington. His duties, which were in connection with the manufacture of aero engines, were carried out with great skill, and he received high commendation for his services.

140, Sulgrave Road, Hammersmith.   T11822C

GEORGE, J. H., Private, 3rd East Surrey Regt.

Volunteering in January 1915, he was shortly afterwards sent overseas. During his service on the Western Front he was in action in many engagements, and was severely wounded at Ypres in May 1915. He was invalided to England, and subsequently discharged in consequence of his injuries in January 1916. He holds the 1914-15 Star, and the General Service and Victory Medals.

131, Wickersley Road, Lavender Hill, S.W.11.   Z2249

GEORGE, W., Private, 10th Middlesex Regiment.

He joined in May 1916, and after his training was sent to Egypt in January 1918. Here he took part in the Palestine Campaign until the following March, when he was captured by the Turks. He was held prisoner until after the Armistice when he was released and returning to England was demobilised in September 1919, holding the General Service and Victory Medals. 140, Sulgrave Road, Hammersmith, W.6.   T11822B

GERMAINE, W., Private, 2/4th King's Own (Royal Lancaster Regiment).

He was mobilised at the outbreak of hostilities, and was immediately sent to France. In this theatre of war he fought in the Retreat from Mons, and in the Battles of Ypres, Hill 60, Loos, Vermelles, the Somme, Vimy Ridge, Bullecourt, Passchendaele, and Cambrai. He was severely wounded at Arras in October 1918, and invalided to England. He was demobilised in May 1919, and holds the Mons Star, and the General Service and Victory Medals.

147, Gordon Road, Nunhead, S.E.15.   Z5965

GERRARD, F., Private, 19th London Regiment.

He joined in November 1916, and in the following month was drafted to France, where he was posted to the Royal West Surrey Regiment. He fought in many battles of note, including those of Lens, Vimy Ridge, Messines and Cambrai. He also took part in the Allied Advance of 1918. He was gassed at Vermelles, and wounded at Valenciennes shortly before the Armistice. He was demobilised in April 1919, and holds the General Service and Victory Medals.

133, Rosemary Road, Peckham, S.E.15.   Z5399

GERRES, J. B., Gunner, R.F.A.

He joined in July 1916, and at the conclusion of his training was engaged on special duties at home until drafted to France in March 1918. Whilst on the Western Front he fought in operations during the German Offensive, and Allied Advance, and was unfortunately killed in action in October of that year. He was entitled to the General Service and Victory Medals.

" Whilst we remember, the Sacrifice is not in vain."

16, Palmerston Street, Battersea, S.W.11.   Z2250

GEYVE, C., Bandsman, 18th (Queen Mary's Own) Hussars.

He joined in June 1916, and at the conclusion of his training served with his unit on special duties at various stations. He did good work, but was unable to secure his transfer overseas before the cessation of hostilities, and was demobilised in May 1919.

45, Mayall Road, Herne Hill, S.E.24.   Z2252B

GEYVE, R. J. G., Bandsman, 18th (Queen Mary's Own) Hussars.

A serving soldier, he was mobilised at the outbreak of war, and was engaged on important duties at various stations with his Squadron. He later proceeded to Germany with the Army of Occupation, and was stationed at Cologne, having been unsuccessful in obtaining his transfer overseas before the cessation of hostilities. He was still serving in 1920.

45, Mayall Road, Herne Hill, S.E.24.   Z2252A

GHENT, E. J., Private, Queen's (Royal West Surrey Regiment).

Volunteering in 1915, he embarked for the Western Front in the same year, and fought in the Battles of Hill 60, Loos, Vimy Ridge and Beaumont-Hamel. He gave his life for the freedom of England in the Battle of the Somme, on August 13th, 1916, and was entitled to the 1914-15 Star, and the General Service and Victory Medals.

" Great deeds cannot die."

34, Gordon Road, Nunhead, S.E.15.   Z6172B

GIBBINS, W R., Sergt., King's Royal Rifle Corps.

Volunteering in April 1915, he served at various stations, where he was engaged in responsible duties until he was drafted to the Western Front in March 1917. Here he fought in many battles, notably on the Somme and at Ypres, and Arras. He was also engaged in the closing campaign of 1918. He returned from France for his demobilisation in February 1919, and holds the General Service and Victory Medals.

9, Loncroft Road, Camberwell, S.E.5.   Z5400

GIBBONS, E. E., Piper, 18th London Regiment (London Irish Rifles).

He was mobilised with the Territorials at the outbreak of war, and drafted to France later in 1914. Whilst on the Western Front he fought at the Battle of Ypres and was gassed. He was also in action at Loos, La Bassée, and Béthune, and was again gassed. He was invalided home, and on recovery was engaged on home duties until demobilised in 1919. He holds the 1914 Star, the General Service and Victory Medals, and the Long Service and Good Conduct Medals.

10, Tasman Road, Landor Road, S.W.9.   Z2253

GIBBS, A. E., Sapper, R.E.

He volunteered in September 1914, and was sent overseas in the following year. Whilst on the Western Front he was engaged on important duties with his unit during the fighting at the Battles of Loos, Ypres, the Somme, Albert, Cambrai, and during the Retreat and Allied Advance of 1918. He was demobilised in January 1919, and holds the 1914-15 Star, and the General Service and Victory Medals.

105, Ingelow Road, Battersea Park, S.W.8.   Z2259B

GIBBS, A. E., Private, Oxfordshire and Buckinghamshire Light Infantry.

He volunteered in May 1915, and in the following September proceeded overseas. During his service on the Western Front he was in action in many battles, including those of La Bassée, Festubert and the Somme, where he was severely wounded. He was invalided to England and after recovery was transferred to the Royal Army Service Corps, and returning to France, did good work with the Mechanical Transport there. He was demobilised in May 1919, and holds the 1914-15 Star, and the General Service and Victory Medals.

37, Dorothy Road, Lavender Hill, S.W.11.   Z2255

GIBBS, F. (M.M.), Sergt., M.G.C.

A serving soldier, having enlisted in 1910, he was drafted to France at the outbreak of hostilities, and fought in the Retreat from Mons and many battles which followed, including those of Ypres, Cambrai and the Retreat and Advance of 1918, and was wounded. He was awarded the Military Medal for his conspicuous gallantry in taking ammunition to the front line trenches under heavy shell fire. After the signing of the Armistice he proceeded to Germany with the Army of Occupation, and was stationed on the Rhine. He was demobilised in 1920, and holds the Mons Star, and the General Service and Victory Medals.

3, Newby Street, Wandsworth Road, S.W.8.   Z1592C

GIBBS, F. A., Private, 22nd London Regt. (Queen's), Acting L/Corporal, M.F.P.

He joined in March 1917, and later in the same year was drafted to Egypt. In this theatre of war he took part in the British Advance through Palestine, and the operations at Beersheba, Gaza, the Jordan and the capture of Jerusalem. He contracted malaria, and was invalided to hospital in Jaffa, and eventually sent to England, where, on recovery, he did excellent work with the Military Police until demobilised in March 1919. He holds the General Service and Victory Medals.

26, Combermere Road, Stockwell, S.W.9.   Z2256

GIBBS, F. T., Sapper, R.E.

He volunteered in June 1915, and later in the same year proceeded to France. He served on mining and other important duties in connection with operations at Loos, St. Eloi, Vimy Ridge, Beaumont-Hamel, Arras, Ypres and during the Retreat and Advance of 1918. He was demobilised in July 1919, and holds the 1914-15 Star, and the General Service and Victory Medals.

33, Patmos Road, Vassall Road, S.W.9.   Z5078

GIBBS, J., Leading Seaman, R.N.

He joined in 1905, and at the outbreak of hostilities was serving in H.M.S. " Astræa," which vessel was engaged during the war on important patrol and coastal defence duties in the English Channel. His ship also took part in the Battle of Jutland and the raid on Zeebrugge, and afterwards proceeded to Africa in 1918. He lost his life when his ship was wrecked off the West Coast of Africa on April 1st, 1919. He was entitled to the 1914-15 Star, and the General Service and Victory Medals.

" Courage, bright hopes, and a myriad dreams, splendidly given."

3, McKerrell Road, Peckham, S.E.15.   Z5769

GIBBS, J. F., Rifleman, King's Royal Rifle Corps.

A serving soldier, he was drafted to France at the outbreak of hostilities and was in action at the Retreat from Mons and the Battles of Le Cateau, the Marne, the Aisne and Ypres. Owing to ill-health he was invalided to England in December 1914, and two months later returned to the Western Front and took part in the fighting at Ypres and St. Eloi. He was sent to Salonika in November 1915, and served on the Struma and Doiran fronts and was present at the capture of Monastir. He contracted malaria and returned to England for hospital treatment, and on recovery in March 1918, was again drafted to the Western Front. He fought on the Somme and was wounded at Arras in the following May. He was sent home and on discharge from hospital served on home duties until demobilised in May 1919. He holds the Mons Star, and the General Service and Victory Medals.

12, Lothian Road, Camberwell New Road, S.W.9.   Z5079

GIBBS, J. F., Sergt., 23rd London Regiment.

Volunteering in August 1914, he was immediately sent to France. In this theatre of war he fought in many battles and was gassed. On recovery he returned to the firing line and joined his Battalion in the fighting during the German Offensive of 1918. He died gloriously on the Field during the second Battle of the Somme in March 1918, and was entitled to the Mons Star, and the General Service and Victory Medals.

" He joined the great white company of valiant souls."

1, Currie Road, Battersea, S.W.11.   Z2257A

GIBBS, R. F. J., Corporal, Middlesex Regiment.

He volunteered in August 1915, and in the following year was drafted to France, where he fought at the Battles of the Somme, Arras, Ypres and Cambrai, and was wounded. In May 1918, during the German Offensive, he was taken prisoner and held in captivity until after the signing of the Armistice. He was then repatriated and subsequently demobilised in October 1919, and holds the General Service and Victory Medals.

12, Newby Street, Wandsworth, Road S.W.8.   Z2258B

GIBBS, T., Private, Bedfordshire Regiment.

He volunteered in 1915, and in the following year proceeded overseas. During his service on the Western Front he fought in the Battles of the Somme, Passchendaele and Messines, and was badly gassed. He was invalided to England, nad on recovery served on home duties until demobilised in 1919. He holds the General Service and Victory Medals.

3, Newby Street, Wandsworth Road, S.W.8.   Z1592B

GIBBS, S. J., 1st Class Stoker, R.N.

He joined the Royal Marine Artillery in November 1917, and at the conclusion of his training was transferred to the Royal Navy and served aboard H.M.S. " Temeraire," and also H.M.S. " Barham." His ship was engaged on important patrol duties with the Grand Fleet in the North Sea, and was present at Scapa Flow, when the German Fleet was interned there. He holds the General Service and Victory Medals, and was still serving in 1920.

12, Newby Street, Wandsworth Road, S.W.8.   Z2258C

GIBBS, W., L/Corporal, 10th Queen's (Royal West Surrey Regiment) and M.G.C.

He volunteered in October 1915, and in the following May was sent overseas. Whilst on the Western Front he fought at Ploegsteert Wood, the Somme and Messines. In 1917 he returned to England and was transferred to the Machine Gun Corps, with which unit he served on special duties at home until drafted to France in January 1918. He was in action in many engagements during the Retreat and Allied Advance of 1918, and after the Armistice returned to England, and was demobilised in January 1919. He holds the General Service and Victory Medals.

128, Wickersley Road, Lavender Hill, S.W.11.   Z2260

GIBBS, W. H. S., Stoker, R.N.

He was serving at the outbreak of hostilities aboard H.M.S. " Boadicea," which vessel was engaged on important patrol duties and took part in the Battle of Jutland, and the Naval operations at the Landing at the Dardanelles, and was also employed on special convoy duties from America to England. He was demobilised in March 1920, and holds the 1914–15 Star, and the General Service and Victory Medals.

12, Newby Street, Wandsworth Road, S.W.8.   Z2258A

GIBBS, W. J., Rifleman., 2/12th London Regiment (Rangers).

He joined in December 1916, and in the following year was sent to the Western Front. In this theatre of war he fought at the Battles of the Somme, Bullecourt, Cambrai, and in the Retreat and Advance of 1918, and was wounded at Epéhy in September of that year. He was demobilised in January 1919, and holds the General Service and Victory Medals.

22, Thorncroft Street, Wandsworth Road, S.W.8.   Z2261

GIBBS, W. J., Private, Hampshire Regiment.

He volunteered at the outbreak of hostilities, and was drafted to India. He was engaged on important duties with his Battalion at Allahabad, Calcutta, Thaly and many other stations, where he did excellent work with the flying column. He contracted malaria and was invalided to hospital, and on recovery rejoined his unit and served until late in 1919, when he returned to England and was demobilised in the following month. He holds the General Service and Victory Medals and the India General Service Medal (with clasp Afghanistan, N.W. Frontier, 1919).

47, New Road, Battersea Park Road, S.W.8.   Z2254

GIBLING, G., Private, 2nd Bedfordshire Regiment.

He joined in July 1917, and later proceeded to India. He was stationed for a time at Karachi and Hyderabad on important duties with his Battalion, and afterwards was engaged in the fighting on the North-West Frontier. He returned to England and was demobilised in January 1920. He holds the General Service and Victory Medals and the India General Service Medal (with clasp Afghanistan, N.W. Frontier, 1919).

33, Aegis Grove, Battersea Park Road, S.W.8.   Z2262

GIBSON, J. W., Chief Petty Officer, R.N.

He joined the Service in 1914, and was posted to H.M.S. " Lowestoft," which ship was engaged at the Battles of Heligoland Bight, the Dogger Bank and Jutland. She also rendered valuable services on patrol and other important duties in the North Sea. He served on his vessel throughout the war. He was demobilised in 1919, being entitled to the 1914–15 Star, and the General Service and Victory Medals.

87, Brayard's Road, Peckham, S.E.15.   Z5401

GIDLEY, F., Special War Worker.

For the whole period of the war he was engaged on important work at Messrs. Evershed and Vignell's Factory, Acton Lane. His duties, which were those of an engineer's pattern maker, were carried out with great skill and efficiency, and he rendered valuable services throughout.

116, Acton Lane, Chiswick, W.4.   6359B

GIDLEY, L. (Mrs.), Special War Worker.

During the war for a period of nearly four years, this lady offered her services and was engaged on work of National importance at Messrs. Wilkinson's Sword Factory, Acton. Her duties were in connection with the manufacture and drilling of swords, and she gave great satisfaction to the authorities.

116, Acton Lane, Chiswick, W.4.   6359A

GILBERT, A. E., Corporal, 2nd Dragoons Guards (Queen's Bays).

A Reservist, he was mobilised at the outbreak of war, and was immediately drafted to the Western Front. Here he fought at Mons, the Aisne, La Bassée, Ypres, Loos, and in many other engagements, until hostilities ceased. After the cessation of hostilities he served with the Army of Occupation in Germany until demobilised in March 1919. He holds the Mons Star, and the General Service and Victory Medals.

4, Pilkington Road, Peckham, S.E.15.   Z5970

GILBERT, C., Private, Leicestershire Regiment.

He joined in October 1916, and proceeding to the Western Front in the following year saw much service in the Somme sector. He died gloriously on the Field of battle at Polygon Wood on September 24th 1917, and was entitled to the General Service and Victory Medals.

" Great deeds cannot die."

18, Russell Grove, Vassal Road, S.W.9.   Z5026B

GILBERT, C. B., Driver, R.A.S.C.

Joining in February 1917, he was drafted to France three months later and served there throughout the war. During this period he was in action in the Battles of Ypres, Lens and Cambrai, and in many engagements in the Retreat and Advance of 1918. He was demobilised in March 1919, and holds the General Service and Victory Medals.

5, Aylesbury Road, Walworth, S.E.17.   Z2265

GILBERT, H. E., Rifleman, 9th London Regiment (Queen Victoria's Rifles).

He joined in 1916, and was sent to France in the same year. In the course of his service he took part in the Battles of the Somme, Arras, Ypres, Passchendaele, Lens, Cambrai and Amiens, and was invalided home in 1918, owing to shell-shock. After treatment he was discharged as medically unfit for further service in 1919, and holds the General Service and Victory Medals.

12, Stockwell Green, S.W.9.   Z2264

GILBERT, J., Bandsman, R.G.A.

Volunteering in September 1914, he embarked for the Western Front in the following year and saw service in the Somme and Ypres sectors, and was invalided home owing to ill-health. On recovery he was sent to Egypt in 1917, and was engaged on important duties in the Soudan until his return home for demobilisation in May 1919. He holds the 1914–15 Star, and the General Service and Victory Medals.

4, Sterndale Road, Wandsworth Road, S.W.8.   Z2263

GILBERT, J. H., Sergt., R.A.S.C.

He volunteered in November 1915, and was drafted overseas a year later. Sent to India he served there for a time and then proceeded to Mesopotamia. In this theatre of war he was engaged on important transport duties and rendered valuable services throughout the course of hostilities. He holds the General Service and Victory Medals, and in 1920 was still serving.

3, Short Road, Chiswick, S.W.4.   5831A

GILBEY, G. E., Private, 1st Royal Fusiliers.

He volunteered in December 1914, when sixteen years of age, and served with his unit until his embarkation for France in August 1916. Whilst on the Western Front he was in action in several important engagements and was wounded in the Battle of Arras on April 13th, 1917. Rejoining his Battalion on recovery, he fought in the Battle of Ypres and was again wounded on September 12th, 1917, and sent home to hospital. He was subsequently invalided out of the Service in September 1918, and holds the General Service and Victory Medals.

1, Southwell Terrace, Lewis Road, Camberwell, S.E.5.   Z6179B

GILES, W. A., Private, 7th (Queen's Own) Hussars.

He was serving in India when war broke out, and was later drafted to Mesopotamia. Whilst there he took part in many important engagements during the British advance, and was present at the capture of Baghdad. He returned home on the cessation of hostilities, and was demobilised in 1919, and holds the General Service and Victory Medals.

52, Linden Gardens, Chiswick, W.4.   T5646A

GILES, H., Private, Royal Sussex Regiment.

Volunteering in March 1915, he completed his training and was engaged on important duties with his unit until his embarkation for India in March 1917. During his service overseas he took part in operations on the North-Western Frontier and returning home in March 1919, was demobilised in the following month. He holds the General Service and Victory Medals and the India General Service Medal (with clasp, Afghanistan, N.W Frontier, 1919).
99, Elsted Street, Walworth, S.E.17.　　Z2267

GILES, T., Gunner, R.G.A.

He volunteered in July 1915, and later in the same year proceeded to the Western Front. Serving in various sectors he was in action in several engagements, including the Battles of Albert, the Ancre and Cambrai, and was seriously wounded on the Somme in 1917. Sent to hospital in England, he was under medical treatment for several months, and was invalided out of the Service in July 1917. He holds the 1914–15 Star, and the General Service and Victory Medals.
16, Gladstone Terrace, Battersea Park Road, S.W.8. Z2266

GILL, J. E., Private, Worcestershire Regiment.

He joined in May 1917, and after being drafted to France in April 1918 took part in much fierce fighting on the Western Front. He gave his life for King and Country on May 28th, 1918, during the Retreat, and was entitled to the General Service and Victory Medals.
"He joined the great white company of valiant souls."
37, Flaxman Road, Camberwell S.E.5.　　Z5969

GILL, S., Private, R.M.L.I.

Having enlisted in 1897, he was mobilised from the Royal Fleet Reserve on the outbreak of war and served afloat on important patrol duties in various waters throughout the course of hostilities, and his ship had several encounters with enemy vessels. He was demobilised in February 1919, and in addition to the China Medal holds the 1914–15 Star, and the General Service and Victory Medals.
15, Wickersley Road, Lavender Hill, S.W.11.　　Z2268B

GILLESPIE, A., Private, R.M.L.I.

Volunteering in the Royal Army Service Corps in October 1914, he was almost immediately sent to France and served on supply duties at Le Havre until transferred to the Royal Marine Labour Corps in November 1915. Engaged with that unit as a winch driver for over two years, he returned to England in January 1918, for training as an infantryman, and served at home on important duties. He was demobilised in February 1919, and holds the 1914 Star, and the General Service and Victory Medals.
30, Pepler Road, Peckham, S.E.15.　　Z3462

GILLETT, H. A., Private, Middlesex Regiment.

Joining in 1917, on attaining military age, he embarked for France in the following year. During his service overseas he fought in the Battle of Arras and in several engagements in the Advance of 1918. After the Armistice he was engaged on guard duties at various prisoners of war camps, and returning home for demobilisation in 1919, holds the General Service and Victory Medals.
74, Park Crescent, Clapham Park Road, S.W.4.　　Z2269

GILLETT, L. C. H., Driver, R.F.A.

He volunteered in January 1916, and proceeding overseas in the following year served on the Western Front until the cessation of hostilities. During this period he was in action at Arras, Beaumont-Hamel, Messines, Lens and in the Battles of Amiens, Bapaume, Havrincourt and other engagements in the Retreat and Advance of 1918. He was demobilised in September 1919, and holds the General Service and Victory Medals.
74, Park Crescent, Clapham Park Road, S.W.4.　　Z2270

GILLETT, W., Driver, Royal Marine Artillery.

Mobilised in August 1914, he was sent with the Naval Division to Belgium shortly afterwards and took part in the landing at Antwerp and was one of the four thousand men not interned or taken prisoner at this engagement. After the withdrawal he was in action in the Battles of Ypres, Hill 60, Festubert and Loos, and was gassed at Ypres in 1916. He returned home and was discharged on account of service in 1916, and holds the 1914 Star, and the General Service and Victory Medals.
58, Robert Street, Brixton Road, S.W.9.　　Z5080

GILLHAM, C., L/Corporal, Tank Corps.

He joined in 1916, and in the same year embarked for the Western Front. In the course of his service in this theatre of war he was engaged in heavy fighting in the Battle of the Somme and in several engagements during the Advance of 1918. Returning to England on the termination of hostilities, he was demobilised in March 1919, and holds the General Service and Victory Medals.
9, Tasman Road, Landor Road, S.W.9.　　Z2271

GILLHAM, H., Sergt., Tank Corps.

He volunteered in September 1914, and in the same year proceeded to France. Serving in various parts of the line he took an active part in the Battles of Ypres, Loos and the Somme. After the Armistice he was sent into Germany with the Army of Occupation and was stationed on the Rhine. Demobilised in March 1919, on his return home, he holds the 1914–15 Star, and the General Service and Victory Medals.
9, Tasman Road, Landor Road, S.W.9.　　Z2272

GILLINGHAM, C. W., Driver, R.F.A.

He volunteered in September 1915, and was shortly afterwards drafted to the Western Front. There he served with his Battery throughout the war and fought in the Battles of Ypres and Loos and was wounded in October 1915. Rejoining his unit he was in action in the Battles of Arras and the Somme and in several other engagements. He returned home at the end of hostilities, and in 1920 was still serving on special duties, and holds the 1914–15 Star, and the General Service and Victory Medals.
1, Graham Road, Chiswick, W.4.　　6577A

GILLINGHAM, F. C., Bombardier, R.H.A.

Volunteering in October 1915, he completed his training and was engaged on important duties with his Battery at various stations on home defence duties. He rendered valuable services, but was unable to secure a transfer to a theatre of war before the cessation of hostilities, and in 1920 was still serving. Whilst on the voyage from America to enlist, aboard s.s. "Iberian," this vessel was sunk by a submarine on July 30th, 1915, but he was fortunately saved.
1, Graham Road, Chiswick, W.4.　　6577B

GILMORE, A. A. J., Guardsman (Signaller) 2nd Scots Guards.

A serving soldier, having enlisted in 1913, he was mobilised on the declaration of war and sent to France shortly afterwards. He took part in heavy fighting in the early engagements of the war, and was wounded in October 1914, in September 1915, and again in June 1917. Returning to the Field he fought in many battles and was killed in action at Cambrai on September 27th, 1918, and was entitled to the 1914 Star, and the General Service and Victory Medals.
"His memory is cherished with pride."
63, Bramfield Road, Wandsworth Common, S.W.11. Z2273

GINN, A., Petty Officer, R.N.

He was serving in the Royal Navy when war was declared and was engaged on important duties in the North Sea and other waters. He was serving in H.M.S. "Yarmouth" when she was engaged in chasing the German raider "Emden," and, later, attached to the Grand Fleet, was in action in the Battle of Jutland. He also served in H.M.S. "Impregnable," "Emblem," and "Whirlwind," and was on special duty at Scapa Flow on the surrender of the German Fleet. He holds the 1914–15 Star, and the General Service and Victory Medals, and in 1920 was still serving.
15, Nursery Row, Walworth, S.E.17.　　Z2274

GINN, F., A.B., Royal Navy.

Joining the Royal Navy in 1911, he was mobilised on the outbreak of hostilities, and took part in the bombardment of the Dardanelles forts and operations covering the Landings on Gallipoli. His ship was also engaged on important patrol and convoy duties in the North Sea and after the Armistice was sent to Russia. He was still serving in 1920, and holds the 1914–15 Star, and the General Service and Victory Medals.
89, East Street, Walworth, S.E.17.　　Z2275A

GINN, J., Private, Middlesex Regiment and Queen's (Royal West Surrey Regiment).

Joining in 1917, he was drafted to the Western Front in the same year and saw service in many parts of the line. He was in action in the Battles of the Somme, Arras and Ypres, and on the conclusion of hostilities was sent into Germany with the Army of Occupation. He holds the General Service and Victory Medals, and in 1920 was still serving.
89, East Street, Walworth, S.E.17.　　Z2275B

GIORGI, E. G. (Miss), Special War Worker.

During the war this lady offered her services for work of National importance and was employed by the Park Royal Munition Factory for eighteen months. Engaged in the Inspection Bond Department, she discharged her duties throughout the term of her service in a thoroughly efficient and capable manner.
39, Annandale Road, Chiswick, W.4.　　5422A

GIORGI, W. M. (Miss), Special War Worker.

Volunteering for work of National importance, this lady rendered valuable services for two years during the war. Employed by the Park Royal Munitions Factory, she was engaged in the filling department for eighteen months and discharged her dangerous duties with care and efficiency. She later worked with the Land Army from August 1918 to January 1919, and obtained two certificates for proficiency in driving.
39, Annandale Road, Chiswick, W.4.　　5422B

GIRDLER, G. S., Rflmn., King's Royal Rifle Corps, Pte., Northamptonshire Regt., M.G.C. and Labour Corps.
Joining in February 1917, he was sent to the Western Front shortly afterwards and served until the cessation of hostilities. During this period he was attached to an anti-aircraft machine gun section for several months and did good work. He fought in several engagements, including that at Fontaine, Le Croiselles and the Battle of Cambrai, and was gassed. He was demobilised in January 1919, and holds the General Service and Victory Medals.
49, Comyn Road, Battersea, S.W.11.   Z2276

GISLINGHAM, A. G. K., Rifleman, 15th Royal Irish Rifles.
He volunteered in December 1915, and after completing his training served with his unit until his embarkation for France with the 13th London Regiment (Kensingtons) in 1917. Whilst overseas he served in the Battles of the Somme, Ypres, Cambrai, and during the Retreat of 1918, and was also engaged on important clerical duties in the orderly room of his Battalion. He returned to England for demobilisation in March 1919, and holds the General Service and Victory Medals.
27, Vicarage Road, Camberwell, S.E.5.   Z2251

GITTINGS, W. J., Sapper, R.E.
He joined in July 1916, and in the same year was sent to Salonika. During his service in the Balkans he was engaged on important duties in connection with operations in the advance across the Vardar and on the Doiran front. Sent to Constantinople he served with the Army of Occupation until his return home late in 1919. He was demobilised in January 1920, and holds the General Service and Victory Medals.
58, Kay Road, Landor Road, S.W.9.   Z2277

GLADMAN, A. F., Lieut., York and Lancaster Regt.
He volunteered in the Dorsetshire Regiment in September 1914, and was drafted overseas in the following March. Serving on the Western Front he fought in many engagements, including the Battles of the Somme, Arras and Ypres, and was twice wounded and sent home. Returning to France on recovery, he was granted a commission in the York and Lancaster Regiment in September 1916, and with that unit took an active part in operations until the end of the war. He was demobilised in February 1919, and holds the 1914-15 Star, and the General Service and Victory Medals.
1, Nunhead Green, Peckham, S.E.15.   Z6171A

GLADMAN, W., Gunner, R.F.A.
He volunteered in February 1915, and proceeding to France in the following July served there for upwards of four years. During this period he was engaged with his Battery in various sectors and fought in the Battles of the Somme, Arras and Ypres. Returning home on the conclusion of hostilities, he was demobilised in February 1919, and holds the 1914-15 Star, and the General Service and Victory Medals.
1, Nunhead Green, Peckham, S.E.15.   Z6171B

GLASS, B., Private, 6th Wiltshire Regiment.
Volunteering in September 1914, he proceeded to the Western Front in the following July and served there for upwards of four years. He fought in the Battles of Loos, Givenchy, Levantie, Richebourg, Messines and in other engagements until the cessation of hostilities. He was demobilised in February 1919, and holds the 1914-15 Star, and the General Service and Victory Medals.
61, Cowan Street, Camberwell, S.E.5.   Z5081

GLASTONBURY, A. J., Private, 1/4th London Regt. (Royal Fusiliers).
He volunteered in March 1915, and was drafted overseas six months later. Serving with his Battalion on the Western Front, he was engaged in heavy fighting in the Battle of Loos, and owing to a serious injury subsequently sustained, returned to England in December 1915. He was invalided out of the Service in March 1916, and holds the 1914-15 Star, and the General Service and Victory Medals.
59, Doddington Grove, Battersea, S.W.11.   Z2278

GLAYSHER, H., Private, 6th Queen's (Royal West Surrey Regiment).
A Territorial, he was mobilised when war broke out and served with his unit until discharged on account of service in 1915. Re-enlisting, he embarked for France in the following year, and was in action in several important engagements, and was wounded at Aveluy Wood in July 1918, and again at Albert in the following September. He returned home for demobilisation in January 1919, and holds the General Service and Victory Medals.
25, Speke Road, Battersea, S.W.11.   Z2279

GLAZBROOK, H., Special War Worker.
He served in the Royal Navy for over seventeen years prior to the war, and volunteered for work of National importance in 1915. In addition to doing very valuable work in connection with recruiting for the Navy and Army, he was of great assistance in raising funds for the Red Cross Society making models of the " Victory," one of which was graciously accepted by H.M. Queen Alexandra, and afterwards sold for the Red Cross for fifty guineas. He holds the Egyptian Medal 1882, and the Khedive's Star, and a letter from H.M. the Queen commending him for his services during the war.
38, St. Julian's Road, Kilburn, N.W.6.   Z23517

GLEASON, A. J. G., Sergt., R.G.A.
A Regular soldier, he was serving in India when war broke out, and was drafted to the Western Front in 1914. He was in action in several engagements and was wounded in the Battle of Arras, and sent to hospital in France. Rejoining his unit he fought in various operations including those during the Advance of 1918. After the Armistice he was engaged on important duties at a dispersal station until discharged in 1919, and holds the 1914 Star, and the General Service and Victory Medals.
109, Villa Street, Walworth, S.E.17.   Z27447C

GLENISTER, J. C., 1st Air Mechanic, R.A.F.
He joined in February 1918, and on the conclusion of his training served with his Squadron at an aerodrome in the Eastern Counties. Engaged on work calling for a high degree of technical knowledge and skill he rendered valuable services, but was unable to secure a transfer overseas before the cessation of hostilities, and was demobilised in February 1919.
107, Union Road, Wandsworth Road, S.W.8.   Z2281

GLOCKLING, G., Rifleman, 8th London Regiment (Post Office Rifles).
Volunteering in September 1914, he completed his training, but owing to a physical disability could not be drafted overseas, and was invalided out of the Service in January 1915. He did not succeed in a second attempt to enter the Army, but rendered valuable service in the Post Office, until the close of hostilities.
1, Atwell Street, Rye Lane, S.E.15.   Z5402

GLOVER, C., Private, Royal Berkshire Regiment.
He volunteered in September 1914, and after completing his training was sent to France. Serving with his Battalion on important duties in various sectors he returned to England to undergo hospital treatment, and was subsequently discharged as physically unfit for further service in August 1920. He holds the 1914-15 Star, and the General Service and Victory Medals.
14, Landseer Street, Battersea, S.W.11.   Z2282

GLOVER, J. F., Gunner, R.F.A.
He volunteered in June 1915, and in the following year embarked for the Western Front, where he served with his Battery in the Battles of St. Eloi and Loos. He gave his life for King and Country at Béthune on April 5th, 1916, and was entitled to the General Service and Victory Medals.
" A costly sacrifice upon the altar of freedom."
7, Sterndale Road, Handsworth Road, S.W.8.   1632C

GLOVER, J. F. (Junior), Private, Royal Sussex Regt.
He joined in July 1918, and on the completion of his training served with his unit on important duties at various stations. He did much good work, but was not successful in obtaining his transfer overseas before hostilities ceased. After the Armistice, he went with the Army of Occupation into Germany and was stationed at Cologne. He was demobilised in March 1919, on his return to England, and holds the General Service and Victory Medals.
7, Sterndale Road, Wandsworth Road, S.W.8.   1632A

GLOVER, J. H., 1st Air Mechanic, R.A.F. (late R.N.A.S.)
He volunteered in 1915, and in the same year was sent to France, where he was employed in erecting hangars for observation balloons and aeroplanes. In 1916 he was drafted to Scotland and served with his Squadron on important duties at Scapa Flow, and in the following year proceeded to the South-East Coast of England, and was engaged at Sheppey until demobilised in 1919. He holds the 1914-15 Star, and the General Service and Victory Medals.
44, Moncrieff Street, Rye Lane, S.E.15.   Z5609

GOATMAN, A. J., Rifleman, 21st London Regiment (1st Surrey Rifles).
Volunteering in 1914, he was engaged on important duties with his Battalion until drafted overseas in 1916. He served on the Western Front and took part in several engagements, and was wounded at Vimy Ridge. Sent home on account of his injuries, he was invalided out of the Service in 1916, and holds the General Service and Victory Medals.
93, Akerman Road, Brixton Road, S.W.9.   Z4457

GODDARD, A. M., Driver, R.F.A.
He volunteered in April 1915, and, sent to France in the same year, served throughout the war. During this period he fought in many battles, including those at Ypres, Arras, and the Somme, and on several occasions horses were shot from under him. Demobilised in June 1919, he holds the 1914-15 Star, and the General Service and Victory Medals.
9, Eastcote Street, Stockwell Green, S.W.9. Z2283

GODDARD, F., L/Corporal, M.G.C.
Joining the King's Royal Rifle Corps in June 1916, he embarked for France three months later, and fought in the Battles of the Somme, Arras, Vimy Ridge, and was wounded at Cambrai, and sent to hospital in England. He was transferred to the Machine Gun Corps on recovery, and returning to the Western Front served in many engagements until the end of hostilities. He was demobilised in December 1918, and holds the General Service and Victory Medals.
40, Pepler Road, Peckham, S.E.15. Z3460

GODDARD, H., Rifleman, 18th London Regiment (London Irish Rifles).
Volunteering in December 1915, he was sent to Egypt in the following year. He fought at Beersheba, and in other battles during the Advance through Palestine, and was in the Guard of Honour at General Allenby's entry into Jerusalem. Owing to illness he was sent to hospital, and on recovery returned to his unit, and was taken prisoner north of Jerusalem. Repatriated after the Armistice he was invalided out of the Service in May 1919, and holds the General Service and Victory Medals.
46, Bolton Street, Camberwell, S.E.5. Z2284

GODDARD, H., Sergt., R.F.A.
Serving in India at the outbreak of hostilities he proceeded to Gallipoli in April 1915, and took part in the first Landing on the Peninsula and in many of the subsequent engagements, and was twice wounded. He was later drafted to Lemnos, and subsequently served in other places in the near East on important duties until the end of the war. In addition to the India General Service Medal, he holds the 1914-15 Star, and the General Service and Victory Medals.
14, Northlands Street, Camberwell, S.E.5. Z6177

GODDARD, H. C., Sergt., R.A.F.
He joined in June 1916, and after completing his training was engaged on important duties with his Squadron in the Eastern Counties. He rendered valuable services, but was unsuccessful in securing a transfer to a theatre of war before the conclusion of hostilities, and was demobilised in February 1919.
14, Sharon Road, Chiswick, W.4. 5845A

GODDARD, R. R., Rflmn., King's Royal Rifle Corps.
He joined in April 1916, and in the same year embarked for the Western Front in various sectors of which he saw much service. He fought in many important engagements including the Battles of the Somme, Vimy Ridge and Arras, and was gassed in 1918 near Arras. Invalided home suffering from the effects of gas poisoning, he was ultimately demobilised in November 1919, and holds the General Service and Victory Medals.
6, Northlands Street, Camberwell, S.E.5. Z6176

GODDEN, C. J., Gunner, R.F.A.
Volunteering in December 1914, he was sent to France in the following year, and after three months' service in the Ypres salient was drafted to Salonika. He was engaged with his Battery in various parts of the Balkans and fought in the advance on the Doiran front, across the Struma, and was in action at the Battle of Monastir. Returning to England in December 1918, he was demobilised in the following month, and holds the 1914-15 Star, and the General Service and Victory Medals.
20, Parkstone Road, Peckham, S.E.15. Z6174

GODDEN, F. E., Sergt., 14th London Regiment (London Scottish).
He joined in December 1916, and was sent overseas in the following year. Serving in various sectors of the Western Front he took an active part in many important engagements, including the Battles of Arras, Ypres, and Passchendaele. He returned home on the conclusion of hostilities, and was demobilised in February 1919, and holds the General Service and Victory Medals.
24, Richford Street, Hammersmith, W.6. 10453B

GODDEN, P. W., Pte., 29th Royal Dublin Fusiliers.
He volunteered in November 1914, and drafted to Gallipoli in the following year fought at the Landing at Suvla Bay, and in other engagements until the Evacuation of the Peninusla. He also served in Egypt and Mesopotamia, and proceeding to France in 1916, took part in several engagements including the Battles of Arras and Ypres. He was killed in action on October 4th, 1917, and was entitled to the 1914-15 Star, and the General Service and Victory Medals.
"He died the noblest death a man may die,
Fighting for God and right and liberty."
24, Richford Street, Hammersmith, W.6. 10453A

GODDEN, W., Private, 2/22nd Queen's (Royal West Surrey Regiment).
Volunteering in 1915, he was drafted in the same year to the Western Front. He served in various sectors and amongst other notable engagements was in action in the Somme Offensive and in the Battles of Arras and Vimy Ridge. Returning to England on the conclusion of hostilities he was discharged in April 1919, as medically unfit for further service, and holds the 1914-15 Star, and the General Service and Victory Medals.
62, Pepler Road, Peckham, S.E.15. Z3459

GODFREY, J., Gunner, R.F.A.
He volunteered in November 1915, and was sent in June of the following year to the Western Front. He served with his Battery in the Battles of the Somme, Beaucourt, Arras, Vimy Ridge, Ypres, Passchendaele, Messines, Lens, Cambrai, and during the Retreat and Advance of 1918. He holds the General Service and Victory Medals, and was demobilised in May 1919.
95, Beckway Street, Walworth, S.E.17. Z2286

GODFREY, H., Private, 8th Royal Sussex Regiment.
He volunteered in September 1914, and embarked for France in the following July. In the course of his service on the Western Front he was engaged in heavy fighting at Albert and Bray, and was buried by a shell explosion in the Battle of the Somme. Sent home owing to shell-shock in April 1916, he was invalided out of the Service in the following November, and holds the 1914-15 Star, and the General Service and Victory Medals.
86, Surrey Lane, Battersea, S.W.11. Z2285

GODFREY, H., Private, Devonshire Regiment.
Volunteering in September 1914, he proceeded to the Western Front on the completion of his training and served with his unit in several engagements. He died gloriously on the Field of battle at Neuve Chapelle from wounds received in action in April 1915, and was entitled to the 1914-15 Star, and the General Service and Victory Medals.
"The path of duty was the way to glory."
37, Benbow Road, Hammersmith, W.6. 10729A

GODFREY, J. E., Bombardier, R.F.A.
Volunteering in May 1915, he was drafted to France in the following December, and served until the end of hostilities. Whilst on the Western Front he was engaged in heavy fighting at Loos, Vimy Ridge, Passchendaele, Cambrai, and in several of the concluding battles of the war, and was gassed. He was demobilised in February 1919, and holds the 1914-15 Star, and the General Service and Victory Medals.
151, Cator Street, Peckham, S.E.15. Z4528C

GODFREY, S. S., Cpl., 2nd Buffs (East Kent Regt.)
He joined in August 1916, and in the following January was sent to Salonika. He saw much service on the Doiran and Struma fronts, and after the cessation of hostilities proceeded to Turkey, and served with the Army of Occupation at Constantinople, and on the Bosphorus. He was demobilised in December 1919, and holds the General Service and Victory Medals.
1, Wivenhoe Road, Peckham, S.E.15. 5974A

GODLEY, W. R., Private, 7th London Regiment.
Volunteering at the outbreak of war, he was sent overseas in March 1915. During his service on the Western Front he took part in engagements at Festubert and Loos, and was severely wounded during the fighting at the Hohenzollern Redoubt in December 1915. He was invalided to England, and after receiving hospital treatment was discharged as medically unfit for further service in August 1916. He holds the 1914-15 Star, and the General Service and Victory Medals.
54, Grenard Road, Peckham, S.E.15. Z5610

GODMAN, F., Corporal, Guards' Machine Gun Regt.
He joined in April 1918, and completing his training, was stationed at various depôts engaged on guard and other important duties with his unit. Owing to ill-health he was unsuccessful in obtaining his transfer overseas, but rendered valuable services, until demobilised in April 1919.
32, Edithna Street, Landor Road, S.W.9. Z2287

GODWIN, W., Private, Labour Corps.
Volunteering in August 1915, he served at various stations with his unit before proceeding to the Western Front in 1917. During his service overseas he was chiefly engaged in the transport of ammunition and supplies in many different sectors. He returned to England and was discharged in August 1918, and holds the General Service and Victory Medals.
14, Sandover Road, Camberwell, S.E.5. Z5403

GOFF, P. C., Rflmn., 21st London Regt. (1st Surrey Rifles) and Private, 2nd East Surrey Regt.
He joined in February 1918, and at the conclusion of his training was engaged on important defence duties with his unit at various stations. In November 1918, he was transferred to the East Surrey Regiment, and was then sent to Scotland, where he did very good work until demobilised in September 1919.
4, Graylands Road, Peckham, S.E.15. Z5972

GOLDING, E., Private, 21st London Regiment.
He volunteered in August 1914, but was discharged on being discovered to be under military age. Joining again, however, at the age of eighteen, he embarked for France in 1917, and fought in the Battles of Ypres and the Somme, and throughout the German Offensive of 1918. He was seriously wounded at Cambrai on September 10th, 1918, during the Allied Advance and returned to England. He was invalided out of the Service, in February 1919, holding the General Service and Victory Medals.
33, Atwell Street, Rye Lane, S.E.15.   Z5404

GOLDSACK, C. P., Rifleman 12th London Regiment (Rangers).
Volunteering in September 1914, he served at various stations until transferred to the Western Front in February 1916. He fought in many engagements of note, including those at Vimy Ridge, Bullecourt, the Somme, Albert, Passchendaele, Ypres, and was in action throughout the German Offensive and Allied Advance of 1918, and was gassed. He was demobilised in March 1919, and holds the General Service and Victory Medals.
135, Tyneham Road, Lavender Hill, S.W.11.   Z2288

GOLDSMITH, J. H., Sapper, R.E.
He volunteered in October 1915, and proceeded to the Western Front in the following February, and served in the forward areas on important duties connected with operations, and was present at many important engagements including those at Arras, the Somme, Ypres, Cambrai, and throughout the Retreat and Advance of 1918. During his service overseas he was twice wounded, and was demobilised in February 1919. He holds the General Service and Victory Medals.
47, Sidney Road, Stockwell Road, S.W.9.   Z2289

GOLDSTONE, A. J., Rflmn., King's Royal Rifle Corps.
Volunteering in May 1915, he embarked for the Balkan theatre of war in the following year. Here he fought in various parts of the line and was engaged in many battles, and was wounded. He suffered from malaria during his service in Salonika, and returning to England was demobilised in June 1919. He holds the General Service and Victory Medals.
11, Hillery Road, Walworth, S.E.17.   Z2290

GOLLEDGE, A. A., Corporal, 3rd County of London Yeomanry (Sharpshooters' Hussars), and King's Royal Rifle Corps.
He volunteered on the declaration of war, and in the following year was sent to Salonika and served in various parts of the line. Later transferred to the King's Royal Rifle Corps he proceeded to Egypt, and was in action in many engagements on the Palestine Front during the British Advance into Syria. He returned to England and was demobilised in February 1919, and holds the 1914-15 Star, and the General Service and Victory Medals.
137, Beresford Street, Camberwell Road, S.E.5.   Z2291

GOLLEDGE, F. E., Sergt., R.A.S.C.
He volunteered in October 1915, and embarked for the Western Front three months later, and served in the Ypres salient on important duties, transporting ammunition and supplies to the front lines. Later he was engaged on repair work in the workshops in the advanced areas, and on the conclusion of hostilities was sent into Germany with the Army of Occupation, and stationed at Cologne. He returned to England, and was demobilised in May 1920, and holds the General Service and Victory Medals.
76, Arthur Road, Brixton Road, S.W.9.   Z4427

GOLLOP, F., Private, 23rd London Regiment.
Volunteering in 1915, he proceeded to France in the following year, and fought in many engagements of note including those at Ypres, the Somme, and Cambrai. In 1917 he returned to England, and was transferred to the R.A.F., and served at Farnham, engaged on important duties until demobilised in 1919. He holds the General Service and Victory Medals.
37, Peardon Street, Wandsworth Road, S.W.8.   Z2292B

GOLLOP, S. E., Rifleman, 6th London Regt. (Rifles).
He joined in 1918, and on completion of his training served at various stations engaged on important duties with his unit. He was unsuccessful in obtaining his transfer overseas prior to the cessation of hostilities, but sent to the Army of Occupation in Germany in 1919, was stationed on the Rhine until the following year. He then returned to England, and was demobilised.
37, Peardon Street, Wandsworth Road, S.W.8.   Z2292A

GOLLOP, W. H., Private, Buffs (East Kent Regt.)
He volunteered in November 1914, and proceeded to France in the following February. During his service overseas he fought at the Battles of Neuve Chapelle and Ypres, and was wounded at Hill 60. On recovery he rejoined his Battalion, and was engaged in severe fighting in various sectors. He was killed in action on August 8th, 1915, and was entitled to the 1914-15 Star, and the General Service and Victory Medals.
"A costly sacrifice upon the altar of freedom." Z2293
11, C Block, Victoria Dwellings, Battersea Park Road, S.W.11.

GOMERSALL, A. G. W., Corporal, 7th Queen's Own (Royal West Kent Regiment and Queen's (Royal West Surrey Regiment).
He joined in March 1918 on attaining military age, and on completion of his training proceeded to the Western Front. He fought in many engagements during the German Offensive and Allied Advance, including those at Albert and Troncs Wood, where he was wounded in August 1918. He was demobilised in 1920, and holds the General Service and Victory Medals.
28, Victoria Terrace, Queen's Road, Battersea Park, S.W.8.   Z2294

GOOCH, H. W., Gunner, R.G.A.
He joined in May 1916, and was drafted to the Macedonian theatre of war in the following year, and was in action in many engagements on the Doiran front. He suffered from malaria during his service overseas, but remained in Salonika until the close of the war. After the Armistice he was sent to Constantinople with the Army of Occupation, and served there for a time. Returning to England, he was demobilised in October 1919, and holds the General Service and Victory Medals.
8, Ulric Street, Camberwell, S.E.5.   Z2295

GOOD, A., Rifleman, King's Royal Rifle Corps.
He volunteered in November 1915, and early in 1916 was sent to France. In this theatre of war he fought at Delville Wood, and the Somme, and was badly gassed in February 1917. After being invalided to England he was subsequently discharged as unfit for further service. He rejoined in the Royal Air Force in August 1919, but unfortunately died in the following December. He held the General Service and Victory Medals.
"His memory is cherished with pride."
26, Ridgeway Road, Loughborough Road, S.W.9.   Z5967

GOOD, H., Private, 7th London Regiment.
Volunteering at the outbreak of war, he was drafted to France in March 1915, and took part in the fighting at the Battles of Ypres Albert, and Festubert, where he was badly gassed in May 1915. He was sent to hospital in Rouen, and after recovery was employed at General Head Quarters until demobilised in November 1918. He holds the 1914-15 Star, and the General Service and Victory Medals.
50, Cronin Road, Peckham, S.E.15.   Z5611

GOODALL, J., R.S.M., Scots Guards.
He enlisted in 1904, and at the outbreak of war proceeded to the Western Front, and was in action in the Retreat from Mons, and at the Battle of Ypres. Owing to ill-health, he was invalided to England in 1916, and received hospital treatment. On recovery he returned to the Western Front and fought with distinction throughout the Retreat and Advance of 1918, and was mentioned in Despatches for devotion to duty in the Field. He was still serving in 1920, and holds the Mons Star, and the General Service and Victory Medals.
12A, Tennyson Street, Wentworth Road, S.W.8.   Z2296

GOODCHILD, A., Rflmn., King's Royal Rifle Corps.
He joined in March 1916, and, sent to France in the following November, was in action in many important engagements, including those at Ypres, and the Somme. He fought throughout the German Offensive and subsequent Allied Advance, and was wounded at Cambrai. He was demobilised in September 1919, and holds the General Service and Victory Medals.
5, Lombard Road, Battersea, S.W.11.   Z2297

GOODE, W., Private, R.A.S.C.
Volunteering in January 1916, he was shortly afterwards drafted to the Western Front. Here he was engaged on important duties connected with the Expeditionary Force Canteens at Béthune, and rendered excellent services. He returned to England and was demobilised in September 1919, and holds the General Service and Victory Medals.
161B, Latchmere Road, Battersea, S.W.11.   Z2298

GOODEN, E. J., Corporal, King's Royal Rifle Corps and Labour Corps.
He volunteered in April 1915, and in the same year proceeded overseas. During his service on the Western Front he fought at Ypres, Loos, Givenchy, Festubert, Hill 60, the Somme, Arras, Messines, the Marne, the Aisne, and in the Retreat and Advance of 1918. He was demobilised in 1919, and holds the 1914-15 Star, and the General Service and Victory Medals.
17, Copeland Avenue, Peckham Rye, S.E.15.   Z5612

GOODENOUGH, F. W., 1st Class Petty Officer, R.N.
He volunteered in August 1914, and was posted to H.M.S. "Astraea," which vessel was engaged on important duties off the coast of German West Africa. His ship also served in Italian waters, and was engaged on patrol and other duties in other seas until the termination of the war. He was demobilised in 1919, and holds the 1914-15 Star, and the General Service and Victory Medals.
48, Kirkwood Road, Nunhead, S.E.15.   Z6170

GOODLIFFE, J. C., Rifleman, King's Royal Rifle Corps and Private, R.M.L.I.
Volunteering in September 1914, he proceeded to the Western Front in the following month and fought in many engagements including that at La Bassée where he was wounded. Returning to England he received hospital treatment and was subsequently invalided out of the Service. Rejoining, however, for a further term of service in 1916, in the Royal Marine Light Infantry he was sent to Russia, and was in action in various sectors, and was again wounded. He was invalided to England and ultimately discharged unfit for further service in 1918. He holds the 1914 Star, and the General Service and Victory Medals.
65, Rollo Street, Battersea, S.W.11.　　　　Z2299A

GOODMAN, E. C., Sergt., 1st East Surrey Regt.
Mobilised and drafted to the Western Front at the outbreak of hostilities he fought in the Retreat from Mons, and the Battle of the Aisne, where he was wounded. On recovery he returned to the front lines, and was in action in various sectors. Later he was sent to the Base, and was engaged on clerical duties on Headquarters Staff at Le Havre until the cessation of hostilities. He was still serving in 1920, and holds the Mons Star, and the General Service and Victory Medals.
27, Bellefields Road, Stockwell Road, S.W.9.　　Z2304

GOODMAN, F. W., Private, Oxfordshire and Buckinghamshire Light Infantry.
He volunteered in December 1914, and was sent to France seven months later, and fought at Loos, St. Eloi, Albert, Vimy Ridge, the Somme, Bullecourt, Ypres, and many other engagements. During his service overseas he was wounded three times, on the last occasion so severely that he returned to England, and after receiving hospital treatment was invalided out of the Service in March 1918. He holds the 1914–15 Star, and the General Service and Victory Medals.
20, Wansey Street, Walworth, S.E.17.　　　　Z2300

GOODMAN, G. (Mrs.), Special War Worker.
This lady volunteered for work of National importance, and from December 1916 until March 1919, was engaged on special duties by the Postal Authorities at the Clapham Post Office, thus releasing a man for service with the Colours. She rendered valuable services and discharged her duties, which were of a very arduous nature, with efficiency and satisfaction.
48, North Street, Clapham, S.W.4.　　　　Z2301

GOODMAN, G., Guardsman, Scots Guards.
Volunteering in 1914, he was drafted to the Western Front in July of the following year and was in action in many parts of the line. He fought in the Battles of Loos and the Somme, and was wounded, but on his recovery rejoined his unit and was engaged in the fierce fighting during the German Offensive and Allied Advance of 1918. He was demobilised in 1919, and holds the 1914–15 Star, and the General Service and Victory Medals.
130, Elmshurst Mansions, Edgeley Road, Clapham, S.W.4.　　　　Z2302

GOODMAN, J. J., Private, Royal Fusiliers.
He volunteered in February 1916, and after his training was stationed at various depôts engaged on important duties until proceeding to France in February 1918. He fought at the Somme, the Aisne, Hangard Wood, and in many other engagements in the Retreat of 1918, and was wounded and gassed in April. He was picked up by the French Army and taken to hospital in the South of France. On recovery he returned home, and was demobilised in February 1919, and holds the General Service and Victory Medals.
97, Wickersley Road, Lavender Hill, S.W.11.　　Z2303

GOODRUM, F. T., Sergt., R.F.A.
A serving soldier, he was mobilised and drafted to the Western Front at the commencement of hostilities, and was in action in the Retreat from Mons, and in many battles including those at La Bassée, and the Somme. Later, transferred to Italy, he fought in various parts of the line and took part in the final operations in this theatre of war. He was demobilised in February 1919, and holds the Mons Star, and the General Service and Victory Medals.
41, Wayford Street, Battersea, S.W.11.　　　　Z2305

GOODSPEED, A., Trpr., 4th (Royal Irish) Dragoon Guards.
A Reservist, he was mobilised in September 1914, and on completion of his training served at various stations on important duties with his unit. He volunteered for service overseas, but was taken ill and admitted into hospital and subsequently died on November 19th, 1914.
"A costly sacrifice upon the altar of freedom."
320, East Street, Walworth, S.E.17.　　　　Z2307B

GOODSPEED, E. (Miss), Special War Worker.
This lady offered her services for work of National importance, and from the commencement of hostilities until March 1919, held a responsible post at Messrs. Turner and Co's Works, Aldgate, engaged on the manufacture of component parts of bombs. She discharged her duties in a most efficient and satisfactory manner.
320, East Street, Walworth, S.E.17.　　　　Z2309

GOODSPEED, B., Private, 12th East Surrey Regt.
He volunteered in June 1915, and embarked for the Western Front in the following May, and fought at Messines, Ypres, the Somme, and Bapaume. In November 1917, transferred to Italy, he was in action in many engagements on the Piave Front. After the cessation of hostilities he was sent into Germany with the Army of Occupation, and served there until he returned to England, and was demobilised in June 1919. He holds the General Service and Victory Medals.
19, Rectory Gardens, Clapham, S.W.4.　　　　Z2308

GOODSPEED, H. (Miss), Special War Worker.
Volunteering for work of National importance in August 1914, this lady was employed at Messrs. Ross and Co.'s Works, Bermondsey, engaged in the manufacture of army equipment of all descriptions until March 1919. She rendered valuable services throughout and gave complete satisfaction.
320, East Street, Walworth, S.E.17.　　　　Z2306

GOODSWEN, A. G., Private, 1st Norfolk Regiment.
Volunteering in December 1914, he was drafted to the Western Front in the following year, and was in action in the Battles of Ypres, Arras, Albert, Givenchy, and Vimy Ridge. He also fought at Béthune, Messines, Bullecourt, and was wounded at Passchendaele, and sent to a Base hospital in France. Later, invalided to England for treatment, he was discharged as medically unfit for further service in November 1918, and holds the 1914–15 Star, and the General Service and Victory Medals.
93, Clayton Road, Peckham, S.E.15.　　　　Z6169

GOODWIN, G., Driver, R.F.A.
He joined in May 1918, and was sent to France in the following August, and fought in many engagements in the closing operations of that theatre of war. After the Armistice, he proceeded into Germany with the Army of Occupation, and served there until his return to England. He was demobilised in May 1919, and holds the General Service and Victory Medals.
36, Loncroft Road, Camberwell, S.E.5.　　　　Z5405

GOOZEE, F. C., Private, Labour Corps.
He volunteered in February 1916, and proceeding to France two months later served in the advanced areas engaged on important duties, and was present at the Battles of Ploegsteert, Vimy Ridge, the Somme, Ypres, and Messines. He was unfortunately killed in the Lens sector on October 4th, 1917, and was entitled to the General Service and Victory Medals.
"His life for his Country."
108, Mina Road, Walworth, S.E.17.　　　　Z2310B

GOOZEE, H. R., Gunner, R.F.A.
Volunteering at the outbreak of war, he embarked for the Western Front almost immediately, and fought in the Retreat from Mons, and at the Battles of the Aisne, the Marne, La Bassée, Ypres I, II, and III., Festubert, Bullecourt, the Marne II, and was in action throughout the German Offensive. He died gloriously on the Field of Battle at Bapaume on August 21st, 1918, during the Allied Advance, and was entitled to the Mons Star, and the General Service and Victory Medals.
"Great deeds cannot die,
They with the Sun and Moon renew their light for ever."
108, Mina Road, Walworth, S.E.17.　　　　Z2310A

GORDON, J., Private, 2nd London Regiment (Royal Fusiliers) and 1st Middlesex Regiment.
A Reservist, he was mobilised and drafted to the Western Front at the commencement of hostilities, and fought in the Retreat from Mons, the Battle of the Somme, and in many other battles. He also was engaged in heavy fighting throughout the Retreat and Advance of 1918, and was wounded and twice gassed. He also saw active service in India and South Africa from 1899–1902, and holds the Queen's South African Medal (with five clasps), the Mons Star, and the General Service and Victory Medals. He was demobilised in March 1919.
10, Rockingham Street, S.E.1.　　　　Z25358

GORDON, W. C., Private, East Surrey Regiment.
Volunteering in February 1915, he proceeded to France in the following year and saw much service in various parts of the line. In 1917, transferred to the Balkan theatre of war, he was in action in many engagements on the Macedonian front. He returned to England, and was demobilised in February 1919, and holds the General Service and Victory Medals.
40, Cambridge Street, Camberwell, S.E.5.　　　Z2311

GORE, W. G. H., Private, Wellington (N.Z.) Infantry Regiment.
He joined in October 1915, and was sent to Egypt in the following January and was engaged on guard and other duties in the Canal zone until May 1916. Transferred to the Western Front, he was in action at Armentières and the Somme, where he was severely wounded and sustained severe injuries to his ears. He received hospital treatment, and was subsequently invalided out of the Service in September 1917, and holds the General Service and Victory Medals.
226, St. James' Road, Old Kent Road, S.E.1.　　26500

GORING, G., Private, 2nd East Surrey Regiment.

He volunteered in December 1914, and embarked for France five months later, and fought in the Battles of Ypres and Loos. Transferred to Egypt, he saw much service, and later was sent to Salonika, and there fought in many engagements on the Balkan front. After the Armistice he proceeded into Turkey with the Army of Occupation and served there until returning to England. He was demobilised in January 1920, and holds the 1914–15 Star, and the General Service and Victory Medals.
16, Horsman Street, Camberwell, S.E.5.　　Z2313

GOSLING, T., Pte., Yorkshire Regt. and Labour Corps.

He joined in November 1916, and completing his training was stationed at various depôts, engaged on important duties with his unit. Owing to ill-health he was unsuccessful in obtaining his transfer to a theatre of war, but rendered excellent services until demobilised in January 1919.
4, Flint Street, Walworth, S.E.17.　　Z2314

GOSNELL, A. J., East Surrey Regiment.

A Reservist, he was mobilised and drafted to the Western Front at the outbreak of hostilities, and was engaged in heavy fighting in the Retreat from Mons. He gave his life for the freedom of England on September 3rd, 1914, and was entitled to the Mons Star, and the General Service and Victory Medals.
" A valiant soldier, with undaunted heart he breasted Life's last hill."
118, Aylesbury Road, Walworth, S.E.17.　　Z2502B

GOSS, B., Pioneer, R.E.

Volunteering in September 1914, he proceeded to the Western front in the following June. He served in the forward areas, being engaged in all kinds of field work on the Somme and at Ypres, Arras, Cambrai and throughout the Retreat and Advance of 1918. He was demobilised in March 1919, but re-enlisted two months later in the Labour Corps for a further period of service. He holds the 1914–15 Star, and the General Service and Victory Medals.
47, Sandover Road, Camberwell, S.E.5.　　Z5406

GOUGH, W. J., Private, 4th Royal Fusiliers.

He joined in December 1917, and, sent to the Western Front in the following July, fought in the Allied Advance, and was wounded. On recovery he rejoined his unit and was taken ill later in the year. Admitted into hospital, he received treatment and subsequently died in October 1918, and is buried in the British Cemetery at Grevillers. He was entitled to the General Service and Victory Medals.
" His memory is cherished with pride."
25, Wycliffe Road, Lavender Hill, S.W.11.　　Z2315

GOULD, A., Private, Royal Fusiliers.

He joined in December 1916, and embarked for France three months later. During his service overseas he fought in various parts of the line, and was in action in many important engagements. He gave his life for King and Country in October 1917, and was entitled to the General Service and Victory Medals.
" And doubtless he went in splendid company."
10, Barmore Street, Battersea, S.W.11.　　Z2319C. Z2320C

GOULD, A. C. (M.M.), Sapper, R.E.

Volunteering in February 1915, and proceeding to France in the same year, he was in action at St. Eloi, the Somme, Lens, Cambrai and in 1917 was mentioned in Despatches. He was awarded the Military Medal for devotion to duty and gallantry in the Field in establishing and maintaining telephonic communication under heavy fire during the Allied Advance in 1918. He was demobilised in January 1919, and holds the 1914–15 Star, and the General Service and Victory Medals.
25, Severus Road, Battersea, S.W.11.　　Z2318C

GOULD, F. A., L/Corporal, M.G.C.

He volunteered in December 1914 at the age of sixteen, and on completion of his training was sent to France, and was in action in many important engagements, including those at Ypres, the Somme and Cambrai, and was twice wounded. He was mentioned in Despatches on April 19th, 1917, for devotion to duty in the Field. He also fought throughout the Retreat and Advance of 1918, and returning to England, was demobilised in May 1919, and holds the 1914–15 Star, and the General Service and Victory Medals.
25, Severus Road, Battersea, S.W.11.　　Z2318A

GOULD, G., Rifleman, King's Royal Rifle Corps.

He joined in March 1918, and completing his training was stationed at various depôts engaged on guard and other important duties with his unit. In March of the following year he was drafted to the Army of Occupation in Germany and served on the Rhine until he returned to England, and was demobilised in November 1919.
10, Barmore Street, Battersea, S.W.11.　　Z2319B. Z2320B

GOULD, H., Private, R.A.S.C. (F.A.)

Volunteering in 1915, and proceeding to France in the following November, he was engaged on important ambulance duties in the front lines during the Battles of St. Eloi, Ploegsteert, Vermelles, Vimy Ridge, Bullecourt, Lens, Bapaume, Havrincourt, and throughout the German Offensive and Allied Advance of 1918. He was demobilised in June 1919, and holds the 1914–15 Star, and the General Service and Victory Medals.
5, Mayall Road, Herne Hill, S.E.24.　　Z2317

GOULD, J. A., Staff-Sergt., R.E.

Volunteering in August 1914, he shortly afterwards proceeded to West Africa and served throughout the period of hostilities in Sierra Leone, and in the capacity of military foreman of works, rendered valuable services. Returning to England he was demobilised in June 1920, and holds the 1914–15 Star, and the General Service and Victory Medals.
25, Severus Road, Battersea, S.W.11.　　Z2318B

GOULD, M. L. (Miss), Special War Worker.

This lady offered her services for work of National importance, and from January 1916 until the following May was engaged on important clerical duties with the Sugar Commission Then, joining the Women's Forestry Corps, she did excellent work discharging her duties in a most efficient and satisfactory manner.
25, Severus Road, Battersea, S.W.11.　　Z2316

GOULDER, L. J. E., L/Corporal, Queen's (Royal West Surrey Regiment).

He volunteered in August 1914, and in the following January embarked for France. During his service on the Western Front he fought in many notable engagements, including those at Ypres in 1915, and the Somme in the following year, in both of which battles he was wounded. On the second occasion he was invalided home to hospital in July 1916, and after prolonged medical treatment, was subsequently discharged as physically unfit for further military duty. He holds the 1914–15 Star, and the General Service and Victory Medals.
7, Lewis Road, Camberwell, S.E.5.　　Z6175

GOULDER, T., Sergt., Rifle Brigade.

He joined in July 1917, and later in the same year proceeded to Egypt. Here he was engaged on important duties at a prisoners' of war camp, and rendered valuable services until 1920, when he returned home and was demobilised in February of that year. He holds the General Service and Victory Medals.
10, Power Street, Wandsworth Road, S.W.8.　　Z2321

GOULSTONE, G. F., Private, 19th London Regt.

He volunteered in August 1914, and served with his Battalion on home service duties until 1916, when he proceeded to the Western Front. He was engaged in heavy fighting in the Battles of the Somme and Ypres, and in the following year was drafted to Egypt, where he was in action during the advance through Palestine, and was present at the fall of Jerusalem. He was afterwards sent to Salonika and fought in many important engagements on the Doiran front, and was wounded during his service overseas. He returned home and was demobilised in February 1919, and holds the General Service and Victory Medals.
15, Trollope Street, Battersea Park, S.W.8.　　Z2323

GOULSTONE, W. G., Private, 5th Royal Fusiliers.

He volunteered in August 1914, and later in the same year was drafted to the Western Front. He played an important part in the fighting at the Battles of Le Cateau, Ypres and Cambrai, and was wounded in 1915. He was, unfortunately, killed in action on the Somme on July 7th, 1916, and was entitled to the 1914–15 Star, and the General Service and Victory Medals.
" Courage, bright hopes, and a myriad dreams, splendidly given."
15, Trollope Street, Battersea Park, S.W.8.　　Z2322

GOURRIET, L. E., 1st Class Stoker, R.N.

He was mobilised in August 1914, and was posted to H.M.S. " Magnificent," aboard which vessel he was engaged on patrol duties in the North Sea and later in convoying troops to the Dardanelles and Salonika. His ship was afterwards employed on salvage duties and submarine warfare in the North Sea until after the close of the war. He was demobilised in December 1919, and holds the 1914–15 Star, and the General Service and Victory Medals.
39, Thornton Street, Stockwell, S.W.9.　　Z2324A

GOVE, J. S., Private, R.A.S.C. (M.T.)

He joined in March 1918, and in the following month proceeded to the Western Front. He was engaged on transport duties with his unit and served during the Retreat and Advance of 1918. On the cessation of hostilities he was sent to Germany with the Army of Occupation and was stationed at Cologne. He was demobilised in July 1920, and holds the General Service and Victory Medals.
15, Bullen Street, Battersea, S.W.11.　　Z2325

GOW, A., A/Sergt., 14th London Regiment (London Scottish).

He volunteered in August 1914, and early in the following year was sent to the Western Front. He took an important part in the Battles of Givenchy and Neuve Chapelle, and proceeded to Salonika in 1916. In this theatre of war he fought in many engagements on the Macedonian front, and returning to England in 1917, was discharged on account of service in September of that year. He holds the 1914-15 Star, and the General Service and Victory Medals.
97, St. Alban's Avenue, Chiswick, W.4. 7965B

GOW, T. A. O., Private, 14th London Regt. (London Scottish), Welch Regt. and Black Watch.

He joined in August 1917, and after completing his training was sent to France in the following year. He took an active part in the Retreat and Advance of 1918, and was wounded in September. He was invalided home, and after recovery was demobilised in January 1919, and holds the General Service and Victory Medals.
97, St. Alban's Avenue, Chiswick, W.4. 7965A

GOWER, C., Gunner, R.F.A.

He volunteered in November 1914, and in the following year proceeded to the Western Front. In this theatre of war he fought in many engagements, including the Battles of the Somme, Arras, Loos, Neuve Chapelle, Armentières, and St. Quentin. He was demobilised in 1919, and holds the 1914-15 Star, and the General Service and Victory Medals.
8, Loris Road, Hammersmith, W.6. 12252

GOWER, E. E. (Mrs.), Special War Worker.

This lady volunteered her services for work of National importance during the war, and from June 1916 until January 1917, was engaged at Woolwich Arsenal as an examiner of cartridge cases. She carried out her various duties to the satisfaction of the authorities.
5, Flinton Street, Walworth, S.E.17. Z2326B

GOWER, W. E. P., Private, 2nd Devonshire Regt.

He volunteered in February 1916, and in May of the following year was sent to France. In this theatre of war he saw much fighting and was in action in the Battles of Bullecourt, Messines, and Ypres. He was, unfortunately killed at the third Battle of Ypres on July 31st, 1917, and was entitled to the General Service and Victory Medals.
" He joined the great white company of valiant souls."
5, Flinton Street, Walworth, S.E.17. Z2326A

GOWERS, W., Stoker, R.N.

He joined in August 1917, and was posted to H.M.S. " Eclipse." He was shortly afterwards transferred to H.M.S. " Hyacinth," which ship was in action in the raids on Zeebrugge and Ostend. He was serving in this vessel when she was sunk, but was fortunately saved. He then joined H.M.S. " Pelages " and served aboard her in the North Sea until discharged in September 1918. He holds the General Service and Victory Medals.
87, Gwynne Road, Battersea, S.W.11. Z1515B

GOWIN, W. C., Sapper, R.E.

He volunteered in September 1914, and in October of the following year was sent to India. He was engaged on important duties at Rangoon and was placed in charge of natives making munitions. He returned to England late in 1917, and in January 1918 was drafted to the Western Front, where he was employed on railway work at Rouen until his demobilisation in March 1919. He holds the General Service and Victory Medals.
128, Sabine Road, Battersea, S.W.11. Z2328

GOWING, J. W., Stoker, R.N.

He was already serving on the outbreak of war aboard H.M.S. " Harpy," which vessel was engaged in convoying troops to France. He was later transferred to H.M.S. " Cornwallis," and was serving in her when she was torpedoed and sunk off Malta in January 1917. He was then posted to H.M.S. " Intrepid," and engaged on convoy duties to Norway and Sweden until the end of the war. He was still serving in 1920 in H.M.S. " Commonwealth," and holds the 1914-15 Star, and the General Service and Victory Medals.
111, Gurney Street, Walworth, S.E.17. Z2329

GRADY, J. T., Rifleman, 2/12th London Regiment (Rangers).

He volunteered in October 1915, and proceeded in the following year to France. In this theatre of war he took a prominent part in the fighting in various parts of the line, and was in action in the Retreat and Advance of 1918, and was severely wounded in August of that year. He was invalided home, and on recovery was discharged unfit for further service in November 1918. He holds the General Service and Victory Medals.
8, Stewart's Road, Battersea Park Road, S.W.8. Z2330

GRADY, S., Gunner, R.F.A.

He volunteered in May 1915, and in the following year was drafted to the Western Front. He was in action in many battles, including those of Ypres, Armentières and Verdun, and was wounded. On recovery he returned to the front lines, and after fighting in many engagements was again wounded in 1917. He was invalided to England and was later sent to France again and fought in the concluding operations of the war. He was demobilised in September 1919, and holds the General Service and Victory Medals.
42, Corunna Road, New Road, South Lambeth, S.W.8. Z2331

GRAFTON, R., Private, Labour Corps.

He joined in July 1917, and after his training served at various stations on important guard duties with his unit. He also rendered valuable services in unloading ships at various ports, but was unable to obtain his transfer overseas before the cessation of hostilities owing to ill-health, and was demobilised in February 1919.
20, Gideon Road, Lavender Hill, S.W.11. Z2332

GRAHAM, H. A., Sergt., R.E.

He volunteered in March 1915, and was shortly afterwards drafted to France. He served for a short period in this theatre of war, and was then transferred to the Macedonian Front, where he took an active part in the fighting on the Vardar and Monastir fronts until the close of the war. Returning home, he was demobilised in July 1919, and holds the General Service and Victory Medals.
5, Tweed Street, Battersea Park Road, S.W.8. Z2333

GRAHAM, R. S. (M.M.), Corporal, R.F.A.

He volunteered in November 1914, and in the following year was sent to France, where he fought at the Somme, Ypres and Arras, and in various other sectors until hostilities ceased. In 1917 he was awarded the Military Medal for bravery and devotion to duty in the Field at Ypres, where he was wounded. He also holds the 1914-15 Star, and the General Service and Victory Medals, and was demobilised in May 1919.
23, Pilkington Road, Peckham, S.E.15. Z5971

GRAINGER, C. H., Sergt., 1st King's (Liverpool Regiment).

A serving soldier, he was mobilised in August 1914, and was almost immediately drafted to France. He fought in the Retreat from Mons and the Battle of Ypres, and was wounded in May 1915. On recovery he was again in action in many engagements, including those on the Somme, and was wounded a second time. He was invalided to England, and in consequence of his injuries, his left hand had to be amputated, and after receiving medical treatment he was discharged as physically unfit for further service in October 1919. He holds the Mons Star, and the General Service and Victory Medals.
50, Dale sStreet, Chiswick, W.4. 5492A

GRAINGER, E., Private, 3rd (King's Own) Hussars.

He enlisted in 1912, and on the outbreak of war was almost immediately sent to France. He was in action in many important engagements, including the Retreat from Mons and the Battles of Ypres, Neuve Chapelle, Loos, the Somme and Messines, where he was wounded, and sent to a Base hospital. On recovery he fought in the Retreat and Advance of 1918, and at the close of the war went to Germany with the Army of Occupation. He returned to England in February 1919, and was still serving in 1920. He holds the Mons Star, and the General Service and Victory Medals.
56, D'Eynsford Road, Camberwell, S.E.5. Z2334B

GRAINGER, G. (M.M.), Pte., Royal Berkshire Regt.

He volunteered in September 1914, and in June of the following year proceeded to France. He fought in many battles, including those of Loos, the Somme, Arras, Cambrai and Messines. He was awarded the Military Medal for conspicuous gallantry and devotion to duty in the Field whilst acting as Battalion runner. He died gloriously on the Field of Battle at Bourlon Wood on March 7th, 1918, and was entitled to the 1914-15 Star, and the General Service and Victory Medals.
" A valiant soldier, with undaunted heart he breasted Life's last hill."
56, D'Eynsford Road, Camberwell, S.E.5. Z2334A

GRAINGER, J. E., Driver, R.F.A.

He volunteered in April 1915, and later in the same year was sent to the Western Front. He fought in many engagements, including the Battles of the Somme, Arras, Vermelles, and was wounded at Beaumont-Hamel in 1916. He was invalided home in December of that year and on recovery served at Winchester for a time. Owing to illness he was again sent to hospital and was eventually discharged as medically unfit for further military service in November 1917. He holds the 1914-15 Star, and the General Service and Victory Medals.
50, D'Eynsford Road, Camberwell, S.E.5. Z2334C

GRAINGER, W., Private, 2nd Queen's Own (Royal West Kent Regiment).
Serving in India at the outbreak of war, engaged on garrison duties with his Battalion, he was later sent to Mesopotamia, where he was engaged in much heavy fighting. He gave his life for the freedom of England in an engagement at Kut in October 1917, and was entitled to the General Service and Victory Medals.
"Whilst we remember the Sacrifice is not in vain."
50, Dale Street, Chiswick, W.4.   5492B

GRANGER, A., Private, 7th Canadian Infantry.
He volunteered in March 1915, and after his training was drafted to England in August of the same year. Proceeding to the Western Front in the following month he was in action at the Battles of Ypres, Arras, Bullecourt, and in the Retreat and Allied Advance of 1918, and was present at the entry into Mons on November 11th, 1918. He was awarded the Belgian Croix de Guerre for conspicuous gallantry displayed in taking a trench at Ypres in August 1916. After the Armistice he served with the Army of Occupation in Germany and was stationed on the Rhine until February 1919. He was then sent to England and was demobilised in July of that year. He also holds the 1914-15 Star, and the General Service and Victory Medals.
29, Caldew Street, Camberwell, S.E.5.   5763A

GRANT, A. J., Private, Queen's Own (Royal West Kent Regiment).
He volunteered in June 1915, and was drafted overseas in the following year. Whilst in France he fought at Vermelles, on the Somme and at Arras, and was severely wounded at Cambrai in 1917. He was sent home to hospital, and after eight months' medical treatment was invalided out of the Service in March of the following year. He holds the General Service and Victory Medals.
46, Parkstone Road, Peckham, S.E.15.   Z6173

GRANT, D., Armourer Sergt., R.A.O.C.
He volunteered in November 1914, and in the following year proceeded with his unit to the Western Front. He was engaged on special duties in various sectors, including those of the Somme, Ypres and Arras, and during his service overseas was attached to the 1st Coldstream Guards and the Middlesex Regiment. He was demobilised in March 1919, and holds the 1914-15 Star, and the General Service and Victory Medals.
71, Sandmere Road, Clapham, S.W.4.   Z2341

GRANT, D., Sergt., Seaforth Highlanders.
Volunteering in August 1914, he was drafted to France in the same year and served throughout the war. During this period he served in various sectors and fought in many engagements, including the Battles of Armentières and Hill 60, and was wounded at Ypres on April 25th, 1915. Returning to England for demobilisation in March 1919, he holds the 1914-15 Star, and the General Service and Victory Medals.
205, Mayall Road, Herne Hill, S.E.24.   Z2336

GRANT, H., L/Corporal, R.A.M.C.
Mobilised from the Army Reserve he was sent to the Western Front in August 1914, and was engaged in convoying wounded soldiers to England. He was sent to Malta in 1915, where he served for two years, and was then drafted to Salonika and engaged on special duties at a Base hospital. He was also on duty in an Italian hospital ship for a time, and did excellent work throughout. He was demobilised in February 1919, and holds the 1914 Star, and the General Service and Victory Medals.
98A, Tennyson Street, Wentworth Road, S.W.8.   Z2342

GRANT, H. E., Private, 1st East Surrey Regiment.
Enlisting in October 1911, he was mobilised on the outbreak of war and proceeded to France in August 1914. He was taken prisoner during the Retreat from Mons on August 23rd, 1914, and suffered many hardships during his captivity, and was sent to Russia with a batch of other prisoners. Released after the Armistice, he returned home very ill and was discharged as medically unfit for further service in December 1919. He holds the Mons Star, and the General Service and Victory Medals.
57, Longhedge Street, Battersea, S.W.11.   Z2339B

GRANT, J. C., Private, Buffs (East Kent Regiment).
He volunteered in September 1914, and proceeding to France in the following year, took part in several important engagements, including the Battles of Ypres, Arras and the Somme, and was severely wounded in July 1916. Sent home to hospital, owing to his injuries, he had his left arm amputated, and was discharged as physically unfit for further service in July 1917. He holds the 1914-15 Star, and the General Service and Victory Medals.
56, Avenue Road, Camberwell, S.E.5.   Z2343A

GRANT, J. W., Driver, R.F.A.
He enlisted as a band boy and was serving in the 8th (King's Royal Irish) Hussars in India at the outbreak of war, and was drafted in January 1915 to the Western Front, on attaining military age. Amongst other engagements he was in action in the Battles of the Somme, the Aisne, and the Marne, and when hostilities ceased, went with the Army of Occupation into Germany and was stationed at Cologne. He was demobilised in July 1919, on his return to England, and holds the General Service and Victory Medals.
56, Avenue Road, Camberwell, S.E.5.   Z2343B

GRANT, J. C., Private, 14th Middlesex Regiment.
Volunteering in July 1915, in the following year he was sent to Mudros and later to Egypt and Salonika. He served with his Battalion on important garrison duties and rendered valuable services until sent home owing to illness in January 1919. After receiving hospital treatment he was invalided out of the Army in April 1919, and holds the General Service and Victory Medals.
44, Doddington Grove, Battersea, S.W.11.   Z2340

GRANT, J. W., Private, R.A.P.C.
He volunteered in August 1915, and on the completion of his training was engaged on important duties at Blackheath. He rendered valuable service, but was not successful in obtaining his transfer overseas, and was discharged on account of service in January 1917. He had served in the 15th London Regiment (Civ. Service Rifles) before the war.
22, Coronation Buildings, S. Lambeth, S.W.8.   Z2338

GRANT, M., Private, 6th Queen's (Royal West Surrey Regiment).
Joining in November 1916, he embarked for France in the following year and served there for upwards of two years. During this period he was in action in many operations until the cessation of hostilities, when he was sent into Germany with the Army of Occupation. He returned home for demobilisation in November 1919, and holds the General Service and Victory Medals.
34, Rockley Road, W. Kensington, W.14.   11813

GRANT, S. E., Sapper, R.E.
He joined in June 1916, and proceeded to Egypt in the same year. He was engaged on important duties in connection with operations at Sollum, Jiffjaffa, Katia, Romani, Jericho, and was wounded in the Battle of Gaza and a second time near Jerusalem. Returning to England after the Armistice, he was demobilised in 1919, and holds the General Service and Victory Medals.
4, Milford Street, Wandsworth Road, S.W.8.   Z2337

GRANT, T. W., Private, 1st Middlesex Regiment and East Surrey Regiment.
Volunteering in August 1914, he was drafted to the Western Front in the same year and fought in several battles, including those of Le Cateau, St. Eloi, Loos, and was severely wounded and sent home. Invalided out of the Service he subsequently re-enlisted and was sent with the Expeditionary Force to Russia, where he served until his return home for demobilisation in April 1920. He holds the 1914-15 Star, and the General Service and Victory Medals.
33, Priory Grove, Lansdowne Road, S.W.8.   Z1187B

GRANT, W., Private, M.G.C.
He volunteered in September 1915, and was sent to France in the following year. He served with his unit in several important engagements and was wounded in the Battle of the Somme in 1916. Returning to the Field on recovery he was unhappily killed in action at the Battle of Messines Ridge on June 7th, 1917, and was entitled to the General Service and Victory Medals.
"The path of duty was the way to glory."
57, Longhedge Street, Battersea, S.W.11.   Z2339A

GRANTHAM, W. H. (M.M.), A.B., Royal Navy, Corporal, 13th East Surrey Regiment, 2nd King's (Liverpool Regiment) and R.A.S.C.
He was serving in the Royal Navy at the outbreak of war, in H.M.S. "Tiger," which vessel took part in the Battle of the Dogger Bank in January 1915, and he was wounded. He was discharged on account of service in the following April and joined the Army two months later, and drafted to France in the same year, fought in the Battles of Arras and the Somme and was again wounded. He was awarded the Military Medal for conspicuous bravery and devotion to duty in the Field. He later served in the R.A.S.C. as an Instructor and was demobilised in February 1919. Four months afterwards he rejoined the Royal Navy, but was discharged unfit for further service in the following year. He holds the 1914-15 Star, and the General Service and Victory Medals.
10, Monkton Street, Kennington, S.E.11.   Z26900

GRASSO, A., Chef, Merchant Service.
He was in the Merchant Service at the outbreak of hostilities and during the war served in hospital and troop ships in the North, Mediterranean and Baltic Seas, the Dardanelles and in many other waters. He saw service in H.M.S. " Briton " and the "Kidonan Castle," and in 1920 was serving in the "Llanstephen Castle." He holds the General Service and Mercantile Marine War Medals.
4, Sudbury Street, Lambeth, S.E.1.   Z26094

GRATER, G. J., Corporal, Royal Fusiliers.
A serving soldier he was stationed in India at the outbreak of war, and in 1915 proceeded to Gallipoli. In this theatre of war he was engaged in heavy fighting at the Landing on the Peninsula and in many battles which followed, and was severely wounded. He was invalided to England, and after receiving medical treatment he was drafted to France and fought in various parts of the line and in the Retreat and Advance of 1918. He was discharged in January 1920, and holds the 1914-15 Star, and the General Service and Victory Medals.
172, East Street, Walworth, S.E.17.   Z3348A

GRATREX, W. J. C., Pte., 8th Buffs (East Kent Regt).
He volunteered in September 1914, and later in that year was drafted to the Western Front, where he fought in the Battles of Ypres, Hill 60, Festubert, Loos, Vermelles and Ploegsteert Wood. He was seriously wounded and died in Boulogne Hospital on April 23rd, 1917. He was buried in the General Cemetery of that place. He was entitled to the 1914-15 Star, and the General Service and Victory Medals.
"His life for his Country."
57, Farmer's Road, Camberwell, S.E.5.   Z2344

GRAVES, W. T., Leading Stoker, R.N.
He joined the Service in January 1915, and was posted to H.M.S. "Killena," which ship was engaged on patrol and other important duties with the Grand Fleet in the North Sea. Later his ship served with the Mediterranean Squadron and rendered excellent services until the cessation of hostilities. He returned to England and was discharged in May 1919, holding the 1914-15 Star, and the General Service and Victory Medals.
61, Goldie Street, Camberwell, S.E.5.   Z5407

GRAVESTOCK, H., Private, 1st East Surrey Regt.
He volunteered in November 1914, and during the same month was drafted to the Western Front. He took an active part in much fighting, and was reported missing at the Battle of Hill 60, on April 25th, 1915, and later was presumed killed in action on that date. He was entitled to the 1914-15 Star, and the General Service and Victory Medals.
"Great deeds cannot die."
46, Stanton Street, Peckham, S.E.15.   Z5246

GRAY, C., Private, 7th East Surrey Regiment.
A serving soldier at the outbreak of war, he was almost immediately drafted to France. He fought in many battles, including those of La Bassée, Ypres, Neuve Chapelle, St. Eloi and Loos, where he sustained severe shell-shock in September 1915. He was invalided home and after hospital treatment was discharged in December 1915 as unfit for further service. He holds the 1914-15 Star, and the General Service and Victory Medals.
13, Broomsgrove Road, Stockwell, S.W.9.   Z4458

GRAY, E. H., Private, Gordon Highlanders.
He joined in October 1916, and after his training in the Queen's (Royal West Surrey Regiment), was drafted to France. After serving there with the Gordon Highlanders, he was invalided home, and was discharged as medically unfit for further service in January 1918. He holds the General Service and Victory Medals.
10, Arden Street, Battersea Park Road, S.W.8.   Z2348

GRAY, F. R., Sergt., East Lancashire Regt. and R.A.F.
He volunteered in December 1914, and saw much fighting on the Western Front, being wounded in May and July 1915 in the Ypres sector. After hospital treatment he served on the embarkation staff at Boulogne, and was later transferred to the R.A.F., serving as an aerial gunner. Returning to England he was trained as a pilot and was still serving in 1920. He holds the 1914-15 Star, and the General Service and Victory Medals.
24, Bramfield Road, Battersea, S.W.11.   Z2345A

GRAY, L. R. R., L/Cpl., 2nd East Lancashire Regt.
A serving soldier he was mobilised on the outbreak of hostilities. Upon his return from Africa he was drafted to France in September 1914. Serving through the early stages of the war he was engaged in heavy fighting in the Battles of Ypres, and Neuve Chapelle. He gave his life for King and Country at Festubert on May 11th, 1915, and was entitled to the 1914 Star, and the General Service and Victory Medals.
"Great deeds cannot die :
They with the Sun and Moon renew their light for ever."
13, Dalby Road, Wandsworth, S.W.18.   Z2345B

GRAY, X. W., Air Mechanic, R.A.F.
He joined in September 1918, on attaining military age, and after completing his training was engaged with his Squadron on important duties in connection with coast defence. He was also engaged on instrument repairing, which called for a high degree of technical knowledge and skill. He was unable to obtain a transfer overseas before the termination of hostilities, and was demobilised in March 1920.
16, Andulus Road, Landor Road, S.W.9.   Z2346

GRAY, S. G. (M.M.), Sergt., 1st Queen's Own (Royal West Kent Regiment).
A Regular, having enlisted in 1912, he was mobilised on the declaration of war and drafted to the Western Front in January 1915. He fought in the Battles of Hill 60, St. Eloi, and was wounded at Carnoy on December 24th, 1916. On recovery he was in action at Villers and Monchy le Preux, and was wounded three times, and invalided home in October 1917, and is now serving in the Army Reserve. Whilst overseas he was awarded the Military Medal for conspicuous bravery and devotion to duty in the Field, and also holds the 1914-15 Star, and the General Service and Victory Medals.
3, Park Grove, Battersea, S.W.11.   Z2347

GREEN, A., Rifleman, Rifle Brigade.
He volunteered in January 1915, and proceeding to France two months later served in the Battles of Neuve Chapelle, St. Eloi, and Hill 60. He was wounded in the second Battle of Ypres, and was removed to a Base hospital, where he unfortunately died from the effects of his injuries on August 9th, 1915. He was entitled to the 1914-15 Star, and the General Service and Victory Medals.
"His life for his Country, his Soul to God."
3, Lothian Road, Camberwell New Road, S.W.9.   Z5083A

GREEN, A. E., Rifleman, King's Royal Rifle Corps.
Joining in January 1916, he was drafted to France two months later, and served throughout the war. He was engaged in heavy fighting at St. Eloi, Albert, Vermelles, Vimy Ridge, on the Somme, and the Ancre. He was later in action in the Battles of Messines, Ypres, Passchendaele, Cambrai, and during the Retreat and Advance of 1918. Owing to medical unfitness for further active service he was employed on guard and other duties. He holds the General Service and Victory Medals, and in 1920 was still serving.
3, Lothian Road, Camberwell New Road, S.W.9.   Z5083C

GREEN, C., Pte., 13th London Regt. (Kensingtons).
Volunteering in May 1915, he embarked for the Western Front after completing his training and served with his unit in various engagements, including the Battles of Ypres. He gave his life for the freedom of England in the Battle of the Somme on July 1st, 1916, and was entitled to the General Service and Victory Medals.
"Steals on the ear the distant triumph song."
10, Porten Road, W. Kensington, W.14.   12228A

GREEN, G. P., 2nd Lieutenant, 3rd Cheshire Regt.
Volunteering in November 1915, he proceeded overseas in September of the following year. During his service on the Western Front he took part in much severe fighting, and was seriously wounded near Albert on October 22nd, 1916. He was taken to the Base Hospital, but unhappily died three days later, and was buried in Warloy Cemetery. He was entitled to the General Service and Victory Medals.
"A costly sacrifice upon the altar of freedom."
73, Gloucester Road, Peckham, S.E.15.   Z5963A

GREEN, H., Sergt., Royal Defence Corps.
He had previously served for 25 years with the Colours and volunteered in October 1915, but being over military age was posted to the Royal Defence Corps, with which unit he served on important guard and escort duties at many stations. He did very good work, and was demobilised in February 1919.
117, Cronin Road, Peckham, S.E.15.   Z5607B

GREEN, H. H., Rifleman, Rifle Brigade.
Volunteering in September 1914, he proceeded to France in the succeeding January. During his service on the Western Front he fought on the Somme, at Arras, Ypres, and in many other engagements. He died gloriously on the Field of Battle on the Somme in June 1917, and was entitled to the 1914-15 Star, and the General Service and Victory Medals.
"Nobly striving,
He nobly fell that we might live."
12, Sears Street, Camberwell, S.E.5.   Z5762

GREEN, H. W., Bombardier, R.F.A.
Volunteering in March 1915, he was drafted to the Western Front in the same year. He was in action at Hill 60, Ypres, the Somme, Loos, and Cambrai, and in November 1917 proceeded to Italy, where he took part in the fighting on the Piave, and was wounded. He returned to France in 1918, and served in the final operations of the war, and was again wounded. He was demobilised in April 1919, and holds the 1914-15 Star, and the General Service and Victory Medals.
117, Cronin Road, Peckham, S E.15.   Z5613

GREEN, J., Rifleman, King's Royal Rifle Corps.

Volunteering in August 1914, he was sent to France in the following December and fought in the Battles of Neuve Chapelle St. Eloi, Hill 60, and Ypres (II). He was wounded in June 1915. Returning to the Western Front in January 1916, he took part in several engagements until again invalided to England owing to wounds. On recovery he proceeded to Ireland, and served there for several months. He was demobilised in February 1919, and holds the 1914-15 Star, and the General Service and Victory Medals.
3, Lothian Road, Camberwell New Road, S.W.9.   Z5083B

GREEN, J. A., Private, 19th Essex Regiment.

He joined in August 1916, and on the conclusion of his training served with his Battalion on important duties in England until discharged on medical grounds in February 1918. Rejoining later, he proceeded to France in August 1919, and was employed on the lines of communication until his demobilisation in March 1920.
11, Pitcairn Street, Wandsworth Road, S.W.8.   Z2349

GREEN, J. H., Driver, R.F.A.

He volunteered in June 1915, and in the following year proceeded to France and saw service in the Ypres and Somme sectors. Drafted to Salonika in 1917, he was in action during the advance across the Struma, and later in the year embarked for Egypt. He took part in the operations on the Red Sea, and also fought at Bethlehem during the Palestine campaign and was wounded near Jerusalem in 1917. Returning to England on the conclusion of hostilities, he was demobilised in 1919, and holds the General Service and Victory Medals.
13 Lollard Street, Kennington, S.E.11.   Z25860

GREEN, S., Gunner, R.F.A.

Volunteering in August 1914, he was drafted to the Western Front in the following May, and served throughout the course of hostilities. During this period he was in action in numerous engagements and was gassed. He returned to England for demobilisation in June 1919, and holds the 1914-15 Star, and the General Service and Victory Medals.
14, Cator Street, Peckham, S.E.15.   Z4459C

GREEN, W., Private, 5th Royal Berkshire Regiment.

He volunteered in August 1914, and served with his Battalion at various stations until his embarkation for France in 1916. In the course of his service overseas he took part in heavy fighting in the Battle of Delville Wood, and several other important engagements. He was unfortunately killed in action in June 1917, during the Battle of Messines, and was entitled to the General Service and Victory Medals.
"Thinking that remembrance, though unspoken, may reach him where he sleeps."
114, Cator Street, Peckham, S.E.15.   Z4459B

GREEN, W., Gunner, R.H.A.

Enlisting in August 1905, he was mobilised at the outbreak of hostilities and immediately drafted to France. During his service on the Western Front he fought in the Retreat from Mons, and the subsequent Battles of Le Cateau, the Marne, The Aisne, Ypres, Loos, Vermelles, the Somme, the Ancre, and Beaumont-Hamel. He returned to England and was demobilised in January 1919, and holds the Mons Star, and the General Service and Victory Medals.
44, Graylands Road, Peckham, S.E.15.   Z5765

GREEN, W. J., Sergt., R.A.M.C.

Serving in the Army when war broke out he was drafted to the Western Front in August 1914. He did excellent work with the Field Ambulance during the Retreat from Mons, the Battles of Ypres, Loos, Cambrai, the Somme, and in numerous engagements until the conclusion of hostilities. Returning home for demobilisation in May 1919, he holds the Mons Star, and the General Service and Victory Medals, and has been placed on the Army Reserve after eight years' service with the Colours.
136, East Surrey Grove, Peckham, S.E.15.   Z5082

GREEN, W. J., Private, 13th London Regiment (Kensingtons).

Volunteering in August 1914, he proceeded to France shortly afterwards and fought during the Retreat from Mons and was wounded. Rejoining his unit he subsequently took part in the Battles of the Somme, Ypres, and Cambrai, and was wounded on another occasion. He died gloriously on the Field of Battle at Aubers Ridge on May 9th, 1915. He was entitled to the Mons Star, and the General Service and Victory Medals.
"Nobly striving,
He nobly fell that we might live."
10, Porten Road, W. Kensington, W.14.   12228B

GREENAWAY, A., Private, 10th Middlesex Regt.

He volunteered in 1915, and was sent overseas in the same year. Serving with his unit in Egypt, he took part in several engagements, but was unfortunately killed in action in March 1917. He was entitled to the 1914-15 Star, and the General Service and Victory Medals.
"He passed out of the sight of men by the path of duty and self-sacrifice."
42, Annandale Road, Chiswick, W.4.   5444C

GREENAWAY, F. G., Special War Worker.

Volunteering for work of National importance, he was employed by His Majesty's Office of Works from 1915 to 1919. During this period he was engaged in the construction of searchlight and gun stations and in the transport of oil and petrol for their use. He discharged his duties in a thoroughly capable and efficient manner.
42, Annandale Road, Chiswick, W.4.   9263

GREENAWAY, G. E., L/Corporal, Queen's (Royal West Surrey Regiment) and M.G.C.

Joining in June 1916, he embarked for the Western Front in the following February, and saw service in various sectors. During his varied service he fought in the Battles of the Somme, Arras, Ypres, Lens, Messines, Passchendaele, and Cambrai. He also took part in the Retreat and Advance of 1918. He was demobilised in October 1919, and holds the General Service and Victory Medals.
43, Heygate Street, Walworth, S.E.17.   Z2350

GREENAWAY, J., Private, Royal Scots Fusiliers.

He volunteered in 1914, and after completing his training was drafted overseas. Serving on the Western Front he was engaged in heavy fighting until wounded at Neuve Chapelle. Sent home owing to his injuries, he was subsequently invalided out of the Army in 1917, and holds the 1914-15 Star, and the General Service and Victory Medals.
40, Church Road, Hammersmith, W.6.   11126A

GREENAWAY, T. E., Gunner, R.F.A.

Volunteering in September 1915, he proceeded to France in the following year and served throughout the war. Engaged with a Trench Mortar Battery he did good work in the Battles of the Somme, Arras, Vimy Ridge, Bullecourt, Cambrai, and Amiens, and in other engagements during the Advance of 1918. He returned home for demobilisation in June 1919, and holds the General Service and Victory Medals.
40, Church Road, Hammersmith, W.6.   11126B

GREENFIELD, E. J., Driver, R.A.S.C.

He volunteered in November 1914, and was engaged on important transport duties at home until drafted to France in June 1916. Transferred to the Royal Fusiliers he served with his Battalion in many important engagements, and at the conclusion of hostilities was sent with the Army of Occupation into Germany, and was stationed at Cologne. Demobilised in January 1919 on his return to England, he holds the General Service and Victory Medals.
23, Birley Street, Battersea, S.W.11.   Z2351A

GREENFIELD, J. A., A.B., Royal Navy.

He was serving in the Royal Navy when war broke out, and was engaged on important duties in H.M.S. "Iron Duke." His ship was in action in the Battles of Heligoland and Jutland, and took an important part in other operations in the North Sea. His ship was also engaged in heavy fighting in the Black Sea. He holds the 1914-15 Star, and the General Service and Victory Medals, and in 1920 was still serving.
23, Birley Street, Battersea, S.W.11.   Z2351B

GREENFIELD, T. G., Rifleman, 13th King's Royal Rifle Corps and Private, Labour Corps.

He volunteered in November 1915, and was sent overseas in the following April. He fought at the Battles of Ypres and the Somme, and was wounded. He was invalided to England where, after receiving hospital treatment, he served on important guard duties at various stations, and was transferred to the Labour Corps. In March 1918, he returned to France, and was employed at Ypres with the Salvage Corps, and did good work until demobilised in April 1919. He holds the General Service and Victory Medals.
65, Graylands Road, Peckham, S.E.15.   Z5766

GREENWAY, H. W., Private, Middlesex Regiment.

Joining in May 1916, he was engaged on important duties with his unit until drafted to France in March 1918. After a period of service on the Western Front, he was sent to Italy, and took part in heavy fighting on the Asiago Plateau, and was sent to hospital owing to an accidental injury. Returning home in February 1919, he was demobilised in the following month, and holds the General Service and Victory Medals.
19, Basnett Road, Lavender Hill, S.W.11.   Z2352

GREENWELL, W., Pte., 3rd (King's Own) Hussars.

Volunteering in the Royal Army Service Corps in January 1915, he completed his training, and served as a driver on important commissariat duties, and was also engaged in the transport of mules to various depôts. He afterwards transferred to the 3rd (King's Own) Hussars, but was, however, unable to obtain a transfer to a theatre of war before hostilities ended. He was demobilised in January 1919.
128, Wells Street, Camberwell, S.E.5.   Z4460B

GREENWOOD, A. S., Sergt., R.F.A.
He volunteered in May 1915, and was engaged on important duties with his Battery at various depôts until his embarkation for France in March 1918. He was in action in the second Battle of the Somme, and was gassed and sent to hospital in France. Returning to the Field on recovery he fought in the Battles of the Marne, Amiens, Bapaume, Havrincourt, and in other engagements during the Advance of 1918. He was demobilised in February 1919, and holds the General Service and Victory Medals.
108, Darwin Street, Walworth, S.E.17.　　Z2355

GREENWOOD, F., Rflmn., 12th London Regiment (Rangers).
Joining in October 1916, he was sent to the Western Front four months later and served in various sectors. He was in action in several engagements and was wounded in the Battle of Bullecourt. Rejoining his unit he fought in the Battles of Ypres and Lens, and was gassed, and invalided home in November 1917. He was discharged as medically unfit for further service in January 1918, and holds the General Service and Victory Medals.
16, Cologne Road, Battersea, S.W.11.　　Z2353

GREENWOOD, T., Corporal, R.A.O.C.
He joined in 1916, and in the same year proceeded to France. During his service on the Western Front he was engaged on special duties in connection with guns and ammunition at Rouen, and also took part in operations during the Retreat and Advance of 1918. He was demobilised in 1919, and holds the General Service and Victory Medals.
29, Patmore Street, Wandsworth Road, S.W.8.　　Z2354

GREENWOOD, T., Private, 4th Royal Fusiliers.
A Regular, having joined in May 1914, was mobilised on the outbreak of hostilities, and sent to France in August 1914. He served in the early battles of the war and fell fighting at Ypres on June 16th, 1915, and was entitled to the 1914 Star, and the General Service and Victory Medals.
"Honour to the immortal dead who gave their youth that the world might grow old in peace."
42, Annandale Road, Chiswick, W.4.　　5444B

GREENWOOD, W., Sergt., 21st London Regiment (1st Surrey Rifles).
He volunteered in April 1915, and embarking for the Western Front in the same year was engaged in heavy fighting in the Battles of the Somme, Arras, and Ypres. Contracting illness whilst overseas he was invalided home in 1917, and after medical treatment served with his unit until discharged as physically unfit for further service in September 1918. He holds the 1914-15 Star, and the General Service and Victory Medals.
75, Somerleyton Road, Coldharbour Lane, S.W.9.　　Z3464A

GREER, R. W., Stoker, Mercantile Marine.
Joining in March 1918, he was posted to H.M.S. "Heroic," and later to H.M.S. "Osiris." These ships were engaged on important duties transporting troops from England and France to Mesopotamia during the war. He did excellent work throughout his service and was demobilised in October 1919, and holds the General Service and Victory Medals.
11, D'Eynsford Road, Camberwell Green, S.E.5.　　Z2356

GREGORY, A. V., A.B., Royal Navy.
He joined the Service in 1910, and at the outbreak of hostilities was aboard H.M.S. "Commonwealth," which ship was engaged on patrol and other important duties in the North Sea throughout the war. His ship frequently passed through mine-infested areas, and had many narrow escapes. He was still serving in 1920, and holds the 1914-15 Star, and the General Service and Victory Medals.
107, St. Alban's Avenue, Chiswick, W.4.　　7964B

GREGORY, F. J., Sapper, R.E.
Volunteering in April 1915, he was later sent to the Western Front and was in action in many important engagements, including those at Vimy Ridge, Passchendaele, Arras, Cambrai, and throughout the German Offensive and Allied Advance in 1918. After the Armistice he proceeded into Germany with the Army of Occupation and served there until 1919. He returned to England, and was demobilised later in that year, and holds the General Service and Victory Medals.
87, Kelmscott Road, Battersea, S.W.11.　　Z3086A

GREGORY, P. B., Private, 10th Middlesex Regiment and 2/19th London Regiment.
Volunteering in August 1914, he served at various stations until embarking for France in 1916. He saw much service in various parts of the line, and was later drafted to Salonika where he fought in many engagements. Transferred to Egypt he was in action on the Palestine front, and was present at the Capture of Jerusalem, and was wounded at Jericho. He took part in the British Advance into Syria, and returning to England was demobilised in September 1919. He holds the General Service and Victory Medals.
107, St. Alban's Avenue, Chiswick, W.4.　　7964C

GREGORY, F. T., Special War Worker.
He offered his services for work of National importance, and throughout the war held a responsible post at Messrs. Wilkinson's Factory, engaged on the manufacture of swords. He rendered valuable services, and discharged his duties in a most efficient and satisfactory manner.
107, St. Alban's Avenue, Chiswick, W.4.　　7964A

GREGORY, W. A., Gunner, R.F.A.
Volunteering in February 1915, he proceeded to the Western Front in the following December, and fought at the Somme, and was severely wounded at Fricourt. Invalided to England, he received hospital treatment, and on recovery served at various stations in England until demobilised in February 1919. He holds the 1914-15 Star, and the General Service and Victory Medals.
38, Mansion Street, Camberwell, S.E.5.　　Z2357

GREGORY, W. S., Private, R.A.M.C.
Volunteering in January 1916, he completed his training and served at various hospitals engaged on important duties attending sick and wounded troops. He was unsuccessful in obtaining his transfer to a theatre of war, but rendered valuable services until demobilised in September 1919.
87, Kelmscott Road, Battersea, S.W.11.　　Z3086B

GREIG, D. L., Gunner, R.F.A.
Volunteering in March 1915, he proceeded to the Western Front in the following January, and was in action on the Somme, and at Arras, Vimy Ridge and Cambrai. Owing to ill-health he was invalided to England, and on recovery returned to France in April 1918, and fought throughout the German Offensive and subsequent Allied Advance. Returning to England after the Armistice he was demobilised in May 1919, and holds the General Service and Victory Medals.
10, Ada Road, Camberwell, S.E.5.　　Z3457

GREW, F. W., Private, Yorkshire Regiment.
He joined in November 1916, and completing his training, served at various depôts with his unit engaged on guard and other important duties. He was unsuccessful in obtaining his transfer overseas prior to the cessation of hostilities, but proceeded to France in April 1919. He did good work, and returning to England was demobilised in November 1919.
11, Dorchester Grove, Chiswick, W.4.　　5395

GREY, S., Corporal, King's (Liverpool Regiment).
He joined in May 1917, and embarked for France in the following January. He fought in many parts of the line during the German Offensive and Allied Advance, and in August 1918 was transferred to Egypt, and was in action in various engagements during the Advance through Palestine into Syria. He returned to England and was demobilised in May 1920, and holds the General Service and Victory Medals.
25, Chumleigh Street, Camberwell, S.E.5.　　Z5084

GRIDLEY, C., Driver, R.F.A.
He volunteered in 1915, and in the same year was drafted to the Western Front. In this theatre of war he was engaged in the fighting at Ypres, Loos, Hill 60, Vimy Ridge, the Somme, Arras, Passchendaele, Cambrai, and in the Retreat and Allied Advance of 1918. He holds the 1914-15 Star, and the General Service and Victory Medals, and was demobilised in 1919.
11, Copeland Avenue, Peckham Rye, S.E.15.　　Z5614

GRIDLEY, H., Stoker Petty Officer, R.N.
He joined the Service prior to the declaration of war, and was serving aboard H.M.S. "Inflexible," which ship took part in various engagements, including the Battles of the Narrows, the Falkland Islands, Jutland and Heligoland Bight. His ship also rendered valuable services engaged on patrol and other important duties in the North Sea until the cessation of hostilities. Owing to ill-health he was discharged in April 1919, and holds the 1914-15 Star, and the General Service and Victory Medals.
195, Mayall Road, Herne Hill, S.E.24.　　Z2358

GRIDLEY, H., Leading Stoker, R.N.
He joined in July 1917, and was posted to H.M. Minesweeper "John Pollard" which vessel was engaged on mine-sweeping and patrol duties off the coast of Ireland. His ship did good work and had many narrow escapes, both from mines and hostile submarines. He was discharged in September 1919, and holds the General Service and Victory Medals.
42, Ballater Road, Acre Lane, S.W.2.　　Z2359

GRIDLEY, H., Rifleman, Royal Irish Rifles.
He joined in June 1916, and proceeded to France in the following January. During his service overseas he was in action in many parts of the line, fighting at Arras, Vimy Ridge, Bullecourt and Messines. He gave his life for King and Country on June 7th, 1917, and was entitled to the General Service and Victory Medals.
"He joined the great white company of valiant souls."
15, Cross Street, Clapham, S.W.4.　　Z2360

GRIEVE, J. F., Rifleman, King's Royal Rifle Corps and Air Mechanic, R.A.F.

He joined in December 1916, and two months later proceeded to France, where he was in action in many important battles, including those of the Somme and Messines, and was badly gassed. Returning to England, he received medical treatment, and on recovery was transferred to the Royal Air Force and served at various aerodromes in England until demobilised in August 1919. He holds the General Service and Victory Medals.

15, Hubert Grove, Landor Road, S.W.9.　　Z2361

GRIFFIN, G. H., Sergt.-Major, 10th Middlesex Regt.

Volunteering in August 1914, he was stationed at various depôts until drafted to the Western Front. He fought in many engagements in France and Flanders, and was in action throughout the German Offensive, and the opening operations of the subsequent Allied Advance of 1918, and was wounded. He returned to England, and was discharged on account of service in October 1918, and holds the General Service and Victory Medals.

1, Beryl Road, Hammersmith, W.6.　　12784B

GRIFFIN, G. T., Corporal, R.E.

Volunteering in June 1915, he was sent to the Western Front later in the same year, and was in action in many parts of the line, and did very good work. He was unfortunately killed in action in the Battle of Arras on July 1st, 1916, and was entitled to the 1914-15 Star, and the General Service and Victory Medals.

"Courage, bright hopes, and a myriad dreams, splendidly given."

37, Banim Street, Hammersmith, W.6.　　11112B

GRIFFIN, G. W., Private, 2/4th Queen's (Royal West Surrey Regiment).

He joined in June 1918, on attaining military age, after having previously done excellent work for three years at Woolwich Arsenal. At the conclusion of his training he served at various stations with his Battalion until after the cessation of hostilities, when he was drafted to Germany with the Army of Occupation. He returned to England and was demobilised in March 1920.

43, Blake's Road, Peckham Grove, S.E.15.　　Z5966

GRIFFIN, J. W., Private, 5th (Royal Irish) Lancers.

Volunteering in August 1914, he proceeded to France in the following year, and fought at the Battles of the Somme, Arras, and those in the Ypres salient. He gave his life for the freedom of England in the Battle of Cambrai on October 29th, 1917, and was entitled to the 1914-15 Star, and the General Service and Victory Medals.

"A valiant soldier, with undaunted heart he breasted Life's last hill."

37, Banim Street, Hammersmith, W.6.　　11112A

GRIFFIN, M. L. (Miss), Special War Worker.

This lady gave up her post to serve her Country and for two years was employed at Messrs. Gwynne's Works, Chiswick, engaged on important duties in connection with the manufacture of aeroplane parts. She rendered valuable services, and gave complete satisfaction throughout.

37, Banim Road, Hammersmith, W.6.　　11112C

GRIFFIN, T. J., Private, 1st Oxfordshire and Buckinghamshire Light Infantry.

Volunteering in February 1916, he was drafted to France in the following year, and saw much fighting in the Ypres salient, and in other parts of the line. In 1917, transferred to Italy, he was in action on the Asiago Plateau and was wounded. On recovery, he returned to the front lines, and fought in the final Allied Advance on the Piave. He returned to England, and was demobilised in March 1919, and holds the General Service and Victory Medals.

6, Westmacott Street, Camberwell, S.E.5.　　Z3458

GRIFFITH, R. S., Driver, R.F.A.

Volunteering in January 1915, he embarked in the following September for the Dardanelles, where he took part in many operations until the Evacuation of the Peninsula. He after served in Egypt and Mesopotamia, where he was engaged in heavy fighting, resulting in the relief of Kut-el-Amara. In 1917 he was invalided to India and later to England, being discharged as medically unfit for further service in September 1918. He holds the 1914-15 Star, and the General Service and Victory Medals.

201, Neate Street, Camberwell, S.E.5.　　Z5408A

GRIFFITHS, A., Private, Royal Inniskilling Fusiliers.

He joined in 1916, and later in that year proceeded to the Western Front, where he fought in many important engagements. He was wounded and taken prisoner on the Somme, and held in captivity in Bavaria until the cessation of hostilities. Repatriated, he was demobilised in 1919, and holds the General Service and Victory Medals.

27, Wilcox Road, Wandsworth Road, S.W.8.　　Z2368

GRIFFITHS, E. W., Private, 10th (Prince of Wales' Own Royal) Hussars.

He volunteered in 1914, and later in the same year embarked for the Western Front. During his service overseas he fought in many parts of the line, and was wounded in the Ypres salient. On recovery he rejoined his Squadron and was in action throughout the Retreat and Advance of 1918. He was demobilised after the Armistice, and holds the 1914-15 Star, and the General Service and Victory Medals.

1, Yeldham Building, Yeldham Road, Hammersmith, W.6.　　12808B

GRIFFITHS, E. J., Sergt., R.A.F.

He volunteered in November 1915, and, sent to France two months later, was stationed at the aerodrome at Pont de Larche, Rouen, in charge of the workshops and stores. He rendered valuable services, and after the cessation of hostilities returned to England. He was demobilised in September 1919, and holds the General Service and Victory Medals.

31, Larcom Street, Walworth, S.E.17.　　Z2363A

GRIFFITHS, F. S., Private, 24th London Regiment (The Queen's).

Volunteering in 1914, he was drafted to the Western Front in the following year, and was in action at the Battles of Ypres, Arras and the Somme. He was severely wounded at High Wood, and returning to England, received hospital treatment, and was ultimately invalided out of the Service in 1916. He holds the 1914-15 Star, and the General Service and Victory Medals.

102, Wilcox Road, Wandsworth Road, S.W.8.　　Z2364

GRIFFITHS, G., Private, 1/24th London Regiment (The Queen's).

He volunteered in May 1915, and embarked for the Western Front later in that year. He was in action in the Ypres salient and the Somme, and was wounded at Loos. Admitted into hospital he received medical treatment, and on recovery returned to the front lines, and fought at Arras, and throughout the German Offensive and Allied Advance of 1918. He was demobilised in February 1919, and holds the 1914-15 Star, and the General Service and Victory Medals.

2, Longhope Place, Monkton Street, Kennington, S.E.11.　　Z26897

GRIFFITHS, J., Gunner, Royal Marine Artillery.

He enlisted in 1901, and was mobilised at the outbreak of hostilities. He landed with the Royal Marines at Ostend on August 27th, 1914, and was stationed there until the following October. He was then sent to Dunkirk, where he served for a time, and in March 1915 proceeded to Egypt, and saw much service there. A year later he was drafted to the Western Front, and was in action on the Somme and in other parts of the line. He joined the Grand Fleet in June 1917, and remained afloat until April 1919. He was still serving in 1920, and holds the 1914 Star, and the General Service and Victory Medals.

14, Currie Road, Battersea, S.W.11.　　Z2366

GRIFFITHS, J., Private, R.A.S.C. (M.T.)

A Reservist, he was mobilised and drafted to France at the outbreak of war, and was engaged on important transport duties during the Retreat from Mons, and the Battles of the Aisne, the Marne, and Ypres (I and II). He was mentioned in Despatches on October 14th, 1914, for devotion to duty in the Field in assisting to defend a position of strategical importance until his Brigade arrived, and whilst on guard duty at Bailleul on November 22nd, 1914, he captured four spies. Owing to ill-health he was invalided to England and subsequently discharged unfit for further service in February 1916. He holds the Mons Star, and the General Service and Victory Medals.

18, Avondale Square, Old Kent Road, S.E.1.　　Z27190

GRIFFITHS, M. (Mrs.), Worker, Q.M.A.A.C.

She joined in August 1917, and was drafted to France in the following January. Stationed at Pont de l'Arche, she was engaged on important duties connected with the repair of aero-engines. She rendered valuable services, and returning to England was demobilised in January 1919, and holds the General Service and Victory Medals.

31, Larcom Street, Walworth, S.E.17.　　Z2363B

GRIFFITHS, S., Corporal, R.F.A.

Volunteering in September 1914, he was drafted to the Western Front in the following year, and was in action at the Battles of Ypres, the Somme, Cambrai and in many other engagements. Transferred to the Balkan theatre of war in 1916, he fought in operations on the Doiran front, and contracting malaria was invalided to hospital in Malta and later to England. He received medical treatment, and on recovery was posted to the Labour Corps, with which unit he served at Woolwich until demobilised in February 1919. He holds the 1914-15 Star, and the General Service and Victory Medals.

20, Montefiore Street, Wandsworth Road, S.W.8.　　Z2365

GRIFFITHS, W. B., Signalman, Royal Navy.

He joined the Service in November 1916, and completing his training served with the Grand Fleet in the North Sea, and later in the Mediterranean and Baltic Seas. His ship rendered valuable services engaged on submarine patrol and other important duties, and frequently had to pass through mine-infested areas. During the war he served in H.M.S. "Queen Elizabeth," H.M.S. "Warspite," H.M.S. "Powerful," H.M.S. "Impregnable," H.M.S. "Ganges" and H.M.S. "Egmont." He was demobilised in November 1919, and holds the General Service and Victory Medals.
10, St. Alphonsus Road, Clapham, S.W.4. Z2367A

GRIFFITHS, W. F., Rifleman, 8th London Regt. (Post Office Rifles) and Rifle Brigade.

Joining in November 1916, he completed his training and served at various depôts with his Battalion on garrison and other important duties. In 1918 he embarked for France and fought in many important engagements during the Retreat and Allied Advance of 1918. He gave his life for King and Country on the Somme early in August 1918, and was entitled to the General Service and Victory Medals.
"Whilst we remember, the Sacrifice is not in vain."
10, St. Alphonsus Road, Clapham, S.W.4. Z2367B

GRIGG, F. W., Sergt., Northamptonshire Regiment.

He volunteered in October 1914, and in the following year was drafted to Egypt. In this theatre of war he served in many engagements, and later was transferred to the Balkan front, where he saw much fighting and remained until the cessation of hostilities. He returned home and was demobilised in March 1919. He had previously seen service during the South African campaign, and holds the King's Medal, the 1914-15 Star, and the General Service and Victory Medals.
45, Wyndham Road, Camberwell, S.E.5. Z2362

GRIGG, L. (Miss), Special War Worker.

This lady volunteered for work of National importance and was engaged for twelve months at Messrs. Llewellyn and Dents' Works, Shepherd's Bush, in the manufacture of carburettors. She did good work and gave complete satisfaction.
78, Rayleigh Road, W. Kennington, W.14. 12071B

GRIGG, T., Private, 7th London Regiment.

He volunteered in February 1915, and on the completion of his training was in the following year drafted to the Western Front. He fought in many sectors until the end of the war, and took an important part in the Battles of Ypres and Cambrai. He returned home and was demobilised in 1919, holding the General Service and Victory Medals.
78, Rayleigh Road, W. Kennington, W.14. 12071A

GRIGG, T. G. W., C.Q.M.S., 12th Royal Sussex Regt.

Volunteering in August 1914, he proceeded overseas in the following March, and during his service on the Western Front was engaged on important duties in many sectors. He was in action at the Battles of Ypres, Festubert, St. Julien, Loos, Vimy Ridge, the Somme, Albert, Arras and Messines, and in the Retreat and Advance of 1918. He returned to England, and was demobilised in December of the same year, and holds the 1914-15 Star, and the General Service and Victory Medals.
1, Lewis Road East, Camberwell, S.E.5. Z6178A

GRIMES, J. W., Bombardier, R.F.A.

He volunteered in May 1915, and later in the same year was sent to the Western Front. In this theatre of war he fought in the Battles of the Somme, Ypres, Vimy Ridge, Messines, and was severely wounded at Passchendaele. He was then sent to hospital in England, and was subsequently invalided out of the Service in December 1917. He holds the 1914-15 Star, and the General Service and Victory Medals.
15, Flaxman Road, Camberwell, S.E.5. Z5968

GRIMMETT, F., Private, R.A.S.C.

He joined in March 1917, and in the following September proceeded to the Western Front. He was engaged in conveying food and munitions to the front line at Ypres, and Cambrai, and did valuable service. He was incapacitated from duty for four months owing to illness, but after rejoining his unit served until demobilised in September 1919. He holds the General Service and Victory Medals.
8, Smyrks Road, Walworth, S.E.17. Z2369

GRIMMOND, J. E., L/Cpl., King's Royal Rifle Corps.

He joined in 1916, and on the completion of his training was in the same year sent to the Western Front. He was in action in several important engagements, including the Battles of Ypres, the Somme, and Arras. and was taken prisoner near Cambrai in 1918. During his ten months' captivity in Germany he worked in an iron foundry. After his release he was demobilised in 1919, and holds the General Service and Victory Medals.
11, Wesley Place, Newington Butts, S.E.11. 26168

GRIMSHAW, W., P.O., R.N.A.S. and Sergt., M.M.G.C.

He volunteered in March 1915, and in the same year was sent to France, where he was engaged on special duties at the Base for eight months. He was then transferred to Russia, and served for this period under Commander Locker-Lampson. After much excellent work along the Baltic and at Archangel he was transferred to the Motor Machine Gun Corps, and drafted to Mesopotamia, where he rendered valuable services for eighteen months. He returned home in consequence of eye trouble and was demobilised in June 1919, holding the 1914-15 Star, the General Service and Victory Medals, and a Russian Decoration.
27, Arlesford Road, Landor Road, S.W.9. Z2370

GRIMSTER, J. H., Private, R.A.S.C. (M.T.)

He volunteered in November 1914, and after completing his training at Grove Park and Woolwich proceeded to France, where he rendered valuable services in connection with many important engagements until hostilities ceased, including those at Ypres and the Somme. He returned home and was demobilised in September 1919, holding the 1914-15 Star, and the General Service and Victory Medals.
97, Ingrave Street, Battersea, S.W.11. Z2371

GRIMWOOD, A. E., Private, 11th Queen's (Royal West Surrey Regiment).

He volunteered in 1915, and after the completion of his training was in the following year on the Western Front. He saw much fighting on the Somme, and in 1917 was transferred to Italy, where he took part in many important operations until the cessation of hostilities. He was then sent with the Army of Occupation to Germany, and on returning home was demobilised in 1919. He holds the General Service and Victory Medals.
49, Edithna Street, Landor Road, S.W.9. Z2372

GRIST, J., Sergt., Loyal North Lancashire Regt.

Having previously served in the Army for twenty two years, he re-enlisted in October 1914, and in 1915 was sent to France. He took an important part in many engagements, and died gloriously on the field of Battle in 1915. He was entitled to the 1914-15 Star, and the General Service and Victory Medals.
"His memory is cherished with pride."
8, Barmore Street, Battersea, S.W.11. Z2374

GRIST, J. A., Private, 10th Queen's (Royal West Surrey Regiment).

He volunteered in September 1915, and was going through his course of training at Battersea, when his health broke down. He was in consequence discharged in the following November as medically unfit for further military service.
112, Stewart's Road, Battersea Park Road, S.W.8. Z2373

GRISTWOOD, J. W., Shoeing-Smith, Surrey Lancers (Queen Mary's Own).

He volunteered in September 1914, and in the following year was drafted to Egypt, where he saw much fighting at the Battle of Mersa Matruh. Afterwards he was transferred to the Western Front and was engaged in many important operations, including those at the Somme, Ypres and Vimy Ridge. After being invalided home owing to serious illness, he was discharged as physically unfit for further service in December 1917. He holds the 1914-15 Star, and the General Service and Victory Medals.
26, Goldsboro Road, Wandsworth Road, S.W.8. Z2375

GRITZMAN, S., Private, Labour Corps.

He joined in June 1918, and two months later was drafted to the Western Front. He was engaged on important duties with his unit, and saw much fighting in the Battles of Cambrai and Ypres in the Advance of 1918. After returning to England he was demobilised in March 1919, and holds the General Service and Victory Medals.
65, Rollo Street, Battersea, S.W.11. Z2299B

GROSVENOR, W. A., Rifleman, 18th London Regt. (London Irish Rifles).

He volunteered in 1915, and in the following year was drafted to the Western Front, where he was engaged in much severe fighting at St. Eloi and other places until the end of 1916. He was then transferred to Salonika and took part in many engagements on the Doiran front. Proceeding afterwards to Egypt, he rendered valuable service there until the cessation of hostilities. He was demobilised in July 1919, and holds the General Service and Victory Medals.
31A, Emu Road, Battersea Park, S.W.8. Z2377

GROUNSELL, E. H., Gunner, R.F.A.

He volunteered in 1915, and later in the same year was sent to the Western Front. In this theatre of war he was engaged in much heavy fighting in the Battles of Loos, the Somme and Ypres, and in the Retreat and Advance of 1918. He was demobilised in 1919, and holds the 1914-15 Star, and the General Service and Victory Medals.
37, Wyvil Road, South Lambeth, S.W.8. Z2378

GROUSE, F. T., Corporal, King's Royal Rifle Corps.
He volunteered in August 1914, and in July of the following year was drafted to France, where he took part in the Battle of the Somme, and was wounded in the third Battle of Ypres in 1917. He was invalided to England and after protracted hospital treatment rejoined his unit, but was unfortunately killed in the Battle of the Marne on July 11th, 1918. He was entitled to the 1914–15 Star, and the General Service and Victory Medals.
" A costly sacrifice upon the altar of freedom."
74, Henley Street, Battersea, S.W.11.	Z2379

GROVE, H. G., A.B., R.N., H.M.S. " Boyne " and " Canterbury."
He volunteered in September 1914, and was posted to H.M.S. " Boyne," in which ship he was engaged on patrol duties in the North Sea, and afterwards in escorting troops to and from the Dardanelles. He also served in Russian waters from September 1918. He was demobilised in April 1919, and holds the 1914–15 Star, and the General Service and Victory Medals.
98, Ferndale Road, Clapham, S.W.4.	Z2380A

GROVER, A. G. F., Driver, R.F.A.
He was mobilised from the Reserve in August 1914, and proceeded almost immediately to the Western Front. He fought in the Retreat from Mons and subsequently in the Battles of Ypres, Hill 60, Loos, the Somme and Cambrai. He was then transferred to the Italian front and took part in the heavy fighting on the Piave until the close of the war. He returned to England and was demobilised in February 1919, holding the Mons Star, and the General Service and Victory Medals.
1, Belham Street, Camberwell, S.E.5.	Z2381

GROVES, C., Private, South Wales Borderers.
Volunteering in November 1914, he embarked for the Western Front in the following year, and fought in many engagements of note, including those at Ypres, the Somme, Bullecourt, Arras and Richebourg, and was wounded. Rejoining his Battalion after recovery, he was in action at Armentières, and was again badly wounded at Messines, He was admitted into hospital, where it was found necessary to amputate his left arm, and returning to England was subsequently invalided out of the Service in March 1919. He holds the 1914–15 Star, and the General Service and Victory Medals.
8, Hilmer Street, West Kensington, W.14.	16922B

GROVES, J. W., Corporal, R.A.S.C.
Volunteering at the outbreak of war, he was drafted to France almost immediately. He served with his unit on important duties during the Retreat from Mons and the Battles of La Bassée, Ypres, Festubert and Arras, and was constantly under shell-fire. He afterwards served on Headquarter Staff until demobilised in March 1919. He holds the Mons Star, and the General Service and Victory Medals.
49, Copeland Road, Peckham Rye, S.E.15.	Z5770

GRUBB, F. J., Rifleman, 8th London Regt. (Post Office Rifles) and Pte., Queen's (Royal West Surrey Regiment).
He volunteered in September 1914, and was sent to France in the following year. He fought at Loos, Festubert, Givenchy, the Somme and throughout the German Offensive and subsequent Allied Advance of 1918. He returned to England and was demobilised in January 1919, and holds the 1914–15 Star, and the General Service and Victory Medals.
40, Steedman Street, Walworth, S.E.17.	Z26175

GULLETT, W. J., L/Cpl., Oxfordshire and Buckinghamshire Light Infantry.
He volunteered in 1915, and was drafted to Mesopotamia later in the same year. He fought in many important engagements, including those at Amara, and Kut, and was in action almost continuously for four years. After a short stay in India he returned to England and was demobilised in 1919, holding the 1914–15 Star, and the General Service and Victory Medals.
57, Hubert Grove, Landor Road, S.W.9.	Z2382

GUNN, A. F., Driver, M.G.C.
Volunteering in May 1915, he was drafted to the Western Front in the following year, and was in action in many parts of the line, especially the Somme. In 1917 he was transferred to Italy, and after much fighting in various sectors took part in the Allied Advance there in 1918. He returned to England and was demobilised in February 1919, and holds the 1914–15 Star, and the General Service and Victory Medals.
5, Dashwood Road, Wandsworth Road, S.W.8.	Z2383

GUNN, A. J., 2nd Corporal, R.E.
Volunteering in May 1915, he embarked for France later in that year, and rendered valuable services at Vimy Ridge, the Somme, and in many engagements throughout the German Offensive and subsequent Allied Advance in 1918. He returned to England and was demobilised in July 1919, and holds the 1914–15 Star, and the General Service and Victory Medals.
6, East Surrey Grove, Peckham, S.E.15.	Z5245

GUNN, H. C., Private, R.A.S.C. (Labour Battalion).
After volunteering in April 1915, and being drafted to France in the following month, he was engaged on very important duties with his Battalion in many sectors, including the Somme, Ypres, and Amiens, and during the Retreat and Advance of 1918. Ne was demobilised in March 1919, and holds the 1914–15 Star, and the General Service and Victory Medals.
69, Dashwood Road, Wandsworth Road, S.W.8.	Z2384

GUNN, E. F., Private, 6th Queen's Own (Royal West Kent Regiment).
He volunteered in May 1915, and after completing his training was engaged on important duties at various depôts with his unit until drafted to the Western Front in January 1918. He fought in many engagements in the German Offensive, but was later taken ill and invalided to England. He unfortunately died in hospital on July 19th, 1918, and was entitled to the General Service and Victory Medals.
" And doubtless he went in splendid company."
153, East Surrey Grove, Peckham, S.E.15.	Z5085

GUNN, J., Pte., Queen's (Royal West Surrey Regt.)
He joined in August 1916, and after completing his training was engaged at various stations on important duties with his unit. He rendered valuable services, but was not successful in obtaining his transfer overseas before the cessation of hostilities, and was demobilised in February 1919.
50, Bellefields Road, Stockwell Road, S.W.9.	Z1538B

GURR, F. W. (M.M.), Cpl., 2/3rd London Regt. (Royal Fusiliers).
Volunteering in April 1915, he was sent to the Western Front shortly afterwards and took a prominent part in the Battles of Ypres, Festubert and Loos. During heavy fighting at Albert he was awarded the Military Medal for conspicuous bravery and devotion to duty in going out alone and capturing a German sniper single handed. He was later wounded in the first Battle of the Somme, and rejoining his unit on recovery fought in the Battles of Vimy Ridge, Ypres, Cambrai, the Somme (II), and Amiens. After the Armistice he was sent into Germany with the Army of Occupation, and returning home for demobilisation in February 1919 holds the 1914–15 Star, and the General Service and Victory Medals.
72, Army Street, Clapham, S.W.4.	Z2386

GUSCOTT, E., Sergt., R.A.O.C.
He volunteered in February 1915, and at the conclusion of his training was sent to France. He was there engaged on special duties as a storeman at various depôts, including Calais, Dunkirk and Dieppe, and did good work. He holds the 1914–15 Star, and the General Service and Victory Medals, and was still serving in 1920.
191, St. George's Road, Peckham, S.E.15.	Z5764

GUY, E. G., 1st Air Mechanic, R.A.F.
He joined in June 1916, and on the completion of his training proceeded to Canada in the following year, and was engaged on important instructional duties in connection with aeroplanes. He rendered valuable services in the training of recruits and returned to England for demobilisation in January 1918.
8, Epple Road, Fulham Road, S.W.6.	X20038

GYDE, W. J. B., Sergt., R.G.A.
He volunteered in November 1914, and drafted to France in March 1916, served throughout the war. During this period he was in action at Dixmude, Ypres, Passchendaele, and was awarded the Belgian Croix de Guerre for conspicuous bravery and devotion to duty in the Field whilst serving under General Rawlinson in the Dixmude sector. He also fought in the Battles of Kemmel Hill, the Marne and the Scarpe, and other engagements during the Retreat and Advance of 1918. He was demobilised in July 1919, and holds the General Servicee and Victory Medals.
53, Bedford Street, Walworth, S.E.17.	Z2387A

H

HACKER, F. G., Private, 13th London Regiment (Kensingtons).
He joined in July 1916, and in the same year was drafted to the Western Front. There he fought at Arras and Givenchy, and was again in action at the Somme and Cambrai during the Retreat and Advance of 1918. Previously to enlisting he was engaged on important duties at the National Shell Filling Factory, Nottingham, where he contracted T.N.T. poisoning, and was nine months under treatment. He was demobilised in February 1919, and holds the General Service and Victory Medals.
9, The Parade, Lambeth Walk, S.E.11.	Z25690

HACKER, W. T., Sergt., King's Royal Rifle Corps.

Mobilised in August 1914, he immediately proceeded to France, where he took part in the Retreat from Mons. He later served with distinction in other important engagements until November 1915, when he was badly wounded in action at Ypres. In consequence he was discharged in August 1916, as medically unfit for further service, and holds the Mons Star, and the General Service and Victory Medals.

10, Ewell Place, Camberwell, S.E.5. 5778B

HACKETT, C., Driver, R.A.S.C. (M.T.)

He volunteered in July 1915, and proceeded to France in the following September. He was attached to the 6th Ammunition Column, and was engaged in conveying supplies up to the line in various sectors, notably the Somme, Ypres, Festubert and Cambrai. After the Armistice he proceeded to Germany with the Army of Occupation and was stationed at Cologne. He was demobilised in June 1919, and holds the 1914-15 Star, and the General Service and Victory Medals.

11, Ulric Street, Camberwell, S.E.5. Z2388

HADDOCK, W. R., Private, R.A.M.C.

He volunteered in November 1914, and in the following year was drafted overseas, first to Mesopotamia and afterwards to Egypt. He was then sent to Salonika and subsequently to Italy. On all these fronts he served on important duties with his Corps, and did excellent work. After the Armistice he was sent to France for a short time until his demobilisation in May 1919. During his voyages the ships in which he was sailing were torpedoed three times, and as a result he suffered severely from shock. He holds the 1914-15 Star, and the General Service and Victory Medals.

29, Langton Street, Vassall Road, S.W.9. Z5086

HADDON, C., 1st Air Mechanic, R.A.F.

He joined in July 1916, and after his training proceeded overseas in the same year. He was engaged on important duties with his Squadron, and was present at various engagements in many sectors of the Western Front. In March 1919 he was demobilised and holds the General Service and Victory Medals.

49, Tabor Road, Hammersmith, W.6. 11553

HADFIELD, W., Special War Worker.

Throughout the course of the war he was engaged on work of National importance at Woolwich Arsenal. He rendered valuable services as a steel tester in connection with the manufacture of guns, and carried out all his duties with care and efficiency.

37, Kimberley Road, Peckham, S.E.15. Z6391B

HADLEY, G. W., L/Cpl., 1st Devonshire Regiment.

A serving soldier, who joined the Royal Warwickshire Regiment in March 1914, he was in 1915 drafted overseas. During his service in France he took part in numerous engagements in various sectors, and after the Armistice proceeded to Germany with the Army of Occupation and was stationed at Cologne. He was demobilised in February 1919, and holds the 1914-15 Star, and the General Service and Victory Medals.

79, Clifton Street, Wandsworth Road, S.W.8. Z2389

HADRILL, W. H. G., Gunner, R.G.A.

He joined in June 1916, and in the same year was drafted to France, where he did valuable service as a signaller in the Battles of the Somme, Arras and Ypres. He was gassed in October 1917, and invalided home until June in the following year. He was then sent to Italy, where he served up to April 1919. After returning home he was demobilised in the following August, and holds the General Service and Victory Medals.

41, Mantua Street, Battersea, S.W.11. Z2390

HAILSTONE, F., Private, R.A.M.C.

He volunteered in May 1915, and in the same year was drafted to France, where he did excellent service with his unit at Loos, Vermelles, the Somme, the Ancre, Lens, and in many engagements in the Retreat and Advance of 1918. After the Armistice he proceeded to Germany with the Army of Occupation, and was stationed at Cologne until demobilised in August 1919. He holds the 1914-15 Star, and the General Service and Victory Medals.

27, Gladstone Terrace, Battersea Park Road, S.W.8. Z2392

HAILSTON, F. W. C., Driver, R.F.A.

He volunteered in September 1914, and in the following June was drafted to France. He served in many sectors, and was severely gassed in the Battle of the Somme in 1916. As a result he was discharged as unfit for further military duty in March 1917. He holds the 1914-15 Star, and the General Service and Victory Medals.

47, Lockington Road, Battersea Park Road, S.W.8. Z2391

HAINES, A. J., Rifleman, King's Royal Rifle Corps.

He joined in May 1918, and after his training was engaged on important duties at various stations. He was unsuccessful in obtaining his transfer overseas during hostilities, but in November 1918 was sent to India, where he was still serving in 1920.

78, Blondel Street, Battersea, S.W.11. Z2622A

HAINES, A., Private, Northumberland Fusiliers.

He joined in August 1916, and after his training, served at various stations until January 1917, when he was drafted to France. Whilst overseas he fought in the third Battle of Ypres and at Passchendaele Ridge and Cambrai. He was afterwards transferred to the Labour Corps, and after the Armistice, proceeded to Germany with the Army of Occupation. He returned home and was demobilised in January 1919, and holds the General Service and Victory Medals.

78, Blondel Street, Battersea, S.W.11. Z2622B

HAINES, A. E., Rflmn., King's Royal Rifle Corps.

Volunteering in May 1915, he was drafted to France in the following March. During his service on the Western Front he took part in much severe fighting, and was buried by a shell explosion. He died gloriously on the Field of Battle in 1916, and was entitled to the General Service and Victory Medals.

" A costly sacrifice upon the altar of freedom."

2, I Block, Victoria Dwellings, Battersea Park Road, S.W.8. Z2393

HAINES, E., Private, 24th London Regt. (Queen's).

He volunteered in August 1914, and in the following year was drafted to Egypt, and afterwards to Palestine, where he served in many engagements, and was present at the Fall of Jerusalem. He was wounded in the East, and on recovery was drafted to France. Whilst in this theatre of war he fought on the Somme, and was severely wounded in September 1918, near Cambrai. After treatment in France and Scotland he was demobilised in February 1919, and holds the 1914-15 Star, and the General Service and Victory Medals.

46, Neville Street, Vauxhall, S.E.11. Z25441

HAINES, F. J., Corporal, 9th London Regiment (Queen Victoria's Rifles).

He volunteered in May 1915, and in the following year was drafted to France. He was in action at the Somme, Ypres and Cambrai, and was severely gassed. He was invalided home and after his recovery was stationed at Blackdown Camp until February 1919, when he was demobilised. He holds the General Service and Victory Medals.

6, The Grove, South Lambeth Road, S.W.8. Z2395

HAINES, W., A.B., R.N., H.M.S. "Sutley," "Cyclops" and "Grange."

He was mobilised in August 1914, and was sent to the North Sea, where he was engaged on important patrol and convoy duties. He was also engaged in similar work in the Mediterranean Sea and off the coasts of Belgium. During the war he was posted to H.M.S. "King Lear," a mystery ship, acting as a submarine decoy, and was also present at Scapa Flow at the surrender of the German Fleet. He was discharged in January 1919, and holds the 1914-15 Star, and the General Service and Victory Medals.

10, Ingleton Street, Brixton Road, S.W.9. Z2394

HAINES, W., Private, Bedfordshire Regiment and Air Mechanic, R.A.F.

He volunteered in October 1914, and in the following year was drafted to France, where he fought at St. Eloi, Hill 60, Ypres, and was severely wounded. After his recovery he again took part in many engagements, and did good service until the cessation of hostilities. In February 1919 he was demobilised and holds the 1914-15 Star, and the General Service and Victory Medals.

25, Kingswood Road, Chiswick, W.4. 6799

HALE, E., Sergt., Royal Fusiliers.

He volunteered in 1914, and after completing his training, was sent to German West Africa. In this theatre of war he saw much service, and unfortunately contracted fever, from which he died in 1917. He was entitled to the General Service and Victory Medals.

" Whilst we remember, the Sacrifice is not in vain."

30, Mundella Road, Wandsworth Road, S.W.8. Z2398B

HALE, E., Private, 8th Middlesex Regiment.

He volunteered in August 1914, and early in the following year was drafted to France. There he took part in the Battles of Neuve Chapelle, Hill 60, Ypres and Loos, and later in the Somme engagements. He fell fighting near Ypres on February 27th, 1918, and was entitled to the 1914-15 Star, and the General Service and Victory Medals.

" A valiant soldier, with undaunted heart he breasted
Life's last hill."

84, Ascalon Street, Battersea Park Road, S.W.8. Z2397B

HALE, E. C., Gunner, R.G.A. (Anti-Aircraft).

He volunteered in August 1914, and after serving on important duties at home was drafted to France in May 1916. He was in action at Ploegsteert Wood, Vimy Ridge, the Somme, Beaumont-Hamel, Arras, Bullecourt, Ypres, Cambrai, Amiens, Havrincourt, and was also present at the entry into Mons on Armistice Day. He was demobilised in February 1919, and holds the General Service and Victory Medals.

5, Glendall Street, Ferndale Road, S.W.9. Z2396

HALE, J., Private, 23rd London Regiment.

He was mobilised at the outbreak of war, and was almost immediately drafted overseas. He gave his life for the freedom of England in the Retreat from Mons, and was entitled to the Mons Star, and the General Service and Victory Medals.

" His life for his Country, his Soul to God."

30, Mundella Road, Wadnsworth Road, S.W.8. Z2398A

HALE, J. W., Special War Worker.

Being under age for military service, he volunteered for work of National importance, and was engaged at the National Projectile Company's Works in the production of 6-inch shells. Just before the Armistice he was called up for military duty, but owing to the conclusion of hostilities he was soon demobilised.

84, Ascalon Street, Battersea Park Road, S.W.8. Z2397A

HALE, W. E., Driver, R.F.A.

He volunteered in April 1915, and in the same year was drafted to France. During his service on the Western Front he did good work as a driver for his Battery at the Somme, Beaumont-Hamel, Arras, Bullecourt, Ypres, Passchendaele, St. Quentin, Bapaume, Le Cateau and many other engagements until the cessation of hostilities. He was demobilised in May 1919, and holds the 1914–15 Star, and the General Service and Victory Medals.

38, Park Place, Clapham Park Road, S.W.4. Z2399

HALES, C. S. S. (D.S.M.), C.P.O., R.N., H.M.S. "Calliope."

A serving sailor, he was sent to the North Sea at the outbreak of war, and in 1915 took part in the Dardanelles expedition. He won the Distinguished Service Medal in this campaign for his bravery and devotion to duty in cutting mines from under the ship. He also served off the coasts of Italy and France, and took part in various engagements in the North Sea, including the Battle of Jutland. He holds, in addition to the Distinguished Service Medal, the 1914–15 Star, the General Service and Victory Medals, the Life Saving Medal and an Italian Decoration. In 1920 he was still serving.

265, Mayall Road, Herne Hill, S.E.24. Z2400

HALES, H. J., Private, 7th Royal Fusiliers.

He joined in February 1918, and in the following July was drafted to France, where he fought in the Albert and Arras sectors, and was twice severely wounded and taken prisoner. In Germany he was in hospital at Minden until after the Armistice, when he was repatriated. He was demobilised in August 1919, and holds the General Service and Victory Medals.

7, Walcorde Avenue, Walworth, S.E.17. 2402

HALES, R., Corporal, 2nd Dorsetshire Regiment.

A serving soldier since May 1910, he proceeded to Mesopotamia in 1914, and served in many important engagements, including those of Amara, Kut-el-Amara, Sanna-i-Yat, the Relief of Kut, and the capture of Baghdad. In 1917 he was sent to Egypt, and in the Advance with General Allenby's Forces through Palestine fought at Gaza and was present at the entry into Jerusalem and the fall of Damascus. He returned home and was demobilised in August 1919, holding the 1914–15 Star, and the General Service and Victory Medals.

8, D'Eynsford Road, Camberwell Green, S.E.5. Z2401

HALEY, T., Private, R.A.V.C.

He volunteered in August 1914, and on the completion of his training proceeded to France in the following November. He rendered valuable service in many sectors, especially round Neuve Chapelle and St. Eloi, and was subsequently transferred to Mesopotamia, where he was engaged on important duties with his unit until the Armistice. After his return home he served in Ireland until his demobilisation in September 1919. He holds the 1914 Star, and the General Service and Victory Medals.

19, Redan Terrace, Camberwell, S.E.5. Z6186

HALFACRE, F. W., Rifleman, 21st London Regt. (1st Surrey Rifles).

He volunteered in November 1915, and in January of the following year was drafted to the Western Front, where he was in action at Vimy Ridge. Afterwards he proceeded to Salonika and served on the Vardar and Struma fronts, before going thence to Egypt. He took part with General Allenby's forces in the Advance into Palestine and was present at the Entry into Jerusalem. In April 1919 he returned home and was demobilised, holding the General Service and Victory Medals.

45, Dalyell Road, Landor Road, S.W.9. Z2403

HALFORD, W. H., Sapper, R.E.

He volunteered in April 1915, and after his training was retained at various stations on important duties in connection with the fixing of searchlights. He rendered valuable services but was unable to obtain his transfer overseas owing to being over age. In February 1919 he was demobilised.

13, Stainforth Road, Battersea, S.W.11. Z2404

HALL, C., Private, Royal Fusiliers.

Volunteering in February 1915, he was drafted on the completion of his training to the Western Front, and was in action at St. Eloi, Loos, Ploegsteert Wood, and Vimy Ridge, and was wounded twice. On July 16th, 1916, he died gloriously on the Field of Battle on the Somme, and was entitled to the 1914–15 Star, and the General Service and Victory Medals.

" The path of duty was the way to glory."

62, St. Andrew's Street, Wandsworth, S.W.8. Z2406

HALL, C. P., Corporal, R.G.A.

He volunteered in September 1914, and after completing his training was drafted to the Western Front, where he was in action at Ypres and in other sectors. In 1915, he proceeded to Salonika and took part in the Balkan campaign, during which he contracted fever and was invalided home. After receiving hospital treatment he was discharged in 1918, as medically unfit for further duty. He holds the 1914 Star, and the General Service and Victory Medals.

5A, Willowbrook Road, Peckham, S.E.15. Z4461

HALL, C. P. (M.M.), Corporal, Rifle Brigade.

Volunteering in August 1914, he was drafted to France on the completion of his training and was in action in many sectors. He was wounded three times. He was twice mentioned in Despatches for gallantry, and was awarded the Military Medal for conspicuous bravery in the Field. In March 1920 he was demobilised, holding in addition to the Military Medal, the 1914–15 Star, and the General Service and Victory Medals.

89, Brackenbury Road, Hammersmith, W.6. 10723

HALL, D., Private, 23rd London Regiment.

Mobilised in August 1914, he proceeded in the following year to France. He fought in many battles, including those of Neuve Chapelle, Givenchy, and the Somme, and was wounded three times. On recovery he returned to the line and fought till the end. In January 1919 he returned home and was demobilised, holding the 1914–15 Star, and the General Service and Victory Medals.

169, Lavender Road, Battersea, S.W.11. Z2407

HALL, D. C. W., Gunner, R.H.A.

He joined in May 1916, and after completing his training proceeded to France and took part in much severe fighting at the Somme, Arras, Cambrai, and in many later battles. On the conclusion of hostilities he was drafted to Germany with the Army of Occupation and served there until demobilised in September 1919. He holds the General Service and Victory Medals.

263, Beresford Street, Camberwell, S.E.5. Z2408B
Z2409B. Z2410B

HALL, E. E., Driver, R.A.S.C. (M.T.)

Volunteering in May 1915, he proceeded to the Western Front four months later and rendered valuable services whilst engaged on important transport duties in the forward areas. He took an active part in engagements on the Somme and during the Retreat and Advance of 1918. Demobilised in January 1919, he holds the 1914–15 Star, and the General Service and Victory Medals.

7, Ewell Place, Camberwell, S.E.5. Z5779

HALL, E. J., Rflmn., 21st London Regt. (1st Surrey Rifles).

Volunteering in July 1915, he proceeded in the following October to the Western Front. There he took part in many engagements, including those at Loos and Vimy Ridge, where he was wounded. On his recovery he returned to the fighting area, but was again wounded at Messines, and sent home. Later he served in Ireland until February 1919, when he was demobilised, hodling the 1914–15 Star, and the General Service and Victory Medals.

10, Charleston Street, Walworth, S.E.17. Z2411A

HALL, E. R., Driver, R.F.A.

He volunteered in February 1915, and in November of the same year embarked for France. Whilst there he fought in many battles, including those of Vimy Ridge, the Somme, Arras, Ypres, Passchendaele, Cambrai, and others until the signing of the Armistice. In January 1919 he was demobilised and holds the 1914–15 Star, and the General Service and Victory Medals.

183, Cator Street, Peckham, S.E.15. Z5087

HALL, E. W., Private, 6th Bn. Royal Fusiliers.

Mobilised on the outbreak of war he was almost immediately drafted to France. He fought in the Retreat from Mons, and the Battles of the Marne, and the Aisne. He was unfortunately killed in action on October 18th, 1914, and was entitled to the Mons Star, and the General Service and Victory Medals.

" Great deeds cannot die."

37, Gwynne Road, Battersea, S.W.11. Z2412

HALL, F., Sergt., Lancashire Fusiliers.

Mobilised on the outbreak of war he at once proceeded to France and fought at Mons, the Marne, and the Aisne, and was wounded. He was invalided to hospital, but on recovery returned to his unit, and after serving at Ypres and Arras was again wounded at Cambrai. He was then sent home and was discharged as medically unfit in February 1918. He holds the Mons Star, and the General Service and Victory Medals.

57, Wellington Road, Stockwell, S.W.9. Z1747B

HALL, F. N., Boatswain, Mercantile Marine.

Throughout the war he served in s.s. " Corinthian " on important transport duties. He was engaged in bringing troops from Canada, and in conveying them to and from France. In 1919 he was demobilised, holding the General Service and the Mercantile Marine War Medals.

9, Medwin Street, Ferndale Road, S.W.4. Z2413

HALL, F. T., Electrical Artificer, R.N.

He volunteered in August 1914, and during the war served on board H.M.S. " King George " and " Blenheim." He was in action in the engagements at the Falklands and at Dogger Bank, and in the Battle of Jutland, and was also engaged on important duties in the North Sea, and off the coasts of Egypt, Malta, Italy and Salonika. On one occasion whilst the guns were being prepared for action he was injured. He holds the 1914-15 Star, and the General Service and Victory Medals, and in 1920 was still serving.

83, Tyneham Road, Lavender Hill, S.W.11. Z2414

HALL, G., A.B., Royal Navy.

He volunteered in March 1915, and was later posted to H.M.S. " Duke of Edinburgh." While in this vessel he took part in the Battle of Jutland, and in several minor engagements. He also served in H.M.S. " Canada " and was engaged in convoy and other important duties in the Atlantic and the North Sea. In September 1919 he was demobilised, holding the 1914-15 Star, and the General Service and Victory Medals.

31, Stanton Street, Peckham, S.E.15. Z5253

HALL, H. A., Private, 10th Middlesex Regt. and 22nd London Regiment (The Queen's).

He volunteered in August 1914, and in the following year proceeded to Gallipoli, where he took part in the landing at Suvla Bay and was wounded. Later he was sent to Egypt, and afterwards served in the Advance through Palestine. He was present in the Battle of Gaza, and at the entry into Jerusalem, and was again wounded. He holds the 1914-15 Star, and the General Service and Victory Medals, and was demobilised in May 1919.

43, Nasmyth Street, Hammersmith, W.6. 11228

HALL, J., Private, R.F.C. and Sherwood Foresters.

Volunteering in June 1915, he proceeded in the following November to the Western Front. There he took part in many notable engagements until hostilities ceased, including those at Albert, the Somme, Vimy Ridge, and St. Quentin. In February 1919 he returned home and was demobilised, holding the 1914-15 Star, and the General Service and Victory Medals.

51, Clovelly Road, Chiswick, W.4. 6372

HALL, J., Private, 2nd East Surrey Regiment.

Volunteering in 1915, he proceeded on the completion of his training to the Western Front. Whilst in this theatre of war he fought in many notable battles until fighting ceased, including that at Armentières. He returned home and was demobilised in March 1919, and holds the General Service and Victory Medals.

75, Darien Road, Battersea, S.W.11. Z2415

HALL, J. F., Private, 3rd London Regt. (Royal Fusiliers).

He joined in April 1917, and after having completed his training was drafted to France in June. He was killed in action on August 13th, 1917, after only six weeks' active service. He was entitled to the General Service and Victory Medals.

" He died the noblest death a man may die,
Fighting for God and right and liberty,"

9, Warrior Road, Camberwell, S.E.5. Z2416

HALL, R., Pte., Royal Fusiliers and R.A.S.C. (M.T.)

He volunteered in December 1914, and after his training was retained for some time on important defence duties with his unit. Later he was drafted to France with the R.A.S.C., and with them was engaged in conveying supplies and ammunition from the Base to the various fighting areas until the conclusion of hostilities. He was demobilised in June 1919, holding the General Service and Victory Medals.

16, Aldbridge Street, Walworth, S.E.17. Z2417

HALL, R. G., Private, Royal Fusiliers.

He joined in January 1918, and after his training was drafted in the same year to the Western Front. There he took part in the fighting at Cambrai, and after being wounded in August, was invalided to England. After being in hospital for a considerable time he was discharged in February 1919, holding the General Service and Victory Medals.

263, Beresford Street, Camberwell, S.E.5. Z2408A
Z2409A. Z2410A

HALL, R. R. P., L/Corporal, R.A.M.C.

Volunteering in September 1915, he was drafted on the completion of his training to the Western Front. There he did valuable work with his unit in many important battles until the conclusion of hostilities, and was wounded. In February 1919 he was demobilised after his return home, and holds the General Service and Victory Medals.

5, Benbow Road, Hammersmith, W.6. 10568

HALL, R. S. (M.M.), Private, R.A.M.C.

Volunteering in February 1915, he proceeded overseas in the same year, and did excellent service in many sectors of the Western Front. He was present at the Battles of the Somme, Ypres, Arras, St. Quentin, Armentières, Amiens, Bapaume, Béthune and many others, and was gassed. He was awarded the Military Medal for conspicuous bravery at Cambrai in bringing in the wounded under heavy shell fire. In addition, he holds the 1914-15 Star, and the General Service and Victory Medals, and was demobilised in May 1919.

57, Pulross Road, Brixton Road, S.W.9. Z2418

HALL, T., Rifleman, King's Royal Rifle Corps.

Joining in April 1916, he proceeded in the following August to the Western Front, where he was in action at the Somme, Arras, Ypres, and was badly wounded at Passchendaele. After hospital treatment in England he was engaged on his recovery on important home duties until demobilised in March 1919. He holds the General Service and Victory Medals.

32, Dalyell Road, Landor Road, S.W.9. Z2419

HALL, W. G., Private, M.G.C.

He joined in August 1917, and after having completed his training was drafted in December of the same year to France. Whilst there he fought in many battles in the Retreat and Advance of the Allies in 1918, including those on the Somme. He gave his life for King and Country on October 31st, 1918, and was entitled to the General Service and Victory Medals.

" A costly sacrifice on the altar of freedom."

19, Cowan Street, Camberwell, S.E.5. Z5088

HALL, W. W., Driver, R.E.

Called up from the Reserve at the outbreak of hostilities, he was quickly drafted to France, and did valuable work with his unit during the Retreat from Mons, and the Battles of the Marne and the Aisne. He also served in many of the important sectors, including those of Festubert, Neuve Chapelle, Hill 60, Loos, the Somme, Arras, Albert and Cambrai, and in the Retreat and Advance of 1918. He was demobilised in March 1919, and holds the Mons Star, and the General Service and Victory Medals.

88, Vaughan Road, Camberwell, S.E.5. Z6253

HALLS, E. A., Special War Worker.

Being under age for the Army he offered his services at the Royal Arsenal, Woolwich, and was employed on work of National importance. He was engaged as an examiner for rifle cartridges, and rendered very valuable services, carrying out his duties in a highly responsible manner.

38, Russell Street, Battersea Park Road, S.W.11. Z2426B

HALLS, J., Private, 23rd London Regiment.

He volunteered in April 1915, and was drafted to the Western Front in the following year. He took part in the Somme Offensive, and the Battles of Arras and Ypres, and also served in the Advance of 1918, during which he sustained severe shell-shock. He was invalided home and in January 1919 was discharged as medically unfit for further service. He holds the General Service and Victory Medals.

49, Bullen Street, Battersea, S.W.11. Z2421

HALLS, M., Private, 1st London Regiment (Royal Fusiliers).

He was mobilised in August 1914, and shortly afterwards was drafted to Malta. In March 1915 he was sent to the Western Front, and took part in the Battles of Hill 60, Ypres, Loos and the Somme. He died gloriously on the Field of Battle on May 3rd, 1917, and was entitled to the 1914-15 Star, and the General Service and Victory Medals.

" A valiant soldier, with undaunted heart he breasted Life's last hill."

49, Bullen Street, Battersea, S.W.11. Z2420

HALSEY, E. L. (M.S.M.), Driver, R.A.S.C. (M.T.)

He joined in April 1916, and in the same month proceeded to the Western Front. Here he was engaged on important duties conveying supplies of food and ammunition to the front lines. He continued to serve in France until 1919, when he returned home and was demobilised. He holds the Meritorious Service Medal, awarded for his consistently good work, and the General Service and Victory Medals.

49, Lintaine Grove, West Kensington, W.14. T16822C

HALSEY, F. H., Private, The Buffs (East Kent Regt.)
He joined in May 1917, and after completing his training served at various stations on important duties with his unit. He rendered valuable services, but was not successful in obtaining his transfer overseas prior to the cessation of hostilities. After the Armistice, however, he was drafted to Germany with the Army of Occupation, and served at Cologne until November 1919, when he returned to England and was demobilised.
62, Chatham Road, Wandsworth Common, S.W.11.
Z2422

HALSEY, G. F. W., Private, 23rd London Regt.
He was mobilised at the outbreak of hostilities, and proceeded to France in March 1915. He took part in the Battles of Hill 60 and Loos, and was also in action at Vimy Ridge, the Somme and Arras. He served in the Retreat and Advance of 1918, and was three times wounded. Returning to England after the cessation of hostilities he was demobilised in February 1919, holding the 1914-15 Star, and the General Service and Victory Medals.
10, Latchmere Grove, Battersea, S.W.11.
Z2423

HALSEY, G. H., Corporal, R.E.
He joined in June 1916, and after having completed his training was drafted to France, where he was engaged on important duties with his unit until after the cessation of hostilities. In February 1919 he returned to England and was demobilised, holding the General Service and Victory Medals.
49, Lintaine Grove, West Kensington, W.14.
T16822B

HALSEY, H. J., Private, M.G.C. (Cavalry).
He was called up from the Reserve on the outbreak of hostilities and was immediately drafted to the Western Front, where he took part in the Retreat from Mons and the Battle of Ypres, and numerous other engagements. In November 1917 he was seriously wounded at Cambrai, and was invalided home. On his recovery he served on important duties at various stations until March 1919, when he was demobilised. He holds the Mons Star, and the General Service and Victory Medals.
49, Lintaine Grove, West Kensington, W.14.
T16822A

HAMBLETON, E. D., Bombardier, R.M.A.
He volunteered in February 1915, and in the same year was drafted to the Western Front, where he took part in the Battles of the Somme, Beaumont-Hamel, Bullecourt, Messines and St. Quentin. After the cessation of hostilities he returned to England, and in June 1919 was demobilised, holding the 1914-15 Star, and the General Service and Victory Medals.
9A, Pope's Road, Brixton Road, S.W.9.
3469

HAMBLIN, C. R., Private, 9th Queen's (Royal West Surrey Regiment).
He joined in August 1918, and had not completed his training in time to proceed overseas prior to the cessation of hostilities. After the Armistice, however, he was drafted to Germany, and served with the Army of Occupation on the Rhine until November 1919, when he returned to England and was demobilised.
33, Southerton Road, Hammersmith, W.6.
11193

HAMES, C. W. R., Sergt., R.F.A.
He enlisted in January 1910, and proceeded to the Western Front in June 1915. He took part in numerous engagements, including those of the Somme, Armentières and Messines, and later was drafted to Italy, where he fought in the campaign against the Austrians. Afterwards returning to France, he served in the Arras and Somme sectors, and was wounded. On the cessation of hostilities he was sent to Germany with the Army of Occupation. He returned home and was demobilised in April 1919, and holds the 1914-15 Star, and the General Service and Victory Medals.
81, Hubert Grove, Landor Road, S.W.9.
Z2424

HAMILTON, R. G., Private, 1st Middlesex Regt.
He volunteered in August 1914, and in the following June was drafted to the Western Front, where he was in action at Laventie, and Béthune. In January 1916 he was invalided home and discharged suffering from bronchitis, but in May of the following year he rejoined and was sent to Ireland, where he served on important guard and police duties until June 1919, when he was demobilised, holding the 1914-15 Star, and the General Service and Victory Medals.
48, Nelson Row, High Street, Clapham, S.W.4.
Z2425

HAMILTON, V., Private, 17th Royal Fusiliers.
He volunteered in 1915, and on completing his training in the following year was drafted to France. There he saw much heavy fighting at Vermelles, the Somme and Ypres. He was reported missing at Cambrai in 1918, and is now presumed to have been killed in action. He was entitled to the General Service and Victory Medals.
" A costly sacrifice upon the altar of freedom."
28, Wivenhoe Road, Peckham, S.E.15.
Z5997

HAMILTON, W., Private, Queen's Own (Royal West Kent Regiment).
He volunteered in August 1914, and in the following year was drafted to the Western Front. Here he took part in numerous engagements, and gave his life for the freedom of England on May 12th, 1917. He was entitled to the 1914-15 Star, and the General Service and Victory Medals.
" Whilst we remember, the Sacrifice is not in vain."
126, Farmer's Road, Camberwell, S.E.5.
Z2427A

HAMLETT, C., Private, The Queen's (Royal West Surrey Regiment).
He joined in 1917, and in the same year was drafted to the Western Front. Here he was in action in numerous engagements and was wounded and gassed. After the cessation of hostilities he went to Germany with the Army of Occupation, with which he served until August 1919, when he returned to England, and was demobilised. He holds the General Service and Victory Medals.
66, Stewart Road, Battersea Park Road, S.W.8.
Z2428

HAMMERTON, W., Private, Hampshire Regiment.
He joined in April 1918, and was shortly afterwards drafted to Russia, where he served at Archangel and was taken prisoner by the Bolshevists. He had only been held in captivity a few weeks in Siberia, when he escaped and returned to his unit. He was demobilised in December 1919, and holds the General Service and Victory Medals.
18, Heaton Road, Peckham, S.E.15.
Z5998A

HAMMOND, A., Private, R.G.A.
He was serving at the outbreak of hostilities, and was drafted to the Western Front, where he took part in the Retreat from Mons, and the Battles of the Marne, the Aisne, Ypres and St. Eloi. He was wounded on October 16th, 1916, during the Somme Offensive, and was invalided to England. On his recovery he returned to France and served in the engagements at Arras, Passchendaele, St. Quentin, Amiens and Cambrai, and was present during the Advance of 1918. After the cessation of hostilities he returned to England, and in September 1919 was demobilised, holding the Mons Star, and the General Service and Victory Medals.
15, Crawshay Road, Stockwell, S.W.9.
Z4462B

HAMMOND, A. E., Private, Queen's (Royal West Surrey Regiment).
He volunteered in August 1914, and proceeded to the Western Front in September of the following year. He took part in the Battles of Loos and Ypres, and was severely wounded in October 1916 during the Somme Offensive. He was invalided home, but on his recovery returned to France, and was killed in the engagement on Vimy Ridge on April 15th, 1917. He was entitled to the 1914-15 Star, and the General Service and Victory Medals.
" His life for his Country."
65, Calmington Road, Camberwell, S.E.5.
Z5409

HAMMOND, A. G., Rifleman, Rifle Brigade.
He volunteered in July 1915, and in September of the following year proceeded to the Western Front, where he took part in the Somme Offensive, and was wounded and invalided home. On his recovery he returned to France and fought at the Battle of Cambrai, where he was again wounded and invalided to hospital in England. Afterwards he was discharged as medically unfit for further service in November 1918, holding the General Service and Victory Medals.
55, Atwell Road, Rye Lane, S.E.15.
Z5410

HAMMOND, A. W., Gunner, R.H.A.
He volunteered in August 1914, and was drafted to the Western Front in the following November. He took part in the Battles of Ypres, Neuve Chapelle, St. Eloi, Hill 60 and Loos, where he was wounded, and was also in action at Albert, Vermelles, Ploegsteert Wood, Vimy Ridge and the Somme, where he was again wounded, having his right leg blown off. He was invalided home, and in November 1918 was discharged as medically unfit for further service, holding the 1914 Star, and the General Service and Victory Medals.
27, Atwell Road, Rye Lane, S.E.15.
Z5411

HAMMOND, C. F. J., Driver, R.A.S.C.
He volunteered in August 1914, and was immediately drafted to the Western Front, where he took part in the Retreat from Mons, and was present at the Battles of the Somme and Ypres. He was severely wounded in June 1917, and was invalided home and in January 1918 was discharged as medically unfit for further service. He holds the Mons Star, and the General Service and Victory Medals.
57, Southerton Road, Hammersmith, W.6.
10709B

HAMMOND, T. W., Sergt.-Major, R.G.A.
He was serving at the outbreak of hostilities, and was drafted to the Western Front in 1914. He took part in the Battles of La Bassée, Ypres, Neuve Chapelle, Festubert, Hill 60, Loos, Lens and Amiens, and also served in the Advance of 1918. He holds the 1914 Star, and the General Service and Victory Medals, and was still serving in 1920.
15, Crawshay Road, Stockwell, S.W.9.
Z4462A

HAMMOND, E., Gunner, R.F.A.

He volunteered in August 1914, and after passing through his course of training was drafted to Salonika, where he did excellent service with his Battery. While on his way to hospital at Malta for treatment for malaria his vessel was torpedoed, but he was saved. After his recovery he was sent to France in 1918, and fought in many important engagements in the Retreat and Advance of that year. He was demobilised in 1919, and holds the 1914-15 Star, and the General Service and Victory Medals.

15, Kirkwood Road, Peckham, S.E.15. Z6181A

HAMMOND, H. (M.M.), Sergt., R.E.

He was mobilised in August 1914, and was immediately drafted to the Western Front, where he took part in the Retreat from Mons, and the Battles of the Marne, the Aisne, Ypres, St. Eloi, Loos and Ploegsteert Wood, and was gassed at Ypres in 1917. He was awarded the Military Medal for conspicuous gallantry at Cambrai in 1918, and also holds the Mons Star, and the General Service and Victory Medals. He was demobilised in July 1919.

21, Russell Street, Brixton Road, S.W.9. Z5251

HAMMOND, W., Rifleman, 16th Rifle Brigade.

He volunteered in May 1915, and in the following year proceeded to France, where he took part in many engagements, including those at Ypres and Cambrai. He was sent to hospital at Etaples, and whilst there, the hospital was bombed, and he was badly gassed and finally sent home. He was demobilised in September 1919, and holds the General Service and Victory Medals.

145, Gloucester Road, Peckham, S.E.15. Z5985A

HAMMOND, W., Private, 10th The Queen's (Royal West Surrey Regiment).

He volunteered in March 1915, and was for some time stationed at Aldershot. He was unable to obtain a transfer overseas, and was sent to Woolwich Arsenal on important munition work until hostilities ceased. He was demobilised in January 1919.

38, Russell Street, Battersea, S.W.11. Z2426A

HAMMOND, W. J., Special War Worker.

During the war he devoted his time to work of National importance. He first rendered valuable services at Messrs. Hooper's, where he was engaged on important work in connection with aircraft, and afterwards at Messrs. Darracq's on similar duties. Finally he accepted a responsible position at Messrs. Gordon Watney's, where his exceptional abilities proved of great value.

83, Grayshott Road, Lavender Hill, S.W.11. Z2429

HAMMOND, W. J., Corporal, 8th Rifle Brigade.

He joined in April 1916, and in the following August was drafted to the Western Front. Here he fought in the Battle of the Somme, and gave his life for the freedom of England on September 16th, 1916. He was entitled to the General Service and Victory Medals.

"Great deeds cannot die."

153, The Grove, Hammersmith, W.6. 10364

HAMPTON, H., Sapper, R.E.

He volunteered in December 1915, and in September of the following year proceeded to France, where he was engaged on special mining duties. He saw much heavy fighting on the Somme and at Arras. On April 21st, 1918, he gallantly laid down his life for King and Country at Aire-sur-Lys, and was entitled to the General Service and Victory Medals.

" He joined the great white company of valiant souls."

53, Albany Road, Camberwell, S.E.5. Z5615

HAMSHAW, A. H., 1st Class Steward, R.N., H.M.S. "P.C. 63."

He volunteered in May 1915, and during his service of over three and a half years rendered valuable services in H.M. Mystery Ships, Destroyers, and other units of the Fleet in the North Sea, Irish Sea, the Dardanelles and Mediterranean. He was demobilised in January 1919, and holds the 1914-15 Star, and the General Service and Victory Medals.

9, Cavendish Grove, South Lambeth, S.W.8. Z2430

HANBURY, W., Sergt., R.E.

Volunteering in November 1914, he crossed to France on the completion of his training and took part in the Battle of Ypres. In 1915 he was transferred to Gallipoli, where he rendered excellent service until the Evacuation. He then returned to France and served on the Somme, Ypres and Arras Fronts until the close of hostilities. He holds the 1914 Star, and the General Service and Victory Medals, and in 1920 was still serving.

98, Haselrigge Road, Clapham, S.W.4. Z2432

HANCE, E. E., Private, 24th London Regt. (Queen's).

Mobilised at the outbreak of hostilities he was at once drafted to France, and took part in the Retreat from Mons. He afterwards fought gallantly at La Bassée, Ypres, Neuve Chapelle, Loos, Vimy Ridge and the Somme. Being severely wounded he was invalided home, and after prolonged hospital treatment was discharged as medically unfit for further service in August 1918. He holds the 1914 Star, and the General Service and Victory Medals.

65, Westmoreland Road, Walworth, S.E.17. Z2433

HANCOCK, A. E., Sergt., King's Royal Rifle Corps.

Volunteering in May 1916, he proceeded to France in March of the following year. He took a prominent part in the Battle of Lens, and many later engagements, and was badly wounded in August 1918. After considerable hospital treatment he was demobilised in February 1919, and holds the General Service and Victory Medals.

37, Elmington Road, Camberwell, S.E.5. Z4451A

HANCOCK, T. J., Gunner, R.G.A.

Volunteering in March 1915, he was sent to France immediately upon completing his training. After taking part in the Battles of Ypres and Loos, he was severely wounded during the Somme Offensive in 1916, and was invalided to hospital in Manchester. On recovery, however, he rejoined his Battery in France, and in August 18th, 1917, was killed in action in the Somme sector. He was entitled to the 1914-15 Star, and the General Service and Victory Medals.

"The path of duty was the way to glory."

131, Kirkwood Road, Peckham, S.E.15. Z6251B

HAND, J. W., Rflmn., 6th London Regt. (Rifles).

He volunteered in January 1912 and proceeded to France with his unit in March 1915. He took part in many engagements of importance, including those at Festubert, Loos, Vermelles, and was invalided home in consequence of many severe wounds. In August 1916 he was discharged as unfit for further service, and holds the 1914-15 Star, and the General Service and Victory Medals.

2, Odell Street, Camberwell, S.E.5. Z5412

HANKIN, L., Private, 2nd Dorsetshire Regiment.

He volunteered in August 1915, and on the completion of his training was drafted to India, where he stayed only a few weeks before proceeding to Mesopotamia in 1916. While there he was engaged on important convoy work and entered Baghdad with the victorious troops. He afterwards took part in the Palestine campaign from Gaza to Damascus. He returned home and was demobilised in April 1919, holding the General Service and Victory Medals.

91, Cobourg Road, Camberwell, S.E.5. Z5414A

HANKIN, T., Air Mechanic, R.A.F.

He joined in February 1916, and after completing his training was engaged on important aeronautical work with his Squadron at various stations. Owing to physical disability he was unable to secure his transfer overseas while hostilities lasted, but he rendered valuable services until his demobilisation in January 1919.

54, Pulross Road, Stockwell, S.W.9. Z2434

HANKIN, W. F., Rflmn., King's Royal Rifle Corps.

Mobilised at the outbreak of war he was quickly sent to France, and fought in the Battles of Mons, the Marne, the Aisne, Ypres, St. Eloi, Hill 60, Loos, Vimy Ridge, the Somme and Passchendaele. In consequence of severe wounds in the hand he was invalided home and was discharged in February 1918. He holds the Mons Star, and the General Service and Victory Medals.

26, Clarence Street, Clapham, S.W.4. Z2435

HANKIN, W. J., Private, East Surrey Regiment.

He joined in February 1916, and proceeded to France in May. He took an active part in the Battles of Ploegsteert Wood, Vimy Ridge, and the Somme, where he was wounded. On his recovery he was drafted to Italy, and served on the Piave front. He then returned to France, where after taking part in many further engagements he was captured. After eight months' captivity he returned home and was demobilised, holding the General Service and Victory Medals.

20, Elwell Road, Clapham, S.W.4. Z2436

HANKS, J., Private, R.A.S.C.

He was mobilised with the Territorial Forces on the outbreak of war and proceeded to France in 1915. After much valuable transport work on the Somme and Ypres Fronts, he was transferred to the R.A.M.C., and was engaged on important duties on hospital trains until the end of the war. After his return home he was demobilised in May 1919, and holds the 1914-15 Star, and the General Service and Victory Medals.

51, Corunna Road, New Road, S.W.8. Z2437

HANLEY, M., Gunner, R.F.A.
He volunteered in January 1915, and in the same year crossed to France. Whilst in this theatre of war he was engaged in the fighting at Hill 60, St. Eloi, Loos, Vimy Ridge, Vermelles, Beaumont-Hamel, Arras, and Ypres, where he was so severely gassed as to necessitate his return to England. He was invalided out of the Service in December 1917, and holds the 1914-15 Star, and the General Service and Victory Medals.
40, Gordon Road, Peckham, S.E.15.   Z6247

HANLON, J., Private, 1st South Wales Borderers.
He re-enlisted in August 1914, and in the following year proceeded to the Dardanelles. After much valuable service there he was invalided home in January 1916, but on his recovery was drafted to Egypt in August. He was engaged for a time at Cairo and Alexandria, and afterwards took part in the campaign in Palestine until hostilities there ceased. After returning home he was demobilised in February 1919, and holds the 1914-15 Star, and the General Service and Victory Medals.
8, Camelia Street, Wandsworth Road, S.W.8.   Z2438

HANNAFORD, L. J., Pte., Royal Welch Fusiliers.
Volunteering in June 1915, he was drafted to France and took part in the Battles of Loos, the Somme, and Ypres, where he was severely wounded. He was invalided home in consequence, and after protracted hospital treatment was discharged in March 1919, as medically unfit for further service. He holds the 1914-15 Star, and the General Service and Victory Medals.
9A, Froude Street, Battersea Park, S.W.8.   Z2439

HANNINGTON, G., Private, 10th Middlesex Regt.
He joined in September 1916, and on the completion of his training was engaged on important coastal defence duties with his unit at various stations. He afterwards did valuable work at the Hertford School of Instruction, but was not successful in securing his transfer to a fighting area while hostilities lasted. He was demobilised in March 1919.
17, Florence Road, Chiswick, W.4.   6579B

HANNINGTON, G. P., Private, R.A.S.C. (M.T.)
He joined in April 1917, and on the completion of his training proceeded to the Western Front, where he did valuable work as a fitter at various depôts behind the lines until his service ceased. He returned home and was demobilised in December 1919, holding the General Service and Victory Medals.
17, Florence Road, Chiswick, W.4.   6579A

HANSON, A. J., Sergt., King's Royal Rifle Corps.
Joining in December 1916, he was retained on special duties in connection with the training of recruits at Wimbledon. Owing to medical unfitness he was not allowed to proceed overseas until 1918, when he was drafted to France. In this theatre of war he served with distinction at Arras, Ypres, the Somme, Amiens and Cambrai, during the Retreat and Advance of that year. He was invalided home suffering from a defective heart in 1919, and was discharged in January of the same year. He holds the General Service and Victory Medals.
23, Parkstone Road, Peckham, S.E.15.   Z5616

HANSON, D. J., Sergt., 1st East Surrey Regiment.
He enlisted in August 1907, and soon after the outbreak of the late war was drafted to the Western Front, where he took a prominent part in the Battles of the Marne, Ypres and the Somme, and many subsequent engagements until hostilities ceased, and was wounded three times. He was demobilised in February 1919, and holds the 1914 Star, and the General Service and Victory Medals.
21, Dorchester Grove, Chiswick, W.4.   5391

HANVEY, H. P., Private, Queen's (Royal West Surrey Regiment).
He joined in December 1917, and on the completion of his training was drafted to the Western Front, where he took part in many important engagements. He fell fighting in the Advance of the Allies on September 21st, 1918, and was entitled to the General Service and Victory Medals.
"His life for his Country, his Soul to God."
10, Benbow Road, Hammersmith, W.6.   10575A

HANVEY, J. R., Petty Officer, R.N.
He joined the Navy in February 1914, and during the late war rendered valuable service at the Dardanelles and in other waters on board H.M.S. "Queen Elizabeth" until hostilities ceased. He holds the 1914-15 Star, and the General Service and Victory Medals, and in 1920 was still serving.
10, Benbow Road, Hammersmith, W.6.   10575B

HANWELL, A. G., A.B., Royal Navy.
He volunteered in January 1915, and on the completion of his training was posted to H.M.S. "Hibernia." In this ship and the "Rowena" he did much valuable patrol and convoy work in the North Sea and the Indian Ocean until the cessation of hostilities. He was demobilised in May 1919, and holds the 1914-15 Star, and the General Service and Victory Medals.
114, Akerman Road, Brixton Road, S.W.9.   Z3465

HARBERT, H. F., Rifleman, 15th Rifle Brigade.
He had served through the South African War, and on the outbreak of hostilities in August 1914 re-enlisted. While stationed at Southend he became seriously ill and unfortunately died of appendicitis on January 6th, 1915.
"The path of duty was the way to glory."
17, Dowlas Street, Camberwell, S.E.5.   Z4463

HARBUTT, W. E., Gunner, R.H.A. and R.G.A.
After volunteering in April 1915, he completed his course of training, and was drafted to Mesopotamia. He served in this important theatre of war until hostilities ceased, taking part in the Relief of Kut, the capture of Baghdad and Mosul, and in many other operations on the Tigris. He was afterwards transferred to the North West Frontier of India, and was actively engaged in several skirmishes with the hill tribes. After his return home he was demobilised in October 1919, and holds the 1914-15 Star, and the General Service, Victory and India General Service Medals (with clasp, Afghanistan, N.W. Frontier, 1919).
31, Manaton Road, Peckham, S.E.15.   Z6386

HARDCASTLE, H., A.B., R.N., H.M.S. "Florida."
He was serving at the outbreak of war and immediately afterwards proceeded with the Naval Division to the Western Front, where he took part in much important fighting. After a short period in France he rejoined his ship and served in the Battle of Heligoland Bight. During this engagement his vessel was sunk and he was taken prisoner. Whilst in captivity he made two unsuccessful attempts to escape, and on being recaptured was confined in No 1 punishment camp. He was in June 1918 sent to Holland and in November to England, and was demobilised in February 1919. He holds the 1914 Star, and the General Service and Victory Medals.
48, Tate Street, Vauxhall, S.E.11.   TZ25167

HARDCASTLE, M., Cpl., 21st Battalion Canadian Overseas Forces.
Volunteering in October 1914, he crossed to the Western Front on the completion of his training and rendered valuable service there. He took an active part in the Battles of Arras, Vimy Ridge, Passchendaele and Amiens, and was gassed and wounded during his service. After much hospital treatment he was discharged in October 1919 as medically unfit for further duty, and holds the General Service and Victory Medals.
79, Akerman Road, Brixton Road, S.W.9.   Z4399A
                                               Z4400A

HARDEN, W., L/Sergt., 20th Middlesex Regiment.
He volunteered in May 1915, and proceeded to the Western Front in the following year, and took part in severe fighting. He was unfortunately killed in action whilst bombing the enemy trenches on the Somme on June 27th, 1916, and was entitled to the General Service and Victory Medals.
"A valiant soldier, with undaunted heart he breasted Life's last hill."
15, Arthur Road, Brixton Road, S.W.9.   Z4464

HARDIE, A., Private, 2nd Royal Fusiliers.
He volunteered in August 1914, and was afterwards drafted to the Dardanelles. He was later transferred to the Western Front, where he took part in many important engagements. He died gloriously on the Field of Battle on July 1st, 1916, and was entitled to the 1914-15 Star, and the General Service and Victory Medals.
"Whilst we remember, the Sacrifice is not in vain."
10, Chancellor's Road, Hammersmith, W.6.   12780A

HARDIE, P. A., Rifleman, Royal Irish Rifles.
He volunteered in August 1914, and was afterwards drafted to the Western Front and took part in severe fighting in various engagements. He was unfortunately killed in action on September 29th, 1916, and was entitled to the 1914-15 Star, and the General Service and Victory Medals.
"Nobly striving,
He nobly fell that we might live."
10, Chancellor's Road, Hammersmith, W.6.   12780B

HARDIMAN, E. M. (Mrs.), Special War Worker.
From 1917 onwards this lady was engaged as a parcel sorter for overseas and town at Victoria. Her duties ,which were of a responsible nature were carried out with great care and accuracy, and she rendered valuable services. She unfortunately had to resign her post through ill-health in 1919.
36, Emu Road, Battersea Park, S.W.8.   Z2441A

HARDIMAN, W. G., Private, 23rd London Regt.
He volunteered in October 1914, and was later transferred to the Royal Defence Corps. He was engaged at various stations on important duties with the 23rd London Regiment and other units. He also rendered valuable service in escorting prisoners fron France to England. He was discharged in August 1918 as medically unfit for further service, and holds the 1914-15 Star, and the General Service and Victory Medals.
12, Barmore Street, Battersea, S.W.11.   Z2128A
                                               Z2129A

HARDIMAN, W. J., Private, Labour Corps.
He joined in 1917, and in the same year was drafted to the Western Front, where he took part in various engagements, including that at Ypres, where he was wounded and invalided home. He was demobilised in 1919, and holds the General Service and Victory Medals.
36, Emu Road, Battersea Park, S.W.8. Z2441B

HARDIMAN, W. T., Rifleman, King's Royal Rifle Corps.
Volunteering in 1915, he was drafted to the Western Front in the same year. He took part in severe fighting on the Somme and at Arras and Ypres. He was wounded and taken prisoner in May 1917, and was held in captivity until after the Armistice. On his release he returned home and was demobilised in 1919, holding the 1914-15 Star, and the General Service and Victory Medals.
50, Barlow Street, Walworth, S.E.17. Z2440

HARDING, A. (Miss), Special War Worker.
This lady was engaged on special work at Messrs. Wilkinson's Sword Factory, Acton Vale, during the whole period of the war. Her duties, which were of a responsible nature were carried out in a highly commendable manner, and she rendered valuable services.
10, Chiswick Common Road, Chiswick, W.4. 8812B

HARDING, A. J., Rifleman, 9th London Regiment (Queen Victoria's Rifles).
He volunteered in November 1914, and in the following year was drafted to the Western Front, where he took part in numerous engagements, including those on the Somme and was severely wounded. He was demobilised in March 1919, holding the 1914-15 Star, and the General Service and Victory Medals.
23, Berrymead Gardens, Acton Green, W.4. 7065B

HARDING, G., Private, 2nd Royal Sussex Regiment.
He attested in 1915, and was called up in 1918, and was sent to France in October of the same year, and served in the Cambrai and St. Julien areas. He afterwards proceeded with the Army of Occupation to Germany, where he served until he was demobilised in September 1919. He holds the General Service and Victory Medals.
47, Verona Street, Battersea, S.W.11. Z2443

HARDING, G. E., Bombardier, R.G.A.
Joining in April 1917 he proceeded to France in the same year. He took part in severe fighting at Arras, Vimy Ridge, Bullecourt, Messines, Ypres, Passchendaele, the Somme, the Aisne and the Marne, and entered Mons with the troops at dawn on Armistice Day. He was discharged in February 1919 in consequence of his services, and holds the General Service and Victory Medals.
12, Prairie Street, Battersea Park, S.W.8. Z2442

HARDING, H., Private, R.A.S.C. (Remount Service).
He volunteered in October 1914, and was drafted to France in the same year. He was engaged at the Remount Depôt in breaking in horses and taking them up to the front lines, and was wounded. He was invalided home and discharged in January 1916, but in March 1917 he re-enlisted in the R.F.A. and later was engaged with the R.F.C., until he was discharged in August of the same year in consequence of his services. He holds the 1914-15 Star, and the General Service and Victory Medals.
18, Calmington Road, Camberwell, S.E.5. Z5415

HARDING, H. W., Private, Middlesex Regiment.
He joined in February 1917, and was drafted to France early in the following year. He took part in the Retreat and Advance of 1918, and was in action at Havrincourt, Cambrai and various other engagements. He was demobilised in November 1919, and holds the General Service and Victory Medals.
3, Shellwood Road, Battersea, S.W.11. Z2444

HARDING, J., Private, R.A.S.C.
He was mobilised in August 1914, and was sent to France shortly afterwards and served at Mons, the Marne, the Aisne, Ypres and Neuve Chapelle. He returned home in the latter part of 1915, but in 1917 proceeded to Italy and was engaged on the Piave front. He was demobilised in 1919, holding the Mons Star, and the General Service and Victory Medals.
50, Bullen Street, Battersea, S.W.11. Z2445

HARDING, J. E., Private, Middlesex Regiment.
He volunteered in August 1914, and served on important duties with his unit until the following year, when he was drafted to France, where he was engaged in various sectors and rendered valuable services. He was demobilised in March 1919, and holds the 1914-15 Star, and the General Service and Victory Medals.
94, Westmoreland Road Walworth, S.E.17. Z2457

HARDING, W., Sergt., R.A.S.C. (M.T.)
He volunteered in September 1914, and after the completion of his training was engaged on important duties as a blacksmith with his unit. He rendered valuable services, but was not successful in obtaining his transfer overseas before the cessation of hostilities. He was demobilised in February 1919.
10, Chiswick Common Road, Chiswick, W.4. 8812A

HARDY, A., Corporal, 15th London Regt. (Civil Service Rifles).
He volunteered in 1915, and after his training was drafted to the Western Front, where he took part in severe fighting on the Somme and was wounded. He was invalided home, and on his recovery was engaged at the London Record Office until he was demobilised in 1919, holding the General Service and Victory Medals.
42, Yeldham Road, Hammersmith, W.6. 12828B

HARDY, A. W., 1st Air Mechanic, R.A.F.
He joined in 1917, and after his training served at various stations on important duties with his Squadron. His work, which demanded a high degree of technical skill, was carried out with great efficiency. He rendered valuable services, but was not successful in obtaining his transfer overseas before the cessation of hostilities. He was demobilised in 1919.
42, Yeldham Road, Hammersmith, W.6. 12828C

HARDY, G., Sergt., Labour Corps.
Volunteering in August 1914, he was drafted to France in the following year. He served in various important engagements, including those on the Somme and at Arras and Ypres, and was wounded. and also took part in the Retreat and Advance of 1918. He was demobilised in February 1920, and holds the 1914-15 Star, and the General Service and Victory Medals.
45, Seaham Street, South Lambeth, S.W.8. Z2446

HARE, C. W., Leading Seaman, R.N.
He enlisted in January 1906, and at the outbreak of war in August 1914 was engaged on important patrol duties with H.M.S. " Vengeance," in the English Channel. In February 1915 he proceeded to the Dardanelles, where he took part in the Naval operations, and in August of that year was transferred to H.M.S. " Jupiter." Later he proceeded to home waters, and was engaged on convoy and submarine chasing duties. He received his discharge in February 1919, and holds the 1914-15 Star, and the General Service and Victory Medals.
87E, Albany Road, Camberwell, S.E.5. Z5774

HARE, J., Private, Royal Fusiliers.
He volunteered in February 1915, and served on important duties with his unit until March 1917, when he was drafted to the Western Front, and took part in numerous engagements. He fell fighting at Bullecourt in June 1917, and was entitled to the General Service and Victory Medals.
" His life for his Country."
1, Currie Road, Battersea, S.W.11. Z2447B

HARE, R., Corporal, 2nd East Surrey Regiment.
He was serving at the outbreak of war, and in January of the following year was sent to France, where he took part in various engagements, and was wounded, and was mentioned in Despatches for gallantry. He died gloriously on the Field of Battle at Hill 60, and was entitled to the 1914-15 Star, and the General Service and Victory Medals.
" Great deeds cannot die."
1, Currie Road, Battersea, S.W.11. Z2447A

HARE, W. E., Driver, R.F.A.
Volunteering in October 1915, he was drafted to France in June of the following year. He took part in numerous engagements, including those on the Somme and at Cambrai. He also served in the Retreat and Advance of 1918. He was demobilised in August 1919, and holds the General Service and Victory Medals.
26, St. John's Hill Grove, Battersea, S.W.11. Z2448

HARFFY, T., Private, Royal Scots.
Volunteering in August 1914, he proceeded in the following year to the Western Front, and was in action on the Somme and at Ypres, Arras and Hill 60. Shortly afterwards he was drafted to Egypt and served in the Advance to Palestine, and was present at the entry into Jerusalem. Later he returned to France, and during the fighting at Cambrai was wounded and invalided home to hospital. In March 1919 he was demobilised, holding the 1914-15 Star, and the General Service and Victory Medals.
16, Tindal Street, Lothian Road, S.W.9. Z5090

HARFIELD, J., Private, R.A.M.C.
He joined in March 1917, and in the following January was drafted to Salonika, where he was engaged on important hospital duties until the conclusion of the war. In February 1920 he was demobilised, holding the General Service and Victory Medals.
97, Beckway Street, Walworth, S.E.17. Z2449

HARGREAVES, A. R. W., Pte., 6th Middlesex Regt.
He joined in May 1917, and in the following month was drafted to France. In this theatre of war he took part in the Battles of Messines, Ypres (III), Passchendaele, Lens, Cambrai and Bapaume, and in the Retreat and Advance of 1918. After the cessation of hostilities he went into Germany with the Army of Occupation. He was demobilised in September 1919, and holds the General Service and Victory Medals.
9, Sturdy Road, Peckham, S.E.15.   Z5999

HARLE, G., Private, 2nd Border Regiment.
Volunteering in August 1914, he was drafted in the following October to the Western Front. There he took part in engagements at La Bassée, Ypres, Neuve Chapelle, St. Eloi, Festubert, Loos, Givenchy and the Somme. Later he proceeded to Italy and was in action on the Asiago Plateau and the Piave. In March 1919 he returned home and was demobilised, holding the 1914-15 Star, and the General Service and Victory Medals.
93, Beckway Street, Walworth, S.E.17.   Z2450

HARLEY, A., Corporal, M.G.C.
He volunteered in 1914, and in December of the same year was drafted to the East. He saw much heavy fighting in Mesopotamia, including the engagements of Amara, Kut, Ctesiphon, Sann-i-Yat, and at the capture of Baghdad, and occupation of Mosul. He returned home and was demobilised in January 1919, and holds the 1914-15 Star, and the General Service and Victory Medals.
42, Wivenhoe Road, Peckham, S.E.15.   Z5980

HARLEY, E., Aircraftsman, R.A.F.
He joined in July 1916, and served in the Airship Section at Wormwood Scrubbs, on important duties in connection with the construction of airships. He rendered valuable services until demobilised in February 1919.
33, Binns Road, Chiswick, W.4.   5453

HARLEY, L. C., Pte., 7th Buffs (East Kent Regt.)
He joined in September 1916, and after the completion of his training was retained on important duties with his unit until May 1918, when he crossed to the Western Front. He afterwards took part in several operation on the Somme and Amiens fronts in the Retreat of the Allies, and in July was badly wounded in the second Battle of the Marne. After considerable hospital treatment in France and England he was discharged in November 1918, as medically unfit for further service. He holds the General Service and Victory Medals.
18, Haymerle Road, Peckham, S.E.15.   Z6394

HARLOW, W. H., Rflmn., Rifle Brigade and Pte., Labour Corps.
Joining in 1917, he completed his course of training in the Isle of Sheppey and other stations, and then proceeded to France, where he took an active part in the Battle of Passchendaele and numerous other engagements of importance in the critical stages of the Retreat and Advance of 1918. After rendering much valuable service he returned home, and was demobilised in April 1919, holding the General Service and Victory Medals.
55, Commercial Road, Peckham, S.E.15.   Z6396

HARMAN, A., Driver, R.F.A., "C" Battery.
He volunteered in 1914, and after having completed his training proceeded overseas in 1916. Whilst in France he fought in many battles, including those on the Somme and at Ypres, and Arras. In 1919 he returned home and was demobilised, holding the General Service and Victory Medals.
9, Orb Street, Walworth, S.E.17.   Z2452

HARMAN, A. R., Driver, R.A.S.C. (H.T.)
He joined in May 1916, and after having completed his training served on important transport duties at various stations with his unit. He also acted as a riding master and rendered valuable services. He was not successful in obtaining his transfer overseas owing to medical unfitness, and in July 1918 was discharged.
71, Waterloo Street, Camberwell, S.E.5.   Z2451

HARMAN, R., Private, R.A.M.C.
He joined in June 1916, and shortly afterwards was sent to France, where he served in various sectors of the Front. He took an active part in the Battles of Cambrai and Ypres, and many other important engagements in this theatre of war, and rendered very valuable services until September 1919, when he was discharged. He holds the General Service and Victory Medals.
7, Denmark Road, Camberwell, S.E.5.   Z5991A

HARMER, A., Pte., 6th West Yorkshire Regiment.
Volunteering in September 1914, he was drafted overseas in the following year. Whilst in France he took part in many notable engagements, including those at Ypres, Festubert, St. Eloi, Bullecourt, Amiens and Epéhy, and after the conclusion of hostilities returned to England and in January 1919 was demobilised, holding the 1914-15 Star, and the General Service and Victory Medals.
56, St. Lawrence Road, Brixton Road, S.W.9.   Z4465

HARMER, A. W., Pte., 10th London Regt. and Rflmn., Cameronians (Scottish Rifles), and 2/13th London Regiment (Kensingtons).
He joined in July 1918, and was after a brief training drafted to the East. He saw much service as a Drummer and Bugler and was also engaged on outpost duties, whilst in Egypt. He returned home and was demobilised in April 1920.
255, Waterloo Road, Lambeth, S.E.1.   Z25071A

HARMER. C., Pte., Queen's (Royal West Surrey Regiment).
Volunteering in September 1914, he proceeded in the following February to France. Whilst in this theatre of war he was in action in many battles, including those of Loos, Vimy Ridge, the Somme, Arras, Messines, Ypres, Cambrai and the Retreat and Advance of 1918. In June 1919 he was demobilised, holding the 1914-15 Star, and the General Service and Victory Medals.
98, Aylesbury Road, Walworth, S.E.17.   Z2453

HARMER, F. A., Pte., 1st Northamptonshire Regt.
He joined in July 1917, on attaining military age, and was drafted to the Western Front in the following year. Whilst there he took part in the fighting at Delville Wood and on the Aisne, where he was taken prisoner. He was held in captivity until January 1919, and then proceeded to Ireland where he remained until September of that year, when he was demobilised. He holds the General Service and Victory Medals.
97, Inville Road, Walworth, S.E.17.   Z27313

HARMER, H. T., Pte., R.A.M.C. and Worcestershire Regiment.
Volunteering in June 1915, he was drafted in the same year to the Western Front, where he served with the R.A.M.C., and was highly commended for bringing in wounded under heavy shellfire. Later he was transferred to the Worcester Regiment and took part in engagements on the Somme and at Arras, where he was wounded. He was invalided home and on his recovery was engaged on important duties until June 1919, when he was demobilised, holding the 1914-15 Star, and the General Service and Victory Medals.
233, Waterloo Road, Lambeth, S.E.1.   25071B

HARMS, S. A., Driver, R.F.A.
He joined in June 1915, and after his training was drafted in March of the following year to France. Whilst in this theatre of war he fought in many important battles, including those of Vimy Ridge, the Somme, Ypres, Lens, Cambrai and the Advance of 1918. In July 1919 he returned home and was demobilised, holding the General Service and Victory Medals.
1, Gonsalva Road, Wandsworth Road, S.W.8.   Z2454B

HARMS, S. T., Corporal, Royal Defence Corps.
He was on the National Reserve at the outbreak of war, and in June 1915 was mobilised. He then served on important defence duties until September 1919, when he was invalided out of the Service.
1, Gonsalva Road, Wandsworth Road, S.W.8.   2454A

HARNDEN, J. L., Private, Middlesex Regiment.
Volunteering in August 1914, he proceeded overseas in the following December. Whilst on the Western Front he fought in many battles, including those of Ypres (where he was wounded), Arras and Messines. Later he was transferred to Italy, but in 1918 returned to France and was again wounded and taken prisoner, being held in captivity until after the Armistice, when he returned home and was demobilised in April 1919, holding the 1914-15 Star, and the General Service and Victory Medals.
91, Rayleigh Road, W. Kensington, W.14.   T12125

HARNDEN, W. G., Private, R.A.M.C.
He volunteered in September 1914, and on the completion of his training was drafted to the Western Front. There he served in many engagements, including those on the Somme and at Arras, Ypres, Cambrai, and did splendid work until the cessation of hostilities. In April 1919 he returned home and was demobilised, holding the 1914-15 Star, and the General Service and Victory Medals.
13, Biscay Road, Hammersmith, W.6.   12797A

HARPER, F. G., Private, 13th London Regiment (Kensingtons).
He volunteered in December 1914, and on the conclusion of his training was retained with his unit on important duties until June 1916, when he was drafted to France. After service in the Vimy and Arras sectors he proceeded to Salonika and did much good work on the Doiran front. In June 1917 he was transferred to Palestine and served under General Allenby at Jaffa, Jerusalem and in other engagements until hostilities ceased. He returned home and was demobilised in June 1919, holding the General Service and Victory Medals.
14, Northlands Street, Coldharbour Lane, S.E.5.   Z6189

HARPER, H., L/Cpl., 24th London Regt. (Queen's).
He volunteered in September 1914, and on the completion of his training served at various stations on important duties with his unit. He rendered valuable services, but was not successful in obtaining his transfer overseas owing to medical unfitness. In January 1919 he was demobilised.
81, Tyneham Road, Battersea, S.W.11.   Z2456

HARPER, T. W. J., Rifleman, 11th King's Royal Rifle Corps.
Joining in October 1916 he served, after his training on important duties in England until March 1918, when he was drafted overseas. Whilst in France he took part in the fighting at Lens and Cambrai and in the Advance of 1918. In February 1919 he returned home and was demobilised, holding the General Service and Victory Medals.
4, Latchmere Street, Battersea, S.W.11.   Z2455

HARRAWAY, S., A.B., Royal Navy.
Already in the Royal Navy at the outbreak of hostilities, he rendered valuable services on board H.M.S. "Chatham" in 1914, when this vessel shelled the German raider "Königsberg" in the Rufiji River in East Africa. Later he did duty on H.M.T.B.D. "Hoste" and "Anzac," and was on board the former vessel when she sank in a collision in the North Sea. He also took part in the Dardanelles operations and eventually received his discharge in January 1920, after twelve years' service. He holds the 1914-15 Star, and the General Service and Victory Medals.   Z5617

HARRINGTON, H. S., Sergt., R.D.C.
Volunteering in November 1914 he served on the completion of his training on important guard and other duties. He rendered valuable services until the cessation of hostilities, when he unfortunately contracted influenza, subsequently dying from the effects in February 1919.
92, Somerleyton Road, Coldharbour Lane, S.W.9.   Z3090

HARRIS, A., Private, 19th London Regiment.
He attested in 1915, and was called up in 1917 and sent to France in February of the following year. During his service on the Western Front he fought in various engagements in the Retreat of 1918, and was taken prisoner. He was held in captivity in Germany until after the Armistice and was subjected to much ill treatment and neglect during this time. In February 1919 he was demobilised, and holds the General Service and Victory Medals.
95, East Surrey Grove, Peckham, S.E.15.   5091B

HARRIS, A. (Mrs.), Special War Worker.
For two years during the war, from 1915 until 1917, this lady held an important position at Woolwich Arsenal, where she was engaged on responsible work in connection with detonators. She rendered valuable services and carried out her duties in a highly commendable manner.
35, Mansion Street, Camberwell, S.E.5.   Z2472A

HARRIS, A., Sergt., R.G.A.
Volunteering in August 1914, he proceeded to France later in the same year and served with distinction in many engagements. He was in action at the Battles of La Bassée, Ypres, Hill 60, the Somme and Cambrai, and after the Armistice was stationed at Cologne with the Army of Occupation until his demobilisation in August 1919. He holds the 1914 Star, and the General Service and Victory Medals.
204, Albert Road, Peckham, S.E.15.   Z5618B

HARRIS, A. L., Corporal, 2nd Duke of Wellington's (West Riding Regiment).
He was serving at the outbreak of war, and in 1915 was drafted to the Western Front, where he fought in the Battle of Hill 60, and was severely wounded. He was invalided home and after his recovery was transferred to munition work in Yorkshire, being especially selected for the duties. Unfortunately he contracted an illness which proved fatal after a few days, and he died on July 5th, 1916. He was entitled to the 1914-15 Star, and the General Service and Victory Medals.
27, Peacock Street, Walworth, S.E.17.   Z26162

HARRIS, A. G., P.O., R.N., H.M.S. "Powerful."
A serving sailor, he was posted to H.M.S. "Arethusa," which was sunk by an enemy mine off the East Coast in February 1916., but fortunately he was saved. He was then engaged in H.M.S. "Powerful" on important and dangerous duties off the Coasts of Belgium and Ireland, and also took part in the engagement at Dogger Bank, and the raid on Zeebrugge. Later he served in Russian waters, and in the Black Sea. In 1920 he was still serving, and holds the 1914-15 Star, and the General Service and Victory Medals.
27, Smyrk's Road, Walworth, S.E.17.   Z2471

HARRIS, C. E., Rifleman, 12th Rifle Brigade.
He volunteered in November 1914, and in the following July proceeded to France. There he fought in various engagements, including that at Laventie, where he was wounded on September 25th, 1915, and invalided home to hospital. He was transferred to the Royal Army Ordnance Corps in October 1916, and was stationed in England until his demobilisation in February 1919. He holds the 1914-15 Star, and the General Service and Victory Medals.
24, Dartnell Road, Camberwell, S.E.5.   Z5416

HARRIS, C. J., Private, Middlesex Regiment and Suffolk Regiment.
He volunteered in July 1915, and in the following year was drafted to France, and served in many important engagements in various sectors of the Western Front. He was mortally wounded in action on October 26th, 1918, and succumbed to his injuries a few hours later. He was entitled to the General Service and Victory Medals.
"Honour to the immortal dead who gave their youth that the world might grow old in peace."
196, South Street, Walworth, S.E.17.   Z2463

HARRIS, C. S., L/Corporal, 1st Queen's Own (Royal West Kent Regiment).
He enlisted in August 1907, and immediately on the outbreak of war in August 1914, was drafted to the Western Front, where he fought in the Retreat from Mons. Later he took part in the Battles of the Marne, the Aisne, Neuve Chapelle, Loos and the Somme, and other engagements until transferred to Italy in 1917. He returned to France in time to serve through the Retreat and Advance of 1918, and in the Battles of Cambrai and Messines. He was demobilised in March 1919, and holds the Mons Star, and the General Service and Victory Medals.
20, Denmark Road, Camberwell, S.E.5.   Z5992

HARRIS, E., Gunner, R.H.A.
Mobilised at the outbreak of war in 1914, he was drafted to the Western Front in the following month and was in action at the Battles of the Marne, the Aisne, Ypres, Neuve Chapelle, Loos, the Somme, Beaumont-Hamel, Arras, Amiens, and Bapaume. He also rendered valuable services during the Advance of 1918, and after the Armistice proceeded to Cologne, where he did duty with the Army of Occupation. He holds the Mons Star, and the General Service and Victory Medals, and was discharged in April 1919.
49C, Lewis Trust Buildings, off Warner Road, Camberwell, S.E.5.   Z5993

HARRIS, E. J., Private, 24th London Regiment (The Queen's).
He joined in March 1916, and in the following June was drafted to France, where he saw much active service. He fought on the Somme, and at Arras, Bullecourt, and Messines, where he was wounded and sent to hospital and remained under treatment for one month. He afterwards rejoined his unit, and was in action at Ypres, Cambrai, the Somme, Amiens, and Bapaume, and was present at the entry into Lille after the evacuation by the Germans. He holds the General Service and Victory Medals and was demobilised in February 1919.
21, Mayall Road, Herne Hill, S.E.24.   Z2464

HARRIS, E. O., L Corporal, Bedfordshire Regt.
He volunteered in September 1914, and was sent to the Western Front. During his service in France he fought in the Battles of Loos, the Somme, Armentières, and was twice wounded, and later taken prisoner at the capture of Vimy Ridge. He was held in captivity in Germany until after the Armistice, when he was released, and returning home was demobilised in 1919. He holds the 1914-15 Star, and the General Service and Victory Medals.
33, Banim Street, Hammersmith, W.6.   11122B

HARRIS, F., Rifleman, 21st London Regiment (1st Surrey Rifles).
He joined in April 1915, and being physically unfit for transfer overseas, was retained on special duties of importance at various stations in England. He was discharged in May 1916, as a result of his indifferent health, having rendered twelve months' valuable services.
204, Albert Road, Peckham, S.E.15.   Z5618A

HARRIS, F., Private, 13th East Surrey Regiment.
He volunteered in July 1915, and in the same year was sent overseas, and during his service in France fought at St. Eloi and Loos, and in various later engagements, He died gloriously on the Field of Battle on August 12th, 1916, and was entitled to the 1914-15 Star, and the General Service and Victory Medals.
"He passed out of the sight of men by the path of duty and self-sacrifice."
13, Yeovil Street, Wandsworth Road, S.W.8.   Z2459A

HARRIS, F., Sergt., M.G.C.

He volunteered in September 1914, and in the following year proceeded to France. There he was in action at Ypres, and on the Somme, and in various other engagements. He was very severely gassed in 1917, and was invalided home to hospital, but unhappily died from the effects on June 10th, 1918. He was entitled to the 1914-15 Star, and the General Service and Victory Medals.

"His memory is cherished with pride."

13, Yeovil Street, Wandsworth Road, S.W.8.   Z2459B

HARRIS, F. J. G., Driver, R.F.A.

He volunteered in October 1915, and in the following year was drafted to France, and whilst in this theatre of war did excellent work as a driver in many engagements. He served on the Somme, and at Arras, and Vimy Ridge, where he was wounded and sustained severe shell-shock. After his recovery he was again in action at Lens, Armentières, Amiens, and Bray, and later was discharged through ill-health in December 1917. He hold the General Service and Victory Medals.

33, Banim Street, Hammersmith, W.6.   11122

HARRIS, F. W., Gunner, R.F.A.

He joined in 1916, and in July of the following year was sent overseas, and during his service in France did excellent work as a Signaller, and fought in the Battle of Cambrai. He gave his life for his King and Country on December 3rd, 1917, and was entitled to the General Service and Victory Medals.

"He died the noblest death a man may die, fighting for God and right and liberty."

87, Tyneham Road, Lavender Hill, S.W.11.   Z2468

HARRIS, G. H., Private, 2nd Dragoons (Royal Scots Greys).

He joined in February 1917, and in the same year was drafted to the Western Front. There he served in many important engagements, including those at Givenchy and Ypres, and in various subsequent operations in the Retreat and Advance of 1918. He was demobilised in March 1919, and holds the General Service and Victory Medals.

17, Medlar Street, Camberwell, S.E.5.   Z2473B

HARRIS, G. T., Sergt., R.G.A.

Volunteering in September 1914, he was drafted to the Dardanelles with the first Expeditionary Force, and played a distinguished part in the Landing on the Gallipoli Peninsula. He saw much heavy fighting in this theatre of war until August 1915, and was then transferred to France in February 1916. There he was present at many important engagements, including those at Messines, Ypres, Lens, Passchendaele, Cambrai, and the Somme, and was in action during the Retreat and Advance of 1918. He holds the 1914-15 Star, and the General Service and Victory Medals, and was demobilised in June, 1919.

26, Heaton Road, Peckham, S.E.15.   Z5782

HARRIS, H., Private, R.A.S.C. and Labour Corps.

He had previously served twelve years in the King's Royal Rifle Corps, and in January 1916 rejoined, and was engaged in the Forage Department on important duties at Woolwich. He rendered valuable services until December 1916, when he was discharged.

93, Minnow Street, Walworth, S.E.17.   Z2458

HARRIS, H., Private, R.A.S.C. (M.T.)

He joined in 1916, and in the following year was drafted to France. There he served on important duties with the motor transport section, and in the ammunition and the supply column. After the Armistice was signed he proceeded to Germany with the Army of Occupation, and was stationed at Cologne until in October 1919, he returned home, and was demobilised. He holds the General Service and Victory Medals.

38, Emu Road, Battersea Park, S.W.8.   Z2461

HARRIS, H., Driver, R.F.A.

He volunteered in February 1915, and did excellent work as a driver until November of the same year when he was discharged on account of his service. He was then engaged in important duties in England with the British Red Cross Society for three years, and rendered valuable services.

47, Gonsalva Road, Wandsworth Road, S.W.8.   Z2460

HARRIS, H., Driver, R.F.A.

He volunteered in 1915, and in the same year was sent overseas. After taking part in several engagements on the Western Front he was severely wounded in action and invalided home to hospital. He died of his injuries on February 5th, 1916, and was entitled to the 1914-15 Star, and the General Service and Victory Medals.

"The path of duty was the way to glory."

21, Medwin Street, Ferndale Road, S.W.4.   Z2462B

HARRIS, H. A., Private, 4th Middlesex Regiment.

He joined in February 1917, and in the same year was drafted overseas. During his service in France he fought at Cambrai, Ypres, Fonquevillers, Bucquoy, and Gommecourt, where he was gassed in June 1918. He was demobilised in December 1919, and holds the General Service and Victory Medals.

21, Medwin Street, Ferndale Road, S.W.4.   Z2462A

HARRIS, H. J., Rifleman, 8th London Regiment (Post Office Rifles).

He volunteered at the outbreak of war, and in 1915, was drafted to the Western Front. Here he fought at Ypres and Festubert and was severely wounded in the latter engagement. He was invalided to the Base, and after his recovery was discharged as medically unfit for further military duty in March 1916. He holds the 1914-15 Star, and the General Service and Victory Medals.

63, Mostyn Road, Brixton Road, S.W.9.   Z3466

HARRIS, J., Private, R.A.M.C.

He had previously served in the West Riding Regiment for twelve years, and at the outbreak of war was above the age for overseas service. Nevertheless he rejoined in August 1915, and for nearly four years was engaged on important duties with his unit at the 5th London General Hospital. He rendered valuable services and was demobilised in April 1919.

94, Coronation Buildings, South Lambeth Road, S.W.8.   Z2467

HARRIS, J. T., Corporal, R.F.A.

He volunteered in October 1914, and was almost immediately drafted to France, where he took part in various engagements including those at Ypres and Loos. In December 1915 he was sent to Salonika, and served in the general offensive on the Doiran front. He contracted malaria, and was invalided home, and later serving at Brighton as an instructor in drill and horse riding to recruits, he was demobilised in April 1919. He holds the 1914 Star, and the General Service and Victory Medals.

55, Neate Street, Camberwell, S.E.5.   Z5092

HARRIS, P. A., Staff Sergt., 21st London Regt. (1st Surrey Rifles).

He volunteered in August 1914, and in the same year was drafted to France, and fought in several early engagements, including that of La Bassée, where he was severely wounded in action. He was invalided home to hospital, subsequently discharged as physically unfit for further military duty in 1915. He holds the 1914 Star, and the General Service and Victory Medals.

35, Mansion Street, Camberwell, S.E.5.   Z2472B

HARRIS, R., Member, W.R.A.F.

She joined in July 1918, and served at first on important duties at home, and was later sent to France in May 1919. She rendered valuable services until September in the same year, when she returned to England, and was demobilised in the following month.

34, Dorchester Grove, Chiswick, W.4.   5583A

HARRIS, R. S., Private, R.A.M.C.

He joined in February 1916, and in the following June was drafted to France, where he served on important duties with the 133rd Field Ambulance at Ypres, St. Quentin, and various subsequent engagements. He was gassed whilst attending to the wounded in 1918, and after a short period of time in hospital in France rejoined his unit until the cessation of hostilities. He holds the General Service and Victory Medals, and was demobilised in January 1919.

12, Caspian Street, Camberwell, S.E.5.   Z5551

HARRIS, R. T., Sapper, R.E.

He volunteered in June 1915, and in the same year was drafted to Salonika, where he took part in the offensives on the Struma and Doiran fronts. He unfortunately contracted malaria and was invalided home in 1917. After recovery he was sent to the Western Front, and was in action in the Somme and Ypres sectors and rendered valuable services during the Retreat and Advance of 1918. He holds the 1914-15 Star, and the General Service and Victory Medals, and was demobilised in September 1919.

41, Philip Road, Peckham, S.E.15.   Z5975

HARRIS, R. W., Pte., Royal Berkshire Regiment, Worcestershire Regiment and R.A.S.C.

He volunteered in September 1914, and in the following year was drafted to France. There he fought in the engagements at Neuve Chapelle, St. Eloi, Hill 60, and Loos, and was subsequently wounded by an enemy sniper whilst conveying rations up the line. He was sent to hospital at Boulogne, and thence to England, and was then transferred to the Royal Army Service Corps with which he was engaged on important duties until demobilised in May 1919. He holds the 1914-15 Star, and the General Service and Victory Medals.

3, Combermere Road, Stockwell, S.W.9.   Z2469

HARRIS, S. A., Private, R.A.O.C.

He had previously joined the Army in September 1911, and at the outbreak of war was drafted overseas. During his service in France he was engaged on important duties in various sectors, and was subsequently killed in action at Ypres, on April 23rd, 1915. He was entitled to the 1914-15 Star, and the General Service and Victory Medals.

"His life for his Country."

37, Benbow Road, Hammersmith, W.6.   10729B

HARRIS, S., Private, Queen's (Royal West Surrey Regiment).

He joined in February 1917, and in the following August was drafted to Egypt proceeding thence through Palestine with General Allenby's Forces. After taking part in several engagements he was present at the entry into Jerusalem. In 1918 he was sent to the Western Front, and fought in many of the later operations, notably at the capture of Soissons, when he was severely wounded. He was invalided home to hospital and discharged in May 1919. He holds the General Service and Victory Medals.

95, East Surrey Grove, Peckham, S.E.15. 5091C

HARRIS, T., Private, 1st East Surrey Regiment.

He had previously served for twelve years in the East Surrey Regiment, and had fought throughout the South African War. At the outbreak of the late war he was mobilised, and in 1915 was drafted to the Dardanelles, where he took part in the Landing at Suvla Bay, and in the subsequent engagements until the Evacuation of the Peninsula. He then proceeded to Egypt and Palestine, and fought in the Great Advance under General Allenby at Gaza, and on the Jordan, and was present at the Fall of Jerusalem. He returned home, and was demobilised in December 1918, and holds the Queen's and King's South African Medals, the Soudan, the 1914-15 Star, and the General Service and Victory Medals.

213, Neate Street, Camberwell, S.E.5. Z5417

HARRIS, T. H., Private, King's Own (Yorkshire Light Infantry).

He volunteered in March 1915, and in the following September was drafted overseas. During his service in France he fought at Loos, and Vimy Ridge, and in the Battles of the Somme, where he was severely wounded in July 1916. He was invalided home to hospital, and after protracted treatment was discharged as physically unfit for further military duty in April 1919. He holds the 1914-15 Star, and the General Service and Victory Medals.

27, Mason Street, Walworth, S.E.7. Z2466

HARRIS, W., Private, 7th London Regiment.

He volunteered in March 1915, and embarked for France in January 1917. During his service on the Western Front he was in action at Arras, Albert, Bullecourt, Ypres, Cambrai, St. Quentin, the Somme, Amiens, and the engagements which followed until the cessation of hostilities. He was demobilised in March 1919, and holds the General Service and Victory Medals. 31, Aldensley Road, Hammersmith, W.6. 10739B

HARRIS, W., Private, 26th Middlesex Regiment.

He attested in November 1915, but was not called up until April 1918. After his training he proceeded to Russia with the Relief Forces in April 1919, and served in the campaign against the Bolshevists until the following October, when he returned home and was demobilised in November 1919. He holds the General Service and Victory Medals.

95, East Surrey Grove, Peckham, S.E.15. 5091A

HARRIS, W., Private, 23rd Middlesex Regiment.

He volunteered in November 1915, and in the following year proceeded to France. After serving in various minor engagements he was reported wounded and missing after an engagement at Armentières. Later he was presumed to have been killed in action on September 13th, 1916. He was entitled to the General Service and Victory Medals.

"He died the noblest death a man may die,
Fighting for God and right and liberty."

65, Neate Street, Camberwell, S.E.5. Z5093B

HARRIS, W., Gunner, R.G.A.

Volunteering at the outbreak of war he was ineligible for service overseas, and did good work at his depôt for four months. He was then discharged from causes due to his service in December 1914.

34, Dorchester Grove, Chiswick, W.4. 5583B

HARRIS, W. C., Corporal, 2nd Middlesex Regiment, Norfolk Regiment and Labour Corps.

He joined in March 1916, and in the following February embarked for France. There he fought at Vimy Ridge, and was afterwards transferred to the Labour Corps and served in many sectors on important duties. He returned home in November 1919, and was discharged as medically unfit for further military duties in the same months. He holds the General Service and Victory Medals.

1, Sheepcote Lane, Battersea, S.W.11. Z2465

HARRIS, W. H., Cpl., 5th Royal Warwickshire Regt.

He joined in May 1917 as a Driver in the Royal Army Service Corps, and was afterwards transferred to the Royal Warwickshire Regiment, with which he proceeded to France in the following month. He took an active part in the Battle of Ypres, and other engagements, and in November was sent to Italy where, he rendered excellent service against the Austrians on the Piave front until the Armistice. After returning to England he was demobilised in February 1919, and holds the General Service and Victory Medals.

108, Kenbury Street, Camberwell, S.E.5. Z5986

HARRIS, W. H., Private, 2nd Queen's (Royal West Surrey Regiment).

He joined in January 1916, and in the same year was drafted to France, and served in many important battles, including those at Hill 60, Ypres, Loos, and Passchendaele Ridge. He returned home in August 1918, and was later sent to Ireland, and afterwards returned to England where he was engaged on guard duties at a detention camp. He was discharged in December 1919, and holds the General Service and Victory Medals.

17, Medlar Street, Camberwell, S.E.5. Z2473A

HARRIS, W. H. G., Bandsman, 8th London Regt. (Post Office Rifles).

He joined the Territorials in February 1914, and was mobilised on the outbreak of war, and sent to France in the following year. Whilst overseas he was in action at La Bassée, and was severely wounded in the Battle of Festubert. He was invalided home to hospital, and discharged as physically unfit for further military duty in May 1916. He was entitled to the 1914-15 Star, and the General Service and Victory Medals.

57, Wilton Avenue, Chiswick, W.4. 5509

HARRIS, W. J., Stoker, R.N., H.M.S. "Theseus."

He joined in February 1916, and was posted to H.M.S. "Theseus," and sent to Russia in October of the following year. He served at Batum, and in various other ports until August 1918, when he returned home and was demobilised. He holds the General Service and Victory Medals.

2, Gayville Road, Wandsworth Common, S.W.11. Z2470

HARRIS, W. T., Captain, R.A.M.C.

He joined in February 1917, and in the following April embarked for Egypt. On the outward voyage the ship in which he was sailing was torpedoed, but he was fortunately rescued. After his arrival in the East he served on important duties throughout the Palestine campaign, and in 1920 was still in the Army. He holds the General Service and Victory Medals.

72, Duke's Avenue, Chiswick, W.4. 5694

HARRISON, A., Driver, R.A.S.C. (M.T.)

He joined in January 1916, and at the conclusion of his training crossed to France. Whilst in this theatre of war he was engaged on duties of an important nature in connection with the transport of supplies to the forward areas, and also as an ambulance driver, conveying the wounded to the Base. He was present at many important battles, including those of the Somme, Arras, Vimy Ridge, and Ypres, and also served in the Retreat and Advance of 1918, during which he did excellent work. He was demobilised in February 1919, and holds the General Service and Victory Medals.

21, Pulross Road, Brixton Road, S.W.9. Z2475

HARRISON, A., Private, 13th Royal Fusiliers.

Volunteering in September 1914, he was drafted to France, where he subsequently fought in several important battles, notably those of Ypres and Loos. He died gloriously on the Field of Battle at Arras in 1917, after three years' service. He was entitled to the 1914 Star, and the General Service and Victory Medals.

"His life for his Country, his Soul to God."

105, Ingrave Street, Battersea, S.W.11. Z2477

HARRISON, A., Gunner, R.N.

Having joined in 1912, he was in the Navy at the outbreak of war, and in the course of his service was on board H.M.S.'s "Indomitable," and "Abercrombie." He was engaged with his ship in the North Sea and the Dardanelles, where he was in action against the "Breslau" and the "Goeben," and also took part in the Battles of Jutland, and the Dogger Bank. In 1916 he served for a time with a landing force at Salonika, and fought in engagements on the Struma front. He holds the 1914-15 Star, and the General Service and Victory Medals, and was still serving in 1920.

82, Somerleyton Road, Coldharbour Lane, S.W.9. Z3089B

HARRISON, A. G., Driver, R.F.A.

Mobilised at the outbreak of hostilities he was quickly drafted to the Western Front, where he served until the war ended. He took an active part in the Retreat from Mons, and the Battles of Ypres, Hill 60, and Loos, and afterwards fought in the Somme, Ypres, Arras, and Cambrai sectors. After the Armistice he went into Germany with the Army of Occupation, and on his return home was demobilised in 1919. He holds the Mons Star, and the General Service and Victory Medals.

50, Caulfield Road, Peckham, S.E.15. Z6393

HARRISON, E., Private, R.A.V.C.

Volunteering in April 1915, he joined in the 23rd Middlesex Regiment, and was later transferred to the Royal Army Veterinary Corps. In the course of his service overseas, which lasted three years, he did valuable work with his unit, and was present at several important battles, at one of which he was wounded. He was demobilised in July 1919, on his return to England, and holds the General Service and Victory Medals.

71, Rayleigh Road, West Kensington, W.14. 12084C

HARRISON, A., Driver, R.A.S.C. (H.T.) and King's Royal Rifle Corps.

He volunteered in August 1914, and served in the King's Royal Rifle Corps but in the following November was discharged owing to physical unfitness. In October 1917, however, he rejoined in the Royal Army Service Corps, and in the following January was drafted to the Western Front. Whilst in this theatre of war he was engaged on duties of an important nature in connection with the transport of supplies, and did valuable work during the Retreat and Advance of 1918. He holds the General Service and Victory Medals, and was demobilised in June 1919, after his return to England.

13, Everett Street, Nine Elms Lane, S.W.8.　　2474

HARRISON, H., Leading Stoker, R.N.

He enlisted in 1910, and during the recent war served on board H.M.S.'s " Royalist," " Duncan," and " Princess Royal." He was engaged with his ship in several Naval actions off the Belgian Coast, and also took part in the Battle of Jutland. He holds the 1914-15 Star, and the General Service and Victory Medals, and was still serving in 1920.

82, Somerleyton Road, Coldharbour Lane, S.W.9.　　Z3089C

HARRISON, J., Gunner, R.F.A.

Volunteering in November 1914, he crossed to France in the following September, and subsequently fought in the Battles of Loos, Albert, Vermelles, Ploegsteert Wood, and the Somme. In February 1917 he was transferred to India, where he was engaged on garrison duties, and during his service there was in hospital for three months suffering from dysentery. He was demobilised in November 1919, after his return to England, and holds the 1914-15 Star, and the General Service and Victory Medals.

7, Halpin Place, Walworth, S.E.17.　　Z2476

HARRISON, R., Private, R.A.S.C.

He volunteered early in 1915, and during his service on the Western Front, which lasted for over three years, was engaged on duties of an important nature in connection with the transport of ammunition to the forward areas. He was demobilised in February 1919, and holds the 1914-15 Star, and the General Service and Victory Medals.

71, Rayleigh Road, West Kensington, W.14.　　12084D

HARRISON, R. H., Gunner, R.G.A.

Volunteering at the commencement of hostilities, he was drafted to the Western Front at the conclusion of his training, and subsequently fought in many important engagements. He gave his life for King and Country at Ypres on August 23rd, 1916, and was entitled to the General Service and Victory Medals.

" Great deeds cannot die,
They with the sun and moon renew their light for ever."
71, Rayleigh Road, West Kensington, W.14.　　12084B

HARRISON, R. J., Private, East Surrey Regiment.

Volunteering in September 1914, he crossed to France early in the following year and fought at Albert and St. Quentin, and in various other sectors. He was reported missing on May 3rd, 1917, after an engagement near Vimy Ridge, but a later report stated that he was killed in action on that date. He was entitled to the 1914-15 Star, and the General Service and Victory Medals.

" He joined the great white company of valiant souls."
71, Rayleigh Road, West Kensington, W.14.　　12084A

HARROLD, C., Pte., Queen's (Royal West Surrey Regiment).

He volunteered in 1914, and until he was sent to France in 1916 was engaged upon duties of an important nature. During his service overseas, he fought in many of the principal engagements, notably the Battles of the Somme and Arras, and in the Retreat and Advance of 1918. On three occasions he was severely wounded, but remained on the Western Front until after the termination of hostilities. He holds the General Service and Victory Medals, and was demobilised in 1919, after his return to England.

7, Urswicke Road, Battersea, S.W.11.　　Z2478

HARROW, F., Signaller, H.A.C.

He volunteered in July 1915, and two years later crossed to France, where he subsequently fought in many important battles, including those of Arras, Ypres, and Cambrai. After the Retreat and Advance of 1918, in which he also took part, he was sent with the Army of Occupation to Germany. He was demobilised in May 1919, on his return to England, and holds the General Service and Victory Medals.

20, Vicarage Road, Camberwell, S.E.5.　　Z2479

HARROW, J. E., Stoker, Merchant Service.

He was in the Merchant Service on the outbreak of hostilities, and during the war served on board the s.s. " Lindale." This ship was engaged on important transport duties, conveying ammunition and stores to the various theatres of war, and he did valuable work until after the cessation of hostilities. He holds the General Service and the Mercantile Marine War Medals.　15, Warhams Street, Camberwell, S.E.5.　　Z2480

HARSANT, A., Driver, R.E.

He was already serving in the Territorials at the outbreak of war in August 1914, and was immediately mobilised. In 1915 he was drafted to the Dardanelles, where he saw much severe fighting on the Gallipoli Peninsula, and after the Evacuation, embarked for France. In this theatre of war he took part in many engagements, including those at Ypres, the Somme and Cambrai, and later in action during the Retreat and Advance of 1918. He holds the 1914-15 Star, and the General Service and Victory Medals, and was demobilised in August 1919.

3, Lidgate Road, Peckham, S.E.15.　　Z5619

HART, A. G., Cpl., 7th Buffs (East Kent Regt.)

Volunteering in August 1914, he crossed to France in the following January. Whilst overseas he fought in many battles, including those of Ypres, and Hill 60. During his service he was blown up by an explosion and was wounded in seventeen places. He was sent to England in August 1915, and in the following February was invalided out of the Service. He holds the 1914-15 Star, and the General Service and Victory Medals.

111A, Cator Street, Peckham, S.E.15.　　Z4466

HART, C. J., Private, Royal Sussex Regiment.

He joined on attaining military age in October 1918, but had not completed his training when hostilities ceased. Afterwards however, he was sent with the Army of Occupation to Germany, and in the course of his service there contracted an illness, which necessitated his being invalided to England. After protracted treatment in Woolwich Hospital, he was sent to Staffordshire, but in October 1919 was again admitted into hospital, and in the following month was invalided out of the Service.

12, Comyn Road, Battersea, S.W.11.　　Z1778　1779A

HART, F. H., Driver, R.A.S.C. (M.T.)

He volunteered in July 1915, and during his service on the Western Front, which lasted for nearly three years, was engaged on important transport duties in many sectors, including those of the Somme, Arras, and Ypres. On one occasion he was severely wounded. He was demobilised in 1918, and holds the 1914-15 Star, and the General Service and Victory Medals.

58, Mordaunt Street, Landor Road, S.W.9.　　Z2482B

HART, F. T. (M.M.), Cpl., 12th Royal Fusiliers.

Volunteering in November 1914, he crossed to France in the following August, and a month later was taken prisoner during the Battle of Loos, where he also won the Military Medal for conspicuous bravery and devotion to duty. In 1917 he, with two other prisoners, escaped from their detention camp at Friederichsfeld, and after making their way to Holland, successfully reached our lines. He was demobilised in March 1919, and holds the 1914-15 Star, and the General Service and Victory Medals.

6, Torrens Street, Ferndale Road, S.W.4.　　Z2481

HART, F. W., Private, 2nd London Regt. (Royal Fusiliers).

Volunteering in May 1915, early in the following year he was sent to the Western Front, where he fought in many battles and was wounded. In 1916 he was invalided to hospital at Netley, but after his recovery returned to France. He was unhappily killed in action on April 24th, 1918, during the German Offensive. He was entitled to the General Service and Victory Medals.

" And doubtless he went in splendid company."
62, Westmacott Street, Camberwell, S.E.5.　　Z5548A

HART, G. A., Private, R.A.S.C. (M.T.)

He volunteered in February 1915, and at the conclusion of his training was sent to the Western Front. Whilst in this theatre of war he served on important transport duties, and was present at engagements at Ypres, Arras, Armentières, Vimy Ridge and Valenciennes, and in the Retreat and Advance of 1918. During his service he was gassed. He was demobilised in December 1918, and holds the 1914-15 Star, and the General Service and Victory Medals.

6, Bolney Street, Dorset Road, S.W.8.　　Z2485A

HART, G. W., Rifleman, 2nd Rifle Brigade.

He joined in May 1917, and on the conclusion of his training was drafted to France, where he was in action at Ypres and the Somme, and was taken prisoner at Villers-Bretonneux in April 1918. After detention at various prison camps in Germany he was repatriated after the Armistice and was demobilised in February 1919, holding the General Service and Victory Medals.

103, Evelina Road, Peckham, S.E.15.　　Z5979

HART, H., Private, R.A.S.C. (M.T.)

Volunteering in November 1914, he was sent to the Western Front early in the following year. During his service overseas he was engaged at Divisional Headquarters, driving the G.O.C., and also did valuable work during the last Retreat and Advance. He holds the 1914-15 Star, and the General Service and Victory Medals, and was demobilised in December 1918.　6, Bolney Street, Dorset Road, S.W.8.　　Z2485B

HART, S., Gunner, R.F.A.

Volunteering at the commencement of hostilities, he was quickly sent to France, and took part in the Retreat from Mons and the Battles of Ypres, the Somme and Cambrai. He died gloriously on the Field of Battle on September 1st, 1918, during the Advance of that year, and was entitled to the Mons Star, and the General Service and Victory Medals.
"A valiant soldier with undaunted heart, he breasted Life's last hill."
21, Bolton Street, Camberwell, S.E.5.   Z2483A

HART, L. Gunner, R.F.A.

He volunteered in January 1915, and in the following September was sent to Egypt and thence to the Dardanelles. He took part in the Landing at Gallipoli and the Battles of Krithia, and after the Evacuation of the Peninsula returned to Egypt. Later he was sent to Mesopotamia, where he did valuable work with his unit at Baghdad and during the operations on the Tigris. In 1917 he was transferred to India in consequence of ill-health caused through strain, and for the remaining period of hostilities was engaged on garrison duty. He was demobilised in November 1919, and holds the 1914-15 Star, and the General Service and Victory Medals.
41, Searles Road, New Kent Road, S.E.1.   Z2484

HART, S. A., Driver, R.A.S.C. (H.T.)

He volunteered in 1915, and during his service in France, which lasted for over three years, was engaged upon duties of an important nature in connection with the transport of supplies to our troops in the forward areas. He was demobilised in 1919, and holds the 1914-15 Star, and the General Service and Victory Medals.
58, Mordaunt Street, Landor Road, S.W.9.   Z2482A

HART, S. H., Gunner, R.F.A.

He volunteered in January 1915, and at the conclusion of his training was drafted to the Western Front, where he fought in several important engagements, including those at Ypres, Loos and Albert. In 1917 he was severely wounded, returning to England in consequence, and in July of the same year was invalided out of the Service. He holds the 1914-15 Star, and the General Service and Victory Medals.
21, Bolton Street, Camberwell. S.E.5.   Z2483B

HART, J. E., Stoker, R.N.

Volunteering at the commencement of hostilities, he was posted to H.M.S. "Aboukir," in which he subsequently lost his life, when she was torpedoed and sunk by a German submarine off the Hook of Holland on September 22nd, 1914. He was entitled to the 1914-15 Star, and the General Service and Victory Medals.
"Whilst we remember, the Sacrifice is not in vain."
185, Cronin Road, Peckham, S.E.15.   Z5418

HARTIGAN, J. S., Dr., R.F.A., 6th London Brigade.

He was serving at the outbreak of war and after being engaged on important duties in England was drafted overseas in the following year. Whilst on the Western Front he fought in many battles, including those of Ypres, Festubert, the Somme, Arras, Vimy Ridge and Cambrai. He was demobilised in February 1919, and holds the 1914-15 Star, and the General Service and Victory Medals.
47, Harvey Road, Camberwell, S.E.5.   Z2486

HARTSHORN, F. H., Cpl., 2nd Battalion Royal Sussex Regiment.

Joining in January 1916 he proceeded overseas in the same year, and whilst in France took part in the fierce fighting in the Ypres sector. He suffered from shell-shock and was invalided to hospital, but on recovery returned to his unit and served until the close of war. He holds the General Service and Victory Medals, and in 1920 was still serving.
69, Speldhurst Road, Chiswick, W.4.   7669

HARVEY, A. J., Private, 23rd London Regiment.

Volunteering in May 1915, he served after his training on important guard and other duties with his unit at various stations. He rendered valuable services, but was not successful in obtaining his transfer overseas owing to medical unfitness. In June 1916 he was discharged.
8, Amies Street, Battersea, S.W.11.   Z2488B

HARVEY, F. J., Private, Queen's Own (Royal West Kent Regiment).

Mobilised at the outbreak of hostilities, he was at once drafted to France and fought with distinction at Mons, Neuve Chapelle and Hill 60. In consequence of a serious wound received in action he was discharged in 1915 as medically unfit for further service. He holds the Mons Star, and the General Service and Victory Medals.
4, Heaton Road, Peckham, S.E.15.   Z5976

HARVEY, H., Private, 7th London Regiment.

He joined in May 1917, and in the following September proceeded to France. There he took part in much of the heavy fighting on the Ypres sector, and at Cambrai, Bapaume and in many other battles, until the conclusion of hostilities. He was severely gassed during his service, and in July 1919 was discharged as medically unfit. He holds the General Service and Victory Medals.
134, Coronation Buildings, S. Lambeth Road, S.W.8.   Z2489

HARVEY, H., Private, 25th London Regt. (Queen's).

He joined in February 1916, and after having completed his training was drafted overseas in the same year. Whilst in France he took part in the fighting at Cambrai, afterwards being engaged on highly important duties behind the lines. In March 1919 he was demobilised, and holds the General Service and Victory Medals.
1, Dartford Street, Walworth, S.E.17.   26227B

HARVEY, H. J., Sapper, R.E. and Labour Corps.

He joined in June 1916, and later in the same year proceeded to France. There he took part in many engagements, including those at Ypres, Albert and St. Quentin. He was severely wounded at Hill 60 and was eventually invalided to England. In due course he returned to the Western Front and was transferred to a Labour Corps at Rouen, but owing to illness was discharged in November 1918 as medically unfit for further service. He holds the General Service and Victory Medals.
2, Tindal Street, Lothian Road, S.W.9.   Z5785

HARVEY, H. V. (M.M.), Corporal, R.F.A.

He volunteered in September 1914, and in the following year was drafted to France. There he served with the 175th Army Brigade, Trench Mortar Batteries, in many battles, including that of Ypres, and was wounded three times and gassed. He was invalided home, but returned to the Western Front on recovery and was awarded the Military Medal for conspicuous gallantry in action. He died gloriously on the field of battle near Valenciennes on November 1st, 1918, and was entitled to the 1914-15 Star, and the General Service and Victory Medals.
"The path of duty was the way to glory."
44, Tindal Street, Lothian Road, S.W.9.   Z5252

(V.C.), HARVEY, J., Private, 22nd London Regt. (Queen's)

He volunteered in November 1914, and was drafted to the Western Front, where during his three and a half years' service he took a prominent part in many important engagements, including those at Loos, High Wood, Messines Ridge and Bourlon Wood, and the Retreat and Advance of 1918. He was awarded the Victoria Cross on September 2nd, 1918, for most conspicuous gallantry and disregard of personal danger during an advance north of Péronne. The advance of his Company was held up by intense machine-gun fire and he at once dashed forward a distance of fifty yards alone through our barrage and, in the face of heavy enemy fire, rushed a machine-gun post, shooting two of the team and bayoneting another. He then destroyed the gun and continued to work his way along the enemy trench, and going forward alone for about two hundred yards, single-handed rushed an enemy dug-out, which contained thirty-seven Germans, and compelled them to surrender. By these acts of great gallantry he saved the company heavy casualties and enabled the whole of the attacking line to advance. Throughout the entire operation he showed the most magnificent courage and determination, and by the splendid example he set to all ranks materially assisted in the success of the operation. In addition he holds the 1914 Star, and the General Service and Victory Medals, and was demobilised in February 1919.
34, Harling Street, Camberwell, S.E.5.   Z5419

HARVEY, J. M., Private, R.D.C.

He was mobilised from the National Reserve in June 1915 and served on important defence duties at various stations with his unit. He was also engaged in guarding German prisoners and rendered valuable service until January 1919, when he was demobilised.
8, Amiens Street, Battersea, S.W.11.   Z2488A

HARVEY, S., Sapper, R.E. and Private, North Staffordshire Regiment.

Volunteering in December 1915, he was drafted on the completion of his training to the Western Front, and with the North Staffordshire Regiment took part in many notable engagements. Later he was invalided home through ill-health, and on recovery was transferred to the R.E. and served on military police duties until demobilised in March 1919. He holds the General Service and Victory Medals.
186, Farmer's Road, Camberwell, S.E.5.   Z2490B

HARVEY, S., 2nd Cook, R.N.

He joined in July 1916 and was at first stationed at Devonport, but afterwards was posted to H.M.S. "Diana," on board which vessel he saw much service. His ship was engaged on important patrol duties in the China Sea and Indian Ocean until May 1919, when she returned to port and he was demobilised, holding the General Service and Victory Medals.
13, Raywood Street, Battersea Park Road, S.W.8. Z2491

HARVEY, T. H., Private, 10th Essex Regiment.

Joining in March 1917, he was drafted to France in the following November, and whilst there took part in various important engagements, including the Retreat and Advance of 1918. He was wounded and gassed and was invalided home to hospital. On his recovery he served in Ireland until January 1920, when he was demobilised, holding the General Service and Victory Medals.
4, Over Place, Princes Road, Kennington, S.E.11. Z25526

HARVEY, W., Private, Duke of Cornwall's Light Infantry and Royal Dublin Fusiliers.

Volunteering in August 1914, he proceeded to France in the following year, and during the fighting at Ypres was wounded and sent home. On recovery he was drafted to Salonika, where he took part in the Balkan campaign and was twice wounded, and thence to Egypt, where he served in the advance to Palestine, and was present at the capture of Jerusalem. He returned home in August 1919, and was demobilised, holding the 1914-15 Star, and the General Service and Victory Medals.   1, Dartford Street, Walworth, S.E.17.   Z26227A

HARVEY, W. (M.S.M.), Sergt., R.E.

Volunteering in August 1914, he was drafted in the following year to France, where he served for about eighteen months and took part in various engagements. He then proceeded to East Africa and served on important duties in the Signal Section until 1918. He was awarded the Meritorious Service Medal for devotion to duty and was twice mentioned in Despatches for conspicuous gallantry. In addition he holds the 1914-15 Star, and the General Service and Victory Medals, and in March 1919 was demobilised.
74, Killyon Road, Wandsworth Road, S.W.8.   Z2487

HARVEY, W. J., Private, R.A.S.C. (M.T.)

Mobilised at the outbreak of war, he almost immediately proceeded to France and served during the Retreat from Mons and in the Battles of the Marne and Aisne. He was also present at many other engagements, including those of Ypres and the Somme, but in March 1917 was invalided home through ill-health. Later he served in Ireland on important duties until discharged as medically unfit in June 1918. He holds the Mons Star, and the General Service and Victory Medals. 10, Winstead Street, Battersea, S.W.11. Z2492

HARWOOD, A. W., Pte., Canadian Overseas Forces.

Having previously served in the South African War, he at once volunteered on the outbreak of war, and in November 1914 proceeded to France. He fought in many battles, including those of Ypres, the Somme, Arras, Cambrai and the Retreat and Advance of 1918, during which time he was twice wounded and gassed. In June 1919 he was demobilised, and holds the 1914-15 Star, and the General Service and Victory Medals.
4, Hopwood Street, Inville Road, Walworth, S.E.17. Z2493B

HARWOOD, C. R., Private, 1st and 2nd London Regiment (Royal Fusiliers).

He joined in December 1917, and after having completed his training proceeded to France. There he fought in many engagements and during the fierce fighting at Arras was wounded on August 27th, 1918. He holds the General Service and Victory Medals, and in 1920 was still serving.
5, Church Path, Acton Green, W.4.   6890A

HARWOOD, J., Private, R.A.S.C.

He joined in March 1917, and after his training served at various stations on important transport and other duties. He rendered valuable services, but was not successful in obtaining his transfer overseas owing to medical unfitness. In June 1919 he was demobilised.
4, Hopwood Street, Walworth, S.E.17.   Z2493A

HARWOOD, J. B., Pte., 24th London Regt. (Queen's).

He volunteered in October 1914, and after the completion of his training was engaged on important duties with his unit at various stations. He rendered valuable services, but was not able to secure his transfer overseas while hostilities continued, and was discharged in August 1916.
11, Lewis Road, Camberwell, S.E.5.   Z6188A

HARWOOD, W., Air Mechanic, R.A.F. (late R.F.C.)

He joined the R.A.S.C. in February 1917, but later was transferred to the R.F.C. In January of the following year he was drafted to France and was engaged on important duties until his discharge in June 1919. He holds the General Service and Victory Medals.
5, Church Path, Acton Green, W.4.   6890B

HARWOOD, J. T., Private, Royal Fusiliers.

Joining in March 1916 he proceeded to France later in that year and took part in many engagements, including the Battle of the Somme, where he was wounded in July. After his recovery he was retained on important home defence duties at various stations until his demobilisation in November 1919. He holds the General Service and Victory Medals.
11, Lewis Road, Camberwell, S.E.5.   Z6188B

HASLAM, P., Private, Royal Berkshire Regiment.

He volunteered at the outbreak of war, and in the following year was drafted to France, where he saw much service. He fought in the Battles of Ypres, Vimy Ridge, Arras and Cambrai, and in many engagements during the Retreat and Advance of 1918. He returned home and was demobilised in January 1919, and holds the 1914-15 Star, and the General Service and Victory Medals.
4, Thorncroft Street, Wandsworth Road, S.W.8.   Z2494

HASS, F., Driver, R.A.S.C. (H.T.)

He volunteered in October 1915, and in the following year proceeded to Salonika. During his service he fought in the advance across the Struma, and in the operations on the Doiran front. He was severely wounded in July 1916, and was consequently invalided home to hospital, and subsequently discharged as physically unfit for further duty in September 1917. He holds the General Service and Victory Medals.
4, Cancell Road, Brixton Road, S.W.9.   Z/5250

HASTIE, W. K., Special War Worker.

For two years during the war he was engaged on work of National importance at Messrs. Wilkinson's Sword Works. He was chiefly employed in the manufacture of bolt cutters for Army swords, and did excellent work. Later, however, he unfortunately was taken ill and died on July 30th, 1918.
14, Redmore Road, Hammersmith, W.6.   11623B

HASTINGS, A., Private, Royal Fusiliers.

He volunteered in May 1915, and in the following year proceeded to France and during his service on the Western Front fought in various engagements. On July 1st 1916 he died gloriously on the field of battle on the Somme, and was entitled to the General Service and Victory Medals.
"A valiant soldier, with undaunted heart, he breasted Life's last hill."
74, Smith Street, Camberwell, S.E.5.   Z2495B

HASTINGS, J., Private, Norfolk Regiment.

Volunteering in May 1915, he proceeded to France in the following year, and served in many important engagements on various sectors of the Western Front until the conclusion of hostilities. In 1920 he was serving in India with the Machine Gun Corps, and he holds the General Service and Victory Medals.
74, Smith Street, Camberwell, S.E.5.   Z2495A

HASTINGS, J. G., Private, R.A.M.C.

He joined in August 1916, and after his training was stationed at a large military hospital at Birmingham. For two years he was engaged on important hospital duties, and in August 1918 was discharged through causes due to his service.
37, Smyrk's Road, Walworth, S.E.17.   Z2159A

HASTWELL, T. E., Flight Sergt., R.A.F.

He volunteered in May 1915, and in the following year was drafted to France. During his service on the Western Front he was engaged with his Squadron at Ypres, Albert, Arras, Armentières, Givenchy, St. Quentin, Bapaume and Béthune. He suffered from ill-health and was for three months under treatment in hospital, and on his recovery was sent home. He was then engaged on important duties at various equipment depôts until his demobilisation in February 1919. He holds the General Service and Victory Medals.
21, Crawshay Road, Stockwell, S.W.9.   Z4467

HATCHER, A. G., Pte., Oxfordshire and Buckinghamshire Light Infantry.

He was mobilised at the outbreak of hostilities, and almost immediately drafted to France. There he took part in the memorable Retreat from Mons, and in the Battles of the Marne and the Aisne. Owing to illness he was then sent home and invalided out of the Service in November 1914. He holds the Mons Star, and the General Service and Victory Medals.
5, Clovelly Road, Chiswick, W.4.   6599

HATFIELD, W., Sergt., 13th London Regiment (Kensingtons).

He volunteered in September 1914, and in the following February proceeded to France. During his service on the Western Front he fought in various engagements, including those at Neuve Chapelle, the Somme, Arras and Cambrai. He gave his life for the freedom of England on August 29th, 1918, and was entitled to the 1914-15 Star, and the General Service and Victory Medals.
"His memory is cherished with pride."
208, Beresford Street, Camberwell Road, S.E.5.   Z2496B

HATFIELD, C. G., Corporal, 13th London Regt. (Kensingtons).
He joined in February 1918, and after his training served at various stations on important duties with the Machine Gun Corps. Later he was transferrred to clerical work, on which he served until his demobilisation in November 1919.
208, Beresford Street, Camberwell Road, S.E.5. Z2496A

HATHAWAY, J., Pte., Queen's (Royal West Surrey Regiment).
He volunteered in February 1915, and after serving on important duties at various stations, was drafted to France in 1917. Whilst overseas he took part in numerous engagements, including those at Ypres and Bapaume, and also was in action in the Advance of 1918, and was twice wounded. He was demobilised in February 1919, and holds the General Service and Victory Medals.
21, Royal Road, Walworth, S.E.17. Z26570

HATLEY, F. L., Drummer, 2nd Bedfordshire Regt.
He was mobilised from the Reserve in August 1914, and in the same year was sent to the Western Front. There he served at Calais, St. Omer and Armentières, from where he was invalided home to undergo an operation. After his recovery he was transferred to the Labour Corps, and was subsequently discharged as medically unfit for further service in March 1916. He holds the Queen's and King's South African Medals, King George's Coronation Medal, the 1914 Star, and the General Service and Victory Medals.
28, Motley Street, Wandsworth Road, S.W.8. Z2497

HATTLE, H., Pte., Queen's (Royal West Surrey Regiment).
He volunteered in 1914, and in 1916 was drafted to the Western Front. Whilst in France he fought on the Somme and at Arras, and in various other engagements, and was severely wounded in action. He was invalided home and was discharged as medically unfit for further duty in December 1917. He holds the General Service and Victory Medals.
154, Stewart's Road, Battersea Park Road, S.W.8. Z2498

HATTON, G. W. T., Sapper, R.E.
He joined in September 1916, and in the same year was sent to the Western Front. There he was engaged on important duties in connection with the operations, and was frequently in the forward areas, notably on the Somme and at Arras. He was very severely wounded at Ypres on October 14th, 1918, and was invalided home to hospital, where he remained for two years under treatment. He was discharged as permanently disabled in 1919, and in the following year was still undergoing treatment. He holds the General Service and Victory Medals.
40, Eastcote Street, Stockwell Green, S.W.9. Z2499

HAUTOT, G., Private, 3rd Royal Fusiliers.
He volunteered in November 1914, and after his training was drafted to France in the following March, and during his service on the Western Front fought at the Battle of Neuve Chapelle. After only six weeks' service in France he fell fighting at Hill 60 on April 14th, 1915, and was entitled to the 1914 15 Star, and the General Service and Victory Medals.
"Thinki g that remembrance, though unspoken, may reach him where he sleeps."
7, Dean's Buildings, Walworth, S.E.17. Z2500B

HAUTOT, J. F., Driver, R.F.A.
He volunteered in August 1915, and in the following May was drafted to France, where he served in many important engagements, including those of the Somme, Albert, Arras, Messines and Ypres. In November 1917 he was sent to Italy, and was in action in various operations against the Austrians until March of the following year, when he returned to France. He then took part in engagements during the Retreat and Advance of 1918, and after the cessation of hostilities returned home and was demobilised in August 1919, holding the General Service and Victory Medals.
7, Dean's Buildings, Walworth, S.E.17. Z2500A

HAVERS, W., Corporal, R.A.S.C. (M.T.)
Volunteering at the commencement of hostilities, he crossed to France after a brief course of training. During his service he was attached to the Signal Section of the Royal Engineers, in which he did valuable work in many important sectors, including those of the Somme, Ypres and Arras. He holds the 1914 Star, and the General Service and Victory Medals, and was demobilised in 1919.
132, Kirkwood Road, S.E.15. Z6246

HAWES, F. R., A.B., R.N., H.M. Monitor "Prince Rupert."
He volunteered at the outbreak of hostilities, and after his training was posted to H.M. Monitor "Prince Rupert." Whilst in this vessel he took part in the bombardment of Zeebrugge, and in the engagement off Ostend. He also served on various important duties until demobilised in February 1919. He holds the 1914-15 Star, and the General Service and Victory Medals.
172, Boyson Road, Walworth, S.E.17. Z2503

HAWES, J. F., Rifleman, 5th London Regiment (London Rifle Brigade).
He joined in July 1917, and in the following April was sent to France, where he saw considerable active service. He gave his life for King and Country at Bapaume on October 12th, 1918, and was entitled to the General Service and Victory Medals.
"Honour to the immortal dead who gave their youth that the world might grow old in peace."
62, St. George's Road, Peckham, S.E.15. Z5420

HAWES, S. S., Pte., Queen's (Royal West Surrey Regiment).
He joined in February 1916, and in the following September was drafted to France. Whilst in this theatre of war he fought at Loos, Albert, the Somme, Arras, Ypres, Lens, Cambrai, and in many engagements in the Retreat and Advance of 1918. He was demobilised in June 1919, and holds the General Service and Victory Medals.
3, High Park Crescent, Aylesbury Road, Walworth, S.E.17. Z2502A

HAWES, W., Private, R.A.S.C.
He volunteered in October 1914, and in the following month was sent to the Western Front, where he served for four and a quarter years. Throughout the war he was engaged on transport duties, conveying food and ammunition supplies to the troops in the front lines, and was present at numerous battles, including those at Ypres, the Somme and Cambrai. He was demobilised in February 1919, and holds the 1914 Star, and the General Service and Victory Medals.
95, Manor Street, Clapham, S.W.4. Z2501

HAWKER, A., Private, 10th Queen's (Royal West Surrey Regiment).
He joined in December 1917, and in the same month was drafted to France. Whilst overseas he took part in many important engagements in the Retreat and Advance of 1918. He was demobilised in October 1919, and holds the General Service and Victory Medals.
22, Congreve Street, Walworth, S.E.17. Z2504B

HAWKER, C., Gunner, R.F.A.
He joined in March 1917, and in the following September was sent overseas. During his service in France he fought in the Battles at Passchendaele, Lens and Cambrai, and in the engagements which followed in the Retreat and Advance of 1918, and was gassed. He was demobilised in September 1919, and holds the General Service and Victory Medals.
22, Congreve Street, Walworth, S.E.17. Z2504A

HAWKER, W. G. (D.S.M.), Stoker, R.N., H.M. Submarine E14.
He was serving in the Navy at the outbreak of war, and was posted to the E14, which torpedoed a German transport, all men on board the submarine being awarded the Distinguished Service Medal for their gallantry in this action. He was then transferred to the E11, and afterwards to the J1. He served in the Dardanelles and in the Sea of Marmora until the cessation of hostilities. In 1920 he was still in the Navy, and holds the 1914-15 Star, and the General Service and Victory Medals.
22, Congreve Street, Walworth, S.E.17. Z2504C

HAWKES, W. H., Driver, R.A.S.C. (M.T.)
Volunteering in April 1915, he was sent to France in the same year. Whilst overseas he served in many battle areas, including those of the Somme, Arras, Ypres, Cambrai and did splendid work with the ammunition column. In September 1918 he was discharged through causes due to his service, and holds the 1914-15 Star, and the General Service and Victory Medals.
12, Nealdon Street, Landor Road, S.W.9. Z2505

HAWKIN, H., Private, Welch Regiment.
He volunteered in February 1915, and in the following October was drafted to France, where during the fighting near Neuve Chapelle he was severely wounded and gassed. He was invalided home, and after hospital treatment was eventually discharged as medically unfit for further duty in June 1918. He holds the 1914-15 Star, and the General Service and Victory Medals.
9, Townsend Street, Walworth, S.E.17. Z1360B

HAWKINS. A. J., Private, 2nd Hampshire Regt.
He was serving in India at the outbreak of war, having enlisted in 1907, afterwards was drafted to Gallipoli, where he fought at Sedd-el-Bahr and in various engagements, and was wounded. After the Evacuation of the Peninsula he was sent to Egypt, where he served for a few months before proceeding to France. He was in action in the Battle of the Somme and many other engagements until the cessation of hostilities. In May 1919 he was demobilised, holding the 1914-15 Star, and the General Service and Victory Medals.
132, Ingrave Street, Battersea, S.W.11. Z2510

HAWKINS, C., Private, 43rd Canadian Infantry.

Volunteering in August 1914, he came to England with the first Canadian Contingent, and was subsequently drafted to the Western Front. Whilst in this theatre of war he fought at Ypres and Vimy Ridge, where he was severely wounded. After treatment, however, he returned to the Field, and took part in engagements on the Somme, at Passchendaele, Lens and Cambrai. He was demobilised in June 1919, and holds the 1914-15 Star, and the General Service and Victory Medals.

113, Commercial Road, Peckham, S.E.15.   Z6243B. Z6244B

HAWKINS, E. G., Sapper, R.E.

Mobilised from the Reserve at the outbreak of war he immediately proceeded to France and served in the memorable Retreat from Mons. He was afterwards engaged on important work in connection with bridge building and laying barbed-wire entanglements, and was gassed and blown up by a mine explosion. He was invalided to England and eventually discharged in June 1918. He holds the Mons Star, and the General Service and Victory Medals.

3, Emu Road, Battersea Park, S.W.8.   Z2507B

HAWKINS, F., Corporal, R.F.A.

He volunteered in September 1914, and after training at Aldershot crossed to France early in 1915. Whilst in this theatre of war he fought at Ypres, Loos, Arras and in many other important engagements, and was later drafted to Salonika and took part in the Balkan campaign. He holds the 1914-15 Star, and the General Service and Victory Medals, and was demobilised in May 1920, after returning to England.

113, Commercial Road, Peckham, S.E.15.   Z6243A
Z6244A

HAWKINS, G. D. (Jun.), Rflmn., 1st Rifle Brigade.

Volunteering in May 1915, he was retained for a time on important duties in England. Later he was drafted to France and fought in numerous engagements in the Retreat and Advance of 1918, especially near Cambrai. After the conclusion of hostilities he proceeded to India and did good service there, and in Mesopotamia until June 1920, when he returned home and was demobilised. He holds the General Service and Victory Medals.

11, Broomsgrove Road, Stockwell Road, S.W.9.   Z2511

HAWKINS, G. D. (Sen.), Driver, R.F.A.

Volunteering in May 1915 he was drafted in the same year to Egypt, where he served for a few months. He then proceeded to France and fought in many battles, including those at the Somme, Ypres, Arras, and in other sectors until the close of the war. In 1919 he returned home and was demobilised, holding the 1914-15 Star, and the General Service and Victory Medals.

29, Broomsgrove Road, Stockwell Road, S.W.9.   Z2512

HAWKINS, G. F. W., Rifleman, Royal Irish Rifles.

Joining in 1916, he proceeded overseas on the completion of his training in the following year. Whilst in France he took part in the fierce fighting in the Ypres sector. In August 1917 he was killed in action at Lens after six months' active service. He was entitled to the General Service and Victory Medals.

"His life for his Country, his Soul to God."

50, Stanley Street, Queen's Road, Battersea Park, S.W.8.
Z2509A

HAWKINS, H., Private, Royal Fusiliers.

He joined in January 1918, and in the following March was drafted to France. Whilst overseas he fought in many notable engagements until hostilities ceased, including those at the Somme, and Grandecourt. In February 1919 he returned home and was demobilised, holding the General Service and Victory Medals.

17, Kingswood Road, Chiswick, W.4.   6802A

HAWKINS, T. C., Staff-Sergt., 25th King's Royal Rifle Corps and 8th Rifle Brigade.

He volunteered in December 1915, and for some time was retained on important duties with his unit until May 1917, when he was drafted to the Western Front. He took part in many important engagements until the end of the war, including those at St. Quentin, Vimy Ridge, Ypres, and Passchendaele, and was wounded. After valuable service with the Army of Occupation in Germany he returned home and was demobilised in November 1919, holding the General Service and Victory Medals.

10, Over Place, off Princes Road, Kennington, S.E.11. Z25523

HAWKINS, T. E., Private, Labour Corps.

Joining in 1916 he proceeded overseas in the following year and served with his Corps on many sectors of the Western Front. He was principally engaged in road making, and rendered valuable services until his demobilisation in March 1919. He holds the General Service and Victory Medals.

50, Stanley Street, Battersea Park, S.W.8.   Z2509B

HAWKINS, T. F., Private, 2nd Rifle Brigade.

He joined in September 1917, and after having completed his training proceeded to France. He took part in numerous engagements of importance, and at Arras was taken prisoner. In Germany he suffered much privation until December 1918, when he was repatriated and demobilised. He holds the General Service and Victory Medals.

30, Rolls Street, Battersea, S.W.11.   Z2506

HAWKINS, W., Private, 23rd London Regiment.

He volunteered in 1915, and after his training was engaged at various stations on important duties with his unit. He rendered valuable services, but was not successful in obtaining his transfer overseas owing to medical unfitness. In 1916 he was discharged, in consequence of illness due to his service.

28, Mundella Road, Wandsworth Road, S.W.8.   Z2508A

HAWTIN, T. S., Driver, R.A.S.C.

Volunteering in 1914, he was drafted overseas in the following year. He served until the cessation of hostilities in various sectors of the Western Front, including the Somme, Ypres, Arras, conveying supplies to the fighting areas. He then proceeded to Germany with the Army of Occupation, and remained there until demobilised in 1919. He holds the 1914-15 Star, and the General Service and Victory Medals.

62, Faraday Street, Walworth, S.E.17.   Z2513

HAYDON, J. C., Pte., 22nd London Regt. (Queen's).

He joined in August 1916, and in the same year was drafted to France. Whilst in this theatre of war he served with distinction in many battles, and was wounded. In March 1918 he gave his life for his King and Country in the second Battle of the Somme. He was entitled to the General Service and Victory Medals.

"Whilst we remember, the Sacrifice is not in vain."

75, Farmer's Road, Camberwell, S.E.5.   1241D

HAYES, A., Private, Lincolnshire Regiment.

Joining in November 1916, he was retained on the completion of his training for important agricultural duties in Lancashire. He rendered valuable services but was not successful in obtaining his transfer overseas before the cessation of hostilities. In February 1919 he was demobilised.

66, Priory Grove, Lansdowne Road, S.W.8.   Z2514

HAYES, C. F., Pte., 1st Duke of Cornwall's Light Infantry.

Volunteering in October 1914, he was drafted in the same year to the Western Front. There he took part in many battles, including those on the Somme Front. He was reported missing after the Battle of Delville Wood, and was presumed killed in action there on July 22nd, 1916. He was entitled to the 1914-15 Star, and the General Service and Victory Medals.

"The path of duty was the way to glory."

40, Riverhall Street, Wandsworth Road, S.W.8.   Z2515B

HAYES, F., Private, 7th City of London Regiment and Tank Corps.

Volunteering in May 1915, he was drafted on the completion of his training to France, where he took part in many engagements, and was wounded in March 1917. Later he was transferred to the Tank Corps, and with them served in the Advance of 1918. In December of that year he returned home, and was eventually demobilised in March 1919, holding the General Service and Victory Medals. Early in 1920 he re-joined the Colours in the Tank Corps.

130, Sulgrave Road, Hammersmith, W.6.   11782

HAYES, S. P., Driver, R.A.S.C.

He joined in 1916, and in the following year was drafted to Russia, where he was engaged on important transport duties in various places, including Archangel and Murmansk. Later he was sent to Ireland, and was stationed at Curragh, and in 1920 was still serving. He holds the General Service and Victory Medals.

5, Riverhall Street, Wandsworth Road, S.W.8.   Z2516

HAYES, W. F., Staff-Sergt. Saddler, R.A.S.C. (H.T.)

He volunteered in April 1915, and for a time was engaged on important instructional duties. In July of the same year he embarked for France and served with the 17th Division, on important work in connection with the repairing of harness. He saw much active service at Ypres, St. Eloi, Armentières, the Somme, Cambrai, and many other places until the cessation of hostilities. He returned home in May 1919, and was demobilised, holding the 1914-15 Star, and the General Service and Victory Medals.

36, Wickersley Road, Lavender Hill, S.W.11.   Z3290A

HAYES, W. G., Rifleman, Rifle Brigade.

He joined in June 1916, and in the following September proceeded to France, where he took part in much severe fighting until November 1916. He was then invalided home through ill-health, but on recovery returned to the fighting area. He was unfortunately killed in action on May 8th, 1918, and was entitled to the General Service and Victory Medals.

"He died the noblest death a man may die."

16, Birley Street, Battersea, S.W.11.   Z2517

HAYMAN, W. L. (M.M.), L/Corporal, R.E.
Volunteering in January 1915, he served for a time on important duties in England, and in February 1917 was drafted to
France where he served with distinction in many battles. He
was awarded the Military Medal for conspicuous bravery in
advancing in the face of great danger in front of the infantry
to erect a bridge, thus enabling the troops to cross, and capturing
five Germans single handed. In addition he holds the General
Service and Victory Medals, and in April 1919 returned home
and was demobilised.
208, Cator Street, Peckham, S.E.15.   Z5094

HAYNES, A. C., Seaman Gunner, R.N.
He volunteered in 1914, and on the conclusion of his training
was posted to H.M.S. "Britannia," in which he fought in the
Battle of Jutland, and was engaged on important escort duties,
chiefly in the North Sea, until her sinking by submarine off
Cape Trafalgar in November 1918. After some months'
service in H.M.S. "Empress of India" in Russian waters he
was transferred to H.M.S. "Dublin," in which in 1920 he was
still serving. He holds the 1914-15 Star, and the General
Service and Victory Medals.
26, Wivenhoe Road, Peckham, S.E.15.   Z5996

HAYNES, F., Gunner (Signaller), R.F.A.
He joined in December 1916, and in the following year was
drafted to the Western Front, where he served on important
duties as a signaller and wireless operator. He was in action
in many engagements, including those at Ypres, Arras, Passchendaele, Bapaume, Amiens, and the Advance of 1918. After
the conclusion of hostilities he was sent to Cologne with the
Army of Occupation, and in 1920 was still serving. He holds
the General Service and Victory Medals.
44, Sussex Road, Caldharbour Lane, S.W.9.   Z3468

HAYNES, F. F., A.B., Royal Navy.
Volunteering in May 1915, he was posted to s.s. "Pavonia,"
in which vessel he served throughout the war. This ship
was principally engaged in conveying troops from New
York to Liverpool, and did splendid work. In November
1918 he was demobilised, holding the General Service and
Victory Medals.
19, Northampton Place, Walworth, S.E.17.   Z2518

**HAYNES, G. J., 2nd Lieut., Royal Fusiliers and
Middlesex Regiment.**
Volunteering in November 1915, he embarked for France
in the following year, and whilst in this theatre of war took
part in many battles and was wounded during the fierce
fighting on the Somme. He was unfortunately killed in action
on June 17th, 1918, and was entitled to the General Service
and Victory Medals.
        "His life for his Country, his Soul to God."
39, Southfield Road, Bedford Park, W.4.   7892B

HAYNES, W., Gunner, R.G.A. and R.F.A.
He joined in June 1916, and in the following year proceeded
overseas. Whilst in France he saw much service on the Somme
and at Menin Road, Cambrai, and in many other sectors,
until the cessation of hostilities. In December 1918 he was
demobilised, holding the General Service and Victory Medals.
39, Southfield Road, Bedford Park, W.4.   7892A

HAYSEY, H. W., Sapper, R.E.
Mobilised at the outbreak of war, he embarked for the Dardanelles early in the following year, and served there until
the Evacuation of the Peninsula. Later he was drafted to
France, and was present at the engagements on the Somme,
and at Ypres and Arras as a telegraphist. In February
1919, he returned home and was demobilised, holding the 1914-
15 Star, and the General Service and Victory Medals.
45, Bonnington Square, South Lambeth Road, S.W.8.
                                                      Z2519A

HAYSEY, R. A. H., Driver, R.E.
Mobilised at the outbreak of war he was drafted overseas
early in the following year. He served on many sectors of
the Western Front as a driver, and also acted as a shoeing
smith during his service, and was present at the fighting on
the Somme, and at Ypres and Arras. In July 1919 he was
demobilised, holding the 1914-15 Star, and the General Service
and Victory Medals.
45, Bonnington Square, South Lambeth Road, S.W.8.
                                                      Z2519B

HAYSOM, A. R., Sapper, R.E.
He volunteered in October 1915, and in the following March
was drafted to France, and during the fighting on the Somme
was wounded. On recovery he returned to the front line,
and was shortly afterwards again severely wounded and
invalided to England. Later, in July 1917, he proceeded to
Mesopotamia, where he served until May 1919, and then
returned home for demobilisation. He holds the General
Service and Victory Medals.
170, Tyneham Road, Lavender Hill, S.W.11.   Z2520

HAYTER, E. M. M. (Mrs.), Special War Worker.
This lady was engaged at Hayes Munition Factory, Middlesex,
in shell filling and other important work. Her duties which
were of a most responsible nature were carried out in a highly
commendable manner and she rendered valuable services
during the war.
52, Linden Gardens, Chiswick, W.4.   T5646C

HAYTER, W., Special War Worker.
He was engaged at Reading, also at Holland Park on the inspection of army boots. His duties, which were of a highly
important character, were carried out with great care and
efficiency, and he rendered valuable services during the war.
52, Linden Gardens, Chiswick, W.4.   T5646B

HAYWARD, F., Private, R.A.O.C.
He joined in January 1916, and in June of the same year
was sent to Egypt. He was engaged on important work
in connection with his branch of the service at various stations,
including Cairo and Alexandria, and rendered valuable services. He was demobilised in September 1919, and holds
the General Service and Victory Medals.
60, St. Philip Street, Battersea Park Road, S.W.8.   Z2521

HAZEL, H. G., Pte., 8th Buffs (East Kent Regt.)
He volunteered in September 1914, and in the following year
was drafted to the Western Front and took part in severe
fighting at Hill 60, Loos, Vimy Ridge, the Somme, Arras,
Messines, and in many other engagements, and was twice
wounded. He was invalided home, but on his recovery
returned to France, and served in the Retreat and Advance
of 1918. He was demobilised in March 1919, and holds
the 1914-15 Star, and the General Service and Victory Medals.
10, Elsted Street, Walworth, S.E.17.   Z2522

HAZELDINE, H. H., Bombardier, R.G.A.
He joined in May 1916, and in the same year was drafted to
Egypt and thence to Palestine, where he took part in many
engagements, including those at Gaza, Beersheba and Jericho,
and was present at the capture of Jerusalem. In 1917 he was
transferred to France, where he was again in action, and was
wounded. He was invalided home, and was discharged as
medically unfit for further service in October 1918. He holds
the General Service and Victory Medals.
18, Venn Street, Clapham, S.W.4.   Z2523

HAZELTINE, G., Gunner, R.F.A.
He was serving in India at the outbreak of war, and shortly
afterwards proceeded to Mesopotamia, and took part in
severe fighting in many engagements. He was taken prisoner
at Kut-el-Amara with General Townshend's forces, and unhappily died in captivity in 1916. He was entitled to the
1914-15 Star, and the General Service and Victory Medals.
        "The path of duty was the way to glory."
2, Huntsman Street, Walworth, S.E.17.   Z2524A

HAZELTINE, J. H., Gunner, R.F.A.
He volunteered in November 1914, and in September of the
following year was sent to France, where he took part in severe
fighting at Loos. In December 1915, he was transferred to
Salonika, and served on the Vardar, Doiran and Struma
fronts. Later he was invalided to Malta with rheumatism,
and thence to England. He was discharged in December
1917, as medically unfit for further service, and holds the
1914-15 Star, and the General Service and Victory Medals.
2, Huntsman Street, Walworth, S.E.17.   Z2524B

HAZZARD, C. J., Rifleman, Rifle Brigade.
Volunteering in January 1915, he went through a course of
training, and afterwards served on important duties with his
unit. He rendered valuable services, but was not successful
in obtaining his transfer overseas owing to being medically
unfit for duty abroad. He was discharged in August 1916.
87, Kinglake Street, Walworth, S.E.17.   Z2526

**HAZZARD, E. T., Private, Queen's (Royal West
Surrey Regiment).**
He joined in September 1916, and served on important duties
with his unit until June 1918, when he was drafted to France,
and took part in the Retreat and Advance of that year. He
was afterwards transferred to the King's Own Scottish
Borderers, and finally was demobilised in February 1919,
holding the General Service and Victory Medals.
3, Etherdon Street, East Street, Walworth, S.E.17.   Z2525

HEAD, A. W. (M.M.), Bombardier (Signaller), R.F.A.
He was mobilised at the outbreak of war, and was shortly
afterwards drafted to France, and took part in severe fighting
at Mons, the Marne, the Aisne and Neuve Chapelle, and
was wounded at Loos. He was awarded the Military Medal
for bravery on the Field in maintaining communication
under heavy fire, and also holds the Mons Star, and the General
Service and Victory Medals. He was demobilised in May
1919.
16, Vicarage Road, Camberwell, S.E.5.   Z2527

HEAD, G., Rflmn., 17th King's Royal Rifle Corps.
He volunteered in May 1915, and in March of the following year was drafted to the Western Front, where he took part in severe fighting. He gave his life for King and Country on the Somme on September 3rd, 1916, and was entitled to the General Service and Victory Medals..
"His life for his Country, his Soul to God."
15, Sheepcote Lane, Battersea, S.W.11.   Z4931C

HEAD, W. M., P.O. Stoker, R.N., H.M.S. "Sentinel."
He volunteered in August 1914, and in the following year proceeded to Gallipoli, where he was engaged with the Fleet. Later, contracting malaria, he was invalided to hospital at Malta. He was afterwards sent to Turkey, where he was still serving in 1920, and holds the 1914-15 Star, and the General Service and Victory Medals.
94, Storhouse Street, Clapham, S.W.4.   Z2528

HEALEY, C., Air Mechanic, R.A.F.
He volunteered in June 1915, and after his training was engaged upon duties of an important nature, which called for much technical knowledge and skill. He was unable to secure his transfer overseas before the termination of hostilities, but nevertheless did valuable work until he was demobilised in May 1919.
43, Carlton Road, Chiswick, W.4.   6362A

HEALEY, A. R., Driver, R.F.A.
He volunteered in December 1914, and served on the Western Front from the following September until 1917, during which time he took part in many notable battles, including those of the Somme and Ypres. He was then sent to Salonika, and did valuable work with his unit in the operations on the Vardar and Doiran fronts. He was demobilised in March 1919, and holds the 1914-15 Star, and the General Service and Victory Medals.
94, Warham Street, Camberwell, S.E.5.   Z2531

HEALEY, C. G., Private, 3rd Royal Fusiliers.
A serving soldier, he was previously in India for two years, and was sent to the Western Front in 1915. A month after his arrival at this theatre of war, he was reported missing, but later it was stated he had been killed in action at Ypres on May 3rd, 1915. He was entitled to the 1914-15 Star, and the General Service and Victory Medals.
"His Life for his Country."
19, Park Place, Clapham Park Road, S.W.4.   Z2530

HEALEY, E. G., Sergt., R.F.A.
He volunteered in September 1914, and early in the following year crossed to France. Whilst in this theatre of war he fought at Loos, the Somme, where in 1916 he was wounded, Messines, Ypres, Epéhy, Merville, Arras and Tournai. Returning to England after the termination of hostilities, he was discharged through ill-health, following his wound in May 1919. He holds the 1914-15 Star, and the General Service and Victory Medals.
24, Kimpton Road, Camberwell, S.E.5.   Z4004B
    Z4005B

HEALEY, J. N., Rifleman, 21st London Regiment (1st Surrey Rifles).
He volunteered in November 1915, and after the completion of his military training was retained from 1916 to 1918, for important munition work at Woolwich Arsenal. He rendered valuable services there, but owing to physical disability was not able to secure his transfer to a fighting front. From 1899 to 1912 he had done good service in the Royal Marine Light Infantry.
161, Kimberley Road, Peckham, S.E.15.   Z6389

HEALEY, W. G., Guardsman, Grenadier Guards.
Joining in May 1917, he was drafted to France in the following year, and was engaged in the fighting in many important sectors, notably those of the Somme, Ypres, Passchendaele, Bapaume and Bullecourt. Towards the close of hostilities, he contracted an illness, and after being in hospital for a time at the Base, was invalided to Torquay, where he underwent protracted treatment. He was demobilised in January 1919, and holds the General Service and Victory Medals.
12, Park Place, Clapham Park Road, S.W.4.   Z2529

HEALEY, W. J., Private, 35th Royal Fusiliers and Queen's (Royal West Surrey Regiment).
After joining, he obtained his training at various stations in England, and in March 1917 crossed to France. Whilst in this theatre of war he was for a time attached to the R.E., engaged on important duties in connection with laying cables, fixing barbed wire entanglements, and other work. He was in action in many important sectors during the Retreat and Advance of 1918, and helped to construct the broad gauge Railway line from Bray to St. Quentin. After the Armistice he returned home and was demobilised in April 1919, holding the General Service and Victory Medals.
24, Kimpton Road, Camberwell, S.E.5.   Z4004C
    Z4005C

HEALEY, S. C. G., Private, 2nd London Regiment.
He joined in March 1917, and during his service on the Western Front took an active part in many important battles, including that of Ypres. He was demobilised in December 1919, after his return to England, and holds the General Service and Victory Medals.
43, Carlton Road, Chiswick, W.4.   6362B

HEARD, B., Private, Bedfordshire Regiment.
He joined in 1918, and after his training was engaged on duties of an important nature with his unit. He was unable to secure his transfer overseas before the termination of hostilities, but afterwards was sent with the Army of Occupation to Germany, where he served for eighteen months. He returned home and was demobilised in January 1920.
44, Park Crescent, Clapham Park Road, S.W.4.   Z2532B

HEARD, F., Private, R.A.V.C.
Joining in June 1916, he was sent to France at the conclusion of his training, and subsequently fought in the Battles of Vimy Ridge and the Somme. In 1917 he returned to England for a time and was later re-drafted to the Western Front, where he served in the Retreat and Advance of 1918, at the end of which he was sent with the Army of Occupation to Germany. He holds the General Service and Victory Medals, and was demobilised in 1920 on his return to England.
44, Park Crescent, Clapham Park Road, S.W.4.   Z2532A

HEARN, A. E., Private, 16th Middlesex Regiment.
He volunteered in March 1915, and at the conclusion of his training was drafted to the Western Front. Whilst in this theatre of war he fought in many of the principal battles, and was severely wounded during the Somme Offensive in in July 1916. He was invalided home and was discharged in 1918, and holds the 1914-15 Star, and the General Service and Victory Medals.
75, St. Philip Street, Battersea Park, S.W.8.   Z2533A

HEARN, C. (M.M.), C.S.M., 2nd Grenadier Guards.
Having enlisted in 1902, he was serving when war broke out, and was immediately drafted to France, where he fought in the Retreat from Mons, and the Battles of Loos, where he was wounded, and Ypres. He gave his life for King and Country during the Somme Offensive on September 15th, 1916. He was posthumously awarded the Military Medal for gallantry and devotion to duty in the Field, and was entitled to the Mons Star, and the General Service and Victory Medals.
107A, Tennyson Street, Wentworth Road, S.W.8.
    Z2537B

HEARN, C. H., Private, Royal Fusiliers.
He joined in June 1917, and after his training was engaged on duties of an important nature as a Lewis Gun Instructor. Although unable to secure his transfer overseas before the termination of hostilities, he did valuable work in this capacity until he was demobilised in January 1919.
11, Medwin Street, Ferndale Road, S.W.4.   Z2534

HEARN, F., Gunner, R.F.A.
He volunteered in January 1915, and after his training saw service in France, Salonika and Mesopotamia. On each of these Fronts he did valuable work with his unit in the capacity of Signaller, taking part in many of the principal engagements. He was serving in Mesopotamia in 1920, and holds the 1914-15 Star, and the General Service and Victory Medals.
1, Sydney Square, Latona Road, Peckham, S.E.15.   Z6245A

HEARN, H. A., Private, Royal Warwickshire Regt.
Joining in February 1917, he was drafted to the Western Front at the conclusion of his training, and was taken prisoner during the German Offensive in March 1918. After his release at the termination of hostilities, he returned to England, and was demobilised in January 1919. He holds the General Service and Victory Medals.
75, St. Philip Street, Battersea Park, S.W.8.   Z2533B

HEARN, J., Shoeing Smith, R.F.A.
Volunteering May 1915, he was sent to France immediately upon completing his training, and subsequently took part in many important engagements. In the course of his service he contracted a severe form of pneumonia, of which unfortunately he died on November 5th, 1918. He was entitled to the 1914-15 Star, and the General Service and Victory Medals.
"And doubtless he went in splendid company."
1, Sydney Square, Latona Road, Peckham, S.E.15.
    Z6245B

HEARN, J., Private, Royal Scots Fusiliers.
He joined in 1916, and after his training was engaged on duties of an important nature at various stations with his unit. He was not successful in obtaining his transfer overseas before the cessation of hostilities, but was afterwards sent to Constantinople, where in 1920 he was still serving.
104, Faraday Street, Walworth, S.E.17.   Z2536

HEARN, L., Private, 1/23rd London Regiment.
Volunteering in May 1915, he crossed to France in the following January, and fought in several engagements. He was unhappily killed in action at Vimy Ridge on May 6th, 1916, and was entitled to the General Service and Victory Medals.
" His memory is cherished with pride."
80, Lavender Road, Battersea, S.W.11. Z2535

HEARN, S., Gunner, R.F.A.
He volunteered in June 1915, and during his service on the Western Front, which lasted for three years, took an active part in many of the principal battles, notably those of Vimy Ridge, the Somme, Ypres, Arras and Cambrai. He holds the General Service and Victory Medals, and was demobilised in March 1919.
70, Vaughan Road, Camberwell, S.E.5. Z6256

HEARNE, F., Special War Worker.
Being ineligible for service with the Colours, he obtained work of National importance at the South Metropolitan Gas Works, where he operated a drilling lathe in connection with the manufacture of munitions. He carried out these important duties with a high degree of efficiency, and rendered valuable services for a considerable period of the war.
21, Loughboro Street, Kennington, S.E.11.
TZ25494B

HEARNE, G. L., Sergt., Buffs (East Kent Regt.)
Mobilised at the outbreak of hostilities, he was drafted to Mesopotamia in 1915, and during his service in that theatre of war, took an active part in many important battles. He was demobilised in 1919, after his return to England, and holds the 1914-15 Star, and the General Service and Victory Medals.
27, Mundella Road, Wandsworth Road, S.W.8. Z2538

HEASMAN, G. H., Sapper, R.E.
He volunteered in February 1915, and in the following September crossed to France, where he was engaged on important duties with the 107th Field Comapny. In December of the same year he was transferred to Salonika, and attached to the 26th Division, did valuable work during operations on the Doiran front, and was twice wounded. He was invalided to a hospital in Malta, and returning to England on his recovery was demobilised in April 1919. He holds the 1914-15 Star, and the General Service and Victory Medals.
51, Pitt Street, Peckham, S.E.15. Z5095

HEATH, A. W., Trooper, Royal Bucks Hussars.
Volunteering at the age of fifteen, in August 1914, he was drafted to France at the conclusion of his training. He subsequently took part in several important engagements in the Somme sector, and whilst in action in 1915, received a severe wound, to which, unhappily, he succumbed in hospital on March 21st, of that year. He was entitled to the 1914 Star, and the General Service and Victory Medals.
7, Alsace Street, Walworth, S.E.17. Z2541

HEATH, E. A., Gunner, R.G.A.
He volunteered in November 1915, and in October of the following year was drafted to Salonika, where he fought in several engagements, including that at Monastir. In 1917 he was transferred to Egypt, and shortly afterwards took part in the Palestine campaign, during which he was engaged in the Battles of Gaza, and the capture of Jerusalem, Jericho and Aleppo. He was demobilised in April 1919, after his return to England, and holds the General Service and Victory Meddals.
11, Palmerston Street, Battersea, S.W.11. Z2539

HEATH, E. M., Rifleman, King's Royal Rifle Corps.
Volunteering in September 1915, he was sent to the Western Front in the following year and there served with distinction until the close of the war in many important engagements. He fought in the Battles of the Somme, Arras, Ypres, St. Quentin, Amiens and many other operations in the Retirement and Advance of the Allies of 1918, and after his return home was demobilised in February 1919. He holds the General Service and Victory Medals.
35, Manaton Road, Peckham, S.E.15. Z6385

HEATH, G. H., Private, 2nd Royal Fusiliers.
He volunteered in February 1915, and after his training was drafted to the Western Front, where he fought at Messines and Dickebusch. In 1916, however, he was invalided to England in consequence of ill-health, and in June of that year was discharged as medically unfit. He holds the 1914-15 Star, and the General Service and Victory Medals.
15, Odell Street, Camberwell, S.E.5. Z5421C

HEATH, H., Rifleman, Rifle Brigade.
Volunteering in February 1915, he was sent to the Western Front at the conclusion of his training. He was subsequently engaged in the fighting in many important sectors and was four times wounded, on the Somme twice and at Passchendaele and St. Quentin. Invalided home, he was for some time in hospital, and in August 1917, was discharged as physically unfit. He holds the 1914-15 Star, and the General Service and Victory Medals.
15, Odell Street, Camberwell, S.E.5. Z5421D

HEATH, H. A., Leading Signalman, R.N.
Having enlisted in March 1913, he was in the Navy when war broke out, and later on board H.M.S. " Inflexible," took part in several engagements, including those off the Falkland Isles, the Dogger Bank and Heligoland Bight. His ship also participated in Naval actions in the Dardanelles, in one of which he was wounded, and covered the Landing of the troops on the Peninsula and also the Evacuation. Later he served with his vessel on important patrol and convoy duties in the North Sea and in 1920 was in Russian waters. He holds the 1914-15 Star, and the General Service and Victory Medals.
15, Odell Street, Camberwell, S.E.5. Z5421B

HEATH, H. S., Special War Worker.
Being ineligible for service with the Colours he obtained work of National importance at the Hendon Aerodrome. He held an important post, and was responsible for the output of fifty workers, of whom he was in charge. On resigning at the termination of hostilities, he was the recipient of a testimonial from Mr. Grahame-White, in recognition of his splendid work.
11, Palmerston Street, Battersea, S.W.11. Z2543

HEATH, J. R., Gunner, R.G.A.
Joining in March 1917, he crossed to France in the following June and took part in several important engagements. He gave his life for the freedom of England in the Battle of Ypres on October 6th, 1917, and was entitled to the General Service and Victory Medals.
" He died the noblest death a man may die,
Fighting for God, and right, and liberty."
35, Overstone Road, Hammersmith, W.6. 10776B

HEATH, T. S., Private, 24th London Regt. (Queen's) and Rifleman, Royal Irish Rifles.
Joining in 1916, he was sent to the Western Front at the conclusion of his training and subsequently fought in many important engagements, notably those on the Somme and at Ypres. During the German Offensive of 1918, he was severely wounded in action at Passchendaele, but after being for a time in hospital at the Base, rejoined his unit and served in the Advance of that year. He was demobilised in 1919, and holds the General Service and Victory Medals.
26, Henshaw Street, Walworth, S.E.17. Z2542

HEATH, W. G., L/Cpl., 16th (The Queen's) Lancers.
A serving soldier, he was sent to the Western Front immediately upon the outbreak of hostilities, and took part in the Retreat from Mons and the Battles of the Marne and the Aisne. He also served in many of the engagements which followed until 1915, when in consequence of his having been severely gassed, he was invalided home. After his recovery he was retained for important home duties until his demobilisation, which took place in March 1919. He holds the Mons Star, and the General Service and Victory Medals.
15, Odell Street, Camberwell, S.E.5. Z5421A

HEATH, W. H., Gunner, R.F.A.
He volunteered in November 1914, and after his training served on the Western Front for over three years. During this time he fought in many important engagements, notably those on the Somme and at Arras, Ypres and Cambrai, and did valuable work with his unit. He was demobilised in February 1919, and holds the 1914-15 Star, and the General Service and Victory Medals.
19, Vicarage Road, Camberwell, S.E.5. Z2540

HEATHFIELD, J. C., Leading Stoker, R.N.
He enlisted in 1913, and during the war served on board H.M. Submarines, C28 and L14. He took part with his vessel in several actions against enemy U-boats, and also served in the North Sea and off the Belgian Coast on patrol and convoy duties. He was discharged in 1920, and holds the 1014-15 Star, and the General Service and Victory Medals.
275, East Street, Walworth, S.E.17. Z2544

HEATHWHITE, C., Rifleman, 16th London Regt. (Queen's Westminster Rifles).
He volunteered in April 1915, and in July 1916 crossed to France. Whilst in this theatre of war, he fought at Vimy Ridge, the Somme, Bullecourt, Messines, Ypres, Passchendaele and Lille, and in August 1918, was wounded during the Advance of that year. After being for a time in hospital at Rouen, he was sent to Stockport, and after protracted treatment, was invalided out of the Service in February 1919. He holds the General Service and Victory Medals.
6, Portland Mansions, Bromell's Road, Clapham, S.W.4. Z2545

HEATON, H., Private, Loyal North Lancashire Regiment, and Driver, M.G.C.
A serving soldier, he was drafted to France at the outbreak of war, and took part in the Retreat from Mons. In 1915 he was severely wounded near Loos, during the heavy fighting for the Hohenzollern Redoubt, and was in consequence invalided home. After his recovery he was sent to Salonika, where he fought in several battles on the Doiran front, and was again wounded. He holds the Mons Star, and the General Service and Victory Medals, and discharged in April 1919.
4, Horsman Street, Camberwell, S.E.5. Z2546

HEAVENS, E., Private, 2/1st London Regt. (Royal Fusiliers).
He joined in March 1916, and at the conclusion of his training was drafted to the Western Front, where he subsequently fought in many important engagements. In April 1917 he was taken prisoner and was in captivity for eighteen months before being repatriated at the termination of hostilities. He was demobilised in February 1919, and holds the General Service and Victory Medals.
138, Speke Road, Battersea, S.W.11.   Z2547A

HEAVENS, J., L/Corporal, 1st London Regt. (Royal Fusiliers).
He volunteered in August 1914, and was sent to Malta, where he served until the following March, when he was drafted to the Western Front. Whilst overseas he took part in several of the principal engagements, and fell fighting in the Somme sector in September 1916. He was entitled to the 1914-15 Star, and the General Service and Victory Medals.
" The path of duty was the way to glory."
138, Speke Road, Battersea, S.W.11.   Z2547B

HEAVENS, O. J., Private, 4th London Regt. (Royal Fusiliers).
He joined in 1917, and after his training, which he obtained at Winchester and Hounslow, was drafted to Mesopotamia, where he did valuable work with his unit, and in 1920 was still serving. He holds the General Service and Victory Medals.
138, Speke Road, Battersea, S.W.11.   Z2547C

HEAYES, A., Private, York and Lancaster Regt.
Joining in 1917, he was drafted to the Western Front at the conclusion of his training, and fought at Ypres and Lens. In November of the same year he was transferred to Italy, and did valuable work with his unit during operations on the Piave, and after the Armistice served at Fiume for a time. At the end of 1918 he was sent to Egypt, where he served until 1920. He was demobilised in January of that year, and holds the General Service and Victory Medals.
42, Hargwyne Street, Stockwell Road, S.W.9.   Z2548A

HEAYES, W., Stoker, R.N.
He joined in December 1917, and during his service was on board the " Thomas Young," the " Urie " and the " Harlech." With his ship, he was engaged on important mine-sweeping and patrol duties in the North Sea, and in conveying food supplies from Norway and Sweden. He was demobilised in May 1919, and holds the General Service and Victory Medals.
42, Hargwyne Street, Stockwell Road, S.W.9.   Z2548B

HECTOR, G. W., Rifleman, Rifle Brigade.
He volunteered on the outbreak of war, and was shortly afterwards drafted to the Western Front. There he took part in many important engagements, including the Battles of Ypres, the Somme and Cambrai and also participated in the Retreat and Advance of 1918. Serving overseas until 1919 he rendered valuable services, and returning home was demobilised in May 1920, holding the 1914 Star, and the General Service and Victory Medals.
1, Montefiore Street, Wandsworth Road, S.W.8.   Z2549A

HECTOR, W. C. H., Private, 7th Royal Fusiliers.
He joined in June 1918, and proceeding to the Western Front took part in the Advance, during which he was severely wounded and taken prisoner. Kept in captivity until after the signing of the Armistice he was then released and sent home, and was eventually discharged in November 1919, holding the General Service and Victory Medals.
1, Montefiore Street, Wandsworth Road, S.W.8.   Z2549B

HEED, G. W., Private, 23rd Middlesex Regiment.
He volunteered in 1915, and after a course of training was drafted to France. There he took part in the Battles of Cambrai, Passchendaele, the Somme, and Arras, and was twice wounded in action. He also served for a time in Italy, and after the Armistice proceeded into Germany with the Army of Occupation. Returning home he was demobilised in 1919, holding the 1914-15 Star, and the General Service and Victory Medals.
72, Rayleigh Road, West Kensington, W.14.   12072A

HEED, J. D., Private, Royal Sussex Regiment.
He joined in June 1918, and proceeded to France shortly after the signing of the Armistice. He did good work whilst employed on various duties with his unit near Ypres, and returning home was demobilised in November 1919.
72, Rayleigh Road, West Kensington, W.14.   12072B

HEED, J. H., Pte., 75th Canadian Light Infantry.
Volunteering in 1915, he proceeded to France in the following year, and took part in the Battles of Vimy Ridge and Ypres. Twice wounded in action before the Battle of Ypres, he was there wounded for the third time, involving the loss of an eye. Evacuated to England, he was eventually demobilised in 1919, holding the General Service and Victory Medals.
72, Rayleigh Road, West Kensington, W.14.   12072C

HEIB, A., Pte., Duke of Cornwall's Light Infantry and Royal Dublin Fusiliers.
He volunteered on the outbreak of war, and was shortly afterwards drafted to France, where he took part in the Retreat from Mons, and the Battle of Ypres. Invalided home on account of ill-health, on recovery he was transferred to the Royal Dublin Fusiliers, and was drafted to Salonika, where after taking a prominent part in several severe engagements, he died on October 8th, 1916, of wounds received in action on the Doiran front. He was entitled to the Mons Star, and the General Service and Victory Medals.
" Whilst we remember the Sacrifice is not in vain."
26, Longcroft Road, Camberwell, S.E.5.   Z5340B

HEIB, C. W., Private, 9th Worcestershire Regt.
Volunteering in August 1914, he was retained at home and rendered valuable services whilst employed on various duties until July 1915, when he was sent to Gallipoli. He had only served in that theatre of war for a short period when he was unhappily killed in action on August 12th, 1915, while taking part in the Landing at Suvla Bay. He was entitled to the 1914-15 Star, and the General Service and Victory Medals.
" His Life for his Country."
26, Longcroft Road, Camberwell, S.E.5.   Z5340C

HEIB, D., Pte., 2nd Queen's (Royal West Surrey Regiment).
Having enlisted in June 1914, he was ordered to France on the outbreak of war, and took part in the Retreat from Mons. He played a prominent part in several severe engagements, but was killed by a sniper near Ypres on December 14th, 1914. He was entitled to the Mons Star, and the General Service and Victory Medals.
" Great deeds cannot die."
26, Longcroft Road, Camberwell, S.E.5.   Z5340D

HEIMERS, R., Private, Royal Fusiliers.
He volunteered in April 1915, and after completing his training was retained at home on important duties until November 1916, when he was drafted to Salonika. In this theatre of war he took part in numerous engagements on the Doiran, Struma and Vardar fronts, and rendered valuable services until he returned home for demobilisation in March 1919, holding the General Service and Victory Medals.
15, Cornbury Street, Walworth, S.E.17.   Z2550

HEMINGTON, H., Driver, R.F.A.
He volunteered in April 1915, and after completing his course of training was drafted to the Western Front later in that year. He did valuable service with his Battery in many engagements of importance, including those at the Somme, Arras, Vimy Ridge, Ypres, Passchendaele, and served throughout the critical operations of 1918. He returned to England and was demobilised in June 1919, holding the 1914-15 Star, and the General Service and Victory Medals.
43, Sunwell Street, Peckham, S.E.15.   Z6387

HEMPSTON, F. W., Pte., 2nd East Surrey Regt.
Volunteering in November 1915, he was drafted to Salonika in the following August. There he played a prominent part in many important engagements, including severe actions on the Struma and Doiran fronts, and during the last Bulgarian Offensive. Returning home, he was demobilised in January 1919, holding the General Service and Victory Medals.
86, Neate Street, Camberwell, S.E.5.   Z5096B

HEMPSTON, G. F., Private, 1/13th London Regt. (Kensingtons).
He volunteered in November 1915, and was despatched in the following year to the Western Front, where he took a prominent part in several engagements, including that at Neuve Chapelle, during his twelve months' active service. He was unhappily killed in action on May 13th, 1917. He was entitled to the General Service and Victory Medals.
" His memory is cherished with pride."
86, Neate Street, Camberwell, S.E.5.   Z5096A

HENDERSON, C., Corporal, R.E.
Joining in May 1916, he was retained on special duties at important stations in England on account of his physical unfitness for service overseas. He did consistently good work during the latter period of hostilities, especially during the frequent air raids on London, and was demobilised in March 1919.
54, Cronin Road, Peckham, S.E.15.   Z5620

HENDERSON, F., Gunner, R.F.A. (T.F.)
He was mobilised with the Territorials in August 1914, and proceeded to France shortly afterwards. There he took part in much severe fighting, including the Battles of Ypres, Loos, Arras and the Somme, and was wounded twice. He was evacuated to England, and after a period in hospital was discharged as medically unfit for further military duties in February 1917, through his wounds. He holds the 1914-15 Star, and the General Service and Victory Medals.
5, Palmerston Street, Camberwell, S.E.5.   Z2551

HENDRY, A. C., Pte., 2nd Queen's (Royal West Surrey Regiment).
He volunteered in October 1914, and was drafted in the following month to France, where he took part in several important engagements, including the Battles of Ypres, Hill 60, and Loos, and was wounded on the Somme. Invalided home he was retained in England until the cessation of hostilities, rendering valuable services at various stations. He was demobilised in September 1919, holding the 1914-15 Star, and the General Service and Victory Medals.
56, Russell Street, Battersea, S.W.11.   Z2552B

HENDRY, A. J., Private, R.A.S.C. (M.T.)
He joined in October 1916, but was retained on home service, owing to the indispensable nature of his work. He was stationed for a period at Grove Park, and afterwards at various other workshops in England, where he rendered valuable service, until he was demobilised in November 1919.
56, Russell Street, Battersea, S.W.11.   Z2553A

HENDRY, C. W., Pte., 10th Queen's (Royal West Surrey Regiment).
He volunteered in November 1915, and was sent to Northampton, where he completed his training. He was unable to obtain his transfer overseas, owing to ill-health, but, nevertheless, rendered valuable services whilst engaged upon agricultural work, until his demobilisation in June 1919.
56, Russell Street, Battersea, S.W.11.   Z2552A

HENDRY, S. G., Private, 53rd Bedfordshire Regt.
He joined in April 1918, and after training at Norwich, proceeded in March 1919 to Antwerp, where he rendered valuable services until he was transferred to the Army of Occupation on the Rhine. In August 1919 he was invalided to England with a severe illness to a hospital in Ripon, and was later discharged as medically unfit for further military duties in February 1920.
56, Russell Street, Battersea, S.W.11.   Z2553B

HENLEY, G., Sergt., Black Watch.
An old soldier, who had been through the South African war, he volunteered in September 1914, and was drafted overseas in the following year. He saw much active service in France, and being severely wounded in the Battle of Loos, was invalided home. He was on his way to England in the hospital ship "Glenart Castle," when it was torpedoed, but he was rescued. He was discharged in September 1917, as unfit for further service, and holds the Queen's and King's South African Medals (with five Bars), the 1914-15 Star, and the General Service and Victory Medals.
73, Fletcher Road, Chiswick, W.4.   6369

HENLEY, W., Rifleman, Rifle Brigade.
He volunteered in 1914, and was sent overseas in the following year. A few days after landing he was in action on the Somme sector of the Western Front, and was wounded and invalided to hospital for a short time. On recovery he served at Ypres, and was again severely wounded and gassed in action. Having become unfit for the front line he was transferred to the Labour Corps, where he gave valuable services till the termination of the war. He was demobilised in 1919, and holds the 1914-15 Star, and the General Service and Victory Medals.
6, Murray Buildings, Burnett Street, Vauxhall, S.E.11.
TX25006

HENNELL, S. A., Private, 1st London Regt. (Royal Fusiliers) and Rifleman, 12th London Regiment (Rangers).
He volunteered in 1915, and after completing his training was drafted to the Western Front, where he took part in the severe fighting on the Somme. He gave his life for King and Country in July 1916, and was entitled to the General Service and Victory Medals.
He died the noblest death a man may die,
Fighting for God, and right, and liberty."
95, Brayards Road, Peckham, S.E.15.   Z5422

HENNESSY, R. A., Driver, R.A.S.C. (M.T.)
Volunteering in February 1915, he shortly afterwards proceeded overseas, and saw service in the Dardanelles. Transferred to Mesopotamia, he took part in the operations surrounding Kut-el-Amara. He was subsequently invalided home, and was discharged on account of his service in December 1916, and holds the 1914-15 Star, and the General Service and Victory Medals.
24, Priory Road, Wandsworth Road, S.W.8.   Z2554

HENSHAW, A., Private, 11th Welch Regiment.
He volunteered in December 1915, and in the following January was drafted overseas. Whilst in Salonika he fought in many important engagements on the Doiran front, and in August 1918 was sent to France, where he did good work with his unit during the concluding operations of the war. He holds the General Service and Victory Medals, and was demobilised in January 1919.
4, Boathouse Walk, Peckham, S.E.15.   Z6261

HENSON, H. T., Private, 3rd Queen's (Royal West Surrey Regiment).
Volunteering in 1915, he served at various stations on important duties with his unit until 1916, when he was discharged on medical grounds. He re-joined in 1917, and was sent to France in May of the following year, and was gassed, wounded, and taken prisoner at Vimy Ridge. He was subsequently repatriated, and was demobilised in March 1919, and holds the General Service and Victory Medals.
125, Chatham Road, Wandsworth Common, Battersea, S.W.11.
Z2555

HENSON, S. C., Private, Queen's (Royal West Surrey Regiment).
He joined in May 1916, and in the following October was drafted to the Western Front, where he fought on the Somme, at Arras, Cambrai, and in the Retreat and Advance of 1918. He did much good work with his unit, and returning home was demobilised in November 1919, and holds the General Service and Victory Medals.
22, Camellia Street, Wandsworth Road, S.W.8.   Z2556

HERBERT, A. G., Farrier-Sergt., R.E.
He volunteered in August 1914, and on the completion of his training, was drafted overseas. He saw much service in Gallipoli and Egypt, and latterly took part in the Advance of 1918 on the Western Front. He proceeded with the Army of Occupation into Germany, and holding the 1914-15 Star, and the General Service and Victory Medals, was still serving in 1920.
93, Rayleigh Road, West Kensington, W.14.   12124A

HERBERT, C. F., Private, Royal Defence Corps.
He joined in July 1918, and after his training, served at various stations on important duties with his unit. He was engaged in coastal defence work, and rendered valuable services in that connection. He was demobilised in January 1919.
167, South Street, Walworth, S.E.17.   Z2558B

HERBERT, C. H., Rifleman, 6th London Regiment (Rifles) and King's Royal Rifle Corps.
He joined in October 1917, and proceeding to France in the following year, took part in the Retreat and Advance of 1918. He was in action on the Somme, at Albert, Bullecourt and Cambrai, and was gassed, and also suffered from shell-shock. Returning home he was demobilised in July 1919, and holds the General Service and Victory Medals.
167, South Street, Walworth, S.E.17.   Z2558A

HERBERT, H., Sapper, R.E.
Volunteering in 1915, he shortly afterwards proceeded to the Western Front, and served at Neuve Chapelle, Loos, on the Somme, at Arras, and in the Advance of 1918. He rendered valuable services with his unit, and was wounded. Returning to England, he was demobilised in 1919, and holds the 1914-15 Star, and the General Service and Victory Medals.
93, Rayleigh Road, West Kensington, W.14.   12124B

HERBERT, H. H., Petty Officer, R.N.
Serving in the Navy before the war, he was mobilised on the outbreak of hostilities, and engaged on important duties with the Dover Patrol. He took part in several destroyer actions in the Channel, and was prominent in the Naval operations covering the Landings at 11 Beach and Suvla Bay. He was in H.M.S. "Irresistible" when she was sunk in the Dardanelles and was mentioned in Despatches for gallant behaviour and coolness under fire. He was subsequently sent to Salonika, and thence to Turkey. He holds the 1914-15 Star, Naval, General Service and the Victory Medals, and in 1920 was still serving.
37, Crozier Street, Lambeth, S.E.1.   Z26079

HERBERT, S., Corporal, R.A.S.C. (M.T.)
He volunteered in October 1914, and was shortly afterwards drafted to the Western Front. There he rendered valuable services as a motor transport driver, serving at Ypres, the Somme, Arras, Amiens and Cambrai. He returned home after the termination of hostilities, and was demobilised in April 1919, holding the 1914 Star, and the General Service and Victory Medals.
10, Arthur Road, Brixton Road, S.W.9.   Z3087

HERBERT, T., Observer, R.A.F.
He volunteered in August 1914, and later proceeding to France, served there during practically the whole period of hostilities. He rendered valuable services whilst engaged with a Bombing Squadron for three years, taking part in numerous raids. Also holding a commission in the Middlesex Regiment, he served in Ireland through the rebellion. He was demobilised in January 1919, holding the 1914-15 Star, and the General Service and Victory Medals.
24, Anley Road, West Kensington, W.14.   11797B

HERBERT, W., Rifleman, Rifle Brigade, and Driver, R.F.A.

He volunteered in June 1916, and served at Winchester and Bordon prior to being transferred to the R.F.A. Proceeding overseas early in 1917 he played a prominent part in many important engagements, including the Battles of Messines, Passchendaele, Ypres, and Cambrai. He fell gloriously on the Field of Battle on September 28th, 1918, and was entitled to the General Service and Victory Medals.
"The path of duty was the way to glory."
120, Tyneham Road, Battersea, S.W.11. Z2557

HERD, C., Gunner, R.F.A.

He was mobilised from the Reserve in August 1914, and proceeded to France in the same year. He took a prominent part in several engagements during his four years' active service and saw much fighting in the Battles of the Marne, the Aisne, Ypres and the Somme. Later, whilst in action at Armentières, he was seriously wounded, and died from the effects on April 9th, 1918. He was buried in Etaples Cemetery and was entitled to the Mons Star, and the General Service and Victory Medals.
"Great deeds cannot die."
25, Alsace Street, Walworth, S.E.17. Z2559A

HERD, C. F., Gunner, R.G.A.

He joined in July 1916, and proceeded in the following year to the Western Front, where he saw much heavy fighting, and acting as a gunner in an Anti-Aircraft Section, took part in several important engagements, including the Battles of the Somme, Ypres, Arras and Cambrai. After the cessation of hostilities he was demobilised in February, 1919 and holds the General Service and Victory Medals.
3, Beech Street, Dorset Road, South Lambeth, S.W.8. Z2560

HERD, E., Private, R.M.L.I.

Volunteering in January 1915, later in that year he proceeded to the Dardanelles, where he took part in the Landing at Suvla Bay. On the Evacuation of Gallipoli, he was transferred to the Western Front, and whilst in this theatre of war saw much severe fighting in various sectors. He gave his life for King and Country on the Somme on April 28th, 1917. He was entitled to the 1914-15 Star, and the General Service and Victory Medals.
"He died the noblest death a man may die,
Fighting for God, and right, and liberty,"
25, Alsace Street, Walworth, S.E.17. Z2559B

HERMAN, S., Guardsman, Coldstream Guards.

Volunteering in February 1915, he went through his course of training, and in the same year proceeded to France. While there he took an active part in numerous engagements of importance, including those at the Somme, Arras, Ypres and Cambrai, in the last of which he was wounded. After his recovery he rejoined his unit and fought in the Retreat and Advance of 1918. He subsequently moved to Cologne with the Army of Occupation, and returned home in 1919. In 1920 he was still in the Army, and holds the 1914-15 Star, and the General Service and Victory Medals.
9B Block, Lewis Trust Buildings, Camberwell, S.E.5. Z5990

HERMITAGE, A., Bombardier, R.F.A.

He volunteered in October 1914, and in August of the following year was drafted to the Western Front, where he saw much severe fighting in the Ypres and Somme sectors. In November 1916 he was invalided home, but on his recovery in the following year sailed in the "Arcadian" for India. He unfortunately lost his life when she was torpedoed in the Mediterranean on April 15th, 1917. He was entitled to the 1914-15 Star, and the General Service and Victory Medals.
"His memory is cherished with pride."
8, Hilmer Street, West Kensington, W.14. 16922A

HERON, A. E., Pte., Essex and Royal Sussex Regts.

He volunteered in 1915, and was stationed in England until 1917, when he was drafted to the Western Front. There he saw much severe fighting and took part in the Battles of Arras, Ypres and the Somme, and many other important engagements until the cessation of hostilities. He was demobilised on his return home in 1919, and holds the General Service and Victory Medals.
257, East Street, Walworth, S.E.17. Z2561

HERRING, A., Pte., 1st Royal Warwickshire Regt.

Two months after joining in May 1918, he was sent to France, where he saw much heavy fighting in various sectors of the Front. He served through the second Battle of Cambrai, and many minor engagements in the Advance of 1918, and on his return to England in March 1919, was demobilised. He holds the General Service and Victory Medals.
207, Cator Street, Peckham, S.E.15. Z5037B

HERROD, G. W., R.S.M., R.G.A.

He volunteered in October 1914, and was engaged on important duties at various stations in England until drafted to the Western Front. There he saw severe fighting and took part in important engagements until the cessation of hostilities, when he proceeded with the Army of Occupation into Germany. He returned home for demobilisation in 1919, and holds the General Service and Victory Medals.
24, Cornwall Grove, Chiswick, W.4. T5612A

HESSELWORTH, F., Gunner, R.F.A.

Shortly after volunteering in March 1915, he proceeded to the Western Front, where he fought in various sectors. He took part in the Battles of Ypres, the Somme, Arras, Vimy Ridge, Bullecourt and Passchendaele, and many other engagements, and was severely gassed whilst in action on the Somme in 1916. He was invalided from the Army in July 1918, and holds the 1914-15 Star, and the General Service and Victory Medals.
4, Broomsgrove Road, Stockwell Road, S.W.9. Z4468

HESSEY, A. V., Special War Worker.

During the period of hostilities he was engaged on work of great National importance at Messrs. Gwynne's, Chiswick, and Messrs. Napiers', Acton. He was employed throughout on responsible duties in connection with the construction of aero-engines, and did much good work, his services being highly valued by his firms.
47, Eastbury Grove, Chiswick, W.4. 5489A

HESSEY, G., Bombardier, R.M.A.

A Reservist, he was called to the Colours in August 1914, and was with the first British Expeditionary Force to land at Ostend. For three years he was engaged as a gun-layer in various sectors of the Western Front, and later served in various waters in a merchantman. He was finally discharged in April 1919, and holds the 1914 Star, and the General Service and Victory Medals.
47, Eastbury Grove, Chiswick, W.4. 5489B

HETHERSAY, W., Private, M.G.C.

He volunteered in 1915, and later in that year was drafted to the Western Front. Whilst in this theatre of war he saw much severe fighting and took part in the Battles of Ypres, the Somme, Arras and Cambrai, and many other important engagements. He died gloriously on the Field of Battle at Cambrai on August 20th, 1918. He was entitled to the 1914-15 Star, and the General Service and Victory Medals.
"Courage, bright hopes, and a myriad dreams, splendidly given."
12, Thurlow Street, Walworth, S.E.17. Z2562

HEWETT, A. E., Gunner, R.F.A.

Volunteering in 1915, he was shortly afterwards drafted to the East. There he was engaged on important garrison duties at Hong Kong until 1918, when he was transferred to the Western Front. He saw much severe fighting in this theatre of war, was invalided home in the same year, and in 1919 was discharged as medically unfit for further service. He holds the General Service and Victory Medals.
297, East Street, Walworth, S.E.17. Z2563

HEWETT, W. E. O., Shoeing-Smith, R.F.A. (attached R.N.D.)

He joined in June 1916, and served at various stations in England until drafted to the Western Front in 1918. There he saw much severe fighting and took part in many important engagements until wounded in action at Valenciennes shortly before the cessation of hostilities. He was invalided from the Army in August 1919, and holds the General Service and Victory Medals.
99, Robertson Street, Wandsworth Road, S.W.8. Z2564

HEWITSON, W., Sergt., R.F.A.

He joined in November 1916, and in the following year proceeded to the Western Front, where he saw severe fighting in various sectors. He fought in the Battles of Arras and Cambrai, and many other important engagements, and took part also in the Retreat and Advance of 1918. He was then sent with the Army of Occupation into Germany, finally returning home for demobilisation in 1919. He holds the General Service and Victory Medals.
50, Frances Street, Battersea, S.W.11. Z2565

HEWITT, E. C., Pte., Middlesex Regt. and Labour Corps.

Joining in November 1916, he was drafted to France shortly afterwards and there fought in various sectors of the Front. He took part in many important engagements in this theatre of war, and was also employed on responsible duties on the lines of communication. He was demobilised on his return to England in December 1918, and holds the General Service and Victory Medals.
2, Bognor Street, Wandsworth Road, S.W.8. Z2566

HEWITT, G., Private, Royal Marine Engineers.
He joined in April 1917, and was engaged on special duties in Chatham and elsewhere during the concluding stages of the war. He rendered valuable services whilst attached to the Royal Navy and was finally demobilised in February 1919.
16, Victory Square, Camberwell, S.E.5.   Z5775

HEWITT, G. S., Pte., 7th Northamptonshire Regt.
Shortly after joining in September 1917, he was sent to the Western Front. Whilst in this theatre of war he took part in many important engagements, and was for some time in hospital suffering from neurasthenia. Later he was invalided to England, and was in hospital until December 1919, when he was discharged as medically unfit for further service. He holds the General Service and Victory Medals.
30, Rollo Street, Battersea, S.W.11.   Z2567

HEWITT, J., Driver, R.A.S.C. (M.T.)
Volunteering in October 1914, he proceeded to the Western Front in the following year, and there served in various sectors. He was chiefly engaged on transport duties, conveying food and ammunition to the forward areas, took an active part in the Advance of 1918, and was twice gassed. Later he served with the Army of Occupation in Germany, before returning home for demobilisation in April 1919. He holds the 1914–15 Star, and the General Service and Victory Medals.
7, Broughton Street, Battersea Park, S.W.8.   Z2568

HEWITT, R., L/Corporal, R.E
He was mobilised in August 1914, and was retained on important duties with his unit at various stations. He was unable to obtain his transfer overseas, owing to injuries received in an accident, and after being for some months in hospital, did good work in the clothing department until May 1919, when he was discharged. He holds the Long Service and Good Conduct Medals.
22A, Cross Street, Clapham, S.W.4.   Z2569A

HEWITT, R. G., A.B., R.N., H.M.S. "Trefoil."
He volunteered at the age of eighteen years in January 1915, and was posted to H.M.S. "Trefoil," an oil-tank, in which he saw service in the English Channel and North Sea. He was also engaged in various other waters, and on one occasion his ship was torpedoed, but he was fortunately among those rescued. He holds the 1914–15 Star, and the General Service and Victory Medals, and in 1920 was still at sea.
223, Cross Street, Clapham, S.W.4.   Z2569B

HEWLETT, E. G., Petty Officer, R.N., H.M.S. "Redgauntlet."
He was already in the Navy when war broke out in August 1914, and served throughout in H.M.S. "Redgauntlet," with a North Sea Cruiser Squadron. He took part in the Battles of Heligoland Bight, Dogger Bank and Zeebrugge, was in destroyer actions off the Belgian coast, Harwich, and in the North Sea, and also fought in many minor engagements. He was discharged in March 1919, and holds the 1914–15 Star, and the General Service and Victory Medals.
113, Mayall Road, Herne Hill, S.E.24.   Z2570

HEWSON, H. F., Driver, R.F.A.
After volunteering in September 1914, he proceeded to France in June 1915, and remained there throughout the rest of the war. He took an active part in many great engagements, including those round Albert, Ypres, the Somme and Cambrai, and in the Offensives of 1918, happily without any injury. He returned home and was demobilised in February 1919, and holds the 1914–15 Star, and the General Service and Victory Medals.
11, Haymerle Road, Peckham, S.E.15.   Z6388

HEYBURN, W. E. J., Driver, R.F.A.
He volunteered in September 1914, and in the following year was sent to Egypt, and thence to Salonika, where he took part in the severe fighting on the Vardar, Struma and Doiran fronts, until hostilities ceased in that area. He was demobilised in January 1919, after his return home, and holds the 1914–15 Star, and the General Service and Victory Medals.
22, Nunhead Green, S.E.15.   Z6184

HEYWARD, A. B., Gunner, R.F.A.
He volunteered in October 1914, and in the following July was drafted to France. There he took part in the Battles of the Somme, Bullecourt, Ypres and Cambrai, and was mentioned in Despatches for conspicuous bravery in the Field. He also fought in the Retreat and Advance of 1918, at Epéhy and Havrincourt. He was badly wounded at Cambrai and unfortunately died the following day on November 7th, 1918. He was entitled to the 1914–15 Star, and the General Service and Victory Medals.   Z3444B
        "Nobly striving, he nobly fell that we might live."
102, Trafalgar Road, Old Kent Road, Peckham, S.E.15.

HIBBARD, F. G., A.B., Merchant Service.
Volunteering in August 1914, he first served on board H.M.H.S. "Galeka," which vessel struck a mine in November 1916, but he was fortunately rescued. He then did duty in the "Saxon" and "Durban Castle," which vessels carried troops to various war zones, and finally served in the "Dunvegan Castle." In July 1918, his ship sank a German Submarine off the shores of America. He was demobilised in March 1919, and holds the General Service and the Mercantile Marine War Medals.
3, Montholme Road, Wandsworth Common. S.W.11.   Z2571

HIBBERT, S., Private, Royal Fusiliers.
He was called up from the Reserve in August 1914, and immediately drafted to France, where he took part in the heavy fighting at the Battles of Mons, the Marne and the Aisne. He gave his life for King and Country at La Bassée on October 18th, 1914, and was entitled to the Mons Star, and the General Service and Victory Medals.
        "His memory is cherished with pride."
83, Lavender Road, Battersea, S.W.11.   Z1741B

HIBBERT, S., Private, East Surrey Regiment.
Having previously served in the South African campaign, he volunteered in September 1914, and in the following March was drafted to France. In this seat of war he took part in many engagements, including the Battles of Loos, Albert, the Somme, Ypres, Cambrai and the Retreat and Advance of 1918, and was wounded in action. He was demobilised in February 1919, and holds the Queen's and King's South African Medals, the 1914–15 Star, and the General Service and Victory Medals.
1, St. John's Hill Grove, Battersea, S.W.11.   Z2572

HIBBLE, G. J., Private, 24th London Regiment (The Queen's).
He joined in September 1916, and on completing his training in the following year proceeded to Egypt. There he took part in many engagements with General Allenby's forces, and fought through the Advance in Palestine at the taking of Jerusalem and other places. He returned home for his demobilisation in February 1920, and holds the General Service and Victory Medals.
18, Tradescant Road, South Lambeth Road, S.W.8.   Z1087B

HIBBLE, W. C., Rifleman, 52nd Rifle Brigade.
He joined in April 1918, on attaining military age, and served at various stations during his training. Owing to the early cessation of hostilities he did not proceed overseas until after the Armistice, when he went to Germany with the Army of Occupation. He was demobilised in February 1920.
16, Faraday Street, Walworth, S.E.17.   2746

HICKEY, A. W., Private, The Queen's (Royal West Surrey Regiment) and Labour Corps.
He joined in March 1916, and was quickly drafted to France. Whilst in this seat of war he took part in much heavy fighting in various sectors of the Front, and was wounded in action. He was demobilised in October 1919, and holds the General Service and Victory Medals.
6, Surrey Terrace, Walworth, S.E.17.   Z2573A

HICKEY, E., Private, 19th London Regiment.
He volunteered in June 1915, and in the following year was drafted to the East. In this seat of operations he saw much fighting in Egypt and Palestine, taking part in the capture of Jerusalem, Jericho, and the Offensive under General Allenby. He contracted malaria, and was for some time in hospital. He returned home and was demobilised in December 1919, and holds the General Service and Victory Medals.
20, Carfax Square, Clapham Park Road, S.W.4.   Z2574

HICKEY, W. E., Mechanic, R.A.F.
He joined in November 1916, on attaining military age and in the following year proceeded to France. In this theatre of war he was engaged on important duties, which called for a high degree of technical skill. After hostilities ceased, he went into Germany with the Army of Occupation. He was demobilised in December 1919, and holds the General Service and Victory Medals.
6, Surrey Terrace, Walworth, S.E.17.   Z2573B

HICKMAN, E., Private, 18th (Queen Mary's Own) Hussars.
He volunteered in October 1914, and after a period of training was drafted to India. There he served on important garrison duties at various stations, including that of Lucknow, and rendered valuable services. He returned home and was demobilised in February 1919, and holds the General Service and Victory Medals.
135, Duke Road, Chiswick, W.4.   5654A

HICKMAN, E. A., Mechanic, R.A.F.

He joined in 1918, and after his training was stationed in Yorkshire on important duties, which demanded a high degree of technical skill. Owing to the early cessation of hostilities, he was unable to obtain a transfer overseas, but, nevertheless, rendered valuable services with his Squadron. He was demobilised in June 1919.

23, Medlar Street, Camberwell, S.E.5.   Z2576

HICKMAN, H. J., Corporal, R.F.A.

He volunteered in November 1914, and in the following year proceeded to France. There he saw much fighting at Loos, St. Quentin, the Somme, Vimy Ridge, Messines, Cambrai, and in the Advance of 1918. He was demobilised in February 1919, and holds the 1914-15 Star, and the General Service and Victory Medals.

3, Pallador Place, Camberwell, S.E.5.   Z2577A

HICKMAN, J. J., Gunner, Royal Marine Artillery.

He joined the Service in January 1902, and throughout the war was engaged on board H.M.S. "Ajax" with the Grand Fleet in the North Sea. He took part in the engagements off Heligoland, and the Falkland Islands, and in the Battle of Jutland. Later his ship was employed in conveying supplies from America to France. In 1920 he was serving in Russia, and holds the 1914-15 Star, and the General Service and Victory Medals.

3, Pallador Place, Camberwell, S.E.5.   Z2577B

HICKMAN, J. J., Private, Labour Corps.

Joining in June 1917, he immediately proceeded to the Western Front, where he served for five months at Boulogne. He was then invalided home, and was attached to the Welch Guards on important duties until February 1918. After serving for a few months in the Record Office of the London Regiment, he was sent to hospital and finally discharged as medically unfit for further service in August 1918. He holds the General Service and Victory Medals.

17, Belleville Road, Battersea, S.W.11.   Z2575

HICKMAN, W. A., Rifleman, 20th Rifle Brigade.

He joined in February 1916, and twelve months later was drafted to the Western Front. Whilst in this theatre of war he took part in many important engagements, including the Battles of Ypres, Cambrai, the Somme and St. Quentin, and also fought in the Retreat and Advance of 1918. He was demobilised on his return to England in February 1919, and holds the General Service and Victory Medals.

44, Harris Street, Camberwell, S.E.5.   Z4469

HICKS, C., Private, Gloucestershire Regiment.

Mobilised in August 1914, he immediately proceeded to the Western Front, where he fought in the Retreat from Mons. Later he took part in the Battles of the Marne, the Aisne, Ypres and Hill 60, was wounded in action at Loos, and invalided home. On his recovery he returned to France, and was wounded a second time on the Somme in 1917. After eight months in hospital he was finally invalided from the Army in May 1918, and holds the Mons Star, and the General Service and Victory Medals.

15, Clarence Street, Clapham, S.W.4.   Z2578

HICKS, F., Sapper, R.E.

He volunteered in September 1915, and after a period of training, served at various stations, where he was engaged on duties of great importance. He was not successful in obtaining his transfer to the Front, but nevertheless, did good work with his unit until March 1919, when he was demobilised.

146, The Grove, Hammersmith, W.6.   10341A

HICKS, F. G., Gunner, R.F.A.

He joined on attaining military age in May 1916, and in the following year proceeded to the Western Front, where he fought in the Battles of Arras, Vimy Ridge, Ypres, Passchendaele and Lens. Later he served for a short time in Italy, returning to France in time to take part in the Retreat and Advance of 1918, and the Battles of the Somme, Amiens, Bapaume and Cambrai. He was twice wounded in action whilst overseas, and on his return home was demobilised in October 1919. He holds the General Service and Victory Medals.

27, Comus Place, Walworth, S.E.17.   Z2579

HICKS, L. (Mrs.), Special War Worker.

This lady gave her services voluntarily at the Wandsworth Bridge Road, Y.M.C.A. Canteen, where she did much good work three days a week for a considerable period of the war. Her services were very highly valued.

146, The Grove, Hammersmith, W.6.   10341B

HICKS, L. L., Private, Royal Fusiliers.

He joined in January 1918, and in the following month proceeded to the Western Front. There he took part in many engagements, including the second Battles of the Somme and Cambrai, and the fourth Battle of Ypres. He was severely wounded in September 1918 during the Advance of that year, and was demobilised in February 1919, holding the General Service and Victory Medals.   Z2580

12, Williams Grove, Aylesbury Road, Walworth, S.E.17.

HICKS, R. H., Capt., R.A.M.C. (Canadian Overseas Forces).

He volunteered at the outbreak of war and proceeded to France with the first Canadian contingent. He rendered valuable services in many of the early battles, and played a distinguished part whilst in charge of the wounded in various sectors of the Front. He was eventually discharged in August 1916, and holds the 1914 Star, and the General Service and Victory Medals.

3, Brackley Terrace, Chiswick, W.4.   5431B

HIGGINS, F. R., Private, 8th Gordon Highlanders.

He joined in May 1917, on attaining military age, and was drafted to France in the following August. There he took part in many engagements, including the first Battle of Cambrai, and the second Battle of the Marne, and was wounded. After the Armistice he proceeded to Germany, where he did duty with the Army of Occupation until his demobilisation in May 1919. He holds the General Service and Victory Medals.

156, Ferndale Road, Clapham, S.W.4.   Z2581/2B

HIGGINS, H. W., Pte., York and Lancaster Regt.

He volunteered in October 1915, and after doing duty in England for a time was sent to France in September 1916. He was in action on the Somme and Ancre fronts, and took part in the Battles of Arras and Bullecourt, and was wounded. After being invalided to England, he returned to the Western Front in January 1918, and acted as a despatch rider with the R.A.F. He was finally demobilised in April 1919, and holds the General Service and Victory Medals.

156, Ferndale Road, Clapham, S.W.4.   Z2581A

HIGGINS, W., L/Corporal, R.A.O.C.

He joined in April 1916, and in the following July proceeded to the Western Front, where he was in charge of ammunition dumps in various important sectors during the course of hostilities. He rendered valuable services, and was often in danger through bombardment by enemy aircraft. He was demobilised in August 1919, and holds the General Service and Victory Medals.

17, Patience Road, Battersea, S.W.11.   Z2582

HIGGS, A., Private, R.A.S.C.

He volunteered in November 1914, and early in the following year was drafted to the Eastern theatre of war, where he saw much service in both Egypt and Salonika. He unfortunately contracted malaria, was invalided to England in March 1918, and was subsequently discharged in February 1919, as medically unfit for further service. He holds the 1914-15 Star, and the General Service and Victory Medals.

12, Sterndale Road, Wandsworth Road, S.W.8.   Z2583

HIGGS, W. R., Private, 23rd London Regiment.

Volunteering in May 1915, he was drafted to France in the following October, after a period of training. In this theatre of war he took part in many important engagements, including the Battles of Loos, Vimy Ridge and the Somme. He was unfortunately killed in action on September 15th, 1916, and was entitled to the 1914-15 Star, and the General Service and Victory Medals.

"A valiant soldier, with undaunted heart he breasted Life's last hill."

13, Benfield Street, Battersea, S.W.11.   Z2584

HIGH, J., Stoker (1st Class), R.N., H.M.S. "Meki."

He was already serving in H.M. Navy at the outbreak of war in August 1914, and did duty in the North and Baltic Seas. He was also engaged in transporting and convoying troops to battle areas, and rendered valuable services during hostilities. In 1920 he was still on the high seas, and holds the 1914-15 Star, and the General Service and Victory Medals.

25, Pensbury Street, Wandsworth Road, S.W.8.   Z2585

HIGH, T. W., Private, R.A.S.C. (M.T.)

He volunteered in September 1914, and was shortly afterwards drafted to France, where he was engaged on important transport duties. He was present at numerous engagements in various sectors throughout the period of hostilities, and after the Armistice returned to England, and was demobilised in March 1919. He holds the 1914 Star, and the General Service and Victory Medals.

37, Montgomery Road, Chiswick, S.W.4.   6901B

HIGNELL, A. S., Private, 3rd Suffolk Regiment.

He joined the Forces in August 1917, after doing duty in France with the Army Canteen Board since the outbreak of war, and was retained with his unit at important stations in England. Owing to his being physically unfit, he was unable to obtain his transfer to a theatre of war, but nevertheless rendered valuable services until the termination of hostilities. He was demobilised in 1919.

20, Frere Street, Battersea, S.W.11.   Z2586

HILDER, A. T., Pte., 25th London Regt. (Cyclists).

Joining in April 1915, he was in due course sent to the Western Front, where he was engaged on special duties. He was present at many important engagements during the course of hostilities, and returning to England was demobilised in February 1919. He holds the General Service and Victory Medals.

8, Carthew Villas, Hammersmith, W.6.   11638B

HILDER, R. E., A.B., R.N., H.M.S. "King George V."
He was mobilised in August 1914, and was engaged on board H.M.S. " King Georve V," and did duty in many waters. He took part in the Battle of Jutland in 1916, and many other engagements of minor importance throughout the course of hostilities. He holds the 1914–15 Star, the General Service (with clasp, Jutland), and Victory Medals, and was demobilised in January 1920.
8, Carthew Villas, Hammersmith, W.6. 11638A

HILEY, J. J., Private, 2/2nd London Regiment (Royal Fusiliers).
Volunteering in 1915, and completing a period of service in England, he was drafted to the Western Front in November 1916, and took an active part in many important engagements. He saw much severe fighting on the Somme and elsewhere, and died gloriously on the Field of Battle at Epéhy on September 10th, 1918. He was entitled to the General Service and Victory Medals.
" Whilst we remember the Sacrifice is not in vain."
30, Medwin Street, Ferndale Road, S.W.4. Z2587

HILKIN, C., Sapper, R.E.
He volunteered in May 1915, and shortly afterwards was drafted to the Western Front, where he made much heavy fighting in various sectors. He also took part in many mining operations and rendered valuable services during hostilities. He holds the 1914–15 Star, and the General Service and Victory Medals, and was discharged in March 1919.
4, North Street, Lambeth, S.E.1. Z24624

HILL, A., Private, R.A.S.C. (M.T.)
He volunteered in October 1915, and in February of the following year was drafted to German East Africa. There he took part in many engagements with native tribesmen, and was engaged principally on the transport of food and ammunition to forward areas. He finally returned to England after the Armistice, and was demobilised in 1919. He holds the General Service and Victory Medals.
7, Totteridge Road, Battersea, S.W.11. Z2592

HILL, A., Private, Northumberland Fusiliers.
He joined in 1917, and was shortly afterwards drafted to France, where he was in action at the Battle of Cambrai. He was also present during the Retreat and Advance of 1918 and was wounded, and later returned to England for demobilisation in 1919. He holds the General Service and Victory Medals.
18, Patmore Street, Wandsworth Road, S.E.8. Z2588A

HILL, A. A., Guardsman, Grenadier Guards.
A Reservist, he was called to the Colours in August 1914, and immediately proceeded to France, where he fought at Mons, Antwerp, Neuve Chapelle, Ypres, Arras, Vimy Ridge and Cambrai, and also served through the Retreat and Advance of 1918. He was gassed and wounded in action and was discharged in February 1919, holding the Mons Star, and the General Service and Victory Medals.
7, Comus Place, Walworth, S.E.17. Z2590

HILL, A. W., Air Mechanic, R.A.F.
He joined in May 1916, and previously to being sent overseas, was engaged on important coast defence work in Yorkshire. In 1917, he was drafted to France and rendered valuable services with an airship section at Dunkirk. He was demobilised in March 1919, and holds the General Service and Victory Medals.
51, Montholme Road, Wandsworth Common, S.W.11.
Z2589

HILL, C. A., Corporal, 1st Grenadier Guards.
He volunteered in October 1914, and in June of the following year was drafted to France, where he played a prominent part in heavy fighting in various sectors. He died gloriously on the Field of Battle at Ypres on March 20th, 1917. He was entitled to the 1914–15 Star, and the General Service and Victory Medals.
" His memory is cherished with pride."
16, Dale Street, Chiswick, W.4. 5375B

HILL, C. L., Sergt., East Surrey Regiment.
Volunteering in August 1914, he proceeded to France in the following May, and served with distinction at the Battles of Ypres, Festubert, Loos and the Somme, where he was badly wounded in action and invalided home. After twelve months under treatment, he returned to the Western Front, but was immediately sent to Italy, and fought on the Piave, and the Asiago Plateaus. He was later transferred again to France, and was in action throughout the Advance of 1918. After the Armistice he proceeded to Germany with the Army of Occupation, and was stationed at Cologne until his demobilisation in March 1919. He holds the 1914–15 Star, and the General Service and Victory Medals.
1, Granville Mansions, Bromell's Road, Clapham, S.W.4.
Z2593

HILL, E., Rifleman, Rifle Brigade.
He joined in July 1917 and in the following month was drafted to France. He gave his life for King and Country on the 16th of August 1917. He was entitled to the General Service and Victory Medals.
" The path of duty was the way to glory."
3, Kinglake Street, Walworth, S.E.17. Z2594/95C

HILL, G. A. (Mrs.), Special War Worker.
During the war this lady gave her time to the making of articles of clothing for sick and wounded soldiers. She worked in connection with the British Red Cross Society, and rendered valuable services.
85, North Street, Wandsworth Road, South Lambeth, S.W.8.
Z2598B

HILL, H. A., Rifleman, Rifle Brigade.
A Reservist, he was called to the Colours in August 1914, and was immediately drafted to the Western Front with the British Expeditionary Force. He took part in the Battle of Mons and the subsequent Retreat, and was also in action at Neuve Chapelle, Ypres, Loos, Arras, and the Battle of the Somme. He was invalided to England in 1917, and finally discharged from the Army in December of that year as medically unfit for further service. He holds the Mons Star, and the General Service and Victory Medals.
16, Odell Street, Camberwell, S.E.5. Z5621

HILL, H. S., Pte., 16th Royal Warwickshire Regt.
He volunteered in September 1915, and three months later proceeded to France, where he rendered valuable services on lines of communication with the R.E. for two years. In November 1917 he was transferred to Italy and fought on the Piave before returning to the Western Front in April 1918. He then served at Havrincourt (where he was wounded in action), Cambrai and other important engagements during the Retreat and Advance, and was demobilised in January 1919. He holds the 1914–15 Star, and the General Service and Victory Medals.
92, Ferndale Road, Clapham, S.W.4. Z2596

HILL, J. G., Private, Labour Corps.
Volunteering in November 1915, he proceeded to the Western Front in the following April, and there rendered valuable services with the 166th Labour Company in the Somme, Vimy Ridge, Messines, Cambrai and Ypres sectors. After the Armistice he carried out important salvage duties until his return home for demobilisation in January 1920, and holds the General Service and Victory Medals.
94, Westmoreland Road, Walworth, S.E.17. Z2597

HILL, J. T., Gunner (Signaller), R.F.A.
Joining in April 1916, he proceeded to Egypt in the following February, and from there took part in the Advance into Palestine. He served at the Battle of Gaza, and at the taking of Jerusalem, Jaffa and Jericho, and contracted malarial fever. Whilst in hospital he also underwent an operation for appendicitis, and was invalided home. Demobilised in September 1919, he holds the General Service and Victory Medals.
85, North Street, Clapham, S.W.4. Z2598A

HILL, J. W., Bombardier, R.F.A.
Volunteering in August 1914, he was sent to France early in the following year, and took part in the severe fighting at Neuve Chapelle, Hill 60, the Somme, Beaumont-Hamel, Ypres, Cambrai and Armentières, and in the Retreat and Advance of 1918. He was demobilised in February 1919, holding the 1914–15 Star, and the General Service and Victory Medals.
127, Flaxman Road, Camberwell, S.E.5. Z6185B

HILL, N. F., 2nd Lieutenant, Royal Naval Division.
He volunteered in August 1914, and in the following year proceeded to Gallipoli, where he took part in the Landing in April 1915, and the subsequent operations until the Evacuation. He was afterwards transferred to France, where he served in many important engagements, including those at the Somme and Cambrai, and was gassed. He was demobilised in February 1919, holding the 1914–15 Star, and the General Service and Victory Medals.
127, Flaxman Road, Camberwell, S.E.5. Z6185A

HILL, R. C. I. (D.S.M.), A.B., Royal Navy.
He volunteered in August 1914, and during the whole period of hostilities rendered valuable services on board H.M. Submarines E 45, E 31, and E 4, also in mine-layers. He was principally engaged on mine-laying duties off the Belgian Coast and was awarded the Distinguished Service Medal for conspicuous bravery and devotion to duty on E 31. Demobilised in April 1920, he also holds the 1914–15 Star, and the General Service and Victory Medals.
13, Willington Road, Stockwell, S.W.9 Z2591

HILL, R. J., Bombardier, R.G.A.

Already serving at the outbreak of war in August 1914, he was retained on important duties with his Battery until June 1916. He was then drafted to France, where he took part in many engagements, and was twice wounded in action. He received his discharge in February 1919, and holds the General Service and Victory Medals.
16, Dale Street, Chiswick, W.4.   5375C

HILL, S. W., Gunner, R.F.A.

Volunteering in August 1914, he proceeded to France three months later, and there took part in the Battles of Ypres, Neuve Chapelle, St. Eloi, Festubert, Loos, the Somme, Arras, Vimy Ridge, Messines, Passchendaele and Cambrai. He also served through the Retreat of 1918, and was wounded in action on the Marne during the subsequent Advance. He was discharged in November 1918, and holds the 1914 Star, and the General Service and Victory Medals.
14, Akers Street, Walworth, S.E.17.   Z2599A

HILL, T. C., Private, 24th Queen's (Royal West Surrey Regiment).

He volunteered in February 1915, and proceeded to France in the following month. He took a prominent part in the Battles of Hill 60, and Givenchy, where he was seriously wounded in May. After three months' treatment in hospital he was evacuated in August, and in February 1916 was discharged as medically unfit for further service. He holds the 1914-15 Star, and the General Service and Victory Medals.
50, Hornby Road, Peckham, S.E.15.   Z5984

HILL, V. N., Ordinary Seaman, R.N.

He volunteered in November 1914, and throughout the war, did good work on board His Majesty's Mine-sweeper " Reindeer," which ship was engaged on dangerous duties in the North Sea and Mediterranean. He was also present at the landing of troops on the Gallipoli Peninsula, and was demobilised in February 1919. He holds the 1914-15 Star, and the General Service and Victory Medals.
18, Burns Road, Battersea, S.W.11.   Z2600

HILL, W., Private, Royal Guernsey Light Infantry.

Joining in April 1916, he was drafted to France in the following June. During his service on the Western Front, he saw much severe fighting in various sectors, and was twice wounded in action. He was demobilised in January 1919, and holds the General Service and Victory Medals.
16, Dale Street, Chiswick, W.4.   5375A

HILL, W. C., Rifleman, Rifle Brigade.

He joined in July 1917, and in March of the following year was drafted to the Western Front, where he took part in heavy fighting near Cambrai and was wounded and taken prisoner on the Somme in May 1918. He unfortunately died of his wounds in September of the same year, whilst in captivity. He was entitled to the General Service and Victory Medals.
" His life for his Country, his Soul to God."
14, Akers Street, Walworth, S.E.17.   Z2599B

HILL, W. J., Driver, R.F.A.

He volunteered in 1914, and early in the following year proceeded to France. Whilst on the Western Front, he was in action at the Battles of Ypres, Loos, the Somme, Arras, Cambrai and the Aisne, and during the Retreat and Advance of 1918. He was demobilised in 1919, and holds the 1914-15 Star, and the General Service and Victory Medals.
18, Patmore Street, Wandsworth, Road, S.W.8.   Z2588B

HILLEARD, A., Driver, R.F.A.

A serving soldier since March 1913, he was sent overseas at the outbreak of war, and was in action in the Retreat from Mons. He also served in the Battles of the Marne, the Aisne and the Somme and in the engagements at Langemarck, Ypres and Kemmel. During his service in France he was also attached to the French and the American Flying Columns in the Noyon sector. He was also in action in the Retreat and Advance of 1918, and was at Charleroi when the Armistice was signed, and was demobilised in the following year. He holds the Mons Star, and the General Service and Victory Medals.
27, Dean's Buildings, Walworth, S.E.17.   Z2601

HILLEARD, R., Driver, R.A.S.C. (M.T.)

He was mobilised at the outbreak of war, and almost immediately drafted to France, where he took part in the Retreat from Mons. He also did excellent work as a driver in the Battles of the Marne, the Aisne and La Bassée. In 1916 he was sent to Mesopotamia and was stationed at Baghdad with General Maude until he died. He was invalided for a time to hospital at Basra with sand-fly fever. In May 1919, he was demobilised after his return to England, and holds the Mons Star, and the General Service and Victory Medals.
11, Northampton Place, Walworth, S.E.17.   Z2602

HILLIER, A. S., Private, Bedfordshire Regiment.

He joined in January 1917, at the age of eighteen years, and in the following year, was drafted to France. He took part in various important engagements in the Retreat and Advance of 1918, and was demobilised in November of the following year. He holds the General Service and Victory Medals.
80, Weybridge Street, Battersea, S.W.11.   Z2603A

HILLIER, F., Trooper, 5th (Princess Charlotte of Wales') Dragoon Guards.

Joining in June 1918, he was sent to Ireland on completion of his training, and was stationed on the Curragh. Although unable to obtain his transfer to a theatre of war, he nevertheless, rendered valuable services with his unit, particularly in several Sinn Fein risings. He was demobilised in October 1919.
176, Bridge Road West, Battersea, S.W.11.   Z2604

HILLIER, J. E., Private, Duke of Cornwall's Light Infantry.

He volunteered in August 1914, and proceeded to France in the following year. He saw much fighting in various sectors of the Western Front, and was invalided home in 1916 suffering from gas poisoning. He was eventually discharged as medically unfit for further service in August of that year, and holds the 1914-15 Star, and the General Service and Victory Medals.
10, Boyton Row, Camberwell, S.E.5.   Z5622A

HILLIER, W. F., Driver, R.F.A.

He volunteered in September 1914, and in the following May was drafted to France. Whilst in this theatre of war he served at Ypres and on the Somme, and in various later engagements. Unhappily, he was killed in action at Arras on May 28th, 1917, and was entitled to the 1914-15 Star, and the General Service and Victory Medals.
" A costly sacrifice upon the altar of freedom."
80, Weybridge Road, Battersea, S.W.11.   Z2603B

HILLIER, W. H., Pte., Duke of Cornwall's Light Infantry.

He volunteered in September 1914, and was drafted to France in the following year. After a short period of service in this theatre of war he proceeded to Salonika and took part in operations on the Vardar, Struma and Doiran fronts. He was mentioned in Despatches, and was also awarded the Serbian Gold Medal for conspicuous gallantry whilst serving in the Bulgarian Offensive of 1918. He also holds the 1914-15 Star, and the General Service and Victory Medals, and was demobilised in May 1919.
10, Boyton Row, Camberwell, S.E.5.   Z5622B

HILLING, A., Rifleman, King's Royal Rifle Corps.

He joined in March 1916, and in the following year proceeded to France. During his service on the Western Front he fought in various engagements, including those on the Somme and at Arras and Cambrai. In March 1918 he was wounded and taken prisoner, and was held in captivity in Germany until January 1919, when he was repatriated, and discharged as unfit for further military duty. He holds the General Service and Victory Medals.
6, Longcroft Road, Camberwell, S.E.5.   Z5423

HILLMAN, A. E., Private, R.A.S.C.

He volunteered in October 1915, at the age of fifty years and was sent to Mesopotamia and later to Egypt. Whilst in the East he did excellent work with his unit for over a year. He returned home suffering from ill-health, and was invalided out of the Service in October 1917. He holds the General Service and Victory Medals.
10, Amies Street, Battersea, S.W.11.   Z2605A

HILLMAN, W. T., Private, Tank Corps.

He volunteered in August 1915, at the early age of fifteen years, and after serving two years in England was drafted to France in 1917. He was first in the Bantams' Regiment and was then transferred to the Tank Corps and fought on the Somme and at Ypres, where he was gassed in 1918. After his recovery, he was again in action in the final Advance. He returned home and was demobilised, but rejoined the Army and in 1920 was still serving. He holds the General Service and Victory Medals.
10, Amies Street, Battersea, S.W.11.   Z2605B

HILLS, E., Corporal, M.F.P.

He joined in November 1916, and after his training in the Yeomanry was retained for important duties at various stations until October 1918, when he was drafted to Italy. While there he was transferred to the Military Foot Police, in which he did much valuable service. After his return home he was demobilised in March 1919, and holds the General Service and Victory Medals.
130, Gloucester Road, Peckham, S.E.15.   Z5983

HILLS, H. W., Driver, R.F.A.
He joined in April 1916, and in the same year was drafted to France. Whilst overseas he did good work as a driver in various engagements, including those on the Somme and at Ypres and Cambrai, and was twice wounded. After the cessation of hostilities he proceeded to Germany with the Army of Occupation, remaining there until January 1920, when he was demobilised. He holds the General Service and Victory Medals.
178, Farmer's Road, Camberwell, S.E.5.   Z2610B

HILLS, J. A., Private, 9th Essex Regiment.
He joined in February 1917, and after serving at various stations on important duties with his unit was drafted to France in August 1918. He fought in heavy fighting on the Somme, and in other engagements until the cessation of hostilities. He was demobilised in January 1919, and holds the General Service and Victory Medals.
4, Westhall Road, Camberwell, S.E.5.   Z2607

HILLS, J. J., A.B., R.N., H.M.S. "Shannon."
He was serving in the Navy at the outbreak of war, having previously enlisted in July 1910. He was posted to H.M.S. "Shannon," and served in this ship with the Grand Fleet in the North Sea on important and dangerous patrol and convoy duties. His vessel also took part in the Battle of Jutland in May 1916. He was discharged in June 1919, and holds the 1914-15 Star, and the General Service and Victory Medals.
173, Farmer's Road, Camberwell, S.E.5.   Z2610A

HILLS, J. T., Rflmn., 1/17th London Regt. (Rifles).
He joined in 1916, and in the same year embarked for France. Whilst on the Western Front he fought in the Battle of the Somme and in an engagements at St. Eloi. He died gloriously on the Field of Battle at Arras in November 1917, and was entitled to the General Service and Victory Medals.
    "And doubtless he went in splendid company."
31, Hargwyne Street, Stockwell Road, S.W.9.   Z2606

HILLS, P. S., Private, R.A.M.C.
He volunteered in February 1916, and in the same year was drafted overseas. During his service in France he was present at many engagements in the Ypres and Somme sectors, and rendered inestimable services in tending the wounded on the battle-fields, and was often under heavy fire. He contracted a serious illness whilst on duty, and was consequently discharged as unfit for further service in July 1919. He holds the General Service and Victory Medals.
6, Hubert Grove, Landor Road, S.W.9.   Z2608

HILLS, T. E., Private, East Surrey Regiment.
He was mobilised at the outbreak of war, and was almost immediately sent to France, where he took part in the Retreat from Mons. He also served in the Battles of the Marne, La Bassée, Ypres, Neuve Chapelle, St. Eloi, Hill 60, and Loos. During these engagements he was twice wounded and also buried by shell explosion, but, after his recovery, he rejoined his unit, and served until the cessation of hostilities. He was discharged in March 1919, and holds the Mons Star, and the General Service and Victory Medals.
97, Robertson Street, Wandsworth Road, S.W.8.   Z2609

HILLYER, H., Rifleman, Royal Irish Rifles.
He joined in August 1916, and in the following December was drafted to France. During his service on the Western Front he fought on the Somme and at Ypres, and was wounded. In 1917 he proceeded to Egypt and advanced with the British Forces under General Allenby through Palestine. He was again wounded in action, but continued to serve throughout the campaign. He returned home and was demobilised in August 1919, and holds the General Service and Victory Medals.
95, Speke Road, Battersea, S.W.11.   Z2611

HILLYER, J. F., 2nd Corporal, R.E.
He was mobilised at the outbreak of war, and was almost immediately drafted to the Western Front, where he took part in the Retreat from Mons. He served also in the Battles of the Marne, the Aisne and Neuve Chapelle. In 1915 he was sent to Salonika and fought throughout the campaign. He was demobilised in February 1919, after his return to England, and holds the Mons Star, and the General Service and Victory Medals.
25, Latchmere Road, Battersea, S.W.11.   Z2612

HILTON, H. T., Private, R.A.S.C.
He volunteered in September 1915, and in the next month was sent to the Western Front. During his service in France, he was in action at Neuve Chapelle, and was afterwards engaged in conveying food supplies and ammunition up to the firing lines until the cessation of hostilities. He was demobilised in March 1919, and holds the 1914-15 Star, and the General Service and Victory Medals.
26, Rollo Street, Battersea, S.W.11.   Z2614

HILTON, F. E., Private, R.A.M.C.
He joined in April 1916, but was ineligible for overseas service. After his training he was engaged on important duties as an orderly at Leeds War Hospital, and rendered valuable services in attending the wounded. He was demobilised in March 1919, after over three years' service.
41, D'Eynsford Road, Camberwell, S.E.5.   Z2613

HIMSWORTH, W., Sergt., R.E.
He volunteered in November 1914, and after being promoted to the rank of Corporal, was drafted to the Western Front in the following year. Whilst in France he was engaged on important duties in the forward areas, at Ypres, on the Somme, and in the first and second Battles of Cambrai. He was twice wounded, at Morval in September 1916, and again on the Scheldt Canal in November 1918. He was promoted to Sergeant in March 1916, and served with distinction throughout his military career. He was demobilised in February 1919, and holds the 1914-15 Star, and the General Service and Victory Medals.
18, Priory Road, Wandsworth Road, S.W.8.   Z2615

HIND, F. G., Chief Petty Officer, R.N., H.M.S. "Zealandia" and "Birmingham."
He volunteered in August 1914, and was posted to H.M.S. "Mohawk," in which vessel he served in the North Sea under Admiral Jellicoe, and fought in the Battle of Heligoland Bight in August 1914. He was also engaged on patrol and convoy duties in the North Sea, and was afterwards transferred to H.M.S. "Zealandia," and sent to the Dardanelles, where he was in action at Suvla Bay, covering the Landing of the troops. His ship returned to the North Sea, where he remained until the conclusion of the war. He then went to Portsmouth on H.M.S. "Birmingham" and sailed for Africa, where in 1920 he was still serving. He holds the 1914-15 Star, and the General Service and Victory Medals.
85, The Chase, Clapham Common, S.W.4.   Z2617B

HIND, A., Private, 1st Northumberland Fusiliers.
A serving soldier at the outbreak of war, he was sent overseas in December 1914. Whilst in France he fought in many important engagements, including those at Neuve Chapelle, St. Eloi, Ypres, Vimy Ridge and the Somme, and various subsequent battles. After the Armistice was signed, he proceeded to Germany with the Army of Occupation, and was stationed at Cologne until February 1919, when he returned home and was demobilised. He holds the 1914-15 Star, and the General Service and Victory Medals.
33, Westhall Road, Camberwell, S.E.5.   Z2616

HIND, H., Gunner, R.F.A.
He volunteered in October 1914, and in the following year proceeded to France. Whilst in this theatre of war he did excellent work as a gunner at Neuve Chapelle, Ypres and Albert. He was severely gassed in action and also suffered from dysentery, and was discharged as medically unfit for further duty in July 1917. He holds the 1914-15 Star, and the General Service and Victory Medals.
70, Neate Street, Camberwell, S.E.5.   Z5097

HIND, H. V., Corporal, 23rd London Regiment.
Volunteering in August 1914, he was sent to the Western Front in January 1916, and during his service in France, fought at Vimy Ridge and on the Somme. He was killed in the heavy fighting at High Wood on September 16th, 1916, and was entitled to the General Service and Victory Medals.
    "Great deeds cannot die."
85, The Chase, Clapham Common, S.W.4.   Z2619A

HIND, N. (Miss), Special War Worker.
During the war this lady volunteered her services and was engaged for over two years at the Army Clothing Department at Pimlico. She did good work in the clerical office from October 1917 until January 1920, and carried out her duties in a commendable manner.
85, The Chase, Clapham Common, S.W.4.   Z2619B

HIND, S. J., Private, 23rd London Regiment.
Volunteering in August 1914, he was drafted to the Western Front in January 1916. During his service in France he fought at Albert, Vimy Ridge, High Wood and on the Somme, and was then invalided home owing to heart trouble. He received medical treatment for about six months, and on recovery served in the Clerical Department of the Record Office at London Wall until his demobilisation in June 1919. He holds the General Service and Victory Medals.
85, The Chase, Clapham Common, S.W.4.   Z2617A

HIND, W. H., Gunner, R.F.A.
He volunteered in October 1914, and in the following August was drafted to the Western Front. During his service in France, he did good work as a gunner at Loos, on the Somme and at Arras. He was wounded in action at Passchendaele in September 1917, and after his recovery fought at Cambrai and in various subsequent engagements until the conclusion of hostilities. He was demobilised in June 1919, and holds the 1914-15 Star, and the General Service and Victory Medals.
18, Vicarage Road, Camberwell, S.E.5.   Z2618

HINDS, E. J., Driver, R.F.A.

He volunteered in January 1915, and in the same year proceeded to France. Whilst in this theatre of war he did good work as a driver in the engagements at Loos, Ypres, the Somme, Arras and Vimy Ridge and in many subsequent battles until the conclusion of hostilities. During his service he was twice wounded, and after the Armistice was signed he advanced into Germany, and was stationed at Cologne, where in 1920 he was still serving. He holds the 1914–15 Star, and the General Service and Victory Medals.
99, Avenue Road, Camberwell, S.E.5.　　　Z2620

HINE, A., Sapper, R.E.

He volunteered in December 1914, and in the following May was drafted to France, and served with the 1st Cavalry Mounted Royal Engineers. Throughout his service overseas, he was engaged on important duties in connection with the operations, and was frequently in the forward areas, notably at Albert, on the Somme, at Ypres and Cambrai. He returned home and was demobilised in January 1919, and holds the 1914–15 Star, and the General Service and Victory Medals.
136, Maysouie Road, Battersea, S.W.11.　　　Z2621

HINE, J., Private, Royal Marine Light Infantry.

He enlisted in September 1901, and at the outbreak of war in August 1914, was posted to a ship of the Royal Navy, and was engaged on important duties with the Northern Patrol. He also served for a time at Scapa Flow, and in June 1919 received his discharge. He holds the 1914–15 Star, and the General Service and Victory Medals.
24, Benbow Road, Hammersmith, W.6.　　　10573A

HINES, A. C., Orderly, St. John Ambulance Brigade.

He volunteered in August 1914, but was ineligible for service overseas. After his training he served on important duties as an orderly at various military hospitals. He rendered valuable services and was discharged on medical grounds in October 1918.
34, Lothian Road, Camberwell New Road, S.W.9.　　　Z5098

HINES, G. H. W., Pte., R.A.S.C. and Labour Corps.

He volunteered in August 1915, and sailed for France in the following October. During his service on the Western Front he was engaged on important duties connected with the transport and served at Calais, Dunkirk, Abbeville and Le Havre. In December 1918 he was sent home and was demobilised in the following March. He holds the 1914–15 Star, and the General Service and Victory Medals.
20, Lisford Street, Peckham, S.E.15.　　　Z5206A

HINES, S. C., L/Corporal, 24th London Regiment (Queen's).

He volunteered at the outbreak of war, and was almost immediately drafted to France, where he served in the Retreat from Mons. He was also in action at Neuve Chapelle and towards the end of 1915, was sent to Egypt. In the following year he proceeded to Salonika, where he contracted malaria, and was invalided home. After his recovery, he was re-drafted to France, and fought on the Somme in the fourth Battle of Ypres and in the engagements which followed until the cessation of hostilities. He was demobilised in February 1919, and holds the Mons Star, and the General Service and Victory Medals.
1, Lock's Square, Walworth, S.E.17.　　　Z2623

HINES, W., Private, Royal Defence Corps.

He volunteered in October 1914, and was retained on important duties for three years. He was principally engaged in guarding German prisoners at various detention camps, including one at the Isle of Man. He was discharged on medical grounds in August 1917, having rendered valuable services.
48, Thorncroft Street, Wandsworth Road, S.W.8.　　　Z2624

HINKLEY, F., Private, R.A.S.C.

He volunteered in April 1915, and in the same year proceeded to the Western Front. There he served in many sectors on important duties in the Army Post Office, and did valuable work. In January 1919 he returned home and was demobilised, holding the 1914–15 Star, and the General Service and Victory Medals.
20, Auckland Road, Battersea, S.W.11.　　　Z2625

HINKLY, G. R., Private, 20th London Regiment.

He joined in February 1916, and in October of the same year was drafted to France and there took part in engagements on the Somme and at Arras, and in various other sectors. Later he was sent to Salonika, where he saw much active service until June 1917, when he was invalided home through ill-health, being subsequently discharged in November of that year. He holds the General Service and Victory Medals.
3, Palmerston Street, Camberwell, S.E.5.　　　Z2626

HINRICH, A. Air Mechanic, R.A.F.

Joining in March 1917, he served, on the completion of his training, on important duties at various stations with his unit. He rendered valuable services, but was not successful in obtaining his transfer overseas before the cessation of hostilities. He was demobilised in March 1919.
18, Waterloo Street, Hammersmith, W.6.　　　12593B

HINRICH, F. J., Private, 18th Middlesex Regiment.

Volunteering in October 1915 he was shortly afterwards drafted to the Dardanelles, serving there until the Evacuation of the Peninsula. Later he was sent to France, and was in action at Ypres, the Somme and in many other engagements until the conclusion of hostilities. During his service he was twice wounded and suffered from trench fever, and was in hospital for some considerable time. He was demobilised in March 1919, and holds the 1914–15 Star, and the General Service and Victory Medals.
18, Waterloo Street, Hammersmith, W.6.　　　12593A

HINSON, A. E., Leading Seaman, R.N.

He was mobilised on the declaration of war, having previously fought in the South African campaign, and was posted to H.M.S. "Prince George." He served in the North Sea until 1915, when his vessel proceeded to the Dardanelles and took part in the Naval operations during that campaign. Shortly afterwards he returned to the North Sea and was engaged on important duties off the coast of Scotland, later going to Italy in H.M.S. "Manxman," and serving there until the end of 1918. He was then invalided to hospital through ill-health, and in February 1919 was discharged as medically unfit. He holds the Queen's South African Medal, the 1914–15 Star, and the General Service and Victory Medals.
20, Medway Street, Horseferry Road, S.W.1.　　　Z24547

HINSON, P. R., Driver, R.F.A.

An ex-soldier, who had already served in His Majesty's Forces for twelve years, he rejoined in January 1917 and completed his training at various stations in England. In the following October he was drafted to France and served in that theatre of war for nearly two years. During that period he played an important part in numerous engagements in different sectors of the Western Front, in particular being in action at Dickebusch, Kemmel Hill and Ypres. He also served in the Retreat and subsequent Advance of 1918, and was with his Battery during the triumphal entry of the British troops into Lille in October. After the cessation of hostilities he returned to England and was demobilised in January 1919. He holds the General Service and Victory Medals.
63, Choumet Grove, Peckham, S.E.15.　　　Z6761

HINTON, F., Rifleman, King's Royal Rifle Corps.

He joined in April 1916, and after having completed his training was drafted to the Western Front. Whilst in this theatre of war he was in action in many engagements, including those at Beaucourt, Arras, Bullecourt and Cambrai and others, until the cessation of hostilities. In November 1919 he was demobilised, and holds the General Service and Victory Medals.
2, Bolingbroke Road, Battersea, S.W.11.　　　Z2628

HINTON, W. G., Rifleman, Rifle Brigade and Private, King's Shropshire Light Infantry.

He joined in January 1917, and in the following May embarked for the Western Front, and was wounded during the fighting at Passchendaele. He was invalided home, but on his recovery he returned to the front line and was again wounded on the Somme. He was sent to hospital in England and after receiving treatment was discharged as medically unfit in April 1919. He holds the General Service and Victory Medals.
5, Sheepcote Lane, Battersea, S.W.11.　　　Z2629

HINXMAN, A. W. (M.M.), Sergt., R.A.S.C. (M.T.)

Volunteering at the outbreak of war, he was drafted, after having completed his training, to the Western Front, where he served for twelve months. Shortly afterwards he was sent to the East and attached to the light armoured car section, did splendid work in Salonika and Egypt, where on October 6th, 1917, he was wounded in an encounter with the Arabs. During his service he was mentioned three times in Despatches for gallantry and was awarded the Military Medal for conspicuous bravery in the Field. In addition he holds the 1914 Star, and the General Service and Victory Medals. He returned to England and was demobilised in 1919.
21, Cornwall Grove, Chiswick, W.4.　　　5483A

HINXMAN, A. W., Pte., 8th North Staffordshire Regt.

He joined in 1917, and after completing his training was drafted to France. He was unfortunately killed in action at Ypres on April 29th, 1917, after three months' active service, and was entitled to the General Service and Victory Medals.
"The path of duty was the way to glory."
21, Cornwall Grove, Chiswick, W.4.　　　5483B

HIRON, A., C.Q.M.S., 11th East Yorkshire Regiment.

He volunteered in July 1915, and in December of the same year was drafted to the Western Front, where he was in responsible charge of prisoners of war camps at Amiens and other places and rendered valuable services. He was demobilised in May 1919, holding the 1914–15 Star, and the General Service and Victory Medals.
115, Flaxman Road, Camberwell, S.E.5.　　　Z6187C

HIRON, F., Rifleman, 21st London Regt. (1st Surrey Rifles).
He volunteered in August 1914, and was sent to France in March of the following year. He took part in the severe fighting at Hill 60 and Loos, and was badly wounded. After being invalided home he was discharged in July 1916 as unfit for further service. He holds the 1914–15 Star, and the General Service and Victory Medals.
115, Flaxman Road, Camberwell, S.E.5.   Z6187B

HIRON, S., Pte., 20th London Regt. and Queen's Own (Royal West Kent Regiment).
He joined in March 1917, and in May of the same year was sent to France. On his way up to the front lines he was severely gassed and was in consequence invalided home. After protracted hospital treatment he was discharged as medically unfit for further service in September 1919, and holds the General Service and Victory Medals.
115, Flaxman Road, Camberwell, S.E.5.   Z6187A

HIRST, A. T., Private, R.A.S.C.
Volunteering in August 1915, he proceeded to France in the same year. Whilst in this theatre of war he served in many notable engagements, including those at Loos, the Somme and Arras, and was wounded. He was discharged in March 1919, but later rejoined, and in 1920 was still serving in India. He holds the 1914–15 Star, and the General Service and Victory Medals.
50, St. Philip Street, Battersea Park, S.W.8.   Z2630

HISLOP, A. (Mrs.), Special War Worker.
From June 1918 until March 1919 this lady was engaged by Messrs. Tillings as a Bus conductress on the Lewisham and Croydon routes, and by so doing released a man for military service. She carried out her trying duties with great care and punctuality.
13, Elam Street, Camberwell, S.E.5.   Z5989B

HISLOP, D. D., Sapper, R.E.
Prior to volunteering in November 1915 he was engaged on important work as a plumber in hospitals. He crossed to the Western Front in 1916 and took part in a number of important engagements, among them Cambrai, where he was badly wounded. After the recovery he returned to the Line and fought in the operations of 1918 from June until the close. He was demobilised in February 1919, and holds the General Service and Victory Medals.
13, Elam Street, Camberwell, S.E.5.   Z5989A

HITCHCOCK, H. S., Private, Royal Berkshire Regt.
He volunteered in August 1914, and after completing his training proceeded to France in the following year. Whilst there he fought in many notable engagements, including those at Neuve Chapelle, Hill 60, and Loos, and was wounded. He was invalided home, and after receiving hospital treatment was discharged as medically unfit in November 1916. He holds the 1914–15 Star, and the General Service and Victory Medals.
45, Rosemary Road, Peckham, S.E.15.   Z5254

HITCHINS, A. J., Private, West Yorkshire Regiment.
Mobilised at the outbreak of war, he served for a considerable time on important duties at the aerodrome at Gosport, but in November 1917 was sent to France. There he served for seven months, but later was taken ill and was invalided home and discharged in June 1918 owing to heart trouble. He holds the General Service and Victory Medals.
64, Beaufoy Road, Lavender Hill, S.W.11.   Z2631

HITCHINS, F., C.Q.M.S., 10th Queen's (Royal West Surrey Regiment).
He volunteered in August 1915, and in the following year was drafted to France. There he took part in many important battles including that of Ypres, and also served in the Retreat and Advance of 1918. Shortly afterwards he was invalided to England through ill-health, and was subsequently discharged in November 1919. He holds the General Service and Victory Medals.
80, Weybridge Road, Battersea, S.W.11.   Z2603C

HITCHINS, J. H., Private, Northumberland Fusiliers.
He joined in August 1916, and in the following year was drafted to the Western Front. There he was in action in many important battles and at Ploegsteert Wood was taken prisoner. He was held in captivity until December 1918, when he was released and subsequently demobilised in February 1919. He holds the General Service and Victory Medals.
7, Love Lane, Stockwell, S.W.9.   Z2632

HITCHINS, M., Signaller, South Wales Borderers.
He volunteered in September 1914, and in the following year was drafted to France, where he served in the Somme sector until November of that year. He then proceeded to the East and served in the Balkan campaign, later going to Malta. During his service he was wounded twice. He returned home and was demobilised in November 1919, holding the 1914-15 Star, and the General Service and Victory Medals.
80, Weybridge Street, Battersea, S.W.11.   Z2603D

HITCHMAN, H., L/Corporal, Norfolk Regiment.
He was serving at the outbreak of war, and in 1915 was drafted to Egypt, going thence to Mesopotamia, where he took part in much of the heavy fighting. He was unfortunately killed in action on April 14th, 1915, and was entitled to the 1914 Star, and the General Service and Victory Medals.
"He died the noblest death a man may die."
46, Barlow Street, Walworth, S.E.17.   Z2633

HOAR, E., Corporal, R.A.F.
Volunteering in 1915, he was drafted in the same year to France, where he served with the Royal Air Force on important duties as a fitter for aeroplanes. In 1916 he proceeded to Italy, and saw much service on the Piave until March 1919, when he returned home and was demobilised. He holds the 1914–15 Star, and the General Service and Victory Medals.
12, Sidney Road, Stockwell Road, S.W.9.   Z2634

HOARE, A., A.B., Royal Navy.
He joined the Navy in August 1908, and during the war served in H.M. Ships "Oratavia" and "Lowestoft." His vessel took part in the sinking of the "Blucher" in January 1915, and later in the Naval operations during the Dardanelles campaign. His ship was also engaged on important patrol duties in the North Sea, and in convoying supplies to the various ports. In September 1919 he was demobilised, holding the 1914–15 Star, and the General Service and Victory Medals.
141, Sabine Road, Battersea, S.W.11.   Z2637

HOARE, A. C., Private, Duke of Cornwall's Light Infantry.
Mobilised at the outbreak of war he was drafted overseas on the completion of his training. Whilst in France he took part in many battles including those on the Somme, and at Arras, St. Quentin, Armentières, Ypres, and Amiens, and was wounded and taken prisoner. Later he was released and discharged on account of his wounds in 1918. He holds the 1914–15 Star, and the General Service and Victory Medals.
66, Bradmore Park Road, Hammersmith, W.6.   10695A

HOARE, A. J., A/C.Q.M.S., Northamptonshire Regt.
Mobilised at the outbreak of hostilities, he was drafted to the Western Front with the first Expeditionary Force, and was wounded during the Retreat from Mons. After a few weeks' treatment he rejoined his unit and was killed in action at Givenchy on December 31st, 1914. He was entitled to the Mons Star, and the General Service and Victory Medals
"His life for his Country, his Soul to God."
42, Phelp Street, Walworth, S.E.17.   Z2664+

HOARE, C. J., Gunner (Signaller), R.F.A.
He volunteered in September 1914, and on the completion of his training was drafted overseas. He took part in many notable engagements on the Western Front, including those at Thiepval, Grandcourt, and Albert. He was invalided home through ill-health, and on recovery served on important home duties until demobilised in April 1919. He holds the General Service and Victory Medals.
41, Thorncroft Street, Wandsworth Road, S.W.8.   Z2635A

HOARE, E., Private, 1/10th London Regiment.
He joined in February 1917, and in the following November was drafted to Egypt, where he took part in numerous engagements during the campaign against the Turks. In April 1920 he returned home and was demobilised holding the General Service and Victory Medals.
141, Sabine Road, Battersea, S.W.11.   Z2636C

HOARE, E. (Miss), Special War Worker.
During the war this lady held an important position at Hayes Munition Factory. Her duties, which were of a clerical nature, were carried out with great care and efficiency.
66, Bradmore Park Road, Hammersmith, W.6.   10695C

HOARE, E. W., Rflmn., King's Royal Rifle Corps.
He joined in 1918, and after a brief training was drafted to France, where he served principally at Dunkirk on important duties until the cessation of hostilities. He then proceeded to Germany with the Army of Occupation, remaining there until demobilised in 1920. He holds the General Service and Victory Medals.
66, Bradmore Park Road, Hammersmith, W.6.   10695B

HOARE, H., Guardsman, 3rd Bn. Grenadier Guards.
He was already serving with the Colours at the outbreak of war in August 1914, and was drafted to the Western Front in the following month. In this theatre of war he took part in the Battles of the Marne, the Aisne, Ypres, Neuve Chapelle, Loos, Festubert, the Somme, Vimy Ridge, Arras, Passchendaele and Bapaume. After the Armistice he proceeded to Cologne, and did duty with the Army of Occupation until his return to England. He holds the 1914 Star, and the General Service and Victory Medals, and in 1920 was still serving in the Army.
40, Greylands Road, Peckham, S.E.15.   Z5781

HOARE, G. E., Driver, R.F.A.

Volunteering in October 1915, he was drafted to the Western Front in the following June and served in this theatre of war for a few months. He then proceeded to Salonika, and took part in the fighting at Monastir, and later to Egypt, where he served in the Advance into Palestine, and was present at the entry into Jerusalem. In June 1919, he returned home and was demobilised holding the General Service and Victory Medals.
141, Sabine Road, Battersea, S.W.11.   2636B

HOARE, S., Stoker, Petty Officer, R.N.

He joined the Navy in June 1908, and at the outbreak of war was posted to H.M.S. "Splendid." On board this ship he took part in the fighting off Heligoland, and in many minor engagements in the North Sea. He was then engaged on important duties until his demobilisation in June 1920. He holds the 1914-15 Star, and the General Service and Victory Medals.
141, Sabine Road, Battersea, S.W.11.   Z2636A

HOARE, W. E., Corporal, R.F.A.

Volunteering in February 1915 he proceeded in the following year to the Western Front, and was in action in the Ypres sector. Shortly afterwards he was drafted to Salonika going thence to Mesopotamia, where he took part in the fighting at Kut-el-Amara. Later he served with General Allenby's Forces in the Advance through Egypt into Palestine, and was present at the entry into Jerusalem. In December 1919, he was demobilised holding the General Service and Victory Medals.
41, Thorncroft Street, Wandsworth Road, S.W.8.   Z2635B

HOBBS, E. J., Corporal, R.F.A.

Volunteering in October 1914, he was drafted in the following March to France, and took part in the fighting at Festubert, Loos, and the Somme, where he was wounded. He was invalided to hospital, and on recovery proceeded to Salonika, but after serving there for a short time contracted malaria, and subsequently died in 1917. He was entitled to the 1914-15 Star, and the General Service and Victory Medals.
         " His life for his Country, his Soul to God."
62, Hargwyne Street, Stockwell Road, S.W.9.   Z2638B

HOBBS, H. J., Private, R.A.V.C.

He volunteered in January 1915, and in the same year was drafted to France. He served principally at Dieppe on important duties with the horses, and whilst there he met with an accident, resulting in the loss of a finger. In May 1919, he returned home, and was demobilised holding the 1914-15 Star, and the General Service and Victory Medals.
52, Henley Street, Battersea, S.W.11.   Z2639

HOBBS, H. W., Private, Tank Corps.

He joined in October 1917, and after his training served at various stations on important duties with his unit. He rendered valuable services but was not successful in obtaining his transfer overseas before the cessation of hostilities. He was demobilised in January 1919.
62, Hargwyne Street, Stockwell Road, S.W.9.   Z2638A

HOBBS, J., Corporal, R.E.

Volunteering in February 1915, he served on the completion of his training at the Dardanelles. Later he was drafted to France where he took part in many notable engagements including those on the Somme, and at Arras, Cambrai, and elsewhere until the conclusion of hostilities. In February 1919, he was demobilised holding the General Service and Victory Medals.
10, Banim Street, Hammersmith, W.6.   11617A

HOBBS, S. (Mrs.), Special War Worker.

During the war this lady was engaged on important duties at Messrs. Blake's. She served there for about three months on the production of 6-pounder shells. Later she took up work on the G.W.R., thereby releasing a man for military service. Her duties which were of an arduous nature were carried out in an efficient manner.
10, Banim Street, Hammersmith, W.6.   11617B

HOBBY, A. H., Private, R.A.S.C. (M.T.)

He volunteered in March 1915, and was sent to the Western Front in the same year. He rendered valuable transport services in numerous engagements including those at Hill 60, Ypres, and Vimy Ridge. In 1917 he was transferred to Italy and was engaged on the Paive and Asiago fronts. He was demobilised in February 1919, holding the 1914-15 Star, and the General Service and Victory Medals.
39, Atwell Road, Peckham, S.E.15.   Z5424

HOBBY, F. J., Private, 23rd London Regiment and East Surrey Regiment.

Volunteering in 1915, he was sent to France in the following year. In the course of his duties he unfortunately met with an accident which necessitated his being invalided home. On his recovery he returned to France, and was engaged on important duties in various sectors. He was demobilised in 1918 and holds the General Service and Victory Medals.
26, Gwynne Road, Battersea, S.W.11.   Z2641

HOBDEN, A. A., Private, 1st Royal Berkshire Regt.

Volunteering in May 1915, he crossed to France in the following October. He was engaged in the fighting in several important sectors, notably that of the Somme, where he was severely wounded in July 1916. After being for a time in hospital in France, he was invalided home, and after rejoining his unit was discharged as medically unfit in March 1917. He holds the 1914-15 Star, and the General Service and Victory Medals.
27, Sydney Square, Latona Road, Peckham, S.E.15.   Z6260

HOBOROUGH, J., Pte., Northumberland Fusiliers.

He joined in August 1916, and was drafted to France in October 1917. Two months later after much valuable service he was proceeding home on leave to bury his child when he was unfortunately killed in an air raid at Boulogne on December 22nd, 1917. He was entitled to the General Service and Victory Medals.
     " Honour to the immortal dead who gave their youth that the
                world might grow old in peace."
61, Warriner Gardens, Battersea, S.W.11.   Z2640

HOCKEY, A. G., Pte., 24th London Regt. (Queen's).

He volunteered on the outbreak of hostilities and after completing his training proceeded in June 1916, to France, where he served at St. Eloi and Arras. In 1916 he was drafted to Salonika, and was stationed on the Doiran and Vardar fronts until March 1917. He then sailed to Egypt, and afterwards took part in the Palestine campaign, in which he was present at Beersheba, Jerusalem, Jericho, and the Advance across the Jordan. He returned to France in June 1918 in time to take part in the engagements at Cambrai, Epéhy, Le Cateau, in the final stages of hostilities. He was demobilised in March 1919, and holds the General Service and Victory Medals.
7, Haymerle Road, Peckham, S.E.15.   Z6383

HOCKEY, W. G., Sapper, R.E.

He volunteered in May 1915, and in July of the same year was drafted to the Western Front. He took part in the operations of Ypres, and being badly injured by a mine explosion was invalided home. In 1918 he volunteered for service in North Russia, and was engaged on important duties at Archangel. He was demobilised in August 1919, holding the 1914-15 Star and the General Service and Victory Medals.
49, Kay Road, Stockwell, S.W.9.   Z2643

HOCKING, S., Stoker, R.N., H.M.S. "Thunderer."

Volunteering in September 1915, he served during the remainder of the war with the Grand Fleet in the North Sea on important patrol and escort duties and rendered valuable services. He was still in the Navy in 1920 and holds the General Service and Victory Medals.
18, Mayall Road, Herne Hill, S.E.24.   Z2644

HOCKLEY, H., Private, Queen's (Royal West Surrey Regiment).

Joining in February 1917 he was sent to the Western Front in the following month. He took part in the severe fighting at the Battle of Arras, and in May of the same year was invalided home suffering from shell-shock. He was discharged as medically unfit for further service in December 1917, and holds the General Service and Victory Medals.
74, Wickersley Road, Lavender Hill, S.W.11.   Z2646A

HOCKLEY, J., Private, R.A.S.C.

He joined in April 1916, and was drafted to France in the following month. He was engaged until hostilities ceased in transport of ammunition and supplies to the lines on the Somme, Arras, Vimy Ridge, Messines, Ypres areas, and many other sectors. He was demobilised in August 1919, and holds the General Service and Victory Medals.
244, East Street, Walworth, S.E.17.   Z2647

HOCKLEY, W. H., Leading Stoker, R.N., H.M.S. "Yarmouth" and "Pembroke."

He joined the Navy in 1907, and was serving in the China Seas at the outbreak of war, and afterwards in all parts of the North Sea with the Grand Fleet. He took part in the Battle of Jutland, and in numerous other engagements of a minor character. He was discharged in January 1917 owing to defective eyesight, and holds the 1914-15 Star, and the General Service and Victory Medals.
54, Goldsboro' Road, Wandsworth Road, S.W.8.   Z2645

HODGE, J., Private, 13th Middlesex Regiment.

Volunteering in February 1915, and completing a period of training, he was sent to the Western Front in the following August, and was in action at the Battles of Loos, Ypres, Béthune, Vimy Ridge, and Arras, and later took part in the Advance of 1918. He eventually returned to England, and was demobilised in May 1919, holding the 1914-15 Star, and the General Service and Victory Medals.
26, New Church Road, Camberwell, S.E.5.   Z5773

HODGE, J. C., Private, R.A.S.C.

He volunteered in July 1915, and almost immediately proceeded to the Western Front, where he was engaged on important transport duties. He was invalided to Ireland owing to severe injuries received in an accident, but in January 1917, returned to France, and was attached to the Canadian Royal Engineers on important railroad construction. He holds the 1914-15 Star, and the General Service and Victory Medals, and was demobilised in November 1918.
26, New Church Road, Camberwell, S.E.5.   Z5772

HODGES, A. J., Private, 3rd Royal Fusiliers.

He joined in December 1917, and in the following year after the completion of his training was drafted to France, where he served in various sectors until fighting ceased. He afterwards proceeded with the Army of Occupation to Germany, where he was still serving in 1920, and holds the General Service and Victory Medals.
43, Rosemary Road, Peckham, S.E.15.   Z5249B

HODGES, C., Special War Worker.

From 1916 until after the close of hostilities he worked for the Projectile Company at Battersea as charge hand over a squad of men engaged in the manufacture of six-inch shells, and was also responsible for the repairing of the lathes and all the necessary tools. He frequently worked at the highest pressure on day and night shifts when the production was urgently needed, and rendered valuable services which were greatly appreciated.
6, Castlemain Road, Peckham, S.E.15.   Z5995

HODGES, J. S., Rifleman, King's Royal Rifle Corps.

He joined in May 1916, and was sent to France in the following year, where he took part in much severe fighting at Arras, Cambrai, and the Somme, and in the Retreat and Advance of 1918. He afterwards proceeded with the Army of Occupation to Germany. He was demobilised in February 1919, after returning home, and holds the General Service and Victory Medals.
64, Mayall Road, Herne Hill, S.E.24.   Z2648

HODGSON, J. W., Sapper, R.E.

He volunteered in January 1915, and in August of the same year was drafted to the Western Front, where he took part in numerous engagements, including those on the Somme, and at Arras, Vimy Ridge, Messines, and Ypres. Whilst in action at Cambrai, he was wounded and taken prisoner, and was repatriated after the termination of hostilities. He was demobilised in March 1919, and holds the 1914-15 Star, and the General Service and Victory Medals.
4, Distin Street, Kennington, S.E.11.   TZ25659

HOGAN, E., Private, 9th Royal Inniskilling Fusiliers.

He volunteered in September 1914, and at the conclusion of his training early in the following year was sent to the Western Front, where he subsequently fought in many important engagements, including that at Arras. Later in consequence of ill-health, he was invalided home, and in September 1916 was discharged as physically unfit. He holds the 1914-15 Star, and the General Service and Victory Medals.
107, Avenue Road, Camberwell, S.E.5.   Z2649A

HOGAN, J. P., Driver, R.A.S.C. (M.T.)

He volunteered in April 1915, and at the conclusion of his training was drafted to the Western Front. Whilst in this theatre of war he was engaged in duties of an important nature in connection with the transport of supplies to the forward areas. He was demobilised in September 1919, after his return to England, and holds the 1914-15 Star, and the General Service and Victory Medals.
107, Avenue Road, Camberwell, S.E.5.   Z2649B

HOGAN, W. C., Private, R.A.M.C.

He volunteered in June 1915, and after his training was engaged on duties of an important nature at various hospitals. He was not successful in obtaining his transfer overseas before the termination of hostilities, but nevertheless did valuable work until he was demobilised in March 1919.
107, Avenue Road, Camberwell, S.E.5.   Z2649C

HOGBEN, F. J., Special War Worker.

Being ineligible for service with the Colours, he was employed at Messrs. Piersons, Forest Hill Road, where he was engaged as a baker for the Government. In addition to this important work, he joined a Volunteer Corps, and throughout the war rendered services of a valuable nature.
11, Lisford Street, Peckham, S.E.15.   Z5099A

HOGG, H. M., Air Mechanic, R.A.F.

He joined in October 1917, and at the conclusion of his training was engaged on important duties which called for much technical knowledge and skill. In 1918 he was sent to the United States, where he did valuable instructional work until November of that year, when he returned to England. After the signing of the Armistice, he was sent to Germany with the Army of Occupation, and was demobilised on his return to England in November 1919.
109, Cobourg Road, Camberwell, S.E.5.   Z5425

HOGG, J. C., Guardsman, Coldstream Guards.

Volunteering in December 1914, he was later drafted to the Western Front, where he fought in the Battles of Loos, Vermelles, Vimy Ridge, and the Somme. He was unfortunately killed whilst in action at Passchendaele, and was entitled to the General Service and Victory Medals.
"Steals on the ear the distant triumph song."
6, Lock's Square, Walworth, S.E.17.   Z2650

HOGG, W. F., Corporal, M.G.C.

He enlisted in the South Staffordshire Regiment in 1909, and was later transferred in turn to the Royal Army Service Corps and the Machine Gun Corps. In 1915 he was drafted to the Western Front, where he was subsequently in action until he was wounded and taken prisoner in May 1917. He was held captive until early in the following year, when owing to an exchange of prisoners, he was repatriated. He was discharged as physically unfit in March 1918, and holds the 1914-15 Star, and the General Service and Victory Medals.
75, St. Philip Street, Battersea Park, S.W.8.   Z2651

HOGGER, A. V. J., L/Corporal, 19th and 2nd London Regiment (Royal Fusiliers).

He joined in October 1918, and at the conclusion of his training was drafted to Egypt, where he was engaged on duties of an important nature. During his service in the East he contracted malaria, and was in consequence for some time in hospital. He was demobilised in March 1920, on his return to England, and holds the General Service and Victory Medals.
75, Chancellor's Road, Hammersmith, W.6.   12794

HOGSTON, G. S., Driver, R.F.A.

After volunteering in October 1914, at the age of fifteen he was sent to France in the following year, and there took part in many severe engagements, including those at Albert, Bray, and the Somme. He was badly wounded in July 1916, and has lost his right foot in consequence of his injuries. After protracted hospital treatment he was discharged in January 1918, as unfit for further service, and holds the 1914-15 Star, and the General Service and Victory Medals.
159, Hollydale Road, Nunhead, S.E.15.   Z6399

HOLBROOK, F., Private, Gloucestershire Regt.

He volunteered in November 1915, and in the following May crossed to France, where he was engaged in the fighting at Loos, and Armentières, and was wounded. In 1917 he was transferred to Mesopotamia, and during his service there contracted a severe form of pneumonia, of which, unhappily, he died. He was entitled to the General Service and Victory Medals.
"The path of duty was the way to glory."
118, Mayall Road, Herne Hill, S.E.24.   Z2686A

HOLDEN, A. W., L/Cpl., 4th Buffs (East Kent Regt.)

He joined in June 1916, and on completing his training in the following May, was drafted to India, where he took part in the fighting on the North West Frontier. He returned home and was demobilised in November 1919, holding the India General Service Medal (with clasp Afghanistan, N.W. Frontier, 1919), and the General Service and Victory Medals.
1, Medwin Street, Ferndale Road, S.W.4.   Z2652B

HOLDEN, J., 1st Class Stoker, R.N.

He was in the Navy at the outbreak of war and throughout hostilities was engaged on board H.M.S. "Cochrane" and H.M. Gunboat "Glow Worm." He served in these vessels in many waters and was wounded whilst on duty by an explosion on an ammunition barge. He was discharged in January 1919, on account of his wounds and holds the 1914-15 Star, and the General Service and Victory Medals.
67, Dashwood Road, Wandsworth Road, S.W.8.   Z2653

HOLDER, H. C., L/Corporal, 9th Devonshire Regt.

He volunteered in March 1915, and in the same year was drafted to France. During his service on the Western Front he fought at Festubert and Loos, and was severely wounded at Ypres, and invalided to hospital at Boulogne, and thence to England. He was subsequently discharged as physically unfit for further service in August 1916, and holds the 1914-15 Star, and the General Service and Victory Medals.
24, Manaton Road, Peckham, S.E.15.   Z6250

HOLDGATE, W., Private, R.A.S.C. (M.T.)

He joined in March 1916, and was immediately drafted to France, where he was engaged with the Mechanical Transport conveying supplies to the forward areas. He took part in engagements at Albert, Vimy Ridge, the Somme (I), Arras, Messines, Ypres (III), Cambrai, the Somme (II), and Bapaume. He was demobilised in January 1919, and holds the General Service and Victory Medals.
157, Chatham Street, Walworth S.E.17.   Z2654

HOLDING, F. E. (Mrs.), Special War Worker.

For two years of the war, this lady was employed at the Anti-Gas Works, New Kent Road, on work of National importance. She was engaged in the manufacture of Anti-Gas Masks, and rendered valuable services whilst carrying out her work in a highly commendable manner.
186, East Street, Old Kent Road, Walworth, S.E.17.   Z2655B

HOLDING, E. R., Private, 2nd London Regiment (Royal Fusiliers).
He volunteered in September 1914, and after three months' training was drafted to Malta, thence to Egypt. Later he was sent to the Dardanelles, where he saw much fighting, but contracted dysentery, and was invalided to Malta. On recovery he saw service in Egypt and then France, was in action during many important engagements, including the Battles of the Somme and Arras, and was badly gassed during the Advance of 1918. He was sent home and later transferred to the Royal Army Pay Corps, in which unit he served at home until his demobilisation in April 1920. He holds the 1914-15 Star, and the General Service and Victory Medals.
186, East Street, Old Kent Road, S.E.17.   Z2655A

HOLDING, J. W. T., Private, M.G.C.
Volunteering in July 1915, he was retained for a time on important duties in England and Ireland, and in September 1916, proceeded to France. There he was soon in action and took part in much heavy fighting in the Somme, Ypres, and Cambrai sectors. He was wounded at Delville Wood and Menin Road, and after recovery, proceeded to Cologne with the Army of Occupation. He holds the General Service and Victory Medals, and was demobilised in May 1919.
32, Sandover Road, Camberwell, S.E.5.   Z5777

HOLDSWORTH, B., Sergt., R.A.S.C.
He volunteered in March 1915, and three months later proceeded to France. There he was engaged on transport work, conveying supplies to the forward areas during the Battles of Ypres, Loos, Vermelles, and Vimy Ridge. Later he was attached to the Headquarter Staff on organising work until hostilities ceased. He was demobilised in June 1919, and holds the 1914-15 Star, and the General Service and Victory Medals.
19, Broadhinton Road, Clapham, S.W.4.   Z2656

HOLE, J., Baker, Merchant Service.
He volunteered for the Navy in 1915, but, owing to medical unfitness, was rejected. In March 1916 he succeeded in joining the Merchant Service, and during his twelve months at sea, served on board H.M.T. " Briton." This vessel was employed in conveying troops to India, Alexandria, Malta, Gibraltar, and Port Said. He then returned home, and was discharged as medically unfit for further duty in September 1917. He holds the General Service and Mercantile Marine War Medals.
93, Latchmere Road, Battersea, S.W.11.   Z2657

HOLGATE, H. J. (Senior), Private, 10th Middlesex Regiment (T.F.)
He volunteered in September 1914, and after a period of training served on important garrison duties at various stations. He was not successful in obtaining a transfer overseas, but rendered valuable services until his discharge in June 1916.
13, Clovelly Road, Chiswick, W.4.   6597B

HOLGATE, H. J. (Junior), Private, 8th Middlesex Regiment (T.F.)
He volunteered in August 1914, and shortly afterwards was sent to Gibraltar, where he served for some months. In 1915 he was drafted to France and took part in the heavy fighting in the Ypres sector and was wounded. He was killed in action on April 25th, 1915, and was entitled to the 1914-15 Star, and the General Service and Victory Medals.
   " His life for his Country, his Soul to God."
13, Clovelly Road, Chiswick, W.4.   6597A

HOLLAND, C., Rifleman, King's Royal Rifle Corps.
He was called up from the Reserve in August 1914, and immediately drafted to France, where he took part in the Retreat from Mons. He was reported missing, but later killed in action in October 1914, and was entitled to the Mons Star, and the General Service and Victory Medals.
   " Whilst we remember, the Sacrifice is not in vain."
7, Park Grove, Battersea, S.W.11.   Z2658

HOLLAND, C., Driver, R.A.S.C.
He volunteered in May 1915, and after his training proceeded to France, where he served in many important engagements, including those at the Somme, Vimy Ridge, and Ypres, and in various subsequent battles. He was demobilised in May 1919, after five years' excellent service, and holds the 1914-15 Star, and the General Service and Victory Medals.
69, Commercial Road, Peckham, S.E.15.   Z6395

HOLLAND, E. G., Sapper, R.E.
Volunteering in August 1914, he was drafted overseas in the following May. During his service in France he was engaged on important duties in connection with the operations, and was frequently in the forward areas, notably at Ypres, Loos, Vimy Ridge, Ploegsteert Wood, and the Somme, where he was wounded in the eye in August 1916. He has since lost the sight of that eye as a result of his wound, and was demobilised in June 1919. He holds the 1914-15 Star, and the General Service and Victory Medals.
80, Evelina Road, Peckham, S.E.15.   Z5978

HOLLAND, F. H., Gunner, R.F.A.
He volunteered in August 1914, and after completing his training served at various stations on important duties. He was not successful in obtaining a transfer overseas owing to his being medically unfit, but rendered valuable service until his discharge in 1917. In 1920 he rejoined the Territorials and was again in the R.F.A.
50, Mostyn Road, Brixton Road, S.W.9.   Z4471

HOLLAND, J., Private, 11th Royal Fusiliers.
He volunteered in August 1914, and was quickly drafted to France. In this theatre of war he took part in many important engagements in various sectors of the Front, including the Battles of Arras and Ypres. He was demobilised in February 1919, and holds the 1914 Star, and the General Service and Victory Medals.
16, Percival Road, Mortlake, S.W.14.   8980B

HOLLIS, J., Private, R.M.L.I., H.M.S. "Constance."
He joined in August 1916, and after his training was posted to H.M.S. " Constance," and whilst in this vessel served on important duties in patrolling the North Sea until the conclusion of hostilities. In 1920 he was still serving, and holds the General Service and Victory Medals.
24, Boathouse Walk, Peckham, S.E.15.   Z6259A

HOLLIS, W., Private, Middlesex Regiment.
He joined in April 1917, and after his training served at various stations on important duties with his unit. He did good work, but was not successful in obtaining his transfer overseas prior to the cessation of hostilities. He was demobilised in January 1919.
24, Boathouse Walk, Peckham, S.E.15.   Z6259B

HOLLOWAY, T., Trooper, 3rd (Prince of Wales') Dragoon Guards and Private, R.A.S.C.
Having previously served in the South African campaign, in which he was wounded, he volunteered in September 1914, and during his training was transferred to the R.A.S.C. Remount Depôt. In 1916 he proceeded to France and was employed on many important duties until his discharge in December 1917. He holds the Queen's and King's South African Medals, and the General Service and Victory Medals.
4, Doctors Street, Walworth, S.E.17.   Z2647I

HOLMAN, W., A.B., R.N., H.M.S. "Queen Elizabeth."
He joined the Navy just before war was declared and throughout hostilities served in H.M.S. " Minotaur " in the North Sea. He took part in the Battle of Jutland and saw much active service during the war. He was present at the surrender of the German Fleet and in 1920 was serving on board H.M.S. " Queen Elizabeth." He holds the 1914-15 Star, and the General Service and Victory Medals.
8, Cologne Road, Battersea, S.W.11.   Z2660

HOLMAN, W. J., Private, Royal Sussex Regiment.
Volunteering in January 1915, he proceeded to France four months later and fought at the Battles of Loos, Vimy Ridge and the Somme, and in engagements at Hill 60, Ypres and Festubert. He was badly wounded whilst acting as a sniper in the Loos sector and was invalided home, but in 1917 returned to the Western Front. He was again in action at the Battles of Arras, Ypres, Passchendaele, Lens and Cambrai, and was wounded a second time. On his recovery he was transferred to the R.A.S.C. and remained in France until his demobilisation in June 1919. He holds the 1914-15 Star, and the General Service and Victory Medals.
21, Elwell Road, Clapham, S.W.4.   Z2659

HOLME, S. E., Sergt., R.F.A.
He was in the Army at the outbreak of war and was immediately drafted to the Western Front. In this theatre of war he took part in many engagements, and was wounded in action at the Battle of Ypres in 1915. In 1920 he was still serving with his Regiment, and holds the 1914 Star, and the General Service and Victory Medals.
35, Atwell Road, Rye Lane, S.E.15.   Z5426

HOLMES, A., Sergt., 7th City of London Regiment.
He was mobilised in August 1914, and in the following year was drafted to the Western Front, where he took part in much heavy fighting in many sectors. He fell in action at High Wood on October 7th, 1916, and was entitled to the 1914-15 Star, and the General Service, Victory and the Long Service and Good Conduct Medals.
   " His memory is cherished with pride."
47, Southfields Road, Bedford Park, W.4.   7786C

HOLMES, C. G., Private, East Surrey Regiment.
He volunteered in May 1915, and in the same year was drafted to France, where he saw much heavy fighting on the Somme, and was wounded and invalided home. On his recovery he returned to the Western Front and was severely wounded in action and died of his wounds shortly afterwards on September 6th, 1918. He was entitled to the 1914-15 Star, and the General Service and Victory Medals.
   " Whilst we remember, the Sacrifice is not in vain."
68, Mark's Road, Camberwell, S.E.5.   Z2663

HOLMES, E. G., Cpl., 7th City of London Regt. and Mechanic, R.A.F.
He volunteered in August 1914, and in the following year proceeded to France. During his service overseas he took part in many engagements, including those at Festubert, Loos, the Somme and Amiens, and was wounded in action. He was demobilised in February 1919, and holds the 1914-15 Star, and the General Service and Victory Medals.
47, Southfield Road, Bedford Park, W.4.   7786B

HOLMES, J. W., Driver, R.A.S.C. (M.T.)
Volunteering in August 1914, he proceeded to France shortly afterwards, and was engaged on important transport duties in various sectors of the Front. He took an active part in many engagements, including the Battles of Ypres, Neuve Chapelle, Loos, Vimy Ridge, the Somme, Arras and Cambrai, and also rendered valuable service during the Retreat and Advance of 1918. He holds the 1914 Star, and the General Service and Victory Medals, and was demobilised in February 1919.
3, Boyton Row, Camberwell, S.E.5.   Z5776

HOLMES, W. E., Mechanic, R.A.F.
He joined in October 1917 at the age of seventeen, and after a period of training proceeded to France, where he saw much heavy fighting in various sectors. After the cessation of hostilities he went into Germany with the Army of Occupation until his demobilisation in October 1919. He holds the General Service and Victory Medals.
47, Southfield Road, Bedford Park, W.4.   7786A

HOLMES, L., Gunner, R.F.A.
He volunteered in December 1914, and in the following September was drafted to France. There he took part in the Battles of Loos, the Somme, Arras, Vimy Ridge and Messines, where he was wounded. On his recovery he returned to the Western Front and fought at Cambrai and in the Retreat and Advance of 1918, was again wounded at Ypres, and was invalided home. In 1920 he was still serving, and holds the 1914-15 Star, and the General Service and Victory Medals.
27, Kinglake Street, Walworth, S.E.17.   Z2662

HOLT, A., Sapper, R.E.
He joined in May 1917, and on completing his training was drafted to France. In this seat of war he took part in the Retreat and Advance of 1918 and was later engaged on special duties until hostilities ceased. He was demobilised in March 1919 and holds the General Service and Victory Medals.
8, Porson Street, Wandsworth Road, S. Lambeth, S.W.8.   Z2664A

HOLT, A. J., Private, R.A.S.C. and Gunner, R.G.A.
He volunteered in April 1915, and was quickly drafted to France, where he served with the R.A.S.C. on important duties. He was employed in conveying supplies to the forward areas during fighting in many sectors and in 1918 was transferred to the R.G.A. He was kicked by a horse, which caused him to be in hospital some time. He was demobilised in March 1919, and holds the 1914-15 Star, and the General Service and Victory Medals.
35, Riverhall Street, Wandsworth Road, S.W.8.   Z2665

HONEYBALL, E., Stoker, R.N.
Already in the Navy at the outbreak of war in August 1914, he served on board H.M.S. " Cornwallis " and " Vanguard " in the North Sea for some time, and was engaged on important convoy and patrol duties. Later he saw service off the shores of Italy whilst transporting troops and supplies. In 1920 he was on board H.M.S. " Sir Thomas Picton " in Turkish waters, and holds the 1914-15 Star, and the General Service and Victory Medals.
26, Bournemouth Road, Rye Lane, S.E.15.   Z5427B

HONEYBALL, E., Private, 22nd London Regiment.
Shortly after joining in 1917 he was drafted to the Western Front, where he saw severe fighting in various sectors. He took part in the Battles of Ypres and the Somme and many other important engagements in this theatre of war, and was gassed whilst in action in the Advance of 1918. After the cessation of hostilities he proceeded to Egypt and was stationed at Alexandria and on the Suez Canal until his return home for demobilisation in January 1920. He holds the General Service and Victory Medals.
26, Bournemouth Road, Rye Lane, S.E.15.   Z5427C

HONEYSETT, A. H., A.B., Royal Navy.
He enlisted in June 1912, and after the outbreak of war in August 1914, served in H.M.S. " Nottingham," and whilst in this vessel fought in the Battles of Heligoland Bight, Dogger Bank and Jutland and many minor engagements. He was in H.M.S. " Nottingham " when this vessel was torpedoed in the North Sea on August 19th, 1916, but was fortunately rescued and later was engaged on mine-sweeping duties in H.M.S. " Marigold," " Dahlia," " Daphne " and " Sunflower." He was finally discharged in June 1920, and holds the Naval General Service Medal (with clasp Persian Gulf), the 1914-15 Star, and the General Service and Victory Medals.
13, Knox Road, Battersea, S.W.11.   Z2666

HONIBROW, R., Private, 7th London Regiment.
He joined in April 1918, and in the following June proceeded to France. Whilst in this theatre of war he fought in many engagements in the Advance of 1918, and after the Armistice proceeded to Germany with the Army of Occupation. He served there until November 1919, when he returned home and was demobilised. He holds the General Service and Victory Medals.
1, Bredon Road, Camberwell, S.E.5.   Z6382C

HONIBROW, S., Cpl., 7th (Queen's Own) Hussars.
He volunteered in January 1915, and in the following August proceeded to the Dardanelles, where he took part in the heavy fighting until the Evacuation. He afterwards saw much service in Egypt, Mesopotamia and India, where he was in action against the Afghans in the risings on the North-West Frontier. He returned home, and was demobilised in December 1919, and holds the 1914-15 Star, the India General Service Medal (with clasp Afghanistan, N.W. Frontier, 1919), and the General Service and Victory Medals.
1, Bredon Road, Camberwell, S.E.5.   Z6382A

HOOK, C., Private, R.M.L.I.
He volunteered in 1914, and saw service in the North Sea and many other waters during the period of activity. He took part in operations at the Dardanelles and fought in the Battle of Jutland and many minor Naval engagements. He was demobilised in 1919, and holds the 1914-15 Star, and the General Service and Victory Medals.
33, Seaham Street, Wandsworth Road, S.W.8.   Z2668

HOOK, E. A., Bandsman, Royal Munster Fusiliers.
He enlisted in April 1907, and immediately on the outbreak of war in August 1914, proceeded to the Western Front, where he fought through the Retreat from Mons. He also took part in the Battles of the Marne, the Aisne, Neuve Chapelle, Hill 60, Loos, the Somme, Arras and Cambrai, served through the Retreat and Advance of 1918, and was wounded in action on five occasions. He holds the Mons Star, and the General Service and Victory Medals, and in 1920 was still with his unit.
7, Cambridge Street, Camberwell, S.E.5.   Z2669

HOOK, W., Private, R.A.M.C.
Joining in August 1916, he was drafted to France early in the following year, and there served as a stretcher-bearer in various sectors of the Front. He took part in the Battles of Arras, Cambrai and the Somme and many other important engagements, and was wounded in action during the Advance of 1918. After the cessation of hostilities he served with the Army of Occupation in Germany, finally returning home for demobilisation in January 1920. He holds the General Service and Victory Medals.
26, Camellia Street, Wandsworth Road, S.W.17.   Z2667

HOOKER, R. E., Private, Bedfordshire Regiment.
He joined in June 1918, and on completion of a period of training was engaged on important duties at various stations. Owing to the early cessation of hostilities, he was unable to obtain his transfer overseas, but, nevertheless, rendered very valuable services with his unit until January 1919, when he was demobilised.
10B, Madron Street, Walworth, S.E.17.   Z2670

HOOKINS, A. E., Sergt., 24th London Regiment (The Queen's) and Military Police.
Six months after volunteering in September 1914, he proceeded to the Western Front, where he saw much heavy fighting. He was wounded in action at Givenchy and after only two months' overseas service was invalided home. On his recovery he was engaged on important duties with the Military Police until 1918, when he returned to France. He was finally demobilised in June 1919, and holds the 1914-15 Star, and the General Service and Victory Medals.
11, Otto Street, Walworth, S.E.17.   Z26228

HOOPER, A. E., Gunner, R.G.A.
He joined in October 1917, and in the following May was drafted overseas. During his service in France he took part in the heavy fighting on the Arras Front and in the second Battle of Cambrai, and was severely wounded. He was invalided home, and after his evacuation from hospital was retained on home defence duties until his demobilisation in January 1919. He holds the General Service and Victory Medals.
134, Hollydale Road, Peckham, S.E.15.   Z6397

HOOPER, B. L., Gunner, R.F.A.
He volunteered in June 1915, and in the following year proceeded to France, where he did excellent work as a gunner in many engagements, including that at Vimy Ridge. In November 1916 he was drafted to Salonika and served on the Doiran front until February 1917, when he was sent to Egypt. He afterwards advanced through Palestine with General Allenby's Forces and was in action at the third Battle of Gaza, and at Jericho and was present at the entry into Jerusalem. He returned home and was demobilised in June 1919, holding the General Service and Victory Medals.
38, Flaxman Road, Camberwell, S.E.5.   Z5987

HOOPER, F., Gunner, R.F.A.

He volunteered in 1915, and later in the same year was drafted to France, where he saw much severe fighting whilst taking part in many important engagements. He died gloriously on the field of battle at Arras in October 1916, and was entitled to the 1914-15 Star, and the General Service and Victory Medals.

" He passed out of the sight of men by the path of duty and self-sacrifice."

12, Lock's Square, Walworth, S.E.17.   Z3285B

HOOPER, J., Gunner, R.G.A.

He joined in February 1917, and in May of that year proceeded to the Western Front. Whilst in this theatre of war he took part in many important engagements, including the Battles of Ypres, Passchendaele, Cambrai, the Somme, the Scarpe and Mons (II), and saw much heavy fighting in the Advance of 1918. He was demobilised on his return home in February 1919, and holds the General Service and Victory Medals.

46, Grant Road, Battersea, S.W.11.   Z2671B

HOOPER, J. A., Driver, R.H.A.

He volunteered in August 1914, and proceeded to France in September of the following year. During his service there he took part in numerous engagements, including those at Festubert, Loos, the Somme, Arras, Vimy Ridge, Ypres and Cambrai. In 1917 he was invalided home for a time, but on recovery rejoined his Battery in France in time for the Retreat and Advance of 1918, and after the Armistice he advanced into Germany with the Army of Occupation. He was demobilised in July 1919, and holds the 1914-15 Star, and the General Service and Victory Medals.

30, Elam Street, Camberwell, S.E.5.   Z5988

HOOPER, J. P., Rifleman, Rifle Brigade.

He joined in June 1916, and in May of the following year was drafted to the Western Front, where in the same month he was taken prisoner whilst in action. He was held in captivity until the cessation of hostilities, and after his return home in January 1919, was engaged in guarding prisoners of war at various stations until August of that year, when he was demobilised. He holds the General Service and Victory Medals.

19, Newcomen Road, Battersea, S.W.11.   Z2672

HOOPER, W. G. A., Private, 7th Royal Fusiliers.

He joined in January 1918, and underwent a period of training prior to being drafted to the Western Front in the following July. There, only a few weeks after landing in France, he fell fighting near Bapaume on August 21st, 1918, during the Allies' last Advance. He was entitled to the General Service and Victory Medals.

"A costly Sacrifice upon the altar of freedom."

46, Grant Road, Battersea, S.W.11.   Z2671A

HOPE, A. G., Private, 25th London Regt. (Cyclists).

He volunteered in November 1915, and in June of the following year was drafted to India, where he served for some time as a 1st Class Male Nurse in various hospitals. During the Rising on the North-Western Frontier he was engaged on special transport duties, and rendered valuable services. He eventually returned to England, and was demobilised in January 1920, holding the India General Service Medal (with clasp, Afghanistan, N.W. Frontier, 1919), and the General Service and Victory Medals.

31, Graylands Road, Peckham, S.E.15.   Z5780

HOPE, A. V., Driver, R.F.A.

Shortly after volunteering in January 1915, he was drafted to the Western Front, where he saw much severe fighting and took part in the Battles of Neuve Chapelle and Ypres. In 1917 he was transferred to Italy but returned to France in time to serve through the Advance of 1918. Later he proceeded with the Army of Occupation into Germany, returning home for demobilisation in May 1919, and holds the 1914-15 Star, and the General Service and Victory Medals.

12, Gonsalva Road, Wandsworth Road, S.W.8.   Z2673

HOPE, J. D., Corporal, Norfolk Regiment.

He volunteered in August 1914, and after serving for a time in England, proceeded to France, where he saw severe fighting in various sectors of the Front. He took part in the Battles of Loos, the Somme, Ypres and Cambrai, and many other important engagements in this theatre of war, and was demobilised on his return home in February 1919, and holds the General Service and Victory Medals.

91, Nasmyth Street, Hammersmith, W.6.   11829A

HOPE, J. G., Gunner, R.F.A.

Shortly after volunteering in 1915, he proceeded to the Western Front, where he saw much heavy fighting. He served through the Battles of Neuve Chapelle, Ypres, Loos, the Somme, Arras, Vimy Ridge, Bullecourt and Cambrai, and many minor engagements, and took part also in the Advance of 1918. He was demobilised on returning to England in 1919, and holds the 1914-15 Star, and the General Service and Victory Medals.

19, Redmore Road, Hammersmith, W.6.   11602C

HOPE, R. (Miss), Special War Worker.

During the period of hostilities this lady was engaged on work of great National importance at the Hayes Filling Factory, Middlesex. There she was employed on the responsible and dangerous duties of a shell-filler and rendered very valuable services throughout.

19, Redmore Road, Hammersmith, W.6.   11602B

HOPES, L. B., Private, 2nd Royal Fusiliers.

Joining in April 1916, he went through his course of training and in the same year crossed to France. He took part in many operations on the Arras front, and was there wounded in 1917. After three months' treatment in England he returned to the lines and fought in the Retreat and Advance of 1918 until badly wounded at Epéhy. On his recovery some months later he was drafted to India, where in 1920 he was still serving, and holds the General Service and Victory Medals.

76, Tappesfield Road, Peckham, S.E.15.   6473

HOPKINS, C., Private, Labour Corps.

Volunteering in August 1914, he was engaged at Aldershot and other stations on important duties with his unit. He rendered valuable services, but on medical grounds was not successful in securing his transfer overseas, and was discharged in August 1916.

132, Gloucester Road, Peckham, S.E.15.   Z5982B

HOPKINS, E. (Mrs.), Special War Worker.

In order to release a man for the Colours, this lady offered her services to Messrs. Lyons, Cadby Hall, where she was engaged on important and responsible duties during the period of hostilities. She did much excellent work and her services proved of great value to the firm.

38, Yeldham Road, Hammersmith, W.6.   12835A

HOPKINS, J. W., Corporal, King's Royal Rifle Corps and M.G.C.

He joined in January 1917, and later in the same year was drafted to the Western Front. Whilst in this theatre of war he took part in many important engagements, including the Battles of Arras, Bullecourt, Ypres, St. Quentin, the Somme and Amiens, and was severely wounded in action at Cambrai. He was demobilised in February 1919, and holds the General Service and Victory Medals.

9, Sedan Street, Walworth, S.E.17.   Z2675

HOPKINS, O. H., Trooper, 1st (Royal) Dragoons.

Mobilised in August 1914, he immediately proceeded to the Western Front, where he took part in the Retreat from Mons. He fought also in the Battles of Ypres, Neuve Chapelle, Loos, the Somme, Arras and Armentières and many other important engagements, and served through the Advance of 1918. He was then sent with the Army of Occupation into Germany, finally returning home for discharge in January 1919. He holds the Mons Star, and the General Service and Victory Medals.

38, Yeldham Road, Hammersmith, W.6.   12835B

HOPKINS, P., Gunner, R.F.A.

After volunteering in November 1914, he underwent a period of training prior to being drafted to France in the following year. There he saw much heavy fighting and took part in the Battles of Loos and the Somme and many other important engagements until severely wounded in action. He was invalided to No. 11 Stationary Hospital, Rouen, and there had his left leg amputated. He was consequently discharged in August 1917, and holds the 1914-15 Star, and the General Service and Victory Medals.

61, Cator Street, Peckham, S.E.15.   Z5100

HOPKINS, R. C., Gunner, R.F.A. and R.G.A.

He volunteered in March 1915, and in the following December was drafted overseas. During his service in France he fought at the Somme, Beaumont-Hamel, Vimy Ridge, Ypres, Passchendalele, Lens, and was wounded. Afterwards he served in the anti-aircraft section at Boulogne until November 1918, when he fell ill. On his recovery he was transferred to the Royal Garrison Artillery and drafted home, where he was engaged on important duties until his demobilisation in March 1919. He holds the 1914-15 Star, and the General Service and Victory Medals.

137A, Coldharbour Lane, Camberwell, S.E.5.   Z6381

HOPKINS, S. G., Private, 23rd London Regiment.

Mobilised with the Territorials in August 1914, he proceeded to France early in the following year and there saw much heavy fighting. After only a few months' service on the Western Front he was severely wounded in action at Festubert and invalided home. He was discharged in June 1916 as medically unfit for further service, and holds the 1914-15 Star, and the General Service and Victory Medals.

2, Morrison Street, Battersea, S.W.11.   Z2674

HOPPE, H., 1st Class Stoker, R.N.

He volunteered in October 1914, and served in H.M.S. "Martin" with the Grand Fleet in the North Sea. He was engaged on various important duties, and on board H.M.S. "Botha," took part in the Battle of Jutland and many minor engagements. He was invalided from the Navy in July 1917, suffering from heart disease, and holds the 1914–15 Star, and the General Service (with two clasps) and Victory Medals.
33, Dean's Buildings, Flint Street, Walworth, S.E.17.   Z2676

HOPSON, H. L., L/Corporal, 9th Queen's (Royal West Surrey Regt.) and Labour Corps.

He volunteered in September 1915, and in the following year was drafted to the Western Front, where he saw much severe fighting in various sectors and took part in many important engagements. He was reported missing and later presumed killed in action on the Somme on March 23rd, 1918, and was entitled to the General Service and Victory Medals.
"Courage, bright hopes, and a myriad dreams, splendidly given."
18, Pulross Road, Brixton Road, S.W.9.   Z2677

HOPTON, H. C. A., L/Corporal, R.A.S.C.

Mobilised in August 1914, he immediately proceeded to the Western Front, where he served through the Battle of, and Retreat from, Mons. He also took an active part in the Battles of the Marne, the Aisne, Hill 60, and Ypres, and many minor engagements, and was wounded at Loos in September 1915. He was invalided home, and on his recovery in the following year proceeded to Salonika, and served on the Vardar and Doiran fronts, and at Monastir. He was discharged on his return home in 1919, and holds the Mons Star, and the General Service and Victory Medals.
5, McKerrell Road, Peckham, S.E.15.   Z5784B

HOPTON, H. W., L/Cpl., 21st London Regt. (1st Surrey Rifles).

He was mobilised in August 1914, and was drafted to the Western Front in time to take part in the Battle of, and Retreat from, Mons. He also served through the Battles of the Marne, La Bassée, Hill 60, and Loos, and many other engagements until invalided home in December 1915. He was then engaged on coastal defence duties in England until January 1919, when he was demobilised, and holds the Mons Star, and the General Service and Victory Medals.
5, McKerrell Road, Peckham, S.E.15.   Z5784C

HOPTON, W. T., Corporal, 7th Royal Fusiliers.

Shortly after volunteering in May 1915, he was drafted to the Western Front, and there saw severe fighting in various sectors. He served through the Battles of Loos, St. Eloi and Albert and many other important engagements until wounded in action at La Bassée in August 1916. He was invalided home, but on recovery returned to France and took part in the Retreat and Advance of 1918. He was demobilised in June 1919, and holds the 1914–15 Star, and the General Service and Victory Medals.
5, McKerrell Road, Peckham, S.E.15.   Z5784A

HORLOCK, H. T., Shoeing Smith, R.A.S.C. (H.T.)

Having previously fought in the Boer War, he re-enlisted in September 1915, and served at various stations, where he was engaged on duties of great importance. He was not successful in obtaining his transfer to the Front, but, nevertheless, rendered very valuable services with his unit until demobilised in February 1919. He holds the Queen's South African Medal.
2, Alsace Street, Walworth, S.E.17.   Z2678

HORN, A. J., Rifleman, Rifle Brigade.

He was serving at the outbreak of war, and in 1914 was drafted to France. Whilst in this theatre of war he fought in engagements on the Somme front and was wounded and taken prisoner at Ypres in May 1915. He was held in captivity in Germany until January 1919, when he was released and repatriated and was subsequently demobilised in the following October. He holds the 1914 Star, and the General Service and Victory Medals.
94, Vaughan Road, Camberwell, S.E.5.   Z6254A. Z6255A

HORN, H. E. H., Petty Officer, R.N., H.M.S. "Prince of Wales."

He joined in April 1916, and was chiefly engaged on important duties at the docks, but also saw service in H.M.S. "Prince of Wales" with the Grand Fleet in the North Sea. Whilst in Scotland he was severely injured in an accident, and as a result was finally invalided from the Navy in December 1918. He holds the General Service and Victory Medals.
210, Beresford Street, Camberwell Road, S.E.5.   Z2680

HORN, R. J., Telegraphist, R.N.

He joined in 1916, and served in H.M.S. "Actaeon" and "Inverness" with the Grand Fleet in the North Sea. He was also stationed for a time at Scapa Flow, and whilst engaged on important duties as wireless operator did much useful work until his demobilisation in January 1920. He holds the General Service and Victory Medals.
56, Acorn Street, Camberwell, S.E.5.   Z2679

HORNBY, A., Sapper, R.E.

Volunteering in May 1915, he proceeded to the Western Front in the following November and there served in various sectors. He took an active part in the Battles of Ypres, Albert, the Somme, Cambrai and Bapaume, and many other important engagements until the cessation of hostilities, and on his return home in July 1919, was demobilised. He holds the 1914–15 Star, and the General Service and Victory Medals.
36, Jardin Street, Camberwell, S.E.5.   Z5101

HORNE, J. S., Trooper, 1/3rd Scottish Horse (Dragoons).

He volunteered in September 1915, and underwent a period of training prior to being drafted to the Western Front. After taking part in many important engagements in this theatre of war he was transferred to Salonika, where he was again in action and was also for a time in hospital suffering from malaria. He returned home for demobilisation in March 1919, and holds the General Service and Victory Medals.
43, Minford Gardens, West Kensington, W.14.   11870A

HORNE, R. J., Pte., Queen's (Royal West Surrey Regiment).

He volunteered in February 1915, and twelve months later was drafted to France. Whilst in this theatre of war he took part in many important engagements, including the Battles of the Somme, Arras, Vimy Ridge, Cambrai and Bapaume, served also through the Retreat and Advance of 1918, and was wounded in action at Amiens. He was demobilised in February 1919, and holds the General Service and Victory Medals.
33, Holden Street, Battersea, S.W.11.   Z2681

HORNETT, H., L/Corporal, M.G.C.

Joining in August 1916, he proceeded to France after four months' training, but was invalided home only a few weeks later. He returned to the Western Front in January 1918, and there saw much severe fighting and took part in many important engagements until May 1918, when he was again sent home suffering from trench fever. He was ultimately demobilised in September 1919, and holds the General Service and Victory Medals.
184, Cator Street, Peckham, S.E.15.   Z5102B

HORNSBY, J., Private, 23rd London Regiment.

He volunteered in February 1915, and in June of the following year proceeded to the Western Front, where he fought at St. Eloi and Vimy Ridge. In December 1916 he was transferred to the East and took part in engagements on the Doiran Vardar and Struma fronts in Salonika, before serving in Egypt. He was also in action in Palestine, where he was present at the capture of Beersheba and Jerusalem and was wounded in November 1917. He returned home, and was invalided from the Army in January 1919, and holds the General Service and Victory Medals.
4, Ashness Road, Battersea, S.W.11.   Z3088

HOROBIN, A. G., Private, R.A.V.C.

He volunteered in November 1915, and in the following December sailed for France, where he was stationed at Le Havre on important duties in attending to the horses. Later he went up to the front lines on September 8th 1916, and was severely wounded during a raid by enemy aircraft at Elverdinghe, near Ypres, and was invalided home and transferred on recovery to the Labour Corps. In February 1917 he again went to France and served there on important duties on the railways until the following September, when he returned to England. He then served on home defence until demobilised in March 1919. He holds the 1914–15 Star, and the General Service and Victory Medals.
52, Hornby Road, Peckham, S.E.15.   Z6262

HORSLEY, C., Air Mechanic, R.A.F.

He joined in March 1917, and shortly afterwards proceeded to France, where he served in a Balloon Section in various sectors of the Front. He took an active part in the Battles of Vimy Ridge, Cambrai, and the Somme, and many other important engagements in this theatre of war, and also served for a time at Dunkirk. He was demobilised on his return home in March 1919, and holds the General Service and Victory Medals.
82, Westmoreland Road, Walworth, S.E.17.   Z2682

HORTON, C. E., Private, 53rd Middlesex Regt. and R.A.S.C.

He joined on attaining military age in April 1918, and after a period of training, was engaged on important duties at various stations. Owing to the early cessation of hostilities, he was unable to obtain his transfer to the Front, but, later was sent with the Army of Occupation to Germany, where he served at Cologne. He finally returned home for demobilisation in May 1920.
4, Myatt Road, Stockwell, S.W.9.   Z4472

HORWOOD, A. E., Corporal, King's Own (Royal Lancaster Regiment).
Mobilised in August 1914, he proceeded to the Western Front in time to take part in the Retreat from Mons. He also fought in the Battles of Neuve Chapelle, Loos, the Somme, Arras, Bullecourt, Armentières, and Amiens, and was twice wounded in action. He was consequently invalided from the Army in 1918, and holds the Mons Star, and the General Service and Victory Medals.
3, Yeldham Buildings, Yeldham Road, Hammersmith, W.6.
12831A

HORWOOD, H. E., Sapper, R.E.
Mobilised in August 1914, he was immediately drafted to the Western Front, where, after fighting in the Retreat from Mons, he took an active part in the Battles of the Marne, the Aisne, Ypres, Neuve Chapelle, Festubert and Loos. In December 1916 he was transferred to Salonika, and there served on the Doiran, Struma, and Vardar fronts, and was for some time in hospital suffering from malaria. He was also stationed at Mudros before returning home to be discharged in December 1918. He holds the Mons Star, and the General Service and Victory Medals.
9, Darwin Buildings, Walworth, S.E.17.
Z2683

HOSE, W., Sapper, R.E. and Private, R.A.S.C., Middlesex Regiment and Labour Corps.
Having attested in November 1915, he was called to the Colours in July of the following year, and after a period of training was engaged on important duties at various stations. Being medically unfit for active service, he was unable to obtain his transfer to the Front, but nevertheless did much useful work until April 1919, when he was demobilised.
17, Manor Street, Clapham, S.W.4.
Z2684

HOSIER, J., Private, Durham Light Infantry.
He volunteered in December 1915, and after a period of training was drafted to the Eastern Theatre of War in the following June. He took part in many engagements on the Struma, Vardar, and Doiran fronts in Salonika, was present at operations in Macedonia, and later was transferred for duty in Russia. He rendered valuable services during hostilities but eventually invalided to England with malaria and finally discharged in October 1919. He holds the General Service and Victory Medals.
109, Chatham Street, Walworth, S.E.17.
Z2685

HOSKIN, A., Driver, R.F.A.
Volunteering in 1914, he was serving at home stations preparatory to his being drafted overseas, when he was severely injured by the kick of a horse whilst training. He consequently had to undergo an operation, and was ultimately discharged in 1916 as physically unfit for further service.
26, Bournemouth Road, Peckham, S.E.15.
Z5427A

HOSKINS, F., Gunner, R.F.A.
He volunteered at the outbreak of war in August 1914, and after undergoing a period of training was drafted to the Western Front in the following year. There he played an important part in many of the early battles, including those of Ypres, and the Somme, and was unfortunately killed in action in July 1916 at Mametz Wood. He was entitled to the 1914-15 Star, and the General Service and Victory Medals.
"His life for his Country, his Soul to God."
28, Mundella Road, Wandsworth Road, S.W.8.
Z2508B

HOSKINS, H., Driver, R.F.A.
He volunteered in September 1914, and in May of the following year was drafted to the Western Front, where he took part in much severe fighting at Loos, the Hohenzollern Redoubt, the Somme, Pozières, Arras, Monchy, and in many other engagements. After being wounded in August 1918, he was invalided home, and was discharged as medically unfit for further services in March 1919. He holds the 1914-15 Star, and the General Service and Victory Medals.
17, Nunhead Crescent, Peckham, S.E.15.
Z6182

HOSKINS, P., Corporal, 12th (Prince of Wales' Royal) Lancers.
Volunteering in August 1914, he was sent to France after a period of training, and played a prominent part in many important engagements throughout hostilities. He saw much heavy fighting in various sectors of the Front, and was wounded in action at Cambrai. After being invalided to England, he was retained with his unit for duty at Cardiff, and was later demobilised in 1919. He holds the 1914-15 Star, and the General Service and Victory Medals.
28, Mundella Road, Wandsworth Road, S.W.8.
Z2508C

HOSKYNS, W. H., Private, County of Middlesex Motor Volunteers.
He joined in November 1917, and was engaged on important duties, conveying the wounded from the stations to hospital, and rendered very valuable services with his unit. He unfortunately died of influenza on October 30th, 1918.
4, New Church Road, Camberwell, S.E.5.
Z5711B

HOSSACK, E. G., Private, R.A.M.C. and R.A.S.C.
He was mobilised with the Territorial Force at the outbreak of war, and in September 1916, after transference to the Royal Army Service Corps, was sent to Italy. There he was engaged on important transport duties throughout the operations on the Piave, and the subsequent engagements, and was on one occasion injured by a kick from a horse. He was demobilised in April 1919, and holds the General Service and Victory Medals.
81, Blake's Road, Peckham Grove, S.E.15.
Z6000

HOTHAM, T. G., L/Corporal, R.E. (I.W.T.)
He volunteered in January 1916, and after undergoing a period of training, was engaged on important transport duties, conveying munitions of war to France. He rendered very valuable services with his unit until February 1919, when he was demobilised, and holds the General Service and Victory Medals.
2, Domville Grove, Camberwell, S.E.5.
Z5623A

HOTHAM, T. W. G., L/Cpl., 10th Royal Fusiliers.
He volunteered in March 1915, and in the following year, proceeded to the Western Front, where he took part in many important engagements, including the Battles of the Somme, Arras, Vimy Ridge, Cambrai, the Aisne and the Marne. He died gloriously on the field of battle at Achiet-le-Grand on August 23rd 1918, and was entitled to the General Service and Victory Medals.
"A costly sacrifice upon the altar of freedom."
2, Domville Grove, Camberwell, S.E.5.
Z5623B

HOUCHIN, W., Leading Aircraftsman, R.A.F.
He volunteered in August 1914, and sailed for France in June 1916. During his service on the Western Front he was engaged on important duties as a winchman on the observation balloons, and in executing general repairs to aeroplanes, and was present at engagements on the Somme, and at Arras, Ypres, Passchendaele, Bullecourt and Cambrai, and finally Mons. After the Armistice he served with the Army of Occupation in Germany, and was stationed on the Rhine until his demobilisation in June 1919. He holds the General Service and Victory Medals.
15, Boat House Walk, Peckham, S.E.15.
Z6242

HOUNSELL, E., Private, Buffs (East Kent Regt.)
He volunteered in September 1914, and early in the following year proceeded to France, where he was soon in action and was wounded in September 1915. In 1916 he was transferred to Salonika, and took part in many engagements, but unfortunately, suffered from repeated attacks of malaria, and was eventually invalided to England and discharged from the Army in March 1919 as medically unfit for further service. He holds the 1914-15 Star, and the General Service and Victory Medals.
21, Thessaly Square, Wandsworth Road, S.E.8.
Z2687

HOUSDEN, A., Private, 24th London Regiment (The Queen's).
He volunteered in August 1914, and after a period of training and service at home, was sent to the Western Front in August 1915. There he took part in many important engagements, including the Battles of the Somme, Vimy Ridge, Arras, and Ploegsteert Wood. He fell fighting at Chérisy on May 3rd, 1917, and was entitled to the 1914-15 Star, and the General Service and Victory Medals.
"Great deeds cannot die."
11, Cunard Street, Camberwell, S.E.5.
Z5103

HOUSE, J. H., L/Corporal, M.G.C.
He joined in February 1917, and in due course was drafted to the Western Front, where he took part in several engagements of importance in 1918. Unfortunately he suffered from shellshock and trench fever, and after being invalided home, completed his service in Ireland. He holds the General Service and Victory Medals, and was demobilised in September 1919.
137, Queen's Road, Walworth, S.E.17.
Z2688B

HOUSE, R. G., Rifleman, 18th London Regiment (London Irish Rifles).
He volunteered in September 1914, and after serving for some time at important stations in England, was drafted to the Western Front in 1917. In this theatre of war he took part in many important battles, including those at Arras, Vimy Ridge and Bullecourt, and died gloriously on the field of battle at Combles on September 2nd, 1918. He was entitled to the General Service and Victory Medals.
"His memory is cherished with pride."
137, Queen's Road, Battersea, S.W.8.
Z2688A

HOUSTON, W. J., Sergt., 3rd London Regiment (Royal Fusiliers).
He volunteered in 1915, and in the following year proceeded to France, where he played a conspicuous part in much heavy fighting on various fronts. He rendered valuable services and was wounded in action at Bullecourt, which wounds necessitated his discharge in June 1917 as physically unfit for further duty. He holds the General Service and Victory Medals.
99, Akerman Road, Brixton Road, S.W.9.
Z4473-4A

HOWARD, C., Private, 9th Bedfordshire Regiment.
After having served with the Colours for several years previous
to the outbreak of war in August 1914, he volunteered in the
following month, and was drafted to France in May 1915.
There he took part in numerous engagements and was twice
wounded and gassed in action. He rendered valuable services
during the Retreat and Advance of 1918, and after the Armistice returned to England, and was demobilised in June 1919.
He holds the 1914-15 Star, and the General Service and Victory
Medals. 9, Chesney Street, Battersea, S.W.11. Z2691A

**HOWARD, C. H., Private, 10th Queen's (Royal
West Surrey Regiment).**
Joining in March 1917, he was sent to France after twelve
months' service in England, and took part in the Retreat and
Advance of 1918. He saw much severe fighting in the Ypres
sector, but owing to ill-health was invalided to England just
before the Armistice, and was finally demobilised in March
1919. He holds the General Service and Victory Medals.
39, Dawlish Street, Wilcox Road, S.W.8. Z2693B

HOWARD, C. H. (Senior), Private, R.A.S.C.
He volunteered in August 1915, and was drafted to the Dardanelles shortly afterwards. He took part in the Landing at
Suvla Bay, and was engaged in unloading lighters and carrying
supplies to the trenches. After the Evacuation of the Peninsula
he was admitted into hospital at Malta and later brought to
England, when he was discharged in July 1918 as physically
unfit for further service. He holds the 1914-15 Star, and the
General Service and Victory Medals.
39, Dawlish Street, Wilcox Road, S.W.8. Z2693A

HOWARD, C. W. J., 1st Air Mechanic, R.A.F.
He volunteered in December 1915, and was drafted to the
Western Front in the following year. In this theatre of war
he took part in many important engagements on the Somme
front. He suffered from septic poisoning whilst in this sector,
and, returning to England in November 1917 was retained with
his Squadron until his demobilisation in May 1919. He holds
the General Service and Victory Medals.
30, Meyrick Road, Battersea, S.W.11. Z2690

**HOWARD, E. H., Pte., 3rd London Regt. (Royal
Fusiliers).**
He re-enlisted in August 1914, having previously served with
the Royal Marines, and did duty at various stations in England
until January 1917, when he was drafted to the Western Front.
There he took part in the Battles of Arras, Bullecourt, Ypres,
Passchendaele, and Cambrai, was wounded and gassed, and
was taken prisoner at St. Quentin in March 1918. Whilst in
captivity he was forced to work in the iron ore mines in Germany, and shortly after his release was demobilised in March
1919. He holds the General Service and Victory Medals.
189, Albert Road, Peckham, S.E.15. Z5783

**HOWARD, F. W., Private, 23rd London Regt. and
R.A.M.C.**
He joined in March 1916, and in the following June was sent
to the Western Front. There he was in action at Vimy Ridge
and the Somme, and after being severely wounded at High
Wood was invalided home to hospital for three months. He
was then retained on home defence, and in February 1918 was
transferred to the Royal Army Medical Corps in which he served
until demobilised in August 1919. He holds the General
Service and Victory Medals.
53, Albert Road, Peckham, S.E.15. 6001A

HOWARD, G. T., Rifleman, Rifle Brigade.
He volunteered in November 1914, and in May of the following
year was drafted to France. He was at once sent up to the
Front line trenches at Armentières, but whilst serving there
fell ill, and was invalided home. After three months' medical
treatment he was discharged as unfit for further military duty
in April 1916. He holds the 1914-15 Star, and the General
Service and Victory Medals.
53, Albert Road, Peckham, S.E.15. 6001C

HOWARD, L., Baker, Merchant Service.
Volunteering at the outbreak of war in August 1914, he did
duty in many vessels, including H.M.T. " Montreal," " Galicia," " Kaiserin," and " Minotaur," conveying troops to
various theatres of war. He rendered valuable services during
the course of hostilities, and his vessel was torpedoed. In 1920
he was still in the Mercantile Marine, and holds the General
Service and the Mercantile Marine War Medals.
182, Grosvenor Terrace, Camberwell, S.E.5. Z2695

HOWARD, W., Gunner, R.G.A.
He enlisted in 1906, and in the following year proceeded to
India, where he was serving at the outbreak of war in August
1914. Later he was drafted to Mesopotamia, and was taken
prisoner during the attempt to relieve Kut. He unfortunately died from dysentery whilst a captive in Turkish hands,
and was entitled to the 1914-15 Star, and the General Service
and Victory Medals.
" He passed out of the sight of men by the path of duty and
self-sacrifice."
18, Holden Street, Battersea, S.W.11. Z2694A

HOWARD, S. R., Pte., 53rd Royal Sussex Regt.
He joined in October 1918, on attaining military age, and was
undergoing a course of training at Aldershot, when he fell a
victim to influenza and died in hospital on the third day of
the following month.
18, Holden Street, Battersea, S.W.11. Z2694B

HOWARD, T. W., Pte., 1/9th Middlesex Regt. (T.F.)
He joined in December 1916, and in due course proceeded to
Mesopotamia, where he took part in many engagements,
including the fighting for the relief of Kut, the subsequent
advance on Baghdad, and the taking of Tekrit. He eventually
returned to England and was demobilised in March 1920,
holding the General Service and Victory Medals.
16, Bolton Street, Camberwell, S.E.5. Z2689

HOWARD, W., Private, R.A.S.C.
He volunteered in April 1915, and in the following year was
drafted to France, where he was engaged in transporting food
and ammunition to forward areas. He was later transferred
to Italy, and took part in engagements on the Asiago and Piave
fronts. He holds the General Service and Victory Medals, and
was demobilised in April 1919.
73, Rayleigh Road, W. Kensington, W.14. 12076B

HOWARD, W. (Jun.), Private, R.A.S.C. (M.T.)
Joining in May 1918 on attaining military age, he was retained
on special duties with his unit at important stations in England.
He was unable to obtain his transfer to a theatre of war during
the period of hostilities, but, nevertheless, rendered valuable
services until his demobilisation in January 1920.
73, Rayleigh Road, W. Kensington, W.14. 12076A

HOWARD, W. E., Private, East Surrey Regiment.
He joined in July 1917, at the age of eighteen years, and in
January of the following year proceeded to India. Whilst in
the East he was engaged on important duties at various
garrison outposts, and after contracting malaria was in hospital
at Agra. He returned home and was demobilised in November
1919, and holds the General Service and Victory Medals.
53, Albert Road, Peckham, S.E.15. 6001B

HOWARD, W. J., Private, R.M.L.I.
He joined on attaining military age in August 1918, and after
a period of training was engaged on important defence duties
at various stations. Owing to the early cessation of hostilities
he saw no active service, but did much useful work, and in
1920 was still with his unit.
11, Camellia Street, Wandsworth Road, S.W.8. Z6292

HOWARTH, H., A.B., Royal Naval Division.
He volunteered in July 1915, and shortly afterwards was drafted
to the Dardanelles, where he saw much severe fighting until the
Evacuation of the Peninsula. He was then transferred to the
Western Front, and after taking part in many important
engagements, was severely wounded in action at Passchendaele. After being for a time in Portsmouth Naval Hospital
he was invalided out in August 1918, and holds the 1914-15
Star, and the General Service and Victory Medals.
21, White Hart Street, Kennington, S.E.11. Z2696

**HOWATT, A., Pte., 1/22nd London Regt. (Queen's,
Bermondsey).**
He joined in August 1916, and five months later proceeded to
the Western Front. Whilst in this theatre of war he took part
in many important engagements, including the Battles of
Arras, Vimy Ridge, and Bullecourt, and was three times
wounded in action on the Ancre, at Ypres, and Cambrai. On
the last occasion he was invalided home and was in hospital
until October 1919, when he was finally discharged as medically
unfit for further service. He holds the General Service and
Victory Medals.
37, Atwell Road, Rye Lane, S.E.15. Z5428

HOWE, H. W., Private, 1st East Yorkshire Regt.
Shortly after volunteering in February 1915, he was drafted
to the Western Front, where he saw severe fighting in various
sectors. He fought in the Battles of the Somme, Ypres,
Armentières, and Cambrai, and many other important engagements, took part also in the Retreat and Advance of 1918, and
was wounded in action in November 1917. He was demobilised in October 1919, and holds the 1914-15 Star, and the
General Service and Victory Medals.
21, Bolton Street, Camberwell, S.E.5. Z2483C

HOWE, W., Driver, R.F.A.
He joined in February 1916, and after a period of training
was drafted to the East. He served for a time in Egypt and
then took part in the Advance into Palestine, where he fought
in the second Battle of Gaza, at Jerusalem, and in the Jordan
Valley. He was in hospital at Cairo for two months suffering
from dysentery, and on his recovery rejoined his Battery and
served in the second Offensive towards Aleppo, under General
Allenby. He was demobilised on his return home in November
1919, and holds the General Service and Victory Medals.
16, Diamond Street, Peckham, S.E.15. Z3472

HOWELL, F. W., Cpl., 3rd King's Royal Rifle Corps.

He was serving at the outbreak of war and in December of the same year was drafted to France, where he took part in the severe fighting at St. Eloi and Ypres. In November 1915 he was transferred to Salonika, where he did valuable service until January 1919, and was in action on the Vardar and Struma fronts. He was demobilised in February 1919, holding the 1914-15 Star, and the General Service and Victory Medals.

18, Nunhead Green, S.E.15.   Z6183

HOWELL, H. (D.C.M., M.M.), Private, Duke of Cornwall's Light Infantry.

He volunteered in August 1914, and was soon drafted to the Western Front where he saw much service. He fought with distinction at La Bassée, Ypres, and St. Eloi, Loos, Arras, Lens, and Cambrai, and in many subsequent engagements in the Retreat and Advance of 1918. He was awarded the Distinguished Conduct Medal and the Military Medal for conspicuous gallantry and devotion to duty in the Field, and was also the recipient of the French Croix de Guerre and Médaille Militaire for distinguished services rendered. He holds in addition the 1914 Star, and the General Service and Victory Medals, and was demobilised in January 1919.

185, Sumner Road, Peckham, S.E.15.   Z6263

HOWELL, L., Private, R.A.S.C.

Volunteering in 1914, he was drafted to Salonika on completion of a period of training in the following year. There he was engaged on important duties at various places for four years, and was finally invalided home suffering from malaria. He was demobilised in 1919, and holds the 1914-15 Star, and the General Service and Victory Medals.

4, Ramsay Road, Acton, W.4.   6283A

HOWELL, W., Private, 4th Lincolnshire Regiment.

He joined in September 1916, and on completing his training was sent to France in February of the following year. He took part in the severe fighting at Arras, Ypres, and Lens, where he was badly wounded. After being invalided home he was discharged in June 1918, owing to his injuries and holds the General Service and Victory Medals.

28, Philip Road, Peckham, S.E.15.   Z6180

HOWELLS, H., Private, R.A.S.C.

He volunteered in February 1916, and in March of the following year proceeded to the Western Front. There he took an active part in engagements in various sectors, including the Battles of Loos, St. Eloi, Albert, Vimy Ridge, Arras, Ypres, and Cambrai, served through the Retreat and Advance of 1918, and was twice gassed. He was demobilised in July, 1919, and holds the General Service and Victory Medals.

19, Heygate Street, Walworth, S.E.17.   Z2697

HOWES, C., Rifleman, 2nd Rifle Brigade.

He joined in March 1917, and in the following January was drafted to the Western Front, where he fought at St. Quentin, and Amiens, and in many other engagements. He was taken prisoner at Villers-Bretonneux, and was held in captivity until the cessation of hostilities, finally being demobilised in November 1919. He holds the General Service and Victory Medals.

15, Doddington Grove, Walworth, S.E.17.   Z2698

HOWES, F. R., L/Corporal, 8th London Regiment (Post Office Rifles).

He joined in February 1916, and shortly afterwards proceeded to the Western Front, where he saw much severe fighting. He took part in the Battles of the Somme, Cambrai, and Ypres, and many minor engagements, and was twice wounded in action—on the Somme in September 1916, and at Albert in August 1917. He was demobilised on his return home in January 1919, and holds the General Service and Victory Medals. 6, Bradmore Chambers, Hammersmith, W.6.   13251C

HOWES, H. J., Private, Labour Corps.

Volunteering in March 1915, he was engaged on special duties at Tring, Aldeburgh, Windsor, Brighton, and other places of importance. Although unable to obtain his transfer overseas, he nevertheless rendered valuable services with his unit until his demobilisation in January 1919.

6, Bradmore Chambers, Hammersmith, W.6.   13251A

HOWES, H. J. (Junior), Sapper, R.E. (R.O.D.)

He joined in June 1916, and was quickly drafted to France, where he rendered valuable services as an engine driver in various sectors and was engaged on the carrying of ammunition and guns to the forward areas. He was demobilised in October 1919, and holds the General Service and Victory Medals.

6, Bradmore Chambers, Hammersmith, W.6.   13251B

HOWES, P. A., Stoker, R.N.

Joining in 1916, he first served on board H.M.S. " Stour " with a destroyer flotilla in the North Sea, took part in important Naval operations, and was wounded. Later he was transferred to H.M.S. " Kellett," which vessel was engaged on the escorting of troops to Mesopotamia. He was demobilised in 1919, and holds the General Service and Victory Medals.

14, Thurlow Street, Walworth, S.E.17.   Z2699

HOWLAND, H., Private, R.A.M.C.

He joined in April 1917, and in the following October, after completing his training, was drafted to France. He was stationed at Calais and rendered valuable services in attendance on the sick and wounded, and in stretcher bearing duties. He returned home and was demobilised in November 1919, and holds the General Service and Victory Medals.

125, Gloucester Road, Peckham, S.E.15.   Z5994

HOWS, H. W. A., Corporal, R.A.S.C.

Volunteering in March 1915, he was retained on important duties in England until January 1917, when he was drafted to France. In this theatre of war he rendered valuable services on the transporting of supplies to the forward areas, and was demobilised in May 1919. He holds the General Service and Victory Medals.

160, Beresford Street, Camberwell Road, S.E.5.   Z2700

HUBBARD, R., Private, Queen's Own (Royal West Kent Regiment).

Mobilised in August 1914, he immediately proceeded to France and fought through the Retreat from Mons. After taking part in other important engagements, he was badly wounded in action at the Battle of Ypres, and was invalided home in November of the same year. He was discharged in August 1915, as medically unfit for further service, and holds the Mons Star, and the General Service and Victory Medals.

121, Grant Road, Battersea, S.W.11.   Z1389B

HUBERT, A. E., Corporal, R.F.A. (D. Battery, 162nd Brigade).

Volunteering in January 1915, he proceeded to the Western Front in November of the same year. Whilst in the theatre of war, he played a prominent part in many important engagements, including the Battles of the Somme (1916 and 1918), Arras, Passchendaele, and Kemmel Hill, and was wounded and gassed in action. Demobilised in March 1919, he holds the 1914-15 Star, and the General Service and Victory Medals.

67, East Surrey Grove, Peckham, S.E.15.   Z5255

HUBERT, G. A. Private, 2nd Royal Scots.

He volunteered in January 1915, and in the following year was sent to France. During his service on the Western Front he fought at Lens, Cambrai, Amiens, the Scarpe, the second Battle of Cambrai, where he was severely wounded in September 1918. He was invalided home in consequence, and discharged in February 1919, holding the General Service and Victory Medals.   11, Whorlton Road, Peckham, S.E.15.   Z5981

HUCKIN, F. C., Sergt., Tank Corps.

Already serving in the Hussars at the outbreak of war, he proceeded to France in August 1914, and took part in the Battle of, and Retreat from, Mons, the Battles of the Marne, the Aisne, and Ypres, where he was badly wounded in November 1914. He was invalided home, but on his recovery was sent to Ireland and served in the Rebellion of April 1916. In the following November he returned to the Western Front, and four months later was transferred to the Cavalry Machine Gun Corps. Later in the same year he was again transferred to the Tank Corps and fought with distinction at Cambrai, and in the Retreat and Advance of 1918. After serving in Germany with the Army of Occupation for a time, he received his discharge in October 1920, and holds the Mons Star, and the General Service and Victory Medals.

109, Honeywell Road, Wandsworth Common, S.W.11.   Z2701

HUCKSTEPP, A. R., Rifleman, 21st London Regt. (1st Surrey Rifles).

He volunteered in August 1915, and four months later proceeded to the Western Front, where he took part in heavy fighting at Loos, Vermelles and Ploegsteert, and fought at the Battles of the Somme, Arras, Vimy Ridge, Bullecourt, Messines, Ypres, Cambrai, Amiens, Bapaume, and Havrincourt. He was demobilised in February 1919, and holds the 1914-15 Star, and the General Service and Victory Medals.

12, Halpin Place, Walworth, S.E.17.   Z2702B

HUCKSTEPP, H. J., Rifleman, 21st London Regt. (1st Surrey Rifles).

He volunteered in August 1915, and four months later proceeded to France, where he took part in heavy fighting at St. Eloi and Vermelles, and was badly wounded in action on the Somme in September 1916. After six months in hospital in England, he returned to the Western Front and fought at the Battles of Vimy Ridge, Bullecourt and Messines. He died gloriously on the Field of Battle at Ypres on September 28th 1917, and was entitled to the 1914-15 Star, and the General Service and Victory Medals.

" Great deeds never die ;
They with the Sun and Moon renew their light for ever."

12, Halpin Place, Walworth, S.E.17.   Z2702A

HUCKSTEPP, C., Rifleman, Rifle Brigade.

He joined in June 1916, and in December of the same year was drafted to France, where he took part in the Battles of Arras, Vimy Ridge, Bullecourt, Messines, Ypres, and Passchendaele, and was badly wounded in action in August 1917. He was invalided home, and after long treatment in hospital at Norwich and Tipperary, was discharged in December 1918 as medically unfit for further service. He holds the General Service and Victory Medals.

12, Halpin Place, Walworth, S.E.17.   Z2703

HUDSON, F. S., Bombardier, R.G.A.

He enlisted in October 1905, and proceeded to India four years later. At the outbreak of war in August 1914 he proceeded thence to the Persian Gulf, and after much severe fighting was eventually taken prisoner in April 1916 at the fall of Kut. He was released from captivity in November 1918, and in April of the following year received his discharge, holding the India General Service Medal, the 1914 Star, and the General Service and Victory Medals.

125, Eversleigh Road, Battersea, S.W.11.   Z2704

HUDSON, H., L/Corporal, 23rd London Regiment.

He joined in April 1917, and after serving on important duties at home was drafted overseas in February of the following year. He was severely wounded during the Retreat of March 1918, and was invalided to hospital, where he remained until returning to England for his demobilisation in July 1919. He holds the General Service and Victory Medals.

28, Nutt Street, Peckham, S.E.15.   Z6264

HUDSON, H. R. (M.M.), Trooper, 2nd County of London Yeomanry (Westminster Dragoons).

Volunteering in August 1914, he proceeded to Egypt in November 1915, and was soon in action at Messa Matruh. Later he fought at Sollum and Rafa, and then took part in the Advance into Palestine, where he served at the capture of Jerusalem and Jericho, and in other important engagements. He was awarded the Military Medal for conspicuous bravery in saving a machine gun under heavy fire, and was eventually demobilised in March 1919. He also holds the 1914-15 Star, and the General Service and Victory Medals.

61, Blondel Street, Battersea, S.W.11.   Z2706

HUDSON, J. W., Private, Queen's (Royal West Surrey Regiment).

He joined in August 1916, and a month later was drafted to France, where he took part in the Battles of the Somme, Arras, Messines, Lens, Ypres, Passchendaele and Cambrai, and other, minor, engagements. He was wounded in action in 1918 and was demobilised in June of the following year. He holds the General Service and Victory Medals.

14, Namur Terrace, Alvey Street, Walworth, S.E.17.   Z2705

HUFFAM, E., Sergt., Labour Corps.

He joined in July 1916, and in the following September was drafted to Salonika, where he rendered valuable services with his unit whilst engaged on the making of roads, railways and dumps. He also saw heavy fighting on the Serres Road and on the Doiran front, and eventually advanced into Bulgaria and thence to Constantinople. Unfortunately he contracted malaria and was invalided from the Army in November 1919. He holds the General Service and Victory Medals.

16, Runham Street, Walworth, S.E.17.   Z2707

HUGALL, F. H., Private, R.A.S.C. (M.T.)

He joined in April 1917, and on being drafted to the Western Front was engaged on important transport duties in the Ypres, Somme and Arras sectors. He did consistently good work with his unit and was discharged early in 1918, holding the General Service and Victory Medals.

57, Tasman Road, Landor Road, S.W.9.   Z2708

HUGGETT, W. A., Corporal, 1st Life Guards.

Having previously been in the Army, he rejoined in August 1914, and was quickly drafted to France, where he served with distinction until the following year, when he was invalided home owing to ill-health. In 1917, however, he proceeded to Italy, where he saw much severe fighting. Demobilised in March 1919, he holds the 1914 Star, and the General Service and Victory Medals.

84, Queen's Road, Battersea Park, S.W.8.   Z2709

HUGGINS, A. R., Private, 19th London Regiment.

Joining in February 1916, he proceeded to France later in the same year, and, after taking part in the heavy fighting at the commencement of the Somme Battle, unfortunately, fell in action on July 8th, 1916. He was entitled to the General Service and Victory Medals.

"He died the noblest death a man may die,
    Fighting for God, and right, and liberty."

20, Westbury Street, Wandsworth Road, S.W.8.   Z2710

HUGHES, E., Private, 24th London Regt. (Queen's).

He volunteered in January 1915, and in the following April proceeded to France, where he took part in the Battles of Hill 60, Ypres and Festubert, before being seriously wounded in action at Loos. He was invalided to hospital at Rouen and unhappily died of his wounds in October 1915. He was entitled to the 1914-15 Star, and the General Service and Victory Medals.

"His memory is cherished with pride."

5, Pallador Place, Camberwell, S.E.5.   Z2712

HUGHES, C., Private, R.A.S.C.

He volunteered in October 1915, and proceeded to Salonika two months later. Whilst in the East he was engaged on important duties with his unit and rendered valuable services, but, at the end of 1916, was invalided home and in January 1917 was discharged as medically unfit for further duty. He holds the General Service and Victory Medals.

136, Stewart's Road, Battersea Park Road, S.W.8. Z2715

HUGHES, H. A., Gunner, R.F.A.

He enlisted in June 1904, and immediately on the outbreak of war in August 1914, proceeded to the Western Front. There, after taking part in the Battle of, and Retreat from, Mons, he fought on the Marne, the Aisne and at Ypres. In May 1915 he was transferred to Mesopotamia, served at Kut and the capture of Amara and then proceeded to Egypt, where he was in action at Sollum and Jiffaffa. After taking part in the three Battles of Gaza, he returned to France in December 1917, and served on the Somme, the Aisne and at Cambrai and was wounded in action in September 1918. He was invalided home and was for a time in hospital before being discharged as medically unfit for further service in January 1919. He holds the Mons Star, and the General Service and Victory Medals.

24, Myatt Road, Stockwell, S.W.9.   Z5786

HUGHES, H. G., Private, 23rd London Regiment.

He joined in March 1916, and was quickly drafted to France, where he fought with his Regiment at the Capture of High Wood. He was unfortunately reported missing on September 16th, 1916 and is now presumed to have been killed in action on that date. He was entitled to the General Service and Victory Medals.

"His life for his Country, his Soul to God."

11, Lavender Road, Battersea, S.W.11.   Z2716

HUGHES, J., Private, 23rd Middlesex Regiment.

He volunteered in April 1915, and proceeded to France in the following year. During his service on the Western Front he took part in many important engagements, including the Battles of the Somme, Messines and Ypres, and was wounded in action. In 1917 he was drafted to Italy and fought on the Piave before returning to France early in 1918. He was gassed during the Retreat of that year and was invalided home, but on his recovery, again proceeded to France and was at Mons on Armistice Day. Demobilised in March 1919, he holds the General Service and Victory Medals.

141, Battersea Bridge Road West, Battersea, S.W.11. Z2717

HUGHES, J., Private, East Surrey Regiment.

He volunteered in 1915, and in the following year was drafted to the Western Front, where he took part in the Battles of the Somme and Ypres. Being badly wounded in the latter engagement, he was invalided home, and on his recovery was retained on important duties in England until his demobilisation in 1919. He holds the General Service and Victory Medals.

20, Crichton Street, Wandsworth Road, S.W.8.   Z2714

HUGHES, M., Sapper, R.E.

He joined in 1917, and later in the same year proceeded to the Western Front, where he served through the Retreat and Advance of 1918. After the Armistice he went to Germany with the Army of Occupation and was stationed at Cologne until his demobilisation in 1919. He holds the General Service and Victory Medals.

2, Raywood Street, Battersea Park Road, S.W.8.   Z2713

HUGMAN, G. T., Pte., Queen's (Royal West Surrey Regiment).

Volunteering in November 1915, he was speedily drafted to France, where he took part in important engagements at Albert and Hill 60 and also fought in the Battles of the Somme, Arras, Ypres, Amiens, Bapaume and St. Quentin and throughout the Retreat and Advance of 1918. He was badly wounded in action during the Advance, and after being invalided home, was discharged in December 1918 as medically unfit for further service. He holds the 1914-15 Star, and the General Service and Victory Medals.

105, Kinglake Street, Walworth, S.E.17.   Z2718

HULL, W. T., Pte., Monmouthshire Regt. and 1st Royal Welch Fusiliers.

Volunteering in May 1915, he was drafted to the Western Front twelve months later. He was severely wounded on the 1st October 1917, and died of his wounds on the following day at the Casualty Clearing Station. He was entitled to the General Service and Victory Medals, and is buried in Belgium.

"His life for his Country, his Soul to God."

4, Newnham Terrace, Hercules Road, S.E.1.   Z24497

HULLAND, G. R., Gunner, R.A.

Mobilised in August 1914, he immediately proceeded to France and fought at Mons. He also took part in the Battles of the Marne, the Aisne, Ypres, Hooge and Loos, and was badly gassed in action in 1917. As a result he was invalided from the Service later in the same year, and holds the Mons Star, and the General Service and Victory Medals.

2, Andulus Road, Landor Road, S.W.9.   Z2719

HULLS, H. G., Pte., Devonshire Regt. and Labour Corps.

He joined in August 1916, and in the following November was drafted to the Western Front, where he rendered valuable services with a Labour Battalion, whilst engaged on the making of roads and bridges and other important duties. He was demobilised on his return home in August 1919, and holds the General Service and Victory Medals.

41, Warham Street, Camberwell, S.E.5.   Z2720

HULME, W., Private, R.A.S.C.

Volunteering in April 1915 he proceeded overseas in the following July. He served in many sectors of the Western Front, and was wounded twice, returning on recovery to his unit. Later in January 1919 he was discharged through heart trouble, and holds the 1914-15 Star, and the General Service and Victory Medals.

102, Duke Road, Chiswick, W.4.   5662B

HUME, J. A., Bandsman, Coldstream Guards.

He enlisted in December 1889 in the Seaforth Highlanders, and at the outbreak of war rejoined in the Coldstream Guards, and with them served in France in many battles until the conclusion of hostilities. Afterwards he was sent to Germany with the Army of Occupation. Having previously served in Egypt and India, he holds the Sudan and the Khedive's Sudan Medals with the Atbara and Khartoum clasps, the 1914 Star, and the General Service and Victory Medals, and in 1920 was still serving.

124, Eversleigh Road, Battersea, S.W.11.   Z2721

HUMPHREY, J., 1st Class Stoker, R.N.

Mobilised at the outbreak of war he was posted to H.M.S. "Halcyon," on board which vessel he served on important duties in the North Sea. His ship also took part in the Battle of Jutland and in several minor engagements off the Belgian Coast. In 1919 he was demobilised, and holds the 1914-15 Star, and the General Service and Victory Medals.

69, Henshaw Street, Walworth, S.E.17.   Z2724

HUMPHREY, S., Rifleman, 8th London Regiment (P.O. Rifles).

Volunteering in March 1915, he was drafted overseas in the same year. Whilst in France he took part in much of the fighting at Ypres, the Somme, Arras and in many other engagements, including the Advance of 1918. He returned home and was demobilised in April 1919, and holds the 1914-15 Star, and the General Service and Victory Medals.

69, Arthur Road, Brixton Road, S.W.9.   Z3473

HUMPHREYS, A. (M.M.), Pte., 2nd South Staffordshire Regiment.

Mobilised in August 1914, he was almost immediately drafted to the Western Front and fought in the Battles of the Marne and Aisne. He also served with the Trench Mortar Batteries in many engagements, including those on the Somme, and was awarded the Military Medal for conspicuous bravery and coolness in remaining at his post when all his company, with the exception of two, had been either wounded or killed. He died gloriously on the Field of Battle at Couechelettes in 1917, and was entitled to the 1914 Star, and the General Service and Victory Medals.

"Great deeds cannot die."

16, Treherne Road, Stockwell, S.W.9.   Z3471

HUMPHREYS, S. J., C.S.M., R.A.S.C. (M.T.)

He volunteered in September 1914, and in the same month proceeded to France, where he served on important duties in the motor transport, conveying food supplies and ammunition up to the lines. He was present at La Bassée, Ypres, the Somme and Arras and in subsequent engagements up to the end of 1917. He was then invalided to England owing to ill-health, and after his recovery was retained on home defence duties. He holds the 1914 Star, and the General Service and Victory Medals, and was demobilised in June 1919.

13, Wroxton Road, Peckham, S.E.15.   Z6252

HUMPHREYS, H., Corporal, 7th Norfolk Regiment.

Joining in April 1916, he was drafted on the completion of his training to France. There he fought in many notable battles, including those on the Somme, and was severely wounded, subsequently being discharged through the effects of his injuries in January 1919. He holds the General Service and Victory Medals.

1, Beryl Road, Hammersmith, W.6.   12784C

HUMPHREYS, W. E., Rifleman, 21st London Regt. (Surrey Rifles).

He joined in May 1916, and in the following December proceeded to France, where he took part in much of the fighting in the Somme sector. He was also in action in many other engagements, including those of Ypres and Cambrai. In January 1919 he returned home and was demobilised, holding the General Service and Victory Medals.

36, Warrior Road, Camberwell, S.E.4.   Z1007B

HUMPHRIES, F. W., Air Mechanic, R.A.F. (late R.F.C.)

He joined in July 1918, and after completing his training served at various stations with his Squadron, on important duties which demanded a high degree of technical skill, preparing planes for sea-service and escort work. He rendered valuable service, but was not successful in obtaining his transfer overseas before the cessation of hostilities. He was demobilised in January 1919.

78, Surrey Lane, Battersea, S.W.11.   Z2725

HUMPHRIES, J. A., Rifleman, Rifle Brigade.

Joining in August 1916 he was drafted on the completion of his training to India. He served in this theatre of war on important duties until the conclusion of hostilities, and in July 1919 returned home and was demobilised. He holds the General Service and Victory Medals.

91, Nasmyth Street, Hammersmith, W.6.   11829B

HUMPHRIES, W. E., L/Corporal, Queen's (Royal West Surrey Regiment).

He volunteered in August 1914, and was drafted to France in the following year. During his service on the Western Front he fought at Hill 60, Ypres, Festubert, Loos, and Arras, where he was severely wounded on April 8th, 1917. He was invalided home to hospital and discharged as physically unfit for further duty in the following December. He holds the 1914-15 Star, and the General Service and Victory Medals.

20, Brabourn Grove, Peckham, S.E.15.   Z6248

HUMPHRIES, W. E., Sergt., King's Own Scottish Borderers.

He enlisted in 1909, and was sent from Egypt to France in 1915. Whilst in this theatre of war he was in action in many engagements, including the Retreat of 1918, during which he was blown up by the explosion of a shell, and severely injured, and sent into hospital at the Base. He was afterwards invalided home, and in November 1918 was discharged as medically unfit, holding the 1914-15 Star, and the General Service and Victory Medals.

11, Belham Street, Camberwell, S.E.5.   Z2722

HUMPHRIES, W. G., Sergt., King's Royal Rifle Corps.

He had previously served in the Royal Navy for several years, but was invalided out in consequence of ill-health. He volunteered in May 1915, and although, owing to physical unfitness, he was unable to secure his transfer overseas did valuable work as a drill Instructor and recruiting sergeant. In the course of his service he crossed to France on several occasions, in charge of reinforcements. He was discharged on medical grounds in October 1917, and holds the General Service and Victory Medals.

29, Mosedale Street, Camberwell, S.E.5.   Z2723

HUMPHRIS, A. H., Private, Royal Defence Corps.

Being ineligible for service abroad owing to physical disability, he joined the Royal Defence Corps in April 1917. In the course of his service he was engaged on various important duties, which included guarding munition factories and German prisoners, and did valuable work until he was discharged in April 1919.

63, Arthur Road, Brixton Road, S.W.9.   Z3467

HUNT, C. H., Sergt., Queen's (Royal West Surrey Regiment).

He volunteered at the commencement of hostilities, and early in 1915 was drafted to the Western Front. Whilst in this theatre of war he fought in many important battles, including those of Ypres, the Somme, Albert and Vimy Ridge. In 1918, he returned to England in consequence of ill-health, and after his recovery was retained for important home duties. He was demobilised in March 1920, and holds the 1914-15 Star, and the General Service and Victory Medals.

6, Thorncroft Street, Wandsworth Road, S.W.8.   Z2726A

HUNT, F. C., Private, 1st Middlesex Regiment.
He volunteered in February 1915, and in the following August crossed to France. Whilst in this theatre of war he fought in several important engagements, notably those on the Somme and at Ypres and Arras and did valuable work with his unit. He holds the 1914-15 Star, and the General Service and Victory Medals, and in 1920 was still serving.
6, Thorncroft Street, Wandsworth Road, S.W.8.　Z2726B

HUNT, E., Private, 11th Yorkshire Regiment.
A serving soldier, he was engaged on special duties until early in 1915, when he was drafted overseas. Whilst on the Western Front he fought on the Somme and at Ypres, Arras, Albert and St. Quentin, and was severely wounded. After being for some time in hospital at Etaples, he was invalided home, but on recovery returned to France and was subsequently wounded at the second Battle of the Somme. He was again sent to England, and after protracted treatment, was stationed at Hartlepool until he was demobilised in March 1919. He holds the 1914-15 Star, and the General Service and Victory Medals.
82, Sussex Road, Coldharbour Lane, S.W.9.　Z2729

HUNT, F. D., A.B., Royal Navy.
Mobilised at the outbreak of hostilities, he was posted to H.M.S. "Glory" and was later transferred to H.M.S. "Vernon." In the course of his service he sailed with his ship to America, and also covered the troops during the Landing at, and the Evacuation of, the Gallipoli Peninsula. Owing to his age, and physical unfitness he was discharged in April 1917, and holds the 1914-15 Star, and the General Service and Victory Medals.
57, Nursery Row, Walworth, S.E.17.　Z2730

HUNT, G., 1st Aircraftsman, R.A.F.
He vounteered in 1915, and after his training was for some time engaged on duties of an important nature at home. In October 1917, however, he crossed to Dunkirk, where he did valuable work until the following December. He then returned to England, and was stationed at Godnamshaw Park, Ashford. Whilst engaged on guard duty at a gas stores a serious explosion occurred, in which the airship he was guarding was blown to pieces, and he was severely injured. He was demobilised in November 1918, and holds the General Service and Victory Medals.
11, Barclay Road, Walham Green, S.W.6.　X19713

HUNT, G., Gunner, R.F.A.
He joined in April 1916, and after his training served in France for nearly three years, during which time he fought in many important battles. He was demobilised in February 1919, and holds the General Service and Victory Medals.
79, Yeldham Road, Hammersmith, W.6.　13242A

HUNT, H., Driver, R.F.A.
He volunteered in August 1914, and in the same month crossed to France, where he served throughout the period of hostilities. During this time he fought in the Retreat from Mons and many of the engagements which followed, including those on the Marne and Aisne and at Ypres, Loos, Festubert, Neuve Chapelle and the Somme, and on one occasion was gassed. After the cessation of hostilities he was drafted to India, where in 1920 he was still serving. He holds the Mons Star, and the General Service and Victory Medals.
78, Grant Road, Battersea, S.W.11.　Z2731A

HUNT, J. W., Private, Northumberland Fusiliers.
He volunteered in October 1914, and early in the following year was sent to the Western Front, where he fought in the Battles of Ypres, the Somme and Cambrai. Later he served for upwards of two years in Malta, engaged on duties of an important nature, and in 1918 returned to France and took part in the concluding operations of the war. Whilst overseas he was wounded on two occasions. He holds the 1914-15 Star, and the General Service and Victory Medals, and was demobilised in January 1919.
26, Stockdale Road, Wandsworth Road, S.W.8.　Z2727

HUNT, R. J., Private, 51st Royal Sussex Regiment.
He joined on attaining military age in March 1917, and at the conclusion of his training was engaged on duties of an important nature. He was unable to secure his transfer to a theatre of war before the termination of hostilities, but afterwards was sent with the Army of Occupation to Germany. He was demobilised in November 1919 on his return to England.
152, Lavender Road, Battersea, S.W.11.　Z2728

HUNTER, C. F., L/Corporal, 23rd Bedfordshire Regt.
He volunteered in January 1915, and after his training served at various stations on important duties with his unit. He rendered valuable service, but owing to being medically unfit for duty abroad was unable to secure his transfer overseas before the cessation of hostilities. He was demobilised in July 1919.
38, Bullen Street, Battersea, S.W.11.　Z2733

HUNTER, J., Driver, R.F.A.
He attested in May 1916, but was not called up until January 1917, and in the following September was drafted to France and was in action at Ypres in October. Later in the year he was sent to Italy and served in the engagements on the Piave, and during this period suffered from malaria. In 1918 he proceeded to Egypt, where he remained until his return home for demobilisation in March 1920. He holds the General Service and Victory Medals.
163, Sabine Road, Battersea, S.W.11.　Z2732

HUNTINGFORD, C. P. W., Driver, R.F.A.
Volunteering in August 1914, he was sent overseas in 1916, and served in various engagements on the Somme. In 1917 he was drafted to Italy and did good work as a driver on the Piave and in subsequent operations until the cessation of hostilities. He was demobilised in July 1919, and holds the General Service and Victory Medals.
13, Willington Road, Stockwell, S.W.9.　Z2734

HUNTLEY, P. R., Corporal, 11th Queen's (Royal West Surrey Regiment).
He volunteered in 1915, and in the same year was drafted to France. During his service in this theatre of war he fought in various engagements in the Somme, Ypres and Arras sectors. Later he was sent to Italy and was in action on the Piave, and was wounded. After his recovery he returned to France and took part in many of the final operations, and after the Armistice proceeded to Germany, whence he was demobilised at the end of 1918. He holds the 1914-15 Star, and the General Service and Victory Medals.
32, Bagshot Street, Walworth, S.W.17.　Z2431A

HUNTLEY, R., Corporal, R.A.S.C. (M.T.)
He volunteered in August 1914, and in the same year was drafted to France. Whilst overseas he was engaged on important duties in connection with the transport, notably on the Somme, at Ypres and in the Retreat of 1918. He was demobilised in the Summer of 1919, and holds the 1914 Star, and the General Service and Victory Medals.
76, South Street, Walworth, S.E.17.　Z2735

HUNTLEY, R., Corporal, R.A.S.C. (H.T.)
He was mobilised at the outbreak of war, and served overseas throughout the war from August 1914 to March 1919. He was present at the Retreat from Mons, and the Battles of the Marne, the Aisne, the Somme, Ypres and Cambrai, and in various subsequent engagements in the Retreat and Advance of 1918. and after the cessation of hostilities returned to England, and was demobilised in March 1919, holding the Mons Star, and the General Service and Victory Medals.
69, Surrey Square, Walworth, S.E.17.　Z2736

HUNTLEY, W., Private, Queen's (Royal West Surrey Regiment), Anti-Aircraft Section.
He volunteered in 1915, having previously served in the Special Constabulary for about six months. He was over age for service overseas, but did good work with the Anti-aircraft Section at various defence stations. He was discharged in 1918.
32, Bagshot Street, Walworth, S.E.17.　Z2431B

HURCOMBE, W. H., Private, 20th Hussars.
He was mobilised at the outbreak of war, and was almost immediately drafted to France, where he took part in the Retreat from Mons. He served also in the Battles of the Marne, the Aisne, Ypres, Hill 60, Armentières, Givenchy, Loos, Lens, Bapaume and Béthune and in various subsequent operations in the Retreat and Advance of 1918. In January of the following year he was demobilised, and holds the Mons Star, and the General Service and Victory Medals.
7, Hillery Road, Walworth, S.E.17.　Z2737

HURLEY, A. W., Private, R.D.C.
He volunteered in November 1914, and served on important duties at Kensington and in Wales, and was later drafted to Ireland, where he was engaged with his unit at various stations. He was demobilised in April 1919.
21, Camellia Street, Wandsworth Road, S.W.8.　21545B

HURLEY, J., Corporal, R.A.S.C.
He volunteered in April 1915, and in the following July was drafted to the Dardanelles, where he served in the Landing at Gallipoli, and in the first, second and third Battles of Krithia, the capture of Chunuk Bair and the Evacuation of the Peninsula in December of the same year. He was sent to Salonika in April 1916, and was present at the general Offensive by the Allies on the Doiran front, the capture of Monastir and the later advance on the Doiran and the operations on the Vardar. He was twice wounded during this period, in April and September of 1917. He returned home and was demobilised in January 1919, and holds the 1914-15 Star, and the General Service and Victory Medals.
6, William's Grove, Walworth, S.E.17.　Z2738

HURST, A., Pte., 24th London Regt. (The Queen's) attached R.A.O.C.

Volunteering in August 1914, he proceeded overseas in 1916, and served on important duties in various sectors of the Western Front. Later he was drafted to Salonika, and subsequently to Egypt, thence to Palestine, where he was present at the engagements at Gaza and Jericho, and at the fall of Jerusalem. He returned home and was demobilised in February 1919, and holds the General Service and Victory Medals.

47, Northway Road, Camberwell, S.E.5.   Z6257

HURST, A. A., Rifleman, 21st London Regiment (1st Surrey Rifles).

He joined in June 1916, and in the following October was sent to the Western Front. During his service in France he was frequently in action, notably on the Somme, at Arras and Ypres. In March 1917 he was invalided home and remained under treatment for about nine months. He rejoined his unit in France early in 1918, and served until the conclusion of hostilities. He was demobilised in September 1919, and holds the General Service and Victory Medals.

18, Wroxton Road, Peckham, S.E.15.   Z6398

HURST, E., Pioneer, R.E. (Gas Corps).

He volunteered in the King's Royal Rifles in December 1915, and in October of the following year after being transferred to the Rifle Brigade, embarked for France. Whilst overseas he was engaged on important duties in connection with the Gas Corps, which he joined in November 1916, notably at Arras and Messines. In June 1917 he was invalided home through ill-health, but rejoined his unit in the succeeding May and was in action at Oppy Wood. He also served in Alsace Lorraine, attached to the American Army, and subsequently in various other parts of the front until demobilisation in October 1919. He holds the General Service and Victory Medals.

7, Reddius Road, Peckham, S.E.15.   Z6384

HURST, H. J., Saddler-Sergt., R.F.A.

A serving soldier, he was soon drafted to France after the outbreak of hostilities, and was in action on the Marne and the Aisne and in the first Battle of Ypres and many subsequent engagements. Whilst serving in the Arras sector he contracted influenza and pneumonia, to which he succumbed on November 3rd, 1918. He was entitled to the 1914 Star, and the General Service and Victory Medals.

"His memory is cherished with pride."

26, Ingleton Street, Brixton Road, S.W.9.   Z2739

HUSK, W. Driver, R.F.A.

He volunteered in January 1915, and in the following August was drafted to France. Whilst in this theatre of war he served in many engagements, including those at Loos, Vermelles, Ploegsteert Wood, Vimy Ridge, the Somme, Messines, Ypres and Menin Road, and was wounded during this period. After the Armistice he advanced into Germany with the Army of Occupation, and was stationed on the Rhine until May 1919, when he returned home and was demobilised. He holds the 1914-15 Star, and the General Service and Victory Medals.

173, Sumner Road, Peckham, S.E.15.   Z6265

HUSSEY, A., Driver, R.A.S.C. (M.T.)

He volunteered in August 1914, and in the following October was drafted to France. There he served on important duties in connection with the Motor Transport, notably at La Bassée, Ypres, Neuve Chapelle, St. Eloi, and Hill 60. He was invalided home to hospital owing to ill-health, and after about three months' treatment was discharged as medically unfit for further military duty in July 1915. He holds the 1914 Star, and the General Service and Victory Medals.

8, Exon Street, Walworth, S.E.17.   Z2740B

HUSSEY, Q. E. (Miss), Special War Worker.

During the war this lady volunteered her services for work of National importance, and was engaged on responsible clerical duties in the Ministry of Munitions, Charing Cross Buildings, in the Machine Tool Department. She rendered valuable services, which were much appreciated, for nearly two years, from March 1917 to January 1919.

8, Exon Street, Walworth, S.E.17.   Z2740A

HUTCHINGS, E., Sapper, R.E.

He joined in February 1918, and in the same year was drafted to Salonika. During his service in this theatre of war he was principally engaged on duties connected with the transport, and was in the front lines during the Vardar operations of 1918. He was demobilised in March of the following year, and holds the General Service and Victory Medals.

12, Tidemore Street, Battersea Park Road, S.W.8.   Z1636B

HUTCHINS, T. W., Private, 10th Middlesex Regt.

He volunteered in November 1915, and on the completion of his training was drafted to India, where he was engaged on important garrison duties at Lucknow until the time of his death on June 15th, 1918.

"The path of duty was the way to glory."

14, Bollo Bridge Road, Acton, W.3.   6384B

HUTCHINS, W. (D.C.M.), Pte., 2nd Royal Irish Regt.

He was mobilised from the Reserve at the outbreak of war, and shortly afterwards was sent to France, where he took part in numerous engagements until hostilities ceased, including those at Mons, the Somme, Ypres and Cambrai. He was awarded the Distinguished Conduct Medal for great bravery in the Field in rescuing his Colonel near Mons in 1914, and also holds the Mons Star, and the General Service and Victory Medals. He was demobilised in May 1919.

3, Northlands Street, Camberwell, S.E.5.   Z6190

HUTCHISON, J. G., Private, Queen's Own (Royal West Kent Regiment).

He volunteered in September 1914, and in the following year was drafted overseas. During his service in France he fought at Ypres and Loos, and in various subsequent engagements. He fell gloriously on the Field of Battle on the Somme in August 1916, and was entitled to the 1914-15 Star, and the General Service and Victory Medals.

"A valiant soldier, with undaunted heart he breasted Life's last hill."

7, Radnor Terrace, South Lambeth Road, S.W.8.   Z2741

HUTT, A. W., Rifleman, King's Royal Rifle Corps.

He joined in April 1917, and in July of the same year was drafted to France. After only two months' active service he was reported missing during the third Battle of Ypres on September 20th, 1917, and was afterwards presumed to have been killed in action on that date. He was entitled to the General Service and Victory Medals.

"He died the noblest death a man may die, Fighting for God, and right, and liberty."

101, Waterloo Street, Camberwell, S.E.5.   Z2742

HUTTON, H. E., Private, R.A.S.C. (M.T.)

He joined in April 1917, but was rejected on medical grounds for overseas service. On the completion of his training he was engaged at the Headquarters Repair Depôt, London, on important duties in connection with the repairing of motor cars. He did excellent work for two years and was demobilised in April 1919.

126, Beresford Street, Camberwell Road, S.E.5.   Z2744

HUTTON, V., Corporal, Bedfordshire Regiment.

He volunteered in April 1915, and in the same year proceeded to India, where he served on important duties at various outposts. He also took part in the engagements on the North West Frontier during the Afghan risings. He returned home and was demobilised in December 1919, and holds the India General Service Medal (with clasp Afghanistan, N.W. Frontier, 1919), the General Service and Victory Medals.

16, Councillor Street, Camberwell, S.E.5.   Z2743

HUXLEY, G., Private, R.A.V.C.

He joined in February 1916, and after his training was engaged at various stations on important duties connected with the care of horses. After over four years' valuable service he was demobilied in May 1919, having been unable to secure a transfer overseas during the period of the war.

45, Gonsalva Road, Wandsworth Road, S.W.8.   Z2745

HUZZEY, H., Staff-Sergt. Shoesmith, R.A.S.C.

He was mobilised at the outbreak of war and was immediately drafted to France, where he served in the Retreat from Mons. He was also present at Ypres, and on the Somme, and in many subsequent engagements and was gassed in action. After his recovery he continued his service until the Armistice was signed, and then proceeded to Germany with the first contingent under General Plumer, remaining there until March 1920, when he returned home and was demobilised. He holds the Mons Star, and the General Service and Victory Medals.

220, Cator Street, Peckham, S.E.15.   Z5104

HYDE, A. G., Private, 10th Queen's (Royal West Surrey Regiment).

He volunteered in August 1915, and after his training was drafted to France in February 1917. Whilst overseas he fought at Ypres and Cambrai, and later was transferred to the Labour Corps, and was engaged on special duties in connection with the interment of the dead. He was demobilised in April 1919, and holds the General Service and Victory Medals.

10, Kennard Street, Battersea, S.W.11.   Z2747

HYDE, E., Private, South Staffordshire Regiment.

He volunteered in December 1915, and until 1917, when he was sent to France, was engaged on important duties at various stations. Whilst overseas he took part in several battles, and was so severely wounded whilst in action at Lens as to necessitate his return to England. After his recovery, however, he was re-drafted to the Western Front, and in 1918 was wounded a second time at Messines. He remained overseas until after the termination of hostilities, and in April 1919 was demobilised, holding the General Service and Victory Medals.

22, Newman Street, Battersea, S.W.11.   Z2746

HYNER, E., Corporal, R.F.A.
Volunteering at the commencement of hostilities, he was quickly drafted to the Western Front, and was severely wounded during the Retreat from Mons. After being in hospital in Paris for three weeks, he rejoined his unit, and subsequently fought in the Battles of Neuve Chapelle, Hill 60, St. Eloi, Ypres, Ploegsteert Wood, Arras and Passchendaele. He was later invalided home in consequence of ill-health, but after two months' treatment in hospital returned to France and served in the concluding stages of the war. He was demobilised in March 1919, and holds the Mons Star, and the General Service and Victory Medals.
39, St. Lawrence Road, Brixton Road, S.W.9. Z4475

I

IBERTSON, A., Gunner, R.G.A.
He joined in April 1916, and proceeding to the Western Front later in the same year, fought in many important engagements, including those at the Somme, Ypres and Lens. He was also in action throughout the German Offensive and Allied Advance of 1918. Returning to England he was demobilised in March 1919, and holds the General Service and Victory Medals.
10, Calmington Road, Camberwell, S.E.5. Z5429

ILES, E., Private, R.A.S.C.
He joined in September 1916, and was sent to Egypt in the following year. During his service in this theatre of war he was employed as a storekeeper in the advanced areas in the Gaza and Jerusalem sectors, and in the Jordan Valley, and was present at many engagements. He returned to England and was demobilised in September 1919, and holds the General Service and Victory Medals.
103, Sandmere Road, Clapham, S.W.4. Z2756

INGARFIELD, C., Gunner, R.F.A.
Volunteering at the outbreak of war he was drafted to France almost immediately and fought in the Retreat from Mons, and at the Battles of the Marne, the Aisne, Neuve Chapelle, Festubert and Loos. Suffering from shell-shock, he was invalided to England, and after receiving hospital treatment, was subsequently discharged unfit for further service in June 1916. He holds the Mons Star, and the General Service and Victory Medals.
66, Acorn Street, Camberwell, S.E.5. Z4440A

INGHAM, G., Sergt.-Drummer, Essex Regiment.
Having previously served in the South African War he re-enlisted in August 1914, and was stationed at various depôts engaged on important duties training recruits of the New Armies. He was unsuccessful in obtaining his transfer to a theatre of war, but rendered valuable services until demobilised in 1919. He holds the Queen's South African Medals (with six bars).
64, Faraday Street, Walworth, S.E.17. Z2748

INGOLD, A. G., Corporal, 3rd Middlesex Regiment.
He was serving at Malta at the outbreak of hostilities, and was immediately drafted to France. In this theatre of war he fought at the Battles of Ypres, Neuve Chapelle, St. Eloi, and Hill 60, and was wounded and gassed. On recovery, he rejoined his Regiment in the Field, and served until the cessation of hostilities. He was demobilised in February 1919, and holds the 1914 Star, and the General Service and Victory Medals.
1, Reddins Road, Peckham, S.E.15. Z6400

INGRAM, A., Trumpeter, R.F.A.
Volunteering in August 1914, he embarked for France in the same month, and was in action in the Retreat from Mons, and in many other battles. In February 1915, he returned to England, and was later sent to Gallipoli and fought in various engagements and was wounded. On recovery he was drafted to Mesopotamia, where he saw much service, until proceeding to Serbia in 1917. There he rendered valuable services as a despatch rider, and was twice wounded, and awarded the Serbian Gold Medal for devotion to duty in the Field. Returning home he was demobilised in 1919, and also holds the Mons Star, and the General Service and Victory Medals.
37, Chryssell Road, Brixton Road, S.W.9. Z5257

INGRAM, A. E., Private, 3rd Worcestershire Regt.
He volunteered and proceeded to France at the outbreak of war, and fought in the Retreat from Mons, and at the Battles of Le Cateau, the Aisne and the Marne. He gave his life for the freedom of England on November 7th, 1914, in the first Battle of Ypres, and was entitled to the Mons Star, and the General Service and Victory Medals.
"Whilst we remember the Sacrifice is not in vain."
56, Dalyell Road, Landor Road, S.W.9. 1127A

INGRAM, J. J. (D.C.M.), L/Corporal, 3rd Coldstream Guards.
Volunteering in August 1914, he proceeded to France in the same month, and fought in the Retreat from Mons, and was wounded near Festubert in November 1914. Returning to his unit on recovery, he took part in further fighting and in January 1915, was awarded the Distinguished Conduct Medal for conspicuous bravery in the Field, in bringing in wounded under heavy fire. He was unfortunately killed in action on July 12th, 1915, and was entitled to the Mons Star and the General Service and Victory Medals.
"He died the noblest death a man may die,
Fighting for God, and right, and liberty."
134, Gloucester Road, Peckham, S.E.15. Z6002

INGRAM, R., Leading Signalman, Royal Navy.
He joined in August 1914, and served in the North Sea with his ship which was in action in the Battle of Jutland, and did good work engaged on patrol and other important duties. During the war he served aboard H.M.S. "Broke," H.M.S. "Neptune" and H.M.S. "Castor." He was demobilised in February 1919, and holds the 1914-15 Star, and the General Service and Victory Medals.
231, Mayall Road, Herne Hill, S.E.24. Z2750

INGRAM, W. J., Cpl., King's Royal Rifle Corps.
Volunteering in May 1915, he was sent to the Western Front in the following February, and fought in the Battles of Loos, Ploegsteert, Vimy Ridge, Bullecourt, Messines and Lens, and was twice wounded. He was badly gassed at the second Battle of the Marne in July 1918, and returned to England. Having received medical treatment he was ultimately invalided out of the Service in December 1918, and holds the General Service and Victory Medals.
56, Dalyell Road, Landor Road, S.W.9. Z1127B

INNS, F. J., Leading Signalman, R.N.
He joined in August 1914, and during his service afloat did good work. He was present at the bombardment of the Dardanelles, and later his ship was engaged on patrol and other important duties. During the war he served aboard H.M.S. "Paladin" and H.M.S. "Renown." He was taken ill, and died on May 22nd, 1918, and was entitled to the 1914-15 Star, and the General Service and Victory Medals.
"His Life for his Country."
13, Elcho Street, Battersea, S.W.11. Z2751

INWOOD, A. E., Leading Telegraphist, R.N.
He joined in March 1915, and was posted to H.M.S. "Glenaven," which ship was engaged on mine-sweeping duties off the French and Belgian Coasts, in the North Sea, and in the English Channel. His vessel rendered valuable services on many occasions, rescuing the crews of torpedoed ships. He was demobilised in May 1919, and holds the 1914-15 Star, and the General Service and Victory Medals.
15, Victory Square, Camberwell, S.E.5. Z5569B

ION, J., Private, Labour Corps.
He volunteered in May 1915, and was drafted to France in January 1916. During his service on the Western Front he was employed with his unit on special duties at Albert, Vermelles, Vimy Ridge, and the Somme, and was constantly under shell fire. He gave his life for King and Country in July 1916, during the first British Offensive on the Somme, and was entitled to the General Service and Victory Medals.
"His memory is cherished with pride."
1, Cross Street, Clapham, S.W.4. Z2752A

IRELAND, F. J., Corporal, R.A.S.C. (M.T.)
He joined in 1917, and was drafted to German East Africa, later in the same year. During his service overseas he fought in many important engagements, and was mentioned in Despatches on September 30th, 1918, for devotion to duty in the Field. He returned to England, and was demobilised in March 1919, and holds the General Service and Victory Medals.
41, Baret Street, Brixton Road, S.W.9. Z5256

IRON, I. H., Corporal, R.F.A.
He volunteered at the outbreak of hostilities, and was immediately sent to France. In this theatre of war he was in action at the Retreat from Mons, and the Battles of La Bassée, Neuve Chapelle, St. Eloi, Hill 60, Ypres, Loos, Vimy Ridge, the Somme, Beaumont-Hamel, Arras, Messines, Lens, Passchendaele, Cambrai and the Retreat and Allied Advance of 1918. He was demobilised in January 1919, and holds the Mons Star, and the General Service and Victory Medals.
26, Hargwyne Street, Stockwell Road, S.W.9. Z2753

IRONSIDE, T. H., A.B., Royal Navy.
He was serving in the Navy at the outbreak of hostilities, and throughout the war served in the North Sea. His ship was in action at the Battle of Jutland, and in various minor engagements, and also did good work engaged on patrol and escort duties. He served aboard H.M.S. "Verdun" and H.M.S "Espeigle," and was still serving in 1920. He holds the 1914-15 Star, and the General Service and Victory Medals.
4, Blendon Row, Walworth, S.E.17. Z2754

IRVING, D., Private, 1/20th London Regiment and Queen's Own (Royal West Kent Regiment).
He volunteered in December 1915, and was drafted overseas in the following year. Serving on the Western Front he was in action in the Battles of Vermelles, Arras, Ypres and Passchendaele, and was wounded and taken prisoner at Ypres in 1917. Released on the signing of the Armistice he was sent to hospital in Belgium and later in Paris, and was then invalided to England, and after receiving medical treatment was demobilised in Januray 1919, and holds the General Service and Victory Medals.
10, Claude Road, Peckham Rye, S.E.15. Z6003

ISAACKS, H. W., L/Corporal, R.E.
He volunteered in February 1915, and was sent to the Western Front later in the same year, and saw much service in various parts of the line. In 1916 he was transferred to Salonika, and was in action on the Vardar front, and later proceeded to Egypt. He took part in many engagements during the Advance through Palestine and Syria, and returning to England was demobilised in 1919. He subsequently died from an illness contracted whilst on service, and was entitled to the 1914-15 Star, and the General Service and Victory Medals.
65, Queen's Road, Battersea Park, S.W.8. Z2755

ISITT, G., Corporal, 2nd Coldstream Guards.
Volunteering in December 1914, he completed his training, and served at the Guards' Depôt at Windsor, engaged on guard and other important duties. He was unsuccessful in obtaining his transfer overseas prior to the cessation of hostilities, but was sent to Russia in April 1919, and took part in various engagements. He returned to England in the following October, and was still serving in 1920. He holds the General Service Medal (with clasp, Russia, 1919).
36, Frank Street, Vauxhall S.E.11. Z25190B

ISITT, J., Signalman, R.N.
He joined the Service in March 1917, and was posted to H.M.S. " Ganges," which ship was engaged on patrol and other important duties in the North, Baltic, and Mediterranean Seas, until the cessation of hostilities. In 1920, he was serving in Home waters, and holds the General Service and Victory Medals.
36, Frank Street, Vauxhall, S.E.11. Z25190A

ISITT, J. E. H., Private, M.G.C.
He volunteered in 1915, and joined the Royal Fusiliers, but discovered as being under age, was discharged. Joining the Machine Gun Corps in 1917, he embarked for France later in the year and was in action in many engagements. He also fought throughout the German Offensive and Allied Advance of 1918, and returning to England at the cessation of hostilities was demobilised in January 1919. He holds the General Service and Victory Medals.
24, Monkton Street, Kennington, S.E.11. Z26896

IVES, A. L., Corporal, R.E.
He joined in May 1916, and embarked for the Western Front in the following January. During his service overseas, he was in action in many important engagements, including those at Vimy Ridge, Ypres and Amiens, and throughout the Retreat and Advance of 1918. He returned to England and was demobilised in September 1919, and holds the General Service and Victory Medals.
100, Battersea Bridge Road, Battersea, S.W.11. Z2759

IVES, C. H., Driver, R.A.S.C.
Joining in October 1916, he proceeded to France two months later, and was engaged on important duties, transporting ammunition and supplies to the front lines. He was present at the Battles of Ypres, Arras, Armentières, Ploegsteert, and at the heavy fighting in the Retreat and Advance of 1918. He was demobilised in November 1919, and holds the General Service and Victory Medals.
134, Cobourg Road, Camberwell, S.E.5. Z5430

IVES, S. S., Private, Sherwood Foresters.
Volunteering in September 1915, he was sent to France in the following February, and fought in many parts of the line. He was unfortunately killed in action at the second Battle of the Somme in March 1918, during the German Offensive, and was entitled to the General Service and Victory Medals.
" He joined the great white company of valiant souls."
34, Charleston Street, Walworth, S.E.17. Z2758B

IVES, T., Private, Tank Corps.
Volunteering in July 1915, he was drafted to the Western Front in the following September, and fought at Albert, the Somme, Beaumont-Hamel, Vimy Ridge, Havrincourt, Lens and Ypres. He was also in action throughout the German Offensive and Allied Advance of 1918, and returning to England was demobilised in February 1919. He holds the 1914-15 Star, and the General Service and Victory Medals.
34, Charleston Street, Walworth, S.E.17. Z2758A

IVIMY, H. J., Sapper, R.E.
He volunteered in June 1915, and was sent to France in the following April. During his service on the Western Front he served with his unit on important duties whilst operations were in progress at Ypres, the Somme, Albert, Vermelles, Vimy Ridge, Bullecourt, Messines, Lens, Cambrai, Arras, Amiens, Bapaume, and during the Retreat and Advance of 1918. He was demobilised in March 1919, and holds the General Service and Victory Medals.
198, Hollydale Road, Peckham, S.E.15. Z6401

IVORY, J. W., Sapper, R.E.
He joined in May 1917, and completing his training was stationed at various depôts engaged on guard and other important duties with his unit. He was unsuccessful in obtaining his transfer overseas prior to the cessation of hostilities, but did good work until demobilised in February 1919.
70, Cator Street, Peckham, S.E.15. Z4476A

IVORY, W. G., Private, 1/2nd Royal Fusiliers.
Volunteering in April 1915, he embarked for France a year later, and during the fighting on the Somme front, was taken prisoner in May 1916. He was held in captivity until after the cessation of hostilities, and was then repatriated in accordance with the terms of the Armistice, and demobilised in January 1919. He holds the General Service and Victory Medals.
70, Cator Street, Peckham, S.E.15. Z4476B

J

JACK, J., Driver, R.E.
He was mobilised from the Reserve at the outbreak of war, and proceeded to France, where he served in the Retreat from Mons and was wounded. He was later engaged on important duties during the Battles of the Marne, the Aisne, La Bassée, Arras, Ypres, the Somme, and many others until hostilities ceased. He then went into Germany with the Army of Occupation, and returning to England was demobilised in February 1919. He holds the Mons Star, and the General Service and Victory Medals.
13, Listowel Street, Stockwell, S.W.9. Z5105

JACKSON, A. H., Private, Manchester Regiment.
Volunteering in August 1914, he was shortly afterwards drafted to France, and took part in the Retreat from Mons, and several other engagements. Whilst engaged in the fighting during the Battle of Neuve Chapelle, he was unfortunately killed in action on March 28th, 1915. He was entitled to the Mons Star, and the General Service and Victory Medals.
" Nobly striving,
He nobly fell that we might live."
47, Thorncroft Street, Wandsworth Road, S.W.8. Z2764A

JACKSON, A. M., Private, M.G.C.
He joined in February 1917, and after a short period of training proceeded to the Western Front, where he served with his unit in various sectors, and fought in many important engagements, including those of Vimy Ridge, and Oppy Wood. He was invalided to England with fever, and on recovery was stationed at Grantham until demobilised in February 1919. He holds the General Service and Victory Medals.
51, Councillor Street, Camberwell, S.E.5. Z2763

JACKSON, C. B., Private, R.A.V.C.
Volunteering in August 1914, he proceeded shortly afterwards to France and saw much heavy fighting, and was present at the Retreat from Mons, and several other important engagements. He rendered valuable services in tending sick and wounded horses. Owing to illness he was invalided to England and unfortunately died. He was entitled to the Mons Star, and the General Service and Victory Medals.
" His memory is cherished with pride."
186, Farmer's Road, Camberwell, S.E.5. Z2490A

JACKSON, D. C., Private, R.A.S.C. (M.T.)
He joined in May 1916, and in the same year was despatched to the Western Front, where he was employed on transport work, taking stores and ammunition to the front lines. During his three years' service overseas, he saw heavy fighting in various sectors, and was in action during the Retreat and Advance of 1918. After the cessation of hostilities he returned to England and was demobilised in September 1919, and holds the General Service and Victory Medals.
25, Gladstone Street, Battersea Park Road, S.W.8. Z2768

JACKSON, E. J., Rflmn., King's Royal Rifle Corps.
He joined in 1917, and was drafted in the following year to the Western Front, where he saw much heavy fighting in various sectors, and took part in the Retreat and Advance of 1918. Later, he proceeded with the Army of Occupation into Germany, and whilst there was transferred to the R.A.S.C. He was demobilised in March 1920, and holds the General Service and Victory Medals.
33, Chalmers Street, Wandsworth Road, S.W.8. Z2766

JACKSON, E. C., Sapper, R.E.

He volunteered in February 1915, and after training for eight months was drafted to the Western Front, where he was attached to the 93rd Field Company. He was engaged on special duties in connection with operations and was under fire in many engagements, including the Battles of the Somme' Ypres, Neuve Chapelle, Arras and Cambrai. After the conclusion of hostilities, he was demobilised in May 1919, and holds the 1914-15 Star, and the General Service and Victory Medals.

130, Harbut Road, Battersea, S.W.11. Z2771

JACKSON, F. S., Driver, R.A.S.C. (H.T.)

Volunteering in March 1915, he proceeded to the Western Front three months later. During his service overseas he was employed on transport duties, and was present at several engagements, including the Battles of Arras, Cambrai, the Somme, and the Retreat and Advance of 1918. He then proceeded with the Army of Occupation into Germany, and attached to the Cavalry Corps did very good work. He was demobilised in June 1919, and holds the 1914-15 Star, and the General Service and Victory Medals.

41, Brisbane Street, Camberwell, S.E.5. Z4477

JACKSON, F. W., Private, 4th Middlesex Regt.

Volunteering in June 1915, he was despatched in the following December to the Western Front, and took a prominent part in the Battles of Ypres, and Arras and was wounded at Loos Evacuated to England, he returned to France on recovery, and served as a Signaller in the Retreat and Advance of 1918. After the cessation of hostilities he returned home and was demobilised in May 1919, holding the 1914-15 Star, and the General Service and Victory Medals.

9, Langley Lane, South Lambeth Road, S.W.8. Z2772

JACKSON, C. J., Corporal, Prince of Wales' (Leinster Regiment).

An ex-soldier, having served in the Boer war, he re-enlisted in January 1915, and proceeded in the following year to the Western Front, where he took a distinguished part in several engagements. During the Battle of the Somme he made the supreme sacrifice, being killed in action on April 12th, 1917. He held the Queen's and King's South African Medals, and was entitled to the General Service and Victory Medals.

" He joined the great white company of valiant souls."

13, Calmington Road, Camberwell, S.E.5. Z5431

JACKSON, G. P., Private, 2/24th London Regt. (Queen's).

He volunteered in May 1915, and after training proceeded in the same year to the Western Front, where he fought in the Battle of Ypres. He was then transferred to Salonika, and engaged in the fighting on the Vardar front. Later, sent to Egypt, he served under General Allenby, and was in action during the Advance through Palestine, and was wounded near Jerusalem. After receiving medical treatment in Egypt he was invalided to England, and subsequently discharged from Netley Hospital in May 1919, as medically unfit for further military service. He holds the 1914-15 Star, and the General Service and Victory Medals.

27, Parkstone Road, Peckham, S.E.15. Z5624

JACKSON, J. J., L/Corporal, R.A.S.C. (M.T.)

Joining in May 1916, he proceeded in the same year to the Western Front, and took an active part in several engagements, including the Battles of the Somme, Ypres, Passchendaele, and was wounded in action at Arras. He was invalided home, and after receiving hospital treatment was transferred to the Labour Corps, with which unit he rendered valuable services in Scotland. He was discharged as medically unfit for further military service in March 1919, and holds the General Service and Victory Medals.

117, Kinglake Street, Walworth, S.E.17. Z2767B

JACKSON, J. W., Pte. (Sig.), 10th Middlesex Regt. and Rifleman, 2nd Cameronians (Scottish Rifles).

He volunteered in March 1915, and proceeded shortly afterwards to the Western Front. In this theatre of war he saw much heavy fighting and took part in several engagements, including the Battles of Vimy Ridge, Lens, the Somme, Cambrai and in the Retreat and Advance of 1918. He was demobilised in February 1919, and holds the General Service and Victory Medals.

6, Dale Street, Chiswick, W.4. 5419A

JACKSON, L. P., Pte., 2nd Lancashire Fusiliers.

He enlisted in June 1914, and at the outbreak of war was drafted with his unit to France, where he played an important part in various engagements, including the Battles of Ypres and Neuve Chapelle. He was unhappily killed in action on October 9th, 1917, and was entitled to the 1914-15 Star, and the General Service and Victory Medals.

" Courage, bright hopes, and a myriad dreams, splendidly given."

6, Dale Street, Chiswick, W.4. 5419B

JACKSON, N. (Mrs.), Special War Worker.

This lady offered her services for work of National importance during the war, and was engaged at Messrs. Ducros' Munition Factory, Acton, from September 1915, until March 1918, during which period she was employed in making shells. She then went to Messrs. Waring and Gillows, Hammersmith, and was engaged on aircraft work until the following December. She rendered valuable services throughout.

116, Dalling Road, Hammersmith, W.6. 11630A

JACKSON, R. D., Private, South Staffordshire Regt.

He joined in January 1917, and proceeding in the same year to the Western Front, took a distinguished part in many important engagements, during his short period of active service. Whilst fighting in the Lens sector he made the supreme sacrifice, being killed in action in October 1917. He was entitled to the General Service and Victory Medals.

" A valiant soldier, with undaunted heart he breasted Life's last hill."

15, Pitcairn Street, Wandsworth Road, S.W.8. Z1201C

JACKSON, R. T., L/Corporal, R.E.

He volunteered in August 1914, and after his training served at various stations on important duties with his unit. Drafted overseas to German East Africa in 1917, he took part in severe fighting during operations in that country, and was unfortunately drowned whilst crossing a river during an engagement with the enemy. He was entitled to the General Service and Victory Medals.

" Thinking that remembrance, though unspoken, may reach him where he sleeps."

5, Mordaunt Street, Landor Road, Stockwell, S.W.9. Z2765

JACKSON, S., Rifleman, 6th Rifle Brigade.

He had previously volunteered for service with the Colours, but was rejected on account of his age. However, he joined in December 1916, and proceeded in the following year to the Western Front, where he took a prominent part in several engagements, including the Battles of Ypres, Cambrai, the Somme, and in the Retreat and Advance of 1918. After the cessation of hostilities he returned home and was demobilised in February 1919, and holds the General Service and Victory Medals.

29, Lavender Road, Battersea, S.W.11. Z2769

JACKSON, S., Private, 10th London Regiment.

He joined in August 1917, and on completion of his training served at various stations on important duties with his unit. He did very good work as a coal porter, but was not successful in securing his transfer overseas before the cessation of hostilities, and was demobilised in October 1919.

4, Neate Street, Camberwell, S.E.5. Z5106

JACKSON, S. T., Gunner, R.G.A.

Volunteering in October 1915, he was unable to obtain his transfer overseas owing to medical unfitness. After completing his training at Aldershot and Deepcut, he was attached to an Anti-aircraft Mobile Section. During raids by hostile aircraft over London, he was one of the successful Battery to bring down enemy machines at Godstone. After the cessation of hostilities, he was demobilised in April 1919, but re-enlisted in the R.G.A. two months later, and proceeded overseas to Gibraltar, where he was still serving in 1920.

59, Meyrick Road, Battersea, S.W.11. Z2770

JACKSON, W., Private, R.A.M.C.

Volunteering in August 1914, he proceeded immediately to France, and rendered valuable services tending the sick and wounded in the Retreat from Mons, and the Battles of the Marne, the Aisne, Ypres, Arras, and the Somme. He was wounded at Festubert, and after receiving hospital treatment at Boulogne was evacuated to England, and discharged from King's College Hospital, London, in November 1917, as medically unfit for further military service. He holds the Mons Star, and the General Service and Victory Medals.

117, Kinglake Street, Walworth, S.E.17. Z2767A

JACKSON, W., L/Corporal, 7th Royal Fusiliers.

He volunteered in March 1915, and proceeded in the same year to the Western Front. He served with his Battalion in many parts of the line, and was engaged in much heavy fighting. Severely wounded during the Battle of Ypres, he was invalided to England, and in consequence of his injuries his left leg had to be amputated. He was discharged as medically unfit for further military service in April 1916, and holds the 1914-15 Star, and the General Service and Victory Medals.

32, Harris Street, Camberwell, S.E.5. 4478-9A

JACKSON, W. J., Shoeing-Smith, 2nd Dragoon Guards (Queen's Bays).

He volunteered in August 1914, and after his training served at various stations on important duties with his unit. Drafted to France in September 1916, he was engaged in various sectors, and saw much heavy fighting. After the cessation of hostilities he returned home and was demobilised in September 1919, and holds the General Service and Victory Medals.

116, Dalling Road, Hammersmith, W.6. 11630B

JACOB, A., Bombardier, R.F.A.

Volunteering in April 1915, he was sent to France in the following November, and served there until hostilities ceased. During this period he was engaged with his Battery in the Battles of Loos, Ploegsteert Wood, Vimy Ridge, the Somme (I and II), Messines, Ypres and Cambrai, and did good work during the Retreat and Advance of 1918. He was demobilised in July 1919, and holds the 1914-15 Star, and the General Service and Victory Medals.

284, Sumner Road, Peckham, S.E.15.　　　Z6006

JACOBS, G. H., Private, Middlesex Regiment.

He joined in September 1916, and after completing his training was engaged on important duties as a telephone operator at home. He rendered valuable services, but owing to medical unfitness for General Service was not successful in obtaining his transfer overseas, and was demobilised in January 1919.

200, Ferndale Road, Stockwell, S.W.9.　　　Z2760

JACOBS, E. G. H., Private, R.A.S.C.

Joining in December 1916, he completed his training and was engaged on important duties in connection with remounts at various Cavalry barracks in England. He did excellent work, but was unable to obtain his transfer to a theatre of war before the conclusion of hostilities, and was demobilised in March 1919.

23, Combermere Road, Stockwell, S.W.9.　　　Z2762

JACOBS, L., Private, Middlesex Regiment.

Joining in July 1916, he proceeded to the Western Front six months later, and was engaged in heavy fighting in the Battles of Arras, Ypres, Messines, Lens, Cambrai and the Somme. Owing 'th illness he was invalided to hospital in England, and after receiving medical treatment for several months, was subsequently discharged in December 1918, as medically unfit for further service, and holds the General Service and Victory Medals.

23, Darwin Street, Walworth, S.E.17.　　　Z2761

JAMES, A. E., Private, 2/13th London Regiment (Kensingtons).

He volunteered in August 1914, and was sent overseas in the following January. Serving in France in many important engagements he was wounded in the Battle of the Somme in September 1916, and invalided home. On recovery he proceeded to Salonika, and after a period of service in the Balkans was drafted to Egypt, where he was in action during the British Advance through Palestine, and was present at the fall of Jerusalem in 1917. He returned to England for demobilisation in March 1919, and holds the 1914-15 Star, and the General Service and Victory Medals.

23, Rowena Crescent, Battersea, S.W.11. -　　　Z2778

JAMES, A. E., Private, Norfolk Regiment and Lancashire Fusiliers.

Joining in 1917, he was drafted overseas in the following year, and served on the Western Front. Whilst in this theatre of war he took part in several engagements during the Advance of 1918, and was severely wounded and sent to England. He received hospital treatment and was subsequently discharged as medically unfit for further service in January 1919, and holds the General Service and Victory Medals.

106, Faraday Street, Walworth, S.E.17.　　　Z2776A

JAMES, A. E. (Mrs.), Special War Worker.

Volunteering for work of National importance during the war this lady was engaged on important duties by the Postal Authorities at the South Eastern district post office from December 1914 to June 1919, thus releasing a man for service with the Colours. Throughout the period of her employment she discharged her responsible duties in a highly capable and efficient manner.

3, Venn Street, Clapham, S.W.4.　　　Z2775B

JAMES, E. A., Corporal, 24th Queen's (Royal West Surrey Regiment).

He volunteered in 1915, and owing to physical unfitness for general service, was engaged on important clerical duties in a Record Office for three years. Drafted to France in 1918, he served in the Somme sector and did valuable work on guard and other duties at various prisoners of war camps. He was demobilised in 1919, and holds the General Service and Victory Medals.

106, Faraday Street, Walworth, S.E.17.　　　Z2776B

JAMES, E. R., Private, 7th London Regiment.

He joined in April 1917, and four months later embarked for the Western Front, where he fought in the Battles of Ypres and Passchendaele, and was gassed. Serving as a sniper he was later in action in the Battle of the Somme, and was again gassed at Combles, near Cambrai, and invalided home in September 1918. Recovering after hospital treatment he served with his unit until demobilised in September 1919, and holds the General Service and Victory Medals.

33, Freedom Street, Battersea, S.W.11.　　　Z2779

JAMES, F., Pte., 22nd London Regt. (The Queen's).

Volunteering in the 21st London Regiment in December 1915, he was sent to France in the following April and was wounded in the Battle of Vimy Ridge a month later, and admitted to hospital. He was transferred to the 2/22nd London Regiment on recovery and drafted to Salonika in December 1916, and after serving for three months proceeded to Egypt. In this theatre of war he fought in the Battles of Gaza, Beyrout and in other engagements during the British Advance through Palestine, and was wounded in the vicinity of Jerusalem in November 1917. Rejoining his unit he served in operations until the close of hostilities, and returned to England in July 1919. He was demobilised two months later and holds the General Service and Victory Medals.

15, Pitt Street, Peckham, S.E.15.　　　Z5258

JAMES, F. W., Driver, R.A.S.C.

He volunteered in April 1915, and in the same year was drafted to Salonika. He served in various parts of the Balkans, and was present in the Advance on the Vardar and at the Battle of Monastir. Sent to the Western Front he was engaged on important duties in connection with the transport of ammunition and supplies to the firing line, and did valuable work during the concluding stages of the war. He was demobilised in April 1919, and holds the 1914-15 Star, and the General Service and Victory Medals.

49, Dorset Road, Clapham Road, S.W.8.　　　Z2780

JAMES, G., 1st Class Stoker, R.N.

He volunteered in August 1914, and was posted to H.M.S. " St. Vincent," which vessel was attached to the Grand Fleet and engaged on important patrol duties in the North Sea. He was transferred in January 1915, to H.M.S. " Amethyst," and three months later proceeded to the Dardanelles, where his ship was heavily bombarded by the Turks, and suffered serious casualties, but he fortunately escaped injury and served aboard this vessel until the end of the war. He holds the 1914-15 Star, and the General Service and Victory Medals, and in 1920 was still serving.

50, Larcom Street, Walworth, S.E.17.　　　Z2777

JAMES, H., Sergt., 24th Queen's (Royal West Surrey Regiment).

A regular soldier, having enlisted in 1887, he was mobilised on the outbreak of war, and was employed as Sergeant Instructor at home. He rendered valuable services in the training of recruits for the New Armies until invalided out of the Service in August 1916. He holds the 3rd India General Service Medal, 1895-98, the Long Service and Good Conduct Medal, and the Territorial Force Efficiency Medal.

10, Milford Street, Wandsworth Road, S.W.8.　　　Z5554A

JAMES, J., Private, East Surrey Regiment.

Volunteering in August 1914, he was sent to France shortly afterwards and fought in the Retreat from Mons, and in the Battles of the Aisne, Le Cateau, La Bassée, Ypres and Neuve Chapelle. He was also in action at St. Eloi, Hill 60, Festubert, Loos, Vimy Ridge, and was wounded and taken prisoner in the Battle of the Somme. He received medical treatment in a prison hospital in Germany, and endured many hardships, and on recovery was made to work in the coal mines until his repatriation in December 1918. He was demobilised in March 1919, and holds the Mons Star, and the General Service and Victory Medals.

320, East Street, Walworth, S.E.17.　　　Z2307A

JAMES, J. H., Private, 2/24th London Regt. (The Queen's).

He volunteered in November 1914, and proceeding to France in the following year was in action in the Battles of Ypres, Loos, Albert and the Somme. In 1916 he was drafted to Salonika and served in operations on the Struma, Vardar and Doiran fronts, and was sent to Egypt in 1917. Taking part in General Allenby's Advance through Palestine, he fought in the Battles of Gaza, Beersheba, in several engagements at Jericho and on the Jordan, and was present at the fall of Jerusalem. Returning to the Western Front in 1918, he served in the final Allied Advance. He was demobilised in February 1919, and holds the 1914-15 Star, and the General Service and Victory Medals.

3, Venn Street, Clapham, S.W.4.　　　Z2775A

JAMES, J. J. J., Driver, R.F.A.

Volunteering in October 1914, he completed his training, and was later drafted to France, where he served throughout the war. During this period he was engaged with his Battery in the Battles of Loos, the Somme, the Ancre, Arras, Ypres, Passchendaele, and Amiens, Le Cateau and other engagements until the end of hostilities. He was demobilised in March 1919, and holds the 1914 Star, and the General Service and Victory Medals.

32, Stainforth Road, Battersea, S.W.11.　　　Z2773

JAMES, J. S. (M.M.), Gunner, R.F.A.

He volunteered in 1915, and in the same year embarked for the Western Front. Serving as a signaller he was in action in the Battles of the Somme and Ypres, and was wounded and sent to a Pase Hospital. On recovery he returned to his Battery, and taking part in the Retreat and Advance of 1918, was awarded the Military Medal for conspicuous bravery and devotion to duty in the Field under heavy shell-fire. He also holds the 1914-15 Star, and the General Service and Victory Medals, and was demobilised in 1919.
187, Stewart's Road, Battersea Park Road, S.W.8. Z4200C

JAMES, S. A., Rifleman, King's Royal Rifle Corps.

Volunteering in March 1915, he embarked for France three months later, and fought in many engagements, including those at Loos, Vimy Ridge, the Somme, and was wounded. Returning to England, he received hospital treatment, and on recovery returned to France and was in action at Bullecourt, Havrincourt and throughout the Retreat and Advance of 1918. He was demobilised in February 1919, and holds the 1914-15 Star, and the General Service and Victory Medals.
5, Nunhead Lane, Peckham, S.E.15. Z6268

JAMES, T., Corporal, 2/2nd Royal Fusiliers.

Volunteering in September 1914, he was engaged on important duties with his Battalion until sent to France in 1916. Serving in various sectors he fought at Bourlon Wood, and in many other engagements and was taken prisoner at Arras in 1918. He was made to work on German guns, and was killed by an explosion of hydrogen on August 6th, 1918, whilst a prisoner of war. He was entitled to the General Service and Victory Medals.
" Courage, bright hopes, and a myriad dreams, splendidly given."
194, Farmer's Road, Camberwell, S.E.5. Z1946B

JAMES, W., Sergt., 3rd Middlesex Regiment.

He volunteered in August 1914, and proceeding to the Western Front in the following year fought in several engagements until wounded in the Battle of Loos. He was invalided to hospital in England, and on recovery, was drafted to Mesopotamia in 1916, and was actively engaged with his unit in fierce fighting in this thratre of operations. He was killed in action on November 18th, 1917, and was entitled to the 1914-15 Star, and the General Service and Victory Medals.
" He joined the great white company of valiant Souls."
84, Avenue Road, Camberwell, S.E.5. Z2042A

JAMES, W., Private, 23rd London Regiment and Rifleman, Royal Irish Rifles.

Volunteering in the 23rd London Regiment in September 1915, he embarked for France three months later, and was engaged in heavy fighting in the Ancre sector, and in the Battle of Vimy Ridge. Sent home owing to illness in February 1917, he received medical treatment, and on recovery was transferred to the Royal Irish Rifles, and sent to Ireland, where he served as a cook until his demobilisation in March 1919. He holds the 1914-15 Star, and the General Service and Victory Medals.
9, Shillwood Road, Battersea, S.W.11. Z2774

JAMESON, F., Private, 3/22nd Queen's (Royal West Surrey Regiment).

He volunteered in August 1914, and at the conclusion of his training was engaged with his Battalion on special duties at many depôts. He did very good work, but on account of his being over military age, was unable to secure his transfer overseas. He was discharged in December 1918.
6, Sears Street, Camberwell, S.E.5. Z5787

JARDINE, E. T., Private, R.A.M.C.

He had previously served in the South African War, and in March 1915 again volunteered. He was afterwards drafted to the Western Front, and did excellent service with his unit in the Battles of Loos, the Somme, Arras, Ypres and Cambrai, and throughout the Retreat and Advance of the Allies in 1918. as far as Cologne. After his return home he was demobilised in February 1919, and holds the 1914-15 Star, and the General Service and Victory Medals.
6, Boyton's Cottages, off New Church Road, Camberwell, S.E.5. Z6492

JARED, G. J., Corporal, R.A.S.C.

A Reservist of the R.F.A., he was mobilised at the outbreak of hostilities, and immediately proceeded to France. Whilst on the Western Front he fought in the Retreat from Mons and the Battles of the Marne, La Bassée and Neuve Chapelle. In March 1915 he was transferred to the Royal Army Service Corps, and was engaged with his unit on important duties, taking supplies to the front line trenches, and did excellent work until the end of the war. He holds the Mons Star, and the General Service and Victory Medals, and was demobilised in March 1919.
14, Palmerston Street, Battersea, S.W.11. Z2781B

JARED, H., Driver, R.H.A.

He was mobilised with the Reservists at the outbreak of hostilities, and drafted to France in November 1914. He served on the Western Front and was in action in many engagements until severely wounded in February 1915. He was invalided to hospital in England, and eventually discharged as medically unfit for further service in the following July. He holds the 1914 Star, and the General Service and Victory Medals.
14, Palmerston Street, Battersea, S.W.11. Z2781C

JARMAN, H. R., L/Corporal, R.F.A.

He volunteered in September 1915, and in the following year proceeded to France, where he fought at the Battle of the Somme and was wounded. He was sent to England for hospital treatment, and on recovery was drafted to Salonika. He was there transferred to the Anti-aircraft Section of the Royal Garrison Artillery. and did good work during the operations on the Vardar front. He holds the General Service and Victory Medals, and was demobilised in July 1919.
19, Pitcairn Street, Wandsworth Road, S.W.8. Z2782

JARRETT, E., Corporal, R.F.A.

He volunteered in April 1915, and in December of the same year was drafted overseas. During his service in France he fought in many engagements, including those on the Somme, at Hill 60, Arras, Vimy Ridge, and was wounded near Passchendaele in October 1917. On recovery he rejoined his Battery and took part in the final operations of the war. He was demobilised in June 1919, and holds the 1914-15 Star, and the General Service and Victory Medals.
11, Sandover Road, Camberwell, S.E.5. Z5432

JARRETT, W. H., Rifleman, Rifle Brigade.

Volunteering in May 1915, he was drafted to France later in the same year. He fought at Ypres and was wounded in June 1916. He received treatment at Le Treport Hospital, and on recovery returned to the firing line, and was in action at Arras, and was again wounded on the Somme. Invalided to England in 1918 he was subsequently demobilised in April 1919, and holds the General Service and Victory Medals.
3, Henry Street, Kennington, S.E.11. Z2454I

JARROLD, E. W., Sergt., 1st Royal Sussex Regt.

He enlisted in 1907, and was serving in India at the outbreak of hostilities. He was engaged with his Battalion on important duties in various parts and fought in the operations on the North West Frontier. After the signing of the Armistice he proceeded to Germany, and in 1920 was still serving with the Army of Occupation on the Rhine. He holds the General Service and Victory Medals, and the India General Service Medal (with clasp Afghanistan, N.W. Frontier, 1919).
25, Haines Street, Battersea Park Road, S.W.8. Z2783B

JARROLD, S., Private, 1st Leicestershire Regt.

He joined in October 1916, and shortly afterwards was sent to France, where he fought at Ypres and was wounded in 1917. On recovery he returned to the front line trenches and was again wounded on the Somme in the following year. He later took part in the Allied Advance and was wounded a third time. After the cessation of hostilities he returned to England and was demobilised, but rejoined shortly afterwards, and in 1920 was serving with his Battalion in Ireland. He holds the General Service and Victory Medals.
25, Haines Street, Battersea Park Road, S.W.8. Z2783A

JARVIS, A. F., Gunner, R.F.A.

Volunteering in June 1915, in the following year he proceeded overseas. During his service on the Western Front he took part in much fighting, and was mortally wounded on the Somme in September 1916. He was taken to a Casualty Clearing Station, where he died on September 14th, and was buried in Doullens Military Cemetery. He was entitled to the General Service and Victory Medals.
" Honour to the immortal dead who gave their youth that the world might grow old in peace."
31, Nursery Row, Walworth, S.E.17. Z2784A

JARVIS, J. F., Private, 4th Middlesex Regiment.

He joined in February 1917, on attaining military age, and after completing his training was engaged on important duties with his unit in the Southern and Eastern Counties. He rendered valuable services, but was unable to secure his transfer to a theatre of war before hostilities were concluded. He was, however, afterwards sent to Gibraltar, where he was still serving in 1920.
28, Pilkington Road, Peckham, S.E.15. Z6008

JARVIS, R. (Saddler), R.F.A.

He volunteered in September 1914, and proceeded to France in the following year. He was engaged with his Battery in the fighting at Hill 60, Loos, Albert Vimy Ridge, the Somme, Beaumont-Hamel, Ypres, Passchendaele, Cambrai, the Sambre and in the Retreat and Allied Advance of 1918. He was demobilised in July 1919, and holds the 1914-15 Star, and the General Service and Victory Medals.
10, McKerrill Road, Peckham, S.E.15. Z5788

JARVIS, R. W., A.B., Royal Navy.
He joined in January 1916, and was posted to H.M.S. " Shakespeare," which vessel was engaged on important patrol and other duties, and was in action at the raids on Zeebrugge and Ostend, and also served off the coasts of Russia and Africa. With his ship he was employed on special work at Scapa Flow, when the German Fleet was interned there. He holds the General Service and Victory Medals, and was still serving in 1920.
58, St. Mark's Road, Camberwell, S.E.5.   Z2785A

JARVIS, W. S., Leading Aircraftsman, R.A.F.
He joined in June 1916, and at the conclusion of his training was engaged on important duties, which demanded a high degree of technical skill. In 1917 he was severely wounded whilst flying during an hostile air raid over London, and two other men in the machine were killed. After the cessation of hostilities he proceeded to Germany, and served with the Army of Occupation until demobilised in November 1919.
31, Nursery Row, Walworth, S.E.17.   Z2784B

JAYES, H., Rifleman, King's Royal Rifle Corps.
A Reservist, he was mobilised at the outbreak of hostilities. and drafted at once to France. He fought in the Retreat from Mons and the Battles of the Marne, the Aisne and Ypres, where he was taken prisoner. He was held captive until April 1918, and was then interned in Holland and served at the Hague until demobilised in March 1919. He holds the Mons Star, and the General Service and Victory Medals.
16, Shorncliffe Road, Walworth, S.E.17.   Z2786

JASPER, J., Saddler, R.F.A.
He volunteered in October 1915, and in March of the following year was sent overseas. Whilst on the Western Front he was engaged in the fighting at Vimy Ridge, Loos, the Somme, Beaumont-Hamel, and was wounded near Arras in 1918. He was sent to hospital in England, and on recovery rejoined his Battery in the firing line, and served until the end of the war. He holds the General Service and Victory Medals, and was demobilised in March 1919.
42, Herring Street, Camberwell, S.E.5.   Z5433

JEAL, C. E., Private, R.A.M.C.
He joined in 1916, and at the conclusion of his training was engaged with his unit on important duties at various stations until drafted to France early in 1918. Whilst on the Western Front he was engaged as an hospital orderly and also served as a stretcher bearer, in the fighting at Ypres and Cambrai during the Retreat and Advance of that year. He was demobilised in February 1919, and holds the General Service and Victory Medals.
19, Longcroft Road, Camberwell, S.E.5.   Z5434

JEAL, H., Private, R.A.S.C.
Volunteering at the outbreak of war he was immediately sent overseas. During his service on the Western Front he served on important duties at Rouen, transporting ammunition and supplies to the forward areas, and did excellent work. He was demobilised in June 1919, and holds the 1914 Star, and the General Service and Victory Medals.
5, Namur Terrace, Walworth, S.E.17.   Z2787

JEE, R. H., Driver, R.F.A.
He volunteered in 1914, and in October of the following year embarked for the Western Front. Whilst in this theatre of war he served with his Battery in many engagements, including the Battles of the Somme, Ypres, Vimy Ridge, and was wounded near Arras in October 1917. He was sent to hospital in England owing to his injuries, and on recovery was retained for duties at home until demobilised in March 1919. He holds the 1914-15 Star, and the General Service and Victory Medals.
49, Camberwell Station Road, S.E.5.   Z6007

JEFCUT, S., Petty Officer, R.N.
He was serving at the outbreak of hostilities in H.M.S. " Eden," which vessel during the war was engaged in escorting transports to France, and also on patrol duties in the North Sea. His ship was rammed by a transport in the English Channel in June 1916, and towed into Le Havre harbour. He was then transferred to H.M.S. " Undaunted," and later served in H.M.S. " Coventry," until after the Armistice. He holds the 1914-15 Star, and the General Service and Victory Medals. and was placed on the Reserve in July 1919.
172, Lavender Road, Battersea, S.W.11.   Z2788

JEFCUT, W. J., Sapper, R.E.
He volunteered in November 1915, and was drafted to France in the following year. Whilst on the Western Front he was engaged with his unit on mining and other special duties during the fighting on the Somme, at Vimy Ridge, Messines and was severely wounded at Beaumont-Hamel, and in consequence lost the sight of an eye. He was sent to hospital in England, and subsequently invalided out of the Service in September 1918. He holds the General Service and Victory Medals.
15, Porson Street, Wandsworth Road, S.W.8.   Z1502B

JEFFERIES, L. W., Private, Royal Fusiliers.
He joined in 1917, and after his training served at various stations on guard and other important duties with his unit. He was unable to secure his transfer to a theatre of war before the cessation of hostilities, but rendered valuable services until his demobilisation, which took place in 1919.
44, Gilbert Road, Kennington, S.E.11.   Z27245

JEFFERIES, S., Private, 1st Devonshire Regiment.
Volunteering in October 1914, he was drafted to Egypt in the following year. There he was engaged with his Battalion in the fighting at Rafa, Gaza, Jaffa, and Jerusalem, during the British Advance through Palestine. He returned to England in 1919, and was demobilised in April of that year, and holds the 1914-15 Star, and the General Service and Victory Medals.   Z5625
17, Copeland Avenue, Peckham Rye, S.E.15.   Z5626

JEFFERY, B., Rifleman, Rifle Brigade.
A Territorial, he was mobilised at the outbreak of hostilities, and served on special duties until sent to France in 1916. Whilst on the Western Front he fought in the Battles of the Somme, Vimy Ridge and Bullecourt and was mortally wounded during the German Offensive in March 1918, and died shortly afterwards. He was entitled to the General Service and Victory Medals, also the Territorial Efficiency, and the Long Service and Good Conduct Medals.
" The path of duty was the way to glory."
55, Coronation Buildings, South Lambeth Road, S.W.8.   Z2789

JEFFERY, C., Private, 23rd Middlesex Regiment.
He joined in October 1918, and after completing his training was employed at various Depôts on important duties with his Battalion. In January 1919, he was drafted overseas, and served with the Army of Occupation in Germany, and was stationed at Cologne until 1920. He then returned to England and was demobilised in July of that year.
19, Ada Road, Camberwell, S.E.5.   Z3474

JEFFERY, M. E., Private, 2/4th Queen's (Royal West Surrey Regiment).
He joined in September 1918, and after his training served at St. Albans with his Battalion. He did good work, but was not able to secure his transfer overseas until after the cessation of hostilities. He was sent to Germany in April 1919 to the Army of Occupation, and was stationed at Cologne. He returned to England in November 1919, and was demobilised in the following month.
21, Park Crescent, Clapham Park Road, S.W.4.   Z2790B

JEFFERY, W. F., Private, 19th Manchester Regt.
Volunteering in January 1916, he was sent overseas in the following year, and during his service in France fought at the Battles of Arras, Messines and Vimy Ridge, and was seriously wounded near Messines. He was invalided to England, and in consequence of his injuries one of his feet had to be amputated. After protracted medical treatment he was discharged as physically unfit for further service in March 1918. He re-enlisted in the Royal Army Pay Corps in the following October, and was employed on clerical duties with that unit until demobilised in February 1919. He holds the General Service and Victory Medals.
21, Park Crescent, Clapham Park Road, S.W.4.   Z2790A

JEFFERY, W. J., Corporal, R.E. (Signal Section).
A Reservist, he was mobilised at the outbreak of hostilities, and drafted to France. In this theatre of war he served in the fighting during the Retreat from Mons, and the Battles of the Marne, the Aisne, Ypres, the Somme and Arras. In December 1915, he proceeded to Salonika, and was engaged on important duties with the 27th Division during the operations at Monastir, and on the Struma front. He was demobilised in February 1919, and holds the Mons Star, and the General Service and Victory Medals.
2, McKerrell Road, Peckham, S.E.15.   Z5789

JEFFS, J. H., L/Corporal, Royal Sussex Regiment.
He joined in June 1918, and later in the same year proceeded to the Western Front, where he took part in the final operations of the war. After the signing of the Armistice he proceeded to Germany with the Army of Occupation and was stationed at Cologne. He was demobilised in March 1920, and holds the General Service and Victory Medals.
17, Rumsey Road, Stockwell Road, S.W.9.   Z2791

JELLETT, E. J., Private, Wiltshire Regiment.
He volunteered in August 1914, and drafted to Gallipoli in the following year fought in the Landing at Suvla Bay, and at the capture of Chunuk Bair. On the Evacuation of the Peninsula he went to Mesopotamia in 1916, and served during the Battle of Kut-el-Amara, in the Relief of Kut, and the capture of Baghdad. He later proceeded to India and was stationed there until his return to England for demobilisation in October 1919. He holds the 1914-15 Star, and the General Service and Victory Medals.
66, Mayall Road, Herne Hill, S.E.24.   Z2792

JELLISS, H., Private, 3rd King's Own (Royal Lancaster Regiment).
Volunteering in August 1914, he proceeded overseas in the following November, and was in action in several engagements, including the Battle of Hill 60, in which he was wounded and taken prisoner on May 8th, 1915. He died from the effects of his injuries at Gettin, Germany, on May 17th, 1915, and was entitled to the 1914 Star, and the General Service and Victory Medals.
"A valiant soldier, with undaunted heart he breasted Life's last hill."
37, Fletcher Road, Chiswick, W.4. 6304B

JELLY, J., Private, 2/9th Durham Light Infantry.
He volunteered in July 1915, and after his training, saw service in Salonika and Mesopotamia, taking part in many of the principal engagements in each of these theatres of war. After three years' service overseas, he returned to England for demobilisation in March 1919, and holds the General Service and Victory Medals.
54, Elliott's Row, St. George's Road, S.E.11. Z26890

JENKINS, A., Rifleman, Rifle Brigade.
Joining in June 1916, he was sent to France in the same year and served with his Regiment in various parts of the line. He took part in many engagements, including those of the Somme and Ypres, and was severely wounded at Arras in April 1917. Evacuated to hospital in England he received medical treatment, and was subsequently invalided out of the Service in June 1918. He holds the General Service and Victory Medals.
10, Humphrey Street, Bermondsey, S.E.1. Z26849

JENKINS, C. F., 2nd Lieutenant, R.A.F.
He joined in June 1917, and on completing his training was engaged with his Squadron on important flying duties in connection with home defence. He rendered valuable services but was not successful in securing his transfer overseas before the cessation of hostilities, and was demobilised in February 1919. 21, Peveril Street, Battersea, S.W.11. Z2793

JENKINS, E. (Mrs.), Special War Worker.
Volunteering for work of National importance this lady was engaged by the Vauxhall Gas Works from January 1918 until April 1919, thus releasing a man for military service. Her work was of an extremely arduous nature throughout the period of her employment and she carried out her duties in a capable and efficient manner.
23, Ayliffe Street, New Kent Road, S.E.1. Z25813

JENKINS, G., Private, 3rd Northamptonshire Regt.
Mobilised in August 1914, he embarked for the Western Front in the following January, and was engaged in heavy fighting in the Battles of Neuve Chapelle, Ypres and Festubert, and was severely wounded in May 1915. Sent to hospital in England owing to his injuries, he received medical treatment and was eventually invalided out of the Army in May 1918. He holds the India General Service Medal (with three clasps) in addition to the 1914-15 Star, and the General Service and Victory Medals.
44, Wye Street, Battersea, S.W.11. Z2794

JENKINS, H. E., Corporal, R.E.
He volunteered in April 1915, and drafted to Egypt three months later was engaged on important duties in connection with supplies. He served in the Battle of Gaza and in other engagements during the British Advance through Palestine, and was present at the fall of Jerusalem. He returned to England for demobilisation in July 1920, and holds the 1914-15 Star, and the General Service and Victory Medals.
10, Councillor Street, Camberwell, S.E.5. Z2795

JENKINS, H. P., Driver, R.F.A.
Volunteering in September 1915, he proceeded to France in the following March, and served with his Battery in the Battles of Albert, the Somme, Arras, Ypres, Messines, Lens and Cambrai. He acted as shoeing-smith, and owing to injuries received through a kick from a horse, was invalided home in 1918, and ultimately discharged as medically unfit for further service in October of the same year. He holds the General Service and Victory Medals.
1, Hotspur Street, Kennington, S.E.11. Z25399

JENKINS, J., Private, Cheshire Regiment.
A Regular, with several years' service in India, he was mobilised on the outbreak of war, and in 1915 embarked for France. There he took part in the Battles of Neuve Chapelle, Ypres and Loos and was wounded. On recovery he was sent in 1916 to Salonika and served in the Advance on the Doiran front, and in other operations in the Balkans until sent to Egypt in the following year. He was in action in several engagements in Palestine, and was present at the entry into Jerusalem. Returning to the Western Front in 1918 he fought in the German Offensive, and was wounded in an engagement in the Allied Advance of that year. He was demobilised in December 1918, and holds the 1914-15 Star, and the General Service and Victory Medals.
23, Gabriel Street, Kennington, S.E.11. Z26695

JENKINS, T., Private, Queen's Own (Royal West Kent Regiment).
Mobilised from the Army Reserve on the declaration of war he was sent to France in August 1914, and fought in the Retreat from Mons, and in other engagements. He gave his life for King and Country at La Bassée on October 25th, 1914. He held the Queen's and King's South African Medals, and was entitled to the Mons Star, and the General Service and Victory Medals.
"Whilst we remember the Sacrifice is not in vain."
16, Sandover Road, Camberwell, S.E.5. Z5317A

JENKINS, W., Private, 11th Middlesex Regiment.
Volunteering in August 1914, he proceeded to the Western Front in the following May, and served there for upwards of four years. During this period he was engaged in heavy fighting in the Battles of Loos, the Somme, Arras, Ypres, Armentières and Cambrai. He was demobilised in February 1919, and holds the 1914-15 Star, and the General Service and Victory Medals.
2, Lansdowne Place, Southwark, S.E.1. Z25609

JENKINS, W. H., Sergt., 5th London Regt. (London Rifle Brigade) and R.A.P.C.
He volunteered in 1915, and on the conclusion of his training was engaged on important coast defence duties at various stations. He also acted as Assistant Company Accountant, and rendered valuable services. He was unsuccessful in obtaining his transfer to a theatre of war before the cessation of hostilities, and was demobilised in March 1919.
33, Burgoyne Road, Stockwell, S.W.9. Z2796

JENKS, J. J., Private, 6th Bedfordshire Regiment.
Volunteering in August 1914, he was drafted overseas in the following year. Whilst on the Western Front he took part in much fighting, and was severely wounded near Cambrai during the Allied Advance of 1918. He was taken to a Base Hospital, and later sent to England, where he received treatment. He was subsequently invalided out of the Service in August 1918, but rejoined in the Royal Army Pay Corps six weeks later. He was sent to Egypt in March 1919, and served on important duties as storekeeper at Cairo until April 1920, when he returned home and was demobilised. He holds the 1914-15 Star, and the General Service and Victory Medals.
1, Nursery Row, Orb Street, Walworth, S.E.17. Z2797A

JENN, L. W., Private, 14th London Regiment (London Scottish).
Joining in March 1916, he proceeded overseas shortly afterwards and served with his Battalion during heavy fighting in the Somme sector. He died gloriously on the Field of Battle at Morlancourt in August 1916, and was entitled to the General Service and Victory Medals.
"His Life for his Country, his Soul to God."
52, Solon Road, Acre Lane, S.W.2. Z2798

JENNER, D., Rifleman, King's Royal Rifle Corps.
He joined in May 1916, and at the conclusion of his training served at various stations on important home defence duties with his Regiment. He did very good work, but owing to medical unfitness was unable to obtain his transfer overseas before the close of the war. He was demobilised in February 1919. Later, contracting illness he unfortunately died on August 6th, 1920.
"His memory is cherished with pride."
26, Elfin Road, Camberwell, S.E.5. Z2799B

JENNER, D. J., Driver, R.F.A.
He volunteered in January 1915, and after six months' training embarked for the Western Front, where he saw much heavy fighting and fought in many engagements, including the Battles of the Somme and Cambrai. In 1917 he proceeded to the Italian Front, and was in action in operations in the Piave and other sectors until the conclusion of hostilities. Returning home in 1919 he was drafted to Ireland, where in 1920 he was still serving. He holds the 1914-15 Star, and the General Service and Victory Medals.
26, Elfin Road, Camberwell, S.E.5. Z2799A

JENNER, H. C., Sapper, R.E.
He joined in February 1917, and landed in France in the following month. He served on special duties in various sectors of the Western Front, and saw much heavy fighting in the Battles of Ypres, Arras, St. Quentin, Passchendaele and during the Retreat and Advance of 1918, and was wounded at Elverdinghe. After the cessation of hostilities he returned home and was demobilised in September 1919. He holds the General Service and Victory Medals.
4, Broughton Street, Battersea Park, S.W.8. Z2800

JENNINGS, R. T., Private, R.A.S.C. (M.T.)
He volunteered in June 1915, and on completing his training was engaged on important duties with his unit at various stations. He did good work as a mechanic, but was unsuccessful in obtaining his transfer overseas owing to medical unfitness for active service, and was demobilised in June 1919.
9, Harris Street, Camberwell, S.E.5. Z4482

JENNINGS, A. E. Rflmn., King's Royal Rifle Corps.
Volunteering in June 1915, he was sent in the following year to the Western Front, and fought in many notable engagements, including the Battles of Ypres, the Somme, Arras and Cambrai. In 1917 he was wounded at Ypres and upon recovery returned to the Field and was taken prisoner at Cambrai on March 21st, 1918. After the cessation of hostilities he was repatriated and subsequently demobilised in March 1919, and holds the General Service and Victory Medals.
11, Westhall Road, Camberwell, S.E.5.   Z2802

JENNINGS, E., Driver, R.F.A.
A Reservist, he was mobilised at the outbreak of war, and shortly afterwards drafted to France, where he fought in several engagements, and was severely wounded in 1917. Evacuated to England, he still remains in hospital suffering from the effects of his wounds. He also served through the South African War, and in addition to the Queen's and King's South African Medals, holds the 1914 Star, and the General Service and Victory Medals.
202, Grosvenor Terrace, Camberwell, S.E.5.   Z2803

JENNINGS, G. J., Private, Northamptonshire Regt.
He joined in March 1916, and after training was in April 1917, sent to the Western Front, where he rendered valuable services with the Labour Corps in the construction of roads and assisting in the transport of ammunition to the front lines. Returning to England on the conclusion of hostilities he was stationed at Nottingham with the Royal Defence Corps, and did further useful work, until demobilised in April 1919. He holds the General Service and Victory Medals.
29, Everett Street, Battersea, S.W.8.   Z2804

JENNINGS, J. H., Sergt.-Major, 2nd Northamptonshire Regiment.
He enlisted in March 1897, and served in the South African War until 1902, and then proceeded to India for a period of four years, he afterwards returned to England and was sent to Malta in 1911, and to Egypt in 1914. In September 1914 he was drafted from Egypt to France, where he fought in several engagements, including the Retreat from Mons, and was wounded in the Battle of Neuve Chapelle. Invalided home for treatment, he returned to the Western Front in 1918, and during the German Offensive of that year was wounded again. Evacuated to England, he received hospital treatment, and upon recovery was discharged in July 1919, as a time-expired man. In addition to the Queen's and King's South African Medals, he holds the Mons Star, and the General Service and Victory Medals.
12, Belham Street, Camberwell, S.E.5.   Z2801

JEPSON, C. J., Engine-Room Artificer, R.N.
He joined in April 1918, and served in H.M.S. PC55, patrolling the Atlantic and convoying troopships and other transports to and from France, and other theatres of war. Prior to joining the Royal Navy he was engaged on work of National importance in connection with the output of munitions. He was demobilised in June 1919, and holds the General Service and Victory Medals.
409, S. Block, Guinness' Buildings, Page's Walk, Grange Road, S.E.1.   Z2625

JESSETT, G. C., Private, 2nd Middlesex Regiment.
He volunteered in October 1914, on attaining military age, and two months later proceeded to the Western Front, where he was unfortunately killed in action in his first engagement on January 22nd, 1915. He was entitled to the 1914–15 Star, and the General Service and Victory Medals.
"He died the noblest death a man may die,
Fighting for God, and right, and liberty."
26, Bromell's Road, Clapham Common, S.W.4.   Z2806B

JESSUP, E. W., Gunner, R.F.A.
He was mobilised from the Reserve in August 1914, and immediately proceeded with his Battery to France, where he saw much heavy fighting and took part in the Retreat from Mons, and the Battles of Ypres, Neuve Chapelle, Loos, Arras, Cambrai and was wounded at Hill 60, and later on the Somme. After the cessation of hostilities he returned to England and was discharged on account of service on April 7th, 1919. He holds the Mons Star, and the General Service and Victory Medals.
45, Acorn Street, Camberwell, S.E.5.   Z4006

JEWELL, A. E., Private, R.A.M.C.
Volunteering in November 1915, he completed his training, and after serving at home for a time was sent to France in January 1917. Whilst on the Western Front he served on special duties at the 3rd General Hospital at Trouville, and did excellent work, tending sick and wounded troops. He holds the General Service and Victory Medals, and was demobilised in July 1919.
5, Warrior Road, Camberwell, S.E.5.   Z1125A

JEWELL, F. W., Shoeing-Smith, R.F.A.
He volunteered in March 1915, and twelve months later proceeded to the Western Front. He fought at the Battles of the Somme, Arras, Ypres, Albert and was gassed during the German Offensive in March 1918. He was demobilised in April 1919, and holds the General Service and Victory Medals.
2, Kennard Street, Battersea, S.W.11.   Z2048B

JEWELL, W., Corporal, R.A.S.C. (M.T.)
Mobilised in August 1914, he was drafted to France, and was engaged with his unit on special duties during the Retreat from Mons, and the Battles of the Marne, the Aisne, Ypres, Arras, Albert, Passchendaele, Dickebusch, Vimy Ridge, Hill 60, Amiens, Armentières, Bullecourt, Delville Wood, Givenchy, and in the Retreat and Advance of 1918. He was demobilised in March 1919, and holds the Mons Star, and the General Service and Victory Medals.
54, Sussex Road, Coldharbour Lane, S.W.9.   Z3475

JIGGINS, H. A., Private, 1st East Surrey Regt.
Volunteering at the outbreak of war, he was almost immediately sent overseas. He fought in the Retreat from Mons, and the subsequent Battles of the Marne, La Bassée and Ypres, where he was wounded. He was sent to hospital at the Base, and two months later rejoined his Battalion in the firing line, and was in action at Ypres and died gloriously on the Field of Battle on May 13th, 1915. He was entitled to the Mons Star, and General Service and Victory Medals.
"A valiant soldier, with undaunted heart he breasted Life's last hill."
20, Grimwade Crescent, Peckham, S.E.15.   Z6403

JOBSON, R., Private, R.A.O.C.
He joined in 1916, and in the same year proceeded to Salonika, where he served on special duties for a period of twelve months. He was then sent to Egypt and was stationed with his unit at Kantara and Ismailia. He returned to England after the cessation of hostilities, and was demobilised in 1919, and holds the General Service and Victory Medals.
215, East Street, Walworth, S.E.17.   Z2809A

JOBSON, W. H., Driver, R.F.A.
He volunteered in 1914, and in the following year was drafted to France. He was in action in many battles, including those of the Somme and Ypres and was wounded near Arras, early in 1916. He was invalided to England and on recovery was sent to Salonika and was engaged in the operations there until demobilised in 1919. He holds the 1914–15 Star, and the General Service and Victory Medals.
215, East Street, Walworth, S.E.17.   Z2809B

JOHNES, C. W., Private, R.M.L.I.
He was serving aboard H.M.S. "Antrim" at the outbreak of hostilities. His ship was then engaged on important convoy duties in the Atlantic Ocean, the North Sea and English Channel, and he was severely wounded in the Raid on Zeebrugge. He was afterwards employed on special duties at Dunkirk until demobilised in April 1919. He holds the 1914–15 Star, and the General Service and Victory Medals.
126, Aylesbury Road, Walworth, S.E.17.   Z2810

JOHNES, G. W., L/Cpl., 7th Buffs (East Kent Regt).
He volunteered in September 1914, and in the following year was drafted to France. During his service on the Western Front he fought in many engagements on the Somme and fell fighting in the Battle of Cambrai on November 20th, 1917. He was entitled to the 1914–15 Star, and the General Service and Victory Medals.
"His life for his Country, his Soul to God."
7, Hillery Road, Walworth, S.E.17.   Z2811A

JOHNSON, A., Driver, R.A.S.C. (M.T.)
He joined in November 1917, and at the conclusion of his training was engaged on important duties, conveying supplies to various parts of England. He did excellent work, but owing to medical unfitness was unable to obtain his transfer overseas, and was in consequence invalided out of the Service in March 1918.
62, Westmacott Street, Camberwell, S.E.5.   Z5548B

JOHNSON, A., Sergt., 7th Norfolk Regiment.
He volunteered in August 1914, and proceeded overseas in the following year. He fought in various sectors of the Western Front, including those of Albert, Loos, Ploegsteert, Ypres and Bullecourt. He was wounded at Pozières and invalided to hospital in England. On recovery he was sent to Ireland, serving on special duties until demobilised in 1919. He holds the 1914–15 Star, and the General Service and Victory Medals. 59, Hubert Grove, Landor Road, S.W.9.   Z2819A

JOHNSON, C. W., Private, Royal Fusiliers.
He joined in February 1917, and two months later was sent to France. In this theatre of war he was in action at the Battles of Messines, Ypres, the Somme, Arras, Lens, Passchendaele, Cambrai and in the Retreat and Advance of 1918, and was twice wounded and gassed. He was demobilised in October 1919, and holds the General Service and Victory Medals. 43, Heygate Street, Walworth, S.E.17.   Z2817

JOHNSON, E., Driver, R.F.A.
Volunteering in 1915, he proceeded overseas in the following
year. Whilst in France he served with his Battery in many
parts of the line, and fought on the Somme, at Bullecourt,
Bapaume, Valenciennes, Grandecourt, and Cambrai. He
was demobilised in 1919, and holds the General Service and
Victory Medals.
59, Hubert Grove, Landor Road, S.W.9.   Z2819B

JOHNSON, F. H., Sapper, R.E.
He volunteered in April 1915, and six months later was
drafted to France. In this theatre of war he was engaged
with his unit on wiring and other special duties, and was
severely wounded on April 20th, 1916. He was taken to
hospital, and on recovery served at various stations on the
Western Front until demobilised in June 1919. He holds
the 1914–15 Star, and the General Service and Victory Medals.
79, Wickersley Road, Lavender Hill, S.W.11.   Z2816

JOHNSON, G., Private, R.A.S.C. (M.T.)
Joining in March 1916, he proceeded to France six months
later. During his service on the Western Front he served
with his unit on special transport duties at Albert, Ypres,
Beaucourt, Arras, the Somme, and did very good work during
the Retreat and Advance of 1918. He holds the General
Service and Victory Medals, and was demobilised in June
1919.
4, Flint Street, Walworth, S.E.17.   Z2818A

JOHNSON, G. F., Sergt., Essex Regiment.
He volunteered at the declaration of war, and was shortly
afterwards sent to France, where he took part in the fighting
at Loos, and was severely wounded. He was invalided to
England, and on recovery was drafted to Egypt. He served
in the British Advance through Palestine and was in action
at the Battles of Gaza, and many other engagements until
the signing of the Armistice. He was demobilised in February
1919, and holds the Queen's and King's South African Medals,
the 1914 Star, and the General Service and Victory Medals.
He has served for twenty-five and a half years with the Colours,
and fought in the South African War.
20, Abyssinia Road, Battersea, S.W.11.   Z2822

JOHNSON, H. T. C., Private, R.A.M.C.
He joined in March 1917, on attaining military age, and after
serving for a time in Ireland was sent to France early in 1918.
With his unit he was employed on special work on hospital
trains, and later was engaged in taking prisoners of war to
Egypt. He also served in hospital ships. After the cessation
of hostilities he proceeded to Germany with the Army of
Occupation, and was stationed on the Rhine. He was demobilised in February 1920, and holds the General Service
and Victory Medals.
26, Cross Street, Clapham, S.W.4.   Z2825

**JOHNSON, H. W., Rifleman, 18th London Regiment
(London Irish Rifles).**
He volunteered in May 1915, at the age of 16 years, and in
the following September was sent to France. In this theatre
of war he was engaged in much fierce fighting, and was severely
wounded at the Battle of Loos in October 1915. He was invalided to hospital, but unhappily his injuries proved fatal,
and he died on November 5th of that year. He was entitled
to the 1914–15 Star, and the General Service and Victory
Medals.
"Courage, bright hopes, and a myriad dreams, splendidly
given."
95, Bridge Road West, Battersea, S.W.11.   Z1621A

JOHNSON, J., Private, 8th Middlesex Regiment.
He volunteered in June 1915, and two months later was
drafted to the Western Front, where he was engaged with
his Battalion in the fighting in various sectors, and was gassed
near Ypres and twice wounded. He was demobilised in
August 1919, and holds the 1914–15 Star, and the General
Service and Victory Medals.
43, Reckitt Road, Chiswick, W.4.   5829C

**JOHNSON, J., Private, Middlesex Regiment and
Air Mechanic, R.A.F.**
He volunteered in 1914, but was shortly afterwards claimed
out owing to his age. He later joined the Royal Air Force
in 1917, and at the conclusion of his training was engaged
on important duties at various stations in England and Ireland, and did excellent work. He was unsuccessful in obtaining his transfer overseas, and was demobilised in December
1918.
26, Stewart's Road, Battersea Park Road, S.W.8.   Z2823

JOHNSON, J. J., Private, 2/19th London Regiment.
He joined in July 1916, and at the conclusion of his training
proceeded to Egypt in November of the same year. He
served with his Battalion in the British Advance through
Palestine and fought in many engagements until the cessation
of hostilities. He was demobilised in January 1920, and holds
the General Service and Victory Medals.
48, Weybridge Street, Battersea, S.W.11.   Z2815

JOHNSON, J., Leading Stoker, R.N.
He was mobilised at the outbreak of hostilities, and served
with the Grand Fleet in the North Sea. His ship was engaged
in the Battles of Jutland, Heligoland Bight, and the Falkland
Islands, and was in action during the operations at the Dardanelles. Aboard H.M.S. "Ajax" he served off the coasts
of Russia, and in 1920 was serving in H.M.S. "Sirdar."
in Italian waters. He holds the 1914–15 Star, and the General
Service and Victory Medals.
10, Ægis Grove, Battersea Park Road, S.W.8.   Z2826A

JOHNSON, J. R., Chief Petty Officer, R.N.
He volunteered in September 1914, and was posted to H.M.S.
"Pembroke," which vessel took part in several engagements
in the English Channel, and was employed on patrol and
convoy duties in the North and Mediterranean Seas. He
holds the 1914–15 Star, and the General Service and Victory
Medals, and in 1920 was serving at Chatham.
93A, Tennyson Street, Wentworth Road, S.W.8.   Z2813C

JOHNSON, J. H., Private, R.A.S.C. (Remounts).
He volunteered in July 1915, and in the same year was sent
to France. Whilst on the Western Front he served at the
Remount Depôt, Le Havre, on special duties, and was also
employed in taking horses up the line. Owing to ill-health
he was invalided to England, and after receiving medical
treatment was discharged as medically unfit for further
service in October 1918. He holds the 1914–15 Star, and
the General Service and Victory Medals.
93A, Tennyson Street, Wentworth Road, S.W.8.   Z2813B

JOHNSON, J. R. W., L/Corporal, R.F.A. and M.F.P.
A Reservist, he was mobilised at the outbreak of hostilities,
and immediately drafted to France. He fought in the Retreat
from Mons, and the Battles of Le Cateau, the Marne, the
Aisne, La Bassée, Neuve Chapelle, Festubert and Loos. In
September 1915 he embarked for Mesopotamia, and was
in action at the Battles of Ctesiphon, and Kut-el-Amara,
and in the attempted reliefs of Kut. He was wounded on the
Tigris in April 1916, and, invalided to England, was transferred
to the Military Foot Police on recovery in May 1918. He
did good work with that unit until demobilised in March
1919. He holds the Mons Star, and the General Service and
Victory Medals.
21, Pepler Road, Peckham, S.E.15.   Z3476

**JOHNSON, J. W., Pte., Queen's (Royal West Surrey
Regiment) and Air Mechanic, R.A.F.**
He volunteered in August 1914, and was immediately sent to
France. There he fought in various engagements and was
severely wounded at Ypres in November 1914. He was invalided to hospital in England and on recovery after prolonged
medical treatment was transferred to the Royal Air Force,
and served on important home duties until demobilised in
February 1919. He holds the 1914 Star, and the General
Service and Victory Medals.
6, Dalyell Road, Landor Road, S.W.9.   Z2820

JOHNSON, W., Private, M.G.C.
He joined in January 1917, and in the following November
proceeded to the Western Front, where he was in action in
many sectors, including those of the Somme and Cambrai. He
was wounded in April 1918, and after receiving treatment
at the Base, was invalided to England, and was in hospital
at Sheffield. He was demobilised in December 1919, and
holds the General Service and Victory Medals.
327, Eversleigh Road, Battersea, S.W.11.   Z2824

JOHNSON, W. E., Corporal, R.A.V.C.
He attested in December 1915, and in the following September
was called up and joined the Royal Army Veterinary Corps.
At the conclusion of his training he served at various stations
on important duties attending to sick and wounded horses,
and also did very good work with the Military Police. He
was demobilised in April 1919.
210, Westmoreland Road, Walworth, S.E.17.   Z2821

JOHNSON, W. E., 1st Class Petty Officer, R.N.
He was mobilised from the Fleet Reserve at the outbreak of
war, and aboard a supply ship did very good work in the
North Sea for some time. He was later engaged on special
anti-aircraft duties at Chatham until the Armistice. He was
demobilised in February 1919, and holds the 1914–15 Star,
and the General Service and Victory Medals.
59A, Emu Road, Battersea Park, S.W.8.   Z2814

**JOHNSON, A. M. (Miss), Nurse, Edmonton Military
Hospital.**
Volunteering for work of National importance, this lady
entered as a probationery nurse at Edmonton Military Hospital
in April 1915, and was later appointed nurse. She rendered
valuable service in this capacity and was mentioned in
Despatches in November 1917 for good work. She died whilst
serving on October 24th, 1918, and was buried in "Heroes'
Corner" in Tottenham Cemetery.
"Her memory is cherished with pride."
93A, Tennyson Street, Wentworth Road, S.W.8.   Z2813A

JOHNSTON, H. E., Sergt., R.F.A.

He volunteered in August 1914, and proceeding to the Western Front in the following year fought in the Battles of Loos, the Somme, Albert, Vimy Ridge, Bullecourt and was wounded at Arras in May 1917 and sent to a Base hospital. Returning to the Field on recovery, he took an active part in several engagements during the Advance of 1918, and was recommended for the Military Medal for working his gun single-handed. He was demobilised in April 1919, and holds the 1914–15 Star, and the General Service and Victory Medals.
48, Clayton Road, Peckham, S.E.15. Z6009A

JOHNSTON, W. E., Private, R.A.M.C.

Volunteering in August 1915, he was drafted to Salonika in the following year and served in the Balkans until the end of the war. During this period he was engaged with the Field Ambulance in the advance across the Struma, Vardar and Doiran fronts, and also carried out important duties in the stores depôt at Salonika. He returned to England for demobilisation in May 1919, and holds the General Service and Victory Medals.
48, Clayton Road, Peckham, S.E.15. Z6009B

JOHNSTONE, R., Corporal, R.E.

He joined in May 1916, and was drafted overseas in the same year. Serving in Egypt he was employed on special duties in connection with operations during the British Advance through Palestine, and was present at many engagements, including the Battle of Gaza and the Fall of Jerusalem. He returned home for demobilisation in February 1920, and holds the General Service and Victory Medals.
54, Stockdale Road, Wandsworth Road, S.W.8. Z2812

JOHNSTONE, S. A., Stoker, R.N.

He joined in January 1916, and at the conclusion of his training was posted to H.M.S. "Redbreast." His ship was employed on important patrol and other duties in the Mediterranean Sea, and was torpedoed whilst serving in the North Sea, but he fortunately was saved. He holds the General Service and Victory Medals, and was still serving in 1920.
4, Stockwell Grove, S.W.9. Z1202A

JOLIN, H., Quarter-Master-Sergt., R.A.S.C.

He volunteered in June 1915, and proceeded overseas in the same month. Serving on the Western Front he was engaged on important transport duties with his unit and owing to illness was sent home in November 1915. Admitted to hospital he was subsequently discharged as medically unfit for further service in August 1916. He had served in the South African War, and in addition to the Queen's and King's Medals for that campaign, holds the 1914–15 Star, and the General Service and Victory Medals.
147A, Wickersley Road, Lavender Hill, S.W.11. Z2827

JOLLEY, F., Driver, R.A.S.C.

He joined in April 1917, and was sent to the Western Front in the same year. He was engaged on important duties in connection with the transport of rations and supplies to the forward areas and did good work during the Retreat and Advance of 1918. When hostilities ended he served at a Base until his return home for demobilisation in January 1920, and holds the General Service and Victory Medals.
3, Victory Square, Camberwell, S.E.5. Z5627B

JOLLEY, W., Private, 1st East Surrey Regiment.

Mobilised on the outbreak of war, he embarked for France shortly afterwards and took part in heavy fighting during the Retreat from Mons and in the Battles of the Marne and the Aisne, and was wounded. On recovery he was sent to Egypt in 1915, and served in operations in the Canal zone. Returning to the Western Front in 1916, he was in action on the Somme and was again wounded. Invalided to England for hospital treatment, he rejoined his unit in the Field and fought in the Battles of Arras and Albert and in subsequent engagements during the Retreat and Advance of 1918. He was demobilised in March 1919, and holds the Mons Star, and the General Service and Victory Medals.
3, Victory Square, Camberwell, S.E.5. Z5627A

JONAS, A. E. (M.M.), Corporal, R.F.A.

Enlisting in 1910, he was serving in South Africa when war broke out and was almost immediately drafted to France. There he fought during the Retreat from Mons and in other notable engagements, and was awarded the Military Medal and two Certificates for conspicuous bravery and devotion to duty in the Field. He was later sent to Italy, where he took part in many operations on the Piave, and was wounded. He holds the Mons Star, and the General Service and Victory Medals, and was demobilised in February 1919.
35, Meyrick Road, Battersea, S.W.11. Z2828

JONES, A. E., Private, M.G.C. (Canadians).

He volunteered in 1915, and in the same year was drafted to the Western Front, where he was engaged in much fighting in the Ypres and Arras sectors. He was reported missing on October 21st, 1916, and was later presumed to have been killed in action on that date. He was entitled to the 1914–15 Star, and the General Service and Victory Medals.
"Whilst we remember the Sacrifice is not in vain."
24, Hollydale Road, Peckham, S.E.15. Z6404A

JONES, A. G., 1st Class Warrant Officer, R.A.O.C.

He volunteered in August 1914, and proceeding to France saw much fighting in the Retreat from Mons and the Battles of the Aisne, the Marne and Poperinghe. During his service overseas he served in many parts of the line and was in action throughout the Retreat and Advance of 1918. He was demobilised in September 1919, and holds the Mons Star, and the General Service and Victory Medals.
20, Crewy's Road, Peckham, S.E.15. Z6269

JONES, A. W., Driver, R.A.S.C. (H.T.)

Joining in February 1918, he proceeded to France in the same year and served until the conclusion of hostilities. During this period he served with the horse transport during the Battles of the Somme and Cambrai, and in the final Allied Advance, and did good work. He returned to England for demobilisation in July 1919, and holds the General Service and Victory Medals.
1, Northall Street, Stockwell, S.W.9. Z2831

JONES, A. W., Corporal, R.E.

He volunteered in August 1915, and in the following year, after completing his course of training, was drafted to France, where he rendered valuable services on the Somme, and at Arras, Ypres, Bullecourt, Armentières, Vimy Ridge, Amiens, St. Quentin and many other operations, almost until hostilities ceased. He was badly gassed during the Advance and was sent to hospital at Boulogne. After his recovery he returned home and was demobilised in January 1919, holding the General Service and Victory Medals.
43, Burchell Road, Peckham, S.E.15. Z6490

JONES, A. W., L/Corporal, 1/2nd London Regt. (Royal Fusiliers).

He was mobilised in August 1914, and was shortly afterwards sent to Malta, when he served until drafted to France in January 1915. Engaged with the Lewis gun section of his platoon, he fought in the Battles of Neuve Chapelle, Loos and the Somme. He gave his life for King and Country at Combles, near Albert, on September 14th, 1916, and was entitled to the 1914–15 Star, and the General Service and Victory Medals.
"A costly sacrifice upon the altar of freedom."
91, Fitzalan Street, Kennington, S.E.11. Z25564B

JONES, C., Rifleman, Rifle Brigade.

He volunteered in December 1914, and in the following year embarked for the Western Front. In the course of his service he was in action in several engagements, and was severely wounded in the Battle of Ypres. Sent home, owing to his injuries, he received hospital treatment and was invalided out of the Army in July 1916. He holds the 1914–15 Star, and the General Service and Victory Medals.
76, South Street, Walworth, S.E.17. Z2838

JONES, E., Private, 2nd Suffolk Regiment.

He volunteered in October 1915, and was engaged on important duties with his Battalion until January 1918, when he was sent to France. He served in several engagements during the German offensive and was taken prisoner in March 1918 at Monchy-le-Prieux. During his captivity he was made to dig trenches and load and unload supplies behind the German lines until repatriated after the Armistice. Owing to illness contracted whilst a prisoner of war, he was admitted to hospital in England, and after treatment was demobilised in April 1919. He holds the General Service and Victory Medals. 34, St. John's Hill Grove, Battersea, S.W.11. Z2832

JONES, F., Driver, R.F.A.

He joined in May 1916, and was drafted to the Western Front in the same year. He served in the Battles of Arras, Ypres, Albert, Vimy Ridge, St. Eloi, Amiens, Bapaume and during the Advance of 1918. He was gassed and wounded twice in the course of operations, and on the second occasion was sent to hospital in France and afterwards to England. He was demobilised in March 1919, and holds the General Service and Victory Medals.
97, Sussex Road, Coldharbour Lane, S.W.9. Z3092

JONES, F. H., Private, 8th Duke of Cornwall's Light Infantry.

He volunteered in 1914, and in the following year proceeded overseas. Whilst on the Western Front he was in action at Hill 60, Loos, Ypres, the Somme and Arras, and in 1917 was drafted to Salonika, where he fought in the engagements on the Doiran front. He returned to England after the cessation of hostilities and was demobilised in 1919. He holds the 1914–15 Star, and the General Service and Victory Medals.
24, Hollydale Road, Peckham, S.E.15. Z6404B

JONES, G., A.B., Royal Navy.

Volunteering in February 1915, he was posted to H.M.S. "King George V," and served in that vessel throughout the war. During this period his ship was engaged on important patrol duties in the North Sea and was in action in several engagements with enemy craft. He was demobilised in January 1919, and holds the 1914–15 Star, and the General Service and Victory Medals.
33, Mundella Road, Wandsworth Road, S.W.8. Z2834B

JONES, G. E. (D.C.M., M.M.), Sergt., 3rd (Prince of Wales') Dragoon Guards.

A Regular, having enlisted in 1900, he was mobilised on the outbreak of war and was almost immediately drafted to France. He took an active part in heavy fighting during the Retreat from Mons and in the Battles of the Marne, the Aisne, Arras, Ypres and Neuve Chapelle, and was also in action in several engagements during the Advance of 1918. He was awarded the Distinguished Conduct Medal and the Military Medal for conspicuous gallantry and devotion to duty in the Field, and was twice wounded in the course of his service. Sent home on account of his injuries, the hospital ship in which he was crossing was torpedoed, but he was fortunately rescued. He was discharged on account of service in April 1919, and holds the Mons Star, and the General Service and Victory Medals.

121, Farmer's Road, Camberwell, S.E.5.　　Z2842

JONES, G. J., Private, R.A.S.C. (M.T.)

Volunteering in March 1915, he was sent later in that year to Egypt, where he was rendered valuable transport services at Alexandria. He was afterwards transferred to the Balkan area and did excellent service of a similar nature at Monastir, and on the Vardar and Struma fronts, until hostilities ceased. He was demobilised in May 1919 after returning to England, and holds the 1914–15 Star, and the General Service and Victory Medals.

33, Burchell Road, Peckham, S.E.15.　　Z6491

JONES, H., Private, Royal Marines.

He joined in 1917, although exempt from military service as a Government worker in the London Docks, and after completing his training was engaged with the Royal Marine Engineers on important coastal defence duties at Shoreham. He rendered valuable services, but was unable to obtain a transfer overseas before the cessation of hostilities, and was demobilised in January 1919.

26, Henshaw Street, Walworth, S.E.17.　　Z2837

JONES, H. W., Rifleman, 21st London Regiment (1st Surrey Rifles).

Volunteering in November 1914, he completed his training, and served at various depôts, engaged on guard and other important duties with his unit. Owing to ill-health he did not obtain his transfer overseas, but rendered valuable services until demobilised in March 1919.

56, Vaughan Road, Camberwell, S.E.5.　　Z6270

JONES, J., Private, 1/2nd London Regiment (Royal Fusiliers).

Joining in March 1916, he embarked for the Western Front in the following year, and serving with his Battalion in many parts of the line was engaged in heavy fighting until taken prisoner on August 17th, 1917. He died two days later, whilst in captivity in Germany, and was entitled to the General Service and Victory Medals.

" His memory is cherished with pride."

25, Evelina Road, Peckham, S.E.15.　　Z6191

JONES, J., Private, R.A.S.C.

He volunteered in August 1914, and in the following March proceeded to the Western Front. He was engaged on important duties in connection with the transport of ammunition and supplies during the Battles of Neuve Chapelle, Festubert, Loos, the Somme, Ypres, Passchendaele, Cambrai and Havrincourt, and in several other engagements. After the Armistice he was sent into Germany with the Army of Occupation, and was stationed on the Rhine. Returning to England for demobilisation in May 1919, he holds the 1914–15 Star, and the General Service and Victory Medals.

70, Wickersley Road, Lavender Hill, S.W.11.　　Z2840

JONES, J., Gunner, R.G.A.

Joining in April 1917, he was drafted to France in the following March, and served with his Battery in the Battles of Ypres and Messines, and was wounded in June 1918. Sent to hospital he rejoined his unit, on recovery and fought during the Advance of 1918. Invalided home owing to illness he received medical treatment, and was demobilised in March 1919. He holds the General Service and Victory Medals.

18, Dartnell Road, Camberwell, S.E.5.　　Z5628

JONES, J., Private, Duke of Cornwall's Light Infantry and Dorsetshire Regiment.

Volunteering in August 1914, he was sent to France two months later and fought in several engagements and was wounded at the Battles of Hill 60 and Festubert. He was invalided to England and after receiving hospital treatment was drafted to Mesopotamia in 1916. He was in action in much of the fighting in the Middle East, and was wounded for the third time at the capture of Baghdad. He later saw service in Egypt and was severely wounded at Damascus. He subsequently died from the effects of his injuries on December 15th, 1918, and was buried at that place. He was entitled to the 1914 Star, and the General Service and Victory Medals.

" The path of duty was the way to glory."

9, Broughton Street, Battersea Park, S.W.8.　　Z2836A

JONES, J., Gunner, R.F.A.

He volunteered in April 1915, and in the same year embarked for France. Serving with the Howitzer Battery he fought in several important engagements, including the Battles of Loos, Ypres, and the Somme. He gave his life for the freedom of England in the Battle of Vimy Ridge, on April 21st, 1917, and was entitled to the 1914–15 Star, and the General Service and Victory Medals.

' Great deeds cannot die : They with the Sun and Moon renew their light for ever."

9, Broughton Street, Battersea Park, S.W.8.　　Z2836B

JONES, P. W., Private, 19th London Regiment.

He volunteered in December 1915, and in the following year proceeded to Salonika. During his service in the Balkans, he was in action in the Advance on the Struma and Doiran fronts, and in the Battle of Monastir. In 1918, he was sent to Egypt, and was engaged in heavy fighting until the Armistice. He returned to England in 1919, and was demobilised in March of that year, and holds the General Service and Victory Medals.

15, Love Lane, Stockwell Road, S.W.9.　　Z2829B

JONES, R., Private, Labour Corps.

He joined in 1916, and drafted to France in the same year was engaged on important duties in various canteens, and rendered valuable services throughout the war. He served in the South African war, and in addition to the Queen's and King's Medals for that campaign, holds the General Service and Victory Medals, and was demobilised in 1919.

69, Lollard Street, Kennington, S.E.11.　　Z25684A

JONES, R. W., Driver, R.F.A.

Volunteering in August 1914, he was shortly afterwards sent to France, and served during the Retreat from Mons, and in many subsequent engagements, including the Battles of the Marne, and the Somme. Owing to illness he was invalided to hospital in England, and on recovery was engaged on home defence duties. He was discharged on account of service in November 1918, and holds the Mons Star, and the General Service and Victory Medals.

10, Dickens Street, Wandsworth Road, S.W.8.　　Z2839

JONES, S. E. A., Corporal, Rifle Brigade.

Mobilised from the Army Reserve on the outbreak of war he embarked for France shortly afterwards, and took part in heavy fighting during the Retreat from Mons, and in the Battle of Le Cateau, and was twice wounded. Sent home on account of his injuries he received hospital treatment, and was subsequently discharged as medically unfit for further service in December 1915. He holds the Mons Star, and the General Service and Victory Medals.

32, Trollope Street, Battersea Park, S.W.8.　　Z2843

JONES, S. H., Private, Welch Regiment.

He volunteered in July 1915, and in the following year was drafted overseas. Serving in Mesopotamia he fought in the Battle of Sanna-i-Yat, in operations in connection with the attempted relief of Kut, at Khan Baghdadie, and in the occupation of Mosul. Returning to England on the termination of hostilities he was demobilised in February 1920, and holds the General Service and Victory Medals.

15, Love Lane, Stockwell Road, S.W.9.　　Z2829A

JONES, T. A., Driver, R.F.A.

Volunteering in January 1915, he was sent to the Western Front four months later and served there throughout the war. During this period he was in action in many important engagements, including the Battles of Loos, and the Somme, and was wounded. After the Armistice he proceeded with the Army of Occupation into Germany and was stationed on the Rhine. He returned home for demobilisation in March 1919, and holds the 1914–15 Star, and the General Service and Victory Medals.

15, Benfield Street, Battersea, S.W.11.　　Z2830A

JONES, W., Private, 23rd London Regiment.

A Territorial, having enlisted in 1912, he was mobilised when war broke out, and proceeding to France in March 1915, served there for over four years. He fought in the Battles of St. Eloi, Festubert, Loos, Vimy Ridge, and during the Retreat of 1918. He was also in action in the Battle of Bapaume, and in several other engagements of the closing stages of the war. Demobilised in May 1919, he holds the 1914–15 Star, and the General Service and Victory Medals.

20, Darley Road, Wandsworth Common, S.W.11.　　Z2835

JONES, W., Pte., 22nd London Regt. (The Queen's).

He was mobilised on the declaration of war, and served at various stations on special duties with his unit, and rendered valuable services. Owing to an accident which incapacitated him for further military service, he was invalided out of the Army in 1917. He was then employed at Woolwich Arsenal on clerical work until the end of the war.

69, Lollard Street, Kennington, S.E.11.　　TZ25684B

JONES, W. F., Private, 4th Gordon Highlanders.

He joined in July 1917, and in the following February was drafted to the Western Front, where he was in action in several engagements during the Retreat and Advance of 1918. On the conclusion of hostilities he was sent into Germany with the Army of Occupation, and served there for upwards of a year. He was demobilised in October 1919, on his return to England, and holds the General Service and Victory Medals.
91, Fitzalan Street, Kennington, S.E.11.　　Z25564A

JONES, W. H., Gunner, R.F.A.

Volunteering in April 1915, and proceeding to France later in the year, he was engaged in heavy fighting on the Somme, at Ypres, Arras, Albert, and Passchendaele. Transferred to Italy in 1917, he fought on the Trentino, the Piave, and the Asiago Plateaux, and was in action in the final Allied Advance in that theatre of war. Returning to England he was demobilised in February 1919, and holds the 1914-15 Star, and the General Service and Victory Medals.
53, Clayton Road, Peckham, S.E.15.　　Z6271

JONES, W. H., Private, 11th Essex Regiment.

He joined in February 1917, and embarked for France in the following January. Whilst overseas he served with his Battalion in various parts of the line, and was engaged in heavy fighting during the Retreat and Advance of 1918. He was killed in action on September 17th, 1918, and was entitled to the General Service and Victory Medals.
"His life for his Country, his Soul to God."
74, Westmacott Street, Camberwell, S.E.5.　　Z3091

JONES, W. R., L/Cpl., 1st South Lancashire Regt.

A Regular soldier, having enlisted in September 1908, he was serving in India when war broke out and in 1917 was drafted to Mesopotamia. He was engaged on special duties as Battalion postman throughout the course of hostilities, and, returning home for demobilisation in November 1919, holds the General Service and Victory Medals.
15, Benfield Street, Battersea, S.W.11.　　Z2830B

JONES, W. T., Rifleman, Rifle Brigade.

He joined in 1916, and whilst serving with his unit at Eastchurch was injured during an hostile air raid in December 1917. On recovery he was sent to France and fought in several important engagements until wounded in the Battle of Cambrai on September 1st, 1918. Sent to hospital in England owing to his injuries, he was discharged in consequence in March 1919, and holds the General Service and Victory Medals.
135, Gordon Road, Nunhead, S.E.15.　　Z6004

JONES, W. T. Private, 1st London Regiment (Royal Fusiliers).

Joining in 1917, in the following year he was sent to the Western Front, and served in various sectors. He was in action in several engagements during the Retreat and Advance of 1918, and contracting illness after the Armistice was admitted to a Base hospital, and later sent to England for treatment. He was subsequently discharged as medically unfit for service in April 1919, and holds the General Service and Victory Medals.
40, Sussex Road, Coldharbour Lane, S.W.9.　　Z2841

JORDAN, H., Corporal, Northumberland Fusiliers.

He enlisted in February 1914, and shortly after the declaration of war was sent to France. He fought in many engagements, including those of the Marne, Loos and Ypres. In 1915, transferred to the Dardanelles, he took part in heavy fighting in that theatre of war and was severely wounded. Invalided to England he received hospital treatment and was discharged unfit for further service in April 1919. He holds the 1914-15 Star, and the General Service and Victory Medals.
33, Gonsalva Road, Wandsworth Road, S.W.8.　　Z2844

JORDAN, J., Private, Cheshire Regiment and Labour Corps, and Air Mechanic, R.A.F.

He joined in November 1917, after five unsuccessful attempts to enlist, and completing his training, served at various stations engaged on important duties with his unit. He was not successful in obtaining his transfer to a theatre of war previous to the cessation of hostilities, but rendered valuable services until discharged in September 1918.
18, Moat Place, Stockwell Road, S.W.9.　　Z2845

JORDAN, J., Private, 1/20th London Regiment.

He volunteered in January 1916, and was drafted to the Western Front in May of the following year. During his service overseas he fought at the Battles of the Somme and Merville and through the German Offensive and Allied Advance of 1918. He returned to England and was demobilised in March 1919, and holds the General Service and Victory Medals.
32, Langton Road, Vassall Road, S.W.9.　　Z5107

JOSLAND, F. C. J., Rifleman, 21st London Regt. (1st Surrey Rifles).

He volunteered in April 1915, and proceeding to France in the same year served in various sectors. He was in action in the Battles of Festubert, Loos, the Somme, Lens, Lys and Cambrai, and in engagements during the Retreat and Advance of 1918. Returning home after the signing of the Armistice he was demobilised in January 1919, and holds the 1914-15 Star, and the General Service and Victory Medals.
38, Parkstone Road, Peckham, S.E.15.　　Z6143B

JOYCE, C. P., Leading Seaman, R.N.R.

A Reservist, he was called up at the outbreak of war, and was sent to Antwerp and served there until the city was captured by the Germans, on which occasion he crossed the Dutch Frontier and was interned in Holland until after the cessation of hostilities, when he was repatriated. He was discharged in February 1920, and holds the 1914 Star, and the General Service and Victory Medals.
9, Perrers Road, Hammersmith, W.6.　　11136A

JUDD, S., Private, M.G.C.

He joined in June 1916, and was sent to France four months later. During his service overseas he fought in many engagements of note, including the Somme, Beaumont-Hamel, Arras, Monchy, and was in action throughout the German Offensive and Allied Advance of 1918, and was wounded. He was demobilised in December 1918, and holds the General Service and Victory Medals.
32, Duffield Street, Battersea, S.W.11.　　Z2807

JOYCE, J. G., Rifleman, 9th London Regiment (Queen Victoria's Rifles).

He joined in August 1916, and embarking for the Western Front in the following year served in many parts of the line, where heavy fighting took place. He gave his life for King and Country at Arras on May 3rd, 1917, and was entitled to the General Service and Victory Medals.
"Great deeds cannot die :
They with the Sun and Moon renew their light for ever."
111, St. Philip Street, Battersea Park, S.W.8.　　Z2846

JUKES, G., Private, 2nd Bedfordshire Regiment.

He volunteered in September 1914, and proceeding to France in the following April fought in many important engagements. He was unfortunately killed in action in June 1915, and was entitled to the 1914-15 Star, and the General Service and Victory Medals.
"He died the noblest death a man may die,
Fighting for God, and right, and liberty."
15, Wickersley Road, Lavender Hill S.W.11.　　Z2268A

JUKES, J. T. A., Sergt., 1st Bedford Regiment.

A Reservist, he was mobilised and sent to France at the outbreak of hostilities, and was in action in the Retreat from Mons, the Battles of La Bassée, Givenchy, Ypres, I and II, and Arras. He was severely wounded at Delville Wood on July 27th, 1916, during the first British Offensive on the Somme, and returning to England received hospital treatment. He was eventually invalided out of the Service in November 1917, and holds the Mons Star, and the General Service and Victory Medals.
25, Dashwood Road, Wandsworth Road, S.W.8.　　Z2808

JUNEMAN, J., Leading Signalman, R.N.

He enlisted in May 1906, and in August 1914 was serving in H.M. Submarine "E. 39," which vessel was engaged on important duties in many waters, including the North and Baltic Seas. In 1918, his ship was in action against the Bolshevist Fleet. He was demobilised in October 1919, and holds the 1914-15 Star, and the General Service and Victory Medals.
3E, Lewis Buildings, Camberwell, S.E.5.　　Z6402

K

KALEY, H., Gunner. R.F.A.

He volunteered in August 1914, and in July of the following year was sent to France. He took part in the severe fighting at Hill 60, Ypres, Vimy Ridge, the Ancre, Passchendaele, and in many engagements in the Retreat and Advance of 1918. He was demobilised in August 1920, after eighteen months' service in Ireland, holding the 1914-15 Star, and the General Service and Victory Medals.
35, Grant Road, Battersea, S.W.11.　　Z2847

KASPER, C. A., Corporal, R.E.

He was serving at the outbreak of war, having enlisted in 1908, and was shortly afterwards sent to France, where he rendered valuable services in numerous engagements, including those at Ypres, Neuve Chapelle, Festubert and Loos. He was afterwards engaged for a time on mining work, and subsequently was employed on special duties at the Base. He was demobilised in March 1919, holding the 1914 Star, and the General Service and Victory Medals.
32, Power Street, Wandsworth Road, S.W.8.　　Z2848

KAVANAUGH, F. J., Corporal, R.M.L.I.

He was serving at the outbreak of war, and joined the Grand Fleet in the North Sea. He was under orders for the Dardanelles and later took part in the Battle of Jutalnd in H.M.S. " Tyne " and in various other engagements until hostilities ceased. In 1920 he was still serving in H.M.S. " Lowestoft " in South African waters, and holds the 1914-15 Star, and the General Service and Victory Medals.

48, Caldew Street, Camberwell, S.E.5. Z5790

KEANE, A. E. (D.C.M.), Sergt.-Major, Military Mounted Police.

Having previously served for twenty-one years he volunteered in September 1914, and in the following year was sent to the Dardanelles, where he fought at the Landing at Suvla Bay, and in many subsequent engagements until the Evacuation. He afterwards proceeded to Egypt and thence to Salonika, where he did gallant service on the Struma front. He returned home for leave, but shortly afterwards was sent to France, and served at Ypres, Valenciennes, St. Quentin, and in many other operations in the Retreat and Advance of 1918. He was mentioned in Despatches by General Sir Charles Monro for gallant and distinguished service with the Mediterranean Expeditionary Force, and was awarded the Distinguished Conduct Medal for his excellent work. He also holds the Soudan (British) and Soudan (Khedive's) Medals, the Queen's and King's South African Medals, the 1914-15 Star, and the General Service, Victory, and Long Service and Good Conduct Medals. He was demobilised in March 1919.

27, Shorncliffe Road, Walworth, S.E.17. Z2849

KEARNS, A. W., L/Corporal, R.A.S.C. (M.T.)

He joined in June 1916, and was drafted to the Western Front in the same month. He was engaged with the water supply column in various sectors of the line, and rendered valuable services. He later proceeded with the Army of Occupation to Germany, and was engaged on clerical duties until demobilised in March 1919. He holds the General Service and Victory Medals.

57, Cronin Road, Peckham S.E.15. Z5629B

KEEBLE, A. L., Private, 22nd London Regiment (Queen's).

He joined in May 1918, and in October of the same year, after the completion of his training, was drafted to the Western Front, where he was engaged in various sectors in Belgium on important duties with his unit. He returned home and was demobilised in June 1919, holding the General Service and Victory Medals.

47, Mordaunt Street, Stockwell, S.W.9. Z2851B

KEEBLE, J., Private, 1st Bedfordshire Regiment.

He volunteered in 1915, and was posted to the 3rd Middlesex Regiment. He was later transferred to the 1st Bedfordshire Regiment, and proceeding to France in May of the same year took part in the Battle of Ypres. He afterwards contracted fever and was invalided home. On his recovery he was drafted to India, where he rendered valuable services until his return home for demobilisation in November 1919. He holds the 1914-15 Star, and the General Service and Victory Medals.

100, Surrey Lane, Battersea, S.W.11. Z2850

KEEBLE, R. W., Private, 2/12th City of London Volunteer Regiment (Anti-Aircraft Section).

He joined the City Volunteer Regiment immediately war broke out, and was attached to the Anti-Aircraft Section. He did excellent service throughout the war, particularly during air-raids, when he was sometimes on duty for twenty-four hours continuously. He was demobilised in 1919.

21, Sunwell Street, Peckham, S.E.15. Z6493

KEEBLE, W. A., Pte., 24th London Regt. (Queen's).

He volunteered in September 1915, and was sent to France in the following year. He took part in the severe fighting at Vimy Ridge, the Somme, the Ancre, Arras, and Messines. He was unfortunately killed in action at Ypres on June 8th, 1917, and was entitled to the General Service and Victory Medals.

" Whilst we remember the Sacrifice is not in vain."

71, Sterndale Road, Wandsworth Road, S.W.8. Z2853

KEEFE, B. J., Driver, R.F.A.

He was serving at the outbreak of war and shortly afterwards proceeded to France, where he took part in the severe fighting at Mons, the Marne, the Aisne, La Bassée, Loos, Albert, the Somme, Arras, and Cambrai, and was twice wounded. He also served with distinction in the Retreat and Advance of 1918. He afterwards volunteered for duty in Russia, and did a year's active service at Archangel. He was demobilised in October 1919, and holds the Mons Star, and the General Service and Victory Medals.

1, High Park Crescent, Aylesbury Road, Walworth, S.E.17. Z2854

KEEFFE, S. W., Private, Seaforth Highlanders.

Volunteering in March 1915, he was sent to France in the following month and took part in the heavy fighting at Ypres and Loos. In 1916 he was transferred to Egypt, and thence to Mesopotamia, where he did excellent service in various engagements, and was wounded. In 1917 he proceeded to India, and was engaged on important garrison duties until his return home for demobilisation in January 1919. He holds the 1914-15 Star, and the General Service and Victory Medals.

128, Aylesbury Road, Walworth, S.E.17. Z2855

KEEN, A. J. (D.C.M.), Sergt., R.G.A. and R.F.A.

He volunteered in April 1915, and in December of the same year crossed to France, where he took part in much severe fighting on the Somme, and was wounded and invalided home. On his recovery he returned to France and served with the R.G.A. in the Retreat and Advance of 1918. He was awarded the Distinguished Conduct Medal for great bravery in the Field, and also holds the 1914-15 Star, and the General Service and Victory Medals. He was demobilised in January 1919.

48, Theatre Street, Battersea, S.W.11. Z2856

KEEN, D., Private, Queen's (Royal West Surrey Regiment) and Labour Corps.

He joined in February 1917, and proceeded to France with the Queen's (Royal West Surrey Regiment) in the same month. He rendered valuable services in the Battles of Vimy Ridge, Ypres and Cambrai, and owing to ill-health returned home and was transferred to the Labour Corps. He was afterwards engaged on various important home duties until demobilised in February 1919. He holds the General Service and Victory Medals.

23, Barmore Street, Battersea, S.W.11. Z2858

KEEN, J. W., Private, 1st East Surrey Regiment.

Volunteering in August 1914, he was sent to the Western Front in November of the same year. He took part in the severe fighting at Hill 60, Vimy Ridge, the Somme, Arras, and in other engagements, and after being severely wounded at Fresnoy in June 1917, was invalided home. He was discharged as medically unfit for further service in February 1918, and holds the 1914 Star, and the General Service and Victory Medals.

132, Dalyell Road, Stockwell, S.W.9. Z2857

KEENAN, A., Wireless Operator, Merchant Service.

He was in the Merchant Service when war broke out, and during the period of hostilities, was engaged in H.M.S. " Vigilant," s.s. " City of Marseilles," and one of H.M. Mine-sweepers. In the course of his service, he was engaged on important mine-sweeping duties in the North Sea and the Mediterranean, and also in H.M.S. " Vigilant " on coastal defence, and did valuable work until demobilised in 1919. He holds the General Service and Victory, and Mercantile Marine War Medals.

19, Neville Street, Vauxhall, S.E.11. Z25571

KEENAN, W. T., Corporal, Middlesex Regiment.

Mobilised at the commencement of hostilities, he was sent to the Western Front, and fought in the Retreat from Mons, and the Battles of the Marne, Le Cateau, and La Bassée. In October 1914, he was severely wounded in action at Ypres, and was invalided to a hospital in England. He returned to France in 1916, and again took part in several important engagements, but was wounded a second time at Messines in June 1917. After his recovery, he rejoined his unit and served in the concluding stages of the war engaged on duties of an important nature on the lines of communication. He was demobilised in March 1919, and holds the Mons Star, and the General Service and Victory Medals.

2, St. James' Grove, Battersea, S.W.11. Z2859

KELLIE, A., Private, R.A.S.C. and Tank Corps.

He joined on attaining military age in July 1916, and a year later was drafted to the Western Front. Whilst in this theatre of war he took part in the fighting at Ypres, Cambrai, the Somme, Amiens, and Bapaume. In October 1918, he was invalided to King's College Hospital, suffering from shell-shock, and was under treatment for some weeks. He was demobilised in February, 1919, and holds the General Service and Victory Medals.

22, Charleston Street, Walworth, S.E.17. Z2860C

KELLIE, J. M., Cpl., 1st Highland Light Infantry.

Volunteering at the commencement of hostilities, he was drafted to France after completing his course of training and was taken prisoner whilst in action near La Bassée in December 1914. For three years, he was in a detention camp at Wittenberg, and in March 1918 was sent to Holland, where he remained until his release at the signing of Armistice. He was demobilised in May 1919, and in 1920 was employed at the British Legation in Holland. He holds the 1914 Star, and the General Service and Victory Medals.

22, Charleston Street, Walworth, S.E.17 Z2860A

KELLIE, T. A., Private, King's Own Royal Lancaster Regiment.
Mobilised at the commencement of hostilities, he was quickly drafted to the Western Front, and soon afterwards gave his life for King and Country at the Battle of Ypres on October 13th, 1914. He was entitled to the 1914 Star, and the General Service and Victory Medals
" The path of duty was the way to glory."
22, Charleston Street, Walworth, S.E.17.   Z2860B

KELLIER, A. J., L/Corporal, Middlesex Regiment.
Joining in January 1918, he was sent to France immediately upon the completion of his training. After taking part in the concluding operations of the war he was sent to Germany with the Army of Occupation, and in 1920 was still serving at Cologne on Regimental postal duties. He holds the General Service and Victory Medals.
85, Westmacott Street, Camberwell, S.E.5.   Z4007B

KELLIER, J., Private, M.G.C.
He volunteered in August 1915, and at the conclusion of his training crossed to France. Hes service in this theatre of war lasted until the termination of hostilities, during which time he took part as a gunner in many of the principal battles. He was demobilised in February 1919, and holds the 1914-15 Star, and the General Service and Victory Medals.
85, Westmacott Street, Camberwell, S.E.5.   Z4007A

KELLIHER, D., Sergt., Grenadier Guards.
He enlisted in January 1897, and before the late war served in Nova Scotia, Jamaica, and in South Africa. After the outbreak of hostilities he was drafted to France, and landed at Zeebrugge in October 1914. In the course of his service, he fought in many of the principal battles, and did most valuable work with his unit overseas until August 1918. He was demobilised in February 1919, and holds the Queen's and King's South African Medals, the Mons Star, and the General Service, Victory, and Long Service, and Good Conduct Medals.
1, Southolm Street, Battersea, S.W.11.   Z2861

KELLOW, F. J., Private, King's (Liverpool Regt.)
He volunteered in November 1915, and until January 1918, when he was drafted to France, was engaged on duties of an important nature with his unit. Whilst overseas, he fought in the second Battles of the Somme, the Aisne, and the Marne, and on September 8th, 1918 he gave his life for the freedom of England at the fourth Battle of Ypres. He was entitled to the General Service and Victory Medals.
" Thinking that remembrance, though unspoken, may reach him where he sleeps."
14, Lingham Street, Clapham Road, S.W.9.   Z2862

KELLY, B., Rifleman, Rifle Brigade.
He volunteered in September 1914, and in the same year was sent to France, where he took part in the severe fighting at Ypres, and in many other important engagements. He was unfortunately killed in action in February 1916, and was entitled to the 1914-15 Star, and the General Service and Victory Medals.
" And doubtless he went in splendid company."
36, Goulden Street, Battersea, S.W.11.   Z2863A

KELLY, G., Private, 9th Royal Sussex Regiment.
He volunteered in February 1915, and in August of the same year was sent to the Western Front, where he took part in the Battles of Loos, the Somme, Arras, Ypres, and Bapaume, and was twice wounded. He was invalided home in consequence and was afterwards transferred to the Labour Corps. He was demobilised in June 1919, holding the 1914-15 Star, and the General Service and Victory Medals.
20, Caspian Street, Camberwell, S.E.5.   TZ5552

KELLY, J., Engine Room Artificer, R.N., H.M.S. "Savage."
He joined in 1916, and during his service in the North Sea and the Mediterranean was engaged on important patrol duties. He was in the " Cornwallis " when that vessel was torpedoed in January 1917, and was discharged later in the same year in consequence of an injury to his eyes, which rendered him unfit for further service. He holds the General Service and Victory Medals.
49, Heaton Road, Peckham Rye, S.E.15.   Z5793

KELLY, J., Rifleman, Rifle Brigade.
He joined in May 1916, and after completing his training was drafted to the Western Front. He took part in the heavy fighting at Bullecourt, and being wounded there was invalided home. On his recovery he returned to France, and while in action on the Somme was again wounded. He was still serving in 1920, and holds the General Service and Victory Medals.
36, Goulden Street, Battersea, S.W.11.   Z2863B

KELLY, T. D., Rifleman, King's Royal Rifle Corps.
He volunteered in 1914, and was sent to France in the following year. He took part in the severe fighting at Ypres, the Somme, Arras, and Cambrai, and was wounded, but afterwards served in the Retreat and Advance of 1918. He was demobilised in 1919 after his return home, holding the 1914-15 Star, and the General Service and Victory Medals.
25, Mundella Road, Wandsworth Road, S.W.8.   Z2864

KELSEY, A., Gunner, R.F.A.
Joining in March 1916, he was sent to France in the same year after the conclusion of his training. He took part in much heavy fighting at the Somme, Ypres and Cambrai, and in other engagements, and in 1918 was transferred to Italy where he was in action on the Piave Front. He was demobilised in March 1919, after his return home, and holds the General Service and Victory Medals.
40, Radnor Terrace, South Lambeth, S.W.8.   Z2865

KEMBLE, B., Private, R.A.M.C.
After having previously volunteered and been rejected five times, he was accepted for service in August 1917, and soon afterwards was drafted to Salonika, where he rendered valuable services in various capacities, chiefly on the Doiran front. After the Armistice he did excellent work in Russia and Constantinople until his return to England. During his service in the East he suffered from malaria. He was demobilised in February 1920, and holds the General Service and Victory Medals.
86, Maysoule Road, Battersea, S.W.11.   Z2866

KEMP, F. M. J., Private, Labour Corps.
Joining in July 1917, he was sent to France in the same year. He was engaged on important duties in various sectors in connection with defence works and road making, and rendered valuable services. He returned home and was demobilised in February 1920, and holds the General Service and Victory Medals.
64, Neate Street, Camberwell, S.E.5.   Z5108

KEMP, G., Private, R.A.S.C. (M.T.)
He volunteered in 1915, and shortly afterwards was sent to France. He was engaged as a motor despatch rider and later as motor ambulance driver, and served in many sectors until hostilities ceased. After the Armistice he was taken ill with appendicitis from which he unfortunately, died, on June 24th, 1919.
" His memory is cherished with pride."
63, Greyhound Road, Fulham, W.6.   T15026A

KEMP, G. H., C.Q.M.S., 21st London Regiment (1st Surrey Rifles).
He was mobilised in August 1914, and in March of the following year crossed to France, where he took a prominent part in the heavy fighting at Givenchy, Vimy Ridge, the Somme, Messines, Passchendaele and Cambrai. He also served in many important engagements in the Retreat and Advance of 1918. He was demobilised in February 1919, holding the 1914-15 Star, and the General Service and Victory Medals.
46, Pepler Road, Peckham, S.E.15.   Z3479

KEMP, H. J., Private, 1st London Regiment (Royal Fusiliers).
He joined in August 1916, and on the completion of his training was drafted to France, where he served with great credit. He took part in the engagements at Vimy Ridge, Arras and Cambrai, and was wounded in August 1918 in the Advance of the Allies. He was demobilised in January 1919, after his return home, and holds the General Service and Victory Medals.
8, Pownall Terrace, Kennington Road, S.E.11.   Z25489

KEMP, J., Private, 42nd Australian Infantry (Queensland).
He volunteered in 1914, and in the following year proceeded to France. He took part in much severe fighting at Ypres and Loos, and being wounded in action was invalided to England. On his recovery he returned to France and fought in the Battles of the Somme, Lens, Passchendaele and Cambrai. He also served in the Retreat and Advance of 1918. He was demobilised in 1919, holding the 1914-15 Star, and the General Service and Victory Medals.
15, Copeland Avenue, Peckham Rye, S.E.15.   Z5630

KEMP, W. C., Corporal, 23rd London Regiment.
Volunteering in May 1915, he was sent to France in the same year. He took part in several engagements and was gassed at the Battle of Loos and invalided home. On his recovery he returned to France and served with distinction throughout the remainder of the war. He was demobilised in April 1919, holding the 1914-15 Star, and the General Service and Victory Medals.
25, Henley Street, Battersea, S.W.11.   Z2867

KEMP, W. H., Private, 22nd London Regiment (Queen's) and Essex Regiment.

He joined in June 1917, and after proceeding to France in the same year took part in the Battle of Cambrai. In consequence of severe illness he was invalided home, and on his recovery was drafted to Egypt, where he remained until April 1920. He then returned home, and was demobilised, holding the General Service and Victory Medals.

21, Milford Street, Wandsworth Road, S.W.8.   Z2868

KEMPTON, F. C., A/Sergt., Royal Welch Fusiliers.

He volunteered in August 1914, and was sent to the Dardanelles in the following year. He took part in the Landing at Suvla Bay, where the 5th Welch were badly cut up. He contracted dysentery and whilst awaiting removal to hospital was wounded by rifle fire. He was afterwards invalided home, and on his recovery proceeded to France. He took part in the Battles on the Somme front, and was twice wounded and contracted trench fever. After being again invalided home, he was discharged on medical grounds in July 1918, holding the 1914–15 Star, and the General Service and Victory Medals.

7, Hubert Grove, Stockwell, S.W.9.   Z2870

KENCH, A., Pte., 24th London Regt. (Queen's).

He volunteered in May 1915, and later in that year, on the conclusion of his training, crossed to France. He took an active part in many operations in the Vimy Ridge and Somme sectors, and was wounded in September 1916. On his return to France in 1917 he fought in the Battles of Messines and Ypres, and was again wounded. After his recovery he remained in England on home duties until his demobilisation in February 1919. He holds the 1914–15 Star, and the General Service and Victory Medals.

20, Cheam Place, off Newchurch Road, Camberwell, S.E.5.
                                          Z6494B Z6495B

KENCH, A. W., Leading Signalman, R.N., H.M.S. "Scout."

He joined the Navy in July 1912, and was serving at the outbreak of war with the Grand Fleet in the North Sea. He took part in the Battles of Heligoland Bight, Falkland Islands, Dogger Bank and Jutland and was engaged on constant patrol work until the war ended. In 1919 he proceeded with the Baltic Fleet to Russia, where he remained until February 1920. He was then invalided home owing to an accident and discharged from further service. He holds the 1914–15 Star, and the General Service and Victory Medals.

13, Cheam Place, Camberwell, S.E.5.   Z5791

KENDALL, D., Gunner, R.G.A.

He volunteered in October 1915, and in January of the following year, after the conclusion of his training, was sent to British East Africa, where he took part in various engagements. In June 1917 he was transferred to France and after being in action at Ypres, Lens, Cambrai and the Somme, also served in the Retreat and Advance of 1918. He fell fighting bravely at Kemmel Hill on August 27th, 1918, and was entitled to the General Service and Victory Medals.

"A costly sacrifice upon the altar of freedom."

43, Charleston Street, Walworth, S.E.17.   Z2872A

KENDALL, W. F. S., Private, R.A.S.C. (Remounts).

He joined in November 1916, and was sent to France in the following year. He served on the Somme and in other sectors and was engaged in breaking in and training remounts until hostilities ceased. After rendering valuable services, he was demobilised in 1919, and holds the General Service and Victory Medals.

108, Hubert Grove, Stockwell, S.W.9.   Z2871

KENNEDY, C. S., Guardsman, Scots Guards.

He was serving at the outbreak of war, having enlisted in 1910, and was sent to France in the same year and took part in heavy fighting at La Bassée, Givenchy and Béthune. He was wounded and taken prisoner in January 1915, and sent to Germany. On his release, after the Armistice, he returned home and was demobilised in January 1919, holding the 1914–15 Star, and the General Service and Victory Medals.

65, Stanley Street, Queen's Road, Battersea Park, S.W.8. Z2873

KENNEDY, H. W., 1st Class Stoker, R.N., H.M.S. "Swift," "Antrim," "Lowestoft" and "Forward."

He joined in 1912, and proceeded with the Grand Fleet to the North Sea on the outbreak of war, being present at the sinking of H.M.S. "Aboukir," "Cressy," and "Hogue." Later he proceeded to the South Atlantic and took part in the Battle of the Falkland Isles. Afterwards he was posted to the Mediterranean station and was in action during the Naval operations in the Dardanelles. He then served on various important duties until June 1919, when he was demobilised. He holds the 1914–15 Star, and the General Service and Victory Medals.

9, Broomgrove Road, Stockwell, S.W.9.   Z4483A

KENNEDY, W., Driver, R.F.A.

He volunteered in August 1914, having previously served in Egypt and India, and was later transferred to the Western Front, where he served in various engagements. He was unfortunately killed in action in Belgium on July 10th, 1917, and was entitled to the 1914–15 Star, and the General Service and Victory Medals.

"His life for his Country, his Soul to God."

27, Cardross Street, Hammersmith, W.6.   11574B

KENSETT, F. S., Pioneer, R.E.

He joined in October 1916, and served on important duties with his unit until 1918, when he was sent to Egypt and thence to Palestine, where he took part in the capture of Jericho and in the offensive under General Allenby. He was demobilised in December 1919, and holds the General Service and Victory Medals.

21, Tindal Street, Lothian Road, S.W.9.   Z5435B

KENSETT, G. T., Private, 14th London Regiment (London Scottish) and Gordon Highlanders.

He joined in October 1917, and was sent to France in the following year and took part in various engagements, including those on the Somme and at Havrincourt, Bapaume, Béthune, and Bullecourt. He afterwards proceeded with the Army of Occupation to Germany, where he served until he was demobilised in October 1919. He holds the General Service and Victory Medals.

21, Tindal Street, Lothian Road, S.W.9.   Z5435A

KENT, A., Rifleman, King's Royal Rifle Corps.

He volunteered in August 1914, and on the completion of his training proceeded to France. During his service on the Western Front he fought in numerous engagements, including the Battle of the Somme, and was reported missing in November 1916. He was later presumed to have been killed in action at that time, and was entitled to the 1914–15 Star, and the General Service and Victory Medals.

"A valiant soldier, with undaunted heart he breasted Life's last hill."

44, Morrison Street, Battersea, S.W.11.   Z2875B

KENT, A., Rifleman, Rifle Brigade.

He volunteered in 1915, and in the same year was drafted to the Western Front. After only a very short period overseas he died gloriously on the Field of Battle at Hooge in September 1915. He was entitled to the 1914–15 Star, and the General Service and Victory Medals.

"He died the noblest death a man may die,
Fighting for God, and right, and liberty."

10, Tennyson Street, Wentworth Road, S.W.8.   Z1238A

KENT, G., A./Q.M.S., R.F.A.

A serving soldier, since 1901, he was on garrison duty in India at the outbreak of war. In 1915 he was drafted to the Dardanelles, and in April of the following year was unfortunately drowned whilst on board a troopship in the Eastern Mediterranean. He was entitled to the 1914–15 Star, and the General Service and Victory Medals.

"The path of duty was the way to glory."

10, Tennyson Street, Wentworth Road, S.W.8.   Z1238D

KENT, G., Air Mechanic, R.A.F.

He joined in October 1916, and after his training was completed, served at various stations on important duties with his unit. He rendered valuable services, but was not successful in obtaining a transfer overseas during the war. He was discharged in consequence of his service in October 1918.

43, Smyrk's Road, Walworth, S.E.17.   Z2874

KENT, S. J., Rifleman, King's Royal Rifle Corps.

He volunteered in November 1915, and proceeded overseas in March of the following year, and during his service in France fought in many engagements. He gave his life for the freedom of England in June 1916, and was entitled to the General Service and Victory Medals.

"A costly sacrifice upon the altar of freedom."

44, Morrison Street, Battersea, S.W.11.   Z2875C

KENT, W., Bandsman, R.M.A.

He enlisted in the Navy in 1902, and at the outbreak of war was posted to H.M.S. "Thunderer" and was sent to the North Sea. Whilst in this vessel he took part in the Battle of Jutland, and was engaged on important and dangerous duties until the cessation of hostilities. He returned to land and was demobilised in February 1919, and holds the 1914–15 Star, and the General Service and Victory Medals.

44, Morrison Street, Battersea, S.W.11.   Z2875A

KENT, W., Driver, R.M.A.

He volunteered in 1915, and after his training was drafted to France, where he served with the Armoured Car Division at Dunkirk. He did good work, but later returned home and was discharged from causes due to his service in 1916. He holds the General Service and Victory Medals.

10, Tennyson Street, Wentworth Road, S.W.8.   Z1238B

KENT, W. J. T., Leading Cook's Mate, R.N., H.M.T.B.D. "Garry," H.M.S. "Forward," "Pembroke," "Actaeon" and "St. George."

A serving sailor, at the outbreak of war he was sent to the North Sea on patrol duties, and was also engaged in convoying food supply ships. Whilst he was in "The Garry" three enemy submarines were sunk by that vessel. After the Armistice he proceeded to Russian waters and fought in the Baltic engagements against the Bolsheviks. He returned home in April 1920, and was invalided out of the Service as medically unfit for further duty. He holds the 1914–15 Star, and the General Service and Victory Medals.
18, Kennington Grove, S.E.11.   Z24587

KENTISH, B. M. (Mrs.), Special War Worker.

For eighteen months during the war this lady held a responsible position at Woolwich Arsenal, where she was engaged on fusing shells, her duties being of a highly dangerous character. Later she was poisoned by T.N.T. powder fumes and was blinded for a fortnight. After her recovery she returned to her work, but again contracted poisoning, her arm being affected, and she was obliged to relinquish her post in 1917. Her courageous efforts were highly appreciated by the authorities.
267, Eversleigh Road, Battersea, S.W.11.   Z2876

KENT-SMITH, B., Driver, R.A.S.C.

He was mobilised at the outbreak of war and was almost immediately drafted to France, where he was wounded in the Retreat from Mons. He served also in the Battles of the Marne, the Aisne, Ypres, Festubert, Loos, the Somme, and in 1917 was again wounded in action in the Ypres sector. He was invalided home in January 1918, and was demobilised in the following year, but subsequently died in February 1920. He was entitled to the Mons Star, and the General Service and Victory Medals.
15, Russell Street, Battersea, S.W.11.   Z2877

KENWARD, H., Rflmn., 6th London Regt. (Rifles).

He volunteered in August 1915, and after his training served in the Band of the 6th London Regiment. He did good work, but owing to ill-health was unable to secure his transfer overseas. Later he was invalided to hospital suffering from nervous debility, and was subsequently discharged as medically unfit for further service in August 1916.
6, Cavour Street, Walworth, S.E.17.   Z26008

KENYON, E., Private, East Surrey Regt. and Labour Corps.

He had previously served with the Colours in India and throughout the South African war. After the outbreak of hostilities in 1914 he was twice rejected for military service on account of an injury he had received whilst in the employ of the South-Eastern Railway Company. Eventually, however, he joined in November 1918 and was drafted to France in the same year. He served on important duties until February 1919, when he returned to England, and was demobilised. He holds the Queen's South African Medal.
36, Eltham Street, Walworth, S.E.17.   Z2878

KEOHANE, D., Sergt., 25th London Regt. (Cyclists).

He volunteered in August 1914, and after his training was sent to the East Coast, where he served on important duties, and was promoted to the rank of Sergeant. In February 1916 he proceeded to India and during his service was in action on the North-West Frontier until November 1919, when he returned home and was demobilised in the following January. He holds the India General Service Medal (with clasp Afghanistan, N.W. Frontier, 1919), the General Service and Victory Medals.
27, Dorothy Road, Lavender Hill, S.W.11.   Z2879A

KERNICK, A., Private, 2nd London Regt. (Royal Fusiliers).

Volunteering in August 1914, he was sent to the Western Front in the same year, and fought in various important engagements, including the first Battle of Ypres. He was afterwards drafted to Malta and thence to Egypt and subsequently to the Dardanelles. After taking part in the Gallipoli operations he proceeded to German East Africa, where he served until the conclusion of hostilities. During his service he was twice wounded, and finally returned to England, and was demobilised in May 1919. He holds the 1914–15 Star, and the General Service and Victory Medals.
47, Thorncroft Street, Wandsworth Road, S.W.8.   Z2764B

KERRIDGE, A. W. J., A.B., R.N., H.M.S. "Empress of India."

He joined the Navy in February 1918, and on the completion of his training was posted to H.M.S. "Empress of India." Whilst in this ship he was sent to Russian waters and fought against the Bolshevik forces until June 1919, when he returned home and was demobilised. He holds the General Service and Victory Medals.
316, East Street, Walworth, S.E.17.   Z2880B

KERRIDGE, C. E., Gunner, R.F.A.

He volunteered in April 1915, and in the following December was drafted to France. There he did excellent work as a gunner in the engagements at St. Eloi, Albert, and Vimy Ridge. He gave his life for his Country in the Battle of the Somme on July 21st, 1916, and was entitled to the 1914–15 Star, and the General Service and Victory Medals.
"He passed out of the sight of men by the path of duty and self-sacrifice."
316, East Street, Walworth, S.E.17.   Z2880A

KERSHAW, G., A.B., R.N., H.M.S. "Endeavour."

He was serving in the Navy at the declaration of hostilities, and was posted to H.M.S. "Endeavour" and served with the Grand Fleet on important patrol duties in the North Sea. Later his ship proceeded to the Dardanelles and was engaged in covering the Landing of the troops at Gallipoli and again when the Peninsula was evacuated in December 1915. He then returned to the North Sea until September 1919, when he was placed on the Reserve. He holds the 1914–15 Star, and the General Service and Victory Medals.
73B, Station Road, Camberwell, S.E.5.   Z6012

KERWOOD, A. E., Private, Royal Sussex Regiment.

He volunteered in February 1915, and after his training served at various stations on important duties with his unit. He did good work, but owing to illness was invalided out of the Service in September of the same year.
108, Cator Street, Peckham, S.E.15.   Z4485

KETTLE, G., Private, R.A.M.C.

He volunteered in January 1916, and after his training was completed, was drafted to Salonika in 1917. Whilst overseas he was engaged on important duties as a hospital orderly conveying the wounded from the various fronts to the hospitals at the Base. He was demobilised in May 1919, and holds the General Service and Victory Medals.
121, Farmer's Road, Camberwell, S.E.5.   Z2881

KEY, H., Rifleman, King's Royal Rifle Corps and Royal Irish Rifles.

He joined in February 1917, and in the same year was drafted to France. During his service on the Western Front he was severely wounded in the Battle of Messines in June 1917. He was invalided to hospital in England, and after his recovery was engaged on important garrison duties at Dover until his demobilisation in January 1919. He holds the General Service and Victory Medals.
1, Sandmere Gardens, Seneca Road, Clapham, S.W.4. Z2882

KEY, H. W., A.B., R.N., H.M. Minesweeper, "L238."

He joined in May 1916, and after his training was completed was posted to H.M. Minesweeper L238 and served in the Adriatic Sea off the Italian coast for three years. His vessel which frequently passed through mine-infested areas had many narrow escapes. He returned home and was demobilised in July 1919, and holds the General Service and Victory Medals.
18, Chatto Road, Battersea, S.W.11.   Z3093

KEYTE, J. G. (M.M.) Sergt., Grenadier Guards.

A serving soldier since 1909, he proceeded to France in October 1915, and took part in various important engagements on the Western Front, notably on the Somme and at Arras and Cambrai. On November 27th, 1917, he was awarded the Military Medal for extreme gallantry at Fontaine Nôtre Dame in leading his Platoon during a series of isolated engagements. He served in the Retreat and Advance of 1918, and in October of that year was invalided home owing to an accident. He holds in addition to the Military Medal the 1914–15 Star, and the General Service and Victory Medals, and in 1920 was still serving.
27, B Block, Lewis Trust Buildings, Camberwell, S.E.5.
                                                 Z6011

KIDD, A., Private, 23rd London Regiment.

Volunteering in February 1915, he was quickly drafted to France and subsequently fought in several engagements. On May 28th of the same year he was unfortunately killed in action at Loos. He was entitled to the 1914–15 Star, and the General Service and Victory Medals.
"A valiant soldier, with undaunted heart he breasted Life's last hill."
30, Bolingbroke Road, Battersea, S.W.11.   Z2883A

KIDD, G., Private, Devonshire Regiment.

He volunteered early in 1915, and at the conclusion of his training was sent to the Western Front. Whilst in this theatre of war he took part in many important engagements, including those at Ypres, Loos and Neuve Chapelle, and in consequence of ill-health was for a time in hospital at the Base. He was demobilised in March 1919, and holds the General Service and Victory Medals.
30, Bolingbroke Road, Battersea, S.W.11.   Z2883B

KIDD, H. W., Private, 10th Queen's (Royal West Surrey Regiment).

He volunteered in January 1915, and at the conclusion of his training was sent to the Western Front, where he fought in the Battles of Loos and Festubert. Later he saw service with his unit in Italy, and did much valuable work on that Front. He was demobilised in March 1919, and holds the 1914-15 Star, and the General Service and Victory Medals.
30, Bolingbroke Road, Battersea, S.W.11. Z2883C

KIDGELL, F. W., Cpl., Queen's (Royal West Surrey Regt.) and Surrey Lancers (Queen Mary's Regt.)

He volunteered in November 1914, and until 1916, when he was drafted to France, was engaged upon duties of an important nature. After fighting in the Battles of Ypres, Vimy Ridge, the Somme and Cambrai, he was drafted to Italy in 1918, and did valuable work with his unit during operations on the Piave. He was demobilised in 1919, and holds the General Service and Victory Medals.
46, Mostyn Road, Brixton Road, S.W.9. Z4486

KIEFER, F., Private, 29th Middlesex Regiment.

Joining in May 1916, he was engaged on important duties at various stations until April 1918, when he was drafted to France. Whilst in this theatre of war he was engaged in constructing roads and other important duties with a Labour Company, and was present at the Battles of Cambrai and Arras. He was demobilised in April 1919, and holds the General Service and Victory Medals.
1, Wivenhoe Road, Peckham, S.E.15. Z5974B

KILBY, L. S., 1st Air Mechanic, R.A.F.

Joining in the 19th London Regiment in June 1916, he was later transferred to a Yeomanry Regiment and whilst serving in the latter, was severely injured in an accident, which resulted in his being retained for home duties. He was then transferred to the R.A.F. and was subsequently engaged on important instructional duties in connection with aerial photography until he was demobilised in September 1917.
30, Birley Street, Battersea, S.W.11. Z2884

KILLASPY, A., Pte., 22nd London Regt. (Queen's).

Joining in June 1917, he crossed to France at the conclusion of his training and during his service in that theatre of war fought in a number of important battles, and was wounded whilst in action at Albert. He was demobilised in February 1919 after his return to England, and holds the General Service and Victory Medals.
8, Lower Bland Street, Great Dover Street, S.E.1. Z2550B

KILLASPY, D. W., Sergt., 22nd London Regiment (Queen's).

He volunteered in September 1914, and in the following March was drafted to France and took part in the Battles of Hill 60, Ypres and Loos. He was unfortunately killed in action at Vimy Ridge in May 1916, and was entitled to the 1914-15 Star, and the General Service and Victory Medals.
"Whilst we remember the Sacrifice is not in vain."
8, Lower Bland Street, Great Dover Street, S.E.1.
TZ25520A

KILLICK, W., Driver, R.F.A.

Volunteering in October 1914, he crossed to France in the following September. Whilst overseas he fought in many important engagements, notably those at Ypres, Loos, Vimy Ridge, the Somme, Arras, Passchendaele, Lens and Cambrai, and also served in the Retreat and Advance of 1918. He holds the 1914-15 Star, and the General Service and Victory Medals, and was demobilised in December 1919.
28, Runham Street, Walworth, S.E.17. Z2199A

KIMBER, W., Private, 6th Queen's (Royal West Surrey Regiment).

He joined in February 1916, and crossing to France in the following month took part in several engagements, including those at Vimy Ridge, the Somme and Arras, where he was wounded. On April 5th, 1918, he gave his life for King and Country whilst in action at Albert, during the German offensive. He was entitled to the General Service and Victory Medals.
"The path of duty was the way to glory."
139, Tyneham Road, Lavender Hill, S.W.11. Z2885

KIMBER, W. H., Private, 9th Essex Regiment.

Joining in May 1917 he was drafted to the Western Front in the following March. Whilst overseas he fought in several important engagements, and was severely wounded in action at Albert during the German Offensive. He was invalided to England, but on his recovery returned to France, and fell fighting at Péronne on September 1st, 1918. He was entitled to the General Service and Victory Medals.
"His life for his Country."
17, Jocelyn Street, Peckham, S.E.15. Z5436

KIMBER, W. J., Sapper, R.E.

He volunteered in December 1914, and in the following year was sent to the Dardanelles, subsequently taking part in the Landing at Suvla Bay and the engagements which followed. After the Evacuation of the Peninsula he was sent to Egypt, where in consequence of his having contracted malaria he was for some time in hospital. After his recovery he was transferred to the Western Front and did valuable work with his unit during operations on the Somme, at Arras, Albert and Passchendaele. In August 1917 he was so severely wounded as to necessitate his return to England, and after protracted treatment at various hospitals, was invalided out of the Service in June 1918. He holds the 1914-15 Star, and the General Service and Victory Medals.
2, Sandmere Gardens, Clapham, S.W.4. Z2886

KINCHLEA, H. A., Private, R.A.S.C.

He joined in November 1916, and at the conclusion of his training was engaged on important duties in the forage section of his unit. He was unable to secure his transfer to a theatre of war before the termination of hostilities, but, nevertheless, did valuable work until he was demobilised in September 1919.
22, Hazlemere Road, Peckham, S.E.15. Z6013A. Z6014A

KINCHLEA, W. T. D., Rfmn., 16th London Regt. (Queen's Westminster Rifles) and Private, Labour Corps.

He joined in September 1916, and after his training was engaged upon duties of an important nature at various stations with his unit. He was unable to secure his transfer overseas before the termination of hostilities, but afterwards served in France from July 1919 until the following October, when he was demobilised.
22, Hazlemere Road, Peckham, S.E.15. 6013B. 6014B

KINDRED, H. W., Driver, R.F.A.

Volunteering in November 1914, he was sent to France in December 1915 and fought in several engagements, notably that at Festubert. He gave his life for the freedom of England in the Battle of the Somme on July 21st, 1916, and was entitled to the 1914-15 Star, and the General Service and Victory Medals.
"His memory is cherished with pride."
43, Maltby Street, Bermondsey, S.E.1. TZ27418A

KINDRED, W. A., A.B., Royal Navy.

He was serving on H.M.S. "Sarna," when war broke out, and was subsequently engaged with this vessel on important transport duties to and from Salonika, France and the United States. On one occasion she was attacked by enemy craft and he was wounded. He holds the 1914-15 Star, and the General Service and Victory Medals, and was serving in 1920.
43, Maltby Street, Bermondsey, S.E.1. Z27418C

KINDRED, W. G., A.B., Royal Navy.

He volunteered in January 1915, and after his training was posted to the s.s. "Vulcan," in which he was engaged for the remaining period of hostilities on submarine patrol duties in the North Sea. He was demobilised in August 1919, and holds the General Service and Victory Medals.
43, Maltby Street, Bermondsey, S.E.1. Z27418B

KING, A. C., Rifleman, 21st London Regiment (1st Surrey Rifles).

He volunteered in April 1915, and in the following year was drafted to the Western Front and took part in heavy fighting at Albert, the Somme, Arras, Messines, Lens and Cambrai. He also served in the Retreat and Advance of 1918. He was demobilised in January 1919, and holds the General Service and Victory Medals.
1, Claude Road, Peckham Rye, S.E.15. Z5795

KING, B., Pte., King's Own Yorkshire Light Infantry.

He volunteered in August 1914, and in the same month was sent to France and was in action at Mons, where he was wounded, Le Cateau, the Aisne, La Bassée, Ypres, Hill 60, Loos, the Somme, Arras, Messines and Cambrai. Later he was taken prisoner and held in captivity until the Armistice, when he was released and returned home and was demobilised in January 1919, holding the Mons Star, and the General Service and Victory Medals.
163, Gloucester Road, Peckham, S.E.15. Z6272

KING, C., Driver, R.F.A.

He volunteered in October 1914, and after his training was sent to France, where he took part in severe fighting on the Somme and in various other engagements. He was later transferred to Salonika and served on the Vardar and Struma fronts. He was demobilised in May 1919, and holds the 1914-15 Star, and the General Service and Victory Medals.
30, Verona Street, Battersea, S.W.11. Z2887

KING, C., Private, 15th Lancashire Fusiliers.
He volunteered in December 1915, and in the following year was drafted to France and took part in heavy fighting at Vimy Ridge, Arras, Ypres and Péronne. He also served in the Retreat and Advance of 1918. He was demobilised in May 1919, and holds the General Service and Victory Medals.
162, South Street, Walworth. S.E.17.   Z2893

KING, C. J., Gunner (Saddler), R.F.A.
He volunteered in October 1914, and in September of the following year was sent to France and was in action at Loos, Vimy Ridge, the Somme, Bullecourt, Bapaume, Passchendaele and Cambrai. He was demobilised in May 1919, and holds the 1914-15 Star, and the General Service and Victory Medals.
189, St. George's Road, Peckham, S.E.15.   Z5792

KING, C. W., Private, East Surrey Regiment.
He was mobilised in August 1914, and was sent to France in April of the following year and took part in heavy fighting at Hill 60, Vimy Ridge, the Somme and in other engagements, and was three times wounded. He was taken prisoner at La Fresnoy, and was held in captivity until after the cessation of hostilities, when he returned home and was demobilised in March 1919. He holds the 1914-15 Star, and the General Service and Victory Medals.
26, Wayford Street, Battersea, S.W.11.   Z2892

KING, D., Leading Stoker, R.N., H.M.S. "Prospin."
He enlisted in 1906, and at the outbreak of war was serving with the Grand Fleet in the North Sea, and was engaged in the transport of ammunition to the Fleet when in action. He also served in the Red Sea and Indian Ocean, and whilst in the East contracted malaria. He was demobilised in April 1919, and holds the 1914-15 Star, and the General Service and Victory Medals.
22, Abercrombie Street, Battersea, S.W.11.   Z2890

KING, E., Private, 12th Royal Fusiliers.
He volunteered in August 1914, and in the following year was drafted to the Western Front, where he took part in numerous engagements, including that at Loos, where he was taken prisoner in 1915. On his release he returned home and was demobilised in February 1919, and holds the 1914-15 Star, and the General Service and Victory Medals.
150, Maysoule Road, Battersea, S.W.11.   Z2901

KING, F. (Miss), Special War Worker.
This lady held a position at Messrs. Ross and Co.'s Munition Factory, Grange Road, Bermondsey, where she was engaged as a rivetter. Her duties which were of a responsible nature were carried out with great care and she rendered valuable services during the war.
338E, East Street, Old Kent Road, S.E.1.   Z2889A

KING, F., Private, 4th (Queen's Own) Hussars.
He volunteered in August 1914, and was sent to Egypt in the same year and thence to Palestine. He afterwards proceeded to Mesopotamia, where he was engaged in various important duties with his unit and rendered valuable services. He was demobilised in March 1919, and holds the 1914-15 Star, and the General Service and Victory Medals.
18, Tradescent Road, South Lambeth Road, S.W.8.   Z1212B

KING, F. J., Corporal, 11th Royal Fusiliers.
Volunteering in March 1915, he was drafted to the Western Front in the following year, and was in action on the Somme, and at Grandcourt. He was wounded in 1917, and was invalided home, and in June 1918, was discharged as medically unfit for further service, holding the General Service and Victory Medals.
41, Stockdale Road, Battersea, S.W.8.   Z1673A

KING, G., Private, 10th Devonshire Regiment.
Volunteering in 1915 he was drafted to the Western Front in the same year, and after taking part in various engagements was transferred to Salonika, where he was again in action, and was twice wounded and invalided home. He was demobilised in 1919, and holds the 1914-15 Star, and the General Service and Victory Medals.
258, Sumner Road, Peckham, S.E.15.   Z5109

KING, G., Rifleman, 21st London Regiment (1st Surrey Rifles).
He volunteered in August 1914, and in the following year was sent to France, where he took part in various engagements. He died gloriously on the Field of Battle on the Somme on September 15th, 1916, and was entitled to the 1914-15 Star, and the General Service and Victory Medals.
"The path of duty was the way to glory."
14, Cambridge Street, Camberwell, S.E.5.   Z2894

KING, H., Private, M.G.C.
He volunteered in 1915, and in the same year was drafted to the Western Front, where he took part in numerous engagements, including that at Ypres. He also served in the Retreat and Advance of 1918. He was demobilised in 1920, and holds the 1914-15 Star, and the General Service and Victory Medals.
9, Candahar Road, Battersea, S.W.11.   Z2899

KING, G. A., Private, M.G.C.
Joining in 1916 he was sent to the Western Front in the same year. He was in action at Vimy Ridge, Ypres, Passchendaele, and Cambrai, and was wounded and gassed. He also served in the Retreat and Advance of 1918, during which he was again wounded. He afterwards proceeded with the Army of Occupation to Germany, where he served until he was demobilised in January 1919. He holds the General Service and Victory Medals.
18, Milford Street, Wandsworth Road, S.W.8.   Z2902

KING, H., Rifleman, 9th King's Royal Rifle Corps.
He volunteered in August 1914, and was sent to France in the same year. He took part in heavy fighting at Loos, the Somme, Arras, Messines, Ypres, Passchendaele, and in other engagements, and also served in the Retreat and Advance of 1918, and was twice wounded. He was later transferred to the Labour Corps, and served at Le Havre until he was demobilised in December 1918, holding the 1914-15 Star, and the General Service and Victory Medals.
12, Porson Street, Wandsworth Road, S.W.8.   Z2891

KING, H. J., Rifleman, Rifle Brigade.
Mobilised at the outbreak of hostilities, he was immediately drafted to France, and fought in the Retreat from Mons, and the Battles of the Marne, the Aisne, and La Bassée. He also took part in a number of the engagements which followed, including those at Ypres, Albert, the Somme, Arras, Lens, Passchendaele, and Cambrai, and the Retreat and Advance of 1918. During his service he was wounded on three occasions, and was also gassed. He holds the Mons Star, and the General Service and Victory Medals., and was demobilised in February 1919.
26, Northampton Place, Walworth, S.E.17.   Z2903A

KING, J., Private, M.G.C.
He joined in 1916, and in March of the following year was drafted to the Western Front and took part in various engagements, including those on the Somme, and at Ypres. He was unfortunately killed in action at the Battle of Cambrai on December 2nd, 1917, and was entitled to the General Service and Victory Medals.
"His life for his Country, his Soul to God."
18, Chatham Road, Battersea, S.W.11.   Z2898

KING, J., Private, Middlesex Regt. and Sapper, R.E.
He volunteered in February 1915, and was sent to France in the same year and took part in various actions, including those at Loos and Messines, and was wounded. He was afterwards transferred to Egypt, and served at Gaza, Jaffa, Beyrout, and the capture of Jerusalem. He was demobilised in 1919, and holds the 1914-15 Star, and the General Service and Victory Medals.
10, The Triangle, Clapham, S.W.4.   Z2895B

KING, J. A. (Mrs.), Special War Worker.
This lady was engaged at Messrs. Spiller and Baker's, Bermondsey, S.E., as a packer. Her duties, which were of an important nature, were carried out with great care, and she rendered valuable services during the war.
338E, East Street, Old Kent Road, S.E.17.   Z2889C

KING, J. F., Private, 2nd London Regiment (Royal Fusiliers).
He was mobilised at the outbreak of war and served on important duties with his unit until December 1917, when he was sent to France and was in action on the Somme, and at Cambrai. He was killed near Cambria on March 21st, 1918, and was entitled to the General Service and Victory Medals.
"Courage, bright hopes, and a myriad dreams, splendidly given."
11, Beech Street, Clapham, S.W.8.   Z2897

KING, L., Special War Worker.
During the war, this lady gave her services as a waitress at a Y.M.C.A. hut at the Elephant and Castle, and carried out these duties with great zeal. She also did much good work in connection with the sale of flags in aid of St. Dunstan's Hostel for blinded soldiers.
128, St. George's Road, Peckham, S.E.15.   Z5631B

KING, N., Leading Seaman, R.N.
He was already in the Navy when war broke out, and subsequently, on board H.M.S. "Northesk," served on important submarine patrol duties in the North Sea and the Dardanelles. His ship also took part in several Naval engagements, including those at the Falkland Isles, and Jutland. He was demobilised in April 1919, and holds the 1914-15 Star, and the General Service and Victory Medals.
196, Albert Road, Peckham, S.E.15.   Z5632

KING, R. J., Gunner, R.G.A.
He joined in December 1916, and after his training was engaged on important duties at various stations with his Battery. He was unable to secure his transfer overseas before the termination of hostilities, but nevertheless did valuable work until January 1919, when he was demobilised.
131, Grant Road, Battersea, S.W.11.   Z1244A

KING, S., Private, Northamptonshire Regiment.
He joined in 1916, and after his training served on the Western Front for upwards of two years. During this time he was engaged in the fighting at Ypres, the Somme, and Arras, and towards the close of hostilities was severely wounded. He was invalided out of the Service in consequence, in 1919, and holds the General Service and Victory Medals.
10, The Triangle, Clapham, S.W.4.   Z2895C

KING, T., Air Mechanic, R.A.F.
He joined at the age of seventeen in August 1917, and crossed to France in November of that year. Whilst overseas he was engaged on duties of an important nature, which called for much technical knowledge and skill, and served at Etaples, Cambrai, Dunkirk, and Nieuport. On one occasion, whilst on duty in one of the forward areas he was wounded, but remained on the Western Front until after the cessation of hostilities. He was still serving in 1920, and holds the General Service and Victory Medals.
338E, East Street, Old Kent Road, S.E.1.   Z2889B

KING, T., Rifleman, 11th London Regt. (Rifles).
He joined in October 1916, and at the conclusion of his training was drafted to the Western Front. Whilst in this theatre of war, he fought at Ypres, Loos, the Somme, and Cambrai, and towards the close of hostilities contracted a severe illness which necessitated his return to England. After his recovery he was sent with the Army of Occupation to Germany. He was demobilised in October 1919, and holds the General Service and Victory Medals.
27, Cobbett Street, Dorset Road, S.W.8.   Z2900

KING, W., Private, 23rd London Regiment.
Volunteering at the commencement of hostilities, he was sent to France at the conclusion of his training and subsequently fought in several battles, notably that of Ypres. He was unfortunately killed in action in April 1915, and was entitled to the 1914-15 Star and the General Service and Victory Medals.
" A costly Sacrifice upon the altar of freedom."
10, The Triangle, Clapham, S.W.4.   Z2895A

KING, W. G., Private, R.A.M.C.
He volunteered in January 1915, and shortly afterwards crossed to France. Whilst in this theatre of war he was engaged on duties of an important nature on the ambulance trains, by one of which he was unfortunately run over and killed in January 1917. He was entitled to the 1914-15 Star, and the General Service and Victory Medals.
" His memory is cherished with pride."
23, Wilcox Road, Wandsworth Road, S.W.8.   Z2888

KING, W. H. (M.M.), Sergt., R.F.A.
He was in the Territorials when war broke out, and was sent to the Western Front in February 1915. Whilst overseas he was engaged in the fighting at Ypres, Loos, the Somme, Passchendaele, and in many other important sectors, and also served in the Retreat and Advance. He was wounded on one occasion, and was awarded the Military Medal for an act of distinguished gallantry in the Field. In addition, he holds the 1914-15 Star, and the General Service and Victory Medals, and at the time of his demobilisation, which took place in February 1919, was undergoing training in England for promotion to commissioned rank.
128, St. George's Road, Peckham, S.E.15.   Z5631A

KINGDON, G. R. (M.M.), Gunner, R.F.A.
He joined in November 1916, and in January of the following year was sent to France, where he was in action on the Somme, and at Ypres, and was wounded twice, and gassed. He was invalided home and discharged as medically unfit for further service in January 1919, and holds the Military Medal awarded for bravery in the Field in saving life, and the General Service and Victory Medals.
5A, Wells Street, Camberwell, S.E.5.   Z5110

KINGETT, A. H., Private, 23rd London Regiment.
He volunteered in 1914, and was sent to France in the following year, and was in action at Ypres, Givenchy, Loos, Beaumont-Hamel, and Cambrai. He also served in the Retreat and Advance of 1918. He was demobilised in June 1919, and holds the 1914-15 Star, and the General Service and Victory Medals.
11, Milford Street, Wandsworth Road, S.W.8.   Z2904

KINGMAN, T., Pte. (The Buffs), East Kent Regt.
He volunteered in September 1914, and in the following year was drafted to France. He took part in severe fighting at Loos and was wounded, and suffered the loss of the sight of his left eye. He was invalided home and discharged as medically unfit for further service in August 1916, and holds the 1914-15 Star, and the General Service and Victory Medals.
78, Nelson Road, High Street, Clapham, S.W.4.   Z2905A

KINGSFORD, F. E. W., Private, East Surrey Regt. and East Lancashire Regt. and Gunner, R.F.A.
He joined in April 1917, and after his training served at various stations on important duties with his unit. He rendered valuable services, but was not successful in obtaining his transfer overseas before the cessation of hostilities. He was discharged as medically unfit for further service in March 1919.
16, Seneca Road, Clapham, S.W.4.   Z1325B

KINGSMILL, G. F., Rifleman, 11th King's Royal Rifle Corps.
He joined in April 1917, and after his training was sent to France, and was in action at Cambrai, the Somme, and Delville Wood. He was wounded at the last place, and invalided home, and was discharged as medically unfit for further service in October 1918. He holds the General Service and Victory Medals.
99, St. George's Road, Peckham, S.E.15.   Z5633

KINSBURY, A., Private, Dorsetshire Regiment.
He was mobilised in August 1914, and was shortly afterwards sent to France. He was in action in severe fighting in the Retreat from Mons, on the Marne, and at La Bassée, and Ypres, and was taken prisoner whilst serving in the La Bassée sector in 1916. On his release he returned home, but was afterwards sent to Germany, where he was still serving in 1920, holding the Mons Star, and the General Service and Victory Medals.
17, Love Lane, Stockwell, S.W.9.   Z2906

KINSEN, E. S, Segt., 77th Chinese Labour Company.
He joined in March 1917, and was sent to France in the same year. He served in various sectors, including Ypres, and was engaged on important duties with his unit and rendered valuable services. He was demobilised in August 1919, and holds the General Service and Victory Medals.
55, Heath Road, Wandsworth Road, S.W.8.   Z2907

KINGSTON, J. M., Bombardier, R.G.A.
He volunteered in October 1914, and served on important duties with his Battery until March 1916, when he was drafted to France, where he took part in numerous engagements, including those on the Somme, and at Vimy Ridge, and Ypres, He afterwards proceeded with the Army of Occupation to Germany, where he served until he was demobilised in February 1919, holding the General Service and Victory Medals.
4, Rita Road, South Lambeth Road, S.W.8.   Z2908

KIPPS, L., Corporal, R.A.S.C
He was mobilised in August 1914, and was shortly afterwards sent to France, where he took part in the Retreat from Mons, and also served at Rheims and Nancy. He was invalided home and discharged in October 1914, and holds the Mons Star, and the General Service and Victory Medals. He subsequently died on October 20th, 1916.
" He joined the great white company of valiant souls."
11, Trafalgar Road, Peckham, S.E.15.   Z3477B

KIRBY, H. J., Rifleman, 11th London Regiment (Finsbury Rifles).
He joined in November 1916, and was sent to the Western Front in the same year. He took part in severe fighting on the Somme, and at Arras, Bullecourt, Ypres, and Cambrai, and contracting trench fever was invalided home, and discharged in April, 1918.   Z2909
32, Trollope Street, Silverthorne Road, Battersea Park, S.W.8.

KIRBY, S. Private, 11th Queen's (Royal West Surrey Regt).
He volunteered in March 1915, and in the following year was sent to the Western Front, where he was in action at Albert, the Somme, Arras, Bullecourt, and Cambrai. He also served in the Retreat and Advance of 1918. He afterwards proceeded with the Army of Occupation to Germany, where he served until he was demobilised in February 1919, holding the General Service and Victory Medals.
49, Russell Street, Brixton Road S.W.9.   Z5259A

KIRBY, S. F., Private, R.A.S.C. (M.T.)
He joined in 1916, and served as a motor driver on important duties with his unit until 1918, when he was sent to France, where he served in various sectors. He afterwards proceeded with the Army of Occupation to Germany, where he served until he was demobilised in August 1919, holding the General Service and Victory Medals.
49, Russell Street, Brixton Road, S.W.9.   Z5259B

KIRK, F. S., Corporal, R.A.O.C.
He volunteered in 1915, and in the following year was drafted to France. He served in the engagement at Vimy Ridge, and was also stationed at Le Havre on important duties. He was employed on special work during the air raid at Etaples, and was afterwards invalided home to hospital and was discharged in March, 1919. He holds the General Service and Victory Medals.
9, Patmore Street, Wandsworth Road, S.W.8.   Z2910

KIRK, F., Private, Royal Sussex Regiment.

He volunteered in September 1914, and on medical grounds was retained on home defence duties until May 1916, when he was drafted to France. He served on the Somme, and was taken prisoner on June 30th, after only about one month's service overseas. He was held in captivity in Germany, enduring many hardships until the day of his death October 30th, 1916. He was entitled to the General Service and Victory Medals.

" Thinking that remembrance, though unspoken, may reach
                    him where he sleeps."

38, Elsted Street, Walworth, S.E.17.   Z2911A

KIRK, J., Driver, R.A.S.C. (M.T.)

He joined in February 1918, having attested two years previously, and after his training served at the London Supply Depôt on important duties connected with the distribution of foodstuffs to the various military hospitals. He did excellent work, but owing to medical reasons was unable to secure a transfer overseas, and was demobilised in December 1919.

107, Barlow Street, Walworth, S.E.7.   Z2912

KIRK, W. H., Private, 16th Canadian Scottish Regt.

He volunteered in November 1914, and arrived on the Western Front in January 1915. During his service in France he fought at Neuve Chapelle, Hill 60, Ypres, Festubert, Loos, and Albert. He was severely wounded in the Battle of the Somme, and succumbed to his injuries a few days later on August 4th, 1916. He was entitled to the 1914-15 Star, and the General Service and Victory Medals.

" Nobly striving,
He nobly fell that we might live."

38, Elsted Street, Walworth, S.E.17.   Z2911B

KITCHIN, A., Private, 1st London Regiment (Royal Fusiliers).

He attested in August 1915, and was called upon in the following August, embarking for France two months later. During his service on the Western Front he fought at Beaumont-Hamel, Vimy Ridge, and Lens, and was wounded at Arras, and invalided home. After his recovery he was transferred to the Machine Gun Corps in January 1918, and was again sent to France, where he was in action in the second Battle of the Marne, and in various subsequent engagements until the conclusion of hostilities. He was sent home and demobilised in January 1919, and holds the General Service and Victory Medals.   16, Russell Street, Battersea, S.W.11.   Z2913

KITCHING, H. W., Sergt., Coldstream Guards.

He was mobilised in August 1914, and was almost immediately drafted to France, and took part in the Retreat from Mons. He also served at La Bassée, Ypres, Loos, the Somme, Arras, Messines, Lens, Passchendaele, Cambrai, and the second Battle of the Somme, and in various later engagements in the Retreat and Advance of 1918. In 1917 he was wounded on one occasion and invalided home to hospital, but rejoined his unit in France after his recovery. He was demobilised in April 1919, and holds the Mons Star, and the General Service and Victory Medals.

68, Brayard's Road, Peckham, S.E.15.   Z5437

KITE, W. H., Gunner, R.G.A.

He joined in July 1916, and in the following September proceeded to France. Whilst in this theatre of war he fought in various engagements in the Somme and Ypres sectors. On October 19th, 1917, he died gloriously on the Field of Battle at Ypres, and was entitled to the General Service and Victory Medals.

" His life for his country, his Soul to God."

20, Abercrombie Street, Battersea, S.W.11.   Z2914

KITSON, W., C.S.M., 1st Royal Fusiliers.

A serving soldier at the outbreak of war he was soon sent to the Western Front, and took part in many important engagements throughout the war. He was in action on the Somme, and at Ypres, Arras, and in numerous subsequent battles, and was wounded during this period. He was demobilised in May 1920, and holds the 1914 Star, and the General Service, Victory and Long Service, and Good Conduct Medals.

78, Geneva Road, Coldharbour Lane, S.W.9.   Z3094A

KORN, W. W., Private, 25th London Regt. (Cyclists).

He volunteered in August 1915, and on the completion of his training was drafted to India in February of the following year. For three months in 1917, he was in action against the Waziris on the North West Frontier, and also served at Amritsar under General Dyer during the riots. He returned home and was demobilised in January 1920, and holds the General Service and Victory Medals.

13, Chip Street, Little Manor Street, Clapham, S.W.4.   Z2915

KNAPMAN, J. F., Driver, R.F.A.

He joined in April 1917, and in the following September proceeded to France. Whilst overseas he did excellent work as a driver in the Ypres salient, at Albert, and in numerous subsequent engagements until the Armistice was signed. He then served on various duties up to the date of his demobilisation in June 1919. He holds the General Service and Victory Medals.   17, Bonsor Street, Camberwell, S.E.5.   Z4487

KNIGHT, A. E., Rifleman, 8th London Regiment (Post Office Rifles) and Private, Labour Corps.

He joined in May 1917, and in the following August was sent overseas. During his service on the Western Front he fought on the Somme, and at Ypres and Cambrai, and in many subsequent engagements in the Retreat and Advance of 1918. Later he was attached to the Royal Army Medical Corps, and finally transferred to the Labour Corps, with which he served until he was demobilised in March 1919. He holds the General Service and Victory Medals.

13, Carew Street, Camberwell, S.E.5.   Z6010

KNIGHT, A. A., Private, R.A.S.C. (M.T.)

He volunteered in August 1914, and in the same month was drafted overseas. Whilst in France he served on important duties in connection with the Motor Transport at Ypres, Neuve Chapelle, St. Eloi, Loos, the Somme, Beaumont-Hamel, Messines, Ypres, Lens, Cambrai, and in the engagements which followed in the Retreat and Advance of 1918. He was mainly engaged throughout this period in conveying ammunition and stores up to the front lines. In March 1919 he was demobilised, and holds the 1914 Star, and the General Service and Victory Medals.

97, Dalyell Road, Landor Road, S.W.9.   Z2916

KNIGHT, C., Gunner, R.G.A. and Sapper, R.E.

He volunteered in October 1914, and in the following year was drafted to France. During his service on the Western Front he was severely wounded while moving guns, and was invalided home to hospital where he was for thirteen weeks under medical treatment. On his recovery he was posted to Headquarters' staff at Woolwich, and then transferred to the Royal Engineers, with whom he was engaged on important duties until demobilised in February 1919. He holds the 1914-15 Star, and the General Service and Victory Medals.

13, Parkstone Road, Peckham, S.E.15.   Z5794

KNIGHT, C., Rifleman, Rifle Brigade.

He volunteered in 1914, and on the completion of his training was sent overseas in the following year. After taking part in several engagements he was reported missing in 1915, and later was presumed to have been killed in action at that time. He was entitled to the 1914-15 Star, and the General Service and Victory Medals.

" And doubtless he went in splendid company."

69, Mordaunt Street, Stockwell, W.S.9.   Z2917

KNIGHT, C. S., Rfimn., Rifle Brigade (Lewis Gunner).

Volunteering in August 1914, he was almost immediately drafted to France, and took part in the Retreat from Mons. He also served at Neuve Chapelle, Hill 60, Hooge, Festubert, Loos, Vimy Ridge, the Somme, and Beaumont-Hamel. Whilst fighting in the Somme sector he fell in action on September 15th, 1916.

" His memory is cherished with pride."

6, Prideaux Road, Landor Road, S.W.9.   Z2918

KNIGHT, E. (M.M.), Rifleman, King's Royal Rifle Corps.

He volunteered in February 1915, and in the same year proceeded to France. During his service on the Western Front he fought with distinction at Ypres, Arras, the Somme, and in the Retreat of March 1918. He was awarded a Certificate for gallantry at the Battle of Hooge in July 1915, and later won the Military Medal for conspicuous bravery and devotion to duty at Arras in April 1917. He was severely wounded and taken prisoner at St. Quentin, and subsequently died of his injuries. He was entitled to the 1914-15 Star, and the General Service and Victory Medals.

" Courage, bright hopes, and a myriad dreams, splendidly
                              given."

79, Grosvenor Terrace, Camberwell, S.E.5.   Z2919

KNIGHT, E., Private, Royal Sussex Regiment.

He joined in 1918, at the age of eighteen years, and after his training was sent to Germany with the Army of Occupation, and served on the Rhine for about six months. In 1920 he was serving with the Royal Warwickshire Regiment, to which he was transferred after his return to England.

3, Landor Road, Clapham, S.W.9.   Z2929

KNIGHT, F. J., Private, M.G.C.

He volunteered in November 1915, and joined the City of London Yeomanry (Rough Riders), and was then transferred to the Lincolnshire Lancers. He was drafted to Egypt in 1915, and served through all the important engagements with General Allenby up to the fall of Jerusalem. He then returned to England, and was afterwards sent to France, where he fought in the fourth Battle of Ypres, and in subsequent engagements until the cessation of hostilities. He was demobilised in April 1919, and holds the 1914-15 Star, and the General Service and Victory Medals.

51, Broughton Street, Battersea Park, S.W.8.   Z2920

KNIGHT, G., Bombardier, R.F.A.

He joined in April 1916, and in the following December was drafted overseas. During his service on the Western Front he fought in the Battles of the Somme, Arras, Vimy Ridge, Ypres, Passchendaele, and Cambrai, and in the engagements which followed in the Retreat and Advance of 1918. After the Armistice he proceeded to Germany with the Army of Occupation, and was stationed at Cologne until September 1919, when he returned home and was demobilised. He holds the General Service and Victory Medals.

14, Elliott Road, Stockwell, S.W.9.   Z5111

KNIGHT, G. H., Private, Queen's (Royal West Surrey Regiment).

He joined in January 1916, and in the following August was sent overseas. Whilst in France he fought on the Somme, and at Arras, and in many subsequent engagements. Later he was drafted to Salonika, where he served until 1919, when he returned home and was demobilised, and holds the General Service and Victory Medals.

19, Cavendish Grove, Wandsworth Road, S.W.8.   Z2921

KNIGHT, G. W., Private, Queen's (Royal West Surrey Regiment).

He joined in 1916, and in the same year was drafted to France. During his service on the Western Front he fought at Ypres and the Somme, and in the third Battle of the Aisne, where he was wounded and taken prisoner. He was held in captivity in Germany until after the Armistice, when he was released and repatriated. He holds the General Service and Victory Medals, and was demobilised in 1918.

41, Brooklands Road, South Lambeth, S.W.8.   Z2922

KNIGHT, J., Corporal, R.N.D. and R.A.F.

He volunteered in August 1914, having previously served, and was almost immediately drafted to France, and was present during the Retreat from Mons. He also fought at Loos, Lens, Ypres, Arras, Cambrai, Bapaume, St. Quentin, and the engagements which followed in the Retreat and Advance of 1918. After the Armistice he returned home, and served with the Royal Air Force prior to being demobilised in February 1920. He holds the Mons Star, and the General Service and Victory Medals.

54, Old Paradise Street, Lambeth, S.E.11.   Z25788

KNIGHT, J. M., Corporal, R.E.

He volunteered in June 1915, and on the completion of his training was promoted to the rank of Corporal. He was drafted to Russia in 1918, and was engaged there on important duties in connection with the operations of the Russian Relief Forces. He returned home and was demobilised in October 1919, and holds the General Service and Victory Medals.

46, Russell Street, Battersea, S.W.11.   Z2924C

KNIGHT, T. E., Rifleman, King's Royal Rifle Corps.

Volunteering in 1914, he was drafted overseas at the latter end of the following year, and during his service in France fought in numerous important engagements. He was in action on the Somme, and at Vimy Ridge, Ypres, Cambrai, and in the second Battle of the Marne, and in various subsequent battles until the conclusion of hostilities. In March 1919 he was demobilised, and holds the 1914-15 Star, and the General Service, and Victory Medals.

47, Wells Place, Camberwell, S.E.5.   Z3478A

KNIGHT, W., Private, Royal Sussex Regiment.

He volunteered in March 1915, and in the same year was drafted to France. Whilst overseas he fought in the Battles of Ypres, and was wounded, and on recovery served in many subsequent engagements until the Armistice was signed. He was then sent to Russia, where he did excellent service against the Bolsheviks. He returned home and was discharged in September 1919, and holds the 1914-15 Star, and the General Service and Victory Medals.

17, St. Philip Street, Battersea Park, S.W.8.   Z2928

KNIGHT, W., Stoker, R.N., H.M.S. " Agamemnon."

He volunteered in August 1915, and after his training was posted to H.M.S. " Europa " and sent to the North Sea. He was later transferred to H.M.S. " Agamemnon," and whilst in this ship fought in the Battle of Jutland and served at Mudros. He was also present at the surrender of the German Fleet, and was demobilised in March 1919. He holds the 1914-15 Star, and the General Service and Victory Medals.

73, Gwynne Road, Battersea, S.W.11.   Z2927B

KNIGHT, W. R., Rifleman, 8th London Regt. (P.O. Rifles).

He joined in May 1916, and in August of the same year was drafted to the Western Front, where he took part in various engagements. He was unfortunately killed in action on October 7th, 1916, and was entitled to the General Service and Victory Medals.

" The path of duty was the way to glory."

10E, Lewis Trust Dwellings, Camberwell, S.E.5.   Z6405

KNIGHTS, G. W., Sergt., 10th London Regiment.

After joining in January 1916, he pursued his course of training and was retained on important duties with his unit until February 1917. In that year he crossed to France and fought with distinction in the Battles of Arras, Bullecourt, Ypres, and Passchendaele, and in 1918 in the severe engagements in the Retirement and Advance of the Allies. After his return home he was demobilised in August 1919, and holds the General Service and Victory Medals.

226, Grosvenor Terrace, Camberwell, S.E.5.   Z2930B

KNIGHTS, R. C., Cpl., 24th London Regt. (Queen's).

He joined in June 1916, and on the completion of his training was drafted to Palestine in June 1917. While there he fought in the series of engagements from Beersheba to the Judean Hills, and afterwards returned to France in time to take part in the Advance of the Allies before the Armistice. He entered Germany with the victorious Army of Occupation, and served at Cologne until his demobilisation in January 1920. He holds the General Service and Victory Medals.

226, Grosvenor Terrace, Camberwell, S.E.5.   Z2930A

KNIGHTS, T. H., Gunner, R.G.A.

He joined in 1916, and after the completion of his training was drafted to the Western Front, where he did valuable service in many engagements, including those at Arras, Ypres, and the Somme. In consequence of gas poisoning and other illness arising out of his service he was discharged in 1919 as medically unfit for further duty. He holds the General Service and Victory Medals.

13, Barlow Street, Walworth, S.E.17.   Z2925B

KNOCKER, F. C., Gunner, R.G.A.

Joining in September 1916, he proceeded to France early in 1917, and then took an active part in many engagements of vital importance, including those at Vimy Ridge, Ypres, Cambrai, the Somme, and in the Retreat and Advance of the Allies in 1918. During his service he was wounded twice. He returned to England and was demobilised in January 1919, holding the General Service and Victory Medals.

17, Vicarage Road, Camberwell, S.E.5.   Z2931

KNOTT, C. T., Private, R.A.S.C. (M.T.)

He volunteered in April 1915, and after his training at Grove Park and Aldershot proceeded to France in the following August. He rendered valuable transport services up to the close of hostilities in numerous engagements of great importance, especially at Ypres, the Somme and Bullecourt. After returning home he was demobilised in February 1919, and holds the 1914-15 Star, and the General Service and Victory Medals.

91, Bridge Road, Battersea Bridge Road, S.W.11.   Z2932

KNOTT, H. W., Private, East Surrey Regiment.

After attesting in December 1915 he was called up for service in October of the following year ; and crossing to France early in 1917 fought in the Battles of Arras, Messines, Ypres, Cambrai, and the Somme. In the last battle he was wounded and captured ; but after nine months' captivity in Germany he was released. He was demobilised in February 1919, and holds the General Service and Victory Medals.

19, Kay Road, Stockwell, S.W.9.   Z2933

KNOTT, T., Corporal, Sherwood Foresters.

He volunteered in April 1915, and after the completion of his training proceeded to France in 1916. He took a prominent part in numerous engagements, including the Somme Offensive and was severely wounded. After prolonged treatment in hospital he was eventually discharged in 1918, as medically unfit for further service. He holds the General Service and Victory Medals.

5, Abyssinia Road, Battersea, S.W.11.   Z2934

KNOWLES, W., Pioneer, R.E.

Volunteering in August 1915, he crossed to France before the end of that year, and there took part in many engagements of importance, including those on the Somme, Ypres, Arras, and Cambrai fronts, and in the Offensives of 1918 up to the cessation of hostilities. After his return home he was demobilised in March 1919, and holds the 1914-15 Star, and the General Service and Victory Medals.

152, Farmer's Road, Camberwell, S.E.5.   Z2935

KNOWLES, W. E., Private, Queen's (Royal West Surrey Regiment).

He volunteered in January 1915, and in June of the same year was sent to France, where he took part in the severe fighting at Loos, Albert, Vimy Ridge, the Somme, Ypres, Arras, Lens, and Cambrai. He also served in the Retreat and Advance of 1918, and was twice wounded. In 1918 he was transferred to Egypt, and after serving there for a time returned to the Western Front and proceeded to Germany with the Army of Occupation. He was demobilised in April 1919, holding the 1914-15 Star, and the General Service and Victory Medals.

22, Townsend Street, Walworth, S.E.17.   Z2936

KNOX, F. A., Private, R.M.L.I.

He was mobilised in August 1914, and proceeded to sea at the outbreak of war and served on H.M. Troopship "Europa," conveying troops to and from India, France, and Australia. At the beginning of 1917 he was transferred to various merchant vessels, on which he served as a gunner until the close of hostilities. He was demobilised in May 1919, holding the 1914-15 Star, and the General Service and Victory Medals.

4, Silcote Road, Camberwell, S.E.5. Z5438

KNOX, W., Sergt., R.A.M.C.

He was mobilised in August 1914, and shortly afterwards was sent to the Western Front. He rendered excellent service at Mons, the Marne, and in many other engagements until 1916 when he came home, and was stationed at Aldershot. He was demobilised in February 1919, holding the Mons Star, and the General Service and Victory Medals, but later re-enlisted and proceeded to North Russia, where he was engaged at Archangel.

12, Neate Street, Camberwell, S.E.5. Z5112A

KNOX, W. G., Private, R.A.M.C.

He enlisted in the Regular Army in March 1919, and in September of the same year was sent to North Russia, where he remained until July of the following year, when he returned home. In 1920 he was still serving with his unit. During the war he was employed on important munition work in the Royal Arsenal, Woolwich, where he rendered valuable services.

12, Neate Street, Camberwell, S.E.5. Z5112B

L

LACEY, R. A. (M.M.), Sergt., R.F.A.

Volunteering in November 1914, he was retained on special duties at various stations, including York, Aldershot, and Norwich, prior to being drafted in 1916 to the Western Front, where he distinguished himself in the Battle of the Somme, and was awarded the Military Medal for conspicuous bravery and devotion to duty in the Field. Later whilst in action at Passchendaele, he was severely gassed and invalided home to England. Upon his recovery he rendered valuable services as a signalling instructor until demobilised in February 1919. In addition to the Military Medal, he holds the General Service and Victory Medals.

30, Cabul Road, Battersea, S.W.11. Z2939

LACEY, W. C., A.B., Royal Navy.

He joined in May 1916, and was posted to H.M.S. "Monarch," which vessel was engaged on important duties patrolling the North Sea. After the cessation of hostilities he was transferred to H.M.S. "Phaeton," and this ship acted as escort at the internment of the German Fleet at Scapa Flow. He was demobilised in March 1919, and holds the General Service and Victory Medals.

39, Warrior Road, Camberwell, S.E.5. Z2938

LACKEY, H. T., Private, 10th Duke of Wellington's (West Riding Regiment).

He joined in September 1916, and in the following year was sent to the Western Front. He served with his Battalion in many parts of the line and fought at the Battles of the Somme and Ypres, and was severely wounded at the Menin Road. Unhappily he died from effects of his wounds on September 21st, 1917, and was buried in Passchendaele Cemetery. He was entitled to the General Service and Victory Medals.

"Thinking that remembrance, though unspoken, may reach
him where he sleeps."

6, Mary's Cottages, Eastcote Street, Stockwell, S.W.9. Z2940

LADBROOK, J., Sub-Inspector, Metropolitan Special Constabulary, Peckham Division.

He joined the Peckham Division of the Metropolitan Special Constabulary in September 1914, and rendered valuable services throughout the war, particularly during air raids. For his efficient work he was promoted to Sub-Inspector before his discharge in July 1919.

9, Bavent Road, Camberwell, S.E.5. Z6474

LADBROOKE, R. W., Rifleman, Rifle Brigade and Private, Labour Corps.

He volunteered in December 1915, and after his training served at various stations on important duties with his unit. He was engaged at the Docks on clerical work and in checking ammunition, medical stores, and supplies prior to their transport overseas. He did good work, but was not successful in securing his transfer overseas owing to medical unfitness and was demobilised in January 1919.

6, Walcot Buildings, Walnut Tree Walk, Kennington, S.E.11. 26993

LADD, W., Sapper, R.E.

Volunteering in February 1915, he proceeded to the Western Front five months later, and was in action in many engagements of note. He rendered valuable services engaged on field work of all descriptions in the front lines. Owing to ill-health he returned to England, and after receiving medical treatment was invalided out of the Service in June 1917. He holds the 1914-15 Star, and the General Service and Victory Medals.

3, Fendick Road, Peckham, S.E.15. Z6274

LADYMAN, W. E., Private, 2nd Lancashire Fusiliers.

Enlisting in 1906, he was mobilised on the outbreak of war and proceeded immediately to France, where he saw much heavy fighting. He fought in the early engagements, and was unhappily killed in action on November 4th, 1914. He was entitled to the 1914 Star, and the General Service and Victory Medals.

"Honour to the immortal dead who gave their youth that the
world might grow old in peace."

23, Ramsay Road, Acton, W.3. 6383A

LAFFAN, J., Private, 19th London Regiment.

Prior to volunteering in December 1915, he was engaged upon Government work, as a machine hand in connection with the production of National stamps. On completing his training he served at various stations on important duties with his Battalion. Owing to illness he was invalided to hospital, and after receiving medical treatment was discharged as medically unfit for further military service in April 1917. He then returned to his former Government occupation and rendered further valuable services.

57, Graylands Road, Peckham, S.E.15. Z5801

LAFFIN, W. N., Private, South Staffordshire Regt. and R.A.S.C.

He joined in September 1915, and after training proceeded to Ireland, and later to the Western Front. In this theatre of war he was engaged in much heavy fighting and fought at the Battles of Ypres, Arras, the Somme, and was gassed at Cambrai. After receiving hospital treatment, he returned to the front lines and served until the cessation of hostilities. He was demobilised in January 1919, and holds the General Service and Victory Medals.

186, St. George's Road, Peckham, S.E.15. Z5799

LAILEY, C. (D.C.M.), Gunner, R.F.A.

Volunteering in August 1914, after previous service with the Colours, he was almost immediately drafted to France, and fought during the Retreat from Mons, and was awarded the Distinguished Conduct Medal on October 31st, 1914, for conspicuous bravery and devotion to duty during the Battle of Ypres. He gave his life for the freedom of England in the Battle of the Somme on September 1st, 1916, and was entitled to the Mons Star, and the General Service and Victory Medals.

"He joined the great white company of valiant souls."

2, Bavent Road, Camberwell, S.E.5. Z6475

LAING, J., L/Corporal, 23rd London Regiment.

He volunteered in May 1915, and after training proceeded in the same year to the Western Front, and was in action in several engagements, including the Battles of Ypres, Arras, Cambrai, Loos. He was unhappily killed in action during the Somme Offensive in July 1916, and was entitled to the General Service and Victory Medals.

"He passed out of the sight of men by the path of duty and
self-sacrifice."

6, Urswicke Road, Battersea, S.W.11. Z2941

LAIT, C. E., Q.M.S., 19th London Regiment.

Volunteering in September 1914, he embarked for France in the following year. During his service overseas he was in action at Givenchy and Loos, where he was wounded. He returned to England and received medical treatment, but on recovery was not passed fit for active service and consequently served at various depôts at home until demobilised in March 1919. He holds the 1914-15 Star, and the General Service and Victory Medals.

39, Evelina Road, Peckham, S.E.15. Z6275

LAKE, D. J., Pte., 6th South Wales Borderers Regt.

He volunteered in March 1915, and after completing his training was drafted in the same year to the Western Front, and fought in several battles, including those at Ypres, Loos, the Somme, and Lens. In November 1917 he was severely wounded in action, and, evacuated to England, received medical treatment at Oxford. On recovery he returned to France in 1918, and served in the concluding operations of the war. He was demobilised in February 1919, and holds the 1914-15 Star, and the General Service and Victory Medals.

24, Pepler Road, Peckham, S.E.15. Z3482

LAKER, L. (Miss), Worker, Q.M.A.A.C.

She volunteered in June 1916, and proceeded to France in March of the following year. During her service on the Western Front, she served at Pont de l'Arche and other stations engaged on special duties in the Officers' Mess. After the cessation of hostilities she returned to England and was demobilised in October 1919, and holds the General Service and Victory Medals. 131, Speke Rd., Battersea, S.W.11. Z2942

LAMB, O. F., Private, R.A.M.C.

He volunteered in October 1914, and in the following May embarked for Egypt, where he served for a time. Later posted to a hospital ship stationed at the Dardanelles, he rendered valuable services attending to the wounded during the Gallipoli campaign, and on the Evacuation of the Peninsula proceeded to Malta. He was afterwards drafted to Salonika, and was engaged on hospital work until invalided home in December 1918, suffering from malaria. After receiving hospital treatment he was demobilised in March 1919, and holds the 1914-15 Star, and the General Service and Victory Medals.

38, Honeywell Road, Wandsworth Common, S.W.11. Z6519B

LAMB, P. W., Bombardier, R.F.A.

Volunteering in May 1915, he was sent to the Western Front later in the same year, and served with his Battery in various parts of the line and fought in the Battles of the Somme, Ypres, Arras, and in the Retreat and Advance of 1918, and was gassed. After hostilities ceased he returned to England, and was demobilised in February 1919. He holds the 1914-15 Star, and the General Service and Victory Medals.

56B, Morat Street, Clapham Road, S.W.9. Z24622

LAMBERT, G., Private, Royal Inniskilling Fusiliers.

He volunteered in March 1915, and embarked for the Western Front in the same year. There he was in action in several engagements, including the Battles of Ypres, Cambrai, the Somme, Loos, Messines Ridge, and during the Retreat and Advance of 1918. After the conclusion of hostilities he returned home for demobilisation in February 1919, and holds the 1914-15 Star, and the General Service and Victory Medals.

12, Stockdale Road, Wandsworth Road, S.W.8. Z2944

LAMBERT, G. S., Driver, R.A.S.C.

He volunteered in August 1914, and in the same year was sent to the Western Front, where he served during the Retreat from Mons, and in the Battles of the Aisne, La Bassée, Ypres, Loos and Arras. Engaged with the Horse Transport he did excellent work until the cessation of hostilities, and returning home for demobilisation in March 1919, he holds the Mons Star, and the General Service and Victory Medals.

27, Sunwell Street, Peckham, S.E.15. Z6476

LAMBERT, H., Rifleman, Rifle Brigade.

He joined in June 1917, and in the following year was drafted to the Western Front, where he fought in several engagements, including the Battle of Cambrai. During the German Offensive he was taken prisoner at St. Emilie in March 1918, and was made to work behind the German lines. On repatriation after the cessation of hostilities he was demobilised in February 1919, and holds the General Service and Victory Medals.

4, New Church Road, Camberwell, S.E.5. Z5797

LAMBERT, T. A., Sergt., 1st East Surrey Regiment.

A Reservist, he was mobilised at the outbreak of war and sent to France in the following year. During his service overseas he was in action in many important engagements, including those at the Somme, Vimy Ridge and Arras. Owing to ill-health he returned to England, and after receiving hospital treatment was discharged unfit for further service in October 1917. He holds the 1914-15 Star, and the General Service and Victory Medals.

78, Vaughan Road, Camberwell, S.E.5. Z6276

LAMBERT, W. A., Private, 37th Middlesex Regt.

Volunteering in 1914, he was drafted to France in the same year and during his five years' service overseas, took a prominent part in many important engagements, including the Battles of Ypres, Vimy Ridge and Arras. He returned to England after the cessation of hostilities, and was demobilised in February 1919, and holds the 1914-15 Star, and the General Service and Victory Medals.

25, Westhall Road, Camberwell, S.E.5. Z2945

LAMBOURNE, G. S., Gunner, R.F.A.

He volunteered in September 1914, and was sent to the Western Front in the following year. There he was engaged in much heavy fighting, including the Battles of Ypres, Arras, Loos, Messines Ridge, Vimy Ridge, Lille, Festubert, Albert, Menin Road, Bapaume, Combles, and in the Retreat and Advance of 1918. After the cessation of hostilities he returned home and was demobilised in January 1919, and holds the 1914-15 Star, and the General Service and Victory Medals.

137, South Street, Walworth, S.E.17. Z2946

LAMBOURNE, W., Rifleman, 13th Rifle Brigade.

He joined in 1916, and in the following year embarked for the Western Front. After six days' service in the trenches he was seriously wounded, whilst taking rations up the line. He was evacuated to England, and owing to the severity of his injuries his left leg had to be amputated, and his left hand became paralysed. He was invalided out of the Service in January 1919, and in 1920 was still in Burnham-on-Crouch Hospital receiving medical treatment. He holds the General Service and Victory Medals.

47, Gladstone Street, Battersea Park Road, S.W.8. Z2947B

LAMBOURNE, W., 2nd Lieut., 12th, 17th and 23rd London Regiments.

Volunteering in September 1914, he was drafted in the following year to the Western Front, where as a Sergeant in the 17th London Regiment he took a distinguished part in several engagements until transferred to Salonika in 1917. After serving in this theatre of war for a time he returned to England for training, having been selected for promotion to commissioned rank. He was gazetted in January 1918, and shortly afterwards proceeded to France, and was actively engaged in the Retreat and Advance of 1918. He was unhappily killed in action at Morlancourt in August of that year, and was entitled to the 1914-15 Star, and the General Service and Victory Medals.

" A costly sacrifice upon the altar of freedom."

47, Gladstone Street, Battersea Park Road, S.W.8. Z2947A

LAMPON, A. E. R., L/Cpl., 2/11th London Regiment (Rifles).

He joined in November 1916, and embarking for France two months later, fought in many parts of the line. He was severely wounded in the Ypres salient on November 6th, 1917, and died from the effects of his injuries the following day. He was entitled to the General Service and Victory Medals.

" Whilst we remember the Sacrifice is not in vain."

15, Alder Street, Peckham, S.E.15. Z6277

LANCASHIRE, A. E., Private, R.A.M.C.

Volunteering in 1915, he was drafted to Mesopotamia in the following year, and served in the forward areas at Baghdad, and also at the Base at Basra, engaged on important duties attending the sick and wounded troops. He rendered valuable services and returning to England was demobilised in 1919. He holds the General Service and Victory Medals.

8, Tisdale Place, Elsted Street, Walworth, S.E.17. Z2949

LANCASHIRE, W. F., Private, Essex Regiment.

He joined in 1918, and proceeding to the Western Front, was in action at the Battles of the Somme, Ypres and Arras during the German Offensive and subsequent Allied Advance of 1918. Returning to England after the cessation of hostilities, he was demobilised in 1920, and holds the General Service and Victory Medals.

8, Tisdale Place, Elsted Street, Walwo,th, S.E.17. Z2949A

LANCASTER, E., Leading Stoker, R.N.

He joined the Service in October 1908, and at the outbreak of war was serving in H.M.S. " Lowestoft," which ship was in action when the " Blucher " was sunk at the Battle of the Dogger Bank. Later he was transferred to H.M.S. " Pembroke " and saw much service during the time this vessel was engaged on patrol and other important duties. He was discharged in June 1920, and holds the 1914-15 Star, and the General Service and Victory Medals.

13, Westmacott Street, Camberwell, S.E.5. Z3481

LANCASTER, E. W., Corporal, R.F.A.

Volunteering in May 1915, he proceeded to France later in the same year, and was in action at the Battles of St. Eloi, Vimy Ridge, Passchendaele, and was wounded and gassed at the second Battle of the Somme in March 1918. On recovery he rejoined his Battery and fought throughout the concluding operations of the war. He was demobilised in May 1919, and holds the 1914-15 Star, and the General Service and Victory Medals.

15, Gaskell Street, Larkhall Lane, S.W.4. Z2948

LANCUM, G. M., Private, 23rd London Regiment.

Volunteering in August 1914, he completed his training and was stationed at Warminster until drafted to the Western Front in 1916. He served in the forward areas as a stretcher-bearer in many engagements, including the Battle of Ypres. In 1917 he was transferred to Salonika, and saw much service there until sent to Egypt later in the same year. He was engaged on important duties in various sectors of the Palestine front, and returning to England was demobilised in March 1919. He holds the General Service and Victory Medals.

8, Newland Terrace, Queen's Row, Walworth, S.E.17. Z2950

LAND, H. J., Gunner, R.F.A.

Volunteering in November 1914, he was sent to the Western Front in the following September, and fought at the Battles of St. Eloi, Albert, Vimy Ridge, Beaumont-Hamel and Bullecourt, where he was severely wounded. Admitted into hospital he subsequently died from the effects of his injuries on May 23rd, 1917, and was entitled to the 1914-15 Star, and the General Service and Victory Medals.

" His life for his Country, his Soul to God."

1, Aldbridge Street, Walworth, S.E.17 Z2951

LANDER, F. W., Private, Royal Fusiliers.

Volunteering in 1915, he was drafted to France later in that year, and was in action in many engagements of note, including those in the German Offensive of 1918. On July 31st, 1918, he was reported missing, and later was presumed to have been killed in action on that date. He was entitled to the 1914–15 Star, and the General Service and Victory Medals.
"And doubtless he went in splendid company."
25, Beckway Street, Walworth, S.E.17. Z2953A

LANDER, M. C., Sergt., R.G.A.

Joining in May 1916, he proceeded to France later and fought at Ypres and the Somme, and was then transferred to Italy. Here he was in action in various parts of the Piave and Asiago fronts. He then was sent to Egypt, and saw considerable service in Palestine during the Advance through the Holy Land into Syria. He was demobilised in November 1919, on his return to England, and holds the General Service and Victory Medals.
56, Gayville Road, Wandsworth Common, S.W.11. Z2952

LANDER, T. E., Private, Dorsetshire Regiment.

He volunteered at the outbreak of hostilities, and was sent to France in November 1914. During his service overseas he was in action in the Ypres salient, and in many other parts of the line. He gave his life for the freedom of England at Ypres on April 10th, 1915, and was entitled to the 1914–15 Star, and the General Service and Victory Medals.
"His life for his Country, his Soul to God."
25, Beckway Street, Walworth, S.E.17. Z2953B

LANDS, W. G., Rifleman, King's Royal Rifle Corps.

He joined in August 1916, and was drafted to the Western Front in the following December. He fought in the Battles of Ypres, Arras, Vimy Ridge, Passchendaele, and many other engagements. Invalided to England in July 1917, he received hospital treatment, and on recovery was transferred to the R.A.O.C., with which unit he rendered valuable services at various stations. He was demobilised in January 1919, and holds the General Service and Victory Medals.
34, Boathouse Walk, Peckham, S.E.15. Z6278

LANE, A., Gunner, R.G.A.

Volunteering in August 1914, he completed his training and was stationed at various depôts until embarking for France in 1916. He saw heavy fighting in the Ypres, Vimy Ridge and Arras sectors, and was in action throughout the Retreat and Advance of 1918. After the Armistice he was sent with the Army of Occupation into Germany, where he was still serving in 1920, and holds the General Service and Victory Medals.
70, Mayall Road, Herne Hill, S.E.24. Z1773B

LANE. A. (Mrs.), Special War Worker.

This lady offered her services for work of National importance, and from November 1916 until September 1918 worked at Woolwich Arsenal, employed as Inspector in the fuse-making department. She rendered valuable services throughout, and discharged her duties in a most efficient and satisfactory manner.
2, Merrick Square, Trinity Street, S.E.1. Z2957C

LANE, A., Private, R.A.M.C.

He volunteered in November 1914, and embarking for France three months later, served in various parts of the line until proceeding to Salonika, where he was engaged on important duties attending the sick and wounded troops. Contracting malaria, he was admitted into hospital and received treatment. On recovery he was drafted to Egypt, and served in many sectors of the Palestine front. He returned to England and was still serving in 1920, and holds the 1914–15 Star, and the General Service and Victory Medals.
2, Merrick Square, Trinity Street, S.E.1. Z2957A

LANE, A., Rflmn., 2/16 London Regiment (Queen's Westminster Rifles).

Volunteering in August 1914, he was sent to the Western Front in the following year. During his service overseas he fought in many engagements, including those at Hill 60, Vimy Ridge, the Somme, Ypres, and was wounded at Kemmel and later at Cambrai. He was in action throughout the German Offensive of 1918, and was gassed in the Allied Advance, and returned to England. He received hospital treatment, and was demobilised in December 1918, and holds the 1914–15 Star, and the General Service and Victory Medals.
49, Longhedge Street, Battersea, S.W.11. Z2954

LANE, C., A.B., Royal Navy.

He joined in June 1915, and conpleting his training at the Crystal Palace was posted to one of H.M. Patrol Boats in the following year. His ship proceeded to the Mediterranean, and operating from Gibraltar, was engaged on important duties. He returned to England and was demobilised in March 1919, and holds the General Service and Victory Medals.
23, Dalyell Road, Landor Road, S.W.9. Z2955

LANE, F., Special War Worker.

He offered his services for work of National importance, and from January 1915, until March 1919, held an important position as time-keeper at Woolwich Arsenal. He rendered valuable services and discharged his duties satisfactorily.
2, Merrick Square, Trinity Street, S.E.1. Z2957B

LANE, H. C. J., Private, 7th Queen's Own (Royal West Kent Regiment).

He volunteered in September 1914, and proceeding to France shortly afterwards, saw heavy fighting at Ypres, Loos, the Somme and Arras. He was severely wounded at the second Battle of the Somme in March 1918, and admitted into hospital. His injuries were so serious, that it was found necessary to amputate one of his arms. He returned to England and was invalided out of the Service in 1918, and holds the 1914 Star, and the General Service and Victory Medals.
175, Mayall Road, Herne Hill, S.E.24. Z2956

LANE, J., Gunner, R.F.A.

Volunteering in November 1914, he embarked for the Western Front in the following year, and fought in the Battles of Loos, Albert, Vermelles, Vimy Ridge, the Somme, Lens, and was in action almost continuously in the Retreat and Advance of 1918. After the Armistice he returned to England and was serving in Ireland in 1920, and holds the 1914–15 Star, and the General Service and Victory Medals.
3, Mina Road, Walworth, S.E.17. Z2958

LANE, W. H., Private, Sherwood Foresters.

Joining in September 1916, he was drafted to France four months later, and took part in many engagements, including those at the Ancre, Bullecourt, Ypres and Cambrai, and was wounded. On recovery he rejoined his Battalion, and fought in various sectors, and was again wounded in the second Battle of the Somme in March 1918. He returned to England, and after receiving hospital treatment, was discharged unfit for further service in July 1918. He holds the General Service and Victory Medals.
65, SNeate treet, Camberwell, S.E.5. Z5093A

LANE, W. R., Cpl., Cameronians (Scottish Rifles).

Mobilised and sent to France at the outbreak of hostilities, he fought in the Retreat from Mons, and in the Battles of the Marne, the Aisne, and Ypres. Owing to ill-health he was invalided to England, and after receiving hospital treatment returned to France. After a further period of service he was again invalided to England, and on recovery was drafted again to the Western Front, and was in action throughout the Allied Advance of 1918. He was demobilised in January 1919, and holds the Mons Star, and the General Service and Victory Medals.
35, Nursery Row, Brandon Street, Walworth, S.E.17. Z2959A

LANGAN, H. (M.M.), Private, Queen's (Royal West Surrey Regiment) and Gunner, R.G.A.

Volunteering in August 1914, he proceeded to France later in that year and fought in the Battles of Festubert, Richebourg, and Loos, where he was wounded. On recovery rejoining his Battalion in the Field, he was in action at Arras, Neuve Chapelle, and various other engagements. He was awarded the Military Medal for conspicuous gallantry and devotion to duty in the Field in repairing telephone wires, and maintaining communication under heavy fire. He was demobilised in February 1919, and also holds the 1914–15 Star, and the General Service and Victory Medals.
79, Commercial Road, Peckham, S.E.15. Z6279

LANGFORD, E. C., Sergt., Royal Fusiliers.

He volunteered in August 1914, and proceeding to the Western Front later in that year, fought in many engagements of note, including those at Ypres, Neuve Chapelle and Arras. He died gloriously on the Field of Battle at Hill 60, on May 15th, 1915, and was entitled to the 1914–15 Star, and the General Service and Victory Medals.
"Courage, bright hopes, and myriad dreams, splendidly given."
90, Somerleyton Road, Coldharbour Lane, S.W.9. Z3055B

LANGHAM, F., Private, R.A.S.C. (M.T.)

Volunteering in 1915, he completed his training and served at various stations engaged on transport and other important duties with his unit. He was unsuccessful in obtaining his transfer overseas, but rendered valuable services until demobilised in 1919.
37, Southville, Wandsworth Road, S.W.8. Z2960

LANGLEY, F. H., Rflmn., King's Royal Rifle Corps.

He volunteered in November 1915, and was sent to France in the following September. He saw much fighting on the Somme front and in the Ypres salient, and in November 1917 was transferred to Italy, where he served on the Piave front until March 1918. Then, returning to the Western Front he was in action throughout the German offensive, and was wounded at Bisseghem during the Allied Advance. He was demobilised in February 1919, and holds the General Service and Victory Medals.
24, D Block, Lewis Trust Buildings, off Warner Road, Camberwell, S.E.5. Z6023

LANGLEY, H. S., Driver, R.A.S.C.
Volunteering in August 1914, in the following October he proceeded to France, where he served in the forward areas transporting supplies to the front lines. He was present at the Battles of Ypres, Hill 60, the Somme, the Ancre, Le Cateau, and saw much service in the Retreat and Advance of 1918. He was demobilised in May 1919, and holds the 1914 Star, and the General Service and Victory Medals.
97, Cronin Road, Peckham, S.E.15. Z5439

LANGLEY, J. A., Air Mechanic, R.A.F.
He joined in February 1918, and completing his training was stationed at Bath Aerodrome, engaged on important duties. He was not successful in obtaining his transfer to a theatre of war prior to the cessation of hostilities, but did good work until demobilised in January 1919.
152, Farmer's Road, Camberwell, S.E.5. Z2961

LANGRIDGE, H., Gunner, R.M.A.
Volunteering in March 1915, in the following November he proceeded to France and served there until the cessation of hostilities. During this period he was in action in various parts of the line and fought in many important engagements. He returned to England and was demobilised in February 1919, and holds the 1914-15 Star, and the General Service and Victory Medals.
16, Cardross Street, Hammersmith, W.6. 11519

LANSDALE, A. P., Private, 2nd London Regiment (Royal Fusiliers).
He joined in May 1916, and three months later was drafted to the Western Front. During his service in this theatre of war he fought in the Battles of Passchendaele, Lens and the Somme, and was taken prisoner on March 21st, 1918. He was held in captivity in Germany until repatriated in December 1918. He then served at home until his demobilisation in September 1919, and holds the General Service and Victory Medals.
29, Manor Street, Clapham, S.W.4. Z2962

LANSDOWN, R. G., Rough Rider, R.A.S.C. (Remounts).
Volunteering in September 1914, he was drafted to the Western Front in the same month and served in the Battles of Ypres, Festubert, Loos, the Somme, Bullecourt, Passchendaele, and during the Retreat and Advance of 1918, and was wounded. After the Armistice he was sent with the Army of Occupation into Germany and stationed on the Rhine. He returned to England for demobilisation in April 1919, and holds the 1914 Star, and the General Service and Victory Medals.
52, Robsart Street, Brixton Road, S.W.9. Z2964

LAPWOOD, W., Pte., 2/5th North Staffordshire Regt.
Joining in September 1916, he proceeded to France in the following February and was in action in the Battles of Arras, Vimy Ridge, Bullecourt, Ypres and Passchendaele. Owing to illness he was invalided to hospital in England in September 1917, and on recovery served with his unit on home service duties until demobilised in February 1919. He holds the General Service and Victory Medals.
9, Glendall Street, Ferndale Road, S.W.9. Z2965

LARNDER, E. C., Pte., 4th (Queen's Own) Hussars.
Enlisting in 1912, he was mobilised when war broke out and shortly afterwards drafted to France. He was engaged in heavy fighting during the Retreat from Mons, and in the Battles of Ypres and Loos, and was severely wounded. Sent home to hospital on account of his injuries, he underwent twenty-six operations, and after prolonged medical treatment was subsequently demobilised in January 1919. He holds the Mons Star, and the General Service and Victory Medals.
29, Mostyn Road, Brixton Road, S.W.9. Z3483

LARTER, A., Driver, R.A.S.C. (M.T.)
He volunteered in May 1915, and two months later proceeded overseas. Engaged on important duties in connection with the transport of rations and supplies to the forward areas, he did good work in many sectors of the Western Front, and was present at the Battles of the Somme, Arras and Cambrai. He was demobilised in January 1919, and holds the 1914-15 Star, and the General Service and Victory Medals.
8, Thorncroft Street, Wandsworth Road, S.W.8. Z2968C

LARTER, A. E., Private, Northamptonshire Regt.
He joined in December 1917, on attaining military age, and early in the following year embarked for the Western Front. There he took part in several important engagements, including the Battles of the Somme, Ypres and Cambrai, and was wounded during the Advance of 1918. Invalided home on account of his injuries, he was discharged in consequence in October 1919, and holds the General Service and Victory Medals.
8, Thorncroft Street, Wandsworth Road, S.W.8. Z2968A

LARTER, A. W., Private, King's Own (Royal Lancaster Regiment).
He volunteered in November 1914, and in the following August was sent to the Western Front. In this theatre of war he fought in several battles, notably those of Loos, Arras, Merveille and the Somme. He died gloriously on the Field of Battle at Monchy on May 12th, 1917, and was entitled to the 1914-15 Star, and the General Service and Victory Medals.
"Steals on the ear the distant triumph song."
8, Thorncroft Street, Wandsworth Road, S.W.8. Z2968B

LARTER, H. G., Sergt., R.A.F. (late R.N.A.S.)
Volunteering in October 1914, he was drafted to France in the same year, and served until the cessation of hostilities. During this period he was engaged as a motor mechanic with his Squadron at Ypres, Arras and other places in the Somme sector. He was also stationed at Dunkirk and did good work on duties of a highly technical nature. He was demobilised in November 1919, and holds the 1914-15 Star, and the General Service and Victory Medals.
51, Villa Street, Walworth, S.E.17. Z2969

LARTER, W. C., Private, 7th London Regiment
He volunteered in 1915, and, drafted to the Western Front in the following year served in various parts of the line. He was in action in many engagements, including the Battles of Ypres, and was wounded at Messines on June 7th, 1917. Admitted to hospital in France on account of his injuries, he was afterwards evacuated to England for medical treatment and ultimately discharged as medically unfit for further service in March 1919. He holds the General Service and Victory Medals.
198, Mayall Road, Herne Hill, S.E.24. Z5113

LASHAM, F., Master at Arms, R.N.
Mobilised on the outbreak of war, he served in H.M.S. "Dragon " throughout the course of hostilities. His ship was engaged on patrol duties in the North Sea and was in action in the Battle of Heligoland Bight, and had several other encounters with enemy craft. After the Armistice this vessel was sent to the Baltic and was torpedoed, but he fortunately escaped injury. He holds the 1914-15 Star, and the General Service and Victory Medals, and in 1920 was still serving.
46, Wansey Street, Walworth, S.E.17. Z2970A

LASSAM, E., Farrier Staff-Sergt., R.A.S.C.
He volunteered in August 1914, and proceeding to the Western Front in the following November served there for over four years. Engaged on important duties with his unit he did good work in numerous engagements, including those at Laventie, La Bassée, Ypres, Passchendaele, Ploegsteert Wood, Vimy Ridge and the Somme. He returned home after the Armistice, was demobilised in February 1919, and holds the 1914 Star, and the General Service and Victory Medals.
36, South Island Place, Brixton Road, S.W.9. Z5261

LAST, H., Private, 8th Queen's (Royal West Surrey Regiment).
Volunteering in December 1915, he was sent to France in the following year and fought in several engagements, including the Battles of the Somme, Ypres and Cambrai, and was wounded three times. Rejoining his unit on recovery he took part in the Retreat of 1918, and fell fighting near St. Quentin on March 21st of that year. He was entitled to the General Service and Victory Medals.
"Thinking that remembrance, though unspoken, may reach him where he sleeps."
42, Gladstone Terrace, Battersea Park Road, S.W.8. Z2972B

LAST, J. B., Corporal, R.G.A.
He volunteered in August 1914, and proceeding to France almost immediately, was engaged in heavy fighting during the Retreat from Mons, and in the Battles of Neuve Chapelle, Ypres, Cambrai and the Somme. He was also in action in several engagements during the Retreat and Advance of 1918, and was gassed a few days before the Armistice. He returned home for demobilisation in February 1919, and holds the Mons Star, and the General Service and Victory Medals.
42, Gladstone Terrace, Battersea Park Road, S.W.8. Z2971

LAST, L., Sapper, R.E.
He volunteered in August 1915, and, drafted overseas in the same year, served in various theatres of war. Whilst in France he was engaged on important duties during the Battles of St. Eloi and Loos, and was sent to Salonika in 1916. After a period of service in the Balkans he proceeded to Egypt and did good work during the British Advance through Palestine, and was present at the Entry into Jerusalem. Returning to England on the conclusion of hostilities he was demobilised in July 1919, and holds the 1914-15 Star, and the General Service and Victory Medals.
42, Gladstone Terrace, Battersea Park Road, S.W.8. Z2972A

LAST, W., A.B., Royal Navy.

Joining in 1916, he was posted to a mine-sweeper, and was engaged on mine-sweeping duties in the North Sea. His ship had several narrow escapes in the discharge of her hazardous duties, and he did valuable work throughout his service. He was demobilised in September 1919, and holds the General Service and Victory Medals.

42, Gladstone Terrace, Battersea Park Road, S.W.8.   Z2972C

LATCHFORD, W. A., Gunner, R.F.A.

He volunteered in April 1915, and later in the same year was drafted to France, where he took part in numerous engagements. He unfortunately died of wounds received in action at Delville Wood on July 27th, 1916, and was entitled to the 1914-15 Star, and the General Service and Victory Medals.

"And doubtless he went in splendid company."

175, South Street, Walworth, S.E.17.   Z3145

LATHWELL, H., L/Corporal, 2nd Welch Regiment.

He volunteered in December 1915, and embarked for the Western Front in the following year. He served in various sectors and fought in several important engagements, in the course of which he was wounded at Messines, and was later gassed in the Battle of St. Quentin. On recovery he served through the Retreat and Advance of 1918, and returning to England for demobilisation in February 1919, holds the General Service and Victory Medals.

212, Beresford Street, Camberwell, S.E.5.   Z2973

LATTER, E. T., Gunner, R.N.V.R.

He volunteered in 1915, and at the conclusion of his training was posted to H.M.S. "Chipana." His ship was engaged on special duties, transporting food supplies between America, Gibraltar, Australia, Egypt, Italy, France and England, and he did very good work. He was demobilised in 1919, and holds the 1914-15 Star, and the General Service and Victory Medals.

103, Kimberley Road, Nunhead, S.E.15.   Z6407

LAUER, A. C., L/Corporal, Royal Fusiliers.

Volunteering in February 1915, he was sent to the Western Front in the following August, and served as a sniper in several engagements, including the Battles of Loos, Arras and Ypres. He gave his life for the freedom of England in the Battle of the Somme, and was entitled to the 1914-15 Star, and the General Service and Victory Medals.

"Nobly striving, he nobly fell that we might live."

127, Ferndale Road, Clapham, S.W.4.   Z2974B

LAUER, A. E., Pte., 14th London Regt. (London Scottish).

He volunteered in 1917, on attaining military age, and in the same year proceeded overseas. Serving on the Western Front he was in action in the Battle of Cambrai and owing to illness was sent home. He received hospital treatment and was discharged as medically unfit for service in 1918, and holds the General Service and Victory Medals.

127, Ferndale Road, Clapham, S.W.4.   Z2974A

LAVER, F. W., Rflmn., King's Royal Rifle Corps.

Volunteering in 1914, he was engaged on important duties with his Battalion until drafted to Salonika in 1916. He took part in several operations in the Balkans, including the Advance across the Vardar, and owing to illness was invalided home to hospital. Discharged on account of service in 1919, he holds the General Service and Victory Medals.

28, Thurlow Street, Wandsworth Road, S.W.8.   4190B

LAW, C., Sergt., Worcestershire Regiment.

He volunteered in August 1914, and was shortly afterwards sent to France, where he served until drafted to Gallipoli in 1915. He fought in the three Battles of Krithia, and in other operations, and on the Evacuation of the Peninsula in 1916 returned to France. There he was in action in the Battles of Beaumont-Hamel, Ypres, St. Julien, the Somme, the Aisne and in the concluding engagements of the war. He was wounded five times whilst overseas, and in 1920 was still serving, and holds the 1914-15 Star, and the General Service and Victory Medals.

69, Killyon Road, Wandsworth Road, S.W.8.   Z2975C

LAW, R. J., Private, Middlesex Regiment.

He joined in March 1918, when of military age, and was engaged on important duties with his unit at various stations, and rendered valuable services. He was unsuccessful in obtaining a transfer to a theatre of war before the termination of hostilities. In 1919, however, he was sent with the Army of Occupation into Germany and served there on outpost and other duties until his return home for demobilisation in 1920.

Doctor Street, Walworth, S.E.17.   Z26469

LAWLESS, F., Lieut., 10th Yorkshire Regiment.

He volunteered in 1914, and in the following year proceeded to France, where he served for upwards of three years. During this period he was engaged on important duties with his unit, and saw much heavy fighting until the conclusion of the war. Returning home after the Armistice, he was demobilised in 1919, and holds the 1914-15 Star, and the General Service and Victory Medals.

13, Montgomery Road, Chiswick, W.4.   6903B

LAWRENCE, F., 1st Air Mechanic, R.A.F.

He joined in April 1916, and was shortly afterwards sent to the Western Front. He served with the Kite Balloon Section in various sectors, and was engaged on important duties, which called for a high degree of technical skill. He was demobilised in 1919, and holds the General Service and Victory Medals.

68, Andulus Road, Landor Road, S.W.9.   Z2977

LAWRENCE, F. W., L/Cpl., Bedfordshire Regiment.

He joined in June 1918, and after his training was stationed at Norwich with his Battalion, but was not able to secure his transfer overseas before the cessation of hostilities. In January 1919, he proceeded to Germany with the Army of Occupation, and served there until his demobilisation in October 1919.

21, Cunard Street, Camberwell, S.E.5.   Z5114B

LAWRENCE, G. W., Pte., 8th East Surrey Regt.

Volunteering in September 1914, he was drafted to France in the following June. He was engaged in heavy fighting on the Somme, and was wounded at Fricourt in February 1916. He was sent to hospital in England, and in the following August was discharged medically unfit for further service. He rejoined in May 1918, and was almost immediately sent to the Western Front, where he served on special duties with his Company during the Retreat and Advance of 1918. He was wounded in November of that year, and after receiving treatment in England he again returned to France, and was employed on various duties until demobilised in February 1920. He holds the 1914-15 Star, and the General Service and Victory Medals.

10, Stanton Street, Peckham, S.E.15.   Z5260

LAWRENCE, H. F., Pte., Queen's (Royal West Surrey Regiment).

He joined in March 1917, and in the same month proceeded overseas. Whilst on the Western Front he was engaged with his unit on important duties at various places, during the fighting at Arras, Lens, Albert and in many other sectors. He returned to Englnad after the cessation of hostilities, and was demobilised in February 1919. He holds the General Service and Victory Medals.

136, Maysoule Road, Battersea, S.W.11.   Z2976

LAWRENCE, R., Pte., Duke of Cornwall's Light Infantry.

He joined in July 1917, and shortly afterwards was sent to the Western Front, where he took part in many engagements, including the actions on the Somme, at Ypres and during the Retreat and Advance of 1918. After the Armistice he remained in France until October 1919, when he returned to England, and was demobilised. He holds the General Service and Victory Medals.

13, Froude Street, Battersea Par,k S.W.8.   Z2978

LAWRENCE, R. C., Gunner, R.F.A.

Volunteering in March 1915, he was sent to France twelve months later, and was in action in various sectors on the Western Front, where he took part in the fierce fighting on the Somme. He died gloriously on the Field of Battle at Delville Wood on July 29th 1916. He was entitled to the General Service and Victory Medals.

"Thinking that remembrance, though unspoken, may reach him where he sleeps."

21, Cunard Street, Camberwell, S.E.5.   Z5114A

LAWRENCE, S. (M.M.), Corporal, 1st London Regt. (Royal Fusiliers).

He volunteered in November 1914, and in March of the following year was drafted to the Western Front, where he fought in the Battle of Ypres and was wounded. On recovery he returned to the firing line and was in action on the Somme and at Cambrai. He was awarded the Military Medal in 1916 for gallantry in the Field, and for the bravery he displayed during a bombing raid, and the capture of an enemy trench with thirty-six prisoners. He was demobilised in March 1919, and also holds the 1914-15 Star, and the General Service and Victory Medals.

8, Lollard Street, Kennsington S.E.11.   TZ25861A

LAY, A. H., Private, 3rd Norfolk Regiment and 7th Leicestershire Regiment.

He joined in May 1917, on attaining military age, and early in the following year was drafted to France, where he was engaged in the fighting during the German Offensive of 1918. On May 27th, 1918, he was reported missing, and was later presumed to have been killed in action on that date. He was entitled to the General Service and Victory Medals.

"He joined the great white company of valiant souls."

165, South Street, Walworth, S.E.17. Z2979

LAY, W. H., Petty Officer, R.N.

Having previously served in the Royal Navy, he was on the outbreak of war, recalled to the Service. He served on various duties with his ship in the North Sea and later went out to German East Africa. In 1920 he was still with his ship on the China station. He holds the 1914-15 Star, and the General Service and Victory Medals.

26, Wyvill Road, Wandsworth Road, S.W.8. Z2980

LAYCOCK, W. L., Driver, R.A.S.C.

A Reservist, he was mobilised in August 1914, and shortly afterwards was sent overseas. During his service on the Western Front he was engaged with his unit on special duties, transporting food supplies and ammunition to the forward areas. In 1918 he was drafted to Egypt, where he contracted malaria and was in hospital for some considerable time. He later returned to England, and was demobilised in February 1919, and holds the 1914 Star, and the General Service and Victory Medals.

20, Mund Street, W. Kensington, W.14. 16921C

LAYEN, T., Rifleman, 21st London Regiment (1st Surrey Rifles).

He volunteered in August 1914, and in the following year proceeded to the Western Front, where he took part in the fighting on the Somme in 1916. He was then sent to Egypt and was in action during the British Advance through Palestine until the capture of Jerusalem. He also saw service in the Balkan campaign, and returned to England after the signing of the Armistice. He was demobilised in May 1919, and holds the 1914-15 Star, and the General Service and Victory Medals.

43, Royal Road, Walworth, S.E.17. Z26569

LAYFIELD, C. T., Sergt., R.E.

He joined in 1916, and at the conclusion of his training was engaged with his unit on special duties at various stations. He did excellent work, but was unsuccessful in obtaining his transfer overseas, and was demobilised in January 1919.

1, Exon Street, Walworth, S.E.17. Z2981

LAYLE, S. F., A.B., Royal Navy.

He volunteered in August 1914, and at the conclusion of his training served with the Grand Fleet in the North Sea. In the course of his service he was engaged with his ship in escorting troops and munitions to Salonika, and other theatres of war. His ship was in constant danger from enemy mines and submarines, and in 1918 was torpedoed. He was demobilised in February 1920, and holds the 1914-15 Star, and the General Service and Victory Medals.

68, St. George's Road, Peckham, S.E.15. Z5440

LAZENBY, F. T., Corporal, Middlesex Regiment.

He attested for service with the Colours in December 1915, and joined in the following May, and in August of that year he proceeded to Singapore. The ship on which he was sailing, s.s. "Tyndareus" was mined off Cape Agulhas, South Africa, but fortunately no lives were lost, and on reaching Singapore, he served with his Battalion on garrison duties until August 1918. He was then drafted to Siberia, where he took part in the fighting against the Bolshevists. He was demobilised in May 1919, and holds the General Service and the Victory Medals.

13, Scylla Road, Peckham, S.E.15. Z6015A

LEA, W. G., Sergt., Loyal North Lancashire Regt.

Volunteering in August 1914, he was sent to France in the following year. During his service on the Western Front he took part in much fighting, and was wounded at Loos, as a consequence of which he was temporarily blinded. He was sent to hospital in England, and was subsequently discharged unfit for further service in August 1917. He holds the 1914-15 Star, and the General Service and Victory Medals.

8, Priory Road, Wandsworth Road, S.W.8. Z2982

LEACH, A., Private, R.A.M.C.

He volunteered in October 1914, and was drafted overseas in the following year. Serving with the Field Ambulance in France he did valuable work in the Battles of Loos, Ypres, Vimy Ridge, the Somme, Bullecourt and Messines. He was unhappily killed in action at Arras on May 16th, 1918, and was entitled to the 1914-15 Star, and the General Service and Victory Medals.

"The path of duty was the way to glory."

6, Burchell Road, Peckham, S.E.15. Z6520

LEACH, A. A., Private, Duke of Cornwall's Light Infantry.

He volunteered in March 1915, and in the following August was sent overseas. Whilst on the Western Front he fought in many engagements, and was severely wounded at Loos in December 1916. He was sent to hospital in England, where he remained for a long period. He was subsequently invalided out of the Service in December 1918. He holds the 1914-15 Star, and the General Service and Victory Medals.

45, Smyrk's Road, Walworth, S.E.17. Z2983B

LEACH, A. T., Rifleman, 9th London Regiment (Queen Victoria's Rifles).

Volunteering in August 1915, he was sent to the Western Front in December of the following year, and fought in several engagements. He was wounded and gassed in the Battle of Arras in April 1917, and sent to hospital. Rejoining his unit on recovery he was in action in the Battles of Vimy Ridge, Lens, Cambrai, the Somme, and in the concluding operations of the war. Demobilised in February 1919, he holds the General Service and Victory Medals.

53, Lower Park Road, Peckham, S.E.15. Z6521

LEACH, J. W., Private, 3rd Middlesex Regiment.

He volunteered in the 17th Lancers in January 1915, but later transferred to the Middlesex Regiment, and at the conclusion of his training served on special duties until drafted to France in May 1917. Whilst in this theatre of war he was engaged in the fighting in the Ypres salient, where he gave his life for King and Country in July 1917. He was entitled to the General Service and Victory Medals.

"Steals on the ear the distant triumph song."

45, Smyrk's Road, Walworth, S.E.17. Z2983A

LEADBEATTER, J. V., Private, 1st Royal Welch Fusiliers.

He volunteered in November 1914, and in the following year was drafted to the Western Front. In this theatre of war he fought in many engagements, including those at Loos, St. Eloi, Albert, Vermelles, and the Somme. He gave his life for the freedom of England during the first British Offensive on the Somme on July 6th, 1916. He was entitled to the 1914-15 Star, and the General Service and Victory Medals.

"And doubtless he went in splendid company."

31, Wivenhoe Road, Peckham, S.E.15. Z6018A

LEADBEATTER, W. H., Bombardier, R.F.A.

Volunteering at the outbreak of hostilities, he was sent overseas in the following year. Whilst in France he fought at Ypres, Ploegsteert Wood, Vimy Ridge, Arras, Bullecourt, Messines, the Somme, Cambrai, and the Retreat and Advance of 1918. He was demobilised in February 1919, and holds the 1914-15 Star, and the General Service and Victory Medals.

31, Wivenhoe Road, Peckham, S.E.15. Z6018B

LEAHEY, J., Private, Worcestershire Regiment.

Prior to August 1914, he had served twenty-one years with the Colours, taking part in the Boer War. He volunteered in October 1915, and was engaged on important defence duties with his Battalion at various stations, and did excellent work. Owing to ill-health he wa invalided to hospital, where he died on October 10th, 1917. He held the Queen's and King's South African Medals.

"His memory is cherished with pride."

27, Park Road, Battersea, S.W.11. Z2984A

LEAHEY, J. J., Private, R.A.M.C.

Volunteering in August 1914, he was almost immediately sent overseas. He was engaged with his unit during the fighting in the Retreat from Mons and many subsequent engagements on the Western Front. He was later sent to Salonika, where he served for a time, and was afterwards drafted to Egypt. He also saw service in Mesopotamia, and returned to England after the signing of the Armistice. He was demobilised in August 1919, and holds the Mons Star, and the General Service and Victory Medals. Owing to ill-health, due to his service, he died shortly after his demobilisation.

"And doubtless he went in splendid company."

27, Park Road, Battersea, S.W.11. Z2984B

LEAHY, T., Private, 6th Royal Fusiliers.

He volunteered in August 1914, and in the following October was drafted to France, where he took part in many engagements and was seriously wounded at Ypres in February 1915. He was invalided to hospital, where it was found necessary to amputate his right arm. He was subsequently discharged unfit for further service in July 1915. He holds the 1914 Star, and the General Service and Victory Medals.

64, Weybridge Street, Battersea, S.W.11. Z2985

LEAKE, F. W., Q.M.S., Royal Scots Fusiliers.

He joined in June 1916, and at the conclusion of his training served on important home duties until drafted to the Western Front early in 1918. He did excellent work on the Commissariat Staff, and was stationed at Dunkirk until after the signing of the Armistice. He was demobilised in October 1919, and holds the General Service and Victory Medals.

4, Roslyn Avenue, Camberwell, S.E.5. Z6406A

LEAKE, R. O., Private (Gunner), M.G.C.

He joined in December 1917, and in the following year proceeded to the Western Front. He fought in engagements on the Somme and during the Retreat and Advance of 1918. He returned to England in September 1918, and served on home duties until demobilised in April 1919. He holds the General Service and Victory Medals.

4, Roslyn Avenue, Camberwell, S.E.5.　　　Z6406B

LEAL, L. R., Private, R.A.S.C. (M.T.)

He volunteered in December 1915, and in March of the following year proceeded overseas. During his service on the Western Front he served on special duties as an engine fitter in many sectors, and did valuable work at Arras, Ypres and the Somme. He was wounded at Ypres in August 1917, and invalided to England. On recovery he was employed on home duties until demobilised in March 1919. He holds the General Service and Victory Medals.

63, Flaxman Road, Camberwell, S.E.5.　　　Z6198

LEAR, F. (Miss), Special War Worker.

During the early part of the war this lady was engaged on important work in connection with the output of munitions. Later, she underwent a course of training at the London Technical School of Engineering, and after passing a number of examinations was appointed to a responsible position with a firm of engineers at Leicester. The services which she rendered in this connection were of the utmost value, and the manner in which she carried out her arduous duties was worthy of high praise.

10, Cunnington Street, Chiswick, W.4.　　　6874A

LEAR, R. (Miss), Special War Worker.

This lady offered her services for work of National importance and for eighteen months was employed at Messrs. Vandervill's Munition Works, as an assembler of grenades. After much valuable service in this capacity she joined the Land Army (Forage Department), where she did excellent work for about two years until demobilised in 1919.

10, Cunnington Street, Chiswick, W.4.　　　6875A

LEAR, T., Pantry Steward, Mercantile Marine.

He joined in January 1918, and was posted to the " Huntsgreen "—a captured German vessel—with which ship he was engaged on important transport duties in the Mediterranean Sea and other waters. His ship was frequently in danger from enemy submarines, but escaped on all occasions. In 1920 he was still serving, and holds the General Service and Mercantile Marine War Medals.

10, Cunnington Street, Chiswick, W.4.　　　6874B

LEAR, T., Gunner, R.F.A.

A Reservist, he was mobilised at the outbreak of war, and in December 1914, was sent to France, where he served for three months, and then proceeded to Gallipoli. In this theatre of war he took part in much fighting until the Evacuation of that Peninsula and was then drafted to Salonika, where he was in action in many engagements. He contracted malaria and was in hospital for some considerable time. After the signing of the Armistice he returned to England, and was demobilised in May 1919. He holds the 1914-15 Star, and the General Service and Victory Medals.

37, Gaskell Street, Larkhall Lane, S.W.4.　　　Z2986

LEAR, W., Cook and Baker, Mercantile Marine.

He joined in February 1915, and during the period of the war rendered valuable services in the " Mahana " and other vessels on important duties, including the transport of troops from Marseilles to North Russia. In January 1918 his vessel, the " Minnetonka," was torpedoed and sunk about 120 miles from Malta, and he was in the sea for many hours before being rescued. He was still serving in 1920, and holds the General Service and the Mercantile Marine War Medals.

10, Cunnington Street, Chiswick, W.4.　　　6875B

LEAR, W., Air Mechanic, R.A.F.

He joined in April 1918, and at the conclusion of his training served with his Squadron at various stations on important duties, which demanded a high degree of technical skill. He did excellent work, but was unable to secure his transfer overseas, and was demobilised in April 1919.

72, Jocelyn Street, Peckham, S.E.15.　　　Z5441

LEAVER, E. J., Rifleman, Royal Irish Rifles.

He joined in January 1917, and on the completion of his training was drafted to the Western Front in the following May, and served in several engagements with his Battalion. He was unfortunately killed in action near Hill 60 in June 1917, and was buried at Messines. He was entitled to the General Service and Victory Medals.

" He passed out of the sight of men by the path of duty and
　　　　self-sacrifice."

64, Maysoule Road, Battersea, S.W.11.　　　Z2988

LEBBY, A., Pte., Queen's (Royal West Surrey Regt).

He volunteered in August 1914 and was sent shortly afterwards to France, where he served throughout the war. He was in action in many important engagements, and was wounded in the Battle of Ypres on November 5th, 1914. Returning to the Field on recovery he served in many operations and was gassed in 1917. He returned home for demobilisation in February 1919, and holds the 1914 Star, and the General Service and Victory Medals. He had previously served in the South African campaign.

15, Henley Street, Battersea, S.W.11.　　　Z2989

LEDGER, P., Rifleman, King's Royal Rifle Corps.

He volunteered in 1915, and in the following year was sent to Salonika. Serving with his Battalion he took part in various operations in the Balkans, including engagements on the Struma and Doiran fronts. He contracted malaria whilst overseas, and returning to England was discharged in consequence in 1919. He holds the General Service and Victory Medals.

12, Bournemouth Road, Rye Lane, S.E.15.　　　Z6197

LEDGERWOOD, F. T., Gunner, R.F.A.

He volunteered in August 1914, and proceeding to France shortly afterwards fought in the Retreat from Mons, and in the Battles of the Marne, and the Aisne. Severely wounded at Ypres in November 1914, he was sent home to hospital, and on recovery returned to the Western Front in the following February. In 1916, he was drafted to Egypt, and was in action in the Battle of Gaza and other engagements during General Allenby's Advance through Palestine. Returning to England for demobilisation in May 1919, he holds the Mons Star, and the General Service and Victory Medals.

58, Burgoyne Road, Stockwell, S.W.9.　　　Z2992A

LEDGERWOOD, J. H., Private, R.A.S.C. (M.T.)

Volunteering in 1915, he embarked for the Western Front in the following year. Serving there for a time, he then proceeded to Italy. There he was engaged on important duties in connection with the transport of rations and supplies to the firing line, and rendered valuable services throughout the war. Returning home on the cessation of hostilities he was discharged on account of service in 1918, and holds the General Service and Victory Medals.

58, Burgoyne Road, Stockwell, S.W.9.　　　Z2992B

LEE, A., Private, 1st Bedfordshire Regiment.

A serving soldier, he was mobilised on the outbreak of war, and almost immediately proceeded to France. There he fought in several important engagements, and was wounded in the Battle of La Bassée on October 27th, 1914. Rejoining his unit on recovery he was drafted to Salonika in November 1915, and saw much service in the Balkans. Owing to illness he was sent home and was subsequently discharged in consequence in June 1917. He holds the 1914 Star, and the General Service and Victory Medals.

35, Overstone Road, Hammersmith, W.6.　　　10776A

LEE, A. A., Driver, R.F.A. and R.A.S.C.

He volunteered in the Royal Field Artillery in August 1914, and on the completion of his training served with his unit at various stations. Sustaining severe injuries through falling from his horse he was admitted to hospital, and later invalided out of the Army. He was then employed on munition work at Woolwich Arsenal until he joined the Royal Army Service Corps. Whilst serving at Southampton he contracted influenza and died on October 20th, 1918. He was buried at Nunhead Cemetery.

" His memory is cherished with pride."

44, Tindal Street, Lothian Road, S.W.9.　　　Z5262

LEE, A. F., Sergt., Grenadier Guards.

He enlisted in January 1910, and was mobilised when war broke out. Proceeding to France in August 1914, he was in action during the Retreat from Mons, and in the Battles of Neuve Chapelle, Ypres, and the Somme, and was wounded in 1916. He was sent to hospital in England and on recovering from his injuries acted as Musketry Instructor until the Armistice. He holds the Mons Star, and the General Service and Victory Medals, and in 1920 was still serving.

39A, Lewis Trust Buildings, Warner Road, Camberwell, S.E.5.
　　　　　Z6024

LEE, A. W., Private, 3rd Middlesex Regiment.

Serving in India at the outbreak of war he was drafted to France in 1914, and took part in the Battles of Loos, Festubert and Ypres, and was wounded in 1915. On recovery he proceeded in the same year to Egypt, and served in that theatre of war in several important engagements. He returned to England for demobilisation in April 1919, and holds the 1914-15 Star, and the General Service and Victory Medals.

60, Weybridge Street, Battersea, S.W.11.　　　Z2999

LEE, B. A., Private, 4th Lancashire Fusiliers.
Joining in May 1916, on the conclusion of his training he was engaged on guard and other important duties with his Battalion at various stations. He rendered valuable services, but was unable to secure his transfer overseas before the cessation of hostilities owing to medical unfitness, and was discharged in consequence in May 1918.
12, Harvey Road, Camberwell, S.E.5. Z2993A

LEE, C. H., L/Corpl., R.A.F., Sherwood Foresters, Royal Warwickshire Regt. and Manchester Regt.
Volunteering in January 1916, he embarked for France in the following year and fought in the Battles of St. Quentin, Ypres, Passchendaele, Messines and Poelcappelle. He was sent to Italy in 1918, and during his service there was in action during the Advance on the Piave. On the termination of hostilities he proceeded to Austria in January 1919, and was engaged on special duties until drafted in the same year to Egypt. Returning home after a period of service at Cairo, Kantara, and other stations, he was demobilised in 1919, and holds the General Service and Victory Medals.
68, Hargwyne Street, Stockwell Road, S.W.9. Z2987

LEE, F. T., Corporal, 1st Royal Fusiliers.
A Regular, having enlisted in 1912, he was serving in Ireland at the outbreak of war and was shortly afterwards sent to France. He took part in several important engagements on the Western Front, and was wounded on the Somme. He died from the effects of his injuries on February 6th, 1917, and was entitled to the 1914 Star, and the General Service and Victory Medals.
" Honour to the immortal dead, who gave their youth that the world might grow old in peace."
67, Priory Grove, Lansdowne Road, S.W.8. Z2996

LEE, G., Private, 10th Canadian Infantry.
Volunteering in August 1914, he proceeded to France on completing his training and served in several parts of the line. He fought in many engagements and was wounded at St. Julien near Ypres on April 23rd, 1915. Sent to hospital in England, on account of his injuries, he was discharged in 1915, as medically unfit for further service, and holds the 1914-15 Star, and the General Service and Victory Medals.
27, Bradmore Park Road, Hammersmith, W.6. 10691B

LEE, G. H., Rifleman, King's Royal Rifle Corps.
He joined in May 1916, and embarking for Salonika three months later was actively engaged in operations in the Balkans. Sent to France early in 1918, he was in action in the Battles of the Somme and Cambrai, and was wounded during the Advance in November 1918. He was discharged as medically unfit for further service in December 1918, and holds the General Service and Victory Medals.
12, Harvey Road, Camberwell, S.E.5. Z2993B

LEE, H., 1st Class Stoker, R.N.
He joined in April 1916, and was posted to H.M.S. " Lucia," which vessel served on patrol duties in the Suez Canal. Proceeding to East Africa in November 1917, his ship was engaged in the bombardment of enemy positions on the coast and assisted in operations with the 3rd King's African Rifles. Returning to England in 1919, owing to ill-health, he was discharged in consequence in 1920, and holds the General Service and Victory Medals.
28, Councillor Street, Camberwell, S.E.5. Z2995

LEE, H. H., Private, 3rd Suffolk Regiment.
He volunteered in January 1915, and three months later embarked for the Western Front, where he served for over three years. During this period he fought in the Battles of the Somme, Ypres, Arras, Festubert, Vimy Ridge, and several other engagements, and was wounded at Festubert in May 1915, and on the Somme in May 1918. Returning to England he was demobilised in March 1919, and holds the 1914-15 Star, and the General Service and Victory Medals.
19, Cavendish Grove, Wandsworth, S.W.8. Z2994

LEE, L. C., Pte., 55th Loyal North Lancashire Regt.
He joined in June 1916, and was sent to France in the following January. During his service on the Western Front, he was engaged in heavy fighting in the Battles of Vimy Ridge and Arras, and was wounded at Bullecourt on May 21st, 1917. Sent home owing to his injuries he returned to the Field on recovery and fought in several engagements during the Retreat and Advance of 1918. He was demobilised in September 1919, and holds the General Service and Victory Medals.
1, Secretan Road, Camberwell, S.E.5. Z5442

LEE, P. S., Rifleman, 8th London Regiment (Post Office Rifles).
He joined in April 1917, and in March of the following year was drafted to the Western Front. There he served in several important engagements until wounded in the Battle of Albert in August 1918. Owing to his injuries he was invalided home for medical treatment and was subsequently demobilised in February 1919. He holds the General Service and Victory Medals. 78, Grayshott Road, Lavender Hill, S.W.11. Z2998

LEE, R. R., Rifleman, Rifle Brigade.
He joined in 1918, and on completing his training was engaged on important duties with his unit at various depôts. He did valuable work, but was unsuccessful in his efforts to secure his transfer to a theatre of war before hostilities ceased, and in 1920 was still serving.
1, Bradmore Road, Hammersmith, W.6. 10691A

LEE, S. A., Gunner, R.G.A.
Volunteering in June 1915, in the following April he was sent to the Western Front, and served with his Battery in various sectors. He was in action in the Battles of the Somme, Arras, Ypres, Vimy Ridge, Passchendaele, Lens, Cambrai, and during the Retreat and Advance of 1918. After the Armistice he proceeded into Germany with the Army of Occupation, and returning home for demobilisation in April 1919, holds the General Service and Victory Medals.
83, Gurney Street, Walworth, S.E.17. Z2997

LEEDHAM, W. C., Private, 20th London Regiment.
He volunteered in October 1915, and proceeded overseas in the following year. During his service on the Western Front he fought in several engagements, including the Battles of Ypres, Arras, the Somme, Vimy Ridge and Passchendaele. He returned home on the cessation of hostilities and was demobilised in 1919, holding the General Service and Victory Medals.
25, Thurlow Street, Walworth, S.E.17. Z3000

LEEK, A. T., Corporal, R.A.F.
Volunteering in the Royal Naval Air Service in July 1915, he served aboard H.M.S. " Glowworm " and other vessels engaged on submarine patrol duties in the North Sea. In February 1916, he was sent to German East Africa, and took part in several operations until his return to duty in the North Sea. He served later as Physical Instructor at No. 8 Balloon Base, Immingham, until demobilised in February 1919, and holds the 1914-15 Star, and the General Service and Victory Medals.
120, Gloucester Road, Peckham, S.E.15. Z6020

LEES, H. E., Private, 7th Northumberland Fusiliers.
He joined in April 1916, and in the following month proceeded to the Western Front. Whilst in this theatre of war he served with his unit in the Somme sector until invalided home, owing to illness in January 1917. He was discharged in the same month as medically unfit for further service, and holds the General Service and Victory Medals.
26, Commercial Road, Peckham, S.E.15. Z6522

LEESON, H., Driver, R.F.A.
Volunteering in August 1914, he embarked for the Western Front in the following year and served there throughout the war. He was in action in the Battles of Ypres and Arras, and was wounded at Beaumont-Hamel in 1916, and sent home to hospital in Leicestershire. Rejoining his Battery on recovery, he took part in several engagements in the Somme sector, and after the Armistice returned to England. He was demobilised in January 1919, and holds the 1914-15 Star, and the General Service and Victory Medals.
42, Wivenhoe Road, Peckham, S.E.15. Z6200

LEETE, E. T., Driver, R.F.A.
He volunteered in January 1915, and sent to France six months later, was engaged in heavy fighting at St. Eloi, Laventie, the Somme, Kemmel Hill, Bullecourt, Lens, Passchendaele, and was in action throughout the German Offensive and subsequent Allied Advance of 1918. He was demobilised in April 1919, and holds the 1914-15 Star, and the General Service and Victory Medals.
114, Brandon Street, Walworth, S.E.17. Z3001

LEGGE, A. J., L/Corporal, Rifle Brigade.
He volunteered in May 1915, and embarking for France in the following August was in action at Albert, Vimy Ridge, the Somme, Arras, Messines, Passchendaele, Lens and throughout the German Offensive and Allied Advance of 1918. During his service overseas he was three times wounded and also gassed. He was demobilised in February 1919, and holds the 1914-15 Star, and the General Service and Victory Medals.
27, Searles Road, New Kent Road, S.E.1. Z3004B

LEIGHTON, H. W., Corporal, R.A.M.C.
Volunteering in September 1914, he completed his training and served at various military hospitals, engaged on important duties attending sick and wounded troops. Owing to ill-health, he did not succeed in obtaining his transfer overseas, but did good work until discharged unfit for further service in April 1918.
112, Brayard's Road, Peckham, S.E.15. Z5443

LEMON, C. E., Private (Gunner), M.G.C.
He volunteered in June 1915, and later in that year was drafted
to France. He was in action at Ypres, Loos, and in many other
engagements. He was reported missing on September 3rd,
1916, on the Somme Front and later was presumed to have
been killed in action on that date. He was entitled to the
1914-15 Star, and the General Service and Victory Medals.
"His life for his country, his Soul to God."
22, Gladstone Terrace, Battersea Park Road, S.W.8.
Z3005B

LEMON, G. M., Rifleman, Rifle Brigade.
Volunteering in May 1915, he proceeded to France later in
the same year. He fought in the Battles of Cambrai, Loos,
Ypres, and in many parts of the line. He was reported missing
on September 3rd, 1916, during the first Battle of the Somme,
and later was presumed to have been killed on that date.
He was entitled to the 1914-15 Star, and the General Service
and Victory Medals.
"Great deeds cannot die."
22, Gladstone Terrace, Battersea Park Road, S.W.8. Z3005A

LENEY, E. P., Private, 5th Dorsetshire Regiment.
He volunteered in May 1915, and later in the year was sent
to the Dardanelles, where he took part in the heavy fighting
then in progress on the Peninsula. In November he contracted
fever, and was invalided to hospital at Malta, and subsequently
died there on November 25th, 1915. He was entitled to the
1914-15 Star, and the General Service and Victory Medals.
"Steals on the ear the distant triumph song."
3, Reform Street, Battersea, S.W.11. Z3006B

LENEY, H. B., Private, Royal Sussex Regiment and R.A.S.C. (M.T.)
He joined in 1916, and drafted to France in April of the following year fought at the Battles of Arras and Ypres, and was
wounded. He returned to England and received hospital
treatment, and on recovery was transferred to the R.A.S.C.
With this unit he rendered excellent services at various depôts
until demobilised in 1919. He holds the General Service and
Victory Medals.
37, Reform Street, Battersea, S.W.11. Z3006A

LENT, C. M., Sergt., Oxfordshire and Buckingham-shire Light Infantry.
Volunteering in August 1914, he completed his training and
served at various stations until embarking for France in July
1917. He was in action in many parts of the line, and fought
in the Retreat of 1918, and was wounded in March. He
returned to England, and after receiving medical treatment,
was discharged unfit for further service in May 1919. He
holds the General Service and Victory Medals. He had
previously served in the South African War.
144, Battersea Park Road, S.W.11. Z3007

LENTON, E. A., Pte., 2/14th London Regt. (London Scottish).
Volunteering in May 1915, and proceeding to France in the
following year he saw much service in many parts of the line.
Transferred to Salonika he fought in several engagements,
and later was sent to Egypt, and served there until returning
to France. He was in action throughout the German Offensive
of 1918, and was unfortunately killed in action on October
4th, during the Allied Advance. He was entitled to the
General Service and Victory Medals.
"Nobly striving,
He nobly fell that we might live."
43, Cologne Road, Battersea, S.W.11. Z3009A

LENTON, E. H., Master Mariner, Merchant Service.
He was serving in the Merchant Service at the commencement
of hostilities, and throughout the war served aboard s.s.
"Inconka," engaged in transporting troops and supplies to
various theatres of war. His ship frequently passed through
mine-infested areas in the discharge of his duties, and had
many narrow escapes. He was still serving in 1920, and holds
the General Service and the Mercantile Marine War Medals.
95, Ferndale Road, Clapham, S.W.4. Z3008

LENTON, W. W., Private, 2nd East Surrey Regiment.
A serving soldier, he was stationed in India at the outbreak
of war, and sent to France in the following year, was engaged
in heavy fighting in various sectors. He gave his life for the
freedom of England in 1915, at Neuve Chapelle, and was entitled to the 1914-15 Star, and the General Service and Victory
Medals.
"Great deeds cannot die:
They with the Sun and Moon renew their light for ever."
43, Cologne Road, Battersea, S.W.11. Z3009B

LENTZ, W. H., Sapper, R.E.
He volunteered in November 1915, and, drafted to France in
the following year, was engaged with his unit on important
duties in the Ypres sector. In 1917 he proceeded to Italy,
and served during the heavy fighting on the Piave, until
the close of the war. He then returned to England and was
demobilised in February 1919, and holds the General Service
and Victory Medals.
34, Church Road, Battersea, S.W.11. . Z3010

LEONARD, E. A., Private, 11th Royal Fusiliers.
Volunteering in September 1914, he proceeded to the Western
Front in the July of the following year. During his service
in this theatre of war he fought in many engagements. He
gave his life for the freedom of England on July 1st, 1916,
during the first British Offensive on the Somme. He was
entitled to the 1914-15 Star, and the General Service and
Victory Medals.
"A costly Sacrifice upon the altar of freedom."
29, Portslade Road, Wandsworth Road, S.W.8. Z3012

LEONARD, E. J., Private, Royal Sussex Regiment.
He volunteered in September 1914, and two months later was
drafted to France. He took part in the fighting at Ypres,
Loos, Vimy Ridge, and the Somme, and was badly wounded.
He was invalided to England, and after receiving hospital
treatment for six months, was discharged medically unfit for
further service in April 1917. He holds the 1914-15 Star,
and the General Service and Victory Medals.
42A, Sutton Buildings, Ixnorth Place, Chelsea, S.W.3.
Z24966

LEONARD, W., L/Corporal, Rifle Brigade.
He joined in May 1918, and after his training served with his
unit at various stations on special duties. He did good work,
but was not successful in obtaining his transfer overseas
before the cessation of hostilities. He was drafted to Germany
with the Army of Occupation in the latter part of 1918,
and was stationed on the Rhine, until demobilised in March
1920.
13, Weybridge Street, Battersea, S.W.11. Z3011

LESLIE, D. A., Rifleman, 1/21st London Regiment (1st Surrey Rifles).
Joining in May 1916, he was drafted three months later to
France. Whilst on the Western Front he was engaged in the
fighting on the Somme, and at Vimy Ridge and Messines,
and did excellent work as a Bomber with his Battalion.
Severely wounded near Messines in June 1917, he was invalided to hospital in England, and was subsequently discharged as medically unfit for further service in August 1919.
He holds the General Service and Victory Medals.
265, Sumner Road, Peckham, S.E.15. Z6022

LESLIE, W., Private, 1/23rd London Regiment.
Volunteering in January 1915, he was sent overseas in the
following March. During his service on the Western Front
he fought at Neuve Chapelle, Hill 60, and Ypres, where he
was badly gassed. He was invalided to hospital, and after
receiving treatment was discharged in August 1915, as medically unfit for further service. He holds the 1914-15 Star,
and the General Service and Victory Medals.
89, Speke Road, Battersea, S.W.11. Z3013

LESTER, F., Sergt., 1st (Royal) Dragoons.
Volunteering at the outbreak of hostilities, he was drafted
overseas in 1915. During his service on the Western Front
he was engaged in the fighting in various sectors, and did
excellent work. After the cessation of hostilities he proceeded
to India, where he served on important garrison duties until
demobilised in November 1919. He holds the 1914-15 Star,
and the General Service and Victory Medals.
38, Tabor Road, Hammersmith, W.6. 11548

LESTER, F. G., Special War Worker.
During the war, for a period of three years, he was engaged on
work of National importance at Woolwich Arsenal. His
duties, which were in connection with the manufacture of parts
for guns, were carried out with great care and skill.
6, Bromell's Road, Clapham, S.W.4. Z3016B

LESTER, F. G., Rifleman, King's Royal Rifle Corps.
He joined in June 1916, and at the conclusion of his training
served at various stations on important duties with his unit.
He did very good work, but owing to ill-health was unable to
secure his transfer overseas, and was in consequence discharged
in February 1918, as medically unfit for further service.
6, Bromell's Road, Clapham, S.W.4. Z3017

LESTER, R. (Jun.), Orderly, British Red Cross Society.
In July 1918, at the age of seventeen years, he joined the
British Red Cross Society, and was sent to France, where he
rendered very valuable services until after the cessation of
hostilities. He was demobilised in January 1919, and holds
a Certificate for consistently good work. He later joined H.M.
Army, and in 1920 was serving in India.
87, Westmoreland Road, Walworth, S.E.17. Z3015B

LESTER, T., Special War Worker.
For a period of five years he was engaged on important work
at the Projectile Company, Battersea, and later at Woolwich
Arsenal. His duties, which were in connection with the manufacture of shells, were carried out in a highly satisfactory
manner, and his work was much appreciated.
6, Bromell's Road, Clapham, S.W.4. Z3016A

LESTER, R., Private, 9th East Surrey Regiment.
He volunteered in October 1914, and twelve months later proceeded overseas. Whilst on the Western Front he fought at Loos, Albert, Vimy Ridge, the Somme, Beaumont-Hamel, Beaucourt, Arras, Messines, Ypres, Passchendaele and Lens. He displayed conspicuous bravery on one occasion at Cambrai, when he killed seven Germans after he had himself been severely wounded. For this deed of valour he was recommended for the Victoria Cross. He was invalided to hospital in England, and in October 1919 was discharged medically unfit for further service. He holds the 1914-15 Star, and the General Service and Victory Medals.
87, Westmoreland Road, Walworth, S.E.17.   Z3015A

LESTER, W., Rifleman, King's Royal Rifle Corps.
He volunteered at the outbreak of hostilities, but owing to ill-health was discharged as medically unfit for further service in November 1914. He was then employed with the Projectile Company, Battersea, as a shell turner until July 1915, and later served until December 1918, with the Townmead Engineering Company, Wandsworth, as a tool setter for munition machines. In the course of his duties he met with a serious accident, resulting in the loss of his right eye. He received high commendation for the services he rendered.
6, Bromell's Road, Clapham, S.W.4.   Z3014

LETIN, R., Leading Seaman, Merchant Service.
He volunteered in September 1915, and at the conclusion of his training was posted to H.M. Motor Launch " 530," which vessel was engaged on patrol duties and mine-sweeping in the Mediterranean and in the English Channel. He was awarded three amounts of prize money for sinking submarines. He was demobilised in September 1919, and holds the General Service and Mercantile Marine War Medals.
40, Mostyn Road, Brixton Road, S.W.9.   Z4412A

LETLEY, C. H., Sergt., R.A.S.C. (M.T.).
He volunteered in June 1915, and after his training with the 22nd London Regiment (Queen's), served on special duties with the Forage Department of the R.A.S.C. He did very good work, but owing to physical unfitness was unable to secure his transfer overseas, and was demobilised in June 1919.
126, Boyson Road, Walworth, S.E.17.   Z3289B

LETT, A. G., L/Corporal, East Surrey Regiment.
He had previously taken part in the Boer War, and at the outbreak of hostilities was serving in India. He was almost immediately drafted to France, where he was engaged in the fighting at Hill 60, Ypres, and Vimy Ridge, and was wounded on four different occasions, and taken prisoner at Cambrai in 1917. He was held in captivity until after the signing of the Armistice, and was then repatriated. He shortly afterwards returned to France, proceeding to Russia, where he was in action against the Bolshevists, and unhappily fell fighting in September 1919. He held the Queen's and King's South African Medals, and was entitled to the 1914 Star, and the General Service and Victory Medals.
"He died the noblest death a man may die,
Fighting for God, and right, and liberty."
30, Stainforth Road, Battersea, S.W.11.   Z3018. Z3019

LEVERENTZ, E., Sergt., 13th Queen's (Royal West Surrey Regiment).
He joined in June 1916, and two months later proceeded overseas. During his service on the Western Front he was chiefly engaged in the Ypres sector in the transport of ammunition to the Artillery. He was gassed in 1917. Returning to England after the cessation of hostilities, he was demobilised in November 1919. He holds the General Service and Victory Medals.
18, Runham Street, Walworth, S.E.17.   Z3020

LEVERETT, B., Sapper, R.E.
He volunteered in October 1915, and in the following year proceeded overseas. Whilst on the Western Front he was engaged with his unit on special duties at Cambrai and Arras, and in the Retreat and Advance of 1918. After the cessation of hostilities he served in Germany with the Army of Occupation, and was stationed at Cologne. He was demobilised in December 1919, and holds the General Service and Victory Medals.
44, Thorncroft Street, Wandsworth Road, S.W.8.   Z3021

LEVERETT, C. W. J., Rifleman, 8th London Regt. (Post Office Rifles) and Private. M.G.C.
Joining in September 1917, he was drafted to France early in the following year. He fought in the Battles of the Somme, and Marne, and also took part in the Retreat and Allied Advance of 1918. He later proceeded to Germany with the Army of Occupation, and served at Cologne. He was demobilised in September 1919, and holds the General Service and Victory Medals.
35, Bellefields Road, Stockwell, S.W.9.   Z3022A

LEVERETT, W. B., Corporal, R.E.
Volunteering in May 1915, he was sent shortly afterwards to France. In this theatre of war he was engaged with his unit in many sectors, including those of the Somme and Ypres. In the following year he proceeded to Italy, where he was in charge of a Field Post Office, and also Postmaster in Rome. He was demobilised in 1919, and holds the 1914-15 Star, and the General Service and Victory Medals.
35, Bellefields Road, Stockwell, S.W.9.   Z3022B

LEVERINGTON, A. T., Driver, R.A.S.C.
He joined in April 1917, and on the completion of his training was sent overseas in August of the same year. Whilst on the Western Front he served at Ypres, Passchendaele, Lens, Cambrai, the Somme, and Lille, being engaged in the transport of supplies and ammunition. Although frequently exposed to danger, he escaped injury, and was demobilised in October 1919, holding the General Service and Victory Medals.
32, Beckway Street, Walworth, S.E.17.   Z3023D

LEVERINGTON, P. E., Signalman, R.N.
He was serving in H.M.S. " Iron Duke " at the outbreak of hostilities, and subsequently took part both in the Battle of Jutland and in the Raid on Zeebrugge. He also was engaged in mine-sweeping and in chasing submarines. He unhappily died on October 31st, 1918. He was entitled to the 1914-15 Star, and the General Service and Victory Medals.
" His life for his Country."
32, Beckway Street, Walworth, S.E.17.   Z3023A

LEVERMORE, S. C., Corporal, R.A.S.C. (M.T.)
Volunteering at the outbreak of hostilities, he was drafted to France in October 1914. He served at Ypres, and in November 1914 was mentioned in Despatches for devotion to duty in the Field. He also took part in the Battles of the Somme, Arras and Cambrai, being chiefly engaged in the transport of the wounded. He was demobilised in April 1919, and holds the 1914 Star, and the General Service and Victory Medals.
137, Warham Street, Camberwell, S.E.5.   Z3024

LEVETT, J., Private, Labour Corps.
He joined in March 1917, and was shortly afterwards drafted to the Western Front. Whilst overseas he was engaged on important duties in connection with operations during the Advance of 1918, and was later employed on exhumation work in various sectors. He was demobilised in October 1919, and holds the General Service and Victory Medals.
89, Tennyson Street, Wentworth Road, S.W.8.   Z3026

LEVETT, J. H., Private, 10th Queen's (Royal West Surrey Regiment).
He volunteered in August 1915, and proceeding overseas in the following May served on the Western Front. There he was engaged in heavy fighting in the Battles of the Somme, Ypres, and other engagements, and later drafted to Italy, took part in operations on the Piave. Returning to the Western Front in 1918, he fought in the Retreat of that year, and was wounded in July. He was demobilised in April 1919, and holds the General Service and Victory Medals.
28, Lockington Road, Battersea Park Road, S.W.11.
                                                  Z3027

LEVETT, S. H., Sergt., 50th Canadian Infantry.
He volunteered in May 1915, and in the following November proceeded to the Western Front. There he was in action in numerous engagements, including the Battles of the Somme and Vimy Ridge, and was wounded. Invalided to England on account of his injuries, he was admitted to hospital, and on recovery served on home duties until demobilised in January 1920. He holds the 1914-15 Star, and the General Service and Victory Medals.
4, Lapfort Place, off Upper Kennington Lane, S.E.11.
                                                  Z25310D

LEVETT, W. L., Private, 13th East Surrey Regt.
Volunteering in July 1915, he was drafted to the Western Front in June of the following year, and served there until the end of the war. During this period he was in action in several engagements, including the Battles of the Somme, Arras and Cambrai. After the Armistice he was sent into Germany with the Army of Occupation, and was stationed at Cologne. Returning to England in 1919, he was demobilised in February of that year, and holds the General Service and Victory Medals.
33, Portslade Road, Wandsworth Road, S.W.8.   Z3025

LEVINGTON, H., Private, 20th London Regiment.
He volunteered in August 1914, when under military age, and was engaged on important duties with his unit until drafted to France in 1916. He saw much service on the Western Front, and was wounded on the Somme. Later sent to Egypt he served there for a time and returning to France accompanied the Army of Occupation into Germany. He holds the General Service and Victory Medals, and in 1920 was serving in India.
25, Smyrk's Road, Walworth, S.E.17.   Z3028

LEVINGTON, M., Private, 20th London Regiment.

Volunteering in September 1914, he was sent to the Western Front three months later, and fought in the Battles of Neuve Chapelle and Ypres, and was wounded. Invalided home on account of his injuries, he was discharged in October 1915, as medically unfit for further service. He re-enlisted, however, in June 1916, and returning to France took part in several engagements until wounded in the Battle of the Somme. Sent home to hospital he was invalided out of the Service in July 1917, and holds the 1914-15 Star, and the General Service and Victory Medals.

25, Smyrk's Road, Walworth, S.E.17.   Z3029

LEVITT, F. G., Corporal, R.E.

He joined in April 1916, and on the completion of his training was engaged on important duties with his unit. He was later attached to the Canadian Forestry Corps, and served as a clerk with this unit. He rendered valuable services, but was unsuccessful in obtaining his transfer overseas before the cessation of hostilities, and was demobilised in November 1919.

2, Clarence Mansions, Bromwell's Road, Clapham. S.W.8.   Z2990

LEWELL, C., Driver, R.F.A.

He volunteered in August 1914, and was almost immediately drafted to France, where he served during the Retreat from Mons and in the Battles of the Marne, Ypres and Loos. He was also in action in the Battles of Passchendaele, Cambrai and the Somme, and after the Armistice was sent into Germany with the Army of Occupation. He returned to England for demobilisation in May 1919, and holds the Mons Star, and the General Service and Victory Medals.

33, Russell Road, Peckham, S.E.15.   Z5313B

LEWER, A. J., Private, 8th Devonshire Regiment.

Volunteering in April 1915, he embarked for France in the following October, and was in action in the Battles of Loos, Albert, Vimy Ridge, the Somme, Messines, Ypres, Passchendaele and Cambrai. In March 1918 he was sent to Italy, and served there in operations on the Asiago and Piave fronts. He was demobilised in February 1919, and holds the 1914-15 Star, and the General Service and Victory Medals.

40, Smyrk's Road, Walworth, S.E.17.   Z3030

LEWIS, A. E., Rifleman, King's Royal Rifle Corps.

He volunteered in July 1915, and proceeding to France in the following year served there until the termination of hostilities. During this period he was engaged on guard and other important duties at prisoners of war camps, as he was unfit for service in the trenches. He was demobilised in March 1919, and holds the General Service and Victory Medals.

9, Shorncliffe Road, Old Kent Road, S.E.1.   Z3032

LEWIS, B., Corporal, East Surrey Regiment.

Volunteering in March 1915, he was sent to France in the following October, and saw much service there until drafted to Italy in 1917. He was in action in several engagements during the Advance on the Piave, and returning to France was taken prisoner in the Battle of Cambrai, and held in captivity in Germany. Repatriated after the Armistice, he was demobilised in January 1919, and holds the 1914-15 Star, and the General Service and Victory Medals.

96, St. George's Road, Peckham, S.E.15.   Z5634

LEWIS, B., Private, Gloucestershire Regiment.

He joined in November 1916, and was drafted overseas in the following year. Serving with his Battalion in Mesopotamia he was in action in several engagements, and was present at the capture of Baghdad. In 1918 he was sent to Russia, and rendered valuable services on the lines of communication until his return to England for demobilisation in December 1919. He holds the General Service and Victory Medals.

35, Lingham Street, Clapham Road, S.W.9.   Z3031

LEWIS, F., Corporal, R.A.S.C.

Joining in November 1916, he was drafted to Salonika in the same year, and did good work in connection with Remounts during operations in the Balkans. On the termination of hostilities, and later served with the Army of Occupation in Turkey, and rendered valuable services. He was demobilised in April 1920, and holds the General Service and Victory Medals.

41, Sterndale Road, Wandsworth Road, S.W.8.   Z3035

LEWIS, F., Sergeant, R.A.S.C. (M.T.)

He volunteered in February 1915, and in the following year proceeded to France. Engaged with the 27th Field Ambulance Company, he rendered valuable services in conveying the wounded to the Casualty Clearing Stations, and was present at the Battle of the Somme, and several engagements during the Retreat and Advance of 1918. After the Armistice he was sent into Germany with the Army of Occupation, and was stationed on the Rhine. Returning home, he was demobilised in May 1919, and holds the General Service and Victory Medals.

30, Gladstone Street, Battersea Park Road, S.W.8.   Z1075B

LEWIS, L., Rifleman, 16th London Regt. (Queen's Westminster Rifles).

Volunteering in August 1914, he was almost immediately sent to France, and taking part in the Retreat from Mons was wounded and invalided home. Returning to the Western Front on recovery he fought in the Battles of Loos, Albert, Vermelles, and was again wounded at Vimy Ridge. Sent to England on account of his injuries he received hospital treatment, and was discharged as medically unfit for further service in November 1917. He holds the Mons Star, and the General Service and Victory Medals.

19, Broadhinton Road, Clapham, S.W.4.   Z3033

LEWIS, S. (M.M.) Private, King's (Liverpool Regt.).

He joined in March 1916, and in the same year proceeding to the Western Front took part in the Battles of the Somme, Beaumont-Hamel and Arras. He was awarded the Military Medal for conspicuous bravery and devotion to duty in bringing in one of his Officers from the enemy lines during the Battle of Cambrai, and was later taken prisoner in the same sector. During his captivity he experienced much ill-treatment at the hands of the enemy, and was injured by a coal truck. Repatriated after the Armistice, he was demobilised in August 1919, and holds the General Service and Victory Medals.

44, Larcom Street, Walworth, S.E.17.   Z3034

LEWIS, W. (D.S.M.), Chief Petty Officer, R.N.

Mobilised on the outbreak of war he was posted to H.M.S. " Bellona," which vessel was engaged on mine-sweeping in the North Sea, and had several narrow escapes whilst carrying out her dangerous duty. He was awarded the Distinguished Service Medal on January 6th, 1916, for conspicuous bravery in saving the lives of two of his comrades at the risk of his own. After serving on several other ships he was transferred to H.M.S. " Bona Dea," and was demobilised in December 1918. He holds the 1914-15 Star, and the General Service and Victory Medals.

3, Frances Street, Battersea, S.W.11.   Z3036

LEWZEY, J. H., Private, 22nd London Regt. (The Queen's).

He joined in August 1916, and after four months' training was drafted to the Western Front, where he fought in many important engagements, including the Battle of Ypres. He was unhappily killed in action at Messines Ridge on June 8th, 1917, and was entitled to the General Service and Victory Medals.

    " The path of duty was the way to glory."

36, Odell Street, Camberwell, S.E.5.   Z5444

LIDDELL, J., Guardsman, Scots Guards.

A serving soldier, he was mobilised and drafted to France shortly after the outbreak of hostilities. Whilst on the Western Front he served with his Battalion in various parts of the line, and fought at the Battles of Givenchy, Neuve Chapelle, Loos, the Somme, Passchendaele, and in the Retreat and Advance of 1918, and was twice gassed. After the Armistice he proceeded with the Army of Occupation into Germany, and was stationed at Cologne. He returned to England in February 1919, and was demobilised in the following month, and holds the 1914-15 Star, and the General Service and Victory Medals.

38, Balaclava Road, Bermondsey, S.E.1.   Z26050

LIFFORD, A. E., Gunner, R.G.A.

He volunteered in August 1915, and after completing his training proceeded five months later to the Western Front. He fought at the Battle of Loos, and was wounded in heavy fighting on the Somme in July 1916. Evacuated to hospital at Leicester he received medical treatment, and on recovery returned to France, and served with his Battery in the concluding operations of the war. He was demobilised in January 1919, and holds the General Service and Victory Medals.

28, Verona Road, Battersea, S.W.11.   Z3037

LIGGITT, O., A.B., Royal Navy.

He volunteered in April 1915, and was posted to H.M.S. " Princess Royal," which vessel was engaged on patrol and other duties in the North Sea. His ship was also in action at the Battles of Jutland and Heligoland Bight, and had other encounters with enemy craft. He holds the 1914-15 Star, and the General Service and Victory Medals, and in 1920 was still serving.

66, Robertson Street, Wandsworth Road, S.W.8.   Z3038

LILL, G. A., Pte., 7th Queen's (Royal West Surrey Regiment).

He volunteered in August 1914, and served at various stations with his unit until sent to the Western Front in 1917. Here he was engaged in many important battles, including those at Arras, Vimy Ridge, Bullecourt and Messines Ridge. He was also in action in the Retreat and Advance of 1918. Demobilised in April 1919, he holds the General Service and Victory Medals.

18, Holyoak Road, Kennington, S.E.11.   Z26577

LILLEY, C., 1st Class Stoker, R.N.

He volunteered in February 1915, and was posted to H.M.S. " Swift," which ship was engaged in escorting troopships to and from the Dardanelles and other theatres of war. He also served in H.M.S. " Liberty " and T.B.4., on submarine patrol duties in various waters. He rendered valuable services throughout, and was demobilised in May 1919. He holds the 1914-15 Star, and the General Service and Victory Medals.

79, Akerman Road, Brixton, S.W.9.   Z4399-4400C

LILLEY, J., Private, R.A.S.C.

He volunteered in March 1915, at the age of fifty-seven, and in the following month proceeded to France. During his service on the Western Front he was stationed at Verdun, engaged in loading and unloading forage and other stores until 1916, when, owing to ill-health, he was invalided home and subsequently discharged as medically unfit for further military service in June 1916. He holds in addition to the Egypt Medal 1882, and the Khedive's Star, the 1914-15 Star, and the General Service and Victory Medals.

1, Miles Cottages, Battersea, S.W.11.   Z3039

LILLEY, J., Rifleman, Royal Irish Rifles.

He joined in June 1917, and on completion of his training with the 45th Training Reserve Battalion at Warminster, he was posted to the Royal Irish Rifles and sent to the Western Front in March of the following year. He saw much heavy fighting during the Retreat and Advance of 1918, and was wounded in action at Roulers in October of that year. Evacuated to England he received hospital treatment, and was subsequently demobilised in December 1919. He holds the General Service and Victory Medals.

26, Abercrombie Street, Battersea, S.W.11.   Z3040

LILLYWHITE, W., Corporal, R.G.A.

Volunteering in September 1914, he was drafted in the following month to France, and fought at the Battles of Ypres, Neuve Chapelle, Festubert, Loos and the Somme. In 1916 he was invalided home owing to ill-health, and after prolonged hospital treatment was eventually discharged on account of service in January 1919. He holds the Mons Star, and the General Service and Victory Medals. Prior to the war he had served for a period of twelve years with the Colours.

102, Westmacott Street, Camberwell, S.E.5.   Z5546

LIM, H., Private, Essex Regiment and Labour Corps.

He joined in May 1917, and in the following month was sent to the Western Front. During his service overseas he was engaged in heavy fighting in the Ypres salient, and contracting shell-shock was invalided to England. He received medical treatment at Bradford Hospital, and on recovery served with the Labour Corps until discharged on account of service in March 1919. He holds the General Service and Victory Medals.

33, Blake's Road, Peckham Grove, S.E.15.   Z6021B

LIM, H., Private, R.A.S.C.

He joined in November 1916, and proceeding to Salonika in the following July was engaged on important transport duties during the Advance on the Doiran front. He served in the bombardment of Dedeayatch, and on the conclusion of hostilities was sent with the Army of Occupation into Turkey, and was stationed at Constantinople. Returning home for demobilisation in December 1919, he holds the General Service and Victory Medals.

107, Gloucester Road, Peckham, S.E.15.   Z6027

LINDFIELD, H. C., Private, 3rd Middlesex Regiment.

He volunteered in February 1915, and in the same year proceeded to the Western Front. Whilst there he fought in the Battles of Loos, Festubert, the Somme, Arras, Béthune, Péronne, Delville Wood, Dickebusch, Cambrai and Armentières and was gassed at Brandhoek, near Poperinghe. Sent to hospital in England he received medical treatment, and was subsequently demobilised in February 1920, and holds the 1914-15 Star, and the General Service and Victory Medals.

23, Moat Place, Stockwell Road, S.W.9.   Z3480

LINDFIELD, J. G., Pte., 3rd East Surrey Regt. and R.A.S.C.

Volunteering in October 1914, he embarked for France in the following year, and served in various sectors. He was in action in the Battles of St. Eloi, Loos, Albert, Beaumont-Hamel, Vimy Ridge, and Bullecourt, and was wounded at Ypres in May 1915. He also fought in the Battles of Lens, the Marne, Le Cateau, and other engagements during the Advance of 1918. Returning to England for demobilisation in February 1919, he holds the 1914-15 Star, and the General Service and Victory Medals.

15, Industry Terrace, Brixton Road, S.W.9.   Z2991A

LINDGREN, L., Driver, R.A.S.C. (M.T.)

He volunteered in January 1915, and in the same year was sent to France. Whilst in this theatre of war he was engaged on important transport duties in the Battles of Ypres, Hill 60, Festubert, Loos, Vimy Ridge, the Somme, Arras, Amiens, and several other engagements until the cessation of hostilities. He was demobilised in February 1919, and holds the 1914-15 Star, and the General Service and Victory Medals.

36, Viceroy Road, Guildford Road, S.W.8.   Z3041

LINDLEY, T., Private, Royal Fusiliers.

Mobilised on the outbreak of war and almost immediately drafted to France he fought in the Retreat from Mons and in the Battles of the Aisne and La Bassée, and was seriously wounded in December 1914. Sent to hospital at home on account of his injuries he received medical treatment, and on recovery served with his unit at various stations until his demobilisation in January 1919. He holds the Mons Star, and the General Service and Victory Medals.

2, Glendall Street, Ferndale Road, S.W.9.   Z3042

LINDSAY, J. W., Rifleman, Rifle Brigade.

He joined in June 1916, and after a period of training was drafted to the Western Front. There he fought in many battles, including those of Arras, Bullecourt, Messines and Ypres, and was wounded twice. He was taken prisoner at Cambrai, and was kept in captivity until the conclusion of hostilities, after which he was released and returned to England. He was demobilised in 1919, and holds the General Service and Victory Medals.

13, St. Mary's Square, Kennington, S.E.11.   Z27232

LINDSEY, P., Air Mechanic, R.A.F.

Joining in July 1917, on the completion of his training he served in the repair shop of his Squadron. He rendered valuable services on work of a highly technical character, but was unsuccessful in obtaining a transfer overseas before the termination of hostilities, owing to medical unfitness. He was demobilised in February 1919.

49, Gilbert Road, Kennington, S.E.11.   Z27244

LINEHAN, W. J., Private, East Lancashire Regt. and Sapper, R.E.

He joined in October 1917, and a year later proceeded to France, where he served until the conclusion of hostilities. He took part in several engagements during the Advance of 1918, and on transfer to the Royal Engineers rendered valuable services as a wire man on the lines of communication. He was demobilised in March 1920, and holds the General Service and Victory Medals.

3, Reckitt Road, Chiswick, W.4.   5602A

LINES, P., L/Corporal, 15th London Regiment (Civil Service Rifles).

Volunteering in June 1915, he was sent overseas in the following year, and took part in heavy fighting in the Battles of Vimy Ridge, Arras, Ypres and Passchendaele. He fell fighting near Ypres in November 1917, and was entitled to the General Service and Victory Medals.

" And doubtless he went in splendid company."

32, Russell Road, Peckham, S.E.15.   Z5445

LINES, R., Private, R.A.S.C.

He volunteered in January 1915, and was drafted overseas in the same year. Stationed at Le Havre he was engaged on important duties in connection with the transport of supplies to the forward areas, and rendered valuable services. Owing to illness he was sent to hospital at home, and was invalided out of the Army in February 1916. He holds the 1914-15 Star, and the General Service and Victory Medals.

72, Sterndale Road, Wandsworth Road, S.W.8.   Z3044

LINFOOT, M. W., Private, York and Lancaster Regt.

Volunteering in September 1915, he embarked for France in the following January, and served there for over three years. During this period he was in action at Loos, and in the Battles of Vimy Ridge, the Somme, Arras, Bullecourt, Ypres and Messines, and was twice wounded, on one occasion being buried by a shell explosion, and only rescued after three days. Sent to England for hospital treatment he returned to the Western Front on recovery, and fought in several engagements during the Retreat and Advance of 1918. He was demobilised in February 1919, and holds the General Service and Victory Medals.

62, Geneva Road, Coldharbour Lane, S.W.9.   Z3096

LINFORD, G. R., Private, Bedfordshire Regiment.

He volunteered in August 1914, and after completing his training was engaged on construction work with his unit at various stations on the East Coast and in Scotland. He rendered valuable services, but owing to defective vision, was unable to obtain his transfer to a theatre of war before the cessation of hostilities, and was demobilised in July 1919.

22, Old Paradise Street, Kennington, S.E.11.   Z25873

LING, A. E., Sergt., R.A.M.C.

Volunteering in September 1914, he proceeded to France on the conclusion of his training, and served with the Field Ambulance in several important engagements, including the Battles of Ypres and the Somme. He was also engaged on important duties in No 11 Field Hospital, and did good work attending to the wounded. Demobilised in May 1919, he holds the 1914–15 Star, and the General Service and Victory Medals.

132, Fort Road, Bermondsey, S.E.1.   Z26294

LING, G., Private, Queen's (Royal West Surrey Regt.).

He joined in February 1917, and in the following month was sent to the Western Front, where he served until the cessation of hostilities. During this period he fought in the Battles of Arras, Vimy Ridge, Messines, Ypres, Passchendaele, Lens and Cambrai, and in the Retreat and Advance of 1918. He was demobilised in December 1919, and holds the General Service and Victory Medals.

85, Beckway Street, Walworth, S.E.17.   Z3045

LINGE, A. J., Corporal, R.E.

He volunteered in July 1915, and in the same year embarked for Egypt. He was engaged on important duties in connection with operations during the Advance through Palestine, and was present at the Battle of Gaza and the fall of Jerusalem. Sent to France in 1918 he served through the Advance of that year, and after the Armistice proceeded into Germany with the Army of Occupation. Returning to England he was demobilised in February 1919, and holds the 1914–15 Star, and the General Service and Victory Medals.

7, Santley Street, Ferndale Road, S.W.4.   4445C

LINGE, H. G., Gunner, R.F.A.

Volunteering in September 1915, he proceeded to France shortly afterwards, and served there throughout the course of hostilities. During this period he was engaged with his Battery in various sectors, and amongst other battles fought in those of Ypres and Loos. He was wounded three times whilst overseas, and sent home to hospital, but on his recovery returned to the Field, and served until the end of the war. He was demobilised in January 1919, and holds the 1914–15 Star, and the General Service and Victory Medals.

7, Santley Street, Ferndale Road, S.W.4.   4445D

LINGHAM, S. E., Gunner, R.F.A.

He volunteered in April 1915, and in the following November embarked for the Western Front. In the course of his service in this theatre of war he was in action in several important engagements, including the Battles of Ypres, Arras and the Somme. Returning to England on the conclusion of hostilities, he was demobilised in May 1919, and holds the 1914–15 Star, and the General Service and Victory Medals.

35, Atwell Road, Rye Lane, S.E.15.   Z5446

LINGLEY, W. J., Special War Worker.

He volunteered for work of National importance, and from 1915 to 1920 was engaged as a mechanic at a London County Council Munition training centre. Employed on work demanding a high degree of technical knowledge and skill he carried out his duties in a thoroughly efficient and capable manner throughout his service.

203, Beresford Street, Camberwell Road, S.E.5.   Z3046

LINGWOOD, J. W., Sergt., 2nd East Surrey Regt.

He enlisted in 1906, and was drafted to France in January 1915. He fought in several engagements and was wounded in the Battle of Hill 60, and sent home to hospital. On recovery he rejoined his Battalion, and was in action in the Battles of the Somme and Ypres, and was gassed during the Advance of 1918. He was demobilised in March 1919, and holds the 1914–15 Star, and the General Service and Victory Medals.

58, Lavender Road, Battersea, S.W.11.   Z3047

LINNELL, E., C.S.M., East Surrey Regiment.

After twenty-one years' previous service with the Colours, he volunteered in September 1914, and acted as an Instructor. He rendered valuable services in the training of recruits for the New Armies, and was discharged in 1915 as medically unfit for further duty.

28, Atherton Street, Battersea, S.W.11.   Z3048

LINSDELL, A., Private, 1st North Staffordshire Regt.

He volunteered in January 1915, and in the same year proceeded to the Western Front. Whilst overseas he took part in several important engagements, including the Battle of the Somme, and was twice gassed. In 1918 he was sent to Russia, and during his service there was recommended for the Russian Order of St. George for conspicuous bravery and devotion to duty in working a machine gun in the face of heavy enemy attacks. He returned to England for demobilisation in July 1919, and holds the 1914–15 Star, and the General Service and Victory Medals.

1, Southwell Terrace, Lewis Road, Camberwell, S.E.5. Z6179A

LINSELL, W. J., Sergt., 4th Coldstream Guards.

Volunteering in November 1914, he was sent to France in the following August, and amongst other important engagements, fought in the Battles of Loos, Ypres, the Somme, Arras, Passchendaele and Beaumont-Hamel, and during the Advance of 1918. On the conclusion of hostilities he proceeded with the Army of Occupation to Germany, and was stationed at Cologne. He was demobilised in April 1919, on his return to England, and holds the 1914–15 Star, and the General Service and Victory Medals.

19, Elmington Road, Camberwell, S.E.5.   Z4439A

LISNEY, J. T., Sergt., 2nd East Surrey Regiment.

He volunteered in September 1914, and proceeding to the Western Front five months later, took part in many engagements in the Ypres salient, and was wounded at Kemmel in July 1915. Transferred to Egypt in January 1916, he saw much service there until sent to Salonika. He was in action on the Struma front and saw heavy fighting in various sectors. Owing to ill-health he returned to England, and was subsequently invalided out of the Service in November 1917. He holds the 1914–15 Star, and the General Service and Victory Medals, and also the Queen's and King's South African Medals for service in the Boer War.

1, Badsworth Road, Camberwell, S.E.5.   Z3049

LIST, R. E., Private, 24th Queen's (Royal West Surrey Regiment).

Volunteering in 1915, he was sent to France later in that year and was in action at Hill 60, Ypres and Loos. Transferred to Salonika in 1916, he fought in many engagements on the Doiran front, and in the following year proceeded to Egypt. He served both on the Western Front and the Palestine front in this theatre of war, and in December 1917 returned to France. He was engaged in heavy fighting during the German Offensive of 1918, and was wounded near Cambrai on October 24th in the Allied Advance. He returned to England and after receiving hospital treatment was demobilised in 1919, holding the 1914–15 Star, and the General Service and Victory Medals.

37, Myatt Road, Stockwell, S.W.9.   Z4488

LITTLE, E., Private, 3rd Norfolk Regt. 7th London Regt. and 20th and 4th Middlesex Regt.

He volunteered in December 1914, but when discovered to be under military age, was discharged in the following August. He joined again in October 1917, and proceeding to France in April 1918, fought at Bapaume, Cambrai, Le Cateau and in many other engagements during the Retreat and Advance of 1918. He was demobilised in March 1919, but re-enlisted in May of the following year for a further period of service. He was finally discharged in October 1920, and holds the General Service and Victory Medals.

92, Cronin Road, Peckham, S.E.15.   Z5447

LITTLEJOHN, A. H., Q.M.S., R.E.

He joined in 1916, and was engaged at various depôts on important duties in connection with the training of the recruits of the New Armies. Owing to medical unfitness, he did not obtain his transfer overseas while hostilities continued, but rendered valuable services until demobilised in 1919.

75, Arthur Road, Brixton Road, S.W.9.   Z4489A

LITTLEJOHN, S. W., Sapper, R.E. and Gunner, R.G.A.

Although exempt from military service, he joined H.M. Forces in 1916, and embarked for France later in that year. He was in action in many parts of the line, and fought at the Somme, Arras, Ypres and Passchendaele. He gave his life for King and Country at Ypres on September 23rd, 1917, and was entitled to the General Service and Victory Medals.

"He joined the great white company of valiant souls."

75, Arthur Road, Brixton Road, S.W.9.   Z4489B

LIVERMORE, H., Colour Sergt., Queen's (Royal West Kent Regt.) and 2nd British West Indian Regiment.

He enlisted in July 1909, and throughout the war was engaged on special duties between the West Indies and Egypt. He rendered valuable services, and in 1920 was serving in the West Indies at Jamaica. He holds the General Service and Victory Medals.

38, Antrobus Road, Chiswick, W.4.   6303

LIVERMORE, W. E., Driver, R.F.A.

He joined in March 1916, and four months later embarked for Mesopotamia, where he saw much service in various sectors. Proceeding later to Egypt he fought in many engagements on the Palestine front, and was transferred to the Western Front in April 1917. On his voyage to France his ship was torpedoed, but fortunately he was saved. He was in action at Vimy Ridge, St. Quentin, Béthune, and throughout the Retreat and Advance of 1918. Returning to England after the cessation of hostilities, he was demobilised in January 1919, and holds the General Service and Victory Medals.

23, Cunnington Street, Chiswick, W.4.   T6298

LIVERSEDGE, A. W., Seaman Gunner, R.N.

He was serving in the Royal Naval Volunteer Reserve previous to the war, and was called up in August 1914, and posted to H.M.S. "Hannibal." After service in the North Sea his ship was ordered to the Dardanelles, and was engaged in the Battle of the Narrows, and in the Landing at Gallipoli. He was wounded in this action, and was invalided to Egypt. On recovery he rejoined his vessel, which returned to England, and saw much service with the Grand Fleet in the North Sea until the close of the war. He was demobilised in February 1919, and holds the 1914–15 Star, and the General Service and Victory Medals.

54, Deverell Street, New Kent Road, S.E.1.　　25642B

LIVERSEDGE, H. Private, 2nd Royal Fusiliers.

He volunteered in August 1915, and later in the same year was drafted to the Western Front, where he took part in many important engagements, including those at Ypres, the Somme and Arras. He also fought in the Retreat and Advance of 1918, and was severely wounded. He was invalided home and discharged in November 1918 as unfit for further service. holding the 1914–15 Star, and the General Service and Victory Medals.

54, Deverell Street, New Kent Road, S.E.1.　　Z25642A

LIVERSEDGE, P., Rifleman, 1/17th King's Royal Rifle Corps.

He joined in June 1917, and embarking for the Western Front in the following March, served in various sectors, where heavy fighting was in progress. He gave his life for King and Country in the German Offensive of 1918, and lies at rest in the British Cemetery at Amiens. He was entitled to the General Service and Victory Medals.

"Courage, bright hopes, and myriad dreams, splendidly given."

54, Deverell Street, New Kent Road, S.E.1.　　25642C

LIVERTON, A. E., Special War Worker.

Ineligible for service with the Colours, he rendered valuable sevrices transporting supplies and stores of all descriptions to various Army Depôts. He was engaged on this work of National importance from August 1914 until December 1918, and received high commendation for the efficient way in which he discharged his duties.

85, Avondale Square, Old Kent Road, S.E.1.　　Z27084

LIVINGSTONE, J., Rifleman, 2nd Rifle Brigade.

Volunteering in June 1915, he was drafted to the Western Front later in that year. During his service overseas he fought at Ypres, Loos, Festubert, the Somme and Lens, and being wounded at Passchendaele was invalided to England. On recovery he returned to France in 1918, and was in action throughout the Retreat and Advance of the Allies. He was demobilised in 1919, and holds the 1914–15 Star, and the General Service and Victory Medals.

33, Mostyn Road, Brixton Road, S.W.9.　　Z3484

LLOYD, A., Corporal, Manchester Regiment.

Joining in 1918, after completing his training, he served with his unit at various stations. He did excellent work, but was unable to obtain his transfer overseas before the cessation of hostilities. After the Armistice, however, he was sent to France in 1919, and was engaged on important duties until his return home for demobilisation in March 1920.

1, Thurlow Street, Wandsworth Road, S.W.9.　　Z3050

LLOYD, A., Corporal, R.A.S.C. (M.T.)

Volunteering in May 1915, he was drafted to the Western Front in the same year, and served there for upwards of four years. During this period he was engaged in the transport of supplies and ammunition to the firing line in the Battles of Ypres, the Somme, Arras, Armentières, and Cambrai, and during the Retreat and Advance of 1918. He was demobilised in January 1919, and holds the 1914–15 Star, and the General Service and Victory Medals.

94, Avenue Road, Camberwell, S.E.5.　　Z3109B

LLOYD, A. E., Private, Royal Fusiliers and Queen's (Royal West Surrey Regiment).

He joined in November 1916, when sixteen years of age, and on the completion of his training served with his unit in the Southern Counties. He was unsuccessful in his efforts to secure a transfer to a theatre of war before the conclusion of hostilities, but was, however, sent into Germany with the Army of Occupation after the Armistice. He returned eo England, and was demobilised in February 1919.

94, Avenue Road, Camberwell, S.E.5.　　Z3109A

LLOYD, C., Officers' Steward, R.N.

Volunteering in July 1915, he served at air stations on the coast until posted to a mine-sweeper engaged on important operations in the North Sea. He was afterwards transferred to H.M.S. "Wessex," which ship was engaged on special duties in the North Sea and the Mediterranean. He was demobilised in July 1920, and holds the General Service and Victory Medals.

11, St. Andrew's Street, Wandsworth Road, S.W.8.　　Z3104

LLOYD, A. S., Private, West Yorkshire Regiment.

He volunteered in August 1914, and in the following June proceeded tr Gallipoli, where he fought in the Landing at Suvla Bay, and was wounded. After the Evacuation of the Peninsula he was sent to France in June 1916, and saw much service in the Somme sector. He gave his life for King and Country in the Battle of the Somme on September 29th, 1916, and was entitled to the 1914–15 Star, and the General Service and Victory Medals.

"Great deeds cannot die:
They with the Sun and Moon renew their light for ever."

11, Albany Road, Camberwell, S.E.5.　　Z5566B

LLOYD, E. A., Private, R.A.S.C.

Volunteering in March 1915, he was drafted to the Western Front in the same month, and after a short period of service was invalided home on account of ill-health. He received hospital treatment for several months, and in April 1916 was discharged as medically unfit for further service. He died on July 28th, 1918, and was entitled to the 1914–15 Star, and the General Service and Victory Medals.

"The path of duty was the way to glory."

228, East Street, Walworth, S.E.17.　　Z3110

LLOYD, G., Sergt., 1st East Surrey Regiment.

He joined in June 1917, and proceeding to France in the same year served throughout the war. He was in action in numerous engagements, including the Battles of Ypres, Lens, Cambrai and those of the Retreat and Advance of 1918. Returning to England after the conclusion of hostilities, he was demobilised in October 1919, and holds the General Service and Victory Medals. 29, Thurlow Street, Wandsworth Road, S.W.8.　　Z3107

LLOYD, H., Rifleman, 21st London Regt. (1st Surrey Rifles).

He volunteered in April 1915, and in the same year embarked for the Western Front. In the course of his service in this theatre of war he fought in several operations, including the Battle of Vermelles, and sustained severe shell-shock. Invalided to hospital in England for treatment he was subsequently discharged as medically unfit for service in August 1917, and holds the 1914–15 Star, and the General Service and Victory Medals.

24, Mordaunt Street, Landor Road, S.W.9.　　Z3106

LLOYD, H. F., Private, M.G.C.

Volunteering in November 1915, he was sent to the Western Front in the following June, and served in various parts of the line until the conclusion of hostilities. He was in action in numerous engagements, including the Battles of the Somme, Vimy Ridge, and Ypres. Returning home after the Armistice, he was demobilised in September 1919, and holds the General Service and Victory Medals.

35, Portslade Road, Wandsworth Road, S.W.8.　　Z3105

LLOYD, W. G., Private, Buffs (East Kent Regiment).

He volunteered in October 1914, and drafted to France in the following year fought in the Battles of Loos and Ypres, and was wounded on the Somme. Returning to his unit on recovery he was wounded in the Battle of Delville Wood, and taken prisoner in January 1917. He was held in captivity until repatriated after the Armistice, and was demobilised in December 1919. He holds the 1914–15 Star, and the General Service and Victory Medals.

1, Dorset Road, Clapham Road, S.W.8.　　Z3108B

LLOYD, W. J., Corporal, R.A.S.C. (M.T.)

Volunteering in June 1915, he proceeded overseas in the same year, and served on the Western Front throughout the war. He was engaged in the transport of ammunition and supplies to the forward areas, whilst heavy fighting was in progress, and for a time served on special duties at General Headquarters. He was demobilised in March 1919, and holds the 1914–15 Star, and the General Service and Victory Medals.

9, Lidgate Road, Peckham, S.E.15.　　Z5800

LLOYD, W. J., L/Corporal, R.E.

He volunteered in August 1914, and after completing his training served with his unit until his embarkation for the Western Front in 1918. He did valuable work in connection with operations during the closing stages of the war, and was engaged on important duties after hostilities ceased. Returning home for demobilisation in March 1920, he holds the General Service and Victory Medals.

1, Dorset Road, Clapham Road, S.W.8.　　Z3108A

LOCHEAD, A. G., Rifleman, Rifle Brigade.

Volunteering in September 1914, he proceeded to France in the following July, and fought in the Battle of Loos and other important engagements until invalided home, owing to illness. Returning to the Western Front in November 1916 he served in the Battles of Beaumont-Hamel, Arras, Vimy Ridge, Messines and Ypres, and was wounded at Arras in October 1917, and sent to England for medical treatment. On recovery he acted as Bombing Instructor, and in September 1918 was sent back to France, and was again wounded at Arras in the following month. On leaving hospital he served with his unit until he was demobilised in February 1919, and holds the 1914–15 Star, and the General Service and Victory Medals.

73, Speke Road, Battersea, S.W.11.　　Z3112

LOCK, C. A., Private, 3rd Cheshire Regiment.

He joined in May 1916, and in the following September embarked for the Western Front. Serving in the Battle of the Somme he was wounded and taken prisoner, and was in hospital in Germany. On recovery he was engaged on farm work until released from captivity after the Armistice. Demobilised in 1919, he holds the General Service and Victory Medals.

50, Park Crescent, Clapham Park Road, S.W.4.　　Z3111

LOCK, C. E. (M.M.), Private, 2nd East Surrey Regt.

Enlisting in July 1910, he was serving in India when war broke out, and shortly afterwards sailed for France. There he was in action in the Battles of Ypres (I.), Loos and the Somme, and was awarded the Military Medal for conspicuous bravery and devotion to duty in the Field. He also fought in the Battles of Armentières, Ypres (II. and III.), and Thiepval, and was four times wounded. Demobilised in July 1919, he holds the 1914 Star, and the General Service and Victory Medals.

104, Ingrave Street, Battersea, S.W.11.　　Z3043

LOCKETT, T. G., Private, East Yorkshire Regiment and M.G.C.

He was serving in India at the outbreak of war, and immediately proceeded to the Western Front, where he fought in the Retreat from Mons, and many subsequent battles, including those at Neuve Chapelle, Ypres, Loos, the Somme, Arras, Cambrai and the Retreat and Advance of 1918, being present at the entry into Mons on November 11th, 1918. He afterwards served in Germany with the Army of Occupation, and was stationed at Cologne. He was demobilised in March 1919, and holds the Mons Star, and the General Service and Victory Medals.

8, Neate Street, Camberwell, S.E.5.　　Z5055B

LOCKWOOD, A., Sergt., 2nd North Staffordshire Regiment.

He enlisted in 1907, and at the outbreak of war was serving in India. He was engaged there during the whole period of hostilities, and took part in many skirmishes on the North West Frontier, and in Afghanistan. He was wounded on one occasion. He holds the 1914-15 Star, the General Service and Victory Medals, and the India General Service Medal (with clasp, Afghanistan, N.W. Frontier, 1919). He was discharged after the Armistice, but re-enlisted in the R.A.S.C., and in 1920 was serving in Turkey.

23, Willcox Road, Wandsworth Road, S.W.8.　　Z3113

LOCKWOOD, G. W., Cpl., King's Royal Rifle Corps.

He volunteered in 1915, and in the same year was drafted overseas. During his service on the Western Front he fought on the Somme and at Arras and Ypres, where he was wounded in 1915. On his recovery he returned to the firing line, and was again wounded at Ypres. After a long period in hospital in England, he was drafted to Ireland, and was finally discharged in January 1919. He holds the 1914-15 Star, and the General Service and Victory Medals.

27, Wilcox Road, Wandsworth Road, S.W.8.　　Z3114

LOCKYER, A. V., Driver, R.F.A.

He volunteered in 1915, and in the same year embarked for the Western Front in several sectors of which he served with his Battery. Amongst other battles he fought in those of Arras, Ypres and the Somme, and was seriously wounded during the Advance of 1918. Sent home to hospital on account of his injuries, he was subsequently invalided out of the Service in 1919, and holds the 1914-15 Star, and the General Service and Victory Medals.

4, Sunwell Street, Peckham, S.E.15.　　Z6477

LOCKYER, E., Sapper, R.E.

Joining in October 1917, he was drafted at the conclusion of his training to London, where he was engaged at the G.P.O. for about twenty months. He was then sent to Egypt, where his duties were in the Postal Section, and subsequently he went to Palestine. He was demobilised in May 1920.

34, Morrison Street, Battersea, S.W.11.　　Z3115

LODER, H. J. (M.S.M.), Staff-Sergt., R.A.M.C.

He enlisted in 1905, and at the oubreak of hostilities was serving in China, where he was engaged with the British Expeditionary Force until May 1920, when he returned to England. He holds the Meritorious Service Medal, for which he was twice recommended, and the General Service and Victory Medals, and was still serving in 1920.

51, Philip Road, Peckham, S.E.15.　　Z6017

LOFTHOUSE, T. W., Corporal, Royal Scots Fusiliers.

A Reservist, he was mobilised at the outbreak of hostilities, and drafted at once to France. He fought in the Retreat from Mons and many subsequent battles, including those of the Marne and the Aisne, and was wounded near Ypres. On recovery he rejoined his unit and fought on the Somme and at Arras and Ypres. He was demobilised in February 1919, and holds the Mons Star, and the General Service and Victory Medals.

22, Vivian Road, Peckham, S.E.15.　　Z6016

LOFTIN, H. F., Flight-Cadet, R.A.F.

Joining in June 1918, he commenced his training as a flight cadet at Hastings. He had made several flights and was nearly qualified as a pilot, when the Armistice was declared. On this account he did not succeed in obtaining his commission and in being drafted overseas, and was demobilised in November 1918.

34, Chumleigh Street, Camberwell, S.E.5.　　Z5635

LOFTUS, F., Rifleman, Rifle Brigade.

He joined in May 1916, and three months later was drafted overseas. Whilst on the Western Front he fought in the Battles of Somme, Beaucourt, the Ancre, Bullecourt (where he was wounded), Ypres III and Passchendaele, being severely wounded at Langemarck. He was invalided to England, and in February 1918 was discharged as medically unfit for further service. He holds the General Service and Victory Medals.

108, Mina Road, Walworth, S.E.17.　　Z3116

LONDON, E., Driver, R.A.S.C.

Joining in 1916, he was sent to Salonika in the same year, where he was engaged with his unit on special duties during the fighting on the Struma front. In January 1919 he was invalided to England, having contracted malaria, and after receiving hospital treatment was demobilised later in that year. He holds the General Service and Victory Medals.

14, Blendon Row, Walworth, S.E.17.　　Z3117

LONG, D. F., Corporal, R.G.A.

Volunteering in August 1914, and proceeding to the Western Front, he fought at the Battles of Ypres, the Somme and in many other engagements of note. In 1917 he was transferred to Egypt and was in action in various sectors on the Palestine front and was present at the capture of Jerusalem. Owing to ill-health he was admitted into hospital and died on January 12th, 1919. He was entitled to the 1914-15 Star, and the General Service and Victory Medals.

"A valiant soldier, with undaunted heart, he breasted life's last hill."

80, Commercial Road, Peckham, S.E.15.　　Z6280

LONG, G. A., Gunner, R.F.A.

He volunteered in June 1915, and at the conclusion of his training was sent in the following January to France. Whilst in this theatre of war he was posted to "C" Battery, 119th Brigade. He fought in the Battles of the Somme and at Messines, Ypres and Passchendaele, and also took part in the final Advance of 1918. He was demobilised in January 1919, and holds the General Service and Victory Medals.

9, Caspian Street, Camberwell, S.E.5.　　Z5448

LONG, J., Private, 10th Queen's (Royal West Surrey Regiment).

He volunteered in November 1915, and in June of the following year proceeded overseas. During his service in France he fought on the Somme, and at Arras, Ploegsteert, Armentières and Cambrai. During this long period of service he was fortunate in escaping injury. He was demobilised in July 1919, and holds the General Service and Victory Medals.

138, Stewart's Road, Battersea Park Road, S.W.8.　　Z3119

LONG, S., 1st Air Mechanic, R.A.F.

He volunteered in February 1915, and at the conclusion of his training served on home defence at many aerodromes. He was engaged upon special duties, which called for a high degree of technical skill. He did excellent work, but was unable to secure his transfer overseas, and was demobilised in September 1920.

29, Lockington Road, Battersea Park Road, S.W.8.　　Z3118B

LONG, S. R., Private, R.A.S.C.

He volunteered in September 1914, and was later drafted to the Western Front, where he was engaged on special duties with his unit in various sectors. Whilst employed in taking horses to the front line trenches he sustained severe injuries, which incapacitated him from service in the trenches. He was demobilised in April 1919, and holds the 1914-15 Star, and the General Service and Victory Medals.

196, Lynton Road, Bermondsey, S.E.1.　　Z26182

LONG, W., Driver, R.H.A.

He joined in December 1917, on attaining military age, and at the conclusion of his training served with his Battery on special duties at various depôts. He did good work, but was unsuccessful in obtaining his transfer overseas, and was serving in 1920 in Ireland.

29, Lockington Road, Battersea Park Road, S.W.8.　　Z3118A

LONGHURST, E. (Mrs.), Special War Worker.

During the war this lady offered her services, and was engaged on important work at the Anti-gas Works, New Kent Road, Southwark. Her duties, which were to examine anti-gas masks, were carried out in a highly satisfactory manner, and she received commendation for her services.

304, East Street, Walworth, S.E.17.　　Z3122B

LONGHURST, G. A., L/Corporal, East Surrey Regt.
Volunteering at the outbreak of hostilities, he was sent overseas in January 1915. He fought at Neuve Chapelle, St. Eloi and Hill 60, where he was wounded. On recovery he took part in the fighting at Loos, Albert, Vimy Ridge and the Somme. He was again wounded, but after six months' hospital treatment he returned to France and was in action at Arras, Bullecourt and Ypres. He also took part in the Retreat and Advance of 1918, during which he was badly gassed. He was demobilised in December 1919, and holds the 1914-15 Star, and the General Service and Victory Medals.
304, East Street, Walworth, S.E.17.　　　Z3120

LONGHURST, H., Private, R.A.S.C.
He volunteered in October 1914, and at the conclusion of his training served with his unit at various stations on important duties. He rendered excellent service, but owing to defective eyesight was unable to secure his transfer to a theatre of war, and was in consequence invalided out of the Service in May 1915.
304, East Street, Walworth, S.E.17.　　　Z3122A

LONGHURST, H. J., Corporal, R.F.A.
He volunteered in November 1914, and after completing his training served on home duties until June 1916, when he was drafted to India. He was engaged with his Battery at Lahore, Rawal Pindi and Bombay, and later took part in the campaign on the North-West Frontier. He was afterwards sent to Mesopotamia and saw much service, and whilst at Bagdhad contracted malaria. On recovery he returned to England and was demobilised in November 1919. He holds the General Service and Victory Medals, and the India General Service Medal (with clasp Afghanistan, N.W. Frontier, 1919).
57, Marcia Road, Bermondsey, S.E.1.　　　Z3121A

LONGHURST, W. (Mrs.), Special War Worker.
During the war this lady offered her services and was engaged on important work at Messrs. Hampton's, Westminster. Her duties, which were in connection with the manufacture of Army equipments, were carried out in a highly satisfactory manner.
57, Marcia Road, Bermondsey, S.E.1.　　　Z3121B

LOOM, G. A., Gunner, R.F.A.
Volunteering in January 1915, he was drafted later in that year to the Western Front, and was in action in several engagements in the Ypres salient. After being transferred to Egypt in the following year, he fought in many parts of the Palestine Front under General Allenby and took part in the Advance through the Holy Land into Syria. Returning to England he was demobilised in March 1919, and holds the 1914-15 Star, and the General Service and Victory Medals.
98, Wilcox Road, Wandsworth Road, S.W.8.　　　Z3124

LOOM, H. R., Driver, R.F.A.
He joined in January 1917, and proceeding to France later in the same year fought in many engagements of note. He was in action throughout the German Offensive and subsequent Allied Advance of 1918, and was present at the entry of the British troops into Lille on October 17th, 1918. He was demobilised in June 1919 after his return home, and holds the General Service and Victory Medals.
47, Bedford Street, Walworth, S.E.17.　　　Z3123A

LORD, E. P. H., C.Q.M.S., 1/4th York and Lancaster Regiment.
He joined in March 1917, and proceeded to the Western Front a year later. He fought with distinction in many important engagements during the German Offensive and Allied Advance of 1918. After the cessation of hostilities he was sent into Germany with the Army of Occupation and was stationed at Cologne until he returned to England, and was demobilised in November 1919. He holds the General Service and Victory Medals.
108, Bramfield Road, Wandsworth Common, S.W.11.　Z3095

LORD, W. T., Special War Worker.
Although he attested under the Derby scheme, he was exempted from military service as he was engaged on work of vital importance at the Charing Cross Electric Light Supply Works. He rendered valuable services throughout the war as a switchboard operator, and discharged his duties most efficiently.
37, Castlemaine Road, Peckham, S.E.15.　　　Z6028

LOVEJOY, C. G., Pte., Australian Imperial Forces.
He joined in July 1917, and proceeded to France in the same year. During his service overseas he fought in many important engagements and was severely wounded. After receiving treatment he was invalided to Australia, but, unfortunately, died near Sydney in November 1918. He was entitled to the General Service and Victory Medals.
"His life for his Country, his soul to God."
7, Medwin Street, Ferndale Road, Clapham, S.W.4.　Z3128

LOVELACE, S. W., L/Cpl., 4th Middlesex Regiment.
Joining in January 1917, and drafted to the Western Front in the same year, he fought in many engagements of note, including those at Ypres and the Somme. He was also in action throughout the Retreat and Advance of 1918, and was wounded. He was demobilised in November 1919, and holds the General Service and Victory Medals.
24, Stanley Street, Battersea Park, S.W.8.　　　Z3129A

LOVELACE, W. G., Rflmn., King's Royal Rifle Corps.
He joined in April 1917, and later in the same year was drafted to the Egyptian Expeditionary Force. During the Palestine campaign he was in action at Gaza and in various other engagements. Owing to ill-health he was admitted into hospital at Alexandria, and later returned to England. He was discharged in January 1919, and holds the General Service and Victory Medals.
24, Stanley Street, Battersea Park, S.W.8.　　　Z3129B

LOVELAND, L. B., Private, Queen's Own (Royal West Kent Regiment).
He volunteered in September 1915, and proceeding to France in October of the following year, fought in the Battles of Arras, Vimy Ridge and Ypres. In January 1918 he was invalided to England on account of serious illness, and after his recovery served at various depôts at home until demobilised in January 1919. He holds the General Service and Victory Medals.
185, Albert Road, Peckham, S.E.15.　　　Z6019

LOVELESS, E., Cook, Merchant Service.
He was in the Merchant Service at the commencement of hostilities, and throughout the war did good work on board various ships, which were engaged in transporting troops and supplies to various theatres of war. He was in the troopship "Annapolis" when she was torpedoed and sunk on April 19th, 1917, off the West coast of Ireland, but he was fortunately saved. He was still serving in 1920, and holds the General Service and Mercantile Marine War Medals.
133, Flaxman Road, Camberwell, S.E.5.　　　Z6199

LOVELL, A. C., Private, 19th (Queen Alexandra's Own Royal) Hussars.
A serving soldier, he was drafted to France at the outbreak of war and fought with distinction in the Retreat from Mons, and in the Battles of the Marne, Ypres, Bullecourt and many other engagements throughout the German Offensive and Allied Advance of 1918, and was gassed. He was demobilised in 1919, and holds the Mons Star, and the General Service and Victory Medals. He also holds the Queen's and King's South African Medals for service in the Boer War.
25, Narford Road, Clapton, E.5.　　　7773B

LOVELL, A. R., Stoker, R.N.
He joined in 1916, and was posted to H.M.S. "Diana," which was engaged on anti-submarine patrol duties in the Indian Ocean. After the Armistice he was sent to China, and served there on important garrison duties. He returned to England, and was demobilised in October 1919, and holds the General Service and Victory Medals.
22, Russell Road, Peckham, S.E.15.　　　Z5449

LOVELL, B., Driver, R.F.A.
Volunteering in November 1914, and proceeding to the Western Front in the following year, he fought in various engagements. Transferred to Salonika in 1916, he was in action in many parts of the line and throughout the final Allied Advance. During his service in the Balkan theatre of war he suffered from malaria. Returning to England he was demobilised in April 1919, and holds the 1914-15 Star, and the General Service and Victory Medals.
7, Sedan Street, Walworth, S.E.17.　　　Z3126B

LOVELL, F., L/Cpl., Queen's Own (Royal West Kent Regiment).
Volunteering in 1915, he proceeded to the Western Front shortly afterwards and fought in the Ypres salient and in the Arras sector. He was reported missing on September 26th, 1915, during the Battle of Loos, and later was presumed to have been killed on that date. He was entitled to the 1914-15 Star, and the General Service and Victory Medals.
"He joined the great white company of valiant souls."
56, Philip Road, Peckham, S.E.15.　　　Z6025

LOVELL, J. W., Guardsman, 2nd Coldstream Guards.
Volunteering in September 1914, he was sent to the Western Front in the following year and was in action at Festubert, Loos, the Somme, Vimy Ridge, Ypres, Passchendaele and throughout the German Offensive and Allied Advance of 1918. After the Armistice he was drafted to Germany with the Army of Occupation, and served there until he returned to England, and was demobilised in March 1919. He holds the 1914-15 Star, and the General Service and Victory Medals.
10, Matthews Street, Battersea, S.W.11.　　　Z3125

LOVELL, S. H. J., Pte., 10th Queen's (Royal West Surrey Regiment).
He joined in June 1918, on attaining military age and after completing his training was drafted to France in October. He did not go into the fighting line during the closing operations of the war, but after the Armistice was sent into Germany with the Army of Occupation, and was still serving there in 1920. He holds the General Service and Victory Medals.
25, Narford Road, Clapton, E.5.　　　7773A

LOVELL, W. G., Private, 11th Essex Regiment.
He volunteered in September 1914, and embarking for France in the following year was in action in many important engagements, including those at Loos, Lens, St. Quentin, St. Eloi and Bullecourt, and was twice gassed. He also served throughout the Retreat and Advance of 1918. He was demobilised in February 1919, and holds the 1914-15 Star, and the General Service and Victory Medals.
7, Sedan Street, Walworth, S.E.17.　　　Z3126A

LOVELOCK, E. T., Sapper, R.E.
He volunteered in 1915, and proceeding to the Dardanelles later in that year took part in the Landing at Suvla Bay and the capture of Chunuk Bair. He was in action in many subsequent engagements, and after the Evacuation of the Peninsula was sent to Mesopotamia. He saw much service here, and was present at the capture of Kut and Bagdhad and the occupation of Mosul. Returning to England, he was demobilised in 1919, and holds the 1914-15 Star, and the General Service and Victory Medals.
30, McKerrell Road, Peckham, S.E.15.　　　Z6026

LOVELOCK, G. H., Gunner, Australian F.A.
He volunteered in August 1914, and being sent in the following year to the Dardanelles, took part in many engagements on the Peninsula. He was unfortunately killed in action on 26th July, 1915, and was entitled to the 1914-15 Star, and the General Service and Victory Medals. He had served thirteen years in the Regular Army prior to emigrating to Australia, and held the Queen's and King's South African Medals for service in the Boer War.
"A costly sacrifice upon the altar of freedom."
198, St. James' Road, Old Kent Road, S.E.1.　　　Z26730

LOVETT, J. A., Driver, R.F.A.
He volunteered in August 1914, and was drafted to the Western Front in February 1916. During his service overseas he saw much fighting in France, and in 1917 was transferred to Italy, where he was in action on the Piave front and in various other sectors, and was wounded and gassed. He returned to England, and was demobilised in April 1919, and holds the General Service and Victory Medals.
51, Bramfield Road, Wandsworth Common, S.W.11.　　Z3127

LOWDEN, G. H., Saddler, R.A.S.C.
Volunteering in March 1915, he was sent to France later in the same year, and was engaged on important duties in the forward areas during the progress of the Battles of Albert, Neuve Chapelle, and Vimy Ridge. He also served throughout the Retreat and Advance of 1918, and returning to England, was demobilised in June 1919. He holds the 1914-15 Star, and the General Service and Victory Medals.
7, Morrison Street, Battersea, S.W.11.　　　Z3130

LOWE, J. A. (O.B.E.), Leading Stoker, R.N.
He volunteered in December 1914, and was posted to H.M.S. "Temeraire." Whilst on board this ship he was appointed to the Order of the British Empire, for bravery in dealing with a fire, in which he was injured. He was invalided for eight months, but on recovery rejoined the same vessel, and served in the North, Mediterranean and Baltic Seas. He was demobilised in April 1919, and holds the 1914-15 Star, and the General Service and Victory Medals.
90, Chatham Street, Walworth, S.E.17.　　　Z3132

LOWE, S. C., Gunner, R.F.A.
He joined in 1918, and completing his training, embarked for the Western Front. He fought in many engagements during the Allied Advance of 1918, and proceeded to Germany with the Army of Occupation after the cessation of hostilities. He was demobilised in 1919, and holds the General Service and Victory Medals. Previous to joining the Colours he was employed at the Projectile Co.'s Works, Battersea, on work of National importance.
83, Wadhurst Road, Wandsworth Road, S.W.8.　　Z1785A

LOWLES, F. J., Private, 6th Northamptonshire Regt.
He joined in August 1917, and embarked for France in the following year. He was in action in many parts of the line, and was wounded at Arras and also at Villers Bretonneux. On recovery he rejoined his unit, and took part in heavy fighting until severely wounded at Péronne. Admitted into hospital he died from his injuries on September 18th, 1918, and was entitled to the General Service and Victory Medals.
"And doubtless he went in splendid company."
4, Edithna Street, Landor Road, S.W.9.　　　Z3133B

LOWLES, G. W., Corporal, R.G.A.
A serving soldier, he was drafted to France at the outbreak of hostilities, and fought in the Retreat from Mons and in the Battles of the Aisne, the Marne, Ypres, Albert, Loos, Kemmel Hill, Gommecourt, Roubaix and Roulers. He was also in action throughout the German Offensive and Allied Advance of 1918. He was demobilised, but rejoined for a further period of service, and was still serving in 1920. He holds the Mons Star, and the General Service and Victory Medals.
4, Edithna Street, Landor Road, S.W.9.　　　Z3133A

LOWLES, H. T., Private, Northumberland Fusiliers.
He joined in August 1916, and proceeding to France in the following year was engaged in heavy fighting at Bullecourt and in many other parts of the line. He served throughout the Retreat and Advance of 1918, and returning to England after the Armistice was demobilised in March 1919, and holds the General Service and Victory Medals.
43, Willington Road, Stockwell, S.W.9.　　　Z3131

LOWNES, H., Private, 6th Middlesex Regiment.
He joined in July 1918, and after completing his training was drafted to the Western Front, where he served in several sectors during the final Allied Advance. After the Armistice he proceeded with the Army of Occupation to Germany, and was stationed at Cologne. He returned home, and was demobilised in January 1920, and holds the General Service and Victory Medals.
38, Thorncroft Street, South Lambeth, S.W.8.　　Z3135B

LOWNES, J., Lieutenant, Duke of Cornwall's Light Infantry and R.A.F.
He volunteered in August 1914, and was sent to the Western Front in the following year. He took part in numerous engagements, including those at Ypres, Loos, the Somme, Arras, Messines, Passchendaele and Cambrai, and was wounded at Hooge and later at Delville Wood. He returned home in 1918, and was transferred to the R.A.F., with which unit he served as a flying officer, and rendered excellent services. He was demobilised in March 1919, holding the 1914-15 Star, and the General Service and Victory Medals.
36, Thorncroft Street, South Lambeth, S.W.8.　　Z3134

LOWNES, W., Driver, R.F.A.
Volunteering in October 1915, he was drafted to France in the following year, and was in action at the Battles of the Somme and Ypres, and in numerous other engagements. In 1918, he was transferred to Italy and served on the Piave front until hostilities ceased. He was demobilised in July 1919, and holds the General Service and Victory Medals.
38, Thorncroft Road, South Lambeth, S.W.8.　　Z3135A

LOWTHER, A. H., Private, Middlesex Regiment.
He volunteered in May 1915, and in November of the same year was drafted to France, where he took part in the severe fighting on the Somme, at Arras, and Cambrai. He contracted appendicitis, and after receiving medical treatment at Boulogne was employed on clerical duties in the offices of the Expeditionary Force Canteen, until demobilised in June 1919. He holds the 1914-15 Star, and the General Service and Victory Medals.
14, Gideon Road, Battersea, S.W.11.　　　Z3137

LOWTHER, M. A., Private, Labour Corps.
He volunteered in September 1915, and was posted to the 11th East Surrey Regiment, with which unit he served for eighteen months. He was then transferred to the Labour Corps, and was engaged at various stations on important duties. He rendered valuable services, but was not successful in obtaining his transfer overseas before the cessation of hostilities. He was demobilised in February 1919.
83, Battersea Bridge Road, Battersea, S.W.11.　　Z3136

LOYE, A., Private, Royal Fusiliers.
He volunteered in August 1914, and in July of the following year was sent to France, where he took part in numerous engagements. He was unfortunately killed in action near Ypres in August 1915, and was entitled to the 1914-15 Star, and the General Service and Victory Medals.
"He joined the great white company of valiant souls."
77, Gaskell Street, Clapham, S.W.4.　　　Z3138A

LOYE, A. M., Air Mechanic, R.A.F.
He joined in January 1918, and after his training served on important duties with his unit. His work which demanded a high degree of technical skill was carried out with great care and efficiency, and he rendered valuable services, but was not successful in obtaining his transfer overseas before the cessation of hostilities. He was still serving in 1920.
77, Gaskell Street, Clapham, S.W.4.　　　Z3138B

LUCAS, P., Rifleman, 21st London Regiment (1st Surrey Rifles).

He volunteered in June 1915, and in the following year was sent to France. During his service on the Western Front he fought in numerous Battles, including those of Albert and Vimy Ridge. Later in 1916 he was transferred to Salonika, and after serving there for a time contracted malaria and rheumatism, and was invalided home. He was discharged in June 1918, as medically unfit for further service, and holds the General Service and Victory Medals.

34, Royal Terrace, Walworth, S.E.17.   Z26199

LUCAS, F., Private, South Staffordshire Regiment.

Volunteering in February 1916, he was sent to France in the same year, and was engaged in severe fighting on the Somme, at Lens and Ypres, and many other places. He was taken prisoner at Bapaume in March 1918, and sent to Germany. On his release he returned home and was demobilised in September 1919, and holds the General Service and Victory Medals.

25, Gladstone Terrace, Battersea Park Road, S.W.8.   Z3139

LUCAS, G. W., Rifleman, 18th London Regiment (London Irish Rifles).

He volunteered in June 1915, and in October of the following year was sent to France, where he took part in numerous engagements, including those at Arras, Messines, Ypres and Cambrai, and was taken prisoner during the German Offensive in March 1918. On his release he returned home and was demobilised in December 1918, and holds the General Service and Victory Medals.

1, Aylesbury Road, Walworth, S.E.17.   Z3141

LUCAS, H., Private, 23rd London Regiment.

He was mobilised in August 1914, and shortly afterwards proceeded to France and was engaged in severe fighting during the Retreat from Mons, and the Battles of the Marne, the Aisne, Ypres, St. Eloi, Hill 60, Loos, Vimy Ridge, the Somme and Passchendaele, and was twice wounded and gassed. He was invalided home and discharged as unfit for further service in November 1918, and holds the Mons Star, and the General Service and Victory Medals.

26, Clarence Street, Clapham, S.W.4.   Z3140

LUCAS, W., Corporal, 12th Hampshire Regiment.

He volunteered in September 1914, and was sent to France in the following year. He fought in numerous engagements, including those at Loos, the Somme, Arras, and Ypres. In 1916 he was drafted to Salonika, and during his service on the Macedonian front contracted malaria. He was demobilised in February 1919, and holds the 1914–15 Star, and the General Service and Victory Medals.

35, Park Place, Clapham Park Road, S.W.4.   Z3142

LUCKETT, H. A., Private, 19th London Regiment.

He volunteered in August 1914, and shortly afterwards was sent to France. Whilst in this theatre of war he was engaged in the fierce fighting at the Battles of Vimy Ridge, the Somme and Ypres, and was wounded. He was later drafted to Egypt, and was aboard H.M.S. "Aragon" when she was torpedoed and sunk in the Mediterranean, but he was fortunately saved. He was demobilised in March 1919, holding the 1914–15 Star, and the General Service and Victory Medals.

31, Waterloo Street, Hammersmith, W.6.   12598B

LUCKINS, J. A., Private, 4th East Surrey Regiment.

He joined in 1916, and after conpleting his training served on important duties with his unit until 1918, when he was drafted to the Western Front. He was in action in numerous engagements during the Retreat and Advance of 1918, including those at Ypres and Cambrai, and was wounded and also suffered from fever. He was demobilised in 1919, holding the General Service and Victory Medals.

32, Amies Street, Battersea, S.W.11.   Z3143

LUDFORD, S. J., Q.M.S., R.A.M.C.

He volunteered in February 1915, and in June of the same year was sent to Egypt, where he remained until the end of the war. During this period he was engaged at various dressing stations on special duties, and rendered valuable services. He was demobilised in August 1920, holding the 1914–15 Star, and the General Service and Victory Medals.

45, Charleston Street, Walworth, S.E.17.   Z3144

LUDLOW, F., Cpl., 22nd London Regt. (Queen's) and Labour Corps.

He volunteered in August 1914, and was drafted to the Western Front in the same year. He was in action at the Battles of Ypres, Fricourt Wood, Neuve Chapelle, Loos, the Somme in 1916, and Arras. He also took part in the Retreat and Advance of 1918, and was three times wounded. He was later transferred to the Labour Corps, with which unit he served until demobilised in March 1919. He holds the 1914–15 Star, and the General Service and Victory Medals.

6, Tinworth Street, Kennington, S.E.11.   TZ24943B

LUDLOW, T. J., Private, Duke of Cornwall's Light Infantry (Labour Corps).

He volunteered in September 1915, and was drafted to the Western Front later in that year. He was in action at the Battles of Ypres, Neuve Chapelle, Loos, Hill 60, the Somme and Arras. He also served throughout the Retreat and Advance of 1918. Holding the 1914–15 Star, the General Service and Victory Medals, he was demobilised in November 1919.

6, Tinworth Street, Kennington, S.E.11.   TZ24943A

LUER, C. F., Private, Labour Corps.

Joining in September 1917, he was sent to France in December of the same year, and served in numerous engagements, including those in the Lens and Arras sectors. He also took part in the Retreat and Advance of 1918, and later proceeded with the Army of Occupation to Germany. He was demobilised in April 1920, and holds the General Service and Victory Medals.

6, Caldew Street, Camberwell, S.E.5.   Z5796

LUFF, A. F. (Jun.), Pte., 2nd South Wales Borderers.

He joined in 1916, on attaining military age, and after completing his training was engaged on important duties with his unit at various depôts. He rendered valuable services, but was unsuccessful in obtaining his transfer overseas, owing to an accident sustained whilst undergoing a course of gas training. He was invalided out of the Service in June 1918.

62, Moncrieff Street, Rye Lane, S.E.15.   Z5636B

LUFF, P. G., Corporal, R.A.V.C.

Volunteering in January 1916, he completed his training and served with his unit on important duties at home. He did excellent work, but was unable to secure his transfer to a theatre of war on account of his age. He was discharged in consequence in June 1918.

62, Moncrieff Street, Peckham, S.E.15.   Z5636A

LUFF, W., Private, 23rd London Regiment.

He volunteered in May 1915, and proceeding to the Western Front in June of the following year served in various sectors until the end of hostilities. During this period he was in action in the Battles of the Somme, Messines, Passchendaele, Cambrai, Havrincourt, and was wounded at Albert in June 1918, and again at Ypres in the following August. Returning home for demobilisation in February 1919, he holds the General Service and Victory Medals.

137, Lavender Road, Battersea, S.W.11.   Z3146

LUKE, J. W., C.S.M., Cheshire Regt. and Queen's Own (Royal West Kent Regiment).

A serving soldier, he was mobilised on the outbreak of war and drafted to France in 1915. In the course of his service on the Western Front he took part in several engagements, and was three times wounded. In consequence of his injuries his left arm was rendered useless and he was invalided out of the Service in May 1919. He holds the 1914–15 Star, and the General Service and Victory Medals.

28, Stewarts Road, Battersea Park Road, S.W.8.   Z3147

LUTMAN, J. (D.C.M.), C.S.M., M.G.C.

A Regular, having enlisted in 1912, he was mobilised on the declaration of war and sent to France shortly afterwards. He was engaged in heavy fighting during the Retreat from Mons, and was wounded. On recovery he fought in the Battles of Ypres and the Somme, and was sent to Egypt in 1917. He served during General Allenby's Advance through Palestine, and amongst other operations was present at the fall of Jerusalem. In the course of his service overseas he was awarded the Distinguished Conduct Medal for conspicuous bravery and devotion to duty in the Field, and was demobilised in December 1918, on his return to England. He also holds the Mons Star, and the General Service and Victory Medals.

107, Heath Road, Wandsworth Road, S.W.8.   Z3148

LUXFORD, A., Driver, Australian Motor Transport.

He volunteered in November 1914, and served with his unit until embarking for the Western Front in 1916. Whilst overseas he was engaged on important transport duties during the Battles of Villers Bretonneux, Ypres, Cambrai, Messines, and the Somme, and in the Retreat and Advance of 1918. Returning to England in 1919, he was demobilised in January 1920, and holds the General Service and Victory Medals.

1, Stockdale Road, Wandsworth Road, S.W.8.   Z3149C

LUXFORD, J., Ordinary Seaman, Merchant Service.

Volunteering in 1915, he served in various vessels engaged on transport and other special work in the Atlantic Ocean, the North Sea and other waters. His ships were torpedoed and sunk on four occasions, but he fortunately was rescued. In 1920, he was still serving in s.s. "Rimutaka," and holds the General Service and the Mercantile Marine War Medals.

1, Stockdale Road, Wandsworth Road, S.W.8.   Z3149D

LUXFORD, W., Cpl., Northumberland Fusiliers.

He volunteered in February 1916, and proceeded overseas in the same year. Sent to Egypt he fought in the Battles of Magdhaba, Rafa, and in several other engagements during the British Advance through Palestine. He returned home for demobilisation in April 1920, and holds the General Service and Victory Medals.
1, Stockdale Road, Wandsworth Road, S.W.8.　　Z3149B

LUXFORD, W., Gunner, R.F.A.

He joined in March 1917, and proceeding to the Western Front in the same year served with his Battery in the Battles of Messines, Ypres, Passchendaele, Lens, Cambrai, and during the Retreat and Advance of 1918. He was wounded in the course of operations, and returning to England was demobilised in 1920, and holds the General Service and Victory Medals.
33, Stockdale Road, Wandsworth Road, S.W.8.　　Z3150

LYE, H. S., Private, Labour Corps.

He joined the Middlesex Regiment in October 1916, and after completing his training served with his unit, and was transferred to the Cheshire Regiment, and later to the Labour Corps. He did excellent work at Stations on the East Coast, and in other parts of England, but was unable to obtain a transfer overseas before the cessation of hostilities. He was demobilised in July 1919.
12, Dickens Street, Wandsworth Road, S.W.8.　　Z3151B

LYGO, F. W., Sergt., R.A.S.C. (M.T.)

He volunteered in August 1915, and on the conclusion of his training was engaged on important transport duties at various depôts. He rendered valuable services but was unsuccessful in obtaining his transfer overseas before the termination of the war, and was demobilised in September 1919.
15, Geneva Terrace, Coldharbour Lane, S.W.9.　　Z4490

LYLE, W., Pte., Duke of Wellington's (West Riding Regiment).

Volunteering in August 1914, he was drafted to France in the following year, and fought in the Battles of Neuve Chapelle, Hill 60, and was gassed. Sent home suffering from gas poisoning he received medical treatment, and was invalided out of the Service in April 1917. He joined the Labour Corps in 1919, and sent to the Western Front in August of that year was engaged as a transport driver under the War Graves Commission until he sustained a severe injury through being kicked by a mule. Returning home in December 1919, he was discharged as physically unfit for further service in the following month. He holds the 1914-15 Star, and the General Service and Victory Medals.
149, Ethelred Street, Kennington, S.E.11.　　TZ24800

LYNCH, A., Gunner, R.F.A.

He volunteered in November 1915, and was sent to the Western Front in the same year. After serving in various sectors of France and Flanders for over a year he returned home and was engaged on important duties with his unit. In 1918, he was drafted to India, and served there until his return to England for demobilisation in December 1919. He holds the General Service and Victory Medals.
103, Ingelow Road, Battersea Park, S.W.8.　　Z1393B

LYNE, J. F. C., Driver, R.F.A.

Volunteering in November 1914, he embarked for Egypt in the following year, and served with his Battery throughout the British Advance through Palestine. During this period he was in action in the Battles of Romani, Gaza (I, II and III), and was present at the capture of Jericho. Returning to England after the Armistice he was demobilised in March 1919, and holds the 1914-15 Star, and the General Service and Victory Medals.
27, Joubert Street, Battersea, S.W.11.　　Z3152

LYNN, E. W., Private, 3rd East Surrey Regiment.

He volunteered in September 1914, and drafted to France shortly afterwards, fought at the Battles of the Marne, Ypres, Hill 60, Loos, Vimy Ridge, and many other engagements. He was severely wounded in the third Battle of Ypres, and invalided to England, received hospital treatment. He was subsequently discharged unfit for further service in August 1918, and holds the 1914 Star, and the General Service and Victory Medals.
110, Paradise Road, Larkhall Lane, S.W.4.　　Z3153

LYNN, F., 1st Class Petty Officer, R.N.

He joined the Service before the declaration of war, and in August 1914, was serving aboard H.M.S. "Kennett," on the China Station. Later he was transferred to H.M.S. "Syke," which vessel was in action at the Dardanelles, and in many other engagements. She also did good work engaged on patrol and other important duties until the cessation of hostilities. He was demobilised in May 1919, and holds the 1914-15 Star, and the General Service and Victory Medals.
97, Westmoreland Road, Walworth, S.E.17.　　Z1961A

LYONS, C., Private, 11th Welch Regiment.

He joined in April 1917, and embarked for Mesopotamia three months later and fought in many important engagements, and was severely wounded in the British Advance of 1917. Admitted into hospital, it was found necessary to amputate his right leg. Returning to England he was invalided out of the Service in October 1918, and holds the General Service and Victory Medals.
41, Warrior Road, Camberwell, S.E.5.　　Z3154

LYONS, C. W. W., Private, 1st East Surrey Regt.

He volunteered in August 1914, and was sent to France in February of the following year. He fought at the Battles of Neuve Chapelle, Hill 60, Loos, Vimy Ridge, St. Eloi, Vermelles, and the Somme, where he was seriously wounded. Invalided to England he received hospital treatment, but died on June 24th, 1917, and was entitled to the 1914-15 Star, and the General Service and Victory Medals.
"He passed out of the sight of men by the path of duty and self-sacrifice."
31, White Square, Clapham, S.W.4.　　Z3156D

LYONS, H., Guardsman, 2nd Coldstream Guards.

Mobilised and sent to France at the commencement of hostilities he was in action in the Retreat from Mons, the Battles of the Marne, the Aisne, Loos, Festubert, Hill 60, Bullecourt, Beaumont-Hamel, Arras, and was wounded on March 27th, 1918, in the German Offensive. Invalided to England he received medical treatment, and was subsequently discharged unfit for further service in January 1919. He holds the Mons Star, and the General Service and Victory Medals.
21, Evelina Road, Peckham, S.E.15.　　Z6162-3B

LYONS, H., Private, Essex Regiment.

Volunteering in February 1916, he was drafted to Egypt in July of the following year, and fought in many engagements on the Palestine front. Transferred to Salonika he was in action on the Vardar, and served throughout the final Allied Advance in this theatre of war. He returned to England, and was demobilised in February 1920, and holds the General Service and Victory Medals.
31, White Square, Clapham, S.W.4.　　Z3156C

LYONS, J., Private, R.A.S.C. (M.T.)

He joined in July 1917, and completing his training served at various stations engaged on important duties with his unit. He was unsuccessful in obtaining his transfer overseas prior to the cessation of hostilities, but rendered valuable services until demobilised in November 1918.
31, White Square, Clapham, S.W.4.　　Z3156A

LYONS, J. (Jun.), Private, Northumberland Fusiliers.

Volunteering in October 1914, and proceeding to France in the same month, he fought in many important engagements including those at Ypres, Neuve Chapelle, Loos, Albert, Vimy Ridge, and was severely gassed at Bullecourt. Invalided to England he received medical treatment and was discharged unfit for further service in November 1917. He holds the 1914 Star, and the General Service and Victory Medals.
31, White Square, Clapham, S.W.4.　　Z3156B

LYONS, T., Private, R.A.S.C.

Volunteering in April 1915, he was drafted to France in the same month, and served in the forward areas engaged on important transport duties. He was present at the Battles of Ypres, Arras, Vimy Ridge, and rendered valuable services throughout. Returning to England he was demobilised in March 1919, and holds the 1914-15 Star, and the General Service and Victory Medals.
74, St. Philip Street, Battersea Park, S.W.8.　　Z3155

M

MABE, W. T., R.S.M., 7th Queen's (Royal West Surrey Regiment).

Having previously served throughout the South African campaign he volunteered in September 1914, and was sent to France in June of the following year. He was in action at Albert, and on the Somme, and was wounded and invalided home. On his recovery he served on important duties until demobilised in July 1919. He holds the Queen's and King's South African Medals, and the 1914-15 Star, and the General Service and Victory Medals.
139, Blakes Road, Peckham, S.E.15.　　Z6047

MACAULAY, J. E., Rifleman, 21st London Regt. (1st Surrey Rifles).

Joining in May 1917 he was drafted to France in the following August. He took part in the severe fighting at Lens, Cambrai, and the Somme, and in numerous engagements in the Retreat and Advance of 1918. He was afterwards allowed to return home on compassionate grounds in November 1918. He was demobilised in January 1919, and holds the General Service and Victory Medals.
22, Dundas Road, Peckham, S.E.15.　　Z6478

MCAULIFFE, W., Private, East Surrey Regiment and Sapper, R.E.

He volunteered in November 1914, and was posted to the Royal Engineers, but was later transferred to the East Surrey Regiment and sent to France in 1915. He took part in various actions, and fell fighting at Delville Wood on August 16th, 1916. He was entitled to the 1914-15 Star, and the General Service and Victory Medals.

"His life for his country, his Soul to God."

55, Speke Road, Battersea, S.W.11.   Z3157

MCBRIDE, J., Corporal, Royal Inniskilling Fusiliers.

He was serving in India at the outbreak of war and proceeded to France in 1915. He took part in severe fighting at Festubert, was wounded and invalided home. On his recovery he returned to France where he was again in action. He was killed on the Somme on July 1st, 1916, and was entitled to the 1914-15 Star, and the General Service and Victory Medals.

"Steals on the ear the distant triumph song."

9, Boyton Road, Camberwell, S.E.5.   Z5637A

MCBRIDE, T., Private, Royal Dublin Fusiliers.

He volunteered in August 1914, having previously served, and was sent to the Dardanelles in the following year. He took part in various actions and, three times wounded, was invalided home and discharged in September 1916. He holds the Queen's and King's South African, and the India General Service Medals, the 1914-15 Star, and the General Service and Victory Medals.

46, Chantry Road, Stockwell, S.W.9.   Z3158

MCBRYDE, A., Pte. (Prince of Wales's Own Royal) Hussars.

Having enlisted in March 1908 he was serving in Africa when was was declared and was sent immediately afterwards to France where he took part in the Retreat from Mons, and the Battles of the Marne and the Aisne. He fell fighting at Ypres in May 1915, and was entitled to the Mons Star, and the General Service and Victory Medals.

"His life for his Country."

181A, Latchmere Road, Battersea, S.W.11.   Z3159

MCCALLA, W. F., Sapper, R.E.

He volunteered in 1915, and in the same year was drafted to the Western Front, where he took part in various engagements, including those on the Somme and at Arras and Ypres. He also served in the Retreat and Advance of 1918. He was demobilised in 1919, and holds the 1914-15 Star, and the General Service and Victory Medals.

84, Somerleyton Road, Coldharbour Lane, S.W.9.   Z3065

MCCALLAN, J., Private, 1st Queen's (Royal West Surrey Regiment).

He volunteered in August 1914, and in the following September was sent to France, where he took part in severe fighting at Ypres, and was wounded and invalided home. He was discharged, owing to his wounds, in February 1915, but rejoined in June 1918 in the Labour Corps with which he served on important duties until he was demobilised in February 1919. He holds the 1914-15 Star, and the General Service and Victory Medals.

27, Stanton Street, Peckham, S.E.15.   Z5267

MCCANN, W., Sapper, R.E.

Volunteering in October 1914 he was sent to France in December of the same year. He was engaged in various sectors on important railway duties, and rendered valuable services. He returned home and was demobilised in June 1919, and holds the 1914-15 Star, and the General Service and Victory Medals.

9, Westbury Street, Wandsworth Road, S.W.8.   Z3160

MCCARTHY, J. E., Pte., 24th London Regt. (Queen's).

He volunteered in August 1914, and in the following March proceeded overseas. Whilst in France he fought at Givenchy and was wounded, but after his recovery rejoined his unit, and was in action on the Somme Front. He gave his life for the freedom of England on September 11th, 1916, in the Battle of the Somme, and is buried at High Wood. He was entitled to the 1914-15 Star, and the General Service and Victory Medals.

"Great deeds cannot die."

10, Warrior Road, Camberwell, S.E.5.   Z3161

MCCARTHY, T. J., Rifleman, Rifle Brigade.

He joined in January 1916, and in the following August was drafted to the Western Front where he saw much service. He fought in the Battle of the Somme, and was wounded and invalided home. After his recovery he rejoined his unit, and served at Havrincourt and Cambrai, where he again was wounded, and sent to hospital in England. He returned to France in June 1918, and was gassed in action, and was afterwards stationed at Doullens until his return home for demobilisation in February 1919. He holds the General Service and Victory Medals.

18, Belham Street, Camberwell S.E.5.   Z3162

MCCARTHY, J. M., Private, 2nd Welch Regiment.

He volunteered in September 1914, having previously served for sixteen years, and was shortly afterwards drafted to France. After taking part in several minor engagements he was severely wounded at Ypres, on May 26th, 1915. He was invalided home to hospital, and discharged as medically unfit for further service in May of the following year, and holds the 1914 Star, and the General Service and Victory Medals.

20, Mansion Street, Camberwell, S.E.5.   Z3163

MCCARTHY, T. E., Corporal, R.F.A.

He volunteered in August 1914, and in the following year was drafted to France. During his service on the Western Front he fought at Ypres, the Somme, and Arras, and was subsequently severely wounded during the Advance of 1918. He was invalided home to hospital, and discharged as physically unfit for further service in September 1918. He holds the 1914-15 Star, and the General Service and Victory Medals.

6, Langley Lane, South Lambeth Road, S.W.8.   Z3164

MCCLEAVE, J., Private, Royal Fusiliers.

He volunteered in August 1914, and was almost immediately drafted to France, and took part in the Retreat from Mons. He also served at Neuve Chapelle, St. Eloi, Ypres, and Cambrai, and in numerous subsequent engagements. He was wounded on four different occasions during his service, and was demobilised in January 1919. He holds the 1914-15 Star, and the General Service and Victory Medals.

32, Cobbett Street, Clapham Road, S.W.8.   Z1473B

MCCLUMPHA, J. H., Member, W.A.A.C.

She joined in January 1917, and was engaged on clerical duties with the 3rd East Surrey Regiment at Dover. In 1918 she was transferred to Colchester, where she was employed as A.P.M.'s Clerk until the following December, and rendered valuable services.

37, Bavent Road, Camberwell, S.E.5.   Z6479

MCCONVELL, A., Private, Durham Light Infantry.

He joined in June 1916, and after his training served at various stations on important duties with his unit. He rendered valuable services, but was not successful in obtaining a transfer overseas before the cessation of hostilities, and was demobilised in February 1919.

28, Bromell's Road, Clapham, S.W.4.   Z2806A

MCDANIEL, G., Pte., 9th Somerset Light Infantry.

He joined in June 1917, at the age of eighteen years, but during the course of his training was found to be physically unfit for military service and consequently was discharged in the following October.

10, Wood Street, Kennington, S.E.11.   TZ25331

MCDANIEL, G., Pte., 24th London Regt. (Queen's).

He volunteered in September 1915, and in November of the following year was drafted to Salonika. Whilst in this theatre of war he served in many engagements, and in 1917 was sent to Egypt where he took part in the Advance through Palestine until the conclusion of the campaign. He was demobilised in March 1919, after his return to England, and holds the General Service and Victory Medals.

30, Ceylon Street, Battersea Park Road, S.W.8.   Z3165

MCDANIEL, J., Pte., 25th City of London Regiment (Cyclists).

He volunteered in November 1915, and after his training served at various stations on important duties with the Cyclists' Corps. Owing to ill-health he was discharged as medically unfit for further service in April 1916.

30, Ceylon Street, Battersea Park Road, S.W.8.   Z3166

MCDERMOTT, J., Rflmn., King's Royal Rifle Corps and 5th London Regt. (London Rifle Brigade) and Pte., Dorsetshire Regt.

He joined in May 1916, and in the same year was sent overseas, and took part in various engagements in the Somme sector. He died gloriously on the Field of Battle on November 5th, 1918, whilst endeavouring to capture a German machine gun. He was entitled to the General Service and Victory Medals.

"The path of duty was the way to glory."

34, Aldred Road, Walworth, S.E.17.   Z26539

MCDONALD, P. W., Corporal, R.E. (I.W.T.)

He volunteered in October 1915, and in January 1916 proceeded to France, where he did valuable work with his unit at Le Havre and Rouen, before being drafted to Italy. After much commendable service there on the Piave front he was transferred to the Balkans to assist the Serbians during their Retreat. Subsequently he went to Mesopotamia where he was engaged in the conveyance of food and supplies on the waterways. After his varied service he returned home and was demobilised in April 1919, and holds the General Service and Victory Medals.

122, Commercial Road, Peckham, S.E.15.   Z6281

MⁱDOUGALL, N. A., Rifleman, 5th London Regt. (London Rifle Brigade).
He joined in November 1916, and after his training served at various stations on important duties with his unit. He was discharged as physically unfit for further service in March 1917.
48, Stansfield Road, Stockwell, S.W.9.   Z3167

McDOWELL, E. A., A.B., R.N., H.M.S. "Tarantula."
He was mobilised at the outbreak of hostilities and posted to H.M.S. "Tarantula," and sent to the North Sea where he served on important and dangerous patrol duties until 1916. He then proceeded to Mesopotamia and was unfortunately killed in action in a gunboat engagement near Baghdad in February 1917. He was entitled to the 1914–14 Star, and the General Service and Victory Medals.
"Great deeds cannot die."
38, Coronation Buildings, S. Lambeth Road, S.W.8.   Z3168A

MACEFIELD, E. S., Sapper, R.E.
He volunteered in October 1915, and crossed to France on completing his training early in the following year. Whilst overseas, he was engaged on duties of an important nature in the forward areas, until he was invalided home. He was discharged as physically unfit for further service in October 1916, and holds the General Service and Victory Medals.
6, Belham Street, Camberwell, S.E.5.   Z3169B

MACEY, J. C., Sapper, R.E.
Joining in 1916, he was drafted to the Western Front early in the following year. During his service, he was attached to the signal section, and did much valuable electrical work in connection with many important engagements, including the Retreat and Advance of 1918, and was gassed. He holds the General Service and Victory Medals, and was demobilised in January 1919.
50, Kelmscott Road, Battersea, S.W.11.   Z3170

MⁱFERRAN, F., Pte., 2nd Royal Warwickshire Regt.
Mobilised in August 1914, he crossed to France a month later. After taking part in the Battles of the Marne, the Aisne, La Bassée, Ypres, Neuve Chapelle, and St. Eloi, he was transferred to Salonika, where he subsequently did good work with his unit during operations on the Struma, Vardar, and Doiran fronts. After the Armistice he saw three months' service in Russia, and was engaged on special duties on the lines of communication. He holds the 1914 Star, and the General Service and Victory Medals, and was demobilised in February 1920.
106, Mina Road, Walworth, S.E.17   Z3171

MⁱGARRICK, A. J., Rifleman, 8th London Regt. (Post Office Rifles).
He volunteered at the commencement of hostilities, and at the conclusion of his training was drafted to the Western Front. Whilst in this theatre of war he fought in the Battles of Ypres, Festubert, the Somme, Arras, and Vimy Ridge, where he was severely wounded. He then returned to England, and after hospital treatment was invalided out of the Service in 1917. He holds the 1914–15 Star, and the General Service and Victory Medals.
4, Hubert Grove, Stockwell, S.W.9.   Z3172

MⁱGEORGE, C. H., Rifleman, Rifle Brigade.
Volunteering in May 1915, he crossed to France four months later and fought at Albert, Vermelles, Ploegsteert Wood, Vimy Ridge, and the Somme, where he was wounded. He was invalided home, but after his recovery rejoined his unit on the Western Front, and died gloriously on the Field of Battle near Arras on May 12th, 1917. He was entitled to the 1914–15 Star, and the General Service and Victory Medals.
"He died the noblest death a man may die,
Fighting for God, and right, and liberty."
78, Nelson Row, High Street, Clapham, S.W.4.   Z2905B

MⁱGEORGE, E. W., Private, East Surrey Regiment.
After volunteering in September 1914, he went through his course of training, and early in 1915 was drafted to France. After only a short period of active service he fell fighting gallantly at Hill 60 in April 1915, and is believed to have been buried at Zonnebeke Cemetery. He was entitled to the 1914–15 Star, and the General Service and Victory Medals.
"The path of duty was the way to glory."
15, Pitcairn Street, Clapham, S.W.8.   Z1201D

MⁱGEORGE, E. W. C., Pte., Buffs (East Kent Regt.)
He joined in February 1917, and after the completion of his training proceeded to France later in the same year. While in this theatre of war he was killed in action later in the year at Passchendaele. He was entitled to the General Service and Victory Medals.
"Nobly striving,
He nobly fell that we might live."
15, Pitcairn Street, Clapham, S.W.8.   Z1201B

MⁱGILL, D., Sapper, R.E.
He joined in July 1916, and on the completion of his training was engaged on important duties with his unit at Richborough. He rendered very efficient services, but was not able to secure his transfer overseas before hostilities ceased, and was demobilised in January 1919.
34, Gladstone Terrace, Battersea Park Road, S.W.8.   Z3173

MⁱGRATH, W. J., C.P.O., R.N., H.M.S. "Prince George."
He joined the Royal Navy in May 1887, and during his service he took part in the China campaign, and the South African War of 1899–02, and was discharged on completion of twenty-one years' service. At the outbreak of the late war he was employed in the Royal Arsenal, Woolwich, as an examiner. In 1916 he re-joined the Navy, and was posted to H.M.S. "Prince George," in which he was engaged in the North Sea on mine sweeping. He was later employed on Police Duties in Ireland. He was demobilised in July 1919, and unfortunately died soon afterwards from concussion of the brain. He was entitled to the China and the Queen's and King's South African Medals, the General Service, the Victory, and the Long Service and Good Conduct Medals.
"His life for his country, his Soul to God."
30, Tyers Street, Upper Kennington Lane, Vauxhall, S.E.11.   Z25145

MACGREGOR, S., Gunner, R.F.A.
Volunteering in April 1915, he proceeded to the Western Front in the following July. While there he took part in many important engagements until 1916, when he was drafted to Mesopotamia. He did excellent service there in many operations until hostilities ceased, and was present at the capture of Baghdad. He was demobilised in May 1919, after his return home, and holds the 1914–15 Star, and the General Service and Victory Medals.
3, Farmer's Road, Camberwell, S.E.5.   Z3174

MⁱGUIRE, S., Sapper, R.E.
He volunteered in February 1915, and proceeded to France in the following October. He rendered valuable services there at Albert, Fricourt, High Wood, and all along the Somme Front, and was very badly wounded in June 1918. After prolonged hospital treatment, during which it was necessary to amputate one of his legs, he was discharged in September 1920 as unfit for further service. He holds the 1914–15 Star, and the General Service and Victory Medals.
25, Benfield Street, Battersea, S.W.11.   Z3175

MACHELL, P. T., 1st Air Mechanic, R.A.F. (late R.N.A.S.)
He joined in September 1916, and after his training served with his Squadron at various stations on important duties, which called for a high degree of technical skill. He rendered valuable services at Lincoln, and with the Coast Defence Squadron, but was not successful in obtaining his transfer overseas before the cessation of hostilities. In February 1919, he was demobilised.
14, Chapter Terrace, Walworth, S.E.17.   Z26773

MACHIN, A. E., Sapper, R.E. (I.W.T.)
He volunteered in September 1915, and was engaged in the transport of ammunition and supplies from Dover to Calais and Dunkirk until June 1917. From that time forward he was employed on similar duties on the rivers and canals in France, and rendered valuable services. He was shelled and bombed several times, happily without injury. He was demobilised in February 1919, holding the 1914–15 Star, and the General Service and Victory Medals.
88A, Lavender Road, Battersea, S.W.11.   Z3177

MACHIN, W. F. C., Private, 5th Wiltshire Regiment.
He volunteered soon after the outbreak of war, and in June 1915 was drafted to Gallipoli. He took a prominent part in several operations of importance there, but has not been heard of since the attack on Chunuk Bair in August, and is believed to have been killed in action at that spot. He was entitled to the 1914–15 Star, and the General Service and Victory Medals.
"He died the noblest death a man may die
Fighting for God, and right, and liberty."
187, Sumner Road, Peckham S.E.15.   Z6282

MⁱHUGH, J. (Sen.), Rifleman, King's Royal Rifle Corps and Private, Bedfordshire Regiment.
He volunteered in 1915, and in the following year was drafted to France where he took an active part in the severe fighting at Ypres, Passchendaele, and Lens. He was then invalided home through illness arising out of his service, and was later demobilised. He holds the General Service and Victory Medals.
2, Stockwell Grove, Stockwell, S.W.9.   Z2711B

McHUGH, J., Private, Royal Sussex Regiment.

Joining in April 1917 he was drafted to France in the same year after finishing his course of training. He served in various sectors but contracting tuberculosis was invalided home. He was discharged in 1919 after prolonged treatment as medically unfit for further service, and afterwards unfortunately died. He was entitled to the General Service and Victory Medals.

"His life for his country, his Soul to God."

2, Stockwell Grove, Stockwell, S.W.9.   Z2711A

McINNES, A. H., Private, Royal Fusiliers.

He joined in November 1918, before the Armistice was signed, and after his training was engaged on important duties with his unit. He rendered valuable services at Stafford until demobilised in March 1919.

2, Kenbury Street, Camberwell, S.E.5.   Z6283

McINNES, R., Pte., R.A.S.C. (M.T.) and Tank Corps.

He volunteered in September 1914, and in the same month was sent to France. On the introduction of tanks he was transferred to the Tank Corps. He took part in numerous engagements of importance, including those at Ypres, Loos, and Cambrai, and was twice wounded. He was demobilised in April 1919, after his return home, and holds the 1914 Star, and the General Service and Victory Medals.

4, Charleston Street, Walworth, S.E.17.   Z3179

McINTOSH, A. J., Private, South Lancashire Regt.

He joined in June 1918, and after his training was engaged in Ireland on important duties in connection with the Sinn Fein troubles. He rendered valuable services there chiefly as a motor-transport driver, but was not successful in obtaining his transfer to a theatre of war before the cessation of hostilities. He was demobilised in October 1920.

17, Scylla Road, Peckham, S.E.15.   Z6029

McIVOR, G. J., Gunner, R.H.A.

He was in the Army before the war, and in September 1914 was sent to the Eastern Mediterranean. He took part in the memorable operations at Suvla Bay and Anzac Cove, and at the end of the campaign was drafted to Egypt, where he served for about twelve months. He was then sent to the Western Front where he was frequently in action, especially during the general Offensive of 1918, and was severely wounded. He was invalided home, and demobilised in February 1919. He holds the 1914-15 Star, and the General Service and Victory Medals.

40, Hurlbutt Place, Walworth, S.E.17.   Z26022

MACKAY, F., Corporal, Duke of Cornwall's Light Infantry.

He was mobilised in August 1914, and in the same year was sent to France, where he saw much service. In the following year he was drafted to Salonika and fought against the Bulgarians in the engagements on the Doiran and Vardar fronts, and was wounded. He was invalided home, and subsequently discharged in February 1919. He holds the 1914 Star, and the General Service and Victory Medals.

77, Acorn Street, Camberwell, S.E.5.   Z5553

MACKAY, F. E., Sergt., 9th London Regiment (Queen Victoria's Rifles).

He joined in July 1916, and after being posted to the 9th London Regiment was transferred to the Intelligence Corps. In November 1916 he was drafted to France and was engaged on important duties on the Armentières front, until after the cessation of hostilities. He was demobilised in October 1919, and holds the General Service and Service Medals.

31, Kersley Street, Battersea, S.W.11.   Z3180

MACKENDER, E., Rflmn., King's Royal Rifle Corps.

He was mobilised in August 1914, and shortly afterwards was sent to France, where he took part in the Retreat from Mons, and in many other engagements, and was wounded. He unfortunately died from his injuries on 29th October 1914, and was entitled to the Mons Star, and the General Service and Victory Medals.

"He joined the great white company of valiant souls."

16, Riverhall Street, South Lambeth, S.W.8.   Z3181

MACKENZIE, D. G., Gunner, R.M.A., H.M.S. "Thunderer."

He was serving at the outbreak of war on H.M.S. "Thunderer" patrolling the North Sea. In 1915 he proceeded to the Dardanelles and was engaged at Cape Helles, Gaba Tepe, Suvla Bay, and other operations until the Evacuation. He then returned home and in April 1916 was sent to France, where he took part in various engagements including that at Arras, and was gassed. After his recovery he was posted to H.M.S. "Shannon," and served in several minor engagements in the North Sea, whilst on patrol duties. He was discharged in May 1918 as medically unfit for further service and holds the 1914-15 Star, and the General Service and Victory Medals.

46, Lavender Road, Battersea, S.W.11.   Z3182

(ϑ.ℭ.) McKENZIE, A., A.B., R.N., H.M.S. "Vindictive."

Having enlisted in December 1913, he proceeded to sea with the Grand Fleet at the outbreak of war, and was engaged on mine-sweeping and patrol duties. He played a distinguished part in the Battle of Jutland, and served in H.M.S. "Vindictive" during the famous raid on Zeebrugge on April 23rd, 1918. After his ship had been riddled with shells, and had lost several marines, he with heroic gallantry took his Lewis-gun into action on the Mole, but was badly wounded, and his gun rendered useless. However, with undaunted courage he fought his way through the enemy with a rifle and bayonet, which he had picked up, and was helped on board his vessel. For this glorious deed of gallantry he was awarded the Victoria Cross. Unfortunately, before he had fully recovered from his wounds he died of influenza on November 3rd, 1918. In addition to the Victoria Cross he was entitled to the 1914-15 Star, and the General Service and Victory Medals.

"Honour to the immortal dead who gave their youth that the world might grow old in peace."

1, Shorncliffe Road, Old Kent Road, S.E.1.   5478

MACKENZIE, W. J. A., Corporal, East Surrey Regt.

He volunteered in September 1914, and in the following year was drafted to France, where he took part in many important engagements including those at Hill 60 and Loos. He was very severely wounded on the Somme on August 13th, 1916, and was sent to hospitals in France and England, where he was under treatment until September 1917, when he was invalided out of the Service. He holds the 1914-15 Star, and the General Service and Victory Medals.

39A, Odell Street, Camberwell, S.E.5.   Z5450

MACKEY, W., Driver, R.F.A.

He volunteered in September 1914, and in the following year was drafted to the Western Front, where he served in various sectors with the remount and observation sections and did much valuable work. He was discharged in consequence of his services in April 1916, and holds the 1914-15 Star, and the General Service and Victory Medals.

20, Nursery Street, Battersea, S.W.8.   Z3183

McKIE, J. H., Gunner, R.F.A.

He was serving in India at the outbreak of war, and later was sent to the Western Front, where he took part in numerous engagements. He was badly wounded at Mount Kemmel, and in consequence lost one of his legs. After being invalided home he was discharged in December 1919, owing to his physical disability and holds the General Service and Victory Medals.

21, Spencer Street, Battersea, S.W.11.   Z2008A

MACKLIN, W., Private, 1st Queen's (Royal West Surrey Regiment).

He volunteered in August 1914, and was immediately drafted to France, where he took part in the fierce fighting at Mons. In the following October he was taken prisoner and sent to Germany, where he remained in captivity for over four years, and suffered many privations. He was released in January 1919, and was demobilised in the following March. He holds the Mons Star, and the General Service and Victory Medals.

10, Willow Street, Bermondsey, S.E.1.   TZ25984

McKOEN, E., Rifleman, Rifle Brigade.

He volunteered in November 1915, and in the following year was sent to France, where he took part in numerous engagements and was wounded at the Somme and at Ypres. He was invalided home and discharged in August 1918, owing to his wounds, holding the General Service and Victory Medals.

14, Rumsey Road, Stockwell, S.W.9.   Z6517B. Z6518B

McLAREN, S., A.B., Royal Naval Division.

He volunteered in November 1914, and was shortly afterwards sent to Egypt, and thence to the Dardanelles, where he took part in severe fighting, and was wounded. He died as a result of his injuries in December 1916, and was entitled to the 1914-15 Star, and the General Service and Victory Medals.

"Great deeds cannot die."

1, Sandford Row, Walworth, S.E.17.   Z3184C

McLEAN, C., Pte., 2nd Highland Light Infantry.

He was mobilised in August 1914, and was shortly afterwards sent to France, where he took part in the severe fighting at Mons, and in the Retreat, and was also in action at Le Cateau and the Aisne. He was killed at the Battle of Ypres on November 13th, 1914, and was entitled to the Mons Star, and the General Service and Victory Medals.

"His memory is cherished with pride."

20, Myatt Road, Brixton, S.W.9.   Z5039D

McLEAN, W. J., Driver, R.H.A.

He volunteered in February 1915, and in the following November was drafted to France, where he served in several engagements, including those at Béthune, the Somme, Arras (where he was wounded) Vimy Ridge, Passchendaele, and St. Quentin. Later he was injured in an accident, and was in hospital for six weeks. He was demobilised in February 1919, and holds the 1914-15 Star, and the General Service and Victory Medals.

71, Mann Street, Walworth, S.E.17.   Z27311

M^CLEOD, A. R., Private, R.A.M.C.
He joined in April 1917, and after his training served at various hospitals on important duties with his unti. He rendered valuable services, but was not successful in obtaining his transfer overseas before the cessation of hostilities. He was demobilised in October 1919.
11, Yelverton Road, Battersea, S.W.11.   Z3185

M^CLOUGHLIN, E., Rifleman, 5th London Regiment (Post Office Rifles).
Having volunteered in 1916, he was sent to the Western Front in the same year, and took part in the Battle of the Somme. He was reported " missing " in August 1916, and is presumed to have been killed in action. He was entitled to the General Service and Victory Medals.
"A costly sacrifice upon the altar of freedom."
13, Henshaw Street, Walworth, S.E.17.   Z3186B

M^CLOUGHLIN, G., Private, Royal Welch Fusiliers.
He volunteered in 1915, and in the same year was drafted to the Western Front, where he took part in many important engagements, including those on the Somme, and at Arras, and Ypres, and was three times wounded. He was demobilised in 1919, and holds the 1914–15 Star, and the General Service and Victory Medals.
13, Henshaw Street, Walworth, S.E.17.   Z3186A

M^CMAHON, C. E., Driver, R.F.A.
Having volunteered in August 1914, he was sent to France in March of the following year and took part in the fighting at St. Eloi, Albert, the Somme, Ypres, Passchendaele and Cambrai. He also served in the Retreat and Advance of 1918. He was demobilised in July 1919, and holds the 1914–15 Star, and the General Service and Victory Medals.
14, Lubeck Street, Battersea, S.W.11.   Z3178

M^CMAHON, J., Corporal, 1st East Surrey Regiment.
He was mobilised in August 1914, and shortly afterwards was sent to France, and took part in the Retreat from Mons, and in other engagements. He was killed in action at La Bassée in January 1915, and was entitled to the Mons Star, and the General Service and Victory Medals.
"He died the noblest death a man may die,
Fighting for God, and right, and liberty."
20, Gonsalva Road, Wandsworth Road, S.W.8   Z3187

M^CMAHON, T. A. J., Pte., 8th Buffs (East Kent Regt.)
He volunteered in August 1914, and in September of the following year was sent to France, where he took part in numerous engagements. He fell fighting on the Somme on August 18th, 1916, and was entitled to the 1914–15 Star, and the General Service and Victory Medals.
"The path of duty was the way to glory."
29, Sheepcote Lane, Battersea, S.W.11.   Z3188

MACMINN, C. L., Sapper, R.E.
He volunteered in 1914, and in the following year was drafted to France, where he took part in various engagements including those at Ypres, Loos, and the Somme, and was wounded. He was demobilised in 1919, and holds the 1914–15 Star, and the General Service and Victory Medals.
2, Saltoun Road, Brixton, S.W.2.   Z3101

M^CNULTY, A. V., C.S.M., M.G.C.
He volunteered in May 1915, and served as an Instructor at various stations with his unit. He rendered valuable services, but was not successful in obtaining his transfer overseas before the cessation of hostilities. He was demobilised in February 1919.
22, Speenham Road, Stockwell, S.W.9.   Z5718B

MADDEN, C. F., Private, Royal Fusiliers.
He joined in May 1918, and in the following September was drafted to the Western Front, where he took part in various engagements in the Advance of 1918, and was wounded at Cambrai. He afterwards served in Egypt and Palestine. He was demobilised in February 1920, and holds the General Service and Victory Medals.
47, Mordaunt Road, Stockwell, S.W.9.   Z2851A

MADDEN, G. A. E., Driver, R.F.A.
He volunteered in August 1914, and in January of the following year proceeded to the Western Front, where he took part in the fighting at St. Eloi, Armentières, Loos, Ploegsteert Wood, Vimy Ridge, the Somme, Passchendaele, Lens, and Cambrai. He also served in the Retreat and Advance of 1918, and after the cessation of hostilities returned home and was demobilised in June 1919, holding the 1914–15 Star, and the General Service and Victory Medals.
100, Stonhouse Street, Clapham, S.W.4.   Z3189B

MADDON, D. M. (Mrs.), Special War Worker.
This lady was engaged at Messrs. Leslie Ray's, Park Place, in the manufacture of accumulator boxes for aeroplanes, and was afterwards with Messrs. C. Peacock, St. Andrew's Street, Wandsworth Road. She carried out her duties with great care and efficiency and rendered valuable services during the war.
100, Stonhouse Street, Clapham, S.W.4.   Z3189A

MAGGS, W. J. C., Rflmn., King's Royal Rifle Corps.
Volunteering in May 1915, he was sent to France in the following year and took part in severe fighting at St. Eloi, Vimy Ridge, the Somme, Arras, Ypres, and Passchendaele, and in numerous other engagements. He also served in the Retreat and Advance of 1918, and was wounded. He was demobilised in January 1919, and holds the General Service and Victory Medals.
96, Kinglake Street, Walworth, S.E.17.   Z3190

MAGMUS, A., Corporal, 109th Labour Corps.
He joined in October 1916, and in January of the following year was drafted to the Western Front, where he served in various engagements, including those on the Somme and at Ypres, where he was wounded and gassed. He was invalided home and was discharged as medically unfit in October 1918, and holds the General Service and Victory Medals.
8, Barmore Street, Battersea, S.W.11.   Z3191

MAGUIRE, W. C., Rflmn., King's Royal Rifle Corps.
Mobilised in August 1914 he was quickly drafted to the Western Front, where he took an active part in many operations of great importance, including those at Mons, Ypres, and the Somme, and was wounded on two occasions. He fell fighting gallantly in April 1917, and was entitled to the Mons Star, and the General Service and Victory Medals.
"The path of duty was the way to glory."
1, Claxton Grove, Hammersmith, W.6.   13535B

MAHER, H., Pte., Queen's (Royal West Surrey Regt.)
He was serving at the outbreak of war and was immediately afterwards sent to France, where he took part in many engagements, including those at Mons, the Marne, the Aisne, Albert, Ypres, and Passchendaele, where he was severely wounded, and lost the sight of one eye. He was invalided home and discharged as medically unfit for further service in April 1918, and holds the Mons Star, and the General Service and Victory Medals.
24, Eltham Street, Walworth, S.E.17.   Z3192

MAHER, H. G., Private, Sherwood Foresters.
He joined in March 1916, and served at various stations on important duties with his unit. Later he became blind from the effects of poison gas used during the course of his training. He was demobilised in March 1919 after exactly three years with the Colours, and in 1920 was at St. Dunstan's Hostel for blinded soldiers.
84, Harris Street, Camberwell, S.E.5.   Z4491

MAHON, G. R., Sapper, R.E.
He volunteered in September 1914, and was first stationed in Ireland and drafted overseas in July of the following year. During his service in France he was frequently engaged in the forward areas whilst operations were in progress, and was later sent to Mesopotamia where he was wounded in action, and also contracted malaria. He was demobilised in April 1919, after his return to England, and holds the 1914–15 Star, and the General Service and Victory Medals.
88, Henley Street, Battersea, S.W.11.   Z3193

MAHONEY, H. W., Sergt., R.A.F.
He joined in July 1916, and after his training served at various stations on important duties which demanded a high degree of technical skill. He did excellent work in aerial defence, but was not successful in obtaining a transfer overseas before the cessation of hostilities, and was demobilised in March 1919.
71, Acorn Street, Camberwell, S.E.5.   Z3194

MAHONEY, J. J., Pte., York and Lancaster Regt.
He joined in August 1917, and in the following year embarked for France. Whilst overseas he served in numerous engagements in the Offensives of 1918, including the Battle of Cambrai, in which he was severely wounded in October. In January of the following year he was demobilised, and holds the General Service and Victory Medals.
60, Evelina Road, Peckham, S.E.15.   Z6284B

MAHONEY, T., Private, Dublin Fusiliers.
He volunteered in October 1914, and was soon drafted to the Western Front, where he took part in the engagements at Ypres, Loos, and Vimy Ridge, and in the Battle of the Somme. He also served throughout the Retreat and during the early part of the Advance of 1918. He was discharged through causes due to his service in October 1918, and holds the 1914–15 Star, and the General Service and Victory Medals.
2, Holyoak Road, Kennington, S.E.11.   Z26579

MAHONEY, T. P., Private, 22nd Queen's (Royal West Surrey Regiment).
He volunteered in September 1914, and in the following year was drafted overseas. Whilst in France he served in various engagements in the Somme sector, and was wounded. He was killed during a raid on the enemy trenches on July 9th, 1916, in the Battle of the Somme, having volunteered to accompany his officer into the German lines. He was entitled to the 1914–15 Star, and the General Service and Victory Medals.
"He died the noblest death a man may die,
Fighting for God, and right, and liberty."
3, Sedan Street, Walworth, S.E.17.   Z3195

MAIDMENT, E. E., Private, R.D.C.

He voluteeerd in October 1914, and after his training served at various stations in Ireland, on important duties with his unit. Owing to his being overage for active service he was unable to proceed overseas, and was demobilised in 1918.
14, Falcon Terrace, Battersea, S.W.11.   Z3196

MAILLARDET, A. A., Pte., West Yorkshire Regt.

He joined in June 1916, and in the following September was drafted to the Western Front. During his service in France he fought on the Somme, and at Arras, Vimy Ridge, Bullecourt, Messines, Ypres, Passchendaele, and Cambrai, and was wounded in action in February 1918. He was invalided home to hospital, and on recovery rejoined his unit in France, and served in various engagements in the Advance of 1918. After the Armistice he proceeded to Germany with the Army of Occupation, and was stationed at Cologne until January 1919, when he was demobilised. He holds the General Service and Victory Medals.
12, Exon Street, Walworth, S.E.17.   Z3197

MAIN, A. W., Corporal, 1st Bedfordshire Lancers.

He volunteered in August 1914, and in the following year was sent to the Dardanelles, where he took part in the Landing at Suvla Bay, and in other engagements until the Evacuation. He was then drafted to Egypt, and afterwards to the Western Front, where he was engaged on important duties as clerk interpreter at the Royal Army Ordnance Corps Depôt. He was discharged in August 1919 as unfit for further military duty owing to heart trouble, and holds the 1914-15 Star, and the General Service and Victory Medals.
20, Brabourn Grove, Peckham, S.E.15.   Z6285

MAIRS, J., Private, R.M.L.I.

He was at Buenos Aires in H.M.S. "Lancaster" at the outbreak of war, and was sent to the North Sea where he served for about three years. He was then transferred to H.M.S. "Prince Eugene" and in this ship was in action in the engagements at Ostend and Zeebrugge. He returned to Barracks in England, and after a course of instruction in motor driving proceeded to France, where he was engaged as driver to the Commodore. He was demobilised in February 1920, and holds the 1914-15 Star, and the General Service and Victory Medals.
26, Winstead Street, Battersea, S.W.11.   Z3198

MALLETT, C., Private, 1st London Regiment (Royal Fusiliers).

He re-enlisted in 1916, having previously served in the East Surrey Regiment for fourteen years, and in the same year proceeded to France. There he fought in the Battle of the Somme, and died gloriously on the Field of action on September 5th, 1916. He was entitled to the General Service and Victory Medals.
"A valiant soldier, with undaunted heart he breasted Life's last hill."
96, Ingrave Street, Battersea, S.W.11.   Z3199A

MALLETT, E., Private, 19th Canadian Regiment.

He volunteered in February, 1915, and came over to England with the first contingent of Canadians. In the same year he proceeded to France, and was in action at Ypres, Vimy Ridge, and the Somme, and in many subsequent engagements until the cessation of hostilities. He was demobilised in 1919. and holds the 1914-15 Star, and the General Service and Victory Medals.
96, Ingrave Street, Battersea, S.W.11.   Z3199B

MALLETT, H., Private, King's Own Yorkshire Light Infantry.

He was mobilised in August 1914, and was almost immediately drafted to France, where he took part in the Retreat from Mons. He also served on the Marne and the Aisne and at La Bassée, Loos, the Somme, and Amiens, and after the Armistice advanced into Germany with the Army of Occupation. Later, he returned home, and on October 17th, 1919, was accidentally killed by being thrown from his horse. He was entitled to the Mons Star, and the General Service and Victory Medals.
18, Patmos Road, Vassall Road, S.W.9.   Z4492

MALLETT, J., Private, 2nd Royal Fusiliers.

A serving soldier since 1913, at the outbreak of war he was drafted to Egypt, where he fought in many engagements against the Turks until 1916, when he was sent to the Western Front. Whilst in France he took part in the heavy fighting in the Battle of the Somme, and gave his life for his King and Country in July 1916. He was entitled to the 1914-15 Star, and the General Service and Victory Medals.
96, Ingrave Street, Battersea, S.W.11.   3199C

MALONEY, C., Private, Labour Corps.

He joined in November 1917, and in the same year was drafted to France. Whilst overseas he was engaged on important duties in various sectors of the Front until March 1920, when he was demobilised after his return home. He holds the General Service and Victory Medals.
70, Faroe Road, West Kensington, W.14.   T12186A

MALONEY, E., Rifleman, 21st London Regt. (1st Surrey Rifles).

He volunteered in April 1915, and on the completion of his training served at various stations on important duties with his unit. He rendered valuable services, but owing to medical reasons, wes discharged in May 1916.
7, Unwin Road, Peckham, S.E.15.   Z6415

MALSTER, W., Rifleman, King's Royal Rifle Corps.

He originally enlisted in 1893, and after seeing service in South Africa and India, was discharged in 1909. At the outbreak of the late war he re-enlisted and being drafted to France in August 1914, fought in the Battle of the Marne, and in many subsequent engagements. In February 1916 he was sent to India, where he was engaged at several camps in guarding Turkish prisoners. Owing to malaria he was invalided home, and on recovery was discharged in August 1918 after four years' service with the Colours in the late war and twenty years altogether. He holds the Queen's and King's South African Medals, the 1914 Star, and the General Service and Victory Medals.
90, Cronin Road, Peckham, S.E.15.   Z5451

MALYON, W. J., Sapper, R.E.

He volunteered in December 1914, and was shortly afterwards drafted to France, where he was engaged on important duties in connection with the operations and was frequently in the forward areas. He was in action at Neuve Chapelle, Ypres and Cambrai and in many later engagements in the Retreat and Advance of 1918. In March of the following year he was demobilised, and holds the 1914-15 Star, and the General Service and Victory Medals.
2, Ridge Street, Camilla Road, Bermondsey, S.E.1.   Z6400

MANESTER, S. H., Private, R.A.M.C.

He volunteered in January 1916, and in the same year was drafted to Mesopotamia. Whilst in this theatre of war he served in the Relief of Kut and at the Capture of Baghdad. From Mesopotamia he was sent to Egypt and was engaged on his medical duties in the Palestine campaign until the Armistice. He was present at the Entry into Jerusalem. Afterwards he was sent to India, where he was retained on important duties until October 1919, when he returned home and was demobilised. He holds the General Service and Victory Medals.
63, Westmacott Street, Camberwell, S.E.5.   Z4008

MANEY, J. A., Pte., 7th Royal Warwickshire Regt.

Volunteering in November 1914 in the R.A.S.C., he was sent to France in the following month and fought at Ypres, Loos, the Somme and Arras. In 1917 he was drafted to Italy, where he took part in the important engagements on the Asiago Plateau, and was wounded in action. He was among the first men to enter Austria, and was mentioned in Despatches for his conspicuous bravery in action on the Italian Front. He was demobilised in February 1919, and holds the 1914-15 Star, and the General Service and Victory Medals.
57, Swan Street, Southwark, S.E.1.   Z25703

MANIGER, L. (Senior), Driver, R.A.S.C.

He re-joined in 1914, and in the same year was drafted to France. During his service on the Western Front he was present in engagements on the Somme, at Arras and Ypres. Owing to being severely gassed he was invalided home and was discharged in 1918 as unfit for further service. He holds the 1914 Star, and the General Service and Victory Medals.
4, Wallis Court, Clapham Park, S.W.4.   Z3200A

MANIGER, L., Rifleman, Rifle Brigade.

He volunteered in 1915, and in the same year was drafted overseas. During his service in France he fought in many important engagements until hostilities ceased, including those at the Somme, Arras and Ypres. After the Armistice he was sent to India, where in 1920 he was still serving. He holds the 1914-15 Star, and the General Service and Victory Medals.
4, Wallis Court, Clapham Park, S.W.4.   Z3200B

MANLEY, J. W., Gunner, R.F.A.

He volunteered in January 1915, and in the following October was drafted to the Western Front. During his service in France he did good work as a gunner at Loos, St. Eloi, Albert, Vimy Ridge, Arras, Messines, Ypres and Cambrai, and in March 1918 was wounded and invalided home. After his recovery he was retained on home duties until demobilised in August 1919. He holds the 1914-15 Star, and the General Service and Victory Medals.
265, Sayer Street, Walworth, S.E.17.   Z3203A

MANLEY, J. W., Gunner, R.G.A.

He volunteered in 1915, and in the same year was drafted to France. Whilst overseas he took an active part in the Battles of Ypres, the Somme and many subsequent engagements in the Retreat and Advance of 1918. After the Armistice he proceeded to Germany with the Army of Occupation, and was stationed at Cologne until 1919, when he returned home and was demobilised. He holds the 1914-15 Star, and the General Service and Victory Medals.
123, New Road, Battersea Park Road, S.W.8.   Z3204

MANLEY, L. (Miss), Special War Worker,
During the war this lady offered her services in order to release a man for military duty, and was engaged on important work as a sorter at the General Post Office. She carried out her work with care and efficiency until September 1920, when she relinquished her post.
265, Sayer Street, Walworth, S.E.17.   Z3203B

MANN, T. H., Private, Buffs (East Kent Regiment).
He joined in October 1916, when only sixteen years of age, and was later drafted to the Western Front, where he served for four months in the Ypres sector. He was then sent home and discharged on account of being under age. On attaining the age of eighteen he re-joined and was again sent to France, and was wounded in action at Albert. He was unfortunately killed in action near Le Cateau on November 1st, 1918, and was entitled to the General Service and Victory Medals.
"His life for his Country, his Soul to God."
34, Doctor Street, Walworth, S.E.17.   Z26468

MANNERS, A., Private, R.A.S.C.
He volunteered in March 1915, and in April of the same year was sent to France, where he served on the Somme and at Arras and Ypres. He also took part in the Retreat and Advance of 1918, and returning to England after the cessation of hostilities was demobilised in March 1919, holding the 1914–15 Star, and the General Service and Victory Medals.
142, Lavender Road, Battersea, S.W.11.   Z1686B

MANNERS, F. W., Private, East Surrey Regiment.
He volunteered in September 1914, and was sent to France in January of the following year. He took part in the severe fighting at Neuve Chapelle, Hill 60, Ploegsteert Wood, Vimy Ridge, the Somme, Arras, Ypres and Cambrai, and was severely wounded and invalided home. He was discharged as medically unfit for further service in January 1919, and holds the 1914–15 Star, and the General Service and Victory Medals.
52, Elsted Street, Walworth, S.E.17.   Z3201

MANNING, C., Gunner, R.F.A.
He joined in 1916, and after his training served at various stations with his Battery. He rendered valuable services, but owing to physical unfitness was not successful in obtaining his transfer overseas before the cessation of hostilities. He was demobilised in January 1919.
37, Lanvanor Road, Peckham, S.E.15.   Z6480

MANNING, C. J. F., Cpl., 9th London Regt. (Queen Victoria's Rifles) and 6th London Regt. (Rifles).
He joined in June 1916, and in the following September was sent to France, where he took part in various engagements, including those on the Somme and at Arras, Messines, Ypres and Passchendaele, and was wounded. On his recovery he returned to France and served in the Retreat and Advance of 1918. He was demobilised in February 1919, and holds the General Service and Victory Medals.
29, Vincent Street, Westminster, S.W.1.   Z23475

MANNING, E. J., Rifleman, 1st Royal Irish Rifles.
Joining in June 1916, he was sent to France in the same year and took part in the fighting on the Somme and at Arras and Ypres, and was wounded and invalided home. He was discharged as medically unfit for further service in May 1918, and holds the General Service and Victory Medals.
179, Gordon Road, Peckham, S.E.15.   Z6031

MANNING, G., Air Mechanic, R.A.F.
He joined in December 1917, and after his training served at various stations on important duties with his Squadron. His work demanded a high degree of technical skill, and he rendered valuable services, but was not successful in obtaining his transfer overseas before the cessation of hostilities. He was demobilised in 1919, but later in the same year re-enlisted in the R.A.S.C. and was sent to France, where he was engaged on burial duties. He was finally demobilised in August 1920.
47, Freedom Street, Battersea, S.W.11.   Z3202

MANNING, G., Gunner, R.F.A.
He volunteered in September 1914, and after his training proceeded to Gallipoli in 1915. Whilst in this theatre of war he took part in the Landing at Cape Helles, and was severely wounded whilst carrying Despatches. He was invalided home and remained under medical treatment until discharged in November 1918 as physically unfit for further military duty. He holds the 1914–15 Star, and the General Service and Victory Medals.
87, Commercial Road, Peckham, S.E.15.   Z6286A

MANNING, H., A.B., R.N., H.M.S. "Devonport" and "Fury."
He joined in February 1916, and after his training was posted to H.M.S. "Devonport." In this and other vessels he was engaged in the Mediterranean and the Atlantic on important and dangerous duties escorting troopships and vessels conveying munition and food supplies, through mine-infested areas and liable to enemy submarine attacks. He was demobilised for causes due to his service in August 1918, and holds the General Service and Victory Medals.
87, Commercial Road, Peckham, S.E.15.   Z6286B

MANS, G. A., Sergt., R.A.S.C. (M.T.)
He joined in May 1916, and after his training served at various stations on important duties with his unit. He was engaged as a motor driver in the transport of supplies and conveying wounded to hospital and rendered valuable services, but was not successful in obtaining his transfer overseas before the cessation of hostilities. He was demobilised in April 1919.
40, Pulross Road, Stockwell, S.W.9.   Z3205

MANSELL, H. (M.M.), Private, Border Regiment.
He was serving in India at the outbreak of war, and in the following year was sent to the Dardanelles and was wounded in the Landing. He afterwards proceeded to France and was in action on the Somme and was again wounded at Thiepval, and suffered the loss of a leg. He was awarded the Military Medal for bravery in the Field in saving a Lewis gun under heavy fire, and also holds the 1914–15 Star, and the General Service and Victory Medals. He was discharged owing to his disability in August 1917.
100, Wadhurst Road, Battersea Park Road, S.W.8.   Z5019A

MANSELL, W., Driver, R.F.A.
He volunteered in 1915, and after his training was drafted to the Western Front and took part in the severe fighting at St. Eloi, Loos, Vimy Ridge, the Somme, Beaumont-Hamel and the Retreat and Advance of 1918, and was twice wounded. He was demobilised in June 1919, and holds the General Service and Victory Medals.
23, Dante Road, Kennington, S.E.11.   Z26685

MANSELL, W. P., Private, R.A.S.C. (M.T.).
He joined in January 1916, and after his training served on important duties with his unit. He was engaged as a motor driver and rendered valuable services, but was not successful in obtaining his transfer overseas before the cessation of hostilities. After the Armistice he proceeded to the Army of Occupation in Germany, where he served until demobilised in June 1919.
57, Akerman Road, Brixton, S.W.9.   Z5205

MANSER, J. J. T., Pte., 53rd Royal Sussex Regt.
He joined in September 1918 on attaining military age, and after his training was drafted with the Army of Occupation to Germany, where he was engaged on important duties with his unit and rendered valuable services. He returned home and was demobilised in March 1920.
168, Rolls Road, Bermondsey, S.E.1.   Z26518

MANSFIELD, F. J., Corporal, 9th East Surrey Regt.
He volunteered in September 1914, and early in the following year was drafted to the Western Front. Whilst in France he fought in many notable engagements, including those at Loos, Ypres, the Somme, Messines, Vimy Ridge and Cambrai, and was wounded in the second Battle of the Somme on March 23rd, 1918. He was invalided home, and after treatment in hospital was demobilised in the following March. He holds the 1914–15 Star, and the General Service and Victory Medals.
1, Roslyn Avenue, Camberwell, S.E.5.   Z6409

MANSFIELD, J., Driver, R.F.A.
He volunteered in December 1915, and served on important duties with his Battery until 1917, when he was sent to France, where he took part in numerous engagements, including those on the Somme and at Villers Bretonneux and Cambrai, and was gassed and invalided home. He was demobilised in June 1919, and holds the General Service and Victory Medals.
62, Hargwynne Street, Stockwell, S.E.9.   Z3206

MANTLE, H. S., Guardsman, 1st Grenadier Guards.
He volunteered in February 1915, and was sent to France in the same year and took part in the severe fighting at St. Eloi, Loos and the Somme, and was severely wounded in eight places, suffering the loss of his right foot. He was invalided home and discharged owing to his physical disability, in July 1917, and holds the 1914–15 Star, and the General Service and Victory Medals.
96, Maysoule Road, Battersea, S.W.11.   Z3207

MANUEL, H., Gunner, R.G.A.
He was serving at the outbreak of war, and in 1915 was sent to France, where he took part in the fighting at Loos, the Somme, Messines, Ypres, Cambrai, and in many other engagements, and was wounded and gassed. He was invalided home in 1918, and discharged in June of that year as medically unfit for further service. He holds the 1914–15 Star, and the General Service and Victory Medals.
8, Pepler Road, Peckham, S.E.15.   Z3488

MANUEL, T., Guardsman, Coldstream Guards.
He joined in June 1917, and in April of the following year was drafted to the Western Front, where he took part in the Retreat and Advance. He was unfortunately killed in action on the Somme on August 21st, 1918, and was entitled to the General Service and Victory Medals.
"He passed out of the sight of men by the path of duty and self-sacrifice."
34, Venn Street, Clapham, S.W.4.   Z3208

MANWARING, A., Pte., 4th Hampshire Regiment and Trooper, Hampshire Dragoons.

He volunteered in June 1915, and was sent to France in the following year. He took part in the fierce fighting at Ypres and in many other engagements, and was twice wounded. He also served for a time in Italy and was invalided home and discharged as medically unfit in February 1919, and holds the General Service and Victory Medals.

23B, Theatre Street, Battersea, S.W.11. Z3209

MARA, E. J., Rifleman, Rifle Brigade and King's Royal Rifle Corps.

He joined in August 1917, and after his training was drafted to France, where he took part in numerous engagements, including those on the Somme, the Lys and the Aisne. He was demobilised in October 1919, and holds the General Service and Victory Medals.

34, Brunnington Square, South Lambeth Road, S.W.8. Z3210

MARCHAM, W. G., Gunner, R.G.A.

Joining in January 1918, he was in the same month sent to France, where he took part in the fierce fighting during the Retreat and Advance of 1918, and was gassed. He returned home, and was demobilised in September 1919, and holds the General Service and Victory Medals.

13, The Grove South, South Lambeth Road, S.W.8. Z3211

MARCHANT, F. J., Trooper, 2nd Dragoon Guards (Queen's Bays).

He volunteered in September 1914, and in the same year was sent to the Western Front, where he was in action at La Bassée, Ypres, Loos, the Somme, Beaumont-Hamel, Bullecourt, Cambrai, and the Retreat and Advance of 1918. He was demobilised in February 1919, and holds the 1914 Star, and the General Service and Victory Medals.

142, Ferndale Road, Clapham, S.W.4. Z3212

MARFLEET, A., Gunner, R.F.A.

Volunteering in April 1915, he was sent to the Western Front early in the following year. Whilst overseas he fought in many of the principal engagements, including those at Vermelles, Vimy Ridge, Ypres, Cambrai, Amiens, and the Sambre, and was demobilised on his return to England in February 1919. He holds the General Service and Victory Medals.

22, Huguenot Road, Peckham Rye, S.E.15. Z6032A

MARFLEET, G. A., Pte., 8th Worcestershire Regt.

Joining in 1916, he was drafted to the Western Front early in the following year. He was subsequently engaged in the fighting at Ypres, Passchendaele, Cambrai and the Somme, and in the Retreat and Advance of 1918, at the conclusion of which he was sent with the Army of Occupation to Germany. He was demobilised in October 1919, and holds the General Service and Victory Medals.

22, Huguenot Road, Peckham Rye, S.E.15. Z6032B

MARFLEET, H. (M.M.), Sergt., 2nd Highland Light Infantry.

Volunteering at the commencement of hostilities, he was quickly drafted to France and took part in the Retreat from Mons. He also fought in many of the engagements which followed, including those on the Marne and at Ypres, La Bassée, Albert, Arras, Messines and Cambrai, and in the Retreat and Advance of 1918. He was awarded the Military Medal for conspicuous bravery and devotion to duty in the Field, and in addition holds the Mons Star, and the General Service and Victory Medals. He was demobilised in July 1919.

28, Wivenhoe Road, Peckham, S.E.15. Z6046

MARGERUM, C., Gunner, R.F.A.

He volunteered in May 1915, and in the same year was drafted overseas. During his service in France he did good work as a gunner at Arras, Ypres, Passchendaele and the Somme, and when the Armistice was signed was serving in Belgium. He was demobilised in January 1919 after his return home, and holds the 1914-15 Star, and the General Service and Victory Medals.

8, Parkstone Road, Peckham, S.E.15. Z6287

MARIE, E., Gunner, R.G.A.

He volunteered early in 1915, and at the conclusion of his training was engaged upon duties of an important nature at various stations with his Battery. Owing to ill-health he was unable to secure his transfer to a theatre of war, but did valuable work until 1918, when he was invalided out of the Service. Unfortunately, he died on February 5th, 1919.

"His memory is cherished with pride."

89, Barlow Street, Walworth, S.E.17. Z3376

MARIE, F. J. (M.M.), Driver, R.F.A.

Volunteering in September 1914, he crossed to France in the following January. During his overseas service he fought in the Battles of Ypres, Loos, Albert, the Somme, Arras, Lens and Cambrai, and in the Retreat and Advance of 1918. In September of that year he was awarded the Military Medal for bravery and devotion to duty in the Field. He holds in addition the 1914-15 Star, and the General Service and Victory Medals, and was demobilised in May 1919.

94, Aylesbury Road, Walworth, S.E.17. Z3213

MARKE, A. T., Rifleman, 3rd King's Royal Rifle Corps.

He joined on attaining military age in May 1918, and at the conclusion of his training was engaged on important duties at various stations. He was unable to secure his transfer overseas before the termination of hostilities, but afterwards was drafted to India, where he was still serving with his unit in 1920.

201, Neate Street, Camberwell, S.E.5. Z5408B

MARKS, C. J., Private, R.A.S.C. (M.T.)

He volunteered in October 1914, and in the following year proceeded to France, where he served in numerous engagements, including those at Albert, the Somme, Arras, Ypres and Passchendaele. He also took part in the Retreat and Advance of 1918, and returning to England after the cessation of hostilities, was demobilised in May 1919, holding the 1914-15 Star, and the General Service and Victory Medals.

1, Burchell Road, Peckham, S.E.15. Z6526

MARKS, R., Rifleman, 21st London Regiment (1st Surrey Rifles).

He joined in October 1916, and until he was drafted to France in 1918, was engaged on important duties at various stations. Whilst overseas he served with the 47th Division, and did valuable work during the Retreat and Advance of 1918, in the course of which he fought in many engagements. He holds the General Service and Victory Medals, and was demobilised in May 1919.

75, Ingelow Road, Battersea Park, S.W.8. Z3214

MARLE, J., Private, 2nd London Regiment (Royal Fusiliers).

He volunteered at the commencement of hostilities, and at the conclusion of a brief course of training was sent to Egypt, where he was engaged on special duties. In 1915, however, he contracted enteric fever and was invalided home in consequence. After his recovery he served with the Military Foot Police at Aldershot until 1916, when he was discharged as physically unfit. He holds the 1914-15 Star, and the General Service and Victory Medals.

62, Saltoun Road, Brixton, S.W.2. Z3100

MARLER, A. F., Pte., 22nd London Regt. (Queen's).

Volunteering in January 1915, he was sent to the Western Front in the same year and subsequently fought at Neuve Chapelle, Loos and Ypres, and in other important engagements. He was, unfortunately, killed during the heavy fighting on the Somme on September 16th, 1916, and was entitled to the 1914-15 Star, and the General Service and Victory Medals.

"Great deeds cannot die."

386, Guinness' Buildings (R Block), Page's Walk, Grange Road, S.E.1. Z26366

MARLEY, G. H., Pte., 10th Queen's Own (Royal West Kent Regiment).

He volunteered in October 1915, and in the same year was drafted overseas. During his service on the Western Front he took part in many engagements at Ypres, Loos, Vimy Ridge, the Somme, Messines, Ypres, Passchendaele and Cambrai. He was taken prisoner in March 1918 and sent to Germany, but escaped in the following October from Stammlager, the Prisoners' Camp, and reported himself to his unit. He was then sent home and demobilised, holding the 1914-15 Star, and the General Service and Victory Medals.

34, Harders Road, Peckham, S.E.15. Z6288B

MARLEY, R., L/Corporal, Royal Defence Corps.

He volunteered in 1915, and being over age for overseas service, joined the Royal Defence Corps, and was sent to Ireland on garrison duty. He was also engaged in guarding German prisoners at various camps and on other important duties. He rendered valuable services until he was demobilised in 1919.

34, Harders Road, Peckham, S.E.15. Z6288A

MARLEY, W. F., Sapper, R.E.

Joining in March 1916, he was drafted to the Western Front at the conclusion of his training. In the following October he was severely wounded whilst in action on the Somme, and after being in hospital at Le Treport for some time, rejoined his unit and served until the termination of hostilities. He was demobilised in May 1919, after his return to England, and holds the General Service and Victory Medals.

21, Hillery Road, Walworth, S.E.17. Z3215

MARLOW, W., Cpl., King's Royal Rifle Corps.
He volunteered in August 1914, and in the same year was drafted to Salonika, where he served in many important engagements, and was twice severely wounded. He was afterwards sent to the Western Front and took part in the Allied Advance of 1918. He holds the 1914 Star, and the General Service and Victory Medals, and was demobilised in February 1919.   Z26898
6, Longhope Place, off Monkton Street, Kennington, S.E.11.

MARLTON, E. E., Private, R.A.O.C.
Joining in March 1917, he was drafted to Egypt at the conclusion of his training. He served under General Allenby in the Palestine campaign, doing valuable work with his unit, and was present at several engagements, including the capture of Jerusalem. He was demobilised in July 1919, and holds the General Service and Victory Medals.
6, Dartford Street, Walworth, S.E.17.   Z26207

MARNEY, A., Private, 6th East Surrey Regt.
He volunteered early in 1915, and after obtaining his training at Aldershot, crossed to France and fought in the Battles of Hill 60, and Ypres. In 1916 he was so severely wounded as to necessitate his return to England, but on his recovery was redrafted to the Western Front and was in action until the cessation of hostilities, when he advanced with the Army of Occupation into Germany. He was demobilised in February 1919, and holds the 1914-15 Star, and the General Service and Victory Medals.
51, Blake's Road, Peckham, S.E.15.   Z6033

MARRABLE, R., Private, Hampshire Regiment.
Volunteering in August 1915, he crossed to the Western Front early in the following year. Whilst overseas he fought in engagements at Albert, Vimy Ridge, the Somme and Ypres, and was severely wounded and gassed. After protracted hospital treatment he was invalided out of the Service in February 1918, and holds the General Service and Victory Medals. 103, Grant Road, Battersea, S.W.11.   Z3216

MARRIAGE, S. J., Sergt., 1st Royal Fusiliers.
A serving soldier, he crossed to France immediately upon the outbreak of hostilities and fought in the Battle of, and Retreat from, Mons. He also took part in many of the subsequent engagements, including those at Le Cateau, the Marne, the Aisne, La Bassée, Ypres, Neuve Chapelle, St. Eloi, Festubert and the Somme. In 1916 he was wounded, but on recovery rejoined his unit and was later wounded a second time at Messines. He was then invalided home, and on being discharged from hospital served on important duties at his depôt until he was demobilised in February 1919. He holds the Mons Star, and the General Service and Victory Medals.
36, Dante Road, Kennington, S.E.11.   Z26687

MARRIOTT, A., Sapper, R.E.
He volunteered in September 1914, and in the following year was sent to the Dardanelles, subsequently taking part in the Landing at Suvla Bay and the engagements which followed. After the Evacuation of the Peninsula, he was drafted to Egypt, where he was for some time in charge of a Helio station. He was transferred to France in 1916, and did valuable work with his unit during the Somme Offensive, in the course of which he was severely wounded at Hangard Wood. Invalided to the Queen's Hospital, Sidcup, he underwent protracted treatment before being demobilised in February 1919. He holds the 1914-15 Star, and the General Service and Victory Medals.   16, Sedan Street, Walworth, S.E.17.   Z3217

MARSDEN, S., Private, R.A.S.C.
He joined in 1916, and in the same year was drafted to the Western Front, where he served in important engagements, including those on the Somme and at Arras, Messines, Ypres, Cambrai and St. Quentin. He also took part in the Retreat and Advance of 1918. He was demobilised in 1919, and holds the General Service and Victory Medals.
24, Elizabeth Street, Walworth, S.E.17.   Z26419

MARSH, A., C.S.M., 10th Devonshire Regiment.
Having previously served for sixteen years, he rejoined the Army on the outbreak of hostilities, and in August 1915 was drafted to the Western Front. Later in the same year he was transferred to Salonika, where he took part in numerous engagements during the Balkan campaign. He gave his life for the freedom of England on February 10th, 1917, and was entitled to the 1914-15 Star, and the General Service and Victory Medals.
    "And doubtless he went in splendid company."
9, Thorncroft Street, Wandsworth Road, S.W.8.   Z3223

MARSH, F. W., Private, Labour Corps.
He joined in February 1917, and in the same year was drafted to France. Here he served at Dunkirk for a time, being present when that town was bombarded by enemy aircraft. Later he was engaged on important duties constructing roads and also interring the dead. During the Retreat of 1918 he took part in the fighting in the Cambrai sector. He holds the General Service and Victory Medals, and was demobilised in October 1919.
13, Fenwick Place, Stockwell, S.W.9.   Z3222

MARSH, C. P., Special War Worker.
An ex-Navy man, he had served in the South African War and holds the Medals for that campaign. At the outbreak of hostilities he volunteered, but was rejected, and after again endeavouring in 1916 to enlist in either the Navy or the Army and being rejected for both, he was engaged at the Metropolitan Gas Works on work of National importance in connection with the output of munitions. After eighteen months' valuable service there he joined the Royal Air Force at Kidbrooke Aerodrome, where he did much excellent work until his health broke down.
1, Sydney House, Latona Road, Peckham, S.E.15.   Z6289A

MARSH, G. S., Private, R.A.S.C. and Duke of Cornwall's Light Infantry.
He volunteered in December 1914, and in the following year was drafted to France and took part in the Battle of Hill 60, in which he was wounded. Later he was transferred to the R.A.S.C. and served as an ambulance driver. He holds the 1914-15 Star, and the General Service and Victory Medals, and in 1920 was still serving.
11, Dickens Street, Wandsworth Road, S.W.8.   Z3221

MARSH, G. W., Gunner, R.F.A.
He volunteered in January 1915, and after completing his training proceeded to France in March of the same year and took part in numerous engagements, including those of the Somme and Passchendaele. In 1918 he was in action at Epéhy and was severely gassed. He returned home and was demobilised in January 1919, and holds the 1914-15 Star, and the General Service and Victory Medals.
185, Merrow Street, Walworth, S.E.17.   Z27117

MARSH, H., Sapper, R.E.
He volunteered in May 1915 and in the same year proceeded to France, where he was in action on the Somme and at Albert and Arras, and took part in the Retreat and Advance of 1918. During his service he was twice wounded, and after the cessation of hostilities was drafted to Germany with the Army of Occupation, with which he served until demobilised in July 1919. He holds the 1914-15 Star, and the General Service and Victory Medals.
11, Westbury Street, Wandsworth Road, S.W.8.   Z3219

MARSH, J. H., Driver, R.F.A.
He volunteered in 1915, and on the completion of his training was sent to France, where he took part in numerous engagements and was twice wounded. After the cessation of hostilities he returned to England in 1919 and was demobilised, holding the 1914-15 Star, and the General Service and Victory Medals.
130, Cranbrook Road, Chiswick, W.4.   8356C

MARSH, L., (Mrs.) Special War Worker.
From 1915 to 1917 this lady was engaged in making soldiers' helmets at her own home. She carried out her duties for two years with care and efficiency, and rendered valuable services.
1, Sydney House, Latona Road, Peckham, S.E.15.   Z6289B

MARSH, T. H., Private, 11th Essex Regiment.
He volunteered in August 1914, and in September of the following year was drafted to the Western Front. Here he took part in numerous engagements, including those at Loos, the Somme and Ypres and was gassed. After the cessation of hostilities he proceeded to Germany with the Army of Occupation, with which he served until demobilised in August 1919. He holds the 1914-15 Star, and the General Service and Victory Medals.
92, Cator Street, St. George's Road, Peckham, S.E.15.   X4493

MARSH, R. E., Sapper, R.E.
He joined in December 1917, and after having completed his training was engaged on important duties with the searchlight section at various stations. He rendered valuable service, but was not successful in procuring his transfer to a theatre of war prior to the cessation of hostilities. He was demobilised in March 1919.
22, Wheatsheaf Lane, South Lambeth Road, S.W.8.   Z3218

MARSHALL, A., Private, M.G.C.
He volunteered in January 1915, and after his training was sent in 1916 to the Western Front, where he took part in numerous engagements, including those on the Somme. He was unfortunately killed by a stray shell on July 30th, 1917, while resting in his dug-out, and was entitled to the General Service and Victory Medals.
    "Honour to the immortal dead who gave their youth that the world might grow old in peace."
48, Denmark Road, Camberwell, S.E.5.   Z6039

MARSHALL, A. E., Trooper, 2nd County of London Yeomanry (Westminster Dragoons).

He volunteered in May 1915, and after completing his training was sent to Egypt in the following year. While overseas he took part in various important engagements in the Canal zone and in Palestine, including those outside Jerusalem and in the Jordan Valley. In 1917 he was transferred to Salonika and fought on the Doiran front. In the following year he was sent to France, where he was in action at Ypres, Armentières, the Retreat and Advance of the Allies. He holds the General Service and Victory Medals, and in February 1919 was demobilised.

6, King Edward Street, Southwark, S.E.1.   Z25050

MARSHALL, A. H., Private, Labour Corps.

Joining in 1917, he was sent to France in the following year. He rendered valuable service in the canteens during the Retreat and Advance of 1918, and afterwards proceeded with the Army of Occupation to Germany. He was demobilised in September 1919 after his return home, and holds the General Service and Victory Medals.

8, Bond Street, South Lambeth Road, S.W.8.   Z3288A

MARSHALL, A. R., Gunner, R.G.A.

He volunteered in May 1915, and in February 1916 was sent to France, where he took part in the severe fighting at Albert, the Somme, Beaumont-Hamel, Arras, Messines, Lens and Cambrai. He also served in the Retreat of 1918, and was gassed near Cambrai. He was demobilised in February 1919, and holds the General Service and Victory Medals.

46, Alfreton Street, Walworth, S.E.17.   Z3227

MARSHALL, B., Member, W.R.A.F.

She joined in June 1918, and was engaged at Walnut Tree Walk, Kennington, as a tinsmith and metal sheet worker. Her duties, which demanded a high degree of skill, were carried out with great efficiency, and she rendered valuable services. She was demobilised in April 1919.

67, The Grove, South Lambeth Road, S.W.8.   Z3230A

MARSHALL, C. (Miss), Special War Worker.

From September 1916 until March 1919 this lady held an important position at Messrs. John Bell, Hill and Lucas' Works, Bermondsey. She was engaged on the manufacture of anti-gas masks and proved herself an expert at the work she had undertaken.

59, Marcia Road, Bermondsey, S.E.1.   Z27265B

MARSHALL, C. J., Pte., 2nd Buffs (East Kent Regt.)

He volunteered in August 1914, and having completed his training proceeded to the Western Front in April of the following year. He took part in several important engagements until hostilities ceased, including those at Ypres, Dickebusch, Festubert, the Somme and Arras, where he was severely wounded. He was also gassed at Ypres. He returned to England and was demobilised in January 1919, and holds the 1914-15 Star, and the General Service and Victory Medals.

15, Stevens Street, Bermondsey, S.E.1.   Z27427

MARSHALL, E., L/Corporal, Queen's (Royal West Surrey Regiment).

He volunteered in January 1915, and in the following April was drafted to the Western Front, where he took part in numerous engagements, including those at Hill 60, Ypres, Festubert and Loos and was wounded. On his recovery he returned to France in September 1916, and was in action at Vimy Ridge, Bullecourt, Messines, Passchendaele and Cambrai, and in the Retreat and Advance of 1918. He was demobilised in April 1919, and holds the 1914-15 Star, and the General Service and Victory Medals.

4, Geneva Terrace, Coldharbour Lane, S.W.9.   Z4494

MARSHALL, E. C., Pte., 1st South Staffordshire Regt.

He was mobilised in Africa in September 1914, and sent to England, and thence to the Western Front, where he took part in numerous engagements. After being severely wounded at Ypres and invalided home, he was discharged in June 1915, owing to his injuries, and holds the 1914-15 Star, and the General Service and Victory Medals.

68, Gayville Road, Battersea, S.W.11.   Z3224

MARSHALL, F. S., Private, H.A.C.

He joined in December 1917, and after his training was retained at the Tower of London, Bisley, and other stations on important duties with his unit. He rendered valuable services, but was not successful in obtaining his transfer overseas before the cessation of hostilities. He was demobilised in May 1919, but at once re-enlisted in the 2nd Devonshire Regiment, and was drafted to India, where he was still serving in 1920.

1, Comber Grove, Camberwell, S.E.5.   Z3226

MARSHALL, G. F., Driver, R.E.

He volunteered in 1915, and served on important duties with his unit until 1917, when he was sent to Egypt. During the campaign in Palestine he rendered valuable services in connection with telegraphic communication in numerous engagements, including those leading up to the capture of Jerusalem. He contracted malaria while in the East, and after being invalided home was discharged, owing to his disability in January 1919. He holds the General Service and Victory Medals.

67, The Grove, South Lambeth Road, S.W.8.   Z3230B

MARSHALL, H., Special War Worker.

From September 1914 until March 1919 he was engaged on important work in connection with the manufacture of soldiers' boots at Messrs. Underwood's Factory, St. George's Road, Peckham. He carried out his duties with great care and efficiency, and throughout rendered valuable services.

59, Marcia Road, Bermondsey, S.E.1.   Z27265A

MARSHALL, H. V., Driver, R.F.A.

Volunteering in May 1915, he was sent to France in December of the same year. He took part in numerous engagements until the cessation of hostilities, including those at Vimy Ridge, the Somme, Ypres and Cambrai, and in the Retreat and Advance of 1918. He was demobilised in March 1919 after returning home, and holds the 1914-15 Star, and the General Service and Victory Medals.

3, Canterbury Place, Lambeth, S.E.11.   Z26962

MARSHALL, J. D., Cpl., North Staffordshire Regt.

He was serving at the outbreak of war, and immediately afterwards was drafted to France, where he took part in the fierce fighting at Mons and in numerous other engagements, including that at Loos, and was twice wounded. He also did valuable service in the Retreat and Advance of 1918. He was still in the Army in 1920, and holds the Mons Star, and the General Service and Victory Medals.

21, Smyrk's Road, Walworth, S.E.17.   Z1470C
                                     Z1471C

MARSHALL, J. D., Pte., 4th Royal Fusiliers and 20th London Regiment.

He joined in September 1917, and in March of the following year was drafted to France, where he took part in the Retreat and Advance of 1918, and was wounded near Albert in August. He was invalided home after hospital treatment, and demobilised in February 1919, holding the General Service and Victory Medals. In July 1919 he re-enlisted in the 4th Royal Fusiliers, and in 1920 was still in the Army.

38, Clovelly Road, Acton Green, Chiswick, W.4.   6607A

MARSHALL, J. J. E., 3rd Middlesex Regt. and 3rd Suffolk Regt.

He volunteered in November 1914, and after completing his training was retained on important duties with his unit until June 1916, when he was sent to France. While there he took part in numerous engagements until the close of hostilities, including those at Arras, Ypres, Cambrai and the Retreat and Advance of 1918, and was twice wounded. He was demobilised in June 1919, and holds the General Service and Victory Medals. He re-enlisted in the Suffolk Regiment in August 1919, and was still serving in 1920.

38, Clovelly Road, Acton Green, Chiswick, W.4.   6607B

MARSHALL, R. W., Rifleman, Rifle Brigade.

He joined in 1916, and after his training was drafted to the Western Front, where he was engaged as a stretcher bearer. He was taken prisoner at Cambrai, and sent to Germany. He is reported to have died in captivity in 1917, and was entitled to the General Service and Victory Medals.

"His memory is cherished with pride."

8, Bond Street, S. Lambeth Road, S.W.8.   Z3228B

MARSHALL, S., Gunner, R.F.A.

Volunteering in November 1914, he was in the following year sent to France, where he took part in numerous engagements, including those at Loos, Gouzeaucourt and Cambrai. He was discharged in 1917 in consequence of his service, and holds the 1914-15 Star, and the General Service and Victory Medals.

129, Amelia Street, Walworth, S.E.17.   Z26153

MARSHALL, W., L/Sergt., King's Royal Rifle Corps.

He volunteered in August 1914, and was retained on important duties with his unit until September 1916, when he was sent to France. While there he was in action at the Somme, Ypres, Passchendaele, and in other engagements, and in September 1917 was transferred to Italy, where he did valuable service until March 1918. He then returned to France and served in the Retreat and Advance of the Allies, particularly at Neuve Eglise and Gouzeaucourt, where he was badly wounded in September 1918. He was also wounded on another occasion. After his evacuation from hospital he was demobilised in April 1919, and holds the General Service and Victory Medals.

11, Chumleigh Street, Camberwell, S.E.5.   Z5115

MARSHALL, W. E., Pioneer, R.E.

He joined in August 1916, and in the same year was sent to Salonika, where he served on several fronts, and was engaged on railway reconstruction. He was in May 1919 transferred to South Russia, where he did excellent work until his return home to be demobilised in October 1919. He holds the General Service and Victory Medals.

79, Gwynne Road, Battersea, S.W.11.   Z3225

MARSHALL, W. H., Private, Royal Welch Fusiliers.

He volunteered in January 1915, and in the following November after completing his training, was drafted to the Western Front. He took an active part in the Battles of Loos, the Somme, Ypres, Cambrai and Armentières, and also served in many engagements during the Retreat and Advance of 1918. He was demobilised in January 1919, after returning home, and holds the 1914-15 Star, and the General Service and Victory Medals.

29, Warrior Road, Camberwell, S.E.5.   Z3229

MARSHAM, J. M., Driver, R.F.A. and Gnr., R.G.A.

Mobilised at the outbreak of hostilities he was quickly drafted to France, and throughout the war did valuable service in many engagements of importance, including those at the Marne, Ypres, Neuve Chapelle, Vimy Ridge, the Somme, Loos, the Ancre, Beaumont-Hamel, and in the Retreat and Advance of 1918. He was discharged in December 1918 as a time-expired man, but rejoined the R.H.A. in May 1919, and in 1920 was serving in Mesopotamia. He holds the 1914 Star, and the General Service and Victory Medals.

23, Comus Place, Walworth, S.E.17.   Z3232C

MARSHAM, R., Private, 51st Royal Sussex Regt.

He joined in July 1918, and on the completion of his training proceeded to France, where he rendered much valuable service. After the Armistice he proceeded to Germany with the Army of Occupation, and remained there engaged on various important duties until his return to England for demobilisation in April 1920. He holds the General Service and Victory Medals.

65, Darien Road, Battersea, S.W.11.   Z3231

MARSON, H. A., Sergt., R.E.

He was mobilised at the outbreak of hostilities, and was at once drafted to France, where he remained until the war ended, and did much valuable service in the Postal Section. He was mentioned in Despatches twice for his consistently excellent work, and holds the 1914 Star, and the General Service and Victory Medals. He was demobilised in March 1919.

24, Graham Road, Chiswick, W.4.   6610

MARTIN, A. E., Private, 3rd Bedfordshire Regt. and King's (Liverpool Regt.)

Joining in July 1917, he proceeded to France early in 1918, and fought through the Retreat and Advance of that year, in the important engagements at Havrincourt, Bullecourt, Cambrai and other places. During the Allied Offensive he was severely wounded, and was eventually invalided home. At an earlier date he gave a transfusion of blood to save the life of a comrade, who was badly injured. In February 1919 he was demobilised, and holds the General Service and Victory Medals.

47, Tindal Street, Brixton, S.W.9.   Z5452

MARTIN, A. H., Private, 3rd and 7th Queen's (Royal West Surrey Regiment).

He joined in May 1916, and at the conclusion of his training was drafted to the Western Front, where he subsequently fought in many engagements, including those at Ypres, Arras, Poelcapelle and the Somme. After the Retreat and Advance of 1918, in which he also took part, he was sent with the Army of Occupation to Germany, where he served for some months. He was demobilised in October 1919, and holds the General Service and Victory Medals.

72, Kirkwood Road, Peckham, S.E.15.   Z6203A

MARTIN, A. P., Gunner, R.G.A.

Volunteering in October 1914, he went through his course of training, and proceeded to France in 1915. While overseas he took an active part with his Battery in numerous battles of great importance, including those at Neuve Chapelle, Ypres, Loos and the Somme, and was badly gassed. He was invalided home in consequence, and in February 1919 was discharged as medically unfit for further service. He holds the 1914-15 Star, and the General Service and Victory Medals.

4, Rosemary Road, Peckham, S.E.15.   Z5453

MARTIN, A. T., Private, 19th (Queen Alexandra's Own Royal) Hussars.

Mobilised at the outbreak of hostilities, he quickly proceeded to the Western Front, and fought at Mons and many other engagements of the greatest importance. Owing to a breakdown in health he was discharged in July 1917 as medically unfit for further military duty. He holds the Mons Star, and the General Service and Victory Medals.

104, Brayard's Road, Peckham, S.E.15.   Z5454

MARTIN, A. T., Rifleman, Rifle Brigade.

He joined in May 1916, and in July of the same year was drafted to the Western Front, where he took part in several engagements of importance, including those at Arras, the Somme and Poperinghe, in which he was wounded. On coming out of hospital he was sent to Ireland and was transferred to the Black Watch, from which Regiment he was demobilised in August 1919. He holds the General Service and Victory Medals.

51, Elim Street, Weston Street, S.E.1.   Z25791

MARTIN, A. W., Driver, R.A.S.C.

He volunteered in 1914, and in the following year after the completion of his training, crossed to France, where he was engaged in the transport service in the Arras, Ypres and Somme areas. In 1916 he was drafted to Salonika and did much valuable work on the Struma and Doiran fronts until he was sent home wounded and gassed. He was discharged in 1917 as medically unfit for further military duty, and holds the 1914-15 Star, and the General Service and Victory Medals.

52, Thurlow Street, Walworth, S.E.17.   Z3233

MARTIN, C., Sapper, R.E.

Mobilised at the outbreak of the war he at once crossed to the Western Front, and took part in the Battles of Mons, the Marne and the Aisne. He also rendered valuable service with his unit at Ypres, Loos, Albert, the Somme, Lens and Cambrai, and in the Retreat and Advance of 1918, and was three times wounded. He was awarded the French Croix de Guerre for saving the life of a French Officer, and also holds the Mons Star, and the General Service and Victory Medals. He was demobilised in December 1918.

20, Alsace Street, Walworth, S.E.17.   Z3236

MARTIN, C., Staff-Sergt., East Surrey and Essex Regts.

He was an old soldier, who originally enlisted in 1885, and served in the Burmese War of 1889, and volunteered at the outbreak of the late war. After being retained on important duties at home for some time he was drafted to Mesopotamia in 1916, and did excellent work at Kut, Baghdad and other places until 1917, when he was invalided to India. After much valuable service, he returned to England and was demobilised in May 1919. He holds the Burmah Medal (1899), and the General Service and Victory Medals.

229, East Street, Walworth, S.E.17.   Z3235

MARTIN, E., Private, Labour Corps and Rflmn., King's Royal Rifle Corps.

He joined in June 1916, and in the following September was drafted to France with the King's Royal Rifle Corps. After taking part in many important engagements he was severely wounded at Cambrai in November 1917. On his recovery he was transferred to the Labour Corps, and in January 1918 was invalided home owing to ill-health. He was retained at various stations on special duties in connection with the repairs of motor lorries, and was discharged as unfit for further service in February 1919. He holds the General Service and Victory Medals.

237, Sumner Road, Peckham, S.E.15.   Z6290

MARTIN, F., Rifleman, Rifle Brigade.

He joined in March 1917, and in the following February, having completed his training, was drafted to France. He took part in several engagements and was wounded and taken prisoner on the Somme front in April. During his captivity in Germany he was employed on farm work until the Armistice, when he was repatriated and rejoined his unit. He afterwards served for a time in Sierra Leone, and on returning home was demobilised in March 1920, holding the General Service and Victory Medals.

8, Stanton Street, Peckham, S.E.15.   Z5265

MARTIN, F. E., Private, R.A.M.C.

Joining in July 1916, he crossed to France six months later, and did excellent service as stretcher-bearer with the 95th Field Ambulance at Arras, Messines, Ypres, Passchendaele, Ploegsteert, the Lys, and many severe engagements in the Retreat and Advance of 1918. He returned home, and was demobilised in 1919, holding the General Service and Victory Medals.

12, Turret Grove, Clapham, S.W.4.   Z3244

MARTIN, G., Sapper, R.E.

He volunteered in March 1915, and on the conclusion of his training in the same year proceeded to France. He afterwards did excellent work with his unit until the close of hostilities, at Loos, St. Eloi, the Somme, Vermelles, Vimy Ridge and in the Retreat and Advance of the Allies in 1918. During his service he was wounded at Vimy Ridge. He returned to England, and was demobilised in February 1919, and holds the 1914-15 Star, and the General Service and Victory Medals.

2, Moat Place, Stockwell, S.W.9.   Z4496

MARTIN, G., Rifleman, Royal Irish Rifles.
He joined in 1916, and in the same year proceeded to the
Western Front. He did gallant service at the Somme and
Ypres, and was reported missing, and has since been presumed
killed in action at Menin Road on August 16th, 1917. He was
entitled to the General Service and Victory Medals.
      " The path of duty was the way to glory."
77, Somerleyton Road, Coldharbour Lane, S.W.9.   Z3490

MARTIN, G., Private, 1st Buffs (East Kent Regt.)
He was mobilised in August 1914, and was immediately
drafted to France, where he took part in the Battles of Mons
and the Marne. While fighting gallantly at the Aisne he was
killed in action on October 8th, 1914. He was entitled to
the Mons Star, and the General Service and Victory Medals.
      " His life for his Country, his Soul to God."
47, B Block Guinness Buildings, Page's Walk, Grange Road,
S.E.1.   Z26823

MARTIN, G. W., L/Corporal, Duke of Cornwall's
    Light Infantry.
He was serving in the Army at the outbreak of war, and was
immediately drafted to France with the first Expeditionary
Force. He took part in the Battles of Mons, the Marne and
the Aisne, and in operations in other sectors. He was wounded
and taken prisoner, and his death is reported to have taken
place at Namur, between January 22nd, 1915, and April
4th, 1916. He was entitled to the Mons Star and the General
Service and Victory Medals.
      " His memory is cherished with pride."
3, Colworth Grove, Walworth, S.E.17.   Z3238

MARTIN, H., Driver, R.F.A.
He joined in 1916, and later in the year on the completion of
his training was drafted to France. He took part with his
Battery in the Battles of the Somme, Ypres and Cambrai,
and in the chief engagements of the Retreat and Advance of
1918 until hostilities ceased. After his return home he was
demobilised in August 1919, and holds the General Service and
Victory Medals.
9, Langley Lane, South Lambeth Road, S.W.8.   Z3239

MARTIN, H. H., Pte., 12th Gloucestershire Regt.
He volunteered in October 1915, and in the following year
after completing his course of training was sent to the Western
Front. After taking part in many important engagements
he was transferred to Italy, where he did much valuable
service in the later stages of the war. After his return to
England he was demobilised in February 1919, and holds the
General Service and Victory Medals.
75, Sulgrave Road, Hammersmith, W.6.   11832

MARTIN, J., Private, 7th London Regiment.
Volunteering in August 1914, he proceeded to the Western
Front in the following year, and took an active part in many
important engagements, including those at Loos, Vimy Ridge,
Ypres, and in the Retreat of the Allies in 1918. During his
service he was wounded three times, at Loos, Ypres and in
the Retreat. After returning to England he was demobilised
in February 1919, and holds the 1914–15 Star, and the General
Service and Victory Medals.
4, Bolton Street, Camberwell, S.E.5.   Z3242A

MARTIN, L. A., Private, 3rd Queen's (Royal West
    Surrey Regiment).
He joined in June 1918, and at the conclusion of his training
was engaged on duties of an important nature with his unit.
Owing to ill-health he was unable to secure his transfer to a
theatre of war, but, nevertheless, did valuable work until
he was demobilised in December 1919.
72, Kirkwood Road, Peckham, S.E.15.   Z6203B

MARTIN, L. M., Rifleman, 21st London Regiment
    (1st Surrey Rifles).
He volunteered in August 1914, and served on important
duties with his unit until 1916, when he was sent to France,
where he took part in the Battle of the Somme, and in many
other engagements. Later in the same year he proceeded to
Salonika, and served in the Balkan campaign. He was afterwards transferred to Egypt, and thence to Palestine, where
he was in many engagements, including those leading up to
the capture of Jerusalem. Whilst in this theatre of war he
contracted malaria and suffered from septic poisoning, and
was sent to hospital in Egypt. He was demobilised in January
1919, and holds the General Service and Victory Medals.
16, Montpelier Road, Peckham, S.E.17.   Z6525

MARTIN, R., Sergt., R.F.A. and R.A.V.C.
He volunteered in 1915, and in the same year was drafted to
France, where he did excellent work with his Battery in many
of the principal engagements, including those at the Somme
and Ypres, and was wounded. He was afterwards transferred
to the R.A.V.C., in which he rendered valuable services until
the cessation of hostilities. He was demobilised in 1919,
and holds the 1914–15 Star, and the General Service and
Victory Medals.
1, Totteridge Street, Battersea, S.W.11.   Z3237A

MARTIN, W., Gunner, R.F.A.
Volunteering in May 1915, he finished his course of training,
and later in that year crossed to France. He took an active
part with his Battery in the engagements at Festubert, Loos,
the Somme, Vimy Ridge, Ypres, and others up to the cessation
of hostilities, and was wounded. After returning to England
he was demobilised in March 1919, and holds the 1914–15 Star,
and the General Service and Victory Medals.
89, Dorset Road, Clapham Road, S.W.8.   Z3234

MARTIN, W. E., Rifleman, King's Royal Rifle
    Corps., and Private, 1st East Surrey Regt.
Volunteering in October 1914, he crossed to the Western
Front in the following year after the conclusion of his training.
He served there until the close of the war, and took part in
in many important engagements. After the Armistice he
re-enlisted for a further period of four years, and was for a
time on duty in Ireland. He holds the 1914–15 Star, and the
General Service and Victory Medals.
15, Cronin Road, Peckham, S.E.15.   Z5455

MARTIN, W. G., Private, 23rd London Regiment.
He volunteered in August 1914, and on completing his training
crossed to France in 1915. He took an active part in many
engagements of importance up to the close of hostilities,
including those at Ypres, Loos, the Ancre, Cambrai and the
Somme, and after fighting bravely through the Retreat and
Advance of 1918, proceeded with the Army of Occupation into
Germany. After his return home he was demobilised in
January 1919, holding the 1914–15 Star, and the General
Service and Victory Medals.
73, Tasman Road, Stockwell, S.W.9.   Z3240

MARTIN, W. H., Cpl., King's Royal Rifle Corps.
He volunteered in 1914, and in the following year after finishing his training was drafted to France. He took an active
part in the Battles of Ypres, Loos, the Somme and Arras,
in the last of which he was badly wounded. After treatment
in England he was retained for home duties until his demobilisation in March 1919. He holds the 1914–15 Star, and the
General Service and Victory Medals.
8, Bond Street, S. Lambeth Road, S.W.8.   Z3241

MARTIN, W. J., Gunner, R.F.A.
He volunteered on the outbreak of hostilities, and in the
following year was sent to France, where he was in action
with his Battery in many important engagements, including
those at Hill 60, Ypres, Festubert, Loos, the Somme and Arras.
In consequence of being severely wounded he was in hospital
for a time in France and England, but on his recovery returned
to the lines, and served until hostilities ceased. He was
demobilised in April 1919, and holds the 1914–15 Star, and
the General Service and Victory Medals.
69, Dorset Road, Clapham Road, S.W.8.   Z3243

MARYAN, E., Stoker Petty Office, Torpedo Boat, "6."
A serving sailor at the outbreak of war he was posted to
Torpedo Boat 6, and served in this vessel for over three years
in the North Sea. He was afterwards transferred to the
Destroyer " Christopher," until the termination of hostilities.
In 1920 he was still in the Navy, and was stationed at Mudros.
He holds the 1914–15 Star, and the General Service and Victory
Medals.
17, Beckway Street, Walworth, S.E.17.   3246

MASH, A., Pte., Queen's (Royal West Surrey Regt.)
He joined in March 1918, and in the following July was drafted
to France. There he took part in many important engagements during the Advance, notably at Menin Road, and Ypres.
After the Armistice he proceeded to Germany with the Army
of Occupation, and was stationed on the Rhine until March
1920, when he was demobilised on his return home. He holds
the General Service and Victory Medals.
9, Foreign Street, Camberwell, S.E.5.   6037A

MASH, F., Gunner, R.F.A.
He was mobilised at the outbreak of war, and was almost
immediately drafted to France, where he took part in the
Retreat from Mons. He also fought in the Battles of the
Marne, the Aisne, Neuve Chapelle, Ypres, Festubert, Loos
and the Somme, and was invalided home suffering from shell-
shock, and deafness. After treatment he was discharged as
medically unfit for further duty in November 1917, and holds
the Mons Star, the General Service and Victory Medals.
9, Foreign Street, Camberwell, S.E.5.   6037B

MASKELL, E. H., Rflmn., King's Royal Rifle Corps.
Volunteering in October 1915, he was drafted to the Western
Front in the following year, and during his service overseas
was engaged in heavy fighting in various sectors. Amongst
the notable battles in which he took part were those on the
Somme and at Arras and Ypres. He also fought in various
engagements during the Retreat and Advance of 1918. He was
demobilised in February 1919, and holds the General Service
and Victory Medals.
85, Monkton Street, Kennington, S.E.11.   Z27361

MASKELL, M. A. (Mrs.), Special War Worker.
For four years, from 1915 to 1919, this lady was engaged at the South Metropolitan Gas Company's Works on important and dangerous duties in connection with the output of munitions. She was employed in the manufacture of the powder for gas shells, and on repairing work, and rendered valuable services. She carried out her duties with skill and efficiency, and when discharged in January 1920 was awarded a War Service Badge.
95, Kimberley Road, Peckham, S.E.15.   Z6416

MASON, A., Pte., 2nd London Regt. (Royal Fusiliers).
He joined the Territorial Force in October 1913, and was mobilised at the outbreak of war. In June 1915 was drafted to the Dardanelles and wounded in the engagement at Cape Helles. He was then sent to Egypt, and after his recovery proceeded to the Western Front, where he was twice wounded and gassed in action. He was invalided home to hospital and was subsequently discharged in February 1919. He holds the 1914-15 Star, and the General Service and Victory Medals.
7, Gray's Place, Hutton Road, Kennington, S.E.11. TZ25465

MASON, C. O. (M.M.), Air Mechanic, R.A.F.
He joined in February 1917, and after his training was drafted to France in the following July, and served with distinction in general observation duties in the Battles of the Somme, Arras, and Cambrai. In 1918 he was sent to Italy, where he was engaged on important duties which demanded a high degree of technical skill. After six weeks' service in this theatre of war, however, he returned to the Western Front and took part with his Squadron in the Advance of 1918. He was awarded the Military Medal for gallantry in action and devotion to duty, and was also decorated with the Croix de Guerre. In addition he holds the General Service and Victory Medals, and was demobilised in November 1919.
8, Latchmore Road, Battersea, S.W.11.   Z3250

MASON, C. S., Sergt., Oxfordshire and Buckinghamshire Light Infantry.
He volunteered in October 1914, and early in the following year proceeded to France. Whilst overseas he fought in the engagements at Ploegsteert Wood, Ypres, and various subsequent operations. He was invalided home with illness, and after his recovery was drafted to India, where he was engaged on important garrison duties until sent home and discharged owing to malaria in March 1918. He holds the 1914-15 Star, and the General Service and Victory Medals.
23, Conderton Road, Camberwell, S.E.5.   Z6291

MASON, F., Rifleman, King's Royal Rifle Corps.
He volunteered in August 1914, and was trained in the Middlesex Regiment, and in 1915 was discharged as medically unfit for military service. He re-enlisted, however, in the following year in the King's Royal Rifle Corps, and in 1917 was drafted to France. Whilst overseas he fought on the Somme, and at Arras, and Cambrai, and in the engagements which followed until the conclusion of hostilities. He was demobilised in March 1919, and holds the General Service and Victory Medals.
37, Portslade Road, Wandsworth Road, S.W.8.   Z3247

MASON, F. A., Bombardier, R.F.A.
He volunteered in November 1914, and after his training was drafted in the following year to the Western Front, where he served in numerous engagements, including those on the Somme, and at Arras, and Cambrai. He was in action also throughout the Retreat and Advance of 1918. He holds the 1914-15 Star, and the General Service and Victory Medals, and in 1920 was still serving in Mesopotamia.
71, Kirkwood Road, Peckham, S.E.15.   Z6202B

MASON, G. E., Private, Queen's Own (Royal West Kent Regiment).
He was mobilised at the outbreak of war, and was almost immediately drafted to France, where he took part in the Retreat from Mons, and also fought at La Bassée, Hill 60, Ypres, and Festubert. In August 1915 he gave his life for the freedom of England, and was entitled to the Mons Star, and the General Service and Victory Medals.
"Nobly striving,
He nobly fell that we might live."
1, Avondale Square, Old Kent Road, S.E.1.   Z27081

MASON, H., Private, King's Own Yorkshire Light Infantry.
He attested in December 1915, and was called up in the following year, and in June 1917 was drafted to the Western Front. Whilst overseas he served in many engagements, including that at Nieuport, where he was blown up by a shell explosion and severely injured. He was invalided home to hospital suffering from shell-shock and heart trouble, and was subsequently discharged in October 1917 as medically unfit for further duty. He holds the General Service and Victory Medals.
41, Castlemaine Road, Peckham, S.E.15.   Z6045

MASON, H. T., L/Corporal, 3rd London Regiment (Royal Fusiliers) and Tank Corps.
He volunteered in September 1914, and in August of the following year was drafted to Gallipoli. Whilst in this theatre of war he was in action at Suvla Bay, and in various subsequent engagements. He was invalided to Malta with enteric fever, and then sent to hospital in England. After his recovery he was retained on home defence until May 1917, when he rejoined his unit in France. There he fought at Ypres and Passchendaele, and was wounded at Cambrai, and invalided home. He then served at various stations on important duties until March 1919, where he was demobilised. He holds the 1914-15 Star, and the General Service and Victory Medals.
47, Mayall Road, Herne Hill, S.E.24.   Z3248

MASON, J., L/Corporal, 6th London Regt. (Rifles).
He was mobilised at the outbreak of war, and was engaged in important duties at various stations for two years. He rendered valuable services, but owing to ill-health was unable to obtain a transfer overseas, and in March 1916 was invalided out of the service.
26, Rita Road, Fentiman Road, S.W.8.   Z3249

MASON, J., Private, R.A.S.C. (Labour Corps).
Volunteering in August 1914, he was almost immediately drafted to France and served in the Retreat from Mons. He did good work in many notable engagements including those at Delville Wood, Arras, Ypres, Passchendaele, St. Julien, Bullecourt, St. Quentin, and in the subsequent operations in the Retreat and Advance of 1918. He was demobilised in February 1919, and holds the Mons Star, and the General Service and Victory Medals.
5, Distin Street, Kennington, S.E.11.   L25784

MASON, L. F., Private, Northamptonshire Regt.
He joined in 1916, and in the following year proceeded to Egypt, and took part in the British Offensive through Palestine under General Allenby. He fought in the Battles of Gaza and the Jordan, and was present at the fall of Jerusalem, and also in the later operations of the campaign until the cessation of hostilities. He holds the General Service and Victory Medals. and in 1920 was serving in India, where he was stationed at Rawal Pindi.
71, Kirkwood Road, Peckham, S.E.15.   Z6202A

MASON, P., Private, R.A.S.C. (M.T.)
He volunteered in 1915, and after his training proceeded to France in the following year. During his service on the Western Front he did good work in the motor transport section, and was present at Ypres, and on the Somme, where he was severely wounded. He was invalided home in 1916, and after his recovery was retained on home defence duties until demobilised in 1919. He holds the General Service and Victory Medals.
6, Patience Road, Battersea, S.W.11.   Z3253

MASON, T., Private, 12th Essex Regiment.
He volunteered in 1915, and in the following year was drafted to France, where he served nearly three years. During this period he took part in numerous engagements in various sectors of the Western Front, and was twice wounded in action. He was demobilised in 1919, and holds the General Service and Victory Medals.
135, Duke Road, Chiswick, W.4.   5654B

MASON, W., Cpl., Black Watch (Royal Highlanders).
He volunteered in 1915, and in the following year embarked for France. During his service on the Western Front he fought at Vimy Ridge, and on the Somme, and in many engagements in the Retreat and Advance of 1918. He holds the General Service and Victory Medals, and was demobilised in February 1919.
21, Pensbury Street, Wandsworth Road, S.W.8.   Z3254

MASON, W. R., C.S.M., R.G.A.
He volunteered in September 1914, having previously served in the Army, and acted as Sergeant-Major in the Signalling Schools at various stations. He also conducted drafts backwards and forwards to France, and rendered valuable services. He was demobilised in February 1919, and holds the General Service and Victory Medals.
100, Ferndale Road, Clapham, S.W.4.   Z3252

MASON, W. T., Driver, R.F.A.
He volunteered in April 1915, and in the same year was drafted to the Western Front. During his service in France he was in action at Ypres, Loos, the Somme, Cambrai, and various subsequent engagements in the Retreat and Advance, and was wounded and severely gassed at Bapaume in August 1918. He was demobilised in the following January, and holds the 1914-15 Star, and the General Service and Victory Medals.
45, Thorncroft Street, Wandsworth Road, S.W.8.   Z3251

MASSINGHAM, W. G., Rifleman, 21st London Regiment (1st Surrey Rifles).
He volunteered in September 1914, and until he was sent to the Western Front nearly three years later, was engaged on home duties. Whilst overseas, he fought in several important battles, and fell fighting at Cambrai on December 9th, 1917. He was entitled to the General Service and Victory Medals. "He passed out of the sight of men by the path of duty and self-sacrifice."
5, Seneca Road, Clapham, S.W.4. Z3255

MASTERS, V., Private, 13th London Regiment (Kensingtons).
He volunteered in November 1914, and almost immediately proceeding to the Western Front took part in severe fighting in many sectors. Amongst the battles in which he was engaged were those of the Somme, Arras, Ypres, Gommecourt and Givenchy. Severely wounded and suffering from shell shock, he was sent to hospital in England, and on recovery served at various stations with his unit until he was demobilised in 1919. He holds the 1914-15 Star, and the General Service and Victory Medals.
22, Phelp Street, Walworth, S.E.17. Z26634

MATHER, W., Private, 2nd East Cheshire Regt.
Volunteering at the commencement of hostilities, he was quickly drafted to the Western Front, where he saw much active service. He fought in the Battles of the Marne, La Bassée, Ypres, Loos, Albert, Vimy Ridge, the Somme, where he was wounded, and in many other important sectors. Later he was wounded a second time, and in consequence was invalided to hospital at Taplow, where he was under treatment for six months. After his recovery he returned to France, and served until the termination of hostilities. He was demobilised in December 1918, and holds the 1914 Star, and the General Service and Victory Medals.
28, Royal Road, Kennington, S.E.11. Z26559

MATHERS, W. J., Corporal, R.A.M.C.
Called up from the Reserve at the outbreak of hostilities, he was subsequently engaged on important duties at various hospitals in England. He was unsuccessful in obtaining his transfer overseas before the termination of hostilities, but nevertheless did much valuable work before being demobilised in August 1919.
105, Cronin Road, Peckham, S.E.15. Z5456

MATHEW, H. H., Private, 201st Labour Corps.
Joining in July 1916, he was sent to Salonika at the conclusion of his training, and did valuable work with his unit during operations on the Doiran front and at Monastir. After three years overseas service he returned to England and was demobilised in September 1919, and holds the General Service and Victory Medals.
14, Moat Place, Stockwell, S.W.9. Z4495

MATHIS, G., Private, 2nd East Surrey Regiment.
Joining in February 1916, he was drafted to Italy at the conclusion of his training, and did valuable work on that front with his unit until he was transferred to France in 1918. In March of that year he was taken prisoner whilst in action at Cambrai, during the German Offensive. Repatriated after the termination of hostilities, he was demobilised in October 1919, and holds the General Service and Victory Medals.
7, Dashwood Road, Wandsworth Road, S.W.8. Z3256A

MATHIS, M., Sapper, R.E.
Volunteering in November 1915, he was drafted to the Western Front in the following April. He was engaged on duties of an important nature in the forward areas, and was present at the Battles of the Somme, Ypres, Cambrai, and was wounded at Arras in November 1917. Returning to England he was invalided out of the Service in November 1918, and holds the General Service and Victory Medals.
7, Dashwood Road, Wandsworth Road, S.W.8. Z3256B

MATHISON, D. G., Private, R.A.S.C. (M.T.)
He volunteered in September 1914, and after his training saw service in France and Italy. On each of these fronts, he did much valuable work, chiefly in connection with the removal of the sick and wounded from the various forward areas. He was demobilised in March 1919, and holds the 1914-15 Star, and the General Service and Victory Medals.
17, Pitcairn Street, Wandsworth Road, S.W.8. Z3257

MATTHEWS, A., Rflmn., King's Royal Rifle Corps.
He volunteered in July 1915, and at the conclusion of his training was engaged on duties of an important nature at various stations. Owing to ill-health he was unable to secure his transfer to a theatre of war, but nevertheless rendered valuable services until he was demobilised in May 1919.
3, Dashwood Road, Wandsworth Road, S.W.8. 3260

MATTHEWS, A., Gunner, R.F.A.
He volunteered in October 1914, and early in the following year crossed to France. His service in this theatre of war lasted until the termination of hostilities, during which time he fought in many important Battles, including those of the Somme, Arras, and the Ancre. He returned to England, and was demobilised in February 1919, and has since died. He was entitled to the 1914-15 Star, and the General Service and Victory Medals.
95, Smith Street, Camberwell, S.E.5. Z3259

MATTHEWS, A. C., Driver, R.F.A.
He volunteered in August 1914, and after completing his training was drafted to the Western Front. In this theatre of war he took part in many engagements, including those at Neuve Chapelle, Loos, Vimy Ridge, the Somme, Arras and Cambrai, and the Advance of 1918. He holds the General Service and Victory Medals, and was discharged at the expiration of his period of service in August 1920.
7, Galena Road, Hammersmith, W.6. 11807B

MATTHEWS, A. H., Private, 7th London Regt.
He volunteered in May 1915, and after his training was drafted to the Western Front, where he subsequently fought in many important engagements. In March 1918, he was severely wounded and taken prisoner, but after the Armistice was repatriated in November of the same year. He holds the General Service and Victory Medals, and was demobilised in February 1919.
18, Yeldham Buildings, Hammersmith, W.6. 10436. 12809

MATTHEWS, C. E., Driver, R.E.
He volunteered in April 1915, and crossed to France in the following October. During his service overseas he did much valuable work in the capacity of driver in the forward areas, and was also in action at several engagements, notably those at Arras, La Bassée, Ypres, and the Somme, where he was so severely wounded as to necessitate his return to England in July 1917. After twelve months' hospital treatment he was invalided out of the Service in August 1918, and holds the 1914-15 Star, and the General Service and Victory Medals.
71, Cardross Street, Hammersmith, W.6. 11187A

MATTHEWS, C. D., Pte., 1/5th South Lancashire Regiment.
Joining in November 1916, he was sent to the Western Front at the conclusion of his training. Whilst overseas he was engaged in the fighting in many important sectors, including those of Ypres, Givenchy and La Bassée, where in August 1918, he was wounded. Returning to England at the termination of hostilities he was demobilised in January 1919, and holds the General Service and Victory Medals.
31, Elmington Road, Camberwell, S.E.5. Z3098

MATTHEWS, F. H., Special War Worker.
Being ineligible for service with the Colours owing to his age, he obtained work of National importance at Messrs. Fermans' Munition Factory, Willesden. He was engaged in the production of hand grenades, and in this capacity did much valuable work during the war.
7, Galena Road, Hammersmith, W.6. 11807C

MATTHEWS, F. J., Driver, R.F.A.
Volunteering early in 1915, he was drafted to the Western Front at the conclusion of his training, and subsequently fought in many notable battles, including those of the Somme, Ypres and Arras. He was demobilised in 1919, after his return to England, and holds the 1914-15 Star, and the General Service and Victory Medals.
37, Orb Street, Walworth, S.E.17. Z3261

MATTHEWS, G., Private, M.G.C.
Mobilised at the outbreak of hostilities, he crossed to France almost immediately, and served in the Retreat from Mons, and the Battles of the Marne, the Aisne (where he was wounded) and Givenchy. He gave his life for King and Country at Beaumont-Hamel on July 12th, 1916, during the Somme Offensive. He was entitled to the Mons Star, and the General Service and Victory Medals.
"A valiant soldier, with undaunted heart he breasted life's last hill."
32, Eltham Street, Walworth, S.E.17. 3262

MATTHEWS, H., Rifleman, 21st London Regiment (1st Surrey Rifles).
He volunteered in April 1915, and on the conclusion of his training was engaged with his unit on important guard duties at various stations. He did much valuable work, but was not successful in securing his transfer overseas while hostilities lasted, and on August 1917, after a serious illness which led to an operation was discharged as medically unfit for further service.
82, Commercial Road, Peckham, S.E.15. Z6292

MATTHEWS, H. W., Driver, R.E.

Volunteering in November 1914, he was drafted to the Western Front in the following year. Whilst overseas, he was engaged as a driver on the light railways, and was present at many engagements, including those at Loos, Festubert, Ypres, Vimy Ridge, and the Somme. He also served during the Retreat of 1918, but towards the end of the subsequent Advance was invalided home in consequence of an illness, and was in hospital for three months. He was discharged as physically unfit for further service in January 1919, and holds the 1914-15 Star, and the General Service and Victory Medals.

7, Galena Road, Hammersmith, W.6.   11807A

MATTHEWS, J., Private, 23rd London Regiment.

Having joined the Territorial Force in March 1911, he was mobilised on the outbreak of war, and was retained for important home duties until March 1915. He then crossed to France and took part in several of the principal engagements, notably those at Givenchy, Loos and Festubert. He returned to England, and was discharged in March 1916, at the conclusion of his period of service, and holds the 1914-15 Star, and the General Service and Victory Medals.

38, Kersley Street, Battersea, S.W.11.   Z3258

MATTHEWS, J. F., Pte., Middlesex Regiment and R.A.M.C.

Although under age for military service, he volunteered in November 1914, and at the conclusion of his training was engaged on important duties until August 1915, when he was claimed out of the Army on account of his youth. In April 1917, however, he re-joined in the R.A.M.C. and was subsequently drafted to North Russia, where he did mcuh valuable work with his unit. He was demobilised in August 1919, and holds the General Service and Victory Medals.

71, Cardross Street, Hammersmith, W.6.   T11187C

MATTHEWS, J. W., Pte., 1st East Surrey Regt.

Volunteering in January 1915, he crossed to France in the following June, and remained on that front for six months, during which time he fought in several engagements, and was wounded at Albert. He was next sent to Salonika, where he again took part in much heavy fighting, and in 1919 was drafted to Russia. He was still serving in 1920, and holds the 1914-15 Star, and the General Service and Victory Medals.

12D, Victoria Dwellings, Battersea, S.W.11.   Z3264

MATTHEWS, S., Corporal R.A.S.C.

Joining early in 1916, he was drafted to German East Africa in June of that year, and subsequently did much valuable work with his unit in connection with the transport of supplies to our troops in the forward areas. During his service however, he contracted a severe form of malaria, of which, unfortunately he died in hospital at Dar-es-Salaam, on March 8th, 1918. He was entitled to the General Service and Victory Medals.

"His memory is cherished with pride."

7, Galena Road, Hammersmith, W.6.   11807A

MATTHEWS, T. A. G., B.S.M., R.H.A.

He was in the Army at the outbreak of war, and was engaged on important training duties with his Battery until October 1917, when he was sent to France. He served with distinction at the Battles of Arras and Bullecourt, but was later invalided home through ill-health, and was discharged as medically unfit for further duty in March 1918. He holds the General Service and Victory Medals.

46, Ansdell Road, Peckham, S.E.15.   Z6482

MATTHEWS, T. G., Cpl., 12th Middlesex Regt.

He volunteered in August 1914, and served on the Western Front from October 1915, until January 1918. During this time he fought in many of the principal engagements, notably those in the Somme sector. He was then invalided home, suffering from shell-shock, and after being for some time in hospital, was invalided out of the Service in January 1919. He holds the 1914-15 Star, and the General Service and Victory Medals. 71, Cardross Street, Hammersmith, W.6.   11187B

MATTHEWS, W., Sapper, R.E.

He joined in the Essex Regiment in June 1916, and was later transferred to the R.E. At the conclusion of his training he was engaged upon duties of an important nature at various stations, and although he was unable to secure his transfer to a theatre of war before the termination of hostilities, did much valuable work. He was demobilised in March 1919.

16, Ruskin Street, Wandsworth Road, S.W.8.   Z3265

MATTHEWS, W. T., Private, Royal Fusiliers and Labour Corps.

He volunteered in January 1915, and crossed to France two months later. During his service overseas, he took an active part in many notable battles, including those of Hill 60, Ypres, Loos, Albert, Vermelles, Ploegsteert Wood, Vimy Ridge, the Somme, Beaumont-Hamel, Arras, Bullecourt and Cambrai, and also did splendid work with his unit during the Allied Retreat and Advance. On one occasion he was wounded. He was demobilised in November 1919, and holds the 1914-15 Star, and the General Service and Victory Medals.

2, Nelson Row, Clapham, S.W.4.   Z3263

MATTINGLY, E. T., Gunner, R.F.A.

He joined in May 1916, and in the following August was drafted to France. Whilst overseas he was in action at the Somme, Beaumont-Hamel, Beaucourt, Arras, Vimy Ridge, Bullecourt and Ypres, where he was severely gassed. He was invalided home, and after about eight months' medical treatment was sent to the depôt at Woolwich, when he remained until discharged as physically unfit for further military duty in January 1919. He holds the General Service and Victory Medals.

51, Barlow Street, Walworth, S.E.17.   Z3266

MATTOCKS, J. W. H., Gunner, R.F.A.

He volunteered in December 1914, and in the following September was drafted to the Western Front, where he served until December of the same year. He then sailed for Salonika, and in this theatre of war did excellent work as a Gunner in the Battles near Monastir, and on the Vardar front, and the engagements which followed until the cessation of hostilities. He was demobilised in January 1919, after his return to England, and holds the 1914-15 Star, and the General Service and Victory Medals.

163, Lavender Road, Battersea, S.W.11.   Z3267

MAULE, H. A. G., 1st Class Petty Officer, Merchant Service, H.M.S. "Iddersley."

He joined in February 1918, and until the close of the war saw much service in the "Iddersley." Whilst in this ship he sailed with cargoes of rations and grain for the horses to and from Europe, Africa, and the Argentine. His vessel frequently passed through mine infested areas, and was in constant danger of being sunk by enemy submarines. He was demobilised in March 1919, and holds the General Service and Mercantile Marine War Medals.

34, Broadhinton Road, Clapham, S.W.4.   Z3269

MAULE, R. W. J., Driver, R.A.S.C. (M.T.)

He volunteered in February 1915, and in the following month was drafted to France. Whilst overseas he was engaged on important motor transport duties in the Somme, Arras, Vimy Ridge, and Ypres areas, and was severely wounded near Arras, when conveying ammunition and stores to the front lines. He was invalided home in consequence, and was discharged in September 1917, as medically unfit for further duty. He holds the 1914-15 Star, and the General Service and Victory Medals.

11, Cleveland Street, Camberwell, S.E.5.   Z3268

MAURICE, T. F., 2nd Lieut., Royal Sussex Regt.

He volunteered in May 1915, and in the same year was drafted to France. During his service overseas he fought at Ypres and Vimy Ridge and was wounded and invalided home to hospital. After his recovery he rejoined his unit in France, and was in action on the Somme and Ancre fronts, and in the engagements which followed until the conclusion of hostilities. He was demobilised in January 1919, and holds the 1914-15 Star, and the General Service and Victory Medals.

23, Tasman Road, Landor Road, S.W.9.   Z3270

MAXWELL, A. E., Private, East Surrey Regiment.

He volunteered in February 1915, and later in the year after completing his training was drafted to France, where he took an active part in many engagements of great importance until the close of hostilities, particularly those on the Somme front. During his service overseas he was gassed on one occasion. He returned to England, and was demobilised in 1919, and holds the 1914-15 Star, and the General Service and Victory Medals.

26, Henshaw Street, Walworth, S.E.17.   Z1108B

MAY, A. E. (M.M.), L/Corporal, King's Royal Rifle Corps and M.G.C.

He volunteered in April 1915, and in the following month was sent to France, where he fought at Hill 60, Hooge and Ypres, and advanced to Arras to relieve the French. He afterwards was in the severe fighting at the Somme, and again at Arras, Grandcourt and Messines Ridge. During his service he was twice wounded and gassed, and was invalided home in August, 1917. He was awarded the Military Medal for distinguished gallantry and devotion to duty on the Field, and also holds the 1914-15 Star, and the General Service and Victory Medals. He was discharged as physically unfit for further military duty in December 1917.

43, Green Lane, Battersea, S.W.11.   3273B

MAY, A. K., Private, M.G.C.

He joined in August 1917, and in February of the following year was drafted to France, where he was engaged in the severe fighting on the Somme, and was reported killed in action at the Battle of St. Quentin on March 26th, 1918. He had in reality been taken prisoner at that time, but afterwards died. He was entitled to the General Service and Victory Medals.

"Whilst we remember, the Sacrifice is not in vain."

46, Chantrey Road, Stockwell, S.W.9.   Z3272A

MAY, C. A. (Mrs.), Special War Worker.

For nearly three years during the war this lady was engaged on important work for the Shell Marketing Company, making petrol containers for aeroplanes. She afterwards worked at the South Western Saw Mills, and made ammunition boxes for shells and cartridges. She served there for nearly a year until the Armistice, and carried out all her exacting duties with great efficiency.

43, Green Lane, Battersea, S.W.11.   Z3273A

MAY, F. G., Rflmn., 11th London Regt. (Rifles).

He volunteered in December 1915, and proceeded to France in the following February. During his service on the Western Front he was engaged in the first line Regimental Transport with his unit, and was in action at Arras, Ypres, and Bullecourt. He was disabled by a severe kick from a mule, and after being invalided home was discharged as medically unfit for further duty in December 1917. He holds the General Service and Victory Medals.

30, Newby Street, Clapham, S.W.8.   Z1944A

MAY, F. J., Private, 3rd East Surrey Regt.

He volunteered at the outbreak of hostilities, and in February of the following year was drafted to France. He gave his life for the freedom of England in his first engagement, at the Battle of Neuve Chapelle on March 16th, 1915, after only about a month's service overseas, and was buried at Kemmel Chateau Military Cemetery. He was entitled to the 1914-15 Star, and the General Service and Victory Medals.

" Courage, bright hopes, and myriad dreams splendidly given."

46, Chantrey Road, Stockwell, S.W.9.   Z3272B

MAY, G., Corporal, R.E.

He volunteered in September 1915, and in the following month was drafted to France. During his service on the Western Front he was engaged on important duties in connection with the operations until fighting ceased, and was frequently in the forward areas, notably on the Somme, Ypres, Arras and Cambrai fronts. He was demobilised in 1919, and holds the 1914-15 Star, and the General Service and Victory Medals.

12, Thorncroft Street, Wandsworth Road, S.W.8.   Z3275

MAY, G., Bombardier, Royal Horse Artillery.

He volunteered in March 1915, and in the same year proceeded to France, where he took part in many important engagements, including those at Loos, the Somme, Arras and Cambrai, and various subsequent operations throughout the Retreat and Advance of 1918. He holds the 1914-15 Star, and the General Service and Victory Medals, and in 1920 was still serving.

1, Bognor Street, Battersea Park Road, S.W.8.   Z1617B

MAY, H., Private, East Surrey Regiment and The Buffs (East Kent Regiment).

He volunteered at the outbreak of war at the age of only sixteen, and after serving at various home stations on important duties was drafted to France in December 1917. Whilst overseas he fought in the second Battles of the Somme, and at the Marne, Amiens and Bapaume. He died gloriously on the field of battle at Havrincourt on September 18th, 1918, and was entitled to the General Service and Victory Medals.

" Honour to the immortal dead, who gave their youth that the world might grow old in peace."

29, Bagshot Street, Walworth, S.E.17.   Z3271

MAY, H. G., Private, Royal Fusiliers.

He joined in 1916, and on the completion of his training was drafted to France. Whilst overseas he served in the Battles of the Somme, Ypres, and Cambrai and in various later engagements. He was invalided home with a seriously poisoned hand, and on his recovery was transferred to the Labour Corps and retained on important duties at several home stations. He was demobilised in November 1919, and holds the General Service and Victory Medals.

15, Montefiore Street, Wandsworth Road, S.W.8.   Z3277

MAY, J. P., Engine Room Artificer, R.N. H.M.S. "Heracles."

He was called up from the Reserve in August 1914, and was in H.M.S. " Intrepid " at the outbreak of war. After much valuable service in the North Sea and the English Channel he was transferred to another vessel and was engaged on important duties for three years in the Far Eastern waters, and the Mediterranean. He returned home after the cessation of hostilities, and was transferred to H.M.S. " Heracles " in which he was still serving in 1920. He holds the 1914-15 Star, and the General Service and Victory Medals.

25, Corunna Road, New Road, S.W.8.   Z3276

MAY, R. F., Rifleman, 18th London Regt. (London Irish Rifles).

He volunteered in May 1915, and in the same year was drafted to France. During his service on the Western Front he fought at Ypres, Loos, the Somme, where he was wounded, Arras and Cambrai, and in the Retreat and Advance of 1918. He was at home on leave when the Armistice was signed, and was demobilised in the following month. He holds the 1914-15 Star, and the General Service and Victory Medals.

1, Bognor Street, Battersea Park Road, S.W.8.   Z1617C

MAY, W. C., Saddler, R.F.A.

He volunteered in November 1915, and in the following January was sent to Egypt, where he served for six months and was in action in several minor engagements. In July 1916, he was drafted to the Western Front, and fought in the Battles of the Somme, Albert, and many subsequent operations in the 1918 Offensive. He entered Mons on Armistice day, and was demobilised in the following January, holding the General Service and Victory Medals.

11, Amies Street, Battersea, S.W.11.   Z3274

MAYBANK, D., Sergt., King's Royal Rifle Corps.

He was mobilised at the outbreak of war, and being almost immediately drafted to France took part in the Retreat from Mons. He also served at the Battles of the Marne, the Aisne, Ypres, the Somme, and in many subsequent engagements. He gave his life for King and Country on the Cambrai front in the Advance of 1918, and was entitled to the Mons Star, and the General Service and Victory Medals.

" A valiant soldier, with undaunted heart he breasted life's last hill."

29, Tasman Road, Landor Road, S.W.9.   Z3278

MAYLE, C. S., Private, 7th London Regiment.

He had previously enlisted in the Territorials in March 1908, and at the outbreak of war volunteered for overseas service. He was retained, however, for important duties as an Army bootmaker, and carried out his arduous work single-handed. After falling seriously ill he was discharged as medically unfit for further duty in April 1915.

21, Cator Street, Peckham, S.E.15.   Z3489

MAYLE, J., Pte., 8th Somerset Light Infantry.

He joined in May 1916, and in the following year sailed for India where he was engaged until 1919 on many important duties. He was in action in several skirmishes with the hill tribes on the Frontier, and contracted malaria whilst overseas. He returned home and was demobilised in 1919, and holds the India General Service Medal (with clasp, Afghanistan N.W. Frontier, 1919), and the General Service and Victory Medals.

47, Lavender Road, Battersea, S.W.11.   Z3279

MAYNARD, L., Gunner, R.F.A.

He volunteered in July 1915, and was drafted to France in the following year. During his service on the Western Front he did good work as a Gunner at St. Eloi, Vimy Ridge, the Ancre, Messines, Ypres, Passchendaele, the second Battle of the Somme, and in many subsequent operations until the conclusion of hostilities. He was demobilised in January 1919, and holds the General Service and Victory Medals.

23, Wivenhoe Road, Peckham, S.E.15.   Z6205

MAYNE, A. Private, 20th London Regiment.

He volunteered in January 1915, having previously served from 1886 until 1903 in the 11th Hussars. He did excellent service at the Royal Arsenal, Woolwich, and at various other stations for over three years, but owing to physical weakness was not drafted overseas, and was invalided out of the Army in March 1918.

97, Flaxman Road, Camberwell, S.E.5.   Z6206

MAYNE, H. W., Rifleman, 9th London Regiment (Queen Victoria's Rifles).

He joined in June 1916, and in the following September was drafted overseas. During his service in France he fought in the engagements at Albert, the Somme, Arras and Lens. He died gloriously on the Field of Battle at Polygon Wood on September 26th, 1917, and was entitled to the General Service and Victory Medals.

" He died the noblest death a man may die, Fighting for God, and right and liberty."

91, Darwin Street, Walworth, S.E.17.   Z3208

MAYNE, J., Air Mechanic, R.A.F.

After having served for about a year in the Special Constabulary he joined the Royal Air Force in 1918, and was engaged as an air mechanic at various stations, including Dublin. His work demanded a high degree of technical skill, and he rendered valuable services, but was not successful in securing his transfer overseas before hostilities ceased. He was demobilised in January 1919.

161, Abbey Street, Bermondsey, S.E.1.   Z27413

MAYO, E. J., Private, R.A.M.C.

He volunteered in September 1914, and in the following year was drafted to France. During his service overseas he was engaged on important duties with his Corps and was present at the Battles of Ypres, Loos, Vimy Ridge, the Somme and Passchendaele. He was wounded and sent to hospital in France, and on his recovery proceeded to Italy, where he served in the operations on the Piave, until the conclusion of hostilities. He holds the 1914-15 Star, and the General Service and Victory Medals, and was demobilised after his return to England in March 1919.

68, Brayards Road, Peckham, S.E.15.   Z5457

MAYO, F., Driver, R.F.A.

He volunteered in April 1915, and in the following year was drafted to France. Whilst overseas he did excellent work as a Driver for the Royal Field Artillery in numerous important engagements, including those at Ypres, Arras, Bullecourt, Messines, Lens, Cambrai, St. Quentin, Bapaume, Combles, and in others in the Retreat and Advance of 1918. He was demobilised in June 1919, and holds the General Service and Victory Medals.

6, Tindal Street, North Brixton, S.W.9.   Z5116B

MAYO, H., Driver, R.F.A.

He volunteered in June 1915, and in the following year was drafted to France. During his service on the Western Front he did excellent work as a Driver at Albert, Ploegsteert Wood, Beaumont-Hamel, Ypres, Passchendaele, Messines, Cambrai, and various subsequent engagements in the Retreat and Advance of 1918. After the Armistice he was engaged on important clerical duties as Battery Clerk near Mons, and was demobilised in July 1919. He holds the General Service and Victory Medals.

6, Tindal Street, North Brixton, S.W.9.   Z5116A

MAYS, C., Pioneer, R.E. (Labour Battalion).

He volunteered in August 1915, at the age of fifty-six, and in the same month proceeded to France. There he was engaged on important duties in connection with the operations and was frequently in the forward areas, notably at Ypres and the Somme. During his service he became seriously ill, and after being sent home was invalided out of the Army in October 1916. He holds the 1914-15 Star, and the General Service and Victory Medals.

39, Urswicke Road, Battersea, S.W.11.   Z3281B

MAYS, J., Gunner, R.F.A.

A serving soldier, he was stationed in India at the outbreak of war, and proceeding to France in December 1914, was in action at Ypres. In December 1915 he was drafted to Salonika, where he took part in the operations on the Doiran and other Balkan fronts. He was sent home and discharged owing to ill-health in April 1919, and holds the 1914-15 Star, and the General Service and Victory Medals.

39, Urswicke Road, Battersea, S.W.11.   Z3281C

MAYS, W., Bombardier, R.H.A.

A serving soldier since 1912, he was in India at the outbreak of war, and in December 1914 came over to the Western Front. Whilst in France he fought at Ypres, Loos, the Somme and Arras, and in many subsequent engagements in the Retreat and Advance of 1918. In the following year he returned to India, where in 1920 he was still serving. He holds the 1914-15 Star, and the General Service and Victory Medals.

39, Urswicke Road, Battersea, S.W.11.   Z3281A

MEACOCK, F. W., Driver, R.A.S.C. (M.T.)

He joined in February 1916, and in the following month was drafted to France. Whilst overseas he was engaged with the Motor Transport section in conveying rations and war materials up to the lines, and returning with the wounded to the Base. He served in many sectors of the Western Front, including those of the Somme, Vimy Ridge, Arras and Cambrai, and after the Armistice proceeded to Germany with the Army of Occupation, remaining until his demobilisation in October 1919. He holds the General Service and Victory Medals.

22, Vaughan Road, Camberwell, S.E.5.   Z6410

MEAD, A. J., Sapper, R.E. (R.O.D.)

He joined in June 1917, and was sent to France in the following year, and took part in numerous engagements, including those on the Somme and at Arras, Vimy Ridge and Cambrai. He later served in the Retreat and Advance of 1918, and returning to England after the cessation of hostilities was demobilised in December 1919, and holds the General Service and Victory Medals.

64, Southville, Wandsworth Road, S.W.8.   Z3284B

MEAD, A. V., Pte., Royal Fusiliers and Labour Corps.

He joined in April 1917, and having completed his training proceeded to France in the following year. He was present at several important engagements, including those on the Somme, and at Ypres and Cambrai, and after the Armistice served with the Army of Occupation in Germany until he was demobilised in October 1919. He holds the General Service and Victory Medals.

117, Grange Road, Bermondsey, S.E.1.   Z27165

MEAD, H., Pte., Queen's (Royal West Surrey Regt).

He volunteered in August 1914, and shortly afterwards was sent to the Western Front, where he took part in numerous engagements. He was unfortunately killed in action on September 28th, 1918, and was entitled to the 1914 Star, and the General Service and Victory Medals.

"Whilst we remember the Sacrifice is not in vain."

5, Prairie Street, Battersea Park, S.W.8.   Z3283

MEAD, H. J. (D.C.M.), Sergt., R.E.

He volunteered in September 1914, and was engaged on Instructional duties until June 1916, when he was sent to France, where he was in action at St. Eloi. He later in the same year proceeded to Salonika, and took part in the Advance on the Doiran. In 1917 he was transferred to Egypt, and thence to Palestine, and served at Beersheba, and in other engagements leading up to the capture of Jerusalem. He was awarded the Distinguished Conduct Medal at Jerusalem for conspicuous bravery in taking out a party to repair a bridge under heavy fire. He also holds the General Service and Victory Medals, and was demobilised in May 1919.

1, Shellwood Road, Battersea, S.W.11.   Z3282

MEAD, N., Air Mechanic, R.A.F.

He joined in 1918, and after his training served on important duties with his Squadron. He was engaged in various parts of Scotland, including Scapa Flow, as an observer and rendered valuable services, but was not successful in obtaining his transfer overseas before the cessation of hostilities. He was demobilised in 1919.

45, Goldsboro Road, Wandsworth Road, S.W.8.   Z3291

MEADER, G. A., Driver, R.F.A.

He volunteered in June 1915, and in the following year was sent to France, where he took part in numerous engagements, including those on the Somme, and at Ypres. He also served in the Retreat and Advance of 1918. He was demobilised in May 1919, and holds the General Service and Victory Medals.

43, Brisbane Street, Camberwell, S.E.5.   Z3099A

MEADER, T. W., Private, Duke of Cornwall's Light Infantry.

Volunteering in August 1914, he was sent to France in February of the following year. After eleven days' fighting he was unfortunately killed in action on February 15th, 1915, and was entitled to the 1914-15 Star, and the General Service and Victory Medals.

"His life for his Country."

43, Brisbane Street, Camberwell, S.E.5.   Z3099B

MEADOWS, W., Drummer, Rifle Brigade.

He joined in July 1917, and in the same year was drafted to India, where he was engaged at various stations on the Frontier on important duties with his unit. He returned home in 1919 and was demobilised in December of that year, and holds the General Service and Victory Medals.

28, D'Eynsford Road, Camberwell, S.E.5.   Z3292

MEADS, M. H., Private, Duke of Cornwall's Light Infantry.

He was serving at the outbreak of war, and was shortly afterwards sent to France, where he was in action at Armentières, Ypres and St. Eloi. In 1915 he was transferred to Salonika, and served on the Doiran front, and was wounded. He was invalided home and was discharged in March 1919, as medically unfit for further service, and holds the 1914-15 Star, and the General Service and Victory Medals.

291, Mayall Road, Herne Hill, S.E.24.   Z4009A

MEALAND, T. (M.C.), 2nd Lieut., 2nd Suffolk Regt.

He volunteered in February 1915, and in the same year was sent to the Western Front, where he took part with distinction in many important engagements and was severely wounded at Arras. On his recovery he served throughout the Retreat and the Advance of 1918, and was again wounded. He won the Military Cross for conspicuous gallantry during an attack, and for displaying marked courage and devotion to duty throughout all operations. He also holds the 1914-15 Star, and the General Service and Victory Medals, and was discharged as medically unfit for further military duty in August 1919.

8, Jerome Place, Walworth, S.E.17.   Z26440

MEALING, G. E., L/Corporal, Royal Scots Fusiliers.

He was mobilised in August 1914, and was immediately afterwards sent to France, where he took part in the severe fighting during the Retreat from Mons and was taken prisoner in September 1914. On his release he returned home and was demobilised in March 1919, and holds the Mons Star, and the General Service and Victory Medals.

47, Aylesbury Road, Walworth, S.E.17.   Z3293

MEARS, J. H., Private, Royal Berkshire Regt.

He was mobilised in August 1914, and was shortly afterwards sent to France, and was in action at Mons and La Bassée. He fell fighting at Zonnebeke on October 26th, 1914, and was entitled to the Mons Star, and the General Service and Victory Medals.

"Great deeds cannot die."

30, Dalyell Road, Stockwell, S.W.   Z3294

MEARS, W. G. (D.C.M.), "King's Sergt.," 13th Middlesex Regiment.

He volunteered in February 1915, and in the same year was drafted to the Western Front, where he took part in numerous engagements, including those at Loos, Ypres and Cambrai, and served in the Retreat and Advance of 1918. He was promoted Sergeant and awarded the Distinguished Conduct Medal for conspicuous gallantry in the Field, and also holds the 1914-15 Star, and the General Service and Victory Medals. He was demobilised in February 1919.

30, Myatt Road, Stockwell, S.W.9.   Z5117

MEDDEMEN, F., Private, Duke of Cornwall's Light Infantry and Tank Corps.

He was mobilised in August 1914, and was immediately sent to France, and was in action at Mons, the Marne, the Aisne, Albert, Ypres, and in many other engagements, and was wounded and invalided home. On his recovery he returned to France, and took part in the fighting at Delville Wood, where he was again wounded. He was sent to hospital in England, and was later transferred to the Tank Corps. He was demobilised in February 1919, and holds the Mons Star, and the General Service and Victory Medals.

8, Sedan Street, Walworth, S.E.17.   Z3295

MEDLEY, A. H., Pte., 2nd East Lancashire Regt.

He was serving at the outbreak of war and shortly afterwards was sent to France, where he was in action during the Retreat from Mons, and at Ypres and Loos. In September 1915, he proceeded to Mesopotamia, and served at Kut and in the capture of Baghdad, and was wounded. He was later drafted to Salonika, where he remained until after the cessation of hostilities, when he returned to England and was transferred to the Army Reserve in October 1920. He holds the Mons Star, and the General Service and Victory Medals.

18, Sandover Road, Camberwell, S.E.5.   Z5458

MEDLYCOTT, E. G., Private, 22nd London Regt. (Queen's).

He volunteered in June 1915, and after his training was drafted to the Eastern Front, where he took an active part as a Lewis gunner in important engagements during the Balkan campaign. He returned home after the cessation of hostilities, and was demobilised in March 1919, holding the General Service and Victory Medals.

264, Lynton Road, Bermondsey, S.E.1.   Z26351

MEE, B. F., Sergt., R.A.S.C. (M.T.)

Joining in June 1916, he went through his course of training, and in 1917 was drafted to Egypt. He afterwards did excellent service in the transport of supplies during the Palestine campaign, and was present at Beersheba, Gaza, Jerusalem, the Jordan and Aleppo. In 1920 he was still in the Army, stationed at Cairo, and holds the General Service and Victory Medals.   23, Russell Grove, Vassall Road, S.W.9.   Z5269A

MEE, O., Private, R.A.S.C. (M.T.)

Volunteering in March 1915, he proceeded in the same year to France, and rendered valuable services in the transport of ammunition and supplies of all kinds to many fields of action until the cessation of hostilities, including Ypres, Neuve Chapelle, the Somme, Albert, Arras, Bullecourt, Armentières, St. Quentin, Amiens and Bapaume. He was demobilised in May 1920, after his return to England, and holds the 1914-15 Star, and the General Service and Victory Medals.

6, Edithna Street, Landor Road, Stockwell, S.W.9.   Z3297

MEE, W. H., Air Mechanic, R.A.F.

He joined in June 1918, when below military age, and on the conclusion of his training was engaged on important duties with his Squadron as a rigger and repairer. He was not successful in securing his transfer overseas before hostilities ceased, but rendered valuable coast defence services until his demobilisation in 1919.

23, Russell Grove, Brixton, S.W.9.   Z5269B

MEECH, W. S., Private, 9th Royal Highlanders (Black Watch).

He volunteered in May 1915, and later in that year on the conclusion of his training was sent to the Western Front. He played a gallant part in many engagements of importance during his short service overseas, and was killed in action near Loos on February 6th, 1916. He was entitled to the General Service and Victory Medals.

"His life for his Country, his Soul to God."

17, Pulross Road, Stockwell, S.W.9.   Z3298

MEEK, G. A., C.Q.M.S., R.A.S.C. (M.T.)

After volunteering in November 1914, he was retained on important duties with his unit until March 1916, when he crossed to France. He remained there until 1920, and did excellent service in various sectors, superintending the distribution and supply of rations to the troops. For his marked efficiency he was promoted Sergeant while still under eighteen and Quarter-Master-Sergeant in the following year. He was demobilised in March 1920, and holds the General Service and Victory Medals.

130, Lollard Street, Kennington, S.E.11.   Z2152

MEEKING, J. A. A., Guardsman, 2nd Grenadier Guards.

He joined in March 1917, at the age of eighteen, and in the following December proceeded to the Western Front. While in this seat of war he took part in numerous important engagements, especially those at the Somme, the Marne, and Amiens, where on August 27th, 1918, he was unfortunately killed. He was entitled to the General Service and Victory Medals.

"A costly Sacrifice upon the altar of freedom."

19, Mann Street, Walworth, S.E.17.   Z27128

MELCHIOR, G., Boy, R.N., H.M.S. "Impregnable."

He volunteered in January 1917, at the age of sixteen, and was engaged for some time on his training ship at Devonport. His health, however, proved unequal to the strain of Naval service and he was consequently discharged in the following September.

7, Eastcote Street, Stockwell Green, S.W.9.   Z3299

MELLARS, G. W., Gunner, R.F.A.

After frequent attempts to join the Army he was accepted for service in November 1916, and on the conclusion of his training was drafted to France in 1917. While overseas he took an active part with his Battery in many notable engagements, including those at Ypres, the Somme, and the Retreat and Advance of 1918. In consequence of being badly gassed he was invalided home, and after considerable hospital treatment was discharged in June 1919, as unfit for further service. He holds the General Service and Victory Medals.

23, Inworth Street, Battersea, S.W.11.   Z3300

MELLING, T. P., Staff-Sergt., Bedfordshire Regt.

He joined in 1918, and afterwards was retained on important duties with his unit. He was not successful in securing his transfer overseas before hostilities ceased, but after the Armistice proceeded to Germany, and did good service at Cologne until he returned to England to be demobilised in March 1920.   33, Brook Street, Kennington, S.E.11.   Z26915

MELTON, R., Private, R.A.S.C. and 1st Hertfordshire Regiment.

He volunteered in August 1914, and after the completion of his training was drafted to France, where he served at Ypres, Festubert, Loos, the Somme, and in many other engagements. Whilst in France he was badly gassed and sent to hospital, but after his recovery rejoined his unit, and was transferred to Italy for about six months. He then returned to France, and stayed there until demobilised in January 1919. He holds the 1914 Star, and the General Service and Victory Medals.

19, Suffield Road, Walworth, S.E.17.   Z26137

MELTON, W. E., Rifleman, 21st London Regiment (1st Surrey Rifles).

He volunteered in May 1915, and after his training was drafted in 1916 to France, where he served on the Somme front, and at Ypres, Arras, Albert, La Bassée, and in the Retreat and Advance of 1918. He was demobilised in January 1919 after his return home, and holds the General Service and Victory Medals.

5, Farnham Royal, Kennington, S.E.11.   Z25883

MENDHAM, L. F., Private, R.A.S.C.

He volunteered in November 1915, and in June of the following year was sent to France, where he did valuable transport work at Le Havre, and other places until the cessation of hostilities. He returned home in December 1918, owing to illness, and was demobilised in the following May. He holds the General Service and Victory Medals.

47, East Surrey Grove, Peckham, S.E.15.   Z5264

MENNISS, W., Private, M.G.C.

He volunteered in November 1914, and after his training was sent to the Western Front in May of the following year. He was in action in the Ypres and Loos sectors and throughout the great Offensive on the Somme in 1916, and afterwards took part in the general Retreat and Advance of 1918. Being severely wounded he was invalided home, and afterwards was demobilised in January 1919. He holds the 1914-15 Star, and the General Service and Victory Medals.

34, Willow Street, Bermondsey, S.E.1.   Z25940

MERCHANT, W. J., Gunner, R.G.A.

After volunteering in July 1915, he went through his course of training and in the following January crossed to France. While overseas he did valuable work with his Battery at Albert, Vermelles, Vimy Ridge, the Somme, Beaumont-Hamel, Arras, Bullecourt, Ypres, Lens, Cambrai, and the chief engagements of the Retreat and Advance of 1918. On one occasion he was much burnt in an accident which occurred while unloading ammunition. He was demobilised in April 1919, and holds the General Service and Victory Medals.

120, Ferndale Road, Clapham, S.W.4.   Z3302

MEREDITH, H., Private, R.A.M.C.

He volunteered in August 1914, and in the same year was drafted to Egypt, and was stationed in the 17th General Hospital at Alexandria on important duties. He was invalided home owing to ill-health, and after six months in hospital died from tuberculosis on December 23rd, 1916. He was entitled to the 1914 Star, and the General Service and Victory Medals.
" A costly sacrifice upon the altar of freedom."
24, Harder's Road, Peckham, S.E.15. Z6294

MERRELL, W. A., Cpl., 1st Northamptonshire Regt.

He volunteered in August 1914, and in June of the following year proceeded to the Western Front. While overseas he took a prominent part in many important engagements, including those at Loos, Albert, Vimy Ridge, the Somme, Messines, Ypres, Cambrai, and in the Retreat and Advance of 1918. He was wounded on three occasions, but after treatment in France returned to his Regiment. He was demobilised in January 1919, and holds the 1914-15 Star, and the General Service and Victory Medals.
5, Kimberley Road, Stockwell, S.W.9. Z3303

MERRION, H. A., Pte., Northumberland Fusiliers.

After volunteering in October 1915, in the Royal West Surrey Regiment he completed his training, and was engaged on important defence duties on the Kentish Coast. He was then transferred to the Northumberland Fusiliers, and sent to Ireland in March 1917, where he assisted in the maintainance of law and order during the riots in the following July. He was not successful in securing his transfer to a foreign front, but rendered valuable service until demobilised in July 1919.
23, Gideon Road, Battersea, S.W.11. Z3304

MERRIOTT, C. J., Private, R.A.M.C.

He was called up from the Reserve on the outbreak of hostilities and was immediately drafted to France. He rendered valuable service with the 5th Field Ambulance at Mons, Ypres, the Somme, and several other engagements, including the Retreat and Advance of 1918, until hostilities ceased. He afterwards went into Germany with the Army of Occupation. On his return home he was demobilised in June 1919, and holds the Mons Star, and the General Service and Victory Medals.
57, Heath Road, Wandsworth Road, S.W.8. Z1970B

MERRITT, A. W., L/Cpl., 7th West Yorkshire Regt.

He joined in September 1916, and after the completion of his course of training was drafted to the Western Front in October 1917. He afterwards saw much service in the Bapaume, Arras, and Cambrai Sectors at the close of 1917, and later was in action at Monchy, Oppy Wood, and Roclincourt. After being absent from the line for some weeks, owing to wounds received at Bucquoy, he rejoined his unit on the Somme front and, in the Advance of the Allies, did gallant service at Ypres and Arras. After the Armistice he was stationed at Douai until his return to England for demobilisation in February 1919. He holds the General Service and Victory Medals.
73, Langton Road, Vassall Road, S.W.9. Z5118

MERRITT, C. J., Private, Welch Regiment.

Joining in 1916 he proceeded to France in 1917. He saw much service on the Arras, Ypres, and Somme Fronts, and fought at Cambrai, and right through the Retreat and Advance of 1918, until the cessation of hostilities. After the Armistice he was sent into Germany with the Army of Occupation, and after much valuable service there returned to England for demobilisation in 1919. He holds the General Service and Victory Medals.
17, Sondes Street, Walworth, S.E.17. 26636

MERRY, F., Private, 23rd London Regiment.

He volunteered at the outbreak of war, and proceeding to France in the following August fought in the Battle of Loos, where he was severely gassed. He was invalided home to hospital where he remained under medical treatment until March 1916, when he was transferred to the Royal Air Force as millwright, and stationed in various places until May 1919. He was then demobilised and holds the 1914-15 Star, and the General Service and Victory Medals.
254, Sumner Road, Peckham, S.E.15. Z6295

MERRYWEATHER, H. C., Cpl., 4th Royal Sussex Regiment.

He volunteered in December 1914, and crossing to France in the following May, was in action until September 1915, when he was severely wounded at Loos. After his recovery he was drafted to Egypt, and later served in the Palestine campaign, during which he fought in the Battles of Gaza, and also took part in the capture of Jerusalem and Jericho. In September 1918, he returned to the Western Front, where he did good work with his unit in the concluding operations of the war, and afterwards advanced into Germany with the Army of Occupation. Nine months later he returned to England, and in September 1919 was demobilised, holding the 1914-15 Star, and the General Service and Victory Medals.
9, Park Grove, Battersea, S.W.11. Z3305

MESSENBIRD, E. A., L/Corporal, 10th Queen's (Royal West Surrey Regiment).

Volunteering in November 1915, he crossed to France in May 1916, and subsequently fought in the Battles of the Somme, Messines, and Passchendaele. In November 1917, he was transferred to Italy, where he did valuable work with his unit during the operations on the Piave. Returning to the Western Front in March 1918, he served in the Retreat and Advance of that year, at the conclusion of which he was sent with the Army of Occupation to Germany. He was demobilised in May 1919, and holds the General Service and Victory Medals.
87, Sabine Road, Battersea, S.W.11. Z3306

MESSENGER, C. R. J., Rifleman, King's Royal Rifle Corps.

He volunteered in September 1914, and immediately upon completing his training was drafted to the Western Front. During his service in this theatre of war he fought in the Battles of Ypres, St. Eloi, and Armentières, where he was so severely wounded, as to necessitate his return to England. After his recovery he was re-drafted to France and took part in engagements at Arras and the Somme, where he was again wounded. Invalided home, he was in hospital for nine months, and in May 1917, was discharged as physically unfit for further service. He holds the 1914-15 Star, and the General Service and Victory Medals.
2, Shillington Street, Battersea, S.W.11. Z3307

MESSENGER, E., Private, Oxfordshire and Buckinghamshire Light Infantry.

He volunteered in May 1915, and at the conclusion of his training proceeded to Mesopotamia, where he served for upwards of three years. During this period he did most valuable work with his unit in various sectors of that Front, including those at Kut, Baghdad, and Ramadieh. He holds the 1914-15 Star, and the General Service and Victory Medals, and was demobilised in January 1919, on his return to England.
1, Walton Terrace, South Lambeth, S.W.8. Z27530

MEASURE, A., L/Corporal, 4th Middlesex Regiment.

Called from the Reserve at the outbreak of war, he immediately crossed to France, and on August 23rd, 1914, was severely wounded and taken prisoner during the Retreat from Mons. In June 1915, however, he was repatriated in an exchange of prisoners, and shortly afterwards was invalided out of the Service. He holds the Mons Star, and the General Service and Victory Medals.
19, Tidemore Street, Battersea Park Road, S.W.8. Z3308

METCALFE, R., Sergt., Cameronians (Scottish Rifles)`

Called from the Reserve at the outbreak of hostilities, he was at once drafted to France and took part in the Retreat from Mons. He also fought in many of the engagements which followed, and died gloriously on the Field of Battle on January 20th, 1916. Prior to the recent war, he had served in the Army for ten years, and had been promoted to the rank of Sergeant for his efficient work. He was entitled to the Mons Star, and the General Service and Victory Medals.
" A valiant soldier, with undaunted heart he breasted Life's last hill."
42, Cooper's Road, Old Kent Road, Bermondsey, S.E.1.
Z27153

METSON, T. H., Gunner, R.F.A.

He volunteered in February 1915, and in the same year was drafted to the Dardanelles, where he took part in the Landing at Suvla Bay, and the engagements which ensued. After the Evacuation of the Peninsula, he was transferred to Mesopotamia, where he fought in engagements at Kut, Baghdad, and Amara. Later he was drafted to France, and did much valuable work with his Battery in the concluding operations of the war. He was demobilised in February 1919, and holds the 1914-15 Star, and the General Service and Victory Medals.
60, Clayton Road, Peckham, S.E.15. Z6043

METTERNICH, W., L/Sergt., R.G.A.

A serving soldier since May 1912, he was sent to India at the outbreak of war, and thence to the Western Front in 1915. During his service in France he was in action at Neuve Chapelle, Loos, Vimy Ridge, the Somme, Arras, Beaumont-Hamel, and Ypres, where he was severely wounded in December 1917. He was sent to hospital in France and Scotland, and after treatment was demobilised in May 1920. He holds the 1914-15 Star, and the General Service and Victory Medals.
133, Kimberley Road, Nunhead, S.E.15. Z6417

MEYERN, J., Pte., Bedfordshire Regt. and R.A.S.C.

He joined on attaining military age in May 1918, and at the conclusion of his training was engaged on important duties at various stations with his unit. In November 1918, he was placed on a draft for foreign service, but owing to the termination of hostilities did not sail. He did valuable work, however, until he was demobilised in January 1920.
88, Somerleyton Road, Coldharbour Lane, S.W.9. Z3102

MICKLEBOROUGH, G., Pte., 4th Royal Fusiliers.
Joining in December 1916, he crossed to France two months later. He was engaged in the fighting at Arras, Vimy Ridge, Bullecourt, Messines, Ypres, Lens and Cambrai, and in March 1918, was taken prisoner during the German Offensive. Repatriated after the termination of hostilities, he returned to England, and was demobilised in February 1919. He holds the General Service and Victory Medals.
1, Torrens Street, Ferndale Road, Clapham, S.W.4.　Z3311

MICKLEFIELD, E., Special War Worker.
Being ineligible for service with the Colours he obtained work of National importance at the Hackney Marsh Munition Factory. He was engaged in the production of six inch shells, and did much valuable work.
16, St. David Street, Falmouth Road, S.E.1.　Z25822

MICKLEFIELD, E., 1st Class Stoker, R.N., H.M.S "Benbow."
He joined in August 1918, and served in H.M.S. " Benbow " with the Grand Fleet in the North Sea under Admiral Beatty. His vessel was engaged until the Armistice on important patrol duties and afterwards escorted the surrendered German Fleet to Scapa Flow. He was demobilised in July 1919, and holds the General Service and Victory Medals.
16, St. David Street, Falmouth Road, S.E.1.　Z25823

MIDDLEDITCH, H.C., Private, R.A.M.C.
He volunteered in August 1914, and at the conclusion of his training was engaged on important duties with his unit at various stations. Owing to physical disability, he was unable to secure his transfer to a theatre of war, but did valuable work until February 1917, when he was invalided out of the Service.
47, Tabor Road, Hammersmith, W.6.　11153

MIDDLEDITCH, H. J., Driver, R.F.A.
Volunteering in September 1914, he crossed to France early in 1915. His service overseas lasted for upwards of three years, during which time he did much valuable work with his Battery in operations in many important sectors, and was wounded on one occasion. He was demobilised in May 1919, and holds the 1914-15 Star, and the General Service and Victory Medals.　35, Tabor Road, Hammersmith, W.6.　11151

MIDDLETON, E., Sergt., R.A.S.C. (H.T.)
He volunteered in January 1915, and crossing to France a year later, served there until the cessation of hostilities. During this time he was engaged on duties of an important nature in connection with the supply of food and ammunition to the forward areas, and was present at Vimy Ridge, the Somme, Arras, Ypres, Passchendaele, and Cambrai. He also served in the Retreat and Advance of 1918, and was demobilised in May of the following year after his return to England. He holds the General Service and Victory Medals.
14, Blake's Road, Peckham, S.E.15.　Z6035

MIDDLETON, E., Private, 22nd Welch Regiment.
He volunteered in December 1915, and early in the following year was drafted to Salonika, where he did valuable work with his unit on the Doiran, Struma, and Vardar fronts, and took part in the capture of Monastir. He was demobilised in November 1919, after his return to England, and holds the General Service and Victory Medals.
26, Tunstall Road, Brixton Road, S.W.9.　Z3313

MIDDLETON, R. F., 1st Class Air Mechanic, R.A.F.
He joined the British Red Cross Society in February 1916, and crossing to France, served there for six months, doing much valuable work. He then returned to England, and joined the Royal Naval Air Service, with which he took part in several Monitor bombardments off the Belgian Coast. Later he was engaged on important duties at various stations in England, and was demobilised in September 1919. He holds the General Service and Victory Medals.
32, Crozier Street, Lambeth, S.E.1.　Z26075

MIDDLETON, S. R. G., Corporal, R.E.
He volunteered in August 1914, and after his training served on the West Coast of Ireland with the searchlight section of the Royal Engineers, and later was transferred to the Government Service on the telephone section. He had previously served for thirteen years in the Navy, and also took part in the Benin Expedition, and was discharged as time-expired in October 1915.
106, Commercial Road, Peckham, S.E.15.　Z6296

MIDDLETON, W. A., Driver, R.F.A.
He volunteered in April 1915, and served on the Western Front from the following November until early in 1919. During this period he fought in the Battles of Vimy Ridge, the Somme, Bullecourt, Arras, and Cambrai, and at the termination of hostilities, advanced with the Army of Occupation into Germany. He holds the 1914-15 Star and the General Service and Victory Medals, and in 1920 was still serving with his Battery at Aldershot.
33, Lockington Road, Battersea Park Road, S.W.8.　Z3312

MIDDLETON, W. J., Sergt., R.E. (I.W.T.)
Volunteering in July 1915, he crossed to France at the conclusion of his training. His service overseas lasted for over three years, and during this time he did much valuable work while in charge of a section of the Inland Water Transport. He was demobilised in January 1919, and holds the 1914-15 Star, and the General Service and Victory Medals.
254, Lynton Road, Bermondsey, S.E.1.　TZ26268

MIDMER, G., Sergt., East Yorkshire Regiment.
A serving soldier, he was in India when war broke out, and embarking in December 1914, arrived in France early in the following year. He was subsequently engaged in the fighting in many important sectors and was severely wounded on the Somme while in charge of a working party. He unfortunately died of his injuries on July 16th, 1916. He was entitled to the 1914-15 Star, and the General Service and Victory Medals.
" Whilst we remember the Sacrifice is not in vain."
42, Sussex Road, Coldharbour Lane, S.W.9.　Z5119

MIDWINTER, W., Private, 2nd Border Regiment.
Mobilised from the Reserve he was sent to France immediately upon the outbreak of hostilities, and took part in the early operations. Shortly afterwards he was severely wounded in action, and on October 4th, 1914, was reported missing after a heavy bombardment of the place to which he had been removed for safety. It is presumed that he died of his wounds. He was entitled to the 1914 Star, and the General Service and Victory Medals.
" Thinking that remembrance, though unspoken, may reach him where he sleeps."
25, Nursery Row, Walworth, S.E.17.　Z3314

MIHELL, J. E., Stoker, R.N., H.M.S. " Toronto " and " Essex."
He joined in 1917, and after his training served on submarine trawlers in the North Sea and off the coasts of Belgium. His ship was also engaged in the great attack on Zeebrugge in 1918. He was demobilised in the following year and holds the General Service and Victory Medals.
49, Sunwell Street, Peckham, S.E.15.　Z6413

MILARICK, C., Pte., 24th London Regt. (Queen's).
He volunteered in August 1914, and in the following year was sent to Salonika, and was engaged on the Vardar and Doiran fronts. In 1916 he was transferred to Egypt, and thence to Palestine, and took part in many engagements including the capture of Jerusalem. In 1918 he proceeded to the Western Front and served in the Retreat and Advance of 1918, and was wounded. He was invalided home and demobilised in February 1919, and holds the 1914-15 Star, and the General Service and Victory Medals.
218, J Block, Guinness' Buildings, Page's Walk, Grange Road, S.E.1.　TZ26370

MILBURN, G. J., Private, R.A.S.C. (M.T.)
Volunteering in April 1915, he was sent to France in the same month. He was engaged in the transport of supplies to the various fronts, including those of Ypres, the Somme, Bullecourt, Arras, and others, and took part in the Retreat and Advance of 1918. He was demobilised in March 1919, and holds the 1914-15 Star, and the General Service and Victory Medals.
133, Wells Street, Camberwell, S.E.5.　Z4497

MILDENHALL, E. W. (D.C.M.), Cpl., Royal Scots.
He was mobilised in August 1914, and sent to France in the same month. He took part in the severe fighting on the Marne, and at Ypres, St. Eloi, Arras, Passchendaele, and the Somme, and in the Retreat and Advance of 1918, and was wounded. He was awarded the Distinguished Conduct Medal for conspicuous bravery on the Somme, in keeping the machine guns in action at a critical period. He also holds the 1914 Star, and the General Service and Victory Medals.
26, Basnett Road, Lavender Hill, S.W.11.　Z3315

MILEHAM, F. W., Bombardier, R.G.A.
He volunteered in November 1914, and after his training served at various stations on important duties with his Battery. Later he unfortunately contracted tuberculosis, which resulted in his death on May 28th, 1916.
" He joined the great white company of valiant souls."
1, Stockdale Road, Wandsworth Road, S.W.8.　Z3149A

MILES (Mrs.), Special War Worker.
This lady offered her services for work of National importance, and for a period of eighteen months held a responsible position at Messrs. Gwynne's Factory, engaged on the manufacture of aeroplane parts. She did good work and discharged her duties in a most efficient and satisfactory manner.
37, Banim Street, Hammersmith, W.6.　11112D

MILES, A. H., Driver, R.F.A.
Volunteering in November 1914, he served on important duties with his Battery until January 1916, when he was drafted to France. He took part in numerous engagements, and in 1918 was wounded and suffered the loss of a leg. He was invalided home and was discharged as physically unfit for further service in May 1919, and holds the General Service and Victory Medals.
60, Bennerley Road, Battersea, S.W.11.   Z3316

MILES, A. V., Driver, R.E.
Volunteering in April 1915 he was sent to France in the same year and took part in many important engagements, including those on the Somme, and at Arras and Ypres, and in the Retreat and Advance of 1918. He was demobilised in June 1919, and holds the 1914-15 Star, and the General Service and Victory Medals.
90, Somerleyton Road, Coldharbour Lane, S.W.9.   Z3103

MILES, R. C., Private, R.A.S.C. (M.T.)
He volunteered in April 1915, and in the same year was sent to the Western Front, where he served in numerous engagements, including those on the Somme, and at Armentières, Arras, Ypres, and Passchendaele. He was demobilised in February 1919, and holds the 1914-15 Star, and the General Service and Victory Medals.
54, Cambridge Street, Camberwell, S.E.5.   Z3317

MILES, T. W., Sergt., 16th (The Queen's) Lancers.
He was mobilised in August 1914, and was shortly afterwards sent to France, where he took part in the severe fighting at Mons, La Bassée, the Somme, Arras, Ypres, and Cambrai. He also served in the Retreat and Advance of 1918, and was wounded. After the Armistice he proceeded with the Army of Occupation to Germany, where he remained until he was demobilised in February 1919, holding the Mons Star, and the General Service and Victory Medals.
69, Brookville Road, Dawes Road, S.W.6.   X20432

MILGATE, J. E. G., Rflmn., King's Royal Rifle Corps.
He joined in June 1917, and in July of the following year was drafted to France, where he took part in numerous engagements during the Advance in 1918. In 1919 he proceeded to India, where he was still serving in 1920, and holds the General Service and Victory Medals.
76, Warriner Gardens, Battersea, S.W.11.   Z3318

MILLAR, A., Sergt., 1st Scots Guards.
He was serving at the outbreak of war and was sent to France in the same year. He took part in the Retreat from Mons, and numerous other engagements including the Battles of Ypres, and the Somme. He also fought in the Retreat and Advance of 1918, and was three times wounded. He was still serving in 1920, and holds the Mons Star, and the General Service and Victory Medals.
107A, Tennyson Street, Wandsworth Road, S.W.8.   Z2537A

MILLARD, A. J., Private, Scots Guards.
After enlisting in Canada and being disbanded he came to England, and re-enlisted in December 1914, and proceeded to France in October of the following year. He was in action at St. Eloi, the Somme, Ypres, and in numerous engagements during the Retreat and Advance of 1918, and was three times wounded. He was demobilised in March 1919, and returned to Canada, holding the 1914-15 Star, and the General Service and Victory Medals.
19, Flaxman Road, Camberwell, S.E.5.   Z6036B

MILLARD, C. E., Private, 3rd East Surrey Regt.
He volunteered in February 1915, and in the following August was sent to France, and was in action at Vimy Ridge, the Somme, and in other engagements. He was wounded on the Somme in 1916, and invalided home, and was demobilised in September 1919, holding the 1914-15 Star, and the General Service and Victory Medals.
63, Coleman Road, Camberwell, S.E.5.   Z4498

MILLARD, H. J. (M.M.), Sergt., 29th Vancouver Regt. and Canadian M.G.C.
He volunteered in November 1914, and proceeded overseas in May 1915, with the 2nd Canadian Expeditionary Force, and in September of the same year arrived on the Western Front. He was in action at Loos, St. Eloi, Vimy Ridge, Ploegsteert, Arras, and Cambrai, and was three times wounded. He was awarded the Military Medal for bravery in the Field, and also holds the 1914-15 Star, and the General Service and Victory Medals. He was demobilised in January 1919, and has since returned to Canada.
19, Flaxman Road, Camberwell, S.E.5.   Z6036A

MILLEN, J. F., Private, 51st Australian Infantry.
He volunteered in March 1915, and proceeded to Gallipoli in the following June, and took part in several engagements. He contracted dysentery and was sent to Egypt, and thence to England. Having been found medically unfit for further service he was sent back to Australia in June 1918, and discharged in October of the same year, holding the 1914-15 Star, and the General Service and Victory Medals.
53, Moncrieff Street, Peckham, S.E.15.   Z5638

MILLER, A., Corporal, (Princess Charlotte of Wales') Dragoon Guard).
He was mobilised in 1914, and was shortly afterwards sent to France where he took part in the severe fighting at Mons, the Marne, the Aisne, Ypres, and Loos. He was wounded at Vermelles in May 1916, and was invalided home. On his recovery he was transferred to the Machine Gun Corps and proceeded to India. He was demobilised in February 1920, and holds the Mons Star, and the General Service and Victory Medals. 53, Barset Road, Peckham, S.E.17.   Z6524

MILLER, A., Driver, R.F.A.
Volunteering in August 1914 he was sent to France in March of the following year, and served in the Battle of the Somme, in which he was severely gassed. Subsequently he was in action at Béthune and Monchy, where he was blown up by shell explosion, and was invalided home. He was discharged as medically unfit for further military duty in August 1917, and holds the 1914-15 Star, and the General Service and Victory Medals.
15, Cronin Road, Peckham, S.E.15.   Z5639

MILLER, A. E., Rifleman, 21st King's Royal Rifle Corps.
He joined in June 1916, having previously attested and having been rejected three times. In August of the same year he landed in France, and fought on the Ancre front, at Beaumont-Hamel, Arras, and Vimy Ridge, and was severely wounded at Messines on June 15th, 1917. He succumbed to his injuries three days later, on June 18th, and was buried at Etaples Military Cemetery. He was entitled to the General Service and Victory Medals.
"Whilst we remember the Sacrifice is not in vain."
10, Myatt Road, Stockwell, S.W.9.   Z4443B

MILLER, A. J., Private, 4th Queen's (Royal West Surrey Regiment, Machine Gun Section).
He joined in March 1918, and in the same year was drafted to France, and served in the Advance in the Somme sector in September 1918. Later he was severely wounded, and was invalided to hospital in England, and after prolonged treatment was discharged as physically disabled for further service in May 1919. He holds the General Service and Victory Medals. 10, Pulross Road, Stockwell, S.W.9.   Z3320

MILLER, C., Driver, R.F.A.
He volunteered in September 1914, and in the following June was drafted overseas. Whilst in France he did good work as a driver at Armentières, Ypres, and the Somme. He was gassed at Ypres in 1917, and subsequently served at Passchendaele, Lens, Cambrai, and in the Retreat and Advance of 1918. He was demobilised in June of the following year and holds the 1914-15 Star, and the General Service and Victory Medals.
20, Flint Street, Walworth, S.E.17.   Z3321

MILLER, F. B., Private, 23rd Middlesex Regiment.
He joined in January 1916, and in the same year was drafted to the Western Front. During his service in France he fought at Vimy Ridge, the Somme, Beaumont-Hamel, Messines, Ypres, and in various engagements in the Retreat and Advance of 1918. He remained in France until November 1919, when he returned home, and was demobilised, and holds the General Service and Victory Medals. [
7, Headley Street, Peckham, S.E.15.   Z6204B

MILLER, G., Private, 11th Suffolk Regiment.
He volunteered in August 1914, and in November of the following year was drafted to France. Whilst overseas he took part in the severe fighting in the Battle of the Somme and was taken prisoner and sent to the Würtenberg prisoners-of-war detention camp. After suffering many hardships at the hands of his captors he died in June 1917. He was entitled to the 1914-15 Star, and the General Service and Victory Medals.
"Thinking that remembrance, though unspoken, may reach him where he sleeps."
59, Ascalon Street, Battersea Park Road, S.W.8.   Z3322

MILLER, G. H., Private, 23rd Middlesex Regiment.
He joined in 1917 as soon as he had attained military age, and in January of the following year was drafted to France. Here he served in various important engagements, including Bapaume and Cambrai, and in the Retreat and Advance of 1918. He remained overseas until 1919 when he returned home and was demobilised, holding the General Service and Victory Medals.
7, Headley Street, Peckham, S.E.15.   Z6204C

MILLER, J., Driver, R.F.A.
He joined in November 1917, and in April of the succeeding year was drafted to France. Whilst overseas he did good work as a driver in numerous engagements, including that of Ypres, and was wounded. After the Armistice was signed he proceeded to Germany with the Army of Occupation, and was stationed at Cologne until February 1920, when he returned home and was demobilised. He holds the General Service and Victory Medals.
7, Benfield Street, Battersea, S.W.11.   Z3326

MILLER, J. G., Private, R.A.S.C.

He volunteered in April 1915, and in the following July was drafted to France. Whilst in this theatre of war he served with the Supply Division, and was present at Armentières, Ypres, Arras, Béthune, and Givenchy, and in other sectors of the Western Front. He was discharged in October 1918, at the age of sixty years, as physically unfit for further military duty, and holds the 1914-15 Star, and the General Service and Victory Medals.
79D Block, Guinness' Buildings, Page's Walk, Bermondsey, S.E.1.   Z26825

MILLER, J. G. R., Private, Queen's (Royal West Surrey Regiment).

He was mobilised at the outbreak of hostilities, and was almost immediately drafted to France, where he took part in the fighting at Mons. He gave his life for the freedom of England during the Retreat, and was entitled to the Mons Star, and the General Service and Victory Medals.
" His life for his Country, his Soul to God."
26, Elizabeth Street, Walworth, S.E.17.   Z26421

MILLER, J. H., Private, The Border Regiment.

A serving soldier since January 1912, he was stationed in India when war was declared, and early in 1915 embarked for Gallipoli. There he fought in various engagements until August 1915, when he gave his life for King and Country during the Landing at Suvla Bay. He was entitled to the 1914-15 Star, and the General Service and Victory Medals.
" He passed out of the sight of men by the path of duty and self-sacrifice."
48, Lingham Street, Clapham Road, S.W.9.   Z3323

MILLER, R., Private, 19th London Regiment.

He joined in May 1916, and in the same year was drafted to France. During his overseas service he fought at Ypres, and was severely gassed in Bourlon Wood. He was invalided to hospital at Etaples, and after his recovery returned to the front lines, and was taken prisoner during the German Offensive in March 1918. He was sent to the Munster prisoners of war detention camp, where he was held in captivity until after the Armistice, when he was released and returned to England. He was demobilised in December 1918, and holds the General Service and Victory Medals.
34, Raywood Street, Battersea Park Road, S.W.8.   Z3319

MILLER, R. C., Private, 23rd Middlesex Regiment.

He joined in February 1916, and in the same year was drafted to France, where he saw much service. He fought in the engagements at Vimy Ridge, the Somme, Beaumont-Hamel, Messines, Ypres, and Cambrai, and in many of the subsequent operations in the Retreat and Advance of 1918. In November 1919 he was demobilised, and holds the General Service and Victory Medals. 7, Headley Street, Peckham, S.E.15.   Z6204A

MILLER, R. T., L/Corporal, 2nd East Surrey Regt.

He joined in June 1916, and in the following November was drafted to Salonika, where he served in many sectors of the Macedonian and Balkan fronts, until the cessation of hostilities. In January 1919 he was sent home, and discharged through ill-health in the following April. He holds the General Service and Victory Medals.
131, Heath Road, Wandsworth Road, S.W.8.   Z3325

MILLER, W. B., Private, East Surrey Regiment.

He joined in November 1916, and in the same month was sent overseas. During his service in France he fought on the Somme, and at the capture of Vimy Ridge, and was in action at Ypres, and Cambrai, where he was severely injured. He was invalided home and discharged as medically unfit for further duty in December 1918, and holds the General Service and Victory Medals.
70, Crescent Road, Clapham, S.W.4.   Z3324

MILLER, W. J., Private, 9th Royal Irish Fusiliers.

He volunteered in June 1915, and in November of the same year proceeded to France. Whilst in this theatre of war he took part in the severe fighting in the Battle of the Somme, and at Cambrai, where he was wounded in October 1917. He was invalided to hospital and sent home in the following December, but rejoined his unit in France after his recovery. He then served in many engagements in the Retreat and Advance of 1918, and was at Courtrai when the Armistice was signed. He holds the 1914-15 Star, and the General Service and Victory Medals, and was demobilised in February 1919.
2, Cheam Place, Camberwell, S.E.5.   Z5803

MILLER, W. R., Sergt.-Major, R.A.S.C. (M.T.)

He joined in 1916, and in the following year was drafted to the East, where he served for three years. Whilst overseas he was present at the Battles of Gaza, and at the memorable entry into Jerusalem, and the Capture of Jericho, and subsequently was stationed at Kantara in charge of the engineers' shops until the conclusion of hostilities. He was demobilised in March 1920 after his return to England, and holds the General Service and Victory Medals.
20, McKerrell Road, Peckham, S.E.15.   Z6042

MILLETT, H., Corporal, R.A.S.C.

He volunteered in 1915, and was drafted to the Western Front in the following year. He was engaged at the rail heads chiefly in the Somme and Ypres sectors, loading and unloading shells and other supplies. He remained on the Western Front until the cessation of hostilities, and after his return to England he was demobilised in 1919, holding the General Service and Victory Medals.
70, Lollard Street, Kennington, S.E.11.   Z25767

MILLETT, J., S.M. (Instructor), R.F.A.

Having previously served throughout the South African Campaign, in which he was wounded, he volunteered in September 1914, and served at Portsmouth and other stations on important duties with the Batteries to which he was attached. He was engaged in instructional duties and rendered valuable services, but was not successful in obtaining his transfer overseas before the cessation of hostilities. He was demobilised in September 1919, and holds the Queen's and King's South African Medals
69, Killyon Road, Wandsworth, Road, S.W.8.   Z2975B

MILLETT, W. J., Sapper, R.E.

He volunteered in December 1914, and after being sent to France in the following year, took part in several engagements. He was unfortunately killed in action on June 26th, 1915, and was buried in a Communal Cemetery near Vermelles. He was entitled to the 1914-15 Star, and the General Service and Victory Medals.
" His memory is cherished with pride."
69, Killyon Road, Wandsworth Road, S.W.8.   Z2975A

MILLICHAP, A. G., Private, R.A.S.C.

He volunteered in November 1915, and in the same year proceeded to France, where he served in the Somme, Ypres, Cambrai, and other sectors, and was engaged in the transport of ammunition and supplies to the front lines. During his service overseas he was wounded. He was discharged in January 1919 in consequence of his services, and holds the 1914-15 Star, and the General Service and Victory Medals.
18, Bolton Street, Camberwell, S.E.5.   Z3328A

MILLICHAP, A. T., Rifleman, Rifle Brigade.

After joining in July 1917, he completed his training, and in the same year proceeded to India, where he was engaged on important duties with his unit at Sialkot in the Punjab, and rendered valuable services. He returned home in 1919, and was demobilised in September of that year, holding the General Service and Victory Medals.
18, Bolton Street, Camberwell, S.E.5.   Z3328B

MILLICHAP, J. A., Gunner, R.F.A.

He volunteered in December 1915, and after being sent to France in the following year was in action at Vimy Ridge and Ypres, where he was badly gassed. On his recovery he returned to the front, and with the 14th Division took part in the Retreat and Advance of 1918. He was demobilised in January 1920, after returning home, and holds the General Service and Victory Medals.
24, Cobbett Street, Dorset Road, S.W.8.   Z3327B

MILLICHAP, J. F., L/Corporal, 9th London Regt. (Queen Victoria's Rifles).

Joining in November 1917, he completed his training and was drafted to France in the same year. He took part with distinction in numerous engagements of importance in the Retreat and Advance of the Allies in 1918. He returned home and was demobilised in September 1919, and holds the General Service and Victory Medals.
18, Bolton Street, Camberwell, S.E.5.   Z3328C

MILLICHAP, J. T., Bombardier, R.F.A.

He volunteered in January 1915, and in the same year was drafted to the Western Front, where he took part in numerous engagements, including those at Festubert, Vimy Ridge, Longueval, Arras, and Ypres. He was later transferred to Italy, and did excellent service on the Piave. Whilst in this theatre of war he met with a severe accident by being thrown from a horse. He was demobilised in December 1919, holding the 1914-15 Star, and the General Service and Victory Medals.
24, Cobbett Street, Dorset Road, S.W.8.   Z3327A

MILLS, A. E., Private, 6th Devonshire Regiment.

He volunteered in August 1914, and in the following March was drafted to France, where he fought in the Battles of Neuve Chapelle, Ypres, and various minor engagements. Early in 1916 he was sent to Mesopotamia, but after a few months' service he succumbed to enteric fever whilst serving on the Tigris on July 28th of the same year. He was entitled to the 1914-15 Star, and the General Service and Victory Medals.
" A costly sacrifice upon the altar of freedom."
47, Wells Place, Camberwell, S.E.5.   Z3486

MILLS, A., Driver, R.F.A.
He volunteered in October 1914, and embarked for France in the following April. Whilst overseas he did excellent work as a driver at Festubert, Vimy Ridge, the Somme, Arras, and Messines, but later, contracting trench fever, he was invalided home. He was discharged as medically unfit for further military duty in November 1917, and holds the 1914-15 Star, and the General Service and Victory Medals.
8, Fendick Road, Peckham, S.E.15.   Z6034

MILLS, E. S., A.B., R.N., H.M.S. "Blenheim."
He was mobilised at the outbreak of hostilities, and was posted to H.M.S. "Hogue" and whilst in this ship took part in the engagement at Heligoland Bight, and was on board when she was torpedoed and sunk in September 1914. Fortunately he was amongst the survivors and subsequently served on various destroyers in the North Sea, and other waters, being in action in the Battle of Jutland in May 1916. He was demobilised in April 1919, and holds the 1914-15 Star, and the General Service and Victory Medals.
24, Ceylon Street, Battersea Park Road, S.W.8.   Z3329

MILLS, F. J., Yeoman of Signals, R.N., H.M.S. "Benbow" and "Royal Sovereign."
He had previously served for nineteen years in the Navy, and in August 1914 was posted to H.M.S. "Benbow," and served with the Grand Fleet. Whilst in this ship he was in action at the Battle of Jutland, and in many subsequent engagements, and was present at the surrender of the German Fleet. He was demobilised in March 1919, and holds the 1914-15 Star, and the General Service and Victory Medals.
40, Porten Road, West Kensington, W.14.   12479A

MILLS, G. C., Corporal, Royal Scots.
He volunteered in March 1915, and in the following February was drafted to France. During his service on the Western Front he was in action at Vimy Ridge, and the Somme, and in the third Battle of Ypres, and at Passchendaele. He was then invalided home owing to ill-health, and after medical treatment was retained on home service until March 1919, when he was demobilised, having completed exactly four years with the Colours. He holds the General Service and Victory Medals.
10, Osborne Street, Walworth, S.E.17.   Z3330

MILLS, G. S., Private, 1st Queen's (Royal West Surrey Regiment).
He volunteered in December 1914, and was drafted to the Western Front in the following year. During his service in France he fought in the Battles of Neuve Chapelle and Ypres, and unhappily was subsequently killed in action in an engagement on May 6th 1916. He was entitled to the 1914-15 Star, and the General Service and Victory Medals.
    "He died the noblest death a man may die,
    Fighting for God, and right, and liberty."
18, St. Oswald's Place, Kennington, S.E.11.   Z25415

MILLS, H., Private, R.A.S.C. (Remounts).
He joined in September 1917, and in the same year was drafted to France, where he served on important duties at the Remount Depôt at Rouen. He was demobilised in November 1919, and holds the General Service and Victory Medals.
45, Dalwood Street, Camberwell, S.E.5.   Z3485C

MILLS, H., Sergt., 2nd Dragoon Guards (Queen's Bays) and Military Police.
He had previously enlisted in December 1901, and at the outbreak of war was mobilised and sent to France with the first contingent of the British Expeditionary Force. He served in the Battles of the Marne, the Aisne, Neuve Chapelle, Ypres, Loos, the Somme, Cambrai, and in many later engagements in the Retreat and Advance of 1918. He finished his active service at Spa, and in 1920 was still with the Military Mounted Police. He holds the 1914 Star, and the General Service and Victory Medals, and King George V's Police Coronation Medal, 1911.
38, Coronation Buildings Road, South Lambeth, S.W.8.
                                                     Z3168B

MILLS, H. A., Special War Worker.
He volunteered his services in September 1914, and for four and a half years was engaged on work of National importance at Messrs. Doughty and Co's, Farringdon Road, Blackfriars. He was employed in the manufacture of stretcher bags, belts, and surgical instruments for military hospitals, and rendered valuable services until January 1919.
70, Willow Walk, Grange Road, Bermondsey, S.E.1.   Z26859

MILLS, H. E., Rifleman, 13th Rifle Brigade.
He joined in August 1916, and after a period of training was drafted to the Western Front, where he served in many engagements in various sectors. He died gloriously on the Field of Battle on April 27th, 1917 and was entitled to the General Service and Victory Medals.
    "Nobly striving,
    He nobly fell that we might live."
13, Cardross Street, Hammersmith, W.6.   11575A

MILLS, I. W. A., Private, 13th London Regt. (Kensingtons).
He volunteered in August 1914, and in the following November was drafted to France. During his service on the Western Front he fought at La Bassée, and was severely wounded in action, and invalided home to hospital. After fifteen months' medical treatment he was discharged as physically unfit for further military duty in July 1916. He holds the 1914 Star, and the General Service and Victory Medals.
73, Meyrick Road, Battersea, S.W.11.   Z3332

MILLS, J., Rifleman, Rifle Brigade.
He joined in November 1916, and on the completion of his training was drafted to France in the following year. After only three months' active service on the Western Front he gave his life for King and Country at the Battle of Cambrai in November 1917. He was entitled to the General Service and Victory Medals.
    "Courage, bright hopes and a myriad dreams splendidly given."
115, Chatham Road, Wandsworth Common, S.W.11.   Z6130B

MILLS, J., Sergt., 7th Royal Fusiliers.
Volunteering in August 1914, he was drafted overseas on the completion of his training. After serving in various important engagements he made the supreme sacrifice in the Battle of Loos on September 28th, 1915. He was entitled to the 1914 Star, and the General Service and Victory Medals.
    "He died the noblest death a man may die,
    Fighting for God, and right, and liberty."
45, Dalwood Street, Camberwell, S.E.5.   Z3485B

MILLS, J. C., Armourer's Crew, R.N., H.M.S. "Pembroke" and "Vanguard."
He volunteered in June 1915, and on the completion of his training was posted to H.M.S. "Pembroke," and served with the Grand Fleet in the North Sea. His ship took part in many engagements, including the Battles of Heligoland Bight and Jutland. He lost his life when H.M.S. "Vanguard" was blown up at Scapa Flow, and all hands perished.
    "He passed out of sight of man by the path of duty and self-sacrifice."
35, Kennington Grove, S.E.11.   Z24832B

MILLS, R. W., Private, M.G.C.
He joined in August 1917, and in the following January was drafted overseas. During his service in France he fought in the second Battle of the Somme, and was wounded in June 1918. He was sent home to hospital, and after his recovery rejoined his unit in France early in the following September, and was again severely wounded in the Advance towards Mons on November 4th, 1918. He was invalided home, and was under treatment in hospital until discharged in April 1919. He holds the General Service and Victory Medals.
14, Harling Street, Camberwell, S.E.5.   Z5459

MILLS, S., Private, 4th Royal Fusiliers.
He volunteered in November 1915, and in October of the succeeding year was drafted to France. Whilst in this theatre of war he took part in the fighting on the Somme, and the Ancre, and at Arras, Ypres, Cambrai, Selle, and the Sambre, and was present at the memorable entry into Mons at dawn on Armistice Day. During his service he was gassed, and after the cessation of hostilities proceeded to Germany with the Army of Occupation. Returning to England in January 1919, he was discharged in the following April, and holds the General Service and Victory Medals.
23, Lambeth Road, S.E.1.   26092

MILLS, S., Gunner, R.G.A.
He was mobilised in August 1914, and in the same month was sent overseas and took part in the Retreat from Mons. He was also in action at the Battles of La Bassée, Ypres, and Neuve Chapelle, and later was severely wounded and gassed. After his recovery he served in many engagements until the conclusion of hostilities, and was demobilised in March 1919. He holds the Mons Star, and the General Service and Victory Medals.
47, Grant Road, Battersea, S.W.11.   Z3333

MILLS, W., Rifleman, 7th King's Royal Rifle Corps.
He joined in December 1916, and in March of the following year was drafted to France. Here he fought in many important battles, including those at Arras, Vimy Ridge, and Messines, where he was gassed and sent home to hospital. On recovery he rejoined his unit on the Western Front in January 1918, but later was reported missing after the engagement at St. Quentin on March 21st, 1918, and is presumed to have been killed in action on that date. He was entitled to the General Service and Victory Medals.
    "His life for his Country, his Soul to God."
9, Mostyn Terrace, Brixton Road, S.W.9.   Z5268

MILLS, W., Private, M.G.C.
He joined early in November 1918, and on the completion of his training was drafted to India, where he was engaged on special duties at various garrison outposts. In 1920 he was still serving.
45, Dalwood Road, Camberwell, S.E.5. Z3485A

MILLS, W. A., Rifleman, 18th London Regiment (London Irish Rifles).
He volunteered in September 1914, and in March of the following year was drafted to France, where he fought in the engagements at Givenchy and Loos. In January 1916 he was invalided home with frost bite, and after prolonged treatment in hospital rejoined his unit in June of the succeeding year. He then served in the Battle of Ypres, and was killed whilst bringing in the wounded, having volunteered for this perilous duty. He was entitled to the 1914-15 Star, and the General Service and Victory Medals.
" Greater love hath no man than this, that a man lay down his life for his friends."
105, Smyrks Road, Walworth, S.E.17. Z2222B

MILLS, W. G., Private, 10th Middlesex Regiment.
Volunteering in August 1914, he was shortly afterwards drafted to India. He served there throughout the war, and during this time was on three occasions invalided to hospital suffering from fever. He returned to England to be demobilised in May 1919, and holds the General Service and Victory Medals.
13, Cardross Street, Hammersmith, W.6. 11575B

MILLS, W. H., Rifleman, 18th London Regiment (London Irish Rifles) and Private, Labour Corps.
He volunteered in 1915, and in the following year was drafted to France. During his service on the Western Front he was engaged in the severe fighting on the Somme and at Arras and Cambrai. He was afterwards transferred to the Labour Corps, and was employed on Graves Registration in France. He was demobilised in 1919, and holds the General Service and Victory Medals.
48, Saltoun Road, Brixton, S.W.2. Z5640

MILLS, W. H. A., Stoker, R.N., H.M.S. " Essex."
He joined in February 1918 at eighteen years of age, and was posted on the completion of his training to H.M.S. " Essex " and sent to the North Sea. His ship took part in several engagements off Scapa Flow, and he was present at the surrender of the German Fleet. In March 1919 he was demobilised, and holds the General Service and Victory Medals.
35, Kennington Grove, S.E.11. Z24832A

MILLSON, W. G., Corporal, R.A.S.C. (M.T.)
Joining in June 1916, he crossed to France two months later, and for upwards of two years did valuable work in connection with the Ambulance Section. In the course of his service he was present at several engagements, notably those at Vimy Ridge, the Somme, Arras, Messines, Ypres, Passchendaele, and Cambrai, and in the Retreat and Advance of 1918. He was demobilised in November 1919, and holds the General Service and Victory Medals.
3, Aylesbury Road, Walworth, S.E.17. Z1475D

MILNE, A., Corporal, Canadian A.S.C.
He volunteered in May 1915, and early in the following year was drafted to the Western Front, where he was subsequently engaged on important duties in connection with the supply of food and stores to the Canadian troops. He was demobilised in June 1919, and holds the General Service and Victory Medals.
27, Heygate Street, Walworth, S.E.17. Z3334

MILNE, A. L., Private, 17th Welch Regiment.
Joining in April 1916, he crossed to France in the following November. Whilst overseas he' fought in many important engagements, including those at Beaumont-Hamel, Arras, Vimy Ridge, Bullecourt, Ypres, Passchendaele, Cambrai, and the Retreat and Advance of 1918. During his service he was wounded and invalided home on two occasions, returning to France on his recovery. He holds the General Service and Victory Medals, and was demobilised in March 1919.
177, Albert Road, Peckham, S.E.15. Z5805A Z6040A

MILNE, F., Sergt., R.A.S.C.
He volunteered in January 1915, and later in that year proceeded to Salonika, where he did excellent service at General Head-quarters. From there he was transferred to Egypt, and was engaged on important duties with his unit until his return to England for demobilisation in January 1919. He holds the 1914-15 Star, and the General Service and Victory Medals.
251, Hollydale Road, Peckham, S.E.15. Z6563

MILNE, J. H., Private, Royal Sussex Regiment.
He joined in March 1916, and until January 1918, when he was sent to France, was engaged on duties of an important nature at various stations. Whilst overseas he fought in many important engagements during the Retreat and Advance of 1918, including those on the Somme and the Aisne, and at the conclusion of hostilities was sent with the Army of Occupation to Germany, where he served in the Royal Army Ordnance Corps. He was demobilised in September 1919, and holds the General Service and Victory Medals.
177, Albert Road, Peckham, S.E.15. Z5805B

MILSOM, E. R., Driver, R.F.A.
He volunteered in April 1915, and in same year was drafted to the Western Front. He took part in heavy fighting at Vermelles, Vimy Ridge, the Somme, Arras, and Passchendaele, and in the Retreat and Advance of 1918. He was demobilised in July 1919, and holds the 1914-15 Star, and the General Service and Victory Medals.
19, Grimscott Street, off Grange Road, Bermondsey, S.E.1.
TZ25971

MILSTEAD, A. W. G., Private, 1st London Regt. (Royal Fusiliers).
Joining in August 1916, he crossed to France four months later, and subsequently took an active part in many important engagements, notably those at Ypres and Arras. He was unfortunately killed in action on March 28th, 1918, during the German Offensive. He is buried in Roclincourt Cemetery in the vicinity of Arras, and was entitled to the General Service and Victory Medals.
" The path of duty was the way to glory."
53, Arthur Road, Brixton Road, S.W.9. Z3491

MILTON, A. (M.M.), Private, Royal Fusiliers.
Joining on attaining military age in November 1917, he crossed to France early in the following year, and took part in the Retreat and Advance of 1918. At the conclusion of hostilities he was sent with the Army of Occupation to Germany, where he was engaged on special duties. During his service he was awarded the Military Medal for conveying wounded into safety under heavy fire, and in addition holds the General Service and Victory Medals. He is now demobilised.
8, Raywood Street, Battersea Park Road, S.W.8. Z3335

MILTON, G., L/Corporal, Lancashire Fusiliers.
Joining in November 1916, he was drafted to France two months later, but was afterwards taken ill during an Advance on that front. After his recovery he was engaged on duties of an important nature with his unit until April 1920, when he returned to England, and was demobilised. He holds the General Service and Victory Medals.
63, Stonhouse Street, Clapham, S.W.4. Z1726B

MIMMS, J. H. W., Sergt., R.A.M.C.
He volunteered in September 1914, and after a period of training proceeded to Gallipoli in the following year. In 1916 he was transferred to France and was engaged on important and dangerous duties in connection with the Field Ambulances, and was twice wounded. On February 1919 he was demobilised and holds the 1914-15 Star, and the General Service and Victory Medals.
250, St. James' Road, Old Kent Road, S.E.1. Z2650

MINEHAN, J., Private, East Surrey Regiment.
He volunteered in June 1915, and in May of the following year was drafted to the Western Front, where he took part in numerous engagements, including those at Ploegsteert Wood, Messines, Ypres, the Somme, and Bapaume. In 1917 he proceeded to Italy and was in action on the Piave. Returning to France he was later sent with the Army of Occupation to Germany. He was demobilised in April 1919, and holds the General Service and Victory Medals.
19, Rectory Gardens, Clapham, S.W.4. Z3336

MIST, G. T., Private, Leicester Regiment.
He joined in 1916, and in the same year was sent to India. He was later transferred to Egypt, and thence to Palestine. Returning to Egypt he was attached to the Royal Army Medical Corps, with which he was engaged on important duties at various stations. He returned home and was demobilised in September 1919, and holds the General Service and Victory Medals.
23, Arden Street, Battersea Park Road, S.W.8. Z3338

MITCHAM, A., Private, 1st London Regiment (Royal Fusiliers).
He joined in August 1916, and after his training served on important duties with his unit until November 1917, when he was drafted to France. Here he took part in the severe fighting at Ypres, Cambrai, and St. Quentin, and in the Retreat and Advance of 1918. He was unfortunately killed in action on November 10th, 1918, and was entitled to the General Service and Victory Medals.
" The path of duty was the way to glory."
2, Newchurch Road, Camberwell, S.E.5. Z5802

MITCHELL, A. C., Private, King's Own Yorkshire Light Infantry.
He volunteered in 1915, and was sent to France in the same year, and took part in numerous engagements, including those at Loos, the Somme, Arras, Ypres, and Cambrai. After the Armistice he proceeded with the Army of Occupation to Germany. He was demobilised in 1919, and holds the 1914-15 Star, and the General Service and Victory Medals.
63, Barlow Street, Walworth, S.E.17.　　Z3341A

MITCHELL, A. G., Private, Queen's (Royal West Surrey Regiment).
He volunteered in 1915, and in the same year was drafted to the Western Front, where he served in the severe fighting on the Somme, and at Arras and Ypres, and was taken prisoner in 1918. On his release he returned home and was demobilised in 1919, and holds the 1914-15 Star, and the General Service and Victory Medals.
63, Barlow Street, Walworth, S.E.17.　　Z3341D

MITCHELL, C. W., Private, Queen's Own (Royal West Kent Regiment) and Essex Regiment.
Volunteering in May 1915, he was sent to France in August of the same year. He took part in numerous engagements, including those at Albert, Vimy Ridge, the Somme, Arras, Bullecourt, Messines, Ypres, St. Quentin, Armentières and Cambrai, and was wounded and invalided home. On his recovery he returned to France, where he again served in much severe fighting, and was wounded for the second time. He was sent to hospital in Scotland, and after his recovery was demobilised in March 1919, holding the 1914-15 Star, and the General Service and Victory Medals.
26, Chatham Street, Walworth, S.E.17.　　Z3339

MITCHELL, F. J., Driver, R.F.A.
He joined in January 1916, and in the same year was sent to Mesopotamia, where he took part in the Relief of Kut and the Capture of Baghdad. In 1917 he proceeded to Egypt and thence to Palestine, and served in many engagements, including that at Gaza and the Capture of Jerusalem. In 1918 he was transferred to France and was engaged in the Retreat and Advance. Afterwards returning home on leave he contracted influenza, of which he unfortunately died on October 22nd, 1918. He was entitled to the General Service and Victory Medals.
"His memory is cherished with pride."
92, Clayton Road, Peckham, S.E.17.　　Z6201A

MITCHELL, G. F., Rflmn., King's Royal Rifle Corps.
He volunteered in March 1915, and in the same year was drafted to the Western Front, where he took part in severe fighting. He was reported missing in September 1915, and is presumed to have been killed in action. He was entitled to the 1914-15 Star, and the General Service and Victory Medals.
"Great deeds cannot die."
They with the Sun and Moon renew their light for ever."
92, Clayton Road, Peckham, S.E.15.　　Z6201B

MITCHELL, J., Driver, R.F.A. (6th London Bde.) and Air Mechanic, R.A.F.
He volunteered in January 1915, and after his training served on important duties with his Battery, but being found medically unfit for service overseas he was discharged in November of the same year. He re-enlisted, however, in December 1917, and was engaged on various duties until he was demobilised in June 1919.
28, Pitman Street, Camberwell, S.E.5.　　Z3343

MITCHELL, J., Private, 17th Lancashire Fusiliers.
He volunteered in August 1915, and was drafted to the Western Front in the following December. He was in action at the Battles of Vimy Ridge, Arras, Messines, Passchendaele, Amiens, Ypres and other engagements, and also in the Advance from Cambrai in 1918. Holding the 1914-15 Star, and the General Service and Victory Medals, he was demobilised in March 1919.
16, Over Place, Princes Road, Kennington, S.E.11. TZ25463

MITCHELL, J., Private, East Surrey Regiment.
He was serving at the outbreak of war, and was shortly afterwards drafted to the Western Front, where he took part in numerous engagements. He was later transferred to Salonika and was in action on the Doiran front, and also saw service in Egypt. He was still serving in 1920, and holds the 1914 Star, and the General Service and Victory Medals.
26, Bognor Street, Battersea Park Road, S.W.8.　　Z1021B

MITCHELL, J. J., Private, R.A.S.C. (M.T.)
He volunteered in August 1914, and was early drafted to the Western Front. He served in various sectors as a despatch rider, and was afterwards transferred to the Repair Depôt. He went to Italy in 1917, and did valuable work transporting supplies. He was demobilised in February 1919, and holds the 1914 Star, and the General Service and Victory Medals.
48, Sturgeon Road, Walworth, S.E.17.　　Z26815

MITCHELL, L. J., Private, M.G.C. (Cavalry).
He volunteered in November 1915, and on the completion of his training was drafted in 1917 to Egypt, whence he took part in the Offensive in Palestine and fought in various important engagements. Early in 1918 he was sent to the Western Front, and served at Etaples and at several other places. He was demobilised in January 1919, and holds the General Service and Victory Medals.
70, Reedworth Street, Kennington, S.E.11.　　Z27256

MITCHELL, N., Driver, R.G.A.
He volunteered in 1915, and in the same year was sent to France, where he took part in numerous engagements, including that on the Somme, and at Arras and Ypres, and in the Retreat and Advance of 1918. He was demobilised in 1919, holding the 1914-15 Star, and the General Service and Victory Medals.
63, Barlow Street, Walworth, S.E.17.　　Z3341B

MITCHELL, S. H., Driver, R.F.A.
He volunteered in January 1915, and in the same year was sent to Salonika, and was in action on the Vardar and Doiran fronts, and in many other engagements. He returned home and was demobilised in February 1919, holding the 1914-15 Star, and the General Service and Victory Medals.
27, Kimpton Street, Camberwell, S.E.5.　　Z3340

MITCHELL, T., Private, Labour Corps.
He volunteered in 1915, and in the same year was drafted to the Western Front. He served in many sectors and was engaged in unloading supplies at the railheads, and in other important duties and rendered valuable services. He returned home and was demobilised in 1919, holding the 1914-15 Star, and the General Service and Victory Medals.
63, Barlow Street, Walworth, S.E.17.　　Z3341C

MITCHELL, W. M., Rflmn., King's Royal Rifle Corps.
Having previously served in the Army he volunteered in 1914, and was sent to France in November of the same year. He took part in numerous engagements, including those at Ypres, Loos and Arras, and was twice wounded and invalided home. He was discharged in June 1916, as medically unfit, and holds the 1914-15 Star, and the General Service and Victory Medals.
13, Henshaw Street, Walworth, S.E.17.　　Z3186C

MITCHIE, A., Bombardier, R.G.A.
He was mobilised in August 1914, and shortly afterwards proceeded to France, where he took part in the Retreat from Mons, and was twice wounded and invalided home. On his recovery he returned to France, and was later sent to Egypt, and thence to Palestine, and served at Jericho and in the Advance to Jerusalem. He was demobilised in February 1919, and holds the Mons Star, and the General Service and Victory Medals.
187, Neate Street, Camberwell, S.E.5.　　Z5460

MITCHINSON, C. F., Private, R.A.O.C.
He joined in 1916, and was drafted to the Western Front, where he served in many engagements, including those at Albert, the Somme, Arras, Messines and Bapaume. He was also in the Retreat and Advance of 1918, and was wounded. He was demobilised in August 1919, and holds the General Service and Victory Medals.
4, Jerome Place, Walworth, S.E.17.　　Z26443

MITCHLEY, B. (M.M.), S.M., 8th London Regiment (Post Office Rifles).
He joined in January 1916, and after completing his training he was sent to France in February of the following year. He took part in numerous engagements, including those at Arras, Bullecourt, Messines and Passchendaele, and was also in the Retreat and Advance of 1918, and was twice wounded and gassed. He was awarded the Military Medal for conspicuous bravery at St. Julien, and also holds the General Service and Victory Medals. He was demobilised in March 1919.
1, Currie Road, Battersea, S.W.11.　　Z2257B

MITCHLEY, B. A. F. (M.M.), C.S.M., 8th London Regiment (Post Office Rifles).
He volunteered in November 1915, and after his training served on important duties with his unit until January 1917, when he was drafted to the Western Front, and was in action at Bullecourt, Ypres and Menin Road, and was three times wounded. He was awarded the Military Medal for conspicuous gallantry at Menin Wood, and also holds the General Service and Victory Medals. He was demobilised in March 1919.
1, Currie Road, Battersea, S.W.11.　　Z3344

MITCHLEY, H. C., Rifleman, 3rd Rifle Brigade.
He was serving at the outbreak of war, and shortly afterwards was sent to France, where he was in action at La Bassée, Ypres, St. Eloi, Loos, Vimy Ridge and the Somme. He was unfortunately killed in action near Passchendaele on December 2nd, 1916, and was entitled to the 1914 Star, and the General Service and Victory Medals.
"His life for his Country, his Soul to God."
12, Shellgate Road, Battersea, S.W.11.　　Z3345

MIZEN, A., Driver, R.F.A. (6th London Brigade).
He volunteered in April 1915, and proceeded to France in June of the following year and was in action at Arras. He was later sent to Salonika and served on the Vardar and Doiran fronts, after which he was transferred to Egypt, and thence to Palestine, and took part in the Advance to Jerusalem. In 1918 he returned to France and was engaged in the Retreat and Advance of 1918. After the Armistice he was sent with the Army of Occupation to Germany. He was demobilised in July 1919, and holds the General Service and Victory Medals.
58, Waterloo Street, Camberwell, S.E.5.   Z3346

MOBBS, W., Rifleman, 12th London Regt. (Rangers) and Pte., R.A.S.C.
Volunteering in January 1916, he proceeded to France a year later. Whilst in this theatre of war he fought at Ypres, and was wounded twice in 1917, and again in the German Offensive of 1918. Evacuated to hospital in England, he was later transferred to the R.A.S.C., with which unit he rendered valuable services until demobilised in March 1919. He holds the General Service and Victory Medals.
20, Luscombe Street, Wandsworth Road, S.W.8.   Z27513

MOGG, J., Private, Royal Warwickshire Regiment.
He volunteered in November 1914, and in the following year was drafted to Gallipoli, where he was engaged in heavy fighting until the Evacuation of the Peninsula. He was then sent to Alexandria, and later proceeding to Mesopotamia was in action at the attempted Relief of Kut-el-Amara, and many other engagements. After the signing of the Armistice he served with the Relief Force in Russia during the Bolshevist risings, and was wounded. He returned to England and was discharged on account of service in May 1919, and holds the 1914-15 Star, and the General Service and Victory Medals.
56, Avenue Road, Camberwell, S.E.5.   Z3350

MOGRIDGE, H., Driver, R.H.A.
Volunteering in September 1914, he was stationed at various depôts after his training, and did very good work with his Battery. Owing to ill-health he was unable to secure his transfer overseas, and was discharged as medically unfit for further service in June 1915.
6, Bonsor Street, Camberwell, S.E.5.   Z4500

MOIR, L. R. R., Leading Stoker, R.N.
He enlisted in March 1912, and at the outbreak of hostilities was serving in H.M.S. " Penelope." His ship was engaged on important patrol and other duties with the Grand Fleet. and took part in the Battle of Heligoland Bight, and was damaged by a mine explosion in September 1914, and again in 1916. He was demobilised in January 1920, and holds the 1914-15 Star, and the General Service and Victory Medals.
12, Newby Street, Wandsworth Road, S.W.8.   Z3351

MONGER, H., Driver, R.E.
Volunteering in January 1915, he was sent overseas in November of that year. During his service on the Western Front he was engaged with his unit in many sectors, including those of Loos, St. Eloi, Albert, the Somme, Arras, Messines and Ypres, and was wounded in November 1917. He was invalided to hospital in England and three months later rejoined his unit in France and served in the Retreat and Advance of 1918. He was demobilised in February 1919, and holds the 1914-15 Star, and the General Service and Victory Medals.
9, Perrer's Road, Hammersmith, W.6.   11136B

MONGER, W., Driver, R.F.A.
He joined in April 1918, and after training and serving at various stations on important duties was drafted to India in October of the following year. He was stationed at several garrison outposts on the Indian Frontier engaged on special duties, and in 1920 was still serving.
22, Perrer's Road, Hammersmith, W.6.   11136C

MONK, J., Rifleman, King's Royal Rifle Corps.
He joined in 1916, and later in the same year was drafted overseas. Whilst in France he fought at Albert, the Somme, Arras and Cambrai, and was severely wounded. He was invalided to England, and whilst in King's College Hospital, H.M. Queen Alexandra graciously autographed his fancy needle work. He holds the General Service and Victory Medals. and was discharged as medically unfit for further service in 1917.
7, Brayard's Road, Peckham, S.E.15.   Z5641-2

MONK, J. C., Private, East Surrey Regiment.
He volunteered in 1915, and in the following year was sent overseas. Whilst on the Western Front he fought in the Battles of the Somme, Ypres and Arras. In March 1917 he was reported missing, and was later presumed to have been killed in action. He was entitled to the General Service and Victory Medals.
" Thinking that remembrance, though unspoken, may reach him where he sleeps."
39, Trafalgar Street, Walworth, S.E.17.   Z27332

MONK, P. W., Driver, R.F.A.
He volunteered in January 1915, and was drafted to France in the following March. Whilst overseas he fought in numerous engagements, including Festubert, Loos, High Wood, Vimy Ridge, Messines, Ypres, Menin Road, Cambrai, Bapaume and Combles. He was demobilised in May 1919, and holds the 1914-15 Star, and the General Service and Victory Medals.
212, Sumner Road, Peckham, S.E.15.   Z6297

MONKHOUSE, W. W., Pte., 1/24th London Regt. (The Queen's).
He volunteered in November 1914, and at the conclusion of his training served on important coastal defence duties until drafted to Ireland in 1915. He was engaged with his Battalion in assisting to quell the Irish Rebellion and did very good work, but was unable to secure his transfer to a theatre of war. Owing to an injury, which he sustained in the course of his duties, he was invalided to hospital in England, and in May 1916 was discharged medically unfit for further service.
55, D'Eynsford Road, Camberwell, S.E.5.   Z3352

MONKS, A., Private, 2nd London Regt. (Royal Fusiliers), R.D.C. and Somerset Light Infantry.
He volunteered in January 1915, and at the conclusion of his training served with the Royal Defence Corps on important guard duties at various prisoners of war camps. He was later transferred to the 6th Somerset Light Infantry, and early in 1918 was drafted to France. In this theatre of war he was engaged in the fighting at Cambrai, and in the Retreat and Advance of 1918. He was demobilised in February 1919, and holds the General Service and Victory Medals.
9, Wincott Street, Kennington, S.E.11.   Z27217

MONKS, G., Private, 7th Gloucestershire Regiment.
He volunteered at the outbreak of hostilities, and in July 1915 was sent to the Dardanelles, where he fought at the Landing at Suvla Bay and in many engagements which followed. In 1916 he was drafted to Mesopotamia, and served at the second Battle of Kut, and was wounded in February 1917. On recovery he rejoined his Battalion in the Field and was in action until the Armistice. He then returned to England and was demobilised in May 1919, and holds the 1914-15 Star, and the General Service and Victory Medals.
264, L Block, Guinness' Buildings, Page's Walk, Grange Road, S.E.1.   Z26418

MONTAGUE, J. T., 1st Class Wireless Operator, R.N.
He volunteered in June 1915, and during his training served in H.M.S. " Arethusa." He was later sent to China and there joined H.M.S. " Venus," which vessel was engaged on patrol and other duties off the coast of India. He was transferred to the wireless section in August 1917, and in 1920 was serving in H.M.S. " Actæon." He holds the General Service and Victory Medals.
569, Battersea Park Road, S.W.11.   Z3310C

MOODY, H., Rflmn., 12th King's Royal Rifle Corps.
He volunteered in August 1914, and in the following year was sent to the Western Front. During his service on the Western Front he fought in many engagements, including those at Neuve Chapelle, St. Eloi, Hill 60, Ypres and Loos, where he was wounded. He was invalided to hospital in England, and on recovery rejoined his unit in the firing line, and was in action in the Retreat and Advance of 1918. He was demobilised in 1919, and holds the 1914-15 Star, and the General Service and Victory Medals.
38, Bedford Street, Walworth, S.E.17.   Z3354A

MOODY, T., Trooper, 3rd Dorset (Queen's Own) Hussars.
Having enlisted in 1913, he was mobilised at the outbreak of hostilities, and served on special duties at home until drafted to Egypt in 1917. Whilst in this theatre of war he was engaged in the fighting during the British Advance through Palestine, and contracted malaria in the Jordan Valley. He returned to England in 1919, and was demobilised in September of the following year. He holds the General Service and Victory Medals.
38, Bedford Street, Walworth, S.E.17.   Z3353

MOODY, W., Rifleman, 6th London Regt. (Rifles) and 1st Rifle Brigade.
He was serving at the outbreak of war, and was drafted to France in January 1916. Whilst on the Western Front he served in various parts of the line and fought at the Battle of the Somme, during which he was wounded in November 1916, and was again severely wounded at Arras in April 1917. He was evacuated to hospital in England and subsequently discharged as medically unfit for further service in November of the same year. He holds the General Service and Victory Medals.
38, Bedford Street, Walworth, S.E.17.   Z3354B

MOON, G. J., Trooper, Royal Horse Guards.

A serving soldier, he was mobilised at the outbreak of war, and in November 1914 was sent to France. He fought in many engagements, including the Battles at Ypres, the Somme, Neuve Chapelle, Loos, Beaumont-Hamel, and Cambrai. He returned to England after the signing of the Armistice, and was demobilised in March 1920, and holds the 1914 Star, and the General Service and Victory Medals.
5, Amies Street, Battersea, S.W.11.   Z3355

MOONE, J. F., Private, 3rd East Surrey Regiment.

He joined in November 1917, on attaining military age, and at the conclusion of his training was engaged with his Battalion on important guard duties at various prisoners of war camps. In March 1918 he proceeded to France, where he served for a year and returning to England was demobilised in April 1919. He holds the General Service and Victory Medals.
61, Mysore Road, Lavender Hill, S.W.11.   Z3356

MOONEY, J., A.B., R.N., H.M. Ships, "Impregnable," "Ajax," "Powerful," and "Pheasant."

He volunteered in 1915, and after his training served with the Grand Fleet in the North Sea on important and hazardous duties. He was transferred finally to H.M.S. "Pheasant," and when this vessel was blown up by a mine explosion he was lost with all hands on board on February 20th, 1916. He was entitled to the 1914-15 Star, and the General Service and Victory Medals.
"His memory is cherished with pride."
23, Mortlock Gardens, Peckham, S.E.15.   Z6298B

MOORE, A., Private, East Surrey Regiment.

He volunteered in November 1914, and at the conclusion of his training served at various stations on important duties with his Battalion. He was seriously wounded during a course of training in bomb throwing and invalided to hospital. He was subsequently discharged as medically unfit for further service in February 1915. He later contracted illness from which he died on October 16th, 1918.
"Whilst we remember the Sacrifice is not in vain."
112, Avenue Road, Camberwell, S.E.5.   Z1012B

MOORE, A. E., Driver, R.A.S.C. (M.T.)

He volunteered in March 1915, and shortly afterwards proceeded to France and served in the Battles of Neuve Chapelle, Ypres, Ploegsteert Wood, the Somme and Cambrai. He was also present at many important engagements in the Retreat and Advance of 1918. In January 1920 he was demobilised, and holds the 1914-15 Star, and the General Service and Victory Medals.
35, Conderton Road, Camberwell, S.E.5.   Z6299A

MOORE, A. E., Special War Worker.

He offered his services for work of National importance during the war and from June 1916 was employed at Messrs. Wilkinson's Sword Factory, Acton. His duties, which were in connection with the straightening and setting of bayonets, demanded a high degree of technical skill, and he rendered valuable services throughout. He was still in the employ of this firm in 1920.
222, Southfield Road, Bedford Park, W.4.   T6885

MOORE, A. W., Private, M.G.C.

He joined in July 1916, and five months later proceeded overseas. During his service on the Western Front he took part in the fighting at Armentières, the Somme, Arras, Ypres, Vimy Ridge, Messines, Bourlon Wood, Albert, Cambrai and the Retreat and subsequent Allied Advance of 1918, and was twice wounded. He was demobilised in February 1919, and holds the General Service and Victory Medals.
29, Odell Street, Camberwell, S.E.5.   Z5461

MOORE, B., Private, Tank Corps.

He joined in June 1916, and later in the same year was sent to France, where he was engaged as a gunner in much severe fighting in various sectors until hostilities ceased, including those of the Somme, Ypres, Arras and Cambrai, and was wounded on two different occasions. He was demobilised in April 1919, and holds the General Service and Victory Medals.
9, Solon New Road, Bedford Road, S.W.4.   Z3364B

MOORE, D., Rifleman, 6th London Regt. (Rifles).

He joined in 1917, and in the same year was sent to the Western Front, where he fought at Ypres and the Somme, and during the German Offensive at Cambrai in 1918, was wounded and taken prisoner. He suffered much during his captivity, and whilst still a prisoner, died later in the same year. He was entitled to the General Service and Victory Medals.
"Courage, bright hopes and a myriad dreams, splendidly given."
9, Solon New Road, Bedford Road, S.W.4.   Z3364A

MOORE, E. C., Private, 5th Middlesex Regiment.

He volunteered in June 1915, and early in the following year after completing his training, was drafted to France, where he took part in numerous engagements of importance. He afterwards was invalided home owing to heart trouble and discharged as medically unfit for further service in February 1919. He holds the General Service and Victory Medals.
5, Cheam Place, off Newchurch Road, Camberwell, S.E.5   Z6483

MOORE, F., Private, 3rd Middlesex Regiment.

Volunteering in November 1914, he proceeded overseas in the following year, and was engaged in the fighting in various sectors of the Western Front, including those of Ypres, Loos, the Somme and Lens, and was badly gassed in 1915. He later was drafted to Salonika and was in action during the Bulgarian Retreat. He also served for a time in Egypt and after his return home was demobilised. He holds the 1914-15 Star, and the General Service and Victory Medals.
56, Linden Gardens, Chiswick, W.4.   T5846

MOORE, G. E., Corporal, R.A.S.C.

He joined in February 1916, and in July of that year was sent to Egypt. In this theatre of war he served on important duties with his unit whilst operations were in progress at El-Arish, Gaza, Jerusalem, Jericho and the Jordan, and later was engaged in transporting food and ammunition to Aleppo. He returned to England, and was demobilised in December 1919, and holds the General Service and Victory Medals.
36, Pepler Road, Peckham, S.E.15.   Z3487

MOORE, G. H., Corporal, R.A.S.C.

He volunteered in April 1915, and at the conclusion of his training served on important transport duties with his unit. He did excellent work, but owing to medical unfitness and on account of being over military age, he was unable to secure his transfer to a theatre of war, and was demobilised in February 1919.
114, Crimsworth Road, Wandsworth Road, S.W.8.   Z3358

MOORE, H., Rifleman, King's Royal Rifle Corps.

He joined in July 1916, and in the following year, after completing his training, proceeded overseas. During his service on the Western Front he fought in many important engagements, including the German Offensive and subsequent Allied Advance of 1918, and was twice wounded. He was demobilised in November 1919, and holds the General Service and Victory Medals.
12, Avenue Road, Camberwell, S.E.5.   Z1012C

MOORE, H. E., Driver, R.A.S.C.

He joined in May 1916, and proceeded to France in the following September. During his service on the Western Front he was engaged with the Motor Transport in conveying rations and supplies up to the lines until the Armistice was signed. He did excellent work and was demobilised in November 1919, and holds the General Service and Victory Medals.
35, Conderton Road, Camberwell, S.E.5.   Z6299B

MOORE, H. T., L/Corporal, R.E.

Volunteering in August 1915, he wa drafted to Egypt early in 1916, and after serving a short while there was sent to the Western Front in April of that year. Whilst in France he was engaged with his unit on special duties during the fighting at the Somme, Arras, Ypres, and Valenciennes. He also served for a time with the French at Verdun. He was demobilised in January 1919, and holds the General Service and Victory Medals.
100, Harris Street, Camberwell, S.E.5.   Z5120A

MOORE, H. W., Sergt., 2nd East Surrey Regiment.

A Reservist, he was mobilised at the outbreak of hostilities, and in April 1915, after being drafted to France fought at Ypres and Loos, and was wounded. In October of the same year he proceeded to Salonika, and was in action on the Vardar and Struma fronts, and after the signing of the Armistice served in Turkey with the Army of Occupation, until he returned to England in August 1920. Later in the same year he was still serving with the Colours, and holds the 1914-15 Star, and the General Service and Victory Medals.
100, Harris Street, Camberwell, S.E.5.   Z5120B

MOORE, J., Sergt., R.A.S.C.

Volunteering in May 1915, he later in the same year proceeded to the Western Front, where, with his unit he was engaged on special duties attached to the Royal Engineers, and did very good work in connection with plate-laying for the railways. Owing to ill-health he was invalided to England and discharged medically unfit for further service in February 1916. He holds the 1914-15 Star, and the General Service and Victory Medals.
3, Hook's Road, Peckham, S.E.15.   Z6523

MOORE, J., Pte., R.A.O.C. and Air Mechanic, R.A.F.

He volunteered in December 1915, and being transferred to the Royal Air Force in 1917, served in the workshops at various aerodromes, and was engaged on duties which called for a high degree of technical skill. He did very good work but was unable to secure his transfer overseas while hostilities continued, and was demobilised in March 1919.
123, Gloucester Road, Peckham, S.E.15. Z6044

MOORE, J. E. (Mrs.), Member, W.R.A.F.

She joined in March 1918, and at the conclusion of her training was engaged as a painter at the R.A.F. (M.T.) Depôt, Kennington, and afterwards at a garage for the issue of petrol to official cars. She rendered valuable services for over a year, and was demobilised in May 1919.
44, Wooler Street, Walworth, S.E.17. Z3360B

MOORE, J. H., Private, R.A.S.C. (M.T.)

Joining in August 1916, he wa sent overseas in the same year. During his service on the Western Front he served with his unit during the fighting at Ypres, Arras, Lens, Loos, Lille, Passchendaele Ridge, Hill 60, Vimy Ridge, St. Quentin, St. Eloi, Bullecourt, Cambrai and in the final Allied Advance of 1918. He was demobilised in December 1918, and holds the General Service and Victory Medals.
17, Hillery Road, Walworth, S.E.17. Z3359

MOORE, J. H., Private, Royal Sussex Regiment.

He volunteered in 1915, and in the same year proceeded overseas. Whilst in France he took part in many battles, including those at Ypres, the Somme and Arras, and in the course of his duties was on two occasions blown up by shell explosion. He returned to England after the cessation of hostilities, and was demobilised in 1919. He holds the 1914-15 Star, and the General Service and Victory Medals.
71, Trafalgar Street, Walworth, S.E.17. Z27334

MOORE, J. L., Private, R.A.S.C. (M.T.)

He volunteered in May 1915, and after serving on important duties at various home stations was drafted to Egypt in February 1918. Whilst overseas he was engaged with the Motor Transport Section in conveying rations, ammunition and stores up to the front lines, and also for a time attached to the Royal Engineers' Signal Section. He was present at the engagements at Jericho, Damascus and Aleppo and in other operations until the cessation of hostilities. He was demobilised in 1919, after his return to England, and holds the General Service and Victory Medals.
157, Kimberley Road, Peckham, S.E.15. Z6418

MOORE, J. W., Private, R.A.M.C.

During the war he was exempted from service with the Colours, being engaged on work of National importance. In July 1918, however, he was called up and served on special duties with his unit. He did good work, but was not successful in obtaining his transfer overseas before hostilities ceased. He was demobilised in January 1919.
6, Geneva Road, Coldharbour Lane, S.W.9. Z3470

MOORE, M., Private, Middlesex Regiment.

A serving soldier, he was mobilised at the outbreak of hostilities and drafted almost immediately to France. In this theatre of war he fought at the Battles of the Marne, Ypres, Neuve Chapelle, Loos, Arras, the Somme and in many other engagements. He later proceeded to Salonika and was in action during the Balkan campaign, and was wounded. He returned to England and was discharged on account of service in February 1919, and holds the 1914 Star, and the General Service and Victory Medals.
52, Avenue Road, Camberwell, S.E.5. Z3362B

MOORE, S. E., Gunner, R.F.A.

He volunteered in March 1915, and in the same year proceeded overseas. Whilst on the Western Front he was engaged in the fighting at the Battle of La Bassée, the Somme and was wounded at Beaumont-Hamel in 1916. He was invalided to hospital in England and on recovery in 1917 was sent to India, where he served on garrison duties until 1919. He then returned to England, and was still serving in 1920, and holds the 1914-15 Star, and the General Service and Victory Medals.
84, Mayall Road, Herne Hill, S.E.24. Z3357

MOORE, T., Private, Royal Berkshire Regiment.

A Reservist, he was mobilised at the outbreak of hostilities, and immediately sent to France, where he fought in the Retreat from Mons, and the subsequent Battles of Le Cateau, the Aisne, La Bassée, Ypres and Neuve Chapelle. Owing to ill-health he was invalided to hospital in England in March 1915, and in January of the following year returned to the Western Front, and was engaged in the fighting at Loos, Albert, Vimy Ridge, the Somme, Arras, Armentières, and in the Advance of 1918. He was demobilised in April 1919, and holds the Mons Star, and the General Service and Victory Medals.
44, Wooler Street, Walworth, S.E.17. Z3360A

MOORE, T., Driver, R.A.S.C. (M.T.)

He volunteered at the oubreak of hostilities, and was immediately sent overseas. He served with his unit during the fighting in the Retreat from Mons, and was employed in transport duties in the Battles of Ypres, the Somme, Vimy Ridge, and many others until the close of the war, and was badly gassed. He was demobilised in October 1919, and holds the Mons Star, and the General Service and Victory Medals.
186, Cator Street, Peckham, S.E.15. Z5121

MOORE, T. E., L/Cpl., King's Royal Rifle Corps.

He volunteered in August 1914, and in February of the following year was sent to France. In this theatre of war he took part in many engagements, and was severely wounded. He was invalided and subsequently discharged as medically unfit for further service in March 1916. He holds the 1914-15 Star, and the General Service and Victory Medals.
54, Beckway Street, Walworth, S.E.17. Z3363

MOORES, W., L/Corporal, R.A.S.C.

He volunteered in December 1914, and in the following year was drafted to the Western Front, where he served for upwards of four years. During this period he was engaged as a motor transport driver and did good work during the Battles of Ypres, Albert, Cambrai. Returning to England after the conclusion of hostilities, he was demobilised in April 1919, and holds the 1914-15 Star, and the General Service and Victory Medals.
19, Stansfield Road, Stockwell Road, S.W.9. Z6196-7B

MORETON, R. V., Private, Labour Corps.

He volunteered in January 1916, and after completing his training served with his unit at home. Engaged on agricultural work he rendered valuable services, but was unable to obtain a transfer overseas before the cessation of hostilities. He was demobilised in January 1919.
10, Milford Street, Wandsworth Road, S.W.8. Z5554C

MOREY, J. W., Rifleman, King's Royal Rifle Corps.

He joined the 6th London Regiment (Rifles) in May 1916, and in the following April proceeded to France, where, attached to the 253rd Tunnelling Coy., R.E., he served during the Battles of Ypres and the Somme. Owing to shell-shock he was sent to hospital at home, and on recovery was transferred to the King's Royal Rifle Corps. Being unfit for further active service he was engaged on guard and other important duties in England until he was demobilised in October 1919. He holds the General Service and Victory Medals.
43, Cronin Road, Peckham, S.E.1.5 Z5462

MOREY, T., Sergt.-Instructor, 2nd County of London Yeomanry (Westminster Dragoons), and R.F.A.

He volunteered in August 1915, and was engaged on important duties with his unit until sent to the Western Front in 1917. Whilst overseas he took an active part in engagements in the Somme, Arras and Ypres sectors and was wounded near Cambrai on September 28th, 1918. Sent home on account of his injuries he received hospital treatment, and was discharged as physically unfit in February 1919. He had also served in South Africa, and in addition to the Queen's and King's Medals for that campaign, holds the General Service and Victory Medals.
21, Russell Grove, Vassal Road, S.W.9. Z5122

MORGAN, A., Trooper, 6th Dragoon Guards (Carabiniers).

He volunteered in August 1914, and after completing his training was engaged on important duties at various depôts with his unit. He did excellent work, but was not successful in securing his transfer overseas before the termination of hostilities, and was demobilised in 1918. He had served with the Colours in India and Egypt, and holds the Queen's and King's Medals for the South African War.
11, Dante Road, Kennington, S.E.11. Z26689

MORGAN, A. E., Private, 1st Duke of Cornwall's Light Infantry.

Mobilised from the Army Reserve on the outbreak of war he proceeded to France shortly afterwards and took part in heavy fighting in the Retreat from Mons, and in the Battles of the Marne and the Aisne. He died gloriously on the Field of Battle at Hill 60 on April 17th, 1915, and was entitled to the Mons Star, and the General Service and Victory Medals.
"A valiant soldier, with undaunted heart he breasted Life's last hill."
32, Edmund Street, Camberwell, S.E.5. Z3365

MORGAN, H. J., Special War Worker.

Ineligible for military service on account of his age, he volunteered for work of National importance and was employed at Woolwich Dockyard from 1916 to 1920. He was engaged on important duties in connection with the packing and despatch to the various theatres of war of military equipment and stores, and throughout his service discharged his duties in a capable and efficient manner.
36, Elliott Road, Stockwell, S.W.9. Z4501

MORGAN, G. F., Gunner, R.F.A.
Volunteering in September 1914, he was employed in conveying prisoners of war from the Western Front until drafted to France in March 1915. He served in the travelling workshops of the Anti-aircraft section, and was seriously injured in November 1915 by the bursting of a gun, which he was repairing. Sent home to hospital he received medical treatment, and on recovery was engaged with his unit on air defence work. He was demobilised in February 1919, and holds the 1914-15 Star, and the General Service and Victory Medals.
41, Stanton Street, Peckham, S.E.15. Z5266

MORGAN, H. W., Rifleman, 15th London Regiment (Civil Service Rifles).
He joined in May 1918, on attaining military age, and was drafted overseas in the following September. Serving on the Western Front he was engaged on important duties until invalided to hospital in England, owing to illness. On recovery he rejoined his unit and was sent with the Army of Occupation to Germany, and was stationed on the Rhine. Returning home for demobilisation in April 1920, he holds the General Service and Victory Medals.
180, Manor Place, Walworth, S.E.17. Z27047

MORILL, H., Private, R.A.S.C. (M.T.)
He joined in February 1917, and in the following June proceeded overseas. During his service in France he was engaged as a tractor driver moving guns into position, and was present at engagements at Ypres and on the Somme, and in various later battles. He was invalided home to hospital with illness, but on recovery rejoined his unit in France, remaining until March 1919, when he was demobilised. He holds the General Service and Victory Medals.
171, Gloucester Road, Peckham, S.E.15. Z6300

MORISON, A. T., Pte., Royal Fusiliers and R.A.S.C.
Enlisting in 1911, he went to France shortly after the outbreak of war. He took part in heavy fighting during the Retreat from Mons, and in the Battle of Ypres, and was wounded. After his recovery he returned to the Western Front and served in the Battles of the Somme and Arras. He was drafted to Italy in 1917, and was in action on the Piave. He served again in France, but after hospital treatment was transferred to the Royal Army Service Corps. Demobilised in 1919, he holds the Mons Star, and the General Service and Victory Medals.
23, Arthur Road, Brixton Road, S.W.9. Z3097

MORLEY, A., Gunner, R.F.A.
He volunteered in 1915, and embarking for the Western Front in the following year served there throughout the war. He was engaged with his Battery in the Battles of the Somme, Ypres and Arras, and in several other operations until the conclusion of hostilities. Returning to England he was demobilised in 1919, but re-engaged for a term of service and was sent to Malta. He holds the General Service and Victory Medals, and in 1920 was still serving.
287, East Street, Walworth, S.E.17. Z3370

MORLEY, D. (Miss), Special War Worker.
Offering her services for work of National importance during the war this lady was engaged from January 1917 to March 1919, in making socks, body-belts, operating garments and other comforts for the sick and wounded, in conjunction with the British Red Cross and Order of St. John. She also served in the Y.M.C.A., Spurgeon's Tabernacle, Walworth, and the troops greatly appreciated her efforts on their behalf.
13, Exon Street, Walworth, S.E.17. Z3368B

MORLEY, D. E. (Miss), Special War Worker.
During the war this lady voluntarily gave her services for work of National importance, and worked in conjunction with the British Red Cross Society and Order of St. John, in making socks, scarves, body-belts and other comforts for the sick and wounded in several hospitals, and also served at the Y.M.C.A., Spurgeon's Tabernacle, Walworth. She rendered valuable services from January 1917 to March 1919, and her efforts on behalf of the troops were greatly appreciated.
13, Exon Street, Walworth, S.E.17. Z3369B

MORLEY, D. W. E., Gunner, R.F.A.
Volunteering in April 1915, he proceeded to the Western Front in the following November. He fought in the Battles of Albert and Vimy Ridge, and was wounded on the Somme on September 1st, 1916. On recovering from the effects of his injuries he was transferred to the Royal Army Service Corps, and was engaged in the transport of ammunition and supplies, and was afterwards stationed at Dieppe. He was demobilised in November 1919, and holds the 1914-15 Star, and the General Service and Victory Medals.
13, Exon Street, Walworth, S.E.17. Z3369A

MORLEY, G. (Miss), Special War Worker.
From January 1917 to March 1919, this lady who offered her services for work of National importance worked in conjunction with the British Red Cross Society and Order of St. John. She devoted her time to the manufacture of socks, scarves, body-belts and other comforts for the use of the sick and wounded in various hospitals, and her voluntary efforts to ameliorate their sufferings, met with success and great appreciation.
13, Exon Street, Walworth, S.E.17. Z3369C

MORLEY, L. V. (Miss) Special War Worker.
During the war this lady voluntarily devoted herself to work in connection with the British Red Cross Society and Order of St. John, and from January 1917 to March 1919 was untiring in her efforts on behalf of the troops. In addition to making comforts of all kinds for the use of the sick and wounded in hospitals. She attended to the material wants of soldiers at the Y.M.C.A., Spurgeon's Tabernacle, Walworth, 13, Exon Street, Walworth, S.E.17. Z3367

MORLEY, Mabel E. (Miss), Special War Worker.
During the war for a period of over two years this lady devoted her time to making comforts, in connection with the British Red Cross Society, and St. John Ambulance Brigade, for the wounded. These garments were distributed to the various military hospitals, and were much appreciated.
13, Exon Street, Walworth, S.E.17. Z3368C

MORLEY, Maud E. (Miss), Special War Worker.
During the war this lady worked from January 1917 to March 1919, in conjunction with the British Red Cross Society and Order of St. John, in making socks, scarves, helmets and similar comforts for the sick and wounded in various hospitals. She also gave a considerable portion of her time to attending the Y.M.C.A., Spurgeon's Tabernacle, Walworth, serving refreshments and entertaining soldiers en route to the Front.
13, Exon Street, Walworth, S.E.17. Z3368A

MORLEY, R., Private, East Surrey Regiment.
He volunteered in September 1914, and proceeding to the Western Front in the following year served in various sectors, until the end of hostilities. He was in action in numerous engagements, and was wounded three times, being invalided to hospital on each occasion. After the Armistice he was sent to Russia in the King's (Liverpool Regiment), and was awarded the Order of St. George (IV Class) by the Russian Government, for conspicuous gallantry and devotion to duty in the Field. He also holds the 1914-15 Star, and the General Service and Victory Medals, and was demobilised in July 1919.
73, Hellingdon Street, Walworth, S.E.17. Z26810

MORLEY, S., Rflmn., 6th King's Royal Rifle Corps.
Joining in May 1916, he was drafted overseas in the same year and saw much service on the Western Front. He fought in the Battles of the Somme, Arras, Vimy Ridge, Lens, and was wounded by a shell explosion near Cambrai in March 1918. Returning to the firing line on recovery he was in action in several engagements during the Advance of 1918. He was demobilised in February 1919, and holds the General Service and Victory Medals.
47, Barlow Street, Walworth, S.E.17. Z3366

MORPHEW, J. J., Private, 20th London Regiment.
Volunteering in September 1914, he embarked for the Western Front in the following March, and served with his Battalion in several engagements. He gave his life for King and Country at Vermelles on June 3rd, 1915, and was buried near the Town. He was entitled to the 1914-15 Star, and the General Service and Victory Medals.
"Great deeds cannot die:
They with the Sun and Moon renew their light for ever."
175, Cator Street, Peckham, S.E.15. Z4502

MORRIS, A., Private, King's Own (Royal Lancaster Regiment).
He volunteered in September 1914, and proceeding to the Western Front five months later, served with his unit throughout the course of hostilities. He fought in the Battles of Ypres, Loos, Vimy Ridge, the Somme, Arras, Passchendaele, Lens, and during the Retreat and Advance of 1918. He returned to England for demobilisation in June 1919, and holds the 1914-15 Star, and the General Service and Victory Medals. 8, High Park Crescent, Walworth, S.E.17. Z3372

MORRIS, A. (M.M.), Sergt., Rifle Brigade.
Volunteering in 1915, he was drafted overseas in the same year, and served on the Western Front. He fought in the Battles of Ypres, the Somme, Bullecourt and Messines, and was wounded and sent to a Base Hospital. He was subsequently taken prisoner in an engagement, but effected his escape. He also took part in the Retreat and Advance of 1918. On one occasion he was awarded the Military Medal for gallantry and devotion to duty in saving the life of one of his officers, and also holds the 1914-15 Star, and the General Service and Victory Medals. He was demobilised in September 1919.
31, Peardon Street, Wandsworth Road, S.W.8. Z3377

MORRIS, B., Gunner, R.F.A.
He volunteered in January 1915, and after completing his training served at various stations on important duties with his Battery. He rendered valuable services, but owing to being medically unfit for duty abroad was unable to secure his transfer overseas before the termination of hostilities. He was demobilised in January 1919.
8, Vaughan Road, Camberwell, S.E.5.   Z6408

MORRIS, C., Private, R.A.M.C.
Joining in 1916, he was sent overseas in the same year, and served as a stretcher bearer in France and Flanders. Proceeding to Salonika he was engaged with the Field Ambulance in several operations during the campaign in the Balkans, and returned to the Western Front, and served through the Retreat and Advance of 1918. He was demobilised in 1919, and holds the General Service and Victory Medals.
202, Alderminster Road, Bermondsey, S.E.1.   Z26256

MORRIS, C. A., Rifleman, Rifle Brigade.
He joined in February 1917, and embarked for the Western Front in the same year. Serving in various parts of the line, he fought in the Battle of the Somme, and during the Retreat and Advance of 1918. He returned home in 1919, and was sent to Mesopotamia, where he was stationed in 1920. He holds the General Service and Victory Medals.
16, Bournemouth Road, Rye Lane, S.E.15.   Z5806B

MORRIS, E., Private, 3rd London Regiment (Royal Fusiliers).
He volunteered in January 1915, and in the following November was drafted to the Western Front. Whilst in France he fought in many engagements, including those at Vimy Ridge, Ploegsteert Wood, the Somme and Cambrai. In September 1918 he was wounded and gassed at Havrincourt, and was invalided home to hospital. On recovery he rejoined his unit and served in England until April 1919, when he was demobilised. He holds the 1914–15 Star, and the General Service and Victory Medals.   11, Unwin Road, Peckham, S.E.15.   Z6419

MORRIS, E. A., Sapper, R.E.
He joined in July 1918, and on completing his training was engaged in the workshops of his unit at Chatham. He did excellent work, but was unable to secure his transfer overseas before the cessation of hostilities, and was demobilised in January 1919.
12, Sugden Street, Camberwell, S.E.5.   Z5804

MORRIS, E. W., Private, 8th Royal Fusiliers.
He volunteered in October 1914, and proceeding to the Western Front in the same year, fought in the Battles of Loos, Arras, the Somme and Albert. Sent to assist in the transport of American troops to the Field, he served at the Base for a time. He subsequently returned to the firing line, and took part in the Advance of 1918. He was demobilised in February 1919, and holds the 1914–15 Star, and the General Service and Victory Medals.
17, Stewarts Road, Battersea Park Road, S.W.8.   Z3378

MORRIS, J., Private, 22nd Queen's (Royal West Surrey Regiment).
Volunteering in 1914, he completed his training, and was engaged on garrison and other important duties with his Battalion. He was not sent overseas owing to physical unfitness for general service, and was discharged in consequence in 1915.   289, East Street, Walworth, S.E.17   Z3371

MORRIS, J., Rifleman, 18th London Regiment (London Irish Rifles).
He volunteered in June 1915, and after completing his training was drafted overseas. Serving on the Western Front he was in action in the Battles of Loos, Vimy Ridge, the Somme, and in several other engagements until the conclusion of hostilities. He was demobilised in December 1918, and holds the 1914–15 Star, and the General Service and Victory Medals.
18, East Surrey Grove, Peckham, S.E.15.   Z5263

MORRIS, J. G., Rfimn., 17th London Regt. (Rifles).
He joined in July 1916, and in the following December was sent to Salonika. After serving in the Advance on Lake Doiran he proceeded to Egypt and was engaged in several operations until drafted to the Western Front in June 1918. He took part in the Advance of 1918, and was seriously wounded in the Battle of the Selle. He was in consequence invalided to hospital in England, and was discharged as medically unfit in May 1920. He holds the General Service and Victory Medals.   55, Russell Street, Battersea, S.W.11.   Z3373

MORRIS, J. T., Private, Bedfordshire Regiment.
Joining in February 1918, he embarked for France in the same year, and was engaged on guard and other important duties at various Prisoner-of-war camps. He did excellent work throughout his service overseas, returning to England for demobilisation in February 1919. He holds the General Service and Victory Medals.
1, Harris Street, Camberwell, S.E.5.   Z4503

MORRIS, L., Private, R.A.S.C., Hampshire Regt. and Loyal North Lancashire Regiment.
Volunteering in August 1914, he was drafted to France in the following year. Stationed at Etaples he was engaged on important duties until invalided home owing to illness. On recovery he was transferred to the Hampshire Regiment, and returning to the Western Front, fought in the Battles of the Somme, Ypres, Passchendaele, Menin Road, and in engagements during the Advance of 1918. He was demobilised in February 1919, and holds the 1914–15 Star, and the General Service and Victory Medals.
44, Liverpool Street, Walworth, S.E.17.   Z27320

MORRIS, S. H., Corporal, Northumberland Fusiliers.
Volunteering in October 1914, in the Royal Warwickshire Regiment, he served in Ireland until transferred to the Northumberland Fusiliers, and drafted to France early in 1918. He fought during the German Offensive and subsequent Allied Advance, and on the conclusion of hostilities was sent into Germany with the Army of Occupation, and was stationed at Cologne. He returned home for demobilisation in February 1919, and holds the General Service and Victory Medals.
99, Thorparch Road, Wandsworth Road, S.W.8.   Z1969D

MORRIS, S. J., Private, 10th Queen's (Royal West Surrey Regiment).
He volunteered in June 1915, and embarking for the Western Front in the following January was in action in several engagements, and was wounded in the Battle of the Somme in July 1916. Sent home on account of his injuries he received hospital treatment, and on recovery returned to France in May 1917. After fighting in the Battle of Cambrai and other engagements he proceeded to Italy in November 1917, and served there until sent back to France in the following March. He was wounded and taken prisoner in April 1918, during the German Offensive, and held in captivity until the Armistice. He was then repatriated and subsequently demobilised in March 1919, and holds the General Service and Victory Medals.
24, Lisford Street, Peckham, S.E.15.   Z5123

MORRIS, S. W., Sergt., Rifle Brigade.
Volunteering in February 1915, he was sent to the Western Front in the following August, and served there until the close of the war. During this period he took part in heavy fighting at the Battles of Loos, Albert, Arras, Ypres, Messines, Cambrai, the Somme, and in the Retreat and Advance of 1918. He was demobilised in February 1919, and holds the 1914–15 Star, and the General Service and Victory Medals.
25, Flint Street, Walworth, S.E.17.   Z3375

MORRIS, T., Sapper, R.E.
Joining in 1917, he completed his training and was engaged on important duties with his unit at various depôts. He did valuable work but was unable to secure his transfer to a theatre of war before the termination of hostilities, and was demobilised in February 1919.
20, Cambridge Street, Camberwell, S.E.5.   Z3374

MORRIS, W. E., Private, 22nd London Regt. (The Queen's) and Norfolk Regt.
Volunteering in June 1915, he proceeded to France a year later, but was sent home after six months' service overseas, as he was under military age, and discharged. Recalled to the Colours when eighteen years of age in January 1917, he returned to the Western Front and fought in the Battles of Arras, Vimy Ridge, Bullecourt, Messines, Cambrai and the Marne (II), and was wounded in July 1918. Invalided to England he received medical treatment, and on recovery was demobilised in January 1919. He holds the General Service and Victory Medals.
269, New Kent Road, S.E.1.   Z27191

MORRIS, W. G., Private, 24th Queen's (Royal West Surrey Regt.) and Manchester Regt.
He volunteered in October 1915, and after his training was completed served with his unit until discharged on medical grounds. Called up later, however, he was posted to the Labour Corps and attached to the Manchester Regiment, was engaged on cookhouse and other duties, and did excellent work until demobilised in June 1919.
39, Olney Street, Walworth, S.E.17.   Z26221

MORRIS, W. H. (M.C.), Lieut., South Wales Borderers.
He volunteered in August 1915, and three months later embarked for the Western Front. There he took a prominent part in the Battles of Loos, St. Eloi, Ploegsteert Wood, Vimy Ridge, Arras, Hazebrouck and the Aisne. During his service he was wounded on the Somme, and gassed at Nieppe Forest, and returned home for treatment on both occasions. He was awarded the Military Cross for conspicuous gallantry and devotion to duty in taking an enemy machine gun position and several prisoners at Nieppe Forest. He was demobilised in May 1920, and also holds the 1914–15 Star, and the General Service and Victory Medals.
47, Chryssell Road, Brixton Road, S.W.9.   Z5270

MORTBY, C., Private (Signaller), 1st Royal Berkshire Regiment.

He was mobilised from the Territorial Force in August 1914, and in the following year was drafted to the Western Front. He took part in the severe fighting during the Somme Offensive in 1916, and the Battles of Arras, Ypres, and Bullecourt. He also served in the Retreat and Advance of 1918, and was gassed. Later proceeding with the Army of Occupation to Germany, he served on the Rhine for a time. Returning home in 1919, he was demobilised in May of that year, and holds the 1914-15 Star, and the General Service and Victory Medals.
16, Shepherds Place, Upper Kennington Lane, S.E.11.
Z25893

MORTIMER, T. H., Private, Middlesex Regiment.

He joined in 1917, and was sent to the Western Front in the same year. Serving with his Battalion in various sectors he took part in several engagements, notably the Battles of Ypres, Passchendaele and in the Retreat and Advance of 1918. On the conclusion of the war he returned home for demobilisation in February 1919, and holds the General Service and Victory Medals.
47, Westmacott Street, Camberwell, S.E.5.
Z4010B

MORTIMER, W. J., Private, Royal Sussex Regt.

He joined in June 1916, on attaining military age, and was drafted in the same year to the Western Front, where he saw much heavy fighting, and fought in the Battles of Ypres, Arras and many other engagements. He made the supreme sacrifice, being killed in action during the final Allied Advance on November 4th, 1918, and was entitled to the General Service and Victory Medals.
"Whilst we remember the Sacrifice is not in vain."
187, Brook Street, Kennington, S.E.11.
Z4524B

MORTON, F., Corporal, R.A.S.C. (M.T.)

Volunteering in 1914, he landed in France with the First Expeditionary Force, and was engaged on important transport duties during the Retreat from Mons, the Battle of Ypres and many other engagements. He also served in the forward areas conveying the wounded from the front lines. After the cessation of hostilities he returned home, and was demobilised in June 1919, and holds the Mons Star, and the General Service and Victory Medals.
183, Gordon Road, Peckham, S.E.15.
Z6030

MORTON, H., Private, 19th Middlesex Regiment.

He volunteered in February 1915, and embarked for France in the same year. He fought in several engagements, including the Battles of Loos, St. Eloi, Vermelles, Vimy Ridge, and was wounded at Guillemont in August 1916. Invalided home to a hospital in Manchester, he received medical treatment and on recovery returned to France in May 1917. Taking part in much heavy fighting, he was unhappily killed in action at Ypres on July 31st, 1917, and was entitled to the 1914-15 Star, and the General Service and Victory Medals.
"His life for his Country, his Soul to God."
119, Mayall Road, Herne Hill, S.E.24.
Z3379

MORTON, R. S., L/Corporal, Middlesex Regiment.

He joined in June 1917, and after completing his training proceeded to the Western Front in the same year. He served with his Battalion in various parts of the line, and fought in many important engagements until the cessation of hostilities. He returned to England in 1919, and was demobilised in February of that year, and holds the General Service and Victory Medals.
40, Tabor Road, Hammersmith, W.6.
11547

MORTON, T. G., L/Corporal, Queen's (Royal West Surrey Regiment).

Joining in 1916, he proceeded in the same year to Mesopotamia, and was engaged in heavy fighting in many engagements, including those at Sanna-i-Yat and the capture of Baghdad. In 1918 he returned to England, and was later drafted to India, where in 1920 he was still serving. He holds the General Service and Victory Medals.
18, Revesby Street, Walworth, S.E.17.
Z3380

MOS, A. C., Driver, R.A.S.C. (H.T.)

Volunteering in November 1914, he proceeded overseas in the following year, and took part in the first Landing at Gallipoli, and during the subsequent heavy fighting was wounded in action. On recovery he embarked for Mesopotamia, and was employed on transport duties in the operations at Kut, (where he was again wounded in 1917), the capture of Baghdad and several other engagements. Drafted to Persia in 1918, and later to Baku in Russia, he did much good work. He returned to England in 1919, and was demobilised in July of that year, and holds the 1914-15 Star, and the General Service and Victory Medals.
10, Russell Grove, Vassall Road, S.W.9.
Z5807

MOSS, A. H., Driver, R.F.A.

He volunteered in April 1915, and in the same year was drafted to France. There he fought with his Battery in many important engagements, including the Battles of the Somme, Beaumont-Hamel, Arras, Messines Ridge, Passchendaele, Nieuport, and was gassed at Kemmel in 1918. On recovery he rejoined his Battery, and served until the end of the war. He returned home for demobilisation in May 1919, and holds the 1914-15 Star, and the General Service and Victory Medals.
62, Maysoule Road, Battersea, S.W.11.
Z3381

MOSS, D., Private, R.A.S.C.

He volunteered in February 1915, and in the following month was drafted to France. Whilst in this theatre of war he was engaged on important transport duties in the Battles of the Somme, Arras, Loos, Lens, and during the Retreat and Advance of 1918, and was gassed. Returning to England on the termination of hostilities, he was demobilised in March 1919, and holds the 1914-15 Star, and the General Service and Victory Medals.
22, Berkley Street, Kennington, S.E.11.
Z25871

MOSS, G., Driver, R.F.A.

After volunteering in May 1915, he completed his training, and in December was sent to France. While on that Front he did excellent service with his Battery in the Battles of the Somme, Messines, Ypres, Passchendaele, Cambrai and the Retreat and Advance of the Allies in 1918. After his return home he was demobilised in June 1919, and holds the 1914-15 Star, and the General Service and Victory Medals.
27, Ledbury Street, Peckham, S.E.15.
Z6562B

MOSS, G., Gunner, R.F.A. (T.M.B.)

He attested in December 1915, and was called up in March 1917. He proceeded to the Western Front two months later, and served with a Trench Mortar Battery in many engagements, including the Battles of Ypres, Passchendaele, Cambrai, the Somme, Villers-Bretonneux, and was wounded. He was invalided home to Stourbridge Hospital, and after recovery was retained on home service duties until after the conclusion of hostilities. He was demobilised in February 1919, and holds the General Service and Victory Medals.
6, Charleston Street, Walworth, S.E.17.
Z3382

MOSS, G. W., Air Mechanic, R.A.F. (Kite Balloon Section).

He joined in June 1917, and on completion of his training proceeded two months later to Mesopotamia, where he served with his Squadron on special duties which called for a high degree of technical skill, and took part in operations during the Advance on Kut. He returned to England in October 1918, and was demobilised in April of the following year, and holds the General Service and Victory Medals.
33, Binns Road, Chiswick, W.4.
5455

MOSS, W. H., Driver, R.F.A.

Volunteering in July 1915, he completed his course of training and was afterwards engaged on general duties at various stations. He was not able to secure his transfer overseas while hostilities continued, and in April 1916 was discharged as medically unfit for further service.
27, Ledbury Street, Peckham, S.E.15.
Z6562A

MOSSMAN, A., Special War Worker.

During the war he was engaged on work of National importance at Woolwich Arsenal, as an electrical switchboard operator from December 1914. He attested under the Derby Scheme, but was exempted as indispensable to the Arsenal, and in 1920 was still working there.
171, Sumner Road, Peckham, S.E.15.
Z6301

MOTHERSOLE, A., Corporal, 3rd County of London Yeomanry (Sharpshooters Hussars) and M.G.C.

Volunteering in May 1915, he embarked for Egypt later in the same year, and was in action in many engagements during the operations following the third Battle of Gaza, and resulting in the capture of Jerusalem. In 1918 he was transferred to Salonika, and later to the Western Front, where he fought throughout the closing operations of the war. He was demobilised in February 1919, and holds the 1914-15 Star, and the General Service and Victory Medals.
4, Carew Street, Camberwell, S.E.5.
Z6038

MOULES, G. W., Bombardier, R.F.A. and Trench Mortar Battery.

He enlisted in February 1914, and was sent to France shortly after the declaration of war. During his service overseas, he fought in many engagements including those at Armentières, Ypres, the Somme, and throughout the Retreat and Advance of 1918, and was three times gassed. After the Armistice he was sent into Germany with the Army of Occupation, and served there until he returned to England, and was demobilised in June 1919. He holds the 1914 Star, and the General Service and Victory Medals.
275, Mayall Road, Herne Hill, S.E.24.
Z3383

MOUNTFORD, E. F., Private, 20th Queen's (Royal West Surrey Regiment).

He volunteered in March 1917, and proceeding to the Western Front was engaged on important duties, attached to Headquarters Staff of the Labour Corps. He was also present at heavy fighting during the Retreat and Advance of 1918, and rendered valuable services throughout. He was demobilised in 1919, and holds the General Service and Victory Medals.

10, Thurlow Street, Walworth, S.E.17. Z3384A

MOUNTFORD, W. C., Private, West Yorkshire Regt.

Joining in 1916, he embarked for France later in the same year, and fought in many important engagements, including the Battle of the Somme. He gave his life for King and Country at Arras in June 1917, and lies at rest in the British Cemetery at Arras. He was entitled to the General Service and Victory Medals.

"He died the noblest death a man may die.
Fighting for God, and right, and liberty."

10, Thurlow Street, Walworth, S.E.17. Z3384B

MOUNTSTEPHENS, J., Chief Petty Officer, R.N.

He joined the Service in 1897, and at the outbreak of war was serving in H.M.S. "Royal Oak," which ship was in action at the Battles of Jutland, and Heligoland Bight. She also did good work with the Grand Fleet in the North Sea, engaged on patrol and other important duties. He was demobilised in January 1919, and holds the 1914-15 Star, and the General Service and Victory Medals. He also holds the Queen's South African Medal with two bars, and the West African Medal (with Clasp Benin).

35, Odell Street, Camberwell, S.E.5. Z5463A

MOUNTSTEPHENS, J. C., A.B., Royal Navy.

He joined in August 1914, and was posted to H.M.S. "Lord Nelson." His hip proceeded to the Mediterranean Sea, and was in action in the Battle of the Narrows, and assisted to cover the Landing of the troops at Gallipoli. She was afterwards engaged on patrol and convoy work in the Mediterranean Sea frequently passing through mine-infested areas in the discharge of her duties, and rendered valuable services throughout. In 1920 he was serving aboard H.M.S. "Valient," and holds the 1914-15 Star, and the General Service and Victory Medals.

35, Odell Street, Camberwell, S.E.5. Z5463B

MOUSLEY, W. F., Private, 1st Queen's (Royal West Surrey Regiment).

A Reservist, he was mobilised at the outbreak of war and shortly afterwards proceeded to France, where he was in action in many engagements, and was wounded. On recovery he rejoined his Battalion, and saw heavy fighting in many parts of the line. He was reported missing, and later to have been killed in action, and was entitled to the 1914 Star, and the General Service and Victory Medals.

"The path of duty was the way to glory."

3, Cyril Street, Walworth, S.E.17. X6225B

MOWER, F. G., Private, 3rd Dorsetshire Regt.

He volunteered in May 1915, and proceeding to the Western Front in the following December, fought in the Battles of the Somme, Bullecourt and Passchendaele. He was also in action in the German Offensive and subsequent Allied Advance of 1918, and was present at the entry into Mons on November 11th, 1918. Suffering from shell-shock he was admitted into hospital, and later returned to England. On recovery he was demobilised in February 1919, and holds the 1914-15 Star, and the General Service and Victory Medals.

11, Darien Road, Battersea, S.W.11. Z3385

MOWFORTH, T., Gunner, R.F.A.

He volunteered in June 1915, and drafted to the Western Front later in that year was in action in many engagements in the Ypres and Arras sectors. He died gloriously on the field of Battle near Ypres on September 20th, 1917, and was buried in the Military Cemetry at Ypres. He was entitled to the 1914-15 Star, and the General Service and Victory Medals.

"Great deeds cannot die :
They with the sun and moon renew their light for ever."

50, Bournemouth Road, Rye Lane, S.E.15. Z5464

MOXEY, D. L. (D.F.M.), Air Mechanic, R.A.F. (late R.N.A.S.)

Volunteering in April 1915, and proceeding to the Western Front he did good work, engaged as an observer. Later he was transferred to Italy and saw much service in this theatre of war. He was awarded the Distinguished Flying Medal for gallantry and devotion to duty in shooting down an Austrian Seaplane at Otranto in September 1918. He returned to England and was discharged on account of service in November 1918, and holds the 1914-15 Star, and the General Service and Victory Medals.

53, Cooks Road, Walworth, S.E.17. Z26785

MOXON, F. W., Gunner, Royal Marine Artillery.

He enlisted in 1913, and at the declaration of war was serving aboard H.M.S. "Benbow." This ship was in action at the Battles of the Dogger Bank and Jutland, and did good work engaged on escort duties between the United States and England, and also served in the Baltic Sea. He was serving in Southern Russia in 1920, and holds the 1914-15 Star, and the General Service and Victory Medals.

16, Ada Road, Camberwell, S.E.5. Z4504

MOYES, S. C. H., Private, 7th Royal Sussex Regt.

He joined in October 1917, on attaining military age, and proceeding to France in the following month was in action at the Battles of the Somme, Ypres, Cambrai and throughout the German Offensive and Allied Advance of 1918. He was still serving in 1920, and holds the General Service and Victory Medals.

10, Nelson's Row, Clapham, S.W.4. Z3386B

MOYES, T. M., Trooper, 4th Australian Light Horse.

He joined in November 1916, and embarking for Egypt three months later saw much service on the Palestine front. He fought in the Battles of Gaza I, II and III, and Jericho and in many engagements during the British Advance through the Holy Land into Syria. He was demobilised in August 1919, and holds the General Service and Victory Medals.

10, Nelson's Row, Clapham, S.W.4. Z3386A

MOYSES, A. E., Rifleman, 21st London Regiment (1st Surrey Rifles).

Mobilised and drafted to France at the outbreak of hostilities, he fought in the Retreat from Mons and at the Battle of Hill 60, where he was wounded in May 1915, and in consequence lost the sight of his right eye. On recovery he returned to France in 1916, and attached to the King's Royal Rifle Corps, and later to the Sherwood Foresters, took part in many engagements, and saw much fighting during the Retreat and Advance of 1918. After the Armistice he proceeded with the Army of Occupation into Germany and served there until he returned to England and was demobilised in May 1919. He holds the Mons Star, and the General Service and Victory Medals. 6, Belham Street, Camberwell, S.E.5. Z3169A

MUIR, A. W., A.B., Royal Navy.

He joined the Service in November 1915, and was posted to H.M.S. "President." Shortly afterwards he returned to shore and served with the Anti-aircraft Guns at Westgate and various other stations until the cessation of hostilities. He rendered valuable services throughout, and was demobilised in January 1919, and holds the General Service and Victory Medals.

19, Radner Terrace, South Lambeth Road, S.W.8. Z3387

MULLAN, B., Private, M.G.C.

Volunteering in August 1914, and drafted to the Western Front later in the same year he fought in many engagements, and was wounded at Neuve Chapelle. On recovery he rejoined his unit and took part in severe fighting, and was again wounded, and also gassed at Ypres. Returning to England he received medical treatment and subsequently died from his injuries at Edinburgh Hospital in August 1917. He was entitled to the 1914-15 Star, and the General Service and Victory Medals.

"And doubtless he went in splendid company."

31, Fort Road, Bermondsey, S.E.1. Z26067

MULLINGS, A., L/Corporal, R.A.O.C.

Joining in February 1918, he proceeded to France five months later, and was engaged on important duties at Le Havre, attached to the Labour Corps. He rendered valuable services throughout, and returning to England, was demobilised in February 1920, and holds the General Service and Victory Medals.

25, Stewarts Road, Battersea Park Road, S.W.8. Z3389

MULLINGS, C., Private, 16th Middlesex Regt. and R.A.S.C.

Volunteering in February 1915, he was sent to France in the following November, and fought at the Battles of Loos, Vimy Ridge, the Somme, Beaumont-Hamel, and was twice wounded. On recovery from the latter wound, he was transferred to the Royal Army Service Corps, and returned to France in 1917. He served in various sectors, engaged on transporting supplies to the front lines and was present at heavy fighting in the Retreat and Advance of 1918. He was demobilised in May 1919, and holds the 1914-15 Star, and the General Service and Victory Medals.

90, De Laune Street, Walworth, S.E.17. Z25931

MULLINGS, R., Private, 6th Middlesex Regiment.

He joined in June 1918, and embarking for France three months later, fought in many engagements during the closing operations of the war. After the Armistice he served in France engaged on important duties until 1919, and then returned to England, and was demobilised in November of that year. He holds the General Service and Victory Medals.

2, Totteridge Road, Battersea, S.W.11. Z3390

MULVANEY, H., Corporal, Queen's (Royal West Surrey Regiment).

A Territorial, he was mobilised in August 1914, and in the following year was sent to the Western Front. Here he took part in heavy fighting at the Battles of Loos, Arras, Ypres, the Somme, and was in action throughout the Retreat and Advance of 1918. He was demobilised in March 1919, and holds the 1914-15 Star, and the General Service and Victory Medals.
96, Rolls Road, Bermondsey S.E.1.   Z26748

MUMFORD, A. T., Cpl., Somerset Light Infantry.

He volunteered in September 1914, and completing his training served at various depôts engaged on important duties until sent to France in November 1917. He fought in many important engagements, including those at Amiens, Ypres, and Cambrai, and saw heavy fighting during the Retreat and Advance of 1918. Wounded and gassed, he returned to England, and after receiving hospital treatment was discharged unfit for further service in January 1919. He holds the General Service and Victory Medals.
42, Rosemary Road, Peckham, S.E.15.   Z5465B

MUMFORD, W., Private, R.A.O.C.

He joined in February 1917, and was drafted to Salonika later in the same year. During his service in this theatre of war he was engaged on important duties at the Base and rendered excellent services. Returning to England he was demobilised in March 1920, and holds the General Service and Victory Medals.
42, Rosemary Road, Peckham, S.E.15.   Z5465A

MUNDAY, A. E., Private, R.A.S.C. and 3rd Somerset Light Infantry.

He joined in December 1916, and was sent to France in the following year. He fought in engagements at the Somme and Ypres, and was wounded and gassed in the second Battle of the Somme in March 1918. On recovery he rejoined his unit, and saw much fighting in the closing stages of the war. After the Armistice he proceeded to Egypt, and was engaged on garrison duty at various stations. He returned to England, and was demobilised in January 1920, and holds the General Service and Victory Medals.
22, Pilkington Road, Peckham, S.E.15.   Z6041

MUNDAY, A. G., Private, R.A.O.C.

He joined in 1917, and completing his training was stationed at Portsmouth, engaged on important duties connected with the shipment of ammunition to various theatres of war. Owing to medical unfitness he did not obtain his transfer overseas, but did excellent work until demobilised in 1919.
57, Elizabeth Street, Walworth, S.E.17.   Z26546

MUNDAY, H. S., Private, East Surrey Regiment.

Joining in 1917, and drafted to the Western Front in February of the following year, he was in action in many important engagements. He was seriously wounded at Albert on March 31st, 1918, during the German Offensive, and returning to England received medical treatment. He was subsequently invalided out of the Service, totally disabled later in 1918, and holds the General Service and Victory Medals.
88, Inville Road, Walworth, S.E.17.   Z27304A

MUNDAY, J., Air Mechanic, R.A.F.

He joined in November 1916, and was drafted to France later in that year. During his service overseas he served at Bray, Landrecies, Le Quesnoy and in many other parts of the line. He saw heavy fighting in the German Offensive and Allied Advance, and returning to England after the cessation of hostilities was demobilised in January 1919. He holds the General Service and Victory Medals.
2, Lapford Place, off Vauxhall Street, Kennington, S.E.11.
25308C

MUNDAY, J. (Jun.), Private, 4th Royal Fusiliers.

He joined in November 1916, and completing his training served at various depôts with his unit engaged on guard and other important duties. He did not obtain his transfer overseas prior to the cessation of hostilities, owing to medical unfitness, but was drafted to Mesopotamia in November 1918, and was still serving there in 1920.
2, Lapford Place, off Vauxhall Street, Kennington, S.E.11.
TZ25308A

MUNDAY, Joseph, Private, M.G.C.

Joining in November 1916, he proceeded to the Western Front shortly afterwards, and was in action at the Battles of Ypres, Arras, the Somme, and throughout the German Offensive and subsequent Allied Advance of 1918. In 1919 he was sent to India, where he was serving in 1920, and holds the General Service and Victory Medals.
2, Lapford Place, off Vauxhall Street, Kennington, S.E.11.
TZ25308B

MUNDAY, L. A., Sapper, R.E.

Joining in 1916, and proceeding to France later in the same year, he served on special duties at the Battles of Albert, Loos, St. Eloi, Arras, Messines, Passchendaele, Lens and the Somme. He rendered valuable services engaged on important field work throughout the Retreat and Advance of 1918, and returning to England was demobilised in 1919. He holds the General Service and Victory Medals.
88, Inville Road, Walworth, S.E.17.   Z27304B

MUNDAY, W. C., Air Mechanic, R.A.F. (late R.F.C.)

He joined in May 1918, and completing his training was stationed at various aerodromes engaged on important duties in connection with the repair of aeroplanes. He did not obtain his transfer overseas prior to the cessation of hostilities, but rendered excellent services until demobilised in March 1919.
56, Trehene Road, Stockwell, S.W.9.   Z4505A

MUNNS, A. C., Private, R.A.O.C.

He joined in 1916, and after his training served at various depôts on important duties with his unit. He rendered valuable services, but owing to his being medically unfit was not able to proceed overseas. He was demobilised in March 1919.
60, Evelina Road, Nunhead, S.E.15.   Z6284A

MUNT, F. C., Pte., 2nd and 3rd Bedfordshire Regt.

He joined in March 1917, and embarked for the Western Front later in the same year. He was in action in many important engagements, including those at the Somme, Ypres, Arras, Passchendaele, and was severely wounded at St. Quentin. Returning to England he received hospital treatment, and was subsequently invalided out of the Service in September 1918. He holds the General Service and Victory Medals.
74, Sussex Road, Coldharbour Lane, S.W.9.   Z3391A

MUNT, W., Gunner, R.F.A.

He enlisted in July 1914, and shortly after the declaration of war, embarked for the Western Front. He was in action in many parts of the line, and was taken prisoner at Le Cateau. He was held in captivity at Sennenlager and various other camps in Germany until after the Armistice, when he was repatriated, and subsequently demobilised in July 1920. He holds the 1914 Star, and the General Service and Victory Medals.
8, Geneva Road, Coldharbour Lane, S.W.9.   Z3492

MUNT, W., Private, Essex Regiment and R.D.C.

He joined in August 1918, at the age of forty-eight, and after his training was transferred to the Royal Defence Corps. He was engaged on guard and other important duties at various prisoners of war camps, and rendered excellent services throughout. He was demobilised in January 1919.
74, Sussex Road, Coldharbour Lane, S.W.9.   Z3391B

MURPHY, A. G., Pte., Devonshire Regt. and M.G.C.

He joined in February 1917, and was later transferred to the Machine Gun Corps, with which unit he proceeded to the Western Front in the following year. After only a short period of active service, he made the supreme sacrifice, being killed in action on March 29th, 1918. He was entitled to the General Service and Victory Medals.
"He passed out of the sight of men by the path of duty and self-sacrifice."
2, Victoria Place, Priory Grove, S.W.8.   Z3392

MURPHY, J., Private, Royal Irish Regiment.

He was mobilised from the Reserve at the outbreak of war, and drafted to France shortly afterwards took part in the Retreat from Mons, and was wounded in the Battle of the Aisne. After receiving medical treatment he returned to the front lines and was unhappily killed in action during the Battle of Neuve Chapelle on March 15th, 1915. He was entitled to the Mons Star, and the General Service and Victory Medals.
"Nobly striving, he nobly fell that we might live."
186, Farmer's Road, Camberwell, S.E.5.   Z1707B

MURPHY, J., Pte., 2nd East Yorkshire Regiment.

He was mobilised from the Reserve at the outbreak of war, and in September 1914, proceeded to France. During his service on the Western Front he fought in the Battles of the Aisne, La Bassée, and Ypres. Owing to ill-health he was invalided home and receiving hospital treatment was subsequently discharged as medically unfit for further military service in February 1916. Unhappily he died on October 14th, 1919, from the effects of an illness contracted whilst on active service and was entitled to the Mons Star, and the General Service and Victory Medals.
"His memory is cherished with pride."
38, Runham Street, Walworth, S.E.17.   Z3593B

MURPHY, J., Private, R.A.S.C.

He volunteered in September 1915, and proceeded in the same month to France, where he was engaged on important transport duties until the Armistice. During this period he served in the forward areas in many parts of the line, and was frequently under shell fire. He then went with the Army of Occupation into Germany and was stationed on the Rhine. Returning to England in April 1919, he was demobilised in the following month, and in addition to the Queen's and King's South African Medals, holds the Mons Star, and the General Service and Victory Medals.

28, Atherton Street, Battersea, S.W.11.   Z3394

MURPHY, R., Sapper, R.E.

He volunteered in November 1914, and after completing his training was sent to the Dardanelles a year later. In this theatre of war he was engaged on special work during the final operations on the Peninsula, and after the Evacuation proceeded to Egypt, and subsequently to Salonika, where he served in engagements during the Advance on the Vardar front in September 1918. Returning home he was demobilised in February 1919, and holds the 1914–15 Star, and the General Service and Victory Medals.

7, Silcote Road, Camberwell, S.E.5.   Z5466

MURPHY, T., Private, 4th Middlesex Regiment.

He was mobilised from the Reserve in August 1914, and proceeded to France with his unit. There he was engaged in heavy fighting in the Retreat from Mons, and the Battles of the Marne, the Aisne, Ypres, and Arras, and was wounded twice at La Bassée and later at the second Battle of the Somme in 1918. After receiving medical treatment he returned to England in 1919, and was invalided out of the Service later in that year. He holds the Mons Star, and the General Service and Victory Medals.

15, Lebanon Street, Walworth, S.E.17.   Z3395

MURPHY, W. J., Gunner, R.F.A. and R.H.A.

Volunteering in December 1914, he was drafted in the following year with his Battery to France, where he took part in many notable engagements, including the Battles of Ypres, Festubert and Loos. Later transferred to the R.H.A. he served with the Army of Occupation in Germany, and was stationed on the Rhine. He subsequently returned to England, and in 1920 was serving at Aldershot. He holds the 1914–15 Star, and the General Service and Victory Medals.

25, Everett Street, Nine Elms Lane, S.W.8.   Z3396

MURRANT, W. H. E., L/Corporal, 1st Queen's Own (Royal West Kent Regiment).

Volunteering in August 1914, he was drafted in the same month to France and was engaged in heavy fighting in the Retreat from Mons, and the Battles of La Bassée and Givenchy, during which engagement he was buried by shell explosion. He gave his life for King and Country at La Bassée on October 26th, 1915, and was entitled to the Mons Star, and the General Service and Victory Medals.

"Great deeds cannot die:
They with the sun and moon renew their light for ever."

53, Lower Park Road, Peckham, S.E.15.   Z6527

MURRAY, A., Rifleman, Rifle Brigade.

He joined in September 1918, and on completion of his training served at various stations on important duties with his Regiment. He did good work but was not able to secure his transfer overseas before the Armistice. Later however, he was drafted to India, and from there to Mesopotamia, where he was still serving in 1920.

1, Carfax Square, Clapham Park Road, S.W.4.   Z3397C

MURRAY, A. E., Gunner, R.F.A.

He volunteered in January 1915, and in the following September was sent to France, where he fought in the Battles of Ypres, Bullecourt, the Somme, Vimy Ridge, Lens, Passchendaele, Cambrai, St. Quentin, Givenchy, Loos, St. Eloi and Albert. He was also in action in the final Retreat and Advance and was present at the entry into Mons at dawn on November 11th, 1918. During his service overseas he was twice wounded, on each occasion returning to England for treatment. He was demobilised in February 1919, and holds the 1914–15 Star, and the General Service and Victory Medals.

1, Carfax Square, Clapham Park Road, S.W.4.   Z3397B

MURRAY, A. J., Stoker, R.N.

He was serving at the outbreak of war aboard H.M.S. "Good Hope," which vessel served with the Grand Fleet in the North Sea and was also in action against the German Squadron off Coronel. He lost his life when the "Good Hope" was sunk in this engagement in November 1914, and was entitled to the 1914–15 Star, and the General Service and Victory Medals.

"The path of duty was the way to glory."

47, Hargwyne Street, Stockwell Road, S.W.9.   Z1637B

MURRAY, D. F. (Mrs.), Special War Worker.

During the war this lady offered her services for work of National importance, and was employed at Woolwich Arsenal from January 1917. She was employed in the danger zone, shell filling, and owing to illness contracted during the performance of her duties she was compelled to relinquish her work in June 1918. She rendered valuable services throughout.

40, Clapham Park Road, S.W.4.   Z3397A

MURRAY, F. C., Private, Labour Corps.

He joined in February 1917, and in the following June proceeded to the Western Front, and engaged on important duties in the forward areas was present during several engagements, including the second Battle of the Somme. He was killed in action on March 21st, 1918, and was entitled to the General Service and Victory Medals.

"His life for his Country, his Soul to God."

36, Neate Street, Camberwell, S.E.5.   Z5124

MURRAY, F. R. (Mrs.), Special War Worker.

Offering her services for work of National importance this lady was engaged by Messrs. Harris and Other, Old Town, Clapham, and was employed in their factory from December 1916 until January 1919. During this period she rendered valuable services in connection with the manufacture of body shields and aeroplane wings, and discharged her duties to the complete satisfaction of her employers.

1, Carfax Square, Clapham Park Road, S.W.4.   Z3398C

MURRAY, G., Ship's Cook, Merchant Service.

He was in the Merchant Service at the outbreak of hostilities, and during the war served in s.s. "Peninsula" in the North Sea and other waters. In the course of her voyages his ship was torpedoed in August 1917, off the Scilly Islands, but he was fortunately rescued. He was discharged in the same month, and holds the General Service and Mercantile Marine War Medals.

96, D Block, Guinness Buildings, Page's Walk, Grange Road, Bermondsey, S.E.1.   Z26831A

MURRAY, L. (Mrs.), Special War Worker.

During the war this lady volunteered for work of National importance and was engaged by the Anti-Gasworks Factory, 130, New Kent Road, S.E.1. from June 1916 until March 1919 Working on tube and gas mask testing, she carried out her responsible duties in an efficent and capable manner.

96, D. Block, Guinness Buildings, Page's Walk, Grange Road, Bermondsey, S.E.1.   Z26831B

MURRAY, R. W., Air Mechanic, R.A.F.

He joined in June 1918, and on the conclusion of his training served with his Squadron at various aerodromes. Engaged on duties connected with the making and repairing of aeroplanes, he carried out his duties, which called for a high degree of technical knowledge and skill, in an efficient manner, but was unable to secure his transfer overseas before hostilities ceased. He was demobilised in August 1919.

1, Carfax Square, Clapham Park Road, S.W.4.   Z3398A

MURRAY, S. V., Private, 1/10th London Regiment.

He volunteered in January 1915, and sent to France in the same year fought in the Battle of Loos. In January 1916, he embarked for Egypt, but during the voyage his ship was wrecked in the Mediterranean with heavy loss of life. Rescued by a Torpedo Boat he was conveyed to Egypt and served during the British Advance through Palestine .He was in action in the Battles of Gaza, Jaffa, Jericho, and was present at the entry of General Allenby into Jerusalem. During his service in the East he contracted malaria, and sent to hospital at Alexandria rejoined his unit on recovery, and served until the signing of the Armistice. He was demobilised in June 1919, on returning to England, and holds the General Service and Victory Medals.

1, Carfax Square, Clapham Park Road, S.W.4.   Z3398B

MURRAY, W., 1st Class Stoker, R.N.

Joining the Royal Navy in 1906, he was mobilised when war broke out and served in H.M.S. "Bedford" and later in H.M.S. "Vanguard." His ship was engaged on important patrol duties in the North Sea and off the Belgian Coast, and was in action in the Battle of Jutland, and in several other encounters with enemy craft. Owing to ill-health he returned to shore and was subsequently invalided out of the Service in March 1919. He holds the 1914–15 Star, and the General Service and Victory Medals.

114, Cator Street, Peckham, S.E.15.   Z4459A

MURRELL, W. L., Private, Duke of Cornwall's Light Infantry.

He volunteered in September 1914, and proceeding to France in the following August served in the Machine Gun section of his Platoon in the Battles of St. Eloi, and the Somme. Severely wounded in August 1916, he was sent to hospital in England and died from the effects of his injuries in August 14th, 1916. He was entitled to the 1914–15 Star, and the General Service and Victory Medals.

"Steals on the ear, the distant triumph song."

74, Wickersley Road, Lavender Hill, S.W.11.   Z2646B

MURROCK, E., Private, North Staffordshire Regt.

He joined in September 1916, and in the same year was drafted overseas. During his service in France he fought at Vimy Ridge and Arras, and was severely wounded at Ypres in 1917. He was invalided home, and after three months' treatment rejoined his unit in France, and was in action in the second Battle of the Somme, and again wounded at Havrincourt. He was sent to hospital in England, and after some months was demobilised in March 1919, holding the General Service and Victory Medals.

59, Tappersfield Road, Nunhead Lane, Peckham, S.E.15.
Z6412

MUSGROVE, A. J., Gunner, R.F.A.

He volunteered in November 1915, and in March of the following year was drafted to France. Whilst in this theatre of war he was in action in almost every sector of the British front, and also served with the French Army on the Marne in 1918, and did excellent work as a Gunner in the Retreat and Advance. He was wounded in September 1918, in the second Battle of Cambrai and invalided to hospital in England, and in the following February was demobilised. He holds the General Service and Victory Medals.

32, Unwin Road, Peckham, S.E.15.
Z6414

MUSGROVE, G. H., Private, 11th Hampshire Regt.

He volunteered in September 1914, and after training in Ireland was drafted to France in November of the following year. Whilst overseas he fought on the Somme, and at Messines, Ypres and Cambrai, but after contracting trench fever was invalided home in November 1917. After prolonged medical treatment in hospital he was transferred to the Royal Army Ordnance Corps, and was engaged on important duties at Woolwich until his demobilisation in March 1919. He holds the 1914-15 Star, and the General Service and Victory Medals.

24, Unwin Road, Peckham, S.E.15.
Z6411

MUSSARED, O. E., Petty Officer, R.N.

He was already serving when war broke out and aboard H.M.S. "Jason" was engaged on special work throughout the course of hostilities. His ship carried out important submarine patrol duties, and was also employed in convoying and escorting vessels across the North Sea. He was blown up by a mine when mine-sweeping, but he was fortunately rescued. Transferred to Torpedo Boat "M. 33," he was serving in this vessel when she was torpedoed the day before the Battle of Jutland. He was discharged on account of service in March 1919, and in addition to the Queen's and King's South African Medals, and the China Medal (1900), he holds the 1914-15 Star, and the General Service and Victory Medals.

9, Kimberley Road, Landor Road, S.W.9.
Z3409

MUSSELBROOK, B., Wireless Operator, Merchant Service.

Joining in December 1916, he was posted to s.s. "Beechleaf," and served as a wireless operator. His ship was engaged on special duties in connection with the supply of oil fuel to vessels of the Royal Navy in Eastern waters, and served in the Persian Gulf, and the Red and Black Seas. He was later transferred to the R.M.S.P. "Somme," aboard which he was still serving in 1920. He holds the General Service and Mercantile Marine War Medals.

17, Stansfield Road, Stockwell Road, S.W.9.
Z3410B

MUSSELBROOK, F., Private, 11th Somerset Light Infantry.

He joined in November 1916, and was drafted in the following year to France, where he served in the transport section of his Battalion. He rendered valuable services during the Battles of Ypres, Lille, Amiens, Epéhy, and the Somme, and in other engagements until the cessation of hostilities. Demobilised in October 1919, he holds the General Service and Victory Medals.

17, Stansfield Road, Stockwell Road, S.W.9.
Z3410A

MUST, H. T. J., Driver, R.A.S.C. (M.T.)

Volunteering in 1914, he embarked for the Western Front in the following year and served in various sectors with his unit. He was engaged with the ammunition supply column and was present at several engagements, including those on the Somme, at Ypres, Arras, Messines, and Valenciennes. After the Armistice he was sent with the Army of Occupation into Germany and stationed at Cologne. He returned home for demobilisation in June 1919, and holds the 1914-15 Star, and the General Service and Victory Medals.

90, Cambridge Street, Camberwell, S.E.5.
Z3412

MUTIMER, J. (M.C., D.C.M.), Captain, R.G.A.

He was serving in the Army when war was declared, and was drafted to France in September 1914. He took a prominent part in the Battles of the Marne, the Aisne, the Somme, Ypres and during the Retreat and Advance of 1918, and was wounded three times. During his service on the Western Front he was awarded the Distinguished Conduct Medal, and later the Military Cross for conspicuous gallantry and devotion to duty in the Field. He also holds the 1914 Star, and the General Service and Victory Medals, and was demobilised in 1919.   59A, Winstead Street, Battersea, S.W.11.
Z3413

MYERS, R., Private, R.A.S.C.

Volunteering in 1915, he embarked for France later in that year, and was engaged on important duties connected with the supply of ammunition to the front lines. He was present at many engagements of note and was almost continuously under fire. Owing to ill-health he returned to England, and after receiving hospital treatment was invalided out of the Service in May 1918. He subsequently died from the effects of illness contracted whilst on service, and was entitled to the 1914-15 Star, and the General Service and Victory Medals.
"His memory is cherished with pride."

124, Trafalgar Street, Walworth, S.E.17.
Z27341

MYERS, W. G., Private, R.A.M.C.

Volunteering in August 1914, he was drafted to France and served in the Retreat from Mons, and in the Battles of Ypres, Neuve Chapelle, Loos and the Somme, engaged on important ambulance duties in the front lines. He was mentioned in Despatches for devotion to duty in attending the wounded under heavy fire. He was unfortunately killed in action on November 6th, 1917, and was entitled to the Mons Star, and the General Service and Victory Medals.

75, Avenue Road, Camberwell, S.E.5.
Z3414

MYERSON, A., Private, The Buffs (East Kent Regt.)

He volunteered in 1915, and proceeding to the Western Front in the following year was in action at the Battles of the Somme, Hill 60, Arras and many other engagements. He fought throughout the German Offensive and Allied Advance of 1918, and returning to England was demobilised in 1920. He holds the General Service and Victory Medals.

15, Lollard Street, Kennington, S.E.11.
Z25859

MYHILL, B., Special War Worker.

He offered his services for work of National importance, and for two years worked at Du Cros' Works, Acton, as a shell-borer. Later he was employed at Messrs. Wilkinsons' Sword Factory, attending to the furnaces for fifteen months. He joined the 3rd Royal Fusiliers in August 1918, but was unable to obtain his transfer overseas prior to the cessation of hostilities. He was sent to the Army of Occupation in Germany, and was still serving there in 1920.

139, Southfield Road, Bedford Park, W.4.
7072A

MYHILL, E. O., Private, Lincolnshire Regiment.

A serving soldier, he was mobilised and drafted to France at the commencement of hostilities, and fought in the Retreat from Mons, and in the Battles of the Aisne, and the Marne. He died gloriously on the field of battle at Neuve Chapelle on March 10th, 1915, and lies buried there. He was entitled to the Mons Star, and the General Service and Victory Medals.
"A valiant soldier, with undaunted heart he breasted Life's last hill."

15, St. Alphonsus Road, Clapham, S.W.4.
Z3415A

MYHILL, F. (Miss), Special War Worker.

This lady offered her services for work of National importance and for two years worked at Messrs. Vanderville's Works, Acton, engaged on the manufacture of hand-grenades. She rendered valuable services, and discharged her duties in a satisfactory and efficient manner.

139, Southfield Road, Bedford Park, W.4.
7072C

MYHILL, H. P., Private, East Surrey Regiment.

He joined in June 1916, and proceeding to France later in that year was in action at the Battles of Arras, Albert, St. Quentin, St. Eloi, Lens, Passchendaele, and was taken prisoner in March 1918, during the German Offensive. He was held in captivity until after the Armistice, and was then repatriated. He was still serving in 1920, and holds the General Service and Victory Medals.

15, St. Alphonsus Road, Clapham, S.W.4.
Z3415B

MYHILL, W., Special War Worker.

He volunteered for work of National importance, and throughout the whole period of the war was employed at Messrs. Du Cros' Works, Acton. He rendered excellent services, engaged on transporting the completed shell cases to the various filling factories, and received high commendation for the efficient way in which he carried out his duties.

139, Southfield Road, Bedford Park, W.4.
7072B

N

NAGLE, H. F., Driver, R.F.A. and A.B., Royal Navy.

He volunteered in January 1915, but was discharged as unfit for military service in the same month. He then joined the Navy in February 1915, and was posted to H.M.S. "Victory," and after one month's service was invalided out of the Service in March.

25, Newland Terrace, Queens Road, Battersea Park, S.W.8.
Z3500

NAPPER, T. A., Driver, R.F.A.

He volunteered in May 1915, and completing his training, served at various stations with his Battery engaged on important duties. He was unsuccessful in obtaining his transfer overseas, but rendered valuable services until demobilised in February 1919.

22, Dawlish Street, Wilcox Road, S.W.8. 3501

NARBOROUGH, C. (Mrs.), Special War Worker.

This lady was employed at Messrs. Vickery's Munition Factory, Southwark, in the manufacture of hand grenades, and afterwards at the British Oxygen Company, Westminster, on important duties. Her work involved a high degree of skill and integrity, and she rendered valuable services during her period of engagement, which extended for over four years.

23, Hinchliffe Street, Westminster, S.W.1. Z23281A

NARBOROUGH, H., Pioneer, Australian I.F.

He volunteered in October 1915, and in the same year proceeded to the Dardanelles, where he served in the final operations on the Peninsula. He was transferred to the Western Front in March 1916, and fought in many engagements, including those on the Somme, at Arras and Passchendaele. He was wounded and invalided home and on recovery served in England until demobilised in March 1920. He holds the 1914-15 Star, and the General Service and Victory Medals.

23, Hinchliffe Street, Westminster, S.W.1. Z23281B

NASH, A. G., Private, Royal Fusiliers.

He joined in June 1915, and was sent to France shortly afterwards. He was in action at the Battles of Loos, Festubert, Hill 60, Ypres, and in many other engagements of note. In attempting to save a comrade he was killed in action on April 26th, 1916, and was entitled to the General Service and Victory Medals.

"A costly Sacrifice upon the altar of freedom."

74, Surrey Lane, Battersea, S.W.11. Z3503

NASH, C., Private, North Staffordshire Regiment and Air Mechanic, R.A.F.

Joining in September 1916, he embarked for the Western Front in the following February, and fought in many notable engagements. He was wounded on the Somme in May 1917, and invalided to England, received hospital treatment. On recovery he rejoined his unit, and in September 1917, was transferred to the R.A.F., and drafted to Egypt. Here he served at various aerodromes engaged on important work until he returned to England, and was demobilised in August 1919. He holds the General Service and Victory Medals.

17, Dane Avenue, Camberwell, S.E.5. Z6420

NASH, C. B., Sergt., R.F.A.

A serving soldier, he was mobilised at the declaration of war, and sent to the Dardanelles in March 1915. He took part in the first Landing at Gallipoli, and in the subsequent fighting until the Evacuation of the Peninsula. Transferred to Egypt in 1916, he saw considerable service at various stations, and proceeded to France in May 1916. He fought at Beaumont-Hamel, Ypres, the Somme, and was gassed at Armentières. On recovery, rejoining his Battery, he fought throughout the Retreat and Advance of 1918, and was present at the entry into Mons on November 11th, 1918. He was demobilised in July 1920, and holds the 1914-15 Star, and the General Service and Victory Medals.

18, Westcott Street, Borough, S.E.1. Z25628

NASH, C. E., Seaman Gunner, Royal Navy.

He joined the Service in June 1914, and was posted to H.M.S. "Calliope" which vessel was in action at the Battles of the Narrows, Zeebrugge, and Jutland. Later transferred to H.M.S. "Tempest," this ship rendered valuable services engaged on patrol, escort and mine-sweeping duties until the cessation of hostilities. He was demobilised in September 1919, and holds the 1914-15 Star, and the General Service and Victory Medals.

3A, Winstead Street, Battersea, S.W.11. Z3502

NASH, J., A.B., Royal Navy.

He joined in August 1914, and was posted o H.M.S. "Repulse." His ship was engaged on important patrol and escort duties with the Grand Fleet in the North Sea, frequently passing through mine-infested areas in the discharge of her duties, and was in action at the raid on Zeebrugge. He was demobilised in January 1919, and holds the 1914-15 Star, and the General Service and Victory Medals.

54, Cambridge Street, Camberwell, S.E.5. Z3504

NASH, J., Private, 3rd Royal Scots Fusiliers and 3rd Argyll and Sutherland Highlanders.

Volunteering in December 1915, and proceeding to the Western Front six months later, he fought in the Battles of the Somme, I and II, Cambrai, Beaumont-Hamel, Havrincourt, and owing to ill-health was invalided to England in 1918. He received hospital treatment, and was subsequently discharged unfit for further service in March 1919. He holds the General Service and Victory Medals.

114, Crown Road, Peckham, S.E.15. Z5467

NASH, P., Driver, R.F.A.

He volunteered in August 1915, and proceeding to the Western front later in that year was in action in many important engagements, including those at Arras, Loos, Lens, Grandcourt, Ypres, Messines and Kemmel. He also saw heavy fighting throughout the Retreat and Advance of 1918, and returning to England after the cessation of hostilities, was demobilised in March 1919. He holds the 1914-15 Star, and the General Service and Victory Medals.

12, Royal Road, Walworth, S.E.17. Z26462

NASH, S. H. W., Private, 3rd East Surrey Regt. and M.G.C.

Volunteering in February 1915, he embarked for France in the following June, and took part in heavy fighting at Armentières, Arras, La Bassée, where he was wounded in July 1915. On recovery he rejoined his unit, and was in action in many parts of the line during 1916 and 1917, and was wounded on three occasions during this time. He also served throughout the German Offensive and Allied Advance of 1918, and returning to England was demobilised in January 1919. He holds the 1914-15 Star, and the General Service and Victory Medals.

165, Gloucester Road, Peckham, S.E.15. Z6302

NASH, W., Sapper, R.E.

Volunteering in September 1915, he was sent to the Western Front in the following year, and was in action in many engagements, including those at Héricourt and Poziéres. He did good work engaged on field work, and served throughout the Retreat and Advance of 1918. Returning home he was demobilised in May 1920, and holds the General Service and Victory Medals.

9, Thurlow Street, Wandsworth Road, S.W.8. Z3505A

NASH, W. G., Gunner, R.G.A.

He joined in March 1917, and later in that year embarked for the Western Front, where he was in action on the Somme, Lens, Cambrai, and during the German Offensive and Allied Advance of 1918. After the Armistice he was sent into Germany with the Army of Occupation and was stationed at Cologne. He was demobilised in September 1919, and holds the General Service and Victory Medals.

9, Thurlow Street, Wandsworth Road, S.W.8. Z3505B

NATION, F. R., Lieutenant, M.G.C.

He volunteered in 1915, and joined the Honourable Artillery Company. In the following year he obtained his commission in the Machine Gun Corps, and later in 1916, proceeded to France. He was in action in various sectors, and served throughout the Retreat and Advance of 1918. After the Armistice he proceeded to Salonika, and later into Turkey with the Army of Occupation, and was stationed at Constantinople until he returned home and was demobilised in August 1919. He holds the General Service and Victory Medals.

20, Moffat Road, Bowes Park, N.13. 5272

NAULDER, F. E., Steward, Royal Navy.

He was serving in the Navy at the outbreak of war, and was posted to H.M.S. "Foresight." This ship was in action at the Dardanelles and was also engaged on mine-sweeping and convoy duties. Later he was transferred to H.M.S. "Nasturtium," which ship did good work in the North Sea, and was present at various actions in the Bight of Heligoland, and at the raid on Zeebrugge in April 1918. He was discharged in January 1920, and holds the 1914-15 Star, and the General Service and Victory Medals.

16, Sunwell Street, Peckham, S.E.15. Z64848B

NAULDER, W. W. Rifleman, Rifle Brigade.

He joined in April 1919, at the age of seventeen, and later in that year was sent to France, and served at various stations, engaged on guard and other important duties with his unit. He rendered valuable services, and returning to England, was demobilised in April 1920.

16, Sunwell Street, Peckham, S.E.15. Z6484A

NAYLER, E. T., Gunner, R.F.A.

Volunteering in January 1915, he was drafted to the Western Front, and was in action in many important Battles, including those of Ypres, Festubert, Hill 60, St. Eloi, Vermelles, Vimy Ridge, Passchendaele and Messines. He also was engaged in heavy fighting during the Retreat and Advance of 1918. He was demobilised in April 1919, and holds the 1914-15 Star, and the General Service and Victory Medals.

11, Grimwade Crescent, Peckham, S.E.15. Z6422

NAYLER, W., Sergt., R.A.V.C.

Mobilised and sent to France at the commencement of hostilities he served throughout the Retreat from Mons, and in many engagements of note. He rendered valuable services attending sick and wounded horses whilst overseas, and saw heavy fighting in the Retreat and Advance of 1918, and was wounded. He was admitted into hospital and after receiving medical treatment rejoined his unit and served in France until demobilised in March 1919. He holds the Mons Star, and the General Service and Victory Medals.

99, Cator Street, Peckham, S.E.15. Z4506

NAYLOR, L., Pte., 2nd Prince of Wales' Leinster Regt.
Joining in June 1916, he proceeded to the Western Front five months later, and fought at the Battle of the Ancre, and in many other engagements of note. In 1917, owing to ill-health, he returned to England, and after receiving medical treatment was invalided out of the Service in May 1917. He holds the General Service and Victory Medals.
13, Longhedge Street, Battersea, S.W.11.   Z3506

NEAL, A., Pte., Queen's (Royal West Surrey Regt.)
Volunteering in August 1914, he embarked for the Western Front, and was engaged in heavy fighting in the Retreat from Mons. He was reported missing during these operations, and later was presumed to have been killed in action. He was entitled to the Mons Star, and the General Service and Victory Medals.
  "A valiant soldier, with undaunted heart he breasted Life's last hill."
105, Yeldham Road, Hammersmith, W.6.   13240C

NEAL, A. C., Private, Royal Berkshire Regiment.
He volunteered in August 1914, and drafted to France, fought in the Retreat from Mons and the Battle of Albert, where he was severely wounded. He was admitted into hospital, and after receiving treatment for twelve months returned to France, and took part in heavy fighting in many parts of the line. He was recommended for the Victoria Cross for most conspicuous gallantry and devotion to duty in the Field. He gave his life for King and Country in November 1917, at the first Battle of Cambrai, and was entitled to the Mons Star, and the General Service and Victory Medals.
  "Whilst we remember the Sacrifice is not in vain."
6, Hurlbutt Cottages, Hurlbutt Place, Walworth, S.E.17.   Z26016

NEAL, J., Private, R.A.S.C. (M.T.)
Volunteering in March 1915, he was sent to Egypt later in that year. Attached to General Headquarters' Staff, he was driver to General Murray, and later served at Jerusalem, Nazareth, Aleppo, and many other places during the Advance through Palestine. Returning to England he was demobilised in June 1919, and holds the 1914-15 Star, and the General Service and Victory Medals.
268, Albert Road, Peckham, S.E.15.   Z6486A

NEAL, J. H., A.B. Royal Navy.
He joined in September 1918, and was posted to H.M.S. "Weymouth," which ship was engaged on patrol and other duties in the North Sea, until the cessation of hostilities. He was then employed on patrol duties in the salving of the German ships sunk at Scapa Flow, and in 1920, was serving at the South Atlantic Station. He holds the General Service and Victory Medals.
268, Albert Road, Peckham, S.E.15.   Z6486B

NEAL, J. H., Pte., London Regt. (Royal Fusiliers).
Joining in March 1916, he proceeded to France later in that year, and fought in many important engagements. He gave his life for the freedom of England whilst on patrol duty on September 8th, 1916, and was entitled to the General Service and Victory Medals.
  "His life for his Country, his Soul to God."
105, Yeldham Road, Hammersmith, W.6.   13240B

NEAL, N., Sergt., 20th London Regiment.
He enlisted in August 1913, and, mobilised at the outbreak of war, was drafted to the Western Front in February 1915. He fought in many engagements of note, including those at Ypres, the Somme, Arras, and was wounded at Passchendaele on September 18th, 1917. He returned to England, and after receiving hospital treatment was stationed at various depôts until discharged unfit for further service in February 1919. He holds the 1914-15 Star, and the General Service and Victory Medals.
11, Cheam Place, Camberwell, S.E.5.   Z6485

NEALE, A. C., Pte, 24th London Regt. (The Queen's).
He volunteered in June 1915, and drafted to France in the following year fought in the Battles of the Somme, Bullecourt, and Cambrai, and was wounded at Ypres. On recovering from his injuries he was transferred to the Tank Corps, with which unit he served during the Retreat and Advance of 1918. Returning home on the conclusion of hostilities he was sent to Ireland and subsequently demobilised in June 1919. He holds the General Service and Victory Medals.
27, Temple Street, Kennington, S.E.11.   Z26973A

NEALE, G. H., Corporal, R.F.A.
He enlisted in 1911, and serving in India when war broke out was immediately drafted to France. There he took part in heavy fighting in the Retreat from Mons, and the Battles of the Marne, the Aisne, the Somme, and was wounded in 1916. On recovery he was later in action in other engagements and was severely wounded at Ypres in 1917, and sent home for medical treatment. Invalided out of the Service in October 1918, he holds the Mons Star, and the General Service and Victory Medals.
26, Totteridge Road, Battersea, S.W.11.   Z3507

NEALE, J., Private, Hampshire Regiment.
Volunteering in 1914, he was drafted to the Western Front in the following year, and served there until after hostilities ceased. During this period he fought in the Battles of Ypres, Loos, Albert, the Somme, Arras, Messines, Cambrai, and in the Retreat and Advance of 1918. Returning home he was demobilised in February 1919, and holds the 1914-15 Star, and the General Service and Victory Medals.
50, Chalmers Street, Wandsworth Road, S.W.8.   Z3508

NEALE, S, Pte., 24th London Regt. (The Queen's).
He volunteered in December 1915, and in the next year was sent overseas. Serving in France he was in action in the "Labyrinth," and was later drafted to the Balkans, where he fought in the Advance on the Vardar, and in the capture of Monastir. He then proceeded to Egypt, and was in action in many operations during the Palestine campaign, and was present at General Allenby's entry into Jerusalem. He was demobilised in February 1919, on returning to England, and holds the General Service and Victory Medals.
26, Temple Street, Kennington, S.E.11.   Z26973B

NEATE, E. H., Gunner, R.M.A.
He was mobilised on the outbreak of war, and embarking for France with the first British Expeditionary Force fought in the Retreat from Mons, and was wounded. On recovery he was posted to a ship in the Grand Fleet and served in the Battles of Heligoland Bight, and the Dogger Bank, and was discharged on account of service in January 1919. He later joined the Royal Air Force in which unit he was still serving in 1920, and holds the Mons Star, and the General Service and Victory Medals.
51, Gonsalva Road, Wandsworth Road, S.W.8.   Z3509B

NEATE, F. L., Private, Suffolk Regiment.
He joined in October 1918, and after completing his training was engaged on important duties with his Battalion, and did good work. He was unable to obtain a transfer to a theatre of war before the termination of hostilities, but was, however, drafted to India after the Armistice, and in 1920 was still serving there.
51, Gonsalva Road, Wandsworth Road, S.W.8.   Z3509C

NEATE, W. G., Sergt., Royal Sussex Regiment.
A serving soldier, having enlisted in 1910, he was mobilised on the outbreak of war and proceeded to France with the First Expeditionary Force. He was in action in many of the principal engagements from the commencement of hostilities until the signing of the Armistice after which he returned to England in 1918. He holds the Mons Star, and the General Service and Victory Medals. and in 1920 was still serving.
51, Gonsalva Road, Wandsworth Road, S.W.8.   Z3509A

NEATH, W. G., L/Corporal, 2nd Queen's (Royal West Surrey Regiment).
He volunteered in February 1915, and in the following January was drafted to the Western Front. Whilst in this theatre of war he fought in the Somme sector, and was taken prisoner in April 1916. Held in captivity in Germany he was repatriated on the conclusion of hostilities, and was demobilised in January 1919, holds the General Service and Victory Medals.
11, Union Grove, Wandsworth Road, S.W.8.   Z3510

NEIGHBOUR, E. D., Sapper, R.E.
Volunteering in August 1915, he completed his training and served with his unit at various stations until sent to the Western Front in 1917. In this theatre of war he was engaged on important duties in connection with operations, and did good work until the cessation of hostilities. Demobilised in June 1919, he holds the General Service and Victory Medals.
45, Bradmore Park Road, Hammersmith, W.6.   10623

NELSON, G., L/Corporal, Queen's Own (Royal West Kent Regiment).
He joined in December 1916, and on completing his training was engaged on important duties with his Battalion until 1918, when he embarked for France. There he took part in several engagements during the Advance of 1918, and on the conclusion of hostilities returned to England. He was demobilised in February 1919, and holds the General Service and Victory Medals.
162, Hillingdon Street, Walworth, S.E.17.   Z26770

NETTLEINGHAM, H. D., Stoker, R.N.
Joining the Royal Navy in 1910, he was mobilised on the outbreak of war and served in several ships during the course of hostilities. After a period of service on patrol duties in the North Sea his ship was sent to the Dardanelles, and was engaged in the bombardment of the forts, and in the other operations until her return home for repairs. On other vessels he took part in the Battle of Jutland, and in the raid on Zeebrugge, where his ship, H.M.S. "Swiftsure," was sunk to close up the entrance to the channel. He holds the 1914-15 Star, and the General Service and Victory Medals, and in 1920 was still serving.
5, Stopford Road, Walworth, S.E.17.   Z26800

NEVE, R. J., Gunner, R.G.A.

He joined in October 1916, and proceeding overseas in the following year served on the Western Front until the termination of hostilities. Engaged with the heavy artillery he fought in several important engagements, including the Battle of the Somme, Arras and Ypres, and returned to England after the Armistice. He was demobilised in September 1919, and holds the General Service and Victory Medals.
66, Mordaunt Street, Landor Road, S.W.9.   Z3511

NEVILLE, E. E., L/Sergt., Queen's Own (Royal West Kent Regiment).

He volunteered in August 1914, and was in the following year drafted to the Western Front, where he took part in the severe fighting at Loos, St. Eloi, and Albert, and was wounded and invalided home. On his recovery he was sent in 1917, to Mesopotamia, where he contracted malaria. He returned home and was discharged in February 1918 in consequence of his services. He holds the 1914-15 Star, and the General Service and Victory Medals.
13, Buchan Road, Peckham, S.E.15.   Z6598

NEW, E., Rifleman, King's Royal Rifle Corps.

Joining in May 1916, he completed his training and served on the East Coast with his unit. In 1917 he was transferred to the Labour Corps, and engaged on important duties at an Army Remount Depôt, and was then sent back to the King's Royal Rifle Corps for further training. Owing to physical unfitness for general service he was not sent overseas, and was discharged in consequence in March 1919.
79, D'Eynesford Road, Camberwell Green, S.E.5.   Z3513

NEW, G. W., Private, 2nd Lancashire Fusiliers.

A serving soldier, he was mobilised on the outbreak of war, and shortly afterwards proceeded to France. There he was in action during the Retreat from Mons, and in the Battles of Le Cateau, La Bassée, Ypres, Festubert, Loos, and in several other engagements. Seriously wounded on March 30th, 1917, in the Ancre sector, he was evacuated to hospital in England, and subsequently discharged as medically unfit for further service in April 1918. He holds the Mons Star, and the General Service and Victory Medals.
104, Abbey Street, Bermondsey, S.E.1.   Z27416

NEW, J. R., Pte., 8th Queen's (Royal West Surrey Regiment).

Volunteering in September 1914, he was sent overseas in the following August, and serving on the Western Front, fought with his Battalion in the Battles of Ypres and Loos, and was wounded and taken prisoner. He received medical treatment at the Kaiserin Hospital, Hamelin, and after three years' captivity in Germany was released after the signing of the Armistice. Demobilised in April 1919, he holds the 1914-15 Star, and the General Service and Victory Medals.
68, Kimberley Road, Nunhead, S.E.15.   Z6529

NEWBON, E. I. (M.S.M.), S.M., R.A.S.C.

Mobilised on the declaration of war and drafted to France shortly afterwards, he served throughout the course of hostilities. During this period he was engaged with the Supply Column in the Retreat from Mons, and in the Battles of the Marne, the Aisne, the Somme, Ypres, and Arras. He was also present at the Battle of Vimy Ridge and was mentioned in Despatches, and awarded the Meritorious Service Medal for consistently good work in the Field. After the Armistice he proceeded into Germany with the Army of Occupation, and was stationed on the Rhine. Returning to England for demobilisation in March 1919, he holds the Mons Star, and the General Service and Victory Medals.
106, Inville Road, Walworth, S.E.17   Z27303

NEWBURY, C. V., Private, 2nd Welch Regiment.

He was mobilised when war broke out, and embarking for France with the first British Expeditionary Force, was engaged in heavy fighting during the Retreat from Mons. Severely wounded and taken prisoner, he was held in captivity in Germany until repatriated on the conclusion of hostilities. He was demobilised in January 1919, and holds the Mons Star, and the General Service and Victory Medals.
40, Crescent Road, Clapham, S.W.4.   Z6208

NEWBY, W., Rflmn., 20th King's Royal Rifle Corps.

He joined in September 1918 on attaining military age, and on the conclusion of his training served at various stations on important duties with his unit. He did good work, but was unsuccessful in securing his transfer overseas before the termination of hostilities. After the Armistice, however, he was sent with the Army of Occupation into Germany, and stationed on the Rhine. He returned to England in 1920, and was discharged on account of service in May of that year.
37, Edithna Street, Landor Road, S.W.9.   Z3514C

NEWCOMBE, E. (Mrs.), Special War Worker.

During the war this lady offered her services for work of National importance, and was employed at the Bond Munition Factory until the Armistice. She was engaged on important duties in connection with the packing of containers of 6-in. shells, and throughout her service discharged her duties in a thoroughly capable and efficient manner.
69, Wadhurst Road, Wandsworth Road, S.W.8.   Z3515

NEWCOMBE, R., L/Corporal, R.A.S.C. (H.T.)

Volunteering in August 1914, he was sent to France shortly afterwards, and served during the Retreat from Mons, and in several other engagements including the Battles of the Marne, the Aisne, Albert, Ypres, and Vimy Ridge. In 1917 he proceeded to Salonika, and was engaged on important transport duties during the Advance on the Struma. Returning to England, he was demobilised in May 1919, and holds the Mons Star, and the General Service and Victory Medals.
12, Shorncliffe Road, Old Kent Road, S.E.1.   Z3516

NEWCOMBE, W. H., Private, East Yorkshire Regt.

He joined in October 1916, and in the following January embarked for the Western Front, where he served in several sectors. He fought in the Battles of Arras and Cambrai, and was wounded and taken prisoner at Armentières on April 11th, 1918. Held in captivity in Germany, and afterwards interned in Switzerland, he returned to England, and was discharged on account of service in April 1919. He holds the General Service and Victory Medals.
55, Philip Street, Peckham, S.E.15.   Z6048

NEWELL, H. R., Pte., 16th (The Queen's) Lancers.

He volunteered in August 1914, and in the same year was drafted overseas. In the course of his service on the Western Front he was in action in several engagements in the Arras and Ypres sectors, and was wounded in 1916 in the Battle of the Somme. Invalided home on account of his injuries, it was found necessary to amputate one of his legs, and after receiving medical treatment he was discharged as physically unfit for further service in 1916. He still suffers from the effects of his wounds, and holds the 1914 Star, and the General Service and Victory Medals.
40, Bournemouth Road, Rye Lane, S.E.15.   Z5468B

NEWELL, W. H., Private, 23rd Royal Fusiliers.

He joined in 1916, and proceeding to France in the following year served there until after hostilities ceased. During this period he fought in the Battles of the Somme, Ypres, and in the Retreat and Advance of 1918. He then went into Germany with the Army of Occupation, and returning home in 1919, was demobilised later in that year. He holds the General Service and Victory Medals.
8, Sunwell Street, Peckham, S.E.15.   Z6487

NEWELL, W. R., Private, M.G.C.

Joining in 1917, he was drafted overseas in the following year, and engaged on important duties with his unit on the Western Front. In the course of operations in the Somme sector he was severely wounded in July 1918, and evacuated to England for hospital treatment, was invalided out of the Service later in that year. He holds the General Service and Victory Medals and in 1920 was still receiving medical treatment.
40, Bournemouth Road, Rye Lane, S.E.15.   Z5468A

NEWHAM, W. F., Corporal, R.G.A.

He joined in May 1916, and three months later embarked for Egypt, where he was engaged in the fighting in operations during the British Advance through Palestine, including those at Gaza, and the capture of Jerusalem. In 1917 he was sent to France and fought in the Battles of the Somme, Arras, Vimy Ridge, and Cambrai. Returning to England on the cessation of hostilities, he was demobilised in November 1919, and holds the General Service and Victory Medals.
26, Sears Street, Camberwell, S.E.5.   Z5808

NEWINGTON, G. H., Private, Royal Fusiliers.

Joining in August 1918, on the completion of his training, he served with his Battalion at various depôts, and did good work. He was not successful in obtaining his transfer overseas before hostilities ceased, but was sent to Germany in 1919. Stationed at Cologne with the Army of Occupation he was engaged on guard and other duties until his return home for demobilisation in March 1920.
37, Comus Place, Walworth, S.E.17.   Z1399B

NEWLAND, A. E. (D.C.M.), Bombardier, R.F.A.

He volunteered in September 1914, and drafted to the Western Front in the following year served in many parts of the line. He fought in several engagements, including the Battles of Ypres, the Somme, Arras, Messines and Cambrai, and was awarded the Distinguished Conduct Medal in April 1916, for conspicuous bravery and devotion to duty in saving a gun and bringing in wounded under heavy fire. He also holds the 1914-15 Star, and the General Service and Victory Medals.
103, Abbey Street, Bermondsey, S.E.1.   Z27414B

NEWLAND, C. V., Gunner, R.G.A.

Volunteering in November 1914, he was sent to Malta in the following year, and after a period of service there proceeded to Italy in 1916. He was in action during the Offensive on the Piave, and in 1918 was drafted to the Western Front, and took part in the Retreat and Advance of that year. Sent home owing to illness, and admitted to hospital he was subsequently demobilised in February 1919, and holds the General Service and Victory Medals.

108, Cronin Road, Peckham, S.E.15.   Z5570A

NEWLAND, E. (Miss), Special War Worker.

During the war this lady offered her services for work of National importance, and in 1916 was engaged on clerical duties in a Government Office at 107, Thames Street, London, E.C., and later at Woolwich Arsenal on work in connection with the manufacture of munitions. She discharged her duties until 1918, in a competent and thoroughly satisfactory manner.

37, Kimberley Road, Nunhead, S.E.15.   Z6391A

NEWLAND, F. E., Special War Worker.

During the war he was engaged on propaganda work in connection with the National War Savings Committee, and toured through England with Cine Motor No. 18. He rendered valuable services, and was untiring in his efforts to stimulate National economy and thrift.

57, Gwynne Road, Battersea, S.W.11.   Z3519

NEWLAND, J., Special War Worker.

He offered his services for work of National importance during the war, and was employed from August 1914 until November 1918, by the Projectile Company, Battersea. He served on casting work, and carried out his duties in a thoroughly efficient and capable manner.

18, Westbury Street, Wandsworth Road, S.W.8.   Z3518

NEWLAND, T., Pte., 4th Royal Sussex Regt.

He joined in January 1917, and in the same year embarked for the Western Front. In the course of his service overseas he was in action in the Battles of Arras, Albert, Lens, Cambrai, and in several other engagements until the termination of hostilities. He returned to England for demobilisation in September 1919, and holds the General Service and Victory Medals.

103, Abbey Street, Bermondsey, S.E.1.   Z27414A

NEWMAN, A., Private, 2nd Bedfordshire Regt.

A Reservist, he was mobilised and drafted to the Western Front in August 1914, and fought in many important engagements in the Retreat from Mons. He died gloriously on the field of Battle in September 1914, and was entitled to the Mons Star, and the General Service and Victory Medals.

"A costly sacrifice upon the altar of freedom."

69, Grant Road, Battersea, S.W.11.   Z3525-6C

NEWMAN, A., Private, R.A.O.C.

He joined the Colours in 1918, and proceeding to France later in that year, was stationed at St. Omer, engaged on important duties with his unit. He rendered valuable services throughout, and returning to England was demobilised in October 1919. He holds the General Service and Victory Medals.

34, Bond Street, South Lambeth Road, S.W.8.   Z3524B

NEWMAN, A. E., Pte., 7th Royal Sussex Regt.

Joining in September 1916, he completed his training, and served at various stations until drafted to France in April 1918. He fought in many important engagements during the Retreat and Advance of 1918, and was wounded at Albert. Returning to England, he received medical treatment, and was subsequently discharged in March 1919. He holds the General Service and Victory Medals.

110, Maysoule Road, Battersea, S.W.11.   Z3525-6D

NEWMAN, C., Pte., 10th Northumberland Fusiliers.

Joining in 1916, and sent to France in February of the following year, he fought in the Battles of the Somme and Ypres, and in many other parts of the line. He was unfortunately killed in action at Lens on September 20th, 1917, and was entitled to the General Service and Victory Medals.

"He died the noblest death a man may die,
Fighting for God, and right, and liberty."

69, Grant Road, Battersea, S.W.11.   Z3525-6B

NEWMAN, C., Private, Dorsetshire Regiment.

Volunteering in 1914, he shortly afterwards embarked for India, where he was engaged on important duties at various garrison towns. Transferred to Egypt he fought in many sectors of the Palestine front, and did good work. He was killed whilst on a bombing raid in November 1917, and was entitled to the 1914-15 Star, and the General Service and Victory Medals.

"The path of duty was the way to glory."

34, Bond Street, South Lambeth Road, S.W.8.   Z3524C

NEWMAN, C. A., Pte., Queen's (Royal West Surrey Regiment).

He joined in March 1917, and embarking for the Western Front later in the same year, was engaged in heavy fighting in many parts of the line. He gave his life for the freedom of England at the Battle of Loos on April 4th, 1917, and was entitled to the General Service and Victory Medals.

"Honour the immortal dead, who gave their youth that the world might grow old in peace."

23, Peacock Street, Walworth, S.E.17.   Z26156A

NEWMAN, E., Private, 11th Suffolk Regiment.

He joined in 1916 ,and after serving in Ireland for a short period was drafted to France in 1917. He fought in many parts of the line, and was in action during the German Offensive, and subsequent Allied Advance of 1918, and was gassed. Returning home, he was demobilised in September 1919, and holds the General Service and Victory Medals.

34, Bond Street, South Lambeth Road, S.W.8.   Z3524A

NEWMAN, E. (Mrs.), Nurse, V.A.D.

This lady offered her services for work of National importance, and engaged on nursing duties with the Voluntary Aid Detachment, rendered valuable services attending to sick and wounded troops at Carlton House Terrace and Middlesex Hospitals. She discharged her duties in a most satisfactory and efficient manner.

206, Beresford Street, Camberwell Road, S.E.5.   Z3522B

NEWMAN, E. E., Private, R.A.S.C.

Volunteering in December 1914, he was drafted to France in the same month, and saw much service in the advanced areas in many parts of the line. Later he served at the Base with the Remount Depôt, and did good work. Owing to ill-health he was invalided to England, and after hospital treatment was discharged unfit for further service in May 1916. He holds the 1914-15 Star, and the General Service and Victory Medals.

15, Alberta Street, Walworth, S.E.17.   Z25937

NEWMAN, E. F., Sergt., 12th London Regiment (Rangers).

He volunteered in September 1914, and after serving at various depôts was sent to the Western Front in January 1917. He was in action at the Battles of Ypres, Amiens, Bullecourt, Beaumont-Hamel, Villers Bretonneux, and in the final Retreat was gassed and wounded in April 1918. He was demobilised in February 1919, and holds the General Service and Victory Medals.

206, Beresford Street, Camberwell, S.E.5.   Z3522A

NEWMAN, E. T., Private, R.A.O.C.

He joined in June 1917, and embarking for the Western Front in the following January, was engaged on important duties in the forward areas. He was present at the Battles of St. Quentin and Cambrai, and at many other important engagements. Returning to England he was demobilised in August 1919, and holds the General Service and Victory Medals.

78, Dalwood Street, Camberwell, S.E.5.   Z3528

NEWMAN, F. J., A.B., Royal Navy.

He joined the Service in 1907, and aboard H.M.S. "Colleen" saw much service, his ship being engaged on patrol and other important duties in the North Sea. Transferred to another vessel he saw much service and was wounded at the Battle of Jutland. Invalided to hospital in Yarmouth, he subsequently died there from the effects of his injuries in March 1919, and was entitled to the 1914-15 Star, and the General Service and Victory Medals.

"Great deeds cannot die."

69, Grant Road, Battersea, S.W.11.   Z3525-6E

NEWMAN, G., Corporal, 1st South Lancashire Regt.

A serving soldier, he was stationed in India at the outbreak of hostilities engaged on important duties at various garrison towns. He was in action during the fighting in Afghanistan in 1919, and was still serving in 1920. He holds the General Service and Victory Medals. and the India General Service Medal (with clasp Afghanistan North Western Frontier, 1919).

39, Horace Street, Wandsworth Road, S.W.8.   Z27519A

NEWMAN, H., Private, M.G.C.

He joined in March 1916, and on completing his training served at various stations engaged on important duties. He was unsuccessful in obtaining his transfer overseas prior to the cessation of hostilities, but rendered valuable services until demobilised in February 1920.

64, Dorothy Road, Lavender Hill, S.W.11.   Z3523

NEWMAN, J., L/Corporal, 21st London Regiment (1st Surrey Rifles).

Volunteering in April 1915, he was sent to the Western Front in the following February, and fought in many engagements, including those at St. Eloi, Vimy Ridge, the Somme, Messines, Passchendaele, and throughout the German Offensive and Allied Advance of 1918. He was demobilised in January 1919, and holds the General Service and Victory Medals.

3, Bagshot Street, Walworth, S.E.17.   Z3520

NEWMAN, J., Private, 8th Yorkshire Regiment.
He joined in January 1917, and embarked for France five months later. During his service overseas he fought at the Battles of Ypres, Passchendaele, and Lens, and was transferred to Italy in November 1917. He was in action on the Piave and Asiago Plateaux, and was killed in action on the Piave on October 27th, 1918. He was entitled to the General Service and Victory Medals.
" His life for his country, his Soul to God."
100, Dalyell Road, Landor Road, S.W.9. Z3527

NEWMAN, J., Private, 24th Queen's (Royal West Surrey Regiment).
He volunteered in 1915, and drafted to France later in that year, served with his Battalion in various parts of the line and fought in many engagements of note. He gave his life for King and Country at the Somme in September 1917, and was entitled to the 1914-15 Star, and the General Service and Victory Medals.
39, Horace Street, Wandsworth Road, S.W.8. Z27519B

NEWMAN, T. C., Private, Somerset Light Infantry.
He volunteered in March 1915, and sent to France in the following October, fought in many important engagements. He was severely wounded on July 31st, 1916, and admitted into hospital subsequently succumbed to his injuries on August 14th. He was entitled to the 1914-15 Star, and the General Service and Victory Medals.
" He joined the great white company of valiant souls."
48, Riverhall Street, Wandsworth Road, S.W.8. Z3529

NEWMAN, W. E., Private, 1/23rd London Regiment.
Volunteering in May 1915, he was sent to the Western Front later in that year, and fought in many important engagements in various parts of the line. He gave his life for King and Country in the Battle of the Somme on October 20th, 1916, and was entitled to the 1914-15 Star, and the General Service and Victory Medals.
" And doubtless he went in splendid company."
69, Grant Road, Battersea, S.W.11. Z3525-6A

NEWMAN, W. F., Corporal, R.E.
He volunteered in February 1915, and proceeding to France twelve months afterwards, was in action in many notable engagements. Owing to ill-health he returned to England, and after receiving medical treatment was finally discharged unfit for further service in March 1919. He holds the General Service and Victory Medals.
39, Green Lane, Battersea, S.W.11. Z3521

NEWSON, A. C., Private, Royal Fusiliers.
He joined in May 1918, and in the following September proceeded to the Western Front, where he was in action in the Allied Advance of 1918, and was wounded near Havrincourt Wood in October. Evacuated to England he received medical treatment at Liverpool Hospital, and afterwards at King's College Hospital, London, from which he was discharged as medically unfit for further military service on October 8th 1919. He holds the General Service and Victory Medals.
55, Harris Street, Camberwell, S.E.5. Z4507

NEWSON, W., Private, 1st East Surrey Regiment.
He joined in 1918, and after completing his training proceeded in the same year to North Russia, where he served under General Ironside, and was in action in several engagements on the Murmansk Coast. Returning to England in 1919, he was later sent to Ireland. In 1920 he was still serving with his Regiment, having embarked for Egypt in that year. He holds the General Service and Victory Medals.
51, Wilcox Road, South Lambeth Road, S.W.8. Z3532

NEWSTEAD, F. J. T., Air Mechanic, R.F.C.
He joined in March 1917, and on completion of his training served at Farnborough on important duties with his unit. He did good work in the aeroplane repair shops, but owing to illness was removed to Brompton Hospital, where he shortly afterwards died on June 24th, 1917.
" A costly sacrifice upon the altar of freedom."
25, Kempsford Road, Kennington, S.E.11. Z27362

NEWSTEAD, J. R., A.B., Royal Navy.
He joined in September 1916, and after training at Devonport was posted to H.M.S. " Glorious," which ship served with the Grand Fleet engaged on patrol and other duties in the North Sea. He was later transferred to H.M.S. " Inflexible," and aboard this vessel was present at Scapa Flow when the German Fleet surrendered and was interned there. He was demobilised in January 1919, and holds the General Service and Victory Medals.
106, Olney Street, Walworth, S.E.17. Z26323

NEWSUM, A. E., Private, 8th Queen's (Royal West Surrey Regt.) and Labour Corps.
Joining in March 1916, he was drifted overseas in the following year, and served in various sectors of the Western Front. In this theatre of war he fought in the Battles of the Somme, Arras, and Bullecourt, and was wounded at Ypres in August 1918. Invalided home on account of his injuries he was transferred to the Labour Corps on recovery, and returned to France, where he served until he was demobilised in March 1919, and holds the General Service and Victory Medals.
41, Howbury Road, Peckham, S.E.15. Z6564

NEWTON, F., Rifleman, 13th Rifle Brigade.
Joining in June 1916, he was sent to France in the following September, and served there for upwards of three years. Whilst on the Western Front he was engaged in heavy fighting in the Battles of the Somme, Arras, Cambrai, and Bapaume, and was wounded in 1917 on the Somme, and again at Bapaume in 1918. He holds the General Service and Victory Medals, and was demobilised in February 1919.
31, Lockington Road, Battersea Park Road, S.W.8. Z3537

NEWTON, G., Private, Suffolk Regiment.
He joined in November 1916, on attaining military age, and embarked for France in the following March. During his service overseas he was in action in the Battles of Arras, Vimy Ridge, Messines, Ypres, and Lens, and was wounded on the Somme, and sent home. His injuries resulted in the loss of the sight of his right eye, but he returned to the Western Front in June 1918, and served until the cessation of hostilities. He was demobilised in February 1919, and holds the General Service and Victory Medals.
90, Nelson's Row, Clapham, S.W.4. Z3535A

NEWTON, G., Gunner, R.F.A.
He was mobilised on the outbreak of war, and almost immediately sent to France, where he served during the Retreat from Mons, and in the Battles of the Marne, and the Aisne, and was wounded three times. He was later in action in the Battles of Ypres and Loos, and was severely wounded near Albert, and sent to hospital in England. After receiving medical treatment he was invalided out of the Service in February 1919, and holds the Mons Star, and the General Service and Victory Medals.
16, Newington Crescent, Walworth, S.E.17. Z26170

NEWTON, H., L/Corporal, 13th London Regiment (Kensingtons).
Volunteering in December 1915, he embarked for the Western Front a year later, and took part in several important engagements, including the Battles of Arras, Ypres, and Cambrai. Severely wounded in August 1917, near Ypres, he was invalided home for medical treatment, and was subsequently demobilised in January 1919, and holds the General Service and Victory Medals.
11, Lockington Road, Battersea Park Road, S.W.8. Z3533

NEWTON, H. C., Private, Royal Welch Fusiliers.
He volunteered in January 1916, and proceeding to the Western Front in the following April fought in the Battles of the Somme, Ypres, Arras, Albert, and Passchendaele. He died gloriously on the Field of Battle at Mericourt on April 25th, 1917, and was entitled to the General Service and Victory Medals.
" Nobly striving,
He nobly fell that we might live."
40, Freemantle Street, Walworth, S.E.17. Z3536A

NEWTON, H. T., Sapper, R.E.
He volunteered in January 1915, and after completing his training was sent to Ireland, where he was engaged on important duties with his unit. He did good work, but owing to physical disability was invalided out of the Army in June 1915. He had previously served in the South African War, and holds the Queen's and King's Medals for those campaigns.
8, Tilson Road, Peckham, S.E.15. Z5644

NEWTON, J. A., Sapper, R.E.
Volunteering in May 1915, in the following December he was drafted to Egypt and served there until sent to France in April 1916. Whilst on the Western Front he was in action in several engagements, including the Battles of Ypres, and Armentières, and on the conclusion of hostilities returned to England. He was demobilised in January 1919, and holds the 1914-15 Star, and the General Service and Victory Medals.
20,, Longville Road, Kennington, S.E.11. Z26723

NEWTON, J. E., Pte., Queen's (Royal West Surrey Regiment).
He volunteered in March 1915, and was drafted overseas in the same year. Serving on the Western Front he was in action in the Battles of Hill 60, Loos, Ypres, Arras, Delville Wood, and the Somme, and during the Retreat and Advance of 1918, and was wounded near Cambrai. Returning to England after the Armistice he was demobilised in February 1919, and holds the 1914-15 Star, and the General Service and Victory Medals.
40, Freemantle Street, Walworth, S.E.17. Z3536B

NEWTON, S. C., Pte., 3rd Royal Sussex Regiment.

Volunteering in July 1915, he completed his training and served with his unit until sent to Woolwich, where he was engaged on important duties in the Store Department. He rendered valuable services but was not sent to a theatre of war owing to physical disability, and was demobilised in May 1919. He had served with the Colours for six years prior to the war, but had purchased his discharge.
204, Hollydale Road, Peckham, S.E.15. Z6423

NEWTON, W. H., Private, R.A.S.C. (M.T.)

A Territorial, he was mobilised on the outbreak of war, but owing to ill-health was discharged in September 1914. Re-joining in 1916, he was sent to the Western Front in the following year, and did good work in the transport of ammunition and supplies to the firing line during the Battle of the Somme. Contracting illness in 1918, he was admitted to hospital in France, and afterwards sent home and was ultimately invalided out of the Service in March 1919. He also served in the Rifle Brigade, and the Royal Fusiliers, and holds the General Service and Victory Medals.
40, Freemantle Street, Walworth, S.E.17. Z3534

NIBLETT, C., Private, 23rd Royal Fusiliers.

He joined in June 1916, and in the following November proceeded overseas. Serving with his Battalion on the Western Front he took part in heavy fighting in several engagements in the Somme sector. He fell fighting near Albert on February 17th, 1917, and was entitled to the General Service and Victory Medals.
" He passed out of the sight of men by the path of duty and self-sacrifice."
34, Heath Road, Wandsworth Road, S.W.8. Z3538

NICHOLAS, A. W., Rifleman, Rifle Brigade.

He volunteered in August 1914, and was drafted in the following year to the Western Front. There he fought in the Battles of Hooge, Loos and Ypres, and was wounded in October 1916, and again in the following October, being invalided to hospital at home on both occasions. Returning to France he was unfortunately killed during the Advance of 1918, and was entitled to the 1914-15 Star, and the General Service and Victory Medals.
" Honour to the immortal dead who gave their youth that the world might grow old in peace."
24, Porson Street, Wandsworth Road, S.W.8. Z3539

NICHOLLS, A., Driver, R.A.S.C.

Volunteering in January 1915, he was drafted to the Western Front in the following June and served with an ammunition supply column in several engagements, including those of Loos and Vimy Ridge. Owing to illness he was invalided home in June 1916, and on recovery proceeded to Egypt a year later. During the British Advance through Palestine he acted as despatch carrier, and was present at the Capture of Jericho, and the fall of Jerusalem. Returning to England on the cessation of hostilities he was demobilised in June 1919, and holds the 1914-15 Star, and the General Service and Victory Medals.
90, Wickersley Road, Lavender Hill, S.W.11. Z3540

NICHOLLS, E., Private, R.M.L.I.

Enlisting in 1902, he was mobilised on the outbreak of war, and served on H.M.S. " Dominion." His ship was engaged on important patrol duties in the North Sea, and was in action in the Battle of the Dogger Bank in which the Blücher was sunk, and other enemy vessels badly damaged. Later he was taken ill and died on October 21st, 1918. He was entitled to the 1914-15 Star, and the General Service and Victory Medals.
" And doubtless he went in splendid company."
54, Vestry Road, Camberwell, S.E.5. Z6528

NICHOLLS, G., Driver, R.A.S.C.

He volunteered in August 1914, and after completing his training was sent to Salonika. During operations in the Balkans he was engaged on important duties in connection with the transport of ammunition and supplies to the forward areas, and did excellent work. Owing to illness he was sent home and demobilised in 1919, and holds the 1914-15 Star, and the General Service and Victory Medals.
23, Bellefields Road, Stockwell Road, S.W.9. Z3542

NICHOLLS, H., Private, 8th Devonshire Regiment.

He volunteered in September 1914, and served with his unit until his embarkation for France in 1916. In the course of his service on the Western Front he fought in several engagements and was wounded in the Battle of the Somme, in July 1916, at Beaumont-Hamel in 1917, and at Ypres later in the same year. He was afterwards sent to Italy, and was in action during the Advance on the Asiago Plateau, and again wounded. Returning home on the cessation of hostilities he was demobilised in January 1919, and holds the General Service and Victory Medals.
7, Auckland Road, Battersea, S.W.11. Z3541

NICHOLLS, G. C., Private, 23rd London Regiment.

He joined in August 1916, and after completing his training served with his Battalion at various depôts on special duties. He did good work, but owing to physical disability he was not successful in securing his transfer overseas, and was invalided out of the Army in January 1917.
11, Seneca Road, Sandmere Road, S.W.4. Z3546

NICHOLLS, R., Sergt.-Major, R.A.F.

Volunteering in August 1914, he proceeded to the Western Front in the following October, and was engaged on observation duties with his Squadron. Shot down over the lines and severely wounded he was sent to hospital in France, and thence home in 1917. On recovery he was engaged on important duties as an Instructor at an aerodrome in England, and rendered valuable services in that capacity. He was mentioned in Despatches on three occasions, and holds the 1914 Star, and the General Service and Victory Medals, and in 1920 was still serving.
32, Mostyn Road, Brixton Road, S.W.9. Z4508

NICHOLS, B. F., Private, R.A.M.C.

He volunteered in August 1914, and almost immediately proceeded to France. There he acted as stretcher bearer and rendered valuable services during the Retreat from Mons, and in the Battles of Neuve Chapelle, Hill 60, Loos, the Somme and Lens. Gassed at Cambrai he was sent home for hospital treatment and invalided out of the Service in November 1917. He holds the Mons Star, and the General Service and Victory Medals.
107, Flaxman Road, Camberwell, S.E.5. Z6209

NICHOLS, P. J., Q.M.S., 8th London Regt. (Post Office Rifles).

A Territorial, he was mobilised when war broke out and proceeded to France in March 1915. Serving with his Battalion in various sectors he was in action in the Battles of Festubert, Loos, Vermelles, and Vimy Ridge, and was later engaged on special duties at the Fourth Corps School. Returning to England for demobilisation in March 1919, he holds the 1914-15 Star, and the General Service and Victory Medals, and the Territorial Efficiency Medal.
25, Mysore Road, Lavender Hill, S.W.11. Z3543

NICHOLSON, C. W., Sergt., R.A.S.C.

Volunteering in 1915, he was drafted overseas in the same year and served at Salonika. He was employed on important clerical duties at the Base during the Balkan Campaign, and on the conclusion of hostilities was sent to Turkey with the Army of Occupation and stationed at Constantinople. He was demobilised in 1919, on his return to England, and holds the 1914-15 Star, and the General Service and Victory Medals.
100, Wilcox Road, Wandsworth Road, S.W.8. Z3544

NICHOLSON, G., Pte., Royal Inniskilling Fusiliers.

He joined in April 1916, and was sent to the Western Front on the completion of his training. Whilst overseas he took part in heavy fighting in several important engagements, and was wounded in the Battle of Messines. On recovery he rejoined his unit, and served in several operations of the closing stages of the war. returning home for demobilisation in February 1919. He holds the General Service and Victory Medals.
21, Church Path, Hammersmith, W.6. 6367A

NICHOLSON, W. J., Pte., 11th Royal Scots Fusiliers.

He volunteered in October 1915, and was engaged on important duties in connection with the coastal defences in the South Eastern Counties until drafted to France in May 1918. He then served with his unit in several operations and returned home on the termination of the war. Demobilised in February 1919, he holds the General Service and Victory Medals.
100, Warriner Gardens, Battersea, S.W.11. Z3545

NIGHTINGALE, B. C., Private, 10th Queen's (Royal West Surrey Regiment).

He joined in February 1917, and in the following month proceeded to the Western Front, where he did good work in the Labour Battalion in various Sectors of the Front. He was present at numerous engagements, including the Battles of Ypres and Arras, and later returning to England was discharged in consequence of his service in September 1919. He holds the General Service and Victory Medals.
48, Binns Road, Chiswick, W.4. 5373A

NIGHTINGALE, P. J., Driver, R.A.S.C. (M.T.)

Volunteering in 1915 he proceeded overseas in the same year and rendered valuable services on transport work in various sectors of the Front, and was gassed. After receiving medical treatment, he was transferred as a driver to the General Headquarter Staff, with which he remained until the cessation of hostilities, when he returned home and was demobilised in 1919. He holds the 1914-15 Star, and the General Service and Victory Medals.
71, Solon New Road, Bedford Road, S.W.4. Z3547A

NIGHTINGALE, F. L., Gunner, R.G.A.

He joined in October 1916 and in March of the following year wa drsafted to the Western Front and was in action at Arras, Messines Ridge, Ypres Passchendaele and Cambrai, where he was taken prisoner in November 1917, and sent to Germany. On his release he returned home and was demobilised in March 1919, and holds the General Service and Victory Medals.

182, Commercial Road, Peckham, S.E.15.   Z6599

NISBET, A. J., Sapper, R.E.

He joined in April 1916, and two months later proceeded overseas. Serving in various sectors of the Western Front, he was engaged on important duties on the lines of communication until the cessation of hostilities. Returning home he was demobilised in September 1919, and holds the General Service and Victory Medals.

50, Havil Street, Camberwell, S.E.5.   Z6531D

NISBET, G. F., Rifleman, 21st London Regiment (1st Surrey Rifles).

He joined in March 1916, and proceeded overseas in the following July. Serving with his Battalion in the Western Front he fought in several sectors and saw much heavy fighting, including the Battles of the Somme, Arras, and made the supreme sacrifice, being killed in action at Cambrai on November 27th, 1917. He was entitled to the General Service and Victory Medals.

"Nobly striving, he nobly fell that we might live."

50, Havil Street, Camberwell, S.E.5.   Z6531A

NISBET, C. J. (M.M.), Private, M.G.C.

Volunteering in November 1915, he served at home as Divisional Cyclist until proceeding to France in 1917. In this theatre of war he was engaged in heavy fighting in many engagements, including those at Menin Road, Zillebeke Achiet-le-Grand, Havrincourt Wood, and Cambrai. On August 21st, 1918, he was awarded the Military Medal for conspicuous bravery whilst acting as runner in delivering Despatches and taking up rations to the Front lines under heavy fire. He also holds the General Service and Victory Medals, and was demobilised in February 1919.

50, Havil Street, Camberwell, S.E.5.   Z6531C

NISBET, T., L/Corporal, 4th Royal Fusiliers.

He enlisted in 1909, and was mobilised on the outbreak of war, and sent to France shortly afterwards. He saw much heavy fighting during the Retreat from Mons, and was seriously wounded in the Battle of Ypres. Invalided to England, he unhappily died in hospital from the effects of his injuries on February 11th, 1915, and was entitled to the Mons Star, and the General Service and Victory Medals.

"He passed out of the sight of men by the path of duty and self-sacrifice."

50, Havil Street, Camberwell, S.E.5.   Z6531B

NISBETT-GARRATT, C., Private, 10th Sherwood Foresters.

He volunteered in October 1915, and in the following March proceeded overseas. Serving with his Battalion in several sectors of the Western Front he took part in heavy fighting in many important engagements. He was killed in action near St. Quentin in March 1918 during the German Offensive, and was entitled to the General Service and Victory Medals.

"Honour to the immortal dead who gave their youth that the world might grow old in peace."

49, Priory Road, Bedford Park, W.4.   6664

NISBETT-GARRATT, S., Pte., 10th Hampshire Regt.

He joined in March 1917, and in the same year proceeded overseas. He served with his unit in several sectors of the Western Front, and was afterwards sent to Salonika. In that theatre of war he saw much heavy fighting on the Doiran and Bulguarian fronts, and later he proceeded with the Army of Occupation to Turkey. On the cessation of hostilities he returned home for demobilisation in March 1920, and holds the General Service and Victory Medals.

49, Priory Road, Bedford Park, W.4.   6663

NISBETT-GARRATT, W., Air Mechanic, R.A.F.

He joined in September 1918, and on completing his training, served with his Squadron at various stations. He was engaged on important duties of a highly technical nature, which required much knowledge and skill, and rendered valuable services, although unsuccessful in obtaining his transfer overseas. He was demobilised in December 1919.

49, Priory Road, Bedford Park, W.4.   6709

NIXON, F., Sergt., 1st East Surrey Regiment.

He volunteered in August 1914, and proceeded to France almost immediately. He fought in the Retreat from Mons, and was wounded, but on recovery rejoined his Battalion, and was in action at Hill 60, Loos, Ypres, Armentières, Messines, and Arras. He was then transferred to the Royal Fusiliers, and served at the Base on guard duties. Returning to England he was demobilised in January 1919, and holds the Mons Star, and the General Service and Victory Medals.

25, Stewarts Road, Battersea Park Road, S.W.8.   Z3548

NIXON, H. A., Private, 2nd Middlesex Regiment.

He enlisted in 1906, and was drafted to the Western Front shortly after the commencement of hostilities. He fought in many important engagements, including those at Ypres, Loos, and Albert, and did good work. He was unfortunately killed in action on the Somme on July 1st, 1916, and was entitled to the 1914 Star, and the General Service and Victory Medals.

"His memory is cherished with pride."

31, Priory Grove, Lansdowne Road, S.W.8.   Z1211B

NIXSON, W. T., Sergt., R.A.S.C. (M.T.) and Tank Corps.

Volunteering in September 1914, he embarked for France two months later, and was in action at La Bassée, the Somme, Bullecourt, Loos, Vimy Ridge, and St. Eloi, and was gassed at Albert in March 1916. On recovery he rejoined his unit and served in many engagements during the Retreat and Advance of 1918. He was demobilised in April 1919, and holds the 1914–15 Star, and the General Service and Victory Medals.

39, Charlotte Street, Old Kent Road, S.E.1.   Z27270

NOAKES, T., Bandsman, 2nd Gordon Highlanders.

He enlisted in October 1904, and served in India and Egypt prior to the outbreak of war. In August 1914 he proceeded to France and fought in the Retreat from Mons, and in the Battles of the Marne, the Aisne, La Bassée, Ypres (I.), Neuve Chapelle, Hill 60, and the Somme. He died gloriously on the Field of Battle at Arras on April 24th, 1917, and was entitled to the Mons Star, and the General Service and Victory Medals.

"Great deeds cannot die, they with the sun and moon renew their light for ever."

31, Dartrey Road, King's Road, S.W.10.   22306D

NOBBS, F. H., Private, Royal Fusiliers and Labour Corps.

Volunteering in January 1915, he was sent to France in March of that year, and fought at Ypres, Arras, and in many other engagements of note. He was also in action throughout the German Offensive and subsequent Allied Advance of 1918, and did good work. He was demobilised in August 1919, and holds the 1914–15 Star, and the General Service and Victory Medals.

73, Gywnne Road, Battersea, S.W.11.   Z2927A

NOCK, W., Gunner, R.F.A.

Volunteering in December 1914, he was sent to France shortly afterwards, and was engaged in heavy fighting in the Battles of Ypres, the Somme, and St. Eloi. He was severely wounded at Loos, and returning to England, received hospital treatment. On recovery he was stationed at various depôts in England, engaged on important duties until demobilised in March 1919. He holds the 1914–15 Star, and the General Service and Victory Medals. 15A, Froude Street, Battersea Park, S.W.8.   Z3549

NOCK, W. G., Private, Royal Fusiliers and Rifleman, 12th London Regt. (Rangers).

Volunteering in September 1914, he was sent to the Dardanelles in the following year, and took part in the landing at Suvla Bay, and in the subsequent engagements until the Evacuation of the Peninsula. Transferred to the Western Front, he fought in many parts of the line, and was unfortunately killed in action on the Somme on September 15th, 1916. He was entitled to the 1914–15 Star, and the General Service and Victory Medals.

7, Hillery Road, Walworth, S.E.17.   Z2811B

NOEL, G. W. (M.M.), L/Corporal, 1/23rd London Regiment.

He volunteered in June 1915, and was drafted to the Western Front four months later. During his service overseas he fought at Ypres, Hill 60, the Somme, and Cambrai, and throughout the Retreat and Advance of 1918. He was awarded the Military Medal for conspicuous gallantry and devotion to duty in the Field, and in addition holds the 1914–15 Star, and the General Service and Victory Medals, and was demobilised in February 1919.

160, Stewart's Road, Battersea Park Road, S.W.8.   Z3550

NOLAN, A., Gunner, R.G.A.

Volunteering in October 1915, he completed his training and served at various stations until proceeding to France in 1917. He fought at Ypres, the Somme, and Passchendaele, and throughout the German Offensive and subsequent Allied Advance of 1918. Returning home he was demobilised in January 1919, and holds the General Service and Victory Medals.

57, Flaxman Road, Camberwell, S.E.5.   Z6049

NOLAN, H. J., Sergt., 24th London Regiment (The Queen's).

He volunteered in June 1915, and was engaged on important duties instructing recruits of the New Armies until drafted to France in December 1917. He took part in heavy fighting during the German Offensive, and was wounded, and on recovery rejoined his unit, and served throughout the Allied Advance. He was demobilised in January 1919, and holds the General Service and Victory Medals.

1, Cavour Street, Walworth, S.E.17.   Z26007

NORBURY, H. J., Gunner, R.F.A.
He volunteered in March 1915, and embarking for France in the following December, fought in many engagements, including those at Neuve Chapelle, Hill 60, Ypres, Vermelles, Vimy Ridge, Bullecourt, Messines and Bapaume. He also saw heavy fighting in the Retreat and Advance of 1918, and during his service overseas was twice wounded. He was demobilised in March 1919, and holds the 1914-15 Star, and the General Service and Victory Medals.
119, Mayall Road, Herne Hill, S.E.24.   Z3551

NORFIELD, T. H., A.B., Royal Navy.
He joined the service at the outbreak of war, and was posted to H.M.S. " Cressy," with which ship he was in action at the Battle of Heligoland Bight, and was engaged on patrol and other important duties. Later transferred to H.M.S. " Ardent " he saw much service, and did good work in the Mediterranean Sea, and in home waters.. Afterwards he fought in the Battle of Jutland, during which he was killed. He was entitled to the 1914-15 Star, and the General Service and Victory Medals.
"His life for his Country, his Soul to God."
38, Mostyn Road, Brixton Road, S.W.9.   Z4509

NORMAN, J., Private, R.A.S.C. (M.T.)
Volunteering in March 1915, later in that year he proceeded to the Western Front, and was engaged on important duties in the forward areas transporting supplies to the front lines. He was present at the Battles of the Somme, Arras, Loos, Lens, Grandcourt, and at many engagements in the Retreat and Advance of 1918. Returning to England he was demobilised in December 1919, and holds the 1994-15 Star, and the General Service and Victory Medals.
22, Royal Road, Walworth, S.E.17.   Z26563

NORMAN, S. G., Sergt., Royal Sussex Regiment.
He volunteered in February 1915, and in the following July was sent to France. During his service in this theatre of war he was mentioned in Despatches for consistently good work at Loos, and was promoted to Corporal. Later on the Somme front he again rendered excellent service and was promoted to Sergeant. He was wounded there, and on his recovery after treatment in England was engaged on home duties until demobilised in May 1919. He holds the 1914-15 Star, and the General Service and Victory Medals.
49, Bedford Street, Walworth, S.E.17.   Z2387B

NORMAN, S. J., L/Corporal, 7th Yorkshire Regt.
He volunteered at the outbreak of hostilities, and in the following year proceeded overseas. Whilst on the Western Front he fought in many engagements of importance, including those at St. Eloi, Ypres and Loos. He gave his life for the freedom of England in the British Offensive on the Somme on July 1st, 1916. He was entitled to the 1914-15 Star, and the General Service and Victory Medals.
"Steals on the ear the distant triumph song."
33, Sterndale Road, Wandsworth, S.W.8.   Z3552

NORMAN, T., Private, R.A.S.C. (M.T.)
He joined in August 1916, and three months later was sent to France. He served in various sectors, doing good work in the transport of supplies during the operations at Ypres, the Somme, and in the Advance of 1918. After the Armistice he proceeded to Germany with the Army of Occupation, and whilst stationed at Cologne was in hospital for a time owing to injuries received in a lorry accident. He was demobilised in October 1919, and holds the General Service and Victory Medals.   11, Paulin Street, Bermondsey, S.E.1.   Z27172

NORMAN, W., Corporal (Shoeing Smith), R.F.A.
He volunteered in May 1915, and later in the same year was sent to the Western Front, where he was in action at Arras, the Somme, Ypres, Passchendaele, St. Quentin, Lille, Cambrai and the Advance of 1918. During his service abroad he contracted dysentery, and was invalided to hospital for a time. He was demobilised in March 1919, and he holds the Queen's and King's South African Medals for his service in the Boer War, and also the 1914-15 Star, and the General Service and Victory Medals.
11, Freemantle Street, Walworth, S.E.17.   Z3553

NORRIS, A. B., Rifleman, 51st Rifle Brigade.
He joined in October 1918, on attaining military age, and on the conclusion of his training was sent to France, and afterwards to Germany, where he did much good work with the Army of Occupation on the Rhine. He returned to England and was demobilised in February 1920.
3A, Willowbrook Road, Peckham, S.E.15.   Z4510

NORRIS, C., L/Cpl., 1st East Surrey Regiment.
He enlisted in 1907, and was serving in India at the outbreak of hostilities. He was afterwards drafted to France, and fought in the engagements at Loos and Ypres. He fell fighting gallantly at Ypres on February 14th, 1915. He was entitled to the 1914-15 Star, and the General Service and Victory Medals.
"A valiant soldier, with undaunted heart he breasted Life's last hill."
8, Creek Street, Battersea, S.W.11.   Z3557A

NORRIS, C. A., Gunner, R.G.A.
Volunteering in 1914, he was drafted to France on the completion of his training in the following year. During his service on the Western Front he was in action at Ypres, the Somme, Arras, Vimy Ridge, Lens, and in many other engagements until hostilities ceased. He was demobilised in June 1919, and holds the 1914-15 Star, and the General Service and Victory Medals.
13, Chatham Street, Walworth, S.E.17.   Z3554

NORRIS, G., Rifleman, Rifle Brigade.
Volunteering in June 1915, he was drafted overseas five months later. Whilst on the Western Front he served in the Ypres sector, but owing to ill-health was invalided to England in the same year. He was discharged as medically unfit for further service in May 1916, and holds the 1914-15 Star, and the General Service and Victory Medals.
157A, Wickersley Road, Lavender Hill, S.W.11.   Z3555

NORRIS, G. S., Private, 20th London Regiment.
He volunteered in August 1914, and served on important duties with his unit until 1916, when he was drafted to the Western Front, where he took part in important engagements. He was later transferred to Salonika and was engaged on patrol duties. He was unfortunately killed in action on April 22nd, 1917, and was entitled to the General Service and Victory Medals.
"Courage, bright hopes, and a myriad dreams splendidly given."
65, Lausanne Road, Peckham, S.E.15.   Z6600

NORRIS, H., Stoker, R.N.
He was mobilised at the outbreak of hostilities, and in H.M.S. " Formidable " served with the Grand Fleet in many waters, and was engaged on patrol duties in the English Channel. On January 1st, 1915, his ship was torpedoed, and he unhappily was drowned. He was entitled to the 1914-15 Star, and the General Service and Victory Medals.
"He joined the great white company of valiant souls."
74, Cambridge Street, Camberwell, S.E.5.   Z3560

NORRIS, H., Driver, R.F.A.
He volunteered in October 1915, and in the same year was sent to France. Whilst in this theatre of war he fought at the Battles of the Somme, Arras, Bullecourt, Albert, Ypres, Passchendaele, Lens, Cambrai, St. Quentin, and many other operations in the Retreat and Advance of 1918. He was demobilised in August 1919, and holds the 1914-15 Star, and the General Service and Victory Medals.
93, Sussex Road, Coldharbour Lane, S.W.9.   Z3558

NORRIS, H. G., Gunner, R.F.A.
Volunteering in January 1915, he proceeded to France in September of that year. He was in action at Loos and various other engagements in that vicinity. He was afterwards drafted to Salonika, where he fought in several important engagements until invalided to England on account of fever. He later returned to the Western Front, where he remained until demobilised in April 1919. He holds the 1914-15 Star, and the General Service and Victory Medals.
3A, Willowbrook Road, Peckham, S.E.15.   Z4511

NORRIS, H. R., Pte., Black Watch and Rflmn., Cameronians (Scottish Rifles).
He volunteered in May 1915, and proceeded overseas in the following year. During his service on the Western Front, he fought at the Somme, Arras and Albert, and was severely wounded in action. He was then invalided to England, and after six months' treatment, was retained on home duties until discharged as medically unfit for further service in August 1918. He holds the General Service and Victory Medals.
17, Fenwick Place, Landor Road, S.W.9.   Z3559

NORRIS, H. W., Private, 5th Essex Regiment.
He joined in June 1916, and on the completion of his training embarked for France on special work with prisoners of war. He afterwards returned to England and was employed on important home duties for the remainder of his service. He was demobilised in January 1919, and holds the General Service and Victory Medals.
92, Alberta Street, Walworth, S.E.17.   Z25916

NORRIS, W., Private, 2nd East Surrey Regiment.
Having enlisted in 1895, he fought in the Boer War, and was mobilised in 1914 at the outbreak of hostilities. He was drafted at once to France, where he was in action during the Retreat from Mons, the Battles of the Marne and Ypres, and many other engagements. He gave his life for King and Country on February 28th, 1916, during a German attack near Loos. In addition to holding the Queen's and King's South African Medals, he was entitled to the Mons Star, and the General Service and Victory Medals.
"A valiant soldier, with undaunted heart he breasted Life's last hill."
8, Creek Street, Battersea, S.W.11.   Z3557B

NORRIS, W., Private, 16th (The Queen's) Lancers.
A serving soldier, he was mobilised at the outbreak of hostilities
and immediately drafted to France, where he fought in the
Retreat from Mons, and the Battles of the Marne, the Aisne,
Ypres, the Somme, and was severely wounded near Cambrai.
He was sent to hospital in England, and in June 1918 was
invalided out of the Service. He holds the Mons Star, and
the General Service and Victory Medals.
8, Broughton Street, Battersea Park, S.W.8.   Z3556

NORTH, F. G., Driver, R.F.A.
He volunteered in September 1915, and was sent to France
in the following year. During his service overseas he was
in action at the Battles of the Somme, Arras, Lens, Ypres,
Passchendaele, Vimy Ridge, and throughout the German
Offensive and subsequent Allied Advance of 1918. He suffered
from malaria whilst serving on the Western Front, and was
demobilised in April 1919. He holds the General Service
and Victory Medals.
28, Grant Road, Battersea, S.W.11.   Z3565

NORTH, A., Gunner, R.F.A., and Pte., 23rd London
    Regiment.
Volunteering in August 1914, and drafted to France a year
afterwards, he fought in many parts of the line. Owing to
ill-health he returned to England, and was discharged unfit
in February 1916. He re-enlisted, however, in the London
Regiment, and proceeded to the Western Front, where he was
in action in many engagements of note. In February 1917,
he was killed by a sniper, and lies at rest at Ypres. He was
entitled to the 1914-15 Star, and the General Service and
Victory Medals.
" Thinking that remembrance, though unspoken, may reach
him where he sleeps."
79, Speke Road, Battersea, S.W.11.   Z3561

NORTH, F. G., Sergt., 25th London Regt. (Cyclists').
Mobilised on the declaration of war, he was stationed at various
Depôts engaged on guard and other important duties with his
unit until 1916. In that year he was sent to India, and assisted
in restoring order in the Riots in 1917 and 1918. He was
in action in Afghanistan and rendered valuable services
throughout. Returning to England, he was demobilised in
January 1920, and holds the General Service and Victory
Medals, the India General Service Medal (with clasp, Afghanistan, North Western Frontier, 1919), and the Territorial
Force Efficiency Medal.
119, Hollydale Road, Peckham S.E.15.   Z6421

NORTH, F. G., Driver, R.A.S.C.
He volunteered in November 1915, and proceeding to France
in the following March was engaged on important transport
duties in the advanced areas. He was present at the Battles
of the Somme, St. Eloi, Arras, and at fierce fighting in the
Retreat and Advance of 1918. After the Armistice he was
sent into Germany with the Army of Occupation, and served
there until he returned to England for demobilisation in
August 1919. He holds the General Service and Victory
Medals.
6, Aulton Place, Kennington, S.E.11.   Z27494

NORTH, F. W., Bombardier, R.G.A.
He joined in June 1916, and completing his training, served
at various stations on important work with his unit. Owing
to defective eyesight he was unable to obtain his transfer to
a theatre of war, but did good work engaged on clerical duties
in the Master Gunner's office until demobilised in July 1919.
5, Rozel Road, Wandsworth Road, S.W.4.   Z3562

NORTH, H., Rifleman, 2/15th London Regt. (Civil
    Service Rifles).
He joined in June 1917, and later in that year was drafted to
the Western Front. He was in action in many important
engagements, including those at Messines, Lens, Passchendaele,
Cambrai, Ypres, Le Cateau, and fought throughout the German
Offensive and Allied Advance of 1918. He was demobilised
in 1919, and holds the General Service and Victory Medals.
132, Mayall Road, Herne Hill, S.E.24.   Z3563

NORTH, W. A., Corporal, King's Royal Rifle Corps.
Volunteering in October 1914, and embarking for France
three months later, he fought at the Battles of Neuve Chapelle,
Hill 60, Ypres, Festubert and Loos. Transferred to Salonika
in October 1915 he was in action in many engagements on the
Vardar, Struma, Monastir and Doiran fronts. He returned
to England on leave, and at the conclusion of his furlough
was drafted to France and was engaged in heavy fighting
throughout the German Offensive and Allied Advance of
1918, and was wounded twice during his service overseas.
He was demobilised in February 1919, and holds the 1914-15
Star, and the General Service and Victory Medals.
99, Mayall Road, Herne Hill, S.E.24.   Z3564

NORTH, H. T., Private, R.A.S.C. (M.T.)
Joining in November 1916, he was drafted to the Western
Front later in that year, and served in the advanced areas
engaged on important duties connected with the transport
of ammunition and supplies. He was present at heavy
fighting on the Somme and in the Retreat and Advance of
1918. He was demobilised in March 1919, and holds the
General Service and Victory Medals.
11, Royal Terrace, Royal Road, Walworth, S.E.17.   Z26334

NORTHAM, G., Rifleman, 6th London Regt. (Rifles).
He volunteered in October 1915, and embarking for France
in the following month, was in action in the Battles of Loos
and St. Eloi. He died gloriously on the Field of Battle on
February 28th, 1916, and was entitled to the 1914-15 Star,
and the General Service and Victory Medals.
" He passed out of sight of men by the path of duty and
self-sacrifice."
31, Ægis Grove, Battersea Park Road, S.W.8.   Z3566

NORTHAM, G. H., Rflmn., 6th London Regt. (Rifles).
Joining in September 1916, he was drafted to the Western
Front in the following December, and was engaged in heavy
fighting in many parts of the line. He was wounded on
February 21st, 1917, at Ypres, and, admitted into hospital,
died from his injuries two days later, and is buried at Poper-
inghe. He was entitled to the General Service and Victory
Medals.   5, Latchmere Road, Battersea, S.W.11.   Z3570

NORTHCOTE, H., L/Corporal, Wiltshire Regiment.
Volunteering in September 1914, he was sent to the Western
Front in the following June, and acting as a sniper, was
in action in many important engagements, including those at
Arras, Ypres, the Somme and Passchendaele, and was twice
wounded. Transferred to India in December 1916, he assisted
to restore order in the rioting at Calcutta and served at various
stations on guard and other important duties. Returning
to England, he was demobilised in July 1919, and holds the
1914-15 Star, and the General Service and Victory Medals.
32, Mordaunt Street, Landor Road, S.W.9.   Z3567

NORTHEAST, W. J., Sapper, R.E.
He enlisted in 1900, and mobilised from the Reserve at the
outbreak of war, was drafted to France shortly afterwards.
He was in action in the Retreat from Mons, and at the Battles
of Ypres, Albert, and the Somme. Later he was employed
with the Railway Operative Department as an engine driver
and on constructional work, and rendered valuable services
until demobilised in April 1919. He holds the 1914-15 Star,
and the General Service and Victory Medals.
159, Harbut Road, Battersea, S.W.11.   Z3568

NORTHFIELD, H. W., A.B., Royal Naval Reserve.
He joined in August 1914, and was posted to H.M.S. " Orawa."
This ship was in action at the Battle of the Falkland Islands
and served in the Pacific, taking an active part in the pursuit
and sinking of the " Dresden." Later he was sent to German
East Africa and fought in many engagements ashore, and was
wounded. Rejoining his ship he served until demobilised
in January 1919. He holds the 1914-15 Star, and the General
Service and Victory Medals.
23, Rowena Crescent, Battersea, S.W.11.   Z3569

NORTHOVER, F. E., Rifleman, 2nd Rifle Brigade.
He joined in May 1916, and embarking for France four months
later was in action at the Battles of the Somme, Arras and
Ypres. In January 1917 he was invalided to England owing
to ill-health, and on recovery returned to France in the following May and fought in many parts of the line. He was also
engaged in heavy fighting in the Retreat and Advance of
1918, and was twice wounded. Returning to England he
was demobilised in August 1919, and holds the General Service
and Victory Medals.
29, Radner Street, Peckham, S.E.15.   Z6530

NORTHWOOD, G., Private, Queen's Own (Royal
    West Kent Regiment).
Volunteering in August 1914, he was sent to France in the
following year and was in action at the Battles of Ypres,
Hill 60, the Somme, Arras and Vimy Ridge. Transferred to
Italy in 1917, he was engaged in heavy fighting on the Piave,
and, returning to France in 1918, fought throughout the
German Offensive and Allied Advance. He was demobilised
in March 1919, and holds the 1914-15 Star, and the General
Service and Victory Medals.
48, Odell Street, Camberwell, S.E.5.   Z5469

NORTON, A., Leading Stoker, R.N.
He joined the Service in 1908, and was serving aboard H.M.S.
" Shannon " at the outbreak of war, which vessel was engaged
on patrol and other important duties in the North Sea. Transferred to H.M.S. " Terror," his ship was in action during the
raids on Zeebrugge and Ostend, and was torpedoed at the
latter place, but fortunately he was saved. He was demobilised in January 1919, and holds the 1914-15 Star, and
the General Service and Victory Medals.
53, Kirkwood Road, Nunhead, S.E.15.   Z6207

NORTON, C., Private, 2/20th London Regiment.

Volunteering in April 1915, and sent to Egypt in the following year, he fought in operations on the Palestine front, including those at Gaza and in the vicinity of Jerusalem. Transferred to France in March 1918, he was engaged in heavy fighting in the Retreat and Advance of 1918, and was wounded at Cambrai in November. Returning to England it was found necessary to amputate one of his legs, and in 1920 he was still receiving treatment at Roehampton Hospital. He holds the General Service and Victory Medals.

56, Parkstone Road, Peckham, S.E.15.　　　　Z6210

NORTON, J. W., Private, M.G.C.

Volunteering in February 1915, he was drafted to the Western Front in the following May. He took part in the fierce fighting at Festubert, Loos, the Somme, Bullecourt, Ypres and other engagements, and also served in the Retreat and Advance of 1918. He was demobilised in March 1919, and holds the 1914–15 Star, and the General Service and Victory Medals.

15, Galleywall Road, Rotherhithe, S.E.16.　　Z6601

NORTON, V., Driver, R.A.S.C.

Volunteering in September 1914, he served at various stations until drafted to the Western Front in 1916, and was engaged on transport duties during heavy fighting in many parts of the line. Transferred to Salonika in 1917, he saw much service there, and contracting malaria was admitted into hospital. He subsequently died on June 15th, 1917, and was entitled to the General Service and Victory Medals.

11, Joubert Street, Battersea, S.W.11.　　　Z3571

NOTLEY, J. A., Corporal, Royal Berkshire Regiment.

He volunteered in September 1914, and in the following year was sent to France. There he took part in much fighting, and was wounded at Loos. On recovery he returned to the firing line and was in action at Albert, the Somme, Arras, Bullecourt and Ypres, and was wounded a second time at Cambrai. He returned to England after the signing of the Armistice, and was demobilised in February 1919. He holds the 1914–15 Star, and the General Service and Victory Medals.

254, Fort Road, Bermondsey, S.E.1.　　　Z26341

NOULTON, G., Sergt., 23rd Lancashire Fusiliers.

Volunteering in November 1914, he was sent overseas in the following year, and was engaged in much fighting on the Western Front. He was in action at Ypres, the Somme and Bullecourt, and was wounded at Cambrai. He was then invalided to England, and on recovery rejoined his Battalion in the front line trenches. He died gloriously on the Field of Battle during the final Allied Advance of 1918. He was entitled to the 1914–15 Star, and the General Service and Victory Medals.

"Whilst we remember the Sacrifice is not in vain."

3, Arden Street, Battersea Park, S.W.8.　　Z3572B

NOULTON, H. C., Driver, R.F.A.

He volunteered in June 1915, and later in the same year was drafted overseas. During his service in France he took part in many engagements, including those on the Somme and at Arras and Cambrai and during the Retreat and Advance of 1918. He was demobilised in February 1919, and holds the 1914–15 Star, and the General Service and Victory Medals.

5, Arden Street, Battersea Park, S.W.8.　　Z3573B

NOULTON, H. J., Private, R.M.L.I.

He volunteered in June 1915, and on the completion of his training was posted to a cruiser squadron. His ship was engaged on special patrol duties off the coast of Russia. In October 1918, the vessel on which he was serving, whilst conveying wounded across the Irish Sea, was torpedoed, but after several hours in the water he, fortunately, was rescued. He was demobilised in February 1920, and holds the General Service and Victory Medals.

5, Arden Street, Battersea Park, S.W.8.　　Z3573A

NOWELL, G. H., L/Corporal, Middlesex Regt. and Wiltshire Regt.

He volunteered in May 1915, and in June of the following year was sent to France. Whilst in this theatre of war he was in action at Loos, Combles, the Somme, Péronne and Bullecourt. He was then transferred to the Wiltshire Regiment, and during the Battle of Le Cateau was wounded in October 1918. He returned to England and was subsequently demobilised in March 1919, and holds the General Service and Victory Medals.

34, Camellia Street, Wandsworth Road, S.W.8.　Z3574

NUNN, A. E., Private, 6th Dorsetshire Regiment.

He volunteered in August 1914, and in the following year proceeded overseas. Whilst in France he was engaged in much fighting at Ypres, Arras, Givenchy and Loos, and was severely wounded at Hooge in October 1915. He was sent to hospital in England and eventually invalided out of the Service in February 1917. He holds the 1914–15 Star, and the General Service and Victory Medals.

5, Sunwell Street, Peckham, S.E.15.　　　Z6488

NUNN, G. H., Private, 11th Queen's (Royal West Surrey Regiment) and Air Mechanic, R.A.F.

He volunteered in July 1915, and in the following May was drafted to France. In this theatre of war he was engaged in the fighting at Ploegsteert Wood, Vimy Ridge, the Somme, Beaumont-Hamel, Arras, Ypres, Cambrai, the Marne, Amiens, Bapaume, Havrincourt, and the final Allied Advance of 1918. Since his demobilisation, which took place in 1919, he has suffered from defective hearing caused by the heavy gunfire. He holds the General Service and Victory Medals.

65, Ferndale Road, Clapham, S.W.4.　　　Z3576

NUNN, W. E., L/Cpl., 22nd London Regiment (The Queen's).

He joined in November 1916, and in the following month was drafted to Egypt, where he took part in the British advance through Palestine, and was in action at Jerusalem and Jericho, and at various other places. He returned to England after the signing of the Armistice, and was demobilised in August 1919, and holds the General Service and Victory Medals.

2, Sandford Row, Walworth, S.E.17.　　　Z3575

NURSE, C., Private, M.G.C.

He joined in October 1916, and in the following year proceeded overseas. During his service on the Western Front he fought in various engagements, and was taken prisoner in March 1918 during the fighting on the Somme. He was held captive until after the signing of the Armistice, when, after repatriation, he served in Ireland on garrison duties until demobilised in September 1919. He holds the General Service and Victory Medals.

28, Cator Street, Peckham, S.E.15.　　　Z4512

NURSE, R., Private, North Staffordshire Regiment.

Volunteering in April 1915, he was drafted to the Dardanelles in the same year and took part in the Landing at Suvla Bay. After the Evacuation of the Peninsula he was sent to Egypt and was stationed at Alexandria for a time. He then proceeded to Mesopotamia and served in the campaign against the Turks until 1917, when he was wounded and invalided home. He was discharged as medically unfit in November of the same year and holds the 1914–15 Star, and the General Service and Victory Medals.

39, Riverhall Street, South Lambeth, S.W.8.　Z3577

NUTLEY, W., Gunner, R.H.A.

Having enlisted in 1908 he was serving in India on the outbreak of war and was later drafted to Mesopotamia, where he took part in the campaign against the Turks and was severely wounded in January 1917. He afterwards succumbed to his injuries, and was entitled to the 1914–15 Star, and the General Service and Victory Medals.

"He joined the great white company of valiant souls."

36, Thurlow Street, Wandsworth Road, S.W.8.　Z3578

NUTTALL, L. M. (Mrs.), Special War Worker.

Being anxious to serve her country this lady took up work of importance at Messrs. John Bell, Hill and Lucas', Bermondsey, where she was engaged in making gas-masks. Later she was employed on the Underground Railway as a lift attendant, thus releasing a man for military duties. She carried out her duties in a highly commendable manner.

50, Mercia Road, Bermondsey, S.E.1.　　Z26388

NYE, C. S., Private, East Surrey Regiment.

He volunteered in September 1914, and was drafted to France in the following March and fought in the Battle of Hill 60. Here he was killed in action in April 1915, and was entitled to the 1914–15 Star, and the General Service and Victory Medals.

"The path of duty was the way to glory."

23, Cairns Road, Battersea, S.W.11.　　Z3579

NYE, H. P., Corporal, 10th Middlesex Regiment.

He volunteered in April 1915, and after having completed his training was sent to France. Here he took part in numerous engagements, and was in action in the Cambrai sector. He returned to England and was demobilised in May 1919, and holds the General Service and Victory Medals.

20, Cornwall Grove, Chiswick, W.4.　　　5610

NYE, P. S., Cpl., 21st London Regt. (1st Surrey Rifles).

He joined in May 1916, and in the same year was drafted to the Western Front, where he took part in numerous engagements, including those on the Somme, and at Arras and Ypres. He returned home and was demobilised in January 1919, and holds the General Service and Victory Medals.

24, Sunwell Street, Peckham, S.E.15.　　Z6602

NYE, T. W., Sapper, R.E.

He volunteered in 1915, and after having completed his training was drafted to France in 1917. He served at Cambrai and on the Somme, and was taken prisoner during the German Offensive of March 1918. He was held in captivity until after the Armistice, when he was released, and returning to England was demobilised in March 1919, holding the General Service and Victory Medals.

59, Park Crescent, Clapham, S.W.4.　　　Z3580

O

OAK, H., Private, Royal Sussex Regiment and Royal Defence Corps.

He joined in June 1916, and was engaged for a time with the Royal Sussex Regiment at Crowborough, on important duties as a storekeeper. He was not successful in securing his transfer overseas, and was afterwards transferred to the Royal Defence Corps, in which he rendered valuable services until his demobilisation in March 1919.

11, Fendick Road, Peckham, S.E.15.   Z6306

OAKLEY, W., Bombardier, R.F.A.

After volunteering on the outbreak of hostilities he completed his training, and in 1915 proceeded to France. While on that front he took an active part in many notable engagements, including those at Ypres, Hill 60, Loos, Vimy Ridge, the Somme, Arras, Cambrai, and in the German and British Offensives of 1918. On one occasion he was wounded. He returned to England and was demobilised in May 1919, holding the 1914-15 Star, and the General Service and Victory Medals.

1, Vaughan Road, Camberwell, :E.5.   Z6424

OATES, A. J., Private, 5th Essex Regiment.

He joined in October 1916, and having completed his course of training crossed to France in August 1917. He took an active part in many important engagements on this Front, including those at Arras, Cambrai and the Somme, and was severely gassed. In consequence of this he was invalided to England and was ultimately discharged in July 1918 as unfit for further duty. He holds the General Service and Victory Medals.

27, Warham Street, Camberwell, S.E.5.   Z3581

O'BRIEN, A. A., Rifleman, Rifle Brigade.

After joining in May 1917, he was drafted to the Western Front in the following month, and took a prominent part in many subsequent operations, including those at Cambrai and the Somme. He was badly wounded in the Cambrai Advance in 1918, and was invalided home in consequence, but on his recovery he was sent to Egypt, where he did much valuable service until his demobilisation in January 1920. He holds the General Service and Victory Medals.

2, Horsman Street, Camberwell, S.E.5.   Z1425B

OCKHAM, A. E., Acting L/Cpl., 51st Queen's (Royal West Surrey Regiment).

After joining in February 1918 he completed his course of training, and was drafted to France in the following August. In the following month he took an active part in engagements at Mont Kemmel, and was so severely wounded and gassed there that after being invalided home he was discharged in October as unfit for further military service. He holds the General Service and Victory Medals.

38, Darby Road, Battersea, S.W.11.   Z3582

OCKMORE, G. J., Private, Royal Fusiliers.

He joined in 1916, and on the completion of his training crossed to France in December. In the following year he fought in the Battle of Arras, and was badly wounded, but on his recovery he returned to the line and took an active part in the Retreat and Advance of the Allies. Being again severely wounded he was invalided home to Mitcham Hospital, from which he was demobilised in February 1919. He holds the General Service and Victory Medals.

10, Larcom Street, Walworth, S.E.17.   Z3583

O'CONNELL, J., Sapper, R.E.

He volunteered in the first week of the war, and after rendering valuable service in a Cavalry unit at Aldershot and other stations until January 1917, was transferred to the R.E. He afterwards did important work as an engineer in dry docks at Poplar and Rotherhithe, but was not successful in obtaining his transfer overseas while hostilities lasted. He was demobilised in March 1919, and has since died of illness contracted during his military service.

58, Wyndham Road, Camberwell, S.E.5.   Z3584

O'CONNELL, P. J., L/Sergt., 4th Irish Guards.

Mobilised in August 1914, he was quickly drafted to France, and there took an active part in the early engagements at Mons, Le Cateau, the Marne and the Aisne. He was afterwards reported missing, and is believed to have been killed in action on November 6th, 1914. He was entitled to the Mons Star, and the General Service and Victory Medals.

"He died the noblest death a man may die,
Fighting for God, and right, and liberty."

95, Bird in Bush Road, Peckham, S.E.15.   Z6532

O'CONNOR, T. W., Rflmn., King's Royal Rifle Corps.

He joined in September 1917, and after finishing his course of training was drafted to the Western Front in March 1918. He did much valuable work as a Signaller during the Retreat and Advance of 1918, especially in the operations at the Somme, Kemmel and Cambrai. After returning to England he was demobilised in October 1919, and holds the General Service and Victory Medals.

94, Vaughan Road, Camberwell, S.E.5.   Z6304

O'CONNOR, G., Private, Army Cyclist Corps and R.A.S.C. (H.T.)

He joined in December 1916, and after the completion of his training was retained at Swindon, Chelmsford and other stations on important duties until 1918, when he was drafted to France and transferred to the R.A.S.C. He unhappily met with a serious accident, for which he was invalided home. He was demobilised in March 1919, and holds the General Service and Victory Medals.

Pulross Road, Brixton Road, S.W.9.   Z3585

ODDY, J. R., Private, 19th London Regiment.

Volunteering in December 1915, he was drafted to France in the following June. Whilst overseas he fought in many engagements, including those at Cambrai, Bourlon Wood, Gavrelle and Arras. Owing to ill-health, he returned to England in March 1918, and was in hospital for a long time. He was invalided out of the Service in March 1919, and holds the General Service and Victory Medals.

24, Kempton Road, Camberwell, S.E.5.   Z4004-5A

O'DONNELL, D., Private, 2nd Queen's (Royal West Surrey Regiment).

Joining in June 1916, he was quickly drafted to the Western Front, where he served with the Labour Battalion of his Regiment in many important engagements, including those at the Somme, Beaumont-Hamel, Arras, Vimy Ridge, Messines, Ypres, Lens and Cambrai. In 1918, owing to being severely gassed, he returned to England, and in October of that year was invalided out of the Service. He holds the General Service and Victory Medals.

24, Little Manor Street, Clapham, S.W.4.   Z3587

OFFORD, C. J. G., Private, R.A.S.C. (H.T.)

He volunteered in January 1915, and later in the year, at the conclusion of his training, was drafted to the Western Front, where he served for upwards of three years. During this time he was engaged on important transport duties in the Somme, Ypres and Arras areas, and did much valuable work. He was also present at several important engagements, and was twice gassed, at Dickebusch and at Albert. After the Retreat and Advance of 1918, in which he also served, he was sent with the Army of Occupation into Germany. He was demobilised in February 1919, and holds the 1914-15 Star, and the General Service and Victory Medals.

135, Kirkwood Road, Nunhead, S:E.15.   Z6303

O'FLAHERTY, W. P., Gunner, R.F.A.

Volunteering in January 1915, he was drafted to France a year later, and was in action on that Front until December 1916, taking part in engagements at Loos, Vermelles, Vimy Ridge and the Somme. He was then transferred to Salonika, and after participating in fighting on the Doiran front, was sent to Egypt. Whilst in the latter theatre of war he was for some time in hospital, suffering from shell-shock. During his service he was wounded, and having returned to England, in January 1918 was invalided out of the Army. He holds the General Service and Victory Medals.

66, Geneva Road, Brixton, S.W.9.   Z5125

O'GRADY, W. A., L/Corporal, M.G.C.

A serving soldier, he was in Ireland when war broke out, and was drafted to the Western Front, where he fought in the Battles of the Aisne, Ypres, St. Eloi and Armentières, and was wounded. He was then invalided home, but on his recovery was sent to Salonika, and subsequently did valuable work with his unit during operations on the Struma and Vardar fronts. He holds the 1914 Star, and the General Service and Victory Medals, and is now on the Reserve.

60, Stainsforth Road, Battersea, S.W.11.   Z3588

O'HARE, H. F., Rifleman, 8th London Regt. (Post Office Rifles).

Volunteering in September 1914, he crossed to France in the following February, and subsequently fought in a number of important engagements. He died gloriously on the Field of Battle at Ypres, on July 19th, 1917, and is buried in a cemetery at Voormezeele, in the vicinity of the place where he was killed. He was entitled to the 1914-15 Star, and the General Service and Victory Medals.

"Honour to the immortal dead, who gave their youth that the world might grow old in peace."

80, Commercial Road, Peckham, S.E.15.   Z6426

O'KEEFE, H. W., Private, R.A.S.C. (M.T.)

He volunteered early in 1915, and after his training was drafted to the Western Front, where he was engaged on important transport duties in the forward areas. In 1916, however, owing to ill-health, he returned to England, and was invalided out of the Service. He holds the General Service and Victory Medals.

12, Tennyson Street, Queen's Road, South Lambeth, S.W.8.   Z3589

OKINES, G., Private, 1st Queen's (Royal West Surrey Regiment).
Volunteering in December 1915, he crossed to France early in the following year. During his overseas service, he fought in many important engagements, including those at Ypres and High Wood, but in 1918 was invalided home and discharged owing to ill-health. He holds the General Service and Victory Medals.
33, Chalmers Street, Wandsworth Road, S.W.8.   Z3590

OKINES, R., Private, 2nd Middlesex Regiment.
Joining in 1918, he was drafted to Egypt at the conclusion of his training, and was engaged on duties of an important nature until the following year. He then returned to England in consequence of ill-health, and in 1920 was invalided out of the Service. He holds the General Service and Victory Medals.
35, Chalmers Road, Wandsworth Road, S.W.8.   Z3591

OKLEY, E. W., Sapper, R.E.
He volunteered early in 1915, and in the follwoing year was drafted to the Western Front. Whilst in this theatre of war he was engaged on important duties in the forward areas, and was present at many battles, notably those of Loos and the Somme. He holds the General Service and Victory Medals. and was demobilised in November 1918.
5, Ingrave Street, Battersea, S.W.11.   Z3592

OLDFIELD, A., Private, East Lancashire Regiment.
A serving soldier, he crossed to France immediately upon the outbreak of war and took part in the Retreat from Mons and the Battles of Le Cateau, the Marne, the Aisne, and Ypres. He also fought at Ploegsteert Wood, the Somme and Beaumont-Hamel, and in the Retreat and Advance of 1918, and did valuable work with his unit throughout the period of hostilities. He holds the Mons Star, and the General Service and Victory Medals, and was demobilised in February 1919.
49, Pitt Street, Peckham, S.E.15.   Z5126

O'LEARY, E., Private, Royal Irish Fusiliers.
Volunteering in January 1915, he was sent to Salonika on completing his training, and did valuable work with his unit during military operations on the Vardar, Struma and Monastir fronts. Whilst in this theatre of war he contracted malaria, and after returning to England was in hospital for ten months. In 1917 he was transferred to Egypt, and later served in the Palestine campaign, taking part in several engagements, including the capture of Jerusalem and Jericho. He was demobilised in July 1919, and holds the 1914-15 Star, and the General Service and Victory Medals.
13, Hollydale Road, Peckham, S.E.15.   Z6489

OLLIFFE, M., Private, Bedfordshire Regiment.
He joined early in 1917, and at the conclusion of his training was drafted to the Western Front, where he fought in several engagements in the Somme sector. In September of the same year he was severely wounded in the vicinity of Ypres, but on recovery rejoined his unit in the Field, and was in action until the termination of hostilities. He was demobilised in November 1919, and holds the General Service and Victory Medals.
77, Henshaw Street, Walworth, S.E.17.   Z3596

OLIVER, C., Private, 1st Hampshire Regiment.
Joining in January 1916, he embarked for Egypt in the following June. Later he served in the Palestine campaign, during which he fought in the first and second Battles of Gaza, where he was severely wounded in October 1917. After his recovery, however, he rejoined his unit in the Field, and was in action until November 1918, when he was again sent to hospital suffering from malaria. He was invalided home in July 1919, and a month later was demobilised. He holds the General Service and Victory Medals.
12, Newcomen Street, Battersea, S.W.11.   Z3593

OLIVER, C. H. G., Sergt., 12th London Regiment (Rangers).
He joined in May 1916, and on the completion of his training was drafted to the Western Front, where he fought on the Somme and at Arras, Ypres and Passchendaele, and in the Retreat and Advance of 1918. He was demobilised in August 1919, and holds the General Service and Victory Medals.
58, Peacock Street, Walworth, S.E.17.   Z26038

OLIVER, G., B.Q.M.S., R.G.A.
He was serving in Malta when war broke out, having enlisted in 1889, and was immediately sent to England, where he was engaged on special duties until March 1915. He then crossed to France, and was subsequently engaged in the fighting at Ypres, Loos and the Somme, and was promoted to the rank of Quarter-Master Sergeant for his efficient work. Unfortunately, he was killed in action on October 2nd, 1918, during the final Advance. He was entitled to the 1914-15 Star, and the General Service and Victory Medals.
    " Whilst we remember the Sacrifice is not in vain."
26, Darley Road, Battersea, S.W.11.   Z3594

OLIVER, G., Private, R.A.M.C.
He volunteered in 1915, and after his training served on the Western Front until 1918. During this time, he did much valuable work with his unit, and among the many notable engagements at which he was present were those at Ypres, the Somme and Arras. He was demobilised in May 1919, and holds the 1914-15 Star, and the General Service and Victory Medals.
10, Cambridge Street, Camberwell, S.E.5.   Z3595

OLIVER, W. R., Private, 10th Royal Fusiliers.
Joining in April 1917, he was drafted to the Western Front at the conclusion of his training. Whilst overseas, he served as a Lewis Gunner, and in this capacity took part in several important engagements, including that at Achiet-Le-Grand, and the Retreat and Advance of 1918, and was wounded. He was demobilised in February 1919, and holds the General Service and Victory Medals.
61, Evelina Road, Peckham, S.E.15.   Z6496

OLLIVER, M., Special War Worker.
This lady was engaged on important work in connection with the production of shells for five months, at the works of Messrs. Daimler, Coventry. For a further period of eighteen months, she served as a cook at the Military Hospital, Milton, Peterboro', and in each of these capacities carried out her duties in a commendable manner.
28, Rockley Road, West Kensington, W.14.   11815B

OLLIVIER, J., Pte., 118th Regiment of Infantry, French Army.
Mobilised at the commencement of hostilities, he proceeded to the Field of Battle immediately upon completing a brief course of training. He fought in the Retreat from Mons and the Battles of the Marne, the Aisne, La Bassée, St. Eloi, Hill 60, Festubert, the Somme and Verdun. On three occasions he was badly gassed, and was in consequence invalided out of the Service in 1918. He holds the Victory Medal, and the Decorations for service in the French Army.
5, St. Mary's Square, Kennington, S.E.11.   27222

OLNEY, C., Private, 12th Middlesex Regiment.
He volunteered in August 1915, and in the following March was drafted to France. During his service there he was engaged in the fighting at Albert, and all along the Somme, and after being buried by shell explosion and gassed was invalided home. He rejoined his unit in France in 1917, and was in action at Passchendaele, and in many subsequent engagements throughout the Retreat and Advance of 1918. He was demobilised in March of the succeeding year, and holds the General Service and Victory Medals.
36, Dawlish Street, South Lambeth, S.W.8.   Z3597

OLNEY, E. H. Private (Signaller), 7th Buffs (East Kent Regiment).
He joined in February 1917, and on the completion of his training was drafted to France. After taking part in several engagements of importance he was captured by the enemy in the Battle of the Somme on March 21st, 1918, and held in captivity in Germany until the cessation of hostilities. He was demobilised after his repatriation in 1919, and holds the General Service and Victory Medals.
45, Chiswick Lane, Chiswick, W.4.   5618A

OLNEY, S. T., Private, Royal Fusiliers.
He joined in November 1916, and after a short training was sent to France, where he took part in various engagements, including those of Vimy Ridge and Ypres, and was wounded. He was invalided to Ireland, and after his recovery rejoined his unit on the Western Front, and in the Retreat of April 1918 was again severely wounded. He was sent home and after a considerable period of medical treatment in hospitals was discharged in 1919. He holds the General Service and Victory Medals.
45, Chiswick Lane, Chiswick, W.4.   5618B

O'NEALE, J., Pte., East Surrey, and Essex Regts.
He was mobilised at the outbreak of war, and was almost immediately drafted to France and fought in the Retreat from Mons, and the Battles of the Marne, Ypres, Hill 60, and Loos, where he was wounded. After his recovery he returned to France in March 1916, and was in action at Vimy Ridge, and the Somme, where he was again wounded. After serving for a time at Aldershot as a Drill Instructor he rejoined his unit on the Western Front in December 1917, and took part in several engagements in the Retreat of 1918, and was a third time severely wounded. He was discharged from hospital as medically unfit for further duty in October 1918. His complete service with the Colours lasted about twenty years, and covered the South African War, in which he was wounded whilst serving in the East Surrey Regiment. He holds the Queen's and King's South African Medals, the Mons Star, and the General Service and Victory Medals.
150, Lavender Road, Battersea, S.W.11.   1768

OLSZEWSKI, L. M., 1st Air Mechanic, R.A.F.
He joined in February 1916, and on the completion of his training was retained at Farnborough and other stations on important duties as an aeroplane draughtsman. He rendered valuable services, but was not successful in securing his transfer to a fighting front. Before the conclusion of hostilities he was undergoing training for promotion to commissioned rank at the time of his demobilisation in December 1918.
29, Alfreton Street, Walworth, S.E.17. Z3598

O'NEILL, A. G. (Miss), Special War Worker.
For over two years of the war this lady rendered valuable services, first in the employ of the General Post Office, and later in the Women's Land Army. She did much good work, but for medical reasons was discharged in August 1918.
37, St. Philip Street, Battersea Park, S.W.8. Z3600B

O'NEILL, M., Sapper, R.E.
He volunteered in September 1914, and in the following year proceeded to France, where he was engaged on important duties in connection with the operations in various sectors of the Western Front. In 1916 he was drafted to Egypt, and was stationed at Alexandria, where he unfortunately died on December 7th, 1918. He was entitled to the 1914–15 Star, and the General Service and Victory Medals.
"His memory is cherished with pride."
37, St. Philip Street, Battersea Park, S.W.8. Z3600A

O'NEILL, M. C., Pte., 10th Queen's (Royal West Surrey Regiment).
He volunteered in August 1915, and in the following year proceeded to France, where he served as a Signaller in many important engagements, including those of the Somme, Vimy Ridge and Ypres. He was wounded, but on his recovery was drafted to Italy, and rendered valuable services there in 1917. Returning later to the Western Front he was again in action in the operations of 1918. After the Armistice he served with the Army of Occupation at Cologne until February 1919, when he returned home and was demobilised. He holds the General Service and Victory Medals.
37, St. Philip Street, Battersea Park, S.W.8. Z3600D

O'NEILL, P., Rifleman, King's Royal Rifle Corps.
He joined in April 1918, on arriving at military age, and received his training at Colchester and other stations. He was not successful in securing his transfer overseas while hostilities continued, but after the Armistice proceeded to Germany with the Army of Occupation, and did much valuable work at Cologne until his return home for demobilisation in March 1920.
53, Villa Street, Walworth, S.E.17. Z3599

O'NEILL, P., Sergt., R.M.L.I.
He was serving at the outbreak of war, having joined in 1910, and took part in the engagements at Heligoland Bight and the Falkland Islands. He was later drafted to the Dardanelles and the Persian Gulf, where his ship was engaged on important and dangerous convoy duties until the cessation of hostilities. He holds the Naval General Service Medal (with Persian Gulf Clasp), the 1914–15 Star, and the General Service and Victory Medals, and in 1920 was still serving in H.M.S. "Lion."
37, St. Philip Street, Battersea Park, S.W.8. Z3600C

ONLEY, W. S., Sergt., Labour Corps.
He first joined the North Staffordshire Regiment in June 1916, and after service in Ireland crossed to France in February 1917. He took part in many important engagements there, notably Arras and Ypres, and was on one occasion blown up by an explosion. He was afterwards transferred to the Labour Corps, in which he did much valuable service. After his return home he was demobilised in November 1919, and holds the General Service and Victory Medals.
5, Danes Road, Camberwell, S.E.5. Z6212A

ORAM, C. G., Private, R.A.M.C.
He joined in November 1917, and after his training was engaged as an orderly in various hospitals, including Guy's and the Prince's Home, Bermondsey. He rendered valuable services, but was not successful in obtaining his transfer overseas before the cessation of hostilities. He was demobilised in March 1919.
21, Trinity Street, Borough, S.E.1. Z25956C

ORAM, D. D. (Miss), Special War Worker.
During the war this lady was engaged at the Ministry of Food Office, 152, Newington Causeway, on clerical work. Her duties which were of a responsible nature were carried out with great care and efficiency.
164, New Kent Road, S.E.1. Z25956B

ORAM, G. L., Corporal, 1st Grenadier Guards.
He joined in March 1918, on attaining military age, and after the completion of his training was engaged on important duties with his unit at various stations. He was not successful however, in securing his transfer overseas before the cessation of hostilities. In 1920 he was still serving and was acting as a Lewis Gun Instructor at the Tower of London.
5, Warrior Road, Camberwell, S.E.5. Z1125B

ORAM, S., Rifleman, 17th London Regt. (Rifles).
He joined in September 1916, and in the following February after the completion of his training proceeded to France, where he took part in many of the important engagements of 1917. During the early stages of the Retreat of 1918, he was unfortunately killed in action on March 25th. He was entitled to the General Service and Victory Medals.
"The path of duty was the way to glory."
37E, Lewis Trust Buildings, Camberwell, S.E.5. Z6425

ORAM, W. J., Gunner, R.G.A.
He joined in March 1916, and after his training was retained at various stations in England and Ireland on important duties with his Battery. He rendered valuable services, but was not successful in obtaining his transfer overseas before the cessation of hostilities. After his demobilisation he re-enlisted and was drafted to India, where he was still serving in 1920.
164, New Kent Road, S.E.1. Z25956A

ORANGO, A., Rifleman, King's Royal Rifle Corps.
He joined in June 1917, and in the following September, after finishing his training was sent to France, where he took part in the important engagements at Cambrai, the Somme, the Lys, the Marne, Amiens, Bapaume and numerous others until fighting ceased. He was demobilised in November 1919, after returning to England, and holds the General Service and Victory Medals.
33, Crozier Street, Lambeth, S.E.1. Z26076

ORCHARD, E. G., Private, 7th Royal Fusiliers.
Mobilised at the outbreak of hostilities he immediately crossed to France in the first Expeditionary Force, and fought gallantly at Mons, and many other subsequent engagements. He fell fighting for King and Country near Bailleul on July 6th, 1917. He was entitled to the Mons Star, and the General Service and Victory Medals.
"A costly sacrifice on the altar of freedom."
21, Redan Terrace, Camberwell, S.E.5. Z6211A

ORCHARD, E. J., Rifleman, Rifle Brigade.
He volunteered in May 1915, and on the completion of his training was drafted to the Western Front, where he took a prominent part in many operations of great importance. He was unhappily killed in action at Messines on July 31st, 1917. He was entitled to the General Service and Victory Medals.
"His life for his Country, his Soul to God."
21, Redan Terrace, Camberwell, S.E.5. Z6211B

ORCHARD, W., Corporal, Rifle Brigade.
Volunteering in May 1915, he went through his course of training, and in the following October proceeded to the Western Front. He fought with distinction in many engagements of importance during his service overseas, and was unfortunately killed at Messines on July 31st, 1917. He was entitled to the 1914–15 Star, and the General Service and Victory Medals.
"He died the noblest death a man may die,
Fighting for God, and right, and liberty."
21, Redan Terrace, Camberwell, S.E.5. Z6211C

ORCHISON, N., Corporal (Farrier), R.A.S.C.
He volunteered in March 1915, and after his training was retained as a Farrier at several R.A.S.C. Depôts until 1917, when he crossed to France. While there he rendered valuable services in his special capacity at St. Omer and other stations until his return to England for demobilisation in June 1919. He holds the General Service and Victory Medals.
47, Gibbon Road, Peckham, S.E.15. Z6603

ORIEL, T., Private, Northumberland Fusiliers.
He volunteered in February 1915, and two months later was drafted to France. During his service overseas he was wounded in action at La Bassée and invalided home, but on his recovery returned to the line and fought in the Battles of the Somme, Arras and Ypres. He fell fighting gallantly on March 21st, 1918, in the early stages of the German Offensive, and was entitled to the General Service and Victory Medals.
"And doubtless he went in splendid company."
57, Goldie Street, Camberwell, S.E.5. Z5470

ORME, J. J., Sapper, R.E.
He volunteered in December 1915, and in the following year after completing his training was drafted to France. He rendered valuable services until the close of hostilities in many sectors, including those of the Somme, Ypres, Passchendaele and Cambrai, and also served through the Offensives of 1918. He was chiefly engaged in bridge building and wire-cutting. After his return home he was demobilised in 1919, and holds the General Service and Victory Medals.
34, Kimberley Road, Nunhead, S.E.15. Z6565

ORRISS, C. (M.M.), Sergt., R.F.A.

Mobilised from the Reserve at the outbreak of hostilities, he was at once drafted to France, and fought at Mons, Ypres, and others of the early operations of the war. In consequence of being gassed at Ypres, he was invalided home, but afterwards returned to the Front and fought with distinction at Vimy Ridge and the leading engagements in the Retreat and Advance of 1918. He was awarded the Military Medal for great gallantry in keeping up telegraphic communications at Vimy Ridge after his Officer was killed, and also holds the Mons Star, and the General Service and Victory Medals. After his return home he was demobilised in February 1919. He had served in India for six years before the war, and at the date of demobilisation had completed thirteen years in the Army.
39, Brooklands Road, Wandsworth Road, S.W.8.   TZ3601

ORRIN, A. C., L/Corporal, Royal Sussex Regiment.

He volunteered in November 1914, and in the following March was drafted to France, where he took part in the severe fighting in many sectors of the front, including Neuve Chapelle and St. Eloi, and was gassed at Loos. On returning to the line he fought in several engagements during the Somme Offensive of 1916, and was unfortunately killed in action on September 9th of that year. During his service overseas he was twice wounded. He holds the 1914-15 Star, and the General Service and Victory Medals.
" His memory is cherished with pride."
13, Pasley Road, Walworth, S.E.17.   Z27037

ORUM, B. V., Gunner, R.F.A.

He volunteered in October 1914, and after completing his training was retained for important work with his Battery until 1916, when he proceeded to France. While overseas he served with distinction as a gunner and signaller in the Battles of the Somme, Albert, Vimy Ridge, Messines and Ypres, when he was wounded. After returning to the line he was again wounded, and subsequently was gassed at Cambrai. After treatment in England at Bristol, and the Royal Hubert Hospital, Woolwich, he was discharged in June 1918, as medically unfit for further service. He holds the General Service and Victory Medals.
17, Combermere Road, Stockwell, S.W.9.   Z3602

OSBALDESTON, S., Rifleman, 21st London Regt. (1st Surrey Rifles).

He joined in November 1917, and after completion of his training was engaged on important duties at various stations in England and Scotland. He was not successful in securing his transfer to a fighting front before hostilities ceased but rendered valuable services as a Signaller and a Guard for German prisoners, until demobilised in September 1919.
28, Philemon House, Gerridge Street, Westminster Bridge Road, S.E.1.   Z25069

OSBORN, A. S., Private, R.A.S.C. (M.T.)

He volunteered in May 1915, and in the same year was sent to France and served on the Somme, Arras, Ypres and Cambrai fronts, being engaged in the transport of ammunition and supplies. He returned home and was demobilised in 1919, holding the 1914-15 Star, and the General Service and Victory Medals.
86, Robertson Street, Wandsworth Road, S.W.8.   Z3603

OSBORN, F., Private, M.G.C. and Queen's Own (Royal West Kent Regt.)

Joining in April 1916, he was drafted in the same year to Mesopotamia, where he took part in numerous engagements, including the capture of Amara and Baghdad. He returned home and was demobilised in March 1919, and holds the General Service and Victory Medals.
2, Longcroft Road, Camberwell, S.E.5.   Z5471

OSBORN, H., Corporal, R.A.F.

He joined in 1916, and after his training served at the School of Aerial Gunnery at New Romney, on important duties with his Squadron. He rendered valuable services, but was not successful in obtaining his transfer overseas before the cessation of hostilities. He was demobilised in 1919.
8, Whellock Road, Chiswick, W.4.   5354A

OSBORN, J., Private, Australian Imperial Force.

He volunteered in February 1915, and served at Gallipoli from the time of the Landing at Suvla Bay until the Evacuation of the Peninsula. He then went to France, and fought in several engagements on the Somme. Later however, he was transferred to Egypt, and was in the Advance through Palestine to Jerusalem. In 1918 he returned to France and took part in the Retreat and Advance. He was demobilised in April 1919, and holds the 1914-15 Star, and the General Service and Victory Medals.
171, Alderminster Road, Bermondsey, S.E.1.   Z26259

OSBORNE, A., Private, Hampshire Regiment.

He volunteered in September 1914, and served on important duties until May 1916, when he was sent to France. There he was in action at Vimy Ridge, the Somme, Lens and Ypres. Later he was invalided home owing to ill-health, and was discharged in December 1918, holding the General Service and Victory Medals.
3, Osborne Street, Walworth, S.E.17.   Z3604

OSBORNE, A. (M.M.), Private, R.A.S.C. (M.T.)

Volunteering in April 1915, he was speedily drafted to the Western Front. There he served with distinction in many engagements, including those at Loos, Albert, Vimy Ridge, Passchendaele, Cambrai, the Somme and the Retreat and Advance of 1918, during which he was wounded. He won the Military Medal for conspicuous gallantry in the Field, and also holds the 1914-15 Star, and the General Service and Victory Medals, and was demobilised in June 1919.
10, Walnut Tree Walk, Kennington, S.E.11.   Z26996

OSBORNE, A. W., Stoker, R.N., H.M.S. "Pembroke."

He volunteered in December 1915, and was posted to H.M.S. " Pembroke " and whilst in this vessel was engaged on important and dangerouw duties in the Mediterranean Sea. During his service he was invalided home for a short period. After the Armistice was signed he served in Russian waters until his demobilisation in May 1920. He holds the General Service and Victory Medals.
1, Cyril Street, Walworth, S.E.17.   Z26226

OSBORNE, F. C., Sergt., R.F.A.

He was serving at the outbreak of war and shortly afterwards was sent to France, and was in action at Mons, Le Cateau, the Marne, the Aisne, La Bassée, Ypres, Neuve Chapelle, Vimy Ridge, Ploegsteert Wood and Dickebusch, and was wounded and gassed. He was then transferred to Italy, and was engaged on the Piave. Afterwards he proceeded to Russia, where he served until September 1918. He was then engaged on important duties until demobilised in December 1919, holding the Mons Star, and the General Service and Victory Medals.
218, Albert Road, Peckham, S.E.15.   Z5645

OSBORNE, R. H., Driver, R.F.A.

Volunteering in November 1915, he was sent to Ireland in the following year and thence to Mesopotamia, where he served in numerous engagements. He was afterwards transferred to France, and was in action on the Cambrai front. Later he unfortunately met with an accident, which necessitated his being invalided home and discharged in April 1919. He holds the General Service and Victory Medals.
295, Mayall Road, Herne Hill, S.E.24.   Z3446A

OTRIDGE, H. J., Driver, R.A.S.C. (H.T.)

He was mobilised in 1914, and shortly afterwards was sent to France, and was present at the engagements at Mons, the Marne, La Bassée, Ypres and Loos. He returned home in 1916, and was discharged on the expiration of his period of service. He holds the Mons Star, and the General Service and Victory Medals.
32, Bagshot Street, Walworth, S.E.17.   Z1457C

OTRIDGE, H. W., Pte. ,24th London Regt. (Queen's).

He volunteered in 1915, and was sent to France in the same year and took part in numerous engagements, including those on the Somme. He was unfortunately killed in action near Hill 60 in 1916, and was entitled to the 1914-15 Star, and the General Service and Victory Medals.
" Steals on the ear, the distant triumph song."
32, Bagshot Street, Walworth, S.E.17.   Z1457B

OTTEN, A., Tpr., 1st Herts Dragoons and Rflmn., King's Royal Rifle Corps.

He joined in March 1918, and in the same year was drafted to France. He served in several sectors, and was engaged in guarding German prisoners and other important duties. He returned home and was demobilised in December 1919, and holds the General Service and Victory Medals.
84, Tyers Street, Vauxhall, S.E.11.   Z25139

OTTEN, A., Private, 13th Middlesex Regiment.

He joined in 1916, and in the following year was drafted to the Western Front, where he took part in numerous engagements, including those at Ypres, Cambrai, and the Somme and was gassed and invalided home. He was discharged as medically unfit in February 1919, and holds the General Service and Victory Medals.
247, Beresford Street, Camberwell, S.E.5.   Z3605

OUSLEY, A., Gunner (Signaller), R.G.A.

He volunteered in June 1915, and served on important duties with his Battery until 1917, when he was sent to France, where he served in numerous engagements, including those in the Retreat and Advance of 1918. He afterwards proceeded with the Army of Occupation to Germany, where he served until he was demobilised in October 1919. He holds the General Service and Victory Medals.
37, South Islands Place, Brixton Road, S.W.9   Z5271

OUTING, E., Private, Bedfordshire Regiment.

He joined in September 1918, and after his training was drafted to the Army of Occupation in Germany, where he was engaged on important duties, until he returned home and was demobilised in March 1920.

79, Albany Road, (Flat No. 6), Camberwell, S.E.5.

Z5646

OVERTON, F., Rifleman, Rifle Brigade.

Joining in 1916, he was sent to France in the same year, and took part in the severe fighting on the Somme, and at Ypres and Cambrai, and was wounded. He was taken prisoner at St. Quentin, and was sent to Germany. On his release he returned home and was demobilised in 1919, and holds the General Service and Victory Medals.

11, Brooklands Road, South Lambeth, S.W.8.

Z3609

OVERTON, J., Private, R.A.O.C.

He joined in July 1918, and after his training served on important duties with his unit. He was engaged as a driller and rendered valuable services, but was not successful in obtaining his transfer overseas before the cessation of hostilities. He was demobilised in January 1919.

27, Lavender Road, Battersea, S.W.11.

Z3607

OVERTON, W. G., Sapper, R.E.

He joined in 1916, and in the following year was drafted to France, and was engaged on special duties with his unit. He later took part in the Retreat and Advance of 1918. He returned home and was demobilised in February 1919, and holds the General Service and Victory Medals.

20, Brooklands Road, South Lambeth, S.W.8.

Z3608

OVERY, J. T., Corporal, R.M.L.I. (Labour Corps).

He joined in May 1917, and after his training was sent to France. He was engaged at Rouen, Le Havre, and other places unloading transports at the Docks, and rendered valuable services. Later he was taken ill and invalided home and was discharged in consequence in March 1919, holding the General Service and Victory Medals.

2, Badsworth Road, Camberwell, S.E.5.

Z3610

OWEN, A. W. (M.M.), Gunner, R.F.A.

He was serving at the outbreak of war, and was almost immediately drafted to France, where he took part in the Retreat from Mons. He also served with distinction at Ypres, and on the Somme, and in various later engagements, and was awarded the Military Medal and bar for his conspicuous gallantry and devotion to duty at Ypres in 1917. He was mortally wounded in the second Battle of the Somme, and succumbed to his injuries in May 1918. He was entitled to the Mons Star, and the General Service and Victory Medals.

"His life for his Country, his Soul to God."

160, Southwark Bridge Road, S.E.1.

Z25195B

OWEN, C., Private, R.A.M.C.

He volunteered in March 1915, and served for two years on important duties in a hospital in England prior to embarking for France in February, 1917. Whilst overseas he was stationed in hospitals at Ypres, Albert, and Amiens, and rendered valuable services. He was demobilised in February 1919, after exactly two years in France, and holds the General Service and Victory Medals.

78, Grayshott Road, Lavender Hill, S.W.11.

Z3611

OWEN, C. C., Sergt.-Major, The Queen's (Royal West Surrey Regiment).

He volunteered in September 1914, and two years later in September 1916, was drafted to France. Whilst in this theatre of war he took part in the fighting on the Somme, and at Arras, Vimy Ridge, Bullecourt, Messines, Ypres, and Passchendaele. In November 1917, he was sent to Italy, where he served for about four months, returning to France in March 1918. He was then in action and wounded in the second Battle of the Somme, and was invalided to hospital at Etaples, and after about four months, medical treatment was sent back to the front lines. He fought on the Marne, and at Amiens, Bapaume, and many subsequent engagements, and after the Armistice advanced into Germany with the Army of Occupation, and was stationed at Cologne. In April 1919 he returned home and was demobilised, holding the General Service and Victory Medals.

8, Flint Street, Walworth, S.E.17

Z1742A

OWEN, G., Private, 3rd (King's Own) Hussars.

He was serving in the Army at the outbreak of hostilities, having enlisted in October 1913, and in January 1915 proceeded to France. While there he took an active part in many engagements of importance, including those at Ypres, Bourlon Wood, Loos, the Somme, Arras, Vimy Ridge, Cambrai, and the Offensives of 1918. During his service he was wounded on two occasions. After his return to England he was transferred to the Reserves in October 1920, and holds the 1914-15 Star, and the General Service and Victory Medals.

32, Catlin Street, Rotherhithe, S.E.16.

Z6604

OWEN, J. J., Private, R.A.S.C. and Labour Corps.

He volunteered in April 1915, at the age of forty-five years, as a special transport worker, having had many years' experience of this work, and proceeded overseas in 1915. He served for three years conveying supplies to the Ypres front, after which period he was invalided home. Owing to ill health, and transferred to the Labour Corps, he was sent to Ireland. He was subsequently discharged as medically unfit for further military duty in October 1918, and holds the 1914-15 Star, and the General Service and Victory Medals.

160, Southwark Bridge Road, S.E.1.

Z25195A

OWEN, J. S., Rifleman, Rifle Brigade.

He joined in June 1916, and in November of the following year was drafted to France. In this theatre of war he fought at Ypres, Dickebusch, Menin Road, Montecourt, and Albert, where he was severely wounded on March 5th, 1918. He was sent home to hospital and was under medical treatment until discharged as physically unfit for further duty in November 1918. He holds the General Service and Victory Medals.

5, Scarsdale Grove, Camberwell, S.E.5.

Z5472

OWEN, L. R. (Mrs.), Special War Worker.

During the war this lady rendered valuable services in the employ of the South Eastern and Chatham Railway Company, and thereby released a man for military service. She was afterwards engaged on important clerical duties at the Ministry of Labour, Bow Street, Strand. Her work in both capacities was carried out in an efficient manner, and she was commended for her patriotic services

8, Hinton Street, Walworth, S.E.17.

Z1742B

OWEN, S., Private, R.A.M.C.

He volunteered in September 1914, and until June 1916 was engaged on hospital duties at Lewisham and other places. He then proceeded to France and was present at the engagements on the Somme, and at Beaumont-Hamel, Arras, Vimy Ridge, Ypres, Lens, and Cambrai. Later he was invalided home suffering from tuberculosis, and was under treatment in hospital until discharged as medically unfit for further duty in May 1918. He holds the General Service and Victory Medals

35, Charleston Street, Walworth, S.E.17.

Z3612

OXFORD, E. G., Gunner, R.F.A.

He volunteered in November 1915, and in June of the following year proceeded to France. During his service on the Western Front he did good work as a gunner in various sectors, including those of the Somme, Arras, Ypres, and Cambrai. He was twice wounded at Arras in April 1917, and again at Ypres in August of the same year. In January 1918 he was drafted to Italy, and took part in the Offensive on the Piave, and in subsequent engagements until the cessation of hostilities. He was sent home from Italy in February 1919, and was then demobilised, and holds the General Service and Victory Medals. and an Italian award.

44, Bengeworth Road, Camberwell, S.E.5.

Z6305

P

PACK, F., Private, Royal Fusiliers.

He volunteered in November 1915, and during his training was injured in an accident which delayed his transfer overseas until 1917, when he was drafted to France. He was only seven weeks on the Western Front before he gave his life for his Country on June 8th, 1917. He was entitled to the General Service and Victory Medals.

"Whilst we remember, the Sacrifice is not in vain."

59, Nursery Row, Orb Street, Walworth, S.E.17.

Z3613

PACKARD, G. T., Driver, R.F.A.

He volunteered in June 1915, and in October of the same year was drafted to the Western Front, where he was engaged on various sectors until hostilities ceased. He served at the Somme, Vimy Ridge, Arras, Ypres, and Cambrai, and was wounded in action in the fighting at Ypres in 1918. He was demobilised in April of the following year, and holds the 1914-15 Star, and the General Service and Victory Medals.

51, Canterbury Place, Lambeth Walk, S.E.11.

Z26964

PACKER, T., Sergt., 23rd Royal Fusiliers.

He volunteered in February 1915, and on the completion of his training was drafted to France. While overseas he met with a serious accident, and was invalided home, and on his recovery was engaged on important special duties in various stations in England until his demobilisation in February 1919. He holds the General Service and Victory Medals.

24, Oakden Street, Kennington, S.E.11.

Z27378

PACKHAM, E. C., Private, R.F.C. and 23rd London Regiment.

He joined in March 1916, and in the following year was drafted to France. Whilst overseas he took part in various engagements, and subsequently fell in action in an engagement on the Cambrai Front, on August 23rd, 1918. He was entitled to the General Service and Victory Medals.

"He died the noblest death a man may die
Fighting for God, and right, and liberty."

71, Aldred Road, Walworth, S.E.17. Z26481

PACKMAN, G. R., Rifleman, Rifle Brigade.

He joined in March 1917, and after his training at Aldershot and other stations was engaged on important duties with his unit. In 1918 he was sent to France, and thence to Germany with the Army of Occupation. After serving for some time on the Rhine he proceeded to Russia, where he was engaged on important frontier duty. He returned home and was demobilised in April 1920, and holds the General Service and Victory Medals. 7, Eversleigh Road, Battersea, S.W.11. Z3614

PADDOCK, G. H., Worker, Q.M.A.A.C. and Member W.R.A.F.

Joining the Q.M.A.A.C. in January 1918, she was transferred some time afterwards to the W.R.A.F., in which force she was engaged on important clerical duties in a branch of the Air Ministry at Earls Court. She did valuable work until she was demobilised in September 1919.

40A, Lewis Buildings, Chelsea, S.W.3. X22659B

PADDOCK, T., Private, Royal Warwickshire Regt. and Somerset Light Infantry.

He volunteered in December 1914, and in the following year was drafted overseas. During his service in France he fought at Loos and the Somme, and was wounded and invalided to hospital. After his recovery he was sent to India in 1917 and served on important garrison duties. He also acted as a hospital orderly in the Afghan Frontier risings, and suffered severely from malaria. He was sent home and demobilised in January 1920, and holds the 1914-15 Star, the India General Service (with clasp Afghanistan N.W. Frontier, 1919), and the General Service and Victory Medals.

40A, Lewis Buildings, Chelsea, S.W.3. X22659A

PADDON, F., Private, 2nd London Regiment (Royal Fusiliers).

He was mobilised in August 1914, and in the same month was drafted to France, where he served in many sectors, and saw much fighting. Amongst the important actions in which he was engaged were those of St. Eloi, Hill 60, Ypres, Loos and the Somme. He gave his life for the freedom of England at Combles on September 17th, 1917, and was entitled to the 1914 Star, and the General Service and Victory Medals.

"The path of duty was the way to glory."

13, Hayles Street, Kennington, S.E.11. Z26883A

PADDON, T., Private, 3rd East Surrey Regiment.

He volunteered in February 1915, and in the same year was drafted to the Western Front. Whilst overseas he took part in the severe fighting at Hill 60, Ypres, Loos, Ploegsteert Wood, and the Somme and was wounded three times in this sector. He also served in the Retreat and Advance of 1918, and was demobilised in February of the following year. He holds the 1914-15 Star, and the General Service and Victory Medals. 48, Southville, Wandsworth Road, S.W.8. Z3615

PADDON, W., Corporal, 8th Royal Berkshire Regt.

He volunteered in August 1914, and after a period of duty as Drill Instructor at the depôt of his unit was drafted to the Western Front in September of the following year. He was unfortunately killed in action at Hulluch on October 13th, 1915, after only a few weeks in France, and was entitled to the 1914-15 Star, and the General Service and Victory Medals.

"A costly sacrifice upon the altar of freedom."

13, Hayles Street, Kennington, S.E.11. Z26883B

PADDON, W. G., Corporal, R.G.A.

He volunteered in August 1914, and in the following December was drafted overseas. After serving in several sectors of the Western Front, where amongst other engagements he was in those of Neuve Chapelle, Festubert, Hulluch and Loos, he was sent to Salonika. In this theatre of war he fought on the Struma, Lake Doiran and in the Advance into Bulgaria, returning on the conclusion of hostilities to England for demobilisation June 1919. He holds the 1914-15 Star, and the General Service and Victory Medals.

13, Hayles Street, Kennington, S.E.11. Z26883C

PADWICK, F., Private, R.A.S.C. (M.T.)

He volunteered in May 1915, and in the same year was drafted to Egypt. Whilst overseas he was engaged on important duties in connection with the Motor Transport in the Suez Canal zone, and the Libyan Desert. He was stabbed in the Egyptian riots at Cairo, and was for some time under medical treatment in the hospital there. In September 1919 he returned home, and was demobilised and holds the 1914-15 Star, and the General Service and Victory Medals.

196, Mayall Road, Herne Hill, S.E.24. Z3616

PAGE, A. (Miss), Special War Worker.

For two years during the war this lady was engaged on important duties as a seamstress at the Royal Army Clothing Department at Park Royal. She carried out her duties with great efficiency, and thoroughness until her resignation in July 1919. 95, Robertson Street, Wandsworth, S.W.8. Z3612C

PAGE, A. A., Private, Royal Fusiliers and Royal Warwickshire Regiment.

He joined in February 1917, at the age of seventeen, and early in the following year was drafted to the Western Front. Whilst overseas he fought at Merville, and gave his life for his King and Country on May 28th, 1918. He was entitled to the General Service and Victory Medals.

"Honour to the immortal dead, who gave their youth that the world might grow old in peace."

13, Gaza Street, Kennington Park Road, S.E.17. Z25925A

PAGE, A. J., Driver, R.F.A.

He volunteered in February 1915, and after his training was engaged on important duties with his Battery until April 1916, when he was discharged as medically unfit for further military service. He died in hospital after his discharge from the effects of the disease arising out of his service.

"His memory is cherished with pride."

95, Robertson Street, Wandsworth Road, S.W.8. Z3621B

PAGE, G., Private, Queen's Own (Royal West Kent Regiment).

He volunteered in September 1914, and in 1916 was drafted to France. Whilst overseas he fought in the Battles of the Somme, Arras, Vimy Ridge and Cambrai, and in the engagements which followed until the cessation of hostilities. He contracted tuberculosis through the exposures of foreign service, and unfortunately died from that disease in hospital in London on February 7th 1919. He was entitled to the General Service and Victory Medals.

"His life for his Country."

20, Radstock Street, Battersea, S.W.11. Z3622

PAGE, G. A., Rifleman, King's Royal Rifle Corps.

He joined in 1917, on attaining military age, and in March of the following year was drafted overseas. During his service on the Western Front he fought in the second Battles of the Somme and Cambrai, and in other engagements in the Offensives of 1918, and after the Armistice advanced into Germany with the Army of Occupation. He served there until January 1919, when he returned home and was demobilised. He holds the General Service and Victory Medals.

23, Cavendish Grove, Wandsworth Road, S.W.8. Z3618

PAGE, H., Sergt., Royal Scots Fusiliers and North Staffordshire Regiment.

He was serving at the outbreak of war, having enlisted in 1911, and was immediately drafted to France, where he took part in the Retreat from Mons. He also served in the Battles of the Marne, the Aisne, La Bassée and Ypres, where he was wounded. After his recovery he was again in action at Loos, the Somme, Lens and Cambrai, and in many subsequent engagements during the Retreat and Advance of 1918. He was demobilised in March 1919, and holds the Mons Star, and the General Service and Victory Medals.

13, Gaza Road, Kennington, S.E.17. Z25925C

PAGE, H., Private, M.G.C.

He volunteered in October 1915, and in the following year was drafted to France. During his service on the Western Front he took part in many engagements of importance in various sectors, and was afterwards sent to Italy, where he fought in the operations on the Piave. Later he proceeded to Russia, and in 1920 was serving in Mesopotamia. He holds the General Service and Victory Medals.

3, Arden Street, Battersea, S.W.8. Z3572A

PAGE, H. E., Pte., 22nd London Regt. (Queen's).

He joined in February 1917, and on the completion of his training was drafted to France. During his service overseas he fought in the Battle of the Somme, and in many other engagements in the Retreat and Advance of 1918. He was demobilised in November 1919 after his return home, and holds the General Service and Victory Medals.

72, Landseer Street, Battersea, S.W.11. Z3617

PAGE, J., Private, East Yorkshire Regiment.

He joined in October 1916, and in the following year proceeded overseas. During his service in France he fought in the Battles of Arras, Vimy Ridge and Passchendaele, and was wounded and taken prisoner at Epéhy, in March 1918. He was sent to Gustrow in Mecklenburg, and was held in captivity until the Armistice. After his repatriation he was demobilised in August 1919, and holds the General Service and Victory Medals.

95, Robertson Street, Wandsworth Road, S.W.8. Z3621A

PAGE, J., Special War Worker.

He offered his services for Government work at the outbreak of war, and for two years was engaged as a carpenter in the erection of temporary buildings, and extensions, at the 3rd London General and St. Thomas' Hospitals. He rendered valuable and skilled services until November 1916.

95, Robertson Street, Wandsworth Road, S.W.8.　　Z3621D

PAGE, R. E., Private, Leicestershire Regiment.

He volunteered in August 1914, and in the following year was sent over to France, where he fought in many important engagements in various sectors. He gave his life for the freedom of England in the Battle of the Somme on September 15th, 1916, and was entitled to the 1914-15 Star, and the General Service and Victory Medals.

" A valiant soldier, with undaunted heart, he breasted Lifes' last hill."

13, Gaza Street, Walworth, S.E.17.　　Z25925B

PAGE, V. L., Bombardier, R.F.A.

He volunteered in January 1915, and later in the same year was drafted to France, where he saw much service. He was in action at Ypres, Loos, the Somme, Arras, Bullecourt and Messines, Lens, and was severely gassed in the Retreat of April 1918, and invalided to hospital in France and England. After his recovery he was retained at Woolwich on garrison duties until his demobilisation in January 1919. He holds the 1914-15 Star, and the General Service and Victory Medals.

57, Clayton Road, Peckham, S.E.15.　　Z6055

PAGE, W., Pte., Duke of Wellington's (West Riding Regiment).

He volunteered in March 1915, and in the following month was drafted to the Dardanelles, where he saw much heavy fighting. He took part in the landing at Gallipoli, the Battles of Krithia, the Landing at Suvla Bay and the Evacuation of the Peninsula. In 1916 he was sent to France and whilst in this theatre of war fought at Loos, Albert, where he was wounded, the Somme and Vimy Ridge. He next proceeded to India, and was stationed for two years at Bombay on important garrison and guard duties. He returned home and was demobilised in May 1919, and holds the 1914-15 Star, and the General Service and Victory Medals.

40, Searles Road, New Kent Road, S.E.1.　　Z3619

PAGE, W. J. F., Pte., 7th Buffs (East Kent Regt).

He joined in September 1917, and after being retained on important duties with his unit proceeded to France early in September of the following year. After taking part in the fighting at Havrincourt and the Scarpe he gave his life for King and Country at Epéhy, in September 1918, He was entitled to the General Service and Victory Medals.

" The path of duty was the way to glory."

65, Palmerston Street, Battersea, S.W.11.　　Z3620

PAICE, A. F., Private, R.A.M.C.

Volunteering in May 1915, he crossed to France at the conclusion of his training, and was subsequently engaged on important duties in connection with the wounded in the forward areas. Later he returned to England, and after being on home service for a year was sent with the Army of Occupation to Germany. He holds the 1914-15 Star, and the General Service and Victory Medals, and in 1920 was still serving.

1, Sterndale Road, Wandsworth Road, S.W.8.　　Z3623A

PAICE, A. W. (M.M.), Cpl., 23rd London Regiment.

Volunteering in May 1915, he served on the Western Front from early in the following year until March 1918. During this time he fought on the Somme and at Albert, and in many other important engagements, and was taken prisoner whilst in action in the Retreat. He was awarded the Military Medal for an act of distinguished gallantry in the Field, and was presented with the decoration by the Mayor of Battersea, at St. George's School, after his repatriation. In addition, he holds the General Service and Victory Medals, and was demobilised in December 1918.

1, Sterndale Road, Wandsworth Road, S.W.8.　　Z3623B

PAILTHORPE, W., Pte., 1/2nd London Regiment.

Joining in April 1917, he was drafted to the Western Front in the following August. He was engaged in the fighting at Cambrai, Arras and Vimy Ridge, and in the Retreat and Advance of 1918, being severely wounded in October of that year. After receiving treatment at the 8th Casualty Clearing Station he rejoined his unit and remained overseas until the termination of hostilities. He holds the General Service and Victory Medals, and was demobilised in October 1919.

66, Cator Street, Peckham, S.E.15.　　Z4513

PAIN, F., Leading Air Mechanic, R.A.F.

Joining in May 1916, he was drafted to France in the following January. During his overseas' service he was engaged on important duties in the mobile motor shops, and did much valuable work in many sectors, including those of the Somme, Albert, Ypres and Arras. Returning to England in 1919 he was demobilised in April of that year, and holds the General Service and Victory Medals.

55, Heygate Street, Walworth, S.E.17.　　Z3624

PAINE, C. H., Corporal, R.A.S.C.

He volunteered in September 1914, and at the conclusion of his training was engaged on duties of an important nature in the Remount Section. Owing to physical disability he was unable to secure his transfer to a theatre of war, but, nevertheless, did valuable work with his unit at various stations until March 1918, when he was invalided out of the Service.

99, Brooke Street, Kennington, S.E.11.　　Z26905

PAINTER, A., Pte.,13th London Regt. (Kensingtons).

He volunteered in April 1915, and served on the Western Front from the following September until after the termination of hostilities. During this time he took an active part in many important battles, notably these of the Somme, Ypres, Arras and Cambrai, and also served in the Retreat and Advance of 1918. He was demobilised in 1919, and holds the 1914-15 Star, and the General Service and Victory Medals.

5, Heaton Road, Peckham, S.E.15.　　Z6063

PAINTER, G. H., Private, R.A.S.C.

He volunteered in June 1915, and after his training was engaged on important duties in connection with the repair of lorries and waggons. He was unable to secure his transfer overseas before the termination of hostilities, but, nevertheless, rendered valuable services with his unit at various stations until he was demobilised in January 1919.

80, Kirkwood Road, Nunhead, S.E.15.　　Z6214

PAINTER, J. H., Rflmn., King's Royal Rifle Corps.

He volunteered in September 1914, and after his training served on the Western Front for four years. During this period he was engaged in the fighting in many important sectors, notably those of the Somme, Arras, and Cambrai, but in the latter part of 1918 was invalided home owing to an injury to his eye, received in an accident whilst on duty. He was discharged as medically unfit for further service in December of that year, and holds the 1914-15 Star, and the General Service and Victory Medals.

50, Lockington Road, Battersea Park Road, S.W.8.　　Z3625

PALGRAVE, L., Lieutenant, R.A.F.

He joined as an air mechanic in the Royal Air Force in 1916, and after training was engaged at various stations on important duties with his Squadron. In the course of his service he won rapid promotion, and was subsequently given a commission for his very efficient work. He was unable to secure his transfer overseas before the termination of hostilities, but until 1919, when he was demobilised, rendered much valuable service.　　Z3632

190, Elmhurst Mansions, Edgeley Road, Clapham, S.W.4.

PALING, F. W., Driver, R.F.A.

He volunteered in December 1914, and after his training was drafted to the Western Front, where he was engaged in the fighting at Ypres, Bapaume, Corbie Wood and the Somme, and was wounded. In 1917 he was transferred to Salonika and did valuable work with his Battery during operations on the Doiran front and in Bulgaria. He was demobilised in February 1919, and holds the 1914-15 Star, and the General Service and Victory Medals.

51, Cooper's Road, Old Kent Road, S.E.1.　　Z26931

PALLANT, C. E., L/Cpl., 11th London Regt. (Rifles).

Joining in February 1916, he was drafted to the Western Front a year later, and subsequently served in many important battles, including those of Arras, Vimy Ridge and Ypres. Unfortunately, he was killed in action at Lens. He was entitled to the General Service and Victory Medals.

" Whilst we remember the Sacrifice is not in vain."

8, Cologne Road, Battersea, S.W.17.　　Z3626

PALMER, A., Private, 2nd East Surrey Regiment.

A serving soldier, he was drafted to the Western Front immediately upon the outbreak of war and took part in the Retreat from Mons. He also fought in many of the engagements which followed, including those at Neuve Chapelle and Ypres, and was wounded twice and gassed. Later he saw service as a stretcher-bearer in Egypt and Salonika and did valuable work in this capacity. He was demobilised in March 1919, and holds the Mons Star, and the General Service and Victory Medals.

16, Barmore Road, Battersea, S.W.11.　　Z1812A

PALMER, A. E. (M.M.), Sergt., Yorkshire Regiment.

He volunteered in September 1914, and early in the following year was drafted to the Western Front, where he took part in fighting on the Somme and at Albert, Arras, Ypres and Passchendaele. In the course of his service he was taken ill and after being for some time in hospital at Etaples was invalided to Torquay. After his recovery, however, he returned to France and took part in the Retreat and Advance of 1918. He was awarded the Military Medal for conspicuous gallantry in rescuing a comrade who was buried by an explosion, and in addition holds the 1914-15 Star, and the General Service and Victory Medals. He was demobilised in April 1919.

19, Clayton Road, Peckham, S.E.15.　　Z6053

PALMER, A. E., Driver, R.A.S.C. (M.T.)

He volunteered in April 1915, and after his training served on the Western Front for three years. During this time he was engaged on important duties in connection with the transport of food and ammunition to the troops in the forward areas, and was present at several engagements, notably those on the Somme and in the Retreat and Advance of 1918. He was demobilised in September 1919 on his return to England, and holds the General Service and Victory Medals.

7, Warrior Road, Camberwell, S.E.5.　　Z3629B

PALMER, B. H., Private, Royal Fusiliers.

Joining in February 1917, he crossed to France a year later. Whilst in this theatre of war he took part in several notable battles and was also engaged on various special duties, which included guarding German prisoners and convoying transports of stores and food. He holds the General Service and Victory Medals, and was demobilised in November 1919.

69, Darwin Street, Walworth, S.E.17.　　Z3630

PALMER, E. W., Private, 13th East Surrey Regt.

Volunteering in August 1915, he was drafted to France in the following June, and first went into action on the Somme, where he was wounded in September 1916. After receiving treatment he rejoined his unit in the Field, and subsequently fought at Beaumont-Hamel, Arras, Passchendaele and Cambrai. Whilst on duty at a signal post at Fleurbaix during the German Offensive, he was called upon by the enemy to surrender, but on answering the challenge was shot dead. He is buried in the vicinity of the place where he was killed, and was entitled to the General Service and Victory Medals.

"Thinking that remembrance, though unspoken, may reach him where he sleeps."

74, Wickersley Road, Lavender Hill, S.W.11.　　Z3631

PALMER, F., Rifleman, King's Royal Rifle Corps.

Joining in June 1916, he was sent to France six months later, and after taking part in heavy fighting on the Ancre front, was taken prisoner whilst in action at Arras in April 1917. Repatriated after the termination of hostilities, he returned to England, and was demobilised in March 1919. He holds the General Service and Victory Medals.

10, Cooper's Road, Old Kent Road, S.E.1.　　Z26929

PALMER, F., Rifleman, King's Royal Rifle Corps and Private, Wiltshire Regiment.

He volunteered early in 1915, and at the conclusion of his training crossed to France. Whilst in this theatre of war he took part in heavy fighting in the Somme, Arras and Ypres sectors, and was severely wounded and taken prisoner at Messines in the German Offensive of 1918. During his captivity which lasted for nine months, he was employed at a foundry until repatriated early in 1919. He was demobilised on his return to England, and holds the 1914–15 Star, and the General Service and Victory Medals.

263, East Street, Walworth, S.E.17.　　Z3627

PALMER, G., Private, Queen's Own (Royal West Kent Regiment).

Volunteering in May 1915, he crossed to France a year later, and subsequently fought in several engagements. On October 2nd, 1917, he died gloriously on the Field of Battle at Arras. He was entitled to the General Service and Victory Medals.

"Courage, bright hopes, and a myriad dreams splendidly given."

7, Warrior Road, Camberwell, S.E.5.　　Z3629A

PALMER, G., L/Corporal, 1/1st Royal Fusiliers.

He joined in May 1916, and at the conclusion of his training, which he obtained at Salisbury, was drafted to the Western Front. Whilst in this theatre of war he took an active part in the operations at Arras, where he was wounded, Cambrai, Vimy Ridge, Croiselles and Bullecourt, and did valuable work with his unit until after the termination of hostilities. He was demobilised in October 1919, and holds the General Service and Victory Medals.

54, Cabul Road, Battersea, S.W.11.　　Z3628

PALMER, H., Q.M., Merchant Service.

He was in the Merchant Service at the outbreak of hostilities, and his ship was subsequently commissioned by the Admiralty for war service. Later, on board the s.s. "Kiaora" he voyaged to and from New Zealand and Australia, engaged on important duties in connection with the transport of troops and supplies, and did much valuable work. He holds the General Service and Mercantile Marine War Medals, and in 1920 was still serving.

47, Philip Road, Peckham, S.E.15.　　Z6051C

PALMER, S., L/Corporal, 4th Middlesex Regiment.

Volunteering at the commencement of hostilities, he was quickly drafted to the Western Front, and was taken prisoner during the Retreat from Mons in August 1914. He was held in captivity until January 1918, when owing to an exchange of prisoners, he was repatriated. He holds the Mons Star, and the General Service and Victory Medals, and was discharged on his return to England.

57, Southerton Road, Hammersmith, W.6.　　10709A

PALMER, J. (M.M.), Sergt., Duke of Wellington's (West Riding Regiment).

He enlisted in March 1907, and when war broke out was serving in India, where he remained throughout the period of hostilities. He took part in the Afghan campaign on the North-West Frontier, and on June 26th, 1919, was awarded the Military Medal for conspicuous gallantry in the Field at Spinbaldak. In addition he holds the General Service, Victory, and India General Service Medals (with clasp Afghanistan, N.W. Frontier, 1919), and was demobilised in December of that year on his return to England.

220, Beresford Street, Camberwell, S.E.5.　　Z1959B

PALMER, T., Bombardier, R.F.A.

Volunteering in October 1914, he crossed to France early in the following year, and served in the Ypres salient until June 1916. He was then transferred to Salonika, and subsequently did valuable work with his Battery during operations on the Struma, Doiran, Vardar and Monastir fronts. He was demobilised in June 1919, and holds the 1914–15 Star, and the General Service and Victory Medals.

6, Silcote Road, Camberwell, S.E.5.　　Z5473

PALMER, W. G., Sapper, R.E.

Volunteering in November 1914, he crossed to France in the same year and was engaged on duties of an important nature in the forward areas. He was also present at the Battles of Neuve Chapelle, Loos and Ypres, and was unhappily killed on September 20th, 1917, during heavy fighting on the Menin Road. He was entitled to the 1914 Star, and the General Service and Victory Medals.

"A costly sacrifice upon the altar of freedom."

381 (R Block), Guinness Buildings, Page's Walk, Grange Road, S.E.1.　　Z26248

PALMER, W. J., Sergt., 2nd London Regt. (Royal Fusiliers).

Mobilised at the outbreak of war, he was sent to Malta in September 1914, and a month later to France. Whilst in this theatre of war he fought in many notable battles, including those of Ypres, Festubert, Loos and Arras, and owing to ill-health was for a time in hospital. After the termination of hostilities he returned to England, but on being demobilised in March 1919, re-enlisted and in 1920 was still serving. He holds the 1914 Star, and the General Service, Victory, and Territorial Force Efficiency Medals.

6, Dartford Street, Walworth, S.E.17.　　Z26206

PALMER, W. M., Pte., 22nd London Regt. (Queen's).

He volunteered at the outbreak of war, and after the completion of his training proceeded to France early in 1915. He fought with distinction in numerous engagements of great importance, almost until the close of hostilities. He was reported missing after an engagement in the Advance of September 1918, and is believed to have been killed in action. He was entitled to the 1914–15 Star, and the General Service and Victory Medals.

"His life for his Country, his Soul to God."

15, Galleywall Road, S. Rotherhithe, S.E.16.　　Z6605

PAMMENT, W. O., L/Corporal, 1st Suffolk Regt.

He was serving at the outbreak of war, and was afterwards drafted to France. After taking part in several engagements of importance in the Ypres salient, he was captured by the enemy in May 1915. During his long captivity in Germany he was interned at Hamelin, Magdeburg and other prisoners' camps, and after returning home in January 1919 was demobilised in the following April. He holds the 1914–15 Star, and the General Service and Victory Medals.

16, South Island Place, Brixton Road, S.W.9.　　Z5276B

PAMPHLET, W. T., Private, 18th Middlesex Regt. and Labour Corps.

He volunteered in May 1915, and was drafted to the Western Front in the same year. He took part in numerous engagements, including those on the Somme and at Ypres, High Wood and Cambrai, and also served in the Retreat and Advance of 1918. During his service overseas he was wounded on five different occasions and was invalided home for a time, but on recovery returned to his unit. He was demobilised in February 1919, and holds the 1914–15 Star, and the General Service and Victory Medals.

45, Westmacott Street, Camberwell, S.E.5.　　Z5550

PARFITT, W., Private, 25th Royal Fusiliers.

Joining in 1916, he was drafted in the same year to France, where he took part in the severe fighting at Vimy Ridge, the Somme, Arras, Ypres and Cambrai, and was in the Retreat and Advance of 1918. After the Armistice he proceeded with the Army of Occupation to Germany. He was demobilised in November 1919, and holds the General Service and Victory Medals.

23, Baker Street, Brixton Road, S.W.9.　　Z5275

PARFITT, G. S., Sapper, R.E.
He volunteered in January 1915, and was sent to France in the same year. He took part in the engagements at St. Eloi, Hill 60, Festubert and Albert, and was wounded on the Somme and invalided home. He was discharged as medically unfit for further service in July 1918, and holds the 1914–15 Star, and the General Service and Victory Medals.
28, Stonhouse Street, Clapham, S.W.4. Z3633B

PARFITT, W. G., L/Corporal, 5th Royal Berkshire Regiment.
He volunteered in September 1914, and was sent to France in the following year. He took part in numerous engagements, including those at St. Eloi, Hill 60, Loos, the Somme, Arras and Ypres, and was wounded and suffered from shell-shock. He was invalided home and discharged as medically unfit for further service in October 1917, and holds the 1914–15 Star, and the General Service and Victory Medals.
28, Stonhouse Street, Clapham, S.W.4. Z3633A

PARISH, E., Private, 3rd London Regt. (Royal Fusiliers).
He volunteered in 1915, and in the same year was drafted to the Western Front, where he took part in the fighting at Hill 60, Festubert, Loos, Ypres, and in many other engagements. He also served in the Retreat and Advance of 1918, and was gassed. He was demobilised in April 1919, holding the 1914–15 Star, and the General Service and Victory Medals.
21, Nursery Street, Battersea Park, S.W.8. Z2011B

PARISH, T. W., Private, R.A.S.C. (M.T.)
Volunteering in August 1914, he was speedily drafted to the Western Front. There he served with distinction in the Battle of Mons and various other engagements. In 1918 he proceeded to Italy, where he saw much active service, and was gassed. He returned to England and was demobilised in February 1919, and holds the Mons Star, and the General Service and Victory Medals.
8, Hurlbutt Place, Walworth, S.E.17. Z26029

PARISH, W., Private, East Surrey Regiment.
He joined in August 1916, and on the completion of his training was drafted to the Western Front, where he took part in the fighting on the Somme, and was wounded during the Retreat from Cambrai. He also served at Arras, and later returned home and was demobilised in February 1919. He holds the General Service and Victory Medals.
202, Alderminster Road, Bermondsey, S.E.1. Z26255

PARK, J., Rifleman, 5th London Regiment (London Rifle Brigade).
He volunteered in August 1915, and after his training was sent to France, and was in action on the Somme and at Cambrai, and in many other engagements. He was, unfortunately, killed in action near Arras on November 4th, 1917, and was entitled to the General Service and Victory Medals.
"And doubtless he went in splendid company."
65, Commercial Road, Peckham, S.E.15. Z6434

PARK, N. J. (M.S.M.), Sapper, R.E.
Volunteering in January 1915, he was in the same year sent to France, where he took part in numerous engagements, including those at Neuve Chapelle, Vimy Ridge, the Somme, Bullecourt and Ploegsteert. He also served in the Retreat and Advance of 1918. He was awarded the Meritorious Service Medal for devotion to duty and also holds the 1914–15 Star, and the General Service and Victory Medals, and was demobilised in June 1919.
73, Hubert Grove, Stockwell, S.W.9. Z2139B

PARKER, A., Sergt., 22nd London Regiment (The Queen's).
He volunteered in August 1914, and in the following year was sent to the Western Front, where he took part in the Battles of Neuve Chapelle, Ypres, Loos, and the offensive on the Somme in 1916. Later in the same year he was drafted to Salonika, and served on the Vardar front in the Balkan campaign. In the following year he went to Egypt and thence to Palestine, where he was in action throughout the offensive under General Allenby, and was present at the entry into Jerusalem. During his service overseas he was gassed and acted for part of the time as Drill Sergeant and Instructor. He returned home and was demobilised in April 1919, and holds the 1914–15 Star, and the General Service and Victory Medals.
7, Willow Street, Bermondsey, S.E.1. Z25949B

PARKER, A. E., Private, R.A.S.C.
He joined in October 1917, and in December of the same year was drafted to the Western Front and served in numerous engagements. He was employed on the transport of ammunition and supplies to the front lines. Returning home after the cessation of hostilities, he was demobilised in January 1919, and holds the General Service and Victory Medals.
71, Mayall Road, Herne Hill, S.E.24. Z3634

PARKER, A. G., Rifleman, 21st London Regiment (1st Surrey Rifles).
He volunteered in January 1915, proceeded to France in the same year and took part in important engagements at Ypres Loos and Festubert. He was wounded on the Somme and again at Beaumont-Hamel, and also at Cambrai in 1917. He returned home, and was demobilised in February 1919, and holds the General Service and Victory Medals.
44 (B Block), Guinness Buildings, Page's Walk, Grange Road, Bermondsey, S.E.1. Z26830

PARKER, A. J., Rifleman, Rifle Brigade.
He was mobilised at the outbreak of war and was shortly afterwards sent to France, and was in action at Le Cateau, where he was wounded, and taken prisoner. He was sent to Germany, and whilst in captivity was taken ill and was eventually exchanged and returned home. He was discharged as medically unfit for further service in February 1916, and holds the Mons Star, and the General Service and Victory Medals.
61, Bennerley Road, Wandsworth Common, S.W.11. Z3636

PARKER, F. L., L/Corporal, 1st Lincolnshire Regt.
He was mobilised in August 1914, and was sent to France immediately afterwards. He died gloriously on the Field of Battle at Mons on August 24th, 1914, and was entitled to the Mons Star, and the General Service and Victory Medals.
"He passed out of the sight of men by the path of duty and self-sacrifice."
21, Harris Street, Camberwell, S.E.5. Z4514A

PARKER, G., Cpl., 22nd London Regt. (Queen's).
He volunteered in September 1914, and in May of the following year was drafted to France, where he took part in numerous engagements, including those at Ypres, Festubert, Loos, Albert, Vimy Ridge, and the Somme, and was wounded. He was invalided home and discharged as medically unfit in October 1917, and holds the 1914–15 Star, and the General Service and Victory Medals.
10B, Madron Street, Walworth, S.E.17. Z3639

PARKER, H., Private, R.A.S.C. (M.T.)
He volunteered in August 1914, and in the same month was sent to France and was engaged on important duties in connection with the operations, being present during the Retreat from Mons, and the Battles of the Marne, the Aisne, Ypres, the Somme, and Arras. He was demobilised in November 1919, holding the Mons Star, and the General Service and Victory Medals.
35, Hargwynne Street, Stockwell Road, S.W.9. Z3640

PARKER, H., Air Mechanic, R.A.F.
He joined in August 1918, and after his training served with his unit on important duties, which demanded a high degree of technical skill. He was under age for overseas service, and was therefore unable to effect a transfer abroad before the cessation of hostilities. He was demobilised in October 1919.
7, Willow Street, Bermondsey, S.E. Z25949A

PARKER, H., Private, 22nd London Regt. (Queen's).
He volunteered in September 1914, and in the following year was sent to France, where he took part in the fighting at Ypres, Festubert, Loos, Albert, the Somme, Arras, Messines, and Vimy Ridge. He later proceeded to Egypt, and thence to Palestine, where he was in action throughout the offensive under General Allenby, and the entry into Jerusalem. He was demobilised in July 1919, and holds the 1914-15 Star, and the General Service and Victory Medals.
10B, Madron Street, Walworth, S.E.17. Z3637

PARKER, H. E., Bombardier, R.G.A.
He joined in January 1916, and after his training served on important duties with his Battery. He rendered valuable services, but was not successful in obtaining his transfer overseas before the cessation of hostilities. He was demobilised in October 1919.
10, Nelson's Row, Clapham, S.W.4. Z3638A

PARKER, H. G., Private, M.G.C.
Joining in August 1917, he was sent to France in the same year, and took part in the fighting at Ypres and Cambrai, and in the Retreat and Advance of 1918. He returned home in October 1919, and was demobilised, holding the General Service and Victory Medals.
16, Brisbane Street, Camberwell, S.E.5. Z3642

PARKER, J., Private, 2nd Suffolk Regiment.
He was serving in Ireland at the outbreak of war, and was immediately sent to France, and took part in the Retreat from Mons, and in other engagements. He was killed in action at Ypres on December 14th, 1914, and was entitled to the Mons Star, and the General Service and Victory Medals.
"Honour to the immortal dead who gave their youth that the world might grow old in peace."
3, Emu Road, Battersea, S.W.8. Z2507A

PARKER, J. W., Trooper, 2nd Life Guards and Household Siege Battery.

He joined in October 1917, and in May of the following year he was drafted to France, where he took part in the Retreat and Advance of 1918, and was in action on numerous occasions and was gassed. He was demobilised in September 1919, and holds the General Service and Victory Medals.
16, Nelson Row, Clapham, S.W.4.   Z3638B

PARKER, P. J., Driver, R.F.A.

He volunteered in October 1915, and in the same year was drafted to Salonika, where he served until the end of the campaign, and took part in numerous engagements. He returned home and was demobilised in March 1919, holding the 1914-15 Star, and the General Service and Victory Medals.
21, Harris Street, Camberwell, S.E.5.   Z4514B

PARKER, R., Bombardier, R.F.A.

He volunteered in January 1915, and was sent to France in the same year and took part in numerous engagements, including those at Loos, the Somme, Arras, Bullecourt, Ypres, and Passchendaele. He also served in the Retreat and Advance of 1918, and was wounded and invalided home. He was demobilised in June 1919, and holds the 1914-15 Star, and the General Service and Victory Medals.
8, New Road, Battersea, S.W.8.   Z1132A

PARKER, R., Gnr., R.F.A. and Pte., Labour Corps.

He volunteered in January 1915, and was sent to France in the same year. He took part in the fighting at Neuve Chapelle and Loos, and was gassed and invalided home. He was afterwards transferred to the Labour Corps, and returned to France, and was wounded on the Somme in 1916. He was then sent to hospital in England, and on his recovery served on important duties until demobilised in March 1919, holding the 1914-15 Star, and the General Service and Victory Medals.
29C, Edmund Street, Camberwell, S.E..   Z3635

PARKER, S. G., Rflmn., King's Royal Rifle Corps.

Joining in June 1916 he was drafted in October of the following year to the Western Front, where he was in action during the German Retreat of 1917, and in the engagements at Vimy Ridge, Beaumont-Hamel, Ypres, and Passchendaele. He was wounded and suffered from trench fever, and was invalided home. On his recovery he returned to France in February 1918, and was again in action on many occasions. He was demobilised in September 1919, and holds the General Service and Victory Medals.
66, Howbury Road, Peckham, S.E.15.   Z6567

PARKER, W., Private, R.A.S.C.

He volunteered in July 1915, and in the following August was sent to the Dardanelles, and was on board H.M.T. "Royal Edward," when that vessel was torpedoed in the Ægean Sea in August 1915. After being in the water for seven hours he was fortunately rescued. He was then present at the Landing at Suvla Bay, and at Chunuk Bair. In 1916 he was transferred to France, and was engaged on important duties at Vermelles, the Somme and Cambrai. He was discharged in March 1918 on compassionate grounds, and holds the 1914-15 Star, and the General Service and Victory Medals.
205, Albert Road, Peckham, S.E.15.   Z5647

PARKER, W. G. M., Private, West Yorkshire Regt.

He volunteered in August 1914, and was sent to France in the same year. He was wounded in action at Neuve Chapelle, and also served on the Somme, and at Amiens, La Bassée, Béthune, Cambrai, and in other engagements. He was later attached to the Royal Engineers for signal duties. He was demobilised in February 1919, holding the 1914 Star, and the General Service and Victory Medals.
31, Clayton Road, Peckham, S.E.15.   Z6054

PARKMAN, R. G. (M.M.), Private, 7th Queen's (Royal West Surrey Regiment).

Joining in June 1916, he crossed to France two months later, and acting as a signaller was in action in engagements at Vimy Ridge, the Somme and Cambrai, and was wounded. He was awarded the Military Medal for conspicuous bravery in repairing wires under heavy fire, which act was the means of maintaining communication and transmitting an important message through to his Battalion. In addition, he holds the General Service and Victory Medals, and was demobilised in September 1919.
57, Morrison Street, Battersea, S.E.11.   Z3643

PARLE, E. W., Air Mechanic, R.A.F. (late R.N.A.S.)

He volunteered in December 1915, and early in the following year, was drafted to Italy. During his service in this theatre of war he was stationed principally at Taranto, where he was engaged on special duties as a rigger. Later he contracted malaria, and after being for some time in hospital at Malta, returned home and was stationed in Scotland until demobilised in May 1919. He holds the General Service and Victory Medals.
67, Flaxman Road, Camberwell, S.E.5.   Z6057B

PARLE, T., Leading Aircraftsman, R.A.F.

He joined in November 1917, and at the conclusion of his training was engaged on important duties, which demanded a high degree of technical skill. Owing to physical disability, he was unable to secure his transfer to a theatre of war, but he nevertheless did valuable work as an aero-engine fitter until January 1920, when he was discharged owing to heart trouble.
67, Flaxman Road, Camberwell, S.E.5.   Z6057A

PARMENTER, A., Rifleman, 13th King's Royal Rifle Corps.

Joining in April 1917, he crossed to France three months later and fought at Ypres and Passchendaele. He was then transferred to the Italian Front, but after four months'service there returned to France and took part in the Retreat of 1918. He also fought in the subsequent Advance, and in November of that year received a severe wound, from which he unhappily died at Albert. He was entitled to the General Service and Victory Medals.
"He passed out of the sight of men by the path of duty and self-sacrifice."
275, Lynton Road, Bermondsey. S.E.1.   Z26509

PARMENTER, A. J., L/Corporal, Norfolk and Essex Regiments.

He volunteered in August 1914, and in the following year was drafted to the Dardanelles, when he took part in the Landing at Suvla Bay, and in several of the engagements which followed. In November 1915, however, he was invalided home from the Peninsula. but on his recovery was transferred to the Essex Regiment, and sent to Mesopotamia. Whilst in this theatre of war he was engaged on important duties, principally at Baghdad, and did valuable work. He was demobilised in July 1919, and holds the 1914-15 Star, and the General Service and Victory Medals.
17, Bengeworth Road, Camberwell, S.E.5.   Z6308A

PARMENTER, E. A., Private, Gloucestershire Regt.

Joining in May 1916, he was sent to France early in the following year, and in July 1917, was severely wounded at the Battle of Ypres. He was invalided to hospital in England, and on his recovery was retained in Northumberland on special duties until he was demobilised in October 1919. He holds the General Service and Victory Medals.
17, Bengeworth Road, Camberwell, S.E.5.   Z6308B

PARNELL, W. E., L/Corporal, 18th London Regt. (London Irish Rifles).

He volunteered in March 1916, and during his service on the Western Front fought at Arras, Messines, Ypres, and in many other important sectors. Later he was invalided home suffering from shell-shock, and in May 1919 was discharged as physically unfit for further service. He holds the General Service and Victory Medals.
21, Viceroy Road, South Lambeth, S.W.8.   Z3644

PARISH, C. E., Private, R.A.S.C.

He volunteered in October 1914, and early in the following year crossed to France, where he was engaged on important duties in connection with the transport of supplies to our troops in the Somme and Arras areas. In the course of his service he was present at many engagements, and on three occasions was wounded. He holds the 1914-15 Star, and the General Service and Victory Medals, and was demobilised in 1919.
9, Broomgrove Road, Stockwell, S.W.9.   Z4483B

PARRISH, W. E., Private, London Regiment (Royal Fusiliers).

He joined in August 1916, and until August 1918, was engaged upon duties of an important nature. Whilst in France he fought at Amiens, Bapaume, Lille, and other engagements in the final Advance and did valuable work until the termination of hostilities. He holds the General Service and Victory Medals, and was demobilised in January 1919.
31, Wooler Street, Walworth, S.E.17.   Z3645

PARRETT, W. H., L/Cpl., King's Royal Rifle Corps.

Volunteering in May 1915, he crossed to France in the following March, and took part in fighting at Ypres, where he was wounded, Vimy Ridge, the Somme, and Arras. On the 12th September, 1917, he was reported missing after an engagement at Epéhy, but it is presumed that he fell in action on that date. He was entitled to the General Service and Victory Medals.
"Thinking that remembrance, though unspoken, may reach him where he sleeps."
198, Albert Road, Peckham, S.E.15.   Z5648A

PARRY, A. H., A.B., R.N., H.M.S. "Pembroke."

He joined in February 1918, and was sent to Chatham, where he was in training. In the course of his service however, he contracted an illness of which he died on May 28th, 1918. He is buried at Gillingham Cemetery.
68, Avenue Road, Camberwell, S.E.5.   Z3362C

PARRY, T., Rifleman, Rifle Brigade.
Joining in September 1916, he was drafted to Egypt at the conclusion of his training. Later he served in the Palestine campaign, during which he took part in the Battles of Gaza, and the capture of Jerusalem and Jericho. Whilst in action near the Jordan, he was severely wounded, and after being invalided home was in hospital for two years. He was demobilised in 1919, and holds the General Service and Victory Medals.
92, Somerleyton Road, Coldharbour Lane, S.W.9.　Z5127

PARRY, W. C., Gunner, R.F.A.
He volunteered in June 1915, and in the following March was drafted to the Western Front. Whilst in this theatre of war he fought in many engagements, notably those at Vimy Ridge, Arras, and Ypres, and was twice wounded. Later he was transferred to Italy, where he was again in action, and was wounded a third time. After being for some time in hospital at Boulogne, he returned to England, and in January 1919 was invalided out of the Service. He holds the General Service and Victory Medals.
86, Gwynne Road, Battersea, S.W.11.　Z3646

PARSONS, A. C., Private, Buffs (East Kent Regt).
Volunteering in 1915 he went through his training, and on its conclusion was drafted to Mesopotamia, where he took an active part in the engagements at Kut and Baghdad, and the occupation of Mosul. After three years' active service on this front he returned to England, and was demobilised in May 1919. He holds the General Service and Victory Medals.
5, Gaza Street, Kennington Park Road, S.E.17.　Z25922A

PARSONS, C. H., Private, Queen's (Royal West Surrey Regiment).
He volunteered in August 1914, and after his training rendered valuable service at various stations with his unit. He was employed on coast defence work, and in guarding railway bridges and munition factories. Owing to ill-health he was unable to secure his transfer to a theatre of war, and in November 1915, was invalided out of the Service.
5, Doctor Street, Walworth, S.E.17.　Z26216

PARSONS, E. J., Private, Middlesex Regiment.
Volunteering in August 1915, was drafted to Egypt at the conclusion of his training, and served on that front until the commencement of the Palestine campaign, in which he took an active part. He was unfortunately killed in action in the operations proceeding the capture of Jerusalem on November 28th, 1917, and was entitled to the 1914-15 Star, and the General Service and Victory Medals.
"The path of duty was the way to glory."
46, Brymer Road, Camberwell, S.E.5.　Z5649B

PARSONS, F. W., Driver, R.F.A.
He volunteered in January 1915, and at the conclusion of his training was sent to France, where he did valuable work with his Battery during military operations, at Loos, the Somme, Ypres, Messines, and Vimy Ridge. He gave his life for King and Country in the operations near Cambrai on August 7th, 1918. He was entitled to the 1914-15 Star, and the General Service and Victory Medals.
"His life for his Country, his Soul to God."
46, Brymer Road, Camberwell, S.E.5.　Z5649A

PARSONS, G., Rifleman, Rifle Brigade.
He volunteered in September 1914, and in the following year was drafted to the Western Front, where he took part in many important engagements, including those at Ypres, Neuve Chapelle, Loos, the Somme, Arras, Messines, Hill 60, and Cambrai. He also served in the Retreat and Advance of 1918, and was wounded. He was demobilised in 1919, and holds the 1914-15 Star, and the General Service and Victory Medals.
24, Elizabeth Street, Walworth, S.E.17.　Z26420

PARSONS, G. F., L/Corporal, Bedfordshire Regt.
Volunteering in August 1914, he crossed to France early in the following year. He was engaged in the fighting at St. Eloi and Arras, and was later wounded at the Battle of Ypres. After his recovery however, he rejoined his unit in the Somme area, and was in action until the termination of hostilities. He was demobilised in February 1919, and holds the 1914-15 Star, and the General Service and Victory Medals.
32, Bellefield Road, Stockwell, S.W.9.　Z3649

PARSONS, J., Private, R.A.V.C.
He volunteered in November 1915, and soon afterwards proceeded to Egypt where he remained until the following July, when he was transferred to Salonika. Whilst in this theatre of war he did much valuable work until after the cessation of fighting, in connection with the care of sick and wounded horses, but in the course of his service became seriously ill, and unhappily died on January 2nd, 1919. He was entitled to the 1914-15 Star, and the General Service and Victory Medals.
"His memory is cherished with pride."
10, New Church Road, Camberwell, S.E.5.　Z5815B

PARSONS, J. H., Pte., 1st New Zealand Forces ((Canterbury).
Volunteering in New Zealand in January 1915, he was drafted to the Dardanelles with the first Australian Contingent, and took part in the Landing at Suvla Bay and the chief engagement which followed. After the Evacuation of the Peninsula, he was invalided to Malta suffering from dysentery, and after his recovery was sent to France. He was unfortunately killed by liquid fire whilst in action in the Somme sector on July 10th, 1916. He was entitled to the 1914-15 Star, and the General Service and Victory Medals.
"A costly sacrifice upon the altar of freedom."
46, Brymer Road, Camberwell, S.E.5.　Z5649C

PARSONS, R., Drummer, Irish Guards.
He was in the Army when war broke out, having enlisted in April 1900, and was engaged on important home duties until December 1917, when he crossed to the Western Front. Whilst in this theatre of war, he was in action in several important engagements, and later saw service in Italy. He holds the General Service and Victory Medals, and in 1920, was still serving.
15, Matthews Street, Battersea, S.W.11.　Z3648

PARSONS, J. W., Private, King's Shropshire Light Infantry.
He was in India when war broke out, having enlisted in 1908, and immediately embarked for England. On December 1914, he was drafted to the Western Front, and took part in several engagements, including that at Ypres, where in April 1915, he was wounded and lost an arm. He was then invalided home, and after being for some time in hospital at Newcastle-on-Tyne, was discharged as physically unfit for further duty in August of the same year. He holds the 1914-15 Star, and the General Service and Victory Medals.
24, Pepler Road, Peckham, S.E.15.　Z3647

PARSONS, T., Driver, R.A.S C. (M.T.)
Joining in June 1916, he crossed to France at the conclusion of his training, and for three years did valuable work with the ammunition column until the end of the war in various important sectors, including those of the Somme, Ypres, and Arras. He was demobilised in 1919 after his return home, and holds the General Service and Victory Medals.
25, Cottage Grove, Stockwell, S.W.9.　Z3650

PARSONS, W., Petty Officer, R.N.
He was already in the Navy when hostilities began, and during the recent war served in turn on board H.M.S.'s "Lion" and "Coquette," which were engaged on important patrol duties with the Grand Fleet in the North Sea. On March 25th, 1916, he was reported missing after his ship had been blown up by a mine, and it is presumed that he was killed on that date with all his comrades, except three. He was entitled to the 1914-15 Star, and the General Service and Victory Medals.
"Whilst we remember the Sacrifice is not in vain."
5, Gaza Street, Kennington Park Road, S.E.17.　Z25922B

PARSONS, W., Sergt., Royal Fusiliers.
He volunteered at the commencement of hostilities, and after his training served on the Western Front, where he fought in several engagements of importance. He died gloriously on the Field of Battle at Neuve Chapelle on March 9th, 1915, and is buried in a military cemetery in Belgium. He was entitled to the 1914 Star, and the General Service and Victory Medals.
"He died the noblest death a man may die,
Fighting for God, and right, and liberty."
81, Trafalgar Street, Walworth, S.E.17.　Z27134-5

PARTLETON, B., Rifleman, 21st London Regt. (1st Surrey Rifles).
Volunteering in July 1915, he was drafted overseas in the same year and saw much service in France and Flanders. He took part in heavy fighting in the Battles of the Somme, and in the Advance of 1918, and was twice wounded and suffered from shell-shock. Invalided home on account of his injuries in November 1918, he received hospital treatment, and was discharged as medically unfit in February 1919. He holds the 1914-15 Star, and the General Service and Victory Medals.
240, Hillington Street, Walworth, S.E.17.　Z26650

PARTLETON, W. C., Private, Queen's (Royal West Surrey Regiment).
He volunteered in 1915, and sent to the Western Front in the following year fought in the Battle of the Somme. In 1917 he proceeded to Italy, and served with his Battalion in operations on the Piave until the cessation of hostilities. Returning home he was demobilised in February 1919, and holds the General Service and Victory Medals.
10, Royal Road, Walworth, S.E.17.　Z26460

PARTRIDGE, G. M., Driver, R.E.

Volunteering in January 1915, he embarked for France in the same year, and served there until the end of the war. During this period he was in action in the Battles of Loos, St. Eloi, Albert, Vermelles, Vimy Ridge, and in several engagements in the Retreat and Advance of 1918. Returning home on the conclusion of hostilities he was demobilised in June 1919, and holds the 1914–15 Star, and the General Service and Victory Medals.

37, Robertson Street, Wandsworth Road, S.W.8.   Z3651

PASBY, A., Driver, R.F.A.

He volunteered in August 1914, and drafted to the Western Front shortly afterwards served with his Battalion in many parts of the line. He was in action in several engagements including the Battles of the Marne, Ypres, Festubert, La Bassée, the Somme, and during the Retreat and Advance of 1918. Owing to an accident which resulted in the loss of the sight of an eye, he was sent to hospital in England, and after receiving treatment was demobilised in January 1919. He holds the 1914 Star, and the General Service and Victory Medals.

23, Gladstone Terrace, Battersea Park Road, S.W.8.   Z3652

PASKELL, A. W., Rifleman, Rifle Brigade.

Volunteering in August 1914, he embarked for France in the same month, and fought in the early operations of the war. Taken prisoner, he effected his escape and rejoining his unit was seriously wounded in the Battle of Loos in September 1915, and sent to hospital in England. On recovery he returned to the Field, and was wounded in the Battle of the Ancre in January 1917, and invalided home. He holds the Mons Star, and the General Service and Victory Medals, and in 1920 was still serving.

9, Auckland Road, Battersea, S.W.11.   Z3653

PATCHING, A. A., Private, 2nd Middlesex Regt.

A Regular, he was serving in India at the outbreak of war, and immediately proceeded to France. There he took part in the Retreat from Mons, and in the Battles of the Marne, the Aisne, La Bassée, Ypres (I, II, and III), and several other important engagements, including those during the Retreat and Advance of 1918. On the termination of hostilities he returned home for demobilisation in February 1919, and holds the Mons Star, and the General Service and Victory Medals.

21, Cornbury Street, Walworth, S.E.17.   Z3654A

PATCHING, B. J., L/Cpl., 6th (Inniskilling) Dragoons.

A serving soldier, he was sent from India to the Western Front shortly after the outbreak of war, and fought in the Retreat from Mons, and the subsequent Battles of the Marne and the Aisne. He was later in action at La Bassée, Loos, Vimy Ridge, and in many engagements during the German Offensive, and subsequent Allied Advance of 1918, which terminated hostilities. He holds the Mons Star, and the General Service and Victory Medals, and was demobilised in January 1919.

21, Cornbury Street, Walworth, S.E.17.   Z3654B

PATCHING, W. J., Pte., 2nd Northamptonshire Regt.

He was mobilised from the Army Reserve on the declaration of war and proceeded to France almost immediately. Taking part in fierce fighting during the Retreat from Mons, he was severely wounded and invalided home in September 1914. After two years' treatment in hospital he was discharged as medically unfit for further service in September 1916, and holds the Mons Star, and the General Service and Victory Medals.

21, Cornbury Street, Walworth, S.E.17.   Z3654C

PATERSON, J. N., Sergt., 1st Grenadier Guards.

Enlisting in June 1912, he was mobilised when war broke out, and proceeding to France soon afterwards took part in heavy fighting during the Retreat from Mons. Owing to wounds received in the Battle of Neuve Chapelle he was sent to England for hospital treatment, and on recovery returned to his unit and fought in the Battles of the Somme, Ypres, Passchendaele. Invalided home on account of ill-health, he was later engaged as a Drill Instructor, and did much good work in that capacity. He was mentioned in Despatches on September 25th, 1916 for gallantry in patrol work, and for securing important information of enemy movements. He was still serving in 1920, and holds the Mons Star, and the General Service and Victory Medals

32A, Lewis Trust Buildings, off Warner Road, Camberwell, S.E.5.   Z6060

PATEY, A. H., Farrier Staff-Sergt., R.G.A.

He volunteered in September 1914, and in the following May proceeded overseas. Serving in several sectors of the Western Front he was in charge of farriers in the forward areas, and was present at several engagements during the Retreat and Advance of 1918. After the Armistice he was sent into Germany with the Army of Occupation, and was stationed on the Rhine. Returning home in December 1919, he was demobilised in the following month, and holds the 1914–15 Star, and the General Service and Victory Medals.

15, Lambeth Square, S.E.1.   Z24844

PATEY, F. J., Air Mechanic, R.A.F.

He joined in May 1917, and in the same year was drafted to the Western Front. There he served with his Squadron, and was engaged on duties of a highly technical nature at various aerodromes. On the conclusion of hostilities he was sent into Germany with the Army of Occupation, and, returning home for demobilisation in November 1919, holding the General Service and Victory Medals.

22, Bond Street, S. Lambeth Road, S.W.8.   Z3656A

PATEY, H. T., Wireless Operator, R.N.

He volunteered in January 1915, and was posted to H.M.S. "Yeovil," which vessel, attached to the Grand Fleet was engaged on important duties in the North Sea. He was subsequently transferred to a mine-sweeper, and served aboard this ship off the Scottish and Irish Coasts. He holds the 1914–15 Star, and the General Service and Victory Medals. and was invalided out of the Service in March 1920.

22, Bond Street, S. Lambeth Road, S.W.8.   Z3655

PATEY, W., Private, Dorsetshire Regiment.

Volunteering in August 1914, he was drafted to France in the following year, and took part in heavy fighting in the Battle of Loos, and was wounded. Sent home to hospital he proceeded to Mesopotamia on recovery, and served there until the end of hostilities. During this period he was in action in several operations including those for the relief of Kut, and the capture of Baghdad. Returning to England for demobilisation in June 1919, he holds the 1914–15 Star, and the General Service and Victory Medals.

125, Fort Road, Bermondsey, S.E.1.   Z26110

PATEY, W. J., Private, R.D.C.

A Reservist, who had fought in South Africa, he was mobilised when war broke out, and owing to ineligibility for general service was posted to the Royal Defence Corps. After completing his training he was engaged on guard duties at the Alexandra Park prisoners of war camp, and also served on special duties at various stations on the coast. He was demobilised in February 1919, and holds the South African Medals.

22, Bond Street, S. Lambeth Road, S.W.8.   Z3656B

PATIENT, F., Gunner, R.G.A.

He volunteered in October 1914, and on completing his training was engaged on important duties with his Battery, and whilst practising bomb-throwing he met with an accident which necessitated the amputation of a leg, and he was discharged in consequence in December 1916.

22, Madron Street, Walworth, S.E.17.   Z3657A

PATIENT, G., Bombardier, R.F.A.

Volunteering in May 1915, he embarked for the Western Front in the same year, and saw service in various parts of the line. He was engaged with his Battery in heavy fighting, and was wounded in the Battle of Ypres in September 1915, and sent home to hospital. Subsequently invalided out of the Service in June 1918, he holds the General Service and Victory Medals.

9, Odell Street, Camberwell, S.E.5.   Z5335A

PATON, H., Corporal, 2nd Scots Guards.

Enlisting in 1897, he had fought in the South African War, and was mobilised in August 1914. In the following October he embarked for France and was in action in the Battle of Ypres. Seriously wounded in this engagement he died from the effects of his injuries on November 25th, 1914. He held the Queen's and King's South African Medals, and was entitled to the 1914 Star, and the General Service and Victory Medals.

"Courage, bright hopes, and a myriad dreams, splendidly given."

26, Peardon Street, Wandsworth Road, S.W.8.   Z3658

PATTEN, E. A., L/Corporal, Royal Fusiliers.

He volunteered in September 1914, and in the following year proceeded to Gallipoli where he fought in operations from the Landing at Suvla Bay until the Evacuation of the Peninsula. Sent to the Western Front in 1916, he took part in many engagements and returned home in 1918, owing to medical unfitness for general service. He was then engaged on military police duties until invalided out of the Service in December 1918. He fought in South Africa and holds the Queen's and King's Medals for that campaign, in addition to the 1914–15 Star, and the General Service and Victory Medals.

19, St. Philip Street, Battersea Park Road, S.W.8.   Z6196A

PATTEN, W. F., Rifleman, King's Royal Rifle Corps.

He volunteered in August 1915, and was sent overseas in the following year. Serving with his Battalion on the Western Front, he was in heavy fighting in the Battle of Ypres and other engagements. He gave his life for King and Country in the Battle of the Somme on September 3rd, 1916, and was entitled to the General Service and Victory Medals.

"A valiant soldier, with undaunted heart, he breasted Life's last hill."

13, Alsace Street, Walworth, S.E.17.   Z3660

PATTEN, F. S., Sergt., 24th London Regiment (The Queen's).

Volunteering in April 1915, he was drafted to France in November of the following year, and serving there for a short time proceeded to Salonika. He took an active part in operations in the Balkans, and was killed by a bomb explosion on January 28th, 1917, when attempting to save the lives of twelve of his men. He was entitled to the General Service and Victory Medals. He had previously served in the South African War with the City Imperial Volunteers, for which he held the Queen's and King's Medals, and received the freedom of the City of London.

"He joined the great white company of valiant souls."

65, Smyrk's Road, Walworth, S.E.17. Z3659

PATTENDEN, R. D., Driver, R.F.A.

He volunteered in September 1914, and proceeding to the Western Front in the following year served there for upwards of four years. During this period he fought in the Battles of the Somme, Ypres (I, II and III), Loos, and was wounded at St. Eloi. He was also in action during the Retreat and Advance of 1918, and on the conclusion of hostilities was sent into Germany with the Army of Occupation. Returning from Cologne he was demobilised in March 1920, and holds the 1914-15 Star, and the General Service and Victory Medals.

17, St. Andrew Street, Wandsworth Road, S.W.8. Z2096B

PATTERSON, G. T., Private, East Yorkshire Regt.

He was mobilised from the Army Reserve when war broke out and drafted to the Western Front shortly afterwards. In the course of his service he was wounded in October 1914, and invalided to hospital in England and returned to France on his recovery. Transferred to the Royal Air Force he served with the Balloon Training section for a time and was then posted to the Labour Corps, with which unit he was engaged on important duties during operations on the Somme. He was demobilised in January 1919, and holds the 1914-15 Star, and the General Service and Victory Medals.

15, Cook's Road, Walworth, S.E.17. Z26666

PATTERSON, W. H. J., Air Mechanic, R.A.F.

He joined in 1917, and proceeding overseas in the same year served with his Squadron until the conclusion of hostilities. During this period he was engaged on special duties in the aeroplane repair shops near Arras and served in the Advance of 1918. Demobilised in February 1919, he holds the General Service and Victory Medals.

12, St. Alban's Street, Kennington, S.E.11. Z26991

PAUL, A., Private, Seaforth Highlanders.

He volunteered in 1915, and drafted to the Western Front in the following year, served in various parts of the line. He fought in the Battles of Ypres, the Somme, Beaumont-Hamel and in the German Offensive and subsequent Advance of 1918. On the cessation of hostilities he was sent to Germany with the Army of Occupation and stationed at Cologne. Returning home he was demobilised in 1918, and holds the General Service and Victory Medals.

25, Crichton Street, Wandsworth Road, S.W.8. Z3662

PAUL, A. J., Private, R.A.S.C. (H.T.)

Volunteering in August 1914, he was sent overseas two months later and serving on the Western Front, was engaged on important duties in connection with the transport of supplies to the forward areas whilst heavy fighting was in progress. He was demobilised in June 1919, and holds the 1914-15 Star, and the General Service and Victory Medals.

35, Danson Road, Walworth, S.E.17. 27007

PAUL, M. J., Private, R.A.S.C.

He volunteered in 1914, and in the same year embarked for France. During his service in this theatre of war he was engaged on important duties at the Base and later acted as a stretcher-bearer during several important engagements, including those at Ypres and the Somme. After hostilities ceased he returned to England and was demobilised in February 1919, and holds the 1914-15 Star, and the General Service and Victory Medals.

26, Raywood Street, Battersea Park Road, S.W.8. Z3661

PAULIZKY, L. T., Private, 13th Royal Fusiliers.

Volunteering in January 1915, he proceeded to the Western Front in the following July and served in various parts of the line. Whilst overseas he fought in several engagements, including the Battles of Loos, the Somme, Beaucourt, Monchy, Arras and was wounded at High Wood in August 1916. Returning home after the Armistice, he was demobilised in February 1919, and holds the 1914-15 Star, and the General Service and Victory Medals.

6, Flint Street, Walworth, S.E.17. Z3663

PAVIER, E., A.B., Royal Navy.

He joined the Service in June 1914, and throughout the war served in the North Sea and off the French coast. His ship was in action in the Battles of Heligoland Bight and Jutland and took part in the bombardment of Dunkirk and in the raid on Zeebrugge. He was demobilised in October 1919, and holds the 1914-15 Star, and the General Service and Victory Medals.

9, Royal Terrace, Royal Road, Walworth, S.E.17. Z26333

PAXTON, F., Private, Queen's Own (Royal West Kent Regiment).

He volunteered in May 1915, and embarking for France five months later, fought at the Battles of Loos, Vimy Ridge and Albert. He gave his life for the freedom of England on September 1st, 1916, in the first British Offensive on the Somme, and was entitled to the 1914-15 Star, and the General Service and Victory Medals.

"Steals on the ear the distant triumph song."

5, Flint Street, Walworth, S.E.17. Z3664

PAXTON, F., Driver, R.E.

Volunteering in March 1915, he was sent to the Western Front in the following August, and was in action in many important engagements, including those at Ypres, Armentières, Hill 60, and the Somme. He was wounded in the Ypres salient in 1917, and returning to England received hospital treatment. Invalided out of the Service in November 1917, he holds the 1914-15 Star, and the General Service and Victory Medals.

18, Bonnington Square, South Lambeth Road, S.W.8. Z3665

PAYNE, A. W., Sergt., 22nd London Regt. (Queen's).

He volunteered in April 1915, and in the following year proceeded to France. After valuable service there, he was transferred to Salonika later in the year and took a prominent part in the subsequent operations on the Vardar and Doiran fronts. In 1917 he crossed to Egypt and afterwards fought in General Allenby's campaign in Palestine at Gaza and outside Jerusalem, when he was badly wounded. He was in consequence sent to hospital in Egypt for treatment. After his return home he was demobilised in May 1919, and holds the General Service and Victory Medals.

16, Parfitt Road, Rotherhithe, S.E.16. Z6640

PAYNE, C., Pte., 24th London Regt. (The Queen's).

He volunteered in May 1915, and completing his training served at various stations engaged on guard and other important duties. Owing to medical unfitness he was unsuccessful in obtaining his transfer overseas prior to the cessation of hostilities, but was sent to France in February 1919, and served there for nearly a year. He returned to England, and was demobilised in February 1920.

82, Westmoreland Road, Walworth, S.E.17. Z3671

PAYNE, C. H., Private, R.A.M.C.

He joined in June 1917, and served at various hospitals engaged on important duties attending the sick and wounded troops. In March 1918 he was sent to France and rendered valuable services at the Chinese Labour Hospital, Le Havre, until demobilised on January 31st, 1919. He holds the General Service and Victory Medals.

29, Nunhead Crescent, Peckham, S.E.15. Z6215

PAYNE, E., Trooper, 7th (Princess Royal's) Dragoon Guards.

He was serving with the Colours when war broke out, and embarking for the Western Front in the following year, was in action in the Battles of Ypres, Arras, and the Somme. In 1917, transferred to Egypt, he fought in many engagements during the British Advance through Palestine into Syria. He returned to England in 1919 and was still serving in 1920, and holds the 1914-15 Star, and the General Service and Victory Medals.

29, Rutland Street, Wilcox Road, S.W.8. Z3674

PAYNE, F. H., Sergt., 2nd Rifle Brigade.

He joined in May 1916, and drafted to the Western Front in the following year, fought in the engagements at Bullecourt, Amiens, Ypres, the Somme and was wounded at Passchendaele on February 17th, 1918. On recovery he rejoined his Battalion and was in action in the opening operations of the German Offensive of 1918. Taken prisoner on May 27th, 1918, he was held in captivity until December and was then repatriated, and demobilised in February 1919. He holds the General Service and Victory Medals.

193, Hollydale Road, Peckham, S.E.15. Z6429

PAYNE, F. J., Pte., The Queen's (Royal West Surrey Regiment).

Volunteering in August 1914, he embarked for France in the following year and fought in many parts of the line. Transferred to Salonika later in 1915, he saw much service in various sectors, fighting on the Doiran and Vardar fronts and in the final operations in that theatre of war. He returned to England and was demobilised in April 1919, and holds the 1914-15 Star, and the General Service and Victory Medals.

10, Kimpton Road, Camberwell, S.E.5 Z3666

PAYNE, F. T., Private, R.A.S.C.

He joined in October 1917, and two months later proceeded to France, where he served in the advanced areas engaged on important transport duties. He was present at the Battles of Ypres and Passchendaele and saw much fighting in the Retreat and Advance of 1918. After the Armistice he was sent into Germany with the Army of Occupation and was stationed at Cologne. He was demobilised in November 1919, and holds the General Service and Victory Medals.

233, Sumner Road, Peckham, S.E.15.   Z6314

PAYNE, F. W., Bombardier, R.F.A.

He volunteered in May 1915, and embarked for the Western Front six months later. During his service overseas he was engaged in heavy fighting at Messines, Ypres, Passchendaele, Cambrai, the Somme, and throughout the German Offensive and Allied Advance of 1918. He was demobilised in June 1919, and holds the 1914–15 Star, and the General Service and Victory Medals.

8, Elwell Road, Larkhall Lane, S.W.4.   Z3673

PAYNE, G., Private, Labour Corps.

Volunteering in February 1916, he proceeded to the Western Front in the following month, and served in the vicinity of Béthune engaged in making and mending roads. He rendered valuable services throughout the fighting in the Retreat and Advance of 1918, and returning home was demobilised in February 1919. He holds the General Service and Victory Medals.

203, Hollydale Street, Peckham, S.E.15.   Z6428

PAYNE, G. R., Rifleman, 11th King's Royal Rifle Corps.

Joining in March 1916, and proceeding to France in the following June, he fought at the Battles of Arras, Vimy Ridge, Ypres, Passchendaele and Cambrai, and was gassed. He was invalided to England in 1917, and after receiving medical treatment returned to France and was engaged in heavy fighting throughout the closing operations of the war. He was demobilised in August 1919, and holds the General Service and Victory Medals.

1, Melon Road, Peckham, S.E.15.   Z6309

PAYNE, G. W., Private, R.A.S.C. (M.T.)

He volunteered in February 1915, and proceeded to France in the following month. He served in the advanced areas transporting ammunition and supplies to the front lines, and did good work throughout the German Offensive and Allied Advance of 1918. He was demobilised in March 1919, and holds the 1914–15 Star, and the General Service and Victory Medals.

45, Merrow Street, Walworth, S.E.17.   Z27116

PAYNE, H. J., Sergt., Rifle Brigade.

Volunteering in September 1914, he was sent to France shortly afterwards, and fought at the Battles of Arras, Givenchy, La Bassée, Ypres and the Somme. He gave his life for King and Country in the Battle of the Somme on September 18th, 1916, and was entitled to the 1914 Star, and the General Service and Victory Medals.

"And doubtless he went in splendid company."

93, Sandmere Road, Clapham, S.W.4.   Z3672B

PAYNE, H. V., Private, R.A.V.C.

He volunteered in February 1916, and embarking for the Western Front in September of the same year, rendered valuable services attending the sick and wounded horses and in training remounts for active service. He returned to England, and was demobilised in June 1919, and holds the General Service and Victory Medals.

39, Dean's Buildings, Flint Street, Walworth, S.E.17. Z3670B

PAYNE, J. R., Private, 11th Queen's (Royal West Surrey Regiment).

He volunteered in November 1915, and in the following year was drafted to the Western Front and fought in various parts of the line. He was severely wounded in action and admitted into No.10 Casualty Clearing Station, subsequently succumbed to his injuries on June 27th, 1917, and lies at rest in the military cemetery at Poperinghe. He was entitled to the General Service and Victory Medals.

"He joined the great white company of valiant souls."

3, Bidwell Street, Peckham, S.E.15.   Z6568

PAYNE, N. G., Driver, R.F.A.

Volunteering in January 1915, he was drafted to France later in that year, and was in action at Arras and in various other sectors. In 1916, transferred to Salonika, he fought in many important engagements and proceeded to Egypt in the following year. He took part in severe fighting during the Advance into Syria and suffered from malaria during his service in this theatre of war. He returned to England and was demobilised in July 1919, and holds the 1914–15 Star, and the General Service and Victory Medals.

93, Sandmere Road, Clapham, S.W.4.   Z3672A

PAYNE, T., Private, R.A.S.C. (H.T.)

Volunteering in December 1914, and embarking for France in the following September, he served in the forward areas on important transport duties and was present at the Battles of the Somme, Albert and Arras. He rendered valuable services throughout, and returning to England owing to ill-health, received hospital treatment. He was subsequently discharged from the Service in June 1917, and holds the 1914–15 Star, and the General Service and Victory Medals.

19, Dean's Buildings, Flint Street, Walworth, S.E.17. Z3669

PAYNE, W., Gunner, R.F.A.

Volunteering in March 1915, he served at various depôts at home until drafted to the Western Front in February 1916. He was engaged in heavy fighting at Albert, Loos, the Somme, Ypres, Arras, Messines, Lens and throughout the Retreat and Advance of 1918. He was demobilised in March 1919, and holds the General Service and Victory Medals.

23, Townsend Street, Walworth, S.E.17.   Z3668

PAYNE, W. A., Pte., Loyal North Lancashire Regt.

A Reservist, he was mobilised at the outbreak of hostilities and sent to France shortly afterwards, was in action in the Retreat from Mons and in the Battles of the Marne. He was unfortunately killed in action at the Battle of the Aisne on October 31st, 1914, and was entitled to the Mons Star, and the General Service and Victory Medals.

"Nobly striving,

He nobly died that we might live."

38, Runham Street, Walworth, S.E.17.   Z3393A

PAYNE, W. F., Special Constable.

Ineligible for services with the Colours, he placed his services at the disposal of his Country and from 1914 until the following year did good work as a Special Constable, generally assisting the police. He discharged his duties efficiently, but was invalided out of the Force in 1915. He subsequently died in 1916.

"His memory is cherished with pride."

17 (A Block), Sutton Buildings, Chelsea, S.W.3. X22983A

PAYNE, W. G., Telegraphist, R.N.

He joined in April 1916, and saw considerable service whilst his ship was engaged on important duties convoying troops and supplies to various theatres of war. In July 1917 his ship was torpedoed and he was wounded. On recovery he was retained on shore and acting as a wireless operator, did good work at Immingham and Dumbarton wireless stations until demobilised in February 1919. He holds the General Service and Victory Medals.

15, St. John's Hill Grove, Battersea, S.W.11.   Z3667

PAYNE, W. H. J., Pte., Northumberland Fusiliers.

Joining in September 1917 at the age of eighteen, he served at various stations at home until embarking for France in October 1918. He fought in engagements during the closing operations of the war, and returning to England in the following year, was demobilised in October 1919, and holds the General Service and Victory Medals.

17, (A Block), Sutton Building, Chelsea, S.W.3. X22983B

PAYS, J. C., Pte., 22nd London Regt. (The Queen's).

He joined in July 1917, and proceeding to the Western Front in the following November, fought in many engagements and was wounded on January 31st, 1918, at Cambrai. On recovery, rejoining his Battalion in the Field, he was in action throughout the German Offensive, and was again wounded on August 22nd at Epéhy during the Allied Advance. He returned to England, and after receiving hospital treatment, was demobilised in February 1919, and holds the General Service and Victory Medals.

39, Stanton Street, Peckham, S.E.15.   Z5274

PEACHEY, H., Private, 2nd East Surrey Regiment.

He was mobilised and proceeded to France at the declaration of war, and fought in the Retreat from Mons, and in the Battles of the Aisne, the Marne, the Somme and Arras and was gassed in the first gas attack. He was later wounded at Cambrai and after receiving hospital treatment rejoined his unit and was in action in the German Offensive and Allied Advance. He was demobilised in February 1919, and holds the Mons Star, and the General Service and Victory Medals.

25, Gladstone Street, Battersea Park Road, S.W.8. Z3675

PEACHEY, H., Driver, R.F.A.

Volunteering in November 1914, he was drafted to France in the following August and saw heavy fighting in the Loos sector. In October 1915, transferred to Salonika, he fought in many parts of the line and later proceeded to Egypt. On the Palestine front he was in action in various engagements during the British Advance through the Holy Land, and returning home was demobilised in May 1919. He holds the 1914–15 Star, and the General Service and Victory Medals.

3, Upper Hall Street, Peckham, S.E.15.   Z6566

PEACHEY, H. A., Private, 10th Royal Fusiliers.
He joined in December 1916, and was sent to the Western Front in the following year. During his service overseas he fought at the Battles of Ypres and Arras, and throughout the German Offensive and subsequent Allied Advance of 1918. After the Armistice he was transferred to the Railway Operative Department of the Royal Engineers and did good work engaged on transporting supplies to the Army of Occupation in Germany. He was demobilised in September 1919, and holds the General Service and Victory Medals.
4, Bolton Street, Camberwell, S.E.5.   Z3242B

PEACHEY, W., Private, R.A.S.C.
Volunteering in May 1915, he embarked for France in the same month and was engaged on important duties in the forward areas. He was present at heavy fighting on the Somme and at Roye and rendered valuable services throughout. Returning to England he was demobilised in April 1919, and holds the 1914-15 Star, and the General Service and Victory Medals.
93, Lockington Road, Battersea Park Road, S.W.8.   Z3683

PEACHMENT, A. T., Private, R.A.S.C. and Sapper, R.E. (R.O.D.)
He volunteered in April 1915, and in the following month proceeded to the Western Front, where he was engaged with his unit in various sectors until transferred to the Railway Operative Department of the Royal Engineers. He did very good work on the railways and returned to England after the cessation of hostilities. He was demobilised in March 1919, and holds the 1914-15 Star, and the General Service and Victory Medals.
52, Hornby Road, Peckham, S.E.15.   Z6313

PEARCE, A., Sapper, R.E.
Joining in October 1916, he was drafted overseas in January of the following year. During his service on the Western Front he was engaged with his unit on special duties, fixing telegraph wires and maintaining the lines of communication at Tournai, Ypres, Lille, Cambrai and in various other sectors until hostilities ceased. He was demobilised in October 1919, and holds the General Service and Victory Medals.
170, Fort Road, Bermondsey, S.E.1.   Z26338

PEARCE, A. D., Gunner, R.G.A.
He volunteered in December 1915, and served on important home duties until drafted to France in 1917. Whilst on the Western Front he took part in engagements at Ypres, the Somme, Cambrai, and during the German Offensive and subsequent Allied Advance of 1918. He was demobilised in February 1919, and holds the General Service and Victory Medals.
44, Andulus Road, Landor Road, S.W.9.   Z3680

PEARCE, C., Gunner (Signaller), R.F.A.
He volunteered in April 1915, and in the same year was sent to the Western Front, where he served in various parts of the line and fought in many important engagements, and was wounded on the Somme and later at Cambrai, and also gassed. On recovery he rejoined his Battery and fought in the final operations of the war. He was demobilised in February 1919, and holds the 1914-15 Star, and the General Service and Victory Medals.
2, Kempsford Road, Kennington, S.E.11.   Z27250

PEARCE, C., Private, 20th London Regiment.
He volunteered in November 1915, and in the following year was drafted to France, where he served on the Somme, and at Arras. Later in 1916 he proceeded to Salonika, and engaged in the fighting in the Balkan campaign, was in action on the Vardar and Doiran fronts. He then proceeded to Egypt and took part in the British Advance through Palestine, and was in action at the Battles of Beersheba, the Jordan Valley and Jerusalem. Early in 1918 he returned to France through Italy, and during the Allied Advance of 1918 was severely wounded in October of that year. He was invalided to hospital in England and eventually discharged as medically unfit for further service in March 1919. He holds the General Service and Victory Medals.
85, St. Paul's Road, Walworth, S.E.17.   Z27062

PEARCE, E. A., Rifleman, Royal Irish Rifles.
He joined in May 1916, and in the same year was drafted to the Western Front, where he served in various parts of the line and was in action in the Battles of Arras and Ypres, and was severely wounded. Invalided to hospital in England, he received medical treatment, and on recovery returned to France and fought at Cambrai, and in the Retreat and Advance of 1918. He was demobilised in November 1919, and holds the General Service and Victory Medals.
15, Opal Street, Kennington, S.E.11.   Z27390

PEARCE, E. W. (Miss), Worker, Q.M.A.A.C.
She joined in August 1918, and on completing her training was drafted to Stonor Camp, Richborough, where she served on important duties as a cook to the Royal Engineers. She rendered valuable services, but was unsuccessful in obtaining her transfer overseas, and was demobilised in January 1920.
13, Elmington Road, Camberwell, S.E.5.   Z3677

PEARCE, G. H., Private, 2nd Royal Fusiliers and Air Mechanic, R.A.F.
Volunteering at the outbreak of hostilities, he was drafted to France in November 1915. Whilst on the Western Front he fought in numerous battles, and was three times wounded and gassed. Owing to ill-health he was invalided to hospital in England, and in February 1919 was discharged as medically unfit for further service. He unhappily died on November 14th, 1919, and was entitled to the 1914-15 Star, and the General Service and Victory Medals.
" Steals on the ear the distant triumph song."
43, East Surrey Grove, Peckham, S.E.15.   Z5273A

PEARCE, J., Private, Devonshire Regt. and R.A.S.C.
He joined the Devonshire Regiment, but being medically unfit for service with the Colours he was shortly afterwards discharged. He rejoined, however, early in 1918 and was posted to the R.A.S.C., and at the conclusion of his training was sent to the Western Front, where he was engaged on special duties until severely wounded during the Allied Offensive of 1918. He was evacuated to hospital in England and subsequently invalided out of the Service in December of the same year. He holds the General Service and Victory Medals.
25, Newland Terrace, Queen's Road, Battersea Park, S.W.8.   Z3679A

PEARCE, S., Corporal (Shoeing-Smith), R.F.A.
He volunteered in October 1914, and in the following year was sent to France. In this theatre of war he was engaged in heavy fighting with his Battery at the Battles of Ypres and Loos, and many other engagements. Owing to ill-health he was sent to England, and in April 1916 was invalided out of the Service. He holds the 1914-15 Star, and the General Service and Victory Medals.
3, Adelaide Place, Peckham, S.E.15.   Z6311

PEARCE, V. T., Private, Royal Fusiliers.
He joined in April 1916, and was shortly afterwards drafted overseas. During his service on the Western Front he saw much fighting and was engaged on special duties in various sectors with his Battalion. He was demobilised in August 1919, and holds the General Service and Victory Medals.
14, Kennard Street, Battersea, S.W.11.   Z3682

PEARCE, W., Air Mechanic, R.A.F.
He volunteered in December 1915, and six months later embarked for France. On the Western Front he was employed as a motor driver, transporting stores and aeroplane parts to various aerodromes and depôts. He also served in the same capacity in Italy from December 1917 until the Armistice. He was demobilised in March 1919, and holds the General Service and Victory Medals.
35, Aldbridge Street, Walworth, S.E.17.   Z3681

PEARCE, W. B., R.S.M., 10th Royal Fusiliers.
A Reservist, he was mobilised at the outbreak of hostilities and drafted to France in 1915. Whilst on the Western Front he fought in many battles, including those at Ypres and on the Somme. He gave his life for the freedom of England in August 1916, during the first British Offensive on the Somme, and was entitled to the 1914-15 Star, and the General Service and Victory Medals.
" Nobly striving,
He nobly fell, that we might live."
25, Newland Terrace, Queen's Road, Battersea Park, S.W.8.
Z3679B

PEARCE, W. E., Pte., 10th R.A.S.C., Labour Corps.
Volunteering in April 1915, he embarked for France in the following May, and was engaged with his unit in various sectors of the Western Front, including those of the Somme, Ypres, Passchendaele, Menin Road, Kemmel and Courtrai, and was frequently under shell fire. He was demobilised in February 1919, and holds the 1914-15 Star, and the General Service and Victory Medals.
34, Henshaw Street, Walworth, S.E.17.   Z3678

PEARCE, W. J., Cpl., Royal Fusiliers and R.A.P.C.
He volunteered for service with the Colours in 1914, but was rejected owing to medical unfitness. He later joined the Royal Fusiliers in July 1917, and after his training was transferred to the R.A.P.C., with which unit he proceeded to France. He served on special clerical duties, and was later sent to Italy, and after the Armistice he was drafted to Turkey, where he remained until 1920. He then returned to England and was demobilised in May of that year. He holds the General Service and Victory Medals.
85, Blake's Road, Peckham Grove, S.E.15.   Z6065

PEARL, C. E., Pte. (Signaller), 8th East Surrey Regt.
He volunteered in May 1915, and in June of the following year was sent to France. There he acted as a signaller and fought in numerous engagements until wounded and taken prisoner during the German Offensive in March 1918. He unhappily died from the effects of his wounds in a German Field Hospital on April 12th of that year. He was entitled to the General Service and Victory Medals.
" Whilst we remember the Sacrifice is not in vain."
80, Cator Street, Peckham, S.E.15.   Z4444A

PEARL, H., Pte., 10th Queen's (Royal West Surrey Regiment).

Volunteering in August 1914, he was shortly afterwards sent to France and fought in the Retreat from Mons, and the subsequent Battle of Ypres, and was wounded. He was again wounded at Festubert and invalided to hospital in England. On recovery in 1915, he returned to the Western Front, and during heavy fighting was wounded a third time on March 1st, 1917. He was evacuated to England, but unhappily succumbed to his injuries a week later, and was entitled to the Mons Star, and the General Service and Victory Medals.

"His life for his country, his Soul to God."

80, Cator Street, Peckham, S.E.15. Z4444B

PEARL, W., Private, 23rd London Regiment.

He volunteered in May 1915, and at the conclusion of his training served with his Battalion on important duties until discharged as medically unfit for further service in December 1915. He was then employed on work of National importance in the British Dye Works, Huddersfield, and later in the Rolling Mills, Southampton, and rendered valuable services until January 1919.

36, Amies Street, Battersea, S.W.11. Z3684B

PEARL, W. A., Private, 13th East Surrey Regt.

He volunteered in August 1915, at the age of 16 years, and served on home duties until drafted to Italy in November 1917. He took part in the fighting on the Piave, and in March of the following year proceeded to the Western Front, and was in action during the German Offensive, and was gassed at Ypres. He also fought in the subsequent Allied Advance and served with the Army of Occupation on the Rhine. In March 1919 he returned to England on furlough and shortly afterwards was drafted to Russia with the Relief Force, and took an active part against the Bolshevists. He holds the General Service and Victory Medals, and in 1920 was still serving with the Colours in England.

36, Amies Street, Battersea, S.W.11. Z3684A

PEARL, W. G. E., Pte. (Sig.), 2nd Royal Fusiliers.

He volunteered in March 1915, and was sent to France in July 1917. Whilst on the Western Front he took part in several engagements, including the Battle of Cambrai on November 30th, 1917, when he was reported missing, and later was presumed to have been killed in action on that date. He was entitled to the General Service and Victory Medals.

"Courage, bright hopes, and a myriad dreams, splendidly given."

13, Unwin Road, Peckham, S.E.15. Z6431

PEARMAIN, P., Sergt., 13th London Regiment (Kensingtons) and Rifle Brigade.

He joined in July 1917, and seven months later proceeded to France, where he was in action in many parts of the line and fought in the Battles of Ypres, Le Cateau and many other engagements during the Retreat and Advance of 1918. He returned to England in 1919, and was demobilised in November of that year, but later re-enlisted for a further period of service, and in 1920 was still serving. He holds the General Service and Victory Medals.

175, Lavender Road, Battersea, S.W.11. Z3686

PEARMAN, J. B., Private, M.G.C.

He joined in June 1916, and after completing his training embarked for France in the following year. During his service in this theatre of war he was engaged in the fighting in many notable battles, including those of Bullecourt, Messines Ridge, Passchendaele and Cambrai. He also served during the Retreat and Advance of 1918, and was wounded and gassed twice. He was demobilised in December 1918, and holds the General Service and Victory Medals.

46, Aliwal Road, Battersea, S.W.11. Z3685

PEARSON, A. H., Private, 18th Middlesex Regt.

He volunteered in February 1915, and five months later was drafted overseas. Serving on the Western Front he was in action in the Battles of Loos, Albert, Ploegsteert Wood, Arras, Messines, and was wounded on the Somme and later at Vimy Ridge. He also fought in the Battles of Cambrai, the Somme (II) and Amiens, and was wounded a third time. Admitted to hospital in France, he was afterwards sent to England for medical treatment, and was ultimately invalided out of the Service in November 1918. He holds the 1914-15 Star, and the General Service and Victory Medals.

5, Charleston Street, Walworth, S.E.17. Z3723

PEARSON, E., Private, Durham Light Infantry.

Volunteering in September 1915, and posted to the Royal Army Cyclists Corps he was later transferred to the Durham Light Infantry and sent to France in April 1916. In the course of his service overseas he fought in several engagements until wounded in the Battle of Cambrai in November 1917. He was invalided home and on recovery served with his unit at home, and was demobilised in February 1919. He holds the General Service and Victory Medals.

20, Lewis Road, Camberwell, S.E.5. Z6145,6379/80C

PEARSON, F. E., Air Mechanic, R.A.F.

Joining in August 1918 on attaining military age, he completed his training and served as a motor driver with his Squadron in the Eastern Counties. He did excellent work, but was unable to obtain a transfer overseas before the conclusion of hostilities, owing to physical disability for general service, and was demobilised in January 1919.

12, Wansey Street, Walworth, S.E.17. Z3689

PEARSON, F. J., Air Mechanic, R.A.F. (late R.N.A.S.)

He joined in March 1917, and on completion of his training was engaged on important duties in connection with the manufacture of gas for use overseas. He rendered valuable services, but was not drafted to a theatre of war owing to age and medical unfitness for general service, and was demobilised in February 1919.

54, St. Paul's Road, Walworth, S.E.17. Z27069

PEARSON, S., L/Corporal, R.G.A.

He volunteered in April 1915, and embarked for France four months later. Engaged with the Caterpillar Section he was in action in the Battles of Loos, the Somme, Bullecourt, Messines, Ypres, Cambrai, and during the Retreat and Advance of 1918. He was wounded in the course of operations, and after the Armistice proceeded into Germany with the Army of Occupation, and was stationed at Bonn. Returning to England, he was demobilised in June 1919, and holds the 1914-15 Star, and the General Service and Victory Medals.

16, Elmington Road, Camberwell, S.E.5. Z3690

PEARSON, W., Private, R.A.M.C.

He joined in January 1917, and drafted to the Western Front in the same year served as a stretcher bearer and hospital orderly at Field dressing stations in the Ypres and the Somme sectors until the cessation of hostilities. He did valuable work throughout, and returning home for demobilisation in November 1919, holds the General Service and Victory Medals.

88, Arthur Road, Brixton Road, S.W.9. Z3691

PEART, A. W., Private, 6th Leicestershire Regt.

He joined in October 1916, and was drafted overseas a month later. Serving with his Battalion on the Western Front he was in action in several engagements, including the Battles of Albert and Passchendaele, and was wounded at Armentières in 1918. Rejoining his unit on recovery he fell fighting at Beaumont-Hamel on July 25th, 1918, and was entitled to the General Service and Victory Medals.

"Whilst we remember the Sacrifice is not in vain."

20, Mordaunt Street, Landor Road, S.W.9. Z3692

PEASNELL, F. A. (M.S.M.), Sergt., Royal Marines.

Mobilised in August 1914, he completed his training and served with his unit in the Southern Counties. He acted as Sergeant Instructor, and rendered valuable services in that capacity in the training and instruction of recruits for the New Armies, and was awarded the Meritorious Service Medal for consistently good work. He was unable to secure his transfer overseas before the conclusion of hostilities, and in 1920 was still serving.

8, Wansey Street, Walworth, S.E.17. Z1658D

PEASNELL, F. G., Corporal (Signaller), R.E.

He volunteered in August 1914, and was sent to France in the same month. Serving as a despatch rider he did valuable work in the forward areas and was present at many important battles. He was unfortunately drowned in May 1918, and was entitled to the 1914 Star, and the General Service and Victory Medals.

"A valiant soldier, with undaunted heart he breasted Life's last hill."

8, Wansey Street, Walworth, S.E.17. Z1658B

PEASNELL, S. W., Sergt., 2nd Middlesex Regt.

Mobilised on the outbreak of war he embarked for France shortly afterwards and took part in heavy fighting in the Retreat from Mons, and the Battles of La Bassée, Ypres (I and II), Hill 60, Loos, Albert and Vimy Ridge. He was reported missing in the first Battle of the Somme, and was later presumed to have been killed in action in August 1916. He was entitled to the Mons Star, and the General Service and Victory Medals.

"Great deeds cannot die."

8, Wansey Street, Walworth, S.E.17. Z1658C

PECK, A. E., Rifleman, 12th Royal Irish Rifles.

He volunteered in November 1915, and proceeding overseas in the following October served with his Battalion on the Western Front. He fought in the Somme Offensive, and the Battles of Messines, Ypres, St. Quentin, and in several engagements during the Retreat and Advance of 1918. After the Armistice he was sent into Germany with the Army of Occupation, and was stationed on the Rhine. Returning to England he was demobilised in November 1919, and holds the General Service and Victory Medals.

3, Bullen Street, Battersea, S.W.11. Z3693

PECK, G. F., Private, Suffolk Regiment.

Volunteering in 1915, he was drafted to the Western Front in October of the same year, and served there until after the Armistice. During this period he was in action in the Battles of the Somme, Arras, and in many engagements in the Retreat and Advance of 1918. He returned home for demobilisation in March 1919, and holds the 1914-15 Star, and the General Service and Victory Medals.

3, Bullen Street, Battersea, S.W.11.　　　　Z3694

PECK, W., Private, R.A.S.C. (M.T.)

He volunteered in February 1915, and was sent to France in the same year. Whilst on the Western Front he was engaged on important transport duties in the forward areas, and was present at the Battles of Ypres and Vimy Ridge, and was gassed and wounded. Invalided home in 1917, on recovering he proceeded to Mesopotamia in September of that year, and served in operations resulting in the capture of Baghdad. He returned home on the conclusion of hostilities and was demobilised in August 1919, and holds the 1914-15 Star, and the General Service and Victory Medals.

30, Urswicke Road, Battersea, S.W.11.　　　　Z3695

PEDDER G. E., Seaman, R.N.

He joined in 1917, when eighteen years of age, and posted to H.M.S. "Donegal" served in that vessel throughout the course of hostilities. His ship was engaged in the Mediterranean and Atlantic in convoying transports from America to England, and to the various theatres of war. He holds the General Service and Victory Medals, and was demobilised in 1919.

98, Faraday Street, Walworth, S.E.17.　　　　Z3696

PEDEL, F. T., Private, 8th Lincolnshire Regiment.

He volunteered in November 1915, and in the following year embarked for the Western Front. During his service in this theatre of war he took part in several important engagements, including the Battles of Ypres, and Bourlon Wood, and was twice wounded. Whilst overseas he submitted to an operation for the transfusion of blood to save the life of a comrade. On the cessation of hostilities he returned to England, was discharged on account of service in April 1919, and holds the General Service and Victory Medals.

97, Smith Street, Camberwell, S.E.5.　　　　Z3697

PEGG, C. H., Sergt., R.F.A.

A Territorial, he was mobilised when war broke out and embarked for France in the following year. In the course of his service overseas he was in action in the Battles of Neuve Chapelle, Ypres, Festubert, Loos, Cambrai, and in several other engagements. He was wounded in the second Battle of the Somme and sent to the Canadian General Hospital at Etaples for treatment, and on recovery fought in the Retreat and Advance of 1918. Returning home after the Armistice he was demobilised in February 1919, and holds the 1914-15 Star, and the General Service and Victory Medals.

12, Edithna Street, Landor Road, S.W.9.　　　　Z3698

PEGLER, F. W. C., Rifleman, 21st London Regt. (1st Surrey Rifles).

Volunteering in August 1914, he was drafted to the Western Front in the following year, and served in several engagements in the Arras sector until sent to Salonika in November 1915. He was in action in the Advance on the Doiran and Vardar fronts, and proceeded to Egypt in 1917. Taking part in the Palestine campaign he fought in the Battles of Gaza and Jericho, was present at the fall of Jerusalem, and was wounded at Amman and invalided home. After receiving treatment in the 1st Southern General Hospital, Bristol, he was demobilised in March 1919, and holds the 1914-15 Star, and the General Service and Victory Medals.

34, Brisbane Street, Camberwell, S.E.5.　　　　Z3699

PEGLEY, C. L., 1st Air Mechanic, R.A.F. (late R.F.C.)

He joined in April 1917, and proceeding overseas in the same year in France until the termination of hostilities. During this period he was engaged as an observer with the Balloon Section at Ypres, Armentières, Arras, and other places, and took part in the Advance of 1918. He was also employed on work of a highly technical nature in the workshops of his Squadron. Demobilised in February 1919, he holds the General Service and Victory Medals.

85, St. Paul's Road, Walworth, S.E.17.　　　　Z27068

PELLANT, W. R., Gunner, R.F.A. and Corporal, Military Mounted Police.

Volunteering in August 1914, he was sent to the Western Front in the following November, and served there for nearly five years. He fought with his Battery in the Battles of Neuve Chapelle, Ypres (II and III), Albert, Lens, Bapaume, and the Somme (I and II), and was invalided home owing to illness. Returning to France on recovery he was transferred to the Military Mounted Police, and was engaged on important duties at the Base until evacuated home. Demobilised in June 1919, he holds the 1914 Star, and the General Service and Victory Medals.　43, Charleston Street, Walworth, S.E.17.　Z3700

PELLETT, R., Pte., 9th Royal Warwickshire Regt.

Volunteering in December 1915 he completed his course of training, and in April 1916, was drafted to Mesopotamia where he rendered valuable service in many important engagements until 1918. He then proceeded to Russia and saw much service in various places until the following year. He returned home and was demobilised in July 1919, holding the General Service and Victory Medals.

30, Anchor Street, Rotherhithe, S.E.16.　　　　Z6641

PELLS, C. W., A.B., Royal Navy.

Joining the Royal Navy in August 1912, he was mobilised on the outbreak of war and served throughout the course of hostilities. His ship was in action in the Battle of Jutland, and took part in the bombardment of enemy positions on the Belgian Coast, and was also engaged on special duties in the White Sea. After the Armistice he was employed with a river flotilla on the Rhine until his return to Portsmouth. He holds the 1914-15 Star, and the General Service and Victory Medals, and in 1920 was still serving.

77, St. George's Road, Peckham, S.E.15.　　　　Z5650A

PELLS, T. F., A.B., Royal Navy.

He joined the Royal Navy in August 1912, and was mobilised when war broke out. His ship was engaged on important duties in the North Sea, and other waters and was in action in the Battles of Heligoland Bight and the Falkland Islands and covered operations in the Landing at Suvla Bay. He also served in a submarine for over a year engaged in laying mines off the German Coast. In 1920 he was still serving, and holds the 1914-15 Star, and the General Service and Victory Medals.

77, St. George's Road, Peckham, S.E.15.　　　　Z5650B

PELLUET, E. A., Sergt., 8th Queen's (Royal West Surrey Regiment).

He volunteered in September 1914, and was sent overseas in the following year. In the course of his service on the Western Front he took an active part in the Battles of Loos, Vimy Ridge, Messines, the Somme, Ypres, and was wounded near Cambrai in October 1918. He was demobilised in February 1919, and holds the 1914-15 Star, and the General Service and Victory Medals.

22, Bolingbroke Road, Battersea, S.W.11.　　　　Z3702

PEMBERTON, W. A., Sapper, R.E. (Signal Section).

He joined in 1916, and in the same year embarked for the Western Front, where as a linesman he served on the lines of communication until sent to Italy. In this theatre of war he rendered valuable services as a despatch rider attached to the General Headquarters Staff, and returned home after the Armistice. Demobilised in November 1919, he holds the General Service and Victory Medals.

17, Este Road, Battersea, S.W.11.　　　　Z3703

PENFOLD, J. G., Private, Bedfordshire Regiment.

Joining in 1917, when eighteen years of age, he completed his training and served with his unit at various depôts. He rendered valuable services but was unable to obtain his transfer overseas before the termination of hostilities. He was, however, sent into Germany with the Army of Occupation, and, returning home was demobilised in September 1919.

40, Melon Road, Peckham, S.E.15.　　　　Z6312

PENMAN, A., Private, M.G.C.

He joined in November 1916, and embarked for Egypt in the following June. In the course of his service he was in action in several operations during the British Advance through Palestine, and was wounded in the third Battle of Gaza. He was also present at General Allenby's entry into Jerusalem, and on the conclusion of hostilities was stationed in Egypt for some time. Returning home he was demobilised in January 1920, and holds the General Service and Victory Medals.

62, Neate Street, Camberwell, S.E.5.　　　　Z5129

PENMAN, R. T., Rifleman, Rifle Brigade.

Joining in November 1916, he proceeded to the Western Front shortly afterwards, and was in action during the Somme Offensive, in the course of which he was wounded. Returning to his unit on recovery he fought in the Battles of Arras, Cambrai, and in several important engagements, during the Retreat and Advance of 1918. After the Armistice he was sent into Germany with the Army of Occupation and returning home from Cologne was demobilised in May 1919. He holds the General Service and Victory Medals.

62, Neate Street, Camberwell, S.E.5.　　　　Z5128

PENNELL, F. J. D., Sergt., R.A.V.C.

He volunteered in April 1915, and drafted to the Western Front in the following year was engaged on important duties attending sick and wounded horses. He saw heavy fighting on the Somme and the Ancre, and was severely wounded on April 2nd, 1917. Admitted into hospital he died from his injuries on the succeeding day and was entitled to the 1914-15 Star, and the General Service and Victory Medals.

"Great deeds cannot die:
They with the Sun and Moon renew their light for ever."

6, Lilford Road, Camberwell, S.E.5.　　　　Z6217

PENNELL, A. E., Cpl., Cape Town Highlanders and 11th Queen's (Royal West Surrey Regt.)

He volunteered in October 1914, and served in many engagements in West Africa until July 1915. He was then attached for duty to H.M. Transport "City of Athens" which ship was engaged on convoy duties from India to the United Kingdom. He volunteered on arrival in England and was sent to France in 1916, fought at Armentières, Bapaume, Havrincourt, and was gassed in July 1916, and wounded later at St. Eloi in July 1917. Returning to England, he received hospital treatment, and on recovery proceeded to Italy in January 1917, and was engaged in heavy fighting on the Piave. Returning to France in the following June he was in action at Ypres, and during the Retreat and Advance of 1918, and suffering from shell-shock was invalided to England. He was subsequently discharged unfit for further service in October 1918, and holds the 1914-15 Star, and the General Service and Victory Medals.
7, Stockwell Grove, S.W.9. Z3701

PENNELL, F., Special War Worker.

He offered his services for work of National importance, and from 1915 until 1920, rendered valuable services in connection with the transport of supplies to various training centres in England. For this work he was exempted from military service, and discharged his duties most efficiently.
47, Sunwell Street, Peckham, S.E.15. Z6432

PENNELL, H. T. N., Pte., 5th Wiltshire Regiment.

He volunteered in August 1914, and embarking for the Dardanelles in the following year was in action at the Landing at Suvla Bay, and in the subsequent fighting until the Evacuation of the Peninsula. Proceeding to Mesopotamia in 1916, he fought at the Battles of Sanna-i-Yat and Kut. He was unfortunately killed in action at Baghdad on March 29th, 1917, and was entitled to the 1914-15 Star, and the General Service and Victory Medals.
"A costly sacrifice upon the altar of freedom."
47, St. Lawrence Road, Brixton Road, S.W.9. Z4515

PENNINGTON, H., Sapper, R.E.

Joining in 1917, he completed his training, and served at various stations with his unit engaged on important duties. Owing to ill-health he was unsuccessful in obtaining his transfer overseas, but rendered valuable services until invalided out of the Service in February 1919.
55, Stainforth Road, Battersea, S.W.11. Z3705

PENNINGTON, T., A.B., Royal Navy.

He was mobilised at the commencement of hostilities, and served aboard H.M.S. "Crozier" with the Grand Fleet in the North Sea, Mediterranean Sea, and the Indian Ocean on mine-sweeping and patrol duties, and rendered valuable services throughout. He was demobilised in 1919, and holds the 1914-15 Star, and the General Service and Victory Medals.
10, Reform Street, Battersea, S.W.11. Z3706

PENNY, W. R., Private, R.A.M.C.

He joined in April 1917, and was posted for duty aboard one of H.M. Hospital Ships. He rendered valuable services attending the sick and wounded troops, whilst his ship was engaged on hospital duties from the various theatres of war to the United Kingdom. He was demobilised in September 1919, and holds the General Service and Victory Medals.
22, Graylands Road, Peckham, S.E.15. Z5816

PENSON, F., L/Corporal, R.A.S.C.

He volunteered in 1914, and completing his training served at various depôts engaged on transport and other important duties with his unit. He was unable to obtain his transfer to a theatre of war, but rendered valuable services until demobilised in March 1919.
56, Cambridge Street, Camberwell, S.E.5. Z3707

PENTON, E. J., Gunner, R.G.A.

Volunteering in January 1915, he embarked for the Western Front in the following August, and served with an anti-aircraft Battery at Abbeville. Later he was engaged in heavy fighting at Lens and Arras, and in the German Offensive and Allied Advance of 1918. He was demobilised in January 1919, and holds the 1914-15 Star, and the General Service and Victory Medals.
3, Warriner Gardens, Battersea, S.W.11. Z3708

PEPPER, S. F., Sergt., M.G.C.

Volunteering in November 1915, in the following month he embarked for South Russia, and served on the Caucasus and Galician fronts with the Armoured Car Brigade. Later he was transferred to the Roumanian theatre of war, and was in action in many engagements. In January 1918, he proceeded to Mesopotamia, and there fought throughout the concluding operations of the war. Returning to England in January 1919, he was admitted into hospital and subsequently died on March 13th, 1919, in Grantham Hospital. He was awarded the Cross of St. George of Russia for devotion to duty in the Field, and was entitled to the 1914-15 Star, and the General Service and Victory Medals.
"His memory is cherished with pride."
5, Pemberton Gardens, Upper Holloway, N.19. 5701B

PEPPER, W. W., Bombardier, R.G.A.

He enlisted in 1910, and mobilised at the outbreak of war was sent to France in March 1915. He fought in many important engagements, including those at Ypres, Loos, Albert, Messines, Lens and was wounded at Hill 60, in August 1917. On recovery he rejoined his Battery and was in action throughout the Retreat and Advance of 1918. He was demobilised in March 1919, and holds the 1914-15 Star, and the General Service and Victory Medals.
118, Aylesbury Road, Walworth, S.E.17. Z3709

PEPPERELL, A. (Mrs.), Special War Worker.

This lady offered her services for work of National importance and from 1915 until 1918 held a responsible position at the Park Royal Munition Works, inspecting fuses. She rendered valuable services throughout and received high commendation for the satisfactory manner in which she discharged her duties.
5, Leghorn Road, Harlesden, N.W.10. 12903B

PEPPERELL, F., Corporal, Royal Fusiliers and Seaforth Highlanders.

He volunteered in 1915, and completing his training served at various stations engaged on guard and other important duties. Although he volunteered for active service, he was unsuccessful in obtaining his transfer overseas, but did good work until demobilised in 1919.
5, Leghorn Street, Harlesden, N.W.10. 12903A

PERCIVAL, G., Private, R.A.S.C. (M.T.)

Volunteering in May 1915, at the age of forty-eight, he was drafted to the Western Front later in that year, and served at Rouen and Le Havre on important duties as packer and loader with the lines of communication. Returning home after the cessation of hostilities he was demobilised in April 1919, and holds the 1914-15 Star, and the General Service and Victory Medals.
8, Hillery Road, Walworth, S.E.17. Z3710B

PERCIVAL, G. S., L/Cpl., 12th East Surrey Regt.

He volunteered in June 1915, and embarking for France in the following year, fought at the Battles of Arras, Albert, Passchendaele, St. Quentin, St. Eloi, Vimy Ridge, the Somme, and was wounded by an explosive bullet on the Menin Road. Returning to England, he received medical treatment and was subsequently demobilised in April 1919. Later he joined the Mercantile Marine, and proceeded to Russia, and served at Archangel until 1920. He holds the General Service and Victory Medals.
8, Hillery Road, Walworth, S.E.17. Z3710A

PERKINS, E., Pte., Bedfordshire and Suffolk Regts.

He joined in August 1916, and sent to the Western Front in the following year, was engaged in heavy fighting at Arras, Messines, Ypres, Lens, Cambrai, and throughout the Retreat and Advance of 1918. He was present at the entry into Mons at daybreak on November 11th, 1918. Returning to England, he was demobilised in October 1919, and holds the General Service and Victory Medals.
12, Malmsey Place, Vauxhall Street, S.E.11. Z25242

PERKINS, F. C., Private, Royal Fusiliers.

He volunteered in 1915, and sailed for France in the following year. During his service overseas he fought at the Battles of Ploegsteert Wood, Loos, the Somme, Arras, and in the German Offensive and Allied Advance of 1918. After the Armistice he was sent into Germany with the Army of Occupation, and served there until 1919. He then returned home and was demobilised in February of that year. He holds the General Service and Victory Medals.
44, Bellefields Road, Stockwell, S.W.9. Z3711

PERKINS, F. J., Q.M.S., 1st Oxfordshire and Buckinghamshire Light Infantry.

He volunteered in November 1915, and later in the same year embarked for Mesopotamia, where he fought at Amara and Kut-el-Amara, and in many other engagements of note. He returned to England and was demobilised in January 1919, and holds the 1914-15 Star, and the General Service and Victory Medals.
36, Rosemary Road, Peckham, S.E.15. Z5474

PERKINS, J. J. F., 2nd Lieutenant, R.A.F.

Volunteering in August 1914, in the R.A.M.C., he was sent to France shortly afterwards, and rendered valuable services engaged on important ambulance duties in the front lines. He was present at many important engagements, including those at Ypres, the Somme, Péronne and Arras. He returned to England in September 1918, and completing his training was gazetted in the Royal Air Force as a Flying Officer in January 1919, and demobilised two months later. He holds the 1914 Star, and the General Service and Victory Medals.
134, Farmer's Road, Camberwell, S.E.5. Z3712

PERKINS, R. (M.M.), Private, Black Watch (Royal Highlanders).
He enlisted in December 1904, and was drafted to France at the outbreak of hostilities. He fought in the Retreat from Mons and at the Battles of the Marne, the Aisne, Ypres and the Somme, where he was awarded the Military Medal for conspicuous gallantry and devotion to duty in the Field. Owing to an accident he was invalided to England and discharged unfit for further service in February 1918. He holds the Mons Star, and the General Service and Victory Medals.
25, Peardon Street, Wandsworth Road, S.W.8. Z3713

PERKINS, W. J., Air Mechanic, R.A.F.
Joining in December 1917, he was sent to France in the following year and was engaged on special duties with the R.A.F. transport at St. Omer. Previous to going to France he did excellent work in the repairing shops at various stations, carrying out all his duties with marked efficiency. He was demobilised in December 1919, and holds the General Service and Victory Medals.
68, Neate Street, Camberwell, S.E.5. Z5131

PERMAN, C., Private, R.A.S.C. (M.T.)
Volunteering in August 1914, he was drafted to the Western Front in the following year and served as a fitter in the workshops of his unit. He did valuable work in various sectors of France and Flanders and took part in the Retreat and Advance of 1918. After the Armistice he went with the Army of Occupation into Germany, and was stationed at Cologne. Demobilised in April 1919 on returning home, he holds the 1914–15 Star, and the General Service and Victory Medals.
4, Cheam Place, Camberwell, S.E.5. Z5817

PERRETT, T. H., Shoeing Smith, R.F.A.
He volunteered in November 1914, and in the following August was sent overseas. Serving in France he acted as a Driver, Shoeing Smith and Gunner, and was in action in the Battles of Loos and other engagements. Wounded and gassed at Bullecourt he was invalided home to hospital, and returning to the Western Front on recovery took part in the Retreat and Advance of 1918. He was discharged on account of service in February 1919, and holds the 1914–15 Star, and the General Service and Victory Medals.
181, Abbey Street, Bermondsey, S.E.1. Z27411

PERRIN, A. H. (Miss), Special War Worker.
Offering her services for work of National importance this lady was employed by Messrs. Peek, Frean & Co., Biscuit Manufacturers, from 1915 to November 1918. She acted as a motor driver and assisted in the distribution of food supplies ordered by Government. She also drove motor cars for Army Surgeons in London, and did valuable work throughout.
227, Lynton Road, Bermondsey, S.E.1. Z26357B

PERRIN, C., Rifleman, King's Royal Rifle Corps.
He volunteered in August 1914, and served with his Battalion until his embarkation in 1916 for the Western Front. In the course of his service in this theatre of war he was in action in several engagements and was seriously wounded in the Battle of Ypres on June 24th, 1917, and died in hospital the same night. He was entitled to the General Service and Victory Medals.
" A costly sacrifice upon the altar of freedom."
227, Lynton Road, Bermondsey, S.E.1. Z26356B

PERRIN, G., Special War Worker.
Volunteering for work of National importance he was employed in October 1914, by Messrs. Clarke & Co, Grange Walk, Bermondsey, and served with that firm until March 1919. During this period he was engaged as a leather dresser in connection with the manufacture of belts, pouches, bandoliers, and other equipment for the troops in the Field. He carried out his duties in a thoroughly capable and efficient manner.
3, Avondale Square, Old Kent Road, S.E.1. Z27201

PERRIN, H., Private, 2nd London Regiment (Royal Fusiliers).
He volunteered in October 1915, and proceeding overseas in the following April served in various sectors of the Western Front. He took part in heavy fighting and was wounded in September 1916, and sent to hospital. Rejoining his unit on recovery he was unfortunately killed in action on May 5th, 1917, near Cambrai, and was entitled to the General Service and Victory Medals.
" He died the noblest death a man may die,
Fighting for God, and right, and liberty."
227, Lynton Road, Bermondsey, S.E.1. Z26356A

PERRIN, S. E. H., Stoker, R.N.
He volunteered in May 1915, and posted to H.M.S. "Latona" served in that vessel throughout the war. During this period his ship was engaged in mine-laying and mine-sweeping duties in the Dardanelles, the Mediterranean, and off the Coasts of Italy and Greece. She had several encounters with enemy vessels in the course of her dangerous duties, and was frequently bombed by aircraft. He was demobilised in June 1919, and holds the 1914–15 Star, and the General Service and Victory Medals.
227, Lynton Road, Bermondsey, S.E.1. Z26357A

PERRING, H., Gunner, R.F.A.
He volunteered in August 1914, and in the following October was drafted overseas. Serving with his Battery in various sectors of the Western Front he was in action in several engagements, including the Battles of Ypres, Arras, and the Somme. On the conclusion of hostilities, he returned to England for demobilisation in March 1919, and holds the 1914 Star, and the General Service and Victory Medals.
24, Barsett Road, Peckham, S.E.15. Z6534

PERROTT, R., Corporal, 3rd Essex Regiment and Yorkshire Regiment.
Volunteering in September 1914, at the age of forty-six, he completed his training and was engaged with his unit on important defence duties on the East Coast until 1918. He was then sent to France and served on guard and other duties at prisoners of war camps for a year. Returning home he was demobilised in January 1919, and holds the General Service and Victory Medals. He had served with the Colours for nearly ten years prior to the war.
1, Hook's Road, Peckham, S.E.15. Z6536A

PERROTT, R. T. (Jun.), Pte., Royal Fusiliers and 25th King's (Liverpool Regiment).
He joined in April 1917, on attaining military age, and embarked for the Western Front in the same year. He took part in heavy fighting in the Ypres salient, in the Battle of the Somme, and in the Retreat and Advance of 1918, and was gassed near Cambrai. Returning to England after the Armistice, he was demobilised in February 1919, and holds the General Service and Victory Medals.
1, Hooks Road, Peckham, S.E.15. Z6536B

PERRY, A., Private, 24th Royal Fusiliers.
A Territorial, he was mobilised when war broke out and proceeded to France in November 1915. In the course of his service overseas, he was in action in several important engagements, including the Battles of the Somme, Arras, Ypres, Vimy Ridge, Péronne and Cambrai, and entered Mons the day the Armistice was signed. He was demobilised in March 1919, and holds the 1914–15 Star, and the General Service and Victory Medals.
10, Bonnington Square, South Lambeth Road, S.W.8. Z3718

PERRY, A. D., C.Q.M.S., 24th London Regt. (The Queen's).
Mobilised in August 1914, he was drafted to France in the following March and fought in the Battles of Neuve Chapelle and Festubert, and was wounded on May 25th, 1915, at Givenchy. Returning to the firing line after treatment at the Base Hospital he was in action in the Battle of Loos, and was invalided home owing to ill-health, in January 1916. On recovery he served as an Instructor at home until his return to the Western Front in July 1918. He was demobilised in February 1919, and holds the 1914–15 Star, and the General Service and Victory Medals.
1, Dowlas Street, Camberwell, S.E.5. Z4516

PERRY, A. E., Private, Shropshire Light Infantry.
A Regular soldier, having enlisted in 1907, he was mobilised on the declaration of war, and drafted to France later in 1914. Whilst overseas he served in the Ypres, Arras and Somme sectors and fought in many notable engagements. He gave his life for King and Country in the Battle of the Somme on July 14th, 1916, and was entitled to the 1914 Star, and the General Service and Victory Medals.
" Steals on the ear the distant triumph song."
45, Edithna Street, Landor Road, S.W.9. Z3715

PERRY, C. A., L/Corporal, 10th Royal Fusiliers.
He joined in April 1917, and in the following December embarked for France. In this theatre of war he took part in several engagements, including those during the Retreat and Advance of 1918, and was wounded at Bucquoy. Sent to hospital at Rouen he returned to his Battalion on recovery and served until the end of hostilities. He holds the General Service and Victory Medals, and was demobilised in February 1919.
52, Broughton Street, Battersea Park, S.W.8. Z3719

PERRY, C. H., Pte., Queen's (Royal West Surrey Regiment).
Joining in March 1917, he was sent overseas in the same year, and saw much service on the Western Front. Amongst other engagements he was in action at the Battle of Arras and Bullecourt, and was severely wounded in a mine explosion in the vicinity of Hill 60. He was admitted to hospital at Etaples, and later evacuated to England, where he was discharged as medically unfit for further service in June 1918. He holds the General Service and Victory Medals.
81, Hargwyne Street, Stockwell, Road S.W.9. Z3716

PERRY, E., Stoker, R.N.
He was serving in H.M.S. "Cheerful" when war broke out, having joined the Royal Navy in November 1911, and did good work throughout the war. His ship was attached to the Grand Fleet, and engaged on important duties in the North Sea and the English Channel. He also served aboard H.M.S. "Doon," "Matchless" and "Courageous" and in 1920 was transferred to H.M.S. "St. Vincent" attached to the Reserve Fleet at Rosyth. He holds the 1914-15 Star, and the General Service and Victory Medals.
5, Bolney Street, Dorset Road, S.W.8.   Z3717

PERRY, F. S., Sergt., Royal Welch Fusiliers.
A serving soldier, having enlisted in September 1910, he was drafted to Gallipoli in 1915, and took part in several operations until the Evacuation of the Peninsula. He was then sent to Gibraltar, where he was engaged on guard and other important duties, and was mentioned in Despatches on August 22nd, 1919, for consistently good work. Demobilised in November 1919, he holds the 1914-15 Star, and the General Service and Victory Medals.
25, Dorchester Grove, Chiswick, W.4.   5379A

PERRY, G., Pte., Queen's (Royal West Surrey Regt.)
Volunteering in 1915, he was drafted overseas in the following year and served on the Western Front until hostilities ceased. He was in action in several engagements in the Ypres salient, and the Battles of Arras, and was wounded in March 1918, during the German Offensive. On recovery he rejoined his Battalion and took part in operations during the concluding stages of the war. He was demobilised in 1919, and holds the General Service and Victory Medals.
59, Bournemouth Road, Rye Lane, S.E.15.   Z5818

PERRY, G., Pte., 1/24th London Regiment (The Queen's).
He volunteered in 1914, and embarked for France in the same year. In the course of his service he fought with his Battalion in many parts of the line, and was wounded and gassed. Owing to his injuries he was sent to hospital in England and after treatment was discharged as medically unfit for further service in 1916. He holds the 1914-15 Star, and the General Service and Victory Medals.
15, Gayville Road, Wandsworth Common, S.W.11.   1793A

PERRY, G. A., Private, 2/4th Lincolnshire Regt.
He joined in March 1917, and four months later proceeded to the Western Front, where he was engaged in heavy fighting in the Battles of Ypres, Passchendaele and Lens. He fell fighting near Albert in October 1917, and was entitled to the General Service and Victory Medals.
"Thinking that remembrance, though unspoken, may reach him where he sleeps."
157, Albert Road, Peckham, S.E.15.   Z5819

PERRY, G. H., Gunner, R.F.A.
Mobilised from the Army Reserve on the outbreak of war he embarked for France with the Original Expeditionary Force, and was in action during the Retreat from Mons. He also fought in the Battles of the Aisne, Ypres, Loos, Arras and the Somme, and in several engagements during the German Offensive, and the subsequent Allied Advance of 1918. After the signing of the Armistice he served at Cologne with the Army of Occupation. He was demobilised in 1919, on his return home, and holds the Mons Star, and the General Service and Victory Medals.
45, Mundella Road, Wandsworth Road, S.W.8.   Z3714

PERRY, G. J., A.B., Royal Navy.
He was serving in the Royal Navy at the outbreak of war in H.M.S. "Achilles." Attached to the Grand Fleet his ship was engaged on important duties in the North Sea. He also served in H.M. Torpedo Boat Destroyer, No. 8, engaged in submarine patrol work, and in conveying troopships and merchant vessels across the Atlantic. In the course of his duties he was wounded by shrapnel in a minor engagement with enemy craft. He holds the 1914-15 Star, and the General Service and Victory Medals, and in 1920 was still serving.
21, Moat Place, Stockwell Road, S.W.9.   Z3720

PERRY, H. J., Pte., 7th Somerset Light Infantry.
He volunteered in December 1914, and after the completion of his training crossed to France early in 1915. He took part in the Battles of Ypres, Festubert, Loos, Vermelles, Vimy Ridge, Arras, Bullecourt, Messines and Cambrai, and was badly wounded and taken prisoner on the Somme in March 1918. He was kept in captivity until the Armistice, and after his return home was demobilised in January 1919. He holds the 1914-15 Star, and the General Service and Victory Medals. 43, Daniel's Road, Peckham, S.E.15.   Z6606

PERRY, H., Guardsman, Coldstream Guards.
He joined in May 1918, and on the conclusion of his training was engaged on important duties with his unit in the Southern Counties. He rendered valuable services, but was unsuccessful in obtaining his transfer to a theatre of war before hostilities ceased, and was demobilised in January 1919.
60H, New Kent Road, S.E.1.   26127

PERRY, J. J., Rifleman, 12th King's Royal Rifle Corps and L/Corporal, Labour Corps.
He volunteered in December 1915, and was drafted to France in September 1916. In the course of the Somme Offensive he was seriously wounded at High Wood, his injuries resulting in the loss of the use of his left arm, and he was discharged as physically unfit for service in May 1917. Rejoining, however, in April 1918, he was posted to the Labour Corps, and was engaged on important duties in Devonshire until demobilised in July 1920. He holds the General Service and Victory Medals.
165, Bird-in-Bush Road, Peckham, S.E.15.   Z6537

PERRY, S., 1st Class Stoker, R.N.
Joining in May 1915, he was posted to H.M.S. "Himalaya," and transferred to H.M.S. "Malaya" in January 1916. His ship was engaged on important patrol duties in the North Sea and attached to the fifth Battle Squadron, was in action in the Battle of Jutland. She was also employed on coast defence duties, and in escorting troopships and merchant vessels to and from Canada and Australia, and landed troops in Ireland at the time of the rebellion. He was still serving in 1920, and was sent to the West Indies in October of that year. He holds the 1914-15 Star, and the General Service and Victory Medals.
67, D'Eynsford Road, Camberwell Green, S.E.5.   Z3722

PESTELL, A. P., Sapper, R.E.
He joined in 1916, and at the conclusion of his training served on important duties at various stations with his unit. Owing to medical unfitness he was unable to secure his transfer overseas, but did good work until discharged from the Service in October 1917.
17, Earl Road, Upper Grange Road, S.E.1.   Z26843B

PESTELL, C. G., Driver, R.F.A.
He volunteered in March 1915, and in the same year proceeded to the Western Front. Whilst in this theatre of war he took part in the fighting in numerous battles, and was three times wounded. He gave his life for King and Country at the Battle of Ypres on November 1st, 1917, and was entitled to the 1914-15 Star, and the General Service and Victory Medals.
"And doubtless he went in splendid company."
17, Earl Road, Upper Grange Road, S.E.1.   Z26843A

PETERS, A. E., Private, 2nd Royal Fusiliers.
He joined in May 1917, and in the following September proceeded to France. In this theatre of war he took part in the fighting in the Ypres sector, and in the following month was reported missing, and was later presumed to have been killed in action on October 26th, 1917. He was entitled to the General Service and Victory Medals.
"His life for his country, his Soul to God."
31, Newcomen Road, Battersea, S.W.11.   Z3725B

PETERS, E. J., Pte., 1st West Yorkshire Regiment.
Joining in February 1917, he proceeded to France in January 1918. Whilst on the Western Front he took part in various engagements during the German Offensive, and unhappily fell fighting on March 21st of that year, having previously been reported as missing. He was entitled to the General Service and Victory Medals.
"A valiant soldier, with undaunted heart he breasted Life's last hill."
165, Beresford Street, Camberwell Road, S.E.5.   Z3726B

PETERS, E. P., L/Corporal, R.A.S.C. (M.T.)
He joined in June 1917, and in the following January was drafted to France. In this theatre of war he served with his unit on important duties, conveying ammunition and supplies to the front line trenches during the German Offensive and subsequent Allied Advance of 1918. He was demobilised in January 1919, and holds the General Service and Victory Medals.
165, Beresford Street, Camberwell Road, S.E.5.   Z3726A

PETERS, F. T., Private, 13th East Surrey Regt.
He volunteered in August 1915, and in the following June was sent overseas. Whilst on the Western Front he fought in many engagements, including those on the Somme, at Arras, Ypres and Cambrai, and was severely gassed in December 1917. Invalided to England, he received medical treatment, and after recovery served on home duties until demobilised in March 1919. He holds the General Service and Victory Medals.
31, Newcomen Road, Battersea, S.W.11.   Z3725C

PETHERICK, E. J. (Mrs.), Special War Worker.
During the war this lady offered her services, and for a period of three years was engaged in the Camberwell Canteen of the Y.M.C.A., where she did very good work, and was awarded the Order of the Red Triangle, and also the London District Badge. She rendered very valuable services throughout.
8, Clayton Road, Peckham, S.E.15.   Z6213

PETITE, H. J., L/Corporal, 13th East Surrey Regt.
He volunteered in January 1916, and in the following year proceeded overseas, having previously done good work as a Drill Instructor after his training. Whilst on the Western Front he fought in many battles, and was wounded at Arras in 1917, again on the Somme early in 1918, and for the third time on the Marne in March 1918, when he was taken prisoner. He was held captive at Altengrabow Camp in Germany until repatriated in February 1919. He was demobilised in the following month, and holds the General Service and Victory Medals.
12, Nursery Street, Wandsworth Road, S.W.8. Z3727

PETRY, C. H., Rifleman, 6th London Regiment (Rifles) and Sapper, R.E.
He joined in July 1917, and after his training was engaged with his unit on important duties at many stations. He did very good work, but owing to medical unfitness was unable to secure his transfer overseas, and was demobilised in 1919.
49, East Lane, Rotherhithe, S.E.16. Z27434

PETTIFOR, W., Sergt., R.A.S.C.
He volunteered in September 1914, and served on home duties until drafted to Egypt in 1917. He was engaged with his unit on special duties, doing work during the British Advance through Palestine, and was present at many engagements, including those resulting in the fall of Jerusalem. He was demobilised in 1919, and holds the General Service and Victory Medals. 102, Barlow Street, Walworth, S.E.17. Z3728

PETTIT, F., Rifleman, Rifle Brigade.
He volunteered in August 1914, and was almost immediately drafted to the Western Front, where he fought in the Retreat from Mons and the subsequent Battles of the Marne, La Bassée, Ypres, and was wounded at Hill 60, in April 1915. He was sent to the Base Hospital, and after recovery rejoined his unit in the fighting line, and was in action at Loos, Vimy Ridge, the Somme, Arras and Ypres. He was demobilised in March 1919, and holds the Mons Star, and the General Service and Victory Medals.
28, Lothian Road, Camberwell New Road, S.W.9. Z5132

PETTIT, F., Driver, R.A.S.C. (M.T.)
He volunteered in December 1914, and in the following year was sent to France. In this theatre of war he was engaged with his unit during the heavy fighting, and at the Battles of the Somme, Ypres, Loos, Neuve Chapelle, St. Quentin, St. Eloi, and Béthune. He later proceeded to Salonika and served on the Struma, Vardar and Doiran fronts. He returned to England after the cessation of hostilities and was demobilised in July 1919, and holds the 1914-15 Star, and the General Service and Victory Medals.
78, Sussex Road, Coldharbour Lane, S.W.9. Z3724

PETTIT, G. J., Private, R.A.S.C.
Volunteering in March 1915, he was almost immediately sent to France. During his service in this theatre of war he was engaged with his unit on important duties in the Ypres, Loos, Vimy Ridge, the Somme, Arras, Passchendaele and Cambrai sectors until the end of the war. He was demobilised in February 1919, and holds the 1914-15 Star, and the General Service and Victory Medals.
130, Aylesbury Road, Walworth, S.E.17. Z1754A

PETTIT, W., Cpl., Cameronians (Scottish Rifles).
Volunteering in January 1915, he was drafted to France in the following October after the completion of his training. He did gallant service in many important engagements until the cessation of hostilities, including those at the Somme, Armentières, Ypres and Passchendaele, and was twice wounded, first on the Somme, and afterwards at Ypres. After this return to England he was demobilised in March 1919, and holds the 1914-15 Star, and the General Service and Victory Medals. 135, Galleywall Road, Rotherhithe, S.E.16. Z6642

PETTITT, S. A., L/Corporal, M.G.C.
He was mobilised at the outbreak of hostilities, and sent to the Dardanelles in April 1915, fought at the first Landing, and in many other engagements until the Evacuation of the Peninsula. He then proceeded to Egypt, and after serving a short time at Alexandria was drafted to the Western Front, where he took part in the fighting on the Somme in 1916, and was wounded. He later returned to the firing line, and was in action during the German Offensive, and subsequent Allied Advance of 1918. He was discharged in December 1918 on account of service, and holds the 1914-15 Star, and the General Service and Victory Medals.
2, Sterndale Road, Wandsworth Road, S.W.8. Z3729

PETTITT, W., Private, York and Lancaster Regt.
Serving in India at the outbreak of hostilities, having enlisted in 1907, he was mobilised and drafted to France in August 1914. During his service in this theatre of war he took part in many engagements on the Somme, and was in action during the German Offensive and subsequent Allied Advance of 1918. He was demobilised in June 1919, and holds the 1914-15 Star, and the General Service and Victory Medals.
18, Hurlbutt Place, Walworth, S.E.17. Z26028

PETTS, G. Q., Private, Buffs (East Kent Regt.)
He volunteered in December 1914, and served on home duties until sent to France in 1916. He was in action at Guillemont, Ypres, and Vimy Ridge, and owing to ill-health was invalided to hospital in England. On recovery he returned to the front line trenches, and fought in the Retreat and Advance of 1918, and was wounded. He was demobilised in February 1919, and holds the General Service and Victory Medals.
14, Methley Street, Kennington, S.E.11. Z26604

PEVERITT, B. W., Musician, Royal Navy.
He joined in October 1899, and at the outbreak of hostilities was serving aboard H.M.S. "Centurion," which ship was engaged on important patrol duties in the North Sea, and took part in the fighting during the Battle of Jutland. He holds, in addition to the 1914-15 Star, and the General Service Medals, the Messina Earthquake Medal, and was demobilised in April 1919.
51, Kingswood Road, Chiswick, W.4. T6794A

PHELPS, W., Private, 3rd East Surrey Regiment.
He volunteered in August 1914, and in the following January was drafted to France. Whilst overseas he fought in the Battle of Neuve Chapelle, and at Loos, where he was very severely wounded. He was invalided home to hospital, and after six months' medical treatment was discharged as physically unfit for further service in December 1915. He holds the 1914-15 Star, and the General Service and Victory Medals.
32, Chumleigh Street, Camberwell, S.E.5. Z5133

PHELPS, W., Private, Queen's Own (Royal West Kent Regiment).
He was mobilised at the outbreak of war, and in the following month was drafted to France, and whilst overseas fought in many engagements, including the Battle of the Somme. He fell fighting at Messines in July 1916, and was entitled to the 1914 Star, and the General Service and Victory Medals.
"He died the noblest death a man may die,
Fighting for God, and right, and liberty."
6, Albion House, Amelia Street, Walworth, S.E.17. Z26131

PHELPS, W. A., Pte., 2nd Royal Warwickshire Regt.
He joined in June 1917, at the age of eighteen years, and after his training was drafted to France in the following May. After only five weeks' service on the Western Front he was unhappily killed in action in June 1918. He was entitled to the General Service and Victory Medals.
"Honour to the immortal dead, who gave their youth that the world might grow old in peace."
41, Sandover Road, Camberwell, S.E.5. Z5475

PHELPS, W. H., Private, East Surrey Regiment.
He volunteered in 1914, and after his training served at various stations on important duties until 1917, when he was drafted to France. Whilst overseas he fought at Arras, Ypres, Passchendaele, Lens and Cambrai, and was severely wounded in action. He was recommended for the Military Medal for his gallant attempts to rescue the fallen under heavy shellfire. He holds the General Service and Victory Medals, and was demobilised in January 1919.
77, Ferndale Road, Clapham, S.W.4. Z3730A

PHILBEY, G., Sergt., 19th London Regiment.
He volunteered in September 1914, and after his training was drafted to France, where he fought in various important engagements, including those at Givenchy, Festubert, and Loos, in which battle he was severely gassed. He was invalided home to hospital, and after his recovery was retained on important instructional duties in England until his demobilisation in February 1919. He holds the 1914 Star, and the General Service and Victory Medals.
23, Gladstone Street, Battersea Park Road, S.W.8. Z3731

PHILCOX, F., Driver, R.F.A.
He volunteered in March 1915, and in June of the same year was drafted to France. During his service on the Western Front he did good work as a driver at Loos, Albert, the Somme, Arras, Vimy Ridge, Messines, Ypres, Lens and Cambrai, and in many subsequent engagements in the Retreat and Advance of 1918. He was demobilised in December 1919, and holds the 1914-15 Star, and the General Service and Victory Medals.
22, Madron Street, Walworth, S.E.17. Z3657B

PHILLIMORE, A. H., Private, Royal Defence Corps.
He volunteered in April 1915, having previously served several years with the Colours in the Hampshire Regiment. He did excellent work at various stations on important duties with his unit, and was demobilised after nearly four years' service in February 1919.
75, Dashwood Road, Wandsworth Road, S.W.8. Z3732B

PHILLIMORE, H. D., Gunner, R.F.A.

He joined in November 1917, on attaining military age, and in June of the following year was drafted to France. During his service overseas he was in action in the Cambrai sector for three months, and was severely wounded in September 1918. He was invalided home to hospital and subsequently discharged through wounds, in February 1919. He holds the General Service and Victory Medals.

75, Dashwood Road, Wandsworth, Road, S.W.8. Z3732A

PHILLIPS, A., Private, Royal Fusiliers.

He volunteered in November 1914, and after his training proceeded to France in the following year. Whilst overseas he fought in various engagements, and was then claimed out as under military age. Later he rejoined and was again sent to the Western Front, and was severely wounded at Ypres, and invalided home to hospital. In 1920 he was still under medical treatment at Tooting Military Hospital, and holds the 1914-15 Star, and the General Service and Victory Medals.

2, Stanley Villas, Gonsova Road, Wandsworth Road, S.W.8. Z3738A

PHILLIPS, A., Sergt., R.F.A.

He volunteered in June 1915, and in the following March was drafted to the Western Front. There he took part in many engagements in the Somme, Arras and Ypres sectors. He was wounded in the Battle of the Somme, and sent home to hospital, rejoining his unit in France after about three months. In March 1918 he was again severely wounded during the German Offensive, and was invalided to hospital in Scotland, whence he was discharged as medically unfit for further military duty in May 1918. He holds the General Service and Victory Medals.

27, Scylla Road, Peckham, S.E.15. Z6050

PHILLIPS, A. F., Gunner, R.F.A.

A serving soldier since 1912, he was drafted first to India and later to Mesopotamia, where he did good work as a gunner in various engagements, including that of Kut-el-Amara. He was taken prisoner with General Townshend's Forces at Kut, and subsequently died of dysentery whilst in captivity. He was entitled to the 1914-15 Star, and the General Service and Victory Medals.

"Thinking that remembrance though unspoken may reach him where he sleeps."

9, Ruskin Street, Wandsworth Road, S.W.8. Z3740

PHILLIPS, D., Cpl., 24th London Regiment (The Queen's) and Royal Defence Corps.

He volunteered in April 1915, and in the following year served on important escort duties conducting German prisoners from France to England. He was also employed with the Military Police at various places, and was stationed in the Isle of Man and Wales. He was demobilised in April 1919, and holds the General Service and Victory Medals.

38, Arthur Road, Brixton Road, S.W.9. Z3733

PHILLIPS, E., Private, 1st East Surrey Regiment.

He was mobilised at the outbreak of war, and was almost immediately drafted to France, where he took part in the memorable Retreat from Mons and in the Battles of the Marne, the Aisne, Neuve Chapelle, Ypres, Festubert and Loos. He was wounded on the Somme in 1916, and after his recovery rejoined his unit. Finally, he fell fighting in the fierce encounter at Arras on March 23rd, 1917, and was entitled to the Mons Star, and the General Service and Victory Medals.

"A valiant soldier, with undaunted heart he breasted Life's last hill."

73, Battersea Bridge Road, Battersea, S.W.11. Z3737A

PHILLIPS, E. A., Private, R.A.M.C.

He volunteered in 1915, and after his training saw much varied service. He was engaged on important duties attending to the wounded on several hospital ships and voyaged to India and Egypt from France. On two occasions the vessels in which he was serving were torpedoed, but fortunately he was rescued. He was demobilised in August 1919, and holds the General Service and Victory Medals.

33, Oakden Street, Kennington, S.E.11. Z27373

PHILLIPS, F., Corporal, South Wales Borderers.

A serving soldier since August 1912, he was sent to France at the outbreak of war, and took part in the Retreat from Mons. He was taken prisoner at Langemarck, and was held in captivity in Germany for over four years. He was released and repatriated after the Armistice, and was demobilised in September 1919. He holds the Mons Star, and the General Service and Victory Medals.

2, Stanley Villas, Gonsova Road, Wandsworth Road, S.W.8. Z3738C

PHILLIPS, G. (M.M.), Private, 13th London Regt. (Kensingtons).

He joined in October 1917, and in the following February was drafted to France, where he fought in many important engagements, including those at Oppy Wood, Croiselles, and Bullecourt. After the Armistice he proceeded to Germany with the Army of Occupation, with which he served until demobilised in October 1919. He was awarded the Military Medal for distinguished gallantry and devotion to duty in the Field, and in addition, holds the General Service and Victory Medals.

10, Luscombe Street, South Lambeth, S.W.8. Z27510

PHILLIPS, G., Gunner, R.F.A.

He was mobilised in August 1914, and was almost immediately drafted to France, where he took part in the Retreat from Mons. He also was in action on the Marne and the Aisne, and at Ypres, Loos, Albert, Arras and Cambrai, and in many subsequent engagements in the Retreat and Advance of 1918. He was demobilised in January 1919, and holds the Mons Star, and the General Service and Victory Medals. Z3738B

2, Stanley Villas, Gonsalva Road, Wandsworth Road, S.W.8.

PHILLIPS, J., Trooper, 2nd Dragoon Guards (Queen's Bays).

He volunteered in August 1914, and in the following year proceeded to France, where he saw much service, and was in action at Loos, Ypres, Cambrai, and in many engagements in the Retreat and Advance of 1918. He was demobilised in January of the following year, and holds the 1914-15 Star, and the General Service and Victory Medals.

2, Stanley Villas, Gonsalva Road, Wandsworth Road, S.W.8. Z3738D

PHILLIPS, J., Private, Labour Corps.

He had previously served for fifteen and a half years in the Army, having fought throughout the South African campaign, and prior to rejoining was engaged on munition work, until re-enlisting in March 1919. He was drafted to France in the same year, and was employed on important exhumation duties until February 1920, when he was demobilised. He holds the Queen's and King's South African Medals.

22, Bognor Street, Battersea Park Road, S.W.8. Z3736A

PHILLIPS, J. H., Private, Hampshire Regiment.

He volunteered in August 1914, and in the following December was drafted overseas. During his service in France he fought at Neuve Chapelle, Loos, Bayonne, Albert, the Somme, and Arras and in various minor engagements. He was seriously injured in an accident with a gun carriage, and was discharged as physically unfit for further duty in August 1917, after exactly three years with the Colours. He holds the 1914 Star, and the General Service and Victory Medals.

22, Bognor Street, Battersea, S.W.8. Z3736B

PHILLIPS, J. W., Driver, R.F.A.

He volunteered in November 1914, and in June of the following year was sent to France, where he served for nearly four years. He was in action at Loos, the Somme, Arras and Ypres, and in many engagements in the Retreat and Advance of 1918, and did excellent work as a driver throughout this period. He was demobilised in February of the ensuing year, and holds the 1914-15 Star, and the General Service and Victory Medals.

156, Rolls Road, Bermondsey, S.E.1. Z26750A

PHILLIPS, W., Driver, R.F.A.

He volunteered in August 1914, and was almost immediately drafted to France, where he served in the Retreat from Mons. He was subsequently engaged at Ypres, and in other important battles, and was afterwards invalided home with severe shell-shock. In March 1916 he was discharged as medically unfit for further duty, and holds the Mons Star, and the General Service and Victory Medals.

16, Landseer Street, Battersea, S.W.11. Z3735A

PHILLIPS, W. F., Private, 1st Duke of Cornwall's Light Infantry.

He had previously enlisted in 1913, and at the outbreak of war was immediately drafted to France. After only a few weeks overseas he died gloriously on the Field of Battle in the Retreat from Mons. He was entitled to the Mons Star, and the General Service and Victory Medals.

"He passed out of the sight of men by the path of duty and self sacrifice."

16, Landseer Street, Battersea, S.W.11. Z3735B

PHILLIPS, W. H., Sergt., Rifle Brigade.

He was mobilised at the outbreak of war, and was almost immediately drafted to France, where he was in action in the Retreat from Mons, and also on the Marne, at La Bassée, Ypres and Loos. In 1916 he was severely wounded and invalided home and discharged as medically unfit for further duty. However, he re-enlisted later, and was finally demobilised in July 1920. He holds the Mons Star, and the General Service and Victory Medals.

39, Orb Street, Walworth, S.E.17. Z3739

PHILLIPS, W. J. V., Pioneer, R.E.
He volunteered in April 1915, in the Middlesex Regiment, and three months later was discharged as medically unfit, owing to defective eyesight. He re-enlisted, however, in the Royal Engineers in January 1917, and was drafted to France in the following month. Whilst overseas he was engaged on important duties in connection with the operations, but in the Summer of 1918 was invalided to hospital in Scotland, owing to ill-health. After four months' medical treatment he was discharged in December 1918. He holds the General Service and Victory Medals.
13, Earl Road, Bermondsey, S.E.1.   Z26841

PHILPOTT, H., Private, Sherwood Foresters.
He joined in September 1916, and in February of the following year was sent to France, where he took part in numerous engagements, including those at Ypres, and Cambrai, and was wounded. He also served in the Retreat and Advance of 1918. He was demobilised in January 1919, and holds the General Service and Victory Medals.
31, Greylands Road, Peckham, S.E.15.   Z5813

PHILPOTT, J., C.P.O., R.N., H.M.S. "Champion."
He volunteered in August 1914, and served with the Grand Fleet in the North Sea, and took part in the Battle of Jutland and in many other engagements. He was demobilised in 1920, and holds the 1914-15 Star, and the General Service and Victory Medals.
31, Chantrey Road, Stockwell Road, S.W.9.   Z3741

PHINBOW, F. W., Rifleman, Rifle Brigade.
He joined in 1916, and was sent to France in the following year, and was in action on the Somme and at Ypres, and took part in the Retreat and Advance of 1918. He returned home in 1919, and was demobilised, holding the General Service and Victory Medals.
9, Heaton Road, Peckham, S.E.15.   Z6064

PHIPPS, C., Gunner, R.H.A.
Joining in 1916, he was sent to France in the following year, and took part in numerous engagements, including those at Messines, Ypres, Lens, St. Quentin, Passchendaele, Cambrai and the Somme. He later proceeded with the Army of Occupation to Germany, where he served until demobilised in 1919. He holds the General Service and Victory Medals.
196, Mayall Road, Herne Hill, S.E.24.   Z3742

PHIPPS, H. T., Private, 15th Middlesex Regiment and 4th East Surrey Regiment.
He joined in May 1916, and served on important duties at various stations with his unit. He was later transferred to the 4th East Surrey Regiment. and rendered valuable service until demobilised in 1919. Owing to being physically unfit for active service he was unable to obtain his transfer abroad.
1, Elizabeth Street, Walworth, S.E.17.   Z26473

PICKARD, G., Gunner, R.F.A.
He volunteered in June 1915, and in the following year was sent to France, where he took part in numerous engagements, including those on the Somme, and at Passchendaele, and was twice wounded. In 1917 he was transferred to Italy, and was in action on the Piave. He served in the campaign against the Austrians until the cessation of hostilities, after which he returned home and was demobilised in February 1919. He holds the General Service and Victory Medals.
99, Thorpach Road, Wandsworth Road, S.W.8.   Z3743

PICKBURN, J. W., Rifleman, Rifle Brigade.
He was serving at the outbreak of war, and in the same year was drafted to the Western Front, where he took part in numerous engagements, including those at Albert, Ypres, Vimy Ridge, Arras, Poperinghe, Béthune and Bapaume. He was also in action in the Retreat and Advance of 1918, and was wounded. He was demobilised in February 1919, but has since re-enlisted, and in 1920 was still serving in the Royal Fusiliers, in France. He holds the 1914 Star, and the General Service and Victory Medals.
21, Loughboro Street, Kennington, S.E.11.   TZ25494A

PICKEN, W. E., Driver, R.F.A.
He volunteered in January 1915, and in June of the following year was sent to the Western Front, and was in action at Hill 60, Ypres, Vimy Ridge, the Somme, Arras, Cambrai and Amiens. He returned home and was demobilised in April 1919, and holds the 1914-15 Star, and the General Service and Victory Medals.
8, Brynmaer Road, Battersea, S.W.11.   Z3744

PICKFORD, J. F., Corporal, R.A.S.C. (M.T.)
Volunteering in April 1915, he was sent to France in the same year, and was engaged on transport duties in the Somme and Ypres Sectors. Through shock he suffered the loss of speech, and was invalided home and discharged as medically unfit for further service in November 1915, holding the 1914-15 Star, and the General Service and Victory Medals.
2, St. Alphonsus Road, Clapham, S.W.4.   Z3745

PICKING, H. J., Private, Royal Sussex Regiment.
He volunteered in November 1915, and was sent to France in the following year, and was in action at Ypres, the Somme and Arras, where he was severely wounded. He was discharged in 1918 owing to his disability and holds the General Service and Victory Medals.
19, Mantua Street, Battersea, S.W.11.   Z3746

PICKSTOCK, P. G., Rifleman, 10th Rifle Brigade.
He joined in June 1916, and in September of the same year was drafted to France, where he took part in numerous engagements, including those at Passchendaele, Lens and Cambrai, and also served in the Retreat and Advance of 1918. He was demobilised in February 1919, and holds the General Service and Victory Medals.
97, Grosvenor Terrace, Camberwell, S.E.5.   Z3288C

PICKSTOCK, T. H., Private, Royal Sussex Regt.
Joining in February 1916, he was sent to France in the following June, and was in action at Kemmel and the Somme. He was wounded at Guillemont, and was invalided home and was discharged as medically unfit for further service in July 1918. He holds the General Service and Victory Medals.
24A, Avenue Road, Camberwell, S.E.5.   Z3288B

PICTON, E. H., Sapper, R.E.
He joined in August 1916, and after his training served on important duties with his unit at various stations on the East Coast. He rendered valuable services, but was not successful in obtaining his transfer overseas before the cessation of hostilities. He was demobilised in February 1919.
41, Heaton Road, Peckham, S.E.15.   Z5820

PIDDOCK, F. D., Corporal, 11th Queen's (Royal West Surrey Regiment).
He volunteered in November 1915, and in the following year was drafted to the Western Front, and was in action on the Somme and the Ancre, and at Arras and Messines. He was then sent to Italy and was engaged on the Piave front, but later returned to France. He fell fighting on the Somme on March 21st, 1918, and was entitled to the General Service and Victory Medals.
"And doubtless he went in splendid company."
32, Aldred Road, Kennington Park, S.E.17.   Z3747

PIERPOINT, J. H., Rflmn., King's Royal Rifle Corps.
Volunteering in June 1915, he was sent to France in the same year. He took part in numerous engagements, including those at Ypres, the Somme, and Arras, and was severely wounded at Messines. He was invalided home and discharged as medically unfit in 1918, and holds the 1914-15 Star, and the General Service and Victory Medals.
53, Henshaw Street, Walworth, S.E.17.   Z3748

PIGDEN, R., Private, R.A.S.C.
He volunteered in June 1915, and after his training was drafted to the Eastern Front, where he served at Salonika and was engaged on the transport of ammunition and supplies to the front lines. Later, owing to ill-health, he was invalided to Malta, and thence home. He was discharged in November 1917 as medically unfit for further service, and holds the General Service and Victory Medals.
85, Grayshott Road, Battersea, S.W.11.   Z3749A

PIGDEN, R., Trimmer, H.M.S. "Rinto" (Mine Sweeper).
He volunteered in August 1914, and was engaged on mine-sweeping duties between the coasts of England and France, during the whole period of the war and rendered valuable services. He was demobilised in April 1919, and holds the General Service and Mercantile Marine War Medals.
85, Grayshott Road, Battersea, S.W.11.   Z3749B

PIGOTT, E. F., Private, 5th Royal Berkshire Regt.
He volunteered in September 1914, and later in the same year proceeded to France, where he was in action at Ypres and Loos, and other engagements. He was reported missing after a night bombing raid in October 1916, and has since been reported as having died of wounds while a prisoner of war in German hands, near Douai, on October 15th, 1916. He was entitled to the 1914 Star, and the General Service and Victory Medals.
"A costly sacrifice upon the altar of freedom."
11, Tisdale Place, Walworth, S.E.17.   Z3750

PIGUET, C. R., Private, R.M.L.I.
He volunteered at the outbreak of hostilities, and was posted to H.M.S. "Sutley." in which he was engaged in the North Sea, on important patrol and escort duties. He also saw much service in other vessels, engaged on defence work, and convoying food and troopships in the Atlantic and Mediterranean and other waters. He was demobilised in April 1919 after valuable service, and holds the 1914-15 Star, and the General Service and Victory Medals.
17, Etherdon Street, East Street, Walworth, S.E.17.   Z4124

PIKE, E., Sergt., R.F.A.
After volunteering in September 1914, he passed through his
course of training, and in 1915 proceeded to the Dardanelles,
where he took part in many engagements, and was wounded.
After his recovery he was drafted to France in December
1917, and fought in the Retreat and Advance of the Allies
in 1918. During his service he did excellent work at Woolwich, as an Instructor in Rough-riding, Physical Training
and Gunnery. He was on duty in Ireland in 1919 and 1920,
and was demobilised in September 1920, holding the 1914-15
Star, and the General Service and Victory Medals.
3, Warrior Road, Camberwell, S.E.5.   Z3751A

**PIKE, E. C., Pte., 2nd Queen's (Royal West Surrey
Regiment).**
He was called from the Reserve in August 1914, and in the
following month crossed to France ,where he took an active
part in the first and second Battle of Ypres, and the engagements at Neuve Chapelle, Loos, Albert, Vimy Ridge, the
Somme, Arras, Messines, Passchendaele, Lens, Cambrai, and
the Retreat and Advance of 1918. After his return home he
was demobilised in August 1919, and holds the 1914 Star,
and the General Service and Victory Medals.
35, Smyrks Road, Walworth, S.E.17.   Z3286C

PIKE, G. G., Private, R.A.M.C.
Volunteering in November 1914, he was sent to the Western
Front in 1915, and rendered valuable services with his Corps
at the Battles of Ypres, the Somme, Arras, Cambrai and many
other important engagements until the close of hostilities.
During his service abroad he was wounded on one occasion.
After his return home he was demobilised in February 1919,
and holds the 1914-15 Star, and the General Service and
Victory Medals.
33, Stansfield Road, Stockwell, S.W.9.   Z3752A

PIKE, H. A., Private, Dorsetshire Regiment.
He joined in July 1917, and in the completion of his training
proceeded to France later in that year. He took an active
part in the Battle of Cambrai and the engagements in the
Retreat and Advance of 1918, and on one occasion was wounded.
After his return home he was demobilised in February 1919,
and holds the General Service and Victory Medals.
33, Stansfield Road, Stockwell, S.W.9.   Z3752B

PIKE, J., Gunner, R.F.A. and R.H.A.
He joined in March 1916, and in the following year was drafted
to the Western Front. There he served with the 2nd Division,
and took a prominent part in engagements at Ypres and Arras.
He also saw valuable service with the Flying Column at
St. Quentin, Péronne and St. Eloi in the Retreat and Advance
of 1918. He was demobilised in April 1920, and holds the
General Service and Victory Medals.
56, Liverpool Street, Walworth, S.E.17.   Z27323

PIKE, J. A., Pte., 12th East Surrey Regiment.
He volunteered in June 1915, and in April of the following
year was drafted to France, where he took part in many
important engagements, including those at Albert, Vimy Ridge,
the Somme, Arras, Messines, Ypres, Lens, Cambrai and the
Retreat and Advance of the Allies in 1918. He was wounded
on one occasion on the Somme front. After returning to
England he was demobilised in June 1919, and holds the
General Service and Victory Medals.
110, Aylesbury Road, Walworth, S.E.17.   Z3754A

PIKE, J. W., Special War Worker.
From the outbreak of hostilities in August 1914 until October
1920 he was engaged on important duties as a storeman
under the Navy and Army Canteens Board, and in this capacity
rendered over six years' valuable services at the Tower of
London and other depôts with the guards. He discharged
his duties throughout this long period with great care and
efficiency.
59B, Lewis Trust Buildings, Camberwell, S.E.5.   Z6427

PIKE, L., Rifleman, King's Royal Rifle Corps.
He volunteered in February 1915, and four months later
on the completion of his training proceeded to France. He
took a prominent part in many engagements of the utmost
importance until the cessation of hostilities, including those
at the Somme, Hooge, Loos, Arras and in the German and
British Offensives of 1918. He was demobilised in March
1919 after his return home and holds the 1914-15 Star, and
the General Service and Victory Medals.
3, Warrior Road, Camberwell, S.E.5.   Z3751B

PIKE, N. F., Private, Bedfordshire Regiment.
He was mobilised at the outbreak of war and soon afterwards
crossed to France, where he took an active part in numerous
operations until hostilities ceased. He was wounded near
Bapaume in 1916, but after his recovery rejoined his unit.
Later he was again wounded and gassed on the Somme in
1918, but after hospital treatment at home was able to return
to the line for the final engagements of the war. He was
demobilised in March 1919, and holds the 1914 Star, and
the General Service and Victory Medals.
54, Ingleton Street, Brixton Road, S.W.9.   Z3844

PIKE, R. J., Guardsman, Coldstream Guards.
He joined in May 1916, and later in the year proceeded to
the Western Front, where he served with distinction in many
of the principal engagements right up to the close of hostilities. During his service overseas he was gassed on two
occasions. After his return home he was demobilised in
December 1919, and holds the General Service and Victory
Medals.
7, Victoria Place, Priory Grove, S.W.8.   Z3753

PIKE, R. T., Gunner, R.G.A.
He joined in December 1916, and on the completion of his
training was engaged on important coast defence duties until
1918, when he was drafted to France. He took part in the
early operations of the Retreat in 1918, and was badly wounded
in April. After hospital treatment in France and at home he
was discharged in consequence of his service in February 1919.
He holds the General Service and Victory Medals.
6, Carew Street, Camberwell, S.E.5.   Z6058

PILBEAM, S. A., Private, 20th London Regiment.
He joined in March 1918, and in the same year was drafted
to France, where he was engaged as signaller at Lille and
various other places during the Advance of 1918. He was
demobilised in February 1919, and holds the General Service
and Victory Medals.
142, Lower Kennington Lane, S.E.11.   Z27532

PILBROW, J., Private, 23rd London Regiment.
He volunteered in August 1915, and in January of the following
year was sent to Salonika, where he took part in several
actions. He was later transferred to Egypt, where he served
in numerous engagements. Afterwards he proceeded to
France, and took part in the heavy fighting during the closing
stages of the war. He was demobilised in January 1919,
and holds the General Service and Victory Medals.
98, Gloucester Road, Peckham, S.E.5.   Z5812

PILCHER, S. G., Gunner, R.F.A.
He volunteered in August 1915, and was sent to France in
the following year, and took part in numerous engagements,
including the Battle of the Somme. He was unfortunately
killed in action on October 22nd, 1916, and was buried near
Albert. He was entitled to the General Service and Victory
Medals.
"He joined the great white company of valiant souls."
13, Elam Street, Camberwell, S.E.5.   Z5989C

PILGRIM, C. R., Gunner, Royal Navy.
He was serving when war broke out, and did valuable work
with the Fleet, cruising in the North Sea and the English
Channel. He was also engaged on submarine patrols in the
Mediterranean and other waters. He holds the 1914-15 Star,
and the General Service and Victory Medals, and the Naval
General Service Medal (with Persian Gulf clasp), and with
thirteen years' service is now on H.M.S. " Neptune."
49, Stangate Buildings, Lambeth, S.E.1.   Z26080B

PILGRIM, L. J., L/Corporal, M.F.P.
He was serving at the outbreak of war, and in 1917 was sent
to the Western Front, and shortly afterwards was wounded
and invalided home. On his recovery he returned to France,
and was engaged in various parts on important duties until
the cessation of hostilities. He holds the General Service
and Victory Medals, and in 1920 was serving in Ireland.
70, Coronation Buildings, Lambeth Road, S.W.8.   Z1644A

PIMM, J. J., Private, Royal Sussex Regiment.
He joined in December, 1917, and proceeded to France in
the following year, and took part in important engagements
during the Retreat and Advance of 1918, including those
on the Somme and at Amiens and Ypres, and was wounded.
Later he was drafted to Egypt, where he contracted malaria,
and was in hospital for a time. On his recovery he rejoined
his unit, however, and continued to serve until February
1920, when he returned to England and was demobilised,
holding the General Service and Victory Medals.
102, Gloucester Road, Peckham, S.E.15.   Z5811

**PINCHBECK, J., Pte., Duke of Cornwall's Light
Infantry.**
Volunteering in September 1914, he was sent to France in
February of the following year, and was in action at St. Eloi,
Hill 60, and Ypres. In November 1915 he was transferred to
Salonika, and was engaged on the Struma front. He was
demobilised in February 1919, and holds the 1914-15 Star,
and the General Service and Victory Medals.
13, Halfpin Place, Walworth, S.E.17.   Z3755

PINCHES, G. E., Sapper, R.E.
He volunteered in August 1914, and after the completion of his training proceeded to Egypt, and served under General Allenby, and was wounded in the Advance on Jerusalem. He was drafted to France in 1918, and served there until demobilised in January 1919. He holds the 1914-15 Star, and the General Service and Victory Medals.
1, Albion House, Amelia Street, Walworth, S.E.17.   Z26133

PINDER, J., Sergt., 1st Northumberland Fusiliers.
He was mobilised in August 1914, and in the same month was sent to France, where he took part in the Retreat from Mons and the 1st Battle of Ypres. He fell fighting at Ypres on June 16th, 1915, and was entitled to the Mons Star, and the General Service and Victory Medals.
" He joined the great white company of valiant Souls."
44, Riverhall Street, S. Lambeth, S.W.8.   Z3756

PINDER, J. H., L/Corporal, 12th Middlesex Regt.
He volunteered in February 1915, and was sent to the Dardanelles in August of the same year. In February 1916 he was transferred to France, and was engaged on the Somme. He was unfortunately killed in action on September 26th, 1916, and was entitled to the 1914-15 Star, and the General Service and Victory Medals.
" Whilst we remember, the Sacrifice is not in vain."
11, Dashwood Road, Wandsworth Road, S.W.8.   Z3757

PINK, E. T., Private, 23rd London Regiment.
Volunteering in May 1915, he was drafted to France in September of the same year, and took part in various engagements including that at Loos. Later he was taken ill, and died at the Clearing Station on November 21st, 1915. He was buried near Béthune, and was entitled to the 1914-15 Star, and the General Service and Victory Medals.
" His life for his country."
53, Darien Road, Battersea, S.W.11.   Z3758A

PINN, Z. T. V., Rfimn., 1/11th London Regt. (Rifles).
He volunteered in November 1915, and on completion of his training was drafted to Egypt, and thence to Palestine, and served in the Battle of Gaza and numerous other engagements. He returned home and was demobilised in February 1919, and holds the General Service and Victory Medals.
61, Elliotts Row, St. George's Road, S.E.11.   Z26885

PINNINGTON, E. F., Rfimn., 2nd Royal Irish Rifles.
He volunteered in 1914, and was sent to France in the following year, and took part in the fierce fighting at Ypres and Festubert. He was unfortunately killed in action in February 1916, and was entitled to the 1914-15 Star, and the General Service and Victory Medals.
" Great deeds cannot die."
37, Wivenhoe Road, Peckham, S.E.15.   Z6052

PIPE, H. S., Sapper, R.E. (Signals).
He volunteered in August 1914, and was sent to France in the following year. He served in many sectors, and was engaged in laying cables and other important duties, and rendered valuable services. He returned home, and was demobilised in November 1919, and holds the 1914-15 Star, and the General Service and Victory Medals.
143, Elmhurst Mansions, Edgley Road, Clapham, S.W.4.   Z3760

PIPER, H. E., 1st Class Stoker, R.N., H.M.S. "Courageous" and "Blanche."
He volunteered in February 1915, and served with the Grand Fleet in the North Sea, where he took part in many engagements, and was also in action at Zeebrugge and Heligoland Bight. He was demobilised in March 1919, and holds the 1914-15 Star, and the General Service and Victory Medals.
4, McKerrel Road, Peckham, S.E.15.   Z5821

PIPER, W. J., Private, 13th Devonshire Regiment.
He joined in June 1916, and on the completion of his course of training at Salisbury Plain and other stations, was retained on important duties with his unit. He was not successful in securing his transfer overseas while hostilities continued, but rendered valuable services at Headquarters until his demobilisation in February 1919.
243, Commercial Road, Peckham, S.E.15.   Z6643

PIPKIN, G., Private, Bedfordshire Regiment.
He volunteered in August 1914, and in the same month was drafted to the Western Front, where he took part in the Battles of Albert and Arras, and was in action at Fricourt. He also served in the Advance of 1918, and was twice wounded. After the cessation of hostilities he returned to England, and in February 1919 was demobilised, holding the 1914 Star, and the General Service and Victory Medals.
8, Chester Buildings, Lomond Grove, Camberwell, S.E.5.   Z5814

PIPPARD, G., Private, Northamptonshire Regt.
He was mobilised at the outbreak of war, and in November 1914 was drafted to the Western Front, and served in many important engagements in various sectors. He was mortally wounded in action on March 18th, 1915, and succumbed to his injuries on the 23rd of the same month. He was entitled to the 1914 Star, and the General Service and Victory Medals.
" A costly sacrifice upon the altar of freedom."
117, Speke Road, Battersea, S.W.11.   Z3759C

PIPPEN, T. F., A.B., Merchant Service.
He was serving in the Merchant Service at the outbreak of hostilities, aboard the Union Castle Liner " Glengorm Castle," which during the war was used as a hospital ship for conveying the wounded from France to England. In 1916 his vessel was sent to the Mediterranean, where she cruised between Salonika and other places until March 1919, when she returned to port, and he was demobilised. He holds the General Service and Mercantile Marine War Medals.
54, Galleywall Road, Rotherhithe, S.E.16.   Z6607

PITCHER, J. E., Sergt., Queen's Own (Royal West Kent Regiment).
He volunteered in September 1914, and in July of the following year was drafted overseas. During his service in France he was in action at Loos, Albert and Vimy Ridge, and was wounded in the Battle of the Somme, and sent home to hospital. After eight months in England he was sent to Italy, where he served for three months, and then returned to the Western Front in time to take part in the Battle of Cambrai. Subsequently he fought on the Somme, and was severely wounded at Amiens and invalided home, and after his recovery was retained on important home defence duties until his discharge in May 1919. He holds the General Service and Victory Medals.
174, East Street, Walworth, S.E.17.   Z3761

PITCHLEY, H., Private, Queen's (Royal West Surrey Regiment).
He volunteered in March 1915, and after his training served at various stations on important duties with his unit. He rendered valuable services, but owing to being medically unfit was not able to secure a transfer overseas, and was demobilised in February 1919.
93, Trafalgar Street, Walworth, S.E.17.   Z27147

PITMAN, G., Sergt., East Surrey Regiment.
He was mobilised at the outbreak of war, and was almost immediately drafted to France, and took part in the Retreat from Mons. He also served in the first Battle of Ypres, and was invalided home owing to ill-health. On recovery he rejoined his unit, and was in action in the Battle of the Somme and in many subsequent engagements in the Retreat and Advance of 1918. He returned home, and was demobilised in February 1919, and holds the Mons Star, and the General Service and Victory Medals.
1, Thessaly Square, Wandsworth Road, S.W.8.   Z3763

PITT, F. J., L/Corporal, 8th Queen's Own (Royal West Kent Regiment) and Military Police.
He volunteered in September 1914, and in the following year was drafted to France, where he saw much service. He was in action at Ypres, Loos, Arras, Vimy Ridge, Lens, Bapaume and Béthune, and in many later engagements. During his service he was twice gassed, on the Somme in 1916, when he was sent to Etaples hospital, and again in the Advance of 1918, when he was invalided home. After his recovery he was transferred to the Military Police, with whom he served until his demobilisation in March 1919. He holds the 1914-15 Star, and the General Service and Victory Medals.
16, Cossall Street, Peckham, S.E.15.   Z6533

PITT, F. W., Driver, R.F.A.
He volunteered in May 1915, and in the following September was drafted to India. During his service in the East he took part in numerous frontier engagements and skirmishes in various places. He returned home and was demobilised in June 1920, and holds the India General Service (with clasp Afghanistan N.W. Frontier, 1919), the General Service and Victory Medals.
96, Maysoule Road, Battersea, S.W.11.   Z3762B

PITT, H. C., Driver, R.F.A.
He volunteered in August 1915, at fourteen years of age, and proceeded to France in December of the same year. He served at Ypres and the Somme, and was then sent back to England owing to his youth, and retained on important duties in home defence until he was discharged in September 1918. He holds the 1914-15 Star, and the General Service and Victory Medals.
96, Maysoule Road, Battersea, S.W.11.   Z3762A

PITT, W. G., Bombardier, R.F.A.
Volunteering in 1915, he was shortly afterwards drafted to the Western Front, where he saw much service. He fought at St. Eloi, Loos, Vimy Ridge, Albert, the Somme, the Ancre, Beaumont-Hamel, Bullecourt, Messines, Ypres and Cambrai, and in various subsequent engagements until the cessation of hostilities. He was demobilised in June 1919, and holds the 1914–15 Star, and the General Service and Victory Medals.
3, Dante Road, Kennington, S.E.11.   Z26913

PITTARD, J., Corporal, R.F.A.
He was mobilised at the outbreak of hostilities, and was almost immediately drafted to France, where he served in the Retreat from Mons, and at La Bassée and Ypres. He was severely gassed at Hill 60, and after his recovery was in action on the Somme, and in many subsequent engagements until the cessation of hostilities. He then advanced into Germany with the Army of Occupation, and was stationed on the Rhine for some time. In 1920 he was still serving at Dover, and holds the Mons Star, and the General Service and Victory Medals.
151, St. George's Road, Peckham, S.E.15.   Z5810

PITTMAN, A. E., Rifleman, 11th London Regiment (Rifles) and 9th London Regt. (Queen Victoria's Rifles).
He joined in November 1916, and in the following year was drafted to France. During his service on the Western Front he fought in various engagements in the Somme and Ypres sectors, and was wounded in the second Battle of the Somme, early in 1918. After six months in hospital at home he rejoined his unit in France in November, and after the cessation of hostilities served with the Army of Occupation in Germany until January 1919, when he was demobilised. He holds the General Service and Victory Medals.
56, Philip Road, Peckham, S.E.15.   Z6061

PLATT, L. T., Private, Northumberland Fusiliers.
He joined in 1916, and in the same year was drafted to the Western Front. During his service in France he was engaged in very heavy fighting at Vimy Ridge, the Ancre, Ypres, Passchendaele, Cambrai and in the second Battle of the Somme. He also took part in various later engagements in the Retreat and Advance of 1918, until the cessation of hostilities. He was demobilised in November 1919, and holds the General Service and Victory Medals.
52, Brook Street, Kennington, S.E.11.   Z26906

PLATTS, T., Private, 1st Leicestershire Regiment.
He was mobilised at the outbreak of war, and in the following October was drafted to France. During his service on the Western Front he fought at St. Eloi, and was wounded in the Battle of Ypres, and invalided to hospital at Boulogne, and thence home. After his recovery he was sent back to France, and took part in various engagements until the cessation of hostilities. He was demobilised in March 1919, and holds the 1914 Star, and the General Service and Victory Medals.
33, Ponsonby Terrace, Grosvenor Road, S.W.1.   Z23199

PLOWRIGHT, J., Rifleman, Rifle Brigade.
He joined in May 1916, and was drafted to France on the completion of his training. After taking part in various engagements he was reported missing, and is believed to have fallen on the Field of Battle in the Somme sector in 1917. He was entitled to the General Service and Victory Medals.
" His life for his Country, his Soul to God."
3, Darien Road, Battersea, S.W.11.   Z3764

PLOWS, C., Private, R.A.M.C.
He joined in May 1916, and after his training served at various stations, including Belfast, on important hospital duties. He was engaged in several Military hospitals as an orderly in the Mental Wards, and carried out his exacting duties with great care and efficiency. He did excellent work, but was not successful in obtaining a transfer overseas, and was demobilised, after more than three years' service in June 1919.
92, Upper Grange Road, Bermondsey, S.E.1.   Z27259

PLOWS, C. D., 1st Class Stoker, R.N.
He volunteered in August 1914, and was engaged on cruising patrol duties with the Grand Fleet in the North Sea. His ship was in action in the Battle of Heligoland Bight, and in many minor engagements, and whilst on H.M.S. " General Crawford " he took part in the bombardment of the enemy positions on the Belgian Coast. Transferred to H.M.S. " Pyramus " he was employed on escort duty in the Persian Gulf and other Eastern waters. In March 1919 he was demobilised, and holds the 1914–15 Star, and the General Service and Victory Medals.
92, Upper Grange Road, Bermondsey, S.E.1.   Z26863

PLOWS, J., Fireman, Mercantile Marine.
He joined in January 1917, and was posted to the " Eaglet," and was engaged on conveying food supplies and other commodities from foreign ports to England. He was demobilised after nearly three years' service, in December 1919, and holds the General Service and the Mercantile Marine War Medals.
92, Upper Grange Road, Bermondsey, S.E.1.   Z27258

PLOWS, W., 1st Class Stoker, R.N.
Volunteering in June 1915, he was posted to H.M.S. " Norman' and whilst in this ship served with the Cruiser Squadron under Admirals Jellicoe and Beatty in the North Sea. He was engaged on patrol duty and in convoying food and troopships to and from the fighting areas, and also took part in an engagement off the coast of Scotland in December 1915. He was discharged through ill-health in September 1918, and holds the 1914–15 Star, and the General Service and Victory Medals.
92, Upper Grange Road, Bermondsey, S.E.1.   Z26865

PLUCKROSE, J., Pte., King's (Liverpool Regt.)
He joined in June 1916, and after serving on important coastal defence duties was drafted to Russia with the Relief Force. At Archangel he was frequently in action against the Bolsheviks during his nine months' service there. He returned to England and was demobilised in July 1919, and holds the General Service and Victory Medals.
217, K Block, Guinness' Buildings, Page's Walk, Bermondsey, S.E.1.   Z26376

PLUMB, B. M. (Mrs.), Special War Worker.
From August 1914 until 1916 this lady was engaged on important duties in connection with the production of friction tubes for machine-guns. Afterwards she was engaged at Messrs. John Bell, Hill and Lucas, Bermondsey, on the inspection of anti-gas masks, and from January 1917 until February 1918 at Woolwich Arsenal, where she served as a cartridge examiner. She did most commendable work in each of these capacities, and was worthy of high praise.
64, Marcia Road, Bermondsey, S.E.1.   Z26383B

PLUMB, G. J., Gunner, R.F.A.
He volunteered in August 1914, and in June of the following year was drafted to the Western Front. Whilst in this theatre of war he took part in many notable battles, including those of Vimy Ridge, the Somme, Messines, Ypres, Thiepval, Armentières, St. Quentin, Amiens, Bapaume, and the Advance of 1918, and was wounded. He was demobilised in December 1919, and holds the 1914–15 Star, and the General Service and Victory Medals.
64, Marcia Road, Bermondsey, S.E.1.   Z26383A

PLUMB, H., Rifleman, Rifle Brigade.
Joining in January 1917, he crossed to France two months later. Whilst overseas, he fought in many important engagements, including those at Arras, Vimy Ridge, Bullecourt, Messines, Ypres, Cambrai, the Somme, Amiens, Bapaume and Havrincourt Wood. He was demobilised in February 1920, and holds the General Service and Victory Medals.
12, Elsted Street, Walworth, S.E.17.   Z3765

PLUMMER, C. W., Air Mechanic. R.A.F.
He volunteered in September 1915, and at the conclusion of his training was engaged on important duties at various stations with his Squadron. He was unable to secure his transfer to a theatre of war before the termination of hostilities, but nevertheless, did valuable work until he was demobilised in January 1919.
19, Trafalgar Road, Peckham, S.E.15.   Z3766

PLUMMER, H., Private, R.A.S.C. (M.T.)
Joining in March 1916, he was drafted to the Western Front, where he was engaged on important transport duties in the forward areas. He served in many important engagements, including those on the Somme, and at Loos, Lens, Grandcourt, Ypres, Cambrai, St. Quentin, and the Retreat and Advance of 1918. He was demobilised in March 1919, and holds the General Service and Victory Medals.
6, Chapter Terrace, Walworth, S.E.17.   Z26766

PLUMMER, R. H., Bombardier, R.F.A.
He volunteered in May 1915, and during his service in France, which lasted for upwards of two years, did valuable work with his Battery during military operations in many important sectors, notably those of Vimy Ridge, the Somme, Arras, Ypres and Cambrai. He holds the General Service and Victory Medals, and was demobilised in February 1919.
180, Beresford Street, Camberwell, S.E.5.   Z3768

PLUMMER, W., Sergt., R.G.A.
He was in the Army when war broke out, having enlisted in September 1913, and was retained for important home duties until early in 1915, when he crossed to France. Whilst in this theatre of war, he took an active part in engagements at Ypres, the Somme, Arras and Cambrai, and was gassed. During the German Offensive of March 1918, he was taken prisoner and was subsequently held captive for nine months. After his repatriation, he rejoined his Battery, and in 1920 was still serving. He holds the 1914–15 Star, and the General Service and Victory Medals.
35, Gladstone Street, Battersea Park Road, S.W.8.   Z3767

POCKETT, G., Sergt., 3rd Rifle Brigade.
Called up from the Reserve at the outbreak of war, he immediately crossed to France, and took part in the Retreat from Mons. He also fought in many of the engagements which followed, notably those at Ypres, Neuve Chapelle, Loos, Hill 60, the Somme, Messines and Cambrai, and the Retreat and Advance of 1918. He was demobilised in January 1919, and holds the Mons Star, and the General Service and Victory Medals.
31, Blake's Road, Peckham, S.E.15. Z6056

POCOCK, A., Air Mechanic, R.A.F. (late R.N.A.S.)
Joining in May 1916, he was drafted to Italy with his Squadron at the conclusion of his training early in the following year. Whilst overseas he was engaged on duties of an important nature, which demanded much technical knowledge and skill, and did valuable work until December 1918, when he returned to England. He was demobilised in July 1919, and holds the General Service and Victory Medals.
19, St. Philip Street, Battersea, S.W.8. Z6196B

POCOCK, C. D., Sergt., King's Own Yorkshire Light Infantry.
A serving soldier, he crossed to France with the first Expeditionary Force, and took part in the Retreat from Mons. At the conclusion of this engagement, he was reported missing, and it is presumed that he was unhappily killed in action. He was entitled to the Mons Star, and the General Service and Victory Medals.
"Great deeds cannot die."
33, Coronation Buildings, Lambeth, S.W.8. Z3770

POLGLAZE, A. T., Gunner, R.H.A.
He joined in 1917, and at the conclusion of his training was engaged on special duties with his Battery at various stations. Owing to his being under age for duty abroad, he was unable to secure his transfer overseas before the termination of hostilities, but did much valuable work and was still serving in 1920.
12, Opal Street, Kennington Lane, S.E.11. Z27394B

POLGLAZE, W., Private, M.G.C.
He joined early in 1919, on attaining military age, and at the conclusion of his training did valuable work with his unit at various stations. He was still serving in 1920.
12, Opal Street, Kennington Lane, S.E.11. Z27394A

POLLARD, A., Q.M.S., Royal Defence Corps.
Volunteering at the commencement of hostilities, he joined in the 21st London Regiment, but later was transferred to the Royal Defence Corps. He subsequently did much valuable work on home defence duties, and after serving for almost five years was discharged in April 1919.
54, Mostyn Road, Brixton Road, S.W.9. Z3771

POLLARD, J., Sergt., Labour Corps.
He joined in 1916, and at the conclusion of his training was engaged on important clerical duties in the Eastern Command. He was unable to secure his transfer overseas before the termination of hostilities, but nevertheless rendered services of a valuable nature before he was discharged in 1919.
82, Meadow Road, Fentiman Road, S.W.8. Z3772

POLLEY, A. J., Private, R.A.S.C. (M.T.)
He joined in December 1917, and after his training served at various stations on important duties with his unit. He rendered valuable services, but on medical grounds was not successful in obtaining his transfer overseas before the cessation of hostilities. He was discharged as unfit for further service in August 1919.
32, Aylesford Street, St. George's Road, S.W.1. Z23490C

POLLEY, D. G., Corporal, Prince of Wales 3rd Yeomanry (Sharpshooters).
He volunteered in March 1915, and was unable to serve overseas as his services at home were indispensable. Until demobilised in November 1919, he was employed throughout the war as electrican in charge of all electrical work on vessels torpedoed, or otherwise damaged in warfare, which were brought into Belfast.
32, Aylesford Street, St. George's Road, S.W.1. Z23490B

POLLEY, F. S., Corporal, King's Royal Rifle Corps.
He volunteered in May 1915, and shortly proceeded to the Western Front, where he took a prominent part in the Battle of Loos. He was severely wounded in this engagement, his injuries resulting in total blindness. Invalided home he was in hospital at Fulham for a considerable time, and later was in training at St. Dunstan's Hostel for twelve months. He was discharged in 1917, on account of his service, and holds the 1914-15 Star, and the General Service and Victory Medals.
32, Aylesford Street, St. George's Road, S.W.1. Z23490A

POLLEY, W. J., Driver, R.F.A.
He volunteered in 1915, and the following year after completing his training was drafted to the Western Front. He did excellent service with his Battery in the Battles of the Somme, Arras, Vimy Ridge, Ypres, Passchendaele, Cambrai, and the Retreat and Advance of 1918. and on one occasion was lost in the woods for five days, but eventually found his way back to his Battery. After his return home he was demobilised in 1919, and holds the General Service and Victory Medals.
5, Thurlow Street, Walworth, S.E.17. Z3773

POLLITT, J. D. F., Engineer, R.N., H.M.S. "Sidmark."
He volunteered in April 1915, and shortly afterwards proceeded to the Dardanelles, where his ship took part in the bombardments and subsequent Evacuation. He was wounded on one occasion, and after the loss of his vessel by torpedo was transferred to the Grand Fleet, in which he served in the North Sea until discharged as medically unfit for further service in September 1917. He holds the 1914-15 Star, and the General Service and Victory Medals.
18, Badsworth Road, Camberwell, S.E.5. Z3774

POLLOCK, A., Stoker, R.N.
He was mobilised in 1914, and throughout the course of hostilities did excellent service in the North Sea. He was in H.M.S. "Highflyer" when she sank a German submarine, and was also in action in H.M.S. "Theseus." He was demobilised in 1919, and holds the 1914-15 Star, and the General Service and Victory Medals.
20, Thurlow Street, Walworth, S.E.17. Z3775B

POLLOCK, M., Private, R.F.A.
He volunteered in 1915, and on the completion of his training crossed to France in the same year. He did gallant service in many engagements, including those of the Somme, Arras and Cambrai, and was severely wounded at Ypres. After eighteen months' hospital treatment he was demobilised in 1919, and holds the 1914-15 Star, and the General Service and Victory Medals.
20, Thurlow Street, Walworth, S.E.17. Z3775A

POLLOCK, S. L., Rifleman, 2nd Rifle Brigade.
Joining in November 1916, he passed through his course of training, and in January 1917 was drafted to France. He did valuable service at Bullecourt, Ypres and the Somme, and was wounded and taken prisoner near St. Quentin in March 1918. During his captivity in German hands he was employed as an orderly until his repatriation. He was demobilised in October 1919, and holds the General Service and Victory Medals 218, Commercial Road, Peckham, S.E.15. Z6608

POMFRET, C., Private, Queen's Own (Royal West Kent Regiment).
Volunteering in November 1915, he was drafted in 1916 to the Western Front, where he was in action in the Ypres salient. He was very severely wounded at Ploegsteert in June 1916, and was in hospital for eighteen months in consequence. He was discharged as unfit for further service in December 1917, but is still under treatment for his wounds in 1920. He holds the General Service and Victory Medals.
5, Tyne Terrace, High Street, Peckham, S.E.15. Z6609B

POMFRET, W. S., Private, Royal Sussex and Hertfordshire Regiments.
He volunteered in December 1915, and after completing his training was sent to the Western Front. He took an active part in many engagements of importance until the cessation of hostilities, including those of the Somme, Arras, Ypres, Passchendaele and Cambrai, and the Retreat and Advance of 1918. After his return to England he was demobilised in March 1919, and holds the General Service and Victory Medals.
5, Tyne Terrace, High Street, Peckham, S.E.15. Z6609A

PONDER, A. E., Private, 4th Royal Fusiliers.
He was serving at the outbreak of hostilities, and in January 1915, proceeded to the Western Front. He took part in many important Battles, including those at the Somme, Arras, Vimy Ridge, Cambrai Kemmel, the Offensives of 1918, and was wounded at the Somme, and suffered from shell-shock. After his return to England he was demobilised in March 1919, and holds the 1914-15 Star, and the General Service and Victory Medals.
34, Harvey Road, Camberwell, S.E.5. Z3776

PONDER, E. C. A., Private, 8th Middlesex Regt.
He joined in February 1917, and in the following December, after completing his training was drafted to the Western Front. He saw much service on the Cambrai and Arras fronts and fought at St. Quentin, and other engagements in the Retreat and Advance of 1918. He was gassed in March and September, and in consequence of the second case was sent to England in October 1918. Two months later he was demobilised, and holds the General Service and Victory Medals.
34, Harvey Road, Camberwell, S.E.5. Z3777

PONTEFRACT, T. H., Private, 1st Royal Scots.

He was mobilised from the Reserve in August 1914, and quickly proceeded to the Western Front, where he took part in many early engagements, including the Retreat from Mons. He was unfortunately killed in action on November 14th, 1914, near Neuve Chapelle, and was entitled to the Mons Star, and the General Service and Victory Medals.

" The path of duty was the way to glory."

8, Elizabeth Street, Walworth, S.E.17.   Z26425

POOK, J., Sergt., King's Royal Rifle Corps.

He was serving at the outbreak of war, and in 1915 was sent to the Western Front, where he fought in the Battles of Ypres, the Somme and Arras. In 1917, he was drafted to Sqlonika, and whilst in this theatre of war suffered severely from malaria. Later he returned to France, and was in action during the Advance of 1918. In 1920 he was still serving with the Colours, and holds the Queen's and King's South African Medals, the 1914 Star, and the General Service and Victory Medals.

43, Gilbert Road, Kennington, S.E.11.   Z27246

POOKE, T., Private, 1st York and Lancaster Regt.

He joined in April 1916, and in the same year was drafted to France. During his service overseas he fought in various engagements, including those on the Somme, and at Arras and Ypres, and was in action during the final Offensive of 1918. He was demobilised in September of the following year, and holds the General Service and Victory Medals.

16, Bournemouth Road, Peckham S.E.15.   Z5806A

POOLE, F. E., Rifleman, King's Royal Rifle Corps.

He joined in February 1916, and in the same year was drafted overseas. After serving in several engagements, he died gloriously on the Field of Battle on the Somme on November 6th, 1916. He was entitled to the General Service and Victory Medals.

" Courage, bright hopes, and a myriad dreams, splendidly given."

2, Aytoun Road, Stockwell, S.W.9.   Z5822A

POOLE, J., Private, 3rd East Surrey Regiment.

He volunteered in October 1914, and in February of the following year was drafted to France, where he saw much service. He fought at Festubert, Loos, the Somme, Ypres and Passchendaele, and was wounded at Chérisy in 1917. After his recovery he took part in various engagements in the Advance of 1918, and was demobilised in February of the following year after exactly four years' overseas service. He holds the 1914-15 Star, and the General Service and Victory Medals.

74, Henley Street, Battersea, S.W.11.   Z2379B

POOLE, R., Private, East Surrey Regiment.

He volunteered in November 1914, but owing to being medically unfit for duty abroad was unable to obtain his transfer overseas. He was engaged at various stations on important work and rendered valuable services until discharged as physically unfit for further duty in January 1916.

2, Aytoun Road, Stockwell, S.W.9.   Z5822B

POOLE, W. F., Private, 8th Middlesex Regiment.

He volunteered in October 1914, and proceeded overseas in the following March. He fought in the Battle of Neuve Chapelle, and in April 15th, 1915, was severely wounded by the explosion of a trench mortar, one of his legs being shattered. He was invalided home and discharged as physically unfit for further service in February 1916. He holds the 1914-15 Star, and the General Service and :Victory Medals.

56, Comber Grove, Camberwell, S.E.5.   Z3778

POOLEY, W. T., Private, R.A.M.C. and Driver, R.F.A.

He joined in 1916, and in the same year was drafted to Egypt, and served with the British forces under General Allenby in the Advance through Palestine. He was engaged on important duties at Gaza, the Jordan, Jerusalem, Beyrout and Tripoli, until the conclusion of the campaign. Afterwards he was sent to Constantinople with the Army of Occupation, but later returned to Egypt and was stationed at Cairo until he proceeded to England to be demobilised in 1919. He holds t. e General Service and Victory Medals.

22, Sunwell Street, Peckham, S.E.15.   Z6535

POORE, F., Rifleman, King's Royal Rifle Corps.

He volunteered in September 1914, and in the following month was drafted to France, where he was frequently engaged in heavy fighting. He served in the first and second Battles of Ypres, and at Loos and Albert, and in the severe fighting on the Somme. He gave his life for his Country on September 3rd, 1916, in an engagement on the Ancre, and was entitled to the 1914 Star, and the General Service and Victory Medals.

" A valiant soldier, with undaunted heart he breasted Life's last hill."

112, Aylesbury Road, Walworth, S.E.17.   Z3796

POORE, E. E. Driver, R.A.S.C. (M.T.)

He joined in August 1916, and in the same year proceeded to France, where he served in various important engagements, including those on the Somme, and at Arras, Ypres, Passchendaele, and Cambrai. He was also present during the Retreat and Advance of 1918, and after the Armistice returned to England and was demobilised in November 1919, holding the General Service and Victory Medals.

24, Albany Street, Camberwell, S.E.5.   Z5651

POPE, A. (M.M.), Sergt., R.F.A.

He was mobilised at the outbreak of war and was almost immediately drafted to France, where he took part in the memorable Retreat from Mons. He also fought with distinction in numerous notable engagements, including those of the Marne, Neuve Chapelle, Ypres, Festubert, Loos, and many subsequent Battles up to the signing of the Armistice. He was wounded during his service, and was awarded the Military Medal for his distinguished gallantry and devotion to duty on the Field. After the cessation of hostilities he proceeded to India with his Regiment, and in 1920 was still serving there. In addition to the Military Medal he holds the Mons Star, and the General Service and Victory Medals.

39, Westbury Street, Wandsworth Road, S.W.8.   Z3780D

POPE, C. J., Rifleman, King's Royal Rifle Corps.

He volunteered in August 1914, and in the same year was drafted to France. After taking part in several important engagements he gave his life for the freedom of England in action on the Somme in 1915. He was entitled to the 1914 Star, and the General Service and Victory Medals.

" Whilst we remember, the Sacrifice is not in vain."

39, Westbury Street, Wandsworth Road, S.W.8.   Z3780C

POPE, G., Corporal, King's Royal Rifle Corps.

He volunteered in June 1915, and after his training served at various stations on important duties with his unit. He rendered valuable services, but was not successful in obtaining a transfer overseas before his discharge.

39, Westbury Street, Wandsworth Road, S.W.8.   Z3780B

POPE, H., Driver, R.F.A. and R.H.A.

He volunteered in September 1915, and in December of the following year proceeded to France, where he saw much active service. He did excellent work as a driver and was in action at Vimy Ridge, Ypres, Passchendaele, Cambrai, the Somme, the Aisne, Amiens, Bapaume and Havrincourt. He was severely wounded whilst conveying ammunition, and assisting the gunners at Wancourt on the Arras front, and was invalided home to hospital in September 1918. His injuries necessitated the amputation of an arm and a leg, and after twelve months in hospital he was discharged as totally disabled in August 1919. He holds the General Service and Victory Medals.

45, Mossbury Road, Battersea, S.W.11.   Z3779

POPE, H., Rifleman, Rifle Brigade.

He volunteered in August 1914, and on the completion of a short training was drafted to France in the same year. During his service overseas he took part in the severe fighting at Hill 60, Ypres, Vermelles, Vimy Ridge, and the Somme, where he was badly wounded in action. He was sent home to hospital and eventually invalided out of the Service in December 1917. He holds the 1914 Star, and the General Service and Victory Medals.

39, Westbury Street, Wandsworth Road, S.W.8.   Z3780A

POPE, J., Corporal, 1st Middlesex Regiment.

He was mobilised at the outbreak of war, and embarked for France in the same month and fought in the Battles of the Marne, and in various minor engagements. He died gloriously on the Field of Battle at Ypres on October 30th, 1914, and was entitled to the 1914 Star, and the General Service and Victory Medals.

" He died the noblest death a man may die, Fighting for God, and right and liberty."

243, Cator Street, Peckham, S.E.15.   Z5134

POPE, J, S., Private, R.A.S.C.

He volunteered in December 1915, and in July of the following year was drafted to France. Whilst overseas he was engaged on special duties with the Expeditionary Force Canteens, and served at various places, including St. Omer, St. Pol and Dunkirk. He was demobilised in November 1919, after nearly four years' service, and holds the General Service and Victory Medals.

60, Galleywall Road, Rotherhithe, S.E.16.   Z6610

POPE, R. W., Rifleman, 15th London Regiment (Civil Service Rifles).

He volunteered in November 1915, and in March of the following year was drafted overseas. During his service in France he took part in many important engagements, until in March 1918 he was severely wounded and gassed in the Retreat. He was sent to hospital at Rouen, and thence to England, where he remained under medical treatment until February 1919, when he was demobilised. He holds the General Service and Victory Medals.

18, Rowena Crescent, Battersea, S.W.11.   Z3781

POPE, W. J., Air Mechanic, R.A.F.
Volunteering in October 1915, he served on important duties with the Royal Army Service Corps, and the Labour Corps in Salonika from 1915 until 1917. He was afterwards transferred to the Royal Air Force, and was engaged on important work which demanded a high degree of technical skill until November 1917, when he was invalided home, owing to ill-health. He was demobilised in January 1919, and holds the 1914-15 Star, and the General Service and Victory Medals.
17, Loncroft Road, Camberwell, S.E.5. Z5476

POPPLE, H., Sergt., 2nd Queen's (Royal West Surrey Regiment).
A serving soldier, he crossed to France immediately upon the outbreak of war, and took part in the Retreat from Mons. He also fought in the Battles of the Marne, the Aisne and Neuve Chapelle, and died gloriously on the Field of Battle at Givenchy on June 8th, 1915. He had previously served in India, and in the South African Campaign, for which he held the Queen's and King's South African Medals, and was entitled to the Mons Stark and the General Service and Victory Medals.
"A valiant soldier, with undaunted heart, he breasted Life's last hill."
38, Ingelow Road, Battersea Park Road, S.W.8. Z3782

PORT, C., Corporal, R.E.
He volunteered in July 1915, and two months later crossed to France. Whilst in this theatre of war he was engaged on duties of an important nature in connection with the light railways in the forward areas, principally at Armentières, and Hazebrouck. In 1916, however, he was invalided home in consequence of ill-health, and on recovery was retained for important home duties until demobilised in February 1919. He holds the 1914-15 Star, and the General Service and Victory Medals. 73B, Queen's Road, Battersea, S.W11. Z3783

PORT, S., Corporal, 9th Essex Regiment.
He volunteered in October 1914, and crossed to France on completing his training in the following May. In the course of his service, he fought in numerous battles, notably those of Loos, the Somme, Arras, Ypres, and Cambrai, and did excellent work with his unit. On August 10th, 1918, he gave his life for the freedom of England during the Advance of that year. He was entitled to the 1914-15 Star, and the General Service and Victory Medals.
"The path of duty was the way to glory."
72, Flaxman Road, Camberwell S.E.5. Z6216

PORTCH, C., Private, R.A.S.C.
He volunteered in April 1915, and at the conclusion of his training was sent to the Western Front, where he was engaged on important duties, and served in various sectors until hostilities ceased, notably those of Albert, the Somme, Messines and Bapaume. He was demobilised in March 1919, and holds the 1914-15 Star, and the General Service and Victory Medals.
182, Albert Road, Peckham, S.E.15. Z5652

PORTER, A., Private, Tank Corps.
He volunteered in November 1915, and until he was drafted to the Western Front in August 1917, was engaged on special home duties. Whilst overseas he fought in many important engagements, including that at Cambrai, where in November 1917, he was wounded, and the Retreat and Advance of 1918. He was demobilised in November 1919, after his return to England, and holds the General Service and Victory Medals.
32, Knowsley Road, Battersea, S.W.11. Z3785

PORTER, A. J., Gunner, R.G.A.
Although under age for military service, he volunteered in September 1915, and at the conclusion of his training was engaged on important duties with his Battery. He did valuable work at various stations in connection with anti-aircraft guns, but on May 21st, 1918, was unfortunately drowned near Hull.
"His memory is cherished with pride."
99, Akerman Road, Brixton, S.W.9. Z4473-4B

PORTER, C., Private, Labour Corps.
He volunteered in August 1915, and rendered valuable service on the Western Front for three years. During this time, he was attached to the Royal Engineers, and did excellent work in the construction of roads and light railways. In 1918, he returned to England in consequence of ill-health, and after being for some time in hospital was invalided out of the Service in November of the same year. He holds the 1914-15 Star, and the General Service and Victory Medals.
153, Ingrave Street, Battersea, S.W.11. Z3784B

PORTER, C. B., Corporal, Royal Army Pay Corps.
He joined in 1917, and after his training was stationed in Scotland, where he was engaged on important clerical duties. Owing to his being under the regulation height for active service, he was unable to secure his transfer overseas while hostilities lasted, but did very good work before he was demobilised in 1919.
2, Russell Grove, Brixton, S.W.9. Z5735B

PORTER, D. T., Rifleman, King's Royal Rifle Corps.
He joined in May 1918, and after his training at Colchester, served on important duties with his unit. He was unable to secure his transfer overseas before the termination of hostilities, but after the Armistice was sent with the Army of Occupation to Germany, where he was engaged for some months on important guard duties. He was demobilised in November 1919.
153, Ingrave Street, Battersea, S.W.11. Z3784C

PORTER, E. E., Driver, R.F.A.
Volunteering in August 1914, he crossed to France in the following July. In the course of his overseas service he fought in many of the principal battles, including those at the Somme, where he was severely wounded and gassed in 1916. After treatment however, he rejoined his Battery in the Field and again went into action at Arras and Cambrai. In 1918, he returned to England, owing to ill-health following his wound and gas-poisoning, and was invalided out of the Service in October of that year. He holds the 1914-15 Star, and the General Service and Victory Medals.
8, Vaughan Road, Camberwell, S.E.5. Z6430

PORTER, E. S. (M.M.), Sergt., 1st Dorsetshire Regt.
Volunteering in March 1915, he was sent to the Western Front in the following year, and took an active part in several engagements, including those of the Somme, Arras, and was wounded and gassed. He was removed to a hospital in Boulogne, but on his recovery rejoined his unit in the Field, and fought in several other battles. In 1918, he was awarded the Military Medal for his gallant conduct in a bombing raid at Hamelincourt, and in August of that year was again wounded during the final Advance. Invalided home, he was in hospitals at Manchester and Stockport for seven months, and was demobilised in March 1919. In addition to the decoration won in the Field, he holds the General Service and Victory Medals.
4, Rozel Street, Clapham, S.W.4. Z3786A

PORTER, F., Private, Middlesex Regiment.
A serving soldier, he crossed to France immediately upon the outbreak of hostilities, and fought in the Retreat from Mons, and the Battles of the Marne, and the Aisne. He also took part in many other engagements in the course of his four years' overseas service, including those at La Bassée, Ypres, Loos, Albert, the Somme, Arras, Messines, Cambrai, and the Retreat and Advance of 1918. Returning to England he was demobilised in May 1919, and holds the Mons Star, and the General Service and Victory Medals.
13, Aylesbury Road, Walworth, S.E.17. Z3641

PORTER, F. C., Gunner, R.G.A.
Joining in May 1916, he was sent to the Western Front at the conclusion of his training. Whilst overseas, he fought in the Battles of the Somme, Ypres, Arras, Passchendaele, Cambrai, and in many important engagements, in the Retreat and Advance of 1918. During his service he was wounded and gassed, but on each occasion, after receiving treatment in hospital was able to rejoin his Battery in the Field. He holds the General Service and Victory Medals, and was demobilised in February 1919.
3, Rozel Road, Clapham, S.W.4. Z3787

PORTER, H. H., Private, 9th East Surrey Regt.
He joined in March 1917, and crossed to France immediately upon completing his training. He fought in several important engagements in the course of his service doing special work as a bomber, and was unfortunately killed in action near Arras on August 6th, 1918, during the Advance of that year. He was entitled to the General Service and Victory Medals.
"Honour to the immortal dead, who gave their youth that the world might grow old in peace."
4, Rozel Road, Clapham, Road S.W.4. Z3786B

PORTER, J. W., Private, R.A.S.C. (Remounts).
He joined in 1916, and at the conclusion of his training was engaged on important duties at the Remount Depôt. In the course of his service he crossed to France on several occasions in charge of horses and ammunition for the front. He did much valuable work until he was demobilised in February 1919, and holds the General Service and Victory Medals.
12, Locks Square, Walworth, S.E.17. Z3285A

PORTER, R. C., Sapper, R.E.
He volunteered in February 1915, and at the conclusion of his training was engaged on duties of a very important nature at various stations with his unit. Owing to ill-health, he was unable to secure his transfer to a theatre of war, but did much valuable work making pontoons and supervising barbwiring, until July 1918, when he was invalided out of the Service.
153, Ingrave Street, Battersea, S.W.11. Z3784A

POSSEE, A. H., Private, M.G.C.

Joining in May 1916, he was sent to France in the following January, after having completed his course of training. While overseas he fought in the Battles of Arras, Vimy Ridge and Cambrai, where he was badly gassed. After treatment in hospital he rejoined his unit and took an active part in the Battle of the Somme, and many subsequent engagements in the Retreat and Advance of 1918. He was demobilised in October 1919, and holds the General Service and Victory Medals.
2, Cunard Street, Camberwell, S.E.5.   Z5136

POTTER, A. S., Private, R.A.S.C. (M.T.)

Volunteering in February 1915, he was afterwards drafted to the East, and in the Gallipoli campaign did excellent service in the second and third Battles of Krithia, and in the Landing at Suvla Bay. After considerable work in Egypt he was transferred to the Western Front and took part in the Retreat and Advance of the Allies in 1918, until hostilities ended. After his return home he was demobilised in March 1919, and holds the 1914-15 Star, and the General Service and Victory Medals.
4, Lingham Street, Clapham Road, S.W.9.   Z3789

POTTER, G. H., Sergt., 2nd Duke of Wellington's (West Riding Regiment).

He was serving in the Army at the outbreak of war, and was immediately drafted to France. He fell fighting for King and Country in the Battle of Mons on August 24th, 1914, and was entitled to the Mons Star, and the General Service and Victory Medals.
"He died the noblest death a man may die,
Fighting for God, and right and liberty."
27, Searles Road, Southwark, S.E.1.   Z3004A

POTTER, J. J., Corporal, R.A.M.C.

He joined in February 1917, and after completing his course of training at Aldershot, Blackpool, and other stations, proceeded through France and Italy to Egypt, where he did much valuable service from 1918 until his return to England for demobilisation in May 1920. He holds the General Service and Victory Medals.
3, Willowbrook Road, Peckham, S.E.15.   Z4517

POTTER, W. F., Rifleman, 12th Rifle Brigade.

He joined in June 1916, and after the completion of his training was retained for important duties with his unit until drafted to France in June 1918. He did much valuable work in the operations in the Somme sector, and afterwards took part in the Advance of the Allies as far as Maubeuge. After his return to England he was demobilised in December 1919, and holds the General Service and Victory Medals.
346, Commercial Road, Peckham, S.E.15.   Z6644

POTTERELL, F. W., A.B., Royal Navy.

He joined in January 1916, and afterwards was engaged in H.M.S. "Anzac" until the cessation of hostilities on important patrol duties in the North Sea, and in escorting troopships across the Channel to the Western Front. He was demobilised in March 1919, and holds the General Service and Victory Medals.
9, Hargwyne Street, Stockwell Road, S.W.9.   Z3790

POTTERVELD, E. A. (M.M.), Private, 6th Royal Berkshire Regiment.

He volunteered in August 1914, and proceeding to France in June of the following year fought in many important engagements. He was awarded the Military Medal for conspicuous gallantry and devotion to duty in the Field, whilst acting as a runner he delivered Despatches at Headquarters under very heavy fire. He was also in action throughout the Retreat and Advance of 1918, and returning to England was demobilised in March 1919. He holds the 1914-15 Star, and the General Service and Victory Medals.   Z3791B
115, Darwins Buildings, Crail Row, Walworth, S.E.17.

POTTERVELD, H. W., A.B., Royal Navy.

He joined the Royal Navy prior to the outbreak of hostilities, and in August 1914, was serving in H.M.S. "Arethusa." His ship was in action at the engagements at the Dogger Bank, Cuxhaven, and Heligoland, where he was wounded. He was aboard H.M.S. "Arethusa" when she was sunk by a mine off the East Coast on February 11th, 1916, but fortunately he was rescued. He saw much service in various ships engaged on patrol and other important duties until the signing of the Armistice. He was still serving in 1920, and holds the 1914-15 Star, and the General Service and Victory Medals.   Z3791A
115, Darwins Buildings, Crail Row, Walworth, S.E.17.

POTTLE, J. W., Gunner, R.F.A.

Joining in November 1916, he embarked for Egypt shortly afterwards, and serving on the Palestine front, fought in many engagements, including those at Rafa, Siwa, Gaza I, II and III, and was present at the capture of Jerusalem. He was also in action throughout the final British Advance into Syria. Returning to England he was demobilised in September 1919, and holds the General Service and Victory Medals. 14, Akers Street, Walworth, S.E.17.   Z3792

POTTS, E. A. (M.C.), 2nd Lieutenant, 10th Royal Fusiliers and Coldstream Guards.

Volunteering in September 1914, he was sent to the Western Front later in that year. During his service overseas he fought at the Battles of Ypres, Arras, La Bassée, Givenchy, and many other engagements of note. He was awarded the Military Cross for conspicuous gallantry and devotion to duty in the Field during the heavy fighting on the Somme in 1918. He was severely wounded on October 8th, 1918, and subsequently died from the effects of his injuries on October 15th. He was entitled to the 1914-15 Star, and the General Service and Victory Medals.
"A valiant soldier, with undaunted heart he breasted Life's last hill."
9, Mordaunt Street, Landor Road, S.W.9.   Z3788A

POTTS, E. W., Guardsman, 1st Coldstream Guards.

Volunteering in September 1914, and proceeding to the Western Front three months later, he was engaged in heavy fighting at Ypres, Arras and Givenchy. Wounded and taken prisoner at Loos he was held in captivity in Germany for twelve months and then interned in Switzerland. In 1918 he was repatriated, and subsequently discharged on account of service in August of thet year. He holds the 1914-15 Star, and the General Service and Victory Medals.
9, Mordaunt Street, Landor Road, S.W.9.   Z3788B

POTTY, E. J., Private, R.A.S.C.

He volunteered in March 1915, and drafted to France in the same month, served in the advanced areas on important duties connected with the supply of ammunition and food to the front lines. He was present at the Battles of Arras, Albert, the Somme, Lens, and did good work. Returning to England in 1918, he was demobilised in March of the following year, and holds the 1914-15 Star, and the General Service and Victory Medals.
90, Maysoule Road, Battersea, S.W.11.   Z3793

POULSON, W. A., Special War Worker.

He offered his services for work of National importance, and from 1915 until 1919 was employed as a fitter at Woolwich Arsenal. He did good work engaged in making tools for the boring and turning of guns, on pattern making for castings, and in repairing machinery. He discharged his duties in a most efficient and satisfactory manner.
23D, Theatre Street, Lavender Hill, S.W.11.   Z3794

POULTER, A. H., Private, R.A.S.C. (M.T.) and Labour Corps.

He volunteered in May 1915, and embarked for France later in the same year. During his service overseas he was engaged on important transport duties in the forward areas, and saw heavy fighting at Ypres, the Somme, Merville and Albert. Transferred to the Labour Corps he did good work in many parts of the line, and served throughout the German Offensive and Allied Advance of 1918. He was demobilised in February 1919, and holds the 1914-15 Star, and the General Service and Victory Medals.
54, Park Place, Clapham Park Road, S.W.4.   Z3795B

POULTER, A. H. (Jun.), Corporal, R.A.S.C. (M.T.)

He volunteered in February 1916, and completing his training served at various stations with his unit, engaged on important duties. Owing to ill-health he was unsuccessful in obtaining his transfer to a theatre of war, but did good work until discharged. After the Armistice he re-enlisted for a further period of service, and in 1920 was serving in Turkey on important ambulance duties.
54, Park Place, Clapham Park Road, S.W.4.   Z3795A

POULTER, F. T., Private, R.A.S.C. (M.T.)

Volunteering in June 1915, and drafted to the Western Front later in that year he served with the Ammunition Column of the 184th Siege Battery, in many engagements. He was present at heavy fighting throughout the Retreat and Advance of 1918, and returning to England after the Armistice was demobilised in June 1919. He holds the 1914-15 Star, and the General Service and Victory Medals.
24, Stainforth Road, Battersea, S.W.11.   Z3796

POULTER, W. H., Private, R.A.M.C.

He joined in 1917, and completing his training served at various hospitals, engaged on important duties attending the sick and wounded troops. He was unsuccessful in obtaining his transfer overseas prior to the cessation of hostilities, but rendered valuable services until demobilised in 1919.
3, Parkville Road, Fulham, S.W.6.   X20489

POULTON, C., Private, R.A.S.C.

He joined in November 1916, and was sent to France in the following March. He served in various sectors, transporting food and ammunition to the front lines, and in 1917, was transferred to Italy. He saw much service on the Aisago Plateau and in the final Allied Advance in that theatre of war. He was demobilised in February 1919, and holds the General Service and Victory Medals.
13, Ambrose Street, Rotherhithe, S.E.16.   Z6645

POVEY, J. H., Private, 5th Middlesex Regiment.
Volunteering in August 1914, he was drafted to the Egyptian Expeditionary Force in the following year, and fought in many engagements, including those at Sollum, Katia, Romani, Siwa, Gaza I and II, and throughout the Advance through Palestine into Syria. He returned to England, and was demobilised in July 1919, and holds the 1914-15 Star, and the General Service and Victory Medals.
19, Ceylon Street, Battersea Park Road, S.W.8. Z3797

POWELL, A. C., Leading Seaman, R.N.
Mobilised in August 1914, from the Reserve, he was posted to H.M.S. "Aboukir," which ship was engaged on patrol and other important duties in the North Sea. She was torpedoed off the Hook of Holland on September 22nd, 1914, and sunk with all hands. The body of Leading Seaman A.C. Powell was recovered and buried with full Naval honours in Holland. He was entitled to the 1914-15 Star, and the General Service and Victory Medals.
"Whilst we remember the Sacrifice in not in vain."
45, Dorothy Road, Lavender Hill, S.W.11. Z3802C

POWELL, A. W., L/Cpl., 1/21st London Regiment (1st Surrey Rifles).
A Territorial, he was mobilised at the declaration of war, and embarked for the Western Front in March 1915, During his service overseas he fought in many important engagements, including those at Festubert and Hill 60. He gave his life for the freedom of England in the Battle of Givenchy in April 1915, and was entitled to the 1914-15 Star, and the General Service and Victory Medals.
"His life for his country, his soul to God."
17, Mosedale Street, Camberwell, S.E.5. Z3798B

POWELL, G., Pte., Royal Fusiliers and Labour Corps.
He joined in April 1917, after being twice previously rejected, and on the conclusion of his training was retained on important duties at various stations. He was not successful in securing his transfer to a fighting front, but did much valuable agricultural work until he fell ill. He unfortunately died at Nottingham on December 2nd, 1918.
"And doubtless he went in splendid company."
43, Stanley Street, Queen's Road, Battersea Park, S.W.8. Z1261B

POWELL, H., Pte., 11th (Prince Albert's Own) Hussars.
He volunteered in August 1914, and proceeded to France almost immediately. He was in action in the Retreat from Mons, at the Battles of La Bassée, Ypres, Hill 60 and was wounded at Loos. On recovery, he rejoined his unit and fought at Ploegsteert, Arras, Lens, Cambrai, and was wounded and gassed in the second Battle of the Somme in the German Offensive of 1918. Returning to England, he received hospital treatment, and was invalided out of the Service in July 1918. He subsequently died in February 1919, and was entitled to the Mons Star, and the General Service and Victory Medals.
"His memory is cherished with pride."
90, Nelson Row, Clapham, S.W.4. Z3585B

POWELL, J., 1st Class Stoker, R.N.
He was serving in the Royal Navy at the commencement of war, and was posted to H.M. Torpedo Boat No. 13. This vessel was engaged on patrol and other important duties in the North Sea and was in action in many engagements with hostile craft. He was killed in action on January 28th, 1916, and was entitled to the 1914-15 Star, and the General Service and Victory Medals.
"A costly sacrifice upon the altar of freedom."
21, Horsman Street, Camberwell, S.E.5. Z3800

POWELL, J., C.S.M., Royal Fusiliers.
He volunteered at the outbreak of war, and proceeding to France shortly afterwards, fought in the Retreat from Mons and the Battles at Ypres, the Somme, Cambrai and throughout the German Offensive and Allied Advance of 1918, and was three times wounded. He was demobilised in January 1919, and holds the 1914-15 Star, and the General Service and Victory Medals.
11, Dorset Road, Clapham Road, S.W.8. Z3804

POWELL, J. H., Pte., Duke of Cornwall's Light Infantry.
He volunteered in March 1915, and embarked for the Western Front later in that year. He was in action at the Battles of the Somme, Arras, Loos, and was transferred to Salonika in 1917. In this theatre of war he fought in many parts of the line, and during his service overseas was wounded. He returned to England and was demobilised in April 1919, and holds the 1914-15 Star, and the General Service and Victory Medals.
4, Danson Road, Walworth, S.E.17. Z27012

POWELL, J. G., Petty Officer, R.A.F. (late R.N.A.S.)
He volunteered in January 1915, and completing his training served at various aerodromes, engaged on important duties with his Squadron. He was unable to obtain his transfer to a theatre of war owing to medical unfitness, and, owing to the same cause, was invalided out of the Service in March 1917. 35, Sulgrave Road, Hammersmith, W.6. 12099

POWELL, J. P., Private, 1st Queen's Own (Royal West Kent Regiment).
Volunteering in September 1914, he was sent to France later in that year and fought in the Ypres salient and in many other parts of the line. Owing to ill-health he returned to England, and after receiving hospital treatment, was discharged unfit for further service in December 1915. He holds the 1914-15 Star, and the General Service and Victory Medals. He had previously served for twelve years with the Colours.
17, Mosedale Street, Camberwell, S.E.5. Z3798A

POWELL, L., A.B., Royal Navy.
He joined in March 1917, and was posted to H.M. Motor Launch No. 252, which vessel was engaged on patrol and other important duties in the North Sea, and took part in the raids on Zeebrugge and Ostend, and also in various minor engagements with enemy craft. He was demobilised in February 1919, and holds the General Service and Victory Medals.
86, Chatham Street, Walworth, S.E.17. Z3806

POWELL, R., L/Corporal, R.A.P.C.
He volunteered in September 1914, and proceeded to France in the following March. He was first stationed at Wimereux and later was sent to Rouen, where he served until after the cessation of hostilities, engaged on important clerical duties. He was demobilised in July 1919, and holds the 1914-15 Star, and the General Service and Victory Medals.
86, Chatham Street, Walworth, S.E.17. Z3805

POWELL, R. E., Rflmn., King's Royal Rifle Corps.
Joining in April 1916, he went through his training at Winchester and three months later was drafted to France. He fought in the Battles of Arras and Messines, but was invalided home through illness arising out of his service. After treatment in several hospitals he was eventually discharged in 1917 as medically unfit for further service. He holds the General Service and Victory Medals.
43, Stanley Street, Queen's Road, Battersea Park, S.W.8. Z1261C

POWELL, W., L/Corporal, 7th Royal Fusiliers.
He enlisted in 1903, and at the outbreak of hostilities was sent to the Western Front. He fought in the Retreat from Mons, and the Battles of the Marne, the Aisne and many other engagements of note. He died gloriously on the field of battle in July 1916 during the first British Offensive on the Somme, and was entitled to the Mons Star, and the General Service and Victory Medals.
"Great deeds cannot die."
92, Westmacott Street, Camberwell, S.E.5. Z5547B

POWELL, W. F., Corporal, M.G.C.
He joined in February 1917, and proceeded to the Western Front six months later. He fought in many parts of the line, and was in action throughout the German Offensive and Allied Advance of 1918. After the Armistice he was sent into Germany with the Army of Occupation and was stationed at Cologne for a time. He was then sent to Ireland, and returning to England was demobilised in September 1919. He holds the General Service and Victory Medals.
46, Warriner Gardens, Battersea, S.W.11. Z3799

POWELL, W. H., Private, R.A.S.C.
Joining in April 1917, he completed his training and served at various depôts with his unit, engaged on important duties as a motor engine fitter in the workshops. He was not successful in obtaining his transfer to a theatre of war prior to the cessation of hostilities, but rendered excellent services until demobilised in September 1919.
46, Warriner Gardens, Battersea, S.W.11. Z3801

POWER, E., Private, 5th Middlesex Regiment.
He volunteered in April 1915, and in the same year was drafted to France. During his service overseas, he was severely gassed in action in the third Battle of Ypres in October 1917, but after his recovery fought in various subsequent engagements until the cessation of hostilities. He was demobilised in April 1919, and holds the 1914-15 Star, and the General Service and Victory Medals.
22, Rumsey Road, Stockwell, S.W.9. Z6560

POWER, F. C., Private, Devonshire Regiment.
He joined in December 1916, and in the following year proceeded to the Western Front. During his service in France he fought in the Battle of Cambrai, and was blown up by a shell explosion and invalided home to hospital. He was subsequently discharged as medically unfit for further service in March 1918, and holds the General Service and Victory Medals. 96, Farmer's Road, Camberwell, S.E.5. Z3808

POYNTER, W. E., Private, Queen's (Royal West Surrey Regiment).

He joined in March 1918, and in the same year was drafted to France, and during his service overseas fought in various engagements. He died gloriously on the field of battle at Ypres on September 28th, 1918, and was entitled to the General Service and Victory Medals.

"He died the noblest death a man may die,
    Fighting for God, and right and liberty."

19, Draycourt Place, Camberwell, S.E.5.   Z4518

PRAGNELL, R., Private, R.A.S.C.

He volunteered in February 1915, and in the following month was drafted to the Dardanelles. During the Gallipoli Campaign he served on important duties in various engagements until the Evacuation of the Peninsula. In 1916 he was sent to the Western Front, and was present at the Battles of the Somme and Cambrai and in many subsequent engagements until the cessation of hostilities. He holds the 1914-15 Star, and the General Service and Victory Medals, and in 1920 was still serving with the Colours.

17, Kingswood Road, Chiswick, W.4.   6802B

PRANGLEY, E., Bandsman, Royal Berkshire Regt.

A serving soldier since May 1903, he was almost immediately sent overseas at the outbreak of hostilities and took part in the Retreat from Mons. He was sent home in September 1914, and until the Armistice was signed was engaged on special duties at various stations. He was discharged in February 1919, but has since re-enlisted in the Scots Guards. He holds the Mons Star, and the General Service and Victory Medals.

45A, Lewis Trust Buildings, off Warner Road, Camberwell, S.E.5.   Z6059

PRANGNELL, H., Private, Duke of Cornwall's Light Infantry.

He joined in June 1917, and after his training was drafted to France in July of the following year. During his service overseas he was wounded at Amiens in August 1918, and in December in the same year was sent home and demobilised. He re-enlisted, however, for another two years, and in 1920 was still serving. He holds the General Service and Victory Medals.

21, Sydney Square, Peckham, S.E.15.   Z6310

PRANKARD, F. G., Rifleman, Rifle Brigade.

Joining in June 1916, he was drafted overseas in the following year and served in various engagements in the Somme, Arras, and Ypres sectors. During this period he was severely wounded and was invalided home to hospital, where he underwent medical treatment for nearly eighteen months. He then rejoined his unit in France and was engaged in guarding German prisoners until the cessation of hostilities. He was demobilised in 1919, and holds the General Service and Victory Medals.

29, Bromgrove Road, Stockwell, S.W.9.   Z3809

PRATT, A., Gunner, R.F.A.

He volunteered in August 1914, and three months later proceeded overseas. During his service in France he did good work as a gunner in the first Battle of Ypres, at Loos and on the Somme, and was wounded. Subsequently he was in action in various engagements until the cessation of hostilities, and was demobilised in March 1919. He holds the 1914 Star, and the General Service and Victory Medals.

92, Waterloo Road, Camberwell, S.E.5.   Z3810

PRATT, C., Rifleman, King's Royal Rifle Corps.

He volunteered in August 1914, and in the same year was drafted to France. During his service on the Western Front he fought in the Battles of Ypres, the Somme and Cambrai, and in various other engagements. He was severely wounded in three places and invalided home to hospital, and after his recovery was transferred to the Royal Army Medical Corps and was stationed for a time at Park Royal. Subsequently he was sent back to France, where he was engaged on important duties until May 1919, when he returned home and was demobilised. He holds the 1914 Star, and the General Service and Victory Medals.

8, Walton Terrace, South Lambeth Road, S.W.8.   Z27526

PRATT, J. H., Private, 3rd Bedfordshire Regt.

He volunteered in September 1914, and in March of the following year was drafted overseas. Whilst in France he fought in the engagements at Hill 60, the Somme and Arras, and was severely wounded in action in May 1917. He was invalided home to hospital, and, subsequently, unfortunately, killed in an enemy air raid on July 22nd, 1917. He was entitled to the 1914-15 Star, and the General Service and Victory Medals.

"Courage, bright hopes, and a myriad dreams, splendidly given."

31, Portslade Road, Wandsworth Road, S.W.8.   Z3812

PRATT, C. W., Rifleman, 8th London Regiment (Post Office Rifles).

He volunteered in September 1915, and two months later was drafted to France. During his service on the Western Front he fought at Vimy Ridge, the Somme, Bullecourt and Messines, and was severely wounded at Passchendaele in September 1917. He was invalided to England, and after many months medical treatment in hospital was discharged as medically unfit for further service in March 1918. He holds the 1914-15 Star, and the General Service and Victory Medals.

50, Doddington Grove, Battersea, S.W.11.   Z3811

PRATT, J., Private, M.G.C.

He joined in September 1916, and in the following year proceeded overseas, and during his service in France fought in many important engagements. He was in action at Vimy Ridge, Bullecourt, Messines, Ypres and Passchendaele and in many subsequent battles in the Retreat and Advance of 1918. Towards the latter end of this year he was in hospital at Rouen on account of illness, and later returned to England and was demobilised in December 1918. He holds the General Service and Victory Medals.

21, Power Street, Wandsworth Road, S.W.8.   Z3813

PRATT, W. C., Corporal, R.A.O.C.

He volunteered in February 1915, and in the same year proceeded to the Western Front. Whilst overseas he served on important duties with his Corps on the Ypres front, and also in the Somme and Arras sectors. After the cessation of hostilities he was sent home and demobilised in June 1919, and holds the 1914-15 Star, and the General Service and Victory Medals.

22, Moncrieff Street, Peckham, S.E.15.   Z5653

PRENDERGAST, A., Gunner, R.G.A.

He joined in December 1916, and in the following year was drafted to France, where he saw much service. He did good work on special duties on the Somme front, at Albert, Arras, Passchendaele, Péronne, Bapaume and Béthune and in the final Advance of 1918. He was demobilised in September of the succeeding year, and holds the General Service and Victory Medals.

31, St. Alphonsus Road, Clapham, S.W.4.   Z3814

PRENTICE, W., Driver, R.A.S.C.

Volunteering in May 1915, he was drafted, on the completion of his training to the Western Front, and whilst in this theatre of war served on important duties in connection with the transport at Arras, Ypres and in various other sectors of France. He afterwards proceeded to Egypt and was stationed at Alexandria, where he was engaged in special work until the Armistice. He returned home and was demobilised in March 1919, and holds the 1914-15 Star, and the General Service and Victory Medals.

2, Warrior Road, Camberwell, S.E.5.   Z3815

PRESTON, C. F., Rifleman, Rifle Brigade.

He joined in May 1918, and in the same year was sent to France and took part in the final Allied Advance of that year. He gave his life for the freedom of England on October 14th near Croiselles, and is buried near by. He was entitled to the General Service and Victory Medals.

"Honour to the immortal dead who gave their youth that the world might grow old in peace."

33, Trollope Street, Battersea Park, S.W.8.   Z3817

PRESTON, E., Private, M.G.C.

He joined in June 1916, and in the same year was drafted to France. During his service in France he fought at Ypres and on the Somme, Arras and Passchendaele and in many subsequent engagements in the Retreat and Advance of 1918. He holds the General Service and Victory Medals, and was demobilised in September 1919.

44, Thorncroft Street, South Lambeth, S.W.8.   Z3819

PRESTON, F., Private, Essex Regiment.

He volunteered in January 1915, and sailed for Gallipoli in April of the same year. Whilst in this theatre of war he took part in the Landing at Suvla Bay, and in the subsequent engagements until the Evacuation of the Peninsula. He then proceeded to Egypt and served at Agagia and in other engagements, but later contracted malaria, he was invalided home to hospital and died on January 16th, 1917. He was entitled to the 1914-15 Star, and the General Service and Victory Medals.

12, Creek Street, Battersea, S.W.11.   Z3818

PRESTON, G. L., Driver, R.F.A.

He was mobilised in 1914, and was almost immediately drafted to France, where he took part in the Retreat from Mons. He also served in the Battles of the Marne, Ypres and Loos, and was wounded on the Somme during the heavy fighting in 1916, whilst conveying ammunition up to the firing line. He was invalided home to hospital, and after his recovery returned to France, and was in action at Arras and in many of the operations in the Retreat and Advance of 1918. He holds the Mons Star, and the General Service and Victory Medals, and was demobilised in 1919.

10, Spring Gardens, Vauxhall Walk, S.E.11.   TZ24449

PRESTNEY, E. W., Private, Royal Sussex Regt.

He volunteered in September 1914, and was drafted overseas in the following year. During his service in France he fought at Ypres, Loos and on the Somme, where he was wounded. He was invalided to hospital in England in July 1916, and was sent back to France after his recovery in the following year, and was in action at Arras, Ypres and Lens, where he was again severely wounded. He returned home and after his discharge from hospital served in England instructing recruits until the cessation of hostilities. He was demobilised in January 1919, and holds the 1914-15 Star, and the General Service and Victory Medals.

4, Burgoyne Road, Stockwell, S.W.9. Z3816

PRETTY, H. G., Sergt., Royal Sussex Regiment.

He volunteered in November 1914, and at the conclusion of his training served with his Battalion on important duties at various stations. He rendered valuable services as an Instructor, but was unsuccessful in obtaining his transfer overseas, and was demobilised in March 1919.

21, Oswin Street, Kennington, S.E.11 Z26703

PRETTY, T. E., Stoker, R.N.

He had previously served many years in the Navy, and was invalided out in 1904. He was mobilised at the outbreak of war, and sent to Portsmouth, where he was engaged on important duties on board the "Victoria and Albert." Owing to medical unfitness he was unable to secure his transfer to sea, and was in consequence discharged unfit for further service in January 1917.

10, Tindall Street, Lothian Road, S.W.9. Z5823

PRICE, A. F., Driver, R.F.A.

He joined in 1917, and in the same year was sent overseas. During his service on the Western Front he fought on the Somme and at Arras and Ypres, and in various other sectors. After the signing of the Armistice he proceeded to Germany with the Army of Occupation, and was stationed on the Rhine, until demobilised in 1919. He holds the General Service and Victory Medals.

23, Orb Street, Walworth, S.E.17. Z3820B

PRICE, C., Pte., Queen's (Royal West Surrey Regt.)

He joined in May 1917, on attaining military age, and was sent overseas in April 1918. Whilst on the Western Front he was in action at Le Cateau, Selle and the Sambre, and was present at the entry into Mons in November 1918. He later proceeded to Germany with the Army of Occupation and was stationed on the Rhine. He was demobilised in January 1920, and holds the General Service and Victory Medals.

56, Geneva Road, Coldharbour Lane, S.W.9. Z3823

PRICE, E. J., Driver, R.A.S.C. (M.T). and Private, R.A.M.C.

He volunteered in January 1915, and later in the same year was sent to Salonika. In this theatre of war he was engaged with his unit on important duties on the Struma and Doiran fronts, also during the final Advance through Bulgaria. He was demobilised in March 1919, and holds the 1914-15 Star, and the General Service and Victory Medals.

95, Avenue Road, Camberwell, S.E.5. Z5306 Z2137B

PRICE, F., Leading Stoker, R.N.

He volunteered in August 1914, and with his ship, H.M.S. "Bellerophon," took part in the Battles of Heligoland Bight and the Dogger Bank, and was then transferred to H.M.S. "Tiger," in which he was serving at the Battle of Jutland. He was later on escort duty at the surrender of the German Fleet at Rosyth and the internment at Scapa Flow. He holds the 1914-15 Star, and the General Service and Victory Medals, and was still serving in 1920.

8, Avondale Square, Old Kent Road, S.E.1. Z27186

PRICE, F., Driver, R.A.S.C. (M.T.)

He volunteered in June 1915, and served on home duties until drafted to East Africa in May 1917. There he was engaged on important transport work, conveying war materials and ration supplies to various parts of the country. He returned to England after the cessation of hostilities, and was demobilised in May 1919. He holds the General Service and Victory Medals.

5, Bavent Road, Camberwell, S.E.5. Z6497

PRICE, F. J., Gunner, R.G.A.

He volunteered in May 1915, and in the following August was sent to France. In this theatre of war he fought in many engagements, including those at Ypres, Festubert, Loos, Albert, the Somme, Arras, Messines, and Cambrai. He was severely wounded in October 1917, and invalided to hospital in England, being subsequently discharged as unfit for further service in October 1918. He holds the 1914-15 Star, and the General Service and Victory Medals.

10, Hopwood Street, Walworth, S.E.17. Z3309A

PRICE, H. H., Private, 3rd Middlesex Regiment.

He volunteered in February 1915, and three months later crossed to France. Whilst in this theatre of war he fought in several important engagements, but after taking part in the Battle of Loos on September 30th, 1915, was reported missing. He was later presumed to have been killed in action on that date. He was entitled to the 1914-15 Star, and the General Service and Victory Medals.

"A costly sacrifice upon the altar of freedom."

14, Riverhall Street, South Lambeth, S.W.8. Z3821

PRICE, H. W., Pte., Loyal North Lancashire Regt. and Suffolk Regt.

Joining in July 1917, he was drafted to France in September of that year. During his service in this theatre of war he was engaged in the fighting in many important sectors, notably that of Ypres, and was also in action in the Retreat and Advance of 1918. He was demobilised in January 1920, and holds the General Service and Victory Medals.

40, Smyrk's Road, Walworth, S.E.17. Z3822B

PRICE, J., Private, 12th Royal Fusiliers.

Volunteering in November 1915, he embarked for France in the following January, and four months later, after taking part in engagements at Loos, St. Eloi and Albert, was severely wounded in action at Vimy Ridge. After receiving hospital treatment in France he was evacuated to England and sent to Leicester Hospital from which he was invalided out of the Service in October 1916. He holds the General Service and Victory Medals.

104, Westmoreland Road, Walworth, S.E.17. Z3825

PRICE, J., Sergt., R.A.S.C.

He volunteered in April 1915, and at the conclusion of his training was engaged on special duties in connection with the hospital medical transport, dealing with 156 hospitals. He was unable to secure his transfer to a theatre of war before the termination of hostilities, but, nevertheless, rendered valuable services until he was demobilised in April 1919.

191, Portland Street, Walworth, S.E.17. Z27118A

PRICE, J. F., Corporal, 1st East Surrey Regiment and 10th Hampshire Regiment.

He was in the Army when war broke out, having enlisted in 1912, and immediately crossed to France, where he fought in the Retreat from Mons and the Battles of the Marne and the Aisne. Owing to a severe wound received in action at La Bassée, he was invalided home to hospital, and on recovery was sent to his depôt at Dover. He was then transferred to the 10th Hampshire Regiment, and in September 1915, was drafted to the Dardanelles. After the Evacuation of the Peninsula he was sent to Salonika, where he fought in many engagements and also took part in the Serbian Retreat. In 1917 he returned to England and in November of that year was discharged. He holds the Mons Star, and the General Service and Victory Medals.

7, Sterndale Road, Wandsworth Road, S.W.8. Z1632C

PRICE, L. A., Corporal, 1st Devonshire Regiment.

Mobilised at the commencement of hostilities, he was quickly drafted to the Western Front, and fought in the Retreat from Mons. He also took part in many of the engagements which followed, including those at Le Cateau, Ypres and Hill 60, where he was seriously wounded. Invalided home, he was for some time in hospital, and after recovery was stationed at Exeter and Devonport. In 1917 he was drafted to Italy and served there for six months, during which time he did valuable work with his unit. He was demobilised in April 1919, and holds the Mons Star, and the General Service and Victory Medals.

124, Abbey Street, Bermondsey, S.E.1. Z27417

PRICE, R. R., Rifleman, King's Royal Rifle Corps.

He joined in August 1917 and after his training was engaged on duties of an important nature at various stations. In the course of his service he was attached to the Royal Scots and Border Regiments, and although unable to secure his transfer overseas before the termination of hostilities he did valuable work until demobilised in December 1919.

40, Smyrk's Road, Walworth, S.E.17. Z3822A

PRICE, W. A., Gunner, R.F.A.

He joined in 1916 and was engaged at home on duties of an important nature until drafted to India in 1918. During his service overseas he served with his Battery on garrison duties at various stations and in 1919 took an active part in the Afghan Campaign on the North-West Frontier, where he did valuable work. He was demobilised in January 1920, and in addition to the General Service and Victory Medals, holds the India General Service Medal (with Clasp, Afghanistan, North-West Frontier, 1919).

10, Heygate Street, Walworth, S.E.17. Z3820A

PRICE, W. E., 1st Air Mechanic, R.A.F. (late R.N.A.S.)

Joining in May 1916 he crossed to France in the following December and served principally at Dunkirk, where he was engaged on important duties, which demanded a high degree of technical skill, and did much valuable work with his Squadron until after the termination of hostilities. He was demobilised in May 1919, and holds the General Service and Victory Medals.

191, Portland Street, Walworth, S.E.17.   Z27118B

PRICE, W. J., Private, 2nd Manchester Regiment.

Joining in February 1916 he was drafted to the Western Front at the conclusion of his training and subsequently took part in several of the principal battles. Unfortunately he was killed in action in the vicinity of St. Quentin during the German Offensive in March 1918, and was entitled to the General Service and Victory Medals.

          " His life for his Country, his soul to God."

54, Sandover Road, Camberwell, S.E.5.   Z5477A

PRICE, W. T., A.B., Royal Navy.

Joining in November 1917 he was posted to H.M.S. " Rowan," which vessel was engaged in the Mediterranean and Ægean Seas. In the course of his service his ship was used as a convoy and troopship, and also as Fleet messenger, and he did valuable work until after the termination of hostilities. He was demobilised in July 1919, and holds the General Service and Victory Medals.

13, Beech Street, Dorset Road, S.W.8.   Z3824

PRIEST, W. F., Private, Royal Fusiliers.

Volunteering early in 1915 he was drafted overseas in May of the following year and during the course of his service on the Western Front fought in many of the principal engagements, and was wounded in action on the Somme in September 1916, and a second time at Vimy Ridge in the following April. After the Retreat and Advance of 1918 he was sent with the Army of Occupation to Germany, and was stationed at Cologne. He was demobilised on returning to England in February 1919, and holds the General Service and Victory Medals.

27, Cambridge Street, Camberwell, S.E.5.   Z3826

PRIGMORE, H., Private, 12th East Surrey Regiment and Highland Light Infantry.

He volunteered in June 1915 and after a period of training proceeded to the Western Front in 1916, where he took part in many important engagements, including those at the Somme, Arras, Ypres, Cambrai, and the Retreat and Advance of 1918. He was transferred to the Highland Light Infantry in which he acted as Signaller and was slightly wounded. In February 1919 he was demobilised, and holds the General Service and Victory Medals.

17, Trothy Road, Bermondsey, S.E.1.   Z27170B

PRIGMORE, N. T., Private, 22nd London Regiment (The Queen's).

He volunteered in September 1914 and after a period of training proceeded to the Western Front in the following year. Whilst overseas he took part in the fighting at Neuve Chapelle and Loos, and was afterwards invalided home and in hospital for some months. On his recovery he was drafted to Salonika in 1917 and afterwards with General Allenby's Forces took part in several engagements in Palestine and was present at the Entry into Jerusalem. He returned to England for his demobilisation in July 1919, and holds the 1914–15 Star, and the General Service and Victory Medals.

17, Trothy Road, Bermondsey, S.E.1.   Z27170A

PRINCE, T. G., Rifleman, Rifle Brigade.

He was serving at the outbreak of war and immediately crossed to France, where he fought in the Battle of Mons and was wounded. On his recovery after treatment in England he returned to his unit and took an active part in the engagements at Ypres, Armentières and the Somme, in which he was again badly wounded. After prolonged treatment in Norfolk War Hospital he was discharged in August 1917, and holds the Mons Star, and the General Service and Victory Medals.

58, St. Mark's Road, Kennington, S.E.5.   Z2785B

PRIOR, E. F., Pte., 5th Northamptonshire Regt.

He first volunteered for service in 1914 but was then rejected on account of his age. In February 1917 however he was accepted and after his training proceeded to the Western Front later in that year. He took an active part in the Battles of Messines and Cambrai, and in the leading operations of the Retreat and Advance of 1918, and remained in France until his demobilisation in May 1919. He holds the General Service and Victory Medals.

29, Harder's Road, Peckham, S.E.15.   Z6307

PRIOR, G. A. (Mrs.), Special War Worker.

In January 1916 this lady volunteered for work of National importance and from that date until January 1919 was engaged on shell-turning at the Projectile Factory, New Road, Battersea. She performed all her duties during her three years' service with the greatest skill and efficiency.

569, Battersea Park Road, Battersea, S.W.11.   Z3310A

PRIOR, G. W. C., Chief Stoker, Royal Navy.

He was serving in H.M.S. " Commonwealth " when war was declared in 1914. He went through the Battles of Heligoland Bight and Dogger Bank and several cruiser actions off the Belgian Coast. In July 1916 he was transferred to H.M.S." Repulse," in which he took part in much valuable patrol work in the North Sea and in many minor engagements. In August 1918 in H.M.S. " Starfish " he was in action in the second Battle of Heligoland Bight and subsequently was engaged on escort and convoy duties until his discharge after highly creditable service in December 1919. He was wounded on one occasion, and holds the 1914–15 Star, the General Service and Victory Medals, as well as the China Medal for services before the late war.

569, Battersea Park Road, S.W.11.   Z3310B

PRIOR, W. H., Private, Queen's (Royal West Surrey Regiment).

Volunteering in 1914 he was drafted after a period of training to the Western Front. There he fought with distinction in the Battles of Neuve Chapelle, Hill 60, Ypres, Festubert, Loos, the Somme, the Aisne and many engagements in the Retreat and Advance of 1918. During his service he was twice wounded. He returned to be demobilised in 1919, and holds the 1914–15 Star, and the General Service and Victory Medals.

24, Richmond Street, Kennington, S.E.11.   Z27000

PRITCHARD, A. (D.S.M.), Leading Seaman, Royal Navy.

He was mobilised at the outbreak of war and was sent to the North Sea, and later to the South Atlantic, where he served under Admiral Craddock and was in action in the engagement at the Falkland Islands. Afterwards he was sent to the Dardanelles and took part in the Landings at Gallipoli and Suvla Bay. On June 21st, 1917, his ship was in action against two enemy submarines, both of which were sunk. He was awarded the Distinguished Service Medal for his gallantry, in this engagement, and holds in addition the 1914–15 Star and the General Service and Victory Medals. He was demobilised in January 1919.

99, Ingelow Road, Battersea Park Road, S.W.8.   Z3828

PRITCHARD, J. T., Private, Queen's (Royal West Surrey Regt.) and 2nd Northamptonshire Regt.

He volunteered in February 1915 at the age of sixteen-and-a-half years and in 1917 was drafted to the Western Front. Whilst overseas he was in action in the Somme sector and at Ypres and Arras, and was gassed. He was taken prisoner at Vimy Ridge in March 1917 and was held in captivity in Germany at Limburg and Metz until his release after the Armistice. He returned home and was demobilised in February 1919, and holds the General Service and Victory Medals.

121, Kinglake Street, Walworth, S.E.17.   Z3827

PROBETS, A., Sapper, R.E., and Private, Labour Corps.

He volunteered in April 1915 in the Royal Engineers and was discharged as medically unfit in the following month. He re-enlisted later, however, in the Labour Corps and in July 1919 was drafted to France, where he did excellent work in connection with the Graves Registration. He returned home and was demobilised in February 1920.

7, Sheepcote Lane, Battersea, S.W.11.   Z3829B

PROBETS, E. (Mrs.), Special War Worker.

For three years during the war this lady rendered valuable services in the employ of the South Metropolitan Gas Works Company and thereby released a man for military service. Her duties were carried out in an efficient and commendable manner until December 1919, when she relinquished her post.

7, Sheepcote Lane, Battersea, S.W.11.   Z3829A

PROCKTER, E. G., Private, 24th London Regiment (Queen's).

He volunteered in September 1914 and after his training was completed was drafted to France in the following March. After taking part in various engagements he was unfortunately killed in action at Festubert on May 25th, 1915. He was entitled to the 1914–15 Star, and the General Service and Victory Medals.

          " Courage, bright hopes, and a myriad dreams splendidly given."

14, Elliott Road, Brixton, S.W.9.   Z5654

PROTHERO, W. W., Stoker Petty Officer, Royal Navy, H.M.S. " Dreadnought " and " Raven."

He was serving in H.M.S. " Dreadnought " at the outbreak of war and was immediately sent to the North Sea. Whilst in this ship he served on dangerous and important patrol duties and took part in various engagements in the North Sea, including the sinking of the U29 in March 1915. Later he was transferred to H.M.S. " Raven " in October 1919 and in the following year was still serving. He holds the 1914–15 Star, and the General Service and Victory Medals.

27, Newcomen Road, Battersea, S.W.11.   Z3830

PRUCE, E., Apprentice, Mercantile Marine.
He joined in February 1917 at the age of fifteen years and was trained as an apprentice at the Nautical Training School at Rotherhithe. On the completion of his training he was posted to the "Milwaukee," with which he served on important duties. In 1920 he was in the "Caterina," and holds the General Service and Mercantile Marine War Medals.
13, Date Street, Walworth, S.E.17. Z27112

PRUCE, L., Signaller, R.F.A.
He volunteered at the outbreak of war and after his training was drafted to the Western Front. During his service in France he fought in the Battle of the Somme and was gassed and wounded in action at Hooge and invalided home. On recovery he rejoined his battery in France and took part in various engagements, including that of Vimy Ridge and in many subsequent battles in the Retreat and Advance of 1918. After the Armistice he advanced into Germany with the Army of Occupation, with which he served until he returned home and was demobilised in April 1919. He holds the General Service and Victory Medals.
13, Date Street, Walworth, S.E.17. Z27111

PRYOR, C., Private, East Surrey Regiment.
He volunteered in November 1914 and after his training proceeded to France in May of the following year. During his service on the Western Front he took part in many engagements and was wounded in the Battle of Loos on October 13th, 1915. He was invalided home to hospital and after some months' treatment was discharged as medically unfit for further service in July 1916. He holds the 1914-15 Star, and the General Service and Victory Medals.
8, Cheam Place, Off Newchurch Road, Camberwell, S.E.5. Z6498

PUDDICK, A. J., Private, 10th Essex Regiment.
He volunteered in December 1915 and in the following year was drafted to the Western Front. During his service in France he fought in various engagements and was wounded near Loos and invalided to hospital at Trouville. After his recovery he rejoined his unit and was in action on the Somme and at Cambrai and in various sectors until the cessation of hostilities. He was demobilised in January 1919, and holds the General Service and Victory Medals.
34, East Surrey Grove, Peckham, S.E.15. Z5272

PUDDEPHATT, A., Private, 1st West Yorkshire Regiment.
A serving soldier at the outbreak of hostilities he was almost immediately drafted to France and fought in the Retreat from Mons, at Le Cateau, La Bassée and the first Battle of Ypres. In this engagement he was severely wounded and lay for three days unattended in a trench until he was found and sent to hospital in France. Later he was invalided home and medically treated in various hospitals, but subsequently died in a sanatorium on April 4th, 1915. He was entitled to the Mons Star, and the General Service and Victory Medals.
"A costly sacrifice upon the altar of freedom."
63, Albert Road, Peckham, S.E.15. Z6066

PUDDEPHATT, E. E., Corporal, Machine Gun Corps.
A serving soldier at the outbreak of war he was immediately sent to France direct from Malta and took part in the Retreat from Mons. He also served at Le Cateau, La Bassée, Ypres, Loos, Albert, Vermelles and Vimy Ridge, and was wounded in the first Battle of the Somme. On recovery he was in action again at Arras, Vimy Ridge, Messines, Bullecourt, Ypres, Cambrai, the Somme, the Marne, Amiens, Bapaume and the second Battle of Cambrai, and during this period was wounded three times and also gassed. He was demobilised in March 1919, and holds the Mons Star, and the General Service and Victory Medals.
63, Albert Road, Peckham, S.E.15. Z6066B

PUDNEY, W., Private, 11th (Prince Albert's Own) Hussars and York and Lancaster Regiment.
He volunteered in August 1914 and after his training was transferred to the York and Lancaster Regiment and sent to Gallipoli. Whilst in this theatre of war he took part in the Landing at Suvla Bay, where he contracted dysentery and was sent to Mudros. Subsequently he proceeded to Salonika and was in action in various engagements on the Balkan front and wounded during the Advance across the Struma. He returned home and was demobilised in March 1919, and holds the 1914-15 Star, and the General Service and Victory Medals.
2, Este Road, Battersea, S.W.11. Z3831

PUGH, C. R., Rifleman, 9th Rifle Brigade.
He volunteered in August 1914 and in April 1915 was sent to the Western Front, where he fought in the second Battle of Ypres. He was also in action at Hooge, where he was severely wounded, and in consequence was invalided home to hospital. He was discharged as medically unfit for further service in 1916, and holds the 1914-15 Star, and the General Service and Victory Medals.
28, Marcia Road, Bermondsey, S.E.1. Z26369A

PUGH, F. T., Sergt., R.F.A.
Volunteering in January 1915 he crossed to France in the following October after eight months' service in the Army Pay Corps. Whilst overseas he was in action at Loos, Albert, Vermelles, Vimy Ridge, the Somme, Beaumont-Hamel, Arras, Bullecourt, Messines, Ypres, Lens and Cambrai. During the second Battle of the Somme in 1918 he was wounded and gassed, and in consequence returned to England. He was invalided out of the Service in April of that year, and holds the 1914-15 Star, and the General Service and Victory Medals.
41, Charleston Street, Walworth, S.E.17. Z3832

PUGH, H., Private, 14th Royal Welch Fusiliers.
He volunteered in November 1914 and served on the Western Front from November 1915 until the cessation of hostilities, during which time he took part in numerous important engagements and did very good work with his unit. He was demobilised in 1919 after his return home, and holds the 1914-15 Star, and the General Service and Victory Medals.
28, Marcia Road, Bermondsey, S.E.1. 26369B

PUGH, T., Private, Northamptonshire Regiment.
He was serving at the outbreak of the war and was sent immediately to France, where he took part in the Retreat from Mons and the Battles of the Marne and the Aisne. He was taken prisoner at La Bassée in October 1914 and was held in captivity until after the cessation of hostilities, during which time he received very harsh treatment at the hands of his captors. He was repatriated and demobilised in January 1919, and holds the Mons Star, and the General Service and Victory Medals.
5B Block, Peabody Buildings, East Lane, Rotherhithe, S.E.16. Z27446

PUGH, T. G., Corporal, R.E.
Volunteering in November 1915 he crossed to France immediately upon completing his training. He was engaged on important duties with his unit in the forward areas and did valuable work during military operations at Ypres, Loos, Arras, Ypres, Lens, Passchendaele and Armentières, where he was severely wounded. After being for some time in hospital at Rouen he returned to England, and early in 1919, after further treatment at the Lewisham Military Hospital, he was invalided out of the Service. He holds the 1914-15 Star, and the General Service and Victory Medals.
18, Heaton Road, Peckham, S.E.15. Z5998B

PULFORD, H. T., 1st Class Stoker, Royal Navy.
Joining in February 1916 he was posted to H.M. Destroyer "Laforey," in which he served with distinction in several engagements in the Dover Patrol. Whilst proceeding to the rescue of a ship in distress in the English Channel his vessel struck a mine and he was unfortunately killed on March 23rd, 1917. He was entitled to the General Service and Victory Medals.
"The path of duty was the way to glory."
183, Battersea Bridge Road, Battersea, S.W.11. Z3833B

PULFORD, L. R., Driver, R.F.A.
He volunteered in February 1915 and crossing to France in the following October after the completion of his training at Tidworth fought in the Battle of Loos and the Somme Offensive of 1916. In September 1917 he was transferred to Italy and during his service in this theatre of war was mentioned in Despatches for conveying supplies to the forward areas under heavy fire. Returning to England in December 1918 he was demobilised in the following March, and holds the 1914-15 Star, and the General Service and Victory Medals.
183, Battersea Bridge Road, Battersea, S.W.11. Z3833A

PULLEN, A., Private, 5th (Royal Irish) Lancers.
Volunteering at the commencement of hostilities he crossed to France in 1914 and took part in several subsequent important battles, notably those of the Somme and Cambrai. Early in 1918 he was wounded and gassed and was in consequence invalided to the Bristol Military Hospital. After his recovery he was stationed in Ireland until he was demobilised in February 1919. He holds the 1914 Star, and the General Service and Victory Medals.
422, Guinness' Buildings, Page's Walk, Grange Road, S.E.1. 26254

PULLEN, A. J., Signalman, Royal Navy.
Volunteering at the outbreak of war he was posted to H.M.S. "Blanche," which was engaged on important duties in the North Sea and the Baltic. In the course of his service he took part in several Naval engagements, including those off the Dogger Bank and Heligoland Bight, where he was wounded. He was later transferred to a submarine and in 1920 he was still serving in the Navy. He holds the 1914-15 Star, and the General Service and Victory Medals.
10, Charleston Street, Walworth, S.E.17. Z2411B

PULLEN, E. J., Pte. (Driver), 52nd Middlesex Regt.
He joined on attaining military age in July 1918 and had only completed his training when hostilities ceased. Afterwards, however, he was sent with the Army of Occupation to Cologne, where he did much valuable service. He was demobilised in March 1920 on his return to England.
10, Charleston Street, Walworth, S.E.17. Z2411C

PULLEN, A. W., Pioneer, R.E.
He joined in July 1916 and during his service on the Western Front, which lasted for upwards of two years, did valuable work with his unit in many important sectors, including those of Beaumont-Hamel, Arras and Vimy Ridge. He also served throughout the Retreat and Advance of 1918. Returning to England after the termination of hostilities he was demobilised in October 1919, and holds the General Service and Victory Medals.   24, Southville, Wandsworth Road, S.W.8.   Z3834

PULLEN, F. A., Private, 10th Queen's (Royal West Surrey Regiment).
He joined in May 1918 and at the conclusion of his training was engaged on important duties at various stations with his unit. He was not successful in obtaining his transfer overseas before the termination of hostilities, but afterwards was sent to France and thence to Germany, where he served with the Army of Occupation for ten months. He was demobilised in October 1919.
33, Gideon Road, Battersea, S.W.11.   Z3835

PULLEN, G. J., Petty Officer, R.N.A.S.
He volunteered in November 1914 and early in the following year was drafted to the Western Front, where he subsequently did excellent work with his Squadron. In May 1915 however he was invalided home and discharged in consequence of ill-health. He holds the 1914-15 Star, and the General Service and Victory Medals.   55, Ivy Crescent, Chiswick, W.4.   5877B

PULLEN, H. G., Sergt., 1st Queen's (Royal West Surrey Regiment).
He volunteered in November 1915 and crossing to France in the following month was in action at Loos, Albert, Vermelles, Ploegsteert Wood, Vimy Ridge, the Somme, Beaumont-Hamel, Arras, Ypres and Passchendaele. He also fought in the Retreat and Advance of 1918 and did much valuable work with his unit until the termination of hostilities. After he returned to England he was demobilised in February 1919, and holds the 1914-15 Star, and the General Service and Victory Medals.
126, Dalyell Road, Stockwell, S.W.9.   Z3836

PULLEN, S., Gunner, R.F.A.
He joined in March 1917 and after his training was engaged on important duties at various stations. He was unable to secure his transfer to a theatre of war before fighting ceased, but nevertheless did much valuable work. On being demobilised in 1917 he re-enlisted and in 1920 was serving in India.
50, Cator Street, Peckham, S.E.15.   Z5307-8A

PULLILG, F. G., Gunner, R.G.A.
He joined in July 1916 and in the same year was drafted to the Western Front, where he served with distinction until the end of the war. He took part in numerous actions of importance, including those in the Retreat and Advance of 1918. He was demobilised in May 1919 after his return home, and holds the General Service and Victory Medals.
9, Gratton Road, West Kensington, W.14.   T12147B

PULLINGER, R. J., Private, R.A.S.C. (Remounts).
Volunteering in September 1914 he was sent to France in the same month and was engaged on important duties during the Retreat from Mons. In January 1915 he unfortunately met with an accident which resulted in his being invalided home. He was discharged in May 1916, holding the Mons Star, and the General Service and Victory Medals. He died as a result of his war services on July 20th, 1920.
"His memory is cherished with pride."
85, Gloucester Road, Peckham, S.E.15.   Z6062

PULLINGER, W. E., Private, R.A.S.C. (M.T.)
He joined in January 1916 and in the following month was sent to France. He was engaged on the Somme and in the Albert and other sectors and was employed in the transport of ammunition and supplies for over three years. He was demobilised in October 1919, and holds the General Service and Victory Medals.
99, Ingrave Street, Battersea, S.W.11.   Z3837

PURDY, G. S., Corporal, 8th London Regiment (Post Office Rifles).
He volunteered in May 1915 and was sent to France in February of the following year. He took part in the fighting on the Somme and after being wounded in September 1916 was invalided home. On his recovery he returned to France and was in action at Vimy Ridge, Messines and Ypres, and was again wounded. He also served later in the Retreat and Advance of 1918. He was demobilised in January 1919, holding the General Service and Victory Medals.
15, Bonsor Street, Camberwell, S.E.5.   Z4519

PURKISS, T. F., Corporal, 5th Royal Fusiliers.
Volunteering in March 1915 he was retained for important duties with his unit until January 1917, when he was drafted to France and was in action at Arras, Vimy Ridge, Ypres, Passchendaele and in many other important engagements until hostilities ceased. He had previously served twelve years in the Rifle Brigade. He was demobilised in January 1919 after his return home, holding the General Service and Victory Medals.
10, Bridgman Road, Acton Green, Chiswick, W.4.   6273

PURLAND, W. W., Gunner, R.F.A.
He volunteered in November 1914 and in September of the following year was sent to France, where he served till the end of the war. He took part in the fighting at Loos, Armentières, the Ancre and many later operations of importance, and was twice wounded. He was demobilised in May 1919, and holds the 1914-15 Star, and the General Service and Victory Medals.
50, Latchmere Road, Battersea, S.W.11.   Z3838

PURSER, W. S. L., Warrant Officer (Sub-Conductor), R.A.O.C.
He volunteered in 1914 and proceeded to the Eastern Front in 1916. He was engaged on highly important duties at various ammunition dumps in Palestine and Mesopotamia and rendered valuable services until hostilities ceased. He contracted malaria while in the East and after being invalided home was demobilised in 1919. He holds the General Service and Victory Medals.
90, Main Street, Walworth, S.E.17.   Z27091

PURSEY, W. A., Air Mechanic, R.A.F.
He volunteered in 1914 in the Royal Fusiliers and afterwards was sent to France, where he was in action at Ypres and the Somme and was wounded. On his recovery he was transferred to the R.A.F. and returned to France, where he was engaged on important duties with his Squadron in various sectors. He was demobilised in 1919 after five years' service, and holds the 1914-15 Star, and the General Service and Victory Medals.
13, Pennack Road, Peckham, S.E.15.   Z3839

PURSSEY, G., Private, East Surrey Regiment.
He volunteered in May 1915 and in February of the following year was sent to France, where he took part in the fierce fighting at Albert, Vimy Ridge, the Somme, Arras, Ypres, Lens, Cambrai and the Offensives of 1918, and was twice wounded. He was demobilised in January 1919 after returning home, and holds the General Service and Victory Medals.
110, Aylesbury Road, Walworth, S.E.17.   Z3754B

PURSSEY, J. A., Private, 23rd London Regiment.
Joining in November 1916 he was sent to France in the following year and was in action at Arras, Messines, Lens and Cambrai, and the Retreat and Advance of 1918, and was wounded. He unfortunately died from the effects of his wounds and war service on January 16th, 1920, and was entitled to the General Service and Victory Medals.
"Whilst we remember the Sacrifice is not in vain."
110, Aylesbury Road, Walworth, S.E.17.   Z3754C

PURTON, C. W., Bombardier, R.F.A.
He volunteered in August 1914 and shortly afterwards was sent to France, where he took part in several engagements of importance, including those at La Bassée, Ypres, Festubert, Loos, Albert, Vimy Ridge, the Somme, Beaumont-Hamel, Messines, Cambrai, and in the Offensives of 1918. Whilst on active service he was badly gassed and in hospital for about two months, but afterwards rejoined his Battery. He was demobilised in January 1919, and holds the 1914 Star, and the General Service and Victory Medals.
12, Empress Street, Walworth, S.E.17.   Z26325

PURVEY, C., Private, R.A.S.C.(Labour Company).
He volunteered in April 1915 and was sent to France in June of the same year. He served in various sectors, including the Somme, Ypres and Cambrai, loading ammunition and supplies and rendering valuable services throughout his period of duty. He was demobilised in February 1919, holding the 1914-15 Star, and the General Service and Victory Medals.
50, Anchor Street, Rotherhithe, S.E.16.   Z6646

PURVEY, F., Gunner, R.F.A., and Private, Labour Corps.
He volunteered in November 1914 and after completing his training was sent to France, where he was in action at Loos, Armentières, the Somme and in other important engagements, and was wounded. He was invalided home in consequence and discharged as medically unfit for further service in September 1917. He holds the 1914-15 Star, and the General Service and Victory Medals.
87, Stainsforth Road, Battersea, S.W.11.   Z3840

PURYER, A. E., Sapper, R.E. (Labour Battalion).
He joined in January 1916 and afterwards was engaged on important duties with his unit at Deptford, shipping munitions and supplies to various theatres of war. He rendered valuable services but was not successful in obtaining his transfer overseas and was discharged in January 1917.
62, Commercial Road, Peckham, S.E.15.   Z6433

PUTNAM, J. G., Private, R.A.S.C. (M.T.)
He volunteered in May 1915 and on the completion of his training was drafted to Salonika, where he rendered valuable transport services in numerous engagements in various sectors of the Front. He was sent home and demobilised in September 1919, and holds the General Service and Victory Medals.
54, Elliott's Row, St. George's Road, S.E.11.   Z26889

PUTTOCK, H., Private, Royal Fusiliers.

He volunteered in 1915 and after completing his training proceeded to the Western Front in the following year. While in this theatre of war he took part in various important engagements, including those on the Somme, at Arras and Ypres, and in the Retreat and Advance of 1918, and was twice wounded. In 1919 he was demobilised, and holds the General Service and Victory Medals.

5, Sondes Street, Walworth, S.E.17. Z27101

PUTTOCK, L. W., L/Corporal, 23rd London Regiment.

He volunteered in May 1915 and on completing his training was sent to France in September of the same year. He was in action at Loos, Vimy Ridge, the Somme, Bullecourt and Ypres. He was twice wounded and was invalided home in consequence. He was demobilised in June 1919, and holds the 1914-15 Star, and the General Service and Victory Medals.

51, Darien Road, Battersea, S.W.11. Z3841

PUTTOCK, T. W., Sapper, R.E.

Volunteering in January 1915 he was drafted to the Western Front in the following year and rendered valuable service in connection with various engagements of importance. He was later transferred to Salonika, where he was engaged until fighting ceased on the Vardar and Doiran fronts. He was demobilised in April 1919 after returning to England, and holds the General Service and Victory Medals.

4, Smyrk's Road, Walworth, S.E.17. Z3842A

PUTZ, H. H., Private, Labour Corps.

He volunteered in November 1915 in the R.F.A. and after three months was transferred on medical grounds to the Labour Corps. In March 1917 he was sent to France and was engaged on important railway and trenching duties with his unit, particularly during the Retreat and Advance of 1918. He was demobilised in February 1919, and holds the General Service and Victory Medals.

112, Beaufoy Road, Battersea, S.W.11. Z3843

PYE, C., Private, 1st East Surrey Regiment.

Joining in June 1917 he was sent to France in the following October and was in action at Cambrai, the Somme, Amiens and other important engagements in the Retreat and Advance of the Allies in 1918. He was demobilised in 1919 after his return home, and holds the General Service and Victory Medals.

9, Copeland Avenue, Peckham, S.E.15. Z5655

PYLE, W. C., Private, R.A.S.C. (M.T.)

He volunteered in December 1915 in the R.A.V.C. and was sent to France in April of the following year. He was engaged in attending to sick and wounded horses and rendered valuable services. He was later transferred to the R.A.S.C. and was employed in the transport of ammunition and supplies to the lines on various fronts. Falling seriously ill he was invalided home and unfortunately died in Westminster Hospital on September 30th, 1920. He was entitled to the General Service and Victory Medals.

"His life for his Country."

98, Cronin Road, Peckham, S.E.15. Z5479

Q

QUAIFE, C. E., Driver, R.H.A.

Joining in 1916 on the completion of his training he was drafted to France, where he was in action on the Somme, at Arras and Vimy Ridge, and many engagements in the Retreat and Advance of 1918. On the cessation of hostilities he proceeded to Germany and was sent home in 1919. Since then he has unhappily died from the effects of gas poisoning. He was entitled to the General Service and Victory Medals.

"The path of duty was the way to glory."

48, Mann Street, Walworth, S.E.17. Z27088

QUAIFE, E., Private, 13th East Surrey Regiment.

After joining in February 1916 he passed through his course of training and in the following May crossed to France. He did gallant service in many important engagements, including those at Vimy Ridge, the Somme, Arras and Ypres. He fell fighting for King and Country at Bourlon Wood on November 26th, 1917, and was buried in France. He was entitled to the General Service and Victory Medals.

"A costly sacrifice upon the altar of freedom."

108, Cronin Road, Peckham, S.E.15. Z5570B

QUANTRILL, C., Sapper, R.E.

He volunteered in August 1914 and after the completion of his training proceeded to France later in the year with 1st West Kent Regiment. While there he fought in the Battle of Neuve Chapelle and was shortly afterwards invalided home. He was subsequently transferred to the R.E. and retained for duties at home until March 1918, when he was discharged in consequence of ill-health. He holds the 1914 Star, and the General Service and Victory Medals.

37, Dalwood Street, Camberwell, S.E.5. Z3845B

QUANTRILL, H. R., Private, R.A.S.C. (M.T.)

He volunteered in December 1915 and after the completion of his course of training was drafted to Mesopotamia, where he did valuable transport service in connection with the Battles of Kut-el-Amara, Baghdad, Ramadieh, Tekrit, Khan Baghdadie and Mosul, and other operations until the cessation of hostilities. After his return home he was demobilised in February 1920, and holds the General Service and Victory Medals.

27, Dalyell Road, Stockwell, S.W.9. Z3846

QUANTRILL, J. C., Sapper, R.E.

He joined in January 1916 and after completing his course of training proceeded to France in the following November and took part in numerous engagements with the 156th Field Company. He was unfortunately killed in action on November 21st, 1917, after much valuable service, for which he was highly commended by his Commanding Officer. He was entitled to the General Service and Victory Medals.

"He died the noblest death a man may die
Fighting for God, and right, and liberty."

37, Dalwood Street, Camberwell, S.E.5. Z3845A

QUAKLEY, C., Rifleman, 18th Rifle Brigade.

He had served through the South African Campaign and was in North Russia when the recent war broke out. He was mobilised in October 1914 and after his course of training was drafted to India in November 1914-15. During his five years' service there he was engaged on important garrison duties at various stations and helped in the suppression of gun-running. He returned home in November 1919 and was demobilised in the following month, holding the Queen's and King's South African Medals, the 1914-15 Star, and the General Service and Victory Medals. 205, Commercial Rd., Peckham, S.E.15. Z6647

QUARRENDON, J. H., Private, R.A.S.C. (M.T.)

He joined in 1916 and after his training proceeded to France later in the year. He rendered valuable services in connection with many engagements, including those at Vimy Ridge, Ypres, Passchendaele, Lens and Cambrai, and was chiefly engaged in conveying ammunition and stores of all kinds to the lines. He returned from France and was demobilised in 1919, holding the General Service and Victory Medals.

29, Wivenhoe Road, Peckham, S.E.15. Z6067

QUARRINGTON, A. B., Private, Oxfordshire and Buckinghamshire Light Infantry (attached R.E.)

He volunteered in September 1914 and in November proceeded to the Western Front, where he did gallant service in many engagements and was unhappily killed by a sniper when coming off mining duty on March 26th, 1915. He was buried at Cambrai, and was entitled to the 1914-15 Star, and the General Service and Victory Medals.

"His memory is cherished with pride." Z6315B

3, Boathouse Walk, Peckham, S.E.15. Z6316B

QUARRINGTON, A. J., Private, 2nd Border Regt.

He was serving at the outbreak of hostilities and sailed for France in January 1915. He fought in the Battles of Hill 60, Ypres, where he was gassed, and Loos, where he was taken prisoner in September 1915 and sent to Germany suffering from shell-shock. After long captivity there he returned to England and was discharged as unfit for further service in April 1919. He holds the 1914-15 Star, and the General Service and Victory Medals. Z6315A

12, Boathouse Walk, Peckham, S.E.15. Z6316A

QUARRINGTON, T. A., Private, 9th Middlesex Regt.

He volunteered in October 1915 and afterwards was sent to India. He was subsequently transferred to Mesopotamia and was in action at Tekrit, Baghdadie and numerous other engagements. He afterwards rendered valuable services in Egypt at Kantara, and in Salonika, Italy and France, and was demobilised in June 1919 on his return to England. He holds the General Service and Victory Medals.

20, Lockington Road, Battersea Park Road, S.W.8. Z3847A

QUARTERMAN, W., Private, 24th London Regiment (Queen's).

He volunteered in September 1914 and after his training was drafted to the Western Front, where he served in many important engagements. He was in action at Festubert, Givenchy and Loos, and afterwards was retained for special duties with the Military Police for the remainder of his service. He took part in the Retreat and Advance of 1918 and in April of the following year was demobilised. He holds the 1914-15 Star, and the General Service and Victory Medals.

190, Lynton Road, Bermondsey, S.E.1. Z26194

QUICK, W., Rifleman, Rifle Brigade.

He was called up from the Reserve at the outbreak of war and at once proceeded to France, where he fought in the Retreat from Mons and the Battles of the Marne, the Aisne, Neuve Chapelle, Ypres, the Somme, Vimy Ridge, and the Retreat and Advance of 1918. During his service overseas he was wounded on four occasions. He returned to England and was demobilised in May 1919, holding the Mons Star, and the General Service and Victory Medals.

92, Westmacott Street, Camberwell, S.E.5. Z5547A

QUICK, W. C., Private, 1st Duke of Cornwall's Light Infantry.

He was serving in Ireland at the outbreak of hostilities and crossing to France at once took part in the Battles of Mons, Le Cateau, the Marne and the Aisne, where he was wounded. After his recovery he rejoined his regiment and fought at Ypres and in other engagements until sent home through illness arising out of his service. He returned to the front in July 1915 and rendered much valuable service until March 1916, when he was again invalided home owing to severe shell-shock. He was discharged five months later as unfit for further service, and holds the Mons Star, and the General Service and Victory Medals.
243, Cator Street, Peckham, S.E.15.	Z5137

QUINNELL, G., Private, R.A.S.C., Duke of Wellington's (West Riding Regiment), and Royal Fusiliers.

Joining in February 1916 in the following year he was drafted to France, where he served on the Somme, at Ypres, Arras, Béthune and contracted trench fever at Cambrai in 1917. He was invalided to Etaples and afterwards to England. On his recovery he returned to France and served in the Retreat and Advance of 1918. He was discharged in February 1919 after his return home, and holds the General Service and Victory Medals.
99, St. Paul's Road, Walworth, S.E.17.	Z26788

R

RACKETT, S., Private, 22nd London Regiment (Queen's) and R.A.S.C.

He joined in May 1905 and was mobilised with the Territorial Force on the outbreak of war. Proceeding to France in March 1915 he took part in various engagements and was severely wounded at the Hohenzollern Redoubt and invalided home in November 1915. On his recovery he was transferred to the Royal Army Service Corps in August 1916 and served on important duties at various home stations until discharged in March 1919. He holds the 1914-15 Star, and the General Service and Victory, and the Long Service and Good Conduct Medals.
17, Cranham Road, Rotherhithe, S.E.16.	Z6648B

RACKETT, W., Private, Northamptonshire Regt.

He joined in June 1916 and on the completion of his training proceeded to the Western Front in November 1917. In the following month he was wounded at Merville and after his recovery was transferred to the Royal Sussex Regiment in March 1918. He was then sent to Russia, where he served until his return home for demobilisation in November 1919. He holds the General Service and Victory Medals, and a Russian decoration.
17, Cranham Road, Rotherhithe, S.E.16.	Z6648A

RADFORD, C. W. H., Private, R.A.S.C. (M.T.)

He volunteered in March 1915 and in the same month was drafted to France. During his four years' service overseas he was in charge of a travelling workshop and rendered valuable services in various sectors of the Front. He was demobilised in May 1919, and holds the 1914-15 Star, and the General Service and Victory Medals.
31, Comyn Road, Battersea, S.W.11.	Z3848

RADFORD, W., Gunner, R.G.A., 95th Siege Battery, Flying Column.

He volunteered in November 1915 and in the following year was drafted to France, where he saw much service. He was in action at Albert, Delville Wood and the Somme, Vimy Ridge, Arras, Ypres, Amiens and Péronne, Bapaume and in many other engagements in the Retreat and Advance of 1918, and did excellent work as a Gunner throughout. Returning to England he was demobilised in February 1919, holding the General Service and Victory Medals.
17, Cossall Street, Peckham, S.E.15.	Z6573

RADMALL, A., Driver, R.F.A.

He joined in April 1917 and in August of the same year was drafted to India. He served on the North-Western Frontier during the Afghan risings and unfortunately died of heatstroke on July 25th, 1919. He was entitled to the General Service, India General Service (with Clasp, Afghanistan, North-West Frontier, 1919) and the Victory Medals.
"His memory is cherished with pride."
31, Dartrey Road, King's Road, Chelsea, S.W.10.	X22306A

RADMALL, A., Private, Labour Corps.

He joined in April 1917 and three weeks later was sent to France, where he was engaged on various important duties in connection with the operations. In October 1919 he was demobilised, and holds the General Service and Victory Medals.
36, Glycena Road, Lavender Hill, S.W.11.	Z2201B

RAEBURN, A. J., Private, R.A.S.C. (M.T.)

He volunteered in March 1915 and in July of the same year was drafted to the Western Front. Whilst overseas he served on important duties in motor transport conveying supplies and ammunition up to the front lines at Ypres, the Somme and Cambrai, and in other sectors of the Front. He was demobilised in January 1919, and holds the 1914-15 Star, and the General Service and Victory Medals.
15, Elim Street, Weston Street, S.E.1.	25843A

RAEBURN, G., Gunner, R.F.A.

He volunteered in May 1915 and after his training was drafted to France and served at Ypres and the Somme, and in various other engagements, and was wounded. Unfortunately he was killed near Cambrai in October 1918, and was entitled to the General Service and Victory Medals.
"The path of duty was the way to glory."
15, Elim Street, Weston Street, S.E.1.	Z25843C

RAEBURN, T. H. (D.C.M.), Sergt., R.F.A.

He was serving at the outbreak of hostilities and in 1914 was drafted to France. Whilst overseas he fought with distinction in the Battles of Ypres, the Somme, Arras and Cambrai. He was awarded the Distinguished Conduct Medal for remaining at his post when in charge of a trench mortar and repairing it under continuous and heavy firing. He holds in addition to the D.C.M., the 1914 Star, and the General Service and Victory Medals. He was demobilised in August, 1920.
15, Elim Street, Weston Street, S.E.1.	25843B

RAINBOW, A. G., Driver, R.A.S.C. (H.T.)

He volunteered in November 1915 and in the following year proceeded to France, where he served at Ypres, the Somme and Arras. In 1917 he was severely injured in an explosion whilst driving a wagon and was sent to hospital in England. After his recovery he was engaged on important duties in connection with food supplies for France at Blackheath until his discharge in February 1919. He holds the General Service and Victory Medals.
2, Irving Grove, Stockwell, S.W.9.	Z3849

RAINES, P., L/Corporal, Machine Gun Corps.

He was serving at the outbreak of war and was almost immediately drafted to France, where he took part in the Retreat from Mons. He also served at La Bassée, Ypres, Nieuport, St. Eloi, Loos, the Somme, Arras and Passchendaele, and was wounded. After the Armistice he proceeded to Germany with the Army of Occupation and was stationed on the Rhine until May 1919, when he was demobilised. He holds the Mons Star, and the General Service and Victory Medals.
17, Wayford Street, Battersea, S.W.11.	Z3851

RALPH, E. W., Guardsman, Grenadier Guards.

He joined in January 1917 and in the following December was drafted to the Western Front. During his service in France he fought at Arras and Ypres, and in many subsequent engagements until the cessation of hostilities. After the Armistice he proceeded to Germany, where he served with the Army of Occupation until November 1919, when he was demobilised. He holds the General Service and Victory Medals.
9, Sedan Street, Walworth, S.E.17.	Z3853

RALPH, F., Corporal, R.F.A.

He was mobilised at the outbreak of war and was almost immediately drafted to France and took part in the Retreat from Mons. He also served at La Bassée, Ypres, Loos, the Somme and various minor engagements. He died gloriously on the field of battle on September 26th, 1916, and was entitled to the Mons Star, and the General Service and Victory Medals.
"Courage, bright hopes, and a myriad dreams splendidly given."
7, Pennack Road, Camberwell, S.E.15.	Z3852A

RAMAGE, H. E. (M.M.), Driver, R.F.A.

He was mobilised at the outbreak of war and was almost immediately drafted to France. Whilst overseas he fought in numerous engagements in various sectors of the Western Front, and during his service was severely wounded on three occasions and invalided to hospital. On recovery he rejoined his unit and in March 1919 proceeded to Russia, where he remained for some months. In 1920 he was serving in India. He was awarded the Military Medal for conspicuous gallantry in action, and also the Croix de Guerre for bravery in the Field. In addition to these decorations he holds the 1914 Star, and the General Service and Victory Medals.
64, Landseer Street, Battersea, S.W.11.	Z3854

RAMSAY, J. W., Private, 1st East Surrey Regiment.

He volunteered in January 1915 and in the following March was drafted to France. After serving for two months in various engagements he was severely wounded in the second Battle of Ypres in May 1915. He was sent to hospital in England and subsequently invalided out of the Service in August 1916. He holds the 1914-15 Star, and the General Service and Victory Medals.
4, Camelia Street, Wandsworth Road, S.W.8.	Z3855

RAMSEY, H., Private, Labour Corps.

He joined in May 1916 and in the same year was drafted to the Western Front and was engaged at Divisional Headquarters on important duties connected with the Sanitary Staff. He also took part in the Retreat and Advance of 1918. He was demobilised in January 1919, and holds the General Service and Victory Medals.

34, Bavent Road, Camberwell, S.E.5.　　　　　　Z6499

RANCE, B. C., Gunner, R.F.A.

He volunteered in March 1915 and in the following December was drafted to the Western Front, where he did excellent work as a Gunner at Ypres, the Somme, the Ancre and Arras. He gave his life for the freedom of England in March 1917, and was entitled to the 1914–15 Star, and the General Service and Victory Medals.

"A valiant soldier with undaunted heart he breasted Life's last hill."

155, Hartington Road, South Lambeth, S.W.8.　　　Z3857B

RANCE, C. F., Rifleman, 6th London Regiment (Rifles).

He volunteered in April 1915 and in the following September was drafted overseas. Whilst in France he fought in many engagements, including those on the Somme and at Arras. He gave his life for King and Country at Vimy Ridge on June 7th, 1917, and was entitled to the 1914–15 Star, and the General Service and Victory Medals.

"He died the noblest death a man can die
Fighting for God, and right, and liberty."

155, Hartington Road, South Lambeth, S.W.8.　　　Z3857A

RANCE, J. W., Sergt., King's Royal Rifle Corps.

He had previously served in the South African War and in May 1915 re-enlisted and was drafted to France in the following March. During his service on the Western Front he fought on the Somme and at Richebourg, Bapaume, Givenchy and in many other engagements until the cessation of hostilities. He was demobilised in March 1919, and holds the General Service and Victory Medals.

155, Hartington Road, South Lambeth, S.W.8.　　　Z3858

RANCE, R., Bombardier, R.F.A.

He volunteered in March 1915 and in the following December was sent to France. During his service overseas he was frequently in action, notably on the Somme, the Ancre, and at Ypres, Arras, Cambrai and Péronne. He was demobilised in March 1919, and holds the 1914–15 Star, and the General Service and Victory Medals.

3, Madrid Place, Dorset Road, South Lambeth, S.W.8.　Z3859

RANCE, W. A., Private, 24th London Regiment (Queen's).

He was mobilised with the Territorial Force at the outbreak of war and after his training served at various stations on important duties with unit. He rendered valuable services until 1915, when he was discharged as medically unfit.

60, Faraday Street, Walworth, S.E.17.　　　　　Z3856

RANDALL, F. H., Gunner, R.F.A.

Having volunteered in March 1915 he was sent to France in the same year and was in action at La Bassée, the Somme and Arras. He was wounded and invalided home and on his recovery returned to France and took part in the Retreat and Advance of 1918. He was demobilised in February 1919, and holds the 1914–15 Star, and the General Service and Victory Medals.

4, Treherne Road, Stockwell, S.W.9.　　　　　Z3860

RANDALL, G. J. W., 1st Class Air Mechanic, R.A.F.

He volunteered in April 1915 and was posted to the 12th London Regiment (Rangers) and served on important duties with his unit until 1917 when he was sent to France. Here he took part in the fighting at Vimy Ridge, Cambrai and the Somme, and was later invalided home owing to a poisoned foot. On his recovery he was transferred to the R.A.F. and proceeded to Russia on wireless duties. He was demobilised in October 1919, and holds the General Service and Victory Medals.

94, Brayard Road, Peckham, S.E.15.　　　　　Z5480

RANDALL, H., Driver, R.F.A.

He volunteered in October 1915 and in June of the following year was drafted to France, where he took part in numerous engagements, including those on the Somme and at Albert, Beaumont-Hamel, Arras, Vimy Ridge, Ypres and Cambrai. He also served in the Retreat and Advance of 1918. He was demobilised in March 1919, and holds the General Service and Victory Medals.

7, Silcote Road, Camberwell, S.E.5.　　　　　Z5481

RANDALL, H., Driver, R.F.A.

Volunteering in November 1914 he was sent to the Western Front in September of the following year and was in action at Loos, Vimy Ridge, the Somme, Arras, Lens and the Marne. He also served in the Retreat and Advance of 1918. He was demobilised in March 1919, and holds the 1914–15 Star, and the General Service and Victory Medals.

4, Treherne Road, Stockwell, S.W.9.　　　　　Z3861

RANDALL, H., Private, R.A.S.C.

Volunteering in November 1915 he was sent to France in the same year and was engaged on important transport duties in many sectors, including those of the Somme, Ypres and Arras. In 1917 he was transferred to Italy and served on the Piave front but later returned to France and took part in the Retreat and Advance of 1918. During his service he was wounded and after the Armistice was sent to Germany, where he served with the Army of Occupation until demobilised in June 1919. He holds the 1914–15 Star, and the General Service and Victory Medals.

54, Paragon Buildings, Rodney Road, Walworth, S.E.17.　Z3862

RANDLE, A. G., Rifleman, 16th London Regiment (Queen's Westminster Rifles).

He volunteered in February 1915 and later in the same year was sent to France, where he took part in various engagements, including those on the Somme. In 1916 he was transferred to Salonika and served on the Serbian front. In the following year he proceeded to Mesopotamia and was in action on many occasions. He was demobilised in September 1919, and holds the 1914–15 Star, and the General Service and Victory Medals.

13, Southfield Road, Bedford Park, W.4.　　　　7792B

RANSOM, A., Private, 10th Queen's (Royal West Surrey Regiment).

He joined in April 1918 and after completing his training was engaged on important duties with his unit until February of the following year, when he was sent to Germany. Here he served with the Army of Occupation until October 1919, when he returned to England and was demobilised.

76, New Road, Battersea Park Road, S.W.8.　　　Z3864

RANSON, A. E., Rifleman, King's Royal Rifle Corps.

Volunteering in August 1914 he was sent to the Western Front in the same year and served in the Ypres Sector and at Dickebusch, Hooge, Kemmel and other places. He was severely wounded in action and was invalided home and discharged as medically unfit for further duty in May 1916. He holds the 1914–15 Star, and the General Service and Victory Medals.

131, Trafalgar Street, Walworth, S.E.17.　　　　Z27143

RANSON, A. R., Rifleman, King's Royal Rifle Corps.

He volunteered in October 1914 and after completing his training was engaged on important duties with his unit and in January 1916 was drafted to Egypt. He was unfortunately drowned in the Suez Canal whilst en route for India on May 9th, 1916, and was entitled to the General Service and Victory Medals.

"Steals on the ear the distant triumph song."

37, Salisbury Row, Walworth, S.E.17.　　　　　Z3863A

RATCLIFFE, C. E., Trooper, Isle of Wight Yeomanry.

He was mobilised in August 1914 and immediately afterwards sent to France, where he was engaged as a despatch rider during the Retreat from Mons and the Battle of Ypres and numerous other engagements and was wounded and invalided home. He was discharged as medically unfit in August 1915, and holds the Mons Star, and the General Service and Victory Medals.

31, Dorothy Road, Battersea, S.W.11.　　　　　Z3865

RAWE, T. W., Private, Queen's Own (Royal West Kent Regiment).

He volunteered in September 1914 and after completing his training was engaged with his unit on important duties. In 1916 he was sent to France and was in action on the Somme and at Ypres. He also took part in the Retreat and Advance of 1918 and after the Armistice proceeded to Germany. Here he served with the Army of Occupation until demobilised in February 1919, holding the General Service and Victory Medals.

166, Albert Road, Peckham, S.E.15.　　　　　Z6072

RAWLINGS, A. H., Corporal, R.A.F.

He joined in May 1916 and in the following year was drafted to the Western Front, where he was engaged in various sectors on important duties with his Squadron. He later proceeded to India, where he was still serving in 1920, holding the General Service and Victory Medals.

37, Stansfield Road, Stockwell, S.W.9.　　　　Z3866

RAWLINGS, G. M., Private, 22nd London Regiment (Queen's).

He volunteered in October 1914 and after his training was sent to France and was in action at Neuve Chapelle, St. Eloi, Hill 60, Ypres, Festubert and Loos, and was wounded. He was later transferred to Salonika and thence to Egypt. He afterwards proceeded to Palestine and took part in the Offensive under General Allenby. He returned home and was discharged as medically unfit for further service in June 1919, holding the 1914–15 Star, and the General Service and Victory Medals.

23, Comus Place, Walworth, S.E.17.　　　　　Z3232A

RAWLINGS, H. A., Bombardier, R.G.A.

He was serving at the outbreak of war and was immediately afterwards sent to France and was in action at Mons, the Marne, the Aisne, La Bassée, Ypres, Neuve Chapelle, Festubert, Loos, Albert, Vimy Ridge, the Somme, Arras, Messines and other engagements and was wounded. Later, owing to ill-health, he was invalided home and was discharged in October 1917, holding the Mons Star, and the General Service and Victory Medals.
93, Beckway Street, Walworth, S.E.17.　　　Z3867

RAWLINGS, H. W., Sergt.-Major, R.G.A.

He joined in 1916 and was sent to France in the same year and took part in the fighting on the Somme and at Albert, Vimy Ridge, Ypres, Passchendaele, Lens and Cambrai, and was twice wounded. He was also in action in the Retreat and Advance of 1918 and later proceeded to Germany, where he served with the Army of Occupation until he was demobilised in 1919, and holds the General Service and Victory Medals.
23, Comus Place, Walworth, S.E.17.　　　Z3232B

RAY, A. J., Rifleman, King's Royal Rifle Corps and Rifle Brigade.

He volunteered in September 1914 and in the following November was drafted to France, where he took part in numerous engagements, including those at Ploegsteert Wood and the Somme, and was wounded. He was invalided home and discharged as medically unfit in August 1915, and holds the 1914 Star, and the General Service and Victory Medals.
281, Sumner Road, Peckham, S.E.15.　　　Z6318

RAY, J. H., Sergt., East Surrey Regiment.

He volunteered in August 1914 and in the following year was sent to France, where he served in action on the Somme and at Ypres and Passchendaele, and in many other important engagements. He also took part in the Retreat and Advance of 1918. He was demobilised in February 1919, and holds the 1914-15 Star, and the General Service and Victory Medals.
110, Ingrave Street, Battersea, S.W.11.　　　Z3868

RAY, W., Leading Seaman, Royal Navy.

He was called up from the Reserve in August 1914 and served on H.M.S. "Cygnet" in the North Sea on highly important patrol and escort duties. When this vessel was torpedoed he was transferred to one of the mystery ships, "Q14." He took part in several engagements and was demobilised in March 1919, holding the General Service and Victory Medals.
41, Cook's Road, Walworth, S.E.17.　　　Z26787

RAYFIELD, E. J., Private, R.A.S.C.

He joined in August 1917 and in the same year proceeded to German East Africa, where he served in many important engagements. He later contracted malaria and was invalided home. On his recovery he was sent to France, where he remained until he returned home and was demobilised in August 1919, holding the General Service and Victory Medals.
44, Commercial Road, Peckham, S.E.15.　　　Z6441

RAYNER, A., Private, 1st Buffs (East Kent Regiment).

He was mobilised in August 1914 and was shortly afterwards sent to France and took part in the fierce fighting at Mons, the Aisne, Armentières and Menin Road, and in numerous other engagements, and was twice wounded. He was discharged as time expired in February 1919, holding the Mons Star, and the General Service and Victory Medals.
108, Brayard's Road, Peckham, S.E.15.　　　Z5482

RAYNER, A., Pioneer, R.E.

He joined in May 1916 and in the same year was drafted to the Western Front, where he took part in numerous engagements, including those on the Somme and at Messines, Ypres and St. Julien, and was wounded. He also served in the Retreat and Advance of 1918 and after the Armistice proceeded to Germany with the Army of Occupation, with which he remained until January 1920, when he was demobilised, holding the General Service and Victory Medals.
23, Motley Street, Battersea, S.W.8.　　　Z3869

RAYNER, C. W. E., Sapper, R.E.

He volunteered in September 1914 and in the following year was drafted to France. He was in action in many important engagements, including those at Loos, Ypres, the Somme, Arras and Cambrai, and was taken prisoner during the Retreat in May 1918. After the Armistice he was released and returning home was demobilised in March 1919, holding the 1914-15 Star, and the General Service and Victory Medals.
105, Ingelow Road, Battersea Park, S.W.8.　　　Z2259A

RAYNER, P., Private, 25th King's (Liverpool Regiment).

He joined in July 1917 and was drafted to France in the following year and was in action at Cambrai and other important engagements during the Advance of 1918. In 1919 he was transferred to Egypt, where he remained until 1920, when he returned home and was demobilised in February of that year, holding the General Service and Victory Medals.
61, Heyford Avenue, South Lambeth Road, S.W.8.　　　Z3870

REA, G. C., Driver, R.F.A.

Volunteering at the outbreak of hostilities he was drafted to the Western Front in March 1915 and fought at the Battles of Loos, Festubert, Vimy Ridge, Cambrai, Ploegsteert, the Somme and throughout the German Offensive and subsequent Allied Advance of 1918. He was demobilised in March 1919, and holds the 1914-15 Star, and the General Service and Victory Medals.
21, Conderton Road, Camberwell, S.E.5.　　　Z6321

READ, A. G., Sapper, R.E.

He volunteered in April 1915 and embarking for Egypt in the following year saw much service there. Later, transferred to Salonika, he was in action in many engagements in various sectors, and was wounded. On recovery he was engaged on important duties connected with the water supply and did good work. He returned to England and was demobilised in May 1919, and holds the General Service and Victory Medals.
129, Chatham Road, Battersea, S.W.11.　　　Z3871

READ, A. J., Private, 8th Buffs (East Kent Regt.)

Volunteering in January 1915 and proceeding to France in the same year he was engaged in heavy fighting in many parts of the line. He gave his life for King and Country in the Battle of the Somme in July 1916, and was entitled to the 1914-15 Star, and the General Service and Victory Medals.
"Great deeds cannot die, they with the sun
and moon renew their light for ever."
20, Birley Street, Battersea, S.W.11.　　　Z3872

READ, E., Private, Highland Light Infantry.

He volunteered in August 1914 and was drafted to France almost immediately. During his service overseas he fought in the Retreat from Mons, the Battle of the Marne and in various other engagements. He was unfortunately killed in action in the first Battle of Ypres on October 23rd, 1914, and was entitled to the Mons Star, and the General Service and Victory Medals.
"Steals on the ear the distant triumph song."
85, Paradise Road, Larkhall Lane, S.W.4.　　　Z3876

READ, E., Sapper, R.E.

Volunteering in April 1915 he was sent to France later in that year and served in the Somme, Ypres and Arras sectors, engaged on important duties with a Mining Company. He was in action throughout the Retreat and Advance of 1918 and, returning to England after the Armistice, was demobilised in November 1919. He holds the 1914-15 Star, and the General Service and Victory Medals.
24, Ingleton Street, Brixton Road, S.W.9.　　　Z4520

READ, G. W., Q.M.S., Northumberland Fusiliers.

Joining in May 1916 and drafted to Mesopotamia four months afterwards he fought in many engagements during the progress of the campaign in this theatre of war and was in action during the final British Advance to Mosul. After the cessation of hostilities he was sent into Turkey with the Army of Occupation and served there until July 1919. He then returned home and was demobilised in the following month. He holds the General Service and Victory Medals.
7, Newby Street, Wandsworth Road, S.W.8.　　　Z3873

READ, W., Sapper, R.E.

He joined in May 1917 and embarking for France later in that year saw heavy fighting in various parts of the line. Transferred to Palestine he was in action in the operations resulting in the capture of Jerusalem and in many other engagements during the Advance into Syria. He returned to England and was demobilised in 1920, and holds the General Service and Victory Medals.　50, Andulus Road, Landor Road, S.W.9.　　　Z1465A

READ, W. J., Sapper, R.E.

Volunteering in May 1915 he was drafted to France later in the same year and was engaged on important duties at Prisoners-of-war Camps and in the advanced areas. Owing to ill-health he returned to England and was invalided out of the service in January 1918, and holds the 1914-15 Star, and the General Service and Victory Medals.
14, Auckland Road, Battersea, S.W.11.　　　Z3287B

READWIN, B., Rifleman, 1st Rifle Brigade.

He volunteered in March 1915 and was sent to the Western Front later in that year. During his service overseas he fought at the Battles of Ypres and the Somme, where he was wounded in 1916. On recovery he rejoined his Battalion and took part in various engagements and was wounded and taken prisoner at Corbie in 1918. He was held in captivity in Germany and later interned in Switzerland and finally repatriated after the Armistice. He was demobilised in April 1919, and holds the 1914-15 Star, and the General Service and Victory Medals.
106, Maysoule Road, Battersea, S.W.11.　　　Z3875

REAVELL, E. W., Sapper, R.E.

He volunteered in August 1914 and later in that year was sent to France, where he saw heavy fighting in the Ypres salient, at Arras, and on the Somme. He was severely wounded and returning to England received hospital treatment. He was ultimately discharged unfit for further service with the Colours in October 1918, and holds the 1914 Star, and the General Service and Victory Medals.
27, Edithna Street, Landor Road, S.W.9.　　　Z3874

REDDECLIFFE, W., Private, R.A.S.C. (M.T.)
He joined in March 1916 and proceeding to the Western Front five months later was engaged on important duties as driver to the Base Commandant at Calais. In this capacity he piloted His Majesty the King during his tour of the Western Front and also drove for the Shah of Persia and General Allenby when they visited France. He was demobilised in December 1919, and holds the General Service and Victory Medals.
132, Glengall Road, Peckham, S.E.15. Z6569

REDDIN, J. F., Private, Labour Corps.
Volunteering in September 1915 he embarked for the Western Front three months later and, engaged on important duties in the front lines, was present at the Battles of Ypres, the Somme and Arras, and saw much fighting in the Retreat and Advance of 1918. He was demobilised in June 1919, and holds the 1914-15 Star, and the General Service and Victory Medals.
61, Paradise Street, Larkhall Lane, S.W.4. TZ25748

REDDING, H., Private, East Surrey Regiment.
Volunteering in November 1914 he served at various depôts until proceeding to Salonika in 1916. He was engaged in heavy fighting in many parts of the line and did good work throughout. Owing to ill-health he returned to England and on discharge from hospital was demobilised in March 1919. He holds the General Service and Victory Medals.
34, Lettson Street, Camberwell, S.E.5. Z6538

REDMILE, G. D., Rifleman, 21st London Regiment (1st Surrey Rifles), and Private, Labour Corps.
Volunteering in February 1915 he was sent to France in the following year and fought at the Battles of Ypres, the Somme and Cambrai. Later in 1917 he was transferred to the Labour Corps and served in the forward areas engaged on important duties throughout many engagements and the Retreat and Advance of 1918. He was demobilised in October 1919, and holds the General Service and Victory Medals.
62, Cranham Road, Rotherhithe, S.E.16. Z6611

REECE, E., Private, 1/5th Lancashire Fusiliers and R.A.S.C.
He joined in June 1916 and was sent to the Western Front in the following year. During his service overseas he fought in many engagements of note in the Ypres, Arras and Somme sectors, and was wounded in March 1918. Returning to England he received hospital treatment and on recovery was transferred to the Royal Army Service Corps. With his unit he served at various depôts at home until demobilised in April 1919. He holds the General Service and Victory Medals.
22, Hollydale Road, Peckham, S.E.15. Z6443

REED, C. H. T., Sapper, R.E.
He joined in March 1916 and in the same year was drafted to German East Africa, where he was engaged on important duties in connection with operations against the enemy forces. Contracting malaria whilst on service he was sent home and invalided out of the Service in September 1918. He died from the effects of his illness in February 1919, and was entitled to the General Service and Victory Medals.
"And doubtless he went in splendid company."
26, Townsend Street, Walworth, S.E.17. Z3878

REED, J. T., Guardsman, 1st Grenadier Guards.
Volunteering in August 1914 he embarked for the Western Front in the same year and fought in the Battles of La Bassée, Ypres, Neuve Chapelle and Loos, and was wounded, gassed and suffered from shell-shock. Sent home owing to his injuries he received hospital treatment and was invalided out of the Service in August 1916. He was entitled to the 1914 Star, and the General Service and Victory Medals.
53, Selden Road, Peckham, S.E.15. Z6649

REED, R., Private, R.A.S.C.
He volunteered in April 1915 and was sent overseas in the same year. He was engaged on important transport duties in the Battles of Hill 60, Ypres, Loos, the Somme, Messines and did good work during the Retreat and Advance of 1918. After the Armistice he proceeded into Germany with the Army of Occupation, returning home for demobilisation in April 1919. He died of a sudden illness a few days later, and was entitled to the 1914-15 Star, and the General Service and Victory Medals.
"His memory is cherished with pride."
12, Oakden Street, Kennington, S.E.11. Z27384

REED, W. T., Corporal, R.G.A.
Volunteering in November 1914 he proceeded overseas in the following year and saw much service on the Western Front. Engaged with his Battery in various parts of the line he fought in numerous engagements, including those on the Somme and at Vimy Ridge and Cambrai, and during the German Offensive and subsequent Allied Advance of 1918. On the conclusion of hostilities he was sent into Germany with the Army of Occupation and was stationed on the Rhine. He was demobilised in March 1920 on returning to England, and holds the 1914-15 Star, and the General Service and Victory Medals.
9, Boyton Row, New Church Road, Camberwell, S.E.5. Z5637B

REES, J. W., Driver, R.F.A.
Volunteering in October 1914 he embarked for France in the following year and after two months' service there he proceeded to Salonika in November 1915. He fought in various parts of the Balkans, taking an active part in several engagements on the Vardar and Struma fronts. He returned home on the cessation of hostilities and was demobilised in March 1919, and holds the 1914-15 Star, and the General Service and Victory Medals.
14, Trafalgar Street, Walworth, S.E.17. Z27488

REEVE, F. A., Sergt., Royal Defence Corps.
Volunteering in December 1914 he was posted to the Royal Defence Corps owing to ineligibility for active service and after training was engaged on guard and other duties at home. He was later sent to Ireland, where he served until his demobilisation in February 1919.
60, Blake's Road, Peckham Grove, S.E.15. Z6073

REEVE, F. S., Private, R.M.L.I.
He volunteered in October 1914 and posted to H.M. Monitor "Prince Eugene" served aboard that vessel during the raid on Zeebrugge. His ship also took part in several engagements off Dunkirk and in the bombardment of enemy positions on the coast of Belgium. He also served in H.M.S. "Ophir," "Agamemnon," "Thames" and in 1920 was serving in H.M.S. "Dragon" on special duty in Danish waters. He holds the 1914-15 Star, and the General Service and Victory Medals.
26, Winstead Street, Battersea, S.W.11. Z3880

REEVE, J. W., Chief Petty Officer, Royal Navy.
Mobilised on the outbreak of hostilities he served in H.M.S. "Hindustan" throughout the course of hostilities. His ship was attached to the Grand Fleet and was engaged on important duties in the North Sea and was present at the surrender and internment of the German Fleet at Scapa Flow. Demobilised in January 1919, he holds the 1914-15 Star, and the General Service and Victory Medals.
36, Stockdale Road, Wandsworth Road, S.W.8. Z3881

REEVES, A. V., Private, Middlesex Regiment.
Joining in 1916 in the following year he proceeded to the Western Front and served with his Battalion in various parts of the line. He was engaged in heavy fighting in the Battles of Vimy Ridge and Ypres, and during the Retreat and Advance of 1918. After the Armistice he was sent with the Army of Occupation into Germany and returning home for demobilisation in January 1919, holds the General Service and Victory Medals.
29, Chalmers Street, Wandsworth Road, S.W.8. Z3879

REEVES, E., Driver, R.A.S.C. (M.T.)
He joined in July 1916 and was drafted overseas in the same year. Serving as a despatch rider he did excellent work in several engagements during the Balkan Campaign, and after the Armistice was sent to France. From there he proceeded into Germany with the Army of Occupation and was stationed at Cologne until his return to England for demobilisation in February 1919. He holds the General Service and Victory Medals.
91, Coburg Road, Camberwell, S.E.5. Z5414B

REEVES, E. M., Private, 11th Queen's (Royal West Surrey Regiment).
He volunteered in November 1915 and sent to France in the following May fought in the Battles of Ploegsteert Wood, the Somme, St. Eloi, Fleurs Wood and was wounded in October 1917. On recovery he proceeded to Italy a month later and served during the British Offensive on the Piave, and returned to the Western Front in February 1918. He was in action in the Battle of Arras and in several engagements during the Retreat and Advance of 1918. On the termination of hostilities he was sent with the Army of Occupation into Germany and stationed at Cologne. He was demobilised in May 1919, and holds the General Service and Victory Medals.
8c, Lewis Trust Buildings, Warner Road, Camberwell, S.E.5. Z6086B

REEVES, F. J., Pioneer, R.E., and Rifleman, Rifle Brigade.
He joined in June 1916 but was shortly afterwards discharged on medical grounds. Re-enlisting later he was sent to the Western Front in 1918 and was engaged on important duties with his unit until admitted to hospital at Etaples owing to illness in 1918. On recovery he served with his Battalion and returned to England for demobilisation in February 1919. He holds the General Service and Victory Medals.
74, Smith Street, Camberwell, S.E.5. Z2495C

REEVES, G. W., Private, 3rd Royal Fusiliers.
He joined in July 1916 and three months later embarked for Salonika. In the course of his service in the Balkans he was engaged in heavy fighting during the Allied Advance across the Struma and Vardar fronts, and was gassed and wounded. On recovery he returned to his Battalion and was sent to Russia on special duty. Returning to England he was demobilised in October 1919, and holds the General Service and Victory Medals.
117, Cronin Road, Peckham, S.E.15. Z5607C

REEVES, R., Private, Middlesex Regiment, Sherwood Foresters, and Trooper Nottinghamshire Hussars (Sherwood Rangers).
He joined in September 1916 and in the following year proceeded to the Western Front. In this theatre of war he fought in the Battles of Ypres, Albert, Passchendaele, Bullecourt, and was wounded at Havrincourt. Admitted to hospital in France on recovery he returned to the firing line and was again wounded at Elverdinghe Wood and sent to the 3rd Canadian Hospital, Doullens, and later to Etaples, where, after undergoing three operations, he was evacuated to England. He was demobilised in February 1919, and holds the General Service and Victory Medals.
48, Sussex Road, Coldharbour Lane, S.W.9. Z1782A

REGAN, F., Rifleman, King's Royal Rifle Corps.
Volunteering in October 1914 he was drafted overseas six months later and served with his Battalion on the Western Front. Whilst overseas he was in action in several important engagements and was wounded in the Battle of Ypres. Sent home to hospital he received medical treatment and was invalided out of the service in October 1916. He holds the 1914-15 Star, and the General Service and Victory Medals.
51, Kingston Street, Walworth, S.E.17. Z27481

REGAN, H., Rifleman, 10th Rifle Brigade.
Joining in June 1916 he was sent overseas in the following November and saw much service on the Western Front. Whilst in this theatre of war he fought in several engagements and was wounded and taken prisoner in November 1917. He died in captivity from the effects of his injuries in the following month, and was entitled to the General Service and Victory Medals.
"He passed out of the sight of men by the path of duty and self-sacrifice."
196, Portland Street, Walworth, S.E.17. Z27342

REGAN, P., Corporal, 7th Royal Fusiliers.
He volunteered in August 1914 and a year later embarked for France. There he was engaged in heavy fighting in the Battles of Loos, Albert, Vimy Ridge, the Somme, Arras, Ypres, Messines, Passchendaele and was wounded at St. Quentin in April 1918. Sent home on account of his injuries, part of his hand having been amputated, he was ultimately invalided out of the service in January 1919, and holds the 1914-15 Star, and the General Service and Victory Medals.
192, Manor Place, Walworth, S.E.17. Z27040

REID, C. A., Private, 5th (Royal Irish) Lancers.
Volunteering in August 1914 he embarked for France two months later and fought in the Battles of Loos, Vermelles, the Somme, Arras, Cambrai and was gassed. He was also in action during the German Offensive and subsequent Allied Advance and entered Mons at dawn on the day the Armistice was signed. Demobilised in May 1919, he holds the 1914 Star, and the General Service and Victory Medals.
54, Grant Road, Battersea, S.W.11. Z3883

REID, E. (Mrs.), Special War Worker.
During the war this lady offered her services and for a period of upwards of twelve months was engaged on important duties as a packer at Messrs. Brittle's Works, thus relieving a man for military duties. Her work was carried out in an efficient manner and she rendered valuable services throughout.
37, Edithna Street, Landor Road, S.W.9. Z3514B

REID, F., Private, Labour Corps.
He joined in December 1917 and on the conclusion of his training was engaged on important clerical duties at the White City, Kensington. He did excellent work but was unable to obtain his transfer to a theatre of war owing to medical unfitness for general service, and was demobilised in 1919.
37, Edithna Street, Landor Road, S.W.9. Z3514A

REID, R. A., Pte., 3rd London Regt. (Royal Fusiliers).
He joined the 21st London Regiment in April 1916 and drafted to France in the following year was transferred to the 3rd London Regiment. Serving with his unit in various parts of the line he was in action in the Battle of Menin Road and was wounded on the Somme in March 1918. Sent to hospital he was stationed at the Base and on recovery served as a motor driver at G.H.Q. Demobilised in November 1919, he holds the General Service and Victory Medals.
44, Blake's Road, Peckham Grove, S.E.15. Z6069

REID, W., Sergt., R.A.S.C. (M.T.)
He volunteered in July 1915 and proceeded to France in the same year. He was engaged on important duties in connection with the transport of ammunition and supplies in the Battles of Arras, Ypres and the Somme, and was gassed. After hospital treatment in France he rejoined his unit and did good work during the Retreat and Advance of 1918, and on the conclusion of hostilities was sent with the Army of Occupation into Germany. Returning from Cologne he was demobilised in January 1919, and holds the 1914-15 Star, and the General Service and Victory Medals.
69, Surrey Square, Walworth, S.E.17. Z3882

REID, W., Private, 20th London Regiment.
Volunteering in June 1915 when over fifty years of age he was discharged on medical grounds in the following month, but joined the Volunteer Training Corps and served with that unit at various stations. He was engaged on guard and other important duties and rendered valuable services until his demobilisation after the Armistice.
26, Lyndhurst Grove, Peckham, S.E.15. Z6540

REID, W. F., Private, R.A.S.C. (M.T.)
He joined in June 1916 and was later drafted overseas. Serving with his unit in various sectors of the Western Front he rendered valuable services in the transport of ammunition and supplies to the forward areas during the Battles of the Somme, Arras, Ypres and Cambrai. He also took part in the Retreat and Advance of 1918 and after the Armistice proceeded into Germany with the Army of Occupation. He was demobilised in November 1919 on his return home, and holds the General Service and Victory Medals.
28, Flaxman Road, Camberwell, S.E.5. Z6221

REITZ, E. J., Private, 6th Worcestershire Regiment.
He joined in June 1917 and after his training crossed to France. During his service in this theatre of war he fought in the Retreat of 1918 and whilst taking part in the subsequent Advance was severely wounded. After receiving treatment at a Base hospital, however, he rejoined his unit in the Field and remained overseas until 1920. He was demobilised on his return to England in October of that year, and holds the General Service and Victory Medals.
100, Eland Road, Lavender Hill, S.W.11. Z3884

RENDER, R. S., Gunner, R.G.A.
Volunteering in June 1915 he was drafted to the Western Front at the conclusion of his training and fought in several engagements At the end of 1916 he was transferred to Salonika and did valuable work with his Battery during operations on the Vardar front. Later he was sent to Palestine, where, under the command of General Allenby he took part in several important battles and in the capture of Jerusalem. Demobilised in March 1919 after his return to England, he holds the General Service and Victory Medals.
17, Bolton Street, Camberwell, S.E.5. Z3885

RESTRICK, A. S., Private, Duke of Cornwall's Light Infantry.
He was serving in China when war broke out and embarking for France arrived in that theatre of war in December 1914. He then took part in several of the principal battles, including that of Ypres and later, owing to a severe injury, which he sustained in an accident, was invalided home. After eighteen months' treatment in hospital he was found to be physically unfit and on these grounds was discharged in June 1918. He holds the 1914 Star, and the General Service and Victory Medals.
53, Russell Street, Battersea, S.W.11. Z3886

REUMEL, F. A., Private, Middlesex Regiment.
He joined in March 1916 and after his training served on the Western Front for upwards of two years. During this period he did important work with his unit in many sectors, notably in those of Ypres, Arras, Provin, Lille, Merville and Lucheux. He was demobilised in 1919 and holds the General Service and Victory Medals.
63, Surrey Square, Walworth, S.E.17. Z3887B

REUMEL, W. J., Gunner, R.F.A.
He volunteered in October 1915 and crossed to France two months later. In the course of his service overseas he was engaged in the fighting at the Hohenzollern Redoubt, on the Somme, at Arras, Ypres and Hooge, and after taking part in the Retreat and Advance of 1918 entered Mons at dawn on November 11th of that year, and was twice wounded. He was demobilised in July 1919, and holds the 1914-15 Star, and the General Service and Victory Medals.
63, Surrey Square, Walworth, S.E.17. Z3887A

REVELL, C., Stoker, Royal Navy.
He joined in January 1918 and was posted to H.M.S. "Devonport" for training. During his service in this ship, however, he contracted an illness and in March of the same year was discharged as physically unfit for further service.
119, Cator Road, Peckham, S.E.15. Z4521

REVELL, H., Private, 1st Queen's (Royal West Surrey Regiment).
Volunteering in January 1915 he was sent to the Western Front five months later and was in action at the Battles of Loos, St. Eloi and Vimy Ridge, and was wounded and taken prisoner during the Somme Offensive in July 1916. Repatriated in December 1918 he was invalided out of the Service in February 1919. He holds the 1914-15 Star, and the General Service and Victory Medals.
26, Myatt Road, Stockwell, S.W.9. Z5138

REVELL, T., Private, 13th Royal Fusiliers.

He volunteered in 1915 and in the following year served on the Western Front, where he took part in several important engagements. He was severely wounded in action in 1917 and died from the effects of his injuries on September 9th of that year. He was entitled to the General Service and Victory Medals.
"The path of duty was the way to glory."
35, The Grange, Bermondsey, S.E.1.   Z27176

REYNOLDS, A., Corporal, Labour Corps.

He joined in May 1916 and at the conclusion of his training was drafted to the Western Front, where he fought in the Somme Offensive, in which he was severely wounded. He was invalided to an hospital in Cirencester and after his recovery was drafted to Egypt, subsequently taking part in the Palestine Campaign. In the course of his service he was attached to the Cambridge, Essex and Norfolk Regiments and was demobilised in June 1919 after his return to England. He holds the General Service and Victory Medals.
10, Brabourn Grove, Peckham, S.E.15.   Z6559

REYNOLDS, A., Sergt.-Major, R.F.A.

He was mobilised at the commencement of hostilities and until he was drafted to France in July 1916 was engaged on important home duties instructing recruits. In the course of his service overseas he did valuable work with his unit during military operations on the Somme, at Beaumont-Hamel, the Ancre, Arras, Vimy Ridge, Bullecourt, Ypres, Lens, Cambrai, Amiens and Bapaume, and was twice wounded. He holds the General Service and Victory Medals, and was demobilised in March 1919.
39, Charleston Street, Walworth, S.E.17.   Z3889

REYNOLDS, C., Gunner, R.F.A.

He volunteered in September 1914 and after his training was drafted to the Western Front, where he fought in engagements on the Somme, at Albert, Arras and Messines. Unfortunately he was killed in action in the vicinity of Ypres in 1917, and was entitled to the 1914-15 Star, and the General Service and Victory Medals.
"The path of duty was the way to glory."
93, Trafalgar Street, Walworth, S.E.17.   Z27136B

REYNOLDS, C., Gunner, R.F.A.

He volunteered in June 1915 and after his training served on the Western Front for upwards of three years. During this time he took an active part in engagements on the Somme, and in the Retreat and Advance of 1918, and was gassed and wounded. He was demobilised in July 1919, and holds the 1914-15 Star, and the General Service and Victory Medals.
93, Trafalgar Street, Walworth, S.E.17.   Z27136A

REYNOLDS, C. B., Sergt., Royal Army Pay Corps.

He volunteered in November 1914 and at the conclusion of his training was engaged on important accountant's duties at various stations, doing much valuable work in this capacity. He was unable to secure his transfer overseas before the termination of hostilities, but nevertheless rendered valuable services until demobilised in February 1920.
162, St. George's Road, Peckham, S.E.15.   Z5825

REYNOLDS, C. H. W., Q.M.S., R.G.A.

Joining in 1916 he was drafted to Egypt early in the following year and did important work with his Battery during operations in Palestine and took part in the Battles of Gaza and the Capture of Jerusalem. In 1918 he was transferred to the Western Front, where he fought in the Retreat and Advance of that year. He was demobilised in 1919 on his return to England, and holds the General Service and Victory Medals.
49, Elliott Road, Brixton, S.W.9.   Z4522

REYNOLDS, F. W., Air Mechanic, R.A.F.

He joined in January 1918 and after his training served on important duties as a motor driver with his Squadron. He did valuable work but was not successful in securing his transfer overseas before hostilities ceased. After the Armistice however he proceeded with the Army of Occupation into Germany and stationed at Cologne, where he obtained his Observer's Brevet, was engaged on observing duties until returning home for demobilisation in December 1919.
2, Eythorne Road, Stockwell, S.W.9.   Z5826A

REYNOLDS, H., Corporal, East Surrey Regiment.

An ex-soldier with a previous record of service in the South African Campaign he volunteered in September 1914 and shortly afterwards crossed to France. Whilst in this theatre of war he fought in many engagements, including those at Neuve Chapelle and Hill 60, and was in action almost continuously until 1916, when a severe wound necessitated his return to England. After protracted hospital treatment he was sent to Yeovil, where he was engaged on important aircraft work until demobilised in December 1918. He holds the Queen's South African Medal, the 1914 Star, and the General Service and Victory Medals.
15, Yeovil Street, Wandsworth Road, S.W.8.   Z3890

REYNOLDS, J. M., Private, R.A.V.C.

Joining in June 1916 he crossed to France three months later. In the course of his overseas service he did much valuable work in connection with the care of sick and wounded horses and was present at several engagements, including those in the Retreat and Advance of 1918. He was discharged on account of service in November of that year, and holds the General Service and Victory Medals.
11, Calmington Road, Camberwell, S.E.5.   Z5483

REYNOLDS, W. C., Private, R.A.V.C.

He volunteered in October 1914 and after his training served on the Western Front for upwards of four years. During this time he did valuable work with his unit in connection with the care of wounded horses, and was in action in the Somme, Ypres and Arras sectors. He was demobilised in March 1919, and holds the 1914 Star, and the General Service and Victory Medals.
1, Tyne Terrace, High Street, Peckham, S.E.15.   Z6612

REYNOLDS, S. G., L/Corporal, R.A.S.C. and Royal Inniskilling Fusiliers.

Volunteering at the commencement of hostilities he was drafted overseas in 1914. During his service on the Western Front he took an active part in many notable battles, including those of Loos, Vimy Ridge, the Somme, Arras and Ypres. Owing to a severe wound received in action, however, he was sent to England early in 1918 and after protracted treatment was invalided out of the Service in October of that year. He holds the 1914 Star, and the General Service and Victory Medals.
82, Aylesbury Road, Walworth, S.E.17.   Z3888

RICE, A., Gunner, R.G.A.

He joined in December 1916 and served at various stations on important duties until March 1918, when he was drafted to France. He fought in the Retreat and Advance until the Armistice and then proceeded with the Army of Occupation into Germany, remaining there until September 1919, when he was demobilised. He holds the General Service and Victory Medals.
24, Cunard Street, Camberwell, S.E.5.   Z5139

RICE, G., Private, Essex Regiment.

He joined in 1918 and after a short period of training proceeded to France and was in action at various places during the operations prior to the Armistice. After the cessation of hostilities he returned to England and was demobilised in 1919, holding the General Service and Victory Medals.
7A, Willowbrook Road, Peckham, S.E.15.   Z4523A

RICE, G., Signalman, Royal Navy.

He joined the Navy in 1917 and served in various ships being employed on convoy duties between America and this country. After rendering valuable service he was demobilised in 1919, and holds the General Service and Victory Medals.
7A, Willowbrook Road, Peckham, S.E.15.   Z4523B

RICE, J., Rifleman, 9th London Regiment (Queen Victoria's Rifles).

He joined in June 1916 and proceeded to France in October of same year. He fought at Arras and Bullecourt and was wounded at Ypres in September 1917. He also served at Passchendaele, Cambrai and Havrincourt, and was again wounded at Albert in August 1918, but continued his service until the Armistice. He then returned home and was demobilised in December 1919, holding the General Service and Victory Medals.
35, Comus Place, Walworth, S.E.17.   Z3891

RICH, C., Chief Petty Officer, Royal Navy.

He was serving in the Mediterranean at the outbreak of hostilities and was present at the Dardanelles during the whole of the operations there, being in action on a number of occasions. He then served in H.M.S. "Swiftsure" until after the Armistice, when he was stationed in home waters for a short time. In 1920 he was in H.M.S. "Hawkins" on the China Station, and holds the 1914-15 Star, and the General Service and Victory Medals.
233, St. George's Road, Peckham, S.E.15.   Z3892

RICH, E. J., Driver, R.E.

He joined in February 1916 and after his training was engaged on important duties at various stations. He rendered valuable services but was unable to obtain his transfer overseas and was discharged as medically unfit in August 1917.
58, Bagshot Street, Walworth, S.E.17.   Z23893B

RICH, H. F., Stoker, Royal Navy.

He volunteered in November 1914 and after a short training joined H.M.S. "Chatham" in May 1915 and proceeded to the Dardanelles and Eastern Mediterranean, where he was in action on several occasions. In 1917 he joined H.M.S. "Ettrick," which was employed on patrol and convoy duties in the North Sea. The vessel was torpedoed and he was unfortunately killed on July 7th, 1917. He was entitled to the 1914-15 Star, and the General Service and Victory Medals.
"His life for his Country, his Soul to God."
58, Bagshot Street, Walworth, S.E.17.   Z3893A

RICHARDS, C. H., Private, Machine Gun Corps.

He joined in March 1917 and proceeded to France later in that year. He fought at Arras, Bullecourt, Cambrai and the Somme, and also served in the Retreat and Advance of 1918 until seriously wounded at Cambrai in September, when he was sent to England and remained in hospital for several months. He was finally discharged in January 1919, holding the General Service and Victory Medals.

9, Shannon Grove, Brixton Road, S.W.9.   Z3896

RICHARDS, G., Gunner, R.G.A.

He joined in August 1916 and proceeded to the Western Front in October of that year. He fought in many engagements, including those at Ypres, Passchendaele and Cambrai, and also served in the Retreat and Advance of 1918. He returned to England and was demobilised in 1919, and holds the General Service and Victory Medals.

94, Lavender Road, Battersea, S.W.11.   Z3898

RICHARDS, H. J., Sergt., 21st County of London Regiment (Surrey Rifles).

He was mobilised with the Territorial Force at the outbreak of hostilities and was retained on important home duties until March 1917, when he proceeded to Salonika and fought in many engagements on that front. At the end of 1917 he was sent to Egypt and took part in the Advance into Palestine, being present at the Capture of Jerusalem and Jericho. He was demobilised in February 1919, and holds the General Service and Victory Medals.

45, Sansom Street, Waterloo Street, Camberwell, S.E.5.   Z3895

RICHARDS, J. K. B., Rifleman, 8th London Regiment (Post Office Rifles).

He was mobilised in August 1914 and was drafted to France in March 1915. He was in action at Hill 60, Ypres and Festubert, and meeting with an accident was severely injured and after being in hospital in France was invalided to England. On his recovery he was engaged on important duties until discharged in September 1918. He holds the 1914–15 Star, and the General Service and Victory Medals.

165, Albert Road, Peckham, S.E.15.   Z5827

RICHARDS, W., Private, Rifle Brigade.

He volunteered in 1914 and proceeded to France in that year. He fought in many engagements, including the Battles of Ypres, the Somme and Arras, and was three times wounded. He was invalided to England and was discharged as medically unfit in March 1918, holding the 1914–15 Star, and the General Service and Victory Medals.

19, Latchmere Street, Battersea, S.W.11.   Z3897

RICHARDSON, A., Private, Royal Fusiliers.

Volunteering in November 1915 he was drafted to France in the following year and fought in the Battles of the Somme, Ypres, Arras, Albert, Passchendaele, St. Quentin, St. Eloi, Bapaume, and throughout the German Offensive and subsequent Allied Advance of 1918. He was demobilised in April 1919, and holds the General Service and Victory Medals.

9, Combermere Road, Stockwell, S.W.9.   Z3899A

RICHARDSON, A., Sergt., Buffs (East Kent Regiment).

He joined in 1916 and in the same year was drafted to the Western Front, where he took part in many important engagements, including those on the Somme and at Albert, where he was wounded. After his recovery he served in the Retreat and Advance of 1918. He was demobilised in 1919, and holds the General Service and Victory Medals.

164, St. James' Road, Old Kent Road, S.E.1.   Z25737

RICHARDSON, F., Private, R.A.S.C. and Oxfordshire and Buckinghamshire Light Infantry.

He enlisted in June 1913 and was stationed at Devonport at the outbreak of hostilities. He was drafted to France in August 1914 and served in the Retreat from Mons and the Battles of Ypres, Neuve Chapelle, Festubert, engaged on important transport duties. He was later transferred to the Oxfordshire and Buckinghamshire Light Infantry and proceeded to Salonika, where he fought in many engagements on the Struma, Doiran and Vardar fronts until the cessation of hostilities. Suffering from malaria he was invalided home late in 1918 and after receiving hospital treatment was discharged in June 1919. He holds the Mons Star, and the General Service and Victory Medals.

40, Wyndham Road, Camberwell, S.E.5.   Z3900

RICHARDSON, F. W. (Junior), Private, 2/2nd London Regiment (Royal Fusiliers).

He joined in December 1917 and embarked for France in the following year. He fought in many engagements, including those at Albert and the Somme, and, severely wounded in the Allied Advance of 1918, returned to England and received hospital treatment. In 1920 he was still serving, and holds the General Service and Victory Medals.

5, Shepherd's Place, Lambeth, S.E.1.   Z25892A

RICHARDSON, F. W., Private, Middlesex Regiment.

Volunteering in September 1914 he proceeded to the Western Front in the following year and fought at the Battles of Neuve Chapelle, Ypres, Arras and was wounded at La Bassée. He returned home and after receiving hospital treatment returned to France and was in action at Ypres, Passchendaele, and in the Retreat and Advance of 1918. He was demobilised in March 1919, and holds the 1914–15 Star, and the General Service and Victory Medals.

5, Shepherd's Place, Lambeth, S.E.1.   Z25892B

RICHARDSON, G., Driver, R.F.A.

Volunteering in January 1915 he was sent to the Western Front in March of the following year and was in action in many important engagements, including those of Arras, Vimy Ridge, the Somme, Passchendaele, and throughout the Retreat and Advance of 1918. He was present at the entry of the British Troops into Mons on November 11th, 1918, and shortly afterwards returned to England. He was demobilised in June 1919, and holds the General Service and Victory Medals.

155, Gloucester Road, Peckham, S.E.15.   Z6324B

RICHARDSON, G. F., Corporal, 4th, 7th and 8th Royal Fusiliers.

He volunteered in December 1914 and after completing his training proceeded to France in the following year. Whilst overseas he fought in the Battles of Hill 60, Ypres, Loos, Vimy Ridge, the Somme, Givenchy and Arras, and was wounded at St. Eloi and Hulluch. He was discharged in 1917 owing to illness consequent upon his wounds, after having had his left leg amputated. He holds the 1914–15 Star, and the General Service and Victory Medals.

36, Relf Road, Peckham, S.E.15.   Z6683

RICHARDSON, J., Private, 24th London Regiment (The Queen's).

Volunteering in June 1915 and proceeding to France later in that year he fought at Messines, Vimy Ridge, Bapaume, Béthune and was gassed at Bourlon Wood. On recovery he rejoined his Battalion and was engaged in heavy fighting in many parts of the line. He was taken prisoner and held in captivity in Prussia at Limburg and Posen until repatriated after the cessation of hostilities in accordance with the terms of the Armistice. He was demobilised in December 1919, and holds the 1914–15 Star, and the General Service and Victory Medals.

9, Combermere Road, Stockwell, S.W.9.   Z3899B

RICHARDSON, J., Private, 1st King's (Liverpool Regiment).

A Reservist he was mobilised and drafted to France at the commencement of hostilities and fought in the Retreat from Mons, and in the subsequent Battles of the Marne, the Aisne and Neuve Chapelle. In 1915 he was reported wounded and missing during the fighting at Richbourg and later to have been killed in action. He was entitled to the Mons Star, and the General Service and Victory Medals.

"Nobly striving, he nobly fell that we might live."

40, Murray Buildings, Burnett Street, Vauxhall, S.E.11.   Z24160

RICHARDSON, J., Private, 7th Middlesex Regiment.

Joining in May 1918 he completed his training and embarked for France shortly afterwards. He was engaged in heavy fighting in many parts of the line during the Allied Advance of 1918, and was wounded. He returned to England and after receiving hospital treatment was invalided out of the Service in March 1919. Previously to joining the Colours he was engaged on work of National importance from the declaration of war. He holds the General Service and Victory Medals.

6, Lilac Place, Vauxhall, S.E.11.   Z24849

RICHARDSON, J., Private, Royal Marine Light Infantry.

He was serving aboard H.M.S. "Weymouth" at the outbreak of war and was wounded in an engagement with hostile craft in August 1914. On recovery he was posted to H.M.S. "Juno," which ship was in action in the Battle of Jutland and did good work engaged on patrol and other important duties with the Grand Fleet in the North Sea until the cessation of hostilities. He was demobilised in March 1920, and holds the 1914–15 Star, and the General Service and Victory Medals.

84, Cabul Road, Battersea, S.W.11.   Z3902

RICHARDSON, P., Sergt., 3rd Coldstream Guards.

A Reservist he was mobilised and sent to France at the outbreak of hostilities and fought in the Retreat from Mons and at the Battles of the Somme, Loos, Ypres (I, II, III) and Givenchy, where he was wounded. On recovery he rejoined his unit and fought throughout the German Offensive and was wounded at Cambrai in October 1918. He was demobilised in May 1919, and holds the Mons Star, and the General Service and Victory Medals.

162, Beresford Street, Camberwell Road, S.E.5.   Z3901

RICHARDSON, P. R., Corporal, Machine Gun Corps.

He joined in December 1916 and embarked for the Western Front in the following March. He fought at the Battles of Ypres, Arras, Vimy Ridge, Armentières and the Somme, and throughout the German Offensive and Allied Advance of 1918. Returning to England he was demobilised in June 1919, and holds the General Service and Victory Medals.

155, Gloucester Road, Peckham, S.E.15. Z6324A

RICHARDSON, R., Gunner, R.G.A.

Joining in November 1917 he was sent to the Western Front in April of the following year and fought in many engagements in the Retreat and Advance of 1918, including those at Messines, Passchendaele and Ypres. He was demobilised in March 1919, and holds the General Service and Victory Medals.

15, Cronin Road, Peckham, S.E.15. Z5656

RICHARDSON, T., Gunner, R.F.A.

Volunteering in June 1915 he embarked for the Western Front in the following March and fought at the Battles of the Somme, Messines, Ypres, Passchendaele, Bapaume and during the German Offensive and subsequent Allied Advance of 1918. He was demobilised in January 1919, and holds the General Service and Victory Medals.

104, Cronin Road, Peckham, S.E.15. Z5484

RICHARDSON, W. H., Sergt., 8th and 9th Rifle Brigade.

He volunteered at the declaration of war and proceeded to France in January 1915. During his service overseas he was in action at the Battles of Neuve Chapelle, St. Eloi, Hill 60, Ypres and Festubert. He was killed in action in the Battle of Loos on September 25th, 1915, and was entitled to the 1914-15 Star, and the General Service and Victory Medals. He held the Queen's and King's South African Medals, and the Egyptian (Khedive's) Medal.

"And doubtless he went in splendid company."

23, Albert Road, Peckham, S.E.15. Z6075

RICHENS, J. W. (M.M.), Company Sergt.-Major, 2nd Wiltshire Regiment.

A serving soldier he was mobilised on the outbreak of war and drafted to France in October 1914. In the course of his service on the Western Front he took an active part in operations at Antwerp and in the Battles of Ypres, Neuve Chapelle, Givenchy, Loos, Albert and was wounded at Trones Wood. He was awarded the Military Medal for conspicuous bravery in capturing a German machine gun single handed during heavy fighting on the Somme and was again wounded. He was evacuated to England and after receiving treatment at Cheltenham Hospital was invalided out of the Service in 1917. He holds the 1914 Star, and the General Service and Victory Medals.

131, Elmhurst Mansions, Edgeley Road, Clapham, S.W.4. Z3903

RICKARD, J., Corporal, R.A.S.C. (M.T.)

He volunteered in March 1916 and in the same year embarked for the Western Front. Engaged on important duties in connection with the transport of ammunition and supplies to the forward areas he was present at the Battles of Ypres, Arras, Albert, Bullecourt, Bapaume and Le Cateau. He also served during the Retreat and Advance of 1918 and, returning home for demobilisation in January 1919, holds the General Service and Victory Medals. 75, Clayton Road, Peckham, S.E.15. Z6071

RICKERBY, F. E., Private, 2/15th Lincolnshire Regt.

He joined in October 1916 and in the following February proceeded to France, where he was in action in the Battles of Ypres, Passchendaele, Cambrai and in several other engagements. Invalided home owing to illness in February 1918 he received medical treatment and on recovery was transferred to the Royal Army Pay Corps and was employed on important duties in the office of the Regimental Paymaster, Nottingham. Demobilised in March 1918, he holds the General Service and Victory Medals.

164, Commerical Road, Peckham, S.E.15. Z6613

RICKS, J., Gunner, R.F.A.

Mobilised from the Army Reserve on the outbreak of war he was sent to France shortly afterwards and fought in the Retreat from Mons and the Battles of the Marne, the Aisne, La Bassée, Ypres, Loos and Albert. He fell fighting on the Somme in July, 1916, and was entitled to the Mons Star, and the General Service and Victory Medals.

"Honour to the immortal dead who gave their youth
That the world might grow old in peace."

35, Smyrk's Road, Walworth, S.E.17. Z3286B

RICKWOOD, G. P., Sergt., 1st Royal Welch Fusiliers.

Serving in India when war broke out, having enlisted in January 1910, he sailed for France in November 1914 and fought in the Battles of Neuve Chapelle, St. Eloi and Hill 60, and was wounded. Sent to hospital in France he was later evacuated to England and on recovery proceeded to Egypt in January 1916. He was in action at Agagia, Sollum, the Battles of Jifjaffa, Gaza (I, II, and III) and was present at the Capture of Jericho and the fall of Jerusalem and returned home after the Armistice. Demobilised in June 1919, he holds the 1914 Star, and the General Service and Victory Medals.

161, Commercial Road, Peckham, S.E.15. Z6614

RICKWOOD, J., Private, North Staffordshire Regiment.

Attesting in April 1916 he was called up five months later and was drafted overseas in February 1917. He served in several sectors of the Western Front and was engaged in heavy fighting in the Battles of Arras, Vimy Ridge, Bullecourt, Messines, Ypres, Lens, the Somme and was wounded at Cambrai. Sent home in March 1918 owing to illness he rejoined his unit on recovery and after the Armistice proceeded into Germany with the Army of Occupation. He was demobilised in September 1919, and holds the General Service and Victory Medals.

173, Albert Road, Peckham, S.E.15. Z6076

RICKWOOD, S. H., Driver, R.F.A.

A serving soldier, having enlisted in October 1911, he was mobilised in August 1914 and sent to France almost immediately, afterwards and was in action during the Retreat from Mons, and in the Battles of La Bassée, Ypres, Vimy Ridge and the Somme. He also took part in several engagements during the Retreat and Advance of 1918, and entered Mons the day the Armistice was signed. Returning home on the conclusion of hostilities he was demobilised in January 1919, and holds the Mons Star, and the General Service and Victory Medals.

161, Commercial Road, Peckham, S.E.15. Z6615

RIDDINGTON, D., Rifleman, 21st London Regiment (1st Surrey Rifles).

Joining in April 1916 he embarked for the Western Front in the same year and saw much service in the Somme sector. He was wounded in September 1916 during the Somme Offensive and sent home to hospital and on recovery rejoined his unit in France. Reported missing on June 10th, 1917, he was later presumed to have been killed in action on that date, and was entitled to the General Service and Victory Medals.

"And doubtless he went in splendid company."

6, Ingleton Street, Brixton Road, S.W.9. Z1762B

RIDDLE, R. V., A.B., Royal Navy.

Volunteering in 1914 he received his training on H.M.S. "Warspite" and "Pembroke" and was posted to H.M.S. "Powerful." His ship was attached to the Grand Fleet and engaged on important duties in the North Sea. She was in action in the Battle of Jutland and was present at Scapa Flow on the surrender and internment of the German Fleet. Discharged on account of service in January 1919, he holds the 1914-15 Star, and the General Service and Victory Medals.

18, Verona Street, Battersea, S.W.11. Z3904

RIDDLES, H. G., A.B., Royal Navy.

He joined in January 1917 and was posted to H.M. Monitor "General Craufurd," which vessel was engaged on patrol duties off the Belgian Coast and took part in operations at Zeebrugge and Ostend. Transferred to H.M.S. "Tara" he served aboard that ship until the Cessation of hostilities and was stationed at Scapa Flow. Demobilised in September 1919, he holds the General Service and Victory Medals.

9, Lothian Road, Camberwell New Road, S.W.9. Z5305

RIDDY, A. E. (D.C.M., M.M.), Sergt., 22nd London Regiment (The Queen's).

A Territorial he volunteered in October 1914 and in the following year was drafted to the Western Front. In the course of his service in this theatre of war he was awarded the Distinguished Conduct Medal for conspicuous bravery and devotion to duty in the Field in the Battle of Messines in June 1917 and the Military Medal for gallant conduct during the Advance of 1918. He died gloriously on the Field of Battle at Lille on October 15th, 1918, and was entitled to the 1914-15 Star, and the General Service and Victory Medals.

"He joined the great white company of valiant souls."

6, Colworth Grove, Walworth, S.E.17. Z3909A

RIDDY, C. G., Sergt., 2nd East Surrey Regiment.

A Regular, having served for six years in India, he was mobilised on the outbreak of war and sent to France shortly afterwards. He took part in heavy fighting in the early stages of hostilities and, reported missing, was found later to have been killed in action on February 14th, 1915, in the Battle of Ypres. He was entitled to the 1914 Star, and the General Service and Victory Medals.

"A valiant soldier, with undaunted heart he breasted
Life's last hill."

6, Colworth Grove, Walworth, S.E.17. Z3909B

RIDER, G. V., Private, R.A.M.C.

After several unsuccessful attempts to enlist he joined in 1917 and was drafted overseas in the following year. Serving with the Field Ambulance he did good work in the Field during the Retreat of 1918, and at the Battle of Cambrai and other engagements in the subsequent Allied Advance. He holds the General Service and Victory Medals, and was demobilised in 1919.

12, McKerrell Road, Peckham, S.E.15. Z5828

RIDEWOOD, G. E., Sergt., 1st West Yorkshire Regiment.

He fought in South Africa and volunteered in October 1914 though over military age. After completing his training he served with his unit and did good work, but owing to ineligibility for general service was not sent to a theatre of war. He was however drafted to Malta in 1915 and was engaged on garrison duties until the termination of hostilities. Returning home he was demobilised in January 1919 and, in addition to Medals for the South African Campaign, holds the General Service Medal.

39, Arthur Road, Brixton Road, S.W.9. Z3905

RIDEWOOD, W. C., Driver, R.A.S.C.

Volunteering in September 1914 he embarked for Mesopotamia in the following year and was engaged on important transport duties. He served in the forward areas in several operations, including the attempts for the relief of Kut and rendered valuable services. Sent home in 1917 he was discharged on account of service in the following year, and holds the 1914-15 Star, and the General Service and Victory Medals.

67, Westmacott Street, Camberwell, S.E.5. Z4011

RIDGE, C., Private, 1st East Surrey Regiment.

Joining in February 1917 on attaining military age he proceeded overseas in the following September and served on the Western Front. He saw heavy fighting in the Ypres salient and, reported missing on October 4th, 1917, was later presumed to have been killed in action on that date. He was entitled to the General Service and Victory Medals.

" Whilst we remember the sacrifice is not in vain."

308, Commercial Road, Peckham, S.E.15. Z6650

RIDGE, H., Rifleman, 3rd Rifle Brigade.

He volunteered in March 1915 and drafted overseas five months later saw much service on the Western Front. He was in action in the Battles of Ypres, St. Eloi, Albert, Vimy Ridge, the Somme, Messines, Lens, Amiens, Havrincourt and in the course of operations was wounded at Ypres, on the Somme, and gassed and wounded for the third time at Ypres. Sent home owing to his injuries he was later engaged on important duties at home and in Ireland. He was demobilised in June 1920, and holds the 1914-15 Star, and the General Service and Victory Medals.

59, Marcia Road, Bermondsey, S.E.1. Z27264A

RIDGE, I. (Mrs.), Special War Worker.

Offering her services for work of National importance this lady was employed by Messrs. John Bell, Hill & Lucas, Tower Bridge Road, Bermondsey, from October 1916 until March 1919. She was engaged in the manufacture of anti-gas masks and throughout the period of her service discharged her duties in a thoroughly capable and efficient manner.

59, Marcia Road, Bermondsey, S.E.1. Z27264B

RIDGEWELL, H. G., C.Q.M.S., 24th London Regiment (The Queen's).

He volunteered in August 1914 and in March of the following year was sent to France. In this theatre of war he fought at the Battles of Festubert, Givenchy, Loos, Vimy Ridge, the Somme, Messines, Passchendaele, Cambrai, Menin Road, and in the Retreat and Allied Advance of 1918. He holds the 1914-15 Star, and the General Service and Victory Medals, and was demobilised in February 1919.

26, Jocelyn Street, Peckham, S.E.15. Z5485

RIDGEWELL, W., Private, R.A.S.C. (M.T.), and Cheshire Regiment.

He volunteered in March 1915 and in the following month was sent to the Western Front, where he was engaged with his unit on transport duties at the Battles of Ypres, Loos, Vimy Ridge, the Somme, Bullecourt, Ypres, Cambrai. Transferred to the Cheshire Regiment early in 1918 he fought in the Retreat and subsequent Allied Advance of that year and was wounded. He was demobilised in February 1919, and holds the 1914-15 Star, and the General Service and Victory Medals.

12, Charleston Street, Walworth, S.E.17. Z3906

RIDINGS, J. J., Trooper, 4th (Royal Irish) Dragoon Guards.

He had previously served in the Boer War and volunteered for service with the Colours in August 1914 and was drafted almost immediately to France. He fought in the Retreat from Mons, and the Battles of the Aisne, La Bassée, Ypres, Neuve Chapelle, St. Eloi, Festubert, Loos, Albert, Vimy Ridge, the Somme, the Ancre, Beaucourt, Arras, Lens, Messines, Passchendaele and Cambrai. Owing to an accident he sustained severe injuries and was evacuated to hospital in England and subsequently discharged unfit for further service in April 1918. He holds the Mons Star, and the General Service and Victory Medals, in addition to the Queen's and King's South African Medals.

99, Smyrk's Road, Walworth, S.E.17. Z3907

RIDLEY, A. W., Private, 1/3rd London Regiment (Royal Fusiliers).

Joining in October 1917 he proceeded to the Western Front in the following May and fought in several engagements in the Ypres salient during the German Offensive. He was unfortunately killed at Cambrai on September 10th, 1918, and was entitled to the General Service and Victory Medals.

" Courage, bright hopes, and a myriad dreams, splendidly given."

10, Upper Hall Street, Peckham, S.E.15. Z6616

RIDLEY, W., 2nd Lieutenant, Bedfordshire Regiment.

He volunteered in September 1914 and in the following year proceeded overseas. Whilst on the Western Front he fought in many engagements, including those on the Somme, at Arras and Cambrai. In September 1918 he returned to England for training for promotion to commissioned rank and was granted a Commission two months later, after which he was engaged on important home duties until demobilised in March 1919. He holds the 1914-15 Star, and the General Service and Victory Medals.

129, Grosvenor Terrace, Camberwell, S.E.5. Z3908

RIDOUT, F. A., Private, 25th London Regiment (Cyclists).

He volunteered in August 1914 and served at home on important duties until drafted to India in 1916. He was engaged on special work with his Battalion and took part in the fighting during the campaign in Afghanistan. He was demobilised in November 1919, and holds the General Service and Victory Medals, and the India General Service Medal (with Clasp, Afghanistan, North-West Frontier, 1919).

2, Eythorn Road, Stockwell Road, S.W.9. Z5826B

RIGGALL, G. J., Private, 2/22nd London Regiment (The Queen's).

He joined in August 1917 and in the following year proceeded to Egypt. He took part in the operations during the British Advance through Palestine and remained in this theatre of war until early in 1920. He then returned to England and was demobilised in February of that year. He holds the General Service and Victory Medals.

126, Boyson Road, Walworth, S.E.17. Z3289A

RIGGALL, W. T., Corporal, Queen's Own (Royal West Kent Regiment) and R.A.P.C.

He volunteered in November 1914, and drafted to the Western Front in June 1917, was in action at the Battles of Ypres, Passchendaele and Cambrai. Sent to Italy in the following November he fought in many engagements on the Piave front and returning to France early in 1918 took part in the fighting at Amiens, Ypres, Cambrai, during the Retreat and Advance of that year. He was demobilised in January 1919, and holds the General Service and Victory Medals.

64, Geneva Road, Coldharbour Lane, S.W.9. Z3910

RIGNALL, W. G., Private, 2nd Middlesex Regiment.

He joined in March 1917 and was sent to France early in the following year. He fought during the German Offensive at Amiens and was taken prisoner in April 1918. He was held captive in Alsace-Lorraine until the signing of the Armistice, when he was one of fifty prisoners of war who marched into the British lines. He returned to England and was demobilised in September 1919. He holds the General Service and Victory Medals.

57, Corunna Road, New Road, S.W.8. Z3911

RILEY, A. C., Driver, R.F.A.

He volunteered in August 1914 and in February of the following year was sent to France. Owing to ill-health he was invalided to the Base hospital, and six months later was sent to Mesopotamia, where he served in many notable engagements with his Battery until he returned to England in 1919. He holds the 1914-15 Star, and the General Service and Victory Medals, and was still serving in 1920.

15, Copeland Avenue, Peckham Rye, S.E.15. Z5657A

RILEY, A. T., Private, 7th East Surrey Regiment.

He volunteered in November 1915 and was drafted to the Western Front in March 1916. He fought in engagements at Arras and Cambrai, and was severely wounded and taken prisoner in November 1917. Held in captivity in Germany for 14 months he was repatriated after the signing of the Armistice and discharged as medically unfit for further service in January 1919. He holds the General Service and Victory Medals.

67, Marlborough Road, Old Kent Road, S.E.1. Z27273

RILEY, F. C., Private, Royal Fusiliers.

A serving soldier he was mobilised at the outbreak of hostilities and sent to France in 1915. He fought in many engagements, including those at Ypres, Loos, Festubert, St. Eloi, the Somme, Arras, Lens, Passchendaele, Cambrai, Amiens, and in the Retreat and Allied Advance of 1918. After the signing of the Armistice he was sent with the Army of Occupation into Germany, where he served for a time. He was demobilised in 1919, and holds the 1914-15 Star, and the General Service and Victory Medals.

15, Copeland Avenue, Peckham Rye, S.E.15. Z5657B

RILEY, H. D., Corporal, Hampshire Regiment.
He volunteered in August 1914 and in February of the following year proceeded overseas. He was engaged in the fighting at the first Landing at Gallipoli and many engagements which followed. Sent to Egypt early in 1916 he served in the British Advance through Palestine and was present at the entry into Jerusalem, and was wounded. He returned to hospital in England and on recovery was discharged medically unfit for further service in November 1918. He holds the 1914-15 Star, and the General Service and Victory Medals.
15, Copeland Avenue, Peckham Rye, S.E.15. Z5657C

RILEY, J. H., Sergt., Dorsetshire Regiment.
He volunteered in September 1914 and in the following year proceeded to the Western Front, where he was in action at the Battles of Ypres and Arras, and was seriously wounded at Ypres, causing him to be partially paralysed. He was evacuated to hospital in England and subsequently discharged unfit for further service in March 1916. He holds the 1914-15 Star, and the General Service and Victory Medals.
25, Tindal Street, Lothian Road, S.W.9. Z5486

RILEY, J. H. S., Gunner, R.F.A.
A serving soldier, having enlisted in 1908, he was mobilised at the outbreak of hostilities and, proceeding to France in February 1915, took part in the fighting at the Battles of Hill 60, La Bassée, Ypres and Loos. Drafted to Salonika in 1916 he was in action in many engagements and was wounded and contracted malaria. He was invalided to England in 1918 and, demobilised in the following year, holds the 1914-15 Star, and the General Service and Victory Medals.
15, Copeland Avenue, Peckham Rye, S.E.15. Z5657D

RINGSHALL, H., Private, 2nd Dorsetshire Regt.
He enlisted in 1904 and was mobilised and drafted to France at the outbreak of hostilities. He fought in the Retreat from Mons and was wounded and returned to England. He received protracted hospital treatment and after many operations died from the effects of his injuries on May 9th, 1920. He was entitled to the Mons Star, and the General Service and Victory Medals.
" Great deeds cannot die, they with the sun and moon
renew their light for ever."
74, Cronin Road, Peckham, S.E.15. Z5658

RINGWOOD, B., Gunner, R.G.A.
Volunteering in October 1914 he was sent to Egypt in 1915 and saw much service on the Palestine front. He fought at the Battles of Gaza (I, II and III) and Jericho, and in operations in the vicinity of Jerusalem, and throughout the British Advance into Syria. He returned to England, and, demobilised in May 1919, holds the 1914-15 Star, and the General Service and Victory Medals.
7, Goldie Street, Camberwell, S.E.5. Z5487

RISELEY, G., Private, R.A.S.C.
He volunteered in May 1915 at the age of fifty-five and was drafted to France in the same month. During his service overseas he was stationed at Dieppe and rendered valuable services in the Stores Depôt. In August 1917 he was invalided to England owing to an accident and after hospital treatment was discharged unfit for further service in the following December. He holds the 1914-15 Star, and the General Service and Victory Medals.
205, Albert Road, Peckham, S.E.15. Z5659

RISELEY, H., Driver, R.A.S.C.
He volunteered in December 1914 and drafted to the Western Front in the following August served in the forward areas on important duties transporting ammunition and supplies to the front lines. He was present at the Battles of Neuve Chapelle, Ypres, Festubert, Vermelles, the Somme and during heavy fighting in the Retreat and Advance of 1918, and was twice wounded. After the Armistice he proceeded into Germany with the Army of Occupation and served there until he returned to England and was demobilised in May 1919. He holds the 1914-15 Star, and the General Service and Victory Medals.
98, Harbut Road, Battersea, S.W.11. Z3912

RIVERS, A. R., Private, 2/2nd London Regiment (Royal Fusiliers).
Volunteering in March 1915 he served at various stations until proceeding to the Western Front in January 1917. He fought in many engagements of note, including those at Arras, Ypres and the Somme, and was severely wounded in October 1917. Returning to England he received hospital treatment and was invalided out of the Service in October 1918. He holds the General Service and Victory Medals.
75, Warham Street, Camberwell, S.E.5. Z3913

RIVETT, W. G., Driver, R.A.S.C. (M.T.)
Mobilised from the Army Reserve in August 1915 he was sent to France almost immediately and served in many parts of the line engaged on important duties connected with the transport of supplies of ammunition and other war material to the front lines. He rendered valuable services throughout, and, demobilised in April 1919, holds the 1914 Star, and the General Service and Victory Medals.
38, Graylands Road, Peckham, S.E.15. Z5829

RIXON, A. J., C.S.M., 18th London Regiment (London Irish Rifles).
A Territorial he was mobilised in August 1914 and proceeding to France in March 1915 fought in the Battles of Loos, Ypres and in many other engagements of note. He was wounded at Loos and on recovery rejoined his Battalion and was in action in various sectors. He gave his life for the freedom of England at Ypres on April 7th, 1917, and was entitled to the 1914-15 Star, and the General Service and Victory Medals.
" He joined the great white company of valiant souls."
1, Bonnington Square, South Lambeth Road, S.W.8. Z3914

RIXON, F., Corporal, 1st King's Royal Rifle Corps.
He volunteered in April 1915 and embarked for France later in the same year. He took part in many engagements and was wounded in September 1915. He returned to England and after receiving hospital treatment rejoined his unit in France and fought in various parts of the line. Injured through a fall of earth, which buried him, he was invalided to England and on recovery was engaged on instructional duties until demobilised in January 1919. He holds the 1914-15 Star, and the General Service and Victory Medals.
25, Harris Street, Camberwell, S.E.5. Z4525

ROACH, J., Private, Labour Corps.
He joined in October 1916 and was sent to the Western Front in the following March. He did good work attached to the Royal Engineers engaged on railway construction and was present at the Battles of Ypres, Arras, Merville, Cambrai, Menin Road and during heavy fighting in the Retreat and Advance of 1918. He was demobilised in March 1919, and holds the General Service and Victory Medals.
86, Galley Wall Road, Rotherhithe, S.E.16. Z6651

ROBARTS, A. P., Private, R.A.P.C. and M.G.C.
Volunteering in December 1914 and later transferred to the Machine Gun Corps he proceeded to France in 1916. He was in action in many important engagements, including those at the Somme, Ypres, Béthune, Amiens, Arras, and fought throughout the German Offensive and Allied Advance of 1918, and was slightly gassed. He was demobilised in January 1919, and holds the General Service and Victory Medals.
44, Clayton Road, Peckham, S.E.15. Z6068

ROBBINS, G. W., Driver, R.H.A.
A serving soldier he was mobilised and drafted to the Western Front shortly after the commencement of hostilities and fought in many engagements. Later transferred to Egypt he saw much service on the Palestine front and was afterwards sent to Mesopotamia, where he took part in various operations. He proceeded to India and later to Russia, and there saw heavy fighting in many parts of the line. He was demobilised in April 1920, and holds the 1914-15 Star, and the General Service and Victory Medals, also the Queen's and King's South African Medals (with five Bars), and the Long Service and Good Conduct Medal.
156, Rolls Road, Bermondsey, S.E.1. Z26750B

ROBBINS, W., Private, Royal Warwickshire Regiment.
Volunteering in June 1915 he was drafted to the Western Front in the following December and fought in many parts of the line. Transferred to Egypt he was in action in many engagements and was killed in action in April 1916, and was entitled to the 1914-15 Star, and the General Service and Victory Medals.
" A valiant soldier, with undaunted heart he breasted
Life's last hill."
129, Westmoreland Road, Walworth, S.E.17. Z27470

ROBERTS, A., Saddler, R.A.S.C.
He volunteered in August 1914 and, sent to France almost immediately, served in the Retreat from Mons, and the Battles of the Aisne, Loos, Neuve Chapelle, the Somme, and throughout the German Offensive and Allied Advance of 1918. He was demobilised in July 1919, and holds the Mons Star, and the General Service and Victory Medals. He also holds the Queen's and King's South African Medals for service in the Boer War.
55, Neate Street, Camberwell, S.E.5. Z5141

ROBERTS, A., 1st Air Mechanic, R.A.F.
He joined in August 1916 and after the completion of his course of training was retained at Farnborough, Wendover and other stations on important duties which called for a high degree of technical skill. He was not successful in securing his transfer overseas while hostilities lasted but rendered valuable services until his demobilisation in February 1919.
2, Lugard Road, Peckham, S.E.15. Z6684

ROBERTS, A., Rifleman, King's Royal Rifle Corps.
Volunteering in August 1914 he landed in France in the same month and fought in the Retreat from Mons and in the Battles of the Somme and Ypres. He was wounded during the German Offensive of 1918 and admitted into hospital. On recovery he returned to the front lines and was in action in many engagements in the Allied Advance and was again wounded. He was demobilised in January 1919, and holds the Mons Star, and the General Service and Victory Medals.
16, Patmore Street, Wandsworth Road, S.W.8. Z3916B

ROBERTS, D., Rifleman, 21st London Regiment (1st Surrey Rifles).

He volunteered in 1914 and served at various depôts until drafted to the Western Front in 1916. During his service overseas he fought in many engagements and did good work throughout. He gave his life for King and Country at Ypres on June 7th, 1917, and was entitled to the General Service and Victory Medals.
"His life for his country."

5, Monkton Street, Kennington, S.E.11. Z26971

ROBERTS, E. A., Driver, R.A.S.C. (H.T.)

He volunteered in 1914 and in the same year was drafted to France, where he served in the forward areas engaged on transport duties. He was present at heavy fighting at Arras, the Somme, Ypres, La Bassée, Loos, Lens, and throughout the Retreat and Advance of 1918. After the Armistice he was sent into Germany with the Army of Occupation and served there until he returned to England and was demobilised in 1919. He holds the 1914 Star, and the General Service and Victory Medals, and also the Queen's and King's South African Medals for service in the Boer War.

259, East Street, Walworth, S.E.17. Z3919A

ROBERTS, E. A. (Junior), Rifleman, Rifle Brigade.

He joined in 1916 and was drafted to the Western Front later in that year. He fought at the Battles of Arras, Ypres and the Somme, where he was blown up by shell explosion and contracted shell-shock. Invalided home he received hospital treatment and was discharged unfit for further service in 1918. He holds the General Service and Victory Medals.

259, East Street, Walworth, S.E.17. Z3919B

ROBERTS, F., Gunner, R.F.A.

He volunteered in April 1915 and was sent to the Western Front in the same year. He fought in many parts of the line, including the Arras sector. Transferred to Salonika in 1916 he was in action on the Struma and Doiran fronts and was drafted to Egypt a year later. Here he was engaged in heavy fighting on the Palestine front and served throughout the Advance into Syria. Returning to England he was demobilised in July 1919, and holds the 1914-15 Star, and the General Service and Victory Medals.

11, Russell Grove, Vassall Road, S.W.9. Z5140B

ROBERTS, F. T., L/Corporal, R.A.S.C. (M.T.)

He joined in September 1916 and embarking for France in the following month served in various sectors on important supply duties. He rendered valuable services throughout and was present at severe fighting during the German Offensive and subsequent Allied Advance of 1918. He was demobilised in May 1919, and holds the General Service and Victory Medals.

32, Mansion Street, Camberwell, S.E.5. Z3921

ROBERTS, G., Corporal, South Lancashire Regiment.

A serving soldier he crossed to France immediately upon the outbreak of war and fought in the Retreat from Mons and the Battles of the Marne and the Aisne, where he was blown up and injured by shell explosion. He was invalided home in December 1914 and after treatment in hospital his hearing was found to have been so badly impaired as to render him unfit for further active service. He was therefore retained on home duties until March 1920, when he was discharged on account of service. He holds the Mons Star, and the General Service and Victory Medals.

125, Akerman Road, Brixton Road, S.W.9. Z5142

ROBERTS, G. (Junior), Private, Welch Regiment and Machine Gun Corps.

Mobilised with the Territorials at the outbreak of war he was drafted to the Western Front in September 1915 and fought in engagements at Loos, Ypres and the Somme. He gave his life for the freedom of England at Limburg on August 27th, 1917, and was entitled to the 1914-15 Star, and the General Service and Victory Medals.

12, Brewer Street, Chelsea, S.W.3. 22680A

ROBERTS, G., Private, Labour Corps.

He volunteered in April 1915 and crossed to France in the same month. Whilst overseas he was engaged in repairing and making roads in the forward areas and served in many sectors, notably those of the Somme and Ypres. He holds the 1914-15 Star, and the General Service and Victory Medals, and was demobilised in March 1919.

12, Brewer Street, Chelsea, S.W.3. X22680B

ROBERTS, G. A., Sergt., Middlesex Regiment.

Volunteering on the outbreak of hostilities he proceeded to France with the first Expeditionary Force and took part in the Retreat from Mons and the Battles of the Marne and the Aisne. He also fought in many of the engagements which followed, including those at Ypres, Loos, the Somme and Arras, and did much valuable work as a bomber, and was wounded three times. He was demobilised in 1919, and holds the Mons Star, and the General Service and Victory Medals

40, Bournemouth Road, Peckham, S.E.15. Z5488A

ROBERTS, G. T., Private, 1/20th London Regiment.

Joining in October 1916 he was sent overseas in the following January and fought in the Battles of Arras, Vimy Ridge, Bullecourt, Ypres, Lens, Cambrai and the Somme, and in March 1918 was taken prisoner during the German Offensive. Working behind the enemy lines he received much ill-treatment at the hands of his captors and was subsequently removed to hospital suffering from dysentery. Repatriated after the termination of hostilities he was demobilised in March 1919, and holds the General Service and Victory Medals.

65, Moncrieff Street, Peckham, S.E.15. Z5660

ROBERTS, H. F., Driver, R.F.A.

He joined in December 1916 and after his training was engaged as an instructor at the Riding School, Salisbury Plain. Owing to ill-health he was unable to secure his transfer to a theatre of war but nevertheless did much valuable work until demobilised in March 1919.

11, Russell Grove, Vassall Road, S.W.9. Z5140A

ROBERTS, H. J., Private, 9th Royal Irish Fusiliers.

He joined in June 1916 and in the following year was drafted to the Western Front, where he took part in numerous engagements, including those at Ypres and the Somme. He also served in the final Retreat, and during the subsequent Advance was unfortunately killed in action at Bailleul on September 4th, 1918. He was entitled to the General Service and Victory Medals.
"A costly sacrifice upon the altar of freedom."

136, Abbey Street, Bermondsey, S.E.1. Z27412

ROBERTS, J., Sapper, R.E., and Private, Labour Corps.

Volunteering in September 1915 he crossed to France at the conclusion of his training and was engaged on duties of an important nature in the forward areas. After being severely wounded at Ypres he was transferred to the Labour Corps and did good work overseas until after the termination of hostilities. He was demobilised in May 1919, and holds the 1914-15 Star, and the General Service and Victory Medals.

79, Silverthorne Road, Battersea Park, S.W.8. Z3918

ROBERTS, J., Driver, R.A.S.C. (M.T.)

An ex-soldier with a previous record of service in the South African War he volunteered in December 1915 and was drafted to the Western Front in the following August. Whilst overseas he served with the Ammunition Column and did very good work in many important sectors. After the Retreat and Advance of 1918 he was sent with the Army of Occupation into Germany and was stationed at Cologne. He was demobilised on his return to England in July 1919, and in addition to the Queen's and King's South African Medals, holds the General Service and Victory Medals.

26, Greylands Road, Peckham, S.E.15. Z5830

ROBERTS, J., Rifleman, King's Royal Rifle Corps.

He volunteered early in 1915 and crossed to France in the same year. In this theatre of war he fought at the Battles of Ypres, Beaumont-Hamel and Loos, and was later invalided home wounded. After recovery he returned to the Western Front and took part in the Retreat and Advance of 1918. He then returned to England and was demobilised in 1919, and holds the 1914-15 Star, and the General Service and Victory Medals.

16, Patmore Street, Wandsworth Road, S.W.8. Z3916A

ROBERTS, J. C., Sergt., R.F.A.

He was serving in India when war broke out and, embarking for France, arrived on this Front in 1914. He took an active part in the Battles of Ypres, Neuve Chapelle, the Somme and Arras, and in 1917 was severely wounded and invalided to England. After recovery he rejoined his Battery in the Field and served in the Advance of 1918. He was discharged in 1919, and holds the 1914 Star, and the General Service and Victory Medals.

85, Wadhurst Road, Battersea Park Road, S.W.8. Z1498A

ROBERTS, T. W., Private, Connaught Rangers.

He volunteered in October 1914 and in the following May crossed to France, where he subsequently took part in several engagements, including those at Ypres and Loos. Later he was transferred to the Eastern front, where he was severely wounded on January 28th, 1916. He died the same day from the effects of his injuries, and was entitled to the 1914-15 Star, and the General Service and Victory Medals.
"He passed out of the sight of men
By the path of duty and self-sacrifice."

13, Totteridge Road, Battersea, S.W.11. 3917A

ROBERTS, W., Stoker, Royal Navy.

Volunteering in January 1915 he was posted to H.M.S. "Repulse," which vessel was engaged on special duties in the North Sea. He also took part with his ship in the Battles of Jutland and Heligoland Bight, and in various Naval engagements off the Belgian Coast, and did valuable work until after the termination of hostilities. He was demobilised in January 1919, and holds the 1914-15 Star, and the General Service and Victory Medals.

25, Willington Road, Stockwell, S.W.9. Z3915

ROBERTS, W. F., Gunner, R.F.A.

Volunteering in January 1915 he was drafted to France at the conclusion of his training, and fought at the Battles of Hill 60, St. Eloi and the Somme, where he was wounded. After treatment at a Base hospital he rejoined his Battery in the Field and took part in engagements at Noyon, Arras, Vimy Ridge, and in the Retreat and Advance of 1918. He holds the 1914-15 Star, and the General Service and Victory Medals, and was demobilised in June, 1919.

23, Hargwyne Street, Stockwell, S.W.9.   Z3920

ROBERTS, W. R., Private, Queen's (Royal West Surrey Regiment).

He enlisted in March 1914 and on the outbreak of war at once proceeded to France, where he fought gallantly at Mons, Ypres, Loos, Vermelles and the Somme. He was wounded on four occasions during his service, but after each one rejoined his unit and continued to serve. He returned to England and was discharged in December 1917 in consequence of his service. He holds the Mons Star, and the General Service and Victory Medals.

111, Verney Road, Rotherhithe, S.E.16.   Z6685

ROBERTS, F. W., Private, Labour Corps.

Volunteering in the 7th London Regiment in November 1915 he was drafted to the Western Front three months later and served there for three years. During this period he was in action in several engagements, including the Battles of Ypres and High Wood, and was afterwards transferred to the Labour Corps. Serving with this unit he did good work during the final stages of the war. He returned home for demobilisation in February 1919, and holds the General Service and Victory Medals.

55, Ascalon Street, Battersea Park Road, S.W.8.   Z3922

ROBERTSON, S., Special War Worker.

Exempt from military service as he was engaged on work of National importance he was employed from June 1916 to November 1918 as a milling machinist in the factory of Messrs. Harvey Du Cros and for a time by Messrs. Vickers Ltd., Erith. He was engaged in the manufacture of shells and cartridge cases and did excellent work throughout the period of his service.

31, Baker Street, Brixton Road, S.W.9.   Z5278

ROBERTSON, T. E., Air Mechanic, R.A.F.

Joining in 1916 he was drafted to France on the completion of his training and served in the workshops at various aerodromes. He carried out highly technical duties in connection with the repairs of damaged aircraft until ill-health necessitated his return to England, and was discharged in consequence in February 1918. He holds the General Service and Victory Medals.

31, Army Street, Clapham, S.W.4.   Z3923

ROBINS, W., Private, 2nd Middlesex Regiment.

He volunteered in August 1914 and was sent to the Western Front three months later. In the course of his service he fought in the Battles of Neuve Chapelle, Vermelles and Loos, and was gassed in September 1915 and invalided home. After hospital treatment he was transferred to the Suffolk Regiment and after being drafted to Italy in 1917 took part in several engagements until hostilities ceased. After returning home he was demobilised in February 1919, and holds the 1914 Star, and the General Service and Victory Medals.

3, Bolney Street, Dorset Road, S.W.8.   Z3924

ROBINSON, A., Private, 3rd (King's Own) Hussars.

He volunteered in August 1914 and in March of the following year embarked for Egypt, where he served in the Canal zone, and was wounded in 1915. Sent home in December 1916, he proceeded to France in the following year and fought in the Battles of Cambrai, Havrincourt, and was wounded in 1918. After the Armistice he was sent into Germany with the Army of Occupation and was stationed at Cologne until his return to England for demobilisation in February 1919. He holds the 1914-15 Star, and the General Service and Victory Medals.

20, Sydney Square, Peckham, S.E.15.   Z6323

ROBINSON, A., Private, Duke of Cornwall's Light Infantry.

Mobilised on the declaration of war he was sent to France with the first British Expeditionary Force. He fell fighting gallantly on August 25th, 1914, during the Retreat from Mons, and was entitled to the Mons Star, and the General Service and Victory Medals.

"Whilst we remember the sacrifice is not in vain."

76, Thurlow Street, Walworth, S.E.17.   Z3926B

ROBINSON, A. H., Private, National Reserve.

Volunteering in 1914 he was engaged on guard and other important duties with his unit at Plumstead. He was ineligible for general service, but did much valuable work until discharged on account of ill-health in 1916.

78, Grant Road, Battersea, S.W.11.   Z2731B

ROBINSON, C. P., Private, R.A.F. (late R.F.C.)

He volunteered in December 1915 and in the following year embarked for Mesopotamia. Serving in the balloon section he did good work in observation and other duties in the attempted relief of Kut, the Battle of Kut-el-Amara and the Capture of Baghdad. Returning home owing to illness in April 1918 he was demobilised a year later and holds the General Service and Victory Medals.

22, Calmington Road, Camberwell, S.E.5.   Z5489

ROBINSON, E. A. C., Sapper, R.E.

Volunteering in 1915 he proceeded overseas in July of the same year and served in France and Flanders throughout the war. Engaged as a telegraphic linesman he rendered valuable services during the Battles of Loos, Vimy Ridge, the Somme and Ypres, and was invalided home for a severe operation. Returning to the Western Front on his recovery he carried out important duties on the lines of communication during the Allied Advance of 1918. On returning home after the Armistice he was demobilised in August 1919, and holds the 1914-15 Star, and the General Service and Victory Medals.

41, Bellefields Road, Stockwell Road, S.W.9.   Z6561A

ROBINSON, F., Stoker, Royal Navy.

He was serving at the outbreak of war in H.M.S. "Monarch," which vessel was attached to the Grand Fleet and engaged on patrol and escort duties in the North Sea. She was in action in the Battles of Heligoland Bight, Dogger Bank and Jutland, and had several narrow escapes when traversing mined areas. He did good work throughout the course of hostilities, holds the 1914-15 Star, and the General Service and Victory Medals, and was still serving in 1920.

33, Mundella Road, Wandsworth Road, S.W.8.   Z2834A

ROBINSON, F., 1st London Regiment (Royal Fusiliers).

A Territorial he was mobilised on the declaration of war and was drafted to France shortly afterwards. Serving as a signaller he took part in heavy fighting in the early engagements of the war and in several subsequent battles, including those of Ypres and Soissons. He was killed in action on October 22nd 1917, at Cambrai, where he was buried, and was entitled to the 1914 Star, and the General Service and Victory Medals.

" His life for his Country."

30, Gladstone Terrace, Battersea Park Road, S.W.8.   Z3928

ROBINSON, F. V., Private, R.A.M.C.

Mobilised on the outbreak of war he was sent to the Western Front in 1914 and served during the Battles of Ypres, St. Eloi and the Somme. Proceeding to Salonika in the next year he was engaged with the Field Ambulance in the Advance on the Struma and the Vardar, and after falling ill was sent to hospital at Malta. After returning home he was demobilised in March 1919, and holds the 1914-15 Star, and the General Service and Victory Medals.

4, Clayton Road, Peckham, S.E.15.   Z6219

ROBINSON, G., Musician, Irish Guards.

A serving soldier, who enlisted in 1901, he was mobilised when war broke out and was engaged on guard and other important duties with his unit. He took part in several marches through England and Ireland in connection with recruiting for the New Armies, and after the Armistice was sent to France on special duties in connection with the Peace celebrations. In 1920 he was still serving with his Battalion.

11, Freedom Street, Battersea, S.W.11.   Z3931

ROBINSON, G., Private, 7th London Regiment.

He joined in November 1916 and embarking for the Western Front two months later was in action in the Battles of Cambrai and Bullecourt, and was wounded in June 1917. Sent home owing to his injuries he received hospital treatment and returning to his unit served in several engagements until invalided to England on account of ill-health in 1918. He was subsequently demobilised in February 1919, and holds the General Service and Victory Medals.

241, St. George's Road, Peckham, S.E.15.   Z3925

ROBINSON, H. T., Sapper, R.E., and 1st Air Mechanic, R.A.F.

Volunteering in August 1914 and proceeding to France almost immediately he was in action in the Retreat from Mons, and the Battles of Loos, Neuve Chapelle, La Bassée and the Somme. Transferred to the Royal Air Force in 1916 he served at various aerodromes engaged on important duties. In 1917 owing to ill-health he returned to England, and was ultimately discharged as unfit for further service in August 1918. He holds the Mons Star, and the General Service and Victory Medals.

37, Lettsom Street, Camberwell, S.E.5.   Z6539

ROBINSON, J., Driver, R.A.S.C.

He volunteered in January 1916 and completing his training was stationed at various depôts engaged on important duties with his unit. He was unsuccessful in obtaining his transfer to a theatre of war prior to the cessation of hostilities, but rendered valuable services until demobilised in December 1918.

15, Everett Street, Nine Elms Lane, S.W.8.   Z392

ROBINSON, J. E., Corporal, 12th East Surrey Regiment.

He volunteered in November 1915 and embarked for France five months later. He was in action in the Battles of Ploegsteert, Vimy Ridge, the Somme, Arras, Messines, Ypres and Lens, and suffering from shell-shock returned to England. He received hospital treatment and was subsequently invalided out of the Service in December 1917. He holds the General Service and Victory Medals.

294, East Street, Walworth, S.E.17.   Z3929

ROBINSON, L. W., Private, 6th Queen's Own (Royal West Kent Regiment).

Volunteering in August 1914 he completed his training and proceeding to the Western Front in the following May served in many parts of the line where heavy fighting was in progress. He died gloriously on the field of battle at Hulluch on October 8th, 1915, and was entitled to the 1914-15 Star, and the General Service and Victory Medals.

"Nobly striving, he nobly fell that we might live."

41, Bellefields Road, Stockwell Road, S.W.9.   Z6561C

ROBINSON, R. H., Private, 6th Dorsetshire Regiment.

Volunteering in August 1914 he was sent to France in the succeeding July and fought at Ypres, the Somme, Arras, Passchendaele, Cambrai, Thiepval and throughout the German Offensive and subsequent Allied Advance of 1918. He was demobilised in February 1919, and holds the 1914-15 Star, and the General Service and Victory Medals.

54, D'Eynsford Road, Camberwell Green, S.E.5.   Z3932

ROBINSON, W. A., Driver, R.F.A.

Prior to the outbreak of war he had served in H.M. Forces and had seen active service in the South African War. He re-enlisted in September 1914 and, drafted to France in the same month, fought at the Marne, the Aisne, the Somme and many other engagements. He also saw heavy fighting in the Retreat and Advance of 1918, and returning to England after the cessation of hostilities was demobilised in April 1919. He rejoined in the Labour Corps in May 1919 and was sent to France with the War Graves Commission, and was engaged on important duties. He was still serving in 1920, and holds the 1914 Star, and the General Service and Victory Medals.

2, Knox Road, Battersea, S.W.11.   Z5704A

ROBINSON, W. J., L/Corporal, 4th Queen's Own (Royal West Kent Regiment).

Volunteering in August 1914 he served at various stations with his unit engaged on guard and other important duties. He was not successful in obtaining his transfer to a theatre of war, but did good work until demobilised in March 1919. He had previously served for twelve years in the 8th Hussars and throughout the Boer War was with the Reserve of Hussars training horses.

41, Bellefields Road, Stockwell Road, S.W.9.   Z6561B

ROBINSON, W. J., Driver, R.F.A.

Volunteering in March 1915 he embarked for the Western Front in the following December, and fought in many engagements of note, including those at the Somme and Ypres. He was unfortunately killed in action at Arras on April 21st, 1917, and was entitled to the 1914-15 Star, and the General Service and Victory Medals.

13, Harris Street, Camberwell, S.E.5.   Z4526A

ROBINSON, W. J., Yeoman of Signals, Royal Navy.

He joined the Service in 1901 and at the outbreak of hostilities was serving in H.M.S. "Ceres," which ship was in action in the Battle of Heligoland Bight and against Bolshevist craft in the Baltic Sea. She also did good work engaged on patrol, convoy, and minelaying duties in the North Sea. At the cessation of hostilities he was serving in H.M.S. "Caledonian," and was still in the Navy in 1920. He holds the 1914-15 Star, and the General Service and Victory Medals.

36, Andulus Road, Landor Road, S.W.9.   Z3930

ROBINSON, W. S., Driver, R.F.A.

He volunteered in 1914 and, drafted to France in the following year, was in action at Arras, the Somme and Ypres. Transferred to Italy in 1916 he fought in many engagements on the Piave front and in the final Allied Advance in this theatre of war. He returned to England and was demobilised in 1919, and holds the 1914-15 Star, and the General Service and Victory Medals.

76, Thurlow Street, Walworth, S.E.17.   Z3926A

ROBSON, A. E., L/Corporal, 1st Rifle Brigade.

He joined in May 1916 and proceeded to France in the following year. He took part in the fighting at Arras, Ypres, Cambrai, the Somme and in many other engagements in the Retreat and Advance of 1918. During his service in this theatre of war he was three times wounded and gassed. He was invalided home, but on his recovery he returned to France. He was demobilised in May 1919, holding the General Service and Victory Medals.

60, Westmacott Street, Camberwell, S.E.5.   Z5549

ROBSON, F., Private, R.A.S.C.

He was mobilised in August 1914 and shortly afterwards was sent to France, where he was engaged on important transport duties during the Retreat from Mons. He was soon afterwards taken ill and invalided home. On his recovery he returned to duty at the Grove Park Depôt, but afterwards fell ill again and unfortunately died in December 1916. He was buried in Nunhead Cemetery, and was entitled to the Mons Star, and the General Service and Victory Medals.

"His memory is cherished with pride."

135, Kimberley Road, Peckham, S.E.15.   Z6440B

ROBSON, F. J., A.B., Royal Navy, H.M.S. "Royal Sovereign."

He joined in June 1918 and during his training served on board H.M.S. "Impregnable." He was afterwards transferred to H.M.S. "Royal Sovereign," and proceeded to Turkey, where he was still serving with the Allied Fleet in 1920.

149, Cator Street, Peckham, S.E.15.   Z4528B

ROBSON, F. W., Gunner, R.F.A.

He volunteered in August 1914 and was engaged with his Battery on important duties until February 1917, when he was drafted to France. He took part in the severe fighting at Arras, Messines, Ypres, Passchendaele, Lens, Cambrai and the Somme. He was killed in action at Villers-Bretoneux on April 24th, 1918. He was entitled to the General Service and Victory Medals.

"Great deeds cannot die :
They with the sun and moon renew their light for ever."

135, Kimberley Road, Peckham, S.E.15.   Z6440A

ROBSON, H., Private, Northamptonshire Regiment.

He was mobilised in August 1914 and after being sent to France in the same month was in action at Mons, Neuve Chapelle, Ypres, Loos and in many other important engagements. He was unfortunately killed in action in May 1916, and was entitled to the Mons Star, and the General Service and Victory Medals.

"The path of duty was the way to glory."

157, Cator Street, Peckham, S.E.15.   Z4527

ROBSON, H. C., Gunner, Royal Marine Artillery.

He was serving at the outbreak of war, having joined in 1903, and was sent to France in the same year. He was engaged as a driver of motor tractors, used for placing guns in position, in many sectors, and was in many engagements during the whole period of the war. He was still serving in 1920, and holds the 1914 Star, and the General Service and Victory Medals.

149, Cator Street, Peckham, S.E.15.   Z4528A

ROBSON, W., Private, Labour Corps.

He was mobilised in August 1914 and was shortly afterwards sent to France, where he rendered valuable service at numerous engagements, including those at Mons, Ypres, Loos, Festubert, the Somme, Lens, Cambrai and Amiens, and other operations in the Retreat and Advance of 1918. He was demobilised in 1919, holding the 1914 Star, and the General Service and Victory Medals. In addition he has a Certificate for bravery in saving two children from drowning in the Surrey Canal, diving for them in full marching order.   Z5641B

7, Brayard's Road, Peckham, S.E.15.   Z5642B

ROCK, H. T., Private, R.A.S.C.

He volunteered in May 1915 and in the same year was drafted overseas. Whilst in France he was engaged at Abbeville, Amiens and other places on important duties in connection with the supply of stores of all kinds until the Armistice. He was demobilised in February 1919, and holds the 1914-15 Star, and the General Service and Victory Medals.

12, Pasley Road, Walworth, S.E.17.   Z27033

ROCKLIFFE, R. C., Bombardier, R.F.A.

He volunteered in March 1915 and later in the same year was sent to France, where he was in action at Vimy Ridge, the Somme, Arras, Bullecourt, Ypres and in numerous other engagements, and was wounded and invalided home. On his recovery he returned to France and took part in the Retreat and Advance of 1918. While serving in France he suffered from trench fever. He was demobilised in June 1919, and holds the 1914-15 Star, and the General Service and Victory Medals.

121, Villa Street, Walworth, S.E.17.   27452A

RODWAY, G. W. F., Rifleman, 13th Rifle Brigade.

He joined in May 1916 and after completing his training was drafted to the Western Front, where he took part in numerous engagements, including that at Ypres. He also served in the Retreat and Advance of 1918, and was wounded. He was commended by his Brigadier-General on the Field for his valiant service in March 1918, and holds the General Service and Victory Medals. He was demobilised in June 1920.

13, Cronin Road, Peckham, S.E.15.   Z5661

ROE, E. W., Constable, Special Constabulary.

He volunteered in August 1914 as a special constable in the Peckham Division and did most valuable work during the air-raids and on numerous other duties throughout the war. He rendered valuable services and was demobilised in June 1919, holding the Special Constabulary Long Service Medal and Star, and a Certificate of Commendation.

45, Castlemain Road, Peckham, S.E.15.   Z6074

ROFF, D., Bombardier, R.F.A.

He was mobilised in August 1914 and was immediately sent to France, where he took part in the severe fighting at Mons, the Marne, the Aisne, La Bassée, Ypres, Neuve Chapelle and St. Eloi. He was unfortunately killed in action by shell fire on May 2nd, 1915, and holds the Mons Star, and the General Service and Victory Medals.

"A costly sacrifice upon the altar of freedom."   Z2594A
3, Kingslake Street, Walworth, S.E.17.   Z2595A

ROFF, J. E., Gunner, R.F.A.

He volunteered in August 1915 and proceeded to France in March of the following year. He took part in many important engagements on the Somme and Albert fronts, but was later invalided home owing to nerve trouble and was engaged on various duties until he was demobilised in March 1919. He holds the General Service and Victory Medals.

27, Warrior Road, Camberwell, S.E.5.   Z3933

ROFFEY, F. C., Driver, R.F.A.

He volunteered in November 1914 and in August of the following year was drafted to the Western Front, where he took part in the Battles of the Somme, Arras and in numerous other engagements in the Retreat and Advance of 1918. He was demobilised in March 1919, and holds the 1914-15 Star, and the General Service and Victory Medals.

24, Horsman Street, Camberwell, S.E.5.   Z3935

ROFFEY, H. A., Private, R.A.S.C.

Volunteering in September 1914 he was sent to France in the same month. He was engaged on important transport duties on many fronts, including those of Mons, the Marne, the Aisne, Ypres, Loos, Albert, Vimy Ridge, the Somme, Lens and Cambrai He also took part in the Retreat and Advance of 1918. He was demobilised in May 1919, and holds the Mons Star, and the General Service and Victory Medals.

92, Crail Row, Walworth, S.E.17.   Z3934

ROFFEY, S., Gunner, R.F.A.

He volunteered in June 1915 and in the same year was drafted to the Western Front, where he took part in many notable engagements, including those at Loos, Ypres, Vimy Ridge, Messines and the Somme, where he was wounded. He also took part in the Retreat and Advance of 1918. He was demobilised in February 1919, and holds the 1914-15 Star, and the General Service and Victory Medals.

10, Nursery Street, Wandsworth Road, S.W.8.   Z3936

ROGER, H. A., Corporal, 7th Middlesex Regiment (Labour Company).

He joined in March 1917 and served first in the 19th London Regiment and later in the M.G.C. He was afterwards transferred to the 7th Middlesex Regiment and in July 1918 was drafted to France, where he was engaged on important duties in various sectors. He returned home in December 1919, and was demobilised, holding the General Service and Victory Medals.

145, Gloucester Road, Peckham, S.E.15.   Z5985B

ROGERS, A., Bombardier, R.F.A.

He was mobilised in August 1914 and being shortly afterwards sent to France was in action at Neuve Chapelle, St. Eloi, Hill 60, Festubert and in many other important engagements. He fell fighting on the Somme on September 13th, 1916, and was entitled to the 1914-15 Star, and the General Service and Victory Medals.

"He died the noblest death a man may die,
Fighting for God, and right, and liberty."

79, Sussex Road, Brixton, S.W.9.   Z3058B

ROGERS, C., Private, 10th Queen's (Royal West Surrey Regiment).

He joined in April 1916 and in the following year was drafted to the Western Front, where he took part in the Battles of Arras, Ypres, Passchendaele, the Somme, Bapaume, St. Quentin and in numerous other engagements in the Retreat and Advance of 1918, and was gassed twice. After the Armistice he proceeded to Germany and on his return was demobilised in September 1919. He holds the General Service and Victory Medals.

79, Sussex Road, Brixton, S.W.9.   Z3058C

ROGERS, H. J., Rifleman, 6th London Regiment (Rifles).

He was mobilised in August 1914 and served with his unit on important duties until 1916, when he was sent to France. There he took part in the Battles of Vimy Ridge, the Somme, Bullecourt and Cambrai, and also served throughout the Retreat and Advance of 1918. He was demobilised in January 1919 after his return home, and holds the General Service and Victory Medals.

35, Stanbury Road, Peckham, S.E.15.   Z6500

ROGERS, J., Private, 2nd Hampshire Regiment.

He joined in November 1916 and in March of the following year was sent to France, where he was in action at Ypres and Cambrai, and was twice wounded. He was unfortunately killed in action at Ypres on May 6th, 1918, and was entitled to the General Service and Victory Medals.

"His life for his country, his soul to God."

18, Buck Street, Dorset Road, S.W.8.   Z3937

ROGERS, W. A., Corporal, R.A.S.C. and Labour Corps.

He volunteered in June 1915 and in the following month was drafted to France, where he was engaged on important transport duties at Ypres and in other sectors. He contracted fever and was invalided home, but after the Armistice he returned to France and proceeded with the Army of Occupation to Germany. He was demobilised in March 1920, and holds the 1914-15 Star, and the General Service and Victory Medals.

47, Crimsworth Road, Wandsworth Road, S.W.8.   Z3938

ROGERSON, D. G., L/Corporal, R.A.S.C. and 2nd Wiltshire Regiment.

He volunteered in May 1915 and was transferred to the 2nd Wiltshire Regiment in 1916 and proceeded to France later in the same year. He took an active part in many engagements, including those on the Somme and at Arras, Bullecourt and Albert, and in the Retreat and Advance of 1918 at Amiens and Cambrai. He returned to England in 1919 and was demobilised in February of that year, holding the General Service and Victory Medals.

36, Manaton Road, Peckham, S.E.15.   Z6317

ROGERSON, J. J., Rifleman, Rifle Brigade.

He joined in 1916 and was drafted to France in March 1917. He fought in various engagements until he was wounded at St. Eloi and sent to hospital in England. On his recovery he was again sent to France in August 1917 and took an active part in operations at Cambrai in November of that year and also in the Retreat of 1918, when he was taken prisoner and sent to Germany. Here he remained in captivity until shortly after the Armistice, when he was repatriated and finally demobilised in January 1919, holding the General Service and Victory Medals.

52, Harris Street, Camberwell, S.E.5.   Z4529

ROLFE, C., L/Corporal, East Surrey Regiment.

He was serving in Ireland on the outbreak of war and was immediately drafted to France and took part in the Retreat from Mons. He also fought at Ypres, the Somme and Arras, where he was wounded and invalided to the Base. On his recovery he returned to his unit and served at Vimy Ridge, where he was again wounded and sent to hospital in England. Later he returned to France and was in action on the Somme and wounded for the third time. He holds the Mons Star, and the General Service and Victory Medals, and was demobilised in December 1919.

2, Milford Street, Wandsworth Road, S.W.8.   Z3939

ROLFE, D. J., Private, Queen's Own (Royal West Kent Regiment).

He volunteered in June 1915 and proceeded to France in May 1916 and fought at Ploegsteert Wood, Vimy Ridge, the Somme, Arras and Ypres. After much valuable service he was invalided home owing to ill-health towards the end of 1917 and finally discharged in that year, holding the General Service and Victory Medals.

18, Selden Road, Peckham, S.E.15.   Z6652

ROLL, S. J., Pioneer, R.E.

He joined in 1918 and after a short training proceeded to France. Here he was engaged on important duties in the transport of food supplies. After the Armistice he returned to England and was demobilised in March 1919, holding the General Service and Victory Medals.

17, Priory Place, Wandsworth Road, S.W.8.   Z3940

ROLLS, H., Private, R.A.F.

He volunteered in 1915 and being unfortunately prevented from service overseas by ill-health rendered valuable services on Home Defence at many stations until he was demobilised in January 1919.

74, Harleyford Road, Kennington, S.E.11.   Z24478

ROLPH, E., Private, R.A.S.C.

He volunteered in 1915 and was drafted to the Dardanelles, where he took part in the Gallipoli Campaign. On the Evacuation of the Peninsula he was drafted to France and served in the La Bassée and other sectors until demobilised in February 1919. He rejoined the Colours, however, in June of the same year and was engaged on interment duties until finally discharged in September 1920, holding the 1914-15 Star, and the General Service and Victory Medals.

5, Chalmers Street, Wandsworth Road, S.W.8.   Z3941

ROMANO, F., Private, Somerset Light Infantry.

He joined in September 1916 and was drafted to France in 1917. Shortly afterwards he was sent to Italy, where he was severely gassed. After a long period in hospital he was invalided home and was discharged as medically unfit in June 1919, holding the General Service and Victory Medals.

23, Anley Road, West Kensington, W.14.   011877

RONALD, J. D., C.S.M., Border Regiment.
Serving at the outbreak of hostilities he was drafted to Gallipoli, where he took part in the Campaign against the Turks and was wounded at Cape Helles. He was sent to hospital at Cairo and afterwards to England. Later he proceeded to France and fought on the Somme and at Beaumont-Hamel and Bullecourt, being again wounded at Passchendaele and invalided home. He was afterwards engaged on important duties in England until he was demobilised in March 1920, holding the 1914-15 Star, and the General Service and Victory Medals.
14, Clayton Road, Peckham, S.E.15. Z6218

ROOD, A. E., Corporal, 2nd East Surrey Regiment.
He was in India on the outbreak of war and as a reservist was called to the Colours and posted to the East Surrey Regiment. Proceeding to France in February 1915 he took an active part in the fighting at St. Eloi, Ypres and Loos. Later he was sent to Salonika and did good service in the operations on the Struma and Vardar fronts up to the time of the Armistice. He was demobilised in May 1919, holding the 1914-15 Star, and the General Service and Victory Medals.
86, Neate Street, Camberwell, S.E.5. Z5057C

ROONEY, J., Rifleman, 8th Rifle Brigade.
He volunteered in April 1915 and was drafted to France in June of that year and took part in the fighting at Loos, where he was wounded and gassed. He was sent to hospital at Netley, where he remained for more than eight months and was then discharged as medically unfit for service in July 1916. Later he died on February 3rd, 1917, and was entitled to the 1914-15 Star, and the General Service and Victory Medals.
"Whilst we remember the Sacrifice is not in vain."
2, Sussex Grove, Brixton, S.W.9. Z4454C

ROOTS, D. J., Gunner, R.F.A.
He volunteered in 1915 and was drafted to France, where he rendered valuable service during the fighting at Ypres, the Somme and Arras. Later, owing to ill-health, he was invalided home and discharged as medically unfit in 1917, holding the 1914-15 Star, and the General Service and Victory Medals.
24, Pilkington Road, Peckham, S.E.15. Z6070

ROSE, A. E., Rifleman, 6th London Regiment (Rifles).
He volunteered in September 1914 and on the completion of his training was drafted to France in 1915. After taking part in many important engagements he was badly wounded in October and unfortunately died at Boulogne Hospital on November 20th, 1915. He was buried in Boulogne Cemetery, and was entitled to the 1914-15 Star, and the General Service and Victory Medals.
"The path of duty was the way to glory."
27, Denmark Road, Camberwell, S.E.5. Z5991B

ROSE, A. J. H., Private, 2nd Royal Fusiliers.
Volunteering in June 1915 he completed his course of training and in the following December was drafted to France. While serving there he took an active part in numerous engagements of importance, including those at Arras, Vimy Ridge, Bullecourt, the Somme and the Retreat and Advance of the Allies in 1918, and was wounded. After his return to England he was demobilised in April 1920, and holds the 1914-15 Star, and the General Service and Victory Medals.
21, Heygate Street, Walworth, S.E.17. Z3945

ROSE, E., Stoker Petty Officer, Royal Navy.
He joined the Navy in 1901 and throughout the course of hostilities rendered excellent service on Submarine K8 in the Mediterranean and the North Seas. He took part in the Battle of the Dogger Bank and in many other operations of importance. He was discharged in May 1920, and holds the 1914-15 Star, the General Service and Victory Medals, and the Naval Long Service and Good Conduct Medal.
23E, Lewis Trust Buildings, Camberwell, S.E.5. Z6436

ROSE, E. F., Private, Buffs and Queen's Own (Royal West Kent Regiment).
He joined in 1916 and after his training was retained on important duties with his unit until June 1918, when he was drafted to France. While overseas he took an active part in the engagements at Ypres and Merville, and in other important operations in the Retreat and Advance of 1918. After his return home he was demobilised at the end of 1918, and holds the General Service and Victory Medals.
92, Stonehouse Street, Clapham, S.W.4. Z3942

ROSE, J., Private, 1st East Surrey Regiment.
He volunteered in December 1914 and having completed his training proceeded to France in March 1915. While overseas he fought in the Battle of Hill 60, and was very severely wounded. After being invalided home he was discharged later in the year as medically unfit for further duty, and holds the 1914-15 Star, and the General Service and Victory Medals.
133, Speke Road, Battersea, S.W.11. Z3944

ROSE, S. T., Gunner, R.F.A.
He volunteered in April 1915 and after a period of training was drafted to the Western Front. While in this theatre of war he took part in numerous battles, including those at Vimy Ridge, the Somme, Arras, Ypres, Passchendaele, Cambrai and the Retreat and Advance of 1918. He holds the General Service and Victory Medals, and in April 1919 was demobilised after his return to England.
37, Charlotte Street, Old Kent Road, S.E.1. Z27269

ROSMELER, W., Private, 23rd London Regt.
He was mobilised at the outbreak of hostilities and after completing his course of training was drafted to France at the end of 1915. While in that theatre of war he took an active part in numerous engagements of importance, including those at the Somme and Ypres, and was severely wounded. He was invalided home in consequence and afterwards was discharged in July 1918 as medically unfit for further service. He holds the 1914-15 Star, and the General Service and Victory Medals.
62, Corunna Road, New Road, S.W.8. Z3946

ROSS, B. G., Corporal, 1st Border Regiment.
He was serving when war broke out and in April 1915 was drafted to the Dardanelles, where he took part in the Landing at Gallipoli and the engagements at Suvla Bay and Chocolate Hill. While there he was twice wounded, but after his recovery proceeded to France and fought at the Somme and Ypres. After a period of valuable service in England he crossed again to France in March 1918, and in the Retreat and Advance of that year did excellent work in the neighbourhood of Lille. He was invalided out of the Service in May 1919, and holds the 1914-15 Star, and the General Service and Victory Medals.
59, Smyrk's Road, Walworth, S.E.17. Z3947

ROSS, D. G., Private, 1st Duke of Cornwall's Light Infantry.
Volunteering in March 1915 he proceeded to France four months later and took an active part in many severe engagements, particularly in the Somme Offensive of 1916. He gave his life for King and Country on September 27th, 1916, on the Somme and was buried in the Citadel Military Cemetery near Albert. He was entitled to the 1914-15 Star, and the General Service and Victory Medals.
"Great deeds cannot die :
They with the sun and moon renew their light for ever."
41, Darren Road, Battersea, S.W.11. Z3948

ROSS, F. J., Driver, R.F.A.
He volunteered in February 1915 and after the completion of his course of training was engaged at Colchester, Aldershot and other stations on important duties with his Battery. He was unable on medical grounds to secure his transfer to a fighting front while hostilities continued, but rendered valuable guard and coastal defence services until his demobilisation in June 1919.
94, Aylesbury Road, Walworth, S.E.17. Z3949

ROSS, G. R., Private, 1st Hampshire Regiment and R.A.S.C. (H.T.)
He volunteered in February 1915 and after completing his training was drafted to the Western Front, where he took an active part in the Battles of Ypres, the Somme, Arras, Albert, Lens, Amiens and Bapaume. In consequence of being severely gassed he was invalided home, but after being transferred to the R.A.S.C. on his recovery was sent again to France in time for the last stages of the Advance of 1918. He was demobilised in June 1919, and holds the 1914-15 Star, and the General Service and Victory Medals.
36, Lugard Road, Peckham, S.E.15. Z6686

ROSS, H., Private, 3rd Border Regiment.
Joining in 1917 he passed through his course of training and later in that year crossed to the Western Front. He took an active part in the Battle of Cambrai, and in the important engagements at the Somme and Ypres in the Offensives of 1918, and was wounded near Ypres. After his return to England he was demobilised in September 1919, and holds the General Service and Victory Medals.
61, Dashwood Road, Wandsworth Road, S.W.8. Z3950

ROSWELL, W. A., Gunner, R.F.A.
He volunteered in 1914 and after the completion of his training was drafted to the Western Front, where he took part in the Battles of Neuve Chapelle, Hill 60, Ypres and Loos. In 1916 he was transferred to Salonika and did excellent service there on the Doiran and Vardar fronts until the close of the war. After his return to England he was demobilised in 1919, and holds the 1914-15 Star, and the General Service and Victory Medals.
60, Meadow Road, Fentiman Road, S.W.8. Z3951

ROULLIER, T. E., Private, 2nd East Surrey Regt.
He volunteered in October 1914 and was soon drafted to the Western Front. While overseas he took an active part in numerous engagements of importance, including those at Ypres and the Somme, and was badly gassed in 1917. After considerable hospital treatment at Cosham and Taplow he was discharged in January 1919, and holds the 1914-15 Star, and the General Service and Victory Medals.
18, Nutt Street, Peckham, S.E.15. Z6319

ROULLIER, A. W., Sergt., 2nd Buffs.
He enlisted in 1898 and served through the South African War and in Singapore and Hong Kong. He was in India when the recent war broke out and was drafted to France in January 1915 where he took part in numerous engagements of importance, including those at Loos, the Somme, Ypres, Arras, and the Retreat and Advance of 1918. After his return home he was demobilised in November 1919, and holds the Queen's and King's South African Medals, the 1914-15 Star, and the General Service and Victory Medals.
11, Haymerle Road, Peckham, S.E.15.   Z6438

ROUS, J. W., Aircraftsman, R.A.F. (late R.N.A.S.)
He joined in September 1916 and after the completion of his training was drafted to the Western Front in November 1917. After valuable service there for a short time he was transferred to the Eastern Mediterranean, where he carried out important duties with the Ægean Sea Squadron at Salonika, the Dardanelles, Mudros, Mytilene and other stations. After his return home he was demobilised in November 1919, and holds the General Service and Victory Medals.
16, Beech Street, South Lambeth, S.W.8.   Z3952

ROUSE, W., Sergt., 5th Bedfordshire Regiment.
He volunteered in November 1915 and after his training was completed was sent to India in the following year. He was afterwards drafted to Mesopotamia and was in action at Kut and in various other engagements. He also served in Persia and subsequently returned to India, and eventually proceeded home, and was demobilised in May 1920. He holds the General Service and Victory Medals.
87A, Ingelow Road, Battersea Park, S.W.8.   Z3953

ROWE, A., Driver, R.F.A.
He volunteered in May 1915 and in the following October sailed for France, where he saw much service. He did good work as a driver on the Somme, and at Messines, Ypres and Cambrai, and in many of the engagements which followed in the Retreat and Advance of 1918. He returned home in August of the following year and was demobilised in January 1920. He holds the 1914-15 Star, and the General Service and Victory Medals.
77, Latchmere Road, Battersea, S.W.11.   Z3954

ROWE, A. E., Private, 16th Middlesex Regiment.
He joined in August 1918 on attaining military age and on the completion of his training was drafted to Germany with the Army of Occupation, with which he served until November 1919, when he returned home and was demobilised.
93, Geneva Road, Coldharbour Lane, S.W.9.   Z4012C

ROWE, B., Private, 22nd London Regt. (Queen's).
He volunteered in August 1915 and in the following December was drafted to France. During his service overseas he fought in many engagements, including those at Vimy Ridge and on the Somme. In 1917 he was severely wounded and invalided home to hospital, but rejoined his unit in France in March of the following year. Whilst holding the line he was again seriously wounded in the following June and invalided to England and subsequently discharged in September 1918. He holds the 1914-15 Star, and the General Service and Victory Medals.
209, Abbey Street, Bermondsey, S.E.1.   Z27445

ROWE, C., Sergt., R.E.
A serving soldier since 1906 he was sent to Malta at the outbreak of hostilities, but was subsequently drafted to France in December 1914. He was engaged on important duties in connection with the operations and was frequently in the forward areas, notably at Neuve Chapelle, Ypres, Loos, the Somme and Armentières. He returned home as time expired just before the Armistice, and holds the 1914-15 Star, and the General Service and Victory Medals.
19, Emu Road, Battersea Park, S.W.8.   Z3956B

ROWE, F. E. A., Rifleman, 11th Rifle Brigade.
He joined in June 1916 and was drafted to France in March of the following year. During his service on the Western Front he took part in numerous engagements, including those at Metz Wood, Havrincourt, Ypres and Cambrai, and many others during the Advance of 1918. He returned to England and was demobilised in February 1919, and holds the General Service and Victory Medals.
30, Ledbury Street, Peckham, S.E.15.   Z6570

ROWE, G. J., A.B., Royal Navy, H.M.S. "Indefatigable."
He was serving at the outbreak of hostilities and was posted to H.M.S. "Indefatigable" and served for a time in the Mediterranean, where his ship took part in the chase of the "Goeben" and "Breslau." Later he was transferred to the North Sea and was in action in the Battle of Jutland. He perished with all on board the H.M.S. "Indefatigable" when she was blown up in the Jutland Battle in May 1916, and was entitled to the 1914-15 Star, and the General Service and Victory Medals.
"He passed out of the sight of men by the path of duty and self-sacrifice."
93, Geneva Road, Brixton, S.W.9.   Z4012A

ROWE, H., Private, Royal Marine Light Infantry.
He volunteered in October 1914 and in April of the following year took part in the Landing at Gallipoli. Whilst in this theatre of war he served in all the engagements of that Campaign until the Evacuation of the Peninsula, and was wounded. In 1916 he was drafted to the Western Front and taken prisoner on the Somme in March 1918 and held in captivity in Germany until the cessation of hostilities. He was demobilised in July of the following year, and holds the 1914-15 Star, and the General Service and Victory Medals.
71, Mayall Road, Herne Hill, S.E.24.   Z3955

ROWE, H. A., Lieutenant, R.A.F.
He volunteered for the Navy in August 1914 and later was transferred to the Royal Naval Air Service and acted as Observer on Aerial Escort and Patrols from England to Dunkirk. He obtained his Commission in May 1918 and afterwards served on important coastal patrol duties in Scotland. He was demobilised in March 1919, and holds the 1914 Star, and the General Service and Victory Medals.
93, Geneva Road, Brixton, S.W.9.   Z4012B

ROWELL, G. J., Sapper, R.E. (R.O.D.)
He joined in August 1916 and on the completion of his training was drafted to the Western Front, where he rendered valuable service in connection with the transport of supplies at Calais, Dieppe, Abbeville, Boulogne and Le Havre, and on the fighting fronts at the Somme, Albert, Ypres, Arras, Passchendaele, Amiens, Bapaume and Poperinghe. He returned home after the close of hostilities and was demobilised in April 1919, holding the General Service and Victory Medals.
5, Burchell Road, Peckham, S.E.15.   Z6501

ROWELL, W., L/Corporal, Royal Warwickshire Regiment.
He volunteered in January 1915 and in the same year was drafted to Egypt. During his service in the East he was stationed at Kantara and Cairo, and in the Suez Canal zone. Later he served in Palestine with General Allenby's Forces and fought at the capture of Jericho and in many subsequent engagements until the conclusion of the campaign, and during his service was wounded and gassed. He returned home and was demobilised in July 1919, and holds the General Service and Victory Medals.
15, Wadding Street, Walworth, S.E.17.   Z3803

ROWLAND, C. L., Private, 2nd Middlesex Regiment.
He joined in August 1918 and after his training was drafted to Egypt in the following June and was engaged on important duties at various stations. In 1920 he was still serving.
11, Haymerle Road, Peckham, S.E.15.   Z6437B

ROWLAND, D. W., Sergt., R.E.
He volunteered at the outbreak of hostilities and in March 1915 was drafted to France as a Sapper in the Royal Engineers. During his service overseas he was engaged on important duties in connection with the operations and was frequently in the forward areas, notably at Ypres and on the Somme. Early in 1918 he returned to England and was promoted to the rank of Sergeant and retained as Drill Instructor to recruits until February 1919, when he was demobilised. He holds the 1914-15 Star, and the General Service and Victory Medals.
40, Camellia Street, South Lambeth, S.W.8.   Z3957A

ROWLAND, H. J., Sapper, R.E.
He volunteered in August 1914 and in the following March was drafted to France, and whilst in this theatre of war was engaged on important duties laying lines and cables until 1917, and was frequently in the front lines. He was twice wounded during this period and was invalided to hospital for some time. He then proceeded to Egypt, where he served until his return home for demobilisation in March 1919. He holds the 1914-15 Star, and the General Service and Victory Medals.
40, Camellia Street, South Lambeth, S.W.8.   Z3957B

ROWLAND, H. W., Private, 3rd Norfolk Regiment.
He joined in April 1916 and after his training served on important duties with his unit on the East Coast. He rendered valuable services but owing to medical reasons was unable to secure a transfer overseas and was invalided out of the service in May 1918.
11, Haymerle Road, Peckham, S.E.15.   Z6437A

ROWLANDS, S. C., Private, R.A.M.C.
He had previously enlisted in the Territorials in 1913 and after the declaration of hostilities was drafted to France in March 1915. During his service overseas he was engaged on important duties as a stretcher-bearer, and was present at the Battles of the Somme, Beaumont-Hamel, Arras and Ypres. He did excellent work throughout in attending to the sick and wounded, and was demobilised in July 1919. He holds the 1914-15 Star, and the General Service and Victory Medals.
94, Eversleigh Road, Battersea, S.W.11.   Z3958

ROWLANDS, W., Stoker, Royal Navy, H.M.S. " Africa."

He volunteered in March 1915 and after his training was posted to H.M.S. " Africa " and sent to the Dardanelles in the following June. After the Evacuation of Gallipoli his ship served for three months in conjunction with the Italian Fleet, and in November 1916 was engaged in conveying troops from Sierra Leone to Cape Town. In November 1918 the " Africa " returned home and he was stationed at Chatham Barracks until his demobilisation in May of the following year. He holds the 1914-15 Star, and the General Service and Victory Medals.

49, Haymerle Road, Peckham, S.E.15.   Z6442

ROWLEY, R., Corporal, East Yorkshire Regiment.

He volunteered in September 1914 and in December of the same year was drafted to France, where he saw much service. He fought at Neuve Chapelle, St. Eloi, Ypres and Loos, and was wounded and buried by the explosion of a shell and invalided to hospital in England. He was demobilised in February 1919, and holds the 1914 Star, and the General Service and Victory Medals.

38, Gideon Road, Battersea, S.W.11.   Z3959

ROWLINSON, E., Gunner, R.F.A.

He joined in March 1916 and in the same year proceeded to France and whilst overseas did excellent work as a gunner in many important battles. On May 1st, 1918 he was killed by an explosion, and was entitled to the General Service and Victory Medals.

"Honour to the immortal dead who gave their youth
that the world might grow old in peace."

6, New Road, Battersea, S.W.8.   Z3960A

ROWLINSON, F., Private, 1st South Wales Borderers.

He was mobilised at the outbreak of hostilities and was almost immediately drafted to France, where he was severely wounded in the Retreat from Mons. After enduring great suffering he died in hospital in England, and was entitled to the Mons Star, and the General Service and Victory Medals.

"A costly sacrifice upon the altar of freedom."

6, New Road, Battersea Park Road, S.W.8.   Z3960B

ROWLINSON, W., Sapper, R.E.

He volunteered in September 1915 and in the following November was drafted overseas. During his service in France he was engaged on important duties in connection with the operations and was frequently in the forward areas, notably on the Somme, where he was wounded, and at Albert, Ypres, Arras, Messines, Lens and Cambrai. He was demobilised in June 1919, and holds the 1914-15 Star, and the General Service and Victory Medals.

35, Heygate Street, Walworth, S.E.17.   Z3961

ROXBY, R., Sapper, R.E.

He volunteered in August 1915 and in the same year was drafted to France, where he was engaged on mine-laying on the Somme. In the following year he was sent to Egypt and served with General Allenby's Forces in Palestine and was present at the engagements at Romani and Gaza, and in many others until the conclusion of the campaign. He was retained in Italy for a short time on his way to England, and was afterwards demobilised in July 1919. He holds the 1914-15 Star, and the General Service and Victory Medals.

19, Emu Road, Battersea Park, S.W.8.   Z3956A

ROYAL, W. H., Private, Royal Fusiliers.

He volunteered in March 1915 at the age of seventeen, and in the following October was drafted to France. Whilst in this theatre of war he fought at Loos, Albert, Vermelles, Vimy Ridge and the Somme, and was wounded and invalided home to hospital. After six weeks he rejoined his unit in France, and was in action at Beaumont-Hamel, and subsequently fell fighting on the Ancre front on February 17th, 1917. He was entitled to the 1914-15 Star, and the General Service and Victory Medals.

"His life for his Country, his soul to God."

17, Wansey Street, Walworth, S.E.17.   Z3962

ROYALS, W. J., Private, Royal Defence Corps.

He volunteered in August 1914 and was stationed on important duties at Alexandra Palace, where he was mainly engaged in guarding German prisoners. He rendered valuable services, but owing to heart trouble was discharged as medically unfit for further duty in November 1916.

1, Yeovil Street, Wandsworth Road, S.W.8.   Z3963

RUBIDGE, D., Bombardier, R.G.A. (384th Siege Battery).

He joined in February 1916 and proceeded to Mesopotamia in the following year, and took an active part in various engagements, including the Capture of Baghdad. After much valuable service he contracted double pneumonia and died at Basra on October 10th, 1918. He was entitled to the General Service and Victory Medals.

"A costly sacrifice upon the altar of freedom."

3, Cunard Street, Camberwell, S.E.5.   Z5143

RUBY, W. S., C.S.M., Machine Gun Corps.

He was serving at the outbreak of hostilities and was engaged on important duties in England until early in 1916, when he proceeded to France. Here he fought in various engagements, including that of Zonnebeke and the fighting on the Somme and at Arras and Ypres. After the Armistice he returned to England and was demobilised in March 1920, holding the General Service and Victory Medals.

205, East Street, Walworth, S.E.17.   Z3964

RUCK, A. A., Sergt. (Observer), R.A.F.

He joined in December 1917 and after a period of training was engaged on important aerial patrol duties in the North Sea Patrol. He was demobilised in October 1920, and holds the General Service and Victory Medals.

52, Crescent Road, Clapham, S.W.4.   Z3965C

RUCK, G. H., Sergt., R.F.A.

He volunteered in September 1914 and after a period of training was drafted to France in the following July. He was engaged in numerous operations at Ypres, St. Eloi and the Somme, and rendered valuable services also in the Retreat, during which he was unhappily killed in action on June 1st, 1918, in the Champagne district. He was entitled to the 1914-15 Star, and the General Service and Victory Medals.

"He joined the great white company of valiant souls."

52, Crescent Road, Clapham, S.W.4.   Z3965A

RUCK, H. F., Gunner, R.F.A.

He volunteered in January 1915 and proceeded to France in the same year and took part in the fighting at Ypres. In 1916 he was sent to Salonika and was in action in various engagements on that front. In the following year he proceeded to Egypt and served in the campaign under General Allenby until the Armistice, after which he returned to England and was demobilised in March 1919, holding the 1914-15 Star, and the General Service and Victory Medals.

52, Crescent Road, Clapham, S.W.   Z3965B

RUDDERHAM, E. R., Officers' Steward, Royal Navy.

He volunteered in August 1914 and was posted for duty with H.M.S. " Hogue " in the North Sea. He unhappily lost his life in that vessel when she was sunk whilst going to the assistance of H.M.S. " Cressy " and " Aboukir," which had been torpedoed by an enemy submarine. He was entitled to the 1914-15 Star, and the General Service and Victory Medals.

"He passed out of the sight of men by the path of duty and
self-sacrifice."

13, Lillieshall Road, Clapham, S.W.4.   Z3966

RUDHALL, H. B. (D.C.M.), Private, 24th London Regiment (The Queen's).

He volunteered in August 1914 and proceeded to France. Here he was actively engaged in various actions, including the Battles of the Somme and Ypres, and was awarded the Distinguished Conduct Medal for gallantry whilst acting as Brigade runner. Unfortunately he was killed in action at Agincourt on December 10th, 1917, and in addition to holding the D.C.M. was entitled to the 1914 Star, and the General Service and Victory Medals.

"Honour to the immortal dead who gave their youth that the
world might grow old in peace."

9, Warrior Road, Camberwell, S.E.5.   Z3967

RUFF, A. J., Private, 23rd London Regiment.

He volunteered in April 1915 and was drafted to France in June of the following year. He was in action at Arras but afterwards owing to ill-health was invalided to hospital and returned to England in March 1918. On his recovery he served at various stations until demobilised in March 1919, holding the General Service and Victory Medals.

44, Honeywell Road, Battersea, S.W.11.   Z3968

RUFFELLS, E. W., 2nd Officer, Mercantile Marine.

He served from 1914 until 1919 in the Atlantic, transporting food, stores and munitions from America to England. After the declaration of war between the United States and Germany he was engaged also in conveying American troops to Europe. He was demobilised in 1919, and holds the Mercantile Marine War Medal, and the General Service Medal.

202, Mayall Road, Herne Hill, S.E.24.   Z3969C

RUFFELLS, H. C., Private, 1st Yorkshire Regiment.

He was serving in India on the outbreak of hostilities and was stationed on the Afghanistan Frontier on outpost duty. During his service he contracted malaria and was in hospital for a time. In 1919 he returned to England and was demobilised, holding the General Service and Victory Medals.

202, Mayall Road, Herne Hill, S.E.24.   Z3969B

RULE, A. L., Rifleman, 7th Rifle Brigade.

He joined in May 1917 and was sent to France in the following August and fought at the Battle of Lens and at Cambrai, where he was wounded. He rendered valuable services in France until 1919, when he returned to England and was demobilised, holding the General Service and Victory Medals.

51, Tyneham Road, Lavender Hill, S.W.11.   Z3970

RULER, G. J., L/Corporal, Rifle Brigade.

He joined in November 1916 and was sent to France in the following month. He saw much fighting at Loos, Vimy Ridge, Albert, the Somme, Arras, Messines, Lens and Cambrai, and also during the Retreat and Advance of 1918, and after valuable service was demobilised in June 1919, holding the General Service and Victory Medals.

2, Townsend Street, Walworth, S.E.17.   Z3971

RUMBOL, W., Gunner, R.G.A.

He joined in March 1918 and in the following month was sent to France, where he took part in the fighting at St. Quentin, Bourlon Wood, Cambrai and other engagements up to the entry into Mons. Afterwards he proceeded to Germany with the Army of Occupation. He was demobilised in November 1919, and holds the General Service and Victory Medals.

174, Grosvenor Terrace, Camberwell, S.E.5.   Z3972

RUSBY, G., Driver, R.F.A.

He was mobilised in August 1914 and immediately proceeded to the Western Front, where he took part in the Battles of Mons, La Bassée, Ypres, Neuve Chapelle, Festubert, Loos, Albert, Vermelles, Vimy Ridge, the Somme, Arras and Lens. In 1917 he was transferred to Italy and was in action on the Piave. He was demobilised in February 1919, and holds the Mons Star, and the General Service and Victory Medals.

131, Westmoreland Road, Walworth, S.E.17.   Z27469

RUSHFORTH, E. W. A., A/Drummer, Scots Guards.

He joined in December 1916 and after his training was engaged on important duties with his unit. He rendered valuable services but was not successful in obtaining his transfer overseas before the cessation of hostilities. He was demobilised in February 1919.

19, Ramsey Road, Stockwell, S.W.9.   Z3973

RUSHTON, A., Private, 2nd Somerset Light Infantry.

Volunteering in August 1914 in the 5th Wiltshire Regiment he proceeded overseas in the following March and fought in the first Landing and in other operations in Gallipoli. On the Evacuation of the Peninsula he was sent to Egypt and later to Mesopotamia, where he took part in several engagements. Proceeding to India he saw much service in actions against the rebel tribes on the North-West Frontier, and on the conclusion of hostilities returned home. Demobilised in January 1920, he holds the 1914-15 Star, the General Service and Victory Medals, and the India General Service Medal (with Clasp, Afghanistan, North-West Frontier, 1919).

45, Melon Road, Peckham, S.E.15.   Z6322

RUSHTON, G. F., Corporal, 34th London Regiment.

He volunteered in August 1914 and after his training was sent to Malta. He was later transferred to the Western Front, where he took part in the severe fighting at Hill 60, Ypres and Loos. He was wounded on the Somme and invalided home, but on his recovery returned to France and was again in action and was gassed. He was demobilised in February 1919, and held the 1914-15 Star, and the General Service and Victory Medals. He was taken ill from the effects of his war service and unfortunately died in King's College Hospital in February 1919.

"Thinking that remembrance, though unspoken, may reach him where he sleeps."

48, Castlemaine Road, Peckham, S.E.15.   Z5831

RUSKIN, B. F., Sergt., R.F.A.

He volunteered in June 1915 and in the same year was drafted to the Western Front, where he took part in numerous severe engagements, including those at Albert, Vimy Ridge, the Somme, Arras and Cambrai. He also served through the Retreat and Advance of 1918 and after the Armistice proceeded to Germany. He was demobilised in February 1919, and holds the 1914-15 Star, and the General Service and Victory Medals.

42, St. Lawrence Road, Brixton Road, S.W.9.   Z4530

RUSSELL, A., Driver, R.F.A.

He volunteered in April 1915 and later in the same year was sent to France, where he took part in numerous engagements of importance, including those at Ypres, Vimy Ridge, the Somme, Albert, Arras, Passchendaele, Lens and Cambrai. He also served in the Retreat and Advance of 1918. He was demobilised in June 1919, and holds the 1914-15 Star, and the General Service and Victory Medals.

24, Northampton Place, Walworth, S.E.17.   Z3976

RUSSELL, A. G., L/Cpl., 17th London Regt. (Rifles).

He joined in March 1917 and in the same year proceeded to France. He was in action at Cambrai, the Somme and in other important engagements in the Retreat and Advance of 1918 and afterwards proceeded with the Army of Occupation to Germany. He was wounded on one occasion during his service overseas. He was demobilised in November 1919, and holds the General Service and Victory Medals.

20, Parfitt Road, Rotherhithe, S.E.16.   Z6653

RUSSELL, A. J., Sapper, R.E.

He joined in April 1917 and after being sent to France in the same year rendered valuable service in numerous engagements, including that at Ypres. In 1918 he was invalided home and after his recovery was engaged on important duties until demobilised in February 1919. He holds the General Service and Victory Medals.

217, Hollydale Road, Peckham, S.E.15.   Z6571

RUSSELL, A. W., Private, 13th Middlesex Regt.

He joined in March 1917 and proceeded to France in the following year. He took an active part as a machine gunner in the fighting on the Somme and Cambrai fronts, and in the Retreat and Advance of 1918, and was twice wounded and invalided home. He was demobilised in September 1919, and holds the General Service and Victory Medals.

54, Manaton Road, Peckham, S.E.15.   Z6439

RUSSELL, C. G., L/Corporal, 23rd London Regt.

He was mobilised in August 1914 and in the following March was sent to France. He was in action at Hill 60, Ypres, Festubert, Loos, and was wounded on the Somme in 1916 and sent to hospital. On his recovery he returned to the front lines and was again wounded during the fighting at Arras. He later took part in the Retreat and Advance of 1918, and was wounded for the third time. He was unfortunately killed in action at Amiens on August 10th, 1918. He was entitled to the 1914-15 Star, and the General Service and Victory Medals.

"He passed out of the sight of men by the path of duty and self-sacrifice."

127, Tyneham Road, Battersea, S.W.11.   Z3977

RUSSELL, E. W., Pte., 24th London Regt. (Queen's).

He volunteered in August 1914 and in the following year was drafted to France, where he took part in numerous engagements, including those at Givenchy and the Somme. He also served in the Retreat and Advance of 1918 with the 47th London Division. He returned home and was demobilised in February 1919, holding the 1914-15 Star, and the General Service and Victory Medals.

30, Treherne Road, Brixton Road, S.W.9.   Z4536

RUSSELL, G. S. W., A.B., Royal Navy.

He volunteered in May 1915 and from that date until the close of hostilities was engaged in H.M.S. "Pembroke" and "Violent" chiefly on patrol and escort duties in the North Sea and off the Belgian Coast. He took part in the action in the Kattegat in 1917 and also did valuable service in Russian waters. He was demobilised in May 1919, and holds the 1914-15 Star, and the General Service and Victory Medals.

72, Barlow Street, Walworth, S.E.17.   Z3975

RUSSELL, H. J., A.B., Royal Fleet Reserve.

He was mobilised in August 1914 and was posted to H.M.S. "Aboukir." He took part in the Battle of Heligoland Bight and was unfortunately drowned in H.M.S. "Aboukir" when that vessel was sunk on September 22nd, 1914. He was entitled to the 1914-15 Star, and the General Service and Victory Medals.

"Steals on the ear the distant triumph song."

9, Park Grove, Battersea, S.W.11.   Z3974

RUSSELL, P. C. W., Ship's Cook, Royal Navy, H.M.S. " Southampton."

He volunteered in 1914 and served with the Grand Fleet in the North Sea. He was later transferred to H.M.S. "Vincent" and took part in the Battle of Jutland and later serving on H.M.S. "Mermaid" when that vessel was disabled in the Channel while engaged on important escort duties. He was demobilised in 1919, and holds the 1914-15 Star, and the General Service and Victory Medals.

42, Yeldham Road, Hammersmith, W.6.   12828A

RUSSELL, S., Driver, R.F.A.

He joined in January 1917 and after being drafted to the Western Front in the same year took part in the severe fighting at Vimy Ridge, Gommecourt, Croiselles and in numerous other engagements in the Retreat and Advance of 1918. He afterwards proceeded with the Army of Occupation to Germany. He was demobilised in February 1919, and holds the General Service and Victory Medals.

53, Calmington Road, Camberwell, S.E.5.   Z5490

RUSSELL, W., Private, 1st East Surrey Regiment.

He was serving in Ireland at the outbreak of war, having enlisted in 1912, and was immediately sent to France. He was in action at Mons, Le Cateau, the Marne, La Bassée, Ypres and Hill 60 where he was wounded. He was then invalided home and later was transferred to the 4th Battalion with which he was engaged on important duties until discharged in July 1916 in consequence of his service. He holds the Mons Star, and the General Service and Victory Medals.

105, Bird in Bush Road, Peckham, S.E.15.   Z6617

RUST, J. J., Sergt., R.E.
Volunteering in July 1915 he was drafted overseas in the following
month and did good work on the Western Front in many parts
of the line. He was present at several engagements, including
those at Armentières, Ypres, Cambrai and the Somme. Owing
to ill-health he was evacuated to England early in 1918 and after
receiving medical treatment was invalided out of the Service
in May of that year. He holds the 1914–15 Star, and the General
Service and Victory Medals.
26, Cambria Road, Camberwell, S.E.5.   Z6435B

RUST, R. T., Private, 2nd Leicestershire Regiment.
A serving soldier he was mobilised when war broke out and,
embarking for France in October 1914, took part in heavy fighting
in the Battles of Neuve Chapelle and Festubert. He gave his
life for King and Country at Loos on September 25th, 1915, and
was entitled to the 1914 Star, and the General Service and Victory
Medals.
                "Great deeds cannot die."
26, Cambria Road, Camberwell, S.E.5.   Z6435A

RUTH, J. A., Special War Worker.
During the war he was engaged on work of National importance
and was employed by Messrs. Bliss & Co., Engineers, Blackfriars,
London, from August 1914 to March 1919. He served as a
turner making parts of engines for aeroplanes and motors, and
carried out his duties to the complete satisfaction of his employers.
180, East Street, Walworth, S.E.17.   Z3979

**RUTLEDGE, H. G. (M.M.), Regimental Sergt.-Major,
R.A.S.C. (M.T.)**
Enlisting in 1905 he was mobilised when war broke out and
drafted to France in August 1914. In the course of his service
on the Western Front he took part in the Retreat from Mons
and was engaged on important duties in the Battles of the Marne,
the Aisne, Festubert, Hill 60, Vimy Ridge, Messines and during
the Retreat and Advance of 1918. He was wounded three times
whilst overseas and was awarded the Military Medal for
conspicuous gallantry and devotion to duty in the Battle of
Ypres in October 1916. He also holds the Mons Star, and the
General Service and Victory Medals, and was demobilised after
the Armistice.
84, Vaughan Road, Camberwell, S.E.5.   Z6320

RYAN, A., Private, R.A.M.C.
Volunteering in August 1914 he was sent to Egypt in the same
year and served in the 17th General Hospital at Alexandria
for a time. He was later attached to the 21st Field Ambulance
and did excellent work at Gaza, Jerusalem and in the Jordan
Valley during the British Advance through Palestine. Whilst
in the East he was transferred to the Royal Air Force, but owing
to illness was sent to hospital for treatment. Returning home
on the conclusion of hostilities he was demobilised in July 1919,
and holds the 1914–15 Star, and the General Service and Victory
Medals.
1, Bidwell Street, Peckham, S.E.15.   Z6572

RYAN, A., Sergt., R.A.S.C.
He volunteered in December 1915 and in the following year
embarked for Mesopotamia. Engaged on important duties as
an accountant he accompanied the Forces in their Advance
from Kut-el-Amara to Baghdad and did good work throughout
the Campaign. Returning home on the termination of hostilities
he was demobilised in June 1919, and holds the General Service
and Victory Medals.
17, Crawshay Road, Stockwell, S.W.9.   Z4531

RYAN, J. A., Private, Bedfordshire Regiment.
He volunteered in 1914 and drafted to the Western Front in the
following year served there until the end of hostilities. During
this period he fought in the Battles of Ypres, the Somme, Beaumont-Hamel, Cambrai and in several engagements in the Retreat
and Advance of 1918. Returning to England after the Armistice
he was demobilised in 1919, and holds the 1914–15 Star, and the
General Service and Victory Medals.
2, Crichton Street, Wandsworth Road, S.W.8.   Z3980

RYAN, J. E., Sapper, R.E.
Volunteering in 1915 he proceeded to Italy in January of the
following year and was engaged on bridge building and other
constructional work in connection with operations in various
parts of the line. He served throughout the course of hostilities
and returning home for demobilisation in February 1919, holds
the General Service and Victory Medals. He served in the
London Regiment prior to the war.
11, Calmington Road, Camberwell, S.E.5.   Z5491

RYAN, P. J., Private, Northamptonshire Regiment.
Volunteering in March 1915 he was sent overseas in the same
year and served on the Western Front. Whilst in this theatre
of war he was attached to a Trench Mortar Battery and fought
in several engagements, including those on the Somme, at Arras,
Messines, Passchendaele, Lens and Cambrai, and was gassed
and wounded in 1918. Invalided home he received protracted
medical treatment and was eventually discharged as medically
unfit for further service in February 1919. He holds the 1914–15
Star, and the General Service and Victory Medals.
4, Danson Road, Walworth, S.E.17.   27006

**RYAN, P. S., Sergt., 21st London Regiment (1st
Surrey Rifles) and Surrey Regiment.**
He volunteered in April 1915 and in the following year embarked
for France. There he took part in the Battles of Ypres, Arras,
Albert, Armentières and was three times wounded and gassed.
After his third wound he returned to England and on recovery
proceeded into Germany with the Army of Occupation and was
stationed on the Rhine. He returned to England for demobilisation in April 1919, and holds the General Service and Victory
Medals.
7, Alsace Street, Walworth, S.E.17.   Z2541B

**RYAN, W. H., Rifleman, Rifle Brigade, and Trooper,
Sussex Dragoons.**
Volunteering in September 1915 he completed his training
and served with his Battalion until sent to Ireland, where he was
engaged on important duties at the Regimental Stores. He
did good work but was unable to obtain his transfer to a theatre
of war before hostilities ceased and was demobilised in February
1919.
15, Hillery Road, Walworth, S.E.17.   3981

RYDER, E. J., Gunner, R.F.A.
Joining in August 1917 he proceeded to the Western Front in
the following March and took part in heavy fighting in several
engagements during the Advance of 1918. After the Armistice
he was sent into Germany with the Army of Occupation and
returning to England for demobilisation in September 1919,
holds the General Service and Victory Medals.
67, Graylands Road, Peckham, S.E.15.   Z5832

RYE, W., Sergt., 1st Norfolk Regiment.
A Regular, having enlisted in 1894, and fought in South Africa,
he was mobilised on the outbreak of war and sent to France
with the original Expeditionary Force in August 1914. He was
in action in the retreat from Mons and in the Battles of Ypres,
Armentières, the Somme and several other important engagements, including those during the Retreat and Advance of 1918.
Returning home after the Armistice he was discharged as time
expired with twenty-four years' service, and holds the Queen's
and King's South African Medals, the Good Conduct and Long
Service Medal in addition to the Mons Star, and the General
Service and Victory Medals.
52A, Chester Street, Kennington, S.E.11.   Z27516

S

SACH, G., Air Mechanic, R.A.F.
He joined in July 1918, and crossing to France at the conclusion of his training, served on important clerical duties
at an aerodrome near Nancy. He did valuable work until
the termination of hostilities, and was demobilised in December
1918, on his return to England. He holds the General Service
and Victory Medals.
28, Edithna Street, Stockwell, S.W.9.   Z3982A

SACH, G. F. W., L/Cpl., 12th London Regt. (Rangers).
He volunteered in February 1915, and after completing his
training served at home until 1917, when he was drafted to
France. Whilst overseas, he fought on the Somme, at Ypres,
Arras, Albert, St. Quentin, St. Eloi and Lille. He also served
in the Retreat of 1918, and on September 21st of that year
was unfortunately killed in the Allied Advance. He was
entitled to the General Service and Victory Medals.
                "Whilst we remember, the sacrifice is not in vain."
28, Edithna Street, Stockwell, S.W.9.   3982B

SADLEP, A. L., Leading Air Mechanic, R.A.F.
Volunteering in August 1915, he crossed to France four months
later. In the capacity of wireless operator, he took part in
engagements at Loos, St. Eloi, Albert, Vermelles, Ploegsteert
Wood, Vimy Ridge, the Somme, Arras, Bullecourt, Messines,
Ypres, Lens, and in the Retreat and Advance of 1918, and
did valuable work until after the termination of hostilities.
He was demobilised in February 1919, and holds the 1914–15
Star, and the General Service and Victory Medals.
85, Dalyell Road, Stockwell, S.W.9.   Z3985

**SADLER, G., Rifleman, 18th London Regt. (London
Irish Rifles).**
He volunteered in November 1915, and early in the following
year was drafted to the Western Front. Whilst in this theatre
of war he served with the British Red Cross Society and
did much valuable work. In 1917, he returned to England
and was engaged on important duties at Blackpool until
demobilised in March 1919. He holds the General Service
and Victory Medals.
4, Kenbury Street, Camberwell, S.E.5.   Z6331

SADLER, G. S., Private, 2nd Middlesex Regiment.
He joined in June 1916, and crossing to France in the following
September, took part in various engagements. He fell fighting
in the Somme sector on March 30th, 1917, and is buried in
the Communal Cemetery Extension at Hendecourt. He was
entitled to the General Service and Victory Medals.
"His life for his country, his soul to God."
3, Burgoyne Road, Stockwell, S.W.9. Z3986

SADLER, J., Sick Berth Attendant, R.N.R.
Mobilised at the outbreak of hostilities, he was first sent to
Portsmouth, and later to the Crystal Palace, where he was
attached to H.M.S. "Victory." He was not successful in
being sent to sea, but nevertheless did valuable work in attending to sick and wounded Naval men until demobilised in
February 1919.
16, Bonsor Street, Camberwell, S.E.5. Z4532

SADLER, W. J. (M.M.), Cpl., Middlesex Regiment.
He was in the Army when war broke out, and had previously
seen service at Malta, and in India. He left Aldershot for
France in August 1914, and subsequently fought in many
important battles, including that of Neuve Chapelle, in which
he was wounded and gassed. In addition to the Military
Medal, which he was awarded for conspicuous bravery in the
Field, he holds the 1914 Star, and the General Service and
Victory Medals, and was discharged in February 1919, on the
completion of a period of service extending over nineteen years.
24, Plough Road, Battersea, S.W.11. Z3984

SAGE, F. W., Corporal, R.A.F.
He joined in January 1916, and was sent to Malta later in the
same year. In 1917 he proceeded to France and carried out
important duties as Squadron Armourer. He took part in the
Retreat and Advance of 1918, during which he did much
work. After the Armistice he was stationed at Dunkirk
until he was demobilised in April 1919, holding the General
Service and Victory Medals.
14, Cutcombe Mansion, Cutcombe Road, Camberwell, S.E.5.
Z6706

SAGE, T., Private, 1/7th Warwickshire Regiment.
Volunteering in February 1916, he crossed to France in the
following year, and fought in engagements at Ypres and
Péronne. In December 1917, he was drafted to Italy, where
he did valuable work with his unit during operations on
the Piave and the Asiago Plateaux. He was demobilised
in February 1919, and holds the General Service and Victory
Medals.
11, Cronin Road, Peckham, S.E.15. Z5492

SAINSBURY, T. A., Sergt., 18th London Regiment
(London Irish Rifles).
He volunteered in 1914, and crossing to France early in the
following year, took part in many of the principal engagements,
including those at Ypres, the Somme, Loos, Lens, and Bourlon
Wood, where he was wounded and gassed. Invalided home,
he underwent protracted treatment at a hospital in Gloucester,
before being demobilised in 1919. He holds the 1914-15 Star,
and the General Service and Victory Medals.
23, Victoria Terrace, Queen's Road, Battersea Park, S.W.8.
Z3987

SAINTY, C. W., Pte., 6th North Staffordshire Regt.
Joining in September 1916, he was drafted to the Western
Front early in the following year, and after taking part in
heavy fighting in the Arras sector, was wounded and taken
prisoner at Bullecourt in 1918. Repatriated after the termination of hostilities, he was demobilised in March 1919, and
holds the General Service and Victory Medals.
69, Hargwyne Street, Stockwell, S.W.9. Z3988

SALES, M. C., Sergt. (Farrier), R.F.A. and R.A.V.C.
He volunteered in October 1914, and, crossing to France,
served with his unit in many important engagements. Later
he was transferred to the Royal Army Veterinary Corps, and
on returning to England was engaged for some time on important duties as an Instructor. He holds the 1914 Star,
and the General Service and Victory Medals, and was demobilised in February 1919.
35, Gladstone Street, Battersea Park, S.W.8. Z4014

SALMON, H. J., Private, M.G.C. (Infantry).
He joined in November 1916, and after the completion of his
training was engaged on important duties with the Royal
Army Service Corps Remounts Department in various parts
of England and Ireland. In April 1918 he was sent to France
with the Machine Gun Corps, and fought in numerous engagements during the Retreat and Advance until after valuable
services he unhappily died at the 4th Casualty Clearing Station
on November 27th, 1918, from illness contracted in the Service.
He was entitled to the General Service and Victory Medals.
"Whilst we remember, the sacrifice is not in vain."
280, Commercial Road, Peckham, S.E.15. Z6705

SALT, H. R., Private, R.A.S.C. (M.T.)
Joining in June 1916, he was drafted overseas in the following
May, and did much valuable work in connection with the
transport of ammunition to the forward areas of the Western
Front, principally on the Somme, and at Dunkirk. In 1918,
he contracted an illness, and in consequence was invalided
home. He was demobilised in February 1919, and holds the
General Service and Victory Medals.
50, Balfern Street, Battersea, S.W.11. Z4015

SALTER, E. H., Private, Middlesex Regiment.
He volunteered early in 1915, and crossing to France in April
of that year fought at the Battles of Ypres, Arras, and the
Somme. On July 1st, 1916, he received a serious wound, to
which he unfortunately succumbed a day later. He was
entitled to the 1914-15 Star, and the General Service and
Victory Medals.
"Great deeds cannot die."
259, East Street, Walworth, S.E.17. Z4017A

SALTER, F., Pte., Queen's (Royal West Surrey
Regiment).
Mobilised from the Reserve at the outbreak of war, he immediately crossed to France, and took part in the Retreat
from Mons, and was taken prisoner at Ypres in October 1914.
After being for four years in a detention camp in Germany, he
was repatriated, and subsequently demobilised in January
1919. He holds the Mons Star, and the General Service and
Victory Medals.
11, Cambridge Street, Camberwell, S.E.5. Z4016

SALTER, G., Private, Middlesex Regiment.
Joining in March 1916, he was drafted to the Western Front
early in the following year, and fought in engagements on the
Somme and at Ypres, where in 1917 he was wounded. He
was then invalided home to hospital, and after recovery
returned to France and served in the concluding operations of
the war. He was demobilised in January 1919, and holds the
General Service and Victory Medals.
16, Alsace Street, Walworth, S.E.17. Z4018

SALTER, L. F., Driver, R.A.S.C. (H.T.)
Volunteering at the outbreak of war, he immediately crossed
to France, and served on important transport duties with his
unit during the Retreat from Mons, and the Battles of the
Marne, the Aisne, Ypres, and many other engagements until
the termination of hostilities. He holds the Mons Star, and
the General Service and Victory Medals, and was demobilised
in 1919. 259, East Street, Walworth, S.E.17, Z4017B

SALTER, W., Gunner, R.G.A.
He volunteered in January 1915, and at the conclusion of his
training served at home until drafted to the Western Front in
March 1917. Whilst in this theatre of war, he fought in several
notable engagements, including those at Armentières and
Ypres. In May 1918, he was severely wounded, but after
treatment, rejoined his unit in the Field, and was in action for
the remaining period of hostilities. He was discharged in
February 1919, owing to ill-health following his wound, and
holds the General Service and Victory Medals.
11, Bredon Road, Camberwell, S.E.5. Z6446

SAMAUELLE, E. J. G., Gunner, R.F.A.
He volunteered at the commencement of hostilities, and
crossing to France in 1915, was so severely wounded at the
Battle of Loos in September of that year, as to necessitate his
return to England. After his recovery, being physically unfit
for further active service, he was engaged on important home
duties until demobilised in 1919. He holds the 1914-15 Star,
and the General Service and Victory Medals.
120, Kimberley Road, Peckham, S.E.15. Z6502A

SAMAUELLE, H. H., Driver, R.F.A.
He volunteered in August 1914, and after his training served
in France for upwards of three years. During this period, he
did valuable work with his unit in many important sectors,
including those of Loos and Ypres, and was for a time in
hospital, undergoing treatment for shell-shock. He was
demobilised in 1919, and holds the 1914-15 Star, and the
General Service and Victory Medals.
120, Kimberley Road, Peckham, S.E.15. Z6502B

SAMS, R. H., Sapper, R.E.
He joined in May 1916, and at the conclusion of his training
was engaged on duties of an important nature at various
stations. He was unable to secure his transfer overseas before
the termination of hostilities, but nevertheless did valuable
work until demobilised in October 1919.
48, Ingelow Road, Battersea Park Road, S.W.8. Z4020

SANDERS, A. W., 1st Air Mechanic, R.A.F.
He joined in May 1916, and during his service on the Western
Front was engaged on duties of an important nature which
called for much technical knowledge and skill. After the
termination of hostilities, he was advanced into Germany with the
Army of Occupation. He was demobilised in December 1919,
and holds the General Service and Victory Medals.
6, Aldbridge Street, Walworth, S.E.17. Z1925B

SANDERS, G., Leading Stoker, R.N.
He was in the Royal Navy when war broke out, having joined in 1909, and during the period of hostilities served in various vessels, including H.M.S. " Black Prince," " Indefatigable " (which was subsequently sunk in the Battle of Jutland), and the " Inflexible." He was engaged with his ship on important duties in the North and Mediterranean Seas, and was also for a time at Scapa Flow. He was demobilised in June 1920, and holds the General Service and Victory Medals.
10, Mawbey Street, South Lambeth Road, S.W.8. Z4021

SANDERS, J. W., Rifleman, Rifle Brigade.
Joining in December 1917, he crossed to France early in the following year, and after taking part in several engagements was so severely wounded and gassed as to necessitate his return to England. After protracted hospital treatment, he was invalided out of the Service in March 1919, and holds the General Service and Victory Medals.
29, Parkstone Road, Peckham, S.E.15. Z5662

SANDERS, T. C. H., Special War Worker.
Being ineligible for service with the Colours, he obtained work of National importance with Messrs. Tuff and House, Woolwich. He was engaged as a transport driver, in connection with the supply of food to our troops at Woolwich and other stations, and did much valuable work in this capacity until after the termination of hostilities.
338c, East Street, Walworth, S.E.17. Z1884A

SANDILAND, H., Gunner, R.F.A.
He volunteered in August 1914, and completing his training, was stationed at various depôts with his unit, engaged on important duties as Brigade tailor. Owing to ill-health he was admitted into hospital, and subsequently invalided out of the Service in April 1915.
13, Elam Street, Camberwell, S.E.5. Z6231

SANDISON, J. C., Q.M.S., R.A.M.C.
He was mobilised at the outbreak of war, and proceeding to Malta in 1915, was engaged on important hospital duties attending the sick and wounded men. Invalided home on account of ill-health, he received hospital treatment, and on recovery was drafted to France. Here he served in the front lines in many engagements on ambulance duties, and saw much fighting in the Retreat and Advance of 1918. He was demobilised in August 1919, and holds the General Service and Victory Medals.
37, Crawshay Road, Stockwell, S.W.9. Z4395B

SANDLE, W., Corporal, R.A.M.C. (F.A.).
Volunteering in January 1915, he was sent to France five months later, and served in the front lines on important ambulance duties in the Battles of the Somme, Ypres, Arras, Passchendaele, Gommecourt, and throughout the German Offensive and subsequent Allied Advance of 1918. He was demobilised in February 1919, and holds the 1914-15 Star, and the General Service and Victory Medals.
91, Smith Street, Camberwell, S.E.5. Z4022

SANCTO, R., Private, York and Lancaster Regt.
Joining in October 1916, he embarked for France in the following June and served in many parts of the line, and was wounded at Ypres in August 1917. He was evacuated to hospital in England, and on recovery returned to the front lines, and was in action in the Battle of Cambrai, and throughout the Retreat and Advance of 1918, and was again wounded in October of that year. He was demobilised in April 1919, and holds the General Service and Victory Medals.
35, Chumleigh Street, Camberwell, S.E.5. Z5144

SANS, H. J., Bombardier, R.F.A.
Volunteering in August 1914, he was sent to the Western Front in the following January, and was in action in many important engagements, including that on the Somme. Transferred to Salonika in 1915, he saw much fighting on the Struma. Owing to ill-health, he returned home, and after receiving hospital treatment was discharged unfit for further service in January 1919. He holds the 1914-15 Star, and the General Service and Victory Medals.
21, Chryssell Road, Brixton Road, S.W.9. Z5285

SANSOM, S. L., Rifleman, 8th London Regiment. (Post Office Rifles).
He joined in March 1917, and embarked for the Western Front in the following August. During his service overseas he fought at Ypres, Abbeville, and later was employed with the Military Police on regulating traffic and other important duties. He was demobilised in October 1919, and holds the General Service and Victory Medals.
11, Etherdon Street, Walworth, S.E.17. Z4023

SARCHFIELD, J., Driver, R.F.A.
Volunteering in March 1915, and later in that year drafted to France he fought in the Battles of Ypres, the Somme, Vimy Ridge, Passchendaele, Arras, Albert, and throughout the Retreat and Advance of 1918. Returning to England, he was demobilised in April 1919, and holds the 1914-15 Star, and the General Service and Victory Medals.
16, Oswyth Road, Camberwell, S.E.5. Z6544

SARGEANT, J., Gunner, R.G.A.
He joined in June 1916, and embarked for France in the following January. He was in action in many important engagements, including those at Arras, Vimy Ridge, Messines, Ypres, Bullecourt, the Somme, Bapaume, Havrincourt, Cambrai I and II, and throughout the Retreat and Advance of 1918. After the Armistice he was sent into Germany with the Army of Occupation, and served there until he returned to England for demobilisation in September 1919. He holds the General Service and Victory Medals.
158, Ferndale Road, Clapham, S.W.4. Z4024

SARGEANT, W., Private, 13th London Regiment (Kensingtons).
He volunteered in November 1914, and shortly afterwards proceeded to the Western Front. During his service overseas, he fought in various parts of the line and rendered excellent services. He gave his life for the freedom of England at Armentières in December 1914, and was entitled to the 1914 Star, and the General Service and Victory Medals.
" Whilst we remember, the sacrifice is not in vain."
3, Yeldham Buildings, Yeldham Road, Hammersmith, W.6. 12831B

SARGENT, G. E., Sapper, R.E.
He volunteered in May 1915, and was sent to France five months later, and was in action at the Battles of Loos, the Somme, Ypres, Arras, and rendered valuable services throughout the German Offensive and Allied Advance of 1918, engaged on field work of all descriptions. He was demobilised in July 1919, and holds the 1914-15 Star, and the General Service and Victory Medals.
30, Nunhead Grove, Peckham, S.E.15. Z6687

SARGENT, W. H., Lieutenant, Royal Fusiliers.
Serving in His Majesty's Forces at the outbreak of war, he proceeded to France, and fought in the Retreat from Mons, and the Battles of the Marne, the Aisne, Ypres, Neuve Chapelle, Loos, the Somme, and throughout the German Offensive and Allied Advance of 1918, and was wounded. In the closing operations of the war he was serving with the American Forces, and after the Armistice he was sent into Germany with the Army of Occupation, and served there until he returned to England for demobilisation in December 1919. He holds the Mons Star, and the General Service and Victory Medals.
102, Warriner Gardens, Battersea, S.W.11. Z4025

SARNEY, H. F., Private, R.A.M.C.
Mobilised at the outbreak of hostilities, and sent to the Western Front in February 1915, he served in the front lines on important ambulance duties in the Battles of Neuve Chapelle, St. Eloi, Hill 60, Ypres, Festubert, Arras, Messines, and did good work throughout the Retreat and Advance of 1918. He was demobilised in January 1919, and holds the 1914-15 Star, and the General Service and Victory Medals.
9, Lothian Road, Camberwell New Road, S.W.9. Z6457

SAUL, A., Shoeing Smith, R.F.A.
He enlisted in 1911, and at the outbreak of hostilities embarked for the Western Front, where he fought in the Retreat from Mons, and the Battles of the Marne, the Aisne, Ypres, and Passchendaele. Owing to ill-health, he returned to England in 1918, and after receiving hospital treatment served at various stations at home until demobilised in April 1919. He holds the Mons Star, and the General Service and Victory Medals.
17, Newcomen Road, Battersea, S.W.11. Z4026

SAUNDERS, C., Corporal, R.A.M.C.
He joined in July 1917, and drafted to Salonika in the following March, rendered valuable services engaged on important duties, attending to sick and wounded troops. He returned to England and was demobilised in January 1920, and holds the General Service and Victory Medals.
50, Sheepcote Lane, Battersea, S.W.11. Z4036B

SAUNDERS, C., Driver, R.A.S.C. (M.T.)
He volunteered in August 1914, and was sent to France almost immediately and fought in the Retreat from Mons, the Battles of Ypres, the Somme, Cambrai, Lens, and was wounded in March 1915. He was on recovery, returned to France and saw heavy fighting in many parts of the line, and throughout the Retreat and Advance of 1918, and was twice wounded. He was demobilised in April 1919, and holds the Mons Star, and the General Service and Victory Medals, in addition to the Sudan (Khedive's) Medal, and the Sudan (British) Medal.
61, Bird-in-Bush Road, Peckham, S.E.15. Z6575

SAUNDERS, E., Driver, R.F.A.
He volunteered in May 1915, and later in that year embarked for the Western Front. During his services overseas he fought in many engagements, including those at Ypres, the Somme, the Ancre, Combles, and was engaged in heavy fighting in the Retreat and Advance of 1918. He was demobilised in June 1919, and holds the 1914-15 Star, and the General Service and Victory Medals.
21, St. Andrew's Street, Wandsworth Road, S.W.8. Z4209B

SAUNDERS, E., Driver, R.F.A.
Volunteering in 1915, he embarked for France in the same year and fought in many engagements. He was in action during the German Offensive and subsequent Allied Advance of 1918, and rendered excellent services throughout. Returning to England he was demobilised in November 1919, and holds the 1914-15 Star, and the General Service and Victory Medals.
50, Sheepcote Lane, Battersea, S.W.11.　　　　Z4036C

SAUNDERS, F., Private, Labour Corps.
He joined in September 1917, and was shortly afterwards drafted to the Western Front, where he served in the forward areas engaged on important duties. He was present at the Battles of Cambrai, the Somme, the Marne, Bapaume, Havrincourt, and at the fighting in the Retreat and Advance of 1918. After the Armistice he was sent into Germany with the Army of Occupation and stationed at Cologne. Returning to England, he was demobilised in November 1919, and holds the General Service and Victory Medals.
314, East Street, Walworth, S.E.17.　　　　Z4034

SAUNDERS, F., L/Cpl., 4th East Surrey Regiment.
Volunteering in December 1915, and proceeding to France in the following October, he fought at the Battles of Arras, Vimy Ridge, the Somme, Albert, Péronne, Passchendaele, and in the German Offensive and Allied Advance of 1918. He was demobilised in April 1919, and holds the General Service and Victory Medals.
29, Verona Street, Battersea, S.W.11.　　　　Z4032

SAUNDERS, G. F., Volunteer Training Corps.
Ineligible for service with the Colours, he joined the Volunteer Training Corps in January 1916, and served with a machine gun battery engaged in the defences of London against hostile aircraft. He rendered valuable services throughout, and was discharged in January 1919.
30, Councillor Street, Camberwell, S.E.5.　　　　Z4028

SAUNDERS, H., Rifleman, 18th London Regiment (London Irish Rifles).
Mobilised at the commencement of the war he embarked for France in 1915, and served in many parts of the line, fighting at Ypres, Loos, and the Somme. He was also in action throughout the German Offensive and Allied Advance of 1918, and was gassed. Returning to England, he was demobilised in March 1919, and holds the 1914-15 Star, and the General Service and Victory Medals.
17, Stanley Street, Battersea Park, S.W.8.　　　　Z4027

SAUNDERS, H. E., Guardsman, Grenadier Guards.
He enlisted in 1904, and shortly after the declaration of war was sent to the Western Front where he served in many parts of the line, fighting at the Battles of Ypres, the Somme, Cambrai, and throughout the German Offensive and subsequent Allied Advance of 1918. After the cessation of hostilities he was sent into Germany with the Army of Occupation and stationed at Cologne. He was still serving in 1920, and holds the 1914 Star, and the General Service and Victory Medals, and also holds the Queen's South African Medal.
135D, Queen's Road, Battersea Park, S.W.8.　　　　Z4030

SAUNDERS, J., Private, Middlesex Regiment.
Joining in February 1917, he was sent to the Western Front eight months later, and was engaged in heavy fighting at Ypres, Arras, and in many other important engagements. Severely wounded in October 1918, during the Allied Advance he returned to England, and after receiving hospital treatment, was discharged unfit for further service in March 1919. He holds the General Service and Victory Medals.
25, Burns Road, Battersea, S.W.11.　　　　Z4031A

SAUNDERS, J. A., Private, M.G.C.
He joined in July 1917, and proceeding to France in the following December, was in action in various sectors. He fought in the Ypres Salient and throughout the German Offensive and subsequent Allied Advance of 1918. He was demobilised in April, 1919, and holds the General Service and Victory Medals.
25, Burns Road, Battersea, S.W.11.　　　　Z4031B

SAUNDERS, J. P., Private, M.G.C.
Joining in May 1918, he completed his training and attached to the Coldstream Guards, was stationed at various depôts engaged on important duties. He was not successful in obtaining his transfer to a theatre of war prior to the cessation of hostilities, but did good work until demobilised in January 1919.
1, Medwin Street, Ferndale Road, S.W.4.　　　　Z4037

SAUNDERS, J. W., Private, 1st Duke of Cornwall's Light Infantry.
Volunteering in 1914, he was sent to the Western Front almost immediately and fought in the Retreat from Mons, and the Battles of the Marne, the Aisne, Ypres, Festubert, Loos, Ploegsteert, and was wounded in October 1918, at Le Pas. Returning to England, he received medical treatment, and was invalided out of the Service in November 1918. He holds the Mons Star, and the General Service and Victory Medals.
33, Daniel's Road, Peckham, S.E.15.　　　　Z6618

SAUNDERS, P., Driver, R.F.A.
He volunteered in 1915, and later in the same year was drafted to the Western Front. During his service overseas he was in action at the Battles of the Somme, Arras, Ypres, where he was wounded in 1917. Returning to England, he received medical treatment, and on recovery was stationed at Ripon, and did good work with the Remount Depôt. He was demobilised in 1919, and holds the 1914-15 Star, and the General Service and Victory Medals.
55, Bagshot Street, Walworth, S.E.17.　　　　Z4033A

SAUNDERS, V. G., Private, M.G.C.
He volunteered in July 1915, and embarking for France in the same year, fought in many important engagements, including those at Vimy Ridge, Arras, Kemmel, Ypres, and was wounded near Vimy Ridge. On recovery, he returned to the Front, and was engaged in heavy fighting during the Retreat and Advance of 1918. He was demobilised in May 1919, and holds the 1914-15 Star, and the General Service and Victory Medals.
63, Stockdale Road, Wandsworth Road, S.W.8.　　　　Z1487A

SAUNDERS, W. H., Pte., 9th York and Lancaster Regiment.
Volunteering in August 1914, he served at various stations until drafted to France in 1916. He was in action in the Battles of Ypres, Cambrai, and was wounded at Martinpuich in October 1916. On recovery he rejoined his Battalion and took part in heavy fighting in various sectors. He gave his life for King and Country on April 8th, 1917, and was entitled to the General Service and Victory Medals.
"Steals on the ear, the distant triumph song."
21, St. Andrew's Street, Wandsworth Road, S.W.8.
　　　　Z4036A. Z4029A

SAVAGE, G. W., Corporal, R.F.A.
He volunteered in August 1914, and was immediately sent to France where he fought in the Retreat from Mons, and the Battles of the Marne, the Aisne, La Bassée, Albert, and Loos. Owing to ill-health he was transferred to the Labour Corps in 1917, and did very good work with this unit, acting as Sergeant. He was demobilised in February 1919, and holds the Mons Star, and the General Service and Victory Medals.
15, Flint Street, Walworth, S.E.17.　　　　Z4038

SAVAGE, L. H., Sergt., 2nd Dorsetshire Regiment.
He had previously served for twelve years with the Colours and re-enlisted in 1916. He was sent to France in the following year and was engaged in much heavy fighting and was severely wounded and gassed in 1917. Evacuated to hospital in England he received medical treatment and on recovery was employed on home duties until demobilised in January 1919. He holds the General Service and Victory Medals.
15, Dashwood Road, Wandsworth Road, S.W.8.　　　　Z4039

SAVILL, A. B., Rifleman, 21st London Regiment (1st Surrey Rifles).
Volunteering in August 1914, he was drafted to France in the following year and fought in the Battles of Ypres, Loos, Vimy Ridge, Festubert, and was wounded in action on the Somme. Invalided to England he received medical treatment and on recovery proceeded to Salonika in 1917, and served in this theatre of war in many engagements. He contracted malaria and after spending some time in hospital was sent to Palestine where he was engaged in operations resulting in the fall of Jerusalem. He returned to the Western Front in July 1918, and took part in the final Allied Advance. He holds the 1914-15 Star, and the General Service and Victory Medals, and in 1920, was still serving.
125, Ferndale Road, Clapham, S.W.4.　　　　Z4041A

SAVILL, A. E., A.B., Royal Navy.
He joined in February 1917, and during his period of service was engaged aboard H.M.S. "Dominion," and H.M.S. "Commonwealth" on special duties as a decoder of signals, whilst convoying food ships to and from Norway, Sweden, and England. He also did good work in charge of a party of gunners at Scapa Flow. He was demobilised in 1919, and holds the General Service and Victory Medals.
125, Ferndale Road, Clapham, S.W.4.　　　　Z4041C

SAVILL, J., Rifleman, 21st London Regiment (1st Surrey Rifles).
He volunteered at the outbreak of hostilities, and sent to France in 1915, fought at the Battles of Ypres, Loos, Vimy Ridge, High Wood, Arras, and was mentioned in Despatches for the gallantry he displayed in rescuing an officer at Ypres. He was severely wounded in action on the Somme, and evacuated to hospital in England, and after receiving protracted hospital treatment served at home until demobilised in January 1919. He holds the 1914-15 Star, and the General Service and Victory Medals.
125, Ferndale Road, Clapham, S.W.4.　　　　Z4041B

SAVORY, E. J., Private, King's (Liverpool Regt.)
He joined in November 1916, and was employed on important duties until sent overseas in May 1918. Whilst on the Western Front he took part in the fierce fighting at Ypres during the German Offensive, and was unhappily killed in action in the subsequent Allied Advance on October 2nd of that year. He was entitled to the General Service and Victory Medals.
" A valiant soldier, with undaunted heart he breasted Life's last hill."
16, St. Philip Street, Battersea Park, S.W.8. Z4042

SAWYER, A. J., Gunner, R.G.A.
He joined in May 1916, and five months later proceeded to the Western Front where he served in the Battles of Arras, Vimy Ridge, Lens, Loos, Amiens, Bapaume, Havrincourt, and Le Cateau. Owing to illness he was taken to hospital at Etaples, and subsequently died on November 13th, 1918. He was entitled to the General Service and Victory Medals.
" His memory is cherished with pride."
23, Poyntz Road, Battersea, S.W.11. Z4045

SAWYER, H. G., Pte., King's Own Scottish Borderers.
He joined in 1916, and later in the same year was sent to France. In this theatre of war he fought at Ypres, and was seriously wounded. He was invalided to hospital in England, and in consequence of his injuries one of his legs had to be amputated. He was discharged unfit for further service in 1917, and holds the General Service and Victory Medals.
12, Archer Street, South Lambeth Road, S.W.8. Z4043

SAWYER, J. H., Private, 6th Wiltshire Regiment.
He joined in June 1916, and in the same year was sent to France, where he fought at the Battles of Ypres, the Somme, Arras, St. Eloi, Albert, Passchendaele, Cambrai, and in the Retreat and subsequent Allied Advance of 1918. After the signing of the Armistice he proceeded to Egypt and took part in the fighting at the Sinai Peninsula, and served at Jerusalem and Magdhaba. He was demobilised in January 1920, and holds the General Service and Victory Medals.
8, Arthur Road, Brixton Road, S.W.9. Z4044

SAYERS, J. G. Bombardier, R.F.A.
He volunteered in April 1915, and in the following November was sent to France. He was in action at the Battles of Arras, Givenchy, the Somme, and Combles. Owing to ill-health he was invalided to England for a time and returned to the Western Front in 1917, but was again evacuated to hospital in England with fever in June 1918, and on recovery was demobilised in December of that year. He unhappily died from the effects of his previous illness on April 11th, 1920, and was entitled to the 1914-15 Star, and the General Service and Victory Medals.
" Whilst we remember, the sacrifice is not in vain."
54, Jocelyn Street, Peckham, S.E.15. Z5493

SCAIFE, T., Private, West Yorkshire Regiment.
A Reservist he was mobilised at the outbreak of hostilities and drafted immediately to France. He fought in the Retreat from Mons, and the subsequent Battles of the Marne, and the Aisne. During much heavy fighting in 1915, he was taken prisoner and suffered many hardships during his captivity in Germany. Repatriated at the signing of the Armistice, he was demobilised in December 1918, and holds the Mons Star, and the General Service and Victory Medals.
73, Battersea Bridge Road, Battersea, S.W.11. Z3737B

SCANLAN, J., 1st Air Mechanic, R.A.F.
He volunteered in August 1914, and proceeded to France with the Queen's Regiment and fought at Mons, where he was wounded, and was invalided home. On recovery he was transferred to the Royal Air Force, and rendered valuable services on the East Coast until he was demobilised in March 1919, holding the Mons Star, and the General Service and Victory Medals.
63, Galleywall Road, Rotherhithe, S.E.16. Z6704

SCANLAN, P. C., Squad Sergt.-Major, 13th Hussars.
He enlisted in 1899, and at the outbreak of hostilities was serving in India. He was drafted to France and took part in the fighting in the Battles of Neuve Chapelle, Ypres, Festubert, Loos, the Somme, Vimy Ridge, and Messines. He returned to England in October 1918, and was discharged on completion of service in August 1920. He holds the 1914-15 Star, and the General Service and Victory Medals, and the Long Service and Good Conduct Medals.
3, Denmark Road, Camberwell, S.E.5. Z6084

SCARLES, F. W., Seaman Gunner, R.N.
A Reservist, he was mobilised in August 1914, and aboard a submarine served with the Grand Fleet in the North Sea, and at Heligoland Bight. Owing to severe shell-shock he was invalided out of the Service in August 1916, and holds the 1914-15 Star, and the General Service and Victory Medals.
29, Horsman Street, Camberwell, S.E.5. Z4046

SCARBOROUGH, E., Corporal, Queen's (Royal West Surrey Regiment).
He had previously served with the City Imperial Volunteers in the Boer War, and in August 1914, volunteered for service with the Colours. He was engaged on important work as an Instructor of recruits for Kitchener's Army until sent to France in June 1917. Whilst on the Western Front he took part in the heavy fighting in the Ypres Salient, and died gloriously on the Field of Battle at Hooge on September 27th, 1917. He held the Queen's and King's South African Medals, and was entitled to the General Service and Victory Medals.
" Nobly striving,
He nobly fell, that we might live."
1, Boyson's Cottages, New Church Road, Camberwell, S.E.5. Z6494-5A

SCHLATTER, H., Private, 23rd London Regiment.
He was mobilised at the outbreak of hostilities, and shortly afterwards proceeded to the Western Front. In this theatre of war he was in action in numerous engagements, including those at La Bassée, Hill 60, Ypres, and Loos. Owing to illness he was invalided to hospital and subsequently discharged as medically unfit for further service in 1916. He holds the 1914 Star, and the General Service and Victory Medals.
69, Westmoreland Street, Grosvenor Road, S.W.1. X24546

SCHLUTER, F. G. H., Private, 7th London Regt.
He joined in 1916, and later in the same year was sent overseas. During his service on the Western Front he fought at the Battles of the Somme, Ypres, Arras, and Cambrai, where he was severely wounded in June 1917. He was evacuated to hospital in England, and subsequently invalided out of the Service in 1919. He holds the General Service and Victory Medals.
4, Andulus Road, Landor Road, S.W.9. Z4047

SCHNEIDER, E., Private, Middlesex Regiment.
Joining in 1916, he was sent to France in the same year. Whilst on the Western Front he took an active part in numerous engagements, including those on the Somme, at Beaumont-Hamel, Arras, Messines, Lens, Passchendaele, and in the Retreat and Allied Advance of 1918. He was demobilised in 1920, and holds the General Service and Victory Medals.
63, Stonhouse Street, Clapham, S.W.4. Z1726A

SCHOFIELD, A. E., Rifleman, Rifle Brigade.
Volunteering in August 1914, he was drafted to the Western Front early in the following year, and was severely wounded near St. Eloi in May 1915. After treatment he again went into action and was wounded on two other occasions, at Guillemont in September 1916, and at Cambrai in November 1917, when he was also taken prisoner. During his captivity he was made to work behind the German lines and suffered much ill-treatment at the hands of his captors. He was repatriated after the Armistice, and subsequently demobilised in July 1919, and holds the 1914-15 Star, and the General Service and Victory Medals.
8c, Lewis Trust Buildings, Camberwell, S.E.5. Z6086A

SCHOLES, B., Rifleman, Rifle Brigade.
He joined in March 1918, and at the conclusion of his training was engaged on important duties with his unit. He was unable to secure his transfer overseas before the termination of hostilities, but afterwards was sent with the Army of Occupation to Germany, where he served on guard and outpost duties. He was demobilised in 1920 on his return to England.
48, Chatto Road, Battersea, S.W.11. Z4050

SCHOLL, A. V., Pte., Loyal North Lancashire Regt.
He volunteered in 1915, and proceeding to France in the following year was engaged in heavy fighting during the Somme Offensive. Taken prisoner in 1917 on the Somme, he was made to load and unload ships, and worked for some time in the engine room of a laundry. During his captivity he was wounded in the face and neck by a German officer, and removed to hospital for treatment. Repatriated after the Armistice he was demobilised in 1919, and holds the General Service and Victory Medals.
74, Buchan Road, Peckham, S.E.15. Z6582

SCHOOL, A. H. V., Bombardier, R.G.A.
Volunteering in October 1914, he was sent to Gibraltar two months later and served on important garrison duties for two years, when he returned to England. In March 1917, he proceeded to the Western Front, and was engaged with his Battery in the Battles of Passchendaele, the Somme, and Cambrai. He was killed in action on March 21st, 1918, during the German Offensive on the Somme, and was entitled to the General Service and Victory Medals.
" His memory is cherished with pride."
112, Gloucester Road, Peckham, S.E.15. Z5838B

SCHOOLING, F. H., Private, 3rd R.M.L.I.

He was serving at the outbreak of war, and was posted to H.M.S. " Triumph" in October 1914, which ship was ordered to China, and after a period of service there sailed for the Dardanelles in February 1915. She was in action in the Battle of the Narrows, and was sunk by a submarine on May 25th, 1915, but he was fortunately rescued and sent to Mudros. Returning home in June 1915, he was posted to H.M.S. " Marshal Ney " two months later, and served in that vessel in several engagements off the Belgian Coast. Transferred to H.M.S. " Terror " in July 1916, his ship was in action with enemy craft at Zeebrugge, Ostend, and off Dover, and was torpedoed during the raid on Dunkirk in March 1918. Rescued again he was sent to Chatham, and from there to Mudros in May 1919. Returning home he was demobilised in April 1920, and holds the 1914–15 Star, and the General Service and Victory Medals.

96, Cator Street, Peckham, S.E.15.   Z4533

SCOVELL, W., Private, Royal Welch Fusiliers.

Joining in November 1916, he was drafted to the Western Front in the following January, and saw service in various sectors. He fought in several engagements including the Battles of Ypres, Arras, and Cambrai, and returned home after the Armistice. Demobilised in February 1919, he holds the General Service and Victory Medals.

101, Galleywall Road, Rotherhithe, S.E.16.   Z6655

SCHULER, B., Rifleman, King's Royal Rifle Corps.

He volunteered in May 1915, and six months later proceeded to the Western Front, where he served throughout the war. Engaged on important duties with his Battalion he took part in various battles and was wounded. On the cessation of hostilities he returned to England and was demobilised in February 1919. He holds the 1914–15 Star, and the General Service and Victory Medals.

29, Kimberley Road, Landor Road, S.W.9.   Z4048

SCIARRETTA, H. I. R., Gunner, R.F.A.

Joining in April 1917, he was sent overseas in the following September, and served in many parts of the Western Front. He was engaged in heavy fighting in the Battles of Passchendaele, Armentières, and was gassed. After the Armistice he was sent into Germany with the Army of Occupation, and returning home for demobilisation in September 1919, holds the General Service and Victory Medals.

38, Honeywell Road, Wandsworth Common, S.W.11.   Z6519A

SCOFIELD, A. C., Special War Worker.

During the whole period of the war he was engaged at Messrs. Clement Talbot's Works, North Kensington, as a fitter. His duties, which were in connection with the construction of aeroplanes, were carried out in a skilful and efficient manner and he rendered valuable services throughout.

31, Parfitt Road, Rotherhithe, S.E.16.   Z6654

SCOFIELD, H., Pte., 11th Queen's (Royal West Surrey Regiment).

Volunteering in June 1915, he embarked for France in May of the following year and served with his Battalion in the Offensive on the Somme. He was killed in action on September 23rd, 1916, and buried at Delville Wood, and was entitled to the General Service and Victory Medals.

"A costly sacrifice upon the altar of freedom."

88, Geneva Road, Coldharbour Lane, S.W.9.   Z3054B

SCOFIELD, H. J., Pte., 20th Lancashire Fusiliers.

Joining in February 1917, and drafted to France in the following September he was engaged in heavy fighting in the Battles of Passchendaele and Lens. He gave his life for King and Country on October 23rd, 1917, and was entitled to the General Service and Victory Medals.

"He died the noblest death a man may die, Fighting for God, and right, and liberty."

15, Abyssinia Road, Battersea, S.W.11.   Z4049B

SCOFIELD, W. T., Gunner, R.F.A.

He volunteered in May 1915, and in the same year proceeded to France, where he served at a base until sent to Salonika. He saw much service with his Battery in the Balkans, and was in action in several engagements during the Allied Offensive on the Vardar and Struma fronts, and returning to England after the Armistice was discharged as medically unfit for further military service. He holds the 1914–15 Star, and the General Service and Victory Medals.

15, Abyssinia Road, Battersea, S.W.11.   Z4049A

SCOGGINS, W., Private, 1/5th Border Regiment.

He joined in August 1916, and embarking for the Western Front seven months later fought in the Battles of the Ancre, Arras, Messines Ypres and Lens. Wounded at Cambrai in January 1918, he was invalided home to hospital, and on recovery returned to France and took part in the Battles of Bapaume, Havrincourt, and in the concluding engagements of the war. He was demobilised in March 1919, and holds the General Service and Victory Medals.

30, Elsted Street, Walworth, S.E.17.   Z4051

SCOTT, A., Corporal, R.A.M.C. and Pioneer, R.E.

He volunteered in September 1914, and was engaged on important duties at home until his embarkation for France in 1916. Serving with the gas section of the Royal Engineers he was engaged on important duties during the Battles of the Somme, Arras, Ypres, and was gassed at Albert. Returning home after the Armistice he was demobilised in June 1919, and holds the General Service and Victory Medals.

24, Edithna Street, Landor Road, S.W.9.   Z4053A

SCOTT, A. F., Petty Officer, R.N.

He was serving at the outbreak of war in H.M.S. " Calypso," which vessel, attached to the Grand Fleet, was engaged on important patrol duties in the North Sea. She was sent to Egypt in 1915, and after a period of service in the Mediterranean and Persian Gulf, proceeded to Italian waters, and later to the Baltic where she was in action against the Bolshevist Fleet. He was demobilised in March 1919, and holds the 1914–15 Star, and the General Service and Victory Medals.

42, Edithna Street, Landor Road, S.W.9.   Z4052

SCOTT, C. G., Private, 1st East Yorkshire Regt.

He joined in May 1916, and in the following July was drafted overseas and fought in several engagements on the Western Front. He was taken prisoner on March 22nd, 1918, during the German Offensive and died in hospital in Germany on May 21st, 1919, and was buried in Dimbeck Cemetery. He was entitled to the General Service and Victory Medals.

"The path of duty was the way to glory."

13, Vaughan Road, Camberwell, S.E.5.   Z6444B

SCOTT, C. H., L/Cpl., 2nd East Surrey Regiment.

A Regular, having enlisted in March 1912, he was serving in India at the outbreak of war and was wounded in an engagement on the North West Frontier in April 1916. Sent home in January 1918, he was engaged on special duties with his unit at various depôts, and in 1920 was still serving. He holds the General Service and Victory Medals.

44, Grenard Road, Peckham, S.E.15.   Z5564–5B

SCOTT, E., Sapper, R.E.

A serving soldier was mobilised on the outbreak of war and proceeding to Gallipoli served in the Landing at Suvla Bay, and in other operations until the Evacuation of the Peninsula. He was sent to Egypt in 1915, and was engaged on special duties on the printing staff at General Headquarters at Cairo. Returning home after hostilities ceased he was demobilised in August 1919, and holds the General Service and Victory Medals.

24, Edithna Street, Landor Road, S.W.9.   Z4053B

SCOTT, E. A., Gunner, R.F.A.

A Territorial he was mobilised on the declaration of war and drafted overseas in June 1915. Serving with his Battery on the Western Front he fought in the Battles of Ypres, Loos, Albert, the Somme, Arras, Messines, Lens, Cambrai, and in several engagements during the Retreat and Advance of 1918. Returning to England after the Armistice he was demobilised in August 1919, and holds the 1914–15 Star, and the General Service and Victory Medals.

47A, Flint Street, Walworth, S.E.17.   Z4060C

SCOTT, F. W., Driver, R.F.A.

Joining in October 1916, he was drafted to the Western Front in the following year and served with his Battery throughout the course of hostilities. During this period he fought in several important engagements, including the Battles of Arras, Ypres, Messines and Passchendaele. On the termination of the war he was sent with the Army of Occupation into Germany and was stationed on the Rhine for a year. Returning to England for demobilisation in March 1920, he holds the General Service and Victory Medals.

33, Verney Road, Rotherhithe, S.E.16.   Z6688

SCOTT, H., Private, Duke of Wellington's (West Riding Regiment).

A serving soldier, having enlisted in February 1912, he was mobilised on the outbreak of war and drafted to France with the First Expeditionary Force. He took part in heavy fighting during the Retreat from Mons, and was wounded at Charleroi. Rejoining his unit on recovery he fought in the Battles of Ypres, Arras, Cambrai, and in several engagements during the Retreat and Advance of 1918, and in the course of operations was wounded at Beaumont-Hamel. He holds the Mons Star, and the General Service and Victory Medals, and was demobilised in May 1919.

17, Priory Road, Wandsworth Road, S.W.8.   Z4054

SCOTT, H. C., Gunner, R.F.A.

Volunteering in April 1915, he was sent to the Western Front in the following December and served there for upwards of four years. During this period he was in action in the Battles of Albert, Vimy Ridge, the Somme, Arras, Passchendaele, Lens, Cambrai, and in the Retreat and Advance of 1918. After the Armistice he returned home and was demobilised in September 1919, and holds the General Service and Victory Medals. 47A, Flint Street, Walworth, S.E.17.   Z4055

SCOTT, H. W., Corporal, R.A.S.C. (M.T.)

He volunteered in April 1915, and embarking for France two months later served as a motor ambulance driver during the Battles of Neuve Chapelle, Festubert and Loos. Transferred to the 69th Siege Battery, Royal Garrison Artillery he fought in several engagements, including those on the Somme, at Albert, Vimy Ridge, Beaumont-Hamel, Arras, Messines, and Bapaume. On the conclusion of hostilities he was sent into Germany with the Army of Occupation, and returning from Cologne for demobilisation in May 1919, holds the 1914–15 Star, and the General Service and Victory Medals.
37, Radnor Street, Peckham, S.E.15.   Z6549

SCOTT, J. O., Private, 2nd London Regiment (Royal Fusiliers).

Joining in September 1917, he embarked for the Western Front in the following March, and took part in the Battles of Amiens and St. Quentin. He gave his life for the freedom of England at Corbie during the final Allied Advance on August 8th, 1918, and was entitled to the General Service and Victory Medals.   "Great deeds cannot die;
They with the Sun and Moon renew their light for ever."
87F, Albany Road, Camberwell, S.E.5.   5663

SCOTT, J. T., L/Corporal, 3rd Bn. Australian I.F.

Volunteering in February 1915, he was sent to Gallipoli in the same year and fought in several engagements from the Landing at Suvla Bay until wounded and sent to hospital. On recovery he proceeded to France, and in the course of operations was wounded again in 1917, and a third time in August 1918. Owing to his injuries he was evacuated to hospital in England for treatment, and was subsequently demobilised in April 1919. He holds the 1914–15 Star, and the General Service and Victory Medals.   88, Surrey Lane, Battersea, S.W.11.   Z4056

SCOTT, L., Private, Labour Corps.

He joined in 1916, and embarking for France in the following year served there until the conclusion of hostilities. During this period he was engaged in making roads in the forward areas, and in unloading ammunition and supplies at the rail head in the Arras sector. He holds the General Service and Victory Medals, and was demobilised in 1919.
37, Mordaunt Street, Landor Road, S.W.9.   Z4057

SCOTT, M., Bombardier, R.F.A.

He volunteered in 1915, and proceeding overseas in the same year served on the Western Front until hostilities ceased. During this period he fought with his Battery in numerous battles, including those in the Ypres salient, at Arras, and on the Somme. Returning to England after the Armistice he was demobilised in 1919, and holds the 1914–15 Star, and the General Service and Victory Medals.
79, Orb Street, Walworth, S.E.17.   Z4058

SCOTT, S. (M.M.), Private, 6th Buffs (East Kent Regiment).

Volunteering in November 1915, he was almost immediately sent to France, and was in action in several engagements. He was wounded at St. Eloi in March 1916, and sent to hospital in England. Returning to his unit on recovery he took part in many operations, was wounded in the Somme Offensive in 1916, and awarded the Military Medal for conspicuous bravery and devotion to duty in the Field. Taken prisoner in 1918, he was held in captivity until repatriated after the Armistice. He also holds the 1914–15 Star, and the General Service and Victory Medals, and was demobilised in February 1919.
59, Harris Street, Camberwell, S.E.17.   4693B

SCOTT, S., Private, Royal Berkshire Regiment.

He volunteered in August 1914, and drafted to France in the following May, served in the Battles of Festubert and Loos, and was wounded in October 1915, and invalided home. Returning to the Western Front in January 1916, he took part in heavy fighting at Vimy Ridge and Delville Wood, and was twice wounded. Sent to England, owing to his injuries, he was discharged in consequence in October 1917, and holds the 1914–15 Star, and the General Service and Victory Medals.
52, Musjid Road, Battersea, S.W.11.   Z4059

SCOTT, S. H., Private, 1/7th London Regiment.

Volunteering in July 1915, he was sent overseas in the following year and served with his Battalion in several engagements in the Somme Sector. Reported missing on October 7th, 1916, he was later presumed to have been killed in action on that date and was entitled to the General Service and Victory Medals.
"His life for his Country, his soul to God."
24, Edithna Street, Landor Road, S.W.9.   Z4053C

SCOTT, S. J., Private, South Wales Borderers.

Volunteering in February 1915, he embarked for France four months later, and was in action in the Battles of Ypres and Festubert, and then proceeded to Salonika. Serving with his Battalion he fought in the advance on the Vardar, the Struma, and Doiran fronts, and was in action at the capture of Monastir. On the termination of hostilities he returned to England for demobilisation in March 1919, and holds the 1914–15 Star, and the General Service and Victory Medals.
47A, Flint Street, Walworth, S.E.17.   Z4060A

SCOTT, W., Sapper, R.E.

He volunteered in January 1915, and proceeding to France in the following year was engaged on special duties in connection with the printing of maps for use in the Field. Later he served with his unit during the Battles of Vimy Ridge, the Somme, Arras, Ypres, Lens, Cambrai, and in the Retreat and Advance of 1918. Demobilised in March 1919, he holds the General Service and Victory Medals.
47A, Flint Street, Walworth, S.E.17.   Z4060B

SCOTT, W. A., Private, M.G.C.

He joined in July 1917, and in the following June was drafted to the Western Front. In this theatre of war he did excellent work with his unit at Vimy Ridge, and in several engagements during the Advance of 1918. After the Armistice he was sent to Palestine, and returning from Kantara for demobilisation in May 1920, holds the General Service and Victory Medals.
13, Vaughan Road, Camberwell, S.E.5.   Z6444A

SCOTT, W. E., Rifleman, 2nd Rifle Brigade.

He joined in February 1916, and later in the same year was sent to France, where he took part in the fierce fighting at Vermelles, Arras, Ypres, and Bullecourt. He was unfortunately reported missing at St. Quentin on May 3rd, 1917, and was presumed to have been killed in action on that date. He was entitled to the General Service and Victory Medals.
"A costly sacrifice upon the altar of freedom."
50, Surrey Road, Peckham Rye, S.E.15   Z6732

SCOTT, W. J., Corporal, M.G.C.

Volunteering in March 1915, he embarked for France three months later and attached to the Welch Regiment, served in the Battle of Loos and was blown up in a mine explosion. On recovery he was sent to Salonika, and was in action in several engagements in the Balkans until admitted to hospital with malaria. Evacuated to England he was subsequently discharged as medically unfit in May 1919, and holds the 1914–15 Star, and the General Service and Victory Medals.
14, Pearson Street, Battersea, S.W.11.   Z4061

SCOTT, W. R., Driver, R.F.A.

A Territorial he was mobilised when war broke out and was sent to France in 1914. He fought in the Battles of Neuve Chapelle, St. Eloi, Hill 60, Ypres, Loos, the Somme, the Ancre, Arras, Messines, Lens and Cambrai, and taking part in the British Advance entered Mons at dawn on November 11th, 1918. He was demobilised in January 1919, and holds the 1914 Star, and the General Service and Victory Medals.
49, Gonsalva Road, Wandsworth Road, S.W.8.   Z4062

SCRIVENER, C., Private, 4th Royal Fusiliers.

He was serving in India at the outbreak of war, and sailing for France in January 1915, fought in the Battle of Ypres, and was wounded and invalided home. Returning to the Field in September of the same year he was in action in the Battle of Loos, and was severely wounded. Sent home for hospital treatment he was subsequently discharged as medically unfit for further service in October 1918, and holds the 1914–15 Star, and the General Service and Victory Medals.
46, Russell Street, Battersea, S.W.11.   Z2924A

SCRIVENER, W. G., Leading Seaman, R.N.

He was serving in H.M.S. "Yarmouth" when war broke out and was engaged on important duties in that vessel throughout the course of hostilities. His ship was sent to German East Africa, and in co-operation with the land forces took part in many engagements, and was also employed in patrolling the African Coast. He holds the 1914–15 Star, and the General Service and Victory Medals, and in 1920 was still serving.
46, Russell Street, Battersea, S.W.11.   Z2924B

SCRIVENER, W. T., Special War Worker.

Ineligible for military service owing to medical unfitness, he volunteered for work of National importance, and was employed by Messrs. Gwynne, Hammersmith, throughout the war, on the manufacture of munitions. During his period of service he carried out his duties in a capable and efficient manner.
3, Hawksmoor Street, Hammersmith, W.6.   14276

SCROGGINS, T. A., Private, 6th Queen's Own (Royal West Kent Regiment).

He volunteered in July 1915, and in the same year proceeded to the Western Front, where he was in action in several engagements in the Ypres salient. Severely wounded in the Battle of Cambrai he was admitted to hospital at Rouen, and later evacuated to England. After convalescence he was discharged as medically unfit for further service in June 1918, and holds the 1914–15 Star, and the General Service and Victory Medals.
30, Cobbett Street, Dorset Road, S.W.8.   Z4063

SCUTT, E. J., Private, 1st Sussex Regiment.
Mobilised in August 1914, he was almost immediately drafted to France and took part in heavy fighting in the Retreat from Mons, and was wounded. He was afterwards in action in the Battles of Neuve Chapelle, Loos, the Somme, and was again wounded in 1916. On recovery he returned to the Field and fought in several engagements and in the German Offensive and subsequent Allied Advance of 1918, and was wounded a third time. He was sent to England and subsequently demobilised in December 1918, and holds the Mons Star, and the General Service and Victory Medals.
2, Fryfar's Farm, Stedham.   Z6335

SEARCH, A. S., Rifleman, 21st London Regiment (1st Surrey Rifles).
He joined in 1917, and in the following year was sent to France and was in action on the Somme. He was also engaged in the Retreat and Advance of 1918. After the Armistice he proceeded with the Army of Occupation to Germany where he served until he was demobilised in February 1919, holding the General Service and Victory Medals.
14, Huguenot Road, Peckham, S.E.15.   Z6090A

SEARCH, H. G., Sergt., 21st London Regiment (1st Surrey Rifles).
He volunteered in April 1915, and was sent to France in the same year and was in action at Loos, Vimy Ridge, the Somme, the Ancre, Messines, Ypres, and Cambrai. He also took part in the Retreat and Advance of 1918. He returned home and was demobilised in February 1919, and holds the 1914-15 Star, and the General Service and Victory Medals.
14, Huguenot Road, Peckham, S.E.15.   Z6090C

SEARCH, H. J., Private, 24th Queen's (Royal West Surrey Regiment.
He volunteered in September 1914, and in the following year was sent to France, where he took part in the fighting at Ypres, Festubert, and Loos, where he was wounded and invalided home. Later he unfortunately died of his injuries in hospital at Chichester in December 1915. He was entitled to the 1914-15, Star, and the General Service and Victory Medals.
"Thinking that remembrance, though unspoken, may reach him where he sleeps."
14, Huguenot Road, Peckham, S.E.15.   Z6090B

SEARLE, A. J., Sergt., R.A.M.C.
He volunteered in August 1914, and in the following year was sent to the Dardanelles, where he served until the Evacuation of Gallipoli. He then proceeded to German East Africa, where he was engaged on important hospital duties until April 1919, when he returned home and was demobilised, holding the 1914-15 Star, and the General Service and Victory Medals.
14, Odell Street, Camberwell, S.E.5.   Z5664B

SEARLE, H., Pte., Royal Sussex Regt. (Labour Batt.)
He volunteered in August 1915, and was sent to France in the same year. He was engaged on the Ypres, Arras, and Somme fronts in repairing roads, and other important duties until November 1919, when he returned home and was demobilised, holding the 1914-15 Star, and the General Service and Victory Medals.
12, Mayall Road, Herne Hill, S.E.24.   Z4064

SEARLE, J., Private, Welch Regiment.
He joined in June 1916, and was sent to Salonika in the same year, and took part in numerous engagements against the Austro-Bulgarian Forces. After the Armistice he returned home and was demobilised in June 1919, holding the General Service and Victory Medals.
48, Keenbury Street, Camberwell, S.E.5.   Z6332

SEARLE, J. F., Private, R.A.S.C.
He volunteered in November 1915, and in the following month was sent to France. He was engaged in the transport of ammunition and supplies to the various fronts including those of Ypres, the Somme, and Arras. He also took part in the Retreat and Advance of 1918. He was demobilised in May 1919, and holds the 1914-15 Star, and the General Service and Victory Medals.
14, Odell Street, Camberwell, S.E.5.   Z5664A

SEARLE, J. J. (D.C.M.), Sergt., 3rd and 4th Rifle Brigade.
He was serving at the outbreak of war, and was immediately afterwards sent to France, and was in action at Mons, St. Eloi, Hill 60, Ypres, Albert, Vimy Ridge, the Somme, Arras, Bullecourt, and in many other engagements, and was wounded and invalided home. He was awarded the Distinguished Conduct Medal for conspicuous gallantry in the Field, and also holds the Mons Star, and the General Service and Victory Medals. He was discharged in March 1918 as medically unfit for further service.
51, East Surrey Grove, Peckham, S.E.15.   Z5281

SEARS, C., L/Corporal, 8th Border Regiment.
He volunteered in November 1915, and at first served in the Yeomanry, but later was posted to the Border Regiment with which he was engaged on important duties until June 1917, when he was sent to the Western Front, where he took part in the fighting at Messines, Ypres, Lens, and Cambrai, the Somme, the Aisne, and the Marne. He also fought in many other engagements during the Retreat and Advance of 1918, and was twice wounded. He was demobilised in February 1919, and holds the General Service and Victory Medals.
78, Geneva Road, Brixton, S.W.9.   Z3094B

SEARS, E., Private, Tank Corps.
He joined in 1917 after having been previously rejected and was sent to France in the following year. He took part in numerous engagements during the Retreat and Advance of 1918, and after the cessation of hostilities returned home, and was demobilised in October 1919, holding the General Service and Victory Medals.
23, Cornwell Road, Peckham, S.E.15.   Z6580

SEATON, J. W., Corporal, 18th London Regiment (London Irish Rifles).
He joined in June 1917, and in the same year was sent to France, where he took part in numerous engagements including that at Beaumont-Hamel. He also served in the Retreat and Advance of 1918. He was demobilised in April 1919, and holds the General Service and Victory Medals.
102, Wadhurst Road, New Road, Battersea Park Road, S.W.8.   Z4065A

SEATON, L. A. (Miss), Special War Worker.
This lady was engaged at the Church Place, Piccadilly Post Office, on important duties. She carried out her work in a most efficient manner and rendered valuable services during the war.   Z4065D
102, Wadhurst Road, New Road, Battersea Park Road, S.W. 8

SEATON, W. H., Private, R.A.S.C.
He volunteered in March 1915, and in the same year was sent to France, and was engaged on important duties in checking stores. Later, owing to ill-health, he was invalided home, but on his recovery returned to France. He was again taken ill however, and was sent to hospital in England, and discharged as medically unfit for further service in May 1918, holding the 1914-15 Star, and the General Service and Victory Medals.
102, Wadhurst Road, Battersea Park Road, S.W.8. Z4065B

SEATON, W. H., Private, 23rd London Regiment.
He volunteered in August 1914, and in the same year was drafted to France and took part in the fighting at Ypres and Loos, where he was wounded. He was invalided home and unfortunately died of his injuries in Dublin in September 1915, and was buried at Nunhead. He was entitled to the 1914-15 Star, and the General Service and Victory Medals.
"Whilst we remember the sacrifice is not in vain."
102, Wadhurst Road, Battersea, S.W.8.   Z4065

SECKER, A. W., Rifleman, Rifle Brigade.
He joined in May 1916, and proceeded to France in September of the same year. He took part in numerous engagements, including those at Ypres and Passchendaele, and was wounded and invalided home. On his recovery he returned to France and served in the Retreat of 1918, during which he was taken prisoner, and sent to Munster Prison Camp. On his release he returned home and was demobilised in March 1919, and holds the General Service and Victory Medals.
23, Brisbane Street, Camberwell, S.E.5.   Z3983B

SECKER, C. E., Private, Bedfordshire Regiment.
He joined in July 1916, and served in the East Surrey Regiment until the following year, when he was transferred to the Bedfordshire Regiment, and was engaged on important duties at various stations with his unit. He rendered valuable services, but was not successful in obtaining his transfer overseas before the cessation of hostilities. He was demobilised in October 1919.
23, Brisbane Street, Camberwell, S.E.5.   Z3983A

SEDGLEY, E. F., Cpl., Royal Horse Guards (M.G.C.)
He volunteered in October 1914, and in the following year was sent to the Western Front, where he was in action at St. Eloi, Loos and Vermelles. He was then sent home for machine gun training, after which he returned to France in May 1917, and was engaged at Ypres, Havrincourt, Epéhy, Cambrai, Le Cateau, and in many other engagements. He was demobilised in May 1919, and holds the 1914-15 Star, and the General Service and Victory Medals.
17, Albert Road, Peckham, S.E.15.   Z6091

SEELEY, A. W., Driver, R.F.A.
He was mobilised in August 1914, and was immediately afterwards sent to France. He was in action at Mons, the Marne, the Aisne, Neuve Chapelle, Givenchy, Hill 60, Festubert, Loos, the Somme, Passchendaele, and in many other engagements. He also took part in the Retreat and Advance of 1918. He was demobilised in April 1919, and holds the Mons Star, and the General Service and Victory Medals.
26, Fenwick Place, Stockwell, S.W.9.   Z1217B

SEELY, W., Gunner, R.F.A.

He volunteered in 1914, and in the following year was sent to France, where he took part in numerous engagements, including those at Ypres, Loos, Armentières, the Somme, Beaumont-Hamel, Lens, where he was wounded and suffered the loss of an eye. He was invalided home and discharged in 1918, as medically unfit for further service, and holds the 1914-15 Star, and the General Service and Victory Medals.
4, Milford Street, Wandsworth Road, S.W.8.　　Z4066

SEIDLER, H. A., L/Cpl., King's Royal Rifle Corps.

He joined in 1916, and in the following year was sent to France, and was engaged in the Ypres sector. He afterwards proceeded to Italy, where he was in action on the Piave. He next returned to France and served in the Retreat and Advance of 1918, and was taken prisoner at Bapaume in August of that year. On his release he returned home and was demobilised in 1919, and holds the General Service and Victory Medals.
64, Arthur Road, Brixton Road, S.W.9.　　Z4534

SELBY, F., Private, Royal Fusiliers.

He volunteered in June 1915, and in the following year was drafted to France, where he was in action at St. Eloi, Albert, Loos, the Somme, Arras, Beaumont-Hamel, Bullecourt, Lens, and in many other engagements. He also took part in the Retreat and Advance of 1918. He was demobilised in April 1919, and holds the General Service and Victory Medals.
3, St. Alphonsus Road, Clapham, S.W.4.　　Z4067

SELF, E. J., Private, R.M.L.I.

He volunteered in August 1914, and was engaged with the Royal Naval Division at Antwerp. Later returning to England he was drafted to H.M.S. "Hermes" being on board her when she was torpedoed at end of October 1914. Fortunately he was saved and afterwards proceeded to German East Africa in January 1915, and took part in various engagements, including the sinking of the German cruiser "Konigsberg." He remained in this theatre of war until 1916, when owing to ill-health he was invalided to England and discharged in June of that year. He holds the 1914 Star, and he General Service and Victory Medals.
57, Vestry Road, Camberwell, S.E.5.　　Z6545

SELF, C., Private, R.A.M.C.

He volunteered in December 1915, and was sent to France in the following year. He went through heavy fighting at Loos, and on the Somme, and was severely wounded, and suffered the amputation of his left leg. He was discharged as physically unfit for further service in November 1918, and holds the General Service and Victory Medals.
64, Southville, Wandsworth Road, S.W.8.　　Z3284C

SELLS, J. J. T., Private, East Surrey Regiment.

He volunteered in May 1915, and after his training was sent to Salonika in 1917, and was in action on the Doiran front, and in various other sectors. Later he was invalided to hospital at Malta with malaria, and later was drafted to France, where he was still serving in 1920. He holds the General Service and Victory Medals.
53, Thorncroft Road, South Lambeth, S.W.8.　　Z4068

SELLWOOD, W. C., L/Corporal, Queen's Own (Royal West Kent Regiment).

He volunteered in February 1915, and was sent to Mesopotamia in that year. He took an active part in the operations for the Relief of Kut. and was wounded at Es Sinn and invalided to the Base at Basra, and later to England. He was discharged in July 1917, and holds the 1914-15 Star, and the General Service and Victory Medals.
23, Rollo Street, Battersea, S.W.11.　　Z4069

SELWOOD, A. (Miss), Special War Worker.

Soon after the outbreak of war this lady accepted an important position with the Reliance Company, Sheen. Here she was engaged on work of a most responsible nature in connection with the manufacture of hand and rifle grenades, and afterwards on 5.9 inch shells. Later, meeting with a serious accident, she was, to her great regret, unable to continue to serve her Country, and was obliged to relinquish her appointment. During the whole of her service she carried out her arduous duties in a most exemplary manner, which was worthy of the highest praise.
59, Winstead Street, Battersea, S.W.11.　　Z4070

SENFT, C., Driver, R.G.A.

He volunteered in June 1915, and was sent to France in the following March, and fought in numerous engagements until the end of 1916, when he was gassed and was sent to hospital in England. On recovery he was engaged on important duties until demobilised in February 1919. He holds the General Service and Victory Medals.
22, Howbury Road, Nunhead, S.E.15.　　Z6586

SENFT, F. W., Private, Duke of Cornwall's Light Infantry.

He joined in November 1916, and proceeded to France in the following February. After fighting in various engagements he was unfortunately killed in action at Monchy on May 8th, 1917. Previous to joining the Duke of Cornwall's Light Infantry he served with the Middlesex Regiment, but was discharged as under age. He was entitled to the General Service and Victory Medals.
"His life for his Country."
27, Ledbury Street, Peckham, S.E.15.　　Z6562

SERVANT, A., Gunner, R.F.A.

He joined in September 1917, and was sent to Ireland for training. He was unable to obtain his transfer to a theatre of war, owing to being medically unfit for duty abroad, but nevertheless did valuable service until he was demobilised in November 1919.　19, Upper Hall Street, Peckham, S.E.15.　　Z6579

SERVANT, H. F., L/Corporal, 7th London Regt.

He volunteered in September 1914, and was sent to France in the following March, and took an active part in many engagements, including those at Givenchy, Festubert and Loos. Unhappily he was killed in action at Loos on September 25th, 1915, and was entitled to the 1914-15 Star, and the General Service and Victory Medals.
"His memory is cherished with pride."
30, Gloucester Road, Peckham, S.E.15.　　Z5837

SETTERS, A., Driver, R.G.A.

He joined in 1916, and was drafted to France in 1917. He fought in many engagements, including those on the Somme, and at Ypres, Arras, and Cambrai, and was also in the Retreat and Advance of 1918. He remained in France until he was demobilised in September 1919, and holds the General Service and Victory Medals.
54, Arthur Road, Brixton Road, S.W.9.　　Z4073

SEWELL, G. A., Private, Royal Sussex and 2nd Middlesex Regiments.

He joined in August 1917, and after his training proceeded to France, where he took part in the Battle of Cambrai, and in the Retreat and Advance of 1918. After the cessation of hostilities he proceeded to Egypt, where he was still serving in 1920. He holds the General Service and Victory Medals.
85, Edmunds Street, Camberwell, S.E.5.　　Z4071

SEWELL, S. G., Gunner, R.G.A.

He volunteered in November 1915, and w s sent to France in May 1917. He fought in many actions, including those at Messines, Ypres, Passchendaele and Cambrai, and also rendered valuable service during the fighting in the Retreat and Advance of 1918. He returned to England and was demobilised in May 1919, holding the General Service and Victory Medals.
23, Gideon Road, Battersea, S.W.11.　　Z4072

SEWELL, W. S. H., Leading Aircraftsman, R.A.F. (late R.F.C.)

He joined in 1917, and proceeded to France in 1918. He took an active part in the fighting during the Retreat and Advance of that year, and after the Armistice served with the Army of Occupation in Germany until he was demobilised in 1920. He holds the General Service and Victory Medals.
28, Bagshot Street, Walworth, S.E.17.　　Z4074

SEXTON, A. J., Shoeing Smith, 4th (Queen's Own) and 8th (Royal Irish) Hussars.

He was mobilised in August 1914, and was sent to France. He took part in the heavy fighting on the Marne, and the Aisne, and at Ypres, Loos, St. Eloi, Lens, Delville Wood and St. Quentin. He was severely gassed, and after much valuable service was sent to England and discharged in June 1917. He had previously taken part in the South African War, and holds the Queen's and King's South African Medals, and the General Service and Victory Medals.
76, Ingleton Street, Stockwell, S.W.9.　　Z1669B

SEYMOUR, R. T. B., Lieutenant, R.G.A.

He joined as a Gunner in 1916, and received his Commission before going to France. He was gassed during the fighting at Proville and was sent to England. On his recovery he was employed on important duties at Dover until he was demobilised in 1919, holding the General Service and Victory Medals.
26, Tennyson Street, Wandsworth Road, S.W.8.　　Z4075

SHACKEL, G. T. (M.M.), Corporal, R.E.

Having joined the Territorial Force in January 1912, he was mobilised and proceeded overseas at the outbreak of war, and served in many important engagements, including those at St. Eloi, Ypres, Festubert, Vermelles, and Vimy Ridge. He was taken prisoner in the second Battle of the Somme on March 23rd, 1918, and held in captivity in Germany until the Armistice, when he was repatriated and subsequently demobilised in April 1919. He was awarded the Military Medal for conspicuous bravery and devotion to duty in the Field, and holds in addition the 1914 Star, and the General Service and Victory Medals, and the Territorial Efficiency Medal.　27, Stainsford Road, Battersea, S.W.11.　　Z4076

SHADBOLT, H. E., Rifleman, 16th London Regt. (Queen's Westminster Rifles).

He joined in October 1916, and in the following March was drafted to France, and was wounded in action at Arras, and invalided to hospital at Etaples. After serving for a short time at the Base he was sent up to the firing line and fought at Ypres and Cambrai. He was demobilised in October 1919, and holds the General Service and Victory Medals.
83, Wickersley Road, Battersea, S.W.11. Z4077

SHAMBLER, H., Gunner, R.F.A.

He volunteered in 1915, and in the same year was drafted to France, where he took part in numerous engagements. He did good work as a Gunner until the cessation of hostilities, after which he returned to England, and in May 1919, was demobilised, holding the 1914-15 Star, and the General Service and Victory Medals.
11, Brooklands Road, Wandsworth Road, S.W.8. Z4078

SHANKS, W. J., Private, R.A.S.C.

He rejoined in November 1914, having previously served in the South African War, and a week later proceeded to the Western Front. During his service in France he was present at the Battles of Neuve Chapelle, Ypres, Loos, the Somme, Arras, and in many subsequent engagements in the Retreat and Advance of 1918. After the Armistice he proceeded to Brussels, where he served until demobilised in April 1919. He holds the Queen's South African Medal, the 1914 Star, and the General Service and Victory Medals.
35, Urswicke Road, Battersea, S.W.11. Z4079

SHAPLEY, C., Rifleman, Rifle Brigade.

He joined in February 1916, and after six months' training was drafted to France. Whilst overseas he fought in the Battle of Arras, and gave his life for his King and Country in April 1917. He was entitled to the General Service and Victory Medals.
" Whilst we remember, the sacrifice is not in vain."
11, Park Grove, Battersea, S.W.11. Z4080A

SHAPLEY, J., Private, Royal Scots.

He volunteered in December 1915, and in the same year was drafted to France, where he served for three years. Whilst overseas he fought at Ypres, Albert, Ploegsteert and Béthune, and was wounded and invalided home to hospital. Later he served with the Relief Force in Russia, until returning to England. He was demobilised in June 1919, and holds the 1914-15 Star, and the General Service and Victory Medals.
11, Park Grove, Battersea, S.W.11. Z4080B

SHAPLEY, J., Rifleman, King's Royal Rifle Corps.

He volunteered in February 1915, and after his training was drafted to France. During his service overseas he fought in the Battle of the Somme, and at Arras, Vimy Ridge and Bullecourt. He gave his life for the freedom of England in August 1918, and was entitled to the 1914-15 Star, and the General Service and Victory Medals.
"' Great deeds cannot die."
11, Park Grove, Battersea, S.W.11. Z4080C

SHARGOOL, J. H., Private, 23rd Middlesex Regt.

He joined in February 1916, and in the same year was drafted to France. During his service overseas he fought in various engagements in the Ypres, Somme, and Arras sectors, and later contracting trench fever was invalided home to hospital. On recovery he rejoined his unit in France in January 1918, and took part in the operations during the Retreat and Advance of that year. He was demobilised in February 1919, and holds the General Service and Victory Medals.
78, Moncrieff Street, Peckham, S.E. 15. Z5665

SHARMAN, S. G., Private, R.A.S.C. (M.T.)

He volunteered in 1914, and after his training served at various stations on important duties as a motor transport driver. In 1916, he was drafted to Ireland, during the risings of that year. He rendered valuable services throughout the war, but was not successful in securing a transfer overseas before the cessation of hostilities, and was demobilised in 1919.
65, Kimberley Road, Peckham, S.E.15. Z6450

SHARP, A. H., Private, 7th Queen's (Royal West Surrey Regiment).

He volunteered in September 1914, and on the completion of his training was drafted to France in June 1917. He was wounded at St. Eloi in the following August, and was invalided home to hospital, but rejoined his unit in France in February 1918. He then took part in the engagements on the Somme, and at Albert, Villers-Bretonneux, and the subsequent operations until the Armistice. He was demobilised in the following March, and holds the General Service and Victory Medals.
35D, Lewis Trust Buildings, Warner Road, Camberwell, S.E.5. Z6087

SHARP, A. A., Gunner, R.F.A.

He volunteered in October 1915, and in the following year was sent to the Eastern Front, where he saw much varied service in Egypt, Salonika, and Macedonia. Later he contracted malaria, and was invalided home and in April 1917 was drafted to France. Whilst in this theatre of war he fought at Ypres and Monchy, and in the defence of Amiens in the Retreat of 1918. He did excellent work as a Gunner throughout his service, and was demobilised in July 1919. He holds the General Service and Victory Medals.
166, South Street, Walworth, S.E.17. Z4081B

SHARP, F. E., Private, 1st London Regiment (Royal Fusiliers).

He volunteered in November 1914, and in the following February was drafted overseas. During his service in France he fought in many engagements, including those at Neuve Chapelle, Hill 60, (where he was wounded), Loos, Vimy Ridge, the Somme, Beaumont-Hamel, (where he was again wounded), Arras, Bullecourt, Messines, Lens and Cambrai, and was severely gassed near Bapaume. He was invalided to England, and after his recovery was demobilised in March 1919. He holds the 1914-15 Star, and the General Service and Victory Medals.
43, Charleston Street, Walworth, S.E.17. Z2872B

SHARP, G., Corporal, 3rd Grenadier Guards.

A serving soldier since 1911, he was stationed at Chelsea Barracks until drafted overseas in 1915. He then took part in the fierce fighting at Loos, and was severely wounded and invalided to hospital at Rouen, where later he succumbed to his injuries. He was entitled to the 1914-15 Star, and the General Service and Victory Medals.
" His life for his Country, his soul to God."
4, Milford Street, Wandsworth Road, S.W.8. Z4082

SHARP, W., Driver, R.F.A.

He volunteered in May 1915, and in August of the same year was drafted to France. During his service overseas he was in action at Ypres, Loos, Albert, the Somme, Arras and Vimy Ridge. In September 1917, he was invalided home owing to ill-health, and was in hospital for two years. He was discharged in November 1919, and holds the 1914-15 Star, and the General Service and Victory Medals.
38, Knowsley Road, Battersea, S.W.11. Z408

SHARP, W. W., Corporal, 1st Royal Fusiliers.

He was serving at the outbreak of hostilities, and was almost immediately drafted to France and took part in the Retreat from Mons. He also was in action in the Battles of the Marne, and the Aisne, and at Armentières, where he was severely wounded. He was sent home to hospital, and after undergoing two years' medical treatment was invalided out of the Service in October 1916, He holds the Mons Star, and the General Service and Victory Medals.
166, South Street, Walworth, S.E.17. Z4081A

SHARPE, F. (M.M.), Private, 7th Queen's (Royal West Surrey Regiment).

He volunteered in November 1914, and in June of the following year was drafted to France. During his service overseas he fought on the Somme, and at Arras, Vimy Ridge, Messines, Ypres, Passchendaele, Lens and Cambrai, and was severely wounded at Villiers-Bretonneux and invalided home to hospital. He was awarded the Military Medal for his conspicuous gallantry and devotion to duty in carrying despatches under heavy shell fire during the fighting at Thiépval, and holds in addition the 1914-15 Star, and the General Service and Victory Medals. He was demobilised in March 1919.
22, Cornbury Street, Walworth, S.E.17. Z4086C

SHARPE, G. W., C.S.M., R.A.S.C. (H.T.)

He volunteered in August 1914, and in the same year was drafted to France. Whilst in this theatre of war he served in various engagements, including those at La Bassée, Ypres and Loos. He was invalided home to hospital with illness, and after convalescence was sent to Egypt, where he was engaged with the British Forces under General Allenby in the Advance through Palestine. He was present at the Battles of Gaza, Beersheba, and Jericho and the fall of Jerusalem, and in numerous subsequent engagements until the cessation of hostilities. In April 1919 he was demobilised, after his return to England, and holds the 1914 Star, and the General Service and Victory Medals.
60, Park Place, Clapham, S.W.4. Z4085

SHARPE, H., Private, 7th Queen's (Royal West Surrey Regiment).

He volunteered in August 1914, and in July of the following year was drafted to France. During his service overseas he fought in various engagements and was severely wounded in the Battle of the Somme in July 1916. He was invalided home to hospital, and after prolonged treatment died as a result of his injuries in August 1917. He was entitled to the 1914-15 Star, and the General Service and Victory Medals.
" A costly sacrifice upon the altar of freedom."
22, Cornbury Street, Walworth, S.E.17. Z4086B

SHARPE, R. H., Guardsman, Scots Guards.
A serving soldier since August 1899, he was almost immediately drafted to France at the outbreak of hostilities, and took part in the Retreat from Mons. He also served in the Battles of the Aisne, the Marne, Loos and the Somme, and in many subsequent engagements. He gave his life for his King and Country on November 20th, 1917, and was entitled to the Mons Star, and the General Service and Victory Medals.
"A valiant soldier, with undaunted heart he breasted Life's last hill."
24, Pitcairn Street, Wandsworth Road, S.W.8.
Z4084

SHARPE, T., Rifleman, King's Royal Rifle Corps.
He joined in May 1918, and after his training served at various stations on important duties with his unit. He was chiefly engaged in guarding railways and rendered valuable services, but owing to the cessation of hostilities was unable to proceed overseas. He was demobilised in November 1919.
22, Cornbury Street, Walworth, S.E.17.
Z4086D

SHARPE, T. A., Private, R.A.S.C. (M.T.)
He volunteered in September 1914, and was almost immediately drafted to France where he served in the Battles of the Marne, the Aisne, St. Eloi, Hill 60, and Loos. He was engaged in conveying food and ammunition up to the front line trenches, throughout his service which lasted until the cessation of hostilities. In February 1919, he was demobilised and holds the 1914-15 Star, and the General Service and Victory Medals.
54, Baker Street, Brixton Road, S.W.9.
Z5283

SHARPE, W., Sergt., 22nd London Regiment (The Queen's).
He was mobilised at the outbreak of war and in March of the following year was drafted overseas, and whilst in France fought in the Battles of St. Eloi, Loos, Vimy Ridge, and the Somme, where he was wounded. He was invalided home to hospital, and after his recovery proceeded to Salonika in February 1917. In this theatre of war he served in the engagements on the Doiran and Vardar fronts until the conclusion of hostilities. He returned home and was demobilised in April 1919, and holds the 1914-15 Star, and the General Service and Victory Medals.
22, Cornbury Street, Walworth, S.E.17.
Z4086A

SHAW, A., Rifleman, 18th London Regt. (London Irish Rifles).
He joined in September 1916, and was drafted to France in the same year. He took part in the Battles of the Somme, Arras, Ypres and Cambrai, and also fought in the Retreat, during which his Corps was highly commended for its efficiency. He fell fighting at Albert on 1st September 1918, and was entitled to the General Service and Victory Medals.
"His memory is cherished with pride."
11, Thurlow Street, Walworth, S.E.17.
Z4090

SHAW, E., Sergt., R.E.
He volunteered in September 1915, and in the same year was drafted to France. Here he served with the Expeditionary Force Canteens at Havre and Boulogne until 1917, when he was transferred to Italy, and was stationed at Taranto on important duties in connection with the transport of stores. He returned to England, and was demobilised in September 1919, holding the 1914-15 Star, and the General Service and Victory Medals.
24, Venn Street, Clapham, S.W.4.
Z4087

SHAW, S. E., Private, 2nd London Regiment (Royal Fusiliers).
He volunteered in September 1914, and in the following December was drafted to Malta, where he served on important duties. Later he contracted malaria and was invalided home, and in February 1919 was discharged. He holds the Territorial Force Medal, and the General Service Medals.
139, Cator Street, Peckham, S.E.15.
Z6341

SHAW, W., Gunner, R.F.A. and Pte., Labour Corps.
He joined in January 1916, and later in the same year was drafted to France, where he was in action at Cambrai and numerous other engagements. Returning to England after the cessation of hostilities he was demobilised in February 1919, holding the General Service and Victory Medals.
39, Thorton Street, Stockwell, S.W.9.
Z2324B

SHEAN, A., Private, Royal Fusiliers.
Joining in November 1916, he was drafted to France in the following year. He took part in numerous engagements of importance, including that at Ypres, where he was wounded. He was invalided home, and after a period in hospital was discharged as medically unfit for further service in August 1918. He holds the General Service and Victory Medals.
12, Barkworth Road, Rotherhithe, S.E.16.
Z6733B

SHEAN, G., Armourer's Crew, R.N., H.M.S. "Himalaya."
He volunteered in August 1915, and for a time served with the Grand Fleet in the North Sea on patrol duties. He later proceeded to German East Africa for convoy duty until fighting ceased. He returned home in 1918, and was demobilised in February of the following year, holding the 1914-15 Star, and the General Service and Victory Medals.
12, Barkworth Road, Rotherhithe, S.E.16.
Z6733A

SHEARMUR, F. G., Rifleman, King's Royal Rifle Corps.
He volunteered in June 1915, and in the following January was sent to France, where he fought in the Battles of Ypres, Arras, and the Somme. During his service overseas he was wounded three times, and on each occasion returned to England for medical treatment. Later, whilst in action, he made the supreme sacrifice being killed at the Battle of Le Cateau on October 1918. He was entitled to the General Service and Victory Medals.
"His life for his Country."
93, Geneva Road, Brixton, S.W.9.
Z4012D

SHEARS, G., Private, Royal Fusiliers.
He joined in 1917, and on completion of his training served with his unit in the Eastern Counties on important duties in connection with coast defence. He rendered valuable services, but was unsuccessful in obtaining his transfer overseas, owing to his medical unfitness, and was demobilised in February 1919.
283, East Street, Walworth, S.E.17.
Z4091

SHEEHAN, F. C., Private, R.A.S.C. (M.T.)
He volunteered in November 1915, and proceeding to Egypt in the following March, was engaged on important transport duties in the Battles of Jiffjaffa, Katia, Magdhaba and Gaza (I, II and III), and during the British Advance through Palestine. He was also present at the fall of Jerusalem, and on the conclusion of hostilities returned to England for demobilisation in June 1919. He holds the General Service and Victory Medals. He had previously served with the motor transports in German West Africa from May 1915, until September 1915, during the operations in that territory under General Botha.
126, Dalyell Road, Stockwell, S.W.9.
Z4092

SHEEHAN, J., Rifleman, 8th London Regiment (Post Office Rifles).
He joined in August 1918, on attaining military age, and on completing his training served at various prisoners' of war camps on guard and other important duties. He did good work, but was unable to secure his transfer overseas before the cessation of hostilities. He was demobilised in January 1919.
50, Stainforth Road, Battersea, S.W.11.
Z4093

SHEEHY, J., Corporal, R.A.S.C. (M.T.)
Volunteering in February 1915, he embarked for France in the same month, and was engaged on important duties transporting ammunition and supplies to the front lines. He rendered excellent services during the Battles of Loos, the Somme, Arras and throughout the Retreat and Advance of 1918, and also served at Marseilles on instructional duties. He was demobilised in February 1919, and holds the 1914-15 Star, and the General Service and Victory Medals.
19, Kinglake Street, Walworth, S.E.17.
Z4095

SHEEHY, J. A., A.B., Royal Navy.
He joined the Service in June 1915, and was posted to H.M.S. "Calypso," which vessel was in action in the Battle of Jutland and engaged on patrol and other important duties in the North and Baltic Seas. After the Armistice he was sent into Germany, and served with the Army of Occupation stationed on the Rhine. He was demobilised in February 1919, and holds the 1914-15 Star, and the General Service and Victory Medals. 19, Kinglake Street, Walworth, S.E.17. Z4094

SHEENHAM, T. G., A.B., Royal Navy.
He joined in June 1916, and during the war served with the Grand Fleet in the North Sea. His ship was engaged on patrol and other duties until blown up by a mine. He was rescued, but found to be suffering from shock was sent to Portsmouth Hospital, and on recovery served in a torpedo boat on escort duties in various waters. After the Armistice he was demobilised in January 1919, and holds the General Service and Victory Medals.
67, Daniel's Road, Peckham, S.E.15.
Z6619

SHEFFIELD, J., Corporal, Military Foot Police.
He had served throughout the South African war, and volunteering at the outbreak of hostilities proceeded to France in 1915, and served in various sectors. Transferred to Egypt late in 1915, he rendered excellent services stationed at Alexandria, Cairo, Port Said and Ismalia. Returning to England he was demobilised in July 1919, and holds the 1914-15 Star, and the General Service and Victory Medals, and also the Queen's South African Medal.
25, Sunwell Street, Peckham, S.E.15.
Z6503

SHELDRAKE, H. G., Private, 23rd London Regt. and Air Mechanic, R.A.F.

Volunteering in October 1914, he served at various stations until embarking for France in September 1916. He was in action at the Battles of the Somme, and Ypres, and was wounded. On recovery he rejoined his Regiment, and was engaged in heavy fighting in many parts of the line, and was again wounded at Ypres. Returning to England, he received medical treatment, and on recovery was transferred to the Royal Air Force, and did good work at various aerodromes until demobilised in October 1919. He holds the General Service and Victory Medals.

3, Sandmere Gardens, Clapham, S.W.4.   Z4096B

SHELDRAKE, V. T., Private, 6th Hampshire, Gloucestershire and 2nd Leicestershire Regts.

He joined in March 1916, and shortly afterwards embarked for India, where after six months' service he contracted malaria and, invalided home received hospital treatment. On recovery he was sent to France, and fought at St. Quentin, St. Eloi, Passchendaele, Messines, Bapaume, and was wounded at Ypres. Discharged from hospital, he rejoined his unit, and was in action throughout the Retreat and Advance of 1918, and proceeded into Germany with the Army of Occupation, and was stationed at Cologne. He was recommended for the Military Medal for conspicuous gallantry and devotion to duty at Cambrai. He was demobilised, but rejoined in 1920, was serving in India. He holds the General Service and Victory Medals.

3, Sandmere Gardens, Clapham, S.W.4.   Z4096A

SHELDRICK, H. G., Pte., Royal Fusiliers and M.G.C.

Volunteering in February 1916, and drafted to France in the following month he was in action in many parts of the line, and was wounded at Kemmel in November 1916. On recovery he rejoined his Regiment and fought at Dickebusch, and was again wounded in August 1917 in the Ypres salient. He returned to England, and after receiving hospital treatment returned to France, and was engaged in heavy fighting in the Retreat and Advance of 1918. He was demobilised in February 1919, and holds the General Service and Victory Medals.

16, Bonsor Street, Camberwell, S.E.5.   Z4535

SHEPHARD, A. F. (Miss), Special War Worker.

During the war this lady held an important appointment at the National Filling Factory, Hayes, where she carried out the arduous duties assigned to her in a manner worthy of the highest praise.

2, Silverlock Street, Rotherhithe, S.E.16.   Z6710

SHEPHARD, A. W., Rifleman, Rifle Brigade.

He volunteered in June 1915, and later in that year proceeded to France and fought in the Battles of Ypres, Arras, Albert, Passchendaele. He was taken prisoner on March 22nd, 1918, in the opening operations of the German Offensive, and held in captivity in Saxony. After the cessation of hostilities he was repatriated in accordance with the terms of the Armistice, and was demobilised in July 1919. He holds the 1914-15 Star, and the General Service and Victory Medals.

7, Alsace Street, Walworth, S.E.17.   Z4097

SHEPHARD, D. (Miss), Special War Worker.

From March until December 1915, this lady was engaged in making respirators at Messrs. Bell's, Old Kent Road. She later took up an important appointment at Woolwich Arsenal, where she did responsible work in connection with munitions, until December 1918. During the whole period of her service she carried out her arduous duties in a manner worthy of the highest praise.

2, Silverlock Street, Rotherhithe, S.E.16.   Z6711

SHEPHARD, S., Sapper, R.E.

Volunteering in May 1915, he embarked for Egypt in the following year, and was in action in many engagements, including those at Siwa, Rafa, Gaza, and in the fighting in the vicinity of Jerusalem and Jericho. Owing to ill-health he returned to England in October 1919, and after hospital treatment was discharged unfit for further service two months later. He holds the General Service and Victory Medals.

30, Mayall Road, Herne Hill, S.E.24.   Z4104

SHEPHERD, A. G., Air Mechanic, R.A.F.

He joined in November 1916, and proceeded to the Western Front in the following October. He did good work as a wireless operator in co-operation with the Artillery in many parts of the line. After the Armistice he was sent into Germany with the Army of Occupation, and was stationed on the Rhine. He returned to England, and was demobilised in November 1919, and holds the General Service and Victory Medals.

17, Acarthus Road, Lavender Hill, S.W.11.   Z4100

SHEPHERD, C., Driver, R.E.

Volunteering in April 1915, he was sent to the Western Front in the following year, and served in the Battles of Arras, Lens, Passchendaele, and the Somme. Transferred to Salonika in December 1916, he saw heavy fighting on the Doiran front, and proceeded to Egypt in July 1917. He was in action in many engagements, including those at Jericho, Amman, Biera and throughout the Advance into Syria. Returning to England he was demobilised in April 1919, and holds the General Service and Victory Medals.

34, Elliott Road, Stockwell, S.W.9.   Z5145

SHEPHERD, C. F., Private, 23rd London Regt.

Volunteering at the outbreak of war, he embarked for France in the March 1915, and fought at Festubert, Givenchy, Loos, the Somme, and Arras, and was wounded. Transferred to Salonika in 1917, he served in many parts of the line and was in action on the Doiran front. Later in 1917, he was sent to Egypt, and saw much fighting during the British Advance through Palestine, and was again wounded. He returned to England, and was demobilised in June 1919, and holds the 1914-15 Star, and the General Service and Victory Medals.

172, Robertson Street, Wandsworth Road, S.W.8.   Z4103A

SHEPHERD, C. J., Private, R.A.S.C. (M.T.)

He joined in July 1918, and completing his training, served at various stations on important duties with his unit. He was unsuccessful in obtaining his transfer overseas prior to the cessation of hostilities, but rendered valuable services until demobilised in February 1920.

125, Battersea Bridge Road, Battersea, S.W.11.   Z4102

SHEPHERD, F. T., Rifleman, 7th Rifle Brigade.

Joining in May 1917, he proceeded to the Western Front in the following August, and fought at Polygon Wood, Passchendaele, Le Cateau, and was taken prisoner at St. Quentin on March 21st, 1918, and held in captivity in Germany. In January 1919 he was repatriated, and subsequently demobilised in October 1919, holding the General Service and Victory Medals.

2, Flinton Street, Walworth, S.E.17.   Z4099

SHEPHERD, G. H., Private, Royal Fusiliers.

He volunteered in November 1915, and drafted to the Western Front in the following year, was in action in many engagements, including those at the Somme and Arras. He gave his life for the freedom of England at Cambrai on November 20th, 1917, and was entitled to the General Service and Victory Medals.

"Nobly striving,
He nobly fell that we might live."

172, Robertson Street, Wandsworth Road, S.W.8.   Z4103B

SHEPHERD, G. W., Private, M.G.C.

Volunteering in April 1915, he was stationed at various depôts until drafted to Egypt in January 1918. He served at Cairo, Ismalia and other places, engaged on important garrison duties, and later was in action in many engagements of note and was wounded in April 1918, near Jaffa. Returning to England he was demobilised in March 1919, and holds the General Service and Victory Medals.

116, Crimsworth Road, Wandsworth Road, S.W.8.   Z4101

SHEPHERD, J., Driver, R.F.A.

He volunteered in January 1916, and embarked for the Western Front in 1917. During his service overseas he fought in many engagements of note, and was engaged in heavy fighting throughout the German Offensive and subsequent Allied Advance of 1918, and was wounded. He was demobilised in December 1919, and holds the General Service and Victory Medals.

172, Robertson Street, Wandsworth Road, S.W.8.   Z4103C

SHEPHERD, J. W., Private, 9th Royal Fusiliers.

Volunteering in August 1914, he was sent to France in the following July, and was engaged in severe fighting at Loos, Albert, St. Eloi, Combles, Vimy Ridge, the Somme, Arras, Havrincourt and throughout the Retreat and Advance of 1918. He later served with the Army of Occupation in Germany, and was stationed at Bonn. He was demobilised in October 1919, and holds the 1914-15 Star, and the General Service and Victory Medals.

2, Flinton Street, Walworth, S.E.17.   Z4098

SHEPHERD, W., Gunner, R.G.A.

He joined in 1916, and embarking for the Western Front in the following year, served in many parts of the line, including the Dixmude sector. He was in action throughout the German Offensive, and subsequent Allied Advance, and returning to England after the cessation of hostilities, was demobilised in 1919. He holds the General Service and Victory Medals.

77, Ferndale Road, Clapham, S.W.4.   Z3730C

SHEPPARD, G., Private, 9th Worcestershire Regt.

He volunteered in October 1914, and sent to Mesopotamia in the following June, fought in many important engagements, including those at Amara and Kut. He was unfortunately killed in action in the second Battle of Kut, and was entitled to the 1914-15 Star, and the General Service and Victory Medals.

" Whilst we remember, the Sacrifice is not in vain."

101, Linden Grove, Nunhead, S.E.15.   Z6656A

SHEPPARD, R., Private, 1st Royal Fusiliers.

A serving soldier, he was drafted to the Western Front at the declaration of war, and fought in the Retreat from Mons, and in the Battles of Le Cateau, the Marne, La Bassée and Ypres. He was unfortunately killed in action in the Ypres salient on February 21st, 1915, and lies buried at Armentières. He was entitled to the Mons Star, and the General Service and Victory Medals.

" A costly sacrifice upon the altar of freedom."

101, Linden Grove, Nunhead, S.E.15.   Z6656B

SHEPPARD, S., L/Corporal, Queen's Own (Royal West Kent Regiment).

He volunteered in September 1915, and drafted to France a year later, was in action in various sectors, and fought in many important engagements. He died gloriously on the Field of Battle in Flanders in January 1917, and was entitled to the General Service and Victory Medals.

" He died the noblest death a man may die,
Fighting for God and right, and liberty."

87, Ilderton Road, Rotherhithe, S.E.16.   Z6689

SHEPPARD, W. W., Private, Queen's Own (Royal West Kent Regiment).

He volunteered in August 1914, and was sent to France in the following year. He was in action at the Battles of Ypres, the Somme, Cambrai, Messines, and was severely wounded at Arras. On recovery he rejoined his Battalion and fought in the Retreat and Advance of 1918. After the cessation of hostilities he proceeded into Germany with the Army of Occupation, and was stationed at Cologne. He was demobilised in April 1919, and holds the 1914-15 Star, and the General Service and Victory Medals.

202, Stewart's Road, Battersea Park Road, S.W.8.   Z4105

SHERRELL, W. J., Sergt., 23rd London Regiment and Hampshire Regiment.

He was mobilised at the outbreak of war, and proceeding in the following year to France, fought in the Battles of Neuve Chapelle, Ypres, the Somme, St. Eloi, St. Quentin, Hill 60, Festubert and Loos. Later he returned home as a time-expired man, but was afterwards recalled to the Colours, and transferred to the Hampshire Regiment, with which he served as a bombing and gas instructor. until he was discharged as medically unfit in April 1918, holding the 1914-15 Star, and the General Service and Victory Medals.

22, Stonhouse Street, Clapham, S.W.4.   Z4107

SHERWOOD, H., Private, R.A.S.C.

He was mobilised on the outbreak of war, and shortly afterwards proceeding to France, took part in the Retreat from Mons and the Battle of Ypres. He was also engaged on important duties in the Battles of the Somme, and in several engagements during the Retreat and Advance of 1918. Returning home after the Armistice, he was demobilised in March 1919, and holds the 1914-15 Star, and the General Service and Victory Medals.

19, Sterndale Road, Wandsworth Road, S.W.8.   Z3296A

SHEWARD, F., Sergt., R.F.A.

He volunteered in September 1914, and was drafted in the following May to France, serving with his Battery in the Battle of Arras, he was wounded, and during the Battle of the Somme in September 1916, was again severely wounded, suffering the amputation of his left arm. He was invalided home and discharged as medically unfit for further military service on March 21st, 1917, and holds the 1914-15 Star, and the General Service and Victory Medals.

33, Cronin Road, Peckham, S.E.15.   Z5666

SHILLUM, J. W., Gunner, R.F.A.

He volunteered in January 1915, and in the following year proceeded to the Western Front, where he saw much service in the Arras sector. In 1916, he was drafted to Salonika, and fought in the Offensive on the Doiran and across the Vardar, until sent to Egypt. Taking part in the British Advance through Palestine under General Allenby, he was in action in several engagements, including the Battles of Beersheba, Jericho, and was present at the fall of Jerusalem. Returning home he was demobilised in April 1919, and holds the General Service and Victory Medals.

95, Sussex Road, Coldharbour Lane, S.W.9.   Z4103

SHILSON, W. H., Special War Worker.

Being ineligible for service with the Colours, he obtained work of National importance at the Woolwich Arsenal, where he was engaged as an electrician. In this capacity he did valuable work during the war for a period extending over four years, and his services were greatly appreciated.

29, Mansion Street, Camberwell, S.E.5.   Z4109A

SHILSON, W. H. (Jun.), Pte., South Lancashire Regt.

He enlisted in July 1914, and at the outbreak of hostilities crossed to France, and fought in the Retreat from Mons, during which he was taken prisoner. During his captivity he was employed in felling timber, and was repatriated after the conclusion of hostilities. He was discharged through causes due to his service in November 1918, and holds the Mons Star, and the General Service and Victory Medals.

29, Mansion Street, Camberwell, S.E.5.   Z4109B

SHIRES, F., Private, R.M.L.I.

Volunteering in January 1915, he was drafted to the Dardanelles in the following August, and served on the Gallipoli Peninsula until the Evacuation. He returned to England and proceeded to India in 1916, where he served for a year. He was then posted to a ship which he joined at Ceylon, and sailed to Russia, his ship being engaged on special duties in the Caspian Sea. He was demobilised in November 1919, and holds the 1914-15 Star, and the General Service and Victory Medals.

5, Vaughan Road, Camberwell, S.E.5.   Z6445

SHIRLEY, J., Corporal, R.A.S.C.

He volunteered in April 1915, and was sent to the Western Front in the following September. Whilst overseas, he was engaged on duties of an important nature in the forward areas, and served in many important engagements, including the Somme Offensive and the Retreat and Advance of 1918. Later, owing to ill-health, he was invalided first to a hospital in Rouen and then to York, where he underwent medical treatment. He was demobilised in February 1919, and holds the 1914-15 Star, and the General Service and Victory Medals.

48, East Lane, Bermondsey, S.E.1.   Z27433

SHOEBRIDGE, H. F., Private, 3rd Queen's Own (Royal West Kent Regiment).

He volunteered in March 1915, and crossing to France in the following year fought at the Battles of Loos, Arras and the Somme, where he was severely wounded in 1916. Invalided home, he was for some time in hospital in Manchester, and on his recovery returned to the Western Front, and was in action until the termination of hostilities. He was demobilised in February 1919, and holds the General Service and Victory Medals.

50, Parkstone Road, Peckham, S.E.15.   Z6227.

SHOLL, E., Signalman, R.N.

Volunteering in January 1916, he was sent to Devonport for training, and was afterwards posted to H.M.S. " Malaya," in which ship he served in the North Sea and took part in the Battle of Heligoland. Later transferred to H.M.S. " Clive," he served aboard this ship in actions off the Belgian Coast, and against the Bolshevists. Owing to ill-health, he returned to shore, and was invalided out of the Service in September 1920. He holds the General Service and Victory Medals.

12, Rosemary Road, Peckham, S.E.15.   Z5494

SHORE, H. G., Sergt., 24th London Regt. (Queen's).

He was mobilised in August 1914, and was drafted to France in the following year. He was in action at Neuve Chapelle, Hill 60, Ypres, Festubert and Loos, and later on duty in the front lines was severely wounded. He unfortunately died of his wounds on December 29th, 1915, and was buried at Abbeville. He was entitled to the 1914-15 Star, and the General Service and Victory Medals.

" He died the noblest death a man may die,
Fighting for God, and right, and liberty."

92, Hall Road, Peckham, Rye, S.E.15.   Z6734

SHORT, H., Gunner, R.G.A.

He volunteered in May 1915, and after his training served on important duties until drafted to France in August 1917. Whilst overseas, he fought in many of the principal engagements, including those of Ypres, Arras, Bullecourt, Messines and Cambrai, and after the Retreat and Advance of 1918, in which he also took part, was sent with the Army of Occupation to Germany. He was demobilised in April 1919, and holds the General Service and Victory Medals.

9, Longhedge Street, Battersea, S.W.11.   Z4110

SHORTER, A. J., L/Corporal, 1st Suffolk Regiment.

He was mobilised at the outbreak of war, and crossing to France, took an active part in the early operations on that Front. Unfortunately, he was killed in action at the Battle of Ypres in 1915, and was entitled to the 1914 Star, and the General Service and Victory Medals.

" The path of duty was the way to glory."

80, Wilcox Road, Wandsworth, Road, S.W.8.   Z4111

SHORTLAND, J. R., Private, Buffs (East Kent Regiment) and Trooper, Derbyshire Dragoons.
He volunteered in September 1915, and at the conclusion of his training was engaged on duties of an important nature at various stations. Despite his efforts, he was unable to secure his transfer to a theatre of war, owing to ill-health, but nevertheless did valuable work until demobilised in March 1919.
71, St. George's Road, Peckham, S.E.15. Z5667

SHORTMAN, S. A., Private, 22nd London Regiment (Queen's).
He joined in August 1916, and proceeding to France three months later, was in action in several engagements, including the Battle of Cambrai. Later he was invalided home, owing to ill-health, but returned to the Western Front on recovery, and served in the concluding operations of the war. On his return to England he was invalided out of the Service in December 1918, and holds the General Service and Victory Medals.
29, Comyn Road, Battersea, S.W.11. Z4112

SHOULT, B. H., Private (Driver), R.A.S.C.
He volunteered in December 1915, and at the conclusion of his training served as a transport driver at various stations. Owing to ill-health, he was unable to obtain his transfer to a theatre of war, but rendered valuable services until May 1919, when he was demobilised.
18, Duffield Street, Battersea, S.W.11. Z4113

SHREEVE, E. T. S., Private, Queen's (Royal West Surrey Regiment) and Middlesex Regiment.
He joined in June 1916, and at the conclusion of his training was drafted to the Western Front. In the capacity of Lewis gunner, he took part in numerous important engagements, and was wounded on three occasions, at Arras and Ypres in 1917, and at Villers-Bretonneux in the following year. Owing to his last wound he was invalided home in April 1918, and after his recovery was demobilised in February 1919. He holds the General Service and Victory Medals.
63, Heyford Avenue, South Lambeth Road, S.W.8. Z4114–5A

SHREEVE, W., Telegraphist, Royal Navy.
He volunteered in January 1915, and after his training was posted to H.M. Submarine H.5, later being transferred to the V.4. Throughout the remaining period of hostilities, he was engaged with his vessel on important patrol duties in the North Sea, and did valuable work. He holds the 1914–15 Star, and the General Service and Victory Medals, and in 1920 was serving on H.M.S. H.27.
63, Heyford Avenue, South Lambeth Road, S.W.8.
Z4114–5B

SHRIMPTON, H. J., Private, Queen's Own (Royal West Kent Regiment).
He volunteered in May 1915, and in the following October was drafted to Egypt, subsequently taking part in engagements at Agayia, Sollum and Magdhaba. In February 1917 he was transferred to Salonika, where he fought on the Vardar and Doiran fronts. Towards the close of his service overseas he contracted malaria, and was for a time in hospital. He was demobilised in May 1919, and holds the 1914–15 Star, and the General Service and Victory Medals.
6, Latchmere Grove, Battersea, S.W.11. Z4117

SHRIMPTON, A. (M.S.M.), Q.M.S., 3rd Coldstream Guards.
Volunteering at the commencement of hostilities, he immediately crossed to France, and fought in the Retreat from Mons and the Battles of the Marne, the Aisne, Le Cateau and Ypres. He also served in many of the engagements which followed, including those at Neuve Chapelle, St. Eloi, Hill 60, Festubert, Loos, Albert, Vimy Ridge, Ploegsteert Wood and the Somme, where he was wounded. Invalided home, he was in hospital for five months, but on recovery returned to France, and was in action until the close of hostilities, when he proceeded with the Army of Occupation to Germany. In the course of his service he was mentioned in Despatches on two occasions, and awarded the Meritorious Service Medal for consistently good work in the Field. He holds in addition, the Mons Star, and the General Service and Victory Medals, and in 1920 was still serving. Z4116
6, Avondale Mansions, Bromell's Road, Clapham, S.W.4.

SHRIVES, A. E., Sapper, R.E.
He volunteered in April 1915, and after his training served on the Western Front for upwards of three years. During this period he was engaged on duties of an important nature in the forward areas, and was present during operations in many sectors, including that of the Somme. He was demobilised in February 1919, and holds the 1914–15 Star, and the General Service and Victory Medals.
8, Tidbury Street, Battersea Park Road, S.W.8. Z4118

SHRIVES, G., Private, 20th Hussars.
He joined on attaining military age in March 1917, and in the following December crossed to France. Whilst in this theatre of war he fought in many important engagements, including the Retreat and Advance of 1918, at the conclusion of which he proceeded with the Army of Occupation to Germany, where he served until October 1919. He was demobilised on his return to England in October 1919, and holds the General Service and Victory Medals.
205, Warham Street, Camberwell, S.E.5. Z6557B

SHRIVES, G., Rifleman, 21st London Regiment (1st Surrey Rifles).
Joining in May 1916, he was drafted to Salonika in the following January, and fought in various parts of the line. Six months later he was transferred to Egypt, and served in the Palestine campaign, during which he took part in the Battles of Gaza and the capture of Beersheba. In March 1918 he was wounded and taken prisoner, and on May 5th of the same year, died whilst in the hands of the enemy. He was entitled to the General Service and Victory Medals.
"Thinking that remembrance, though unspoken, may reach him where he sleeps."
205, Warham Street, Camberwell, S.E.5. Z6557A

SHRUBSOLE, A. E. J., Private, 1st London Regt. (Royal Fusiliers).
He enlisted in August 1913, and was serving in Malta when war broke out. Drafted to France in 1915, he fought in the Battles of Ypres and the Somme, and in several engagements during the German Offensive of 1918. Seriously wounded in an engagement in the Allied Retreat he was sent home and invalided out of the Service in March 1918. Re-enlisting in September 1919, he was discharged as medically unfit two months later, and holds the 1914–15 Star, and the General Service and Victory Medals.
5, Chalmers Street, Wandsworth Road, S.W.8. Z4119

SIBLEY, A. J., Corporal, 3rd London Regiment (Royal Fusiliers).
A Territorial, he was mobilised on the declaration of war, and drafted to Malta in 1914, served on garrison duties until his embarkation for France in the following year. He took part in heavy fighting at Thiépval, St. Quentin and on the Somme, and was killed in action at Arras in April 1916, and was entitled to the 1914–15 Star, and the General Service and Victory Medals.
"Steals on the air the distant triumph song."
9, Kingswood Road, Chiswick, W.4. T6299A

SIBLEY, C., Bombardier, R.G.A.
He joined in June 1916, and was sent overseas in the same year. Serving with his Battery in various sectors of the Western Front he fought in numerous engagements, including the Battles of the Somme, Arras, Ypres, and those during the Retreat and Advance of 1918, and was gassed. He returned to England for demobilisation in February 1919, and holds the General Service and Victory Medals.
44, Mansion Street, Camberwell, S.E.5. Z4122

SIBLEY, G. H., L/Corporal, 9th London Regiment (Queen Victoria's Rifles).
Volunteering in December 1915, he embarked for the Western Front in the following year, and served with his Battalion in the Battles of the Somme, Arras, Ypres, Passchendaele, Lens and Bullecourt. He was also in action during the German Offensive and subsequent Allied Advance of 1918, and was gassed and invalided home. After receiving hospital treatment he was discharged as medically unfit for further service in March 1919, and holds the General Service and Victory Medals.
37, Arthur Road, Brixton Road, S.W.9. Z4120

SIBLEY, J. J., Pte., 7th London Regt. and M.G.C.
Joining in July 1917, he served with his unit at home and transferred to the Machine Gun Corps, embarked for India in February 1918. In the course of his service overseas he was in action in several engagements on the North West Frontier of India. Returning home, he was demobilised in April 1919, and holds the General Service and Victory Medals, and the India General Service Medal (with clasp, Afghanistan, N.W. Frontier, 1919).
46, Pulross Road, Brixton Road, S.W.9. Z4123

SIBLEY, W., L/Corporal, Dorsetshire Regiment.
Volunteering in September 1914, he was sent to Gallipoli in November 1915, and served in operations until the Evacuation of the Peninsula, when he proceeded to France in January 1916. During his service on the Western Front he fought in the Battles of the Somme, Ypres, and was wounded at Combles in November 1916, and at Cambrai a year later. Returning home after the Armistice, he was demobilised in May 1919, and holds the 1914–15 Star, and the General Service and Victory Medals.
71, Latchmere Road, Battersea, S.W.11. Z4121

SIDDALL, L., Private, H.A.C.

He joined in June 1918, and after completing his training was engaged on important duties with his unit at home., He did valuable work but was unsuccessful in obtaining his transfer to a theatre of war before hostilities ceased, and was demobilised in October 1919.

76, Hatfield Road, Bedford Park, W.4.   7419B

SIDE, E. T., Rifleman, 9th King's Royal Rifle Corps.

Joining in October 1916, he proceeded overseas in the following year, and served on the Western Front. He was in heavy fighting in the Ypres sector, and also fought in the Battles of Arras, Bullecourt and Lens. He died gloriously on the field of battle at St. Quentin in March 1918, and was entitled to the General Service and Victory Medals.

"Thinking that remembrance, though unspoken, may reach him where he sleeps."

61, Howbury Road, Peckham, S.E.15.   Z6583

SIEGERT, G., L/Corporal, 30th Middlesex Regiment.

He joined in June 1916, and in the following March embarked for the Western Front, where he served until after the Armistice. He fought in the Battles of Ypres, Passchendaele, Courtrai and in several other engagements, and was stationed in Belgium after hostilities ceased. Returning home for demobilisation in September 1919, he holds the General Service and Victory Medals.

201, Commercial Road, Peckham, S.E.15.   Z6657

SILVESTER, J. Private, East Surrey Regiment.

He volunteered in January 1916, and three months later proceeded to India. He was engaged on guard and other duties with his unit, and assisted to quell riots in 1917. He was later transferred to the Military Foot Police, and served in that unit until his return home for demobilisation in November 1919. He holds the General Service Medal.

11, Barmore Street, Battersea, S.W.11.   Z4125

SILVESTER, W., Rifleman, 8th and 10th King's Royal Rifle Corps.

Volunteering in August 1915, he was sent to the Western Front in the following October, and fought in the capture of Guillemont, and was wounded at Ypres. Rejoining his unit on recovery he was in action in the Somme Offensive and the Battle of Cambrai, and was taken prisoner during an enemy counter attack. He was repatriated after the Armistice, and was demobilised in March 1919, and holds the 1914-15 Star, and the General Service and Victory Medals.

22, Rumsey Road, Stockwell Road, S.W.9.   Z5717A

SIMFIELD, D. J., Private, 4th Royal Fusiliers.

He volunteered in November 1914, and was sent to France in the same year. He took part in the heavy fighting at Ypres, Loos and St. Eloi, where in March 1916 he was wounded. After his recovery he was again seriously wounded at Delville Wood in July 1916, and was invalided home and discharged in January 1917, holding the 1914-15 Star, and the General Service and Victory Medals.

8, Selden Road, Nunhead, S.E.15.   Z6707

SIMMONDS, G. F., Driver, R.F.A.

He volunteered in November 1914, and in the following year embarked for France. There he was engaged with his Battery in the Battles of Arras, Ypres, Albert, St. Eloi, Armentières and also fought during the Retreat and Advance of 1918. He was demobilised in February 1919, and holds the 1914-15 Star, and the General Service and Victory Medals.

69, Clayton Road, Peckham, S.E.15.   Z6079

SIMONDS, S., Rifleman, 6th London Regt. (Rifles).

He volunteered in 1914, and was sent to France in the following year. He took part in the severe fighting at Ypres, Festubert and Loos, where he was wounded. After being invalided home he was discharged in 1917 as medically unfit for further service. He holds the 1914-15 Star, and the General Service and Victory Medals.

24, Surrey Road, Peckham Rye, S.E.15.   Z6735

SIMMONS, C., Private, R.A.M.C.

After making several unsuccessful attempts to enlist he joined the R.A.M.C. in June 1918, and completing his training was posted to the Hospital Ship "Panama." She was engaged in conveying the sick and wounded from Le Havre to Southampton, and brought the first convoy of British prisoners of war home from Holland. He holds the General Service and Victory Medals, and was demobilised in November 1919.

25, Khyber Road, Battersea, S.W.11.   Z4127

SIMMONS, F. G., Gunner (Signaller), R.G.A.

Joining in June 1916, he was drafted to France in the following December, and served with his Battery in several engagements, including those in the Ypres salient and on the Somme. He was also in action in the Battle of St. Quentin and other operations during the Advance of 1918, and after the Armistice was sent into Germany with the Army of Occupation. Returning from Cologne he was demobilised in October 1919 and holds the General Service and Victory Medals.

4, Draycourt Place, Camberwell, S.E.5.   Z4538

SIMMONS, F. W. (M.M.), Private, Somerset Light Infantry.

He was mobilised in August 1914, and proceeded to France in the same month. He took part in the Retreat from Mons, and was in action on the Marne, and at Neuve Chapelle, Hill 60, Ypres and Loos. the Somme, Arras, Messines, Cambrai and the Retreat and Advance of 1918, rendering much good service. After the Armistice he returned to England and was demobilised in July 1919. He holds the Military Medal, awarded for gallantry in the Field, and the Mons Star, and the General Service and Victory Medals.

51, Verney Road, Rotherhithe, S.E.16.   Z6712

SIMMONS, G., Rifleman, 8th Rifle Brigade.

He joined in June 1916, and embarking for the Western Front in the following December served in various sectors until the conclusion of hostilities. He fought in the Battles of Arras, Messines and was gassed at Ypres in October 1917, and sent home for treatment. Proceeding to France on recovery in March 1918, he was in action in several engagements in the final stages of the war, and returning to England for demobilisation in February 1919, holds the General Service and Victory Medals.

157, Hill Street, Peckham, S.E.15.   Z6621

SIMMONS, H. R., Private, R.A.S.C.

Volunteering in July 1915, he was drafted to France in the same year, and served in various parts of the line until the end of hostilities. He was engaged on important duties in connection with the transport of ammunition and supplies to the forward areas and was present at the Battles of Ypres, Cambrai and the Somme. Returning to England for demobilisation in March 1919, he holds the 1914-15 Star, and the General Service and Victory Medals.

21, Ingelow Road, Battersea Park, S.W.8.   Z4129A

SIMMONS, H. R. (Jun.), Rifleman, 2/8th London Regiment (Post Office Rifles).

He joined in February 1917, and sent overseas in the same year saw much service on the Western Front. Engaged with his Battalion in heavy fighting he was reported missing on March 21st, 1918 during the German Offensive and was later presumed to have been killed in action on that date. He was entitled to the General Service and Victory Medals.

"Nobly striving,
He nobly fell that we might live."

21, Ingelow Road, Battersea Park, S.W.8.   Z4129B

SIMMONS, J. J., Driver, R.F.A.

He volunteered in January 1915, and embarking for the Western Front in the following August, fought in the Battles of Loos, St. Eloi, the Somme, Vimy Ridge, Ploegsteert Wood and Ypres. Proceeding to Italy in November 1917, he served with his Battery in several engagements during the operations on the Piave and the Asiago Plateaux. Returning to England in 1919, he was demobilised in April of that year and holds the 1914-15 Star, and the General Service and Victory Medals.

4, Elmington Road, Camberwell, S.E.5.   Z4126

SIMMONS, L. C., Private, Royal Fusiliers.

He joined in November 1918, on attaining military age, and on the completion of his training was engaged on important duties with his unit. He rendered valuable services, but contracting cerebro-spinal meningitis, died after a brief illness on March 20th, 1919.

"His memory is cherished with pride."

40, Nunhead Grove, Peckham, S.E.15.   Z6690

SIMMONS, W. A., Private, 3rd Middlesex Regiment.

Volunteering in November 1914, he proceeded to the Western Front in the following year and took part in heavy fighting in the Battles of Neuve Chapelle, St. Eloi, Hill 60, Loos, and was sent tn 1916, to Salonika. He was in action in several engagements on the Vardar, the Struma, and Doiran fronts, and was present at the capture of Monastir. On the conclusion of operations he returned to England and was demobilised in August 1919, and holds the 1914-15 Star, and the General Service and Victory Medals.

38, Tindal Street, Lothian Road, S.W.9.   Z5287

SIMMONS, W. S., Sergt., 12th (Prince of Wales's Royal) Lancers and M.G.C.

He volunteered in August 1914, and served with his unit at home until his embarkation in 1916, for the Western Front. Whilst in this theatre of war he was in action in the Battles of Arras, Ypres, and the Somme, and was wounded during the German Offensive of 1918. Returning to the Field on recovery he fought in several engagements in the Allied Advance, which concluded the war. He was demobilised in March 1919, and holds the General Service and Victory Medals.

11, Nealdon Street, Landor Road, S.W.9.   Z4128

SIMPSON, A., Rifleman, Rifle Brigade.

He joined in August 1917, on attaining military age, and was sent in the following May to the Western Front. Serving with his unit, he was in action at the Battles of the Somme, Amiens, Bapaume, and in other engagements during the Retreat and Advance of 1918, and was wounded in September. On recovery he went with the Army of Occupation into Germany, and returning to England in 1919 was demobilised in October of that year. He holds the General Service and Victory Medals.

28, Dalyell Road, Stockwell, S.W.9. Z4130B

SIMPSON, F., C.Q.M.S., R.E.

He volunteered in April 1915, and in the following March proceeded to France. He was engaged on important duties, during the Battles of Albert, Vermelles, the Somme, Arras, Beaumont-Hamel and Bullecourt, and was invalided home in April 1919, owing to illness. After medical treatment in Lewisham Hospital he was discharged as medically unfit for further military service in September 1918. He holds the General Service and Victory Medals.

22A, Broadhinton Road, Clapham, S.W.4. Z4131

SIMPSON, G. T., Driver, R.A.S.C. (M.T.)

Volunteering in February 1915, he was sent to the Western Front six months later, and did very good work engaged in conveying the sick and wounded from the front lines, and in transporting stores and ammunition to the forward areas, during the Battles of the Somme, Vimy Ridge, Ypres, Poperinghe and Cambrai. After the cessation of hostilities he returned home and was demobilised in April 1919, holding the 1914-15 Star, and the General Service and Victory Medals.

58, Foreign Street, Camberwell, S.E.5. Z6083

SIMPSON, H. E., Private, 20th London Regiment.

He joined in March 1916, and proceeded four months later to the Western Front. During his service in this theatre of war, he fought in operations on the Somme, and was wounded. Evacuated to England he received protracted medical treatment at Manchester Hospital, and on recovery returned to France, and was in action at the Battle of Cambrai. Taken prisoner during the German Offensive in March 1918, he died whilst a prisoner of war on June 12th, 1918. He was entitled to the General Service and Victory Medals.

"A costly sacrifice upon the altar of freedom."

28, Dalyell Road, Stockwell, S.W.9. Z4130A

SIMPSON, H. W., Corporal, Middlesex Regiment.

He joined in May 1916, and shortly afterwards proceeded overseas, and serving with his Battalion in various sectors of the Western Front was engaged in the fighting in many battles, including those of Ypres, Arras, the Somme, Ploegsteert, Armentières, Beaumont-Hamel and Bapaume. On the cessation of hostilities he returned home for demobilisation in May 1919, and holds the General Service and Victory Medals.

33, Wyndham Road, Camberwell, S.E.5. Z4132B

SIMPSON, S. G., Private, 7th London Regiment.

Volunteering in May 1915, he was sent in the following February to the Western Front, and fought in many notable engagements, until wounded and taken prisoner during operations at Vimy Ridge. Whilst in captivity he was sent to Westphalia, and made to work in the coal mines. After the Armistice he was repatriated and demobilised in January 1919, and holds the General Service and Victory Medals.

33, Wyndham Road, Camberwell, S.E.5. Z4132C

SIMPSON, W., L/Corporal, 12th (Prince of Wales' Royal) Lancers.

He joined in July 1918, on attaining military age, and after completing his training, served at various stations on important duties with his Regiment. He did good work, but was unable to secure his transfer overseas before the cessation of hostilities. In February 1919, he proceeded to Germany to the Army of Occupation, and was stationed at Cologne until the following August. Returning home he served for a short period in Ireland, and was demobilised in October 1919.

31, Sandover Road, Camberwell, S.E.5. Z5495

SIMPSON, W. C., Sergeant, R.E.

Volunteering in May 1915, he landed in France two months later and served with his unit in various parts of the line, employed on special duties in connection with operations, and was present at the Battles of Ypres, Arras, the Somme, Beaumont-Hamel, Ploegsteert, Bapaume, and entered Mons at dawn on November 11th, 1918. After the Armistice he served with the Army of Occupation in Germany, and was stationed at Cologne. Returning home in 1920 he was demobilised in February of that year, and holds the 1914-15 Star, and the General Service and Victory Medals.

33, Wyndham Road, Camberwell, S.E.5. Z4132A

SIMMS, J., Private, King's Own (Royal Lancaster Regiment) and Labour Corps.

He joined in August 1917, and was sent in the same year to the Western Front, where he fought in many notable engagements, including the Battles of the Somme, Arras, Bapaume, Bullecourt, Givenchy, and in the Retreat and Advance of 1918. After the Armistice, he served on guard and other duties at various prisoners of war camps until he returned to England for demobilisation in November 1919. He holds the General Service and Victory Medals.

12, Content Street, Walworth, S.E.17. Z4133

SIMS, H. F., Sergt., R.F.A.

Volunteering in November 1914, he was drafted shortly afterwards to France, and served with his Battery in many notable engagements, including the Battles of Ypres, Festubert, Loos, Vermelles, the Somme, Arras, Vimy Ridge, Beaumont-Hamel, Bapaume, and in the Retreat and Advance of 1918. On the conclusion of hostilities he was stationed at Béthune, until returning home for demobilisation in June 1919. He holds the 1914-15 Star, and the General Service and Victory Medals.

5, Scarsdale Terrace, Camberwell, S.E.5. Z5147

SINCLAIR, H., Private, R.A.S.C. (M.T.)

He volunteered in January 1915, and at the conclusion of his training was drafted to Egypt. He was engaged on important duties in connection with the transport of stores and ammuntion to the forward areas, and was stationed principally at Alexandria and Cairo. Later, he returned to England, suffering from shell-shock, and received treatment in hospital at Bristol. Crossing to France after his recovery he served in a similar capacity on the Somme, at Cambrai and Lens, and did valuable work with his unit until the termination of hostilities. He was demobilised in 1919, and holds the 1914-15 Star, and the General Service and Victory Medals.

21, Kirkwood Road, Peckham, S.E.15. Z6224

SINCLAIR, T., Private, 1st London Regiment (Royal Fusiliers).

He joined in August 1917, and during his service on the Western Front, fought in many important attacks in the Arras and Cambrai sectors, and was wounded three times. He holds the General Service and Victory Medals, and was demobilised in February 1919, after his return to England.

230, Albert Road, Peckham, S.E.15. Z5668-9-70B

SINCLAIR, W., Rifleman, Rifle Brigade and King's Royal Rifle Corps.

Joining in 1916, he crossed to France at the conclusion of his training and subsequently fought in the Battles of the Somme, Arras and Ypres. During the Retreat of 1918, the whole of his Battalion was captured, but he, together with six others succeeded in making their escape, and served in the Advance which followed. He was demobilised in 1919, and holds the General Service and Victory Medals.

15, Kirkwood Road, Peckham, S.E.15. Z6181B

SINFIELD, W., Sapper, R.E.

He joined in August 1916, and at the conclusion of his training was engaged upon duties of an important nature with his unit at various stations. Owing to ill-health, he was unable to secure his transfer to a theatre of war, but nevertheless did valuable work until demobilised in January 1919.

37, Selden Road, Nunhead, S.E.15. Z6658

SINGER, W., Rifleman, 2/6th London Regiment and King's Royal Rifle Corps.

He volunteered in May 1915, and after his training was engaged on important duties at various stations until January 1917, when he crossed to France. Four months later, however, after taking part in fighting at Bullecourt, he was reported missing, but a later report stated that he was killed in action on May 17th, 1917. He was entitled to the General Service and Victory Medals.

"Steals on the ear, the distant triumph song."

67, Warner Road, Camberwell, S.E.5. Z6504

SINGFIELD, F., Driver, R.F.A.

Volunteering in August 1914, he crossed to France in the following May, and took part in operations at Loos, Hill 60, Festubert Givenchy, Arras, Messines, and Vimy Ridge. After the Retreat and Advance of 1918, in which he also served, he entered Mons at dawn on November 11th, and later proceeded with the Army of Occupation to Germany. He was demobilised in January 1919, and holds the 1914-15 Star, and the General Service and Victory Medals.

12, Ægis Grove, Battersea Park Road, S.W.8. Z4134

SINGFIELD, F. W. H., Q.M.S., 23rd London Regt.

Mobilised with the Territorials at the commencement of hostilities, he proceeded to France early in 1915, and was actively engaged in the fighting at the Battles of Loos, Givenchy, Vimy Ridge, and Arras, and many others in the German Offensive of 1918. He fell in action at Bullecourt on July 29th, 1918, and was entitled to the 1914-15 Star, and the General Service and Victory Medals.

"A valiant soldier, with undaunted heart he breasted Life's last hill."

7, Dashwood Road, Wandsworth Road, S.W.8. Z4135

SINGFIELD, H., Private, Queen's Own (Royal West Kent Regiment).

He volunteered in June 1915, and crossing to France, fought in engagements at Loos, St. Eloi and Ploegsteert Wood, and was wounded. Owing to his being under military age he was sent to England and discharged, but on attaining the age of eighteen rejoined, and was again drafted to the Western Front. He was subsequently in action until the close of hostilities, and was gassed at Kemmel Hill in July 1918. In the following year he proceeded to India, where in 1920 he was still serving, and holds the General Service and Victory Medals.

12, Ægis Grove, Battersea Park Road, S.W.8.   Z4134B

SINGLETON, R. H., Sergt., 1st Loyal North Lancashire Regiment.

He volunteered in November 1915, and at the conclusion of his training was drafted to the Western Front. Whilst in this theatre of war he did good work with his unit in operations on the Somme, at Ypres, Arras, Albert, Passchendaele, Armentières, Béthune, Bapaume, and in the Retreat of 1918. During the subsequent Advance he contracted fever, and after being for a time in hospital at Rouen was invalided home. He was discharged as medically unfit for further service in August of that year, and holds the General Service and Victory Medals.

61, Sussex Road, Coldharbour Lane, S.W.9.   Z4136

SINNBERG, F. T., Private, 18th Middlesex Regt.

He joined up at eighteen years of age in June 1917, and proceeded to the Western Front in the following April. He took part in the Retreat and Advance of 1918, and in the fighting at Bapaume, Havrincourt, Epéhy, Cambrai, Ypres, and Le Cateau, and after the Armistice returned to England and was demobilised, holding the General Service and Victory Medals.

25, Nutbrook Street, Peckham, S.E.15.   Z6713

SIVETER, J. S., A.B., Royal Navy.

He joined in June 1917, and after training was posted to H.M.S. "Valiant," later being transferred to H.M.S. "Douglas." His ship was engaged on important duties with the Grand Fleet in the North Sea, and also served with the Dover patrol, during raids on Zeebrugge and Ostend. He was discharged on account of service in February 1919, and holds the General Service and Victory Medals.

71, Silverthorne Road, Battersea Park, S.W.8.   Z4137

SKELTON, E., Gunner, R.F.A.

He volunteered in May 1915, and served on the Western Front from the following December until the conclusion of hostilities. During this period he fought in actions on the Somme, at Arras, Vimy Ridge, Messines, Ypres, Passchendaele, Lens, and in the Retreat and Advance of 1918. He returned to England and was demobilised in July 1919, and holds the 1914-15 Star, and the General Service and Victory Medals.

15, Massinger Street, Walworth, S.E.17.   Z4138

SKELTON, G. H. Gunner, R.F.A.

He volunteered in March 1915, and crossing to France in the following December, took part in the Somme Offensive, the Battles of Arras, Ypres, and Passchendaele, and in the final Retreat, and was wounded at Menin Road, in May 1918 In the following August, he was transferred to India, and in 1919, served in the Afghan campaign on the North West Frontier. He was demobilised in November of that year, and in addition to the 1914-15 Star, and the General Service and Victory Medals, holds the India General Service Medal (with clasp, Afghanistan, N.W. Frontier, 1919).

10, Lime Tree Terrace, Pitt Street, Peckham, S.E.15. Z5148

SKIDMORE, J., A.B., Royal Navy.

Mobilised in July 1914, he was posted to the Grand Fleet in the North Sea, and subsequently took part with his ship in the Battles of Heligoland, Jutland, the Dogger Bank and other Naval actions. Later transferred to H.M.S. "Mary Rose." he was rescued when this vessel after a gallant fight, was sunk by a German Naval Force in the North Sea, on October 17th, 1917, whilst on convoy duty. He was demobilised in March 1919, and holds in addition to the 1914-15 Star, and the General Service and Victory Medals, the Long Service and Good Conduct Medals.

29, Gonsalva Road, Wandsworth Road, S.W.8.   Z4141

SKILTON, A., Private, 17th Middlesex Regiment.

He volunteered in January 1916, and in the following June, after completing his course fo training, proceeded to the Western Front, and took part in many important engagements, including those of the Somme, the Ancre and Arras, where he was severely wounded in April 1917. He was in consequence discharged in the following November as unfit for further duty, and holds the General Service and Victory Medals.

12, Temple Road, Chiswick, W.4.   6081

SKINGLE, E., Sergt. (Instructor), R.G.A. and Tank Corps.

He first enlisted in 1889, and after serving with the Colours until 1892, was discharged, but later served through the South African Campaign. In September 1914, he volunteered for further service, and in June 1915, crossed to France. Attached to a Trench Mortar Battery, he took an active part in many notable engagements, including those at Armentières, Hooge, Hill 60, Ypres and Polygon Wood. In October 1915, he was promoted to the rank of Sergeant for good work in the Field, and on two occasions was buried as the result of shell fire, fortunately escaping without injury. Owing to ill-health, he was invalided home in June 1916, and after recovery was engaged for six months in testing guns at Woolwich, and then as an Instructor in the Tank Corps. Later, however, he contracted an illness, to which unfortunately he succumbed on May 18th, 1918, and was entitled to the 1914-15 Star, and the General Service and Victory Medals.

"Great deeds cannot die :
They with the sun and moon, renew their light for ever."

158, St. George's Road, Peckham, S.E.15.   Z5836B

SKINGLE, E. G., L/Cpl., 1/4th Northamptonshire Regiment.

He joined on attaining military age in January 1918, and at the conclusion of his training was drafted to the Western Front, where he fought in the Retreat of that year, during which he was taken prisoner in April. For a time he was employed behind the enemy lines, and was later sent into Germany. After his repatriation, he was drafted to Egypt, and was engaged on important duties there until January 1920, when he returned to England, and was demobilised. He holds the General Service and Victory Medals.

158, St. George's Road, Peckham, S.E.15.   Z5836A

SKINNER, A., Drummer and Bugler, Sherwood Foresters.

He was mobilised on the outbreak of war, and drafted to the Western Front, where he took part in the Retreat from Mons, and was severely wounded. Unfortunately he succumbed to his injuries on November 17th, 1914, and lies buried at Estaires. He was entitled to the Mons Star, and the General Service and Victory Medals.

"Steals on the ear the distant triumph song."

62, Henry Street, Kennington, S.E.11.   Z24730

SKINNER, E. J., Rifleman, 18th London Regiment (London Irish Rifles).

Joining in September 1916, he crossed to France in the following January and was in action in many important sectors, notably those of Vimy Ridge, Bullecourt, Messines, Ypres, Passchendaele, Lens and Cambrai. He also fought in the Retreat and Advance of 1918, during which he did good work with his unit, and remained overseas until the conclusion of hostilities. He was demobilised in February 1919, and holds the General Service and Victory Medals.

4, Wroxton Road, Peckham, S.E.15.   Z6329

SKINNER, F. J., Private, M.G.C.

He joined in January 1917, and during his service on the Western Front, fought at Arras, Bapaume, Cambrai, and in other important parts of the line. Whilst overseas, he was wounded and suffered from shell-shock, but after treatment remained in France, until after the conclusion of hostilities. He was demobilised in October 1919, and holds the General Service and Victory Medals.

3, Middleton Road, Battersea, S.W.11.   Z4142

SKINNER, G. V., Private, R.A.S.C. (M.T.)

He joined in December 1916, and after his training was engaged on important transport duties at various stations. He did valuable work, but owing to ill-health was unable to secure his transfer overseas, and in April 1918, was invalided out of the Service.

59A, Winstead Street, Battersea, S.W.11.   Z4143

SKINNER, L. T., Ship's Cook, R.N.

He volunteered in September 1915, and after training with the "Pembroke" at Chatham, was posted to H.M.S. "Shannon." This vessel was engaged on important convoy and escort duties in the North Sea and the Atlantic, and also took part in several Naval engagements. He was demobilised in February 1919, and holds the General Service and Victory Medals.

29, St. Alphonsus Road, Clapham, S.W.4.   Z4144

SKIPPER, G., Private, 18th Middlesex Regiment.

Joining in July 1917, he proceeded overseas in the following year, and during his service on the Western Front took part in the fighting at Vimy Ridge, Courcelles, Corbie, and the Somme. He also fought in the German Offensive of 1918, and was wounded in May of that year. After the Armistice he served at Péronne and Cambrai, and returned to England for demobilisation in December 1920. He holds the General Service and Victory Medals.

51, Sunwell Street, Peckham, S.E.15.   Z6453

SKIPPER, L., Private, 3rd Bedfordshire Regiment.
He joined in March 1917, and at the conclusion of his training served with his unit on important duties at various depôts. He did good work, but was not successful in obtaining his transfer overseas, and was demobilised in 1919.
57D, Hubert Grove, Landor Road, S.W.9.   Z4145

SKIPPER, W. E., Private, 5th Middlesex Regiment and Bedfordshire Regiment.
He volunteered in November 1915, and in March of the following year embarked for India. He served at Delhi for a considerable time, and was engaged on special guard and other duties at the Forts and outposts during the riots there. He returned to England after the cessation of hostilities and was demobilised in June 1919. He holds the General Service and Victory Medals.
260, Sumner Road, Peckham, S.E.15.   Z5149

SKOTTOW, F., Trooper, 9th (Queen's Royal) Lancers.
He volunteered in August 1914, and in the following November was drafted to France. He fought at the Battles of Ypres, Neuve Chapelle, Festubert, Loos, St. Eloi, Ploegsteert Wood, Vimy Ridge, the Somme and Beaumont-Hamel. Owing to ill-health he was sent to hospital in England, and on recovery served on special duties in Ireland at the Curragh. He was demobilised in February 1919, and holds the 1914-15 Star, and the General Service and Victory Medals.
12, Lothian Road, Camberwell New Road, S.W.9.   Z5150

SKUDDER, E. T., Rifleman, 21st London Regiment (1st Surrey Rifles).
He volunteered in June 1915, and on completing his training was sent in the following year to the Western Front, where he played an important part in several battles, including those of Hill 60, Ypres, II, Loos and Vimy Ridge. He was unhappily killed in action at Cambrai, during the Allied Advance in October 1918, and was entitled to the General Service and Victory Medals.
" Honour to the immortal dead, who gave their youth that the world might grow old in peace."
10, Clarence Street, Clapham, S.W.4.   Z4140

SKUDDER, T., Shoeing-Smith, R.F.A.
He volunteered in November 1915, and on completion of his training was engaged on important duties with his Battery at various depôts. He rendered valuable services, but owing to severe injuries sustained from the kick of a horse he was admitted into hospital, and subsequently invalided out of the Army as medically unfit for further military service in February 1917.
78, Barset Road, Peckham, S.E.15.   Z6584

SLADE, A. T., Private, Middlesex Regiment.
Volunteering in August 1914, he was shortly afterwards sent to France. In this theatre of war he fought in many battles, including those at Neuve Chapelle, Ypres, Hill 60, the Somme, Arras, the Marne, Vimy Ridge, and Messines, and was twice wounded. He returned to England after the cessation of hostilities, and demobilised in March 1919, holds the 1914-15 Star, and the General Service and Victory Medals.
61, Farmer's Road, Camberwell, S.E.5.   Z4146

SLADE, G. F. W., Private, R.A.S.C. (M.T.)
He volunteered in November 1914, but owing to medical unfitness was discharged from the Service shortly afterwards. He rejoined in July 1915, and sent to France in March 1917, served in various sectors of the Western Front as a driver in the Mechanical Transport. He was engaged in taking the guns up to the firing line during the Retreat and Advance of 1918, and was constantly under heavy shell fire. He was demobilised in May 1919, and holds the General Service and Victory Medals.
57, Duffield Street, Battersea, S.W.11.   Z4147

SLADE, H., Air Mechanic, R.A.F.
He joined in May 1916, and at the conclusion of his training was engaged with his Squadron at various aerodromes, as a fitter, and later on clerical duties, in the Pay Office at Farnborough. He rendered valuable services, but was unable to secure his transfer overseas, and was demobilised in September 1919.
24, Sedan Street, Walworth, S.E.17.   Z4148

SLADE, T. A., Battery Sergt.-Major, R.F.A.
Enlisting in June 1908, he was mobilised at the outbreak of hostilities, and sent to France. He fought in the Retreat from Mons, and the subsequent Battles of the Marne, the Aisne, Neuve Chapelle, Festubert, Loos, Vimy Ridge, the Somme, Arras, Albert, Cambrai, and in the final Retreat and Advance of 1918. He holds the Mons Star, and the General Service and Victory Medals, and was demobilised in January 1919.
115, Farmer's Road, Camberwell, S.E.5.   Z4149

SLADE, T. H., Private, 2/2nd London Regt. (Royal Fusiliers).
He volunteered in February 1916, and in the following January was sent to France. In this theatre of war he fought in many engagements, including those on the Ancre, at Arras, Vimy Ridge, and Messines, where he was reported missing on June 16th, 1917. He was later presumed to have been killed in action on that date, and was entitled to the General Service and Victory Medals.
" The path of duty was the way to glory."
64, Royal Road, Walworth, S.E.17.   Z26613

SLANEY, W., Gunner, R.F.A.
He volunteered in January 1915, and in the following year was drafted to the Western Front, where he took part in the fighting at the Battles of Ypres, the Somme, and Cambrai. He proceeded to India in 1918, and served there on special duties at Delhi and other stations until his return to England for demobilisation in March 1919. He holds the General Service and Victory Medals.
4, Hayles Street, Kennington S.E.11.   Z26618

SLATER, A., Rifleman, Rifle Brigade.
Mobilised from the Army Reserve on the outbreak of war, he was drafted to France shortly afterwards, and took part in heavy fighting in the Retreat from Mons, and in the Battles of La Bassée and Ypres. He was severely wounded in this last engagement, and in consequence of his injuries his right arm had to be amputated, and after two months' hospital treatment in France he was evacuated to England. Discharged as physically unfit in 1915 after twelve years' service with the Colours, he holds the Mons Star, and the General Service and Victory Medals.
11B, Peabody Terrace, Ebury Bridge Road, Pimlico Road, S.W.1.   Z3496A

SLATER, A. W., Driver, R.A.S.C.
Joining in May 1917, he was sent overseas in the same year, and serving on the Western Front was engaged on important transport duties in the forward areas and was present at the Battle of the Somme and in several engagements during the Retreat and Advance of 1918. He was killed in action at Bapaume on September 10th, 1918, and was entitled to the General Service and Victory Medals.
" He passed out of the sight of men by the path of duty and self-sacrifice."
54, Sandover Road, Camberwell, S.E.5.   Z5477B

SLATER, H. W., Private, Shropshire Light Infantry.
A serving soldier, he was mobilised when war broke out, and drafted to France in November 1914, was in action with his Battalion in several important engagements, including those in the Ypres salient, and was wounded near Ypres in 1915. Sent home on account of his injuries he was invalided out of the Service in March 1916, and holds the 1914 Star, and the General Service and Victory Medals.
35, Canterbury Place, Lambeth Walk,, S.E.11.   Z27207

SLATER, J., Rifleman, King's Royal Rifle Corps.
Joining in December 1916, he embarked for the Western Front in the following May, and was engaged on important duties with his Battalion until invalided home owing to illness. Returning to France on recovery he was found to be medically unfit for general service and was again sent home, and later transferred to the Royal Air Force. He served with his Squadron, doing good work until demobilised in October 1919, and holds the General Service and Victory Medals.
15, Lillington Street, Vauxhall Bridge Road, S.W.1. Z23312

SLATER, W. G., Private, R.A.M.C.
After several unsuccessful attempts to enlist he volunteered for military service in June 1915, and posted to the Royal Army Medical Corps proceeded to France in January 1916, and served as a stretcher-bearer in several engagements, and was badly gassed near Messines in the following year. Removed to hospital he died from the effects of gas poisoning five days after admission in June 1917. He was entitled to the General Service and Victory Medals.
" And doubtless he went in splendid company."
11, Peabody Terrace, Ebury Bridge Road, Pimlico Road, S.W.1.   Z3496C

SLATER, W. T. (M.M.), Private, Royal Inniskilling Fusiliers.
He volunteered in September 1914, and after serving with his unit in England and Ireland was drafted to France a year later. Whilst on the Western Front he fought in several engagements, including the Battles of Ypres, and the Somme, and was awarded the Military Medal in 1918, for conspicuous gallantry and devotion to duty during the Battle of Cambrai. Demobilised in February 1919, he later rejoined the Army, and in 1920 was serving with the M.G.C. at Shorncliffe. He holds the 1914-15 Star, and the General Service and Victory Medals.
7, Sydney Square, Peckham, S.E.15.   Z6336

SLATTER, C., Sergt., 5th Royal Irish Fusiliers.

Mobilised from the Army Reserve on the outbreak of war, and almost immediately sent in the Bedfordshire Regiment to the Western Front, he fought in the Retreat from Mons, and in the Battles of the Marne, the Aisne, La Bassée and Ypres, and was wounded at Hill 60 in April 1915. Invalided home on account of his injuries he was transferred on recovery to the Royal Irish Fusiliers in September 1915, and sailed for Mudros in the following November. Drafted to Salonika a month later he took part in the Retreat from Serbia, the Advance on the Vardar and the Struma, the capture of Monastir and other operations in the Balkans, and in June 1917 proceeded to Egypt. After serving in the Battles of Rafa, Gaza, Beersheba, and other engagements in the Palestine campaign leading to the fall of Jerusalem, and the capture of Aleppo, he returned to France. There he was in action at Amiens, Bapaume, and was wounded at Havrincourt in September 1918. Demobilised in January 1919, he holds the Mons Star, and the General Service and Victory Medals.
20, Ledbury Street, Peckham, S.E.15.   Z6576

SLATTER, W., Private, 2nd Royal Sussex Regt.

He volunteered in November 1915, and proceeding to the Western Front in the following August served with his Battalion in many important engagements until invalided home owing to illness in 1917. On recovery he returned to France in January 1918, and was in action in the second Battle of the Somme, and severely wounded. Admitted to hospital in France he was later sent to the Dover hospital and suffered the amputation of his right leg. He died from the effects of his wounds in June 1918, and was entitled to the General Service and Victory Medals.
" He joined the great white company of valiant Souls."
11B, Peabody Terrace, Ebury Bridge Road, Pimlico Road, S.W.1.   Z3496B

SLATTER, W. H., Pioneer, R.E.

He joined in October 1916, and in the same year embarked for Salonika. Engaged on important duties during operations in the Balkans he saw heavy fighting during the Advance across the Vardar, and was present at the capture of Monastir. On the conclusion of hostilities he returned home for demobilisation in February, 1919, and holds the General Service and Victory Medals.
20, Lockington Road, Battersea Park Road, S.W.8.   Z3847B

SLEDMAR, T. G., Gunner, R.G.A.

Volunteering in December 1915, he was drafted to the Western Front in the following year, and served until the end of the war. During this period he fought in several battles, including those at Ypres, Arras, Albert, Armentières, Bullecourt and on the Somme, and was gassed at Cambrai. After treatment at a Base Hospital he returned to his Battery, and carried out his duties during the final stages of hostilities. Demobilised in February 1919, he holds the General Service and Victory Medals.
18, Shorncliffe Road, Old Kent Road, S.E.1.   Z4150

SLEET, A. H., Corporal, R.E.

Volunteering in the Royal Naval Division in December 1914, he was sent to Gallipoli in the following February and fought in the Landing at Cape Helles and other operations on the Peninsula. Owing to illness he was invalided home in February 1916, and on recovery was in the following August transferred to the Royal Engineers, and served with the Signal Section of that Corps at General Head-quarters until demobilised in April 1920. He holds the 1914–15 Star, and the General Service and Victory Medals
4, Elmington Terrace, Camberwell, S.E.5.   Z4151

SLINGER, W. J., Corporal, R.E.

He joined in 1916, after having served on the railways at home, and was drafted to France in the same year. He was engaged on important work in the Railway Operative Division of his Corps, and carried out duties in connection with the handling and despatch of military stores until the conclusion of hostilities. He was demobilised in August 1919, and holds the General Service and Victory Medals.
23, Pitcairn Street, Wandsworth Road, S.W.8.   Z4152

SLOCOMBE, R., Rifleman, Rifle Brigade.

He joined in August 1918, and after completing his training was engaged on important duties with his Battalion at home. He did good work, but was unable to obtain his transfer overseas before hostilities ended. He was, however, sent to Germany with the Army of Occupation in 1919, and served on guard and other duties until his return to England for demobilisation in April 1920.
59, Blake's Road, Peckham Grove, S.E.15.   Z6092

SLOUGH, F., Driver, R.H.A. and R.F.A.

Joining in December 1916, he was sent overseas a year later and saw service on the Western Front. He took part with his Battery in the Battles of the Somme II, Bapaume, Ypres, and Cambrai, and on the conclusion of hostilities returned to England. Demobilised in February 1919, he holds the General Service and Victory Medals.
41, Seaton Street, Cheyne Walk, S.W.10.   X24696

SLOUGH, J. A., Private, 24th Queen's (Royal West Surrey Regiment).

He volunteered in September 1914, and embarking for the Western Front in the following year served in the Somme sector until sent to Salonika. After a period of service in the Balkans he proceeded to Egypt, and taking part in the British Advance through Palestine was in action on the Jordan, and before Jerusalem. Returning home after the Armistice he was demobilised in July 1919, and holds the General Service and Victory Medals.
28, Berryfield Road, Walworth, S.E.17.   Z27490

SLOUGH, J. R., Private, R.A.S.C.

Volunteering in March 1915, he proceeded overseas in the same year and saw much service on the Western Front. Attached to the Indian Cavalry he was engaged on important duties in connection with the transport of ammunition, rations, and other supplies to the firing line during the Battles of the Somme and Vimy Ridge. On the conclusion of hostilities he returned to England for demobilisation in 1919, and holds the 1914–15 Star, and the General Service and Victory Medals.
20, Chryssell Road, Brixton Road, S.W.9.   Z5286

SLUMAN, A. J. (M.C.), 2nd Lieut., 2nd Rifle Brigade.

Volunteering in March 1915 he proceeded in the following year to the Western Front and fought in many important engagements, including the Battles of Ypres, Passchendaele, Ploegsteert, and Beaumont-Hamel. He was recommended for a commission, and returned to England for training and was gazetted a 2nd Lieutenant. Returning to France he was wounded at Cambrai during the German Offensive in March 1918, and was awarded the Military Cross for conspicuous bravery and devotion to duty. Evacuated to England, he was demobilised in March 1919, after receiving medical treatment at Devizes Hospital in Wiltshire. In addition to the Military Cross, he holds the General Service and Victory Medals.
24, Stonhouse Street, Clapham, S.W.4.   Z4153

SLUMAN, G. E., Sergt., Wiltshire Regiment.

He volunteered in August 1914, and proceeded overseas in the following year to the Dardanelles, where he fought in the Landing at Suvla Bay. Wounded in a subsequent engagement he was sent to the Victorian War Hospital in Egypt for treatment, and on recovery proceeded to Mesopotamia. There he was in action in the Battles of Kut-el-Amara, Mosul, and Ctesiphon, and present at the capture of Baghdad. Contracting malarial fever he was invalided to India, later returning home for demobilisation in May 1919. He holds the 1914–15 Star, and the General Service and Victory Medals.
20, Stonhouse Street, Clapham, S.W.4.   Z4154

SLYDEL, E., Guardsman, Grenadier Guards.

Joining in June 1917, he completed his training and served with his unit at home engaged on special duties in canteens and officers' mess. He was unsuccessful in obtaining his transfer overseas, but nevertheless did much good work until the cessation of hostilities, and was demobilised in May 1919.
41, Aylesbury Road, Walworth, S.E.17.   Z4155

SMALE, E. J., Private, Canadian Highlanders.

He volunteered in August 1914, while still in Canada, and after completing his course of training reached France in April 1915. He was reported missing three weeks later after the Battle of Festubert, and is believed to have been killed in that engagement on May 20th. He was entitled to the Canadian War Medal, the 1914–15 Star, and the General Service and Victory Medals.
" A costly sacrifice upon the altar of freedom."
46, Wansey Road, Walworth, S.E.17.   Z2970B

SMALE, H. G., Sapper, R.E.

He came from America to fight for his Country, and joined in January 1916. After the completion of his training he was retained on important duties with his unit at various stations, but on account of physical disability was not transferred to a fighting front while hostilities continued. After much valuable coastal defence services he was demobilised in February 1919, and afterwards returned to America.
17, Nunhead Crescent, Peckham, S.E.15.   Z6226

SMALE, J., Private, 6th Devonshire Regiment.

He volunteered in September 1914, and after the completion of his training was drafted to India, and later to Mesopotamia. After taking part in numerous engagements of great importance there he was transferred to Salonika, where he rendered much valuable service for a period of eight months. During his service in the East he suffered from malaria. After his return home he was demobilised in June 1919, and holds the 1914–15 Star, and the General Service and Victory Medals.
25, Tradescant Road, S. Lambeth Road, S.W.8.   Z4156

SMALE, R. W. V., L/Corporal, R.A.S.C. (M.T.)
Mobilised at the outbreak of hostilities he was quickly sent to France, and rendered valuable transport service at Mons, the Marne, the Aisne, La Bassée, and Givenchy. He was wounded in 1916 near St. Venant, and in consequence was invalided home, but after his recovery returned to France, and again did good work for a short time. He then returned home and was demobilised in 1916 in consequence of his service, holding the Mons Star, and the General Service and Victory Medals.
36, Pasley Road, Walworth, S.E.17. Z27027

SMALL, A. V., Leading Seaman, R.N.
He was called up from the Reserve on the outbreak of war, and was posted to H.M.S. "Lord Nelson," in which he was in action in the Battles of Heligoland Bight, Dogger Bank, and Jutland. He afterwards took part in the important operations at the Dardanelles, and subsequently did good work at Chatham. In 1920 he was still serving, and holds the 1914-15 Star, and the General Service and Victory Medals.
29, Darien Road, Battersea, S.W.11. Z4159

SMALL, F. E., Driver, R.F.A.
He volunteered in October 1915, and after the completion of his training was retained on important duties with his Battery until January 1917, when he crossed to France. While there he did excellent work in the Battles of Arras, Ypres, and Messines, and in many other important engagements until hostilities ended. After his return home he was demobilised in February 1919, and holds the General Service and Victory Medals.
14, Grace's Road, Camberwell, S.E.5. Z6543

SMALL, G., Gunner, R.G.A.
He was called up from the Reserve on the declaration of war, and until 1917 was engaged on important coastal defence duties in Cornwall, and other parts of the country. He was afterwards drafted to Mesopotamia, where he took part in the capture of Baghdad, and other important engagements until hostilities ceased. In consequence of illness he returned to England, and in February 1919 was demobilised, holding the General Service and Victory Medals.
25, Chalmers Street, Wandsworth Road, S.W.8. Z4158

SMALL, W., Gunner, R.F.A.
Volunteering in June 1915, he completed his training, and in March 1916 was drafted to the Western Front, where he was engaged in the Battles of the Somme, Ypres, Passchendaele, Cambrai, and many operations in the Retreat and Advance of 1918. In 1917 he was wounded and gassed. After his return to England he was demobilised in May 1919, and holds the General Service and Victory Medals.
29, Westhall Road, Camberwell, S.E.5. Z4157

SMALLWOOD, F., L/Corporal, R.A.S.C. (M.T.)
He joined in May 1917, and at once crossed to France. He did much valuable service at the Battles of Messines, Ypres, Passchendaele, Cambrai, and the engagements in the Retreat and Advance of the Allies up to August 1918. He then returned to England, and was retained for duty at the N.A.C.B. Head quarters until his demobilisation in June 1919. He holds the General Service and Victory Medals.
25, Mayall Road, Herne Hill, S.E.24. Z4160B

SMALLWOOD, S. G., Pte., 8th (King's Royal Irish) Hussars.
He joined in October 1916, and having completed his training embarked for France in November 1917. He took an active part in many important engagements in the Offensives of the following year, including those at Amiens, Bapaume, Havrincourt, Cambrai, and Le Cateau, and after his return to England was demobilised in February 1919, holding the General Service and Victory Medals.
25, Mayall Road, Herne Hill, S.E.24. Z4160A

SMART, F., Sergt., 21st London Regt. (1st Surrey Rifles) and 5th West Yorkshire Regt.
After volunteering in May 1915, he went through his course of training, and in the following year proceeded to the Western Front. He took a prominent part in many important engagements, including those at Arras, Ypres, Cambrai, and the Retreat and Advance of 1918, and was wounded both at Ypres and at Cambrai. After much valuable service he returned home and was demobilised in March 1919. He holds the General Service and Victory Medals.
50, Acorn Street, Camberwell, S.E.5. Z4539

SMART, M. (Miss), Special War Worker.
From October 1914 until January 1919 this lady held an important position at Messrs. Carr and Son's Factory, Bermondsey. She was engaged on arduous work in connection with the supply of sand bags for the troops, and throughout her long period of service carried out her duties in a highly commendable manner.
37, Page's Walk, Grange Road, S.E.1. Z26283

SMART, J. J., Pte., King's Own Scottish Borderers.
He volunteered in September 1914, and in November of the following year proceeded to France, where he took an active part in the Battle of Albert, and was wounded at Vimy Ridge. After treatment in England he returned to the line, and was again wounded at Ypres. On his recovery he was engaged on duties at the Base in France for six months, and subsequently fought in the Retreat and Advance of 1918. In consequence of a wound received at Thiepval in August 1918, he was invalided home and afterwards was retained for light duties until his demobilisation in February 1919. He holds the 1914-15 Star, and the General Service and Victory Medals.
150, Hollydale Road, Peckham, S.E.15. Z6455

SMART, S. (Miss), Special War Worker.
From January 1915 until December 1918, this lady was engaged on highly important work, as a dry cell battery binder, at the Atlas Carbon Company's Works, Southwark Bridge. She carried out her responsible work with care and efficiency, and earned the highest commendation for her services.
37, Page's Walk, Grange Road, S.E.1. Z26286

SMART, W., B.S.M., R.G.A.
He was already serving at the outbreak of war, and at once proceeded to the Western Front. He took a prominent part in numerous engagements, including the Retreat from Mons, the Marne, the Aisne, La Bassée, Ypres, Neuve Chapelle, Hill 60, Festubert, Loos, Vimy Ridge, the Somme, and several others. He was mentioned in Despatches for his conspicuous conduct in the Field, and was recommended for recognition. Invalided home he was still serving in 1920, and holds the Mons Star, and the General Service and Victory Medals.
37, Pages Walk, Grange Road, S.E.1. Z26276

SMEATH, A. J., Corporal, R.E. (I.W.T.)
He volunteered in August 1914, and early in the following year was drafted to the Western Front where he rendered valuable services in connection with many important engagements until hostilities ceased, and was wounded. He was invalided home and demobilised in April 1919, holding the 1914-15 Star, and the General Service and Victory Medals.
26, Marcia Road, Bermondsey, S.E.1. Z26317

SMEE, W. H., Private, R.A.M.C.
He joined in June 1916, and after completing his training was engaged on important duties at various hospitals. He was not successful in securing his transfer overseas, but rendered valuable services until his discharge in 1917.
1, Totteridge Road, Battersea, S.W.11. Z3237B

SMITH, A., Gunner, R.G.A.
He volunteered in May 1915, and proceeded to France in the following January. He took an active part in the fighting at Vimy Ridge and on the Somme, and in the Ypres and Arras sectors, rendering much valuable service until he was demobilised in April 1919. He holds the General Service and Victory Medals.
19, Nunhead Green, S.E.15. Z6328

SMITH, A., Corporal, West Yorkshire Regiment.
He volunteered in December 1914, and in 1917 was sent to the Western Front, where he took part in numerous important engagements, including that at Arras, and served throughout the Retreat and Advance of 1918. He was blown up by a shell explosion at Arras, where he was acting as Quarter-master, and invalided home to hospital where he died on December 5th, 1918. He was entitled to the General Service and Victory Medals.
"And doubtless he went in splendid company."
226, Fort Road, Bermondsey, S.E.1. Z26320

SMITH, A., Rifleman, 6th London Regt. (Rifles).
He joined in 1916, and was sent to France in the same year and took an active part in many engagements, including those at Vermelles, Ploegsteert Wood, Vimy Ridge, Bullecourt, and Cambrai, and also in the heavy fighting during the Retreat and Advance of 1918. In October of that year he was invalided to England suffering from shell-shock, and in 1919 was discharged as medically unfit. He holds the General Service and Victory Medals.
33, Lanvanor Road, Peckham, S.E.15. Z6503B

SMITH, A., Private, R.A.S.C. and Labour Corps.
He volunteered in May 1915, and was sent to France in the same month and served in the Labour Corps at Ypres, Lille, Cambrai, and various other places, being engaged on road repairing and other important and dangerous duties. He returned to England and was demobilised in March 1919, holding the 1914-15 Star, the General Service and Victory Medals.
40, Blake's Road, Peckham, S.E.15. Z6081A

SMITH, A., Private, R.A.M.C.
He joined the Royal Army Medical Corps in April 1920, and after having completed his training was engaged on important duties. He was still serving at the end of 1920, having enlisted for a period of seven years with the Colours and five with the Reserve.
62, Albany Road, Camberwell, S.E.5. Z5671B

SMITH, A., Private, The Queen's (Royal West Surrey Regiment).

He volunteered in March 1915, and proceeded to France in the following November. He was in action in numerous engagements, and was severely wounded at Delville Wood, having his right hand blown off. He was invalided to England and was discharged in February 1917, holding the 1914-15 Star, and the General Service and Victory Medals.

35, Kennard Road, Battersea, S.W.11.   Z4177

SMITH, A. E., Rifleman, 9th London Regiment (Queen's Westminster Rifles).

He joined in March 1917, and was sent to France in the following year. He fought in numerous engagements, including those at Arras and Oppy Wood, where he was wounded, and was invalided to England. He was discharged physically unfit for further service in November 1919, and holds the General Service and Victory Medals.

64, Southville, S.W.8.   3284A

SMITH, A. E., Private, 24th London Regt. (Queen's).

He was serving at the outbreak of war, and was sent to France in 1915. He took part in numerous engagements, until January 1st, 1917, when he was unhappily killed in action in the Ancre sector. He was awarded the 1914-15 Star, and the General Service and Victory Medals.

"His memory is cherished with pride."

238, Hillingdon Street, Walworth, S.E.17.   Z26616

SMITH, A. E., Private, R.A.S.C. (M.T.)

He volunteered in May 1915, and after his training proceeded to France in June 1916. He was present at numerous engagements, including those on the Somme, and at Beaumont-Hamel, Arras, Bullecourt, Ypres, Passchendaele, Cambrai, Amiens, Bapaume, and Havrincourt, and in the Retreat and Advance of 1918, being employed in the transport service to the front lines. In November 1918 he was seriously injured in an accident and invalided to England, and was discharged as physically unfit in August 1920, holding the General Service and Victory Medals.

58, Wansey Street, Walworth, S.E.17.   Z4198

SMITH, A. E., Private, 7th South Staffordshire Regt.

He joined in 1916, and was sent to the Western Front in 1917. He fought in various engagements, including those at Ypres, and Cambrai, where he was severely wounded in October 1918, and was invalided to England. He was discharged in 1919, and holds the General Service and Victory Medals.

104, Barlow Street, Walworth, S.E.17.   Z4202

SMITH, A. E., Private, 13th East Surrey Regiment.

He joined in December 1915, and proceeded to France in November 1917. He fought in various engagements, including those at Bullecourt and Armentières, and also took part in the Retreat and Advance of 1918. He returned to England, and was demobilised in April 1919, and holds the General Service and Victory Medals.

68, Acorn Street, Camberwell, S.E.5.   Z4197

SMITH, A. E., Private, Queen's Own (Royal West Kent Regiment).

He volunteered in May 1915, and was drafted to France later in that year. He was in action on numerous occasions until he was unhappily killed near Hill 60 on January 5th, 1916. He was entitled to the 1914-15 Star, and the General Service and Victory Medals.

"He died the noblest death a man may die,
Fighting for God, and right, and liberty."

57, Evelina Road, Peckham, S.E.15.   Z6222B

SMITH, A. J., Private, 1st London Regiment (Royal Fusiliers).

He was mobilised in August 1914, and was engaged on important duties with his unit until April 1918, when he was drafted to the Western Front, and took part in the severe fighting at Bapaume, the Scarpe and Cambrai, during the Retreat and Advance of 1918. He returned home and was demobilised in February 1919, holding the General Service and Victory Medals.

53, Duffield Street, Battersea, S.W.11.   Z4171

SMITH, A. J., Private, R.A.S.C., Bedfordshire Regt. and 5th London Regt. (London Rifle Brigade).

He joined in 1918, and after his training was engaged at various stations with his unit on important duties. He rendered valuable services, but was not successful in obtaining his transfer overseas before the cessation of hostilities. He was demobilised in 1919.

104, Barlow Street, Walworth, S.E.17.   Z4202B

SMITH, B., W., Driver, R.F.A.

He volunteered in April 1915 and took his course of training for overseas service at Camberwell and Tidworth. He unfortunately fell ill and died on November 16th, 1915.

"The path of duty was the way to glory."

9, Camellia Street, Wandsworth Road, S.W.8.   Z4179

SMITH, A. J., Rifleman, Royal Irish Rifles.

He volunteered in August 1915, and in the following December was drafted to France, where he took part in the severe fighting at Albert, Vimy Ridge, the Somme, Arras, Messines, Passchendaele and Cambrai. He was also engaged in the Retreat and Advance of 1918, and was wounded and gassed. He was demobilised in February 1919, and holds the 1914-15 Star and the General Service and Victory Medals.

27, Smyrk's Road, Walworth, S.E.17.   Z4178B

SMITH, A. J., Sapper, R.E.

He volunteered in May 1915, and after his training was drafted to France, where he served at the Somme and Loos. Later he was sent to Salonika, and took part in many engagements on the Doiran front. He afterwards advanced into Bulgaria, and remained there until sent home for demobilisation in April 1919. He holds the 1914-15 Star, and the General Service and Victory Medals.

42, Hutton Road, Kennington, S.E.11.   Z25520

SMITH, A, P., Sergt., R.A.S.C. (M.T.)

He volunteered in April 1915, and in the same year was sent to the Western Front. He was attached to the 51st (Highland) Division, and took a prominent part in several important engagements, including those in the Somme area, and in the Retreat and Advance of 1918. He was demobilised in May 1919, and holds the 1914-15 Star, and the General Service and Victory Medals.

77, Whellock Road, Chiswick, W.4.   7519

SMITH, A. R., L/Corporal, Royal Sussex Regiment.

He joined in June 1918, and after completing his training was engaged at various stations on important duties with his unit. He rendered valuable services, but was not successful in obtaining his transfer overseas before the cessation of hostilities. He was discharged in May 1919, as unfit for further service, owing to ear trouble.

2, Ewell Place, Camberwell, S.E.5.   Z5833

SMITH, A. T., Rifleman, Rifle Brigade.

Joining in June 1916 he was sent to France later in the same year and was in action at Vimy Ridge, the Somme, Arras, Passchendaele, Lens, and in other engagements. He was wounded during his service overseas, but after his recovery took part in the Retreat and Advance of 1918. He was demobilised in January 1919, and holds the General Service and Victory Medals.

41, Sunwell Street, Peckham, S.E.15.   Z6452

SMITH, A. V., Private, 14th Worcestershire Regt.

He joined in November 1916, and was engaged on important duties with his unit until 1918, when he was drafted to France. He took an active part in many important engagements during the Offensive of 1918, especially in the Battles of the Marne and Ypres, and after the Armistice was engaged on important guard and demobilisation duties at Le Havre and Dieppe. After being invalided home he was demobilised in November 1919, and holds the General Service and Victory Medals.

57, Evelina Road, Nunhead, S.E.15.   Z6222A

SMITH, A. V., Private, Royal Dublin Fusiliers.

He was serving in India at the outbreak of war, and in the following year proceeded to Gallipoli, where he took part in numerous engagements and was wounded and invalided to Malta. In 1916 he was transferred to France and was in action at Ypres, Poperinghe and Arras, and was twice wounded and gassed. He returned home and was demobilised in March 1919, holding the 1914-15 Star, and the General Service and Victory Medals.

153, East Surrey Grove, Peckham S.E.15.   Z5152

SMITH, A. V., Corporal, Royal Sussex Regiment.

He joined in June 1917, and after a period of training was drafted to the Western Front, where he took part in the Advance of 1918. At the conclusion of hostilities he returned to England, and was discharged in November 1919 as unfit for further duty. He holds the General Service and Victory Medals.

192, Hillingdon Street, Walworth, S.E.17.   Z26615

SMITH, A. W., L/Corporal, Queen's Own (Royal West Kent Regiment).

He volunteered in November 1915, and after a period of training was sent to France. He took part in several important engagements, including the Battle of the Somme, and was gassed. Invalided home, he was demobilised in April 1919, holding the General Service and Victory Medals.

44, Fielding Road, Bedford Park, Chiswick, W.4.   7900

SMITH, B., Private, M.G.C.

He joined in July 1917, and in the following May was drafted to France, where he took part in much heavy fighting in the Offensive of 1918, and was wounded. He later proceeded to Germany with the Army of Occupation, and returning home was demobilised in September 1919, holding the General Service and Victory Medals.

28, Quick Road, Chiswick, W.4.   5828

SMITH, B. J. (D.C.M.), R.S.M., M.G.C.

He volunteered in September 1914, and after crossing to France played a conspicuous part in several important engagements. He was awarded the Distinguished Conduct Medal for bravery and devotion to duty, and was mentioned in Dispatches in September 1916. He was demobilised in March 1919, and holds in addition to the Distinguished Conduct Medal, the 1914-15 Star, and the General Service and Victory Medals.
38A, Mill Hill Grove, Acton, W.3.   7192

SMITH, C., Pte., 1st Loyal North Lancashire Regt.

Mobilised at the outbreak of hostilities he was immediately drafted to the Western Front where he fought at Mons, the Aisne, Neuve Chapelle, Hill 60, Festubert, Loos, the Somme, Messines, Vimy Ridge, Cambrai, and in the great Offensive of 1918. He was twice mentioned in Despatches for his excellent work as a signaller, and was gassed three times. Upon his return home he was demobilised in February 1919 after seventeen years' active service, and holds the Mons Star, the General Service and Victory Medals, and the Delhi Durbar Medal.
84, Vaughan Street, Camberwell, S.E.5.   Z6330

SMITH, C., Driver, R.F.A.

He volunteered in April 1915, and proceeding to France in the following December, took an active part in the heavy fighting at Aire, Béthune, Crouy, and the Somme, and was wounded at Fricourt. After his evacuation from hospital he returned to the line and suffered from shell-shock at Mametz. He again rejoined his Battery and served with distinction in many engagements until the close of hostilities. He was demobilised in June 1919, and holds the 1914-15 Star, and the General Service and Victory Medals.
10, New Church Road, Camberwell, S.E.5.   Z5815A

SMITH, C., Private, M.G.C.

He volunteered in September 1914, and after his training was retained on important duties with his unit until 1916 when he proceeded to France. He was gassed and temporarily blinded in the Battle of Vimy Ridge, and after being invalided home was found unfit for further overseas service owing to defective sight. He was demobilised in January 1919, and holds the General Service and Victory Medals.
22, East Surrey Grove, Peckham, S.E.15.   Z5279

SMITH, C., Sergt., 5th The Buffs (East Kent Regt).

He volunteered in December 1914, and was shortly after drafted to Mesopotamia. He played a distinguished part in many important engagements on this Front, and was mentioned in Despatches on November 2nd, 1917. He was invalided home and discharged on account of his service in October 1918.
34A, Rothschild Road, Chiswick, W.4.   6771

SMITH, C. B., L/Corporal, Queen's (Royal West Surrey Regiment).

He volunteered in September 1914, and after being retained on important duties until 1916 was drafted to France. After taking part in many engagements he fell in action in the great Somme Offensive on September 15th, 1916. He was entitled to the General Service and Victory Medals.
"His life for his Country, his Soul to God."
33, Gladstone Terrace, Battersea Park Road, S.W.8.   Z4180

SMITH, C. F., Gunner, R.F.A.

Mobilised at the outbreak of war he at once proceeded to France and took an active part in the Battles of Mons, the Marne, the Aisne, La Bassée, Loos, and several engagements on the Arras Front. After being discharged as a time-expired man, he was again called up in 1917, and subsequently was retained on important duties in England until demobilised in January 1919. He holds the Mons Star, and the General Service and Victory Medals.
68, Daniel's Road, Peckham, S.E.15.   Z6659

SMITH, C. H., Sergt., 2nd East Lancashire Regiment.

He was serving in the Army at the outbreak of hostilities and was retained for important instructional duties. He was not successful in obtaining his transfer overseas while hostilities continued, but rendered valuable services until his death from phthisis in March 1917.
"The path of duty was the way to glory."
11, Blewitt Street, Walworth, S.E.17.   Z4195

SMITH, C. J., Rifleman, Rifle Brigade.

Having volunteered in March 1915, he crossed to France six weeks later and took an active part in numerous engagements of great importance until the close of hostilities, including those at Albert, Vimy Ridge and the Somme. On being wounded in action in 1917 he came home, but on his recovery returned to France. He was again wounded at Ypres. He was demobilised in January 1919, and holds the 1914-15 Star, and the General Service and Victory Medals.
149, Lavender Road, Battersea, S.W.11.   Z4181

SMITH, C. J., Trooper, 2nd Life Guards (Cyclist Section).

He volunteered in November 1914, and having completed his training proceeded to France in 1915. He took an active part in many notable engagements, including those of Loos, the Somme, Ypres, Albert and the Retreat and Advance of 1918. He was killed while fighting gallantly at Bray on August 23rd, 1918, and was entitled to the 1914-15 Star, and the General Service and Victory Medals.
"He joined the great white company of valiant souls."
27, Elam Street, Camberwell, S.E.5.   Z6230A

SMITH, D. (D.S.M.), 1st Class Petty Officer, R.N.

He joined the Navy in 1912, and throughout the war did excellent service with the Grand Fleet in the North Sea in H.M.S. "Undaunted." He took a prominent part in many important engagements, including those at Heligoland Bight, where his boat was torpedoed, and at Jutland, and also did much valuable patrol work. In December 1918 he proceeded to North Russia, where he was frequently in action at Archangel against the Bolshevists until October 1919. He was mentioned in Despatches three times by Admiral Sykes, was awarded the Distinguished Service Medal for his gallantry in action, and was recommended for the Russian Order of St. George. In 1920 he was still in the Navy, and holds in addition to the Distinguished Service Medal, the 1914-15 Star, and the General Service and Victory Medals.
9, Sugden Street, Camberwell, S.E.5.   Z6541

SMITH, E., Bombardier, R.F.A.

He volunteered in April 1915, and in the following December proceeded to the Western Front, where he was in action at Albert, Vimy Ridge, the Somme, Arras, Bullecourt, Messines, Ypres, Passchendaele, Cambrai, Amiens and other important engagements in the great Offensive of 1918. He also did valuable work while overseas as Pay Sergeant. After returning home he was demobilised in June 1919, and holds the 1914-15 Star, and the General Service and Victory Medals.
57, Aldbridge Street, Walworth, S.E.17.   Z4183

SMITH, E. B., Driver, R.A.S.C. (M.T.)

Volunteering in January 1915, he was drafted in the same year to the Western Front, where he did excellent work conveying stores of all kinds to the various fronts. He also was engaged in transporting the wounded from the lines after the Battles of Ypres, Loos, Armentières and other engagements. In consequence of severe shell-shock, he was invalided home and was subsequently discharged in August 1917, as unfit for further service. He holds the 1914-15 Star, and the General Service and Victory Medals.
64, Denmark Road, Camberwell, S.E.5.   Z6085

SMITH, E. D., Private, 10th Middlesex Regiment.

He volunteered in 1915, and was drafted to the Eastern Front. He took part in various operations of importance in the Offensive in Palestine under General Allenby, and fought in the Battle of Gaza, and was present at the Entry into Jerusalem. He returned home and was demobilised in 1919, and holds the General Service and Victory Medals.
16, Chiswick Common Road, Chiswick, W.4.   5355

SMITH, E. H., Driver, R.F.A.

He volunteered in December 1914, and in the following year was drafted to Salonika, where he took part in the Balkan campaign. He was in action on the Struma and was wounded, and in 1917 was invalided home suffering from malaria. He was discharged in February 1919, and holds the 1914-15 Star, and the General Service and Victory Medals.
20, Northall Street, Stockwell, S.W.9.   Z4166

SMITH, E. W., L/Corporal, Royal Welch Fusiliers.

He volunteered in November 1915, and in the following year proceeded to France. While overseas he took part in various engagements on the Western Front, including those on the Somme and at Arras, Bullecourt and Cambrai. In June 1917 he was wounded during an encounter at Mametz Wood and again in the following August near Ypres. He was demobilised in February 1919, and holds the General Service and Victory Medals.
46, Reedworth Street, Kennington, S.E.11.   Z27351

SMITH, F., Gunner, R.F.A.

He joined in April 1915, and proceeded to France in the following December and was in action on the Somme and the Ancre and at Arras and Ypres. Later he was gassed and invalided home, and was discharged in June 1919, holding the 1914-15 Star, and the General Service and Victory Medals.
61, Cranham Road, South Bermondsey, S.E.16.   Z6660

SMITH, F., Sergt., M.G.C.

He was mobilised from the Reserve in August 1914, and immediately afterwards was sent to France, where he took part in the severe fighting at Mons, the Marne, the Aisne, Ypres and Loos, where he was severely wounded. He was then invalided home, and on his recovery was engaged on important instructional duties until demobilised in March 1919. He holds the Mons Star, and the General Service and Victory Medals. 17, Beddome Street, Walworth, S.E.17. Z4210

SMITH, F., Bombardier, R.F.A.

He volunteered in 1915, and in the following year was sent to France, where he took part in numerous engagements, including those at the Somme, Ypres, Cambrai and in the Retreat and Advance of 1918. He was wounded on one occasion, and was demobilised in 1919, holding the General Service and Victory Medals.

187, Stewart's Road, Battersea Park Road, S.W.8. Z4200D

SMITH, F., Special War Worker.

From March 1915 to September 1917 he was engaged on work of National importance as a shell-turner at the Projectile Company's Factory, Battersea, and afterwards was employed in a like capacity for over a year at Messrs. Ducros' Works, Acton. Throughout his service he performed his duties in a highly efficient and commendable manner.

116, Dalling Road, Hammersmith, W.6. 11630C

SMITH, F., C.Q.M.S., Royal Irish Rifles.

Having previously served in the South African campaign, he volunteered in August 1914, and was sent to Ireland on instructional duties. In 1915 he was drafted to Gallipoli, where he was in action on many occasions. He later proceeded to Salonika and took part in the operations round Ghevgali during the Serbian Retreat and on the Doiran front. He was later invalided home and discharged as medically unfit for further service in July 1917. He holds the Queen's South African Medal (with five clasps), the 1914–15 Star, and the General Service and Victory Medals.

1, Arlington Grove, Camberwell, S.E.5. Z5151

SMITH, F., Corporal, Scots Guards.

He was mobilised, at the outbreak of the war and was immediately sent to France, where he took part in the Retreat from Mons and the Battles of the Marne, the Aisne, Neuve Chapelle, Hill 60, Festubert and Loos, where he was badly wounded. He was then invalided to England and was discharged in 1915 as medically unfit for further service. He holds the Mons Star, and the General Service and Victory Medals. 22, Oakden Street, Kennington, S.E.11. Z27380

SMITH, F. A., Cpl., Queen's (Royal West Surrey Regt.)

He joined in August 1916, and on the completion of his training served at Tunbridge Wells on important duties with his unit. He rendered valuable service, but was unsuccessful in obtaining his transfer overseas before the cessation of hostilities. He was demobilised in February 1919.

38, Weston Road, Chiswick, W.4. 5844

SMITH, F. A., Private, Connaught Rangers.

He volunteered in October 1914, and was shortly afterwards sent to Ireland. He was drafted thence to the Western Front, and was in action at the Battle of Loos. Transferred to Mesopotamia, he was wounded in an engagement with the Turks, and also contracted malaria. He was sent to hospital in India and on recovery proceeded to Egypt and Palestine, where he was in action at Gaza, Jaffa, Jericho, and was with General Allenby in his triumphant entry into Jerusalem. Holding the 1914–15 Star, and the General Service and Victory Medals, he was demobilised in March 1919.

10, Hudson Terrace, Earl Street, Westminster, S.W.1. Z23482

SMITH, F. B., Corporal, Rifle Brigade.

He volunteered in September 1915, at the age of sixteen, and after completing his training was drafted to France and was in action on the Somme, and at Ypres and Lens. He was wounded and invalided home. On his recovery he returned to France and was again wounded and sent home. He returned to France for the third time and fought gallantly in numerous engagements there till the cessation of hostilities. He was demobilised in 1919, and holds the 1914–15 Star, and the General Service and Victory Medals.

27, Ivy Crescent, Chiswick, W.4. 6036

SMITH, F. C., Sergt., 21st London Regiment (1st Surrey Rifles).

Having previously served in the South African campaign, he volunteered in August 1914, and in the following year was sent to France, where he took part in numerous engagements, including those at Neuve Chapelle, Givenchy, Loos, Vimy Ridge, the Somme, Ypres and many others in the offensives of 1918. He served for a time in the 34th K.R.R.C. and was also engaged in guarding prisoners of war. He was demobilised in February 1919, and holds the Queen's South African Medal, the 1914–15 Star, and the General Service and Victory Medals.

268, Commercial Road, Peckham, S.E.15. Z6661

SMITH, F. E., L/Cpl., 6th Royal Welch Fusiliers.

He volunteered in November 1915, and in December of the following year was drafted to the East. He saw much active service in Egypt, Palestine, Salonika, Bulgaria and Constantinople. Contracting malaria, he returned to England for demobilisation in November 1919, and holds the General Service and Victory Medals. He still suffers from heart trouble brought on by his war service.

3, Humphrey Street, Old Kent Road, S.E.1. Z26838

SMITH, F. E., Private, 3rd London Regiment (Royal Fusiliers).

He joined in 1916, and in the following year was drafted to France, where he took part in many important engagements, including that at Ypres. He was badly wounded and invalided home in consequence and discharged in 1919 as unfit for further duty. He holds the General Service and Victory Medals.

77, Arthur Road, Brixton Road, S.W.9. Z4163

SMITH, F. F., Private, Northumberland Fusiliers.

He volunteered in March 1915, and after his training was drafted to the Western Front, where he took part in numerous engagements of importance and was taken prisoner at St. Quentin. On his release after the Armistice he returned home, and was demobilised in January 1919, holding the General Service and Victory Medals.

28, Spencer Street, Battersea, S.W.11. Z4207C

SMITH, F. J. (Mrs.), Special War Worker.

This lady was engaged for eighteen months by the Government as a telephone operator at the Victoria and Hop Exchanges. The manner in which she performed her duties under very trying night conditions during the air raids, gave great satisfaction, and she was commended for her valuable services.

24, St. George's Road, Peckham, S.E.15. Z5496A

SMITH, F. J., Sapper, R.E.

He volunteered in January 1915, and after completing his training was sent to France, where he was engaged as an engine driver. He was later transferred to Salonika and served on important duties connected with his branch of the Service. On contracting fever, he was invalided home, and was discharged in March 1919. He holds the 1914–15 Star, and the General Service and Victory Medals.

100, Ingrave Street, Battersea, S.W.11. Z4205

SMITH, F. L., Corporal, 6th Middlesex Regiment.

Joining in March 1916, he was drafted to the Western Front in the same year and took part in the fighting at Albert, the Somme, Arras, Bullecourt, Ypres, Cambrai and in many important engagements in the Retreat and Advance of 1918. He was demobilised in November 1919 after returning home, and holds the General Service and Victory Medals.

49, Parkstone Road, Peckham, S.E.15. Z5673

SMITH, F. W., Sergt., Durham Light Infantry.

He joined in May 1916, and in December of the same year was sent to France, where he was in action at Messines, Ypres and Passchendaele, and was twice wounded. In December 1917 he proceeded to Italy and served with distinction on the Piave and Asiago fronts. He was demobilised in November 1919, and holds the General Service and Victory Medals.

48, St. George's Road, Peckham, S.E.15. Z5497B

SMITH, F. W., 1st Air Mechanic, R.A.F.

Joining in March 1916, he was sent to France in the same year and was engaged on important duties with his Squadron on the Somme, at St. Quentin, the Hindenburg Line and other places. He also did valuable service during the Retreat and Advance of 1918. He returned home and was demobilised in April 1919, holding the General Service and Victory Medals.

26, Rozel Road, Clapham, S.W.4. Z4209

SMITH, G., Private, Welch Regiment.

He volunteered in December 1915, and in the following year proceeded to France, and fought in the Battles of Ypres, the Somme, Vermelles and Cambrai. He was also frequently in action in the Retreat and Advance of 1918, and returned home and was demobilised in January of the following year. He holds the General Service and Victory Medals.

43, Caulfield Road, Peckham, S.E.15. Z6449

SMITH, G., Sergt., Queen's Own (Royal West Kent Regiment).

A serving soldier, he was in India at the outbreak of hostilities and was drafted to Mesopotamia in 1914, and served in this theatre of war until the Armistice. During this period he fought in many engagements and was present at the Capture of Baghdad in March 1917. He returned home and was demobilised in 1919, and holds the 1914–15 Star, and the General Service and Victory Medals.

38, Bournemouth Road, Peckham, S.E.15. Z5498B

SMITH, G., Private, King's Own (Yorkshire Light Infantry).

He was mobilised at the outbreak of war, and was soon afterwards drafted to France and took part in the Retreat from Mons, and the Battles of La Bassée, Ypres (where he was wounded), and Hill 60 (where he was again wounded). After his recovery he fought at Loos, Albert and Vimy Ridge, and was then invalided home and discharged as medically unfit for further service. He holds the Mons Star, and the General Service and Victory Medals.

40, Pardoner Street, Tabard Street, S.E.1. Z25740

SMITH, G., Sapper, R.E.

He had previously served in the South African war, and volunteered in August 1914, and in the following year was drafted to the Western Front. Whilst in France he was engaged on important duties in connection with the operations and was frequently in the forward areas, notably at Arras, Ypres and Cambrai, and in various subsequent battles in the Retreat and Advance of 1918. He was invalided home with trench feet in November 1918, and was discharged as medically unfit for further duty in February of the following year. He holds the Queen's and King's South African Medals (with five bars), the 1914-15 Star, and the General Service and Victory Medals.
158, Weston Street, Bermondsey, S.E.1.   Z25794

SMITH, G., Driver, R.A.S.C.

He had previously served in the South African War, and in August 1914 was mobilised and shortly afterwards sent to France. Whilst overseas he was engaged on important duties with his unit and was present at the Battles of the Marne, the Aisne, Ypres, Loos, the Somme and Arras. Later he was wounded and gassed in action, and in 1918 was invalided out of the Service. He holds the Queen's and King's South African Medals, the 1914 Star, and the General Service and Victory Medals.
1, Horse and Groom Court, off Walworth Road, S.E.17. Z26145

SMITH, G. A., Private, Queen's (Royal West Surrey Regiment) and Labour Corps.

He joined in February 1917, and after his training proceeded to France with the Labour Corps later in the same year. He served on important duties in several engagements, and was unfortunately killed near Ypres on December 30th, 1917. He was entitled to the General Service and Victory Medals.
" His memory is cherished with pride."
4, Arden Street, Battersea Park Road, S.W.8.   Z4184

SMITH, G. A., Private, 2nd Essex Regiment.

He volunteered in August 1915, and in the same year was drafted to France. Whilst overseas he fought in the Battle of the Somme, and was wounded and in hospital for some months. After his recovery he rejoined his unit, and was gassed and wounded at Arras, and subsequently invalided home to hospital, where he again remained for some months. In 1920 he was serving at Malta, and holds the 1914-15 Star, and the General Service and Victory Medals.
39, Ancill Street, Fulham, W.6.   13868B

SMITH, G. E., Private, Sherwood Foresters and East Surrey Regiment.

He joined in 1916, and after his training served at various stations on important duties with his unit. He was mainly engaged in garrison and coastal defence duties and rendered valuable services. Owing to medical reasons he was unable to proceed overseas, and was demobilised in 1919.
9, Mays Place, Peckham, S.E.15.   Z6078

SMITH, G. J., L/Corporal, R.E.

He volunteered in April 1915, and was almost immediately drafted to France, where he was engaged on important duties in connection with the operations, and was frequently in the forward areas. He also served on the trains conveying munitions and food supplies to various units in the firing line. Later he proceeded to Italy, where he was engaged on duties of a similar nature until his demobilisation in 1918. He holds the 1914-15 Star, and the General Service and Victory Medals.   19, Wayford Street, Battersea, S.W.11.   Z4168

SMITH, G. P., Sapper, R.E.

He was mobilised at the outbreak of war and was almost immediately drafted to France, and served in the Retreat from Mons and at Le Cateau, Festubert, Loos, and many subsequent engagements. Throughout the war he was almost continuously in action and was frequently engaged on important duties in the forward areas whilst operations were in progress. He was demobilised in January 1919, and holds the Mons Star, and the General Service and Victory Medals. 28, Spencer Street, Battersea, S.W.11.   Z4207A

SMITH, G. S., Private, Lincolnshire Regiment.

He joined in July 1916, and after his training was drafted to France in the following year, and served at Arras, Ypres, Lens, Cambrai and Rheims. He died gloriously on the Field of Battle when in action in an engagement in April 1918, and was entitled to the General Service and Victory Medals.
" The path of duty was the way to glory."
31, Buchan Road, Peckham, S.E.15.   Z6622

SMITH, G. T., Private, 6th Worcestershire Regiment.

He joined in January 1916, and in the same year was drafted to France. During his service overseas he was severely wounded near Ypres and invalided home. Rejoining his unit in France after his recovery, he fought on the Somme, but later contracted fever and was again invalided to England. After treatment in hospital he was retained on garrison duties at home until his demobilisation in April 1919. He holds the General Service and Victory Medals.
13, Combermere Road, Stockwell, S.W.9.   Z4185

SMITH, G. W. (M.S.M.), Staff-Sergt., Queen's Own (Royal West Kent Regiment).

He volunteered in November 1914, after having previously served in the South African War, and in India. In 1916 he was sent to the Western Front, where he took part in various engagements, including those at Ypres, the Somme, Arras, Cambrai and in the Advance in 1918, and was wounded. He was awarded the Meritorious Service Medal for his excellent work in France, and also holds the Queen's and King's South African Medals, the India General Service Medal, and the General Service and Victory Medals. He was demobilised in January 1919.
14, Collingwood Street, Chelsea, S.W.3.   TX22696

SMITH, G. W., L/Corporal, 23rd London Regiment.

He was mobilised in August 1914, and was afterwards retained on important duties with his unit until July 1916, when he crossed to France. He fought gallantly at the Somme, Messines, Passchendaele, Cambrai, and through the Retreat and Advance of 1918, until hostilities ceased. He was demobilised after his return home in February 1919, and holds the General Service and Victory Medals.
70, Bennerley Road, Wandsworth Common, S.W.11.   Z4537

SMITH, G. W., Gunner, R.F.A.

He was called up from the Reserve on the outbreak of hostilities, and was quickly drafted to France, where he did excellent service at Mons and in numerous other engagements of importance until the cessation of fighting. After returning home he was demobilised in 1919, holding the Mons Star, and the General Service and Victory Medals.
26, Victoria Terrace, Queen's Road, Battersea Park, S.W.8. Z4173.

SMITH, H., Special War Worker.

He was exempted from military service on account of the importance of his skilled work, and throughout the war was engaged on aeroplane construction at Messrs. Barker's Factory, Shepherd's Bush. His expert knowledge was greatly appreciated.
122, Acton Lane, Chiswick, W.4.   6361

SMITH, H., Pte., Duke of Cornwall's Light Infantry.

He volunteered in August 1914, and after his training was drafted to the Western Front in February 1915. While overseas he took a gallant part in various engagements and was unfortunately killed by shell fire at Ypres on February 11th, 1916. He was entitled to the 1914-15 Star, and the General Service and Victory Medals.
" A costly sacrifice upon the altar of freedom."
7, Brodie Street, Old Kent Road, S.E.1.   Z27399

SMITH, H., Driver, R.A.S.C.

He joined in March 1917, and was drafted to the Western Front in the following May. He rendered valuable service with his Corps until October 1918, when he returned to England on special leave, but contracting influenza, he unhappily died at home on November 6th, 1918. He was entitled to the General Service and Victory Medals.
" His life for his Country, his Soul to God."
19, Adam Street, New Kent Road, S.E.1.   Z25402

SMITH, H., Rifleman, 21st London Regiment (1st Surrey Rifles).

Volunteering in September 1915, he proceeded in 1916 first to France and afterwards to Salonika. After valuable services on both these fronts, he was transferred to Egypt and subsequently took part in General Allenby's victorious campaign through Palestine, during which he was present at the Entry into Jerusalem. After his return home he was demobilised in February 1919, and holds the General Service and Victory Medals.
126, Farmer's Road, Camberwell, S.E.5.   Z2427B

SMITH, H., Driver, R.A.S.C. (M.T.)

He was serving at the outbreak of hostilities, and at once crossed to the Western Front, where he was engaged on important transport duties conveying food and munitions to various sectors, until wounded at Arras. He was then invalided home, and when convalescent was employed on agricultural work at Swanley until his discharge in May 1919. He holds the 1914 Star, and the General Service and Victory Medals.
7, Smyrks Road, Walworth, S.E.17.   Z4169

SMITH, H. A., Private, 11th (Prince Albert's Own) Hussars.

He volunteered in October 1915, and in May of the following year was drafted to the Western Front, where he took a prominent part in many engagements, including those at the Somme and Beaumont-Hamel, Grandicourt, Messines, Kemmel, and in the Retreat and Advance of 1918. He was discharged in February 1919, and holds the General Service and Victory Medals.
155, Brook Street, Kennington, S.E.11.   Z26619.

SMITH, H. E., Private, M.G.C.

He joined in June 1916, and after the completion of his course of training was drafted to India, where he was engaged on important duties at various stations. He was still serving there in 1920, and holds the General Service and Victory Medals.
27, Smyrk's Road, Walworth, S.E.17.   Z4178A

SMITH, H. E., Pte., 23rd London Regt. and R.A.S.C.

He volunteered in September 1914, and after the completion of his training was retained on important duties with his unit until 1916, when he was drafted to France. He took an active part in the Battles of the Somme, Arras, Vimy Ridge, Messines, Ypres and in the Retreat and Advance of 1918, in which he was wounded. After his return home he was demobilised in January 1919, and holds the General Service and Victory Medals.
44, Ingelow Road, Battersea Park, S.W.8.   Z1190B

SMITH, H. G., Private, R.A.M.C.

He volunteered in 1915, and after the completion of his training was engaged on important duties in military hospitals at Blackpool and other places. He was not successful in securing his transfer overseas, but rendered valuable services until he was injured in an air raid, when his ambulance was blown up. After a year in hospital he was discharged in 1918, but still feels the ill-effects of the shell-shock.
24A, Pasley Road, Walworth, S.E.17.   Z27026

SMITH, H. H., Private, 23rd London Regiment.

He volunteered in September 1914, and was sent to France in the following March. He served in various sectors and in numerous engagements including those at Loos and Givenchy, until he was later invalided home owing to ill-health. He was discharged as medically unfit for further service in 1916, and holds the 1914-15 Star, and the General Service and Victory Medals.
124, Stewart's Road, Battersea Park Road, S.W.8.   Z4203B

SMITH, H. J., Rifleman, 2nd Rifle Brigade.

He joined in September 1918, and after his training was engaged on important duties at various stations. He rendered valuable services until January 1920, when, owing to ill-health he was discharged as medically unfit.
302, Commercial Road, Peckham, S.E.15.   Z6662A

SMITH, H. J., Sergt., R.A.M.C.

He volunteered in November 1914, having previously served in the Boer War, and proceeded to France in the following June. Here he was attached to the 38th Field Ambulance and was present at numerous engagements, including those at Armentières, Loos, Arras and the Somme, and rendered valuable service until demobilised in February 1919. He holds the 1914-15 Star, and the General Service and Victory Medals.
111, Lavender Sweep, Battersea, S.W.11.   Z4204

SMITH, H. L., Bombardier, R.F.A.

He volunteered in March 1915, and was sent to France in the following January and fought at Vimy Ridge, Armentières, and the Somme, and was gassed at Ypres in September 1917. After his recovery he was in action at Cambrai and during the Retreat and Advance of 1918 rendered valuable services. He returned to England and was demobilised in January 1919, and holds the General Service and Victory Medals.
43, Rosemary Road, Peckham, S.E.15.   Z5249A

SMITH, H. L., Sapper, R.E.

He volunteered in September 1914, and on the conclusion of his course of training was drafted to the Western Front. While there he did much excellent work with his unit in many sectors up to the close of the war, and was wounded on the Somme and at Cambrai. After his return home he was demobilised in February 1919, holding the 1914-15 Star, and the General Service and Victory Medals.
58, Eastbury Grove, Chiswick, W.4.   5591

SMITH, H. O., Private, Royal Fusiliers.

He joined in April 1916, and proceeded to France in December of the following year. He took an active part in the fighting at Arras and on the Somme, and at Amiens, Cambrai and Ypres during the Retreat and Advance of 1918. After the Armistice he returned to England and was demobilised in January 1919, holding the General Service and Victory Medals.
36, Wyndham Road, Camberwell, S.E.5.   Z4196

SMITH, H. P. (M.M.), Pte., 1st Hampshire Regt.

He volunteered in March 1915, and after his training was sent to Gallipoli and took part in the Landing. Later he was wounded and on his recovery he was sent to France in February 1916. Here he saw much fighting on the Somme and at Arras, and fought in the Retreat and Advance of 1918, rendering good service until he was demobilised in March 1919, holding the 1914-15 Star, and the General Service and Victory Medals.
90, Abercrombie Street Battersea, S.W.11.   Z4161

SMITH, H. S., Rifleman, Rifle Brigade.

Volunteering in August 1914, he was shortly afterwards drafted to the Western Front, where he took part in many notable battles, and was killed in action during the fierce fighting on the Somme. He was entitled to the 1914 Star, and the General Service and Victory Medals.
"He died the noblest death a man may die
Fighting for God, and right, and liberty."
7A, Guinness' Buildings, Pages Walk, Grange Road, S.E.1.
                                                       Z26853

SMITH, H. V., Sergt., 2nd Royal Fusiliers.

He was serving in India when war broke out, and in 1915 was sent to the Dardanelles. Here he took part in the Landing at Gallipoli during which he was unfortunately killed on April 25th, 1915. He was entitled to the 1914-15 Star, and the General Service and Victory Medals.
"The path of duty was the way to glory."
129, Blakes Road, Peckham, S.E.15.   Z6093

SMITH, H. W., Air Mechanic, R.A.F.

Joining in 1917, he served on the completion of his training, on important duties which demanded a high degree of technical skill. He rendered valuable service until demobilised in 1919.
187, Stewarts Road, Battersea Park Road, S.W.8.   Z4200B

SMITH, J., Private, R.M.L.I.

He joined in January 1917, and on the completion of his training was engaged in the construction of floating towers for the Navy, and on other important duties. He rendered valuable services, but was not successful in obtaining his transfer overseas before the cessation of hostilities. He was demobilised in November 1919.
302, Commercial Road, Peckham, S.E.15.   Z6662B

SMITH, J., Stoker, R.N.D.

Mobilised at the outbreak of war he was shortly afterwards drafted overseas, and took part in the operations at Antwerp. After the British retirement he crossed the Dutch Frontier, and was interned in Holland until after the cessation of hostilities. In 1918 he was repatriated and discharged, holding the 1914 Star, and the General Service and Victory Medals.
6, Faraday Street, Walworth, S.E.17.   27459

SMITH, J., Sergt., 1st Coldstream Guards.

Volunteering in September 1914, he proceeded in the following April to France, where during the severe fighting at Ypres, he was wounded. He was invalided home, and on recovery returned to the Western Front and took part in many engagements including those on the Somme, and at Vimy Ridge, and Ypres, and in the Retreat and Advance of 1918 during which he was again wounded. After receiving hospital treatment he was demobilised in February 1919, and holds the 1914-15 Star, and the General Service and Victory Medals.
34, St. George's Road, Peckham, S.E.15.   Z5499

SMITH, J., Corporal, R.F.A.

Volunteering in August 1914, he proceeded in the following November to France, and was in action at La Bassée, Ypres, Neuve Chapelle, Hill 60, Loos, and many other important engagements. Shortly afterwards he was drafted to Egypt and served there until the conclusion of hostilities. He returned home and was demobilised in February 1920, holding the 1914 Star, and the General Service and Victory Medals.
84, Cabul Road, Battersea, S.W.11.   Z4186

SMITH, J., Private, R.A.S.C.

Though forty-seven years of age he volunteered in December 1914, and in the following month proceeded to France, where he did valuable transport work on many different sectors of the front right up to the cessation of hostilities. After returning to England he was demobilised in February 1919, and holds the 1914-15 Star, and the General Service and Victory Medals.
118A, Acton Lane, Chiswick, W.4.   6365

SMITH, J., Private, East Yorkshire Regiment.

He volunteered in April 1915, and after having completed his training was drafted to the Western Front. There he was in action in many engagements including those of St. Quentin, Cambrai, and Arras, where he was wounded on December 2nd, 1917. He was invalided to hospital, on recovery serving on home defence duties until demobilised in March 1919. He holds the General Service and Victory Medals.
8, Spencer Street, Battersea, S.W.11.   Z4164

SMITH, J., Trooper, 5th Dragoon Guards.

Volunteering in February 1914, he proceeded overseas in the same year, and whilst in France fought in many notable engagements including those of Ypres, the Somme, and Arras. He gave his life for King and Country in the Retreat of 1918 on March 25th, and was entitled to the 1914-15 Star, and the General Service and Victory Medals.
"His memory is cherished with pride."
2, Mawbey Street, South Lambeth, S.W.8.   Z4188

SMITH, J., Gunner, R.F.A.
He volunteered in March 1915, and in the following July was drafted to France, and was in action at Loos, Vimy Ridge, the Somme, and Beaumont-Hamel. In July 1917 he was invalided to hospital with trench fever, and on recovery returned to his unit, but after a few months in the fighting area he was again taken ill, and returned home, and was demobilised in January 1919, holding the 1914-15 Star, and the General Service and Victory Medals.
40, Benfield Street, Battersea, S.W.11.   Z4187

SMITH, J., Sapper, R.E.
He joined at the age of fourteen as a cadet sapper, and was stationed at the Duke of York's Barracks, Chelsea, engaged on guarding bridges, and other important duties. He was demobilised in February 1920, but has since re-enlisted in the Royal Garrison Artillery.
14, Caroline Place, Chelsea, S.W.3.   X24221

SMITH, J. A., Corporal, Royal Scots Fusiliers.
Mobilised at the outbreak of war he was almost immediately drafted overseas. Whilst in France he took part in many important engagements, including the Retreat from Mons, and the Battles of the Marne, the Aisne, La Bassée, Neuve Chapelle, Ypres, Loos, and Albert Later he was invalided home through ill-health, and in September 1918 was discharged as medically unfit, holding the Mons Star, and the General Service and Victory Medals.
27, Tracey Street, Kennington, S.E.11.   Z25479

SMITH, J. C., Stoker, R.N.
Volunteering in December 1914, he was posted to H.M.S. " Africa," and in this ship saw much service. His vessel was engaged on important patrol and other duties, and also served off the coasts of Africa and Russia. He holds the 1914-15 Star, and the General Service and Victory Medals, and was still serving in 1920.
33 Urswicke Road, Battersea, S.W.11.   Z4208A

SMITH, J. E., Private, 5th Wiltshire Regiment.
He volunteered in August 1914, and after a period of training in the following June proceeded to the Dardanelles, where he only remained for a short time before he was killed in action on June 23rd, 1915. He was entitled to the 1914-15 Star, and the General Service and Victory Medals.
   " Steals on the ear the distant triumph song."
7, Brodie Street, Old Kent Road, S.E.1.   27400

SMITH, J. E., Chief Petty Officer, R.N., H.M.S. " Bruce."
He was serving at the outbreak of war, having joined in 1904, and throughout the period of hostilities was engaged on important patrol duties with the Grand Fleet in the North Sea, being present at the Battle of Jutland. He was highly commended for his excellent service by Admiral Beatty, and holds the 1914-15 Star, and the General Service and Victory Medals. He was still serving in 1920.
33, Urswicke Road, Battersea, S.W.11.   Z4208B

SMITH, J. F., Rifleman, 11th London Regt. (Rifles).
He joined in December 1916, and after his training was drafted to Egypt in the following March. He was reported missing after the Battle of Gaza and is presumed to have been killed in action on April 19th, 1917. He was entitled to the General Service and Victory Medals.
   " His memory is cherished with pride."
40, Blake's Road, Peckham, S.E.15.   Z6081B

SMITH, J. F., Gunner, R.F.A.
He was serving at the outbreak of war, having enlisted in May 1914, and was immediately drafted to France, where he took part in the Retreat from Mons, and the Battles of the Marne, the Aisne, Ypres, Loos, the Somme, and Arras. He was taken prisoner during the German Offensive in March 1918, and was held in captivity until after the Armistice. He was then released and repatriated, and in May 1920 was demobilised, holding the Mons Star, and the General Service and Victory Medals. 9, Mays Place, Peckham, S.E.15.   Z6077

SMITH, J. G., Stoker Petty Officer, R.N.
He was serving at the outbreak of hostilities, and in the course of his valuable service in H.M.S. " Cheerful," " Doon," " Vittoria," and " Q12 " went through many exciting engagements. In January 1917 his vessel was in action with a German submarine and sank her, and three months later the " Q12," on which he was then serving was sunk. In 1919 his vessel the " Vittoria," was destroyed by a Bolshevist submarine in the Gulf of Finland, but he was rescued by H.M.S. " Abdiel." After his return to England he was demobilised in September 1919, and holds the 1914-15 Star, and the General Service and Victory Medals.
15, Ivy Crescent, Chiswick, W.4.   6042

SMITH, J. H., Leading Seaman, R.N., H.M.S. " Dido " and " Llewellyn."
He volunteered in 1915, and throughout the remaining period of hostilities served on important convoy duties in the North Sea. He returned to port in 1919, and was demobilised, holding the 1914-15 Star, and the General Service and Victory Medals. 55, Bagshot Street, Walworth, S.E.17.   24033C

SMITH, J. H., Rflmn., 12th London Regt. (Rangers).
He volunteered in September 1914, and after completing his training was drafted in the following year to the Western Front, where he served until 1916. He took part in many important engagements and was severely wounded, in consequence of which he was invalided home and ultimately discharged in February 1919. He holds the 1914-15 Star, and the General Service and Victory Medals.
17, St. Alban's Avenue, Chiswick, W.4.   7880

SMITH, J. H., Private, R.A.S.C. (M.T.)
He volunteered in May 1915, and after the completion of his training proceeded to France, where for fifteen months he did valuable transport work at Rouen and in many important sectors of the line, especially those of Arras and Messines. He was discharged in January 1918 in consequence of his service, and holds the General Service and Victory Medals.
4, Leamore Street, Hammersmith, W.6.   12574

SMITH, J. H., 1st Class Petty Officer, R.N., H.M.S. " Lowestoft."
He was serving at the outbreak of war, having joined in 1905, and was engaged in the transport of troops to France, until contracting rheumatic fever, he was invalided to hospital and later discharged in October 1914 as physically unfit for further service. He holds the 1914-15 Star, and the General Service and Victory Medals.
10, Ewell Place, Camberwell, S.E.5.   5778A

SMITH, J. R., Corporal, R.A.S.C.
He joined in January 1917, and proceeding to Egypt in the following month, served in the Offensive in Palestine with General Allenby's Forces. He was engaged on important transport duties throughout the campaign, and was present at the three Battles of Gaza, the Entry into Jerusalem, and the captures of Jericho, Tripoli, and Aleppo. He returned home and was demobilised in August 1919, and holds the General Service and Victory Medals.
51, Attwell Road, Peckham, S.E.15.   Z5500

SMITH, J. T., Engineer, Mercantile Marine and Minesweeping Service.
He volunteered in January 1915, and was posted to H.M. Trawlers " Wisteria " and " Osprey." Whilst in these vessels he was engaged in dangerous minesweeping operations in the Irish Sea and English Channel, and subsequently on convoy and transport duties until December 1916. He was then discharged as medically unfit for further duty, and holds the 1914-15 Star, and the General Service and Victory Medals.
35, Cook's Road, Walworth, S.E.17.   Z26784

SMITH, J. W., Stoker, R.N.
He joined the Navy in September 1900, and at the outbreak of war was called up and posted to H.M.S. " Seahorse." Whilst on board this ship he served with the Grand Fleet in various waters on patrol and other duties until the cessation of hostilities. He was demobilised in February 1919, and holds the 1914-15 Star and the General Service and Victory Medals.
48, Earl Road, Upper Grange Road, S.E.1.   Z26851

SMITH, L., Driver, R.F.A.
He volunteered in January 1915, and in the same year proceeded overseas. During his service in France he did good work as a driver with his Battery at Ypres, Loos, the Somme,. Cambrai, Arras, and in many subsequent engagements until the Armistice. He then proceeded to Germany with the Army of Occupation and remained there until his return home in April 1919, when he was demobilised. He holds the 1914-15 Star, and the General Service and Victory Medals.
22, Crescent Road, Clapham, S.W.4.   Z4162

SMITH, L. E., Rifleman, 9th London Regiment (Queen Victoria's Rifles).
He joined in June 1916, and in the following September was drafted to France. Whilst overseas he served in many sectors of the Front with the Lewis Machine Gun Section, and was in action at the Somme and Lens. He gave his life for King and Country near Loos on August 18th, 1917, and was entitled to the General Service and Victory Medals.
   " He died the noblest death a man may die,
    Fighting for God, and right, and liberty."
29, Southampton Street, Camberwell, S.E.5.   Z4540

SMITH, L. E., Rflmn., Cameronians (Scottish Rifles).
He joined in November 1918 before attaining military age, and after his course of training was engaged upon important duties with his unit. He was not able to be drafted overseas while hostilities continued, but rendered valuable services until his demobilisation in August 1920.
28, Spencer Street, Battersea, S.W.11.   Z4207B

SMITH, L. T., Private, R.A.F.
He joined in June 1917 at the age of forty-six, and on this account was retained on home defence duties. He rendered valuable service at various stations with his Squadron and was demobilised in January 1919.
12K, Victoria Dwellings, Battersea Park Road, S.W.8.   Z4165

SMITH, M. J., Sergt., Queen's Own Oxfordshire Hussars (M.G. Section).
He volunteered in February 1915, and was employed for a time in Ireland as Instructor at Curragh Camp. He was then drafted to the Western Front, where he took an active part in the Battles of the Somme, and was in the heavy fighting at Ypres, Arras, Albert, Amiens, Vimy Ridge, and St. Quentin. He also took part in the Retreat and Advance of 1918 in which he was severely wounded. He was invalided home and discharged as unfit for further service in December 1919, holding the 1914-15 Star, and the General Service and Victory Medals.
76, Aldred Road, Walworth, S.E.17.   Z26484

SMITH, M. M., Private, 2nd Essex Regiment.
Volunteering in April 1915, on the completion of his training he served on the Western Front, and took part in the fighting at Arras, Ypres, and Lens. He was unfortunately killed in action near Arras in June 1918 during the Allied Retreat whilst acting as a stretcher bearer for his Regiment. He was recommended for bravery on the Field in rescuing his Colonel under heavy fire, and was entitled to the General Service and Victory Medals.
"Greater love hath no man than this, that a man lay down his life for his friends"
156, Lynton Road, Bermondsey, S.E.1.   Z26192

SMITH, M. W., Corporal, 2nd London Regt. (Royal Fusiliers).
He volunteered in October 1914, and after his training was drafted to France in April 1916. During his service on the Western Front he fought at the Somme and Cambrai, when he was taken prisoner in 1917. He unfortunately died whilst a captive in the hands of the Germans in July 1918, and was entitled to the General Service and Victory Medals.
"Thinking that remembrance though unspoken may reach him where he sleeps."
124, Stewarts Road, Battersea Park Road, S.W.8.   Z4230A

SMITH, O. A., Private, R.A.S.C.
He volunteered in April 1915, and in the same year was drafted to France. During his service overseas he was engaged in loading up munitions, and was in charge of a detachment of South African natives and Chinese coolies. Unfortunately his health broke down, and he was invalided out of the Service in January 1919. He had previously served in the South African War, and holds the Queen's and King's South African Medals (with five clasps), and also the 1914-15 Star, and the General Service and Victory Medals.
28, Knowsley Road, Battersea, S.W.11.   Z4199

SMITH, P. A., Sergt., 21st London Regt. (1st Surrey Rifles).
Volunteering in August 1914, he was drafted overseas in the following year and served at St. Eloi, Ypres, Loos, Ploegsteert Wood, Arras, Lens, and Cambrai. He also took an active part in various engagements in the Retreat and Advance of 1918, and after the Armistice proceeded to Germany with the Army of Occupation, remaining there until January 1919, when he returned to England and was demobilised. He holds the 1914-15 Star, and the General Service and Victory Medals.
38, Offley Road, Brixton Road, S.W.9.   Z5501

SMITH, P. H., Corporal, South Lancashire Regiment.
A serving soldier since February 1912, he was immediately drafted to France at the outbreak of hostilities, and served throughout the war. He was in action in all the early engagements including the memorable Retreat from Mons and the Battles of La Bassée, Ypres, and Hill 60, and in many others until hostilities ceased. During his service he was wounded. He was demobilised in March 1919, and holds the Mons Star, and the General Service and Victory Medals.
30, Wayford Street, Battersea, S.W.11.   Z4189

SMITH, R., Rifleman, Rifle Brigade.
He joined in January 1916, and in September of the same year proceeded to France, where he served in various engagements, including those of Ypres, the Somme, and Arras. He was discharged owing to ill-health in June 1917, as medically unfit for further service, and holds the General Service and Victory Medals.
62, Albany Road, Camberwell, S.E.5.   Z5672

SMITH, R. F., Trooper, 2nd Life Guards.
He joined in January 1917, and proceeded overseas in the following October. He was stationed at Etaples when the severe German air raid took place, and the hospital was bombed. He also served in several engagements in the Offensives of 1918, including that of Le Cateau in October, when he was seriously gassed. He was invalided home and unfortunately died of the effects of gas poisoning on December 8th, 1918. He was entitled to the General Service and Victory Medals.
"A costly sacrifice upon the altar of freedom."
27, Elam Street, Camberwell, S.E.5.   Z6230B

SMITH, R., Corporal, R.A.S.C. (M.T.)
He volunteered in November 1915, and in the following February was drafted to the Western Front. Whilst in France he did valuable transport service on many fronts until hostilities ceased, including those of the Somme and Arras. He was demobilised in August 1919, and holds the General Service and Victory Medals.
30, Weston Road, Chiswick, W.4.   6026

SMITH, R. G. (M.M.), Private, R.A.M.C.
He volunteered in July 1915, and in the following October was drafted to France, where he served with distinction with the Field Ambulance, and in various hospitals until the cessation of hostilities. He won the Military Medal for his great courage and devotion to duty, and was highly commended by his commanding officer for his conduct at Maricourt on March 25th, 1918. He holds in addition the 1914-15 Star, and the General Service and Victory Medals, and was demobilised in May 1919.
48, St. George's Road, Peckham, S.E.15.   Z5497A

SMITH, S., Pte., Queen's (Royal West Surrey Regt.)
He joined in September 1918, and after his training was engaged at various stations on important duties with his unit. He rendered valuable services, but was not successful in obtaining his transfer overseas before the cessation of hostilities. He was demobilised in January 1920.
198, Albert Road, Peckham, S.E.15.   Z5648C

SMITH, S., Gunner, R.F.A.
He volunteered in 1915, and in the following year was drafted to France, where he took part in numerous engagements, including those on the Somme, where he was badly gassed and invalided home. On his recovery he returned to France and was in action at Arras and Ypres. He also served in the Retreat and Advance of 1918. He was demobilised in June 1919, and holds the General Service and Victory Medals.
35, Bournemouth Road, Peckham, S.E.15.   Z5842B

SMITH, S., Rifleman, King's Royal Rifle Corps.
Joining in 1916 he was drafted to France in the same year and took part in the severe fighting on the Somme, and at Arras and Ypres. He also served in the Retreat and Advance of 1918, and was three times wounded and suffered from frost bite. He was demobilised in 1919, and holds the General Service and Victory Medals.
63, Henshaw Street, Walworth, S.E.17.   Z4212

SMITH, S. A., Rifleman, Rifle Brigade.
He volunteered in September 1914, and after completing his training was engaged with his unit at various stations on important duties until he was drafted to India, where he was stationed until he returned home, and was demobilised in May 1919, holding the General Service and Victory Medals.
16, Este Road, Battersea, S.W.11.   Z4167

SMITH, S. E., Private, R.A.S.C.
He was mobilised at the outbreak of war, and in the following year was sent to France, where he was engaged on important duties on the Somme, Arras, Ypres, and Cambrai fronts, and was gassed. He was afterwards transferred to the Sherwood Foresters, with which he served until he was discharged in March 1919 as medically unfit, holding the 1914-15 Star, and the General Service and Victory Medals.
11, Union Grove, Wandsworth, S.W.8.   Z4182

SMITH, S. F., Gunner, R.F.A.
He attested in November 1915, but owing to his being engaged as foreman on important work connected with aeroplanes he was not called up until March 1918. After training he was sent to France in July of the same year, and took part in the severe fighting at Ypres and Mount Kemmel. He proceeded with the Army of Occupation to Germany after the Armistice, and served at Cologne until he was demobilised in September 1919, holding the General Service and Victory Medals.
24, St. George's Road, Peckham, S.E.15.   Z5496B

SMITH, S. G., Private, R.A.S.C. (M.T.)
He volunteered in October 1914, and in the same month was drafted to France. He was engaged in many sectors, including that of Ypres, in the transport of ammunition and supplies to the front lines. He also took part in the Retreat and Advance of 1918. He was demobilised in April 1919, and holds the 1914 Star, and the General Service and Victory Medals.
31, Pentridge Street, Peckham, S.E.15.   Z5674

SMITH, S. G., A/Staff-Sergt., R.A.O.C.
He joined in October 1916, and in the following year was sent to France and was engaged on important duties at Calais, Boulogne and elsewhere. He was later sent home, but after the Armistice was drafted to Germany with the Army of Occupation, and served there until he was demobilised in April 1920, holding the General Service and Victory Medals.
28, Thurlow Street, Wandsworth Road, S.W.8.   4190A

SMITH, S. H., Private, R.A.S.C. (M.T.)
He volunteered in September 1914, and after completing his training was drafted to Egypt. Later he was transferred to the Western Front, where he was engaged in various sectors on important transport duties. He returned home and was demobilised in April 1919, and holds the General Service and Victory Medals.
65, Faroe Road, West Kensington, W.14. 12453A

SMITH, S. R., Sapper, R.E.
He joined in 1918, and after completing his training was engaged on important duties with his unit. He rendered valuable services, but was not successful in obtaining his transfer overseas before the cessation of hostilities. He was demobilised in 1919.
33, Lanvanor Road, Peckham, S.E.15. Z6505A

SMITH, S. T., Telegraphist, R.N., H.M.S. "Pembroke."
He joined in December 1917, and was engaged as a wireless operator on H.M.S. "Manx King," "Queen," and other vessels in the Mediterranean, Adriatic, and Italian waters on mine-sweeping duties. He returned home and was demobilised in January 1919, holding the General Service and Victory Medals.
1, Draycourt Place, Camberwell, S.E.5. Z4542A

SMITH, T., Gunner, R.G.A.
Joining in January 1916 he was sent to France in the same year and was in action at St. Eloi, Albert, Vermelles, Beaumont-Hamel, Vimy Ridge, the Somme, Messines, Passchendaele, and Cambrai. He also took part in the Retreat and Advance of 1918. He was demobilised in June 1919, and holds the General Service and Victory Medals.
7, Harders Road, Peckham, S.E.15. Z6326

SMITH, T. E., Private, 20th London Regiment.
He joined in 1917, and after completing his training was drafted to the Western Front in the same year. He took part in many important engagements, including those at Arras, Ypres, and Passchendaele, and was wounded in the Somme Offensive of 1918, while carrying despatches. Returning home he was demobilised in 1919, and holds the General Service and Victory Medals.
12, Wesley Place, S.E.11. Z26179

SMITH, T. G., Private, R.A.M.C.
He enlisted in June 1912, and at the outbreak of war was sent to France, where he fought in the Retreat from Mons, the Battles of the Marne, the Aisne, Valenciennes, Cambrai, the Somme, and throughout the German Offensive and Allied Advance of 1918. During his service overseas he was twice gassed, and returning to England after the Armistice was demobilised in February 1919. He holds the Mons Star, and the General Service and Victory Medals.
187, Heath Road, Wandsworth Road, S.W.8. Z4211

SMITH, T. H., Private, 3rd Queen's (Royal West Surrey Regiment).
He joined in August 1916, and was drafted to France shortly afterwards. He did much valuable work at Dunkirk and Nieuport, and after taking part in many important engagements in 1917, was in action throughout the German Offensive and subsequent Allied Advance of 1918. Returning to England he was demobilised in March 1919, and holds the General Service and Victory Medals.
79, D'Eynsford Road, Camberwell, S.E.5. Z4201

SMITH, T. J., Private, 7th Yorkshire Regiment.
He joined in April 1917, and embarking for France four months later, saw much service in many parts of the line, including the Ypres salient. He also fought throughout the Retreat and Advance of 1918, and returning home after the cessation of hostilities, was demobilised in February 1919. He holds the General Service and Victory Medals.
70, Tyers Street, Kennington, S.E.11. Z25153

SMITH, T. W., Gunner (Signaller), R.F.A.
Volunteering in September 1914, he embarked for the Western Front in the following March, and was in action at Festubert, Loos, Vimy Ridge, the Somme, and was wounded at Messines. Returning to England he received hospital treatment at Exeter, and on his recovery served at various stations until demobilised in January 1919. He holds the 1914–15 Star, and the General Service and Victory Medals.
20, Lisford Street, Peckham, S.E.15. Z5206C

SMITH, W., Pioneer, R.E.
He volunteered in December 1915, and shortly afterwards was drafted to Salonika, where he was in action in many engagements on the Vardar, Struma and Doiran fronts. Being transferred to Egypt he rendered valuable services while engaged on important transport duties, and returning to England after the Armistice was demobilised in March 1919. He holds the General Service and Victory Medals.
82, Neate Street, Camberwell, S.E.5. Z5502

SMITH, W., Driver, R.F.A.
Joining in March 1917, he embarked later in that year for the Western Front, and was in action in the Battles of the Somme, Ypres, Arras and throughout the German Offensive and Allied Advance of 1918. After the Armistice, proceeding into Germany with the Army of Occupation, he served there until he returned to England and was demobilised in 1919. He holds the General Service and Victory Medals.
38, Bournemouth Road, Peckham, S.E.15. Z5498A

SMITH, W., Private, Queen's (Royal West Surrey Regiment) and M.G.C.
He joined in August 1916, and after being drafted to the Western Front in the following April fought at Messines, Ypres, Passchendaele, Lens, Cambrai, Amiens and throughout the Retreat and Advance of 1918. He was demobilised in September 1919, after his return home, and holds the General Service and Victory Medals.
50, Alfreton Street, Walworth, S.E.17. Z4191

SMITH, W., Private, 6th Somerset Light Infantry.
Volunteering in June 1915, he embarked for the Western Front in the following October, and was engaged in the heavy fighting at Albert, Arras, Loos, and was wounded at Ypres in March 1916. On his recovery he rejoined his unit, and fought in the British Offensive on the Somme, and was wounded and taken prisoner at Ypres in August 1916. During his captivity he suffered greatly from privation. Repatriated after the Armistice, he was demobilised in March 1919, and holds the 1914–15 Star, and the General Service and Victory Medals.
146, St. George's Road, Peckham, S.E.15. Z5835

SMITH, W., Corporal, Scots Guards.
He joined in June 1917, and proceeding to the Western Front in the succeeding month, was in action in many important engagements, including those at Arras, Ypres, and Cambrai. Invalided to England in February 1918, owing to ill-health, he received hospital treatment and was subsequently demobilised in July 1919. He holds the General Service and Victory Medals.
246, The Grove, Hammersmith, W.6. 10737

SMITH, W., Driver, R.A.S.C.
A serving soldier, he was mobilised and drafted to France at the outbreak of war, and served in the Retreat from Mons, in the Battles of La Bassée, Neuve Chapelle, Loos, Vimy Ridge, and throughout the German Offensive and Allied Advance of 1918. After the Armistice he was engaged on important transport duties until transferred to the Reserve in January 1919. He holds the Mons Star, and the General Service and Victory Medals.
198, Albert Road, Peckham, S.E.15. Z5648B

SMITH, W., Gunner, R.H.A.
He enlisted in November 1907, and at the declaration of war was sent to the Western Front. He was in action in the Retreat from Mons, and in the Battles of Neuve Chapelle, Loos, Festubert, Ypres, and was badly wounded on the Somme in 1916. After being invalided to England he received protracted hospital treatment and was ultimately discharged as unfit for further service in 1918. He holds the Mons Star, and the General Service and Victory Medals.
86, Buchan Road, Peckham, S.E.15. Z6546

SMITH, W., Gunner, R.G.A.
He volunteered in December 1915, and embarked for Salonika in the following year. During his service overseas he fought in many engagements of note and was wounded. Suffering from malaria he returned to England, and after receiving hospital treatment was invalided out of the Service in November 1918. He holds the General Service and Victory Medals.
2, Warrior Road, Camberwell, S.E.5. Z4170

SMITH, W., Gunner, R.F.A.
He volunteered in March 1915, and after completing his training was sent to the Western Front, where he fought in the Battles of Ypres, the Somme, Arras, Vimy Ridge and Bullecourt. He also took part in heavy fighting during the German Offensive and Allied Advance of 1918, and returned to England in 1919. He was demobilised in March of that year, and holds the General Service and Victory Medals.
81, Nursery Road, Brixton Road, S.W.9. Z4194

SMITH, W., Guardsman, Coldstream Guards.
He was mobilised in August 1914, and was immediately drafted to the Western Front, where he saw service at Mons and in the heavy fighting that followed. He was twice wounded and sent to the Base. On his recovery he subsequently took part in the Advance of 1918. He returned to England and was demobilised, but has since rejoined, and was still serving in 1920. He holds the Mons Star, and the General Service and Victory Medals.
5, Camberwell Gate, Walworth, S.E.17. Z26204

SMITH, W., Private, M.G.C.
He joined in 1916, and was sent to France in the same year. He fought at the Somme, Arras, and Ypres, where he was gassed. On his recovery he returned to the line and took part in many engagements of the Retreat and Advance until the Armistice. He was demobilised in 1920, holding the General Service and Victory Medals.
55, Bagshot Street, Walworth, S.E.17.   Z4033B

SMITH, W., Private, R.A.S.C. (Remounts).
He joined in February 1916, and after completion of his training was engaged on important duties in the Remount department in various parts of England. He rendered valuable services, but was unable to obtain his transfer overseas before the cessation of hostilities, and was demobilised in May 1919.
18, Carfax Square, Clapham, S.W.4.   Z4172

SMITH, W. A., Pte., 1st Scottish Rifles (Cameronians).
He enlisted in July 1914, and embarking for the Western Front at the outbreak of war fought in the Retreat from Mons, and at the Battles of Le Cateau and the Somme, where he was wounded. On recovery he proceeded to Egypt, and was in action in many engagements during the British Advance through Palestine and was twice wounded. He returned to England and was demobilised in February 1919, and holds the Mons Star, and the General Service and Victory Medals.
70, Cornbury Road, Rotherhithe, S.E.16.   Z6763

SMITH, W. D., Private, Middlesex Regiment.
He volunteered in 1915, and in the following year after the completion of his training proceeded to the Western Front, where he took part in numerous engagements of importance, including those at Arras, Bullecourt, Vimy Ridge, St. Quentin, Amiens and Cambrai. After his return home he was demobilised in February 1919, and holds the General Service and Victory Medals.
38A Block, Sutton Buildings, Chelsea, S.W.3.   X22992

SMITH, W. F., Private, H.A.C.
He volunteered in 1915, and was sent to France in October 1916. He fought in numerous engagements, including those at Ypres, Passchendaele, Vermelles, Ploegsteert Wood Beaumont-Hamel, and the Somme. He proceeded to Italy in 1917, and after fighting heavily on the Piave front fell in action there, on October 23rd, 1918. He was buried at Tezze Cemetery in Italy. He was entitled to the General Service and Victory Medals.
"A costly sacrifice upon the altar of freedom."
63, Smith Street, Camberwell, S.E.5.   Z4175

SMITH, W. F., Private, 2nd Royal Sussex Regiment.
He joined in June 1918, and for several months was engaged on important duties with his unit at various stations. He was unable to secure his transfer overseas before the cessation of hostilities, but afterwards proceeded to Germany, where he rendered valuable services until his return to England for demobilisation in March 1920.
20, Lisford Street, Peckham, S.E.15.   Z5206B

SMITH, W. G., Rifleman, 21st London Regiment (1st Surrey Rifles).
He volunteered in April 1915, and proceeded to France in October of that year, where he fought in many important engagements, including those at Arras, La Bassée, Oppy Wood and Cambrai. After rendering much valuable service he was unfortunately killed in action at Bourlon Wood on December 4th, 1917. He was entitled to the 1914-15 Star, and the General Service and Victory Medals.
"The path of duty was the way to glory."
1, Draycott Place, Camberwell, S.E.5.   Z4542B

SMITH, W. G. N., Private, 2nd London Regiment (Royal Fusiliers).
He joined in March 1916, and later in that year proceeded to France. He took an active part in the heavy fighting at the Somme, Ypres and Arras, where he was wounded in 1917. On his recovery he returned to the front line and did much valuable work until he was reported wounded and missing after the Battle of Cambrai on November 30th, 1917. Since that date he has been presumed killed in action. He was entitled to the General Service and Victory Medals.
"His life for his Country, his Soul to God."
155, Kirkwood Road, Peckham, S.E.15.   Z6325

SMITH, W. H., Corporal, Grenadier Guards and Canadian Mounted Rifles.
He volunteered in 1915, and was drafted in June of the following year to the Western Front, where he served with distinction at the Somme, Vimy Ridge and Lens, and was mentioned in Despatches in July 1917, for gallantry in the Field. On August 25th, 1917, he was severely wounded in the fierce fighting at Lens, and unfortunately died two days later. He was entitled to the General Service and Victory Medals.
"A valiant soldier, with undaunted heart he breasted Life's last hill."
42, Cunnington Street, Chiswick, W.4.   6876

SMITH, W. H., Sergt., R.F.A.
He volunteered in 1915, and was sent to France in that year. After fighting gallantly at Ypres, the Somme, and Bullecourt, he was unhappily killed in action on July 2nd, 1917, and was buried in France. He was entitled to the 1914-15 Star, and the General Service and Victory Medals.
"And doubtless he went in splendid company."
187, Stewart's Road, Battersea, S.W.8.   Z4200A

SMITH, W. H., Gunner, R.G.A.
He volunteered in August 1915, and after his training was drafted to the Western Front, where he was in action at Ypres, the Somme, Arras, and many operations in the Retreat and Advance of 1918. During his service overseas he was wounded on three occasions. He returned home and was demobilised in 1919, holding the 1914-15 Star, and the General Service and Victory Medals.
31, Neville Street, Vauxhall, S.E.11.   Z25574

SMITH, W. H., Gunner, R.F.A.
He volunteered in 1915, and was shortly afterwards sent to France. After taking part in many engagements of importance he was unfortunately killed in action near Arras, and was buried in Arras Cemetery. He was entitled to the 1914-15 Star, and the General Service and Victory Medals.
"His life for his Country."
22, Cambridge Street, Camberwell, S.E.5.   Z4176

SMITH, W. J., Private, Labour Corps.
He joined in June 1918, and proceeded to France in the following month. He did much valuable work there for several months, after which he returned to England, and was demobilised in April 1919. He holds the General Service and Victory Medals.
62, Albany Road, Camberwell, S.E.5.   Z5671A

SMITH, W. J., Gunner (Fitter), R.G.A.
He joined in 1916, and after the completion of his training was engaged on important duties with his unit at Lydd, and other stations. He rendered valuable services, but was unable to obtain his transfer to a foreign front before the cessation of hostilities. He was demobilised in January 1919.
34, Clayton Road, Peckham, S.E.15.   Z6080

SMITH, W. J., Bombardier (Shoeing Smith), R.F.A.
He volunteered in 1915, and after his training was sent to France. He took part in many important engagements, including those at the Somme, Ypres, Arras, and in the Advance and Retreat of the Allies in 1918. After returning to England he was demobilised in January 1919, and holds the 1914-15 Star, and the General Service and Victory Medals.
83, Westmacott Street, Camberwell, S.E.5.   Z4541

SMITH, W. J., Rifleman, Rifle Brigade.
He joined in May 1916, and after completing his training proceeded to France. After taking part in many operations in the Somme Offensive, he was seriously injured while off duty and after protracted hospital treatment was discharged in February 1919, as unfit for further military duty. He holds the General Service and Victory Medals.
22, Aldbridge Street, Walworth, S.E.17.   Z4192

SNAPES, W., Pte., Northumberland Fusiliers and M.G.C.
He was mobilised in August 1914, and was almost immediately drafted to France, where he took part in many of the early operations including the Retreat from Mons, and the Battles of La Bassée, Ypres, Neuve Chapelle and Loos. Subsequently he fought on the Somme, and at Arras and Ypres, and was severely wounded at Cambrai in 1917. He was invalided home to hospital and discharged as medically unfit for further duty in October of the following year. He holds the Mons Star, and the General Service and Victory Medals.
175, Mayall Road, Herne Hill, S.E.24.   Z4213

SNELL, A. J., Private, 2nd Royal Berkshire Regt.
Volunteering in August 1914, he sailed for France in the following November, and whilst overseas fought in several early engagements, including that of Neuve Chapelle. He died gloriously on the Field of Battle at Festubert in May 1915, and was entitled to the 1914 Star, and the General Service and Victory Medals.
"Courage, bright hopes, and a myriad dreams splendidly given."
65, Graylands Road, Peckham, S.E.15.   Z5840B

SNELL, B. C., Private, 7th Norfolk Regiment.
He volunteered in March 1915, at the age of fifteen years, and sailed for France in the following August. Whilst overseas he took part in numerous engagements, including those at Vimy Ridge, and the Battle of the Somme, where he was wounded in July 1916. He was invalided home to hospital, and after his recovery was retained on home service duties at various stations. In January 1920 he embarked for India, where he was still serving in 1920. He holds the 1914-15 Star, and the General Service and Victory Medals.
65, Graylands Road, Peckham, S.E.15.   Z5840A

SNELL, F., Driver, R.G.A.
He volunteered in 1915, and in the following February was drafted to the Western Front. Whilst overseas he was engaged on important duties in transporting ammunition, and also served in the Royal Field Artillery for nearly a year in the Somme sectors. He was invalided home owing to ill-health in January 1917, and after a period in hospital returned to France in the following October, and served on the Ypres Front and in many engagements in the Retreat and Advance of 1918. He returned home in March of the following year and was discharged in October, holding the 1914-15 Star, and the General Service and Victory Medals.
12, Landseer Street, Battersea, S.W.11. Z1298B

SNELL, S. E., 2nd Lieutenant, R.A.F.
He was already serving at the outbreak of war, and in 1916 was sent to Egypt, where he took a prominent part in the Palestine Offensive under General Allenby. He was in action at all three Battles of Gaza, and was present at the fall of Jerusalem, and in the operations at Aleppo. In 1918 he returned to England, and was demobilised, but has since rejoined in the Scots Guards, and was still serving in 1920. He holds the General Service and Victory Medals.
176, Fort Road, Bermondsey, S.E.1. Z26321

SNELGROVE, C. H., Private, Royal Fusiliers.
He joined in June 1916, and after his training was completed served at various stations on important duties with his unit. He rendered valuable services, but owing to medical reasons, was unable to secure a transfer overseas before the cessation of hostilities. He was demobilised in March 1919.
89, Ranelagh Road, Pimlico, S.W.1. TZ26158

SNELLING, C., Private, Dorsetshire Regiment.
He joined in March 1917, and in the following year was drafted overseas. Whilst in France he fought on the Somme, and was wounded at Albert in 1918, and was invalided home to hospital. He remained under treatment for several months, after which he was demobilised in February 1919, holding the General Service and Victory Medals.
6, Halstead Street, Stockwell, S.W.9. Z4214

SNELLING, C. (Mrs.), Special War Worker.
For two years during the war this lady was engaged on important duties in the employ of the London General Omnibus Company. She carried out her arduous work in a most efficient manner, and her services were highly appreciated.
39, Kempton Road, Camberwell, S.E.5. Z4217B

SNELLING, C. C., Driver, R.F.A.
He volunteered in April 1915, and in the same year was drafted overseas, and took part in many notable engagements, including those at Loos, the Somme, Vimy Ridge, Messines and Ypres. He also served throughout the Retreat and Advance of 1918, and after the Armistice was signed proceeded to Germany with the Army of Occupation. He returned home and was demobilised in February 1919, and holds the 1914-15 Star, and the General Service and Victory Medals.
39, Kimpton Road, Camberwell, S.E.5. Z4217A

SNELLING, G. R., Pte., 22nd London Regt. (Queen's).
He was mobilised in August 1914, and in the following April was drafted to France. During his service overseas he fought in several important engagements, and was severely wounded in action at Givenchy in December 1915. He was invalided home to hospital, and was under medical treatment until discharged as physically unfit for further duty in August 1916. He holds the 1914-15 Star, and the General Service and Victory Medals.
36, St. George's Road, Peckham, S.E.15. Z5503

SNELLING, J. L., Private, R.A.S.C. (M.T.)
He volunteered in April 1915, and in the same year was drafted to the Western Front, where he served on important duties in connection with the Motor Transport in various sectors. He was present in engagements at Ypres, Loos, the Somme and Cambrai, and in many subsequent actions until the Armistice, after which he advanced into Germany with the Army of Occupation, with which he served until he returned home and was demobilised in April 1919. He holds the 1914-15 Star, and the General Service and Victory Medals.
49, Motley Street, Wandsworth Road, S.W.8. Z4215

SNELLING, S., Private, 25th Middlesex Regiment.
He joined in May 1916, and after his training was drafted to Singapore. Whilst en route, the "Tindarus," on board which ship he sailed, was torpedoed, but he was fortunately saved. In June 1918 he was sent to Siberia and landed at Vladivostock, and served with Colonel John Ward, M.P., being attached to General Koltchak's forces. Later, owing to ill-health, he was invalided home and was demobilised in July 1919. He holds the General Service and Victory Medals, and a Russian decoration.
9, Hubert Grove, Stockwell, S.W.9. Z4216

SNOOK, A. E., Ordinary Seaman, Mercantile Marine.
He joined in April 1918, and served on the oil ship "Teakol" for nine months, being engaged in supplying oil to the Fleet. He has since joined the Royal Navy, and was still serving in 1920. He holds the General Service and the Mercantile Marine War Medals.
46, Cator Street, Peckham, S.E.15. Z4543

SNOOK, A. S., Bombardier, R.F.A.
He was mobilised in August 1914, and was sent to the Western Front in the same month, and was in action at Mons, and the Marne, and in many other important engagements. In January 1916, he was transferred to Salonika, where he was again engaged in severe fighting. He unfortunately died of bronchial pneumonia on December 17th, 1918, and was buried at Sesargol Cemetery, Greece. He was entitled to the Mons Star, and the General Service and Victory Medals.
"His life for his Country."
30, Temple Road, Acton Green, W.4. 6084A

SOAR, L. H. S., Private, Lancashire Fusiliers and Durham Light Infantry.
Joining in July 1916, he was sent to France in the same year and took part in the fighting at Messines and Ypres, where he was wounded. He also took part in the Retreat and Advance of 1918. He returned home and was demobilised in November 1919, holding the General Service and Victory Medals.
4, Cornbury Road, Rotherhithe, S.E.16. Z6736

SOILLEUX, W. H., Rflmn., 6th London Regt. (Rifles).
He joined in May 1917, and shortly afterwards proceeded to France, where he took part in severe fighting on the Arras front. He was wounded and taken prisoner in November 1917, and was held in captivity for one year. On his return to England he was in charge of German prisoners at various camps. He was demobilised in November 1919, and holds the General Service and Victory Medals.
16, Willow Street, Bermondsey, S.E.1. Z25944

SOLLIS, L. H., Rifleman, King's Royal Rifle Corps.
He volunteered in May 1915, but unfortunately during the course of his training at Winchester his health broke down, and he was, in consequence, discharged as medically unfit for further service in September of the same year.
16, St. John's Hill Grove, Battersea, S.W.11. Z4218

SOLMAN, H. T., Private, 23rd London Regiment.
He volunteered in April 1915, and was sent to France in June of the following year and was in action on the Somme, and at Ypres, Passchendaele and Cambrai. He also took part in the Retreat and Advance of 1918. During his service overseas he suffered from shell-shock, and was in hospital for a time. He was demobilised in February 1919, and holds the General Service and Victory Medals.
31, Newcomen Road, Battersea, S.W.11. Z3725A

SOLOMON, H. W., Private, Durham Light Infantry.
Joining in June 1916, he was sent to France later in the same year and took part in the fighting on the Somme, and at Cambrai and in many other important engagements, and was three times wounded. He was taken prisoner near Cambrai in March 1918, and held in captivity until after the Armistice. On his release he returned home and was demobilised in February 1919, and holds the General Service and Victory Medals.
17, Catlin Street, Rotherhithe, S.E.16. Z6623

SOMERFORD, H., Private, 17th Middlesex Regiment and M.G.C.
He volunteered in April 1915, and in the following year was sent to France, where he took part in numerous engagements, including those on the Somme, and at Ypres, Cambrai and Armentières, and was twice wounded. He was demobilised in March 1919, and holds the General Service and Victory Medals.
77, Akerman Road, Brixton Road, S.W.9. Z4544

SOMERFORD, S., Rifleman, 16th London Regiment (Queen's Westminster Rifles).
He volunteered in March 1915, and proceeded to France in the following year and took part in the fighting on the Somme, and at Beaumont-Hamel, and in other engagements. Later he contracted pleurisy and was invalided to the Base, and subsequently sent home and discharged as medically unfit for further service in August 1918, holding the General Service and Victory Medals.
6, Senate Street, Nunhead, S.E.15. Z6663

SOMERVILLE, E. A., Rifleman, Rifle Brigade and Northamptonshire Regiment.
He volunteered is November 1914, and after his training served at various stations on important duties with his unit. He rendered valuable services, but was not successful in obtaining his transfer overseas, and was discharged in 1916.
60, Standard Street, Union Road, S.E.1. Z25423

SONNEX, G., Private, 14th London Regt. (London Scottish).
He volunteered in July 1915, and later in the same year was sent to France, where he took part in numerous engagements, including those on the Somme, and at Arras, and Ypres. After the Armistice he proceeded with the Army of Occupation to Germany, and served there until he was demobilised in October 1919, holding the 1914–15 Star, and the General Service and Victory Medals.
19, Mayall Road, Herne Hill, S.E.24.   Z4219

SONNEX, W., Bandsman, King's Royal Rifle Corps.
He volunteered in October 1915, and served at various stations on important duties with his unit until 1918, when he was drafted to France. Later in the same year he proceeded with the Army of Occupation into Germany, and in 1920 was still serving. He holds the General Service and Victory Medals.
5, Ontario Street, Southwark, S.E.1.   Z25202

SOPER, A., Sergt., R.F.A.
He volunteered in April 1915, and in the same year was sent to the Western Front, and took part in the severe fighting in the Somme, and Albert sectors, and was wounded. He unfortunately died of his injuries at Doullens on September 23rd, 1916, and was buried in the British Cemetery at Warlencourt near Albert. He was entitled to the 1914–15 Star, and the General Service and Victory Medals.
" Great deeds cannot die."
17, Relf Road, Peckham, S.E.15.   Z6691

SOPER, A., Private, 10th Queen's (Royal West Surrey Regiment).
He joined in October 1916, and served at various stations until sent to France in 1918. He was in action throughout the German Offensive and Allied Advance of 1918, and was invalided to England early in November 1918. He received treatment and was demobilised in January 1919, and holds the General Service and Victory Medals.
52, Cornbury Road, Rotherhithe, S.E.16.   Z6764

SOPER, E. F., Worker, Q.M.A.A.C.
She volunteered for service in July 1918, and was engaged on important duties with her Corps at Caterham and Wimbledon until October 1919, when she was demobilised, after doing much valuable work.
26, Cornwall Grove, Chiswick, W.4:   5611

SOPER, G., Private, 24th Queen's (Royal West Surrey Regt.) and Royal Irish Fusiliers.
He joined in March 1916, and after a brief training proceeded to the Western Front, where he took part in heavy fighting in the Somme sector, at Arras and Ypres, and was wounded. In 1918 he was killed in action, and was entitled to the General Service and Victory Medals.
35, Newport Street, Kennington, S.E.11.   Z25857

SOPER, J. (M.M.), Rflmn., 8th London Regt. (P.O. Rifles).
He volunteered in December 1915, and in January 1917 was drafted to the Western Front, where he took part in various engagements, including those at Arras, Bullecourt, Passchendaele, Havrincourt, and others. He also served in the Retreat and Advance of 1918. He was wounded and awarded the Military Medal for bravery in the Field, on September 20th, 1917. He was invalided home and discharged as unfit for further service in February 1920, and holds in addition, the 1914–15 Star, and the General Service and Victory Medals.
31, Suffield Road, Walworth, S.E.17.   Z26555

SOULSBY, A. E., Corporal, R.M.L.I.
He volunteered in 1914, and throughout the period of hostilities served in the North Sea. He took part in the Battles of Heligoland Bight, Jutland and Zeebrugge, and also served at the bombardment of Ostend, and after the Armistice was at Constantinople for a time. He was demobilised in February 1919, and holds the 1914–15 Star, and the General Service and Victory Medals.
24, Kirkwood Road, Peckham, S.E.15.   Z6225

SOUTER, W., Driver, R.F.A.
He enlisted in 1871, and afterwards served in South Africa, and took part in the Zulu Campaign of 1877–9. He also served in Basutoland with the Diamond Field with General Lord Chelmsford, and finished up at Pretoria in 1880. On the outbreak of the Great War he volunteered his services, but was rejected owing to his age, and was highly complimented for his patriotism. He holds the South African Medal 1877–79.
64, Galleywall Road, South Bermondsey, S.E.16.   Z6762

SOUTH, H. J., Gunner, R.F.A.
He volunteered in May 1915, and in the same year was drafted to the Western Front, where he was in action at Hill 60, Loos, Vimy Ridge, the Somme, Arras, Ypres, and Cambrai. He also served in the Retreat and Advance of 1918. He was demobilised in June 1919, and holds the 1914–15 Star, and the General Service and Victory Medals.
5, Neate Street, Camberwell, S.E.5.   Z5153B

SOUTH, J. W., Private, Royal Fusiliers and Labour Corps.
He joined in February 1916, and in the following May was sent to France, where he took part in the fighting at Vimy Ridge, the Somme, Arras, Ypres, and Cambrai, where he was wounded and buried by an explosion. After being rescued he was invalided home and discharged as medically unfit for further service in February 1918, and holds the General Service and Victory Medals.
5, Neate Street, Camberwell, S.E.5.   Z5153A

SOUTH, W., Private, R.A.S.C.
He joined in April 1916, and in the same month was sent to France, where he was engaged in various sectors on important transport duties. Later, owing to ill-health, he was invalided home, and was discharged as medically unfit in October 1918, holding the General Service and Victory Medals.
41, Dawlish Street, South Lambeth, S.W.8.   Z4220A

SOUTH, W. C., Gunner, R.F.A.
He volunteered in October 1914, and in the following year was sent to France, where he took part in numerous engagements. In 1916, he was transferred to Salonika, and was engaged in the fierce fighting on the Doiran front. He later contracted malaria, and was invalided home. He was demobilised in February 1919, and holds the 1914–15 Star, and the General Service and Victory Medals.
41, Dawlish Street, South Lambeth, S.W.8.   Z4220B

SOUTHAM, A. E., Sergt., 6th London Regt. (Rifles).
He was mobilised with the Territorial Force at the outbreak of war, and proceeded to France in 1915. Here he fought at Neuve Chapelle, Festubert and Givenchy. Later he returned to England and was discharged as time expired, but rejoined in May 1917, and was engaged on important duties until finally demobilised in January 1919, holding the 1914–15 Star, and the General Service and Victory Medals.
46, Villa Street, Walworth, S.E.17.   Z27317

SOUTHGATE, F., Rifleman, 1st Rifle Brigade.
Mobilised in August 1914, he was sent to the Western Front almost immediately and fought in the early engagements. He was taken prisoner at Le Cateau on 26th August, 1914, and held in captivity in Germany at Doberitz and other camps until after the Armistice. After his repatriation he was demobilised in February 1919, and holds the Mons Star, and the General Service and Victory Medals.
169, Lynton Road, Bermondsey, S.E.1.   Z26269

SOUTHGATE, H., Corporal, 3rd County of London Yeomanry (Sharpshooters).
He volunteered in September 1914, and on the conclusion of his training was drafted to the East, where he served for three years in the Balkans, Egypt and Palestine. He took part in all the leading engagements in the Palestine campaign under General Allenby, including those near Gaza, Jerusalem, and Nazareth, and after his return home he was demobilised in February 1919, holding the General Service and Victory Medals.
87, Fielding Road, Bedford Park, W.4.   7650

SOWTEN, G. E., Sapper, R.E.
He joined the 7th London Regiment, and was discharged, but rejoined in the R.E. in May 1918. Completing his training, he served at various stations engaged on important duties with his unit. He was unsuccessful in obtaining his transfer overseas prior to the cessation of hostilities, but afterwards was sent to the Army of Occupation in Germany in 1919. Returning to England he was demobilised in November 1919.
54, Henley Street, Battersea, S.W.11.   Z4221

SPACKMAN, E. S., Corporal, R.F.A.
He volunteered in June 1915, and after being drafted to France in the following March was in action at the Somme, Arras, Cambrai and Bullecourt, where he was wounded. On his recovery he rejoined his Battery and saw heavy fighting in many sectors. He was taken prisoner at Cambrai in March 1918, in the opening operations of the German Offensive. Repatriated in accordance with the terms of the Armistice he was demobilised in February 1919, and holds the General Service and Victory Medals.
14, Thorncroft Street, Wandsworth Road, S.W.8.   Z4223

SPACKMAN, H., Pte., East Surrey Regiment and Royal Scots.
He volunteered in February 1915, and in the following August proceeded to France, where he fought in many parts of the line. Discovered to be under military age he returned to England and served at various stations until drafted again to France. He was unfortunately killed in action on March 23rd, 1918, in the opening stages of the German Offensive, and was entitled to the 1914–15 Star, and the General Service and Victory Medals.
" His life for his Country."
4, Park Road, Battersea, S.W.11.   Z4222A

SPACKMAN, J. O., Driver, R.A.S.C.
Volunteering in March 1915, he embarked for France later in that year and served at Le Havre and in the forward areas at Cambrai and other places, engaged on important transport duties with the 47th Division. In 1918 he met with an accident, and broke his leg. After returning to England he received hospital treatment, and served at various depôts until demobilised in 1919. He holds the 1914-15 Star, and the General Service and Victory Medals.
4, Park Road, Battersea, S.W.11. Z4222B

SPALDING, A. J., Rifleman, Royal Irish Rifles.
He joined in December 1916, and proceeded to France in the following June. During his service overseas he fought at Ypres, Lens, and in many other important engagements. He died gloriously on the Field of Battle on August 16th, 1917, and was entitled to the General Service and Victory Medals.
"Whilst we remember, the sacrifice is not in vain."
44, Selden Road, Nunhead, S.E.15. Z6664

SPALDING, W., Driver, R.F.A.
He joined in May 1916, and was sent to the Western Front in the following year, but shortly afterwards was invalided to England on account of injuries received in an accident. On his recovery he returned to France, and fought at the Somme, Arras, Bullecourt, Ypres, Passchendaele, Lens, Cambrai and throughout the Retreat and Advance of 1918. He was demobilised in February 1919, and holds the General Service and Victory Medals.
4, Seneca Road, Clapham, S.W.4. Z4224

SPALL, T. G., Leading Cook's Mate, R.N.
He joined the Service in December 1912, and during the war served in H.M.S. "Shannon" H.M.S. "Clematis," and H.M.S. "Royal Oak." He was in action in the Battle of Jutland, and in many other engagements, and did good work on patrol and other important duties. Later he served in the Red Sea, and went to Constantinople with the Allied Fleet in November 1918. He rendered valuable services throughout, and was still serving in 1920. He holds the 1914-15 Star, and the General Service and Victory Medals.
23, Lubeck Street, Battersea, S.W.11. Z4225

SPARKES, A., Private, Royal Fusiliers.
Volunteering in September 1914, he embarked for France in the following May, and served in many parts of the line, fighting at Ypres, and Loos. Owing to ill-health he returned to England, and after receiving hospital treatment was discharged in January as unfit for further military service. He holds the 1914-15 Star, and the General Service and Victory Medals.
27, Kimpton Road, Camberwell, S.E.5. Z4226

SPARKS, C. V., L/Corporal, East Surrey Regt.
He joined in 1916, and embarked for the Western Front in November of that year. He was engaged in the heavy fighting at the Somme, Arras, Cambrai, and was mentioned in Despatches for devotion to duty in the Field in carrying messages under heavy shell fire. He was taken prisoner at Fleurbaix in April 1918, and was held in captivity for seven months, during which he was forced to work in the Dortmund coal-pits. He was repatriated and demobilised at the end of 1918, and holds the General Service and Victory Medals.
99, Stonhouse Street, Clapham, S.W.4. Z4228

SPARKS, H. G., Private, 14th London Regiment (London Scottish).
Volunteering in January 1916, and proceeding to France in the following September he was in action in many important engagements, and was three times wounded. He gave his life for King and Country on March 28th, 1918, in the opening operations of the German Offensive, and was entitled to the General Service and Victory Medals.
"Great deeds cannot die.
They with the Sun and Moon renew their light for ever."
10, St. John's Hill Grove, Battersea, S.W.11. Z4227

SPARKS, R., Trooper, 6th (Inniskilling) Dragoons.
He joined in July 1918, on attaining military age, and after completing his training, served at various stations with his unit engaged on important duties. He was unsuccessful in obtaining his transfer to a theatre of war prior to the cessation of hostilities, but was drafted to the Army of Occupation in Germany in 1919, and was stationed at Cologne, where he was still serving in 1920. Z24482B
6, Cromwell House, Vauxhall Walk, Vauxhall, S.E.11.

SPARKSMAN, A., A.B., R.N., H.M.S. "Ajax."
He was mobilised in August 1914, and served with the Grand Fleet for the whole period of the war. He was in the supporting forces at the actions of Heligoland Bight and the Dogger Bank, and was also engaged in the Battle of Jutland. He was demobilised in February 1919, and holds the 1914-15 Star, and the General Service and Victory Medals.
258, Albert Road, Peckham, S.E.15. Z5844

SPAUGHTON, A, H., Driver, R.F.A.
He volunteered in March 1915, and in November of the same year was drafted to the Western Front, where he took a prominent part in many important engagements, including those at Loos, Vimy Ridge, on the Somme, Arras, Ypres, Messines, St. Quentin, Amiens and in the Advance of 1918. He was demobilised in March 1919, and holds the 1914-15 Star, and the General Service and Victory Medals.
23, Rolls Road, Bermondsey, S.E.1. Z26624

SPEAR, F. J., Private, 6th Wiltshire Regiment.
He volunteered in September 1914, and in the next year went to the Western Front. He took part in several important engagements, including those at Neuve Chapelle, Hill 60, Ypres, Festubert, Loos, Vimy Ridge, the Somme, the Ancre and St. Quentin. He was wounded and gassed and was taken prisoner during the German Offensive of 1918. He was demobilised after his repatriation in February 1919, and holds the 1914-15 Star, and the General Service and Victory Medals.
3, Walnut Tree Walk, Kennington, S.E.11. Z26998

SPEARING, T., Private, 7th London Regiment.
Joining in September 1916, he was shortly afterwards drafted to France, where he took part in the fighting at Ypres, during which he was killed in action in February 1917. He was entitled to the General Service and Victory Medals.
"His life for his Country."
15, Rosetta Street, South Lambeth Road, S.W.8. Z27493

SPEARPOINT, E. E. (Mrs.), Special War Worker.
This lady was engaged at Messrs. Lucas and Bell's, Tower Bridge Road, in the manufacture of gas masks. She carried out her duties in a most efficient manner, and rendered valuable services during the war.
66, Delaford Road, Rotherhithe, S.E.16. Z6737

SPEARS, C. W., Pte., 2nd Buffs (East Kent Regt.)
He was mobilised in September 1914, and proceeded to France in January 1915. He fought at St. Eloi and Hill 60, where he was wounded, and after his recovery was in action in various other engagements, and was again wounded near Ypres. Later he took part in the fighting at Passchendaele and Cambrai, where he was wounded for the third time and invalided home. He returned to France later, and took part in the Advance of 1918, and after the Armistice served with the Army of Occupation in Germany until he was demobilised in February 1919. Previously to the late war he served in the South African campaign, and holds the Queen's and King's South African Medals and the 1914-15 Star, and the General Service and Victory Medals.
59, Tyneham Road, Lavender Hill, S.W.11. Z4229

SPEED, A., Gunner, R.F.A.
He volunteered in April 1915, and after his training was sent to France, where he took part in severe fighting around Ypres, Messines, and various other places, and was gassed at Albert. Invalided to England, he was demobilised in February 1919, and holds the 1914-15 Star, and the General Service and Victory Medals.
55, Fort Road, Bermondsey, S.E.1. Z26066

SPEED, C. J., Private, 2nd Leicester Regiment.
He was serving at outbreak of hostilities, and was sent to France in 1914. There he was engaged in various sectors until 1915, when he proceeded to Egypt, and later to Mesopotamia, where he took part in the operations against the Turks, including those at Baghdad. Unfortunately his health broke down, and he was invalided home and discharged as medically unfit in April 1918. He holds the 1914 Star, and the General Service and Victory Medals.
6, Bolton Street, Camberwell, S.E.5. Z4230

SPEED, H. D., Sapper, Royal Marine Engineers.
He joined in May 1917, and after his training served at various stations on important duties with his unit. He rendered valuable services, but was not successful in obtaining his transfer overseas before the cessation of hostilities. He was demobilised in March 1919.
51, Basuto Road, Parson's Green, S.W.6. X19963

SPEER, H. G., A.B., R.N., H.M.S. "Powerful."
He volunteered in September 1915, and after his training was sent with the Grand Fleet to the North Sea, and took part in the Battle of Jutland in May of the following year. He also served in H.M. Ships "Furious," "Andes" and "Tactician," and in 1920 was engaged on mine-sweeping duties in H.M.S. "Mistley." He holds the General Service and Victory Medals.
12, Alder's Street, Walworth, S.E.17. Z2200B

SPEER, T. G., Driver, R.A.S.C.
He joined in September 1916, and in the following month was drafted to Salonika, and served on important transport duties on the Offensive on the Doiran front, the Advance across the Struma, and the recapture of Monastir. In 1917 he was sent to Egypt, and was present at numerous engagements in the Advance through Palestine, including those at Gaza, Jerusalem, Jericho, Tripoli and Aleppo. He returned home and was demobilised in December 1919, and holds the General Service and Victory Medals.
12, Akers Street, Walworth, S.E.17. Z2200A

SPELLER, H., Private, R.A.S.C.

He volunteered in April 1915, and in the same year was drafted overseas, and during his service in France was present at the Battles of Hill 60, Ypres, Festubert, Loos, Vimy Ridge and Cambrai. In August 1918, he was wounded in the Somme sector, and invalided home, and was subsequently discharged as medically unfit for further duty in December 1918. He holds the 1914-15 Star, and the General Service and Victory Medals.

10, Lindo Street, Nunhead, S.E.15.   Z6692B

SPELLER, H., Private, 19th London Regiment.

He joined in March 1917, and in April of the following year was drafted to France, where he served at Albert. Later owing to ill-health, he was invalided home to hospital, but in April 1919 was drafted to the East, and was engaged on important duties at Aleppo, Beyrout, Alexandria and Kantara. He returned home and was demobilised in April 1920, and holds the General Service and Victory Medals.

30, Hatcham Road, New Cross, Peckham, S.E.15.   Z6692A

SPENCE, W. J., Private, R.A.O.C.

He joined in December 1916, and after his training served for some time in the Army Cyclist Corps. He was subsequently transferred to the Royal Army Ordnance Corps, and was engaged on important duties in connection with stores at various stations. He rendered valuable services, but owing to being medically unfit for duty abroad, was unable to obtain a transfer overseas, and was demobilised in February 1919, 3,

3, Sydney House, Latona Road, Peckham, S.E.15.   Z6339

SPENCER, A., Private, M.G.C.

He volunteered in December 1915, and after his training embarked for France in 1917. Whilst serving on the Western Front he was in action at Arras, Ypres and Cambrai, and was with his unit at the entry into Mons at dawn on Armistice Day. During his period of service overseas he was wounded, and returning to England after the cessation of hostilities he was demobilised in February 1919, holding the General Service and Victory Medals.

72, Speke Road, Battersea, S.W.11.   Z4231

SPENCER, A. E., Private, Lincolnshire Regiment.

He volunteered in December 1915, and in February of the following year was sent to France, where he took part in numerous engagements, and was badly gassed. He was invalided home, and was discharged owing to gas poisoning in June 1917, and holds the General Service and Victory Medals. He later unfortunately died on April 8th, 1918.

"Whilst we remember, the sacrifice is not in vain."

59, Reculver Road, Rotherhithe, S.E.16.   Z6738

SPENCER, C. W., Private, R.M.L.I.

He joined in June 1916, and after his training was posted to H.M.S. "Roxburgh." Throughout his service his vessel was engaged on important and dangerous convoy duties, escorting ships between America, Canada and France. His vessel was several times attacked by enemy submarines, and on one occasion sank a U-boat. He holds the General Service and Victory Medals, and in 1920 was serving in H.M.S. "Sandhurst.

37, Darwin Street, Walworth, S.E.17.   Z4232

SPENCER, E., Private, R.A.S.C. (M.T.)

He volunteered in January 1916, and in the same year was drafted to France, where he was engaged on important transport duties in various sectors of the Western Front, notably those of Ypres, the Somme, Arras and Cambrai. After the Armistice he proceeded to Germany with the Army of Occupation and in 1920 was still serving there. He holds the General Service and Victory Medals.

37, Barnet Road, Peckham, S.E.15.   Z6547

SPENCER, F. D., Deck Hand, H.M.S. "Jeannette II."

He joined in May 1918, and after his training was posted to H.M.S. "Jeannette II," and was sent to the Mediterranean Sea. During his service he was engaged on important duties with the Auxiliary Patrols off Gibraltar. He was demobilised in February 1919, and holds the General Service and Victory Medals.

21, Spencer Street, Battersea, S.W.11.   Z2008B

SPENCER, G. A., Rifleman, 21st Rifle Brigade.

He volunteered in November 1914, and after his training proceeded to Egypt in January 1916. During his service in the East he fought at Katia and in various subsequent engagements, until just prior to the Armistice, when he embarked for India. Here he served until November 1919, when he returned home and was demobilised, holding the General Service and Victory Medals.

86, Backworth Road, South Bermondsey, S.E.16.   Z6693

SPENCER, H. J., Driver, R.A.S.C. (M.T.)

He joined in June 1916, and in the same year was drafted overseas. Whilst in France he was engaged on important motor transport duties, and was present at many battles, including those on the Somme, and at Ypres and Arras. Later owing to ill-health he was invalided to England in 1918, and demobilised in the following year. He holds the General Service and Victory Medals.

22, Ingleton Street, Brixton Road, S.W.9.   Z4233

SPENCER, W. R., C.Q.M.S., 2nd Rhodesian Regt.

He volunteered in 1914, having previously been in the Rhodesian Railway Service. After his training he proceeded to East Africa, where he was promoted to the rank of Quarter Master Sergeant as a result of his excellent work. He contracted black water fever, and died in hospital on June 12th, 1916, and was entitled to the 1914-15 Star, and the General Service and Victory Medals.

"His life for his Country, his Soul to God."

44, Heaton Road, Peckham, S.E.15.   Z5841

SPICER, F. J., Driver, R.F.A. and Corporal, R.A.F.

He volunteered in March 1915, and after his training served at various stations on important duties with his unit. In 1916 he was sent to Ireland, where he was on duty during the Irish Rising in Dublin. He rendered valuable services, and was demobilised in February 1919.

53, Edithna Street, Landor Road, S.W.9.   Z4236

SPICER, G. A. S., L/Corporal, R.E.

He was mobilised with the 23rd London Regiment at the outbreak of war, and was shortly afterwards transferred to the Royal Engineers. In October 1915, he crossed to France, and was engaged on important duties in connection with the operations at Ypres, Arras, Etaples, Vimy Ridge, Cambrai and various other places. In October 1918 he was invalided home to hospital owing to ill-health, and was discharged in the following January. He holds the 1914-15 Star, and the General Service and Victory Medals.

22, Wycliffe Road, Battersea, S.W.11.   Z4235

SPICER, W. H., Private, Labour Corps.

He joined in November 1916, and trained in the Royal Field Artillery, but was afterwards transferred to the Labour Corps. During his service on the Western Front he was engaged on important duties in various sectors, until the cessation of hostilities. In February 1919 he was demobilised, and holds the General Service and Victory Medals.

21, Blondel Street, Battersea, S.W.11.   Z4234

SPIESS, H. W., Private, Labour Corps.

He joined in 1916, and in the same year was drafted to France, and served on important duties on various parts of the Front, including Albert, Vimy Ridge, Vermelles, Arras, Ypres, and the Somme. After the cessation of hostilities he returned home and was demobilised in August 1919. He holds the General Service and Victory Medals.

4, Oakden Street, Kennington, S.E.11.   Z27376

SPINKS, J. C., Driver, R.F.A.

He volunteered at the outbreak of war, and in March 1915 was drafted to France. During his service he did excellent work as a driver in many notable engagements, including those of Ypres, the Somme, Arras, Cambrai and various subsequent battles in the Retreat and Advance of 1918. He was demobilised in January of the following year, and holds the 1914-15 Star, and the General Service and Victory Medals.

69, Westmacott Street, Camberwell, S.E.5.   Z4545

SPOHR, J. W., Private, Middlesex Regiment.

He joined in June 1917, and was first attached to the Military Police, and stationed at Winchester. He sailed for France in November 1918, and was engaged whilst overseas on important salvage duties. He was demobilised in March 1919, and holds the General Service and Victory Medals.

8, Palmerston Street, Battersea, S.W.11.   Z4237

SPOONER, G. J., Rifleman, 5th London Regiment (London Rifle Brigade).

He joined in April 1917, and in March of the following year embarked for France. Whilst overseas he served in the Arras sector, and on August 29th, 1918, gave his life for the freedom of England at Bazancourt. He was entitled to the General Service and Victory Medals.

"The path of duty was the way to glory."

1, Theatre Street, Lavender Hill, S.W.11.   Z4238

SPOONER, W. C., Private, Middlesex Regiment.

He volunteered in December 1915, and after his training served at various stations on important duties with his unit. He rendered valuable services, but owing to being medically unfit was not able to secure a transfer overseas, and was demobilised in March 1919.

51, Edithna Street, Stockwell, S.W.9.   Z4239

SPRADBROW, A. A., Sergt., R.E.

He volunteered in May 1915, and in the following year was drafted to France, where he was severely wounded in action in an engagement at Ypres in 1916, and was invalided to hospital at Etaples. After his recovery he rejoined his unit and fought in the Battles of the Somme and Arras, and was again wounded at Cambrai, and subsequently took part in the Advance of 1918, and was gassed. After a short period in hospital at Calais he was demobilised in February 1919. He holds the General Service and Victory Medals.

6, Treherne Road, Stockwell, S.W.9.   Z4240

SPRADBROW, W. E., Private, R.A.M.C.

He volunteered in October 1915, and in the following year was drafted to the East. For a time he was stationed at Cairo, and later took part in the Advance into Palestine, and was present at the entry into Jerusalem. He returned to England, and was demobilised in October 1919, holding the General Service and Victory Medals.

24, Camberwell Gate, Walworth S.E.17.   Z26201

SPRATLING, J. F., Cpl., King's Royal Rifle Corps.

He volunteered in June 1915, and in March of the following year was drafted to France, where he served on important duties in connection with the commissariat for nearly three years. He was demobilised in February 1919, and holds the General Service and Victory Medals.

35, Cornwall Road, Peckham, S.E.15.   Z6578

SPRATT, E. A., Private, Middlesex Regiment.

Volunteering in February 1915, he proceeded to France in the same year, and served in the Ypres and Arras sectors. He was drafted in the following year to Salonika, and was in action on the Doiran front, and in the Advance across the Struma, and in various subsequent engagements until the conclusion of hostilities. He was sent to Turkey, and was stationed at Constantinople until April 1919, when he returned home and was demobilised. He holds the 1914–15 Star, and the General Service and Victory Medals.

26 Ingleton Street, Brixton Road, S.W.9.   Z4242

SPRATT, W., Rifleman, 1st Rifle Brigade.

He joined in July 1916, and in May of the following year was drafted to France. During his service overseas he took part in the heavy fighting at Messines, and in the third Battle of Ypres. He died gloriously on the Field of Battle at Passchendaele on October 4th, 1917, and was entitled to the General Service and Victory Medals.

"He died the noblest death a man may die,
Fighting for God, and right, and liberty."

11A, Sheepcote Lane, Battersea, S.W.11.   Z4241

SPREADBURY, F. A., Private, M.G.C. and 24th London Regiment (The Queen's).

He had joined the Territorial Force in January 1914, and after the outbreak of war served at several stations on important duties. In 1916 he proceeded to France, and after taking part in various engagements was severely wounded at Vimy Ridge. He was invalided to hospital, and succumbed to his injuries a week later, and is buried at the Military Cemetery at Etaples. He was entitled to the General Service and Victory Medals.

"He passed out of the sight of men by the path of duty and self-sacrifice."

34, Hutton Road, Kennington, S.E.1.   Z25521

SPRING, H. S., Pioneer, R.E.

He was serving at outbreak of hostilities, and was almost immediately sent to France. After the heavy fighting at Ypres on November 12th, 1914, he was reported missing, and since has been presumed to have fallen in that battle. He was entitled to the 1914 Star, and the General Service and Victory Medals.

"Nobly striving.
He nobly fell that we might live."

2, Lugard Road, Peckham, S.E.15.   Z6694

SPRING, J., Private, M.G.C.

He enlisted in March 1913, and drafted to the Western Front on the declaration of war, fought in the Retreat from Mons, and at Loos, Neuve Chapelle, Hill 60, the Somme and Cambrai. He was taken prisoner in 1917, and was repatriated when the exchange of prisoners took place just before the Armistice. He was still serving in 1920, and holds the Mons Star, and the General Service and Victory Medals.

70, Reculver Road, Rotherhithe, S.E.16.   Z6765

SPRINGALL, C. E., Gunner, R.F.A.

He volunteered in March 1915, and after his training was sent to France in August of that year. He fought in many engagements including those at Ypres, Loos, the Somme, Vimy Ridge and Beaumont-Hamel, and also throughout the great Retreat and Advance of 1918. He rendered much valuable service and after the Armistice returned to England and was demobilised in February 1919. He holds the 1914–15 Star, and the General Service and Victory Medals.

38, Mossbury Road, Battersea, S.W.11.   Z4243

SPRINGETT, C., Cpl., 6th London Regt. (Rifles).

He volunteered in August 1914, and in the following March was sent to the Western Front, where he took a prominent part in many engagements, and was wounded five times. He was killed in action at the Battle of Vimy Ridge on May 22nd, 1916. He was entitled to the 1914–15 Star, and the General Service and Victory Medals.

"Great deeds cannot die:
They with the Sun and Moon renew their light for ever."

191, Alderminster Road, Bermondsey, S.E.1.   Z26243

SPROUSE, C. L., Corporal, R.F.A.

He volunteered in December 1915, and after his training was drafted to France in January 1917. He took part in many engagements of importance until the close of hostilities, including those at Ypres, the Ancre, the Somme and the great Offensive of 1918. After the Armistice he proceeded to Germany with the Army of Occupation and did good service there until October 1919, when he returned to England and was demobilised. He holds the General Service and Victory Medals.

52, Farm Street, Southwark, S.E.1.   Z25352

SPURDEN, H., Gunner, R.F.A.

He volunteered in January 1915, and was sent to France in the same year. He saw much service there on various fronts until in 1917 he was drafted to Salonika, where he did good work. Later he proceeded to Egypt and served in Palestine under General Allenby, who presented him with a Certificate for saving a comrade's life at great risk to his own. He was demobilised in March 1919, holding the 1914–15 Star, and the General Service and Victory Medals.

12, Moat Place, Stockwell, S.W.9.   Z4244A

SPURDEN, W., Driver, R.F.A.

He volunteered in 1914, and after his training was sent to France in 1915, where he was in action at Armentières and other places. In 1916 he was drafted to Salonika and took an active part in the operations on the Vardar and other fronts. In the following year he proceeded to Egypt and subsequently fought with distinction at the River Jordan and in other important engagements in General Allenby's Palestine campaign. During his service he was twice mentioned in Despatches for his excellent work. He was demobilised in February 1919, and holds the 1914–15 Star, and the General Service and Victory Medals.

291, Mayall Road, Brixton, S.W.9.   Z4009B

SPURDEN, W., Gunner, R.F.A.

He volunteered in January 1915, and was sent to France later in that year. He was in action there in many sectors until in 1917 he proceeded to the Balkan front, where he took an active part in many operations of importance. Later he was drafted to Egypt and served throughout General Allenby's Palestine campaign until the Armistice. He was demobilised in March 1919, and holds the 1914–15 Star, and the General Service and Victory Medals.

12, Moat Place, Stockwell, S.W.19.   Z4244B

SPURRIER, J., Saddler, R.A.V.C.

He volunteered in November 1915, and after completing his course of training was drafted to France in the following year. He was employed on important duties at Rouen as a saddler until the Armistice, and was afterwards stationed at Charleroi until demobilised in April 1919. He holds the General Service and Victory Medals.

1A, Clifton Square, Peckham, S.E.15.   Z6088

SQUIRES, E. H., Sapper, R.E.

He volunteered in November 1915, and was drafted to France in the following year. He took a prominent part in the operations on the Somme and at Ypres, and in 1917 he was drafted to the Balkan front, where he rendered good service on the Struma front. He proceeded to Egypt afterwards and served under General Allenby in his Palestine campaign. He was wounded during these operations, and after recovery was sent to Turkey in Asia. He returned to England and was demobilised in August 1919. holding the General Service and Victory Medals.

93, Barlow Street, Walworth, S.E.17.   Z4245

SQUIRES, E. J., L/Corporal, Royal Welch Fusiliers.

He joined in April 1916, and after his training was employed on important duties with his unit in various parts of the East Coast. He rendered valuable services, but was unable to obtain his transfer overseas owing to ill-health. He was demobilised in January 1919.

74, Gibbon Road, Nunhead, S.E.15.   Z6715

SQUIRES, W. S., Sapper, R.E.

He volunteered in March 1915, and was drafted to the Western Front in the following January. He was in action at the Battles of the Somme, Ypres, Passchendaele, Poperinghe and Hazebrouck. He also took part in the Retreat and Advance of 1918 and was wounded. When he was returning home on the Hospital Ship "Donegal," the ship was torpedoed, but he was rescued by the destroyer "Jackal." On his recovery he returned to France and went with the Army of Occupation into Germany. Holding the General Service and Victory Medals, he was demobilised in April 1919.

15, Courtenay Street, Kennington, S.E.11.   Z25595

SQUIRES, F., Driver, R.A.S.C. (M.T.)
He volunteered in February 1915, and was drafted to France shortly afterwards. He rendered valuable service in the engagements at Festubert, Ploegsteert Wood, Vimy Ridge and Ypres, and in 1917 proceeded to Italy, where he did good work at Genoa, on the Piave and at other places until after the Armistice. He returned to England and was demobilised in February 1919, holding the 1914-15 Star, and the General Service and Victory Medals.
11, Trafalgar Road, Peckham, S.E.15.   Z3477A

SQUIRRELL, C., L/Corporal, M.G.C.
He was mobilised in August 1914, and took part with the R.H.A. and M.G.C. in the Battle of, and Retreat from, Mons, the Battles of La Bassée, Hill 60, Ypres, Loos, Albert, the Somme, Beaumont-Hamel, Arras and the Retreat and Advance of 1918. After rendering much valuable service, he was demobilised in 1919, and holds the Mons Star, and the General Service and Victory Medals.
12, Industry Terrace, Brixton Road, S.W.9.   Z4246

STACEY, B. H. (M.C.), Captain, 19th Middlesex Regt.
Volunteering in December 1914, he joined the ranks as a Private, and in the following year proceeded to the Western Front, where he took part in many engagements, including those at Neuve Chapelle, Ypres, Loos, Albert, Vimy Ridge, the Somme, Arras, Messines, Lens and Cambrai. In 1917 he was transferred to Italy and played a distinguished part in action on the Piave front. He returned to France in 1918 and was again in action in the final operations on that front. During his service he was wounded on one occasion in 1918. He was awarded the Military Cross for great gallantry in the Field in 1917, and in addition holds the 1914-15 Star, and the General Service and Victory Medals. He was demobilised in June 1919.
3/49, Sancroft Street, Kennington, S.E.11.   Z25284

STACEY, J.C., Pte., Duke of Cornwall's Light Infty.
Serving at the outbreak of war, he was at once sent to France and took an active part in the severe fighting at Mons, the Somme, Ypres, Cambrai, and many other places until the Armistice. He was demobilised in May 1919 after returning to England, and holds the Mons Star, and the General Service and Victory Medals.
78, Vaughan Road, Camberwell, S.E.5.   Z6333

STACEY, S. F., Private, 1st Northamptonshire Regt.
He joined in May 1916, and was drafted to the Western Front in December of that year. He took an active part in the Battles of the Somme and Passchendaele, and also served in Belgium at the Dunes and on the Yser. He suffered from shell-shock in 1917 after being buried beneath débris for many hours, and was discharged as unfit for further service in November 1918. He holds the General Service and Victory Medals.
24, Lilford Road, Camberwell, S.E5.   Z6228

STACEY, W., Rifleman, Rifle Brigade.
He joined in 1916, and being sent to France in the same year, took part in the Battle of the Somme, where he was wounded. On his recovery he was again wounded at Ypres in the following September and sent to England. After his recovery he was employed on important duties in England, guarding prisoners of war, and was eventually invalided out of the Army in March 1919. He holds the General Service and Victory Medals.
6, Atwell Street, Peckham, S.E.15.   Z5504

STADDON, J. J. ,Private, R.A.M.C.
He volunteered in August 1914, and after completing his course of training was drafted to the Western Front in the following year, attached to the R.F.A. as a stretcher-bearer. He rendered valuable services in many important engagements including those of Festubert, Loos, Vimy Ridge, Ypres, the Somme, Messines, Cambrai, Bapaume and other operations in the Offensive of 1918. During his service he was twice gassed, first at Festubert and later at the Somme. After his return home he was discharged in consequence of his service in March 1919, and holds the 1914-15 Star, and the General Service and Victory Medals.
99, Battersea Bridge Road, Battersea, S.W.11.   Z4247

STADELMAN, W. W., Private, Duke of Cornwall's Light Infantry.
He was mobilised from the Reserve in August 1914, and proceeding at once to France took part in the Retreat from Mons, and the Battles of Ypres, the Somme, and numerous other engagements until August 16th, 1917. He was unfortunately killed in action on that date, and was entitled to the Mons Star, and the General Service and Victory Medals.
"He joined the great white company of valiant souls."
24, Church Path, Hammersmith, W.6.   Z019393A

STADLER, A., Corporal, 21st London Regiment (1st Surrey Rifles).
He volunteered in May 1915, and was sent overseas in the same year. He was in action at Ypres, Givenchy, Loos, the Somme, Vimy Ridge and Albert, and was severely wounded. He was sent to England in consequence, and on his recovery was engaged on important guard duties in England until he was demobilised in April 1919. He holds the 1914-15 Star, and the General Service and Victory Medals.
248, Albert Road, Peckham, S.E.15.   Z5845B

STADLER, E. W., Rifleman, 18th London Regiment (London Irish Rifles).
He volunteered in September 1914, and proceeded overseas in the following year after the completion of his training. He fought gallantly in several engagements on the Western Front, and was unhappily killed in the Battle of Loos on September 25th, 1915. He was entitled to the 1914-15 Star, and the General Service and Victory Medals.
"His life for his Country."
248, Albert Road, Peckham, S.E.15.   Z5845A

STADLER, S. M., Sergt., 18th London Regiment (London Irish Rifles).
He was mobilised from the Reserve in August 1914, and was sent overseas in the following year. He took a prominent part in many engagements, including those at Ypres, Loos, Albert, Givenchy and Vimy Ridge, until he was discharged, owing to defective sight and heart trouble in February 1916. He holds the 1914-15 Star, and the General Service and Victory Medals.
248, Albert Road, Peckham, S.E.15.   Z5845C

STAERCK, T. J., Driver, R.A.S.C.
He volunteered in August 1914, and was sent to France shortly after. He rendered valuable transport services on many fronts, supplying ammunition to the front lines at Ypres, Festubert, Loos, the Somme, Ploegsteert Wood, Cambrai and Passchendaele, and also through the Retreat and Advance of 1918. He came to England and was demobilised in May 1919, and holds the 1914-15 Star, and the General Service and Victory Medals.
9, Lavender Road, Battersea, S.W.11.   Z4248

STAFFORD, A. J., Air Mechanic, R.A.F. (late R.N.A.S.)
He was engaged on important Government work and unable to serve until 1918, when he joined the R.N.A.S. He was engaged with his Squadron in England doing valuable work, but did not succeed in obtaining his transfer overseas before the cessation of hostilities. He was demobilised in February 1919.
7, Alvey Street, Walworth, S.E.17.   Z16667B

STAFFORD, D. N., Gunner, R.F.A.
He volunteered in November 1914, and was sent to France in the following year. He fought in numerous engagements, including those at the Somme, Arras, and Ypres, and also took an active part in the Retreat and Advance of 1918. After the Armistice he returned to England and was demobilised in 1919, holding the 1914-15 Star, and the General Service and Victory Medals.
10, Andulus Road, Stockwell, S.W.9.   Z4249B

STAFFORD, D. S., Telegraphist, R.N.V.R.
He joined in May 1917, and after his training was employed in the Auxiliary Patrol Service in the North Sea, and off the Belgian coast. He also did much valuable escort work until the fighting ceased. His vessel was torpedoed in July 1918, but he was rescued. He was demobilised in February of the following year, and holds the General Service and Victory Medals.
10, Andulus Road, Clapham, S.W.9.   Z4249C

STAFFORD, W. M., Sergt., R.F.A.
He volunteered in August 1914, and in the following year was sent to France, where he was in action at Ypres, Arras, the Somme, Givenchy, Béthune, La Bassée, and other places. He was wounded on two occasions, but continued to serve in France until the end of the war. After his return to England he was demobilised in 1919, holding the 1914-15 Star, and the General Service and Victory Medals.
10, Andulus Road, Stockwell, S.W.9.   Z4249A

STAGG, C., Gunner, R.F.A.
He volunteered in May 1915, and later in the same year was sent to France, where he took part in numerous engagements, and was gassed at Ypres. He also served in the Retreat and Advance of 1918. He returned home in March 1920, and was demobilised, holding the 1914-15 Star, and the General Service and Victory Medals.
25, Dawlish Street, South Lambeth, S.W.8.   Z4250

STAGG, D., Private, 10th London Regiment

He joined in March 1917, and in the following month was drafted to Egypt. Here he served in the operations against the Turks, during the Palestine offensive. He was killed in action on November 11th, 1917, and was entitled to the General Service and Victory Medals.

"His memory is cherished with pride."

34, East Lane, Rotherhithe, S.E.16. Z27429

STAGG, F. C., Rifleman, 21st London Regt. (1st Surrey Rifles).

He joined in January 1916, and in the following year proceeded to France, where he took part in numerous engagements, including those on the Somme, and at Arras, Vimy Ridge and Ypres. He also served in the Retreat and Advance of 1918. He was demobilised in October 1919, and holds the General Service and Victory Medals.

19, Calmington Road, Camberwell, S.E.5. Z5505B

STAGG, M. W., Gunner, R.G.A

He volunteered in 1915, and in the following year was drafted to the Western Front, where he took part in the fighting on the Somme, and at Arras, Ypres, Givenchy, and in other engagements. He also served in the Retreat and Advance of 1918. He was demobilised in 1919, and holds the General Service and Victory Medals.

4, Sondes Street, Walworth, S.E.17. Z27099B

STAGG, R. E., Rifleman, 21st London Regt. (1st Surrey Rifles).

Volunteering in May 1915, he was sent to France in the same year. He took part in numerous engagements, including those on the Somme, and at Arras and Vimy Ridge, where he was twice wounded and was invalided home. On his recovery he was drafted to Salonika, and served in the Balkan campaign. In 1917 he was transferred to Egypt, and thence to Palestine, where he was engaged in the Advance on Jerusalem under General Allenby, and was again wounded. He was demobilised in August 1919, and holds the 1914–15 Star, and the General Service and Victory Medals.

19, Calmington Road, Camberwell, S.E.5. Z5505A

STAGG, W. E., Corporal, Royal Fusiliers.

He volunteered in 1914, and in the following year was sent to the Dardanelles. During the operations at Gallipoli he contracted dysentery and was invalided to Egypt. Later, in 1916, he was transferred to France, and was engaged in the Somme, Ypres and Arras sectors, and was twice wounded. He was invalided home and was discharged in 1918 as medically unfit for further service, holding the 1914–15 Star, and the General Service and Victory Medals.

4, Sondes Street, Walworth, S.E.17. Z27099A

STAINER, F. G., Pte., 6th Somerset Light Infantry.

Joining in June 1916, and proceeding to France in the following October he fought in many engagements, including those at Arras and Ypres. Owing to ill-health he was invalided to England, and on recovery rejoined his unit in France, and saw heavy fighting in many parts of the line. Invalided home in November 1917, he received protracted medical treatment and was demobilised in August 1919. He holds the General Service and Victory Medals.

174, Ivydale Road, Nunhead, S.E.15. Z6766

STAINES, A., Rifleman, Rifle Brigade.

He was mobilised in August 1914, and was shortly afterwards sent to France and took part in the fighting on the Marne and the Aisne, and at La Bassée, and was wounded in October 1914, and invalided home. On his recovery he returned to France, and was in action at Neuve Chapelle. He fell fighting at Armentières on March 4th, 1915, and was entitled to the 1914 Star, and the General Service and Victory Medals.

"Great deeds cannot die."

98, Smyrks Road, Walworth, S.E.17. Z1676B

STALLARD, G., Private, H.A.C.

Joining in May 1916, he was sent to France later in the same year and shortly afterwards was transferred to Italy and served on the Piave front, where he took part in numerous engagements. He returned home and was demobilised in February 1919, holding the General Service and Victory Medals.

47, Chantry Road, Stockwell, S.W.9. Z4251A

STALLWOOD, H., Guardsman, 2nd Grenadier Guards.

He volunteered in August 1914, and in January of the following year was sent to France and took part in the fighting at Neuve Chapelle, Ypres, Festubert and Loos, where he was buried by the explosion of a shell and was not rescued for eight hours. He was later in action at Albert, Vermelles, Vimy Ridge and Arras. He afterwards contracted trench fever and was invalided home, and discharged as medically unfit for further service in September 1917, holding the 1914–15 Star, and the General Service and Victory Medals.

17, Mayall Road, Herne Hill, S.E.24. Z4252

STAMMERS, A. A., Rifleman, King's Royal Rifle Corps.

He was serving at the outbreak of war, and was immediately sent to France, where he took part in numerous engagements, including those at Mons, the Marne the Aisne, the Somme and Ypres, where he was wounded and invalided home. On his recovery he returned to France and was again wounded in action. He was demobilised in January 1919, and holds the Queen's and King's South African Medals, (with six clasps), the Mons Star, and the General Service and Victory Medals.

18, Runham Street, Walworth, S.E.17. Z4254

STAMMERS, J., Rifleman, Royal Irish Rifles.

He joined in March 1916, and in the following June was drafted to France, where he took part in numerous engagements, including those on the Somme, the Ancre, and at Beaumont-Hamel and Beaucourt, and was wounded and invalided home. He later returned to France, but owing to his injuries was again sent home. He was demobilised in October 1919, and holds the General Service and Victory Medals.

290, East Street, Walworth, S.E.17. Z4255

STAMMERS, J. H., Stoker, R.N., H.M.S. "Wallace."

He volunteered in 1914, and served with the Grand Fleet in the North Sea, where he was engaged on patrol duties. He was also in the Atlantic on convoy work in H.M.S. "Achilles" for a time. He was still serving in 1920, and holds the 1914–15 Star, and the General Service and Victory Medals.

19, Ceylon Street, Battersea Park Road, S.W.8. Z4253

STANBOROUGH, B., Pte., 23rd East Surrey Regt.

Joining in August 1916, he proceeded to the Western Front five months later, and fought at Arras, Vimy Ridge, Messines, Ypres, Passchendaele, Lens and Cambrai. He gave his life for the freedom of England on December 4th, 1917, and was entitled to the General Service and Victory Medals.

"And doubtless he went in splendid company."

18, Smyrk's Road, Walworth, S.E.17. Z4257

STANBOROUGH, P., Pte., R.A.S.C. and Gordon Highlanders.

He was mobilised in August 1914, and in the following month was drafted to France with the R.A.S.C. After valuable service at Mons, and in many later battles, he was in 1916 transferred to the Gordon Highlanders and fought on the Somme. After much good work later in Salonika he crossed to Egypt, and was in action on the Palestine front and was wounded. On his recovery he was sent to Italy, and served there until 1918, when he returned to France. He fought in the Retreat and Advance of that year, and was wounded, He was demobilised in March 1919, and holds the Mons Star, and the General Service and Victory Medals.

6, Benfield Road, Battersea, S.W.11. Z4546

STANBRIDGE, G., Corporal, R.A.S.C. (M.T.)

He joined in June 1916, and on the completion of his training served at various depôts with his unit engaged on instructional and other important duties. He was not successful in obtaining his transfer overseas prior to the signing of the Armistice, but rendered valuable services until demobilised in October 1919.

88, Southfield Road, Bedford Park, W.4. 7790.

STANBURY, T. J., Sergt., R.E.

He volunteered in July 1915, and later in that year was drafted to the Western Front, where he was engaged on important duties on the supply and hospital trains from the Base to the Front. He rendered excellent services throughout, and returning to England was demobilised in October 1919. He holds the 1914–15 Star, and the General Service and Victory Medals.

3, Yeovil Street, Wandsworth Road, S.W.8. Z4258

STANDEN, C., Private, Tank Corps.

He joined in September 1916, and was retained on important duties at various stations in England until sent to Russia in 1918. In this theatre of war he was engaged in much heavy fighting in many parts of the line and did good work throughout. He returned to England after the cessation of hostilities and was still serving in 1920. He holds the General Service and Victory Medals.

16, Clarence Street, Clapham, S.W.4. Z4259

STANDEN, E. T., Rflmn., King's Royal Rifle Corps.

Volunteering in January 1915, he embarked for the Western Front in the following September, and fought in many engagements of note. He was severely wounded at Loos in 1916, losing his left eye, and returned to England. After a protracted course of hospital treatment he was ultimately invalided out of the Service in October 1917, and holds the 1914–15 Star, and the General Service and Victory Medals.

41, North Street, Lambeth, S.E.1. Z26098

STANDIN, A. G., L/Corporal, R.E.
He volunteered in June 1915, and in the same year proceeded to France, where he rendered valuable services with his unit at Ypres, the Somme, and in the Retreat and Advance of 1918. He was badly gassed on one occasion, and in November 1918 was demobilised, holding the 1914–15 Star, and the General Service and Victory Medals.
4, Horace Street, Wandsworth Road, S.W.8.　Z27522

STANDIVAN, F., Private, 19th London Regiment.
He joined in April 1917, and was sent to France later in that year. He fought in the Cambrai sector, and did good work until he was severely gassed at Bourlon Wood, in November 1917. He was invalided to England and discharged in November 1919, as unfit for further service. He holds the General Service and Victory Medals.
70, Maxted Road, Peckham, S.E.15.　Z6779

STANDWAN, A. H., Rifleman, 5th London Regt. (London Rifle Brigade).
On attaining military age in February 1918, he joined the Colours, and after completing his training was engaged at various depôts on guard and other important duties with his unit. He rendered valuable services throughout, but did not obtain his transfer to a theatre of war, although he had volunteered for active service, and was demobilised in December 1919.
70, Henshaw Street, Walworth, S.E.17.　Z4260

STANHOPE, R. A., Bombardier, R.F.A.
Volunteering at the outbreak of war, and sent to France in March 1915, he was in action in the Battles of Ypres, Loos, and the Somme, where he was wounded in September, 1916. On his recovery he rejoined his Battery, and fought at Arras and in the German Offensive and Allied Advance of 1918. He was demobilised in May 1919 after returning home and holds the 1914–15 Star, and the General Service and Victory Medals.
87, Grosvenor Terrace, Camberwell, S.E.5.　Z4261

STANLEY, C. H. M., Private, 23rd Middlesex Regt.
He joined in August 1917, on attaining military age, and was sent to France in the following April. He fought in many engagements in the Retreat and Advance of 1918, including those at the Marne and the Aisne, and was badly wounded and gassed. After his recovery he rejoined his unit and was sent into Germany with the Army of Occupation and was stationed on the Rhine, until he returned to England for demobilisation in October 1919. He holds the General Service and Victory Medals.
67, Meyrick Road, Battersea, S.W.11.　Z4263

STANLEY, G. A., Driver, M.G.C.
He volunteered in March 1915, and in the following January was sent to France, where he was in action at Vimy Ridge, and in many engagements in the Ypres salient. He also fought in the German Offensive and Allied Advance of 1918, and was wounded at Nesle. He was demobilised in January 1919, after returning home, and holds the General Service and Victory Medals.
25, Ingrave Street, Battersea, S.W.11.　Z4262

STANLEY, J. W., 1st Class Stoker, R.N.
A Reservist, he was mobilised at the commencement of hostilities and throughout the war served in different ships with the Grand Fleet in the North Sea. His ship was in action at the Battles of Heligoland Bight, Dogger Bank and Jutland. He was in H.M.S. "Antrim" when she was torpedoed, and fortunately he was saved. He also saw much service in vessels engaged on patrol and other important duties. He was demobilised in February 1919, and holds the 1914–15 Star, and the General Service and Victory Medals.
210, Rolls Road, Bermondsey, S.E.1.　Z26492

STANMORE, W., Private, R.A.S.C. (M.T.)
Joining in 1916, he was in the following year drafted to the Egyptian Expeditionary Force, and was engaged on important transport duties at Cairo and other places. He rendered valuable services, and returning to England was demobilised in January 1920. He holds the General Service and Victory Medals.
37, Rutland Street, South Lambeth, S.W.8.　Z4264

STANNARD, A., Private, Queen's (Royal West Surrey Regt.) and Suffolk Regt.
He joined in September 1918, and after completing his training served at Colchester and other stations on important duties with his unit. He rendered valuable garrison services, but on account of his age did not obtain his transfer overseas prior to the cessation of hostilities. He was demobilised in February 1919.
24, Stannary Street, Kennington Road, S.E.11.　Z24714

STANNARD, E. H., Private, 2nd Queen's (Royal West Surrey Regiment).
An old soldier who had served through the South African War, he volunteered in 1915, and after completing his training was retained at various depôts with his unit engaged on important guard and other duties. Owing to ill-health he did not obtain his transfer to a theatre of war, and was ultimately invalided out of the Army in 1917, after twenty-five years' Colour Service. He holds the Queen's and King's South African Medals.
29, Trott Street, Battersea, S.W.11.　Z2691B

STANNARD, H. E., Sergt., Lancashire Fusiliers.
He enlisted in 1912, and after being mobilised at the outbreak of war, was sent to the Dardanelles in 1915. Here he was in action in many engagements and after the Evacuation of the Peninsula was transferred to France, where he fought in many operations round Ypres, and in the German and Allied Offensives of 1918. He was unfortunately killed in action during the Advance on August 8th, 1918, and was entitled to the 1914–15 Star, and the General Service and Victory Medals.
"The path of duty was the way to glory."
29, Trott Street, Battersea, S.W.11.　Z4256A

STANNARD, H. G., Private, 2nd Queen's (Royal West Surrey Regiment).
He joined in November 1917, as soon as he reached military age, and embarking for the Western Front in the following year, fought in many engagements in the German Offensive and Allied Advance and was gassed and wounded. After the cessation of hostilities he returned to England, but later was drafted to India, where he was serving in 1920. He holds the General Service and Victory Medals.
29, Trott Street, Battersea, S.W.11.　Z4256C

STANNARD, W., Private, R.A.M.C.
He joined in July 1916, and proceeding to the Western Front in the following year was engaged on important ambulance duties in the front lines during the Battles of Ypres, the Somme and Arras, and was wounded. On his recovery he rejoined his unit, and saw much fighting in the Retreat and Advance of 1918, and was again wounded. Invalided to England, he received hospital treatment and afterwards was sent to Mesopotamia, where he was serving in 1920. He holds the General Service and Victory Medals.
29, Trott Street, Battersea, S.W.11.　Z4256B

STANNETT, A., Private, 23rd London Regiment and Rifleman, Rifle Brigade.
Volunteering in June 1915, and embarking for France five months later, he was in action in many engagements of note and was wounded at Vimy Ridge in 1916. After hospital treatment he returned to France in December 1916, and in the same month was transferred to Egypt. He was afterwards engaged in the heavy fighting near Jerusalem, and in many other sectors during the British Advance into Syria. In November 1918 he proceeded to India and served at various garrison towns until he returned home and was demobilised in November 1919. He holds the 1914–15 Star, and the General Service and Victory Medals.
23, Barmore Street, Battersea, S.W.11.　Z1586A

STANTON, A. A., Sergt., Royal Fusiliers.
A Reservist, he was mobilised at the outbreak of war, and sent to Malta, where he served for six months and was then drafted to France. He was in action in the Battles of Ypres and the Somme, and was badly gassed and blinded at Bourlon Wood. Invalided home he received treatment, and on recovery returning to the Western Front, fought throughout the Retreat and Advance of 1918. After the Armistice he was sent into Germany with the Army of Occupation and served on the Rhine until he returned to England and was demobilised in March 1920. He holds the 1914–15 Star, and the General Service and Victory Medals.
28, Raywood Street, Battersea Park Road, S.W.8.　Z4265

STANTON, J., Special War Worker.
He was the first man to volunteer at the Mortlake Recruiting Office on the outbreak of hostilities, but being rejected on medical grounds was engaged on munition work. He was employed for eighteen months as a moulder in a factory at Poplar, and gave great satisfaction by his marked skill in his work.
12, Quick Road, Chiswick, W.4.　5674

STANTON, W., Private, Royal Fusiliers.
Volunteering in December 1914, he was drafted to the Dardanelles in the following August and was in action almost continuously until invalided to England owing to ill-health. On his recovery he proceeded to France and fought in the first British Offensive on the Somme and was wounded at Béthune. He returned to England and was discharged as unfit for further service in June 1917. He holds the 1914–15 Star, and the General Service and Victory Medals.
21, Granfield Street, Battersea, S.W.11.　Z4266

STAPLES, C., Private, 32nd M.G.C.
He joined in September 1916, and in the following month was sent to France, where he served on the Somme, at Cambrai, Passchendaele, Messines, Vimy Ridge, Arras, and also in the Retreat and Advance of 1918, during which he was wounded. He was demobilised in March 1920, and holds the General Service and Victory Medals.
8, Suffield Road, Walworth, S.E.17.   Z26142

STAPLES, W., 1st Class Stoker, R.N.
He was in the Navy at the outbreak of war and on board H.M.S. "Queen Mary" served with the Grand Fleet in the North Sea. His ship was present during the fighting at Heligoland and also took a prominent part in the Battle of Jutland, during which he was killed. He was entitled to the 1914-15 Star, and the General Service and Victory Medals.
    "His life for his Country, his Soul to God."
47, Wells Place, Camberwell, S.E.5.   Z3478B

STAPLETON, G. C., Private, South Lancashire Regt.
He enlisted in 1912, and at the outbreak of war proceeded to France, and took part in the Retreat from Mons, and the Battles of the Marne and Aisne, and La Bassée. He was also in action at Ypres, Neuve Chapelle, Loos, and the Somme, and was wounded three times, being subsequently discharged on account of his injuries in December 1917. He holds the Mons Star, and the General Service and Victory Medals.
33, Bennerley Road, Battersea, S.W.11.   Z4267

STAPLETON, J., A.B., R.N., H.M.S. "Prince Eugene."
He joined in July 1915, and on board his ship served with the Grand Fleet in the North Sea. Later he was posted to H.M.S. "Vindictive" and in this vessel took part in the bombardment of Zeebrugge, and afterwards was engaged on important duties until his demobilisation in January 1919. He holds the 1914-15 Star, and the General Service and Victory Medals.
41, Craham Road, Rotherhithe, S.E.16.   Z6665

STAPLETON, S. E., Private, R.A.V.C.
Joining in May 1917, he was drafted overseas in the same year, and served principally at Le Havre and Calais tending sick and wounded horses. After the Armistice he proceeded to Germany with the Army of Occupation. In June 1919 he returned home and was discharged on account of ill-health. He holds the General Service and Victory Medals.
123, Brayard's Road, Peckham, S.E.15.   Z5506

STARK, J., Pte., 5th Royal Warwickshire Regt.
He volunteered in January 1915, and after having completed his training was drafted overseas. He saw much active service in France and Italy, and also served with the Royal Army Ordnance Corps. He returned home in June 1919, and was demobilised holding the 1914-15 Star, and the General Service and Victory Medals.
43, Minford Gardens, West Kensington, W.14.   11870B

STEBBIN, F. J., Private, R.A.S.C.
Volunteering in November 1915 he was drafted in the following January to the Western Front where he served for two and a half years. He was present at many engagements including those on the Somme, and in the Retreat and Advance of 1918. In March 1919 he returned home and was demobilised and holds the General Service and Victory Medals.
57, Camelia Street, Wandsworth Road, S.W.8.   Z4315

STEEL, E. (Mrs.), (née Woodman), Special War Worker.
From March 1916 until 1917 this lady did valuable work in connection with munitions at Messrs. Vickery's, Old Kent Road, and later at the Arsenal on the production of cartridges. Afterwards she was engaged on important duties at the Air Ministry until 1918. Her good work was worthy of the highest commendation.
200, Commercial Road, Peckham, S.E.15.   6624A

STEEL, J., Corporal, Guards' Machine Gun Regt.
Volunteering in September 1914 he was drafted on the completion of his training to France and served there in many important engagements with the Grenadier Guards. Later he was transferred to the Guards' Machine Gun Regiment, with which he did much valuable work until he was wounded and invalided home in 1918. After being in hospital for some time he was demobilised in March 1919, holding the 1914-15 Star, and the General Service and Victory Medals.
200, Commercial Road, Peckham, S.E.15.   6624B

STEELE, S., Private, East Surrey Regiment.
Volunteering in May 1915 he was engaged after the completion of his training on important duties at various stations with his unit. He rendered valuable services but was not successful in obtaining his transfer overseas before the cessation of hostilities. In September 1919 he was demobilised.
30, Gonsolva Road, Wandsworth Road, S.W.8.   Z4269

STEELE, W. T., Gunner, R.F.A.
Volunteering at the outbreak of hostilities he was drafted to France in 1916, and whilst on the Western Front was in action during the fighting at the Battles of Ploegsteert-Wood, Vimy Ridge, the Somme, and Beaumont-Hamel. Owing to ill-health he was sent to hospital at Le Havre and on recovery was employed there as a shoemaker until demobilised in July 1919. He holds the General Service and Victory Medals.
22, Myatt Road, Stockwell, S.W.9.   Z5154

STEEMSON, G., Private, Royal Warwickshire Regt.
Joining in June 1917, in March of the following year he proceeded overseas and during his service on the Western Front fought in many engagements in the German Offensive and Allied Advance. After the signing of the Armistice he returned to England and was demobilised in February 1920, and holds the General Service and Victory Medals.
35, Auckland Road, Battersea, S.W.11.   Z4272

STEER, G., Private, Royal Fusiliers.
He joined in August 1916, and in the following April embarked for the Western Front. There he took part in many important battles including those of Arras, Bullecourt, Cambrai, St. Quentin, Amiens, Bapaume, and the Advance of 1918 during which time he was severely gassed and wounded. On his recovery he was drafted to Germany with the Army of Occupation, remaining there until November 1919, when he was demobilised. He holds the General Service and Victory Medals.
95, North Street, Wandsworth Road, Clapham, S.W.4.   Z4270

STEER, G. S., Gunner, R.F.A.
He was serving at the outbreak of war, but was not successful in obtaining his transfer overseas. He was engaged on various important duties with his unit at different stations and rendered valuable services until discharged in September, 1918.
39, Kingston Street, Walworth, S.E.17.   Z27477

STEER, J., Rifleman, 9th London Regt. (Queen Victoria's Rifles).
He joined in August 1916, and in the following December embarked for France. He fought in many engagements, including those on the Somme, and at Arras where he was wounded and taken prisoner, subsequently succumbing to his injuries whilst in captivity. He was entitled to the General Service and Victory Medals.
    "His life for his Country, 'his soul to God."
66, Sheepcote Lane, Battersea, S.W.11.   Z4211

STEER, T. H., Sergt., Rifle Brigade.
He volunteered in January 1915, and in June of the same year proceeded to the Western Front, and was in action on the Somme, and at Ypres. Later contracting trench fever he died on January 1st, 1917, and was entitled to the General Service and Victory Medals.
    "Whilst we remember, the sacrifice is not in vain."
28, Annandale Road, Chiswick, W.4.   5441B

STEER, W. (M.S.M.), Sergt., 7th Norfolk Regt.
Volunteering in January 1915 he was drafted in the following June to the Western Front, where he saw much active service. He fought at Arras, Ypres, the Somme, and Cambrai, and was awarded the Meritorious Service Medal for devotion to duty. In addition he holds the 1914-15 Star and the General Service and Victory Medals, and was demobilised in March 1919.
28, Annandale Road, Chiswick, W.4.   5441A

STEER, W., Driver, R.A.S.C. (M.T.)
He volunteered in March 1915, and in the same year was drafted overseas. He served in many sectors of the Western Front, and was present in engagements at Ypres, Loos, Vimy Ridge, the Somme, and Cambrai, and in the Retreat and Advance of 1918. He returned to England, and was demobilised in April 1919, holding the 1914-15 Star, and the General Service and Victory Medals.
141, Denmark Road, Camberwell, S.E.5.   Z5889B

STEGGLE, G., Private, 1st Wiltshire Regiment.
He joined in February 1917, and was drafted to France in the following month. In this theatre of war he fought in many important engagements and during the Retreat from Cambrai, was unhappily killed in action on April 16th, 1918. He was entitled to the General Service and Victory Medals.
    "A valiant soldier, with undaunted heart he breasted Life's last hill."
63, Fitzalan Street, Kennington, S.E.11.   Z25672

STEINBERG, A., Private, 30th Middlesex Regiment.
He joined in July 1916, and on the conclusion of his training was drafted to the Western Front where he took part in many important engagements, including those at Arras, Cambrai, Bapaume, and in the Retreat and Advance of 1918. After his return to England he was demobilised in December 1919, and holds the General Service and Victory Medals.
37, Cranbrook Road, Chiswick, W.4.   5352

STEMSON, W., Private, Northumberland Fusiliers.
He volunteered in October 1914, and two months later was sent to France where he was in action in various engagements until contracting pneumonia in February 1915, he was invalided to hospital in Rouen. On recovery he returned to England on leave, and then proceeded to India and later to Mesopotamia and Egypt, where he served on garrison duties, being unfit for service in the trenches. He was demobilised in April 1919, and holds the 1914–15 Star, and the General Service and Victory Medals.
17, White Square, Clapham, S.W.4. Z4273

STENNETT, F. G., Rifleman, 10th Rifle Brigade.
He volunteered in November 1914, and after a period of training proceeded to France in the following year. He took part in several engagements and was killed in action on the Somme. He rendered valuable services, and was entitled to the 1914–15 Star, and the General Service and Victory Medals.
" Great deeds cannot die."
13, Hutton Road, Kennington, S.E.11. Z25270

STENNING, C., Trooper, 1st Surrey Lancers (Queen Mary's Regiment).
He volunteered in 1914, and in the following year was sent to France, where he fought in many engagements including those at Ypres. He was later drafted to Salonika, and was in action on the Struma front, and in many other sectors. He was demobilised in 1919, and holds the 1914–15 Star, and the General Service and Victory Medals.
21, Chatto Road, Battersea, S.W.11. Z4274A

STENNING, F. J., Private, M.G.C.
He joined in March 1917, and in the following August was drafted to France. In this theatre of war he fought at the Battles of Ypres, Passchendaele, Cambrai, St. Quentin, and in March 1918, was taken prisoner, and held in captivity until January 1919. He was then repatriated and later sent to Egypt where he served on garrison duties until his return to England for demobilisation in February 1920. He holds the General Service and Victory Medals.
80, Cabul Road, Battersea, S.W.11. Z4275

STENNING, S. G., Driver, R.A.S.C.
He volunteered in 1915, and at the conclusion of his training proceeded to the Western Front. He served with his unit on important duties in the Somme and other sectors, and was frequently under heavy shell fire. He returned to England after the cessation of hostilities, and was demobilised in 1919. He holds the 1914–15 Star, and the General Service and Victory Medals.
21, Chatto Road, Battersea, S.W.11. Z4274B

STENNING, T., Private, 23rd London Regiment.
A Territorial, having enlisted in 1913, he was mobilised at the outbreak of hostilities, and drafted to France in 1915. He was in action at the Battles of Loos, Ypres, and in various other engagements until evacuated to hospital in England, suffering from shell-shock. He was subsequently invalided out of the Service in December 1917, and holds the 1914–15 Star, and the General Service and Victory Medals.
21, Chatto Road, Battersea, S.W.11. Z4274D

STENNING, W. J., Private, 23rd London Regiment.
He volunteered in 1914, and in the following year was sent to France. In this theatre of war he was engaged in much heavy fighting, and was seriously wounded in action. He was invalided to hospital in England, and his injuries proved so severe as to necessitate the amputation of a leg, but he died after the operation in 1919. He was entitled to the 1914–15 Star, and the General Service and Victory Medals.
" Whilst we remember, the sacrifice is not in vain."
21, Chatto Road, Battersea, S.W.11. Z4274C

STEPHENS, A. E., Rflmn., King's Royal Rifle Corps.
He joined in August 1916, and in the following November was drafted to France. Whilst overseas he took part in the fighting at Vimy Ridge, Arras, Ypres, and Lens, and in October 1917, was unfortunately killed in action at Menin Road. He was entitled to the General Service and Victory Medals.
" A valiant soldier, with undaunted heart, he breasted Life's last hill."
94, Avondale Square, Old Kent Road, S.E.1. Z27082

STEPHENS, B., Lieut., R.A.S.C. and Labour Corps (Chinese).
Volunteering at the commencement of hostilities, he was drafted overseas, and served in the Retreat from Mons and the Battles of the Marne, the Aisne, La Bassèe, Ypres, Neuve Chapelle, St. Eloi, Hill 60, Festubert, and Loos. He also did valuable work with his unit during operations at Albert, Vimy Ridge, the Somme, Arras, Bullecourt, Messines, Ypres, Passchendaele, Cambrai, Amiens, Bapaume, and Havrincourt Wood, and in the Allied Advance of 1918. Returning to England after the termination of hostilities he was demobilised in January 1920, and holds the Mons Star, and the General Service and Victory Medals.
84, Chatham Street, Walworth, S.E.17. Z4276

STEPHENS, C., Driver, R.F.A.
He volunteered in August 1914, and crossing to France in the following January was in action until July 1915. He was then transferred to Salonika and subsequently served throughout the Balkan campaign. Whilst in the East, he contracted malaria, and was for a time in hospital. He was demobilised in May 1919, and holds the 1914–15 Star, and the General Service and Victory Medals.
20, Henry Street, Battersea, S.W.11. Z4277

STEPHENS, L., Private, 2/6th West Yorkshire Regt.
Joining in January 1917, he crossed to France in the same month and took part with his unit in several notable engagements, including that at Bullecourt. In December of that year he returned to England, and was afterwards engaged on duties of an important nature at the War Office until demobilised in July 1919. He holds the General Service and Victory Medals.
437, Battersea Park Road, Battersea, S.W.11. Z4278

STEPHENS, W. T., Rifleman, 5th London Regiment (London Rifle Brigade).
He joined in January 1917, and was sent to France in the following March. He fought in the Battle of Arras, and was taken prisoner of war there in May. After a long and trying captivity he was repatriated in January 1919, and was engaged on important duties guarding London Docks until August of the same year, when he proceeded to Egypt. After rendering valuable services at Headquarters there he returned to England, and was demobilised in March 1920. He holds the General Service and Victory Medals.
10, Abbeyfield Road, Rotherhithe, S.E.16. Z6780

STEPHENSON, S., Private, M.G.C.
He joined in April 1917, and at the conclusion of his training was drafted to the Western Front. Whilst in this theatre of war he fought in many parts of the line, and did good work with his unit during the Retreat and Advance of 1918. He was demobilised in June 1920, after his return to England, and holds the General Service and Victory Medals.
6, Landseer Street, Battersea, S.W.11. Z4279

STEPHENSON, H. E., Trooper, Duke of Lancaster's Own Dragoons.
He joined in November 1916, and was sent to France in the following year. He took part in numerous engagements, including those at Arras, Vimy Ridge, Bullecourt, the Hindenburg Line, Ypres, and Passchendaele and afterwards served at Rouen and Dunkirk with the Military Police. He was later transferred to the Royal Welch Fusiliers, and did good service in the Retreat and Advance of 1918. He was demobilised in June 1919, and holds the General Service and Victory Medals.
108, Lugard Road, Peckham, S.E.15. Z6739

STEPHENSON, W. H., A.B., R.N., H.M.D. " Ocean Gleaner."
He joined in July 1918, and after his training was engaged on convoy duties between Liverpool and Port Said. Later he served in various ships in the North Sea on important minesweeping duties, and did much valuable work. He holds the General Service and Victory Medals, and was demobilised in June 1919.
28, Cooper's Road, Old Kent Road, S.E.1. Z27157

STEPTOE, F. W., Private, R.A.S.C. (M.T.)
He volunteered in November 1915, and after his training was engaged on duties of an important nature with his unit. In the course of his service, he contracted bronchitis, from which illness he unfortunately died in March 1916.
" His memory is cherished with pride."
104, Stonhouse Street, Clapham, S.W.4. Z4280

STERRY, H. R., Private, Manchester Regiment.
He volunteered in August 1914, and after his training, served on the Western Front for upwards of four years. During this period, he fought in engagements at Ypres, Hill 60, Festubert, Albert, the Somme, Beaumont-Hamel, Arras, and in the Retreat and Advance of 1918, and on two occasions was severely wounded. He holds the 1914- Star, and the General Service and Victory Medals. and was demobilised in January, 1919.
4, Industry Terrace, Brixton, S.W.9. Z4139

STEVENS, B. R., Pte., R.F.A. and Royal Fusiliers.
Volunteering in January 1915, he embarked for France in March of the following year, and took part in the Somme Offensive, in which he was severely wounded in July 1916. After treatment at one of the Base hospitals however, he rejoined his unit in the Field and fought at Messines, Passchendaele, and Lens, where in August 1917, he was again wounded. Whilst still in action in this sector, a few days later, he received a third wound, to which unhappily he succumbed at the 5th General Hospital, Hardelot. He was entitled to the General Service and Victory Medals.
" A costly sacrifice upon the altar of freedom."
70, Plough Road, Battersea, S.W.11. Z1564B

STEVENS, A.. W, Private, 5th East Surrey Regt.
He volunteered in October 1914, and after his training embarked for India, Later, he was transferred to Mesopotamia, where he fought in several important engagements, subsequently returning to India. He was discharged in October 1918, through causes due to his service, and holds the General Service and Victory Medals.
35, Auckland Road, Battersea S.W.11.   Z4285

STEVENS, B. W., Private, 1st Canadian Infantry.
Volunteering in August 1914, he was sent to France early in the following year, and was in action at the Battles of Ypres, Loos, the Somme, Arras, Passchendaele Ridge, and Cambrai. After the Retreat and Advance of 1918, in which he also served, he proceeded with the Army of Occupation to Germany, and was engaged on important duties at Cologne. He was demobilised in 1919, and holds the 1914–15 Star, and the General Service and Victory Medals.
2, Nigel Buildings, Nigel Road, Peckham, S.E.15.   Z6695

STEVENS, C. A., Private, 2nd Manchester Regiment.
A serving soldier, he crossed to France with the first British Expeditionary Force, and was wounded in the fighting at Mons. He was invalided home, but returned to the Western Front shortly afterwards, and was unfortunately killed in the subsequent Retreat from that sector. He was entitled to the Mons Star, and the General Service and Victory Medals.
"His life for his Country, his soul to God."
9, St. Philip Street, Battersea Park, S.W.8.   Z1962C

STEVENS, C. E., Corporal, Queen's (Royal West Surrey Regiment)
Volunteering in January 1916, he embarked for France in the following May, and was in action on that front until April 1917. In 1918, he was transferred to Egypt and thence to Palestine, where he took part in several engagements, including the Capture of Jerusalem. Later, returning to the Western Front he fought in several battles during the Retreat and Allied Advance, and was wounded twice. He holds the General Service and Victory Medals, and was demobilised in March 1919.
173, Albany Road, Camberwell, S.E.5.   Z5675

STEVENS, F., Gunner, R.F.A.
He volunteered at the commencement of hostilities, and proceeded with his Battery to France in November 1914. In the course of his service overseas, he fought in many notable battles and was severely wounded on three occasions. He was invalided home and discharged in August 1917, but re-enlisted for home service and did good work at various stations until November 1918, when he was invalided out of the Service. He holds the 1914 Star, and the General Service and Victory Medals.
271, Sumner Road, Peckham, S.E.15.   Z6082

STEVENS, F., Driver, R.F.A.
He volunteered in 1914, and in the following year embarked for Salonika, where he served with his Battery for upwards of three years. During this period he was in action in operations on the Vardar and Struma fronts, and was for a time in hospital suffering from malaria. He was demobilised in February 1919, and holds the 1914–15 Star, and the General Service and Victory Medals.
47, Gibbon Road, Nunhead, S.E.15.   Z6625

STEVENS, F. G. (D.C.M.), Rifleman, Cameronians (Scottish Rifles).
Mobilised on the declaration of war, he proceeded to France, and fought in the Retreat from Mons, and the Battles of the Marne, the Aisne, Loos, and Ypres. He was awarded the Distinguished Conduct Medal for conspicuous bravery and devotion to duty in the Field. After being in action in the Somme Sector, where he was wounded, he was reported missing, but later was presumed to have been killed in action on June 20th, 1916. He was entitled to the Mons Star, and the General Service and Victory Medals.
"A valiant soldier, with undaunted heart, he breasted Life's last hill."
101, Grant Road, Battersea, S.W.11.   Z4281C

STEVENS, G., Sapper, R.E.
He volunteered in 1915, and at the conclusion of his training was sent to the Western Front, where he served with his unit on important duties in the forward areas. Owing to a severe wound, he returned to England early in 1918, and after treatment was invalided out of the Service later in that year. He holds the General Service and Victory Medals.
22, Crichton Street, Wandsworth Road, S.W.8.   Z4284

STEVENS, G., Rifleman, Rifle Brigade.
He volunteered in 1914, and at the completion of his training served with his unit at various stations on special duties. He did very good work, but owing to physical unfitness was unable to secure his transfer overseas, and owing to ill-health was discharged from the Service in 1916.
297, East Street, Walworth, S.E.17.   Z4282

STEVENS, G. E., Corporal, Royal Sussex Regt.
He volunteered in March 1915, and six months later was drafted to the Western Front. He took part in the fighting at Loos, Vimy Ridge, and the Somme, and died gloriously on the Field of Battle during an engagement in the First British Offensive on the Somme, on August 20th, 1916. He was entitled to the 1914–15 Star, and the General Service and Victory Medals.
"And doubtless he went in splendid company."
172, East Street, Walworth, S.E.17.   Z3348B

STEVENS, G. W., Private, Queen's Own (Royal West Kent Regiment).
He volunteered in September 1914, and in the following year proceeded overseas. Whilst on the Western Front he was in action at the Battles of Ypres, Arras, Albert, Passchendaele, St. Quentin, St. Eloi, Vimy Ridge, Beaumont-Hamel, Messines, Bullecourt, Hill 60, Loos, Lille, and Lens, and was severely gassed on the Somme in 1918. He received treatment at a Base hospital, and on recovery was engaged on important guard duties at the Prisoners of War Camp, Boulogne, until demobilised in April 1919. He holds the 1914–15 Star, and the General Service and Victory Medals.
16, Manaton Road, Peckham, S.E.15.   Z6327

STEVENS, H., Driver, R.F.A. and R.E.
A Reservist, he was mobilised at the outbreak of hostilities, and proceeding to France, fought in the Retreat from Mons, and the subsequent Battles of La Bassée. He later took part in the fighting in the Arras sector, and in 1918 was transferred to the Royal Engineers, with which unit he did very good work in the final operations of the war. He was demobilised in February 1919, and holds the Mons Star, and the General Service and Victory Medals.
115, Chatham Road, Wandsworth Common, S.W.11. Z6130A

STEVENS, H. C., L/Cpl., 7th Northamptonshire Regt.
He volunteered in September 1914, and in the following August was drafted to France. In the course of his service in this theatre of war he fought in the Battles of Festubert, Loos, Ypres, and the Somme. He gave his life for King and Country at Messines on June 23rd, 1917, and was entitled to the 1914–15 Star, and the General Service and Victory Medals.
"Honour to the immortal dead who gave their youth that the world might grow old in peace."
101, Grant Road, Battersea, S.W.11.   Z4281A

STEVENS, J., Private, R.A.S.C.
Volunteering in March 1915, he was sent to the Western Front a month later and served in various sectors until the termination of hostilities. During this period he was engaged on important duties at various ammunition dumps, and did good work in the transport of supplies to the firing line during the Battles of the Somme, Messines, and St. Quentin. Demobilised in March 1919, he holds the 1914–15 Star, and the General Service and Victory Medals.
27, Northland Street, Camberwell, S.E.5.   Z6229

STEVENS, J., Signalman, R.N.
Joining in March 1917, he was posted to H.M.S. "Neptune," which ship was engaged on important patrol and convoy duties in the North Sea, in the course of which she was in action against enemy destroyers and submarines off the Dogger Bank. He also served in H.M.S. "Osiris" and "Dragon," which were employed on convoy duties in the Atlantic and the Baltic Sea, and took part in operations against the Bolshevik forces at Riga. Demobilised in April 1920 he holds the General Service and Victory Medals.
36, Bournemouth Road, Rye Lane, S.E.15.   Z5507

STEVENS, R. H., Rifleman, 16th London Regt. (Queen's Westminster Rifles).
He volunteered in November 1915, and in the following July embarked for the Western Front where he served in engagements in the Ypres salient and in the Arras sector. Taken prisoner in February 1917, he was employed on clerical and other duties during his captivity in Germany and repatriated after the Armistice, was demobilised in February 1919. He holds the General Service and Victory Medals.
94, Sussex Road, Coldharbour Lane, S.W.9.   Z4283

STEVENS, T. H., Private, 23rd London Regt. and East Surrey Regt.
Volunteering in October 1914, he proceeded to France in the following January and took part in heavy fighting until wounded in the Battle of Hill 60. Sent home for medical treatment he returned to the Field on recovery, and served with his Battalion in several important engagements. Severely wounded on August 22nd, 1918, he died from the effects of his injuries two days later, and was entitled to the 1914–15, Star and the General Service and Victory Medals.
"Courage, bright hopes, and a myriad dreams, splendidly given."
96, St. Philip Street, Battersea Park, S.W.8.   Z1962B

STEVENS, W. C., Private, 7th Dorsetshire Regt.

He volunteered in September 1914, and drafted to France in the following year fought in the Battles of Festubert and Loos, and in other parts of the line. He gave his life for the freedom of England in the Battle of the Somme on July 7th, 1916, and was entitled to the 1914-15 Star, and the General Service and Victory Medals.

" And doubtless he went in splendid company."

101, Grant Road, Battersea, S.W.11.   Z4281B

STEVENS, W. E. (M.M.), Sergt., 2nd Royal Berkshire Regiment.

Volunteering in August 1914, he crossed to the Western Front shortly afterwards, and was engaged in heavy fighting in the Battles of La Bassée, Arras, Ypres, Vimy Ridge, Lens, and Cambrai. During his service overseas he was wounded at Albert on July 1st, 1916, and was awarded the Military Medal on March 4th, 1917 for conspicuous bravery and devotion to duty on the Somme, in holding the enemy at bay for over five hours with bombs and a Lewis gun, causing them to retire. He also holds the 1914-15 Star, and the General Service and Victory Medals, and was demobilised in January 1920.

21, Caspian Street, Camberwell, S.E.5.   Z5508

STEVENS, W. G. R., L/Cpl., 1st Royal Dublin Fusiliers.

A Regular, he was serving in India on the outbreak of war, and was sent to Gallipoli in 1915. He was engaged in heavy fighting in the first Landing on the Peninsula, and gave his life for King and Country on May 11th, 1915, and was entitled to the 1914-15 Star, and the General Service and Victory Medals.

" He joined the great white company of valiant souls."

28, Lurgan Street, Hammersmith, W.6.   T13540A

STEVENS, W. H., Rifleman, 21st London Regt. (1st Surrey Rifles).

He volunteered in October 1915, and three months later proceeded overseas. After a period of service in France during which he took part in fierce fighting at Loos, he was sent to Egypt in April 1916. Serving in the British Advance through Palestine he was in action in the Battles of Jifjaffa, Katia, Gaza (I, II, and III), and was present at the fall of Jerusalem, and the capture of Jericho and Aleppo. After the Armistice he returned home for demobilisation in July 1919, and holds the General Service and Victory Medals.

9, Lothian Road, Camberwell New Road, S.W.9.   Z6458

STEVENS, W. J., Corporal, R.F.A.

Volunteering in September 1914, he embarked for France in the following August and served in the Battles of Loos. Three months later he was sent to Salonika and took part in the Advance on the Struma and the capture of Monastir, and was wounded on the Doiran front, and invalided to hospital at Malta in September 1917, and later to England. Proceeding to the Western Front on recovery in January 1918, he was in action in several engagements during the Retreat and Advance of that year, and entered Mons on the morning of November 11th, 1918. He was demobilised in February 1919, and holds the 1914-15 Star, and the General Service and Victory Medals.

70, Stanley Street, Ferndale Road, Clapham, S.W.4. Z4286

STEVENSON, J. L., Pte., 6th Royal Welch Fusiliers.

He joined in April 1917, and after serving in Ireland was drafted to France. Whilst in this theatre of war he took part in various engagements including the second Battle of Cambrai, in which he was severely wounded. He was invalided to hospital in Wales, and was subsequently demobilised in January 1919. He holds the General Service and Victory Medals.

13, Cook's Road, Walworth, S.E.17.   Z26538

STEVENSON, L. J., Rifleman, 17th London Regt. (Rifles).

He joined in September 1916, and in the same year was drafted to Salonika, and fought in several engagements in the Balkan campaign. In 1917 he was sent to Egypt, and took part in the advance into Palestine with General Allenby's Forces, being present at the fighting on the Jordan and at the fall of Jerusalem. In the following year he proceeded to the Western Front, and was in action in the Retreat and Advance of 1918. He was demobilised in November 1919, and holds the General Service and Victory Medals.

13, Cook's Road, Walworth, S.E.17.   Z26535

STEVENTON, C. A. (M.M.), Driver, R.F.A.

He volunteered in October 1914, and was engaged with his Battery on important duties until January 1916, when he was sent to the Western Front, and took part in the fighting at Vimy Ridge, the Somme, Arras, Messines, and Ypres. He also served with distinction in the Retreat and Advance of 1918, and was awarded the Military Medal for bravery in the Field in assisting to save the guns on March 21st, 1918. He also holds the General Service and Victory Medals, and was demobilised in May 1919.

39, Cornbury Road, Rotherhithe, S.E.16.   Z6740

STEVES, I. A., Private, 23rd London Regiment.

Volunteering in August 1915, he proceeded to France in the following December and served in the Battle of the Somme, and at Ypres, and in various subsequent engagements. He was wounded in 1916, and on recovering was again frequently in action until the cessation of hostilities. He was demobilised in January 1919, and holds the General Service and Victory Medals. 23, Abyssinia Road, Battersea, S.W.11. Z4287

STEVSON, S., Gunner, R.F.A.

He was mobilised at the outbreak of war and was almost immediately drafted to France and took part in the Retreat from Mons. He also served on the Marne, and the Aisne, and at Ypres, St. Eloi, Hill 60, Festubert, Loos, Albert, and the Somme, and in many engagements in the Retreat and Advance of 1918. During his service he was twice wounded and gassed, and was in hospital for a time. He was demobilised in June 1919, and holds the Mons Star, and the General Service and Victory Medals.

5, Bishop's Terrace, Kennington, S.E.11.   Z27227

STEWARD, J., Signaller, R.F.A.

He volunteered in September 1914, and after his training was completed was drafted to France. During his service on the Western Front he took part in many engagements in various sectors, and was twice wounded in action. He returned home and was demobilised in March 1919, and holds the General Service and Victory Medals.

47, Philip Road, Peckham, S.E.15.   Z6051A

STEWART, F. A., Gunner, R.F.A.

He volunteered in August 1915, in the Royal Army Medical Corps, and in November of the same year served on H.M.H.S. " Mauretania," which was plying between Mudros and England. Later, he was transferred to the Field Ambulance, and was drafted to Egypt in April 1916, and engaged on important duties in the Palestine campaign at Jericho and Jerusalem until September 1918. He then volunteered for duty with the Royal Field Artillery, and completed his services in the Palestine campaign as a gunner. He returned home and was demobilised in March 1919, and holds the 1914-15 Star, and the General Service and Victory Medals.

42, Lavender Road, Battersea, S.W.11.   Z4288

STEWART, C., Driver, R.F.A.

He volunteered in December 1914, and was drafted to France in the following June. He took a prominent part in the heavy fighting at Loos, Ypres, Armentières, Arras, the Somme, and Bapaume, and other important engagements in the Retreat and Advance of 1918. He was demobilised in April 1919, and holds the 1914-15 Star, and the General Service and Victory Medals. 3, Warndon Street, Rotherhithe, S.E.16. Z6781

STEWART, J., Private, 14th Welch Regiment.

Volunteering in March 1915, he proceeded to the Western Front in the following August. Whilst overseas he took part in numerous engagements, including those at Loos, Vimy Ridge, the Somme, the Ancre, Arras, and the second Battle of the Marne. Unfortunately he was killed by a sniper at Bapaume in 1918, and was entitled to the 1914-15 Star, and the General Service and Victory Medals.

" Courage, bright hopes, and a myriad dreams, splendidly given."

4, Alice Street, Tower Bridge Road, S.E.1.   Z25842

STEWART, J., Air Mechanic, R.A.F.

He joined in February 1918, and after training as an aero-engine fitter proceeded to France in the following April. He served with the Independent Air Force at Nancy, and was chiefly engaged in maintaining bombing machines in good repair. After the Armistice was signed he was attached to the Army of Occupation and stationed at Cologne until December 1919, when he returned home, and was demobilised. He holds the General Service and Victory Medals.

190, Grosvenor Terrace, Camberwell, S.E.5.   Z4289

STEWART, M. H., Gunner, R.G.A.

He volunteered in August 1914, and in February of the following year was drafted to France, where he saw much service. He was in action at Ypres, Loos, Vimy Ridge, the Somme, Arras, Passchendaele, Lens, and Cambrai, and in many subsequent engagements in the Retreat and Advance of 1918. After the Armistice was signed he proceeded to Germany remaining until January 1919, when he returned home, and was demobilised. He holds the 1914-15 Star, and the General Service and Victory Medals.

63, Melon Road, Peckham, S.E.15.   Z6258

STICKLES, F. C., 1st Class Stoker, R.N., H.M.S. " Ostrich."

He volunteered in August 1914, and after his training was posted to H.M.S. " Ostrich," and served with the Grand Fleet in the North Sea. Whilst in this vessel he took part in the Battle of Heligoland Bight, and rendered valuable services in rescuing members of the crew of H.M.S. " Pathfinder." On January 1915, he was invalided out of the Service as medically unfit for further duty. He holds the 1914-15 Star, and the General Service and Victory Medals.

79, Great Bland Street, Great Dover Street, S.E.1. Z25367

STILL, F. W., Private, 23rd London Regiment.
He was mobilised in August 1914, and crossed to France in March of the following year. Whilst overseas he served at Givenchy and Festubert, and on account of ill-health was then invalided home to hospital. After his recovery he was engaged on important coastal defence duties until discharged as unfit for further service in June 1916. He holds the 1914-15 Star and the General Service and Victory Medals.
66, Wickersley Road, Lavender Hill, S.W.11.   Z4290

STILL, S. J., Driver, R.A.S.C. (M.T.)
He volunteered in August 1914, and after his training was drafted to France, and served in various sectors of the Western Front as a motor transport driver until 1918. He was engaged in conveying ammunition and food supplies to the troops, and was present at the Battles of the Somme, Arras, Ypres, and Cambrai. He was demobilised in February 1919, after four and a half years' service with the Colours, and holds the 1914-15 Star, and the General Service and Victory Medals.
80, Robertson Street, Wandsworth Road, S.W.8.   Z4291

STIMPSON, W. S., Private, R.A.S.C.
He volunteered in June 1915, and after his training was drafted to Gallipoli, where he served on important duties in connection with food supplies for the troops. Later he proceeded to Egypt, where he was engaged in similar work for three and a half years. He returned home and was demobilised in June and holds the 1914-15 Star and the General Service and Victory Medals.
105, Yeldham Road, Hammersmith, W.6.   T13240A

STOAKLEY, W. H., Gunner, R.G.A.
Joining in 1916, he was shortly afterwards drafted to the Western Front, where he served in many important engagements including those at Arras, Vimy Ridge, Messines, Ypres, and Passchendaele. He also took part in various operations in the Retreat and Advance of 1918, and after the Armistice proceeded to Germany with the Army of Occupation. He returned home and was demobilised in August 1919, and holds the General Service and Victory Medals.
19, Dante Road, Kennington S.E.11.   Z26623

STOCKER, S., Guardsman, Coldstream Guards.
Volunteering in July 1915 he embarked for France in the following June, and took part in the heavy fighting in the Battle of the Somme, and was wounded. He was invalided home to hospital, and after his recovery rejoined his unit in France, but subsequently contracted fever, and was sent back to hospital in England. After many months' illness he was discharged as medically unfit for further duty in July 1918. He holds the General Service and Victory Medals.
51, Duffield Street, Battersea, S.W.11.   Z2642

STOCKING, S. J., Private, Lincolnshire Regiment.
Volunteering in August 1914, he was drafted overseas in the following month and took part in many of the early engagements, including the Battles of the Marne, the Aisne and Ypres. He was severely wounded at Loos on September 11th, 1915, and succumbed to his injuries on the 27th of that month. He was entitled to the 1914 Star and the General Service and Victory Medals.
"A costly sacrifice upon the altar of freedom."
13, Henshaw Street, Walworth, S.E.17.   Z3186D

STOCKLEY, P. C., C.P.O., R.N., H.M.S. "Gibraltar."
A serving sailor since 1909, he was posted to H.M.S. "Lord Nelson" and served with the Grand Fleet throughout the duration of hostilities. His ship was sent to the Dardanelles and was engaged in covering the Landing and Evacuation of the troops. He did excellent work throughout as a Petty Officer, and in 1920 was serving on H.M.S. "Gibraltar" at Portland with the Home Fleet. He holds the 1914-15 Star, and the General Service and Victory Medals.
48, Broughton Street, Battersea, S.W.8.   Z1713B

STOCKTON, A. L., Corporal, R.F.A.
He volunteered in February 1915, and in the same year was drafted overseas. During his service in France he did good work as a gunner in the Armentières sector, and was severely wounded and gassed in action. He was subsequently invalided home and afterwards was demobilised in 1919. He holds the 1914-15 Star, and the General Service and Victory Medals.
20, Rumsey Road, Stockwell, S.W.9.   Z4548C Z4549C

STOCKTON, F., Telegraphist, R.N., H.M.S. "Peony."
He joined in March 1917, and after his training was posted to H.M.S. "Endymion" and sent to the Mediterranean Sea. During his service he was on two occasions on board vessels which were blown up, but fortunately was rescued. He was discharged in February 1920 as medically unfit for further service, and holds the General Service and Victory Medals.
20, Rumsey Road, Stockwell, S.W.9.   Z4548D Z4549D

STOCKTON, H., Gunner, R.F.A.
He volunteered in February 1915, and in the same year was drafted to France, where he did excellent work as a gunner in the Armentières sector. He was severely wounded in action during an engagement, and subsequently succumbed to his injuries in 1915, and was buried at Bailleul. He was entitled to the 1914-15 Star, and the General Service and Victory Medals.
"He joined the great white company of valiant souls."
20, Rumsey Road, Stockwell, S.W.9.   Z4548B Z4549B

STOCKTON, H. M. S., Gunner, R.F.A.
He volunteered in February 1915, and in the same year was drafted to France. During his service overseas he did good work as a gunner in many engagements, including that at Armentières. He gave his life for King and Country early in 1916, and was entitled to the 1914-15 Star, and the General Service and Victory Medals.
"The path of duty was the way to glory."
20, Rumsey Road, Stockwell, S.W.9.   Z4548A Z4549A

STOCKWELL, F., Private, Manchester Regiment.
He volunteered in September 1914, and in 1916 proceeded to France. He saw much heavy fighting at the Somme, Deville Wood, Arras, Vimy Ridge, Messines, Bullecourt, Ypres and Cambrai, and was wounded. Subsequently his health broke down, and after having rendered much valuable service he was discharged as medically unfit in January 1918. He holds the General Service and Victory Medals.
101, North Road, Wandsworth Road, S.W.4.   Z4292A

STOCKWELL, G., Private, M.G.C.
He volunteered in August 1914, and was sent to France in the following year. He was in action at Loos, the Hohenzollern Redoubt, Ovillers, the Somme, Monchy, Pozières, Arras and in many other engagements until the cessation of hostilities, and was gassed on one occasion. He was demobilised in March 1919, and holds the 1914-15 Star, and the General Service and Victory Medals.
78, Evelena Road, Nunhead, S.E.15.   Z6223

STOCKWELL, J. (Mrs.), Special War Worker.
This lady was engaged for over two years of the war on work of National importance at the Projectile Company's Factory at Clapham, as an examiner of shells for the Admiralty. During the whole of this period she carried out her responsible duties in a manner worthy of the highest praise.
101, North Street, Clapham, S.W.4.   Z4292B

STOCKWELL, V. G., Air Mechanic, R.A.F.
He joined in September 1917, and after his training served at Aldershot and other stations in England with his unit. He rendered valuable services, but was unable to obtain his transfer overseas while hostilities continued, and was discharged on account of ill-health in October 1918.
4, Goldsboro' Road, Wandsworth Road, S.W.8.   Z4293

STOFFELL, C. E., Pte., 2nd Royal Sussex Regt.
Serving at the outbreak of hostilities he was at once sent to France and took part in the Battle of Mons and was wounded. He remained at the Front, however, rendering valuable services, until in the Battle of La Bassée, he was unhappily killed. He was entitled to the Mons Star, and the General Service and Victory Medals.
"Great deeds cannot die."
4, Bonar Road, Peckham, S.E.15.   Z6456

STOFFELL, C. F., Cpl., 2nd Durham Light Infantry.
He volunteered in September 1914, and after completing his training proceeded to Salonika, where he took part in many important engagements on the Vardar and other fronts until the war ended. He was demobilised in March 1919 after his return home, and holds the General Service and Victory Medals.
30, Graces Road, Camberwell, S.E.5.   Z6542

STOKES, A. J., Driver, R.A.S.C. (M.T.)
He volunteered in 1915, and in that year proceeded to France. He served with the ammunition columns in various sectors of the line, including Ypres, Arras and the Somme and rendering valuable services until the close of the war. He was demobilised in 1919 after his return home, and holds the 1914-15 Star, and the General Service and Victory Medals.
5, Russell Grove, Brixton, S.W.9.   Z5155

STOKES, E., Sergt., Worcestershire Regiment.
He was mobilised in August 1914, and crossing at once to France fought at Mons, the Marne and the Aisne, where he was mentioned in Despatches for gallantry in the Field. He also served at La Bassée, Ypres, Neuve Chapelle, Festubert and Loos. He was mentioned in Despatches on no fewer than six occasions, and was severely wounded, and was sent to England. After having rendered much valuable service he was discharged in September 1916 as unfit for further military duty, and holds the Mons Star, and the General Service and Victory Medals.
55, Army Street, Clapham, S.W.4.   Z4296

STOKES, A. J., Rifleman, 5th London Regiment (London Rifle Brigade).

He joined in 1918, and was sent to France in August of that year. He fought on the Somme front and in many engagements until the conclusion of the war. After returning to England he was demobilised in November 1919, and holds the General Service and the Victory Medals.

18, Thurlow Street, S.E.17. Z4295B

STOKES, H. C., Private, Royal Fusiliers.

He joined in January 1916, and on the conclusion of his training was drafted to France and afterwards to Italy, on both of which fronts he rendered valuable services in many engagements of importance up to the close of hostilities, and was wounded. After his return to England he was demobilised in April 1919, holding the General Service and Victory Medals.

45, Ramsay Road, Acton, W.. . 6392

STOKES, J. A. (M.M.), Gunner, R.F.A.

He was already serving at the outbreak of war, and was immediately drafted to France, where he took part in the Retreat from Mons, the Battles of the Marne, the Aisne, Neuve Chapelle, Loos, Ypres and the Somme Offensive of 1916 and Arras. He was sent to Italy in 1918, and was in action with the gun which beat the world's record for quick firing. Whilst in France he was awarded the Military Medal for great bravery in the Field, and was both wounded and gassed. He was demobilised in February 1919, and holds in addition to the Military Medal, the Mons Star, and the General Service and Victory Medals.

68, Holyoak Road, Kennington, S.E.11. Z24709

STOKES, W., Private, R.A.M.C.

He volunteered in February 1915, and was sent to Malta in that year. In the following year he was sent to France and did excellent work at the 44th Casualty Clearing Station during the remainder of the war. He went to Germany with the Army of Occupation in December 1918, and was still serving in 1920. He holds the General Service and the Victory Medals.

61, Broughton Street, Battersea, S.W.8. Z4294

STOKES, W. A., Rifleman, 3rd Rifle Brigade.

He volunteered in April 1915, and was sent to France four months later. He fought gallantry at Ypres and Loos, where he was unhappily killed by a sniper on October 29th, 1915, after rendering valuable sevices to his Country. He was buried at Hollebeke in Belgium, and was entitled to the 1914–15 Star, and the General Service and Victory Medals.

"His life for his Country, his Soul to God."

18, Thurlow Street, S.E.17. Z4295

STONE, H. N., Pte., King's Own (Royal Lancaster Regiment).

He volunteered in September 1914, and was sent to France a year later. He first served in the Somme area and later in that year was drafted to Salonika, where he took an active part in the operations on the Doiran and Vardar fronts. In 1917 he came back to France and rendered much valuable service in the Battle of Cambrai and the Retreat and Advance of 1918. He was demobilised in March 1919, and holds the 1914–15 Star, and the General Service and Victory Medals.

16, Cronin Road, Peckham, S.E.15. Z5676A

STONE, C. W., Private, R.A.S.C.

An old soldier, who had served through the Boer War, volunteered in 1915, and was afterwards drafted to the Western Front, where he rendered valuable service at the Somme, Ypres, and in the Retreat and Advance of 1918. He was invalided home through illness brought on by his service overseas, and during his convalescence was unfortunately injured in a motor lorry accident. He was demobilised in November 1919, and holds the Queen's and King's South African Medals with five clasps, the Kimberley Star, and the General Service and Victory Medals.

96, Rolls Road, Bermondsey, S.E.1. Z26611

STONE, J. A., Private, 5th Yorkshire Regiment.

He joined in July 1916, and after his training was engaged on important duties with his unit until in April 1918 he was sent to France. He fought gallantly in many engagements until July of that year, when he was wounded and taken prisoner whilst fighting on the Marne. He unfortunately died from results of his wound in a German hospital on July 26th, 1918. He was entitled to the General Service and Victory Medals.

"His memory is cherished with . pride."

16, Cronin Road, Peckham, S.E.15. Z5676B

STONE, W. D., Private, 23rd Royal Fusiliers.

He joined as soon as he attained military age in September 1918, and after the completion of his training was sent to Germany with the Army of Occupation. He rendered valuable service there until March 1920, when he returned home and was demobilised.

9, Alford Road, Union Grove, Wandsworth, S.W.8. Z4298

STONE, W. H. J., Gunner, R.G.A.

He joined in May 1916, and was drafted to France later in that year. He took part in various engagements, including those at Ypres, the Somme, Guillemont, the Ancre, Arras, Vimy Ridge, Messines and Cambrai, and throughout the Retreat and Advance of 1918. He was demobilised in February 1919 after his return home, and holds the General Service and Victory Medals.

70, Ingelow Road, Battersea Park Road, S.W.8. Z4297

STONEHAM, C. J., Sapper, R.E. (Volunteers).

He joined in September 1917, and was engaged on important duties in the construction of the London defences. He rendered valuable services until discharged in July 1918.

3, Fendick Road, Peckham, S.E.15. Z6340A

STONEHAM, H., Private, 1st King's Own Yorkshire Light Infantry.

He joined in March 1916, and was sent to France in the following October. During his service overseas he fought in many engagements of note, and was in almost continuous fighting throughout the Retreat and Advance of 1918. After the Armistice he was sent into Germany with the Army of Occupation and served there until November 1919. He was then drafted to Mesopotamia and later to India, where he was serving in 1920. He holds the General Service and Victory Medals.

3, Fendick Road, Peckham, S.E.15. Z6340B

STONELL, C. E., Sergt., 8th London Regt. (Post Office Rifles).

He joined in June 1916, and in the following year embarked for France, where he fought in many important engagements, including the Battles of the Somme and Lens, and was in action throughout the German Offensive and Allied Advance of 1918. After the Armistice he was drafted into Germany with the Army of Occupation and served there until he returned to England and was demobilised in September 1919. He holds the General Service and Victory Medals.

7, Tunstall Road, Brixton, S.W.9. Z4301A

STONELL, F. H., Private, R.A.S.C.

Joining in December 1917, and proceeding to the Western Front in the following year, he served in the forward areas, engaged on important duties transporting ammunition and supplies to the front lines throughout the Retreat and Advance of 1918. He was demobilised in November 1919, and holds the General Service and Victory Medals.

7, Tunstall Road, Brixton, S.W.9. Z4301B

STONELL, T., Gunner, R.F.A.

Volunteering in June 1915, he was drafted to Egypt early in the following year, and after serving there for a few months was transferred to Salonika. In this theatre of war he was in action in many engagements on the Doiran, Monastir, Struma and Vardar fronts, and later was sent to Russia. Here he saw much service in various sectors, and returning home was demobilised in May 1919. He holds the General Service and Victory Medals.

77, Mayall Road, Herne Hill, S.E.24. Z4300

STONER, W. F., Private, Royal Welch Fusiliers.

Volunteering in March 1915, he embarked for France in the following January and was in action at Mametz Wood, the Somme, Vimy Ridge, Ypres and throughout the German Offensive and subsequent Allied Advance of 1918. He was demobilised in March 1919, and holds the General Service and Victory Medals.

16, Kitson Road, Camberwell, S.E.5. Z4302

STONES, W., Gunner, R.F.A.

Volunteering in September 1914, three months later he was drafted to France and fought at Neuve Chapelle, Ypres, Loos, Vimy Ridge, the Somme and Bapaume, and was gassed. Returning to England he received hospital treatment, and on recovery rejoined his Battery in France and took part in heavy fighting until the cessation of hostilities. He was demobilised in May 1919, and holds the 1914–15 Star, and the General Service and Victory Medals.

56, Elsted Street, Walworth, S.E.17. Z4299

STOPES, G., Private, R.A.S.C. (M.T.)

He volunteered in November 1915, and proceeding to France in the following year served on the Somme, and at Arras, Messines, Lens and Passchendaele, and was transferred to Italy in 1917. Here he was engaged on important duties in many parts of the line, and returned to France in 1918 and saw much fighting in the Retreat and Advance of that year. He was demobilised in January 1919, and holds the General Service and Victory Medals.

38, Nigel Buildings, Nigel Road, Peckham, S.E.15. Z6696

STOPP, F. G., Corporal, 2/5th East Lancashire Regt
He joined in October 1916, and was drafted to the Western Front in the following January. During his service overseas he fought in many important engagements, including those at Ypres and St. Quentin, where he was taken prisoner in 1918. Repatriated in December of the same year he was ultimately demobilised in September 1919, and holds the General Service and Victory Medals.
27, Haymerle Road, Peckham, S.E.15. Z6574

STORER, A. E., Air Mechanic, R.A.F.
He joined in June 1917, and completing his training served at various aerodromes engaged on important repair duties as a carpenter. He was unsuccessul in obtaining his transfer overseas prior to the cessation of hostilities, but rendered valuable services until demobilised in February 1919.
46, Northway Road, Camberwell, S.E.5. Z6334B

STORER, E. W., Sergt., R.A.F.
Volunteering in December 1915, he completed his training and served at various aerodromes in England and Scotland on important duties. He did good work connected with the repair of woodwork for airships, but did not obtain his transfer to a theatre of war. He was demobilised in February 1919. 46, Northway Road, Camberwell, S.E.5. Z6334A

STORER, S. J., Air Mechanic, R.A.F.
Joining in 1917, he underwent a course of training and was stationed at various aerodromes. He rendered valuable services, engaged on duties connected with repairs to aircraft, but was not sent overseas prior to the cessation of hostilities. He was demobilised in March 1919.
46, Northway Road, Camberwell, S.E.5. Z6334C

STORY, E. F., Rifleman, Rifle Brigade.
Joining in January 1918, and in the following August proceeding to France, he fought at Amiens, Bapaume, Havrincourt, Arras, the Scarpe and in many engagements during the Allied Advance of 1918, and was wounded. He was demobilised in June 1919, and holds the General Service and Victory Medals.
72, Page's Walk, Old Kent Road, S.E.1. Z26288

STORKEY, J. H., Special War Worker.
He offered his services for work of National importance and from August 1914 until March 1919 was employed in the Royal Army Clothing Department on important duties. He rendered valuable services and discharged his duties in a most satisfactory and efficient manner.
31A, Prairie Street, Battersea Park, S.W.8. Z4303

STORY, S., Private, R.A.M.C.
A Reservist, he was mobilised and sent to France at the outbreak of war, and served in the Retreat from Mons, in the Battles of the Marne, the Aisne, Ypres and La Bassée. In 1917 he was transferred to German East Africa and did good work there at various hospitals until the cessation of hostilities. Returning to England, he was demobilised in 1919, and holds the Mons Star, and the General Service and Victory Medals.
4, Jerome Place, Hillingdon Street, Walworth, S.E.17. Z26442

STOVOLD, A. W., Corporal, R.A.S.C.
Volunteering in August 1914, he was sent to France shortly afterwards and served in many engagements, including those at Ypres, Arras, Albert, Bapaume, Loos, Verdun and Armentières. He was engaged on important transport duties throughout the Retreat and Advance of 1918, and after the Armistice proceeded into Germany with the Army of Occupation and was stationed at Cologne. He was demobilised in July 1919, and holds the 1914-15 Star, and the General Service and Victory Medals.
14, Hillery Road, Walworth, S.E.17. Z4305

STOW, R. W., Private, Royal Marines.
He joined in May 1918, and after his training was stationed at Shoreham, engaged on important duties connected with the construction of the Mystery Towers. He was unsuccessful in obtaining his transfer overseas prior to the cessation of hostilities, but did good work until demobilised in February 1919. 19, Fenwick Place, Stockwell, S.W.9. Z4304

STRACHAM, W. H., Bombardier, R.F.A.
He volunteered in 1914, and in the following year was drafted to the Western Front. There he took a prominent part in many notable engagements, including those at Loos, Vimy Ridge, the Somme, Arras and Ypres. He also served at Le Cateau and other engagements in the Offensives of 1918. He returned to England and was demobilised in 1919, and holds the 1914-15 Star, and the General Service and Victory Medals.
37, Trafalgar Street, Walworth Road, S.E.17. Z27325

STRANGE, R. C., Private, 23rd London Regiment.
He volunteered in July 1915, and in the following year was sent to Palestine, where he took part in numerous engagements, including those at Beersheba, Gaza, Jaffa, the Jordan, Beyrout and in those leading up to the capture of Jerusalem, and was twice wounded. He was demobilised in August 1919, after returning home, and holds the General Service and Victory Medals.
11, St. Andrew Street, Wandsworth Road, S.W.8. Z4306

STRATFORD, C., Private, R.A.S.C. (H.T.)
He volunteered in 1915, and in the same year proceeded to the Western Front, where he was engaged on important duties with the horse transport at Ypres, the Somme, Arras and various other important engagements. Later he was transferred to Italy, where he saw much active service until demobilised in 1919. He holds the 1914-15 Star, and the General Service and Victory Medals.
26, Inville Road, Walworth, S.W.17. Z27455

STREET, A. J., Private, R.A.M.C. (6th London Field Ambulance).
He volunteered in August 1914, and was engaged with his unit on important duties until 1916, when he was drafted to France. After valuable service there in the same year he was transferred to Salonika, where he served in many important engagements. He afterwards proceeded to Palestine and was in the Advance to Jerusalem and the chief operations on that front. He was twice mentioned in Despatches for his excellent work. After his return home he was demobilised in December 1919, and holds the General Service and Victory Medals.
11, St. Philip Street, Battersea, S.W.8. Z4307

STREET, A. R., Private, R.A.M.C.
He volunteered in September 1915, and after his training was drafted to Gallipoli. He was engaged as stretcher bearer and in many other important duties in this theatre of war and rendered valuable services. He also did excellent service as a hospital orderly. He was demobilised in May 1919, and holds the 1914-15 Star, and the General Service and Victory Medals.
21, Peveril Street, Battersea, S.W.11. 2032B

STREET, A. R., Private, R.A.M.C.
Volunteering in September 1914, he proceeded in July of the following year to the Dardanelles and did much good work there until the Evacuation of the Peninsula. He was then drafted to Egypt, and served in the Palestine Advance as a stretcher bearer, tending the wounded until returning home for demobilisation in May 1919. He holds the General Service and Victory Medals.
21, Peveril Street, Battersea, S.W.11. 2032B

STREET, E. S., Private, R.A.M.C. (6th London Field Ambulance).
He was mobilised at the outbreak of hostilities and was quickly sent to France, where throughout the whole course of the war he rendered excellent service in all the chief engagements. He was wounded on one occasion and gassed twice. After returning to England he was demobilised in December 1919, and holds the 1914 Star, and the General Service and Victory Medals, and the Territorial Long Service Medal.
11, St. Philip Street, Battersea, S.W.8. Z4307A

STREETLY, E., Sergt., 1st Royal Berkshire Regt.
He volunteered in August 1914, and was afterwards sent to France, where he took part in numerous engagements of great importance. He was unfortunately killed in action at Festubert in May 1915, and was entitled to the 1914-15 Star, and the General Service and Victory Medals.
" And doubtless he went in splendid company."
24, Rollo Street, Battersea, S.W.11. Z4308B

STREETLY, W., Private, 7th Norfolk Regiment.
He joined in December 1917, and after his training was drafted to the Western Front, where he took part in numerous engagements. He was invalided to hospital owing to eye trouble and remained there until December 1919, when he was discharged owing to his disability. He holds the General Service and Victory Medals.
24, Rollo Street, Battersea, S.W.11. Z4308A

STREETON, G. F. S., Sapper, R.E.
He joined in August 1916, and later in the same year was sent to France, where he served in the special company that was responsible for the manufacture of gas. He took part in numerous engagements, including that at Ypres, where he was wounded in 1917. After his recovery he returned to his unit in France and did excellent work on the Ypres salient, and was again wounded. On returning home he was demobilised in May 1919, and holds the General Service and Victory Medals.
51, Castlemain Road, Peckham, S.E.15. Z5834

STRETTEN, T., Private, 5th Royal Fusiliers.
He volunteered in March 1915, and after his training rendered valuable service at various stations in connection with coast defences and patrol duty. He was unable to obtain his transfer overseas before the cessation of hostilities, and was demobilised in December 1919.
46, Somerset Road, Chiswick, W.4. 7633

STRIBBLING, B., Sergt., Royal Inniskilling Fusiliers.
He volunteered in September 1914, and after being sent to the Dardanelles in the following year took part in the Landing at Suvla Bay, and was badly wounded. In 1916 he was transferred to France, where he was gassed and blown up. After a long period in hospital he was placed in charge of the Chinese Labour Corps at the Base. He was demobilised in July 1919, and holds the 1914-15 Star, and the General Service and Victory Medals.
7, Chatham Street, Walworth, S.E.17. Z4309

STRICKLAND, A., Private, Duke of Wellington's (West Riding Regiment).
He joined in November 1917, and after completing his training was drafted to the Western Front, where he took part in numerous engagements in the Ypres and Somme areas and the Offensives of 1918, and was wounded. He returned home, and was afterwards sent to India, where he was still serving in 1920. He holds the General Service and Victory Medals.
11, Motley Street, Battersea, S.W.8. Z4310

STRICKLAND, J. D., Sapper, R.E.
He volunteered in July 1915, and on completing his training was sent to France, where he took part in many important engagements. He rendered valuable service with his unit on the Somme in 1916 and 1917, and in the various operations in the Advance of 1918. He was demobilised in June 1919 after his return home, and holds the 1914-15 Star, and the General Service and Victory Medals.
4, Dawson Road, Walworth, S.E.17. Z27013

STRINGER, E. W., Rifleman, 21st London Regt. (1st Surrey Rifles).
He volunteered in April 1915, and in January of the following year was sent to France, where he took part in the Battle of the Somme and in numerous other engagements. He was unfortunately killed in action on the Somme front on September 15th, 1916, and was entitled to the General Service and Victory Medals.
"His life for his Country, his Soul to God."
33, Sandover Road, Camberwell, S.E.5. Z5509

STRINGER, J. A., Private, Labour Corps (Royal Fusiliers).
He joined in June 1916, and in the following month was drafted to France, where he rendered valuable services in numerous engagements, and was wounded. He was invalided home and discharged as medically unfit for further service in July 1917, holding the General Service and Victory Medals.
27, Cork Street, Camberwell, S.E.5. Z4590A Z4591A

STRINGER, J. T., Sapper, R.E.
He joined in September 1917, and after his training was engaged at various stations on important duties with his unit. He was employed on Inland Water Transport duties and also as a guard for German prisoners of war, and rendered valuable services, but was not successful in obtaining his transfer overseas before the cessation of hostilities. He was demobilised in January 1919.
33, Bellefields Road, Stockwell Road, S.W.9. Z4311

STRIPP, F. W., Sergt., R.A.F. (late R.N.A.S.)
He joined in 1916, and proceeded to France in August of that year. He was stationed at Dunkirk with the air defence and bombing Squadrons and was in action on a number of occasions. During the Retreat and Advance he served at Amiens and Le Cateau, and was present at the entry into Mons. He rendered valuable services, and was demobilised in April 1919, holding the General Service and Victory Medals.
5, Amott Road, Peckham, S.E.15. Z6716

STRONG, A. D., L/Corporal, M.G.C.
Mobilised in August 1914, he was at once sent to France, and fought in the Retreat from Mons, at the Marne, Ypres, Loos, Arras, and was wounded near Ypres in November 1917. On his recovery he rejoined his unit and was in action at Cambrai, the Somme, and in many engagements in the Retreat and Advance of 1918. He was demobilised in January 1919, and holds the Mons Star, and the General Service and Victory Medals.
68, Copeland Road, Peckham, S.E.15. Z5677

STRONG, C. W., Sergt.-Drummer, 24th London Regiment (The Queen's).
Mobilised at the commencement of hostilities, he was retained at various depôts with his unit engaged on important duties. Owing to ill-health he was not successful in obtaining his transfer overseas, but did excellent work, especially in connection with entertainments for the troops until demobilised in March 1919.
27, Lothian Road, Camberwell New Road, S.W.9. Z5282

STRONG, C. W., Driver, R.F.A.
He was mobilised in August 1914, and shortly afterwards embarked for the Western Front, where he fought in many important engagements. He died gloriously on the field of battle on September 24th, 1917, and was entitled to the 1914 Star, and the General Service and Victory Medals.
"He joined the great white company of valiant souls."
58, Beryl Road, Hammersmith, W.6. 13431

STRONG, H., Sergt., R.A.F.
Volunteering in 1915, he was sent to France later in that year and served at various aerodromes as a fitter. In 1917, on being transferred to Egypt, he was stationed at Cairo and Alexandria, and after much excellent work there proceeded to India in 1918, where he was employed on highly important duties with his Squadron at Lahore and Bombay. He was demobilised in 1919, on his return to England, and holds the 1914-15 Star, and the General Service and Victory Medals.
122, Kimberley Road, Peckham, S.E.15. Z6506

STRONG, L. G., Private, 24th Queen's (Royal West Surrey Regiment).
He enlisted in September 1913, and after the commencement of hostilities was retained at various stations until drafted to France in 1917. He fought in many engagements in the Cambrai front, and was present in the heavy fighting in the British Offensive against the Hindenburg Line. Later in 1917 he returned to England suffering from shell-shock, and after protracted hospital treatment was discharged in March 1919. He holds the General Service and Victory Medals.
30, Newby Street, Wandsworth Road, S.W.8. Z4312

STRONG, S. J., Private, Hampshire Regiment.
He joined in 1917, and after completing his training was engaged at various stations on important duties with his unit. Owing to ill-health, he did not obtain his transfer to a theatre of war prior to the cessation of hostilities, but rendered valuable services as a guard for prisoners of war until finally discharged as unfit for further service in April 1919.
52, Henshaw Street, Walworth, S.E.17. Z4313

STUART, A. F., 1st Class Stoker, R.N., H.M.S. "Rattlesnake."
He was serving at the outbreak of hostilities and was engaged in escorting troopships to different parts of the Mediterranean. He afterwards took part in the Naval operations at the Dardanelles from the first Landing to the Evacuation, and subsequently was engaged on patrol duties. After being transferred to H.M.S. "Grasshopper" in 1917, he rendered valuable service in the Atlantic until discharged in March 1919. He holds the 1914-15 Star, and the General Service and Victory Medals.
49, Rollo Road, Battersea, S.W.11. Z4314

STUART, C. F., Rflmn., King's Royal Rifle Corps.
He joined in May 1916, and in the following December was sent to France. He took part in numerous engagements and was badly wounded near Ypres in March 1917. He was invalided home, and after a long period in hospital was transferred to the Royal Army Pay Corps. He was still serving in 1920, and holds the General Service and Victory Medals.
15, Suffield Road, Walworth, S.E.17. 26155

STUART-ADAMS, P. N., Bombardier, R.F.A.
He volunteered in June 1915, and was drafted to the Western Front in the following March. He took an active part in the Battles of the Somme and Passchendaele, and was severely wounded near Ypres, in consequence of which he underwent fourteen operations and had one of his legs amputated. After protracted treatment in hospital at Shepherd's Bush and Roehampton he was ultimately discharged in March 1920, holding the General Service and Victory Medals.
24, Rephidim Street, Weston Street, S.E.1. Z25498

(V.C.) STUBBS. F. E., Sergt., 1st Lancashire Fusiliers.
Volunteering in August 1914, he embarked for the Dardanelles in April of the following year, and played a distinguished part in the Landing in Gallipoli on the 25th of that month. His unit being met by a devastating fire from hidden machine guns, Sergeant Stubbs rushed forward, regardless of personal danger, and cut the wire entanglements. It was entirely owing to his splendid initiative that the most formidable obstacles were overcome, the cliff gained, and the position consolidated. In the performance of this gallant act of self-sacrifice and devotion to duty, Sergeant Stubbs fell mortally wounded. He was mentioned in General Sir Ian Hamilton's Despatches, bearing date August 5th, 1915, and was posthumously awarded the Victoria Cross. In a letter to his mother announcing this award, Sir Ian Hamilton writes:—
"I am to express to you the King's high appreciation of these services and to add that His Majesty trusts that their public acknowledgment may be of some consolation in your bereavement." He was entitled, in addition to the Victoria Cross, to the 1914-15 Star, and the General Service and Victory Medals.
"Greater love hath no man than this, that a man lay down his life for his friends."
19, Huguenot Road, Peckham Rye, S.E.15. Z6089

STUBBS, R. B., Private, Royal Sussex Regiment.

He joined in April 1917, and in the following year after completing his training was sent to the Western Front, where he took part in numerous engagements in the Retreat of 1918, and was wounded near Loos. After his recovery he rendered valuable services first at Newhaven and subsequently in the Demobilisation Staff at the Crystal Palace, until himself demobilised in September 1919. He holds the General Service and Victory Medals.

290, Commercial Road, Peckham, S.E.15. Z6666-7B

STUBBS, R. G., Staff-Sergt., 22nd London Regt. (Queen's).

He was mobilised in August 1914, and being sent to France in the following year took a prominent part in the fighting at Neuve Chapelle, Festubert, Loos, and in many other engagements. He returned home and was discharged in April 1916 in consequence of his services, holding the 1914-15 Star, and the General Service and Victory Medals.

290, Commercial Road, Peckham, S.E.15. Z6666-7A

STUCKEY, F. (D.S.M.), P.O. (Wireless), R.N., H.M. Monitor " 27."

He was in the Navy at the outbreak of war and served with the Grand Fleet in the North Sea. He took part in numerous engagements throughout the war including the Battles of Heligoland Bight and Jutland. In 1919 he was sent to Russia on Monitor 27, and while serving there was awarded the Distinguished Service Medal in August for his great gallantry. He also holds the 1914-15 Star, and the General Service and Victory Medals, and was still serving in 1920.

58, Hollydale Road, Peckham, S.E.15. Z6454

STUDD, W. R., Sergt., R.A.M.C.

He volunteered in September 1914, and after completing his training was sent to France in February 1916. He was engaged on various duties connected with his corps in the Battles of the Somme, Arras, and Ypres, and in the leading operations in the Retreat and Advance of 1918. He was demobilised in May 1919, and holds the General Service and Victory Medals.

38, Mantua Street, Battersea, S.W.11. Z4316

STUDMAN, R., Driver, R.A.S.C. (H.T.)

He volunteered in December 1915, and after his training served at various stations on important duties with his unit. He rendered valuable services, but on account of his medical unfitness was not successful in obtaining his transfer overseas before the fighting ceased. He was demobilised in April 1919.

27, Crozier Street, Lambeth, S.8. Z26073

STUNELL, R. G., Pte., 8th Somerset Light Infantry.

He joined in January 1917, and in the same year after completing his training was sent to France, where he took part in the fighting at Arras and Bullecourt, and was severely wounded at Messines. He was invalided home in consequence, and discharged, owing to his wounds in December 1917. He holds the General Service and Victory Medals.

14, Anstey Road, Peckham, S.E.15. Z6697

STURTON, J. R., Private, R.A.O.C.

He volunteered in August 1914, and after completing his training was drafted to the Western Front, where he rendered much valuable service with his unit in various sectors until the close of hostilities. He was demobilised in March 1919, after his return to England, and holds the 1914-15 Star, and the General Service and Victory Medals.

21, Leythe Road, Acton, W.3. 6635

STUTELEY, H. A. (M.M.), L/Cpl., R.E. (Signals).

He volunteered in May 1915, and in February of the following year was sent to France, where he took part in numerous engagements including those at Arras, Ypres, and the Offensives of 1918, and was wounded. He was awarded the Military Medal at Heudicourt for holding the line of communication and rescuing a wounded comrade. He also holds the General Service and Victory Medals, and was demobilised in January 1919. 42, Vicarage Road, Camberwell, S.E.5. Z4317

STYLES, A., Rflmn., 8th London Regt. (P.O. Rifles).

He volunteered in October 1914, and in the following year was drafted to the Western Front, where he took part in the Battles of Hill 60, and was wounded at Loos. On his recovery he was detained for service at Farnborough until 1918, when he returned to France and fought in the Retreat and Advance of the Allies. He was demobilised in July 1919, and holds the 1914-15 Star, and the General Service and Victory Medals.

15, McKerrell Road, Peckham, S.E.15. Z5843B

STYLES, A., Sapper, R.E.

He volunteered in February 1915, and after his training was drafted to German East Africa, where he was engaged on important duties as a telegraph linesman, and took part in several engagements. He was invalided home with malaria in 1918, and was demobilised in January 1919, holding the General Service and Victory Medals.

29, Rosetta Street, South Lambeth Road, S.W.8. Z27499

STYLES, E., Private, 2nd Wiltshire Regiment.

He volunteered in August 1914, and in the following year was drafted to the Western Front, where he took part in numerous engagements of importance including those at Hill 60, Festubert, Loos, the Somme, Arras, Ypres, Cambrai, and the Retreat and Advance of 1918. He was demobilised in April 1919, and holds the 1914-15 Star, and the General Service and Victory Medals.

15, McKerrell Road, Peckham, S.E.15. Z5843A

STYLES, J., Private, 2nd Middlesex Regiment.

He volunteered in September 1914, and in the following month was drafted to France where he took part in the Battles of La Bassée, Ypres, Neuve Chapelle, St. Eloi, Vimy Ridge, and Albert, and was wounded at the Somme. He was invalided home, and after much hospital treatment was discharged as medically unfit for further service in July 1916. He holds the 1914 Star, and the General Service and Victory Medals.

25, North Street, Clapham, S.W.4. Z4318

STYLES, S. W., A.B., R.N., H.M.S. " Aurora."

He joined in June 1916, and saw much service with the Harwich Force under Commodore Tyrwhitt, and later with the Grand Fleet in the North Sea. He was also present at the surrender of the German Fleet after the Armistice. He was demobilised in March 1919, and holds the General Service and Victory Medals.

52, Beaufoy Road, Battersea, S.W.11. Z4319

STYLES, W., Gunner, R.F.A.

He was mobilised in August 1914, and was immediately sent to France where he was in action in the Retreat from Mons, and the Battles of the Aisne, La Bassée, Hill 60, Loos, Vimy Ridge, the Somme, Passchendaele, Cambrai, and was badly gassed at Vermelles. He unhappily died from the effects of the poisoning at Treport on May 18th, 1918, and was entitled to the Mons Star and the General Service and Victory Medals.

" His memory is cherished with pride."

15, McKerrell Road, Peckham, S.E.15. Z5843C

STYLES, W. J., Driver, R.A.S.C. (M.T.)

He joined in November 1915, and in the following February proceeded to Egypt, where he served until August 1916. Upon being transferred to Salonika he was engaged in conveying supplies to the 28th Division on the Struma front, and also took part in the pursuit of the retreating Bulgarians at the close of the war. He was sent home and demobilised in April 1919, and holds the General Service and Victory Medals.

18, Pratt Street, Kennington, S.E.11. Z27358

SUDD, C. F., Private, R.F.A.

Volunteering in August 1915, he was drafted to France four months later, and fought in the Battles of the Somme, Messines, Passchendaele, Grandcourt, and was gassed at Bapaume. On recovery he rejoined his unit and shortly afterwards transferred to Italy, fought in many parts of the line and took part in the final Allied Advance in this theatre of war in 1918. He returned to England after the Armistice, and was still serving in 1920. He holds the 1914-15 Star, and the General Service and Victory Medals.

46, Hutton Road, Kennington, S.E.11. Z25519

SUGDEN, E. J., Pte., 22nd London Regt. (Queen's).

Mobilised at the outbreak of hostilities he was drafted to France in the following year, and took a prominent part in the fighting at Loos, Albert, and Vermelles. In 1916 he was seriously injured while in the trenches, and was sent to England. After his recovery he was again drafted to France where he rendered much valuable service, but was unhappily killed in action in the Ypres sector on May 10th, 1917. He was buried at Bedford House Cemetery, near Ypres, and was entitled to the 1914-15 Star, and the General Service and Victory Medals.

" His Life for his Country, his Soul to God."

13, Sandison Street, Peckham, S.E.18. Z6782

SUGG, J. W., Private, The King's (Liverpool Regt.)

A serving soldier, he was stationed in India at the outbreak of war and was retained for duty in that country, and saw active service on the North-Western Frontier. He also did good work whilst stationed at various garrison towns, engaged on important duties. Suffering from malaria, he was invalided to England, and after receiving medical treatment was discharged as unfit for further service in August 1916. He holds the General Service and Victory Medals.

13, Nunhead Grove, Peckham, S.E.15. Z6668

SULLIVAN, A., Private, 1st Lincolnshire Regiment.

A Reservist, having previously served in the South African campaign, he was mobilised at the declaration of war, and sent to France in September 1914. He fought in the closing stages of the Retreat from Mons, in the Battles of the Marne, the Aisne, Ypres, Neuve Chapelle, Arras, and Messines, and throughout the German Offensive and Allied Advance of 1918. He was demobilised in February 1919, and holds the Queen's South African Medal, the Mons Star, and the General Service and Victory Medals.

186, Commercial Road, Peckham, S.E.15. Z6626

SULLIVAN, G. E., Driver, R.F.A.

Volunteering in August 1914, and embarking for France in the succeeding year, he was in action in many important engagements, including those at Ypres, the Somme, Arras, and Vimy Ridge. He also fought throughout the German Offensive of 1918, and was gassed in August 1918, during the Allied Advance. Retreating to England he was demobilised in 1919, and holds the 1914–15 Star, and the General Service and Victory Medals.
49, Sunwell Street, Peckham, S.E.15.　　　Z6451

SULLIVAN, G. W., Rflmn., King's Royal Rifle Corps.

Joining in October 1916, later in that year he proceeded to the Western Front, where he was engaged in heavy fighting in many parts of the line, and was gassed. On recovery he returned to the front and fought in many engagements. He was severely wounded on June 17th, 1917 on the Somme, and admitted into hospital, and died from his injuries on June 29th He was entitled to the General Service and Victory Medals.
"Great deeds cannot die."
11, Nealdon Street, Stockwell, S.W.9.　　　Z4320

SULLIVAN, J., Private, Royal Fusiliers.

He joined in September 1916, and in the same year was drafted to the Western Front. He took part in the engagements on the Somme, and on the Ancre, and was seriously wounded at Bullecourt. He was sent home for treatment and discharged as unfit for further service in February 1919. He holds the General Service and Victory Medals.
14, Barrett Road, Walworth, S.E.17.　　　Z27015

SULLIVAN, J., Private, Royal Fusiliers.

He volunteered in October 1915, and sent to the Western Front two months later, fought in the Battles of St. Eloi, and Vimy Ridge. He laid down his life for the freedom of land on the Somme on July 4th, 1916, and was entitled to the 1914–15 Star, and the General Service and Victory Medals.
"A costly sacrifice upon the altar of freedom."
3, Kinglake Street, Walworth, S.E.17.　　　Z2594–5B

SULLIVAN, J., L/Corporal, Rifle Brigade.

Volunteering in May 1915, he embarked for France in the following September, and was in action at Hooge, St. Eloi, Ploegsteert, and was wounded at Messines in April 1916. Returning to England he received hospital treatment, and after his recovery was transferred to the Royal Army Service Corps, and served at various stations until demobilised in May 1919. He holds the 1914–15 Star, and the General Service and Victory Medals.
34, Wooler Street, Walworth, S.E.17.　　　Z4322

SULLIVAN, J. H., L/Cpl., King's Royal Rifle Corps.

He volunteered in December 1915, and was drafted to the Western Front in the following October. During his service overseas, he fought in various sectors and was wounded on the Somme in 1917. Returning home, he received medical treatment, and on recovery served at various depôts on important duties until demobilised in March 1919. He holds the General Service and Victory Medals.
64, Cabul Road, Battersea, S.W.11.　　　Z4321

SULLIVAN, S., Private, 13th London Regiment (Kensingtons).

He joined in April 1916, and was drafted to the Western Front in the following year. He fought in many engagements, including the first Battle of the Somme, and suffering from shell-shock returned to England. After receiving hospital treatment, he rejoined his unit in France in March 1917, and saw much fighting. He was taken prisoner in the second Battle of the Somme in 1918, but escaped in November of that year, and rejoined the British Forces at Mons on November 11th. Returning home he was demobilised in September 1919, and holds the General Service and Victory Medals.
2, Rephidim Street, Weston Street, S.E.1.　　　Z25711

SULLIVAN, W. J., Private, 11th Somerset Light Infantry.

Joining in November 1916, he completed his training, and stationed at various depôts was engaged on important duties with his unit. Owing to medical unfitness, he was not eligible for active service, but rendered excellent services until ultimately invalided out of H.M. Forces in October 1918.
56, Howbury Road, Nunhead, S.E.15.　　　Z6585B

SULLIVAN, W. J. (Jun.), Private, Queen's (Royal West Surrey Regiment).

He joined in July 1917, and was drafted to France in the following year. During his service overseas he fought in many engagements in the Retreat of 1918, and in the opening phases of the Allied Advance. He gave his life for King and Country on August 24th, 1918, and was entitled to the General Service and Victory Medals.
"The path of duty was the way to glory."
56, Howbury Road, Nunhead, S.E.15.　　　Z6585A

SUMMERFIELD, A. E., A.B., Royal Naval Reserve.

He was called up from the reserve at the outbreak of hostilities and during the war served on various ships which were engaged on patrol, escort, and mine-sweeping duties. He saw service in the North and Mediterranean Seas, and off the coast of Ireland and rendered valuable services throughout. He was demobilised in August 1920, and holds the 1914–15 Star, and the General Service and Victory Medals.
24, Havelock Terrace, Battersea Park Road, S.W.8.　　　Z4324B

SUMMERFIELD, B., Cpl., 18th London Regiment (London Irish Rifles).

He was mobilised in August 1914, and drafted to the Western Front in the following February served in the Loos, Givenchy, and Hill 60 sectors. In March 1915 he returned to England and was discharged as time-expired. Called up again in July 1916 he proceeded to Salonika, and fought in many engagements of note. He was unfortunately killed in action on May 7th, 1917, and was entitled to the 1914–15 Star, and the General Service and Victory Medals.
"Steals on the ear the distant triumph song."
31, Radnor Street, Peckham, S.E.15.　　　Z6548B

SUMMERFIELD, E. E., Cpl., Royal Irish Rifles.

He joined in 1916, and later in the same year was sent to the Western Front, where he fought in many important engagements, including the Battle of the Somme. He was reported missing in heavy fighting at Lens in 1917, and later was presumed to have been killed in action. He was entitled to the General Service and Victory Medals.
"Honour to the immortal dead, who gave their youth that the world might grow old in peace."
24, Havelock Terrace, Battersea, S.W.8.　　　Z4324A

SUMMERFIELD, F., Sergt., 3rd Dorsetshire Regt. and 3rd Prince of Wales Leinster Regt.

He enlisted in April 1914, and mobilised at the outbreak of war served at various depôts on instructional duties until transferred to the Leinster Regiment, and was drafted to France in November 1916. He was engaged in heavy fighting in many parts of the line and was severely wounded on April 12th, 1917. Returning to England he received protracted hospital treatment, but died from his injuries on June 1st, 1918, and was entitled to the General Service and Victory Medals.
"Nobly striving.
He nobly fell that we might live."
31, Radnor Street, Peckham, S.E.15.　　　Z6548A

SUMMERFIELD, G. E. T. (M.M.), Cpl., R.G.A.

He volunteered in August 1914, and proceeding to the Western Front in the following April was in action in the Battles of Ypres, Loos, St. Eloi, Albert, Vermelles, the Somme, Messines, and throughout the Retreat and Advance of 1918. He was awarded the Military Medal for conspicuous gallantry and devotion to duty in the Field. He was demobilised in April 1919, and holds the 1914–15 Star, and the General Service and Victory Medals. 12, Gurney Street, Walworth, S.E.17.　Z4323

SUMMERS, A., Sapper, R.E.

Mobilised in August 1914, he embarked for France in the following January, and was in action at St. Eloi, Festubert, Hill 60, Loos, Vimy Ridge, the Somme, Messines, Passchendaele and throughout the Retreat and Advance of 1918. During his service overseas he was wounded at Festubert in May 1915. He was demobilised in February 1919, and holds the 1914–15 Star, and the General Service and Victory Medals.
16, Haymerle Road, Peckham, S.E.15.　　　Z6447

SUMMERS, J. R., Private, R.A.S.C. (M.T.)

He volunteered in March 1915, and later in that year was sent to France, where he fought in many engagements of note, including those on the Somme, and at Arras, Ypres, St. Quentin, Bapaume, Lens, and Bourlon Wood. He was also in action throughout the German Offensive and Allied Advance of 1918, and returning home after the Armistice was demobilised in May 1919. He holds the 1914–15 Star, and the General Service and Victory Medals.
Edward Cottage, Park Place, Clapham, S.W.4.　　　Z4325

SUMMERSBY, W. T., Pte., 1st Queen's (Royal West Surrey Regiment).

Mobilised at the commencement of hostilities, he was drafted to France and fought in the Retreat from Mons, and in the engagements on the Marne, and Aisne, and at Ypres, Loos, and the Somme. He made the supreme sacrifice, being killed in action between Arras and Messines in 1917, and was entitled to the Mons Star, and the General Service and Victory Medals.
"Whilst we remember the sacrifice is not in vain."
3, Gye Street, Kennington, S.E.11.　　　Z24354

SUMPTON, G. A., Air Mechanic, R.A.F.

He joined in May 1917, and later in that year was drafted to France, where he served at various aerodromes in the Somme, Arras, and Ypres sectors, and also was stationed at Dunkirk. He rendered valuable services throughout, and returning home was demobilised in February 1919, and holds the General Service and Victory Medals.
30, Henshaw Street, Walworth, S.E.17.　　　Z4326

SURGUY, A., Sergt., M.G.C.

Volunteering in October 1915, he was drafted to the Western Front in the following year, and fought in the Battles of the Somme, Arras, Ypres, Passchendaele, St. Quentin, and Béthune. Early in 1918 he was severely wounded and lost the use of his left arm, and invalided home, and received hospital treatment. He was subsequently discharged as unfit for further service in October 1918, and holds the General Service and Victory Medal.
15, South Island Place, Stockwell, S.W.9.   Z5284

SUSSEX, E. J. J., L/Corporal, Royal Scots.

Volunteering in January 1915, at the age of fifteen, he was sent to the Western Front in February of the following year, and fought in many parts of the line. He was gassed at Vimy Ridge, and admitted into hospital received treatment on recovery, he rejoined his unit, and was in action in various engagements in the German Offensive of 1918. Suffering from shell-shock he returned to England, and on recovery was stationed at various depôts engaged on important duties. He was still serving in 1920, and holds the General Service and Victory Medals.
9, Auckland Road, Battersea, S.W.11.   Z4327

SUSSEX, J. C., Private, R.A.S.C. (M.T.)

He joined in May 1917, and embarking for the Western Front in the following month, was engaged on important transport duties in the forward areas. Later he served as a driver of tractors employed in conveying the heavy guns into action. He was present at the Battles of Arras, Vimy Ridge, and Cambrai, and at heavy fighting in the Retreat and Advance of 1918, and was gassed. He was demobilised in May 1919, and holds the General Service and Victory Medals.
1, Auckland Road, Battersea, S.W.11.   Z4328

SUTHERLAND, C. F., Sapper, R.E.

Volunteering in January 1915, later in that year he was sent to the Western Front, and was engaged in heavy fighting in many parts of the line, including the Ypres salient. He died gloriously on the field of battle on the Somme on November 11th, 1916, and was entitled to the 1914-15 Star, and the General Service and Victory Medals.
" He joined the great white company of valiant souls."
13, Mosedale Street, Camberwell, S.E.5.   Z4332

SUTHERLAND, F. N., Sapper, R.E.

He volunteered in January 1915, and was drafted to the Western Front six months later. He rendered excellent services engaged on important duties in the front lines in the Battle of the Somme, and various other engagements. During his service overseas he was twice wounded, on the latter occasion in August 1918. He returned home, and was demobilised in January 1919, and holds the 1914-15 Star, and the General Service and Victory Medals.
6, Cheam Place, Camberwell, S.E.5.   Z6508

SUTTON, A., Pioneer, R.E.

Volunteering in August 1915, later in that year he was drafted to France where he was in action in the Battles of Vimy Ridge, the Somme, and the Ancre. He laid down his life for the freedom of England at Neuve Chapelle on November 28th, 1916, and was entitled to the 1914-15 Star, and the General Service and Victory Medals. He had also served throughout the South African War.
" A costly sacrifice upon the altar of freedom."
38, Sterndale Road, Battersea, S.W.8.   Z4333

SUTTON, E. E., Private, 3rd Buffs (East Kent Regt.)

He joined in August 1916, and completing his training was stationed at various depôts engaged on important duties with his unit. He was unsuccessful in obtaining his transfer to a theatre of war prior to the cessation of hostilities, but rendered excellent services until demobilised in March 1919.
36, Pentridge Street, Peckham, S.E.15.   Z5678

SUTTON, J., Chief Petty Officer, R.N.

He joined in August 1914, and throughout the war served in various ships which were engaged on convoy and other important duties. His ship was also engaged on transporting supplies to the Grand Fleet in the North Sea. He rendered excellent services throughout, and was demobilised in February 1919, and holds the 1914-15 Star, and the General Service and Victory Medals.
79, Avenue Road, Camberwell, S.E.5.   Z4334

SWABEY, C. F. J., Private, R.A.M.C.

He joined in May 1917, and in the following February was drafted to the Italian theatre of war. During his service overseas he was engaged at various hospitals on important duties attending the sick and wounded troops, and did good work. Returning to England he was demobilised in February 1919, and holds the General Service and Victory Medals.
83, Great Bland Street, Southwark, S.E.1.   Z25644

SWAFFER, F. W., L/Corporal, Rifle Brigade and Essex Regiment.

He joined in December 1916, and embarking for the Western Front in the following year fought at Arras, Ypres, and the Somme. He was severely wounded at St. Quentin, and returning to England received hospital treatment. On recovery, he served at various depôts on important duties until demobilised in March 1919.
13, Moat Place, Stockwell, S.W.9.   Z4335

SWAFFIELD, F. R., Driver, R.A.S.C. (M.T.)

Mobilised in August 1914, he was drafted to the Western Front and served throughout the Retreat from Mons. Later he was engaged on important duties, transporting ammunition and supplies to the front lines and saw much fighting in the Ypres salient. In 1916 he returned to England and was discharged in March of that year as time expired. He holds the Mons Star, and the General Service and Victory Medals.
34, Odell Street, Camberwell, S.E.5.   Z5510B

SWAFFIELD, F. W. T., Sergt., 3rd London Regt. (Royal Fusiliers).

He enlisted in 1912, and at the commencement of hostilities was sent to Malta, and later in 1914 proceeded to France, where he fought at Festubert and Loos, and was wounded at Neuve Chapelle. He returned to England, and after receiving hospital treatment was transferred to the South African Rifles, and drafted to German East Africa, where he served throughout the campaign in that territory. In 1920 he was serving with the Cape Mounted Police in Rhodesia, and holds the 1914 Star, and the General Service and Victory Medals.
34, Odell Street, Camberwell, S.E.5.   Z5510A

SWAFFIELD, T. O., Rifleman, 16th London Regt. (Queen's Westminster Rifles).

He volunteered in January 1916, and was drafted to the Western Front shortly afterwards. He was engaged in severe fighting in many parts of the line, and was in action in numerous battles of note. He gave his life for the freedom of England on September 10th, 1916 on the Somme, and was entitled to the General Service and Victory Medals.
" Great deeds cannot die."
12, Montgomery Road, Chiswick, W.4.   6899

SWALE, H. T., Corporal, R.E. (R.O.D.)

He volunteered in January 1916, and in the same year was sent to the Western Front, where he was engaged on important duties as a wire-man, establishing and maintaining telephonic communication in the front lines. He also did good work employed on mining operations. Later he met with an accident and fractured his right arm, and returning to England received hospital treatment and was subsequently invalided out of the Service in November 1919. He holds the General Service and Victory Medals.
230, Albert Road, Peckham, S.E.15.   Z5668-9-70A

SWALE, W., Private, Durham Light Infantry.

He volunteered in September 1914, and in the following year was drafted to France. During his service overseas he fought at Festubert, Ypres, Albert, Vimy Ridge, and was blown up by a shell explosion in July 1916. Returning home, he received medical treatment, and on recovery was sent to Russia, where he was in action in many important engagements. Returning to England he was demobilised in March 1919, and holds the 1914-15 Star, and the General Service and Victory Medals.
153, Hollydale Road, Peckham, S.E.15.   Z6507

SWALLOW, H., Gunner, R.G.A.

He joined in June 1916, and in the following December proceeded to Salonika, and fought in many important engagements on the Monastir, Doiran and Vardar fronts. He rendered valuable services throughout, and returning home after the cessation of hostilities was demobilised in November 1919, and holds the General Service and Victory Medals.
5, Flint Street, Walworth, S.E.17.   Z4336

SWAN, F. J., Q.M.S., R.A.S.C.

Mobilised in August 1914, he was sent to the Western Front and served in the Retreat from Mons, and in the Battles of Neuve Chapelle and Hill 60. He rendered valuable services throughout, and was killed in action in the second Battle of the Marne in 1918. He was entitled to the Mons Star, and the General Service and Victory Medals.
" A valiant soldier with undaunted heart he breasted Life's last hill."
27, Meyrick Road, Battersea, S.W.11.   Z4337

SWANN, H., 1st Air Mechanic, R.A.F.

He joined in December 1916, and was sent to the Western Front in November of the following year. He served at various aerodromes on important duties in the sail-making department, and did good work throughout. He was demobilised in March 1919, and holds the General Service and Victory Medals.
22, Greylands Road, Peckham, S.E.15.   Z5839

SWEENEY, G., Private, Middlesex and Essex Regts.
He volunteered in August 1914, and proceeded to France in the following year. He took part in numerous engagements and rendered much valuable service until August 27th, 1918, when he unhappily fell in action at Bapaume. He was entitled to the 1914-15 Star, and the General Service and Victory Medals.
"He died the noblest death a man may die,
Fighting for God, and right, and liberty."
40, Hutton Road, Lambeth, S.E.11.   Z6556C

SWEENEY, P. J., Private, 1st Middlesex Regiment.
He volunteered in August 1914, and proceeded to France shortly afterwards. He fought in many engagements and did much good work until he was unhappily killed in action at Beaumont-Hamel on November 3rd, 1916. He was entitled to the 1914-15 Star, and the General Service and Victory Medals.
"A valiant soldier, with undaunted heart he breasted Life's last hill."
40, Hutton Road, Lambeth, S.E.11.   Z6556B

SWEENEY, W. H., Guardsman, Irish Guards.
He volunteered in August 1914, and proceeded to France shortly afterwards, and served in numerous engagements. He was wounded at the Battle of Loos and invalided to England. On his recovery he was again sent to France and rendered valuable services until he was again wounded at the Battle of Cambrai. Later he unfortunately died of his injuries on April 19th, 1917, and was buried at Tooting. He was awarded the 1914 Star, and the General Service and Victory Medals.
"His life for his Country, his soul to God."
15, Farmer's Road, Camberwell, S.E.5.   Z6556A

SWEET, H., Artificer, R.N., H.M.S. "Venus."
He was serving at the outbreak of war, and was engaged on important duties in many waters, principally in the Indian Ocean. He rendered valuable services throughout the war, and was still serving in 1920. He holds the 1914-15 Star, and the General Service and Victory Medals.
35, Montgomery Road, Chiswick, W.4.   6900

SWEETING, A. W., Bombardier, R.F.A.
He volunteered in May 1915, and was sent to France later in that year. He took part in many battles, including those on the Somme and at Arras, Ypres and Cambrai, and rendered much valuable service until he was demobilised in January 1919, holding the 1914-15 Star, and the General Service and Victory Medals.
21, Wells Place, Camberwell, S.E.5.   Z4338

SWEETLAND, C. P., Rifleman, Rifle Brigade.
He joined in June 1916, and later in that year was sent to France, where he served until drafted to Salonika. Here he fought in various engagements on the Doiran and Struma fronts, and did good work until returning to England, he was demobilised in November 1919. He holds the General Service and Victory Medals.
99, Meyrick Road, Battersea, S.W.11.   Z4339

SWETMAN, F. W., Private, Royal Fusiliers.
He volunteered in September 1915, and after his training was drafted to France, where he took part in the Somme Offensive, and served at Beaucourt, Grandcourt, Kemmel, Ypres, Bapaume, Cambrai, and in the Retreat and Advance of 1918. He was demobilised in October 1919 after returning home, and holds the General Service and Victory Medals.
31, Berkley Street, Kennington, S.E.11.   Z25869

SWEETMAN, H. Private, 2nd London Regt. (Royal Fusiliers).
He joined in September 1916, and after his training was sent to France, where he took a part in numerous engagements. After valuable service he was unhappily killed in action at Passchendaele on October 26th, 1917. He was entitled to the General Service and Victory Medals.
"And doubtless he went in splendid company."
54, Russell Street, Battersea, S.W.11.   Z4340

SWIFT, S., Rifleman, Rifle Brigade.
He volunteered in May 1915, and was drafted to France early in the following year. He fought in numerous engagements, including those of St. Eloi, Vimy Ridge and the Somme, where he was severely wounded. He was invalided home and after hospital treatment was discharged as physically unfit for further service in September 1917. He holds the General Service and Victory Medals.
44, Bellefields Road, Stockwell, S.W.9.   Z4341

SWINN, T. W., Private, R.A.S.C.
He volunteered in November 1914, and was soon sent to France, where he did much valuable work in transporting supplies of all kinds to numerous sectors of the line. He was kicked by a horse and after being invalided home was discharged in February 1916, as unfit for further military service. He holds the 1914-15 Star, and the General Service and Victory Medals.
141, Sulgrave Road, Hammersmith, W.6.   11778

SWOISH, C. S., Driver, R.F.A.
He volunteered in June 1915, and in the following February proceeded to France, where he took part in numerous engagements, and was in action on the Somme and at Vimy Ridge and Ypres, where he was wounded. He was invalided home and in December 1917 was discharged as medically unfit for further service, holding the General Service and Victory Medals.
29, Brisbane Street, Camberwell, S.E.5.   Z4342

SYCAMORE, J. J., Fitter, R.F.A.
He volunteered in August 1914, and proceeded to France in the following year. He was in action in many engagements, including those on the Somme and at Arras and Ypres, and was severely wounded and suffered the loss of his right eye. He was invalided home, and was discharged as medically unfit in September 1917. He holds the 1914-15 Star, and the General Service and Victory Medals.
1, Hillery Road, Walworth, S.E.17.   Z4343

SYDENHAM, A. W., Rifleman, King's Royal Rifle Corps.
He volunteered in August 1915, and on the completion of his training was drafted to France in 1916. He took part in many engagements in the Arras and Somme sectors, but owing to ill-health was invalided home and subsequently discharged in October 1916, as medically unfit for further military service. He holds the General Service and Victory Medals.
34, Saville Road, Chiswick, W.4.   6666

SYKES, C. T. R., Gunner, R.F.A.
He volunteered in November 1914, and proceeded to France in the following year. He fought at Ypres, Festubert, Loos, the Somme, Cambrai and numerous other engagements, and also served in the Retreat and Advance of 1918. After the Armistice he returned to England and was demobilised in June 1919, holding the 1914-15 Star, and the General Service and Victory Medals.
6, Stanley Street, Battersea Park, S.W.8.   Z4344B

SYKES, F. T. W., L/Corporal, The Queen's (Royal West Surrey Regiment).
He volunteered in November 1915, and proceeded to France in the following year. He fought at Ypres, Cambrai and the Somme, and in numerous other actions, and rendered much valuable service. He was unhappily killed in action at Poperinghe on May 9th, 1918, and is buried at that place. He was entitled to the General Service and Victory Medals.
"Steals on the ear the distant triumph song."
6, Stanley Street, Battersea Park, S.W.8.   Z4344A

SYMES, F., Driver, R.E.
He volunteered in September 1914, and later was drafted to France, where he served at Arras. In 1917 he was sent to the Balkan front, and fought in many of the important actions there. Later he proceeded to Egypt and did much good work during the Palestine campaign. He was demobilised in June 1919, and holds the General Service and Victory Medals.
22, Ceylon Street, Battersea, S.W.8.   Z4345B

SYMES, W. E., Sergt., 1st Coldstream Guards.
He volunteered in September 1914, and in the following January was drafted to the Western Front, where he was in action at La Bassée. Later, owing to ill-health he was invalided home and on his recovery served on important duties until discharged in January 1919. He holds the 1914-15 Star, and the General Service and Victory Medals.
22, Ceylon Street, Battersea, S.W.8.   Z4345A

SYMMONS, F. (Jun.), Private, Middlesex Regiment.
He joined in September 1918, but was unable to obtain his transfer overseas before the cessation of hostilities, but rendered valuable service until he was demobilised in February 1919. Since that date he has rejoined, and in 1920 was serving with the R.H.A. in India.
16, Sussex Road, Coldharbour Lane, S.W.9.   Z4346A

SYMMONS, F., Pte., 3rd Devonshire and Bedfordshire Regiments.
He volunteered in April 1915, and was sent to France in that year. He fought on the Somme and at Givenchy and later proceeded to Mesopotamia, where he took part amongst other engagements, in the relief of Kut. Afterwards he was drafted to India and attached to the Bedfordshire Regiment, was engaged on important duties until demobilised in November 1919. He holds the 1914-15 Star, and the General Service and Victory Medals.
16, Sussex Road, Coldharbour Lane, S.W.9.   Z4346B

SYMONDS, H., Rifleman, Royal Irish Rifles.
He joined in June 1916, and in the following month was sent to France, where he took part in the fighting on the Somme and later in the Retreat and Advance of 1918. Contracting fever he returned to England and was demobilised in February 1919. He holds the General Service and Victory Medals.
36, Berkley Street, Kennington, S.E.11.   Z25867

SYMONDS, J. W., Private, 23rd London Regt.
He volunteered in September 1914, and was after his training drafted to France, where he took part in many engagements, including the Battles of Loos, in which he was both gassed and wounded. He was sent to England, and on his recovery was employed on important duties at various stations until demobilised in March 1919, holding the 1914-15 Star, and the General Service and Victory Medals.
8, Pitcairn Street, Clapham, S.W.8. Z4347

SYRETT, R., Private, 1st Welch Regiment.
Serving at the outbreak of war he was sent to France and took part in the Retreat from Mons and the fighting at Hill 60, Ypres and other places. He was severely wounded at Loos and was invalided to England and discharged as medically unfit in March 1916. He re-enlisted, however, in April 1919, and served in France until March 1920, when he was demobilised, holding the Mons Star, and the General Service and Victory Medals.
10, Ledbury Street, Peckham, S.E.15. Z6577

SYRETT, T. H., C.S.M., 11th Essex Regiment.
He volunteered in September 1914, and in the following year was drafted to the Western Front. There he served with distinction in many battles, including those of Neuve Chapelle, Festubert and Loos, where he was severely wounded. He was invalided to England, and on recovery acted as an instructor until demobilised in 1919. He holds the 1914-15 Star, and the General Service and Victory Medals.
34, Oakden Street, Kennington, S.E.11. Z27211

T

TADMAN, W., Private, 14th Queen's (Royal West Surrey Regiment).
He joined in August 1916, and after his training was drafted to Salonika, where he took part in many engagements on the Doiran, Struma, and Vardar fronts. He contracted malaria and was in hospital during his service in the East. He was demobilised after his return to England in June 1919 and holds the General Service and Victory Medals.
63, Sussex Road, Coldharbour Lane, S.W.9. Z4348

TAGG, F. (Miss), Special War Worker.
During the war this lady offered her services at King's College Hospital, and was engaged for a year and a half in attending to the wounded in the Recreation Room and helping the disabled. She gave all her available time to this valuable work, and her patriotic services were much appreciated.
68, Harris Street, Camberwell, S.E.5. Z4481

TAIT, G T., Private, Labour Corps.
He volunteered in July 1915, and in the following November crossing to France was engaged on important duties in various parts of the line. In 1917 he was drafted to Italy, where he did valuable work for seven months, returning to France in June 1918. He then became seriously ill, and after being invalided home, was demobilised in January 1919. He holds the 1914-15 Star, and the General Service and Victory Medals.
56, Blake's Road, Peckham, S.E.15. Z6103

TALBOT, F., Corporal, 9th Rifle Brigade.
He volunteered in November 1914, and in the following August was drafted to France. After only one month's service overseas he was reported missing after the Battle of Loos, and was presumed to have been killed in action on September 25th, 1915. He was entitled to the 1914-15 Star, and the General Service and Victory Medals.
"He died the noblest death a man may die,
Fighting for God, and right, and liberty."
35, Granfield Street, Battersea, S.W.11. Z4350B

TALBOT, F., Rifleman, 10th London Regt. (London Irish Rifles).
He was mobilised at the outbreak of war, and was drafted to France in March 1915. During his service on the Western Front he was in action at Ypres, Givenchy, Festubert and Loos, and was severely wounded in the heavy fighting on the Somme in September 1916. He was invalided home to hospital and was subsequently demobilised in June 1919. He holds the 1914-15 Star, and the General Service and Victory Medals.
35, Granfield Street, Battersea, S.W.11. Z4350A

TALBOT, F. P., C.S.M., Royal Berkshire Regiment.
Volunteering in September 1914, he proceeded overseas in February of the following year. During his service in France he took a prominent part in various engagements, including the Battles of Loos and the Somme, where he was very severely wounded. He was sent to hospital at Calais, where his right leg was amputated, and after being invalided home he was discharged in August 1919, as unfit for further service. He holds the 1914-15 Star, and the General Service and Victory Medals.
77, Verney Road, Bermondsey, S.E.16. Z6698

TALBOT, S. B., Corporal, R.E.
He volunteered in October 1915, and was engaged in important duties on boats plying between England and France. He met with an accident in 1918 when he fell from his ship into the sea and was severely injured. After being invalided to hospital he was subsequently demobilised in February 1919, and holds the General Service and Victory Medals.
10, Corunna Road, New Road, S.W.8. Z4349

TALLEY, W. E., Private, Somerset Light Infantry.
He volunteered in October 1914, and in 1916 was drafted to France, where he was in action at the Somme, Arras, Ypres, and Soissons. He proceeded later to Salonika and took part in the operations on the Doiran front and in the capture of Monastir. In 1917 he was sent to Palestine and fought in numerous engagements in that campaign. On being re-drafted to France he fought with distinction in the Retreat and Advance of 1918. He was demobilised in the following January, and holds the General Service and Victory Medals.
19A, Froude Street, Battersea Park, S.W.8. Z4351

TALMADGE, W. G., Corporal, R.E.
He joined in February 1917, in the Inland Water Transport Section of the Royal Engineers, and was retained for important clerical duties until March 1918, when he proceeded to Mesopotamia. He was then engaged on important duties at the Army Post Office at Basra and other places and did excellent work until March 1920, when he returned home and was demobilised. He holds the General Service and Victory Medals.
57, Bramfield Road, Battersea, S.W.11. Z4352

TANNER, C. G., Private, 7th (Queen's Own) Hussars and Gloucestershire Regiment.
He volunteered in January 1915, and in the following August proceeded to the Dardanelles and afterwards to Egypt and Salonika. Whilst in these theatres of war he took an active part in many engagements of importance until the conclusion of hostilities. He returned home and was demobilised in February 1920, and holds the 1914-15 Star, and the General Service and Victory Medals.
1, Bredon Road, Camberwell, S.E.5. Z6382B

TANNER, C. W., Sapper, R.E.
He joined in February 1917, and in the following month was drafted to the Western Front. During his service in France he was engaged on important duties as an Army cook, and was present at the Somme, Bullecourt, Cambrai and St. Quentin. He was also stationed for a time at Le Havre, Boulogne and Rouen. He returned home and was discharged on account of his service in March 1918, and holds the General Service and Victory Medals.
2, Freemantle Street, Walworth, S.E.17. Z4353

TANNER, D. S., Rifleman, 21st London Regt. (1st Surrey Rifles).
He joined in May 1916, and after his training was drafted to France, where he served in various engagements in the Somme sector. Owing to serious illness he was sent home to hospital, where he received treatment for about a year. He was invalided out of the Army as medically unfit for further duty in March 1918, and holds the General Service and Victory Medals.
17, Hubert Grove, Landor Road, S.W.9. Z4355

TANNER, F. J., C.Q.M.S., 2nd Middlesex Regiment and Royal Defence Corps.
A serving soldier at the outbreak of war, he was immediately drafted to France and took part in the Retreat from Mons and the Battles of the Marne, the Aisne, Neuve Chapelle, Ypres and Loos. He was severely wounded on the Somme, and after his recovery was transferred to the Royal Defence Corps, and engaged on important duties as an instructor. He was discharged in April 1919, having served thirteen years with the Colours, and died two months later from illness contracted whilst in the Army. He was entitled to the Mons Star, and the General Service and Victory Medals.
"He passed out of the sight of men by the path of duty and self-sacrifice."
15, Glyn Street, Vauxhall, S.E.11. Z24463

TANNER, G. A., Sergt.-Major, R.F.A.
He was mobilised at the outbreak of war and immediately proceeding overseas took part in the memorable Retreat from Mons, in which he was severely wounded. He was sent to hospital at the Base and then to England, and in March 1915 rejoined his battery in France. He served with distinction in many important engagements, including those at Neuve Chapelle, Hill 60, Ypres, Loos, the Somme, Arras, Cambrai and numerous later operations, finishing his fighting at Mons on Armistice Day. He was demobilised on November 30th, 1918, and holds the Mons Star, and the General Service and Victory Medals.
20, D'Eynsford Road, Camberwell, S.E.5. Z4356B

TANNER, G. F., Private, 9th Royal Irish Fusiliers.

He joined in 1916, and after his training proceeded to France later in the same year. Whilst overseas he fought in the Somme, Ypres and Arras sectors in various engagements. He died gloriously on the field of battle at Langemarck on August 16th, 1917, and was entitled to the General Service and Victory Medals.

"Nobly striving,
"He nobly fell that we might live."

48, Bournemouth Road, Peckham, S.E.15.　　　Z5511

TANNER, J. H., Driver, R.F.A.

He joined in April 1917, and in January of the following year was drafted to the Western Front. Whilst overseas he was in action in many engagements on the Amiens and Cambrai sectors and was gassed. He was invalided home in May 1918, and subsequently discharged as medically unfit for further service in the following September. He holds the General Service and Victory Medals.

4, Barmore Street, Battersea, S.W.11.　　　Z4354

TANNER, R. W., Sergt., Rifle Brigade.

Attesting in November 1915, he was called up for training in February of the following year and proceeded overseas in May. During his service in France he was wounded at Givenchy and invalided home to hospital. After his recovery he rejoined his unit and was in action at Messines, Ypres, Lens, Passchendaele, Cambrai, the Somme, the Aisne, Amiens, Bapaume, Havrincourt and in the engagements which followed until the cessation of hostilities. After the Armistice he advanced into Germany with the Army of Occupation and remained there until October of the following year, when he returned home and was demobilised. He holds the General Service and Victory Medals.

35, Chryssell Road, Brixton, S.W.9.　　　Z5291

TANNER, T. R., Staff-Sergt., R.F.A.

He was mobilised at the outbreak of war and was immediately drafted to France, where he took part in the Retreat from Mons. He also served in many other early engagements, including that of Neuve Chapelle, in which he was wounded. After his recovery he returned to the line, and was in action at Hill 60, Ypres, Loos, the Somme, Vimy Ridge, Arras and Cambrai, and in many subsequent battles in the Retreat and Advance of 1918, concluding with the memorable entry into Mons on Armistice Day. He was demobilised in December 1918, and holds the Mons Star, and the General Service and Victory Medals.

20, D'Eynsford Road, Camberwell, S.E.5.　　　Z4356A

TANT, W. E., L/Corporal, 10th Royal Fusiliers.

He volunteered in April 1915, and in March 1916 was drafted to the Western Front, where he took part in much heavy fighting in numerous engagements, including that of Arras. He was killed in action on April 10th, 1917, near Monchy and was buried near the Cambrai-Feuchy Road. He was entitled to the General Service and Victory Medals.

"His life for his Country, his Soul to God."

8, Reckitt Road, Chiswick, W.4.　　　5493

TANTON, H. W., Corporal, R.G.A.

Volunteering in October 1915, he proceeded to France in March of the following year and served at Albert and many other important engagements until hostilities ceased. He acted as Observer for his Battery when in co-operation with aircraft, and did excellent work throughout his service. He holds the General Service and Victory Medals, and the Italian Military Medal in commemoration of the excellent services rendered by his Battery on that front. He was demobilised in March 1919.

108, St. George's Road, Peckham, S.E.15.　　　Z5847

TAPP, S. J. M., Private, R.A.M.C.

He joined in 1916 and served on important duties in England until March 1918, when he proceeded overseas. In France he was principally engaged on the Red Cross trains, tending the sick and wounded and did valuable work. He returned to England, and was demobilised in June 1919, and holds the General Service and Victory Medals.

60, Ilderton Road, Rotherhithe, S.E.15.　　　Z6741

TAPPENDEN, G. A., Corporal, R.F.A. and Air Mechanic, R.A.F. (late R.F.C.)

Mobilised at the outbreak of war he proceeded overseas in the following year, and whilst in France was in action at Ypres and in various other engagements, and was wounded. Mobilised at the outbreak of war he proceeded overseas in the following year, and whilst in France was in action at Ypres, and in various other engagements, and was wounded. Later he was sent home as time expired, and was discharged, but afterwards rejoined in the R.F.C. He returned to the fighting area, and was engaged on important duties with his unit until demobilised in February 1919. He holds the 1914-15 Star, and the General Service and Victory Medals.

16, Russell Road, Peckham, S.E.15.　　　Z5512

TARGETT, H. C., Rifleman, Rifle Brigade, 28th London Regt. (Artists Rifles) and Pte., R.A.S.C.

Volunteering in November 1915, he embarked for France in the following February, and whilst there saw much active service on the Somme and elsewhere. Later he was transferred to the Rifle Brigade, and five weeks afterwards was reported missing on March 23rd, 1918. He is presumed to have been killed in action and was entitled to the General Service and Victory Medals.

"His memory is cherished with pride."

30, Brayards Road, Peckham, S.E.15.　　　Z5513

TARRANT, A. G., Corporal, R.E.

Volunteering in October 1914, he was drafted to France in August of the following year, and served in that theatre of was as gas chemist until September 1916. He was present at many engagements, including those at Loos and the Somme. He then returned to England and did valuable research work at University College, and at various munition factories until January 1919, when he was demobilised. He holds the 1914-15 Star, and the General Service and Victory Medals.

9, Beamfield Road, Wandsworth Common, S.W.11.　　　Z4357

TARRANT, H. L., Private, R.A.V.C.

He volunteered in April 1915, and proceeded to France in the same year, and served with the Mobile Section attached to the 37th Division. He rendered much valuable service in the Arras sector until invalided to England owing to ill-health. On his recovery he was sent to the Balkan front, where he served, until contracting malaria he was invalided home and was discharged in 1918. He holds the 1914-15 Star, and the General Service and Victory Medals.

8, Oldfield Road, Rotherhithe, S.E.16.　　　Z6783

TARRANT, J. T., Private, R.A.S.C. (M.T.)

He volunteered in February 1915, and early in the following year was sent to France. There he saw much service and was present at engagements on the Somme, and at Arras, Messines and Ypres. He also served in the Retreat and Advance of 1918, and later seriously injured his wrist in an accident. In May 1919 he was demobilised and holds the General Service and Victory Medals.

63, Darwin Street, Walworth, S.E.17.　　　Z4358

TASKER, A. E., Private, East Surrey Regiment.

He joined in 1917, on attaining military age, and in the same year was drafted to the Western Front, where he took part in many engagements, including those at Ypres and Cambrai. He returned home and was demobilised in 1919, and holds the General Service and Victory Medals.

23, Mortlake Gardens, Peckham, S.E.15.　　　Z6298A

TASKER, W. J., Private, East Surrey Regiment.

Mobilised at the outbreak of war, he almost immediately proceeded to France and took part in the memorable Retreat from Mons. He also fought in many other engagements, including those at La Bassée and Ypres, and was buried and wounded by the explosion of a shell at Hill 60. During his service he was wounded five times in all, and in 1916 was discharged as medically unfit. He holds the Mons Star, and the General Service and Victory Medals.

73, East Surrey Grove, Peckham, S.E.15.　　　Z5288

TATTERSALL, F. S. (Miss), Special War Worker.

From May 1916 until January 1919 this lady was engaged on important clerical duties at the Quasi-Arc Coy., Ltd., Government Contractors, Caxton House. She did most valuable work, and the manner in which she carried out her responsible duties was worthy of the highest commendation.

52, Westmoreland Road, Walworth, S.E.17.　　　Z1256C

TATTERSALL, G. F., Private, Middlesex Motor Volunteers.

He joined in May 1918, and after his training served at various stations on transport and other important duties with his unit. He rendered valuable services until after the cessation of hostilities, and was demobilised in March 1919.

52, Westmoreland Road, Walworth, S.E.17.　　　Z1256B

TATTERSALL, G. J., Special War Worker.

From January 1915 until 1919 he was engaged on important work at Messrs. Higgs and Hills', Kennington, on the manufacture of various parts of aeroplanes. He carried out his duties in an efficient and highly commendable manner.

52, Westmoreland Road, Walworth, S.E.17.　　　Z4361

TATTERSALL, R. J., L/Cpl., 18th London Regt. (London Irish Rifles).

Volunteering in August 1914, he proceeded overseas in the following year, and served with the 47th Division in many sectors of the Western Front. He fought at Givenchy, and Festubert, and fell in action on September 25th, 1915. He was entitled to the 1914-15 Star, and the General Service and Victory Medals.

"He died the noblest death a man may die,
Fighting for God, and right, and liberty."

36, Treherne Road, Stockwell, S.W.9.　　　Z4685

TATTERSALL, W. A., Private, 2nd London Regt. (Royal Fusiliers).

He volunteered in August 1914, and in the following year embarked for France, where he saw much active service, and was wounded. He was invalided home, but on recovery returned to the fighting area, and serving until the Armistice in many engagements. He holds the 1914–15 Star, and the General Service and Victory Medals, and was demobilised in February 1919.

37, Smith Street, Camberwell, S.E.5. Z4360

TAVENDER, C. H., Private, Loyal North Lancashire Regiment.

A serving soldier since August 1907, he was mobilised at the outbreak of war, and later drafted to German East Africa. He was wounded during the campaign and invalided home in January 1917. After his recovery he was sent to Palestine, and served in many important engagements, returning to England in July 1918. He next proceeded to France and took part in the final operations, and was wounded at St. Quentin and invalided home to hospital. In January 1919 he was discharged as medically unfit, and holds the 1914–15 Star, and the General Service and Victory Medals.

190, Southwark Bridge Road, S.E.1. Z25196

TAVENER, E., Private, Duke of Wellington's (West Riding Regiment).

He had previously enlisted in the Middlesex Regiment in 1904, and had served in India. In 1914 he was drafted to Egypt, and afterwards to Gallipoli, where he was present at the Landing and in subsequent engagements until the Evacuation of the Peninsula. He then returned to Egypt, and was in action during the first attack on the Suez Canal. Afterwards he served in Mesopotamia for a time, and on the cessation of hostilities proceeded to India, and was stationed on the Afghan frontier during the native risings. In 1920 he was still serving, and holds the 1914–15 Star, and the General Service and Victory Medals, and the India General Service Medal (with clasp Afghanistan N.W. Frontier, 1919).

36, Park Grove, Battersea, S.W.11. Z4363

TAVENER, W. E., Gunner, R.H.A.

He volunteered in October 1915, and in May of the following year was drafted to France, where he was found to be physically unfit for the front lines, and was engaged on important duties at the Base. In October 1916 he was sent to England and transferred to the Labour Corps, and served with his unit until February 1918, when he was discharged as medically unfit for further duty. He holds the General Service and Victory Medals.

565, Battersea Park Road, S.W.11. Z4362

TAVNER, A. E., A.B., R.N., H.M.S. "Dirk."

He joined in July 1917, and after his training was posted to H.M.S. "Dirk," and sent to the North Sea. After serving on important and dangerous patrol duties he lost his life when his ship was torpedoed and sunk by enemy action in 1918. He was entitled to the General Service and Victory Medals.

"Honour to the immortal dead, who gave their youth that the world might grow old in peace."

143, Silwood Street, Rotherhithe, S.E.16. Z6742

TAYLER, H. C., Sergt., Tank Corps.

Volunteering in August 1914, he proceeded overseas in the same year, and during his four years' active service took part in many important engagements, and was twice wounded. He was demobilised in February 1919, and holds the 1914 Star, and the General Service and Victory Medals.

23, Nursery Street, Wandsworth Road, S.W.8. Z4364C

TAYLER, M. P., Rifleman, 18th London Regiment (London Irish Rifles).

He volunteered in 1914, and was drafted to the Western Front in the following year. During his service overseas he took part in numerous engagements, and after the cessation of hostilities returned to England and in February 1919 was demobilised, holding the 1914–15 Star, and the General Service and Victory Medals.

23, Nursery Street, Wandsworth Road, South Lambeth, S.W.8. Z4364A

TAYLER, S. P., Corporal, 24th M.G.C.

He enlisted in 1916, and after his training served at various stations on important duties until January 1918, when he proceeded overseas. During his service in France he took part in many engagements in the Retreat and Advance of 1918. He was discharged on account of service in February 1919, and holds the General Service and Victory Medals.

23, Nursery Street, Wandsworth Road, S.W.8. Z4364B

TAYLERSON, L., Leading Stoker, H.M.S. "Nith."

He had previously enlisted in the Navy in 1909, and at the outbreak of war was posted to H.M.S. "Nith" and sent to the North Sea. His ship was in action in various engagements and towed the "Marlborough" in after the Battle of Jutland. He also served in convoying merchant ships laden with cargoes of supplies for the Army and Navy. After the Armistice he proceeded to Russia and was engaged on the ice-breaking vessels and rendered valuable services. He was awarded the Russian Order of St. George on September 24th, 1919, and holds the 1914–15 Star, and the General Service and Victory Medals. In 1920 he was still serving on H.M.S. 'Commonwealth."

58, Hollydale Road, Peckham, S.E.15. Z6464

TAYLOR, A., Drummer, Argyll and Sutherland Highlanders.

He joined in May 1917, when only fifteen years of age, and in January of the following year was drafted to the Western Front, where he was engaged on important duties with his unit until December 1919. Returning then, he was transferred to the 2nd East Surrey Regiment, and was still serving in 1920. He holds the General Service and Victory Medals.

1, Kimberley Road, Stockwell, S.W.9. Z4382C

TAYLOR, A., Rifleman, 11th London Regt. (Rifles).

He volunteered in December 1915, and in the following year was drafted to France, where he was in action at Albert, Vermelles and Vimy Ridge and was badly wounded at Bullecourt. He was invalided home and afterwards discharged owing to his wounds in February 1918. He holds the General Service and Victory Medals.

66, Dalyell Road, Stockwell, S.W.9. Z4369

TAYLOR, A. A., Joiner, R.N., H.M.S. "Colossus."

He volunteered in 1914, and after his training was retained for a time on H.M.S. "Crescent" at Rosyth for special work. He later proceeded to sea in H.M.S. "Colossus" and was engaged on important patrol and other duties with the Grand Fleet until he cessation of hostilities. In 1920 he was still serving and holds the 1914–15 Star, and the General Service and Victory Medals.

17, Latchmere Road, Battersea, S.W.11. Z4367

TAYLOR, A. H., Driver, R.F.A.

He volunteered in April 1915, and during the course of his training his health broke down. After being sent to hospital he was found to be medically unfit for further service, and was discharged in November 1915.

45, Dorothy Road, Battersea, S.W.11. Z3802B

TAYLOR, A. J., Private, 3rd Welch Regiment.

He joined in March 1917, and later in the same year completing his training was drafted to France, where he was in action on the Somme, and was wounded in May 1915 on the Aisne. He was invalided home and discharged owing to his disability in December 1918. He holds the General Service and Victory Medals.

47, Verona Street, Battersea, S.W.11. Z4687

TAYLOR, A. J., Pte., 24th London Regt. (Queen's).

Volunteering in February 1915, he was sent to France in the following year and took part in numerous engagements, including those at the Somme and Arras. In 1917, he was transferred to Salonika, where he was in action on the Vardar and Doiran fronts. Later in the same year he proceeded to Egypt and took part in the Advance to Jerusalem, his being the first Battalion to enter the Holy City. In 1918 he returned to France, and was engaged in the Retreat and Advance of that year, and was twice wounded. He was demobilised in July 1919, and holds the General Service and Victory Medals.

4, Colworth Grove, York Street, Walworth, S.E.17. Z4366

TAYLOR, A. S., Leading Signalman, R.N., H.M.S. "Barham."

He was serving in 1914, and on the declaration of war joined the Grand Fleet in the North Sea in H.M.S. "Barham." He took a prominent part in the Battles of Heligoland Bight and Jutland, as a leading Signalman, and also saw service in the Baltic. He was still in the Navy in 1920, and holds the 1914–15 Star, and the General Service and Victory Medals.

17, Latchmere Road, Battersea, S.W.11. Z4368

TAYLOR, A. W., Private, 2nd London Regt. (Royal Fusiliers).

Volunteering in August 1915, he was after a short training drafted to France, where he took part in much severe fighting in various sectors of the Front, including the Battles of Neuve Chapelle, Loos and Ypres. • He was killed whilst in action at Combles on September 24th, 1916, and was entitled to the 1914–15 Star, and the General Service and Victory Medals.

"The path of duty was the way to glory."

50, Tate Street, Kennington, S.E.11. Z25168

TAYLOR, B. H., Rflmn., King's Royal Rifle Corps.
Volunteering in June 1915, he was drafted to France in the following year and was in action at Ypres, Albert and Arras. He was unfortunately killed in action on the Somme front, on July 27th, 1917, and was entitled to the General Service and Victory Medals.
" He died the noblest death a man may die,
Fighting for God, and right, and liberty."
48, Tindal Street, Lothian Road, S.W.9.   Z5293B

TAYLOR, C., Gunner, R.F.A.
Volunteering in August 1914, he was drafted in October of the same year to the Western Front, where he was in action in many important engagements, including those at Ypres, Neuve Chapelle, Festubert, Loos, Albert, the Somme, Beaumont-Hamel, Arras, Messines, Ypres, Cambrai and Somme II. He returned to England in May 1918, and was demobilised in February 1919. He holds the 1914 Star, and the General Service and Victory Medals.
87, Mann Street, Walworth, S.E.17.   Z27310

TAYLOR, C., Sergt., R.M.L.I.
Though anxious to join the Colours during the recent war, he was unable to do so owing to physical disability and throughout the course of hostilities rendered valuable services on the L. & S.W. Railway. As a young man he was in the R.M.L.I. from September 1877 until January 1884, and did much gallant service in the Gordon Relief Expedition at the Battles of El Teb and Tamaai, for which he holds the Egyptian Medal and the Khedive Star.
10, Comyn Road, Battersea, S.W.11.   Z4377B

TAYLOR, C. A., Private, Queen's Own (Royal West Kent Regiment).
He joined in October 1916, and after a period of training proceeded to France in the following year. While overseas he took part in numerous engagements, including that of Ypres. In November 1917, he was transferred for a short time to Italy, and there suffered from trench fever. Later, he returned to France and took part in the heavy fighting of 1918, until the cessation of hostilities, after which he was attached to the Army of Occupation, and sent to Germany. In October 1919, he returned to England for his demobilisation and holds the General Service and Victory Medals.
190, Abbey Street, Bermondsey, S.E.1.   Z27443

TAYLOR, C. H., Private, 7th Norfolk Regiment.
He volunteered in October 1914, and in May of the following year was sent to France, where he took part in numerous engagements of importance. He was wounded at Loos, and invalided home, but on his recovery returned to France. He was in action at the Somme and Vermelles, and was again wounded and sent home. He was discharged in August 1917, owing to his disabilities, and holds the 1914-15 Star, and the General Service and Victory Medals.
25, Secretan Road, Camberwell, S.E.5.   Z5515

TAYLOR, C. P., Trooper, 6th Dragoon Guards (Carabiniers).
Volunteering in August 1914, he was sent in the following year to the Western Front, where he took part in numerous engagements, including those at Ypres, Arras, the Marne, Amiens, Cambrai, and in the 1918 Offensives. After the Armistice he proceeded with the Army of Occupation to Germany. He was demobilised in September 1919, and holds the 1914-15 Star, and the General Service and Victory Medals.
13, Tunstall Road, Brixton Road, S.W.9.   Z4365

TAYLOR, E., Driver, R.F.A.
He volunteered in 1915, and in the same year was sent to France where he took part in the fighting at Hill 60, Ypres, the Somme, and in numerous other engagements. He afterwards proceeded to Italy, but returning to France, fought gallantly in the Retreat and Advance of 1918. He was demobilised in February 1920, and holds the 1914-15 Star, and the General Service and Victory Medals.
39, Stainforth Road, Battersea, S.W.11.   Z4381

TAYLOR, E. C., Gunner, R.M.A.
He joined in July 1917, and was undergoing training at Southsea for foreign service when he met with a serious accident, which badly impaired his sight. After considerable medical treatment he was discharged in May 1918, as unfit for further military duty.
10, Comyn Road, Battersea, S.W.11.   Z4377A

TAYLOR, E. E., Private, East Surrey Regiment.
Joining in March 1917, he was sent to France in the same year He took part in the severe fighting at Albert, Arras, Bullecourt, the Somme, and many other engagements, and was wounded at Cambrai. After the Armistice he proceeded with the Army of Occupation to Germany, and on his return home was demobilised in March 1920, holding the General Service and Victory Medals.
55, Mordaunt Street, Stockwell, S.W.9.   Z4370

TAYLOR, E. T., Trooper, 4th (Royal Irish) Dragoon Guards.
He joined in March 1917, and after his training served at Tidworth on important duties with his unit. He rendered valuable services, but owing to being under age was not successful in obtaining his transfer overseas before the cessation of hostilities. He was demobilised in 1919.
98, Stonhouse Street, Clapham, S.W.4.   Z4371

TAYLOR, E. W., Cpl., R.A.F. (School of Instruction).
He joined in 1916, and after his training served at various stations on important duties with his Squadron. He was engaged in testing and repairing aero-engines, and rendered valuable services, but was not successful in obtaining his transfer overseas before the cessation of hostilities. He was demobilised in 1919.
71, Solon New Road, Bedford Park, S.W.4.   Z3547C

TAYLOR, G., Saddler-Corporal, R.F.A.
Volunteering in September 1914, he proceeded in June of the following year to France, where he took part in numerous engagements of importance. In November 1917, he was transferred to Italy, and was in action on the Piave front. He later returned to France and served at the Somme, the Marne, Amiens, and other engagements in the Retreat and Advance of 1918. He was demobilised in January 1919, and holds the 1914-15 Star, and the General Service and Victory Medals.
112, Gloucester Road, Peckham, S.E.15.   Z5838A

TAYLOR, G., Gunner, R.F.A.
He joined in 1918, and after completing his training was engaged on important duties with his Battery until February of the following year, when he was drafted to Germany. After much valuable service at Cologne he returned home and was still serving in 1920.
10, Elliott Road, Stockwell, S.W.9.   Z5156B

TAYLOR, G., Private, 1st Northamptonshire Regt.
Mobilised in August 1914, he was immediately sent to France, where he was in action during the Retreat from Mons, and the Battles of the Marne, and the Aisne, where he was severely wounded. He was invalided home and after a long period in hospital was discharged as medically unfit for further service in April 1916. He holds the Mons Star, and the General Service and Victory Medals.
5, Calmington Road, Camberwell, S.E.5.   Z5514

TAYLOR, G. A., Rifleman, Rifle Brigade.
He volunteered in September 1914, and after completing his training was engaged with his unit on important duties until September 1917, when he was drafted to the Western Front. He was only a few weeks in France, when he was severely wounded at the Battle of Cambrai. He was invalided home in consequence and after some months' treatment in hospital was discharged owing to his wounds in February 1919. He holds the General Service and Victory Medals.
140, Aylesbury Road, Walworth, S.E.17.   Z2165A

TAYLOR, G. H., Pte., R.M.L.I., H.M.S. "Chatham" and "Hannibal."
He volunteered in August 1914, and saw much service in the North Sea, the Mediterranean and the Dardanelles, where he was engaged on patrol and convoy duties during the whole period of the war. He rendered valuable services and was once wounded. He was demobilised in 1919, and holds the 1914-15 Star, and the General Service and Victory Medals.
8, Nealdon Street, Landor Road, S.W.9.   Z4375B

TAYLOR, G. V. A., Private, R.A.S.C. (M.T.)
Volunteering in April 1915, he proceeded in the following month to France, and was engaged on important transport duties in connection with numerous engagements, including those at Ypres, Loos, Vimy Ridge, the Somme, Passchendaele and Cambrai. He was afterwards employed in driving a petrol tank for supplying aeroplanes and motors. He was demobilised in February 1919, after much valuable work, and holds the 1914-15 Star, and the General Service and Victory Medals.
33, Costa Street, Peckham, S.E.15.   Z6717

TAYLOR, G. W., Private, R.A.V.C.
He volunteered in December 1914, and in the same month was drafted to France, where he was engaged on important duties with his unit at Rouen. Heart trouble interfered much with his work, and he was frequently in hospital, until April 1919, when he was placed in Class W. Reserve. He was called up for service again in the following September, but was found unequal to the strain of Army duties and was soon discharged. He holds the 1914-15 Star, and the General Service and Victory Medals.
146, Lavender Road, Battersea, S.W.11.   Z4376

TAYLOR, H. (M.M.), Rifleman, King's Royal Rifle Corps.

He volunteered in August 1914, and in the following November was drafted to the Western Front, where he took a prominent part in numerous engagements until March 1918. He was then taken prisoner in the Retreat and sent to Germany. On his release he returned home and was demobilised, but rejoining shortly afterwards was sent to Russia, where he did excellent service until he came home and was demobilised. He was awarded the Military Medal for conspicuous gallantry while serving in France and was awarded a clasp for his bravery on the Field in Russia. He also holds the Mons Star, and the General Service and Victory Medals.

172, St. George's Road, Peckham, S.E.15.   Z5729C

TAYLOR, H. J., Driver, R.F.A.

After volunteering in November 1914, he was engaged on important duties with his Battery until January 1916, when he was drafted to France. He took part in several operations, and was later transferred to the Headquarters Staff of the R.E. He was unfortunately killed in action near Ypres on August 3rd, 1916, and was entitled to the General Service and Victory Medals.

"The path of duty was the way to glory."

45, Dorothy Road, Battersea, S.W.11.   Z3802A

TAYLOR, J., Private, 10th Queen's (Royal West Surrey Regiment).

He volunteered in July 1915, and in January of the following year was sent to France, where he took part in numerous engagements of importance. He was later invalided home, and on his recovery was retained on important duties with his unit until demobilised in May 1919. He holds the General Service and Victory Medals.

8, Goulden Street, Battersea, S.W.11.   Z4379

TAYLOR, J., Private, Duke of Cornwall's Light Infantry.

He volunteered in December 1914, and was soon drafted to France. He was in action at Hill 60, Ypres, Loos, Vimy Ridge, the Somme, Arras, Messines, Passchendaele, Lens and Cambrai, and also served in the Retreat and Advance of 1918. He was demobilised in 1919, after returning home, and holds the 1914-15 Star, and the General Service and Victory Medals.

10, Elliott Road, Brixton S.W.9.   Z5156A

TAYLOR, J. H., Private, R.A.S.C. (M.T.)

He volunteered in June 1915, and proceeding to France in the same year was engaged in the Somme, Arras and Ypres sectors on important duties in connection with the packing and transport of ammunition and supplies until hostilities ceased. He returned home and was demobilised in 1919, holding the 1914-15 Star, and the General Service and Victory Medals.

9, Nealdon Street, Stockwell, S.W.9.   Z4375A

TAYLOR, J. H. Private, 23rd Middlesex Regiment.

He joined in 1918, on attaining military age, and after the conclusion of his training was retained on important duties with his unit. He was not successful in securing his transfer overseas while hostilities continued, but after the Armistice proceeded to Germany with the Army of Occupation. He returned home and was demobilised in March 1920.

42, Creold Road, Hammersmith, W.6.   14497

TAYLOR, J. W., Private, Middlesex Regiment.

He volunteered in August 1914, and after completing his training was engaged with his unit on important duties at various stations. He rendered valuable services, but was not successful in obtaining his transfer overseas owing to his medical unfitness for active service. He was discharged in June 1918.

33, Gaskell Street, Walworth, S.E.4.   Z1695A

TAYLOR, J. W., Rifleman, Rifle Brigade.

He volunteered in September 1914, and in February of the following year was drafted to the Western Front, where he was in action at Hill 60. He was reported missing at Ypres on May 12th, 1915, and was presumed to have been killed in action on that date. He was entitled to the 1914-15 Star, and the General Service and Victory Medals.

"Steals on the ear, the distant triumph song."

172, East Street, Walworth, S.E.17.   Z4380

TAYLOR, L. H., Sapper, R.E.

Joining in February 1917, he was drafted to France in April of the same year. He was engaged on important duties at the ammunition dumps and served in this theatre of war until September 1919. He was demobilised in November of the same year, and holds the General Service and Victory Medals.

53, Brynmaer Road, Battersea, S.W.11.   Z4372

TAYLOR, O., L/Cpl., 9th London Regt. (Queen Victoria's Rifles).

He volunteered in 1915, and in the following year was sent to France, where he took part in numerous engagements, including those at the Somme and Ypres. He was unfortunately killed in action at Cambrai in 1917, and was entitled to the General Service and Victory Medals.

"Thinking that remembrance, though unspoken, may reach him where he sleeps."

71, Solon New Road, Bedford Road, S.W.4.   Z3547B

TAYLOR, R., Rflmn., 6th London Regt. (Rifles).

He joined in June 1916, and later in the same year proceeded to the Western Front. Here he was in action on the Somme, and at Beaumont-Hamel, Messines, Passchendaele, and was severely wounded at Cambrai. On December 4th, 1917 he unfortunately died of his injuries at Rouen. He was entitled to the General Service and Victory Medals.

"His memory is cherished with pride."

34, Gordon Road, Peckham, S.E.15.   Z6172A

TAYLOR, S. F., Air Mechanic, R.A.F.

He joined in August 1918, and after completing his training was engaged at various stations on important duties with his Squadron. His work which demanded much technical skill was carried out with great efficiency, and he rendered valuable services, but was not successful in obtaining his transfer overseas before the cessation of hostilities. He was demobilised in February 1919.

4, Costa Street, Peckham, S.E.15.   Z6718

TAYLOR, S. J., Sapper, R.E.

He volunteered in October 1914, and later in the same year was sent to France, where he took part in numerous engagements until hostilities ended, including those at the Somme, Messines and Passchendaele. He was chiefly engaged in the construction of railways and bridges, and rendered valuable services. He was demobilised in January 1919, and holds the 1914-15 Star, and the General Service and Victory Medals.

33, Silverthorne Road, Wandsworth Road, S.W.8.   Z4374

TAYLOR, T., Private, 19th London Regiment.

He joined in May 1917, and in August of the same year after the completion of his training was drafted to the Western Front, where he was in action at Lens and Cambrai, and was badly gassed at Bourlon Wood. He unhappily died from the effects of gas poisoning on December 7th, 1917, and was entitled to the General Service and Victory Medals.

"He passed out of the sight of men by the path of duty and self-sacrifice."

36, Dalyell Road, Stockwell, S.W.9.   Z4373

TAYLOR, W., Private, 3rd Worcestershire Regt.

He volunteered in August 1914, and after completing his training was drafted in May 1915 to the Western Front, where he took part in numerous engagements of importance. In April 1917 he was seriously wounded by a sniper and unhappily died from the effects on December 9th, 1917. He was entitled to the 1914-15 Star, and the General Service and Victory Medals.

"His life for his Country, his soul to God."

37A, Southfield Road, Bedford Park, W.4.   7787

TAYLOR, W. A., Special War Worker.

Being overage for military service he was engaged as a civilian clerk at the R.A.S.C. Supply Depôt, Aldershot, throughout the war. His duties, which were of a most important nature and entailed long hours of work, were carried out in a most efficient manner and he rendered valuable services. In 1920 he was still serving.

1, Kimberley Road, Stockwell, S.W.9.   Z4382A

TAYLOR, W. H. (M.M.), Sergt., Royal Fusiliers and M.G.C.

He volunteered in March 1915, and in the following year was drafted to France, where he took part in the fighting at Albert, the Somme, Arras, Ypres, Passchendaele, Bapaume, Delville Wood, and in numerous other engagements in the Retreat and Advance of 1918, and was wounded twice and gassed. He was invalided home in consequence, and after a period in hospital was discharged as medically unfit for further service in May 1919. He was awarded the Military Medal for conspicuous bravery in the Field, and also holds the General Service and Victory Medals.

48, Tindal Street, Lothian Road, S.W.9.   Z5293A

TAYLOR, W. R., Assistant Steward, Mercantile Marine.

He joined the Army in February 1915, but owing to being under age was discharged in the following May. Next month he joined the Mercantile Marine, and was engaged on the s.s. "Westpoint," "Corinthian" and "Carpathian," in the transport of stores and troops between Canada and Europe. He was on board the s.s. "Westpoint" when that vessel was torpedoed, and was eighteen hours in the water before being rescued. He was discharged in 1918, in consequence of his services, and holds the Mercantile Marine War Medal, and the General Service Medal. 1, Kimberley Road, Stockwell, S.W.9.   Z4382B

TAYNTON, J. H., Private, R.A.S.C.
He volunteered in August 1915, and was sent to France in the same year. He did much valuable work in taking supplies to the troops in the front line and was engaged at Ypres, Cambrai and other places, and in the Retreat and Advance of 1918, and subsequently proceeded into Germany with the Army of Occupation. He was demobilised in May 1919, and holds the 1914-15 Star, and the General Service and Victory Medals.
53, Thorncroft Street, South Lambeth, S.W.8. Z4383A

TAYNTON, J. T., Sergt., 1st Rifle Brigade.
He joined in 1917, and was employed on important duties with his unit. He rendered valuable services, but was unable to obtain his transfer overseas before the Armistice. In 1919 he was sent to Palestine and in the following year was serving at Baghdad.
53, Thorncroft Street, South Lambeth, S.W.8. Z4383B

TEAR, A. T., Shoeing-Smith, R.A.S.C.
He volunteered in April 1915, and was at first engaged on important duties in England with his unit. Later he proceeded to Russia, and served at Batum and other places. He returned to England and was demobilised in June 1919, and holds the General Service and Victory Medals.
22, Sandover Road, Camberwell, S.E.5. Z5516

TEBBUT, W., Rifleman, Rifle Brigade.
He volunteered in December 1915, and was sent to France in the following year. He took part in the fighting on the Somme, and at Arras, Ypres and Passchendaele, and on March 21st, 1918 was taken prisoner and sent to Germany. Here he remained in captivity until December 1918, when he was released and sent to England. In August 1919 he was demobilised, and holds the General Service and Victory Medals.
26, Moncrieff Street, Peckham, S.E.15. Z5679

TEBWORTH, T. A., Sergt., R.A.S.C.
He was mobilised on the outbreak of war, and was drafted to France early in 1915. He took part in the operations at Ypres, Armentières, Béthune, the Somme, Arras, and Messines, and in the Retreat and Advance of 1918, and after the Armistice served with the Army of Occupation in Germany until demobilised in May 1919. He holds the 1914-15 Star, and the General Service and Victory Medals.
46, Camelia Street, Wandsworth Road, S.W.8. Z4384

TEE, W. J., Bombardier, R.F.A.
He volunteered in 1915, and in the following year was drafted to the Western Front and took part in engagements at Ypres, Festubert, the Somme and Arras. After the cessation of hostilities he returned home and in 1919 was demobilised, holding the General Service and Victory Medals.
79, Orb Street, Walworth, S.E.17. Z4385

TEESDALE, E., Corporal, 3rd Lincolnshire Regt.
He volunteered in September 1914, and after his training was employed on important duties in various parts of England and Ireland. He rendered valuable services, but was unable to obtain his transfer to a theatre of war, owing to being over-age for duty abroad. He was demobilised in November 1919.
37, Dashwood Road, Wandsworth Road, S.W.8. Z4386

TELFER, A. G., Writer, Royal Navy.
He volunteered in 1915, and was sent to sea in the following year. He served in the North Sea, on ships engaged in convoy duties between England and Denmark until the cessation of hostilities, when he was employed on important duties at Portsmouth. He was demobilised in May 1919, and holds the General Service and Victory Medals.
29A, Goldboro' Road, Wandsworth Road, S.W.8. Z4387

TELLING, W. H., Corporal, R.A.O.C.
He joined in July 1916, and after completing his training rendered valuable services on the Western Front until the conclusion of hostilities. He then went to Germany with the Army of Occupation, and was stationed on the Rhine until his return home for demobilisation in October 1919. He holds the General Service and Victory Medals.
21, Ashbourne Grove, Chiswick, W.4. 5501

TEMPLE, E. C., 1st Air Mechanic, R.A.F. (late R.N.A.S.)
He joined in 1916, and after his training was engaged on special duties which demanded a high degree of technical skill. He was injured by a fragment of shell during an air raid on one occasion. He rendered valuable services, but was not successful in obtaining a transfer overseas before his demobilisation in February 1919.
60, Coomer Road, Fulham, S.W.6. 16179

TEMPLE, W., Bombardier, R.G.A.
Serving in India when war broke out he was drafted to Egypt, and served on the shores of the Red Sea. Here he rendered much valuable service until the cessation of hostilities, when he was invalided home suffering from malaria. He was discharged in November 1919, and holds the 1914-15 Star, and the General Service and Victory Medals.
133, Chatham Road, Battersea, S.W.11. Z4551

TEMPLEMAN, G. W. (M.M.), Gunner, R.F.A.
He volunteered in August 1914, and was sent to France in the following year. He fought in numerous engagements, including those at Ypres, Loos, the Somme and Arras, and was awarded the Military Medal for bravery in the Field. He was demobilised in February 1919, and holds in addition to the Military Medal, the 1914-15 Star, and the General Service and Victory Medals.
74, Lothian Road, Camberwell New Road, S.W.9. Z5157

TENNANT, G., Sergt., R.F.A.
He volunteered in September 1914, and was sent to France in the following year. He took part in numerous engagements, including the Battle of Ypres, and rendered much valuable service until October 2nd, 1917, when he was unfortunately severely wounded, and shortly afterwards died. He was entitled to the 1914-15 Star, and the General Service and Victory Medals.
"His life for his Country."
7, Pennack Road, Camberwell, S.E.5. Z3852B

TENNANT, W. H., Bombardier, R.G.A.
He volunteered in November 1914, and was sent to France in the following year. He fought at Vimy Ridge, the Somme, and Passchendaele, and in numerous other engagements, until at the close of hostilities he came home, and was demobilised in January 1919, holding the 1914-15 Star, and the General Service and Victory Medals.
30, Gloucester Road, Peckham, S.E.15. Z5732A

TEOBALDO, J., Driver, R.F.A.
He volunteered in September 1914, and after his training was drafted to Salonika, where he took part in the Balkan campaign. He was in action on the Doiran and Struma fronts, and at Monastir, and after the cessation of hostilities returned to England and was demobilised in March 1919, holding the 1914-15 Star, and the General Service and Victory Medals.
52, Grant Road, Battersea, S.W.11. Z4552

TEPPER, R. C., Private, Middlesex and Queen's (Royal West Surrey) Regiments.
He joined in September 1916, and later in that year he was sent to the Balkan front. Here he fought in the campaign against the Austro-Bulgarian forces and took part in most of the important actions. He rendered valuable services, but later unfortunately contracted malaria and died on December 23rd, 1918. He was entitled to the General Service and the Victory Medals.
"He joined the great white company of valiant souls."
17, Seneca Road, Clapham, S.W.4. Z4553

TERRETT, A. G., Private, 24th London Regiment (The Queen's).
He volunteered in April 1915, and after training was sent to France. He fought at Arras, Vimy Ridge, Bullecourt, Messines, Ypres, and the Somme, rendering much valuable service. Unhappily he was killed in action at Albert in April 1918, and was entitled to the General Service and Victory Medals. Z4554B
"And doubtless he went in splendid company."
16, Peabody Estate, Rodney Road, Walworth, S.E.17.

TERRETT, T. C., Private, 22nd London Regiment (The Queen's).
He joined in January 1917, and was sent to France in the same year. He fought at Cambrai, the Somme, at Bapaume and Havrincourt, where he was wounded and taken prisoner. After having suffered many hardships whilst in captivity he was released and sent to England and invalided out of the Service in January 1920. He holds the General Service and Victory Medals. Z4554A
16, Peabody Buildings, Rodney Street, Walworth, S.E.17.

TERREY, E. L., Bombardier, R.F.A.
He joined in January 1917, and in the following month was drafted to the Western Front, where he took part in numerous important engagements, including that at Poperinghe, and was wounded and gassed. He was demobilised in 1919, and holds the General Service and Victory Medals.
72, Reedworth Street, Kennington, S.E.11. Z27205B

TERREY, T. J., Sergt., R.G.A.
He joined in November 1916, but was not successful in obtaining his transfer overseas before the cessation of hostilities. He was engaged on important duties at various stations and rendered valuable services. He was demobilised in January 1919.
72, Reedworth Street, Kennington, S.E.11. Z27205A

TERRY, A., Corporal, R.F.A.
He volunteered in August 1915, and was sent to France in the following year. He was in action in various sectors and rendered good service until being seriously injured in an accident he was invalided to England and discharged as medically unfit in August 1916. He holds the General Service and Victory Medals.
38, Barkworth Road, Rotherhithe, S.E.16. Z6719

TERRY, G., Private, 4th London Regiment (Royal Fusiliers).
He joined in June 1916, and first served with the R.F.C., from which he transferred and was drafted to France with the London Regiment in 1917. He took part in the fighting in the Lens sector, and was reported missing, and is presumed to have been killed in action on October 26th, 1917. He was entitled to the General Service and Victory Medals.
"A costly sacrifice upon the altar of freedom."
16, Chip Street, Clapham, S.W.4.   Z4555

TERRY, H. A., Private, 2nd East Lancashire Regt.
Serving at the outbreak of hostilities he was drafted to France shortly afterwards, and fought at La Bassée, Ypres, and numerous other engagements. He rendered valuable services until January 4th, 1915, when he was unhappily killed in action. He was entitled to the 1914 Star, and the General Service and Victory Medals.
"Great deeds cannot die."
64, St. Andrews Street, Wandsworth Road, S.W.8.   Z4556

TERRY, J. H., Rifleman, King's Royal Rifle Corps.
He joined in May 1918, and was sent to France shortly afterwards. He took part in the Advance of that year, and in operations until the Armistice, after which he returned to England and was demobilised in November 1919. He holds the General Service and Victory Medals.
14, Reculver Road, Rotherhithe, S.E.16.   Z6743

TERRY, R., Sapper, R.E.
He joined in June 1917, and proceeded to France in the following year. He served in various sectors including those of Vimy Ridge, the Somme, Cambrai, Ypres and Havrincourt, where he was gassed. He was invalided home and after his recovery was demobilised in February 1919. He holds the General Service and Victory Medals.
31, Delaford Road, Rotherhithe, S.E.16.   Z6744

THACKER, G. R., Private, Royal Sussex Regiment.
He volunteered in January 1915, and was sent overseas in the same year. He fought in various sectors of the front, rendering valuable services at Loos, St. Eloi, and the Somme where he was unhappily killed in July 1916. He was entitled to the 1914-15 Star, and the General Service and Victory Medals.
"His memory is cherished with pride."
45, Russell Street, Brixton Road, S.W.9.   Z5292B

THACKER, J. H., Sapper, R.E.
He volunteered in 1915, in the 22nd London Regiment, and after training was employed on important duties in various parts of the country. Later he was transferred to the R.E., and served in Ireland. He was unable to obtain his transfer to a theatre of war owing to being medically unfit, but nevertheless, rendered valuable services until he was demobilised in March 1919.
7, Abbeyfield Road, Rotherhithe, S.E.16.   Z6784

THACKER, R. W., Driver, R.F.A.
He volunteered in January 1915, and was sent overseas in the same year. He fought at Festubert and Loos, and was wounded and gassed at Ypres. Invalided to England he was eventually discharged as physically unfit for further service in 1917. He holds the 1914-15 Star, and the General Service and Victory Medals.
45, Russell Street, Brixton Road, S.W.9.   Z5292A

THACKER, T., Private, M.G.C.
He volunteered in September 1915, and was sent to France early in the following year. He took part in the fighting at Vermelles, Vimy Ridge, Arras, Messines, Ypres and Passchendaele, doing much valuable work. He also served through the Retreat and Advance of 1918. After the cessation of hostilities he returned to England, and was demobilised in February 1919, holding the General Service and Victory Medals.
18, New Church Road, Camberwell, S.E.5.   Z5846

THACKHAM, J. W., Private, Royal Fusiliers.
He joined in May 1917, and was sent to France later in that year. He fought at Passchendaele and on the Somme and in numerous other engagements. Unfortunately he was killed by a bomb on May 31st, 1918, and was entitled to the General Service and Victory Medals.
"And doubtless he went in splendid company."
175, South Street, Walworth, S.E.17.   Z3145B

THAIN, W. F., Gunner, R.F.A.
He volunteered in September 1914, and was almost immediately sent to France, where he took part in numerous important engagements up to the cessation of hostilities, and was wounded in the leg. He was demobilised in January 1919, after his return home, and holds the 1914 Star, and the General Service and Victory Medals.
10, Dale Street, Chiswick, W.4.   8099

THATCHER, W. C. (M.M.), Pte., 8th Middlesex Regt.
He volunteered in April 1915, and on the completion of his training was drafted to France. During his service overseas he fought with distinction at Ypres, Loos, Bullecourt and the Somme, and was awarded the Military Medal for distinguished bravery and devotion to duty on the Field at Cambrai on November 7th, 1918. He also holds the 1914-15 Star, and the General Service and Victory Medals, and was demobilised in March 1919.
30, Caithness Road, West Kensington, W.14.   12439

THIRGOOD, A. J., Private, 7th London Regiment.
He volunteered in June 1915, and on the completion of his training proceeded to France, where he did good work in various sectors of the Western Front. He gave his life for his King and Country on January 28th, 1916, and was entitled to the 1914-15 Star, and the General Service and Victory Medals.
"Great deeds cannot die."
20, Brackley Terrace, Chiswick, W.4.   5435

THIRKELL, J. W., Sergt., R.A.S.C.
He volunteered in September 1914, and in the same year proceeded to France, and served in many important engagements at Ypres, Loos, the Somme, Arras, Messines, Lens and Cambrai. He was wounded in 1915, and was invalided to hospital at Rouen for some months. In April 1920 he returned home and was demobilised and holds the 1914 Star, and the General Service and Victory Medals.   Z4559
1, Anns Buildings, Aylesbury Road, Walworth, S.E.17.

THIXTON, R. G., Sergt., R.A.M.C.
He joined in March 1916, and in the following July was drafted to Mesopotamia, where he served for about six months. He was afterwards posted to a hospital ship, on which he voyaged to Mesopotamia, India, Egypt, South Africa, and France, and rendered valuable services to the wounded on board. He was stationed for a time at Alexandria, and then returned to England, and was demobilised in March 1920. He holds the General Service and Victory Medals.
34, Riverhall Street, South Lambeth, S.W.8.   Z4560

THOLE, P. N., Corporal, R.F.A.
He volunteered in March 1915, and in February of the following year was drafted to France. Whilst overseas he served at the Battles of Vimy Ridge, the Somme, Beaumont-Hamel, and Ypres, and was wounded at Passchendaele Ridge in 1917. After his recovery he rejoined his unit at Kemmel Hill, and was subsequently transferred to hospital in France, and England. He was demobilised in May 1919, and holds the General Service and Victory Medals.
75, Wickersley Road, Battersea, W.S.11.   Z4557

THOMAS, A. (M.M.), Bombardier, R.F.A.
He volunteered in January 1915, and in the following September was drafted to the Western Front. During his service in France he fought with distinction on the Somme and at Arras, Vimy Ridge, Ypres and Cambrai, and in 1917 was awarded the Military Medal for conspicuous gallantry and devotion to duty in conveying ammunition up to the lines under heavy fire. After the Armistice he proceeded to India, where he served about a year, returning to England for demobilisation in December 1919. He holds in addition to the Military Medal, the 1914-15 Star, and the General Service and Victory Medals. 26, Kitson Road, Camberwell, S.E.5.   Z4564

THOMAS, A. G., Gunner, R.F.A.
He had previously enlisted in November 1909, and at the outbreak of hostilities was almost immediately drafted to France, and took part in the Retreat from Mons. He also served on the Marne, and Aisne, and at Ypres, and was wounded at the Battle of the Somme in July 1916. Subsequently he was sent to Mesopotamia, and was in action at the capture of Baghdad, and at Samara. After the Armistice he proceeded to Russia, and fought at Baku. He returned home and was demobilised in June 1919, and holds the Mons Star, and the General Service and Victory Medals.
33, Gloucester Road, Peckham, S.E.15.   Z6097

THOMAS, A. J., Private, 26th Royal Fusiliers.
He joined in March 1918, on the attainment of military age, and proceeded to France in the following June. Whilst overseas he fought in the Battle of Cambrai in 1918, and after the Armistice was signed advanced into Germany with the Army of Occupation. He remained abroad until March 1920, when he returned home, and was demobilised, holding the General Service and Victory Medals.
40, McKerrell Road, Peckham, S.E.15.   Z6101

THOMAS, A. M. (Miss), Special War Worker.
For three years during the war this lady was engaged on important duties at Woolwich Arsenal. Her work which was of a responsible and dangerous nature consisted in the manufacture and filling of shells and detonators. She carried out her duties with great care and efficiency until after the cessation of hostilities, when she was discharged in January 1919.
21, Verney Road, Rotherhithe, S.E.16.   Z6699A

THOMAS, C. J., Sergt., 2nd London Regt. (Royal Fusiliers).
Volunteering in January 1915, he proceeded to France in the following year, and took part in the fighting in several important engagements, including that of the Somme. In May 1916 he was severely wounded in the vicinity of Cambrai, and was invalided home to hospital. He was discharged as medically unfit for further duty in June 1917, and holds the General Service and Victory Medals.
36, Cambria Road, Camberwell, S.E.5.   Z6459

THOMAS, C. W., Sapper, R.E.
Volunteering in February 1915, he was drafted to the Western Front before the end of the year. During his service overseas, which lasted four years, he did most commendable work with his unit in many important sectors, and was present at several of the principal engagements. He was demobilised after his return to England in February 1919, and holds the 1914–15 Star, and the General Service and Victory Medals.
32, Leythe Road, Acton, W.3.   6640

THOMAS, D. H. J., A.B., Royal Navy.
He was mobilised at the commencement of hostilities, and was posted to H.M.S. " Euryalus," which vessel took part in the Battle of Heligoland Bight, and was also engaged at the Dardanelles. During the latter part of his service his ship was employed on important mine-sweeping duties. He was demobilised in January 1919, and holds the 1914–15 Star, and the General Service and Victory Medals.
14, St. Elmo Road, Shepherd's Bush, W.12.   8691

THOMAS, D. M., Rifleman, 18th King's Royal Rifle Corps.
He joined in February 1918, and in the following month was drafted to the Western Front, and was in action in various sectors during the Offensive of that year. After the Armistice he proceeded to Germany and was stationed on the Rhine until February 1920, when he returned home and was demobilised. He holds the General Service and Victory Medals.
14, Vauxhall Buildings, Dolland Street, S.E.11.   Z25250B

THOMAS, E., Private, 14th (King's) Hussars.
He was mobilised in August 1914, and was almost immediately drafted to France, and took part in the Retreat from Mons. He also served at Le Cateau and in various later engagements, until April 1917, when he returned to England, and was discharged as overage. He holds the Queen's and King's South African Medals, the Mons Star, and the General Service and Victory Medals.
11, Barmore Street, Battersea, S.W.11.   Z4566

THOMAS, E. G., Private, East Surrey Regiment.
He joined in July 1918, at the age of eighteen years, and trained in Scotland. Afterwards he served on important duties, but was unable to proceed overseas owing to the conclusion of hostilities. He was demobilised in January 1919.
21, Verney Road, Bermondsey, S.E.16.   Z6699B

THOMAS, E. H., Pte., The Queen's (Royal West Surrey Regiment).
He volunteered in August 1914, and was sent to France in the same year. He fought at Ypres and Festubert, and was unhappily killed in action at Loos in September 1915. He was entitled to the 1914 Star, and the General Service and Victory Medals.
  "And doubtless he went in splendid company."
9, Whorlton Road, Peckham, S.E.15.   Z6095

THOMAS, E. M. S., Pte., Labour Corps and King's Own Yorkshire Light Infantry.
He joined in November 1916, and after his training was in the following month drafted to the Western Front, where he took part in the Retreat and Advance of 1918, and was killed in action near Rheims on July 20th 1918. He was entitled to the General Service and Victory Medals.
  "His life for his Country, his Soul to God."
14, Vauxhall Buildings, Dolland Street, Kennington, S.E.11.
                                                        Z25250A

THOMAS, F. G., Private, The Queen's Own (Royal West Kent Regiment).
He was called up from the Reserve in August 1914, and proceeded to France with the original Expeditionary Force. He fell fighting at Mons in the endeavour to stem the onslaught of greatly superior numbers, and was entitled to the Mons Star, and the General Service and Victory Medals.
  "Great deeds cannot die."
6, Cancel Street, S.E.17.   Z27107

THOMAS, H., Private, R.A.M.C.
He joined in April 1917, and was drafted to France in the following year. Whilst overseas he rendered valuable service in the hospitals at Rouen, St. Omer and various other places. He returned to England after the cessation of hostilities and was demobilised in August 1919, holding the General Service and Victory Medals.
16, Kirkwood Road, Peckham, S.E.15.   Z6232

THOMAS, G. H., Sapper, R.E.
Volunteering in November 1915, he went through his course of training, after which he served for the remaining period of hostilities on the Western Front. Whilst in this theatre of war he did excellent work with his unit in numerous important sectors, was wounded at Arras in 1916, and a second time at Ypres, during the Advance of 1918. Returning to England, he was demobilised in January 1919, and holds the General Service and Victory Medals.
20, Steele Road, Acton Green, W.4.   6403

THOMAS, H., Private, East Surrey Regiment.
He joined in March 1915, and was drafted to France in June of the same year. He fought at Loos, where he was gassed, and after his recovery took part in the fighting at St. Eloi, Vermelles, Ploegsteert Wood and Vimy Ridge. Later he was invalided home through ill-health, and was discharged as medically unfit for further service in June 1916. He holds the 1914–15 Star, and the General Service and Victory Medals.
95, Albert Road, Peckham, S.E.15.   Z5680

THOMAS, H., A.B., Royal Navy.
He volunteered in February 1915, and being posted to H.M.S. " Ebro " was employed on important duties in connection with the blockade of Germany. After two years he was transferred to H.M.S. " Calliope." He did good work protecting mine sweepers, and in cruising and patrol duties in many seas. He was demobilised in February 1919, and holds the 1914–15 Star, and the General Service and Victory Medals.
24, Cooper's Road, Old Kent Road, S.E.1.   Z27262

THOMAS, H. C., Pte., The Queen's (Royal West Surrey Regiment).
He volunteered in September 1914, and was drafted to France in the following year. He fought at Neuve Chapelle, Hill 60, and Ypres, and rendered much valuable service. Unhappily he was killed in action at Loos in December 1915. He was entitled to the 1914–15 Star, and the General Service and Victory Medals.
  " His life for his Country, his soul to God."
9, Townsend Street, Wandsworth, S.E.17.   Z4562

THOMAS, J., L/Corporal, 12th Bedfordshire Regt.
He joined in May 1916, and after his training was engaged on important duties with his unit at various stations. He rendered valuable services, but was not successful in obtaining his transfer overseas prior to the cessation of hostilities. He was demobilised in March 1919.
15, Montpelier Road, Hammersmith, W.6.   13272

THOMAS, J. A., L/Cpl., 8th East Surrey Regiment.
Volunteering in September 1914, he was drafted to the Western Front in the following year, and was in action at Ypres, Loos, the Somme and Arras, and was mentioned in Despatches for conspicuous gallantry. He was taken prisoner in May 1917, and held in captivity until after the Armistice, when he was released and repatriated. He was demobilised in December 1918, and holds the 1914–15 Star, and the General Service and Victory Medals.
7, Woods Road, Peckham, S.E.15.   Z6669

THOMAS, J. R., Sergt., King's Royal Rifle Corps.
Serving at outbreak of war he was sent to France almost immediately, and took part in the Battle of Mons and the fighting on the Marne and Aisne, assisting to stem the advance of the enemy. He also fought in the Battles of Neuve Chapelle and Loos, rendering much valuable service. He was seriously wounded at Ypres in November 1915, and was invalided to England. On his recovery he was employed on important work at Winchester for a time, but later was discharged as medically unfit, owing to his injuries in June 1916. He holds the Mons Star, and the General Service and Victory Medals.
21, Verney Road, Bermondsey, S.E.16.   Z6699C

THOMAS, L. T., Gnr., R.F.A., Rflmn., 21st London Regt. (1st Surrey Rifles), and Sapper, R.E.
Serving at the outbreak of war, he was drafted to France in 1916, and took part in the Battles of the Somme, Arras and Ypres. Later he was taken prisoner during the Advance at Cambrai in 1918, but within a short time escaped and rejoined his unit. During his service overseas he was three times wounded and twice gassed. He returned to England after the cessation of hostilities, and was demobilised in August 1919, holding the General Service and Victory Medals.
90, Sussex Road, Brixton, S.W.9.   Z4567A

THOMAS, M. (Mrs.), Special War Worker.
During the period of hostilities this lady devoted her time to war work. She was at first engaged at Petersfield in doing all she could for the comfort of the wounded soldiers, and later came to London to take up an important appointment with the Bakerloo Tube Coy. She continued her work here until July 1919, when she relinquished her position.
90, Sussex Road, Coldharbour Lane, S.W.9.   4567B

THOMAS, S. W., Driver, R.F.A.
He joined in November 1916, and was sent to the Eastern Front in the following year. He took part in much of the fighting during the Palestine campaign. and was present at the capture of Jerusalem and Beersheba. He rendered much valuable service and returned to England, and was demobilised in September 1919, holding the General Service and Victory Medals.
137, Akerman Road, Brixton Road, S.W.9. . Z5158

THOMAS, W., Private, Labour Corps.
He volunteered in 1915, and during his service in France, which lasted for eighteen months, was engaged in conveying ammunition to many of the forward areas, including those of Arras and Cambrai. He was demobilised in July 1919, and holds the General Service and Victory Medals.
14, Clovelly Road, Chiswick, W.4. 6602

THOMAS, W. C., Bombardier, R.F.A.
He volunteered in 1915, and was sent to France in that year. He fought at Ypres, Festubert, St. Eloi, the Somme, Arras, Cambrai and St. Quentin, and rendered valuable service. He also took part in the Retreat and Advance of 1918, and returning home was demobilised in 1919, holding the 1914-15 Star, and the General Service and Victory Medals.
4, Walconde Avenue, Walworth, S.E.17. Z4561

THOMAS, W. G., Sergt., Royal Engineers.
He volunteered in 1915, and was sent to the Western Front in that year. He took part in the heavy fighting on the Somme and at Arras and Ypres, and also served in the Retreat and Advance of 1918. After the Armistice he proceeded with the Army of Occupation to Turkey, and was still serving in 1920. He holds the 1914-15 Star, and the General Service and Victory Medals.
82, Somerleyton Road, Brixton, S.W.9. Z3089A

THOMAS, W. G., Rifleman, 18th London Regiment (London Irish Rifles).
He volunteered in February 1915, and in the following year was drafted to the Western Front, and took part in the Battle of the Somme. Later he proceeded to Salonika and served in the Balkan campaign. Afterwards transferred to Mesopotamia he fought in the operations against the Turks, and finally being sent to Palestine he was with General Allenby's Forces at Jerusalem, and shortly afterwards was killed in action. He was entitled to the General Service and Victory Medals.
"His memory is cherished with pride."
19, Cologne Road, Battersea, S.W.11. Z4565

THOMPSON, A., Private, R.A.O.C.
Volunteering in July 1915, he was sent to the Western Front in January of the following year, and rendered excellent service in the Battles of the Somme, Arras, Messines, Ypres, and in many engagements during the German Offensive and Allied Advance of 1918. He was mentioned in Despatches for gallantry in the Field, in maintaining a constant supply of ammunition to the guns under heavy fire. He was demobilised in May 1919, and holds the General Service and Victory Medals
60, Commercial Road, Peckham, S.E.15. Z6463

THOMPSON, E. G. B., Driver, R.F.A.
He volunteered in November 1916, and was retained at various stations on important duties, until he proceeded to the Western Front in January 1918. He was in action in many engagements of note, and did good work in connection with the transport of ammunition to his Battery. He made the supreme sacrifice on April 19th, 1918, and was buried at Poperinghe. He was entitled to the General Service and Victory Medals.
"Courage, bright hopes, and myriad dreams, splendidly given."
70, Maysoule Road, Battersea, S.W.11. Z4572

THOMPSON, G. C., Private, R.A.S.C. (M.T.)
Volunteering in May 1915, he was sent to France in the same year, and served at Le Havre with his unit, engaged on important duties as a baker. Owing to ill-health he returned to England, and on his recovery was drafted to India, and later to Mesopotamia. He rendered excellent services throughout, and was demobilised in July 1919 on his return to England. He holds the 1914-15 Star, and the General Service and Victory Medals.
1, Nursery Road, Orb Street, Walworth, S.E.17. Z2797B

THOMPSON, G. W., Gunner, R.F.A.
He volunteered in April 1915, and two months later embarked for the Western Front, where he fought in many engagements, including those at Loos, and the Somme. He was killed in action on the Somme on July 30th, 1916, and was entitled to the 1914-15 Star, and the General Service and Victory Medals.
"Whilst we remember, the Sacrifice is not in vain."
146, Abbey Street, Bermondsey, S.E.1. Z27420

THOMPSON, H. W., Sapper, R.E.
He volunteered in March 1915, and after being drafted to Mesopotamia in the following year, was in action in many engagements of note. He also saw much service with the armoured trains in this theatre of war, and did valuable work throughout. Whilst in the East he suffered much from malaria. Returning to England after the cessation of hostilities he was demobilised in April 1920, and holds the General Service and Victory Medals.
344, Ivydale Road, Peckham, S.E.15. Z6745

THOMPSON, H. W., Driver, R.F.A.
Volunteering in September 1915, and later in the same year drafted to France, he fought at the Somme, Ypres, Arras, Albert, and in various other engagements. He laid down his life for King and Country near Lens, on September 28th, 1917, and was entitled to the 1914-15 Star, and the General Service and Victory Medals.
"A costly sacrifice upon the altar of freedom."
10, Sussex Road, Coldharbour Lane, S.W.9. Z4571

THOMPSON, J. W., Leading Stoker, R.N.
He joined the Navy in 1912, and throughout the recent war did excellent service in submarines J1 and K6. He was on duty for some time in the North Sea, but was after transferred to Mediterranean waters, chiefly around Gibraltar. He was still serving in 1920, and holds the 1914-15 Star, and the General Service and Victory Medals.
5, Sterndale Road, Wandsworth Road, S.W.8. Z4569

THOMPSON, R., Private, R.A.S.C.
Volunteering in January 1915, he was drafted to the Western Front in the following October, and was engaged on important duties in the advanced areas, transporting ammunition and supplies to the front lines. He served in the Battles of Loos, Albert, the Somme, Beaucourt, Messines, Lens, and throughout the Retreat and Advance of 1918. He was demobilised in May 1919, and holds the 1914-15 Star, and the General Service and Victory Medals. He also served in the South African War.
10, Flint Street, Walworth, S.E.17. Z2818B

THOMPSON, T., Bombardier, R.G.A.
He joined in June 1916, and embarking for the Western Front a year later was in action at Arras, Ypres, Kemmel, and in many other engagements. He also fought throughout the German Offensive and Allied Advance of 1918, and returning to England after the Armistice was demobilised in October 1919, and holds the General Service and Victory Medals.
57, Bonnington Square, South Lambeth Road, S.W.8. Z4570

THOMPSON, W. H., Private, Royal Sussex Regt.
He joined in July 1917, and after completing his training served at various stations with his unit engaged on important duties in the armourer's shop. Owing to ill-health, he was not successful in obtaining his transfer to a theatre of war, but rendered excellent services until demobilised in December 1919.
14, Akers Street, Walworth, S.E.17. Z2599A

THOMSON, D. J., Bombardier, R.F.A.
He enlisted in 1913, being drafted to France at the commencement of hostilities, fought in the Retreat from Mons, and at the Battles of the Marne, the Aisne, Arras, Ypres, and Loos. He was badly gassed, and after receiving hospital treatment in England was subsequently invalided out of the Service in March 1918. He holds the Mons Star, and the General Service and Victory Medals.
10, Nealdon Street, Stockwell, S.W.9. Z4573

THOMSON, W., Sapper, R.E.
He joined in June 1918, and after his training was retained at various depôts, engaged on important duties. He was unsuccessful in procuring his transfer to a theatre of war prior to the cessation of hostilities, but rendered excellent agricultural services in North Wales until demobilised in December 1918.
324, East Street, Walworth, S.E.17. Z4568

THOMSON, W. J., Sergt., 2nd Lincolnshire Regt.
He volunteered in August 1914, and until the time of his discharge in September 1918 rendered most valuable services as an Instructor in bombing to the recruits of the New Armies. He was unsuccessful in obtaining his transfer to a theatre of war, as his services at home were indispensable.
10, Marryat Street, Hammersmith, W.6. 12497

THORN, F., Private, Somerset Light Infantry.
He volunteered in September 1914, and a year later, after the completion of his training, embarked for the Western Front, where he saw service in many parts of the line. He fought throughout the German Offensive of 1918, and was wounded in July 1918, during the opening stages of the Allied Advance. He was demobilised in February 1919, and holds the 1914-15 Star, and the General Service and Victory Medals.
51, Dale Street, Chiswick, W.4. 5451

THORN, G. Private, 25th King's (Liverpool Regt.).
He joined the Colours in February 1917, and later in that year proceeded to France, where he was engaged in heavy fighting in various sectors. He was wounded at Vlamertinghe in December 1917, and after the cessation of hostilities was drafted to Egypt, where he served on guard and other important duties. Returning home, he was demobilised in March 1920, and holds the General Service and Victory Medals.
36, Aytoun Road, Brixton Road, S.W.9. Z4574A

THORN, L., Air Mechanic, R.A.F.
He joined in June 1918, and on completing his training as a rigger, served at various aerodromes. He did not obtain his transfer io a theatre of war prior to the cessation of hostilities, but was sent to Germany in January 1919, and served with the Army of Occupation at Cologne. He was demobilised in October 1919.
36, Aytoun Road, Brixton Road, S.W.9. Z4574B

THORNBER, E., L/Corporal, 8th Royal Fusiliers.
Volunteering in September 1914, he embarked for the Western Front shortly afterwards. During his service overseas he fought in various parts of the line, and was in action at Arras and many other engagements of note. He was unfortunately killed in action at Cambrai on November 20th, 1917, and was entitled to the 1914-15 Star, and the General Service and Victory Medals.
"The path of duty was the way to glory."
33, Bridgeman Road, Chiswick, W.4. 6617

THORNE, C., Gunner, R.F.A.
He joined in May 1916, and in the following year was drafted to France. Here he fought in the Battles of Dickebusch, Ypres, Cambrai, Gouzeaucourt, St. Quentin, and throughout the German Offensive and subsequent Allied Advance of 1918. He was demobilised in September 1919, after his return home, and holds the General Service and Victory Medals.
41, Avenue Road, Camberwell, S.E.5. Z4575

THORNE, J. D., Pte., East Surrey Regiment and Queen's (Royal West Surrey Regiment).
Joining in March 1916, he was drafted to the Western Front in the following February, and fought in many engagements, including those at Messines, Passchendaele, the Somme and Ypres. Returning home after the Armistice, he was invalided out of the Service in April 1919, and holds the General Service and Victory Medals.
16, Abbeyfield Road, Rotherhithe, S.E.16. Z6785

THORNE, W., L/Corporal, R.A.S.C. (M.T.)
A Reservist, he was mobilised and sent to France at the outbreak of hostilities and was engaged on important duties transporting ammunition and supplies to the firing line throughout the Retreat from Mons. He was also engaged on similar duties in the Battles of the Marne, the Aisne, Loos, the Somme, Armentières, Bullecourt, Cambrai, and during the Retreat and Advance of 1918. He was demobilised in July 1919, and holds the Mons Star, and the General Service and Victory Medals.
3, Albert Cottages, Park Place, Clapham, S.W.4. Z4576

THORNCROFT, F. G., Driver, R.F.A.
He volunteered in April 1915, and on completing his training, was sent to the Western Front in the following September. He was in action at the Somme, Ypres, Arras, Cambrai and in many other sectors. He was gassed during the heavy fighting in 1918, and returning home after the Armistice, was demobilised in February 1919. He holds the 1914-15 Star, and the General Service and Victory Medals.
209, Warham Street, Camberwell, S.E.5. Z4577

THORNTON, A. J. J., Private, 7th Royal Fusiliers.
Volunteering in March 1915, he was retained at various stations for important duties until he proceeded to France in January 1917. He took part in the severe fighting on the Arras Front, and was severely wounded there in April 1917. He returned to England, and after receiving much hospital treatment was invalided out of the Service in January 1919. He holds the General Service and Victory Medals.
25, Calmington Road, Camberwell, S.E.5. Z5517

THORNTON, R. L., Corporal, R.A.M.C.
He volunteered in June 1915, and later in that year was drafted to Malta, where he was engaged on important duties as a stretcher bearer in the hospitals. Owing to ill-health, he was invalided to England, and after hospital treatment, was discharged as unfit for further service in June 1917. He holds the General Service and Victory Medals.
1, Cottage Grove, Stockwell, S.W.9. Z6682

THOROGOOD, W. F., Gunner, R.F.A.
He joined in August 1916, and in the following December embarked for France, where he saw much active service. He fought in many engagements, including those of Arras, Vimy Ridge, Messines, Ypres, Passchendaele, Lens, Cambrai, and the Retreat and Advance of 1918, during which time he was gassed. He also acted as Pay Sergeant. He returned home and was demobilised in March 1920, holding the General Service and Victory Medals.
57, Smyrk's Road, Walworth, S.E.17. Z4578

THORP, W. G., Private, 23rd London Regiment.
He enlisted in May 1912, at the age of sixteen, and was retained until 1916 on important duties in England. He was then drafted to France, but was shortly afterwards sent to the East, where he saw much active service in Salonika, and Palestine. He fought in the Battles of Gaza and Bethlehem, but owing to ill-health returned to England, and was demobilised in June 1919, holding the General Service and Victory Medals.
24, Birley Street, Battersea, S.W.11. Z4579

THORPE, A., Private, 23rd London and 5th Leicestershire Regiments.
Mobilised at the outbreak of war he was engaged for some time on important duties in England. Afterwards he embarked for France, and there took part in many notable engagements, including those of St. Eloi, Albert, Arras, Ypres, Passchendaele, and Cambrai and was unhappily killed near Bapaume whilst putting up barbed wire entanglements in February 1918. He was entitled to the General Service and Victory Medals.
"He died the noblest death a man may die,
Fighting for God, and right, and liberty."
53, Wycliffe Road, Battersea, S.W.11. Z4580B Z4581B

THORPE, C. H., 1st Class Stoker, R.N.
He volunteered in 1915, and was posted to H.M.S. "Comet," in which ship he served on important and dangerous duties in the North Sea. On August 3rd, 1918, his vessel was torpedoed, and he was drowned. He was entitled to the 1914-15 Star, and the General Service and Victory Medals.
"His memory is cherished with pride."
4, Banim Street, Hammersmith, W.6. 11123A

THORPE, E., L/Cpl., 1st London Regt. (Royal Fusiliers).
Joining in May 1916, he proceeded in the following February to the Western Front, where he took part in many notable engagements, including those at Arras, Ypres, Cambrai and the Retreat and Advance of 1918, and on Armistice Day was wounded and shell shocked. He was invalided to England, and after lengthy hospital treatment was discharged in December 1919. He holds the General Service and Victory Medals.
53, Wycliffe Road, Battersea, S.W.11. Z4580-1A

THREADER, A. C., L/Cpl., 13th Middlesex Regt.
He joined in May 1917, and in the following January, after his training, embarked for France, where he took part in numerous engagements during the German and Allied Offensives of 1918, up to the entry into Mons in November. Later he was drafted to Constantinople and was engaged on special duties with the Military Foot Police. He returned home and was demobilised in May 1920, and holds the General Service and Victory Medals.
53, Haymerle Road, Peckham, S.E.15. Z6465

THRING, S. D., Private, 11th Queen's (Royal West Surrey Regiment).
Volunteering in October 1915, he embarked for France in May of the following year. Whilst in this theatre of war he fought in many engagements, and was unfortunately killed in action in the Somme Offensive on September 17th, 1916. He was entitled to the General Service and Victory Medals.
"A costly sacrifice upon the altar of freedom."
35, Portslade Road, Wandsworth Road, S.W.8. Z4582

THUMWOOD, C., Stoker, R.N.
He volunteered in August 1914, and served in H.M.S. "Falmouth," "Courageous" and "Victory," which were engaged on important duties in the North Sea, with the Grand Fleet. He took part in many important engagements, and was on board the "Falmouth" when she was torpedoed in August 1916. He was fortunately saved, and in 1920 was still serving. He holds the 1914-15 Star, and the General Service and Victory Medals.
42, Stainforth Road, Battersea, S.W.11. Z4583

THUMBWOOD, J., Gunner, R.F.A.
Volunteering in June 1915, he was sent overseas in the following November, and whilst in France served with distinction in many notable engagements. He took part in the fighting at Vimy Ridge, the Somme, Arras, Messines, Ypres, Cambrai and the Retreat and Advance of 1918, and did splendid work in carrying messages under fire. He was mentioned in Despatches for conspicuous gallantry in tending the wounded under heavy shell-fire at Thiepval, and also holds the 1914-15 Star, and the General Service and Victory Medals. In 1919 he was demobilised.
44, Elmhurst Mansions, Edgeley Road, Clapham, S.W.4. Z4584

THUNDER, L. C., Driver, R.A.S.C. (H.T.), (M.T.)
He volunteered in August 1914, and served until 1916 on important home duties. He then proceeded to France, but after much service at Le Havre was sent back to England owing to being under military age. He then served at Woolwich, and whilst there met with an accident with runaway horses, which necessitated his being in hospital for over three months. In April 1919 he was demobilised, and holds the General Service and Victory Medals, but he has since then re-enlisted.
60, Salcott Road, Wandsworth Common, S.W.11.   Z4585

THURGOOD, F. W., Pte., The Buffs (East Kent Regiment).
Mobilised at the outbreak of war he immediately proceeded to France, and fought gallantly in the Retreat from Mons, and in the Battles of the Marne and Aisne. He also took part in the severe fighting at Ypres, and was unhappily killed in action at Loos in September 1915. He was entitled to the Mons Star, and the General Service and Victory Medals.
" He passed out of the sight of men by the path of duty and self-sacrifice."
11, Arlesford Road, Stockwell, S.W.9.   Z4586

THURGOOD, G. J., Private, Royal Fusiliers.
He volunteered in December 1915, and in the following year was drafted to France, where he was in action in many engagements, and also served as Battalion stretcher-bearer. He fought at Arras, Passchendaele and Cambrai, and was wounded twice and gassed. He returned to England for hospital treatment, and in 1919 was demobilised, holding the General Service and Victory Medals.
194, Mayall Road, Herne Hill, S.E.24.   Z4558

THURLEY, G. J., 1st Air Mechanic, R.A.F. (late R.F.C.)
He joined in October 1917, and after his training served with his Squadron at various stations. He was engaged on important duties which called for a high degree of technical skill, and rendered valuable services, but was unable to secure his transfer overseas before the cessation of hostilities. He was demobilised in November 1919.
4, Delorne Street, Fullham, S.W.6.   14272

THURSTON, A. J., Rflmn., King's Royal Rifle Corps.
He joined in March 1916, and was drafted to the Western Front in the following July. He was in action in engagements on the Somme, and at Arras, and Bullecourt, and was wounded and taken prisoner in August 1917. He died whilst in captivity on November 13th, 1917, and was entitled to the General Service and Victory Medals.
" Great deeds cannot die."
54, Fawcett Road, Rotherhithe, S.E.16.   6786B

THURSTON, A. J., 1st Aircraftsman, R.A.F. (Kite Balloon Section).
He joined in April 1916, and in the following December embarked for France, where he served on important observation duties. He saw much service at Nieppe in the Ypres sector, and did valuable work until January 1919, when he returned home and was demobilised. He holds the General Service and Victory Medals.
8, Chryssell Road, Brixton Road, S.W.9.   Z5290

THURSTON, G., Air Mechanic, R.A.F.
He joined in September 1918, and after his training was sent to Ireland, where he was engaged on important duties, which required much technical skill. He rendered valuable services, and was demobilised in March 1919.
43, Havil Street, Camberwell, S.E.5.   Z4587

THURSTON, G. A., L/Corporal, 24th London Regt. (Queen's).
Mobilised at the outbreak of war he almost immediately proceeded overseas, and fought in the Retreat from Mons and in the Battles of the Marne and the Aisne. He also took part in many other engagements, including those at Ypres, the Somme, Passchendaele, Cambrai and the Retreat and Advance of 1918, during which time he was wounded and gassed twice. He returned to England, and was demobilised in January 1919, and holds the Mons Star, and the General Service and Victory Medals.
27, Radnor Terrace, South Lambeth, S.W.8.   Z27503

THURSTON, H., Private, M.G.C.
He joined in June 1917, and after training was sent to France in the following year. He fought in the Retreat and Advance of 1918, being in action on the Somme and at Vimy Ridge, and Cambrai. After the cessation of hostilities he returned to England, and in October 1919 was demobilised, holding the General Service and Victory Medals.
54, Fawcett Road, Rotherhithe, S.E.16.   Z6786A

THURSTON, W. C., Private, R.A.S.C. (M.T.)
He volunteered in October 1914, and after a short training was drafted to the Western Front. He rendered valuable transport service there in various sectors for over four years, and returning to England after hostilities ceased was demobilised in April 1919. He holds the 1914-15 Star, and the General Service and Victory Medals.
23, Purcell Crescent, Fulham, S.W.6.   15162

THWAITES, E. C., Rifleman, 8th London Regt. (Post Office Rifles).
He joined in 1916, and proceeded to the Western Front later in that year. He took part in the heavy fighting at Vimy Ridge, Arras, Bullecourt and Ypres, where he was severely wounded, and was sent to hospital in England. After his recovery he was employed on important duties at his depôt until demobilised in 1919, and holds the General Service and Victory Medals.
8, Wingfield Street, Peckham, S.E.15.   Z6787

THYNNE, L. G., Pte., 2nd Royal Fusiliers and Rflmn., 16th London Regt. (Queen's Westminster Rifles).
Volunteering in August 1914, he proceeded to Malta in the following December, and there served for a few months. He was then sent to Egypt, but in October 1915 was transferred to Gallipoli, where he saw much service until the Evacuation. On returning to Egypt he took part in a number of minor engagements until April 1916, when he was drafted to France in time for our Offensive on the Somme. He was reported missing after the operations at Leuze Wood, on September 15th, and afterwards was presumed to have been killed there when only nineteen years of age. He was entitled to the 1914-15 Star, and the General Service and Victory Medals.
" The path of duty was the way to glory."
35, Arnott Road, Peckham, S.E.15.   Z6812

TIBBALS, A. G., 1st Class Stoker, R.N.
He joined in June 1915, and was posted to H.M.S. " Courageous," which ship was engaged on patrol and other important duties with the Grand Fleet in the North Sea, and also assisted to cover the raid on Zeebrugge in April 1918. He rendered valuable services throughout, and was still serving in 1920. He holds the 1914-15 Star, and the General Service and Victory Medals.
23, Fawcett Road, Rotherhithe, S.E.16.   Z6767

TIBBALS, J. E., Private, 6th South Wales Borderers.
Joining in November 1916, and after serving at various stations he was drafted to the Western Front in December of the following year. He fought in many important engagements, including those on the Somme and at Achiet le Grand, and was wounded at Ploegsteert in April 1918. Returning to England he received hospital treatment, and after the Armistice was sent to Germany with the Army of Occupation, and served there until he returned home and was demobilised in August 1919. He holds the General Service and Victory Medals.
45, Reculver Road, Rotherhithe, S.E.16.   Z6768

TIBBLE, G. S., Driver, R.F.A.
He volunteered in September 1914, and was immediately sent to France, where he served at Mons, and was severely wounded and invalided home. He was discharged as medically unfit in February 1915, but four days later re-enlisted, and took part in numerous engagements, including those on the Somme and at Arras and Ypres. He also fought in the Retreat and Advance of 1918, and after the Armistice was drafted to India, where he was still serving in 1920. He holds the Mons Star, and the General Service and Victory Medals.
21, Trafalgar Street, Walworth, S.E.17.   Z27331

TICEHURST, C. H., Private, 24th London Regt. (Queen's).
He joined in November 1916, and later in the same year was drafted to France, where he took part in the fighting at Vimy Ridge, Bullecourt, Messines and Ypres, and was wounded and sent to hospital. On his recovery he returned to the front lines, and was again in action and gassed. He was invalided home, and was later transferred to the R.A.M.C. In 1919 he was sent to Egypt, and was engaged as orderly on a hospital train until November of that year, when he returned to England, and was demobilised, holding the General Service and Victory Medals.
104, Darwin Street, Walworth, S.E.17.   Z4588

TIEMAN, C., Rifleman, Rifle Brigade.
He volunteered in August 1914, and in October of the same year was drafted to France, where he was in action at La Bassée, Ypres, Neuve Chapelle, Hill 60 and Loos, where he was wounded. He was invalided home and was discharged as medically unfit in December 1915, but re-enlisted in November 1917, and was engaged on important duties at Falmouth until he was demobilised in March 1919, holding the 1914 Star, and the General Service and Victory Medals.
13, Glendall Street, Ferndale Road, S.W.9.   Z4589

TILBURY, A. V., Corporal, R.F.A.
He volunteered in March 1915, and was sent to France in October of the same year. He took part in the fighting at Loos, St. Eloi, Vimy Ridge, the Somme, Arras, Bullecourt, Messines, Ypres, Passchendaele, Cambrai, and in numerous other engagements, and also served in the Retreat and Advance of 1918. During his service in France he was engaged for a time as an engine driver on the railways, and on the occasion of the visit of King George V. to France he was the driver of the Royal train. He was demobilised in February 1919, and holds the 1914 Star, and the General Service and Victory Medals.
2, Springrice Road, Heather Green Lane, Catford, S.E.6.
Z4592

TILBURY, R. R., Private, R.A.S.C. (M.T.)
He volunteered in September 1914, and in the following year was drafted to France, where he was engaged on important transport duties at Arras, Ypres, Cambrai, and many other engagements, and was wounded. He returned home in January 1919, and was demobilised holding the 1914-15 Star, and the General Service and Victory Medals.
63, Masbro Road, W. Kensington, W.14.
12027

TILLETT, H. A., Sergt., 8th London Regiment (Post Office Rifles.)
He was mobilised in August 1914, and sent to France in February of the following year. He took part in the fighting at Ypres, Loos, Vimy Ridge, the Somme and Cambrai and also served in the Retreat and Advance of 1918. He was demobilised in November 1919, and holds the 1914-15 Star, and the General Service and Victory Medals.
106, St. George's Grove, Peckham, S.E.15.
Z5682

TILLEY, F. J., A.B., R.N., H.M.S. "Tirade."
He joined in June 1917, and served with the Grand Fleet in the North Sea. He took part in the Battles of Heligoland Bight, and Zeebrugge, and was also engaged on patrol duties. He was demobilised in February 1919, and holds the General Service and Victory Medals.
73, Waterloo Street, Camberwell, S.E.5.
Z4593

TILLEY, A. W., Rifleman, 18th London Regiment (London Irish Rifles).
Volunteering in August 1915, he was sent to France in the following year, and took part in numerous engagements, including those on the Somme and at High Wood and Ypres. He was wounded and invalided home, but on his recovery proceeded to Egypt in 1917, and thence to Palestine, where he was in action at Jericho, and was again wounded. He was demobilised in July 1919, and holds the General Service and Victory Medals.
32, Burns Road, Battersea, S.W.11.
Z4594

TILLEY, J. A., Sergt., 6th London Regt. (Rifles).
He volunteered in May 1915, and in the following year was sent to France, where he was in action at Vimy Ridge, the Somme, Ypres and Cambrai. He also served in the Retreat and Advance of 1918, and was three times wounded. He was demobilised in February 1919, and holds the General Service and Victory Medals.
81, Bavent Road, Camberwell, S.E.5.
Z6509

TILLEY, W. G., Gunner, R.G.A.
He volunteered in October 1915, and in August of the following year was drafted to Egypt and thence to Palestine. He was in action at Beersheba and also served in the Advance on Jerusalem. He later contracted malaria and was sent to hospital at Deir-el-Bela. He returned home and was demobilised in March 1919, and holds the General Service and Victory Medals.
13, Lisford Street, Peckham, S.E.15.
Z5159

TILLEY, W. H., Sergt., R.A.S.C.
Volunteering in April 1915, he was sent to the Western Front in the same year, and was engaged on important transport duties on the Somme and at Messines, Ypres, Cambrai, St. Quentin and in the Retreat and Advance of 1918. He was demobilised in March 1919, and holds the 1914-15 Star and the General Service and Victory Medals.
22, Wheatsheaf Terrace, S. Lambeth, S.W.8.
Z4595

TILLIN, A. F., Private, King's Own (Royal Lancaster Regiment).
He joined in May 1916, and later in the same year was sent to Salonika, where he took part in numerous engagements, including those on the Doiran front. During his service in this theatre of war he was wounded and also suffered from dysentery and malaria. He returned home and was demobilised in August 1919, and holds the General Service and Victory Medals.
185, Sumner Road, Peckham, S.E.15.
Z6346

TILLING, A. G., Gunner, R.F.A.
Volunteering in 1915, he was sent to France in the same year and was in action on the Somme and at Ypres. He fell fighting at Armentières in 1917, and was entitled to the General Service and Victory Medals.
"And doubtless he went in splendid company."
82, Wilcox Road, Wandsworth Road, S.W.8.
Z4597B

TILLING, C. E., Private, 13th Royal Fusiliers.
He volunteered in January 1915, and in June of the same year was drafted to France, where he took part in the fighting at Ypres, Loos and the Somme. He was wounded and invalided home, and on his recovery he was engaged on important duties with his unit until he was demobilised in 1919, holding the 1914-15 Star, and the General Service and Victory Medals.
88, Abercrombie Street, Battersea, S.W.11.
Z4596A

TILLING, R. J., Gunner, R.F.A.
He volunteered in June 1915, and later in the same year proceeded to France, where he was in action at Ploegsteert Wood, St. Eloi, Albert, the Somme, Arras, Vimy Ridge, Ypres, Passchendaele, Lens, and in many other engagements, and also took part in the Retreat and Advance of 1918. He was demobilised in February 1919, and holds the 1914-15 Star, and the General Service and Victory Medals.
85, Stonhouse Street, Clapham, S.W.4.
Z4598

TILLING, S. J., Pte., 10th Queen's (Royal West Surrey Regiment).
Volunteering in 1915, he was retained on important duties with his unit until 1917, when he was transferred to the Labour Corps, and drafted to France, where he served during the severe fighting at Cambrai, and in the Retreat and Advance of 1918. He was demobilised in 1919, and holds the General Service and Victory Medals.
82, Wilcox Road, Wandsworth Road, S.W.8.
Z4597A

TILLING, T. B., L/Corporal, R.E.
He joined in May 1916, and in the following month was drafted to France, where he took part in numerous engagements, including those on the Somme and at Arras. He also served in the Retreat and Advance of 1918. He was demobilised in October 1919, and holds the General Service and Victory Medals.
88, Abercrombie Street, Battersea, S.W.11.
Z4596B

TILLMAN, A. G., Private, East Surrey Regiment.
He was mobilised at the outbreak of war, and was immediately sent to the Western Front, where he took part in the fighting at Mons and the Marne and Aisne. He was unfortunately killed in action near Ypres on April 20th, 1915, and was buried in Ypres Cemetery. He was entitled to the Mons Star, and the General Service and Victory Medals.
"Courage, bright hopes, and a myriad dreams splendidly given."
22, Pasley Road, Walworth, S.E.17.
Z27028

TILLMAN, H. G., 2nd Corporal, R.E.
He was serving at the outbreak of war in a line regiment, and was engaged in British and German East Africa under General Smuts from 1914 till 1917, when he was sent to Egypt and transferred to the R.E. He was employed as a locomotive driver on the Egyptian Railways, and rendered valuable services. He was discharged in April 1919, and holds the 1914-15 Star, and the General Service and Victory Medals.
26, Longhedge Street, Battersea, S.W.11.
Z4599

TILLYER, R. J., Private, Devonshire Regiment.
He was serving at the outbreak of war, and shortly afterwards was sent to France, where he took part in the fighting at Loos, the Somme and in other important engagements, and was three times wounded. He was invalided home and discharged as medically unfit for further service in March 1917, and holds the 1914-15 Star, and the General Service and Victory Medals.
115, Farmer's Road, Camberwell, S.E.5.
Z1666A

TILSON, F. H., Smith, R.A.S.C.
He volunteered in November 1914, and was sent to France in the following month. He was engaged on the repair of lorries and other important duties in many sectors, including those of Ypres, Albert, Bullecourt, and Passchendaele, and rendered valuable services. He returned home and was demobilised in May 1919, and holds the 1914-15 Star, and the General Service and Victory Medals.
269, Commercial Road, Peckham, S.E.15.
Z6670

TILT, C., Private, R.A.S.C. (M.T.)
Volunteering in May 1915, he proceeded overseas in the same year. He served in many sectors of the Western Front, conveying supplies and ammunition to the various fighting areas until the conclusion of hostilities. He then returned home in April 1919, and was demobilised, holding the 1914-15 Star, and the General Service and Victory Medals.
2A, Lingham Street, Stockwell, S.W.9.
Z4600

TILTMAN, P., Corporal, R.F.A.
He was mobilised at the outbreak of war, and afterwards proceeded to the Western Front, where he served until 1919. In this theatre of war he took part in many important engagements until hostilities ceased. He holds the 1914–15 Star, and the General Service and Victory Medals, and also the Territorial Efficiency Medal, and was demobilised in February 1919, after his return to England.
42, Delorme Street, Hammersmith, W.6. 14084

TILY, B., L/Corporal, King's Royal Rifle Corps.
He volunteered in June 1915, and in September of the same year was drafted to France. He took part in many engagements, including those at Loos, Vimy Ridge, the Somme, Arras, Bullecourt, and Messines, and also served in the Retreat and Advance of 1918, during which he was gassed and was in hospital at Le Havre. He was discharged in February 1919, and holds the 1914–15 Star, and the General Service and Victory Medals.
191, Albert Road, Peckham, S.E.15. Z5851

TIMBS, J., Private, Connaught Rangers.
Mobilised at the outbreak of war, he was shortly afterwards drafted to the Western Front and fought during the Retreat from Mons. He was also in action in many other battles, including those of La Bassée, Neuve Chapelle and Hill 60, and was unfortunately killed in action at Ypres on April 26th, 1915. He was entitled to the Mons Star, and the General Service and Victory Medals.
"His life for his Country, his Soul to God."
69, Saltoun Road, Brixton, S.W.2. Z4601

TIMMINS, C., Gunner, R.F.A.
Volunteering in April 1915, he proceeded overseas in February of the following year, and was severely wounded during the fighting at Passchendaele and invalided home. On recovery he returned to the Western Front and served there in many engagements until hostilities ceased. In February 1919 he was demobilised, holding the General Service and Victory Medals.
27, Dorothy Road, Lavender Hill, S.W.11. Z2879B

TIMMS, E. J., Pte., 3rd Queen's (Royal West Surrey Regt.), 16th Essex Regt. and Labour Corps.
He joined in October 1916, and after his training served with the 438th Agricultural Company on various important farming duties. Later he was transferred to the 3rd Queen's, but was not successful in obtaining his transfer overseas before the cessation of hostilities. He was demobilised in September 1919.
30, Shorncliffe Road, Walworth, S.E.17. Z4603

TIMMS, F. H., Pte., 14th South Lancashire Regt.
Joining in November 1917, he embarked for France early in the following year, and whilst in this theatre of war took part in many engagements with the 54th Division. At Bullecourt he was severely gassed in September 1918 and on recovery served on important duties until returning to England for demobilisation in March 1919. He holds the General Service and Victory Medals.
270, Albert Road, Peckham, S.E.15. Z5721A

TIMMS, T., A.B., Royal Navy.
He joined in November 1916, and was posted to H.M.S. "Douai" (Battle Cruiser), in which ship he served on important patrol duties in the North Sea. Later he was present at the surrender of the German Fleet at Scapa Flow, and was engaged on dangerous work until demobilised in June 1919. He holds the General Service and Victory Medals.
11, Runham Street, Walworth, S.E.17. Z4602

TIMS, T. R., Private, R.A.S.C.
Volunteering in April 1915, he was drafted in the following March to the Western Front. He served in many notable battles, including those of St. Eloi, Vimy Ridge, the Somme, Messines, Ypres, Lens and Cambrai, until the conclusion of hostilities, after which he returned to England and in July 1919 was demobilised, holding the General Service and Victory Medals.
9, Chip Street, Clapham, S.W.4. Z4604

TIMSON, A., Private, R.A.S.C.
Volunteering in 1915 he was shortly afterwards drafted to German East Africa, where he served on important duties until invalided to England. Later he proceeded to France and did valuable work with his unit in many sectors of the Front. He was demobilised in 1919, and holds the General Service and Victory Medals.
13, Patmore Street, Wandsworth Road, S.W.8. Z4605

TINDALL, T. (Senior), Private, R.D.C.
He volunteered in June 1915, and after the completion of his course of training was engaged on home garrison duties in various parts of the country until after the cessation of hostilities. He continued to render valuable services until his demobilisation in March 1919.
3, Broughton Street, Battersea Park, S.W.8. Z4606B

TINDALL, T., Sergt., R.G.A. and R.E.
Serving at the outbreak of hostilities he was sent to France with the R.G.A. in the following year. He fought at Festubert and Loos, where he was wounded. After his recovery he was in action at Arras and Cambrai, and in the Retreat and Advance of 1918. After the Armistice he was drafted to Egypt, where in 1920 he was serving with the R.E. (Wireless Section). He holds the 1914–15 Star, and the General Service and Victory Medals.
3, Broughton Street, Battersea Park, S.W.8. Z4606A

TINDALL, W., Private, R.M.L.I.
He was serving at the outbreak of hostilities, and during the war was engaged in various ships on patrol duties in the North Sea and in North Russian waters. In 1918 he proceeded to France and did much valuable work with the R.G.A. He was demobilised in September 1919 and holds the 1914–15 Star, and the General Service and Victory Medals.
3, Broughton Street, Battersea Park, S.W.8. Z4606C

TINDELL (Mrs.), Special War Worker.
During a large part of the war this lady was engaged on important work in connection with the manufacture of munitions at the Projectile Works, Battersea. She carried out her responsible duties during the whole of the period in a manner worthy of the highest praise.
4, New Road, Battersea Park Road, S.W.8. Z4607B

TINDELL, A., Pte., Middlesex Regt. (Labour Batt.)
He volunteered in January 1915, and after his training was drafted to the Western Front. During his service in this seat of war he took an active part in much heavy fighting and was severely wounded at the Battle of Ypres in 1917. He holds the General Service and Victory Medals, and was demobilised in February 1919.
51, Angel Road, Hammersmith, W.6. 12616

TINDELL, V., Bombardier, R.F.A.
He was mobilised in August 1914, and was sent to France almost immediately. He took part in the Retreat from Mons and in the important engagements at Antwerp, Neuve Chapelle, Ypres, the Somme, Arras and Vimy Ridge, and was wounded. He rendered valuable services with the French Mortar Batteries and also with the Heavy Batteries, and played a gallant part in the Retreat and Advance of 1918. He was demobilised in February 1919, and holds the Mons Star, the General Service and Victory Medals.
4, New Road, Battersea Park Road, S.W.8. Z4607A

TINKER, E. A. J., Pte., 25th London Regt. (Cyclists).
He joined in June 1916, and later in that year embarked for India, where he saw active service against the hostile tribes in Afghanistan on the North-Western Frontier. He also assisted to restore order during the Amritsar riots, and returning home was demobilised in January 1920. He holds the General Service and Victory Medals.
102, Kenbury Street, Camberwell, S.E.5. Z6099

TINSON, E. F., Private, R.A.S.C.
He joined in November 1916, and was drafted to the Western Front later in that year. During his service in this theatre of war he rendered valuable services in many engagements of note, including those at Cambrai, Ypres and the Somme. He was severely wounded and returned to England, but unfortunately died from the effects of his injuries in February 1919. He was entitled to the General Service and Victory Medals.
"The path of duty was the way to glory."
5, Motley Street, Battersea, S.W.8. Z4608

TINWORTH, J., L/Corporal, Queen's (Royal West Surrey Regiment).
Mobilised and drafted to the Western Front at the outbreak of war, he fought throughout the Retreat from Mons, and in many of the subsequent engagements. In May 1915 he was severely wounded in the Battle of Festubert, and after being admitted into hospital died from his injuries on May 15th. He was entitled to the Mons Star, and the General Service and Victory Medals.
"A valiant soldier, with undaunted heart he breasted Life's last hill."
40, Avenue Road, Camberwell, S.E.5. Z1563B

TIPLER, A. T., Gunner, R.F.A. and Pte., R.A.V.C.
He joined the Royal Field Artillery in December 1916, and was transferred to the Royal Army Veterinary Corps on proceeding to France in June 1917. He served in the forward areas as a transport driver with his battery, and was present in the heavy fighting at Ypres and Cambrai, and throughout the Retreat and Advance of 1918. After the Armistice he was sent into Germany with the Army of Occupation and served at Cologne until he returned home for demobilisation in August 1919. He holds the General Service and Victory Medals.
4, The Grove, South Lambeth Road, S.W.8. Z4609

TIPPEN, J. W., Private, Lincolnshire Regiment.
He enlisted in May 1914, and being drafted to the Western front at the declaration of war was engaged in the fierce fighting in the Retreat from Mons, and was severely wounded. He unfortunately succumbed to his injuries on November 16th, 1914, and was entitled to the Mons Star, and the General Service and Victory Medals.
" Whilst we remember, the Sacrifice is not in vain."
6, Etton Street, Hammersmith, W.6.   15138

TITCHMARSH, A. H., Rifleman, 16th London Regiment (Queen's Westminster Rifles).
Volunteering in December 1915, he was drafted to Egypt in the following year, and fought in many engagements on the Palestine front, including those at Magdhaba, Gaza, and in the vicinity of Jerusalem. He was also in action throughout the final British Advance into Syria, and, returning home after the cessation of hostilities, was demobilised in April 1919. He holds the General Service and Victory Medals.
3, Chantrey Road, Stockwell Road S.W.9.   Z4611

TITTERTON, H., Corporal, R.A.F.
He joined in March 1916, and on completing his training was retained at various aerodromes engaged on guard and other important duties. Being unfit for duty overseas, he did not obtain his transfer to a theatre of war, but rendered valuable services until demobilised in April 1919. He subsequently died from the effects of his service on September 24th, 1919.
" His memory is cherished with pride."
44, Alfreton Street, Walworth, S.E.17.   Z4610B

TITTERTON, J. G., Pte., Buffs (East Kent Regt.)
He volunteered in September 1914, and afterwards was drafted to France in the following April was in action in the Battle of Hill 60, and was wounded. On his recovery he rejoined his Battalion and fought at Festubert and Loos, and in various parts of the line. He was unfortunately killed in action near Loos in March 1916, and was entitled to the 1914–15 Star, and the General Service and Victory Medals.
" His life for his Country."
44, Alfreton Street, Walworth, S.E.17.   Z4610A

TOBAR, R., Gunner, R.F.A.
Volunteering in September 1914, he embarked for France in the following year, and with a sector of anti-aircraft guns saw much service in various parts of the line, especially in the Somme, Ypres and Cambrai sectors. In 1917 he went to Italy and did good work on various fronts, and returning to France in 1918, served throughout the Retreat and Advance of that year. He was demobilised in February 1919, holding the 1914–15 Star, and the General Service and Victory Medals. He afterwards died on June 26th, 1920.
" His memory is cherished with pride."
60, Masboro Road, West Kensington, W.14.   12223

TOBY, F. A., 1st Air Mechanic, R.A.F. (late R.N.A.S.)
Volunteering in 1915, he completed his training and was retained at Chingford and other aerodromes on important duties as a blacksmith. He was unsuccessful in obtaining his transfer overseas, as his services were considered indispensable, and rendered excellent services until demobilised in June 1919.
10, Cologne Road, Battersea, S.W.11.   Z4612

TODD, E. R., Driver, R.F.A.
Volunteering in November 1914, he was sent to France a year later, and fought in many engagements, including the Battle of Albert. Transferred to Salonika he was engaged in much heavy fighting in many parts of the line and did good work. He gave his life for King and Country on May 6th, 1918, and was entitled to the 1914–15 Star, and the General Service and Victory Medals.
" Great deeds cannot die."
25, Coopers Road, Old Kent Road, S.E.1.   Z27405

TODD, R., Sergt., M.F.P. and Intelligence Corps.
He joined in March 1916, and on completing his training was engaged at various stations on important duties with the Military Foot Police. He was afterwards transferred to the Intelligence Corps, in which he rendered most valuable services in various parts of the Country. He was not successful in securing his transfer overseas before fighting ceased, but did excellent work until demobilised in July 1919.
53, Lettsom Street, Camberwell, S.E.5.   Z6550

TOLLITT, W. H., Private, 22nd London Regiment (The Queen's).
He volunteered in December 1915, and was engaged on important duties at various depôts until embarking for France in November 1917. He was in action at Bourlon Wood during the first Battle of Cambrai, and also fought throughout the German Offensive and subsequent Allied Advance of 1918. He was demobilised in February 1919, after returning to England, and holds the General Service and Victory Medals.
7, Odell Street, Camberwell, SE..5.   Z5518

TOLSON, H. J., Bombardier, R.G.A.
He volunteered in May 1915, and was sent to France in the following year. He fought at Albert, the Somme, Messines, Passchendaele, and in many other sectors, and rendered valuable services in the operations until the Armistice. He then returned to England and was demobilised in February 1919, holding the General Service and Victory Medals.
6, Reedham Street, Peckham, S.E.18.   Z6788

TOLSON, R., Bandsman, R.G.A., and Scots Guards.
He enlisted in the R.G.A. in September 1911, and throughout the war was engaged at various depôts on important duties. He was unsuccessful in obtaining his transfer to a theatre of war, but rendered valuable services throughout. In 1920 he was still serving at Wellington Barracks with his unit.
21, Eversleigh Road, Battersea, S.W.11.   Z4613

TOLWORTHY, A., 2nd Corporal, R.E.
He volunteered in August 1914, and proceeding to the Dardanelles in the following year took part in the Landing at Suvla Bay, and was badly wounded. Returning to England he received hospital treatment and was discharged as unfit for further service in 1916. Later he went to America, and there received further treatment for his injuries, and having completely recovered joined the American Tank Corps, and proceeded to France, where he fought in many engagements in the closing stages of the war. He holds the 1914–15 Star, and the General Service and Victory Medals, and also was awarded the Royal Humane Society's Medal for saving a man from drowning at Gallipoli.
26, Graham Road, Chiswick, W.4.   6613C

TOMBS, A. E., Private, R.A.M.C.
He joined in February 1917, and after completing his training embarked for the Western Front, where he was engaged as an Orderly at the 8th General Hospital. He rendered valuable services throughout, and returning to England after the Armistice, was demobilised in July 1919. He holds the General Service and Victory Medals.
11, Bonar Road, Peckham, S.E.15.   Z6461

TOMKINS, H., Trooper, Nottinghamshire Hussars (Sherwood Rangers).
Volunteering at the outbreak of war and proceeding to the Western Front shortly afterwards, he fought in many engagements of importance, including the Battles of Loos, Albert, Vimy Ridge, and the Somme. In September 1916, he was transferred to Mesopotamia and saw much service at Kut, Baghdad, and in many parts of the line. Returning to England, he was demobilised in April 1919, and holds the 1914–15 Star, and the General Service and Victory Medals. He was recommended for the Military Medal for conspicuous gallantry and devotion to duty in the Field.
140, Westmoreland Road, Walworth, S.E.17.   Z4614

TOMLINS, B., A/Sergt., 2nd and 5th West Yorkshire Regiment.
A Reservist, he was mobilised and sent to the Western Front at the commencement of the war, and fought in the Retreat from Mons, the Battles of the Marne, the Aisne, La Bassée and Ypres, and was wounded. Returning to England, he received hospital treatment, and on his recovery proceeded to Gallipoli, where he was in action in the Landing at Suvla Bay, and in many subsequent engagements. Owing to ill-health, he was invalided to Malta and England, and after his recovery served as an Instructor at various depôts until discharged as unfit for further service in April 1919. He holds the Mons Star, and the General Service and Victory Medals.
44, Clayton Road, Peckham, S.E.15.   Z6096

TOMLINS, G., Private, 25th London Regt. (Cyclists).
He joined in March 1916, and later in that year was drafted to the Western Front, where he fought in many engagements, and was severely wounded in the Battle of Messines in June 1917. He returned to England, and after receiving medical treatment, was invalided out of the Service in October 1917. He holds the General Service and Victory Medals.
42, Manaton Road, Peckham, S.E.15.   Z6344

TOMLINSON, A., Pte., Sherwood Foresters (Notts and Derby Regiment).
He joined in September 1916, and in the following February was sent to France. While there he fought at Poperinghe, and in many other important engagements. He was transferred to the Labour Corps and did good work in the clothing depôt until his return home after the Armistice. He was demobilised in February 1919, and holds the General Service and Victory Medals.
27, Melon Road, Peckham, S.E.15.   Z6362B

TOMLINSON, C. F. T., Pte., 11th Queen's (Royal West Surrey Regiment).
He volunteered in November 1914, and was sent to France four months later. During his service overseas he fought at Arras, Ypres, Cambrai, and on the Somme, and was wounded. He gave his life for the freedom of England in the second Battle of the Aisne in May 1916. He was entitled to the 1914-15 Star, and the General Service and Victory Medals.
"A costly sacrifice upon the altar of freedom."
48, Pepler Road, Peckham, S.E.15.   Z4615

TOMLINSON, E. W., Private, R.A.S.C.
He volunteered at the outbreak of war, and embarking immediately for France served throughout the Retreat from Mons and the Battles of the Marne, the Aisne, La Bassée, Ypres, the Somme, and Arras. After much valuable transport service at Dunkirk he returned to the front lines and saw heavy fighting in the Allied Advance of 1918. He was demobilised in 1919, after his return home, and holds the Mons Star and the General Service and Victory Medals.
6, Thornton Street, Brixton Road, S.W.9.   Z4616C

TOMLINSON, F., Saddler, R.F.A.
He volunteered in January 1915, and in June of the following year proceeded to the Western Front, where he fought at St. Eloi. Transferred to Salonika in December 1916, he saw much fighting in various parts of the line, and in the following March was sent to Egypt. In the later Palestine campaign he was in action at the Battles of Gaza, Beersheba, and in the vicinity of Jerusalem, and served throughout the final British Advance. Suffering from malaria he returned to England, and after receiving medical treatment was invalided out of the Service in January 1919. He holds the General Service and Victory Medals.
90, Blake's Road, Peckham, S.E.15.   Z6104B

TOMLINSON, F. (M.M.), Sergt., R.E.
Volunteering in October 1915, he was sent to France in the following year, and was in action in many engagements and rendered valuable services in all descriptions of Field work until almost the close of hostilities. He was wounded in August 1918. He was awarded the Military Medal for conspicuous gallantry and devotion to duty in the Field, and also holds the General Service and Victory Medals. He was demobilised in June 1919.
12, Dickens Street, Battersea Park, S.W.8.   Z3151A

TOMLINSON, H. R., Private, R.A.S.C.
He volunteered in November 1915, and being drafted to Egypt in the following year served at Sollum and Katia. After being transferred to Salonika in August 1916, he saw considerable service on the Monastir, Doiran and Vardar fronts, and took part in the final Allied Advance in the Balkans. On returning home he was demobilised in May 1919, and holds the General Service and Victory Medals.
6, Thornton Street, Brixton, S.W.9.   Z4616A

TOMLINSON, R. R., Private, R.M.L.I.
He joined in June 1916, and in the following year his ship was sent to the Mediterranean Sea, where she was engaged on patrol and other important duties. He was in action in the engagement at the Dardanelles with the "Goeben" and "Breslau" in which the latter was sunk. Later after being stationed in Greece on important guard duties he was invalided home with shell-shock, and was discharged unfit for further service in August 1919. He holds the General Service and Victory Medals.
112, Albert Road, Peckham, S.E.15.   Z6102

TOMLINSON, W. A. (M.M.) Sergt., R.A.S.C.
Volunteering at the outbreak of war and proceeding at once to the Western Front, he served in the Retreat from Mons, and in the Battles of the Marne, the Aisne, La Bassée, Ypres, the Somme and Arras. He was awarded the Military Medal for gallantry and devotion to duty in the Field in materially assisting to save a convoy in the Retreat of 1918. He saw much fighting in the later Allied Advance, and returning to England after the Armistice was demobilised in 1919. He holds the Mons Star, and the General Service and Victory Medals.
6, Thornton Street, Brixton, S.W.9.   Z4616B

TOMLINSON, W. B., A.B., Royal Navy and Pte., 3rd Dorsetshire Regt. and R.A.S.C.
He was serving in the Navy at the outbreak of war and was discharged in December 1914. Volunteering for the Army in April 1915 he sailed for Egypt in the following month, and whilst serving on the Palestine front fought in many engagements including the Battles of Rafa and Gaza. He was wounded at Ludd in 1917, and invalided to England. He was subsequently discharged in July 1917, but rejoined in the Royal Army Service Corps, and did good service until demobilised in July 1919. He holds the 1914-15 Star, and the General Service and Victory Medals.
90, Blakes Road, Peckham, S.E.15.   Z6104A

TOMPKINS, E. W., Cpl., Duke of Cornwall's Light Infantry.
He was mobilised at the outbreak of war, and in the following year was drafted to France. During his service overseas he fought in many important engagements, including those of Hill 60, Ypres, Festubert, Loos, the Somme, and Arras, and was wounded in action. After his recovery he served in the Advance of 1918, at Amiens and Bapaume, and was twice gassed. Returning to England after the cessation of hostilities he was demobilised in January 1919, and holds the 1914-15 Star, and the General Service and Victory Medals.
77, Avenue Road, Camberwell, S.E.5.   Z1629B

TOMS, E., Private, R.A.M.C.
He volunteered in February 1915, and after his training was completed was drafted to German East Africa, where he served until the cessation of hostilities. He was engaged throughout on important duties in connection with his Corps, and after suffering from malaria was invalided home, and subsequently discharged as medically unfit for further duty in April 1919. He holds the 1914-15 Star, and the General Service and Victory Medals.
70, Bramber Road, W. Kensington, W.14.   16230

TONGUE, W., Gunner, R.G.A.
He volunteered in August 1915, and in April of the following year was drafted to France and served on the Ancre, and at Arras, Vimy Ridge, Messines, Ypres, and Passchendaele. He was gassed at Ypres in 1917, and wounded at Cambrai during the Advance of the following year. In March 1919 he was demobilised, and holds the General Service and Victory Medals.
9, Burns Road, Battersea, S.W.11.   Z4617

TONKIN, H., Rifleman, King's Royal Rifle Corps.
He joined in May 1917, and in the same year was drafted overseas. During his service in France he fought at Arras, Menin Road, the Scarpe, and the Sambre, and after the Armistice proceeded to Germany with the Army of Occupation, remaining abroad until January 1920, when he returned to England and was demobilised. He holds the General Service and Victory Medals.
46, Eastcote Street, Stockwell Green, S.W.9.   Z4618

TONKINS, J. H., Driver, R.F.A.
He volunteered in April 1915, and sailed for France in the following October. He did good work as a driver at Loos, and on the Somme, and in several other engagements. Whilst on leave early in 1917 he was taken ill and was invalided to hospital, and after receiving treatment was discharged as medically unfit for further service in March 1918. He holds the 1914-15 Star, and the General Service and Victory Medals.
16, Cator Street, Peckham, S.E.15.   Z4688

TOOKE, W., Corporal, R.M.L.I.
He was mobilised in August 1914, and in the following month was sent to Belgium, where he served at Antwerp with the Naval Division. In February 1915 he was drafted to the Dardanelles and took part in the Landing at Suvla Bay, and in the second Battle of Krithia, when he was wounded. He was sent to hospital in Egypt, and after receiving treatment there for about three months was invalided to hospital in England. On recovery he served for a time on home defence duties, and in March 1919, was discharged as physically unfit for further service having lost the use of his left hand. He holds the 1914 Star, and the General Service and Victory Medals.
55, Lillieshall Road, Clapham, S.W.4.   Z4619

TOOP, A., Private, Royal Sussex Regiment.
He joined in April 1918, and after the completion of his training was sent to Germany with the Army of Occupation. Whilst overseas he was engaged on important garrison and other duties until April 1920, when he returned to England and was discharged.
4, Gaskell Street, Larkhall Lane, S.W.4.   Z4620

TOOP, C. A., Sergt., M.G.C.
He was mobilised at the outbreak of hostilities, and in the same year was drafted to France. During his service on the Western Front he fought with distinction in numerous engagements, and was wounded three times. He returned home after the conclusion of the war, was demobilised in March 1919, holding the 1914 Star, and the General Service and Victory Medals.
50, Priory Grove, Lansdowne Road, S.W.8.   Z4621B

TOOP, T. W., Stoker, R.N., H.M.S. "Leander."
He joined in 1916, and after his training was posted to H.M.S. "Leander" and served with the Grand Fleet in the North Sea under Admirals Jellicoe and Beatty, until the conclusion of hostilities. His ship was engaged in many encounters with the enemy, and he did excellent work throughout his service. He was discharged in 1919, and holds the General Service and Victory Medals.
50, Priory Grove, Lansdowne Road, S.W.8.   Z4621A

TOOTH, M. C. (Miss), Special War Worker.

During the war this lady offered her services for work of National importance, and was engaged at Messrs. Hewlett and Blondeau's Aeroplane Works at Leagrave, Bedfordshire. Her duties consisted in the splicing and upholstering of aeroplane parts, and she rendered valuable services until June 1920, when she relinquished her post after over three years' service.

71, Blake's Road, Peckham, S.E.15.   Z6105B

TOPHAM, T. H., A.B., Royal Navy.

He was mobilised in August 1914, and in the same month was sent to the North Sea, where he served with the Grand Fleet in numerous engagements. He also was present during the attempted forcing of the Dardanelles. He was afterwards transferred to the Mercantile Marine, and was posted to a minesweeper, and did excellent work until November 1919, when he was demobilised. He holds the 1914–15 Star, and the General Service and Victory Medals.

26, Melon Road, Peckham, S.E.15.   Z6098

TOPPING, A. G., Private, 37th Royal Fusiliers.

He joined in June 1916, and was almost immediately drafted to the Western Front. During his service in France he fought at Albert, the Somme, Arras, Bullecourt, and Cambrai, and in many later engagements in the Retreat and Advance of 1918, and was with the troops at the entry into Mons on Armistice Day. He was demobilised in April 1919, and holds the General Service and Victory Medals.

257, Mayall Road, Herne Hill, S.E.24.   Z3997A. Z3998A

TORODE, A., C.S.M., Royal Munster Fusiliers.

He had previously served throughout the South African War, and in February 1915 voluntarily re-enlisted. Whilst in France he saw active service in various sectors, and was promoted from Private to the rank of Company Sergeant-Major in recognition of his excellent work. He was demobilised in May 1919, and holds the Queen's and King's South African Medals, and the General Service and Victory Medals.

28, Bayonne Road, Fulham, W.6.   14507

TORODE, W., Gunner, R.G.A.

He joined in November 1917, having previously served in the Boer War, but on account of being medically unfit for duty abroad was not sent overseas. He rendered valuable service, however, at various anti-aircraft stations, with his unit until January 1919, when he was demobilised. He holds the Queen's and King's South African Medals.

51, Parkstone Road, Peckham, S.E.15.   Z5683

TOSDEVINE, J., Gunner, R.G.A.

He was mobilised at the outbreak of war, and was almost immediately drafted to France where he took part in the Retreat from Mons. He was also in action at Ypres, Vimy Ridge, Béthune, Lens, Bapaume, and many other engagements up to the signing of the Armistice in November 1918. He was demobilised in the following March, and holds the Mons Star, and the General Service and Victory Medals.

15, Danson Road, Walworth, S.E.17.   Z27022

TOSSELL, J., Private, Royal Fusiliers.

He joined in 1916, and in the same year was drafted to France and took part in the heavy fighting in the Battle of the Somme. He was severely wounded at Albert in 1916, and invalided home to hospital, where he underwent prolonged medical treatment. He was demobilised in May 1919, and holds the General Service and Victory Medals.

30, Thurlow Street, Walworth, S.E.17.   Z4622

TOTHAM, H., Driver, R.E.

He volunteered in August 1914, having previously fought in the Boer War, and was drafted to Egypt in the following year. Whilst in this theatre of war he was engaged on important duties at Alexandria, and Cairo, and in the Suez Canal zone, and at Kantara. Later he served in the British Offensive in Palestine, and was present at the Battles of Gaza and at the Fall of Jerusalem. He returned to England and was demobilised in 1919, and holds the Queen's and King's South African Medals, and the 1914–15 Star, the General Service and Victory Medals.

7, The Triangle, Clapham, S.W.4.   Z4623

TOTMAN, W., Driver, R.F.A.

He volunteered in 1914, and in September of that year was drafted to France, and did excellent work as a driver in many early engagements, including those at La Bassée, Ypres, Hill 60, and Festubert. He was severely wounded in the vicinity of Ypres in February 1916, and was sent home to hospital. After receiving medical treatment for about a year, he was invalided out of the Service in April 1917. He holds the 1914 Star, and the General Service and Victory Medals.

95C, Tappesfield Road, Peckham, S.E.15.   Z6510

TOWLER, B., Private, R.A.S.C. (M.T.)

Mobilised at the outbreak of war he was drafted to the Western Front and served at the Retreat from Mons and the Battle of Neuve Chapelle. Later he was attached to the Headquarters Staff as a despatch rider until November 1915, when he was sent to Mesopotamia. Here he was present at engagements at Kut and Baghdad, and was wounded. After the cessation of hostilities he returned to England, and in May 1919 was demobilised, holding the Mons Star, and the General Service and Victory Medals.

22, Selden Road, Nunhead, S.E.15.   Z6671

TOWN, F., R.S.M., R.A.S.C.

Volunteering in August 1915 he was sent overseas in the same year, and whilst in France was engaged on important duties in connection with Canteens at various places including Etaples, where he was stationed during the severe enemy air raids. In 1919 he was sent to Boulogne, where he remained until May of the following year, when he returned home and was demobilised. He holds the 1914–15 Star, and the General Service and Victory Medals.

33, Langton Street, Brixton, S.W.9.   Z5160

TOWNS, E. W. H., Private, Queen's (Royal West Surrey Regiment).

He joined in September 1916, and in the following year proceeded to France, where he served for part of his time on important duties as a stretcher bearer until early in 1918, when he was drafted to Italy for a short period. He returned to the Western Front in the same year, and fought in the Retreat and Advance of 1918 until the cessation of hostilities. He was demobilised in March of the following year, and holds the General Service and Victory Medals.

57E, Lewis Trust Buildings, Camberwell, S.E.5.   Z6460

TOWNS, H., Gunner, R.F.A.

He was mobilised at the outbreak of hostilities, and was almost immediately drafted to France where he took part in the Retreat from Mons. During the whole period of the war he remained on the Western Front, and was in action in many engagements, and was wounded. In March 1919 he was demobilised, and holds the Mons Star, and the General Service and Victory Medals.

60, Rayleigh Road, West Kensington, W.14.   12423

TOWNSEND, A. C. (D.C.M.), Private, Royal Scots Fusiliers.

He was mobilised at the outbreak of war, and was almost immediately drafted to France, where he was in action in the Retreat from Mons. He took part also in the Battles of the Marne, the Aisne, Ypres, St. Eloi, Hill 60, Hooge, Ploegsteert Wood, and was severely wounded. He was invalided home to hospital, and after his recovery rejoined his unit in France in January 1917, and subsequently fought at Messines, Ypres, Passchendaele, and in many engagements in the Retreat and Advance of 1918. He was mentioned in Despatches for his courage and devotion to duty at Hooge when he held single-handed the fifth line of German trenches, and was also awarded the Distinguished Conduct Medal for this gallant deed. After the Armistice he proceeded to Germany with the Army of Occupation, and was stationed on the Rhine until demobilised in March 1919. He holds in addition to the Distinguished Conduct Medal, the Mons Star, and the General Service and Victory Medals.

105, Cator Street, Peckham, S.E.15.   Z4689

TOWNSEND, C., Bandsman, South Staffordshire Regt.

A serving soldier since January 1913, he was sent overseas in 1917, and took part in heavy fighting in the Somme sector, and was severely wounded. After eighteen months' medical treatment in hospital he recovered, and in 1920 was still serving, being stationed in Ireland. He holds the General Service and Victory Medals.

31, Broomsgrove Road, Stockwell Road, S.W.9.   Z5203B

TOWNSEND, D., Private, 1st East Surrey Regt.

He volunteered in August 1914, and shortly afterwards was drafted to France, and fought in the first Battle of Ypres, where he was wounded. He was sent home to hospital, and after treatment rejoined his unit on the Western Front, and was again wounded in action. He gave his life for the freedom of England in an engagement in 1915, and was entitled to the 1914 Star, and the General Service and Victory Medals.

"His life for his Country, his Soul to God."

31, Broomsgrove Road, Stockwell Road, S.W.9.   Z5203A

TOWNSEND, J. W., Driver, 1st East Surrey Regt.

He volunteered in 1914, and in the same year was drafted to France, where he took part in many engagements in the Ypres, Somme and Arras sectors. In 1916 he was sent to Italy and did good work as a driver until the cessation of hostilities, notably in the operations on the Piave and the Asiago Plateau. He returned home and was demobilised in 1919, and holds the 1914 Star, and the General Service and Victory Medals.

31, Broomsgrove Road, Stockwell Road, S.W.9.   Z5203C

TOWNSEND, J., Sergt., East Surrey, Regiment.
A serving soldier since March 1909, he was stationed in India at the outbreak of war and was drafted to France in September 1914. He was in action at Ypres and Festubert, where he was wounded, and after his recovery he again fought and was wounded at the Capture of Vimy Ridge in March 1917. On rejoining his unit he served in the Retreat and Advance and was a third time severely wounded in August 1918. He was invalided home to hospital, and was discharged as medically unfit for further duty in November of the same year. He holds the 1914 Star, and the General Service and Victory Medals.
72, Flaxman Road, Camberwell, S.E.5. Z6233

TOWNSEND, S. C., Private, 22nd Middlesex and The Queen's (Royal West Surrey) Regiments.
He volunteered in July 1915, and was drafted to France in the following year and fought in numerous engagements, including those at High Wood and Ploegsteert, being engaged on important bombing and patrol work. He was also in action at Messines, Bullecourt, and at Passchendaele, rendering valuable services. In November 1917 he was sent to Italy and was engaged in the offensive on the Piave and other operations on that Front. After the cessation of hostilities he returned to England and in March 1919 was demobilised, holding the General Service and Victory Medals.
67, Cornbury Road, Rotherhithe, S.E.16. Z6789

TOWNSEND, W. J., Pte., 4th East Surrey Regt.
Volunteering in December 1914, he embarked for France in the following year, and whilst overseas saw much active service. He fought in the engagements at St. Eloi, Albert, Vimy Ridge and Passchendaele, and in September 1917 was drafted to Italy, where he was in action on the Piave. He then returned to the Western Front in January 1918, and served in the second Battles of the Somme and Cambrai. He was demobilised in February 1919, and holds the 1914-15 Star, and the General Service and Victory Medals.
31, Broomsgrove Road, Stockwell Road, S.W.9. Z4690

TOWNSEND, W. R., Pte., 8th East Surrey Regt.
He volunteered in September 1914, and was later drafted to India. In 1916 he was sent to Burmah, where he was engaged on important duties with his unit. He remained there until he was invalided home through ill-health and discharged as medically unfit in September 1918, holding the General Service and Victory Medals.
67, Cornbury Road, Rotherhithe, S.E.16. Z6790

TOZE, E., Sapper, R.E.
He was mobilised at the outbreak of hostilities and was almost immediately drafted to France and served in the Retreat from Mons. He was also present in the engagements at La Bassée, Ypres, Neuve Chapelle, Albert, the Somme, Arras, Cambrai and in many subsequent operations in the Retreat and Advance of 1918. In February 1919 he was demobilised, and holds the Mons Star, and the General Service and Victory Medals.
11, Little Manor Street, Clapham, S.W.4. Z4625

TOZEE, C. G., Sergt., King's Own (Royal Lancaster Regiment).
He was mobilised at the outbreak of hostilities, and was almost immediately sent overseas and fought in the Retreat from Mons. He was also in action at La Bassée and in the first Battle of Ypres and died gloriously on the Field at Armentières on May 28th, 1915. He was entitled to the Mons Star, and the General Service and Victory Medals.
"He died the noblest death a man may die."
Fighting for God, and right, and liberty."
10, Stockwell Green, S.W.9. Z4624

TOZER, A. G., Pte., 22nd London Regt. (The Queen's).
He volunteered in February 1916, and in the following year embarked for France. Whilst overseas he was engaged on important signalling duties at Cambrai, St. Quentin and Amiens, and in various operations which followed in the Advance of 1918, and was wounded. He was demobilised in January 1919, and holds the General Service and Victory Medals.
24, Porson Street, Wandsworth Road, S.W.8. Z4626

TOZER, F., Corporal, R.A.F.
He volunteered in August 1914, and after his training was sent to Gallipoli in the Seaplane Carrier "Ben-ma-Chree," which was afterwards sunk off the Turkish Coast in January 1917. He took part in the bombardment of Dedeagatch in January 1916, and was transferred to the "Arcadian" in April 1917, after a period in hospital. His ship was torpedoed in the same month, and he was then sent to England, where he remained until posted to H.M.S. "Louvain." In January 1918 his vessel was again torpedoed in the Ægean Sea, but he was fortunately rescued, and served, until demobilised, in March 1919, at various stations in the Balkan Peninsula. He holds the 1914-15 Star, and the General Service and Victory Medals.
98, Winstanley Road, Battersea, S.W.11. Z4627

TOZER, E. A., Drummer, City of London Volunteers.
He volunteered in 1916, and rendered valuable service with the City of London Volunteers at their Headquarters at St. Bride Street, London, until discharged in 1918.
6, Arlesford Road, Stockwell, S.W9. Z3342B

TOZER, J., Private, 8th Norfolk Regiment.
He volunteered in November 1914, and sailed for France in the following January. Whilst overseas he fought at Hill 60, Ypres, the Somme (where he was wounded), and Bullecourt, and was again wounded in the Battle of Messines. He rejoined his Regiment in time to take part in the fighting at Passchendaele in July 1917, and was also in action at the second Battle of the Somme and at Le Cateau. In February 1919 he was demobilised, and holds the 1914-15 Star, and the General Service and Victory Medals.
57, Cronin Road, Peckham, S.E.15. Z5629A

TRACEY, W. E., Rifleman, 8th London Regiment (Post Office Rifles).
He joined in September 1916, and was drafted in the same month to France, where he served with the R.E. in many sectors of the Front, especially at Ypres, the Somme and Arras, until hostilities ceased. He was demobilised in October 1919 after returning home, and holds the General Service and Victory Medals.
1, Russell Street, Battersea, S.W.11. Z4628

TRAER, J. T., Aircraftsman, R.A.F.
Volunteering in December 1915, he was retained on the completion of his training at Cranwell and various other stations with his unit. He was principally engaged in fitting the machines with wireless apparatus. He rendered valuable services, but was not successful in obtaining his transfer overseas before the conclusion of hostilities. He was demobilised in March 1919.
56, Cranham Road, Rotherhithe, S.E.16. Z6672

TRANGMAR, H. J. F., O.S., Royal Navy.
Volunteering in 1915, he was posted after his training to H.M.S. "Raglan," and while with this ship took an active part in the Dardanelles Expedition. He was also engaged in the North Sea and off the Belgian Coast on important convoy duties. In August 1915 he was accidentally drowned and was entitled to the 1914-15 Star, and the General Service and Victory Medals.
"His memory is cherished with pride."
24, Faraday Street, Walworth, S.E.17. Z27462B

TRANGMAR, R. S., Bombardier, R.F.A. and R.G.A.
Volunteering in 1915 he was drafted in the following year to the Western Front, and whilst in this theatre of war took part in the fighting at the Somme, Cambrai, and in the Retreat and Advance of 1918. In 1919 he returned to England, and was demobilised, holding the General Service and Victory Medals.
24, Faraday Street, Walworth, S.E.17. Z27462A

TRANTER, A. J., Gunner, R.F.A.
He volunteered in April 1915, and in the following October embarked for France, where he was in action in many important engagements. He died gloriously on the Field of Battle at Poperinghe in July 1917, where he was buried, and was entitled to the 1914-15 Star, and the General Service and Victory Medals.
"Whilst we remember, the Sacrifice is not in vain."
67, Duffield Street, Battersea, S.W.11. Z4629

TRAVERS, A. L. R., L/Corporal, R.A.S.C. (M.T.)
Volunteering in 1914, he was drafted after the completion of his training to France, where he was engaged for over four years in many sectors of the Front. He did valuable work in the conveyance of supplies of all kinds by motor transport until he returned to England for his demobilisation in 1919. He holds the 1914-15 Star, and the General Service and Victory Medals.
13, Montgomery Road, Chiswick, W.4. 6903A

TRAVERS, C. F., Sergt., Canadian Pioneers (1st Contingent).
He volunteered in 1915, and after his training proceeded to France. Whilst in this theatre of war he took part in many notable engagements, but, unfortunately, contracted fever. On his recovery he was transferred to the Canadian Postal Section, where he served until demobilised in 1919. He holds the General Service and Victory Medals.
13, Montgomery Road, Chiswick, W.4. 6903C

TRAYNOR, P., Guardsman, Irish Guards.
He volunteered in 1914, and after crossing to the Western Front, saw much heavy fighting in many parts of the line. He took part in the Battles of Neuve Chapelle, Loos, the Somme, Arras, Ypres, Armentières and Cambrai, and was also in action in the Retreat and Advance of 1918. After the cessation of hostilities he was sent with the Army of Occupation into Germany, and was stationed at Cologne. He holds the 1914-15 Star, and the General Service and Victory Medals. and was still serving with his unit in 1920.
24, Archel Road, West Kensington, W.14. 16484

TREADWELL, F. G., Rifleman, 9th London Regt. (Queen Victoria's Rifles).

He joined in October 1916, and after the completion of his training crossed to France in the following January. He took part in much severe fighting from that date until the cessation of hostilities, and was present at the Battles of Ypres and Albert and in the Retreat and Advance of 1918. During his service he was wounded on one occasion. After returning home he was demobilised in April 1919, and holds the General Service and Victory Medals.

6, Barmore Street, Battersea, S.W.11. Z4630

TREANOR, F., Q.M. and Hon. Captain, Northumberland Fusiliers.

Mobilised at the outbreak of war, he proceeded overseas in the following January. Whilst in France he took part in the Battles of the Somme and Ypres, and was gassed and invalided to hospital in England. On his recovery he returned to his unit and was in action at Cambrai and in the Advance of 1918. He was afterwards stationed at Le Havre until demobilised in November 1919. He holds the 1914-15 Star, and the General Service and Victory Medals.

41, Elmington Road, Camberwell, S.E.5. Z4631

TREAVISH, J., Private, 3rd Middlesex Regiment.

He volunteered in October 1914, and in the following August was sent to France, where he served for a time and was in action at Loos. Afterwards he was drafted to the East and took part in the fighting on the Vardar, Doiran and Struma fronts, and was present at the Capture of Monastir. He returned home in March 1919, and was demobilised, holding the 1914-15 Star, and the General Service and Victory Medals.

18, Blewitt Street, Walworth, S.E.17. Z4634

TREAYS, E., Private, 19th London Regiment.

He volunteered in 1915, and in the following year was drafted to the Balkans and took part in the fighting on the Doiran front. Later he was engaged with General Allenby's Forces in the Advance from Egypt into Palestine and was present at the Battles of Gaza, the Entry into Jerusalem, and the Capture of Aleppo. He afterwards served in Egypt until demobilised in October 1919. He holds the General Service and Victory Medals.

22, McKerrell Road, Peckham, S.E.15. Z6100

TREDWIN, A., Private, 11th Royal Fusiliers.

Volunteering in October 1914, he embarked in the following year for France, after the completion of his training, and fought in the Ypres and Arras sectors. He was unhappily killed when going into action on the Somme on July 1st, 1916, and was buried near Albert. He was entitled to the 1914-15 Star, and the General Service and Victory Medals.

"He died the noblest death a man may die,
Fighting for God, and right, and liberty."

3, Mordaunt Street, Stockwell, S.W.9. Z4632

TREE, A., Private, 2nd South Lancashire Regt.

He enlisted in 1912, and being drafted to France at the outbreak of war fought in the memorable Retreat from Mons and in the Battles of the Marne and the Aisne. He was reported missing after the fighting at La Bassée, but was later presumed to have been killed in action there on October 24th, 1914. He was entitled to the Mons Star, and the General Service and Victory Medals.

"His life for his Country, his Soul to God."

20, Myatt Road, Stockwell, S.W.9. Z5039B

TREE, J. G., Private, Queen's (Royal West Surrey Regiment).

He volunteered in August 1914, and in the following year after completing his training was drafted to the Western Front, where he saw much active service in the Ypres, Somme, and Arras sectors, and in other engagements until hostilities ceased. He was demobilised in February 1919, and holds the 1914-15 Star, and the General Service and Victory Medals.

64, Howbury Road, Nunhead, S.E.15. Z6588B

TREVENNA, W., Rifleman, 21st London Regiment (1st Surrey Rifles).

He volunteered in August 1914, and in the same year embarked for France, where he served for about three months. He was then drafted to the East and saw much active service in Salonika, Mesopotamia, Egypt and Palestine, and was wounded. He also suffered from malaria whilst in the East. He returned home and was demobilised in July 1919, and holds the 1914-15 Star, and the General Service and Victory Medals.

69, The Grove, South Lambeth, S.W.8. Z4633

TREW, H. P., L/Corporal, R.E.

Volunteering in August 1914, he proceeded to France on the completion of his training, and was in action on the Somme and at Arras, and was wounded. He was invalided home, but on his recovery in 1918 returned to the fighting area and took part in the Retreat and Advance of that year. He was unfortunately taken ill again and sent home, and on August 8th, 1919, died. He was entitled to the General Service and Victory Medals.

"Whilst we remember, the Sacrifice is not in vain."

149, St. George's Road, Peckham, S.E.15. Z5848

TRIANCE, G. T., Pte., Loyal North Lancashire Regt.

He volunteered in September 1914, and in the following year was sent to France, where he took part in the fierce fighting at Ypres and Loos. In 1916 he was transferred to Egypt, and joining the expedition into Palestine, was engaged in the operations preceding the entry into Jerusalem and the Battle of Jericho. In 1918 he returned to France and served in the Retreat and Advance of that year. During his service overseas he was three times wounded. He was demobilised in December 1918, and holds the 1914-15 Star, and the General Service and Victory Medals.

28, Alfreton Street, Walworth, S.E.17. Z4635

TRIANCE, J. R., Private, 2nd Queen's (Royal West Surrey Regiment).

He was serving at the outbreak of war and was immediately sent to France, where he was in action at Mons, the Marne, the Aisne, La Bassée, Ypres, Loos, Albert, the Somme, Vimy Ridge, Arras, Lens and Cambrai. He took part in the Retreat and Advance of 1918. He was demobilised in January 1919 after returning home, and holds the Mons Star, and the General Service and Victory Medals.

28, Alfreton Street, Walworth, S.E.17. Z4636

TRIANCE, W. H., Rifleman, Rifle Brigade and Pte., M.G.C.

He joined in February 1917, and in the same month was sent to France, where he took part in the Battles of Passchendaele and Cambrai, and in the Retreat and Advance of 1918. He was demobilised in September 1919, after returning home, and holds the General Service and Victory Medals.

23, Alfreton Street, Walworth, S.E.17. Z4637

TRIGG, F., Rifleman, 15th London Regiment (Civil Service Rifles).

He volunteered in November 1915, and in the following year was sent to Salonika. After much service there he was transferred to Egypt, and afterwards to Palestine, where he was in action at Gaza and on the Jordan. He also served in the Advance on Jerusalem, under General Allenby, and was wounded. In 1918 he proceeded to the Western Front, and took part in the Retreat and Advance of that year. He was demobilised in November 1918, and holds the General Service and Victory Medals.

14, Edithna Street, Stockwell, S.W.9. Z4638

TRIGGS, A. A., Private, 5th Middlesex Regiment.

He joined in February 1917, and in the following April was drafted to the Western Front, where he was in action at Arras, Vimy Ridge, Messines, Ypres, Lens and Cambrai, and was severely wounded. After a period of hospital treatment and convalescence he was discharged as medically unfit for further service in March 1919, and holds the General Service and Victory Medals.

96, Westmoreland Road, Walworth, S.E.17. Z4639

TRIGGS, H. (M.S.M.), 1st Class Air Mechanic, R.A.F. (late R.F.C.)

He volunteered in 1915, and later in the same year proceeded to France, where he was engaged at Albert, the Somme, Messines, Ypres and Armentières. In 1918 he was transferred to Italy, and served on the Piave front. He was employed as a wireless operator attached to the R.F.A. and while in France was awarded the Meritorious Service Medal for consistent work and devotion to duty on the Somme in 1916. He also holds the 1914-15 Star, and the General Service and Victory Medals, and was demobilised in January 1919.

122, Kimberley Road, Peckham, S.E.15. Z6511A

TRIGGS, W. J., 1st Class Air Mechanic, R.A.F.

He joined in 1917, and after completing his training was engaged at various stations on important duties with his Squadron. He was employed as a draughtsman, and rendered valuable service, but was not successful in obtaining his transfer overseas, before the cessation of hostilities. He was demobilised in October 1919.

122, Kimberley Road, Peckham, S.E.15. Z6511B

TRIMLETT, H. J., Special War Worker.
Throughout the period of the war he was engaged at Messrs. Shaw and Kilburn's, Wardour Street, in the manufacture of parts for aero-engines, and in shell making. His duties, which demanded a high degree of technical skill, were carried out with great efficiency, and he rendered valuable services.
49, Lillieshall Road, Clapham, S.W.4. Z4640

TRIMMINGS, W. A., Private, Loyal North Lancashire Regiment.
He was serving at the outbreak of war, and was immediately sent to France, where he was in action at Mons, Neuve Chapelle, Vimy Ridge, the Somme, Arras, Passchendaele, and the Retreat and Advance of 1918. He was wounded at Cambrai in October, and invalided home. He was discharged in March 1919, in consequence of his wounds, and holds the Mons Star, and the General Service and Victory Medals.
57, Dashwood Road, Wandsworth, Road, S.W.8. Z4641

TRINDER, D. F., Private, R.M.L.I.
He was serving in the North Sea, when war broke out, and in August 1915 was on board the armed liner "India," when she was torpedoed. He also served on a mine-laying trawler. He afterwards was taken prisoner near Norway, and was detained there for three years. During this period he rendered valuable services at the British Consulate, and after the Armistice was engaged with the International Commission in Slesvig. He was demobilised in July 1920, and holds the 1914-15 Star, and the General Service and Victory Medals.
23, Pearman Street, Westminster Bridge Road, S.E.1. TZ24662

TRINDER, E. J., Rifleman, Rifle Brigade.
He volunteered in March 1915, and after completing his training was drafted to France, where he was in action in the Somme and Ypres sectors. After much gallant work he was sent home and discharged in October 1916 in consequence of his services, and holds the 1914-15 Star, and the General Service and Victory Medals.
3, Zulu Cottages, Ship Lane, Hammersmith, W.6. 13794

TRODD, G. J., Rifleman, 8th Rifle Brigade.
He volunteered in April 1915, and in the following year was drafted to France, where he took part in the severe fighting on the Somme. He was reported missing on October 23rd, 1916, after but a few weeks' service overseas, and was presumed to have been killed in action on that date. He was entitled to the General Service and Victory Medals.
"Whilst we remember, the Sacrifice is not in vain."
2, Sussex Grove, Loughborogh Park, S.W.9. Z4454B

TRODD, W., Private, R.A.S.C. (M.T.)
He volunteered in January 1915, and in the same month was sent to France. He was engaged on important transport duties in connection with numerous engagements, including those at Neuve Chapelle, Hill 60, Festubert, Loos, Albert, Vermelles, Ploegsteert Wood, Vimy Ridge, and the Somme, where he was blown up near an ammunition dump. He was invalided home with shell-shock which affected his memory, and was discharged as medically unfit for further services in August 1917. He holds the 1914-15 Star, and the General Service and Victory Medals.
2, Eaton Road, Loughborough Park, S.W.9. Z4691

TROKE, H. O., Rifleman, Rifle Brigade.
Joining in October 1916, he was engaged with his unit on important duties until February 1918, when he was sent to France. He was wounded and taken prisoner in the following month during the Retreat. On his release he returned home and was later drafted to India, where he was still serving in 1920. He holds the General Service and Victory Medals.
10, Alfreton Street, Walworth, S.E.17. Z4642B

TROKE, R. W., Rifleman, Rifle Brigade.
He joined in September 1918, on attaining military age, and after his training was engaged at various stations on important duties with his unit. He rendered valuable services, but was not successful in obtaining his transfer overseas owing to his medical unfitness. He was demobilised in November 1919.
10, Alfreton Street, Walworth, S.E.17. Z4642A

TROOD, C. W. C., Sergt., R.F.A.
Volunteering in 1914, he was speedily drafted to the Western Front, where he took a prominent part in various engagements, including those at the Somme, Courbraix and Villers Bretonneux. Shortly afterwards he proceeded to Salonika, and saw much active service on the Vardar and Doiran fronts, and was wounded and invalided to Malta. On his recovery he returned to Salonika and remained there until April 1919, when he was demobilised. He holds the 1914-15 Star, and the General Service and Victory Medals.
82, Inville Road, Walworth, S.E.17. Z27300

TROTT, G. W., Captain's Steward, R.N., H.M.S. "Galatea," "Paxton," and Mystery Ship Q "25"
He was serving at the outbreak of war, and was engaged with the Grand Fleet in the North Sea, in which he took part in the Battles of Heligoland Bight and Jutland, and in other important engagements. He was on board H.M.S. "Paxton" when that vessel was torpedoed by an enemy submarine off the Irish Coast, the captain and officers being taken prisoners and the remainder of the crew being sunk on March 20th, 1917. He was entitled to the 1914-15 Star, and the General Service and Victory Medals.
"His life for his Country."
1A, Combermere Road, Stockwell, S.W.9. Z4643

TROUGHTON, A. E., 1st Air Mechanic, R.A.F.
He joined in 1916, and after his training was engaged with his Squadron on important duties. He was employed on clerical work and rendered valuable services, but was not successful in obtaining his transfer overseas before the cessation of hostilities, owing to his medical unfitness. He was demobilised in 1919.
75, Philip Road, Peckham, S.E.15. Z6094

TROUGHTON, G. W., L/Cpl., King's Royal Rifle Corps.
Joining in May 1916, he was sent to France in October of the same year, after completing his training, and was in action at Arras, Vimy Ridge, Messines, Ypres, Passchendaele, Lens and Cambrai, where he was taken prisoner, and sent to Germany. On his release he returned home and was demobilised in December 1919, holding the General Service and Victory Medals. 52, Cornbury Street, Walworth, S.E.17. Z4644-5B

TROUGHTON, H. J., Rflmn., King's Royal Rifle Corps.
He volunteered in April 1915, and later in the same year, after the completion of his training, was sent to France, where he took part in numerous engagements, and was wounded. He served in the Retreat and Advance of 1918, and after the Armistice he proceeded to Germany, and later to Russia. On his return home he was sent to Ireland, where he was still serving in 1920. He holds the 1914-15 Star, and the General Service and Victory Medals.
52, Cornbury Street, Walworth, S.E.17. Z4644-5A

TROWER, F. G., Driver, R.F.A.
He was mobilised from the Reserve in August 1914, and was immediately sent to France, where he took part in the fighting in the Retreat from Mons and at Ypres, St. Eloi, Hill 60, Albert, the Somme and Vimy Ridge. He was badly wounded at Ypres in 1917, and lost his arm in consequence. He was invalided home and discharged on April 1st, 1920, owing to his disability, holding the Mons Star, and the General Service and Victory Medals.
96, Wycliffe Road, Battersea, S.W.11. Z4646

TRUE, L., Gunner, R.F.A.
He volunteered in August 1914, and in the following year was drafted to France, where he took part in the fighting at Ypres, the Somme and the Ancre. Later he was wounded and invalided home, but on his recovery returned to France, where he was taken prisoner in May 1917, and sent to Germany. On his release he returned home and was demobilised in 1919, holding the 1914-15 Star, and the General Service and Victory Medals.
101, Eugenia Road, Rotherhithe, S.E.16. Z6810

TRUE, T. W., Private, 5th Leicestershire Regiment.
He volunteered in October 1915, and after completing his training was drafted to the Western Front, where he took a prominent part in numerous engagements of importance right up to the cessation of hostilities. He was demobilised in February 1919, after returning home, and holds the General Service and Victory Medals.
8, Hawksmoor Street, Hammersmith, W.6. 14273

TRUELOVE, W. A., 1st Air Mechanic, R.A.F.
He joined in July 1917, and after his training was engaged in Scotland on important duties with his Squadron. His work, which demanded a high degree of technical skill was carried out with great efficiency and he rendered valuable services, but was not successful in obtaining his transfer overseas before the cessation of hostilities owing to his medical unfitness. He was demobilised in February 1919
47, Vicarage Road, Camberwell, S.E.5. Z4647

TRUSLOW, H. G. T. (M.M.), Private, M.G.C.
Joining in May 1916, he went through his course of training, and subsequently proceeded to France. After taking part in many engagements of importance he was severely wounded at Passchendaele. On his recovery after hospital treatment in England he was transferred to the R.A.O.C., in which he did valuable service until demobilised in February 1919. He was awarded the Military Medal for conspicuous gallantry in the Field at Passchendaele, and also holds the General Service and Victory Medals.
15, Cornick Street, Rotherhithe, S.E.16. Z6813

TRUSSLER, A. E., Gunner, R.F.A.
He joined in 1918, and after his training was engaged on important duties at various stations until February 1920, when he was drafted to India and served in Secunderabad.
29, Crimsworth Road, Wandsworth Road, S.W.8.   Z4648A

TRUSSLER, J. C., Private, M.G.C.
He joined in 1916, and was drafted to France in the following year. He took part in the Retreat and Advance of 1918, and after the Armistice proceeded to Germany, where he served with the Army of Occupation until 1919, when he returned to England, and was demobilised, holding the General Service and Victory Medals.
29, Crimsworth Road, Wandsworth Road, S.W.8.   Z4649B

TRUSSLER, R. W., A.B., Royal Navy.
Serving at the outbreak of hostilities, having joined in 1913, he was with H.M.S. "Russell" in the Mediterranean station in August 1914. He was engaged on important duties with his ship until he lost his life, when she was sunk on April 27th, 1916. He was entitled to the 1914-15 Star, and the General Service and Victory Medals.
"Whilst we remember, the Sacrifice is not in vain."
29, Crimsworth Road, Wandsworth Road, S.W.8.   Z4649C

TRY, T. E., Private, Middlesex Regt. and R.A.O.C.
Volunteering in January 1915, he was drafted to France later in the same year, and was engaged with his unit on important duties in various sectors of the Front. He was present during a number of the principal battles of the war, and after the cessation of hostilities returned to England, and was demobilised in March 1919, holding the 1914-15 Star, and the General Service and Victory Medals.
68, Rothschild Road, Chiswick, W.4.   6282

TUBBS, W., Sapper, Royal Marine Engineers.
He joined in June 1918, having previously endeavoured to enlist and having been rejected, and after his training was engaged on important duties at various stations. He rendered valuable service but was unable to procure his transfer abroad prior to the conclusion of hostilities. He was demobilised in March 1919.
58, Pulford Street, Pimlico, S.W.1.   Z23237

TUBBY, A. E., Leading Seaman, R.N., H.M.S. "Gretna."
He was serving at the outbreak of war, and proceeded with his ship to the Dardanelles, being present at the Landing of the troops at Gallipoli. Later he was transferred for duty in the North Sea and English Channel, where he was engaged on convoying hospital ships from France. On one occasion his ship was blown up whilst attempting to rescue the survivors of "The Salta," but fortunately he was saved. He also served on mine-sweeping duties in Russian waters for a time. After a total of eighteen years' service he was demobilised in May 1919, holding the Messina Earthquake Medal and the 1914-15 Star, and the General Service and Victory Medals.
42, Dieppe Street, West Kensington, W.14.   X27557

TUBBY, A. H., Leading Seaman, R.N., H.M.S. "Gretna."
He volunteered in 1914, and later was sent with his ship to the Dardanelles and took part in the bombardment of the Turkish positions at Gallipoli. He was afterwards posted for duty with the P26, patrol ship, in the North Sea, and was on board that vessel when she was sunk, but fortunately was rescued and landed at Le Havre, where he was in hospital for some time. On his recovery he served with H.M.S. "Gretna" on mine-sweeping duties. He holds the 1914-15 Star, and the General Service and Victory Medals. and was demobilised in 1919.
42, Dieppe Street, West Kensington, W.14.   16425

TUCK, F., Private, Labour Corps.
He joined in 1917, and was sent to France in that year. He served on the Somme and at Ypres, doing much valuable work, and was also present during the Retreat and Advance of 1918. He was demobilised in December 1919, and holds the General Service and Victory Medals.
35, Bournemouth Road, S.E.15.   Z5842A

TUCKER, E. A., Sergt., R.A.F.
He volunteered in November 1915, and after the completion of his training was drafted to France in the following year. While overseas he rendered valuable services with the 35th Squadron at Arras, and other places, and was badly wounded. He was invalided home in consequence and was still undergoing treatment at Reading Hospital when the Armistice was signed. He was demobilised in February 1919, and holds the General Service and Victory Medals.
36, Oglander Road, Peckham, S.E.15.   Z6807

TUCKER, E. A., Rifleman, Rifle Brigade.
He volunteered in February 1915, and was drafted to France in the following year, and took part in much of the heavy fighting. During this time he was wounded on three occasions, the last being in May 1918, when he was invalided to England and discharged in March 1919, as medically unfit for further service. He holds the General Service and Victory Medals.
117, Spike Road, Battersea, S.W.11.   Z3759B

TUCKER, H. W., 1st Air Mechanic, R.A.F.
He joined in December 1915, and after his training was employed on important work at various stations. In 1917 he proceeded to France and rendered valuable services at various places until after the cessation of hostilities, when he returned to England, and was demobilised in June 1919, holding the General Service and Victory Medals.
44, Granfield Road, Battersea, S.W.11.   Z4650

TUCKER, J. (M.M.), Gunner, R.F.A.
He volunteered in August 1915, and after having completed his training was drafted to France, where he took part in numerous engagements. He was twice mentioned in Despatches for conspicuous gallantry at Ploegsteert, and at Messines, and was awarded the Military Medal for bravery in the Field. He also holds the General Service and Victory Medals, and was demobilised in February 1919.
6, Perrers Road, Hammersmith, W.6.   11133

TUCKER, J. R. H., L/Cpl., 8th Lancashire Fusiliers.
He joined in June 1916, and proceeded to France later in the same year. He took part in much of the heavy fighting in the Ypres sector, and rendered valuable service. Unhappily he was killed in action at Messines in June 1917, and was entitled to the General Service and Victory Medals.
"And doubtless he went in splendid company."
51, Reculver Road, Rotherhithe, S.E.16.   Z6746

TUCKER, W. H., Private, 8th East Surrey Regt.
He joined in July 1917, and proceeded to France in the following year. He fought on the Somme, and at Amiens, Bourlon Wood, Mametz Wood, Albert and Armentières, and did much good work. After the Armistice he returned to England, and was demobilised in April 1920. He holds the General Service and Victory Medals.
117, Spike Road, Battersea, S.W.11.   Z3759A

TUCKWELL, J. T., Private, 21st Canadian Regt.
He volunteered in Canada in September 1914, and after his training proceeded to the Western Front in the following year. Whilst in this theatre of war he took part in many battles, including those on the Somme, and at St. Eloi, and Vimy Ridge, where he was severely wounded, and lost his left arm in consequence. He was in hospital at Ramsgate during the bombardment there, and was discharged in 1917 as medically unfit for further service. He holds the 1914-15 Star, and the General Service and Victory Medals.
17, Shorncliffe Road, Walworth, S.E.17.   Z4651

TUME, E., Pte., Queen's (Royal West Surrey Regt.)
Mobilised at the outbreak of war he immediately proceeded to France, and fought in the Retreat from Mons, and in the Battles of the Marne, the Aisne, La Bassée, Ypres, Neuve Chapelle, St. Eloi, Festubert, Loos, Vimy Ridge, the Somme, Arras, Messines, Passchendaele, and the Retreat and Advance of 1918. He was demobilised in April 1919, after returning home, and holds the Mons Star, and the General Service and Victory Medals.
95, Beckway Street, Walworth, S.E.17.   Z4652

TUNESI, J. (M.M.), Gunner, R.F.A.
Volunteering in August 1914, he embarked in the following July for the Western Front. There he served as a signaller in many important engagements including those on the Somme, at Vimy Ridge, Arras, Ypres, and in the Retreat and Advance of 1918, and was wounded. He was awarded the Military Medal for conspicuous gallantry at Vimy Ridge in April 1917, and in addition holds the 1914-15 Star, and the General Service and Victory Medals. He was demobilised in August 1920.
14, Cross Street, Clapham, S.W.4.   Z4654

TUNESI, R., Gunner, R.F.A.
He joined in 1916, and in the same year was drafted to France where he saw much service on the Somme, at Ypres, Arras, and in various other sectors until hostilities ceased. In 1919 he returned home and was demobilised holding the General Service and Victory Medals.
10, Pleasant Place, Clapham Park, S.W.4.   Z4653

TUNKS, C. G., Pte., Queen's (Royal West Surrey Regt.)
He joined in December 1916, and on the completion of his training was drafted overseas. He saw much active service in many important engagements on various fronts in France and Italy until hostilities ceased, and returned home in February 1919, for demobilisation. He holds the General Service and Victory Medals.
61, Devonshire Road, Chiswick, W.4.   8097

TUNNACLIFFE, J. (M.M.), Sergt., R.F.A.
He volunteered in April 1915, and in the following December embarked for France, where he took a prominent part in many important engagements. He was in action at Cambrai, the Somme, the Ancre, Arras, and the Offensives of 1918, and was once wounded and gassed. In October 1918, he was awarded the Military Medal for conspicuous bravery in the Field at Maubeuge, and also holds the Mons Star, and the General Service and Victory Medals. He was demobilised in July 1919.
58, Darley Road, Battersea, S.W.11. Z4655

TUPPER, H. T., Petty Officer, R.N.
He had been in the Navy for twelve years before the war, and at the outbreak of hostilities was posted to H.M.S. "Monmouth" in the North Sea. His ship took part in the Battle of Coronel, off the Chilian Coast, and on November 1st, 1914, was sunk with all her crew by superior German forces. He was entitled to the 1914–15 Star, the General Service, and Victory Medals, and the Naval Long Service Medal.
"His life for his Country, his Soul to God."
3, Porson Street, Battersea, S.W.8. Z2664B

TURBEN, A. J., Private, 1st Batt. Dorsethire Regt.
Volunteering in August 1914, he crossed in the same year to France, where he took part in many engagements of importance. In 1915 he was drafted to Salonika, and was in action against the Bulgarians. Later he saw much service with the Egyptian Expeditionary Force until hostilities ceased. During his service he was wounded on one occasion. He returned home and was demobilised in July 1919, and holds the 1914 Star, and the General Service and Victory Medals.
2, Hawksmoor Street, Hammersmith, W.6. 14274

TURNBULL, D. E., Private, 2nd London Regt. (Royal Fusiliers).
Mobilised at the outbreak of war he was sent to Egypt in August of the following year, and afterwards was drafted to the Dardanelles, where he saw much active service. After the Evacuation of the Peninsula he proceeded to France, and took part in the Battles of the Somme, Arras, Messines, Cambrai, and in other engagements until hostilities ceased. He was demobilised in March 1919, and holds the 1914–15 Star, and the General Service and Victory Medals.
100, Vaughan Road, Camberwell, S.E.5. Z6345

TURNER, A., Corporal, 2nd Queen's (Royal West Surrey Regiment).
Having previously served in India and South Africa, he was mobilised at the outbreak of war, and quickly proceeded to France where he took part in many engagements until December 1914. He was then unfortunately invalided home through ill-health, but after his recovery served with the Royal Engineers on important constructional work at Chatham, and other stations until demobilised in March 1919. He holds the 1914 Star, and the General Service and Victory Medals.
193, Sumner Road, Peckham, S.E.15. Z6347

TURNER, A., Private, R.A.S.C. (M.T.)
Volunteering in April 1915, he was drafted in the following month to the Western Front, where he was engaged on important transport duties at Neuve Chapelle, Hill 60, Ypres, Festubert, Loos, Albert, and other places until the cessation of hostilities. In June 1919, he was demobilised after much valuable service and holds the 1914–15 Star, and the General Service and Victory Medals.
26, Baker Street, Brixton Road, S.W.9. Z5289

TURNER, A. (M.M.), Cpl., 2nd East Lancashire Regt.
Mobilised at the outbreak of war he was shortly afterwards drafted to France, and there fought in the memorable Retreat from Mons. He was in action in many other engagements including those at Ypres, Neuve Chapelle, Loos, the Somme, Cambrai, and was twice wounded. During the Advance of 1918 he was taken prisoner, and held in captivity until after the Armistice. For conspicuous gallantry in the Field he was awarded the Military Medal, and also holds the Mons Star, and the General Service and Victory Medals. He was demobilised in March 1919.
50, Thorncroft Street, Wandsworth, S.W.8. Z4664

TURNER, A., Sapper, R.E. (I.W.T.)
He joined in 1917, and in the same year embarked for France, where he did valuable transport work on the waterways around Béthune, Armentières, Dunkirk, and Calais until hostilities were concluded. In 1919 he was demobilised after his return home, and holds the General Service and Victory Medals.
13, Ingate Terrace, Queen's Road, S.W.8. Z4659

TURNER, A. E., Private, 2nd Royal Fusiliers.
Mobilised from the Reserve at the outbreak of war he almost immediately proceeded to France, and there took part in the Retreat from Mons. He was also in action on the Somme and at Arras, and was twice wounded. In 1917 he was discharged on account of his injuries, and holds the Mons Star, and the General Service and Victory Medals.
64, Heath Road, Wandsworth Road, S.W.8. Z4674

TURNER, A. W., Rflmn., 12th Royal Irish Rifles.
He joined in August 1917, and in the same year was drafted to the Western Front. There he was in action in the Ypres, Somme, and Arras sectors, and was wounded at Le Cateau on October 25th in the Advance of the Allies. He was invalided home and after receiving hospital treatment was discharged as medically unfit for further service in May 1919. He holds the General Service and Victory Medals.
19, Atwell Street, Peckham, S.E.15. Z5519

TURNER, C., Pte., Queen's (Royal West Surrey Regt).
Joining in March 1917 he embarked for France in the same year, and whilst in this theatre of war took part in many important engagements. He was severely wounded in the second Battle of the Somme, and after being invalided home was discharged as medically unfit in March 1918. He holds the General Service and Victory Medals.
47, Smith Street, Camberwell, S.E.5. Z4670

TURNER, C. E., Corporal, Dorsetshire Regiment.
He volunteered in September 1914, and after his training was drafted to the East. He was in action in Mesopotamia, and also took part with General Allenby's Forces in the Advance through Egypt into Palestine. During his service he was wounded and invalided to India, but on his recovery he returned to Egypt. In June 1919 he came home to be demobilised and holds the General Service and Victory Medals.
76, Sterndale Road, Wandsworth Road, S.W.8. Z4672A

TURNER, C. J. (Sen.), Private, R.A.M.C.
He joined in August 1917, and after his training was engaged at various stations on important duties with his unit. He rendered valuable services but was not successful in obtaining his transfer overseas before the cessation of hostilities. He was demobilised in February 1919.
21, Beaufoy Road, Battersea, S.W.11. Z4656A. Z4657A

TURNER, C. J., L/Corporal, 23rd London Regiment.
Volunteering in August 1915, he was drafted to France in the following March, and whilst in this theatre of war served in many engagements. He was in action at Vimy Ridge, the Somme, Arras, and Passchendaele, and afterwards proceeded to the East. There he saw much fighting, and was later present at the Capture of Jerusalem. He was wounded while in Palestine, and on his recovery was sent to the Western Front, where he did excellent service until demobilised in February 1919. In August he re-enlisted in the 2nd Northamptonshire Regiment, and in 1920 was serving in India. He holds the General Service and Victory Medals.
21, Beaufoy Road, Battersea, S.W.11. Z4656B. Z4657B

TURNER, C. W., Sergt., R.F.A.
He was on Indian service at the outbreak of war, and in September 1915 landed in France, where he afterwards saw much heavy fighting. He was in action at Albert, the Somme, Arras, and Vimy Ridge, and was gassed. He was unfortunately killed in action near Ypres in April 1917, and was entitled to the 1914–15 Star, and the General Service and Victory Medals.
"The path of duty was the way to glory."
12, Flint Street, Walworth, S.E.17. Z4671B

TURNER, D., Sergt., East Lancashire Regiment.
He enlisted in 1906, and at the outbreak of war was immediately sent to France, where he fought in the Retreat from Mons. He was also in action in many other engagements, including those at Ypres, and Neuve Chapelle, Vimy Ridge, and the Somme, and was severely wounded. In 1916 he was discharged on account of his service, but re-enlisted in 1918 for service in Russia. He was awarded the French Military Medal for conspicuous gallantry in the Field, and also holds the Mons Star, and the General Service and Victory Medals.
19, Raywood Street, Battersea Park Road, S.W.8. Z4668

TURNER, E., Special War Worker.
From the beginning of 1915 until the close of the war he was engaged in the works of Messrs. Cole and Sons, Hammersmith, on important duties in the construction of various parts for aeroplanes. He carried out his duties in a highly efficient manner and gave entire satisfaction.
21, Binns Road, Chiswick, W.4. 5369

TURNER, F., Private, 1st and 4th Wiltshire Regt.
He volunteered in October 1914, and shortly afterwards was sent to Egypt where for some months he served at Khartoum. Returning to Lower Egypt he was in action on the Suez Canal in February 1915, and later fought in the Battles of Agayia, Sollum, Jifjaffa, and El Fasher, on the Western Egyptian front. Transferred to the Sinai front he fought at Romani, Magdhaba, and advancing into Palestine, took part in the engagements at Gaza, and in the vicinity of Jerusalem. He saw much fighting in the final British Advance into Syria, and returning home after the cessation of hostilities was demobilised in September 1919. He holds the 1914–15 Star, and the General Service and Victory Medals.
7, Blewett Street, Walworth, S.E.17. Z4667

TURNER, E., Private, R.A.S.C. (M.T.) and the King's Own (Yorkshire Light Infantry).
He volunteered in September 1915, and after his training was retained at various stations on important duties with his unit. He rendered valuable services, but was not successful in obtaining his transfer overseas owing to ill-health. He was discharged as medically unfit for further duty in January 1918.
129, Villa Street, Walworth, S.E.17.　　27451

TURNER, F., Bombardier, R.F.A.
He joined in October 1916, and after a period of training was engaged at Woolwich on important clerical and instructional duties. He rendered valuable services, but was not successful in obtaining his transfer to a fighting front owing to medical unfitness. He was demobilised in November 1919.
50, Liverpool Street, Walworth, S.E.17.　　Z27322

TURNER, F., Private, Suffolk Regiment.
Volunteering in October 1915, he was drafted in the following June to France, where he was engaged in the heavy fighting in the Battles of the Somme, and Arras, and was wounded at Cambrai in 1917. He returned to the line after his recovery and fought gallantly in the Retreat and Advance of 1918. He was unhappily killed in action on September 27th, and was entitled to the General Service and Victory Medals.
"His life for his Country, his Soul to God."
118, Kimberley Road, Peckham, S.E.15.　　Z6512

TURNER, F. H., Rifleman, 18th King's Royal Rifle Corps.
He joined in March 1918, and after a short period of training was sent to France. There he took an active part in the chief engagements of the Retreat and Advance of 1918 until hostilities ceased. He was demobilised in October 1919, after his return home, and holds the General Service and Victory Medals.
41, Park Grove, Battersea, S.W.11.　　Z4616

TURNER, G. A., Rifleman, 13th Rifle Brigade.
Volunteering in 1915 he was drafted in the following year to the Western Front, and fought in many important battles, including those in the Somme, Ypres, and Arras sectors. He was unfortunately killed in action on May 8th, 1918, during the Retreat, and was entitled to the General Service and Victory Medals.
"Great deeds cannot die;
They with the Sun and Moon renew their light for ever."
128, Kirkwood Road, Peckham, S.E.15.　　Z6343

TURNER, G. W., Q.M.S., R.A.M.C.
Volunteering in August 1914, he was retained for a time on important duties in England. In 1916 he crossed to France, and was engaged in tending the sick and wounded at the 54th Hospital, and did valuable work. Whilst overseas he suffered from several attacks of fever. He was demobilised in April 1919, but in July volunteered for service in Russia, where he was promoted to his present rank. He holds the General Service and Victory Medals.
7, Lombard Road, Battersea, S.W.11.　　Z4669

TURNER, G. T., Rflmn., King's Royal Rifle Corps.
Joining in May 1916 he was drafted to France in the following year. Whilst in this theatre of war he was in action on the Somme front, and at Messines, Lens, Passchendaele, Cambrai, and the Retreat and Advance of 1918. After hostilities ceased he was sent with the Army of Occupation into Germany, where he served until demobilised in December 1919. He holds the General Service and Victory Medals.
12, Flint Street, Walworth, S.E.17.　　Z4671A

TURNER, H. H., A.B., Royal Navy.
He joined in September 1917, and was posted to H.M.S. "Cyclops," in which ship he served with the 1st Battle Squadron on important patrol and cruising duties in the North Sea until hostilities ceased. He was demobilised in April 1919, and holds the General Service and Victory Medals.
110, Gloucester Road, Peckham, S.E.15.　　Z5849

TURNER, J. B., Private, R.M.L.I. (Labour Corps).
Joining in March 1916, he proceeded overseas soon afterwards, and served at Le Havre, Marseilles, Dunkirk, Rouen, and other places. He was chiefly engaged in loading and un-loading supplies, and did valuable work for three years. In March 1919, he returned home and was demobilised, holding the General Service and Victory Medals.
76, Sterndale Road, Battersea, S.W.8.　　Z4672B

TURNER, J. W., Driver, R.F.A.
Mobilised at the outbreak of war he was soon drafted to France, and took part in the Retreat from Mons, and in the battles of the Marne, and the Aisne. He was also in action at Hill 60, Loos, the Somme, Arras, and in the Retreat and Advance of 1918, and was wounded. He was demobilised in 1919 after returning to England, and holds the Mons Star, and the General Service and Victory Medals.
13, Totteridge Road, Battersea, S.W.11.　　Z3917B

TURNER, L., Private, Royal Welch Fusiliers.
Volunteering in April 1915, he was drafted in the same year to the Western Front, and whilst there saw much heavy fighting. He was in action at Ypres, the Somme, Arras, Vimy Ridge, Passchendaele, and many other engagements, and was wounded. He was invalided home early in 1918, and was discharged in August of that year on account of his injuries. He holds the 1914-15 Star, and the General Service and Victory Medals.
43, Kenbury Street, Camberwell, S.E.5.　　Z6462

TURNER, J. R., Sapper, R.E.
He joined in August 1917, and after his training served at Devonport and other stations on important garrison and coastal defence duties. He also did valuable work as a despatch rider, but was not successful in obtaining his transfer overseas before the conclusion of hostilities. He was demobilised in November 1919.
36, Hichisson Road, Peckham, S.E.15.　　Z6747

TURNER, R. E., Private, R.A.S.C.
He volunteered in September 1914, and in the same month proceeded to France, where he did valuable transport work on many sectors of the Front. During the fierce fighting on the Somme in the German Offensive, he was wounded and succumbed to his injuries on May 2nd, 1918. He was entitled to the 1914 Star, and the General Service and Victory Medals.
"Whilst we remember the Sacrifice is not in vain."
28, Duddington Grove, S.W.11.　　Z4660

TURNER, R. G., Rifleman, 21st London Regiment (1st Surrey Rifles).
He enlisted in January 1913, and being mobilised at the outbreak of war proceeded to France in the following March. Whilst in this theatre of war he saw much heavy fighting at Festubert, Loos, and Vimy Ridge, and was badly wounded during the Battle of the Somme. He was invalided to England, and after receiving hospital treatment was discharged as medically unfit for further service in June 1917. He holds the 1914-15 Star, and the General Service and Victory Medals.
25, Chumleigh Street, Camberwell, S.E.5.　　Z5520

TURNER, S., Private, R.A.S.C., Royal Sussex Regiment and Labour Corps.
He volunteered in December 1915, and was sent to Ireland for the completion of his training. In 1917 he proceeded to France and there took part in many engagements, including those on the Somme front, and in the Retreat of 1918 during which he was gassed. He was invalided home, and after much hospital treatment was demobilised in March 1919, holding the General Service and Victory Medals.
49, Mossbury Road, Battersea, S.W.11.　　Z4658

TURNER, T., Driver, R.F.A.
Volunteering in September 1914 he embarked for France in the following March, and whilst in this theatre of war saw much service. He took part in many engagements, including those at Ypres, Festubert, Loos, Vimy Ridge, the Somme, Arras, Messines, Passchendaele, Cambrai, and the Retreat and Advance of 1918. He was invalided home through ill-health and in November 1918 was discharged as unfit for further duty. He holds the 1914-15 Star, and the General Service and Victory Medals. 20, Smyrks Road, Walworth, S.E.17.　　Z4662

TURNER, T. F. C., Air Mechanic, R.A.F.
He joined in 1917, and after his training was retained at various stations on important duties as a rigger, which required much technical skill. He rendered valuable services but was not successful in obtaining his transfer overseas before the cessation of hostilities. He was demobilised in 1919.
10, Santley Street, Ferndale Road, S.W.4.　　Z4666

TURNER, T. H., Private, R.A.M.C.
He volunteered in February 1915, and after completing his training served as a Royal Army Medical Corps orderly on vessels travelling between France and England with the wounded, until the close of the war. He did valuable work until he was demobilised in February 1919, and holds the General Service and Victory Medals.
40, Clovelly Road, Chiswick, W.4.　　6608

TURNER, T. P., Pte., Queen's (Royal West Surrey Regiment).
He joined in March 1916, and in the following month was drafted to France, where he saw much service, and was in action at Bapaume, Arras, Ypres, Cambrai, and many other engagements until hostilities ceased. He returned home and was demobilised in February 1919, and holds the General Service and Victory Medals.
64A, Queen's Road, Battersea, S.W.11.　　Z4663

TURNER, W., Private, R.A.S.C.
Volunteering in November 1914, he proceeded on the completion of his training to the Western Front. There he rendered valuable transport service at many engagements, including those of Cambrai, Armentières, and Ypres. He returned to England and was demobilised in November 1919, and holds the 1914-15 Star, and the General Service and Victory Medals.
48, Beaumont Road, Chiswick, W.4.　　7002

TURNER, W. C., Corporal, R.F.A.
Volunteering in May 1915 he proceeded overseas in the following March, and whilst in France saw much heavy fighting. He was in action at Yyres, the Somme, Arras, and other operations until hostilities ceased, and did valuable work in maintaining the supplies of ammunition for the guns engaged. He was demobilised in February 1919, after returning home, and holds the General Service and Victory Medals.
54, Santley Street, Ferndale Road, S.W.4.   Z4665

TURNEY, C., Rifleman, King's Royal Rifle Corps.
He volunteered in August 1914, and in May of the following year was sent to France, where he took part in the severe fighting at Ypres, Loos, and the Somme, and was wounded. In November 1917, he was transferred to Italy and was in action on the Piave, but in 1918 he returned to France, where he served until after the Armistice. He was demobilised in January 1919, and holds the 1914–15 Star, and the General Service and Victory Medals.
13, Mansion Street, Camberwell, S.E.5.   Z4675

TURPIN, J. L., Private, 3rd Suffolk Regiment.
He joined in May 1916, and in January of the following year was sent to Egypt, and thence to Palestine, where he took part in numerous engagements, including that at Jaffa, and the capture of Jerusalem. He was demobilised in July 1919, and holds the General Service and Victory Medals.
19, Union Grove, Wandsworth Road, S.W.8.   Z4676

TURPIN, W. E., Gunner, R.G.A.
He joined in January 1917, and in the following May was sent to France, where he took part in the fighting at Bullecourt and Messines. Later he was transferred to Italy, where he was unfortunately killed in action on May 30th, 1918, and was buried at Montechiaro. He was entitled to the General Service and Victory Medals.
  " Great deeds cannot die."
15, Elwell Road, Clapham, S.W.4.   Z4677

TURVEY, F. H., Driver, R.F.A.
He was mobilised in August 1914, and was immediately afterwards sent to France, where he took part in the fighting at Mons, Le Cateau, the Marne, the Aisne, Ypres, Hill 60, St. Eloi, Vermelles, the Somme, the Ancre, Arras, Vimy Ridge, Messines, Passchendaele, and in numerous other engagements. He also served in the Retreat and Advance of 1918, and after the Armistice proceeded to Germany with the Army of Occupation. He was demobilised in March 1919, and holds the Mons Star, and the General Service and Victory Medals.
61, Graylands Road, Peckham, S.E.15.   Z5850

TUTT, G., Guardsman, Coldstream Guards.
He volunteered in September 1914, and in January of the following year was sent to France, where he was in action at Neuve Chapelle, Loos, and the Somme. After being disabled through frost bite he was invalided home and discharged in September 1917. He holds the 1914–15 Star, and the General Service and Victory Medals.
51, Dawlish Street, South Lambeth, S.W.8.   Z4678

TUTTON, T. W., Private, 6th Duke of Cornwall's Light Infantry.
He volunteered in April 1915, and later in the same year was drafted to France, where he took part in numerous engagements, including those at Arras and Ypres, and was three times wounded, and was invalided home. On his recovery he was sent to Egypt and thence to Palestine, where he served until 1919, when he returned home and was demobilised in July of that year, holding the 1914–15 Star, and the General Service and Victory Medals.
39, Lockington Road, Battersea Park Road, S.W.8.   Z4679

TYE, J. H., Private, 13th Royal Fusiliers.
He volunteered in November 1914, and in February of the following year was sent to France, where he was in action at Loos, Ypres, and Passchendaele. He was wounded on the Somme in August 1916, and was sent to hospital at Boulogne, where he unfortunately died of his injuries on August 26th 1916, and was entitled to the 1914–15 Star and the General Service and Victory Medals.
  " His memory is cherished with pride."
53, Darien Road, Battersea, S.W.11.   Z3758B

TYERS, C. H., Gunner, R.G.A.
He joined in December 1916, and after completing his training was engaged on anti-aircraft duties in London, and afterwards on similar work in Paris. He later took part in the fighting on the Somme, and at Arras, and Ypres, and also served in the Retreat and Advance of 1918. He was demobilised in November 1919, and holds the General Service and Victory Medals.
42, Aldridge Street, Walworth, S.E.17.   Z4680B

TYERS, G. W. A., Private, M.G.C.
Joining in June 1916, he was drafted to France later in the same year and took part in the fighting at Albert, Arras, and Ypres, and was at Etaples when the hospitals were bombed by enemy aircraft. He was demobilised in March 1919, and holds the General Service and Victory Medals.
48, Aldridge Street, Walworth, S.E.17.   Z4680D

TYLER, F., Gunner, R.F.A.
He was serving at the outbreak of war, and was shortly afterwards sent to France, where he took part in numerous engagements, including those at Mons, Ypres, and the Somme. He fell fighting on the Somme on July 19th, 1916, and was entitled to the Mons Star, and the General Service and Victory Medals.
  " A costly sacrifice upon the altar of freedom."
7, Parfitt Road, S. Rotherhithe, S.E.16.   Z6673

TYLER, H. J., Flight Sergt., R.A.F.
After joining in June 1916, and completing his training he was drafted to France later in the same year. He was engaged at St. Omer and Nancy as a rigger, and also served on the ferrying of machines from England to France. After the Armistice he proceeded to Germany with the Army of Occupation. He was mentioned in Despatches for good work during raids, and holds the General Service and Victory Medals, and was demobilised in June 1919.
27, Park Crescent, Clapham, S.W.4.   Z4681

TYLER, W. R., Sapper, R.E. (I.W.T.)
He joined in May 1918, and in the following month was drafted to France, where he was engaged on the canals in the transport of ammunition and supplies to the various fronts, and rendered valuable services. He returned home and was demobilised in May 1919, and holds the General Service and Victory Medals.
71, Peckham Park Road, Peckham, S.E.15.   Z6700

TYLER, W. S., Private, 12th Middlesex Regiment.
He joined in May 1916, and three months later embarked for the Western Front, where he was engaged in heavy fighting in many parts of the line, including the Arras sector. He gave his life for the freedom of England on June 12th, 1917, and was entitled to the General Service and Victory Medals.
  " His life for his Country, his Soul to God."
3, Edale Road, Rotherhithe, S.E.16.   Z6769

TYRRELL, E. J., Private, 24th Queen's (Royal West Surrey Regiment).
Joining in 1916 he was drafted to the Western Front in the same year, and took part in the heavy fighting on the Somme, and at Arras and Ypres. In 1917 he was transferred to Salonika, and afterwards proceeded to Egypt, and thence to Palestine, where he was wounded. In 1918 he returned to France and was unfortunately killed in action on the Somme on September 18th of that year. He was entitled to the General Service and Victory Medals.
  " He died the noblest death a man may die,
    Fighting for God, and right, and liberty."
11, Beddome Street, Walworth, S.E.17.   Z4682

TYRRELL, T., A.B., R.N., H.M.S. "Pembroke."
He was serving at the outbreak of war and was on H.M.S. " Swiftsure " in the Suez Canal engagements of 1915, and later in the attempt to force the Narrows. He was afterwards at the Landing at Gallipoli, and was in action at Anzac, Cape Helles, and Suvla Bay, and took part in the Evacuation in 1916, being mentioned in Despatches for gallantry. He was next engaged on patrol duties, and then was transferred to T.B.D. " Ettrick " and was engaged on escort duties and whilst so employed was wounded. He afterwards served on H.M.S. " Lord Nelson," and finally with the Fleet at Constantinople. He was demobilised in June 1920, and holds the Naval General Service Medal (with Persian Gulf Clasp), the 1914–15 Star, and the General Service and Victory Medals.
18, Stainforth Road, Battersea, S.W.11.   Z4683

TYSON, J., Private, Royal Defence Corps.
Joining in July 1916, he was engaged on important work at the docks in loading and unloading barges and was also for a time employed on special guard duties. He rendered valuable services until demobilised in January 1919.
37, Salisbury Row, Walworth, S.E.17.   Z3863B

U

UNDERWOOD, D., Pte., 4th (Queen's Own) Hussars.
Prior to the war he served throughout the South African Campaign, and again answering the call to the Colours volunteered in May 1915. He was sent to Ireland, and shortly afterwards met with an accident, and subsequently died from his injuries on June 21st 1915. He held the Queen's and King's South African Medals.
  " His memory is cherished with pride."
25, Barmore Street, Battersea, S.W.11.   Z4692

UNDERWOOD, F., Corporal, 2nd Manchester Regt.
He enlisted in November 1908, and at the outbreak of war was stationed in India. Proceeding to France he fought in many parts of the line in the opening stages of the war. He was severely wounded at La Bassée, and returning to England died from his injuries, and is buried in Netley Hospital Cemetery. He was entitled to the 1914 Star, and the General Service and Victory Medals.
"Whilst we remember, the sacrifice is not in vain."
59, Harris Street, Camberwell, S.E.5. 4693A

UNDERWOOD, G. D., Driver, R.F.A.
He volunteered in April 1915, and in the following December was drafted to France. He served in many important engagements, and, attached to a Trench Mortar Battery, was in action in the Somme Offensive of 1916, during the course of which he was reported missing on August 16th, 1916, and later was presumed to have been killed on that date. He was entitled to the 1914-15 Star, and the General Service and Victory Medals.
"The path of duty was the way to glory."
19, Boathouse Walk, Peckham, S.E.15. Z6348

UNDERWOOD, H., Gunner, R.F.A.
Volunteering in November 1914, in the following March, he was sent to France, and fought in many important engagements including the Battle of Loos. In September 1916 transferred to Salonika he was in action on the Struma Doiran and Monastir fronts, and returned to France in September 1918. He was engaged in heavy fighting in the closing stages of the war, and returning home after the Armistice was demobilised in June 1919. He holds the 1914-15 Star, and the General Service and Victory Medals.
23, Delaford Road, Rotherhithe, S.E.16. Z6720

UNDERWOOD, J. W., Private, 12th Devonshire Regiment and Labour Corps.
He volunteered in 1915, and embarking for the Western Front in the following year fought in many important engagements, including those at Vermelles, Ploegsteert, Vimy Ridge, and Ypres. He was also in action throughout the German Offensive and Allied Advance of 1918. He was demobilised in 1919, and holds the General Service and Victory Medals.
35, Stanbury Road, Peckham, S.E.15. Z6573

UPTON, A. E., Corporal, R.A.S.C. (M.T.)
He volunteered in April 1915, and two months later was drafted to France, where he was engaged on important transport duties in the forward areas. He served in the engagements at Albert, Ploegsteert, the Ancre, and throughout the Retreat of 1918. In the concluding phases of the Allied Advance he was invalided to England owing to ill-health, and after receiving treatment served at various depôts until demobilised in May 1919. He holds the 1914-15 Star, and the General Service and Victory Medals.
29, Elmington Road, Camberwell, S.E.5. Z4694

UPTON, H., Rifleman, Rifle Brigade.
He joined in April 1918, and completing his training served at various stations, engaged on guard and other important duties with his unit. He was unsuccessful in obtaining his transfer to a theatre of war prior to the cessation of hostilities, but rendered excellent services until demobilised in September 1919.
133, Coburg Road, Camberwell, S.E.5. Z5521

UTTING, G., Private, 11th Royal Sussex Regiment.
He joined in May 1917, and later proceeded to Northern Russia, where he served in many parts of the line, and rendered valuable services throughout. Returning to England he was demobilised in November 1919, and holds the General Service and Victory Medals. 32, Spencer Street, Battersea, S.W.11. Z4695

UWINS, G. R., Private, 14th London Regt. (London Scottish).
Joining in February 1917, he embarked for France in the following September and was engaged in heavy fighting in many parts of the line, including the Lens sector. He was reported wounded and missing on November 24th 1917, during the first Battle of Cambrai, and later was presumed to have been killed on that date. He was entitled to the General Service and Victory Medals.
"Great deeds cannot die,
They with the sun and moon renew their light for ever."
46, Nutbrook Street, Peckham, S.E.15. Z6791

V

VAAL, G. F., Private, R.A.S.C.
He joined in September 1916, and after a period of training was sent in 1918 to the Western Front, where he served in many engagements. He was present at Albert, Méricourt, and other places, and later was invalided home owing to ill-health. Afterwards he served on home defence duties until demobilised in August 1919. He holds the General Service and Victory Medals.
6, Kempsford Road, Kennington, S.E.11. Z27365A

VAAL, H. M., Private, R.A.S.C.
He volunteered in May 1915, and in the same year was sent to the Western Front where he saw much service. He was present at engagements, at St. Eloi, Loos, and the Somme, and also served throughout the Retreat and Advance of 1918. After the signing of the Armistice he went to Germany with the Army of Occupation, and in 1920 was still serving at Cologne. He holds the 1914-15 Star, and the General Service and the Victory Medals.
6, Kempsford Road, Kennington, S.E.11. Z27365B

VAINES, A. L., R.S.M., R.E.
He had previously served in the Middlesex Regiment in India and China, and at the outbreak of hostilities was recalled from the Army Reserve and transferred to the Royal Engineers. As he was medically unfit for overseas service he was retained on important garrison duties at various stations. He was highly commended for his excellent work, and was demobilised in February 1919.
61, Morrison Street, Battersea, S.W.11. Z4696

VALENTINE, A., Sapper, R.E.
He volunteered in August 1914, and proceeded to France in the following year. Whilst overseas he was engaged on important duties in connection with the operations and was frequently in the forward areas, notably at Givenchy, Ypres, Festubert and Loos, where he was gassed in action. After his recovery he was present again at engagements at Béthune, Ypres, and many others which followed in the Retreat and Advance of 1918. He was demobilised in February 1919, and holds the 1914-15 Star, and the General Service and Victory Medals.
3, Lewis Road, Camberwell, S.E.5. Z6349

VALLANCE, C., Private, K.O.Y.L.I.
He was serving at the outbreak of war, and was almost immediately drafted to the Western Front, where he took part in the Retreat from Mons. He also fought in the Battle of Neuve Chapelle, and was severely wounded and invalided home to hospital. After treatment, however, he returned to France and served there until 1919, when he was demobilised, holding the Mons Star, and the General Service and Victory Medals.
27, Ernest Street, Bermondsey, S.E.1. Z27278

VALLANCE, F., Trooper, Royal Bucks Hussars and Private, M.G.C.
Volunteering in September 1915, he proceeded to Egypt in the following year and served in various operations in this theatre of war. In 1918, whilst en route for the Western Front, his ship, H.M.T. "Leasome Castle" was torpedoed, but he was fortunately rescued and landed in France. He then took part in much of the heavy fighting in the Advance of 1918, serving with the Machine Gun Corps until hostilities ceased. In February 1919 he was demobilised, and holds the General Service and Victory Medals.
14, Odell Street, Camberwell, S.E.5. Z5684

VANDENBOSCH, F. E., Private, Queen's (Royal West Surrey Regiment).
He was mobilised at the outbreak of war and was almost immediately drafted to France, where he took part in the memorable Retreat from Mons. He also fought at La Bassée and Ypres, and was wounded and invalided to hospital at Versailles, where he subsequently died of his injuries in January 1915. He was entitled to the Mons Star, and the General Service and Victory Medals.
"A costly sacrifice upon the altar of freedom."
1, Brayards Road, Peckham, S.E.15. Z5522

VARDELL, T., Driver, R.A.S.C. (M.T.)
Volunteering in October 1914, he was drafted to the Western Front in the following year, and whilst in France was engaged on important duties in connection with the Motor Transport in the Ypres, Somme and Cambrai sectors. He was afterwards sent to Italy, where he served on the Piave with the transport waggons, conveying food and ammunition up the front lines. In June 1919, he was demobilised, and holds the 1914-15 Star, and the General Service and Victory Medals.
67, Meadow Road, South Lambeth, S.W.8. Z4697

VARNDELL, B., Bombardier, R.G.A.
He joined in July 1916, and proceeded overseas in the following January. Whilst in France he fought at Arras, where he was wounded in May 1917, and on his recovery took part in the third Battle of Ypres, in which he was again wounded in August of the same year. He was invalided home to hospital, and after his recovery rejoined his Battery in France, and was in action on the Somme. He gave his life for his King and Country in the second Battle of Cambrai on September 27th, 1918, and was entitled to the General Service and Victory Medals.
"A valiant soldier, with undaunted heart he breasted Life's last hill."
77, Cranham Road, Rotherhithe, S.E.16. Z6674

VAUGHAN, C. H. L., Driver, R.E.

He volunteered in September 1914, and on the completion of his training proceeded to France in March of the following year. Whilst in France he did good work as a driver, notably at Festubert, Loos, and the Somme, and in the Ypres sector, where he remained nearly a year. He also served at Arras and Bourlon Wood, and in many engagements in the Retreat and Advance of 1918, and entered Lille with the victorious troops on October 28th, 1918. After the Armistice he remained in France until his demobilisation in June 1919, and holds the 1914-15 Star, and the General Service and Victory Medals.

33, Bullen Street, Battersea, S.W.11.   Z4698

VAUGHAN, L. C., Private, 7th Royal Fusiliers.

He volunteered in September 1914, and in the following year was drafted to France. During his service on the Western Front, he fought at Ypres, the Somme, Arras and Cambrai, and was wounded. After treatment in hospital he rejoined his Regiment, and served in various engagements until the cessation of hostilities. He was demobilised in February 1919, and holds the 1914-15 Star, and the General Service and Victory Medals.

78, Coronation Buildings, South Lambeth Road, S.W.8.
Z4699

VAUGHAN, R. J., Private, Middlesex Regiment.

He was mobilised in August 1914, and was almost immediately drafted to the Western Front. During the memorable Retreat from Mons he was wounded and taken prisoner on August 23rd, and was sent to Germany. Whilst in captivity he was engaged in agricultural duties until after the Armistice was signed, when he was released and repatriated. He was demobilised in December 1918, and holds the Mons Star, and the General Service and Victory Medals.

48, Stockdale Road, Wandsworth Road, S.W.8.   Z4700

VEASEY, C., Quartermaster, Mercantile Marine.

He was serving in the Mercantile Marine on convoy ships conveying stores until he attained the age of eighteen years, when he was transferred to the s.s. " Earl of Forfar." He lost his life when his ship was blown up at Archangel on November 8th, 1916, and was entitled to the General Service and Mercantile Marine War Medals.

" Honour to the immortal dead, who gave their youth that the world might grow old in peace."

53, Cork Street, Camberwell, S.E.5.   Z1789A

VEASEY, H., Driver, R.A.S.C. (M.T.)

He joined in October 1916, and proceeded to France in January of the following year. Whilst overseas he did good work as a driver in the Motor Transport section in many engagements, including those at Arras, Vimy Ridge, Bullecourt, the Somme, and Armentières. He was present at the entry into Mons on Armistice Day, and afterwards advanced into Germany with the Army of Occupation and was stationed at Cologne until October 1919, when he returned to England and was demobilised. He holds the General Service and Victory Medals.

5, Danes Road, Camberwell, S.E.5.   Z6212B

VEASEY, J. R., Private, 1st Royal Fusiliers.

A serving Soldier since 1913, he proceeded to France at the outbreak of war and took part in the Retreat from Mons and in the Battles of the Marne, the Aisne, Ypres and Loos. He was severely wounded in action on the Somme, and was invalided home to hospital and discharged as medically unfit for further duty in April 1918. He rejoined, however, in the Labour Corps in 1919, and again proceeded to France, where he was engaged on important duties with his unit until demobilised in 1920. He holds the Mons Star, and the General Service and Victory Medals.

53, Cork Street, Camberwell, S.E.5.   Z1789B

VEITCH, G., C.Q.M.S., 6th Buffs (East Kent Regt.)

Volunteering in September 1914, he was drafted to France in the following year, and served in numerous important engagements, including those at Ypres, Arras, Lens, Béthune, Bapaume and Amiens. He was chiefly engaged in conveying food and ammunition up to the firing lines until returning to England on leave in 1917. He was then, on account of his age, retained on home service and employed in the Army Pay Office until demobilised in April 1919. He holds the 1914-15 Star, and the General Service and Victory Medals.

43, St. Alphonsus Road, Clapham, S.W.4.   Z4701

VENABLES, J. B., Pte., 16th Lancashire Fusiliers.

Volunteering in July 1915, he crossed to France in the following year and fought in the Battles of Vimy Ridge, the Somme, where he was wounded. After his recovery he was again in action at Passchendaele, and was wounded at Festubert in 1917, and again in the Retreat in March of the following year. He also served on the Sambre Canal, and after the Armistice proceeded to Germany, remaining there until March 1919, when he returned home and was demobilised. He holds the General Service and Victory Medals.

7, Reedham Street, Peckham, S.E.15.   Z6792

VENES, H., Private, 2nd Northamptonshire Regt.

He joined in May 1917, and in April of the following year proceeded to France, where he saw considerable service. He took part in the engagements on the Somme, and at Villers-Bretonneux, Amiens, and the Marne, and was also in action at St. Eloi and Albert. After the Armistice was signed he advanced into Germany, and subsequently was engaged in escorting German prisoners from France to their own country. He was demobilised in November 1919, and holds the General Service and Victory Medals.

28, Benfield Street, Battersea, S.W.11.   Z4702

VENN, G., L/Corporal, R.A.S.C.

He volunteered in October 1914, and was drafted to the Western Front in December of the following year. During his service in France he was engaged on important duties in the vicinity of La Bassée and Albert, and was severely wounded in August 1916. He was invalided home to hospital, and after medical treatment was discharged in February 1917, as physically unfit for further duty. He holds the 1914-15 Star, and the General Service and Victory Medals.

12, Luscombe Street, Wandsworth Road, S.W.8.
Z27512

VENN, L. F., Gunner, R.F.A.

He volunteered in April 1915, and in December of the same year was drafted to France. Whilst overseas he fought on the Somme, and was wounded in August 1916, and after his recovery was again wounded in action at Ploegsteert in May 1917. Later, he served at Ypres with the Salvage Corps, and was afterwards stationed at Rouen until May 1919, when he was sent home and demobilised. He holds the 1914-15 Star, and the General Service and Victory Medals.

19, Conder'on Road, Camberwell, S.E.5.   Z6350

VENNER, H. T., Corporal, 2nd Queen's (Royal West Surrey Regiment).

He volunteered in September 1914, and in the same year was drafted to France, where he served in various engagements in different sectors of the Western Front, acting as a sniper. In 1915, he was wounded in action, and in 1917 was taken prisoner during the Battle of Cambrai. He was held in captivity until December 1918, when he was repatriated and demobilised, holding the 1914 Star, and the General Service and Victory Medals.

11, Tidbury Street, Battersea Park Road, S.W.8.   Z4703

VENT, J. R., Private, Northumberland Fusiliers.

He was mobilised at the outbreak of war, and was almost immediately drafted to France, where he took part in the Retreat from Mons, and the Battle of the Marne. He was afterwards sent to the Dardanelles, and served throughout the Gallipoli Campaign until the Evacuation of the Peninsula. He next proceeded to Mesopotamia, and during his service was twice wounded in action, and subsequently discharged as medically unfit for further duty in January 1918. He holds the Mons Star, and the General Service and Victory Medals.

55, Cork Street, Camberwell, S.E.5.   Z1998B

VERCOE, T. (D.C.M.), R.S.M., Black Watch (Royal Highlanders).

He enlisted in 1897, and at the outbreak of hostilities was sent to the Western Front, where he fought in the Retreat from Mons, and in the Battles of the Marne, and the Aisne, and was wounded during the latter engagement. On recovery he rejoined his Regiment, and saw heavy fighting in the Ypres, Arras and Somme sectors. He was awarded the Distinguished Conduct Medal for gallantry and devotion to duty in the Field, and was in action throughout the Retreat and Advance of 1918. He was demobilised in November 1919, and holds in addition to the Distinguished Conduct Medal, the Mons Star, the General Service and Victory Medals, and the Long Service and Good Conduct Medals.

6, Nealdon Street, Stockwell, S.W.9.   Z4704

VERRAN, O. V., Private, 13th London Regiment (Kensingtons).

He volunteered in September 1914, and in the following year landed in France. Shortly afterwards, however, he was invalided to England, owing to ill-health, and received hospital treatment. On recovery, he was posted to an anti-aircraft Battery, and rendered valuable services until his demobilisation in February 1919. He holds the 1914-15 Star, and the General Service and Victory Medals.

82, Sandmere Road, Clapham, S.W.4.   Z1767B

VERRILLS, F., Rifleman, 16th London Regiment (Queen's Westminster Rifles).

He joined in April 1917, and four months later was sent to France with the 6th London Regiment and fought in many parts of the line, and was gassed at Arras in March 1918. On recovery, he rejoined his Battalion and was in action throughout the Allied Advance. He was demobilised in December 1919, and holds the General Service and Victory Medals.

6, Goldie Street, Camberwell, S.E.5.   Z5523

VESTEY, H. A., Gunner, R.F.A.

He joined in May 1917, and in the following August was sent to France. During his service overseas he fought in many parts of the line, and was almost continuously in action during the German Offensive and subsequent Allied Advance of 1918, and was wounded. He was demobilised in October 1919, and holds the General Service and Victory Medals.
130, Robertson Street, Wandsworth Road, S.W.8.   Z4705

VIAN, E., Chief Gunner, Merchant Service.

Volunteering at the outbreak of war, he was posted to the oil tanker " Winnetago," in which he was engaged throughout the period of hostilities,conveying oil from America to England. He holds the General Service and Mercantile Marine War Medals, and was demobilised in January 1919.
69, St. Olaf's Road, Munster Road, Fulham, S.W.6.   X20477

VICARY, F. J., Sergt., R.F.A.

Volunteering in October 1914, he embarked for the Western Front in the following July, and was in action in the Battle of Loos, and in many other engagements of note. He was unfortunately killed in action at the Battle of the Somme in 1916, and was entitled to the 1914-15 Star, and the General Service and Victory Medals.
" His life for his Country, his Soul to God."
34, Joubert Street, Battersea, S.W.11.   Z4706

VICK, F. W. H., Driver, R.F.A.

He enlisted in 1909, and was sent to France shortly after the outbreak of hostilities. He fought in the Battles of Ypres, and the Somme, and was invalided home in 1916, owing to an accident which occurred in the discharge of his duty. On recovery, he returned to France in May 1917, and took part in heavy fighting in many sectors, and was in action throughout the Retreat and Advance of 1918. He was demobilised in March 1919, and holds the 1914 Star, and the General Service and Victory Medals.
39, East Surrey Grove, Peckham, S.E.15.   Z5294

VICKERS, T. J., Private, R.A.S.C.

He volunteered in January 1915, and shortly afterwards was sent to France, where he served on important transport duties in the advanced areas. He was present at the Battles of Neuve Chapelle, Hill 60, Loos, St. Eloi, Albert, Vermelles, Vimy Ridge, Passchendaele, and at heavy fighting in the Retreat and Advance of 1918. He was demobilised in April 1919, and holds the 1914-15 Star, and the General Service and Victory Medals.
30, Moat Place, Stockwell, S.W.9.   Z4707

VICKERY, E., Corporal, R.A.S.C. (M.T.)

He volunteered in September 1915, and later in that year was drafted to East Africa. In this theatre of war he served as a motor transport driver in many parts of the line and rendered valuable services. Returning to England in August 1918, he was demobilised early in 1919, and holds the 1914-15 Star, and the General Service and Victory Medals.
28, Flaxman Road, Camberwell, S.E.5.   Z6234

VICKERY, S. H., Rifleman, 21st London Regt. (1st Surrey Rifles) and Pte., 9th Royal Sussex Regt.

He volunteered in April 1915, and completing his training served at various stations, and was discharged in the following December. Rejoining in April 1917, he embarked for France in January 1918, and was in action in many engagements of note. He was taken prisoner at Chaulnes and held in captivity until after the Armistice. Repatriated in December 1918, he was demobilised in February 1919, and holds the General Service and Victory Medals.
122, Glengall Road, Peckham, S.E.15.   Z6589

VIGOR, F., Rifleman, 21st London Regiment (1st Surrey Rifles).

He volunteered in January 1915, and shortly afterwards drafted to the Western Front, was in action in the Battles of Neuve Chapelle and Ypres. Suffering from shell-shock, he was invalided to England, and after receiving hospital treatment returned to France in November 1915. He laid down his life on the field of honour at Loos in December 1915, and was entitled to the 1914-15 Star, and the General Service and Victory Medals.
" Great deeds cannot die "
24, Haines Street, Battersea Park Road, S.W.8.   Z4708B

VIGOR, J. G., A.B., Royal Navy.

He joined the Service in 1916, and was posted to H.M.S. " Morsby " and later was sent to East Africa, where he saw much fighting on land. He was awarded the Croix de Guerre for conspicuous gallantry and devotion to duty in the Field. He rejoined his ship, which then proceeded to home waters, and was engaged on patrol and other important duties off the coasts of Ireland, until the cessation of hostilities. He was demobilised in March 1919, and holds the African General Service Medal, and the General Service and Victory Medals.
24, Haines Street, Battersea Park Road, S.W.8.   Z4708A

VINALL, C. A., Private, R.A.S.C. (M.T.)

He volunteered in March 1915, and later in that year was sent to the Western Front, where he served in the forward areas and was engaged on important transport duties. He was present at the Battles of Loos, the Somme, Ypres, Lens, and at severe fighting in the Retreat and Advance of 1918. He was demobilised in June 1919, and holds the 1914-15 Star, and the General Service and Victory Medals.
27, Phelps Street, Walworth, S.E.17.   Z26642

VINCENT, E. H., Cpl., 13th Durham Light Infantry.

He joined in February 1917, and later in that year was sent to the Western Front, and was in action at Ypres and Passchendaele, where he was wounded. On recovery he rejoined his unit and fought in many engagements during the German Offensive, and in the opening stages of the Allied Advance, and was gassed at Ypres in September 1918. After receiving hospital treatment, he returned to the front lines and saw much service until the cessation of hostilities. He was demobilised in November 1919, and holds the General Service and Victory Medals.   17, Claude Road, Peckham, S.E.15.   Z5853

VINCENT, G., L/Corporal, 5th Royal Sussex Regt.

He joined in June 1918, at the age of seventeen, and completing his training, served at various stations on important duties with his unit. He was unsuccessful in obtaining his transfer overseas prior to the cessation of hostilities, but was later sent into Germany with the Army of Occupation. He was demobilised in March 1919.
16, Relf Road, Peckham, S.E.15.   Z6721

VINCENT, H., Driver, R.A.S.C. (M.T.)

He volunteered in September 1914, and six months later embarked for France, where he served on important duties, transporting ammunition and supplies to the front lines. He was present at many important engagements, but owing to ill-health was invalided to England. He received hospital treatment, and ultimately was discharged in March 1918. He holds the 1914-15 Star, and the General Service and Victory Medals.   30, Gloucester Road, Peckham, S.E.15.   Z5831B

VINCENT, H., Private, Royal Fusiliers.

He joined in June 1916, and in the following January was drafted to the Western Front, where he was in action in the Battles of Vimy Ridge, Messines, Ypres, Passchendaele, Lens and was wounded and taken prisoner in the first Battle of Cambrai. He was held in captivity until after the Armistice and then was repatriated. He was demobilised in December 1918, and holds the General Service and Victory Medals.
2, Massinger Street, Walworth, S.E.17.   Z4709A

VINCENT, J., A.B., Royal Navy.

He joined in July 1917, but being under age was retained on shore duties after completing his training. Later he was posted to H.M.S. " Malaya " and in 1920 was still serving aboard that ship. He holds the General Service Medal.
2, Massinger Street, Walworth, S.E.17.   Z4709C

VINCENT, R., Private, Buffs (East Kent Regiment).

He joined in 1916, and later in that year proceeded to the Western Front and fought in many parts of the line, including the Cambrai sector. During the first Battle of the Somme, he was taken prisoner and held in captivity until after the cessation of hostilities. Repatriated, he was demobilised in December 1918, and holds the General Service and Victory Medals.   5, Danson Road, Walworth, S.E.17.   Z27019

VINCENT, R., Rifleman, Rifle Brigade.

He volunteered in August 1914, and four months later was sent to France. During his service overseas he fought in many important engagements, and did good work. He gave his life for the freedom of England on March 12th, 1915, during the Battle of Neuve Chapelle, and was entitled to the 1914-15 Star, and the General Service and Victory Medals.
" Steals on the ear the distant triumph song."
2, Massinger Street, Walworth, S.E.17.   Z4709B

VINE, F. A., Corporal, 2nd Leicestershire Regiment.

He enlisted in 1908, and at the outbreak of war was serving in India. Drafted to France shortly after the commencement of hostilities he was engaged in heavy fighting in many parts of the line, and was severely wounded in the Battle of Neuve Chapelle. He returned to England, and after receiving protracted hospital treatment, was invalided out of the Service in July 1916. He holds the 1914 Star, and the General Service and Victory Medals.
176, Robertson Street, Wandsworth Road, S.W.8.   Z4710

VINING, T. H., Gunner, R.H.A.

He volunteered in January 1915, and later in the same year embarked for the Western Front. Here he was engaged in severe fighting in many parts of the line, and rendered valuable services. Owing to ill-health he was invalided to hospital, and after receiving treatment was discharged unfit for further service in October 1919. He holds the 1914-15 Star, and the General Service and Victory Medals.
30, Atherton Street, Battersea, S.W.11.   Z4711

VIZARD, A. H. T., Leading Seaman, R.N.D.

He volunteered in September 1914, and was posted to the Drake Battalion of the Royal Naval Division. In the following April he proceeded to Gallipoli and fought in many engagements. He gave his life for King and Country at Cape Helles in June 1915, and was entitled to the 1914-15 Star, and the General Service and Victory Medals.
"Thinking that remembrance, though unspoken, may reach him where he sleeps."
131, Honeywell Road, Battersea, S.W.11.   Z4712A

VIZARD, E. C., Sergt., Australian I.F.

He volunteered in January 1916, and later in that year landed in Egypt, where he saw considerable service for nine months. Proceeding to France he was in action in many important engagements, including the Battle of the Somme. He was severely wounded at Bapaume in 1917, and invalided to England received hospital treatment, but died from his injuries in October 1918. He was entitled to the General Service and Victory Medals.
"He passed out of the sight of men by the path of duty and self-sacrifice."
131, Honeywell Road, Battersea, S.W.11.   Z4712B

VOGAN, A. W., Private, Labour Corps.

He joined in June 1917, and was sent to the Western Front in the following year. He did good work whilst engaged on important duties in the forward areas, and was gassed near Bapaume. He returned home, and on recovery was attached to the Royal Army Pay Corps, and served at various stations until demobilised in February 1919. He holds the General Service and Victory Medals.
1, Medwin Street, Ferndale Road, S.W.4.   Z2652A

VOICE, C. G., Private, 1st London Regt. (Royal Fusiliers and 2/24th London Regt. (The Queen's).

He volunteered in August 1914, and two years later was drafted to the Western Front, where he fought in the first British Offensive on the Somme. Transferred to Egypt in 1917 he was in action in the vicinity of Jerusalem, and in many other engagements. He returned to France in 1918, and served throughout the Allied Advance. He was demobilised in March 1919, and holds the General Service and Victory Medals.
32, Edmunds Street, Camberwell, S.E.5.   Z4713

VOKES, W., Pioneer, R.E.

He volunteered in January 1915, and landed in France in the following December. He was in action in the Loos sector, and was gassed at Verdun in February 1916. Invalided to England, he received protracted hospital treatment, but died from the effects of gas poisoning on November 15th, 1917. He was entitled to the 1914-15 Star, and the General Service and Victory Medals.
"And doubtless he went in splendid company."
32, Heaton Road, Peckham, S.E.15.   Z5852

VOLKERT, J., Gunner, R.F.A.

Volunteering in August 1915, and proceeding to France in the following March, he fought in the Battles of Vimy Ridge, the Somme, Ypres, Cambrai and throughout the German Offensive and subsequent Allied Advance of 1918. He was demobilised in January 1919, and holds the General Service and Victory Medals.
7, Dashwood Road, Wandsworth Road, S.W.8.   Z4714

VOYCE, A., Driver, R.A.S.C. (M.T.)

He volunteered in April 1915, and in the same month embarked for the Western Front. He was present at the Battles of Ypres, Loos, the Somme and did good work. Transferred to Italy in 1917, he served on the Piave front during the Austrian Offensive, and was engaged in important transport duties. Early in 1918 he returned to France and saw much service during the Retreat and Advance of 1918. He was demobilised in June 1919, and holds the 1914-15 Star, and the General Service and Victory Medals.
106, Farmer's Road, Camberwell, S.E.5.   Z4715

W

WADE, A., Rifleman, 18th London Regiment (London Irish Rifles).

Joining in August 1916, he was drafted to France in October of the same year, and was in action at Messines, Ypres, Passchendaele and Cambrai, and was wounded and invalided home. On his recovery he was engaged on important duties on the East Coast. He was demobilised in January 1919, and holds the General Service and Victory Medals.
6, Reddins Road, Peckham, S.E.15.   6467

WADE, W. E., Special War Worker.

He was engaged at Messrs. Wade Bros.,Taband Street, Borough S.E., in the manufacture of barrels, in which to transport explosives overseas. He carried out his duties in a most efficient manner, and rendered valuable services during the war.
88, Chatham Street, Walworth, S.E.17.   Z4716B

WAGER, D. K., Gunner, R.F.A.

He volunteered in August 1914, and was sent to France in the same month. He took part in the fighting at Neuve Chapelle, the Loos, Somme, Arras and Messines, and later contracting rheumatic fever was invalided home and discharged as medically unfit for further service in November 1916, holding the 1914 Star, and the General Service and Victory Medals.
12, Wayford Street, Battersea, S.W.11.   Z4718

WAGER, W. T., A.B., R.N., H.M.S. "Canterbury."

He volunteered in August 1914, and served with the Grand Fleet in the North Sea, and took part in the Battles of Heligoland Bight, Jutland, Zeebrugge and several other engagements. He was also engaged in the transport of troops to the Dardanelles. He was demobilised in February 1919, and holds the 1914-15 Star, and the General Service and Victory Medals.
39, Darwin Street, Walworth, S.E.17.   Z4717

WAGHORN, E., Sergt., M.G.C.

Volunteering in August 1914, he was sent to France in March of the following year, and was in action at St. Eloi, Festubert, Loos and other engagements. He was wounded and invalided home in June 1916, and after his recovery was engaged on various important duties until 1918, when he was sent to Russia. Here he remained until July 1919, when he returned home, and was demobilised, holding the 1914-15 Star, and the General Service and Victory Medals.
184, Cator Street, Peckham, S.E.15.   Z5102A

WAITE, H., Special War Worker.

He was engaged at Bournemouth Road, Rye Lane, Peckham, in the manufacture of munitions for the Admiralty and rendered valuable services. He was also a member of the Volunteer Training Corps from 1914 to 1919.
2, Nelson Square, Commercial Road, Peckham, S.E.15. Z6701

WAITE, H., Driver, R.F.A.

He volunteered in September 1914, and after completing his training was drafted to the Western Front in the following year. He was in action at Kemmel, Loos, Ypres and Messines, and was later transferred to Salonika, where he was engaged on the Doiran and Struma fronts. Afterwards he was sent to Turkey, and served there until he was demobilised in March 1919, holding the 1914-15 Star, and the General Service and Victory Medals.
11, Heath Road, Wandsworth Road, S.W.8.   Z4719

WAITE, T. B., Rifleman, 1st Rifle Brigade.

He joined in May 1918, and was in training when the Armistice was signed. In 1919 he was drafted to Mesopotamia, where he was still serving in 1920.
6A, Victory Square, Camberwell, S.E.5.   Z5685A

WAITE, T. G., Private, Royal Munster Fusiliers and M.G.C.

Volunteering in September 1914, he was sent to the Dardanelles in the following year, and took part in the operations there up to the Evacuation. He was then transferred to Salonika and served in the Serbian Retreat, and was engaged on the Vardar, Doiran and Struma fronts, and in the last Offensive in the Balkans. Later, contracting malaria he was invalided home, and was discharged as medically unfit for further service in February 1919. He holds the 1914-15 Star, and the General Service and Victory Medals.
6A, Victory Square, Camberwell, S.E.5.   Z5685B

WAKE, H., Private, R.A.S.C.

Volunteering in April 1915, he was drafted to France later in the same year, and was stationed at Havre, Rouen, Boulogne and Abbeville, being engaged on important duties with the printing section. Later, contracting pneumonia, he was invalided home, and was demobilised in January 1919, holding the 1914-15 Star, and the General Service and Victory Medals.
47, Marlborough Road, Old Kent Road, S.E.1.   Z27275

WAKEFIELD, A., Private, R.A.F.

Joining in September 1917, after completing his training he was engaged in the Shetland Islands on important duties with his Squadron. He was employed in building aeroplane hangars, and rendered valuable services, but was not successful in obtaining his transfer to a theatre of war before the cessation of hostilities. He was demobilised in February 1919.
30, Graylands Road, Peckham, S.E.15.   Z5858

WAKEFIELD, A. W., Driver, R.F.A.

He was mobilised in August 1914, and in the same month was sent to France, where he took part in the fighting in the Retreat from Mons and on the Marne and Aisne and at Neuve Chapelle, Ypres, Festubert, Vimy Ridge, the Somme, Arras, Messines, Cambrai and in other engagements. He also served in the Retreat and Advance of 1918. He was demobilised in April 1919, and holds the Mons Star, and the General Service and Victory Medals. Z5161B

6, Arlington Grove, Neate Street, Camberwell, S.E.5.

WAKEFIELD, J., Corporal, R.A.S.C. (M.T.)

Volunteering in September 1915, he was sent to France in the following month. and was engaged at Vimy Ridge, the Somme, Arras and Ypres on important duties with the supply section. Later, he unfortunately met with an accident, and was invalided home. On his recovery he was employed on important Postal duties until demobilised in May 1920. He holds the 1914–15 Star, and the General Service and Victory Medals. 54, Delaford Road, Rotherhithe, S.E.16. Z6751

WAKEFIELD, J. W., Pte., Royal Irish Fusiliers.

He joined in September 1917, and in the following year was drafted to France, where he took part in the Retreat and Advance of 1918, and was severely wounded in September of that year. He was invalided home and discharged owing to his injuries in June 1919, holding the General Service and Victory Medals. Z5161A

6, Arlington Grove, Neate Street, Camberwell, S.E.5.

WAKELING, E. H., Sergt., 24th London Regiment (Queen's).

He volunteered in September 1914, and in the following year was drafted to France, where he took part in numerous engagements, including those at Passchendaele and Givenchy. Later owing to ill-health he was invalided home and was discharged as medically unfit in August 1919, holding the 1914–15 Star, and the General Service and Victory Medals. 2, Beckway Street, Walworth, S.E.17. Z4721

WAKEMAN, T., Corporal, R.A.S.C.

He was mobilised with the Royal Fusiliers in August 1914, and immediately sent to France, where he took part in numerous engagements. He returned home and was discharged as time-expired in 1915, but rejoined in 1916, and was posted to the R.A.S.C. Later whilst en route for Egypt on board H.M.S. Transport " Arcadian," the vessel was torpedoed on April 15th, 1917, and he was unfortunately killed. He was entitled to the 1914 Star, and the General Service and Victory Medals.

"He joined the great white company of valiant souls."
10, Ægis Grove, Battersea Park Road, S.W.8. Z2826B

WALBRIDGE, E. W., Stoker, R.N., H.M.S. "Botha."

He volunteered in October 1914, and served with the Dover Patrol. Later his ship was mined and torpedoed, but fortunately he was unhurt, and afterwards took part with the Fleet in the Bombardment of Ostend, and was severely wounded. He was still serving on H.M.S. " Tryard " in 1920, and holds the 1914–15 Star, and the General Service and Victory Medals. 112, Kirkwood Road, Peckham, S.E.15. Z6355B

WALBRIDGE, H., Stoker, R.N., H.M.S. "Bellerophon."

He joined in 1916, and served in the North Sea with the Grand Fleet. He took part in the Battle of Jutland and was also for a time engaged in conveying troops to France. He was demobilised in 1919, and holds the General Service and Victory Medals. 112, Kirkwood Road, Peckham, S.E.15. Z6355A

WALDING, C. H., Private, Duke of Cornwall's Light Infantry.

Volunteering in May 1915, he was sent to France later in the same year, and took part in numerous engagements. He was unfortunately killed in action on September 10th, 1916, and was entitled to the 1914–15 Star, and the General Service and Victory Medals.

"His life for his Country, his Soul to God."
87B, Albany Road, Camberwell, S.E.5. Z5686

WALE, T., Private, R.A.S.C.

Joining in 1916, and after completing his training he was sent to France, where he was engaged at the Remount Depôt, being employed in the training of horses. He rendered valuable services until demobilised in October 1919, and holds the General Service and Victory Medals. 7, Trafalgar Road, Camberwell, S.E.5. Z4723

WALES, G. F., Corporal, 10th Hampshire Regiment.

He joined in December 1916, and in March of the following year was drafted to Mesopotamia, where he took part in numerous engagements, including that at Mosul. He also served in Egypt, Salonika and the Dardanelles, and was demobilised in July 1920, holding the General Service and Victory Medals. 18, Charleston Street, Walworth, S.E.17. Z4724

WALKER, A. E., Private, 10th Queen's (Royal West Surrey Regiment).

He volunteered in October 1915, and in May of the following year was drafted to France, where he fought in many important engagements, including those at the Somme, Ypres, Arras and High Wood. He was also in action in the chief operations in the Retreat and Advance of 1918, and after the Armistice proceeded to Germany, where he remained until invalided home in 1919. He was demobilised in March of that year, and holds the General Service and Victory Medals. 21, Newcomen Road, Battersea, S.W.11. Z4726

WALKER, A. H., Fireman, Mercantile Marine.

He had served in the Mercantile Marine since 1910, and at the outbreak of war was engaged on the " Miltydes " in the North Sea. During his war service he was engaged on important duties in many seas, constantly passing through mine-infested areas, and exposed to the danger of being torpedoed by enemy action. He holds the General Service and the Mercantile Marine War Medals, and in 1920 was still serving. 168, Lavender Road, Battersea, S.W.11. Z4732

WALKER, A. V., Air Mechanic, R.A.F.

He volunteered in August 1914, in the 13th London Regiment and after six weeks was discharged. He re-enlisted in 1915 in the 21st London Regiment, and was in training in various parts of England until December in the same year. He was then transferred to the Royal Flying Corps, and served at various stations on important duties as an aero-engine fitter. Owing to medical unfitness he was unable to proceed overseas during the war, and after doing much good work with his Squadron was demobilised in January 1919. Z6118

7, Pomfret Road, Camberwell, S.E.5.

WALKER, C. A., Rifleman, 11th and 17th London Regiment (Rifles).

He was mobilised at the outbreak of war, and proceeded to Gallipoli in August 1915. He took part in the Landing at Suvla Bay, but was invalided home in October, and discharged as medically unfit in March 1916. He re-enlisted in the 17th London Regiment in May 1917, and was drafted to France in the following month. Whilst in this theatre of war he fought at Messines, Ypres, Passchendaele and Cambrai, and in the Retreat and Advance of 1918, and was wounded at Bray in August 1918. He was invalided home and demobilised in the following February, holding the 1914–15 Star, and the General Service and Victory Medals. 29, Haymerle Road, Peckham, S.E.15. Z6555

WALKER, E., Corporal, R.F.A.

He was mobilised in August 1914, and soon afterwards drafted to the Western Front. During his service in France he fought at La Bassée, Ypres, Neuve Chapelle, St. Eloi, Hill 60, Loos, Vimy Ridge, the Somme, Beaumont-Hamel, Messines, Passchendaele, Cambrai and the second Battle of the Somme. He was severely wounded in the spine, and invalided home to King George's Hospital, and was afterwards discharged as totally disabled in February 1919. In 1920 he was still a patient in a Nursing Home. He holds the 1914 Star, and the General Service and Victory Medals. 99, Geneva Road, Coldharbour Lane, S.W.9. Z4725

WALKER, E., Rifleman, 18th London Regiment (London Irish Rifles).

He volunteered in February 1914, and in the following February was drafted to France. Whilst overseas he fought in the Battles of Loos and the Somme, and was gassed at Delville Wood and invalided home. After his recovery he was drafted to Egypt and later to Salonika. and served on the Balkan front in many important engagements. He suffered from malaria during his service in the East. He was demobilised in September 1920, and holds the 1914–15 Star, and the General Service and Victory Medals. Z4729

24B Block, Victoria Dwellings, Battersea Park Road, S.W.8.

WALKER, E. W., Private, E.F.C. attached R.A.S.C.

He enlisted in 1916, and was engaged at various stations on important duties with the Expeditionary Force Canteens, attached to the Royal Army Service Corps. He also worked for a time as a checker on the large liners at Liverpool, but unfortunately became seriously ill. He was then sent to hospital and died on July 12th, 1917.

"His memory is cherished with pride."
143, Tyneham Road, Battersea, S.W.11. Z4730

WALKER, G. T., Private, 23rd London Regiment.

Having enlisted in the Territorials in 1909, he was mobilised at the outbreak of war, and drafted to France in March 1915. He rendered excellent service as a despatch rider, and road controller at Festubert, Givenchy and Loos. In the course of his duties he met with a serious accident, and being sent home was invalided out of the Service in September 1917. Since his discharge he has joined the Volunteers, and in 1920 was acting as Staff Sergeant with the Royal Army Medical Corps. He holds the 1914–15 Star, and the General Service and Victory Medals. 178, Bridge Road West, Battersea, S.W.11. Z4731

WALKER, H., Trooper, 2nd and 3rd County of London Yeomanry (Westminster Dragoons and Sharpshooters).

He joined in November 1916, and after his training was sent to Ireland and stationed at Curragh Camp and other places, where he served during many raids in the Irish risings. He rendered valuable services, but owing to ill-health was unable to proceed overseas during the war. He was demobilised in February 1919.

46, Rosenthorpe Road, Peckham Rye, S.E.15.　　Z6770

WALKER, P. S., Rifleman, 21st County of London (1st Surrey Rifles).

He joined in October 1916, and in August of the following year was drafted to France. He was then sent up the line and took part in the fierce fighting in the Ypres salient, where he was killed in action on November 4th, 1917. He was entitled to the General Service and Victory Medals.

"He passed out of the sight of men by the path of duty and self-sacrifice."

40, Riverhall Street, Wandsworth Road, S.W.8.　　Z2515A

WALKER, S., Sergt., 3rd Queen's (Royal West Surrey Regiment).

He volunteered in the R.E. in August 1914, and proceeding to France in the following month served in the Battles of the Aisne, Ypres, Loos and other engagements. In October 1916 he was invalided home through ill-health, and was discharged as unfit for further military duty in December 1917. He holds the 1914 Star, and the General Service and Victory Medals.

115, Bird-in-Bush Road, Peckham, S.E.15.　　Z6593

WALKER, W., Sergt., 2nd London Regiment (Royal Fusiliers).

He was mobilised at the outbreak of war, and was immediately drafted to Malta. He was shortly afterwards sent to the Western Front and fought in the Battles of Ypres, Festubert and Loos. Being severely wounded and gassed in this sector he was invalided home in September 1915, and after receiving medical treatment in various hospitals for eight months was discharged as unfit for further military duties in May 1916. He holds the 1914-15 Star, and the General Service and Victory Medals.

17, Wansey Street, Walworth, S.E.17.　　Z4727

WALKER, W. D., A.B. (Cook), R.N.

A serving sailor at the outbreak of war he was posted to H.M.S. "Monarch," and sent to the North Sea with the Grand Fleet. During his service his ship took part in the Battle of Jutland, and in the bombardment of Zeebrugge. For part of the time he was in H.M. Destroyer "Crusader," and was engaged on important duties in various waters until the cessation of hostilities. He holds the 1914-15 Star, and the General Service and Victory Medals, and in 1920 was still serving.

39, Portslade Road, Wandsworth Road, S.W.8.　　Z4728

WALL, A., Private, 1st Middlesex Regiment.

He was serving at the outbreak of war, and being immediately drafted to France fought in the Retreat from Mons, He was wounded there on August 26th, 1914, taken prisoner, and and was in captivity in various camps in Germany for over four and a half years. He was repatriated in March 1919, and discharged in the same month. He holds the Delhi-Durbar Medal, the Mons Star, and the General Service and Victory Medals.

28, Reynolds Road, Peckham Rye, S.E.15.　　Z6748-9B

WALL, B., Private, 23rd Middlesex Regiment.

He joined in August 1918, and after his training was completed was sent to Germany with the Army of Occupation in 1919. He was engaged on important duties as a driver with the Horse Transport Section of the Royal Army Service Corps, and was stationed at Cologne. He rendered valuable services until April 1920, when he returned home and was demobilised

28, Reynolds Road, Peckham Rye, S.E.15.　　Z6748A
　　　　　　　　　　　　　　　　　　　　　　Z6749A

WALL, G., Sapper, R.E.

He volunteered in October 1914, in the King's Royal Rifle Corps, and was afterwards transferred to the Royal Field Artillery, and later to the Royal Army Service Corps Labour Battalion. In April 1915 he was drafted to France, where he served four months at various places, including Etaples. He was then invalided home for reasons of health and discharged in the following December. He rejoined in November 1916 in the Royal Engineers, and was again sent to France, and after serving in several engagements suffered severe shell-shock in June 1917, and was evacuated to England. After medical treatment in various hospitals for many months he was discharged as medically unfit for further duty in August 1918. He holds the 1914-15 Star, and the General Service and Victory Medals, and in 1920 was still a patient in hospital.

72, Bird-in-Bush Road, Peckham, S.E.15.　　Z6553

WALL, G. J., Sapper, R.E.

He was mobilised at the outbreak of war, and proceeded to France in March 1915. Whilst overseas he was engaged on important duties in connection with the operations at Loos, the Somme, Arras, Vimy Ridge, Ypres and Cambrai. He was afterwards sent to the Base, and was engaged in driving a travelling crane, until the cessation of hostilities. He was demobilised in January 1919, and holds the 1914-15 Star, and the General Service and Victory Medals.

14, Longcroft Road, Camberwell, S.E.5.　　Z5687

WALL, P., Private, 13th York and Lancaster Regt.

He volunteered in November 1915, and after his training was found to be medically unfit and discharged in July 1916. He succeeded in rejoining in July of the following year, and being sent to France in February 1918, served in the important engagements at Nieppe Forest, Bailleul and other places in the Retreat and Advance of that year. He was demobilised from St. Omer in June 1919, and holds the General Service and Victory Medals.

28, Reynold's Road, Peckham Rye, S.E.15.　　Z6748-9C

WALL, T., Private, East Surrey Regiment.

He joined in 1916, and in the same year was drafted to France. During his service overseas he fought in the Battles of the Somme, Arras, Ypres, and Cambrai, and later in the Retreat and Advance of 1918 until the cessation of hostilities. He was demobilised in 1919 after returning home, and holds the General Service and Victory Medals.

77, Hargwyne Street, Stockwell, S.W.9.　　Z1381A

WALLACE, A. A., Private, 3rd Welch Regiment.

He volunteered in August 1915, and in the following December was drafted to France. Whilst overseas he took part in the severe fighting on the Somme, and died gloriously in the Field of Battle at Albert in September 1916. He was entitled to the 1914-15 Star, and the General Service and Victory Medals.

"He died the noblest death a man may die,
Fighting for God, and right, and liberty."

29A, Crimsworth Road, Wandsworth Road, S.W.8.　　Z4733B

WALLACE, J. G., Artificer, M.G.C.

He volunteered in November 1915, and in the following year was drafted to France, where he served for three years. During this period he fought in many important engagements, and was at Etaples when the Germans bombed the hospitals. He also served throughout the Retreat and Advance of 1918, and after the Armistice proceeded to Germany with the Army of Occupation. He was demobilised in March 1919, and holds the General Service and Victory Medals.

29A, Crimsworth Road, Wandsworth Road, S.W.8.　　Z4733A

WALLACE, W., Private, Queen's Own (Royal West Kent Regiment).

Volunteering in August 1914, he proceeded overseas in the following November. He fought in the first Battle of Ypres, and in several other engagements, and gave his life for King and Country in March 1915. He was entitled to the 1914 Star, and the General Service and Victory Medals.

"Nobly striving,
He nobly fell that we might live."

43, Harris Street, Camberwell, S.E.5.　　Z3489A

WALLAKER, E., Air Mechanic, R.A.F. (late R.N.A.S.)

He joined in March 1917, and after his training served at various stations on important duties with his unit. He rendered valuable services, but was not successful in obtaining his transfer overseas before the cessation of hostilities. He was demobilised in February 1919.

9, Crawshay Road, Stockwell, S.W.9.　　Z4734

WALLDER, R. T., Sergt., 2nd London Regiment (Royal Fusiliers).

In 1891 he joined the Volunteers, and at the outbreak of war was drafted to Malta, where he served for some time on important duties. Later he was transferred to the Western Front and took part in the fighting at Armentières, on the Somme, at Arras and Ypres. He was invalided home through ill-health, and was subsequently discharged in January 1918 through causes due to his service. He holds the 1914-15 Star, and the General Service and Victory Medals.

187, Portland Street, Walworth, S.E.17.　　Z27348

WALLER, B., Private, 2/5th Lincolnshire Regiment.

He enlisted in December 1913, and at the outbreak of war was drafted to the Western Front. He took part in the fighting at Ypres, on the Somme and in many other engagements, including that of Arras, where he was killed in action on April 5th, 1918. He was entitled to the 1914 Star, and the General Service and Victory Medals.

"Great deeds cannot die."

70, St. Andrew Street, Wandsworth Road, S.W.8.　　Z4736B

WALLER, C. F., Private, Labour Corps.

He attested in March 1916, but was not called up until the following January. After having completed his training he served at various stations on important clerical duties with his unit. He rendered valuable services, but was not successful in obtaining his transfer overseas before hostilities ceased. He was demobilised in January 1919.

99, Atherley Road, Peckham, S.E.15. Z6771

WALLER, H. H., Private, Queen's (Royal West Surrey Regiment).

Volunteering in August 1914, he embarked in the following year for France, where he saw much service. He was in action at Neuve Chapelle, St. Eloi, Festubert, Loos and in many other engagements. Later he was invalided home through ill-health, and in June 1917 was discharged on account of his service. He holds the 1914-15 Star, and the General Service and Victory Medals.

19, Motley Street, Battersea, S.W.8. Z4735

WALLER, W., Driver, R.F.A. and Gunner, R.G.A.

Volunteering in November 1915, he proceeded on the completion of his training, to Salonika, where he saw much active service. He took part in many engagements in the Balkans, including those on the Vardar front. He returned home and was discharged as unfit for further service in 1919, and holds the General Service and Victory Medals.

10, Rosemary Road, Peckham, S.E.15. Z5524

WALLER, W. J., Sapper, R.E.

He enlisted in October 1911, and at the outbreak of war was sent to France, where he took part in the Retreat from Mons and the Battles of Le Cateau, Ypres, and the Somme. He was also in action during many other engagements, including the Retreat and Advance of 1918. He was demobilised in August 1920, and holds the Mons Star, and the General Service and Victory Medals.

70, St. Andrews Street, Wandsworth Road, S.W.8. Z4736A

WALLIKER, A. P., Bombardier, R.F.A.

A Reservist, he was mobilised at the outbreak of war, and was shortly afterwards sent to France, where he took part in the Battles of the Marne, La Bassée and Armentières. He was wounded and invalided home, but on recovery he returned to the fighting area and was severely gassed and was again sent home. Later he was drafted to Salonika and remained there until returning home for demobilisation in April 1919. He holds the 1914 Star, and the General Service and Victory Medals.

17, Amies Street, Battersea, S.W.11. Z4737

WALLINGTON, C. H., C.S.M., Norfolk Dragoons (The King's Own Royal Regiment).

A Reservist, he was mobilised at the outbreak of war and sent to France, where he took part in the memorable Retreat from Mons. He was in action in many other engagements, including those at Ypres, on the Somme, at Arras, and was twice wounded. He was invalided to England and on recovery served on important home duties until demobilised in March 1919. He holds the Mons Star, and the General Service and Victory Medals.

51, Silverlock Street, Rotherhithe, S.E.16. Z6722

WALLIS, E. A., L/Corporal, 11th Royal Scots.

Volunteering in June 1915, he was drafted in the same year to the Western Front, and was in action in many battles. He took part in the fighting at Loos, Vimy Ridge, on the Somme and was wounded. He was invalided home and after receiving hospital treatment was demobilised in December 1918. He holds the 1914-15 Star, and the General Service and Victory Medals.

27, Dorset Road, Coldharbour Lane, S.W.8. Z4739A

WALLIS, F. G., Private, 1/6th East Surrey Regt.

He joined in April 1916, and in the following November embarked for France. He was in action in many engagements, including those at Beaumont-Hamel, Arras, Vimy Ridge, and Bullecourt, and was seriously wounded. He was invalided home, and after being in hospital some considerable time, succumbed to his injuries on October 6th, 1919, and was entitled to the General Service and Victory Medals.

"His life for his Country, his Soul to God."

13, Scylla Road, Peckham, S.E.15. Z6015B

WALLIS, G., Private, 3rd Royal Fusiliers.

He volunteered in November 1914, and in May of the following year embarked for France, where he was wounded during the fighting at Ypres. On recovery he proceeded to Salonika, and there was in action on the Doiran and Struma fronts. He contracted fever, and after being in hospital for some considerable time was demobilised in March 1919. He holds the 1914-15 Star, and the General Service and Victory Medals.

100, Wickersley Road, Lavender Hill, S.W.11. Z4740

WALLIS, H., Private, 2nd London Regiment (Royal Fusiliers).

Mobilised at the outbreak of war, he was sent to Malta, where he served for about five months. He then proceeded to France and fought in many engagements, including those of Neuve Chapelle, Ypres, Loos, Armentières, and was wounded twice, and also gassed. He was demobilised in December 1918, and holds the 1914-15 Star, and the General Service and Victory Medals.

27, Dorset Road, Clapham Road, S.W.8. Z4739B

WALLIS, J. F. J., Rifleman, Rifle Brigade.

He volunteered in March 1915, and in the same year was drafted overseas. Whilst in France he fought in many notable engagements, including those of Ypres and on the Somme, and was wounded twice and also gassed. He was invalided home, and on recovery proceeded to Mesopotamia, where in 1920 he was still serving. He holds the 1914-15 Star, and the General Service and Victory Medals.

1, Lewis Road, East Camberwell, S.E.5. Z6178B

WALLIS, T. G., Corporal, 5th Bedfordshire Regt.

He volunteered in March 1915, at the age of thirteen, but was shortly afterwards discharged on account of his age. Subsequently he enlisted on three different occasions, each time being discharged after a short period of service. Later he served in the Mercantile Marine, on important mine sweeping duties, and also in bringing troops from America to France, and did valuable work. He was finally discharged in September 1917, and holds the General Service and Victory Medals.

118, Blake's Road, Peckham, S.E.15. Z6128A

WALLIS, T. W., 1st Air Mechanic, R.A.F.

Volunteering in 1915, he completed his training and served at various stations on important duties with his Squadron. He did valuable work, but was not successful in obtaining his transfer overseas owing to his services being indispensable. In April 1919 he was demobilised.

28, Reform Street, Battersea, S.W.11. Z4738

WALLIS, W. D., Corporal, 3rd East Surrey Regt.

He volunteered in August 1915, and on two subsequent occasions, each time being discharged after a short period of service on account of his being under age. Later he rejoined in the Dorset Regiment, and went to France, where he saw much service, but was sent home and transferred to the East Surrey Regiment, with which he served on important duties until demobilised in May 1919. He holds the General Service and Victory Medals.

118, Blake's Road, Peckham, S.E.15. Z6128B

WALLIS, W. G., Pte., 24th London Regt. (Queen's) and R.D.C.

He volunteered in October 1914, and after his training served on important guard and defence duties at various stations. He rendered valuable services, but was not able to obtain his transfer overseas on account of ill-health, and in October 1916 was discharged.

118, Blake's Road, Peckham, S.E.15. Z6128C

WALMSLEY, F., B.S.M., R.F.A.

He had previously served for eight years in India, and re-joining in November 1916, he was drafted in the following March to the Western Front. There he took part in many notable engagements, including those of Cambrai and Arras, and was also in charge of a gas section and did much good work. After hostilities ceased he proceeded to Germany with the Army of Occupation, serving there until demobilised in November 1919. He holds the General Service and Victory Medals.

48, Basnett Road, Lavender Hill, S.W.11. Z4741

WALSH, E. S., Private, R.M.L.I.

He enlisted in January 1904, and at the outbreak of war was serving in H.M.S. "Princess Royal." On board this ship he took part in the engagements off the Heligoland Bight, at the Dogger Bank and in the Battle of Jutland, later being engaged on important patrol duties in the North Sea until June 1918. He was then drafted to France, and during the fierce fighting at Cambrai in September 1918 was wounded and invalided home. On recovery he served on home duties until demobilised in September 1920. He holds the 1914-15 Star, and the General Service and Victory Medals.

42, Palmerston Street, Battersea, S.W.11. Z4742

WALSH, J., Private, 1st Royal Munster Fusiliers.

He enlisted in 1894, and was stationed in India at the outbreak of war, in 1915 being drafted to Gallipoli. There he took part in the fighting at Krithia and was severely wounded at Suvla Bay. He was invalided home and after receiving hospital treatment was discharged as medically unfit in December 1916. He holds the General Service and Victory Medals.

15, Arthur Road, Brixton, S.W.9. Z4464B

WALSH, J., Pte., Queen's (Royal West Surrey Regt.)
He enlisted in 1890, and at the outbreak of war went to France with the British Expeditionary Force, and took part in the Retreat from Mons. He was also in action in many other engagements, including those at Neuve Chapelle. In 1917 he was invalided home through ill-health and was discharged as medically unfit. Having previously served in India and South Africa, he holds the India General Service Medal, the Queen's and King's South African Medals, the Mons Star, and the General Service and Victory Medals.
10, Milford Street, Clapham, S.W.8. Z5554B

WALSH, T., Pte., King's Shropshire Light Infantry.
He joined in January 1916, and on the completion of his training was drafted to France. There he fought in many notable battles, including those of Ypres and Cambrai. In September 1919 he returned home and was demobilised, holding the General Service and Victory Medals.
13, Biscay Road, Hammersmith, W.6. 72797B

WALSH, W. T., Driver, R.F.A.
Mobilised at the outbreak of war he was soon afterwards drafted to the Western Front. Whilst there he took part in many important battles, including those of the Marne, La Bassée, Ypres, Neuve Chapelle, Hill 60, and the Somme, where he was wounded, He was invalided home and subsequently succumbed to his injuries on September 13th, 1916, and was entitled to the 1914 Star, and the General Service and Victory Medals.
" His life for his Country, his Soul to God."
5, Nunhead Lane, Peckham, S.E.15. Z6356

WALTERS, F. T., Gunner, R.G.A.
Volunteering in November 1915, he embarked for France in the following year. Whilst there he was in action in many battles and died gloriously fighting for King and Country on October 14th, 1918. He was entitled to the General Service and Victory Medals.
" Great deeds cannot die."
25, Alexandra Road, West Kensington, W.14. 12088B

WALTERS, H. J., Private, R.A.S.C.
Mobilised at the outbreak of war he was speedily drafted to France, and there served during the Retreat from Mons, and the Battle of the Marne. He was also in action in many other engagements until hostilities ceased, and in March 1919 returned home and was demobilised. He holds the Mons Star, and the General Service and Victory Medals.
25, Alexandra Road, West Kensington, W.14. 12088A

WALTHAM, J. H., Trooper, Surrey Lancers (Queen Mary's Regiment).
Mobilised at the commencement of hostilities he served at various stations until drafted to Salonika in August 1916. He fought in many important engagements and later was transferred to Russia, where he saw much service. He returned home and was demobilised in July 1919, and holds the General Service and Victory Medals.
42, Mann Street, Walworth, S.E.17. Z4743

WALTON, A. J., Pte., 8th and 9th Royal Fusiliers.
He volunteered in February 1915, and shortly afterwards embarked for the Western Front, where he was in action in many important engagements at Ypres, Albert, Vimy Ridge, and the Somme, and was wounded at Loos. On recovery he rejoined his unit and was engaged in heavy fighting in the Retreat and Advance of 1918. He was demobilised in January 1919, and holds the 1914-15 Star, and the General Service and Victory Medals.
260, Albert Road, Peckham, S.E.15. Z5863

WALTON, C. H. A., Cpl., 2nd South Wales Borderers.
He was mobilised in August 1914, and in the following April embarked for the Dardanelles. During his service overseas he took part in the Landing at Gallipoli, and was reported missing on April 26th, 1915, during the first Battle of Krithia. Later he was presumed to have been killed on that date. He was entitled to the 1914-15 Star, and the General Service and Victory Medals.
" He joined the great white company of valiant souls."
7, Santley Street, Ferndale Road, S.W.4. Z4744

WALTON, W. H., Sergt., 22nd London Regiment (The Queen's).
He was mobilised at the outbreak of hostilities, and in 1916 was sent to the Western Front, where he fought in the first British Offensive on the Somme. Transferred to Salonika, he saw much service in this theatre of war, and in 1917 proceeded to Egypt. He was in action in many parts of the line and served throughout the final British Advance into and through Syria. Returning to England, he was demobilised in March 1919, and holds the General Service and Victory Medals.
44, Lugard Road, Peckham, S.E.15. Z6723

WAND, W., Driver, R.F.A.
He volunteered in August 1914, and in March of the following year was drafted to the Western Front, where he took part in various engagements, including those at Ypres, Loos, Albert, the Somme and Arras. He also served in the Retreat and holds the 1914-15 Star, and the General Service and Victory Medals.
20, Kingston Street, Walworth, S.E.17. Z27485

WANNEL, G. H., Pte., Queen's (Royal West Surrey Regiment).
He volunteered in August 1914, and in May of the following year embarked for France. He was in action at Loos, Vermelles, Ploegsteert, Arras and Givenchy, and throughout the German Offensive and Allied Advance of 1918. He was demobilised in March 1919, and holds the 1914-15 Star, and the General Service and Victory Medals.
33, Runham Street, Walworth, S.E.17. Z4745A

WANNEL, G. H. H., Private, 2nd Middlesex Regt.
Volunteering in February 1915, and drafted to France in the following June, he fought in many parts of the line. He was unfortunately killed in action on the Somme front on July 1st, 1916, and was entitled to the 1914-15 Star, and the General Service and Victory Medals.
" His memory is cherished with pride."
33, Runham Street, Walworth, S.E.17. Z4745B

WARD, A. C., Corporal, 1/13th London Regt. (Kensingtons).
Volunteering in February 1916, shortly afterwards he was sent to the Western Front, and fought in the first Battle of the Somme. Owing to ill-health he was invalided home in October 1916. On recovery he served at various home stations until October 1918, and then proceeded to France, and fought throughout the closing operations of the war. He was demobilised in February 1919, and holds the General Service and Victory Medals.
4, Crawshay Road, Stockwell, S.W.9. Z5163

WARD, A. E., Sapper, R.E.
He volunteered in January 1915, and in the following November was drafted to the Western Front. During the whole of his service overseas he served in the Loos sector, and was wounded severely in 1916, whilst working between the lines. Returning home he received hospital treatment and was discharged as unfit for further service in June 1916. He holds the 1914-15 Star, and the General Service and Victory Medals.
6, Ingrave Street, Battersea, S.W.11. Z4753

WARD, A. W., Corporal, M.G.C.
He volunteered in 1915, and in the following year embarked for France, where he served in the Ypres salient for some months before proceeding to Egypt. On the Palestine front he fought at Magdhaba, Rafa, Gaza, and throughout the British Advance into Syria. Returning to England, he was demobilised in October 1919, and holds the General Service and Victory Medals.
106 Copeland Road, Peckham Rye, S.E.15. Z5688

WARD, C., Private, 3rd Middlesex Regiment.
He volunteered in August 1914, and in the following April was sent to France, where he fought in many engagements of note. He gave his life for the freedom of England on May 10th, 1915, and was entitled to the 1914-15 Star, and the General Service and Victory Medals.
" Great deeds cannot die."
132, Gloucester Road, Peckham, S.E.15. Z5982A

WARD, C., Rifleman, King's Royal Rifle Corps.
He volunteered in March 1915, and in the following year was sent to the Western Front and fought in many parts of the line. In 1917 he was transferred to Salonika, and here he was engaged in heavy fighting in various sectors and was wounded. After the Armistice he returned home and was demobilised in March 1919. He holds the General Service and Victory Medals. 12, Banim Street, Hammersmith, W.6. 11615D

WARD, F., Private, 1st East Surrey Regiment.
He enlisted in July 1913, and at the declaration of war was sent to France, and fought in the Retreat from Mons, at the Battles of the Marne, La Bassée and Ypres, and was invalided home in December 1914, suffering from frost-bite. It was found necessary to amputate his left leg, and after five years' treatment in hospital to amputate the toes of his right foot. He was discharged as medically unfit in October 1920, and holds the Mons Star, and the General Service and Victory Medals. 80, Cronin Road, Peckham, S.E.15. Z5689

WARD, F., Private, Bedfordshire Regiment.
He joined in 1917, and in the following year was sent to the Western Front, and was engaged in heavy fighting throughout the German Offensive and Allied Advance of 1918. After the Armistice he proceeded to Germany with the Army of Occupation, and served there until he returned home and was demobilised in 1920. He holds the General Service and Victory Medals. 15, Beddome Street, Walworth, S.E.17. Z4746

WARD, G., Rifleman, King's Royal Rifle Corps.
Joining in 1917, and shortly afterwards drafted to the Western Front, he fought in many important engagements and was gassed and twice wounded. Later he was sent to Egypt, and saw considerable service there. After the Armistice he proceeded into Turkey with the Army of Occupation and was still serving there in 1920. He holds the General Service and Victory Medals.
12, Banim Street, Hammersmith, W.6.   11615A

WARD, G., Private, 1/4th Oxfordshire and Buckinghamshire Light Infantry,
Volunteering in August 1914, he served at various depôts until proceeding to the Western Front in February 1916. He fought in the Battles of Ypres, Bullecourt and Passchendaele, and was transferred to Italy in November 1917. He was in action in many engagements on the Piave front, and in various other sectors until the cessation of hostilities. Returning home he was demobilised in February 1919, and holds the General Service and Victory Medals.
24, Birley Street, Battersea, S.W.11.   Z4747

WARD, H. A., Private, R.A.S.C.
He volunteered in June 1915, and was almost immediately drafted to the Western Front, where he served chiefly with the R.O.D. He was also present at engagements at Ypres, the Somme and Festubert, and on one occasion was blown up by the explosion of a shell and severely gassed. He returned home and after receiving hospital treatment was discharged as medically unfit in March 1917. He holds the 1914-15 Star, and the General Service and Victory Medals.
88, Horne Road, Battersea, S.W.11.   Z1215B

WARD, H. J., Private, 3rd East Surrey Regt.
Joining in May 1918, he proceeded to the Western Front in the following September, and was in action at Epéhy, Cambrai, Le Cateau, and several other important engagements during the final Allied Advance. After the cessation of hostilities he was sent into Germany with the Army of Occupation and served at Cologne. Returning home he was demobilised in January 1920, and holds the General Service and Victory Medals.
67, Stuart Road, Peckham, S.E.15.   Z6750

WARD, H. W., Leading Seaman, R.N.
He volunteered in August 1914, and during the war saw much service both in home waters and abroad. He saw active service in Russia, and he served on four different ships, which were all torpedoed in the Mediterranean. He was demobilised in March 1919, and holds the 9114-15 Star, and the General Service and Victory Medals.
12, Banim Street, Hammersmith, W.6.   11615B

WARD, H. W., Private, R.A.S.C.
He joined in March 1916, and completing his training was stationed at various depôts engaged on important duties with his unit. Owing to ill-health he was unsuccessful in obtaining his transfer overseas, but rendered excellent services until invalided out in August 1917.
7 Flat, 158, Queen's Road, Battersea Park, S.W.8.   Z4750

WARD, J., Private, Royal Welch Fusiliers.
He joined in 1916, and later in the same year landed in France. During his service overseas, he fought in the Battles of the Somme and Arras, and was severely wounded at Ypres in 1917. He was in hospital seven months, and then rejoining his Battalion was in action throughout the Retreat and Advance of 1918. He was demobilised in 1919, and holds the General Service and Victory Medals.
123, Barlow Street, Walworth, S.E.17.   Z4754

WARD, J., Gunner, R.F.A.
Volunteering in November 1914, ten months later he embarked for the Western Front, where he was in action in heavy fighting in many engagements. He fought at Loos, Albert, Beaumont-Hamel, Messines, Lens, Havrincourt, and throughout the Retreat and Advance of 1918, and was twice wounded and gassed. He was demobilised in February 1919, and holds the 1914-15 Star, and the General Service and Victory Medals.
72, Nelson Row, Clapham, S.W.4.   Z4752

WARD, J. F. (M.M.), Corporal, R.F.A.
He enlisted in August 1913, and at the outbreak of hostilities was sent to France. He fought in the Retreat from Mons, and the Battle of the Aisne, and was wounded on September 15th, 1914. On recovery he rejoined his Battery and was in action at La Bassée, Ypres, Neuve Chapelle, Loos, and the Somme, and was wounded. On his discharge from hospital he returned to the Front and fought throughout the Retreat and Advance of 1918. He was awarded the Military Medal for gallantry and devotion to duty in the Field, and in addition holds the Mons Star, and the General Service and Victory Medals, and was demobilised in January 1920.
9, Meyrick Road, Battersea, S.W.11.   Z4794

WARD, J. H., Private, R.A.S.C. (M.T.)
Joining in 1917, later in that year he was sent to German East Africa, and saw heavy fighting in many parts of the line until the conclusion of that campaign. He returned home and was demobilised in April 1919, and holds the General Service and Victory Medals.
12, Banim Street, Hammersmith, W.6.   11615C

WARD, J. S., Gunner, R.G.A. and R.F.A.
Volunteering in April 1915, later in the same year he embarked for France and served in many parts of the line fighting on the Somme, and at Ypres, Armentières, Vimy Ridge, and Lens, and throughout the Retreat and Advance of 1918. He was demobilised in July 1919, and holds the 1914-15 Star, and the General Service and Victory Medals.
18, Russell Grove, Vassell Road, S.W.9.   Z5164

WARD, J. W., Leading Stoker, R.N.
He joined the Service in 1910, and at the outbreak of war was in H.M.T.B.D. "Flying Fish." Later he was posted to H.M.S. "Myosotis," which ship was engaged on important duties off the Irish Coast. On September 9th, 1917, she was torpedoed and he was wounded. Returning to England he received hospital treatment and was invalided out of the Service in April 1919. He holds the 1914-15 Star, and the General Service and Victory Medals.
17, Knox Road, Battersea, S.W.11.   Z4748

WARD, J. W., Private, 19th London Regiment.
He joined in July 1916, and in January of the following year was sent to the Western Front. He was severely wounded in the Battle of the Ancre, and invalided to hospital in Boulogne, and subsequently died there on February 1st, 1917. He was entitled to the General Service and Victory Medals.
"Courage, bright hopes, and a myriad dreams splendidly given."
90, Henley Street, Battersea, S.W.11.   Z1906B

WARD, P. T. S., Private, 22nd London Regiment (Queen's).
He attested in December 1915, and was called up in June 1916, but on account of his medical unfitness for active service was not sent overseas, but was engaged in the danger zone building at Woolwich Arsenal until he was demobilised in January 1919. His duties, which were of a most important nature, were carried out with great care and efficiency.
8, Mossington Road, Rotherhithe, S.E.16.   Z6802

WARD, T. W., Driver, R.A.S.C.
Volunteering in February 1916, shortly afterwards he proceeded to Mesopotamia, and served on important transport duties in many parts of the line. Transferred to Egypt, he was present at many engagements of note, and rendered excellent services throughout the final British Advance into Syria. He returned to England and was demobilised in February 1919, and holds the General Service and Victory Medals.
2, Walter Terrace, South Lambeth, S.W.8.   Z27529

WARD, W. (M.M.), Sergt., 2nd Grenadier Guards.
He enlisted in May 1909, and proceeding to France at the commencement of hostilities, fought in the Retreat from Mons, and was wounded. On recovery he rejoined his Battalion, and was in action at Ypres and Festubert, where he was again wounded. He received treatment and returning to the front lines was engaged in heavy fighting in the Somme, Arras and Cambrai sectors, and during the Retreat and Advance of 1918, and was wounded in August 1918. Returning home he received treatment and on recovery rejoined his unit in March 1919, and was still serving in 1920. He was awarded the Military Medal for conspicuous gallantry and devotion to duty in the Field, and also holds the Mons Star, and the General Service and Victory Medals.
12B, Block, Lewis Trust Buildings, Camberwell, S.E.5.   Z6121

WARD, W. A., Rifleman, 6th Rifle Brigade.
He joined in June 1918, and completing his training served at various stations engaged on guard and other important duties, but was unsuccessful in obtaining his transfer to a theatre of war prior to the cessation of hostilities. Later he was taken ill and died on December 2nd, 1918, aged eighteen years.
"His memory is cherished with pride."
53, Goldie Street, Camberwell, S.E.5.   Z5525

WARD, W. C., Driver, R.A.S.C.
He enlisted in May 1911, and at the commencement of war was sent to France, where he served throughout the Retreat from Mons, and was present during the severe fighting in the Ypres and the Somme sectors. In 1917, transferred to Italy, he served on the Piave and the Asiago Plateau, engaged on important transport duties. He rendered excellent services during the final Allied Advance in 1918, and returning home was demobilised in March 1919. He holds the Mons Star, and the General Service and Victory Medals.
174, Farmer's Road, Camberwell, S.E.5.   Z4751

WARD, W. D., Private, R.M.L.I.
He joined in February 1917, and served at various stations on important duties with his unit until the cessation of hostilities. In August 1919 he was drafted to Russia and saw heavy fighting in many sectors. He returned to England, and was demobilised in 1920, and holds the General Service and Victory Medals. 22, Kingston Street, Walworth, S.E.17.   Z27475

WARD, W. G., Private, 13th Duke of Wellington's (West Riding Regiment).
He joined in March 1916, and completing his training served at various stations until proceeding to the Western Front in 1918. He was in action in many important engagements during the Retreat and Advance of 1918, and returning home after the Armistice was demobilised in September 1919, and holds the General Service and Victory Medals. 19, Credon Road, Rotherhithe, S.E.16.   Z6724

WARDE, J. E., Driver, R.A.S.C. (M.T.)
Volunteering in December 1915, he had previously been engaged on special Secret Service work and was sent to Egypt in the following year. He served on important duties connected with food supplies, but later owing to illness was invalided to hospital. On his recovery he was employed on clerical work until demobilised in April 1919, and holds the General Service and Victory Medals. 63, Treherne Road, Stockwell, S.W.9.   Z4755

WARDEN, J. W., Tpr., Fife and Forfar Dragoons.
He volunteered in 1915, but during his training his health broke down and he was discharged as physically unfit for further service later in the same year. 14, Crichton Street, Wandsworth Road, S.W.8.   Z4756

WARE, E. F., Corporal, R.A.V.C.
Volunteering in November 1914, he was drafted to France in the following month. He served in many sectors and was engaged as Corporal dresser in attendance on sick and wounded horses. In November 1917, he was transferred to Italy, where he was engaged on similar duties. He later returned to France, and there remained until demobilised in April 1919. He holds the 1914–15 Star, and the General Service and Victory Medals. 13, Victoria Road, Peckham, S.E.15.   Z6814

WARE, F. W., Private, R.A.S.C.
Joining in April 1915 he was sent to France in the same year, and was engaged on important transport duties at Loos, the Somme, Arras, Ypres, and Dunkirk. He later proceeded with the Army of Occupation to Germany, where he remained until he was demobilised in April 1919, holding the 1914–15 Star, and the General Service and Victory Medals. 13, Barlow Street, Walworth, S.E.17.   Z2925A

WARE, J., Driver, R.E.
He volunteered in April 1915, and whilst training met with an accident, sustaining a fracture of his thigh. He received hospital treatment, but on recovery was not deemed physically fit for further service with the Colours, and consequently was invalided out in July 1916. 126, Keeton's Road, Rotherhithe, S.E.16.   Z6824

WARE, J. S., Private, R.A.M.C.
He joined in 1916, and after completing his training was drafted to France, where he was engaged at Le Havre and on the Somme in attending to the sick and wounded. He also served on exhumation duties. He was demobilised in September 1919, and holds the General Service and Victory Medals. 48, Halstead Street, Brixton Road, S.W.9.   Z4757

WARE, T., Private, R.A.S.C.
Volunteering in September 1914 he was drafted to France in the following year. He was engaged on important transport duties at Ypres, where he was wounded in May 1915, and was invalided home. On his recovery he returned to France, and was present at engagements at Loos, St. Eloi, the Somme, Ypres, Passchendaele, Amiens and Bapaume, and later proceeded to Germany with the Army of Occupation. He was demobilised in March 1919, and holds the 1914–15 Star, and the General Service and Victory Medals. 28, Atherton Street, Battersea, S.W.11.   Z4759

WARE, W., Private, Royal Fusiliers.
He joined in June 1916, and in the following month was sent to the Western Front. He was engaged in various sectors with the Labour Corps in the repair of roads and other important duties and rendered valuable services. He was demobilised in September 1919, and holds the General Service and Victory Medals. 30, Runham Street, Walworth, S.E.17.   Z4758

WAREHAM, Louise, Special War Worker.
This lady was engaged for four years by the London United Tramways Company, Chiswick Branch. Her duties which were of an important nature were carried out in a most efficient manner, and she rendered valuable services during the war. 27, Askew Crescent, Shepherds Bush, W.12.   5488C

WAREHAM, E. E., Private, Royal Fusiliers.
He was mobilised in August 1914, and was shortly afterwards sent to France, where he took part in the Battle of Mons, and was wounded. He was afterwards transferred to Salonika, where he was again in action, and during his service in this theatre of war contracted malaria. He returned home and was demobilised in February 1919, holding the Mons Star, and the General Service and Victory Medals. 47, Eastbury Grove, Chiswick, W.4.   5488A

WAREHAM, F. A. G., Rifleman, Rifle Brigade.
After joining in April 1916, and completing his training he was sent to France, where he took part in numerous engagements including that at Arras. He was wounded and invalided home, and on his recovery was drafted to Salonika, where he was again in action and was taken prisoner by the Bulgarians. He unfortunately died in captivity. He was entitled to the General Service and Victory Medals.
"His memory is cherished with pride."
47, Eastbury Grove, Chiswick, W.4.   5488B

WAREHAM, S., Corporal, 5th Royal Fusiliers.
He volunteered in June 1917, and in the following September was drafted to France, where he took part in numerous engagements, including those at Ypres and Cambrai. He also served in the Retreat and Advance of 1918, and afterwards proceeded with the Army of Occupation to Germany. He was demobilised in October 1919, and holds the General Service and Victory Medals. 58, Rosemary Road, Peckham, S.E.15.   Z5298

WARING, E. C. T., Private, Tank Corps.
He joined in January 1916, and after completing his training was drafted to the Western Front, where he took part in numerous engagements and was wounded and invalided home. He was discharged in March 1918, owing to his injuries, and holds the General Service and Victory Medals. 117, Brackenbury Road, Hammersmith, W.6.   11163

WARMINGTON, E., Private, Royal Fusiliers and Labour Corps.
Joining in February 1916, he was drafted to France in the following month and took part in numerous engagements. He also served in the Retreat and Advance of 1918. He returned home and was demobilised in January 1919, holding the General Service and Victory Medals. 30, Choumert Square, Peckham, S.E.15.   Z6793A

WARMINGTON, J., Special War Worker.
He was engaged at Messrs. Vickery's, Old Kent Road, and was employed in the fitting and drilling of Mills' hand grenades. His duties were carried out in an efficient manner and he rendered valuable services during the war. 30, Choumert Square, Peckham, S.E.15.   Z6793B

WARNE, E. S., Rifleman, 21st London Regiment (1st Surrey Rifles).
He joined in 1916, and in the same years proceeded to France, where he took part in various engagements, including those in the Somme sector. In 1917 he was drafted to Egypt, and was attached to General Allenby's Forces in Palestine. He returned to England for demobilisation in 1919, and holds the General Service and Victory Medals. 1, Fairford Grove, Kennington, S.E.11.   Z27398

WARNER, A. R. W., Private, Labour Corps.
Joining in March 1917 he was drafted to France in the following month, and was engaged on important work in numerous engagements, including those on the Somme and at Arras, Ypres, and Cambrai. He also took part in the Retreat and Advance of 1918, and after the Armistice proceeded with the Army of Occupation to Germany. He was demobilised in February 1919, and holds the General Service and Victory Medals. 46, Denmark Road, Camberwell, S.E.5.   Z6123

WARNER, C. H., Pioneer, R.E.
He volunteered in August 1915, and later in the same year was drafted to France, where he took part in numerous engagements, including those at Loos, St. Eloi, the Somme and Ypres. He returned home and was demobilised in April 1920, holding the 1914–15 Star, and the General Service and Victory Medals. 11, Dorset Road, Clapham Road, S.W.8.   Z4760

WARNER, F., Private, 16th Queen's (Royal West Surrey Regiment).
He joined in March 1918, and after his training was found unfit for active service, and was transferred to the R.A.O.C., with which he was engaged on important duties until discharged in July 1919 as medically unfit for further service. 85, Arthur Road, Brixton Road, S.W.9.   Z4761B

WARNER, H., L/Corporal, 20th Middlesex Regt.
Having previously served for twenty-four years in the Buffs (East Kent Regiment) he voluntarily re-enlisted in June 1918, and was sent to France, where he took part in the Advance of 1918. He returned home and was demobilised in February 1919, holding the Queen's and King's South African and the General Service and Victory Medals. 85, Arthur Road, Brixton, S.W.9.   Z476A

WARNER, J., Private, R.A.S.C. (Remount Depôt).
He volunteered in October 1914, and in the same year was drafted to the Western Front, where he was engaged on the Somme and at Arras and Ypres in conducting horses to the front to replace those killed. He was later transferred to Italy, and after the Armistice was employed on important duties in Austria. He was demobilised in July 1919, and holds the 1914-15 Star, and the General Service and Victory Medals.
18, Treherne Road, Stockwell, S.W.9. Z4762

WARNOCK, B. W., Private, Labour Corps.
He joined in October 1916, and after his training served on important duties until 1918, when he was drafted to France, and took part in the Retreat and Advance of that year. He also served in the Suffolk, Middlesex and East Surrey Regiments. He was demobilised in January 1919, and holds the General Service and Victory Medals.
52, Tranton Road, Rotherhithe, S.E.16. Z6825

WARR, G. W., Rifleman, King's Royal Rifle Corps, Private, Royal Fusiliers and Sapper, R.E.
After joining in May 1916, he went through a course of training and was then engaged on important duties with his unit until 1918, when he was sent to France, where he took part in the Retreat and Advance of that year. He was demobilised in October 1919, and holds the General Service and Victory Medals.
103, Sandmere Road, Clapham, S.W.4. Z2084A

WARR, W., Gunner, R.G.A.
He was mobilised in August 1914, and was drafted to France with the original Expeditionary Force. He served in numerous notable engagements throughout the war, and during this period was seriously injured in an accident with a horse. He was demobilised in March 1919, and holds the 1914 Star, and the General Service and Victory Medals.
3, Cyril Street, Walworth, S.E.17. Z26225A

WARREN, A. A., Private, 23rd Royal Fusiliers.
Volunteering in December 1915, he was drafted to France in the following year and was in action at St. Eloi, Vimy Ridge, Arras, Ypres and Béthune. He returned home and was demobilised in September 1919, and holds the General Service and Victory Medals.
216, Stewart's Road, Battersea Park Road, S.W.8. Z4763

WARREN, A. J., Corporal, 8th London Regiment (Post Office Rifles).
He joined in January 1917, and was sent to France in the same year and took part in the fighting in numerous actions. He was taken prisoner in March 1918, and sent to Germany. On his release he returned home and was demobilised in November 1919, holding the General Service and Victory Medals.
13, Neate Street, Camberwell, S.E.5. Z5165A

WARREN, F. E., Air Mechanic, R.A.F.
He volunteered in July 1915, and was engaged on important duties with his Squadron until 1917, when he was drafted to Italy, where he was wounded in action and invalided home. He unfortunately died in Netley Hospital from the effects of his injuries on October 8th, 1918, and was entitled to the General Service and Victory Medals.
"The path of duty was the way to glory."
8, Medlar Street, Camberwell, S.E.5. Z4764A

WARREN, J., Private, Labour Corps.
Volunteering in March 1915, he was drafted to the Western Front in the same year and was engaged on important duties in the transport of ammunition and supplies to the various fronts. He was demobilised in March 1919, and holds the 1914-15 Star, and the General Service and Victory Medals. He re-enlisted, however, in June 1919, and returned to France, where he was employed in re-burying the dead until 1920.
24, Mund Street, W. Kensington, W.14. 16433

WARREN, J. J., Private, 15th Middlesex Regiment.
He joined in June 1916, and after his training was engaged on important duties with his unit. He rendered valuable services, but was not successful in obtaining his transfer overseas owing to being medically unfit for duty abroad. He was discharged in June 1917.
13, Neate Street, Camberwell, S.E.5. Z5165C

WARREN, R. C., Private, Royal Fusiliers.
He joined in September 1916, and was posted to the Sussex Dragoons and was later transferred to the Royal Sussex Regiment. He was sent to France in May 1917, and then joined the Royal Fusiliers. He was in action at Vimy Ridge, Messines and Passchendaele, and was wounded and invalided home. On his recovery he returned to his unit. He was demobilised in September 1919, and holds the General Service and Victory Medals.
29, Stanton Street, Peckham, S.E.15. Z5299

WARREN, S. C., Driver, R.F.A.
He volunteered in January 1915, and in the same year was sent to France, where he took part in the fighting at Loos, Vimy Ridge, the Somme and Arras, and was severely gassed in April 1916. He also served in the Retreat and Advance of 1918. He was demobilised in April 1919, and holds the 1914-15 Star, and the General Service and Victory Medals.
13, Neate Street, Camberwell, S.E.5. Z5165B

WARREN, W. E., Sapper, R.E.
He joined in July 1916, and was engaged on the East Coast on important duties with his unit. He rendered valuable services, but was not successful in obtaining his transfer overseas before the cessation of hostilities. He was demobilised in March 1919.
8, Medlar Street, Camberwell, S.E. Z4764B

WARRY, H., Sergt., R.E.
He volunteered in February 1915, and in the same year was drafted to the Western Front. He was engaged on Inland Water Transport duties throughout his service in France and did excellent work. He was demobilised in May 1919, and holds the 1914-15 Star, and the General Service and Victory Medals.
8, Thessaly Square, Wandsworth Road, S.W.8. Z4765

WARWICK, E. C., Rifleman, Rifle Brigade.
He volunteered in July 1915, and in the same year proceeded overseas. Whilst in France he fought and was severely wounded in the Battle of Ypres. After being invalided home, and receiving medical treatment in several military hospitals, he was discharged as physically unfit for further duty in November 1918. He holds the 1914-15 Star, and the General Service and Victory Medals.
15, Calmington Road, Camberwell, S.E.5. Z5526A

WARWICKER, W., Special War Worker.
He was in the employ of the London, Brighton and South Coast Railway Company at the outbreak of war, and throughout the course of hostilities was engaged on work of the utmost importance in connection with the transport of munitions and food supplies, and rendered valuable services.
23, Calmington Road, Camberwell, S.E.5. Z5527

WASHER, A. T., Bombardier, R.F.A.
Volunteering in September 1915, he proceeded overseas in the following July and was in action at the Somme and Vermelles. He was wounded in the third Battle of Ypres in July 1917, and was invalided home to hospital. After several months in England he rejoined his Battery in France and served with distinction in various engagements in the operations of 1918 until the Armistice was signed. He was demobilised in February 1919, and holds the General Service and Victory Medals.
12, Claude Road, Peckham, S.E.15. Z5864

WASHER, W. A., Sergt., R.E.
He was mobilised at the outbreak of war, and almost immediately was drafted to France, where he served in the Retreat from Mons. Being wounded, he was sent home, but after a few weeks rejoined his unit and was again wounded at La Bassée. After medical treatment he was discharged as unfit for further service in August 1915. He rejoined, however, in the following July and was retained on important duties at Chepstow until the cessation of hostilities. In February 1919, he was demobilised and holds the Mons Star, and the General Service and Victory Medals.
3, Rushcroft Road, Brixton, S.W.2. Z4766

WATERMAN, A., Private, 1st Royal Fusiliers.
Volunteering in September 1914, he was drafted overseas in the following year, on the completion of his training. After taking part in various engagements he gave his life for the freedom of England at Ypres on July 16th, 1916. He was entitled to the 1914-15 Star, and the General Service and Victory Medals.
"His life for his Country, his Soul to God."
26, Kay Road, Stockwell, S.W.9. Z4767

WATERS, A., Driver, R.F.A.
Volunteering in August 1914, he crossed to France in the following April and was engaged on important duties as a driver at Hill 60, Ypres, Festubert and Loos, where he suffered shell-shock. After medical treatment for about three months he rejoined his Battery and was present in the engagements at Ploegsteert Wood, the Somme, Passchendaele, Cambrai, and at many of the operations in the Retreat and Advance of 1918. He was demobilised in February 1919, and holds the 1914-15 Star, and the General Service and Victory Medals.
10, Barmore Road, Battersea, S.W.11. Z2319A. Z2320A

WATERS, J., Driver, R.F.A.
He volunteered in November 1914, and in the following September was drafted overseas. During his service in France he fought at the Somme, Vimy Ridge, Arras and Cambrai and the chief engagements in 1918, and was wounded in action. He was demobilised in February 1919 after his return home, and holds the 1914-15 Star, and the General Service and Victory Medals.
28, Pitman Street, Camberwell, S.E.5. Z4768

WATERS, W., Private, 4th East Surrey Regiment.

He volunteered in September 1914, and in the following year was drafted overseas and fought in the Battles of Ypres, Festubert, Loos, and Vimy Ridge, where he was wounded and gassed in May 1916. He was invalided home to hospital and after several months' treatment rejoined his unit in France and served on the Somme and in the Retreat and Advance of 1918. In February 1919 he was demobilised and holds the 1914–15 Star, and the General Service and Victory Medals.

49, Waghorn Street, Peckham, S.E.15.   Z6725

WATERS, W., Special War Worker.

Throughout the war he was engaged on special work for the Government, and was employed in the manufacture of boilers for various munition factories. He rendered valuable services and the skilled manner in which he carried out his duties was much appreciated.

67, Banim Street, Hammersmith, W.6.   11118B

WATERS, W. C., Private, 13th London Regiment (Kensingtons).

Volunteering at the outbreak of war, he was sent to the Western Front in the following year, and whilst in France fought in the Battle of the Somme and in various other engagements. He was then drafted to Salonika and thence to Egypt and took part in the British Advance through Palestine. During his service in the East he was in action at Jaffa and Jericho, and was with General Allenby's Forces at the Entry into Jerusalem. He was demobilised after his return to England in July 1919, and holds the 1914–15 Star, and the General Service and Victory Medals.

47, Banim Street, Hammersmith, W.6.   11118A

WATES, J., Rifleman, Rifle Brigade.

Volunteering in March 1915, he was drafted to the Western Front in the same year, and whilst overseas fought in various engagements in the Somme, Ypres, and Arras sectors. He was wounded and gassed at Arras in May 1917, and sent to hospital at Tréport for treatment. After his recovery he was engaged on important duties at Le Havre until demobilised in January 1919. He holds the 1914–15 Star, and the General Service and Victory Medals.

29, Moat Place, Stockwell, S.W.9.   Z4769

WATKINS, A. E., Private, R.A.V.C.

He joined in November 1916, and after his training served at various stations on important veterinary duties. He did excellent work in the care of horses until the cessation of hostilities, and was demobilised in February 1919.

75, Kirkwood Road, Peckham, S.E.15.   Z6238

WATKINS, A. L., 1st Air Mechanic, R.A.F. (late R.N.A.S.)

He joined in November 1917, and served in the Royal Naval Air Service on board H.M.S. "Comus," and "Revenge," with the first Battle Squadron. He also took part in several air raids over enemy territory, and after the Armistice was present at the sinking of the German Fleet at Scapa Flow. He was demobilised in December 1919, and holds the General Service and Victory Medals.

104, Battersea Bridge Road, Battersea, S.W.11.   Z4770

WATKINS, B., Rifleman, 21st London Regiment (1st Surrey Rifles).

He volunteered in August 1914, and after his training served at various stations on important duties with his unit. In 1916 he was awaiting orders to embark for France when he unfortunately contracted pneumonia, from which he died in hospital on April 1st of the same year.

"Thinking that remembrance, though unspoken, may reach him where he sleeps."

103, Peckham Park Road, Peckham, S.E.15. Z6708B Z6709B

WATKINS, C., Private, Royal Defence Corps.

He joined in January 1917, and was engaged at various stations on important clerical duties. He rendered valuable service until March 1919, when he was demobilised.

103, Peckham Park Road, Peckham, S.E.15. Z6708/9A

WATKINS, E. G., Sergt., R.A.O.C.

He volunteered in March 1915, and in the following year was drafted to France. During his service on the Western Front he was present at many engagements and also served in the Retreat and Advance of 1918. He was mentioned in Despatches for his good work, and in August 1919 returned home and was demobilised, holding the General Service and Victory Medals.

24, Priory Road, South Lambeth, S.W.8.   Z2064B

WATKINS, E. J., Private, Northumberland Fusiliers.

He joined in 1916, and in January of the following year was drafted to Egypt, and stationed at Cairo. Later he was with General Allenby's Forces in the Offensive in Palestine, and saw much service throughout that campaign. He returned home and was demobilised in August 1919, and holds the General Service and Victory Medals.

19, Prairie Street, Battersea Park, S.W.8.   Z4772

WATKINS, J., Private, 22nd Royal Fusiliers.

He had previously served throughout the South African campaign, and in September 1914 voluntarily re-enlisted. In the following year he was drafted overseas and fought in many notable engagements, including those at Ypres, the Somme, Arras and Cambrai, and in various operations in the Retreat and Advance of 1918. He was twice wounded during this period, and was invalided home and discharged in February 1919. He holds the Queen's and King's South African Medals (with three bars), the 1914–15 Star, and the General Service and Victory Medals.

11, Mansion Street, Camberwell, S.E.5.   Z4771

WATKINS, N. (Mrs.), Special War Worker.

During the war this lady was engaged on important duties at Messrs. Du Cros' Munition Factory at Acton Vale, where she was employed on responsible work in connection with the output of shells. The manner in which she executed her work was worthy of the highest praise, and her services were of the utmost value.

44A, Rothschild Road, Chiswick, W.4.   6285

WATKINS, W. F., Shoeing-Smith (Signaller), R.F.A.

He volunteered in September 1914, and was drafted in August of the following year to the Western Front. Whilst in France he served with his Battery, which was attached to the Guards' Brigade, in the Battles of Loos, Vermelles, and the Somme, where he was wounded in September 1916. After his recovery he fought at Arras, Ypres, Passchendaele and Cambrai, and in many subsequent engagements in the Retreat and Advance of 1918, reaching Maubeuge on the morning of Armistice Day. He afterwards proceeded to Germany with the Army of Occupation, remaining there until April 1919, when he returned to England, and was demobilised. He holds the 1914–15 Star, and the General Service and Victory Medals.

24, St. George's Road, Peckham, S.E.15.   Z5496B

WATLING, E. A., Private, East Surrey Regiment.

He volunteered in September 1914, and in the following January was drafted to France. There he took part in the fighting at Neuve Chapelle, Hill 60 and Ypres, and was wounded and invalided home. On recovery he returned to the firing line and was in action in many other engagements, and was again wounded and taken prisoner. He was held in captivity until after the Armistice, when he was released and demobilised in January 1919. He holds the 1914–15 Star, and the General Service and Victory Medals.

55, Atwell Road, Peckham, S.E.15.   Z4773 Z5528

WATMORE, A., Sergt., 7th Yorkshire Regiment.

He volunteered in September 1914, and was sent to France in the following year, and was in action at Loos, Albert, Vimy Ridge, the Somme, Arras, Messines, Ypres and Cambrai. He also took part in the Retreat and Advance of 1918, and was wounded. He was demobilised in January 1919, and holds the 1914–15 Star, and the General Service and Victory Medals..

114, Keetons Road, Rotherhithe, S.E.16.   Z6826

WATSON, A. W., Petty Officer, R.N.

He joined the Navy in 1898 and served in H.M. Ships "Lancaster" "Lion" and "Russell." At the outbreak of war his vessel was engaged on important duties in the North Sea and later was in action at Zeebrugge. In August 1917 he was severely wounded and subsequently succumbed to his injuries. He was entitled to the 1914–15 Star, and the General Service and Victory Medals.

"A costly sacrifice upon the altar of freedom."

13, Stanley Street, Battersea, S.W.8.   Z1509A

WATSON, C. D., Sergt., 17th King's Royal Rifle Corps.

Volunteering in June 1915, he embarked for France in the following January, and whilst in this theatre of war took part in many battles, including those of Loos, St. Eloi, Albert and Vimy Ridge. He gave his life for the freedom of England in the Battle of the Somme on September 3rd, 1916, and was entitled to the General Service and Victory Medals.

"Great deeds cannot die:

"They with the Sun and Moon renew their light for ever."

2, Osborne Street, Walworth, S.E.17.   Z4776A

WATSON, E., Private, 9th Royal Fusiliers.

Mobilised at the outbreak of war, he was shortly afterwards drafted to France. There he was in action in many sectors of the Front, and was taken prisoner. During his service he was wounded five times and gassed on three occasions. In January 1919, having been released, he returned home and was demobilised, holding the 1914 Star, and the General Service and Victory Medals.

31, Binns Road, Chiswick, W.4.   5370C

WATSON, E. A., Sergt., Queen's (Royal West Surrey Regiment).

Volunteering in 1915, he proceeded on the completion of his training to France, where after twelve months' service he was wounded. He was invalided home and in August 1918 was discharged as medically unfit. He holds the General Service and Victory Medals.

49, Eastbury Grove, Chiswick, W.4.   5607

WATSON, G., Driver, R.A.S.C.
Joining in April 1916, he embarked for France in the following August, and whilst in this theatre of war was present during much heavy fighting. He was principally engaged with the food and ammunition Supply Column, and served in many sectors of the Front. In October 1919 he was demobilised, and holds the General Service and Victory Medals. Prior to enlistment he was engaged at Woolwich Arsenal on the production of shells.
21, Graylands Road, Peckham, S.E.15.   Z5857

WATSON, G. (M.M.), Pte., 3rd Australian Division.
Volunteering in 1915, he was in the same year drafted to France, where he fought with distinction in many battles and was mentioned in Despatches, and awarded the Military Medal for conspicuous gallantry in the Field. He died gloriously on the Field of Battle on April 24th, 1918, and was entitled to the 1914-15 Star, and the General Service and Victory Medals.
    " His life for his Country, his Soul to God."
13, Stanley Street, Battersea, S.W.8.   Z1509B

WATSON, G. H., Sergt.-Major, M.G.C.
He volunteered in April 1915, and served on important duties in England until 1917. He then proceeded to France and took part in many notable engagements until hostilities ceased. In July 1919 he was demobilised, and holds the General Service and Victory Medals.
31, Binns Road, Chiswick, W.4.   5370B

WATSON, H., Sergt., 18th Middlesex Regiment and Labour Corps.
He volunteered in April 1915, and in the following year was drafted to France, where he took part in many important engagements. He returned home and was demobilised in February 1919, and holds the General Service and Victory Medals.   31, Binns Road, Chiswick, W.4.   5370A

WATSON, H. J., Gunner, R.G.A.
Joining in 1916, he served on the completion of his training on important coastal defence duties. He rendered valuable services, but was not successful in obtaining his transfer overseas owing to medical unfitness. He was demobilised in February 1919.
37, Sansom Street, Camberwell, S.E.5.   Z4775

WATSON, H. R., Bombardier, R.G.A. and R.F.A.
Volunteering in 1915, he embarked in the same year for France. Whilst in this theatre of war he fought in many notable battles and was twice wounded and gassed, on recovery returning to his unit. He came home and was demobilised in May 1919, and holds the 1914-15 Star, and the General Service and Victory Medals.
11, Pearson Street, Battersea, S.W.11.   Z4779C

WATSON, H. W., Private, Queen's Own (Royal West Kent Regiment).
Volunteering in May 1915, he was drafted, after having completed his training, to India. There he served at various stations, and took part in the suppression of the rioting. In 1919 he returned to England, and was demobilised in May of that year, holding the General Service and Victory Medals. 2, Osborne Street, Walworth, S.E.17.   Z4776B

WATSON, J., Sergt., Bedfordshire Regiment.
Mobilised at the outbreak of war, having previously fought in the South African campaign, he proceeded overseas in September 1914, and whilst in France took part in many notable engagements. He gave his life for the freedom of England in the Battle of the Somme on July 1st, 1916. He held the Queen's and King's South African Medals (with seven bars), and was entitled to the 1914 Star, and the General Service and Victory Medals.
    " His memory is cherished with pride."
23, Nunhead Grove, Nunhead, S.E.15.   Z6675

WATSON, J., Private, 1st Royal Fusiliers.
Mobilised at the outbreak of war he was shortly afterwards drafted to France, and there fought in the Retreat from Mons and in the Battles of the Marne and the Aisne. He was also in action in many other engagements, including those at La Bassée, Ypres and Loos. After the cessation of hostilities he returned home, and was demobilised in 1919, holding the Mons Star, and the General Service and Victory Medals.
117, Barlow Street, Walworth, S.E.17.   Z1028B

WATSON, J. C., Pte., Australian Imperial Forces.
He volunteered in August 1914, and in the following year was sent to Gallipoli, where he took part in the Landing and Evacuation at Suvla Bay, and saw much fighting. Shortly afterwards he proceeded to France, and was in action in many sectors of the Front. During his service he was wounded three times, and in August 1917 was discharged on account of his injuries. He holds the 1914-15 Star, and the General Service and Victory Medals.
13, Stanley Street, Battersea Park, S.W.8.   1509D

WATSON, J. H. (O.B.E.), Captain, R.A.O.C.
He was in the Army at the outbreak of war, and embarked for France in August 1914. There he served in the memorable Retreat from Mons and in many other notable engagements until hostilities ceased. He did valuable work and was mentioned three times in Despatches and appointed an Officer of the Order of the British Empire for consistently good work. In addition he holds the Mons Star, and the General Service and Victory Medals, and in 1920 was still serving.
40, Lavender Sweep, Battersea, S.W.11.   Z4778

WATSON, J. L., Private, 16th Batt. Australian Imperial Forces.
He joined the Australian Imperial Forces and after his training proceeded to France and served in many notable engagements. He was unhappily killed in action in the Advance of 1918 on July 4th, and was entitled to the General Service and Victory Medals.
    " He died the noblest death a man may die,
        Fighting for God, and right, and liberty."
11, Pearson Street, Battersea, S.W.11.   Z4779B

WATSON, R. M. (M.C.), Lieutenant, Leicestershire Regiment and R.H.A.
Receiving his commission in July 1915 he proceeded to Egypt in the following March. Here he took part in the repulse of the Turkish attacks in the Sinai Peninsula, and later in the victorious Advance through the Holy Land. He was in action at Romani, Rafa and Gaza, where he was wounded and on recovery fought at Beersheba, Beit-ur-el-Foka, and was present at the entry into Damascus on October 1st, 1918, and later was stationed at Beirut. He was awarded the Military Cross for distinguished gallantry in July 1917, and in addition holds the General Service and Victory Medals. Returning to England he was demobilised in February 1919.
7, Gloucester Terrace, W.2.   Z6831

WATSON, R. W., Sapper, 2/3rd London Field Coy., R.E.
Volunteering in November 1914, he proceeded to France in the following June, and served with the 47th Division. He took part in many important engagements, including those at Loos, the Somme, and Vimy Ridge, and was wounded. He returned home in March 1919, and was demobilised, holding the 1914-15 Star, and the General Service and Victory Medals.
20, Matthews Street, Battersea, S.W.11.   Z4774A

WATSON, S., Sergt., R.G.A.
A Reservist, he was mobilised at the outbreak of war, and sent to France, where he fought in the Retreat from Mons. He was also in action at La Bassée, Neuve Chapelle, St. Eloi, the Somme and many other battles until hostilities ceased. He was demobilised in 1919, and holds the Mons Star, and the General Service and Victory Medals.
11, Pearson Street, Battersea, S.W.11.   Z4779A

WATSON, T. O., Bombardier, R.F.A.
Volunteering in May 1915, he embarked in the following October for France, where he saw much heavy fighting. He was in action in many battles, including that of the Somme, and was wounded. In September 1919 he returned home and was demobilised, holding the 1914-15 Star, and the General Service and Victory Medals.
17, Dale Street, Chiswick, W.4.   5336

WATSON, W., Private, 7th East Surrey Regiment.
He volunteered in September 1914, and in April of the following year was drafted to France. Whilst there he fought in many notable engagements, including those at Hulluch and Loos, and was killed in action on October 8th, 1915. He was entitled to the 1914-15 Star, and the General Service and Victory Medals.
    " Whilst we remember, the Sacrifice is not in vain."
20, Matthews Street, Battersea, S.W.11.   Z4774B

WATSON, W. A., A.B., Royal Navy.
He joined in 1916, and was posted to H.M.S. " Royal Oak," in which vessel he served with the Grand Fleet in the North Sea on important duties. His ship was also present during the fighting off Heligoland Bight. After the Armistice he was with the Fleet at Constantinople, and holding the General Service and Victory Medals was still serving in 1920.
13, Anchor Street, Rotherhithe, S.E.16.   Z6676

WATSON, W. N., Rifleman, Rifle Brigade.
Volunteering in 1915, he was drafted to the Western Front in the following year, and whilst in this theatre of war fought in many battles. He was in action on the Somme, and at Arras and Ypres, and gave his life for the freedom of England at Sanctuary Wood, on August 17th, 1917. He was entitled to the General Service and Victory Medals.
    " His life for his Country, his Soul to God."
20, Mina Road, Walworth, S.E.17.   Z4777

WATSON, W. E., Special War Worker.

He served from 1916 until 1918, with the King's Norton Metal Coy., on important transport duties. He was principally engaged in conveying shells to and from the works, and rendered valuable services.

54, Nigel Buildings, Nigel Road, Peckham, S.E.15. Z6726

WATT, T. G., L/Corporal, R.E.

Volunteering in September 1915, he was drafted to France in May of the following year. Whilst overseas he was engaged on important duties in connection with the operations and was frequently in the front lines, notably on the Somme, and at Arras, Messines, and Cambrai. On October 11th, 1918, he was unfortunately killed whilst employed on tunnelling at Hazebrouck, and was entitled to the General Service and Victory Medals.

"The path of duty was the way to glory."

42, Anchor Street, Rotherhithe, S.E.16. Z6677

WATTS, A. (Mrs.), Special War Worker.

During the war this lady was engaged for over three years on important duties at Messrs. Hyams and Co's., Southwark Bridge, where she was employed on responsible work in connection with the manufacture of Army uniforms. She rendered valuable services, and carried out her duties with efficiency and to the entire satisfaction of the firm.

8A, Chatham Street, Walworth, S.E.17. Z4785B

WATTS, A. F., Rifleman, 16th Rifle Brigade.

He joined in May 1916, and in August of the same year was drafted to France, where he served in various sectors of the Western Front, including that of the Somme. Later he was invalided home with trench fever, and on his recovery did guard duty in Ireland for a time until he rejoined his unit in France in 1918. He then took part in several engagements in the Retreat and Advance, but again contracting fever was sent to hospital in England, and eventually demobilised in January 1919. He holds the General Service and Victory Medals.

4, Culvert Place, Battersea, S.W.11. Z4782

WATTS, A. S., Rifleman, King's Royal Rifle Corps.

He volunteered in July 1915, and after his training was completed was drafted to France where he took part in many important engagements in various sectors. He died gloriously on the Field of Battle at Cambrai on November 30th, 1917, and was entitled to the General Service and Victory Medals.

"Great deeds cannot die."

2, Claybrooke Road, Fulham, S.W.6. 13425B

WATTS, A. W., Private, Suffolk Regiment and Shoeing-Smith, R.A.S.C.

He was serving at the outbreak of war, and in 1915 was drafted to France. During his service overseas he fought in various engagements, and was twice wounded. After his recovery he was transferred to the Royal Army Service Corps, and was engaged on important duties in different sectors of the Western Front. He was demobilised in February 1919, and holds the 1914-15 Star, and the General Service and Victory Medals.

89, Antrobus Road, Chiswick, W.4. 6043

WATTS, E. L. (Miss), Special War Worker.

In January 1916, this lady volunteered her services, and was accepted for duty at Woolwich Arsenal where she was engaged on important and dangerous work in the filling factory, assembling shells and manufacturing T.N.T. powder. After rendering valuable services for eighteen months she was discharged in July 1917. She then took a responsible position at Messrs. Horne Bros., Commercial Road, where she was engaged until the Armistice on work connected with the output of Army uniforms. She rendered excellent service throughout.

64, Delaford Road, Rotherhithe, S.E.16. Z6752

WATTS, H., Private, Labour Corps.

He joined in March 1917, and in the following October was drafted to France. During his service overseas he was engaged on important duties with the Labour Corps, and was present at Ypres and the Somme, and in many subsequent engagements until the cessation of hostilities. He was demobilised in May 1919, and holds the General Service and Victory Medals.

43, Silverthorne Road, Wandsworth Road, Battersea, S.W.8. Z4783

WATTS, H. J., Stoker, R.N.

He volunteered in January 1915, and was posted to H.M.S. "King Edward VII," which vessel saw much service in the North Sea, engaged on patrol and other important duties. On January 6th 1916, she was sunk by a mine off the North Coast of Scotland, but fortunately he was saved. He was then posted to H.M.T.B.D. "Ness," which was in action in the Battle of Jutland, and rendered excellent services whilst patrolling and escorting in the North Sea. He was present at the surrender of the German Fleet at Scapa Flow, and was demobilised in February 1919, holding the 1914-15 Star, and the General Service and Victory Medals.

8A, Chatham Street, Walworth, S.E.17. Z4785A

WATTS, V., Private, Essex Regiment.

He volunteered in August 1914, and after his training was found to be medically unfit and discharged in August of the following year. However, he rejoined in March 1917, and was sent overseas in the succeeding year. Whilst in France he fought in the second Battle of the Somme, and in the Retreat and Advance. He was demobilised in March 1919, and holds the General Service and Victory Medals.

11, Kersley Street, Battersea, S.W.11. Z4781

WATTS, W., Air Mechanic, R.A.F. (late R.F.C.)

He volunteered in the Grenadier Guards in April 1915, and was subsequently discharged as medically unfit in the following October. He then joined the 25th London Regiment (Cyclists) and after serving on important duties at various stations was again discharged on medical grounds. He enlisted, however, for the third time in March 1917 in the Royal Flying Corps, and was engaged on responsible work for his Squadron until February 1919, when he was demobilised after two years' service.

30, Chumleigh Street, Camberwell, S.E.5. Z5166

WATTS, W. J., Gunner, R.F.A.

He volunteered in August 1914, and in the following July was drafted to France. During his service overseas he took part in numerous engagements, including those at Loos, Vimy Ridge, the Somme, Albert (where he was wounded), Ypres, Lens, and Cambrai. He was also in action in the Retreat and Advance of 1918, and was again wounded and sent to hospitals in France and England. He was discharged in November 1919, and holds the 1914-15 Star, and the General Service and Victory Medals.

28, Caldew Street, Camberwell, S.E.5. Z5690

WATTS, W. J., Sergt., 12th Rifle Brigade.

He volunteered in November 1915, and was drafted to the Western Front in 1917. During his service in France he fought in many important engagements, including those at Arras, Ypres, and Cambrai, and many subsequent operations in the Retreat and Advance of 1918. After the Armistice he proceeded to Germany with the Army of Occupation, with which he served until demobilised in February 1919. He holds the 1914-15 Star, and the General Service and Victory Medals.

53, Tasman Road, Stockwell, S.W.9. Z47.0

WAUGH, G. E. J., Private, 23rd East Surrey Regt.

He volunteered in August 1914, and in March of the following year was drafted to France. Whilst overseas he fought at Neuve Chapelle, St. Eloi, Hill 60 and Ypres, and was mentioned in Despatches for the courage and skill which he displayed in connecting a wire from a German trench to a British trench. He gave his life for King and Country at the Battle of Loos on October 1st, 1915, and was entitled to the 1914-15 Star, and the General Service and Victory Medals.

"Honour to the immortal dead, who gave their youth that the world might grow old in peace."

77, Ferndale Road, Clapham, S.W.4. Z3730D

WAUGH, R. F., Signalman, R.N., H.M.S. "Witley."

He joined in 1917, and was posted to H.M.S. "Witley" and sent to the North Sea, where his ship was engaged on important patrol duties until the cessation of hostilities. After the Armistice he was engaged at Scapa Flow on guard duty over the German Fleet, and whilst on this service sustained a severe injury to his knee in an accident. He was invalided to hospital at Queensferry and discharged as physically unfit for further duty in March 1919. He holds the General Service and Victory Medals.

77, Ferndale Road, Clapham, S.W.4. Z3730B

WAY, W. R., Driver, R.F.A.

Volunteering in July 1915, he was sent to France in March of the following year, and whilst overseas did good work as a driver in many sectors of the Western Front. He served on the Somme, and at Arras, and Ypres, and in various later engagements until the cessation of hostilities. He was demobilised in May 1919, and holds the General Service and Victory Medals.

94, Beresford Street, Camberwell, S.E.5. Z4786

WEATHERLEY, W., Private, 1st Wiltshire Regt.

He volunteered in August 1914, and in the following year was drafted to Salonika, where he fought on the Doiran, Vardar, and Monastir fronts in many engagements. Later he was transferred to Italy, and after serving there for some months proceeded to France and was engaged in heavy fighting in the closing stages of the war. He was sent into Germany with the Army of Occupation and served there until he returned home, and was demobilised in February 1919. He holds the 1914-15 Star, and the General Service and Victory Medals.

25, Arlesford Road, Stockwell, S.W.9. Z4787

WEAVER, C. W. J., Special War Worker.

From January 1915, to June 1919 he was engaged upon work of great importance at the Hibernia Wharf, London Bridge, where he was employed in heavy transport work. He also acted very efficiently as crane-driver to vessels loading munitions and war supplies of all kinds.

20, Arnott Street, New Kent Road, S.E.1. Z25419B

WEAVER, E. C., Bombardier, R.F.A.

He volunteered in August 1915, and in the following March proceeded to the Western Front, where he fought in many engagements of note, including those at Vimy Ridge, the Somme, Arras, and Ypres. He served throughout the heavy fighting in the German Offensive and subsequent AlliedAdvance of 1918, and after the Armistice returned home and was demobilised in June 1919, holding the General Service and Victory Medals.
59, Lothian Road, Camberwell, New Road, S.W.9.　Z5302

WEAVER, F. W., Private, M.G.C.

Joining in January 1917, he landed in Egypt later in the same year and was drafted to the Palestine Front. He fought in the first, second, and third Battles of Gaza, was present at the Capture of Jerusalem, and served throughout the British Advance into Syria. Returning home, he was demobilised in March 1919, and holds the General Service and Victory Medals. 57, Farmer's Road, Camberwell, S.E.5.　Z4788

WEAVER, G., Private, Devonshire Regt., R.A.S.C., and Labour Corps.

He joined in October 1916, and was sent to the Western Front in the following year. He was engaged in heavy fighting in many parts of the line and fought throughout the Retreat and Advance of 1918. After the Armistice he proceeded into Germany with the Army of Occupation and served there until demobilised in March 1919. He holds the General Service and Victory Medals.
9, Ambrose Street, Rotherhithe, S.E.16.　Z6678B

WEAVER, M. (Mrs.), Special War Worker.

This lady offered her services for work of National importance, and from June 1916 until December 1918 did good work at Messrs. Isaac Walton's Factory, Newington Causeway, and at Messrs. Thwaites Factory, engaged on the manufacture of gas masks. She rendered valuable services throughout and discharged her duties most efficiently.
20, Arnott Street, Southwark, S.E.1.　Z25419A

WEAVER, W., Private, Labour Corps.

He joined in October 1918, and did not complete his training until after the cessation of hostilities. Proceeding to France in November 1918 he served at various places engaged on important salvage work. He returned to England and was demobilised in February 1919.
9, Ambrose Street, Rotherhithe, S.E.16.　Z6678A

WEAVER, W. E., Sergt., Royal Fusiliers.

A reservist, he was mobilised at the commencement of hostilities and sent to France. He fought in the Retreat from Mons, the Battles of the Marne, the Aisne, Hill 60, Ypres, the Somme, Arras, and throughout the German Offensive and Allied Advance of 1918. Later contracting trench fever he was invalided to England, and after receiving hospital treatment was discharged in February 1919. He holds the Mons Star, and the General Service and Victory Medals.
23, Alsace Street, Walworth, S.E.17.　1748B

WEBB, A. E., Gunner, R.F.A.

He joined in January 1917 on attaining military age and served at various stations until drafted to the Western Front in March 1918. He was killed in action on April 18th of that year, during the second Battle of the Somme, and was entitled to the General Service and Victory Medals.
"Honour to the immortal dead who gave their youth, that the world might grow old in peace."
18, Kimberley Road, Stockwell, S.W.9.　Z4794B

WEBB, A. E., Private, Queen s Own (Royal West Kent Regiment).

Volunteering in August 1914, three months' later he embarked for India, where he served for twelve months, and was then invalided home suffering from fever. On recovery he served at various stations and later was sent to France. He fought in many important engagements and was in action throughout the Retreat and Advance of 1918. After the Armistice he proceeded with the Army of Occupation into Germany, and was stationed at Cologne. He was demobilised in April 1919, and holds the General Service and Victory Medals.
17, Elfin Road, Camberwell, S.E.5.　Z4798

WEBB, A. E., Private, R.A.S.C. (M.T.)

He joined in May 1916, and later in that year was sent to France. He served in the advanced areas in many parts of the line, including the Arras sector, engaged on important duties transporting ammunition and supplies to the forward areas. He also saw much fighting in the Retreat and Advance of 1918. He was demobilised in February 1919, and holds the General Service and Victory Medals.
4, Chantrey Road, Stockwell Road, S.W.9.　Z4792

WEBB, A. S. G., Gunner, R.G.A.

Volunteering in June 1915, he embarked for France in the following March and was engaged in heavy fighting on the Somme, and at Arras, and throughout the German Offensive and Allied Advance of 1918. He was demobilised in September 1919, and holds the General Service and Victory Medals.
19, Belham Street, Camberwell, S.E.5.　Z4800

WEBB, A. F. Private, East Surrey Regiment.

He volunteered in October 1914, and in the following year was sent to the Western Front, where he fought at Loos, Albert, the Somme, Arras, and Ypres, and during the German Offensive, and subsequently Allied Advance of 1918. He was demobilised in February 1919, and holds the 1914-15 Star, and the General Service and Victory Medals.
37, Yeldham Road, Hammersmith, W6　2805B

WEBB, A. G., Gunner, R.F.A.

He joined in August 1917, and four months later was drafted to the Western Front. He fought on the Somme during the German Offensive of 1918, and was taken prisoner on May 27th, of that year. He was held in captivity until after the Armistice, and then repatriated in December 1918. He was demobilised in October of the following year, and holds the General Service and Victory Medals.
2, Silcote Road, Camberwell, S.E.5.　Z5531

WEBB, B., Driver, R.A.S.C. (H.T.)

Volunteering in November 1915, and drafted to France in the following February, he served in the advanced areas transporting ammunition and supplies to the front lines. He was present at heavy fighting at Vimy Ridge, the Somme, and Arras, and throughout the Retreat and Advance of 1918, during which he acted as driver of a field ambulance for three months. He was demobilised in October 1919, and holds the General Service and Victory Medals.
1, Borland Road, Peckham Rye, S.E.15.　Z6753B

WEBB, C. E., Pioneer, R.E.

He volunteered in August 1915, and in the following month landed in France. During his service he was in action on the Somme, and at Cambrai, and did excellent work on road construction and various kinds of field work. Suffering from shell-shock he was invalided to England in November 1917, and was ultimately discharged in 1918. He holds the 1914-15 Star, and the General Service and Victory Medals.
24, Mosedale Street, Camberwell Green, S.E.5.　Z4802

WEBB, D. A. (Miss), Special War Worker.

This lady volunteered for work of National importance, and from 1914 until after the cessation of hostilities was employed at Messrs. Blake's Munition Works, Hurlingham. She was engaged in the manufacture of T.N.T., work of a very dangerous nature, and discharged her duties in a most satisfactory and efficient manner. She holds a Certificate in recognition of her services.
15, Barmore Street, Battersea, S.W.11.　Z4801B

WEBB, E., Private, R.A.S.C.

Volunteering in July 1915, he completed his training and served at various stations with his unit engaged on important duties. Owing to ill-health he was not successful in obtaining his transfer to a theatre of war, but rendered valuable services until demobilised in March 1919.
47, Rosemary Road, Peckham, S.E.15.　Z5532

WEBB, E. E., Rifleman, 1st Royal Irish Rifles.

He joined in June 1916, and in the following May embarked for the Western Front, where he saw much service in many parts of the line, fighting at Messines and Passchendaele, where he was wounded. On recovery he rejoined his unit and was in action in various engagements. He was taken prisoner at St. Quentin in March 1918, and held in captivity until December of the same year. Then, repatriated, he was demobilised in October 1919, and holds the General Service and Victory Medals.　1, Borland Road, Peckham Rye, S.E.15.　Z6753A

WEBB, F. R. G., Rifleman, 18th King's Royal Rifle Corps.

He joined in June 1916, and later in that year proceeding to Salonika, fought in many engagements on the Struma and other fronts. Early in 1918 he was invalided home suffering from malaria and received hospital treatment. On recovery he was drafted to France, and was engaged in heavy fighting during the final operations of the war. He was demobilised in September 1919, and holds the General Service and Victory Medals.　51, Rowena Crescent, Battersea, S.W.11.　Z4796B

WEBB, G. H., Pte., 5th Oxfordshire and Buckinghamshire Light Infantry.

He joined in January 1915, and in the following October embarking for France, was in action at Loos, Arras, Ypres, Passchendaele, and throughout the German Offensive and Allied Advance of 1918. During his service overseas he was twice wounded, and returning home after the cessation of hostilities was demobilised in January 1919. He holds the 1914-15 Star, and the General Service and Victory Medals.
10, Newcomen Road, Battersea, S.W.11.　Z4797

WEBB, J., Rifleman, King's Royal Rifle Corps.

He joined in September 1916, and served at various depôts on important duties until sent to the Western Front in February 1918. He fought at Albert, and was taken prisoner in the second Battle of the Somme on March 21st, and held in captivity until the following December. Repatriated after the Armistice he was demobilised in October 1919, and holds the General Service and Victory Medals.
55, Calmington Road, Camberwell, S.E.5.　Z5529

WEBB, H. A., Private, Middlesex Regiment.
Volunteering in May 1915 and sailing for France in the succeeding month, he served in many parts of the line, and later was invalided home owing to ill-health. On recovery he returned to France and was in action in various engagements of note. He was unfortunately killed on October 28th, 1916, during the Battle of the Somme, and was entitled to the 1914–15 Star, and the General Service and Victory Medals.
" A valiant soldier, with undaunted heart he breasted Life's last hill."
15, Barmore Street, Battersea, S.W.11. Z4801A

WEBB, J., Private, 4th Royal Fusiliers.
He enlisted in 1911, and was sent to France at the commencement of hostilities. He fought in the Retreat from Mons, the Battles of the Marne, the Aisne, and Ypres, and was wounded at Armentières in February 1915. On recovery he rejoined his unit, and was in action in many parts of the line and was again wounded. He also fought throughout the Retreat and Advance of 1918, and after the Armistice was sent into Germany with the Army of Occupation, and stationed at Cologne. He was demobilised in January 1919, and holds the Mons Star, and the General Service and Victory Medals.
216, Steward's Road, Battersea Park Road, S.W.8. Z4793

WEBB, J. R., L/Corporal, R.A.S.C. (M.T.)
He volunteered in August 1914, and four months later proceeded to the Western Front, where he served in the forward areas on important duties, transporting ammunition and supplies to the front lines. He was present at the Battles of La Bassée, Festubert, Vimy Ridge, the Somme, Ypres, and Messines, and throughout the Retreat and Advance of 1918. He was demobilised in February 1919, and holds the 1914–15 Star, and the General Service and Victory Medals.
180, Westmoreland Road, Walworth, S.E.17. Z4799

WEBB, L. J., Private, 23rd London Regiment.
He volunteered in May 1915, and drafted to the Western Front in the same year was engaged in heavy fighting in many parts of the line. He gave his life for the freedom of England during the first Battle of the Somme on September 16th, 1916, and was entitled to the 1914–15 Star, and the General Service and Victory Medals.
" His life for his Country."
51, Rowena Crescent, Battersea, S.W.11. Z4796A

WEBB, R. A., L/Corporal, 23rd London Regiment.
He volunteered in February 1915, and in June of the following year was sent to the Western Front. He was in action in the first Battle of the Somme and was wounded at Albert and returned to England. On recovery he was drafted to Salonika, and after a few months' service there proceeded to Egypt. On the Palestine front he fought in many engagements and gave his life for King and Country on December 13th, 1917. He was entitled to the General Service and Victory Medals.
" Whilst we remember, the Sacrifice is not in vain."
130, Battersea Bridge Road, Battersea, S.W.11. Z4789

WEBB, R. J., Pte., R.A.V.C., Gunner, R.F.A. and L/Corporal, King's Own (Royal Lancaster Regt).
He volunteered in January 1915, and proceeding to France in the same month served in various sectors engaged on important duties attending the sick and wounded horses. Later he was transferred to the Royal Field Artillery and saw much service. Posted to the Lancaster Regiment he fought throughout the Retreat and Advance of 1918, and after the cessation of hostilities returned home and was demobilised in February 1919, and holds the 1914–15 Star, and the General Service and Victory Medals.
58, Cabul Road, Battersea, S.W.11. Z4795

WEBB, R. J., Private, R.A.S.C.
He attested in March 1915, and called to the Colours in August of the following year was drafted to France in September 1916. He served in the Battles of Arras, Messines, Ypres and Lens, and throughout the Retreat and Advance of 1918, engaged on important transport duties. He was demobilised in February 1919, and holds the General Service and Victory Medals. 18, Kimberley Road, Stockwell, S.W.9. Z4794A

WEBB, T., 1st Class Petty Officer, R.N.
He joined in 1915, and until the following year saw much service in the North Sea, his ship being engaged on patrol and other important duties. From 1916 until the cessation of hostilities his ship was employed on supply duties between England and Archangel. He was demobilised in 1919, and holds the 1914–15 Star, and the General Service and Victory Medals.
28, Tennyson Street, Wentworth Road, S.W.8. Z4791

WEBB, T. G., A.B., Royal Navy.
He joined the Navy in 1903, and during the war served in the North Sea on various ships, including H.M.S. " Tribune," being engaged on convoy and patrol duties. Later he was for a time with the Royal Naval Air Service, and also served in Russia before being demobilised in September 1919. He holds the 1914–15 Star, and the General Service and Victory Medals. 53, Stockdale Road, Wandsworth Rd., S.W.8. Z1064B

WEBB, T. H., Gunner, R.F.A.
He joined in October 1916, and in the following January embarked for France, where he was in action at the Battles of Arras, Ypres, the Somme, and throughout the German Offensive of 1918. He was wounded in October 1918, during the Allied Advance, and returning home received hospital treatment. He was ultimately invalided out of the Service in April 1919, and holds the General Service and Victory Medals.
31, Longcroft Road, Camberwell S.E.5. Z5530

WEBB, T. J., Private, 4th Middlesex Regiment.
He re-enlisted at the outbreak of war, having previously served, and was almost immediately drafted to France, where he took part in the memorable Retreat from Mons. He also served in the Battles of the Marne, the Aisne and Ypres, and was severely wounded in September 1915. He was invalided home to hospital and was under medical treatment for over a year and was discharged as unfit for further service in August 1916. He holds the Mons Star, and the General Service and Victory Medals.
18, Basing Road, Peckham, S.E.15. Z6827

WEBB, T. W., Private, Royal Scots.
A serving soldier, he was stationed in India when war was declared. Proceeding almost immediately to France he fought at Ypres, and in many other engagements, and in 1915 was transferred to Salonika. Here he saw much fighting in many parts of the line and took part in the final Allied Advance in the Balkans in 1918. In 1919 he was sent to Russia and served there until 1919, when he returned home and was demobilised. He holds the 1914 Star, and the General Service and Victory Medals.
37, Yeldham Road Hammersmith, W.6. 12805A

WEBB, W. (M.M., M.S.M.), Q.M.S., Canadian Field Artillery.
He volunteered at the outbreak of war and in February 1915 was sent to France. During his service overseas he was in action in the Battles of Ypres, Loos, the Somme, Messines and throughout the Retreat and Advance of 1918. He was awarded the Military Medal for gallantry in the Field, the Meritorious Service Medal for devotion to duty, and the Belgian Croix de Guerre for consistently good work and efficiency. He was demobilised in April 1919, and holds the 1914–15 Star, and the General Service and Victory Medals.
46, Saltoun Road, Brixton, S.W.2. Z4790

WEBB, W. A. J., Air Mechanic, R.A.F.
He joined in January 1917, and completing his training served at various aerodromes, engaged on important duties with his Squadron. He was unsuccessful in obtaining his transfer overseas prior to the cessation of hostilities, but rendered valuable services until demobilised in November 1919.
9, Silverlock Street, Rotherhithe, S.E.16. Z6727

WEBB, W. C., Private, Royal Defence Corps.
Ineligible for active service with the Colours, he joined the Royal Defence Corps in November 1914, and was engaged on guard duties at prisoners of war camps, and on various other important work. Later he contracted pneumonia whilst on service and died on November 21st, 1918.
" His memory is cherished with pride." Z6514A
9, Boyton Cottages, New Church Road, Camberwell, S.E.5.

WEBB, W. H., Rifleman, Rifle Brigade.
He joined in March 1918, and in the following August was drafted to France, and was in action in many engagements during the concluding stages of the Allied Advance. Returning to England after the Armistice he was demobilised in November 1919, and holds the General Service and Victory Medals.
9, Boyton Cottages, New Church Road, Camberwell, S.E.5. Z6514B

WEBBER, R., Sapper, R.E.
Volunteering in June 1915, he was later in the same year sent to the Dardanelles, where he served till the Evacuation. In 1917 he was transferred to France, where he took part in numerous engagements, including those at Cambrai and the Somme He was unfortunately killed in action on March 22nd, 1918, and was entitled to the 1914–15 Star, and the General Service and Victory Medals.
" Whilst we remember, the Sacrifice is not in vain."
98, Ferndale Road, Clapham, S.W.4. Z2380C

WEBBER, W., Private, R.A.S.C. and Rifleman, 16th London Regiment (Queen's Westminster Rifles).
He volunteered in September 1914, and in March of the following year was sent to France, where he was engaged at Neuve Chapelle, St. Eloi, Hill 60, Ypres, Festubert and Loos. In 1916 he was transferred to Egypt and thence to Palestine and took part in the capture of Jerusalem. In 1918 he returned to France and served in the Retreat and Advance of that year. He was demobilised in February 1919, and holds the 1914–15 Star, and the General Service and Victory Medals.
98, Ferndale Road, Clapham, S.W.4. Z2380B

WEBBER, L., Worker, Q.M.A.A.C.
Having previously served in the V.A.D. as a Nurse, she joined Q.M.A.A.C. in 1917, and was engaged on important duties at various stations until February 1919, when she was demobilised after having rendered valuable service.
52, Avenue Road, Camberwell, S.E.5.　　Z3362A

WEBSTER, C., A.B., R.N., H.M.S. "Hind."
He joined in 1916, and during his service voyaged to Italy, Gibraltar, Malta, Mesopotamia, India, South Africa and Egypt. He also took part in various actions in the North Sea in 1918. He was demobilised in 1919, and holds the General Service and Victory Medals.
145, Gordon Road, Peckham, S.E.15.　　Z6111

WEBSTER, C. W., Driver, R.F.A.
He joined in November 1918, and after completing his training was in the following year drafted to Mesopotamia, where he was engaged on important duties. During his service he suffered from fever, and was in hospital for a time. He was still serving in 1920.
20, Selden Road, Nunhead, S.E.15.　　Z6679A

WEBSTER, E. T., Gunner, R.F.A.
Volunteering in June 1915, he was sent to France early in the following year, and took part in the fighting on the Somme, and at Vimy Ridge and Ypres. He fell fighting on June 19th, 1917, and was entitled to the General Service and Victory Medals.
"His life for his Country."
32, Cornwall Road, Peckham, S.E.15.　　Z6592

WEBSTER, G. G., Pte., Queen's (Royal West Surrey Regt.) and Labour Corps.
He volunteered in 1915, and was drafted to France in the following year. He was in action at Vimy Ridge the Somme, Arras, Messines, Ypres, Passchendaele, Lens, Cambrai and Béthune and also served in the Retreat and Advance of 1918. He was demobilised in March 1919, and holds the General Service and Victory Medals.
20, Selden Road, Nunhead, S.E.15.　　Z6679B

WEBSTER, J., Pte., Queen's (Royal West Surrey Regiment).
He joined in May 1916, and later in the same year was sent to France, where he was in action at Arras, Vimy Ridge and Bullecourt, and was wounded. He was returning home on H.M.S. "Donegal," when that vessel was torpedoed and he was unfortunately drowned on April 17th, 1917, and was entitled to the General Service and Victory Medals.
"He joined the great white company of valiant souls."
25, Charleston Street, Walworth, S.E.17.　　Z4805A

WEBSTER, J., Private, R.A.S.C. (M.T.)
Having volunteered in March 1915, he was drafted to France in the same year, and was engaged on important transport duties at Albert, the Somme, Ypres, Poperinghe and Béthune. He unfortunately met with an accident at Corbeil, and was invalided home. He was discharged in July 1916 as medically unfit for further service, and holds the 1914-15 Star, and the General Service and Victory Medals.
5, Hillery Road, Walworth, S.E.17.　　Z4803

WEBSTER, S., Driver, R.F.A.
He volunteered in June 1915, and later in the same year was drafted to the Western Front, where he took part in numerous engagements. He returned home and was demobilised in February 1919, holding the 1914-15 Star, and the General Service and Victory Medals. He later unfortunately contracted an illness of which he died in April 1920.
"The path of duty was the way to glory."
25, Charleston Street, Walworth, S.E.17.　　Z4805C

WEBSTER, T., Corporal, Queen's (Royal West Surrey Regiment).
He volunteered in October 1914, and was engaged as Instructor in signalling until December 1916, when he was drafted to France, where he took part in the fighting at Vimy Ridge, Bullecourt, and Messines. He was unfortunately killed in action on June 21st 1917, and was entitled to the General Service and Victory Medals.
"A costly sacrifice upon the altar of freedom."
25, Charleston Street, Walworth, S.E.17.　　Z4805B

WEBSTER, W., Private, 12th Gloucestershire Regt.
He joined in January 1917, and was engaged in training remounts and taking them to France. He was afterwards transferred to the 12th Gloucestershire Regiment and in January 1918 was sent to Italy, and was in action on the Piave. He later proceeded to France, where he took part in numerous engagements. Afterwards contracting an illness he was invalided home, and on recovery was demobilised in January 1919, holding the General Service and Victory Medals.
25, East Surrey Grove, Peckham, S.E.15.　　Z5533

WEBSTER, W., Private, Royal Welch Fusiliers.
Volunteering in August 1915, he was sent to France in the following year. He took part in the fighting at Arras and Cambrai, and also served in the Retreat and Advance of 1918. Later owing to ill-health he was invalided home and discharged as medically unfit in October 1918, holding the General Service and Victory Medals.
32, Harris Street, Camberwell, S.E.5.　　4478B, 4479B

WEBSTER, W., Gunner, R.F.A.
Volunteering in April 1915, he was sent to France later in the same year, and was in action on the Somme and at Delville Wood, Arras, Ypres and Cambrai. Later he was invalided home as a result of having been buried in a shell hole for three days. He was demobilised in February 1919, and holds the 1914-15 Star, and the General Service and Victory Medals.
49, Harvey Road, Camberwell Green, S.E.5.　　Z4804

WEEDON, A. S., C.Q.M.S., R.A.S.C. (M.T.)
He volunteered in August 1914, and was shortly afterwards sent to France, where he was engaged on important transport duties in the Retreat from Mons, and at La Bassée, Ypres, Neuve Chapelle, Hill 60, Festubert, Loos, the Somme and Arras. He was later invalided home with rheumatic fever. On his recovery in 1917 he proceeded to Egypt, and then to Palestine, and served at Gaza, Jerusalem, Haifa and Damascus. Whilst in this theatre of war he contracted malaria, and was in hospital for a time. He was demobilised in June 1919, and holds the Mons Star, and the General Service and Victory Medals. 60, Heaton Road, Peckham, S.E.15.　　Z5859

WEEDON, H., Pte., Queen's (Royal West Surrey Regiment).
He was mobilised in August 1914, and immediately sent to France and took part in the Retreat from Mons. He was wounded at Ypres in October 1914, taken prisoner and sent to Germany. On his release he returned home, and was demobilised in March 1919, holding the Mons Star, and the General Service and Victory Medals.
18, Horsman Street, Camberwell, S.E.5.　　Z4806

WEEDON, H., Private, Royal Fusiliers.
He was serving at the outbreak of war, and in the following year was sent to Gallipoli and took part in the Landing at Suvla Bay, and other important engagements. Later he was wounded and invalided to France and shortly afterwards was reported missing during the Battle of the Somme on July 13th, 1916. He is presumed to have been killed in action on that date, and was entitled to the 1914-15 Star, and the General Service and Victory Medals.
"A costly sacrifice upon the Altar of freedom."
63, Kenbury Street, Camberwell, S.E.5.　　Z6359A

WEEDON, R. J., Private, Middlesex Regiment.
He was serving at the outbreak of war and was sent to France in the following November, and was in action at Loos, Ypres, the Somme, Arras, and in many other important engagements, and was twice wounded. He later returned home and was engaged on important defence duties, and after the Armistice proceeded with the Army of Occupation to Germany. He also served in Russia for a time against the Bolshevist Forces. He was still serving in 1920, and holds the 1914 Star, and the General Service and Victory Medals.
63, Kenbury Road, Camberwell, S.E.5.　　Z6359A

WEEKLY, J. W., Pte., 22nd London Regt. (Queen's).
He volunteered in September 1914, and was engaged with his unit on important duties until June 1916, when he was sent to France and was in action on the Somme, and at Arras. In December of the same year he was transferred to Salonika, and was engaged on the Vardar and Doiran fronts. In August 1917 he proceeded to Egypt and thence to Palestine, where he took part in the fighting at Rafa, the three Battles of Gaza, and the Capture of Jerusalem. He was demobilised in May 1919, and holds the General Service and Victory Medals.
425, Southwark Park Road, Rotherhithe, S.E.16.　　Z6815

WEEKS, A. E., Pte., R.A.M.C. and Cheshire Regt.
He volunteered in November 1915, and soon afterwards was sent to Ireland, where he was engaged on hospital duties during the Irish Risings of 1916. He was next drafted to Malta, and served there in the same capacity until September 1917, when he was transferred to the Cheshire Regiment and proceeded to Salonika. Whilst in this theatre of war he fought in the engagements on the Vardar front until the cessation of hostilities. He was demobilised in April 1919, after his return to England, and holds the General Service and Victory Medals.
196, Hollydale Road, Peckham, S.E.15.　　Z6471

WEEKS, C. W., Sergt., Queen's (Royal West Surrey Regiment).
He was mobilised at the outbreak of war, and was immediately drafted to France, where he took part in the Retreat from Mons. He also fought in the Battles of the Marne, Ypres, Loos, Vimy Ridge, the Somme, Arras, Lens, and in many later engagements in the Retreat and Advance of 1918. He was demobilised in the following year, and holds the Mons Star, and the General Service and Victory Medals.
77, Henshaw Street, Walworth, S.E.17.　　Z4807

WEIGHT, W., Sapper, R.E.

He volunteered in 1915, and in the same year was drafted overseas, and served on important duties in connection with the operations in the Battle of the Somme. He was later sent to Salonika, where he was engaged in many of the fighting areas, and on April 29th, 1917 was reported missing. He was subsequently presumed to have been killed in action on that date, and was entitled to the 1914-15 Star, and the General Service and Victory Medals.

"Thinking that remembrance, though unspoken, may reach him where he sleeps."

12, Blendon Row, Walworth, S.E.17.　　　　Z4808

WEISS, A. E., Private, London Regiment.

He joined in December 1917, and owing to blindness of one eye was prevented from proceeding overseas. He served on important clerical duties at Headquarters at Whitehall, and with th Civil Service Rifles at Wimbledon, and in Scotland with the Argylle and Sutherland Highlanders. He rendered valuable services, and was demobilised in March 1919.

11, New James Street, Nunhead, S.E.15.　　　　Z6109

WELCH, C. H., Private, Oxfordshire and Buckinghamshire Light Infantry and Sapper, R.E.

He was mobilised from the Reserve at the outbreak of hostilities and was almost immediately drafted to France, where he served in the Retreat from Mons, and in the Battles of Le Cateau, the Marne, and was wounded on the Aisne in September 1914. He was invalided home, and after his recovery sailed for Egypt in August 1915. Whilst on the Eastern Front he took part in the engagement at El Fasher, and was present at the entry into Jerusalem in the Palestine campaign in December 1917. He was then transferred to the Royal Engineers, and was engaged on important duties as an electrician until he returned home for demobilisation in July 1919. He holds the Mons Star, and the General Service and Victory Medals.

52, Stanton Street, Peckham. S.E.15.　　　　Z5300

WELCH, C. M. (Mrs.), Special War Worker.

During the war this lady devoted her time to assisting as a waitress at the Censorship Department Dining Hall, Kingsway. The services which she rendered in this connection were greatly appreciated.

29, Mordaunt Street, Brixton S.W.9.　　　　Z4809B

WELCH, H., Private, R.A.S.C.

He joined in September 1916, and after his training was sent to Mesopotamia in the same year. Whilst in this theatre of war he was engaged on important transport duties in the Persian Gulf zone, at Kut, and was present in the operations at Baghdad, Ramadieh and Tekrit. He returned home and was demobilised in March 1920, and holds the General Service and Victory Medals.

15, Walton Terrace, South Lambeth, S.W.8.　　　　Z27531

WELCH, J., Corporal, R.G.A.

He joined the Army in 1908, and was stationed at Malta, when war was declared. He was immediately drafted to France, and took part in the Retreat from Mons, and in the first Battle of Ypres, where he was injured in a wagon accident. He was invalided home, and after his recovery, being sent to Egypt in May 1916, served with distinction in the Advance through Palestine. He fought in the Battles of Gaza and Beersheba, and was present at the fall of Jerusalem and in the subsequent engagements until the conclusion of the campaign. He returned to England and was demobilised in April 1919, and holds the Mons Star, and the General Service and Victory Medals.

80, Bird-in-Bush Road, Peckham, S.E.15.　　　　Z6552

WELCH, J. A., Sapper, R.E.

He volunteered in September 1915, and in the following November proceeded to France, where he was engaged on important duties in connection with the operations at Béthune, Arras, Vimy Ridge, Ypres, Lens, Cambrai, and in various later engagements until the cessation of hostilities. He was demobilised in February 1919, and holds the 1914-15 Star, and the General Service and Victory Medals.

27, D'Eynsford Road, Camberwell Green, S.E.5.　　Z4811

WELCH, W., Rifleman, King's Royal Rifle Corps.

He joined in June 1917, and in the following May was drafted to France, where he was engaged in many operations of importance in the Retreat and Advance of 1918, during which he was wounded and gassed in August. In February 1920 he was demobilised after returning home, and holds the General Service and Victory Medals.

36, Runham Street, Walworth, S.E.17.　　　　Z4817

WELCH, W. H., Corporal, R.A.S.C.

He volunteered several times in the early stages of the war, but owing to physical weakness was not accepted until January 1917. After his training he was drafted to France, and later to Italy. He did excellent work as a cook with the Royal Army Service Corps in both theatres of war, and was demobilised after over three years' service in April 1920. He holds the General Service and Victory Medals.

29, Mordaunt Street, Landor Road, S.W.9.　　　　Z4809

WELCH, J. W., L/Corporal, Queen's (Royal West Surrey Regiment).

He was mobilised from the Reserve at the outbreak of war, and being almost immediately drafted to France took part in the Retreat from Mons, and in the Battles of the Marne, the Aisne and La Bassée. He died gloriously in action near Ypres on October 23rd, 1914, and was entitled to the Mons Star, and the General Service and Victory Medals.

"He died the noblest death a man may die,
Fighting for God, and right, and liberty."

118, Aylesbury Road, Walworth, S.E.17.　　　　Z4810

WELLER, G. H., Sergt., 7th London Regiment.

He volunteered in August 1914, and after his training was drafted to France. Whilst overseas he fought in the Battle of the Somme and was wounded, and after his recovery was in action at Arras, Bullecourt and Ypres, where he was again wounded. He subsequently served in many engagements in the Offensive of 1918, and was demobilised in February 1919. He holds the General Service and Victory Medals.

64, Nasmyth Street, Hammersmith, W.6.　　　　11828A

WELLER, J. A., Gunner, R.F.A.

He volunteered in January 1915, and after the completion of his training was drafted to the Western Front and later to Salonika. Whilst overseas he did excellent work as a gunner in both these theatres of war until the cessation of hostilities. He returned home and was demobilised in June 1919, and holds the General Service and Victory Medals.

64, Nasmyth Street, Hammersmith, W.6.　　　　11828B

WELLER, K. (Mrs.), Special War Worker.

During the war this lady devoted her time to assisting at the Dining Hall of the Censorship Department at Kingsway. She rendered valuable services which were greatly appreciated.

6, Arlesford Road, Stockwell, S.W.9.　　　　Z3342C

WELLER, P. R., Corporal, 5th Lancashire Fusiliers.

He joined in 1916, and in the following year was drafted to France, where he fought in the Battles of Messines, Ypres, Passchendaele, Cambrai and the Somme. He served also in many other engagements in the Retreat and Advance of 1918, and was at Ypres when the Armistice was signed. He remained in France until February 1919, when he was demobilised, and holds the General Service and Victory Medals.

21A, Surrey Road, Peckham Rye, S.E.15.　　　　Z6773

WELLER, T. F., Private, 11th Queen's (Royal West Surrey Regiment).

He volunteered in November 1915, and proceeded to France in the following May. After taking part in numerous engagements he was killed in action on the Somme Front. He was entitled to the General Service and Victory Medals.

"His life for his Country."

6, Arlesford Road, Stockwell, S.W.9.　　　　Z3342D

WELLER, W., Private, R.A.S.C.

He joined in June 1916, and after his training served at various stations on important transport duties with his unit. He was chiefly engaged in the distribution of food supplies to the various camps in the districts in which he was stationed. He rendered valuable services, but was unable to secure a transfer overseas before the cessation of hostilities and was afterwards demobilised.

43, Kingston Street, Walworth, S.E.17.　　　　Z27479

WELLING, B. J., Sergt., R.A.F. (late R.N.A.S.)

He volunteered in August 1915, and in the following October was first sent to Imbros and Mudros. After valuable service there he was for seven months afloat in the "Empress," in the Ægean Sea. He afterwards did excellent work in Macedonia and other parts of the Balkan front until hostilities ceased. He was demobilised in February 1919, and holds the 1914-15 Star, and the General Service and Victory Medals.

106, Hall Road, Peckham Rye, S.E.15.　　　　Z6754

WELLS, C., Rifleman, King's Royal Rifle Corps.

He joined in 1917, and after his training was drafted to France in the following year. He was in action in several engagements in the Retreat of 1918, and lost his speech for a time through being badly gassed. After eleven weeks' active service he gave his life for the freedom of England in June 1918. He was entitled to the General Service and Victory Medals.

"Courage, bright hopes, and a myriad dreams splendidly given."

28, Meyrick Road, Battersea, S.W.11.　　　　Z4814C

WELLS, H., Gunner, R.F.A.

He enlisted in 1909, and at the outbreak of hostilities was serving in India, where he remained for nearly three years on garrison duties. He was then drafted to Mesopotamia in March 1917, and fought in the engagements at Samara and Tekrit. In March 1918 he proceeded to Palestine and served under General Allenby in his Offensive on Tripoli and Aleppo. Whilst in the East he suffered intermittently from malaria. He returned to England in March 1919, when he was demobilised, and holds the General Service and Victory Medals. 40, Choumert Square, Peckham, S.E.15.　　Z6795

WELLS, F. A., Private, Royal Fusiliers.

He was serving in India at the outbreak of war, and was brought to England in December 1914, and sent to France in the following January. In the next month he was severely wounded in action on the Aisne front, and invalided home to hospital, where he remained under medical treatment for twelve months. He then rejoined his unit in France, and after being again severely wounded on the Somme on August 14th, 1916, was sent to the 6th General Hospital at Rouen. He died from his injuries on August 15th, and is buried in the Cemetery in Rouen. He was entitled to the 1914-15 Star, and the General Service and Victory Medals.
" A valiant soldier with undaunted heart, he breasted Life's last hill."
47, Bedford Street, Walworth, S.E.17.   Z3123B

WELLS, J., Drummer, South Wales Borderers.

He enlisted in 1905, and had served five years in India. In August 1914, he was mobilised from the Reserve, and was almost immediately drafted to France, where he took part in the Retreat from Mons. He fought also in the Battles of the Marne the Aisne, and in many subsequent engagements, and was wounded three times during his service overseas. He holds the Mons Star, and the General Service and Victory Medals, and in 1920 was still serving with the Colours.
28, Meyrick Road, Battersea, S.W.11.   Z4814A

WELLS, J., Rifleman (Signaller), King's Royal Rifle Corps.

He volunteered in June 1915, and in the same year was drafted to the Western Front. During his service in France he fought in the Battles of the Somme, Albert, Delville Wood, Ypres and Cambrai, and was wounded during the Allied Advance in September 1918. He also went through a severe enemy air-raid at St. Omer. He was demobilised in March 1919, and holds the 1914-15 Star, and the General Service and Victory Medals.
31, Tidemore Street, Stewart's Road, Battersea, S.W.8.Z2034B

WELLS, J. H., 1st Air Mechanic, R.A.F.

He joined in September 1917, at forty-eight years of age, and served at Gosport as a fabric worker for the Royal Air Force. He was also engaged on important coastal defence duties, and was attached to the Torpedo Squadron. He rendered valuable service, but was not successful in securing his transfer overseas while hostilities continued. He was demobilised in January 1919.
6, Prideaux Road, Stockwell, S.W.9.   Z4812

WELLS, J. H., Corporal, 1st Dorsetshire Regiment.

He was serving at the outbreak of hostilities, and was immediately drafted to France, where he took part in the Retreat from Mons, and was wounded. He also served at Ypres, Hill 60, and in the heavy fighting in the Somme area, where he was taken prisoner in May 1916. He was sent to Germany until after the Armistice, when he was repatriated. He was demobilised in June 1919, and holds the Mons Star, and the General Service and Victory Medals.
20, Ceylon Street, Battersea Park Road, S.W.8.   Z4813

WELLS, T. A., Private, 1st Queen's (Royal West Surrey Regiment).

A soldier since April 1901, he had fought in the South African campaign, and served in India and Persia for ten years. In September 1914 he was drafted to France, and took part in the early engagements, and was taken prisoner at Ypres. He was interned in Germany from October 1914 to December 1918, when he was repatriated. In April of the following year he was discharged after nineteen years' service with the Colours, and holds the Queen's South African Medal (with three clasps), the Mons Star, and the General Service and Victory Medals.
21, Azenby Road, Peckham, S.E.15.   Z6796

WELLS, W., Rflmn., 5th King's Royal Rifle Corps.

He joined in March 1917, and in the following December, on being drafted to France was in action at Ypres, Cambrai, Epéhy and Lens. He was wounded in the second Battle of the Somme in March 1918, and was invalided to hospital at Abbeville. After the Armistice he proceeded to Germany with the Queen Victoria's Rifles, and was stationed at Cologne. On returning to England he was transferred to the Royal Army Ordnance Corps, and subsequently demobilised in November 1919. He holds the General Service and Victory Medals.
18, Nelson Square, Peckham, S.E.15.   Z6703

WELLS, W. C. F., Pte., 2nd East Surrey Regiment.

He enlisted in January 1907, and had served in India and Burmah. Soon after the outbreak of hostilities he sailed from India to France, and arrived on the Western Front in January 1915. He fought at Neuve Chapelle, and Loos, and was gassed in the second Battle of Ypres, and afterwards saw much valuable service in Egypt and Salonika until the conclusion of hostilities. He was discharged in February 1918, and holds the 1914-15 Star, and the General Service and Victory Medals.
28, Meyrick Road, Battersea, S.W.11   Z4814B

WELLS, W. A., Private, 7th London Regiment.

He joined in June 1916, and in August of the same year was drafted to the Western Front, where he fought in the Battles of the Somme, Arras, Vimy Ridge, Ypres and Cambrai and in many later engagements until the cessation of hostilities. He was demobilised in September 1919, after returning home, and holds the General Service and Victory Medals.
74, Crimsworth Road, Wandsworth Road, S.W.8.   Z4815

WELSH, M. A., Gunner, R.F.A. and Corporal, R.E.

He volunteered in September 1914, and a year later was drafted to France, where he served as a gunner with the Royal Field Artillery, and was in action at Vermelles. He was subsequently transferred to the Royal Engineers, and was engaged on important electrical duties, chiefly at St. Omer. In May 1919 he was demobilised, and holds the 1914-15 Star, and the General Service and Victory Medals.
73, Mayall Road, Herne Hill, S.E.24.   Z4816

WENHAM, F. C., Gunner, R.F.A.

He volunteered in August 1914, and after having completed his training served at various stations on important duties with his Battery. He rendered valuable services, but was not successful in obtaining his transfer overseas before the cessation of hostilities. In 1919 he was demobilised.
5, Avondale Road, Peckham.   Z6828

WENN, B. W., Private, Sherwood Foresters.

Joining in September 1916, he was drafted overseas in the following year, and served in many sectors of the Western Front, with the Trench Mortar Batteries. He was in action at Ypres, and the Somme, and in the Advance of 1918, during which he was buried by the explosion of a shell and severely injured. After receiving hospital treatment he was demobilised in January 1919, holding the General Service and Victory Medals.   19, Relf Road, Peckham, S.E.15.   Z6728

WENN, J. J., Private, Middlesex Regiment.

He volunteered in January 1915, and in the same year proceeded overseas. Whilst in France he was in action in many engagements, including those at Neuve Chapelle, Hill 60, Ypres, Loos, the Somme, Beaumont-Hamel and Dickebusch, where he was wounded. On recovery he returned to his unit and served until hostilities ceased. He was demobilised in February 1919, and holds the 1914-15 Star, and the General Service and Victory Medals.
76, Maxted Road, Peckham, S.E.15.   Z6797

WENN, T. J., L/Corporal, 21st London Regiment (1st Surrey Rifles).

Joining in November 1916, he was sent in the following year to France, where he served for about seven months, and took part in the fierce fighting at Ypres. Shortly afterwards he proceeded to the East and saw service in Salonika, Egypt, and Palestine, where he was in action at Gaza, Jericho and Tripoli, and was present at the entry into Jerusalem. He returned home in August 1919, and was demobilised, holding the General Service and Victory Medals.
76, Maxted Road, Peckham, S.E.15.   Z6798

WENTZELL, H., Driver, R.A.S.C.

He volunteered in September 1914, and in the same year was drafted to the Western Front, where he saw much service. He was present at the Battles of the Somme, Ypres, and Arras and many other engagements until the conclusion of hostilities. He then returned home and was discharged on account of his service in 1919, and holds the 1914-15 Star, and the General Service and Victory Medals.
78, Henshaw Street, Walworth, S.E.17.   Z4818

WERREN, E. R., Driver, R.F.A.

Volunteering in November 1915, he was drafted in the following year to the Western Front, and saw much heavy fighting. He took part in the Battles of the Somme and Cambrai, and in the Retreat and Advance of 1918, and in December of that year returned to England. He was demobilised in February 1919, and holds the General Service and Victory Medals.
8, Kenbury Street, Camberwell, S.E.5.   Z6358

WESCOTT, F., Pte., Queen's Own (Royal West Kent Regiment).

He volunteered in September 1914, and in the following year was sent to the Western Front, and served in many sectors. He was in action at Hill 60, and was blown up by the explosion of a shell. Invalided home he was discharged on account of his injuries in December 1915, and died from the effects in April 1919. He was entitled to the 1914-15 Star, and the General Service and Victory Medals.
" His memory is cherished with pride."
43, Bournemouth Road, Peckham, S.E.15.   Z5751A

WESSON, W. H., Pte., 7th Leicestershire Regiment.

He joined in May 1916, and was drafted in September of the following year to France. He served with the 21st Division in many sectors, and was in action at Epéhy, Arras, Albert and Ypres. He was in hospital for a time on account of illness, but on recovery returned to his unit, and served until hostilities ceased. In July 1919 he was demobilised, and holds the General Service and Victory Medals.
20, Coopers Road, Old Kent Road, S.E.1.   Z27261

WEST, G. S. T., Corporal, R.A.S.C.
Joining in August 1916, he was sent on the completion of his training to Egypt, and there served on important duties at the Supply Depôt, Alexandria, and various other stations. He rendered valuable services until October 1919, when he returned to England for demobilisation. He holds the General Service and Victory Medals.
147, Beresford Street, Camberwell, S.E.5. Z4821

WEST, H., Corporal, 9th London Regiment (Queen Victoria's Rifles).
Volunteering in October 1915, he proceeded in the following year to France. There he took part in many notable engagements, including those on the Somme, and at Arras, Ypres, Cambrai, and also fought in the Retreat and Advance of 1918. He returned home and was demobilised in February 1919, and holds the General Service and Victory Medals.
39, Deans Buildings, Flint Street, Walworth, S.E.17. Z3670A

WEST, J., Private, Royal Defence Corps.
Volunteering in October 1914, he served on important guard duties, being in charge of German prisoners at various stations. He rendered valuable services until demobilised in March, 1919.
4, Broughton Street, Battersea Park, S.W.8. Z4822C

WEST, J. F., Gunner, R.F.A.
He volunteered in August 1915, and on the completion of his training was drafted to France. He took part in the fighting at Vimy Ridge, Ypres and Cambrai, and in many other engagements, and also served in the Advance of 1918, and was blown up by an exploding shell. He was invalided home and after receiving hospital treatment was discharged in March 1919. He holds the 1914–15 Star, and the General Service and Victory Medals.
4, Broughton Street, Battersea Park, S.W.8. Z4822A

WEST, J. G., Sergt., 2nd Queen's (Royal West Surrey Regiment).
Volunteering in August 1914, he proceeded in the same year to the Western Front. There he took part in many notable engagements, including those at Neuve Chapelle, Hill 60, Ypres, Festubert, Loos and Delville Wood, and was promoted Sergeant for bravery in the Field. He gave his life for the freedom of England in the Battle of the Somme on July 14th, 1916, and was entitled to the 1914 Star, and the General Service and Victory Medals.
"The path of duty was the way to glory."
4, Broughton Street, Battersea Park, S.W.8. Z4822B

WEST, P. H., Rifleman, Rifle Brigade.
Joining in July 1916, he was sent in the following June to the Western Front. He was in action on the Somme, and at Arras, and Ypres, and was wounded in August 1917. He returned to his unit on recovery, and took part in the fighting until killed in action on August 31st, 1918. He was entitled to the General Service and Victory Medals.
"A valiant soldier, with undaunted heart he breasted Life's last hill." Z6254B
94, Vaughan Road, Camberwell, S.E.5. Z6255B

WEST, R., Driver, R.F.A.
He volunteered in August 1914, and in the following February embarked for France, where he saw much service. He was in action at Neuve Chapelle, Hill 60, Ypres, Loos and Beaumont-Hamel, and was severely gassed and invalided home. On recovery he returned to the fighting line, but was sent to England in November 1917, and in December of the following year was discharged as medically unfit. He holds the 1914–15 Star, and the General Service and Victory Medals.
21, Amies Street, Battersea, S.W.11. Z4823

WEST, T. W., Private, R.A.M.C.
He joined in August 1916, and in March of the following year embarked for France. There he served in many battles, including those of Vimy Ridge, Arras, Bullecourt, Messines, Ypres and Cambrai, and was also present during the Retreat and Advance of 1918. He returned home and was demobilised in February 1919, and holds the General Service and Victory Medals. 8, Torrens Street, Clapham, S.W.4. Z4820

WEST, W., Private, R.A.S.C. (M.T.)
He joined in May 1917, and after his training was drafted to Mesopotamia, where he saw much service, and was present during the fighting at Kut and Baghdad, and in various other engagements. Later, contracting malaria, he was in hospital for some considerable time. He returned to England and was demobilised in March 1920, and holds the General Service and Victory Medals.
100, Lugard Road, Peckham, S.E.15. Z6760

WEST, W., 1st Air Mechanic, R.A.F.
He joined in May 1916, and in the same year proceeded to France. There he served with his Squadron in many sectors, and took part in the Retreat and Advance of 1918. He returned home in February 1919, and was demobilised holding the General Service and Victory Medals.
63, Goldie Street, Camberwell, S.E.5. Z5534

WEST, W. B., Rifleman, King's Royal Rifle Corps.
Volunteering in October 1914, he proceeded, after having completed his training, to the Western Front. There he was in action at Ypres, Arras, Armentières and many other engagements until hostilities ceased. He was demobilised in 1919, and holds the 1914–15 Star, and the General Service and Victory Medals.
98, Rayleigh Road, West Kensington, W.14. 12047A

WESTACOTT, A. H., Corporal, R.F.A.
A Reservist, he was mobilised at the outbreak of war, and sent to France, where he took part in the Retreat from Mons and in the Battles of the Marne and Aisne. He was also in action at Ypres, St. Quentin, Armentières, Amiens and Bapaume and during the Advance of 1918. In May 1919 he was demobilised and holds the Mons Star, and the General Service and Victory Medals.
41, Parkstone Road, Peckham, S.E.15. Z5692

WESTBROOK, C. A., Private, Welch Regiment.
Joining in August 1916, he proceeded overseas in the following December. During his service on the Western Front he took part in numerous engagements, including those of the Somme and Cambrai, and was wounded and gassed. After receiving hospital treatment he was discharged in October 1918 as medically unfit. He holds the General Service and Victory Medals.
60, Barkworth Road, Rotherhithe, S.E.11. 6729B

WESTBROOK, S. W., Private, 3rd London Regiment (Royal Fusiliers).
He joined in November 1917, and in the following April was drafted to France. Whilst in this theatre of war he was in action on the Somme, and at Cambrai, and was wounded. He returned home and was demobilised in January 1919, and holds the General Service and Victory Medals.
60, Barkworth Road, Rotherhithe, S.E.16. 6729A

WESTCOTT, S. B., Trooper, 4th Dragoon Guards.
He enlisted in 1908, and at the outbreak of war was drafted to the Western Front. During the fighting in Alsace he was severely wounded and subsequently succumbed to his injuries on November 7th, 1914. He was entitled to the 1914 Star, and the General Service and Victory Medals.
"Whilst we remember, the sacrifice is not in vain."
32, Priory Road, South Lambeth, S.W.8. Z4824

WESTHROP, W. C., Private, M.G.C.
He joined in May 1917, on attaining military age, and in the following December embarked for France. There he took part in many engagements, including those of the Somme, the Marne, Amiens, Bapaume, Havrincourt, Cambrai, and Ypres, and was wounded and sent into hospital. On recovery he returned to his unit and remained in the fighting area until demobilised in February 1919. He holds the General Service and Victory Medals.
4, Elsted Street, Walworth, S.E.17. Z4825

WESTLAKE, F. L., Trooper, Norfolk Dragoons (The King's Own Royal Regiment).
He joined in June 1916, and after having completed his training was drafted to Egypt, where he saw much active service. In March 1918, he proceeded to France and there took part in many engagements, including that of Ploegsteert Wood, remaining in this theatre of war until October 1919, when he was demobilised. He holds the General Service and Victory Medals.
22, Unwin Road, Peckham, S.E.15. Z6468

WESTLAKE, V. J., Gunner, R.F.A.
A Reservist, he was mobilised and sent to France at the outbreak of war, and was in action during the Retreat from Mons. He was severely injured by a kick from a horse, and invalided home. Later he was sent to the East and took part in the fighting at Gallipoli, and in Salonika and Egypt, whilst there contracting malaria. He was invalided home and on recovery was again drafted to France, and served with the 50th Division, until February 1919, when he was demobilised. He holds the Mons Star, and the General Service and Victory Medals.
25, Bedford Street, Walworth, S.E.17. Z4826

WESTLEY, E., Private, Queen's (Royal West Surrey Regiment).
He volunteered in November 1914, but was shortly afterwards discharged. He re-enlisted, however, in November 1915, and in the following year was sent to France, where he was in action on the Somme and at Ypres, Albert, Passchendaele, and in numerous other engagements. He was wounded and buried by an explosion at Gommecourt, but later returned to the fighting line and was again wounded at Cambrai in 1918, and invalided home. He was demobilised in March 1919, and holds the General Service and Victory Medals.
65, Azenby Road, Peckham, S.E.15. Z6805

WESTON, A. E. V., Gunner, R.F.A.

Volunteering in August 1914, he embarked in the following year for France. There he took part in much of the heavy fighting at Loos, the Somme, and in many other engagements. He was unhappily killed in action on September 5th, 1918, and was entitled to the 1914-15 Star, and the General Service and Victory Medals.

"The path of duty was the way to glory."

62, Smith Street, Camberwell, S.E.5.   Z4828

WESTON, A. R., Private, Border Regiment.

Volunteering in 1915, he proceeded overseas in the following year and whilst in France saw much heavy fighting. He was in action at Ypres, the Somme and Passchendaele, where he was wounded. After receiving hospital treatment he was discharged in 1919, as medically unfit. He holds the General Service and Victory Medals.

12, Crichton Street, Wandsworth Road, S.W.8.   Z4827

WESTON, W. G. H., Private, 3rd Bedfordshire Regt.

He volunteered in May 1915, and in the same year was drafted to India, where he served for nearly four years. He took part in the suppression of the Afghanistan risings, and in various minor engagements until returning home for demobilisation in September 1919. He holds the 1914-15 Star, and the General Service and Victory Medals, the India General Service Medal (with clasp, Afghanistan, N.W. Frontier, 1919).

128, Albert Road, Peckham, S.E.15.   Z6125

WESTWOOD, A. W. W., Sergt., Gordon Highlanders.

He volunteered in 1915, and was drafted in November of the following year to France, where he saw much heavy fighting on the Arras front. In February 1917, he was invalided home through ill-health, and after receiving hospital treatment was discharged as medically unfit in December of that year. He holds the General Service and Victory Medals.

21, Nigel Road, Peckham, S.E.15.   Z6704

WETHERILL, H., Private, Middlesex and East Surrey Regiments.

A serving soldier, he was drafted to France shortly after the commencement of hostilities and was in action in many engagements, including those at Ypres, and the Somme, where he was wounded in July 1916. Returning to England, he received protracted hospital treatment and was finally invalided out of the Service in December 1917. He holds the 1914 Star, and the General Service and Victory Medals.

37, Mayall Road, Herne Hill, S.E.24.   Z4829

WEYMAN, A. G., Private (Signaller), 2nd Queen's (Royal West Surrey Regiment).

Volunteering in January 1915, he was drafted to the Western Front in the same year and served at the Battle of Loos, where he was gassed and invalided home. On recovery he returned to France in September 1916, and fought at Messines, and other engagements. He also took part in the Allied Advance of 1918, during which he was in action in the Cambrai sector. At one time during his period of service overseas he was with the British Forces in Italy. Ye holds the 1914-15 Star, and the General Service and Victory Medals, and was demobilised in March 1919.

38, Villa Street, Walworth, S.E.17.   Z27316C

WEYMAN, A. T., Private, Labour Corps.

Joining in November 1917, immediately on attaining military age, he was on the completion of his training, employed on important duties at various stations. He rendered valuable service, but owing to being medically unfit for duty abroad was not successful in obtaining his transfer overseas. He was demobilised in March 1919.

38, Villa Street, Walworth, S.E.17.   Z27316B

WEYMAN, J., L/Corporal, 24th London Regt. (The Queen's), Air Mechanic, R.A.F. and 2nd Lieut., Rifle Brigade.

He volunteered in August 1914, and proceeded to the Western Front in the following year, and took part in the fighting at Givenchy, where he was wounded. He was invalided home, and on recovery was transferred to the R.F.C., and later to the Rifle Brigade, in which he was eventually commissioned. He was demobilised in February 1919, and holds the 1914-15 Star, and the General Service and Victory Medals.

38, Villa Street, Walworth, S.E.17.   TZ27316A

WHALEBONE, J. R., Private, 22nd London Regt. (Queen's).

Having volunteered in November 1914, he was drafted to France in the following year and was in action at Loos, Vimy Ridge, the Somme, Messines, Ypres and Cambrai. He also took part in the Retreat and Advance of 1918. He was demobilised in January 1919, and holds the 1914-15 Star, and the General Service and Victory Medals.

11, Lillington Street, Rotherhithe, S.E.16.   Z6816

WHALEY, W. J., Bombardier, R.F.A. and Private, Labour Corps.

He volunteered in 1915, and completing his training served at various depôts with his unit engaged on important duties. Medically unfit for service abroad, he did not obtain his transfer to a theatre of war, and was ultimately invalided out in 1918. Rejoining in the Labour Corps in 1919, he was sent to France, and there was employed on important salvage work. He was demobilised in 1920.

53, Gonsalva Road, Wandsworth Road, S.W.8.   Z4830

WHALEY, W. J., Private, Seaforth Highlanders.

He volunteered at the declaration of war, and early in 1915 was sent to France. He fought at the Battle of Neuve Chapelle and saw much service in various parts of the line. Later in 1915 he was invalided home owing to ill-health, and on recovery served at different stations until demobilised in January 1919. He holds the 1914-15 Star, and the General Service and Victory Medals.

1, Dashwood Road, Wandsworth Road, S.W.8.   Z4831

WHATLEY, C. W., Sapper, R.E.

He joined in 1916, and completing his training, served at various depôts on important duties on the inland waterways and docks. He did not obtain his transfer to a theatre of war, but rendered excellent services until demobilised in February 1919.   18, Westmacott Street, Camberwell, S.E.5.   Z4832

WHATLEY, R. A., Cpl. (Fitter), R.A.F. (late R.F.C.)

Volunteering in December 1915, he completed his training and was stationed at various aerodromes with his Squadron engaged on important duties fitting and testing aero-engines. He was unsuccessful in obtaining his transfer overseas, but rendered excellent service until demobilised in January 1919.

15, Hillery Road, Walworth, S.E.17.   Z4833

WHEATLAND, F. E. (Mrs.), Special War Worker.

This lady offered her services for work of National importance and from June 1916 until December 1917 was employed by the London County Council Tramway Company as a Conductress, thus releasing a man for service with the Colours. She rendered valuable services and discharged her duties in a most efficient and satisfactory manner.

310, East Street, Walworth, S.E.17.   Z4835B

WHEATLAND, H. G., Corporal, R.A.S.C. (M.T.)

He volunteered in January 1915, and drafted to the Western Front in the same month was engaged on important transport duties in the forward areas. He was present at heavy fighting at Loos, the Somme, Arras, Passchendaele and Bullecourt, and throughout the Retreat and Advance of 1918. After the Armistice proceeding into Germany with the Army of Occupation, he served at Cologne until he returned home and was demobilised in May 1919. He holds the 1914-15 Star, and the General Service and Victory Medals.

310, East Street, Walworth, S.E.17.   Z4835A

WHEATLAND, R. W., Sergt., R.H.A.

A serving soldier, at the outbreak of war he was stationed in India, and was in action on the North Western Frontier in August 1915. He was engaged on guard duties at various stations. In May 1918, proceeding to France he fought throughout the Allied Advance and after the Armistice was sent into Germany with the Army of Occupation and served there until demobilised in February 1919. He holds the General Service and Victory Medals.

25, Gideon Road, Battersea, S.W.11.   Z4834

WHEATLEY, C., Private, Labour Corps.

Joining in February 1917, in the same month he was sent to France and for some time was employed at various depôts loading and unloading supplies. He served throughout the Retreat and Advance of 1918 engaged in the front lines on trench digging and rendered valuable services. He was demobilised in May 1919, and holds the General Service and Victory Medals.

1, Duffield Street, Battersea, S.W.11.   Z4836

WHEDDON, A. H. J., Private, 16th (The Queen's) Lancers.

A serving soldier, he proceeded to France in August 1914, and fought in the Retreat from Mons and in the Ypres, Arras, and Somme sectors. He was in action throughout the Retreat of 1918, and during the opening stages of the Allied Advance. In September 1918, owing to ill-health, he returned home and after receiving hospital treatment served at various stations until demobilised in January 1919. He holds the Mons Star, the General Service and Victory Medals.

11, Sturdy Road, Peckham, S.E.15.   Z6129

WHEELER, J., Private, Labour Corps.

He volunteered at the outbreak of war and completing his training served at various depôts with his unit engaged on guard and other important duties. He was unable to obtain his transfer overseas prior to the cessation of hostilities, but rendered excellent services until demobilised in February 1919.

33, Candahar Road, Battersea, S.W.11.   Z4839

WHEELER, J., Driver, R.F.A.

He volunteered in April 1915, and after serving at various depôts embarked for the Western Front in January 1918. He fought in many engagements during the Retreat and Advance of 1918, including those at Le Cateau, the Sambre and Bapaume, and was wounded. He was demobilised in April 1919, and holds the General Service and Victory Medals.
71, Blakes Road, Peckham, S.E.15. Z6105A

WHEELER, J. A., Rifleman, Rifle Brigade and Private, Labour Corps.

He volunteered in December 1915, and two months later was sent to the Western Front, where he was in action in the Battles of Vimy Ridge, the Somme, Arras, Bullecourt, and Ypres, and was wounded at Passchendaele. On recovery he rejoined his unit and was engaged in heavy fighting in various sectors, and was wounded again at the second Battle of Cambrai and returned home. After receiving hospital treatment he served at various stations until demobilised in March 1919. He holds the General Service and Victory Medals.
24, Dalyell Road, Landor Road, S.W.9. Z4842

WHEELER, J. H., Private, R.A.S.C.

He volunteered in November 1914, and in the same month embarked for France. He served in the advanced areas engaged on important duties driving a lorry for the Air-line section of the Royal Engineers and did good work. He served throughout the German Offensive and Allied Advance of 1918, and after the Armistice was sent into Germany with the Army of Occupation, and was stationed at Cologne. He was demobilised in March 1919, and holds the 1914 Star, and the General Service and Victory Medals.
40, Camelia Street, Wandsworth Road, S.W.8. Z4838

WHEELER, S. W., Stoker, R.N.

He joined the Service in August 1914, and was posted to H.M.S. "Red Gauntlet" which ship was in action in the Battle of Heligoland Bight and in the raid on Zeebrugge, and in various destroyer engagements. He also did good work engaged on patrol and other important duties in the North Sea. Later he was blown up by an explosion and invalided to hospital where he received treatment. He was subsequently discharged as unfit for further service in November 1918, and holds the 1914-15 Star, and the General Service and Victory Medals.
24, Mayall Road, Herne Hill, S.E. 24. Z4840

WHEELER, W., Driver, R.E.

He volunteered in October 1915, and proceeding to France in the following June was engaged on field work of all descriptions in the Advanced areas during the progress of the Battles of Arras, Ypres, Passchendaele and Cambrai. He was present at heavy fighting throughout the Retreat and Advance of 1918, and after the cessation of hostilities was sent into Germany with the Army of Occupation and served there until he returned to England and was demobilised in July 1919. He holds the General Service and Victory Medals.
1, Verona Street, Battersea, S.W.11. Z4841

WHELAN, F., Sergt., Highland Light Infantry.

He joined in 1906, and was serving at the outbreak of hostilities when he was almost immediately drafted to France. He took part in the Retreat from Mons, and in the Battles of the Marne, the Aisne, Ypres and Arras, and was killed in action in the Retreat on March 26th, 1918. He was entitled to the Mons Star, and the General Service and Victory Medals.
"He passed out of the sight of men by the path of duty and self-sacrifice."
70, Westmacott Street, Camberwell, S.E.5. Z3059C

WHELAN, L. (Mrs.), Special War Worker.

During the war this lady was engaged for over a year on important duties at Messrs. Du Cros' Munition Works, Acton Vale. Her work was in connection with the output of shells, and she rendered valuable services, which were highly appreciated.
50, Rothschild Road Chiswick, W.4. 6291A

WHELAN, W., Corporal, R.E.

He volunteered in May 1915, and served for upwards of four years with the Egyptian Expeditionary Force. During this period he was engaged on important duties in connection with the operatons, and was frequently in the forward areas. He was twice wounded, and was mentioned in Despatches for his gallantry in action and devotion to duty. He holds the 1914-15 Star, and the General Service and Victory Medals, and was demobilised after his return to England in July 1919.
50, Rothschild Road, Chiswick, W.4. 6291B

WHETLOR, C., Gunner, R.H.A.

A serving soldier at the outbreak of hostilities he was immediately drafted to France and took part in the Retreat from Mons. He was in the famous L Battery, which was badly cut up during the Retreat and was one of the few survivors. Afterwards he took part in many engagements, and in 1917 was severely wounded in action and invalided home to hospital. After his recovery he was stationed at Woolwich and engaged on important duties until demobilised in March 1919. He holds the Mons Star, and the General Service and Victory Medals. 21, Cranbrook Road, Chiswick, W.4. 5408B

WHETSTONE, J. A., Sapper, R.E.

He volunteered in November 1915, and was drafted to France in No. 1 Special Company in the next month. Whilst overseas he was engaged on important duties in connection with the operations until hostilities ceased, notably at the Somme, Arras and Cambrai. He returned to England after the Armistice, and was demobilised in March 1919. He holds the 1914-15 Star, and the General Service and Victory Medals.
98, Kenbury Street, Camberwell, S.E.5. Z6241

WHETSTONE, W. T., Private, Queen's (Royal West Surrey Regiment).

He joined in February 1916, and in the same year was drafted to France. During his service overseas he fought in many important engagements in various sectors of the Western Front until the cessation of hostilities. He returned home and was demobilised in March 1919, and holds the General Service and Victory Medals.
110, Kenbury Street, Camberwell, S.E.5. Z6116

WHICHER, H., Private, 3rd and 4th London Regt. (Royal Fusiliers) and R.D.C.

He joined in 1916, and after his training was drafted in 1917 to France. He took an active part in many important engagements, including those at Ypres, Passchendaele, Lens, Cambrai, and the second Battle of the Somme. He was wounded in the Offensive of 1918, and after being sent to hospital at Rouen was invalided home. He was subsequently transferred to the Royal Defence Corps, and engaged on important duties until February 1919, when he was discharged. He holds the General Service and Victory Medals.
112, Mayall Road, Herne Hill, S.E.24. Z4843

WHIDDETT, G. F., Private, 2nd King's Shropshire Light Infantry.

He joined in July 1916, and in the following October was drafted to Salonika. Whilst in this theatre of war he took part in the recapture of Monastir, and in the operations on the Doiran and Struma fronts. In 1917, he contracted malaria and dysentery and was sent to hospital at the Base, and afterwards at Malta. In October 1919 he was demobilised, and holds the General Service and Victory Medals.
131, Wickersley Road, Battersea, S.W.11. 4837

WHILEY, F., Private, East Surrey Regiment.

He volunteered at the outbreak of hostilities, and in the following year after completing his training was drafted to France. After taking part in many important engagements with the 18th Division, he fell gloriously on the field of battle in the storming of Montauban on July 1st, 1916. He was entitled to the 1914-15 Star, and the General Service and Victory Medals. 11, Odell Street, Camberwell, S.E.5. Z5535-8A

WHILEY, F. J., Private, 16th (Sussex Yeomanry) Royal Sussex Regiment.

He joined in February 1917, and after his training was completed proceeded to Egypt in July 1917. He served with the British Forces in their Advance through Palestine, and was present at the fall of Jerusalem. In April 1918 he was drafted to the Western Front, but owing to malaria was invalided home two months later. After medical treatment in hospital he was discharged in January 1919, and holds the General Service and Victory Medals.
117, Sabine Road, Battersea, S.W.11. Z4844-5A

WHILEY, J. E., Rifleman, Rifle Brigade.

He volunteered in December 1915, and in June of the following year was drafted to France. Whilst overseas he served at the Somme, Ypres and Lens, but having contracted fever was invalided home. He rejoined his unit in France in May 1918, and fought in various engagements in the Advance of that year until the cessation of hostilities. He was demobilised in September 1919, and holds the General Service and Victory Medals. 109, Grayshott Road, Battersea, S.W.11. Z4844-5B

WHITAKER, C., Private, 2nd London Regt. (Royal Fusiliers).

He joined in May 1917, and in the same year after completing his training was drafted to France. Whilst overseas he fought gallantly in the third Battle of Ypres, and died gloriously near Passchendaele on October 26th, 1917. He was entitled to the General Service and Victory Medals.
"His life for his Country, his soul to God."
9, Copeland Road, Peckham, S.E.15. Z5556B

WHITBREAD, W. J., Gunner, R.G.A.

He volunteered in October 1914, and in the same year was drafted to France, where he served in numerous important engagements, including those at St. Eloi, Ypres and Festubert. In the latter part of 1915, he was sent to Salonika and took part in many operations in the Advance across the Struma, and the Offensives on the Doiran and Vardar fronts. Having contracted malaria and dysentery he was invalided to hospital at the Base, and afterwards to Malta and England. In June 1918 he was discharged as medically unfit for further service and holds the 1914-15 Star, and the General Service and Victory Medals.
4, Alsace Street, Walworth, S.E.17. Z4846

WHITBY, A. J., Private, Royal Berkshire Regiment.
He volunteered at the outbreak of war, and on the completion of his training crossed to France in May of the following year. After fighting in several minor engagements he died gloriously on the Field of Battle at Loos on September 25th, 1915. He was entitled to the 1914-15 Star, and the General Service and Victory Medals.
"A costly sacrifice upon the altar of freedom."
69, Smyrk's Road, Walworth, S.E.17. Z3842C

WHITBY, E., Air Mechanic, R.A.F.
He joined in December 1917, and after his training was drafted to Salonika, where he was engaged on important duties in connection with the repairs of aeroplanes. He was also employed in guarding Turkish prisoners. He was subsequently sent to Egypt, where he rendered valuable services until the cessation of hostilities. He holds the General Service and Victory Medals, and in 1920 was still with the Royal Air Force in Egypt.
69, Symrk's Road, Walworth, S.E.17. Z3842D

WHITBY, J. F., Corporal, Royal Berkshire Regt.
He volunteered at the outbreak of war, and in March of the following year was drafted to France. During his service overseas he fought at St. Eloi, Ypres, Festubert, Loos, Vimy Ridge, and the Somme, where he was badly wounded and gassed. After his recovery he returned to France and was again in action at Messines, Ypres, Passchendaele, Lens, Cambrai, and in many subsequent engagements in the Retreat and Advance of 1918. He was wounded again during this period. He was demobilised in January 1919, and holds the 1914-15 Star, and the General Service and Victory Medals.
69, Smyrk's Road, Walworth, S.E.17. Z3842B

WHITCOMB, A., Private, 20th London Regt. and Queen's Own (Royal West Kent Regiment).
He joined in January 1917, and early in the following year was drafted to France, where he took part in the severe fighting at Arras and was blown up by the explosion of a shell and sustained severe shock. He was invalided home, and after a period in hospital was discharged as medically unfit for further service in January 1918, holding the General Service and Victory Medals.
40, Dilston Grove, Rotherhithe, S.E.16. Z6817A

WHITCOMB, J., Stoker, R.N., H.M.S. "Moon."
He was serving at the outbreak of war and was posted for duty with the Grand Fleet in the North Sea. He was engaged on patrol work and also took part in the Battles of Heligoland Bight and Jutland, and in two destroyer actions of 1916 and 1917. After the Armistice he proceeded to Constantinople, where he was still serving in 1920, and holds the 1914-15 Star, and the General Service and Victory Medals.
40, Dilston Grove, Rotherhithe, S.E.16. Z6817B

WHITCOMBE, H., Rifleman, Rifle Brigade.
He volunteered in November 1914, and after his training was finished was drafted to France in the following April. Whilst overseas he fought at Ypres and other engagements, and was severely wounded, and invalided home to hospital. After considerable medical treatment he was discharged in May 1916, as medically unfit for further military service and holds the 1914-15 Star, and the General Service and Victory Medals.
18 Chatto Road, Battersea, S.W.11. Z4847

WHITE, A. (Mrs.), Special War Worker.
From March 1918 until April of the following year this lady held an important position at Messrs. Napier's, Acton. She was engaged on work in connection with the production of aeroplanes, and carried out her duties in a thoroughly efficient manner.
123, The Grove, Hammersmith, W.6. 10360A

WHITE, A., Gunner, R.F.A.
He was in the Army at the outbreak of war and was drafted to France in August 1914. He took part in the fighting in the Retreat from Mons, and at Ypres, the Somme and Cambrai, and in many other engagements, including the Advance of 1918, and was gassed. He returned home and was demobilised in March 1919, and holds the Mons Star, and the General Service and Victory Medals.
1, Acorn Street, Camberwell, S.E.5. Z4849D

WHITE, A., A.B., Royal Navy.
He joined in 1916, and was posted to H.M.S. "Kilkeel," in which ship he was engaged on important duties for two years. He saw service in many waters and in 1919 was demobilised, holding the General Service and Victory Medals.
21, Cranbrook Road, Chiswick, W.4. 5408A

WHITE, A. H., Leading Seaman, R.N., H.M.T.B. 20.
He was serving at the outbreak of war and was engaged with the Dover Patrol in escorting troop and food ships during the whole period of the war. He was demobilised in March 1919, and holds the 1914-15 Star, and the General Service and Victory Medals.
3, Rudford Road, Rotherhithe, S.W.16. Z681

WHITE, A. R., Air Mechanic, R.A.F.
He joined in February 1917, and after his training proceeded overseas. Whilst in France he saw much service on the Somme sector and did valuable work with the gas plant. In August 1918 he met with an accident necessitating his undergoing an operation. He returned home for demobilisation in June 1919, and holds the General Service and Victory Medals.
3, Northall Street, Stockwell, S.W.9. Z4861

WHITE, C. F., Air Mechanic, R.A.F.
Joining in June 1916, he embarked for France in the following May, and whilst in this theatre of war did much good work. He saw active service on the Somme, and during the Retreat of 1918, and was wounded. After receiving hospital treatment he was discharged in December 1918, and holds the General Service and Victory Medals.
114, Aylesbury Road, Walworth, S.E.17. Z4853

WHITE, C. H., L/Corporal, R.A.M.C. and 2nd Northumberland Fusiliers.
He volunteered in May 1915, and in February of the following year was sent to Egypt, going thence to Salonika. Whilst in this theatre of war he contracted an illness and was invalided to Malta. On recovery, returning to the Macedonian front he was killed in action by a bomb on February 15th, 1918, and was entitled to the General Service and Victory Medals.
"His life for his Country, his soul to God."
63, Broadwater Road, Bruce Grove, Tottenham. N.17. Z5545B

WHITE, C. W., L/Corporal, 3rd Hampshire Regt.
He volunteered in June 1915, and in the following year was drafted to the Western Front, where be took part in numerous engagements including those at Albert, Vimy Ridge, the Somme, Arras and Amiens. He also served in the Retreat and Advance of 1918, and was gassed. He was demobilised in March 1919, and holds the General Service and Victory Medals.
5, New Place, Rotherhithe, S.E.16. Z6829

WHITE, C. W., L/Corporal, 6th Dorset Regiment.
Volunteering in September 1914, he proceeded to the Western Front in the following year. Whilst in this theatre of war he took part in much of the fighting on the Somme and was wounded, and whilst serving at Arras contracted fever and was invalided home. On recovery he returned to the fighting area, and was unfortunately killed in action during the Retreat on March 23rd, 1918. He was entitled to the 1914-15 Star, and the General Service and Victory Medals.
"He died the noblest death a man may die, Fighting for God, and right, and liberty."
91, Neate Street, Camberwell, S.E.5. Z5170

WHITE, D. (Mrs.), Special War Worker.
From January 1918 until early in the following year this lady held an important position at the Metropolitan Gas Works. She was employed as a fitter's mate, and did much good work.
17, Sydney Square, Peckham, S.E.15. Z6364

WHITE, D. G. J., Driver, R.A.S.C. (M.T.)
Joining in February 1917, he proceeded overseas in the following May, and saw much service on the Arras front. During an air-raid at St. Omer he was wounded and invalided to hospital at Dundee, later being discharged on account of his injuries in December 1918. He holds the General Service and Victory Medals.
14, Ewell Place, Camberwell, S.E.5 Z5855B

WHITE, E., Private, East Surrey Regiment.
He volunteered in August 1914, and in the same year proceeded overseas. Whilst in France he was in action in many engagements, including those at Hill 60, and in the Retreat and Advance of 1918. He returned home and was demobilised in February 1919, and holds the 1914-15 Star, and the General Service and Victory Medals.
1, Acorn Street, Camberwell, S.E.5. Z4849C

WHITE, E., Gunner, R.F.A.
Volunteering in May 1915, he was drafted in the following year to Salonika. Whilst in this theatre of war he took part in the fighting on the Doiran, Vardar and Struma fronts, and later contracting malarial fever was invalided to England, and in March 1919 discharged as medically unfit, holding the General Service and Victory Medals.
83, Akerman Road, Brixton Road, S.W.9. Z4851

WHITE, E. H., Rifleman, King's Royal Rifle Corps.
He joined in March 1917, and in the following November proceeded to France, where he saw much heavy fighting. He was present at many engagements, and in August 1918 was wounded and invalided home. After receiving treatment at various hospitals he was transferred to the R.A.O.C., with which he served until demobilised in December 1919. He holds the General Service and Victory Medals.
108, Hollydale Road, Peckham, S.E.15. Z6551

WHITE, E. G., Driver, R.F.A.
Volunteering in August 1915, he embarked in January of the following year for France. There he took part in the fighting at Vimy Ridge, the Somme, Arras, Ypres, Cambrai, Armentières, St. Quentin and Amiens, and also served in the Advance of 1918. He was demobilised in January 1919, and holds the General Service and Victory Medals.
16, Carfax Square, Clapham, S.W.4.   Z4860A

WHITE, E. J., L/Cpl., 1st Bn. East Surrey Regt.
Mobilised at the outbreak of hostilities he proceeded to France with the original Expeditionary Force, and took part in the Retreat from Mons and in the Battles of the Aisne and La Bassée, and was wounded. In February 1916 he was discharged as time-expired, and later served at Woolwich Arsenal on munitions until July of that year. He then re-enlisted and returned to the fighting area, and was killed in action at Zillebeke on July 13th, 1917. He was entitled to the Mons Star, and the General Service and Victory Medals.
"His life for his Country, his soul to God."
11, Odell Street, Camberwell, S.E.5.   Z5535/6/7/8C

WHITE, F., Private, Middlesex Regiment.
Volunteering in May 1915, he embarked in the same year for France, where he took part in many notable engagements, and was wounded. Later was killed in action on May 2nd, 1916, and was entitled to the 1914-15 Star, and the General Service and Victory Medals.
"Whilst we remember, the sacrifice is not in vain."
1, Acorn Street, Camberwell, S.E.5.   Z4849B

WHITE, F., Rifleman, King's Royal Rifle Corps.
Mobilised at the outbreak of war he was almost immediately drafted to France. There he was in action in the Retreat from Mons, and in the Battles of Le Cateau and La Bassée. He was taken prisoner at Ypres in November, 1914, and held in captivity until hostilities ceased. He then returned to England, and was demobilised in February 1919, and holds the Mons Star, and the General Service and Victory Medals.
1, Cross Street, Clapham, S.W.4.   Z2752A

WHITE, F., Driver, R.F.A.
He volunteered in May 1915, and after having completed his training proceeded to France in the following November. Whilst in this theatre of war he took part in many engagements, including those at Loos, Vimy Ridge, the Somme, Beaumont-Hamel, Arras, Ypres, and Cambrai, and was present at the entry into Mons in November 1918. He holds the 1914-15 Star, and the General Service and Victory Medals, and in May 1919 was demobilised.
133, Cator Street, Peckham, S.E.15.   Z4850

WHITE, F. B., Pte., 22nd London Regt. (Queen's) and M.G.C.
He volunteered in August 1914, and in the following March was drafted to France. There he was in action at Hill 60, Ypres, Festubert and Loos, and was invalided home through ill-health. In 1917 he was sent to Mesopotamia and served in that theatre of war until hostilities ceased. He returned home, and was demobilised in March 1919, and holds the 1914-15 Star, and the General Service and Victory Medals.
56, Cornbury Street, Rotherhithe, S.E.16.   Z6774

WHITE, F. W., Driver, R.F.A.
Volunteering in August 1914, he proceeded on the completion of his training to the Western Front, where he saw much service. He was in action at Neuve Chapelle, Loos, Armentières and Cambrai, and in many other engagements until hostilities ceased, and was twice wounded. He returned home and was demobilised in 1919, holding the 1914-15 Star, and the General Service and Victory Medals.
22, Blacks Road, Hammersmith, W.6.   12618B

WHITE, G., Corporal, King's Royal Rifle Corps.
He volunteered at the outbreak of hostilities, and in December 1914 proceeded overseas. Whilst in France he saw much heavy fighting, and was severely wounded at High Wood, and in October 1916 died from his injuries. He was entitled to the 1914-15 Star, and the General Service and Victory Medals.
"His memory is cherished with pride."
16, Alexandra Road, W. Kensington, W.14.   12085B

WHITE, G., Pte., Queen's (Royal West Surrey Regt.)
Joining in May 1916, he was drafted, after a brief training to the Western Front, and was killed in action during the fighting at Armentières on July 12th of that year. He was entitled to the General Service and Victory Medals.
"The path of duty was the way to glory."
32, Milford Street, Wandsworth Road, S.W.8.   Z4848A

WHITE, G. B. (Miss), Special War Worker.
From December 1916 until May of the following year this lady was engaged on important work in making body shields for the Army at Messrs. Harris's, Clapham. She carried out her duties in a thoroughly efficient manner.
16, Carfax Square, Clapham, S.W.4.   Z4860B

WHITE, G. F., Gunner, R.H.A.
Having previously served in the South African campaign and in India, he rejoined in May 1916 and was engaged on important duties with his Battery. He also served with the Scottish Rifles and the 1st Cameron Highlanders. He rendered valuable services, but was not successful in obtaining his transfer overseas before the cessation of hostilities. He was demobilised in September 1919, and holds the Queen's South African Medal.
55, Victoria Road, Peckham, S.E.15.   Z681

WHITE, H., Bombardier, R.F.A.
Volunteering in August 1914, he proceeded in the same year to the Western Front, where he took part in many engagements, being in action at Festubert, Loos, St. Eloi, Albert, Vimy Ridge, Messines, Ypres and Cambrai. In March 1919 he returned home and was demobilised, holding the 1914-15 Star, and the General Service and Victory Medals.
138, Dalyell Road, Stockwell, S.W.9.   Z4857

WHITE, H., Pte., 1st Middlesex Regt. (Labour Corps).
He joined in June 1916, and in the following year was drafted to France, and served in many sectors of the Front in loading and unloading ammunition and on other important duties. He was present at the Battles of Arras, Ypres and Cambrai, and served until hostilities ceased. He was demobilised in September 1919, and holds the General Service and Victory Medals.
39, Portslade Road, Wandsworth Road, S.W.8.   Z4863

WHITE, H., Private, R.A.S.C.
Volunteering in March 1915, he was drafted in the same month to France, where he served on important duties. He was engaged in loading lorries and on important work in connection with the ammunition dumps, and rendered valuable service. During the Retreat of March 1918 he was wounded and invalided home, and after receiving hospital treatment was discharged as medically unfit in July of that year. He holds the 1914-15 Star, and the General Service and Victory Medals.
25, Winstanley Road, Battersea, S.W.11.   Z4862

WHITE, H. (Miss), Special War Worker.
During the war this lady held an important position at Messrs. Waring and Gillows. She was engaged in the manufacture of military equipment, and carried out her duties in a highly commendable manner.
22, Blacks Road, Hammersmith, W.6.   12618A

WHITE, H., Corporal, R.A.F. and King's Royal Rifle Corps.
He volunteered in 1914, and served at first with the R.A.F. Later he was transferred to the King's Royal Rifle Corps, and with them saw service in France. Unfortunately, he was killed in action and was entitled to the General Service and Victory Medals.
"His life for his Country, his soul to God."
21, Cranbrook Road, Chiswick, W.4.   5408C

WHITE, H., Gunner, R.F.A.
Joining in April 1916, he proceeded in the same year to France. Whilst in this theatre of war he was in action at Arras, Cambrai, Ploegsteert Wood and Vimy Ridge, and in many other engagements, including the Retreat and Advance of 1918. He returned home in January 1919, and was demobilised, holding the General Service and Victory Medals.
32, Milford Street, Wandsworth, S.W.8.   Z4848C

WHITE, H. D. Y., Sergt., 3rd Queen's (Royal West Surrey Regiment).
He joined in February 1916, and after his training served at various stations on important duties with his unit. He rendered valuable services, but was not successful in obtaining his transfer overseas owing to medical unfitness. He was demobilised in July 1919.
12, Parker Road, Bermondsey, S.E.1.   Z27436

WHITE, H. R., Bombardier, R.F.A. and Private, 6th Dorset Regiment.
He volunteered in August 1914, but was shortly afterwards discharged as medically unfit. Later he joined the R.F.A., and was drafted to France in March 1916. Whilst in this theatre of war he fought in many engagements, including those on the Somme and at Arras and the Marne, and also served in the Retreat and Advance of 1918, and was wounded and gassed. He returned home in February 1919, and was demobilised, holding the General Service and Victory Medals.
24, Reddins Road, Peckham, S.E.15.   Z6590

WHITE, J. (M.M.), Sergt.-Major, R.F.A.
Volunteering in October 1914, he was sent to France in the following year. He took part in numerous engagements, and was awarded the Military Medal for conspicuous gallantry in the Field for delivering ammunition under heavy shell fire. He also holds the General Service and Victory Medals, and was demobilised in March 1919.
65, Kenbury Street, Camberwell, S.E.5.   Z6117

WHITE, J., A.B., R.N.V.R.
He joined in July 1917, and served for two years on the East Coast defences. He rendered valuable services, but was not successful in obtaining his transfer to a ship. He was demobilised in October, 1919, and holds the General Service Medal. 26, Burgoyne Road, Stockwell, S.W.9.   Z4868

WHITE, J., L/Corporal, Royal Scots Fusiliers.
He was serving at the outbreak of war and immediately proceeded to France, and was in action in the Retreat from Mons and at Ypres, where he was wounded, and Festubert, where he was again wounded, and was sent to hospital at Rouen. He later returned to the front line and took part in the fighting at Neuve Chapelle, Ypres and in other important engagements. He also served in the Retreat and Advance of 1918. He was demobilised in November 1919, and holds the Mons Star, and the General Service and Victory Medals. 23, Riverhall Street, Wandsworth Road, S W 8   Z4866

WHITE, J. H., 1st Class Stoker, R.N., H.M.S. "Lapwing."
He was serving at the outbreak of war, and was engaged with the Grand Fleet in the North Sea He took part in the Battle of Heligoland Bight and was also in action at the Dogger Bank and in the Destroyer engagement of March 1915. Later he served in the Mediterranean and at the Dardanelles. He was demobilised in April 1919, and holds the 1914-15 Star and the General Service and Victory Medals. 2, Northway Road, Camberwell, S.E.5.   Z6466

WHITE, J. R., Private, R.A.S.C. (M.T.)
He joined in February 1917, and in the following June was sent to German East Africa, where he was engaged on important transport duties in many parts. He was, unfortunately killed in action on November 8th, 1917, and was entitled to the General Service and Victory Medals.
"A costly sacrifice upon the altar of freedom." 94, Aylesbury Road, Walworth, S.E.17.   Z4859

WHITE, L., A.B., R.N., H.M.S. "Lancaster."
He joined in May 1918, and proceeded to Vancouver, British Columbia, to join his ship. He was engaged in patrolling the Western coast of America as far south as Chili, and after the cessation of hostilities returned to England and was demobilised in June 1919, holding the General Service and Victory Medals. 29, Dilston Grove, Rotherhithe, S.E.16.   Z6820

WHITE, L., Private, 2nd Royal Fusiliers.
He volunteered in June 1915, and in the following November was drafted to the Western Front, where he took part in various engagements in the Somme sector on July 1st, 1916. He was killed in action and was entitled to the 1914-15 Star, and the General Service and Victory Medals.
"His life for his Country." 54, Reedworth Street, Kennington, S.E.11.   Z27353

WHITE, L. E., Gunner, R.G.A.
He was serving at the outbreak of war, and in the following November was sent to France and was in action during the Retreat from Mons and at La Bassée, Ypres, Loos and the Somme. He was wounded at Ypres in February 1918 and invalided home. On his recovery he was drafted to West Africa. He was still serving in 1920, and holds the Mons Star, and the General Service and Victory Medals. 14, Elwell Place, Camberwell, S.E.5.   Z5855A

WHITE, L. H., Corporal, R.A.S.C.
He was serving at the outbreak of war, and was immediately sent to France, where he was engaged on important transport duties during the Retreat from Mons and in numerous other engagements. After the Armistice he proceeded with the Army of Occupation to Germany. He was discharged in August 1919, and holds the Mons Star, and the General Service and Victory Medals. 47, Westmacott Street, Camberwell, S.E.5.   Z4010A

WHITE, M., Special War Worker.
He was engaged at the Projectile Electric Engineering Company and was employed in the manufacture of tools for shell-making. His duties, which demanded a high degree of technical skill, were carried out with great efficiency, and he rendered valuable services during the war. 21, Morrison Street, Battersea, S.W.11.   Z4854

WHITE, M. E. (Miss), Special War Worker.
This lady was engaged at Messrs. Harris's, Old Town, Clapham, in the manufacture of body shields and aeroplane wings. Her duties, which were of an important nature, were carried out in a most commendable manner, and she rendered valuable services during the war. 16, Carfax Square, Clapham, S.W.4.   Z4860C

WHITE, R., Sapper, R.E.
He volunteered in August 1914, and was engaged with his unit on important duties until September 1916, when he was drafted to France, where he took part in numerous engagements. He returned home, and was demobilised in April 1919, holding the General Service and Victory Medals. 123, The Grove, Hammersmith, W.6.   10360B

WHITE, O., Private, East Surrey Regiment.
He volunteered in 1914, and in the following year was sent to France, where he took part in the fighting at Loos, the Somme, Ypres and numerous other engagements. He was gassed and wounded and was invalided home and discharged as medically unfit for further service in October 1918. He holds the 1914-15 Star, and the General Service and Victory Medals. 42, Chatham Street, Battersea, S.W.11.   Z4855

WHITE, R. H., Sergt., Queen's (Royal West Surrey Regiment).
Having volunteered in September 1914, he was sent to the Dardanelles in the following year. He took part in the Landing at Suvla Bay and was wounded and invalided home. On his recovery he was engaged with his unit on important duties until May 1917, when he proceeded to France, where he served in the Retreat and Advance of 1918. He was demobilised in March 1919, and holds the 1914-15 Star, and the General Service and Victory Medals. 10, Clayton Road, Peckham, S.E.15.   Z6235

WHITE, S., Rifleman, King's Royal Rifle Corps.
He was serving at the outbreak of war and was immediately afterwards sent to France, where he took part in the fighting at Mons, Ypres and the Somme. He was wounded and invalided home, and was discharged in December 1916, on account of his injuries, and holds the Mons Star, and the General Service and Victory Medals. 12, Blewett Street, Walworth, S.E.17.   Z4852

WHITE, S., Sapper, R.E.
Joining in June 1917, he was sent to France in the following year and took part in the Retreat and Advance of 1918. After the Armistice he proceeded with the Army of Occupation to Germany. He returned home, and was demobilised in October 1919, holding the General Service and Victory Medals. 71, Cobourg Road, Camberwell, S.E.5.   Z5539

WHITE, S. E., Rifleman, Rifle Brigade.
He volunteered in May 1915, and later in the same year was drafted to France, and was in action at St. Eloi and the Somme. He was afterwards sent home, but returning to France in December 1916 he took part in the fighting at Arras and in other engagements. He died gloriously on the field of battle at Lens in 1917, and was entitled to the 1914-15 Star, and the General Service and Victory Medals.
"Great deeds cannot die. They with the sun and moon renew their light for ever." 62, Wyndham Road, Camberwell, S.E.5.   Z4865

WHITE, S. G., A.B., R.N., H.M.S. "Strathnethey" (Trawler 112).
He volunteered in October 1914, and served with the Grand Fleet in the North Sea. His vessel was standing by H.M.S. "Natal" when she blew up and he sustained severe shock. He was discharged as medically unfit for further service in January 1917, and holds the 1914-15 Star, and the General Service and Victory Medals. He was later employed on T.N.T. work at Greenwich. 11, Odell Street, Camberwell, S.E.5.   Z5535/6/7/8

WHITE, T., Sergt., R.A.S.C.
After volunteering in March 1915, he was sent to France in September of the same year. He was engaged on important transport duties on the Somme and at Arras, St. Eloi, Bullecourt, Cambrai and Bapaume. He also took part in the Retreat and Advance of 1918. He was demobilised in June 1919, and holds the 1914-15 Star, and the General Service and Victory Medals. 38, Nealdon Street, Stockwell, S.W.9.   Z4867

WHITE, T., Driver, R.F.A.
He volunteered in January 1915, and was drafted to France in the following year. and was transferred to Salonika, where he was in action on the Vardar and Doiran fronts. In 1917 he proceeded to Egypt and thence to Palestine and took part in the Advance and the capture of Jerusalem. He was demobilised in February 1919, and holds the General Service and Victory Medals. 32, Milford Street, Wandsworth Road, S.W.8.   Z4848D

WHITE, W., Stoker, R.N., H.M.S. "Forward."
He was serving at the outbreak of war, and was sent to the Mediterranean. He was later engaged on escort duties in the North Sea until the Armistice. He was demobilised in January 1919, and holds the 1914-15 Star, and the General Service and Victory Medals 10, Chalmers Street, Wandsworth Road, S.W.8.   Z4858

WHITE, W., Private, Royal Scots.
He joined in February 1916, and in the same year proceeded to France, where he took part in numerous engagements. He was unfortunately killed in action on April 22nd, 1918, during the Retreat of that year, and was entitled to the General Service and Victory Medals.
"His life for his Country, his soul to God." 1, Acorn Street, Camberwell, S.E.5.   Z4849A

WHITE, W., 1st Class Air Mechanic, R.A.F.
Joining in April 1916, he was posted to the 34th Royal Fusiliers and sent to France in the same year. He was later transferred to the Pioneer Battalion and was engaged on important duties on the Somme. He afterwards returned home and joined the R.A.F. with which he served until he was discharged in October 1918. He holds the General Service and Victory Medals.
11, Odell Street, Camberwell, S.E.5. Z5535/6/7/8

WHITE, W. A. C., Pte., King's Shropshire Light Infantry.
He volunteered in October 1914, and in 1916 was sent to France with the R.A.S.C. He was later in the same year invalided home, owing to ill-health. On his recovery he proceeded to Salonika and was transferred to the King's Shropshire Light Infantry and took part in the operations on the Vardar and Struma fronts. Contracting malaria, he was invalided home, and was demobilised in March 1919, holding the General Service and Victory Medals.
32, Milford Street, Wandsworth Road, S.W.8. Z4848B

WHITE, W. E., Pte., Northumberland Fusiliers.
After joining in May 1916, he was drafted to France in August of the same year and was in action on the Somme and at Arras, Ypres and in many other important engagements, and was wounded and invalided home. He was demobilised in February 1919, and holds the General Service and Victory Medals.
15, Vicarage Road, Church Street, Camberwell, S.E.5. Z4856

WHITE, W. F., Private, 2nd Hampshire Regiment.
Joining in May 1916, he was sent to the Western Front in the same year and took part in numerous engagements. In 1917 he was wounded and invalided home, but on his recovery returned to France. He was unfortunately killed in action on the Somme on March 11th, 1918, and was entitled to the General Service and Victory Medals.
"Steals on the ear the distant triumph song."
26, St. Mary's Road, Oxford. Z5545A

WHITE, W. J., Private, 8th East Surrey Regiment.
Joining in May 1918, he was sent to France in the following September and took part in the Advance of that year. He was unfortunately killed in action at Le Cateau on October 23rd, 1918, and was entitled to the General Service and Victory Medals.
"A valiant soldier, with undaunted heart he breasted life's last hill."
79, Danby Street, Peckham, S.E.5. Z6806

WHITE, W. J., Sapper, R.E.
He volunteered in October 1914, and in the following year was drafted to the Western Front, where he took part in numerous engagements. He was killed in action at Mametz Wood on August 9th, 1915, and was entitled to the 1914-15 Star, and the General Service and Victory Medals.
"And doubtless he went in splendid company."
99, Fletcher Road, Chiswick, W.4. 6376

WHITEHALL, E., Private, 1st Royal Fusiliers.
A serving soldier at the outbreak of hostilities, he was drafted to France in 1914, and took part in much severe fighting, including the first and second Battles of Ypres. He was wounded in action in September 1915, and invalided home. After lengthy medical treatment he was discharged as physically unfit for further service in July 1916. He holds the 1914 Star, and the General Service and Victory Medals.
11, Dashwood Road, Wandsworth Road, S.W.8. Z4870

WHITEHALL, W., Private, 3rd East Surrey Regt.
He was mobilised from the Reserve in 1914, and was shortly afterwards drafted to the Western Front, where he played a gallant part in the Battle of Hill 60, Ypres and the Somme, and was wounded. He was transferred to the 10th Royal Fusiliers, and was shortly afterwards killed in action at Hulluch on March 3rd, 1917. He was entitled to the 1914 Star, and the General Service and Victory Medals.
"A valiant soldier, with undaunted heart he breasted life's last hill."
20, Dashwood Road, Wandsworth Road, S.W.8. Z4869

WHITEHEAD, B. C., Air Mechanic, R.A.F.
He volunteered in September 1914, and after his training was retained on important duties with his Squadron until March 1916, when he was drafted to India and served as a fitter and engine tester during the remainder of his service. He also did much valuable aircraft work in Afghanistan during the risings of the tribesmen there. He returned home and was discharged in January 1920, and holds the General Service and Victory Medals, and the India General Service Medal (with clasp Afghanistan N.W. Frontier, 1919).
12, Gurney Street, Walworth, S.E.17. Z4871

WHITEHEAD, F. J., Private, 10th London Regt.
He joined in 1916, and after his training was drafted to Egypt. He took part in the British Advance through Palestine under General Allenby and was present at the Battles of Gaza, the entry into Jerusalem, and the capture of Aleppo. During his service he contracted malaria, from which he still suffers, and in August 1919 he was demobilised after his return to England. He holds the General Service and Victory Medals.
26, Randall Street, Battersea, S.W.11. Z2054B

WHITEHEAD, H., Driver, R.F.A.
After being mobilised from the Reserve in August 1914, he was immediately drafted to France and took part in the Retreat from Mons, and in the Battle of Ypres. After serving in many subsequent engagements, he was invalided home through ill-health in October 1915, and was discharged in January of the following year as medically unfit for further duty, after thirteen years' service with the Colours. He holds the Mons Star, and the General Service and Victory Medals.
43, Ernest Street, Bermondsey, S.E.1. Z27280

WHITEHEAD, J., Private, R.A.V.C.
He volunteered in August 1915, and in the following year was drafted to the Western Front. Whilst in this theatre of war he was engaged on important veterinary duties in the Somme, Bapaume and Havrincourt areas, and was wounded near Ypres in February 1917. After his recovery he proceeded to Salonika, where he did valuable service with his unit until the cessation of hostilities. He was demobilised after his return to England in February 1919, and holds the General Service and Victory Medals.
47, Philip Road, Peckham, S.E.15. Z6051B

WHITEHEAD, J. S., Staff-Sergt., R.A.S.C. (M.T.)
He volunteered in May 1915, and in the following year was drafted to Egypt, where he was engaged on special duties as Staff-Sergeant in charge of the workshops at the Base Depôt. He afterwards returned home, and rendered excellent service at various stations in charge of motors, and the repair of caterpillar tractors. During this period he was injured in the course of his duties, and in consequence was discharged as medically unfit for further service in December 1918. He holds the General Service and Victory Medals.
51, Credon Road, Rotherhithe, S.E.16. Z6730

WHITEHOUSE, J. J., Rifleman, King's Royal Rifle Corps.
He joined in June 1916, and after being drafted to the Western Front in the same year took part in the severe fighting at the Somme, Arras and Ypres. He gave his life for the freedom of England near Vimy Ridge on June 24th, 1917, and was entitled to the General Service and Victory Medals.
"He died the noblest death a man may die, Fighting for God, and right, and liberty."
35, Henshaw Street, Walworth, S.E.17. Z3388B

WHITEING, N. (Mrs.), Special War Worker.
During the war this lady was engaged on important duties in connection with Continental traffic at the South Eastern and Chatham Railway Station, Victoria, and thus released a man for military service. She rendered valuable services, and carried out her duties with efficiency until May 1919, when she relinquished her position in favour of a demobilised soldier.
28, Sussex Road, Coldharbour Lane, S.W.8. Z4872A

WHITEING, W. J., Private, 23rd London Regiment.
He joined in August 1916, and in the same year was drafted to France. During his service on the Western Front he fought in many important engagements, including those at Arras, Albert, Vimy Ridge, Ypres, Messines and Lens, and in the Retreat of 1918, and was taken prisoner. After his repatriation from Germany he was engaged in guarding German prisoners at Feltham detention camp until May 1919, when he was demobilised. He holds the General Service and Victory Medals.
28, Sussex Road, Coldharbour Lane, S.W.9. Z4872B

WHITEMAN, A. E., Private, Royal Fusiliers.
He joined in 1916, and in the same year was drafted to France, where he was in action at Ypres and Menin Road, and was wounded twice and gassed. He was taken prisoner in October 1917, and sent to Germany. On his release he returned home, and was demobilised in February 1919, and holds the General Service and Victory Medals.
63, Raymouth Road, Rotherhithe, S.E.16. Z6808

WHITEMAN, J. C., Sergt., Headquarter Staff attd. Queen's Own (Royal West Kent Regiment).
He volunteered in February 1915, and in the same year was drafted to Gallipoli, where he took part in the Landing at Suvla Bay in August of the same year. Owing to an illness contracted on active service he was invalided home to hospital and after medical treatment for some months was attached to the Headquarters Staff at Chatham, where he was engaged on important duties until February 1919. He was then demobilised and holds the 1914-15 Star, and the General Service and Victory Medals.
16, South Island Place, Stockwell, S.W.9. Z5276A

WHITING, A. A., Private, 2nd London Regiment (Royal Fusiliers).

Joining in March 1917, he was drafted in August of the same year to France. During his service overseas he fought in many engagements of importance, and was wounded in action. He gave his life for King and Country on March 21st, 1918, in the early stages of the enemy offensive, and was entitled to the General Service and Victory Medals.

"Courage, bright hopes, and a myriad dreams splendidly given."

57, Greylands Road, Peckham, S.E.15.   Z5856

WHITING, B., Gunner, R.F.A.

He volunteered in May 1915, and in December of the same year was drafted to France. He took an active part in the Battles of Vimy Ridge, the Somme, Messines, Ypres, Passchendaele and Cambrai, and was wounded. He afterwards served in the Retreat and Advance of 1918, notably at Havrincourt and Amiens. He was mentioned in Despatches for his gallantry and devotion to duty at Ypres in August 1917, and holds the 1914-15 Star, and the General Service and Victory Medals. He was demobilised in January 1919.

9, Jocelyn Street, Peckham, S.E.15.   Z5225A

WHITING, G., Gunner, R.G.A.

He joined in August 1916, and crossed to France in the following January. Whilst overseas he did good work as a Gunner at Arras, Ypres and Passchendaele, and in various engagements in the Retreat and Advance of 1918. After the Armistice he proceeded to Germany with the Army of Occupation, and was stationed on the Rhine until September 1919, when he was demobilised on his return to England. He holds the General Service and Victory Medals.

87, Bird-in-Bush Road, Peckham, S.E.15.   Z6591

WHITING, W. J., Sapper, R.E.

He was mobilised in 1914, and was almost immediately drafted to France, where he took part in the Retreat from Mons. He was also present at the Battles of the Marne, the Aisne, St. Eloi, Albert, Ypres, Loos, and the Somme, and whilst engaged on important duties in connection with the operations was wounded three times and shell-shocked. He was invalided home, and after medical treatment was discharged in January 1919, as unfit for further service. He holds the 1914-15 Star, and the General Service and Victory Medals.

29, Tidemore Street, Battersea Park, S.W.8.   Z4873

WHITLOCK, E. A., Bombardier (Signaller), R.F.A.

He volunteered in April 1915, and in the same year proceeded to France, and was in action at Hill 60, Loos, the Somme, Ypres and Cambrai. He also served throughout the Retreat and Advance of 1918. He was demobilised in April 1919, after four years' excellent service, and holds the 1914-15 Star, and the General Service and Victory Medals.

27, Horsman Street, Camberwell, S.E.5.   Z4875

WHITLOCK, H. E., Rifleman, 1st King's Royal Rifle Corps.

He enlisted in March 1913, and on the outbreak of war proceeded to France, where he took part in many engagements, including the first Battle of Ypres, and was wounded in action. He was invalided home, and in 1915, having rejoined his unit in France was again wounded at Festubert. He was again sent home to hospital, and after treatment was discharged as unfit for further service in June 1916. He holds the 1914 Star, and the General Service and Victory Medals.

57, Elmington Road, Camberwell, S.E.5.   Z3442B

WHITLOCK, H. L., A.B., R.N., H.M.S. "Sefton."

He joined in January 1916, and after his training served with the Grand Fleet in the North Sea. He was principally engaged on patrol duties on board a Destroyer, and in escorting convoys between America and English ports. He holds the General Service and Victory Medals, and in 1920 was still serving.

57, Elmington Road, Camberwell, S.E.5.   Z3442A

WHITLUM, H. F., Private, R.A.S.C. (M.T.)

Volunteering in January 1915, later in that year he embarked for Egypt and was engaged on important duties driving an ambulance in the advanced areas, and was present at many engagements, including those at Gaza and Beersheba. Later he was engaged as a driver to General Allenby and rendered valuable services throughout. Suffering from malaria he was invalided to hospital, and on his recovery, rejoined his unit and served until he returned home and was demobilised in June 1919. He holds the 1914-15 Star, and the General Service and Victory Medals.

30, Loughboro' Street, Kennington, S.E.11.   Z25469

WHITMARSH, J. H. F., Leading Cook's Mate, R.N.

He joined the Service in January 1915, and was posted to H.M.S. "Theseus." This ship was in action at the Battle of the Narrows, and took part in the bombardment of the Dardanelles. Later she rendered valuable services engaged on patrol and other important duties in the Mediterranean Sea until the cessation of hostilities. After the Armistice he was transferred to H.M.S. "Lancaster" and in 1920 was still serving on the Pacific Station. He holds the 1914-15 Star, and the General Service and Victory Medals.

39, Cronin Road, Peckham, S.E.15.   Z5540

WHITMORE, J., Rflmn., Rifle Brigade and Private, M.G.C.

He volunteered in August 1914, and in the following year, landing in France, was engaged in the heavy fighting at Vimy Ridge, the Somme, Bullecourt, Ypres, Lens, Cambrai, and throughout the Retreat and Advance of 1919. He was demobilised in December 1919 after returning home, and holds the 1914-15 Star, and the General Service and Victory Medals.

27, Melon Road, Peckham, S.E.15.   Z6362A

WHITNEY, G. A., Leading Seaman, R.N.

He joined the Service in 1899, and at the outbreak of war was serving in H.M.S. "Electra." This ship did good work on patrol and other important duties in the North Sea throughout the war. In 1918 he was discharged in consequence of his service and was transferred to the Royal Fleet Reserve. He holds the 1914-15 Star, and the General Service and Victory Medals.

9, Park Grove, Battersea, S.W.11.   Z4877

WHITNEY, H. V., Sergt., R.A.S.C. (M.T.)

He volunteered in August 1914, and proceeding to France in the same month served throughout the Retreat from Mons, and the Battles of La Bassée, Ypres, and in the Arras sector. He rendered valuable services throughout engaged on the transport of ammunition and supplies to the front lines, and returning home in 1916 was discharged on account of his service in June 1916. He holds the Mons Star, and the General Service and Victory Medals.

31, Arlesford Road, Landor Road, S.W.9.   Z4876

WHITSEY, B., Private, Essex Regiment.

A serving soldier, he proceeded to France shortly after the outbreak of hostilities, and fought in many engagements of note, including the Battles of the Somme. After being transferred to Egypt, he was in action in many parts of the line in Palestine and took part in the final British Advance into Syria. During his service overseas he was wounded three times. After returning home he was demobilised in June 1919, and holds the 1914 Star, and the General Service and Victory Medals.

186, Albert Road, Peckham, S.E.15.   Z5693

WHITSEY, G. R., 1st Class Stoker, R.N.

He was serving in the Navy at the outbreak of war, and during the war served on H.M.S. "Hussar" and "Beaver." He saw active service at the Dardanelles after his ship had been engaged on the escort of troopships to that theatre of war, and later his vessel was employed on important duties in the North Sea. His vessel was torpedoed, but he fortunately was rescued, and after the cessation of hostilities returned to England, and was demobilised in March 1919. He holds the 1914-15 Star, and the General Service and Victory Medals.

76. St. George's Road, Peckham, S.E.15.   Z5541

WHITTAKER, J. C., Private, M.G.C.

He joined in 1916, and in the following year embarked for France, where he was engaged in the heavy fighting in the Ypres sailent, and in many other sectors. He also fought throughout the German Offensive and subsequent Allied Advance of 1918, and returning home after the Armistice was demobilised in November 1919. He holds the General Service and Victory Medals.

32, Avenue Road, Camberwell, S.E.5.   Z4878A

WHITTAKER, P. D., Pte., 52nd Bedfordshire Regt.

He joined in May 1917, and was drafted to France later in the same year. During his service overseas he was in action in many parts of the line and did excellent work during the German Offensive and Allied Advance of 1918. He was demobilised in March 1919, and holds the General Service and Victory Medals.

32, Avenue Road, Camberwell, S.E.5.   Z4878B

WHOWALL, A. G., Cpl., 7th Duke of Wellington's (West Riding Regt.) and 29th Durham Light Infantry.

After joining in 1916, and later in the same year being drafted to France, he fought at Ypres, Vimy Ridge, Bullecourt, Passchendaele, and in many engagements during the enemy Offensive and subsequent Allied Advance of 1918. After returning home he was demobilised in 1919, and holds the General Service and Victory Medals.

1, Cerise Street, Peckham, S.E.15.   Z5694

WHYBROW, J. S. R., Private, R.M.L.I.

He joined in June 1917, and was posted to H.M.S. "Iris." This ship took part in the raid on Zeebrugge in 1917, and later was engaged in escorting the American troops across the Western Ocean. Proceeding to the Mediterranean, he landed in Egypt and assisted to restore order in the riots in Cairo in 1919, being wounded there. He was invalided home, and after hospital treatment was discharged in February 1920. He holds the General Service and Victory Medals.

60, Chatham Road, Battersea, S.W.11.   Z4879

WHYLAND, M. J. (Miss), Worker, Q.M.A.A.C.
She volunteered in September 1915, and later in the year was sent to France. While stationed at Pont-de-l'Arche, she rendered excellent services and went through several air-raids during her service on the Western Front. Returning home after the cessation of hostilities she was demobilised in September 1915, and ho!ds the 1914-15 Star, and the General Service and Victory Medals.
40, Bournemouth Road, Peckham, S.E.15. Z5488B

WICKEN, T. J., Private, 19th Middlesex Regiment.
Joining in 1916, and proceeding to France later in that year he was in action in the first British Offensive on the Somme, and was wounded. On his recovery he rejoined his Battalion and fought in many engagements of note and was severely gassed at Arras in 1917. After treatment in England he subsequently died on September 17th, 1917. He was entitled to the General Service and Victory Medals.
"Great deeds cannot die."
131, Kirkwood Road, Peckham, S.E.15. Z6251C

WICKEN, W., Chief Petty Officer, R.N.
Volunteering in August 1914, he was posted to H.M.S. "Amethyst," which ship was engaged on patrol and other important duties in the early days of the war and did good work. In 1915 she proceeded to the Dardanelles, and was in action in the Battle of the Narrows, during the course of which he was killed. He was entitled to the 1914-15 Star, and the General Service and Victory Medals.
"His life for his Country."
131, Kirkwood Road, Peckham, S.E.15. Z6251A

WICKENDEN, C. A. J., Pte., 4th Leicestershire Regt.
He joined in September 1916, and in the following February was sent to France He fought at Ypres, Cambrai, and many engagements of note and was twice wounded and gassed. He was taken prisoner at Bullecourt in April 1918, and was held in captivity in Germany for nine months. After his repatriation he was demobilised in March 1919, and holds the General Service and Victory Medals.
9, Ancill Street, Hammersmith, W.6. 13738B

WICKENDEN, J., Rifleman, 4th King's Royal Rifle Corps.
He volunteered in August 1914, and after completing his training was engaged at various stations with his unit on guard and other important duties. Owing to ill-health he was unsuccessful in obtaining his transfer overseas and through the same cause was invalided out of the Service in March 1915.
30, Canal Bank, Peckham, S.E.15. Z6367

WICKENDEN, J. W., Private, 16th Royal Welch Fusiliers.
Joining in April 1916, he proceeded to the Western Front shortly afterwards and fought in the first Battle of the Somme, where he was wounded. On recovery he rejoined his unit, and was in action in many later operations. He was unfortunately killed in action on February 25th, 1917, and was entitled to the General Service and Victory Medals.
"Steals on the ear, the distant triumph song."
9, Ancill Street, Hammersmith, W.6. 13738A

WICKENS, A., Driver, R.F.A.
Volunteering in November 1915, he completed his training, and stationed at various depôts, was engaged on transport and other important duties with his unit. Being medically unfit he did not obtain his transfer to a theatre of war, but rendered valuable services until demobilised in August 1919.
27, Wyvil Road, Wandsworth Road, S.W.8. Z4881B

WICKENS, H. C., Driver, R.F.A.
After volunteering in 1914, and completing his training he served at various stations with his battery engaged on important duties. He was unsuccessful in obtaining his transfer overseas and falling seriously ill, died in hospital at Mill Bank in 1918.
"His memory is cherished with pride."
27, Wyvil Road, Wandsworth Road, S.W.8. Z4881A

WICKENS, W., Rifleman, Rifle Brigade.
He volunteered in April 1915, and embarking for the Western Front in May of the following year, fought in the Battles of Vimy Ridge, the Somme, Delville Wood, and Arras. On May 3rd 1917 he was reported wounded and missing after the heavy fighting at Bullecourt, and later was presumed to have been killed in action on that date. He was entitled to the General Service and Victory Medals.
"And doubtless he went in splendid company."
9, Lavender Road, Battersea, S.W.11. Z4880

WICKHAM, H., Corporal, R.E.
He joined the Training Reserve in December 1916, and on completing his course was transferred to the Royal Engineers, but owing to ill-health did not proceed overseas prior to the Armistice. In November 1918 he proceeded to France, and was engaged on important duties in various sectors. After returning home he was demobilised in November 1919.
7, Pratt Street, Lambeth Road, S.E.1. Z27355

WICKINS, W. H., Private, Royal Irish Fusiliers.
He joined in September 1916, and in the following March was sent to the Western Front where he fought in many engagements of note, and was wounded at Poperinghe in July 1915. On his recovery he rejoined his unit and was engaged in heavy fighting in many sectors, and was again wounded in October 1917 at Ypres. After medical treatment and returning to the firing line he was in action throughout the Retreat and Advance of 1918. He was demobilised in January 1919, and holds the General Service and Victory Medals.
1, Thorncroft Street, Wandsworth Road, S.W.8. Z4882

WICKS, P. F., A.B., Royal Navy.
He joined the Service in September 1916, and was posted to H.M.S. "Erin" which was engaged on patrol and other important duties in the North Sea, and took an active part in the raid on Zeebrugge in April 1918. He was present at Scapa Flow when the German Fleet surrendered, and was demobilised in March 1919. He holds the General Service and Victory Medals.
85, Gwynne Road, Battersea, S.W.11. Z4883

WIFFEN, W. J., Pte., 2nd Oxfordshire and Buckinghamshire Light Infantry.
He enlisted in June 1905, and at the outbreak of hostilities was sent to France. He fought in the Retreat from Mons, and the Battles of the Marne, the Aisne, La Bassée, and was wounded at Richbourg on May 15th, 1915. On recovery he rejoined his Battalion and was in action at Vimy Ridge, the Somme, Cambrai, and throughout the German Offensive and Allied Advance of 1918. He served at Cologne with the Army of Occupation after the Armistice, and was demobilised in March 1919, holding the Mons Star, and the General Service and Victory Medals.
267, Mayall Road, Herne Hill, S.E.24. Z4884

WIGG, R. E., Corporal, 9th London Regt. (Queen Victoria's Rifles).
Volunteering in August 1914, in the following November he was drafted to France and fought at Ypres, Hill 60, and in many other engagements. He was reported missing at Gommecourt on July 1st, 1916, and later was presumed to have been killed in action on that date. He was entitled to the 1914 Star, and the General Service and Victory Medals.
"Great deeds cannot die,
They with the sun and moon, renew their light for ever."
21, Ingelow Road, Battersea Park, S.W.8. Z4885

WIGGINS, A. E., Sapper, R.E.
He joined in May 1917, and was drafted to the Western Front in August of the same year. He was employed at the Base on important constructional duties and rendered valuable services. He was not sent to the front lines owing to ill-health and returning home after the Armistice was demobilised in November 1919. He holds the General Service and Victory Medals.
66, Hall Road, Peckham Rye, S.E.15. Z6755

WIGGINS, J. W., A.B., Royal Navy.
He joined in March 1917, and was posted to H.M.S. "The Royalist," which ship was engaged on the dangerous task of mine laying, and had many narrow escapes in the discharge of her duties. After the Armistice she rendered valuable services conveying supplies and ammunition to Russia. He was demobilised in March 1919, and holds the General Service and Victory Medals.
1, Charleston Street, Walworth, S.E.17. Z4887

WIGGINS, T. H., Sergt., Lancashire Fusiliers
He joined in 1916, and embarking for the Western Front in September of the same year fought in many parts of the line, including the Arras, Ypres, and Cambrai sectors. He also was in action throughout the Retreat and Advance of 1918, and was wounded and gassed. After the cessation of hostilities he was stationed at Cologne with the Army of Occupation. After returning home he was demobilised in September 1919, and holds the General Service and Victory Medals.
83, Farmer's Road, Camberwell, S.E.5. Z4886B

WIGGINS, W. J., Driver, R.A.S.C. (M.T.)
He joined in 1916, and in the following year was sent to Mesopotamia, and served in the advanced areas on important duties transporting ammunition and supplies to the front lines. He was present at many engagements of note, and rendered excellent services throughout. Returning to England he was demobilised in February 1920, and holds the General Service and Victory Medals.
73, Farmer's Road, Camberwell, S.E.5. Z4886A

WIGGS, S. A., Rifleman, King's Royal Rifle Corps.
He joined in June 1918 on attaining military age, and on completing his training served at various stations with his unit, engaged on important duties. Owing to ill-health, he was not successful in obtaining his transfer overseas prior to the cessation of hostilities, but rendered excellent services until demobilised in April 1919.
179, Albert Road, Peckham, S.E.15. Z5860B

WIGGS, R. J., Private, M.G.C.

He joined in May 1916, and four months later proceeding to the Western Front, and fought in the Battles of Vimy Ridge, Arras, Bullecourt Messines, Ypres, Cambrai, and in many engagements during the opening stages of the German Offensive of 1918, and was once wounded. He gave his life for King and Country on April 24th, 1918, and was entitled to the General Service and Victory Medals.

"Whilst we remember, the sacrifice is not in vain."

179, Albert Road, Peckham, S.E.15.　　　　Z5860A

WIGLEY, H., Sergt.-Major, Duke of Wellington's (West Riding Regiment).

A reservist, he was mobilised at the commencement of hostilities and almost immediately was drafted to the Western Front. He fought in the Retreat from Mons. On his recovery he rejoined his unit and was engaged in heavy fighting in many sectors until transferred to the Eastern theatre of war. Here he saw much service and rendered valuable service until the cessation of hostilities, and was wounded. After returning home he was demobilised in April 1919, and holds the Mons Star, and the General Service and Victory Medals.

4, Russel Street, Battersea, S.W.11.　　　　Z4888

WIGLEY, W. G., Private, R.A.S.C. (M.T.)

He joined in January 1917, and in the following month sailed for German East Africa where he saw much service until the close of the campaign in this theatre of war, engaged on transport duties. After returning to England he was demobilised in December 1919, and holds the General Service and Victory Medals.

6, Ostend Place, Walworth, S.E.17.　　　　Z26150B

WILCOCKS, A., Private, 23rd London Regiment.

He volunteered in 1914, and later in that year was sent to the Western Front, where he fought in the Battles of Ypres and Hill 60. He was severely wounded at Givenchy in May 1915, and returning to England received hospital treatment, and was ultimately invalided out of the Service in 1915. He holds the 1914 Star, and the General Service and Victory Medals.

3, Elwell Road, Clapham, S.W.4.　　　　Z4889

WILCOX, J., Driver, R.F.A.

He volunteered in 1914, and in the succeeding year landed in France, where he was in action on the Somme, Arras, and Ypres, and Cambrai fronts, and was twice wounded. In 1917 after being transferred to Italy he saw much fighting on the Piave, and took part in the final Allied Advance in that theatre of war in 1918. He was demobilised in 1920, and holds the 1914-15 Star, the General Service and Victory Medals.

35, Henshaw Street, Walworth, S.E.17.　　　　Z4891

WILCOX, P., Private, 1st King's Shropshire Light Infantry.

He joined in February 1918 at the age of fourteen, and after completing his training was stationed at various depôts engaged on important duties. He did not obtain his transfer overseas prior to the cessation of hostilities, but was drafted to Egypt in November 1919, where he served as a bandsman. He was still serving there in 1920.

26, Delaford Road, Rotherhithe, S.E.16.　　　　Z6731

WILCOX, W. E. H., Ordinary Seaman, Mercantile Marine.

He joined in February 1917, and was posted to H.M.T. "Arcadian," engaged in conveying troops to various fronts. This ship was torpedoed in the Mediterranean on April 15th, 1917, and unfortunately he was drowned. He was entitled to the General Service and Mercantile Marine War Medals.

"A costly sacrifice upon the altar of freedom."

3, Riley Street, Bermondsey, S.E.1.　　　　Z27428

WILCOXON, G., Rifleman, King's Royal Rifle Corps.

He volunteered in March 1915, and in June of the succeeding year, after crossing to the Western Front, fought in the first Battle of the Somme. Owing to ill-health he returned to England in September 1916, and on his recovery rejoined his unit in France in August of the following year. He was engaged in much heavy fighting, and after being severely wounded at Loos, was invalided home. On his discharge from Hospital he was transferred to the Royal Scots Fusiliers and with this Regiment served till demobilised in February 1919. He holds the General Service and Victory Medals.

83, Battersea Bridge Road, Battersea, S.W.11.　　　　Z4800B

WILCOXON, H. C., Q.M.S., East Surrey Regiment.

A Reservist, he was mobilised at the outbreak of hostilities and until October 1918 rendered valuable services at various depôts engaged on important duties. He was then sent to France and saw much service in the closing stages of the Allied Advance. He was demobilised in March 1919, and holds the General Service and Victory Medals.

83, Battersea Bridge Road, Battersea, S.W.11.　　　　Z4890A

WILD, A. J., Private, Border Regiment.

Volunteering in August 1914, he proceeded to France in the following year, and fought in many engagements of note, including the Battle of the Somme, and was wounded three times. He was severely wounded at St. Quentin, and after hospital treatment in England was ultimately invalided out of the Service in June 1917. He holds the 1914-15 Star, and the General Service and Victory Medals.

32, Shorncliffe Road, Walworth, S.E.17.　　　　Z4892A

WILD, C. G., Private, Leicestershire Regiment.

Mobilised from the Reserve at the declaration of war, he embarked for France and fought in the Retreat from Mons, the Battle of Ypres, and in many other engagements. He was reported missing on September 15th, 1916, during the first Battle of the Somme, and later was presumed to have been killed in action on that date. He was entitled to the 1914-15 Star, and the General Service and Victory Medals.

"Nobly striving, he nobly fell that we might live."

32, Shorncliffe Road, Walworth, S.E.17.　　　　Z4892C

WILD, D., Rifleman, King's Royal Rifle Corps.

He joined in April 1916, and proceeding to France three months later fought in the Battles of Arras, Vimy Ridge, Bullecourt, Messines, and Ypres. He gave his life for the freedom of England on August 24th, 1917, and was entitled to the General Service and Victory Medals.

"Courage, bright hopes, and a myriad dreams splendidly given."

88, Chatham Street, Walworth, S.E.17.　　　　Z4716A

WILD, J., Pte., Queen's Own (Royal West Kent Regt.)

He joined in August 1917, and in the following year was sent to the Western Front, where he fought at Arras, Albert, and throughout the German Offensive, and subsequent Allied Advance of 1918. He afterwards served in Germany with the Army of Occupation, until, returning to England, he was demobilised in September 1919. He holds the General Service and Victory Medals.

32, Shorncliffe Road, Walworth, S.E.17.　　　　Z4892B

WILDER, J. H., Sergt., 10th Hampshire Regiment.

He enlisted in June 1911, and at the outbreak of war was serving in India. He then returned to England and shortly afterwards was drafted to France. He served there in many engagements including the second Battle of Ypres, where he was wounded. On his recovery he was sent to the Macedonian front and rendered valuable services until the victorious conclusion of the campaign in this theatre of war. On returning home he was demobilised in March 1919, and holds the 1914 Star, and the General Service and Victory Medals. and also a Serbian Decoration.

49, Gonsalva Road, Battersea Park, S.W.8.　　　　Z4893

WILDING, C. F., Driver, R.A.S.C. (M.T.)

Volunteering in October 1914, he was sent to France in the same month, and served in the forward areas, transporting ammunition and supplies to the lines. He was present at the Battles of Ypres, Vimy Ridge, the Somme, Arras, Messines, and in the heavy fighting in the Retreat and Advance of 1918. After the cessation of hostilities he served in Germany with the Army of Occupation until he returned home, and was demobilised in March 1919. He holds the 1914 Star, and the General Service and Victory Medals.

19, Brymer Road, Camberwell, S.E.5.　　　　Z5695

WILDY, D. B., Private, R.A.S.C.

He volunteered in March 1915, and served at various stations until he proceeded to the Western Front in March 1917. He served in the forward areas on important transport duties, and was present at the Battles of Messines, Ypres, Cambrai, and at many engagements in the Retreat and Advance of 1918. He was at the entry into Mons on November 11th, 1918, and returning to England shortly after the Armistice was demobilised in December 1918. He died on May 12th, 1920 from the effects of an illness contracted whilst on active service, and was entitled to the General Service and Victory Medals.

"His memory is cherished with pride."

1, Danes Cottages, Camberwell, S.E.5.　　　　Z6115

WILKIN, E. J., L/Corporal, 10th Royal Fusiliers and 5th Middlesex Regiment.

He was serving in the Mercantile Marine at the commencement of hostilities on s.s. "Arsova." This ship was engaged in transporting troops from Great Britain and the Colonies to various theatres of war and in conveying the sick and wounded to the United Kingdom. He joined the Army in November 1915, and later in that year was sent to France, where he was engaged in heavy fighting in various sectors, and was wounded and invalided home. On his recovery he was transferred to the Middlesex Regiment, and after returning to France fought in many engagements of note. He was taken prisoner during the German Offensive of 1918, and held in captivity until the cessation of hostilities, during which he was engaged on important medical duties. After his repatriation he was demobilised in February 1919, and holds the 1914-15 Star, the General Service, the Mercantile Marine War, and Victory Medals.

15, Clayton Buildings, Little East Street, Lollard Street, Kennington, S.E.11.　　　　25663B

WILKIN, G. A., Private, 3rd Royal Fusiliers.

He volunteered in July 1915, and in the following November proceeded to Gallipoli and fought in many engagements until the Evacuation of the Peninsula. He was then drafted to Egypt, and served there for a few weeks before proceeding to France, where he fought in the first Battle of the Somme, and was severely wounded. After protracted hospital treatment he was invalided out of the Service in February 1918. He holds the 1914-15 Star, and the General Service and Victory Medals.

15, Clayton Buildings, Little East Street, Lollard Street, Kennington, S.E.11. 25663A

WILKIN, J., Private, Royal Fusiliers.

He volunteered in June 1915, and in September of that year proceeding to the Western Front, was in action in the Battle of Loos, and in various other important engagements. He gave his life for King and Country in August 1916, during the first Battle of the Somme, and was entitled to the 1914-15 Star, the General Service and Victory Medals.

"His life for his Country."

26, Wyvil Road, South Lambeth Road, S.W.8. Z4895

WILKINS, A., Rifleman, 13th Rifle Brigade.

Joining in November 1917, he afterwards was drafted to the Western Front, where he fought at Gommecourt and in many other parts of the line. He was unfortunately killed in action on April 3rd 1918, during the German Offensive, and was entitled to the General Service and Victory Medals.

"Great deeds cannot die."

45, Warrior Road, Camberwell, S.E.5. Z3347A

WILKINS, A. E. V., L/Corporal, Royal Irish Rifles.

Volunteering in February 1916, he proceeded to Salonika in January of the following year, and fought in many engagements of note on the Struma and other fronts. In 1918, after being transferred to Egypt, he was in action in various parts of the line on the Palestine front, and served at Gaza, and throughout the final British Advance into Syria. After the Armistice he was stationed in Cairo, and assisted to restore order during the riots there in 1919. After returning home he was demobilised in September 1919, and holds the General Service and Victory Medals.

101, Battersea Bridge Road, Battersea, S.W.11. Z4896

WILKINS, J. H., Private, 7th Sherwood Foresters.

He joined in October 1916, and in February of the following year was sent to France, where he took part in numerous engagements. He was taken prisoner in March 1918, and sent to Essen, where he was compelled to work in the coal mines. On his release he returned home and was demobilised in March 1919, holding the General Service and Victory Medals.

45, Warrior Road, Camberwell, S.E.5. Z3347D

WILKINS, R. V., Corporal, R.E.

Having joined in April 1916 he was sent to France in the same year. He took part in numerous engagements, including those on the Somme, and at Arras, Albert, Bullecourt, Armentières, and Béthune. He also served in the Retreat and Advance of 1918. He was demobilised in February 1919, and holds the General Service and Victory Medals.

27, Clayton Road, Peckham, S.E.15. Z5861

WILKINS, T. E., Rifleman, Rifle Brigade.

He joined in June 1916, and later in the same year was sent to France. He was shortly afterwards invalided home with frost bite. On his recovery he returned to the Western Front in July 1917, and took part in numerous engagements and was gassed. He was again sent home and after a period in hospital was discharged as medically unfit for further service in July 1918, holding the General Service and Victory Medals.

45, Warrior Road, Camberwell, S.E.5. Z3347C

WILKINSON, A., Private, 16th Royal Sussex Regt.

He joined in February 1917, and in the same year was drafted to Egypt, and thence to Palestine, where he was in action at Gaza, and took part in the Advance, and the Capture of Jerusalem. In April 1918 he was transferred to the Western Front, and was engaged in the Retreat and Advance of that year, and was wounded near Albert. He was invalided home and discharged as medically unfit for further service in October 1919, holding the General Service and Victory Medals.

3, Bennerley Road, Battersea, S.W.11. Z4897

WILKINSON, B., A.B., R.N., H.M.S. "Barham."

He was serving on H.M.S. "Galatea" at the outbreak of war and was afterwards transferred to H.M.S. "Barham," and was engaged with the Grand Fleet in the North Sea. He took part in the Battle of Jutland, and later proceeded in H.M.S. "Glory" to North Russia. Finally he served in Patrol Boat 46 until September 1920, when he was demobilised holding the 1914-15 Star, and the General Service and Victory Medals.

13, Russell Street, Battersea, S.W.11. Z4898

WILKINSON, G., Sergt., R.A.V.C. and 12th (Prince of Wales' Royal) Lancers.

He was mobilised in August 1914 with the 12th (Prince of Wales' Royal) Lancers, and was immediately sent to France, where he took part in the fighting at Mons, and in the Retreat. He was also in action at Ypres, Neuve Chapelle, Hill 60, the Somme, Arras, and Cambrai, and in the Retreat and Advance of 1918. He was demobilised in February 1919, and holds the Mons Star, and the General Service and Victory Medals.

38, Dalwood Street, Camberwell, S.E.5. Z4899

WILKINSON, G. F., Gunner, R.F.A.

He volunteered in August 1914, and was engaged with his Battery on important duties until 1916, when he was drafted to France, where he took part in the fighting at St. Eloi, Vimy Ridge, the Somme, and Ypres. In 1917 he was transferred to Salonika, where he was again in action, and was wounded and invalided home. He was discharged owing to his injuries in March 1918, and holds the General Service and Victory Medals.

105, Avenue Road, Camberwell, S.E.5. Z4900

WILKINSON, G. G., Sergt., R.A.S.C. (Supply Section).

He volunteered in September 1914, and in 1916 was sent to France and was engaged on important duties at Arras. He was next transferred to Salonika, and served on the Struma front, and later proceeded to Egypt and thence to Palestine. He returned home in July 1919, and was demobilised holding the General Service and Victory Medals.

12, Ramsey Road, Stockwell, S.W.9. Z6517-8A

WILKINSON, J. H., 1st Air Mechanic, R.A.F.

After having previously been employed on work of National importance he joined in February 1918, and was engaged at various stations with his Squadron on important duties. He served as a motor driver and rendered valuable services, but was not successful in obtaining his transfer overseas before the cessation of hostilities. He was demobilised in January 1919.

72, Delaford Road, Rotherhithe, S.E.16. Z6775

WILKINSON, W., L/Cpl., 1st Queen's Own (Royal West Kent Regiment).

He volunteered in August 1914, and later in the same year was sent to France, where he took part in the fighting at Ypres, the Somme and Cambrai, and was twice wounded. After the Armistice he returned home, but in 1919 proceeded to Egypt, and thence to India, and was stationed at Agra, where he was still serving in 1920, holding the 1914 Star, and the General Service and Victory Medals.

53, Councillor Street, Camberwell, S.E.5. Z4901

WILKS, W. J., Pte., Queen's (Royal West Surrey Regiment).

Joining in February 1917 he was sent to France in the following month, and took part in numerous engagements. He was unfortunately killed by a shell in a dug-out at Havrincourt Wood on December 30th, 1917, and was entitled to the General Service and Victory Medals.

"He joined the great white company of valiant souls."

4, Larcom Street, Walworth, S.E.17. Z4894

WILLARD, C., Private, East Surrey Regiment.

He volunteered in November 1914, and after his training was engaged on important duties at various stations with his unit. He rendered valuable services, but was not successful in obtaining his transfer overseas owing to being medically unfit for duty abroad. He was discharged in March 1916.

5, Opal Street, Kennington Lane, S.E.11. Z27391

WILLCOX, A., Driver, R.F.A.

He volunteered in November 1915, and early in the following year was sent to France, where he was in action at Albert, St. Eloi, Vimy Ridge, the Somme, Beaumont-Hamel, Arras, Messines, Ypres, Cambrai, and numerous other engagements. He also served in the Retreat and Advance of 1918. He was demobilised in August 1919, and holds the General Service and Victory Medals.

188, East Street, Walworth Road, S.E.17. Z4903A

WILLCOX, G., Rifleman, Rifle Brigade.

Joining in June 1917, he was sent to France later in the same year, and took part in numerous engagements. He fell fighting at Cambrai on November 30th, 1917, and was entitled to the General Service and Victory Medals.

"Whilst we remember the Sacrifice is not in vain."

188, East Street, Walworth Road, S.E.17. Z4903B

WILLCOX, H., Driver, R.F.A.

He volunteered in September 1914, and in March of the following year was sent to France, where he was in action at St. Eloi, Hill 60, Ypres, Festubert, Albert, Vimy Ridge, the Somme, Arras, Messines and in numerous other engagements, and was wounded and invalided home. In 1918 on his recovery he proceeded to Russia, where he served until August 1919, when he returned home, and was demobilised, holding the 1914-15 Star, and the General Service and Victory Medals.

188, East Street, Walworth Road, S.E.17. Z4902A

WILLCOX, H., Trooper, Royal Canadian Dragoons.
He volunteered in June 1915, and proceeded to France in May 1917. He took part in the fighting at Vimy Ridge, the Somme, Messines, Ypres, Cambrai, Amiens, and Bapaume. and also served in the Retreat and Advance of 1918. He was demobilised in May 1919, and holds the General Service and Victory Medals.
188, East Street, Walworth Road, S.E.17. Z4902B

WILLCOX, W. T., Private, R.A.S.C. (M.T.)
He volunteered in April 1915, and in the following August was sent to Salonika, where he was engaged on important transport duties on the Vardar and Struma fronts. He returned home and was demobilised in April 1919, and holds the 1914–15 Star, and the General Service and Victory Medals.
103, Smyrk's Road, Walworth, S.E.17. Z1909B

WILLETT, J. T., 1st Air Mechanic, R.A.F. (late R.N.A.S.)
Joining in November 1916, he was engaged, after having completed his training, on important patrol duties with the Grand Fleet in the North Sea. He rendered valuable service until demobilised in November 1919, and holds the General Service and Victory Medals.
95, Scylla Road, Nunhead, S.E.15. Z6108

WILLEY, A., Private, 3rd Norfolk Regt. and Labour Corps.
He volunteered in February 1915, and proceeded in the following November to France. There he served, attached to the Labour Corps, in many sectors of the front, and was present at the Battles of Albert, Arras, Ypres, and numerous other engagements until hostilities ceased. He came home in September 1919, and was demobilised, holding the 1914–15 Star, and the General Service and Victory Medals.
33, Blakes Road, Peckham, S.E.15. Z6021A

WILLEY, A. C., Sergt., Scots Guards.
He volunteered in 1914, and after having completed his training was drafted overseas in the same year. Whilst in France he took part in numerous engagements and fell in action at Festubert in May 1915. He was entitled to the General Service and Victory Medals.
"His life for his Country, his Soul to God."
98, Rayleigh Road, West Kensington, W.14. 12047B

WILLEY, C., Driver, R.A.S.C.
He joined in February 1916, and after completing his training served on important transport duties at various stations with his unit. He rendered valuable services, but was not successful in obtaining his transfer overseas before hostilities ceased. In March 1919 he was demobilised.
128, Wells Street, Camberwell, S.E.5. Z4460A

WILLIAMS, A., Sergt., R.F.A.
He volunteered in 1915, and in the same year proceeded to the Western Front, where he was severely gassed in action in an early engagement and was invalided home. On his recovery he returned to France and took part in the Battles of Vimy Ridge, Messines, Ypres, Passchendaele, Cambrai, and the second Battle of the Somme, where he was taken prisoner in March 1918. He was held in captivity in Germany until after the Armistice, when he was released and demobilised in December 1919. He holds the 1914–15 Star, and the General Service and Victory Medals.
26, Oakden Street, Kennington, S.E.11. Z27371

WILLIAMS, A., Corporal, Royal Fusiliers.
Volunteering in August 1914, he was drafted to France in the same year, and after taking part in various engagements of great importance was unhappily killed in action in September 1917. He was entitled to the 1914–15 Star, and the General Service and Victory Medals.
"Whilst we remember, the Sacrifice is not in vain."
46, Ingrave Street, Battersea, S.W.11. Z4905B

WILLIAMS, A.. Private, R.A.M.C.
He joined in 1916, and in the same year after completing his training proceeded to France where he was engaged on important medical duties in various sectors, notably at Ypres. After three years on the Western Front he was demobilised in October 1919, and holds the General Service and Victory Medals.
2, Belham Street, Camberwell, S.E.5. Z4907A

WILLIAMS, A. A., Signal Boy, R.N., H.M.S. "Defence."
He volunteered in November 1914, and was trained at Devonport. He was then posted to H.M.S. "Defence," and served with the Grand Fleet in the North Sea. His ship took part in the Battle of Jutland, and he lost his life at seventeen years of age when she was sunk in action on May 31st, 1916. He was entitled to the 1914–15 Star, and the General Service and Victory Medals.
"Honour to the immortal dead who gave their youth that the world might grow old in peace."
31, Park Place, Clapham, S.W.4. Z4906

WILLIAMS, A., Private, Royal Fusiliers.
He joined in 1916, and in the same year proceeded to France, where he took part in many important engagements, including those on the Ancre front, and at Arras and Beaumont-Hamel. He also served in the Retreat and Advance of 1918, and after the Armistice was sent to Germany with the Army of Occupation. In August 1920, after his return home he was demobilised and holds the General Service and Victory Medals.
3, Belham Street, Camberwell, S.E.5. Z4907B

WILLIAMS, A. J. (M.M.), Rflmn., 16th Rifle Brigade.
He joined in January 1917, and in the following month proceeded to the Western Front. During his service overseas he fought with distinction at Arras, Ypres, and the Somme, and in many later engagements in the Retreat and Advance of 1918. He was awarded the Military Medal for conspicuous gallantry in action, when he captured an enemy machine gun that was holding up the Allied Advance in September 1920. He holds, in addition to the Military Medal, the General Service, and Victory Medals, and was demobilised.in January 1919.
1A, Barkworth Road, Rotherhithe, S.E.16. Z6756

WILLIAMS, C., Private (Signaller), Essex Dragoons.
He joined in June 1917, at the age of eighteen years, and after his training served at various stations on important duties with his unit. In January 1918 he was drafted to Ireland, where he rendered valuable services, but was not successful in obtaining his transfer overseas before the cessation of hostilities. He was demobilised in September 1919.
122, Hartington Road, South Lambeth, S.W.8. Z4913B

WILLIAMS, C. H., L/Corporal, 1st East Surrey Regt.
He was mobilised at the outbreak of war, having served in the South African Campaign, and was almost immediately drafted to France, where he took part in the Retreat from Mons. He also served in numerous later engagements, including those of the Aisne, La Bassée, Ypres, Neuve Chapelle, Hill 60, Loos, Ploegsteert Wood, the Somme, Beaumont-Hamel, Arras, and Messines. He was wounded at Passchendaele, and after his recovery continued his service in the Retreat and Advance of 1918. He was discharged in November of the same year, and holds the Queen's and King's South African Medals, the Mons Star, and the General Service and Victory Medals.
14, Hargwyne Street, Stockwell Road, S.W.9. Z4904

WILLIAMS, E., Private, R.M.L.I.
He was in the Royal Marines at the outbreak of hostilities, and was sent to the North Sea where he served on the "Black Prince" and "Queen Mary." He was afterwards engaged on Destroyers in convoying ships carrying troops, munitions and supplies to the various theatres of war until the cessation of hostilities. In February 1919 he was discharged, after having completed sixteen years' service, and holds the 1914–15 Star, and the General Service and Victory Medals.
279, Sumner Road, Peckham, S.E.15. Z6366

WILLIAMS, E., Private, Oxfordshire and Buckinghamshire Light Infantry.
He was mobilised at the outbreak of war, and was almost immediately sent to France, where he fought in the Retreat from Mons, and the Battles of the Marne, the Aisne, Ypres, Festubert, Loos, and the Somme, and was gassed. He subsequently gave his life for King and Country in action in June 1917, and was entitled to the Mons Star, and the General Service and Victory Medals.
"Nobly striving.
He nobly fell that we might live."
46, Ingrave Street, Battersea, S.W.11. Z4905A

WILLIAMS, E., Rifleman, Rifle Brigade.
He volunteered in 1915, and in the same year was drafted to the Western Front. Whilst overseas he fought in the Battles of the Somme, Arras, and Ypres, and was later invalided home through ill-health. After his recovery he was retained on home duties, and was mainly engaged in guarding German prisoners, and in coastal defence. He was discharged on account of service in 1918, and holds the 1914–15 Star, and the General Service and Victory Medals.
26, Faraday Street, Walworth, S.E.17. Z27463

WILLIAMS, E. H., Private, 2nd Royal Fusiliers.
Volunteering in May 1915, he was drafted to France in January of the following year. Whilst overseas he fought in various parts of the Somme front until June in the same year, when he was invalided home through ill-health and discharged. He holds the General Service and Victory Medals, and in 1920 was still undergoing medical treatment.
34, Lockington Road, Battersea Park Road, S.W.8. Z4915

WILLIAMS, E. J., Private, 23rd Middlesex Regt.
He joined in March 1916, and after being retained on important duties at various stations was drafted to France in March 1918, took part in various engagements of importance in the Retreat and Advance of that year, and was gassed and in hospital in France during this period. After the Armistice he proceeded to Germany with the Army of Occupation, and was stationed at Cologne until 1919, when he returned home, and was demobilised. He holds the General Service and Victory Medals.
44, Kimberley Road, Nunhead, S.E.15. Z6594

WILLIAMS, E. W., Driver, R.F.A.
He volunteered in March 1915, and in December of the same year embarked for France. During his service on the Western Front he did good work as a driver in many engagements, including those of Vimy Ridge, the Somme, Arras, Ypres, Messines, and Cambrai. He also served throughout the Retreat and Advance of 1918, and was demobilised in April of the following year. He holds the 1914-15 Star, and the General Service and Victory Medals.
20, Harris Street, Camberwell, S.E.5. Z4526B

WILLIAMS, E. W., Stoker, R.N., H.M.S. " Lion."
He volunteered in April 1915, and served with the 6th Middlesex Regiment in France in August of the same year. Whilst on the Western Front he fought in various engagements, including the Battle of Loos, and was wounded at Vermelles, and invalided home. Subsequently he was discharged in April 1916. In September 1917 he joined the Royal Navy, and was posted to H.M.S. " Lion," and whilst in this vessel served at Scapa Flow, and in other home waters and was present when the German Fleet surrendered. He was demobilised in May 1919, and holds the 1914-15 Star, and the General Service and Victory Medals.
27, East Surrey Grove, Peckham, S.E.15. Z5296

WILLIAMS, F. M. (Mrs.), Special War Worker.
For more than a year during the war this lady was engaged on important duties in the employ of the General Post Office at Wynne Road Sorting Office, thus releasing a man for the Army. She rendered valuable services, but was obliged to resign on account of ill-health in April 1918.
8, Pulross Road, Stockwell, S.W.9. 4912A

WILLIAMS, F. S., Private, 22nd London Regiment (The Queen's).
He joined in June 1917, and in the same year was drafted to France. During his service on the Western Front he fought in many engagements in the Retreat and Advance of 1918, his duties consisting chiefly in rifle-bombing, and was twice wounded. After the Armistice he proceeded to Germany, and was stationed at Cologne until December 1919, when he returned home, and was demobilised. He holds the General Service and Victory Medals.
73, St. Mark's Road, Camberwell, S.E.5. Z4909

WILLIAMS, G. C., Private, 1st London Regiment (Royal Fusiliers).
Volunteering in November 1914, he was drafted overseas in the following year. Whilst in France he fought at St. Eloi, Ypres, Loos, Vermelles, and the Somme until December 1916, when he was sent to Italy. In this theatre of war he took part in various operations on the Piave, and died gloriously on the Field of Battle in December 1917. He was entitled to the 1914-15 Star, and the General Service and Victory Medals.
" Thinking that remembrance, though unspoken may
reach him where he sleeps."
52, Mayall Road, Herne Hill, S.E.24. Z6239

WILLIAMS, H., Special War Worker.
For over three years during the war he held an important position at Woolwich Arsenal, where he was engaged on shell fusing. He was afterwards promoted to the post of an Inspector. He rendered valuable services until after the Armistice was signed, and in 1920 was serving in the Naval Division of the Royal Arsenal.
63, Gloucester Road, Peckham, S.E.15. Z6126

WILLIAMS, H , Sergt., South Wales Borderers and Labour Corps.
He was mobilised from the Reserve in 1914, and was almost immediately drafted to the Western Front, where he took part in the Retreat from Mons. He also served in the Battles of the Marne, and the Aisne, and after being severely wounded at Ypres, was invalided home. In 1917 he was sent to Salonika where he saw much valuable service until the cessation of hostilities. He was demobilised after his return to England in 1919, and holds the Mons Star, and the General Service and Victory Medals.
61, Barlow Street, Walworth, S.E.17. Z4914

WILLIAMS, H. G., Private, Buffs (East Kent Regiment) and Middlesex Regiment.
He volunteered in October 1915, and in the following year was drafted to the Western Front. Whilst in France he took part in many engagements, including those at the Somme, Ypres, and Arras. Owing to dysentery he was invalided home in 1918, and after his recovery was retained on important duties at Southampton, Portsmouth, and Liverpool docks until demobilised in March 1919. He holds the General Service and Victory Medals.
19, Trafalgar Street, S.E.17. Z27327A

WILLIAMS, J., Private, R.D.C.
Volunteering in November 1914, he completed his training, and was afterwards engaged on important defence duties on the East Coast. He also served in Ireland in the wireless station in County Galway, and did consistently good work, until demobilised in January 1919.
21, D'Eynsford Road, Camberwell, S.E.5. Z4908A

WILLIAMS, H. C. V., Private, 13th Royal Canadian Highlanders.
After coming home from Canada and joining in September 1916, he proceeded to France in the following year. Whilst there he took part in many engagements, including those at Vimy Ridge, and Hill 70, and was twice wounded. He died of his injuries on August 24th, 1917, and was buried near St. Omer. He was entitled to the General Service and Victory Medals.
" Whilst we remember, the sacrifice is not in vain."
22, Farmer's Road, Camberwell, S.E.5. Z4911

WILLIAMS, H. J., Sergt., R.A.S.C. (M.T.)
He volunteered in August 1914, and later in the same month was drafted to France. During his service there he was responsible under the General Headquarters' Staff for the conveyance of troops, food, and ammunition up to the front lines. He was present at Mons, the Marne, La Bassée, Ypres, Loos, Albert, the Somme, Arras, Lens, and Cambrai, and in many other engagements. In June 1918 he was invalided home with malaria, and was discharged as medically unfit for further service in the following month. He holds the Mons Star, and the General Service and Victory Medals.
17, Freemantle Street, Walworth, S.E.17. Z4910

WILLIAMS, H. S. (M.M.), Sergt., Grenadier Guards.
Mobilised at the outbreak of hostilities he immediately proceeded to France and fought in the Retreat from Mons. He was also in action at Ypres, Neuve Chapelle, the Somme, Arras, Cambrai and many engagements in the Retreat and Advance of 1918. After the cessation of hostilities he went with the Army of Occupation into Germany, and was stationed for a time at Cologne. He was awarded the Military Medal for conspicuous bravery in the Field at Passchendaele in 1917, and in addition holds the Mons Star, and the General Service and Victory Medals. In January 1919 he returned home and was demobilised.
22, Redan Terrace, Camberwell, S.E.5. Z6240

WILLIAMS, J., Private, R.A.M.C.
He joined in March 1917, and on the completion of his training was drafted to Salonika, where he saw much service. Whilst in the East he was principally engaged on important duties in the Military hospitals, and suffered from malaria and dysentery. In February 1920 after his return home he was demobilised, holding the General Service and Victory Medals.
56, Lugard Road, Peckham, S.E.15. Z6759

WILLIAMS, J. A., Private, East Surrey Regiment.
He was mobilised from the Reserve in August 1914, and in the same month was drafted to the Western Front, where he saw much heavy fighting. He was in action at Mons, Ypres, Neuve Chapelle, Hill 60, and many later engagements, and was wounded three times. After receiving hospital treatment he was discharged in September 1917, but later died from the effects of his injuries. He was entitled to the Mons Star, and the General Service and Victory Medals.
" He passed out of the sight of men by the path of duty and
self-sacrifice."
21, D'Eynsford Road, Camberwell, S.E.5. Z4908B

WILLIAMS, J. E., Gunner, R.G.A.
He joined in October 1916, and in the following year after completing his training embarked for the Western Front. There he was in action at Ypres, Bullecourt, Messines, the Somme, Bapaume, Amiens, and in many other engagements, including the Retreat and Advance of 1918. In September 1919 after he returned home he was demobilised, holding the General Service and Victory Medals.
20, Manaton Road, Peckham, S.E.15. Z6354

WILLIAMS, L. J., Corporal, 24th London Regiment (Queen's).
He volunteered in September 1914, and in the following March proceeded to the Western Front. In this theatre of war he took part in many notable engagements, including those at Loos, Vimy Ridge, the Somme, Arras, Passchendaele, Cambrai, and was wounded. During the German Offensive in March 1918 he was taken prisoner and held in captivity until hostilities ceased. In February 1919 he was demobilised and holds the 1914-15 Star, and the General Service and Victory Medals.
122, Hartington Road, South Lambeth, S.W.8. Z4913A

WILLIAMS, M. W. (M.M.), Driver, R.F.A.
Mobilised at the outbreak of hostilities he was immediately drafted to France, where he served with distinction in many battles. He was in action in the Retreat from Mons, and at La Bassée, Ypres, Loos, Vimy Ridge, on the Somme, and was awarded the Military Medal for conspicuous bravery and coolness in the Field. Later he proceeded to Italy and served there some time with the Italian Army. He returned to France and did excellent work with his Battery until demobilised in March 1919. In addition to the Military Medal he also holds the Mons Star, and the General Service and Victory Medals.
267, Sumner Road, Peckham, S.E.15. Z6114

WILLIAMS, T., Sergt., Oxfordshire and Buckinghamshire Light Infantry.

He was in the Army at the outbreak of war, and at once proceeding to France fought in the Retreat from Mons, and in the Battles of the Marne, the Aisne, Ypres, Arras, Passchendaele, Cambrai, and many others in the Retreat and Advance of 1918, and was wounded. He returned to England for demobilisation in March 1919, and holds the Queen's and King's South African Medals for service during the Boer War, the Mons Star, and the General Service and Victory Medals.
8, Pulross Road, Stockwell, S.W.9. Z4912B

WILLIAMS, W., Corporal, R.F.A.

He volunteered in October 1914, and on the completion of his training proceeded to France in the following June. While in that theatre of war he fought with distinction in the 40th Division, which was highly commended for its bravery and self-sacrifice in numerous battles of importance, including those of Loos, Ypres, and the Retreat and Advance of 1918. He was very severely wounded in action on October 11th, 191°, and died for King and Country ten days later. He was entitled to the 1914-15 Star, and the General Service and Victory Medals.
"A valiant soldier, with undaunted heart he breasted life's last hill."
13, Radstock Street, Battersea, S.W.11. Z4917

WILLIAMSON, J., Private, R.A.S.C. (M.T.)

He joined in 1916, and was engaged on important duties with his unit until 1918, when he was sent to France, where he served on the Aisne and Marne, and at Amiens, Albert, Bapaume, Havrincourt, Le Cateau, and Mons. After the Armistice he proceeded with the Army of Occupation to Germany, where he served until he was demobilised in 1919, holding the General Service and Victory Medals.
202, Mayall Road, Herne Hill, S.E.24. Z3969A

WILLIAMSON, R., Gunner, R.F.A.

Volunteering in August 1914 he was sent to France in September of the following year and took part in the fighting at Loos, Vimy Ridge, the Somme and Cambrai, and was twice gassed. He also served in the Retreat and Advance of 1918. He was demobilised in 1919, and holds the 1914-15 Star, and the General Service and Victory Medals. Afterwards, however, he re-enlisted for a further period of twelve months, and was finally demobilised in August 1920.
50, Cator Street, Peckham, S.E.15. Z53078B

WILLIAMSON, T., Private, Royal Welch Fusiliers and Rifleman, 18th London Regiment (London Irish Rifles).

He joined in October 1916, and after his training was drafted to the Western Front, where he took part in the fighting at Ypres, and in other important engagements, and was at Etaples when the hospital was bombed. He returned home and was demobilised in March 1919, holding the General Service and Victory Medals. 4, Spencer Street, Battersea S.W.11. Z4918

WILLICOMBE, H. (D.C.M.), L/Cpl., Rifle Brigade.

He volunteered in August 1914, and early in the following year was sent to France, where he took part in numerous engagements, including those at Loos, the Somme, Arras, and Ypres, and was engaged as a stretcher bearer. He was unfortunately killed in action on April 4th, 1917. He was awarded the Distinguished Conduct Medal for conspicuous gallantry in the Field, and also the Belgian Croix de Guerre, and in addition was entitled to the 1914-15 Star, and the General Service and Victory Medals.
"He passed out of the sight of men by the path of duty and self-sacrifice."
22, Bengeworth Road, Camberwell, S.E.5. Z6359B

WILLINGHAM, G., Private, R.A.S.C. (M.T.)

Volunteering in May 1915, later in the same year he was sent to France, where he was engaged as a steam engine driver on the transport of supplies at Albert, Calais, Boulogne, Etaples, and Armentières. He was demobilised in 1919, and holds the 1914-15 Star, and the General Service and Victory Medals.
21, Nealdon Street, Landor Road, Stockwell, S.W.9. Z4919

WILLIS, C. T., L/Cpl., 2nd King's Royal Rifle Corps.

He was serving at the outbreak of war, and was shortly afterwards sent to the Western Front, where he took part in the fighting at Ypres, and the Somme. He was unfortunately killed in action on August 22nd, 1916, and was entitled to the 1914 Star, and the General Service and Victory Medals.
"Courage, bright hopes, and a myriad dreams, splendidly given."
55, Motley Street, Wandsworth Road, S.W.8. Z4923

WILLIS, C. V., Sergt., R.A.O.C., R.F.A. and Sherwood Foresters.

He was mobilised in August 1914, and was immediately sent to France, where he was in action during the Retreat from Mons, and at Ypres, and Cambrai. He also took part in the Retreat and Advance of 1918. He was demobilised in February 1919, and holds the Mons Star, and the General Service and Victory Medals. 31, Nealdon Street, Stockwell, S.W.9. Z4921

WILLIS, F. E., Rifleman, King's Royal Rifle Corps.

He volunteered in August 1915, and in the following year was sent to France, where he took part in the fighting at Vimy Ridge, the Somme, and in many other important engagements. He also served in the Retreat and Advance of 1918, and was wounded five times, and buried alive for six days. He was demobilised in April 1919, and holds the General Service and Victory Medals.
4, Benfield Street, Battersea, S.W.11. Z4924

WILLIS, F. W., Private, Labour Corps.

He volunteered in 1915, and after his training was engaged on important duties at various stations with his unit. He rendered valuable services, but was not successful in obtaining his transfer overseas before the cessation of hostilities on account of his medical unfitness for active service. He was demobilised in 1919.
22, Northall Street, Stockwell, S.W.9. Z1704B

WILLIS, J. W., Private, 11th East Surrey Regt. and Labour Corps.

Joining in June 1916, after completing his training he was engaged at various stations on important duties with his unit. He was not successful in obtaining his transfer overseas owing to being medically unfit for duty abroad, but rendered valuable service until he was demobilised in September, 1919.
1, Sandmere Gardens, Seneca Road, Clapham, S.W.4. Z4922

WILLIS, L. P., Private, 11th Royal Scots.

He joined in January 1916, and in the following year was drafted to France. Shortly afterwards whilst engaged in the St. Julien Sector with a working party he was severely wounded. He was sent to hospital at Boulogne, and was later invalided home. After protracted hospital treatment he was discharged as medically unfit for further service in June 1920, and holds the General Service and Victory Medals.
82, Surrey Lane, Battersea, S.W.11. Z4925

WILLIS, R. C., Tpr., 1st (King's) Dragoon Guards.

He was serving at the outbreak of war and was immediately afterwards sent to France, and was in action at Mons, Le Cateau, the Marne, the Aisne, La Bassée, Ypres, Neuve Chapelle, Beaumont-Hamel, the Somme and Arras. He also took part in the Retreat and Advance of 1918, and was twice wounded. He was invalided home in November 1918, and discharged as medically unfit for further service, holding the Mons Star, and the General Service and Victory Medals.
10, Sussex Grove, Loughborough Park, S.W.9. Z4920

WILLIS, T., L/Corporal, Royal Fusiliers.

He was serving in India at the outbreak of war, and was immediately sent home and thence to France. He took part in the Battle of La Bassée, and was severely wounded and gassed and invalided to England. After a long period in hospital he was discharged as medically unfit for further service in December 1918, holding the 1914 Star, and the General Service and Victory Medals.
9, Danson Road, Walworth, S.E.17. Z27020

WILLIS, T. J., Corporal, Royal Fusiliers.

Volunteering in January 1915, he was sent to the Dardanelles in April of the same year. Whilst serving against the Ottoman Forces, he contracted malaria and was invalided home. On his recovery he was drafted to Ireland, where he remained until 1917, when he proceeded to France, where he was transferred to the Labour Corps and engaged on important duties at Etaples until he was demobilised in March 1919. He holds the 1914-15 Star, and the General Service and Victory Medals.
1A, Wooler Street, Walworth, S.E.17. Z4926

WILMOTT, F. G., Private, 2/13th London Regiment (Kensingtons).

He volunteered in January 1915, and after having completed his training was drafted overseas. He saw much active service on the Western Front and fought at Vimy Ridge. Later, proceeding to the East, he took part in much of the fighting in Palestine, being in action on the Jordan. He returned home and was demobilised in July 1919, and holds the General Service and Victory Medals.
97, Queen Street, Hammersmith, W.6. 12791A

WILLMOTT, W. J., Private, 8th Devonshire Regt.

He volunteered in April 1915, and after his training embarked for France. There he was in action at Loos, the Somme and Arras, and was wounded. Later he proceeded to the East and took part in the fighting at Kut, and in various other important engagements in Mesopotamia. Returning home he was demobilised in June 1919, holding the 1914-15 Star, and the General Service and Victory Medals.
97, Queen Street, Hammersmith, W.6. Z12791B

WILLOUGHBY, A. E., Private, Royal Fusiliers.

He joined in May 1917, and after his training served at various stations on important duties with his unit. He rendered valuable services, but was not successful in obtaining his transfer overseas owing to being under age for duty abroad. In December 1918 he was demobilised. Prior to his enlistment he was engaged in the production of munitions at Woolwich Arsenal.
42, Tindal Street, Lothian Road, S.W.9. Z5304

WILLOUGHBY, F., Rflmn., 21st King's Royal Rifle Corps.
He volunteered in September 1915, and in the following November proceeded to France. There he took part in many engagements and was killed during a heavy bombing raid on May 28th, 1916, at Etaples. He was mentioned in Despatches for devotion to duty in November 1915, and was entitled to the 1914–15 Star, and the General Service and Victory Medals.
"His life for his Country, his soul to God."
12, Cator Street, Peckham, S.E.15. Z4927

WILLS, A. E., Private, R.M.L.I.
Joining in January 1916, he embarked for France on the completion of his training. Whilst in this theatre of war he saw much fighting, and on March 27th, 1918, was unhappily killed in action. He was entitled to the General Service and Victory Medals.
"Whilst we remember, the sacrifice is not in vain."
69, Beryl Road, Hammersmith, W.6. 13350B

WILLS, C., Corporal, R.A.M.C.
Volunteering in April 1915, he proceeded on the completion of his training to France, where he served on important duties for about two years. In December 1917 he was discharged through causes due to his service, and holds the 1914–15 Star, and the General Service and Victory Medals.
69, Beryl Road, Hammersmith, S.W.6. 13350A

WILLS, W. T., Gunner, R.F.A.
He was in the Army at the outbreak of hostilities, and in March 1915 embarked for France. There he took part in the heavy fighting in many sectors of the Front, including the Somme and Ypres, and on September 15th, 1916, was wounded. He was sent home, and after receiving hospital treatment was discharged on account of his injuries in April 1917. He holds the 1914–15 Star, and the General Service and Victory Medals.
18, Rita Road, S. Lambeth, S.W.8. Z4928

WILMORE, E., Guardsman, 2nd Scots Guards.
He joined in April 1916, and in the following year embarked for France. Whilst there he fought in many engagements and on two occasions was buried by the explosion of a shell, and later was wounded. He was sent into hospital at the Base, and thence to England, and after receiving treatment was discharged in October 1919. He holds the General Service and Victory Medals.
206, Eversleigh Road, Battersea, S.W.11. Z4929

WILSON, A., Private, Australian Imperial Forces.
He was serving in Australia at the outbreak of war and came over to England with his Regiment in January 1915. Later he was drafted to Egypt, where he remained for about four months. He then proceeded to France, and fought in the engagements on the Somme and at Vimy Ridge, Messines, and Ypres, where he was gassed. He was demobilised in November 1919, and holds the General Service and Victory Medals.
15, Sheepcote Lane, Battersea, S.W.11. Z4931A

WILSON, A., Corporal, 2nd Royal Fusiliers.
He had previously joined in 1906, and at the outbreak of war was drafted to the Dardanelles and took part in the Landing at Gallipoli and in the subsequent operations until the conclusion of the campaign. In 1916 he returned home and was later sent to France and fought in various engagements, including those at Vimy Ridge and the Somme. He gave his life for King and Country at Arras whilst on duty at an observation post on May 31st, 1917. He was entitled to the 1914–15 Star, and the General Service and Victory Medals.
"He died the noblest death a man may die,
Fighting for God, and right, and liberty."
15, Sheepcote Lane, Battersea, S.W.11. Z4931B

WILSON, A., Private, R.A.S.C. (M.T.)
Volunteering in April 1915, he was drafted to France in the same year and saw much service. He was engaged on important transport duties, and was present at engagements at Hill 60, Ypres, Armentières, Passchendaele, Béthune and Messines. In 1917 he proceeded to Italy and served on similar duties until the cessation of hostilities. He returned home and was demobilised in March 1919, and holds the 1914–15 Star, and the General Service and Victory Medals.
14, Pulross Road, Stockwell, S.W.9. Z4932

WILSON, A. W., Private, East Surrey Regiment.
He was mobilised in August 1914, and was almost immediately drafted to France, where he took part in the Retreat from Mons. He also served in the first Battle of Ypres, and was wounded and invalided home, but on recovery rejoined his unit in France. He was wounded on two further occasions, and was subsequently discharged as medically unfit for further duty in November 1918. He holds the Mons Star, and the General Service and Victory Medals.
18, Tradescant Road, South Lambeth, S.W.8. Z1212D

WILSON, E. (M.C.), Lieutenant, R.F.A., Middlesex Regiment and R.F.A. (late R.F.C.)
He volunteered at the outbreak of war, and after his training proceeded to France, where he served with distinction in many sectors of the Western Front, both as an infantry officer and an observer in the Royal Air Force. He took a prominent part in various raids and attacks on German trenches and ammunition dumps. In 1918 he was drafted to Egypt, and whilst in the East did excellent work during the operations until the conclusion of hostilities. He was wounded during his service, and was awarded the Military Cross for conspicuous bravery and devotion to duty in 1917. In addition to the Military Cross he holds the General Service and Victory Medals, and was demobilised in April 1919, after returning to England.
89, Sandmere Road, Clapham, S.W.4. Z4934

WILSON, E. E., Gunner, R.F.A.
He enlisted in March 1903, and in January 1915 was drafted to France. Whilst overseas he was in action at Neuve Chapelle, Armentières and Loos, and was later severely gassed at Passchendaele in November 1917. He was invalided home suffering from gas poisoning and shell-shock, and after his recovery was retained on home defence duties until demobilised in March 1919. He holds the 1914–15 Star, and the General Service and Victory Medals.
2, Scarsdale Grove, Camberwell, S.E.5. Z5167

WILSON, F. R., L/Corporal, R.A.S.C. (M.T.)
He volunteered in October 1914, and in the following year was drafted to France, where he served at Loos and in several later engagements. He then proceeded to Salonika and whilst in this theatre of war was employed with the Red Cross on the Doiran front at an advanced dressing station. Afterwards he was sent to Egypt and was present at the Battles of Gaza. He returned home and was demobilised in July 1919, and holds the 1914–15 Star, and the General Service and Victory Medals.
6, Medlar Street, Camberwell, S.E.5. Z4937

WILSON, G. F., Private, Royal Fusiliers and Labour Corps.
He joined in June 1916, and in the same month was drafted to France. Whilst overseas he was engaged on important duties in road construction at Calais, Rouen and many other places on the Western Front. He suffered from fever during his service and returned home and was demobilised in November 1919. He holds the General Service and Victory Medals.
20, Nutt Street, Peckham, S.E.15. Z6361

WILSON, G. J., Staff-Sergt., R.A.S.C.
He was mobilised in August 1914, and in the same year was drafted to France with the Rifle Brigade. He was soon afterwards discharged as time-expired, but rejoined in the Royal Army Service Corps and proceeded to the Dardanelles and was present at the Landings at Cape Helles and Suvla Bay. Later he returned to France and was severely gassed, and after treatment in hospital was discharged as medically unfit for further duty in June 1917. He holds the 1914 Star, and the General Service and Victory Medals.
247, Hollydale Road, Peckham, S.E.15. Z6596

WILSON, H. F., 1st Class Stoker, R.N., H.M.S. "Erebus."
Volunteering in May 1915, he was posted to N.M.S. "Erebus," and took part in the bombardment of the Belgian Coast. Later an explosion occurred on board his vessel, whilst in action with an enemy ship, and he was blown up and gassed. He was afterwards transferred to H.M.S. "Forward" and served with the Ægean Squadron until demobilised in September 1919. He holds the 1914–15 Star, and the General Service and Victory Medals.
407, Southwark Park Road, Rotherhithe, S.E.16. Z6821

WILSON, H. J., Gunner, R.F.A.
He was serving in the Regular Army at the outbreak of war, and was almost immediately drafted to France, where he took part in the Retreat from Mons, and in the Battles of Le Cateau, the Marne, the Aisne, La Bassée and Ypres. He was also in action at Neuve Chapelle, St. Eloi, Hill 60, Festubert, Loos, Ploegsteert Wood, Vimy Ridge, the Somme, the Ancre, Beaumont-Hamel, Messines, Passchendaele, Bapaume and the fourth Battle of Ypres, and in many other engagements. He holds the Mons Star, and the General Service and Victory Medals, and was demobilised in February 1920. Z4940
62, Westmoreland Road, Walworth, S.E.17.

WILSON, R., Private, Manchester Regiment.
He joined in May 1916, and in the following year was drafted to France. Whilst overseas he fought at Arras, Bullecourt, Ypres and St. Quentin, and was twice wounded, and also suffered from trench fever. He returned home, and was demobilised in April 1919, and holds the General Service and Victory Medals.
8, Colvin Street, Hammersmith, W.6. 14488B

WILSON, J., Corporal, 1st Middlesex Regiment.
He was mobilised at the outbreak of war, and was almost immediately drafted to France and fought in the Retreat from Mons, where he was wounded. After his recovery he was in action at Ypres and on the Somme and in many other engagements. He gave his life for the freedom of England on April 20th, 1917, and was entitled to the Mons Star, and the General Service and Victory Medals.
"A valiant soldier, with undaunted heart he breasted life's last hill."
3, Bonnington Square, S.W.8. Lambeth.   Z4936

WILSON, M. E. (Mrs.), Special War Worker.
During the war this lady was engaged on important work at the Pimlico Wheel Works, Fulham. She rendered valuable services and carried out her arduous duties with care and efficiency.
8, Colvin Street, Hammersmith, W.6.   14488A

WILSON, R. R., Private, Northumberland Fusiliers.
He joined in 1917, and after his training was completed, proceeded to France later in the same year. After taking part in several engagements, he was unhappily killed whilst on his way up to the front line trenches in 1918. He was entitled to the General Service and Victory Medals.
"He passed out of the sight of men by the path of duty and self-sacrifice."
31, Wayford Street, Battersea, S.W.11.   Z4942

WILSON, S. J., Rflman., 17th King's Royal Rifle Corps.
He volunteered in May 1915, and in the following March was drafted to France. During his service on the Western Front he fought at Givenchy, Ypres, Festubert and Vimy Ridge, and also took part in several raids on the enemy's trenches and in many engagements during the Retreat and Advance of 1918. He holds the General Service and Victory Medals, and was demobilised in February 1920.
9, Ann's Buildings, Aylesbury Road, Walworth, S.E.17. Z4941

WILSON, T., Gunner, R.F.A.
He volunteered in February 1915, and in the same year was drafted to the Dardanelles and served in the Landing at Gallipoli on April 25th, 1915. During his service in this theatre of war he was wounded, and after the Evacuation of the Peninsula proceeded to Salonika, and took part in the Balkan operations. He gave his life for King and Country in June 1917, and was entitled to the 1914–15 Star, and the General Service and Victory Medals.
"His life for his Country, his soul to God."
18, Tradescant Road, South Lambeth, S.W.8.   Z1212C

WILSON, T. H., Corporal, R.A.S.C. and R.M.L.I.
He volunteered in April 1915, and after his training was drafted to France in the same year. During his service he was engaged on important duties with the Royal Army Service Corps, and was frequently under shell fire whilst unloading ammunition at the various dumps. Later he was transferred to the Royal Marine Light Infantry and subsequently sent home and demobilised in December 1919. He holds the 1914–15 Star, and the General Service and Victory Medals.
35, Stainford Road, Battersea, S.W.11.   Z4938

WILSON, W., Special War Worker.
He offered his services for special war work in November 1915, and during the period of hostilities was engaged in packing books for despatch to troops at the Front, at Messrs. Chatto, Windus & Co., Publishers, St. Martin's Lane, W.C. He rendered valuable services until April 1919.
62, Westmoreland Road, Walworth, S.E.17.   Z4935

WILSON, W. C., A.B., R.N., H.M.S. "Venus."
He volunteered in October 1915, and after his training was posted to H.M.S. "Vivid," and later to H.M.S. "Venus," in which ship he proceeded to India. He served for two years in the East and then returned to England. In August 1918 he sailed for Russia, where the "Venus" was in action on several occasions against the Bolshevists. Returning to home waters in December of the same year, he was transferred to H.M.S. "Dolphin," in which vessel he was still serving in 1920. He holds the General Service and Victory Medals.
8, Sydney Square, Latona Road, Peckham, S.E.15.   Z6363

WILSON, W. J., Private, Border Regiment.
A serving soldier since December 1907, he was sent to France in 1914 with the Bedfordshire Regiment. He fought at the first Battle of Ypres and was wounded twice at that place. He was invalided home, and in November 1915 was transferred to the Border Regiment, and served at various stations on important home defence duties until discharged as medically unfit for further service in June 1917. He holds the 1914 Star, and the General Service and Victory Medals.
30, Prairie Street, Battersea Park, S.W.8.   Z4933

WILTCHER, J. (Senior), Private, Queen's Own (Royal West Kent Regiment).
He joined in November 1916, and was sent to India in the same year. He was engaged at various stations on important police and garrison duties and rendered valuable services. He returned home and was demobilised in May 1919, holding the General Service and Victory Medals.
10, Mostyn Terrace, Brixton Road, N. Brixton. S.W.9. Z5301A

WILTCHER, J. (Jun.), Rflmn., 21st London Regt. (1st Surrey Rifles).
He volunteered in September 1914, and was engaged on important duties until May 1916, when he was sent to France. He was in action at Vimy Ridge and the Somme, and later in the same year, after being transferred to Salonika, served on the Doiran front. In 1917 he proceeded to Egypt and thence to Palestine, where he took part in the Battle of Gaza and also in the capture of Jerusalem. He was badly wounded and after being invalided home was discharged as medically unfit for further service in December 1918. He holds the General Service and Victory Medals.
10, Mostyn Terrace, Brixton Road, N. Brixton, S.W.9. Z5301B

WILTON, A. W., Private, Oxfordshire and Buckinghamshire Light Infantry.
He was rejected in 1914, when he first volunteered, but was accepted in 1916. After the completion of his training he was drafted in the following year to Salonika, where he rendered much valuable service until the close of hostilities. At the Armistice he proceeded to Turkey with the Army of Occupation and after his return home was demobilised in February 1920. He holds the General Service and Victory Medals.
43, Wilcox Road, Wandsworth Road, S.W.8.   Z4943

WILTSHIER, F. C., Gunner, R.F.A.
After volunteering in April 1915, he was drafted to Egypt in the same year, and served under the Duke of Westminster in his armoured car attack upon the Senussi. He was afterwards transferred to France, where he took part in the fighting on the Somme, but was then sent home as being under age. He was demobilised in February 1919, holding the 1914–15 Star, and the General Service and Victory Medals.
27, Burns Road, Battersea, S.W.11.   Z4945A

WILTSHIER, F. J., Private, Royal Defence Corps.
He joined in 1916, and after his training was sent to Douglas in the Isle of Man, where he was engaged on important duties. While serving there he became seriously ill, and unhappily died on March 31st, 1917.
"His memory is cherished with pride."
27, Burns Road, Battersea, S.W.11.   Z4945B

WILTSHIRE, G. A., Pte., 13th East Surrey Regt.
Volunteering in August 1915, he was sent to France in June of the following year. He took part in the Battles of Vimy Ridge, the Somme and in many other important engagements up to the Retreat and Advance of 1918. He was demobilised in February 1919, after returning home, and holds the General Service and Victory Medals.
11, Seldon Street, Battersea Park Road, S.W.8.   Z4944

WILTSHIRE, W., Private, 11th Queen's (Royal West Surrey Regt.)
He volunteered in August 1915, and in the following year after being drafted to France, was in action on the Somme and at Ypres. He was wounded at Armentières, and invalided home but on his recovery in 1917 he was sent to Italy, and took part in the severe fighting on the Piave. He later proceeded to Malta, and after returning home was demobilised in February 1919, holding the General Service and Victory Medals.
42, Mayall Road, Herne Hill, S.E.24.   Z4930

WINDSOR, J. H., Bombardier, R.F.A.
He volunteered in October 1914, and in the following September was sent to France, where he served on the Loos and Arras fronts. Soon afterwards he proceeded to Salonika, where he was again in action and did valuable service until 1918. He then returned home, and was discharged in December 1918, in consequence of his services, holding the 1914–15 Star, and the General Service and Victory Medals.
12, Horsman Street, Camberwell, S.E.5.   Z4946

WINFIELD, G. H., Private, 2nd London Regiment (Royal Fusiliers).
He was mobilised in August 1914, and on completing his training was sent to Gallipoli in the following year. He took part in the Landing, the three Battles of Krithia, the Landing at Suvla Bay and the Evacuation. He afterwards proceeded to Egypt and in 1916 to France. He was unfortunately killed in the Battle of the Somme on July 1st, 1916, and was entitled to the 1914–15 Star, and the General Service and Victory Medals.
"Whilst we remember, the sacrifice is not in vain."
131, Grant Road, Battersea, S.W.11.   Z1244D

WINFIELD, C. H. R., Sergt., 2nd London Regt. (Royal Fusiliers).

He was mobilised in August 1914, and in the following year proceeded to France, where he took part in the fighting at Ypres, the Somme, Arras, and many other engagements until hostilities ceased, and was twice wounded. He returned home, and was demobilised in 1919, holding the 1914-15 Star, and the General Service and Victory Medals.

65, Paragon Buildings, Walworth, S.E.17. Z4947

WINFIELD, T., Air Mechanic, R.A.F.

He joined the Labour Corps in October 1916, and being drafted to Salonika in the same month was engaged on the Doiran front on important duties with the R.A.S.C. On returning home in October 1918 he was transferred to the R.A.F., and served as cook at the School of Observation at Aldborough until he was demobilised in January 1919, holding the General Service and Victory Medals.

131, Grant Road, Battersea, S.W.11. Z1244C

WINFIELD, W. G., Private, R.A.S.C. (Remounts).

Volunteering in May 1915, he was sent to Salonika in the following November with the Remount Section in which he rendered valuable services. He unfortunately contracted malaria in the East, and after being invalided home was discharged in July 1918, owing to his disability. He holds the 1914-15 Star, and the General Service and Victory Medals.

49, Beaufoy Road, Battersea, S.W.11. Z4948

WINGATE, R., Private, Dorsetshire Regiment.

Volunteering in September 1914, he was sent to France in the same year, and was in action at Neuve Chapelle, Ypres, Festubert, Loos and in many other important engagements. He was seriously wounded at Loos and after being invalided home was discharged, owing to his injuries, in April 1916, holding the 1914-15 Star, and the General Service and Victory Medals. He later died from the effects of his injuries at Belmont Hospital, Sutton, Surrey.

" His life for his Country, his soul to God."

61, Westmacott Street, Camberwell, S.E.5. Z4949

WINGROVE, E. J., Private, R.A.S.C.

He was serving at the outbreak of war, and was shortly afterwards sent to France, where he was engaged on important transport duties during the Retreat from Mons and in numerous other engagements throughout the course of hostilities. After the Armistice he proceeded with the Army of Occupation to Germany. He was demobilised in May 1919, and holds the Mons Star, and the General Service and Victory Medals.

72, Sheepcote Lane, Battersea, S.W.11. Z4950

WINGROVE, W., Stoker, R.N., H.M.S. " Vulcan."

He joined in September 1917, and served at first at Chatham and Devonport. He was engaged on H.M.S. " Roxburgh " in convoying food and troopships across the Atlantic. He was afterwards transferred to H.M.S. " Vulcan " and was still serving in that ship in 1920. He holds the General Service and Victory Medals.

19, Pitt Street, Peckham, S.E.15. Z5735A

WINKWORTH, G., Rifleman, Rifle Brigade.

He was serving at the outbreak of war, having enlisted in 1912, a. d was immediately afterwards sent to France, where he took part in the Retreat from Mons. He was badly wounded and taken prisoner whilst a patient in hospital. After long illness in Germany he was sent to Switzerland in July 1916, and repatriated to England in November 1917. He was discharged in October 1918, in consequence of his injuries, and holds the Mons Star, and the General Service and Victory Medals.

20, Kennard Street, Battersea, S.W.11. Z4951B

WINKWORTH, J. A. A., Private, R.A.M.C.

He volunteered in November 1915, and after his training was engaged on important duties at the Military Hospital, Prees Heath Camp, Salop, in attending to the sick and wounded. He rendered valuable services, but was not successful in obtaining his transfer overseas before the cessation of hostilities. He was demobilised in February 1919.

20, Kennard Street, Battersea, S.W.11. Z4951A

WINNING, J., Sapper, R.E.

Volunteering in January 1915, he was sent to France later in the same year and was present at numerous engagements, including those at Vimy Ridge, Arras, Ypres and Cambrai. During his service in France he was wounded seven times and twice gassed. He was demobilised in March 1919, after rendering valuable services and holds the 1914-15 Star, and the General Service and Victory Medals.

52, Doddington Grove, Battersea, S.W.11. Z4952

WINSLADE, E., Pte., Essex Regt. and Labour Corps.

He joined in November 1916, and after his training was engaged at various stations on important duties with his unit. He rendered valuable services but was not successful in obtaining his transfer overseas before the cessation of hostilities. He was discharged in March 1919.

66, Mysore Road, Battersea, S.W.11. Z4953

WINSLEY, W., Corporal, R.F.A.

Volunteering in August 1915, he went through a course of training, and was afterwards engaged on important duties with his Battery until 1917, when he was drafted to France. He took part in the severe fighting at Béthune and in many other important engagements, but having contracted fever was invalided home. On his recovery he was transferred to the Royal Berkshire Regiment, with which he did valuable home service until his demobilisation in October 1919. He holds the General Service and Victory Medals.

11, Montefiore Street, Wandsworth Road, S.W.8. Z1050B

WINSLOW, H. H., Private, R.A.S.C. (M.T.)

He joined in January 1916, and was immediately sent to Salonika, where he was engaged on important transport duties on the Vardar, Doiran, Struma and Monastir fronts until hostilities ceased. Whilst in this theatre of war he contracted malaria, which frequently caused his detention in hospital. He returned home, and was demobilised in February, 1919 holding the General Service and Victory Medals.

181, Albert Road, Peckham, S.E.15. Z6112

WINSPEAR, F. W., Rifleman, King's Royal Rifle Corps.

Having volunteered in November 1915, he was drafted to France in April of the following year, and was in action at Vermelles, Ploegsteert Wood, Vimy Ridge, the Somme, Arras, Bullecourt, Messines, Ypres, Lens, and Cambrai, and was twice wounded. After being invalided home he was retained on important duties with his unit until demobilised in February 1919. He holds the General Service and Victory Medals.

72, Darwin Buildings, Barlow Street, Walworth, SE..17. Z4955

WINSPEAR, W., Rifleman, Rifle Brigade.

Joining in 1916, he was drafted to France in the same year, and took part in the Battles of the Somme, Arras and Ypres. He was invalided home in 1918 through ill-health, and was afterwards transferred to the R.A.F., in which he was engaged on important duties until 1919. He was then demobilised, holding the General Service and Victory Medals.

61, Bagshot Street, Walworth, S.E.17. Z4954

WINSTANLEY, R. A., Private, Queen's (Royal West Surrey Regiment).

Having volunteered in October 1915, he proceeded to France in the following year, and was in action at Ploegsteert Wood, Vimy Ridge, the Somme, Beaumont-Hamel, Ypres, Passschendaele and Cambrai. In 1917, he was transferred to Italy, where he saw much service on the Piave front. In September 1918 he returned to France and took part in the final engagements of the struggle. He was demobilised in March 1919, and holds the General Service and Victory Medals.

6, Cross Street, Clapham, S.W.4. Z4956

WINTER, A. J., Pte., Australian Imperial Forces.

He volunteered in Australia in 1915, and in the following year proceeded to Egypt, and thence to France. He was in action on the Somme and Ypres fronts in many important operations, but after falling seriously ill was invalided home and discharged in July 1917. He holds the General Service and Victory Medals.

27, Mawbey Street, South Lambeth Road, S.W.8. Z4958B

WINTER, E. C., Private, Royal Berkshire Regiment.

He volunteered in September 1914, and was engaged on important duties with his unit until 1916, when he was drafted to France. He took part in much of the fighting on the Somme front, and later in the same year was transferred to Salonika, where he was again in action. He was afterwards sent to Malta, and from there invalided home with dysentery. On his recovery he served as an Artificer with the Cyclist Corps until demobilised in January 1919, holding the General Service and Victory Medals.

27, Mawbey Street, South Lambeth, S.W.8. Z4958A

WINTER, E. E., L/Cpl., King's Royal Rifle Corps.

Having volunteered in August 1914, he was drafted to France in January of the following year and took part in the fighting at Neuve Chapelle, Hill 60, Ypres, Festubert, Vermelles, Vimy Ridge and the Somme. He was reported missing on the Somme on August 24th, 1916, and was presumed to have been killed in action on that date. He was entitled to the 1914-15 Star, and the General Service and Victory Medals.

" Great deeds cannot die."

49, Kimberley Road, Stockwell, S.W.8. Z4957

WINTER, H. E., Rifleman, 17th London Regiment (Rifles).

Joining in April 1916, he was in the same year drafted to France, where he took part in the fighting at Vimy Ridge, Arras, Ypres and Cambrai and was gassed. He was invalided home in consequence and discharged in December 1918, as medically unfit for further service. He holds the General Service and Victory Medals.

15, Flaxman Road, Camberwell, S.E.5. Z6119

WINTER, J., Special War Worker.
He was engaged at the food supply depôt, L.B. & S.C. Railway, Willow Walk, Bermondsey, as a checker, under Colonel Edmundson. His duties, which were of a highly important and responsible nature, were carried out with great care and efficiency, and he rendered valuable services throughout the war.
43, East Surrey Grove, Peckham, S.E.15.   Z5273B

WINTER, W., Private, Queen's (Royal West Surrey Regiment).
Volunteering in September 1914, he proceeded to France in the following year and took part as stretcher bearer in the fighting at Givenchy and numerous other engagements, and was gassed. He was invalided home and discharged as medically unfit for further service in February 1916, holding the 1914-15 Star, and the General Service and Victory Medals. He died from the effects of his war services on April 26th, 1917.
"He joined the great white company of valiant souls."
158, Farmer's Road, Camberwell, S.E.5.   Z4959

WINTER, W. H., Corporal, 10th Rifle Brigade and King's Royal Rifle Corps.
He joined in June 1917, and in the following year was drafted to the Western Front, where he took part in the fighting at Lens, Oppy Wood, Arras, Cambrai and in many other engagements during the Retreat and Advance of 1918, and was once wounded. He was demobilised in November 1919, and holds the General Service and Victory Medals.
57, Edithna Street, Stockwell, S.W.9.   Z4960

WINTERFLOOD, A. H., Pioneer, R.E.
Volunteering in February 1915, and drafted to the Western Front in April of the following year, he was engaged on important duties with the Field Postal Section in the forward areas, and rendered excellent services. After the Armistice he was sent to Germany with the Army of Occupation and served at Cologne, until returning home, he was demobilised in July 1919. He holds the General Service and Victory Medals.
90, Neate Street, Camberwell, S.E.5.   Z5171B

WINTERFLOOD, C. E. (M.M.), Sergt., 12th London Regiment (Rangers).
Volunteering in January 1916, a year later he embarked for the Western Front, and was in action in many important engagements. He was awarded the Military Medal on September 9th, 1917, for conspicuous gallantry and devotion to duty in the Field, and a few days later, on September 26th, was killed in action during the heavy fighting on the Menin Road. In addition to holding the Military Medal he was entitled to the General Service and Victory Medals.
"A costly sacrifice upon the altar of freedom."
90, Neate Street, Camberwell, S.E.5.   Z5171C

WINTERFLOOD, W. P., Bandsman, Middlesex Regt.
Joining in June 1916, he was sent to the Western Front later in the same year and saw much fighting in various sectors. Transferred to Salonika in the following year he fought in many important engagements and in 1918 was drafted to Egypt. On the Palestine front he was engaged in heavy fighting throughout the Advance into Syria and rendered excellent services. Returning home, he was demobilised in August 1919, and holds the General Service and Victory Medals.
90, Neate Street, Camberwell, S.E.5.   Z5171A

WINTERS, A., Private, 24th London Regiment (The Queen's).
Volunteering in August 1914, in the following year he was sent to France and fought in many engagements of note. Transferred to Salonika he was in action on various fronts during the Balkan campaign. Later he proceeded to Mesopotamia, and took part in the concluding operations of the campaign in this theatre of war. Returning home he was demobilised in March 1919, and holds the 1914-15 Star, and the General Service and Victory Medals.
6, Horsman Street, Camberwell, S.E.5.   Z4962

WINTERS, H. G., Corporal, 4th London Regiment (Royal Fusiliers) and Queen's Own (Royal West Kent Regiment).
Volunteering in September 1914, he proceeded to Malta shortly afterwards, and on completing his training was drafted to France. Here he fought in the Battles of Neuve Chapelle, Festubert and Loos, but later owing to ill-health returned home. After receiving hospital treatment he was stationed in Ireland on garrison duties until demobilised in February 1919. He holds the 1914-15 Star, the General Service and Victory Medals.
1, Alsace Street, Walworth, S.E.17.   Z4961

WINTERS, F., Private, 3/24th London Regiment (The Queen's).
Volunteering in May 1915, he completed his training and served at various depôts engaged on recruiting and other important duties. He was unsuccessful in obtaining his transfer overseas owing to ill-health, but rendered valuable services until discharged in September 1916, as unfit for further military duty.
51, Denmark Road, Camberwell, S.E.5.   Z6122

WINUP, T. S., Sergt., 6th London Regt. (Rifles).
Volunteering in June 1915, he embarked for the Western Front seven months later and was in action on the Somme, and at Bullecourt, Ypres and Cambrai. He also fought throughout the German Offensive and subsequent Allied Advance of 1918, and was slightly gassed. He was demobilised in March 1919, and holds the General Service and Victory Medals.
29, Ernest Street, Bermondsey, S.E.1.   Z27277

WINYARD, F., A.B., Royal Navy.
He joined in June 1915, and was posted to H.M.S. "Achilles," and on board this vessel served in the North Sea for two years. Transferred to H.M.T.B.D. "Scrouge" he rendered excellent services whilst his ship was engaged on patrol and other important duties and was present at the action with a German raider in March 1916. He then joined H.M.S. "Vindictive" which was sent to the Baltic and served in those waters till the cessation of hostilities. He was demobilised in January 1920, and holds the 1914-15 Star, and the General Service and Victory Medals.
38, Lavender Road, Battersea, S.W.11.   Z4963

WISBEY, T. W., Private, Duke of Cornwall's Light Infantry.
He volunteered in September 1914, and in the succeeding February was sent to the Western Front. He fought in many engagements of note and was severely wounded during the first Battle of the Somme on September 14th, 1916. Admitted into hospital he died from his injuries two days later, and was entitled to the 1914-15 Star, and the General Service and Victory Medals.
"The path of duty was the way to glory."
59, Cowan Street, Camberwell, S.E.5.   Z5168

WISE, J., Pioneer, R.E.
Volunteering in June 1915, he was sent to France later in the same month and served in the front lines engaged on important duties during heavy fighting on the Somme, and in other parts. He also served throughout the Retreat and Advance of 1918, and returning home after the cessation of hostilities, was demobilised in April 1919, and holds the 1914-15 Star, and the General Service and Victory Medals.
107, Coronation Buildings, South Lambeth Road, S.W.8.   Z4964

WISE, S., Cpl., 2nd London Regt. (Royal Fusiliers).
He enlisted in May 1914, and at the outbreak of war was serving at Malta. Proceeding to the Western Front, he fought in the Battles of Le Cateau, Ypres, Neuve Chapelle, Hill 60, and in many other engagements of note, and was wounded on the Somme. In 1918 he was invalided to England suffering from gas poisoning, and after receiving hospital treatment served at various depôts until demobilised in November 1919. He holds the 1914 Star, and the General Service and Victory Medals.
21, Montefiore Street, Wandsworth Road, S.W.8.   Z1288D

WISE, W. St. G., A.B., Royal Navy.
He joined in June 1915, and was posted to H.M.S. "Russell," which ship served in the North Sea on patrol and other duties, and later proceeded to the Mediterranean. She was sunk by a mine off Malta on April 27th, 1916, but fortunately he was saved. Later he was sent to German East Africa, and was present at the fall of Dar-es-Salaam. Shortly afterwards he joined H.M.S. "Queen Elizabeth" and served on board her until the cessation of hostilities. He was still serving in 1920, and holds the 1914-15 Star, and the General Service and Victory Medals.
54, Moncrieff Street, Peckham, S.E.15.   Z6107

WISEMAN, C., Gunner, R.F.A.
Joining in April 1918, shortly afterwards he embarked for the Western Front, where he fought in many engagements during the German Offensive and subsequent Allied Advance of 1918. After the Armistice he was sent into Germany with the Army of Occupation and served there until he returned home and was demobilised in October 1919. He holds the General Service and Victory Medals.
33, Middleton Road, Battersea, S.W.11.   Z4965

WISEMAN, W., Gunner R.F.A.
Volunteering in November 1915, in the following year he proceeded to the Macedonian theatre of war and fought in many important engagements on the Monastir and Doiran fronts. In 1917, owing to ill-health he was admitted into hospital and later returned home. After receiving treatment he was ultimately invalided out of the Service in January 1918. He holds the General Service and Victory Medals.
35, Stanley Street, Battersea Park, S.W.8. Z4966

WISTOW, E. G., Corporal, R.H.A.
He was mobilised in August 1914, and shortly afterwards was sent to France, where he took part in the fighting at Mons, the Marne, the Aisne, Ypres, Neuve Chapelle, St. Eloi, Hill 60, Vimy Ridge and St. Quentin and was gassed. In 1917 he was transferred to Italy and was in action on the Piave, but in the following year returned to France and served in the Retreat and Advance of 1918. He afterwards proceeded with the Army of Occupation to Germany. He was demobilised in May 1919, and holds the Mons Star, and the General Service and Victory Medals.
22, Azenby Road, Peckham, S.E.15. Z6830

WITCHELL, T. A., Private, R.A.S.C. (M.T.)
Volunteering in August 1914, he was drafted to the Western Front two months later and served in the forward areas engaged on important duties as a fitter with the travelling workshops. He was present at many important engagements and served in many parts of the line. Owing to ill-health he was invalided to England in February 1919, and after receiving treatment served at various stations until demobilised in March 1919. He holds the 1914 Star, and the General Service and Victory Medals.
73, Grayshott Road, Battersea, S.W.11. Z4967

WITHALL, E. S., Driver, R.A.S.C. (M.T.)
He joined in November 1916, and in the following year was drafted to France engaged on important work in the forward areas, transporting ammunition and supplies to the front lines. He rendered excellent services throughout the Retreat and Advance of 1918, and returning home after the Armistice, was demobilised in May 1919. He holds the General Service and Victory Medals.
208, Beresford Street, Camberwell, S.E.5. Z4968

WITHAM, A., Rifleman, 3rd Rifle Brigade.
Joining in September 1916, he proceeded to Salonika late in the following year and fought in many engagements, including the second Battle of the Vardar. Transferred to South Russia, he served at Batoum and Tiflis, and in 1919 returned to England. In 1920 he was serving in Ireland and holds the General Service and Victory Medals.
57, Evelina Road, Nunhead, S.E.15. Z6237

WITHAM, W., Gunner, R.G.A.
He joined in October 1916, and served at various depôts, until embarking for France in 1918. He fought at Cambrai, Valenciennes, and in many other engagements during the Retreat and Advance of 1918. After the Armistice, proceeding into Germany with the Army of Occupation, he served at Cologne. He was demobilised in October 1919, and holds the General Service and Victory Medals.
61, Camilla Road, Rotherhithe, S.E.16. Z6236

WITHERS, E. C., Bombardier, R.F.A.
He enlisted in April 1913, and was sent to the Western Front in 1915. During his service overseas he fought in the Battles of Albert, Ploegsteert, Vimy Ridge, the Somme, Ypres, Passchendaele, and throughout the German Offensive and subsequent Allied Advance of 1918. After the Armistice he served with the Army if Occupation in Germany until he returned to England and was demobilised in June 1920. He holds the 1914-15 Star, and the General Service and Victory Medals.
6, Crichton Street, Wandsworth Road, S.W.8. Z4969

WITHERS, F., Guardsman, Grenadier Guards.
Joining in January 1918, three months later he proceeded to the Western Front, and served in many parts of the line, engaged in severe fighting throughout the German Offensive and Allied Advance, to victory. After the cessation of hostilities he was sent to Germany with the Army of Occupation and served there for some months. Returning to England he was demobilised in 1919, and holds the General Service and Victory Medals.
4, Corunna Road, New Road, S.W.8. Z4970A

WITHERS, F., Rflmn., Rifle Brigade, and Pte., R.A.S.C.
He joined in May 1916, and later in that year landed in France, where he fought in many important engagements. Owing to ill-health he returned to England and received hospital treatment. On recovery he was transferred to the Royal Army Service Corps, with which he served until August 1919, when he was discharged as medically unfit. He holds the General Service and Victory Medals.
4, Corunna Road, New Road, S.W.8. Z4970B

WITHERS, T., Sergt., R.F.A.
Volunteering in September 1914, in the following May he was drafted to the Western Front. Here he saw much service at Loos, Ploegsteert, Vimy Ridge, the Somme, Arras and Ypres, and was engaged in heavy fighting during the Retreat and Advance of 1918. He was demobilised in June 1919, and holds the 1914-15 Star, and the General Service and Victory Medals.
24, Ingrave Street, Battersea, S.W.11. Z4971

WITNEY, W. G., Sergt., Middlesex and North Staffordshire Regiments.
Volunteering in 1915, in the following year he sailed for France, and was in action in the first Battle of the Somme and at Arras and many other engagements of note. He was wounded and taken prisoner in the German Offensive of 1918, and was held in captivity until after the Armistice. Repatriated he was demobilised in February 1919, and holds the General Service and Victory Medals.
7, Russell Grove, Vassall Road, S.W.9. Z5169

WITTS, G., Private, R.A.S.C.
He volunteered in April 1915, and in the same year proceeded to the Western Front. Whilst overseas he was employed on various duties, including those of loading and unloading ships at Boulogne until the signing of the Armistice. He holds the 1914-15 Star, the General Service and Victory Medals, and was demobilised in March 1919.
14, Wilsons Road, Hammersmith, W.6. 16413

WITTS, W. F., L/Corporal, 1st Royal Inniskilling Fusiliers.
Volunteering in September 1915, he completed his training and served at various depôts until drafted to the Western Front in 1918. He fought in the Battles of the Somme, Amiens, Cambrai and Ypres, during the Retreat and Advance of 1918, and was present at the entry into Mons. at dawn on November 11th, 1918. He was demobilised in March 1919, and holds the General Service and Victory Medals.
95, Aylesbury Road, Walworth, S.E.17. Z4972

WOOD, A. A., Sergt., 15th London Regt. (Civil Service Rifles).
Volunteering in November 1915, he proceeded on the completion of his training to the Western Front, and was severely wounded during the fierce fighting on the Somme in 1916. On his recovery he served as a physical Training Instructor until demobilised in February 1919. He holds the General Service and Victory Medals.
24, Handforth Road, Brixton Road, S.W.9. Z5303

WOOD, A. A., Air Mechanic, R.A.F.
He joined in January 1917, and on the completion of his training served on important instructional duties with his unit at various stations. He rendered valuable services, but was not successful in obtaining his transfer overseas before the conclusion of hostilities. Prior to enlistment he was employed as a sheet metal worker, and did much valuable work in that capacity. He was demobilised in October 1919.
23, Peacock Street, Walworth, S.E.17. Z26156B

WOOD, A. J., Driver, R.F.A.
Volunteering in May 1915, he embarked for France in March 1917, and whilst in this theatre of war saw much heavy fighting. He was in action at Arras, Vimy Ridge, Passchendaele and Amiens, and later, transferred to the Labour Corps, and attached to the R.E. did much valuable work on the railways until the conclusion of war. He returned home and was demobilised in January 1919, and holds the General Service and Victory Medals.
101, Avenue Road, Camberwell, S.E.5. Z4975

WOOD, A. J., Corporal, East Surrey Regiment.
Volunteering in November 1914, he proceeded in the following December to France, and there fought in the Battles of Ypres and Loos, where he was wounded in September 1915. On recovery he was drafted to Salonika, and whilst in the East took part in many engagements, until hostilities ceased. He returned home in March 1919, and was demobilised. Having previously served in the South African War he holds the Queen's and King's South African Medals, the 1914-15 Star, and the General Service and Victory Medals.
2, Longcroft Road, Camberwell, S.E.5. Z5542

WOOD, C., Driver, R.F.A.
Volunteering in 1914, he embarked for France in the following year, and whilst in this theatre of war fought in many notable engagements, including those at Loos and Ypres. In 1916 he was invalided to hospital through ill-health, and on recovery was sent to the Base, where he served on important duties until the conclusion of hostilities. In 1919 he was demobilised, and holds the 1914-15 Star, and the General Service and Victory Medals.
13, Lebanon Street, Walworth, S.E.17. Z4978A

WOOD, C. E., Private, Queen's Own (Royal West Kent Regiment).

He volunteered in October 1914, and in the following March was sent to the Western Front. There he fought at Ypres, Festubert and Loos, where he was buried for nine hours by the explosion of a shell. He was invalided home and after receiving hospital treatment was discharged as medically unfit in July 1917. He holds the 1914–15 Star, and the General Service and Victory Medals.

37, Kinglake Street, Walworth, S.E.17.　　Z4976

WOOD, C. R., Private, R.A.S.C. (Remounts).

He joined in November 1916, and in the following year was drafted overseas. He served in many sectors of the Western Front, including those of Arras and Vimy Ridge. At the cessation of hostilities he was in hospital at Dieppe, through ill-health, and in May 1919 came home and was demobilised. He holds the General Service and Victory Medals.

23, Nealdon Street, Stockwell, S.W.9.　　Z4977

WOOD, C. W. (Jnr.), Pte., Northumberland Fusiliers.

He volunteered in 1914, and in the same year proceeded to the Western Front, and served for two years in conveying remounts to the various fighting areas. He was then transferred to the Northumberland Fusiliers, and with them took part in many battles, including those of Ypres, Arras, the Somme, and St. Quentin, where he was wounded. He was sent into hospital and after receiving treatment was discharged as medically unfit in 1919. He holds the 1914 Star and the General Service and Victory Medals.

13, Lebanon Street, Walworth, S.E.17.　　Z4978B

WOOD, E., 1st Class Petty Officer, R.N.

He was in the Navy at the outbreak of hostilities, and served on board H.M.S. "Marlborough" throughout the war, on important patrol duties. His ship was also in various minor engagements in the English Channel, and did much good work. In September 1920 he was demobilised and holds the 1914–15 Star, and the General Service and Victory Medals.

79, Mayall Road, Herne Hill, S.E.24.　　Z4973A

WOOD, E. A., Private, Labour Corps.

He joined in 1916, and in the same year was drafted to the Western Front. There he served in many sectors and did good work in making roads, and on other important duties until hostilities ceased. He returned home and was demobilised in 1919, holding the General Service and Victory Medals.　　31, Smith Street, Camberwell, S.E.5.　　Z4979

WOOD, E. G., Rifleman, King's Royal Rifle Corps.

He enlisted in February 1913, and at the outbreak of war was drafted to France and fought in the Retreat from Mons, and in the Battles of the Marne and Aisne. He was also in action at Neuve Chapelle, Ypres, the Somme and Messines, and served in the Retreat and Advance of 1918, during which time he was wounded. He came home and was demobilised in February 1919, holding the Mons Star, and the General Service and Victory Medals.

43, Foreign Street, Camberwell, S.E.5.　　Z6120

WOOD, E. J., Driver, R.F.A.

Volunteering in December 1915, he proceeded in the following year to the Western Front. There he saw much heavy fighting and was in action at Cambrai and numerous other engagements, and served after hostilities ceased on important duties until demobilised in September 1919. He holds the General Service and Victory Medals.

10, East Surrey Grove, Peckham, S.E.15.　　Z5295

WOOD, F. M., Private, Royal Sussex Regiment.

He joined in 1916, and in the same year proceeded to France, where during the fighting on the Somme he was taken prisoner. Whilst in captivity he was forced to work in the German lines in connection with the supply of ammunition. In 1919 he was released and returned home for demobilisation. He holds the General Service and Victory Medals.

47, Park Crescent, Clapham, S.W.4.　　Z4974

WOOD, F. M. A. (Mrs.), Special War Worker.

During the war this lady took over her husband's work thus releasing him for military service. Her duties, which were of a clerical nature, were carried out with great care and efficiency. From June 1918 until May of the following year she was engaged on important work in connection with munitions at Messrs. Priddy's Hard, Gosport, where she rendered valuable services.　　Z4982C
11, J. Peabody Estate, Rodney Road, Walworth, S.E.17.

WOOD, F. S., Private, 2nd King's Shropshire Light Infantry.

Volunteering in August 1914, he proceeded to France in January of the following year, and during the fierce fighting at Ypres was wounded. He was invalided home, but on recovery returned to the firing line, and was again wounded in the Battle of the Somme. He was sent home and after being in hospital for over a year was discharged in April 1919. He holds the 1914–15 Star, and the General Service and Victory Medals.　　44, Commercial Road, Peckham, S.E.15.　　Z6469

WOOD, F. W., Sapper, R.E.

He volunteered in June 1915, and on the completion of his training proceeded to the Western Front, where he was in action in many notable battles. He served as a bomb-thrower and did much valuable work. Unfortunately he was killed in action whilst carrying Despatches, and was entitled to the General Service and Victory Medals.

"His memory is cherished with pride."

56, Gwynne Road, Battersea, S.W.11.　　Z4980

WOOD, H., Gunner, R.G.A.

He joined in April 1916, and in the same year was sent to Eygpt and was in action at Gaza. In 1917 he was transferred to France, where he took part in the fighting at Cambrai. He afterwards proceeded with the Army of Occupation to Germany where he served until returning home. He was demobilised in December 1919, holding the General Service and Victory Medals. 155, Abbeyfield Road, Rotherhithe, S.E.16. Z6809

WOOD, H. J., Gunner, R.F.A.

Joining in October 1916, he embarked in the same year for the Western Front. There he was in action on the Somme, and at Ypres, Arras, Passchendaele, Armentières, Bapaume, and in many other engagements, including the Retreat and Advance of 1918, during which he was gassed. After the cessation of hostilities he was in hospital through illness, and in August 1919 was demobilised, holding the General Service and Victory Medals.

43, Parkstone Road, Peckham, S.E.15.　　Z5696

WOOD, J., Corporal, Grenadier Guards.

He joined in 1916, and in the following year was drafted overseas. Whilst in France he saw much service and was in action during the Advance of 1918, afterwards proceeding to Germany with the Army of Occupation. In 1919 he returned to England and was demobilised, holding the General Service and Victory Medals.

8, Archer Street, Lambeth Road, S.W.8.　　Z4981

WOOD, J., Private, Tank Corps.

A Reservist, he was mobilised and sent to France at the outbreak of war, and served during the memorable Retreat from Mons. Amongst other engagements he was in action at those of Ypres, Loos, the Somme, and also served in the Advance of 1918, during which time he was wounded. Returning home he was demobilised in February 1919, and holds the Mons Star, and the General Service and Victory Medals.

11, East Surrey Grove, Peckham, S.E.15.　　Z5297

WOOD, J., Sapper, R.E.

He joined in May 1917, and after his training served at various stations on important defence duties. He also acted as a despatch rider and signaller during his period of service, but he was not successful in obtaining his transfer overseas before the cessation of hostilities. In November 1919 he was demobilised.

56, Neate Street, Camberwell, S.E.5.　　Z5172A

WOOD, J. H., Petty Officer (Gunner), R.N.

Mobilised at the outbreak of hostilities he was posted to H.M.S. "Vernon," which vessel was stationed in Portsmouth Harbour. Whilst he was engaged on experimental diving an accidental explosion took place, and he sustained severe shock from which he died on September 26th, 1917. He was entitled to the 1914–15 Star, and the General Service and Victory Medals.

"Whilst we remember, the sacrifice is not in vain."

11, J. Peabody Estate, Rodney Road, Walworth, S.E.17.　　Z4982A

WOOD, J. H., 1st Class Stoker, R.N.

He joined in January 1916, and was posted to H.M.S. "Fearless" in which vessel he served with the Grand Fleet in the North Sea. On one occasion his ship collided with a submarine, but fortunately he escaped without serious injury. Later he was present at the surrender of the German Fleet at Scapa Flow, and in July 1919 was demobilised. He holds the General Service and Victory Medals. 11, J. Peabody Estate, Rodney Road, Walworth, S.E.17.　　Z4982B

WOOD, J. W., A.B., Royal Navy.

He was in the Navy at the outbreak of hostilities and served in H.M.T.B.D. "Tourmaline" and H.M.S. "Monarch." His ship took part in the fighting off Heligoland Bight and in the Battle of Jutland, later being engaged on various important duties until hostilities ceased. Shortly afterwards he was sent into hospital owing to illness and died shortly afterwards on March 26th, 1920.

"And doubtless he went in splendid company."

56, Neate Street, Camberwell, S.E.5.　　Z5172B

WOOD, M. M., Bandsman, Royal Marines.

Mobilised at the outbreak of war he was posted to H.M.S. "Queen Mary" and served in this ship in the Naval engagements off Heligoland Bight and off the Dogger Bank. He unfortunately lost his life when "The Queen Mary" was sunk, during the Battle of Jutland in May 1916. He was entitled to the 1914–15 Star, and the General Service and Victory Medals.

"His life for his Country, his soul to God."

79, Mayall Road, Herne Hill, S.E.24.　　Z4973B

WOOD, R. B., Private, Royal Fusiliers.

Mobilised in August 1914, he was in the following month drafted to Malta, later going to Egypt, and taking part in the fighting on the banks of the Suez Canal. In May 1916 he returned to Malta, and was engaged on important duties guarding prisoners of war. Amongst those under his charge were the crew of "The Emden." He returned to England in March 1919, and was demobilised, holding the 1914-15 Star, the General Service, Victory, and Long Service and Good Conduct Medals.

55, Blondel Street, Battersea, S.W.11.   Z4983

WOOD, S. G., Pte., 20th London and 10th Somerset Regts. and Sapper, R.E.

He joined in March 1916, and in April of the following year proceeded to France, where he saw much service. He did valuable work at Dunkirk with the R.E. on the railways, and on various other duties until hostilities ceased. In October 1919 he returned home and was demobilised, holding the General Service and Victory Medals.

31, Secretan Road, Camberwell, S.E.5.   Z5543

WOOD, T., Sergt., 22nd London Regt. (Queen's).

He was mobilised at the outbreak of war and served on important duties until 1916, when he was sent to France, where he was in action at Vimy Ridge. Afterwards he was transferred to Salonika, where he fought in the Balkan Campaign, and in 1918 proceeded to Egypt. Having served there for twelve months he unfortunately contracted pneumonia, from which he died later. He was buried at Alexandria, and was entitled to the General Service and Victory Medals.

"He joined the great white company of valiant souls."

30, Dilston Grove, Rotherhithe, S.E.16.   Z6822

WOOD, W., Pte., Highland Light Infantry, Suffolk Regiment and Labour Corps.

He volunteered in June 1915, and in the following September proceeded to France. There he was in action at Loos, St. Eloi and Givenchy, and during the fighting on the Somme was severely wounded. After receiving treatment at various hospitals he was discharged in June 1918 as medically unfit. He holds the 1914-15 Star, and the General Service and Victory Medals.   118, Mayall Road, Brixton, S.E.24.   Z2686B

WOODBRIDGE, E. J., Sergt., M.G.C.

He joined in February 1917, and after his training served with his Corps in many important engagements on the Western Front until fighting ceased. After the Armistice he proceeded to Germany with the Army of Occupation and was engaged on important duties on the Rhine. In 1920 he was still serving and holds the General Service and Victory Medals.

40, Studland Street, Hammersmith, W.6.   12459B

WOODBRIDGE, J. T., Cpl., Army Remount Depot.

He volunteered in April 1915, having previously served in the South African Campaign, and was engaged for nearly three years on important duties in the Remount establishment at Kettering. He rendered valuable services, but was not successful in obtaining a transfer overseas during hostilities and was discharged in March 1918. He holds the Queen's and King's South African Medals.

40, Studland Street, Hammersmith, W.6.   12459A

WOODGATE, G. W., Private, 22nd London Regt. (Queen's).

Mobilised in August 1914, he was soon drafted to France and fought in the Battles of the Marne and the Aisne, and was wounded at Ypres. Afterwards he served at the Somme, Arras and Bullecourt, and in July 1917 was sent to Egypt, and took part in the Offensive in Palestine with the British Forces under General Allenby. He was in action at Gaza and Jericho, and was present at the Entry into Jerusalem, and in the subsequent engagements until the conclusion of the campaign. He returned home and was demobilised in September 1919, and holds the 1914 Star, and the General Service and Victory Medals.

3, Thornton Street, Brixton, S.W.9.   Z4984

WOODGATE, J. H., Corporal, 1st Life Guards.

He was mobilised at the outbreak of war, and was immediately drafted to France, where he took part in the Retreat from Mons. He fought also on the Marne, the Aisne, La Bassée, Ypres, and in many subsequent engagements, including those at the Somme, Arras and Cambrai. He was badly wounded in action in May 1918, during the Retreat of the Allies, and was demobilised in March of the following year. He holds the Mons Star, and the General Service and Victory Medals.

25, Flint Street, Walworth, S.E.17.   Z4987

WOODGATE, L. C. H., Private, R.A.M.C.

He volunteered in August 1915, and after his training was first engaged on important duties at Nottingham Hospital. He was next sent to Malta in 1916, and two years later proceeded to Mesopotamia with the 41st Field Ambulance. His duties consisted in conveying wounded men from the lines to the hospital, and he did excellent work throughout. He returned home and was demobilised in March 1919, and holds the General Service and Victory Medals.

21, Gorst Road, Battersea, S.W.11.   Z4985

WOODGATE, W. G., Private, 24th London Regt. (The Queen's).

Volunteering in August 1914, he proceeded overseas in the same year, and whilst on the Western Front fought at La Bassée, Ypres, Givenchy, Festubert, and was wounded at Loos. He was invalided home and being fit until May 1917, when he was drafted to Salonika, and afterwards to Egypt. He then took part in the British Advance through Palestine, and was present at the entry into Jerusalem. He returned home and was demobilised in September 1919, and holds the 1914 Star, and the General Service and Victory Medals.

32, Warrior Road, Camberwell, S.E.5.   Z4986

WOODHOUSE, A. W., Rifleman, 21st London Regt. (1st. Surrey Rifles).

He joined in July 1916, and after his training was engaged on important special duties at his depôt. He did excellent work, but was not successful in obtaining a transfer overseas before the cessation of hostilities, and was discharged in 1918, in consequence of his service.

67, Westmacott Street, Camberwell, S.E.5.   Z4988

WOODHOUSE, I. E., Sapper, R.E.

He volunteered in 1915, and in the same year was drafted to Gallipoli. He was engaged on important duties in connection with the operations and was present at the Battle of Krithia, the Landing at Suvla Bay, and in the Evacuation of the Peninsula. In 1916 he was sent to the Western Front and was present at the engagements at the Somme, Ypres, and in September 1918 was wounded at Cambrai, and invalided home. After his recovery he remained on home service until his demobilisation in 1919. He holds the 1914-15 Star, and the General Service and Victory Medals.

18, Caulfield Road, Peckham, S.E.15.   Z6470

WOODIN, A. W., Private, Labour Corps.

He joined in March 1916, and was at first retained on home service owing to being overage and medically unfit. He was passed for duty overseas in 1917, and was sent to France, where he was engaged on important duties until the cessation of hostilities. He then proceeded to Germany with the Army of Occupation, and was stationed on the Rhine until demobilised in 1919. He holds the General Service and Victory Medals.   135, Gordon Road, Peckham, S.E.15.   Z6110

WOODLEY, H. F., Gunner, R.G.A.

He joined in June 1917, and in the same year was drafted to the Western Front. He was wounded at Ypres in November 1917, and after his recovery was engaged on the Somme and Arras sectors, and was gassed in October 1918, in the final operations of the Advance. He was subsequently demobilised in September 1919, and holds the General Service and Victory Medals.

40, Moncreiff Street, Peckham, S.E.15.   Z5697

WOODMAN, A., Private, 5th Royal Fusiliers.

He volunteered in November 1914, and in September of the following year was drafted to the Dardanelles where he served gallantly until the Evacuation of the Peninsula. In May 1916 he was sent to France and took part in the fierce fighting in the Battle of the Somme on July 1st, 1916, when he was reported missing. He was afterwards presumed to have been killed in action on that date and was entitled to the 1914-15 Star, and the General Service and Victory Medals.

"A costly sacrifice upon the altar of freedom."

14, Quick Road, Chiswick, W.4.   5671C

WOODMAN, C. E., Rifleman, King's Royal Rifle Corps.

He was serving at the outbreak of hostilities and was almost immediately drafted to France where he fought in the Retreat from Mons. He also took part in the severe fighting at Neuve Chapelle, Loos, the Somme, Vimy Ridge, the Ancre, and Passchendaele, and was severely wounded in action at Cambrai in November 1917. He was sent home to hospital and invalided out of the Service in July 1918, holding the Mons Star, and the General Service and Victory Medals.

29, Portslade Road, Wandsworth Road, S.W.8.   Z4990

WOODMAN, C. J., Private, Queen's Royal (West Surrey Regt.)

He joined in June 1918, and after his training was engaged at his depôt on important duties with his unit. He rendered valuable services, but was not successful in obtaining a transfer overseas before the termination of hostilities, and was demobilised in December 1918.

200, Commercial Road, Peckham, S.E.15.   6624C

WOODMAN, F., Gunner, R.F.A.

He joined in 1916, and was drafted first to India, and afterwards to Mesopotamia. Whilst in this theatre of war did good work as a gunner in many important engagements. Subsequently he proceeded to France, and took part in much of the heavy fighting in the Advance of 1918. He holds the General Service and Victory Medals, and was demobilised in 1919.

133, New Road, Battersea Park Road, S.W.8.   Z2214B

WOODMAN, E. D. (Mrs.), Special War Worker.
During the war this lady was engaged at Messrs. Blake's Munition Factory on important and dangerous duties connected with the output of shells. After six months' service there she contracted T.N.T. poisoning and subsequent to her recovery worked for a time at the Royal Flying Corps Station at Hendon. She was afterwards engaged at the Du Cros Factory, Acton Vale, on special work for two and a half years. Her patriotic services throughout were much appreciated.
72, Chiswick Lane, Chiswick, W.4.   5622A

WOODMAN, J. T., L/Corporal, 7th London Regt.
He volunteered in September 1914, and after his training was drafted to the Western Front, where he saw much service. He fought in many engagements of importance, notably at Ypres and the Somme, and was four times wounded. He was demobilised in April 1919, after his return to England, and holds the 1914–15 Star, and the General Service and Victory Medals.
72, Chiswick Lane, Chiswick, W.4.   5622B

WOODMAN, T., Private, 5th Royal Fusiliers and 19th London Regiment.
Volunteering in November 1914, he proceeded to the Western Front in October of the following year and took part in many engagements until December of the same year when he was wounded in action. After his recovery he rejoined his unit, and after serving in various sectors of France was severely wounded again in July 1916. He holds the 1914–15 Star, and the General Service and Victory Medals, and in 1920 was still serving.
14, Quick Road, Chiswick, W.4.   5671B

WOODMAN, T., Private, Duke of Cornwall's Light Infantry.
Volunteering in 1914 he was drafted to France in the following year, and whilst there fought in numerous engagements, including those at Ypres, the Somme, Arras, Delville Wood, Wancourt and Cambrai. He was sent home early in 1918, but later returned to France and was frequently in action in the Retreat and Advance of 1918. He holds the 1914–15 Star, and the General Service and Victory Medals, and was demobilised in 1919.
133, New Road, Battersea Park Road, S.W.8.   Z2214C

WOODMAN, W., Corporal 1st Royal Fusiliers.
He was serving at the outbreak of war and being almost immediately drafted to France, took part in the Retreat from Mons, and in the Battles of Le Cateau, the Marne, and La Bassée. He died gloriously on the field in the Ypres sector on March 3rd, 1915, and was buried at Armentières. He was entitled to the Mons Star, and the General Service and Victory Medals.
"His life for his Country, his soul to God."
101, Linden Grove, Nunhead, S.E.15.   Z6656C

WOODROUGH, F., Bombardier, R.F.A.
He was serving at the outbreak of war and shortly afterwards was sent to France, where he took part in the severe fighting in the Retreat from Mons, and the Battles of the Marne, Ypres, and Neuve Chapelle, and was wounded and invalided home. He was later engaged on important duties with his Battery until demobilised in February 1919. He holds the Mons Star, and the General Service and Victory Medals.
84, Abbeyfield Road, Rotherhithe, S.E.16   Z6803A

WOODROUGH, M. (Mrs.), Special War Worker.
This lady was engaged at Petwood Convalescent Hospital, Woodhall, Lincoln, as ward-maid, attending to the sick and wounded. Her duties were carried out in a most commendable manner and she rendered valuable services during the war.
84, Abbeyfield Road, Rotherhithe, S.E.16.   Z6803B

WOODROW, F., Gunner, R.F.A.
He joined in May 1916, and in the same year was drafted to Mesopotamia, where he served with the Relief Forces at Kut-el-Amara, and was in action at Baghdad. He contracted malaria in the East, and was afterwards sent home. While awaiting his draft for France he was again taken ill, and was invalided to hospital where he was still a patient at the signing of the Armistice. He afterwards qualified as an N.C.O. cook. He was demobilised in August 1919, and holds the General Service and Victory Medals.
38, Pulross Road, Stockwell, S.W.9.   Z4991

WOODROW, F., Private, 1st Queen's Own (Royal West Kent Regiment).
He was mobilised from the Reserve at the outbreak of war, and in the following month embarked for France and fought in the Battles of the Marne, the Aisne, Ypres, Hill 60, and Loos. He was severely wounded on the Somme in July 1916, and was invalided home. After lengthy medical treatment he was discharged as physically unfit for further service in April 1917. He holds the 1914 Star, and the General Service and Victory Medals.
2, Fendick Road, Peckham, S.E.15.   Z6113

WOODROW, J. J., Rifleman, 18th London Regt. (London Irish Rifles).
He joined in September 1916, and in the same year was drafted to the Western Front. After taking part in many important engagements he died gloriously on the Field of Battle at Arras on April 7th, 1917. He was entitled to the General Service and Victory Medals.
"Nobly striving,
He nobly fell that we might live."
49, Rylston Road, Fulham, S.W.6.   16184B

WOODROW, T. M., A.B., Royal Navy.
He joined in July 1918, and after his training was posted to H.M.S. "Peterborough," and whilst in this vessel was engaged on important duties in many waters. During his service he was transferred to H.M.S. "Powerful," and in 1920 was still serving. He holds the General Service and Victory Medals.
49, Rylston Road, Fulham, S.W.6.   16184A

WOODROW, W. W. A., Sergt., R.F.A. and R.G.A.
He volunteered in September 1914, and in the following July was drafted to France where he saw much service. He was in action at Ypres, Armentières, Albert, Vimy Ridge, the Somme, Bullecourt, and Lens, and was wounded and invalided home suffering from fever in 1917. In September of the same year he sailed for German East Africa, but having contracted malaria very severely was sent home on the Hospital Ship "Guildford Castle," which was torpedoed on reaching the Bristol Channel on March 10th, 1918. He was fortunately rescued and was demobilised in February of the following year. He holds the 1914–15 Star, and the General Service and Victory Medals.
76, Gwynne Road, Battersea, S.W.11.   Z4992

WOODRUFF, W., Private, 7th Northumberland Fusiliers.
He joined in August 1916, and after his training was engaged at various stations on important duties with his unit. He was later transferred to the Army Reserve, and employed on the production of munitions until the cessation of hostilities. He was demobilised in March 1919.
29, Ægis Grove, Battersea Park Road, S.W.8.   Z4993

WOODS, A. W., Private, 3rd Essex Regiment.
He was mobilised at the outbreak of war and after being drafted to France was engaged on special duties at the Base until November 1914, when he went up the line and took part in many operations including those round Ypres. He was wounded at Ploegsteert Wood, and invalided home but rejoined his unit in France in 1915. Later in the same year he proceeded to the Dardanelles and served in the Evacuation of Gallipoli. He returned to the Western Front, and was wounded in the Battle of the Somme in 1916. He was then invalided home, and was discharged in March 1917 as medically unfit for further duty. He holds the 1914–15 Star, and the General Service and Victory Medals.
45, Cornbury Road, Rotherhithe, S.E.16.   Z6758

WOODS, C. H., Private, R.A.S.C. Labour Corps.
He volunteered in 1914, and in the following year was drafted to France. During his service overseas he was engaged on important duties in various sectors, and suffered severely from shell-shock. He was invalided home and discharged as medically unfit for further duty in December 1918. He holds the 1914–15 Star, and the General Service and Victory Medals.
30, Sheepcote Lane, Battersea, S.W.11.   Z4994B

WOODS, C. J. L., Sapper, R.E.
He volunteered in April 1915, and in the following year was drafted to France. During his service on the Western Front he was engaged on important duties in connection with many operations, notably at Ypres, Arras, and the Somme. In 1917 he proceeded to Italy, and after valuable service there returned to France in the following year. After the Armistice he advanced into Germany with the Army of Occupation, and served there until June 1919, when he returned home and was demobilised. He holds the General Service and Victory Medals.
77, Somerleyton Road, Coldharbour Lane, S.W.9.   Z3464B

WOODS, F. L., Gunner, R.G.A.
He was mobilised from the Reserve at the outbreak of hostilities, and was immediately drafted to the Western Front, where he served in the Retreat from Mons, and in the Battles of the Marne and Ypres. He was then sent to Salonika, and afterwards took part in the operations of the Allies on the Doiran and Struma fronts. He next proceeded to Egypt in December 1916, and did good work as a gunner under General Allenby in his advance on Palestine. He was in action on the Gaza front, and was present at the Fall of Jerusalem, and the Capture of Tripoli and Aleppo. He returned home and was demobilised in February 1919, holding the Mons Star, and the General Service and Victory Medals.
34, Waghorn Street, Peckham, S.E.15.   Z6799

WOODS, C. R., Bombardier, R.F.A.
He was mobilised from the Reserve in August 1914, and was almost immediately drafted to France where he took part in the Retreat from Mons, and in many subsequent battles. In 1916 he was sent to Salonika, and from thence to Egypt. After valuable service in these fronts he returned to France in time to take part in the general Allied Advance of 1918. He was demobilised in May of the following year after returning home, and holds the Mons Star, and the General Service and Victory Medals.
27, Royal Road, Walworth, S.E.17.   Z26571

WOODS, E., Private, R.A.S.C. (Remounts).
He joined in October 1916, after unsuccessful attempts to volunteer earlier, and after his training was engaged at various remount depôts on important duties with his unit. He rendered valuable services but was unable, owing to medical reasons, to obtain a transfer overseas, and was demobilised in September 1919.
22, Moncreiff Street, Peckham, S.E.15.   Z5698

WOODS, F. T., Private, 25th King's (Liverpool Regt.)
He joined in August 1917, and in April of the following year being drafted to France, fought in several engagements in the Retreat, and was taken prisoner in May 1918. He was kept at work behind the German lines until sent to a detention camp in September, where he remained until his release in January 1919. He proceeded to Egypt in September of the same year, and was stationed at Port Said. After his return to England he was demobilised in May 1920, and holds the General Service and Victory Medals.
200, Albany Road, Camberwell, S.E.5.   Z5699

WOODS, H., Private (Driver), R.A.M.C. (M.T.)
He joined in June 1916, and in the same month was sent to France where he did excellent work as a motor transport driver and served at Albert, the Somme, and Arras. Unfortunately he became ill and was invalided to hospital at Abbeville, and afterwards to England. After receiving further medical treatment he was discharged as physically unfit for further duty in January 1917. He holds the General Service and Victory Medals.
40, Rowena Crescent, Battersea Park Road, S.W.11. Z4995

WOODS, J. T., Sapper, R.E.
He volunteered in November 1915, and after his training was drafted in 1917 to Italy. During his service in this theatre of war he was engaged in the forward areas during many operations, notably on the Piave, in the Italian Retreat and Advance, until hostilities ceased. He returned home and was demobilised in February 1919, and holds the General Service and Victory Medals.
77, Somerleyton Road, Brixton, S.W.9.   Z3464C

WOODS, W. A., Sergt., R.F.A.
He was mobilised from the Reserve at the outbreak of hostilities, and was at first sent to Ireland and soon after to France where he served in the Retreat from Mons. He also took part in the heavy fighting on the Somme in 1916, and in numerous subsequent engagements until the termination of the war, including the Retreat and Advance of 1918. He returned home in 1919, and in the following year was still serving. He holds the Mons Star, and the General Service and Victory Medals.
3, Danson Road, Walworth, S.E.17.   Z27018

WOODS, W. J. (M.M.), Corporal, East Surrey Regt.
He volunteered in August 1914, and on being sent to France in the following year fought with distinction at Ypres, Festubert, Loos, the Somme, and many other engagements of great importance. He was wounded three times during his service, and was awarded the Military Medal for conspicuous gallantry and devotion to duty in the Field. He holds in addition to the Military Medal, the 1914–15 Star, and the General Service and Victory Medals, and was demobilised in 1919.
30, Sheepcote Lane, Battersea, S.W.11.   Z4994A

WOODWARD, J. T., Private, R.A.S.C. (M.T.)
He joined in 1916, and after his training served at various stations on important duties with his unit. He was principally engaged in breaking in mules for army use, and rendered valuable services for three years. He was demobilised in 1919, but unfortunately died six months later from the effects of illness contracted in his service.
" His memory is cherished with pride."
85, Barlow Street, Walworth, S.E.17.   Z4996

WOOLDRIDGE, A., Gunner, R.F.A.
He volunteered in December 1914, and was engaged with his Battery on important duties until January 1916, when he was sent to France and took part in the fighting at Albert, Vermelles, Ploegsteert Wood, Vimy Ridge, the Somme, Arras, Bullecourt, Ypres, Cambrai, and in numerous other engagements. He was demobilised in January 1919, and holds the General Service and Victory Medals.
90, Nelson Row, High Street, Clapham, S.W.4.   Z4997

WOOLFORD, P. L., 6th Middlesex Regiment.
Having volunteered in January 1915 he was sent to France in the following April and was in action at Armentières, Hill 60, Ypres, and many other important engagements and was wounded. He was later transferred to the Tank Corps, with which he served until demobilised in June 1919, and holds the 1914–15 Star, and the General Service and Victory Medals.
45, Sansom Street, Camberwell, S.E.5.   Z4998

WOOLLARD, A. J., Sergt., R.A.V.C.
He volunteered in 1915, having previously served in the Boer War, and in the same year was drafted to the Western Front, and was present at engagements on the Somme, and at Arras, and Ypres. He was afterwards employed on important duties at Boulogne until May 1919, when he returned home and was demobilised, holding the 1914–15 Star, and the General Service and Victory Medals.
194, Beresford Street, Camberwell, S.E.5.   Z4999

WOOLLARD, H. W., Sapper, R.E.
Volunteering in 1915, he was sent to the Western Front, where he was employed on important duties constructing trenches. Later he contracted dysentery, and was in hospital for some time. He holds the 1914–15 Star and the General Service and Victory Medals, and was demobilised in December 1919.
3, Lintaine Grove, West Kensington, W.14.   16811

WOOLLETT, E. J., Pte., Royal Sussex Regiment.
Having volunteered in 1915 he was sent to the Western Front, where he was in action at Loos, the Somme, and Arras. He also took part in the Retreat and Advance of 1918, and was twice wounded. He was demobilised in 1919, and holds the 1914–15 Star, and the General Service and Victory Medals.
3, Urswicke Road, Battersea, S.W.11.   Z5000

WOOLLEY, A., Corporal R.G.A.
He volunteered in June 1915, and was engaged on important duties with his Battery until 1917, when he was drafted to France, and was in action at Lens, and other important engagements, and was wounded and gassed. He was invalided home, but on his recovery returned to France and took part in further fighting. He was demobilised in February 1919, and holds the General Service and Victory Medals.
196, Ivydale Road, Nunhead, S.E.15.   Z6776

WOOLLEY, A. T., L/Corporal, Royal Fusiliers.
Volunteering in August 1914, he was drafted to France in the following year and took part in the fighting on the Somme, and at Arras, Messines, Ypres, Lens, and in several other engagements. He also served in the Retreat and Advance of 1918, and was three times wounded. He was recommended for a French decoration for saving life at a village fire, and holds the 1914–15 Star, and the General Service and Victory Medals, and was demobilised in March 1919.
33, Thorncroft Street, South Lambeth S.W.8.   Z5001

WOOLLEY, D., C.S.M., 9th Border Regiment.
He volunteered in September 1914, and was sent to France in the following year. Later he was transferred to Salonika and was in action on the Doiran and other Fronts. He was afterwards invalided home through illness and discharged as medically unfit for further service in October 1918, holding the 1914–15 Star, and the General Service and Victory Medals.
112, Stewart's Road, Battersea Park Road, S.W.8.   Z5002

WOOLVETT, A., Special War Worker.
Being physically unfit for military service he was engaged in London on responsible work in connection with railway materials. His duties, which were of a highly important nature, were carried out in an efficient manner, and he rendered valuable services during the war.
18, Delaford Road, Rotherhithe, S.E.16.   Z6757A

WOOLVETT, L. (Mrs.), Special War Worker.
This lady was engaged at Woolwich Arsenal for twelve months in shell-filling. Her work which was of a responsible and dangerous nature was carried out with great care and efficiency and she rendered valuable services.
18, Delaford Road, Rotherhithe, S.E.16.   Z6757B

WOOTTON, C. W., Cpl., 2nd East Surrey Regt.
Volunteering in December 1914 he was drafted to France in the same month, and was in action at Ypres and Loos. In 1915 he was transferred to Salonika, where he contracted malaria and was invalided home. On his recovery he was engaged on important duties until he was demobilised in February 1919, holding the 1914–15 Star, and the General Service and Victory Medals.
46, Chantry Road, Stockwell, S.W.9.   Z5003

WORBOYS, E., Private, Labour Corps.
Having been previously rejected he joined in 1918, and was engaged on important duties at Aldershot. He rendered valuable services, but was not successful in obtaining his transfer overseas before the cessation of hostilities. He was demobilised in 1919.
15, Broomgrove Road, Stockwell, S.W.9.   Z5162

WORBOYS, E. F., Pte., 2nd Devonshire Regt. and 1st Hertfordshire Regt.

Volunteering in May 1915, at fifteen and a half years of age he was sent to France in the following December, and was in action on the Somme, where he was severely wounded and invalided home. On his recovery he returned to the Western Front in 1917, and took part in the fighting on the Somme, and at Ypres and Cambrai, and was again wounded and sent home. He was demobilised in March 1919, and holds the 1914–15 Star and the General Service and Victory Medals.
64, Howbury Road, Peckham, S.E.15.   Z6588A

WORDEN, W. J., Private, Royal Fusiliers.

He volunteered in January 1915, and in July of the same year was sent to France, where he took part in the fighting at Loos, Vimy Ridge, the Somme, and Ypres. He was wounded and gassed, and was buried by an explosion. On being rescued he was sent to hospital, but shortly afterwards returned to the fighting line, where he was again in action. He was demobilised in February 1919, and holds the 1914–15 Star, and the General Service and Victory Medals.
74, Grant Road, Battersea, S.W.11.   Z5004

WORDSWORTH, T. M., Staff-Sergt.-Major, R.A.S.C.

He volunteered in December 1914, and was sent to France in the following year, and was engaged on important duties in the Somme and Ypres Sectors. In 1916 he was transferred to Salonika and served on the Doiran Front with the Brigade Headquarters of the 85th and 28th Divisions. He was demobilised in 1919, but afterwards re-enlisted a further period of twelve months. He holds the 1914–15 Star, and the General Service and Victory Medals.
37, Crawshay Road, Brixton, S.W.9.   Z4395A

WORMULL, A. G. H., Private, 7th London Regt.

Joining in October 1916 he was sent to France in the following year and took part in numerous important engagements. He was unfortunately killed in action at Arras on November 10th, 1917, and was buried in Gloucester Farm Cemetery. He was entitled to the General Service and Victory Medals.
"A costly sacrifice upon the altar of freedom."
25, Brymer Road, Camberwell, S.E.5.   Z5700

WORRELL, G., L/Corporal, Tank Corps.

He volunteered in December 1915, and after completing his training was drafted to the Western Front, where he took part in the fighting at Messines, Havrincourt, and Amiens. On one occasion his tank received a direct hit which caused numerous casualties, but fortunately he was uninjured. He was demobilised in February 1919, and holds the General Service and Victory Medals.
14, Goulden Street, Battersea, S.W.11.   Z5005

WORTH, S. C., Driver, R.F.A.

He volunteered in March 1915, and later in the same year was sent to France, where he was in action at Vermelles, Ploegsteert Wood, Vimy Ridge, the Somme, Arras, Messines, Ypres, Passchendaele, and Cambrai. He also took part in the Retreat and Advance of 1918, and returning home after the Armistice was demobilised in January 1919, holding the 1914–15 Star, and the General Service and Victory Medals.
19, Nunhead Green, S.E.15.   Z6357

WOTTON, W. J. (M.M.), Pte., Royal Scots Fusiliers.

Volunteering in October 1915, he was sent to Egypt in the same year, and was in action on the Suez Canal, and in Palestine. In 1918 he was transferred to France, where he took part in further fighting, and after the Armistice he proceeded with the Army of Occupation to Germany. He was awarded the Military Medal for bravery in the Field, and also holds the 1914–15 Star, and the General Service and Victory Medals, and was demobilised in September 1919.
81, Abbeyfield Road, Rotherhithe, S.E.16.   Z6800

WRAY, E. A., Private, 13th East Surrey Regiment.

He volunteered in July 1915, and was engaged with his unit on important duties until April 1918, when he was drafted to France and took part in the fighting on the Somme, and in several other engagements. He was severely wounded and invalided home, and on recovery was transferred to the Buffs (East Kent Regiment). He was demobilised in June 1919, and holds the General Service and Victory Medals.
61, Beaufoy Road, Lavender Hill, S.W.11.   Z1195–6B

WRAY, W. R., Driver, R.A.S.C. (H.T.)

He was mobilised in August 1914, and in the following month was sent to France and was attached to the London Scottish. He took part in the memorable charge which that Regiment made, and was also present at the engagements at La Bassée, and the Ancre. He was later posted to the Anti-Aircraft Section, and whilst serving with them was severely gassed, and suffered with trench fever and dysentery. He was invalided home, and on recovery was transferred to the Tank Corps, and remained with that unit until demobilised in February 1919. He holds the 1914 Star, and the General Service and Victory Medals.
61, Beaufoy Road, Lavender Hill, S.W.11.   Z1195–6C

WRAY, F. F., Private, 9th East Surrey Regiment.

He joined in March 1918, and was sent to France later in the same year and was in action at Bapaume, the Scarpe, Havrincourt, and Le Cateau. After the Armistice he proceeded with the Army of Occupation to Germany, where he served until demobilised in April 1920. He holds the General Service and Victory Medals.
23, Auckland Road, Battersea, S.W.11.   Z5006

WRELTON, S., Private, 33rd Middlesex Regiment.

Having volunteered in August 1914, he was sent to France early in the following year and took part in the fighting at Neuve Chapelle, Hill 60, Ypres, Festubert, and in many other engagements, and was severely wounded. He was invalided home and suffered the amputation of two of his fingers. After a period in hospital he was discharged as medically unfit for further service in May 1916, and holds the 1914–15 Star, and the General Service and Victory Medals.
32, Lothian Road, Camberwell New Road, S.W.9.   Z5173

WREN, F., Corporal, R.F.A.

Having previously served in the Army he re-joined in August 1914, and in October of the same year was sent to France, and was in action at Ypres, where he was wounded. He was invalided home and discharged on account of his injuries in August 1916, and holds the 1914 Star, and the General Service and Victory Medals.
30, Cowan Street, Camberwell, S.E.5.   Z5174

WREN, I. T., Driver, R.F.A.

Volunteering in June 1915, he was drafted to France in the same year and took part in the fighting at St. Eloi, Albert, the Somme, Arras, Bullecourt, Ypres, Passchendaele, and in numerous other engagements. He was invalided home on account of ill-health, but on his recovery returned to France and served in the Retreat and Advance of 1918. He was demobilised in February 1919, and holds the 1914–15 Star, and the General Service and Victory Medals.
28, Manaton Road, Peckham, S.E.15.   Z6353

WRIGHT, A., Corporal, Tank Corps.

He volunteered in 1914, and proceeded to the Western Front with the Royal Sussex Regiment in the following year, and fought in various parts of the line. Later on being transferred to the Tank Corps he was in action in many engagements, including the first Battle of Cambrai. He gave his life for the freedom of England in the opening stages of the German Offensive of 1918, and was entitled to the 1914–15 Star, and the General Service and Victory Medals.
"His life for his Country, his soul to God."
35, Yeovil Street, Wandsworth Road, S.W.8.   Z5007

WRIGHT, A. E., Private, Royal Fusiliers.

He enlisted in 1913, and shortly after the declaration of war, was sent to the Western Front. He fought in many important engagements, and was severely wounded in the second Battle of Ypres. After being admitted into hospital, he died from his injuries on June 16th, 1915, and was entitled to the 1914–15 Star, the General Service and Victory Medals.
"Steals on the ear the distant triumph song."
62, Ancill Street, Hammersmith, W.6.   14005B

WRIGHT, A. J., Rifleman, 5th London Regiment (Rifle Brigade) and Sapper, R.E.

He volunteered in October 1914, and in the following year embarked for the Western Front. Here he served in various parts of the line fighting in many engagements of note, and was wounded and twice gassed. Later he was transferred to the Royal Engineers, and rendered valuable services until the cessation of hostilities. He was still serving in 1920, and holds the 1914–15 Star, and the General Service and Victory Medals.
19, Hollydale Road, Peckham, S.E.15.   Z6515

WRIGHT, A. W., Rifleman, King's Royal Rifle Corps.

He joined in February 1917, and shortly afterwards was drafted to France where he fought at Ypres, Passchendaele, and Lens. Transferred to Italy, he saw heavy fighting in various sectors, and returned to France in 1918. He was in action in many engagements during the Retreat and Advance of 1918, and during his service overseas was six times wounded and gassed. He was demobilised in February 1919, and holds the General Service and Victory Medals.
32, Beckway Street, Walworth, S.E.17.   Z3023B

WRIGHT, C., Cpl., 2nd Loyal North Lancashire Regt.

He enlisted in 1909, and was serving in India at the commencement of hostilities. Shortly afterwards he was drafted to German East Africa, and fought in many engagements, and was present at the fall of Dar-es-Salaam. Later he was sent to Egypt and served in various operations and then proceeded to France. Here he was in action in the Retreat and Advance of 1918, and after the Armistice served in Germany with the Army of Occupation. He was transferred to the Reserve in April 1919, and holds the 1914–15 Star, and the General Service and Victory Medals.
295, Sumner Road, Peckham, S.E.15.   Z6365

WRIGHT, A. W., Rifle Brigade.
He joined in November 1918, and after completing his training was engaged on important duties with his unit. He did not obtain his transfer overseas prior to the cessation of hostilities, but rendered excellent services until demobilised in 1919.
28, Averill Street, Hammersmith, W.6. 13996A

WRIGHT, C., Rfimn., 6th London Regt. (Rifles).
He joined in April 1917, and two months later was sent to the Western Front, where he fought in the Battles of Ypres, Passchendaele, the Somme, and throughout the German Offensive and subsequent Allied Advance of 1918. After the Armistice he served at Cologne with the Army of Occupation, and after returning home was demobilised in February 1919. He holds the General Service and Victory Medals.
9, Darwin Street, Walworth, S.E.17. Z5011A

WRIGHT, C. A., Sapper, R.E.
Volunteering in November 1914, he was sent to France in the following April, and served in the front lines on important duties. Wounded in June 1915, he returned to England, and after receiving hospital treatment rejoined his unit in France in July 1917, and served near Arras and in many other parts of the line. Owing to ill-health he was invalided home in October 1917, and on recovery was stationed at various home depôts until demobilised in January 1919. He holds the 1914-15 Star, and the General Service and Victory Medals.
40, Church Road, Battersea, S.W.11. Z5015

WRIGHT, C. A., Sergt, R.A.M.C.
He volunteered in February 1915, and was engaged on important duties at various stations until embarking for Mesopotamia in October 1917. Here he rendered valuable services as stretcher-bearer and later as ward-master at various hospitals engaged on important duties attending the sick and wounded troops until the cessation of hostilities. He returned to England and was demobilised in March 1920, holding the General Service and Victory Medals.
128, Harbut Road, Battersea, S.W.11. Z5008

WRIGHT, E. F., Stoker, R.N.
He joined in January 1918, and until the cessation of hostilities served on mine-sweeping duties in the North Sea in His Majesty's Mine-sweepers "Snowdrift" and "Eaglet," and later served in H.M.S. "Vivid." He rendered valuable services throughout, and was demobilised in February 1919, holding the General Service and Victory Medals.
32, Beckway Street, Walworth, S.E.17. Z3023C

WRIGHT, F., Pte., Queen's (Royal West Surrey Regt).
A Reservist, he was mobilised at the commencement of hostilities, and proceeded to France. He fought in the Retreat from Mons, and the Battles of Le Cateau, the Marne, the Aisne, La Bassée, and Ypres I. He gave his life for the freedom of England on January 16th, 1915, and was entitled to the Mons Star, and the General Service and Victory Medals.
"Nobly striving.
He nobly fell that we might live."
9, Darwin Street, Walworth, S.E.17. Z5011B

WRIGHT, F. J., Private, 2nd King's Shropshire Light Infantry.
Volunteering in August 1914, he was drafted to the Western Front in the following year, and after being in action at Ypres, Festubert, Loos, was badly gassed at Ypres in 1916. Invalided to England he received hospital treatment and subsequently was discharged as unfit for further service in February 1917. He holds the 1914-15 Star, and the General Service and Victory Medals. 19, Huguenot Road, Peckham Rye, S.E.15. Z6106A

WRIGHT, G. H., Pte., Loyal North Lancashire Regt.
He volunteered in 1915, and later in that year embarked for the Western Front. He was engaged in much heavy fighting in many parts of the line, and in the Battle of Ypres was so severely wounded as to necessitate the amputation of both legs. He was invalided out of the Service in 1917, and holds the 1914-15 Star, and the General Service and Victory Medals.
28, Averill Street, Hammersmith, W.6. 13996B

WRIGHT, G. W., Gunner, R.F.A.
Volunteering in August 1914, he proceeded to France in September of the following year. He was attached for a time to the Headquarter Staff, and was in action in many engagements of note in various sectors. He gave his life for King and Country in July 1916, during the British Offensive on the Somme, and was entitled to the 1914-15 Star, the General Service and Victory Medals.
"His life for his Country, his soul to God."
8, F Block, Victoria Dwellings, Battersea Park Road, Battersea, S.W.11. Z5012

WRIGHT, H., Corporal, R.E.
Volunteering in January 1915, he landed three months later in France, where he was in action in many important engagements, and was severely wounded at Ypres in 1917. He lost an arm in consequence of his injuries, and was demobilised in April 1919. He holds the 1914-15 Star, and the General Service and Victory Medals.
23, Cairns Road, Battersea, S.W.11. Z2923

WRIGHT, H. C., Private, 8th East Surrey Regt.
Volunteering in January 1915, and drafted in the following year to the Western Front, he fought at St. Eloi, the Somme, Arras, and was taken prisoner at Cambrai in March 1918 during the German Offensive. He was held in captivity until after the Armistice, and then was repatriated. He was still serving in 1920, and holds the General Service and Victory Medals.
19, Huguenot Road, Peckham Rye, S.E.15. Z6106B

WRIGHT, H. E., L/Cpl., 2nd East Surrey Regt.
He joined in February 1917 at the age of seventeen, and later in the same year proceeded to the Western Front, but on being discovered to be under military age was sent back to England in 1918. Later in that year he proceeded to Egypt and served at various stations on important garrison duties, until drafted to Constantinople. He was awarded the French Croix-de-Guerre for excellent services in assisting to restore order during the unrest in Stamboul in June 1920. He was still serving in 1920, and holds the General Service and Victory Medals.
9, Sunwell Street, Peckham, S.E.15. Z6516-7A

WRIGHT, H. T., Rfimn., 6th London Regt. (Rifles).
He enlisted in 1912, and mobilised at the commencement of hostilities was drafted to France in 1915. He was in action at Givenchy, and in many other parts of the line, and was severely wounded in the Battle of Loos on September 27th, 1915. He unfortunately died from his injuries on the following day, and was entitled to the 1914-15 Star, the General Service and Victory Medals.
"He passed out of the sight of men by the path of duty and self-sacrifice."
9, Sunwell Street, Peckham, S.E.15. Z6516-7B

WRIGHT, H. T. G., Private, R.A.V.C.
After volunteering in February 1916, he embarked later in the same year for the Western Front, where he was engaged on important duties attending the sick and wounded horses. In 1917 on being transferred to Salonika, he rendered excellent services while employed on similar duties until the cessation of hostilities. Returning home, he was demobilised in August 1919, and holds the General Service and Victory Medals.
62, Ancill Street, Hammersmith, W.6. 14005A

WRIGHT, J. F., Sergt., R.E.
He volunteered in February 1915, and in June of the following year was drafted to France, where he did excellent work in many parts of the line. In 1917, on being transferred to Salonika, he was engaged in various sectors, and in 1918 proceeded to Egypt. On the Palestine front he was employed on important duties throughout the British Advance into Syria, and rendered excellent services throughout. He was present at the entry into Jerusalem. Returning home he was demobilised in June 1919, and holds the General Service and Victory Medals.
23, Fawcett Road, Rotherwithe, S.E.16. Z6778

WRIGHT, J. H., Private, 4th Lincolnshire Regt.
Joining in September 1916, and in the following year embarking for France, he fought at the Battles of Vimy Ridge, Bullecourt, Ypres, Lens, Cambrai, the Somme, and throughout the German Offensive and Allied Advance of 1918. After returning to England he was demobilised in February 1919, and holds the General Service and Victory Medals.
229, Hollydale Road, Peckham, S.E.15. Z6595

WRIGHT, L. G., Private, East Surrey Regiment.
He volunteered in August 1915, and on completing his training was sent to France in the succeeding year. During his service overseas he fought at St. Eloi, the Somme, Vimy Ridge, Ypres, Cambrai, and was engaged in much heavy fighting during the German Offensive and subsequent Allied Advance of 1918. He was demobilised in May 1919 after his return to England, and holds the General Service and Victory Medals.
39, Sterndale Road, Wandsworth Road, S.W.8. Z5013

WRIGHT, P. A., Private, 23rd London Regiment.
Volunteering in March 1915, and drafted to France in July of the following year, he fought in the Battles of the Somme, Arras, and Ypres, and was wounded. On his recovery he rejoined his unit and saw much heavy fighting throughout the Retreat and Advance of 1918, and was present at the entry of the British troops into Lille. He returned to England shortly after the Armistice, and was demobilised in February 1919, holding the General Service and Victory Medals.
19, Horsman Street, Camberwell, S.E.5. Z1024B

WRIGHT, S., Pte., 13th London Regt. (Kensingtons).
Joining in October 1916, he embarked in the following month for the Western Front, and fought in the Battles of Arras, Vimy Ridge, Ypres, Passchendaele, and Cambrai, and was wounded. On his recovery he rejoined his Battalion, and was in action in many engagements during the Allied Advance of 1918. He was demobilised in February 1919, and holds the General Service and Victory Medals.
76, Grant Road, Battersea, S.W.11. Z5016

WRIGHT, R. C., Private, 11th Royal Fusiliers.

He volunteered in September 1915, and in the following year was sent to France, where he took part in numerous engagements, including those on the Somme, and at Arras, Ypres, and Lens, and was wounded. He was demobilised in January 1919, and holds the General Service and Victory Medals.
314, Southwark Park Road, Rotherhithe, S.E.16.   Z6801

WRIGHT, R. O., Rifleman, Rifle Brigade.

He joined in March 1918, and on completing his training was engaged at various depôts on important duties with his unit. He was unsuccessful in obtaining his transfer to a theatre of war prior to the cessation of hostilities, but in September 1919 proceeded to Mesopotamia, and in 1920 was serving on the Tigris.
18, Bengeworth Road, Camberwell, S.E.5.   Z6360B

WRIGHT, S. E., Special War Worker.

He volunteered for work of National importance at the age of fifteen, and during the last month of the war was engaged on important agricultural duties in Lincolnshire. He also rendered valuable services during air raids as a bugler.
9, Sunwell Street, Peckham, S.E.15.   Z6516-7D

WRIGHT, S. T., Gunner, R.F.A.

He volunteered in May 1915, and in the following December was drafted to France, where he fought in the Battles of Vimy Ridge, the Somme, Arras, Messines, Lens, Cambrai, and throughout the Retreat and Advance of 1918. He was demobilised in April 1919, and holds the 1914-15 Star, the General Service and Victory Medals. After demobilisation he was engaged with the Royal Defence Corps as an interpreter for German prisoners of war.
7, Beckway Street, Walworth, S.E.17.   Z5014

WRIGHT, T., Pte., South Wales Borderers and R.A.S.C. (M.T.)

Volunteering in March 1915, he embarked for the Dardanelles in the following September, and fought in many engagements until the Evacuation of the Peninsula. Being then transferred to Egypt he served there for some months, and afterwards proceeded to France. He fought at the Somme, Arras, Ypres, Soissons, and throughout the Retreat and Advance of 1918. Returning home he was transferred to the Royal Army Service Corps, and in 1920 was still serving. He holds the 1914-15 Star, and the General Service and Victory Medals.
92, Trafalgar Road, Peckham, S.E.15.   Z5009

WRIGHT, T. J., Corporal, East Surrey Regiment.

He volunteered in October 1915, and embarked for India in the following February. During his service in this Country, he was stationed at various garrison towns, and was engaged on guard and other important duties. Returning to England after the Armistice he was demobilised in March 1919, and holds the General Service and Victory Medals.
18, Bengeworth Road, Camberwell, S.E.5.   Z6360A

WRIGHT, W., Rflmn., King's Royal Rifle Corps.

Joining in September 1916, he was sent to France in the following year, and fought in many engagements of note. He was wounded and taken prisoner at Cambrai in November 1917, and was held in captivity at various camps until January 1919. After being repatriated he was demobilised in October of that year, and holds the General Service and Victory Medals.
4, South Island Place, Stockwell, S.W.9.   Z5217/8A

WRIGHT, W., Private, Middlesex Regiment.

A Reservist, he was mobilised in October 1914, and was engaged at various depôts on guard and other important duties with his unit. Owing to ill-health he was unsuccessful in obtaining his transfer overseas prior to the cessation of hostilities, but rendered valuable services until demobilised in February 1919.
39, Earl Road, Bermondsey, S.E.1.   Z26835

WRIGHT, W., Pte., 2nd Northumberland Fusiliers.

He enlisted in August 1911, and shortly after the outbreak of war was sent to France, where he fought in many engagements, including those of Ypres and Loos and was wounded at Zillebeke. Late in 1915 he was drafted to Salonika, and until the cessation of hostilities was engaged in this theatre of war in heavy fighting on the Struma and in many other parts of the line. Returning to England he was demobilised in May 1919, and holds the 1914-15 Star, and the General Service and Victory Medals.
3, Mawbey Street, S. Lambeth Road, S.W.8.   Z5010

WRIGHT, W. A., L/Corporal, 1st Royal Fusiliers.

He enlisted in May 1914, and shortly after the commencement of hostilities was sent to France. He fought at Armentières, and was wounded there, but on recovery rejoined his unit and was in action at Loos, the Somme, Arras, Messines, Ypres and throughout the German Offensive and Allied Advance of 1918. He was demobilised in March 1919, and holds the 1914 Star, and the General Service and Victory Medals.   9, Sunwell Street, Peckham, S.E.15.   Z651/67C

WRIGHT, W. F., Gunner, R.F.A.

Volunteering in August 1914, he was drafted to Salonika in the following March, and fought in many engagements of note on the Struma, Doiran and Monastir fronts, and was wounded. Invalided to hospital in Egypt he received treatment, and on recovery rejoined his Battery in the Macedonian theatre of war. He was engaged in heavy fighting on the Vardar and took part in the final Allied Advance. Returning home, he was demobilised in January 1919, and holds the 1914-15 Star, and the General Service and Victory Medals.
44, Crewys Road, Peckham, S.E.15.   Z6352

WRIGHT, W. W., Rflmn., King's Royal Rifle Corps.

He volunteered in May 1915, and in June of the following year was drafted to the Western Front. He fought in many engagements, including the Battle of the Somme, and was wounded and taken prisoner in 1917 in Flanders. Repatriated in accordance with the terms of the Armistice he was demobilised in February 1919, and holds the General Service and Victory Medals.
15, Sears Street, Camberwell, S.E.5.   Z5854

WRIST, E., Private, 16th Royal Sussex Regiment.

Joining in April 1916, he proceeded in the same year to the Western Front, where he took part in much of the fighting. Amongst other engagements he was in action at those of Loos, Vimy Ridge and the Ancre and was three times wounded, on one occasion being buried for several hours by the explosion of a shell. In February 1919 he returned to England and was demobilised, holding the General Service and Victory Medals.
21, Priory Grove, South Lambeth, S.W.8.   Z5017

WYATT, A. E., Sapper, R.E.

Volunteering early in 1915, he proceeded overseas in the same year and served in many sectors of the Western Front. He was in action on the Somme and at Arras and Cambrai and did much valuable work with his unit until 1918, when he was severely gassed. He was invalided to England and after receiving hospital treatment was demobilised in January 1919, holding the 1914-15 Star, and the General Service and Victory Medals.
50, Silverthorne Road, Wandsworth Road, S.W.8.   Z5018

WYATT, F., Corporal, R.F.A.

He joined in November 1916, and for a time served on special duties in England. Later, however, he was drafted to France and took part in the Advance of 1918, afterwards proceeding to Germany with the Army of Occupation. He returned home in February 1920 and was demobilised. Having previously served in the Boer War, he holds the Queen's and King's South African Medals and the General Service and Victory Medals.
100, Wadhurst Road, Battersea, S.W.8.   Z5019B

WYATT, H. J., Sergt., Canadian Overseas Forces.

Joining in September 1916, he served on the completion of his training on important clerical duties in the shipping offices of various hospitals arranging for the men to be sent back to Canada. He rendered valuable services, but was not successful in obtaining his transfer to a fighting front before hostilities ceased. In 1919 he was demobilised.
52, Solon Road, Acre Lane, S.W.2.   Z5020A

WYATT, M. A. M. (Mrs.), Worker, Q.M.A.A.C.

She joined in January 1918, and served on important duties at Wimbledon Common Camp in the officers' mess, until February 1919, when she was demobilised after having rendered valuable services.
40, Averill Street, Hammersmith, W.6.   14173A

WYATT, S. H. C., L/Corporal, 11th Queen's (Royal West Surrey Regiment).

He joined in September 1917, and on the completion of his training was sent to France, where he was in action on the Somme and at Ypres. Shortly afterwards he proceeded to Italy, remaining there for about two months, at the end of which time he returned to France and took part in many engagements, including the Advance of 1918, during which time he was gassed. After hostilities ceased he went with the Army of Occupation into Germany and served there until his demobilisation in September 1919. He holds the General Service and Victory Medals.
26, Holden Street, Battersea, S.W.11.   Z5021

WYATT, T. F., Rifleman, King's Royal Rifle Corps.

He joined in February 1916, and in the following June embarked for France. There he was in action on the Ancre and at Arras and Beaumont-Hamel. He was then invalided into hospital through ill-health, but on recovery returned to the fighting line. He gave his life for King and Country in the engagement at Bourlon Wood on November 20th, 1917, and was entitled to the General Service and Victory Medals.
"A valiant soldier, with undaunted heart, he breasted Life's last hill."
52, Solon Road, Acre Lane, S.W.2.   Z5020B

WYATT, T. H., Rifleman, Rifle Brigade.

Volunteering in 1914, he sailed, on the completion of his training for Salonika, where he saw much service, and was wounded. He was invalided home, but on recovery proceeded to France, and in this theatre of war took part in many battles, including those on the Somme, and at Ypres, Arras and Cambrai. He also served in the Advance of 1918, and after the cessation of hostilities returned to England in January 1919, and was demobilised, holding the 1914-15 Star, and the General Service and Victory Medals.
45, Averill Street, Fulham, W.6. 14173B

WYETH, W. E. W., Gunner, R.F.A.

Joining in April 1917, he embarked in the same year for France, and whilst there fought in various engagements, including those at Messines, Cambrai, Passchendaele and Bapaume. After the Armistice he went with the Army of Occupation into Germany, returning home for demobilisation in March 1919. He holds the General Service and Victory Medals.
274, Albert Road, Peckham, S.E.15. Z5862

WYKES, C. J., A.B., Royal Navy.

He joined in July 1915, and was posted to H.M.S. " Courageous," in which vessel he served with the Grand Fleet in the North Sea. He did much good work until demobilised in July 1920, and holds the 1914-15 Star, and the General Service and Victory Medals.
106, Crimsworth Road, Wandsworth Road, S.W.8. Z5023

WYLES, E., Private, 1st Royal Berkshire Regiment.

He was serving at the outbreak of war, and was sent to France in November 1914. He took part in the fighting at La Bassée, Festubert, Loos and the Somme, where he was wounded and invalided home. He was afterwards transferred to the Labour Corps and finally to the Royal Defence Corps, with which he served until demobilised in December 1918. He holds the 1914 Star, and the General Service and Victory Medals.
427, Southwark Park Road, Rotherhithe, S.E.16.
Z6823

WYNIGER, E. G., Rflmn., King's Royal Rifle Corps and Rifle Brigade, and Pte., Labour Corps.

He joined in June 1916, and after having completed his training proceeded to France. There he was in action at Lens, Béthune, Ypres and in many other engagements, including the Retreat of 1918, during which he was wounded. He was invalided home and after receiving hospital treatment was discharged in February 1919. He holds the General Service and Victory Medals.
82, Mysore Road, Battersea, S.W.11. Z4002B

WYRILL, C. A., Gunner, R.F.A.

He volunteered in August 1914, and after his training was drafted to Salonika in 1916. During his service in the Balkan campaign he did good work as a gunner in the offensive on the Doiran front and in the Advance across the Struma. He was wounded in action in 1918, and also suffered from malaria. He returned home and was demobilised in February 1919, and holds the General Service and Victory Medals.
84, Somerleyton Road, Coldharbour Lane, S.W.9. Z5024

WYRRILL, J., Sapper, R.E.

He volunteered in March 1915, and was sent overseas in the latter part of the same year. Whilst in France he was engaged on important duties in connection with the operations, and was frequently in the forward areas. He was present at engagements at Loos, Vimy Ridge, Arras, Bullecourt, Ypres and Cambrai, and in the second Battle of the Somme, and was also at the memorable entry into Mons at dawn on Armistice Day. He was then sent home, and demobilised in the following January, holding the 1914-15 Star, and the General Service and Victory Medals.
47, Chantrey Road, Stockwell Road, S.W.9. Z4251B

Y

YALDEN, F., Pte., Essex Regt. and R.A.S.C. (M.T.)

He volunteered in September 1914, and in June of the following year proceeded to the Western Front and served in the Somme sector until December 1915, when he was transferred to the Royal Army Service Corps, as a motor mechanic. He was engaged in the Transport Section going to and from the lines for some time, and was then stationed at Marseilles, and later Rouen and Paris. He was demobilised in June 1919, and holds the 1914-15 Star, and the General Service and Victory Medals.
87, Ingrave Street, Battersea, S.W.9. Z5175

YARDLEY, S. W., Gunner, R.G.A.

He joined in May 1917, and was at first engaged with the R.F.C. on home defence duties. In July 1918 he was drafted to France and served in the Anti-Aircraft Section on the lines of communication at Abancourt, where he was present at the time of the explosion of a great ammunition dump, when three hundred men were killed. He afterwards proceeded to Germany with the Army of Occupation and was stationed at Cologne with the Mobile Anti-Aircraft Battery. He returned home, and was demobilised in February 1920, and holds the General Service and Victory Medals.
40, Doddington Grove, Walworth, S.E.17. Z5176

YARHAM, R. J., Driver, R.F.A.

He volunteered in August 1914, and was drafted to France in February 1916. During his service overseas he did good work as a driver on the Somme, and at Arras, Ypres, Cambrai, and in many subsequent engagements in the Retreat and Advance of 1918. He was demobilised in July 1919, and holds the General Service and Victory Medals.
87, Eugenia Road, Rotherhithe, S.E.16. Z6811A

YARHAM, W. G., L/Corporal, Middlesex Regiment.

He volunteered in 1914, and in the following year was sent to the Western Front and fought in the Battle of Loos, and was wounded. He was invalided home to hospital and after six weeks' medical treatment was sent to Mesopotamia, where he was in action at Kut, the Capture of Baghdad and at Ramadieh. He was subsequently sent to India, from where he returned to England, and was demobilised in November 1919, holding the 1914-15 Star, and the General Service and Victory Medals, and the India General Service Medal (with clasp Afghanistan N.W. Frontier, 1919).
87, Eugenia Road, South Bermondsey, S.E.16. Z6811B

YARROW, C., Private, 2nd Eastern Ontario Regt.

He volunteered in October 1914, and in the following year was sent to the Western Front, where he fought at Ypres and Givenchy, and was wounded. He was invalided to hospital at Etaples, but on recovery rejoined his unit and was again in action and wounded a second time and sent home to hospital. He was afterwards engaged on clerical duties at the Clearing Depôt at Shorncliffe, until demobilised in May 1919. He holds the 1914-15 Star, and the General Service and Victory Medals.
24, Pulross Road, Stockwell, S.W.9. Z5178

YATES, E. S., Gunner, R.F.A.

He joined in March 1916, and in the following September was drafted to France. During his service overseas he did good work as a gunner in many engagements, including those on the Somme and at Arras, Messines, Ypres and Cambrai. He was invalided home owing to illness in January 1918, and demobilised in February of the following year. He holds the General Service and Victory Medals.
15, Cambria Road, Camberwell, S.E.5. Z6472

YATES, J., Gunner, R.G.A.

He joined in June 1916, and in the following January was drafted to France, and whilst in this theatre of war did good work as a gunner in the Battles of Arras, Messines, Ypres, Lens and Cambrai. He also served throughout the Retreat and Advance of 1918, and was gassed. He was demobilised in January 1919, and holds the General Service and Victory Medals.
19, Darwin Street, Walworth, S.E.17. Z5179

YEARLING, W., Private, R.A.S.C. (M.T.)

He volunteered in August 1914, and in the following month was sent to the Western Front, and saw service at La Bassée and Ypres. In January 1915 he proceeded to Egypt and was stationed at Cairo and Alexandria, engaged on important duties with the Motor Transport Section until April 1916, when he returned to England and was subsequently discharged on account of ill-health. He had previously fought in the South African War, and holds the Medals for that campaign, the 1914 Star, and the General Service and Victory Medals.
3, Aldensley Road, Hammersmith, W.6. 10739A

YEATES, A. E., Sergt., M.G.C.

He volunteered in August 1914, and in the same year embarked for France, where he was engaged in many important battles, including those at Ypres, the Somme and Arras. He was wounded three times and was invalided home and subsequently demobilised in February 1919. He holds the 1914-15 Star, and the General Service and Victory Medals.
18, Thurlow Street, Walworth, S.E.17. Z5180

YEATES, A. W., Private, M.G.C.

He volunteered in November 1915, and in the following year was drafted to France. During his service overseas he fought at Ypres, Arras, Albert, Passchendaele, Béthune, Lens, Bapaume, and in many other engagements in the Retreat and Advance of 1918. He was demobilised in January of the following year, and holds the General Service and Victory Medals.
35, Nursery Row, Orb Street, Walworth, S.E.17. L2959B

YELLOP, W., Private, R.M.L.I.

He was mobilised in 1914, and was almost immediately sent to Belgium, and took part with the Naval Division in the Defence of Antwerp. In 1915 he was drafted to the Dardanelles, but, later, owing to illness was invalided to hospitals in Malta and thence to England in October 1915. He was afterwards engaged in submarine patrol duties in the North Sea and off the coast of Iceland until the cessation of hostilities. He returned home, and was demobilised in February 1919, and holds the 1914-15 Star, and the General Service and Victory Medals.

20, Meadow Place, South Lambeth Road, S.W.8.　　Z5181

YENDELL, W. J., Stoker, R.N., H.M.S. "Tower."

A serving sailor since 1912, he was at sea when war was declared, and in 1915 was transferred from his ship to H.M.S. "Hydra." He was on board this vessel when she was lost off the Irish coast in 1915. Fortunately, however, he was saved and was then posted to H.M.S. "Tower," with which he was present at the Battle of Jutland on May 31st, 1916. Afterwards he served in the North Sea and the English Channel on important patrol duties, and was at Scapa Flow at the surrender of the German Fleet in 1918. He returned home, and was discharged as time-expired in July 1919, and holds the 1914-15 Star, and the General Service and Victory Medals.

9, Corunna Road, New Road, S.W.8.　　Z5182

YEOMANS, H., L/Corporal, R.A.S.C. (M.T.)

He volunteered in September 1914, and in the same year was drafted to France, where he was engaged on important duties in connection with the Motor Transport and served in many sectors of the Western Front. He was afterwards transferred to the motor ambulances and continued his service until the Armistice was signed. Later he returned home and was invalided to hospital owing to illness, and was discharged in January 1919 after four and a half years with the Colours. He holds the 1914 Star, and the General Service and Victory Medals.　　92, Trafalgar Road, Peckham, S.E.15.　　Z5183

YOCKNEY, J. H., Air Mechanic, R.A.F.

He joined in July 1916, and after his training served at various stations on important duties which demanded a high degree of technical skill. He rendered valuable services, but was not successful in obtaining a transfer overseas before the cessation of hostilities owing to being medically unfit for duty abroad. He was discharged in April 1918.

7, Charleston Street, Walworth, S.E.17.　　Z5184

YORK, A. W., Driver, R.F.A.

Volunteering in January 1915, he was drafted overseas in the following June. During his service in France he was engaged on important duties as a driver and was in action at Loos, the Somme, Ploegsteert Wood, Vimy Ridge, Passchendaele and Cambrai. In the latter part of 1917 he contracted trench fever and was in hospital for a time, but on recovery rejoined his unit and served until March 1919, when he was demobilised. He holds the 1914-15 Star, and the General Service and Victory Medals.

39, Nealdon Street, Landor Road, S.W.9.　　Z5185

YORK, J., Private, 19th London Regiment.

He joined in November 1916, and in February of the following year was drafted to France. During his service overseas he fought in the Battles of the Somme, Arras and Cambrai, and died gloriously on the Field of Battle at Lillers in September 1918.

"He died the noblest death a man may die,
Fighting for God, and right, and liberty."

41, Anchor Street, Rotherhithe, S.E.16.　　Z6680

YORKE, A. J., Cpl., 18th (Queen Mary's Own) Hussars and R.A.S.C.

He was mobilised at the outbreak of war, and in the same year was drafted to France. During his service on the Western Front he was in action at Ypres, Albert, Arras, Bapaume, Béthune and Amiens, and was afterwards transferred to the Royal Army Service Corps, and was mainly engaged on important transport duties. He was demobilised in February 1919, and holds the 1914-15 Star, and the General Service and Victory Medals.

24, Tindal Street, North Brixton, S.W.9.　　Z5866

YOUDALE, W. H., Captain, 1st Border Regiment.

He volunteered in September 1914, and proceeding to France in the May of following year, was in action at Ypres, where he was wounded. He afterwards took part in the severe fighting in the Ypres, Arras and Somme areas with the Duke of Cornwalls Light Infantry. He came home and on completing his training in an O.T.C. was gazetted to a commission, and returned to France. He was wounded during the fighting at St. Quentin and was again invalided home, but rejoined his unit in March 1918, and fought throughout the Retreat and Advance of that year. He afterwards proceeded to Cologne with the Army of Occupation and remained there until demobilised in May 1919. He holds the 1914-15 Star, and the General Service and Victory Medals.

113, Commercial Road, Peckham, S.E.15.　　Z62434C

YOUELL, A. G., Sapper, R.E.

He joined in February 1916, and after being sent to France in the following year was engaged at Ypres. He was later transferred to Italy, but returning to France did excellent service in the Retreat and Advance of 1918. He afterwards went to Germany with the Army of Occupation. He was demobilised in September 1919, and holds the General Service and Victory Medals.

16, Amies Road, Battersea, S.W.11.　　Z5186

YOUNG, A., Private, R.A.S.C.

He joined in November 1916, and after his training served at various stations on important duties with his unit. He rendered valuable services, but owing to ill-health was not successful in obtaining his transfer overseas before the cessation of hostilities. He had previously served in the 8th London Regiment (P.O. Rifles).

1, Kimberley Road, Stockwell, S.W.9.　　Z5200A

YOUNG, A., Saddler, R.F.A.

He joined in January 1915, and was drafted to France in the following year. He rendered excellent service at Vimy Ridge, the Somme, Arras, Bullecourt, Ypres, Cambrai and many later engagements. He returned home and was demobilised in March 1919, holding the General Service and Victory Medals.

17, Irving Grove, Stockwell, S.W.9.　　Z5198

YOUNG, A. A., Private, 2nd Royal Fusiliers.

Joining in June 1916 at the age of seventeen, he was sent to France in October of the same year and took part in the fighting on the Ancre front and at Beaumont-Hamel and Beaucourt. He was then sent home on account of being under age, but returned to France in August 1918, and was in action at Havrincourt, Epéhy and Cambrai. After the Armistice he proceeded with the Army of Occupation to Germany. He was demobilised in February 1919, and holds the General Service and Victory Medals.

103, Westmoreland Road, S.E.17.　　Z5190B

YOUNG, A. E., Rifleman, 21st London Regiment (1st Surrey Rifles).

He volunteered in August 1914, and after being sent to France in the same year took part in the fighting at Ypres and Loos. He was afterwards engaged on important duties in various sectors until hostilities ceased. He was demobilised in January 1919 on his return home and holds the 1914-15 Star, and the General Service and Victory Medals.

31, Mundella Road, Wandsworth Road, S.W.8.　　Z5191

YOUNG, C., Private, Royal Scots.

He volunteered in August 1914, and was drafted to France in the same year. He was in action at St. Eloi, Hill 60, Ypres, Ploegsteert Wood, the Somme, Beaumont-Hamel, Arras, Messines and in many other engagements in the Retreat and Advance of 1918, and was wounded. He was demobilised in March 1919, and holds the 1914 Star, and the General Service and Victory Medals.

3, Carpenters Cottages, Clapham, S.W.4.　　Z5201

YOUNG, E. J., L/Corporal, Royal Sussex Regiment.

Having previously served for twelve years in the above Regiment, he re-enlisted in August 1914, and was sent to France, where he took part in the Battle of Loos, and was wounded whilst acting as a despatch bearer. During his earlier service he was engaged in the South African campaign. He was demobilised in January 1919, and holds the Queen's and King's South African Medals, the 1914-15 Star, and the General Service and Victory Medals.

24, Viceroy Road, Guildford Road, S.W.8.　　Z5197

YOUNG, F. W. G., Sergt., R.A.O.C.

Having volunteered in March 1915, he was sent to France later in the same year and was engaged on important duties with his Corps on many sectors, including the Somme, Ypres, Bapaume, Armentières and Passchendaele. He was wounded in action near Ypres in 1917. He was demobilised in July 1919, and holds the 1914-15 Star, and the General Service and Victory Medals.

34, Ceylon Street, Battersea Park Road, S.W.8.　　Z5193

YOUNG, G., Corporal, R.E.

Volunteering in September 1914 he was sent in March 1916 to France, where he was engaged on highly important duties as a despatch rider in various sectors, including the Somme and Ypres, and in the latter part of the war as King's Messenger. He was injured during his service owing to an accident to his machine. He was demobilised in August 1919, and holds the General Service and Victory Medals.

48, Vicarage Road, Camberwell, S.E.5.　　Z5196

YOUNG, H. L., Driver, R.A.S.C.

He joined in January 1916, and after completing his training was drafted to the Western Front, where he was engaged on important duties conveying the wounded from the firing line to hospital. He also went through the Retreat and Advance of 1918. He was demobilised in February 1919, and holds the General Service and Victory Medals.

9, Carpenters Cottages, Clapham, S.W.4.　　Z5194

YOUNG, J., Private, 6th Dorsetshire Regiment.
Volunteering in August 1914, he proceeded to France later in that year, and fought at Ypres, Festubert and Loos. He gave his life for the freedom of England at Mametz Wood on July 7th, 1916, during the first Battle of the Somme, and was entitled to the 1914-15 Star, and the General Service and Victory Medals.
"And doubtless he went in splendid company."
105, Dorset Road, Clapham Road, S.W.8.   Z5199A

YOUNG, J. T., Pte., 10th Queen's (Royal West Surrey Regt.)
He volunteered in January 1916, and later in that year proceeded to France. During his service overseas he fought at Ploegsteert, the Somme and in many other engagements of note. Owing to ill-health he was invalided home, and after receiving hospital treatment was discharged as medically unfit for further service in January 1918. He holds the General Service and Victory Medals.
105, Dorset Road, Clapham Road, S.W.8.   Z5199B

YOUNG, P., Sapper, R.E.
He volunteered in June 1915, and in the following December landed in France, and was in action at Loos, Vermelles, and Vimy Ridge. Transferred to Salonika in 1916, he was engaged on important duties during heavy fighing on the Struma, Vardar and Doiran fronts, and took part in the final Allied Advance in this theatre of war in 1918. Returning to England he was demobilised in January 1919, and holds the 1914-15 Star, and the General Service and Victory Medals.
1, Kimberley Road, Stockwell, S.W.9.   Z5200B

YOUNG, P. G., Private, 11th Devonshire Regiment.
Volunteering in June 1915, and proceeding to France in June of the following year he was engaged in heavy fighting in many parts of the line. He gave his life for King and Country in September 1916, during the first British Offensive on the Somme, and was entitled to the General Service and Victory Medals.
"Courage, bright hopes, and a myriad dreams splendidly given."
36, Longhedge Street, Battersea, S.W.11.   Z5195

YOUNG, R., Private, Labour Corps.
He joined in July 1916, and on conclusion of his training was engaged on important agricultural duties at various places. He was unsuccessful in obtaining his transfer to a theatre of war prior to the signing of the Armistice, but rendered valuable services until demobilised in February 1919.
8, Ewell Place, Camberwell, S.E.5.   Z5865

YOUNG, R. W., Gunner, R.F.A.
He volunteered in October 1914, and in the following August embarked for the Western Front. He was in action at the Battles of Vimy Ridge, and the Somme, and in many other engagements of note. He also fought throughout the German Offensive and Allied Advance of 1918, and returning home after the Armistice was demobilised in March 1919, holding the 1914-15 Star, and the General Service and Victory Medals.
11, Lisford Street, Peckham, S.E.15.   Z5099B

YOUNG, S. F., Private, Royal Gloucester Hussars.
Joining in April 1916, he was engaged with his unit on important duties until September 1918, when he was sent to Palestine, and served in the final operations in that theatre of war. He returned home and was demobilised in December 1919, and holds the General Service and Victory Medals.
28, Nutbrook Street, Peckham Rye, S.E.15.   Z6804

YOUNG, T. W., L/Cpl., 1st East Surrey Regiment.
A serving soldier he was engaged on important duties, at various stations until drafted to France in June 1916. He then fought at Vimy Ridge, the Somme, and Armentières, and was taken prisoner at Passchendaele. He was held in captivity until after the cessation of hostilities and was then repatriated. He was still serving in 1920, and holds the General Service and Victory Medals.
1, Massinger Street, Walworth, S.E.17.   Z5189

YOUNG, W. G., Private, 2nd London Regt. (Royal Fusiliers) and 13th London Regt. (Kensingtons).
Volunteering in September 1914, he was sent to Malta shortly afterwards, and in the following year proceeded to Gallipoli, and fought in many engagements until the Evacuation of the Peninsula. Transferred to Egypt in 1916, he served there for some months and then embarked for France. Here he was in action in the first Battle of the Somme and other battles of note and in 1917 was sent to Salonika, and fought on the Doiran front. Proceeding to Egypt later in 1917 he took part in the British Advance into Syria, and rendered excellent services. He returned home and was demobilised in April 1919, holding the 1914-15 Star, and the General Service and Victory Medals.
27, Gladstone Street, Battersea Park Road, S.W.8.   Z5192

YOUNG, W. G., Driver, R.F.A.
He volunteered in September 1914, and shortly afterwards was sent to France, where he fought in the Battles of the Marne, the Aisne, and other engagements of note. Later in 1915, he proceeded to Salonika, and was engaged in heavy fighting on the Doiran, Struma and Vardar fronts, until the close of the War. Returning home, he was demobilised in February 1919, and holds the 1914 Star, and the General Service and Victory Medals.
16, Mayall Road, Herne Hill, S.E.24.   Z5187

YOUNG, W. J., Private, Duke of Cornwall's Light Infantry and Gunner, R.F.A.
Mobilised and drafted to France at the outbreak of war, he fought in the Retreat from Mons, and the Battles of the Marne, the Aisne, La Bassée and Ypres. Transferred to Salonika he was in action in many engagements and was taken prisoner. Six months later he escaped and after many privations rejoined his unit, which shortly afterwards proceeded to Russia. He saw much service in this country, and returning to England was demobilised in June 1919. He holds the Mons Star, and the General Service and Victory Medals.
103, Westmoreland Road, Walworth, S.E.17.   Z5190A

Z

ZIMMERMAN, E. N., Private, Middlesex Regiment.
Joining in 1917, later he landed in France and fought in the Battles of Ypres and Passchendaele. He also took part in severe fighting throughout the German Offensive and subsequent Allied Advance of 1918. He was demobilised in October 1919, and holds the General Service and Victory Medals.
16, Pennack Road, Peckham, S.E.15.   Z5202B

ZIMMERMAN, G. R., Private, Middlesex Regiment.
He joined in 1918, and on completing his training served at various depôts with his unit, engaged on guard and other important duties. He did not obtain his transfer overseas prior to the Armistice, but shortly after the cessation of hostilities was sent to France, and rendered valuable services engaged on salvage work. He was demobilised in February 1919.
16, Pennack Road, Peckham, S.E.15.   Z5202A

ZOLLER, F. J., Private, Labour Corps.
Volunteering in February 1915, later in that year he embarked for the Western Front, where he served in the advanced areas in many parts of the line. He was present at the Battles of Ypres, and was severely wounded. He returned to England, and after receiving hospital treatment was ultimately invalided out of the Service in August 1919. In 1920, however, he was still undergoing treatment for his injuries, and holds the 1914-15 Star, and the General Service and Victory Medals.
64, Vaughan Road, Camberwell, S.E.5.   Z6368

Printed in the United Kingdom
by Lightning Source UK Ltd.
127374UK00001B/103-200/A